RALPH P. BARRETT

Frequency Analysis of English Usage:

Lexicon and Grammar

Frequency Analysis of English Usage:

Lexicon and Grammar

W. Nelson Francis and
Henry Kučera

with the assistance of

Andrew W. Mackie

Houghton Mifflin Company • Boston

All correspondence and inquiries should be directed to
Reference Division, Houghton Mifflin Company
Two Park Street, Boston, Massachusetts 02108

Library of Congress Cataloging in Publication Data

Francis, W. Nelson (Winthrop Nelson), 1910-
Frequency Analysis of English Usage.

Bibliography: p.
1. English language—United States. 2. English language—Word frequency. 3. English language—Grammatical categories. I. Kučera, Henry. II. Mackie, Andrew W., 1956- . III. Title.
PE2839.F7 420'.973 82-901
ISBN 0-395-32250-2 AACR2

Printed in the United States of America

Contents

Tables

Preface

Work on the Brown Corpus has been going on for nearly twenty years, since its inception in 1962. During that time a large number of people—mostly academic colleagues and students—have been involved, each one making some contribution leading ultimately to the work presented here. It is not possible to name them all here, but we wish to acknowledge our debt individually to those whose work and advice have been of special value. The following list, incomplete though it is, shows the extent of our debt.

To workers on the original corpus: Anne Robb Taylor, Loretta Felice, Mary Lois Marckworth, Henry Hall Peyton, Jr., Robert Staudte, Jr.

To the originators of the tagging system: Gerald M. Rubin and Barbara Greene Levine.

To subsequent workers on the tagging, especially Patricia Strauss and Sandra Pierce Brenckle.

To colleagues abroad who have not only used the corpus but advised us on its development: Geoffrey Leech, Jan Svartvik, Stig Johansson, Jostein Hauge, Knut Hofland, and Randolph Quirk.

We owe a special debt to Andrew Mackie, whose ingenuity, skill, and industry produced the programs that have made the lemmatization a largely automatic operation. He also developed the programs needed to prepare the text for computerized composition.

The original corpus was prepared under a Research Grant of the Cooperative Research Program of the U.S. Office of Education. The present work was made possible through the assistance of a research grant from the National Endowment for the Humanities. Some aspects of the work were partially supported by a grant to Brown University from the Alfred P. Sloan Foundation. Working space, computer time, and other facilities have been supplied by Brown University.

Providence, Rhode Island, May 1982

W. Nelson Francis

Henry Kučera

Introduction

This volume presents the results of a lexical and grammatical analysis of a one-million-word corpus of present-day American English, originally assembled at Brown University in 1963-64 and thus commonly referred to by researchers interested in text analysis as the Brown Corpus. The Brown Corpus, which was compiled with the view of making it broadly representative of current edited American English, contains selections from five hundred samples belonging to fifteen different genres of writing. The genres range from newspaper reportage to technical writing, and from philosophical essays to various kinds of fiction. Section I of this book gives a detailed description of the composition of the corpus.

The original hope of the compilers of the Brown Corpus, namely that it would provide a source of contemporary English texts in computer-accessible form for further research as well as serve as a standard of comparison for studies of other texts, has been fulfilled beyond expectation. At the present time, nearly two hundred copies of the corpus text and more than seventy copies of the word-frequency lists derived from the corpus have been made available on computer tapes to institutions and individuals all over the world. The book by Henry Kučera and W. Nelson Francis, *Computational Analysis of Present-Day American English* (Providence: Brown University Press, 1967), which provided much of this information in printed form, and which has exhausted two printings since its first publication, has been widely cited by linguists, psychologists, computer scientists, and others. The frequency tables presented in that publication have—at least for some purposes—replaced older lists such as that of Thorndike and Lorge. In addition to that, the Brown Corpus has also served as the basis of numerous studies about the English language and as a model for the construction of other corpora. A bibliography of these studies, listing fifty-seven items, was published in *ICAME News* No. 2: Bergen, 1979:9-12. A briefer bibliography will be found at the end of this book.

This degree of interest among scholars from several disciplines has encouraged us to prepare for publication the results of our subsequent research based on the Brown Corpus, which has been concerned primarily with the grammatical analysis of the entire one million words of the text. The aim of our most recent work has been to make the retrieval and the presentation of both lexical and grammatical information from the corpus possible in a linguistically more sophisticated and thus more useful form. In the course of this work, all of the million-odd words of the corpus have been "tagged," each word being given a specific grammatical designator. This tagging procedure, which was semiautomatic, assigned each running word (i.e., each word token) an unambiguous symbol based on a taxonomy of eighty-seven grammatical categories. A detailed description of the principles of this tagging is presented in Section II. This book thus represents the first results of the research based on the grammatically analyzed corpus.

The information in this volume is presented in seven sections, some or all of which may be of special interest to individual readers. Sections I and II, however, are necessary prerequisites for the understanding and use of the subsequent sections. In Section I, we define, first of all, the terminology used in the rest of the volume, and present a detailed description of our data base. Section II provides an explanation of the grammatical taxonomy utilized in our tagging procedure, a complete list with illustrations of the eighty-seven grammatical symbols used, and a discussion of the difficulties that English presents for a taxonomic grammatical analysis.

Sections III and IV present two frequency lists organized around the notion of a *lemma*. A lemma, in our study, is defined as a set of lexical forms having the same stem and belonging to the same major word class, differing only in inflection and/or spelling. In the frequency lists presented in Section III, all the forms belonging to each individual lemma are given along with their grammatical symbols and their frequency of occurrence under the base form of the lemma. This list is ordered alphabetically. Section IV presents the list of lemmas, represented by their base form, in descending order of their frequency of occurrence. Besides the actual lemma frequency, an adjusted frequency, which takes into account the distribution of the lemma among the fifteen genres of the corpus, is also given. The rationale for this adjusted frequency and the method of computing it can be found in the introduction to Section IV. This is thus a rank list, with the most frequent lemma having rank 1, the next more frequent rank 2, and so on. The rank list is organized in two parallel columns, one based on actual frequency and the other on adjusted frequency. Because the rank of low-frequency words is of little interest—since the particular rank ordering of such low-frequency items is largely idiosyncratic to a particular text—we have not included any lemmas with adjusted frequency of less than five in this list. However, as explained in the Concluding Remarks to this volume, the complete information, including the rank of low-frequency words, is available on computer-readable magnetic tapes.

Sections V and VI summarize the grammatical results of our analysis. In Section V, we give the information about the frequency and distribution of the grammatical classes in the corpus, including a statistical measure of the significance of the distribution of individual word classes in the fifteen different genres of the corpus. In Section VI, we discuss sentence length in the corpus in relation to sentence complexity, which is defined essentially in terms of predicate/argument structure, and the distribution of passive and active constructions, as well as the various verbal forms of tense and aspect in the corpus and its genres. Again, complete information about the distribution of these sentential parameters in the fifteen genres is given. Both the lexical and the grammatical presentations in this volume include information about the properties of the individual genres and thus offer data for the study of stylistic differences among the types of writing represented in the corpus.

The Concluding Remarks provide further information about the computer tapes available to those readers who may wish to retrieve additional lexical and grammatical information from the corpus with the aid of a digital computer.

I

The Data Base

Terminology

The following terminology will be used in this book. It implies the theoretical basis for the procedures of sorting, classifying and counting which have been used.

Graphic word: a string of contiguous alphanumeric characters with space on either side; may include hyphens and apostrophes but no other punctuation marks.

Tag: a string of capital letters and/or symbols indicating the grammatical category to which a graphic token is assigned. The full list of tags is given in Table 1.2.

Grammatical word: a graphic word together with its tag.

Lexical word or **lexeme:** one or more grammatical words forming a lexical unit—i.e., filling a single grammatical position and having a unitary meaning. Normally the constituents of a lexeme are contiguous, but in a few cases—e.g., two-part verbs—they may be separated.

Word class: a set of grammatical words having the same tag.

Major word class: a set of word classes including base forms and their inflectional variants; i.e., a part of speech.

Lemma: a set of grammatical words having the same stem and/or meaning and belonging to the same major word class, differing only in inflection and/or spelling. Inflection is overtly marked by affixes, stem changes, or suppletion. In a few cases it is not overtly marked but is signaled by syntactic features (e.g., subject-verb concord).

Base form: the member of a lemma consisting of stem alone without inflection.

Inflectional variant: a member of a lemma differing from the other members by inflection.

Spelling variant: a grammatical word constituting the same lexical word as another grammatical word from which it differs only in nonsignificant variation in spelling. When a base form or inflectional variant has two or more spelling variants, one has been chosen as the *standard form*, from which the others are considered to be deviant. The form chosen as standard is normally that listed as such by American dictionaries. If more than one are so listed, the one having the highest frequency in this corpus is chosen.

Compound: a lexical word analyzable into constituents which are themselves lexical words. In English, compounds may take three different graphic forms: *solid*, in which the constituents make up a continuous string without space or hyphen; *hyphenated*, in which the constituents are separated by hyphens but no space; *open*, in which the constituents are separated by space. In this work, solid and hyphenated compounds are treated as single grammatical words, while open compounds are treated as series of two (or more) grammatical words. Open compounds are thus not identified as such.

Merged word: a graphic word other than a compound, whose constituents are lexical words, one or both of which are given reduced graphic form to indicate phonological reduction in speech, e.g., *he'll, 'tis, gonna*. These are given the tags of both constituents joined by + and are listed under both relevant lemmas.

Pseudo-word: a graphic word which is not recognizable as a lexeme, usually because it is formally a hyphenated compound one or both of whose constituents are constituents of open compounds. Most of these involve proper names: *Charles MacArthur-Helen Hayes*, for example, contains the pseudo-word *MacArthur-Helen*.

Pseudo-words have been separated into their constituents for purposes of the lemmatized lists and frequency counts in this book. They have been left unchanged in the running text of the corpus available on tape.

Entry: the heading for a lemma. It is identical with the base form, even though the base form may not appear in the corpus; for example, only the plural form *trolls* appears and not the base form *troll*, but the entry is still *troll*. In pronouns, where all forms are inflectionally marked, the entry form is the nominative singular. For inflected foreign words the entry form is the nominative singular of nouns or the infinitive of verbs, except that if only one form occurs it serves as the entry.

The Data Base

The data base from which the frequency lists and other material in this book are derived is the tagged version of the Standard Corpus of Present-Day American English, commonly known as the Brown Corpus. This corpus was compiled and prepared for computer use at Brown University in 1963-64, under the direction of W. Nelson Francis, on a grant from the U. S. Office of Education (Francis 1964a).

The corpus consists of approximately 1,014,000 graphic words of running text, all of which was first printed in the United States in the year 1961. The text is divided into five hundred samples of about two thousand words each, which are assigned to fifteen categories or genres, as listed below in Table 1.1.

Table 1.1: Composition of Corpus

	Daily	Weekly	Total
I. Informative Prose			374 Samples
A. Press: Reportage	Daily	Weekly	Total
Political	10	4	14
Sports	5	2	7
Society	3	0	3
Spot News	7	2	9
Financial	3	1	4
Cultural	5	2	7
Total			44
B. Press: Editorial	Daily	Weekly	Total
Institutional	7	3	10
Personal	7	3	10
Letters to the Editor	5	2	7
Total			27
C. Press: Reviews	14	3	17
Total			17
D. Religion			
Books			7
Periodicals			6
Tracts			4
Total			17
E. Skills and Hobbies			
Books			2
Periodicals			34
Total			36
F. Popular Lore			
Books			23
Periodicals			25
Total			48
G. Belles Lettres, Biography, Memoirs, etc.			
Books			38
Periodicals			37
Total			75
H. Miscellaneous			
Government Documents			24
Foundation Reports			2
Industry Reports			2
College Catalog			1
Industry House Organ			1
Total			30
J. Learned			
Natural Sciences			12
Medicine			5
Mathematics			4
Social and Behavioral Sciences			14
Political Science, Law, Education			15
Humanities			18
Technology and Engineering			12
Total			80
II. Imaginative Prose			126 Samples
K. General Fiction			
Novels			20
Short Stories			9
Total			29
L. Mystery and Detective Fiction			
Novels			20
Short Stories			4
Total			24
M. Science Fiction			
Novels			3
Short Stories			3
Total			6
N. Adventure and Western Fiction			
Novels			15

Short Stories........................ 14
Total........................... 29

P. Romance and Love Story
Novels............................ 14
Short Stories...................... 15
Total........................... 29

R. Humor
Novels............................ 3
Essays, etc........................ 6
Total........................... 9

GRAND TOTAL................ 500

The samples represent a wide range of styles and varieties of prose. Verse was not included on the ground that it presents special linguistic problems different from those of prose. (Short verse passages quoted in prose samples are kept, however.) Drama was excluded as being the imaginative re-creation of spoken discourse, rather than true written discourse. Fiction was included, but no samples were admitted which consisted of more than 50% dialogue. Samples were chosen for their representative quality rather than for any subjectively determined excellence. The use of the term *standard* in the title of the corpus does not in any way mean that it was put forward as standard English; it merely expresses the hope that this corpus would become a standard source of data for various studies of present-day American English. Since the preparation and input of data is a major bottleneck in computer work, the intent was to make available a carefully chosen and prepared body of material of considerable size in standardized format. It was further hoped that the corpus might prove to be a standard in setting a pattern for the preparation and presentation of further bodies of data in English or in other languages. This hope has been in part realized by the preparation of the Lancaster-Oslo-Bergen (LOB) Corpus of Present-Day British English, which replicates as closely as possible the form and content of the Brown Corpus (Leech and Leonard 1974, Johansson 1980c). A similar corpus of Indian English is being undertaken at Shivaji University in Kolhapur (Shastri 1980).

The selection of material to be included followed a two-phased procedure: an initial subjective classification and decision as to how many samples of each category would be used, followed by a random selection of the actual samples within each category. The list of main categories and their subdivisions was drawn up at a conference held at Brown University in February 1963. Participants in the conference were John B. Carroll, W. Nelson Francis, Philip B. Gove, Henry Kučera, Patricia O'Connor, and Randolph Quirk. The participants also independently gave their opinions as to the number of samples there should be in each category. These figures were averaged to obtain the preliminary set of figures used. A few changes were later made on the basis of experience gained in making the selections. Finer subdivision was based on proportional amounts of actual publication during 1961.

Most of the genres listed in Table 1.1 are self-explanatory, with the possible exceptions of E. Skills and Hobbies; F. Popular Lore; and G. Belles Lettres, etc. Topics dealt with in selections included in these categories are as follows:

E. Skills and Hobbies

Bodybuilding
Gardening
Aviation
High Fidelity Sound
Dog Raising
Boats, Boatbuilding
Model Railroading
Hot Rod Racing
Oil Heating
Horse Racing
Guns
Stagecoaching
Photography
Travel
Barbecue Cooking
Needlework
Pottery
Carpentry
Covered Bridges
Swimming Pools
Air Conditioning
Watercolor
Gymnastics
Electronics
Cattle Raising
Interior Decorating
Signboards

F. Popular Lore

Body Language
Recent History
Popular Psychology
Education
Sex
Health Fraud
Orthodontics
Part-time Farming
Birth Control
Folklore
Popular Geology
Foreign Policy
Popular Sociology
Oenology
Popular Culture
Tourism

G. Belles Lettres, Biography, Memoirs, etc.

Social Ethics	National Culture	History
Political Theory	Literary Criticism	Aesthetics
Anthropology	Choreography	History of Science
	Biography and Autobiography	

It will be seen that there is some overlap of subject matter between the latter two categories. The distinctions between them were made principally on the basis of the level of sophistication, education, and specialization of the presumed audience. The level of Popular Lore, as the title indicates, was that of the high-circulation, more or less sensational, popular press. That of Belles Lettres was that of the more serious-minded and selective upper middlebrow press. Category J. Learned, which also includes some of the same subject matter, was drawn largely from learned and professional journals, books, and monographs.

Full information on each individual sample in the corpus is given in the manual which has been prepared to accompany the corpus tape (Francis and Kučera 1979).

A volume of studies of word frequency and distribution based on this corpus was published by the present authors in 1967 (Kučera and Francis 1967). The larger part of this volume consists of two lists giving the frequencies of all graphic words (types) occurring in the corpus, one alphabetical and the other rank-ordered. Although these lists have had wide use, they have two rather serious shortcomings:

1. Graphic words are sorted and counted simply on the basis of their graphic form, without regard to their lexical status. This means that homographs are not distinguished but are counted together. The frequency figure given for *will*, for example, includes the totals for the modal auxiliary (future-tense marker), the lexical verb meaning 'to wish, desire, and bequeath,' and the noun designating 'purpose, desire,' or 'a document expressing intent to bequeath.'

2. All graphic words are treated as separate types, so that variant forms, whether inflectional variants or variant spellings, are counted and listed separately; that is, the lists are not lemmatized.

The frequency lists of the present volume are intended to correct these shortcomings, specifically by disambiguating homographs and grouping variant forms of a lemma together under a single entry. The method chosen for accomplishing this is *tagging;* that is, assigning to each graphic word a tag or symbol indicating the grammatical category to which it belongs. There are eighty-seven such tags, listed in Table 1.2. The criteria by which they have been assigned are described in detail in Section II. Here we may note that the assigning of a tag to each graphic-word token in the corpus has identified them as grammatical-word tokens, and therefore has facilitated both the disambiguation of homographs and the assembling of lemmas, both of which have been done largely automatically by computer. Specifically, two grammatical words consisting of the same graphic word but different tags are treated as distinct types and so counted. Likewise, grammatical words belonging to the same major word class and sharing the same stem are grouped together as members of a lemma. Frequency counts can thus be given not only for the separate grammatical words but for the lemma as a whole.

Table 1.2: List of Tags

TAG	DESCRIPTION	EXAMPLES
.	sentence closer	*. ; ? !*
(	left parenthesis	*([*
)	right parenthesis	*)]*
*	*not, -n't*	
--	dash	
,	comma	
:	colon	
ABL	pre-qualifier	*quite, rather*
ABN	pre-quantifier	*half, all*
ABX	pre-quantifier, double conjunction	
AP	post-determiner	*many, next*
AT	article	*a, the, no*

Table 1.2: List of Tags (cont.)

TAG	DESCRIPTION	EXAMPLES
BE	*be*	
BED	*were*	
BEDZ	*was*	
BEG	*being*	
BEM	*am, -'m*	
BEN	*been*	
BER	*are, -'re*	
BEZ	*is, -'s*	
CC	coordinating conjunction	*and, or*
CD	cardinal numeral	*two, 2*
CS	subordinating conjunction	*if, although*
DO	*do*	
DOD	*did*	
DOZ	*does*	
DT	singular determiner	*this, that*
DTI	singular or plural determiner	*some, any*
DTS	plural determiner	*these, those*
DTX	determiner, double conjunction	*either, neither*
EX	*there* (existential)	
FW	foreign word (hyphenated ahead)	
HL	word in headline (hyphenated after)	
HV	*have*	
HVD	*had* (past tense), *-'d*	
HVG	*having*	
HVN	*had* (past participle)	
HVZ	*has, hath, -'s*	
IN	preposition	
JJ	adjective	
JJR	comparative adjective	
JJS	semantically superlative adj.	*chief, main, top*
JJT	morphologically superlative adj.	
MD	modal auxiliary	*can, may, could*
NC	cited word (hyphenated after)	
NN	singular or mass noun	
NN$	possessive singular noun	
NNS	plural noun	
NNS$	possessive plural noun	
NP	singular proper noun	
NP$	possessive singular proper noun	
NPS	plural proper noun	
NPS$	possessive plural proper noun	
NR	adverbial noun	*home, west, tomorrow*
NR$	possessive adverbial noun	
NRS	plural adverbial noun	
OD	ordinal numeral	*second, 2nd*
PN	nominal pronoun	*everybody, nothing*
PN$	possessive nominal pronoun	
PP$	possessive personal pronoun	*my, your, our*
PP$$	second possessive personal pronoun	
PPL	singular reflexive personal pronoun	*myself, herself*
PPLS	plural reflexive pronoun	*ourselves, themselves*
PPO	objective personal pronoun	*me, us, him*
PPS	3rd. sg. nominative pronoun	*he, she, it*
PPSS	other nominative pronoun	*I, we, they*
QL	qualifier	*very, too, extremely*
QLP	post-qualifier	*enough, indeed*
RB	adverb	
RBR	comparative adverb	
RBT	superlative adverb	

Table 1.2: List of Tags (cont.)

TAG	DESCRIPTION	EXAMPLES
RN	nominal adverb	*here, then*
RP	adverb or particle	*across, off, up*
TL	word in title (hyphenated after)	
TO	infinitive marker	*to*
UH	interjection, exclamation	
VB	verb, base form	
VBD	verb, past tense	
VBG	verb, present participle, gerund	
VBN	verb, past participle	
VBZ	verb, 3rd singular present	
WDT	wh- determiner	*what, which*
WP$	possessive wh- pronoun	*whose*
WPO	objective wh- pronoun	*whom, which, that*
WPS	nominative wh- pronoun	*who, which, that*
WQL	wh- qualifier	*how*
WRB	wh- adverb	*how, when*

II

Tagging Procedures

Since the primary purpose of tagging the Brown Corpus was to facilitate automatic or semiautomatic syntactic analysis, the rationale for the tagging is basically syntactic, though some morphological distinctions with little syntactic significance have been recognized. On the whole, the taxonomy is traditional and should be transparent to the grammarian, but in some areas some arbitrary distinctions and classifications have been made that may not be immediately obvious. These will be explained here. Particular problems result from two characteristics of English: (1) the absence of a consistent system of overt marking of word-class constituency, and (2) the ease with which words may be shifted from one class to another without morphological change (functional shift).

A full account of the procedures of the automatic phase of the tagging is presented in *Automatic grammatical tagging of English* (Greene and Rubin 1971). These procedures resulted in the accurate tagging of 77% of the corpus. The remaining 23% was completed manually by a series of persons over a period of nearly ten years. Inevitably some errors and inconsistencies remain in spite of several complete proofreadings and constant correction of errors as they are found. It is felt that those errors that may have survived would be so few as not to affect the statistical value of the frequency lists.

The full list of eighty-seven tags is given in Table 1.2 above. They are of five kinds:

1. Major form classes (parts of speech): noun, common and proper; verb; adjective; adverb; in short, the open lexical classes. Where these words have inflectional variants, the first two characters of the tag indicate the word class and subsequent characters the inflection. Thus, for common nouns:

NN = base form (singular)
NN$ = singular possessive form
NNS = plural form
NNS$ = plural possessive form

Similarly, VB indicates the verb base form (whether infinitive or present tense other than 3rd singular), and VBZ, VBD, VBN, and VBG indicate the inflectional variants. Comparative and superlative morphologically marked forms of adjectives and adverbs have been indicated the same way: JJ, JJR, JJT and RB, RBR, and RBT. However, in the lemmatized lists these adjective and adverb forms have been treated as derivational rather than inflectional, so that each has a separate entry.

2. Function words: determiners, prepositions, conjunctions, pronouns, etc.; the closed lexical and grammatical classes. Various types of pronouns have been distinguished, and those which have inflectional variants are so marked; thus PPS indicates the 3rd person singular subject forms *he*, *she*, etc.; PPSS all other subject forms, *I*, *we*, *you*, etc.; PPO the object forms *him*, *them*, etc.; PP$ the possessive forms *his*, *their*, etc.; and PP$$ the second possessive (nominal) forms *his*, *theirs*, etc. The tags for *wh-* words, both interrogative and relative, begin with W.

3. Certain important individual words: *not*, existential as distinct from adverbial *there*, the infinitive marker *to*, the forms of the verbs *be*, *have*, and *do* (except the present and past participles *doing* and *done*),

whether auxiliary or full verbs.

4. Punctuation marks of syntactic significance: four kinds of sentence or main clause closers (. ; ? !) have all been tagged by a period symbol. Quotation marks have been disregarded. These punctuation marks have not been included in the frequency lists but their totals are given in Section V.

5. Four designator tags: these are hyphenated to the regular grammatical tags, indicating that the word belongs to a special form of discourse. FW hyphenated before the regular tag indicates a foreign word; normally words are so designated only if some typographical indication of their status, such as italics, is given in the original text. HL hyphenated after the regular tag indicates that the word occurs in a newspaper headline or other type of heading. NC hyphenated after the regular tag indicates that the word is used metalinguistically, i.e., simply as a cited word rather than in its normal grammatical use; usually, though not always, the text gives it some typographical marking. TL hyphenated after the regular tag indicates that the word occurs in a title or name (other than a personal name or other proper noun). See *Capitalized Words, Titles, and Proper Nouns* below.

Of the 87 tags, 6 designate punctuation marks, 4 designate types of discourse, and 77 designate word classes. Of the word classes, 45 are base forms, hence potential lemma entries, while 32 are inflectional variants, hence subordinate forms. It may seem that a system of 45 "parts of speech" is rather overspecified. This remains to be tested by extensive automated parsing routines on strings of tags. Meanwhile simpler systems can be made by collapsing various sets of tags together; for example, VB can be substituted for BE, HV, DO, and even MD, thus creating a single class of verbs and reducing the number of different forms by 17; or, all tags beginning with A can be replaced by DT, thus creating a single set of pre-adjectival components of noun phrases. In general, we felt it better to over- than to underspecify.

The Noun Phrase

The model for this consists of a head preceded by a determiner sector and a modifier sector. The center of the determiner sector is the determiner itself, of which three basic kinds are recognized: articles *a/an* and *the*, tagged AT; deictics *this, that, another, each*, tagged DT, with the plurals *these, those* tagged DTS, and the duals *either, neither*, which may also function as parts of correlative conjunctions, tagged DTX; quantifiers *some, any*, not marked for number, tagged DTI. Preceding the determiner are the pre-quantifiers *all, half*, tagged ABN, and *both*, tagged ABX, since it may also be part of a correlative conjunction. Between the determiner and the modifier position, various elements may appear: a set of post-determiners, tagged AP, most of which are quantifiers such as *many, more, most, several, single*, with some particularizers such as *past, next, same, only;* cardinal and ordinal numerals, tagged CD and OD respectively; possessive nouns and pronouns, all having tags ending in $. The modifier sector may have positive, comparative, or superlative adjectives, tagged JJ, JJR, JJS, and JJT, and present and past participles, tagged VBG and VBN. Adjectives may be modified by qualifiers, such as *rather, very, too*, tagged QL, or post-modified by the post-qualifiers *enough, indeed*, tagged QLP. In general, adverbs in *-ly* immediately preceding and clearly qualifying an adjective or adverb are commonly tagged QL rather than the general adverb tag RB. Examples are *exceedingly, sufficiently, terribly, unusually*. The concept "qualifier" has thus been rather broadly understood. Those interested in the frequencies of specific words of this sort are warned that their totals must be derived from two separate entries in the lists. The ratio of frequencies between the two classifications varies widely, depending on the semantic and idiomatic nature of the adverb. The following exemplify this range.

Word	*QL Tags*	*RB Tags*
extremely	47	3
sufficiently	26	16
unusually	5	6
practically	10	43
possibly	0	61

Certain adjectives which are semantically superlative and thus never compared are given the tag JJS; examples are *chief, head, main, principal, top*.

A difficult taxonomic problem is posed by the fact that in English a large variety of lexemes may appear as noun-modifiers between the determiner sector and the noun head. The tagging system makes provision for three kinds: adjectives, participles, and nominals. The problem lies in the fact that by compounding (open, hyphenated, or closed), suffixation, or simple adjunction, English permits a bewildering variety of lexemes, many of them nonce constructions, to fill this position. Especially difficult are words or compounds with the suffixes *-ed* and *-ing*. The following rules have been followed:

1. hyphenated words which are legitimate noun phrases without the hyphen have been tagged NN; thus *long-range, high-energy.*

2. single words or hyphenated compounds ending in *-ed* or *-ing* which are bona fide verbs when the ending is removed have been tagged VBN (past participle) or VBG (present participle) respectively; thus *untied, down-graded, outdistancing, double-crossing.* An exception is that when one of these words is modified by a qualifier it is considered an adjective and tagged JJ, as in *very tired, rather entertaining.*

3. words normally nouns appearing in the immediate prenominal position are considered noun adjuncts and tagged NN; thus *army officer, weather report.*

4. all other words in the modifier position are tagged JJ. This means that the class of adjectives is the residual class, and is thus a large and miscellaneous one. Among the curiosities it includes are:

Words ending in *-type*: *sandwich-type*

Noun-adjective combinations: *fancy-free, screw-loose, shoulder-high*

Noun-present participle combinations: *run-scoring, sales-building, law-abiding*

Noun-past participle combinations: *home-made, rock-strewn* (both of these also occur solid)

Noun-noun + *-ed* combinations: *shirt-sleeved, bowlegged*

Adjective-noun + *-ed* combinations: *short-skirted, slim-waisted*

Miscellaneous combinations: *show-offy, signal-to-noise, smash-'em-down, snob-clannish, topsy-turvy, to-the-death, tongue-in-cheek, too-simple-to-be-true, unique-ingrown-screwedup, round-the-clock, day-after-day.*

Both *high-power* and *high-powered* occur in the corpus; the procedures outlined above tag the former of these NN and the latter JJ.

In the head position, common nouns are tagged NN, or NNS, NN$, and NNS$ for inflected forms. Even if not morphologically marked, plurals are tagged NNS on the basis of the syntactic context. If this is not clear, as in *He caught the fish,* the word is considered singular and so tagged, unless the discourse context indicates that plural is intended, as in *He caught the fish. After he had cleaned them . . .* Words ending in suffixed *-ing,* even if clearly derived from verbs, are tagged as nouns if they occur in such unequivocally nominal positions as after a determiner or an attributive adjective. Thus in *The skiing is good here* and *The battle was marked by hard fighting, skiing* and *fighting* will be tagged NN. Likewise *-ing* words with plural inflections are tagged as nouns, as in *The shirt was still dirty after three washings.* Otherwise, *-ing* words in nominal syntactic functions are considered gerunds and tagged VBG; this tag is used for both gerunds and participles. Thus the following:

My	PP$
duty	NN
was	BEDZ
raising	VBG
the	AT
flag	NN

My	PP$
duty	NN
was	BEDZ
the	AT
raising	NN
of	IN
the	AT
flag	NN

Capitalized nouns serving solely as names are considered proper nouns and are tagged NP. Other words, whether capitalized or not, which appear as constituents of names or titles are given their normal tags to which the discourse tag TL is joined by a hyphen. See *Capitalized Words, Titles, and Proper Nouns* below.

Pronouns

Personal pronouns have tags beginning with PP, followed by one or more characters indicating case, concord, and sometimes number. All subject forms which concord with the base form of the verb in the present are tagged PPSS, regardless of person and number. Those that concord with the *-s* form of the verb are tagged PPS. Forms in object function, whether or not morphologically marked, are tagged PPO. First possessives (*my, our*) are tagged PP$; second (nominal) possessives (*mine, ours*) are tagged PP$$. Reflexive/intensive pronouns are tagged PPL if singular and PPLS if plural, with no distinction for case. Interrogatives and relatives begin with WP; subject forms are tagged WPS and object forms WPO.

Indefinite pronouns, i.e., compounds of *any-*, *every-*, *no-*, and *some-*, are tagged PN, or PN$ if they have the possessive suffix *'s.*

So-called demonstrative pronouns—*this, that,* etc.—are treated as free-standing determiners and tagged accordingly: DT, DTI, DTS. The colloquial use of *them* as a plural demonstrative, which occurs occasionally in the dialogue of fictional samples, is tagged DTS rather than PPO.

The Verbal Phrase

Verbs in the base form, regardless of syntactic function, are tagged VB. The inflected forms of normal verbs are marked with the suffix tags Z (3rd person singular), D (past tense), N (past participle) and G (present participle/gerund), attached directly to the VB tag. Morphologically unmarked forms like *hit, cast, set, run* are tagged according to their syntactic use. Nonstandard usages such as *seen* and *done* as past-tense forms are tagged according to their syntax, not their morphology. All modal auxiliaries are tagged MD; therefore *could, might, should, would* are considered base forms, not past-tense forms of *can, may, shall, will,* and have their own separate entries. The verbs *be, have,* and *do,* whether functioning as auxiliaries or full verbs, have the special tags BE, HV, and DO, with inflectional variants (exceptions: *doing* and *done* are tagged VBG and VBN). This permits the ready identification and analysis of verb phrases in the corpus. The archaic forms *art* and *hast* are tagged as base forms, while *hath* and other forms in *-th* are tagged as 3rd singular (HVZ, VBZ). Contracted forms of auxiliaries forming merged words with pronominal or nominal subjects have their regular tags joined to the subject tag by +; thus *I'm, John's,* and *you'll* are tagged PPSS+BEM, NP+BEZ or NP+HVZ, and PPSS+MD respectively. Contracted negatives have the tag for *not,* *, immediately following the verb tag; thus *don't* and *can't* are tagged DO* and MD*. Other merged words, appearing mostly in dialogue, are similarly treated; thus *gonna* and *gotta* are tagged VBG+TO and VBN+TO respectively.

Words consisting of a verbal stem and the suffixes *-ing* and *-ed* (*-en,* etc.) once again present problems when they occur in predicate position after a form of *be.* In the case of *-ing* forms, they normally form part of a progressive aspect verb phrase; however, in some cases they may function simply as predicate adjectives. This ambiguity of function is most obvious in the case of a set of transitive verbs normally taking human objects: *entertain, interest, charm, please,* etc. If there is an expressed object, these are tagged VBG, as in *The Duchess was entertaining Alice at tea, The girl was charming the audience with her singing;* if there is no object, the tag is JJ, as in *The girl was charming.* In certain cases, however, a generalized object can be understood, so that *The Duchess was entertaining last evening* is ambiguous. In such cases the tag has been assigned on the basis of the overall meaning of the passage. In the case of words with verbal stem and past-participial ending, the ambiguity lies between a true passive, in which the form is tagged VBN, and a stative description, in which case it is tagged JJ. If an agent phrase with *by* or an instrumental phrase introduced by *with* is present, there is no ambiguity; thus *The dish was broken by the baby* and *The town was devastated with dynamite* are clearly passives, but *The dish was broken* and *The town was devastated* are ambiguous. Conversely, in the absence of an agentive or instrumental phrase, the presence of a qualifier indicates the stative (adjectival) interpretation, as in *The dish was badly broken* and *The town was totally devastated.* If neither of these determining factors is present, the choice of tag has been determined by the overall sense of the passage.

A special case of the adjective versus participle problem is presented by words with the prefix *un-.* This is actually two prefixes, one reversing the directionality of the verbal action and the other negating the verbal state (Marchand 1969:201-07). The procedure here has been to remove the suffix; if the result is a bona fide verb, the prefix is the reversative one and the form is tagged VBG or VBN; if the result is not a bona fide verb, the prefix is the negative one and the form is tagged JJ. This may be viewed as a problem in the order of immediate constituents; if the participial suffix is applied to the verb stem before the *un-*, the form is an adjective; if the *un-* is applied first, the form is a participle. Some examples:

VBG	JJ
unclasping	unending
unfolding	unpromising
unpacking	unvarying

The words in the left hand column derive from the verbs *unclasp, unfold,* and *unpack* by the addition of *-ing,* while those in the right hand column derive from the forms *ending, promising,* and *varying* by prefixing *un-.* Most words of this sort belong exclusively to one set or the other, but there are a few exceptions such as *unsettled, unfastened, untied, unlocked,* which can be ambiguous, as in *The door was unlocked.* Usually the ambiguity is resolved by an adverbial phrase, as in

The door was unlocked all night. (JJ)
The door was unlocked by the janitor. (VBN)

If no such disambiguation is present, the correct parsing has been deduced from the larger context.

Adverbials

The general tag for adverbs is RB, with RBR and RBT for derived comparatives and superlatives. As stated above, the comparative and superlative forms are treated as base forms with their own entries. Adverbs in *-ly* used as qualifiers have been discussed above under *Noun Phrase.* Certain adverbs, mostly temporal or locative, which often function as nominals have been denominated "locative adverbs" and tagged RN; among them are *here, then, indoors.* Conversely, locative and temporal nouns which often function adverbially have been denominated "adverbial nouns" and tagged NR; examples are *home, east, Tuesday.*

In the case of phrasal or two-part verbs, the attempt was at first made to distinguish between adverbs (*hold out your hand*) and particles (*hold out for more money*). It was found, however, that this necessitated a large number of arbitrary decisions, which might confuse or mislead those using the corpus. It was decided instead to consider this a semantic rather than a taxonomic problem, and to give the "portmanteau" tag RP (for 'either adverb or particle') to the ten words *about, across, down, in, off, on, out, over, through, up* except when they function as prepositions, in which case they receive the normal preposition tag IN.

Connectives

Coordinating conjunctions. (*and, or,* etc.) are tagged CC and subordinators (*since, because, if*) CS. Prepositions are tagged IN. The connectives *like* and *than* are tagged CS or IN depending on the surface construction, in spite of the claim by some normative grammmarians that *like* is always a preposition and *than* always a conjunction. The word *to* is tagged TO when it is used as the infinitive marker.

Pseudo-words

In order to eliminate a fairly large number of misleading entries, all pseudo-words (as defined in Section I above) have been eliminated from the lemmatized lists by the simple device of disregarding the hyphen. Thus in the example given in Section I, *Charles MacArthur-Helen Hayes,* the hyphen has been disregarded and the whole phrase treated as four rather than three word tokens. A special problem has been presented by the prefixes (or proclitics) *ex-, non-, post-, pre-* when they are hyphenated to open compounds, as in *ex-prison guard, non-church members, post-World War 2,* and *pre-Civil War.* When these hyphens are disregarded, the prefixes are left as free-standing words. In such cases they have been tagged as adjectives (JJ). It should be emphasized that this has been done only in making the lemmatized lists; the hyphens still appear in the running text of the corpus.

Capitalized Words, Titles, and Proper Nouns

The conventions of non-sentence-initial capitalization in English are complex and to a considerable degree variable, unlike most other aspects of the writing system. This has presented a problem in tagging, which has been disposed of, if not settled, by arbitrary rules. These have been made as objective as possible, but there still remain cases where judgment is necessary and hence inconsistency is possible. The aim has been to identify capitalized uses as much as possible, but also to associate capitalized words with their lower-case alternatives. This has been done by means of the tags NP (with its inflected variants NP$, NPS, and NPS$) and TL. The former of these is a primary tag and the latter a secondary tag hyphenated to primary tags. The following procedures have been observed:

1. Sentence-initial capitals have been reduced to lower case for all words except those identified as bearing capitals when not sentence-initial.

2. Random capitalization occurring in quotations from older sources or semi-literate writers has been preserved but without recognition by tag. The following sentence from Sample G38, a quotation from Defoe, illustrates eighteenth-century practice:

> If they Could Draw that young Gentleman into Their Measures They would show themselves quickly, for they are not asham'd to Say They want Onely a head to Make a beginning.

The capitalized words in passages of this sort have been given their normal tags, but the spellings are preserved as variants in the lemmatized list.

3. The same practice has been followed with German nouns, commonly capitalized. They receive the tag FW-NN.

4. Words identifiable as "proper nouns," that is, nouns used to name specific individuals, types, or groups, are tagged NP (NPS for plurals; NP$ and NPS$ for singular and plural possessives). Examples:

John	NP
F.	NP
Kennedy's	NP$
daughter	NN
Caroline	NP
The	AT
Smiths	NPS
are	BER
Presbyterians	NPS

5. Words occurring as constituents of titles, e.g., of books, plays, corporations, government agencies, etc., are given their normal tag with the addition of the hyphenated tag TL. In most cases these words are capitalized, except for function words such as prepositions, conjunctions, and sometimes pronouns. Some examples:

the	AT
United	VBN-TL
States	NNS-TL
of	IN-TL
America	NP-TL
Gulliver's	NP$-TL
Travels	NNS-TL
the	AT
Protestant	JJ-TL
Episcopal	JJ-TL
Church	NN-TL

It is to be noted that in some languages—French, for example—words in titles are often not capitalized:

Recherches	FW-NNS-TL
sur	FW-IN-TL
l'identite	FW-AT+NN-TL
des	FW-IN+AT-TL
forces	FW-NNS-TL
chimiques	FW-JJ-TL
et	FW-CC-TL
electriques	FW-JJ-TL

(Note that no accent marks are coded in the corpus.)

6. A problem is presented by names of persons and places which are homographs (and often cognates) of common words. Somewhat arbitrarily, the following procedures have been followed:

a. Names of persons have all been tagged NP, regardless of their etymological status:

	Gen.	NN-TL
	Thomas	NP
	Power	NP
compare	Georgia	NP-TL
	Power	NN-TL
	Company	NN-TL

b. Geographical terms and other descriptive words forming parts of place-names are given their basic tags followed by -TL:

the	AT
Mississippi	NP-TL
River	NN-TL
the	AT
Great	JJ-TL
Smoky	JJ-TL
Mountains	NNS-TL

c. Proper names forming parts of place names are tagged NP. See *Mississippi River* above.

d. The titles *Mr.*, *Mrs.*, and *Miss* have been tagged NP.

e. Other titles of persons which also occur as common nouns, adjectives, etc., have been given their regular tags plus -TL:

Mayor	NN-TL
William	NP
B.	NP
Hatfield	NP
Secretary	NN-TL
General	JJ-TL
Dag	NP
Hammarskjold	NP

f. Foreign and/or exotic titles not appearing as common nouns, etc., in the corpus have been tagged NP:

Signora	NP
Ferraro	NP

Since in the lemmatized lists words with hyphenated tags are listed as variants of normal words, the user may count them or not as he wishes. Words tagged NP are listed as separate entries, together with their variant forms (NP$, NPS, NPS$), variant spellings, and variants with hyphenated tags. In the alphabetized list they follow their homographs with regular tags.

Miscellaneous Items

The existential subject *there* has been tagged EX and thus is distinguished from the homonymous adverb, which is tagged RN. Exclamations of various sorts, which have no syntactic function, are tagged UH; they occur mostly in the dialogue of the fictional samples. The symbol $, appended to noun and pronoun tags to mark possessive forms (e.g., *John's*, in *John's book*, would be tagged NP$) may occur with other tags as well, to indicate the use of the *-s* enclitic in marking phrasal possession. Thus *Great's*, in *Alexander the Great's army*, would be tagged JJ$-TL. This usage is considered to be a variant form (rather than an inflection) of words other than nouns and pronouns, and is indicated in the lemmatized list by the double, rather than single, indentation of the form. The word *not* is tagged *, which is joined directly to the verb tag in the case of merged forms like *isn't* BEZ*. Numerals expressed in figures, as *23* and *4th*, are tagged CD and OD respectively in the tagged corpus, but they have not been included in the lemmatized lists; those interested in their frequencies can derive them from Kučera and Francis 1967.

III

Alphabetical Frequency List

The units whose distribution and frequency are given in this and the following list are *grammatical words*, as defined in Section I above. Each distinctive grammatical word, including spelling variants, is considered a separate type and is separately counted. Subtotals are given for each inflectional and spelling variant, and totals for each lemma. Counts are given as three numbers separated by hyphens; the first number of from one to five digits is the number of tokens in the entire corpus; the second number of two digits is the number of genres in which the form appears; the third number of three digits is the number of samples in which it appears. Thus 276-13-195 indicates that the form appears 276 times in the entire corpus and that it appears in 13 of the 15 genres and 195 of the 500 samples. These counts, therefore, give information about distribution as well as frequency.

The form of a lemma is shown below. It is arranged as follows:

1. The first line is the *entry*, consisting of the entry word (always a base form) at the left margin, followed by its grammatical definition if the lemma contains variants or by its tag if it consists only of a base form. Total frequency and distribution figures for the lemma are given in the right hand column. All parts of the entry line are in boldfaced type.

2. The lines with single indentation are the inflectional variants of the lemma, with their tags and counts. The base form, if it occurs, comes first, followed by the inflectional forms. Only those inflectional forms which actually occur in the corpus are listed.

3. The lines with double indentation list first the spelling variants of the inflectional forms under which they fall, followed next by examples having hyphenated tags (e.g., NN-HL), and then by merged words which include the inflectional variant under which they are listed.

4. The lines with triple indentation give spelling variants of merged and hyphenated forms.

5. The column of figures to the right of the tags gives the counts for each individual grammatical word and total counts for lemmas (in bold face).

6. The last column is not part of the lemma; it is used in this example to identify the types of items illustrated.

Sample Lemma

get	**verb**	**1486-15-344**	entry
get	VB	742-15-273	base form
git	VB	4-04-004	variant spelling
get	VB-HL	2-02-002	word in headline
get	VB-NC	1-01-001	cited form
Get	VB-TL	4-03-004	word in title
gets	VBZ	64-12-047	inflectional variant
gets	VBZ-HL	2-01-002	word in headline
got	VBD	338-14-164	inflectional variant
Got	VBD-TL	1-01-001	word in title
got	VBN	140-12-086	inflectional variant
gotten	VBN	16-08-013	variant inflection
Got	VBN-TL	3-02-003	word in title
gotta	VBN+TO	5-04-004	merged word
getting	VBG	162-15-122	inflectional variant
gettin'	VBG	1-01-001	spelling variant
getting	VBG-HL	1-01-001	word in headline

Word	Tag	Frequency
a	**article**	**23073-15-500**
a	AT	22944-15-500
a	AT-HL	60-08-037
a	AT-NC	8-01-001
A	AT-TL	54-10-038
a	AT-TL	1-01-001
A	AT-TL-HL	4-02-003
wanna	+AT	2-01-002
a	**foreign**	**6-05-006**
a	FW-IN	5-04-005
a	FW-IN-TL	1-01-001
A	**prop. noun**	**50-02-019**
A	NP	30-02-013
A	NP-HL	20-02-010
a.	**JJ**	**1-01-001**
a.	**noun**	**2-02-002**
a.	NN	1-01-001
a.	NNS	1-01-001
A.	**prop. noun**	**110-09-053**
A.	NP	103-09-053
A.	NP-HL	7-01-001
A.A.U.	**prop. noun**	**2-01-002**
A.A.U.	NP	0-00-000
A.A.U.	NP-TL	1-01-001
A.A.U.'s	NP$	1-01-001
A.B.	**NP**	**3-02-003**
A.D.	**RB**	**10-03-006**
A.I.D.	**NP**	**1-01-001**
A.K.C.	**NP**	**1-01-001**
A.L.A.M.	**NP**	**13-01-001**
a.m.	**adverb**	**40-10-025**
a.m.	RB	27-05-014
A.M.	RB	13-08-011
A.M.A.	**prop. noun**	**4-03-003**
A.M.A.	NP	3-02-002
A.M.A.	NP-TL	1-01-001
a-gracious	**UH**	**1-01-001**
a-la-Aristotle	**RB**	**1-01-001**
a-tall	**RB**	**1-01-001**
a-wing	**RB**	**1-01-001**
A-1	**adjective**	**2-02-002**
A-1	JJ	1-01-001
A-1	JJ-TL	1-01-001
aaa-ee	**UH**	**1-01-001**
aaawww	**UH**	**1-01-001**
aah	**UH**	**1-01-001**
Aaron	**NP**	**7-06-006**
aback	**RB**	**2-02-002**
abandon	**NN**	**2-02-002**
abandon	**verb**	**47-13-039**
abandon	VB	15-06-013
abandoned	VBD	5-05-005
abandoned	VBN	20-09-019
abandoning	VBG	7-06-007
abandonment	**NN**	**10-05-010**
abaringe	**NN**	**1-01-001**
abasement	**NN**	**2-02-002**
abate	**verb**	**1-01-001**
abated	VBD	1-01-001
Abatuno	**NP**	**1-01-001**
Abbas	**prop. noun**	**3-01-001**
Abbas	NP	2-01-001
Abbas's	NP$	1-01-001
Abbe	**NP**	**5-02-002**
abbey	**noun**	**7-04-005**
abbey	NN	1-01-001
Abbey	NN-TL	6-04-005
abbot	**noun**	**2-01-002**
abbot	NN	1-01-001
Abbot	NN-TL	1-01-001
Abbott	**NP**	**2-01-001**
abbreviate	**verb**	**1-01-001**
abbreviate (cont.):		
abbreviated	VBN	1-01-001
abbreviation	**noun**	**2-02-002**
abbreviation	NN	1-01-001
abbreviations	NNS	1-01-001
ABC	**NP**	**1-01-001**
Abdallah	**NP**	**1-01-001**
abdomen	**NN**	**6-05-006**
abdominal	**JJ**	**4-03-003**
abdominis	**NN**	**1-01-001**
abduction	**NN**	**1-01-001**
Abe	**NP**	**3-03-003**
abed	**RB**	**1-01-001**
Abel	**prop. noun**	**21-03-004**
Abel	NP	20-03-004
Abel's	NP$	1-01-001
Abell	**NP**	**1-01-001**
Abelson	**NP**	**1-01-001**
aber	**FW-CC**	**1-01-001**
Abernathy	**prop. noun**	**3-01-001**
Abernathy	NP	2-01-001
Abernathys	NPS	1-01-001
abrrant	**JJ**	**5-02-003**
aberration	**noun**	**9-03-006**
aberration	NN	3-03-003
aberrations	NNS	5-01-002
abberations	NNS	1-01-001
abet	**verb**	**4-04-004**
abetted	VBD	2-02-002
abetted	VBN	2-02-002
abeyance	**NN**	**3-02-003**
abhor	**verb**	**1-01-001**
abhorred	VBD	1-01-001
abhorrent	**JJ**	**1-01-001**
abide	**verb**	**14-07-013**
abide	VB	6-04-006
Abide	VB-TL	1-01-001
abides	VBZ	2-02-002
abiding	VBG	5-05-005
Abigail	**NP**	**2-01-001**
Abilene	**prop. noun**	**2-01-001**
Abilene	NP	1-01-001
Abilene	NP-TL	1-01-001
ability	**noun**	**87-12-059**
ability	NN	74-12-054
abilities	NNS	13-06-010
abject	**JJ**	**3-03-003**
abjection	**NN**	**1-01-001**
abjectly	**QL**	**1-01-001**
Ablard	**NP**	**2-01-001**
ablate	**verb**	**1-01-001**
ablated	VBN	1-01-001
ablation	**NN**	**2-01-001**
ablaze	**RB**	**3-03-003**
able	**adjective**	**217-15-167**
able	JJ	216-15-167
hable	JJ	1-01-001
abler	**JJR**	**2-01-002**
ably	**RB**	**2-02-002**
Abner	**NP**	**1-01-001**
abnormal	**JJ**	**3-03-003**
abnormality	**noun**	**1-01-001**
abnormalities	NNS	1-01-001
abnormally	**QL**	**1-01-001**
aboard	**IN**	**8-05-007**
aboard	**RB**	**17-08-011**
abode	**NN**	**4-02-003**
abolish	**verb**	**10-05-009**
abolish	VB	8-05-007
abolished	VBN	2-02-002
abolition	**noun**	**10-06-008**
abolition	NN	7-05-006

abolition (cont.):		
Abolition	NN	1-01-001
Abolition	NN-TL	2-02-002
abolitionist	**noun**	**5-03-003**
abolitionist	NN	1-01-001
abolitionists	NNS	3-03-003
Abolitionists	NNS-TL	1-01-001
aboriginal	**JJ**	**1-01-001**
aborigine	**noun**	**15-02-003**
aborigine	NN	7-01-002
aborigines	NNS	8-02-002
abortion	**noun**	**7-06-007**
abortion	NN	5-05-005
abortion	NN-NC	1-01-001
abortions	NNS	1-01-001
abortive	**JJ**	**3-02-003**
abound	**verb**	**5-04-005**
abound	VB	1-01-001
abounds	VBZ	1-01-001
abounded	VBD	2-02-002
abounding	VBG	1-01-001
about	**prep.**	**1242-15-367**
about	IN	1236-15-365
'bout	IN	1-01-001
bout	IN	1-01-001
about	IN-HL	2-02-002
About	IN-TL	2-02-002
about	**RP**	**574-15-249**
about-face	**verb**	**2-01-002**
about-faced	VBD	2-01-002
above	**IN**	**188-15-127**
above	**JJ**	**22-04-017**
above	**RB**	**86-12-052**
above-mentioned	**JJ**	**2-02-002**
above-noted	**JJ**	**1-01-001**
above-water	**JJ**	**1-01-001**
aboveground	**adjective**	**3-02-002**
aboveground	JJ	1-01-001
above-ground	JJ	1-01-001
aboveground	JJ-HL	1-01-001
Abra	**NP**	**1-01-001**
Abraham	**prop. noun**	**6-05-005**
Abraham	NP	5-04-004
Abraham	NP-TL	1-01-001
Abrams	**NP**	**1-01-001**
abrasion-resistant	**JJ**	**1-01-001**
abreaction	**NN**	**2-01-002**
abreast	**RB**	**5-04-005**
abridge	**verb**	**1-01-001**
abridged	VBN	1-01-001
abridgment	**NN**	**1-01-001**
abroad	**adverb**	**52-10-032**
abroad	RB	48-10-029
abroade	RB	1-01-001
abroad	RB-HL	3-02-003
abrogate	**verb**	**1-01-001**
abrogated	VBN	1-01-001
abrupt	**JJ**	**18-10-015**
abruptly	**RB**	**18-05-014**
abruptness	**NN**	**1-01-001**
abscess	**noun**	**3-01-001**
abscesses	NNS	3-01-001
abscissa	**NN**	**1-01-001**
absence	**noun**	**56-13-043**
absence	NN	53-12-040
absences	NNS	3-03-003
absent	**JJ**	**26-09-019**
absent	**verb**	**3-03-003**
absent	VB	2-02-002
absented	VBD	1-01-001
absent-minded	**JJ**	**3-03-003**
absent-mindedly	**adverb**	**4-03-003**
absent-mindedly	RB	3-02-002
absentmindedly	RB	1-01-001
absentee	**NN**	**1-01-001**
absenteeism	**NN**	**1-01-001**
absentia	**NN**	**1-01-001**
absently	**RB**	**6-03-005**
absinthe	**NN**	**1-01-001**
absolute	**JJ**	**29-09-023**
absolute	**noun**	**4-04-004**
absolute	NN	1-01-001
absolutes	NNS	3-03-003
absolutely	**QL**	**17-08-013**
absolutely	**RB**	**10-08-009**
absoluteness	**NN**	**2-01-001**
absolution	**NN**	**2-01-002**
absorb	**verb**	**41-12-031**
absorb	VB	13-08-011

absorb (cont.):		
absorbs	VBZ	1-01-001
absorbed	VBD	2-02-002
absorbed	VBN	22-08-016
absorbing	VBG	3-03-003
absorbency	**NN**	**1-01-001**
absorber	**NN**	**1-01-001**
absorption	**noun**	**14-04-010**
absorption	NN	12-04-009
absorptions	NNS	2-01-001
absorptive	**JJ**	**1-01-001**
abstain	**verb**	**2-02-002**
abstain	VB	1-01-001
abstaining	VBG	1-01-001
abstention	**NN**	**5-03-004**
abstinence	**NN**	**1-01-001**
abstract	**adjective**	**30-08-020**
abstract	JJ	27-07-017
abstract	JJ-HL	1-01-001
Abstract	JJ-TL	2-02-002
abstract	**noun**	**5-03-004**
abstract	NN	1-01-001
abstracts	NNS	3-02-002
Abstracts	NNS-TL	1-01-001
abstract	**verb**	**9-02-003**
abstract	VB	3-01-001
abstracted	VBD	1-01-001
abstracted	VBN	2-01-001
abstracting	VBG	3-01-001
abstractedness	**NN**	**1-01-001**
abstraction	**noun**	**23-03-011**
abstraction	NN	13-02-006
Abstraction	NN-TL	3-02-002
abstractions	NNS	7-03-007
abstractionism	**NN**	**1-01-001**
abstractionist	**noun**	**3-01-001**
abstractionists	NNS	2-01-001
Abstractionists	NNS-TL	1-01-001
abstractive	**JJ**	**1-01-001**
abstractly	**RB**	**1-01-001**
abstractor	**noun**	**1-01-001**
abstractors	NNS	1-01-001
abstruseness	**noun**	**1-01-001**
abstrusenesses	NNS	1-01-001
absurd	**JJ**	**17-07-017**
absurdity	**noun**	**10-07-009**
absurdity	NN	8-07-008
absurdities	NNS	2-02-002
absurdly	**RB**	**1-01-001**
abundance	**NN**	**13-09-011**
abundant	**JJ**	**9-06-008**
abundantly	**QL**	**2-02-002**
abuse	**noun**	**22-09-013**
abuse	NN	13-07-009
Abuse	NN-TL	2-01-001
abuses	NNS	7-04-004
abuse	**verb**	**8-07-008**
abuse	VB	3-03-003
abused	VBN	5-04-005
abusive	**JJ**	**1-01-001**
abutment	**noun**	**1-01-001**
abutments	NNS	1-01-001
abysmal	**JJ**	**2-02-002**
abyss	**NN**	**4-04-004**
Abyssinian	**prop. noun**	**1-01-001**
Abyssinians	NPS	1-01-001
acacia	**NN**	**3-01-001**
academic	**JJ**	**53-10-026**
academic	**noun**	**5-04-004**
academic	NN	3-03-003
academics	NNS	2-01-001
academically	**RB**	**5-02-003**
academicianship	**noun**	**1-01-001**
academicianship	NN	0-00-000
Academicianship	NN-TL	1-01-001
academy	**noun**	**28-09-018**
academy	NN	6-03-004
academeh	NN	1-01-001
Academy	NN-TL	18-08-013
academies	NNS	3-03-003
Acadia	**prop. noun**	**1-01-001**
Acadia	NP	0-00-000
Acadia	NP-TL	1-01-001
Acala	**NP**	**5-01-001**
Acapulco	**NP**	**1-01-001**
Accacia	**NP**	**4-01-001**
Accademia	**NP**	**1-01-001**
Accardo	**NP**	**1-01-001**
accede	**verb**	**2-02-002**

Word	Tag	Frequency
accede (cont.):		
accede	VB	1-01-001
acceded	VBN	1-01-001
accelerate	**verb**	**24-08-021**
accelerate	VB	5-03-005
accelerated	VBD	1-01-001
accelerated	VBN	12-06-012
accelerating	VBG	6-05-005
acceleration	**noun**	**19-05-009**
acceleration	NN	17-05-009
accelerations	NNS	2-01-001
accelerator	**noun**	**8-04-004**
accelerator	NN	5-04-004
accelerators	NNS	3-01-001
accelerometer	**noun**	**25-01-001**
accelerometer	NN	17-01-001
accelerometers	NNS	8-01-001
accent	**noun**	**14-09-014**
accent	NN	9-06-009
accents	NNS	5-04-005
accent	**verb**	**3-03-003**
accented	VBN	3-03-003
accenting	**NN**	**1-01-001**
accentual	**JJ**	**1-01-001**
accentuate	**verb**	**5-03-005**
accentuate	VB	1-01-001
accentuates	VBZ	1-01-001
accentuated	VBN	3-03-003
accept	**verb**	**193-14-126**
accept	VB	72-12-048
accepts	VBZ	6-04-006
accepted	VBD	28-12-026
accepted	VBN	67-10-054
Accepted	VBN-TL	1-01-001
accepting	VBG	19-09-019
acceptability	**NN**	**2-01-001**
acceptable	**JJ**	**21-07-016**
acceptance	**NN**	**49-11-038**
accepting	**JJ**	**2-02-002**
access	**noun**	**25-09-017**
access	NN	23-09-017
access	NN-HL	1-01-001
accesses	NNS	1-01-001
accessibility	**NN**	**2-02-002**
accessible	**JJ**	**5-04-005**
accession	**noun**	**1-01-001**
accessions	NNS	1-01-001
accessory	**noun**	**8-06-007**
accessory	NN	1-01-001
accessories	NNS	7-06-007
accident	**noun**	**41-14-029**
accident	NN	33-14-023
accidents	NNS	8-06-007
accidental	**JJ**	**9-05-006**
accidental-war	**JJ**	**1-01-001**
accidentally	**RB**	**6-06-006**
acclaim	**NN**	**4-02-004**
acclaim	**verb**	**5-04-005**
acclaims	VBZ	1-01-001
acclaimed	VBD	1-01-001
acclaimed	VBN	3-03-003
acclamation	**NN**	**1-01-001**
acclimatize	**verb**	**1-01-001**
acclimatized	VBN	1-01-001
accolade	**noun**	**3-03-003**
accolade	NN	2-02-002
accolades	NNS	1-01-001
accommodate	**verb**	**19-10-016**
accommodate	VB	14-09-013
accommodates	VBZ	2-01-001
accommodated	VBN	1-01-001
accommodating	VBG	2-02-002
accommodation	**noun**	**10-05-009**
accommodation	NN	1-01-001
accommodations	NNS	8-05-007
accomodations	NNS	1-01-001
accompaniment	**noun**	**11-05-009**
accompaniment	NN	8-05-006
accompaniments	NNS	3-02-003
accompanist	**noun**	**2-01-002**
accompanist	NN	1-01-001
accompanists	NNS	1-01-001
accompany	**verb**	**63-14-056**
accompany	VB	8-04-007
accompanies	VBZ	1-01-001
accompanied	VBD	8-05-008
accompanied	VBN	29-11-028
accompanying	VBG	17-07-015
accomplice	**noun**	**3-02-003**

Word	Tag	Frequency
accomplice (cont.):		
accomplice	NN	2-02-002
accomplices	NNS	1-01-001
accomplish	**verb**	**71-14-055**
accomplish	VB	23-08-019
accomplish	VB-HL	1-01-001
accomplishes	VBZ	1-01-001
accomplished	VBD	4-04-004
accomplished	VBN	39-12-034
accomplishing	VBG	3-03-003
accomplished	**JJ**	**1-01-001**
accomplishment	**noun**	**17-10-014**
accomplishment	NN	7-06-007
accomplishments	NNS	10-06-008
accord	**NN**	**7-04-006**
accord	**verb**	**9-07-009**
accord	VB	2-02-002
accords	VBZ	1-01-001
accorded	VBN	4-04-004
according	VBG	2-01-002
accordance	**NN**	**20-07-017**
according	**IN**	**128-14-090**
according	**RB**	**10-02-007**
accordingly	**RB**	**31-06-023**
accordion	**NN**	**1-01-001**
accost	**verb**	**3-02-003**
accosted	VBD	1-01-001
accosted	VBN	1-01-001
accosting	VBG	1-01-001
account	**noun**	**120-13-082**
account	NN	87-13-064
aconte	NN	1-01-001
account	NN-HL	2-02-002
account	NN-NC	1-01-001
accounts	NNS	28-10-022
accounts	NNS-HL	1-01-001
account	**verb**	**49-11-039**
account	VB	27-10-024
accounts	VBZ	9-06-008
accounted	VBD	4-03-003
accounted	VBN	1-01-001
accounting	VBG	8-07-008
accountability	**NN**	**4-02-003**
accountable	**JJ**	**1-01-001**
accountant	**noun**	**3-02-003**
accountant	NN	2-02-002
accountants	NNS	1-01-001
accounting	**NN**	**4-02-004**
accouterment	**noun**	**1-01-001**
accouterments	NNS	1-01-001
accredit	**verb**	**2-02-002**
accredited	VBN	2-02-002
accreditation	**NN**	**7-01-001**
accretion	**noun**	**5-03-003**
accretion	NN	3-02-002
accretions	NNS	2-01-001
accrue	**verb**	**11-03-005**
accrues	VBZ	1-01-001
accrued	VBD	1-01-001
accrued	VBN	2-01-001
accruing	VBG	7-02-002
acculturate	**verb**	**1-01-001**
acculturated	VBN	1-01-001
acculturation	**NN**	**1-01-001**
accumulate	**verb**	**18-04-018**
accumulate	VB	3-03-003
accumulates	VBZ	2-02-002
accumulated	VBN	10-04-010
accumulating	VBG	3-02-003
accumulation	**NN**	**11-06-010**
accuracy	**noun**	**36-07-021**
accuracy	NN	35-07-020
Accuracy	NN-TL	1-01-001
accurate	**JJ**	**35-10-033**
accurately	**RB**	**24-08-019**
accusation	**noun**	**6-06-006**
accusation	NN	3-03-003
accusations	NNS	3-03-003
accuse	**verb**	**45-10-035**
accuse	VB	10-06-008
accuses	VBZ	2-01-002
accused	VBD	5-03-005
accused	VBN	20-08-016
accusing	VBG	8-05-007
accusingly	**RB**	**2-02-002**
accustom	**verb**	**15-10-014**
accustomed	VBN	15-10-014
ace	**noun**	**19-04-008**
ace	NN	14-04-006

Word	Tag	Frequency
ace (cont.):		
Ace	NN-TL	1-01-001
aces	NNS	3-02-002
aces	NNS-HL	1-01-001
acetate	**NN**	**7-02-003**
acetone	**NN**	**4-01-002**
acetonemia	**NN**	**3-01-001**
Acey	**NP**	**3-01-001**
Achaean	**prop. noun**	**2-01-001**
Achaeans	NPS	1-01-001
Achaeans'	NPS$	1-01-001
ache	**NN**	**3-02-003**
ache	**verb**	**11-08-010**
ache	VB	1-01-001
aches	VBZ	1-01-001
ached	VBD	3-03-003
aching	VBG	6-05-006
Acheson	**prop. noun**	**3-01-001**
Acheson	NP	2-01-001
Acheson's	NP$	1-01-001
achieve	**verb**	**133-12-099**
achieve	VB	51-09-040
achieves	VBZ	5-05-005
achieved	VBD	12-05-008
achieved	VBN	50-11-046
achieving	VBG	14-07-014
achieving	VBG-HL	1-01-001
achievement	**noun**	**84-10-041**
achievement	NN	57-07-025
Achievement	NN-TL	8-02-003
achievements	NNS	19-09-016
Achilles	**NP**	**1-01-001**
acid	**JJ**	**3-03-003**
acid	**noun**	**17-05-010**
acid	NN	10-03-006
acids	NNS	7-03-005
acid-fast	**JJ**	**1-01-001**
acidity	**NN**	**1-01-001**
acidulous	**JJ**	**1-01-001**
Ackerly	**NP**	**1-01-001**
acknowledge	**verb**	**27-11-026**
acknowledge	VB	12-07-012
acknowledges	VBZ	2-02-002
acknowledged	VBD	3-03-003
acknowledged	VBN	9-06-008
acknowledging	VBG	1-01-001
acknowledgment	**noun**	**5-04-005**
acknowledgment	NN	2-02-002
acknowledgement	NN	2-01-002
acknowledgments	NNS	1-01-001
acolyte	**NN**	**1-01-001**
acorn	**noun**	**1-01-001**
acorns	NNS	1-01-001
acourse	**RB**	**1-01-001**
acoustic	**JJ**	**1-01-001**
acoustical	**adjective**	**3-02-002**
acoustical	JJ	2-02-002
acoustical	JJ-HL	1-01-001
acoustically	**RB**	**1-01-001**
acoustics	**NNS**	**1-01-001**
acquaint	**verb**	**15-10-014**
acquaint	VB	3-03-003
acquainted	VBN	12-08-011
acquaintance	**NN**	**9-05-009**
acquiesce	**verb**	**4-02-003**
acquiesce	VB	3-02-003
acquiesced	VBN	1-01-001
acquiescence	**noun**	**6-03-006**
acquiescence	NN	5-02-005
acquiesence	NN	1-01-001
acquire	**verb**	**66-12-045**
acquire	VB	27-09-024
acquires	VBZ	2-01-002
acquired	VBD	8-06-008
acquired	VBN	18-07-018
acquiring	VBG	11-04-005
acquisition	**noun**	**20-06-009**
acquisition	NN	17-05-006
aquisition	NN	1-01-001
acquisitions	NNS	2-02-002
acquisitiveness	**NN**	**1-01-001**
acquit	**verb**	**2-02-002**
acquitted	VBN	2-02-002
acquittal	**NN**	**2-01-002**
acre	**noun**	**54-11-022**
acre	NN	10-05-006
acres	NNS	42-10-015
Acres	NNS-TL	2-01-002
acre-foot	**noun**	**1-01-001**

Word	Tag	Frequency
acre-foot (cont.):		
acre-feet	NNS	1-01-001
acreage	**NN**	**11-07-009**
acrid	**JJ**	**1-01-001**
acrobacy	**NN**	**1-01-001**
acrobat	**noun**	**1-01-001**
acrobats	NNS	1-01-001
acrobatic	**JJ**	**2-02-002**
acrobatics	**NN**	**1-01-001**
Acropolis	**NP**	**6-01-001**
across	**prep.**	**258-15-166**
across	IN	256-15-164
across	IN-HL	2-02-002
across	**RP**	**24-09-021**
across-the-board	**JJ**	**1-01-001**
acrylic	**NN**	**11-01-001**
ACS	**NP**	**1-01-001**
act	**noun**	**237-14-097**
act	NN	92-13-066
Act	NN	2-01-001
act	NN-HL	1-01-001
Act	NN-TL	114-07-026
acts	NNS	26-08-021
Acts	NNS-TL	2-02-002
act	**verb**	**159-15-100**
act	VB	74-14-053
acts	VBZ	11-04-009
acted	VBD	11-08-010
acted	VBN	7-06-007
acting	VBG	50-12-038
acting	VBG-HL	1-01-001
Acting	VBG-TL	5-03-003
ACTH	**NP**	**1-01-001**
acting	**NN**	**5-03-005**
acting-President	**noun**	**1-01-001**
acting-President	NN	0-00-000
Acting-President	NN-TL	1-01-001
actinometer	**NN**	**1-01-001**
action	**noun**	**359-15-166**
action	NN	289-15-141
action	NN-HL	1-01-001
Action	NN-TL	1-01-001
actions	NNS	68-11-049
action-oriented	**JJ**	**1-01-001**
action-packed	**JJ**	**1-01-001**
activate	**verb**	**8-04-005**
activate	VB	2-02-002
activated	VBN	5-03-003
activating	VBG	1-01-001
activation	**NN**	**7-02-002**
active	**adjective**	**88-12-059**
active	JJ	87-12-059
Active	JJ-TL	1-01-001
active	**noun**	**8-01-001**
actives	NNS	8-01-001
actively	**QL**	**1-01-001**
actively	**adverb**	**11-06-011**
actively	RB	10-06-010
actively	RB-HL	1-01-001
activism	**NN**	**2-02-002**
activity	**noun**	**231-15-110**
activity	NN	114-12-061
activity	NN-HL	2-02-002
activities	NNS	107-13-058
activities	NNS-HL	3-01-002
Activities	NNS-TL	5-03-004
actor	**noun**	**40-08-022**
actor	NN	24-06-014
actor's	NN$	1-01-001
actors	NNS	15-07-012
actor-crooner	**noun**	**1-01-001**
actor-crooner	NN	0-00-000
Actor-Crooner	NN-TL	1-01-001
actress	**noun**	**9-06-007**
actress	NN	5-04-004
Actress	NN-TL	1-01-001
actresses	NNS	3-03-003
actual	**JJ**	**99-10-061**
actuality	**noun**	**10-04-009**
actuality	NN	8-03-007
actualities	NNS	2-01-002
actually	**QL**	**1-01-001**
actually	**RB**	**165-15-128**
actuarial	**JJ**	**1-01-001**
actuarially	**RB**	**1-01-001**
actuate	**verb**	**3-02-003**
actuate	VB	1-01-001
actuated	VBN	2-01-002
acumen	**NN**	**1-01-001**

Word	Tag	Frequency
acute	**JJ**	**13-08-013**
acutely	**QL**	**3-02-003**
acutely	**RB**	**2-02-002**
ad	**foreign**	**7-06-007**
ad	FW-IN	6-06-006
Ad	FW-IN-TL	1-01-001
ad	**noun**	**14-08-010**
ad	NN	4-03-003
ads	NNS	10-07-009
ad-lib	**NN**	**1-01-001**
Ada	**prop. noun**	**21-01-002**
Ada	NP	17-01-002
Ada's	NP$	4-01-001
adage	**NN**	**3-03-003**
adagio	**noun**	**4-01-002**
adagio	NN	2-01-001
Adagio	NN-TL	1-01-001
adagios	NNS	1-01-001
Adair	**prop. noun**	**3-01-001**
Adair	NP	2-01-001
Adair's	NP$	1-01-001
Adam	**prop. noun**	**46-05-009**
Adam	NP	44-05-009
Adam's	NP$	2-02-002
adamant	**JJ**	**5-04-005**
adamantly	**QL**	**1-01-001**
Adame	**NP**	**1-01-001**
Adamo	**NP**	**1-01-001**
Adams	**prop. noun**	**46-09-012**
Adams	NP	42-09-012
Adams'	NP$	3-01-001
Adams's	NP$	1-01-001
Adamson	**NP**	**1-01-001**
adapt	**verb**	**20-08-020**
adapt	VB	5-04-005
adapted	VBD	1-01-001
adapted	VBN	12-06-012
adapting	VBG	2-02-002
adaptable	**JJ**	**2-02-002**
Adaptaplex	**prop. noun**	**1-01-001**
Adaptaplex	NP	0-00-000
Adaptaplex	NP-TL	1-01-001
adaptation	**noun**	**17-09-011**
adaptation	NN	10-07-009
adaptations	NNS	7-03-003
adapter	**noun**	**3-02-002**
adapter	NN	1-01-001
adapters	NNS	2-01-001
adapting	**NN**	**1-01-001**
Adcock	**NP**	**1-01-001**
add	**verb**	**291-15-188**
add	VB	88-12-063
adds	VBZ	10-05-010
added	VBD	81-14-066
added	VBN	90-13-069
added	VBN-HL	1-01-001
adding	VBG	21-10-019
add-on	**JJ**	**1-01-001**
Addabbo	**prop. noun**	**2-01-001**
Addabbo	NP	0-00-000
Addabbo	NP-HL	2-01-001
addict	**noun**	**5-03-004**
addict	NN	0-00-000
Addict	NN-HL	1-01-001
addicts	NNS	4-02-003
addict	**verb**	**3-03-003**
addicted	VBN	3-03-003
addiction	**NN**	**3-03-003**
adding	**NN**	**1-01-001**
Addison	**NP**	**1-01-001**
addition	**noun**	**151-14-103**
addition	NN	141-13-098
addition	NN-HL	1-01-001
additions	NNS	9-05-009
additional	**adjective**	**120-11-085**
additional	JJ	118-11-083
additional	JJ-HL	2-02-002
additionally	**RB**	**5-05-005**
additive	**noun**	**7-02-002**
additive	NN	2-01-001
additive	NN-HL	1-01-001
additives	NNS	4-02-002
addle-brained	**JJ**	**1-01-001**
address	**noun**	**86-12-039**
address	NN	68-10-033
Address	NN-TL	1-01-001
addresses	NNS	16-05-009
addresses	NNS-HL	1-01-001
address	**verb**	**40-11-034**

Word	Tag	Frequency
address (cont.):		
address	VB	8-05-007
addresses	VBZ	4-03-003
addressed	VBD	7-05-007
addressed	VBN	12-05-010
addressing	VBG	9-05-008
addressee	**noun**	**1-01-001**
addressees	NNS	1-01-001
adduce	**VB**	**1-01-001**
Ade	**NP**	**1-01-001**
Adele	**NP**	**2-02-002**
Adelia	**NP**	**5-01-001**
Adelos	**NP**	**1-01-001**
Adenauer	**prop. noun**	**5-02-003**
Adenauer	NP	4-02-003
Adenauer's	NP$	1-01-001
adenoma	**noun**	**1-01-001**
adenomas	NNS	1-01-001
adept	**JJ**	**4-04-004**
adequacy	**NN**	**3-03-003**
adequate	**JJ**	**66-10-052**
adequately	**QL**	**2-02-002**
adequately	**RB**	**14-05-014**
Aderhold	**prop. noun**	**1-01-001**
Aderholds	NPS	1-01-001
adhere	**verb**	**10-05-010**
adhere	VB	4-02-004
adheres	VBZ	1-01-001
adhered	VBD	1-01-001
adhered	VBN	4-03-004
adherence	**NN**	**9-05-008**
adherent	**JJ**	**1-01-001**
adherent	**noun**	**6-04-005**
adherent	NN	1-01-001
adherents	NNS	5-04-004
adhesion	**NN**	**2-02-002**
adhesive	**JJ**	**2-01-001**
adhesive	**noun**	**6-02-005**
adhesive	NN	4-02-003
adhesives	NNS	2-01-002
adieu	**FW-UH**	**1-01-001**
adios	**FW-UH**	**1-01-001**
Adios	**NP**	**10-01-001**
adipic	**JJ**	**1-01-001**
Adirondack	**prop. noun**	**3-03-003**
Adirondack	NP	1-01-001
Adirondack	NP-TL	1-01-001
Adirondacks	NPS	1-01-001
adjacent	**JJ**	**12-05-009**
adjectival	**JJ**	**3-01-002**
adjective	**noun**	**6-04-006**
adjective	NN	2-02-002
adjectives	NNS	4-02-004
adjoin	**verb**	**17-08-015**
adjoins	VBZ	2-02-002
adjoined	VBD	2-02-002
adjoining	VBG	12-07-011
adjoining	VBG-HL	1-01-001
adjourn	**verb**	**4-03-004**
adjourns	VBZ	1-01-001
adjourned	VBD	2-02-002
adjourning	VBG	1-01-001
adjournment	**NN**	**4-03-003**
adjudge	**verb**	**2-02-002**
adjudged	VBN	1-01-001
adjudging	VBG	1-01-001
adjudicate	**VB**	**1-01-001**
adjudication	**NN**	**4-02-002**
adjunct	**noun**	**7-04-004**
adjunct	NN	6-04-004
adjuncts	NNS	1-01-001
adjust	**verb**	**62-14-036**
adjust	VB	16-09-014
adjusts	VBZ	2-02-002
adjusted	VBD	3-02-002
adjusted	VBN	21-08-015
adjusted	VBN-HL	1-01-001
Adjusted	VBN-TL	8-01-001
adjusting	VBG	10-05-006
adjusting	VBG-HL	1-01-001
adjustable	**JJ**	**2-02-002**
adjustment	**noun**	**55-09-029**
adjustment	NN	30-07-019
adjustment	NN-HL	4-01-002
Adjustment	NN-TL	1-01-001
adjustments	NNS	17-07-011
adjustments	NNS-HL	3-01-001
Adlai	**NP**	**7-05-006**
Adler	**NP**	**3-01-001**

Word	Tag	Frequency
Admassy	**prop. noun**	**4-01-001**
Admassy	NP	2-01-001
Admassy's	NP$	2-01-001
administer	**verb**	**22-08-018**
administer	VB	3-02-003
administers	VBZ	1-01-001
administered	VBD	1-01-001
administered	VBN	13-07-010
administering	VBG	4-03-004
administration	**noun**	**169-09-066**
administration	NN	104-09-040
adminstration	NN	1-01-001
Administration	NN-TL	58-07-030
administration's	NN$	3-02-003
Administration's	NN$-TL	3-01-003
administrative	**adjective**	**53-07-031**
administrative	JJ	50-07-028
Administrative	JJ-TL	3-02-003
administratively	**RB**	**1-01-001**
administrator	**noun**	**20-07-017**
administrator	NN	14-06-012
Administrator	NN-TL	1-01-001
administrators	NNS	5-05-005
admirable	**JJ**	**10-05-009**
admirably	**QL**	**1-01-001**
admirably	**RB**	**5-04-005**
admiral	**noun**	**1-01-001**
admirals	NNS	1-01-001
admiralty	**NN**	**1-01-001**
admiration	**NN**	**10-05-007**
admire	**verb**	**32-13-029**
admire	VB	10-08-010
admires	VBZ	1-01-001
admired	VBD	9-06-009
admired	VBN	8-04-006
admiring	VBG	4-04-004
admirer	**noun**	**5-05-005**
admirer	NN	3-03-003
admirers	NNS	2-02-002
admiringly	**RB**	**1-01-001**
admissible	**JJ**	**9-02-002**
admission	**noun**	**36-08-020**
admission	NN	33-08-019
admissions	NNS	2-02-002
Admissions	NNS-TL	1-01-001
admit	**verb**	**91-15-065**
admit	VB	37-12-033
admits	VBZ	2-01-002
admitted	VBD	25-10-022
admitted	VBN	19-08-015
admitting	VBG	8-05-008
admittance	**NN**	**1-01-001**
admittedly	**RB**	**3-03-003**
admix	**verb**	**1-01-001**
admixed	VBN	1-01-001
admonish	**verb**	**3-03-003**
admonished	VBD	2-02-002
admonishing	VBG	1-01-001
admonishment	**noun**	**1-01-001**
admonishments	NNS	1-01-001
admonition	**noun**	**4-02-004**
admonition	NN	1-01-001
admonitions	NNS	3-02-003
Adnan	**NP**	**1-01-001**
ado	**noun**	**4-01-001**
ado	NN	0-00-000
Ado	NN-TL	4-01-001
adobe	**NN**	**2-01-001**
adolescence	**NN**	**18-03-003**
adolescent	**JJ**	**3-02-002**
adolescent	**noun**	**19-03-005**
adolescent	NN	9-02-003
adolescent's	NN$	3-01-001
adolescents	NNS	7-02-003
Adolf	**prop. noun**	**4-01-002**
Adolf	NP	3-01-001
Adolf	NP-TL	1-01-001
Adolphus	**NP**	**1-01-001**
Adoniram	**NP**	**6-01-001**
Adonis	**NP**	**1-01-001**
adopt	**verb**	**71-11-052**
adopt	VB	13-06-012
adopts	VBZ	2-02-002
adopted	VBD	11-04-010
adopted	VBN	33-09-027
adopted	VBN-HL	1-01-001
adopting	VBG	11-06-010
adoption	**NN**	**11-05-009**
adorable	**JJ**	**3-02-003**

Word	Tag	Frequency
adore	**verb**	**5-02-004**
adore	VB	2-01-002
adores	VBZ	1-01-001
adored	VBD	1-01-001
adored	VBN	1-01-001
adorn	**verb**	**3-03-003**
adorn	VB	1-01-001
adorns	VBZ	1-01-001
adorned	VBN	1-01-001
Adrar	**NP**	**1-01-001**
adrenal	**JJ**	**1-01-001**
adrenal	**NN**	**1-01-001**
Adrian	**NP**	**4-02-002**
Adrianople	**NP**	**1-01-001**
Adriatic	**NP**	**3-01-001**
Adrien	**NP**	**2-01-001**
adrift	**RB**	**1-01-001**
adroit	**JJ**	**1-01-001**
adroitness	**NN**	**1-01-001**
adsorb	**verb**	**4-01-001**
adsorbs	VBZ	1-01-001
adsorbed	VBN	3-01-001
adulation	**NN**	**1-01-001**
adult	**JJ**	**1-01-001**
adult	**noun**	**47-10-027**
adult	NN	24-07-015
adults	NNS	23-09-018
adulterate	**verb**	**1-01-001**
adulterated	VBN	1-01-001
adulterer	**noun**	**2-01-001**
adulterers	NNS	2-01-001
adulterous	**JJ**	**1-01-001**
adultery	**noun**	**3-03-003**
adultery	NN	2-02-002
Adultery	NN-TL	1-01-001
adulthood	**NN**	**3-02-002**
advance	**JJ**	**1-01-001**
advance	**noun**	**60-11-043**
advance	NN	41-11-030
Advance	NN-TL	2-01-001
advances	NNS	17-08-014
advance	**verb**	**71-12-053**
advance	VB	15-08-014
advances	VBZ	1-01-001
advanced	VBD	9-05-008
advanced	VBN	42-09-031
advancing	VBG	4-04-004
advanced	**adjective**	**2-02-002**
advanced	JJ	0-00-000
Advanced	JJ-TL	2-02-002
advancement	**noun**	**11-05-010**
advancement	NN	9-05-008
Advancement	NN-TL	1-01-001
advancements	NNS	1-01-001
advantage	**noun**	**101-13-067**
advantage	NN	73-12-052
advantages	NNS	26-09-019
advantages	NNS-HL	2-02-002
advantageous	**JJ**	**5-04-005**
advantageously	**RB**	**1-01-001**
advent	**NN**	**5-03-005**
Adventist	**prop. noun**	**2-01-002**
Adventists	NPS	1-01-001
Adventists'	NPS$	1-01-001
adventitious	**JJ**	**1-01-001**
adventure	**noun**	**27-11-025**
adventure	NN	13-05-011
adventures	NNS	12-09-012
Adventures	NNS-TL	2-02-002
adventure	**verb**	**2-02-002**
adventure	VB	1-01-001
adventuring	VBG	1-01-001
adventurer	**noun**	**1-01-001**
adventurers	NNS	1-01-001
adventurous	**JJ**	**5-03-004**
adverb	**noun**	**3-02-003**
adverb	NN	1-01-001
adverbs	NNS	2-02-002
adverbial	**JJ**	**2-01-002**
adversary	**noun**	**8-05-007**
adversary	NN	5-04-005
adversaries	NNS	3-03-003
adverse	**JJ**	**11-06-010**
adversely	**RB**	**3-02-003**
adversity	**NN**	**2-02-002**
advertise	**verb**	**49-13-029**
advertise	VB	3-03-003
advertises	VBZ	1-01-001
advertised	VBD	3-03-003

Word	Tag	Frequency
advertise (cont.):		
advertised	VBN	6-03-004
advertising	VBG	34-11-021
advertising	VBG-HL	2-02-002
advertisement	**noun**	**5-04-004**
advertisement	NN	2-02-002
advertisements	NNS	3-02-002
advertiser	**noun**	**6-02-002**
advertiser	NN	0-00-000
Advertiser	NN-TL	1-01-001
advertisers	NNS	5-01-001
advertising	**NN**	**14-07-009**
advertising-conscious	**JJ**	**1-01-001**
advice	**noun**	**52-14-041**
advice	NN	50-14-040
advice	NN-HL	1-01-001
Advice	NN-TL	1-01-001
advisability	**NN**	**4-03-003**
advisable	**JJ**	**1-01-001**
advise	**verb**	**47-12-041**
advise	VB	8-06-008
Advise	VB-TL	1-01-001
advises	VBZ	2-02-002
advised	VBD	17-08-015
advised	VBN	16-08-016
advising	VBG	3-03-003
advisedly	**RB**	**1-01-001**
advisement	**NN**	**2-01-001**
adviser	**noun**	**24-06-018**
adviser	NN	6-03-005
advisor	NN	1-01-001
advisers	NNS	12-04-011
advisors	NNS	5-02-003
advisory	**adjective**	**22-07-012**
advisory	JJ	8-06-007
Advisory	JJ-TL	14-03-006
advisory	**NN**	**2-01-002**
advocacy	**NN**	**3-02-002**
advocate	**noun**	**12-06-008**
advocate	NN	5-03-005
advocate	NN-HL	1-01-001
Advocate	NN-TL	5-01-001
advocates	NNS	1-01-001
advocate	**verb**	**14-06-014**
advocate	VB	4-02-004
advocated	VBD	2-01-002
advocated	VBN	2-02-002
advocating	VBG	6-05-006
Aegean	**JJ**	**6-01-001**
Aegean	**prop. noun**	**9-02-002**
Aegean	NP	8-02-002
Aegean	NP-HL	1-01-001
aegis	**NN**	**1-01-001**
aeon	**NN**	**1-01-001**
aerate	**verb**	**11-02-002**
aerate	VB	1-01-001
aerates	VBZ	1-01-001
aerated	VBN	9-01-001
aeration	**NN**	**7-02-002**
aerator	**NN**	**11-01-001**
aerial	**JJ**	**8-03-006**
aerial	**noun**	**1-01-001**
aerials	NNS	1-01-001
Aerobacter	**NP**	**1-01-001**
aerobic	**JJ**	**1-01-001**
aerodynamic	**JJ**	**1-01-001**
aerogenes	**NP**	**1-01-001**
aeronautical	**JJ**	**1-01-001**
aeronautics	**noun**	**2-02-002**
aeronautics	NN	0-00-000
Aeronautics	NN-TL	2-02-002
aerosol	**noun**	**11-01-001**
aerosol	NN	7-01-001
areosol	NN	1-01-001
aerosols	NNS	3-01-001
aerosolize	**verb**	**3-01-001**
aerosolized	VBN	3-01-001
aerospace	**noun**	**4-01-001**
aerospace	NN	0-00-000
Aerospace	NN-TL	4-01-001
Aeschbacher	**prop. noun**	**2-01-001**
Aeschbacher	NP	1-01-001
Aeschbacher's	NP$	1-01-001
Aeschylus	**NP**	**4-02-002**
aesthete	**noun**	**1-01-001**
aesthetes	NNS	1-01-001
aesthetic	**JJ**	**24-04-017**
aesthetic	**NN**	**2-01-001**
aeternitatis	**FW-NN$**	**1-01-001**

Word	Tag	Frequency
afar	**adv. noun**	**2-02-002**
afar	RN	1-01-001
afar	RN-HL	1-01-001
affable	**JJ**	**1-01-001**
affair	**noun**	**117-13-084**
affair	NN	33-12-030
affairs	NNS	62-11-052
Affairs	NNS-TL	22-06-010
affaire	**foreign**	**2-02-002**
affaire	FW-NN	0-00-000
Affaire	FW-NN-TL	1-01-001
affaires	FW-NNS	0-00-000
Affaires	FW-NNS-TL	1-01-001
affect	**verb**	**93-13-070**
affect	VB	33-10-029
Affect	VB	1-01-001
affects	VBZ	18-10-015
affected	VBD	4-03-004
affected	VBN	32-09-027
affecting	VBG	5-04-005
affectation	**NN**	**1-01-001**
affectingly	**RB**	**1-01-001**
affection	**noun**	**22-10-022**
affection	NN	18-09-018
affections	NNS	4-03-004
affectionate	**JJ**	**6-05-006**
affectionately	**RB**	**3-03-003**
afferent	**JJ**	**1-01-001**
affiance	**verb**	**1-01-001**
affianced	VBN	1-01-001
affidavit	**noun**	**2-02-002**
affidavits	NNS	2-02-002
affiliate	**noun**	**1-01-001**
affiliates	NNS	1-01-001
affiliate	**verb**	**7-07-007**
affiliated	VBN	7-07-007
affiliation	**noun**	**9-05-008**
affiliation	NN	4-02-004
affiliations	NNS	5-04-005
affinity	**noun**	**6-04-006**
affinity	NN	5-04-005
affinities	NNS	1-01-001
affirm	**verb**	**21-08-015**
affirm	VB	12-06-008
affirms	VBZ	1-01-001
affirmed	VBD	4-04-004
affirmed	VBN	2-02-002
affirming	VBG	2-02-002
affirmation	**noun**	**5-04-005**
affirmation	NN	4-03-004
affirmations	NNS	1-01-001
affirmative	**JJ**	**4-02-003**
affirmatively	**RB**	**1-01-001**
affix	**verb**	**15-04-004**
affix	VB	1-01-001
affixed	VBN	14-03-003
afflict	**verb**	**8-03-008**
afflicted	VBN	8-03-008
affliction	**noun**	**2-02-002**
affliction	NN	1-01-001
afflictions	NNS	1-01-001
affluence	**NN**	**4-03-004**
affluent	**JJ**	**2-02-002**
afford	**verb**	**58-12-050**
afford	VB	40-12-034
affords	VBZ	5-03-005
afforded	VBD	4-03-004
afforded	VBN	7-05-007
affording	VBG	2-02-002
affront	**NN**	**2-01-001**
affront	**verb**	**2-02-002**
affronted	VBN	1-01-001
affronting	VBG	1-01-001
affy	**verb**	**1-01-001**
affied	VBD	1-01-001
afghan	**NN**	**1-01-001**
Afghan	**prop. noun**	**3-02-002**
Afghan	NP	2-01-001
Afghans	NPS	1-01-001
aficionado	**NN**	**1-01-001**
afield	**RB**	**1-01-001**
afire	**JJ**	**1-01-001**
aflame	**JJ**	**3-03-003**
afloat	**RB**	**7-04-005**
afoot	**RB**	**1-01-001**
aforementioned	**JJ**	**2-02-002**
aforesaid	**JJ**	**1-01-001**
aforesaid	**RB**	**1-01-001**
aforethought	**RB**	**1-01-001**

Word	Tag	Frequency
afraid	**adjective**	**57-12-043**
afraid	JJ	56-12-042
afraid	JJ-NC	1-01-001
Afranio	**NP**	**1-01-001**
afresh	**RB**	**2-02-002**
Africa	**prop. noun**	**45-10-028**
Africa	NP	31-10-023
Africa	NP-HL	1-01-001
Africa	NP-TL	13-04-010
African	**adjective**	**24-11-017**
African	JJ	23-11-017
African	JJ-TL	1-01-001
African	**prop. noun**	**8-05-007**
African	NP	0-00-000
African	NP-TL	4-03-004
Africans	NPS	4-03-003
Afrika	**foreign**	**1-01-001**
Afrika	FW-NP	0-00-000
Afrika	FW-NP-TL	1-01-001
Afrique	**foreign**	**1-01-001**
Afrique	FW-NP	0-00-000
Afrique	FW-NP-TL	1-01-001
Afro-Asian	**JJ**	**4-01-001**
Afro-Cuban	**JJ**	**1-01-001**
aft	**JJ**	**2-01-001**
aft	**RB**	**3-03-003**
after	**sub. conj.**	**360-15-205**
after	CS	358-15-204
aftuh	CS	1-01-001
After	CS-TL	1-01-001
after	**prep.**	**699-15-319**
after	IN	697-15-319
After	IN-TL	1-01-001
after	IN-TL	1-01-001
after	**RB**	**11-07-011**
after-duty	**JJ**	**1-01-001**
after-effect	**noun**	**1-01-001**
after-effects	NNS	1-01-001
after-hours	**JJ**	**1-01-001**
after-school	**JJ**	**1-01-001**
aftermath	**NN**	**4-03-004**
afternoon	**noun**	**122-12-083**
afternoon	NN	106-12-075
afternoon's	NN$	3-03-003
afternoons	NNS	13-09-011
afterward	**RB**	**16-07-014**
afterwards	**RB**	**14-09-014**
again	**adverb**	**580-15-287**
again	RB	572-15-286
agayne	RB	1-01-001
agin	RB	2-02-002
again	RB-HL	3-02-003
Again	RB-TL	2-01-001
against	**prep.**	**625-15-268**
against	IN	622-15-267
against	IN-HL	1-01-001
against	IN-TL	2-01-001
against	**RB**	**2-02-002**
Agamemnon	**prop. noun**	**3-02-002**
Agamemnon	NP	1-01-001
Agamemnon	NP-TL	1-01-001
Agamemnon's	NP$	1-01-001
agate	**noun**	**1-01-001**
agates	NNS	1-01-001
Agatha	**NP**	**2-01-002**
age	**FW-NN**	**1-01-001**
age	**noun**	**275-15-140**
age	NN	214-15-123
Age	NN-TL	10-04-005
ages	NNS	38-10-024
Ages	NNS-TL	13-05-010
age	**verb**	**24-09-018**
age	VB	2-02-002
aged	VBN	18-08-013
aging	VBG	4-04-004
age-and-sex	**NN**	**2-01-001**
age-old	**JJ**	**5-04-004**
aged-care	**NN**	**1-01-001**
Agee	**NP**	**1-01-001**
ageless	**JJ**	**2-02-002**
agency	**noun**	**118-11-060**
agency	NN	48-10-030
Agency	NN-TL	7-04-006
Agency	NN-TL-HL	1-01-001
agencies	NNS	61-08-034
Agencies	NNS-TL	1-01-001
agenda	**noun**	**5-04-005**
agenda	NN	4-03-004
agenda	NNS	1-01-001
agent	**noun**	**84-12-048**
agent	NN	44-09-026
agent's	NN$	1-01-001
agents	NNS	39-08-026
Aggie	**prop. noun**	**4-02-002**
Aggie	NP	2-01-001
Aggies	NPS	2-01-001
agglomerate	**VB**	**2-01-001**
agglomeration	**NN**	**3-01-002**
agglutinate	**verb**	**1-01-001**
agglutinating	VBG	1-01-001
agglutination	**NN**	**4-01-001**
agglutinin	**noun**	**8-01-001**
agglutinin	NN	6-01-001
agglutinins	NNS	2-01-001
aggravate	**verb**	**5-05-005**
aggravate	VB	1-01-001
aggravates	VBZ	1-01-001
aggravated	VBD	1-01-001
aggravated	VBN	2-02-002
aggregate	**JJ**	**6-03-005**
aggregate	**NN**	**2-01-002**
aggregation	**noun**	**2-01-001**
aggregation	NN	1-01-001
aggregations	NNS	1-01-001
aggression	**noun**	**13-07-012**
aggression	NN	10-07-010
aggressions	NNS	3-01-002
aggressive	**JJ**	**17-09-014**
aggressively	**RB**	**2-02-002**
aggressiveness	**NN**	**5-02-003**
aggressor	**NN**	**2-02-002**
aggrieve	**verb**	**3-02-002**
aggrieved	VBN	3-02-002
aghast	**JJ**	**1-01-001**
agile	**JJ**	**2-02-002**
agilely	**RB**	**1-01-001**
agility	**NN**	**3-02-003**
agitate	**verb**	**3-03-003**
agitate	VB	1-01-001
agitated	VBN	1-01-001
agitating	VBG	1-01-001
agitation	**NN**	**6-06-006**
agitator	**noun**	**2-02-002**
agitator	NN	1-01-001
agitators	NNS	1-01-001
agleam	**JJ**	**1-01-001**
Agnes	**NP**	**1-01-001**
Agnese	**prop. noun**	**6-02-002**
Agnese	NP	4-01-001
Agnese	NP-TL	2-01-001
agnomen	**NN**	**1-01-001**
agnostic	**noun**	**1-01-001**
agnostics	NNS	1-01-001
ago	**RB**	**246-15-163**
Agoeng	**NP**	**1-01-001**
Agonale	**NP**	**1-01-001**
Agone	**prop. noun**	**2-01-001**
Agone	NP	0-00-000
Agone	NP-TL	2-01-001
agonize	**verb**	**3-02-003**
agonizes	VBZ	2-02-002
agonized	VBN	1-01-001
agonizing	**JJ**	**3-03-003**
agony	**noun**	**10-07-010**
agony	NN	9-06-009
agonies	NNS	1-01-001
agrarian	**JJ**	**6-01-002**
agrarian	**NN**	**2-01-001**
agree	**verb**	**150-15-093**
agree	VB	51-12-040
agrees	VBZ	11-06-009
agreed	VBD	52-12-045
agreed	VBN	29-10-020
agreeing	VBG	7-05-006
agreeable	**adjective**	**11-05-007**
agreeable	JJ	8-05-007
Agreeable	JJ-TL	3-01-001
agreeableness	**NN**	**1-01-001**
agreeably	**RB**	**1-01-001**
agreed-on	**JJ**	**1-01-001**
agreed-upon	**JJ**	**1-01-001**
agreement	**noun**	**121-11-051**
agreement	NN	79-10-044
agreement	NN-HL	1-01-001
Agreement	NN-TL	26-02-003
agreements	NNS	15-07-011
agricolas	**FW-NNS**	**1-01-001**
agricultural	**adjective**	**38-07-018**

Word	Tag	Frequency
agricultural (cont.):		
agricultural	JJ	35-07-018
Agricultural	JJ-TL	3-02-002
agriculturally	**RB**	**1-01-001**
agriculture	**noun**	**24-07-019**
agriculture	NN	13-06-012
Agriculture	NN-TL	10-05-008
agriculture's	NN$	0-00-000
Agriculture's	NN$-TL	1-01-001
Agrippa	**NP**	**1-01-001**
Agrobacterium	**NP**	**1-01-001**
ague	**NN**	**1-01-001**
ah	**UH**	**14-07-013**
ahah	**exclam.**	**2-02-002**
ahah	UH	1-01-001
ahah-	UH	1-01-001
ahead	**adverb**	**109-15-081**
ahead	RB	108-15-081
ahead	RB-HL	1-01-001
ahem	**UH**	**1-01-001**
Ahmad	**prop. noun**	**3-02-002**
Ahmad	NP	1-01-001
Ahmad's	NP$	2-02-002
Ahmet	**prop. noun**	**3-01-001**
Ahmet	NP	1-01-001
Ahmet	NP-TL	2-01-001
Ahmiri	**NP**	**1-01-001**
Ahrens	**NP**	**1-01-001**
Ai	**prop. noun**	**1-01-001**
Ai	NP	0-00-000
Ai	NP-TL	1-01-001
AIA	**NP**	**1-01-001**
aid	**noun**	**129-10-063**
aid	NN	101-10-057
aid	NN-HL	4-02-002
Aid	NN-TL	3-02-002
aids	NNS	20-07-008
aids	NNS-HL	1-01-001
aid	**verb**	**46-10-036**
aid	VB	22-06-018
aids	VBZ	6-01-001
aided	VBD	2-02-002
aided	VBN	9-07-009
aiding	VBG	6-03-006
Aiding	VBG-TL	1-01-001
aid-to-education	**NN**	**1-01-001**
Aida	**NP**	**1-01-001**
aide	**noun**	**13-07-011**
aide	NN	8-06-007
Aide	NN-TL	1-01-001
aides	NNS	4-02-003
aide-de-camp	**FW-NN**	**1-01-001**
Aiken	**prop. noun**	**1-01-001**
Aiken	NP	0-00-000
Aiken	NP-TL	1-01-001
Aikin	**NP**	**1-01-001**
ail	**verb**	**2-02-002**
ailing	VBG	2-02-002
aileron	**noun**	**1-01-001**
ailerons	NNS	1-01-001
Ailey	**prop. noun**	**4-01-001**
Ailey	NP	2-01-001
Ailey's	NP$	2-01-001
ailment	**noun**	**10-04-005**
ailment	NN	4-03-003
ailments	NNS	6-02-003
aim	**noun**	**40-10-036**
aim	NN	27-09-025
aims	NNS	13-06-012
aim	**verb**	**42-11-034**
aim	VB	10-05-008
aims	VBZ	3-02-002
aimed	VBD	10-05-009
aimed	VBN	14-07-013
aiming	VBG	5-02-005
aimless	**JJ**	**5-05-005**
aimlessly	**RB**	**1-01-001**
AIMO	**NP**	**1-01-001**
Ainsley	**NP**	**1-01-001**
Ainsworth	**NP**	**1-01-001**
Ainu	**prop. noun**	**2-01-001**
Ainu	NP	1-01-001
Ainus	NPS	1-01-001
air	**noun**	**260-15-131**
air	NN	216-15-113
air	NN-HL	2-02-002
Air	NN-TL	39-09-021
airs	NNS	3-02-003
air	**verb**	**2-02-002**
air (cont.):		
aired	VBD	1-01-001
aired	VBN	1-01-001
air-cell	**NN**	**1-01-001**
air-conditioned	**JJ**	**1-01-001**
air-conditioning	**NN**	**2-02-002**
air-drift	**noun**	**1-01-001**
air-drifts	NNS	1-01-001
air-to-surface	**JJ**	**1-01-001**
airborne	**JJ**	**7-04-007**
aircraft	**noun**	**71-10-019**
aircraft	NN	59-10-015
Aircraft	NN-TL	5-04-004
aircraft's	NN$	0-00-000
Aircraft's	NN$-TL	1-01-001
aircraft	NNS	6-03-003
airdrop	**noun**	**1-01-001**
airdrops	NNS	1-01-001
Airedale	**prop. noun**	**1-01-001**
Airedale	NP	0-00-000
Airedale	NP-TL	1-01-001
airfield	**noun**	**11-03-004**
airfield	NN	5-03-004
airfields	NNS	6-02-002
airflow	**NN**	**1-01-001**
airframe	**noun**	**2-02-002**
airframe	NN	1-01-001
air-frame	NN	1-01-001
airily	**RB**	**2-02-002**
airless	**JJ**	**2-02-002**
airlift	**NN**	**1-01-001**
airline	**noun**	**8-04-006**
airline	NN	2-02-002
airline's	NN$	0-00-000
Airline's	NN$-TL	1-01-001
airlines	NNS	2-02-002
Airlines	NNS-TL	3-01-001
airlock	**NN**	**1-01-001**
airmail	**NN**	**4-01-001**
airman	**noun**	**2-02-002**
airman's	NN$	1-01-001
airmen	NNS	1-01-001
Airpark	**NP**	**1-01-001**
airplane	**noun**	**21-12-014**
airplane	NN	11-08-009
airplanes	NNS	10-05-006
airport	**noun**	**23-09-014**
airport	NN	11-06-008
Airport	NN-TL	8-04-005
airports	NNS	4-02-003
airspeed	**NN**	**1-01-001**
airstrip	**noun**	**3-03-003**
airstrip	NN	2-02-002
airstrips	NNS	1-01-001
airway	**noun**	**6-03-003**
airways	NNS	4-01-001
Airways	NNS-TL	2-02-002
airy	**JJ**	**7-05-007**
aisle	**NN**	**6-05-005**
ajar	**RB**	**2-01-002**
akin	**JJ**	**10-07-010**
Akita	**NP**	**1-01-001**
Akron	**NP**	**1-01-001**
aku	**NN**	**1-01-001**
al	**foreign**	**1-01-001**
al	FW-AT	0-00-000
Al	FW-AT-HL	1-01-001
Al	**prop. noun**	**16-05-009**
Al	NP	14-05-009
Al's	NP$	2-02-002
Alabama	**prop. noun**	**29-08-016**
Alabama	NP	15-07-011
Alabama	NP-TL	5-03-004
Ala.	NP	6-01-004
Ala.	NP-HL	1-01-001
Alabamas	NPS	2-01-001
Alabaman	**prop. noun**	**2-01-001**
Alabaman	NP	0-00-000
Alabamian	NP	1-01-001
Alabamans	NPS	1-01-001
alabaster	**NN**	**3-02-003**
Alacrity	**NP**	**2-01-001**
Alai	**prop. noun**	**1-01-001**
Alai	NP	0-00-000
Alai	NP-TL	1-01-001
Alain	**NP**	**1-01-001**
Alamein	**prop. noun**	**1-01-001**
Alamein	NP	0-00-000
Alamein	NP-TL	1-01-001

Word	Tag	Frequency
Alamo	**NP**	**1-01-001**
Alamogordo	**NP**	**1-01-001**
Alan	**NP**	**5-02-003**
alarm	**noun**	**15-09-013**
alarm	NN	14-08-012
alarms	NNS	1-01-001
alarm	**verb**	**11-08-011**
alarm	VB	2-02-002
alarmed	VBN	8-06-008
alarming	VBG	1-01-001
alarmingly	**RB**	**2-02-002**
alarmist	**JJ**	**1-01-001**
alas	**UH**	**10-08-010**
Alaska	**prop. noun**	**22-05-008**
Alaska	NP	21-05-008
Alaska	NP-HL	1-01-001
Alastor	**prop. noun**	**4-01-001**
Alastor	NP	0-00-000
Alastor	NP-TL	4-01-001
Alba	**NP**	**1-01-001**
Albacore	**NP**	**1-01-001**
Albania	**NP**	**3-02-002**
Albanian	**JJ**	**2-01-001**
Albanian	**prop. noun**	**2-01-001**
Albanians	NPS	2-01-001
Albany	**prop. noun**	**11-07-009**
Albany	NP	6-04-005
Albany	NP-TL	5-04-004
albeit	**CS**	**2-02-002**
Albers	**NP**	**1-01-001**
Albert	**prop. noun**	**29-08-024**
Albert	NP	27-07-022
Albert	NP-TL	2-02-002
Alberto	**NP**	**2-01-001**
albicans	**NP**	**1-01-001**
Albright	**prop. noun**	**6-01-001**
Albright	NP	3-01-001
Albright's	NP$	2-01-001
Albrights'	NPS$	1-01-001
album	**noun**	**8-03-005**
album	NN	6-02-004
albums	NNS	2-01-001
albumin	**NN**	**10-01-002**
alchemy	**NN**	**1-01-001**
Alcibiades	**NP**	**1-01-001**
Alcinous	**prop. noun**	**1-01-001**
Alcinous'	NP$	1-01-001
alcohol	**noun**	**15-05-007**
alcohol	NN	13-05-007
alcohols	NNS	2-01-001
alcoholic	**JJ**	**3-03-003**
alcoholic	**noun**	**4-03-003**
alcoholics	NNS	4-03-003
alcoholism	**NN**	**1-01-001**
Alcorn	**NP**	**2-02-002**
Alcott	**prop. noun**	**1-01-001**
Alcott's	NP$	1-01-001
alcove	**noun**	**5-01-001**
alcoves	NNS	5-01-001
Alden	**NP**	**2-01-001**
alderman	**noun**	**3-02-002**
alderman	NN	1-01-001
aldermen	NNS	1-01-001
Aldermen	NNS	1-01-001
Aldo	**NP**	**1-01-001**
Aldridge	**NP**	**1-01-001**
ale	**NN**	**1-01-001**
Alec	**prop. noun**	**30-01-001**
Alec	NP	25-01-001
Alec's	NP$	5-01-001
aleck	**NN**	**2-02-002**
Alemagna	**NP**	**1-01-001**
alert	**JJ**	**25-10-024**
alert	**NN**	**3-02-003**
alert	**verb**	**13-10-013**
alert	VB	5-05-005
alerts	VBZ	1-01-001
alerted	VBD	1-01-001
alerted	VBN	2-02-002
alerting	VBG	4-03-004
alertly	**RB**	**1-01-001**
alertness	**NN**	**2-02-002**
Alessio	**NP**	**1-01-001**
Alex	**prop. noun**	**40-03-004**
Alex	NP	30-03-004
Alex's	NP$	10-01-001
Alexander	**prop. noun**	**48-10-022**
Alexander	NP	44-10-020
Alexander	NP-TL	1-01-001
Alexander (cont.):		
Alexander's	NP$	3-02-002
Alexandre	**NP**	**2-01-001**
Alexandria	**prop. noun**	**4-03-003**
Alexandria	NP	3-02-002
Alexandria	NP-TL	1-01-001
Alexei	**NP**	**1-01-001**
Alexeyeva	**NP**	**1-01-001**
Alexis	**NP**	**2-01-001**
Alf	**NP**	**2-01-001**
Alfa	**NP**	**1-01-001**
Alfonso	**NP**	**1-01-001**
Alfred	**prop. noun**	**55-05-013**
Alfred	NP	52-05-013
Alfred's	NP$	3-01-001
Alfredo	**NP**	**3-02-002**
alfresco	**NN**	**2-02-002**
alga	**noun**	**7-02-002**
algae	NNS	7-02-002
algaecide	**NN**	**1-01-001**
algebra	**NN**	**2-01-001**
algebraic	**JJ**	**1-01-001**
algebraically	**RB**	**3-01-001**
Alger	**NP**	**1-01-001**
Algeria	**NP**	**2-01-001**
Algerian	**adjective**	**4-02-003**
Algerian	JJ	1-01-001
Algerian	JJ-TL	3-02-002
Algerian	**NP**	**1-01-001**
alginate	**noun**	**1-01-001**
alginates	NNS	1-01-001
Algol	**prop. noun**	**3-01-001**
Algol	NP	0-00-000
Algol	NP-TL	3-01-001
algorithm	**NN**	**1-01-001**
Aliah	**NP**	**1-01-001**
alias	**NN**	**1-01-001**
alibi	**noun**	**9-04-005**
alibi	NN	8-03-004
alibis	NNS	1-01-001
Alice	**NP**	**14-05-006**
Alicia	**NP**	**4-01-001**
alien	**JJ**	**14-08-013**
alien	**noun**	**5-02-003**
alien	NN	2-02-002
aliens	NNS	2-02-002
aliens	NNS-HL	1-01-001
alienate	**verb**	**9-04-009**
alienate	VB	2-02-002
alienates	VBZ	1-01-001
alienated	VBN	6-04-006
alienation	**noun**	**22-02-004**
alienation	NN	20-02-004
alienation	NN-NC	2-01-001
Alienus	**prop. noun**	**1-01-001**
Alienus	NP	0-00-000
Alienus	NP-TL	1-01-001
alight	**JJ**	**2-02-002**
alight	**VB**	**1-01-001**
align	**verb**	**9-05-005**
align	VB	2-02-002
aligned	VBN	6-02-002
aligning	VBG	1-01-001
alignment	**noun**	**5-02-004**
alignment	NN	4-02-004
alignments	NNS	1-01-001
alike	**JJ**	**6-04-006**
alike	**RB**	**14-08-014**
alimony	**NN**	**2-02-002**
aliquot	**noun**	**1-01-001**
aliquots	NNS	1-01-001
Alison	**NP**	**1-01-001**
alius	**foreign**	**10-05-007**
alia	FW-NNS	1-01-001
al	FW-NNS	8-03-005
al.	FW-NNS	1-01-001
alive	**JJ**	**57-13-048**
Alix	**prop. noun**	**3-01-001**
Alix	NP	2-01-001
Alix's	NP$	1-01-001
alizarin	**NN**	**1-01-001**
alkali	**noun**	**6-02-003**
alkali	NN	4-01-002
alkalis	NNS	2-01-001
alkaline	**JJ**	**2-01-002**
alkaloid	**noun**	**1-01-001**
alkaloids	NNS	1-01-001
alkylarysulfonate	**noun**	**1-01-001**
alkylarysulfonate	NN	0-00-000

Word	Tag	Frequency
alkylarysulfonate (cont.):		
alkylarysulfonate	NN-HL	1-01-001
alkylbenzenesulfonate	**noun**	**1-01-001**
alkylbenzenesulfonates	NNS	1-01-001
all	**pre-quant.**	**2758-15-489**
all	ABN	2746-15-489
all	ABN-HL	4-03-004
all	ABN-NC	1-01-001
All	ABN-TL	7-03-004
all	**qualifier**	**242-15-154**
all	QL	241-15-154
aw	QL	1-01-001
all	**RB**	**2-02-002**
all-American	**JJ**	**2-01-002**
all-American-boy	**JJ**	**1-01-001**
all-automatic	**JJ**	**1-01-001**
all-college	**JJ**	**1-01-001**
all-consuming	**JJ**	**1-01-001**
all-county	**JJ**	**1-01-001**
all-female	**JJ**	**1-01-001**
all-important	**JJ**	**5-03-004**
all-inclusive	**JJ**	**1-01-001**
all-knowing	**JJ**	**1-01-001**
all-lesbian	**JJ**	**1-01-001**
all-married	**JJ**	**1-01-001**
all-Negro	**JJ**	**6-01-001**
all-night	**JJ**	**1-01-001**
all-out	**JJ**	**6-04-005**
all-over	**JJ**	**1-01-001**
all-pervading	**JJ**	**1-01-001**
all-powerful	**JJ**	**2-01-002**
all-purpose	**JJ**	**1-01-001**
all-round	**JJ**	**1-01-001**
all-something-or-the-other	**JJ**	**1-01-001**
all-star	**adjective**	**1-01-001**
all-star	JJ	0-00-000
All-Star	JJ-TL	1-01-001
all-time	**JJ**	**3-03-003**
all-too-brief	**JJ**	**1-01-001**
all-victorious	**JJ**	**1-01-001**
all-weather	**JJ**	**2-02-002**
all-white	**JJ**	**5-03-003**
all-woman	**JJ**	**1-01-001**
Alla	**NP**	**2-02-002**
Allah	**NP**	**1-01-001**
Allan	**NP**	**4-03-004**
allay	**VB**	**1-01-001**
allegation	**noun**	**5-03-004**
allegations	NNS	5-03-004
allege	**verb**	**14-06-012**
allege	VB	1-01-001
alleged	VBD	2-01-002
alleged	VBN	8-05-006
alleging	VBG	3-03-003
allegedly	**QL**	**2-02-002**
allegedly	**RB**	**2-02-002**
Allegheny	**prop. noun**	**2-02-002**
Allegheny	NP	0-00-000
Allegheny	NP-TL	1-01-001
Alleghenies	NPS	1-01-001
allegiance	**noun**	**5-04-005**
allegiance	NN	4-03-004
allegiances	NNS	1-01-001
allegoric	**JJ**	**2-02-002**
allegorical	**JJ**	**3-02-002**
allegory	**NN**	**3-03-003**
Allegretti	**NP**	**1-01-001**
allegro	**foreign**	**1-01-001**
allegro	FW-JJ	0-00-000
Allegro	FW-JJ-TL	1-01-001
allegro	**JJ**	**1-01-001**
Allemand	**foreign**	**1-01-001**
Allemand	FW-JJ	0-00-000
Allemands	FW-JJ-TL	1-01-001
Allen	**prop. noun**	**21-08-018**
Allen	NP	15-06-014
Allen	NP-TL	5-03-003
Allen's	NP$	1-01-001
allergic	**JJ**	**2-02-002**
allergy	**noun**	**2-02-002**
allergy	NN	1-01-001
allergies	NNS	1-01-001
alleviate	**verb**	**6-04-006**
alleviate	VB	5-03-005
alleviating	VBG	1-01-001
alleviation	**NN**	**2-01-001**
alley	**noun**	**9-05-007**
alley	NN	8-04-006
alleys	NNS	1-01-001

Word	Tag	Frequency
alleyway	**noun**	**1-01-001**
alleyways	NNS	1-01-001
alliance	**noun**	**22-06-014**
alliance	NN	14-03-007
Alliance	NN-TL	6-06-006
alliance's	NN$	1-01-001
alliances	NNS	1-01-001
alligator	**NN**	**4-02-002**
alligatored	**JJ**	**1-01-001**
Allison	**prop. noun**	**2-01-001**
Allison	NP	1-01-001
Allison's	NP$	1-01-001
alliteration	**NN**	**1-01-001**
alliterative	**JJ**	**1-01-001**
allocable	**JJ**	**3-01-001**
allocate	**verb**	**8-04-006**
allocate	VB	2-02-002
allocate	VB-HL	1-01-001
allocated	VBD	2-02-002
allocated	VBN	3-03-003
allocation	**noun**	**19-04-008**
allocation	NN	16-04-008
allocation	NN-HL	1-01-001
allocations	NNS	2-01-001
allons	**FW-VB**	**1-01-001**
allot	**verb**	**13-06-009**
allot	VB	1-01-001
allotted	VBD	2-02-002
allotted	VBN	8-05-005
alloted	VBN	1-01-001
allotting	VBG	1-01-001
allotment	**noun**	**49-02-002**
allotment	NN	39-02-002
allotments	NNS	6-01-001
allotments	NNS-HL	2-01-001
Allotments	NNS-TL	2-01-001
allow	**verb**	**209-13-132**
allow	VB	72-13-060
'low	VB	1-01-001
allows	VBZ	19-08-016
allowed	VBD	21-08-019
allowed	VBN	64-12-044
allowed	VBN-HL	1-01-001
allowing	VBG	31-09-027
allowable	**JJ**	**5-03-003**
allowance	**noun**	**41-09-016**
allowance	NN	16-08-012
allowances	NNS	23-05-007
allowances	NNS-HL	2-01-001
alloy	**noun**	**7-03-004**
alloy	NN	3-02-002
allay	NN	1-01-001
alloys	NNS	3-01-001
Allstate	**prop. noun**	**5-01-001**
Allstates	NPS	3-01-001
Allstates	NPS-TL	1-01-001
Allstates'	NPS$	1-01-001
Allstates-Zenith	**NP**	**1-01-001**
allude	**verb**	**3-01-003**
alludes	VBZ	1-01-001
alluded	VBN	1-01-001
alluding	VBG	1-01-001
allure	**NN**	**1-01-001**
allure	**verb**	**1-01-001**
alluring	VBG	1-01-001
allurement	**NN**	**1-01-001**
allusion	**noun**	**8-04-008**
allusion	NN	3-03-003
allusions	NNS	5-03-005
allusiveness	**NN**	**1-01-001**
ally	**noun**	**39-06-022**
ally	NN	9-04-007
allies	NNS	23-06-016
allies	NNS-HL	1-01-001
Allies	NNS-TL	6-04-005
ally	**verb**	**29-08-016**
allied	VBN	10-06-009
Allied	VBN-TL	19-04-008
alma	**JJ**	**1-01-001**
Alma	**NP**	**6-01-001**
Almaden	**NP**	**1-01-001**
Almagest	**prop. noun**	**4-01-001**
Almagest	NP	0-00-000
Almagest	NP-TL	4-01-001
almanac	**noun**	**1-01-001**
almanac	NN	0-00-000
Almanac	NN-TL	1-01-001
almighty	**adjective**	**2-01-001**
almighty	JJ	0-00-000

Word	Tag	Frequency
almighty (cont.):		
Almighty	JJ-TL	2-01-001
Almighty	**NP**	**3-02-002**
almond	**noun**	**4-01-001**
almond	NN	1-01-001
almonds	NNS	3-01-001
almost	**qualifier**	**157-15-119**
almost	QL	156-15-119
Almost	QL-TL	1-01-001
almost	**adverb**	**276-15-185**
almost	RB	275-15-185
'most	RB	1-01-001
aloe	**noun**	**2-01-001**
aloes	NNS	2-01-001
aloft	**RB**	**3-03-003**
Alokut	**NP**	**1-01-001**
alone	**adjective**	**8-05-008**
alone	JJ	7-05-007
Alone	JJ-TL	1-01-001
alone	**RB**	**187-15-138**
aloneness	**NN**	**2-02-002**
along	**IN**	**198-15-132**
along	**adverb**	**157-14-127**
along	RB	156-14-127
along	RB-HL	1-01-001
alongside	**IN**	**10-06-010**
alongside	**RB**	**5-05-005**
aloof	**JJ**	**2-02-002**
aloof	**RB**	**3-03-003**
aloofness	**NN**	**1-01-001**
alors	**FW-RB**	**2-02-002**
aloud	**RB**	**13-06-010**
Alp	**prop. noun**	**2-02-002**
Alps	NPS	1-01-001
Alps	NPS-TL	1-01-001
Alpers	**NP**	**2-01-001**
Alpert	**prop. noun**	**6-01-001**
Alpert	NP	5-01-001
Alperts	NPS	1-01-001
Alpha	**NP**	**6-02-002**
alpha-beta-gammas	**FW-NNS**	**1-01-001**
alphabet	**NN**	**2-01-001**
alphabetic	**JJ**	**1-01-001**
alphabetical	**JJ**	**4-03-004**
alphabetize	**verb**	**1-01-001**
alphabetized	VBN	1-01-001
Alpharetta	**NP**	**1-01-001**
Alphonse	**NP**	**1-01-001**
already	**QL**	**2-02-002**
already	**adverb**	**272-15-192**
already	RB	271-15-191
alreadeh	RB	1-01-001
Alsatian	**foreign**	**1-01-001**
Alsatian	FW-JJ	0-00-000
Alsatian	FW-JJ-TL	1-01-001
Alsatian	**prop. noun**	**3-02-002**
Alsatian	NP	2-01-001
Alsatians	NPS	1-01-001
Alsing	**NP**	**1-01-001**
also	**adverb**	**1070-15-383**
also	RB	1066-15-380
allso	RB	1-01-001
also	RB-HL	2-01-001
Also	RB-TL	1-01-001
Alsop	**NP**	**3-02-002**
Altairian	**prop. noun**	**1-01-001**
Altairians	NPS	1-01-001
altar	**noun**	**5-04-004**
altar	NN	4-03-003
Altar	NN-TL	1-01-001
Altenburg	**prop. noun**	**4-01-001**
Altenburg	NP	0-00-000
Altenburg	NP-TL	4-01-001
alter	**verb**	**42-12-032**
alter	VB	15-08-013
alters	VBZ	1-01-001
altered	VBD	2-02-002
altered	VBN	20-08-015
altering	VBG	4-03-004
alter-ego	**NN**	**1-01-001**
alter-parent	**noun**	**1-01-001**
alter-parents	NNS	1-01-001
alteration	**noun**	**14-05-010**
alteration	NN	7-04-005
alterations	NNS	7-03-005
altercation	**NN**	**1-01-001**
Alterman	**NP**	**1-01-001**
alternate	**JJ**	**9-03-005**
alternate	**NN**	**1-01-001**

Word	Tag	Frequency
alternate	**verb**	**3-03-003**
alternate	VB	1-01-001
alternated	VBD	1-01-001
alternating	VBG	1-01-001
alternately	**RB**	**7-07-007**
alternation	**NN**	**2-02-002**
alternative	**JJ**	**9-07-009**
alternative	**noun**	**42-09-026**
alternative	NN	25-07-016
alternatives	NNS	17-08-014
alternatively	**RB**	**3-01-003**
Althaus	**NP**	**1-01-001**
Althea	**NP**	**1-01-001**
although	**sub. conj.**	**323-15-197**
although	CS	321-15-195
altho	CS	2-01-002
altitude	**NN**	**4-03-003**
altitude-azimuth-mounted	**JJ**	**1-01-001**
alto	**NN**	**2-02-002**
Alto	**prop. noun**	**2-02-002**
Alto	NP	1-01-001
Alto	NP-TL	1-01-001
altogether	**QL**	**4-02-004**
altogether	**RB**	**26-10-024**
Alton	**NP**	**2-02-002**
altruism	**NN**	**1-01-001**
altruistically	**RB**	**1-01-001**
alum	**NN**	**1-01-001**
aluminum	**NN**	**18-05-012**
alumna	**noun**	**1-01-001**
alumnae	NNS	1-01-001
alumnus	**noun**	**9-03-003**
alumni	NNS	4-03-003
Alumni	NNS-TL	5-01-001
alundum	**NN**	**1-01-001**
Alusik	**prop. noun**	**3-01-001**
Alusik	NP	1-01-001
Alusik's	NP$	2-01-001
Alva	**NP**	**2-02-002**
Alvarez	**NP**	**3-02-002**
Alvear	**NP**	**1-01-001**
alveolar	**JJ**	**9-01-002**
alveolus	**noun**	**5-01-003**
alveolus	NN	1-01-001
alveoli	NNS	4-01-003
Alvin	**prop. noun**	**6-03-005**
Alvin	NP	5-03-005
Alvin	NP-HL	1-01-001
Alvise	**NP**	**2-01-001**
always	**QL**	**2-02-002**
always	**RB**	**456-15-240**
always-present	**JJ**	**1-01-001**
Alwin	**NP**	**2-02-002**
AM	**NP**	**1-01-001**
AMA	**NP**	**1-01-001**
Amadee	**prop. noun**	**5-01-001**
Amadee	NP	3-01-001
Amadee	NP-TL	1-01-001
Amadee's	NP$	1-01-001
Amadeus	**NP**	**1-01-001**
Amado	**NP**	**1-01-001**
amalgamate	**verb**	**1-01-001**
amalgamated	VBN	1-01-001
amalgamation	**NN**	**1-01-001**
amanuensis	**NN**	**1-01-001**
Amaral	**NP**	**1-01-001**
amass	**VB**	**2-02-002**
amassing	**NN**	**1-01-001**
amateur	**JJ**	**8-04-008**
amateur	**noun**	**19-07-009**
amateur	NN	15-06-008
Amateur	NN-TL	2-02-002
amateurs	NNS	2-01-001
amateurish	**JJ**	**3-03-003**
amateurishness	**NN**	**1-01-001**
amatory	**JJ**	**1-01-001**
amaze	**verb**	**14-07-014**
amaze	VB	3-03-003
amazed	VBD	1-01-001
amazed	VBN	10-06-010
amazement	**NN**	**10-08-009**
amazing	**JJ**	**20-09-020**
amazingly	**QL**	**1-01-001**
amazingly	**RB**	**2-02-002**
amazon	**noun**	**1-01-001**
amazons	NNS	1-01-001
Amazon	**NP**	**2-01-001**
ambassador	**noun**	**29-07-016**
ambassador	NN	9-05-005

Word	Tag	Frequency
ambassador (cont.):		
Ambassador	NN-TL	13-04-010
ambassador's	NN$	1-01-001
ambassadors	NNS	6-04-005
ambassador-at-large	**noun**	**1-01-001**
ambassador-at-large	NN	0-00-000
Ambassador-at-Large	NN-TL	1-01-001
ambassador-designate	**noun**	**1-01-001**
ambassador-designate	NN	0-00-000
Ambassador-designate	NN-TL	1-01-001
amber	**JJ**	**3-02-002**
ambiance	**NN**	**1-01-001**
ambidextrous	**JJ**	**1-01-001**
ambiguity	**noun**	**18-04-010**
ambiguity	NN	9-04-004
ambiguity	NN-HL	2-02-002
ambiguities	NNS	7-03-007
ambiguous	**JJ**	**22-06-016**
ambition	**noun**	**34-12-027**
ambition	NN	19-09-016
ambitions	NNS	15-06-013
ambitious	**JJ**	**16-08-014**
ambitiously	**RB**	**1-01-001**
ambivalence	**NN**	**5-03-005**
ambivalent	**JJ**	**6-05-006**
amble	**verb**	**2-02-002**
ambled	VBD	1-01-001
ambling	VBG	1-01-001
Ambler	**NP**	**1-01-001**
Ambrose	**NP**	**1-01-001**
ambrosial	**JJ**	**1-01-001**
ambulance	**noun**	**7-03-005**
ambulance	NN	6-03-004
ambulances	NNS	1-01-001
ambulatory	**JJ**	**1-01-001**
ambuscade	**NN**	**1-01-001**
ambush	**noun**	**6-03-004**
ambush	NN	5-02-003
ambushes	NNS	1-01-001
ambush	**verb**	**4-03-003**
ambush	VB	2-01-001
ambushed	VBN	2-02-002
Ameaux	**NP**	**2-01-001**
Amelia	**prop. noun**	**2-01-001**
Amelia's	NP$	2-01-001
amen	**adjective**	**7-02-002**
amen	JJ	0-00-000
Amen	JJ-TL	7-02-002
amen	**UH**	**12-02-003**
amenable	**JJ**	**3-02-003**
amend	**verb**	**17-05-012**
amend	VB	2-02-002
amended	VBD	3-03-003
amended	VBN	11-01-006
amending	VBG	1-01-001
amendment	**noun**	**31-05-017**
amendment	NN	17-03-011
Amendment	NN-TL	6-03-005
amendment's	NN$-HL	1-01-001
amendments	NNS	4-03-004
Amendments	NNS-TL	3-02-002
Amenitskii	**NP**	**1-01-001**
America	**prop. noun**	**217-13-100**
America	NP	121-13-071
America	NP-TL	73-11-032
America's	NP$	22-08-022
Americas	NPS	1-01-001
American	**adjective**	**535-14-197**
American	JJ	418-14-163
american	JJ	1-01-001
American	JJ-HL	3-03-003
American	JJ-TL	113-12-076
American	**prop. noun**	**128-14-072**
American	NP	31-10-024
American	NP-TL	3-01-002
American's	NP$	1-01-001
Americans	NPS	91-12-053
Americans	NPS-TL	2-02-002
American-Jewish	**JJ**	**1-01-001**
American-Negro	**prop. noun**	**3-01-001**
American-Negro	NP	0-00-000
American-Negro	NP-TL	3-01-001
American-trained	**JJ**	**1-01-001**
Americana	**prop. noun**	**5-04-004**
Americana	NP	4-03-003
Americana	NP-HL	1-01-001
amethystine	**NN**	**4-01-001**
amiable	**JJ**	**2-02-002**
amicable	**JJ**	**1-01-001**
amicably	**RB**	**1-01-001**
amicus	**foreign**	**4-02-002**
amicam	FW-NN	0-00-000
Amicam	FW-NN-TL	1-01-001
amici	FW-NNS	2-01-001
Amici	FW-NNS-TL	1-01-001
amid	**IN**	**14-06-013**
amide	**NN**	**1-01-001**
amidst	**IN**	**3-02-003**
amigo	**FW-NN**	**2-01-001**
amine	**noun**	**1-01-001**
amines	NNS	1-01-001
amino	**NN**	**1-01-001**
Amis	**NP**	**1-01-001**
amiss	**JJ**	**2-02-002**
amity	**NN**	**1-01-001**
ammo	**NN**	**4-02-002**
ammoniac	**JJ**	**1-01-001**
ammonium	**NN**	**1-01-001**
ammunition	**noun**	**18-05-009**
ammunition	NN	17-05-009
Ammunition	NN-TL	1-01-001
Amonasro	**NP**	**2-01-001**
among	**IN**	**369-15-214**
amongst	**IN**	**4-04-004**
amoral	**JJ**	**2-02-002**
amorality	**NN**	**1-01-001**
amorist	**NN**	**1-01-001**
amorous	**JJ**	**2-02-002**
amorphous	**JJ**	**6-03-005**
amorphously	**RB**	**1-01-001**
amortization	**NN**	**3-01-002**
amortize	**VB**	**2-01-001**
Amory	**NP**	**1-01-001**
Amos	**prop. noun**	**3-02-002**
Amos	NP	2-01-001
Amos	NP-TL	1-01-001
amount	**noun**	**166-12-087**
amount	NN	141-11-080
amount	NN-HL	1-01-001
amounts	NNS	24-08-019
amount	**verb**	**56-14-045**
amount	VB	30-12-026
amounts	VBZ	20-08-019
amounted	VBD	2-02-002
amounted	VBN	3-03-003
amounting	VBG	1-01-001
amp	**NN**	**1-01-001**
amphetamine	**noun**	**1-01-001**
amphetamines	NNS	1-01-001
amphibious	**JJ**	**1-01-001**
amphibology	**NN**	**1-01-001**
amphitheater	**NN**	**1-01-001**
ample	**JJ**	**16-09-015**
amplification	**NN**	**2-01-002**
amplifier	**noun**	**7-03-003**
amplifier	NN	6-02-002
amplifiers	NNS	1-01-001
amplify	**verb**	**8-03-004**
amplify	VB	1-01-001
amplified	VBN	6-02-002
amplifying	VBG	1-01-001
amplitude	**NN**	**6-02-004**
amply	**QL**	**2-02-002**
amply	**RB**	**2-02-002**
amputate	**verb**	**1-01-001**
amputated	VBN	1-01-001
Amra	**NP**	**1-01-001**
Amsterdam	**prop. noun**	**3-02-002**
Amsterdam	NP	2-01-001
Amsterdam	NP-TL	1-01-001
Amt	**FW-NN**	**1-01-001**
amulet	**noun**	**2-02-002**
amulet	NN	1-01-001
amulets	NNS	1-01-001
amuse	**verb**	**12-07-012**
amuse	VB	3-02-003
amused	VBD	5-04-005
amused	VBN	4-03-004
amusedly	**RB**	**1-01-001**
amusement	**noun**	**9-06-008**
amusement	NN	7-05-006
amusements	NNS	2-02-002
amusing	**JJ**	**14-07-012**
amusingly	**QL**	**1-01-001**
amusingly	**RB**	**1-01-001**
Amy	**prop. noun**	**15-04-005**
Amy	NP	14-04-005
Amy	NP-TL	1-01-001

an	**article**	**3727-15-498**
an	AT	3707-15-498
an	AT-HL	13-06-012
an	AT-NC	1-01-001
An	AT-TL	6-03-004
Ana	**NP**	**1-01-001**
Anabaptist	**prop. noun**	**2-01-001**
Anabaptist	NP	1-01-001
Anabaptists	NPS	1-01-001
Anabel	**NP**	**1-01-001**
anachronism	**noun**	**5-04-005**
anachronism	NN	3-03-003
anachronisms	NNS	2-02-002
anachronistically	**RB**	**1-01-001**
anaconda	**noun**	**20-02-002**
anaconda	NN	12-01-001
anaconda	NN-HL	1-01-001
Anaconda	NN-TL	1-01-001
anaconda's	NN$	2-01-001
anacondas	NNS	4-01-001
anaerobic	**JJ**	**1-01-001**
anaesthesia	**NN**	**1-01-001**
anagram	**NN**	**1-01-001**
analeptic	**JJ**	**2-01-001**
analogous	**JJ**	**8-05-007**
analogously	**RB**	**2-02-002**
analogue	**noun**	**2-02-002**
analogue	NN	1-01-001
analogues	NNS	1-01-001
analogy	**noun**	**17-06-014**
analogy	NN	12-05-011
analogy	NN-HL	1-01-001
analogies	NNS	4-03-004
analysis	**noun**	**121-09-056**
analysis	NN	101-09-051
analysis	NN-HL	7-02-005
analyses	NNS	12-02-008
analyses	NNS-HL	1-01-001
analyst	**noun**	**16-04-007**
analyst	NN	7-02-003
analyst's	NN$	3-03-003
analysts	NNS	6-03-004
analytic	**JJ**	**16-02-004**
analytical	**adjective**	**9-03-005**
analytical	JJ	5-03-005
Analytical	JJ-TL	4-01-001
analytically	**RB**	**1-01-001**
analyticity	**NN**	**1-01-001**
Analytrol	**NP**	**1-01-001**
analyzable	**JJ**	**1-01-001**
analyze	**verb**	**36-09-032**
analyze	VB	10-05-010
analyzes	VBZ	2-02-002
analyzed	VBD	1-01-001
analyzed	VBN	12-04-012
analysed	VBN	2-01-001
analyzed	VBN-HL	1-01-001
analyzing	VBG	8-05-007
analyzer	**noun**	**1-01-001**
analyzer	NN	0-00-000
Analyzer	NN-TL	1-01-001
Anania	**NP**	**1-01-001**
anaplasmosis	**NN**	**1-01-001**
anaprapath	**NN**	**1-01-001**
anarchic	**JJ**	**1-01-001**
anarchical	**JJ**	**2-01-002**
anarchist	**NN**	**1-01-001**
anarchist-adventurer	**noun**	**1-01-001**
anarchist-adventurers	NNS	1-01-001
anarchy	**NN**	**7-04-005**
anastomosis	**noun**	**7-01-001**
anastomosis	NN	1-01-001
anastomoses	NNS	6-01-001
anastomotic	**JJ**	**1-01-001**
Anatole	**NP**	**1-01-001**
anatomic	**JJ**	**1-01-001**
anatomical	**JJ**	**5-03-004**
anatomical	**noun**	**5-01-001**
anatomical	NN	4-01-001
anatomicals	NNS	1-01-001
anatomically	**RB**	**2-01-001**
anatomy	**NN**	**9-07-007**
Ancel	**NP**	**1-01-001**
ancestor	**noun**	**13-07-011**
ancestor	NN	7-05-007
ancestors	NNS	6-05-005
ancestral	**JJ**	**5-04-005**
ancestry	**NN**	**8-05-008**
anchor	**noun**	**17-07-013**

anchor (cont.):

anchor	NN	15-07-011
anchors	NNS	2-01-002
anchor	**verb**	**11-05-011**
anchored	VBD	1-01-001
anchored	VBN	9-05-009
anchoring	VBG	1-01-001
anchorage	**NN**	**1-01-001**
anchorite	**JJ**	**1-01-001**
Anchorite	**NP**	**1-01-001**
anchoritism	**NN**	**1-01-001**
anchovy	**NN**	**1-01-001**
ancient	**adjective**	**68-15-054**
ancient	JJ	62-14-050
Ancient	JJ-TL	6-03-004
ancient	**noun**	**2-02-002**
ancient	NN	1-01-001
ancients	NNS	1-01-001
anciently	**RB**	**1-01-001**
ancillary	**JJ**	**2-02-002**
Ancistrodon	**NP**	**1-01-001**
and	**co. conj.**	**28872-15-500**
and	CC	28543-15-500
'n'	CC	1-01-001
'n'	CC-TL	1-01-001
an	CC	12-01-001
an'	CC	8-04-005
and	CC-HL	102-09-067
and	CC-NC	1-01-001
And	CC-TL	69-09-047
and	CC-TL	133-15-081
and	CC-TL-HL	1-01-001
And	CC-TL-HL	1-01-001
and/or	**CC**	**17-05-012**
Andean	**JJ**	**2-01-002**
Anderlini	**NP**	**1-01-001**
Anders	**NP**	**2-01-001**
Andersen	**NP**	**1-01-001**
Anderson	**prop. noun**	**17-04-008**
Anderson	NP	12-04-007
Anderson	NP-TL	1-01-001
Anderson's	NP$	4-02-004
Andover	**prop. noun**	**3-03-003**
Andover	NP	2-02-002
Andover	NP-TL	1-01-001
Andre	**NP**	**3-02-003**
Andrea	**prop. noun**	**4-02-002**
Andrea	NP	3-02-002
Andrea	NP-TL	1-01-001
Andrei	**prop. noun**	**20-01-001**
Andrei	NP	18-01-001
Andrei's	NP$	2-01-001
andrena	**noun**	**5-01-001**
andrena	NN	1-01-001
andrenas	NNS	4-01-001
Andrena	**NP**	**6-01-001**
Andres	**NP**	**1-01-001**
Andrew	**NP**	**12-04-011**
Andrews	**NP**	**2-02-002**
Androfski	**NP**	**3-01-001**
Andromache	**prop. noun**	**1-01-001**
Andromache	NP	0-00-000
Andromache	NP-TL	1-01-001
Andrus	**prop. noun**	**13-01-001**
Andrus	NP	12-01-001
Andruses	NPS	1-01-001
Andy	**prop. noun**	**37-03-004**
Andy	NP	33-03-004
Andy's	NP$	4-01-001
anecdotal	**JJ**	**1-01-001**
anecdote	**noun**	**13-07-011**
anecdote	NN	9-05-008
anecdotes	NNS	4-03-003
anemia	**NN**	**5-01-001**
anemic	**JJ**	**1-01-001**
anesthetic	**noun**	**2-02-002**
anesthetic	NN	1-01-001
anesthetics	NNS	1-01-001
anesthetically	**RB**	**1-01-001**
anesthetize	**verb**	**1-01-001**
anesthetized	VBN	1-01-001
anew	**RB**	**6-05-005**
angel	**noun**	**45-11-024**
angel	NN	9-05-007
Angel	NN-TL	9-04-004
angels	NNS	10-08-009
Angels	NNS-TL	14-04-006
angel's	NN$	0-00-000
Angel's	NN$-TL	3-02-002

Word	Tag	Count
Angeles	**prop. noun**	**51-11-032**
Angeles	NP	40-11-024
Angeles	NP-TL	8-05-006
Angeles'	NP$	3-02-003
angelic	**JJ**	**2-01-001**
angelica	**NN**	**1-01-001**
Angelico	**NP**	**1-01-001**
Angelina	**NP**	**4-01-001**
Angell	**NP**	**1-01-001**
Angelo	**prop. noun**	**10-02-003**
Angelo	NP	8-02-003
Angelo's	NP$	2-01-001
anger	**NN**	**48-10-030**
anger	**verb**	**1-01-001**
angered	VBN	1-01-001
Angie	**NP**	**17-01-001**
angle	**noun**	**61-08-020**
angle	NN	50-08-017
angles	NNS	11-03-006
angle	**verb**	**2-02-002**
angle	VB	1-01-001
angling	VBG	1-01-001
Angleterre	**FW-NP**	**1-01-001**
Anglia	**prop. noun**	**1-01-001**
Anglia	NP	0-00-000
Anglia	NP-TL	1-01-001
Anglican	**adjective**	**11-02-003**
Anglican	JJ	9-02-003
Anglican	JJ-TL	2-01-001
Anglican	**prop. noun**	**2-02-002**
Anglicans	NPS	2-02-002
Anglicanism	**NP**	**1-01-001**
Anglo-American	**JJ**	**2-01-001**
Anglo-American	**prop. noun**	**1-01-001**
Anglo-Americans	NPS	1-01-001
Anglo-Jewish	**JJ**	**1-01-001**
Anglo-Protestant	**JJ**	**1-01-001**
Anglo-Saxon	**adjective**	**20-03-005**
Anglo-Saxon	JJ	19-03-005
Anglo-Saxon	JJ-TL	1-01-001
Anglo-Saxon	**prop. noun**	**3-02-003**
Anglo-Saxon	NP	2-02-002
Anglo-Saxons	NPS	1-01-001
Anglophilia	**NN**	**1-01-001**
Anglophobia	**NN**	**1-01-001**
Angola	**NP**	**3-02-002**
angriest	**JJT**	**1-01-001**
angrily	**RB**	**7-05-007**
angry	**JJ**	**45-10-036**
Angst	**FW-NN**	**2-01-001**
anguish	**NN**	**8-06-008**
anguish	**verb**	**2-02-002**
anguished	VBN	2-02-002
angular	**JJ**	**16-04-008**
Anhalt-Bernburg	**prop. noun**	**1-01-001**
Anhalt-Bernburg	NP	0-00-000
Anhalt-Bernburg	NP-TL	1-01-001
anhemolyticus	**NP**	**1-01-001**
Anhwei	**NP**	**1-01-001**
anhydrous	**JJ**	**1-01-001**
anhydrously	**RB**	**1-01-001**
aniline	**NN**	**1-01-001**
animal	**noun**	**129-14-059**
animal	NN	68-12-037
animal's	NN$	3-02-003
animals	NNS	55-12-033
Animals	NNS-TL	3-01-001
animal-like	**JJ**	**1-01-001**
animate	**JJ**	**1-01-001**
animate	**verb**	**6-05-006**
animated	VBN	5-04-005
anemated	VBN	1-01-001
animation	**NN**	**2-01-001**
animism	**NN**	**1-01-001**
animize	**verb**	**1-01-001**
animized	VBN	1-01-001
animosity	**NN**	**3-03-003**
anion	**noun**	**2-01-002**
anion	NN	1-01-001
anions	NNS	1-01-001
anionic	**adjective**	**10-01-003**
anionic	JJ	9-01-003
anionic	JJ-HL	1-01-001
anionic	**noun**	**1-01-001**
anionics	NNS	1-01-001
anise	**NN**	**2-01-001**
aniseikonic	**adjective**	**2-01-001**
aniseikonic	JJ	1-01-001
aniseikonic	JJ-HL	1-01-001

Word	Tag	Count
anisotropy	**NN**	**1-01-001**
Anita	**NP**	**2-02-002**
Ankara	**prop. noun**	**1-01-001**
Ankara	NP	0-00-000
Ankara	NP-HL	1-01-001
ankle	**noun**	**15-07-013**
ankle	NN	8-06-006
ankles	NNS	7-06-007
ankle-deep	**JJ**	**2-02-002**
Ann	**prop. noun**	**31-06-011**
Ann	NP	26-05-009
Ann	NP-TL	3-02-002
Ann's	NP$	2-01-001
Anna	**NP**	**7-04-005**
annal	**noun**	**4-02-003**
annals	NNS	4-02-003
Annamorena	**NP**	**1-01-001**
Annapolis	**prop. noun**	**7-02-002**
Annapolis	NP	3-02-002
Annapolis	NP-HL	3-01-001
Annapolis	NP-TL	1-01-001
Anne	**prop. noun**	**46-07-015**
Anne	NP	37-05-012
Anne	NP-HL	1-01-001
Anne	NP-TL	4-03-003
Anne's	NP$	3-02-002
Anne's	NP$-TL	1-01-001
annee	**foreign**	**1-01-001**
annee	FW-NN	0-00-000
annee	FW-NN-TL	1-01-001
annex	**VB**	**1-01-001**
Annie	**NP**	**1-01-001**
annihilate	**VB**	**1-01-001**
annihilation	**NN**	**6-05-005**
Annisberg	**NP**	**1-01-001**
Anniston	**prop. noun**	**18-02-002**
Anniston	NP	17-02-002
Anniston's	NP$	1-01-001
anniversary	**noun**	**22-12-018**
anniversary	NN	18-12-015
Anniversary	NN-TL	3-03-003
anniversaries	NNS	1-01-001
announce	**verb**	**116-15-085**
announce	VB	18-07-015
announces	VBZ	3-03-003
announced	VBD	53-13-045
announced	VBN	35-10-028
announcing	VBG	7-05-007
announcement	**noun**	**30-09-023**
announcement	NN	24-08-020
announcements	NNS	6-05-005
announcer	**noun**	**4-03-004**
announcer	NN	2-02-002
announcer's	NN$	1-01-001
announcers	NNS	1-01-001
annoy	**verb**	**10-06-010**
annoy	VB	2-02-002
annoys	VBZ	1-01-001
annoyed	VBD	1-01-001
annoyed	VBN	6-04-006
annoyance	**noun**	**10-06-009**
annoyance	NN	9-06-009
annoyances	NNS	1-01-001
annoying	**JJ**	**6-04-006**
annual	**adjective**	**92-11-060**
annual	JJ	89-11-060
Annual	JJ-TL	3-01-001
annual	**NN**	**1-01-001**
annually	**RB**	**14-06-011**
annum	**NN**	**3-03-003**
annunciate	**verb**	**1-01-001**
annunciated	VBN	1-01-001
anode	**noun**	**78-01-002**
anode	NN	75-01-002
anode	NN-HL	2-01-001
anodes	NNS	1-01-001
anomalous	**JJ**	**1-01-001**
anomaly	**noun**	**2-02-002**
anomaly	NN	1-01-001
anomalies	NNS	1-01-001
anomic	**JJ**	**1-01-001**
anomie	**NN**	**1-01-001**
anonymity	**NN**	**2-02-002**
anonymous	**JJ**	**17-06-011**
anorexia	**NN**	**1-01-001**
anorthic	**JJ**	**1-01-001**
another	**sing. det.**	**690-15-348**
another	DT	681-15-348
'nother	DT	1-01-001

another (cont.):		
another's	DT$	5-05-005
another	DT-HL	2-01-002
Another	DT-HL	5-05-005
Anouilh	**NP**	**1-01-001**
Anselm	**prop. noun**	**1-01-001**
Anselm's	NP$	0-00-000
Anselm's	NP$-TL	1-01-001
Anselmo	**NP**	**1-01-001**
Ansley	**NP**	**1-01-001**
Anson	**NP**	**1-01-001**
answer	**noun**	**145-15-104**
answer	NN	106-15-081
answer	NN-HL	3-02-003
answers	NNS	36-11-027
answer	**verb**	**133-14-101**
answer	VB	43-12-042
ansuh	VB	1-01-001
answers	VBZ	8-06-008
answered	VBD	47-12-042
answered	VBN	20-10-019
answering	VBG	14-09-014
answerable	**JJ**	**1-01-001**
ant	**noun**	**13-05-009**
ant	NN	6-04-005
ants	NNS	7-04-006
Anta	**NP**	**5-01-001**
antagonism	**noun**	**11-04-006**
antagonism	NN	9-04-004
antagonisms	NNS	2-02-002
antagonist	**noun**	**7-01-002**
antagonist	NN	3-01-002
antagonists	NNS	4-01-001
antagonistic	**JJ**	**4-04-004**
antagonize	**verb**	**2-01-002**
antagonize	VB	1-01-001
antagonized	VBN	0-00-000
antagonised	VBN	1-01-001
Antarctica	**NP**	**1-01-001**
Antares	**NP**	**1-01-001**
ante	**NN**	**2-02-002**
ante	**RB**	**1-01-001**
ante-bellum	**JJ**	**3-02-003**
anteater	**NN**	**1-01-001**
antecedent	**noun**	**3-03-003**
antecedent	NN	1-01-001
antecedents	NNS	2-02-002
antelope	**NN**	**7-02-002**
antenna	**noun**	**17-04-006**
antenna	NN	13-03-003
antennae	NNS	3-03-003
antennas	NNS	1-01-001
anterior	**JJ**	**5-02-003**
anterior	**noun**	**1-01-001**
anteriors	NNS	1-01-001
Anthea	**NP**	**3-01-001**
anthem	**noun**	**2-02-002**
anthem	NN	0-00-000
Anthem	NN-TL	1-01-001
anthems	NNS	1-01-001
anthology	**noun**	**4-01-002**
anthology	NN	3-01-001
Anthology	NN-TL	1-01-001
Anthony	**prop. noun**	**17-07-010**
Anthony	NP	15-07-009
Anthony	NP-TL	1-01-001
Anthony's	NP$	1-01-001
anthropological	**JJ**	**1-01-001**
anthropological-religious	**JJ**	**1-01-001**
anthropologist	**noun**	**4-03-004**
anthropologist	NN	2-02-002
anthropologists	NNS	2-02-002
anthropology	**noun**	**7-04-007**
anthropology	NN	6-03-006
Anthropology	NN-TL	1-01-001
anthropomorphic	**JJ**	**1-01-001**
anti	**IN**	**1-01-001**
anti-A	**JJ**	**4-01-001**
anti-aircraft	**JJ**	**2-01-001**
anti-American	**JJ**	**2-02-002**
Anti-Americanism	**NN**	**1-01-001**
anti-assignment	**JJ**	**1-01-001**
anti-authoritarian	**JJ**	**1-01-001**
anti-B	**JJ**	**4-01-001**
anti-Castro	**JJ**	**1-01-001**
anti-Catholic	**JJ**	**1-01-001**
anti-Catholicism	**NN**	**1-01-001**
anti-Christian	**JJ**	**1-01-001**
anti-clericalism	**NN**	**1-01-001**
anti-Colmer	**JJ**	**1-01-001**
anti-Communism	**NN**	**1-01-001**
anti-Communist	**adjective**	**8-03-006**
anti-Communist	JJ	6-01-004
Anti-Communist	JJ	2-02-002
anti-Communist	**noun**	**1-01-001**
anti-Communists	NNS	1-01-001
anti-democratic	**JJ**	**1-01-001**
anti-discrimination	**JJ**	**1-01-001**
anti-discriminatory	**JJ**	**1-01-001**
anti-freeze	**NN**	**1-01-001**
anti-French	**JJ**	**3-02-002**
anti-human	**JJ**	**2-01-001**
anti-infective	**JJ**	**2-01-001**
anti-intellectual	**JJ**	**3-02-003**
anti-intellectualism	**NN**	**1-01-001**
anti-Kennedy	**JJ**	**1-01-001**
anti-liquor	**JJ**	**1-01-001**
anti-missile	**JJ**	**1-01-001**
anti-monopoly	**JJ**	**4-01-001**
anti-Nazi	**JJ**	**2-02-002**
anti-Negro	**JJ**	**1-01-001**
anti-Newtonian	**JJ**	**1-01-001**
anti-organization	**JJ**	**2-01-001**
anti-party	**JJ**	**5-01-001**
anti-personality	**JJ**	**1-01-001**
anti-polio	**JJ**	**1-01-001**
anti-recession	**JJ**	**1-01-001**
anti-Rh	**JJ**	**1-01-001**
anti-secrecy	**JJ**	**2-01-001**
anti-semite	**noun**	**5-01-001**
anti-semite	NN	1-01-001
Anti-Semite	NN	1-01-001
anti-Semites	NNS	3-01-001
anti-Semitic	**JJ**	**4-01-001**
anti-Semitism	**NN**	**23-02-002**
anti-slavery	**adjective**	**13-03-003**
anti-slavery	JJ	11-02-002
antislavery	JJ	1-01-001
anti-slavery	JJ-HL	1-01-001
anti-Soviet	**JJ**	**2-01-001**
anti-trust	**adjective**	**27-04-004**
anti-trust	JJ	26-03-003
antitrust	JJ	1-01-001
antibiotic	**noun**	**2-01-002**
antibiotic	NN	1-01-001
antibiotics	NNS	1-01-001
antibody	**noun**	**21-01-002**
antibody	NN	12-01-001
antibodies	NNS	9-01-002
antic	**JJ**	**1-01-001**
antic	**noun**	**4-03-004**
antics	NNS	4-03-004
anticipate	**verb**	**38-13-035**
anticipate	VB	11-08-011
anticipates	VBZ	2-02-002
anticipated	VBD	4-04-004
anticipated	VBN	19-08-017
anticipating	VBG	2-02-002
anticipation	**noun**	**23-08-017**
anticipation	NN	20-06-014
anticipations	NNS	3-03-003
anticipatory	**JJ**	**1-01-001**
anticoagulation	**NN**	**1-01-001**
anticus	**FW-JJ**	**1-01-001**
antidote	**NN**	**2-02-002**
Antietam	**NP**	**2-02-002**
antifundamentalist	**NN**	**1-01-001**
antigen	**noun**	**12-01-001**
antigen	NN	11-01-001
antigen	NN-HL	1-01-001
Antigone	**NP**	**1-01-001**
antihistorical	**JJ**	**1-01-001**
Antinomian	**prop. noun**	**1-01-001**
Antinomians	NPS	1-01-001
antipathy	**NN**	**4-04-004**
antiphonal	**JJ**	**1-01-001**
antipodes	**NNS**	**1-01-001**
antiquarian	**JJ**	**1-01-001**
antiquarian	**noun**	**1-01-001**
antiquarians	NNS	1-01-001
antiquate	**verb**	**3-02-003**
antiquated	VBN	3-02-003
antiquated	**JJ**	**1-01-001**
antique	**JJ**	**4-02-003**
antique	**noun**	**11-06-007**
antique	NN	8-05-005
antiques	NNS	3-02-003
antiquity	**noun**	**4-03-004**

antiquity (cont.):		
antiquity	NN	2-02-002
Antiquity	NN-TL	1-01-001
antiquities	NNS	1-01-001
antiredeposition	**NN**	**1-01-001**
antiseptic	**JJ**	**4-02-004**
antiseptic	**NN**	**2-02-002**
antiserum	**noun**	**6-01-002**
antiserum	NN	4-01-001
antisera	NNS	2-01-002
antisocial	**JJ**	**2-02-002**
antisubmarine	**adjective**	**8-02-002**
antisubmarine	JJ	5-01-001
anti-submarine	JJ	3-02-002
antithesis	**NN**	**3-02-003**
antithetical	**JJ**	**1-01-001**
antithyroid	**adjective**	**7-01-001**
antithyroid	JJ	6-01-001
antithyroid	JJ-HL	1-01-001
Antler	**NP**	**3-01-001**
Antoine	**prop. noun**	**4-02-002**
Antoine	NP	1-01-001
Antoine's	NP$	3-01-001
Antoinette	**NP**	**1-01-001**
Anton	**NP**	**2-01-002**
Antone	**NP**	**1-01-001**
Antonini	**NP**	**1-01-001**
Antonio	**NP**	**6-03-005**
Antony	**NP**	**2-02-002**
anvil	**NN**	**1-01-001**
anxiety	**noun**	**43-07-017**
anxiety	NN	37-07-016
anxiety	NN-HL	2-01-001
Anxiety	NN-TL	2-01-001
Anxiety	NN-TL-HL	1-01-001
anxieties	NNS	1-01-001
anxiety-released	**JJ**	**1-01-001**
anxious	**JJ**	**29-11-022**
anxiously	**RB**	**9-06-007**
any	**sg/pl det.**	**1335-15-431**
any	DTI	1328-15-431
ani	DTI	2-01-001
anye	DTI	1-01-001
enny	DTI	1-01-001
any	DTI-HL	2-01-002
Any	DTI-TL	1-01-001
any	**QL**	**12-06-012**
any	**RB**	**1-01-001**
anybody	**nom. pro.**	**45-13-039**
anybody	PN	42-13-037
anybody'd	PN+MD	1-01-001
anybody's	PN$	2-02-002
anyhow	**RB**	**20-09-016**
anylabel	**noun**	**1-01-001**
anylabel	NN	0-00-000
anylabel	NN-NC	1-01-001
anymore	**RB**	**5-04-005**
anyone	**nom. pro.**	**146-15-111**
anyone	PN	140-15-105
anyone's	PN$	6-04-006
anyplace	**RB**	**1-01-001**
anything	**nom. pro.**	**281-15-167**
anything	PN	279-15-166
anythin	PN	1-01-001
Anything	PN-TL	1-01-001
anytime	**RB**	**1-01-001**
anyway	**RB**	**46-10-039**
anyways	**RB**	**1-01-001**
anywhere	**adverb**	**39-12-033**
anywhere	RB	38-12-032
Anywhere	RB-TL	1-01-001
Anzilotti	**NP**	**1-01-001**
aorta	**NN**	**3-02-002**
Aouelloul	**NP**	**1-01-001**
AP	**prop. noun**	**14-01-006**
AP	NP	4-01-002
AP	NP-HL	10-01-005
Apache	**prop. noun**	**6-02-004**
Apache	NP	0-00-000
'pache	NP	1-01-001
Apaches	NPS	4-02-002
Apache	NPS	1-01-001
Apalachicola	**NP**	**1-01-001**
Aparicio	**NP**	**1-01-001**
apart	**RB**	**57-12-051**
apartheid	**FW-NN**	**1-01-001**
apartheid	**NN**	**2-02-002**
apartment	**noun**	**98-12-042**
apartment	NN	79-12-038
apartment (cont.):		
Apartment	NN-TL	2-02-002
apartments	NNS	15-06-009
apartments	NNS-HL	1-01-00
Apartments	NNS-TL	1-01-001
apartment-building	**JJ**	**1-01-001**
apathetic	**JJ**	**1-01-001**
apathy	**NN**	**3-02-002**
ape	**NN**	**3-03-003**
Apergillus	**NP**	**1-01-001**
aperture	**NN**	**8-03-004**
apex	**NN**	**4-03-004**
Aphrodite	**NP**	**1-01-001**
apiece	**RB**	**2-02-002**
aplomb	**NN**	**1-01-001**
apocalypse	**noun**	**2-02-002**
apocalypse	NN	1-01-001
Apocalypse	NN-TL	1-01-001
apocalyptic	**adjective**	**5-04-0**
apocalyptic	JJ	3-03-003
Apocalyptic	JJ-TL	2-01-001
Apocrypha	**NP**	**1-01-001**
apocryphal	**JJ**	**1-01-001**
apogee	**NN**	**2-02-002**
Apollinaire	**NP**	**2-01-001**
Apollo	**prop. noun**	**6-05-005**
Apollo	NP	2-02-002
Apollo	NP-TL	3-02-002
Apollo's	NP$	1-01-001
Apollonian	**JJ**	**1-01-001**
apologetic	**JJ**	**2-02-002**
apologetic	**NN**	**1-01-001**
apologetically	**RB**	**6-05-006**
Apologia	**NP**	**1-01-001**
apologist	**NN**	**1-01-001**
apologize	**verb**	**6-05-006**
apologize	VB	1-01-001
apologized	VBD	4-04-004
apologized	VBN	1-01-001
apology	**noun**	**8-02-007**
apology	NN	2-01-001
apologie	NN	0-00-000
Apologie	NN-TL	1-01-001
Apology	NN-TL	1-01-001
apologies	NNS	4-02-004
apostate	**noun**	**1-01-001**
apostates	NNS	1-01-001
apostle	**noun**	**4-03-004**
apostle	NN	2-02-002
apostles	NNS	1-01-001
Apostles	NNS-TL	
apostolic	**JJ**	**4-02-002**
apothecary	**NN**	**3-01-001**
apotheosis	**NN**	**1-01-001**
App	**NP**	**1-01-001**
Appalachian	**prop. noun**	**2-02-002**
Appalachian	NP	0-00-000
Appalachian	NP-TL	1-01-001
Appalachians	NPS	1-01-001
appall	**verb**	**2-02-002**
appalled	VBN	2-02-002
appalling	**JJ**	**9-06-009**
appallingly	**QL**	**1-01-001**
Appaloosa	**prop. noun**	**1-01-001**
Appaloosas	NPS	1-01-001
appanage	**NN**	**1-01-001**
apparatus	**noun**	**29-08-018**
apparatus	NN	27-08-017
apparatus	NN-HL	2-01-002
apparel	**noun**	**3-02-002**
apparel	NN	2-01-001
Apparel	NN-TL	1-01-001
apparel	**verb**	**1-01-001**
appareled	VBN	1-01-001
apparency	**NN**	**1-01-001**
apparent	**JJ**	**57-13-052**
apparently	**QL**	**1-01-001**
apparently	**RB**	**124-15-099**
apparition	**NN**	**3-03-003**
appeal	**noun**	**72-11-042**
appeal	NN	48-11-031
Appeal	NN-TL	5-03-003
appeals	NNS	13-05-008
App.	NNS	0-00-000
App.	NNS-TL	1-01-001
Appeals	NNS-TL	5-03-005
appeal	**verb**	**27-09-022**
appeal	VB	10-05-009
appeals	VBZ	1-01-001

Word	Tag	Frequency
appeal (cont.):		
appealed	VBD	10-04-008
appealed	VBN	3-02-003
appealing	VBG	3-03-003
appealing	**JJ**	**11-05-010**
appear	**verb**	**353-15-205**
appear	VB	117-13-082
appears	VBZ	84-09-063
appeared	VBD	118-15-087
appeared	VBN	17-10-017
appearing	VBG	16-09-016
appearin'	VBG	1-01-001
appearance	**noun**	**71-13-062**
appearance	NN	57-13-050
appearances	NNS	14-06-014
appease	**verb**	**5-05-005**
appease	VB	2-02-002
appeased	VBN	2-02-002
appeasing	VBG	1-01-001
appeasement	**NN**	**3-03-003**
appellant	**FW-VB**	**1-01-001**
append	**verb**	**2-02-002**
appended	VBN	2-02-002
appendage	**noun**	**1-01-001**
appendages	NNS	1-01-001
appendix	**noun**	**11-02-005**
appendix	NN	0-00-000
Appendix	NN-TL	10-02-005
appendices	NNS	0-00-000
appendixes	NNS	0-00-000
Appendixes	NNS-TL	1-01-001
appestat	**NN**	**5-01-001**
appetite	**noun**	**14-06-010**
appetite	NN	11-04-007
appetites	NNS	3-02-003
appetizing	**JJ**	**2-01-001**
Appian	**prop. noun**	**1-01-001**
Appian	NP	0-00-000
Appian	NP-TL	1-01-001
applaud	**verb**	**11-07-011**
applaud	VB	5-05-005
applauded	VBD	1-01-001
applauded	VBN	3-03-003
applauding	VBG	2-02-002
applause	**NN**	**14-07-012**
applause-happy	**JJ**	**1-01-001**
apple	**noun**	**15-04-007**
apple	NN	8-04-006
apple	NN-HL	1-01-001
apples	NNS	6-02-002
apple-tree	**NN**	**1-01-001**
Appleby	**NP**	**1-01-001**
applejack	**NN**	**1-01-001**
Appleton	**NP**	**1-01-001**
appliance	**noun**	**13-04-006**
appliance	NN	5-02-002
appliances	NNS	8-04-006
applicability	**NN**	**2-02-002**
applicable	**JJ**	**18-06-015**
applicant	**noun**	**18-07-009**
applicant	NN	8-03-004
applicants	NNS	10-05-006
application	**noun**	**93-11-050**
application	NN	63-11-041
application	NN-HL	1-01-001
Application	NN-TL	4-01-002
applications	NNS	25-06-015
applicator	**NN**	**1-01-001**
applique	**noun**	**1-01-001**
appliques	NNS	1-01-001
apply	**verb**	**210-14-112**
apply	VB	56-08-044
applies	VBZ	19-06-017
applied	VBD	22-10-018
applied	VBN	84-11-052
applying	VBG	28-08-022
applying	VBG-HL	1-01-001
appoint	**verb**	**50-12-040**
appoint	VB	6-05-006
appoints	VBZ	1-01-001
appointed	VBD	8-06-008
appointed	VBN	34-12-028
appointing	VBG	1-01-001
appointee	**noun**	**7-05-005**
appointee	NN	2-02-002
appointees	NNS	5-03-003
appointment	**noun**	**34-10-027**
appointment	NN	27-08-021
Appointment	NN-TL	1-01-001
appointment (cont.):		
appointments	NNS	6-05-006
apportion	**verb**	**9-03-004**
apportion	VB	1-01-001
apportioned	VBN	8-03-003
apportionment	**noun**	**11-01-001**
apportionment	NN	9-01-001
apportionments	NNS	2-01-001
appraisal	**noun**	**10-06-010**
appraisal	NN	8-05-008
appraisals	NNS	2-02-002
appraise	**verb**	**6-03-006**
appraise	VB	4-02-004
appraised	VBN	1-01-001
appraising	VBG	1-01-001
appraiser	**noun**	**1-01-001**
appraisers	NNS	1-01-001
appraisingly	**RB**	**1-01-001**
appreciable	**JJ**	**5-03-005**
appreciably	**QL**	**3-02-003**
appreciably	**RB**	**4-01-004**
appreciate	**verb**	**39-14-034**
appreciate	VB	26-11-023
appreciates	VBZ	1-01-001
appreciated	VBD	6-03-006
appreciated	VBN	5-05-005
appreciating	VBG	1-01-001
appreciation	**noun**	**23-12-020**
appreciation	NN	22-11-019
appreciations	NNS	1-01-001
appreciative	**JJ**	**2-02-002**
appreciatively	**RB**	**2-02-002**
apprehend	**verb**	**3-03-003**
apprehend	VB	1-01-001
apprehended	VBN	2-02-002
apprehension	**noun**	**16-09-014**
apprehension	NN	11-08-010
apprehensions	NNS	5-04-004
apprehensively	**RB**	**4-03-004**
apprentice	**noun**	**18-07-009**
apprentice	NN	14-06-007
Apprentice	NN-TL	1-01-001
apprentices	NNS	3-02-002
apprentice	**verb**	**1-01-001**
apprenticed	VBN	1-01-001
apprenticeship	**NN**	**2-02-002**
approach	**noun**	**125-14-080**
approach	NN	104-14-074
approach	NN-HL	3-01-001
Approach	NN-TL	1-01-001
approaches	NNS	17-08-014
approach	**verb**	**95-15-075**
approach	VB	15-09-015
approaches	VBZ	8-04-006
approached	VBD	32-10-029
approached	VBN	13-07-012
approaching	VBG	27-13-023
approachable	**JJ**	**1-01-001**
appropriate	**JJ**	**67-10-048**
appropriate	**verb**	**15-04-010**
appropriate	VB	1-01-001
appropriates	VBZ	1-01-001
appropriated	VBD	1-01-001
appropriated	VBN	10-04-007
appropriating	VBG	2-02-002
appropriately	**QL**	**1-01-001**
appropriately	**RB**	**4-04-004**
appropriateness	**NN**	**2-02-002**
appropriation	**noun**	**14-04-011**
appropriation	NN	4-03-004
Appropriation	NN-TL	1-01-001
appropriations	NNS	8-03-006
Appropriations	NNS-TL	1-01-001
approval	**NN**	**51-09-042**
approve	**verb**	**56-10-036**
approve	VB	14-06-012
approves	VBZ	1-01-001
approved	VBD	12-06-010
approved	VBN	28-07-021
approving	VBG	1-01-001
approvingly	**RB**	**2-02-002**
approximate	**adjective**	**9-03-007**
approximate	JJ	8-03-007
approximate	JJ-NC	1-01-001
approximate	**verb**	**7-05-007**
approximate	VB	2-02-002
approximated	VBD	2-02-002
approximated	VBN	3-02-003
approximately	**QL**	**6-04-005**

Word	Tag	Frequency
approximately	**adverb**	**65-07-040**
approximately	RB	60-07-040
approximately	RB-HL	5-01-001
approximation	**noun**	**10-04-009**
approximation	NN	7-02-006
approximations	NNS	3-03-003
apricot	**NN**	**1-01-001**
April	**prop. noun**	**71-11-041**
April	NP	68-11-040
april	NP	1-01-001
April	NP-HL	2-01-001
apron	**noun**	**8-05-007**
apron	NN	7-05-006
aprons	NNS	1-01-001
apropos	**JJ**	**1-01-001**
apse	**noun**	**1-01-001**
apses	NNS	1-01-001
apt	**JJ**	**15-06-014**
aptitude	**noun**	**4-02-004**
aptitude	NN	3-02-003
aptitudes	NNS	1-01-001
aptly	**QL**	**1-01-001**
aptly	**RB**	**3-03-003**
aptness	**NN**	**1-01-001**
aqua-lung	**NN**	**1-01-001**
Aquacutie	**NP**	**1-01-001**
aquam	**FW-NN**	**1-01-001**
aqueduct	**noun**	**1-01-001**
aqueducts	NNS	1-01-001
aqueous	**JJ**	**14-01-004**
Aquidneck	**NP**	**2-01-001**
Aquinas	**prop. noun**	**2-02-002**
Aquinas	NP	1-01-001
Aquinas	NP-TL	1-01-001
Arab	**prop. noun**	**4-03-003**
Arab	NP	1-01-001
Arab	NP-TL	1-01-001
Arabs	NPS	1-01-001
Arabs'	NPS$	1-01-001
arabesque	**NN**	**1-01-001**
Arabia	**NP**	**1-01-001**
Arabian	**adjective**	**2-02-002**
Arabian	JJ	1-01-001
Arabian	JJ-TL	1-01-001
Arabian	**prop. noun**	**1-01-001**
Arabians	NPS	1-01-001
Arabian-American	**adjective**	**1-01-001**
Arabian-American	JJ	0-00-000
Arabian-American	JJ-TL	1-01-001
Arabic	**adjective**	**6-05-005**
Arabic	JJ	5-04-004
arabic	JJ	1-01-001
arable	**JJ**	**3-03-003**
Araby	**NP**	**1-01-001**
arak	**NN**	**1-01-001**
Aransas	**NP**	**1-01-001**
Arapacis	**NP**	**2-01-001**
Arata	**NP**	**1-01-001**
Arbeitskommando	**prop. noun**	**1-01-001**
Arbeitskommando	NP	0-00-000
Arbeitskommando	NP-TL	1-01-001
arbiter	**NN**	**5-02-004**
arbitrarily	**RB**	**5-03-005**
arbitrary	**adjective**	**22-07-019**
arbitrary	JJ	21-07-018
Arbitrary	JJ	1-01-001
arbitrate	**verb**	**4-01-003**
arbitrate	VB	3-01-002
arbitrated	VBN	1-01-001
arbitration	**NN**	**2-02-002**
Arbogast	**prop. noun**	**3-01-001**
Arbogast	NP	2-01-001
Arbogast	NP-HL	1-01-001
Arbor	**NP**	**1-01-001**
arboreal	**JJ**	**1-01-001**
Arbuckle	**prop. noun**	**6-01-001**
Arbuckle	NP	5-01-001
Arbuckle's	NP$	1-01-001
arc	**foreign**	**1-01-001**
arc	FW-NN	0-00-000
Arc	FW-NN-TL	1-01-001
arc	**noun**	**48-08-012**
arc	NN	40-08-012
arcs	NNS	8-01-001
arcade	**noun**	**5-03-003**
arcade	NN	3-03-003
arcades	NNS	2-01-001
arcaded	**JJ**	**1-01-001**
arch	**noun**	**16-06-010**

Word	Tag	Frequency
arch (cont.):		
arch	NN	10-03-005
Arch	NN-TL	1-01-001
arches	NNS	5-04-004
arch	**verb**	**15-06-010**
arch	VB	1-01-001
arches	VBZ	2-02-002
arched	VBD	2-02-002
arched	VBN	9-04-005
arching	VBG	1-01-001
Arch	**NP**	**1-01-001**
arch-heretic	**NN**	**1-01-001**
arch-opponent	**NN**	**1-01-001**
archaeological	**JJ**	**8-02-002**
archaeologist	**noun**	**1-01-001**
archaeologists	NNS	1-01-001
archaeology	**noun**	**11-03-004**
archaeology	NN	10-03-004
Archaeology	NN-TL	1-01-001
archaic	**JJ**	**5-02-003**
archaism	**NN**	**1-01-001**
archaize	**verb**	**1-01-001**
archaized	VBD	1-01-001
archangel	**noun**	**4-02-002**
archangel	NN	0-00-000
Archangel	NN-TL	3-01-001
archangels	NNS	1-01-001
archbishop	**noun**	**9-03-004**
archbishop	NN	2-01-001
Archbishop	NN-TL	6-03-003
archbishops'	NNS$	0-00-000
Archbishops'	NNS$-TL	1-01-001
archdiocese	**NN**	**1-01-001**
archenemy	**noun**	**2-02-002**
archenemy	NN	1-01-001
arch-enemy	NN	1-01-001
archeological	**JJ**	**1-01-001**
archery	**NN**	**1-01-001**
archfool	**NN**	**1-01-001**
Archimedes	**NP**	**1-01-001**
archipelago	**noun**	**2-01-001**
archipelago	NN	1-01-001
Archipelago	NN-TL	1-01-001
architect	**noun**	**33-10-022**
architect	NN	19-07-015
Architect	NN-TL	3-01-001
architect's	NN$	2-02-002
architects	NNS	8-04-006
architects'	NNS$	1-01-001
architectonic	**JJ**	**1-01-001**
architectural	**JJ**	**8-05-005**
architecture	**noun**	**12-07-010**
architecture	NN	11-07-009
architectures	NNS	1-01-001
archive	**noun**	**4-04-004**
archives	NNS	2-02-002
Archives	NNS-TL	2-02-002
archtype	**NN**	**1-01-001**
Archuleta	**NP**	**1-01-001**
Arcilla	**NP**	**1-01-001**
arclike	**JJ**	**1-01-001**
Arco	**NP**	**1-01-001**
Arctic	**adjective**	**2-01-001**
Arctic	JJ	1-01-001
Arctic	JJ-TL	1-01-001
Arctic	**NP**	**2-01-001**
arcus	**NN**	**1-01-001**
Arden	**prop. noun**	**3-02-002**
Arden	NP	0-00-000
Arden	NP-TL	3-02-002
ardent	**JJ**	**11-06-009**
Ardent	**NP**	**1-01-001**
Ardmore	**NP**	**1-01-001**
ardor	**NN**	**3-02-002**
arduous	**JJ**	**4-03-004**
area	**noun**	**562-14-196**
area	NN	318-14-144
area	NN-HL	1-01-001
Area	NN-TL	5-05-005
area's	NN$	2-01-001
areas	NNS	234-10-119
areas	NNS-HL	2-02-002
area-wide	**JJ**	**2-01-002**
areaway	**noun**	**1-01-001**
areaways	NNS	1-01-001
arena	**noun**	**10-04-009**
arena	NN	7-01-006
arenas	NNS	3-03-003
Arenula	**NP**	**1-01-001**

Arequipa	**NP**	**1-01-001**
Ares	**NP**	**1-01-001**
ARF	**NP**	**1-01-001**
Argentina	**NP**	**1-01-001**
Arger	**NP**	**3-01-001**
Argiento	**NP**	**13-01-001**
Argive	**JJ**	**1-01-001**
argon	**NN**	**7-01-001**
Argonaut	**prop. noun**	**1-01-001**
Argonauts	NPS	1-01-001
Argos	**NP**	**1-01-001**
argot	**NN**	**1-01-001**
argue	**verb**	**78-14-055**
argue	VB	29-07-021
argues	VBZ	10-06-007
argued	VBD	17-08-015
argued	VBN	12-08-011
arguing	VBG	10-06-008
argument	**noun**	**78-12-058**
argument	NN	63-11-048
arguments	NNS	15-08-013
argumentation	**NN**	**1-01-001**
Arhat	**prop. noun**	**2-01-001**
Arhat	NP	1-01-001
Arhats	NPS	1-01-001
Ariadne	**NP**	**3-02-002**
Arianism	**NP**	**1-01-001**
Arianist	**prop. noun**	**2-01-001**
Arianist	NP	1-01-001
Arianists	NPS	1-01-001
Aricara	**prop. noun**	**5-01-001**
Aricaras	NPS	5-01-001
arid	**JJ**	**2-02-002**
aridity	**NN**	**2-02-002**
Arigato	**FW-UH**	**1-01-001**
Arimathea	**prop. noun**	**2-01-001**
Arimathea	NP	0-00-000
Arimathea	NP-TL	2-01-001
arise	**verb**	**75-14-055**
arise	VB	28-09-025
arises	VBZ	14-08-013
arose	VBD	18-09-015
arisen	VBN	4-03-003
arising	VBG	11-05-009
Aristide	**NP**	**2-01-001**
aristocracy	**NN**	**4-04-004**
aristocrat	**noun**	**2-02-002**
aristocrats	NNS	2-02-002
aristocratic	**JJ**	**4-02-004**
aristocratically	**RB**	**1-01-001**
Aristotelean-Thomistic	**JJ**	**1-01-001**
Aristotelian	**JJ**	**2-01-002**
Aristotle	**prop. noun**	**27-02-005**
Aristotle	NP	20-02-004
Aristotle	NP-HL	1-01-001
Aristotle's	NP$	6-01-002
arithmetic	**noun**	**8-04-005**
arithmetic	NN	5-03-004
Arithmetic	NN-TL	3-01-001
arithmetical	**JJ**	**1-01-001**
arithmetize	**verb**	**1-01-001**
arithmetized	VBN	1-01-001
Arizona	**prop. noun**	**14-07-012**
Arizona	NP	8-06-008
Ariz.	NP	5-01-004
Arizona	NP-TL	1-01-001
Arkabutla	**prop. noun**	**1-01-001**
Arkabutla	NP	0-00-000
Arkabutla	NP-TL	1-01-001
Arkansas	**prop. noun**	**19-06-011**
Arkansas	NP	13-06-010
Arkansas	NP-TL	5-03-004
Arkansas'	NP$	1-01-001
Arleigh	**NP**	**1-01-001**
Arlen	**prop. noun**	**14-01-001**
Arlen	NP	13-01-001
Arlen's	NP$	1-01-001
Arlene	**prop. noun**	**27-02-002**
Arlene	NP	26-02-002
Arlene's	NP+BEZ	1-01-001
Arlington	**prop. noun**	**4-02-002**
Arlington	NP	2-01-001
Arlington	NP-TL	2-02-002
arm	**noun**	**217-15-119**
arm	NN	92-12-059
Arm	NN-TL	1-01-001
arm's	NN$	3-03-003
arms	NNS	113-15-083
arms	NNS-HL	3-02-002
arm (cont.):		
Arms	NNS-TL	5-04-005
arm	**verb**	**61-10-035**
arm	VB	1-01-001
armed	VBN	34-08-027
Armed	VBN-TL	24-04-008
Armed	VBN-TL-HL	2-01-002
arm-elevation	**NN**	**6-01-001**
arm-levitation	**NN**	**2-01-001**
arm-rise	**NN**	**1-01-001**
armada	**noun**	**1-01-001**
armada's	NN$	0-00-000
Armada's	NN$-TL	1-01-001
armadillo	**NN**	**2-01-001**
Armageddon	**NP**	**1-01-001**
armament	**noun**	**5-03-004**
armament	NN	1-01-001
armaments	NNS	4-02-003
armata	**NP**	**2-01-001**
Armbro	**prop. noun**	**1-01-001**
Armbro	NP	0-00-000
Armbro	NP-TL	1-01-001
armchair	**noun**	**6-05-006**
armchair	NN	4-03-004
armchairs	NNS	2-02-002
Armenian	**JJ**	**1-01-001**
Armentieres	**prop. noun**	**1-01-001**
Armentieres	NP	0-00-000
Armentieres	NP-TL	1-01-001
armful	**NN**	**1-01-001**
armhole	**noun**	**3-01-001**
armhole	NN	1-01-001
armhole	NN-HL	2-01-001
Armide	**NP**	**1-01-001**
Armistead	**prop. noun**	**1-01-001**
Armisteads	NPS	1-01-001
armistice	**noun**	**4-01-003**
armistice	NN	2-01-002
Armistice	NN-TL	2-01-001
armload	**NN**	**1-01-001**
armoire	**NN**	**1-01-001**
Armond	**NP**	**1-01-001**
armor	**NN**	**4-02-004**
armor	**verb**	**3-03-003**
armored	VBN	3-03-003
armory	**noun**	**2-01-001**
armory	NN	0-00-000
Armory	NN-TL	1-01-001
armory's	NN$	1-01-001
Armour	**NP**	**2-01-001**
armpit	**noun**	**3-03-003**
armpit	NN	2-02-002
armpits	NNS	1-01-001
arms-making	**NN**	**1-01-001**
Armstrong	**NP**	**6-03-004**
army	**noun**	**152-14-069**
army	NN	56-11-037
army	NN-HL	2-02-002
Army	NN-TL	74-10-035
army's	NN$	0-00-000
Army's	NN$-TL	5-02-004
armies	NNS	14-04-006
Armies	NNS-TL	1-01-001
arnica	**NN**	**1-01-001**
Arnold	**prop. noun**	**22-05-012**
Arnold	NP	20-05-011
Arnold's	NP$	2-02-002
Arnold-Foster	**NP**	**1-01-001**
Arnolphe	**NP**	**5-01-001**
aroma	**noun**	**5-04-005**
aroma	NN	3-03-003
aromas	NNS	2-02-002
aromatic	**adjective**	**3-02-002**
aromatic	JJ	2-01-001
aromatick	JJ	1-01-001
around	**prep.**	**327-15-192**
around	IN	326-15-191
'round	IN	1-01-001
around	**adverb**	**240-14-141**
around	RB	235-14-138
'round	RB	4-02-003
Around	RB-TL	1-01-001
arousal	**NN**	**3-03-003**
arouse	**verb**	**30-11-027**
arouse	VB	5-03-005
arouses	VBZ	2-02-002
aroused	VBD	5-04-004
aroused	VBN	15-10-015
arousing	VBG	3-02-003

Word	Tag	Frequency
Arp	**NP**	**6-02-002**
arpeggio	**noun**	**1-01-001**
arpeggios	NNS	1-01-001
arrack	**NN**	**1-01-001**
Arragon	**prop. noun**	**1-01-001**
Arragon	NP	0-00-000
Arragon	NP-TL	1-01-001
arraign	**verb**	**3-03-003**
arraigned	VBD	2-02-002
arraigning	VBG	1-01-001
arrange	**verb**	**71-15-058**
arrange	VB	10-06-009
arranges	VBZ	1-01-001
arranged	VBD	11-08-011
arranged	VBN	33-08-027
arranging	VBG	16-10-014
arrangement	**noun**	**72-13-058**
arrangement	NN	34-12-028
arrangements	NNS	38-12-034
arranger	**noun**	**1-01-001**
arrangers	NNS	1-01-001
array	**NN**	**11-05-011**
array	**verb**	**2-01-002**
arrayed	VBN	2-01-002
arrear	**noun**	**6-04-004**
arrears	NNS	6-04-004
arrest	**noun**	**16-05-011**
arrest	NN	13-05-010
arrests	NNS	3-02-002
arrest	**verb**	**27-11-019**
arrest	VB	6-05-005
arrested	VBD	4-03-004
arrested	VBN	15-05-011
arresting	VBG	2-02-002
arresting	**JJ**	**3-02-003**
Arrington	**NP**	**1-01-001**
arrival	**noun**	**26-12-026**
arrival	NN	23-11-023
arrivals	NNS	3-02-003
arrive	**verb**	**108-15-085**
arrive	VB	24-09-021
arrives	VBZ	7-06-007
arrived	VBD	43-12-038
arrived	VBN	19-13-018
arriving	VBG	15-08-014
arrogance	**NN**	**3-03-003**
arrogant	**JJ**	**2-02-002**
arrogantly	**RB**	**1-01-001**
arrogate	**VB**	**1-01-001**
arrow	**noun**	**20-05-005**
arrow	NN	13-02-002
Arrow	NN-TL	1-01-001
arrows	NNS	6-03-003
arrowed	**JJ**	**1-01-001**
arrowhead	**noun**	**2-02-002**
arrowhead	NN	0-00-000
Arrowhead	NN-TL	1-01-001
arrowheads	NNS	1-01-001
arroyo	**NN**	**3-01-001**
arsenal	**NN**	**3-03-003**
arsenic	**NN**	**1-01-001**
Arshinkoff	**NP**	**1-01-001**
arside	**NN**	**1-01-001**
arsine	**noun**	**1-01-001**
arsines	NNS	1-01-001
arson	**NN**	**2-01-001**
art	**noun**	**262-14-088**
art	NN	179-14-065
art	NN-HL	1-01-001
Art	NN-TL	15-08-011
art's	NN$	0-00-000
Art's	NN$-TL	1-01-001
arts	NNS	43-10-023
Arts	NNS-TL	23-07-017
Art	**prop. noun**	**8-03-006**
Art	NP	6-03-006
Art	NP-TL	1-01-001
Art's	NP$	1-01-001
art-filled	**JJ**	**1-01-001**
art-historian	**NN**	**1-01-001**
art-shop	**NN**	**1-01-001**
arte	**foreign**	**5-02-002**
arte	FW-NN	0-00-000
Arte	FW-NN-TL	4-02-002
arte's	FW-NN$	0-00-000
Arte's	FW-NN$-TL	1-01-001
Artemis	**prop. noun**	**1-01-001**
Artemis	NP	0-00-000
Artemis	NP-TL	1-01-001

Word	Tag	Frequency
arterial	**JJ**	**7-02-002**
arteriolar	**JJ**	**3-01-001**
arteriolar	**NN**	**1-01-001**
arteriole	**noun**	**2-01-001**
arterioles	NNS	2-01-001
arteriolosclerosis	**NN**	**2-01-001**
arteriosclerosis	**NN**	**1-01-001**
artery	**noun**	**68-04-007**
artery	NN	51-03-005
artery's	NN$	1-01-001
arteries	NNS	16-04-005
artful	**JJ**	**1-01-001**
artfully	**RB**	**4-03-004**
artfulness	**NN**	**1-01-001**
arthritis	**noun**	**3-02-002**
arthritis	NN	2-02-002
Arthritis	NN-TL	1-01-001
Arthur	**prop. noun**	**52-09-029**
Arthur	NP	44-09-028
Arthur	NP-TL	7-01-001
Arthur's	NP+BEZ	1-01-001
article	**noun**	**99-11-053**
article	NN	47-10-031
article	NN-HL	5-01-001
Article	NN-TL	16-05-006
articles	NNS	30-09-022
Articles	NNS-TL	1-01-001
articulate	**JJ**	**6-04-006**
articulate	**verb**	**4-03-004**
articulate	VB	2-02-002
articulated	VBN	2-02-002
articulation	**noun**	**2-02-002**
articulation	NN	1-01-001
articulations	NNS	1-01-001
Artie	**NP**	**8-01-001**
artifact	**noun**	**1-01-001**
artifacts	NNS	1-01-001
artifice	**NN**	**1-01-001**
artificer	**NN**	**1-01-001**
artificial	**JJ**	**17-08-017**
artificiality	**NN**	**1-01-001**
artificially	**RB**	**6-04-005**
artillerist	**NN**	**1-01-001**
artillery	**noun**	**11-05-010**
artillery	NN	9-04-008
Artillery	NN-TL	2-02-002
artisan	**foreign**	**1-01-001**
artisans	FW-NNS	0-00-000
Artisans	FW-NNS-TL	1-01-001
artisan	**noun**	**3-02-003**
artisan	NN	2-02-002
artisans	NNS	1-01-001
artist	**noun**	**125-12-051**
artist	NN	54-10-033
artist	NN-HL	1-01-001
Artist	NN-TL	2-02-002
artist's	NN$	7-03-005
artists	NNS	46-09-025
Artists	NNS-TL	9-04-005
artists'	NNS$	5-05-005
Artists'	NNS$-TL	1-01-001
artist-author	**NN**	**1-01-001**
artist-nature	**NN**	**1-01-001**
artistic	**JJ**	**33-09-019**
artistically	**RB**	**5-03-005**
artistry	**NN**	**3-02-003**
Artkino	**NP**	**1-01-001**
artless	**JJ**	**2-02-002**
Artur	**NP**	**1-01-001**
Arturo	**NP**	**2-02-002**
arty	**JJ**	**1-01-001**
Arundel	**prop. noun**	**5-01-001**
Arundel	NP	3-01-001
Arundel	NP-TL	2-01-001
Arvey	**NP**	**1-01-001**
aryl	**NN**	**1-01-001**
arylesterase	**noun**	**4-01-001**
arylesterase	NN	3-01-001
arylesterases	NNS	1-01-001
as	**sub. conj.**	**6029-15-500**
as	CS	6018-15-500
's	+CS	3-01-001
as	CS-HL	7-05-006
as	CS-TL	1-01-001
as	**IN**	**121-14-098**
as	**QL**	**1101-15-426**
as	**RB**	**3-02-002**
as-it-were	**RB**	**1-01-001**
asbestos	**NN**	**1-01-001**

asbestos-cement	**NN**	**1-01-001**
ascend	**verb**	**7-06-007**
ascend	VB	1-01-001
ascended	VBD	2-01-002
ascending	VBG	4-04-004
ascendancy	**NN**	**1-01-001**
ascent	**NN**	**1-01-001**
ascertain	**verb**	**11-04-011**
ascertain	VB	7-04-007
ascertained	VBD	1-01-001
ascertained	VBN	3-01-003
ascertainable	**JJ**	**1-01-001**
ascetic	**NN**	**1-01-001**
asceticism	**NN**	**1-01-001**
Asch	**NP**	**1-01-001**
Aschenbach	**NP**	**1-01-001**
ascribe	**verb**	**7-04-007**
ascribe	VB	1-01-001
ascribes	VBZ	1-01-001
ascribed	VBD	1-01-001
ascribed	VBN	4-03-004
aseptic	**JJ**	**1-01-001**
ash	**noun**	**17-08-013**
ash	NN	8-04-007
Ash	NN-TL	3-02-002
ashes	NNS	6-05-005
ash-blonde	**JJ**	**1-01-001**
ash-can	**noun**	**1-01-001**
ash-can	NN	0-00-000
Ash-Can	NN-TL	1-01-001
ashamed	**adjective**	**17-08-016**
ashamed	JJ	16-07-015
asham'd	JJ	1-01-001
ashen	**JJ**	**2-02-002**
Asher	**NP**	**1-01-001**
Asheville	**prop. noun**	**2-01-001**
Asheville	NP	1-01-001
Asheville	NP-TL	1-01-001
Ashikaga	**NP**	**1-01-001**
Ashley	**NP**	**1-01-001**
Ashman	**NP**	**1-01-001**
Ashmolean	**adjective**	**1-01-001**
Ashmolean	JJ	0-00-000
Ashmolean	JJ-TL	1-01-001
ashore	**RB**	**6-03-004**
ashtray	**noun**	**1-01-001**
ashtrays	NNS	1-01-001
Asia	**prop. noun**	**44-11-032**
Asia	NP	25-10-019
Asia	NP-TL	19-07-016
Asian	**adjective**	**10-05-008**
Asian	JJ	9-05-007
Asian	JJ-TL	1-01-001
Asian	**prop. noun**	**1-01-001**
Asians	NPS	1-01-001
Asiatic	**JJ**	**1-01-001**
aside	**adverb**	**67-15-060**
aside	RB	66-15-059
Aside	RB-TL	1-01-001
Asilomar	**prop. noun**	**1-01-001**
Asilomar	NP	0-00-000
Asilomar	NP-HL	1-01-001
Asimov	**prop. noun**	**1-01-001**
Asimov's	NP$	1-01-001
asinine	**JJ**	**2-02-002**
ask	**verb**	**612-15-253**
ask	VB	123-15-090
ask	VB-HL	2-02-002
Ask	VB-TL	3-01-001
asks	VBZ	17-10-015
asks	VBZ-HL	1-01-001
asked	VBD	300-15-157
asked	VBN	97-14-077
asked	VBN-HL	1-01-001
asking	VBG	67-13-056
askin'	VBG	1-01-001
askance	**RB**	**1-01-001**
askew	**RB**	**1-01-001**
Askington	**prop. noun**	**6-01-001**
Askington	NP	5-01-001
Askington's	NP$	1-01-001
asleep	**JJ**	**3-02-003**
asleep	**RB**	**27-08-019**
asocial	**JJ**	**1-01-001**
asparagus	**NN**	**1-01-001**
aspect	**noun**	**111-13-080**
aspect	NN	47-11-038
aspects	NNS	61-10-048
aspects	NNS-HL	2-02-002
aspect (cont.):		
Aspects	NNS-TL	1-01-001
aspen	**NN**	**2-01-001**
Aspencade	**prop. noun**	**3-01-001**
Aspencade	NP	1-01-001
Aspencades	NPS	2-01-001
asphalt	**NN**	**3-03-003**
aspirant	**noun**	**4-03-004**
aspirant	NN	2-01-002
aspirants	NNS	2-02-002
aspiration	**noun**	**15-06-012**
aspiration	NN	3-02-003
aspirations	NNS	12-05-009
aspire	**verb**	**6-02-006**
aspire	VB	3-02-003
aspires	VBZ	1-01-001
aspired	VBD	1-01-001
aspiring	VBG	1-01-001
aspirin	**NN**	**3-03-003**
ASPIS	**foreign**	**1-01-001**
ASPIS	FW-NN	0-00-000
ASPIS	FW-NN-NC	1-01-001
ass	**noun**	**8-06-008**
ass	NN	5-05-005
asses	NNS	2-02-002
Asses	NNS	1-01-001
assai	**foreign**	**1-01-001**
assai	FW-RB	0-00-000
assai	FW-RB-TL	1-01-001
assail	**verb**	**8-05-008**
assail	VB	3-03-003
assailed	VBN	4-04-004
assailing	VBG	1-01-001
assailant	**noun**	**3-02-003**
assailant	NN	2-02-002
assailants	NNS	1-01-001
Assam	**NP**	**2-01-001**
assassin	**noun**	**7-05-006**
assassin	NN	6-04-005
assassins	NNS	1-01-001
assassinate	**verb**	**1-01-001**
assassinated	VBN	1-01-001
assassination	**NN**	**4-03-003**
assault	**noun**	**18-06-015**
assault	NN	14-05-011
assault	NN-NC	1-01-001
assaults	NNS	3-02-003
assault	**verb**	**8-04-007**
assaults	VBZ	1-01-001
assaulted	VBD	3-02-003
assaulted	VBN	3-03-003
assaulting	VBG	1-01-001
assay	**NN**	**1-01-001**
assay	**verb**	**3-01-002**
assayed	VBN	1-01-001
assaying	VBG	2-01-002
assemblage	**noun**	**4-04-004**
assemblage	NN	3-03-003
assemblages	NNS	1-01-001
assemble	**verb**	**39-11-029**
assemble	VB	8-05-007
assemble	VB-HL	1-01-001
assembled	VBD	7-05-007
assembled	VBN	17-09-014
assembling	VBG	6-05-006
assembly	**noun**	**61-10-036**
assembly	NN	21-07-015
assembly	NN-HL	1-01-001
Assembly	NN-TL	28-08-018
assemblies	NNS	6-04-005
Assemblies	NNS-TL	5-01-001
assent	**NN**	**4-04-004**
assent	**verb**	**3-02-003**
assented	VBD	2-02-002
assented	VBN	1-01-001
Asser	**NP**	**1-01-001**
assert	**verb**	**44-07-029**
assert	VB	19-04-014
asserts	VBZ	5-03-005
asserted	VBD	11-06-010
asserted	VBN	5-04-005
asserting	VBG	4-04-004
assertion	**noun**	**10-05-010**
assertion	NN	7-05-007
assertions	NNS	3-03-003
assertive	**JJ**	**2-02-002**
assertiveness	**NN**	**1-01-001**
assess	**verb**	**25-07-016**
assess	VB	6-05-005

Word	Tag	Frequency
assess (cont.):		
assessed	VBN	9-07-008
assessing	VBG	10-03-005
assessment	**noun**	**30-05-013**
assessment	NN	22-05-009
assesment	NN	1-01-001
assessment	NN-HL	1-01-001
assessments	NNS	6-04-006
assessor	**noun**	**24-03-003**
assessor	NN	2-01-001
assessor's	NN$	1-01-001
assessors	NNS	20-03-003
assessors'	NNS$	1-01-001
asset	**noun**	**18-04-010**
asset	NN	5-03-005
assets	NNS	13-04-007
assiduity	**NN**	**1-01-001**
assign	**verb**	**84-11-046**
assign	VB	18-06-014
assigns	VBZ	4-02-004
assigned	VBD	2-02-002
assigned	VBN	51-10-031
assigning	VBG	9-05-009
assignee	**NN**	**2-01-001**
assignment	**noun**	**80-10-027**
assignment	NN	58-08-021
assignment	NN-HL	4-02-002
assignments	NNS	18-07-012
assimilate	**verb**	**6-04-006**
assimilate	VB	2-02-002
assimilated	VBN	4-04-004
assimilation	**noun**	**8-04-004**
assimilation	NN	6-04-004
assimilation	NN-HL	1-01-001
Assimilation	NN-TL	1-01-001
Assiniboia	**NP**	**2-01-001**
Assiniboine	**NP**	**2-01-001**
assist	**noun**	**5-04-005**
assist	NN	4-03-004
assists	NNS	1-01-001
assist	**verb**	**36-09-030**
assist	VB	21-06-018
Assist	VB-TL	1-01-001
assisted	VBD	3-03-003
assisted	VBN	4-04-004
assisting	VBG	6-04-006
assisting	VBG-HL	1-01-001
assistance	**noun**	**87-08-035**
assistance	NN	83-08-035
assistance	NN-HL	3-01-001
Assistance	NN-TL	1-01-001
assistant	**adjective**	**15-07-015**
assistant	JJ	6-05-006
Assistant	JJ-TL	9-04-009
assistant	**noun**	**32-08-026**
assistant	NN	21-06-017
assistants	NNS	11-05-010
associate	**JJ**	**4-02-004**
associate	**noun**	**21-11-020**
associate	NN	3-03-003
Associate	NN-TL	4-03-003
associates	NNS	12-09-012
Associates	NNS	1-01-001
Associates	NNS-TL	1-01-001
associate	**verb**	**74-10-056**
associate	VB	10-08-010
associates	VBZ	1-01-001
associated	VBD	3-03-003
associated	VBN	55-09-040
Associated	VBN-TL	3-02-003
associating	VBG	2-01-002
association	**noun**	**168-14-084**
association	NN	46-10-031
assn.	NN	0-00-000
Assn.	NN-TL	2-01-001
ass'n	NN	0-00-000
Ass'n	NN-TL	2-01-001
Association	NN-TL	85-11-047
Association	NN-TL-HL	1-01-001
association's	NN$	1-01-001
associations	NNS	27-08-021
Associations	NNS-TL	3-02-003
associations'	NNS$	0-00-000
ass'ns'	NNS$	0-00-000
Ass'ns'	NNS$-TL	1-01-001
associatively	**RB**	**1-01-001**
assonance	**NN**	**1-01-001**
assort	**verb**	**2-02-002**
assorted	VBN	2-02-002
assortment	**NN**	**1-01-001**
assuage	**verb**	**2-02-002**
assuaged	VBN	2-02-002
assume	**verb**	**160-15-112**
assume	VB	63-13-050
assumes	VBZ	8-04-008
assumed	VBD	28-12-026
assumed	VBN	44-09-038
assuming	VBG	17-08-015
assumption	**noun**	**64-08-041**
assumption	NN	38-07-029
assumption	NN-HL	3-01-001
assumptions	NNS	22-05-016
assumptions	NNS-HL	1-01-001
assurance	**noun**	**22-11-020**
assurance	NN	19-11-018
assurances	NNS	3-03-003
assure	**verb**	**92-14-074**
assure	VB	37-10-032
assures	VBZ	6-04-006
assured	VBD	16-07-015
assured	VBN	23-12-023
assuring	VBG	10-07-010
assuredly	**RB**	**4-03-003**
Assyrian	**JJ**	**1-01-001**
Assyrian	**prop. noun**	**1-01-001**
Assyrian	NP	0-00-000
Assyrian	NP-TL	1-01-001
Assyriology	**NP**	**1-01-001**
Astaire	**prop. noun**	**1-01-001**
Astaires	NPS	1-01-001
Astarte	**NP**	**1-01-001**
aster	**noun**	**1-01-001**
asters	NNS	1-01-001
Asteria	**NP**	**2-01-001**
asterisk	**noun**	**2-01-001**
asterisks	NNS	2-01-001
asteroid	**NN**	**1-01-001**
asteroidal	**JJ**	**1-01-001**
asthma	**NN**	**1-01-001**
Astin	**NP**	**1-01-001**
astonish	**verb**	**6-04-006**
astonished	VBD	1-01-001
astonished	VBN	5-04-005
astonishing	**JJ**	**8-05-008**
astonishingly	**QL**	**4-04-004**
astonishingly	**RB**	**2-02-002**
astonishment	**NN**	**5-04-005**
Astor	**prop. noun**	**2-01-001**
Astor	NP	1-01-001
Astor	NP-TL	1-01-001
astound	**verb**	**3-03-003**
astound	VB	1-01-001
astounded	VBN	2-02-002
astounding	**JJ**	**5-04-005**
Astra	**NP**	**1-01-001**
astral	**JJ**	**1-01-001**
astray	**RB**	**3-03-003**
astride	**IN**	**3-03-003**
astringency	**NN**	**1-01-001**
astringent	**JJ**	**1-01-001**
astronaut	**noun**	**2-01-002**
astronaut	NN	1-01-001
Astronaut	NN-TL	1-01-001
astronomer	**NN**	**1-01-001**
astronomical	**JJ**	**6-05-006**
astronomically	**QL**	**1-01-001**
astronomy	**NN**	**24-06-006**
astrophysics	**noun**	**3-02-002**
astrophysics	NN	2-02-002
astrophysics	NN-HL	1-01-001
astute	**JJ**	**1-01-001**
astuteness	**NN**	**1-01-001**
Astwood	**NP**	**1-01-001**
asunder	**RB**	**1-01-001**
asylum	**noun**	**1-01-001**
asylum	NN	0-00-000
Asylum	NN-TL	1-01-001
asymmetric	**JJ**	**2-01-001**
asymmetrically	**RB**	**2-01-001**
asymmetry	**NN**	**1-01-001**
asymptotic	**JJ**	**1-01-001**
asymptotically	**RB**	**1-01-001**
asynchrony	**NN**	**2-01-001**
at	**prep.**	**5377-15-500**
at	IN	5353-15-500
att	IN	2-01-001
at	IN-HL	8-04-008
at	IN-NC	4-01-001

Word	Tag	Frequency
at (cont.):		
At	IN-TL	3-03-003
at	IN-TL	4-03-004
lookit	+IN	3-02-002
at-bat	**noun**	**1-01-001**
at-bats	NNS	1-01-001
atavistic	**JJ**	**1-01-001**
Aterman	**NP**	**1-01-001**
Athabascan	**prop. noun**	**14-01-001**
Athabascan	NP	13-01-001
Ath.	NP	1-01-001
Athalie	**prop. noun**	**2-01-001**
Athalie	NP	1-01-001
Athalie	NP-TL	1-01-001
Athearn	**prop. noun**	**1-01-001**
Athearn	NP	0-00-000
Athearn	NP-TL	1-01-001
atheist	**noun**	**3-03-003**
atheists	NNS	3-03-003
atheistic	**JJ**	**1-01-001**
Athena	**NP**	**1-01-001**
Athenian	**JJ**	**2-01-002**
Athenian	**prop. noun**	**4-01-001**
Athenians	NPS	4-01-001
Athens	**prop. noun**	**8-04-006**
Athens	NP	7-03-005
Athens	NP-TL	1-01-001
atheromatous	**JJ**	**1-01-001**
athlete	**noun**	**16-07-012**
athlete	NN	8-05-007
Athlete	NN-TL	1-01-001
athlete's	NN$	1-01-001
athletes	NNS	5-03-004
athletes'	NNS$	1-01-001
athletic	**adjective**	**18-06-009**
athletic	JJ	13-06-008
Athletic	JJ-TL	5-03-003
athleticism	**NN**	**1-01-001**
athletics	**noun**	**9-04-005**
athletics	NN	4-03-003
athletics	NN-HL	1-01-001
athletics	NNS	2-02-002
Athletics	NNS-TL	2-01-001
Atkinson	**NP**	**2-02-002**
Atlanta	**prop. noun**	**39-06-011**
Atlanta	NP	31-06-010
Atlanta	NP-TL	4-01-002
Atlanta's	NP$	4-01-002
Atlantes	**FW-NPS**	**1-01-001**
Atlantic	**adjective**	**30-07-015**
Atlantic	JJ	16-04-006
Atlantic	JJ-HL	1-01-001
Atlantic	JJ-TL	13-06-008
Atlantic	**prop. noun**	**10-05-008**
Atlantic	NP	4-04-004
Atlantic	NP-TL	6-03-004
Atlantica	**NP**	**1-01-001**
Atlantis	**NP**	**2-02-002**
atlas	**noun**	**3-01-001**
atlas	NN	0-00-000
Atlas	NN-TL	3-01-001
Atlas	**NP**	**9-03-004**
Atlee	**NP**	**1-01-001**
atmosphere	**noun**	**84-14-062**
atmosphere	NN	79-14-061
atmospheres	NNS	5-02-003
atmospheric	**adjective**	**9-03-004**
atmospheric	JJ	8-03-004
atmospheric	JJ-HL	1-01-001
atom	**noun**	**78-08-013**
atom	NN	37-07-009
atom's	NN$	1-01-001
atoms	NNS	39-04-008
atoms	NNS-HL	1-01-001
atom-like	**JJ**	**1-01-001**
atomic	**adjective**	**46-09-025**
atomic	JJ	38-09-022
atomic	JJ-HL	3-02-002
Atomic	JJ-TL	5-02-004
atomisation	**NN**	**1-01-001**
atonally	**RB**	**1-01-001**
atone	**VB**	**1-01-001**
atonement	**NN**	**2-01-001**
atop	**IN**	**3-03-003**
atop	**RB**	**3-03-003**
ATP	**NP**	**1-01-001**
Atreus	**NP**	**2-02-002**
atrociously	**QL**	**1-01-001**
atrocity	**noun**	**2-02-002**
atrocity (cont.):		
atrocities	NNS	2-02-002
atrophic	**JJ**	**3-01-001**
atrophy	**NN**	**4-01-001**
atrophy	**verb**	**1-01-001**
atrophied	VBN	1-01-001
atta	**UH**	**2-02-002**
attach	**verb**	**44-13-032**
attach	VB	14-08-011
attaches	VBZ	2-02-002
attached	VBD	3-03-003
attached	VBN	22-10-019
attaching	VBG	3-02-003
attachment	**noun**	**9-07-009**
attachment	NN	5-04-005
attachments	NNS	4-03-004
attack	**noun**	**97-11-053**
attack	NN	78-11-046
attack	NN-HL	2-02-002
attacks	NNS	17-06-013
attack	**verb**	**63-14-049**
attack	VB	24-09-019
attacks	VBZ	3-03-003
attacks	VBZ-HL	2-01-002
attacked	VBD	12-08-011
attacked	VBN	13-08-012
attacking	VBG	9-06-009
attacker	**noun**	**10-05-006**
attacker	NN	6-04-004
attacker's	NN$	1-01-001
attackers	NNS	3-03-003
attain	**verb**	**35-09-028**
attain	VB	20-08-018
attains	VBZ	1-01-001
attained	VBD	5-03-005
attained	VBN	3-02-002
attaining	VBG	6-03-005
attainment	**noun**	**10-07-010**
attainment	NN	9-06-009
attainments	NNS	1-01-001
Attakapas	**NP**	**2-01-001**
attempt	**noun**	**102-13-082**
attempt	NN	71-13-061
attempts	NNS	30-10-029
attempts	NNS-HL	1-01-001
attempt	**verb**	**87-14-067**
attempt	VB	24-10-021
attempts	VBZ	7-04-006
attempted	VBD	18-07-016
attempted	VBN	15-08-014
attempting	VBG	23-10-021
attend	**verb**	**119-12-081**
attend	VB	52-11-039
attend	VB-HL	2-01-002
attends	VBZ	6-04-006
attended	VBD	24-09-022
attended	VBN	12-07-011
attending	VBG	23-09-022
attendance	**NN**	**12-06-009**
attendant	**JJ**	**5-02-005**
attendant	**noun**	**14-07-010**
attendant	NN	7-03-004
attendants	NNS	7-06-006
attention	**noun**	**180-15-129**
attention	NN	179-15-129
attentions	NNS	1-01-001
attentive	**JJ**	**5-03-005**
attentively	**RB**	**1-01-001**
attest	**verb**	**7-05-007**
attest	VB	2-02-002
attested	VBD	2-02-002
attested	VBN	2-02-002
attesting	VBG	1-01-001
Attic	**JJ**	**1-01-001**
attic	**noun**	**15-09-010**
attic	NN	14-08-009
Attic	NN-TL	1-01-001
Attica	**NP**	**1-01-001**
Attilio	**NP**	**1-01-001**
attire	**NN**	**6-05-005**
attire	**verb**	**1-01-001**
attired	VBN	1-01-001
attis	**FW-NN**	**1-01-001**
attitude	**noun**	**155-14-096**
attitude	NN	105-14-071
attitude	NN-HL	2-02-002
attitudes	NNS	48-10-041
Attlee	**NP**	**1-01-001**
Attopeu	**NP**	**1-01-001**

attorney	**noun**	**81-10-036**
attorney	NN	27-07-019
atty.	NN	0-00-000
Atty.	NN-TL	4-02-004
Attorney	NN-TL	38-07-020
attorney's	NN$	2-01-001
Attorney's	NN$-TL	1-01-001
attorneys	NNS	8-02-007
Attorneys	NNS-TL	1-01-001
attract	**verb**	**51-15-042**
attract	VB	19-10-016
attracts	VBZ	3-03-003
attracted	VBD	11-09-011
attracted	VBN	14-08-013
attracting	VBG	4-04-004
attraction	**noun**	**24-12-021**
attraction	NN	15-09-013
attractions	NNS	9-05-008
attractive	**adjective**	**40-13-033**
attractive	JJ	39-13-032
attactive	JJ	1-01-001
attractively	**RB**	**1-01-001**
attributable	**JJ**	**7-03-005**
attribute	**noun**	**15-04-009**
attribute	NN	4-02-004
attributes	NNS	9-04-006
attributes	NNS-HL	2-01-001
attribute	**verb**	**24-08-019**
attribute	VB	2-02-002
attributes	VBZ	1-01-001
attributed	VBD	6-05-006
attributed	VBN	12-06-010
attributing	VBG	3-03-003
attrition	**NN**	**5-03-005**
Attu	**NP**	**1-01-001**
attune	**verb**	**3-02-003**
attuned	VBN	3-02-003
atune	**JJ**	**1-01-001**
Atwells	**prop. noun**	**1-01-001**
Atwells	NP	0-00-000
Atwells	NP-TL	1-01-001
atypical	**JJ**	**1-01-001**
Auberge	**foreign**	**1-01-001**
Auberge	FW-NN	0-00-000
Auberge	FW-NN-TL	1-01-001
Aubrey	**prop. noun**	**2-01-001**
Aubrey	NP	0-00-000
Aubr.	NP-TL	1-01-001
Aubrey's	NP$	1-01-001
auburn	**JJ**	**1-01-001**
Auburn	**NP**	**1-01-001**
auction	**NN**	**4-01-002**
auctioneer	**noun**	**2-02-002**
auctioneer	NN	1-01-001
auctioneer's	NN$	1-01-001
audacity	**NN**	**3-03-003**
audible	**JJ**	**4-04-004**
audibly	**RB**	**1-01-001**
audience	**noun**	**131-14-055**
audience	NN	115-14-047
audiences	NNS	16-07-013
audio	**JJ**	**1-01-001**
audio	**NN**	**1-01-001**
audio-visual	**JJ**	**4-02-003**
audit	**noun**	**5-02-003**
audit	NN	4-02-002
audits	NNS	0-00-000
Audits	NNS-TL	1-01-001
audit	**verb**	**3-02-003**
audited	VBN	2-02-002
auditing	VBG	1-01-001
audition	**noun**	**4-02-003**
audition	NN	2-01-002
auditions	NNS	2-01-001
audition	**verb**	**2-01-001**
audition	VB	1-01-001
auditioning	VBG	1-01-001
auditor	**noun**	**5-02-002**
auditor	NN	1-01-001
auditors	NNS	4-01-001
auditorium	**noun**	**14-07-010**
auditorium	NN	8-06-007
Auditorium	NN-TL	6-02-004
audivi	**FW-VBD**	**1-01-001**
Audrey	**NP**	**1-01-001**
Audubon	**prop. noun**	**5-03-003**
Audubon	NP	0-00-000
Audubon	NP-TL	5-03-003
Auerbach	**prop. noun**	**1-01-001**

Auerbach (cont.):		
Auerbach's	NP$	1-01-001
auf	**foreign**	**2-01-002**
auf	FW-IN	0-00-000
auf	FW-IN-TL	2-01-002
augen	**FW-NNS**	**1-01-001**
augment	**verb**	**12-08-011**
augment	VB	2-02-002
augmented	VBD	4-02-003
augmented	VBN	5-04-005
augmenting	VBG	1-01-001
augur	**verb**	**1-01-001**
augurs	VBZ	1-01-001
august	**JJ**	**1-01-001**
August	**prop. noun**	**77-12-050**
August	NP	52-11-041
Aug.	NP	12-03-011
Aug.	NP-HL	13-01-001
Augusta	**prop. noun**	**7-01-001**
Augusta	NP	4-01-001
Augusta	NP-TL	2-01-001
Augusta's	NP$	1-01-001
Augustan	**JJ**	**1-01-001**
Augustin	**NP**	**1-01-001**
Augustine	**prop. noun**	**5-03-005**
Augustine	NP	3-03-003
Augustine	NP-TL	1-01-001
Augustine's	NP$	1-01-001
Augustus	**NP**	**4-04-004**
aujourd'hui	**FW-NR**	**1-01-001**
aunt	**noun**	**27-09-017**
aunt	NN	8-06-007
Aunt	NN-TL	14-06-009
aunt's	NN$	1-01-001
aunts	NNS	4-04-004
Auntie	**NP**	**3-02-002**
aura	**NN**	**1-01-001**
aural	**JJ**	**1-01-001**
aurally	**RB**	**2-02-002**
Aurelius	**NP**	**2-02-002**
Aureomycin	**NP**	**5-01-001**
Aurora	**prop. noun**	**2-01-002**
Aurora	NP	1-01-001
Aurora	NP-TL	1-01-001
Auschwitz	**NP**	**1-01-001**
auspice	**noun**	**6-06-006**
auspices	NNS	6-06-006
auspicious	**JJ**	**1-01-001**
auspiciously	**RB**	**1-01-001**
austere	**JJ**	**5-04-005**
austerely	**RB**	**1-01-001**
austerity	**NN**	**1-01-001**
Austin	**prop. noun**	**20-04-011**
Austin	NP	11-03-009
Austin	NP-HL	6-01-002
Austin	NP-TL	1-01-001
Austin's	NP$	2-02-002
Australia	**NP**	**11-08-009**
Australian	**JJ**	**4-02-003**
Australian	**NP**	**5-01-001**
australite	**noun**	**1-01-001**
australites	NNS	1-01-001
Austria	**NP**	**4-02-004**
Austrian	**JJ**	**4-02-002**
authentic	**JJ**	**20-09-015**
authentically	**RB**	**2-02-002**
authenticate	**verb**	**2-02-002**
authenticate	VB	1-01-001
authenticated	VBN	1-01-001
authentication	**noun**	**2-01-001**
authentication	NN	1-01-001
authentications	NNS	1-01-001
authenticator	**NN**	**1-01-001**
authenticity	**NN**	**8-03-004**
author	**noun**	**77-11-048**
author	NN	44-09-036
Author	NN-TL	2-01-001
author's	NN$	7-04-006
authors	NNS	23-04-010
authors'	NNS$	1-01-001
authoritarian	**JJ**	**5-03-005**
authoritarianism	**NN**	**2-01-002**
authoritative	**JJ**	**8-07-007**
authoritatively	**RB**	**1-01-001**
authority	**noun**	**135-14-082**
authority	NN	83-12-055
Authority	NN-TL	10-04-008
authority's	NN$	0-00-000
Authority's	NN$-TL	3-02-002

Word	Tag	Frequency
authority (cont.):		
authorities	NNS	39-09-026
authorization	**noun**	**8-02-004**
authorization	NN	2-01-002
authorizations	NNS	6-02-003
authorize	**verb**	**49-08-024**
authorize	VB	5-04-005
authorizes	VBZ	2-02-002
authorized	VBD	4-03-004
authorized	VBN	33-06-013
authorizing	VBG	5-04-004
authorship	**NN**	**3-03-003**
autism	**NN**	**2-01-001**
autistic	**JJ**	**13-01-001**
auto	**noun**	**26-10-016**
auto	NN	21-07-013
Auto	NN-TL	1-01-001
autos	NNS	4-04-004
Auto-Europe	**prop. noun**	**1-01-001**
Auto-Europe	NP	0-00-000
Auto-Europe	NP-TL	1-01-001
auto-limitation	**NN**	**1-01-001**
autobiographic	**JJ**	**1-01-001**
autobiographical	**JJ**	**3-03-003**
autobiography	**noun**	**5-03-005**
autobiography	NN	4-03-004
Autobiography	NN-TL	1-01-001
Autocoder	**NP**	**10-01-001**
autocollimator	**noun**	**5-01-001**
autocollimator	NN	4-01-001
autocollimator	NN-HL	1-01-001
autocracy	**noun**	**4-01-001**
autocracies	NNS	1-01-001
Autocracies	NNS-TL	3-01-001
autocrat	**noun**	**1-01-001**
autocrats	NNS	1-01-001
autocratic	**JJ**	**1-01-001**
autofluorescence	**NN**	**3-01-001**
autograph	**NN**	**3-02-002**
autoloader	**noun**	**4-01-002**
autoloader	NN	3-01-001
autoloaders	NNS	0-00-000
auto-loaders	NNS	1-01-001
automate	**verb**	**3-03-003**
automate	VB	1-01-001
automated	VBN	2-02-002
automatic	**adjective**	**39-10-022**
automatic	JJ	38-09-021
Automatic	JJ-TL	1-01-001
automatic	**NN**	**1-01-001**
automatically	**RB**	**36-12-027**
automation	**NN**	**6-05-006**
automaton	**NN**	**1-01-001**
automobile	**noun**	**74-11-030**
automobile	NN	41-10-022
automobile	NN-HL	3-01-001
Automobile	NN-TL	6-02-002
automobiles	NNS	24-08-011
automotive	**JJ**	**8-03-004**
autonavigator	**NN**	**1-01-001**
autonomic	**JJ**	**11-01-001**
autonomic-somatic	**JJ**	**2-01-001**
autonomy	**NN**	**18-06-008**
autopsy	**NN**	**2-02-002**
autopsy	**verb**	**2-02-002**
autopsy	VB	1-01-001
autopsied	VBN	1-01-001
autosuggestibility	**NN**	**1-01-001**
autumn	**NN**	**22-08-014**
autumn-touched	**JJ**	**1-01-001**
autumnal	**JJ**	**1-01-001**
aux	**foreign**	**1-01-001**
aux	FW-IN+AT	0-00-000
aux	FW-IN+AT-TL	1-01-001
auxiliary	**JJ**	**5-04-005**
auxiliary	**noun**	**5-04-004**
auxiliary	NN	1-01-001
Auxiliary	NN-TL	1-01-001
auxiliaries	NNS	1-01-001
Auxiliaries	NNS-TL	2-01-001
avail	**NN**	**1-01-001**
avail	**verb**	**6-04-005**
avail	VB	3-03-003
availed	VBD	2-01-001
availing	VBG	1-01-001
availability	**noun**	**23-06-015**
availability	NN	21-06-015
availabilities	NNS	2-01-002
available	**adjective**	**246-14-118**
available (cont.):		
available	JJ	243-14-118
avaliable	JJ	1-01-001
Available	JJ-TL	2-01-001
avalanche	**NN**	**1-01-001**
avant	**JJ**	**1-01-001**
avant-garde	**JJ**	**1-01-001**
avant-garde	**NN**	**5-02-003**
avarice	**NN**	**2-02-002**
avaricious	**JJ**	**1-01-001**
AVC	**NP**	**1-01-001**
avec	**foreign**	**1-01-001**
avec	FW-IN	0-00-000
avec	FW-IN-TL	1-01-001
avenge	**verb**	**4-02-004**
avenge	VB	2-01-002
avenging	VBG	2-02-002
Aventine	**prop. noun**	**1-01-001**
Aventine	NP	0-00-000
Aventine	NP-TL	1-01-001
Aventino	**NP**	**1-01-001**
avenue	**noun**	**73-12-043**
avenue	NN	7-03-005
av.	NN	0-00-000
Av.	NN-TL	9-02-003
ave.	NN	0-00-000
Ave.	NN-TL	13-03-008
Avenue	NN-TL	39-11-027
avenues	NNS	5-04-005
average	**adjective**	**64-11-041**
average	JJ	63-10-040
Average	JJ-TL	1-01-001
average	**noun**	**71-12-052**
average	NN	61-12-047
averages	NNS	10-03-007
average	**verb**	**26-06-012**
average	VB	5-02-002
averaged	VBD	13-03-005
averaging	VBG	8-04-007
averaging	**NN**	**1-01-001**
Averell	**NP**	**2-02-002**
aversion	**NN**	**2-01-002**
avert	**verb**	**7-05-006**
avert	VB	1-01-001
averted	VBD	2-02-002
averted	VBN	1-01-001
averting	VBG	3-03-003
Avery	**NP**	**1-01-001**
aviary	**NN**	**1-01-001**
aviation	**noun**	**5-03-004**
aviation	NN	2-02-002
Aviation	NN-TL	3-03-003
aviator	**noun**	**4-02-002**
aviator	NN	3-02-002
aviators	NNS	1-01-001
avid	**JJ**	**1-01-001**
avidity	**NN**	**1-01-001**
avidly	**RB**	**1-01-001**
Avis	**NP**	**1-01-001**
Aviv	**NP**	**1-01-001**
avocado	**noun**	**16-02-002**
avocado	NN	9-01-001
Avocado	NN-TL	1-01-001
avocados	NNS	6-01-001
avocation	**NN**	**1-01-001**
avoid	**verb**	**91-14-077**
avoid	VB	58-14-049
avoids	VBZ	3-03-003
avoided	VBD	7-06-007
avoided	VBN	11-05-011
avoided	VBN-HL	1-01-001
avoiding	VBG	11-06-011
avoidance	**NN**	**8-06-008**
Avon	**NP**	**1-01-001**
avow	**verb**	**2-02-002**
avowed	VBN	2-02-002
aw	**UH**	**2-01-002**
await	**verb**	**26-10-023**
await	VB	9-05-007
awaits	VBZ	3-02-003
awaited	VBD	6-04-006
awaited	VBN	1-01-001
awaiting	VBG	7-04-006
awake	**JJ**	**11-05-010**
awake	**RB**	**7-05-007**
awake	**verb**	**11-07-010**
awake	VB	1-01-001
Awake	VB-TL	1-01-001
awoke	VBD	9-06-008

awaken	**verb**	**13-07-012**
awaken	VB	7-04-006
awakens	VBZ	1-01-001
awakened	VBD	1-01-001
awakened	VBN	3-03-003
awakening	VBG	1-01-001
awakening	**noun**	**3-03-003**
awakening	NN	2-02-002
Awakening	NN-TL	1-01-001
award	**noun**	**60-06-018**
award	NN	35-06-014
award	NN-HL	1-01-001
Award	NN-TL	7-01-002
awards	NNS	16-03-006
awards	NNS-HL	1-01-001
award	**verb**	**22-07-016**
award	VB	3-03-003
awarded	VBD	2-02-002
awarded	VBN	15-06-012
awarding	VBG	2-01-001
awarding	**NN**	**1-01-001**
aware	**JJ**	**84-14-068**
awareness	**NN**	**32-09-026**
awash	**JJ**	**1-01-001**
away	**adverb**	**458-15-243**
away	RB	453-15-242
'way	RB	1-01-001
awaye	RB	1-01-001
Away	RB-TL	3-01-002
awe	**NN**	**5-05-005**
awe	**verb**	**5-05-005**
awed	VBN	5-05-005
awe-inspiring	**JJ**	**1-01-001**
awesome	**JJ**	**4-04-004**
awful	**JJ**	**14-08-013**
awful	**QL**	**3-02-003**
awfully	**QL**	**10-05-007**
awfulness	**NN**	**2-02-002**
awhile	**RB**	**4-03-004**
awkward	**JJ**	**11-05-008**
awkwardly	**RB**	**5-05-005**
awkwardness	**NN**	**1-01-001**
awning	**noun**	**2-02-002**
awnings	NNS	2-02-002
AWOC	**NP**	**1-01-001**
awry	**JJ**	**2-02-002**
axe	**noun**	**19-05-013**
axe	NN	6-02-004
ax	NN	5-02-004
Ax	NN-TL	1-01-001
axes	NNS	7-04-005
axial	**JJ**	**2-02-002**
axially	**RB**	**1-01-001**
axiological	**JJ**	**1-01-001**
axiom	**noun**	**3-02-002**
axiom	NN	1-01-001
axioms	NNS	1-01-001
Axioms	NNS-TL	1-01-001
axiomatic	**JJ**	**3-03-003**
axis	**noun**	**38-05-009**
axis	NN	34-04-008
Axis	NN-TL	4-01-001
axle	**noun**	**6-02-003**
axle	NN	5-02-002
axles	NNS	1-01-001
aya	**noun**	**1-01-001**
aya	NN	0-00-000
aya	NN-NC	1-01-001
aye	**noun**	**1-01-001**
ayes	NNS	1-01-001
aye	**RB**	**1-01-001**
aye-yah-ah-ah	**UH**	**1-01-001**
Aylesbury	**NP**	**2-01-002**
Ayres	**prop. noun**	**1-01-001**
Ayres'	NP$	1-01-001
Aysshom	**NP**	**1-01-001**
Ayub	**NP**	**1-01-001**
azalea	**noun**	**5-02-002**
azalea	NN	2-01-001
azaleas	NNS	3-02-002
Azerbaijan	**prop. noun**	**1-01-001**
Azerbaijan	NP	0-00-000
Azerbaijan	NP-TL	1-01-001
Azusa	**NP**	**1-01-001**

B

b	**noun**	**10-05-007**
b	NN	1-01-001
B	NN-TL	5-05-005
B	NN-TL-HL	4-01-002
B	**prop. noun**	**53-03-019**
B	NP	34-03-013
B	NP-HL	19-02-010
B.	**prop. noun**	**79-08-041**
B.	NP	66-08-041
B.	NP-TL	10-02-002
B.'s	NP$	3-01-002
B.A.	**NP**	**2-02-002**
B.B.C.	**prop. noun**	**2-01-001**
B.B.C.	NP	1-01-001
B.B.C.'s	NP$	1-01-001
B.C.	**prop. noun**	**20-05-007**
B.C.	NP	19-05-007
B.C.	NP-TL	1-01-001
B.D.	**NP**	**1-01-001**
B.S.	**NP**	**1-01-001**
B&O	**prop. noun**	**1-01-001**
B&O	NP	0-00-000
B&O	NP-TL	1-01-001
B'dikkat	**prop. noun**	**22-01-001**
B'dikkat	NP	21-01-001
B'dikkat's	NP$	1-01-001
ba-a-a	**UH**	**1-01-001**
Babatunde	**NP**	**1-01-001**
babbit	**verb**	**1-01-001**
babbiting	VBG	1-01-001
Babbitt	**NP**	**2-02-002**
babble	**verb**	**2-02-002**
babbled	VBD	2-02-002
Babcock	**NP**	**1-01-001**
babe	**noun**	**3-03-003**
babes	NNS	3-03-003
Babe	**prop. noun**	**8-03-005**
Babe	NP	7-03-004
Babe (cont.):		
Babe	NP-TL	1-01-001
babel	**NN**	**1-01-001**
Babel	**NP**	**2-01-001**
Babin	**NP**	**3-01-001**
baby	**noun**	**80-12-045**
baby	NN	57-11-035
Baby	NN-TL	5-02-003
baby's	NN$	6-02-003
babies	NNS	12-06-009
Baby-dear	**NP**	**2-01-001**
baby-sitter	**NN**	**1-01-001**
babyhood	**NN**	**1-01-001**
Babylon	**NP**	**2-02-002**
Babylonian	**JJ**	**2-02-002**
Babylonian	**prop. noun**	**2-02-002**
Babylonians	NPS	2-02-002
Baccarat	**NP**	**1-01-001**
Bacchus	**NP**	**1-01-001**
Bach	**NP**	**4-04-004**
bachelor	**noun**	**10-05-007**
bachelor	NN	4-03-004
Bachelor	NN-TL	2-02-002
bachelors	NNS	4-01-001
bachelor-type	**JJ**	**1-01-001**
baci	**FW-NN**	**1-01-001**
Bacillus	**NP**	**2-02-002**
back	**adjective**	**29-10-021**
back	JJ	27-09-019
Back	JJ-TL	2-02-002
back	**noun**	**190-13-104**
back	NN	177-12-097
back	NN-HL	1-01-001
backs	NNS	12-09-011
back	**adverb**	**734-15-279**
back	RB	730-15-278
back	RB-HL	2-01-002
Back	RB-TL	2-02-002

Word	Tag	Frequency
back	**verb**	**57-12-044**
back	VB	25-09-023
backs	VBZ	1-01-001
backs	VBZ-HL	2-02-002
backed	VBD	21-08-016
backed	VBN	3-03-003
backing	VBG	5-05-005
back-issue	**NN**	**1-01-001**
back-lighted	**JJ**	**1-01-001**
backbend	**noun**	**3-01-001**
backbend	NN	1-01-001
backbends	NNS	1-01-001
backbends	NNS-HL	1-01-001
backbone	**NN**	**4-04-004**
backdrop	**NN**	**2-02-002**
backer	**noun**	**4-01-002**
backers	NNS	4-01-002
background	**noun**	**74-12-056**
background	NN	66-12-051
background	NN-HL	1-01-001
backgrounds	NNS	7-06-007
backing	**NN**	**3-03-003**
backlash	**NN**	**1-01-001**
backlog	**NN**	**5-02-002**
backpack	**NN**	**1-01-001**
backside	**NN**	**1-01-001**
backstage	**RB**	**2-01-001**
backstairs	**RB**	**1-01-001**
backstitch	**noun**	**2-01-001**
backstitch	NN	1-01-001
backstitch	NN-HL	1-01-001
backstitch	**verb**	**3-01-001**
backstitch	VB	2-01-001
backstitching	VBG	0-00-000
backstitching	VBG-HL	1-01-001
backward	**JJ**	**5-04-005**
backward	**adverb**	**17-09-016**
backward	RB	16-09-015
Backward	RB-TL	1-01-001
backwards	**RB**	**2-02-002**
backwater	**JJ**	**1-01-001**
backwoods	**JJ**	**1-01-001**
backwoods	**NNS**	**4-02-002**
backwoods-and-sand-hill	**JJ**	**1-01-001**
backyard	**noun**	**6-05-006**
backyard	NN	1-01-001
back-yard	NN	1-01-001
Backyard	NN-TL	1-01-001
backyards	NNS	3-03-003
bacon	**NN**	**8-04-007**
Bacon	**NP**	**2-02-002**
bacterial	**JJ**	**14-02-003**
bacterium	**noun**	**8-03-006**
bacteria	NNS	8-03-006
bad	**adjective**	**134-15-085**
bad	JJ	133-15-084
bad	JJ-HL	1-01-001
bad	**noun**	**5-03-005**
bad	NN	4-03-004
bads	NNS	1-01-001
bad	**RB**	**4-02-004**
bad-fitting	**JJ**	**1-01-001**
Baden-Baden	**NP**	**1-01-001**
badge	**noun**	**6-05-006**
badge	NN	5-04-005
badges	NNS	1-01-001
badge-toter	**NN**	**1-01-001**
badger	**verb**	**1-01-001**
badgering	VBG	1-01-001
badinage	**NN**	**1-01-001**
Badlands	**NPS**	**1-01-001**
badly	**QL**	**3-03-003**
badly	**RB**	**31-12-028**
badly-needed	**JJ**	**1-01-001**
badman	**noun**	**1-01-001**
badmen	NNS	1-01-001
badminton	**NN**	**1-01-001**
badness	**NN**	**9-02-002**
Badrawi	**NP**	**1-01-001**
Badura-Skoda	**NP**	**1-01-001**
Baer	**NP**	**5-01-001**
Baffin	**prop. noun**	**1-01-001**
Baffin	NP	0-00-000
Baffin	NP-TL	1-01-001
baffle	**verb**	**6-05-005**
baffle	VB	1-01-001
baffled	VBD	1-01-001
baffled	VBN	4-03-003
baffler	**noun**	**1-01-001**
baffler (cont.):		
bafflers	NNS	0-00-000
Bafflers	NNS-TL	1-01-001
baffling	**JJ**	**4-04-004**
bag	**noun**	**51-08-031**
bag	NN	41-08-028
bags	NNS	10-04-006
bag	**verb**	**2-02-002**
bag	VB	1-01-001
bagged	VBD	1-01-001
bagatelle	**noun**	**1-01-001**
bagatelles	NNS	0-00-000
Bagatelles	NNS-TL	1-01-001
baggage	**NN**	**4-03-003**
baggy	**JJ**	**4-03-003**
Bagh	**NP**	**1-01-001**
Bagley	**NP**	**1-01-001**
bagpipe	**NN**	**1-01-001**
bah	**UH**	**1-01-001**
Bahi	**NP**	**1-01-001**
Bahia	**prop. noun**	**1-01-001**
Bahia	NP	0-00-000
Bahia	NP-TL	1-01-001
bail	**noun**	**7-03-004**
bail	NN	6-03-004
bail	NN-HL	1-01-001
bail	**verb**	**2-01-001**
bailing	VBG	2-01-001
bailey	**noun**	**1-01-001**
bailey	NN	0-00-000
bayly	NN	1-01-001
Bailey	**prop. noun**	**3-02-003**
Bailey	NP	1-01-001
Bailey	NP-TL	2-02-002
bailiff	**noun**	**9-01-001**
bailiff	NN	6-01-001
Baileefe	NN	2-01-001
bayleefe	NN	1-01-001
bailing	**NN**	**1-01-001**
Bailly	**NP**	**3-01-001**
Baines	**NP**	**1-01-001**
Baird	**NP**	**4-02-003**
bait	**noun**	**2-02-002**
bait	NN	1-01-001
Bait	NN-TL	1-01-001
bait	**verb**	**1-01-001**
baited	VBN	1-01-001
bake	**adjective**	**2-01-001**
bake	JJ	1-01-001
Bake	JJ-TL	1-01-001
bake	**verb**	**15-05-009**
bake	VB	3-02-002
bakes	VBZ	1-01-001
baked	VBD	1-01-001
baked	VBN	7-04-005
baking	VBG	3-02-002
Bake	**NP**	**7-01-001**
bake-off	**noun**	**3-01-001**
bake-off	NN	0-00-000
Bake-off	NN-TL	1-01-001
Bake-Off	NN-TL	1-01-001
bake-offs	NNS	1-01-001
bake-oven	**NN**	**1-01-001**
baker	**NN**	**2-02-002**
Baker	**prop. noun**	**34-03-010**
Baker	NP	33-03-009
Baker	NP-TL	1-01-001
Bakersfield	**NP**	**1-01-001**
bakery	**NN**	**2-01-002**
Bakhtiari	**NP**	**1-01-001**
baking	**NN**	**1-01-001**
baklava	**FW-NN**	**1-01-001**
Baku	**NP**	**1-01-001**
Bal	**NP**	**1-01-001**
Balafrej	**prop. noun**	**5-01-001**
Balafrej	NP	4-01-001
Balafrej	NP-TL	1-01-001
Balaguer	**prop. noun**	**3-01-001**
Balaguer	NP	2-01-001
Balaguer's	NP$	1-01-001
balance	**noun**	**83-12-044**
balance	NN	80-12-043
balance	NN-HL	2-01-002
balances	NNS	1-01-001
balance	**verb**	**32-11-026**
balance	VB	8-03-008
balanced	VBD	1-01-001
balanced	VBN	21-09-016
balancing	VBG	2-02-002

balance-of-payments	**NN**	**1-01-001**
balance-wise	**RB**	**1-01-001**
balancing	**NN**	**2-01-002**
Balcolm	**NP**	**1-01-001**
balcony	**noun**	**7-04-006**
balcony	NN	5-03-004
balconies	NNS	2-02-002
bald	**JJ**	**4-03-004**
Bald	**NP**	**1-01-001**
balding	**JJ**	**2-02-002**
baldness	**NN**	**2-01-001**
Baldrige	**NP**	**4-01-001**
Baldwin	**NP**	**2-01-002**
Baldy	**NP**	**1-01-001**
bale	**noun**	**8-02-003**
bale	NN	5-01-002
bales	NNS	3-02-002
baleful	**JJ**	**1-01-001**
Balenciaga	**NP**	**1-01-001**
Bales	**NP**	**1-01-001**
Bali	**NP**	**2-02-002**
Balinese	**NP**	**1-01-001**
balk	**verb**	**4-04-004**
balks	VBZ	1-01-001
balked	VBD	2-02-002
balking	VBG	1-01-001
Balkan	**prop. noun**	**4-04-004**
Balkan	NP	2-02-002
Balkans	NPS	2-02-002
balkanize	**verb**	**2-01-001**
balkanize	VB	0-00-000
Balkanize	VB-TL	1-01-001
Balkanizing	VBG	0-00-000
Balkanizing	VBG-TL	1-01-001
balkiness	**NN**	**1-01-001**
ball	**noun**	**123-12-041**
ball	NN	103-12-034
Ball	NN-TL	3-03-003
balls	NNS	17-08-014
ball	**verb**	**2-02-002**
balled	VBN	1-01-001
balling	VBG	1-01-001
Ball	**prop. noun**	**5-02-003**
Ball	NP	3-01-002
Ball	NP-HL	1-01-001
Ball's	NP$	1-01-001
ball-carrier	**noun**	**1-01-001**
ball-carriers	NNS	1-01-001
ball-hawking	**JJ**	**1-01-001**
ballad	**noun**	**16-05-011**
ballad	NN	7-04-007
Ballad	NN-TL	1-01-001
ballads	NNS	7-03-005
ballards	NNS	1-01-001
Ballard	**NP**	**1-01-001**
ballast	**NN**	**2-02-002**
ballerina	**noun**	**2-02-002**
ballerina	NN	1-01-001
ballerinas	NNS	1-01-001
Ballestre	**NP**	**2-01-001**
ballet	**foreign**	**4-02-003**
ballet	FW-NN	1-01-001
Ballet	FW-NN-TL	3-02-002
ballet	**noun**	**45-10-017**
ballet	NN	29-10-015
Ballet	NN-TL	11-03-006
Ballet	NN-TL-HL	1-01-001
ballets	NNS	4-03-003
balletomane	**NN**	**1-01-001**
ballfield	**noun**	**1-01-001**
ballfields	NNS	1-01-001
ballgown	**noun**	**1-01-001**
ballgowns	NNS	1-01-001
ballistic	**adjective**	**17-03-006**
ballistic	JJ	15-03-004
Ballistic	JJ-TL	2-02-002
ballistics	**NNS**	**1-01-001**
balloon	**noun**	**13-09-011**
balloon	NN	9-06-007
Balloon	NN-TL	1-01-001
balloons	NNS	3-03-003
balloon	**verb**	**1-01-001**
ballooning	VBG	1-01-001
ballot	**noun**	**14-04-011**
ballot	NN	12-04-010
ballots	NNS	2-02-002
ballplayer	**noun**	**8-02-002**
ballplayer	NN	5-02-002
ballplayers	NNS	3-01-001
ballroom	**noun**	**8-02-005**
ballroom	NN	7-02-005
Ballroom	NN-TL	1-01-001
ballyhoo	**NN**	**1-01-001**
ballyhooey	**NN**	**1-01-001**
balm-of-Gilead	**NN**	**1-01-001**
balmy	**JJ**	**2-02-002**
balsam	**noun**	**1-01-001**
balsams	NNS	1-01-001
Baltic	**adjective**	**1-01-001**
Baltic	JJ	0-00-000
Baltic	JJ-TL	1-01-001
Baltic	**prop. noun**	**2-02-002**
Baltic	NP	0-00-000
Baltic	NP-TL	2-02-002
Baltimore	**prop. noun**	**24-09-017**
Baltimore	NP	14-08-012
Baltimore	NP-TL	8-04-006
Baltimore's	NP$	2-01-001
Baltimorean	**NP**	**1-01-001**
balustrade	**NN**	**3-02-003**
Balzac	**NP**	**2-02-002**
BAM	**NP**	**4-01-001**
Bambi	**NP**	**1-01-001**
ban	**NN**	**6-04-006**
ban	**verb**	**4-03-004**
ban	VB	1-01-001
bans	VBZ	1-01-001
banned	VBN	2-02-002
banal	**JJ**	**2-01-002**
banana	**noun**	**5-03-004**
banana	NN	4-03-004
bananas	NNS	1-01-001
Banbury	**NP**	**1-01-001**
Bancroft	**prop. noun**	**6-02-002**
Bancroft	NP	5-02-002
Bancroft's	NP$	1-01-001
band	**noun**	**64-13-043**
band	NN	44-13-032
Band	NN-TL	9-04-006
bands	NNS	11-05-010
band	**verb**	**3-03-003**
banded	VBN	2-02-002
banding	VBG	1-01-001
bandage	**noun**	**7-04-004**
bandage	NN	4-03-003
bandages	NNS	3-01-001
bandage	**verb**	**4-02-003**
bandaged	VBN	4-02-003
bandaging	**noun**	**1-01-001**
bandaging	NN	0-00-000
Bandaging	NN-TL	1-01-001
Bandish	**NP**	**1-01-001**
bandit	**noun**	**6-04-004**
bandit	NN	3-02-002
bandits	NNS	3-03-003
banditos	**FW-NNS**	**1-01-001**
bandoleer	**noun**	**1-01-001**
bandoleers	NNS	1-01-001
Bandon	**NP**	**1-01-001**
bandstand	**NN**	**5-02-003**
bandwagon	**NN**	**1-01-001**
bandwidth	**NN**	**1-01-001**
baneful	**JJ**	**1-01-001**
Banfield	**NP**	**1-01-001**
bang	**noun**	**6-04-005**
bang	NN	3-03-003
bangs	NNS	3-01-002
bang	**exclam.**	**3-02-002**
bang	UH	2-01-001
bannnnnng	UH	1-01-001
bang	**verb**	**10-06-010**
bang	VB	2-02-002
bangs	VBZ	1-01-001
banged	VBD	4-03-004
banging	VBG	3-03-003
Bang-Jensen	**prop. noun**	**31-01-001**
Bang-Jensen	NP	25-01-001
Bang-Jensen's	NP$	6-01-001
bang-sash	**noun**	**1-01-001**
bang-sashes	NNS	1-01-001
banging	**NN**	**1-01-001**
bangish	**JJ**	**1-01-001**
Bangkok	**NP**	**1-01-001**
bangle	**noun**	**1-01-001**
bangles	NNS	0-00-000
Bangles	NNS-TL	1-01-001
Bangs	**NP**	**2-01-001**
Bani	**NP**	**1-01-001**

Word	Tag	Frequency
banish	**verb**	**13-05-009**
banish	VB	4-02-002
banishes	VBZ	1-01-001
banished	VBD	1-01-001
banished	VBN	6-02-004
banishing	VBG	1-01-001
banishment	**NN**	**1-01-001**
banister	**noun**	**7-04-005**
banister	NN	5-04-004
banisters	NNS	2-02-002
banjo	**NN**	**1-01-001**
Banjo	**NP**	**1-01-001**
bank	**noun**	**110-10-044**
bank	NN	54-10-030
Bank	NN-TL	29-05-011
banks	NNS	19-09-014
Banks	NNS-TL	8-03-003
bank	**verb**	**7-07-007**
banks	VBZ	1-01-001
banked	VBD	1-01-001
banked	VBN	3-03-003
banking	VBG	2-02-002
banker	**noun**	**20-06-012**
banker	NN	4-03-003
Banker	NN-TL	1-01-001
bankers	NNS	12-04-008
Bankers	NNS-TL	3-01-003
banker-editor	**NN**	**1-01-001**
Bankhead	**NP**	**1-01-001**
bankrupt	**adjective**	**3-02-002**
bankrupt	JJ	2-02-002
bankrupt	JJ-HL	1-01-001
bankrupt	**VB**	**2-02-002**
bankruptcy	**NN**	**8-05-006**
Banks	**prop. noun**	**10-01-001**
Banks	NP	6-01-001
Banks	NP-TL	3-01-001
Banks's	NP$	1-01-001
banner	**noun**	**10-06-010**
banner	NN	6-03-006
Banner	NN-TL	2-02-002
banners	NNS	2-02-002
banning	**NN**	**1-01-001**
banquet	**noun**	**9-05-007**
banquet	NN	6-03-004
banquets	NNS	3-03-003
banqueting	**noun**	**1-01-001**
banquetings	NNS	1-01-001
banshee	**noun**	**3-03-003**
banshee	NN	1-01-001
banshees	NNS	2-02-002
banter	**NN**	**5-02-002**
banter	**verb**	**2-02-002**
bantered	VBN	1-01-001
bantering	VBG	1-01-001
Bantu	**JJ**	**1-01-001**
Bantu	**prop. noun**	**3-01-001**
Bantus	NPS	3-01-001
baptism	**noun**	**5-03-003**
baptism	NN	4-02-002
baptisms	NNS	1-01-001
baptismal	**JJ**	**1-01-001**
baptist	**adjective**	**1-01-001**
baptist	JJ	0-00-000
Baptist	JJ-TL	1-01-001
Baptist	**prop. noun**	**21-07-013**
Baptist	NP	10-04-005
Baptist	NP-TL	6-05-006
Baptist's	NP$	0-00-000
Baptist's	NP$-TL	1-01-001
Baptists	NPS	4-03-003
Baptiste	**NP**	**1-01-001**
baptistery	**NN**	**1-01-001**
baptize	**verb**	**12-04-006**
baptized	VBN	12-04-006
bar	**noun**	**116-14-037**
bar	NN	68-11-025
bar	NN-HL	1-01-001
Bar	NN-TL	10-06-008
bars	NNS	35-09-014
bars	NNS-HL	1-01-001
Bars	NNS-TL	1-01-001
bar	**verb**	**17-10-014**
bar	VB	2-02-002
bar	VB-HL	1-01-001
bars	VBZ	3-02-003
barred	VBD	2-02-002
barred	VBN	6-05-006
barring	VBG	3-02-002

Word	Tag	Frequency
bar-buddy	**NN**	**1-01-001**
Bar-H	**NP**	**1-01-001**
Baraclough	**NP**	**1-01-001**
Barataria	**NP**	**1-01-001**
barb	**noun**	**2-02-002**
barbs	NNS	2-02-002
barb	**verb**	**10-06-007**
barbed	VBN	10-06-007
Barbara	**prop. noun**	**10-03-007**
Barbara	NP	9-03-006
Barbara	NP-HL	1-01-001
barbarian	**noun**	**5-02-004**
barbarian	NN	1-01-001
barbarians	NNS	3-01-003
Barbarians	NNS-TL	1-01-001
barbaric	**JJ**	**1-01-001**
barbarous	**JJ**	**1-01-001**
barbecue	**noun**	**15-03-003**
barbecue	NN	12-03-003
barbecues	NNS	2-01-001
barbecues	NNS-HL	1-01-001
barbecue	**verb**	**3-01-001**
barbecue	VB	1-01-001
barbecued	VBN	1-01-001
barbecued	VBN-HL	1-01-001
barbed	**JJ**	**1-01-001**
barbed-wire	**NN**	**1-01-001**
barbell	**NN**	**5-01-001**
barber	**noun**	**5-04-004**
barber	NN	3-03-003
barber	NN-HL	1-01-001
barber's	NN$	1-01-001
Barber	**NP**	**4-01-002**
barbital	**NN**	**1-01-001**
barbiturate	**NN**	**1-01-001**
Barbour	**prop. noun**	**1-01-001**
Barbour	NP	0-00-000
Barbour	NP-TL	1-01-001
Barbudo	**prop. noun**	**1-01-001**
Barbudos	NPS	1-01-001
Barco	**prop. noun**	**26-01-001**
Barco	NP	18-01-001
Barco's	NP$	8-01-001
Barcus	**prop. noun**	**5-01-001**
Barcus	NP	3-01-001
Barcus	NP-HL	1-01-001
Barcus'	NP$	1-01-001
bard	**noun**	**5-02-002**
bard	NN	3-01-001
bards	NNS	2-02-002
Bardall	**NP**	**1-01-001**
Bardell	**NP**	**1-01-001**
bare	**JJ**	**28-10-025**
bare	**VB**	**1-01-001**
bare-armed	**JJ**	**1-01-001**
barefoot	**JJ**	**4-03-004**
barefoot	**RB**	**3-02-002**
barefooted	**adjective**	**2-02-002**
barefooted	JJ	1-01-001
bare-footed	JJ	1-01-001
barely	**QL**	**6-04-006**
barely	**RB**	**25-11-024**
barest	**JJT**	**3-03-003**
barfly	**noun**	**1-01-001**
barflies	NNS	1-01-001
bargain	**noun**	**9-07-008**
bargain	NN	7-06-007
bargains	NNS	2-02-002
bargain	**verb**	**4-03-003**
bargain	VB	0-00-000
bargen	VB	1-01-001
bargains	VBZ	1-01-001
bargaining	VBG	1-01-001
bargaining	VBG-HL	1-01-001
bargain-priced	**JJ**	**1-01-001**
bargaining	**NN**	**16-05-010**
barge	**noun**	**8-06-007**
barge	NN	5-04-004
barges	NNS	3-03-003
barge	**verb**	**4-03-003**
barge	VB	2-02-002
barging	VBG	2-01-001
Bari	**prop. noun**	**15-02-002**
Bari	NP	14-02-002
Bari's	NP$	1-01-001
Baringer	**NP**	**1-01-001**
baritone	**NN**	**5-03-004**
barium	**NN**	**1-01-001**
bark	**NN**	**13-05-011**

Word	Tag	Frequency
bark	**VB**	**1-01-001**
barkeep	**NN**	**1-01-001**
Barker	**prop. noun**	**8-02-003**
Barker	NP	5-02-003
Barker	NP-TL	3-01-001
barking	**NN**	**2-01-001**
barley	**NN**	**6-02-003**
barn	**noun**	**33-09-020**
barn	NN	29-09-017
barns	NNS	4-02-004
barn-burner	**noun**	**1-01-001**
barn-burner's	NN$	1-01-001
Barnaba	**NP**	**1-01-001**
Barnard	**prop. noun**	**6-03-003**
Barnard	NP	4-02-002
Barnard	NP-TL	1-01-001
Barnard's	NP$	1-01-001
Barnes	**NP**	**9-02-007**
Barnet	**NP**	**1-01-001**
Barnett	**NP**	**11-01-002**
Barney	**NP**	**8-02-002**
barnful	**noun**	**1-01-001**
barnsful	NNS	1-01-001
barnstormer	**NN**	**1-01-001**
Barnumville	**NP**	**4-01-001**
barnyard	**noun**	**2-02-002**
barnyard	NN	1-01-001
barnyards	NNS	1-01-001
barometric	**JJ**	**1-01-001**
baron	**noun**	**3-03-003**
baron	NN	2-02-002
barons	NNS	1-01-001
baroness	**NN**	**1-01-001**
baronial	**JJ**	**1-01-001**
barony	**NN**	**1-01-001**
baroque	**adjective**	**11-04-007**
baroque	JJ	9-04-005
Baroque	JJ-TL	2-02-002
baroreceptor	**NN**	**1-01-001**
Barr	**NP**	**1-01-001**
barrack	**noun**	**4-04-004**
barrack	NN	1-01-001
barracks	NN	2-02-002
barracks	NNS	1-01-001
barrage	**NN**	**5-05-005**
Barre	**prop. noun**	**5-01-001**
Barre	NP	4-01-001
Barre	NP-TL	1-01-001
Barre-Montpelier	**adjective**	**1-01-001**
Barre-Montpelier	JJ	0-00-000
Barre-Montpelier	JJ-TL	1-01-001
barrel	**noun**	**32-10-020**
barrel	NN	23-08-014
bar'l	NN	1-01-001
barrels	NNS	8-05-007
barrel	**VB**	**1-01-001**
barrel-vaulted	**JJ**	**1-01-001**
barrel-wide	**JJ**	**1-01-001**
barren	**adjective**	**7-05-007**
barren	JJ	6-04-006
Barren	JJ-TL	1-01-001
Barrett	**NP**	**1-01-001**
Barrette	**NP**	**1-01-001**
barricade	**noun**	**6-04-005**
barricade	NN	2-02-002
barricades	NNS	4-03-003
barricade	**VB**	**1-01-001**
barrier	**noun**	**26-09-021**
barrier	NN	9-06-009
barriers	NNS	17-08-015
Barrington	**NP**	**2-01-002**
Barrow	**NP**	**1-01-001**
Barry	**NP**	**3-03-003**
Barrymore	**prop. noun**	**1-01-001**
Barrymores	NPS	1-01-001
Barsac	**prop. noun**	**1-01-001**
Barsacs	NPS	1-01-001
Barstow	**NP**	**3-01-001**
bartender	**NN**	**6-02-003**
Barth	**NP**	**5-01-001**
Bartha	**NP**	**1-01-001**
Bartholf	**prop. noun**	**1-01-001**
Bartholf	NP	0-00-000
Bartholf	NP-TL	1-01-001
Bartleby	**prop. noun**	**2-01-001**
Bartleby	NP	0-00-000
Bartleby	NP-TL	2-01-001
Bartlett	**NP**	**3-02-002**
Bartok	**NP**	**1-01-001**
Bartol	**NP**	**1-01-001**
Bartoli	**prop. noun**	**1-01-001**
Bartoli's	NP$	1-01-001
Barton	**prop. noun**	**28-01-001**
Barton	NP	25-01-001
Barton's	NP$	3-01-001
bas	**foreign**	**1-01-001**
bas	FW-RB	0-00-000
Bas	FW-RB-TL	1-01-001
bas-relief	**noun**	**5-02-002**
bas-relief	NN	3-01-001
bas-reliefs	NNS	2-01-001
Bascom	**NP**	**3-01-001**
base	**JJ**	**5-03-004**
base	**noun**	**102-13-051**
base	NN	76-13-045
Base	NN-TL	7-03-003
bases	NNS	19-08-014
base	**verb**	**130-12-093**
base	VB	3-02-003
bases	VBZ	4-03-004
based	VBD	3-02-003
based	VBN	116-12-084
basing	VBG	4-04-004
base-runner	**NN**	**1-01-001**
base-stealing	**JJ**	**1-01-001**
baseball	**noun**	**62-09-016**
baseball	NN	54-09-015
Baseball	NN-TL	3-01-002
baseball's	NN+BEZ	1-01-001
baseball's	NN$	3-01-002
baseballs	NNS	1-01-001
baseballite	**noun**	**1-01-001**
baseballite	NN	0-00-000
baseballight	NN	1-01-001
Basel	**NP**	**2-02-002**
baseless	**JJ**	**1-01-001**
baseline	**NN**	**1-01-001**
baseman	**noun**	**4-02-002**
baseman	NN	3-02-002
Baseman	NN-TL	1-01-001
basement	**noun**	**33-08-011**
basement	NN	31-08-010
basements	NNS	2-01-001
baser	**JJR**	**1-01-001**
Bashaw	**NP**	**2-01-001**
bashful	**JJ**	**2-02-002**
Bashir	**NP**	**1-01-001**
Basho	**prop. noun**	**1-01-001**
Basho's	NP$	1-01-001
basic	**adjective**	**171-10-096**
basic	JJ	165-10-094
basic	JJ-HL	5-03-005
Basic	JJ-TL	1-01-001
basically	**QL**	**1-01-001**
basically	**RB**	**19-07-016**
basics	**NNS**	**1-01-001**
Basie	**NP**	**1-01-001**
Basil	**prop. noun**	**3-02-002**
Basil	NP	1-01-001
Basil's	NP$	2-01-001
basileis	**FW-NN**	**1-01-001**
basin	**noun**	**7-06-006**
basin	NN	5-05-005
Basin	NN-TL	1-01-001
Basin	NN-TL-HL	1-01-001
basis	**noun**	**184-14-112**
basis	NN	183-14-112
basis	NN-HL	1-01-001
bask	**verb**	**3-03-003**
basked	VBD	1-01-001
basking	VBG	2-02-002
basket	**noun**	**19-08-013**
basket	NN	15-08-011
basket	NN-HL	2-01-001
baskets	NNS	2-01-001
basketball	**noun**	**9-04-008**
basketball	NN	8-04-008
Basketball	NN-TL	1-01-001
basketball-playing	**JJ**	**1-01-001**
Basler	**NP**	**1-01-001**
Baslot	**NP**	**2-01-001**
basophilic	**JJ**	**2-01-001**
bass	**JJ**	**1-01-001**
bass	**noun**	**16-07-011**
bass	NN	15-06-010
basses	NNS	1-01-001
Bassi	**prop. noun**	**2-01-001**
Bassi	NP	1-01-001

Word	Tag	Frequency
Bassi (cont.):		
Bassis	NPS	1-01-001
bassinet	**NN**	**1-01-001**
basso	**FW-NN**	**1-01-001**
Basso	**NP**	**1-01-001**
Bast	**NP**	**1-01-001**
bastard	**noun**	**27-05-012**
bastard	NN	12-04-008
bastard's	NN+BEZ	1-01-001
bastards	NNS	14-05-005
baste	**verb**	**2-01-001**
basting	VBG	2-01-001
Bastianini	**NP**	**1-01-001**
bastion	**NN**	**2-02-002**
bat	**noun**	**18-07-012**
bat	NN	13-06-009
bats	NNS	5-03-005
bat	**verb**	**23-07-013**
bat	VB	5-03-004
bats	VBZ	1-01-001
batted	VBD	1-01-001
batted	VBN	1-01-001
batting	VBG	15-05-010
Batavia	**NP**	**3-01-001**
batch	**NN**	**5-04-005**
Batchelder	**NP**	**1-01-001**
bateau	**NN**	**2-01-001**
Bates	**prop. noun**	**7-04-004**
Bates	NP	4-03-003
Bates	NP-TL	2-01-001
Bates'	NP$	1-01-001
bath	**noun**	**31-11-020**
bath	NN	26-10-018
baths	NNS	4-04-004
baths	NNS-HL	1-01-001
Bath	**prop. noun**	**1-01-001**
Bath	NP	0-00-000
Bath	NP-TL	1-01-001
Bathar-on-Walli	**prop. noun**	**1-01-001**
Bathar-on-Walli	NP	0-00-000
Bathar-on-Walli	NP-TL	1-01-001
bathe	**verb**	**26-07-020**
bathe	VB	4-04-004
bathed	VBD	1-01-001
bathed	VBN	6-03-006
bathing	VBG	15-06-012
bather	**noun**	**1-01-001**
bathers	NNS	1-01-001
bathos	**NN**	**1-01-001**
bathrobe	**NN**	**3-02-003**
bathroom	**noun**	**19-07-014**
bathroom	NN	18-07-013
bathrooms	NNS	1-01-001
bathtub	**noun**	**5-05-005**
bathtub	NN	4-04-004
bathtubs	NNS	1-01-001
Bathyran	**JJ**	**1-01-001**
Bathyran	**prop. noun**	**2-01-001**
Bathyrans	NPS	2-01-001
Batista	**prop. noun**	**10-02-003**
Batista	NP	7-02-002
Batista's	NP$	3-02-003
baton	**NN**	**5-04-005**
Baton	**prop. noun**	**5-04-004**
Baton	NP	4-03-003
Baton	NP-HL	1-01-001
battalion	**noun**	**4-02-003**
battalion	NN	2-02-002
Battalion	NN-TL	1-01-001
battalions	NNS	1-01-001
batten	**noun**	**18-01-002**
batten	NN	3-01-001
battens	NNS	15-01-002
Battenkill	**prop. noun**	**4-01-001**
Battenkill	NP	2-01-001
Battenkill	NP-TL	2-01-001
batter	**noun**	**4-03-003**
batter	NN	2-02-002
batter's	NN$	1-01-001
batters	NNS	1-01-001
batter	**verb**	**11-06-011**
battered	VBD	2-02-002
battered	VBN	7-05-007
battering	VBG	2-01-002
battery	**noun**	**22-09-012**
battery	NN	16-06-008
batterie	NN	1-01-001
Battery	NN-TL	2-01-001
batteries	NNS	3-01-002

Word	Tag	Frequency
battery-powered	**JJ**	**2-01-001**
battle	**noun**	**91-14-060**
battle	NN	75-13-051
battle	NN-HL	1-01-001
Battle	NN-TL	8-05-006
battles	NNS	7-06-007
battle	**verb**	**6-04-006**
battle	VB	3-02-003
battling	VBG	3-02-003
battle-ax	**NN**	**1-01-001**
battle-cry	**NN**	**1-01-001**
battle-shattered	**JJ**	**1-01-001**
battlefield	**noun**	**7-05-006**
battlefield	NN	5-04-005
battlefields	NNS	2-01-001
battlefront	**NN**	**1-01-001**
battleground	**NN**	**2-02-002**
battlement	**noun**	**1-01-001**
battlements	NNS	1-01-001
batwing	**noun**	**1-01-001**
batwings	NNS	1-01-001
bauble	**noun**	**2-02-002**
bauble	NN	1-01-001
baubles	NNS	0-00-000
Baubles	NNS-TL	1-01-001
Baudelaire	**NP**	**1-01-001**
Bauer	**NP**	**1-01-001**
Bauer-Ecsy	**NP**	**1-01-001**
Bauhaus	**NP**	**1-01-001**
Baullari	**NP**	**3-01-001**
Baum	**NP**	**2-01-001**
Bavaria	**prop. noun**	**3-02-002**
Bavaria	NP	2-01-001
Bavaria	NP-TL	1-01-001
bawdy	**JJ**	**3-03-003**
bawl	**verb**	**3-03-003**
bawled	VBD	2-02-002
bawling	VBG	1-01-001
bay	**noun**	**60-13-030**
bay	NN	19-08-012
Bay	NN-TL	39-11-020
bays	NNS	2-01-002
bay	**verb**	**3-02-002**
bayed	VBD	2-02-002
bayed	VBN	1-01-001
Bayaderka	**NP**	**1-01-001**
Bayanihan	**NP**	**1-01-001**
Bayerische	**foreign**	**1-01-001**
Bayerische	FW-JJ	0-00-000
Bayerische	FW-JJ-TL	1-01-001
Bayezit	**prop. noun**	**2-01-001**
Bayezit	NP	1-01-001
Bayezit	NP-TL	1-01-001
baying	**NN**	**1-01-001**
Baylor	**prop. noun**	**3-01-001**
Baylor	NP	2-01-001
Baylor's	NP$	1-01-001
bayonet	**noun**	**9-03-004**
bayonet	NN	6-02-002
bayonets	NNS	3-01-002
Bayou	**prop. noun**	**2-01-001**
Bayou	NP	0-00-000
Bayou	NP-TL	2-01-001
Bayreuth	**prop. noun**	**4-03-003**
Bayreuth	NP	1-01-001
Bayreuth	NP-HL	1-01-001
Bayreuth	NP-TL	2-02-002
bazaar	**noun**	**8-04-006**
bazaar	NN	5-03-003
Bazaar	NN-TL	2-02-002
bazaars	NNS	1-01-001
BBB	**NP**	**1-01-001**
be	**verb**	**39175-15-500**
be	BE	6361-15-499
be	BE-HL	13-06-007
Be	BE-TL	1-01-001
am	BEM	226-15-120
am	BEM-NC	2-01-001
'm	+BEM	269-13-112
Ahm	+BEM	1-01-001
ain't	BEM*	9-03-004
are	BER	4372-15-453
ah	BER	1-01-001
art	BER	6-03-003
are	BER-HL	11-04-004
are	BER-NC	5-01-002
Are	BER-TL	6-02-004
're	+BER	280-14-117
're	+BER-NC	2-01-001

Word	Tag	Frequency
be (cont.):		
're	+BER-TL	1-01-001
waddya	+BER	1-01-001
aren't	BER*	35-11-033
ain't	BER*	12-06-010
aren't	BER*-NC	1-01-001
is	BEZ	10066-15-485
ys	BEZ	1-01-001
is	BEZ-HL	30-08-012
is	BEZ-NC	5-01-001
Is	BEZ-TL	7-03-005
is	BEZ-TL	1-01-001
's	+BEZ	872-15-212
's	+BEZ-HL	3-03-003
's	+BEZ-NC	12-01-001
's	+BEZ-TL	6-03-004
'tis	+BEZ	2-02-002
isn't	BEZ*	97-13-065
ain't	BEZ*	19-07-013
'tain't	+BEZ*	1-01-001
haint	+BEZ*	1-01-001
was	BEDZ	9806-15-465
Was	BEDZ	1-01-001
was	BEDZ-NC	8-01-001
was	BEDZ-HL	1-01-001
wasn't	BEDZ*	154-13-083
were	BED	3283-15-453
wuh	BED	1-01-001
were	BED-NC	3-01-001
weren't	BED*	22-08-020
been	BEN	2470-15-477
Been	BEN-TL	2-02-002
being	BEG	681-15-329
bein	BEG	1-01-001
bein'	BEG	2-01-001
beinge	BEG	2-01-001
Be	**UH**	**1-01-001**
Bea	**NP**	**2-02-002**
beach	**noun**	**74-13-039**
beach	NN	33-11-019
Beach	NN-TL	27-06-019
beaches	NNS	14-06-009
beach	**verb**	**1-01-001**
beaching	VBG	1-01-001
Beach	**NP**	**1-01-001**
beach-drift	**NN**	**1-01-001**
beachhead	**noun**	**3-03-003**
beachhead	NN	2-02-002
beach-head	NN	1-01-001
beacon	**NN**	**5-04-005**
bead	**noun**	**5-05-005**
bead	NN	1-01-001
beads	NNS	3-03-003
Beads	NNS-TL	1-01-001
bead	**verb**	**1-01-001**
beaded	VBN	1-01-001
beadle	**NN**	**1-01-001**
Beadle	**prop. noun**	**5-01-002**
Beadle	NP	3-01-001
Beadles	NPS	1-01-001
Beadles'	NPS$	1-01-001
beadsman	**NN**	**1-01-001**
beady	**JJ**	**1-01-001**
beaker	**noun**	**3-01-001**
beaker	NN	2-01-001
beakers	NNS	1-01-001
Beale	**prop. noun**	**2-02-002**
Beale	NP	1-01-001
Beale	NP-TL	1-01-001
Beall	**NP**	**2-01-001**
Beallsville	**NP**	**1-01-001**
beam	**noun**	**33-08-017**
beam	NN	19-06-010
beam	NN-HL	1-01-001
beams	NNS	13-05-008
beam	**verb**	**6-05-006**
beaming	VBG	6-05-006
Beam	**NP**	**1-01-001**
Beame	**prop. noun**	**3-01-001**
Beame	NP	2-01-001
Beame	NP-HL	1-01-001
bean	**noun**	**13-05-008**
bean	NN	4-02-003
beans	NNS	9-04-006
Bean	**NP**	**1-01-001**
bear	**noun**	**24-07-012**
bear	NN	10-05-008
Bear	NN-TL	3-02-002
bear	NNS	1-01-001

Word	Tag	Frequency
bear (cont.):		
Bears	NNS-TL	9-01-002
bear's	NN$	0-00-000
Bear's	NN$-TL	1-01-001
bear	**verb**	**211-15-126**
bear	VB	43-14-038
bears	VBZ	17-07-014
bore	VBD	14-08-013
born	VBN	101-14-060
borne	VBN	8-07-008
born	VBN-HL	8-01-001
born	VBN-NC	1-01-001
Born	VBN-TL	2-02-002
bearing	VBG	17-10-014
bear-like	**JJ**	**1-01-001**
beard	**noun**	**31-08-018**
beard	NN	25-07-015
Beard	NN-TL	1-01-001
beards	NNS	5-04-005
beard	**verb**	**7-06-006**
bearded	VBD	1-01-001
bearded	VBN	6-05-005
bearded	**JJ**	**3-02-002**
Bearden	**prop. noun**	**9-01-001**
Bearden	NP	4-01-001
Beardens	NPS	5-01-001
beardless	**JJ**	**1-01-001**
beardown	**JJ**	**1-01-001**
Beardslee	**NP**	**1-01-001**
Beardsley	**prop. noun**	**1-01-001**
Beardsley's	NP$	1-01-001
bearer	**NN**	**4-04-004**
bearing	**noun**	**14-10-013**
bearing	NN	8-07-008
bearings	NNS	6-05-005
bearish	**JJ**	**2-01-001**
beast	**noun**	**10-07-009**
beast	NN	7-07-007
beasts	NNS	2-02-002
bestes	NNS	1-01-001
beasty	**noun**	**1-01-001**
beasties	NNS	1-01-001
beat	**adjective**	**5-01-002**
beat	JJ	4-01-001
Beat	JJ-TL	1-01-001
beat	**noun**	**26-08-012**
beat	NN	23-08-011
Beat	NN-TL	0-00-000
Beat	NN-TL-HL	1-01-001
beats	NNS	1-01-001
beat	NNS	1-01-001
beat	**verb**	**66-13-054**
beat	VB	25-10-023
beats	VBZ	3-03-003
beat	VBD	12-05-011
beaten	VBN	15-08-014
beat	VBN	1-01-001
beating	VBG	10-04-010
beat-up	**JJ**	**1-01-001**
Beatie	**NP**	**4-01-001**
beatific	**JJ**	**1-01-001**
beatification	**NN**	**1-01-001**
beating	**noun**	**5-04-004**
beating	NN	3-02-002
beatings	NNS	2-02-002
Beatitude	**prop. noun**	**1-01-001**
Beatitudes	NPS	1-01-001
beatnik	**noun**	**11-03-003**
beatnik	NN	7-03-003
beatniks	NNS	4-01-001
Beatrice	**NP**	**7-03-004**
beau	**NN**	**1-01-001**
Beau	**NP**	**1-01-001**
Beauchamps	**NP**	**1-01-001**
Beauclerk	**NP**	**8-01-001**
Beaujolais	**NP**	**2-01-001**
Beaulieu	**NP**	**1-01-001**
Beaumont	**prop. noun**	**3-02-003**
Beaumont	NP	2-02-002
Beaumont	NP-TL	1-01-001
beauteous	**JJ**	**1-01-001**
beautiful	**adjective**	**127-15-080**
beautiful	JJ	124-15-079
Beautiful	JJ-TL	3-02-002
beautifully	**QL**	**2-02-002**
beautifully	**RB**	**14-08-013**
beautifully-built	**JJ**	**1-01-001**
beautifully-tapered	**JJ**	**1-01-001**
beautify	**verb**	**2-02-002**

Word	Tag	Frequency
beautify (cont.):		
beautify	VB	1-01-001
beautifying	VBG	1-01-001
beauty	**noun**	**77-13-048**
beauty	NN	68-13-043
beauty	NN-HL	1-01-001
Beauty	NN-TL	2-02-002
beauty's	NN$	0-00-000
Beauty's	NN$-TL	1-01-001
beauties	NNS	5-03-005
beauty-idiom	**NN**	**1-01-001**
beaux-arts	**foreign**	**1-01-001**
beaux-arts	FW-NNS	0-00-000
Beaux-Arts	FW-NNS-TL	1-01-001
beaver	**NN**	**2-01-002**
Beaver	**NP**	**1-01-001**
beavertail	**NN**	**1-01-001**
Beaverton	**prop. noun**	**6-02-003**
Beaverton	NP	5-02-002
Beaverton	NP-TL	1-01-001
bebop	**NN**	**1-01-001**
becalm	**verb**	**1-01-001**
becalmed	VBN	1-01-001
because	**sub. conj.**	**712-15-301**
because	CS	708-15-301
because	CS-HL	4-01-001
because	**RB**	**171-12-122**
Beccaria	**NP**	**2-01-001**
Bechhofer	**NP**	**1-01-001**
Beck	**NP**	**1-01-001**
Becket	**NP**	**2-02-002**
Beckett	**prop. noun**	**10-01-001**
Beckett	NP	6-01-001
Beckett's	NP$	4-01-001
Beckman	**NP**	**1-01-001**
beckon	**verb**	**12-08-011**
beckon	VB	1-01-001
beckons	VBZ	3-03-003
beckoned	VBD	6-04-006
beckoned	VBN	1-01-001
beckoning	VBG	1-01-001
beckoning	**NN**	**1-01-001**
Beckstrom	**NP**	**3-01-001**
Beckworth	**NP**	**4-01-001**
become	**verb**	**765-15-328**
become	VB	235-15-156
becomes	VBZ	104-10-074
becometh	VBZ	1-01-001
became	VBD	246-15-151
become	VBN	124-15-096
becoming	VBG	54-13-051
becomin'	VBG	1-01-001
becoming	**NN**	**3-02-002**
bed	**noun**	**139-13-076**
bed	NN	127-13-070
beds	NNS	12-06-010
bed	**verb**	**1-01-001**
bedded	VBN	1-01-001
bed-hop	**verb**	**1-01-001**
bed-hopped	VBD	1-01-001
bed-time	**NN**	**1-01-001**
bed-type	**JJ**	**1-01-001**
bedazzle	**verb**	**1-01-001**
bedazzled	VBN	1-01-001
bedazzlement	**NN**	**1-01-001**
bedbug	**noun**	**1-01-001**
bedbugs	NNS	1-01-001
bedding	**NN**	**3-02-002**
Bede	**NP**	**3-01-001**
bedfast	**JJ**	**1-01-001**
Bedford	**prop. noun**	**2-02-002**
Bedford	NP	0-00-000
Bedford	NP-TL	2-02-002
bedground	**NN**	**1-01-001**
bedlam	**NN**	**1-01-001**
bedpost	**NN**	**1-01-001**
bedraggled	**JJ**	**1-01-001**
bedridden	**JJ**	**2-02-002**
bedroom	**noun**	**57-10-037**
bedroom	NN	52-10-034
bedroom's	NN$	1-01-001
bedrooms	NNS	4-03-004
bedside	**NN**	**5-05-005**
bedspread	**NN**	**2-01-002**
bedspring	**noun**	**1-01-001**
bedsprings	NNS	1-01-001
bedstraw	**NN**	**1-01-001**
bedtime	**NN**	**4-04-004**
bee	**noun**	**27-07-009**

Word	Tag	Frequency
bee (cont.):		
bee	NN	10-04-004
Bee	NN-TL	1-01-001
bee's	NN$	1-01-001
bees	NNS	15-05-005
Bee-Hunter	**NP**	**1-01-001**
Beebe	**prop. noun**	**5-03-003**
Beebe	NP	4-03-003
Beebe's	NP$	1-01-001
beebread	**NN**	**7-01-001**
beech	**noun**	**6-02-002**
beech	NN	2-01-001
Beech	NN-TL	4-01-001
Beecher	**NP**	**2-01-001**
beef	**noun**	**32-07-012**
beef	NN	26-07-012
beef	NN-HL	5-01-001
beef's	NN$	1-01-001
beef	**verb**	**1-01-001**
beefed	VBN	1-01-001
beef-fat	**NN**	**1-01-001**
beef-feeding	**JJ**	**1-01-001**
beef-hungry	**JJ**	**1-01-001**
beefed-up	**JJ**	**2-02-002**
beefsteak	**NN**	**1-01-001**
beefy	**JJ**	**1-01-001**
beehive	**NN**	**1-01-001**
beep	**noun**	**7-01-001**
beep	NN	4-01-001
beeps	NNS	3-01-001
beer	**noun**	**36-11-024**
beer	NN	35-11-023
beers	NNS	1-01-001
beer-cooling	**NN**	**1-01-001**
beer-runner	**noun**	**2-01-001**
beer-runner	NN	1-01-001
beer-runners	NNS	1-01-001
beer-running	**NN**	**1-01-001**
Beesemyers	**NP**	**1-01-001**
beet	**noun**	**2-02-002**
beets	NNS	2-02-002
Beethoven	**prop. noun**	**13-03-005**
Beethoven	NP	9-02-004
Beethoven	NP-TL	3-01-002
Beethoven's	NP$	1-01-001
beetle	**noun**	**1-01-001**
beetles	NNS	1-01-001
beetling	**JJ**	**2-01-001**
befall	**verb**	**3-02-003**
befall	VB	2-01-002
befell	VBD	1-01-001
befit	**verb**	**2-02-002**
befits	VBZ	1-01-001
befitting	VBG	1-01-001
befog	**verb**	**1-01-001**
befogged	VBN	1-01-001
before	**sub. conj.**	**450-15-266**
before	CS	447-15-264
'fore	CS	1-01-001
befoh	CS	1-01-001
before	CS-HL	1-01-001
before	**prep.**	**408-15-221**
before	IN	406-15-220
beefore	IN	1-01-001
Before	IN-TL	1-01-001
before	**RB**	**160-14-112**
beforehand	**RB**	**2-02-002**
befoul	**verb**	**1-01-001**
befouled	VBN	1-01-001
befuddle	**verb**	**4-02-003**
befuddles	VBZ	1-01-001
befuddled	VBD	1-01-001
befuddled	VBN	1-01-001
befuddling	VBG	1-01-001
beg	**verb**	**34-11-027**
beg	VB	11-07-010
begs	VBZ	1-01-001
begged	VBD	13-05-010
begging	VBG	9-06-008
beget	**verb**	**6-03-004**
beget	VB	1-01-001
begotten	VBN	5-02-003
beggar	**noun**	**5-03-005**
beggar	NN	2-02-002
beggar's	NN$	1-01-001
beggars	NNS	2-02-002
beggary	**NN**	**1-01-001**
begging	**NN**	**1-01-001**
begin	**verb**	**583-15-278**

Word	Tag	Frequency
begin (cont.):		
begin	VB	84-14-070
begins	VBZ	55-11-042
began	VBD	312-15-177
begun	VBN	51-13-048
beginning	VBG	81-13-063
beginner	**noun**	**6-03-004**
beginner	NN	1-01-001
beginner's	NN$	2-01-002
beginners	NNS	1-01-001
beginners'	NNS$	1-01-001
beginners'	NNS$-HL	1-01-001
beginning	**noun**	**92-13-074**
beginning	NN	83-12-066
beginnings	NNS	9-06-009
Begley	**NP**	**2-01-001**
begrudge	**VB**	**2-02-002**
beguile	**verb**	**3-03-003**
beguile	VB	1-01-001
beguiled	VBN	2-02-002
beguiling	**JJ**	**3-02-003**
behalf	**NN**	**21-06-018**
Behan	**NP**	**1-01-001**
behave	**verb**	**32-12-028**
behave	VB	13-07-013
behaves	VBZ	2-01-002
behaved	VBD	10-08-009
behaved	VBN	3-02-002
behaving	VBG	4-03-003
behavior	**noun**	**100-11-047**
behavior	NN	95-11-046
behaviour	NN	3-01-001
Behavior	NN-TL	1-01-001
behaviors	NNS	1-01-001
behavioral	**JJ**	**3-02-002**
behaviorally	**RB**	**1-01-001**
behead	**verb**	**1-01-001**
beheading	VBG	1-01-001
behind	**prep.**	**231-15-138**
behind	IN	229-15-137
behahn	IN	1-01-001
behynde	IN	1-01-001
behind	**NN**	**2-01-002**
behind	**RB**	**27-10-025**
behold	**verb**	**8-05-007**
behold	VB	4-02-003
beholds	VBZ	1-01-001
beheld	VBD	3-03-003
behoove	**verb**	**1-01-001**
behooves	VBZ	1-01-001
Beiderbecke	**NP**	**1-01-001**
beige	**JJ**	**1-01-001**
Beige	**prop. noun**	**1-01-001**
Beige's	NP$	1-01-001
being	**noun**	**66-13-048**
being	NN	27-13-020
Being	NN-TL	3-03-003
beings	NNS	36-09-027
Beirut	**NP**	**1-01-001**
Beismortier	**NP**	**1-01-001**
Bekkai	**NP**	**1-01-001**
bel	**FW-JJ**	**3-02-002**
Bel	**NP**	**1-01-001**
Bel-Air	**NP**	**1-01-001**
Bela	**NP**	**1-01-001**
belabor	**verb**	**1-01-001**
belaboring	VBG	1-01-001
belaboring	**NN**	**1-01-001**
Belafonte	**NP**	**1-01-001**
Belanger	**NP**	**1-01-001**
Belasco	**prop. noun**	**2-01-001**
Belasco	NP	0-00-000
Belasco	NP-TL	2-01-001
belated	**adjective**	**2-02-002**
belated	JJ	1-01-001
belated	JJ-HL	1-01-001
belatedly	**RB**	**1-01-001**
belch	**NN**	**2-02-002**
belch	**verb**	**5-02-004**
belched	VBD	4-02-003
belching	VBG	1-01-001
belching	**NN**	**1-01-001**
belfry	**NN**	**1-01-001**
Belge	**foreign**	**2-01-001**
Belge	FW-JJ	0-00-000
Belge	FW-JJ-TL	2-01-001
Belgian	**adjective**	**14-05-005**
Belgian	JJ	13-05-005
Belgian	JJ-TL	1-01-001
Belgian	**prop. noun**	**22-02-002**
Belgians	NPS	22-02-002
Belgium	**NP**	**2-02-002**
belie	**verb**	**3-02-003**
belied	VBD	3-02-003
belief	**noun**	**87-13-052**
belief	NN	64-13-042
beliefs	NNS	23-08-016
believable	**JJ**	**1-01-001**
believably	**RB**	**1-01-001**
believe	**verb**	**336-15-195**
believe	VB	200-15-130
believes	VBZ	43-11-030
believeth	VBZ	2-01-001
believed	VBD	52-12-041
believed	VBN	25-11-024
believing	VBG	14-07-013
believer	**noun**	**9-05-009**
believer	NN	4-03-004
believers	NNS	5-04-005
belittle	**verb**	**1-01-001**
belittling	VBG	1-01-001
bell	**noun**	**23-08-019**
bell	NN	14-05-013
Bell	NN-TL	1-01-001
bells	NNS	6-03-004
Bells	NNS-TL	2-02-002
Bell	**prop. noun**	**3-03-003**
Bell	NP	1-01-001
Bell	NP-TL	2-02-002
Bella	**NP**	**2-01-001**
Bellamy	**prop. noun**	**1-01-001**
Bellamy's	NP$	1-01-001
bellboy	**noun**	**6-02-003**
bellboy	NN	4-01-002
bellboys	NNS	2-02-002
belle	**noun**	**1-01-001**
belles	NNS	1-01-001
Belle	**NP**	**1-01-001**
Belletch	**NP**	**2-01-001**
Belleville	**NP**	**1-01-001**
bellhop	**noun**	**1-01-001**
bellhops	NNS	1-01-001
bellicosity	**NN**	**1-01-001**
belligerence	**NN**	**2-02-002**
belligerent	**JJ**	**5-04-005**
belligerently	**RB**	**1-01-001**
Bellini	**NP**	**3-02-003**
Bellman	**NP**	**2-01-001**
bellow	**noun**	**3-03-003**
bellow	NN	2-02-002
bellows	NNS	1-01-001
bellow	**verb**	**9-06-009**
bellows	VBZ	1-01-001
bellowed	VBD	6-04-006
bellowing	VBG	2-02-002
Bellow	**prop. noun**	**3-01-002**
Bellow	NP	2-01-001
Bellow's	NP$	1-01-001
Bellows	**prop. noun**	**6-02-002**
Bellows	NP	5-01-001
Bellows	NP-TL	1-01-001
bellwether	**noun**	**1-01-001**
bellwethers	NNS	1-01-001
Bellwood	**NP**	**1-01-001**
belly	**noun**	**25-08-013**
belly	NN	23-08-012
bellies	NNS	2-02-002
bellyfull	**NN**	**1-01-001**
Belmont	**prop. noun**	**2-02-002**
Belmont	NP	1-01-001
Belmont	NP-TL	1-01-001
belong	**verb**	**88-14-069**
belong	VB	37-13-032
belongs	VBZ	22-08-016
belonged	VBD	14-08-012
belonged	VBN	3-03-003
belonging	VBG	12-07-012
belonging	**noun**	**5-05-005**
belonging	NN	1-01-001
belongings	NNS	4-04-004
beloved	**JJ**	**18-09-015**
below	**IN**	**80-13-058**
below	**RB**	**65-10-047**
belowground	**JJ**	**2-01-001**
Belshazzar	**NP**	**1-01-001**
belt	**noun**	**36-12-023**
belt	NN	27-12-020
Belt	NN-TL	2-01-002

belt (cont.):		
belts	NNS	7-03-005
belt	**verb**	**3-02-003**
belts	VBZ	1-01-001
belted	VBD	2-02-002
belt-driven	**JJ**	**1-01-001**
belting	**NN**	**1-01-001**
Belton	**NP**	**2-01-001**
Belvedere	**NP**	**2-02-002**
Belvidere	**NP**	**2-01-001**
Belzec	**NP**	**1-01-001**
bemadden	**verb**	**1-01-001**
bemaddening	VBG	1-01-001
Beman	**NP**	**1-01-001**
bemoan	**verb**	**2-02-002**
bemoan	VB	1-01-001
bemoans	VBZ	1-01-001
Ben	**prop. noun**	**22-11-015**
Ben	NP	18-10-014
Ben	NP-TL	3-02-002
Ben's	NP$	1-01-001
Ben-Gurion	**NP**	**1-01-001**
Ben-hadad	**NP**	**1-01-001**
bench	**noun**	**42-10-024**
bench	NN	27-09-018
Bench	NN-TL	7-01-002
benches	NNS	8-06-007
bench	**verb**	**3-02-002**
bench	VB	1-01-001
benched	VBN	2-01-001
benchmark	**noun**	**2-01-001**
benchmarks	NNS	2-01-001
bend	**noun**	**13-07-011**
bend	NN	8-04-007
Bend	NN-TL	4-02-003
bends	NNS	1-01-001
bend	**verb**	**50-12-035**
bend	VB	12-05-009
bends	VBZ	1-01-001
bent	VBD	14-06-012
bent	VBN	17-10-016
bending	VBG	6-04-005
bending	**NN**	**1-01-001**
beneath	**IN**	**55-12-038**
beneath	**RB**	**2-02-002**
Benedick	**NP**	**3-01-001**
Benedictine	**JJ**	**1-01-001**
benediction	**noun**	**3-02-003**
benediction	NN	2-01-002
Benediction	NN-TL	1-01-001
benefactor	**noun**	**6-04-004**
benefactor	NN	3-03-003
Benefactor	NN-TL	1-01-001
benefactor's	NN$	1-01-001
Benefactor's	NN$-TL	1-01-001
beneficence	**NN**	**1-01-001**
beneficent	**adjective**	**1-01-001**
beneficent	JJ	0-00-000
beneficient	JJ	1-01-001
beneficial	**JJ**	**11-04-008**
beneficiary	**noun**	**5-02-004**
beneficiary	NN	1-01-001
Beneficiary	NN	1-01-001
beneficiaries	NNS	3-02-003
benefit	**noun**	**75-12-038**
benefit	NN	42-12-027
Benefit	NN-TL	1-01-001
benefits	NNS	31-07-017
benefits	NNS-HL	1-01-001
benefit	**verb**	**24-09-022**
benefit	VB	20-08-018
benefits	VBZ	1-01-001
benefited	VBN	3-02-003
Benelux	**NP**	**2-01-001**
Benesi	**NP**	**1-01-001**
Benet	**prop. noun**	**4-03-003**
Benet	NP	2-02-002
Benet's	NP$	1-01-001
Benets	NPS	1-01-001
benevolence	**NN**	**4-04-004**
benevolent	**JJ**	**2-02-002**
Bengal	**prop. noun**	**4-02-002**
Bengal	NP	2-02-002
Bengal	NP-TL	2-02-002
Bengali	**JJ**	**1-01-001**
benighted	**JJ**	**2-02-002**
benign	**JJ**	**1-01-001**
Benington	**NP**	**7-01-001**
Benita	**NP**	**1-01-001**
Benjamin	**NP**	**12-06-010**
Bennett	**NP**	**1-01-001**
Bennington	**prop. noun**	**4-02-002**
Bennington	NP	2-02-002
Bennington	NP-TL	2-01-001
Benny	**NP**	**4-03-003**
Benoit	**NP**	**1-01-001**
Benson	**prop. noun**	**18-03-003**
Benson	NP	17-03-003
Benson's	NP$	1-01-001
bent	**NN**	**3-02-003**
bent-arm	**noun**	**1-01-001**
bent-arm	NN	0-00-000
Bent-Arm	NN-TL	1-01-001
Bentham	**NP**	**2-01-002**
Bentley	**prop. noun**	**3-02-002**
Bentley	NP	2-01-001
Bentleys	NPS	1-01-001
Benzedrine	**NP**	**1-01-001**
Benzell	**NP**	**1-01-001**
benzene	**NN**	**2-01-001**
Beowulf	**prop. noun**	**15-01-001**
Beowulf	NP	1-01-001
Beowulf	NP-TL	13-01-001
Beowulf's	NP$	1-01-001
bequeath	**verb**	**2-02-002**
bequeathed	VBN	2-02-002
bequest	**noun**	**8-03-003**
bequest	NN	5-02-002
bequests	NNS	3-03-003
berate	**verb**	**3-03-003**
berated	VBD	1-01-001
berated	VBN	2-02-002
Berche	**NP**	**1-01-001**
Berea	**NP**	**1-01-001**
bereavement	**noun**	**5-03-004**
bereavement	NN	4-03-003
bereavements	NNS	1-01-001
bereft	**JJ**	**2-02-002**
berg	**noun**	**1-01-001**
bergs	NNS	1-01-001
Berg	**prop. noun**	**1-01-001**
Berg's	NP$	1-01-001
Bergamaschi	**NP**	**1-01-001**
Berger	**prop. noun**	**20-02-003**
Berger	NP	15-02-003
Berger's	NP$	5-02-003
Bergson	**NP**	**1-01-001**
beribboned	**JJ**	**1-01-001**
beriberi	**NN**	**2-02-002**
Beringer	**NP**	**1-01-001**
Berkeley	**prop. noun**	**1-01-001**
Berkeley	NP	0-00-000
Berkeley	NP-TL	1-01-001
Berkely	**NP**	**2-01-001**
Berkman	**NP**	**1-01-001**
Berkshire	**prop. noun**	**2-02-002**
Berkshires	NPS	2-02-002
Berle	**NP**	**4-02-002**
Berlin	**prop. noun**	**80-09-027**
Berlin	NP	43-09-022
Brelin	NP	1-01-001
Berlin	NP-HL	1-01-001
Berlin	NP-TL	31-04-009
Berlin's	NP$	3-02-002
Berlin's	NP$-TL	1-01-001
Berliner	**prop. noun**	**1-01-001**
Berliners	NPS	0-00-000
Berliners	NPS-TL	1-01-001
Berlioz	**NP**	**1-01-001**
Berlitz	**NP**	**1-01-001**
Berman	**prop. noun**	**7-02-002**
Berman	NP	6-02-002
Berman's	NP$	1-01-001
Bermuda	**NP**	**9-05-005**
Bern	**NP**	**5-01-001**
Bernadine	**prop. noun**	**1-01-001**
Bernadine's	NP$	0-00-000
Bernadine's	NP$-TL	1-01-001
Bernard	**prop. noun**	**9-03-009**
Bernard	NP	8-03-008
Bernard	NP-TL	1-01-001
Bernardine	**NP**	**1-01-001**
Bernardo	**NP**	**1-01-001**
Berne	**prop. noun**	**1-01-001**
Berne	NP	0-00-000
Berne	NP-TL	1-01-001
Bernet	**NP**	**1-01-001**
Bernhard	**NP**	**1-01-001**

Word	Tag	Frequency
Bernhardt	**NP**	**2-02-002**
Bernie	**NP**	**1-01-001**
Berniece	**NP**	**1-01-001**
Bernini	**prop. noun**	**3-02-002**
Bernini	NP	1-01-001
Bernini's	NP$	2-01-001
Bernoulli	**NP**	**2-01-001**
Bernstein	**NP**	**1-01-001**
Bernz-O-Matic	**NP**	**1-01-001**
Beronio	**NP**	**1-01-001**
Berra	**prop. noun**	**3-01-002**
Berra	NP	2-01-001
Berra's	NP$	1-01-001
Berrellez	**NP**	**1-01-001**
berry	**noun**	**5-04-004**
berry	NN	3-02-002
berries	NNS	2-02-002
Berry	**prop. noun**	**7-02-004**
Berry	NP	6-02-004
Berry's	NP$	1-01-001
Bert	**NP**	**1-01-001**
Berteros	**NP**	**1-01-001**
berth	**noun**	**4-03-004**
berth	NN	3-03-003
Berth	NN-TL	1-01-001
Bertha	**NP**	**5-03-003**
Berthelier	**NP**	**1-01-001**
Bertie	**NP**	**1-01-001**
Berto	**prop. noun**	**4-01-001**
Berto	NP	3-01-001
Berto's	NP$	1-01-001
Bertoia	**NP**	**1-01-001**
Berton	**NP**	**1-01-001**
Bertorelli	**NP**	**1-01-001**
Bertrand	**NP**	**1-01-001**
Beryl	**NP**	**3-03-003**
beryllium	**NN**	**1-01-001**
beseech	**VB**	**1-01-001**
beset	**verb**	**9-08-009**
besets	VBZ	1-01-001
beset	VBD	1-01-001
beset	VBN	6-06-006
besetting	VBG	1-01-001
beside	**IN**	**78-11-055**
besides	**IN**	**31-10-028**
besides	**RB**	**35-13-033**
besiege	**verb**	**4-04-004**
besiege	VB	1-01-001
besieged	VBN	2-02-002
besieging	VBG	1-01-001
besieger	**noun**	**2-01-001**
besiegers	NNS	2-01-001
besmirch	**verb**	**3-03-003**
besmirch	VB	1-01-001
besmirched	VBD	1-01-001
besmirching	VBG	1-01-001
bespeak	**verb**	**2-02-002**
bespeak	VB	1-01-001
bespeaks	VBZ	1-01-001
bespectacled	**JJ**	**2-02-002**
Bess	**prop. noun**	**3-02-003**
Bess	NP	1-01-001
Bess	NP-TL	2-02-002
Bessarabia	**NP**	**2-02-002**
Besset	**NP**	**1-01-001**
Bessie	**NP**	**1-01-001**
best	**sup. adj.**	**292-15-197**
best	JJT	289-15-195
best	JJT-HL	3-03-003
best	**QL**	**3-02-003**
best	**RBT**	**51-13-043**
best	**verb**	**2-02-002**
best	VB	1-01-001
bested	VBN	1-01-001
Best	**prop. noun**	**5-04-004**
Best	NP	3-02-002
Best	NP-TL	1-01-001
Best's	NP$	1-01-001
best-educated	**JJT**	**1-01-001**
best-gaited	**JJT**	**1-01-001**
best-hearted	**JJT**	**1-01-001**
best-known	**JJT**	**1-01-001**
best-looking	**JJT**	**1-01-001**
best-preserved	**JJT**	**1-01-001**
best-selling	**adjective**	**2-02-002**
best-selling	JJ	1-01-001
bestselling	JJ	1-01-001
best-tempered	**JJT**	**1-01-001**
Bester	**NP**	**1-01-001**
bestial	**JJ**	**1-01-001**
Bestimmung	**foreign**	**1-01-001**
Bestimmung	FW-NN	0-00-000
Bestimmung	FW-NN-TL	1-01-001
bestow	**verb**	**9-05-009**
bestow	VB	2-02-002
bestowed	VBD	3-03-003
bestowed	VBN	4-03-004
bestowal	**NN**	**4-03-004**
bestseller	**noun**	**4-03-003**
bestseller	NN	2-01-001
best-seller	NN	1-01-001
bestsellers	NNS	0-00-000
best-sellers	NNS	1-01-001
bestubbled	**JJ**	**1-01-001**
bet	**noun**	**9-08-008**
bet	NN	6-05-005
bets	NNS	3-03-003
bet	**verb**	**18-08-016**
bet	VB	13-07-012
bet	VBD	1-01-001
betting	VBG	3-03-003
betting	VBG-HL	1-01-001
Beta	**NP**	**2-01-002**
Betancourt	**NP**	**2-01-002**
bete	**FW-NN**	**1-01-001**
betel-stained	**JJ**	**1-01-001**
Beth	**prop. noun**	**5-04-004**
Beth	NP	4-03-003
Beth	NP-TL	1-01-001
Bethel	**NP**	**1-01-001**
bethink	**verb**	**1-01-001**
bethought	VBD	1-01-001
Bethlehem	**prop. noun**	**1-01-001**
Bethlehem	NP	0-00-000
Bethlehem	NP-TL	1-01-001
betide	**VB**	**2-01-002**
betray	**verb**	**16-05-014**
betray	VB	4-04-004
betrays	VBZ	3-02-003
betrayed	VBD	6-04-006
betrayed	VBN	2-02-002
betraying	VBG	1-01-001
betrayal	**NN**	**6-04-005**
betrayer	**NN**	**1-01-001**
betroth	**verb**	**1-01-001**
betrothed	VBN	1-01-001
betrothal	**NN**	**1-01-001**
Betsey	**NP**	**2-01-001**
Betsy	**NP**	**1-01-001**
better	**comp. adj.**	**238-14-157**
better	JJR	233-14-155
better	JJR-HL	3-01-003
Better	JJR-TL	2-02-002
better	**QL**	**4-04-004**
better	**RBR**	**166-15-112**
better	**verb**	**7-05-006**
better	VB	6-04-005
bettering	VBG	1-01-001
better-remembered	**JJR**	**1-01-001**
better-than-average	**JJ**	**1-01-001**
betterment	**NN**	**3-02-003**
betting	**NN**	**1-01-001**
betty	**noun**	**1-01-001**
betties	NNS	1-01-001
Betty	**prop. noun**	**5-02-003**
Betty	NP	4-02-003
Betty's	NP$	1-01-001
between	**prep.**	**729-15-316**
between	IN	725-15-316
between	IN-HL	1-01-001
Between	IN-TL	3-03-003
between	**RB**	**1-01-001**
bevel	**noun**	**1-01-001**
bevels	NNS	1-01-001
bevel	**verb**	**5-01-001**
bevel	VB	2-01-001
beveled	VBN	3-01-001
beveling	**NN**	**1-01-001**
beverage	**noun**	**9-04-005**
beverage	NN	5-03-004
beverages	NNS	4-02-002
Beverly	**prop. noun**	**14-05-007**
Beverly	NP	5-03-003
Beverly	NP-TL	9-04-006
Bevo	**NP**	**2-01-001**
bevor	**FW-CS**	**1-01-001**
bevy	**NN**	**3-02-003**
bewail	**VB**	**1-01-001**

Word	Tag	Frequency
beware	**VB**	**3-03-003**
bewhiskered	**JJ**	**1-01-001**
bewilder	**verb**	**7-03-007**
bewilders	VBZ	1-01-001
bewildered	VBD	1-01-001
bewildered	VBN	5-03-005
bewilderedly	**RB**	**1-01-001**
bewilderingly	**RB**	**1-01-001**
bewilderment	**NN**	**3-03-003**
bewitch	**verb**	**3-03-003**
bewitched	VBN	2-02-002
bewitching	VBG	1-01-001
Bexar	**NP**	**1-01-001**
Bey	**NP**	**6-01-001**
Beyeler	**NP**	**2-01-001**
beyond	**prep.**	**163-15-121**
beyond	IN	162-15-120
Beyond	IN-TL	1-01-001
beyond	**adverb**	**12-07-012**
beyond	RB	9-05-009
Beyond	RB-TL	3-02-003
beyond-normal	**JJ**	**1-01-001**
BG	**NP**	**1-01-001**
bi-monthly	**JJ**	**1-01-001**
Bianco	**NP**	**1-01-001**
bias	**noun**	**9-03-006**
bias	NN	8-03-006
biases	NNS	1-01-001
bib	**NN**	**2-02-002**
Bibb	**NP**	**1-01-001**
bible	**noun**	**1-01-001**
bibles	NNS	1-01-001
Bible	**prop. noun**	**59-11-028**
Bible	NP	46-11-025
Bible	NP-TL	13-03-006
Bible-emancipated	**JJ**	**1-01-001**
Bible-loving	**JJ**	**1-01-001**
Biblical	**adjective**	**18-06-010**
Biblical	JJ	15-05-007
biblical	JJ	3-02-003
Biblically	**QL**	**1-01-001**
bibliographical	**JJ**	**1-01-001**
bibliography	**noun**	**4-02-003**
bibliography	NN	1-01-001
Bibliography	NN-TL	1-01-001
bibliographies	NNS	2-01-001
bibliophile	**noun**	**1-01-001**
bibliophiles	NNS	1-01-001
bicameral	**JJ**	**1-01-001**
bicarbonate	**NN**	**1-01-001**
biceps	**noun**	**4-02-002**
biceps	NN	3-01-001
bicep	NN	1-01-001
bicker	**verb**	**2-02-002**
bickering	VBG	2-02-002
bickering	**NN**	**1-01-001**
biconcave	**JJ**	**1-01-001**
bicycle	**noun**	**7-04-005**
bicycle	NN	5-03-004
bicycles	NNS	2-02-002
bicycle-auto	**JJ**	**1-01-001**
bid	**noun**	**19-06-011**
bid	NN	12-06-010
Bid	NN-TL	1-01-001
bids	NNS	5-02-003
bids	NNS-HL	1-01-001
bid	**verb**	**10-07-008**
bid	VB	7-05-005
bade	VBD	1-01-001
bid	VBD	1-01-001
bid	VBN	1-01-001
bidder	**noun**	**5-04-005**
bidder	NN	2-02-002
bidders	NNS	3-03-003
bidding	**NN**	**7-03-003**
Biddle	**NP**	**1-01-001**
biddy	**noun**	**1-01-001**
biddies	NNS	1-01-001
bide	**VB**	**1-01-001**
bien	**FW-UH**	**1-01-001**
biennial	**JJ**	**1-01-001**
biennium	**NN**	**1-01-001**
Bienville	**NP**	**9-01-001**
Bierce	**NP**	**1-01-001**
Bietnar	**NP**	**1-01-001**
bifocal	**JJ**	**1-01-001**
bifocal	**noun**	**2-02-002**
bifocals	NNS	2-02-002
Bifutek-san	**NP**	**1-01-001**

Word	Tag	Frequency
big	**adjective**	**359-15-182**
big	JJ	319-15-173
big	JJ-HL	3-02-003
Big	JJ-TL	37-09-016
Big	**NP**	**1-01-001**
big-boned	**JJ**	**1-01-001**
big-business	**NN**	**1-01-001**
big-chested	**JJ**	**1-01-001**
big-daddy	**NN**	**1-01-001**
big-game	**NN**	**1-01-001**
big-large	**adjective**	**1-01-001**
big-large	JJ + JJ	0-00-000
big-large	JJ + JJ-NC	1-01-001
big-league	**NN**	**1-01-001**
big-shouldered	**JJ**	**1-01-001**
big-stage	**NN**	**1-01-001**
big-ticket	**NN**	**1-01-001**
big-town	**NN**	**1-01-001**
bigger	**JJR**	**34-12-026**
biggest	**JJT**	**24-11-023**
bigot	**noun**	**1-01-001**
bigots	NNS	1-01-001
bigoted	**JJ**	**1-01-001**
bigotry	**NN**	**2-02-002**
bijouterie	**FW-NN**	**1-01-001**
bikini	**noun**	**1-01-001**
bikinis	NNS	1-01-001
bilateral	**JJ**	**2-02-002**
bile	**NN**	**3-02-002**
bilge	**NN**	**2-01-001**
bilharziasis	**NN**	**1-01-001**
bilinear	**JJ**	**1-01-001**
bilingual	**JJ**	**1-01-001**
bilk	**verb**	**2-02-002**
bilked	VBN	2-02-002
bill	**noun**	**133-14-061**
bill	NN	78-13-038
Bill	NN-TL	8-03-004
bill's	NN$	2-02-002
bills	NNS	45-11-027
bill	**verb**	**3-02-003**
billed	VBN	3-02-003
Bill	**prop. noun**	**62-12-035**
Bill	NP	56-10-030
Bill	NP-TL	1-01-001
Bill's	NP + HVZ	0-00-000
Bill's	NP + HVZ-NC	1-01-001
Bill's	NP$	2-02-002
Bills	NPS	2-01-001
billboard	**noun**	**3-01-001**
billboard	NN	1-01-001
billboards	NNS	1-01-001
billboards	NNS-HL	1-01-001
billet	**noun**	**2-02-002**
billet	NN	1-01-001
billets	NNS	1-01-001
billiard	**NN**	**1-01-001**
Billie	**NP**	**3-02-002**
Billiken	**prop. noun**	**4-01-001**
Billiken	NP	1-01-001
Billiken	NP-TL	1-01-001
Billikens	NPS	2-01-001
billing	**NN**	**4-04-004**
Billings	**NP**	**1-01-001**
billion	**CD**	**62-08-016**
billion	**noun**	**7-04-004**
billions	NNS	7-04-004
billow	**noun**	**1-01-001**
billows	NNS	1-01-001
billow	**verb**	**1-01-001**
billowed	VBD	1-01-001
Billy	**prop. noun**	**26-06-012**
Billy	NP	23-06-011
Billy	NP-TL	3-01-002
Bimini	**NP**	**1-01-001**
bimolecular	**JJ**	**1-01-001**
bimonthly	**JJ**	**1-01-001**
bin	**noun**	**11-03-006**
bin	NN	9-03-004
bins	NNS	2-02-002
bind	**NN**	**2-02-002**
bind	**verb**	**51-12-044**
bind	VB	2-02-002
binds	VBZ	2-01-002
bound	VBD	5-03-004
bound	VBN	31-12-031
bound	VBN-HL	1-01-001
binding	VBG	10-06-007
binder	**noun**	**3-02-002**

binder (cont.):		
binder	NN	1-01-001
binders	NNS	2-01-001
binding	**JJ**	**1-01-001**
binding	**NN**	**9-02-003**
bindle	**NN**	**1-01-001**
Bing	**NP**	**2-02-002**
binge	**NN**	**1-01-001**
bingle	**noun**	**1-01-001**
bingles	NNS	0-00-000
bingles	NNS-HL	1-01-001
Bini	**NP**	**1-01-001**
binoculars	**NNS**	**2-02-002**
binomial	**adjective**	**36-01-001**
binomial	JJ	32-01-001
binomial	JJ-HL	3-01-001
binomial	JJ-NC	1-01-001
binuclear	**JJ**	**1-01-001**
bio-	**JJ**	**1-01-001**
bio-assay	**NN**	**2-01-001**
bio-dynamic	**adjective**	**1-01-001**
bio-dynamic	JJ	0-00-000
Bio-Dynamic	JJ-TL	1-01-001
bio-medical	**JJ**	**1-01-001**
bio-medicine	**NN**	**2-01-001**
biochemical	**JJ**	**3-02-003**
biographer	**noun**	**2-02-002**
biographer	NN	1-01-001
biographers	NNS	1-01-001
biographical	**JJ**	**4-01-004**
biography	**NN**	**13-07-009**
biologic	**JJ**	**1-01-001**
biological	**adjective**	**20-04-007**
biological	JJ	19-04-007
biological	JJ-HL	1-01-001
biologically	**RB**	**1-01-001**
biologist	**noun**	**4-02-004**
biologist	NN	2-02-002
biologists	NNS	2-01-002
biology	**NN**	**7-05-007**
biophysical	**adjective**	**2-02-002**
biophysical	JJ	1-01-001
biophysical	JJ-HL	1-01-001
biophysicist	**NN**	**1-01-001**
biopsy	**noun**	**3-01-001**
biopsy	NN	2-01-001
biopsies	NNS	1-01-001
biosynthesize	**verb**	**1-01-001**
biosynthesized	VBN	1-01-001
bipartisan	**JJ**	**2-02-002**
biplane	**NN**	**2-01-001**
biracial	**JJ**	**1-01-001**
birch	**noun**	**2-02-002**
birch	NN	1-01-001
birches	NNS	1-01-001
Birch	**prop. noun**	**1-01-001**
Birch	NP	0-00-000
Birch	NP-TL	1-01-001
birch-paneled	**JJ**	**1-01-001**
bird	**noun**	**83-11-048**
bird	NN	25-10-022
bird's	NN$	1-01-001
birds	NNS	48-11-030
Birds	NNS-TL	9-02-003
Bird	**prop. noun**	**8-03-003**
Bird	NP	6-03-003
Birds'	NPS$	2-01-001
bird-brain	**NN**	**1-01-001**
birdbath	**NN**	**1-01-001**
birdie	**noun**	**5-01-001**
birdie	NN	3-01-001
birdies	NNS	2-01-001
birdie	**verb**	**5-01-001**
birdie	VB	1-01-001
birdied	VBD	2-01-001
birdied	VBN	2-01-001
Birdie	**NP**	**1-01-001**
birdlike	**JJ**	**1-01-001**
Birdwhistell	**NP**	**1-01-001**
Birdwood	**NP**	**1-01-001**
birefringence	**NN**	**3-01-001**
Birgit	**NP**	**1-01-001**
Birgitta	**NP**	**1-01-001**
Birkhead	**NP**	**3-01-001**
Birmingham	**prop. noun**	**13-06-008**
Birmingham	NP	10-06-006
Birmingham	NP-HL	1-01-001
Birmingham	NP-TL	2-02-002
Birnbaum	**NP**	**1-01-001**

birth	**noun**	**70-11-034**
birth	NN	47-11-029
birth	NN-HL	16-01-001
Birth	NN-TL	3-02-003
births	NNS	4-03-004
birth	**verb**	**1-01-001**
birthed	VBN	1-01-001
birth-control	**noun**	**5-02-002**
birth-control	NN	4-01-001
birthcontrol	NN	1-01-001
birth-prevention	**NN**	**2-01-001**
birthday	**NN**	**18-09-018**
birthplace	**NN**	**6-03-004**
birthright	**NN**	**1-01-001**
Biscayne	**prop. noun**	**2-01-001**
Biscayne	NP	1-01-001
Biscayne	NP-TL	1-01-001
biscuit	**noun**	**7-06-007**
biscuit	NN	2-02-002
biscuits	NNS	5-04-005
bishop	**noun**	**20-06-011**
bishop	NN	5-03-003
Bishop	NN-TL	8-03-005
bishops	NNS	5-03-004
Bishops	NNS-TL	1-01-001
bishops'	NNS$	1-01-001
Bishop	**NP**	**5-04-004**
bishopry	**NN**	**1-01-001**
Bishopsgate	**NP**	**2-01-001**
Bismarck	**prop. noun**	**2-02-002**
Bismarck	NP	1-01-001
Bismark	NP-TL	1-01-001
bison	**NN**	**1-01-001**
bisque	**NN**	**6-01-001**
bit	**noun**	**105-13-073**
bit	NN	93-13-066
bits	NNS	12-07-011
bit-like	**JJ**	**1-01-001**
bitch	**noun**	**8-03-005**
bitch	NN	6-02-004
bich	NN	1-01-001
bitches	NNS	0-00-000
biches	NNS	1-01-001
bite	**noun**	**9-05-005**
bite	NN	3-03-003
bites	NNS	6-03-003
bite	**verb**	**26-11-022**
bite	VB	7-05-007
bites	VBZ	2-02-002
bit	VBD	7-04-007
bitten	VBN	3-03-003
bit	VBN	1-01-001
biting	VBG	6-04-005
biter	**NN**	**1-01-001**
bitter	**JJ**	**53-12-048**
bitterest	**JJT**	**2-02-002**
bitterly	**QL**	**2-02-002**
bitterly	**RB**	**14-09-013**
bitterness	**NN**	**18-08-016**
bitters	**NNS**	**1-01-001**
bittersweet	**JJ**	**1-01-001**
bivouac	**NN**	**5-02-004**
biwa	**FW-NN**	**9-01-001**
Bix	**NP**	**1-01-001**
biz	**NN**	**2-01-002**
bizarre	**JJ**	**7-04-006**
Bizerte	**NP**	**3-01-001**
Bizet	**prop. noun**	**1-01-001**
Bizet's	NP$	1-01-001
Bjerre	**prop. noun**	**1-01-001**
Bjerre's	NP$	1-01-001
blab	**verb**	**1-01-001**
blabbed	VBD	1-01-001
Blaber	**NP**	**1-01-001**
black	**adjective**	**165-14-088**
black	JJ	149-14-085
Black	JJ-TL	16-04-008
black	**noun**	**11-07-010**
black	NN	9-06-008
blacks	NNS	2-02-002
black	**verb**	**4-04-004**
black	VB	1-01-001
blacked	VBN	3-03-003
Black	**prop. noun**	**35-05-008**
Black	NP	28-05-008
Black's	NP+BEZ	1-01-001
Black's	NP$	5-02-002
Blacks	NPS	1-01-001
black-and-orange	**JJ**	**1-01-001**

Word	Tag	Frequency
black-and-yellow	**JJ**	**1-01-001**
black-ball	**verb**	**1-01-001**
black-balled	VBN	1-01-001
black-bearded	**JJ**	**1-01-001**
black-body	**NN**	**4-01-001**
black-clad	**JJ**	**1-01-001**
black-crowned	**JJ**	**1-01-001**
black-eyed	**JJ**	**1-01-001**
black-haired	**JJ**	**1-01-001**
black-market	**NN**	**1-01-001**
black-tipped	**JJ**	**1-01-001**
blackberry	**NN**	**1-01-001**
Blackberry	**NP**	**2-01-001**
blackbird	**noun**	**1-01-001**
blackbirds	NNS	1-01-001
blackboard	**NN**	**2-01-001**
blacked-in	**JJ**	**1-01-001**
blacken	**verb**	**5-03-004**
blackened	VBN	5-03-004
blackening	**NN**	**1-01-001**
blackest	**JJT**	**1-01-001**
Blackfoot	**prop. noun**	**2-01-001**
Blackfeet	NPS	2-01-001
blacking	**NN**	**1-01-001**
blackjack	**NN**	**2-01-001**
blackmail	**NN**	**2-02-002**
blackmail	**verb**	**1-01-001**
blackmailed	VBN	1-01-001
blackmailer	**NN**	**2-01-001**
Blackman	**NP**	**15-01-001**
Blackmer	**NP**	**3-01-001**
blackness	**NN**	**5-04-005**
blackout	**noun**	**5-04-004**
blackout	NN	4-04-004
blackout	NN-HL	1-01-001
blacksmith	**NN**	**2-02-002**
Blackstone	**NP**	**1-01-001**
Blackwell	**prop. noun**	**5-01-001**
Blackwell	NP	3-01-001
Blackwell's	NP+BEZ	1-01-001
Blackwells	NPS	1-01-001
blade	**noun**	**26-10-018**
blade	NN	14-06-010
blades	NNS	12-08-010
Blaine	**NP**	**2-02-002**
Blair	**prop. noun**	**1-01-001**
Blair	NP	0-00-000
Blair	NP-TL	1-01-001
Blake	**NP**	**6-03-003**
Blakey	**NP**	**3-02-002**
blame	**NN**	**11-07-009**
blame	**verb**	**32-13-031**
blame	VB	23-11-023
blamed	VBD	5-05-005
blamed	VBN	2-02-002
blaming	VBG	2-02-002
Blanc	**NP**	**1-01-001**
blanch	**verb**	**5-02-002**
blanched	VBN	1-01-001
blanching	VBG	4-01-001
Blanchard	**prop. noun**	**4-02-004**
Blanchard	NP	2-01-002
Blanchard's	NP$	1-01-001
Blanchard's	NP$-TL	1-01-001
blanche	**JJ**	**1-01-001**
Blanche	**prop. noun**	**25-03-004**
Blanche	NP	23-03-003
Blanche	NP-TL	1-01-001
Blanche's	NP$	1-01-001
bland	**JJ**	**3-02-003**
blandly	**QL**	**1-01-001**
blandly	**RB**	**1-01-001**
blandness	**NN**	**1-01-001**
blank	**JJ**	**11-06-008**
blank	**noun**	**6-04-005**
blank	NN	3-02-003
blanks	NNS	3-02-002
blanket	**noun**	**39-11-026**
blanket	NN	29-10-018
blankets	NNS	10-05-008
blanket	**verb**	**3-03-003**
blanket	VB	1-01-001
blankets	VBZ	1-01-001
blanketed	VBN	1-01-001
Blanton	**NP**	**1-01-001**
blare	**verb**	**2-01-002**
blared	VBD	1-01-001
blaring	VBG	1-01-001
Blasingame	**NP**	**3-01-001**
blaspheme	**verb**	**1-01-001**
blasphemed	VBD	1-01-001
blasphemous	**JJ**	**5-02-004**
blasphemy	**noun**	**6-02-003**
blasphemy	NN	4-02-003
blasphemies	NNS	2-01-001
blast	**noun**	**16-07-011**
blast	NN	11-05-008
blast	NN-HL	1-01-001
blasts	NNS	4-04-004
blast	**verb**	**9-04-009**
blast	VB	3-03-003
blasted	VBD	3-03-003
blasted	VBN	1-01-001
blasting	VBG	2-02-002
blastdown	**NN**	**1-01-001**
blatancy	**NN**	**1-01-001**
blatant	**JJ**	**2-02-002**
Blatz	**prop. noun**	**10-01-001**
Blatz	NP	9-01-001
Blatz's	NP$	1-01-001
Blauberman	**NP**	**2-01-001**
Blaustein	**NP**	**1-01-001**
blaze	**NN**	**4-03-004**
blaze	**verb**	**11-05-009**
blaze	VB	3-02-003
blazed	VBD	2-02-002
blazing	VBG	6-03-005
blazer	**NN**	**1-01-001**
blazon	**VB**	**1-01-001**
bleach	**verb**	**7-03-005**
bleached	VBN	5-02-003
bleaching	VBG	2-02-002
bleacher	**noun**	**5-04-005**
bleachers	NNS	5-04-005
bleacher-type	**JJ**	**1-01-001**
bleak	**adjective**	**10-06-010**
bleak	JJ	9-06-009
Bleak	JJ-TL	1-01-001
bleakly	**RB**	**3-03-003**
bleary	**JJ**	**2-02-002**
bleat	**noun**	**2-02-002**
bleat	NN	1-01-001
bleats	NNS	1-01-001
bleat	**verb**	**1-01-001**
bleating	VBG	1-01-001
bleb	**noun**	**1-01-001**
blebs	NNS	1-01-001
Bleckley	**NP**	**1-01-001**
bleed	**verb**	**18-06-014**
bleed	VB	2-02-002
bled	VBD	2-01-002
bled	VBN	1-01-001
bleeding	VBG	13-05-010
bleeding	**noun**	**4-03-004**
bleeding	NN	3-03-003
bleedings	NNS	1-01-001
Bleeker	**prop. noun**	**1-01-001**
Bleeker	NP	0-00-000
Bleeker	NP-TL	1-01-001
bleep	**noun**	**1-01-001**
bleeps	NNS	1-01-001
blemish	**noun**	**3-03-003**
blemish	NN	2-02-002
blemishes	NNS	1-01-001
blend	**noun**	**7-04-006**
blend	NN	5-03-005
blends	NNS	2-02-002
blend	**verb**	**9-07-008**
blend	VB	4-03-003
blended	VBD	2-02-002
blended	VBN	2-02-002
blending	VBG	1-01-001
Blenheim	**NP**	**5-01-001**
bless	**verb**	**26-11-023**
bless	VB	9-04-008
blessed	VBN	11-07-010
blest	VBN	3-03-003
Blessed	VBN-TL	2-02-002
blessing	VBG	1-01-001
blessing	**noun**	**12-05-009**
blessing	NN	9-05-008
blessings	NNS	3-02-002
Blevins	**prop. noun**	**3-01-001**
Blevins	NP	2-01-001
Blevins'	NP$	1-01-001
blight	**NN**	**2-02-002**
blight	**verb**	**3-03-003**
blighted	VBD	1-01-001

Word	Tag	Frequency
blight (cont.):		
blighted	VBN	2-02-002
Blimp	**NP**	**1-01-001**
blind	**adjective**	**43-12-033**
blind	JJ	42-12-032
blind	JJ-HL	1-01-001
blind	**noun**	**6-04-005**
blind	NN	3-02-002
blinds	NNS	3-03-003
blind	**verb**	**7-03-007**
blind	VB	1-01-001
blinded	VBN	4-03-004
blinding	VBG	2-02-002
blindfold	**verb**	**3-02-003**
blindfolded	VBN	2-01-002
blind-folded	VBN	1-01-001
blindly	**RB**	**8-07-008**
blindness	**NN**	**12-05-008**
blink	**verb**	**13-07-011**
blink	VB	4-03-003
blinked	VBD	6-04-006
blinking	VBG	3-03-003
blinker	**noun**	**1-01-001**
blinkers	NNS	1-01-001
blip	**noun**	**1-01-001**
blips	NNS	1-01-001
Blish	**prop. noun**	**1-01-001**
Blish's	NP$	1-01-001
bliss	**NN**	**4-04-004**
blissful	**JJ**	**4-03-004**
blissfully	**RB**	**2-02-002**
blister	**noun**	**4-03-003**
blister	NN	2-02-002
blisters	NNS	2-02-002
blister	**verb**	**3-02-002**
blister	VB	1-01-001
blistered	VBN	2-01-001
blithe	**JJ**	**2-01-002**
blithely	**RB**	**3-02-003**
blitz	**noun**	**4-03-004**
blitz	NN	2-02-002
Blitz	NN-TL	1-01-001
blitzes	NNS	1-01-001
blizzard	**noun**	**8-04-004**
blizzard	NN	7-04-004
blizzards	NNS	1-01-001
bloat	**NN**	**8-01-001**
bloat	**verb**	**3-03-003**
bloated	VBN	3-03-003
blob	**NN**	**2-02-002**
bloc	**NN**	**10-05-008**
Bloch	**NP**	**2-02-002**
block	**noun**	**98-14-043**
block	NN	61-14-035
blocks	NNS	37-11-016
block	**verb**	**20-09-018**
block	VB	5-04-005
blocked	VBD	5-03-005
blocked	VBN	7-05-007
blocking	VBG	3-03-003
block-buster	**NN**	**1-01-001**
blockade	**noun**	**16-02-002**
blockade	NN	13-02-002
blockade	NN-HL	3-01-001
blockade	**verb**	**2-01-001**
blockading	VBG	2-01-001
blockage	**noun**	**1-01-001**
blockages	NNS	1-01-001
blockhouse	**NN**	**1-01-001**
blocky	**JJ**	**2-02-002**
Blois	**NP**	**1-01-001**
bloke	**noun**	**2-02-002**
bloke	NN	1-01-001
blokes	NNS	1-01-001
Blomdahl	**NP**	**2-01-001**
blonde	**adjective**	**25-08-021**
blonde	JJ	14-06-013
blond	JJ	11-05-009
blonde	**noun**	**10-03-005**
blonde	NN	6-02-003
blonde's	NN$	3-02-002
blondes	NNS	1-01-001
blonde-haired	**JJ**	**1-01-001**
blonde-headed	**JJ**	**1-01-001**
blood	**noun**	**122-14-070**
blood	NN	119-13-067
Blood	NN-TL	2-02-002
bloods	NNS	1-01-001
blood	**verb**	**1-01-001**
blood (cont.):		
blooded	VBN	1-01-001
blood-bought	**JJ**	**1-01-001**
blood-chilling	**JJ**	**1-01-001**
blood-filled	**JJ**	**1-01-001**
blood-flecked	**JJ**	**1-01-001**
blood-flow	**NN**	**1-01-001**
blood-kinship	**NN**	**1-01-001**
blood-lust	**NN**	**1-01-001**
blood-soaked	**JJ**	**1-01-001**
blood-specked	**JJ**	**1-01-001**
blood-thirsty	**JJ**	**1-01-001**
bloodhound	**noun**	**2-02-002**
bloodhounds	NNS	2-02-002
bloodiest	**JJT**	**1-01-001**
bloodless	**JJ**	**3-02-003**
bloodlust	**NN**	**1-01-001**
bloodroot	**NN**	**1-01-001**
bloodshed	**NN**	**3-03-003**
bloodshot	**JJ**	**1-01-001**
bloodspot	**noun**	**1-01-001**
bloodspots	NNS	1-01-001
bloodstain	**noun**	**1-01-001**
bloodstains	NNS	1-01-001
bloodstained	**adjective**	**2-02-002**
bloodstained	JJ	1-01-001
blood-stained	JJ	1-01-001
bloodstream	**NN**	**4-03-003**
bloody	**JJ**	**8-06-008**
bloom	**noun**	**11-05-008**
bloom	NN	8-05-006
blooms	NNS	3-02-003
bloom	**verb**	**17-07-008**
bloom	VB	3-02-002
bloomed	VBD	6-05-005
blooming	VBG	8-03-004
Bloom	**NP**	**1-01-001**
Bloomfield	**NP**	**1-01-001**
blooming	**NN**	**2-01-001**
bloop	**noun**	**1-01-001**
bloops	NNS	1-01-001
blossom	**noun**	**10-04-007**
blossom	NN	3-02-003
blossoms	NNS	7-04-006
blossom	**verb**	**4-03-003**
blossom	VB	3-02-002
blossomed	VBD	1-01-001
Blossom	**NP**	**1-01-001**
blot	**noun**	**8-05-005**
blot	NN	5-05-005
blots	NNS	3-02-002
blot	**verb**	**7-03-006**
blot	VB	1-01-001
blots	VBZ	1-01-001
blotted	VBD	1-01-001
blotted	VBN	2-02-002
blotting	VBG	2-01-001
blot-appearance	**NN**	**1-01-001**
blot-like	**JJ**	**1-01-001**
blouse	**noun**	**2-02-002**
blouse	NN	1-01-001
blouses	NNS	1-01-001
blow	**noun**	**28-12-024**
blow	NN	25-12-023
blows	NNS	3-03-003
blow	**verb**	**52-12-040**
blow	VB	8-07-007
blows	VBZ	5-05-005
blew	VBD	12-05-010
blown	VBN	9-07-009
blowing	VBG	18-08-012
blower	**noun**	**5-02-002**
blower	NN	4-02-002
blowers	NNS	1-01-001
blowfish	**NNS**	**1-01-001**
blowing	**NN**	**1-01-001**
blown-up	**JJ**	**1-01-001**
blowup	**NN**	**1-01-001**
blubber	**NN**	**1-01-001**
bludgeon	**NN**	**2-02-002**
bludgeon	**VB**	**1-01-001**
blue	**adjective**	**126-14-078**
blue	JJ	84-13-064
Blue	JJ-TL	42-08-017
blue	**noun**	**37-10-019**
blue	NN	15-09-010
blues	NNS	12-04-008
Blues	NNS-TL	10-02-004
Blue	**NP**	**2-01-001**

Word	Tag	Frequency
blue-black	**JJ**	**2-02-002**
blue-collar	**JJ**	**1-01-001**
blue-draped	**JJ**	**1-01-001**
blue-eye	**noun**	**1-01-001**
blue-eyes	NNS	1-01-001
blue-eyed	**JJ**	**3-01-003**
blue-green	**JJ**	**3-03-003**
blue-uniformed	**JJ**	**1-01-001**
blueberry	**noun**	**2-02-002**
blueberry	NN	1-01-001
blueberries	NNS	1-01-001
Bluebird	**NP**	**1-01-001**
bluebonnet	**noun**	**1-01-001**
bluebonnets	NNS	1-01-001
bluebook	**NN**	**1-01-001**
bluebush	**NN**	**1-01-001**
bluefish	**NNS**	**1-01-001**
blueprint	**noun**	**3-02-003**
blueprint	NN	1-01-001
blueprints	NNS	2-02-002
blueprint	**verb**	**1-01-001**
blueprints	VBZ	1-01-001
bluestocking	**NN**	**1-01-001**
bluff	**JJ**	**1-01-001**
bluff	**noun**	**11-07-008**
bluff	NN	7-05-005
bluffs	NNS	4-04-004
bluff	**verb**	**1-01-001**
bluffing	VBG	1-01-001
bluing	**NN**	**1-01-001**
bluish	**JJ**	**2-01-002**
Blum	**NP**	**2-01-001**
Blumberg	**NP**	**3-02-003**
Blume	**NP**	**1-01-001**
Blumenthal	**NP**	**1-01-001**
blunder	**noun**	**3-03-003**
blunder	NN	2-02-002
blunders	NNS	1-01-001
blunder	**verb**	**2-02-002**
blundered	VBN	2-02-002
blundering	**noun**	**1-01-001**
blunderings	NNS	1-01-001
blunt	**adjective**	**7-05-007**
blunt	JJ	6-05-006
blunt	JJ-HL	1-01-001
blunt	**verb**	**4-03-004**
blunt	VB	2-01-002
blunts	VBZ	1-01-001
blunted	VBN	1-01-001
blunter	**JJR**	**1-01-001**
bluntly	**QL**	**1-01-001**
bluntly	**RB**	**7-05-007**
bluntness	**NN**	**2-01-001**
blur	**NN**	**2-02-002**
blur	**verb**	**7-07-007**
blur	VB	1-01-001
blurred	VBD	1-01-001
blurred	VBN	5-05-005
blurry	**JJ**	**1-01-001**
blurt	**verb**	**3-02-003**
blurted	VBD	2-02-002
blurted	VBN	1-01-001
blush	**noun**	**1-01-001**
blushes	NNS	1-01-001
blush	**verb**	**12-07-009**
blush	VB	1-01-001
Blush	VB-TL	1-01-001
blushed	VBD	4-03-004
blushed	VBN	2-02-002
blushing	VBG	4-04-004
bluster	**NN**	**1-01-001**
bluster	**verb**	**1-01-001**
blustered	VBD	1-01-001
blustery	**JJ**	**1-01-001**
Bluthenzweig	**NP**	**1-01-001**
blutwurst	**FW-NN**	**1-01-001**
Blyth	**prop. noun**	**1-01-001**
Blyth	NP	0-00-000
Blyth	NP-TL	1-01-001
BMEWS	**NP**	**1-01-001**
Bo	**NP**	**1-01-001**
boa	**noun**	**7-01-001**
boa	NN	6-01-001
boa	NN-HL	1-01-001
Boadicea	**NP**	**1-01-001**
Boal	**NP**	**1-01-001**
boar	**NN**	**1-01-001**
board	**noun**	**285-15-093**
board	NN	166-13-065

Word	Tag	Frequency
board (cont.):		
board	NN-HL	2-02-002
Board	NN-TL	66-09-026
board's	NN$	4-02-003
Board's	NN$-TL	1-01-001
boards	NNS	43-14-025
Boards	NNS-TL	3-01-001
board	**verb**	**15-10-015**
board	VB	4-03-004
board	VB-NC	1-01-001
boards	VBZ	1-01-001
boarded	VBD	2-02-002
boarded	VBN	3-03-003
boarding	VBG	4-04-004
boarder	**NN**	**1-01-001**
boarding	**NN**	**1-01-001**
boarding-home	**NN**	**1-01-001**
boardinghouse	**noun**	**1-01-001**
boardinghouses	NNS	1-01-001
boast	**NN**	**1-01-001**
boast	**verb**	**18-09-013**
boast	VB	7-05-005
boasts	VBZ	2-01-002
boasted	VBD	5-05-005
boasted	VBN	1-01-001
boasting	VBG	3-03-003
boastfully	**RB**	**1-01-001**
boasting	**noun**	**1-01-001**
boastings	NNS	1-01-001
boat	**noun**	**123-13-030**
boat	NN	69-11-024
boat	NN-NC	1-01-001
Boat	NN-TL	2-01-001
boat's	NN+HVZ	1-01-001
boats	NNS	48-09-011
boats	NNS-HL	2-01-001
boat	**verb**	**17-05-006**
boating	VBG	16-04-005
boating	VBG-HL	1-01-001
boatel	**noun**	**2-01-001**
boatel	NN	1-01-001
boatels	NNS	1-01-001
boater	**noun**	**1-01-001**
boaters	NNS	1-01-001
boathouse	**noun**	**1-01-001**
boathouses	NNS	1-01-001
boating	**NN**	**6-02-002**
boatload	**noun**	**2-02-002**
boatload	NN	1-01-001
boatloads	NNS	1-01-001
boatman	**noun**	**4-01-001**
boatman	NN	3-01-001
boatmen	NNS	1-01-001
Boats	**NP**	**1-01-001**
boatsman	**noun**	**1-01-001**
boatsmen	NNS	1-01-001
boatswain	**noun**	**4-03-003**
boatswain	NN	3-02-002
boatswain's	NN$	0-00-000
bo'sun's	NN$	1-01-001
boatyard	**noun**	**3-02-002**
boatyard	NN	0-00-000
boat-yard	NN	1-01-001
boatyards	NNS	2-01-001
Boaz	**NP**	**2-01-001**
bob	**verb**	**5-02-005**
bobbed	VBD	2-02-002
bobbing	VBG	3-02-003
Bob	**prop. noun**	**41-07-018**
Bob	NP	39-06-017
Bob	NP-TL	1-01-001
Bob's	NP$	0-00-000
Bob's	NP$-TL	1-01-001
Bobbie	**prop. noun**	**24-01-001**
Bobbie	NP	22-01-001
Bobbie's	NP$	2-01-001
bobbin	**noun**	**1-01-001**
bobbins	NNS	1-01-001
bobbin-to-cone	**JJ**	**1-01-001**
bobble	**noun**	**1-01-001**
bobbles	NNS	0-00-000
bobbles	NNS-HL	1-01-001
Bobbsey	**prop. noun**	**2-01-001**
Bobbsey	NP	0-00-000
Bobbsey	NP-TL	2-01-001
bobby	**NN**	**2-01-002**
Bobby	**NP**	**21-03-006**
bobby-sock	**noun**	**1-01-001**
bobby-sox	NNS	1-01-001

Word	Tag	Counts
bobby-soxer	**NN**	**1-01-001**
Bock	**NP**	**1-01-001**
bockwurst	**FW-NN**	**1-01-001**
BOD	**NP**	**1-01-001**
bode	**verb**	**1-01-001**
bodes	VBZ	1-01-001
Bodenheim	**NP**	**1-01-001**
Bodhisattva	**NP**	**1-01-001**
bodice	**NN**	**2-02-002**
bodied	**JJ**	**1-01-001**
bodily	**adjective**	**3-03-003**
bodily	JJ	2-02-002
Bodily	JJ-TL	1-01-001
bodily	**RB**	**4-04-004**
Bodin	**NP**	**2-02-002**
Bodleian	**prop. noun**	**1-01-001**
Bodleian	NP	0-00-000
Bodleian	NP-TL	1-01-001
body	**noun**	**342-15-164**
body	NN	271-15-137
Body	NN	1-01-001
Body	NN-TL	4-03-004
body's	NN$	3-02-002
bodies	NNS	63-13-046
body	**verb**	**1-01-001**
bodies	VBZ	1-01-001
body-building	**adjective**	**1-01-001**
body-building	JJ	0-00-000
body-building	JJ-HL	1-01-001
body-tissue	**NN**	**1-01-001**
bodybuilder	**noun**	**8-01-001**
bodybuilder	NN	6-01-001
bodybuilders	NNS	2-01-001
bodybuilding	**NN**	**1-01-001**
bodyguard	**NN**	**1-01-001**
bodyweight	**NN**	**1-01-001**
Boehmer	**NP**	**1-01-001**
Boeing	**prop. noun**	**3-02-002**
Boeing	NP	2-02-002
Boeing	NP-TL	1-01-001
Boeotian	**JJ**	**1-01-001**
bog	**verb**	**2-01-002**
bog	VB	1-01-001
bogged	VBN	1-01-001
Bogartian	**JJ**	**1-01-001**
bogey	**noun**	**7-03-003**
bogey	NN	5-02-002
bogeys	NNS	2-02-002
bogey	**verb**	**2-01-001**
bogeyed	VBD	2-01-001
bogey-symbol	**NN**	**1-01-001**
bogeyman	**noun**	**1-01-001**
bogeymen	NNS	1-01-001
boggle	**verb**	**1-01-001**
boggled	VBD	1-01-001
Boggs	**NP**	**1-01-001**
bogus	**JJ**	**3-01-001**
bogy	**noun**	**3-02-002**
bogy	NN	2-01-001
bogies	NNS	1-01-001
Bohart	**NP**	**1-01-001**
Boheme	**prop. noun**	**1-01-001**
Boheme	NP	0-00-000
Boheme	NP-TL	1-01-001
Bohemian	**NP**	**1-01-001**
Bohlen	**NP**	**1-01-001**
boil	**noun**	**6-05-006**
boil	NN	5-04-005
boils	NNS	1-01-001
boil	**verb**	**27-10-022**
boil	VB	7-06-007
boils	VBZ	1-01-001
boiled	VBD	1-01-001
boiled	VBN	9-05-007
boiling	VBG	9-05-008
boiler	**noun**	**3-03-003**
boiler	NN	2-02-002
boilers	NNS	1-01-001
boiler-burner	**NN**	**1-01-001**
bois	**FW-NN**	**1-01-001**
Bois	**NP**	**1-01-001**
Boisbriant	**NP**	**1-01-001**
Boismassif	**NP**	**1-01-001**
Boissoneault	**NP**	**1-01-001**
boisterous	**JJ**	**1-01-001**
boite	**foreign**	**2-02-002**
boite	FW-NN	0-00-000
boite	FW-NN-TL	1-01-001
boites	FW-NNS	1-01-001
Boland	**NP**	**1-01-001**
bold	**adjective**	**21-08-021**
bold	JJ	20-08-020
Bold	JJ-TL	1-01-001
bolder	**JJR**	**2-02-002**
boldest	**JJT**	**1-01-001**
boldly	**RB**	**8-06-008**
boldness	**noun**	**3-02-002**
boldness	NN	2-02-002
boldness	NN-HL	1-01-001
Bolet	**NP**	**1-01-001**
Bolger	**NP**	**2-01-001**
Bolingbroke	**prop. noun**	**2-01-001**
Bolingbroke	NP	1-01-001
Bolingbroke's	NP$	1-01-001
Boliou	**prop. noun**	**2-01-001**
Boliou	NP	0-00-000
Boliou	NP-TL	2-01-001
Bolivar	**NP**	**1-01-001**
Bolivia	**NP**	**1-01-001**
Bolker	**NP**	**2-01-001**
bolo	**NN**	**1-01-001**
bologna	**NN**	**1-01-001**
Bologna	**NP**	**1-01-001**
Bolovens	**prop. noun**	**1-01-001**
Bolovens	NP	0-00-000
Bolovens	NP-TL	1-01-001
Bolshevik	**prop. noun**	**2-02-002**
Bolsheviks	NPS	1-01-001
Bolsheviks	NPS-TL	1-01-001
Bolshevism	**NP**	**1-01-001**
Bolshevistic	**JJ**	**1-01-001**
Bolshoi	**prop. noun**	**1-01-001**
Bolshoi	NP	0-00-000
Bolshoi	NP-TL	1-01-001
bolster	**NN**	**1-01-001**
bolster	**verb**	**4-04-004**
bolster	VB	2-02-002
bolstered	VBN	1-01-001
bolstering	VBG	1-01-001
bolt	**noun**	**9-05-009**
bolt	NN	8-05-008
bolts	NNS	1-01-001
bolt	**verb**	**10-07-010**
bolt	VB	2-02-002
bolted	VBD	3-02-003
bolted	VBN	4-03-004
bolting	VBG	1-01-001
bolt-action	**NN**	**3-01-001**
Boltzmann	**NP**	**1-01-001**
bomb	**noun**	**68-11-026**
bomb	NN	33-10-022
bombs	NNS	35-06-008
bomb	**verb**	**7-04-005**
bomb	VB	3-01-001
bombed	VBD	1-01-001
bombing	VBG	3-03-003
bombard	**verb**	**1-01-001**
bombarding	VBG	1-01-001
bombardment	**NN**	**1-01-001**
bombastic	**JJ**	**1-01-001**
Bombay	**NP**	**1-01-001**
bomber	**noun**	**32-06-009**
bomber	NN	8-03-003
bomber's	NN$	1-01-001
bombers	NNS	22-06-007
bombers'	NNS$	0-00-000
Bombers'	NNS$-TL	1-01-001
bombing	**noun**	**4-03-004**
bombing	NN	2-02-002
bombings	NNS	2-02-002
bombproof	**adjective**	**4-02-002**
bombproof	JJ	3-01-001
bomb-proof	JJ	1-01-001
bombus	**noun**	**4-01-001**
bombus	NN	2-01-001
Bombus	NN-TL	2-01-001
bon	**foreign**	**3-02-002**
bon	FW-JJ	2-01-001
bonne	FW-JJ	0-00-000
Bonne	FW-JJ-TL	1-01-001
bona	**FW-JJ**	**1-01-001**
bonanza	**noun**	**2-01-001**
bonanza	NN	1-01-001
Bonanza	NN-TL	1-01-001
Bonaparte	**NP**	**1-01-001**
Bonaventure	**NP**	**2-01-001**
bond	**noun**	**90-08-032**
bond	NN	42-06-019

Word	Tag	Frequency
bond (cont.):		
bond	NN-HL	1-01-001
bonds	NNS	46-07-017
bonds	NNS-HL	1-01-001
bond	**verb**	**3-03-003**
bonded	VBN	2-02-002
bonding	VBG	1-01-001
Bond	**prop. noun**	**3-02-002**
Bond	NP	2-01-001
Bond	NP-TL	1-01-001
bondage	**NN**	**3-02-002**
Bondi	**NP**	**3-01-001**
bondsman	**noun**	**2-02-002**
bondsman	NN	1-01-001
bondsman's	NN$	1-01-001
bone	**noun**	**53-11-037**
bone	NN	33-11-026
bones	NNS	20-08-015
bone-deep	**JJ**	**1-01-001**
bone-weary	**JJ**	**2-02-002**
Bonenfant	**NP**	**1-01-001**
Bonfiglio	**NP**	**1-01-001**
bonfire	**noun**	**4-03-003**
bonfire	NN	3-03-003
bonfires	NNS	1-01-001
bong	**UH**	**6-01-001**
bongo	**NN**	**1-01-001**
Bonham	**NP**	**1-01-001**
bonheur	**FW-NN**	**1-01-001**
Bonhoeffer	**NP**	**1-01-001**
Bonhoffer	**NP**	**1-01-001**
Boniface	**prop. noun**	**5-01-001**
Boniface	NP	4-01-001
Boniface's	NP$	1-01-001
Bonito	**NP**	**1-01-001**
bonjour	**FW-UH**	**1-01-001**
Bonn	**prop. noun**	**9-03-005**
Bonn	NP	5-03-004
Bonn	NP-HL	1-01-001
Bonn's	NP$	3-01-001
Bonner	**NP**	**6-01-001**
bonnet	**noun**	**3-02-003**
bonnet	NN	2-02-002
Bonnet	NN-TL	1-01-001
Bonnie	**NP**	**1-01-001**
Bonnor	**NP**	**4-01-001**
Bontempo	**NP**	**2-02-002**
bonus	**NN**	**2-02-002**
bony	**JJ**	**7-04-004**
bonze	**noun**	**2-01-001**
bonzes	NNS	2-01-001
boo	**noun**	**2-01-001**
boos	NNS	2-01-001
boo	**VB**	**1-01-001**
boobify	**VB**	**1-01-001**
booboo	**NN**	**1-01-001**
booby	**JJ**	**2-01-001**
booby	**NN**	**2-02-002**
booby-trap	**NN**	**1-01-001**
boogie	**noun**	**2-02-002**
boogie	NN	1-01-001
Boogie	NN-TL	1-01-001
book	**noun**	**292-15-140**
book	NN	175-15-094
book	NN-HL	1-01-001
Book	NN-TL	17-04-011
book's	NN$	3-02-003
books	NNS	94-14-064
books	NNS-HL	1-01-001
Books	NNS-TL	1-01-001
book	**verb**	**7-03-005**
booked	VBN	7-03-005
Book	**NP**	**4-01-001**
book-burning	**JJ**	**1-01-001**
book-lined	**JJ**	**1-01-001**
book-review	**NN**	**1-01-001**
book-selection	**NN**	**1-01-001**
bookcase	**noun**	**3-02-002**
bookcase	NN	2-01-001
bookcases	NNS	1-01-001
booker	**noun**	**2-01-001**
booker	NN	1-01-001
bookers	NNS	1-01-001
Booker	**NP**	**2-02-002**
bookie	**noun**	**3-01-001**
bookies	NNS	3-01-001
booking	**noun**	**7-01-001**
booking	NN	6-01-001
bookings	NNS	1-01-001
bookish	**JJ**	**1-01-001**
bookkeeping	**NN**	**5-03-004**
booklet	**noun**	**3-01-003**
booklet	NN	1-01-001
booklets	NNS	2-01-002
booklist	**noun**	**1-01-001**
booklists	NNS	1-01-001
bookseller	**NN**	**1-01-001**
bookshelf	**noun**	**4-03-004**
bookshelf	NN	1-01-001
bookshelves	NNS	3-02-003
Bookwalter	**NP**	**1-01-001**
boom	**NN**	**8-06-008**
boom	**verb**	**2-02-002**
boomed	VBD	1-01-001
booming	VBG	1-01-001
boom-boom-boom	**UH**	**1-01-001**
boomerang	**NN**	**1-01-001**
boomerang	**verb**	**1-01-001**
boomerangs	VBZ	1-01-001
boomtown	**NN**	**1-01-001**
boon	**JJ**	**1-01-001**
boon	**NN**	**2-02-002**
Boone	**NP**	**2-01-001**
Boonton	**prop. noun**	**1-01-001**
Boonton	NP	0-00-000
Boonton	NP-HL	1-01-001
boor	**noun**	**1-01-001**
boors	NNS	1-01-001
boorish	**JJ**	**1-01-001**
boost	**noun**	**11-06-009**
boost	NN	10-06-009
boosts	NNS	1-01-001
boost	**verb**	**11-05-010**
boost	VB	5-02-005
boosted	VBD	2-02-002
boosted	VBN	1-01-001
boosting	VBG	3-03-003
booster	**NN**	**1-01-001**
boot	**noun**	**30-09-024**
boot	NN	9-08-009
Boot	NN-TL	1-01-001
boots	NNS	19-06-015
Boots	NNS-TL	1-01-001
boot	**verb**	**4-04-004**
boot	VB	3-03-003
booted	VBN	1-01-001
boot-wearer	**NN**	**1-01-001**
booth	**noun**	**7-03-007**
booth	NN	4-02-004
booths	NNS	3-03-003
Booth	**NP**	**3-02-002**
Boothby	**NP**	**1-01-001**
Bootle	**prop. noun**	**3-01-001**
Bootle	NP	2-01-001
Bootle's	NP$	1-01-001
bootleg	**verb**	**1-01-001**
bootlegging	VBG	1-01-001
bootlegger	**noun**	**3-02-003**
bootlegger	NN	1-01-001
bootleggers	NNS	2-01-002
booty	**noun**	**3-02-002**
booty	NN	2-01-001
Booty	NN	1-01-001
booze	**NN**	**4-04-004**
bop	**NN**	**3-02-002**
Borak	**NP**	**1-01-001**
borate	**noun**	**1-01-001**
borates	NNS	1-01-001
borax	**NN**	**1-01-001**
Bordeaux	**prop. noun**	**3-02-002**
Bordeaux	NP	2-01-001
Bordeau	NP	1-01-001
Bordel	**NP**	**2-01-001**
Borden	**prop. noun**	**21-01-001**
Borden	NP	20-01-001
Bordens	NPS	1-01-001
border	**noun**	**30-13-025**
border	NN	14-11-014
Border	NN-TL	6-03-004
borders	NNS	10-04-008
border	**verb**	**9-05-008**
borders	VBZ	2-02-002
bordered	VBN	2-01-001
bordering	VBG	5-03-005
borderland	**noun**	**1-01-001**
borderlands	NNS	1-01-001
borderline	**NN**	**3-03-003**
Bordner	**NP**	**1-01-001**

Word	Tag	Frequency
bore	**noun**	**4-02-003**
bore	NN	3-02-003
bores	NNS	1-01-001
bore	**verb**	**26-10-022**
bore	VB	7-05-005
bores	VBZ	1-01-001
bored	VBD	3-03-003
bored	VBN	11-06-010
boring	VBG	4-04-004
boredom	**NN**	**11-05-010**
borer	**NN**	**1-01-001**
Borglum	**NP**	**2-01-001**
boring	**NN**	**1-01-001**
Boris	**prop. noun**	**13-01-001**
Boris	NP	9-01-001
Boris	NP-TL	1-01-001
Boris'	NP$	3-01-001
Borland	**NP**	**1-01-001**
born	**JJ**	**1-01-001**
Borneo	**prop. noun**	**1-01-001**
Borneo	NP	0-00-000
Borneo	NP-TL	1-01-001
Bornholm	**NP**	**1-01-001**
Boron	**NP**	**1-01-001**
borough	**noun**	**7-04-004**
borough	NN	3-03-003
Borough	NN-TL	2-01-001
boroughs	NNS	2-02-002
Borrioboola-Gha	**NP**	**1-01-001**
Borromini	**prop. noun**	**3-01-001**
Borromini	NP	1-01-001
Borromini's	NP$	2-01-001
borrow	**verb**	**31-11-023**
borrow	VB	9-06-009
borrows	VBZ	1-01-001
borrowed	VBD	5-03-005
borrowed	VBN	8-06-008
borrowed	VBN-HL	1-01-001
borrowing	VBG	7-04-004
borrower	**NN**	**2-02-002**
borrowing	**NN**	**1-01-001**
Bosch	**NP**	**2-02-002**
Bosco	**NP**	**1-01-001**
Bosis	**prop. noun**	**7-01-001**
Bosis	NP	6-01-001
Bosis'	NP$	1-01-001
Bosler	**NP**	**1-01-001**
Bosley	**NP**	**1-01-001**
bosom	**noun**	**9-06-008**
bosom	NN	8-05-007
bosoms	NNS	1-01-001
Bosphorus	**NP**	**5-01-001**
boss	**noun**	**28-11-022**
boss	NN	18-09-014
Boss	NN-TL	2-02-002
boss's	NN$	3-02-003
bosses	NNS	5-05-005
boss	**verb**	**1-01-001**
bossed	VBN	1-01-001
bossman	**NN**	**1-01-001**
Bostitch	**NP**	**1-01-001**
Boston	**prop. noun**	**63-12-035**
Boston	NP	49-12-031
Boston	NP-HL	1-01-001
Boston	NP-TL	11-06-009
Boston's	NP$	2-02-002
Bostonian	**prop. noun**	**2-02-002**
Bostonian	NP	0-00-000
Bostonian	NP-HL	1-01-001
Bostonians	NPS	1-01-001
botanical	**JJ**	**1-01-001**
botanist	**noun**	**2-01-001**
botanists	NNS	2-01-001
botany	**NN**	**3-02-002**
both	**ABX**	**731-15-337**
bother	**verb**	**45-13-040**
bother	VB	22-09-022
bothers	VBZ	3-03-003
bothered	VBD	7-05-006
bothered	VBN	7-06-007
bothering	VBG	6-04-006
bothersome	**JJ**	**1-01-001**
Bottega	**NP**	**1-01-001**
Bottineau	**NP**	**1-01-001**
bottle	**noun**	**90-09-031**
bottle	NN	76-08-024
bottles	NNS	14-08-012
bottle	**verb**	**5-03-005**
bottles	VBZ	1-01-001

Word	Tag	Frequency
bottle (cont.):		
bottled	VBN	3-03-003
bottling	VBG	1-01-001
bottleneck	**noun**	**3-03-003**
bottleneck	NN	2-02-002
bottlenecks	NNS	1-01-001
bottom	**JJ**	**3-02-002**
bottom	**noun**	**93-13-051**
bottom	NN	77-12-047
bottom	NN-HL	1-01-001
Bottom	NN-TL	7-02-002
bottoms	NNS	8-04-005
bottom-living	**JJ**	**1-01-001**
bottomless	**JJ**	**1-01-001**
botulinal	**JJ**	**1-01-001**
botulinum	**NP**	**1-01-001**
bouanahsha	**foreign**	**1-01-001**
bouanahsha	FW-VB	0-00-000
bouanahsha	FW-VB-NC	1-01-001
Boucher	**NP**	**2-02-002**
boucle	**NN**	**1-01-001**
bouffant	**JJ**	**2-02-002**
bouffe	**FW-JJ**	**1-01-001**
bough	**noun**	**6-03-004**
bough	NN	2-01-001
boughs	NNS	4-03-004
Bougie	**NP**	**1-01-001**
boulder	**noun**	**11-04-005**
boulder	NN	6-02-002
boulder	NN-HL	1-01-001
Boulder	NN-TL	1-01-001
boulders	NNS	3-02-002
Boulder	**prop. noun**	**2-01-002**
Boulder	NP	1-01-001
Boulder	NP-TL	1-01-001
boulevard	**foreign**	**2-01-001**
boulevard	FW-NN	0-00-000
Boulevard	FW-NN-TL	2-01-001
boulevard	**noun**	**15-07-009**
boulevard	NN	2-02-002
blvd.	NN	0-00-000
Blvd.	NN-TL	4-01-003
Boulevard	NN-TL	7-03-003
boulevards	NNS	2-02-002
Boulez	**NP**	**1-01-001**
Boulle	**NP**	**1-01-001**
boun	**FW-NN**	**1-01-001**
Boun	**NP**	**4-02-002**
bounce	**NN**	**4-02-003**
bounce	**verb**	**28-08-018**
bounce	VB	4-03-003
bounced	VBD	13-05-010
bounced	VBN	3-03-003
bouncing	VBG	8-04-005
bouncing	**NN**	**1-01-001**
bouncy	**JJ**	**1-01-001**
bound	**noun**	**13-08-009**
bound	NN	3-02-002
bounds	NNS	10-07-008
bound	**verb**	**13-07-010**
bound	VB	2-02-002
bounded	VBD	2-02-002
bounded	VBN	7-04-005
bounding	VBG	2-02-002
boundary	**noun**	**30-08-016**
boundary	NN	15-05-007
boundary	NN-HL	1-01-001
boundaries	NNS	14-07-011
boundless	**JJ**	**2-02-002**
bounty	**NN**	**3-02-002**
bouquet	**noun**	**5-03-003**
bouquet	NN	4-02-002
bouquets	NNS	1-01-001
bourbon	**NN**	**4-03-003**
Bourbon	**prop. noun**	**10-03-003**
Bourbon	NP	3-02-002
Bourbon	NP-TL	1-01-001
Bourbons	NPS	6-01-001
Bourcier	**NP**	**3-01-001**
bourgeois	**noun**	**3-02-003**
bourgeois	NN	2-01-002
Bourgeois	NN-TL	1-01-001
bourgeoisie	**NN**	**1-01-001**
Bourguiba	**NP**	**1-01-001**
Bourn	**prop. noun**	**1-01-001**
Bourn	NP	0-00-000
Bourn	NP-TL	1-01-001
bout	**noun**	**7-04-006**
bout	NN	4-02-003

Word	Tag	Frequency
bout (cont.):		
bouts	NNS	3-03-003
bout-de-souffle	**FW-NN**	**1-01-001**
Boutflower	**NP**	**1-01-001**
Bouton	**NP**	**2-01-001**
Bouvardier	**NP**	**1-01-001**
Bouvier	**NP**	**1-01-001**
bovine	**JJ**	**1-01-001**
bovine	**noun**	**2-02-002**
bovine	NN	1-01-001
bovines	NNS	1-01-001
bow	**noun**	**13-07-010**
bow	NN	11-07-010
bows	NNS	2-01-002
bow	**verb**	**13-08-013**
bow	VB	3-02-003
bows	VBZ	1-01-001
bowed	VBD	6-06-006
bowed	VBN	1-01-001
bowing	VBG	2-01-002
Bow	**prop. noun**	**1-01-001**
Bow	NP	0-00-000
Bow	NP-TL	1-01-001
Bowan	**NP**	**1-01-001**
Bowden	**NP**	**2-01-002**
Bowdoin	**NP**	**1-01-001**
bowel	**noun**	**1-01-001**
bowels	NNS	1-01-001
bower	**NN**	**1-01-001**
Bowers	**NP**	**1-01-001**
Bowes	**NP**	**1-01-001**
Bowie	**prop. noun**	**1-01-001**
Bowie	NP	0-00-000
Bowie	NP-HL	1-01-001
bowing	**NN**	**1-01-001**
bowl	**noun**	**26-09-017**
bowl	NN	20-08-012
Bowl	NN-TL	3-03-003
bowls	NNS	3-03-003
Bowman	**NP**	**3-02-002**
bowstring	**NN**	**1-01-001**
box	**noun**	**82-15-047**
box	NN	64-14-036
Box	NN-TL	4-03-004
boxes	NNS	14-06-013
box	**verb**	**4-03-004**
box	VB	2-02-002
boxed	VBN	2-02-002
box-sized	**JJ**	**1-01-001**
boxcar	**noun**	**8-02-002**
boxcar	NN	6-02-002
boxcars	NNS	2-01-001
boxed-in	**JJ**	**1-01-001**
Boxell	**NP**	**4-01-001**
boxer	**NN**	**1-01-001**
Boxford	**prop. noun**	**1-01-001**
Boxford	NP	0-00-000
Boxford	NP-TL	1-01-001
Boxwood	**prop. noun**	**1-01-001**
Boxwood	NP	0-00-000
Boxwood	NP-TL	1-01-001
boxy	**JJ**	**1-01-001**
boy	**noun**	**409-13-155**
boy	NN	235-13-112
bawh	NN	2-01-001
bhoy	NN	1-01-001
boy	NN-HL	2-01-002
boy	NN-NC	1-01-001
Boy	NN-TL	4-03-003
boy's	NN$	16-08-013
boys	NNS	136-11-067
bawhs	NNS	1-01-001
boies	NNS	1-01-001
Boys	NNS-TL	7-04-005
boys'	NNS$	3-02-003
boy	**UH**	**2-02-002**
boy-friend	**noun**	**1-01-001**
boy-friend	NN	0-00-000
boy-furiendo	NN	1-01-001
boy-manager	**NN**	**1-01-001**
boy-meets-girl	**NN**	**1-01-001**
boy-name	**NN**	**1-01-001**
boyar	**noun**	**1-01-001**
boyars	NNS	1-01-001
Boyce	**NP**	**1-01-001**
boycott	**NN**	**7-02-002**
boycott	**verb**	**2-02-002**
boycott	VB	1-01-001
boycotted	VBN	1-01-001

Word	Tag	Frequency
Boyd	**NP**	**5-03-004**
Boyer	**NP**	**2-01-001**
boyhood	**NN**	**5-03-004**
boyish	**JJ**	**4-04-004**
Boylston	**NP**	**1-01-001**
brace	**noun**	**13-06-008**
brace	NN	9-04-005
braces	NNS	4-03-003
brace	**verb**	**8-07-008**
brace	VB	1-01-001
brace	VB-HL	1-01-001
braced	VBD	1-01-001
braced	VBN	4-03-004
bracing	VBG	1-01-001
Brace	**prop. noun**	**4-02-002**
Brace	NP	2-02-002
Brace	NP-TL	1-01-001
Brace's	NP$	1-01-001
bracelet	**NN**	**1-01-001**
brachium	**noun**	**1-01-001**
brachii	NN$	1-01-001
bracing	**NN**	**2-01-001**
Bracken	**NP**	**1-01-001**
bracket	**noun**	**3-02-003**
bracket	NN	1-01-001
brackets	NNS	2-02-002
brackish	**JJ**	**3-03-003**
brad	**NN**	**1-01-001**
Bradbury	**prop. noun**	**2-01-001**
Bradbury's	NP$	2-01-001
Braddock-against-the-Indians	**JJ**	**1-01-001**
Braden	**NP**	**1-01-001**
Bradford	**NP**	**5-02-004**
Bradley	**prop. noun**	**5-03-003**
Bradley	NP	4-02-002
Bradley's	NP$	0-00-000
Bradley's	NP$-TL	1-01-001
Brady	**NP**	**1-01-001**
bradykinin	**FW-NN**	**1-01-001**
brae	**noun**	**1-01-001**
brae	NN	0-00-000
Brae	NN-TL	1-01-001
brag	**NN**	**1-01-001**
brag	**verb**	**4-04-004**
brag	VB	1-01-001
bragged	VBD	2-02-002
bragging	VBG	1-01-001
Bragg	**NP**	**2-01-001**
braggadocio	**NN**	**1-01-001**
Brahmaputra	**NP**	**2-01-001**
Brahms	**prop. noun**	**8-02-004**
Brahms	NP	6-02-003
Brahms	NP-TL	1-01-001
Brahms'	NP$	0-00-000
Brahm's	NP$	1-01-001
Brahmsian	**JJ**	**2-02-002**
braid	**noun**	**1-01-001**
braids	NNS	1-01-001
braid	**verb**	**2-02-002**
braided	VBN	1-01-001
braiding	VBG	1-01-001
Braille	**NP**	**1-01-001**
Brailsford	**NP**	**1-01-001**
brain	**noun**	**64-12-033**
brain	NN	44-12-021
Brain	NN-TL	1-01-001
brain's	NN$	1-01-001
brains	NNS	18-08-014
brain-racking	**adjective**	**1-01-001**
brain-racking	JJ	0-00-000
brain-wracking	JJ	1-01-001
Brainard	**prop. noun**	**1-01-001**
Brainards	NPS	1-01-001
brainwashing	**NN**	**1-01-001**
brainy	**JJ**	**1-01-001**
brake	**noun**	**9-04-006**
brake	NN	2-02-002
brakes	NNS	7-03-005
Brakke	**NP**	**1-01-001**
Bramante	**prop. noun**	**1-01-001**
Bramante's	NP$	1-01-001
bramble	**noun**	**1-01-001**
brambles	NNS	1-01-001
bran	**NN**	**1-01-001**
branch	**noun**	**63-11-034**
branch	NN	28-10-017
Branch	NN-TL	2-02-002
branches	NNS	33-10-019
branch	**verb**	**5-03-005**

Word	Tag	Frequency
branch (cont.):		
branch	VB	2-02-002
branched	VBN	2-02-002
branching	VBG	1-01-001
Branch	**NP**	**1-01-001**
Branchville	**NP**	**1-01-001**
brand	**noun**	**20-08-014**
brand	NN	16-07-011
brands	NNS	4-02-004
brand	**QL**	**1-01-001**
brand	**verb**	**3-03-003**
branded	VBN	2-02-002
branding	VBG	0-00-000
brandin'	VBG	1-01-001
brand-new	**JJ**	**2-02-002**
Brandeis	**NP**	**1-01-001**
Brandel	**NP**	**3-01-001**
Brandenburg	**prop. noun**	**2-02-002**
Brandenburg	NP	1-01-001
Brandenburg	NP-TL	1-01-001
brandish	**verb**	**5-04-005**
brandishing	VBG	5-04-005
Brandon	**prop. noun**	**10-02-002**
Brandon	NP	8-02-002
Brandon's	NP$	2-01-001
Brandt	**prop. noun**	**11-02-004**
Brandt	NP	10-02-004
Brandt's	NP$	1-01-001
brandy	**NN**	**7-05-007**
Brandywine	**NP**	**7-01-001**
Brannon	**prop. noun**	**30-01-001**
Brannon	NP	29-01-001
Brannon's	NP$	1-01-001
Branum	**NP**	**1-01-001**
Braque	**prop. noun**	**14-02-002**
Braque	NP	9-01-001
Braque's	NP$	4-01-001
Braques	NPS	1-01-001
brash	**JJ**	**1-01-001**
brashness	**NN**	**1-01-001**
brass	**noun**	**19-09-015**
brass	NN	18-09-014
Brass	NN-TL	1-01-001
brass-bound	**JJ**	**1-01-001**
Brassbound	**prop. noun**	**1-01-001**
Brassbound's	NP$	1-01-001
Brassica	**NP**	**1-01-001**
brassiere	**NN**	**2-02-002**
Brassnose	**NP**	**12-01-001**
Brasstown	**NP**	**1-01-001**
brassy	**JJ**	**2-02-002**
bratwurst	**FW-NN**	**1-01-001**
Braud	**NP**	**1-01-001**
Braun	**NP**	**1-01-001**
bravado	**NN**	**5-04-005**
Bravado	**NP**	**2-01-001**
brave	**adjective**	**21-10-018**
brave	JJ	18-10-016
Brave	JJ-TL	3-02-002
brave	**noun**	**5-02-005**
brave	NN	0-00-000
Brave	NN-TL	1-01-001
braves	NNS	0-00-000
Braves	NNS-TL	3-01-003
braves'	NNS$	0-00-000
Braves'	NNS$-TL	1-01-001
brave	**verb**	**5-04-005**
brave	VB	2-02-002
braved	VBN	1-01-001
braving	VBG	2-02-002
bravely	**RB**	**4-04-004**
braver	**JJR**	**2-02-002**
bravery	**NN**	**4-03-004**
bravest	**JJT**	**1-01-001**
bravest-feathered	**JJ**	**1-01-001**
bravo	**UH**	**1-01-001**
bravura	**NN**	**1-01-001**
brawl	**noun**	**2-02-002**
brawl	NN	1-01-001
brawle	NN	1-01-001
brawl	**verb**	**1-01-001**
brawling	VBG	0-00-000
braweling	VBG	1-01-001
bray	**verb**	**1-01-001**
braying	VBG	1-01-001
brazen	**JJ**	**1-01-001**
brazenly	**RB**	**1-01-001**
brazenness	**NN**	**1-01-001**
brazier	**NN**	**1-01-001**
brazil	**NN**	**2-01-001**
Brazil	**NP**	**6-04-006**
Brazilian	**JJ**	**3-03-003**
Brazilian	**NP**	**1-01-001**
Brazos	**NP**	**2-01-001**
breach	**NN**	**6-06-006**
breach	**verb**	**2-02-002**
breaching	VBG	2-02-002
bread	**noun**	**41-11-020**
bread	NN	40-11-020
bread	NN-HL	1-01-001
breadth	**NN**	**7-04-007**
break	**noun**	**26-10-023**
break	NN	22-10-020
break	NN-HL	1-01-001
breaks	NNS	3-02-003
break	**verb**	**228-15-156**
break	VB	65-13-061
breaks	VBZ	9-06-009
broke	VBD	66-13-055
brok	VBD	1-01-001
Broke	VBD-TL	1-01-001
broken	VBN	60-12-051
brooken	VBN	1-01-001
broken	VBN-NC	3-01-001
breaking	VBG	21-10-020
breakin	VBG	1-01-001
break-even	**JJ**	**2-02-002**
break-neck	**JJ**	**1-01-001**
breakable	**noun**	**1-01-001**
breakables	NNS	1-01-001
breakage	**NN**	**1-01-001**
breakaway	**noun**	**2-02-002**
breakaway	NN	1-01-001
break-away	NN	1-01-001
breakdown	**noun**	**16-07-013**
breakdown	NN	13-05-010
breakdowns	NNS	3-03-003
breaker	**noun**	**2-02-002**
breaker	NN	1-01-001
breakers	NNS	1-01-001
breakfast	**noun**	**55-11-033**
breakfast	NN	53-11-032
breakfasts	NNS	2-02-002
breakfast	**verb**	**2-02-002**
breakfasted	VBD	2-02-002
breakfast-table	**NN**	**1-01-001**
breaking	**NN**	**4-03-003**
breaking-out	**NN**	**1-01-001**
breakoff	**NN**	**1-01-001**
breakthrough	**noun**	**8-06-007**
breakthrough	NN	4-04-004
break-through	NN	1-01-001
Breakthrough	NN-TL	2-01-001
breakthroughs	NNS	1-01-001
breakup	**noun**	**4-04-004**
breakup	NN	3-03-003
breakups	NNS	1-01-001
breakwater	**noun**	**3-03-003**
breakwater	NN	2-02-002
breakwaters	NNS	1-01-001
breast	**noun**	**20-08-013**
breast	NN	11-07-008
breasts	NNS	9-04-006
Breasted	**NP**	**6-01-001**
breastwork	**noun**	**1-01-001**
breastworks	NNS	1-01-001
breath	**noun**	**54-12-036**
breath	NN	51-12-034
Breath	NN-TL	2-01-002
breaths	NNS	1-01-001
breathe	**verb**	**31-13-028**
breathe	VB	7-05-007
breathes	VBZ	2-02-002
breathed	VBD	9-08-009
breathing	VBG	12-07-012
breathing	VBG-HL	1-01-001
breather	**NN**	**1-01-001**
breathing	**NN**	**8-05-007**
breathless	**JJ**	**5-05-005**
breathlessly	**RB**	**1-01-001**
breathtaking	**adjective**	**6-05-006**
breathtaking	JJ	3-03-003
breath-taking	JJ	3-03-003
breathy	**JJ**	**1-01-001**
Breckenridge	**prop. noun**	**1-01-001**
Breckenridge's	NP$	1-01-001
breech	**noun**	**2-02-002**
breeches	NNS	1-01-001

breech (cont.):		
britches	NNS	0-00-000
Britches	NNS-TL	1-01-001
breed	**noun**	**15-05-011**
breed	NN	13-05-010
Breed	NN-TL	1-01-001
breeds	NNS	1-01-001
breed	**verb**	**6-05-006**
breed	VB	3-03-003
bred	VBN	1-01-001
breeding	VBG	2-02-002
Breed	**prop. noun**	**2-02-002**
Breed	NP	0-00-000
Breed's	NP+BEZ	1-01-001
Breed's	NP$	1-01-001
Breeding	**prop. noun**	**5-02-002**
Breeding	NP	4-02-002
Breeding	NP-HL	1-01-001
breeze	**noun**	**17-12-015**
breeze	NN	14-10-012
Breeze	NN-TL	1-01-001
breezes	NNS	2-02-002
breezy	**JJ**	**1-01-001**
Bregman	**NP**	**1-01-001**
Bremerton	**NP**	**1-01-001**
Bremsstrahlung	**FW-NN**	**1-01-001**
Brendan	**NP**	**1-01-001**
Brennan	**NP**	**3-01-001**
Brenner	**prop. noun**	**13-02-002**
Brenner	NP	10-02-002
Brenner's	NP$	3-01-001
Brest	**NP**	**1-01-001**
Brest-Silevniov	**prop. noun**	**1-01-001**
Brest-Silevniov	NP	0-00-000
Brest-Silevniov	NP-TL	1-01-001
Breton	**NP**	**1-01-001**
Brett	**NP**	**4-02-002**
Breuer	**NP**	**1-01-001**
Brevard	**prop. noun**	**5-01-001**
Brevard	NP	4-01-001
Brevard	NP-TL	1-01-001
Breve	**NP**	**1-01-001**
brevet	**adjective**	**1-01-001**
brevet	JJ	0-00-000
Brevet	JJ-TL	1-01-001
brevity	**NN**	**3-03-003**
brew	**NN**	**2-02-002**
brew	**verb**	**2-01-001**
brewed	VBN	1-01-001
brewing	VBG	1-01-001
Brew	**NP**	**2-02-002**
brewer	**noun**	**2-01-002**
brewer's	NN$	1-01-001
brewers	NNS	1-01-001
brewery	**noun**	**2-02-002**
brewery	NN	1-01-001
Brewery	NN-TL	1-01-001
Brian	**NP**	**5-01-001**
briar	**noun**	**1-01-001**
briar	NN	0-00-000
Briar	NN-TL	1-01-001
bribe	**noun**	**1-01-001**
bribes	NNS	1-01-001
bribe	**verb**	**4-04-004**
bribe	VB	1-01-001
bribed	VBD	2-02-002
bribed	VBN	1-01-001
briber	**noun**	**1-01-001**
bribers	NNS	1-01-001
bric-a-brac	**NN**	**2-02-002**
Brice	**NP**	**1-01-001**
brick	**noun**	**24-09-016**
brick	NN	18-09-016
bricks	NNS	6-03-003
Bricker	**NP**	**1-01-001**
bricklayer	**noun**	**3-02-002**
bricklayers	NNS	3-02-002
bricklaying	**NN**	**3-03-003**
Bricktop	**NP**	**1-01-001**
bridal	**JJ**	**1-01-001**
bridal	**NN**	**1-01-001**
bride	**noun**	**40-08-015**
bride	NN	32-08-013
Bride	NN-TL	1-01-001
bride's	NN$	5-02-002
brides	NNS	2-02-002
bride-gift	**NN**	**1-01-001**
bridegroom	**noun**	**5-03-004**
bridegroom	NN	3-03-003

bridegroom (cont.):		
bridegroom's	NN$	2-01-001
bridesmaid	**noun**	**2-02-002**
bridesmaids	NNS	2-02-002
Bridewell	**prop. noun**	**1-01-001**
Bridewell	NP	0-00-000
Bridewell	NP-TL	1-01-001
bridge	**noun**	**117-13-033**
bridge	NN	79-12-023
Bridge	NN	3-01-001
Bridge	NN-TL	11-03-006
Bridge	NN-TL-HL	1-01-001
bridges	NNS	21-05-009
bridges	NNS-HL	1-01-001
Bridges	NNS-TL	1-01-001
bridge	**verb**	**5-05-005**
bridge	VB	4-04-004
bridges	VBZ	1-01-001
bridged-T	**JJ**	**1-01-001**
bridgehead	**NN**	**2-02-002**
Bridgeport	**NP**	**1-01-001**
Bridges	**NP**	**2-02-002**
Bridget	**prop. noun**	**22-01-001**
Bridget	NP	21-01-001
Bridget's	NP$	1-01-001
Bridgewater	**NP**	**1-01-001**
bridgework	**NN**	**1-01-001**
bridle	**NN**	**1-01-001**
brief	**adjective**	**64-14-053**
brief	JJ	63-14-052
Brief	JJ-TL	1-01-001
brief	**noun**	**10-06-008**
brief	NN	8-05-007
brief	NN-HL	1-01-001
briefs	NNS	1-01-001
brief	**verb**	**3-03-003**
briefed	VBN	2-02-002
briefing	VBG	1-01-001
briefcase	**NN**	**1-01-001**
briefer	**JJR**	**1-01-001**
Briefer	**NP**	**1-01-001**
briefest	**JJT**	**1-01-001**
Brieff	**NP**	**1-01-001**
briefing	**NN**	**1-01-001**
briefly	**RB**	**38-14-036**
briefly-illumed	**JJ**	**1-01-001**
Brien	**NP**	**1-01-001**
brig	**NN**	**1-01-001**
brigade	**noun**	**4-03-004**
brigade	NN	1-01-001
Brigade	NN-TL	2-02-002
brigades	NNS	1-01-001
brigadier	**noun**	**8-06-006**
brigadier	NN	5-04-004
brig.	NN	0-00-000
Brig.	NN-TL	1-01-001
Brigadier	NN-TL	2-02-002
Brigadoon	**NP**	**1-01-001**
Brigantine	**NP**	**1-01-001**
Briggs	**NP**	**1-01-001**
Brighetti	**NP**	**1-01-001**
bright	**adjective**	**81-13-059**
bright	JJ	77-13-058
Bright	JJ-TL	3-02-002
Bright	JJ-TL-HL	1-01-001
Bright	**prop. noun**	**8-01-001**
Bright	NP	4-01-001
Bright	NP-TL	2-01-001
Bright's	NP$	2-01-001
bright-eyed	**JJ**	**2-01-002**
bright-green	**JJ**	**1-01-001**
bright-looking	**JJ**	**1-01-001**
brighten	**verb**	**3-03-003**
brightens	VBZ	1-01-001
brightened	VBD	2-02-002
brighter	**JJR**	**8-07-008**
brightest	**JJT**	**2-02-002**
brightest	**RBT**	**2-02-002**
brightly	**QL**	**2-02-002**
brightly	**RB**	**4-04-004**
brightness	**NN**	**18-04-008**
brilliance	**NN**	**4-03-004**
brilliant	**JJ**	**50-12-036**
brilliantly	**QL**	**2-02-002**
brilliantly	**RB**	**7-05-007**
brim	**NN**	**4-04-004**
brim	**verb**	**1-01-001**
brimmed	VBN	1-01-001
brimful	**JJ**	**1-01-001**

Word	Tag	Frequency
Brindisi	**NP**	**1-01-001**
brindle	**NN**	**1-01-001**
bring	**verb**	**488-15-281**
bring	VB	158-13-131
brynge	VB	1-01-001
brings	VBZ	39-10-031
brings	VBZ-HL	1-01-001
brought	VBD	133-14-103
brought	VBD-HL	1-01-001
brought	VBN	119-15-099
bringing	VBG	36-13-033
bringing	**NN**	**2-01-002**
brink	**NN**	**3-03-003**
Brinkley	**NP**	**1-01-001**
brinkmanship	**NN**	**1-01-001**
Brinsley	**NP**	**1-01-001**
Brisbane	**NP**	**3-01-002**
brisk	**JJ**	**7-06-007**
brisker	**JJR**	**1-01-001**
briskly	**RB**	**5-04-005**
briskness	**NN**	**1-01-001**
bristle	**noun**	**5-03-003**
bristle	NN	2-02-002
bristles	NNS	3-02-002
bristle	**verb**	**8-06-007**
bristle	VB	1-01-001
bristles	VBZ	1-01-001
bristled	VBD	3-02-003
bristling	VBG	3-03-003
Bristol	**prop. noun**	**4-03-004**
Bristol	NP	3-02-003
Brestowe	NP	1-01-001
Britain	**prop. noun**	**61-09-029**
Britain	NP	41-09-021
Britain	NP-TL	14-05-009
Britain's	NP$	6-04-006
Britannic	**JJ**	**1-01-001**
Britannica	**foreign**	**1-01-001**
Britannica	FW-JJ	0-00-000
Britannica	FW-JJ-TL	1-01-001
British	**adjective**	**101-13-054**
British	JJ	84-12-043
British	JJ-HL	1-01-001
British	JJ-TL	16-07-015
British	**NPS**	**17-07-010**
British-American	**JJ**	**1-01-001**
British-born	**JJ**	**1-01-001**
Britisher	**NP**	**1-01-001**
Briton	**prop. noun**	**2-02-002**
Briton	NP	1-01-001
Britons	NPS	1-01-001
Brittany	**NP**	**2-01-001**
Britten	**prop. noun**	**3-01-003**
Britten	NP	2-01-002
Britten	NP-TL	1-01-001
brittle	**JJ**	**3-03-003**
broach	**verb**	**3-03-003**
broach	VB	1-01-001
broached	VBN	2-02-002
broad	**adjective**	**83-13-068**
broad	JJ	82-13-067
Broad	JJ-TL	1-01-001
Broad	**NP**	**1-01-001**
broad-brimmed	**JJ**	**3-03-003**
broad-nibbed	**JJ**	**1-01-001**
broad-scale	**JJ**	**1-01-001**
broadcast	**noun**	**18-07-009**
broadcast	NN	11-05-007
broadcasts	NNS	7-04-004
broadcast	**verb**	**11-07-010**
broadcast	VBD	1-01-001
broadcast	VBN	4-03-004
broadcasting	VBG	2-02-002
broadcasting	VBG-HL	1-01-001
Broadcasting	VBG-TL	3-01-003
broadcaster	**noun**	**2-01-001**
broadcasters	NNS	0-00-000
Broadcasters	NNS-TL	2-01-001
broadcasting	**noun**	**5-03-004**
broadcasting	NN	3-02-003
broadcastings	NNS	2-01-001
broaden	**verb**	**22-08-018**
broaden	VB	8-03-006
broadens	VBZ	2-01-002
broadened	VBD	3-03-003
broadened	VBN	4-03-003
broadening	VBG	5-03-005
broadening	**NN**	**4-02-003**
broader	**JJR**	**19-07-014**
broadest	**JJT**	**1-01-001**
broadly	**QL**	**2-01-002**
broadly	**RB**	**5-04-005**
broadside	**JJ**	**1-01-001**
broadside	**NN**	**1-01-001**
broadside	**RB**	**1-01-001**
Broadway	**prop. noun**	**25-08-018**
Broadway	NP	21-08-017
Broadway	NP-HL	1-01-001
Broadway	NP-TL	2-02-002
Broadway's	NP$	1-01-001
brocade	**NN**	**3-02-003**
brocaded	**JJ**	**1-01-001**
broccoli	**NN**	**1-01-001**
brochure	**noun**	**4-03-003**
brochure	NN	2-02-002
brochures	NNS	2-02-002
brockle	**NN**	**1-01-001**
Brocklin	**prop. noun**	**3-01-001**
Brocklin	NP	2-01-001
Brocklin's	NP$	1-01-001
Brod	**NP**	**1-01-001**
Brodbeck	**NP**	**1-01-001**
Brodie	**NP**	**10-01-001**
Broeg	**NP**	**1-01-001**
Broglie	**NP**	**1-01-001**
Broglio	**prop. noun**	**3-01-001**
Broglio	NP	2-01-001
Broglio's	NP$	1-01-001
broil	**NN**	**1-01-001**
broil	**verb**	**3-02-002**
broil	VB	1-01-001
broiled	VBN	2-02-002
broiler	**NN**	**2-02-002**
broke	**JJ**	**5-03-005**
broken-backed	**JJ**	**1-01-001**
broken-down	**JJ**	**1-01-001**
broken-nosed	**JJ**	**1-01-001**
brokenly	**RB**	**1-01-001**
broker	**noun**	**5-03-003**
broker	NN	1-01-001
brokers	NNS	4-02-002
brokerage	**NN**	**2-02-002**
Bromfield	**prop. noun**	**1-01-001**
Bromfield's	NP$	1-01-001
bromide	**noun**	**1-01-001**
bromides	NNS	1-01-001
Bromley	**NP**	**1-01-001**
bromphenol	**NN**	**1-01-001**
bronchial	**JJ**	**29-01-001**
bronchiolar	**JJ**	**1-01-001**
bronchiole	**noun**	**13-01-001**
bronchiole	NN	4-01-001
bronchioles	NNS	9-01-001
bronchiolitis	**NN**	**1-01-001**
bronchus	**noun**	**7-01-002**
bronchus	NN	4-01-001
bronchi	NNS	3-01-002
bronco	**noun**	**7-02-002**
bronco	NN	0-00-000
bronc	NN	3-01-001
broncos	NNS	0-00-000
broncs	NNS	1-01-001
Broncs	NNS-TL	2-01-001
Broncos	NNS-TL	1-01-001
Bronislaw	**NP**	**1-01-001**
Bronx	**prop. noun**	**9-05-005**
Bronx	NP	8-04-004
Bronx	NP-TL	1-01-001
bronze	**JJ**	**3-03-003**
bronze	**NN**	**8-07-007**
bronze	**verb**	**1-01-001**
bronzed	VBN	1-01-001
bronzy-green-gold	**JJ**	**1-01-001**
brood	**noun**	**12-04-005**
brood	NN	9-04-005
broods	NNS	3-01-002
brood	**verb**	**15-08-015**
brooding	VBG	14-07-014
Brooding	VBG-TL	1-01-001
broody	**JJ**	**2-02-002**
brook	**noun**	**3-02-003**
brook	NN	1-01-001
Brook	NN-TL	2-02-002
brook	**verb**	**1-01-001**
brooked	VBD	1-01-001
Brooke	**prop. noun**	**2-02-002**
Brooke	NP	1-01-001
Brooke	NP-TL	1-01-001

Word	Tag	Frequency
Brookfield	**prop. noun**	**2-01-001**
Brookfield	NP	1-01-001
Brookfield	NP-TL	1-01-001
Brooklyn	**prop. noun**	**30-07-013**
Brooklyn	NP	13-07-011
Brooklyn	NP-TL	16-03-003
Brooklyn's	NP$	1-01-001
Brookmeyer	**prop. noun**	**1-01-001**
Brookmeyer's	NP$	1-01-001
Brookmont	**NP**	**1-01-001**
Brooks	**prop. noun**	**17-05-007**
Brooks	NP	16-05-007
Brooks's	NP$	1-01-001
broom	**NN**	**2-02-002**
Broome	**prop. noun**	**1-01-001**
Broome	NP	0-00-000
Broome	NP-TL	1-01-001
broth	**NN**	**3-03-003**
brothel	**noun**	**3-03-003**
brothel	NN	1-01-001
brothels	NNS	2-02-002
brother	**noun**	**135-14-077**
brother	NN	71-11-042
Brother	NN-TL	2-02-002
brother's	NN$	10-06-007
brothers	NNS	37-13-031
brethren	NNS	7-04-006
brethren	NNS-HL	1-01-001
brothers	NNS-HL	1-01-001
Brothers	NNS-TL	3-03-003
brothers'	NNS$	2-01-001
bros.'	NNS$	0-00-000
Bros.'	NNS$-TL	1-01-001
brother-in-law	**NN**	**5-04-004**
brotherhood	**noun**	**6-05-006**
brotherhood	NN	5-05-005
Brotherhood	NN-TL	1-01-001
brotherly	**JJ**	**2-02-002**
Broun	**NP**	**3-02-002**
brow	**noun**	**11-05-011**
brow	NN	6-05-006
brows	NNS	5-04-005
browbeat	**verb**	**1-01-001**
browbeaten	VBN	1-01-001
brown	**adjective**	**66-12-047**
brown	JJ	62-11-045
Brown	JJ-TL	4-01-002
brown	**NN**	**4-03-004**
brown	**verb**	**1-01-001**
browning	VBG	1-01-001
Brown	**prop. noun**	**129-10-027**
Brown	NP	68-08-016
Brown	NP-TL	38-07-010
Brown's	NP$	22-05-005
Brown's	NP$-TL	1-01-001
brown-black	**JJ**	**1-01-001**
brown-edged	**JJ**	**1-01-001**
brown-paper	**NN**	**1-01-001**
Brownapopolus	**prop. noun**	**1-01-001**
Brownapopolus	NP	0-00-000
Brownapopolus	NP-TL	1-01-001
Browne	**NP**	**1-01-001**
Brownell	**NP**	**1-01-001**
Browning	**prop. noun**	**9-05-006**
Browning	NP	5-03-003
Browning	NP-TL	1-01-001
Browning's	NP$	2-02-002
Brownings	NPS	1-01-001
brownish	**JJ**	**1-01-001**
Brownlow	**NP**	**2-01-001**
browny	**JJ**	**1-01-001**
browny-haired	**JJ**	**2-01-001**
browse	**verb**	**1-01-001**
browsing	VBG	1-01-001
Broxodent	**NP**	**2-01-001**
Bruce	**NP**	**4-03-004**
brucellosis	**NN**	**1-01-001**
Bruckmann	**NP**	**1-01-001**
Bruckner	**prop. noun**	**7-01-001**
Bruckner	NP	4-01-001
Bruckner's	NP$	3-01-001
Bruegel	**NP**	**1-01-001**
Bruhn	**NP**	**1-01-001**
bruise	**noun**	**10-05-005**
bruise	NN	2-01-001
bruises	NNS	8-04-004
bruise	**verb**	**10-06-010**
bruise	VB	1-01-001
bruised	VBN	7-04-007
bruise (cont.):		
bruising	VBG	2-02-002
bruit	**verb**	**1-01-001**
bruited	VBN	1-01-001
Brumby	**prop. noun**	**2-01-001**
Brumby	NP	1-01-001
Brumby	NP-TL	1-01-001
Brumidi	**prop. noun**	**17-01-001**
Brumidi	NP	10-01-001
Brumidi	NP-TL	1-01-001
Brumidi's	NP$	6-01-001
Brumidi-Costaggini	**NP**	**1-01-001**
brunch	**noun**	**1-01-001**
brunches	NNS	1-01-001
brunette	**noun**	**1-01-001**
brunettes	NNS	1-01-001
Bruno	**NP**	**1-01-001**
brunt	**NN**	**1-01-001**
brush	**noun**	**36-10-025**
brush	NN	29-09-022
brushes	NNS	7-05-006
brush	**verb**	**38-11-030**
brush	VB	13-07-011
brushed	VBD	14-08-013
brushed	VBN	6-04-005
brushing	VBG	5-03-005
Brush	**prop. noun**	**2-02-002**
Brush	NP	1-01-001
Brush	NP-TL	1-01-001
Brush-off	**prop. noun**	**2-01-001**
Brush-off	NP	1-01-001
Brush-off's	NP$	1-01-001
brushcut	**NN**	**1-01-001**
brushfire	**NN**	**2-02-002**
brushing	**NN**	**2-01-001**
brushlike	**JJ**	**1-01-001**
brushwork	**NN**	**1-01-001**
brushy	**JJ**	**2-01-001**
brusquely	**RB**	**1-01-001**
Brussels	**prop. noun**	**3-02-002**
Brussels	NP	2-01-001
Brussels	NP-TL	1-01-001
brutal	**JJ**	**7-06-006**
brutality	**noun**	**14-06-012**
brutality	NN	13-06-011
brutalities	NNS	1-01-001
brutalize	**verb**	**1-01-001**
brutalized	VBN	1-01-001
brutally	**QL**	**1-01-001**
brutally	**RB**	**1-01-001**
brute	**JJ**	**1-01-001**
brute	**NN**	**5-04-005**
Bruxelles	**NP**	**1-01-001**
Bryan	**prop. noun**	**14-05-007**
Bryan	NP	12-05-007
Bryan's	NP$	2-02-002
Bryant	**NP**	**1-01-001**
Bryce	**prop. noun**	**2-02-002**
Bryce	NP	1-01-001
Bryce	NP-TL	1-01-001
Bryn	**prop. noun**	**2-01-001**
Bryn	NP	0-00-000
Bryn	NP-TL	2-01-001
Bryson	**NP**	**1-01-001**
Buaford	**NP**	**1-01-001**
bubble	**noun**	**25-10-012**
bubble	NN	12-08-008
bubbles	NNS	13-06-006
bubble	**verb**	**6-06-006**
bubbles	VBZ	1-01-001
bubbled	VBD	1-01-001
bubbled	VBN	1-01-001
bubbling	VBG	3-03-003
bubbly	**JJ**	**1-01-001**
Bubenik	**NP**	**1-01-001**
Buber	**NP**	**1-01-001**
Buc	**prop. noun**	**2-01-001**
Bucs	NPS	0-00-000
Bucs	NPS-HL	1-01-001
Bucs'	NPS$	1-01-001
Bucer	**NP**	**1-01-001**
Buchanan	**NP**	**2-02-002**
Bucharest	**NP**	**1-01-001**
Buchenwald	**NP**	**1-01-001**
Buchheister	**NP**	**6-01-001**
buck	**noun**	**10-04-009**
buck	NN	5-03-005
Buck	NN-TL	1-01-001
bucks	NNS	4-02-004

Word	Tag	Frequency
buck	**verb**	**5-04-004**
bucked	VBN	1-01-001
bucking	VBG	4-03-003
Buck	**prop. noun**	**15-05-006**
Buck	NP	14-05-006
Buck's	NP$	1-01-001
buckaroo	**noun**	**1-01-001**
buckaroos	NNS	1-01-001
buckboard	**NN**	**2-01-001**
Buckenham	**NP**	**1-01-001**
bucket	**noun**	**11-04-008**
bucket	NN	7-04-006
buckets	NNS	4-02-003
bucket-shop	**NN**	**1-01-001**
Buckhannon	**NP**	**1-01-001**
Buckhead	**NP**	**1-01-001**
Buckhorn	**prop. noun**	**1-01-001**
Buckhorn	NP	0-00-000
Buckhorn's	NP+BEZ	1-01-001
bucking-up	**NN**	**1-01-001**
buckle	**noun**	**4-03-003**
buckle	NN	2-02-002
buckles	NNS	2-02-002
buckle	**verb**	**6-04-006**
buckle	VB	3-02-003
buckled	VBD	1-01-001
buckled	VBN	1-01-001
buckling	VBG	1-01-001
buckle-on	**JJ**	**1-01-001**
Buckley	**prop. noun**	**7-02-002**
Buckley	NP	6-02-002
Buckley	NP-HL	1-01-001
Buckman	**prop. noun**	**1-01-001**
Buckman	NP	0-00-000
Buckman	NP-NC	1-01-001
Buckra	**prop. noun**	**2-01-001**
Buckra	NP	0-00-000
Buckra	NP-TL	2-01-001
Bucks	**prop. noun**	**2-02-002**
Bucks	NP	0-00-000
Bucks	NP-HL	1-01-001
Bucks	NP-TL	1-01-001
buckshot	**NN**	**1-01-001**
buckskin	**noun**	**9-02-002**
buckskin	NN	7-01-001
buckskin's	NN$	1-01-001
buckskins	NNS	1-01-001
buckwheat	**NN**	**1-01-001**
Bucky	**NP**	**1-01-001**
bucolic	**adjective**	**2-02-002**
bucolic	JJ	1-01-001
buccolic	JJ	1-01-001
bud	**noun**	**7-04-005**
bud	NN	2-02-002
buds	NNS	5-04-004
bud	**verb**	**4-03-003**
bud	VB	2-02-002
budded	VBD	1-01-001
budding	VBG	1-01-001
Bud	**NP**	**5-03-005**
Budapest	**prop. noun**	**8-04-005**
Budapest	NP	5-03-004
Budapest	NP-TL	3-02-002
Budd	**NP**	**5-02-002**
Buddha	**prop. noun**	**8-03-004**
Buddha	NP	6-02-003
Buddha	NP-TL	2-02-002
Buddhism	**NP**	**9-03-004**
Buddhist	**adjective**	**3-02-003**
Buddhist	JJ	0-00-000
Buddhist	JJ-TL	3-02-003
Buddhist	**prop. noun**	**3-02-002**
Buddhist	NP	1-01-001
Buddhists	NPS	2-01-001
buddy	**noun**	**17-05-009**
buddy	NN	11-05-008
buddy	NN-HL	1-01-001
buddies	NNS	5-03-004
Buddy	**NP**	**1-01-001**
budge	**VB**	**3-03-003**
budget	**noun**	**62-07-024**
budget	NN	53-07-023
budget	NN-HL	3-02-003
Budget	NN-TL	1-01-001
budgets	NNS	5-03-004
budget	**verb**	**8-05-007**
budget	VB	2-02-002
budgeted	VBN	2-02-002
budgeting	VBG	4-03-004

Word	Tag	Frequency
budget-altering	**JJ**	**1-01-001**
budget-making	**JJ**	**1-01-001**
budget-wise	**JJ**	**1-01-001**
budgetary	**adjective**	**3-02-003**
budgetary	JJ	2-01-002
Budgetary	JJ-TL	1-01-001
budgeting	**NN**	**3-01-002**
Budieshein	**NP**	**1-01-001**
Budlong	**NP**	**1-01-001**
Budweiser	**prop. noun**	**1-01-001**
Budweisers	NPS	1-01-001
Budzyn	**NP**	**1-01-001**
Buell	**prop. noun**	**2-02-002**
Buell	NP	1-01-001
Buell's	NP$	1-01-001
Buena	**prop. noun**	**1-01-001**
Buena	NP	0-00-000
Buena	NP-TL	1-01-001
buenas	**foreign**	**1-01-001**
buenas	FW-JJ	0-00-000
Buenas	FW-JJ-TL	1-01-001
bueno	**FW-UH**	**1-01-001**
buff	**JJ**	**3-02-002**
buff	**noun**	**3-03-003**
buff	NN	2-02-002
buffs	NNS	1-01-001
buffalo	**noun**	**10-03-006**
buffalo	NN	7-03-004
Buffalo	NN-TL	1-01-001
buffalo	NNS	1-01-001
buffaloes	NNS	1-01-001
Buffalo	**prop. noun**	**7-04-006**
Buffalo	NP	5-03-004
Buffalo	NP-TL	2-02-002
buffer	**NN**	**16-02-004**
buffer	**verb**	**4-01-001**
buffered	VBN	4-01-001
buffet	**noun**	**6-03-006**
buffet	NN	5-03-005
buffets	NNS	1-01-001
buffet	**verb**	**3-03-003**
buffet	VB	1-01-001
buffeted	VBN	2-02-002
buffeting	**noun**	**1-01-001**
buffetings	NNS	1-01-001
buffoon	**noun**	**2-01-002**
buffoon	NN	1-01-001
buffoons	NNS	1-01-001
bug	**noun**	**7-05-005**
bug	NN	3-01-001
bugs	NNS	4-04-004
bug	**verb**	**6-04-004**
bugs	VBZ	1-01-001
bugged	VBD	1-01-001
bugged	VBN	1-01-001
bugging	VBG	3-01-001
Bug	**prop. noun**	**1-01-001**
Bug	NP	0-00-000
Bug	NP-TL	1-01-001
Bugatti	**NP**	**1-01-001**
bugeyed	**JJ**	**1-01-001**
bugger	**noun**	**1-01-001**
buggers	NNS	1-01-001
buggy	**noun**	**7-04-005**
buggy	NN	6-04-004
buggies	NNS	1-01-001
bugle	**noun**	**2-02-002**
bugle	NN	1-01-001
Bugle	NN-TL	1-01-001
bugler	**NN**	**1-01-001**
Bugs	**NP**	**3-02-002**
Buick	**NP**	**3-02-002**
build	**NN**	**2-02-002**
build	**verb**	**249-15-143**
build	VB	82-14-055
build	VB-HL	2-01-001
builds	VBZ	7-05-006
built	VBD	21-13-020
built	VBN	81-13-055
Built	VBN-TL	1-01-001
building	VBG	54-13-044
buildin'	VBG	1-01-001
build-better-for-less	**JJ**	**1-01-001**
build-up	**noun**	**6-04-006**
build-up	NN	4-03-004
buildup	NN	2-02-002
builder	**noun**	**60-06-015**
builder	NN	26-04-008
builder	NN-HL	1-01-001

Word	Tag	Frequency
builder (cont.):		
Builder	NN-TL	2-02-002
builder's	NN$	2-02-002
builders	NNS	25-04-009
Builders	NNS-TL	2-01-001
builders'	NNS$	2-01-001
builder-dealer	**JJ**	**1-01-001**
builder/active	**JJ**	**1-01-001**
building	**noun**	**187-14-096**
building	NN	94-13-063
bldg.	NN	0-00-000
Bldg.	NN-TL	3-03-003
Building	NN-TL	12-05-011
building's	NN$	2-01-001
buildings	NNS	75-12-043
buildings	NNS-HL	1-01-001
built-detergent	**NN**	**1-01-001**
built-in	**adjective**	**4-04-004**
built-in	JJ	3-03-003
builtin	JJ	1-01-001
built-soap	**NN**	**1-01-001**
Bul'ba	**NP**	**1-01-001**
bulb	**noun**	**10-06-009**
bulb	NN	7-04-006
bulbs	NNS	3-02-003
Bulba	**prop. noun**	**2-01-001**
Bulba	NP	0-00-000
Bulba	NP-TL	2-01-001
Bulgaria	**NP**	**1-01-001**
bulge	**noun**	**5-05-005**
bulge	NN	4-04-004
Bulge	NN-TL	1-01-001
bulge	**verb**	**6-05-006**
bulged	VBD	3-02-003
bulging	VBG	3-03-003
bulk	**JJ**	**3-02-002**
bulk	**NN**	**13-09-012**
bulk	**verb**	**2-02-002**
bulks	VBZ	1-01-001
bulked	VBD	1-01-001
bulkhead	**noun**	**2-01-001**
bulkhead	NN	1-01-001
bulkheads	NNS	1-01-001
bulky	**JJ**	**9-05-008**
bull	**noun**	**16-08-011**
bull	NN	14-08-011
bulls	NNS	2-02-002
bull-like	**JJ**	**1-01-001**
bull-necked	**JJ**	**1-01-001**
bull-roaring	**JJ**	**1-01-001**
bull-session	**noun**	**2-01-001**
bull-sessions	NNS	2-01-001
bull's-eye	**noun**	**16-02-002**
bull's-eye	NN	10-02-002
bull's-eyes	NNS	6-01-001
bulldoze	**VB**	**1-01-001**
bullet	**noun**	**49-09-025**
bullet	NN	26-08-017
Bullet	NN-TL	2-01-002
bullets	NNS	21-07-013
bullet-riddled	**JJ**	**1-01-001**
bulletin	**noun**	**21-08-012**
bulletin	NN	7-05-007
Bulletin	NN-TL	11-03-004
bulletins	NNS	3-02-003
bulletin	**verb**	**2-01-001**
bulletins	VBZ	1-01-001
bulletined	VBD	0-00-000
bulletin'd	VBD	1-01-001
Bullfinch	**NP**	**1-01-001**
bullhide	**NN**	**1-01-001**
bullish	**JJ**	**1-01-001**
Bulloch	**NP**	**2-01-001**
bullshit	**NN**	**1-01-001**
bullshit	**UH**	**1-01-001**
bullshit	**VB**	**1-01-001**
bullwhacker	**noun**	**1-01-001**
bullwhackers	NNS	1-01-001
bully	**JJ**	**1-01-001**
bully	**noun**	**3-03-003**
bully	NN	2-02-002
bullies	NNS	1-01-001
bully	**verb**	**3-03-003**
bully	VB	1-01-001
bullies	VBZ	1-01-001
bullying	VBG	1-01-001
bullyboy	**noun**	**1-01-001**
bullyboys	NNS	1-01-001
Bultmann	**prop. noun**	**11-01-001**

Word	Tag	Frequency
Bultmann (cont.):		
Bultmann	NP	4-01-001
Bultmann's	NP$	7-01-001
bulwark	**NN**	**5-05-005**
bum	**JJ**	**1-01-001**
bum	**noun**	**7-03-005**
bum	NN	5-02-003
bums	NNS	2-02-002
bum	**VB**	**1-01-001**
bumblebee	**noun**	**13-02-002**
bumblebee	NN	2-01-001
bumble-bee	NN	1-01-001
bumblebees	NNS	9-01-001
Bumblebees	NNS-TL	1-01-001
Bumbry	**NP**	**1-01-001**
bumming	**NN**	**1-01-001**
bump	**noun**	**2-02-002**
bump	NN	1-01-001
bumps	NNS	1-01-001
bump	**verb**	**9-06-007**
bump	VB	4-04-004
bumped	VBD	2-02-002
bumping	VBG	2-02-002
bumpin	VBG	1-01-001
bumper	**noun**	**3-03-003**
bumper	NN	2-02-002
bumpers	NNS	1-01-001
bumptious	**JJ**	**1-01-001**
bun	**noun**	**9-02-002**
bun	NN	1-01-001
buns	NNS	8-01-001
bunch	**noun**	**18-09-015**
bunch	NN	17-09-014
buncha	NN+IN	1-01-001
bunch	**verb**	**5-05-005**
bunched	VBD	1-01-001
bunched	VBN	4-04-004
Bundestag	**NP**	**1-01-001**
bundle	**noun**	**26-09-013**
bundle	NN	18-08-011
bundle	NN-HL	1-01-001
bundles	NNS	7-04-005
bundle	**verb**	**4-03-003**
bundle	VB	1-01-001
bundled	VBN	3-03-003
Bundy	**NP**	**2-02-002**
bungalow	**NN**	**1-01-001**
bungle	**verb**	**1-01-001**
bungled	VBD	1-01-001
bunk	**noun**	**35-06-010**
bunk	NN	18-04-006
bunks	NNS	17-05-007
bunker	**NN**	**3-01-002**
bunker	**verb**	**1-01-001**
bunkered	VBN	1-01-001
bunkmate	**noun**	**2-01-001**
bunkmate	NN	1-01-001
bunkmates	NNS	1-01-001
Bunny	**NP**	**1-01-001**
bunt	**NN**	**2-01-002**
bunt	**VB**	**1-01-001**
bunter	**noun**	**2-01-002**
bunter	NN	1-01-001
bunters	NNS	1-01-001
Bunyan	**NP**	**2-02-002**
buoy	**noun**	**1-01-001**
buoys	NNS	1-01-001
buoy	**verb**	**1-01-001**
buoyed	VBN	1-01-001
buoyancy	**NN**	**1-01-001**
buoyant	**JJ**	**2-02-002**
Burbank	**NP**	**2-02-002**
Burch	**prop. noun**	**3-01-001**
Burch	NP	2-01-001
Burch's	NP$	1-01-001
Burckhardt	**NP**	**1-01-001**
burden	**noun**	**50-11-044**
burden	NN	43-11-040
burdens	NNS	7-05-007
burden	**verb**	**5-02-005**
burden	VB	1-01-001
burdened	VBN	4-02-004
burdensome	**JJ**	**1-01-001**
bureau	**foreign**	**1-01-001**
bureau	FW-NN	0-00-000
Bureau	FW-NN-TL	1-01-001
bureau	**noun**	**44-11-029**
bureau	NN	17-07-013
Bureau	NN-TL	25-07-015

bureau (cont.):		
bureaus	NNS	2-02-002
bureaucracy	**noun**	**10-04-007**
bureaucracy	NN	7-02-005
bureaucracies	NNS	3-02-002
bureaucrat	**noun**	**2-02-002**
bureaucrat	NN	1-01-001
bureaucrats	NNS	1-01-001
bureaucratic	**JJ**	**3-02-002**
bureaucratization	**NN**	**1-01-001**
Buren	**NP**	**2-01-001**
Burford	**NP**	**1-01-001**
burgeon	**verb**	**5-04-005**
burgeoned	VBD	1-01-001
burgeoning	VBG	4-03-004
Burger	**NP**	**1-01-001**
burgess	**noun**	**1-01-001**
burgesses	NNS	0-00-000
Burgesses	NNS	1-01-001
Burgess	**NP**	**2-01-002**
Burghardt	**NP**	**1-01-001**
Burgher	**NP**	**1-01-001**
Burghley	**NP**	**1-01-001**
burglar	**noun**	**3-03-003**
burglar	NN	1-01-001
burglars	NNS	2-02-002
burglarproof	**JJ**	**1-01-001**
burglary	**NN**	**4-02-003**
burgomaster	**noun**	**1-01-001**
burgomaster's	NN$	1-01-001
Burgundian	**JJ**	**1-01-001**
Burgundy	**prop. noun**	**7-02-002**
Burgundy	NP	5-02-002
Burgundy	NP-TL	1-01-001
Burgundies	NPS	1-01-001
Buri	**NP**	**3-01-001**
burial	**NN**	**11-05-010**
Burke	**prop. noun**	**11-03-006**
Burke	NP	7-03-005
Burke's	NP$	1-01-001
Burkes	NPS	2-01-001
Burkes'	NPS$	1-01-001
Burke-Rostagno	**prop. noun**	**1-01-001**
Burke-Rostagno	NP	0-00-000
Burke-Rostagno	NP-HL	1-01-001
Burkette	**NP**	**1-01-001**
burl	**NN**	**2-01-001**
Burle	**NP**	**1-01-001**
Burleson	**NP**	**1-01-001**
burlesque	**JJ**	**1-01-001**
burlesque	**noun**	**2-02-002**
burlesque	NN	1-01-001
burlesques	NNS	1-01-001
burley	**NN**	**1-01-001**
Burlingame	**NP**	**1-01-001**
Burlingham	**NP**	**2-01-001**
Burlington	**prop. noun**	**7-01-001**
Burlington	NP	5-01-001
Burlington	NP-TL	1-01-001
Burlington's	NP$	1-01-001
burly	**JJ**	**3-03-003**
Burma	**prop. noun**	**17-06-006**
Burma	NP	15-06-006
Burma	NP-HL	1-01-001
Burma	NP-TL	1-01-001
Burman	**prop. noun**	**4-02-002**
Burman	NP	2-01-001
Burman's	NP$	1-01-001
Burmans	NPS	1-01-001
Burmese	**JJ**	**2-02-002**
Burmese	**NPS**	**2-01-001**
burn	**noun**	**18-04-007**
burn	NN	5-03-004
burns	NNS	13-03-004
burn	**verb**	**103-14-071**
burn	VB	10-06-009
burne	VB	1-01-001
burns	VBZ	2-02-002
burned	VBD	15-06-012
burned	VBN	25-11-023
burnt	VBN	5-03-005
Burnt	VBN-TL	1-01-001
burning	VBG	42-12-029
Burning	VBG	1-01-001
Burning	VBG-TL	1-01-001
burned-out	**JJ**	**1-01-001**
burner	**noun**	**2-02-002**
burners	NNS	2-02-002
Burnes	**NP**	**1-01-001**

Burnet	**NP**	**2-01-001**
Burnham	**prop. noun**	**2-02-002**
Burnham	NP	1-01-001
Burnham's	NP$	1-01-001
burning	**noun**	**7-05-006**
burning	NN	5-04-004
burnings	NNS	2-02-002
burnish	**verb**	**1-01-001**
burnished	VBN	1-01-001
Burns	**prop. noun**	**9-03-004**
Burns	NP	8-02-003
Burns's	NP$	1-01-001
Burnside	**prop. noun**	**16-03-003**
Burnside	NP	6-02-002
Burnside	NP-TL	1-01-001
Burnside's	NP$	4-01-001
Burnsides	NPS	4-01-001
Burnsides'	NPS$	1-01-001
Burnsides	**NP**	**1-01-001**
burnt-red	**JJ**	**1-01-001**
burr	**noun**	**3-03-003**
burr	NN	2-02-002
burrs	NNS	1-01-001
Burr	**prop. noun**	**6-02-003**
Burr	NP	2-02-002
Burr	NP-TL	3-01-001
Burr's	NP$	1-01-001
burr-headed	**JJ**	**1-01-001**
Burro	**NP**	**1-01-001**
burrow	**noun**	**5-02-002**
burrow	NN	3-02-002
burrows	NNS	2-01-001
burrow	**verb**	**3-03-003**
burrow	VB	1-01-001
burrowed	VBD	1-01-001
burrowing	VBG	1-01-001
bursitis	**NN**	**1-01-001**
burst	**noun**	**11-06-009**
burst	NN	10-06-009
bursts	NNS	1-01-001
burst	**verb**	**37-12-032**
burst	VB	9-07-009
bursts	VBZ	0-00-000
bursts	VBZ-HL	1-01-001
burst	VBD	11-07-011
burst	VBN	3-02-003
bursting	VBG	13-06-013
Burt	**NP**	**1-01-001**
Burton	**prop. noun**	**17-02-002**
Burton	NP	13-01-001
Burton	NP-TL	2-01-001
Burton's	NP$	2-01-001
bury	**verb**	**24-09-020**
bury	VB	5-04-005
buries	VBZ	1-01-001
buried	VBD	3-02-003
buried	VBN	15-06-012
Bury	**prop. noun**	**1-01-001**
Bury	NP	0-00-000
Bury	NP-TL	1-01-001
bus	**noun**	**42-09-023**
bus	NN	34-08-020
buses	NNS	7-04-004
busses	NNS	1-01-001
busboy	**NN**	**2-01-001**
Busch	**prop. noun**	**2-01-001**
Busch	NP	0-00-000
Busch	NP-TL	2-01-001
bush	**noun**	**20-08-011**
bush	NN	10-03-004
bushes	NNS	10-07-008
Bush	**NP**	**4-02-002**
bushel	**noun**	**5-03-003**
bushel	NN	1-01-001
bushels	NNS	4-02-002
Bushell	**NP**	**3-01-001**
Bushnell	**NP**	**1-01-001**
bushwhack	**verb**	**1-01-001**
bushwhacked	VBD	1-01-001
bushwhacking	**adjective**	**1-01-001**
bushwhacking	JJ	0-00-000
bushwhackin'	JJ	1-01-001
busier	**JJR**	**1-01-001**
busiest	**JJT**	**2-02-002**
busily	**RB**	**8-06-007**
business	**noun**	**412-15-167**
business	NN	359-15-163
business	NN-HL	8-04-006
Business	NN-TL	26-07-009

Word	Tag	Frequency
business (cont.):		
businesses	NNS	19-06-011
business-like	**JJ**	**1-01-001**
business-minded	**JJ**	**1-01-001**
businessman	**noun**	**24-09-019**
businessman	NN	9-04-008
businessmen	NNS	15-08-012
buss	**NN**	**1-01-001**
bust	**noun**	**9-02-002**
bust	NN	5-02-002
Bust	NN-TL	1-01-001
busts	NNS	3-01-001
bust	**verb**	**5-04-005**
bust	VB	1-01-001
busted	VBN	3-03-003
busting	VBG	0-00-000
bustin'	VBG	1-01-001
Bustard	**NP**	**1-01-001**
Buster	**NP**	**3-02-002**
bustle	**NN**	**2-02-002**
bustle	**verb**	**2-02-002**
bustling	VBG	1-01-001
bustlin'	VBG	1-01-001
busy	**adjective**	**57-14-048**
busy	JJ	56-13-047
busy	JJ-NC	1-01-001
busy	**verb**	**2-02-002**
busy	VB	1-01-001
busied	VBD	1-01-001
busy-work	**NN**	**1-01-001**
busyness	**NN**	**1-01-001**
but	**co. conj.**	**4226-15-489**
but	CC	4218-15-489
butt	CC	2-01-001
but	CC-HL	3-03-003
but	CC-NC	3-01-001
but	**IN**	**131-15-105**
but	**RB**	**26-06-023**
butane	**NN**	**1-01-001**
butcher	**noun**	**7-01-001**
butcher	NN	2-01-001
Butcher	NN-TL	5-01-001
butcher	**verb**	**1-01-001**
butchered	VBN	1-01-001
Butcher	**NP**	**1-01-001**
butchery	**NN**	**5-02-002**
butler	**noun**	**4-03-003**
butler	NN	2-02-002
butlers	NNS	2-02-002
Butler	**prop. noun**	**4-03-004**
Butler	NP	3-03-003
Butlers	NPS	1-01-001
butt	**noun**	**11-06-011**
butt	NN	7-03-007
butts	NNS	4-04-004
butt	**verb**	**7-02-002**
butt	VB	2-01-001
butts	VBZ	1-01-001
butted	VBN	3-01-001
butting	VBG	1-01-001
Butt	**NP**	**1-01-001**
Butte	**prop. noun**	**1-01-001**
Butte	NP	0-00-000
Butte	NP-TL	1-01-001
butter	**NN**	**27-06-012**
butterfat	**NN**	**1-01-001**
butterfly	**noun**	**3-02-003**
butterfly	NN	2-01-002
butterflies	NNS	1-01-001
butternut	**NN**	**1-01-001**
Butterwyn	**NP**	**1-01-001**
buttery	**JJ**	**1-01-001**
buttock	**noun**	**1-01-001**
buttocks	NNS	1-01-001
button	**noun**	**20-07-009**
button	NN	10-03-004
buttons	NNS	10-05-006
button	**verb**	**1-01-001**
buttoned	VBN	1-01-001
Button	**prop. noun**	**1-01-001**
Button's	NP$	1-01-001
button-down	**JJ**	**2-02-002**
buttonhole	**noun**	**1-01-001**
buttonholes	NNS	1-01-001
buttress	**noun**	**1-01-001**
buttresses	NNS	1-01-001
buttress	**verb**	**1-01-001**
buttressed	VBN	1-01-001
Buttrick	**NP**	**1-01-001**

Word	Tag	Frequency
butyl-lithium	**NN**	**1-01-001**
butyrate	**NN**	**9-01-001**
buxom	**JJ**	**1-01-001**
Buxtehude	**NP**	**1-01-001**
Buxton	**NP**	**1-01-001**
buy	**NN**	**1-01-001**
buy	**verb**	**162-13-094**
buy	VB	68-12-041
bye	VB	1-01-001
Buy	VB-TL	1-01-001
buys	VBZ	11-06-008
bought	VBD	32-11-026
bought	VBN	24-10-023
buying	VBG	23-10-019
buyin'	VBG	1-01-001
buying	VBG-HL	1-01-001
buyer	**noun**	**10-06-008**
buyer	NN	2-02-002
buyer's	NN$	2-02-002
buyers	NNS	5-04-005
buyers'	NNS$	1-01-001
buying	**noun**	**7-04-005**
buying	NN	6-03-004
byinge	NN	1-01-001
buzz	**noun**	**6-03-003**
buzz	NN	4-02-002
buzzes	NNS	2-02-002
buzz	**verb**	**9-06-008**
buzz	VB	1-01-001
buzzed	VBD	2-02-002
buzzing	VBG	6-03-005
Buzz	**prop. noun**	**9-01-001**
Buzz	NP	8-01-001
Buzz's	NP$	1-01-001
buzz-buzz-buzz	**UH**	**1-01-001**
by	**prep.**	**5246-15-498**
by	IN	5221-15-498
bi	IN	2-01-001
by	IN-HL	17-05-008
by	IN-NC	4-01-001
by	IN-TL	2-02-002
by	**RB**	**61-14-054**
by-law	**noun**	**2-01-001**
by-laws	NNS	2-01-001
by-passing	**JJ**	**1-01-001**
by-product	**noun**	**10-05-008**
by-product	NN	3-02-003
byproduct	NN	2-02-002
by-products	NNS	2-02-002
byproducts	NNS	3-02-002
by-road	**noun**	**1-01-001**
by-roads	NNS	1-01-001
By-the-Sea	**NP**	**1-01-001**
by-way	**noun**	**1-01-001**
by-ways	NNS	1-01-001
Bye	**UH**	**1-01-001**
Byer-Rolnick	**prop. noun**	**1-01-001**
Byer-Rolnick	NP	0-00-000
Byer-Rolnick	NP-TL	1-01-001
bygone	**adjective**	**3-03-003**
bygone	JJ	2-02-002
by-gone	JJ	1-01-001
byline	**NN**	**1-01-001**
Bylot	**NP**	**1-01-001**
bypass	**noun**	**2-02-002**
bypass	NN	1-01-001
by-pass	NN	1-01-001
bypass	**verb**	**6-05-006**
bypass	VB	2-02-002
bypasses	VBZ	0-00-000
by-passes	VBZ	1-01-001
bypassed	VBD	1-01-001
bypassed	VBN	0-00-000
by-passed	VBN	1-01-001
bypassing	VBG	0-00-000
by-passing	VBG	1-01-001
Byrd	**prop. noun**	**12-06-007**
Byrd	NP	9-06-007
Byrd's	NP$	3-02-002
Byrnes	**NP**	**2-01-001**
Byron	**prop. noun**	**20-06-008**
Byron	NP	16-04-006
Byron's	NP$	4-03-003
Byronic	**JJ**	**1-01-001**
Byronism	**NP**	**1-01-001**
bystander	**NN**	**1-01-001**
Bystrzyca	**prop. noun**	**1-01-001**
Bystrzyca	NP	0-00-000
Bystrzyca	NP-TL	1-01-001

Word	Tag	Frequency
byword	**noun**	**2-02-002**
byword	NN	1-01-001
by-word	NN	1-01-001
Byzantine	**JJ**	**5-03-003**
Byzantium	**NP**	**1-01-001**
Byzas	**NP**	**1-01-001**

C

Word	Tag	Frequency
C	**prop. noun**	**45-05-021**
C	NP	27-05-015
C	NP-HL	17-02-010
C	NP-TL	1-01-001
C.	**prop. noun**	**92-10-054**
C.	NP	90-09-052
C.	NP-TL	2-02-002
C.A.I.P.	**NP**	**1-01-001**
C.C.B.	**NP**	**2-01-001**
C.C.N.Y.	**NP**	**1-01-001**
c'est	**FW-DT+BEZ**	**2-01-001**
c'mon	**exclam.**	**4-03-003**
c'mon	UH	3-03-003
'mon	UH	1-01-001
cab	**noun**	**15-05-008**
cab	NN	12-05-007
cab's	NN$	2-01-001
cabs	NNS	1-01-001
cabana	**noun**	**6-03-003**
cabana	NN	3-01-001
Cabana	NN-TL	1-01-001
cabanas	NNS	2-01-001
cabaret	**NN**	**1-01-001**
cabbage	**NN**	**4-02-003**
cabdriver	**NN**	**1-01-001**
cabin	**noun**	**30-11-016**
cabin	NN	21-08-011
Cabin	NN-TL	2-02-002
cabins	NNS	7-04-005
cabinet	**noun**	**22-08-017**
cabinet	NN	12-06-009
Cabinet	NN-TL	5-04-004
cabinets	NNS	5-04-004
cabinetmaker	**noun**	**1-01-001**
cabinetmakers	NNS	1-01-001
cable	**noun**	**6-04-006**
cable	NN	3-02-003
Cable	NN-TL	1-01-001
cables	NNS	2-02-002
cable	**verb**	**3-02-003**
cable	VB	2-02-002
cabled	VBD	1-01-001
Cable	**NP**	**1-01-001**
Cabot	**prop. noun**	**3-02-002**
Cabot	NP	2-02-002
Cabot's	NP$	1-01-001
Cabrini	**prop. noun**	**4-01-001**
Cabrini	NP	3-01-001
Cabrini	NP-TL	1-01-001
cacao	**NN**	**1-01-001**
cache	**NN**	**1-01-001**
cackle	**verb**	**3-02-003**
cackled	VBD	3-02-003
cackly	**JJ**	**1-01-001**
Cacophonist	**NN**	**1-01-001**
cacophony	**NN**	**1-01-001**
cadaver	**NN**	**1-01-001**
cadaverous	**JJ**	**1-01-001**
Caddy	**NP**	**1-01-001**
cadence	**NN**	**2-02-002**
cadenza	**NN**	**3-02-003**
Cadesi	**NP**	**1-01-001**
cadet	**noun**	**4-04-004**
cadet	NN	2-02-002
Cadet	NN-TL	2-02-002
Cadillac	**prop. noun**	**11-05-007**
Cadillac	NP	8-03-004
Cadillac	NP-TL	1-01-001
Cadillacs	NPS	2-02-002
cadmium	**NN**	**2-02-002**
cadre	**NN**	**3-03-003**
Cady	**NP**	**27-01-001**
Caesar	**NP**	**6-04-005**
Caetani	**NP**	**2-01-001**
cafe	**noun**	**25-10-016**
cafe	NN	15-07-010
Cafe	NN-TL	5-05-005
cafe (cont.):		
cafes	NNS	4-02-002
cafes	NNS-HL	1-01-001
cafeteria	**noun**	**17-05-006**
cafeteria	NN	14-05-005
Cafeteria	NN-TL	1-01-001
cafeterias	NNS	2-02-002
Cafritz	**NP**	**1-01-001**
Cagayan	**NP**	**1-01-001**
cage	**noun**	**11-05-007**
cage	NN	9-05-006
cages	NNS	2-01-001
cage	**verb**	**1-01-001**
caged	VBN	1-01-001
cagey	**JJ**	**2-02-002**
Cahill	**NP**	**1-01-001**
cahoots	**NNS**	**1-01-001**
Cain	**prop. noun**	**2-02-002**
Cain	NP	1-01-001
Cain	NP-TL	1-01-001
Cairns	**NP**	**1-01-001**
Cairo	**NP**	**5-02-003**
Cairoli	**NP**	**1-01-001**
Caius	**NP**	**1-01-001**
cake	**noun**	**16-08-012**
cake	NN	13-08-011
cakes	NNS	3-02-002
cake	**verb**	**2-01-002**
caked	VBN	2-01-002
Cal	**NP**	**1-01-001**
Cal-Neva	**NP**	**1-01-001**
Calabria	**NP**	**2-01-001**
calamitous	**JJ**	**2-02-002**
calamity	**noun**	**5-03-003**
calamity	NN	2-02-002
Calamity	NN-TL	2-01-001
calamities	NNS	1-01-001
calcification	**NN**	**1-01-001**
calcify	**verb**	**1-01-001**
calcified	VBN	1-01-001
calcium	**NN**	**11-04-008**
calculable	**JJ**	**1-01-001**
calculate	**verb**	**46-10-031**
calculate	VB	4-03-004
calculated	VBD	2-01-001
calculated	VBN	33-08-023
calculating	VBG	7-06-007
calculation	**noun**	**22-06-014**
calculation	NN	12-04-010
calculations	NNS	10-04-007
calculator	**noun**	**1-01-001**
calculators	NNS	1-01-001
calculus	**noun**	**1-01-001**
calculi	NNS	1-01-001
Calcutta	**NP**	**4-01-001**
Calder	**NP**	**2-01-001**
Calderone	**NP**	**6-01-001**
Caldwell	**prop. noun**	**5-02-002**
Caldwell	NP	3-02-002
Caldwell's	NP$	2-02-002
Caleb	**NP**	**1-01-001**
Calenda	**NP**	**5-01-001**
calendar	**noun**	**39-07-013**
calendar	NN	28-06-012
calendars	NNS	10-02-002
calendars	NNS-HL	1-01-001
calf	**noun**	**17-08-010**
calf	NN	8-05-007
Calf	NN-TL	3-01-001
calves	NNS	4-02-002
calves	NNS-HL	2-01-001
calf's-foot	**NN**	**1-01-001**
calfskin	**NN**	**1-01-001**
Calhoun	**prop. noun**	**11-03-004**
Calhoun	NP	10-03-004
Calhoun's	NP$	1-01-001
caliber	**noun**	**13-04-006**

Word	Tag	Frequency
caliber (cont.):		
caliber	NN	8-03-004
calibre	NN	2-01-002
calibers	NNS	3-01-001
calibrate	**verb**	**4-03-004**
calibrated	VBN	3-03-003
calibrating	VBG	1-01-001
calibration	**noun**	**7-02-002**
calibration	NN	6-02-002
calibrations	NNS	1-01-001
caliche-topped	**JJ**	**1-01-001**
calico	**NN**	**2-02-002**
California	**prop. noun**	**88-15-046**
California	NP	44-12-030
Cal.	NP	1-01-001
Calif.	NP	18-04-007
Calif.	NP-HL	1-01-001
California	NP-TL	21-08-013
California's	NP$	2-01-002
California's	NP$-TL	1-01-001
Californian	**prop. noun**	**1-01-001**
Californians	NPS	1-01-001
Caligula	**NP**	**1-01-001**
calimala	**foreign**	**1-01-001**
calimala	FW-NN	0-00-000
Calimala	FW-NN-TL	1-01-001
calinda	**NN**	**2-01-001**
caliper	**noun**	**3-01-001**
caliper	NN	2-01-001
calipers	NNS	1-01-001
caliph	**noun**	**1-01-001**
caliphs	NNS	1-01-001
calisthenics	**NNS**	**4-03-004**
call	**noun**	**76-15-056**
call	NN	49-14-039
Call	NN	3-01-001
call	NN-HL	1-01-001
Call	NN-TL	1-01-001
calls	NNS	22-07-015
call	**verb**	**627-15-298**
call	VB	134-14-099
calls	VBZ	44-10-035
calls	VBZ-HL	3-01-003
called	VBD	165-14-114
called	VBN	236-15-156
calling	VBG	44-12-042
callin'	VBG	1-01-001
call-back	**noun**	**1-01-001**
call-backs	NNS	1-01-001
callable	**JJ**	**1-01-001**
Callan	**NP**	**1-01-001**
Callas	**NP**	**2-02-002**
caller	**noun**	**5-04-004**
caller	NN	2-02-002
callers	NNS	3-02-002
calligrapher	**noun**	**1-01-001**
calligraphers	NNS	1-01-001
calligraphy	**NN**	**1-01-001**
calling	**NN**	**1-01-001**
callous	**JJ**	**7-05-007**
callous	**verb**	**2-02-002**
calloused	VBN	2-02-002
callously	**RB**	**1-01-001**
callousness	**NN**	**2-02-002**
callus	**noun**	**1-01-001**
calluses	NNS	1-01-001
calm	**JJ**	**22-11-021**
calm	**NN**	**7-04-006**
calm	**verb**	**14-09-013**
calm	VB	6-05-006
calmed	VBD	3-02-003
calmed	VBN	3-03-003
calming	VBG	2-02-002
calmer	**comp. adj.**	**2-02-002**
calmer	JJR	1-01-001
Calmer	JJR-NC	1-01-001
calmest	**JJT**	**1-01-001**
calmly	**RB**	**11-06-009**
calmness	**NN**	**2-02-002**
caloric	**JJ**	**3-01-001**
calorie	**noun**	**8-02-003**
calorie	NN	1-01-001
calories	NNS	7-02-002
calorie-heavy	**JJ**	**1-01-001**
calorimeter	**NN**	**2-01-001**
calorimetric	**JJ**	**1-01-001**
Caltech	**prop. noun**	**2-01-001**
Caltech	NP	1-01-001
Caltech's	NP$	1-01-001

Word	Tag	Frequency
Calude	**NP**	**1-01-001**
calumniate	**verb**	**1-01-001**
calumniated	VBN	1-01-001
calumny	**NN**	**1-01-001**
Calvary	**NP**	**2-01-001**
calve	**verb**	**3-01-001**
calving	VBG	3-01-001
Calvin	**NP**	**4-02-002**
Calvinist	**adjective**	**1-01-001**
Calvinist	JJ	0-00-000
Calvinist	JJ-TL	1-01-001
calypso	**NN**	**1-01-001**
cam	**noun**	**1-01-001**
cams	NNS	1-01-001
Cam	**NP**	**1-01-001**
camaraderie	**NN**	**2-02-002**
Camaret	**NP**	**4-01-001**
Cambodia	**prop. noun**	**2-02-002**
Cambodia	NP	1-01-001
Cambodia's	NP$	1-01-001
Cambridge	**prop. noun**	**15-07-011**
Cambridge	NP	12-06-009
Cambridge	NP-TL	3-03-003
Cambridgeport	**NP**	**1-01-001**
Camden	**prop. noun**	**2-02-002**
Camden	NP	1-01-001
Camden	NP-TL	1-01-001
camel	**noun**	**2-02-002**
camel	NN	1-01-001
camels	NNS	1-01-001
camellia	**noun**	**1-01-001**
camellias	NNS	1-01-001
Camelot	**NP**	**1-01-001**
cameo	**noun**	**2-02-002**
cameo	NN	0-00-000
Cameo	NN-TL	1-01-001
cameos	NNS	1-01-001
cameo-like	**JJ**	**1-01-001**
camera	**noun**	**46-12-025**
camera	NN	34-11-017
Camera	NN-TL	2-02-002
camera's	NN+BEZ	1-01-001
cameras	NNS	9-07-008
cameraman	**noun**	**1-01-001**
cameramen	NNS	1-01-001
Cameron	**NP**	**1-01-001**
Cami	**NP**	**1-01-001**
Camilla	**NP**	**2-02-002**
Camille	**NP**	**1-01-001**
Camilo	**NP**	**1-01-001**
camouflage	**NN**	**2-02-002**
camouflage	**verb**	**3-02-003**
camouflage	VB	1-01-001
camouflaged	VBN	2-02-002
camp	**noun**	**92-10-041**
camp	NN	65-10-030
camp	NN-NC	2-01-001
Camp	NN-TL	6-02-003
camp's	NN$	1-01-001
camps	NNS	18-07-013
camp	**verb**	**20-03-005**
camp	VB	1-01-001
camped	VBN	1-01-001
camping	VBG	18-01-003
Camp	**NP**	**1-01-001**
camp-made	**JJ**	**1-01-001**
campagna	**FW-NN**	**1-01-001**
Campagnoli	**NP**	**1-01-001**
campaign	**noun**	**94-12-041**
campaign	NN	75-12-033
Campaign	NN-TL	1-01-001
campaign's	NN$	1-01-001
campaigns	NNS	17-07-013
campaign	**verb**	**12-05-008**
campaign	VB	5-03-004
campaigned	VBD	4-03-004
campaigning	VBG	3-02-002
Campaigne	**NP**	**1-01-001**
campaigner	**noun**	**2-01-001**
campaigners	NNS	2-01-001
campaigning	**NN**	**1-01-001**
Campbell	**NP**	**4-03-004**
camper	**noun**	**12-01-001**
camper	NN	3-01-001
campers	NNS	8-01-001
campers	NNS-HL	1-01-001
campfire	**NN**	**2-01-002**
campground	**noun**	**5-01-001**
campground	NN	2-01-001

Word	Tag	Frequency
campground (cont.):		
Campground	NN-TL	1-01-001
campgrounds	NNS	2-01-001
camping-out	**JJ**	**1-01-001**
Campitelli	**NP**	**2-01-001**
campmate	**NN**	**1-01-001**
Campo	**NP**	**1-01-001**
Campobello	**prop. noun**	**1-01-001**
Campobello	NP	0-00-000
Campobello	NP-TL	1-01-001
campsite	**noun**	**2-01-001**
campsites	NNS	1-01-001
campsites	NNS-HL	1-01-001
campus	**noun**	**34-07-016**
campus	NN	29-07-012
campus	NN-HL	2-02-002
Campus	NN-TL	2-01-002
campuses	NNS	1-01-001
Camusfearna	**NP**	**4-01-001**
can	**modal aux.**	**2192-15-425**
can	MD	1758-15-401
c'n	MD	1-01-001
kin	MD	1-01-001
can	MD-HL	2-02-002
can	MD-NC	1-01-001
Can	MD-TL	1-01-001
cannot	MD*	258-14-150
can't	MD*	169-14-106
cain't	MD*	1-01-001
can	**noun**	**12-07-008**
can	NN	7-05-005
cans	NNS	5-03-003
can	**verb**	**14-04-004**
can	VB	2-01-001
canned	VBN	5-03-003
canned	VBN-HL	1-01-001
canning	VBG	6-02-002
Canada	**prop. noun**	**35-11-027**
Canada	NP	30-09-022
Canada	NP-HL	1-01-001
Canada	NP-TL	3-03-003
Canada's	NP$	1-01-001
Canadian	**adjective**	**6-05-006**
Canadian	JJ	3-03-003
Canadian	JJ-TL	3-02-003
Canadian	**prop. noun**	**4-03-003**
Canadian	NP	1-01-001
Canadian's	NP$	1-01-001
Canadians	NPS	2-02-002
canal	**noun**	**4-03-004**
canal	NN	0-00-000
Canal	NN-TL	3-03-003
canals	NNS	1-01-001
Canandaigua	**NP**	**1-01-001**
Canaveral	**prop. noun**	**1-01-001**
Canaveral's	NP$	0-00-000
Canaveral's	NP$-TL	1-01-001
cancel	**verb**	**17-10-012**
cancel	VB	7-04-005
cancels	VBZ	1-01-001
canceled	VBD	1-01-001
canceled	VBN	5-03-003
cancelled	VBN	1-01-001
canceling	VBG	1-01-001
cancelling	VBG	1-01-001
cancellation	**NN**	**2-02-002**
cancer	**noun**	**24-07-009**
cancer	NN	20-06-007
Cancer	NN-TL	3-02-003
cancers	NNS	1-01-001
Cancer	**prop. noun**	**2-02-002**
Cancer	NP	0-00-000
Cancer	NP-TL	2-02-002
cancer-ridden	**JJ**	**1-01-001**
candid	**JJ**	**3-03-003**
candidacy	**NN**	**6-03-005**
candidate	**noun**	**73-10-030**
candidate	NN	34-09-020
candidates	NNS	38-08-017
candidates'	NNS$	1-01-001
candidate-picking	**JJ**	**1-01-001**
Candide	**NP**	**1-01-001**
candidly	**RB**	**2-02-002**
candle	**noun**	**23-08-015**
candle	NN	16-06-010
candle	NN-HL	1-01-001
Candle	NN-TL	1-01-001
candles	NNS	5-03-004
candlelight	**noun**	**1-01-001**
candlelight (cont.):		
candlelight	NN	0-00-000
Candlelight	NN-TL	0-00-000
Candlelight	NN-TL-HL	1-01-001
candlestick	**noun**	**1-01-001**
candlestick	NN	0-00-000
Candlestick	NN-TL	1-01-001
candlewick	**NN**	**1-01-001**
candor	**noun**	**3-03-003**
candor	NN	2-02-002
candour	NN	1-01-001
candy	**noun**	**18-07-013**
candy	NN	15-06-011
candy	NN-HL	1-01-001
candies	NNS	2-02-002
cane	**noun**	**13-07-009**
cane	NN	12-07-009
cane's	NN+BEZ	1-01-001
Caneli	**NP**	**1-01-001**
Canestrani	**NP**	**1-01-001**
canine	**NN**	**1-01-001**
canister	**noun**	**3-01-001**
canister	NN	2-01-001
canisters	NNS	1-01-001
canker	**NN**	**1-01-001**
cannery	**noun**	**15-02-002**
cannery	NN	14-01-001
canneries	NNS	0-00-000
Canneries	NNS-TL	1-01-001
cannibal	**noun**	**2-01-001**
cannibal	NN	0-00-000
Cannibal	NN-TL	1-01-001
cannibals	NNS	1-01-001
cannibalistic	**JJ**	**1-01-001**
Canning	**prop. noun**	**1-01-001**
Canning	NP	0-00-000
Canning	NP-TL	1-01-001
cannon	**noun**	**4-02-004**
cannon	NN	3-02-003
cannon	NNS	1-01-001
Cannon	**NP**	**3-02-002**
cannonball	**NN**	**1-01-001**
canny	**JJ**	**2-01-001**
canoe	**noun**	**8-06-006**
canoe	NN	5-04-004
Canoe	NN-TL	1-01-001
canoes	NNS	2-02-002
canoe	**VB**	**1-01-001**
canon	**noun**	**11-05-007**
canon	NN	4-02-003
Canon	NN-TL	1-01-001
canons	NNS	6-04-004
canonist	**JJ**	**1-01-001**
canonize	**verb**	**2-02-002**
canonized	VBN	2-02-002
canopy	**NN**	**2-01-001**
cant	**NN**	**1-01-001**
cant	**verb**	**2-02-002**
canted	VBN	1-01-001
canting	VBG	1-01-001
cantaloupe	**NN**	**1-01-001**
canteen	**NN**	**2-01-001**
Canteloube	**NP**	**1-01-001**
canter	**NN**	**1-01-001**
canter	**verb**	**1-01-001**
cantered	VBD	1-01-001
Canterbury	**prop. noun**	**4-03-003**
Canterbury	NP	0-00-000
Canterbury	NP-TL	4-03-003
canticle	**noun**	**1-01-001**
canticle	NN	0-00-000
Canticle	NN-TL	1-01-001
cantilever	**noun**	**1-01-001**
cantilevers	NNS	1-01-001
cantle	**noun**	**1-01-001**
cantles	NNS	1-01-001
canto	**FW-NN**	**3-02-002**
Cantonese	**NP**	**1-01-001**
cantonment	**NN**	**1-01-001**
Cantor	**NP**	**2-01-001**
Canute	**NP**	**1-01-001**
canvas	**noun**	**27-12-020**
canvas	NN	19-11-016
canvases	NNS	8-04-005
canvass	**NN**	**2-02-002**
canvass	**verb**	**2-02-002**
canvass	VB	1-01-001
canvassed	VBN	1-01-001
canvasser	**noun**	**2-01-001**

Word	Tag	Frequency
canvasser (cont.):		
canvassers	NNS	2-01-001
canvassing	**NN**	**1-01-001**
canyon	**noun**	**14-05-009**
canyon	NN	6-02-005
Canyon	NN-TL	6-03-003
canyons	NNS	2-02-002
canyonside	**NN**	**1-01-001**
cap	**noun**	**22-10-019**
cap	NN	17-08-015
caps	NNS	5-05-005
cap	**verb**	**6-03-004**
cap	VB	3-01-001
caps	VBZ	1-01-001
capped	VBD	1-01-001
capped	VBN	1-01-001
Cap	**NP**	**7-03-003**
cap-and-ball	**NN**	**1-01-001**
capability	**noun**	**36-06-016**
capability	NN	14-04-005
capabilities	NNS	22-05-012
capable	**JJ**	**66-14-050**
capably	**QL**	**1-01-001**
capacious	**JJ**	**1-01-001**
capacitance	**NN**	**1-01-001**
capacitor	**noun**	**3-02-003**
capacitor	NN	2-02-002
capacitors	NNS	1-01-001
capacity	**noun**	**88-14-056**
capacity	NN	83-14-052
capacities	NNS	5-03-005
cape	**noun**	**24-10-017**
cape	NN	3-03-003
Cape	NN-TL	17-09-013
capes	NNS	4-03-004
Capek	**prop. noun**	**1-01-001**
Capek's	NP$	1-01-001
Capellan	**JJ**	**1-01-001**
capello	**foreign**	**1-01-001**
capello	FW-NN	0-00-000
Capello	FW-NN-TL	1-01-001
caper	**noun**	**7-03-003**
caper	NN	1-01-001
Caper	NN-TL	5-01-001
capers	NNS	1-01-001
caper	**verb**	**1-01-001**
capering	VBG	1-01-001
capercailzie	**NN**	**1-01-001**
Capet	**NP**	**2-01-001**
Capetown	**NP**	**1-01-001**
capillary	**NN**	**8-01-004**
Capistrano	**NP**	**1-01-001**
capita	**NNS**	**16-03-003**
capital	**JJ**	**2-02-002**
capital	**noun**	**90-10-041**
capital	NN	78-10-036
capital	NN-HL	2-02-002
Capital	NN-TL	3-03-003
capital's	NN$	3-02-002
capitals	NNS	4-02-002
capital-gain	**noun**	**1-01-001**
capital-gains	NNS	1-01-001
capitalism	**noun**	**14-06-010**
capitalism	NN	10-04-008
capitalism	NN-NC	1-01-001
Capitalism	NN-TL	3-02-002
capitalist	**adjective**	**2-02-002**
capitalist	JJ	1-01-001
Capitalist	JJ	1-01-001
capitalist	**noun**	**7-06-006**
capitalist	NN	4-03-003
capitalists	NNS	2-02-002
capitalists'	NNS$	1-01-001
capitalist-democratic	**JJ**	**1-01-001**
capitalistic	**JJ**	**2-01-002**
capitalize	**verb**	**6-05-005**
capitalize	VB	4-04-004
capitalizing	VBG	2-02-002
capitol	**noun**	**22-05-012**
capitol	NN	1-01-001
Capitol	NN-TL	21-05-011
Capitoline	**prop. noun**	**1-01-001**
Capitoline	NP	0-00-000
Capitoline	NP-TL	1-01-001
capitulate	**verb**	**2-01-002**
capitulated	VBD	2-01-002
capitulation	**NN**	**2-01-001**
Capo	**NP**	**2-01-001**
Capone	**prop. noun**	**7-02-003**

Word	Tag	Frequency
Capone (cont.):		
Capone	NP	6-02-002
Capone's	NP$	1-01-001
Capote	**NP**	**1-01-001**
Cappy	**prop. noun**	**13-01-001**
Cappy	NP	12-01-001
Cappy's	NP$	1-01-001
capricious	**JJ**	**1-01-001**
Capricorn	**prop. noun**	**1-01-001**
Capricorn	NP	0-00-000
Capricorn	NP-TL	1-01-001
capsicum	**NN**	**1-01-001**
capstan	**NN**	**1-01-001**
capsule	**noun**	**8-06-006**
capsule	NN	5-04-004
capsules	NNS	3-02-002
captain	**noun**	**99-10-027**
captain	NN	45-10-018
cap'n	NN	1-01-001
capt.	NN	0-00-000
Capt.	NN-TL	5-02-004
Captain	NN-TL	40-08-013
captain's	NN$	6-04-004
Captain's	NN$-TL	1-01-001
captains	NNS	1-01-001
captaincy	**NN**	**1-01-001**
caption	**noun**	**1-01-001**
captions	NNS	1-01-001
captious	**JJ**	**1-01-001**
captivate	**verb**	**2-02-002**
captivated	VBD	1-01-001
captivated	VBN	1-01-001
captivating	**JJ**	**2-02-002**
captive	**JJ**	**3-03-003**
captive	**noun**	**4-03-004**
captive	NN	2-02-002
captives	NNS	2-02-002
captivity	**NN**	**4-03-003**
captor	**noun**	**2-01-002**
captors	NNS	2-01-002
capture	**noun**	**5-03-005**
capture	NN	4-03-004
captures	NNS	1-01-001
capture	**verb**	**33-11-027**
capture	VB	13-07-013
captures	VBZ	1-01-001
captured	VBD	2-01-002
captured	VBN	15-09-012
capturing	VBG	2-02-002
car	**noun**	**393-14-101**
car	NN	270-13-078
car	NN-HL	1-01-001
Car	NN-TL	3-03-003
car's	NN$	7-05-005
cars	NNS	112-13-048
carabao	**FW-NN**	**1-01-001**
Caracas	**NP**	**1-01-001**
caramel	**NN**	**1-01-001**
Carausius	**NP**	**1-01-001**
Caravaggio	**NP**	**2-02-002**
caravan	**noun**	**5-04-004**
caravan	NN	3-03-003
caravans	NNS	2-02-002
Caravan	**prop. noun**	**6-01-001**
Caravan	NP	5-01-001
Caravan's	NP$	1-01-001
caraway	**NN**	**2-02-002**
carbide	**NN**	**2-01-001**
carbine	**noun**	**8-04-005**
carbine	NN	6-02-003
carbines	NNS	2-02-002
carbohydrate	**NN**	**1-01-001**
Carboloy	**NP**	**2-01-001**
carbon	**noun**	**32-03-007**
carbon	NN	28-03-007
carbon	NN-HL	1-01-001
Carbon	NN-TL	1-01-001
carbons	NNS	2-01-001
carbon-halogen	**NN**	**1-01-001**
carbon-14	**NN**	**1-01-001**
carbonate	**noun**	**1-01-001**
carbonates	NNS	1-01-001
Carbondale	**prop. noun**	**2-01-001**
Carbondale	NP	1-01-001
Carbondale	NP-TL	1-01-001
Carbone	**prop. noun**	**1-01-001**
Carbones	NPS	1-01-001
carbonyl	**NN**	**2-01-001**
carborundum	**NN**	**1-01-001**

Word	Tag	Frequency
carboxy-labeled	**JJ**	**1-01-001**
carboxymethyl	**NN**	**1-01-001**
carcass	**noun**	**8-06-006**
carcass	NN	7-05-005
carcasses	NNS	1-01-001
carcinoma	**NN**	**1-01-001**
card	**noun**	**61-13-033**
card	NN	26-09-018
cards	NNS	32-11-020
cards	NNS-HL	1-01-001
Cards	NNS-TL	2-02-002
Card	**prop. noun**	**1-01-001**
Cards	NPS	1-01-001
cardamom	**NN**	**1-01-001**
cardboard	**NN**	**5-04-005**
cardiac	**JJ**	**1-01-001**
cardinal	**JJ**	**7-06-007**
cardinal	**noun**	**16-07-010**
cardinal	NN	1-01-001
Cardinal	NN-TL	7-05-006
cardinals	NNS	3-02-003
Cardinals	NNS-TL	5-02-003
cardiomegaly	**NN**	**1-01-001**
cardiovascular	**JJ**	**1-01-001**
cardiovasculatory	**adjective**	**1-01-001**
cardiovasculatory	JJ	0-00-000
Cardiovasculatory	JJ-TL	1-01-001
care	**noun**	**89-15-064**
care	NN	86-15-062
kare	NN	0-00-000
Kare	NN-TL	1-01-001
care	NN-HL	1-01-001
cares	NNS	1-01-001
care	**verb**	**108-15-067**
care	VB	75-14-050
cares	VBZ	7-06-007
Cares	VBZ-TL	1-01-001
cared	VBD	9-07-008
cared	VBN	6-04-006
caring	VBG	10-06-009
careen	**verb**	**2-02-002**
careened	VBD	1-01-001
careening	VBG	1-01-001
career	**noun**	**82-13-053**
career	NN	67-13-046
carreer	NN	1-01-001
careers	NNS	14-07-011
career-bound	**JJ**	**1-01-001**
careerism	**NN**	**1-01-001**
carefree	**adjective**	**10-04-007**
carefree	JJ	9-04-007
care-free	JJ	1-01-001
careful	**JJ**	**62-14-056**
carefully	**RB**	**87-13-069**
carefulness	**NN**	**1-01-001**
careless	**adjective**	**8-06-008**
careless	JJ	7-06-007
Careless	JJ-TL	1-01-001
carelessly	**RB**	**3-03-003**
carelessness	**NN**	**2-02-002**
caress	**noun**	**5-03-003**
caresses	NNS	5-03-003
caress	**verb**	**10-05-009**
caress	VB	1-01-001
caressed	VBD	3-02-002
caressed	VBN	1-01-001
caressing	VBG	5-03-005
caretaker	**NN**	**1-01-001**
careworn	**JJ**	**1-01-001**
Carey	**prop. noun**	**5-01-003**
Carey	NP	4-01-003
Carey	NP-HL	1-01-001
Cargill	**prop. noun**	**1-01-001**
Cargill's	NP$	1-01-001
cargo	**noun**	**7-04-005**
cargo	NN	6-04-005
Cargo	NN-TL	1-01-001
Caribbean	**prop. noun**	**7-05-005**
Caribbean	NP	6-04-004
Caribbean	NP-TL	1-01-001
caricature	**NN**	**1-01-001**
caricature	**verb**	**2-02-002**
caricature	VB	1-01-001
caricatured	VBN	1-01-001
caricaturist	**NN**	**1-01-001**
Carl	**prop. noun**	**45-07-014**
Carl	NP	41-07-014
Carl's	NP$	4-01-001
Carla	**prop. noun**	**17-03-003**
Carla (cont.):		
Carla	NP	15-03-003
Carla's	NP$	2-01-001
Carleton	**prop. noun**	**30-02-002**
Carleton	NP	12-01-001
Carleton	NP-TL	17-01-001
Carleton's	NP$	1-01-001
Carletonian	**NP**	**1-01-001**
Carlisle	**NP**	**1-01-001**
Carlo	**prop. noun**	**2-02-002**
Carlo	NP	1-01-001
Carlo	NP-TL	1-01-001
carload	**noun**	**4-03-003**
carload	NN	3-02-002
carloads	NNS	1-01-001
carloading	**NN**	**1-01-001**
Carlson	**NP**	**3-02-002**
Carlyle	**prop. noun**	**1-01-001**
Carlyle's	NP$	1-01-001
Carmack	**NP**	**2-01-001**
Carmen	**prop. noun**	**2-01-002**
Carmen	NP	1-01-001
Carmen	NP-TL	1-01-001
Carmer	**prop. noun**	**13-01-001**
Carmer	NP	10-01-001
Carmer's	NP$	3-01-001
Carmichael	**NP**	**2-02-002**
Carmine	**prop. noun**	**2-02-002**
Carmine	NP	1-01-001
Carmine	NP-TL	1-01-001
Carmody	**NP**	**2-01-001**
carnal	**JJ**	**2-02-002**
carnality	**NN**	**1-01-001**
Carnarvon	**prop. noun**	**1-01-001**
Carnarvon's	NP$	0-00-000
Carnarvon's	NP$-TL	1-01-001
carne	**FW-NN**	**3-01-001**
Carnegey	**NP**	**2-01-001**
Carnegie	**prop. noun**	**9-04-006**
Carnegie	NP	3-02-002
Carneigie	NP	1-01-001
Carnegie	NP-TL	5-02-004
Carnegie-Illinois	**NP**	**1-01-001**
Carney	**NP**	**1-01-001**
carnival	**noun**	**9-05-006**
carnival	NN	2-02-002
Carnival	NN-TL	7-04-004
Carnochan	**NP**	**1-01-001**
carob	**FW-NN**	**1-01-001**
carol	**noun**	**1-01-001**
carols	NNS	0-00-000
Carols	NNS-TL	1-01-001
Carol	**NP**	**2-01-001**
Caroli	**NP**	**3-01-001**
Carolina	**prop. noun**	**27-07-016**
Carolina	NP	8-02-002
Carolina	NP-TL	17-06-014
Carolina's	NP$	1-01-001
Carolinas	NPS	1-01-001
Caroline	**NP**	**2-02-002**
Carolingian	**JJ**	**1-01-001**
Carolinian	**prop. noun**	**3-02-002**
Carolinians	NPS	2-01-001
Carolinians	NPS-TL	1-01-001
Carolyn	**NP**	**1-01-001**
Caron	**NP**	**1-01-001**
carouse	**verb**	**1-01-001**
carousing	VBG	1-01-001
carousing	**NN**	**1-01-001**
carp	**verb**	**2-02-002**
carping	VBG	2-02-002
Carpathian	**prop. noun**	**1-01-001**
Carpathians	NPS	1-01-001
carpenter	**noun**	**11-05-006**
carpenter	NN	6-03-003
carpenter's	NN$	1-01-001
carpenters	NNS	3-03-003
carpenters'	NNS$	1-01-001
Carpenter	**prop. noun**	**2-01-001**
Carpenter's	NP$	2-01-001
Carpentier	**NP**	**1-01-001**
carpentry	**NN**	**4-03-003**
carpet	**noun**	**17-08-011**
carpet	NN	13-06-009
carpets	NNS	4-03-003
carpet	**verb**	**3-02-003**
carpeted	VBN	3-02-003
carpeting	**NN**	**2-02-002**
carping	**NN**	**1-01-001**

Word	Tag	Frequency
carport	**NN**	**2-01-002**
Carr	**NP**	**2-02-002**
Carrara	**NP**	**1-01-001**
Carraway	**NP**	**3-01-001**
carre	**foreign**	**1-01-001**
carre	FW-NN	0-00-000
Carre	FW-NN-TL	1-01-001
Carre	**NP**	**1-01-001**
Carrel	**NP**	**1-01-001**
Carreon	**prop. noun**	**2-01-001**
Carreon	NP	1-01-001
Carreon's	NP$	1-01-001
carriage	**noun**	**17-06-012**
carriage	NN	11-04-007
carriages	NNS	5-05-005
Carriages	NNS	1-01-001
carriage-step	**NN**	**1-01-001**
Carrie	**NP**	**1-01-001**
carrier	**noun**	**20-09-012**
carrier	NN	9-06-006
carriers	NNS	10-06-008
carriers	NNS-HL	1-01-001
carrier-based	**JJ**	**1-01-001**
carrier-current	**JJ**	**1-01-001**
Carroll	**NP**	**17-04-008**
carrot	**noun**	**5-03-004**
carrot	NN	1-01-001
carrots	NNS	3-02-002
Carrots	NNS-TL	1-01-001
carrozza	**FW-NN**	**1-01-001**
Carruthers	**NP**	**5-02-003**
carry	**verb**	**304-15-197**
carry	VB	88-13-075
carries	VBZ	22-09-020
carried	VBD	60-10-049
carried	VBN	65-11-053
carrying	VBG	69-14-058
carrying	**NN**	**2-01-002**
carryover	**noun**	**13-03-003**
carryover	NN	11-02-002
carryover	NN-HL	1-01-001
carryovers	NNS	1-01-001
Carson	**NP**	**2-02-002**
Carsten	**NP**	**1-01-001**
cart	**noun**	**9-06-006**
cart	NN	4-03-003
carts	NNS	5-03-003
cart	**verb**	**2-01-002**
cart	VB	1-01-001
carted	VBN	1-01-001
carte	**NN**	**1-01-001**
cartel	**noun**	**1-01-001**
cartels	NNS	1-01-001
Carter	**prop. noun**	**8-06-006**
Carter	NP	7-05-005
Carters	NPS	1-01-001
Cartesian	**JJ**	**1-01-001**
Carthage	**NP**	**1-01-001**
Carthago	**FW-NP**	**1-01-001**
cartilage	**NN**	**2-02-002**
carton	**noun**	**1-01-001**
cartons	NNS	1-01-001
cartoon	**noun**	**9-05-007**
cartoon	NN	3-03-003
cartoons	NNS	6-04-005
cartoonist	**noun**	**4-02-002**
cartoonist	NN	3-01-001
cartoonists	NNS	1-01-001
cartridge	**noun**	**11-04-007**
cartridge	NN	6-03-004
cartridges	NNS	5-04-004
cartwheel	**noun**	**2-02-002**
cartwheels	NNS	2-02-002
Carty	**NP**	**1-01-001**
Caruso	**NP**	**2-02-002**
Carvalho	**NP**	**2-02-002**
carve	**verb**	**23-08-020**
carve	VB	3-02-003
carved	VBN	14-07-013
carving	VBG	6-04-004
carved-out-of-solid	**JJ**	**1-01-001**
carven	**JJ**	**1-01-001**
carver	**NN**	**1-01-001**
Carvey	**NP**	**5-01-001**
carving	**noun**	**2-02-002**
carvings	NNS	2-02-002
Carwood	**prop. noun**	**3-01-001**
Carwood	NP	2-01-001
Carwood's	NP$	1-01-001

Word	Tag	Frequency
caryatid	**noun**	**1-01-001**
caryatides	NNS	1-01-001
Casals	**NP**	**1-01-001**
Casanova	**NP**	**2-01-001**
Casassa	**NP**	**2-02-002**
Casbah	**prop. noun**	**3-01-001**
Casbah	NP	2-01-001
Casbah	NP-TL	1-01-001
Casca	**NP**	**1-01-001**
cascade	**verb**	**6-03-003**
cascade	VB	1-01-001
cascades	VBZ	1-01-001
cascaded	VBN	1-01-001
cascading	VBG	3-01-001
case	**noun**	**503-15-235**
case	NN	349-15-196
case	NN-HL	4-03-004
Case	NN-TL	2-02-002
cases	NNS	146-14-093
cases	NNS-HL	2-02-002
case	**verb**	**3-03-003**
case	VB	2-02-002
cased	VBD	1-01-001
Case	**prop. noun**	**6-02-004**
Case	NP	4-02-003
Case	NP-TL	1-01-001
Case's	NP$	1-01-001
case-by-case	**JJ**	**1-01-001**
case-hardened	**JJ**	**1-01-001**
case-history	**NN**	**2-01-002**
case-to-case	**JJ**	**1-01-001**
casebook	**NN**	**1-01-001**
casein	**NN**	**1-01-001**
casework	**NN**	**13-01-001**
caseworker	**noun**	**1-01-001**
caseworkers	NNS	1-01-001
Casey	**prop. noun**	**25-03-007**
Casey	NP	23-03-007
Casey's	NP$	2-01-001
cash	**noun**	**32-11-024**
cash	NN	31-11-023
Cash	NN-HL	1-01-001
cash	**verb**	**3-02-002**
cash	VB	2-02-002
cashed	VBD	1-01-001
Cash	**NP**	**2-01-001**
cashew	**noun**	**1-01-001**
cashews	NNS	1-01-001
cashmere	**NN**	**2-02-002**
casino	**noun**	**3-03-003**
casino	NN	1-01-001
Casino	NN-TL	1-01-001
casino's	NN$	1-01-001
cask	**noun**	**2-02-002**
cask	NN	1-01-001
casks	NNS	1-01-001
casket	**noun**	**1-01-001**
caskets	NNS	1-01-001
Cassiopeia	**NP**	**1-01-001**
Cassite	**JJ**	**1-01-001**
Cassius	**NP**	**1-01-001**
cassocked	**JJ**	**1-01-001**
cast	**noun**	**26-09-016**
cast	NN	23-07-013
casts	NNS	3-03-003
cast	**verb**	**28-12-025**
cast	VB	6-03-005
casts	VBZ	3-02-003
cast	VBD	4-04-004
cast	VBN	12-06-010
casting	VBG	3-03-003
cast-iron	**NN**	**1-01-001**
Castaneda	**NP**	**2-01-001**
castanet	**noun**	**1-01-001**
castanets	NNS	1-01-001
caste	**NN**	**3-03-003**
caster	**noun**	**1-01-001**
casters	NNS	1-01-001
castigate	**verb**	**2-01-002**
castigates	VBZ	1-01-001
castigated	VBD	1-01-001
castigation	**NN**	**1-01-001**
Castillo	**NP**	**1-01-001**
casting	**NN**	**1-01-001**
castle	**noun**	**12-05-012**
castle	NN	6-04-006
Castle	NN-TL	2-02-002
castles	NNS	3-03-003
Castles	NNS-TL	1-01-001

Word	Tag	Frequency
castor	**NN**	**2-01-001**
castorbean	**noun**	**2-01-001**
castorbean	NN	1-01-001
castorbeans	NNS	1-01-001
Castro	**prop. noun**	**39-05-016**
Castro	NP	31-05-014
Castro	NP-TL	1-01-001
Castro's	NP$	5-04-004
Castros	NPS	2-01-002
Castro-held	**JJ**	**1-01-001**
Castroism	**NP**	**2-01-001**
casual	**JJ**	**22-12-021**
casual	**noun**	**1-01-001**
casuals	NNS	1-01-001
casually	**RB**	**13-07-013**
casualty	**noun**	**6-04-005**
casualty	NN	2-01-001
Casualty	NN-TL	1-01-001
casualties	NNS	3-02-003
cat	**noun**	**42-10-025**
cat	NN	20-09-013
cat	NN-NC	2-01-001
Cat	NN-TL	1-01-001
cat's	NN$	1-01-001
cats	NNS	17-06-010
Cats	NNS-TL	1-01-001
cat-like	**JJ**	**1-01-001**
cataclysmic	**JJ**	**1-01-001**
catalogue	**noun**	**16-09-011**
catalogue	NN	8-05-006
catalog	NN	1-01-001
Catalog	NN-TL	2-01-001
catalogues	NNS	3-03-003
catalogs	NNS	2-01-001
catalogue	**verb**	**4-04-004**
catalogued	VBD	1-01-001
catalogued	VBN	3-03-003
catalyst	**noun**	**5-02-002**
catalyst	NN	3-02-002
catalysts	NNS	2-01-001
catalytic	**JJ**	**2-02-002**
catapult	**verb**	**4-04-004**
catapults	VBZ	1-01-001
catapulted	VBD	1-01-001
catapulted	VBN	1-01-001
catapulting	VBG	1-01-001
catastrophe	**noun**	**16-09-014**
catastrophe	NN	10-07-010
Catastrophe	NN-TL	1-01-001
catastrophes	NNS	5-03-004
catastrophic	**JJ**	**5-03-003**
catastrophically	**QL**	**1-01-001**
catastrophically	**RB**	**1-01-001**
Catatonia	**NP**	**7-01-001**
catch	**noun**	**5-05-005**
catch	NN	3-03-003
catch	NN-HL	1-01-001
catches	NNS	1-01-001
catch	**verb**	**146-14-103**
catch	VB	39-12-033
catchee	VB	1-01-001
catches	VBZ	1-01-001
caught	VBD	54-11-043
caught	VBN	44-13-040
catching	VBG	7-04-007
catcher	**noun**	**19-04-006**
catcher	NN	16-03-004
Catcher	NN-TL	1-01-001
catcher's	NN$	1-01-001
catchers	NNS	1-01-001
catching	**NN**	**2-02-002**
catchup	**NN**	**1-01-001**
catchword	**noun**	**1-01-001**
catchwords	NNS	1-01-001
catchy	**JJ**	**1-01-001**
Cate	**prop. noun**	**2-01-001**
Cate's	NP$	1-01-001
Cate's	NP$-TL	1-01-001
catechism	**NN**	**2-02-002**
catechize	**VB**	**1-01-001**
catecholamine	**noun**	**1-01-001**
catecholamines	NNS	1-01-001
categorical	**JJ**	**3-01-003**
categorically	**RB**	**1-01-001**
categorize	**verb**	**3-03-003**
categorize	VB	1-01-001
categorized	VBN	1-01-001
categorizing	VBG	1-01-001
category	**noun**	**47-10-034**
category (cont.):		
category	NN	23-08-017
categories	NNS	24-07-021
cater	**verb**	**7-05-007**
cater	VB	3-02-003
catered	VBD	1-01-001
catering	VBG	3-03-003
Cater	**NP**	**1-01-001**
caterer	**noun**	**1-01-001**
caterer's	NN$	1-01-001
caterpillar	**noun**	**2-01-002**
caterpillar	NN	1-01-001
caterpillars	NNS	1-01-001
catfish	**noun**	**2-01-001**
catfish	NN	0-00-000
Catfish	NN-TL	2-01-001
catharsis	**NN**	**5-03-004**
cathedral	**noun**	**11-06-011**
cathedral	NN	6-04-006
Cathedral	NN-TL	2-02-002
cathedrals	NNS	3-03-003
Cather	**prop. noun**	**1-01-001**
Cather	NP	0-00-000
Catheter	NP	1-01-001
Catherine	**prop. noun**	**7-04-005**
Catherine	NP	5-04-005
Catherine's	NP$	2-01-001
Catherwood	**NP**	**2-01-001**
catheter	**NN**	**2-01-001**
cathode	**NN**	**10-01-002**
cathodoluminescent	**JJ**	**4-01-001**
cathodophoretic	**JJ**	**1-01-001**
Catholic	**adjective**	**83-08-021**
Catholic	JJ	74-08-020
Catholic	JJ-TL	9-04-007
Catholic	**prop. noun**	**35-06-012**
Catholic	NP	1-01-001
Catholics	NPS	32-06-010
Catholics	NPS-TL	1-01-001
Catholics'	NPS$	1-01-001
Catholicism	**noun**	**8-03-004**
Catholicism	NN	6-03-003
Catholicism	NN-TL	2-01-002
Cathy	**prop. noun**	**21-02-002**
Cathy	NP	20-02-002
Cathy's	NP$	1-01-001
Catinari	**prop. noun**	**1-01-001**
Catinari	NP	0-00-000
Catinari	NP-TL	1-01-001
catkin	**noun**	**7-01-001**
catkin	NN	2-01-001
catkins	NNS	5-01-001
catlike	**JJ**	**1-01-001**
Caton	**prop. noun**	**1-01-001**
Caton's	NP$	1-01-001
Catskill	**prop. noun**	**7-04-004**
Catskill	NP	5-02-002
Catskills	NPS	2-02-002
catsup	**NN**	**3-01-002**
Catt	**NP**	**4-01-001**
cattaloe	**NN**	**1-01-001**
cattle	**noun**	**97-09-020**
cattle	NNS	94-09-020
cattle	NNS-HL	3-01-001
cattle-car	**NN**	**1-01-001**
cattleman	**noun**	**3-02-002**
cattlemen	NNS	3-02-002
Caucasian	**JJ**	**1-01-001**
Caucasus	**NP**	**1-01-001**
caucus	**noun**	**3-01-001**
caucus	NN	2-01-001
caucuses	NNS	1-01-001
caucus	**verb**	**1-01-001**
caucusing	VBG	1-01-001
Cauffman	**NP**	**1-01-001**
cauliflower	**NN**	**1-01-001**
causal	**JJ**	**6-01-001**
causally	**RB**	**1-01-001**
causative	**JJ**	**1-01-001**
cause	**noun**	**109-14-076**
cause	NN	78-13-061
causes	NNS	28-08-021
causes	NNS-HL	2-01-001
Causes	NNS-TL	1-01-001
cause	**verb**	**186-15-124**
cause	VB	52-11-042
causes	VBZ	27-08-019
caused	VBD	39-14-034
caused	VBN	51-10-039

Word	Tag	Frequency
cause (cont.):		
causing	VBG	17-09-016
cause-and-effect	**JJ**	**2-02-002**
causing	**NN**	**1-01-001**
cauterize	**VB**	**1-01-001**
caution	**noun**	**18-07-013**
caution	NN	13-07-012
caution	NN-HL	5-01-001
caution	**verb**	**8-06-007**
caution	VB	1-01-001
cautions	VBZ	1-01-001
cautioned	VBD	6-05-005
cautious	**JJ**	**10-06-010**
cautiously	**RB**	**9-04-009**
Cav	**prop. noun**	**2-01-001**
Cav	NP	0-00-000
Cav	NP-TL	1-01-001
Cav's	NP$	0-00-000
Cav's	NP$-TL	1-01-001
cavalcade	**noun**	**1-01-001**
cavalcades	NNS	1-01-001
cavaliere	**foreign**	**1-01-001**
cavaliere	FW-NN	0-00-000
Cavaliere	FW-NN-TL	1-01-001
Cavallini	**prop. noun**	**1-01-001**
Cavallinis	NPS	1-01-001
cavalry	**noun**	**26-06-008**
cavalry	NN	16-05-006
Cavalry	NN-TL	10-03-004
cavalryman	**noun**	**1-01-001**
cavalrymen	NNS	1-01-001
Cavanagh	**prop. noun**	**2-01-001**
Cavanagh	NP	1-01-001
Cavanagh	NP-HL	1-01-001
cave	**noun**	**15-08-011**
cave	NN	9-05-007
caves	NNS	5-04-004
Caves	NNS-TL	1-01-001
cave	**verb**	**3-02-002**
caved	VBN	1-01-001
caving	VBG	1-01-001
cavin	VBG	1-01-001
cave-like	**JJ**	**1-01-001**
caveat	**NN**	**1-01-001**
caveman	**noun**	**2-01-002**
cavemen	NNS	1-01-001
cave-men	NNS	1-01-001
cavern	**noun**	**2-02-002**
cavern	NN	1-01-001
caverns	NNS	0-00-000
Caverns	NNS-TL	1-01-001
cavernous	**JJ**	**1-01-001**
caviar	**NN**	**1-01-001**
cavity	**noun**	**13-04-005**
cavity	NN	12-03-004
cavities	NNS	1-01-001
cavort	**verb**	**3-02-002**
cavort	VB	1-01-001
cavorted	VBD	1-01-001
cavorting	VBG	1-01-001
cavorting	**NN**	**1-01-001**
caw	**verb**	**1-01-001**
cawing	VBG	1-01-001
cayenne	**NN**	**2-01-001**
cc.	**NNS**	**4-02-002**
cease	**verb**	**32-11-030**
cease	VB	15-06-015
ceases	VBZ	3-03-003
ceased	VBD	8-06-008
ceased	VBN	4-04-004
ceasing	VBG	2-02-002
cease-fire	**NN**	**7-02-004**
ceaseless	**JJ**	**3-02-003**
ceaselessly	**RB**	**1-01-001**
Cecil	**NP**	**1-01-001**
Cecilia	**NP**	**3-02-003**
Cedar	**prop. noun**	**1-01-001**
Cedar	NP	0-00-000
Cedar	NP-TL	1-01-001
cedar-roofed	**JJ**	**1-01-001**
Cedric	**NP**	**3-03-003**
Cedvet	**NP**	**1-01-001**
Ceecee	**NP**	**2-01-001**
Ceil	**NP**	**1-01-001**
ceiling	**noun**	**32-10-022**
ceiling	NN	31-10-022
ceilings	NNS	1-01-001
Celebes	**prop. noun**	**1-01-001**
Celebes	NP	0-00-000

Word	Tag	Frequency
Celebes (cont.):		
Celebes	NP-TL	1-01-001
celebrant	**noun**	**2-02-002**
celebrants	NNS	2-02-002
celebrate	**verb**	**25-11-022**
celebrate	VB	4-03-004
celebrates	VBZ	2-02-002
celebrated	VBD	5-05-005
celebrated	VBN	9-07-009
celebrating	VBG	5-05-005
celebration	**noun**	**17-10-016**
celebration	NN	14-08-013
Celebration	NN-TL	1-01-001
celebrations	NNS	2-02-002
celebrity	**noun**	**6-04-004**
celebrity	NN	3-01-001
celebrities	NNS	3-03-003
celerity	**NN**	**1-01-001**
celery	**NN**	**4-03-004**
celestial	**JJ**	**8-03-004**
Celia	**NP**	**1-01-001**
celiac	**JJ**	**1-01-001**
Celie	**prop. noun**	**2-01-001**
Celie	NP	1-01-001
Celie's	NP+HVZ	1-01-001
cell	**noun**	**146-10-026**
cell	NN	65-06-018
cells	NNS	81-06-013
cell-free	**JJ**	**4-01-001**
cellar	**noun**	**27-07-010**
cellar	NN	26-07-010
cellars	NNS	1-01-001
cellist	**noun**	**2-02-002**
cellist	NN	1-01-001
Cellist	NN-TL	1-01-001
cellophane	**NN**	**1-01-001**
cellular	**JJ**	**3-02-002**
cellulose	**noun**	**11-02-004**
cellulose	NN	10-02-004
celluloses	NNS	1-01-001
Celso	**NP**	**1-01-001**
Celtic	**JJ**	**7-01-002**
Cemal	**NP**	**1-01-001**
cement	**noun**	**10-06-010**
cement	NN	9-05-009
Cement	NN-TL	1-01-001
cement	**verb**	**5-04-004**
cement	VB	1-01-001
cemented	VBN	4-03-003
cement-and-glass	**JJ**	**1-01-001**
cemetery	**noun**	**15-06-010**
cemetery	NN	11-05-007
Cemetery	NN-TL	4-04-004
Cennini	**NP**	**1-01-001**
Cennino	**NP**	**1-01-001**
censor	**noun**	**1-01-001**
censors	NNS	1-01-001
censor	**verb**	**3-02-003**
censors	VBZ	1-01-001
censored	VBN	2-02-002
censorial	**JJ**	**1-01-001**
censorship	**NN**	**5-02-004**
censure	**noun**	**5-03-005**
censure	NN	3-03-003
censures	NNS	2-01-002
censure	**verb**	**1-01-001**
censured	VBD	1-01-001
census	**noun**	**14-04-006**
census	NN	8-03-004
Census	NN-TL	3-02-002
censuses	NNS	3-01-001
cent	**noun**	**181-12-064**
cent	NN	155-11-052
cents	NNS	26-09-015
centenary	**NN**	**1-01-001**
centennial	**noun**	**8-06-007**
centennial	NN	3-03-003
Centennial	NN-TL	3-03-003
Cen-Tennial	NN-TL	2-01-001
center	**JJ**	**3-03-003**
center	**noun**	**261-15-128**
center	NN	176-15-097
centre	NN	2-01-001
Center	NN-TL	36-10-023
center's	NN$	1-01-001
Center's	NN$-TL	1-01-001
centers	NNS	44-09-027
centers	NNS-HL	1-01-001
center	**verb**	**34-10-026**

Word	Tag	Count
center (cont.):		
center	VB	9-04-007
centers	VBZ	7-04-006
centered	VBD	5-03-005
centered	VBN	9-04-006
centering	VBG	4-04-004
center-fire	**NN**	**1-01-001**
center-punch	**VB**	**2-01-001**
centering	**NN**	**1-01-001**
centerline	**NN**	**1-01-001**
Centigrade	**NP**	**1-01-001**
centimeter	**noun**	**23-02-005**
centimeter	NN	2-01-001
centimeter-	NN	1-01-001
cm.	NN	5-02-003
centimeters	NNS	8-01-001
cm.	NNS	7-01-002
central	**adjective**	**165-12-084**
central	JJ	108-12-063
central	JJ-HL	1-01-001
Central	JJ-TL	56-10-029
central	**noun**	**2-01-001**
central's	NN$	0-00-000
Central's	NN$-TL	2-01-001
central-city	**NN**	**2-01-001**
centrale	**foreign**	**1-01-001**
centrale	FW-JJ	0-00-000
Centrale	FW-JJ-TL	1-01-001
Centralia	**NP**	**1-01-001**
centrality	**noun**	**4-01-001**
centrality	NN	0-00-000
centrality	NN-HL	1-01-001
Centrality	NN-TL	3-01-001
centralization	**NN**	**4-03-003**
centralize	**verb**	**11-05-008**
centralized	VBD	1-01-001
centralized	VBN	8-04-005
centralizing	VBG	2-02-002
centrally	**QL**	**1-01-001**
centrally	**RB**	**5-01-004**
Centredale	**NP**	**1-01-001**
centric	**JJ**	**1-01-001**
centrifugal	**adjective**	**1-01-001**
centrifugal	JJ	0-00-000
centrifugal	JJ-HL	1-01-001
centrifugation	**NN**	**2-01-002**
centrifuge	**NN**	**2-01-001**
centrifuge	**verb**	**8-01-001**
centrifuged	VBN	7-01-001
centrifuging	VBG	1-01-001
centrist	**NN**	**1-01-001**
cents-per-hour	**JJ**	**2-01-001**
centum	**NN**	**6-01-002**
centuries-old	**JJ**	**2-02-002**
century	**noun**	**254-15-107**
century	NN	183-15-082
century	NN-HL	1-01-001
Century	NN-TL	23-08-015
century	NN-TL	1-01-001
centuries	NNS	46-10-031
Cepheus	**NP**	**1-01-001**
ceramic	**JJ**	**9-04-005**
ceramics	**NN**	**3-03-003**
cereal	**noun**	**21-02-003**
cereal	NN	16-02-003
cereal	NN-HL	1-01-001
cereals	NNS	4-01-002
cerebellum	**NN**	**1-01-001**
cerebral	**adjective**	**8-05-005**
cerebral	JJ	7-04-004
Cerebral	JJ-TL	1-01-001
cerebrate	**verb**	**1-01-001**
cerebrated	VBN	1-01-001
ceremonial	**adjective**	**3-03-003**
ceremonial	JJ	2-02-002
Ceremonial	JJ-TL	1-01-001
ceremonially	**RB**	**1-01-001**
ceremoniously	**RB**	**1-01-001**
ceremony	**noun**	**32-11-027**
ceremony	NN	18-08-017
ceremonies	NNS	13-06-011
ceremonies	NNS-HL	1-01-001
Cerise	**NP**	**1-01-001**
certain	**AP**	**92-04-046**
certain	**FW-JJ**	**1-01-001**
certain	**adjective**	**221-15-152**
certain	JJ	220-15-151
ceartaine	JJ	1-01-001
certainly	**RB**	**143-14-107**

Word	Tag	Count
certainty	**NN**	**21-08-014**
certificate	**noun**	**8-07-007**
certificate	NN	7-06-006
certificates	NNS	1-01-001
certification	**NN**	**3-02-002**
certify	**verb**	**14-04-006**
certify	VB	5-02-002
certifies	VBZ	1-01-001
certified	VBN	7-03-004
certifying	VBG	1-01-001
certiorari	**NN**	**2-02-002**
certitude	**noun**	**1-01-001**
certitudes	NNS	1-01-001
cerulean	**JJ**	**1-01-001**
Cerv	**NP**	**5-01-001**
Cervantes	**prop. noun**	**2-01-001**
Cervantes	NP	1-01-001
Cervantes'	NP$	1-01-001
cervelat	**NN**	**1-01-001**
Cervetto	**NP**	**1-01-001**
Cesare	**NP**	**1-01-001**
cesium-137	**NN**	**3-01-001**
cessation	**NN**	**1-01-001**
cession	**NN**	**1-01-001**
Cestre	**NP**	**2-01-001**
cetera	**foreign**	**5-04-004**
cetera	FW-NNS	4-03-003
ceteras	FW-NNS	1-01-001
Ceylon	**NP**	**5-04-004**
Ceyway	**NP**	**1-01-001**
Cezanne	**prop. noun**	**4-04-004**
Cezanne	NP	2-02-002
Cezanne's	NP$	1-01-001
Cezannes	NPS	1-01-001
cf.	**VB**	**8-02-003**
Ch'an	**NP**	**2-01-001**
Ch'in	**NP**	**2-01-001**
cha-cha	**noun**	**1-01-001**
cha-chas	NNS	1-01-001
Chablis	**NP**	**1-01-001**
Chabrier	**prop. noun**	**4-01-001**
Chabrier	NP	2-01-001
Chabrier's	NP$	2-01-001
Chadroe	**NP**	**1-01-001**
Chadwick	**NP**	**2-01-001**
chafe	**verb**	**3-03-003**
chafe	VB	1-01-001
chafing	VBG	2-02-002
chaff	**verb**	**1-01-001**
chaffing	VBG	1-01-001
Chaffey	**NP**	**1-01-001**
chagrin	**NN**	**4-04-004**
Chahar	**NP**	**1-01-001**
Chaikoff	**NP**	**2-01-001**
chain	**noun**	**60-12-031**
chain	NN	46-10-025
chain	NN-HL	2-02-002
Chain	NN-TL	2-01-001
chains	NNS	9-07-007
chains	NNS-HL	1-01-001
chain-reaction	**NN**	**1-01-001**
chainlike	**JJ**	**1-01-001**
chair	**noun**	**89-13-062**
chair	NN	64-13-047
chair	NN-NC	2-01-001
chairs	NNS	23-10-020
chairing	**NN**	**1-01-001**
chairman	**noun**	**77-09-046**
chairman	NN	48-07-031
chmn.	NN	0-00-000
Chmn.	NN-TL	1-01-001
Chairman	NN-TL	19-05-015
chairmen	NNS	9-04-006
chairmanship	**noun**	**2-02-002**
chairmanship	NN	1-01-001
chairmanships	NNS	1-01-001
chaise	**NN**	**1-01-001**
Chalidale	**NP**	**2-01-001**
chalk	**NN**	**2-02-002**
chalk	**verb**	**2-02-002**
chalk	VB	1-01-001
chalked	VBN	1-01-001
chalk-white	**JJ**	**1-01-001**
chalky	**JJ**	**1-01-001**
challenge	**noun**	**23-11-020**
challenge	NN	21-11-018
Challenge	NN-TL	1-01-001
challenges	NNS	1-01-001
challenge	**verb**	**29-10-026**

Word	Tag	Frequency
challenge (cont.):		
challenge	VB	14-08-014
challenges	VBZ	3-03-003
challenged	VBD	4-04-004
challenged	VBN	5-02-005
challenging	VBG	3-03-003
challenger	**NN**	**1-01-001**
challenging	**JJ**	**9-08-009**
Chalmer	**prop. noun**	**1-01-001**
Chalmers	NPS	1-01-001
Chalon-sur-Saone	**NP**	**1-01-001**
chamber	**noun**	**55-09-030**
chamber	NN	31-07-014
Chamber	NN-TL	15-07-010
chambers	NNS	8-05-008
Chambers	NNS-TL	1-01-001
chamber	**verb**	**1-01-001**
chambered	VBN	1-01-001
Chamberlain	**NP**	**1-01-001**
chambermaid	**noun**	**4-03-003**
chambermaid	NN	3-02-002
chambermaids	NNS	1-01-001
Chambers	**NP**	**2-02-002**
chambre	**foreign**	**6-02-002**
chambre	FW-NN	4-01-001
Chambre	FW-NN-TL	1-01-001
chambre's	FW-NN$	1-01-001
chamfer	**NN**	**2-01-001**
chamois	**NN**	**1-01-001**
champ	**noun**	**1-01-001**
champs	NNS	1-01-001
Champ	**NP**	**1-01-001**
champagne	**NN**	**13-05-006**
Champassak	**NP**	**2-01-001**
champion	**noun**	**31-07-015**
champion	NN	18-06-010
Champion	NN-TL	3-02-003
Champion	NN-TL-HL	1-01-001
champions	NNS	8-03-007
champions	NNS-HL	1-01-001
champion	**verb**	**2-01-002**
champion	VB	1-01-001
champions	VBZ	1-01-001
championship	**noun**	**9-04-006**
championship	NN	8-04-006
championships	NNS	1-01-001
Champlain	**prop. noun**	**3-02-002**
Champlain	NP	0-00-000
Champlain	NP-TL	3-02-002
champs	**foreign**	**2-02-002**
champs	FW-NNS	0-00-000
Champs	FW-NNS-TL	2-02-002
chance	**JJ**	**1-01-001**
chance	**noun**	**152-15-117**
chance	NN	127-15-097
chance	NN-HL	1-01-001
chances	NNS	24-13-023
chance	**verb**	**4-02-004**
chance	VB	1-01-001
chanced	VBD	2-02-002
chanced	VBN	1-01-001
Chance	**NP**	**1-01-001**
chancel	**NN**	**1-01-001**
chancellor	**noun**	**14-05-007**
chancellor	NN	6-04-004
Chancellor	NN-TL	8-04-006
Chancellorsville	**NP**	**1-01-001**
chancery	**noun**	**3-01-002**
chancery	NN	2-01-002
chanceries	NNS	1-01-001
chandelier	**noun**	**4-02-004**
chandelier	NN	3-01-003
chandeliers	NNS	1-01-001
chandelle	**VB**	**1-01-001**
Chandler	**prop. noun**	**34-07-008**
Chandler	NP	32-07-007
Chandler's	NP$	2-02-002
change	**noun**	**284-15-143**
change	NN	161-15-088
change	NN-HL	2-01-002
changes	NNS	118-12-073
changes	NNS-HL	1-01-001
Changes	NNS-TL	2-02-002
change	**verb**	**225-15-155**
change	VB	76-15-061
change	VB-HL	1-01-001
changes	VBZ	10-06-008
changed	VBD	26-12-024
changed	VBN	69-14-060

Word	Tag	Frequency
change (cont.):		
changing	VBG	41-10-034
changing	VBG-HL	1-01-001
Changing	VBG-TL	1-01-001
change-over	**NN**	**2-01-002**
changeable	**adjective**	**5-01-001**
changeable	JJ	4-01-001
changeable	JJ-HL	1-01-001
changing	**NN**	**1-01-001**
channel	**noun**	**38-10-019**
channel	NN	9-05-007
Channel	NN-TL	6-04-004
channels	NNS	23-07-008
channel	**verb**	**4-03-004**
channel	VB	1-01-001
channeled	VBN	3-03-003
channel-type	**JJ**	**2-01-001**
Channing	**prop. noun**	**6-01-001**
Channing	NP	5-01-001
Channing's	NP$	1-01-001
chanson	**noun**	**2-01-001**
chansons	NNS	2-01-001
chant	**noun**	**4-04-004**
chant	NN	1-01-001
chants	NNS	3-03-003
chant	**verb**	**9-07-008**
chant	VB	1-01-001
chanted	VBD	3-03-003
chanted	VBN	3-03-003
chanting	VBG	2-02-002
chanter	**NN**	**1-01-001**
chantey	**NN**	**2-01-001**
chantier	**FW-NN**	**1-01-001**
Chantilly	**NP**	**1-01-001**
chaos	**NN**	**17-07-011**
chaotic	**JJ**	**5-03-005**
chap	**noun**	**3-03-003**
chap	NN	2-02-002
chaps	NNS	1-01-001
chapel	**noun**	**22-07-017**
chapel	NN	10-05-009
Chapel	NN-TL	10-05-009
chapels	NNS	2-02-002
chapel-like	**JJ**	**1-01-001**
Chapelle	**prop. noun**	**1-01-001**
Chapelles	NPS	1-01-001
chaperon	**noun**	**2-02-002**
chaperon	NN	1-01-001
chaperone	NN	1-01-001
chaperone	**verb**	**1-01-001**
chaperoned	VBN	1-01-001
chaplain	**noun**	**6-05-005**
chaplain	NN	3-03-003
Chaplain	NN-TL	2-01-001
chaplains	NNS	1-01-001
Chaplin	**NP**	**3-02-002**
Chapman	**NP**	**6-01-004**
Chappell	**NP**	**1-01-001**
chapter	**noun**	**97-14-049**
chapter	NN	38-09-027
ch.	NN	1-01-001
Ch.	NN-TL	3-02-002
chap.	NN	3-01-001
chapter	NN-HL	6-05-006
Chapter	NN-TL	27-05-013
Chapter	NN-TL-HL	2-02-002
chapter's	NN$	1-01-001
chapters	NNS	12-05-010
Chapters	NNS-TL	4-02-003
char	**verb**	**2-02-002**
char	VB	1-01-001
charred	VBN	1-01-001
character	**noun**	**154-14-093**
character	NN	117-14-082
Character	NN-TL	1-01-001
characters	NNS	36-08-022
character-education	**NN**	**1-01-001**
characteristic	**JJ**	**44-07-034**
characteristic	**noun**	**76-08-049**
characteristic	NN	24-06-020
characteristics	NNS	50-06-032
characteristics	NNS-HL	2-01-001
characteristically	**RB**	**7-04-006**
characterization	**noun**	**10-04-009**
characterization	NN	8-04-008
characterizations	NNS	2-02-002
characterize	**verb**	**32-08-023**
characterize	VB	6-04-006
characterizes	VBZ	4-03-004

Word	Tag	Frequency
characterize (cont.):		
characterized	VBD	6-04-005
characterized	VBN	15-05-013
characterizing	VBG	1-01-001
charcoal	**NN**	**14-03-005**
charcoal	**verb**	**1-01-001**
charcoaled	VBN	1-01-001
charcoal-broiled	**JJ**	**1-01-001**
Chardon	**NP**	**1-01-001**
charge	**noun**	**151-13-092**
charge	NN	104-13-071
charge	NN-HL	1-01-001
charge	NN-NC	1-01-001
Charge	NN-TL	1-01-001
charges	NNS	43-10-030
charges	NNS-HL	1-01-001
charge	**verb**	**82-12-052**
charge	VB	15-07-011
charges	VBZ	1-01-001
charged	VBD	17-07-014
charged	VBN	38-10-025
charged	VBN-HL	2-01-002
charging	VBG	8-06-008
chargin'	VBG	1-01-001
charge-a-plate	**NN**	**1-01-001**
charge-excess	**NN**	**3-01-001**
chargeable	**JJ**	**1-01-001**
chariot	**NN**	**3-03-003**
charisma	**NN**	**1-01-001**
charitable	**JJ**	**5-05-005**
charitably	**RB**	**1-01-001**
charity	**noun**	**12-06-009**
charity	NN	8-05-005
charities	NNS	4-03-004
charlatan	**noun**	**1-01-001**
charlatans	NNS	1-01-001
Charlayne	**NP**	**4-01-001**
Charles	**prop. noun**	**104-12-057**
Charles	NP	88-12-055
Charles	NP-TL	8-02-003
Charles'	NP$	7-04-004
Charles's	NP$	1-01-001
Charleston	**NP**	**2-02-002**
Charley	**prop. noun**	**9-03-005**
Charley	NP	5-02-004
Charley	NP-TL	3-01-001
Charley's	NP$	1-01-001
Charlie	**prop. noun**	**50-09-015**
Charlie	NP	45-09-014
Charlie	NP-TL	3-01-001
Charlie's	NP$	2-01-001
charlotte	**NN**	**1-01-001**
Charlotte	**prop. noun**	**15-04-005**
Charlotte	NP	12-04-005
Charlotte's	NP$	3-01-001
Charlottesville	**prop. noun**	**3-03-003**
Charlottesville	NP	2-02-002
Charlottesville	NP-TL	1-01-001
charm	**noun**	**25-09-022**
charm	NN	23-09-020
charms	NNS	2-02-002
charm	**verb**	**5-05-005**
charm	VB	2-02-002
charmed	VBD	1-01-001
charmed	VBN	2-02-002
Charm	**NP**	**1-01-001**
charmer	**noun**	**1-01-001**
charmer	NN	0-00-000
Charmer	NN-TL	1-01-001
charming	**JJ**	**24-10-021**
charmingly	**QL**	**1-01-001**
Charnock	**NP**	**1-01-001**
chart	**noun**	**30-08-021**
chart	NN	16-07-013
Chart	NN-TL	5-01-002
charts	NNS	9-05-009
chart	**verb**	**11-05-006**
chart	VB	1-01-001
charted	VBN	6-04-005
charting	VBG	4-02-002
chartaceos	**FW-JJ**	**1-01-001**
charter	**noun**	**37-08-018**
charter	NN	20-06-009
charter	NN-HL	1-01-001
Charter	NN-TL	12-04-006
charters	NNS	3-03-003
Charters	NNS-TL	1-01-001
charter	**verb**	**4-03-004**
chartered	VBN	4-03-004
charting	**noun**	**4-02-002**
charting	NN	3-02-002
chartings	NNS	1-01-001
chartist	**noun**	**3-01-001**
chartist	NN	2-01-001
chartists	NNS	1-01-001
Chartres	**NP**	**2-01-002**
chartroom	**NN**	**2-01-001**
chase	**noun**	**7-04-005**
chase	NN	5-02-003
chase	NN-HL	1-01-001
Chase	NN-TL	1-01-001
chase	**verb**	**7-05-007**
chase	VB	4-04-004
chased	VBN	1-01-001
chasing	VBG	2-02-002
Chase	**prop. noun**	**9-02-004**
Chase	NP	4-01-002
Chase	NP-TL	3-01-002
Chases	NPS	2-01-001
chasing	**NN**	**1-01-001**
chasm	**NN**	**2-02-002**
chassis	**NN**	**1-01-001**
chastisement	**NN**	**2-02-002**
chastity	**NN**	**2-02-002**
chat	**NN**	**3-03-003**
chat	**verb**	**6-04-006**
chat	VB	2-02-002
chatted	VBD	2-02-002
chatting	VBG	2-02-002
chateau	**foreign**	**1-01-001**
chateau	FW-NN	0-00-000
Chateau	FW-NN-TL	1-01-001
Chateau	**NP**	**2-01-001**
Chatham	**prop. noun**	**3-01-002**
Chatham	NP	2-01-002
Chatham	NP-TL	1-01-001
Chattanooga	**NP**	**3-03-003**
chatte	**FW-NN**	**1-01-001**
chattel	**noun**	**1-01-001**
chattels	NNS	1-01-001
chatter	**NN**	**6-04-005**
chatter	**verb**	**8-07-008**
chatter	VB	1-01-001
chattered	VBD	3-03-003
chattering	VBG	4-04-004
chattering	**NN**	**2-01-002**
chatty	**JJ**	**1-01-001**
Chaucer	**NP**	**1-01-001**
chauffeur	**noun**	**5-03-004**
chauffeur	NN	4-03-004
chauffeur's	NN$	1-01-001
chauffeur	**verb**	**1-01-001**
chauffeured	VBN	1-01-001
chauffeur-driven	**JJ**	**2-01-001**
chaulmoogra	**NN**	**1-01-001**
Chauncey	**NP**	**2-02-002**
Chautauqua	**NP**	**1-01-001**
Chaves	**NP**	**1-01-001**
Chavez	**prop. noun**	**4-01-001**
Chavez	NP	3-01-001
Chavez'	NP$	1-01-001
Chavis	**NP**	**2-01-001**
chaw	**NN**	**1-01-001**
Che	**NP**	**1-01-001**
cheap	**JJ**	**23-10-020**
cheap	**RB**	**1-01-001**
cheap-money	**NN**	**1-01-001**
cheaper	**JJR**	**10-05-008**
cheaper	**RBR**	**1-01-001**
cheaply	**RB**	**3-02-002**
cheat	**verb**	**7-06-007**
cheat	VB	1-01-001
cheat	VB-NC	1-01-001
cheated	VBN	4-04-004
cheating	VBG	1-01-001
Cheat	**NP**	**1-01-001**
check	**noun**	**53-14-035**
check	NN	36-12-027
check	NN-HL	1-01-001
checks	NNS	15-09-013
checks	NNS-HL	1-01-001
check	**verb**	**88-12-056**
check	VB	51-10-035
checks	VBZ	1-01-001
checked	VBD	10-05-009
checked	VBN	21-08-017
checking	VBG	4-02-003
checkin'	VBG	1-01-001

Word	Tag	Frequency
check-out	**NN**	**1-01-001**
checkbook	**NN**	**5-03-003**
checker	**NN**	**1-01-001**
checking	**NN**	**1-01-001**
Checkit	**NP**	**1-01-001**
checklist	**NN**	**3-03-003**
checkup	**NN**	**2-02-002**
Cheddi	**NP**	**1-01-001**
cheek	**noun**	**33-09-026**
cheek	NN	20-07-016
cheeks	NNS	13-06-012
cheekbone	**noun**	**6-03-006**
cheekbone	NN	1-01-001
cheekbones	NNS	5-03-005
cheer	**noun**	**10-07-009**
cheer	NN	6-04-005
cheers	NNS	4-03-004
cheer	**verb**	**6-03-006**
cheer	VB	2-02-002
cheere	VB	1-01-001
cheered	VBD	1-01-001
cheered	VBN	1-01-001
cheering	VBG	1-01-001
cheerful	**JJ**	**10-06-010**
cheerfully	**RB**	**5-04-005**
cheerfulness	**NN**	**1-01-001**
cheerleader	**noun**	**1-01-001**
cheerleaders	NNS	1-01-001
cheery	**JJ**	**3-02-003**
cheese	**NN**	**9-07-008**
cheesecloth	**NN**	**1-01-001**
cheetah	**NN**	**1-01-001**
cheetal	**NN**	**1-01-001**
chef	**noun**	**9-04-007**
chef	NN	8-04-006
Chef	NN-TL	1-01-001
Chehel	**NP**	**1-01-001**
Chekhov	**NP**	**2-02-002**
chelas	**FW-NNS**	**1-01-001**
Chelmno	**NP**	**1-01-001**
chemical	**adjective**	**7-03-006**
chemical	JJ	5-01-004
Chemical	JJ-TL	2-02-002
chemical	**noun**	**57-08-022**
chemical	NN	36-08-019
chemical	NN-HL	17-02-002
chemicals	NNS	4-04-004
chemically	**RB**	**5-04-005**
chemische	**foreign**	**4-01-001**
chemische	FW-JJ	0-00-000
Chemische	FW-JJ-TL	4-01-001
chemise	**NN**	**1-01-001**
chemist	**noun**	**5-05-005**
chemist's	NN$	1-01-001
chemists	NNS	4-04-004
chemistry	**noun**	**17-08-014**
chemistry	NN	13-08-012
chemistry	NN-HL	3-01-003
chemistries	NNS	1-01-001
Chen	**NP**	**3-01-001**
Cheng	**NP**	**1-01-001**
Chennault	**prop. noun**	**1-01-001**
Chennault's	NP$	1-01-001
Chenoweth	**NP**	**3-01-001**
cherish	**verb**	**23-11-020**
cherish	VB	5-04-004
cherished	VBD	4-04-004
cherished	VBN	12-08-012
cherishing	VBG	2-02-002
Cherkasov	**NP**	**3-01-001**
Chernishev	**NP**	**1-01-001**
Cherokee	**JJ**	**1-01-001**
Cherokee	**prop. noun**	**2-02-002**
Cherokee	NP	1-01-001
Cherokees	NPS	1-01-001
cherry	**JJ**	**1-01-001**
cherry	**noun**	**6-04-005**
cherry	NN	1-01-001
Cherry	NN-TL	3-01-002
cherries	NNS	2-02-002
Cherry	**NP**	**1-01-001**
cherry-flavored	**JJ**	**1-01-001**
cherub	**noun**	**1-01-001**
cherubim	NNS	1-01-001
Cherwell	**NP**	**1-01-001**
Ches	**NP**	**1-01-001**
Chesapeake	**prop. noun**	**4-02-003**
Chesapeake	NP	1-01-001
Chesapeake	NP-TL	3-02-002

Word	Tag	Frequency
Cheshire	**NP**	**1-01-001**
Chesly	**NP**	**1-01-001**
chess	**NN**	**3-03-003**
chest	**noun**	**57-12-035**
chest	NN	53-12-033
chests	NNS	4-04-004
chest-back-lat-shoulder	**JJ**	**1-01-001**
chest-back-shoulder	**JJ**	**1-01-001**
Chester	**prop. noun**	**10-05-009**
Chester	NP	6-04-006
Chester	NP-TL	4-03-004
Chesterton	**NP**	**1-01-001**
chestnut	**noun**	**7-05-007**
chestnut	NN	1-01-001
Chestnut	NN-TL	4-03-004
chestnuts	NNS	2-02-002
Chevalier	**NP**	**1-01-001**
chevaux	**FW-NNS**	**1-01-001**
Chevrolet	**prop. noun**	**4-03-003**
Chevrolet	NP	3-03-003
Chevrolet	NP-TL	1-01-001
Chevy	**NP**	**1-01-001**
chew	**verb**	**16-07-010**
chew	VB	2-02-002
chewed	VBD	4-02-003
chewing	VBG	10-06-008
chewing	**NN**	**3-02-003**
Cheyenne	**prop. noun**	**5-02-003**
Cheyenne	NP	2-01-001
Cheyennes	NPS	3-02-002
Chi	**NP**	**1-01-001**
chi-chi	**NN**	**1-01-001**
Chiang	**NP**	**4-03-003**
Chiaromonte	**NP**	**1-01-001**
Chiba	**NP**	**1-01-001**
chic	**JJ**	**7-03-007**
Chicago	**prop. noun**	**108-11-048**
Chicago	NP	62-09-033
Chicago	NP-HL	8-02-002
Chicago	NP-TL	28-09-017
Chicago's	NP$	9-05-006
Chicago's	NP$-TL	1-01-001
Chicago-style	**JJ**	**1-01-001**
Chicagoan	**prop. noun**	**1-01-001**
Chicagoans	NPS	1-01-001
chicanery	**NN**	**1-01-001**
chick	**noun**	**4-02-002**
chick	NN	3-02-002
chicks	NNS	1-01-001
Chickasaw	**prop. noun**	**4-01-001**
Chickasaws	NPS	4-01-001
chicken	**noun**	**49-12-029**
chicken	NN	33-12-022
Chicken	NN-TL	3-02-002
chickens	NNS	13-04-008
chicken	**VB**	**1-01-001**
Chico	**NP**	**2-02-002**
chide	**verb**	**4-04-004**
chide	VB	2-02-002
chided	VBD	1-01-001
chiding	VBG	1-01-001
chief	**sem. sup.**	**66-11-054**
chief	JJS	58-11-048
Chief	JJS-TL	8-05-008
chief	**noun**	**62-10-034**
chief	NN	28-09-020
Chief	NN-TL	25-05-014
chief's	NN$	1-01-001
Chief's	NN$-TL	2-01-002
chiefs	NNS	3-03-003
Chiefs	NNS-TL	3-01-002
chiefdom	**noun**	**2-01-001**
chiefdom	NN	1-01-001
chiefdoms	NNS	1-01-001
chiefly	**RB**	**22-07-018**
chieftain	**noun**	**5-04-004**
chieftain	NN	4-04-004
chieftains	NNS	0-00-000
Chieftains	NNS-TL	1-01-001
chien	**FW-NN**	**1-01-001**
Chien	**NP**	**8-02-002**
Chieti	**NP**	**1-01-001**
chigger	**noun**	**1-01-001**
chiggers	NNS	1-01-001
chignon	**NN**	**1-01-001**
chilblain	**noun**	**2-01-001**
chilblains	NNS	2-01-001
child	**noun**	**620-15-183**
child	NN	209-14-088

Word	Tag	Frequency
child (cont.):		
child	NN-NC	1-01-001
child's	NN$	32-09-015
children	NNS	346-15-131
children	NNS-HL	4-03-004
Children	NNS-TL	5-03-004
children's	NNS$	21-06-015
Children's	NNS$-TL	2-02-002
Child	**prop. noun**	**4-02-002**
Child	NP	3-01-001
Child's	NP$	1-01-001
child-bearing	**JJ**	**1-01-001**
child-cloud	**NN**	**1-01-001**
child-face	**NN**	**1-01-001**
child-rearing	**NN**	**1-01-001**
childbirth	**NN**	**3-03-003**
Childe	**NP**	**1-01-001**
childhood	**noun**	**55-08-023**
childhood	NN	50-08-022
childhood's	NN$	0-00-000
Childhood's	NN$-TL	5-01-001
childish	**JJ**	**11-06-009**
childishly	**RB**	**2-01-001**
childishness	**NN**	**4-03-003**
childless	**JJ**	**1-01-001**
childlike	**JJ**	**4-02-004**
Chile	**NP**	**1-01-001**
chili	**FW-NN**	**3-01-001**
chili	**NN**	**3-01-001**
chill	**JJ**	**1-01-001**
chill	**noun**	**15-08-015**
chill	NN	13-06-013
chills	NNS	2-02-002
chill	**verb**	**12-07-010**
chilled	VBD	2-02-002
chilled	VBN	5-03-004
chilling	VBG	5-04-005
chillier	**JJR**	**1-01-001**
chilly	**JJ**	**5-04-004**
chime	**noun**	**1-01-001**
chimes	NNS	1-01-001
chimera-chasing	**JJ**	**1-01-001**
chimique	**foreign**	**1-01-001**
chimique	FW-JJ	0-00-000
chimiques	FW-JJ-TL	1-01-001
chimney	**noun**	**10-06-007**
chimney	NN	5-03-004
chimney	NN-NC	2-01-001
chimneys	NNS	3-03-003
chin	**noun**	**25-08-019**
chin	NN	23-08-018
chins	NNS	2-02-002
chin	**verb**	**4-01-001**
chin	VB	2-01-001
chinning	VBG	1-01-001
chinning	VBG-HL	1-01-001
chin-up	**noun**	**2-01-001**
chin-up	NN	1-01-001
chin-ups	NNS	1-01-001
chin-up	**VB**	**1-01-001**
china	**NN**	**6-03-005**
China	**prop. noun**	**66-11-024**
China	NP	54-11-023
China	NP-TL	9-04-005
China's	NP$	3-02-002
Chinaman	**NP**	**1-01-001**
chine	**noun**	**5-01-001**
chines	NNS	5-01-001
Chinese	**adjective**	**38-10-021**
Chinese	JJ	35-09-019
Chinese	JJ-HL	1-01-001
Chinese	JJ-NC	1-01-001
Chinese	JJ-TL	1-01-001
Chinese	**prop. noun**	**18-05-009**
Chinese	NP	1-01-001
Chinese	NP-NC	1-01-001
Chinese	NPS	16-04-007
Chinese-inspired	**JJ**	**1-01-001**
Chinese-Soviet	**JJ**	**1-01-001**
Ching	**NP**	**5-02-002**
chink	**verb**	**1-01-001**
chinked	VBN	1-01-001
chinless	**JJ**	**2-01-001**
Chion	**NP**	**1-01-001**
chip	**noun**	**19-04-007**
chip	NN	16-04-004
chip	NN-HL	1-01-001
chips	NNS	2-02-002
chip	**verb**	**10-06-008**

Word	Tag	Frequency
chip (cont.):		
chipped	VBD	1-01-001
chipped	VBN	3-03-003
chipping	VBG	6-04-004
Chip-o	**prop. noun**	**1-01-001**
Chip-o's	NPS	1-01-001
Chippendale	**NP**	**1-01-001**
chipper	**JJ**	**1-01-001**
Chips	**NP**	**1-01-001**
chiropractor	**noun**	**2-01-001**
chiropractor	NN	1-01-001
chiropractor's	NN$	1-01-001
chirp	**verb**	**1-01-001**
chirped	VBD	1-01-001
chirping	**NN**	**1-01-001**
chisel	**noun**	**5-03-005**
chisel	NN	4-02-004
chisels	NNS	1-01-001
chisel	**verb**	**2-02-002**
chiseled	VBN	2-02-002
Chisholm	**prop. noun**	**3-01-002**
Chisholm	NP	1-01-001
Chisholm	NP-TL	2-01-001
Chiuchow	**NP**	**1-01-001**
chivalrous	**JJ**	**2-02-002**
chivalry	**NN**	**2-02-002**
chive	**noun**	**2-01-002**
chive	NN	1-01-001
chives	NNS	1-01-001
chivy	**verb**	**1-01-001**
chivying	VBG	1-01-001
chloride	**noun**	**6-03-003**
chloride	NN	5-03-003
chlorides	NNS	1-01-001
chlorine	**NN**	**33-02-002**
chlorine-carbon	**NN**	**1-01-001**
chlorothiazide	**NN**	**2-01-001**
chlorpromazine	**NN**	**1-01-001**
chlortetracycline	**NN**	**1-01-001**
chock	**noun**	**1-01-001**
chocks	NNS	1-01-001
chockfull	**JJ**	**1-01-001**
chocolate	**NN**	**9-06-007**
Choctaw	**JJ**	**1-01-001**
Choctaw	**prop. noun**	**3-01-001**
Choctaws	NPS	3-01-001
choice	**JJ**	**5-03-005**
choice	**noun**	**121-13-077**
choice	NN	104-13-069
chouise	NN	1-01-001
choice	NN-HL	2-02-002
Choice	NN-TL	2-02-002
choices	NNS	11-06-008
choices	NNS-HL	1-01-001
choicest	**JJT**	**2-02-002**
choir	**noun**	**9-05-006**
choir	NN	4-03-004
Choir	NN-TL	4-02-002
choir's	NN$	1-01-001
choke	**verb**	**22-09-018**
choke	VB	9-05-006
choked	VBD	4-02-004
choked	VBN	3-02-003
choking	VBG	6-05-006
choking	**NN**	**1-01-001**
chole	**FW-NN**	**1-01-001**
cholelithiasis	**NN**	**1-01-001**
cholera	**NN**	**1-01-001**
cholesterol	**noun**	**21-03-003**
cholesterol	NN	18-03-003
cholesterol	NN-HL	3-03-003
cholesterol-rich	**JJ**	**1-01-001**
cholinesterase	**NN**	**1-01-001**
chomp	**NN**	**1-01-001**
choose	**verb**	**177-15-120**
choose	VB	50-14-039
chooses	VBZ	8-06-008
chose	VBD	37-10-029
chosen	VBN	71-12-059
choosing	VBG	11-07-010
choosy	**JJ**	**1-01-001**
chop	**noun**	**5-04-005**
chop	NN	2-02-002
chops	NNS	3-03-003
chop	**verb**	**9-05-007**
chop	VB	1-01-001
chopped	VBD	1-01-001
chopped	VBN	2-01-001
chopping	VBG	5-03-005

Word	Tag	Frequency
Chopin	**prop. noun**	**3-02-003**
Chopin	NP	2-02-002
Chopin's	NP$	1-01-001
chopper	**NN**	**1-01-001**
choppy	**JJ**	**3-02-002**
choral	**adjective**	**2-02-002**
choral	JJ	1-01-001
Choral	JJ-TL	1-01-001
Chorale	**NP**	**1-01-001**
chord	**noun**	**13-06-012**
chord	NN	7-06-006
chords	NNS	6-03-006
chore	**noun**	**23-12-022**
chore	NN	7-05-007
chores	NNS	16-10-015
choreograph	**verb**	**5-01-003**
choreographed	VBN	5-01-003
choreographer	**noun**	**9-02-003**
choreographer	NN	5-02-002
choreographers	NNS	4-02-002
choreographic	**JJ**	**3-01-003**
choreography	**NN**	**3-02-002**
chorine	**noun**	**2-01-001**
chorines	NNS	2-01-001
choring	**NN**	**1-01-001**
chortle	**verb**	**4-04-004**
chortled	VBD	3-03-003
chortling	VBG	1-01-001
chorus	**noun**	**20-10-015**
chorus	NN	17-09-013
Chorus	NN-TL	1-01-001
choruses	NNS	2-02-002
chorus	**verb**	**1-01-001**
chorused	VBD	1-01-001
Chou	**NP**	**2-01-001**
chouse	**verb**	**1-01-001**
chousing	VBG	0-00-000
chousin'	VBG	1-01-001
chow	**NN**	**2-02-002**
chowder	**noun**	**2-02-002**
chowder	NN	1-01-001
chowders	NNS	1-01-001
Chris	**NP**	**12-02-003**
Chrissake	**UH**	**1-01-001**
Christ	**exclam.**	**6-03-004**
Christ	UH	2-02-002
kee-reist	UH	1-01-001
Keeeerist	UH	1-01-001
keerist	UH	1-01-001
krist	UH	1-01-001
Christ	**prop. noun**	**115-11-032**
Christ	NP	86-10-027
Christ	NP-HL	2-01-001
Christ	NP-TL	7-04-004
Christ's	NP$	8-05-006
Christ's	NP$-TL	12-01-001
Christ-like	**JJ**	**1-01-001**
christen	**verb**	**2-01-002**
christened	VBD	1-01-001
christened	VBN	1-01-001
Christendom	**prop. noun**	**3-03-003**
Christendom	NP	1-01-001
Christendom	NP-TL	2-02-002
christening	**NN**	**1-01-001**
Christi	**NP**	**2-01-001**
Christian	**adjective**	**131-12-037**
Christian	JJ	114-10-031
Christian	JJ-TL	17-08-011
Christian	**prop. noun**	**32-09-022**
Christian	NP	13-06-012
Christians	NPS	17-07-010
Christians'	NPS$	0-00-000
Christians'	NPS$-TL	2-01-001
Christiana	**prop. noun**	**9-01-001**
Christiana	NP	8-01-001
Christiana	NP-TL	1-01-001
Christianity	**prop. noun**	**31-06-015**
Christianity	NP	30-06-014
Christianity	NP-TL	1-01-001
christianize	**verb**	**1-01-001**
christianizing	VBG	1-01-001
Christiansen	**NP**	**2-01-001**
Christie	**NP**	**2-01-002**
Christine	**prop. noun**	**3-01-001**
Christine	NP	2-01-001
Christine's	NP$	1-01-001
Christmas	**prop. noun**	**27-11-019**
Christmas	NP	25-10-018
Christmas	NP-TL	2-02-002

Word	Tag	Frequency
Christmas-season	**JJ**	**1-01-001**
Christmastime	**NP**	**2-01-001**
Christopher	**prop. noun**	**6-04-006**
Christopher	NP	5-03-005
Christophers'	NPS$	1-01-001
Christsake	**VB**	**1-01-001**
Christy	**NP**	**1-01-001**
chromatic	**JJ**	**9-03-004**
chromatic	**noun**	**1-01-001**
chromatics	NNS	1-01-001
chromatogram	**NN**	**1-01-001**
chromatographic	**JJ**	**3-01-002**
chromatography	**noun**	**9-01-002**
chromatography	NN	8-01-002
chromatography	NN-HL	1-01-001
chrome	**NN**	**4-02-002**
chrome	**verb**	**1-01-001**
chromed	VBN	1-01-001
chromic	**JJ**	**1-01-001**
chromium	**NN**	**4-01-001**
chromium-plated	**JJ**	**1-01-001**
chromium-substituted	**JJ**	**1-01-001**
Chromspun	**NP**	**1-01-001**
chronic	**JJ**	**11-03-009**
chronically	**QL**	**1-01-001**
chronicle	**noun**	**8-03-007**
chronicle	NN	4-02-004
Chronicle	NN-TL	1-01-001
chronicles	NNS	1-01-001
Chronicles	NNS-TL	1-01-001
chronicle's	NN$	0-00-000
Chronicle's	NN$-TL	1-01-001
chronicle	**verb**	**1-01-001**
chronicled	VBN	1-01-001
chronicler	**noun**	**1-01-001**
chroniclers	NNS	1-01-001
chronological	**JJ**	**7-04-005**
chronologically	**RB**	**2-02-002**
chronology	**NN**	**5-04-005**
chrysanthemum	**noun**	**1-01-001**
chrysanthemums	NNS	1-01-001
Chrysler	**prop. noun**	**4-04-004**
Chrysler	NP	2-02-002
Chrysler	NP-TL	1-01-001
Chrysler's	NP$	1-01-001
chubby	**JJ**	**2-02-002**
chuck	**noun**	**7-02-003**
chuck	NN	6-02-003
chuck	NN-HL	1-01-001
chuck	**VB**	**3-02-002**
Chuck	**NP**	**4-03-003**
chuck-a-luck	**NN**	**1-01-001**
chuckle	**noun**	**4-04-004**
chuckle	NN	3-03-003
chuckles	NNS	1-01-001
chuckle	**verb**	**10-06-009**
chuckle	VB	2-02-002
chuckled	VBD	8-04-007
chuff	**verb**	**1-01-001**
chuffing	VBG	1-01-001
chug	**verb**	**2-02-002**
chugging	VBG	2-02-002
chum	**NN**	**1-01-001**
chumminess	**NN**	**1-01-001**
chump	**NN**	**1-01-001**
Chung	**NP**	**1-01-001**
chunk	**noun**	**7-04-005**
chunk	NN	2-02-002
chunks	NNS	4-03-003
chunks	NNS-HL	1-01-001
chunky	**JJ**	**1-01-001**
church	**noun**	**451-14-092**
church	NN	223-13-067
church	NN-HL	3-02-002
Church	NN-TL	120-08-038
Church	NN-TL-HL	1-01-001
church's	NN$	2-02-002
Church's	NN$-TL	6-04-005
churches	NNS	83-10-029
Churches	NNS-TL	13-03-006
Church	**prop. noun**	**2-01-001**
Church	NP	1-01-001
Church	NP-HL	1-01-001
church-state	**NN**	**2-02-002**
churchgoer	**noun**	**1-01-001**
churchgoers	NNS	1-01-001
churchgoing	**JJ**	**2-02-002**
churchgoing	**NN**	**1-01-001**
Churchill	**prop. noun**	**14-05-006**

Word	Tag	Frequency
Churchill (cont.):		
Churchill	NP	12-04-004
Churchill's	NP$	2-02-002
Churchillian	**JJ**	**1-01-001**
churchly	**JJ**	**1-01-001**
churchman	**noun**	**3-02-002**
churchmen	NNS	3-02-002
churchyard	**noun**	**8-02-002**
churchyard	NN	6-02-002
Churchyard	NN-TL	2-01-001
churn	**verb**	**4-04-004**
churns	VBZ	1-01-001
churned	VBD	1-01-001
churning	VBG	2-02-002
churning	**NN**	**1-01-001**
chute	**NN**	**2-02-002**
chutney	**NN**	**1-01-001**
ciao	**FW-UH**	**1-01-001**
Ciardi	**NP**	**1-01-001**
Cibula	**prop. noun**	**1-01-001**
Cibula's	NP$	1-01-001
cicada	**noun**	**1-01-001**
cicadas	NNS	1-01-001
Cicero	**prop. noun**	**6-01-002**
Cicero	NP	5-01-001
Cicero's	NP$	1-01-001
Ciceronian	**JJ**	**1-01-001**
Ciciulla	**NP**	**1-01-001**
Cicognani	**NP**	**1-01-001**
cider	**NN**	**2-01-001**
cieca	**foreign**	**1-01-001**
cieca	FW-NN	0-00-000
Cieca	FW-NN-TL	1-01-001
cigar	**noun**	**12-07-010**
cigar	NN	10-06-009
cigars	NNS	2-02-002
cigarette	**noun**	**38-09-029**
cigarette	NN	25-08-020
cigaret	NN	1-01-001
cigarettes	NNS	12-05-011
ciliate	**noun**	**1-01-001**
ciliates	NNS	1-01-001
ciliated	**JJ**	**3-01-001**
cilium	**noun**	**1-01-001**
cilia	NNS	1-01-001
Cimabue	**prop. noun**	**2-01-002**
Cimabue	NP	1-01-001
Cimabue's	NP$	1-01-001
Cimoli	**NP**	**1-01-001**
cinch	**noun**	**4-03-004**
cinch	NN	3-02-003
cinches	NNS	1-01-001
Cincinnati	**prop. noun**	**9-02-006**
Cincinnati	NP	7-02-005
Cincinnati	NP-HL	1-01-001
Cincinnati	NP-TL	1-01-001
cinder	**noun**	**4-03-003**
cinder	NN	2-01-001
cinders	NNS	2-02-002
cinema	**NN**	**3-03-003**
Cinemactor	**NP**	**1-01-001**
cinematic	**JJ**	**3-01-001**
Cinerama	**NP**	**1-01-001**
cinq	**FW-CD**	**1-01-001**
cipher	**noun**	**2-01-002**
ciphers	NNS	2-01-002
cipher	**VB**	**1-01-001**
Cipolla	**NP**	**1-01-001**
Cipriani	**prop. noun**	**1-01-001**
Cipriani's	NP$	1-01-001
circa	**adverb**	**3-03-003**
circa	RB	1-01-001
ca.	RB	2-02-002
circle	**noun**	**91-12-063**
circle	NN	55-09-037
cir.	NN	0-00-000
Cir.	NN-TL	1-01-001
circle	NN-HL	1-01-001
Circle	NN-TL	2-02-002
circles	NNS	32-11-027
circle	**verb**	**13-05-012**
circle	VB	2-01-001
circled	VBD	9-05-009
circling	VBG	2-01-002
circonscription	**foreign**	**2-01-001**
circonscription	FW-NN	1-01-001
circonscriptions	FW-NNS	1-01-001
circuit	**noun**	**27-10-017**
circuit	NN	19-09-012

Word	Tag	Frequency
circuit (cont.):		
Circuit	NN-TL	4-02-004
circuits	NNS	4-03-003
circuitous	**JJ**	**1-01-001**
circuitry	**NN**	**1-01-001**
circular	**adjective**	**18-06-010**
circular	JJ	17-06-009
circular	JJ-HL	1-01-001
circular	**noun**	**3-02-002**
circular	NN	1-01-001
Circular	NN-TL	2-01-001
circularity	**NN**	**2-01-001**
circulate	**verb**	**11-07-010**
circulate	VB	2-02-002
circulated	VBD	2-02-002
circulated	VBN	2-02-002
circulating	VBG	5-04-004
circulation	**NN**	**16-10-015**
circulatory	**JJ**	**2-02-002**
circumcision	**NN**	**1-01-001**
circumference	**NN**	**3-02-003**
circumlocution	**NN**	**1-01-001**
circumpolar	**JJ**	**1-01-001**
circumscribe	**verb**	**3-01-003**
circumscribed	VBN	1-01-001
circumscribing	VBG	2-01-002
circumscription	**noun**	**1-01-001**
circumscriptions	NNS	1-01-001
circumspect	**JJ**	**3-03-003**
circumspection	**NN**	**1-01-001**
circumspectly	**RB**	**1-01-001**
circumstance	**noun**	**99-14-079**
circumstance	NN	12-10-012
Circumstance	NN-TL	3-01-001
circumstances	NNS	84-13-068
circus	**noun**	**7-05-006**
circus	NN	6-04-005
Circus	NN-TL	1-01-001
cistern	**NN**	**2-02-002**
citation	**noun**	**6-03-006**
citation	NN	5-02-005
citations	NNS	1-01-001
cite	**verb**	**44-10-034**
cite	VB	7-04-006
cites	VBZ	9-04-007
cites	VBZ-HL	1-01-001
cited	VBD	11-05-011
cited	VBN	12-09-011
cited	VBN-HL	1-01-001
citing	VBG	3-02-002
citizen	**noun**	**120-14-067**
citizen	NN	28-10-022
Citizen	NN-TL	2-02-002
citizen's	NN$	2-02-002
citizens	NNS	79-13-049
citizens	NNS-HL	1-01-001
Citizens	NNS-TL	6-02-003
citizens'	NNS$	0-00-000
Citizens'	NNS$-TL	2-01-001
citizenry	**NN**	**3-02-003**
citizenship	**NN**	**3-02-003**
cito	**FW-RB**	**1-01-001**
citrated	**JJ**	**1-01-001**
Citroen	**prop. noun**	**1-01-001**
Citroen	NP	0-00-000
Citroen	NP-TL	1-01-001
citron	**NN**	**1-01-001**
citrus	**NN**	**1-01-001**
city	**noun**	**521-15-173**
city	NN	262-14-112
city	NN-HL	2-02-002
City	NN-TL	128-14-074
City	NN-TL-HL	1-01-001
city's	NN$	20-09-013
City's	NN$-TL	1-01-001
cities	NNS	107-12-048
city-bred	**adjective**	**2-02-002**
city-bred	JJ	1-01-001
citybred	JJ	1-01-001
city-dweller	**NN**	**1-01-001**
city-owned	**JJ**	**1-01-001**
city-trading	**NN**	**1-01-001**
city-wide	**adjective**	**3-03-003**
city-wide	JJ	2-02-002
citywide	JJ	1-01-001
cityscape	**noun**	**2-02-002**
cityscapes	NNS	2-02-002
Ciudad	**NP**	**3-01-002**
civic	**adjective**	**23-10-021**

Word	Tag	Frequency
civic (cont.):		
civic	JJ	19-10-018
Civic	JJ-TL	4-02-003
civil	**adjective**	**94-10-055**
civil	JJ	44-08-026
civil	JJ-HL	1-01-001
Civil	JJ-TL	49-09-035
civil-right	**noun**	**1-01-001**
civil-rights	NNS	1-01-001
civilian	**adjective**	**16-05-009**
civilian	JJ	15-04-008
Civilian	JJ-TL	1-01-001
civilian	**noun**	**10-07-010**
civilian	NN	8-07-008
civilians	NNS	2-02-002
Civilian-groups	**NP**	**1-01-001**
civility	**NN**	**1-01-001**
civilization	**noun**	**46-09-027**
civilization	NN	39-09-026
Civilization	NN-TL	3-01-003
civilizations	NNS	4-03-003
civilizational	**JJ**	**8-01-002**
civilize	**verb**	**12-06-010**
civilized	VBN	11-06-009
civilizing	VBG	1-01-001
clad	**JJ**	**7-04-007**
cladding	**NN**	**1-01-001**
claim	**noun**	**124-10-044**
claim	NN	69-10-028
claims	NNS	46-09-025
claims	NNS-HL	1-01-001
Claims	NNS-TL	8-02-002
claim	**verb**	**99-14-073**
claim	VB	28-07-024
Claim	VB-TL	1-01-001
claims	VBZ	18-07-016
claims	VBZ-HL	1-01-001
claimed	VBD	25-09-022
claimed	VBN	10-05-007
claiming	VBG	16-10-016
claimant	**noun**	**13-03-004**
claimant	NN	8-03-003
claimants	NNS	5-02-002
Clair	**NP**	**2-01-001**
clairaudiently	**RB**	**1-01-001**
Claire	**NP**	**16-03-003**
clairvoyance	**NN**	**1-01-001**
clairvoyant	**JJ**	**1-01-001**
clam	**noun**	**5-04-005**
clam	NN	3-03-003
clams	NNS	2-02-002
clamber	**verb**	**7-03-006**
clambered	VBD	6-03-005
clambering	VBG	1-01-001
clammy	**JJ**	**2-02-002**
clamor	**NN**	**1-01-001**
clamor	**verb**	**4-04-004**
clamor	VB	1-01-001
clamors	VBZ	1-01-001
clamored	VBD	1-01-001
clamoring	VBG	1-01-001
clamorous	**JJ**	**1-01-001**
clamp	**noun**	**6-02-002**
clamps	NNS	6-02-002
clamp	**verb**	**11-06-009**
clamped	VBD	6-05-006
clamped	VBN	2-02-002
clamping	VBG	2-02-002
clamping	VBG-HL	1-01-001
clamshell	**NN**	**1-01-001**
clan	**NN**	**2-02-002**
clandestine	**JJ**	**1-01-001**
clang	**NN**	**1-01-001**
clang	**verb**	**1-01-001**
clanged	VBD	1-01-001
clank	**verb**	**1-01-001**
clanking	VBG	1-01-001
clannish	**JJ**	**1-01-001**
clannishness	**NN**	**1-01-001**
clap	**noun**	**2-01-002**
clap	NN	1-01-001
claps	NNS	1-01-001
clap	**verb**	**9-04-009**
claps	VBZ	1-01-001
clapped	VBD	4-02-004
clapping	VBG	4-02-004
clapping	**NN**	**2-02-002**
Clara	**NP**	**3-03-003**
Clare	**NP**	**1-01-001**
Clarence	**NP**	**8-05-007**
claret	**JJ**	**1-01-001**
claret	**noun**	**4-02-002**
claret	NN	3-02-002
clarets	NNS	1-01-001
clarification	**NN**	**5-03-005**
clarify	**verb**	**25-08-020**
clarify	VB	13-05-010
clarifies	VBZ	1-01-001
clarified	VBD	1-01-001
clarified	VBN	7-04-007
clarifying	VBG	3-02-003
clarinet	**NN**	**1-01-001**
clarity	**NN**	**28-09-020**
Clark	**prop. noun**	**36-08-013**
Clark	NP	33-07-011
Clark	NP-TL	2-02-002
Clark's	NP$	1-01-001
Clarke	**prop. noun**	**2-02-002**
Clarke	NP	1-01-001
Clarke's	NP$	1-01-001
clash	**noun**	**7-06-007**
clash	NN	5-05-005
clashes	NNS	2-02-002
clash	**verb**	**1-01-001**
clashed	VBD	1-01-001
clasp	**verb**	**7-05-006**
clasped	VBD	2-01-002
clasped	VBN	1-01-001
clasping	VBG	4-04-004
class	**noun**	**292-14-090**
class	NN	164-14-064
class	NN-HL	2-02-002
Class	NN-TL	40-06-008
class'	NN$	0-00-000
Class'	NN$-TL	1-01-001
classes	NNS	76-09-036
Classes	NNS-TL	9-01-001
class	**verb**	**3-02-003**
class	VB	1-01-001
classed	VBN	2-02-002
class-biased	**JJ**	**1-01-001**
Class-D	**NP**	**1-01-001**
classic	**JJ**	**31-09-025**
classic	**noun**	**14-08-010**
classic	NN	5-04-004
classics	NNS	9-07-007
classical	**adjective**	**33-10-024**
classical	JJ	28-10-022
Classical	JJ-TL	5-02-002
classically	**RB**	**2-02-002**
Classicist	**NP**	**1-01-001**
classiest	**JJT**	**1-01-001**
classification	**noun**	**25-05-014**
classification	NN	20-05-012
classification	NN-HL	1-01-001
classifications	NNS	4-03-003
classification-angle	**NN**	**1-01-001**
classificatory	**JJ**	**1-01-001**
classifier	**noun**	**1-01-001**
classifiers	NNS	1-01-001
classify	**verb**	**21-07-015**
classify	VB	6-03-006
classified	VBN	14-06-010
classifying	VBG	1-01-001
classless	**JJ**	**1-01-001**
classmate	**noun**	**7-05-006**
classmate	NN	3-02-003
classmates	NNS	4-04-004
classroom	**noun**	**23-06-010**
classroom	NN	18-06-007
classrooms	NNS	5-04-004
clatter	**NN**	**1-01-001**
clatter	**verb**	**7-05-007**
clatter	VB	1-01-001
clattered	VBD	5-04-005
clattering	VBG	1-01-001
clattery	**JJ**	**1-01-001**
Claude	**prop. noun**	**12-05-006**
Claude	NP	11-05-006
Claude's	NP$	1-01-001
Claudia	**prop. noun**	**1-01-001**
Claudia's	NP$	1-01-001
Claudio	**NP**	**1-01-001**
Claus	**NP**	**2-02-002**
clause	**noun**	**13-04-008**
clause	NN	9-03-006
clauses	NNS	4-02-002
claustrophobia	**NN**	**1-01-001**

Word	Tag	Frequency
claw	**noun**	**4-04-004**
claw	NN	1-01-001
claws	NNS	3-03-003
claw	**verb**	**3-03-003**
clawed	VBN	2-02-002
clawing	VBG	1-01-001
clay	**noun**	**91-09-015**
clay	NN	85-09-012
Clay	NN-TL	5-04-004
clays	NNS	1-01-001
Clay	**NP**	**10-05-007**
clay-mining	**NN**	**1-01-001**
Clayton	**prop. noun**	**30-03-008**
Clayton	NP	24-02-007
Clayton	NP-TL	3-02-002
Clayton's	NP$	3-01-002
clean	**JJ**	**48-10-037**
clean	**noun**	**1-01-001**
clean	NN	0-00-000
Clean	NN-TL	1-01-001
clean	**RB**	**1-01-001**
clean	**verb**	**58-11-040**
clean	VB	18-09-015
clean	VB-HL	1-01-001
cleans	VBZ	1-01-001
cleaned	VBD	3-03-003
cleaned	VBN	13-07-013
cleaning	VBG	21-08-014
cleaning	VBG-HL	1-01-001
clean-shaven	**JJ**	**1-01-001**
clean-top	**JJ**	**1-01-001**
clean-up	**NN**	**1-01-001**
cleaner	**JJR**	**4-03-004**
cleaner	**noun**	**13-06-007**
cleaner	NN	4-03-003
Cleaner	NN-TL	1-01-001
cleaners	NNS	8-04-004
cleaning	**NN**	**15-05-007**
cleanly	**RB**	**2-01-001**
cleanse	**verb**	**4-03-004**
cleansed	VBD	1-01-001
cleansing	VBG	3-03-003
cleansing	**NN**	**1-01-001**
Cleanth	**NP**	**1-01-001**
cleanup	**noun**	**1-01-001**
cleanups	NNS	1-01-001
clear	**JJ**	**196-15-136**
clear	**RB**	**9-05-008**
clear	**verb**	**48-14-037**
clear	VB	14-07-011
clears	VBZ	1-01-001
cleared	VBD	13-06-011
cleared	VBN	9-06-007
cleared	VBN-HL	1-01-001
clearing	VBG	10-07-009
clear-channel	**JJ**	**2-01-001**
clear-cut	**JJ**	**6-04-006**
clear-headed	**JJ**	**1-01-001**
clearance	**NN**	**4-04-004**
clearer	**comp. adj.**	**15-07-012**
clearer	JJR	14-07-012
clearer	JJR-HL	1-01-001
clearing	**NN**	**6-04-006**
clearly	**QL**	**6-03-006**
clearly	**RB**	**122-14-100**
clearness	**NN**	**2-02-002**
Clearwater	**NP**	**1-01-001**
cleat	**NN**	**1-01-001**
cleavage	**NN**	**2-01-001**
cleave	**verb**	**2-02-002**
cleaved	VBN	1-01-001
cleft	VBN	1-01-001
Cleburne	**prop. noun**	**1-01-001**
Cleburne's	NP$	1-01-001
cleft	**noun**	**2-02-002**
cleft	NN	1-01-001
clefts	NNS	1-01-001
Clemence	**NP**	**1-01-001**
Clemenceau	**NP**	**2-02-002**
clemency	**NN**	**2-01-001**
Clemens	**prop. noun**	**4-03-003**
Clemens	NP	2-02-002
Clemens'	NP$	2-01-001
Clement	**NP**	**1-01-001**
Clemente	**prop. noun**	**3-02-002**
Clemente	NP	2-02-002
Clemente	NP-TL	1-01-001
Clements	**NP**	**3-02-003**
clench	**verb**	**7-06-007**
clench (cont.):		
clench	VB	1-01-001
clenches	VBZ	1-01-001
clenched	VBD	1-01-001
clenched	VBN	4-03-004
Cleota	**prop. noun**	**1-01-001**
Cleota's	NP$	1-01-001
Clerfayt	**NP**	**7-01-001**
clergy	**noun**	**12-04-008**
clergy	NN	10-04-007
clergy	NNS	2-02-002
clergyman	**noun**	**17-06-010**
clergyman	NN	10-05-007
clergyman's	NN$	1-01-001
clergymen	NNS	6-03-004
cleric	**NN**	**1-01-001**
clerical	**JJ**	**9-05-008**
clerical-lay	**JJ**	**1-01-001**
clericis	**foreign**	**1-01-001**
clericis	FW-NNS	0-00-000
Clericis	FW-NNS-TL	1-01-001
clerk	**noun**	**45-09-022**
clerk	NN	33-09-017
clerk's	NN$	5-02-002
clerks	NNS	6-03-005
Clerks	NNS-TL	1-01-001
clerk	**verb**	**2-02-002**
clerk	VB	1-01-001
clerking	VBG	1-01-001
Cleva	**NP**	**1-01-001**
Cleveland	**prop. noun**	**17-06-010**
Cleveland	NP	16-06-009
Cleveland	NP-HL	1-01-001
clever	**adjective**	**17-08-016**
clever	JJ	16-08-016
Clever	JJ-TL	1-01-001
cleverly	**RB**	**4-03-004**
cleverness	**NN**	**3-03-003**
Cliburn	**NP**	**3-01-001**
cliche	**noun**	**11-04-009**
cliche	NN	6-03-005
cliches	NNS	5-03-004
click	**noun**	**3-03-003**
click	NN	2-02-002
clicks	NNS	1-01-001
click	**verb**	**9-06-008**
clicks	VBZ	1-01-001
clicked	VBD	5-03-005
clicked	VBN	3-03-003
clicking	**NN**	**1-01-001**
client	**noun**	**33-08-015**
client	NN	15-06-009
client's	NN$	7-03-003
clients	NNS	10-05-008
clients'	NNS$	1-01-001
client-service	**NN**	**1-01-001**
clientele	**NN**	**3-03-003**
cliff	**noun**	**11-05-009**
cliff	NN	8-04-006
Cliff	NN-TL	1-01-001
cliffs	NNS	2-02-002
Cliff	**NP**	**2-01-001**
cliffhanging	**JJ**	**1-01-001**
Clifford	**NP**	**5-04-005**
Clifton	**NP**	**3-03-003**
climactic	**JJ**	**4-02-003**
climate	**noun**	**27-10-025**
climate	NN	26-10-024
climates	NNS	1-01-001
climax	**noun**	**14-04-013**
climax	NN	13-04-012
climaxes	NNS	1-01-001
climax	**verb**	**3-03-003**
climax	VB	1-01-001
climaxed	VBD	1-01-001
climaxed	VBN	1-01-001
climb	**noun**	**2-02-002**
climb	NN	1-01-001
climbs	NNS	1-01-001
climb	**verb**	**65-10-044**
climb	VB	11-07-009
climbed	VBD	41-08-032
climbed	VBN	3-03-003
climbing	VBG	10-06-009
climbing	**NN**	**1-01-001**
clime	**noun**	**1-01-001**
climes	NNS	1-01-001
clinch	**noun**	**1-01-001**
clinches	NNS	1-01-001

Word	Tag	Frequency
clinch	**verb**	**3-02-003**
clinch	VB	2-02-002
clinched	VBD	1-01-001
clincher	**NN**	**1-01-001**
cling	**verb**	**30-09-028**
cling	VB	6-06-006
clings	VBZ	3-03-003
clung	VBD	13-07-012
clung	VBN	1-01-001
clinging	VBG	7-06-007
clinic	**noun**	**5-03-003**
clinic	NN	3-02-002
clinics	NNS	2-02-002
clinical	**JJ**	**27-05-011**
clinically	**RB**	**1-01-001**
clinico-pathologic	**adjective**	**3-01-001**
clinico-pathologic	JJ	0-00-000
Clinico-pathologic	JJ-TL	3-01-001
clink	**verb**	**1-01-001**
clinked	VBD	1-01-001
Clint	**NP**	**4-01-003**
Clinton	**NP**	**3-01-002**
clip	**noun**	**8-05-007**
clip	NN	6-04-006
clips	NNS	2-02-002
clip	**verb**	**3-02-003**
clipped	VBD	2-01-002
clipped	VBN	1-01-001
Clipper	**prop. noun**	**1-01-001**
Clipper	NP	0-00-000
Clipper	NP-TL	1-01-001
clipping	**noun**	**4-04-004**
clippings	NNS	4-04-004
clique	**noun**	**3-03-003**
clique	NN	2-02-002
cliques	NNS	1-01-001
Clive	**NP**	**1-01-001**
cloak	**NN**	**3-02-003**
cloakroom	**noun**	**1-01-001**
cloakrooms	NNS	1-01-001
clobber	**verb**	**3-03-003**
clobber	VB	1-01-001
clobbers	VBZ	1-01-001
clobbered	VBD	1-01-001
clock	**noun**	**28-10-020**
clock	NN	19-08-014
clock	NN-HL	1-01-001
clocks	NNS	8-05-006
clock	**verb**	**1-01-001**
clocked	VBN	1-01-001
clocking	**NN**	**1-01-001**
clockwise	**RB**	**3-03-003**
clockwork	**NN**	**1-01-001**
clod	**noun**	**5-04-004**
clod	NN	1-01-001
clods	NNS	4-03-003
cloddishness	**NN**	**1-01-001**
clodhopper	**noun**	**1-01-001**
clodhoppers	NNS	1-01-001
clog	**verb**	**6-04-006**
clog	VB	2-02-002
clogged	VBD	1-01-001
clogged	VBN	1-01-001
clogging	VBG	2-02-002
cloister	**noun**	**1-01-001**
cloisters	NNS	1-01-001
clomp	**verb**	**1-01-001**
clomped	VBD	1-01-001
clonic	**JJ**	**1-01-001**
close	**JJ**	**80-14-074**
close	**NN**	**16-08-010**
close	**QL**	**2-02-002**
close	**RB**	**97-14-079**
close	**verb**	**174-15-109**
close	VB	39-12-026
closes	VBZ	6-04-004
closed	VBD	39-12-034
closed	VBN	66-12-045
closed	VBN-HL	1-01-001
closing	VBG	23-10-019
close-in	**JJ**	**1-01-001**
close-up	**noun**	**4-03-004**
close-up	NN	2-02-002
close-ups	NNS	0-00-000
closeups	NNS	2-02-002
Close-up	**NP**	**2-01-001**
closed-circuit	**JJ**	**1-01-001**
closed-door	**JJ**	**2-01-001**
closely	**QL**	**1-01-001**
closely	**RB**	**65-12-048**
closely-packed	**JJ**	**1-01-001**
closeness	**NN**	**1-01-001**
closer	**JJR**	**18-09-017**
closer	**RBR**	**43-13-033**
closest	**JJT**	**9-07-009**
closet	**noun**	**18-05-014**
closet	NN	16-05-013
closets	NNS	2-01-002
closet	**verb**	**1-01-001**
closeted	VBN	1-01-001
closeup	**JJ**	**1-01-001**
closing	**NN**	**5-03-005**
Clostridium	**NP**	**1-01-001**
closure	**NN**	**1-01-001**
clot	**NN**	**2-02-002**
clot	**verb**	**2-02-002**
clot	VB	1-01-001
clotted	VBN	1-01-001
cloth	**noun**	**43-10-025**
cloth	NN	42-10-024
Cloth	NN-TL	1-01-001
cloth-of-gold	**NN**	**1-01-001**
clothbound	**JJ**	**1-01-001**
clothe	**verb**	**6-06-006**
clothe	VB	1-01-001
clothed	VBN	5-05-005
clothes	**NNS**	**89-12-054**
clothesbrush	**NN**	**1-01-001**
clotheshorse	**NN**	**2-01-001**
clothesline	**noun**	**2-02-002**
clothesline	NN	1-01-001
clotheslines	NNS	1-01-001
clothier	**NN**	**1-01-001**
clothing	**NN**	**20-10-019**
cloture	**NN**	**1-01-001**
cloud	**noun**	**64-15-036**
cloud	NN	25-10-016
Cloud	NN-TL	2-01-002
clouds	NNS	33-13-023
Clouds	NNS-TL	4-01-001
cloud	**verb**	**7-06-006**
clouds	VBZ	1-01-001
clouded	VBD	1-01-001
clouded	VBN	4-04-004
clouded	VBN-HL	1-01-001
Cloud	**NP**	**1-01-001**
cloudburst	**NN**	**3-03-003**
Cloudcroft	**NP**	**1-01-001**
cloudless	**JJ**	**2-02-002**
cloudy	**JJ**	**2-02-002**
clout	**NN**	**1-01-001**
Clov	**NP**	**1-01-001**
clove	**noun**	**3-01-002**
clove	NN	1-01-001
cloves	NNS	2-01-002
clover	**NN**	**16-01-001**
clown	**noun**	**6-06-006**
clown	NN	3-03-003
clown's	NN$	1-01-001
clowns	NNS	2-02-002
clowning	**NN**	**1-01-001**
cloy	**verb**	**3-03-003**
cloying	VBG	3-03-003
club	**noun**	**178-14-071**
club	NN	69-13-038
Club	NN-TL	73-12-041
Club	NN-TL-HL	3-03-003
club's	NN$	7-03-006
Club's	NN$-TL	2-02-002
clubs	NNS	19-08-015
Clubs	NNS-TL	5-02-003
club	**verb**	**2-02-002**
clubbed	VBN	2-02-002
clubhouse	**noun**	**5-02-004**
clubhouse	NN	4-01-003
Clubhouse	NN-TL	1-01-001
clubroom	**noun**	**1-01-001**
clubrooms	NNS	1-01-001
cluck	**noun**	**3-02-002**
cluck	NN	2-02-002
clucks	NNS	1-01-001
cluck	**verb**	**3-03-003**
clucks	VBZ	1-01-001
clucked	VBD	1-01-001
clucking	VBG	1-01-001
Cluck	**NP**	**1-01-001**
clue	**noun**	**25-11-025**
clue	NN	15-08-015

clue (cont.):		
clues	NNS	10-07-010
clump	**noun**	**8-04-006**
clump	NN	4-02-003
clumps	NNS	4-03-004
clumsily	**RB**	**1-01-001**
clumsy	**JJ**	**6-05-006**
Clurman	**NP**	**2-01-001**
cluster	**noun**	**13-07-010**
cluster	NN	8-05-007
clusters	NNS	5-04-005
cluster	**verb**	**10-05-009**
cluster	VB	5-03-005
clustered	VBD	1-01-001
clustered	VBN	3-03-003
clustering	VBG	1-01-001
clustering	**NN**	**1-01-001**
clutch	**noun**	**6-04-006**
clutch	NN	4-04-004
clutches	NNS	2-02-002
clutch	**verb**	**17-06-016**
clutch	VB	1-01-001
clutches	VBZ	1-01-001
clutched	VBD	5-04-005
clutched	VBN	2-02-002
clutching	VBG	8-04-008
clutter	**verb**	**2-02-002**
cluttered	VBN	2-02-002
Clyde	**NP**	**2-02-002**
Clyfford	**NP**	**1-01-001**
co-author	**NN**	**1-01-001**
co-chairman	**noun**	**2-02-002**
co-chairmen	NNS	2-02-002
co-educational	**JJ**	**1-01-001**
co-extinction	**NN**	**1-01-001**
co-occur	**verb**	**1-01-001**
co-occurring	VBG	1-01-001
co-op	**noun**	**3-02-002**
co-op	NN	1-01-001
Co-op	NN-TL	1-01-001
co-ops	NNS	1-01-001
co-opt	**verb**	**1-01-001**
co-opting	VBG	1-01-001
co-optation	**noun**	**9-01-001**
co-optation	NN	8-01-001
co-optation	NN-HL	1-01-001
co-signer	**noun**	**1-01-001**
co-signers	NNS	1-01-001
co-star	**NN**	**1-01-001**
coach	**noun**	**30-05-009**
coach	NN	18-05-009
coach	NN-HL	1-01-001
Coach	NN-TL	5-01-002
coach's	NN$	1-01-001
coaches	NNS	5-02-005
coach	**verb**	**5-02-003**
coaching	VBG	5-02-003
coaching	**NN**	**1-01-001**
coachman	**noun**	**5-02-002**
coachman	NN	3-01-001
coachmen	NNS	2-01-001
coachwork	**NN**	**1-01-001**
coagulate	**verb**	**1-01-001**
coagulating	VBG	1-01-001
coal	**noun**	**40-10-012**
coal	NN	27-07-008
coal	NN-HL	1-01-001
Coal	NN-TL	4-03-003
coals	NNS	8-03-003
coal-black	**JJ**	**2-02-002**
coal-like	**JJ**	**1-01-001**
coal-railroad	**NN**	**1-01-001**
coalesce	**verb**	**3-03-003**
coalesce	VB	1-01-001
coalesces	VBZ	1-01-001
coalesced	VBD	1-01-001
coalescence	**NN**	**1-01-001**
coalition	**NN**	**15-04-008**
coarse	**JJ**	**10-07-009**
coarsely	**RB**	**1-01-001**
coarsen	**verb**	**1-01-001**
coarsened	VBN	1-01-001
coarseness	**NN**	**1-01-001**
coast	**noun**	**67-14-044**
coast	NN	32-11-022
coast	NN-HL	2-02-002
Coast	NN-TL	26-10-021
Coast	NN-TL-HL	1-01-001
coasts	NNS	6-04-005

coast	**verb**	**3-02-002**
coasted	VBD	2-02-002
coasted	VBN	1-01-001
coast-to-coast	**NN**	**1-01-001**
coastal	**adjective**	**4-03-004**
coastal	JJ	3-02-003
Coastal	JJ-TL	1-01-001
coastline	**NN**	**1-01-001**
coat	**noun**	**52-09-026**
coat	NN	42-09-023
coats	NNS	10-04-006
coat	**verb**	**6-02-005**
coat	VB	1-01-001
coated	VBN	4-02-003
coating	VBG	1-01-001
Coates	**NP**	**2-01-001**
coating	**noun**	**47-03-006**
coating	NN	35-03-004
coatings	NNS	12-02-003
coattail	**noun**	**1-01-001**
coattails	NNS	1-01-001
coax	**verb**	**5-03-005**
coax	VB	1-01-001
coaxed	VBD	1-01-001
coaxed	VBN	2-02-002
coaxing	VBG	1-01-001
coaxial	**JJ**	**1-01-001**
cobalt	**NN**	**2-02-002**
cobalt-60	**NN**	**1-01-001**
Cobb	**prop. noun**	**19-02-002**
Cobb	NP	17-01-001
Cobb	NP-TL	1-01-001
Cobb's	NP$	1-01-001
cobbler	**noun**	**1-01-001**
cobbler's	NN$	1-01-001
cobblestone	**noun**	**2-02-002**
cobblestone	NN	1-01-001
cobblestones	NNS	1-01-001
Coble	**NP**	**1-01-001**
cobra	**NN**	**3-02-003**
cobweb	**noun**	**1-01-001**
cobwebs	NNS	1-01-001
Coca-Cola	**prop. noun**	**2-02-002**
Coca-Cola	NP	1-01-001
Co-cola	NP	1-01-001
cocaine	**NN**	**1-01-001**
coccidioidomycosis	**NN**	**1-01-001**
coccidiosis	**NN**	**1-01-001**
cochannel	**NN**	**5-01-001**
Cochran	**NP**	**1-01-001**
cock	**NN**	**5-02-003**
cock	**verb**	**6-04-006**
cocked	VBD	4-03-004
cocked	VBN	2-02-002
cockatoo	**NN**	**1-01-001**
cockeyed	**JJ**	**1-01-001**
cockier	**JJR**	**1-01-001**
cockpit	**noun**	**17-07-008**
cockpit	NN	16-06-007
cockpits	NNS	1-01-001
cockroach	**noun**	**2-01-002**
cockroaches	NNS	2-01-002
cocktail	**noun**	**27-09-016**
cocktail	NN	23-09-015
cocktail	NN-HL	2-02-002
cocktails	NNS	2-01-002
cocky	**JJ**	**3-02-003**
coco	**NN**	**1-01-001**
cocoa	**noun**	**3-02-002**
cocoa	NN	2-01-001
cocao	NN	1-01-001
coconut	**noun**	**10-03-005**
coconut	NN	6-03-003
Coconut	NN-TL	1-01-001
coconuts	NNS	3-01-002
coconut-containing	**JJ**	**1-01-001**
cocoon	**NN**	**3-02-002**
cocopalm	**NN**	**1-01-001**
Cocteau	**NP**	**2-02-002**
cocu	**FW-NN**	**1-01-001**
cod	**noun**	**6-04-005**
cod	NN	1-01-001
Cod	NN-TL	5-03-004
Coddington	**NP**	**2-01-001**
coddle	**verb**	**2-01-002**
coddled	VBN	2-01-002
code	**noun**	**55-11-026**
code	NN	22-08-012
Code	NN-TL	16-04-007

Word	Tag	Frequency
code (cont.):		
codes	NNS	17-07-010
code	**verb**	**5-02-003**
code	VB	1-01-001
coded	VBN	1-01-001
coding	VBG	3-01-001
codetermine	**verb**	**1-01-001**
codetermines	VBZ	1-01-001
codfish	**NN**	**1-01-001**
codification	**NN**	**3-01-001**
codify	**verb**	**1-01-001**
codified	VBN	1-01-001
Cody	**NP**	**1-01-001**
Coe	**NP**	**5-01-001**
coed	**noun**	**2-02-002**
coed	NN	1-01-001
coeds	NNS	1-01-001
coeditor	**noun**	**1-01-001**
coeditors	NNS	1-01-001
coefficient	**noun**	**6-02-005**
coefficient	NN	3-02-003
coefficients	NNS	3-02-003
coerce	**verb**	**3-02-003**
coerce	VB	2-02-002
coerced	VBN	1-01-001
coercion	**NN**	**4-04-004**
coercive	**JJ**	**2-01-002**
coexist	**VB**	**1-01-001**
coexistence	**noun**	**12-05-007**
coexistence	NN	11-04-006
co-existence	NN	1-01-001
coexistent	**JJ**	**1-01-001**
cofactor	**noun**	**1-01-001**
cofactors	NNS	1-01-001
coffee	**noun**	**78-10-036**
coffee	NN	76-10-034
Coffee	NN-TL	2-02-002
coffee-house	**noun**	**2-01-001**
coffee-house	NN	1-01-001
Coffee-House	NN-TL	1-01-001
coffeecup	**NN**	**1-01-001**
coffeepot	**NN**	**2-02-002**
coffer	**noun**	**1-01-001**
coffers	NNS	1-01-001
coffin	**NN**	**6-04-005**
Coffin	**NP**	**1-01-001**
cog	**noun**	**1-01-001**
cogs	NNS	1-01-001
cogently	**RB**	**1-01-001**
cognac	**NN**	**4-02-002**
cognate	**JJ**	**1-01-001**
cognitive	**JJ**	**2-02-002**
cognizance	**NN**	**2-02-002**
cognizant	**JJ**	**2-02-002**
Cohen	**NP**	**3-02-003**
cohere	**VB**	**1-01-001**
coherence	**NN**	**1-01-001**
coherent	**JJ**	**5-05-005**
cohesion	**NN**	**6-04-005**
cohesive	**adjective**	**11-03-004**
cohesive	JJ	10-03-004
cohesive	JJ-HL	1-01-001
cohesively	**RB**	**1-01-001**
cohesiveness	**NN**	**1-01-001**
Cohn	**NP**	**4-02-002**
cohort	**noun**	**1-01-001**
cohorts	NNS	1-01-001
coiffure	**NN**	**1-01-001**
coil	**noun**	**8-03-004**
coil	NN	6-02-003
coils	NNS	2-02-002
coil	**verb**	**2-01-002**
coiled	VBD	1-01-001
coiling	VBG	1-01-001
coin	**noun**	**18-08-014**
coin	NN	9-07-009
coins	NNS	9-06-007
coin	**verb**	**4-03-004**
coin	VB	1-01-001
coined	VBD	1-01-001
coined	VBN	2-02-002
coincide	**verb**	**24-07-019**
coincide	VB	12-05-009
coincides	VBZ	5-02-003
coincided	VBD	6-05-006
coinciding	VBG	1-01-001
coincidence	**noun**	**13-07-012**
coincidence	NN	11-07-010
coincidences	NNS	2-02-002
coincidental	**JJ**	**1-01-001**
coke	**NN**	**2-01-001**
Coke	**prop. noun**	**3-02-002**
Coke	NP	2-01-001
Cokes	NPS	1-01-001
Colavito	**NP**	**1-01-001**
colchicum	**NN**	**1-01-001**
Colcord	**prop. noun**	**3-01-001**
Colcord	NP	1-01-001
Colcord's	NP$	2-01-001
cold	**adjective**	**147-13-091**
cold	JJ	139-13-087
Cold	JJ-TL	8-04-004
cold	**noun**	**24-09-015**
cold	NN	22-08-013
colds	NNS	2-02-002
cold	**RB**	**2-01-001**
cold-blooded	**JJ**	**1-01-001**
cold-bloodedly	**RB**	**1-01-001**
cold-war	**NN**	**1-01-001**
colder	**JJR**	**5-04-005**
coldest	**JJT**	**4-02-004**
coldly	**RB**	**8-06-008**
coldness	**NN**	**4-03-004**
Cole	**prop. noun**	**2-01-001**
Cole	NP	1-01-001
Cole's	NP$	1-01-001
Colee	**NP**	**1-01-001**
Colefax	**NP**	**1-01-001**
Coleman	**NP**	**2-02-002**
Coleridge	**prop. noun**	**3-01-003**
Coleridge	NP	1-01-001
Coleridge's	NP$	2-01-002
Coles	**NP**	**1-01-001**
Coletta	**NP**	**1-01-001**
Colfax	**prop. noun**	**1-01-001**
Colfax	NP	0-00-000
Colfax	NP-TL	1-01-001
colicky	**JJ**	**1-01-001**
Coliseum	**prop. noun**	**1-01-001**
Coliseum	NP	0-00-000
Coliseum	NP-TL	1-01-001
collaborate	**verb**	**11-05-007**
collaborate	VB	2-02-002
collaborated	VBD	5-02-003
collaborated	VBN	4-02-003
collaboration	**NN**	**12-03-008**
collaborator	**noun**	**5-04-004**
collaborator	NN	1-01-001
collaborators	NNS	4-04-004
collage	**noun**	**17-01-001**
collage	NN	15-01-001
collages	NNS	2-01-001
collagen	**NN**	**3-01-001**
collapse	**NN**	**6-04-006**
collapse	**verb**	**18-10-017**
collapse	VB	1-01-001
collapses	VBZ	1-01-001
collapsed	VBD	10-06-009
collapsed	VBN	3-03-003
collapsing	VBG	3-03-003
collapsible	**JJ**	**1-01-001**
collar	**JJ**	**1-01-001**
collar	**noun**	**14-08-012**
collar	NN	13-08-012
collars	NNS	1-01-001
collar	**verb**	**4-04-004**
collar	VB	3-03-003
collared	VBN	1-01-001
collar-to-collar	**JJ**	**1-01-001**
collarbone	**NN**	**1-01-001**
collate	**verb**	**1-01-001**
collated	VBN	1-01-001
collation	**NN**	**1-01-001**
colleague	**noun**	**32-09-022**
colleague	NN	9-05-007
colleagues	NNS	23-09-018
collect	**verb**	**78-15-060**
collect	VB	16-11-016
collects	VBZ	5-04-005
collected	VBD	7-04-007
collected	VBN	36-09-029
Collected	VBN-TL	1-01-001
collecting	VBG	13-08-011
collectible	**JJ**	**1-01-001**
collection	**noun**	**92-14-046**
collection	NN	82-14-042
collection	NN-HL	1-01-001
Collection	NN-TL	1-01-001

Word	Tag	Frequency
collection (cont.):		
collections	NNS	8-05-008
collective	**adjective**	**31-08-019**
collective	JJ	30-08-018
collective	JJ-HL	1-01-001
collective	**NN**	**1-01-001**
collective-bargaining	**NN**	**1-01-001**
collectively	**RB**	**4-03-004**
collector	**noun**	**16-08-010**
collector	NN	7-03-003
Collector	NN-TL	1-01-001
collector's	NN$	0-00-000
Collector's	NN$-TL	1-01-001
collectors	NNS	7-04-006
college	**noun**	**308-14-085**
college	NN	164-13-056
college	NN-HL	4-03-004
College	NN-TL	99-10-033
college's	NN$	1-01-001
College's	NN$-TL	1-01-001
colleges	NNS	39-09-022
college-educated	**JJ**	**1-01-001**
college-oriented	**JJ**	**1-01-001**
collegian	**noun**	**1-01-001**
collegians	NNS	1-01-001
collegiate	**adjective**	**4-03-004**
collegiate	JJ	3-02-003
Collegiate	JJ-TL	1-01-001
colles	**FW-JJ**	**1-01-001**
Collett	**NP**	**1-01-001**
collide	**verb**	**1-01-001**
collided	VBD	1-01-001
collie	**NN**	**2-02-002**
collimate	**verb**	**1-01-001**
collimated	VBN	1-01-001
Collingwood	**NP**	**2-01-001**
Collins	**prop. noun**	**7-03-007**
Collins	NP	6-03-006
Collins'	NP$	1-01-001
Collinsville	**NP**	**1-01-001**
collision	**noun**	**9-07-007**
collision	NN	7-05-005
collisions	NNS	2-02-002
colloidal	**JJ**	**2-01-001**
colloquial	**JJ**	**2-02-002**
colloquium	**NN**	**2-01-001**
colloquy	**NN**	**1-01-001**
collusion	**NN**	**3-02-002**
Collyer	**prop. noun**	**1-01-001**
Collyer	NP	0-00-000
Collyer	NP-TL	1-01-001
Colman	**prop. noun**	**4-02-002**
Colman	NP	3-01-001
Colmans	NPS	1-01-001
Colmer	**prop. noun**	**7-01-001**
Colmer	NP	6-01-001
Colmer's	NP$	1-01-001
Cologne	**prop. noun**	**9-03-004**
Cologne	NP	6-03-004
Cologne	NP-TL	3-01-001
Colombia	**NP**	**1-01-001**
Colombian	**JJ**	**1-01-001**
Colombian	**NP**	**1-01-001**
colon	**NN**	**2-01-001**
colonel	**noun**	**47-07-024**
colonel	NN	11-03-008
col.	NN	0-00-000
Col.	NN-TL	7-05-005
Colonel	NN-TL	26-06-015
colonel's	NN$	2-02-002
colonels	NNS	1-01-001
colonial	**adjective**	**21-08-015**
colonial	JJ	14-07-011
Colonial	JJ-TL	7-04-004
colonial	**noun**	**1-01-001**
colonials	NNS	1-01-001
colonialism	**NN**	**4-03-003**
colonialist	**NN**	**1-01-001**
colonist	**noun**	**2-01-002**
colonists	NNS	1-01-001
colonists'	NNS$	1-01-001
colonize	**verb**	**1-01-001**
colonized	VBD	1-01-001
Colonna	**NP**	**2-02-002**
colonnade	**NN**	**3-01-001**
colonnaded	**adjective**	**2-02-002**
colonnaded	JJ	1-01-001
collonaded	JJ	1-01-001
Colonus	**NP**	**1-01-001**
colony	**noun**	**36-09-015**
colony	NN	28-07-010
colony's	NN$	1-01-001
colonies	NNS	7-07-007
color	**noun**	**184-14-099**
color	NN	131-14-085
color	NN-HL	2-02-002
Color	NN-TL	2-02-002
colors	NNS	47-11-031
colors	NNS-HL	1-01-001
Colors	NNS-TL	1-01-001
color	**verb**	**44-11-027**
color	VB	5-04-004
colors	VBZ	3-03-003
colored	VBN	30-10-020
coloured	VBN	1-01-001
Colored	VBN-TL	1-01-001
coloring	VBG	4-02-002
color-TV	**NN**	**2-01-001**
Colorado	**prop. noun**	**16-07-013**
Colorado	NP	9-06-009
Colo.	NP	2-01-001
Colorado	NP-TL	4-04-004
Colorado's	NP$	1-01-001
Colorama	**NP**	**1-01-001**
coloration	**NN**	**2-01-001**
coloratura	**NN**	**2-02-002**
colored	**noun**	**1-01-001**
coloreds	NNS	1-01-001
colorful	**JJ**	**22-07-018**
coloring	**noun**	**4-04-004**
coloring	NN	3-03-003
colorin'	NN	1-01-001
colorless	**JJ**	**3-02-003**
colossal	**adjective**	**4-03-004**
colossal	JJ	3-03-003
collosal	JJ	1-01-001
Colosseum	**NP**	**2-01-001**
Colossian	**prop. noun**	**1-01-001**
Colossians	NPS	0-00-000
Colossians	NPS-TL	1-01-001
colossus	**noun**	**2-02-002**
colossus	NN	1-01-001
Colossus	NN-TL	1-01-001
colour-print	**noun**	**1-01-001**
colour-prints	NNS	1-01-001
Colquitt	**prop. noun**	**2-01-001**
Colquitt	NP	0-00-000
Colquitt	NP-HL	1-01-001
Colquitt	NP-TL	1-01-001
colt	**noun**	**21-04-005**
colt	NN	13-02-002
colts	NNS	6-03-003
Colts	NNS-TL	2-01-001
Colt	**prop. noun**	**6-03-005**
Colt	NP	4-03-004
Colt	NP-TL	1-01-001
Colt's	NP$	1-01-001
coltish	**JJ**	**1-01-001**
Coltsman	**prop. noun**	**1-01-001**
Coltsman	NP	0-00-000
Coltsman	NP-TL	1-01-001
Columbia	**prop. noun**	**20-07-013**
Columbia	NP	4-02-002
Columbia	NP-TL	16-06-011
columbine	**noun**	**1-01-001**
columbines	NNS	1-01-001
Columbus	**prop. noun**	**14-07-012**
Columbus	NP	8-05-007
Columbus	NP-TL	6-05-006
column	**noun**	**107-13-046**
column	NN	59-12-033
column	NN-HL	1-01-001
Column	NN-TL	11-02-002
columns	NNS	31-09-018
Columns	NNS-TL	5-02-002
column-shaped	**JJ**	**1-01-001**
columnist	**noun**	**7-04-007**
columnist	NN	4-03-004
Columnist	NN-TL	1-01-001
columnists	NNS	2-01-002
Colvin	**prop. noun**	**1-01-001**
Colvin's	NP$	1-01-001
Colzani	**NP**	**1-01-001**
coma	**noun**	**1-01-001**
comas	NNS	1-01-001
Comanche	**NP**	**1-01-001**
comb	**NN**	**6-03-005**
comb	**verb**	**5-05-005**

Word	Tag	Frequency
comb (cont.):		
combed	VBD	3-03-003
combed	VBN	1-01-001
combing	VBG	1-01-001
combat	**FW-NN**	**1-01-001**
combat	**NN**	**22-08-013**
combat	**verb**	**6-05-006**
combat	VB	4-04-004
combatted	VBN	1-01-001
combating	VBG	1-01-001
combat-inflicted	**JJ**	**1-01-001**
combat-tested	**JJ**	**1-01-001**
combatant	**JJ**	**1-01-001**
combatant	**noun**	**2-02-002**
combatant	NN	1-01-001
combatants	NNS	1-01-001
Combe	**NP**	**1-01-001**
Combellack	**NP**	**2-01-001**
combinable	**JJ**	**1-01-001**
combination	**noun**	**76-12-055**
combination	NN	57-12-043
combinations	NNS	19-08-016
combine	**NN**	**2-02-002**
combine	**verb**	**72-09-057**
combine	VB	15-06-012
combines	VBZ	7-06-007
combined	VBD	6-04-006
combined	VBN	33-08-029
Combined	VBN-TL	1-01-001
combining	VBG	10-05-009
combo	**NN**	**4-03-004**
Combs	**NP**	**1-01-001**
combustible	**noun**	**1-01-001**
combustibles	NNS	1-01-001
combustion	**NN**	**12-03-003**
come	**verb**	**1561-15-396**
come	VB	431-15-242
com	VB	1-01-001
comest	VB	1-01-001
come	VB-HL	1-01-001
come	VB-NC	2-01-001
Come	VB-TL	5-03-003
c'mon	VB+RP	1-01-001
comes	VBZ	135-14-102
cometh	VBZ	1-01-001
Comes	VBZ-TL	2-01-001
came	VBD	618-15-260
came	VBD-NC	4-01-001
come	VBN	191-15-143
coming	VBG	160-14-121
a-coming	VBG	2-01-001
comin	VBG	3-01-001
comin'	VBG	0-00-000
Comin'	VBG-TL	1-01-001
comminge	VBG	1-01-001
coming	VBG-HL	1-01-001
come-uppance	**NN**	**1-01-001**
comeback	**NN**	**2-02-002**
comedian	**noun**	**7-05-007**
comedian	NN	4-03-004
Comedian	NN-TL	1-01-001
comedians	NNS	2-02-002
comedie	**foreign**	**16-01-002**
comedie	FW-NN	1-01-001
Comedie	FW-NN-TL	13-01-001
comedie's	FW-NN$	0-00-000
Comedie's	FW-NN$-TL	2-01-001
comedy	**noun**	**41-08-019**
comedy	NN	38-08-017
Comedy	NN-TL	1-01-001
comedies	NNS	2-01-001
comely	**JJ**	**1-01-001**
Comenico	**NP**	**1-01-001**
comer	**NN**	**1-01-001**
comet	**noun**	**4-03-003**
comet	NN	1-01-001
Comet	NN-TL	1-01-001
comets	NNS	2-02-002
comet's-tail	**NN**	**1-01-001**
cometary	**JJ**	**1-01-001**
comfort	**noun**	**46-14-037**
comfort	NN	41-14-034
comforts	NNS	5-03-003
comfort	**verb**	**11-09-010**
comfort	VB	2-02-002
comforted	VBN	1-01-001
comforting	VBG	8-08-008
comfortable	**JJ**	**37-12-033**
comfortably	**RB**	**12-07-011**
comic	**JJ**	**7-05-006**
comic	**noun**	**3-03-003**
comic	NN	2-02-002
comics	NNS	0-00-000
Comics	NNS-TL	1-01-001
comically	**RB**	**2-01-002**
comico-romantico	**JJ**	**1-01-001**
Cominform	**NP**	**1-01-001**
coming	**noun**	**16-10-016**
coming	NN	12-06-012
comin'	NN	2-02-002
Coming	NN-TL	1-01-001
comings	NNS	1-01-001
comique	**foreign**	**1-01-001**
comique	FW-JJ	0-00-000
Comique	FW-JJ-TL	1-01-001
Comiskey	**NP**	**1-01-001**
comma	**NN**	**2-02-002**
command	**noun**	**74-13-033**
command	NN	48-13-025
Command	NN-TL	14-05-008
commands	NNS	12-03-005
command	**verb**	**39-12-031**
command	VB	10-05-009
commands	VBZ	3-03-003
commanded	VBD	10-04-009
commawnded	VBD	1-01-001
commanded	VBN	5-04-004
commanding	VBG	9-04-008
Commanding	VBG-TL	1-01-001
Command	**prop. noun**	**1-01-001**
Command's	NP$	1-01-001
commandant	**NN**	**1-01-001**
commandeer	**verb**	**2-02-002**
commandeered	VBN	1-01-001
commandeering	VBG	1-01-001
commander	**noun**	**35-10-022**
commander	NN	23-09-017
cmdr.	NN	0-00-000
Cmdr.	NN-TL	1-01-001
commander	NN-HL	1-01-001
Commander	NN-TL	4-02-003
commanders	NNS	5-04-004
Commanders	NNS-TL	1-01-001
commander-in-chief	**noun**	**4-01-002**
commander-in-chief	NN	3-01-001
Commander-in-Chief	NN-TL	1-01-001
commanding	**NN**	**1-01-001**
commandment	**NN**	**2-01-002**
commando	**NN**	**2-02-002**
commando-trained	**JJ**	**1-01-001**
commemorate	**verb**	**6-02-004**
commemorate	VB	2-02-002
commemorates	VBZ	1-01-001
commemorated	VBN	2-02-002
commemorating	VBG	1-01-001
commence	**verb**	**18-10-016**
commence	VB	2-01-002
commences	VBZ	1-01-001
commenced	VBD	6-04-006
commenced	VBN	1-01-001
commencing	VBG	8-07-008
commencement	**noun**	**4-02-002**
commencement	NN	3-02-002
commencements	NNS	1-01-001
commend	**verb**	**15-09-013**
commend	VB	7-03-006
comend	VB	1-01-001
commends	VBZ	1-01-001
commended	VBD	1-01-001
commended	VBN	3-03-003
commending	VBG	2-02-002
commendable	**JJ**	**5-04-005**
commendation	**NN**	**1-01-001**
commensurate	**JJ**	**4-03-004**
comment	**noun**	**64-14-049**
comment	NN	35-13-028
comments	NNS	27-09-022
comments	NNS-HL	1-01-001
Comments	NNS-TL	1-01-001
comment	**verb**	**31-11-028**
comment	VB	7-05-006
comments	VBZ	1-01-001
commented	VBD	16-07-015
commented	VBN	2-02-002
commenting	VBG	5-04-005
commentary	**noun**	**11-05-008**
commentary	NN	5-04-005
Commentary	NN-TL	3-01-001

commentary (cont.):		
commentaries	NNS	2-02-002
Commentaries	NNS-TL	1-01-001
commentator	**noun**	**5-03-005**
commentator	NN	3-03-003
commentators	NNS	2-02-002
commercant	**foreign**	**1-01-001**
commercant	FW-NN	0-00-000
Commercants	FW-NNS-TL	1-01-001
commerce	**noun**	**58-06-030**
commerce	NN	17-05-008
commerce	NN-NC	1-01-001
Commerce	NN-TL	40-06-023
commercial	**JJ**	**59-08-035**
commercial	**noun**	**12-04-007**
commercial	NN	2-02-002
commercials	NNS	10-03-006
commercialism	**NN**	**1-01-001**
commercialization	**NN**	**1-01-001**
commercially	**RB**	**11-04-010**
Commie	**prop. noun**	**2-02-002**
Commies	NPS	2-02-002
commingle	**verb**	**1-01-001**
commingled	VBN	1-01-001
commiserate	**VB**	**1-01-001**
commissary	**noun**	**2-02-002**
commissary	NN	1-01-001
Commissary	NN-TL	1-01-001
commission	**noun**	**117-09-053**
commission	NN	27-09-021
Commission	NN-TL	76-08-032
commission's	NN$	2-02-002
Commission's	NN$-TL	1-01-001
commissions	NNS	9-06-008
Commissions	NNS-TL	2-01-001
commission	**verb**	**2-02-002**
commissioned	VBN	2-02-002
Commission-controlled	**JJ**	**1-01-001**
commissioner	**noun**	**36-08-025**
commissioner	NN	6-02-005
Commissioner	NN-TL	12-05-009
Commissioner	NN-TL-HL	1-01-001
commissioners	NNS	11-04-007
Commissioners	NNS-TL	5-05-005
commissioner's	NN$	0-00-000
Commissioner's	NN$-TL	1-01-001
commit	**JJ**	**1-01-001**
commit	**verb**	**50-13-041**
commit	VB	15-09-013
commits	VBZ	2-02-002
committed	VBD	4-04-004
committed	VBN	24-10-020
committing	VBG	5-05-005
commitment	**noun**	**29-08-023**
commitment	NN	13-07-011
committment	NN	1-01-001
commitments	NNS	15-07-012
committee	**noun**	**188-10-070**
committee	NN	82-09-039
Committee	NN-TL	86-09-043
committee's	NN$	1-01-001
Committee's	NN$-TL	1-01-001
committees	NNS	15-06-012
Committees	NNS-TL	3-02-002
committeeman	**noun**	**5-02-002**
committeeman	NN	0-00-000
Committeeman	NN-TL	1-01-001
committeemen	NNS	2-02-002
Committeemen	NNS-TL	2-01-001
committeewoman	**NN**	**2-01-001**
commodity	**noun**	**28-07-010**
commodity	NN	7-03-004
commodities	NNS	20-06-009
Commodities	NNS-TL	1-01-001
commodore	**noun**	**3-01-001**
commodore	NN	0-00-000
Commodore	NN-NC	1-01-001
Commodore	NN-TL	2-01-001
common	**adjective**	**211-14-126**
common	JJ	201-14-123
common	JJ-HL	2-02-002
Common	JJ-TL	8-04-004
common	**noun**	**16-09-010**
common	NN	7-07-007
commons	NN	1-01-001
Common	NN-TL	5-01-001
commons	NNS	0-00-000
Commons	NNS-TL	3-02-002
common-sense	**JJ**	**1-01-001**
common-sense	**NN**	**1-01-001**
commoner	**JJR**	**1-01-001**
commoner	**noun**	**1-01-001**
commoners	NNS	1-01-001
commonest	**JJT**	**1-01-001**
commonly	**RB**	**29-07-021**
commonness	**NN**	**1-01-001**
commonplace	**JJ**	**13-07-013**
commonplace	**noun**	**4-03-004**
commonplace	NN	2-01-002
commonplaces	NNS	2-02-002
Commonweal	**prop. noun**	**3-02-002**
Commonweal	NP	2-02-002
Commonweal	NP-TL	1-01-001
commonwealth	**noun**	**8-04-006**
commonwealth	NN	2-01-001
Commonwealth	NN-TL	5-03-004
commonwealths	NNS	1-01-001
commotion	**NN**	**6-06-006**
communal	**JJ**	**4-03-003**
commune	**noun**	**8-03-004**
commune	NN	2-02-002
Commune	NN-TL	1-01-001
communes	NNS	5-02-002
commune	**VB**	**1-01-001**
Communese	**NP**	**5-01-001**
communicate	**verb**	**22-07-016**
communicate	VB	13-06-011
communicated	VBN	3-03-003
communicating	VBG	6-05-005
communicating	**NN**	**1-01-001**
communication	**noun**	**95-12-050**
communication	NN	66-11-035
communication	NN-HL	1-01-001
communications	NNS	25-08-018
communications	NNS-HL	1-01-001
Communications	NNS-TL	2-01-002
communicational	**JJ**	**2-01-001**
communicative	**JJ**	**6-03-005**
communicator	**noun**	**5-02-002**
communicator	NN	3-01-001
communicator's	NN$	1-01-001
communicators	NNS	1-01-001
communion	**noun**	**11-05-010**
communion	NN	10-05-009
Communion	NN-TL	1-01-001
communique	**noun**	**1-01-001**
communiques	NNS	1-01-001
communism	**noun**	**74-09-024**
communism	NN	38-05-009
communism	NN-NC	1-01-001
Communism	NN-TL	31-08-015
Communisn	NN-TL	1-01-001
communism's	NN$	1-01-001
Communism's	NN$-TL	2-02-002
Communist	**adjective**	**24-04-009**
Communist	JJ	21-04-009
Communist	JJ-HL	1-01-001
Communist	JJ-TL	2-01-002
communist	**noun**	**112-08-034**
communist	NN	5-04-004
Communist	NN-TL	68-06-031
communists	NNS	0-00-000
Communists	NNS-TL	39-08-024
Communist-inspired	**JJ**	**1-01-001**
Communist-led	**JJ**	**2-02-002**
Communist-type	**JJ**	**1-01-001**
communistic	**adjective**	**2-02-002**
communistic	JJ	1-01-001
Communistic	JJ	1-01-001
community	**noun**	**275-12-095**
community	NN	217-12-082
community	NN-HL	2-02-002
Community	NN-TL	12-06-008
community's	NN$	3-03-003
communties	NNS	41-09-026
communize	**VB**	**1-01-001**
commutation	**NN**	**1-01-001**
commutator-like	**JJ**	**1-01-001**
commute	**verb**	**19-04-007**
commute	VB	10-01-001
commutes	VBZ	2-01-001
commuted	VBD	1-01-001
commuted	VBN	1-01-001
commuting	VBG	5-03-004
commuter	**NN**	**10-01-001**
compact	**JJ**	**9-06-007**
compact	**noun**	**4-03-003**
compact	NN	3-02-002

Word	Tag	Frequency
compact (cont.):		
compacts	NNS	1-01-001
compactly	**RB**	**1-01-001**
compagnie	**foreign**	**1-01-001**
compagnie	FW-NN	0-00-000
Compagnie	FW-NN-TL	1-01-001
companion	**noun**	**27-10-024**
companion	NN	19-09-018
companions	NNS	8-04-007
companionable	**JJ**	**1-01-001**
companionship	**NN**	**4-04-004**
companionway	**NN**	**1-01-001**
company	**noun**	**453-15-134**
company	NN	218-15-090
co.	NN	0-00-000
Co.	NN-TL	48-08-024
company	NN-HL	1-01-001
Company	NN-TL	71-12-033
company's	NN+BEZ	2-02-002
company's	NN+HVZ	1-01-001
company's	NN$	17-05-010
Company's	NN$-TL	7-04-005
Comany's	NN$-TL	1-01-001
companies	NNS	87-10-035
company-paid	**JJ**	**1-01-001**
company-wide	**JJ**	**1-01-001**
comparable	**JJ**	**41-07-037**
comparative	**adjective**	**17-04-014**
comparative	JJ	16-03-013
comparative	JJ-HL	1-01-001
comparatively	**QL**	**12-05-012**
comparatively	**RB**	**3-02-002**
compare	**verb**	**114-13-085**
compare	VB	28-08-026
compares	VBZ	6-03-006
compared	VBD	10-06-008
compared	VBN	61-11-047
comparing	VBG	9-05-008
comparison	**noun**	**54-10-042**
comparison	NN	48-10-038
comparisons	NNS	6-03-005
compartment	**noun**	**12-07-009**
compartment	NN	11-06-008
compartments	NNS	1-01-001
compass	**NN**	**12-05-008**
compass	**VB**	**1-01-001**
compassion	**NN**	**5-05-005**
compassionate	**JJ**	**2-02-002**
compassionately	**RB**	**2-02-002**
compatibility	**noun**	**1-01-001**
compatibility	NN	0-00-000
compatability	NN	1-01-001
compatible	**JJ**	**16-05-014**
compatriot	**noun**	**2-02-002**
compatriot	NN	1-01-001
compatriots	NNS	1-01-001
compel	**verb**	**25-08-022**
compel	VB	4-03-004
compels	VBZ	2-02-002
compelled	VBD	1-01-001
compelled	VBN	17-08-015
compelling	VBG	1-01-001
compelling	**JJ**	**7-04-007**
compendium	**NN**	**1-01-001**
compensate	**verb**	**10-05-010**
compensate	VB	3-02-003
compensates	VBZ	1-01-001
compensated	VBN	4-03-004
compensating	VBG	2-02-002
compensation	**noun**	**20-07-017**
compensation	NN	17-07-014
compensations	NNS	3-03-003
compensatory	**JJ**	**3-03-003**
compete	**verb**	**41-08-034**
compete	VB	23-08-021
competes	VBZ	1-01-001
competed	VBD	2-02-002
competing	VBG	15-08-014
competence	**NN**	**18-07-012**
competency	**NN**	**1-01-001**
competent	**JJ**	**21-11-019**
competently	**RB**	**5-03-005**
competition	**noun**	**63-11-031**
competition	NN	56-11-031
competition	NN-HL	1-01-001
Competition	NN-TL	6-01-001
competitive	**JJ**	**31-04-020**
competitively	**RB**	**2-02-002**
competitor	**noun**	**13-07-011**
competitor (cont.):		
competitor	NN	3-03-003
competitors	NNS	10-07-008
Compeyson	**NP**	**2-01-001**
compilation	**noun**	**13-03-005**
compilation	NN	10-03-005
compilation	NN-HL	1-01-001
compilations	NNS	2-01-002
compile	**verb**	**15-05-010**
compile	VB	1-01-001
compiled	VBD	2-02-002
compiled	VBN	8-04-006
compiling	VBG	4-02-003
compiler	**noun**	**7-01-001**
compiler	NN	5-01-001
Compiler	NN-TL	2-01-001
complacency	**NN**	**4-04-004**
complacent	**JJ**	**1-01-001**
complain	**verb**	**41-11-036**
complain	VB	11-06-010
complains	VBZ	3-02-002
complained	VBD	21-07-020
complained	VBN	1-01-001
complaining	VBG	5-04-005
complainant	**NN**	**1-01-001**
complaint	**noun**	**22-08-021**
complaint	NN	14-05-013
complaints	NNS	8-06-008
complaisance	**NN**	**1-01-001**
complaisant	**JJ**	**1-01-001**
complement	**noun**	**21-04-007**
complement	NN	19-04-007
complements	NNS	2-01-001
complement	**verb**	**3-03-003**
complement	VB	2-02-002
complementing	VBG	1-01-001
complementary	**JJ**	**4-04-004**
complete	**adjective**	**163-15-109**
complete	JJ	161-15-108
complete	JJ-HL	2-01-002
complete	**verb**	**107-14-076**
complete	VB	19-08-016
completes	VBZ	5-03-005
completed	VBD	6-04-006
completed	VBN	63-13-051
compleated	VBN	1-01-001
completing	VBG	13-09-011
completely	**QL**	**47-10-040**
completely	**RB**	**63-12-048**
completely-restored	**JJ**	**1-01-001**
completeness	**NN**	**4-03-003**
completion	**noun**	**64-06-021**
completion	NN	36-06-020
Completion	NN-TL	21-01-001
completions	NNS	3-01-001
Completions	NNS-TL	4-01-001
complex	**JJ**	**59-09-047**
complex	**noun**	**38-08-018**
complex	NN	31-08-016
Complex	NN-TL	1-01-001
complexes	NNS	6-02-002
complex-valued	**JJ**	**1-01-001**
complexion	**noun**	**7-04-007**
complexion	NN	6-04-006
complection	NN	1-01-001
complexity	**noun**	**18-08-014**
complexity	NN	13-08-011
complexity	NN-HL	1-01-001
complexities	NNS	4-02-003
compliance	**NN**	**6-03-005**
complicate	**verb**	**33-11-029**
complicate	VB	2-02-002
complicated	VBD	1-01-001
complicated	VBN	29-09-025
complicating	VBG	1-01-001
complication	**noun**	**9-06-009**
complication	NN	4-03-004
complications	NNS	5-04-005
complicity	**NN**	**7-02-003**
compliment	**noun**	**7-05-007**
compliment	NN	3-03-003
compliments	NNS	4-03-004
compliment	**verb**	**3-02-003**
complimented	VBN	2-02-002
complimenting	VBG	1-01-001
complimentary	**JJ**	**2-02-002**
comply	**verb**	**14-09-013**
comply	VB	5-05-005
complied	VBD	2-02-002

comply (cont.):		
complied	VBN	4-03-003
complying	VBG	3-03-003
component	**noun**	**80-07-040**
component	NN	25-04-018
components	NNS	54-06-028
Components	NNS-TL	1-01-001
comport	**verb**	**2-02-002**
comport	VB	1-01-001
comported	VBD	1-01-001
comportment	**NN**	**1-01-001**
compose	**verb**	**50-11-039**
compose	VB	6-05-005
composes	VBZ	2-01-001
composed	VBD	4-02-004
composed	VBN	36-09-030
composing	VBG	2-02-002
composer	**noun**	**46-07-017**
composer	NN	31-06-014
composer's	NN$	1-01-001
composers	NNS	12-05-009
Composers	NNS-TL	1-01-001
composers'	NNS$	1-01-001
composer-pianist-conductor	**NN**	**1-01-001**
composing	**NN**	**1-01-001**
composite	**JJ**	**10-02-005**
composite	**noun**	**7-03-004**
composite	NN	3-02-003
Composite	NN-TL	3-01-001
composites	NNS	1-01-001
composition	**noun**	**35-08-023**
composition	NN	25-07-019
compositions	NNS	10-03-006
compositional	**JJ**	**1-01-001**
compost	**NN**	**8-02-002**
composure	**NN**	**4-04-004**
compote	**NN**	**1-01-001**
compound	**noun**	**24-06-009**
compound	NN	9-05-006
compounds	NNS	15-02-004
compound	**verb**	**16-07-013**
compound	VB	2-02-002
compounds	VBZ	1-01-001
compounded	VBN	12-07-011
compounding	VBG	1-01-001
compound-engine	**NN**	**1-01-001**
comprehend	**verb**	**10-05-008**
comprehend	VB	5-04-005
comprehended	VBD	1-01-001
comprehended	VBN	1-01-001
comprehending	VBG	3-02-003
comprehension	**NN**	**7-05-007**
comprehensive	**JJ**	**19-06-013**
comprehensively	**QL**	**1-01-001**
comprehensively	**RB**	**1-01-001**
compress	**noun**	**2-02-002**
compresses	NNS	2-02-002
compress	**verb**	**13-07-011**
compress	VB	2-02-002
compresses	VBZ	1-01-001
compressed	VBD	1-01-001
compressed	VBN	8-05-007
compressing	VBG	1-01-001
compressibility	**NN**	**1-01-001**
compression	**noun**	**8-02-002**
compression	NN	6-02-002
compression	NN-HL	2-02-002
compressive	**JJ**	**2-01-002**
compressor	**NN**	**2-01-001**
comprise	**verb**	**25-09-022**
comprise	VB	11-05-010
comprises	VBZ	3-02-003
comprised	VBD	3-03-003
comprised	VBN	5-04-004
comprising	VBG	3-02-003
compromise	**noun**	**18-06-012**
compromise	NN	16-06-012
Compromise	NN-TL	1-01-001
compromises	NNS	1-01-001
compromise	**verb**	**8-05-008**
compromise	VB	3-02-003
compromised	VBD	1-01-001
compromised	VBN	1-01-001
compromising	VBG	3-03-003
compromising	**NN**	**1-01-001**
Compson	**NP**	**4-01-001**
comptroller	**noun**	**4-02-002**
comptroller	NN	0-00-000
Comptroller	NN-TL	4-02-002

compulsion	**noun**	**9-05-008**
compulsion	NN	8-05-007
compulsions	NNS	1-01-001
compulsive	**JJ**	**10-04-004**
compulsive	**noun**	**4-01-001**
compulsives	NNS	4-01-001
compulsively	**RB**	**3-03-003**
compulsivity	**noun**	**13-01-001**
compulsivity	NN	10-01-001
compulsivity	NN-HL	3-01-001
compulsory	**JJ**	**7-05-006**
computation	**noun**	**8-06-007**
computation	NN	5-05-005
Computation	NN-TL	2-01-001
computations	NNS	1-01-001
computational	**JJ**	**1-01-001**
compute	**verb**	**41-06-015**
compute	VB	7-04-005
computes	VBZ	2-01-001
computed	VBN	21-05-010
computing	VBG	7-03-005
computing	VBG-HL	2-01-001
Computing	VBG-TL	2-01-001
computer	**noun**	**18-05-010**
computer	NN	13-04-006
computers	NNS	5-04-005
comrade	**noun**	**14-04-005**
comrade	NN	4-03-003
comrades	NNS	10-04-005
comradeship	**NN**	**2-01-001**
Comroe	**NP**	**1-01-001**
Comus	**NP**	**2-01-001**
con	**foreign**	**4-01-002**
con	FW-IN	3-01-001
con	FW-IN-TL	1-01-001
con	**JJ**	**2-02-002**
con	**noun**	**2-02-002**
con	NN	1-01-001
cons	NNS	1-01-001
con	**verb**	**2-02-002**
conned	VBN	1-01-001
conning	VBG	1-01-001
Conan	**NP**	**2-01-002**
Conant	**prop. noun**	**10-04-004**
Conant	NP	7-04-004
Conant's	NP$	0-00-000
Conant's	NP$-HL	3-01-001
concave	**JJ**	**4-02-003**
conceal	**verb**	**18-08-016**
conceal	VB	7-05-007
conceals	VBZ	2-02-002
concealed	VBD	1-01-001
concealed	VBN	7-06-007
concealing	VBG	1-01-001
concealment	**NN**	**2-02-002**
concede	**verb**	**23-09-020**
concede	VB	8-06-008
concedes	VBZ	1-01-001
conceded	VBD	5-05-005
conceded	VBN	6-05-006
conceding	VBG	3-03-003
concededly	**RB**	**1-01-001**
conceit	**noun**	**2-02-002**
conceits	NNS	2-02-002
conceivable	**JJ**	**11-06-010**
conceivably	**RB**	**10-06-010**
conceive	**verb**	**45-12-039**
conceive	VB	14-07-014
conceives	VBZ	2-02-002
conceived	VBD	7-06-007
conceived	VBN	20-09-018
conceiving	VBG	2-02-002
concentrate	**noun**	**6-04-004**
concentrate	NN	1-01-001
concentrates	NNS	5-03-003
concentrate	**verb**	**49-10-038**
concentrate	VB	10-05-010
concentrates	VBZ	2-02-002
concentrated	VBD	1-01-001
concentrated	VBN	29-06-022
concentrating	VBG	7-05-007
concentration	**noun**	**56-10-032**
concentration	NN	46-10-028
concentration	NN-HL	1-01-001
concentrations	NNS	9-03-008
concentration-camp	**NN**	**1-01-001**
concentric	**JJ**	**2-01-001**
concept	**noun**	**112-09-059**
concept	NN	83-09-046

Word	Tag	Frequency
concept (cont.):		
concept	NN-HL	2-01-001
concepts	NNS	27-07-018
conception	**noun**	**41-08-028**
conception	NN	32-07-023
conceptions	NNS	9-04-007
conceptual	**JJ**	**4-02-003**
conceptuality	**NN**	**2-01-001**
conceptualization	**NN**	**1-01-001**
conceptually	**RB**	**1-01-001**
concern	**noun**	**115-13-074**
concern	NN	84-13-066
concern	NN-HL	2-01-002
concerns	NNS	29-06-014
concern	**verb**	**161-14-119**
concern	VB	12-07-011
concerns	VBZ	14-10-014
concerned	VBD	4-03-004
concerned	VBN	131-12-099
concerning	**IN**	**62-11-043**
concert	**foreign**	**1-01-001**
concerts	FW-NNS	0-00-000
Concerts	FW-NNS-TL	1-01-001
concert	**noun**	**64-09-027**
concert	NN	35-07-020
Concert	NN-TL	4-04-004
concerts	NNS	21-04-011
Concerts	NNS-TL	4-02-003
Concert-Disc	**NP**	**1-01-001**
concertante	**foreign**	**1-01-001**
concertante	FW-JJ	0-00-000
Concertante	FW-JJ-TL	1-01-001
concerted	**JJ**	**3-02-003**
concertina	**NN**	**1-01-001**
concertmaster	**NN**	**1-01-001**
concerto	**noun**	**18-05-009**
concerto	NN	6-03-004
Concerto	NN-TL	5-03-005
concerto's	NN$	1-01-001
concertos	NNS	5-03-005
concerti	NNS	1-01-001
concession	**noun**	**10-05-010**
concession	NN	3-02-003
concessions	NNS	7-04-007
concessionaire	**noun**	**9-03-003**
concessionaire	NN	2-01-001
concessionaires	NNS	7-02-002
Concetta	**prop. noun**	**3-01-001**
Concetta	NP	1-01-001
Concetta's	NP$	2-01-001
Conchita	**NP**	**5-01-001**
concierge	**NN**	**2-01-001**
conciliate	**VB**	**1-01-001**
conciliator	**NN**	**1-01-001**
conciliatory	**JJ**	**2-02-002**
concise	**JJ**	**1-01-001**
conciseness	**NN**	**1-01-001**
conclave	**NN**	**2-02-002**
conclude	**verb**	**60-13-053**
conclude	VB	16-08-015
concludes	VBZ	4-03-004
concluded	VBD	21-09-018
concluded	VBN	11-08-010
concluding	VBG	7-05-007
concluding	VBG-HL	1-01-001
conclusion	**noun**	**95-12-069**
conclusion	NN	57-12-047
conclusion	NN-NC	2-01-001
conclusions	NNS	36-10-028
conclusive	**JJ**	**11-06-008**
conclusively	**RB**	**7-03-006**
concoct	**verb**	**1-01-001**
concocted	VBN	1-01-001
Concord	**prop. noun**	**10-03-003**
Concord	NP	9-03-003
Concord	NP-TL	1-01-001
Concordance	**NP**	**1-01-001**
concordant	**JJ**	**2-01-001**
concorde	**foreign**	**1-01-001**
concorde	FW-NN	0-00-000
Concorde	FW-NN-TL	1-01-001
concrete	**JJ**	**20-07-018**
concrete	**noun**	**28-09-009**
concrete	NN	26-09-009
concrete	NN-HL	1-01-001
Concrete	NN-TL	1-01-001
concretely	**RB**	**2-01-002**
concretistic	**JJ**	**2-01-002**
concretistic-seeming	**JJ**	**1-01-001**

Word	Tag	Frequency
concur	**verb**	**9-05-008**
concur	VB	4-03-004
concurs	VBZ	3-02-003
concurred	VBD	2-02-002
concurrence	**NN**	**4-04-004**
concurrent	**JJ**	**7-03-006**
concurrently	**RB**	**1-01-001**
concussion	**NN**	**1-01-001**
condemn	**verb**	**30-07-022**
condemn	VB	4-02-003
condemns	VBZ	3-01-002
condemned	VBD	6-04-005
condemned	VBN	13-07-011
condemning	VBG	4-03-004
condemnation	**NN**	**7-03-005**
condemnatory	**JJ**	**1-01-001**
condensation	**noun**	**7-02-004**
condensation	NN	6-02-004
condensation	NN-HL	1-01-001
condense	**verb**	**11-04-008**
condense	VB	1-01-001
condensed	VBN	9-03-006
condensing	VBG	1-01-001
condenser	**NN**	**1-01-001**
condescend	**verb**	**2-01-001**
condescending	VBG	2-01-001
condescension	**NN**	**2-01-001**
condiment	**noun**	**2-02-002**
condiments	NNS	2-02-002
condition	**noun**	**271-14-143**
condition	NN	86-14-065
condition	NN-HL	2-01-002
Condition	NN-TL	2-01-001
conditions	NNS	177-12-097
condicions	NNS	1-01-001
conditions	NNS-HL	2-02-002
Conditions	NNS-TL	1-01-001
condition	**verb**	**24-06-012**
condition	VB	1-01-001
conditioned	VBD	1-01-001
conditioned	VBN	19-06-008
conditioning	VBG	3-02-003
conditional	**JJ**	**3-02-002**
conditioner	**noun**	**18-04-004**
conditioner	NN	12-03-003
conditioner	NN-HL	1-01-001
conditioners	NNS	4-02-002
conditioners	NNS-HL	1-01-001
conditioning	**NN**	**11-04-005**
Condliffe	**NP**	**1-01-001**
condolence	**noun**	**1-01-001**
condolences	NNS	1-01-001
condone	**verb**	**1-01-001**
condoned	VBN	1-01-001
conducive	**JJ**	**2-02-002**
conduct	**noun**	**36-11-028**
conduct	NN	34-11-026
Conduct	NN-TL	1-01-001
conducts	NNS	1-01-001
conduct	**verb**	**91-10-053**
conduct	VB	20-07-013
conducts	VBZ	3-01-001
conducted	VBD	14-07-011
conducted	VBN	41-09-029
conducting	VBG	13-08-012
conduction	**NN**	**2-01-001**
conductivity	**noun**	**5-02-004**
conductivity	NN	4-02-004
conductivity	NN-HL	1-01-001
conductor	**noun**	**28-06-014**
conductor	NN	24-05-012
Conductor	NN-TL	1-01-001
conductor's	NN$	2-02-002
conductors	NNS	1-01-001
conduit	**noun**	**1-01-001**
conduit	NN	0-00-000
Conduit	NN-TL	1-01-001
cone	**noun**	**15-03-004**
cone	NN	13-03-004
cones	NNS	2-02-002
cone	**verb**	**2-01-001**
coning	VBG	2-01-001
cone-sphere	**NN**	**2-01-001**
Conestoga	**NP**	**2-01-002**
Coney	**prop. noun**	**3-01-002**
Coney	NP	0-00-000
Coney	NP-TL	3-01-002
confabulate	**verb**	**1-01-001**
confabulated	VBN	1-01-001

confabulation	**noun**	**4-01-001**
confabulation	NN	3-01-001
confabulations	NNS	1-01-001
confederacy	**noun**	**9-03-004**
confederacy	NN	2-02-002
confederacy	NN-HL	1-01-001
Confederacy	NN-TL	6-02-003
confederate	**adjective**	**13-03-005**
confederate	JJ	0-00-000
Confederate	JJ-TL	12-03-005
Confederate	JJ-TL-HL	1-01-001
confederate	**noun**	**3-03-003**
confederate	NN	0-00-000
Confederate	NN-TL	1-01-001
confederates	NNS	1-01-001
Confederates	NNS-TL	1-01-001
confederation	**noun**	**5-01-003**
confederation	NN	1-01-001
Confederation	NN-TL	3-01-002
confederations	NNS	1-01-001
confer	**verb**	**10-08-010**
confer	VB	3-03-003
confers	VBZ	1-01-001
conferred	VBD	1-01-001
conferred	VBN	4-04-004
conferring	VBG	1-01-001
conferee	**noun**	**2-02-002**
conferees	NNS	2-02-002
conference	**noun**	**122-12-059**
conference	NN	61-10-034
Conference	NN-TL	35-08-015
conference's	NN$	1-01-001
conferences	NNS	21-08-018
conferences	NNS-HL	1-01-001
Conferences	NNS-TL	3-02-002
confess	**verb**	**25-08-020**
confess	VB	11-05-009
'fess	VB	1-01-001
confesses	VBZ	3-02-002
confessed	VBD	6-05-006
confessed	VBN	1-01-001
confessing	VBG	3-03-003
confession	**noun**	**19-07-015**
confession	NN	16-06-012
Confession	NN-TL	1-01-001
confessions	NNS	1-01-001
Confessions	NNS-TL	1-01-001
confessional	**noun**	**3-01-001**
confessional	NN	2-01-001
confessionals	NNS	1-01-001
confessor	**NN**	**1-01-001**
confidant	**NN**	**1-01-001**
confidante	**NN**	**1-01-001**
confide	**verb**	**13-07-013**
confide	VB	3-03-003
confided	VBD	7-04-007
confided	VBN	1-01-001
confiding	VBG	2-02-002
confidence	**noun**	**58-12-046**
confidence	NN	56-12-045
confidence	NN-HL	1-01-001
confidences	NNS	1-01-001
confident	**adjective**	**17-08-017**
confident	JJ	16-07-016
cohnfidunt	JJ	1-01-001
confidential	**JJ**	**6-05-006**
confidentiality	**NN**	**1-01-001**
confidentially	**RB**	**4-04-004**
confidently	**RB**	**2-02-002**
configuration	**noun**	**10-04-008**
configuration	NN	7-02-005
configurations	NNS	3-03-003
confine	**noun**	**7-05-007**
confines	NNS	7-05-007
confine	**verb**	**21-06-019**
confine	VB	2-02-002
confined	VBD	1-01-001
confined	VBN	15-06-013
confining	VBG	3-03-003
confinement	**noun**	**8-06-007**
confinement	NN	7-06-007
confinements	NNS	1-01-001
confirm	**verb**	**41-12-037**
confirm	VB	16-07-015
confirms	VBZ	3-02-003
confirmed	VBD	8-07-008
confirmed	VBN	12-07-012
confirming	VBG	2-02-002
confirmation	**NN**	**7-05-007**
confiscate	**verb**	**3-02-003**
confiscated	VBN	2-02-002
confiscating	VBG	1-01-001
conflagration	**NN**	**1-01-001**
conflict	**noun**	**58-11-046**
conflict	NN	48-10-039
conflict	NN-HL	1-01-001
conflict's	NN$	1-01-001
conflicts	NNS	8-05-008
conflict	**verb**	**12-06-010**
conflict	VB	3-03-003
conflicts	VBZ	1-01-001
conflicting	VBG	8-04-007
confluent	**JJ**	**1-01-001**
conform	**verb**	**18-09-017**
conform	VB	10-06-010
conforms	VBZ	5-03-005
conformed	VBD	1-01-001
conformed	VBN	2-02-002
conformance	**NN**	**2-02-002**
conformation	**noun**	**4-03-003**
conformation	NN	3-02-002
conformations	NNS	0-00-000
conformations	NNS-HL	1-01-001
conformational	**JJ**	**1-01-001**
conformational	**NN**	**1-01-001**
conformist	**JJ**	**1-01-001**
conformist	**noun**	**5-03-003**
conformist	NN	2-02-002
conformists	NNS	3-02-002
conformity	**NN**	**16-04-007**
confound	**verb**	**3-02-003**
confounded	VBD	1-01-001
confounded	VBN	1-01-001
confounding	VBG	1-01-001
confrere	**noun**	**1-01-001**
confreres	NNS	1-01-001
confront	**verb**	**55-13-049**
confront	VB	8-06-008
confronts	VBZ	5-03-005
confronted	VBD	5-04-004
confronted	VBN	27-11-027
confronting	VBG	10-06-010
confrontation	**noun**	**17-06-008**
confrontation	NN	8-06-007
confrontation	NN-HL	1-01-001
Confrontation	NN-TL	7-01-001
confrontations	NNS	1-01-001
Confucian	**adjective**	**2-01-002**
Confucian	JJ	0-00-000
Confucian	JJ-TL	2-01-002
Confucian	**NP**	**1-01-001**
Confucianism	**NP**	**3-02-002**
Confucius	**NP**	**2-02-002**
confuse	**verb**	**52-12-045**
confuse	VB	5-04-005
confuses	VBZ	1-01-001
confused	VBD	4-03-003
confused	VBN	40-12-035
confusing	VBG	1-01-001
confusin'	VBG	1-01-001
confusing	**JJ**	**1-01-001**
confusion	**noun**	**48-12-042**
confusion	NN	44-12-039
confusions	NNS	4-02-004
confute	**verb**	**1-01-001**
confuted	VBN	0-00-000
Confuted	VBN-TL	1-01-001
Cong	**NP**	**1-01-001**
Congdon	**NP**	**1-01-001**
congeal	**verb**	**4-04-004**
congealed	VBD	2-02-002
congealed	VBN	2-02-002
congenial	**JJ**	**7-04-007**
congeniality	**NN**	**1-01-001**
congenital	**JJ**	**1-01-001**
congest	**verb**	**2-02-002**
congested	VBN	2-02-002
congestion	**NN**	**6-04-004**
congestive	**JJ**	**2-01-002**
Congo	**prop. noun**	**60-04-010**
Congo	NP	52-03-009
Congo	NP-HL	1-01-001
Congo	NP-TL	6-04-004
Congo's	NP$	1-01-001
Congolese	**adjective**	**7-02-002**
Congolese	JJ	4-02-002
Congolese	JJ-TL	3-01-001
Congolese	**prop. noun**	**5-01-001**

Word	Tag	Frequency
Congolese (cont.):		
Congolese	NP	1-01-001
Congolese	NPS	4-01-001
congratulate	**verb**	**7-04-007**
congratulate	VB	4-02-004
congratulated	VBN	3-02-003
congratulation	**noun**	**8-06-007**
congratulation	NN	1-01-001
congratulations	NNS	7-05-006
congratulatory	**JJ**	**2-02-002**
congregate	**verb**	**3-02-003**
congregate	VB	2-02-002
congregated	VBD	1-01-001
congregation	**noun**	**65-08-015**
congregation	NN	45-06-011
congregation	NN-HL	1-01-001
Congregation	NN-TL	1-01-001
congregations	NNS	18-03-006
congregational	**adjective**	**14-04-005**
congregational	JJ	7-01-001
Congregational	JJ-TL	7-03-004
Congregational-Baptist	**JJ**	**2-01-001**
Congregationalism	**prop. noun**	**1-01-001**
Congregationalism	NP	0-00-000
Congregationalism	NP-TL	1-01-001
Congregationalist	**prop. noun**	**5-01-001**
Congregationalist	NP	2-01-001
Congregationalists	NPS	3-01-001
congress	**noun**	**3-02-003**
congress	NN	2-01-002
congress'	NN$	0-00-000
Congress'	NN$-TL	1-01-001
Congress	**prop. noun**	**153-09-056**
Congress	NP	126-09-050
Congress	NP-HL	2-01-002
Congress	NP-TL	21-06-016
Congress	NP-TL-HL	1-01-001
Congress'	NP$	2-01-001
Congresses	NPS	1-01-001
congressional	**adjective**	**22-06-017**
congressional	JJ	14-04-009
Congressional	JJ-TL	8-06-008
congressman	**noun**	**32-07-017**
congressman	NN	6-02-002
Congressman	NN-TL	14-05-010
Congressman	NN-TL-HL	1-01-001
congressman's	NN$	1-01-001
congressmen	NNS	9-05-006
Congressmen	NNS-TL	1-01-001
congresswoman	**noun**	**2-01-001**
congresswoman	NN	0-00-000
Congresswoman	NN-TL	1-01-001
Congresswoman	NN-TL-HL	1-01-001
congruence	**NN**	**11-01-001**
congruent	**JJ**	**3-02-003**
conic	**NN**	**2-01-001**
conjecture	**noun**	**5-03-005**
conjecture	NN	3-03-003
conjectures	NNS	2-02-002
conjecture	**verb**	**1-01-001**
conjectured	VBN	1-01-001
conjoin	**verb**	**3-02-003**
conjoined	VBN	3-02-003
conjugal	**JJ**	**3-02-002**
conjugate	**noun**	**24-01-002**
conjugate	NN	10-01-001
conjugates	NNS	13-01-002
conjugates	NNS-HL	1-01-001
conjugate	**verb**	**6-01-001**
conjugated	VBN	5-01-001
conjugating	VBG	1-01-001
conjugation	**NN**	**1-01-001**
conjunction	**noun**	**17-07-015**
conjunction	NN	16-06-014
conjunctions	NNS	1-01-001
conjure	**verb**	**5-04-005**
conjure	VB	1-01-001
conjures	VBZ	2-02-002
conjured	VBD	1-01-001
conjured	VBN	1-01-001
Conlow	**NP**	**1-01-001**
Connall	**NP**	**1-01-001**
Connally	**prop. noun**	**8-01-002**
Connally	NP	6-01-001
Connally	NP-HL	1-01-001
Connally	NP-TL	1-01-001
Conneaut	**NP**	**1-01-001**
connect	**verb**	**44-14-039**
connect	VB	3-03-003

Word	Tag	Frequency
connect (cont.):		
connects	VBZ	2-02-002
connected	VBD	4-04-004
connected	VBN	29-11-028
connecting	VBG	6-03-005
Connecticut	**prop. noun**	**21-09-019**
Connecticut	NP	13-06-012
Conn.	NP	3-03-003
Connecticut	NP-HL	1-01-001
Connecticut	NP-TL	3-03-003
Connecticut's	NP$	1-01-001
connection	**noun**	**86-15-068**
connection	NN	68-14-057
connexion	NN	2-01-001
connection	NN-HL	1-01-001
connections	NNS	15-09-013
connective	**JJ**	**2-02-002**
connective	**NN**	**1-01-001**
Connell	**NP**	**1-01-001**
Connelly	**NP**	**1-01-001**
Connie	**NP**	**1-01-001**
connivance	**NN**	**1-01-001**
conniver	**NN**	**1-01-001**
connoisseur	**noun**	**6-05-005**
connoisseur	NN	3-02-002
connoisseur	NN-HL	1-01-001
connoisseurs	NNS	2-02-002
Connolly	**prop. noun**	**1-01-001**
Connolly's	NP$	1-01-001
Connor	**NP**	**1-01-001**
connotation	**noun**	**8-05-008**
connotation	NN	5-03-005
connotations	NNS	3-03-003
connote	**verb**	**2-02-002**
connote	VB	1-01-001
connotes	VBZ	1-01-001
conquer	**verb**	**10-07-007**
conquer	VB	4-03-003
conquered	VBD	1-01-001
conquered	VBN	2-02-002
conquering	VBG	1-01-001
Conquering	VBG-TL	2-01-001
conqueror	**noun**	**3-02-003**
conqueror	NN	1-01-001
conquerors	NNS	2-02-002
conquest	**noun**	**11-05-008**
conquest	NN	8-04-006
Conquest	NN-TL	1-01-001
conquests	NNS	2-02-002
conquete	**foreign**	**2-01-001**
conquete	FW-NN	1-01-001
Conquete	FW-NN-TL	1-01-001
Conrad	**prop. noun**	**12-02-003**
Conrad	NP	10-02-003
Conrad's	NP$	2-01-001
consanguineous	**JJ**	**1-01-001**
consanguineously	**RB**	**1-01-001**
consanguinity	**NN**	**2-01-001**
conscience	**noun**	**41-09-022**
conscience	NN	38-09-021
Conscience	NN	1-01-001
Conscience	NN-TL	1-01-001
consciences	NNS	1-01-001
conscientious	**JJ**	**10-06-008**
conscionable	**JJ**	**1-01-001**
conscious	**JJ**	**46-13-039**
consciously	**RB**	**12-08-012**
consciousness	**noun**	**30-09-019**
consciousness	NN	29-09-018
consciousness	NN-NC	1-01-001
conscript	**NN**	**1-01-001**
conscript	**verb**	**2-02-002**
conscripted	VBN	2-02-002
conscription	**NN**	**2-02-002**
consecration	**NN**	**1-01-001**
consecutive	**JJ**	**10-04-008**
conseil	**foreign**	**2-01-001**
conseil	FW-NN	0-00-000
Conseil	FW-NN-TL	2-01-001
consensus	**NN**	**7-03-006**
consent	**NN**	**15-06-010**
consent	**verb**	**7-05-007**
consent	VB	1-01-001
Consent	VB-TL	1-01-001
consented	VBD	2-01-002
consented	VBN	2-02-002
consenting	VBG	1-01-001
consequence	**noun**	**65-13-050**
consequence	NN	30-09-025

Word	Tag	Count
consequence (cont.):		
consequences	NNS	35-10-027
consequent	**JJ**	**7-02-006**
consequential	**JJ**	**1-01-001**
consequently	**RB**	**31-09-025**
conservation	**noun**	**13-06-010**
conservation	NN	7-05-007
conservation	NN-HL	1-01-001
Conservation	NN-TL	5-03-004
conservationist	**NN**	**1-01-001**
conservatism	**NN**	**10-03-004**
conservative	**JJ**	**28-06-023**
conservative	**noun**	**7-04-006**
conservative	NN	3-03-003
conservatives	NNS	4-02-003
conservative-liberal	**JJ**	**1-01-001**
conservatively-cravated	**JJ**	**1-01-001**
conservatory	**noun**	**3-02-003**
conservatory	NN	1-01-001
Conservatory	NN-TL	2-01-002
conserve	**verb**	**6-04-004**
conserve	VB	3-03-003
conserves	VBZ	1-01-001
conserving	VBG	2-02-002
consider	**verb**	**317-14-187**
consider	VB	127-13-091
considers	VBZ	15-06-014
considered	VBD	31-10-027
considered	VBN	120-13-089
considering	VBG	24-10-021
considerable	**JJ**	**96-12-078**
considerably	**QL**	**22-10-021**
considerably	**RB**	**22-10-021**
considerate	**JJ**	**4-03-004**
considerately	**RB**	**2-02-002**
consideration	**noun**	**81-10-057**
consideration	NN	49-10-044
considerations	NNS	28-06-021
consderations	NNS	1-01-001
considerations	NNS-HL	3-02-003
considering	**prep.**	**24-11-021**
considering	IN	23-10-020
considerin'	IN	1-01-001
consign	**verb**	**3-02-003**
consign	VB	2-01-002
consigned	VBD	1-01-001
consist	**verb**	**109-14-071**
consist	VB	17-07-015
consists	VBZ	43-09-033
consisted	VBD	22-10-017
consisted	VBN	2-02-002
consisting	VBG	23-08-020
consisting	VBG-HL	2-01-001
consistence	**NN**	**1-01-001**
consistency	**NN**	**18-08-016**
consistent	**JJ**	**28-07-025**
consistently	**adverb**	**20-07-019**
consistently	RB	19-07-018
consisently	RB	1-01-001
consisting	**IN**	**2-02-002**
consolation	**NN**	**3-03-003**
console	**noun**	**4-02-002**
consoles	NNS	4-02-002
console	**verb**	**3-02-003**
consoled	VBD	1-01-001
consoled	VBN	1-01-001
consoling	VBG	1-01-001
consolidate	**verb**	**10-06-009**
consolidate	VB	2-02-002
consolidated	VBN	5-02-004
Consolidated	VBN-TL	1-01-001
consolidating	VBG	2-02-002
consolidation	**NN**	**9-03-004**
consonance	**NN**	**1-01-001**
consonant	**JJ**	**1-01-001**
consonant	**noun**	**6-01-002**
consonant	NN	2-01-001
consonants	NNS	4-01-002
consonantal	**JJ**	**9-01-002**
consort	**noun**	**1-01-001**
consort	NN	0-00-000
Consort	NN-TL	1-01-001
consort	**verb**	**3-03-003**
consorted	VBD	1-01-001
consorting	VBG	2-02-002
conspicuous	**JJ**	**6-05-006**
conspicuously	**QL**	**1-01-001**
conspicuously	**RB**	**7-05-007**
conspiracy	**noun**	**24-06-012**

Word	Tag	Count
conspiracy (cont.):		
conspiracy	NN	22-06-012
conspiracies	NNS	2-02-002
conspirator	**noun**	**4-03-004**
conspirators	NNS	4-03-004
conspiratorial	**JJ**	**1-01-001**
conspire	**verb**	**6-04-006**
conspire	VB	1-01-001
conspires	VBZ	1-01-001
conspired	VBD	2-02-002
conspired	VBN	1-01-001
conpired	VBN	1-01-001
constable	**noun**	**2-02-002**
constable	NN	0-00-000
Constable	NN-TL	1-01-001
constables	NNS	1-01-001
Constable	**prop. noun**	**5-01-001**
Constable	NP	4-01-001
Constable's	NP$	1-01-001
Constance	**NP**	**1-01-001**
constancy	**NN**	**5-02-003**
constant	**adjective**	**61-12-052**
constant	JJ	59-12-052
constant	JJ-HL	2-02-002
constant	**noun**	**19-03-008**
constant	NN	9-02-004
Constant	NN-TL	1-01-001
constants	NNS	4-03-004
constants	NNS-HL	5-01-001
constant-temperature	**NN**	**1-01-001**
Constantin	**NP**	**1-01-001**
Constantine	**prop. noun**	**8-03-003**
Constantine	NP	5-02-002
Constantine	NP-TL	3-02-002
Constantino	**NP**	**1-01-001**
Constantinople	**prop. noun**	**3-02-003**
Constantinople	NP	2-02-002
Constantinople	NP-TL	1-01-001
Constantinos	**NP**	**1-01-001**
constantly	**RB**	**41-11-040**
constatation	**NN**	**1-01-001**
constellation	**noun**	**5-02-003**
constellation's	NN$	1-01-001
constellations	NNS	4-02-003
consternation	**NN**	**1-01-001**
constituency	**noun**	**4-02-002**
constituency	NN	3-02-002
constituencies	NNS	1-01-001
constituent	**noun**	**15-07-009**
constituent	NN	5-02-004
constituents	NNS	10-07-007
constitute	**verb**	**54-09-043**
constitute	VB	29-06-028
constitutes	VBZ	11-05-011
constituted	VBD	8-05-007
constituted	VBN	3-02-003
constituting	VBG	3-03-003
constitution	**noun**	**53-05-020**
constitution	NN	11-04-011
constitution	NN-HL	1-01-001
Constitution	NN-TL	35-05-011
Constitution	NN-TL-HL	2-01-001
constitutions	NNS	2-01-002
Constitutions	NNS-TL	2-01-001
constitutional	**adjective**	**26-07-019**
constitutional	JJ	24-07-015
consitutional	JJ	1-01-001
Constitutional	JJ	1-01-001
constrain	**verb**	**3-03-003**
constrained	VBN	2-02-002
constraining	VBG	1-01-001
constraint	**NN**	**2-01-001**
constrict	**verb**	**3-03-003**
constricted	VBD	1-01-001
constricted	VBN	1-01-001
constricting	VBG	1-01-001
constricting	**JJ**	**1-01-001**
constriction	**noun**	**4-03-003**
constriction	NN	3-02-002
constrictions	NNS	1-01-001
constrictor	**noun**	**7-01-001**
constrictor	NN	5-01-001
constrictor	NN-HL	1-01-001
constrictors	NNS	1-01-001
construct	**verb**	**56-11-039**
construct	VB	12-04-011
constructed	VBD	2-02-002
constructed	VBN	35-09-026
constructing	VBG	7-05-007

construction	**noun**	**98-12-051**
construction	NN	91-10-047
construction	NN-HL	2-02-002
Construction	NN-TL	1-01-001
constructions	NNS	4-03-003
constructional	**JJ**	**1-01-001**
constructive	**JJ**	**15-08-013**
constructively	**RB**	**2-02-002**
construe	**verb**	**8-04-006**
construe	VB	1-01-001
construed	VBD	1-01-001
construed	VBN	5-02-003
construing	VBG	1-01-001
consul	**noun**	**3-01-003**
consul	NN	1-01-001
Consul	NN-TL	2-01-002
consular	**JJ**	**1-01-001**
consulate	**NN**	**1-01-001**
consult	**verb**	**41-11-034**
consult	VB	11-08-011
consulted	VBD	6-04-006
consulted	VBN	10-06-008
consulted	VBN-HL	1-01-001
consulting	VBG	10-05-009
Consulting	VBG-TL	3-01-001
consultant	**noun**	**19-04-010**
consultant	NN	11-03-006
Consultant	NN-TL	1-01-001
consultants	NNS	7-03-005
consultation	**noun**	**12-07-012**
consultation	NN	9-07-009
consultation	NN-HL	1-01-001
consultations	NNS	2-02-002
consultative	**JJ**	**1-01-001**
consume	**verb**	**21-09-016**
consume	VB	2-02-002
consumes	VBZ	1-01-001
consumed	VBD	1-01-001
consumed	VBN	12-06-008
consuming	VBG	5-04-005
consumer	**noun**	**48-08-018**
consumer	NN	38-08-016
consumer's	NN$	1-01-001
consumers	NNS	9-06-008
consummate	**JJ**	**3-01-003**
consummate	**verb**	**4-03-004**
consummated	VBD	1-01-001
consummated	VBN	3-02-003
consummately	**RB**	**1-01-001**
consummation	**NN**	**4-01-001**
consumption	**NN**	**18-06-012**
consumptive	**JJ**	**3-01-001**
contact	**noun**	**79-13-047**
contact	NN	54-12-036
contact	NN-HL	1-01-001
contacts	NNS	23-07-014
Contacts	NNS-TL	1-01-001
contact	**verb**	**15-05-007**
contact	VB	4-01-001
contact	VB-HL	4-01-001
contacts	VBZ	1-01-001
contacted	VBD	2-02-002
contacted	VBN	2-02-002
contacting	VBG	2-01-002
contadini	**FW-NNS**	**2-02-002**
contagion	**NN**	**2-02-002**
contagious	**JJ**	**2-02-002**
contain	**verb**	**188-15-103**
contain	VB	45-12-037
contains	VBZ	38-07-028
contained	VBD	35-10-021
contained	VBN	25-10-023
containing	VBG	45-08-033
container	**noun**	**14-07-012**
container	NN	10-07-008
containers	NNS	4-03-004
containment	**noun**	**2-02-002**
containment	NN	1-01-001
Containment	NN-TL	1-01-001
contaminate	**verb**	**5-03-004**
contaminate	VB	1-01-001
contaminated	VBN	3-02-002
contaminating	VBG	1-01-001
contamination	**NN**	**4-02-003**
contemplate	**verb**	**19-08-017**
contemplate	VB	7-04-007
contemplates	VBZ	1-01-001
contemplated	VBN	5-05-005
contemplating	VBG	5-03-004

contemplate (cont.):		
Contemplating	VBG-TL	1-01-001
contemplation	**NN**	**6-06-006**
contemplative	**adjective**	**1-01-001**
contemplative	JJ	0-00-000
contemplative	JJ-HL	1-01-001
contemporary	**adjective**	**59-10-037**
contemporary	JJ	58-10-037
contemporary	JJ-HL	1-01-001
contemporary	**noun**	**11-05-010**
contemporary	NN	5-03-005
contemporaries	NNS	6-04-006
contempt	**NN**	**15-08-014**
contemptible	**JJ**	**2-02-002**
contemptuous	**JJ**	**6-05-006**
contemptuously	**RB**	**2-02-002**
contend	**verb**	**24-07-021**
contend	VB	6-03-006
contends	VBZ	5-04-004
contended	VBD	6-03-005
contended	VBN	6-04-006
contending	VBG	1-01-001
contender	**NN**	**2-02-002**
contendere	**foreign**	**1-01-001**
contendere	FW-VB	0-00-000
contendere	FW-VB-NC	1-01-001
content	**JJ**	**9-06-009**
content	**noun**	**57-11-043**
content	NN	41-07-030
contents	NNS	16-07-014
content	**verb**	**12-08-010**
content	VB	3-02-002
contented	VBN	8-06-007
contenting	VBG	1-01-001
contentedly	**RB**	**1-01-001**
contention	**noun**	**11-04-008**
contention	NN	9-04-007
contentions	NNS	2-02-002
contentment	**NN**	**1-01-001**
contest	**noun**	**32-08-022**
contest	NN	22-08-016
Contest	NN-TL	2-01-001
contests	NNS	8-06-007
contest	**verb**	**5-04-005**
contest	VB	2-02-002
contested	VBD	1-01-001
contested	VBN	2-02-002
contestant	**noun**	**5-05-005**
contestants	NNS	5-05-005
context	**noun**	**37-05-022**
context	NN	34-05-021
context	NN-HL	1-01-001
contexts	NNS	2-02-002
contiguous	**JJ**	**1-01-001**
continence	**NN**	**1-01-001**
continent	**noun**	**24-10-023**
continent	NN	11-06-011
Continent	NN-TL	6-04-006
continents	NNS	7-06-007
continental	**adjective**	**19-07-014**
continental	JJ	4-04-004
Continental	JJ-TL	15-05-010
continentally	**RB**	**1-01-001**
contingency	**noun**	**8-06-006**
contingency	NN	3-03-003
contingencies	NNS	5-04-004
contingent	**noun**	**4-02-004**
contingent	NN	3-02-003
contingents	NNS	1-01-001
contingent-fee	**NN**	**2-01-001**
continual	**JJ**	**5-03-004**
continually	**RB**	**25-10-024**
continuance	**NN**	**6-05-006**
continuation	**noun**	**18-06-011**
continuation	NN	16-06-011
continuation	NN-HL	1-01-001
Continuation	NN-TL	1-01-001
continue	**verb**	**342-15-203**
continue	VB	107-13-085
continues	VBZ	41-08-032
continued	VBD	83-15-063
continued	VBN	50-11-040
continuing	VBG	61-10-051
continuity	**noun**	**27-06-015**
continuity	NN	25-06-015
continuities	NNS	2-02-002
continuo	**FW-JJ**	**1-01-001**
continuous	**JJ**	**44-10-032**
continuously	**RB**	**23-08-021**

Word	Tag	Frequency
continuum	**noun**	**7-03-006**
continuum	NN	5-03-005
continuum	NN-HL	2-02-002
contort	**verb**	**3-02-003**
contorted	VBN	3-02-003
contortion	**NN**	**1-01-001**
contour	**noun**	**21-07-015**
contour	NN	6-03-005
contours	NNS	15-07-012
contour	**verb**	**1-01-001**
contouring	VBG	1-01-001
contour-obliterating	**JJ**	**1-01-001**
contraband	**NN**	**1-01-001**
contrabass	**NN**	**1-01-001**
contraception	**NN**	**4-01-001**
contraceptive	**JJ**	**1-01-001**
contraceptive	**noun**	**4-01-001**
contraceptives	NNS	4-01-001
contract	**noun**	**73-11-039**
contract	NN	54-09-030
contracts	NNS	18-09-014
contracts	NNS-HL	1-01-001
contract	**verb**	**21-08-016**
contract	VB	6-05-006
contracts	VBZ	4-04-004
contracts	VBZ-HL	1-01-001
contracted	VBD	4-02-003
contracted	VBN	4-03-004
contracting	VBG	2-02-002
contract-negotiation	**NN**	**1-01-001**
contracting	**NN**	**1-01-001**
contraction	**noun**	**12-03-004**
contraction	NN	11-03-004
contraction	NN-HL	1-01-001
contraction-extension	**NN**	**1-01-001**
contractor	**noun**	**10-03-005**
contractor	NN	6-03-004
contractor's	NN$	1-01-001
contractors	NNS	2-01-001
contractors'	NNS$	1-01-001
contractual	**JJ**	**7-02-003**
contradict	**verb**	**8-06-008**
contradict	VB	4-04-004
contradicts	VBZ	2-02-002
contradicted	VBD	1-01-001
contradicted	VBN	1-01-001
contradiction	**noun**	**18-07-014**
contradiction	NN	13-07-010
contradictions	NNS	4-01-004
Contradictions	NNS-TL	1-01-001
contradictorily	**RB**	**2-01-002**
contradictory	**JJ**	**1-01-001**
contradistinction	**NN**	**1-01-001**
contralto	**NN**	**1-01-001**
contraption	**noun**	**1-01-001**
contraptions	NNS	1-01-001
contrariety	**noun**	**1-01-001**
contrarieties	NNS	1-01-001
contrarily	**RB**	**1-01-001**
contrary	**JJ**	**41-10-034**
contrary	**NN**	**11-08-010**
contrary-to-reality	**JJ**	**1-01-001**
contrast	**noun**	**78-13-056**
contrast	NN	69-12-052
contrasts	NNS	9-06-007
contrast	**verb**	**22-08-019**
contrast	VB	5-02-004
contrasts	VBZ	2-01-002
contrasted	VBN	4-02-004
contrasting	VBG	11-07-010
contretemps	**NN**	**2-02-002**
contribute	**verb**	**108-12-081**
contribute	VB	44-08-037
contributes	VBZ	10-07-009
contributed	VBD	24-08-021
contributed	VBN	15-09-015
contributing	VBG	15-08-014
contribution	**noun**	**67-11-053**
contribution	NN	36-09-032
Contribution	NN-TL	1-01-001
contributions	NNS	28-08-025
contribs	NNS	1-01-001
contributions	NNS-HL	1-01-001
contributor	**noun**	**8-05-007**
contributor	NN	2-02-002
contributors	NNS	6-05-006
contributory	**JJ**	**1-01-001**
contrite	**JJ**	**1-01-001**
contrition	**NN**	**1-01-001**

Word	Tag	Frequency
contrivance	**noun**	**1-01-001**
contrivances	NNS	1-01-001
contrive	**verb**	**5-04-005**
contrive	VB	1-01-001
contrived	VBN	3-03-003
contriving	VBG	1-01-001
control	**noun**	**220-14-109**
control	NN	182-14-099
control	NN-HL	3-01-003
Control	NN-TL	10-05-006
controls	NNS	24-07-017
Controls	NNS-TL	1-01-001
control	**verb**	**95-13-073**
control	VB	28-08-023
controls	VBZ	5-05-005
controlled	VBD	5-04-005
controlled	VBN	34-10-033
controlling	VBG	23-09-021
controller	**noun**	**14-04-008**
controller	NN	1-01-001
Controller	NN-TL	8-02-004
controller's	NN$	1-01-001
Controller's	NN$-TL	1-01-001
controllers	NNS	3-03-003
controversial	**JJ**	**12-05-008**
controversialist	**noun**	**1-01-001**
controversialists	NNS	1-01-001
controversy	**noun**	**30-09-023**
controversy	NN	26-09-022
controversies	NNS	4-02-002
contusion	**noun**	**1-01-001**
contusions	NNS	1-01-001
Convair	**NP**	**1-01-001**
convalesce	**verb**	**1-01-001**
convalescing	VBG	1-01-001
convalescence	**NN**	**1-01-001**
convection	**NN**	**2-01-001**
convene	**verb**	**2-02-002**
convened	VBD	2-02-002
convenience	**noun**	**22-07-018**
convenience	NN	19-06-016
convenience	NN-HL	1-01-001
conveniences	NNS	2-02-002
convenient	**JJ**	**22-07-018**
convenient-type	**JJ**	**1-01-001**
conveniently	**RB**	**7-05-007**
convening	**NN**	**2-02-002**
convent	**NN**	**4-02-004**
convention	**noun**	**37-10-023**
convention	NN	23-09-016
Convention	NN-TL	5-04-004
conventions	NNS	9-03-007
conventional	**JJ**	**51-09-035**
conventional-type	**JJ**	**1-01-001**
conventionality	**NN**	**1-01-001**
conventionalize	**verb**	**1-01-001**
conventionalized	VBN	1-01-001
conventionally	**RB**	**1-01-001**
converge	**verb**	**4-02-003**
converge	VB	3-01-002
converged	VBD	1-01-001
conversant	**JJ**	**1-01-001**
conversation	**noun**	**60-13-043**
conversation	NN	50-12-037
conversations	NNS	10-06-009
conversational	**JJ**	**3-03-003**
converse	**NN**	**2-02-002**
converse	**verb**	**4-04-004**
converse	VB	3-03-003
conversing	VBG	1-01-001
conversely	**RB**	**9-04-007**
conversion	**noun**	**27-08-020**
conversion	NN	20-07-014
Conversion	NN-TL	1-01-001
conversions	NNS	6-05-005
conversion-by-renovation	**NN**	**1-01-001**
convert	**noun**	**8-03-004**
convert	NN	3-03-003
converts	NNS	5-03-004
convert	**verb**	**31-09-025**
convert	VB	9-06-009
converted	VBD	2-02-002
converted	VBN	18-09-014
converting	VBG	2-02-002
convertible	**JJ**	**7-03-003**
convertible	**noun**	**3-03-003**
convertible	NN	2-02-002
Convertible	NN-TL	1-01-001
convex	**JJ**	**1-01-001**

Word	Tag	Frequency
convexity	**NN**	**1-01-001**
convey	**verb**	**27-09-023**
convey	VB	13-07-012
conveys	VBZ	4-03-004
conveyed	VBD	3-03-003
conveyed	VBN	6-04-005
conveying	VBG	1-01-001
Conveyance	**NN**	**1-01-001**
conveyor	**NN**	**3-03-003**
convict	**noun**	**10-05-007**
convict	NN	5-03-004
convict's	NN$	1-01-001
convicts	NNS	4-03-003
convict	**verb**	**16-07-013**
convict	VB	1-01-001
convicted	VBD	1-01-001
convicted	VBN	13-07-011
convicting	VBG	1-01-001
conviction	**noun**	**70-12-055**
conviction	NN	50-12-042
convictions	NNS	20-06-017
convince	**verb**	**57-13-048**
convince	VB	4-03-004
convinced	VBD	7-07-007
convinced	VBN	43-13-037
convincing	VBG	3-02-003
convincing	**JJ**	**8-05-007**
convincingly	**RB**	**2-02-002**
convivial	**JJ**	**1-01-001**
convocation	**noun**	**4-01-001**
convocation	NN	0-00-000
Convocation	NN-TL	3-01-001
convocations	NNS	0-00-000
Convocations	NNS-TL	1-01-001
convolute	**verb**	**1-01-001**
convoluted	VBN	1-01-001
convoy	**NN**	**3-02-003**
convulse	**verb**	**1-01-001**
convulsed	VBD	1-01-001
convulsion	**noun**	**1-01-001**
convulsions	NNS	1-01-001
convulsive	**JJ**	**3-02-002**
convulsively	**RB**	**3-03-003**
Conway	**NP**	**1-01-001**
Conyers	**prop. noun**	**3-01-001**
Conyers'	NP$	3-01-001
coo	**verb**	**1-01-001**
cooing	VBG	1-01-001
Cooch	**prop. noun**	**2-01-001**
Cooch	NP	1-01-001
Cooch	NP-HL	1-01-001
cook	**noun**	**22-10-016**
cook	NN	12-07-011
cook's	NN$	1-01-001
Cook's	NN$-TL	1-01-001
cooks	NNS	8-04-004
cook	**verb**	**50-12-031**
cook	VB	14-07-009
cooked	VBD	2-02-002
cooked	VBN	8-05-005
cooking	VBG	26-10-021
Cook	**prop. noun**	**21-05-008**
Cook	NP	19-04-007
Cook	NP-TL	2-02-002
Cooke	**NP**	**3-01-001**
cooked-over	**JJ**	**1-01-001**
cookfire	**NN**	**1-01-001**
cookie	**noun**	**10-05-008**
cookie	NN	3-02-002
cookie's	NN$	0-00-000
coosie's	NN$	1-01-001
cookies	NNS	6-03-006
cooking	**NN**	**6-04-006**
cool	**JJ**	**50-12-031**
cool	**NN**	**2-02-002**
cool	**RB**	**1-01-001**
cool	**verb**	**59-09-020**
cool	VB	7-02-004
cools	VBZ	2-01-002
cooled	VBD	3-03-003
cooled	VBN	13-04-008
cooled	VBN-HL	1-01-001
cooling	VBG	33-04-008
Cool	**NP**	**2-01-001**
coolant	**NN**	**4-02-002**
cooler	**JJR**	**7-05-006**
cooler	**noun**	**9-03-005**
cooler	NN	5-02-002
coolers	NNS	4-02-004

Word	Tag	Frequency
coolest	**sup. adj.**	**4-02-002**
coolest	JJT	3-02-002
coolest	JJT-HL	1-01-001
coolheaded	**JJ**	**1-01-001**
Coolidge	**prop. noun**	**33-03-003**
Coolidge	NP	26-03-003
Coolidge's	NP$	2-01-001
Coolidges	NPS	3-01-001
Coolidges'	NPS$	2-01-001
cooling	**noun**	**9-02-004**
cooling	NN	8-02-003
Cooling	NN-TL	1-01-001
cooling-heating	**JJ**	**1-01-001**
coolly	**RB**	**5-05-005**
coolness	**noun**	**6-03-004**
coolness	NN	5-02-003
coolnesses	NNS	1-01-001
Coombs	**NP**	**9-03-003**
Coons	**NP**	**3-01-001**
coop	**noun**	**4-03-004**
coop	NN	3-02-003
coops	NNS	1-01-001
coop	**verb**	**2-02-002**
cooped	VBN	2-02-002
Cooper	**prop. noun**	**17-06-006**
Cooper	NP	12-04-004
Cooper's	NP$	2-02-002
Coopers	NPS	3-03-003
cooperate	**verb**	**28-11-024**
cooperate	VB	11-06-010
co-operate	VB	4-04-004
cooperates	VBZ	1-01-001
co-operates	VBZ	1-01-001
cooperated	VBD	0-00-000
co-operated	VBD	1-01-001
cooperated	VBN	2-02-002
cooperating	VBG	7-05-006
co-operating	VBG	1-01-001
cooperation	**noun**	**51-10-037**
cooperation	NN	36-08-029
co-operation	NN	12-06-008
Cooperation	NN-TL	3-02-003
cooperative	**adjective**	**24-06-012**
cooperative	JJ	16-06-009
co-operative	JJ	4-01-002
Co-operative	JJ-TL	1-01-001
cooperative	JJ-HL	1-01-001
Cooperative	JJ-TL	2-01-001
cooperative	**noun**	**13-03-004**
cooperative	NN	1-01-001
co-operative	NN	1-01-001
Co-operative	NN-TL	1-01-001
cooperatives	NNS	3-02-002
cooperatives	NNS-HL	1-01-001
Cooperatives	NNS-TL	6-01-001
Cooperman	**NP**	**2-01-001**
coordinate	**JJ**	**1-01-001**
coordinate	**noun**	**7-02-005**
coordinate	NN	2-01-001
coordinates	NNS	5-02-004
coordinate	**verb**	**30-07-021**
coordinate	VB	7-05-006
co-ordinate	VB	1-01-001
coordinates	VBZ	1-01-001
co-ordinates	VBZ	1-01-001
coordinated	VBN	14-04-009
co-ordinated	VBN	1-01-001
coordinating	VBG	4-03-004
co-ordinating	VBG	1-01-001
coordination	**noun**	**17-06-010**
coordination	NN	15-06-008
co-ordination	NN	2-02-002
coordinator	**noun**	**6-02-004**
coordinator	NN	5-01-003
co-ordinator	NN	1-01-001
Coosa	**prop. noun**	**2-01-001**
Coosa	NP	0-00-000
Coosa	NP-TL	2-01-001
cop	**noun**	**32-06-018**
cop	NN	14-04-008
Cop	NN-TL	1-01-001
cops	NNS	17-03-011
cope	**verb**	**30-09-025**
cope	VB	21-09-020
copes	VBZ	1-01-001
coping	VBG	8-04-006
Copeland	**NP**	**2-02-002**
Copenhagen	**prop. noun**	**6-01-001**
Copenhagen	NP	4-01-001

Copenhagen (cont.):		
Copenhagen	NP-TL	2-01-001
Copernican	**JJ**	**8-01-001**
Copernicus	**prop. noun**	**19-01-002**
Copernicus	NP	13-01-002
Copernicus'	NP$	6-01-001
Copernicus-the-astronomer	**NP**	**1-01-001**
coping	**noun**	**1-01-001**
copings	NNS	1-01-001
copious	**JJ**	**1-01-001**
copiously	**RB**	**1-01-001**
Copland	**NP**	**2-02-002**
Copley	**NP**	**1-01-001**
copolymer	**noun**	**2-01-001**
copolymers	NNS	1-01-001
copolymers	NNS-HL	1-01-001
Copp	**NP**	**1-01-001**
copper	**JJ**	**1-01-001**
copper	**noun**	**12-06-011**
copper	NN	11-06-011
Copper	NN-TL	1-01-001
coppery	**JJ**	**2-02-002**
copra	**NN**	**2-02-002**
copy	**noun**	**54-12-030**
copy	NN	36-11-023
copies	NNS	18-07-012
copy	**verb**	**6-05-006**
copy	VB	2-02-002
copied	VBD	1-01-001
copied	VBN	2-02-002
copying	VBG	1-01-001
copybook	**noun**	**1-01-001**
copybooks	NNS	1-01-001
copyright	**noun**	**1-01-001**
copyrights	NNS	1-01-001
copywriter	**NN**	**1-01-001**
coquette	**NN**	**2-01-002**
coral	**noun**	**4-03-003**
coral	NN	1-01-001
Coral	NN-TL	3-02-002
Coral	**NP**	**1-01-001**
coral-colored	**JJ**	**1-01-001**
Corault	**NP**	**1-01-001**
Corbin	**NP**	**1-01-001**
Corcoran	**prop. noun**	**2-02-002**
Corcoran	NP	1-01-001
Corcoran	NP-TL	1-01-001
cord	**noun**	**8-06-008**
cord	NN	6-05-006
cords	NNS	2-02-002
cord	**verb**	**1-01-001**
corded	VBN	1-01-001
Corder	**NP**	**2-01-001**
cordial	**JJ**	**6-06-006**
Cordier	**prop. noun**	**1-01-001**
Cordier's	NP$	1-01-001
cordon	**FW-NN**	**1-01-001**
cordon	**NN**	**1-01-001**
corduroy	**noun**	**2-02-002**
corduroy	NN	1-01-001
corduroys	NNS	1-01-001
core	**noun**	**44-09-023**
core	NN	41-09-022
cores	NNS	3-01-002
core	**VB**	**2-02-002**
core-jacket	**NN**	**1-01-001**
Corelli	**NP**	**2-01-002**
coriander	**NN**	**1-01-001**
Corinth	**prop. noun**	**1-01-001**
Corinth	NP	0-00-000
Corinth	NP-TL	1-01-001
Corinthian	**adjective**	**5-04-004**
Corinthian	JJ	4-03-003
Corinthian	JJ-TL	1-01-001
Corinthian	**prop. noun**	**3-01-002**
Corinthians	NPS	2-01-001
Corinthians	NPS-TL	1-01-001
Coriolanus	**prop. noun**	**1-01-001**
Coriolanus	NP	0-00-000
Coriolanus	NP-TL	1-01-001
cork	**noun**	**10-04-004**
cork	NN	9-04-004
corks	NNS	1-01-001
cork	**verb**	**2-01-001**
corked	VBN	2-01-001
corker	**noun**	**1-01-001**
corkers	NNS	1-01-001
corkscrew	**NN**	**3-03-003**
corn	**noun**	**38-09-021**

corn (cont.):		
corn	NN	32-09-020
corne	NN	2-01-001
Corn	NN-TL	2-02-002
corns	NNS	2-01-001
corn-belt	**NN**	**1-01-001**
cornbread	**NN**	**1-01-001**
Corne	**NP**	**2-01-001**
Corneilus	**NP**	**1-01-001**
Cornell	**prop. noun**	**5-04-004**
Cornell	NP	3-03-003
Cornell	NP-TL	2-02-002
Cornell-Dubilier	**NP**	**1-01-001**
corner	**noun**	**134-15-075**
corner	NN	113-15-062
corner-	NN	1-01-001
Corner	NN-TL	2-02-002
corners	NNS	18-10-016
corner	**verb**	**2-02-002**
cornered	VBN	1-01-001
cornering	VBG	1-01-001
corner-post	**noun**	**1-01-001**
corner-posts	NNS	1-01-001
cornerstone	**NN**	**3-03-003**
cornfield	**NN**	**1-01-001**
corniest	**JJT**	**1-01-001**
Corning	**NP**	**1-01-001**
cornmeal	**NN**	**2-02-002**
cornstarch	**NN**	**1-01-001**
cornucopia	**NN**	**1-01-001**
Cornwall	**NP**	**1-01-001**
Cornwallis	**NP**	**2-01-001**
corny	**JJ**	**1-01-001**
corollary	**noun**	**5-02-004**
corollary	NN	2-01-002
corollary	NN-HL	2-01-001
corollaries	NNS	1-01-001
corona	**NN**	**1-01-001**
Coronado	**prop. noun**	**2-01-002**
Coronado	NP	1-01-001
Coronado	NP-TL	1-01-001
coronary	**JJ**	**4-02-002**
coronary	**noun**	**4-01-001**
coronary	NN	3-01-001
coronaries	NNS	0-00-000
coronaries	NNS-HL	1-01-001
coronation	**noun**	**1-01-001**
coronation	NN	0-00-000
Coronation	NN-TL	1-01-001
coroner	**noun**	**9-03-005**
coroner	NN	5-03-004
coroner's	NN$	4-01-002
corp	**noun**	**1-01-001**
corp	NN	0-00-000
Corp	NN-TL	1-01-001
corporal	**noun**	**4-03-003**
corporal	NN	2-02-002
Corporal	NN-TL	2-01-001
corporate	**adjective**	**19-07-014**
corporate	JJ	18-07-014
corporate	JJ-HL	1-01-001
corporation	**noun**	**131-08-039**
corporation	NN	70-06-017
Corporation	NN	1-01-001
corp.	NN	0-00-000
Corp.	NN-TL	11-04-008
Corporation	NN-TL	19-06-014
corporation's	NN$	5-02-002
corporations	NNS	24-05-009
Corporations	NNS-TL	1-01-001
corporeal	**JJ**	**1-01-001**
corporeality	**NN**	**1-01-001**
corps	**FW-NN**	**7-02-004**
corps	**noun**	**103-13-039**
corps	NN	19-09-016
Corps	NN-TL	81-10-027
Corps	NN-TL-HL	3-01-001
corpse	**noun**	**12-07-011**
corpse	NN	7-04-007
corpses	NNS	5-05-005
corpsman	**NN**	**1-01-001**
corpulence	**NN**	**1-01-001**
corpus	**foreign**	**2-02-002**
corpus	FW-NN	1-01-001
corporis	FW-NN$	1-01-001
corpus	**NN**	**4-02-002**
Corpus	**NP**	**2-01-001**
corpuscular	**JJ**	**1-01-001**
corpuscular-radiation	**NN**	**1-01-001**

Word	Tag	Frequency
corral	**NN**	**4-03-003**
corral	**verb**	**2-02-002**
corral	VB	1-01-001
corralling	VBG	1-01-001
correct	**adjective**	**40-12-031**
correct	JJ	39-12-031
Correct	JJ-TL	1-01-001
correct	**verb**	**21-09-018**
correct	VB	12-07-010
corrected	VBD	3-03-003
corrected	VBN	6-04-006
correction	**noun**	**7-06-007**
correction	NN	3-03-003
correction	NN-HL	1-01-001
Correction	NN-TL	1-01-001
corrections	NNS	2-02-002
correctly	**RB**	**13-07-013**
correctness	**NN**	**3-03-003**
Correggio	**NP**	**1-01-001**
correlate	**verb**	**8-05-007**
correlate	VB	3-02-002
correlated	VBN	3-03-003
correlating	VBG	2-02-002
correlation	**noun**	**18-04-011**
correlation	NN	16-04-011
correlations	NNS	2-01-002
correlatively	**RB**	**1-01-001**
correspond	**verb**	**26-06-021**
correspond	VB	7-04-007
corresponds	VBZ	6-02-006
corresponded	VBD	4-03-004
corresponding	VBG	9-04-007
correspondence	**NN**	**25-10-019**
correspondent	**noun**	**17-07-012**
correspondent	NN	12-07-010
correspondents	NNS	5-04-004
corresponding	**JJ**	**29-07-020**
correspondingly	**RB**	**2-02-002**
Corrette	**NP**	**1-01-001**
corridor	**noun**	**19-06-013**
corridor	NN	17-05-011
corridors	NNS	2-02-002
corroborate	**verb**	**5-03-005**
corroborate	VB	2-01-002
corroborated	VBD	1-01-001
corroborated	VBN	1-01-001
corroborating	VBG	1-01-001
corroborees	**FW-NNS**	**2-01-001**
corrode	**verb**	**2-02-002**
corrode	VB	1-01-001
corroding	VBG	1-01-001
corrosion	**NN**	**4-03-003**
corrosive	**JJ**	**4-04-004**
corrugate	**verb**	**4-03-003**
corrugated	VBN	4-03-003
corrugation	**noun**	**1-01-001**
corrugations	NNS	1-01-001
corrupt	**JJ**	**7-05-006**
corrupt	**verb**	**6-02-003**
corrupt	VB	1-01-001
corrupts	VBZ	1-01-001
corrupted	VBN	2-01-001
corrupting	VBG	2-01-001
corrupter	**NN**	**1-01-001**
corruptible	**JJ**	**5-03-005**
corrupting	**NN**	**1-01-001**
corruption	**NN**	**14-06-010**
corsage	**NN**	**1-01-001**
Corsi	**NP**	**1-01-001**
Corsia	**NP**	**1-01-001**
Corso	**NP**	**7-01-001**
cortege	**NN**	**1-01-001**
cortex	**NN**	**7-01-002**
cortical	**JJ**	**3-01-002**
cortically	**RB**	**1-01-001**
cortico-fugal	**JJ**	**2-01-001**
cortico-hypothalamic	**JJ**	**2-01-001**
corticosteroid	**noun**	**1-01-001**
corticosteroids	NNS	1-01-001
corticotropin	**NN**	**1-01-001**
Cortlandt	**NP**	**3-01-001**
cosec	**NN**	**1-01-001**
cosily	**RB**	**1-01-001**
cosmetic	**noun**	**8-05-007**
cosmetic	NN	1-01-001
cosmetics	NNS	7-05-006
cosmic	**JJ**	**18-08-013**
cosmical	**JJ**	**1-01-001**
Cosmo	**NP**	**1-01-001**

Word	Tag	Frequency
cosmological	**JJ**	**2-02-002**
cosmologist	**noun**	**2-01-001**
cosmologists	NNS	2-01-001
cosmology	**noun**	**3-02-002**
cosmology	NN	2-02-002
Cosmology	NN-TL	1-01-001
cosmopolitan	**JJ**	**2-02-002**
cosmopolitanism	**NN**	**2-01-001**
cosmos	**NN**	**3-03-003**
cosponsor	**verb**	**3-02-003**
cosponsors	VBZ	1-01-001
cosponsored	VBN	2-02-002
Cossack	**prop. noun**	**7-01-002**
Cossack	NP	2-01-002
Cossack	NP-TL	1-01-001
Cossacks	NPS	4-01-001
cost	**noun**	**349-12-078**
cost	NN	177-11-065
cost	NN-HL	4-04-004
Cost	NN-TL	4-01-001
costs	NNS	156-09-040
costs	NNS-HL	8-04-006
cost	**verb**	**62-12-044**
cost	VB	29-09-023
coste	VB	1-01-001
costs	VBZ	12-05-010
cost	VBD	10-07-008
cost	VBN	5-05-005
costing	VBG	5-03-003
cost-accounting	**NN**	**1-01-001**
cost-billing	**NN**	**1-01-001**
cost-data	**NN**	**2-01-001**
cost-finding	**JJ**	**1-01-001**
cost-of-living	**NN**	**3-01-001**
cost-plus	**NN**	**1-01-001**
cost-raising	**JJ**	**2-01-001**
Costaggini	**prop. noun**	**8-01-001**
Costaggini	NP	7-01-001
Costaggini's	NP$	1-01-001
costing	**NN**	**1-01-001**
costive	**JJ**	**1-01-001**
costlier	**JJR**	**1-01-001**
costly	**JJ**	**16-09-015**
costume	**noun**	**28-08-019**
costume	NN	10-06-008
costumes	NNS	18-05-013
costume	**verb**	**1-01-001**
costumed	VBN	1-01-001
cotillion	**noun**	**2-01-001**
cotillion	NN	1-01-001
Cotillion	NN-TL	1-01-001
Cotman	**NP**	**1-01-001**
Cott	**NP**	**1-01-001**
cottage	**noun**	**25-11-019**
cottage	NN	19-11-015
cottages	NNS	6-04-006
Cotten	**prop. noun**	**5-01-001**
Cotten	NP	4-01-001
Cotten's	NP$	1-01-001
cotter	**NN**	**1-01-001**
Cotter	**prop. noun**	**1-01-001**
Cotter's	NP$	1-01-001
cotton	**noun**	**36-08-019**
cotton	NN	30-08-016
Cotton	NN-TL	6-02-004
Cotton	**prop. noun**	**3-02-002**
Cotton	NP	2-02-002
Cotton's	NP$	1-01-001
cotton-growing	**JJ**	**1-01-001**
cottonmouth	**NN**	**1-01-001**
cottonseed	**NN**	**1-01-001**
Cotty	**NP**	**1-01-001**
couch	**noun**	**13-07-010**
couch	NN	12-06-009
couches	NNS	1-01-001
couch	**verb**	**2-02-002**
couched	VBD	1-01-001
couched	VBN	1-01-001
cough	**NN**	**3-01-002**
cough	**verb**	**8-04-007**
cough	VB	4-03-004
coughed	VBD	2-02-002
coughing	VBG	2-02-002
coughing	**NN**	**1-01-001**
Coughlin	**prop. noun**	**7-02-002**
Coughlin	NP	5-01-001
Coughlin	NP-TL	1-01-001
Coughlin's	NP$	1-01-001
could	**modal aux.**	**1782-15-399**

Word	Tag	Frequency
could (cont.):		
could	MD	1598-15-396
colde	MD	3-01-001
could	MD-HL	3-03-003
could've	MD+HV	1-01-001
coulda	MD+HV	1-01-001
couldn't	MD*	175-11-092
coudn	MD*	1-01-001
Coulomb	**NP**	**1-01-001**
Coulson	**NP**	**1-01-001**
council	**noun**	**115-10-049**
council	NN	28-04-012
Council	NN-TL	75-10-040
council's	NN$	2-01-002
Council's	NN$-TL	4-02-003
councils	NNS	4-03-004
Councils	NNS-TL	2-01-001
councilman	**noun**	**5-02-002**
councilman	NN	0-00-000
Councilman	NN-TL	5-02-002
councilwoman	**noun**	**1-01-001**
councilwoman	NN	0-00-000
Councilwoman	NN-TL	1-01-001
counsel	**NN**	**16-06-011**
counsel	**verb**	**9-06-007**
counsel	VB	1-01-001
counseled	VBD	2-02-002
counseled	VBN	1-01-001
counseling	VBG	5-04-004
counseling	**noun**	**5-04-005**
counseling	NN	4-04-004
Counseling	NN-TL	1-01-001
counselor	**noun**	**7-04-005**
counselor	NN	4-04-004
counselors	NNS	3-01-002
count	**noun**	**31-10-022**
count	NN	18-09-013
Count	NN-TL	5-03-004
counts	NNS	8-04-005
count	**verb**	**65-14-054**
count	VB	26-12-025
counts	VBZ	6-04-006
counted	VBD	11-08-010
counted	VBN	6-04-006
counting	VBG	12-05-011
countin'	VBG	4-02-002
countenance	**NN**	**6-04-006**
counter	**noun**	**32-08-016**
counter	NN	24-04-009
counters	NNS	8-05-008
counter	**RB**	**5-03-005**
counter	**verb**	**4-04-004**
counter	VB	2-02-002
countered	VBD	2-02-002
counter-balanced	**JJ**	**1-01-001**
counter-clockwise	**RB**	**1-01-001**
counter-drill	**VB**	**1-01-001**
counter-effort	**noun**	**1-01-001**
counter-efforts	NNS	1-01-001
counter-escalation	**NN**	**1-01-001**
counter-move	**noun**	**1-01-001**
counter-moves	NNS	1-01-001
counter-offensive	**NN**	**1-01-001**
counter-success	**noun**	**1-01-001**
counter-successes	NNS	1-01-001
counteract	**verb**	**8-03-008**
counteract	VB	4-02-004
counteracted	VBD	1-01-001
counteracted	VBN	1-01-001
counteracting	VBG	2-02-002
counterattack	**noun**	**3-01-002**
counterattack	NN	2-01-001
counter-attack	NN	1-01-001
counterattack	**VB**	**1-01-001**
counterbalance	**NN**	**1-01-001**
counterbalance	**verb**	**3-03-003**
counterbalance	VB	1-01-001
counterbalanced	VBN	1-01-001
counterbalancing	VBG	1-01-001
counterchallenge	**VB**	**1-01-001**
counterfeit	**JJ**	**1-01-001**
counterflow	**JJ**	**1-01-001**
counterman	**NN**	**1-01-001**
counterpart	**noun**	**20-04-013**
counterpart	NN	9-04-008
counterparts	NNS	11-04-008
counterpoint	**NN**	**5-03-004**
counterpoint	**verb**	**1-01-001**
counterpointing	VBG	1-01-001
counterproposal	**NN**	**1-01-001**
countervail	**verb**	**1-01-001**
countervailing	VBG	1-01-001
countian	**NN**	**1-01-001**
counting	**noun**	**1-01-001**
counting	NN	0-00-000
countin'	NN	1-01-001
countless	**JJ**	**14-10-014**
country	**noun**	**491-15-192**
country	NN	311-15-160
countrey	NN	1-01-001
country	NN-HL	1-01-001
Country	NN-TL	12-05-009
country's	NN$	15-06-012
countries	NNS	148-11-053
Countries	NNS-TL	3-01-001
country-squirehood	**NN**	**1-01-001**
countryman	**noun**	**8-04-008**
countryman	NN	1-01-001
countriman	NN	1-01-001
countrymen	NNS	5-04-005
Countrymen	NNS-TL	1-01-001
countryside	**NN**	**7-06-007**
countrywide	**JJ**	**2-02-002**
county	**noun**	**192-13-071**
county	NN	71-10-035
county	NN-HL	1-01-001
County	NN-TL	82-13-043
county	NN-TL	1-01-001
county's	NN$	1-01-001
County's	NN$-TL	1-01-001
counties	NNS	31-09-019
Counties	NNS-TL	4-02-002
county-wide	**JJ**	**2-01-002**
coup	**FW-NN**	**2-02-002**
coup	**noun**	**4-03-004**
coup	NN	2-02-002
coups	NNS	2-02-002
coup-proof	**JJ**	**1-01-001**
Coupal	**NP**	**1-01-001**
coupe	**NN**	**2-02-002**
Couperin	**NP**	**5-01-001**
couple	**noun**	**136-15-090**
couple	NN	122-15-084
couple's	NN$	1-01-001
couples	NNS	13-08-010
couple	**verb**	**21-07-015**
coupled	VBD	3-03-003
coupled	VBN	10-04-010
coupled	VBN-HL	1-01-001
coupling	VBG	7-03-003
coupler	**noun**	**9-01-001**
coupler	NN	5-01-001
couplers	NNS	3-01-001
couplers	NNS-HL	1-01-001
coupling	**NN**	**2-01-001**
coupon	**noun**	**2-02-002**
coupon	NN	1-01-001
coupons	NNS	1-01-001
courage	**NN**	**32-11-028**
courageous	**JJ**	**4-04-004**
courageously	**RB**	**3-02-003**
Courbet	**NP**	**1-01-001**
Courcy	**NP**	**3-01-001**
coureurs	**FW-NNS**	**1-01-001**
courier	**noun**	**1-01-001**
courier	NN	0-00-000
Courier	NN-TL	1-01-001
Courier-Journal	**prop. noun**	**1-01-001**
Courier-Journal	NP	0-00-000
Courier-Journal	NP-TL	1-01-001
course	**noun**	**527-15-270**
course	NN	464-15-259
coahse	NN	1-01-001
Course	NN-TL	1-01-001
courses	NNS	60-09-021
Courses	NNS-TL	1-01-001
course	**verb**	**1-01-001**
coursing	VBG	1-01-001
court	**noun**	**286-13-074**
court	NN	113-12-045
ct.	NN	0-00-000
Ct.	NN-TL	1-01-001
court	NN-HL	3-02-003
Court	NN-TL	109-11-035
court	NN-TL	3-01-001
court's	NN$	2-02-002
Court's	NN$-TL	6-03-004
courts	NNS	44-10-021

Word	Tag	Frequency
court (cont.):		
Courts	NNS-TL	5-03-003
court	**verb**	**6-04-005**
court	VB	2-02-002
courts	VBZ	1-01-001
courted	VBN	1-01-001
courting	VBG	2-02-002
court-appointed	**JJ**	**1-01-001**
court-length	**JJ**	**1-01-001**
Court-packing	**NN**	**1-01-001**
Courtenay	**NP**	**4-01-001**
courteous	**JJ**	**6-04-005**
courteously	**RB**	**3-02-002**
courtesan	**NN**	**2-02-002**
courtesy	**noun**	**7-05-007**
courtesy	NN	6-05-006
courtesy	NN-HL	1-01-001
courthouse	**NN**	**3-01-001**
courtier	**noun**	**10-04-007**
courtier	NN	2-01-002
Courtier	NN-TL	3-01-001
courtiers	NNS	4-04-004
cowrtiers	NNS	1-01-001
courting	**NN**	**1-01-001**
courtliness	**NN**	**1-01-001**
courtly	**JJ**	**2-01-002**
Courtney	**NP**	**1-01-001**
Courtrai	**NP**	**1-01-001**
courtroom	**NN**	**2-01-002**
courtship	**NN**	**2-02-002**
courtyard	**noun**	**9-06-007**
courtyard	NN	8-06-006
courtyards	NNS	1-01-001
cousin	**noun**	**65-11-024**
cousin	NN	13-09-012
c'un	NN	0-00-000
C'un	NN-TL	1-01-001
cozen	NN	0-00-000
Cozen	NN-TL	1-01-001
Cousin	NN-TL	39-04-006
cousin's	NN$	1-01-001
cousins	NNS	9-06-007
cousins'	NNS$	1-01-001
cousin-wife	**NN**	**1-01-001**
Couturier	**NP**	**1-01-001**
Couve	**NP**	**1-01-001**
cove	**noun**	**3-03-003**
cove	NN	1-01-001
Cove	NN-TL	1-01-001
coves	NNS	1-01-001
covenant	**noun**	**4-03-003**
covenant	NN	3-03-003
covenants	NNS	1-01-001
Covent	**prop. noun**	**2-01-002**
Covent	NP	0-00-000
Covent	NP-TL	2-01-002
Coventry	**NP**	**1-01-001**
cover	**noun**	**52-11-036**
cover	NN	34-11-025
Cover	NN-TL	1-01-001
covers	NNS	17-09-014
cover	**verb**	**202-15-129**
cover	VB	53-12-041
covers	VBZ	15-06-013
covered	VBD	14-09-014
covered	VBN	90-13-058
covering	VBG	30-12-027
coverage	**NN**	**25-06-015**
coverall	**NN**	**2-01-001**
covering	**noun**	**4-03-004**
covering	NN	2-01-002
coverings	NNS	2-02-002
coverlet	**NN**	**2-02-002**
covert	**JJ**	**2-02-002**
covertly	**RB**	**1-01-001**
covet	**verb**	**6-05-006**
covet	VB	1-01-001
coveted	VBN	4-04-004
coveting	VBG	1-01-001
covetousness	**NN**	**2-02-002**
Covington	**NP**	**2-02-002**
cow	**noun**	**46-10-017**
cow	NN	28-08-011
Cow	NN-TL	1-01-001
cow's	NN$	1-01-001
cows	NNS	16-05-008
cow-people	**NNS**	**1-01-001**
coward	**NN**	**4-02-003**
Coward	**prop. noun**	**7-03-003**
Coward (cont.):		
Coward	NP	4-03-003
Coward's	NP$	3-01-001
cowardice	**NN**	**2-02-002**
cowardly	**JJ**	**2-02-002**
cowardly	**RB**	**1-01-001**
cowbird	**noun**	**5-01-001**
cowbird	NN	1-01-001
cowbirds	NNS	3-01-001
cowbirds'	NNS$	1-01-001
cowboy	**noun**	**21-07-009**
cowboy	NN	16-06-007
cowboy's	NN$	1-01-001
cowboys	NNS	4-04-004
cower	**verb**	**1-01-001**
cowering	VBG	1-01-001
Cowessett	**NP**	**2-01-001**
cowhand	**noun**	**6-02-002**
cowhand	NN	4-02-002
cowhand'd	NN+MD	1-01-001
cowhands	NNS	1-01-001
cowhide	**NN**	**1-01-001**
Cowley	**NP**	**2-01-001**
cowling	**NN**	**1-01-001**
cowman	**noun**	**3-02-002**
cowman	NN	2-01-001
cow-man	NN	1-01-001
coworker	**noun**	**4-03-004**
coworkers	NNS	2-02-002
co-workers	NNS	2-02-002
cowpony	**NN**	**1-01-001**
cowpuncher	**NN**	**1-01-001**
Cox	**NP**	**5-02-004**
coxcomb	**noun**	**1-01-001**
coxcombs	NNS	1-01-001
coy	**JJ**	**4-03-004**
coyly	**RB**	**1-01-001**
coyness	**NN**	**2-02-002**
coyote	**noun**	**2-01-002**
coyote	NN	1-01-001
coyotes	NNS	1-01-001
cozier	**JJR**	**1-01-001**
cozy	**adjective**	**2-02-002**
cozy	JJ	1-01-001
cosy	JJ	1-01-001
Cr--spe	**prop. noun**	**1-01-001**
Cr--spe	NP	0-00-000
Cr--spe	NP-TL	1-01-001
crab	**noun**	**2-02-002**
crabs	NNS	2-02-002
crabapple	**NN**	**1-01-001**
crabbed	**JJ**	**1-01-001**
crack	**JJ**	**1-01-001**
crack	**noun**	**17-07-014**
crack	NN	11-04-009
cracks	NNS	6-04-005
crack	**verb**	**41-11-032**
crack	VB	9-08-009
cracks	VBZ	1-01-001
cracked	VBD	11-05-010
cracked	VBN	6-04-006
cracking	VBG	13-06-010
cracking	VBG-HL	1-01-001
cracker	**noun**	**4-02-003**
crackers	NNS	4-02-003
cracker-box	**NN**	**1-01-001**
cracking	**QL**	**1-01-001**
crackle	**NN**	**2-02-002**
crackle	**verb**	**2-02-002**
crackles	VBZ	1-01-001
crackled	VBD	1-01-001
crackling	**NN**	**1-01-001**
crackpot	**noun**	**3-03-003**
crackpot	NN	1-01-001
crackpots	NNS	2-02-002
Craddock	**NP**	**1-01-001**
cradle	**noun**	**8-04-004**
cradle	NN	5-03-003
Cradle	NN-TL	2-01-001
cradles	NNS	1-01-001
cradle	**verb**	**3-03-003**
cradled	VBD	1-01-001
cradled	VBN	2-02-002
craft	**noun**	**25-10-018**
craft	NN	22-10-015
crafts	NNS	3-02-003
Craft	**NP**	**1-01-001**
craft-industrial	**JJ**	**1-01-001**
crafter	**NN**	**1-01-001**

Word	Tag	Frequency
craftsman	**noun**	**7-04-007**
craftsman	NN	2-02-002
craftsman's	NN$	1-01-001
craftsmen	NNS	4-04-004
craftsmanship	**NN**	**5-04-005**
crafty	**JJ**	**1-01-001**
crag	**noun**	**2-02-002**
crags	NNS	2-02-002
craggy	**JJ**	**1-01-001**
Craig	**prop. noun**	**3-03-003**
Craig	NP	2-02-002
Craig's	NP$	1-01-001
cram	**verb**	**3-02-003**
crammed	VBN	3-02-003
Cramer	**NP**	**1-01-001**
cramp	**noun**	**4-03-003**
cramp	NN	2-02-002
cramps	NNS	2-01-001
cranberry	**noun**	**1-01-001**
cranberries	NNS	1-01-001
crane	**noun**	**2-02-002**
crane's	NN$	1-01-001
cranes	NNS	0-00-000
Cranes	NNS-TL	1-01-001
crane	**VB**	**1-01-001**
Crane	**prop. noun**	**5-04-004**
Crane	NP	4-03-003
Crane's	NP$	1-01-001
cranelike	**JJ**	**1-01-001**
crank	**NN**	**1-01-001**
crankshaft	**NN**	**1-01-001**
cranky	**JJ**	**1-01-001**
cranny	**noun**	**2-02-002**
crannies	NNS	2-02-002
Cranston	**NP**	**16-03-004**
crap	**NN**	**2-02-002**
crap	**UH**	**1-01-001**
crash	**JJ**	**2-02-002**
crash	**noun**	**15-08-011**
crash	NN	14-08-011
crashes	NNS	1-01-001
crash	**verb**	**23-08-018**
crash	VB	4-02-004
crashed	VBD	7-05-007
crashed	VBN	5-04-004
crashing	VBG	7-04-007
crasher	**NN**	**1-01-001**
crass	**JJ**	**2-02-002**
crassest	**JJT**	**1-01-001**
crassness	**NN**	**1-01-001**
crate	**noun**	**4-03-003**
crate	NN	2-01-001
crates	NNS	2-02-002
crater	**noun**	**7-03-003**
crater	NN	2-01-001
craters	NNS	5-03-003
crater	**verb**	**1-01-001**
cratered	VBN	1-01-001
crave	**verb**	**5-04-005**
crave	VB	2-02-002
craved	VBD	1-01-001
craved	VBN	1-01-001
craving	VBG	1-01-001
craven	**JJ**	**1-01-001**
Craven	**NP**	**1-01-001**
craving	**NN**	**1-01-001**
Crawford	**prop. noun**	**3-02-002**
Crawford	NP	2-01-001
Crawford	NP-TL	1-01-001
crawl	**noun**	**4-04-004**
crawl	NN	2-02-002
crawls	NNS	2-02-002
crawl	**verb**	**37-08-024**
crawl	VB	9-05-006
crawled	VBD	17-07-014
crawled	VBN	3-03-003
crawling	VBG	8-03-006
crawlspace	**NN**	**1-01-001**
crayon	**noun**	**1-01-001**
crayons	NNS	1-01-001
craze	**NN**	**2-01-002**
craze	**verb**	**3-03-003**
crazed	VBN	2-02-002
crazing	VBG	1-01-001
crazily	**RB**	**4-03-004**
crazy	**adjective**	**34-12-028**
crazy	JJ	32-12-027
Crazy	JJ-TL	2-01-001
crazy-wonderful	**JJ**	**1-01-001**

Word	Tag	Frequency
creak	**NN**	**1-01-001**
creak	**verb**	**11-04-007**
creaks	VBZ	1-01-001
creaked	VBD	6-02-003
creaking	VBG	4-03-004
creaking	**NN**	**1-01-001**
cream	**JJ**	**2-02-002**
cream	**noun**	**19-08-011**
cream	NN	17-08-010
cream	NN-HL	1-01-001
creams	NNS	1-01-001
cream	**verb**	**1-01-001**
creamed	VBN	1-01-001
creamer	**noun**	**4-01-001**
creamer	NN	3-01-001
creamer	NN-HL	1-01-001
creamery	**noun**	**1-01-001**
creamery	NN	0-00-000
Creamery	NN-TL	1-01-001
creamy	**JJ**	**1-01-001**
crease	**noun**	**2-02-002**
crease	NN	1-01-001
creases	NNS	1-01-001
crease	**verb**	**2-02-002**
creased	VBN	2-02-002
create	**verb**	**177-14-111**
create	VB	54-11-046
creates	VBZ	13-07-012
created	VBD	18-12-016
created	VBN	63-10-041
creating	VBG	29-11-027
creation	**noun**	**50-10-038**
creation	NN	44-10-034
creation	NN-HL	2-01-002
creations	NNS	3-03-003
creations	NNS-HL	1-01-001
creative	**JJ**	**49-09-028**
creatively	**RB**	**3-03-003**
creativeness	**NN**	**1-01-001**
creativity	**NN**	**9-03-005**
creativity-oriented	**JJ**	**1-01-001**
creator	**noun**	**16-06-012**
creator	NN	5-03-004
creator	NN-HL	1-01-001
Creator	NN-TL	8-04-007
creators	NNS	2-01-001
creature	**noun**	**35-13-027**
creature	NN	15-08-013
creatures	NNS	20-09-016
creche	**NN**	**1-01-001**
credential	**noun**	**2-02-002**
credentials	NNS	2-02-002
credibility	**NN**	**1-01-001**
credible	**JJ**	**2-01-002**
credibly	**RB**	**1-01-001**
credit	**noun**	**67-12-039**
credit	NN	53-12-035
credit	NN-HL	1-01-001
Credit	NN-TL	8-01-001
credits	NNS	5-02-004
credit	**verb**	**16-07-014**
credit	VB	2-02-002
credits	VBZ	2-02-002
credited	VBD	2-02-002
credited	VBN	10-06-009
creditable	**JJ**	**4-04-004**
creditor	**noun**	**2-02-002**
creditors	NNS	1-01-001
creditors	NNS-HL	1-01-001
credo	**noun**	**8-03-005**
credo	NN	7-02-004
Credo	NN-TL	1-01-001
credulity	**NN**	**3-03-003**
credulous	**JJ**	**1-01-001**
credulousness	**NN**	**1-01-001**
creed	**noun**	**9-06-007**
creed	NN	6-04-004
Creed	NN-TL	2-02-002
creeds	NNS	1-01-001
creedal	**JJ**	**1-01-001**
creek	**noun**	**15-06-011**
creek	NN	8-04-007
Creek	NN-TL	6-05-005
creeks	NNS	1-01-001
creek-filled	**JJ**	**1-01-001**
Creek-Turn	**NP**	**5-01-001**
creep	**NN**	**3-03-003**
creep	**verb**	**27-09-022**
creep	VB	7-04-007

Word	Tag	Frequency
creep (cont.):		
creeps	VBZ	1-01-001
crept	VBD	9-06-008
crept	VBN	2-02-002
creeping	VBG	8-07-008
creeper	**noun**	**3-02-002**
creeper	NN	1-01-001
creepers	NNS	2-01-001
creepers	**exclam.**	**1-01-001**
creepers	UH	0-00-000
Creepers	UH-TL	1-01-001
creepy	**JJ**	**1-01-001**
Creighton	**NP**	**3-02-002**
cremate	**verb**	**2-02-002**
cremate	VB	1-01-001
cremated	VBN	1-01-001
Creole	**NP**	**1-01-001**
Creon	**NP**	**1-01-001**
crepe	**NN**	**1-01-001**
crescendo	**NN**	**2-02-002**
crescent	**noun**	**2-02-002**
crescent	NN	1-01-001
Crescent	NN-TL	1-01-001
crest	**noun**	**15-05-010**
crest	NN	12-04-008
crests	NNS	3-02-002
crested	**JJ**	**1-01-001**
crestfallen	**JJ**	**1-01-001**
Creston	**prop. noun**	**2-01-001**
Creston	NP	1-01-001
Creston's	NP$	1-01-001
Cretaceous	**prop. noun**	**1-01-001**
Cretaceous	NP	0-00-000
Cretaceous	NP-TL	1-01-001
crevice	**noun**	**3-02-002**
crevice	NN	2-01-001
crevices	NNS	1-01-001
crew	**noun**	**39-10-022**
crew	NN	36-09-020
crew's	NN$	1-01-001
crews	NNS	2-02-002
crewcut	**NN**	**1-01-001**
crewel	**NN**	**2-01-001**
crewman	**noun**	**1-01-001**
crewmen	NNS	1-01-001
crib	**noun**	**8-04-004**
crib	NN	5-02-002
cribs	NNS	3-02-002
cricket	**noun**	**4-04-004**
cricket	NN	2-02-002
crickets	NNS	2-02-002
Cricket	**NP**	**1-01-001**
crime	**noun**	**49-12-032**
crime	NN	32-12-023
crime	NN-HL	1-01-001
Crime	NN-TL	2-01-001
crimes	NNS	13-06-011
Crimes	NNS-TL	1-01-001
Crimea	**NP**	**1-01-001**
Crimean	**adjective**	**2-01-002**
Crimean	JJ	1-01-001
Crimean	JJ-TL	1-01-001
criminal	**adjective**	**15-07-011**
criminal	JJ	10-06-009
criminal	JJ-NC	1-01-001
Criminal	JJ-TL	4-01-001
criminal	**noun**	**15-05-008**
criminal	NN	9-05-005
criminals	NNS	6-03-005
criminality	**NN**	**4-03-003**
crimson	**JJ**	**5-05-005**
crimson	**NN**	**3-03-003**
crimson	**verb**	**1-01-001**
crimsoning	VBG	1-01-001
cringe	**verb**	**5-03-005**
cringed	VBD	2-02-002
cringing	VBG	3-02-003
crinkle	**noun**	**1-01-001**
crinkles	NNS	1-01-001
Crip	**NP**	**2-01-001**
cripple	**NN**	**1-01-001**
cripple	**verb**	**12-09-012**
crippled	VBN	5-05-005
Crippled	VBN-TL	1-01-001
crippling	VBG	6-06-006
Cris	**NP**	**1-01-001**
crisis	**noun**	**102-12-041**
crisis	NN	76-12-034
crisis	NN-HL	1-01-001

Word	Tag	Frequency
crisis (cont.):		
Crisis	NN-TL	4-01-002
crises	NNS	21-07-013
crisis-oriented	**JJ**	**1-01-001**
crisis-to-crisis	**JJ**	**1-01-001**
crisp	**JJ**	**4-03-003**
crisp	**NN**	**4-02-004**
Crispin	**NP**	**1-01-001**
crisply	**RB**	**1-01-001**
crispness	**NN**	**2-01-001**
criss-cross	**JJ**	**1-01-001**
criss-crossed	**JJ**	**2-01-001**
criss-crossing	**NN**	**1-01-001**
crisscross	**verb**	**2-02-002**
crisscrossed	VBN	1-01-001
criss-crossed	VBN	1-01-001
Cristo	**prop. noun**	**1-01-001**
Cristo	NP	0-00-000
Cristo	NP-TL	1-01-001
criterion	**noun**	**22-08-017**
criterion	NN	9-06-008
criterion	NN-HL	2-02-002
criteria	NNS	11-04-008
critic	**noun**	**53-10-040**
critic	NN	25-09-025
critic's	NN$	0-00-000
Critic's	NN$-TL	1-01-001
critics	NNS	26-08-021
critics'	NNS$	1-01-001
critical	**adjective**	**58-10-042**
critical	JJ	57-10-041
Critical	JJ-TL	1-01-001
critical-intellectual	**JJ**	**1-01-001**
criticality	**noun**	**5-01-001**
criticality	NN	0-00-000
criticality	NN-HL	5-01-001
critically	**QL**	**1-01-001**
critically	**RB**	**4-03-004**
criticism	**noun**	**51-09-043**
criticism	NN	39-07-033
Criticism	NN-TL	1-01-001
criticisms	NNS	11-06-010
criticize	**verb**	**20-07-014**
criticize	VB	4-03-004
criticized	VBD	3-02-003
criticized	VBN	8-05-006
criticized	VBN-HL	3-02-003
criticizing	VBG	2-01-002
critique	**NN**	**1-01-001**
Crittenden	**NP**	**3-01-001**
critter	**noun**	**4-02-003**
critter	NN	1-01-001
critters	NNS	3-02-002
croak	**noun**	**2-02-002**
croak	NN	1-01-001
croaks	NNS	1-01-001
croak	**verb**	**2-01-001**
croaked	VBD	1-01-001
croaking	VBG	0-00-000
croakin	VBG	1-01-001
croaking	**NN**	**1-01-001**
crochet	**VB**	**1-01-001**
crocked	**JJ**	**1-01-001**
crocketed	**JJ**	**1-01-001**
Crockett	**NP**	**1-01-001**
crocodile	**NN**	**1-01-001**
crofter	**noun**	**1-01-001**
crofters	NNS	1-01-001
Croix	**NP**	**1-01-001**
Crombie	**prop. noun**	**12-01-001**
Crombie	NP	11-01-001
Crombie's	NP$	1-01-001
Cromwell	**prop. noun**	**22-05-005**
Cromwell	NP	18-05-005
Cromwell	NP-TL	3-01-001
Cromwell's	NP$	1-01-001
Cromwellian	**JJ**	**1-01-001**
crone	**NN**	**2-01-001**
crony	**noun**	**2-02-002**
cronies	NNS	2-02-002
crook	**noun**	**5-04-005**
crook	NN	3-03-003
crooks	NNS	2-02-002
crooked	**JJ**	**3-03-003**
croon	**verb**	**3-02-003**
crooned	VBD	2-01-002
crooning	VBG	1-01-001
crop	**noun**	**37-08-017**
crop	NN	20-07-014

crop (cont.):		
crops	NNS	17-06-009
crop	**verb**	**7-05-007**
crops	VBZ	1-01-001
cropped	VBD	1-01-001
cropped	VBN	4-04-004
cropping	VBG	1-01-001
Crosby	**prop. noun**	**8-05-005**
Crosby	NP	5-02-002
Crosby's	NP$	2-02-002
Crosbys	NPS	1-01-001
cross	**JJ**	**1-01-001**
cross	**noun**	**29-11-028**
cross	NN	18-10-018
Cross	NN-TL	10-07-009
crosses	NNS	1-01-001
cross	**verb**	**84-13-056**
cross	VB	25-10-017
crosses	VBZ	3-01-002
crossed	VBD	26-08-020
crossed	VBN	16-06-012
crossing	VBG	14-09-014
Cross	**NP**	**1-01-001**
cross-cultural	**JJ**	**1-01-001**
cross-examination	**NN**	**1-01-001**
cross-eyed	**JJ**	**1-01-001**
cross-fertilization	**NN**	**1-01-001**
cross-fertilize	**verb**	**1-01-001**
cross-fertilized	VBN	1-01-001
cross-legged	**JJ**	**2-02-002**
cross-licensing	**JJ**	**4-01-001**
cross-purpose	**noun**	**1-01-001**
cross-purposes	NNS	1-01-001
cross-section	**NN**	**5-04-004**
cross-sectional	**JJ**	**4-02-003**
cross-striation	**noun**	**2-01-001**
cross-striations	NNS	2-01-001
cross-top	**NN**	**1-01-001**
cross-writing	**NN**	**1-01-001**
crossbar	**noun**	**1-01-001**
crossbars	NNS	1-01-001
crossing	**noun**	**8-07-008**
crossing	NN	7-06-007
crossings	NNS	1-01-001
Crossman	**NP**	**2-01-001**
Crosson	**prop. noun**	**4-01-001**
Crosson	NP	2-01-001
Crosson's	NP+HVZ	1-01-001
Crosson's	NP$	1-01-001
crossover	**NN**	**1-01-001**
crossroad	**noun**	**12-06-009**
crossroads	NNS	12-06-009
crossroad	**verb**	**1-01-001**
crossroading	VBG	1-01-001
crosswalk	**NN**	**1-01-001**
crossways	**RB**	**1-01-001**
crosswise	**RB**	**1-01-001**
crotchety	**JJ**	**1-01-001**
crouch	**NN**	**2-02-002**
crouch	**verb**	**22-06-015**
crouch	VB	2-01-002
crouched	VBD	10-04-008
crouched	VBN	6-03-004
crouching	VBG	3-03-003
crouchin'	VBG	1-01-001
Crouch	**prop. noun**	**4-01-001**
Crouch	NP	3-01-001
Crouch's	NP$	1-01-001
croupier	**NN**	**1-01-001**
crow	**noun**	**2-02-002**
crow	NN	1-01-001
crows	NNS	1-01-001
crow	**verb**	**5-03-005**
crowed	VBD	2-02-002
crowing	VBG	2-01-002
a-crowing	VBG	1-01-001
Crow	**prop. noun**	**2-02-002**
Crow	NP	1-01-001
Crows	NPS	1-01-001
crowbait	**NN**	**1-01-001**
crowd	**noun**	**63-13-049**
crowd	NN	50-13-037
Crowd	NN-TL	1-01-001
crowds	NNS	12-08-012
crowd	**verb**	**39-13-034**
crowd	VB	2-02-002
crowded	VBD	8-04-006
crowded	VBN	24-12-024
crowding	VBG	5-04-005

Crowder	**NP**	**2-01-001**
crowing	**NN**	**1-01-001**
crown	**noun**	**19-08-011**
crown	NN	16-06-008
Crown	NN-TL	2-02-002
crowns	NNS	1-01-001
crown	**verb**	**11-08-010**
crown	VB	1-01-001
crowned	VBN	7-05-006
crowning	VBG	3-03-003
Croydon	**prop. noun**	**1-01-001**
Croydon	NP	0-00-000
Croydon	NP-TL	1-01-001
Crozier	**NP**	**1-01-001**
crucial	**adjective**	**30-11-024**
crucial	JJ	29-11-024
crucial	JJ-HL	1-01-001
crucially	**RB**	**1-01-001**
crucible	**noun**	**1-01-001**
crucible	NN	0-00-000
Crucible	NN-TL	1-01-001
crucifix	**NN**	**3-02-002**
crucifixion	**NN**	**1-01-001**
crucify	**verb**	**4-04-004**
crucified	VBD	1-01-001
crucified	VBN	1-01-001
crucifying	VBG	2-02-002
crude	**JJ**	**15-08-014**
crudely	**RB**	**2-02-002**
crudest	**JJT**	**1-01-001**
crudity	**noun**	**2-02-002**
crudity	NN	1-01-001
crudities	NNS	1-01-001
cruel	**JJ**	**15-07-014**
cruelest	**JJT**	**1-01-001**
cruelly	**RB**	**4-04-004**
cruelty	**NN**	**13-08-013**
cruise	**noun**	**2-02-002**
cruise	NN	1-01-001
cruises	NNS	1-01-001
cruise	**verb**	**6-05-006**
cruising	VBG	6-05-006
Cruise	**NP**	**1-01-001**
cruiser	**noun**	**6-04-005**
cruiser	NN	4-03-003
cruisers	NNS	2-02-002
cruising	**NN**	**1-01-001**
Crumb	**NP**	**3-01-001**
crumble	**verb**	**7-05-007**
crumble	VB	1-01-001
Crumble	VB-TL	1-01-001
crumbled	VBD	1-01-001
crumbled	VBN	2-02-002
crumbling	VBG	2-02-002
crumbly	**JJ**	**1-01-001**
Crumley	**NP**	**1-01-001**
Crumlish	**NP**	**1-01-001**
crummy	**JJ**	**3-02-002**
Crump	**NP**	**1-01-001**
crumple	**verb**	**4-03-004**
crumpled	VBD	1-01-001
crumpled	VBN	3-03-003
crunch	**NN**	**1-01-001**
crunch	**UH**	**1-01-001**
crunch	**verb**	**1-01-001**
crunched	VBD	1-01-001
crupper	**NN**	**2-02-002**
crus	**foreign**	**4-01-001**
crus	FW-NNS	1-01-001
Crus	FW-NNS-TL	3-01-001
crusade	**noun**	**9-06-006**
crusade	NN	4-04-004
Crusade	NN-TL	4-01-001
crusades	NNS	0-00-000
Crusades	NNS-TL	1-01-001
crusade	**verb**	**1-01-001**
crusading	VBG	1-01-001
crusader	**noun**	**3-02-003**
crusader	NN	1-01-001
crusaders	NNS	0-00-000
Crusaders	NNS-TL	2-01-002
crush	**noun**	**3-03-003**
crush	NN	2-02-002
Crush	NN-TL	1-01-001
crush	**verb**	**17-10-014**
crush	VB	1-01-001
crushed	VBD	2-02-002
crushed	VBN	8-06-006
crushing	VBG	6-05-006

crusher	**noun**	**2-02-002**
crusher	NN	1-01-001
crushers	NNS	1-01-001
crushing	**NN**	**1-01-001**
crust	**NN**	**1-01-001**
crutch	**noun**	**7-05-006**
crutch	NN	1-01-001
crutches	NNS	6-05-005
crux	**NN**	**2-02-002**
Cruz	**NP**	**8-01-001**
cry	**noun**	**35-10-022**
cry	NN	30-10-020
cries	NNS	5-03-004
cry	**verb**	**64-12-045**
cry	VB	18-06-017
cries	VBZ	1-01-001
cried	VBD	25-09-021
cried	VBN	5-04-004
crying	VBG	15-07-014
cryostat	**NN**	**1-01-001**
crypt	**NN**	**1-01-001**
cryptic	**JJ**	**3-02-003**
cryptographic	**JJ**	**1-01-001**
crystal	**noun**	**31-07-011**
crystal	NN	17-06-008
crystal	NN-HL	1-01-001
Crystal	NN-TL	5-02-002
crystals	NNS	8-02-003
crystalline	**JJ**	**5-02-003**
crystallite	**noun**	**4-01-002**
crystallite	NN	1-01-001
crystallites	NNS	3-01-002
crystallization	**noun**	**3-02-002**
crystallization	NN	2-02-002
crystallization	NN-HL	1-01-001
crystallize	**verb**	**4-03-003**
crystallize	VB	1-01-001
crystallized	VBN	1-01-001
crystallizing	VBG	2-02-002
crystallographer	**noun**	**1-01-001**
crystallographers	NNS	1-01-001
crystallographic	**adjective**	**5-01-001**
crystallographic	JJ	4-01-001
Crystallographic	JJ-TL	1-01-001
crystallography	**noun**	**2-02-002**
crystallography	NN	1-01-001
Crystallography	NN-TL	1-01-001
CSF	**NP**	**1-01-001**
CTA	**NP**	**1-01-001**
cub	**noun**	**1-01-001**
cub's	NN$	1-01-001
Cub	**prop. noun**	**2-02-002**
Cubs	NPS	2-02-002
Cuba	**prop. noun**	**49-09-020**
Cuba	NP	43-08-019
Cuba	NP-HL	3-02-002
Cuba	NP-TL	1-01-001
Cuba's	NP$	2-02-002
Cuban	**JJ**	**13-03-007**
Cuban	**prop. noun**	**11-03-007**
Cuban	NP	6-02-005
Cubans	NPS	5-02-003
Cuban-American	**NP**	**1-01-001**
cubbyhole	**NN**	**1-01-001**
cube	**noun**	**5-03-004**
cube	NN	1-01-001
cubes	NNS	4-03-004
cube	**verb**	**1-01-001**
cubed	VBN	1-01-001
cubic	**adjective**	**20-04-004**
cubic	JJ	15-03-003
cu.	JJ	5-01-001
Cubism	**prop. noun**	**11-01-001**
Cubism	NP	8-01-001
Cubism	NP-TL	3-01-001
cubist	**adjective**	**6-01-002**
cubist	JJ	1-01-001
Cubist	JJ-TL	5-01-001
cubist	**noun**	**2-02-002**
cubist	NN	1-01-001
cubists	NNS	1-01-001
cuckoo-bumblebee	**NN**	**1-01-001**
cud	**NN**	**1-01-001**
Cuddleback	**prop. noun**	**1-01-001**
Cuddleback	NP	0-00-000
Cuddleback	NP-TL	1-01-001
cudgel	**noun**	**2-02-002**
cudgels	NNS	2-02-002
Cudkowicz	**NP**	**1-01-001**

Cudmore	**NP**	**1-01-001**
cue	**noun**	**3-02-002**
cues	NNS	3-02-002
cue-phrase	**NN**	**1-01-001**
cuff	**noun**	**3-02-003**
cuff	NN	1-01-001
cuffs	NNS	2-02-002
cufflink	**noun**	**1-01-001**
cufflinks	NNS	1-01-001
cuirassier	**noun**	**1-01-001**
cuirassiers	NNS	1-01-001
cuisine	**FW-NN**	**1-01-001**
Culbertson	**NP**	**1-01-001**
culminate	**verb**	**11-07-011**
culminate	VB	2-02-002
culminates	VBZ	5-04-005
culminated	VBD	2-02-002
culminating	VBG	2-02-002
culmination	**NN**	**4-03-003**
Culmone	**prop. noun**	**1-01-001**
Culmone	NP	0-00-000
Culmone	NP-HL	1-01-001
culpas	**FW-NNS**	**1-01-001**
culprit	**noun**	**4-03-004**
culprit	NN	2-02-002
culprits	NNS	2-02-002
cult	**noun**	**15-07-010**
cult	NN	11-05-007
cults	NNS	4-04-004
culte	**FW-NN**	**1-01-001**
cultist	**NN**	**2-02-002**
cultivate	**verb**	**16-07-014**
cultivate	VB	3-03-003
cultivates	VBZ	1-01-001
cultivated	VBD	2-02-002
cultivated	VBN	8-06-007
cultivating	VBG	2-01-002
cultivation	**NN**	**4-03-004**
cultural	**adjective**	**55-09-032**
cultural	JJ	49-09-030
cultural	JJ-HL	1-01-001
Cultural	JJ-TL	5-03-004
culturally	**RB**	**5-03-005**
culture	**noun**	**71-11-041**
culture	NN	56-09-033
Culture	NN-TL	2-02-002
culture's	NN$	1-01-001
cultures	NNS	12-06-010
culture	**verb**	**4-02-003**
cultured	VBN	4-02-003
culture-Protestantism	**NP**	**1-01-001**
Culver	**prop. noun**	**3-01-001**
Culver	NP	2-01-001
Culvers	NPS	1-01-001
cumara	**NN**	**1-01-001**
Cumbanchero	**prop. noun**	**1-01-001**
Cumbancheros	NPS	1-01-001
Cumberland	**prop. noun**	**3-03-003**
Cumberland	NP	2-02-002
Cumberland	NP-TL	1-01-001
cumbersome	**JJ**	**3-02-003**
Cumhuriyet	**NP**	**1-01-001**
cumin	**NN**	**1-01-001**
cumulate	**VB**	**1-01-001**
cumulative	**adjective**	**13-06-009**
cumulative	JJ	12-06-009
cumulative	JJ-HL	1-01-001
cumulus	**NN**	**1-01-001**
Cunard	**prop. noun**	**6-01-001**
Cunard	NP	4-01-001
Cunard	NP-TL	1-01-001
Cunard's	NP$	1-01-001
cunning	**JJ**	**3-03-003**
cunning	**NN**	**2-01-002**
Cunningham	**prop. noun**	**7-02-002**
Cunningham	NP	5-02-002
Cunningham's	NP$	2-02-002
cunningly	**RB**	**3-03-003**
cup	**noun**	**58-10-029**
cup	NN	43-10-022
Cup	NN-TL	1-01-001
cups	NNS	14-07-011
cup	**verb**	**5-04-005**
cup	VB	1-01-001
cupped	VBD	2-02-002
cupped	VBN	2-02-002
cupboard	**noun**	**4-03-004**
cupboard	NN	2-02-002
cupboards	NNS	2-02-002

Word	Tag	Frequency
cupful	**NN**	**3-01-001**
Cupply	**NP**	**3-01-001**
cur	**NN**	**1-01-001**
curative	**JJ**	**1-01-001**
curator	**NN**	**2-02-002**
curb	**noun**	**15-06-011**
curb	NN	12-05-009
curbs	NNS	3-02-002
curb	**verb**	**4-03-003**
curb	VB	1-01-001
curbing	VBG	3-02-002
curbside	**JJ**	**1-01-001**
curbside	**NN**	**2-02-002**
curd	**noun**	**3-03-003**
curd	NN	2-02-002
curds	NNS	1-01-001
curdle	**verb**	**1-01-001**
curdling	VBG	1-01-001
cure	**noun**	**19-04-011**
cure	NN	16-04-010
cures	NNS	3-02-003
cure	**verb**	**20-07-010**
cure	VB	12-06-008
cured	VBD	1-01-001
cured	VBN	6-03-003
curing	VBG	1-01-001
cure-all	**NN**	**4-02-002**
curettage	**NN**	**1-01-001**
Curia	**NP**	**3-01-001**
curiae	**foreign**	**3-01-001**
curiae	FW-NN$	2-01-001
Curiae	FW-NN$-TL	1-01-001
Curie	**NP**	**2-02-002**
Curie-Weiss	**NP**	**1-01-001**
curio	**NN**	**2-01-001**
curiosity	**NN**	**23-10-020**
curious	**JJ**	**46-14-037**
curiously	**RB**	**11-06-011**
curl	**noun**	**1-01-001**
curls	NNS	1-01-001
curl	**verb**	**17-08-014**
curl	VB	2-02-002
curled	VBD	6-04-006
curled	VBN	7-05-006
curling	VBG	1-01-001
Curling	VBG-TL	1-01-001
curly	**JJ**	**5-03-005**
currant	**noun**	**2-02-002**
currant	NN	1-01-001
currants	NNS	1-01-001
currency	**noun**	**15-06-007**
currency	NN	8-06-006
currency	NN-HL	4-01-001
currencies	NNS	3-01-002
current	**adjective**	**84-11-063**
current	JJ	81-11-063
current	JJ-HL	2-02-002
Current	JJ-TL	1-01-001
current	**noun**	**29-08-014**
current	NN	20-07-010
currents	NNS	9-04-007
currently	**RB**	**34-09-029**
curricular	**JJ**	**2-02-002**
curriculum	**noun**	**20-06-013**
curriculum	NN	16-05-010
curricula	NNS	3-03-003
curriculums	NNS	1-01-001
curry	**NN**	**1-01-001**
Curry	**prop. noun**	**2-01-001**
Curry	NP	1-01-001
Currys	NPS	1-01-001
curse	**noun**	**10-08-010**
curse	NN	7-05-007
curses	NNS	3-03-003
curse	**verb**	**23-08-021**
curse	VB	4-03-003
cursed	VBD	7-05-007
cursed	VBN	4-03-004
cursing	VBG	8-05-008
cursory	**JJ**	**4-03-004**
curt	**JJ**	**1-01-001**
Curt	**prop. noun**	**39-01-001**
Curt	NP	31-01-001
Curt's	NP$	8-01-001
curtail	**verb**	**6-04-006**
curtail	VB	4-04-004
curtailed	VBN	2-01-002
curtain	**noun**	**21-10-018**
curtain	NN	11-06-009
curtain (cont.):		
Curtain	NN-TL	2-02-002
curtains	NNS	8-05-008
curtain-raiser	**NN**	**1-01-001**
curtained	**JJ**	**1-01-001**
Curtin	**NP**	**1-01-001**
Curtis	**NP**	**3-02-002**
Curtiss	**prop. noun**	**2-02-002**
Curtiss	NP	1-01-001
Curtiss	NP-TL	1-01-001
curtly	**RB**	**2-02-002**
curtness	**NN**	**1-01-001**
curtsey	**verb**	**1-01-001**
curtseyed	VBD	1-01-001
curvaceously	**RB**	**1-01-001**
curvature	**NN**	**5-01-003**
curve	**noun**	**64-09-017**
curve	NN	45-05-012
curves	NNS	19-05-008
curve	**verb**	**11-05-009**
curved	VBD	1-01-001
curved	VBN	6-03-005
curving	VBG	4-04-004
Cury	**prop. noun**	**3-02-002**
Cury	NP	2-01-001
Cury	NP-TL	1-01-001
Curzon	**prop. noun**	**8-02-002**
Curzon	NP	3-02-002
Curzon	NP-TL	2-01-001
Curzon's	NP$	3-01-001
Cusa	**prop. noun**	**1-01-001**
Cusa	NP	0-00-000
Cusa	NP-TL	1-01-001
cushion	**noun**	**8-04-004**
cushion	NN	6-04-004
cushions	NNS	2-02-002
cushion	**verb**	**4-02-003**
cushion	VB	2-02-002
cushioning	VBG	2-01-001
cushioning	**NN**	**2-02-002**
Cushman	**NP**	**1-01-001**
cusp	**NN**	**2-01-001**
Custer	**prop. noun**	**6-01-001**
Custer	NP	5-01-001
Custer's	NP$	1-01-001
custodial	**JJ**	**1-01-001**
custodian	**NN**	**3-03-003**
custody	**NN**	**2-02-002**
custom	**adjective**	**4-02-003**
custom	JJ	1-01-001
Custom	JJ-TL	3-01-002
custom	**noun**	**28-08-020**
custom	NN	10-05-010
customs	NNS	17-08-011
Customs	NNS-TL	1-01-001
custom-design	**NN**	**1-01-001**
custom-make	**VB**	**1-01-001**
customarily	**RB**	**4-03-004**
customary	**JJ**	**14-10-014**
customer	**noun**	**69-12-037**
customer	NN	24-08-014
customer	NN-HL	3-03-003
customer's	NN$	1-01-001
customers	NNS	38-11-023
customers	NNS-HL	2-01-001
customers'	NNS$	1-01-001
customer-cost	**NN**	**1-01-001**
customhouse	**noun**	**1-01-001**
customhouse	NN	0-00-000
Customhouse	NN-TL	1-01-001
cut	**noun**	**35-08-021**
cut	NN	17-07-012
cut	NN-HL	2-01-002
cuts	NNS	16-05-010
cut	**verb**	**245-15-117**
cut	VB	87-15-056
cut	VB-HL	1-01-001
cuts	VBZ	14-08-014
cut	VBD	25-11-021
cut	VBN	60-14-047
cutting	VBG	56-07-021
cutting	VBG-HL	1-01-001
Cutting	VBG-TL	1-01-001
cut-and-dried	**JJ**	**1-01-001**
cut-down	**JJ**	**1-01-001**
cut-glass	**NN**	**1-01-001**
cut-to-a-familiar-pattern	**JJ**	**1-01-001**
cutback	**NN**	**1-01-001**
cute	**JJ**	**5-03-004**

Word	Tag	Frequency
cutest	**JJT**	**1-01-001**
cutlass	**NN**	**1-01-001**
cutlet	**noun**	**1-01-001**
cutlets	NNS	1-01-001
cutoff	**noun**	**2-02-002**
cutoff	NN	1-01-001
cut-off	NN	1-01-001
cutout	**noun**	**1-01-001**
cutouts	NNS	1-01-001
cutter	**noun**	**11-03-003**
cutter	NN	4-02-002
cutters	NNS	6-03-003
cutters'	NNS$	1-01-001
cutthroat	**NN**	**1-01-001**
cutting	**noun**	**9-04-006**
cutting	NN	8-03-005
cuttings	NNS	1-01-001
cutting-edge	**NN**	**1-01-001**
Cyclades	**NPS**	**1-01-001**
cycle	**noun**	**30-09-026**
cycle	NN	24-07-021
cycles	NNS	6-05-006
cycle	**verb**	**2-02-002**
cycles	VBZ	1-01-001
cycled	VBN	1-01-001
cyclical	**JJ**	**1-01-001**
cyclist	**NN**	**8-01-001**
cyclohexanol	**NN**	**1-01-001**
cyclorama	**NN**	**1-01-001**
Cycly	**NP**	**1-01-001**
cygne	**foreign**	**1-01-001**
cygne	FW-NN	0-00-000
Cygne	FW-NN-TL	1-01-001
cylinder	**noun**	**27-02-003**
cylinder	NN	18-02-003
cylinder's	NN$	2-01-001
cylinders	NNS	7-01-001
cylindrical	**adjective**	**11-02-006**
cylindrical	JJ	9-02-006
cylindrical	JJ-HL	2-01-001
Cynewulf	**NP**	**3-01-001**
cynic	**noun**	**3-03-003**
cynics	NNS	3-03-003
cynical	**JJ**	**9-05-006**
cynically	**RB**	**1-01-001**
cynicism	**NN**	**4-03-003**
Cynthia	**NP**	**2-02-002**
cypress	**noun**	**7-05-005**
cypress	NN	5-04-004
Cypress	NN-TL	2-01-001
cypress-like	**JJ**	**1-01-001**
Cyprian	**NP**	**1-01-001**
Cyr	**NP**	**1-01-001**
Cyril	**NP**	**1-01-001**
Cyrus	**NP**	**4-03-003**
cyst	**noun**	**3-02-002**
cysts	NNS	3-02-002
cytolysis	**NN**	**1-01-001**
cytoplasm	**NN**	**4-01-002**
czar	**noun**	**1-01-001**
czar	NN	0-00-000
Czar	NN-TL	1-01-001
czarina	**noun**	**5-01-001**
czarina	NN	0-00-000
Czarina	NN-TL	2-01-001
czarina's	NN$	0-00-000
Czarina's	NN$-TL	3-01-001
czarship	**noun**	**1-01-001**
czarship	NN	0-00-000
Czarship	NN-TL	1-01-001
Czechoslovakia	**NP**	**5-04-004**
Czerny	**NP**	**1-01-001**

D

Word	Tag	Frequency
D	**prop. noun**	**28-06-016**
D	NP	13-06-009
D	NP-HL	15-02-009
D.	**prop. noun**	**65-09-046**
D.	NP	63-08-045
D.	NP-TL	2-02-002
D.A.	**prop. noun**	**3-02-002**
D.A.	NP	2-01-001
D.A.	NP-TL	1-01-001
D.C.	**NP**	**25-07-013**
D.J.	**NP**	**1-01-001**
D.O.A.	**JJ**	**1-01-001**
D.W.	**prop. noun**	**2-01-001**
D.W.	NP	1-01-001
D.W.	NP-HL	1-01-001
D-night	**NP**	**1-01-001**
D'Albert	**NP**	**4-01-001**
D'Amours	**NP**	**1-01-001**
d'Argent	**foreign**	**1-01-001**
d'Argent	FW-IN+NN	0-00-000
D'Argent	FW-IN+NN-TL	1-01-001
D'Arlay	**NP**	**1-01-001**
d'art	**foreign**	**2-02-002**
d'art	FW-IN+NN	1-01-001
D'Art	FW-IN+NN-TL	1-01-001
D'Artaguette	**NP**	**3-01-001**
D'Aumont	**NP**	**1-01-001**
d'Eiffel	**foreign**	**1-01-001**
d'Eiffel	FW-IN+NP	0-00-000
d'Eiffel	FW-IN+NP-TL	1-01-001
d'entretenir	**FW-TO+VB**	**1-01-001**
d'etat	**FW-IN+NN**	**2-02-002**
d'hotel	**FW-IN+NN**	**1-01-001**
d'identite	**FW-IN+NN**	**1-01-001**
d'un	**FW-IN+AT**	**1-01-001**
d'Yquem	**foreign**	**1-01-001**
d'Yquem	FW-IN+NP	0-00-000
d'Yquem	FW-IN+NP-TL	1-01-001
Da	**NP**	**9-02-003**
da-da-da-dum	**UH**	**1-01-001**
dab	**verb**	**3-02-003**
dabbed	VBD	1-01-001
dabbing	VBG	2-01-002
dabble	**verb**	**4-03-004**
dabbles	VBZ	1-01-001
dabbled	VBD	1-01-001
dabbling	VBG	2-02-002
dabbler	**NN**	**1-01-001**
dabhumaksanigalu'ahai	**FW-VB**	**1-01-001**
Dachshund	**FW-NN**	**1-01-001**
dactyl	**noun**	**2-01-001**
dactyls	NNS	1-01-001
Dactyls	NNS-TL	1-01-001
dad	**noun**	**15-04-009**
dad	NN	2-02-002
Dad	NN-TL	13-04-007
Dadaism	**NP**	**1-01-001**
daddy	**noun**	**6-04-006**
daddy	NN	2-01-002
Daddy	NN-TL	2-02-002
daddy's	NN+BEZ	0-00-000
Daddy's	NN+BEZ-TL	1-01-001
daddy's	NN$	0-00-000
Daddy's	NN$-TL	1-01-001
Dade	**prop. noun**	**3-02-002**
Dade	NP	0-00-000
Dade	NP-TL	2-02-002
Dade's	NP$	1-01-001
Daer	**prop. noun**	**5-01-001**
Daer	NP	0-00-000
Daer	NP-TL	5-01-001
daffodil	**noun**	**1-01-001**
daffodils	NNS	1-01-001
Dag	**NP**	**7-03-005**
dagger	**noun**	**1-01-001**
daggers	NNS	0-00-000
dagers	NNS	1-01-001
daggerman	**NN**	**1-01-001**
Dailey	**NP**	**1-01-001**
daily	**adjective**	**67-13-039**
daily	JJ	44-12-034
Daily	JJ-TL	23-05-006
daily	**RB**	**55-09-025**
daintily	**RB**	**1-01-001**
dainty	**JJ**	**3-03-003**
dainty-legged	**JJ**	**1-01-001**

Word	Tag	Frequency
daiquiri	**noun**	**1-01-001**
daiquiris	NNS	0-00-000
dack-rihs	NNS	1-01-001
dairy	**noun**	**19-04-005**
dairy	NN	16-04-005
dairy	NN-HL	3-01-001
dairy-oh	**UH**	**1-01-001**
dais	**noun**	**3-03-003**
dais	NN	2-02-002
daises	NNS	1-01-001
daisy	**noun**	**3-02-003**
daisies	NNS	3-02-003
Dakota	**prop. noun**	**7-04-005**
Dakota	NP	0-00-000
Dak.	NP	1-01-001
Dakota	NP-TL	6-04-005
dale	**noun**	**2-02-002**
dale	NN	0-00-000
Dale	NN-TL	1-01-001
dales	NNS	1-01-001
Dale	**NP**	**4-02-002**
Daley	**NP**	**2-02-002**
Dali	**NP**	**1-01-001**
Dallas	**prop. noun**	**58-05-010**
Dallas	NP	43-04-008
Dallas	NP-HL	2-02-002
Dallas	NP-TL	13-03-005
Dallas-based	**JJ**	**1-01-001**
Dallas-headquartered	**JJ**	**1-01-001**
Dalles	**prop. noun**	**1-01-001**
Dalles	NP	0-00-000
Dalles	NP-TL	1-01-001
Dalloway	**NP**	**3-01-001**
Dalton	**prop. noun**	**5-02-004**
Dalton	NP	4-02-004
Dalton's	NP$	1-01-001
Daly	**NP**	**1-01-001**
Dalzell	**NP**	**1-01-001**
dam	**noun**	**5-05-005**
dam	NN	2-02-002
dams	NNS	3-03-003
dam	**verb**	**1-01-001**
dammed	VBD	1-01-001
dam-up	**verb**	**1-01-001**
dammed-up	VBN	1-01-001
damage	**noun**	**30-08-021**
damage	NN	27-08-019
demage	NN	1-01-001
damage	NN-HL	1-01-001
damages	NNS	1-01-001
damage	**verb**	**17-10-014**
damage	VB	5-04-004
damages	VBZ	2-01-001
damaged	VBD	5-04-005
damaged	VBN	2-02-002
damaging	VBG	3-03-003
Damas	**NP**	**1-01-001**
Damascus	**NP**	**3-02-002**
dame	**NN**	**1-01-001**
Dame	**prop. noun**	**6-02-003**
Dame	NP	3-01-002
Dame	NP-TL	3-02-002
damn	**adjective**	**15-04-011**
damn	JJ	13-03-009
dam	JJ	1-01-001
dam'	JJ	1-01-001
damn	**NN**	**4-03-003**
damn	**QL**	**2-01-001**
damn	**UH**	**3-03-003**
damn	**verb**	**33-08-025**
damn	VB	10-05-010
damned	VBN	19-08-015
dam	VBN	1-01-001
damed	VBN	2-01-001
damning	VBG	1-01-001
damnation	**NN**	**3-02-002**
damnit	**exclam.**	**8-03-007**
damnit	UH	1-01-001
dammit	UH	7-03-006
Damon	**NP**	**1-01-001**
damp	**JJ**	**16-08-012**
dampen	**verb**	**6-05-006**
dampen	VB	2-02-002
dampened	VBD	1-01-001
dampened	VBN	2-02-002
dampening	VBG	1-01-001
dampness	**NN**	**2-02-002**
damsel	**NN**	**1-01-001**
Dan	**prop. noun**	**30-03-006**

Dan (cont.):

Word	Tag	Frequency
Dan	NP	26-02-005
Dan	NP-TL	1-01-001
Dan's	NP$	3-01-001
Dana	**prop. noun**	**6-02-002**
Dana	NP	2-01-001
Dana	NP-TL	1-01-001
Dana's	NP$	3-01-001
Danaher	**NP**	**2-01-001**
Danbury	**prop. noun**	**1-01-001**
Danbury	NP	0-00-000
Danbury	NP-TL	1-01-001
dance	**noun**	**94-13-036**
dance	NN	66-13-031
dance	NN-HL	1-01-001
Dance	NN-TL	6-01-004
dances	NNS	19-07-011
dances	NNS-HL	1-01-001
Dances	NNS-TL	1-01-001
dance	**verb**	**59-11-042**
dance	VB	17-08-012
dances	VBZ	2-02-002
danced	VBD	8-05-007
danced	VBN	2-01-001
dancing	VBG	29-08-026
Dancing	VBG-TL	1-01-001
dance-theatre	**NN**	**1-01-001**
dancelike	**JJ**	**1-01-001**
dancer	**noun**	**63-09-022**
dancer	NN	31-07-011
dancers	NNS	30-08-016
Dancers	NNS-TL	1-01-001
dancers'	NNS$	1-01-001
Danchin	**NP**	**1-01-001**
dancing	**NN**	**13-03-006**
dandelion	**NN**	**1-01-001**
dandily	**RB**	**1-01-001**
dandy	**JJ**	**2-02-002**
Dandy	**prop. noun**	**16-01-001**
Dandy	NP	15-01-001
Dandy's	NP$	1-01-001
Dane	**prop. noun**	**6-04-005**
Dane	NP	2-02-002
Danes	NPS	4-03-003
Danehy	**NP**	**1-01-001**
dang	**JJ**	**1-01-001**
dang	**verb**	**1-01-001**
danged	VBN	1-01-001
danger	**noun**	**86-12-065**
danger	NN	68-12-053
danger	NN-HL	2-02-002
dangers	NNS	16-07-015
dangerous	**JJ**	**46-12-041**
dangerously	**RB**	**3-03-003**
dangle	**verb**	**7-04-007**
dangle	VB	1-01-001
dangled	VBD	2-01-002
dangling	VBG	4-03-004
Daniel	**prop. noun**	**17-08-010**
Daniel	NP	15-08-010
Dan'l	NP	1-01-001
Daniel's	NP$	1-01-001
Daniels	**NP**	**2-01-001**
Danish	**adjective**	**8-04-003**
Danish	JJ	7-03-003
Danish	JJ-TL	1-01-001
dank	**JJ**	**1-01-001**
Dannehower	**NP**	**1-01-001**
Danny	**prop. noun**	**7-03-004**
Danny	NP	6-03-004
Danny's	NP$	1-01-001
dans	**foreign**	**1-01-001**
dans	FW-IN	0-00-000
dans	FW-IN-TL	1-01-001
danseur	**NN**	**1-01-001**
Dante	**prop. noun**	**3-03-003**
Dante	NP	2-02-002
Dante's	NP$	1-01-001
Danube	**prop. noun**	**3-03-003**
Danube	NP	2-02-002
Danube	NP-TL	1-01-001
Danubian	**NP**	**1-01-001**
Danville	**NP**	**1-01-001**
Danzig	**NP**	**1-01-001**
Daphne	**NP**	**1-01-001**
dapper	**JJ**	**6-05-005**
Dappertutto	**NP**	**1-01-001**
dapple	**verb**	**1-01-001**
dappled	VBN	1-01-001

Word	Tag	Count
darbuka	**NN**	**1-01-001**
dare	**MD**	**5-04-004**
dare	**verb**	**45-12-037**
dare	VB	16-09-015
dares	VBZ	3-03-003
dared	VBD	7-04-004
dared	VBN	7-06-007
daring	VBG	11-05-009
darin'	VBG	1-01-001
Dare-Base	**NP**	**1-01-001**
Dares	**NP**	**2-01-001**
daring	**NN**	**1-01-001**
Darius	**NP**	**1-01-001**
dark	**adjective**	**160-14-094**
dark	JJ	149-14-089
Dark	JJ-TL	10-05-005
Dark	JJ-TL-HL	1-01-001
dark	**NN**	**22-09-016**
Dark	**NP**	**3-02-002**
dark-blue	**JJ**	**1-01-001**
dark-brown	**JJ**	**1-01-001**
dark-gray	**JJ**	**1-01-001**
dark-green	**JJ**	**1-01-001**
dark-haired	**adjective**	**3-03-003**
dark-haired	JJ	2-02-002
darkhaired	JJ	1-01-001
dark-skinned	**JJ**	**1-01-001**
darken	**verb**	**11-08-010**
darkened	VBD	5-03-004
darkened	VBN	2-02-002
darkening	VBG	4-03-004
darker	**JJR**	**2-02-002**
darkest	**JJT**	**2-02-002**
darkling	**adjective**	**2-02-002**
darkling	JJ	1-01-001
Darkling	JJ-TL	1-01-001
darkly	**RB**	**2-01-002**
darkness	**NN**	**43-10-031**
Darlene	**NP**	**1-01-001**
darling	**adjective**	**5-05-005**
darling	JJ	4-04-004
darlin'	JJ	1-01-001
darling	**NN**	**8-05-008**
Darling	**prop. noun**	**6-01-001**
Darling	NP	4-01-001
Darling	NP-TL	1-01-001
Darling's	NP$	1-01-001
darn	**NN**	**1-01-001**
darn	**verb**	**5-04-005**
darn	VB	2-02-002
darned	VBN	3-03-003
darned	**QL**	**1-01-001**
Darnell	**NP**	**1-01-001**
Darrell	**NP**	**1-01-001**
Darrow	**NP**	**1-01-001**
dart	**verb**	**7-05-007**
darted	VBD	6-04-006
darting	VBG	1-01-001
Dartmouth	**prop. noun**	**33-03-005**
Dartmouth	NP	26-03-005
Dartmouth	NP-TL	4-01-001
Dartmouth's	NP$	3-01-001
Darwen	**NP**	**1-01-001**
Darwin	**prop. noun**	**2-02-002**
Darwin	NP	1-01-001
Darwin's	NP$	1-01-001
Darwinism	**NP**	**2-01-002**
das	**foreign**	**2-02-002**
das	FW-AT	0-00-000
Das	FW-AT-TL	1-01-001
das	FW-AT-TL	1-01-001
dash	**noun**	**11-05-010**
dash	NN	10-05-009
dashes	NNS	1-01-001
dash	**verb**	**14-07-011**
dash	VB	1-01-001
dashes	VBZ	1-01-001
dashed	VBD	4-04-004
dashed	VBN	3-02-002
dashed	VBN-HL	1-01-001
dashing	VBG	4-02-003
dashboard	**NN**	**2-02-002**
Dashiell	**NP**	**3-01-001**
Dashwood	**prop. noun**	**1-01-001**
Dashwood	NP	0-00-000
Dashwood	NP-TL	1-01-001
data-handling	**NN**	**1-01-001**
data-processing	**JJ**	**1-01-001**
data-processing	**NN**	**1-01-001**

Word	Tag	Count
date	**noun**	**120-14-073**
date	NN	97-13-063
Date	NN-TL	1-01-001
dates	NNS	22-09-016
date	**verb**	**36-09-023**
date	VB	5-04-005
dates	VBZ	8-06-008
dated	VBN	19-05-008
dating	VBG	4-04-004
dateline	**verb**	**4-01-001**
datelined	VBN	4-01-001
datum	**noun**	**174-10-049**
datum	NN	1-01-001
data	NN	75-10-038
data	NN-HL	2-02-002
data	NNS	84-05-021
data	NNS-HL	5-01-001
Data	NNS-TL	7-02-004
daub	**verb**	**1-01-001**
daubed	VBD	1-01-001
daughter	**noun**	**91-13-053**
daughter	NN	72-12-043
Daughter	NN-TL	1-01-001
daughter's	NN$	4-03-003
daughters	NNS	14-07-011
daunt	**verb**	**2-02-002**
daunt	VB	1-01-001
daunted	VBN	1-01-001
dauntless	**adjective**	**2-02-002**
dauntless	JJ	1-01-001
Dauntless	JJ-TL	1-01-001
dauphin	**NN**	**1-01-001**
Dauphine	**NP**	**1-01-001**
Davao	**NP**	**1-01-001**
Dave	**prop. noun**	**32-04-008**
Dave	NP	31-04-008
Dave's	NP$	1-01-001
davenport	**NN**	**2-01-001**
Davenport	**NP**	**2-01-001**
David	**prop. noun**	**55-10-029**
David	NP	46-10-024
David	NP-TL	5-03-004
David's	NP$	3-02-002
David's	NP$-TL	1-01-001
Davidson	**prop. noun**	**5-03-003**
Davidson	NP	3-03-003
Davidson's	NP$	2-01-001
Davis	**prop. noun**	**29-05-013**
Davis	NP	26-04-012
Davis	NP-TL	1-01-001
Davis'	NP$	2-02-002
davit	**noun**	**1-01-001**
davits	NNS	1-01-001
Davy	**prop. noun**	**3-02-003**
Davy	NP	2-02-002
Davy's	NP$	1-01-001
dawn	**noun**	**26-09-021**
dawn	NN	25-09-020
Dawn	NN-TL	1-01-001
dawn	**verb**	**4-02-004**
dawn	VB	1-01-001
dawns	VBZ	1-01-001
dawning	VBG	2-02-002
Dawn	**NP**	**1-01-001**
Dawson	**NP**	**1-01-001**
day	**noun**	**1077-15-351**
day	NN	629-15-271
Day	NN-TL	44-12-029
Day	NN-TL-HL	4-01-001
day's	NN$	14-08-013
days	NNS	377-15-214
days	NNS-HL	1-01-001
Days	NNS-TL	6-04-004
days'	NNS$	2-02-002
Day	**prop. noun**	**13-05-006**
Day	NP	12-04-005
Day's	NP$	1-01-001
day-after-day	**JJ**	**2-02-002**
day-by-day	**JJ**	**3-02-003**
day-to-day	**JJ**	**3-02-003**
day-watch	**NN**	**2-01-001**
daybed	**NN**	**1-01-001**
daybreak	**NN**	**1-01-001**
daydream	**verb**	**1-01-001**
daydreamed	VBD	1-01-001
daydreaming	**NN**	**1-01-001**
daylight	**noun**	**17-08-016**
daylight	NN	15-08-014
daylight's	NN$	1-01-001

Word	Tag	Frequency
daylight (cont.):		
daylights	NNS	1-01-001
daytime	**JJ**	**13-02-002**
daytime	**noun**	**5-04-004**
daytime	NN	4-04-004
Daytime	NN-TL	1-01-001
daytime	**RB**	**1-01-001**
daze	**verb**	**4-03-004**
dazed	VBD	1-01-001
dazed	VBN	3-02-003
dazzle	**verb**	**13-07-012**
dazzle	VB	1-01-001
dazzles	VBZ	1-01-001
dazzled	VBN	2-02-002
dazzling	VBG	9-06-008
dazzler	**NN**	**1-01-001**
de	**foreign**	**67-12-039**
de	FW-IN	40-09-021
De	FW-IN	9-04-007
De	FW-IN-TL	12-07-010
de	FW-IN-TL	6-05-006
De	**prop. noun**	**56-11-034**
De	NP	54-11-034
de	NP	2-02-002
de-iodinase	**NN**	**1-01-001**
de-iodinate	**verb**	**4-01-001**
de-iodinate	VB	1-01-001
de-iodinated	VBN	1-01-001
de-iodinating	VBG	2-01-001
de-iodination	**NN**	**1-01-001**
De-Kooning	**NP**	**1-01-001**
deacon	**noun**	**6-02-003**
deacon	NN	2-02-002
Deacon	NN-TL	3-01-002
deacons	NNS	0-00-000
Deacons	NNS-TL	1-01-001
deactivate	**verb**	**1-01-001**
deactivated	VBN	1-01-001
deactivation	**NN**	**2-01-002**
dead	**adjective**	**166-15-098**
dead	JJ	163-15-098
dead	JJ-HL	2-02-002
Dead	JJ-TL	1-01-001
dead	**noun**	**6-03-004**
dead	NN	2-02-002
Dead	NN-TL	4-02-002
dead	**QL**	**1-01-001**
dead	**RB**	**1-01-001**
dead-end	**NN**	**1-01-001**
dead-weight	**NN**	**1-01-001**
deaden	**verb**	**1-01-001**
deadened	VBN	1-01-001
deadhead	**noun**	**1-01-001**
deadheads	NNS	1-01-001
deadliest	**JJT**	**2-02-002**
deadline	**noun**	**7-04-007**
deadline	NN	6-04-006
deadlines	NNS	1-01-001
deadliness	**NN**	**2-02-002**
deadlock	**noun**	**10-03-006**
deadlock	NN	8-03-006
deadlock	NN-HL	2-01-002
deadly	**adjective**	**19-09-017**
deadly	JJ	18-08-016
deadly	JJ-HL	1-01-001
deadness	**NN**	**1-01-001**
deadweight	**NN**	**1-01-001**
Deadwood	**NP**	**1-01-001**
DEAE	**NP**	**1-01-001**
deaf	**adjective**	**12-06-007**
deaf	JJ	11-06-007
Deaf	JJ-TL	1-01-001
deafen	**verb**	**1-01-001**
deafened	VBN	1-01-001
deal	**noun**	**99-14-074**
deal	NN	90-14-069
Deal	NN-TL	8-03-005
deals	NNS	1-01-001
deal	**verb**	**124-13-090**
deal	VB	41-11-037
deal	VB-HL	1-01-001
deal	VB-NC	3-01-001
deals	VBZ	14-05-013
dealt	VBD	8-06-008
dealt	VBN	14-04-012
dealing	VBG	43-10-037
dealer	**noun**	**60-09-022**
dealer	NN	23-05-013
dealer	NN-HL	1-01-001

Word	Tag	Frequency
dealer (cont.):		
Dealer	NN-TL	1-01-001
dealer's	NN$	2-01-001
dealers	NNS	30-07-015
dealers'	NNS$	0-00-000
dealers'	NNS$-HL	1-01-001
Dealers'	NNS$-TL	2-01-001
dealership	**noun**	**1-01-001**
dealerships	NNS	1-01-001
dealing	**noun**	**7-05-007**
dealings	NNS	7-05-007
dean	**noun**	**18-05-011**
dean	NN	13-05-009
Dean	NN-TL	4-03-004
deans	NNS	1-01-001
Dean	**prop. noun**	**25-07-012**
Dean	NP	23-07-012
Dean's	NP$	2-01-001
Deane	**NP**	**1-01-001**
dear	**JJ**	**45-10-033**
dear	**NN**	**8-03-005**
dear	**UH**	**1-01-001**
Dearborn	**prop. noun**	**2-02-002**
Dearborn	NP	0-00-000
Dearborn	NP-TL	2-02-002
dearer	**JJR**	**1-01-001**
dearest	**JJT**	**2-02-002**
Dearie	**NP**	**1-01-001**
dearly	**RB**	**4-04-004**
dearth	**NN**	**3-03-003**
death	**noun**	**284-15-134**
death	NN	264-15-127
death	NN-HL	2-01-002
Death	NN-TL	9-04-009
Death	NN-TL-HL	1-01-001
deaths	NNS	8-05-007
death-like	**JJ**	**1-01-001**
death-locked	**JJ**	**1-01-001**
death-trap	**NN**	**1-01-001**
death-wish	**NN**	**1-01-001**
death's-head	**adjective**	**2-01-001**
death's-head	JJ	0-00-000
Death's-Head	JJ-TL	2-01-001
deathbed	**NN**	**2-02-002**
deathly	**QL**	**1-01-001**
deathward	**JJ**	**1-01-001**
Deauville	**NP**	**2-01-001**
deb	**noun**	**2-02-002**
debs	NNS	2-02-002
debacle	**NN**	**3-03-003**
debatable	**JJ**	**1-01-001**
debate	**noun**	**36-09-021**
debate	NN	30-09-017
debates	NNS	6-03-005
debate	**verb**	**10-06-009**
debate	VB	2-02-002
debated	VBD	1-01-001
debated	VBN	4-03-004
debating	VBG	2-02-002
Debating	VBG-TL	1-01-001
debating	**NN**	**1-01-001**
debauchery	**NN**	**2-02-002**
Debby	**NP**	**1-01-001**
debenture	**noun**	**6-01-001**
debentures	NNS	6-01-001
debilitate	**verb**	**2-02-002**
debilitated	VBN	2-02-002
debilitating	**JJ**	**2-02-002**
debility	**NN**	**2-01-001**
debonair	**JJ**	**1-01-001**
Debonnie	**NP**	**3-01-001**
Debora	**NP**	**2-01-001**
debris	**NN**	**8-05-006**
debt	**noun**	**25-08-020**
debt	NN	13-06-013
debts	NNS	11-05-008
Debts	NNS-TL	1-01-001
debt-free	**JJ**	**1-01-001**
debunk	**verb**	**1-01-001**
debunking	VBG	1-01-001
debunking	**NN**	**1-01-001**
debut	**NN**	**14-03-010**
debut	**verb**	**3-01-002**
debuts	VBZ	1-01-001
debuting	VBG	2-01-001
debutante	**noun**	**5-02-003**
debutante	NN	4-02-002
Debutante	NN-TL	1-01-001
decade	**noun**	**80-11-048**

Word	Tag	Frequency
decade (cont.):		
decade	NN	46-10-026
decades	NNS	34-08-026
decadence	**NN**	**2-02-002**
decadent	**JJ**	**2-02-002**
decant	**verb**	**5-01-001**
decanted	VBN	2-01-001
decanting	VBG	3-01-001
decathlon	**noun**	**1-01-001**
decathlon	NN	0-00-000
Decathlon	NN-TL	1-01-001
Decatur	**NP**	**1-01-001**
decay	**noun**	**12-05-009**
decay	NN	11-05-008
Decay	NN-TL	1-01-001
decay	**verb**	**11-07-009**
decay	VB	2-01-001
decays	VBZ	1-01-001
decayed	VBD	1-01-001
decayed	VBN	3-03-003
decaying	VBG	4-04-004
Decca	**NP**	**3-02-002**
deceased	**JJ**	**6-05-006**
deceased	**NN**	**4-03-003**
decedent	**NN**	**2-01-001**
deceit	**noun**	**3-03-003**
deceit	NN	2-02-002
deceit's	NN$	1-01-001
deceitful	**JJ**	**1-01-001**
deceive	**verb**	**8-05-008**
deceive	VB	1-01-001
deceives	VBZ	1-01-001
deceived	VBD	1-01-001
deceived	VBN	4-03-004
deceiving	VBG	1-01-001
decelerate	**VB**	**1-01-001**
deceleration	**NN**	**2-01-001**
December	**prop. noun**	**79-11-050**
December	NP	62-10-044
Dec.	NP	17-04-008
decency	**noun**	**11-07-011**
decency	NN	10-07-010
decencies	NNS	1-01-001
decent	**JJ**	**20-08-019**
decently	**RB**	**1-01-001**
decentralization	**NN**	**1-01-001**
decentralize	**verb**	**1-01-001**
decentralizing	VBG	1-01-001
deception	**NN**	**1-01-001**
deceptive	**JJ**	**4-04-004**
deceptively	**RB**	**1-01-001**
decertify	**VB**	**1-01-001**
DeCicco	**NP**	**1-01-001**
decide	**verb**	**205-15-143**
decide	VB	40-12-037
decides	VBZ	12-08-011
decided	VBD	105-14-080
decided	VBN	36-12-031
deciding	VBG	12-06-009
decidedly	**RB**	**4-03-004**
decimal	**noun**	**4-01-001**
decimal	NN	3-01-001
decimals	NNS	1-01-001
decimeter-wave-length	**NN**	**1-01-001**
decision	**noun**	**173-14-079**
decision	NN	119-14-062
decisions	NNS	52-10-036
decisions	NNS-HL	2-02-002
decision-making	**NN**	**1-01-001**
decisional	**JJ**	**1-01-001**
decisive	**JJ**	**19-06-017**
decisively	**RB**	**5-02-005**
decisiveness	**NN**	**2-02-002**
deck	**noun**	**28-08-012**
deck	NN	21-07-011
Deck	NN-TL	1-01-001
decks	NNS	6-02-002
deck	**verb**	**2-02-002**
deck	VB	1-01-001
decked	VBN	1-01-001
decking	**NN**	**2-01-001**
declaim	**verb**	**2-01-002**
declaimed	VBD	2-01-002
declamatory	**JJ**	**1-01-001**
declaration	**noun**	**26-08-018**
declaration	NN	8-06-006
declaration	NN-HL	1-01-001
Declaration	NN-TL	15-05-010
declarations	NNS	2-02-002
declarative	**adjective**	**8-01-001**
declarative	JJ	7-01-001
declarative	JJ-HL	1-01-001
declarative	**NN**	**1-01-001**
declare	**verb**	**95-12-067**
declare	VB	8-05-008
declares	VBZ	11-07-009
declared	VBD	52-10-040
declared	VBN	14-07-014
declaring	VBG	10-06-010
declination	**noun**	**1-01-001**
declinations	NNS	1-01-001
decline	**noun**	**26-07-020**
decline	NN	24-07-019
declines	NNS	2-02-002
decline	**verb**	**37-10-035**
decline	VB	7-04-006
declines	VBZ	4-04-004
declined	VBD	15-08-014
declined	VBN	2-02-002
declining	VBG	9-06-009
declivity	**NN**	**2-02-002**
decolletage	**NN**	**1-01-001**
decompose	**verb**	**5-02-003**
decompose	VB	1-01-001
decomposes	VBZ	2-01-001
decomposing	VBG	2-02-002
decomposition	**noun**	**14-01-003**
decomposition	NN	12-01-003
decomposition	NN-HL	2-01-001
decompression	**NN**	**1-01-001**
decor	**NN**	**4-03-004**
decorate	**verb**	**12-06-010**
decorate	VB	2-01-002
decorated	VBD	1-01-001
decorated	VBN	5-04-005
decorating	VBG	4-03-003
decoration	**noun**	**16-09-014**
decoration	NN	8-06-007
decorations	NNS	8-05-007
decorative	**JJ**	**8-04-006**
decorativeness	**NN**	**1-01-001**
decorator	**noun**	**9-05-006**
decorator	NN	5-05-005
decorators	NNS	3-02-003
Decorators	NNS-TL	1-01-001
decorous	**JJ**	**1-01-001**
decorticate	**verb**	**1-01-001**
decorticated	VBN	1-01-001
decorum	**NN**	**2-02-002**
decrease	**noun**	**6-02-004**
decrease	NN	5-02-004
decreases	NNS	1-01-001
decrease	**verb**	**31-08-021**
decrease	VB	10-06-010
decreases	VBZ	7-01-005
decreased	VBD	6-02-004
decreased	VBN	2-01-002
decreasing	VBG	6-02-006
decree	**noun**	**7-03-004**
decree	NN	3-03-003
decrees	NNS	4-02-003
decree	**verb**	**3-03-003**
decrees	VBZ	1-01-001
decreed	VBD	1-01-001
decreeing	VBG	1-01-001
decrement	**NN**	**2-01-001**
decry	**verb**	**6-04-005**
decry	VB	2-01-002
decries	VBZ	0-00-000
decries	VBZ-HL	1-01-001
decried	VBD	2-02-002
decrying	VBG	1-01-001
dedicate	**verb**	**25-10-024**
dedicates	VBZ	2-02-002
dedicated	VBD	2-02-002
dedicated	VBN	21-09-021
dedication	**noun**	**21-09-017**
dedication	NN	20-09-017
Dedication	NN-TL	1-01-001
dedifferentiate	**verb**	**1-01-001**
dedifferentiated	VBN	1-01-001
deduce	**verb**	**10-04-009**
deduce	VB	3-02-003
deduced	VBD	2-02-002
deduced	VBN	4-02-004
deducing	VBG	1-01-001
deduct	**verb**	**17-02-003**
deduct	VB	12-01-001

deduct (cont.):		
deducted	VBD	1-01-001
deducted	VBN	3-01-002
deducting	VBG	1-01-001
deductibility	**NN**	**1-01-001**
deductible	**adjective**	**6-03-005**
deductible	JJ	5-03-004
deductable	JJ	1-01-001
deductible	**noun**	**1-01-001**
deductibles	NNS	1-01-001
deduction	**noun**	**23-05-007**
deduction	NN	9-05-007
Deduction	NN-TL	3-01-001
deductions	NNS	10-02-002
deductions	NNS-HL	1-01-001
deductive	**JJ**	**3-03-003**
deed	**noun**	**14-09-013**
deed	NN	7-06-007
deeds	NNS	7-06-007
deed	**verb**	**2-02-002**
deed	VB	1-01-001
deeds	VBZ	1-01-001
Deegan	**prop. noun**	**24-01-001**
Deegan	NP	22-01-001
Deegan's	NP$	2-01-001
deem	**verb**	**17-07-013**
deem	VB	1-01-001
deemed	VBD	3-03-003
deemed	VBN	12-06-009
deeming	VBG	1-01-001
deep	**adjective**	**87-15-065**
deep	JJ	85-15-063
deep	JJ-HL	1-01-001
Deep	JJ-TL	1-01-001
deep	**noun**	**7-02-002**
deep	NN	0-00-000
Deep	NN-TL	6-02-002
deeps	NNS	1-01-001
deep	**RB**	**16-10-015**
deep-eyed	**JJ**	**1-01-001**
deep-sea	**JJ**	**2-01-001**
deep-seated	**JJ**	**2-02-002**
deep-set	**JJ**	**3-03-003**
deep-sounding	**JJ**	**1-01-001**
deep-tendon	**NN**	**1-01-001**
deepen	**verb**	**3-02-003**
deepen	VB	1-01-001
deepened	VBD	1-01-001
deepened	VBN	1-01-001
deepening	**NN**	**1-01-001**
deeper	**JJR**	**29-12-026**
deeper	**RBR**	**8-05-007**
deepest	**JJT**	**12-07-011**
deepest	**RBT**	**1-01-001**
deeply	**QL**	**10-04-009**
deeply	**RB**	**29-13-027**
deer	**noun**	**13-06-008**
deer	NN	3-02-002
Deer	NN-TL	5-02-002
deer	NNS	5-03-004
deerskin	**noun**	**3-01-001**
deerskins	NNS	3-01-001
Deerstalker	**NP**	**6-01-001**
def	**FW-NN**	**1-01-001**
defacing	**NN**	**1-01-001**
default	**NN**	**2-02-002**
default	**verb**	**1-01-001**
defaulted	VBN	1-01-001
defeat	**noun**	**26-08-019**
defeat	NN	21-08-017
Defeat	NN-TL	3-01-001
defeats	NNS	2-02-002
defeat	**verb**	**25-09-022**
defeat	VB	7-03-006
defeated	VBD	5-04-005
defeated	VBN	10-06-009
defeating	VBG	3-03-003
defeatism	**NN**	**1-01-001**
defeatist	**noun**	**1-01-001**
defeatists	NNS	1-01-001
defecate	**verb**	**1-01-001**
defecated	VBN	1-01-001
defect	**noun**	**16-07-013**
defect	NN	3-03-003
defects	NNS	13-07-010
defection	**NN**	**2-02-002**
defective	**JJ**	**7-05-006**
defend	**verb**	**56-11-048**
defend	VB	21-07-021

defend (cont.):		
defends	VBZ	2-02-002
defends	VBZ-HL	2-02-002
defended	VBD	9-05-009
defended	VBN	9-05-008
defending	VBG	13-07-013
defendant	**noun**	**17-03-006**
defendant	NN	6-02-003
defendant's	NN$	1-01-001
defendants	NNS	10-02-004
defender	**noun**	**9-04-009**
defender	NN	3-01-003
defenders	NNS	6-04-006
defense	**noun**	**180-13-071**
defense	NN	125-11-052
defence	NN	1-01-001
defense	NN-HL	1-01-001
Defense	NN-TL	41-06-022
defenses	NNS	12-09-010
defenseless	**JJ**	**3-03-003**
defensible	**JJ**	**3-02-003**
defensive	**JJ**	**17-06-013**
defensiveness	**NN**	**2-01-001**
defer	**verb**	**3-03-003**
defer	VB	1-01-001
deferred	VBN	1-01-001
deferring	VBG	1-01-001
deference	**NN**	**5-05-005**
deferent	**noun**	**3-01-001**
deferent	NN	2-01-001
deferents	NNS	1-01-001
deferment	**noun**	**2-02-002**
deferment	NN	1-01-001
deferments	NNS	1-01-001
defiance	**NN**	**7-04-007**
defiant	**JJ**	**3-02-003**
defiantly	**RB**	**2-02-002**
deficiency	**noun**	**21-06-013**
deficiency	NN	11-05-007
deficiencies	NNS	10-04-007
deficient	**JJ**	**3-03-003**
deficit	**noun**	**13-05-008**
deficit	NN	11-05-008
deficit	NN-HL	1-01-001
deficits	NNS	1-01-001
definable	**JJ**	**1-01-001**
define	**verb**	**81-10-054**
define	VB	19-07-016
define	VB-HL	1-01-001
Define	VB-TL	7-01-001
defines	VBZ	5-04-005
defined	VBD	1-01-001
defined	VBN	38-05-028
defining	VBG	10-06-010
definite	**JJ**	**37-14-036**
definitely	**RB**	**21-09-019**
definition	**noun**	**44-08-030**
definition	NN	35-08-025
definition	NN-HL	2-01-002
Definition	NN-TL	1-01-001
definitions	NNS	5-03-005
definitions	NNS-HL	1-01-001
definition-specialization	**NN**	**2-01-001**
definitive	**JJ**	**5-04-005**
deflate	**verb**	**1-01-001**
deflated	VBN	1-01-001
defocus	**verb**	**2-01-001**
defocusing	VBG	2-01-001
Defoe	**NP**	**3-01-002**
DeForest	**NP**	**1-01-001**
deformation	**NN**	**5-01-002**
deformational	**JJ**	**1-01-001**
deformity	**noun**	**4-03-003**
deformity	NN	3-02-002
deformities	NNS	1-01-001
defraud	**VB**	**2-01-001**
defray	**VB**	**2-02-002**
defrost	**VB**	**1-01-001**
deft	**JJ**	**2-02-002**
deftness	**NN**	**1-01-001**
defunct	**JJ**	**3-02-002**
defy	**verb**	**13-07-012**
defy	VB	7-05-007
defied	VBD	2-02-002
defied	VBN	2-02-002
defying	VBG	2-02-002
degas	**verb**	**1-01-001**
degassed	VBN	1-01-001
Degas	**NP**	**1-01-001**

degenerate	**verb**	**1-01-001**
degenerated	VBD	1-01-001
degeneration	**NN**	**1-01-001**
deglycerolize	**verb**	**1-01-001**
deglycerolized	VBN	1-01-001
degradation	**NN**	**2-02-002**
degrade	**verb**	**3-03-003**
degrade	VB	1-01-001
degraded	VBN	1-01-001
degrading	VBG	1-01-001
degree	**noun**	**148-14-090**
degree	NN	125-14-081
degrees	NNS	23-05-016
DeGroot	**NP**	**1-01-001**
DeHaviland	**NP**	**1-01-001**
dehumanize	**verb**	**2-02-002**
dehumanize	VB	1-01-001
dehumanized	VBN	0-00-000
dehumanised	VBN	1-01-001
dehumidify	**verb**	**1-01-001**
dehumidified	VBN	1-01-001
dehydrate	**verb**	**1-01-001**
dehydrated	VBN	1-01-001
dehydration	**NN**	**1-01-001**
Dei	**foreign**	**2-01-001**
Dei	FW-NN$	0-00-000
Dei	FW-NN$-TL	2-01-001
Dei	**NP**	**5-02-002**
deification	**NN**	**1-01-001**
deign	**verb**	**1-01-001**
deigned	VBD	1-01-001
deity	**noun**	**4-03-004**
deity	NN	1-01-001
diety	NN	1-01-001
deities	NNS	2-02-002
deja	**FW-RB**	**7-01-001**
dejectedly	**RB**	**1-01-001**
dejection	**NN**	**1-01-001**
dejeuner	**foreign**	**2-01-002**
dejeuner	FW-NN	1-01-001
dejeuners	FW-NNS	1-01-001
DeKalb	**prop. noun**	**7-01-002**
DeKalb	NP	2-01-001
DeKalb	NP-HL	1-01-001
DeKalb	NP-TL	3-01-001
DeKalb's	NP$	1-01-001
del	**foreign**	**1-01-001**
del	FW-IN+AT	0-00-000
del	FW-IN+AT-TL	1-01-001
Del	**prop. noun**	**10-05-005**
Del	NP	9-05-005
Del	NP-HL	1-01-001
Delahanty	**NP**	**1-01-001**
Delancy	**NP**	**1-01-001**
Delaney	**NP**	**3-02-002**
Delano	**NP**	**1-01-001**
Delaware	**prop. noun**	**29-07-010**
Delaware	NP	16-04-005
Del.	NP	1-01-001
Delaware	NP-TL	11-05-006
Delawares	NPS	1-01-001
delay	**noun**	**15-07-014**
delay	NN	13-07-013
delays	NNS	2-01-001
delay	**verb**	**34-10-027**
delay	VB	8-07-008
delays	VBZ	1-01-001
delayed	VBD	6-04-006
delayed	VBN	19-07-013
delectation	**NN**	**1-01-001**
delegate	**noun**	**21-04-010**
delegate	NN	4-02-003
delegates	NNS	14-03-007
Delegates	NNS-TL	2-01-001
delegates'	NNS$	0-00-000
Delegates'	NNS$-TL	1-01-001
delegate	**verb**	**10-06-008**
delegate	VB	4-03-003
delegated	VBN	4-03-004
delegating	VBG	2-02-002
delegation	**noun**	**13-05-012**
delegation	NN	11-05-010
delegations	NNS	2-02-002
delenda	**FW-VBG**	**1-01-001**
Delhi	**prop. noun**	**5-04-005**
Delhi	NP	1-01-001
Delhi	NP-TL	4-04-004
Delia	**NP**	**1-01-001**
deliberate	**adjective**	**15-09-015**

deliberate (cont.):		
deliberate	JJ	14-09-014
deliberate	JJ-NC	1-01-001
deliberately	**RB**	**30-10-026**
deliberation	**noun**	**9-05-006**
deliberation	NN	2-01-001
deliberations	NNS	7-05-005
delicacy	**noun**	**7-04-007**
delicacy	NN	5-04-005
delicacies	NNS	2-02-002
delicate	**JJ**	**27-13-027**
delicate-beyond-description	**JJ**	**1-01-001**
delicately	**RB**	**2-01-001**
delicately-textured	**JJ**	**1-01-001**
delicious	**JJ**	**4-03-004**
deliciously	**RB**	**1-01-001**
delicti	**FW-NN**	**1-01-001**
delight	**noun**	**29-07-025**
delight	NN	27-07-024
delights	NNS	2-02-002
delight	**verb**	**20-10-020**
delight	VB	2-02-002
delights	VBZ	1-01-001
delighted	VBD	1-01-001
delighted	VBN	15-10-015
delighting	VBG	1-01-001
delightful	**JJ**	**26-08-017**
delightfully	**QL**	**2-02-002**
delightfully	**RB**	**2-02-002**
delimit	**verb**	**2-02-002**
delimit	VB	1-01-001
delimits	VBZ	1-01-001
delineament	**noun**	**1-01-001**
delineaments	NNS	1-01-001
delineate	**verb**	**3-01-002**
delineated	VBN	1-01-001
delineating	VBG	2-01-001
delineation	**NN**	**3-03-003**
delinquency	**noun**	**7-04-005**
delinquency	NN	5-04-005
Delinquency	NN-TL	2-01-001
delinquent	**JJ**	**3-01-002**
delinquent	**noun**	**6-04-006**
delinquent	NN	3-03-003
delinquents	NNS	3-03-003
delirium	**NN**	**3-02-002**
deliver	**verb**	**71-13-060**
deliver	VB	18-09-015
delivre	VB	1-01-001
delivers	VBZ	6-04-005
delivered	VBD	13-08-013
delivered	VBN	24-10-022
delivering	VBG	9-06-009
deliverance	**NN**	**2-02-002**
delivery	**noun**	**19-10-013**
delivery	NN	16-09-011
delivery	NN-NC	1-01-001
Delivery	NN-TL	2-02-002
dell	**noun**	**4-02-002**
dell	NN	3-01-001
dells	NNS	0-00-000
Dells	NNS-TL	1-01-001
dell'	**foreign**	**1-01-001**
dell'	FW-IN+AT	0-00-000
dell'	FW-IN+AT-TL	1-01-001
dell'	**NP**	**1-01-001**
Dell'Arca	**prop. noun**	**1-01-001**
Dell'Arca	NP	0-00-000
Dell'Arca	NP-TL	1-01-001
della	**foreign**	**2-01-001**
della	FW-IN+AT	0-00-000
Della	FW-IN+AT-TL	2-01-001
Della	**prop. noun**	**4-01-001**
Della	NP	3-01-001
Della	NP-TL	1-01-001
delle	**NP**	**1-01-001**
Deller	**NP**	**2-01-001**
Dellwood	**prop. noun**	**1-01-001**
Dellwood	NP	0-00-000
Dellwood	NP-TL	1-01-001
Delmore	**NP**	**1-01-001**
Delon	**NP**	**2-01-001**
Deloris	**NP**	**1-01-001**
delouse	**verb**	**1-01-001**
deloused	VBN	1-01-001
Delphi	**NP**	**1-01-001**
delphic	**JJ**	**1-01-001**
Delphine	**prop. noun**	**14-01-001**
Delphine	NP	12-01-001

Word	Tag	Frequency
Delphine (cont.):		
Delphine's	NP$	2-01-001
Delray	**prop. noun**	**1-01-001**
Delray	NP	0-00-000
Delray	NP-TL	1-01-001
delta	**noun**	**1-01-001**
deltas	NNS	1-01-001
Delta	**NP**	**7-02-005**
deltoid	**noun**	**3-01-001**
deltoid	NN	1-01-001
deltoids	NNS	2-01-001
delude	**verb**	**6-02-004**
delude	VB	2-01-002
deluded	VBD	1-01-001
deluded	VBN	2-01-001
deluding	VBG	1-01-001
deluge	**NN**	**4-04-004**
deluge	**verb**	**1-01-001**
deluged	VBD	1-01-001
delusion	**NN**	**2-02-002**
deluxe	**adjective**	**2-01-001**
deluxe	JJ	1-01-001
Deluxe	JJ-TL	1-01-001
deluxer	**NN**	**1-01-001**
delve	**verb**	**2-02-002**
delving	VBG	2-02-002
Delvin	**NP**	**1-01-001**
demagnification	**NN**	**1-01-001**
demagogue	**noun**	**1-01-001**
demagogues	NNS	1-01-001
demand	**noun**	**123-11-070**
demand	NN	77-09-042
demand	NN-HL	3-03-003
demands	NNS	43-11-036
demand	**verb**	**92-13-073**
demand	VB	22-11-020
demands	VBZ	12-06-010
demanded	VBD	33-11-028
demanded	VBN	9-07-009
demanding	VBG	16-09-014
demander	**NN**	**1-01-001**
demanding	**JJ**	**2-01-002**
demanding	**NN**	**1-01-001**
demandingly	**RB**	**1-01-001**
demarcate	**verb**	**1-01-001**
demarcated	VBN	1-01-001
demarcation	**NN**	**2-01-002**
demean	**verb**	**1-01-001**
demeans	VBZ	1-01-001
demeanor	**NN**	**2-02-002**
dement	**verb**	**1-01-001**
demented	VBN	1-01-001
Demetrius	**NP**	**1-01-001**
demi-monde	**NN**	**1-01-001**
demineralization	**NN**	**1-01-001**
demise	**NN**	**4-04-004**
democracy	**noun**	**25-05-016**
democracy	NN	22-05-014
Democracy	NN-TL	2-01-002
democracies	NNS	1-01-001
Democrat	**prop. noun**	**54-06-024**
Democrat	NP	13-04-009
Democrats	NPS	39-06-018
Democrats	NPS-TL	1-01-001
Democrats'	NPS$	0-00-000
Democrats'	NPS$-HL	1-01-001
democratic	**adjective**	**109-08-038**
democratic	JJ	42-08-023
Democratic	JJ	2-02-002
Democratic	JJ-TL	65-05-018
Democratic-endorsed	**JJ**	**2-01-001**
Democratic-sponsored	**JJ**	**1-01-001**
democratique	**foreign**	**1-01-001**
democratique	FW-JJ	0-00-000
Democratique	FW-JJ-TL	1-01-001
democratization	**NN**	**2-02-002**
democratize	**VB**	**3-01-003**
Demodocus	**NP**	**1-01-001**
demographic	**JJ**	**12-02-002**
demographie	**foreign**	**1-01-001**
demographie	FW-NN	0-00-000
Demographie	FW-NN-TL	1-01-001
demographique	**foreign**	**1-01-001**
demographique	FW-JJ	0-00-000
demographiques	FW-JJ-NC	1-01-001
demography	**NN**	**3-01-001**
demolish	**verb**	**4-04-004**
demolished	VBN	4-04-004
demolition	**NN**	**1-01-001**
demon	**noun**	**17-06-008**
demon	NN	4-03-003
Demon	NN-TL	5-01-001
demon's	NN$	0-00-000
Demon's	NN$-TL	1-01-001
demons	NNS	7-03-004
demon-ridden	**JJ**	**1-01-001**
demoniac	**JJ**	**2-02-002**
demonstrable	**JJ**	**3-02-003**
demonstrably	**RB**	**2-02-002**
demonstrate	**verb**	**73-08-052**
demonstrate	VB	28-07-024
demonstrates	VBZ	6-03-005
demonstrated	VBD	9-05-009
demonstrated	VBN	24-05-020
demonstrating	VBG	6-05-005
demonstration	**noun**	**29-09-023**
demonstration	NN	25-09-020
demonstrations	NNS	4-02-003
demonstrative	**noun**	**1-01-001**
demonstratives	NNS	1-01-001
demonstrator	**noun**	**1-01-001**
demonstrators	NNS	1-01-001
DeMontez	**NP**	**1-01-001**
demoralization	**NN**	**1-01-001**
demoralize	**verb**	**7-03-005**
demoralize	VB	3-02-003
demoralizes	VBZ	2-01-001
demoralized	VBN	1-01-001
demoralizing	VBG	1-01-001
demote	**verb**	**1-01-001**
demoted	VBD	1-01-001
demur	**verb**	**1-01-001**
demurred	VBD	1-01-001
demure	**JJ**	**3-03-003**
demurrer	**NN**	**2-02-002**
Demus	**NP**	**1-01-001**
demythologization	**NN**	**6-01-001**
demythologize	**verb**	**5-01-001**
demythologize	VB	2-01-001
demythologized	VBN	2-01-001
demythologizing	VBG	1-01-001
den	**noun**	**3-02-003**
den	NN	2-01-002
dens	NNS	1-01-001
denial	**noun**	**22-10-017**
denial	NN	18-09-013
denials	NNS	4-04-004
Denmark	**NP**	**4-03-003**
Dennis	**NP**	**3-03-003**
Denny	**prop. noun**	**3-01-001**
Denny	NP	2-01-001
Denny's	NP$	1-01-001
denominate	**verb**	**1-01-001**
denominated	VBN	1-01-001
denomination	**noun**	**25-05-009**
denomination	NN	8-04-005
denomination's	NN$	2-01-001
denominations	NNS	15-03-005
denominational	**JJ**	**9-04-005**
denominationally	**RB**	**1-01-001**
denominator	**noun**	**1-01-001**
denominators	NNS	1-01-001
denote	**verb**	**25-04-012**
denote	VB	4-02-004
denotes	VBZ	7-01-003
denoted	VBD	2-02-002
denoted	VBN	7-01-003
denoting	VBG	5-02-003
denouement	**NN**	**2-02-002**
denounce	**verb**	**17-08-017**
denounce	VB	5-04-005
denounces	VBZ	1-01-001
denounced	VBD	2-02-002
denounced	VBN	5-04-005
denouncing	VBG	4-03-004
dense	**JJ**	**9-07-009**
densest	**JJT**	**1-01-001**
densitometry	**NN**	**1-01-001**
density	**noun**	**33-08-016**
density	NN	31-08-016
densities	NNS	2-01-002
Densmore	**NP**	**1-01-001**
dent	**NN**	**1-01-001**
dent	**verb**	**3-02-003**
dented	VBD	1-01-001
denting	VBG	2-02-002
Dent	**NP**	**1-01-001**
dental	**JJ**	**12-04-004**

Word	Tag	Frequency
dentist	**noun**	**19-06-008**
dentist	NN	12-04-006
dentist's	NN$	3-01-001
dentists	NNS	4-02-002
dentistry	**NN**	**1-01-001**
Denton	**prop. noun**	**4-01-002**
Denton	NP	2-01-001
Denton	NP-HL	1-01-001
Denton	NP-TL	1-01-001
denture	**noun**	**1-01-001**
dentures	NNS	1-01-001
denude	**verb**	**1-01-001**
denuded	VBN	1-01-001
denunciation	**noun**	**6-06-006**
denunciation	NN	4-04-004
denunciations	NNS	2-02-002
Denver	**prop. noun**	**17-05-010**
Denver	NP	14-04-009
Denver	NP-TL	2-02-002
Denver's	NP$	1-01-001
Denver-area	**JJ**	**1-01-001**
Denverite	**NP**	**1-01-001**
deny	**verb**	**109-14-072**
deny	VB	46-11-039
deny	VB-HL	1-01-001
denies	VBZ	6-04-006
denied	VBD	10-08-010
denied	VBN	37-07-022
denying	VBG	9-08-009
denying	**noun**	**2-02-002**
denying	NN	1-01-001
denyin'	NN	1-01-001
deodorant	**NN**	**2-01-001**
Deor	**prop. noun**	**1-01-001**
Deor	NP	0-00-000
Deor	NP-TL	1-01-001
depart	**verb**	**28-12-025**
depart	VB	7-05-007
departs	VBZ	1-01-001
departs	VBZ-HL	1-01-001
departed	VBD	5-05-005
departed	VBN	4-02-004
departing	VBG	10-07-010
department	**noun**	**272-13-089**
department	NN	63-12-037
dept.	NN	1-01-001
dept.	NN-HL	1-01-001
Dept.	NN-TL	3-03-003
Department	NN-TL	162-10-060
department's	NN$	2-02-002
Department's	NN$-TL	15-04-007
departments	NNS	25-06-014
departmental	**JJ**	**1-01-001**
departure	**noun**	**24-11-022**
departure	NN	17-08-015
departures	NNS	7-06-007
DePaul	**prop. noun**	**2-02-002**
DePaul	NP	0-00-000
DePaul	NP-TL	2-02-002
depend	**verb**	**106-11-081**
depend	VB	45-09-036
depends	VBZ	49-11-043
depended	VBD	9-05-009
depending	VBG	3-03-003
dependable	**JJ**	**8-05-007**
dependence	**noun**	**12-04-010**
dependence	NN	11-04-010
dependence	NN-HL	1-01-001
dependency	**NN**	**3-02-002**
dependent	**JJ**	**39-08-032**
dependent	**noun**	**3-01-003**
dependent	NN	1-01-001
dependents	NNS	2-01-002
depending	**IN**	**29-07-027**
depersonalization	**NN**	**2-02-002**
depersonalize	**verb**	**1-01-001**
depersonalized	VBN	1-01-001
Depew	**NP**	**4-01-001**
depict	**verb**	**17-07-012**
depict	VB	3-02-003
depicted	VBD	2-02-002
depicted	VBN	6-02-003
depicting	VBG	6-04-005
depiction	**NN**	**1-01-001**
depletion	**NN**	**6-03-003**
deplorable	**JJ**	**2-02-002**
deplorably	**QL**	**1-01-001**
deplore	**verb**	**6-04-005**
deplore	VB	1-01-001

Word	Tag	Frequency
deplore (cont.):		
deplores	VBZ	3-02-002
deplored	VBD	2-02-002
deploy	**verb**	**4-03-003**
deployed	VBD	1-01-001
deployed	VBN	2-01-001
deploying	VBG	1-01-001
deployment	**NN**	**1-01-001**
deport	**VB**	**1-01-001**
deportee	**noun**	**2-01-001**
deportees	NNS	2-01-001
depose	**verb**	**3-02-002**
depose	VB	1-01-001
deposed	VBD	1-01-001
deposed	VBN	1-01-001
deposit	**noun**	**14-08-010**
deposit	NN	7-05-005
deposit	NN-HL	1-01-001
deposits	NNS	6-04-005
deposit	**verb**	**11-05-007**
deposit	VB	1-01-001
deposited	VBN	10-05-007
deposition	**noun**	**6-03-003**
deposition	NN	3-03-003
depositions	NNS	3-01-001
depositor	**noun**	**1-01-001**
depositors	NNS	1-01-001
depot	**noun**	**14-04-006**
depot	NN	3-02-003
Depot	NN-TL	10-02-002
depots	NNS	1-01-001
Deppy	**NP**	**2-01-001**
deprave	**verb**	**2-02-002**
depraved	VBN	2-02-002
depravity	**noun**	**4-02-004**
depravity	NN	3-02-003
depravities	NNS	1-01-001
deprecatory	**JJ**	**1-01-001**
depreciation	**NN**	**13-05-009**
depredation	**noun**	**3-03-003**
depredations	NNS	3-03-003
depress	**verb**	**13-07-011**
depress	VB	1-01-001
depresses	VBZ	1-01-001
depressed	VBD	1-01-001
depressed	VBN	10-05-009
depressant	**noun**	**1-01-001**
depressants	NNS	1-01-001
depressing	**JJ**	**5-05-005**
depressingly	**RB**	**2-02-002**
depression	**noun**	**27-08-020**
depression	NN	23-08-019
Depression	NN-TL	1-01-001
depressions	NNS	3-02-002
depressor	**noun**	**1-01-001**
depressors	NNS	1-01-001
deprivation	**noun**	**2-01-002**
deprivation	NN	1-01-001
deprivations	NNS	1-01-001
deprive	**verb**	**14-08-012**
deprive	VB	3-03-003
deprived	VBD	1-01-001
deprived	VBN	7-03-006
depriving	VBG	3-03-003
depth	**noun**	**72-12-043**
depth	NN	53-07-032
depths	NNS	19-10-016
DePugh	**NP**	**3-01-001**
deputize	**verb**	**1-01-001**
deputized	VBN	1-01-001
deputy	**adjective**	**5-03-005**
deputy	JJ	1-01-001
Deputy	JJ-TL	4-03-004
deputy	**noun**	**27-05-013**
deputy	NN	10-04-007
Deputy	NN-TL	2-02-002
deputy's	NN$	2-01-001
deputies	NNS	12-05-008
deputies	NNS-HL	1-01-001
Dequindre	**prop. noun**	**2-01-001**
Dequindre	NP	1-01-001
Dequindre	NP-TL	1-01-001
der	**foreign**	**1-01-001**
der	FW-AT	0-00-000
der	FW-AT-TL	1-01-001
der	**NP**	**1-01-001**
derail	**noun**	**1-01-001**
derails	NNS	1-01-001
derange	**verb**	**2-02-002**

derange (cont.):		
deranged	VBN	2-02-002
derangement	**NN**	**1-01-001**
deras	**foreign**	**1-01-001**
deras	FW-PP$	0-00-000
deras	FW-PP$-TL	1-01-001
derby	**noun**	**7-04-005**
derby	NN	4-01-002
Derby	NN-TL	3-03-003
derelict	**noun**	**2-02-002**
derelict	NN	1-01-001
derelicts	NNS	1-01-001
dereliction	**NN**	**2-01-002**
derision	**NN**	**4-03-004**
derisively	**RB**	**1-01-001**
derivation	**noun**	**5-03-005**
derivation	NN	4-03-004
derivations	NNS	1-01-001
derivative	**NN**	**1-01-001**
derive	**verb**	**65-10-044**
derive	VB	13-05-012
derives	VBZ	9-06-009
derived	VBD	1-01-001
derived	VBN	38-09-025
deriving	VBG	4-02-004
derogate	**VB**	**1-01-001**
derogatory	**JJ**	**1-01-001**
derrick	**NN**	**3-01-002**
derriere	**NN**	**1-01-001**
dervish	**noun**	**4-03-004**
dervish	NN	0-00-000
Dervish	NN-TL	1-01-001
dervishes	NNS	3-03-003
des	**foreign**	**8-05-007**
des	FW-IN+AT	1-01-001
Des	FW-IN+AT-TL	6-05-005
des	FW-IN+AT-TL	1-01-001
Descartes	**NP**	**2-01-001**
descend	**verb**	**24-11-023**
descend	VB	4-03-004
descends	VBZ	2-02-002
descended	VBD	4-03-004
descended	VBN	4-04-004
descending	VBG	10-07-009
descendant	**noun**	**7-04-007**
descendant	NN	2-01-002
descendants	NNS	4-04-004
descendents	NNS	1-01-001
descent	**noun**	**11-07-011**
descent	NN	10-06-010
Descent	NN-TL	1-01-001
describe	**verb**	**200-14-124**
describe	VB	41-10-036
describes	VBZ	22-09-017
described	VBD	28-08-022
described	VBN	92-08-064
describing	VBG	17-08-015
description	**noun**	**64-12-040**
description	NN	52-10-035
description	NN-HL	1-01-001
Description	NN-TL	1-01-001
descriptions	NNS	10-03-007
descriptive	**adjective**	**7-01-005**
descriptive	JJ	6-01-004
Descriptive	JJ-TL	1-01-001
desecrate	**verb**	**1-01-001**
desecrated	VBN	1-01-001
desecration	**NN**	**1-01-001**
desegregate	**verb**	**7-02-002**
desegregate	VB	0-00-000
desegregate	VB-HL	1-01-001
desegregated	VBN	6-02-002
desegregation	**noun**	**40-04-005**
desegregation	NN	37-04-005
desegregation	NN-HL	2-01-001
Desegregation	NN-TL	1-01-001
desegregation-from-court-order	**NN**	**1-01-001**
desensitize	**verb**	**1-01-001**
desensitized	VBN	1-01-001
desert	**noun**	**21-12-015**
desert	NN	13-09-011
desert	NN-HL	1-01-001
Desert	NN-TL	4-02-002
deserts	NNS	3-03-003
desert	**verb**	**20-08-018**
desert	VB	3-02-003
deserts	VBZ	2-02-002
deserted	VBD	1-01-001
deserted	VBN	14-06-012
desertion	**NN**	**2-02-002**
deserve	**verb**	**40-13-032**
deserve	VB	12-06-010
deserves	VBZ	16-07-016
deserved	VBD	10-09-010
deserved	VBN	2-02-002
deserving	**JJ**	**2-02-002**
design	**noun**	**136-12-053**
design	NN	105-10-042
design	NN-HL	2-01-002
Design	NN-TL	3-03-003
designs	NNS	25-07-017
designs	NNS-HL	1-01-001
design	**verb**	**122-12-082**
design	VB	4-03-003
designs	VBZ	2-02-002
designed	VBD	9-06-008
designed	VBN	98-12-071
designed	VBN-HL	1-01-001
designing	VBG	8-06-008
design-conscious	**JJ**	**1-01-001**
design-side	**NN**	**1-01-001**
designate	**NN**	**2-01-001**
designate	**verb**	**24-08-023**
designate	VB	3-03-003
designates	VBZ	1-01-001
designated	VBD	4-03-004
designated	VBN	13-07-013
designating	VBG	3-02-003
designation	**noun**	**5-04-005**
designation	NN	4-03-004
designations	NNS	1-01-001
designer	**noun**	**33-06-014**
designer	NN	18-04-008
designer's	NN$	1-01-001
designers	NNS	10-04-008
Designers	NNS-TL	4-02-002
designing	**NN**	**1-01-001**
desirability	**NN**	**2-02-002**
desirable	**JJ**	**36-09-029**
desire	**noun**	**88-14-074**
desire	NN	68-14-062
desires	NNS	20-10-018
desire	**verb**	**71-12-056**
desire	VB	11-06-011
dessier	VB	1-01-001
desires	VBZ	4-02-004
desired	VBD	9-06-009
desired	VBN	41-08-031
desiring	VBG	5-05-005
desirous	**JJ**	**1-01-001**
desk	**noun**	**69-11-047**
desk	NN	65-10-044
desks	NNS	4-02-003
Deslonde	**NP**	**2-01-001**
Desmond	**NP**	**1-01-001**
desolate	**JJ**	**6-05-006**
desolation	**noun**	**6-05-006**
desolation	NN	4-03-004
Desolation	NN-TL	1-01-001
desolations	NNS	1-01-001
DeSoto	**prop. noun**	**1-01-001**
DeSoto	NP	0-00-000
DeSoto	NP-TL	1-01-001
despair	**NN**	**20-09-018**
despair	**verb**	**4-02-004**
despair	VB	1-01-001
despairing	VBG	3-02-003
despairing	**NN**	**1-01-001**
despairingly	**RB**	**4-02-004**
desperado	**noun**	**1-01-001**
desperadoes	NNS	1-01-001
desperate	**JJ**	**26-08-021**
desperately	**QL**	**1-01-001**
desperately	**RB**	**20-09-020**
desperation	**NN**	**7-05-007**
Despina	**NP**	**1-01-001**
despise	**verb**	**12-05-011**
despise	VB	7-05-007
despises	VBZ	1-01-001
despised	VBD	2-01-002
despised	VBN	1-01-001
despising	VBG	1-01-001
despite	**IN**	**104-13-077**
despoil	**verb**	**2-02-002**
despoiled	VBN	1-01-001
despoiling	VBG	1-01-001
despoiler	**noun**	**1-01-001**
despoilers	NNS	1-01-001

despondency	**NN**	**2-02-002**
despondent	**JJ**	**2-02-002**
despot	**noun**	**3-03-003**
despot	NN	2-02-002
despots	NNS	1-01-001
despotism	**NN**	**5-04-004**
Desprez	**NP**	**1-01-001**
despues	**FW-RB**	**1-01-001**
dessert	**noun**	**9-05-007**
dessert	NN	7-04-005
desserts	NNS	2-02-002
destination	**NN**	**9-07-007**
destine	**verb**	**9-07-009**
destined	VBN	9-07-009
destiny	**noun**	**25-07-020**
destiny	NN	22-07-018
destinies	NNS	3-01-003
destitute	**JJ**	**2-02-002**
destroy	**verb**	**104-12-065**
destroy	VB	48-10-030
destroyed	VBD	8-05-008
destroyed	VBN	31-10-025
destroying	VBG	17-07-015
destroyer	**noun**	**5-03-005**
destroyer	NN	2-02-002
destroyers	NNS	3-02-003
destruction	**NN**	**38-11-026**
destructive	**JJ**	**25-07-017**
desuetude	**NN**	**1-01-001**
desultory	**JJ**	**1-01-001**
desynchronize	**verb**	**1-01-001**
desynchronizing	VBG	1-01-001
detach	**verb**	**13-07-012**
detach	VB	1-01-001
detached	VBD	1-01-001
detached	VBN	11-06-010
detachable	**JJ**	**2-02-002**
detachment	**NN**	**4-04-004**
detail	**noun**	**128-15-084**
detail	NN	70-13-050
Detail	NN-TL	1-01-001
details	NNS	57-12-049
detail	**verb**	**53-11-046**
detail	VB	1-01-001
detailed	VBN	52-11-045
detain	**verb**	**2-02-002**
detain	VB	1-01-001
detained	VBD	1-01-001
detect	**verb**	**28-09-021**
detect	VB	10-05-010
detected	VBN	12-02-008
detecting	VBG	6-05-006
detectable	**JJ**	**8-03-005**
detection	**NN**	**13-04-008**
detective	**noun**	**72-08-016**
detective	NN	47-07-010
Detective	NN-TL	5-03-003
detective's	NN$	3-02-002
detectives	NNS	16-06-009
Detectives	NNS-TL	1-01-001
detector	**noun**	**5-03-003**
detector	NN	2-01-001
detector	NN-HL	1-01-001
detectors	NNS	2-02-002
detente	**noun**	**2-01-001**
detente	NN	1-01-001
detente	NN-HL	1-01-001
detention	**noun**	**2-02-002**
detention	NN	1-01-001
Detention	NN-TL	1-01-001
deter	**VB**	**1-01-001**
detergency	**NN**	**3-01-001**
detergent	**noun**	**29-04-005**
detergent	NN	24-03-004
detergent	NN-HL	1-01-001
detergents	NNS	4-02-002
deteriorate	**verb**	**8-04-008**
deteriorate	VB	1-01-001
deteriorates	VBZ	1-01-001
deteriorated	VBD	1-01-001
deteriorated	VBN	3-03-003
deteriorating	VBG	2-02-002
deterioration	**NN**	**3-02-003**
determinability	**NN**	**1-01-001**
determinable	**JJ**	**1-01-001**
determinant	**noun**	**3-02-003**
determinant	NN	1-01-001
determinants	NNS	2-01-002
determinate	**JJ**	**1-01-001**

determination	**noun**	**41-10-035**
determination	NN	38-10-032
determination	NN-HL	1-01-001
determinations	NNS	2-01-002
determinative	**JJ**	**1-01-001**
determine	**verb**	**274-15-141**
determine	VB	107-12-067
determines	VBZ	14-05-014
determined	VBD	7-05-006
determined	VBN	112-14-077
determining	VBG	33-08-027
determing	VBG	1-01-001
determinedly	**QL**	**1-01-001**
determinedly	**RB**	**1-01-001**
determinism	**NN**	**1-01-001**
deterministic	**JJ**	**7-02-002**
deterrence	**NN**	**1-01-001**
deterrent	**noun**	**8-05-007**
deterrent	NN	7-05-007
deterrent	NN-HL	1-01-001
detest	**verb**	**4-03-003**
detest	VB	1-01-001
detested	VBD	2-02-002
detested	VBN	1-01-001
detestable	**JJ**	**2-01-002**
detestation	**NN**	**1-01-001**
detonate	**verb**	**4-03-003**
detonated	VBD	1-01-001
detonated	VBN	2-01-001
detonating	VBG	1-01-001
detonation	**NN**	**3-02-002**
detour	**noun**	**1-01-001**
detours	NNS	1-01-001
detour	**verb**	**2-02-002**
detoured	VBD	1-01-001
detoured	VBN	1-01-001
detract	**VB**	**1-01-001**
detractor	**noun**	**2-02-002**
detractor	NN	1-01-001
detractors	NNS	1-01-001
detribalize	**VB**	**1-01-001**
detriment	**NN**	**2-02-002**
detrimental	**JJ**	**4-03-003**
Detroit	**prop. noun**	**22-07-016**
Detroit	NP	17-07-014
Detroit	NP-TL	4-02-002
Detroit's	NP$	1-01-001
deus	**FW-NP**	**1-01-001**
deuterate	**verb**	**1-01-001**
deuterated	VBN	1-01-001
Deutsch	**NP**	**1-01-001**
Deutsche	**foreign**	**1-01-001**
Deutsche	FW-JJ	0-00-000
Deutsche	FW-JJ-TL	1-01-001
deux	**FW-CD**	**4-01-002**
devastate	**verb**	**9-07-009**
devastate	VB	1-01-001
devastated	VBD	1-01-001
devastated	VBN	2-02-002
devastating	VBG	5-04-005
devastatingly	**RB**	**1-01-001**
devastation	**NN**	**2-02-002**
develop	**verb**	**322-15-165**
develop	VB	89-13-065
develops	VBZ	11-07-011
developed	VBD	43-10-036
developed	VBN	127-13-081
developing	VBG	51-09-036
Developing	VBG-TL	1-01-001
developer	**noun**	**7-02-003**
developer	NN	5-02-002
developers	NNS	2-01-002
development	**noun**	**377-12-129**
development	NN	306-12-119
development	NN-HL	4-02-004
Development	NN-TL	23-05-015
developments	NNS	43-10-032
developments	NNS-HL	1-01-001
developmental	**JJ**	**9-03-004**
Devens	**prop. noun**	**1-01-001**
Devens	NP	0-00-000
Devens	NP-TL	1-01-001
Dever	**NP**	**1-01-001**
Devery	**NP**	**2-01-001**
Devey	**prop. noun**	**6-01-001**
Devey	NP	5-01-001
Devey's	NP$	1-01-001
deviance	**NN**	**2-01-001**
deviant	**JJ**	**3-01-003**

Word	Tag	Frequency
deviant	**noun**	**2-02-002**
deviants	NNS	2-02-002
deviate	**verb**	**3-03-003**
deviate	VB	1-01-001
deviated	VBN	1-01-001
deviating	VBG	1-01-001
deviation	**noun**	**18-05-010**
deviation	NN	14-04-008
deviations	NNS	4-02-004
device	**noun**	**92-14-050**
device	NN	53-13-030
device	NN-HL	2-01-002
devices	NNS	37-09-027
devil	**noun**	**32-09-021**
devil	NN	18-07-012
devil	NN-HL	2-02-002
Devil	NN-TL	5-04-005
devil's	NN$	3-02-003
Devil's	NN$-TL	2-02-002
devils	NNS	2-01-001
devil's-food	**NN**	**1-01-001**
devilish	**JJ**	**3-03-003**
devious	**JJ**	**1-01-001**
devise	**verb**	**25-08-023**
devise	VB	8-05-008
devised	VBD	2-02-002
devised	VBN	14-08-014
devising	VBG	1-01-001
devisee	**NN**	**1-01-001**
devoid	**JJ**	**6-05-006**
Devol	**NP**	**3-01-001**
Devonshire	**NP**	**1-01-001**
devote	**verb**	**76-13-055**
devote	VB	15-09-012
devoted	VBD	14-07-012
devoted	VBN	37-12-030
devoting	VBG	10-06-006
devotedly	**RB**	**1-01-001**
devotee	**noun**	**3-03-003**
devotees	NNS	3-03-003
devotion	**noun**	**21-10-016**
devotion	NN	19-10-016
devotions	NNS	2-02-002
devotional	**JJ**	**1-01-001**
devour	**verb**	**3-02-002**
devour	VB	2-02-002
devoured	VBN	1-01-001
devout	**JJ**	**4-03-003**
devoutly	**RB**	**1-01-001**
dew	**NN**	**3-02-002**
dewar	**noun**	**1-01-001**
dewars	NNS	1-01-001
dewdrop	**noun**	**1-01-001**
dewdrops	NNS	1-01-001
Dewey	**NP**	**3-03-003**
DeWitt	**NP**	**1-01-001**
dewy-eyed	**JJ**	**1-01-001**
dexamethasone	**NN**	**2-01-001**
Dexedrine	**NP**	**1-01-001**
Dexter	**prop. noun**	**4-03-003**
Dexter	NP	2-02-002
Dexter	NP-TL	1-01-001
Dexter's	NP$	1-01-001
dexterity	**NN**	**1-01-001**
dextrous	**JJ**	**2-02-002**
dextrous-fingered	**JJ**	**1-01-001**
Dey	**NP**	**1-01-001**
Dharma	**prop. noun**	**1-01-001**
Dharma	NP	0-00-000
Dharma	NP-TL	1-01-001
di	**foreign**	**1-01-001**
di	FW-IN	0-00-000
di	FW-IN-TL	1-01-001
Di	**prop. noun**	**21-04-006**
Di	NP	18-04-006
Di	NP-TL	3-01-001
di-iodotyrosine	**NN**	**5-01-001**
diabetes	**NN**	**4-03-003**
diabetic	**JJ**	**2-01-001**
diabolical	**JJ**	**1-01-001**
diachronic	**JJ**	**1-01-001**
Diaghileff	**NP**	**1-01-001**
diagnometer	**NN**	**1-01-001**
diagnosable	**JJ**	**1-01-001**
diagnose	**verb**	**6-04-005**
diagnose	VB	3-03-003
diagnosed	VBD	1-01-001
diagnosed	VBN	1-01-001
diagnosing	VBG	1-01-001
diagnosing	**NN**	**1-01-001**
diagnosis	**noun**	**14-06-011**
diagnosis	NN	12-05-010
Diagnosis	NN-TL	1-01-001
diagnoses	NNS	0-00-000
Diagnoses	NNS-TL	1-01-001
diagnostic	**JJ**	**8-03-006**
diagnostic	**NN**	**2-02-002**
diagnostician	**noun**	**2-01-002**
diagnosticians	NNS	2-01-002
diagonal	**JJ**	**4-01-001**
diagonal	**noun**	**1-01-001**
diagonals	NNS	1-01-001
diagonalizable	**JJ**	**14-01-001**
diagonally	**RB**	**4-03-003**
diagram	**noun**	**18-07-010**
diagram	NN	10-05-007
diagrams	NNS	8-06-006
diagram	**verb**	**1-01-001**
diagrammed	VBN	1-01-001
dial	**noun**	**2-02-002**
dial	NN	1-01-001
dials	NNS	1-01-001
dial	**verb**	**4-03-004**
dialed	VBD	2-01-002
dialed	VBN	1-01-001
dialing	VBG	1-01-001
dialect	**noun**	**14-07-010**
dialect	NN	10-05-007
dialects	NNS	4-03-004
dialectic	**noun**	**8-02-006**
dialectic	NN	6-01-005
dialectics	NNS	2-01-001
dialectical	**JJ**	**1-01-001**
dialectically	**RB**	**1-01-001**
dialogue	**noun**	**14-05-011**
dialogue	NN	12-05-009
dialogues	NNS	1-01-001
Dialogues	NNS-TL	1-01-001
dialysis	**NN**	**12-01-001**
dialyze	**verb**	**4-01-002**
dialyzed	VBN	4-01-002
diameter	**noun**	**53-05-018**
diameter	NN	43-05-018
dia.	NN	4-01-001
diameter	NN-HL	2-01-001
diameters	NNS	4-02-003
diametric	**JJ**	**1-01-001**
diametrically	**QL**	**1-01-001**
diametrically	**RB**	**1-01-001**
diamond	**noun**	**15-05-008**
diamond	NN	8-04-006
diamonds	NNS	7-04-005
diamond-studded	**JJ**	**1-01-001**
Dian	**prop. noun**	**1-01-001**
Dian's	NP$	1-01-001
Diana	**NP**	**7-02-002**
Diane	**prop. noun**	**18-02-002**
Diane	NP	14-02-002
Diane's	NP$	4-02-002
diaper	**noun**	**3-03-003**
diapers	NNS	3-03-003
diaphanous	**JJ**	**1-01-001**
diaphragm	**noun**	**8-03-003**
diaphragm	NN	7-02-002
diaphragms	NNS	1-01-001
diaphragmic	**JJ**	**2-01-001**
diapiace	**FW-VBZ**	**1-01-001**
Diario	**NP**	**2-01-001**
diarrhea	**noun**	**12-02-002**
diarrhea	NN	7-01-001
diarrhoea	NN	3-01-001
diorah	NN	1-01-001
Dyerear	NN	1-01-001
diary	**noun**	**6-06-006**
diary	NN	3-03-003
Diary	NN-TL	1-01-001
diaries	NNS	2-02-002
diathermy	**NN**	**1-01-001**
diathesis	**NN**	**1-01-001**
diatom	**noun**	**1-01-001**
diatoms	NNS	1-01-001
diatomic	**JJ**	**2-01-001**
dice	**VB**	**1-01-001**
dicendi	**FW-VBG**	**1-01-001**
dichondra	**NN**	**1-01-001**
dichotomy	**NN**	**1-01-001**
dick	**noun**	**1-01-001**
dicks	NNS	1-01-001

Word	Tag	Frequency
Dick	**prop. noun**	**20-06-012**
Dick	NP	18-06-011
Dick's	NP$	2-02-002
Dicke	**NP**	**1-01-001**
Dickens	**prop. noun**	**18-06-008**
Dickens	NP	15-06-007
Dickens	NP-TL	1-01-001
Dickens'	NP$	2-01-001
Dickey	**prop. noun**	**4-01-001**
Dickey	NP	3-01-001
Dickey's	NP$	1-01-001
Dickinson	**NP**	**1-01-001**
Dicks	**prop. noun**	**1-01-001**
Dicks	NP	0-00-000
Dicks	NP-TL	1-01-001
Dickson	**NP**	**3-01-001**
dictate	**noun**	**5-04-005**
dictates	NNS	5-04-005
dictate	**verb**	**14-05-013**
dictate	VB	3-02-003
dictates	VBZ	4-03-004
dictated	VBD	1-01-001
dictated	VBN	4-02-003
dictating	VBG	2-02-002
dictator	**noun**	**11-06-008**
dictator	NN	4-03-003
Dictator	NN-TL	3-02-003
dictators	NNS	3-03-003
dictators	NNS-HL	1-01-001
dictatorial	**JJ**	**1-01-001**
dictatorship	**NN**	**13-05-010**
diction	**NN**	**6-02-004**
dictionary	**noun**	**59-05-008**
dictionary	NN	55-03-005
Dictionary	NN-TL	2-02-002
dictionary's	NN$	1-01-001
dictionaries	NNS	1-01-001
dictum	**NN**	**4-04-004**
diddle	**UH**	**1-01-001**
diddle	**verb**	**1-01-001**
diddling	VBG	1-01-001
Didi	**NP**	**1-01-001**
die	**foreign**	**7-04-006**
die	FW-AT	4-02-004
Die	FW-AT-TL	3-03-003
die	**FW-NN**	**1-01-001**
die	**noun**	**23-08-011**
die	NN	8-03-003
dice	NNS	12-06-007
dies	NNS	2-02-002
dice	NNS-HL	1-01-001
die	**verb**	**183-15-108**
die	VB	57-13-039
dies	VBZ	9-05-008
died	VBD	63-14-046
died	VBN	23-11-021
dying	VBG	30-10-022
Dying	VBG-TL	1-01-001
die-dead	**verb**	**1-01-001**
die-dead	VB + JJ	0-00-000
die-dead	VB + JJ-NC	1-01-001
die-up	**NN**	**1-01-001**
Diego	**NP**	**5-02-003**
diehard	**JJ**	**1-01-001**
diehard	**noun**	**1-01-001**
diehards	NNS	1-01-001
diem	**noun**	**2-02-002**
diem	NN	1-01-001
Diem	NN-TL	1-01-001
Dienbienphu	**NP**	**1-01-001**
Dies	**NP**	**1-01-001**
diesel	**NN**	**1-01-001**
diet	**noun**	**24-09-014**
diet	NN	20-08-012
Diet	NN-TL	1-01-001
diets	NNS	3-03-003
dietary	**adjective**	**6-02-004**
dietary	JJ	5-02-004
dietary	JJ-HL	1-01-001
dieter	**noun**	**1-01-001**
dieters	NNS	1-01-001
dietetic	**adjective**	**1-01-001**
dietetic	JJ	0-00-000
Dietetic	JJ-TL	1-01-001
diethylaminoethyl	**NN**	**2-01-002**
diethylstilbestrol	**NN**	**4-01-001**
Dietrich	**prop. noun**	**5-03-003**
Dietrich	NP	4-03-003
Dietrich	NP-TL	1-01-001

Word	Tag	Frequency
diety	**noun**	**1-01-001**
Deity	NN	0-00-000
Diety	NN-TL	1-01-001
Dieu	**foreign**	**2-02-002**
Dieu	FW-NP	1-01-001
Dieux	FW-NPS	0-00-000
Dieux	FW-NPS-TL	1-01-001
differ	**verb**	**42-09-034**
differ	VB	18-07-016
differs	VBZ	10-04-009
differed	VBD	12-07-010
differed	VBN	1-01-001
differing	VBG	1-01-001
difference	**noun**	**228-14-117**
difference	NN	147-14-093
diffrunce	NN	1-01-001
difference	NN-HL	1-01-001
differences	NNS	78-06-046
differences	NNS-HL	1-01-001
different	**JJ**	**312-15-181**
different-color	**JJ**	**1-01-001**
differentiability	**NN**	**2-01-001**
differentiable	**JJ**	**3-01-001**
differential	**JJ**	**13-01-006**
differential	**NN**	**3-03-003**
differentiate	**verb**	**8-03-006**
differentiate	VB	2-02-002
differentiated	VBD	1-01-001
differentiated	VBN	4-02-003
differentiating	VBG	1-01-001
differentiation	**NN**	**8-03-008**
differently	**RB**	**16-10-014**
difficile	**FW-JJ**	**1-01-001**
difficult	**JJ**	**161-15-127**
difficulty	**noun**	**123-14-087**
difficulty	NN	77-14-060
difficulties	NNS	46-10-039
diffidence	**NN**	**2-02-002**
diffraction	**NN**	**7-02-004**
Diffring	**NP**	**1-01-001**
diffuse	**JJ**	**3-03-003**
diffuse	**verb**	**7-03-006**
diffuse	VB	1-01-001
diffuses	VBZ	1-01-001
diffused	VBN	2-02-002
diffusing	VBG	3-02-002
diffusely	**RB**	**1-01-001**
diffuser	**noun**	**1-01-001**
diffusers	NNS	1-01-001
diffusion	**NN**	**24-03-005**
dig	**NN**	**1-01-001**
dig	**verb**	**32-12-025**
dig	VB	9-07-008
digs	VBZ	1-01-001
dug	VBD	7-06-007
dug	VBN	8-06-008
digging	VBG	7-06-007
Digby	**prop. noun**	**8-01-001**
Digby	NP	7-01-001
Digby's	NP$	1-01-001
digest	**noun**	**3-03-003**
digest	NN	1-01-001
Digest	NN-TL	2-02-002
digest	**verb**	**3-03-003**
digested	VBN	1-01-001
digesting	VBG	2-02-002
digestible	**JJ**	**1-01-001**
digestive	**JJ**	**3-03-003**
digger	**NN**	**2-01-001**
Digges	**NP**	**1-01-001**
DiGiorgio	**NP**	**1-01-001**
digit	**NN**	**1-01-001**
digital	**JJ**	**6-02-004**
digitalis	**NN**	**1-01-001**
digitalization	**NN**	**1-01-001**
dignify	**verb**	**8-06-007**
dignify	VB	1-01-001
dignified	VBN	7-05-006
dignitary	**noun**	**3-03-003**
dignitaries	NNS	3-03-003
dignity	**NN**	**35-12-026**
digress	**VB**	**1-01-001**
digression	**noun**	**1-01-001**
digressions	NNS	1-01-001
diisocyanate	**NN**	**1-01-001**
Dijon	**NP**	**1-01-001**
dilapidate	**verb**	**3-03-003**
dilapidated	VBN	3-03-003
dilatation	**NN**	**3-02-002**

Word	Tag	Frequency
dilate	**verb**	**6-02-002**
dilate	VB	2-01-001
dilates	VBZ	1-01-001
dilated	VBN	2-02-002
dilating	VBG	1-01-001
dilation	**NN**	**2-02-002**
dilemma	**noun**	**27-09-018**
dilemma	NN	25-09-018
dilemmas	NNS	2-02-002
dilettante	**NN**	**1-01-001**
diligence	**NN**	**3-03-003**
diligent	**JJ**	**2-02-002**
diligently	**RB**	**1-01-001**
dill	**NN**	**1-01-001**
Dill	**prop. noun**	**14-01-001**
Dill	NP	11-01-001
Dill's	NP$	3-01-001
Dillinger	**NP**	**1-01-001**
Dillon	**prop. noun**	**11-04-005**
Dillon	NP	8-04-005
Dillon	NP-TL	3-01-001
Dilthey	**NP**	**1-01-001**
diluent	**noun**	**1-01-001**
diluents	NNS	1-01-001
dilute	**JJ**	**1-01-001**
dilute	**verb**	**9-03-007**
diluted	VBN	6-02-005
diluting	VBG	3-03-003
dilution	**NN**	**7-01-003**
DiLuzio	**NP**	**1-01-001**
Dilworth	**NP**	**1-01-001**
Dilys	**NP**	**1-01-001**
dim	**JJ**	**19-07-016**
DiMaggio	**prop. noun**	**6-02-004**
DiMaggio	NP	5-02-003
Dimaggio	NP	1-01-001
Diman	**prop. noun**	**2-01-001**
Diman	NP	1-01-001
Diman's	NP$	1-01-001
dime	**noun**	**7-05-007**
dime	NN	4-03-004
dimes	NNS	2-01-002
Dimes	NNS-TL	1-01-001
dimension	**noun**	**44-11-028**
dimension	NN	14-09-012
dimensions	NNS	30-07-020
dimension	**verb**	**3-01-002**
dimension	VB	1-01-001
dimensioning	VBG	2-01-001
dimensional	**JJ**	**11-02-004**
dimensionally	**RB**	**1-01-001**
dimensioning	**NN**	**1-01-001**
dimer	**noun**	**1-01-001**
dimers	NNS	1-01-001
dimesize	**JJ**	**1-01-001**
dimethylglyoxime	**NN**	**2-01-001**
diminish	**verb**	**24-08-021**
diminish	VB	3-01-003
diminishes	VBZ	3-02-003
diminished	VBD	1-01-001
diminished	VBN	9-05-007
diminishing	VBG	8-05-008
diminution	**NN**	**1-01-001**
diminutive	**JJ**	**3-02-003**
Dimitri	**NP**	**2-02-002**
dimly	**RB**	**12-06-012**
dimly-outlined	**JJ**	**1-01-001**
din	**NN**	**1-01-001**
dine	**verb**	**32-11-026**
dine	VB	2-02-002
dines	VBZ	1-01-001
dined	VBD	2-02-002
dined	VBN	1-01-001
dining	VBG	26-10-022
Dineen	**NP**	**1-01-001**
dinghy	**NN**	**1-01-001**
dingo	**NN**	**1-01-001**
dingy	**JJ**	**5-04-005**
dingy-looking	**JJ**	**1-01-001**
Dinh	**NP**	**1-01-001**
dining	**noun**	**2-01-002**
dining	NN	1-01-001
Dining	NN-TL	1-01-001
dining-room	**NN**	**1-01-001**
dinner	**noun**	**100-13-067**
dinner	NN	91-13-061
dinners	NNS	9-07-009
dinnertime	**NN**	**3-02-002**
dinnerware	**NN**	**1-01-001**

Word	Tag	Frequency
dinosaur	**noun**	**2-02-002**
dinosaur	NN	1-01-001
dinosaurs	NNS	1-01-001
Dinsmore	**NP**	**1-01-001**
diocesan	**JJ**	**5-01-001**
diocese	**NN**	**1-01-001**
DIOCS	**NP**	**1-01-001**
Diodati	**NP**	**1-01-001**
Dion	**NP**	**1-01-001**
Dionie	**NP**	**1-01-001**
Dionigi	**prop. noun**	**1-01-001**
Dionigi	NP	0-00-000
Dionigi	NP-TL	1-01-001
Dionysian	**JJ**	**2-01-001**
Dionysus	**NP**	**1-01-001**
Dior	**NP**	**1-01-001**
diorama	**noun**	**1-01-001**
dioramas	NNS	1-01-001
dioxalate	**NN**	**1-01-001**
dioxide	**NN**	**2-02-002**
dip	**noun**	**5-04-005**
dip	NN	4-04-004
dips	NNS	1-01-001
dip	**verb**	**6-05-006**
dip	VB	2-02-002
dipped	VBD	3-03-003
dipping	VBG	1-01-001
diphosphopyridine	**NN**	**1-01-001**
diplomacy	**NN**	**17-07-013**
diplomat	**noun**	**12-06-010**
diplomat	NN	5-05-005
diplomat's	NN$	1-01-001
diplomats	NNS	6-03-004
diplomatic	**JJ**	**28-08-020**
dipole	**JJ**	**5-01-002**
dipole	**noun**	**1-01-001**
dipoles	NNS	1-01-001
dipper	**NN**	**6-01-002**
Dipylon	**prop. noun**	**3-01-001**
Dipylon	NP	1-01-001
Dipylon	NP-HL	1-01-001
Dipylon	NP-TL	1-01-001
dire	**JJ**	**1-01-001**
direct	**adjective**	**114-14-079**
direct	JJ	108-14-078
direct	JJ-HL	3-01-002
Direct	JJ-TL	3-01-001
direct	**RB**	**3-02-003**
direct	**verb**	**94-13-071**
direct	VB	14-08-014
directs	VBZ	5-03-005
directed	VBD	10-07-010
directed	VBN	58-11-042
directing	VBG	7-05-007
direct-sum	**NN**	**2-01-001**
direction	**foreign**	**1-01-001**
direction	FW-NN	0-00-000
Direction	FW-NN-TL	1-01-001
direction	**noun**	**163-15-093**
direction	NN	132-14-081
Direction	NN-TL	1-01-001
directions	NNS	25-11-017
directions	NNS-HL	1-01-001
Directions	NNS-TL	4-02-002
directional	**JJ**	**8-06-007**
directionality	**NN**	**1-01-001**
directionally	**RB**	**1-01-001**
directive	**noun**	**6-05-005**
directive	NN	2-02-002
directives	NNS	4-03-003
directivity	**NN**	**1-01-001**
directly	**QL**	**8-03-004**
directly	**RB**	**133-13-099**
directness	**NN**	**4-03-004**
director	**noun**	**121-14-063**
director	NN	76-13-043
Director	NN-TL	25-06-017
director's	NN$	1-01-001
directors	NNS	18-08-015
Directors	NNS-TL	1-01-001
director-general	**NN**	**1-01-001**
directorate	**NN**	**4-02-002**
directorship	**NN**	**1-01-001**
directory	**noun**	**7-04-006**
directory	NN	4-04-004
Directory	NN-TL	3-01-002
directrice	**noun**	**1-01-001**
directrices	NNS	1-01-001
dirge	**NN**	**2-02-002**

Word	Tag	Frequency
Dirion	**NP**	**1-01-001**
Dirksen	**NP**	**3-02-003**
Diron	**NP**	**1-01-001**
dirt	**NN**	**43-10-027**
dirt-catcher	**NN**	**1-01-001**
dirty	**JJ**	**36-09-028**
disability	**noun**	**7-06-007**
disability	NN	5-05-005
disabilities	NNS	2-02-002
disable	**verb**	**14-05-006**
disable	VB	1-01-001
disabled	VBN	10-03-003
disabling	VBG	3-01-002
disabuse	**VB**	**2-02-002**
disadvantage	**noun**	**13-05-011**
disadvantage	NN	4-02-004
disadvantages	NNS	7-05-007
disadvantages	NNS-HL	2-01-001
disaffect	**verb**	**1-01-001**
disaffected	VBN	1-01-001
disaffection	**NN**	**1-01-001**
disaffiliate	**VB**	**1-01-001**
disaffiliated	**JJ**	**1-01-001**
disaffiliation	**noun**	**1-01-001**
disaffiliation	NN	0-00-000
disaffiliation	NN-NC	1-01-001
disagree	**verb**	**12-05-010**
disagree	VB	7-02-005
disagrees	VBZ	2-02-002
disagreed	VBD	3-02-003
disagreeable	**JJ**	**1-01-001**
disagreement	**noun**	**13-05-012**
disagreement	NN	11-05-011
disagreements	NNS	2-02-002
disallow	**verb**	**1-01-001**
disallowed	VBD	1-01-001
disappear	**verb**	**54-11-050**
disappear	VB	11-07-010
disappears	VBZ	3-03-003
disappeared	VBD	21-10-021
disappeared	VBN	14-07-013
disappearing	VBG	5-04-005
disappearance	**NN**	**8-04-008**
disappoint	**verb**	**15-06-014**
disappointed	VBN	15-06-014
disappointing	**JJ**	**7-06-007**
disappointment	**noun**	**17-09-017**
disappointment	NN	15-09-015
disappointments	NNS	2-02-002
disapprobation	**NN**	**1-01-001**
disapproval	**NN**	**15-05-011**
disapprove	**verb**	**9-06-009**
disapprove	VB	4-04-004
disapproves	VBZ	1-01-001
disapproved	VBD	3-03-003
disapproved	VBN	1-01-001
disapprovingly	**RB**	**1-01-001**
disarm	**verb**	**8-05-006**
disarm	VB	2-02-002
disarmed	VBN	3-01-001
disarming	VBG	3-02-003
disarmament	**noun**	**11-06-010**
disarmament	NN	10-06-009
Disarmament	NN-TL	1-01-001
disarrange	**verb**	**1-01-001**
disarranged	VBN	1-01-001
disarray	**NN**	**2-01-002**
disassemble	**VB**	**1-01-001**
disassembly	**NN**	**1-01-001**
disaster	**noun**	**30-09-024**
disaster	NN	26-08-021
disasters	NNS	4-04-004
disastrous	**JJ**	**16-08-015**
disband	**verb**	**2-02-002**
disbanded	VBD	1-01-001
disbanded	VBN	1-01-001
disbelief	**NN**	**6-05-005**
disbelieve	**verb**	**4-03-003**
disbelieve	VB	1-01-001
disbelieves	VBZ	1-01-001
disbelieved	VBD	1-01-001
disbelieving	VBG	1-01-001
disburse	**verb**	**1-01-001**
disbursed	VBN	1-01-001
disbursement	**noun**	**4-02-003**
disbursement	NN	2-01-001
disbursements	NNS	2-02-002
discard	**verb**	**9-07-009**
discard	VB	1-01-001
discard (cont.):		
discarded	VBD	1-01-001
discarded	VBN	7-06-007
discern	**verb**	**8-06-008**
discern	VB	4-03-004
discerned	VBN	2-02-002
discerning	VBG	2-02-002
discernible	**adjective**	**9-05-008**
discernible	JJ	8-05-007
discernable	JJ	1-01-001
discernment	**NN**	**1-01-001**
discharge	**noun**	**25-07-011**
discharge	NN	16-07-011
discharges	NNS	9-01-001
discharge	**verb**	**15-08-014**
discharge	VB	3-03-003
discharged	VBD	1-01-001
discharged	VBN	8-06-007
discharging	VBG	3-03-003
disciple	**noun**	**9-05-009**
disciple	NN	4-02-004
disciples	NNS	5-04-005
discipleship	**NN**	**2-01-001**
disciplinary	**adjective**	**1-01-001**
disciplinary	JJ	0-00-000
Disciplinary	JJ-TL	1-01-001
discipline	**noun**	**29-11-025**
discipline	NN	25-11-023
disciplines	NNS	4-04-004
discipline	**verb**	**14-06-014**
discipline	VB	2-02-002
disciplined	VBD	3-03-003
disciplined	VBN	8-05-008
disciplining	VBG	1-01-001
disclaim	**verb**	**1-01-001**
disclaimed	VBD	1-01-001
disclaimer	**NN**	**1-01-001**
disclose	**verb**	**24-10-022**
disclose	VB	9-05-009
discloses	VBZ	1-01-001
disclosed	VBD	7-03-006
disclosed	VBN	7-04-006
disclosure	**noun**	**6-03-005**
disclosure	NN	2-01-001
disclosures	NNS	4-03-004
discoid	**JJ**	**1-01-001**
discolor	**verb**	**2-02-002**
discolors	VBZ	1-01-001
discolored	VBN	1-01-001
discomfort	**NN**	**7-04-006**
disconcert	**VB**	**1-01-001**
disconcerting	**JJ**	**4-03-004**
disconcertingly	**QL**	**1-01-001**
disconnect	**verb**	**4-03-004**
disconnected	VBN	4-03-004
discontent	**NN**	**8-06-007**
discontented	**JJ**	**1-01-001**
discontinuance	**NN**	**1-01-001**
discontinue	**verb**	**9-05-009**
discontinue	VB	2-02-002
discontinued	VBD	2-01-002
discontinued	VBN	5-03-005
discontinuity	**NN**	**4-01-001**
discontinuous	**JJ**	**3-02-002**
discord	**NN**	**1-01-001**
discordantly	**RB**	**2-02-002**
discorporate	**JJ**	**1-01-001**
discorporate	**verb**	**2-01-001**
discorporate	VB	1-01-001
discorporated	VBN	1-01-001
discount	**noun**	**13-06-010**
discount	NN	8-05-008
discounts	NNS	5-04-004
discount	**verb**	**7-05-007**
discount	VB	4-02-004
discounted	VBD	2-02-002
discounting	VBG	1-01-001
discourage	**verb**	**25-09-023**
discourage	VB	9-07-009
discouraged	VBD	1-01-001
discouraged	VBN	14-07-012
discouraging	VBG	1-01-001
discouragement	**NN**	**3-03-003**
discouraging	**JJ**	**4-03-004**
discours	**foreign**	**1-01-001**
discours	FW-NN	0-00-000
Discours	FW-NN-TL	1-01-001
discourse	**noun**	**11-06-009**
discourse	NN	7-05-007

Word	Tag	Frequency
discourse (cont.):		
Discourse	NN-TL	2-01-001
discourses	NNS	2-02-002
discourse	**VB**	**1-01-001**
discourteous	**JJ**	**2-02-002**
discover	**verb**	**123-15-102**
discover	VB	40-11-039
discovers	VBZ	3-03-003
discovered	VBD	30-13-028
discovered	VBN	43-12-037
discovering	VBG	7-07-007
discoverer	**NN**	**1-01-001**
discovery	**noun**	**55-12-030**
discovery	NN	34-10-023
discovery	NN-HL	1-01-001
Discovery	NN-TL	10-01-001
discoveries	NNS	10-06-009
discredit	**NN**	**2-02-002**
discredit	**verb**	**3-02-003**
discredited	VBN	3-02-003
discreet	**JJ**	**3-03-003**
discreetly	**RB**	**2-02-002**
discrepancy	**noun**	**16-06-011**
discrepancy	NN	11-05-008
discrepancies	NNS	4-04-004
discrepancies	NNS-HL	1-01-001
discrete	**JJ**	**7-03-005**
discretion	**NN**	**14-04-010**
discretionary	**adjective**	**2-01-001**
discretionary	JJ	1-01-001
discretionary	JJ-HL	1-01-001
discriminate	**verb**	**6-04-006**
discriminate	VB	1-01-001
discriminating	VBG	5-03-005
discriminating	**JJ**	**2-02-002**
discrimination	**NN**	**23-08-013**
discriminatory	**JJ**	**3-03-003**
discursiveness	**NN**	**1-01-001**
discuss	**verb**	**113-14-085**
discuss	VB	28-10-026
discusses	VBZ	4-02-002
discussed	VBD	18-11-017
discussed	VBN	47-11-038
discussing	VBG	16-08-016
discussant	**NN**	**1-01-001**
discussion	**noun**	**126-13-078**
discussion	NN	89-11-059
discussion	NN-HL	5-01-004
discussions	NNS	32-10-023
disdain	**NN**	**2-02-002**
disdain	**verb**	**4-03-004**
disdain	VB	1-01-001
disdains	VBZ	1-01-001
disdaining	VBG	2-02-002
disdainful	**JJ**	**2-02-002**
disease	**noun**	**72-11-025**
disease	NN	52-10-021
disease	NN-HL	1-01-001
diseases	NNS	16-08-009
Diseases	NNS-TL	3-01-001
diseased	**JJ**	**1-01-001**
disembody	**verb**	**1-01-001**
disembodied	VBN	1-01-001
disenfranchise	**verb**	**1-01-001**
disenfranchised	VBN	1-01-001
disenfranchisement	**NN**	**2-01-001**
disengage	**VB**	**1-01-001**
disengagement	**NN**	**1-01-001**
disentangle	**VB**	**2-01-001**
disfavor	**NN**	**1-01-001**
disfigure	**verb**	**5-03-005**
disfigured	VBD	2-02-002
disfigured	VBN	3-03-003
disgrace	**NN**	**3-03-003**
disgrace	**verb**	**1-01-001**
disgraced	VBN	1-01-001
disgraceful	**JJ**	**1-01-001**
disgruntle	**verb**	**1-01-001**
disgruntled	VBN	1-01-001
disguise	**NN**	**2-01-002**
disguise	**verb**	**15-06-015**
disguise	VB	3-02-003
disguises	VBZ	1-01-001
disguised	VBD	2-02-002
disguised	VBN	9-04-009
disgust	**NN**	**1-01-001**
disgust	**verb**	**6-05-006**
disgusted	VBN	6-05-006
disgusting	**JJ**	**4-04-004**

Word	Tag	Frequency
dish	**noun**	**36-11-021**
dish	NN	15-08-011
Dish	NN-TL	1-01-001
dishes	NNS	19-09-013
dishes	NNS-HL	1-01-001
dish	**verb**	**2-02-002**
dishes	VBZ	1-01-001
dished	VBD	1-01-001
disharmony	**NN**	**1-01-001**
dishearten	**verb**	**3-03-003**
dishearten	VB	2-02-002
disheartening	VBG	1-01-001
dishevel	**verb**	**2-01-002**
disheveled	VBN	2-01-002
dishonest	**JJ**	**3-02-003**
dishonesty	**NN**	**2-02-002**
dishonor	**NN**	**2-02-002**
dishonor	**verb**	**2-02-002**
dishonored	VBN	1-01-001
dishonoring	VBG	0-00-000
dishonouring	VBG	1-01-001
dishwasher	**noun**	**1-01-001**
dishwashers	NNS	1-01-001
dishwater	**NN**	**1-01-001**
disillusion	**verb**	**3-03-003**
disillusioned	VBN	2-02-002
disillusioning	VBG	1-01-001
disillusionment	**NN**	**3-03-003**
DiSimone	**NP**	**1-01-001**
disinclination	**NN**	**2-01-002**
disintegrate	**verb**	**3-03-003**
disintegrate	VB	2-02-002
disintegrating	VBG	1-01-001
disintegration	**NN**	**5-04-005**
disintegrative	**JJ**	**1-01-001**
disinter	**verb**	**1-01-001**
disinterred	VBN	1-01-001
disinterest	**noun**	**3-03-003**
disinterest	NN	2-02-002
disinterest	NN-HL	1-01-001
disinterested	**JJ**	**5-04-005**
disjoint	**verb**	**1-01-001**
disjointed	VBN	1-01-001
disk	**noun**	**42-07-015**
disk	NN	25-03-006
disc	NN	6-02-004
disks	NNS	4-04-004
discs	NNS	7-05-006
disk	**verb**	**1-01-001**
disking	VBG	1-01-001
dislike	**noun**	**8-05-008**
dislike	NN	7-05-007
dislikes	NNS	1-01-001
dislike	**verb**	**22-09-020**
dislike	VB	7-04-007
dislikes	VBZ	3-03-003
disliked	VBD	11-05-010
disliking	VBG	1-01-001
dislocate	**verb**	**1-01-001**
dislocated	VBN	1-01-001
dislocation	**noun**	**3-02-003**
dislocation	NN	1-01-001
dislocations	NNS	2-02-002
dislodge	**verb**	**3-03-003**
dislodge	VB	2-02-002
dislodged	VBD	1-01-001
disloyal	**JJ**	**2-02-002**
disloyalty	**NN**	**2-02-002**
dismal	**JJ**	**8-07-008**
dismally	**RB**	**2-01-002**
dismay	**NN**	**5-05-005**
dismay	**verb**	**1-01-001**
dismayed	VBN	1-01-001
dismaying	**JJ**	**3-02-003**
dismember	**verb**	**2-02-002**
dismembered	VBD	2-02-002
dismemberment	**NN**	**2-01-002**
dismiss	**verb**	**23-14-021**
dismiss	VB	5-03-004
dismisses	VBZ	1-01-001
dismissed	VBD	7-05-007
dismissed	VBN	7-06-007
dismissing	VBG	3-02-003
dismissal	**NN**	**7-04-005**
dismount	**verb**	**7-03-005**
dismounted	VBD	3-02-002
dismounted	VBN	2-02-002
dismounting	VBG	2-01-002
Disneyland	**NP**	**1-01-001**

Word	Tag	Frequency
disobedience	**NN**	**7-01-001**
disobedient	**JJ**	**2-01-001**
disobey	**verb**	**5-05-005**
disobeyed	VBD	1-01-001
disobeyed	VBN	3-03-003
disobeying	VBG	1-01-001
disorder	**noun**	**14-04-009**
disorder	NN	7-03-004
disorders	NNS	7-03-005
disorder	**verb**	**3-02-003**
disordered	VBN	3-02-003
disorderliness	**NN**	**1-01-001**
disorderly	**JJ**	**3-02-003**
disorganization	**NN**	**1-01-001**
disorganize	**verb**	**5-04-005**
disorganized	VBN	5-04-005
disorient	**verb**	**1-01-001**
disoriented	VBN	1-01-001
disown	**verb**	**3-02-003**
disown	VB	1-01-001
disowned	VBD	1-01-001
disowned	VBN	1-01-001
disparagement	**NN**	**2-02-002**
disparate	**JJ**	**4-03-004**
disparity	**noun**	**3-03-003**
disparity	NN	2-02-002
disparities	NNS	1-01-001
dispassionate	**JJ**	**1-01-001**
dispassionately	**RB**	**3-03-003**
dispatch	**noun**	**9-03-008**
dispatch	NN	6-02-006
dispatches	NNS	3-02-002
dispatch	**verb**	**12-06-009**
dispatch	VB	2-01-001
dispatched	VBD	2-01-001
despatched	VBD	1-01-001
dispatched	VBN	3-03-003
despatched	VBN	1-01-001
dispatching	VBG	3-03-003
dispel	**verb**	**12-06-009**
dispel	VB	3-03-003
dispell	VB	1-01-001
dispelled	VBD	1-01-001
dispelled	VBN	7-04-006
dispensary	**NN**	**1-01-001**
dispensation	**NN**	**3-02-003**
dispense	**verb**	**7-05-006**
dispense	VB	4-04-004
dispensed	VBN	2-02-002
dispensing	VBG	1-01-001
dispenser	**noun**	**2-02-002**
dispenser	NN	1-01-001
dispensers	NNS	1-01-001
dispersal	**NN**	**1-01-001**
disperse	**verb**	**10-06-008**
disperse	VB	2-02-002
dispersed	VBD	1-01-001
dispersed	VBN	6-02-004
dispersing	VBG	1-01-001
dispersement	**NN**	**1-01-001**
dispersion	**NN**	**3-02-003**
displace	**verb**	**7-05-007**
displace	VB	3-03-003
displaces	VBZ	1-01-001
displaced	VBN	2-02-002
displacing	VBG	1-01-001
displacement	**noun**	**23-04-010**
displacement	NN	22-04-010
displacement	NN-HL	1-01-001
display	**noun**	**44-11-026**
display	NN	29-11-023
displays	NNS	15-05-007
display	**verb**	**45-10-039**
display	VB	12-10-012
displays	VBZ	6-04-006
displayed	VBD	8-04-007
displayed	VBN	13-07-013
displaying	VBG	6-04-006
displease	**verb**	**7-04-005**
displeased	VBN	7-04-005
displeasure	**NN**	**4-04-004**
disposal	**NN**	**20-09-018**
dispose	**verb**	**23-09-020**
dispose	VB	5-04-004
disposed	VBD	4-04-004
disposed	VBN	14-06-013
disposition	**noun**	**14-08-014**
disposition	NN	13-08-013
dispositions	NNS	1-01-001
dispossess	**verb**	**2-02-002**
dispossessed	VBN	2-02-002
dispossession	**NN**	**1-01-001**
disproportionate	**JJ**	**2-02-002**
disproportionately	**RB**	**1-01-001**
disprove	**verb**	**4-03-004**
disprove	VB	3-02-003
disproving	VBG	1-01-001
disputable	**JJ**	**1-01-001**
dispute	**noun**	**37-06-017**
dispute	NN	30-06-013
disputes	NNS	7-04-005
dispute	**verb**	**7-05-006**
dispute	VB	4-03-003
disputes	VBZ	0-00-000
disputes	VBZ-HL	1-01-001
disputed	VBN	2-02-002
disqualify	**verb**	**2-02-002**
disqualify	VB	1-01-001
disqualified	VBN	1-01-001
disquiet	**NN**	**1-01-001**
disquieting	**JJ**	**1-01-001**
disquietude	**NN**	**1-01-001**
disquisition	**noun**	**1-01-001**
disquisition	NN	0-00-000
Disquisition	NN-TL	1-01-001
disregard	**NN**	**4-03-004**
disregard	**verb**	**9-07-008**
disregard	VB	2-02-002
disregarded	VBD	3-03-003
disregarded	VBN	1-01-001
disregarding	VBG	3-03-003
disrepair	**NN**	**2-01-002**
disreputable	**JJ**	**1-01-001**
disrepute	**NN**	**2-02-002**
disrespect	**NN**	**2-01-002**
disrobe	**VB**	**1-01-001**
disrupt	**verb**	**13-07-012**
disrupt	VB	5-03-005
disrupts	VBZ	1-01-001
disrupted	VBD	2-02-002
disrupted	VBN	3-03-003
disrupting	VBG	2-02-002
disruption	**noun**	**4-03-003**
disruption	NN	3-02-002
disruptions	NNS	1-01-001
disruptive	**JJ**	**4-02-002**
dissatisfaction	**noun**	**10-06-009**
dissatisfaction	NN	9-06-008
dissatisfactions	NNS	1-01-001
dissatisfy	**verb**	**6-04-005**
dissatisfied	VBN	6-04-005
dissect	**VB**	**1-01-001**
dissection	**NN**	**3-02-002**
dissemble	**verb**	**1-01-001**
dissembling	VBG	1-01-001
disseminate	**verb**	**7-02-003**
disseminated	VBN	6-02-003
disseminating	VBG	1-01-001
dissemination	**NN**	**2-02-002**
dissension	**noun**	**4-03-004**
dissension	NN	3-02-003
dissensions	NNS	1-01-001
dissent	**noun**	**6-04-006**
dissent	NN	4-03-004
dissents	NNS	2-02-002
dissent	**verb**	**4-03-004**
dissent	VB	1-01-001
dissented	VBD	1-01-001
dissenting	VBG	1-01-001
dissenting	VBG-HL	1-01-001
dissenter	**noun**	**2-02-002**
dissenter	NN	1-01-001
dissenters	NNS	1-01-001
disservice	**NN**	**1-01-001**
dissident	**JJ**	**1-01-001**
dissimilar	**JJ**	**3-03-003**
dissimulation	**NN**	**1-01-001**
dissipate	**verb**	**3-03-003**
dissipated	VBD	1-01-001
dissipated	VBN	1-01-001
dissipating	VBG	1-01-001
dissociate	**verb**	**1-01-001**
dissociated	VBN	1-01-001
dissociation	**NN**	**4-02-003**
dissolution	**noun**	**4-03-004**
dissolution	NN	3-03-003
dissolutions	NNS	1-01-001
dissolve	**NN**	**1-01-001**

Word	Tag	Count
dissolve	**verb**	**23-08-018**
dissolve	VB	5-04-005
dissolved	VBN	15-05-011
dissolving	VBG	2-02-002
dissolving	VBG-HL	1-01-001
dissonance	**noun**	**1-01-001**
dissonances	NNS	1-01-001
dissuade	**VB**	**3-02-003**
distal	**JJ**	**9-01-003**
distally	**RB**	**1-01-001**
distance	**noun**	**127-15-080**
distance	NN	107-14-074
distance	NN-NC	1-01-001
distances	NNS	19-06-010
distant	**JJ**	**37-11-031**
distantly	**RB**	**1-01-001**
distaste	**NN**	**8-06-008**
distasteful	**JJ**	**1-01-001**
distastefully	**RB**	**2-02-002**
distension	**NN**	**1-01-001**
distil	**verb**	**12-05-006**
distil	VB	1-01-001
distilled	VBN	8-04-005
Distilled	VBN-TL	2-01-001
distilling	VBG	1-01-001
distillation	**NN**	**3-02-002**
distiller	**noun**	**2-02-002**
distiller	NN	1-01-001
distillers	NNS	1-01-001
distinct	**JJ**	**42-11-033**
distinction	**noun**	**56-12-039**
distinction	NN	41-12-031
distinctions	NNS	15-04-011
distinctive	**JJ**	**20-05-018**
distinctively	**QL**	**2-01-001**
distinctly	**QL**	**1-01-001**
distinctly	**RB**	**11-06-011**
distinguish	**verb**	**71-13-056**
distinguish	VB	19-04-014
distinguishes	VBZ	5-02-004
distinguished	VBD	1-01-001
distinguished	VBN	40-13-034
distinguishing	VBG	6-03-006
distinguishable	**JJ**	**4-01-002**
distinguished	**adjective**	**1-01-001**
distinguished	JJ	0-00-000
Distinguished	JJ-TL	1-01-001
distort	**verb**	**15-05-015**
distort	VB	4-02-004
distorted	VBD	1-01-001
distorted	VBN	10-03-010
distortable	**JJ**	**1-01-001**
distortion	**noun**	**9-05-007**
distortion	NN	7-03-005
distortions	NNS	2-02-002
distract	**verb**	**8-05-006**
distract	VB	2-02-002
distracted	VBD	3-03-003
distracted	VBN	2-02-002
distracting	VBG	1-01-001
distractedly	**RB**	**1-01-001**
distraction	**noun**	**4-04-004**
distraction	NN	3-03-003
distractions	NNS	1-01-001
distraught	**JJ**	**1-01-001**
distress	**noun**	**16-06-012**
distress	NN	15-06-011
distresses	NNS	1-01-001
distress	**verb**	**4-03-003**
distressed	VBN	4-03-003
distressing	**JJ**	**7-05-007**
distribute	**verb**	**39-11-028**
distribute	VB	6-04-006
distributes	VBZ	2-02-002
distributed	VBD	2-02-002
distributed	VBN	24-07-015
distributed	VBN-HL	1-01-001
distributing	VBG	3-03-003
distributing	VBG-HL	1-01-001
distribution	**noun**	**95-08-039**
distribution	NN	78-08-037
distribution	NN-HL	7-02-003
distributions	NNS	10-03-006
distributive	**adjective**	**2-02-002**
distributive	JJ	1-01-001
Distributive	JJ-TL	1-01-001
distributor	**noun**	**12-03-005**
distributor	NN	7-02-003
distributor's	NN$	1-01-001

Word	Tag	Count
distributor (cont.):		
distributors	NNS	3-02-003
Distributors	NNS-TL	1-01-001
distributorship	**NN**	**1-01-001**
district	**noun**	**176-10-061**
district	NN	77-10-040
dist.	NN	0-00-000
Dist.	NN-TL	3-02-002
District	NN-TL	58-08-029
districts	NNS	35-06-013
districts	NNS-HL	2-02-002
Districts	NNS-TL	1-01-001
distrust	**NN**	**4-04-004**
distrust	**verb**	**4-04-004**
distrust	VB	2-02-002
distrusted	VBD	1-01-001
distrusted	VBN	1-01-001
disturb	**verb**	**38-10-034**
disturb	VB	10-06-008
disturbed	VBD	4-04-004
disturbed	VBN	22-10-021
disturbing	VBG	2-01-002
disturbance	**noun**	**13-04-010**
disturbance	NN	10-04-009
disturbances	NNS	3-01-003
disturber	**NN**	**1-01-001**
disturbing	**JJ**	**14-07-012**
disturbingly	**RB**	**1-01-001**
disunion	**NN**	**1-01-001**
disunite	**verb**	**1-01-001**
disunited	VBN	1-01-001
disunity	**NN**	**3-03-003**
ditch	**noun**	**12-04-008**
ditch	NN	9-03-005
Ditch	NN-TL	1-01-001
ditches	NNS	2-01-002
ditcher	**NN**	**1-01-001**
dites	**FW-VB**	**1-01-001**
Ditmar	**NP**	**1-01-001**
Ditmars	**NP**	**2-01-001**
ditty	**noun**	**4-02-002**
ditty	NN	1-01-001
ditties	NNS	3-02-002
diurnal	**JJ**	**5-02-002**
diva	**NN**	**1-01-001**
divan	**noun**	**7-04-004**
divan	NN	6-03-003
divans	NNS	1-01-001
divan-like	**JJ**	**1-01-001**
DiVarco	**NP**	**1-01-001**
dive	**noun**	**24-05-009**
dive	NN	20-04-007
dives	NNS	4-02-004
dive	**verb**	**11-05-010**
dive	VB	3-02-002
dived	VBD	4-03-004
dived	VBN	1-01-001
diving	VBG	3-03-003
diver	**noun**	**3-02-002**
diver	NN	1-01-001
divers	NNS	2-02-002
diverge	**verb**	**1-01-001**
diverging	VBG	1-01-001
divergence	**NN**	**2-02-002**
divergent	**adjective**	**6-05-006**
divergent	JJ	5-04-005
divergent	JJ-HL	1-01-001
divers	**JJ**	**1-01-001**
diverse	**JJ**	**13-05-013**
diversification	**noun**	**3-01-002**
diversification	NN	2-01-002
diversification	NN-HL	1-01-001
diversify	**verb**	**7-04-005**
diversified	VBN	4-04-004
Diversified	VBN-TL	3-01-001
diversion	**noun**	**11-06-010**
diversion	NN	7-04-006
diversions	NNS	4-03-004
diversionary	**JJ**	**1-01-001**
diversity	**noun**	**14-03-007**
diversity	NN	13-02-006
diversities	NNS	1-01-001
divert	**verb**	**7-07-007**
divert	VB	1-01-001
diverted	VBN	3-03-003
diverting	VBG	3-03-003
divertimento	**noun**	**2-02-002**
divertimento	NN	1-01-001
Divertimento	NN-TL	1-01-001

divest	**VB**	**1-01-001**
divestiture	**NN**	**4-01-001**
divide	**verb**	**83-12-062**
divide	VB	14-07-010
divides	VBZ	6-01-002
divided	VBD	11-07-011
divided	VBN	44-10-039
divided	VBN-HL	1-01-001
dividing	VBG	7-05-007
dividend	**noun**	**14-05-010**
dividend	NN	6-04-005
dividends	NNS	8-04-006
divider	**NN**	**1-01-001**
divination	**NN**	**3-01-001**
divine	**adjective**	**32-08-020**
divine	JJ	27-07-018
divine	JJ-HL	1-01-001
Divine	JJ-TL	4-03-004
divine	**NN**	**2-02-002**
divine	**verb**	**1-01-001**
divining	VBG	1-01-001
Divine	**prop. noun**	**1-01-001**
Divine's	NP$	1-01-001
divinely	**RB**	**3-03-003**
diving	**noun**	**2-02-002**
diving	NN	1-01-001
Diving	NN-TL	1-01-001
divinity	**noun**	**10-05-005**
divinity	NN	2-02-002
Divinity	NN-TL	5-02-002
divinities	NNS	3-02-002
divisible	**JJ**	**4-01-001**
division	**noun**	**124-09-054**
division	NN	69-09-039
division	NN-HL	1-01-001
Division	NN-TL	37-05-015
division's	NN$	0-00-000
Division's	NN$-TL	2-01-001
divisions	NNS	15-06-010
divisional	**JJ**	**2-01-001**
divisive	**JJ**	**5-05-005**
divorce	**NN**	**23-09-013**
divorce	**verb**	**14-08-014**
divorce	VB	6-05-006
divorced	VBD	2-01-002
divorced	VBN	6-05-006
divorcee	**NN**	**2-02-002**
divulge	**verb**	**1-01-001**
divulging	VBG	1-01-001
Dixie	**prop. noun**	**1-01-001**
Dixie	NP	0-00-000
Dixie	NP-TL	1-01-001
Dixiecrat	**prop. noun**	**1-01-001**
Dixiecrats	NPS	1-01-001
Dixieland	**prop. noun**	**3-02-003**
Dixieland	NP	1-01-001
Dixieland	NP-TL	2-01-002
Dixon	**NP**	**3-02-002**
dizzily	**RB**	**1-01-001**
dizziness	**NN**	**1-01-001**
dizzy	**JJ**	**4-03-004**
Dizzy	**NP**	**1-01-001**
Djakarta	**NP**	**1-01-001**
Django	**prop. noun**	**5-01-002**
Django	NP	4-01-001
Django's	NP$	0-00-000
Django's	NP$-TL	1-01-001
Djangology	**NP**	**2-01-001**
Dnieper	**NP**	**1-01-001**
do	**verb**	**4367-15-484**
do	DO	1350-15-395
doo	DO	2-02-002
dost	DO	1-01-001
do	DO-HL	4-04-004
do	DO-NC	2-01-001
Do	DO-TL	5-03-004
d'you	DO+PPSS	1-01-001
don't	DO*	484-14-176
doan	DO*	1-01-001
don't	DO*-HL	3-01-002
howda	+DO	1-01-001
whaddya	+DO	1-01-001
does	DOZ	467-15-249
does	DOZ-HL	16-02-002
Does	DOZ-TL	2-01-001
doesn't	DOZ*	87-13-069
don't	DOZ*	2-02-002
Doesn't	DOZ*-TL	1-01-001
's	+DOZ	1-01-001
do (cont.):		
did	DOD	1043-15-324
done	DOD	4-01-002
did	DOD-NC	1-01-001
didn't	DOD*	400-14-144
didn	DOD*	2-01-001
Didn't	DOD*-TL	1-01-001
'd	+DOD	7-03-006
whyn't	+DOD*	1-01-001
done	VBN	314-15-198
done	VBN-HL	1-01-001
doing	VBG	159-15-122
doin	VBG	2-01-001
doin'	VBG	1-01-001
do	**noun**	**1-01-001**
do	NN	0-00-000
Do	NN-TL	1-01-001
Do	**NP**	**1-01-001**
do-good	**JJ**	**1-01-001**
do-gooder	**noun**	**2-02-002**
do-gooder	NN	1-01-001
do-gooders	NNS	1-01-001
do-it-yourself	**JJ**	**5-03-004**
Doaty	**prop. noun**	**14-01-001**
Doaty	NP	8-01-001
Doaty's	NP$	6-01-001
Dobbins	**NP**	**1-01-001**
Dobbs	**NP**	**1-01-001**
Doberman	**NP**	**1-01-001**
doble	**FW-JJ**	**1-01-001**
Doc	**NP**	**19-03-005**
Docherty	**NP**	**9-01-001**
docile	**JJ**	**4-04-004**
docilely	**RB**	**1-01-001**
dock	**noun**	**7-04-005**
dock	NN	6-03-004
docks	NNS	1-01-001
dock	**verb**	**3-02-002**
dock	VB	2-01-001
docked	VBN	1-01-001
docket	**verb**	**1-01-001**
docketed	VBN	1-01-001
dockside	**NN**	**2-01-001**
doctor	**noun**	**349-15-108**
doctor	NN	87-11-041
doc	NN	1-01-001
dr.	NN	0-00-000
Dr.	NN-TL	190-13-068
Dr.	NN-TL-HL	2-02-002
Doctor	NN-TL	13-07-007
doctor's	NN+BEZ	1-01-001
doctor's	NN$	17-05-009
doctors	NNS	28-10-019
do(c)ters	NNS	1-01-001
docters	NNS	1-01-001
drs.	NNS	0-00-000
Drs.	NNS-TL	5-03-003
doctors	NNS-HL	1-01-001
Doctors	NNS-TL	1-01-001
doctors'	NNS$	1-01-001
doctor	**verb**	**4-04-004**
doctored	VBN	4-04-004
doctorate	**NN**	**1-01-001**
doctrinaire	**JJ**	**1-01-001**
doctrinaire	**NN**	**1-01-001**
doctrinal	**JJ**	**3-02-002**
doctrinally	**RB**	**1-01-001**
doctrine	**noun**	**51-06-027**
doctrine	NN	39-05-024
Doctrine	NN-TL	7-02-003
doctrines	NNS	5-03-004
document	**noun**	**30-09-023**
document	NN	11-05-009
documents	NNS	16-08-014
Documents	NNS-TL	3-02-002
document	**verb**	**8-05-008**
document	VB	2-02-002
documented	VBD	1-01-001
documented	VBN	5-04-005
documentary	**JJ**	**1-01-001**
documentary	**noun**	**5-03-003**
documentary	NN	3-02-002
documentaries	NNS	2-01-001
documentary-type	**JJ**	**1-01-001**
documentation	**NN**	**3-02-003**
Dodd	**NP**	**1-01-001**
dodge	**NN**	**2-02-002**
dodge	**verb**	**8-04-006**
dodge	VB	4-03-003

Word	Tag	Count
dodge (cont.):		
dodged	VBD	2-01-002
dodging	VBG	2-02-002
Dodge	**prop. noun**	**6-03-004**
Dodge	NP	3-01-002
Dodge	NP-TL	2-02-002
Dodge's	NP$	1-01-001
Dodger	**prop. noun**	**6-01-004**
Dodger	NP	1-01-001
Dodgers	NPS	5-01-004
Dodington	**NP**	**1-01-001**
Doe	**NP**	**1-01-001**
doer	**noun**	**1-01-001**
doers	NNS	1-01-001
Doerner	**prop. noun**	**1-01-001**
Doerner's	NP$	1-01-001
doff	**verb**	**1-01-001**
doffing	VBG	1-01-001
dog	**noun**	**147-12-047**
dog	NN	71-11-026
Dog	NN-TL	5-03-003
dog's	NN$	2-02-002
dogs	NNS	68-11-026
Dogs	NNS-TL	1-01-001
dog	**verb**	**1-01-001**
dogs	VBZ	1-01-001
dog-eared	**JJ**	**1-01-001**
dog-pin	**NN**	**1-01-001**
Dogberry	**NP**	**1-01-001**
dogged	**JJ**	**2-02-002**
doggedly	**RB**	**2-02-002**
doggone	**UH**	**1-01-001**
doghouse	**NN**	**1-01-001**
dogleg	**NN**	**1-01-001**
dogma	**noun**	**6-05-006**
dogma	NN	4-04-004
dogmas	NNS	2-01-002
dogmatic	**JJ**	**4-03-004**
dogmatically	**RB**	**2-02-002**
dogmatism	**NN**	**4-03-003**
Dogtown	**prop. noun**	**9-01-001**
Dogtown	NP	5-01-001
Dogtown	NP-TL	4-01-001
dogtrot	**NN**	**1-01-001**
dogumenti	**FW-NNS**	**1-01-001**
dogwood	**NN**	**1-01-001**
Dohnanyi	**NP**	**1-01-001**
doing	**noun**	**10-07-008**
doing	NN	4-04-004
doings	NNS	6-04-004
Dolan	**NP**	**2-01-001**
dolce	**foreign**	**5-01-002**
dolce	FW-JJ	0-00-000
Dolce	FW-JJ-TL	5-01-002
doldrum	**noun**	**1-01-001**
doldrums	NNS	1-01-001
dole	**verb**	**2-02-002**
dole	VB	1-01-001
doled	VBD	1-01-001
doleful	**JJ**	**1-01-001**
doll	**noun**	**22-05-009**
doll	NN	10-05-008
dolls	NNS	12-03-004
dollar	**noun**	**144-14-078**
dollar	NN	44-10-031
Dollar	NN-TL	2-01-001
dollars	NNS	96-14-058
dollars	NNS-HL	1-01-001
dollars'	NNS$	1-01-001
dollar-and-cents	**JJ**	**1-01-001**
dollar-sign	**NN**	**1-01-001**
dollarette	**NN**	**1-01-001**
dollars-and-cents	**NNS**	**1-01-001**
Dolley	**prop. noun**	**3-01-001**
Dolley	NP	2-01-001
Dolley	NP-TL	1-01-001
dolly	**noun**	**1-01-001**
dollies	NNS	1-01-001
Dolly	**NP**	**4-01-001**
Dolmabahce	**prop. noun**	**1-01-001**
Dolmabahce	NP	0-00-000
Dolmabahce	NP-TL	1-01-001
Dolores	**NP**	**20-02-002**
dolphin	**noun**	**5-04-004**
dolphin	NN	1-01-001
dolphins	NNS	2-02-002
Dolphins	NNS-TL	2-01-001
doltish	**JJ**	**1-01-001**
domain	**noun**	**12-04-011**

Word	Tag	Count
domain (cont.):		
domain	NN	9-04-009
domains	NNS	3-02-002
dome	**noun**	**25-08-012**
dome	NN	17-07-008
domes	NNS	7-04-005
domes	NNS-HL	1-01-001
dome	**verb**	**2-02-002**
domed	VBN	2-02-002
Domesday	**prop. noun**	**1-01-001**
Domesday	NP	0-00-000
Domesday	NP-TL	1-01-001
domestic	**adjective**	**62-10-035**
domestic	JJ	59-10-035
Domestic	JJ-TL	3-01-001
domestic	**NN**	**1-01-001**
domestically	**RB**	**1-01-001**
domesticity	**NN**	**1-01-001**
domi	**FW-RB**	**1-01-001**
domicile	**NN**	**1-01-001**
domicile	**verb**	**1-01-001**
domiciled	VBN	1-01-001
Domicilium	**prop. noun**	**1-01-001**
Domicilium	NP	0-00-000
Domicilium	NP-TL	1-01-001
Domina	**foreign**	**2-01-001**
Domina	FW-NN	0-00-000
Domina	FW-NN-TL	1-01-001
Domina	FW-NN-TL-NC	1-01-001
dominance	**NN**	**11-04-008**
dominant	**JJ**	**65-06-026**
dominantly	**RB**	**1-01-001**
dominate	**verb**	**37-09-029**
dominate	VB	8-07-008
dominates	VBZ	7-03-005
dominated	VBD	5-03-005
dominated	VBN	15-07-014
dominating	VBG	2-02-002
domination	**NN**	**15-06-010**
domineer	**verb**	**2-02-002**
domineering	VBG	2-02-002
Dominic	**NP**	**1-01-001**
Dominican	**JJ**	**8-01-004**
Dominican	**prop. noun**	**6-02-003**
Dominican	NP	0-00-000
Dominican	NP-TL	6-02-003
dominion	**noun**	**8-04-007**
dominion	NN	7-03-006
Dominion	NN-TL	1-01-001
Dominique	**NP**	**1-01-001**
Domitian	**prop. noun**	**1-01-001**
Domitian's	NP$	1-01-001
Domokous	**NP**	**2-01-001**
don	**NN**	**1-01-001**
don	**verb**	**4-03-004**
donned	VBD	3-02-003
donning	VBG	1-01-001
Don	**NP**	**22-07-015**
don't-know's	**NNS**	**1-01-001**
Donald	**NP**	**20-06-011**
Donaldson	**NP**	**2-01-002**
donate	**verb**	**12-08-009**
donate	VB	3-02-002
donates	VBZ	1-01-001
donated	VBD	1-01-001
donated	VBN	5-05-005
donated	VBN-HL	1-01-001
donating	VBG	1-01-001
donation	**noun**	**4-03-004**
donation	NN	2-02-002
donations	NNS	2-01-002
Donato	**NP**	**1-01-001**
Donizetti	**prop. noun**	**1-01-001**
Donizetti's	NP$	1-01-001
donkey	**NN**	**1-01-001**
Donna	**NP**	**4-01-001**
Donnay	**NP**	**3-01-001**
Donnell	**NP**	**1-01-001**
Donnelly	**NP**	**1-01-001**
Donner	**NP**	**1-01-001**
Donnybrook	**NP**	**4-01-001**
donor	**noun**	**10-03-003**
donor	NN	5-03-003
donors	NNS	5-01-001
Donovan	**NP**	**7-01-001**
Dookiyoon	**NP**	**2-01-001**
Dooley	**prop. noun**	**2-02-002**
Dooley	NP	0-00-000
Dooley	NP-HL	1-01-001

Word	Tag	Frequency
Dooley (cont.):		
Dooleys	NPS	1-01-001
Doolin	**prop. noun**	**7-01-001**
Doolin	NP	6-01-001
Doolin's	NP$	1-01-001
Doolittle	**prop. noun**	**3-01-001**
Doolittle	NP	2-01-001
Doolittle's	NP$	1-01-001
doom	**noun**	**4-03-004**
doom	NN	3-02-003
dooms	NNS	1-01-001
doom	**verb**	**10-05-009**
doomed	VBD	2-02-002
doomed	VBN	8-04-007
doomsday	**NN**	**1-01-001**
door	**noun**	**348-14-141**
door	NN	312-13-124
doors	NNS	35-13-029
doors	NNS-HL	1-01-001
door-frame	**NN**	**1-01-001**
door-fronted	**JJ**	**1-01-001**
door-to-door	**NN**	**1-01-001**
doorbell	**NN**	**2-02-002**
doorkeeper	**NN**	**1-01-001**
doorknob	**NN**	**3-03-003**
doorman	**noun**	**7-04-006**
doorman	NN	4-03-004
doormen	NNS	3-02-003
doorstep	**NN**	**3-01-002**
doorway	**noun**	**18-08-015**
doorway	NN	15-07-012
doorways	NNS	3-03-003
dope	**NN**	**2-02-002**
dope	**verb**	**1-01-001**
doped	VBN	1-01-001
dope-ridden	**JJ**	**1-01-001**
Doppler	**NP**	**1-01-001**
Dora	**NP**	**2-02-002**
Dorado	**NP**	**4-02-002**
Doran	**NP**	**2-01-001**
Dorcas	**NP**	**1-01-001**
Doren	**prop. noun**	**1-01-001**
Dorens	NPS	1-01-001
Dorenzo	**NP**	**1-01-001**
Doria	**NP**	**2-02-002**
Doric	**JJ**	**4-02-002**
Doris	**prop. noun**	**6-04-004**
Doris	NP	5-04-004
Doris'	NP$	1-01-001
dormant	**adjective**	**5-04-004**
dormant	JJ	4-04-004
dormant	JJ-HL	1-01-001
dormitory	**noun**	**6-05-006**
dormitory	NN	2-02-002
dormitories	NNS	4-03-004
Dorothy	**NP**	**3-03-003**
Dorr	**NP**	**3-01-001**
Dorset	**prop. noun**	**8-01-001**
Dorset	NP	4-01-001
Dorset	NP-TL	4-01-001
Dorsey	**NP**	**1-01-001**
Dos	**NP**	**1-01-001**
dosage	**noun**	**8-01-002**
dosage	NN	4-01-001
dosages	NNS	4-01-002
dose	**noun**	**24-08-013**
dose	NN	11-07-009
doses	NNS	13-05-006
dose	**verb**	**2-01-001**
dosed	VBN	2-01-001
Dostoevsky	**prop. noun**	**3-02-002**
Dostoevsky	NP	2-02-002
Dostoevsky's	NP$	1-01-001
dot	**noun**	**22-06-010**
dot	NN	11-05-007
dots	NNS	11-04-006
dot	**verb**	**5-04-005**
dot	VB	2-02-002
dotted	VBN	2-02-002
dotting	VBG	1-01-001
dote	**verb**	**2-02-002**
doting	VBG	2-02-002
dotting	**NN**	**1-01-001**
double	**adjective**	**39-12-031**
double	JJ	36-12-029
double-	JJ	1-01-001
double	JJ-HL	1-01-001
Double	JJ-TL	1-01-001
double	**noun**	**14-02-004**

Word	Tag	Frequency
double (cont.):		
double	NN	10-02-004
doubles	NNS	4-01-003
double	**RB**	**3-02-003**
double	**verb**	**25-08-023**
double	VB	5-04-005
doubles	VBZ	1-01-001
doubles	VBZ-HL	1-01-001
doubled	VBD	4-02-004
doubled	VBN	7-03-007
doubling	VBG	7-05-006
double-bogey	**verb**	**1-01-001**
double-bogeyed	VBD	1-01-001
double-breasted	**JJ**	**2-02-002**
double-cross	**verb**	**1-01-001**
double-crossed	VBD	1-01-001
double-crosser	**NN**	**1-01-001**
double-crossing	**NN**	**1-01-001**
double-entendre	**NN**	**2-01-001**
Double-Figure	**NP**	**1-01-001**
double-glaze	**VB**	**1-01-001**
double-header	**noun**	**2-01-002**
double-header	NN	1-01-001
doubleheader	NN	1-01-001
double-married	**JJ**	**1-01-001**
double-meaning	**NN**	**1-01-001**
double-stage	**noun**	**3-01-001**
double-stage	NN	2-01-001
double-stage	NN-HL	1-01-001
double-step	**noun**	**3-01-001**
double-step	NN	2-01-001
double-step	NN-HL	1-01-001
double-strength	**JJ**	**1-01-001**
double-talk	**NN**	**1-01-001**
double-valued	**JJ**	**2-01-001**
double-wall	**noun**	**4-01-001**
double-wall	NN	3-01-001
double-wall	NN-HL	1-01-001
doubloon	**NN**	**1-01-001**
doubly	**QL**	**2-02-002**
doubly	**RB**	**2-02-002**
doubt	**noun**	**115-15-093**
doubt	NN	97-15-083
doubte	NN	1-01-001
doubt	NN-HL	1-01-001
doubts	NNS	16-09-015
doubt	**verb**	**28-13-025**
doubt	VB	16-11-015
doubted	VBD	9-05-009
doubting	VBG	3-03-003
doubtful	**adjective**	**22-10-021**
doubtful	JJ	21-10-020
Doubtful	JJ-TL	1-01-001
doubtfully	**RB**	**2-02-002**
doubtingly	**RB**	**1-01-001**
doubtless	**RB**	**13-08-012**
douce	**foreign**	**1-01-001**
douce	FW-JJ	0-00-000
Douce	FW-JJ-TL	1-01-001
Doug	**NP**	**1-01-001**
dough	**NN**	**13-06-006**
Doughnuttery	**NP**	**1-01-001**
Douglas	**prop. noun**	**23-06-015**
Douglas	NP	19-06-015
Douglas	NP-TL	4-01-001
Douglass	**NP**	**9-01-001**
dour	**JJ**	**2-02-002**
dourly	**RB**	**1-01-001**
douse	**verb**	**1-01-001**
doused	VBD	1-01-001
Dousman	**NP**	**2-01-001**
dove	**noun**	**4-03-003**
dove	NN	3-02-002
doves	NNS	1-01-001
Dove	**NP**	**1-01-001**
Dover	**prop. noun**	**4-02-002**
Dover	NP	3-02-002
Dover	NP-TL	1-01-001
dovetail	**VB**	**1-01-001**
Dow	**NP**	**4-03-003**
Dow-Jones	**NP**	**1-01-001**
dowager	**noun**	**1-01-001**
dowager	NN	0-00-000
Dowager	NN-TL	1-01-001
dowel	**NN**	**2-01-001**
dowel	**verb**	**1-01-001**
doweling	VBG	1-01-001
dower	**NN**	**1-01-001**
Dowex-2-chloride	**NP**	**6-01-001**

Word	Tag	Frequency
Dowguard	**NP**	**1-01-001**
Dowling	**prop. noun**	**1-01-001**
Dowling's	NP$	1-01-001
down	**IN**	**192-13-113**
down	**JJ**	**1-01-001**
down	**noun**	**4-02-003**
down	NN	1-01-001
downs	NNS	3-02-002
down	**adv./part.**	**698-15-280**
down	RP	695-15-278
down	RP-HL	1-01-001
Down	RP-TL	2-02-002
down	**verb**	**8-06-007**
down	VB	2-02-002
downed	VBD	2-02-002
downed	VBN	3-03-003
downing	VBG	1-01-001
Down	**prop. noun**	**1-01-001**
Down	NP	0-00-000
Down	NP-TL	1-01-001
down-and-out	**JJ**	**1-01-001**
down-and-outer	**noun**	**1-01-001**
down-and-outers	NNS	1-01-001
down-payment	**noun**	**1-01-001**
down-payments	NNS	1-01-001
down-to-earth	**JJ**	**5-04-005**
downbeat	**noun**	**1-01-001**
downbeat	NN	0-00-000
Downbeat	NN-TL	1-01-001
downcast	**JJ**	**2-02-002**
Downers	**prop. noun**	**1-01-001**
Downers	NP	0-00-000
Downers	NP-HL	1-01-001
downfall	**noun**	**5-05-005**
downfall	NN	4-04-004
Downfall	NN-HL	1-01-001
downgrade	**verb**	**4-03-004**
downgrade	VB	1-01-001
downgraded	VBN	3-03-003
downhill	**JJ**	**2-02-002**
downhill	**RB**	**4-04-004**
downpayment	**NN**	**1-01-001**
downpour	**NN**	**3-03-003**
downright	**JJ**	**3-03-003**
downright	**QL**	**6-04-005**
Downs	**NP**	**2-02-002**
downstairs	**NN**	**1-01-001**
downstairs	**RB**	**11-04-011**
downstream	**JJ**	**1-01-001**
downstream	**RB**	**4-04-004**
downtalking	**JJ**	**1-01-001**
downtown	**adv. noun**	**41-09-017**
downtown	NR	40-09-017
downtown	NR-HL	1-01-001
downtrend	**NN**	**1-01-001**
downtrodden	**JJ**	**2-02-002**
downturn	**NN**	**2-02-002**
downward	**adjective**	**8-05-007**
downward	JJ	7-05-007
downward	JJ-HL	1-01-001
downward	**RB**	**8-07-008**
downwind	**JJ**	**1-01-001**
downwind	**RB**	**2-01-001**
dowry	**NN**	**2-02-002**
Doxiadis	**NP**	**1-01-001**
Doyle	**prop. noun**	**6-03-005**
Doyle	NP	4-03-003
Doyle's	NP$	2-01-002
doze	**verb**	**8-04-008**
dozed	VBD	4-03-004
dozed	VBN	1-01-001
dozing	VBG	3-02-003
dozen	**noun**	**63-13-056**
dozen	NN	52-12-047
dozens	NNS	11-07-010
drab	**JJ**	**5-04-004**
drab-haired	**JJ**	**1-01-001**
Draco	**NP**	**1-01-001**
draft	**noun**	**26-09-013**
draft	NN	15-09-010
Draft	NN-TL	8-02-002
drafts	NNS	3-02-002
draft	**verb**	**10-05-010**
draft	VB	1-01-001
drafted	VBD	2-02-002
drafted	VBN	3-02-003
drafting	VBG	4-03-004
draftee	**noun**	**2-02-002**
draftee	NN	1-01-001
draftee (cont.):		
draftees	NNS	1-01-001
drafter	**noun**	**1-01-001**
drafters	NNS	1-01-001
drafting	**NN**	**2-01-002**
drafty	**JJ**	**2-02-002**
drag	**NN**	**5-04-005**
drag	**verb**	**40-11-030**
drag	VB	10-06-010
dragged	VBD	8-04-007
dragged	VBN	7-06-007
dragging	VBG	15-06-014
dragger	**NN**	**1-01-001**
dragnet	**noun**	**2-02-002**
dragnet	NN	1-01-001
Dragnet	NN-TL	1-01-001
dragon	**noun**	**3-03-003**
dragon	NN	1-01-001
dragons	NNS	1-01-001
Dragons	NNS-TL	1-01-001
Dragonetti	**NP**	**1-01-001**
dragoon	**verb**	**1-01-001**
dragooned	VBD	1-01-001
Dragoslav	**NP**	**1-01-001**
drain	**noun**	**15-04-005**
drain	NN	11-04-005
drains	NNS	4-01-001
drain	**verb**	**16-05-011**
drain	VB	7-03-004
drains	VBZ	1-01-001
drained	VBD	3-02-003
drained	VBN	4-03-004
draining	VBG	1-01-001
drainage	**NN**	**13-07-009**
draining	**NN**	**2-02-002**
Drake	**NP**	**2-02-002**
dram	**NN**	**1-01-001**
drama	**noun**	**49-11-035**
drama	NN	43-11-030
dramas	NNS	6-04-006
drama-filled	**JJ**	**1-01-001**
dramatic	**JJ**	**63-12-049**
dramatical	**JJ**	**1-01-001**
dramatically	**RB**	**10-05-008**
dramatics	**NN**	**1-01-001**
dramatist	**noun**	**3-03-003**
dramatist	NN	2-02-002
dramatists	NNS	1-01-001
dramatization	**NN**	**1-01-001**
dramatize	**verb**	**6-04-005**
dramatize	VB	3-03-003
dramatizes	VBZ	2-02-002
dramatizing	VBG	1-01-001
drape	**noun**	**1-01-001**
drapes	NNS	1-01-001
drape	**verb**	**9-07-009**
draped	VBD	3-03-003
draped	VBN	6-06-006
draper	**noun**	**3-02-002**
draper	NN	1-01-001
drapers	NNS	2-01-001
Draper	**NP**	**3-01-001**
drapery	**noun**	**6-04-005**
drapery	NN	2-02-002
draperies	NNS	4-03-004
drastic	**JJ**	**11-06-009**
drastically	**QL**	**2-01-001**
drastically	**RB**	**8-07-008**
draught	**noun**	**4-04-004**
draught	NN	2-02-002
draughts	NNS	2-02-002
draughty	**JJ**	**1-01-001**
draw	**NN**	**10-05-005**
draw	**verb**	**222-15-145**
draw	VB	46-13-040
draws	VBZ	14-09-013
drew	VBD	63-10-050
drewe	VBD	1-01-001
drawn	VBN	70-14-065
drawing	VBG	27-10-026
drawin'	VBG	1-01-001
draw-file	**VB**	**2-01-001**
drawback	**NN**	**2-02-002**
drawbridge	**NN**	**1-01-001**
drawer	**noun**	**13-08-011**
drawer	NN	8-05-008
drawers	NNS	5-05-005
drawing	**adjective**	**1-01-001**
drawing	JJ	0-00-000

Word	Tag	Count
drawing (cont.):		
Drawing	JJ-TL	1-01-001
drawing	**noun**	**33-09-024**
drawing	NN	12-04-011
drawings	NNS	21-07-014
drawing-room	**noun**	**3-02-002**
drawing-room	NN	2-02-002
drawing-rooms	NNS	1-01-001
drawl	**NN**	**2-02-002**
drawl	**verb**	**4-03-004**
drawled	VBD	3-02-003
drawling	VBG	1-01-001
drawn-back	**JJ**	**1-01-001**
drawn-out	**JJ**	**1-01-001**
dread	**JJ**	**1-01-001**
dread	**NN**	**8-06-007**
dread	**verb**	**2-02-002**
dreaded	VBD	1-01-001
dreaded	VBN	1-01-001
dreadful	**JJ**	**10-06-010**
dreadfully	**RB**	**1-01-001**
Dreadnought	**NP**	**6-01-001**
dream	**noun**	**88-15-040**
dream	NN	48-10-021
dream	NN-HL	1-01-001
Dream	NN-TL	11-03-003
dreams	NNS	26-12-017
Dreams	NNS-TL	2-01-002
dream	**verb**	**45-10-035**
dream	VB	11-05-011
dreams	VBZ	2-02-002
dreamed	VBD	7-06-006
dreamt	VBD	1-01-001
dreamed	VBN	12-08-012
dreaming	VBG	11-06-010
dreamin	VBG	1-01-001
dream-ridden	**JJ**	**1-01-001**
Dreamboat	**NP**	**1-01-001**
dreamer	**NN**	**2-02-002**
dreamless	**JJ**	**1-01-001**
dreamlessly	**RB**	**1-01-001**
dreamlike	**JJ**	**2-01-002**
dreamy	**JJ**	**4-03-004**
dreariness	**NN**	**1-01-001**
dreary	**JJ**	**6-05-006**
Dred	**NP**	**1-01-001**
dreg	**noun**	**4-03-003**
dregs	NNS	4-03-003
Dreiser	**prop. noun**	**3-02-003**
Dreiser	NP	1-01-001
Dreiser's	NP$	1-01-001
Dreisers	NPS	1-01-001
drench	**verb**	**1-01-001**
drenched	VBN	1-01-001
Dresbach	**prop. noun**	**5-01-001**
Dresbach	NP	1-01-001
Dresbach's	NP$	2-01-001
Dresbachs	NPS	1-01-001
Dresbachs'	NPS$	1-01-001
dress	**noun**	**63-13-041**
dress	NN	53-11-035
dresses	NNS	10-05-009
dress	**verb**	**67-10-040**
dress	VB	14-06-011
dressed	VBD	10-05-010
dressed	VBN	26-07-020
dressing	VBG	17-08-010
dresser	**noun**	**3-02-002**
dresser	NN	1-01-001
dressers	NNS	2-01-001
dressing	**noun**	**6-04-005**
dressing	NN	5-04-004
dressings	NNS	1-01-001
dressy	**JJ**	**2-01-001**
Drew	**prop. noun**	**5-02-002**
Drew	NP	2-02-002
Drew	NP-TL	3-01-001
Drexel	**prop. noun**	**11-02-003**
Drexel	NP	2-01-001
Drexel	NP-TL	8-02-002
Drexel's	NP$	1-01-001
drib-drool	**NN**	**1-01-001**
dribble	**verb**	**1-01-001**
dribbled	VBD	1-01-001
dried-out	**JJ**	**1-01-001**
dried-up	**JJ**	**1-01-001**
drier	**JJR**	**2-02-002**
drift	**noun**	**19-04-008**
drift	NN	15-04-006
drift (cont.):		
drifts	NNS	4-03-003
drift	**verb**	**27-11-020**
drift	VB	3-02-003
drifts	VBZ	1-01-001
Drifts	VBZ-TL	1-01-001
drifted	VBD	5-04-005
drifted	VBN	4-04-004
drifting	VBG	11-06-009
driftin	VBG	1-01-001
driftin'	VBG	1-01-001
drill	**noun**	**21-05-006**
drill	NN	17-03-004
drills	NNS	4-03-003
drill	**verb**	**30-05-008**
drill	VB	16-02-003
drilled	VBN	5-02-004
drilling	VBG	7-04-005
drilling	VBG-HL	2-01-001
drilling	**NN**	**1-01-001**
drink	**noun**	**75-11-039**
drink	NN	56-09-032
drinks	NNS	18-07-012
drinks	NNS-HL	1-01-001
drink	**verb**	**93-11-054**
drink	VB	25-07-018
drink	VB-NC	1-01-001
drinks	VBZ	3-02-003
drank	VBD	19-06-015
drunk	VBD	1-01-001
druncke	VBD	1-01-001
drinking	VBG	35-10-027
a-drinking	VBG	1-01-001
drinking	VBG-NC	7-01-001
drinker	**noun**	**5-04-004**
drinker	NN	3-02-002
drinkers	NNS	2-02-002
Drinkhouse	**NP**	**1-01-001**
drinking	**NN**	**6-04-004**
drip	**noun**	**2-02-002**
drip	NN	1-01-001
drip-	NN-HL	1-01-001
drip	**verb**	**14-06-012**
drips	VBZ	1-01-001
dripped	VBD	5-03-004
dripped	VBN	1-01-001
dripping	VBG	7-05-006
drive	**noun**	**60-12-043**
drive	NN	48-12-038
Drive	NN-TL	10-05-006
Drive	NN-TL-HL	1-01-001
drives	NNS	1-01-001
drive	**verb**	**203-14-122**
drive	VB	46-14-043
drahve	VB	1-01-001
drives	VBZ	5-04-004
drove	VBD	58-10-046
driven	VBN	44-11-031
drove	VBN	2-01-001
driving	VBG	47-11-040
drive-in	**JJ**	**1-01-001**
drive-in	**noun**	**4-03-003**
drive-in	NN	3-02-002
Drive-in	NN-TL	1-01-001
drive-yourself	**JJ**	**1-01-001**
driver	**noun**	**79-12-028**
driver	NN	48-10-019
Driver	NN-TL	1-01-001
driver's	NN$	5-02-003
drivers	NNS	24-09-013
drivers'	NNS$	1-01-001
driveway	**noun**	**15-08-013**
driveway	NN	14-08-012
driveways	NNS	1-01-001
driving	**noun**	**6-04-005**
driving	NN	5-03-004
Driving	NN-TL	1-01-001
drizzle	**NN**	**5-02-002**
drizzle	**verb**	**2-01-001**
drizzling	VBG	2-01-001
drizzly	**JJ**	**1-01-001**
dromozoa	**NNS**	**5-01-001**
dromozootic	**JJ**	**1-01-001**
drone	**noun**	**5-04-004**
drone	NN	3-03-003
drones	NNS	2-01-001
Dronk	**prop. noun**	**3-01-001**
Dronk	NP	2-01-001
Dronk's	NP$	1-01-001

Word	Tag	Count
droop	**verb**	**3-03-003**
droop	VB	1-01-001
drooped	VBD	1-01-001
drooping	VBG	1-01-001
drop	**JJ**	**1-01-001**
drop	**noun**	**34-10-025**
drop	NN	24-10-020
drops	NNS	10-06-006
drop	**verb**	**159-15-105**
drop	VB	34-12-032
drops	VBZ	8-04-007
dropped	VBD	76-15-060
dropped	VBN	25-11-024
dropping	VBG	16-09-015
drop-block	**NN**	**1-01-001**
droplet	**noun**	**3-01-002**
droplets	NNS	3-01-002
dropout	**noun**	**3-02-002**
dropouts	NNS	3-02-002
dropping	**noun**	**1-01-001**
droppings	NNS	1-01-001
dross	**NN**	**4-02-004**
drought	**noun**	**8-04-005**
drought	NN	5-03-004
drouth	NN	1-01-001
droughts	NNS	2-02-002
drought-seared	**JJ**	**1-01-001**
drove	**noun**	**3-01-002**
drove	NN	2-01-001
droves	NNS	1-01-001
drover	**noun**	**1-01-001**
drovers	NNS	1-01-001
drown	**verb**	**14-10-014**
drown	VB	3-03-003
drowns	VBZ	1-01-001
drowned	VBD	4-04-004
drowned	VBN	2-02-002
drowning	VBG	4-04-004
drowse	**verb**	**2-02-002**
drowsed	VBD	1-01-001
drowsing	VBG	1-01-001
drowsily	**RB**	**1-01-001**
drowsy	**JJ**	**1-01-001**
drudgery	**NN**	**1-01-001**
drug	**noun**	**69-06-014**
drug	NN	20-06-009
Drug	NN-TL	4-03-003
drug's	NN$	1-01-001
drug's	NN$-HL	16-01-001
drugs	NNS	27-04-008
drugs	NNS-HL	1-01-001
drug	**verb**	**6-03-005**
drugged	VBN	5-03-005
drugging	VBG	1-01-001
Druggan-Lake	**NP**	**1-01-001**
drugless	**JJ**	**1-01-001**
drugstore	**noun**	**6-01-002**
drugstore	NN	5-01-001
drugstores	NNS	1-01-001
Druid	**NP**	**1-01-001**
drum	**noun**	**26-09-019**
drum	NN	10-07-010
Drum	NN-TL	1-01-001
drums	NNS	15-06-009
drum	**verb**	**6-05-006**
drummed	VBD	2-01-002
drumming	VBG	4-04-004
drumlin	**NN**	**1-01-001**
drummer	**noun**	**4-03-004**
drummer	NN	2-02-002
drummer's	NN$	1-01-001
drummers	NNS	1-01-001
drunk	**adjective**	**26-08-020**
drunk	JJ	24-08-019
druncke	JJ	1-01-001
Drunk	JJ	1-01-001
drunk	**noun**	**13-06-009**
drunk	NN	10-06-008
drunks	NNS	3-02-003
drunk-and-disorderly	**noun**	**1-01-001**
drunk-and-disorderlies	NNS	1-01-001
drunkard	**noun**	**7-04-006**
drunkard	NN	3-03-003
drunkard's	NN$	0-00-000
Drunkard's	NN$-TL	1-01-001
drunkards	NNS	3-02-002
drunken	**JJ**	**6-04-006**
drunkenly	**RB**	**4-04-004**
drunkenness	**NN**	**4-03-004**

Word	Tag	Count
drunker	**JJR**	**2-02-002**
Drury	**prop. noun**	**3-02-002**
Drury	NP	0-00-000
Drury	NP-TL	3-02-002
druther	**RB**	**1-01-001**
dry	**adjective**	**53-10-039**
dry	JJ	52-10-039
dry	JJ-HL	1-01-001
dry	**verb**	**72-12-034**
dry	VB	15-05-008
dries	VBZ	1-01-001
dried	VBD	6-05-006
dried	VBN	21-09-017
dried	VBN-HL	1-01-001
drying	VBG	24-06-011
dryin'	VBG	2-01-001
drying	VBG-HL	2-01-001
dry-dock	**NN**	**1-01-001**
dry-eyed	**JJ**	**1-01-001**
dry-gulching	**noun**	**1-01-001**
dry-gulching	NN	0-00-000
dry-gulchin'	NN	1-01-001
dryer	**noun**	**8-03-003**
dryer	NN	2-01-001
drier	NN	1-01-001
dryer	NN-HL	2-01-001
dryers	NNS	0-00-000
driers	NNS	3-01-001
Dryfoos	**prop. noun**	**3-01-001**
Dryfoos	NP	2-01-001
Dryfoos'	NP$	1-01-001
drying	**NN**	**3-02-002**
dryly	**RB**	**4-03-004**
dryness	**NN**	**2-02-002**
drywall	**NN**	**3-01-001**
drywall	**VB**	**1-01-001**
du	**foreign**	**10-05-008**
du	FW-IN+AT	2-01-002
Du	FW-IN+AT-TL	8-05-006
Du	**prop. noun**	**60-07-009**
Du	NP	58-06-007
du	NP	1-01-001
Du	NP-TL	1-01-001
dual	**JJ**	**9-05-009**
dual-channel	**JJ**	**1-01-001**
dual-ladder	**JJ**	**1-01-001**
dual-road-up	**JJ**	**1-01-001**
dualism	**NN**	**1-01-001**
duality	**noun**	**1-01-001**
dualities	NNS	1-01-001
Duane	**NP**	**1-01-001**
dub	**verb**	**4-03-004**
dubbed	VBD	1-01-001
dubbed	VBN	3-03-003
Dubin	**NP**	**1-01-001**
dubious	**JJ**	**7-05-007**
Dublin	**NP**	**2-02-002**
Dubois	**NP**	**1-01-001**
Dubovskoi	**NP**	**1-01-001**
duces	**FW-VB**	**1-01-001**
duchess	**noun**	**1-01-001**
duchess	NN	0-00-000
Duchess	NN-TL	1-01-001
duck	**noun**	**6-05-006**
duck	NN	2-02-002
ducks	NNS	4-03-004
duck	**verb**	**15-07-014**
duck	VB	7-05-006
ducked	VBD	5-04-005
ducking	VBG	3-02-003
Duclos	**NP**	**7-02-002**
duct	**noun**	**7-02-003**
duct	NN	1-01-001
ducts	NNS	6-02-003
ductwork	**NN**	**1-01-001**
dud	**noun**	**2-02-002**
dud	NN	1-01-001
duds	NNS	1-01-001
Dudley	**NP**	**1-01-001**
duds	**pl. noun**	**1-01-001**
duds	NNS	0-00-000
duds'd	NNS+MD	1-01-001
due	**adjective**	**116-13-072**
due	JJ	112-13-071
due	JJ-HL	3-02-003
Due	JJ-TL	1-01-001
due	**NN**	**7-06-007**
due	**RB**	**19-07-017**
duel	**noun**	**6-02-003**

Word	Tag	Frequency
duel (cont.):		
duel	NN	3-01-002
Duel	NN-TL	2-01-001
duels	NNS	1-01-001
duel	**verb**	**2-01-001**
dueling	VBG	2-01-001
duet	**noun**	**2-02-002**
duet	NN	1-01-001
duets	NNS	1-01-001
duffel	**NN**	**3-01-001**
duffer	**noun**	**3-01-001**
duffer	NN	1-01-001
duffers	NNS	2-01-001
Duffy	**NP**	**2-02-002**
Dufresne	**prop. noun**	**2-01-001**
Dufresne	NP	1-01-001
Dufresne's	NP$	1-01-001
Dugan	**NP**	**2-01-001**
dugout	**NN**	**7-01-001**
Duhagon	**NP**	**1-01-001**
duke	**noun**	**12-06-008**
duke	NN	2-01-001
Duke	NN-TL	6-03-003
duke's	NN$	1-01-001
Duke's	NN$-TL	1-01-001
dukes	NNS	0-00-000
Dukes	NNS-TL	2-02-002
Duke	**NP**	**3-02-002**
dulcet	**JJ**	**1-01-001**
dull	**adjective**	**27-10-026**
dull	JJ	26-10-025
dull	JJ-NC	1-01-001
dull	**verb**	**4-04-004**
dulls	VBZ	1-01-001
dulled	VBD	1-01-001
dulled	VBN	2-02-002
dull-gray	**JJ**	**1-01-001**
duller	**JJR**	**2-02-002**
Dulles	**prop. noun**	**10-04-004**
Dulles	NP	9-04-004
Dulles's	NP$	1-01-001
dullest	**JJT**	**2-02-002**
dullness	**NN**	**1-01-001**
dully	**RB**	**3-02-003**
duly	**RB**	**10-05-007**
Dumas	**NP**	**1-01-001**
dumb	**JJ**	**14-06-009**
dumbbell	**noun**	**3-01-001**
dumbbell	NN	2-01-001
dumbbells	NNS	1-01-001
Dummkopf	**FW-NN**	**1-01-001**
dummy	**JJ**	**3-02-002**
dummy	**noun**	**1-01-001**
dummies	NNS	1-01-001
Dumont	**prop. noun**	**10-02-002**
Dumont	NP	8-02-002
Dumont	NP-TL	2-01-001
dump	**noun**	**2-02-002**
dump	NN	1-01-001
dumps	NNS	1-01-001
dump	**verb**	**14-06-013**
dump	VB	3-03-003
dumped	VBD	7-03-006
dumped	VBN	2-02-002
dumping	VBG	2-01-002
dumping	**NN**	**2-02-002**
Dumpty	**NP**	**1-01-001**
dun	**NN**	**1-01-001**
Dunbar	**prop. noun**	**4-02-002**
Dunbar	NP	2-01-001
Dunbar	NP-TL	2-02-002
Duncan	**NP**	**4-01-001**
Dundeen	**NP**	**1-01-001**
dune	**noun**	**9-04-005**
dune	NN	1-01-001
dunes	NNS	7-03-004
dunes	NNS-HL	1-01-001
dung	**noun**	**2-02-002**
dung	NN	1-01-001
Dung	NN-TL	1-01-001
dungeon	**NN**	**2-02-002**
dunk	**VB**	**1-01-001**
Dunkel	**NP**	**2-01-001**
Dunkirk	**NP**	**2-02-002**
Dunlop	**NP**	**1-01-001**
Dunn	**prop. noun**	**7-04-004**
Dunn	NP	6-04-004
Dunn's	NP$	1-01-001
Dunn-Atherton	**NP**	**1-01-001**

Word	Tag	Frequency
Dunne	**NP**	**4-01-001**
Dunston	**NP**	**1-01-001**
dupe	**verb**	**1-01-001**
duped	VBN	1-01-001
duplex	**JJ**	**1-01-001**
duplicable	**JJ**	**1-01-001**
duplicate	**JJ**	**3-02-002**
duplicate	**NN**	**1-01-001**
duplicate	**verb**	**4-04-004**
duplicate	VB	2-02-002
duplicated	VBN	2-02-002
duplication	**NN**	**8-05-006**
Dupont	**prop. noun**	**6-02-002**
Dupont	NP	0-00-000
DuPont	NP	4-01-001
Dupont	NP-HL	1-01-001
Duponts	NPS	1-01-001
Duque	**NP**	**1-01-001**
durability	**NN**	**2-02-002**
durable	**JJ**	**12-07-011**
Durante	**NP**	**2-02-002**
duration	**noun**	**12-06-012**
duration	NN	11-06-011
durations	NNS	1-01-001
Duren	**prop. noun**	**2-01-001**
Duren	NP	1-01-001
Duren	NP-HL	1-01-001
Durer	**NP**	**2-02-002**
duress	**NN**	**1-01-001**
during	**prep.**	**588-15-266**
during	IN	583-15-264
durin'	IN	3-01-001
during	IN-HL	1-01-001
During	IN-TL	1-01-001
Durkheim	**NP**	**3-01-002**
Durkin	**NP**	**2-01-001**
Durlach	**NP**	**1-01-001**
Durocher	**NP**	**1-01-001**
Durrell	**prop. noun**	**1-01-001**
Durrell's	NP$	1-01-001
Durwood	**NP**	**1-01-001**
dusk	**NN**	**9-03-007**
dusky	**JJ**	**2-02-002**
Dussa	**NP**	**1-01-001**
Dusseldorf	**NP**	**3-01-002**
dust	**noun**	**68-13-035**
dust	NN	65-12-033
Dust	NN-TL	2-02-002
dusts	NNS	1-01-001
dust	**verb**	**9-06-008**
dust	VB	3-03-003
dusted	VBN	1-01-001
dusting	VBG	4-03-003
dustin'	VBG	1-01-001
dust-settling	**JJ**	**1-01-001**
dust-swirling	**JJ**	**1-01-001**
dust-thick	**JJ**	**1-01-001**
dustbin	**NN**	**1-01-001**
dusting	**NN**	**2-01-001**
dusty	**JJ**	**16-07-013**
dusty-green	**JJ**	**1-01-001**
dusty-slippered	**JJ**	**1-01-001**
Dutch	**adjective**	**11-04-006**
Dutch	JJ	5-02-002
Dutch	JJ-TL	6-04-005
Dutch	**prop. noun**	**4-03-004**
Dutch	NP	3-02-003
Dutch	NP-TL	1-01-001
Dutchess	**prop. noun**	**2-02-002**
Dutchess	NP	0-00-000
Dutchess	NP-TL	2-02-002
Dutchman	**prop. noun**	**1-01-001**
Dutchman	NP	0-00-000
Dutchman	NP-TL	1-01-001
dutifully	**RB**	**2-02-002**
Dutton	**prop. noun**	**2-02-002**
Dutton	NP	1-01-001
Dutton	NP-TL	1-01-001
duty	**noun**	**95-14-069**
duty	NN	61-14-046
duties	NNS	33-10-026
Duties	NNS-TL	1-01-001
Duverger	**NP**	**1-01-001**
DuVol	**NP**	**1-01-001**
Duyvil	**NP**	**1-01-001**
Dvorak	**NP**	**1-01-001**
dwarf	**noun**	**3-03-003**
dwarf	NN	2-02-002
dwarfs	NNS	1-01-001

dwarf	**verb**	**4-03-004**
dwarf	VB	2-02-002
dwarfs	VBZ	1-01-001
dwarfed	VBN	1-01-001
dwell	**verb**	**15-07-014**
dwell	VB	8-05-007
dwells	VBZ	1-01-001
dwelt	VBD	1-01-001
dwelling	VBG	5-03-005
dweller	**noun**	**4-04-004**
dweller	NN	2-02-002
dwellers	NNS	2-02-002
dwelling	**noun**	**15-07-010**
dwelling	NN	8-05-005
dwellings	NNS	7-04-006
Dwight	**NP**	**12-07-011**
dwindle	**verb**	**8-08-008**
dwindle	VB	2-02-002
dwindled	VBD	2-02-002
dwindling	VBG	4-04-004
Dwor'	**NP**	**1-01-001**
Dwyer	**prop. noun**	**4-01-001**
Dwyer	NP	3-01-001
Dwyer's	NP$	1-01-001
dye	**verb**	**5-04-005**
dyed	VBN	4-03-004
dyeing	VBG	1-01-001
Dyer	**NP**	**3-02-003**
dying	**NN**	**3-03-003**
Dyke	**NP**	**1-01-001**
Dylan	**NP**	**11-02-003**
Dynafac	**NP**	**4-01-001**
dynamic	**JJ**	**20-05-013**
dynamic	**noun**	**5-02-004**
dynamic	NN	1-01-001
dynamics	NNS	4-02-004
dynamical	**JJ**	**1-01-001**
dynamically	**QL**	**1-01-001**
dynamite	**NN**	**5-04-004**
dynamite	**verb**	**1-01-001**
dynamited	VBN	1-01-001
dynamo	**NN**	**2-02-002**
dynast	**noun**	**3-01-001**
dynasts	NNS	0-00-000
Dynasts	NNS-TL	3-01-001
dynastic	**JJ**	**3-02-002**
dynasty	**noun**	**6-02-002**
dynasty	NN	5-01-001
dynasties	NNS	1-01-001
dynode	**noun**	**1-01-001**
dynodes	NNS	1-01-001
dysentery	**NN**	**1-01-001**
dyspeptic	**JJ**	**1-01-001**
dysplasia	**NN**	**1-01-001**
dystopia	**noun**	**10-01-001**
dystopia	NN	2-01-001
dystopias	NNS	8-01-001
dystopian	**JJ**	**7-01-001**
dystrophy	**NN**	**2-02-002**

E

E	**prop. noun**	**23-03-012**
E	NP	13-03-005
E	NP-HL	10-02-009
e.	**adjective**	**1-01-001**
e.	JJ	0-00-000
E.	JJ-TL	1-01-001
E.	**prop. noun**	**85-09-052**
E.	NP	83-09-051
E.	NP-HL	1-01-001
E.	NP-TL	1-01-001
e.g.	**adverb**	**32-07-022**
e.g.	RB	31-07-021
e.g.	RB-HL	1-01-001
E.G.T.	**NP**	**2-01-001**
E.O.	**NP**	**1-01-001**
E.T.	**NP**	**1-01-001**
each	**sing. det.**	**878-15-320**
each	DT	877-15-320
each	DT-HL	1-01-001
Eades	**NP**	**1-01-001**
eager	**JJ**	**27-09-027**
eagerly	**RB**	**13-07-011**
eagerness	**NN**	**3-03-003**
eagle	**noun**	**12-06-007**
eagle	NN	4-04-004
Eagle	NN-TL	1-01-001
eagle's	NN$	0-00-000
Eagle's	NN$-TL	1-01-001
eagles	NNS	1-01-001
Eagles	NNS-TL	5-01-001
ear	**noun**	**67-12-052**
ear	NN	29-10-025
ears	NNS	37-11-032
Ears	NNS	1-01-001
ear-muff	**noun**	**1-01-001**
ear-muffs	NNS	0-00-000
Ear-Muffs	NNS-TL	1-01-001
eardrum	**noun**	**1-01-001**
eardrums	NNS	1-01-001
eared	**JJ**	**1-01-001**
earl	**noun**	**3-02-003**
earl	NN	1-01-001
Earl	NN-TL	2-02-002
Earl	**NP**	**9-03-005**
earlier	**JJR**	**76-12-060**
earlier	**RBR**	**70-12-055**
earliest	**JJT**	**22-09-020**
early	**adjective**	**254-15-159**
early	JJ	241-15-155
early	JJ-HL	2-02-002
early (cont.):		
Early	JJ-TL	11-04-004
early	**RB**	**107-13-089**
Early	**NP**	**5-01-001**
early-morning	**NN**	**1-01-001**
early-season	**NN**	**1-01-001**
earmark	**verb**	**1-01-001**
earmarked	VBN	1-01-001
earn	**verb**	**45-10-033**
earn	VB	15-06-013
earn	VB-HL	1-01-001
earns	VBZ	2-02-002
earned	VBD	9-05-007
earned	VBN	9-07-009
earning	VBG	9-07-009
earned-run	**NN**	**1-01-001**
earnest	**JJ**	**15-09-014**
earnest	**NN**	**3-03-003**
earnestly	**RB**	**13-08-012**
earnestness	**NN**	**3-03-003**
earning	**noun**	**19-05-012**
earnings	NNS	19-05-012
Earp	**NP**	**1-01-001**
earphone	**noun**	**1-01-001**
earphones	NNS	1-01-001
earring	**noun**	**3-02-002**
earrings	NNS	3-02-002
earsplitting	**JJ**	**2-02-002**
earth	**noun**	**167-15-065**
earth	NN	116-14-056
earth	NN-HL	1-01-001
Earth	NN-TL	33-03-006
earth's	NN$	11-07-008
Earth's	NN$-TL	6-02-002
earth-bound	**JJ**	**1-01-001**
earth-touching	**JJ**	**1-01-001**
Earth-week	**noun**	**2-01-001**
Earth-week	NN	1-01-001
Earth-weeks	NNS	1-01-001
earthenware	**NN**	**1-01-001**
earthly	**JJ**	**6-02-003**
Earthman	**prop. noun**	**6-01-003**
Earthmen	NPS	5-01-003
Earthmen's	NPS$	1-01-001
earthmoving	**NN**	**1-01-001**
earthquake	**noun**	**18-03-003**
earthquake	NN	9-02-002
earthquakes	NNS	9-02-002
earthworm	**NN**	**1-01-001**
earthy	**JJ**	**10-06-010**

Word	Tag	Frequency
ease	**noun**	**28-08-024**
ease	NN	27-07-023
ease	NN-HL	1-01-001
ease	**verb**	**25-10-021**
ease	VB	14-09-012
eased	VBD	2-02-002
eased	VBN	6-03-005
easing	VBG	3-02-003
easel	**NN**	**5-02-003**
easement	**noun**	**4-01-001**
easement	NN	2-01-001
easements	NNS	2-01-001
easier	**comp. adj.**	**45-12-032**
easier	JJR	44-12-031
easier	JJR-HL	1-01-001
easier	**RBR**	**6-06-006**
easiest	**JJT**	**7-04-006**
easily	**QL**	**3-02-003**
easily	**RB**	**104-15-083**
east	**adjective**	**98-12-043**
east	JJ	1-01-001
East	JJ-TL	95-11-041
East	JJ-TL-HL	2-02-002
east	**adv. noun**	**85-13-059**
east	NR	41-10-029
East	NR-TL	44-12-033
east-west	**adjective**	**7-03-004**
east-west	JJ	3-01-001
East-West	JJ-TL	4-02-003
Easter	**prop. noun**	**11-07-010**
Easter	NP	10-07-009
Easter	NP-TL	1-01-001
eastern	**adjective**	**32-11-027**
eastern	JJ	11-08-010
Eastern	JJ-TL	21-09-017
easterner	**noun**	**1-01-001**
easterners	NNS	0-00-000
Easterners	NNS-TL	1-01-001
Easthampton	**NP**	**1-01-001**
Eastland	**NP**	**1-01-001**
Eastman	**NP**	**1-01-001**
eastward	**RB**	**4-04-004**
Eastwick	**prop. noun**	**5-01-001**
Eastwick	NP	1-01-001
Eastwick	NP-TL	4-01-001
easy	**JJ**	**111-15-095**
easy	**RB**	**13-06-010**
easy-to-operate	**JJ**	**1-01-001**
easy-to-reach	**JJ**	**1-01-001**
easy-to-spot	**JJ**	**1-01-001**
easygoing	**adjective**	**2-02-002**
easygoing	JJ	1-01-001
easy-going	JJ	1-01-001
eat	**verb**	**122-14-077**
eat	VB	58-13-041
eat	VB-NC	2-01-001
Eat	VB-TL	1-01-001
eats	VBZ	2-02-002
ate	VBD	16-06-013
et	VBD	1-01-001
eaten	VBN	12-08-011
eating	VBG	29-11-024
eating	VBG-HL	1-01-001
eatable	**JJ**	**1-01-001**
eatable	**noun**	**1-01-001**
eatables	NNS	1-01-001
eater	**noun**	**1-01-001**
eaters	NNS	1-01-001
eating	**noun**	**3-02-003**
eating	NN	2-01-002
eatings	NNS	1-01-001
Eaton	**NP**	**2-01-001**
eats	**noun**	**1-01-001**
eats	NN	0-00-000
Eats	NN-TL	1-01-001
eave	**NN**	**1-01-001**
ebb	**verb**	**4-04-004**
ebb	VB	1-01-001
ebbs	VBZ	1-01-001
ebbing	VBG	2-02-002
Ebbetts	**prop. noun**	**1-01-001**
Ebbetts	NP	0-00-000
Ebbetts	NP-TL	1-01-001
Eben	**NP**	**1-01-001**
Eber	**NP**	**1-01-001**
ebony	**NN**	**3-01-001**
Ebony	**NP**	**1-01-001**
ebullient	**JJ**	**3-03-003**
eccentric	**JJ**	**10-04-008**
eccentric	**noun**	**3-02-003**
eccentric	NN	1-01-001
eccentrics	NNS	2-02-002
eccentricity	**noun**	**5-04-005**
eccentricity	NN	4-03-004
eccentricities	NNS	1-01-001
ecclesiastical	**adjective**	**9-04-008**
ecclesiastical	JJ	8-03-007
Ecclesiastical	JJ-TL	1-01-001
echelon	**noun**	**3-01-001**
echelon	NN	2-01-001
echelons	NNS	1-01-001
echo	**noun**	**15-08-014**
echo	NN	6-03-006
Echo	NN-TL	1-01-001
echoes	NNS	8-07-008
echo	**verb**	**12-09-012**
echo	VB	3-03-003
echoed	VBD	7-06-007
echoing	VBG	2-02-002
Eckart	**NP**	**1-01-001**
Eckenfelder	**NP**	**2-01-001**
eclat	**NN**	**1-01-001**
eclectic	**JJ**	**3-02-003**
eclectically	**RB**	**1-01-001**
eclipse	**noun**	**6-03-005**
eclipse	NN	2-02-002
eclipses	NNS	4-03-003
eclipse	**verb**	**2-02-002**
eclipsed	VBD	1-01-001
eclipsing	VBG	1-01-001
ecliptic	**NN**	**3-02-002**
ecole	**foreign**	**1-01-001**
ecole	FW-NN	0-00-000
Ecole	FW-NN-TL	1-01-001
ecological	**JJ**	**2-02-002**
economic	**adjective**	**243-11-086**
economic	JJ	222-10-082
economic	JJ-HL	1-01-001
Economic	JJ-TL	20-05-010
economical	**JJ**	**22-04-016**
economically	**RB**	**11-07-010**
economics	**noun**	**17-07-016**
economics	NN	13-07-013
Economics	NN-TL	4-02-003
economist	**noun**	**12-05-011**
economist	NN	6-03-005
economist's	NN$	1-01-001
economists	NNS	5-04-005
economize	**verb**	**5-03-004**
economize	VB	3-02-003
economizing	VBG	2-02-002
economy	**JJ**	**1-01-001**
economy	**noun**	**85-09-051**
economy	NN	78-09-049
economies	NNS	7-03-006
ecstasy	**NN**	**6-04-006**
ecstatic	**JJ**	**4-04-004**
Ecuador	**NP**	**1-01-001**
ecumenical	**adjective**	**29-02-002**
ecumenical	JJ	26-02-002
ecumenical	JJ-HL	2-02-002
Ecumenical	JJ-TL	1-01-001
ecumenicist	**noun**	**1-01-001**
ecumenicists	NNS	1-01-001
ecumenist	**noun**	**2-01-001**
ecumenist	NN	1-01-001
ecumenists	NNS	1-01-001
Ed	**NP**	**13-05-009**
Eddie	**prop. noun**	**31-06-008**
Eddie	NP	30-06-008
Eddie's	NP$	1-01-001
eddy	**noun**	**1-01-001**
eddies	NNS	0-00-000
Eddies	NNS-TL	1-01-001
Eddy	**prop. noun**	**2-01-001**
Eddy	NP	1-01-001
Eddy	NP-TL	1-01-001
Eddyman	**NP**	**1-01-001**
edema	**NN**	**2-01-001**
edematous	**JJ**	**1-01-001**
Eden	**NP**	**9-06-006**
edentulous	**JJ**	**1-01-001**
Edgar	**NP**	**2-02-002**
Edgardo	**NP**	**1-01-001**
edge	**noun**	**114-13-071**
edge	NN	76-13-055
Edge	NN-TL	1-01-001
edges	NNS	37-10-021

Word	Tag	Frequency
edge	**verb**	**12-06-007**
edge	VB	1-01-001
edged	VBD	7-04-004
edging	VBG	4-03-003
Edgerton	**prop. noun**	**1-01-001**
Edgerton's	NP$	1-01-001
Edgewater	**prop. noun**	**2-02-002**
Edgewater	NP	0-00-000
Edgewater	NP-TL	2-02-002
edgewise	**RB**	**1-01-001**
edging	**NN**	**1-01-001**
edgy	**JJ**	**2-02-002**
edible	**JJ**	**5-02-002**
edifice	**NN**	**3-01-002**
edify	**verb**	**2-02-002**
edified	VBD	1-01-001
edifying	VBG	1-01-001
Edison	**prop. noun**	**4-02-002**
Edison	NP	3-02-002
Edison's	NP$	1-01-001
edit	**verb**	**12-05-008**
edit	VB	2-01-002
edited	VBD	1-01-001
edited	VBN	6-03-003
editing	VBG	3-03-003
Edith	**NP**	**4-03-004**
editing	**NN**	**2-02-002**
edition	**noun**	**47-09-020**
edition	NN	36-09-015
Edition	NN-TL	1-01-001
editions	NNS	9-04-006
Editions	NNS-TL	1-01-001
editor	**noun**	**100-13-032**
editor	NN	44-12-023
ed.	NN	1-01-001
editor	NN-HL	33-01-003
editor's	NN$	4-03-003
editors	NNS	18-05-012
editorial	**JJ**	**4-04-004**
editorial	**noun**	**48-06-022**
editorial	NN	38-06-016
editorials	NNS	10-05-009
editorialist	**NN**	**1-01-001**
editorially	**RB**	**2-01-002**
editorship	**NN**	**1-01-001**
Edmonia	**NP**	**1-01-001**
Edmund	**NP**	**2-02-002**
Edna	**NP**	**3-03-003**
Eduard	**NP**	**1-01-001**
educate	**verb**	**31-11-025**
educate	VB	7-06-007
educated	VBN	21-10-017
educating	VBG	3-03-003
education	**noun**	**215-12-069**
education	NN	174-12-063
education	NN-HL	4-02-003
Education	NN-TL	36-07-019
educations	NNS	1-01-001
educational	**adjective**	**70-09-036**
educational	JJ	65-09-034
educational	JJ-HL	2-02-002
Educational	JJ-TL	3-02-003
educator	**noun**	**17-05-006**
educator	NN	10-03-003
educator's	NN$	1-01-001
educators	NNS	6-04-005
Edward	**prop. noun**	**53-07-024**
Edward	NP	41-06-022
Ed.	NP	2-01-001
Edw	NP	1-01-001
Edward	NP-TL	4-03-003
Edward's	NP$	5-01-001
Edwardes	**NP**	**1-01-001**
Edwards	**NP**	**3-03-003**
Edwin	**NP**	**11-07-011**
Edwina	**NP**	**1-01-001**
Edythe	**prop. noun**	**16-01-001**
Edythe	NP	14-01-001
Edythe's	NP$	2-01-001
eel	**NN**	**2-01-001**
eerie	**JJ**	**2-02-002**
eerily	**RB**	**2-02-002**
efface	**verb**	**1-01-001**
effaces	VBZ	1-01-001
effect	**noun**	**307-15-158**
effect	NN	197-15-126
ee-faket	NN	1-01-001
effects	NNS	106-12-063
affects	NNS	1-01-001

Word	Tag	Frequency
effect (cont.):		
effects	NNS-HL	2-02-002
effect	**verb**	**32-09-027**
effect	VB	16-08-015
effecte	VB	1-01-001
effected	VBD	1-01-001
effected	VBN	10-06-009
effected	VBN-HL	1-01-001
effecting	VBG	3-01-003
effecting	**noun**	**1-01-001**
effecting	NN	0-00-000
effectinge	NN	1-01-001
effective	**adjective**	**129-10-089**
effective	JJ	128-10-089
effective	JJ-HL	1-01-001
effectively	**RB**	**37-10-034**
effectiveness	**NN**	**32-08-025**
effectual	**JJ**	**1-01-001**
effectuate	**VB**	**2-01-001**
effeminate	**JJ**	**1-01-001**
effete	**JJ**	**1-01-001**
efficacious	**JJ**	**2-02-002**
efficaciously	**RB**	**2-01-001**
efficacy	**NN**	**9-04-005**
efficiency	**noun**	**53-09-029**
efficiency	NN	48-09-028
efficiency	NN-HL	2-02-002
efficiencies	NNS	3-02-002
efficient	**JJ**	**32-13-026**
efficiently	**RB**	**8-04-008**
Effie	**NP**	**1-01-001**
effloresce	**VB**	**1-01-001**
effluent	**noun**	**19-01-001**
effluent	NN	18-01-001
effluents	NNS	1-01-001
effluvium	**NN**	**1-01-001**
effort	**noun**	**272-14-162**
effort	NN	145-14-107
efforts	NNS	127-13-084
effortless	**JJ**	**1-01-001**
effortlessly	**RB**	**1-01-001**
effusive	**JJ**	**1-01-001**
egalitarianism	**noun**	**2-01-002**
egalitarianism	NN	1-01-001
Egalitarianism	NN-TL	1-01-001
Egerton	**NP**	**1-01-001**
egg	**noun**	**47-10-023**
egg	NN	12-04-006
eggs	NNS	35-10-021
egg	**verb**	**1-01-001**
egged	VBN	1-01-001
egg-hatching	**JJ**	**1-01-001**
egg-sized	**JJ**	**1-01-001**
egghead	**NN**	**1-01-001**
eggshell	**NN**	**1-01-001**
Egils	**NP**	**1-01-001**
ego	**noun**	**14-07-011**
ego	NN	13-07-011
ego's	NN$	1-01-001
ego-adaptive	**JJ**	**1-01-001**
egocentric	**JJ**	**1-01-001**
Egon	**NP**	**1-01-001**
egotism	**NN**	**3-01-002**
egotist	**noun**	**3-02-002**
egotist	NN	2-02-002
egotist's	NN$	1-01-001
egregiously	**QL**	**1-01-001**
egret	**noun**	**1-01-001**
egrets	NNS	1-01-001
Egypt	**NP**	**14-06-012**
Egyptian	**JJ**	**5-02-003**
Egyptian	**prop. noun**	**3-01-003**
Egyptians	NPS	3-01-003
eh	**exclam.**	**8-05-008**
eh	UH	7-04-007
Eh	UH-TL	1-01-001
Ehlers	**NP**	**1-01-001**
Eichmann	**prop. noun**	**20-03-003**
Eichmann	NP	13-03-003
Eichmann	NP-TL	1-01-001
Eichmann's	NP$	6-01-001
eidetic	**JJ**	**1-01-001**
eight	**card. num.**	**104-15-073**
eight	CD	101-15-071
Eight	CD-TL	3-02-002
eight-and-a-half-foot	**JJ**	**1-01-001**
eight-bar	**JJ**	**1-01-001**
eight-by-ten	**CD**	**1-01-001**
eight-foot	**JJ**	**1-01-001**

Word	Tag	Frequency
eight-inch	**JJ**	**2-01-001**
eight-thirty	**CD**	**1-01-001**
eight-week	**JJ**	**1-01-001**
eight-year	**JJ**	**1-01-001**
eighteen	**CD**	**17-07-016**
eighteen-year-old	**NN**	**1-01-001**
eighteenth	**ord. num.**	**23-08-019**
eighteenth	OD	18-06-015
eighteenth-	OD	1-01-001
Eighteenth	OD-TL	4-03-003
eighteenth-century	**JJ**	**4-03-003**
eighteenth-century	**NN**	**1-01-001**
eighth	**ord. num.**	**23-10-013**
eighth	OD	16-07-009
eighth	OD-HL	1-01-001
Eighth	OD-TL	6-04-005
eighty	**CD**	**11-05-009**
eighty	**noun**	**2-02-002**
eighties	NNS	1-01-001
Eighties	NNS-TL	1-01-001
eighty-fifth	**OD**	**2-01-001**
eighty-five	**CD**	**2-02-002**
eighty-four	**card. num.**	**4-03-003**
eighty-four	CD	1-01-001
Eighty-Four	CD-TL	3-02-002
eighty-nine	**CD**	**1-01-001**
eighty-one	**CD**	**1-01-001**
eighty-seventh	**ord. num.**	**2-01-001**
eighty-seventh	OD	0-00-000
Eighty-seventh	OD-TL	2-01-001
eighty-sixth	**OD**	**5-01-001**
eighty-three	**CD**	**3-02-002**
eighty-year-old	**JJ**	**1-01-001**
Eileen	**prop. noun**	**29-04-004**
Eileen	NP	26-04-004
Eileen's	NP$	3-01-001
ein	**foreign**	**3-01-002**
ein	FW-AT	2-01-002
eine	FW-AT	1-01-001
Einsatzkommandos	**FW-NNS**	**1-01-001**
Einstein	**prop. noun**	**6-04-005**
Einstein	NP	3-03-003
Einstein's	NP$	3-02-002
Einsteinian	**JJ**	**1-01-001**
Eire	**NP**	**2-02-002**
Eisenhower	**prop. noun**	**62-08-023**
Eisenhower	NP	45-07-019
Eisenhhower	NP	0-00-000
Eisenhhower	NP-TL	1-01-001
Eisenhower	NP-HL	1-01-001
Eisenhower	NP-TL	4-02-003
Eisenhower's	NP$	11-05-009
Eisler	**NP**	**1-01-001**
either	**CC**	**189-14-145**
either	**dt./d. cj.**	**64-13-056**
either	DTX	63-13-055
ether	DTX	1-01-001
either	**RB**	**32-11-028**
either-or	**JJ**	**1-01-001**
ejaculate	**verb**	**3-03-003**
ejaculated	VBD	3-03-003
eject	**verb**	**3-02-003**
eject	VB	1-01-001
ejected	VBN	2-01-002
ejection	**NN**	**2-01-001**
Ekaterinoslav	**prop. noun**	**1-01-001**
Ekaterinoslav	NP	0-00-000
Ekaterinoslav	NP-TL	1-01-001
Ekberg	**NP**	**1-01-001**
eke	**verb**	**2-01-001**
eked	VBN	2-01-001
Ekstrohm	**prop. noun**	**27-01-001**
Ekstrohm	NP	26-01-001
Ekstrohm's	NP$	1-01-001
Ekwanok	**prop. noun**	**1-01-001**
Ekwanok	NP	0-00-000
Ekwanok	NP-TL	1-01-001
el	**foreign**	**2-01-001**
el	FW-AT	0-00-000
El	FW-AT-TL	2-01-001
El	**prop. noun**	**18-04-007**
El	NP	17-03-006
El	NP-TL	1-01-001
elaborate	**JJ**	**26-09-024**
elaborate	**verb**	**10-04-010**
elaborate	VB	6-03-006
elaborates	VBZ	1-01-001
elaborated	VBN	3-02-003
elaborately	**QL**	**2-01-002**

Word	Tag	Frequency
elaborately	**RB**	**4-04-004**
elaboration	**NN**	**2-02-002**
Elaine	**prop. noun**	**23-04-004**
Elaine	NP	22-04-004
Elaine's	NP$	1-01-001
elan	**NN**	**1-01-001**
elapse	**verb**	**7-04-006**
elapse	VB	1-01-001
elapses	VBZ	1-01-001
elapsed	VBD	1-01-001
elapsed	VBN	4-03-003
elastic	**JJ**	**7-05-006**
elasticity	**noun**	**5-01-002**
elasticity	NN	4-01-002
elasticity	NN-HL	1-01-001
elate	**verb**	**3-03-003**
elated	VBN	3-03-003
elation	**NN**	**2-02-002**
Elba	**NP**	**1-01-001**
elbow	**noun**	**17-07-015**
elbow	NN	7-05-006
Elbow	NN-TL	3-02-002
elbows	NNS	7-03-007
elbow	**verb**	**1-01-001**
elbowing	VBG	1-01-001
Elburn	**prop. noun**	**1-01-001**
Elburn	NP	0-00-000
Elburn	NP-HL	1-01-001
elder	**comp. adj.**	**9-05-007**
elder	JJR	8-05-006
Elder	JJR-TL	1-01-001
elder	**noun**	**14-05-008**
elder	NN	1-01-001
Elder	NN-TL	4-01-001
elders	NNS	9-04-006
Elder	**NP**	**1-01-001**
elderly	**JJ**	**13-09-013**
eldest	**JJT**	**5-03-004**
Eldon	**NP**	**2-02-002**
Eleanor	**prop. noun**	**10-05-008**
Eleanor	NP	9-04-007
Eleanor	NP-TL	1-01-001
Eleazar	**NP**	**2-01-001**
Elec	**prop. noun**	**11-01-001**
Elec	NP	9-01-001
Elec's	NP$	2-01-001
elect	**verb**	**42-10-029**
elect	VB	8-04-007
elected	VBD	2-02-002
elected	VBN	30-09-023
elected	VBN-HL	1-01-001
electing	VBG	1-01-001
election	**noun**	**128-10-037**
election	NN	74-09-029
Election	NN-TL	3-03-003
elections	NNS	51-04-009
elective	**noun**	**1-01-001**
electives	NNS	1-01-001
elector	**noun**	**5-04-004**
elector	NN	0-00-000
Elector	NN-TL	2-02-002
electors	NNS	3-02-002
electoral	**adjective**	**13-03-003**
electoral	JJ	11-01-001
Electoral	JJ-TL	2-02-002
electorate	**NN**	**1-01-001**
Electra	**NP**	**1-01-001**
electress	**noun**	**1-01-001**
electress	NN	0-00-000
Electress	NN-TL	1-01-001
electric	**adjective**	**60-14-037**
electric	JJ	51-14-030
electric	JJ-HL	2-01-002
Electric	JJ-TL	7-03-006
electric	**noun**	**9-03-005**
electric	NN	3-01-001
electric	NN-HL	1-01-001
Electric	NN-TL	4-02-003
electric's	NN$	0-00-000
Electric's	NN$-TL	1-01-001
electric-sewer-water	**NN**	**1-01-001**
electric-utility	**NN**	**1-01-001**
electrical	**adjective**	**46-08-019**
electrical	JJ	40-08-018
electrical	JJ-HL	1-01-001
Electrical	JJ-TL	5-02-002
electrically	**RB**	**2-02-002**
electricity	**NN**	**26-08-016**
electrification	**noun**	**1-01-001**

Word	Tag	Frequency
electrification (cont.):		
electrification	NN	0-00-000
Electrification	NN-TL	1-01-001
electrifying	**JJ**	**1-01-001**
electrique	**foreign**	**1-01-001**
electrique	FW-JJ	0-00-000
electriques	FW-JJ-TL	1-01-001
electro-magnetic	**JJ**	**1-01-001**
electrocardiogram	**NN**	**1-01-001**
electrocardiograph	**NN**	**2-01-001**
electrode	**NN**	**5-01-002**
electrodynamics	**NN**	**1-01-001**
electrolysis	**NN**	**1-01-001**
electromagnet	**NN**	**1-01-001**
electromagnetism	**noun**	**1-01-001**
electromagnetism	NN	0-00-000
electromagnetism	NN-HL	1-01-001
electromyography	**NN**	**1-01-001**
electron	**noun**	**40-04-010**
electron	NN	29-03-009
electrons	NNS	11-03-004
electron-microscopical	**JJ**	**1-01-001**
electronic	**adjective**	**68-08-014**
electronic	JJ	63-08-013
electronic	JJ-HL	2-02-002
Electronic	JJ-TL	3-02-003
electronically	**adverb**	**1-01-001**
electronically	RB	0-00-000
electronically	RB-HL	1-01-001
electronics	**noun**	**32-03-006**
electronics	NN	28-03-005
electronics	NN-HL	1-01-001
Electronics	NN-TL	3-01-002
electronography	**NN**	**1-01-001**
electrophoresis	**noun**	**5-01-002**
electrophoresis	NN	4-01-002
electrophoresis	NN-HL	1-01-001
electrophorus	**NN**	**1-01-001**
electroshock	**noun**	**3-01-001**
electroshock	NN	2-01-001
electroshocks	NNS	1-01-001
electrostatic	**JJ**	**9-02-002**
electrotherapist	**NN**	**1-01-001**
elegance	**noun**	**11-05-009**
elegance	NN	9-05-009
elegance	NN-HL	1-01-001
elegances	NNS	1-01-001
elegant	**adjective**	**14-07-011**
elegant	JJ	13-06-010
Elegant	JJ-TL	1-01-001
elegantly	**RB**	**1-01-001**
elegiac	**JJ**	**2-02-002**
elegy	**noun**	**2-02-002**
elegy	NN	1-01-001
elegies	NNS	0-00-000
Elegies	NNS-TL	1-01-001
element	**noun**	**159-12-073**
element	NN	52-12-032
elements	NNS	104-10-051
elements	NNS-HL	2-01-002
Elements	NNS-TL	1-01-001
elemental	**JJ**	**11-06-009**
elementary	**adjective**	**19-06-016**
elementary	JJ	17-06-014
Elementary	JJ-TL	2-01-002
elementary-school	**NN**	**6-02-002**
Elena	**NP**	**3-01-001**
elephant	**noun**	**18-09-013**
elephant	NN	7-05-005
elephant's	NN$	1-01-001
elephants	NNS	10-06-008
elephantine	**JJ**	**1-01-001**
elevate	**verb**	**12-07-012**
elevates	VBZ	1-01-001
elevated	VBN	10-07-010
Elevated	VBN-TL	1-01-001
elevation	**NN**	**3-02-002**
elevator	**NN**	**12-07-011**
eleven	**CD**	**40-13-034**
eleventh	**OD**	**4-03-004**
eleventh-floor	**NN**	**1-01-001**
elfin	**JJ**	**1-01-001**
Elgin	**NP**	**1-01-001**
Eli	**prop. noun**	**4-02-002**
Eli	NP	2-02-002
Eli's	NP$	2-01-001
elicit	**verb**	**10-04-007**
elicit	VB	3-02-003
elicits	VBZ	1-01-001
elicit (cont.):		
elicited	VBD	3-03-003
elicited	VBN	3-03-003
eligibility	**noun**	**4-01-002**
eligibility	NN	3-01-001
eligibility	NN-HL	1-01-001
eligible	**JJ**	**14-04-010**
Eligio	**NP**	**1-01-001**
Elijah	**NP**	**1-01-001**
eliminate	**verb**	**67-10-055**
eliminate	VB	26-06-025
eliminates	VBZ	4-04-004
eliminated	VBD	6-05-006
eliminated	VBN	16-07-016
eliminating	VBG	15-08-013
elimination	**noun**	**10-05-009**
elimination	NN	9-04-008
eliminations	NNS	1-01-001
Elinor	**NP**	**3-01-002**
Elios	**NP**	**1-01-001**
Eliot	**NP**	**4-02-003**
Elisabeth	**prop. noun**	**3-02-002**
Elisabeth	NP	2-01-001
Elisabeth	NP-TL	1-01-001
Elisha	**NP**	**1-01-001**
elite	**JJ**	**1-01-001**
elite	**noun**	**12-07-008**
elite	NN	11-06-007
Elite	NN-TL	1-01-001
Elizabeth	**prop. noun**	**15-09-014**
Elizabeth	NP	13-08-012
Elizabeth	NP-TL	2-02-002
Elizabethan	**JJ**	**7-03-003**
Elizabethan	**prop. noun**	**2-01-002**
Elizabethans	NPS	2-01-002
elk	**noun**	**2-02-002**
elk	NN	1-01-001
elks	NNS	0-00-000
Elks	NNS-TL	1-01-001
ell	**NN**	**1-01-001**
Ella	**NP**	**1-01-001**
Ellamae	**NP**	**1-01-001**
Ellen	**NP**	**10-05-006**
Ellie	**NP**	**1-01-001**
Elliott	**prop. noun**	**5-05-005**
Elliott	NP	4-04-004
Elliott	NP-TL	1-01-001
ellipse	**noun**	**2-02-002**
ellipses	NNS	2-02-002
ellipsis	**NN**	**1-01-001**
ellipsoid	**noun**	**5-01-001**
ellipsoid	NN	1-01-001
ellipsoids	NNS	4-01-001
elliptical	**JJ**	**1-01-001**
Ellis	**NP**	**7-04-004**
Ellison	**prop. noun**	**1-01-001**
Ellison's	NP$	1-01-001
Ellsworth	**NP**	**1-01-001**
Ellwood	**NP**	**1-01-001**
elm	**noun**	**4-03-004**
elm	NN	2-02-002
Elm	NN-TL	1-01-001
elms	NNS	1-01-001
Elman	**NP**	**5-02-002**
Elmer	**prop. noun**	**6-03-003**
Elmer	NP	2-02-002
Elmer	NP-TL	4-01-001
Elmira	**NP**	**1-01-001**
Eloi	**prop. noun**	**1-01-001**
Eloi	NP	0-00-000
Eloi	NP-TL	1-01-001
Eloise	**NP**	**1-01-001**
elongate	**verb**	**5-04-005**
elongated	VBN	5-04-005
elongation	**NN**	**3-01-001**
elope	**verb**	**1-01-001**
eloped	VBD	1-01-001
eloquence	**NN**	**2-01-002**
eloquent	**JJ**	**11-08-011**
eloquently	**RB**	**2-02-002**
else	**adverb**	**185-14-133**
else	RB	176-14-125
else's	RB$	9-06-009
elsewhere	**NN**	**3-02-003**
elsewhere	**RB**	**42-11-036**
Elsie	**NP**	**4-03-004**
Elsinore	**NP**	**2-01-001**
Eluard	**NP**	**2-01-001**
eluate	**noun**	**2-01-001**

Word	Tag	Frequency
eluate (cont.):		
eluate	NN	1-01-001
eluates	NNS	1-01-001
elucidate	**verb**	**1-01-001**
elucidated	VBN	1-01-001
elucidation	**NN**	**1-01-001**
elude	**verb**	**5-05-005**
eludes	VBZ	1-01-001
eluded	VBD	2-02-002
eluding	VBG	2-02-002
elusive	**JJ**	**2-02-002**
elusiveness	**NN**	**1-01-001**
elute	**verb**	**1-01-001**
eluted	VBN	1-01-001
elution	**NN**	**4-01-001**
Elvis	**NP**	**2-02-002**
Elysees	**NP**	**2-02-002**
emaciate	**verb**	**2-02-002**
emaciated	VBN	2-02-002
emaciated	**JJ**	**1-01-001**
emanate	**verb**	**3-03-003**
emanated	VBD	1-01-001
emanating	VBG	2-02-002
emanation	**noun**	**3-03-003**
emanation	NN	2-02-002
emanations	NNS	1-01-001
emancipate	**verb**	**4-02-003**
emancipate	VB	2-02-002
emancipated	VBN	2-01-001
emancipation	**noun**	**14-04-005**
emancipation	NN	8-04-004
Emancipation	NN	1-01-001
Emancipation	NN-TL	5-02-003
Emanuel	**NP**	**1-01-001**
Emanuele	**NP**	**2-01-001**
emasculate	**verb**	**1-01-001**
emasculated	VBD	1-01-001
emasculation	**NN**	**1-01-001**
embalmer	**noun**	**1-01-001**
embalmers'	NNS$	1-01-001
embankment	**NN**	**4-03-003**
Embarcadero	**NP**	**1-01-001**
embargo	**NN**	**2-02-002**
embark	**verb**	**7-05-007**
embark	VB	5-03-005
embarked	VBD	1-01-001
embarked	VBN	1-01-001
embarrass	**verb**	**19-10-019**
embarrassed	VBD	1-01-001
embarrassed	VBN	7-05-007
embarrassing	VBG	11-08-011
embarrassingly	**QL**	**1-01-001**
embarrassment	**NN**	**8-05-008**
embassy	**noun**	**24-05-011**
embassy	NN	9-04-004
Embassy	NN-TL	8-05-007
embassies	NNS	7-03-003
embattle	**verb**	**1-01-001**
embattled	VBN	1-01-001
embed	**verb**	**4-04-004**
embedded	VBN	4-04-004
embellish	**verb**	**1-01-001**
embellished	VBN	1-01-001
embezzle	**verb**	**2-02-002**
embezzle	VB	1-01-001
embezzling	VBG	1-01-001
embezzlement	**NN**	**1-01-001**
embitter	**verb**	**1-01-001**
embittered	VBN	1-01-001
emblematic	**JJ**	**3-01-001**
embodiment	**noun**	**11-05-009**
embodiment	NN	9-05-009
embodiment	NN-HL	1-01-001
embodiments	NNS	1-01-001
embody	**verb**	**14-06-013**
embody	VB	1-01-001
embodies	VBZ	3-03-003
embodied	VBD	1-01-001
embodied	VBN	6-04-006
embodying	VBG	3-03-003
embolden	**verb**	**2-02-002**
emboldened	VBN	2-02-002
emboss	**verb**	**1-01-001**
embossed	VBD	1-01-001
embouchure	**NN**	**1-01-001**
embrace	**noun**	**6-05-006**
embrace	NN	5-04-005
embraces	NNS	1-01-001
embrace	**verb**	**18-09-016**

Word	Tag	Frequency
embrace (cont.):		
embrace	VB	8-05-008
embraces	VBZ	3-03-003
embraced	VBD	4-03-003
embracing	VBG	3-02-003
embracing	**NN**	**1-01-001**
embroider	**verb**	**5-02-003**
embroidered	VBN	5-02-003
embroidery	**noun**	**5-02-002**
embroidery	NN	4-01-001
embroideries	NNS	1-01-001
embroil	**verb**	**1-01-001**
embroiled	VBN	1-01-001
embryo	**NN**	**1-01-001**
embryonic	**JJ**	**2-02-002**
emcee	**NN**	**1-01-001**
emerald	**noun**	**9-05-005**
emerald	NN	2-02-002
Emerald	NN-TL	1-01-001
emeralds	NNS	4-02-002
emeralds	NNS-NC	2-01-001
emerge	**verb**	**68-14-056**
emerge	VB	18-08-016
emerges	VBZ	9-06-009
emerged	VBD	23-12-021
emerged	VBN	3-03-003
emerging	VBG	15-05-010
emergence	**NN**	**3-02-003**
emergency	**noun**	**46-11-032**
emergency	NN	33-11-026
Emergency	NN-TL	6-04-004
emergencies	NNS	7-06-006
emergent	**JJ**	**2-02-002**
emeritus	**adjective**	**3-02-002**
emeritus	JJ	2-02-002
Emeritus	JJ-TL	1-01-001
Emerson	**prop. noun**	**10-05-007**
Emerson	NP	8-05-007
Emerson's	NP$	2-02-002
emigrant	**noun**	**2-01-001**
emigrant	NN	0-00-000
Emigrant	NN-TL	2-01-001
emigrate	**verb**	**2-01-002**
emigrated	VBN	1-01-001
emigrating	VBG	1-01-001
emigration	**NN**	**1-01-001**
Emil	**NP**	**1-01-001**
Emile	**prop. noun**	**7-01-001**
Emile	NP	5-01-001
Emile's	NP$	2-01-001
Emilio	**NP**	**1-01-001**
eminence	**NN**	**4-04-004**
eminent	**JJ**	**9-07-009**
eminently	**QL**	**3-02-003**
eminently	**RB**	**1-01-001**
Eminonu	**prop. noun**	**1-01-001**
Eminonu	NP	0-00-000
Eminonu	NP-TL	1-01-001
emissary	**noun**	**3-02-002**
emissary	NN	2-02-002
emissaries	NNS	1-01-001
emission	**NN**	**32-01-003**
emit	**verb**	**5-03-005**
emit	VB	1-01-001
emitted	VBD	2-02-002
emitted	VBN	1-01-001
emitting	VBG	1-01-001
Emma	**prop. noun**	**12-04-004**
Emma	NP	10-04-004
Emma's	NP$	2-01-001
Emmanuel	**NP**	**1-01-001**
Emmerich	**NP**	**2-01-002**
Emmert	**NP**	**2-01-001**
Emmett	**prop. noun**	**6-03-003**
Emmett	NP	5-03-003
Emmett's	NP$	1-01-001
Emory	**prop. noun**	**14-01-001**
Emory	NP	4-01-001
Emory	NP-TL	10-01-001
emotion	**noun**	**77-10-040**
emotion	NN	34-08-024
emotions	NNS	43-08-026
emotional	**adjective**	**68-08-030**
emotional	JJ	67-08-030
emotional	JJ-HL	1-01-001
emotionalism	**NN**	**2-01-002**
emotionality	**NN**	**1-01-001**
emotionally	**adverb**	**13-06-010**
emotionally	RB	11-06-009

Word	Tag	Frequency
emotionally (cont.):		
emotionally	RB-NC	2-01-001
empathy	**NN**	**1-01-001**
Empedocles	**NP**	**2-01-002**
emperor	**noun**	**26-07-012**
emperor	NN	7-02-003
Emperor	NN-TL	12-05-008
emperor's	NN$	2-02-002
Emperor's	NN$-TL	1-01-001
emperors	NNS	2-02-002
Emperors	NNS-TL	2-01-001
emphasis	**noun**	**60-10-050**
emphasis	NN	58-10-049
emphases	NNS	2-01-002
emphasize	**verb**	**45-12-040**
emphasize	VB	20-09-019
emphasizes	VBZ	3-02-002
emphasized	VBD	9-07-009
emphasized	VBN	9-06-009
emphasizing	VBG	4-03-004
emphatic	**JJ**	**2-02-002**
emphatically	**QL**	**1-01-001**
emphatically	**RB**	**2-02-002**
emphysema	**NN**	**4-01-002**
emphysematous	**JJ**	**1-01-001**
empire	**noun**	**26-06-020**
empire	NN	9-03-008
Empire	NN-TL	13-05-010
empires	NNS	4-03-003
empirical	**JJ**	**23-04-009**
empirically	**RB**	**5-03-003**
empiricism	**NN**	**2-01-002**
employ	**NN**	**3-02-002**
employ	**verb**	**77-12-061**
employ	VB	9-05-009
employs	VBZ	9-06-006
employed	VBD	6-06-006
employed	VBN	43-09-036
employing	VBG	10-04-010
employee	**noun**	**109-09-040**
employee	NN	23-05-007
employe	NN	1-01-001
employee	NN-HL	1-01-001
employee's	NN$	1-01-001
employees	NNS	66-08-025
employes	NNS	17-03-012
employee-contributed	**JJ**	**1-01-001**
employer	**noun**	**34-09-019**
employer	NN	15-08-013
employers	NNS	17-05-010
employers'	NNS$	1-01-001
Employers'	NNS$-TL	1-01-001
employment	**noun**	**48-09-027**
employment	NN	44-09-026
Employment	NN-TL	3-02-002
employments	NNS	1-01-001
empower	**verb**	**4-03-004**
empower	VB	1-01-001
empowered	VBN	2-02-002
empowering	VBG	1-01-001
emptier	**JJR**	**2-02-002**
emptiness	**NN**	**2-02-002**
empty	**JJ**	**64-13-050**
empty	**verb**	**12-07-011**
empties	VBZ	3-03-003
emptied	VBD	3-03-003
emptied	VBN	5-03-005
emptying	VBG	1-01-001
emulate	**verb**	**4-03-004**
emulate	VB	3-03-003
emulated	VBN	1-01-001
emulsify	**verb**	**1-01-001**
emulsified	VBN	1-01-001
emulsion	**NN**	**1-01-001**
en	**foreign**	**7-05-007**
en	FW-IN	5-04-005
En	FW-IN-TL	2-02-002
En-lai	**prop. noun**	**2-01-001**
En-lai	NP	1-01-001
En-lai's	NP$	1-01-001
enable	**verb**	**57-13-048**
enable	VB	23-09-020
enables	VBZ	9-06-009
enabled	VBD	10-08-010
enabled	VBN	2-02-002
enabling	VBG	13-05-011
enact	**verb**	**23-08-018**
enact	VB	7-05-006
enacted	VBD	2-02-002

Word	Tag	Frequency
enact (cont.):		
enacted	VBN	10-04-006
enacting	VBG	4-04-004
enactment	**NN**	**7-04-006**
enamel	**NN**	**1-01-001**
enamel	**verb**	**3-02-003**
enamelled	VBN	1-01-001
enameling	VBG	2-02-002
encamp	**verb**	**2-01-001**
encamp	VB	1-01-001
encamped	VBN	1-01-001
encampment	**NN**	**3-03-003**
encase	**verb**	**1-01-001**
encased	VBD	1-01-001
encephalitis	**NN**	**1-01-001**
encephalographic	**JJ**	**1-01-001**
enchain	**verb**	**1-01-001**
enchained	VBN	1-01-001
enchant	**verb**	**6-05-006**
enchant	VB	1-01-001
enchanted	VBN	5-04-005
enchanting	**JJ**	**9-04-005**
enchantingly	**RB**	**1-01-001**
enchantment	**NN**	**3-03-003**
encipher	**verb**	**1-01-001**
enciphered	VBN	1-01-001
encircle	**verb**	**3-03-003**
encircle	VB	1-01-001
encircled	VBD	1-01-001
encircled	VBN	1-01-001
enclave	**noun**	**1-01-001**
enclaves	NNS	1-01-001
enclose	**verb**	**14-07-012**
encloses	VBZ	1-01-001
enclosed	VBD	3-03-003
enclosed	VBN	8-04-007
inclosed	VBN	1-01-001
enclosing	VBG	1-01-001
enclosure	**NN**	**7-06-006**
encomium	**noun**	**1-01-001**
encomiums	NNS	1-01-001
encompass	**verb**	**8-03-008**
encompass	VB	4-03-004
encompasses	VBZ	1-01-001
encompassed	VBN	3-02-003
encore	**noun**	**1-01-001**
encores	NNS	1-01-001
encounter	**noun**	**19-07-015**
encounter	NN	14-07-014
encounter	NN-HL	1-01-001
encounters	NNS	4-03-003
encounter	**verb**	**47-13-040**
encounter	VB	13-08-013
encounters	VBZ	4-04-004
encountered	VBD	12-07-010
encountered	VBN	18-08-017
encourage	**verb**	**95-13-056**
encourage	VB	46-10-033
encourages	VBZ	5-04-005
encouraged	VBD	5-05-005
encouraged	VBN	24-10-023
encouraging	VBG	13-07-013
encouraging	VBG-HL	2-01-001
encouragement	**NN**	**14-08-014**
encouraging	**JJ**	**8-05-007**
encouragingly	**RB**	**1-01-001**
encroach	**verb**	**4-03-004**
encroach	VB	1-01-001
encroached	VBD	1-01-001
encroaching	VBG	2-02-002
encroachment	**NN**	**5-04-005**
encrust	**verb**	**2-02-002**
encrusted	VBN	2-02-002
encumber	**verb**	**2-02-002**
encumbered	VBN	2-02-002
encumbrance	**noun**	**1-01-001**
encumbrances	NNS	1-01-001
encyclopedia	**noun**	**3-02-002**
encyclopedia	NN	1-01-001
encylopedia	NN	1-01-001
encyclopedias	NNS	1-01-001
encyclopedic	**JJ**	**1-01-001**
end	**noun**	**423-15-249**
end	NN	359-15-220
end	NN-HL	3-03-003
End	NN-TL	7-02-003
ends	NNS	54-11-038
end	**verb**	**140-14-097**
end	VB	40-11-033

Word	Tag	Frequency
end (cont.):		
ends	VBZ	13-07-010
ended	VBD	41-10-035
Ended	VBD-TL	1-01-001
ended	VBN	18-07-014
ending	VBG	27-07-021
end-product	**NN**	**2-01-001**
end-to-end	**JJ**	**1-01-001**
end-use	**JJ**	**2-01-002**
endanger	**verb**	**5-03-005**
endanger	VB	1-01-001
endangered	VBN	1-01-001
endangering	VBG	3-03-003
endear	**verb**	**3-02-002**
endeared	VBD	2-02-002
endeared	VBN	1-01-001
endearing	**JJ**	**3-03-003**
endearment	**noun**	**3-03-003**
endearment	NN	1-01-001
endearments	NNS	2-02-002
endeavor	**noun**	**14-06-012**
endeavor	NN	5-04-005
endeavour	NN	1-01-001
endevor	NN	1-01-001
Endeavor	NN-TL	1-01-001
endeavors	NNS	5-04-004
endeavours	NNS	1-01-001
endeavor	**verb**	**5-03-005**
endeavor	VB	1-01-001
endeavored	VBD	1-01-001
endeavored	VBN	1-01-001
endeavoring	VBG	2-02-002
endgame	**noun**	**1-01-001**
endgame	NN	0-00-000
Endgame	NN-TL	1-01-001
ending	**noun**	**7-03-005**
ending	NN	4-02-004
endings	NNS	3-01-001
endless	**JJ**	**20-11-017**
endlessly	**RB**	**7-07-007**
endogamous	**JJ**	**1-01-001**
endogamy	**NN**	**3-01-001**
endogenous	**JJ**	**1-01-001**
endorse	**verb**	**12-06-011**
endorse	VB	6-04-006
endorsed	VBD	1-01-001
indorsed	VBD	1-01-001
endorsed	VBN	3-03-003
endorsing	VBG	1-01-001
endorsement	**NN**	**2-02-002**
endosperm	**NN**	**1-01-001**
endothelial	**JJ**	**1-01-001**
endothermic	**JJ**	**2-01-002**
endow	**verb**	**10-05-010**
endow	VB	2-02-002
endows	VBZ	1-01-001
endowed	VBN	7-04-007
endowment	**noun**	**6-03-005**
endowment	NN	2-02-002
endowments	NNS	4-03-003
endpoint	**noun**	**1-01-001**
endpoints	NNS	1-01-001
endurable	**JJ**	**2-02-002**
endurance	**NN**	**16-07-012**
endure	**verb**	**31-09-025**
endure	VB	8-06-008
endures	VBZ	2-02-002
endured	VBD	4-03-003
endured	VBN	7-04-006
enduring	VBG	10-05-008
enduringly	**RB**	**1-01-001**
enemy	**noun**	**123-14-049**
enemy	NN	88-11-035
enemy's	NN$	8-04-004
enemies	NNS	27-12-020
enemy-Jew	**NN**	**2-01-001**
energetic	**JJ**	**11-05-011**
energetically	**RB**	**2-02-002**
energize	**verb**	**2-02-002**
energizes	VBZ	1-01-001
energized	VBN	1-01-001
energy	**noun**	**111-14-051**
energy	NN	94-14-044
energy	NN-HL	2-02-002
Energy	NN-TL	4-02-003
energies	NNS	10-03-007
energies	NNS-HL	1-01-001
enervate	**verb**	**2-02-002**
enervating	VBG	2-02-002
enervation	**NN**	**1-01-001**
enfant	**FW-NN**	**1-01-001**
Enfield	**NP**	**1-01-001**
enforce	**verb**	**35-10-026**
enforce	VB	8-05-005
enforce	VB-HL	1-01-001
enforces	VBZ	1-01-001
enforced	VBN	20-10-020
enforcing	VBG	5-04-004
enforceable	**JJ**	**2-01-002**
enforcement	**NN**	**19-05-009**
enforcer	**noun**	**1-01-001**
enforcers	NNS	1-01-001
engage	**verb**	**66-13-050**
engage	VB	14-08-013
engages	VBZ	1-01-001
engaged	VBD	5-04-005
engaged	VBN	42-10-035
engaging	VBG	4-02-003
engagement	**noun**	**30-10-023**
engagement	NN	22-10-018
engagements	NNS	8-04-007
engages	**FW-NNS**	**5-02-002**
engages	**FW-VBN**	**1-01-001**
engaging	**JJ**	**4-02-004**
engagingly	**RB**	**1-01-001**
engender	**verb**	**11-06-011**
engender	VB	2-01-002
engendered	VBN	9-05-009
Engh	**NP**	**1-01-001**
engine	**noun**	**69-11-024**
engine	NN	48-10-021
engine	NN-HL	1-01-001
Engine	NN-TL	1-01-001
engine's	NN$	2-01-001
engines	NNS	17-06-009
engineer	**noun**	**78-09-024**
engineer	NN	36-07-012
engineer	NN-HL	2-01-001
Engineer	NN-TL	4-01-001
engineers	NNS	27-07-013
Engineers	NNS-TL	6-02-002
engineers'	NNS$	3-02-002
engineer	**verb**	**32-06-013**
engineering	VBG	32-06-013
engineering	**noun**	**14-05-007**
engineering	NN	9-04-006
Engineering	NN-TL	5-03-003
engineering-management	**NN**	**2-01-001**
Engisch	**NP**	**1-01-001**
England	**prop. noun**	**157-15-068**
England	NP	94-13-048
Eng.	NP	1-01-001
England	NP-TL	61-12-026
England's	NP$	1-01-001
Englander	**prop. noun**	**8-03-005**
Englander	NP	0-00-000
Englander	NP-TL	5-03-005
Englanders	NPS	0-00-000
Englanders	NPS-TL	3-01-001
Engle	**prop. noun**	**1-01-001**
Engle's	NP$	1-01-001
English	**adjective**	**109-14-047**
English	JJ	101-13-045
English	JJ-TL	8-04-005
English	**prop. noun**	**86-15-052**
English	NP	63-15-042
English	NP-TL	9-04-006
English	NPS	14-04-008
English-born	**JJ**	**1-01-001**
English-dialogue	**JJ**	**1-01-001**
English-Dutch	**JJ**	**1-01-001**
English-Scottish-French	**JJ**	**1-01-001**
English-speaking	**JJ**	**2-02-002**
Englishman	**prop. noun**	**23-04-007**
Englishman	NP	9-03-004
Englishman	NP-TL	6-01-001
Englishmen	NPS	8-02-003
Englishy	**JJ**	**1-01-001**
engrave	**verb**	**4-03-004**
engraved	VBN	4-03-004
engraver	**NN**	**1-01-001**
engraving	**noun**	**3-03-003**
engraving	NN	2-02-002
engravings	NNS	1-01-001
engross	**verb**	**2-02-002**
engrossed	VBN	2-02-002
engrossing	**JJ**	**4-02-004**
engulf	**verb**	**7-05-007**

Word	Tag	Count
engulf (cont.):		
engulfs	VBZ	1-01-001
engulfed	VBD	2-02-002
engulfed	VBN	3-03-003
engulfing	VBG	1-01-001
enhance	**verb**	**12-05-011**
enhance	VB	5-04-005
enhances	VBZ	1-01-001
enhanced	VBN	5-02-005
enhancing	VBG	1-01-001
enigma	**NN**	**4-04-004**
enigmatic	**JJ**	**2-01-002**
enjoin	**verb**	**6-04-004**
enjoin	VB	1-01-001
enjoined	VBD	1-01-001
enjoined	VBN	4-03-003
enjoinder	**NN**	**1-01-001**
enjoy	**verb**	**128-15-103**
enjoy	VB	44-13-038
enjoys	VBZ	10-07-009
enjoyed	VBD	36-10-030
enjoyed	VBN	21-10-020
enjoying	VBG	17-09-016
enjoyable	**JJ**	**2-02-002**
enjoyment	**NN**	**21-07-020**
enlarge	**verb**	**17-07-016**
enlarge	VB	7-05-007
enlarged	VBD	1-01-001
enlarged	VBN	6-05-006
enlargd	VBN	1-01-001
enlarging	VBG	2-02-002
enlargement	**noun**	**5-04-005**
enlargement	NN	4-03-004
enlargements	NNS	1-01-001
enlarging	**NN**	**1-01-001**
enlighten	**verb**	**8-07-008**
enlighten	VB	1-01-001
enlightened	VBN	7-06-007
enlightening	**JJ**	**3-03-003**
enlightenment	**NN**	**2-01-002**
enlist	**verb**	**17-08-016**
enlist	VB	5-04-005
enlists	VBZ	1-01-001
enlisted	VBD	5-04-005
enlisted	VBN	6-03-005
enlistment	**NN**	**1-01-001**
enliven	**verb**	**2-02-002**
enlivened	VBN	2-02-002
enmesh	**verb**	**2-02-002**
enmeshed	VBN	2-02-002
enmity	**noun**	**2-02-002**
enmity	NN	1-01-001
enmities	NNS	1-01-001
Ennis	**NP**	**1-01-001**
Enoch	**NP**	**1-01-001**
enormity	**NN**	**1-01-001**
enormous	**JJ**	**37-12-036**
enormously	**QL**	**5-03-005**
enormously	**RB**	**4-04-004**
Enos	**NP**	**1-01-001**
enough	**post-det.**	**181-15-134**
enough	AP	178-15-132
'nough	AP	1-01-001
nuf	AP	1-01-001
enough	AP-HL	1-01-001
enough	**post-qual.**	**247-15-169**
enough	QLP	246-15-168
'nuff	QLP	1-01-001
enough	**RB**	**6-04-006**
enough	**verb**	**1-01-001**
enough	VB	0-00-000
'nuff	VB-NC	1-01-001
enquetes	**foreign**	**1-01-001**
enquetes	FW-NNS	0-00-000
enquetes	FW-NNS-NC	1-01-001
Enquirer	**NP**	**1-01-001**
enrage	**NN**	**1-01-001**
enrage	**verb**	**1-01-001**
enraged	VBD	1-01-001
enrapture	**verb**	**1-01-001**
enraptured	VBN	1-01-001
enrich	**verb**	**8-05-008**
enrich	VB	5-04-005
enriched	VBN	2-01-002
enriching	VBG	1-01-001
enrichment	**NN**	**3-02-003**
Enrico	**prop. noun**	**2-02-002**
Enrico	NP	1-01-001
Enrico	NP-TL	1-01-001

Word	Tag	Count
Enright	**prop. noun**	**4-01-001**
Enright	NP	3-01-001
Enright's	NP$	1-01-001
Enrique	**NP**	**1-01-001**
enroll	**verb**	**15-06-009**
enroll	VB	5-03-004
enrolled	VBD	2-02-002
enrolled	VBN	7-04-006
enrolling	VBG	1-01-001
enrollee	**noun**	**1-01-001**
enrollees	NNS	1-01-001
enrollment	**noun**	**8-05-008**
enrollment	NN	6-04-006
enrollments	NNS	2-02-002
ensconce	**verb**	**2-02-002**
ensconced	VBD	1-01-001
ensconced	VBN	1-01-001
ensemble	**foreign**	**1-01-001**
ensemble	FW-NN	0-00-000
Ensemble	FW-NN-TL	1-01-001
ensemble	**noun**	**13-04-009**
ensemble	NN	9-02-006
Ensemble	NN-TL	1-01-001
ensembles	NNS	3-03-003
ensign	**noun**	**3-01-001**
ensign	NN	0-00-000
Ensign	NN-TL	3-01-001
Ensign	**NP**	**1-01-001**
enslave	**verb**	**3-02-002**
enslave	VB	2-01-001
enslaved	VBN	1-01-001
enslavement	**NN**	**2-02-002**
enslaving	**NN**	**1-01-001**
Ensolite	**NP**	**1-01-001**
ensue	**verb**	**13-09-013**
ensue	VB	2-02-002
ensues	VBZ	2-02-002
ensued	VBD	4-03-004
ensued	VBN	1-01-001
ensuing	VBG	4-04-004
ensure	**verb**	**11-05-010**
ensure	VB	8-05-007
ensures	VBZ	1-01-001
ensuring	VBG	2-02-002
entail	**verb**	**13-08-012**
entail	VB	5-05-005
entails	VBZ	8-06-007
entanglement	**NN**	**1-01-001**
enter	**verb**	**213-14-145**
enter	VB	78-12-064
enters	VBZ	13-06-013
entered	VBD	76-13-056
entered	VBN	21-09-016
enter'd	VBN	1-01-001
entering	VBG	24-10-023
enterotoxemia	**NN**	**1-01-001**
enterprise	**noun**	**45-07-028**
enterprise	NN	31-07-024
enterprises	NNS	14-06-009
enterprising	**JJ**	**5-04-005**
enterprisingly	**RB**	**1-01-001**
entertain	**verb**	**34-11-022**
entertain	VB	14-08-011
entertained	VBD	4-02-002
entertained	VBN	7-07-007
enterteyned	VBN	1-01-001
entertaining	VBG	8-04-006
entertainer	**noun**	**5-04-005**
entertainer	NN	2-01-002
entertainers	NNS	3-03-003
entertaining	**JJ**	**4-01-004**
entertainment	**noun**	**32-09-021**
entertainment	NN	28-09-018
entertainment	NN-HL	1-01-001
entertainments	NNS	3-03-003
enthalpy	**NN**	**2-01-001**
enthrall	**verb**	**2-02-002**
enthralled	VBN	1-01-001
enthralling	VBG	1-01-001
enthralling	**JJ**	**2-02-002**
enthrone	**verb**	**1-01-001**
enthrones	VBZ	1-01-001
enthusiasm	**noun**	**29-12-027**
enthusiasm	NN	28-12-026
enthusiasms	NNS	1-01-001
enthusiast	**noun**	**5-05-005**
enthusiast	NN	2-02-002
enthusiasts	NNS	3-03-003
enthusiastic	**JJ**	**24-11-024**

enthusiastically	**RB**	**5-03-004**
entice	**verb**	**1-01-001**
enticing	VBG	1-01-001
enticement	**noun**	**1-01-001**
enticements	NNS	1-01-001
entire	**adjective**	**149-14-114**
entire	JJ	148-14-113
entire	JJ-HL	1-01-001
entirely	**QL**	**30-10-027**
entirely	**RB**	**61-14-050**
entirety	**NN**	**7-04-007**
entitle	**verb**	**65-11-041**
entitle	VB	5-03-003
entitles	VBZ	4-03-004
entitled	VBD	2-02-002
entitled	VBN	54-10-035
entity	**noun**	**21-08-015**
entity	NN	10-07-010
entities	NNS	11-04-008
entomb	**verb**	**1-01-001**
entombed	VBN	1-01-001
entomologist	**NN**	**1-01-001**
entourage	**NN**	**4-03-004**
entrance	**NN**	**57-12-036**
entrance	**verb**	**3-03-003**
entranced	VBN	3-03-003
entranceway	**NN**	**1-01-001**
entrant	**NN**	**2-02-002**
entreat	**verb**	**3-01-002**
entreat	VB	1-01-001
entreated	VBD	2-01-002
entrench	**verb**	**5-03-005**
entrenched	VBD	1-01-001
entrenched	VBN	4-02-004
entrepreneur	**noun**	**7-01-003**
entrepreneur	NN	6-01-003
entrepreneurs	NNS	1-01-001
entropy	**NN**	**4-01-001**
entropy-increasing	**JJ**	**1-01-001**
entrust	**verb**	**5-04-004**
entrust	VB	2-02-002
entrusted	VBN	2-02-002
entrusting	VBG	1-01-001
entry	**noun**	**45-12-022**
entry	NN	24-11-018
entry	NN-HL	1-01-001
Entry	NN-TL	1-01-001
entries	NNS	18-04-007
entries	NNS-HL	1-01-001
entry-limit	**NN**	**1-01-001**
entry-limited	**JJ**	**1-01-001**
entry-limiting	**JJ**	**2-01-001**
Entwhistle	**NP**	**1-01-001**
entwine	**verb**	**2-02-002**
entwined	VBN	2-02-002
enumerate	**verb**	**2-01-002**
enumerated	VBN	2-01-002
enumeration	**NN**	**1-01-001**
enunciate	**verb**	**2-02-002**
enunciate	VB	1-01-001
enunciated	VBD	1-01-001
enunciation	**NN**	**1-01-001**
envelop	**verb**	**2-02-002**
enveloping	VBG	2-02-002
envelope	**noun**	**24-06-016**
envelope	NN	21-06-013
envelopes	NNS	3-02-003
envenom	**verb**	**1-01-001**
envenomed	VBN	1-01-001
Enver	**NP**	**4-02-002**
enviable	**JJ**	**4-04-004**
enviably	**RB**	**1-01-001**
envious	**JJ**	**1-01-001**
enviously	**RB**	**1-01-001**
environ	**verb**	**1-01-001**
environing	VBG	1-01-001
environment	**noun**	**47-07-026**
environment	NN	43-07-025
environments	NNS	4-02-003
environmental	**JJ**	**7-02-005**
environs	**NNS**	**4-04-004**
envisage	**verb**	**2-02-002**
envisages	VBZ	1-01-001
envisaged	VBN	1-01-001
envision	**verb**	**9-05-009**
envision	VB	3-02-003
envisions	VBZ	2-01-002
envisioned	VBD	3-03-003
envisioned	VBN	1-01-001

envoy	**noun**	**1-01-001**
envoys	NNS	1-01-001
envy	**NN**	**4-03-004**
envy	**verb**	**8-06-008**
envy	VB	3-03-003
envied	VBD	5-04-005
Enzo	**NP**	**1-01-001**
enzymatic	**JJ**	**4-01-003**
enzyme	**noun**	**17-03-005**
enzyme	NN	6-03-004
enzymes	NNS	11-02-004
eosinophilic	**JJ**	**1-01-001**
epaulet	**noun**	**1-01-001**
epaulets	NNS	1-01-001
Eph	**NP**	**1-01-001**
ephemeral	**JJ**	**4-03-004**
Ephesian	**prop. noun**	**5-01-001**
Ephesians	NPS	0-00-000
Ephesians	NPS-TL	5-01-001
Ephesus	**NP**	**2-02-002**
epic	**JJ**	**4-03-004**
epic	**noun**	**16-02-003**
epic	NN	14-02-003
epics	NNS	2-01-002
epicenter	**NN**	**3-01-001**
epicure	**NN**	**2-02-002**
Epicurean	**NP**	**1-01-001**
Epicurus	**NP**	**1-01-001**
epicycle	**noun**	**7-01-001**
epicycle	NN	1-01-001
epicycles	NNS	6-01-001
epicyclical	**JJ**	**1-01-001**
epicyclically	**RB**	**1-01-001**
epidemic	**noun**	**13-04-005**
epidemic	NN	11-04-005
epidemics	NNS	2-01-001
epidemiological	**adjective**	**1-01-001**
epidemiological	JJ	0-00-000
Epidemiological	JJ-TL	1-01-001
epidermis	**NN**	**2-02-002**
epigenetic	**JJ**	**1-01-001**
epigram	**noun**	**2-02-002**
epigrams	NNS	2-02-002
epigrammatic	**JJ**	**1-01-001**
epigraph	**noun**	**2-01-002**
epigraph	NN	1-01-001
Epigraph	NN-TL	1-01-001
epileptic	**JJ**	**3-03-003**
epilogue	**NN**	**1-01-001**
epiphany	**noun**	**3-02-002**
epiphany	NN	2-01-001
Epiphany	NN-TL	1-01-001
epiphyseal-diaphyseal	**JJ**	**2-01-001**
epiphysis	**NN**	**5-01-001**
Episcopal	**adjective**	**6-04-005**
Episcopal	JJ	1-01-001
Episcopal	JJ-TL	5-04-005
episode	**noun**	**18-10-014**
episode	NN	12-09-011
episodes	NNS	6-05-005
epistemology	**NN**	**3-02-002**
epistle	**noun**	**1-01-001**
epistles	NNS	0-00-000
Epistles	NNS-TL	1-01-001
epistolatory	**JJ**	**1-01-001**
epitaph	**noun**	**4-02-002**
epitaph	NN	1-01-001
Epitaph	NN-TL	3-01-001
epithet	**noun**	**9-02-003**
epithet	NN	2-01-001
epithets	NNS	7-02-002
epitome	**NN**	**2-01-002**
epitomize	**verb**	**5-03-005**
epitomize	VB	1-01-001
epitomizes	VBZ	1-01-001
epitomized	VBD	1-01-001
epitomized	VBN	2-02-002
epoch	**NN**	**6-03-005**
epoch-making	**JJ**	**1-01-001**
epoxy	**NN**	**2-02-002**
Eppler	**NP**	**1-01-001**
Epsilon	**NP**	**1-01-001**
epsom	**NN**	**1-01-001**
Epsom	**NP**	**1-01-001**
Epstein	**prop. noun**	**1-01-001**
Epstein	NP	0-00-000
Epstein	NP-TL	1-01-001
equal	**adjective**	**83-14-065**
equal	JJ	82-14-064

Word	Tag	Frequency
equal (cont.):		
equal	JJ-HL	1-01-001
equal	**noun**	**2-02-002**
equal	NN	1-01-001
equals	NNS	1-01-001
equal	**verb**	**14-06-010**
equal	VB	6-04-006
equals	VBZ	7-03-003
equalled	VBN	1-01-001
equality	**NN**	**12-06-010**
equalization	**NN**	**1-01-001**
equalize	**VB**	**1-01-001**
equalizer	**noun**	**1-01-001**
equalizers	NNS	1-01-001
equalizing	**NN**	**1-01-001**
equally	**QL**	**33-11-027**
equally	**RB**	**29-11-025**
equanimity	**NN**	**2-02-002**
equate	**verb**	**15-04-008**
equate	VB	7-01-003
Equate	VB-TL	1-01-001
equated	VBD	3-02-002
equated	VBN	2-02-002
equating	VBG	2-02-002
equating	**NN**	**1-01-001**
equation	**noun**	**49-05-019**
equation	NN	33-05-014
eq.	NN	0-00-000
Eq.	NN-TL	2-01-001
eqn.	NN	3-01-001
equations	NNS	10-02-006
eqns.	NNS	1-01-001
equator	**noun**	**3-03-003**
equator	NN	1-01-001
Equator	NN-TL	2-02-002
equatorial	**JJ**	**1-01-001**
equidistant	**JJ**	**1-01-001**
equidistantly	**RB**	**1-01-001**
equilibrate	**verb**	**2-01-002**
equilibrated	VBN	2-01-002
equilibrium	**noun**	**14-04-009**
equilibrium	NN	13-03-008
equilibriums	NNS	1-01-001
equine	**noun**	**2-01-001**
equine	NN	1-01-001
equines	NNS	1-01-001
Equinox	**prop. noun**	**2-01-001**
Equinox	NP	0-00-000
Equinox	NP-TL	2-01-001
equip	**verb**	**37-09-028**
equip	VB	1-01-001
equipped	VBN	36-09-027
equipment	**noun**	**167-14-078**
equipment	NN	162-14-078
equipment	NN-HL	5-04-004
equipotent	**JJ**	**1-01-001**
equipping	**NN**	**1-01-001**
equitable	**JJ**	**11-05-007**
equitably	**RB**	**2-02-002**
equity	**noun**	**7-04-004**
equity	NN	5-04-004
Equity	NN-TL	2-01-001
equivalence	**NN**	**4-02-003**
equivalent	**JJ**	**36-10-024**
equivalent	**noun**	**18-08-013**
equivalent	NN	10-06-009
equivalents	NNS	8-04-005
equivalent-choice	**NN**	**1-01-001**
equivocal	**JJ**	**1-01-001**
era	**noun**	**34-11-025**
era	NN	29-11-023
Era	NN-TL	1-01-001
era's	NN$	2-01-002
eras	NNS	2-01-002
eradicate	**VB**	**2-02-002**
eradication	**NN**	**3-01-001**
erase	**verb**	**5-03-004**
erase	VB	1-01-001
erased	VBN	2-02-002
erasing	VBG	2-02-002
eraser	**noun**	**3-02-002**
eraser	NN	2-01-001
erasers	NNS	1-01-001
Erasmus	**prop. noun**	**1-01-001**
Erasmus's	NP$	1-01-001
Erde	**foreign**	**1-01-001**
Erde	FW-NN	0-00-000
Erde	FW-NN-TL	1-01-001
Erdmann	**prop. noun**	**1-01-001**

Word	Tag	Frequency
Erdmann (cont.):		
Erdmann's	NP$	1-01-001
Erdos	**NP**	**2-01-001**
ere	**CS**	**1-01-001**
erect	**JJ**	**8-04-005**
erect	**verb**	**27-06-020**
erect	VB	5-03-004
erects	VBZ	1-01-001
erected	VBD	3-03-003
erected	VBN	15-06-011
erecting	VBG	3-02-003
erection	**noun**	**5-03-004**
erection	NN	4-02-003
Erection	NN-TL	1-01-001
ergotropic	**JJ**	**1-01-001**
Erhart	**NP**	**3-01-001**
Eric	**NP**	**3-03-003**
Erich	**NP**	**4-02-003**
Erickson	**NP**	**1-01-001**
Erie	**NP**	**2-02-002**
Erik	**NP**	**2-02-002**
Erikson	**prop. noun**	**9-01-001**
Erikson	NP	6-01-001
Erikson's	NP$	3-01-001
Erlenmeyer	**NP**	**1-01-001**
Ernest	**NP**	**10-03-004**
Ernie	**prop. noun**	**19-02-003**
Ernie	NP	18-02-003
Ernie's	NP$	1-01-001
Ernst	**NP**	**5-03-003**
erode	**verb**	**4-03-004**
eroded	VBD	1-01-001
eroded	VBN	3-03-003
eromonga	**noun**	**1-01-001**
eromonga	NN	0-00-000
eromonga	NN-NC	1-01-001
Eromonga	**NP**	**9-01-001**
Eros	**prop. noun**	**2-01-001**
Eros	NP	1-01-001
Eros	NP-TL	1-01-001
erosion	**NN**	**6-04-005**
erotic	**JJ**	**8-02-004**
erotica	**NNS**	**1-01-001**
erotically	**RB**	**1-01-001**
err	**verb**	**5-03-005**
err	VB	1-01-001
errs	VBZ	0-00-000
errs	VBZ-HL	1-01-001
erred	VBD	1-01-001
erred	VBN	2-02-002
errand	**NN**	**7-03-005**
erratic	**JJ**	**3-02-003**
erratically	**RB**	**1-01-001**
Errol	**NP**	**1-01-001**
erroneous	**JJ**	**4-04-004**
erroneously	**RB**	**1-01-001**
error	**noun**	**80-11-048**
error	NN	34-08-025
error	NN-HL	2-02-002
errors	NNS	42-10-028
errors	NNS-HL	1-01-001
Errors	NNS-TL	1-01-001
ersatz	**FW-NN**	**2-02-002**
Erskine	**NP**	**1-01-001**
erudite	**JJ**	**3-03-003**
erudition	**NN**	**1-01-001**
erupt	**verb**	**11-06-010**
erupt	VB	2-01-002
erupts	VBZ	1-01-001
erupted	VBD	5-04-005
erupted	VBN	2-02-002
erupting	VBG	1-01-001
eruption	**NN**	**2-02-002**
Ervin	**NP**	**2-01-002**
Erwin	**NP**	**1-01-001**
erysipelas	**NN**	**1-01-001**
erythroid	**JJ**	**1-01-001**
escadrille	**foreign**	**1-01-001**
escadrille	FW-NN	0-00-000
Escadrille	FW-NN-TL	1-01-001
escalation	**noun**	**7-02-002**
escalation	NN	6-02-002
escalation	NN-HL	1-01-001
escapade	**noun**	**3-03-003**
escapade	NN	1-01-001
escapades	NNS	2-02-002
escape	**noun**	**24-10-018**
escape	NN	18-09-014
escape	NN-HL	1-01-001

Word	Tag	Frequency
escape (cont.):		
Escape	NN-TL	2-02-002
escape's	NN$	0-00-000
Escape's	NN$-TL	1-01-001
escapes	NNS	2-02-002
escape	**verb**	**69-13-057**
escape	VB	44-12-038
escapes	VBZ	2-02-002
escaped	VBD	8-06-008
escaped	VBN	10-06-010
escaping	VBG	5-04-005
escapee	**noun**	**1-01-001**
escapees	NNS	1-01-001
escapist	**NN**	**1-01-001**
escheat	**NN**	**2-01-001**
eschew	**verb**	**4-04-004**
eschew	VB	1-01-001
eschews	VBZ	1-01-001
eschewed	VBN	1-01-001
eschewing	VBG	1-01-001
escort	**noun**	**6-04-005**
escort	NN	5-04-005
escorts	NNS	1-01-001
escort	**verb**	**11-07-010**
escort	VB	4-02-003
escorted	VBD	4-03-004
escorted	VBN	1-01-001
escorting	VBG	2-02-002
escritoire	**NN**	**2-01-001**
escutcheon	**noun**	**3-03-003**
escutcheon	NN	2-02-002
escutcheons	NNS	1-01-001
Eshleman	**NP**	**1-01-001**
Eskimo	**prop. noun**	**5-02-002**
Eskimo	NP	3-02-002
Eskimos	NPS	2-01-001
Esmarch	**NP**	**2-01-001**
Esnard	**prop. noun**	**1-01-001**
Esnards	NPS	1-01-001
esoteric	**JJ**	**4-03-003**
ESP	**NP**	**1-01-001**
Espagnol	**FW-JJ**	**1-01-001**
Espanol	**FW-NP**	**1-01-001**
especially	**qualifier**	**21-07-020**
especially	QL	20-06-019
Especially	QL-TL	1-01-001
especially	**RB**	**141-15-111**
Esperanza	**prop. noun**	**1-01-001**
Esperanza	NP	0-00-000
Esperanza	NP-TL	1-01-001
espionage	**NN**	**5-03-005**
esplanade	**NN**	**3-01-001**
espousal	**NN**	**1-01-001**
espouse	**verb**	**4-03-004**
espouses	VBZ	1-01-001
espoused	VBD	1-01-001
espoused	VBN	1-01-001
espousing	VBG	1-01-001
esprit	**FW-NN**	**6-02-003**
Esquire	**NP**	**3-03-003**
essay	**noun**	**27-07-019**
essay	NN	19-05-013
essays	NNS	8-04-006
essay	**verb**	**2-02-002**
essayed	VBD	1-01-001
essayed	VBN	1-01-001
essayist	**noun**	**1-01-001**
essayists	NNS	1-01-001
esse	**foreign**	**2-01-001**
esse	FW-VB	1-01-001
esse	FW-VB-NC	1-01-001
essence	**noun**	**17-08-016**
essence	NN	15-07-014
essences	NNS	2-02-002
essential	**adjective**	**78-13-058**
essential	JJ	77-13-057
essential	JJ-HL	1-01-001
essential	**noun**	**5-04-005**
essential	NN	3-03-003
essentials	NNS	2-02-002
essentially	**QL**	**8-03-007**
essentially	**RB**	**39-09-036**
Essex	**prop. noun**	**12-04-005**
Essex	NP	7-02-003
Essex	NP-TL	5-03-003
est	**FW-BEZ**	**3-02-003**
establish	**verb**	**195-13-126**
establish	VB	58-09-043
establishes	VBZ	4-03-004
establish (cont.):		
established	VBD	9-07-009
established	VBN	98-11-079
established	VBN-HL	1-01-001
establishing	VBG	25-06-019
establishing	**NN**	**1-01-001**
establishment	**noun**	**60-13-050**
establishment	NN	52-12-043
establishments	NNS	8-06-007
estate	**noun**	**56-11-036**
estate	NN	48-11-033
Estate	NN-TL	3-01-001
estates	NNS	4-03-004
estates	NNS-HL	1-01-001
esteem	**NN**	**5-03-005**
esteem	**verb**	**3-02-003**
esteemed	VBD	2-01-002
esteemed	VBN	1-01-001
Estella	**prop. noun**	**5-01-001**
Estella	NP	4-01-001
Estella's	NP$	1-01-001
Estep	**prop. noun**	**1-01-001**
Estep	NP	0-00-000
Estep	NP-TL	1-01-001
ester	**noun**	**1-01-001**
esters	NNS	1-01-001
esterase	**noun**	**2-01-001**
esterases	NNS	1-01-001
esterases	NNS-HL	1-01-001
Estes	**NP**	**1-01-001**
Esther	**NP**	**9-02-002**
Estherson	**NP**	**1-01-001**
esthetic	**JJ**	**3-03-003**
esthetics	**noun**	**4-02-004**
esthetics	NN	3-02-003
aesthetics	NN	1-01-001
estimate	**noun**	**53-10-040**
estimate	NN	26-08-021
Estimate	NN-TL	4-01-001
estimates	NNS	23-07-020
estimate	**verb**	**79-10-049**
estimate	VB	9-05-008
estimates	VBZ	1-01-001
estimated	VBD	8-03-005
estimated	VBN	57-10-038
estimated	VBN-HL	2-02-002
estimating	VBG	2-02-002
estimation	**NN**	**4-03-003**
estrange	**verb**	**4-03-004**
estranged	VBD	1-01-001
estranged	VBN	2-02-002
estranging	VBG	1-01-001
estrangement	**NN**	**1-01-001**
estuary	**noun**	**1-01-001**
estuaries	NNS	1-01-001
et	**foreign**	**29-11-021**
et	FW-CC	19-08-015
et	FW-CC-TL	10-05-006
Eta	**NP**	**4-01-001**
etcetera	**adverb**	**67-10-045**
etcetera	RB	9-02-002
etc.	RB	58-09-043
etch	**verb**	**2-02-002**
etched	VBD	1-01-001
etched	VBN	1-01-001
eternal	**adjective**	**29-09-021**
eternal	JJ	26-08-019
Eternal	JJ-TL	3-03-003
eternity	**NN**	**6-05-005**
etes	**FW-BER**	**1-01-001**
Ethan	**prop. noun**	**4-02-002**
Ethan	NP	0-00-000
Ethan	NP-TL	4-02-002
ethanol	**NN**	**1-01-001**
Ethel	**NP**	**3-02-003**
ether	**noun**	**1-01-001**
ethers	NNS	1-01-001
ethereal	**JJ**	**3-03-003**
ethic	**noun**	**18-06-015**
ethic	NN	4-02-004
ethics	NN	6-03-005
ethics	NNS	7-04-006
ethics	NNS-HL	1-01-001
ethical	**JJ**	**29-06-017**
ethically	**RB**	**2-02-002**
ethicist	**noun**	**3-02-002**
ethicist	NN	2-02-002
ethicists	NNS	1-01-001
ethics	**noun**	**5-03-003**

Word	Tag	Frequency
ethics (cont.):		
ethics	NN	0-00-000
Ethics	NN-TL	5-03-003
Ethiopian	**prop. noun**	**1-01-001**
Ethiopians	NPS	1-01-001
ethnic	**JJ**	**13-06-008**
ethos	**NN**	**4-03-004**
ethyl	**NN**	**4-02-002**
etiquette	**noun**	**3-03-003**
etiquette	NN	2-02-002
etiquette	NN-HL	1-01-001
Etruscan	**JJ**	**1-01-001**
Ettore	**NP**	**1-01-001**
Etude	**prop. noun**	**1-01-001**
Etudes	NPS	1-01-001
etymological	**JJ**	**1-01-001**
eucalyptus	**NN**	**1-01-001**
Euclid	**prop. noun**	**2-01-001**
Euclid's	NP$	2-01-001
Eugene	**prop. noun**	**27-05-009**
Eugene	NP	25-05-009
Eugene's	NP$	2-01-001
Eugenia	**NP**	**15-01-001**
eugenic	**JJ**	**1-01-001**
eulogize	**verb**	**2-02-002**
eulogize	VB	1-01-001
eulogized	VBN	1-01-001
eulogizer	**noun**	**1-01-001**
eulogizers	NNS	1-01-001
EUMMELIHS	**FW-JJ**	**1-01-001**
euphemism	**NN**	**1-01-001**
euphoria	**NN**	**2-02-002**
euphoric	**JJ**	**1-01-001**
Eurasian	**JJ**	**1-01-001**
Euratom	**NP**	**1-01-001**
Euripides	**NP**	**3-01-001**
Europe	**prop. noun**	**121-13-057**
Europe	NP	93-13-050
Europe	NP-HL	1-01-001
Europe	NP-TL	24-08-013
Europe's	NP$	3-02-003
European	**adjective**	**59-08-030**
European	JJ	50-08-027
European	JJ-TL	9-02-004
European	**prop. noun**	**7-05-006**
European	NP	2-01-001
Europeans	NPS	5-05-005
Europeanish	**JJ**	**1-01-001**
Europeanization	**NN**	**1-01-001**
Europeanize	**verb**	**1-01-001**
Europeanized	VBN	1-01-001
Eurydice	**NP**	**2-01-001**
Eustis	**NP**	**3-01-001**
eutectic	**NN**	**1-01-001**
eva	**noun**	**1-01-001**
eva	NN	0-00-000
eva	NN-NC	1-01-001
evacuate	**verb**	**4-03-004**
evacuate	VB	1-01-001
evacuated	VBN	3-02-003
evacuation	**NN**	**5-04-005**
evade	**verb**	**5-05-005**
evade	VB	1-01-001
evades	VBZ	1-01-001
evaded	VBD	1-01-001
evaded	VBN	1-01-001
evading	VBG	1-01-001
Evadna	**NP**	**3-01-001**
evaluate	**verb**	**31-06-026**
evaluate	VB	13-05-011
evaluated	VBN	11-03-010
evaluating	VBG	7-03-006
evaluation	**noun**	**36-05-022**
evaluation	NN	29-04-018
evaluation	NN-HL	2-01-002
evaluations	NNS	5-04-004
evaluative	**JJ**	**1-01-001**
evangelical	**adjective**	**5-02-003**
evangelical	JJ	4-01-002
Evangelical	JJ	1-01-001
Evangelicalism	**NP**	**1-01-001**
evangelism	**noun**	**9-02-003**
evangelism	NN	7-02-003
Evangelism	NN-TL	2-01-001
evangelist	**noun**	**2-02-002**
evangelist	NN	1-01-001
evangelists	NNS	1-01-001
Evans	**NP**	**10-03-004**
Evanston	**NP**	**7-02-002**

Word	Tag	Frequency
Evansville	**prop. noun**	**1-01-001**
Evansville	NP	0-00-000
Evansville	NP-HL	1-01-001
evaporate	**verb**	**3-03-003**
evaporate	VB	1-01-001
evaporated	VBD	1-01-001
evaporated	VBN	1-01-001
evaporation	**NN**	**2-02-002**
evaporative	**JJ**	**1-01-001**
evasion	**noun**	**2-02-002**
evasion	NN	1-01-001
evasions	NNS	1-01-001
evasive	**JJ**	**5-04-005**
eve	**noun**	**11-06-010**
eve	NN	5-04-005
Eve	NN-TL	6-04-005
Eve	**NP**	**8-02-002**
Evegeni	**NP**	**1-01-001**
Evelyn	**NP**	**4-03-004**
even	**JJ**	**25-08-015**
even	**QL**	**119-15-105**
even	**RB**	**997-15-372**
even	**VB**	**28-10-026**
even-handed	**JJ**	**1-01-001**
evening	**noun**	**149-14-089**
evening	NN	128-14-082
Evening	NN-TL	5-04-004
evening's	NN$	1-01-001
evenings	NNS	15-10-014
evenly	**RB**	**4-03-004**
Evensen	**NP**	**1-01-001**
evensong	**NN**	**1-01-001**
event	**noun**	**182-14-119**
event	NN	81-12-062
events	NNS	100-14-068
Events	NNS-TL	1-01-001
eventfully	**RB**	**1-01-001**
eventual	**JJ**	**11-07-010**
eventuality	**noun**	**2-01-002**
eventuality	NN	1-01-001
eventualities	NNS	1-01-001
eventually	**adverb**	**55-14-047**
eventually	RB	52-13-045
eventshahleh	RB	1-01-001
eventshah-leh	RB-NC	1-01-001
evenutally	RB	1-01-001
eventuate	**VB**	**1-01-001**
ever	**QL**	**7-04-006**
ever	**RB**	**337-15-206**
ever-changing	**JJ**	**5-04-005**
ever-existent	**JJ**	**1-01-001**
ever-expanding	**JJ**	**3-03-003**
ever-growing	**JJ**	**2-01-001**
ever-increasing	**JJ**	**2-01-002**
ever-loving	**adjective**	**1-01-001**
ever-loving	JJ	0-00-000
ever-lovin'	JJ	1-01-001
ever-present	**JJ**	**6-05-006**
ever-tightening	**JJ**	**1-01-001**
Everest	**prop. noun**	**2-02-002**
Everest	NP	1-01-001
Everest	NP-TL	1-01-001
Everett	**NP**	**3-03-003**
everglade	**noun**	**1-01-001**
everglades	NNS	0-00-000
Everglades	NNS-TL	1-01-001
evergreen	**adjective**	**1-01-001**
evergreen	JJ	0-00-000
Evergreen	JJ-TL	1-01-001
everlasting	**JJ**	**8-04-006**
everlastingly	**RB**	**1-01-001**
evermounting	**JJ**	**1-01-001**
every	**article**	**492-15-275**
every	AT	490-15-274
ever'	AT	1-01-001
Every	AT-TL	1-01-001
everybody	**nom. pro.**	**77-14-059**
everybody	PN	71-14-055
ever'body	PN	1-01-001
everybody's	PN$	4-04-004
everybody	PN-NC	1-01-001
everyday	**adjective**	**13-07-009**
everyday	JJ	12-07-009
every-day	JJ	1-01-001
everyone	**nom. pro.**	**98-14-073**
everyone	PN	94-14-071
everyone's	PN$	4-02-004
everything	**nom. pro.**	**188-15-123**
everything	PN	185-15-122

Word	Tag	Frequency
everything (cont.):		
everything's	PN+BEZ	3-03-003
everywhere	**NN**	**4-04-004**
everywhere	**adverb**	**43-12-038**
everywhere	RB	42-12-037
Everywhere	RB	1-01-001
evict	**verb**	**2-02-002**
evicted	VBN	2-02-002
evidence	**noun**	**208-14-124**
evidence	NN	203-14-120
evidences	NNS	4-03-004
evidences	NNS-HL	1-01-001
evidence	**verb**	**14-05-013**
evidence	VB	1-01-001
evidenced	VBN	12-05-011
evidencing	VBG	1-01-001
evident	**JJ**	**56-12-043**
evidential	**JJ**	**1-01-001**
evidently	**RB**	**25-09-019**
evil	**JJ**	**39-09-018**
evil	**noun**	**42-11-024**
evil	NN	33-10-019
evils	NNS	9-05-006
evildoer	**noun**	**1-01-001**
evildoers	NNS	1-01-001
evince	**verb**	**1-01-001**
evinced	VBN	1-01-001
evocation	**noun**	**3-02-003**
evocation	NN	1-01-001
evocations	NNS	2-01-002
evocative	**JJ**	**2-02-002**
evoke	**verb**	**19-05-016**
evoke	VB	6-03-006
evokes	VBZ	5-03-004
evoked	VBD	2-02-002
evoked	VBN	5-03-005
evoking	VBG	1-01-001
evolution	**noun**	**14-04-011**
evolution	NN	12-03-010
Evolution	NN-TL	2-02-002
evolutionary	**JJ**	**4-03-003**
evolutionist	**noun**	**1-01-001**
evolutionists	NNS	1-01-001
evolve	**verb**	**16-06-014**
evolve	VB	5-03-005
evolves	VBZ	1-01-001
evolved	VBD	2-02-002
evolved	VBN	6-03-006
evolving	VBG	2-02-002
Evzone	**NP**	**1-01-001**
EWC	**NP**	**1-01-001**
Ewe	**NP**	**1-01-001**
Ewen	**NP**	**1-01-001**
ex	**FW-IN**	**2-02-002**
ex	**JJ**	**7-03-006**
ex-bandit	**noun**	**1-01-001**
ex-bandits	NNS	1-01-001
ex-Communist	**noun**	**1-01-001**
ex-Communist	NN	0-00-000
ex-Communist	NN-TL	1-01-001
ex-convict	**noun**	**2-02-002**
ex-convict	NN	1-01-001
ex-convicts	NNS	1-01-001
ex-fighter	**NN**	**1-01-001**
ex-gambler	**NN**	**1-01-001**
ex-Governor	**noun**	**1-01-001**
ex-Governor	NN	0-00-000
ex-Gov.	NN	1-01-001
ex-Justice	**NN**	**1-01-001**
ex-liberal	**noun**	**2-01-001**
ex-liberals	NNS	2-01-001
ex-marine	**NN**	**1-01-001**
ex-mayor	**NN**	**1-01-001**
ex-musician	**NN**	**1-01-001**
ex-Oriole	**NP**	**1-01-001**
ex-President	**noun**	**3-03-003**
ex-President	NN	2-02-002
ex-Presidents	NNS	1-01-001
ex-schoolteacher	**NN**	**1-01-001**
ex-singer	**NN**	**1-01-001**
ex-Tory	**NP**	**1-01-001**
ex-Yankee	**NP**	**1-01-001**
exacerbate	**verb**	**3-03-003**
exacerbates	VBZ	1-01-001
exacerbated	VBN	2-02-002
exacerbation	**noun**	**4-03-003**
exacerbation	NN	3-02-002
exacerbations	NNS	1-01-001
exact	**JJ**	**27-11-023**

Word	Tag	Frequency
exact	**verb**	**5-03-005**
exacts	VBZ	2-02-002
exacted	VBD	1-01-001
exacting	VBG	2-01-002
exact-size	**JJ**	**1-01-001**
exactly	**QL**	**6-04-006**
exactly	**RB**	**97-15-081**
exaggerate	**verb**	**25-08-021**
exaggerate	VB	8-05-007
exaggerated	VBN	13-07-013
exaggerating	VBG	4-03-004
exaggeration	**noun**	**6-05-006**
exaggeration	NN	5-05-005
exaggerations	NNS	1-01-001
exalt	**verb**	**9-05-009**
exalt	VB	1-01-001
exalted	VBD	1-01-001
exalted	VBN	6-04-006
exalting	VBG	1-01-001
exaltation	**noun**	**2-02-002**
exaltation	NN	1-01-001
exaltations	NNS	1-01-001
examination	**noun**	**38-09-025**
examination	NN	28-08-021
examiantion	NN	1-01-001
examination	NN-HL	1-01-001
examinations	NNS	8-05-007
examine	**verb**	**70-13-056**
examine	VB	33-10-031
examines	VBZ	1-01-001
examined	VBD	11-08-011
examined	VBN	17-08-015
examining	VBG	7-04-007
examinin'	VBG	1-01-001
examiner	**noun**	**15-06-010**
examiner	NN	6-05-005
Examiner	NN-TL	8-03-004
examiners	NNS	0-00-000
Examiners	NNS-TL	1-01-001
example	**noun**	**345-15-176**
example	NN	286-15-165
example	NN-HL	5-02-003
Example	NN-TL	1-01-001
examples	NNS	50-09-039
examples	NNS-HL	3-01-002
exasperate	**verb**	**3-03-003**
exasperate	VB	1-01-001
exasperated	VBN	2-02-002
exasperating	**JJ**	**1-01-001**
exasperatingly	**QL**	**1-01-001**
exasperation	**NN**	**5-04-005**
exboyfriend	**NN**	**1-01-001**
excavation	**noun**	**4-04-004**
excavation	NN	3-03-003
excavations	NNS	1-01-001
exceed	**verb**	**39-08-026**
exceed	VB	18-05-010
exceeds	VBZ	10-04-009
exceeded	VBD	2-02-002
exceeded	VBN	3-03-003
exceeding	VBG	6-03-006
exceedingly	**QL**	**6-04-006**
exceedingly	**RB**	**2-02-002**
excel	**verb**	**2-02-002**
excel	VB	1-01-001
excels	VBZ	1-01-001
excellence	**FW-NN**	**2-02-002**
excellence	**noun**	**14-06-008**
excellence	NN	13-05-007
excellences	NNS	1-01-001
excellency	**noun**	**2-02-002**
excellency	NN	0-00-000
Excellency	NN-TL	2-02-002
excellent	**JJ**	**68-13-055**
excellently	**QL**	**1-01-001**
excellently	**RB**	**4-03-004**
excelsin	**NN**	**1-01-001**
excelsior	**noun**	**4-02-002**
excelsior	NN	1-01-001
Excelsior	NN-TL	3-01-001
except	**prep.**	**174-15-133**
except	IN	173-15-132
'cept	IN	1-01-001
except	**RB**	**7-04-006**
except	**VB**	**1-01-001**
excepting	**prep.**	**2-02-002**
excepting	IN	1-01-001
'ceptin'	IN	1-01-001
exception	**noun**	**66-12-050**

Word	Tag	Freq
exception (cont.):		
exception	NN	40-12-033
exceptions	NNS	26-07-021
exceptional	**JJ**	**19-06-012**
exceptionally	**QL**	**7-05-007**
exceptionally	**RB**	**1-01-001**
excerpt	**noun**	**11-03-006**
excerpt	NN	6-02-003
excerpts	NNS	5-03-004
excess	**JJ**	**19-07-012**
excess	**noun**	**26-09-024**
excess	NN	22-07-020
excess	NN-HL	1-01-001
excesses	NNS	3-02-003
excessive	**JJ**	**30-10-024**
excessively	**QL**	**2-02-002**
excessively	**RB**	**1-01-001**
exchange	**noun**	**72-11-038**
exchange	NN	56-11-031
exchange	NN-HL	1-01-001
Exchange	NN-TL	10-07-008
exchanges	NNS	5-04-004
exchange	**verb**	**13-07-010**
exchange	VB	3-03-003
exchanged	VBD	2-02-002
exchanged	VBN	5-03-003
exchanging	VBG	3-02-003
exchequer	**noun**	**5-01-001**
exchequer	NN	1-01-001
Exchequer	NN-TL	4-01-001
excise	**NN**	**4-02-003**
excise	**verb**	**1-01-001**
excised	VBN	1-01-001
excitability	**NN**	**4-01-001**
excitatory	**JJ**	**4-01-001**
excite	**verb**	**28-13-026**
excite	VB	3-03-003
excited	VBD	2-02-002
excited	VBN	21-11-020
exciting	VBG	2-02-002
excitedly	**RB**	**7-05-007**
excitement	**noun**	**32-11-027**
excitement	NN	31-11-026
Excitement	NN	1-01-001
exciting	**JJ**	**27-11-022**
exclaim	**verb**	**20-08-018**
exclaim	VB	1-01-001
exclaims	VBZ	1-01-001
exclaimed	VBD	14-07-013
exclaiming	VBG	4-03-004
exclamation	**noun**	**8-03-004**
exclamation	NN	6-03-004
exclamations	NNS	2-01-001
exclude	**verb**	**21-08-017**
exclude	VB	7-05-007
excludes	VBZ	3-02-002
excluded	VBN	8-06-008
excluding	VBG	3-03-003
excluding	**prep.**	**13-02-007**
excluding	IN	12-02-007
excluding	IN-HL	1-01-001
exclusion	**noun**	**8-03-006**
exclusion	NN	7-03-005
exclusions	NNS	1-01-001
exclusive	**JJ**	**27-12-025**
exclusive	**NN**	**1-01-001**
exclusively	**QL**	**3-03-003**
exclusively	**RB**	**21-08-018**
exclusiveness	**NN**	**3-02-002**
excommunicate	**verb**	**4-03-004**
excommunicated	VBN	4-03-004
excoriate	**VB**	**1-01-001**
excretion	**NN**	**1-01-001**
excruciating	**JJ**	**2-02-002**
excursion	**noun**	**4-04-004**
excursion	NN	2-02-002
excursions	NNS	2-02-002
excursus	**NN**	**1-01-001**
excusable	**JJ**	**1-01-001**
excuse	**noun**	**23-07-021**
excuse	NN	22-07-020
excuses	NNS	1-01-001
excuse	**verb**	**11-07-011**
excuse	VB	6-06-006
'scuse	VB	1-01-001
excuses	VBZ	1-01-001
excused	VBD	2-02-002
excused	VBN	1-01-001
exec	**NN**	**2-01-001**
execute	**verb**	**22-09-021**
execute	VB	7-04-007
executed	VBD	1-01-001
executed	VBN	13-07-013
executing	VBG	1-01-001
execution	**noun**	**18-09-015**
execution	NN	13-07-011
execution	NN-NC	1-01-001
Execution	NN-TL	1-01-001
executions	NNS	3-02-002
executioner	**noun**	**3-03-003**
executioner	NN	2-02-002
executioner's	NN$	0-00-000
Executioner's	NN$-TL	1-01-001
executive	**adjective**	**15-06-012**
executive	JJ	10-05-009
Executive	JJ-TL	5-03-004
executive	**noun**	**50-10-036**
executive	NN	36-09-027
Executive	NN-TL	4-01-002
executive's	NN$	0-00-000
Executive's	NN$-TL	1-01-001
executives	NNS	7-06-007
Executives	NNS-TL	2-02-002
executor	**noun**	**4-02-003**
executor	NN	2-01-002
executors	NNS	2-01-001
exegete	**noun**	**1-01-001**
exegete	NN	0-00-000
Exegete	NN-TL	1-01-001
exemplar	**NN**	**2-01-002**
exemplify	**verb**	**6-04-006**
exemplify	VB	2-02-002
exemplifies	VBZ	1-01-001
exemplified	VBN	3-02-003
exempt	**JJ**	**4-04-004**
exempt	**VB**	**1-01-001**
exemption	**noun**	**10-04-005**
exemption	NN	7-03-004
exemption	NN-HL	1-01-001
exemptions	NNS	2-02-002
exercise	**noun**	**54-11-023**
exercise	NN	35-09-014
exercises	NNS	18-06-011
exercises	NNS-HL	1-01-001
exercise	**verb**	**50-11-040**
exercise	VB	23-10-021
exercises	VBZ	4-03-003
exercised	VBD	7-04-007
exercised	VBN	11-06-010
exercising	VBG	5-04-005
exercising	**NN**	**1-01-001**
exert	**verb**	**29-09-021**
exert	VB	11-08-011
exerts	VBZ	3-02-002
exerted	VBD	3-02-003
exerted	VBN	10-03-007
exerting	VBG	2-02-002
exertion	**noun**	**2-02-002**
exertion	NN	1-01-001
exertions	NNS	1-01-001
exhale	**verb**	**3-03-003**
exhaled	VBD	2-02-002
exhaling	VBG	1-01-001
exhaust	**NN**	**5-05-005**
exhaust	**verb**	**21-11-020**
exhaust	VB	2-02-002
exhausts	VBZ	1-01-001
exhausted	VBD	3-02-003
exhausted	VBN	12-10-011
exhausting	VBG	3-03-003
exhaustible	**JJ**	**1-01-001**
exhaustingly	**RB**	**1-01-001**
exhaustion	**NN**	**1-01-001**
exhaustive	**JJ**	**2-01-002**
exhaustively	**RB**	**1-01-001**
exhibit	**noun**	**26-06-013**
exhibit	NN	12-05-009
exhibit	NN-HL	1-01-001
exhibits	NNS	12-03-005
Exhibits	NNS-TL	1-01-001
exhibit	**verb**	**31-08-025**
exhibit	VB	12-06-010
exhibits	VBZ	3-03-003
exhibited	VBD	4-02-003
exhibited	VBN	6-06-006
exhibiting	VBG	6-02-004
exhibition	**noun**	**25-07-019**
exhibition	NN	21-06-015

exhibition (cont.):		
Exhibition	NN-TL	1-01-001
exhibitions	NNS	3-03-003
exhibitor	**noun**	**1-01-001**
exhibitors	NNS	1-01-001
exhilarate	**verb**	**1-01-001**
exhilarated	VBN	1-01-001
exhilarating	**JJ**	**2-02-002**
exhort	**verb**	**1-01-001**
exhorting	VBG	1-01-001
exhortation	**noun**	**1-01-001**
exhortations	NNS	1-01-001
exhumation	**noun**	**1-01-001**
exhumations	NNS	1-01-001
exhusband	**NN**	**1-01-001**
exigency	**noun**	**2-02-002**
exigencies	NNS	2-02-002
exile	**noun**	**5-05-005**
exile	NN	4-04-004
exiles	NNS	1-01-001
exile	**verb**	**3-03-003**
exiled	VBD	1-01-001
exiled	VBN	1-01-001
exiling	VBG	1-01-001
exist	**verb**	**202-14-124**
exist	VB	59-10-050
exists	VBZ	42-09-035
exits	VBZ	1-01-001
existed	VBD	27-10-024
existed	VBN	13-07-012
existing	VBG	60-09-042
existence	**noun**	**107-12-066**
existence	NN	106-12-066
existence	NN-HL	1-01-001
existent	**JJ**	**4-02-002**
existent	**NN**	**1-01-001**
existential	**JJ**	**9-02-004**
Existentialism	**NP**	**1-01-001**
existentialist	**noun**	**3-03-003**
existentialist	NN	2-02-002
existentialists	NNS	0-00-000
Existentialists	NNS-TL	1-01-001
exit	**NN**	**7-04-007**
exodus	**noun**	**4-03-004**
exodus	NN	3-03-003
Exodus	NN-TL	1-01-001
exogamous	**JJ**	**1-01-001**
exogamy	**NN**	**2-01-001**
exonerate	**verb**	**3-02-003**
exonerate	VB	2-01-002
exonerated	VBN	1-01-001
exoneration	**NN**	**2-01-001**
exorbitant	**JJ**	**1-01-001**
exorcise	**VB**	**1-01-001**
exothermic	**JJ**	**1-01-001**
exotic	**JJ**	**7-06-007**
expand	**verb**	**64-13-051**
expand	VB	13-07-011
expands	VBZ	2-02-002
expands	VBZ-HL	1-01-001
expanded	VBD	7-05-007
expanded	VBN	13-05-012
expanding	VBG	28-11-025
expandable	**JJ**	**6-02-003**
expanse	**NN**	**5-05-005**
expansion	**noun**	**50-10-033**
expansion	NN	47-10-033
expansions	NNS	3-01-002
expansion-contraction	**NN**	**1-01-001**
expansionist	**NN**	**1-01-001**
expansive	**JJ**	**1-01-001**
expansively	**RB**	**1-01-001**
expansiveness	**NN**	**3-03-003**
ExPe	**NP**	**1-01-001**
expect	**verb**	**335-14-194**
expect	VB	108-14-081
expects	VBZ	22-09-021
expected	VBD	30-09-025
expected	VBN	153-14-103
expected	VBN-HL	4-02-004
expecting	VBG	18-07-018
expectable	**JJ**	**1-01-001**
expectancy	**NN**	**4-04-004**
expectant	**JJ**	**3-03-003**
expectantly	**RB**	**2-02-002**
expectation	**noun**	**34-10-024**
expectation	NN	11-08-011
expectations	NNS	16-07-014
Expectations	NNS-TL	7-01-001

expectedly	**RB**	**1-01-001**
expediency	**NN**	**2-02-002**
expedient	**JJ**	**6-05-006**
expedient	**NN**	**1-01-001**
expedite	**verb**	**2-02-002**
expediting	VBG	2-02-002
expedition	**noun**	**21-09-014**
expedition	NN	14-07-008
Expedition	NN-TL	1-01-001
expeditions	NNS	6-04-005
expeditious	**JJ**	**2-02-002**
expeditiously	**RB**	**1-01-001**
expel	**verb**	**8-05-008**
expel	VB	2-02-002
expelled	VBD	1-01-001
expelled	VBN	4-03-004
expelling	VBG	1-01-001
expend	**verb**	**13-06-012**
expend	VB	1-01-001
expended	VBD	2-02-002
expended	VBN	10-05-009
expendable	**JJ**	**1-01-001**
expenditure	**noun**	**55-08-024**
expenditure	NN	10-06-009
Expenditure	NN-TL	1-01-001
expenditures	NNS	44-07-016
expense	**noun**	**97-13-064**
expense	NN	50-10-044
expenses	NNS	47-11-029
expensive	**JJ**	**44-10-035**
experience	**noun**	**306-15-132**
experience	NN	258-15-116
experiences	NNS	48-11-034
experience	**verb**	**82-12-060**
experience	VB	18-06-015
experiences	VBZ	5-04-004
experienced	VBD	9-06-009
experienced	VBN	43-12-036
experiencing	VBG	7-03-006
experienced	**JJ**	**1-01-001**
experiential	**JJ**	**4-02-002**
experientially	**RB**	**1-01-001**
experiment	**noun**	**122-09-048**
experiment	NN	52-09-027
experiment	NN-HL	3-01-001
experiment	NN-NC	1-01-001
experiments	NNS	65-07-027
experiments	NNS-HL	1-01-001
experiment	**verb**	**20-05-012**
experiment	VB	7-04-007
experimented	VBD	2-02-002
experimented	VBN	4-03-004
experimenting	VBG	7-03-004
experimental	**adjective**	**38-06-022**
experimental	JJ	33-06-020
experimental	JJ-HL	5-01-004
experimentalism	**NN**	**1-01-001**
experimentally	**RB**	**8-03-007**
experimentation	**noun**	**14-06-010**
experimentation	NN	13-06-010
experimentations	NNS	1-01-001
experimenter	**noun**	**9-05-006**
experimenter	NN	5-03-003
experimenters	NNS	4-04-004
expert	**JJ**	**11-06-011**
expert	**noun**	**57-13-042**
expert	NN	19-10-016
experts	NNS	38-09-027
expertise	**NN**	**3-03-003**
expertly	**RB**	**2-02-002**
expiate	**verb**	**1-01-001**
expiating	VBG	1-01-001
expiation	**NN**	**2-02-002**
expiration	**NN**	**3-01-002**
expire	**verb**	**7-05-007**
expire	VB	1-01-001
expires	VBZ	1-01-001
expired	VBD	4-04-004
expired	VBN	1-01-001
explain	**verb**	**177-15-125**
explain	VB	63-15-054
Explain	VB-TL	1-01-001
explains	VBZ	19-07-018
explains	VBZ-HL	1-01-001
explained	VBD	61-13-047
explained	VBN	18-09-018
explained	VBN-HL	1-01-001
explaining	VBG	13-09-013
explanation	**noun**	**58-15-042**

Word	Tag	Frequency
explanation (cont.):		
explanation	NN	42-12-031
explanation	NN-HL	1-01-001
explanations	NNS	15-10-012
explanatory	**JJ**	**4-03-004**
explicable	**JJ**	**4-01-002**
explicit	**JJ**	**24-07-019**
explicitly	**RB**	**6-03-005**
explicitness	**NN**	**1-01-001**
explode	**verb**	**22-10-016**
explode	VB	6-05-006
explodes	VBZ	1-01-001
exploded	VBD	4-03-004
exploded	VBN	4-02-002
exploding	VBG	7-05-005
exploding-wire	**NN**	**1-01-001**
exploit	**noun**	**5-04-005**
exploit	NN	1-01-001
exploits	NNS	4-04-004
exploit	**verb**	**18-07-016**
exploit	VB	8-05-008
exploited	VBD	2-02-002
exploited	VBN	7-05-007
exploiting	VBG	1-01-001
exploitation	**NN**	**5-04-005**
exploiter	**noun**	**1-01-001**
exploiters	NNS	1-01-001
exploration	**noun**	**26-07-014**
exploration	NN	21-07-013
exploration	NN-HL	1-01-001
Exploration	NN-TL	3-02-002
explorations	NNS	1-01-001
exploratory	**adjective**	**4-02-003**
exploratory	JJ	3-02-003
exploratory	JJ-HL	1-01-001
explore	**verb**	**29-11-025**
explore	VB	12-08-011
explores	VBZ	1-01-001
explored	VBD	2-02-002
explored	VBN	9-05-009
exploring	VBG	5-04-005
explorer	**noun**	**7-05-006**
explorer	NN	3-03-003
Explorer	NN-TL	1-01-001
explorers	NNS	3-03-003
explosion	**noun**	**16-09-014**
explosion	NN	15-09-014
explosion	NN-HL	1-01-001
explosive	**JJ**	**16-08-016**
explosive	**noun**	**4-03-004**
explosive	NN	1-01-001
explosives	NNS	3-03-003
explosively	**RB**	**1-01-001**
exponent	**noun**	**2-01-001**
exponents	NNS	2-01-001
exponential	**JJ**	**1-01-001**
export	**noun**	**19-05-009**
export	NN	7-03-006
Export	NN-TL	1-01-001
exports	NNS	11-04-005
export	**verb**	**6-02-004**
export	VB	2-01-001
exported	VBN	3-02-003
exporting	VBG	1-01-001
export-import	**adjective**	**14-01-001**
export-import	JJ	0-00-000
Export-Import	JJ-TL	14-01-001
exporter	**noun**	**1-01-001**
exporters	NNS	1-01-001
expose	**NN**	**1-01-001**
expose	**verb**	**47-13-037**
expose	VB	7-04-006
exposes	VBZ	2-02-002
exposed	VBD	4-04-004
exposed	VBN	30-12-025
exposing	VBG	4-03-004
exposit	**verb**	**1-01-001**
exposited	VBN	1-01-001
exposition	**noun**	**7-05-005**
exposition	NN	4-03-003
Exposition	NN-TL	2-02-002
expositions	NNS	1-01-001
expository	**JJ**	**1-01-001**
exposure	**noun**	**27-09-017**
exposure	NN	24-09-017
exposure	NN-HL	1-01-001
exposures	NNS	2-02-002
exposure-time	**NN**	**1-01-001**
expound	**verb**	**3-02-003**

Word	Tag	Frequency
expound (cont.):		
expounded	VBD	1-01-001
expounded	VBN	1-01-001
expounding	VBG	1-01-001
express	**JJ**	**5-03-005**
express	**noun**	**10-06-008**
express	NN	7-04-006
Express	NN-TL	3-02-002
express	**verb**	**135-15-097**
express	VB	27-11-021
expresses	VBZ	8-04-008
expresses	VBZ-HL	1-01-001
expressed	VBD	24-08-021
expressed	VBN	51-10-044
expressing	VBG	24-10-022
expressible	**JJ**	**1-01-001**
expression	**noun**	**94-12-063**
expression	NN	78-11-056
expression	NN-HL	1-01-001
expressions	NNS	15-06-012
expressionism	**noun**	**3-03-003**
expressionism	NN	2-02-002
Expressionism	NN-TL	1-01-001
expressionist	**noun**	**4-03-003**
expressionist	NN	2-02-002
expressionists	NNS	2-01-001
expressionistic	**JJ**	**1-01-001**
expressionless	**JJ**	**2-01-002**
expressive	**JJ**	**7-05-006**
expressiveness	**noun**	**2-01-002**
expressiveness	NN	1-01-001
expressivness	NN	1-01-001
expressly	**RB**	**3-03-003**
expressway	**noun**	**11-02-002**
expressway	NN	2-01-001
expressway	NN-HL	1-01-001
Expressway	NN-TL	7-02-002
expressways	NNS	0-00-000
Expressways	NNS-TL	1-01-001
expropriate	**verb**	**1-01-001**
expropriated	VBN	1-01-001
expulsion	**NN**	**4-02-003**
expunge	**VB**	**1-01-001**
expunging	**NN**	**1-01-001**
expurgation	**NN**	**1-01-001**
exquisite	**JJ**	**3-03-003**
exquisitely	**QL**	**2-02-002**
exquisitely	**RB**	**1-01-001**
exquisiteness	**NN**	**1-01-001**
extant	**JJ**	**5-03-003**
extempore	**RB**	**1-01-001**
extemporize	**VB**	**1-01-001**
extend	**verb**	**127-13-097**
extend	VB	29-08-024
extend	VB-HL	2-02-002
extends	VBZ	12-08-011
extended	VBD	12-07-011
extended	VBN	43-10-038
extending	VBG	29-09-027
extendible	**noun**	**1-01-001**
extendibles	NNS	1-01-001
extension	**noun**	**44-09-024**
extension	NN	34-08-021
extension	NN-HL	1-01-001
Extension	NN-TL	1-01-001
extensions	NNS	6-06-006
extensions	NNS-HL	2-01-001
extensive	**JJ**	**44-10-034**
extensively	**RB**	**10-05-008**
extensor	**noun**	**1-01-001**
extensor	NN	0-00-000
Extensor	NN-TL	1-01-001
extent	**NN**	**110-10-072**
extenuate	**verb**	**4-04-004**
extenuate	VB	1-01-001
extenuating	VBG	3-03-003
exterior	**JJ**	**5-02-004**
exterior	**noun**	**4-03-004**
exterior	NN	3-02-003
exteriors	NNS	1-01-001
exterminate	**verb**	**4-04-004**
exterminate	VB	2-02-002
exterminating	VBG	1-01-001
exterminatin'	VBG	1-01-001
extermination	**NN**	**1-01-001**
extern	**NN**	**1-01-001**
external	**adjective**	**43-09-026**
external	JJ	40-08-025
external	JJ-HL	2-02-002

external (cont.):		
External	JJ-TL	1-01-001
externalization	**NN**	**1-01-001**
externally	**RB**	**2-01-001**
extinct	**JJ**	**1-01-001**
extinction	**NN**	**3-03-003**
extinguish	**verb**	**2-02-002**
extinguish	VB	1-01-001
extinguished	VBN	1-01-001
extirpate	**verb**	**2-01-001**
extirpated	VBN	1-01-001
extirpating	VBG	1-01-001
extra	**JJ**	**48-14-039**
extra	**noun**	**1-01-001**
extras	NNS	1-01-001
extra	**QL**	**2-02-002**
extra-curricular	**JJ**	**1-01-001**
extra-sensory	**JJ**	**3-02-002**
extra-thick	**JJ**	**1-01-001**
extract	**noun**	**4-03-004**
extract	NN	1-01-001
extracts	NNS	3-03-003
extract	**verb**	**19-06-015**
extract	VB	5-04-004
extracts	VBZ	1-01-001
extracted	VBD	2-02-002
extracted	VBN	7-04-005
extracting	VBG	4-02-004
extraction	**NN**	**5-04-005**
extractor	**noun**	**3-02-002**
extractor	NN	0-00-000
extractor	NN-HL	2-01-001
extractors	NNS	1-01-001
extralegal	**JJ**	**1-01-001**
extramarital	**JJ**	**1-01-001**
extraneous	**JJ**	**3-02-003**
extraneousness	**NN**	**1-01-001**
extraordinarily	**QL**	**1-01-001**
extraordinarily	**RB**	**2-02-002**
extraordinary	**JJ**	**31-10-028**
extrapolate	**verb**	**6-03-003**
extrapolate	VB	1-01-001
extrapolates	VBZ	1-01-001
extrapolated	VBN	4-02-002
extrapolation	**noun**	**5-02-003**
extrapolation	NN	4-01-002
extrapolations	NNS	1-01-001
extraterrestrial	**JJ**	**3-02-002**
extravagant	**JJ**	**5-05-005**
extravaganza	**noun**	**1-01-001**
extravaganzas	NNS	1-01-001
extreme	**JJ**	**53-09-044**
extreme	**noun**	**18-08-015**
extreme	NN	9-06-008
extremes	NNS	9-07-008
extremely	**QL**	**47-08-038**
extremely	**RB**	**3-03-003**
extremis	**FW-NNS**	**1-01-001**
extremist	**noun**	**4-03-003**
extremists	NNS	4-03-003
extremity	**noun**	**5-04-005**
extremity	NN	4-03-004
extremities	NNS	1-01-001
extricate	**VB**	**2-02-002**
extrovert	**NN**	**1-01-001**
extrude	**verb**	**10-02-003**
extruded	VBN	9-02-003
extruding	VBG	1-01-001
extruder	**NN**	**1-01-001**
exuberance	**NN**	**2-02-002**
exuberant	**JJ**	**7-04-007**
exuberantly	**RB**	**2-01-002**
exude	**verb**	**2-02-002**
exuded	VBD	2-02-002
exultantly	**QL**	**1-01-001**
exultation	**NN**	**3-03-003**
eye	**noun**	**524-15-196**
eye	NN	119-13-074
Eye	NN-TL	3-02-002
eyes	NNS	394-15-161
eies	NNS	1-01-001
Eyes	NNS-TL	7-01-001
eye	**verb**	**13-06-010**
eyed	VBD	7-03-006
eyeing	VBG	4-04-004
eying	VBG	2-02-002
eye-beaming	**noun**	**1-01-001**
eye-beamings	NNS	1-01-001
eye-deceiving	**JJ**	**1-01-001**
eye-filling	**JJ**	**1-01-001**
eye-gouging	**JJ**	**1-01-001**
eye-machine	**NN**	**1-01-001**
eye-strain	**NN**	**1-01-001**
eye-to-eye	**RB**	**1-01-001**
eye-undeceiving	**JJ**	**2-01-001**
eyeball	**noun**	**3-03-003**
eyeball	NN	2-02-002
eyeballs	NNS	1-01-001
eyebrow	**noun**	**13-07-011**
eyebrow	NN	4-04-004
eyebrows	NNS	9-04-007
eyed	**adjective**	**1-01-001**
eyed	JJ	0-00-000
eyd	JJ	1-01-001
eyeful	**NN**	**1-01-001**
eyeglass	**noun**	**3-03-003**
eyeglasses	NNS	3-03-003
eyelash	**noun**	**1-01-001**
eyelashes	NNS	1-01-001
eyelet	**noun**	**1-01-001**
eyelets	NNS	1-01-001
eyelid	**noun**	**8-05-006**
eyelid	NN	1-01-001
eyelids	NNS	7-05-005
eyepiece	**NN**	**1-01-001**
eyesight	**NN**	**1-01-001**
eyewitness	**NN**	**2-02-002**
Eyke	**NP**	**1-01-001**
Ezra	**NP**	**2-02-002**

F

F	**prop. noun**	**22-02-008**
F	NP	17-02-004
F	NP-HL	5-02-004
F.	**NP**	**59-08-040**
F.B.I.	**NP**	**2-02-002**
F.D.R.	**NP**	**3-02-002**
F.R.	**NP**	**2-01-001**
F.S.C.	**NP**	**1-01-001**
Faber	**prop. noun**	**7-01-001**
Faber	NP	5-01-001
Faber's	NP$	2-01-001
Fabian	**NP**	**4-01-001**
fable	**noun**	**4-02-002**
fable	NN	2-01-001
fables	NNS	2-01-001
fabled	**JJ**	**4-04-004**
fabric	**noun**	**44-08-015**
fabric	NN	15-06-008
fabrics	NNS	26-04-008
fabrics	NNS-HL	3-01-001
fabricate	**verb**	**3-02-002**
fabricate	VB	1-01-001
fabricated	VBN	1-01-001
fabricating	VBG	1-01-001
fabrication	**NN**	**8-03-004**
Fabricius	**NP**	**1-01-001**
fabulous	**JJ**	**6-04-006**
facade	**noun**	**8-05-007**
facade	NN	7-04-006
facades	NNS	1-01-001
facaded	**JJ**	**1-01-001**
face	**noun**	**379-15-178**
face	NN	319-15-158
Face	NN-TL	1-01-001
faces	NNS	58-11-047
faces	NNS-HL	1-01-001
face	**verb**	**152-15-114**
face	VB	51-14-042
faces	VBZ	12-07-011
Faces	VBZ-TL	1-01-001

Word	Tag	Frequency
face (cont.):		
faced	VBD	22-11-021
faced	VBD-HL	1-01-001
faced	VBN	31-11-031
facing	VBG	34-13-031
face-lifting	**NN**	**1-01-001**
face-saving	**JJ**	**4-02-003**
face-to-face	**JJ**	**2-02-002**
face-to-face	**RB**	**1-01-001**
face-to-wall	**RB**	**1-01-001**
faceless	**JJ**	**1-01-001**
facet	**noun**	**11-07-009**
facet	NN	2-02-002
facets	NNS	9-05-007
facet-plane	**noun**	**4-01-001**
facet-plane's	NN$	1-01-001
facet-planes	NNS	3-01-001
facetious	**adjective**	**1-01-001**
facetious	JJ	0-00-000
Facetious	JJ-TL	1-01-001
facetiously	**RB**	**1-01-001**
facial	**JJ**	**2-01-002**
facile	**JJ**	**1-01-001**
facilitate	**verb**	**9-04-008**
facilitate	VB	5-04-005
facilitates	VBZ	2-02-002
facilitated	VBN	1-01-001
facilitating	VBG	1-01-001
facilitatory	**JJ**	**1-01-001**
facility	**noun**	**111-12-059**
facility	NN	11-05-009
facilities	NNS	93-11-055
facilities	NNS-HL	7-04-005
faciunt	**FW-VB**	**1-01-001**
facsimile	**NN**	**1-01-001**
facsiport	**NN**	**1-01-001**
fact	**noun**	**534-15-255**
fact	NN	446-15-233
fact	NN-HL	1-01-001
facts	NNS	85-15-068
facts	NNS-HL	2-02-002
faction	**noun**	**11-05-009**
faction	NN	5-04-005
factions	NNS	5-02-004
Factions	NNS-TL	1-01-001
facto	**FW-NN**	**7-04-005**
factor	**noun**	**176-11-090**
factor	NN	70-10-051
factor	NN-HL	1-01-001
factors	NNS	103-10-059
factors	NNS-HL	2-01-002
factor	**verb**	**1-01-001**
factors	VBZ	1-01-001
factory	**noun**	**56-11-029**
factory	NN	25-09-015
Factory	NN-TL	7-02-002
factories	NNS	23-10-017
Factories	NNS-TL	1-01-001
factory-to-you	**noun**	**1-01-001**
factory-to-you	NN	0-00-000
Factory-to-You	NN-TL	1-01-001
factual	**JJ**	**7-05-007**
faculty	**noun**	**78-10-021**
faculty	NN	73-09-018
faculties	NNS	5-04-004
fad	**noun**	**3-03-003**
fad	NN	2-02-002
fads	NNS	0-00-000
fads	NNS-HL	1-01-001
fade	**NN**	**1-01-001**
fade	**verb**	**24-10-021**
fade	VB	1-01-001
faded	VBD	8-04-007
faded	VBN	10-08-009
fading	VBG	5-04-005
fade-in	**JJ**	**1-01-001**
fadeout	**NN**	**1-01-001**
Fagan	**NP**	**1-01-001**
Faget	**prop. noun**	**6-01-001**
Faget	NP	4-01-001
Faget	NP-HL	1-01-001
Faget's	NP$	1-01-001
Fahey	**NP**	**1-01-001**
Fahrenheit	**prop. noun**	**1-01-001**
Fahrenheit	NP	0-00-000
Fahrenheit	NP-TL	1-01-001
fail	**verb**	**142-15-106**
fail	VB	37-11-032
fails	VBZ	13-07-013
fail (cont.):		
fails	VBZ-HL	1-01-001
failed	VBD	52-11-041
failed	VBN	22-12-020
failing	VBG	17-06-014
fail-safe	**JJ**	**1-01-001**
failure	**noun**	**93-13-060**
failure	NN	87-13-056
failure	NN-HL	1-01-001
failure	NN-NC	1-01-001
failures	NNS	4-03-004
faim	**FW-NN**	**1-01-001**
Fain	**NP**	**1-01-001**
faint	**JJ**	**25-09-024**
faint	**verb**	**1-01-001**
fainted	VBN	1-01-001
faintest	**JJT**	**3-02-003**
faintly	**RB**	**7-05-006**
fair	**adjective**	**70-13-053**
fair	JJ	62-13-046
faier	JJ	1-01-001
fair	JJ-HL	1-01-001
Fair	JJ-TL	6-05-006
fair	**noun**	**10-05-008**
fair	NN	4-02-004
Fair	NN-TL	3-02-003
fair's	NN$	0-00-000
Fair's	NN$-TL	2-01-001
fairs	NNS	1-01-001
fair	**RB**	**2-02-002**
fair	**verb**	**2-01-001**
fairing	VBG	2-01-001
fair-looking	**JJ**	**1-01-001**
fair-priced	**adjective**	**1-01-001**
fair-priced	JJ	0-00-000
fair-priced	JJ-HL	1-01-001
fair-sized	**JJ**	**2-02-002**
fair-weather	**NN**	**2-02-002**
Fairbrother	**prop. noun**	**2-01-001**
Fairbrothers	NPS	2-01-001
Fairchild	**NP**	**2-02-002**
fairest	**JJT**	**1-01-001**
Fairfax	**prop. noun**	**2-01-001**
Fairfax	NP	1-01-001
Fairfax	NP-TL	1-01-001
fairgoer	**noun**	**1-01-001**
fairgoers	NNS	1-01-001
fairing	**NN**	**1-01-001**
Fairless	**prop. noun**	**1-01-001**
Fairless	NP	0-00-000
Fairless	NP-TL	1-01-001
fairly	**QL**	**50-11-045**
fairly	**RB**	**8-06-007**
Fairmont	**prop. noun**	**2-01-001**
Fairmont	NP	1-01-001
Fairmont	NP-TL	1-01-001
Fairmount	**NP**	**2-01-001**
fairness	**NN**	**6-04-006**
Fairview	**NP**	**3-01-001**
fairway	**noun**	**7-01-002**
fairway	NN	5-01-002
fairways	NNS	2-01-001
fairy	**noun**	**6-05-005**
fairy	NN	2-02-002
faery	NN	1-01-001
Fairy	NN-TL	1-01-001
fairies	NNS	2-02-002
fairy-land	**NN**	**1-01-001**
fairy-tale	**NN**	**1-01-001**
faith	**noun**	**110-15-056**
faith	NN	102-15-053
faith	NN-HL	2-01-001
Faith	NN-TL	3-02-003
faiths	NNS	3-03-003
Faith	**NP**	**4-01-001**
faithful	**JJ**	**10-06-008**
faithful	**noun**	**2-02-002**
faithful	NN	1-01-001
faithful	NNS	0-00-000
Faithful	NNS-TL	1-01-001
faithfully	**RB**	**5-04-005**
fake	**JJ**	**8-02-003**
fake	**NN**	**1-01-001**
fake	**verb**	**3-03-003**
fake	VB	1-01-001
faked	VBN	2-02-002
faker	**NN**	**1-01-001**
falcon	**noun**	**5-02-002**
falcon	NN	2-02-002

Word	Tag	Count
falcon (cont.):		
Falcon	NN-TL	2-01-001
falcons'	NNS$	0-00-000
Falcons'	NNS$-TL	1-01-001
Falegnami	**NP**	**1-01-001**
fall	**noun**	**94-14-057**
fall	NN	71-14-047
fall	NN-HL	1-01-001
Fall	NN-TL	8-03-003
fall's	NN$	1-01-001
falls	NNS	4-03-004
Falls	NNS-TL	9-05-006
fall	**verb**	**239-15-171**
fall	VB	66-13-060
Fall	VB-TL	1-01-001
falls	VBZ	19-10-019
fell	VBD	87-13-070
fallen	VBN	33-11-031
Fallen	VBN-TL	1-01-001
falling	VBG	31-09-025
Falling	VBG-TL	1-01-001
Fall-in	**NP**	**2-01-001**
Falla	**prop. noun**	**1-01-001**
Falla's	NP$	1-01-001
fallacious	**JJ**	**1-01-001**
fallacy	**NN**	**1-01-001**
fallible	**JJ**	**1-01-001**
falling	**NN**	**1-01-001**
falloff	**noun**	**2-02-002**
falloff	NN	1-01-001
fall-off	NN	1-01-001
fallout	**noun**	**32-03-009**
fallout	NN	29-03-007
fallout	NN-HL	2-01-002
fallouts	NNS	0-00-000
fall-outs	NNS	1-01-001
fallow	**JJ**	**1-01-001**
Falmouth	**prop. noun**	**1-01-001**
Falmouth	NP	0-00-000
Falmouth	NP-TL	1-01-001
false	**adjective**	**28-08-025**
false	JJ	27-08-024
false	JJ-NC	1-01-001
false	**RB**	**1-01-001**
false-fronted	**JJ**	**1-01-001**
falsehood	**noun**	**4-02-002**
falsehood	NN	2-02-002
falsehoods	NNS	2-01-001
falsify	**verb**	**3-03-003**
falsify	VB	2-02-002
falsifying	VBG	1-01-001
falsity	**NN**	**3-01-002**
Falstaff	**prop. noun**	**1-01-001**
Falstaff	NP	0-00-000
Falstaff	NP-TL	1-01-001
falter	**verb**	**6-05-006**
falter	VB	2-02-002
falters	VBZ	1-01-001
faltered	VBD	3-03-003
fame	**noun**	**19-08-012**
fame	NN	17-08-012
Fame	NN-TL	1-01-001
fames	NNS	1-01-001
famed	**JJ**	**5-04-005**
familial	**JJ**	**4-04-004**
familiar	**adjective**	**73-14-062**
familiar	JJ	72-14-062
familar	JJ	1-01-001
familiarity	**noun**	**14-08-012**
familiarity	NN	13-08-011
familarity	NN	1-01-001
familiarly	**RB**	**1-01-001**
familiarness	**NN**	**1-01-001**
Familism	**NP**	**1-01-001**
familistical	**JJ**	**1-01-001**
famille	**FW-NN**	**1-01-001**
family	**noun**	**405-15-172**
family	NN	314-15-147
family	NN-HL	1-01-001
Family	NN-TL	16-04-005
family's	NN$	6-03-003
families	NNS	66-11-043
families	NNS-HL	1-01-001
Families	NNS	1-01-001
family-community	**NN**	**1-01-001**
family-oriented	**JJ**	**1-01-001**
family-welfare	**NN**	**1-01-001**
famine	**NN**	**3-02-003**
famous	**JJ**	**89-14-062**

Word	Tag	Count
fan	**noun**	**34-08-019**
fan	NN	14-06-012
fan's	NN$	1-01-001
fans	NNS	19-08-011
fan	**verb**	**13-06-011**
fan	VB	4-03-003
fans	VBZ	2-02-002
fanned	VBD	4-02-003
fanning	VBG	3-02-003
fanatic	**noun**	**2-01-002**
fanatics	NNS	2-01-002
fanatical	**JJ**	**2-02-002**
fanaticism	**NN**	**4-03-003**
fancier	**JJR**	**1-01-001**
fanciful	**JJ**	**2-02-002**
fancy	**JJ**	**6-04-005**
fancy	**NN**	**7-06-007**
fancy	**verb**	**7-04-007**
fancy	VB	3-03-003
fancies	VBZ	1-01-001
fancied	VBD	2-01-002
fancying	VBG	1-01-001
fancy-free	**JJ**	**1-01-001**
Faneuil	**prop. noun**	**1-01-001**
Faneuil	NP	0-00-000
Faneuil	NP-TL	1-01-001
fanfare	**NN**	**1-01-001**
fang	**noun**	**2-02-002**
fangs	NNS	2-02-002
fanning	**NN**	**1-01-001**
Fanning	**NP**	**1-01-001**
Fanny	**NP**	**3-03-003**
Fanshawe	**NP**	**1-01-001**
fantasia	**noun**	**2-02-002**
fantasia	NN	1-01-001
Fantasia	NN-TL	1-01-001
fantasist	**NN**	**1-01-001**
fantastic	**JJ**	**20-09-018**
fantastically	**QL**	**1-01-001**
fantastically	**RB**	**1-01-001**
fantasy	**noun**	**18-05-007**
fantasy	NN	12-02-003
Fantasy	NN-TL	2-01-001
fantasies	NNS	4-03-003
fantod	**noun**	**1-01-001**
fantods	NNS	1-01-001
far	**adjective**	**41-12-036**
far	JJ	35-12-030
Far	JJ-TL	6-04-006
far	**QL**	**131-13-098**
far	**adverb**	**254-15-184**
far	RB	253-15-184
Far	RB-TL	1-01-001
far-away	**JJ**	**1-01-001**
far-famed	**JJ**	**1-01-001**
far-flung	**JJ**	**1-01-001**
far-off	**JJ**	**1-01-001**
far-out	**JJ**	**1-01-001**
far-ranging	**JJ**	**1-01-001**
far-reaching	**JJ**	**4-03-004**
far-sighted	**JJ**	**1-01-001**
farce	**noun**	**4-03-004**
farce	NN	3-02-003
farces	NNS	1-01-001
Fardulli	**prop. noun**	**1-01-001**
Fardulli's	NP$	1-01-001
fare	**noun**	**10-05-010**
fare	NN	7-04-007
fares	NNS	3-01-003
fare	**verb**	**2-01-002**
faring	VBG	2-01-002
farewell	**noun**	**13-09-013**
farewell	NN	11-08-011
Farewell	NN-TL	2-01-002
farewell	**exclam.**	**1-01-001**
farewell	UH	0-00-000
farewell	UH-NC	1-01-001
farfetched	**JJ**	**3-02-003**
Fargo	**NP**	**2-02-002**
Farina	**NP**	**1-01-001**
Farley	**NP**	**1-01-001**
farm	**noun**	**137-14-045**
farm	NN	110-13-038
farm	NN-HL	2-01-001
Farm	NN-TL	9-02-002
farms	NNS	16-08-012
farm	**verb**	**16-03-006**
farm	VB	3-02-002
farmed	VBD	1-01-001

Word	Tag	Frequency
farm (cont.):		
farming	VBG	11-02-003
farming	VBG-HL	1-01-001
farmer	**noun**	**67-09-030**
farmer	NN	23-08-012
farmer's	NN$	7-04-006
farmers	NNS	31-08-018
Farmers	NNS-TL	2-01-001
farmers'	NNS$	4-02-002
Farmer-in-the-Dell	**NP**	**1-01-001**
farmer-type	**JJ**	**1-01-001**
farmhouse	**noun**	**9-03-004**
farmhouse	NN	8-03-004
farmhouses	NNS	1-01-001
farming	**NN**	**4-02-002**
Farmington	**NP**	**1-01-001**
farmland	**noun**	**2-02-002**
farmland	NN	1-01-001
farmlands	NNS	1-01-001
farmwife	**noun**	**1-01-001**
farmwife's	NN$	0-00-000
Farmwife's	NN$-TL	1-01-001
Farnese	**prop. noun**	**3-02-002**
Farnese	NP	1-01-001
Farnese	NP-TL	1-01-001
Farneses	NPS	1-01-001
Farnum	**NP**	**1-01-001**
Farnworth	**NP**	**1-01-001**
faro	**NN**	**4-02-002**
Farouk	**NP**	**5-01-001**
Farr	**NP**	**1-01-001**
Farrar	**NP**	**1-01-001**
Farrell	**prop. noun**	**7-04-005**
Farrell	NP	6-04-005
Farrells	NPS	1-01-001
farther	**QL**	**9-04-006**
farther	**RBR**	**23-08-020**
farthest	**JJT**	**2-02-002**
farthest	**RBT**	**1-01-001**
Farvel	**NP**	**1-01-001**
fascicle	**noun**	**3-01-001**
fascicles	NNS	3-01-001
fasciculation	**noun**	**1-01-001**
fasciculations	NNS	1-01-001
fascinate	**verb**	**11-06-011**
fascinate	VB	3-03-003
fascinates	VBZ	1-01-001
fascinated	VBD	2-02-002
fascinated	VBN	5-04-005
fascinating	**JJ**	**20-09-018**
fascinatingly	**RB**	**1-01-001**
fascination	**NN**	**6-05-006**
Fascio-Communist	**NP**	**1-01-001**
Fascism	**NP**	**3-02-003**
Fascist	**JJ**	**2-02-002**
Fascist	**prop. noun**	**2-01-001**
Fascists	NPS	2-01-001
fashion	**noun**	**70-14-052**
fashion	NN	64-14-049
fashion	NN-HL	1-01-001
Fashion	NN-TL	1-01-001
fashions	NNS	3-03-003
Fashions	NNS-TL	1-01-001
fashion	**verb**	**13-07-012**
fashion	VB	3-02-002
fashions	VBZ	1-01-001
fashioned	VBD	4-03-004
fashioned	VBN	3-03-003
fashioning	VBG	2-02-002
fashionable	**JJ**	**12-07-010**
fast	**JJ**	**31-12-025**
fast	**NN**	**1-01-001**
fast	**QL**	**1-01-001**
fast	**adverb**	**45-11-039**
fast	RB	43-11-037
fast	RB-HL	2-02-002
fast-closing	**JJ**	**2-01-001**
fast-firing	**JJ**	**1-01-001**
fast-frozen	**JJ**	**1-01-001**
fast-grossing	**JJ**	**1-01-001**
fast-growing	**JJ**	**1-01-001**
fast-moving	**JJ**	**1-01-001**
fast-opening	**JJ**	**2-01-001**
fast-spreading	**JJ**	**1-01-001**
fasten	**verb**	**19-06-011**
fasten	VB	4-03-004
fastens	VBZ	1-01-001
fastened	VBD	2-02-002
fastened	VBN	12-05-006

Word	Tag	Frequency
fastening	**noun**	**2-01-001**
fastening	NN	1-01-001
fastenings	NNS	1-01-001
faster	**JJR**	**5-04-005**
faster	**RBR**	**13-09-013**
fastest	**JJT**	**6-05-005**
fastest	**RBT**	**1-01-001**
fastidious	**JJ**	**3-03-003**
fat	**JJ**	**47-12-030**
fat	**noun**	**33-06-011**
fat	NN	13-06-008
fat's	NN+BEZ	1-01-001
fats	NNS	17-03-004
fats	NNS-HL	2-01-001
fat-soluble	**JJ**	**1-01-001**
fatal	**JJ**	**19-07-015**
fatalist	**noun**	**1-01-001**
fatalists	NNS	1-01-001
fatality	**noun**	**3-03-003**
fatality	NN	1-01-001
fatalities	NNS	2-02-002
fatally	**QL**	**1-01-001**
fatally	**RB**	**3-03-003**
fatboy	**noun**	**1-01-001**
fatboy	NN	0-00-000
fatboy	NN-NC	1-01-001
fate	**noun**	**36-11-029**
fate	NN	29-10-022
Fate	NN-TL	4-04-004
fates	NNS	3-03-003
fateful	**JJ**	**3-02-003**
father	**noun**	**240-15-122**
father	NN	162-15-094
fathuh	NN	1-01-001
Father	NN-TL	20-07-012
father's	NN+BEZ	1-01-001
father's	NN$	37-09-031
fathers	NNS	10-07-010
Fathers	NNS-TL	9-03-005
father	**verb**	**3-03-003**
father	VB	1-01-001
fathered	VBD	2-02-002
father-and-son	**JJ**	**1-01-001**
father-brother	**NN**	**1-01-001**
father-confessor	**NN**	**1-01-001**
Father-God	**NP**	**1-01-001**
father-murder	**NN**	**1-01-001**
fatherly	**JJ**	**1-01-001**
fathom	**noun**	**1-01-001**
fathoms	NNS	1-01-001
fathom	**VB**	**3-01-002**
fatigue	**noun**	**13-07-012**
fatigue	NN	11-06-011
fatigues	NNS	2-01-001
fatigue	**verb**	**3-03-003**
fatigued	VBN	3-03-003
Fatima	**prop. noun**	**1-01-001**
Fatima	NP	0-00-000
Fatima	NP-TL	1-01-001
Fatso	**NP**	**1-01-001**
fatten	**verb**	**3-02-002**
fatten	VB	1-01-001
fattening	VBG	1-01-001
fattening	VBG-HL	1-01-001
fatter	**JJR**	**3-03-003**
fatty	**JJ**	**7-03-003**
fatuous	**JJ**	**2-02-002**
faucet	**NN**	**1-01-001**
Faulkner	**prop. noun**	**30-02-003**
Faulkner	NP	21-02-003
Faulkner's	NP$	9-01-001
Faulknerian	**JJ**	**1-01-001**
fault	**noun**	**29-11-024**
fault	NN	22-09-018
faults	NNS	7-05-007
fault	**verb**	**1-01-001**
faulted	VBN	1-01-001
faultless	**JJ**	**1-01-001**
faulty	**JJ**	**8-04-006**
fauna	**NNS**	**1-01-001**
Fauntleroy	**prop. noun**	**1-01-001**
Fauntleroy	NP	0-00-000
Fauntleroy	NP-TL	1-01-001
Faust	**prop. noun**	**6-01-001**
Faust	NP	3-01-001
Faust	NP-TL	1-01-001
Faust's	NP$	2-01-001
Faustian	**JJ**	**1-01-001**
Fausto	**NP**	**1-01-001**

Word	Tag	Count
Faustus	**prop. noun**	**2-01-002**
Faustus	NP	1-01-001
Faustus	NP-TL	1-01-001
fauteuil	**NN**	**1-01-001**
favor	**noun**	**63-14-053**
favor	NN	55-13-048
favour	NN	2-01-002
favors	NNS	6-04-006
favor	**verb**	**49-09-030**
favor	VB	23-07-014
favors	VBZ	4-03-004
favored	VBD	7-05-005
favored	VBN	11-06-008
favoring	VBG	4-02-004
favorable	**JJ**	**33-09-027**
favorably	**QL**	**1-01-001**
favorably	**RB**	**13-05-011**
favore	**FW-NN**	**1-01-001**
favorer	**NN**	**1-01-001**
favorite	**JJ**	**37-10-028**
favorite	**noun**	**16-09-015**
favorite	NN	4-04-004
favorites	NNS	10-07-010
Favorites	NNS-TL	2-01-001
favoritism	**NN**	**4-02-003**
Favre	**prop. noun**	**6-01-001**
Favre	NP	5-01-001
Favre's	NP$	1-01-001
Fawcett	**NP**	**1-01-001**
Fawkes	**prop. noun**	**4-01-001**
Fawkes	NP	1-01-001
Fawkes	NP-TL	3-01-001
fawn	**NN**	**1-01-001**
fawn	**verb**	**2-02-002**
fawned	VBN	1-01-001
fawning	VBG	1-01-001
fawn-colored	**JJ**	**1-01-001**
Fay	**NP**	**3-02-002**
Fayette	**prop. noun**	**4-03-003**
Fayette	NP	2-01-001
Fayette	NP-TL	2-02-002
faze	**VB**	**1-01-001**
Fazio	**NP**	**1-01-001**
FDA	**NP**	**1-01-001**
Fe	**NP**	**7-02-002**
fealty	**NN**	**1-01-001**
fear	**noun**	**141-13-068**
fear	NN	96-13-058
feare	NN	1-01-001
Fear	NN-TL	1-01-001
fears	NNS	43-07-016
fear	**verb**	**53-14-040**
fear	VB	28-11-020
fear	VB-HL	2-02-002
fears	VBZ	3-02-003
fears	VBZ-HL	1-01-001
feared	VBD	10-09-010
feared	VBN	4-03-003
fearing	VBG	5-04-005
fear-filled	**JJ**	**1-01-001**
fear-maddened	**JJ**	**1-01-001**
fearful	**JJ**	**13-08-012**
fearfully	**RB**	**4-03-004**
fearless	**adjective**	**7-04-005**
fearless	JJ	6-04-004
Fearless	JJ-TL	1-01-001
fearlessly	**RB**	**2-02-002**
fearsome	**JJ**	**1-01-001**
feasibility	**NN**	**3-01-003**
feasible	**JJ**	**15-06-011**
feast	**noun**	**5-03-004**
feast	NN	3-02-003
feasts	NNS	2-02-002
feast	**verb**	**1-01-001**
feasting	VBG	1-01-001
feat	**noun**	**9-05-008**
feat	NN	6-04-006
feats	NNS	3-03-003
feather	**noun**	**19-09-015**
feather	NN	5-02-002
feathers	NNS	14-07-013
feather	**verb**	**5-04-004**
feather	VB	1-01-001
feathered	VBD	1-01-001
feathered	VBN	3-03-003
feather-like	**JJ**	**1-01-001**
featherbed	**noun**	**1-01-001**
featherbed	NN	0-00-000
featherbed	NN-HL	1-01-001
featherbed	**verb**	**1-01-001**
featherbedding	VBG	1-01-001
Feathertop	**prop. noun**	**14-01-001**
Feathertop	NP	12-01-001
Feathertop's	NP$	2-01-001
featherweight	**noun**	**1-01-001**
featherweight	NN	0-00-000
Featherweight	NN-TL	1-01-001
feathery	**JJ**	**1-01-001**
feature	**noun**	**105-14-072**
feature	NN	29-09-025
Feature	NN-TL	1-01-001
features	NNS	74-11-050
features	NNS-HL	1-01-001
feature	**verb**	**24-07-019**
feature	VB	7-04-006
features	VBZ	5-03-005
featured	VBD	3-03-003
featured	VBN	5-02-004
featuring	VBG	4-04-004
featureless	**JJ**	**2-02-002**
febrile	**JJ**	**1-01-001**
February	**prop. noun**	**67-10-039**
February	NP	45-10-029
Feb.	NP	14-04-010
Feb.	NP-HL	6-02-004
February's	NP$	2-02-002
fecund	**JJ**	**1-01-001**
fecundity	**NN**	**1-01-001**
federal	**adjective**	**247-11-067**
federal	JJ	113-08-036
federal	JJ-HL	3-02-002
fed.	JJ-HL	1-01-001
Federal	JJ-TL	127-10-040
Federal	JJ-TL-HL	3-03-003
Federal	**prop. noun**	**2-02-002**
Federals	NPS	1-01-001
Feds	NPS	1-01-001
federal-question	**NN**	**1-01-001**
federal-right	**NN**	**1-01-001**
federal-state	**NN**	**2-01-001**
federalism	**NN**	**2-02-002**
federalist	**noun**	**1-01-001**
federalist	NN	0-00-000
Federalist	NN-TL	1-01-001
federalize	**VB**	**1-01-001**
federation	**noun**	**15-06-012**
federation	NN	3-01-001
Federation	NN-TL	12-05-011
Federico	**NP**	**1-01-001**
fedora	**NN**	**2-02-002**
fee	**noun**	**45-07-019**
fee	NN	16-06-011
fees	NNS	28-07-013
fees	NNS-HL	1-01-001
fee-per-case	**JJ**	**1-01-001**
fee-per-day	**JJ**	**1-01-001**
feeble	**JJ**	**8-06-008**
feebly	**RB**	**2-02-002**
feed	**noun**	**65-05-008**
feed	NN	59-05-008
feed	NN-HL	1-01-001
feeds	NNS	4-02-002
feeds	NNS-HL	1-01-001
feed	**verb**	**132-13-057**
feed	VB	45-08-017
feed	VB-HL	16-01-001
Feed	VB-TL	1-01-001
feeds	VBZ	7-06-007
fed	VBD	8-06-008
fed	VBN	33-11-022
feeding	VBG	20-06-011
feeding	VBG-HL	2-01-002
feed-lot	**NN**	**2-01-001**
feedback	**NN**	**4-01-004**
feeder	**noun**	**2-01-001**
feeder	NN	1-01-001
feeder	NN-HL	1-01-001
feeding	**noun**	**5-04-004**
feeding	NN	4-03-003
feedings	NNS	1-01-001
feeding-pain	**NN**	**2-01-001**
feel	**NN**	**15-08-014**
feel	**verb**	**643-15-264**
feel	VB	201-15-135
feels	VBZ	45-11-036
felt	VBD	302-13-149
felt	VBN	54-13-049
feeling	VBG	41-10-029

feeler	**noun**	**2-02-002**
feelers	NNS	2-02-002
Feeley	**NP**	**3-01-001**
feeling	**noun**	**192-14-115**
feeling	NN	131-14-090
feelings	NNS	61-12-035
feeling-state	**NN**	**1-01-001**
Feeney	**NP**	**1-01-001**
feign	**verb**	**2-02-002**
feigned	VBN	1-01-001
feigning	VBG	1-01-001
feint	**NN**	**1-01-001**
feint	**VB**	**1-01-001**
Feis	**prop. noun**	**1-01-001**
Feis	NP	0-00-000
Feis	NP-TL	1-01-001
Felice	**prop. noun**	**5-01-001**
Felice	NP	4-01-001
Felice's	NP$	1-01-001
felicitous	**JJ**	**1-01-001**
felicity	**noun**	**5-04-005**
felicity	NN	3-03-003
felicities	NNS	2-02-002
Felicity	**NP**	**1-01-001**
feline	**JJ**	**2-02-002**
Felix	**prop. noun**	**32-05-006**
Felix	NP	30-05-006
Felix's	NP$	2-01-001
fell	**JJ**	**1-01-001**
fell	**verb**	**8-06-007**
fell	VB	4-03-004
felled	VBD	1-01-001
felled	VBN	1-01-001
felling	VBG	2-02-002
Fellini	**NP**	**2-01-001**
fellow	**JJ**	**1-01-001**
fellow	**noun**	**90-15-071**
fellow	NN	61-14-054
feler	NN	1-01-001
fella	NN	6-02-005
feller	NN	1-01-001
Fellow	NN-TL	1-01-001
fellows	NNS	13-09-012
fellas	NNS	1-01-001
fellers	NNS	1-01-001
Fellows	NNS-TL	5-01-001
fellow-countryman	**NN**	**1-01-001**
fellow-craftsman	**noun**	**1-01-001**
fellow-craftsmen	NNS	1-01-001
fellow-creature	**noun**	**1-01-001**
fellow-creatures	NNS	1-01-001
fellow-employee	**noun**	**1-01-001**
fellow-employees	NNS	1-01-001
fellow-man	**noun**	**1-01-001**
fellow-men	NNS	1-01-001
fellowfeeling	**NN**	**1-01-001**
fellowship	**noun**	**39-08-014**
fellowship	NN	27-05-009
Fellowship	NN-TL	8-03-004
Fellowship	NN-TL-HL	1-01-001
fellowships	NNS	0-00-000
Fellowships	NNS-TL	3-02-002
felon	**noun**	**3-01-002**
felon	NN	1-01-001
felons	NNS	2-01-002
felonious	**JJ**	**2-02-002**
felony	**NN**	**1-01-001**
Felske	**NP**	**1-01-001**
felt	**NN**	**1-01-001**
female	**JJ**	**20-06-015**
female	**noun**	**50-12-025**
female	NN	30-11-020
female's	NN$	3-02-002
females	NNS	17-04-009
feminine	**JJ**	**10-06-009**
femininity	**NN**	**2-02-002**
feminist	**NN**	**1-01-001**
femme	**foreign**	**2-02-002**
femme	FW-NN	1-01-001
femmes	FW-NNS	0-00-000
Femmes	FW-NNS-TL	1-01-001
fen	**noun**	**1-01-001**
fens	NNS	1-01-001
fence	**noun**	**46-10-024**
fence	NN	30-10-019
fences	NNS	16-06-008
fence	**verb**	**4-03-003**
fenced	VBN	3-02-002
fencing	VBG	1-01-001

fence-line	**noun**	**4-01-001**
fence-line	NN	3-01-001
fence-line	NN-HL	1-01-001
fencing	**NN**	**3-02-002**
fender	**noun**	**5-04-004**
fender	NN	4-03-003
fenders	NNS	1-01-001
fennel	**NN**	**2-01-001**
Fenster	**NP**	**1-01-001**
fenugreek	**NN**	**1-01-001**
Fenway	**prop. noun**	**1-01-001**
Fenway	NP	0-00-000
Fenway	NP-TL	1-01-001
Fenwick	**NP**	**1-01-001**
Ferber	**NP**	**1-01-001**
Ferdinand	**NP**	**2-02-002**
Ferdinando	**NP**	**1-01-001**
Fergeson	**NP**	**1-01-001**
Ferguson	**prop. noun**	**9-04-004**
Ferguson	NP	7-04-004
Ferguson's	NP$	2-01-001
Fergusson	**NP**	**1-01-001**
Feringa	**NP**	**1-01-001**
Ferlenghetti	**NP**	**1-01-001**
fermate	**FW-VB**	**1-01-001**
ferment	**noun**	**2-01-001**
ferment	NN	1-01-001
ferment	NN-HL	1-01-001
ferment	**verb**	**5-02-002**
fermented	VBN	4-01-001
fermenting	VBG	1-01-001
fermentation	**noun**	**4-03-004**
fermentation	NN	3-03-003
fermentations	NNS	1-01-001
fern	**noun**	**2-01-002**
fern	NN	1-01-001
ferns	NNS	1-01-001
Fernand	**NP**	**1-01-001**
Fernberger	**NP**	**1-01-001**
fernery	**NN**	**1-01-001**
ferocious	**JJ**	**2-02-002**
ferociously	**RB**	**2-02-002**
ferocity	**NN**	**2-02-002**
Ferraro	**prop. noun**	**5-01-001**
Ferraro	NP	2-01-001
Ferraros	NPS	3-01-001
Ferrell	**NP**	**3-01-001**
ferret	**verb**	**2-02-002**
ferret	VB	1-01-001
ferreted	VBD	1-01-001
Ferris	**NP**	**2-02-002**
Ferro	**NP**	**2-01-001**
ferromagnetic	**JJ**	**2-01-001**
ferry	**noun**	**12-06-007**
ferry	NN	2-02-002
Ferry	NN-TL	9-04-004
ferries	NNS	1-01-001
ferry	**verb**	**1-01-001**
ferried	VBN	1-01-001
fertile	**JJ**	**5-05-005**
fertility	**NN**	**10-03-004**
fertilize	**verb**	**3-01-002**
fertilized	VBN	3-01-002
fertilizer	**noun**	**7-05-005**
fertilizer	NN	4-04-004
fertilizers	NNS	3-01-001
fervent	**JJ**	**5-02-005**
fervently	**RB**	**2-02-002**
fervor	**noun**	**5-03-005**
fervor	NN	4-03-004
fervors	NNS	1-01-001
fester	**verb**	**1-01-001**
festering	VBG	1-01-001
festival	**noun**	**31-09-020**
festival	NN	12-07-012
Festival	NN-TL	16-04-012
festivals	NNS	2-02-002
festivals	NNS-HL	1-01-001
festive	**JJ**	**2-02-002**
festivity	**noun**	**8-05-006**
festivities	NNS	8-05-006
festivus	**FW-JJ**	**2-01-001**
fetch	**verb**	**7-04-005**
fetch	VB	6-04-005
fetching	VBG	1-01-001
fetching	**JJ**	**2-02-002**
fete	**noun**	**3-02-002**
fete	NN	0-00-000
Fete	NN-TL	2-01-001

Word	Tag	Frequency
fete (cont.):		
fetes	NNS	1-01-001
fete	**verb**	**3-01-003**
fete	VB	1-01-001
feted	VBN	2-01-002
fetid	**JJ**	**2-02-002**
fetish	**NN**	**2-01-002**
fetishize	**VB**	**1-01-001**
Feuchtwanger	**NP**	**2-01-001**
feud	**noun**	**3-02-003**
feud	NN	1-01-001
feuds	NNS	2-02-002
feudal	**JJ**	**6-02-003**
feudalism	**NN**	**1-01-001**
feudalistic	**JJ**	**1-01-001**
Feuermann	**NP**	**1-01-001**
fever	**NN**	**19-08-011**
fevered	**JJ**	**1-01-001**
feverish	**JJ**	**4-04-004**
feverishly	**RB**	**3-03-003**
Feversham	**prop. noun**	**1-01-001**
Feversham	NP	0-00-000
Feversham	NP-TL	1-01-001
few	**post-det.**	**601-15-311**
few	AP	600-15-311
few	AP-NC	1-01-001
fewer	**post-det.**	**30-09-025**
fewer	AP	29-09-025
fewer	AP-HL	1-01-001
fewer	**JJR**	**3-02-003**
Feyer	**prop. noun**	**1-01-001**
Feyer's	NP$	1-01-001
Ffortescue	**NP**	**1-01-001**
fiance	**NN**	**1-01-001**
fiasco	**NN**	**4-04-004**
fiat	**NN**	**4-03-004**
Fiat	**prop. noun**	**10-02-002**
Fiat	NP	4-01-001
Fiat	NP-TL	5-01-001
Fiats	NPS	1-01-001
fiber	**noun**	**50-06-008**
fiber	NN	25-03-004
fiber	NN-HL	2-01-001
fibers	NNS	23-05-007
fiber-coupled	**adjective**	**4-01-001**
fiber-coupled	JJ	3-01-001
fiber-coupled	JJ-HL	1-01-001
fiber-photocathode	**NN**	**1-01-001**
fiberglass	**noun**	**5-02-002**
fiberglass	NN	0-00-000
fiberglas	NN	1-01-001
Fiberglas	NN-TL	4-01-001
fibrin	**NN**	**2-01-001**
fibrocalcific	**JJ**	**1-01-001**
fibrosis	**NN**	**6-01-001**
fibrous	**adjective**	**5-02-003**
fibrous	JJ	4-02-002
fibrous	JJ-HL	1-01-001
fiche	**FW-NN**	**1-01-001**
Fichte	**NP**	**1-01-001**
fickle	**JJ**	**1-01-001**
fiction	**NN**	**46-06-019**
fiction-writer	**noun**	**1-01-001**
fiction-writer's	NN$	1-01-001
fiction-writing	**NN**	**1-01-001**
fictional	**JJ**	**13-04-007**
fictitious	**JJ**	**2-02-002**
fictive	**JJ**	**1-01-001**
fiddle	**noun**	**3-02-002**
fiddle	NN	2-01-001
fiddles	NNS	1-01-001
fiddlesticks	**exclam.**	**1-01-001**
fiddlesticks	UH	0-00-000
Fiddlesticks	UH-NC	1-01-001
fiddling	**NN**	**1-01-001**
fide	**FW-NN**	**1-01-001**
Fidel	**NP**	**7-02-004**
fidelity	**noun**	**8-04-004**
fidelity	NN	7-04-004
Fidelity	NN-TL	1-01-001
Fiedler	**prop. noun**	**10-01-001**
Fiedler	NP	9-01-001
Fiedler's	NP$	1-01-001
fiefdom	**NN**	**1-01-001**
field	**noun**	**333-15-153**
field	NN	242-15-117
field	NN-HL	1-01-001
Field	NN-TL	21-05-012
fields	NNS	69-13-054

Word	Tag	Frequency
field	**verb**	**6-04-004**
field	VB	2-02-002
fields	VBZ	1-01-001
fielded	VBD	1-01-001
fielding	VBG	1-01-001
fielding	VBG-HL	1-01-001
Field	**prop. noun**	**10-04-006**
Field	NP	6-03-004
Field	NP-TL	2-02-002
Field's	NP$	2-01-001
field-flattening	**JJ**	**2-01-001**
field-hand	**noun**	**1-01-001**
field-hands'	NNS$	1-01-001
field-sequential	**JJ**	**1-01-001**
fielder	**noun**	**6-04-004**
fielder	NN	3-02-002
fielder's	NN$	1-01-001
fielders	NNS	2-02-002
fielding	**NN**	**1-01-001**
fieldmouse	**noun**	**1-01-001**
fieldmice	NNS	1-01-001
Fields	**NP**	**2-02-002**
fieldstone	**NN**	**1-01-001**
fieldwork	**NN**	**2-01-001**
fiend	**NN**	**3-03-003**
fiendish	**JJ**	**1-01-001**
fierce	**JJ**	**8-06-008**
fiercely	**RB**	**4-02-003**
fierceness	**NN**	**1-01-001**
fiercest	**JJT**	**1-01-001**
fiery	**JJ**	**7-05-007**
fiesta	**NN**	**1-01-001**
Fife	**prop. noun**	**1-01-001**
Fife	NP	0-00-000
Fife	NP-TL	1-01-001
fifteen	**CD**	**56-13-048**
fifteen-mile	**JJ**	**1-01-001**
fifteen-minute	**JJ**	**3-03-003**
fifteen-sixteenths	**NNS**	**1-01-001**
fifteenth	**ord. num.**	**9-04-008**
fifteenth	OD	7-03-006
Fifteenth	OD-TL	2-01-002
fifteenth-century	**NN**	**1-01-001**
fifth	**ord. num.**	**37-11-031**
fifth	OD	23-09-019
Fifth	OD-TL	14-09-012
fifth	**RB**	**1-01-001**
fifth-century	**NN**	**1-01-001**
fiftieth	**OD**	**1-01-001**
fifty	**CD**	**68-14-056**
fifty	**noun**	**12-04-006**
fifties	NNS	7-04-005
Fifties	NNS-TL	5-01-001
fifty-cent	**JJ**	**2-02-002**
fifty-dollar	**JJ**	**1-01-001**
fifty-fifth	**ord. num.**	**2-01-001**
fifty-fifth	OD	0-00-000
Fifty-fifth	OD-TL	2-01-001
fifty-fifty	**JJ**	**1-01-001**
fifty-five	**CD**	**2-02-002**
fifty-four	**CD**	**1-01-001**
fifty-nine	**CD**	**1-01-001**
fifty-ninth	**ord. num.**	**2-02-002**
fifty-ninth	OD	1-01-001
Fifty-ninth	OD-TL	1-01-001
fifty-odd	**CD**	**2-01-001**
fifty-one	**CD**	**1-01-001**
fifty-pound	**JJ**	**1-01-001**
fifty-seven	**CD**	**1-01-001**
fifty-third	**OD**	**1-01-001**
fifty-three	**CD**	**2-02-002**
fifty-two	**CD**	**2-02-002**
fifty-year	**JJ**	**1-01-001**
fig	**NN**	**2-01-001**
Figaro	**prop. noun**	**1-01-001**
Figaro	NP	0-00-000
Figaro	NP-TL	1-01-001
fight	**noun**	**58-12-046**
fight	NN	54-11-044
fight	NN-HL	1-01-001
fights	NNS	3-03-003
fight	**verb**	**155-15-094**
fight	VB	43-13-038
fights	VBZ	3-03-003
fought	VBD	23-09-018
Fought	VBD	1-01-001
fought	VBN	22-09-020
fighting	VBG	54-13-044
fightin'	VBG	1-01-001

Word	Tag	Frequency
fight (cont.):		
Fighting	VBG-TL	8-02-002
fighter	**noun**	**25-10-018**
fighter	NN	9-06-008
fighters	NNS	14-08-011
Fighters	NNS-TL	2-01-002
fighting	**NN**	**10-06-008**
figment	**NN**	**2-02-002**
Figone	**NP**	**2-01-001**
figural	**JJ**	**1-01-001**
figurative	**JJ**	**5-03-004**
figure	**noun**	**389-15-150**
figure	NN	151-14-090
fig.	NN	15-03-005
Fig.	NN-TL	55-02-012
Fig.	NN-TL-HL	1-01-001
Figure	NN-TL	38-03-015
figures	NNS	100-15-070
figs.	NNS	10-03-004
Figs.	NNS-TL	9-02-005
Figures	NNS-TL	10-02-003
figure	**verb**	**53-12-040**
figure	VB	20-10-019
figger	VB	3-01-001
figures	VBZ	3-03-003
figured	VBD	15-07-012
figgered	VBD	1-01-001
figured	VBN	6-05-006
figuring	VBG	5-04-005
figurine	**noun**	**1-01-001**
figurines	NNS	1-01-001
figuring	**NN**	**1-01-001**
Fike	**prop. noun**	**2-01-001**
Fike	NP	1-01-001
Fike	NP-HL	1-01-001
fil	**foreign**	**1-01-001**
fil	FW-NN	0-00-000
Fil	FW-NN-TL	1-01-001
Fil	**NP**	**1-01-001**
filagree	**NN**	**1-01-001**
filament	**noun**	**2-02-002**
filament	NN	1-01-001
filaments	NNS	1-01-001
filbert	**noun**	**3-02-002**
filbert	NN	1-01-001
filberts	NNS	2-01-001
filch	**verb**	**1-01-001**
filched	VBD	1-01-001
file	**noun**	**59-11-026**
file	NN	44-10-020
File	NN-TL	3-01-001
files	NNS	12-07-009
file	**verb**	**87-10-032**
file	VB	30-06-008
file	VB-HL	3-01-001
File	VB-TL	1-01-001
files	VBZ	1-01-001
filed	VBD	12-06-011
filed	VBN	21-05-013
filing	VBG	18-03-007
filing	VBG-HL	1-01-001
filet	**noun**	**1-01-001**
filets	NNS	1-01-001
filial	**JJ**	**1-01-001**
filibuster	**noun**	**4-02-002**
filibuster	NN	3-02-002
filibusters	NNS	1-01-001
filigree	**NN**	**1-01-001**
filigreed	**JJ**	**1-01-001**
Filipino	**JJ**	**1-01-001**
Filipino	**prop. noun**	**2-02-002**
Filipino	NP	1-01-001
Filipinos	NPS	0-00-000
Filipinos	NPS-HL	1-01-001
Filippo	**NP**	**2-02-002**
fill	**verb**	**184-14-134**
fill	VB	49-14-041
fill	VB-HL	1-01-001
fills	VBZ	5-04-005
filled	VBD	31-10-026
filled	VBN	68-14-057
filde	VBN	1-01-001
filling	VBG	27-10-021
filling	VBG-NC	1-01-001
Filling	VBG-TL	1-01-001
fill-in	**noun**	**3-01-002**
fill-in	NN	1-01-001
fill-ins	NNS	2-01-001
fille	**foreign**	**8-03-003**

Word	Tag	Frequency
fille (cont.):		
fille	FW-NN	6-01-001
filles	FW-NNS	2-02-002
filler	**NN**	**1-01-001**
filling	**noun**	**10-03-005**
filling	NN	7-03-004
fillings	NNS	3-01-001
fillip	**NN**	**1-01-001**
filly	**noun**	**10-02-002**
filly	NN	9-02-002
fillies	NNS	1-01-001
film	**noun**	**127-13-043**
film	NN	91-13-033
film	NN-HL	2-01-001
Film	NN-HL	1-01-001
Film	NN-TL	1-01-001
film's	NN$	1-01-001
films	NNS	31-08-018
film	**verb**	**6-03-003**
film	VB	1-01-001
filmed	VBN	4-02-002
filming	VBG	1-01-001
filmdom	**noun**	**1-01-001**
filmdom	NN	0-00-000
Filmdom	NN-TL	1-01-001
filmstrip	**noun**	**1-01-001**
filmstrips	NNS	1-01-001
filmy	**JJ**	**1-01-001**
filter	**noun**	**12-04-009**
filter	NN	8-03-005
filters	NNS	4-03-004
filter	**verb**	**11-05-009**
filter	VB	1-01-001
filtered	VBD	1-01-001
filtered	VBN	5-03-005
filtering	VBG	4-02-003
filtering	**NN**	**2-01-001**
filth	**NN**	**2-02-002**
filthy	**JJ**	**7-05-007**
fin	**noun**	**7-04-005**
fin	NN	2-02-002
fins	NNS	5-04-005
fin	**verb**	**1-01-001**
finned	VBD	1-01-001
final	**AP**	**9-01-005**
final	**adjective**	**146-15-102**
final	JJ	142-15-101
final	JJ-HL	1-01-001
Final	JJ-TL	3-01-001
final	**noun**	**11-03-003**
final	NN	1-01-001
finals	NNS	2-01-001
finals	NNS-HL	1-01-001
Finals	NNS-TL	7-01-001
finale	**NN**	**6-05-005**
finalist	**noun**	**2-01-002**
finalist	NN	1-01-001
finalists	NNS	1-01-001
finality	**NN**	**4-03-003**
finally	**RB**	**191-15-144**
Finan	**NP**	**1-01-001**
finance	**noun**	**19-10-016**
finance	NN	9-07-009
Finance	NN-TL	4-03-003
finances	NNS	6-05-005
finance	**verb**	**55-09-026**
finance	VB	18-06-013
financed	VBN	15-07-012
financed	VBN-HL	1-01-001
financing	VBG	20-05-010
financing	VBG-HL	1-01-001
financial	**adjective**	**86-11-051**
financial	JJ	83-11-050
financial	JJ-HL	2-01-002
Financial	JJ-TL	1-01-001
financially	**RB**	**8-06-008**
financier	**NN**	**2-01-001**
financing	**noun**	**13-05-009**
financing	NN	12-05-008
Financing	NN-TL	1-01-001
Finberg	**NP**	**2-01-001**
find	**NN**	**3-03-003**
find	**verb**	**1033-15-380**
find	VB	397-15-244
finds	VBZ	58-12-048
finds	VBZ-HL	1-01-001
found	VBD	268-15-165
found	VBN	267-15-167
finding	VBG	42-14-038

Word	Tag	Frequency
finder	**noun**	**3-03-003**
finder	NN	2-02-002
finders	NNS	0-00-000
Finders	NNS-TL	1-01-001
finding	**noun**	**45-09-029**
finding	NN	11-05-011
findings	NNS	33-08-021
findings	NNS-HL	1-01-001
fine	**adjective**	**150-15-103**
fine	JJ	141-15-098
Fine	JJ-TL	9-06-008
fine	**noun**	**8-04-008**
fine	NN	6-03-006
fines	NNS	2-02-002
fine	**RB**	**5-04-004**
fine	**verb**	**5-04-005**
fine	VB	1-01-001
fined	VBN	4-03-004
fine-boned	**JJ**	**1-01-001**
fine-chiseled	**JJ**	**1-01-001**
fine-drawn	**JJ**	**1-01-001**
fine-feathered	**JJ**	**1-01-001**
fine-featured	**JJ**	**1-01-001**
fine-grained	**JJ**	**1-01-001**
fine-looking	**JJ**	**5-02-002**
fine-point	**NN**	**1-01-001**
fine-tooth	**NN**	**1-01-001**
finely	**QL**	**1-01-001**
finely	**RB**	**3-02-003**
finely-spun	**JJ**	**1-01-001**
fineness	**NN**	**1-01-001**
finer	**JJR**	**2-02-002**
finest	**JJT**	**16-06-014**
Fing	**NP**	**2-01-001**
finger	**noun**	**106-14-073**
finger	NN	40-13-033
fingers	NNS	66-12-050
finger	**verb**	**4-04-004**
fingered	VBD	2-02-002
Fingered	VBD-TL	1-01-001
fingering	VBG	1-01-001
finger-held	**JJ**	**1-01-001**
finger-paint	**VB**	**1-01-001**
finger-post	**NN**	**2-01-001**
finger-sucking	**NN**	**1-01-001**
finger-tip	**noun**	**1-01-001**
finger-tips	NNS	1-01-001
fingering	**noun**	**1-01-001**
fingerings	NNS	1-01-001
fingernail	**noun**	**2-02-002**
fingernails	NNS	2-02-002
fingerprint	**noun**	**10-01-003**
fingerprint	NN	6-01-002
fingerprints	NNS	4-01-002
fingerprint	**verb**	**1-01-001**
fingerprinting	VBG	1-01-001
fingertip	**noun**	**2-02-002**
fingertips	NNS	2-02-002
finial	**NN**	**1-01-001**
finicky	**JJ**	**1-01-001**
finish	**noun**	**16-08-014**
finish	NN	15-07-013
finishes	NNS	1-01-001
finish	**verb**	**120-15-086**
finish	VB	24-10-019
finishes	VBZ	1-01-001
finished	VBD	31-11-026
finished	VBN	54-12-045
finished	VBN-NC	2-01-001
finishing	VBG	7-04-007
finishing	VBG-HL	1-01-001
finisher	**NN**	**1-01-001**
finishing	**NN**	**1-01-001**
finite	**JJ**	**10-02-005**
finite	**NN**	**1-01-001**
finite-dimensional	**JJ**	**4-01-001**
Fink	**prop. noun**	**5-02-002**
Fink	NP	4-02-002
Fink's	NP$	1-01-001
Finland	**NP**	**2-01-002**
Finley	**NP**	**2-02-002**
Finn	**prop. noun**	**2-02-002**
Finn	NP	1-01-001
Finns	NPS	1-01-001
Finnegan	**NP**	**2-01-001**
Finney	**prop. noun**	**5-01-001**
Finney	NP	3-01-001
Finney's	NP$	2-01-001
Finnish	**JJ**	**1-01-001**

Word	Tag	Frequency
Finnsburg	**NP**	**1-01-001**
Finot	**NP**	**1-01-001**
Fiorello	**NP**	**4-01-001**
Fiori	**NP**	**1-01-001**
fir	**NN**	**2-01-002**
fire	**noun**	**195-14-104**
fire	NN	159-14-089
fire	NN-HL	1-01-001
Fire	NN-TL	16-08-013
fire's	NN+BEZ	2-01-001
fires	NNS	16-07-011
Fires	NNS-TL	1-01-001
fire	**verb**	**78-12-042**
fire	VB	10-06-010
Fire	VB-TL	1-01-001
fired	VBD	19-08-015
fired	VBN	25-10-015
firing	VBG	23-10-017
fire-colored	**JJ**	**1-01-001**
fire-fighting	**JJ**	**2-02-002**
fire-resistant	**JJ**	**1-01-001**
firearm	**noun**	**7-02-003**
firearms	NNS	6-02-002
Firearms	NNS-TL	1-01-001
firebreak	**noun**	**1-01-001**
firebreaks	NNS	1-01-001
firebug	**NN**	**1-01-001**
firecracker	**noun**	**4-03-003**
firecracker	NN	1-01-001
firecrackers	NNS	2-02-002
fire-crackers	NNS	1-01-001
firehouse	**noun**	**1-01-001**
firehouses	NNS	1-01-001
firelight	**NN**	**2-02-002**
fireman	**noun**	**6-04-005**
fireman	NN	1-01-001
firemen	NNS	5-03-004
fireplace	**noun**	**7-04-007**
fireplace	NN	6-04-006
fireplaces	NNS	1-01-001
firepower	**NN**	**1-01-001**
fireside	**noun**	**1-01-001**
fireside	NN	0-00-000
Fireside	NN-TL	1-01-001
fireworks	**NNS**	**5-04-005**
firing	**NN**	**1-01-001**
firm	**JJ**	**50-13-036**
firm	**noun**	**116-11-043**
firm	NN	59-10-032
firm's	NN$	2-01-001
firms	NNS	55-08-023
firma	**FW-JJ**	**1-01-001**
firmer	**JJR**	**6-04-005**
firmly	**QL**	**1-01-001**
firmly	**RB**	**48-11-041**
firmness	**NN**	**4-04-004**
first	**ord. num.**	**1031-15-387**
first	OD	978-15-383
first	OD-HL	2-02-002
first	OD-NC	1-01-001
First	OD-TL	50-11-032
first	**adverb**	**330-15-216**
first	RB	327-15-214
first	RB-HL	3-03-003
first-aid	**NN**	**1-01-001**
First-Born	**NP**	**1-01-001**
first-class	**JJ**	**5-04-005**
first-class	**NN**	**1-01-001**
first-degree	**NN**	**1-01-001**
first-family	**noun**	**1-01-001**
first-families	NNS	1-01-001
first-floor	**NN**	**1-01-001**
first-hand	**JJ**	**3-03-003**
first-level	**NN**	**2-01-001**
first-order	**NN**	**1-01-001**
first-place	**NN**	**1-01-001**
first-rate	**JJ**	**4-03-003**
first-run	**NN**	**1-01-001**
firsthand	**NN**	**1-01-001**
Firzite	**NP**	**1-01-001**
fiscal	**adjective**	**120-05-026**
fiscal	JJ	115-05-025
fiscal	JJ-HL	4-01-001
Fiscal	JJ-TL	1-01-001
fish	**noun**	**33-12-023**
fish	NN	30-12-022
Fish	NN-TL	1-01-001
fish	NNS	1-01-001
fishes	NNS	1-01-001

Word	Tag	Frequency
fish	**verb**	**30-10-018**
fishes	VBZ	1-01-001
fishing	VBG	29-09-017
Fish	**NP**	**3-01-001**
fisher	**noun**	**1-01-001**
fishers	NNS	1-01-001
Fisher	**prop. noun**	**5-03-004**
Fisher	NP	4-03-004
Fisher	NP-TL	1-01-001
fisherman	**noun**	**14-06-009**
fisherman	NN	5-04-004
fisherman's	NN$	2-01-002
fishermen	NNS	7-03-004
fishery	**NN**	**1-01-001**
fishing	**noun**	**3-02-003**
fishing	NN	1-01-001
Fishing	NN-TL	2-01-002
fishing-boat	**NN**	**1-01-001**
Fishkill	**NP**	**1-01-001**
fishmonger	**noun**	**1-01-001**
fishmongers	NNS	1-01-001
fishpond	**NN**	**1-01-001**
Fisk	**NP**	**2-02-002**
Fiske	**NP**	**5-01-001**
fission	**NN**	**5-02-002**
fissure	**verb**	**1-01-001**
fissured	VBN	1-01-001
fist	**noun**	**39-10-024**
fist	NN	25-08-018
fists	NNS	14-07-009
fist	**verb**	**1-01-001**
fisted	VBD	1-01-001
fist-fighting	**NN**	**1-01-001**
Fistoulari	**prop. noun**	**1-01-001**
Fistoulari's	NP$	1-01-001
fit	**adjective**	**9-05-007**
fit	JJ	8-05-006
Fit	JJ	1-01-001
fit	**noun**	**18-08-015**
fit	NN	14-08-012
fit	NN-HL	1-01-001
fits	NNS	3-03-003
fit	**verb**	**91-14-068**
fit	VB	38-11-029
fit	VB-HL	1-01-001
fits	VBZ	10-07-009
fitted	VBD	5-04-005
fit	VBD	1-01-001
fitted	VBN	15-08-014
fit	VBN	11-07-011
fitting	VBG	10-06-007
Fitch	**NP**	**1-01-001**
fitful	**JJ**	**1-01-001**
fitfully	**RB**	**1-01-001**
fitness	**NN**	**8-05-006**
fittest	**JJT**	**2-02-002**
fitting	**JJ**	**5-02-002**
fitting	**noun**	**3-01-003**
fitting	NN	2-01-002
fittings	NNS	1-01-001
Fitzgerald	**NP**	**6-03-003**
Fitzhugh	**NP**	**1-01-001**
Fitzroy	**NP**	**1-01-001**
five	**card. num.**	**287-15-165**
five	CD	264-15-164
five	CD-HL	3-02-003
Five	CD-TL	20-03-005
five	**noun**	**2-01-001**
fives	NNS	2-01-001
five-a-week	**JJ**	**1-01-001**
five-and-a-half	**CD**	**1-01-001**
five-and-dime	**NN**	**1-01-001**
five-and-twenty	**CD**	**1-01-001**
five-cent	**JJ**	**2-02-002**
five-column	**JJ**	**1-01-001**
five-coordinate	**JJ**	**1-01-001**
five-day	**JJ**	**1-01-001**
five-days-a-week	**JJ**	**1-01-001**
five-Element	**noun**	**2-01-001**
five-Elements	NNS	0-00-000
Five-Elements	NNS-TL	2-01-001
five-fold	**RB**	**1-01-001**
five-foot	**JJ**	**1-01-001**
five-gallon	**JJ**	**2-02-002**
five-hundred	**CD**	**1-01-001**
five-hundred-dollar	**JJ**	**1-01-001**
five-hundred-year-old	**JJ**	**1-01-001**
five-member	**JJ**	**1-01-001**
five-minute	**JJ**	**1-01-001**
five-month	**JJ**	**2-01-002**
five-ply	**JJ**	**1-01-001**
five-round	**JJ**	**1-01-001**
five-seventeen	**CD**	**1-01-001**
five-volume	**JJ**	**1-01-001**
five-year	**JJ**	**4-03-004**
fix	**NN**	**1-01-001**
fix	**verb**	**109-15-075**
fix	VB	13-07-013
fixed	VBD	12-06-010
fixed	VBN	73-15-049
fixed	VBN-HL	2-01-001
fixing	VBG	9-08-009
fixation	**noun**	**1-01-001**
fixations	NNS	1-01-001
fixer	**noun**	**1-01-001**
fixers	NNS	1-01-001
fixing	**NN**	**2-02-002**
fixture	**noun**	**6-04-005**
fixture	NN	3-03-003
fixtures	NNS	3-01-002
fizzle	**verb**	**1-01-001**
fizzled	VBD	1-01-001
fjord	**noun**	**2-01-002**
fjords	NNS	2-01-002
flag	**noun**	**18-07-013**
flag	NN	15-07-011
flags	NNS	3-01-003
flag	**verb**	**3-01-001**
flag	VB	1-01-001
flags	VBZ	2-01-001
flag-stick	**NN**	**1-01-001**
flag-waver	**noun**	**1-01-001**
flag-wavers	NNS	1-01-001
flagellate	**verb**	**1-01-001**
flagellated	VBN	1-01-001
flagellation	**NN**	**1-01-001**
flageolet	**NN**	**1-01-001**
Flagler	**prop. noun**	**1-01-001**
Flagler's	NP$	1-01-001
flagpole	**noun**	**1-01-001**
flagpoles	NNS	1-01-001
flagrant	**JJ**	**3-03-003**
flagrantly	**RB**	**1-01-001**
flail	**NN**	**1-01-001**
flail	**verb**	**4-02-004**
flailed	VBD	1-01-001
flailing	VBG	3-01-003
flair	**NN**	**8-05-007**
flake	**noun**	**4-04-004**
flakes	NNS	4-04-004
flake	**VB**	**1-01-001**
flaky	**JJ**	**2-02-002**
flamboyant	**JJ**	**3-02-003**
flamboyantly	**RB**	**1-01-001**
flame	**noun**	**27-11-018**
flame	NN	13-08-011
flames	NNS	12-06-008
flames	NNS-HL	1-01-001
Flames	NNS-TL	1-01-001
flame	**verb**	**11-07-010**
flame	VB	4-03-004
flamed	VBD	1-01-001
flaming	VBG	5-04-005
Flaming	VBG-TL	1-01-001
flame-thrower	**noun**	**1-01-001**
flame-throwers	NNS	1-01-001
flammable	**JJ**	**1-01-001**
Flanagan	**NP**	**1-01-001**
Flanders	**NP**	**2-01-001**
flange	**NN**	**2-02-002**
flank	**NN**	**2-02-002**
flank	**verb**	**6-05-006**
flanked	VBD	2-02-002
flanked	VBN	3-03-003
flanking	VBG	1-01-001
Flannagan	**prop. noun**	**11-01-001**
Flannagan	NP	7-01-001
Flannagans	NPS	3-01-001
Flannagans'	NPS$	1-01-001
flannel	**noun**	**5-03-005**
flannel	NN	4-03-004
flannels	NNS	1-01-001
flap	**verb**	**8-05-007**
flapped	VBD	4-03-003
flapping	VBG	4-04-004
flapper	**noun**	**2-02-002**
flapper	NN	1-01-001
flappers	NNS	1-01-001

Word	Tag	Frequency
flare	**noun**	**8-05-005**
flare	NN	3-03-003
flares	NNS	5-02-002
flare	**verb**	**9-07-009**
flares	VBZ	1-01-001
flared	VBD	3-02-003
flared	VBN	2-02-002
flaring	VBG	3-03-003
flash	**noun**	**24-11-018**
flash	NN	14-09-011
flash	NN-HL	1-01-001
flashes	NNS	9-05-007
flash	**verb**	**28-08-021**
flash	VB	6-05-006
flashed	VBD	12-04-010
flashed	VBN	3-03-003
flashed	VBN-HL	1-01-001
flashing	VBG	6-03-004
flash-bulb	**noun**	**1-01-001**
flash-bulbs	NNS	1-01-001
flashback	**NN**	**1-01-001**
flashlight	**NN**	**8-04-006**
flashlight-type	**JJ**	**1-01-001**
flashy	**JJ**	**3-03-003**
flask	**NN**	**5-01-002**
flat	**adjective**	**52-12-037**
flat	JJ	51-11-036
flat	JJ-TL	1-01-001
flat	**noun**	**13-08-009**
flat	NN	10-05-006
flats	NNS	3-03-003
flat	**QL**	**1-01-001**
flat	**RB**	**4-04-004**
flat-bed	**noun**	**4-01-001**
flat-bed	NN	2-01-001
flat-bed	NN-HL	2-01-001
flat-bottomed	**JJ**	**4-02-002**
flat-footed	**JJ**	**1-01-001**
flat-topped	**JJ**	**1-01-001**
flathead	**NN**	**1-01-001**
flatiron	**noun**	**2-01-001**
flatiron	NN	1-01-001
flatiron	NN-HL	1-01-001
flatland	**NN**	**1-01-001**
flatly	**RB**	**7-06-006**
flatness	**noun**	**9-01-001**
flatness	NN	8-01-001
flatnesses	NNS	1-01-001
flatten	**verb**	**9-07-008**
flatten	VB	1-01-001
flattened	VBD	2-02-002
flattened	VBN	4-03-004
flattening	VBG	2-02-002
flatter	**verb**	**9-07-009**
flatter	VB	1-01-001
flattered	VBD	2-02-002
flattered	VBN	5-04-005
flattering	VBG	1-01-001
flatteringly	**QL**	**1-01-001**
flattery	**NN**	**3-02-003**
flattest	**JJT**	**1-01-001**
flatulence	**NN**	**1-01-001**
flatus	**NN**	**2-01-001**
flaunt	**verb**	**3-02-003**
flaunted	VBD	2-02-002
flaunting	VBG	1-01-001
flautist	**noun**	**2-01-001**
flautist	NN	1-01-001
flautist's	NN$	1-01-001
flavor	**noun**	**18-06-012**
flavor	NN	16-06-012
flavors	NNS	2-02-002
flavor	**verb**	**3-02-002**
flavored	VBN	2-02-002
flavoring	VBG	1-01-001
flavoring	**noun**	**2-01-001**
flavoring	NN	1-01-001
flavorings	NNS	1-01-001
Flavus	**NP**	**1-01-001**
flaw	**noun**	**4-04-004**
flaw	NN	3-03-003
flaws	NNS	1-01-001
flawless	**JJ**	**2-02-002**
flax	**NN**	**3-01-001**
flaxen	**JJ**	**1-01-001**
flaxseed	**NN**	**3-01-002**
flea	**noun**	**4-04-004**
flea	NN	0-00-000
Flea	NN-TL	2-02-002

Word	Tag	Frequency
flea (cont.):		
fleas	NNS	2-02-002
fleawort	**NN**	**1-01-001**
fleck	**NN**	**1-01-001**
fleck	**verb**	**1-01-001**
flecked	VBN	1-01-001
Fledermaus	**foreign**	**1-01-001**
Fledermaus	FW-NN	0-00-000
Fledermaus	FW-NN-TL	1-01-001
fledgling	**noun**	**5-04-004**
fledgling	NN	3-03-003
fledglings	NNS	2-01-001
flee	**verb**	**40-11-029**
flee	VB	1-01-001
flees	VBZ	1-01-001
fled	VBD	22-10-018
fled	VBN	6-05-005
fleeing	VBG	10-06-008
fleet	**JJ**	**1-01-001**
fleet	**noun**	**16-07-011**
fleet	NN	11-05-009
Fleet	NN-TL	3-01-001
fleet's	NN$	0-00-000
Fleet's	NN$-TL	1-01-001
fleets	NNS	1-01-001
fleet	**verb**	**5-03-003**
fleeting	VBG	4-03-003
fleeting	VBG-HL	1-01-001
Fleet	**NP**	**2-01-001**
fleetest	**JJT**	**1-01-001**
fleeting	**JJ**	**2-02-002**
Fleischman	**NP**	**2-01-001**
Fleischmanns	**NP**	**3-01-001**
Fleisher	**prop. noun**	**2-02-002**
Fleisher	NP	1-01-001
Fleisher's	NP$	1-01-001
Flem	**NP**	**2-01-001**
Fleming	**prop. noun**	**3-03-003**
Fleming	NP	2-02-002
Flemings	NPS	1-01-001
Flemish	**JJ**	**5-02-003**
flesh	**NN**	**52-09-034**
fleshy	**JJ**	**2-02-002**
Fletcher	**prop. noun**	**7-03-003**
Fletcher	NP	6-02-002
Fletcher	NP-TL	1-01-001
flex	**NN**	**1-01-001**
flex	**verb**	**3-02-003**
flex	VB	1-01-001
flexed	VBD	2-01-002
flexibility	**NN**	**16-04-010**
flexible	**adjective**	**25-06-017**
flexible	JJ	24-06-016
flexible	JJ-HL	1-01-001
flexural	**adjective**	**5-01-001**
flexural	JJ	4-01-001
flexural	JJ-HL	1-01-001
flick	**noun**	**2-02-002**
flick	NN	1-01-001
flicks	NNS	1-01-001
flick	**verb**	**6-03-005**
flicked	VBD	5-02-004
flicking	VBG	1-01-001
Flick	**NP**	**1-01-001**
flicker	**NN**	**1-01-001**
flicker	**verb**	**3-02-003**
flicker	VB	1-01-001
flickered	VBD	2-02-002
flier	**noun**	**2-02-002**
flier	NN	1-01-001
Flier	NN-TL	1-01-001
flight	**noun**	**60-13-037**
flight	NN	43-13-032
Flight	NN-TL	3-03-003
flights	NNS	14-08-010
flimsy	**JJ**	**2-01-002**
flimsy	**noun**	**1-01-001**
flimsies	NNS	1-01-001
flinch	**verb**	**1-01-001**
flinching	VBG	1-01-001
fling	**verb**	**17-04-013**
fling	VB	2-02-002
flng	VB	1-01-001
flung	VBD	9-03-008
flung	VBN	5-02-004
flint	**NN**	**1-01-001**
Flint	**NP**	**3-01-001**
flintless	**JJ**	**1-01-001**
flip	**noun**	**1-01-001**

flip (cont.):		
flips	NNS	1-01-001
flip	**verb**	**8-05-007**
flip	VB	3-03-003
flipped	VBD	3-02-003
flipping	VBG	2-02-002
Flip	**NP**	**1-01-001**
flippant	**JJ**	**1-01-001**
flipper	**noun**	**1-01-001**
flippers	NNS	1-01-001
flirt	**verb**	**2-02-002**
flirt	VB	1-01-001
flirted	VBD	1-01-001
flirtation	**NN**	**2-02-002**
flirtatious	**JJ**	**1-01-001**
flit	**verb**	**1-01-001**
flitting	VBG	1-01-001
Flite-King	**prop. noun**	**1-01-001**
Flite-King	NP	0-00-000
Flite-King	NP-TL	1-01-001
float	**verb**	**23-10-021**
float	VB	3-02-003
floats	VBZ	1-01-001
floated	VBD	6-04-006
floated	VBN	1-01-001
floating	VBG	12-07-012
floater	**NN**	**1-01-001**
floating-load	**NN**	**1-01-001**
floc	**NN**	**3-01-001**
flocculate	**verb**	**1-01-001**
flocculated	VBN	1-01-001
flocculation	**NN**	**1-01-001**
flock	**noun**	**11-05-008**
flock	NN	6-03-006
Flock	NN-TL	3-01-001
flock's	NN$	0-00-000
Flock's	NN$-TL	1-01-001
flocks	NNS	1-01-001
flock	**verb**	**4-03-004**
flock	VB	1-01-001
flocked	VBD	2-02-002
flocking	VBG	1-01-001
floe	**noun**	**2-02-002**
floe	NN	1-01-001
floes	NNS	1-01-001
flog	**verb**	**3-03-003**
flog	VB	1-01-001
flogged	VBD	2-02-002
flood	**noun**	**24-11-017**
flood	NN	15-07-011
Flood	NN-TL	2-01-002
flood's	NN$	1-01-001
floods	NNS	6-06-006
flood	**verb**	**13-07-013**
flood	VB	2-02-002
flooded	VBD	5-04-005
flooded	VBN	4-04-004
flooding	VBG	2-02-002
flood-lighted	**JJ**	**1-01-001**
flood-ravaged	**JJ**	**1-01-001**
floodhead	**noun**	**1-01-001**
floodheads	NNS	1-01-001
floodlight	**NN**	**1-01-001**
floodlight	**verb**	**1-01-001**
floodlit	VBN	1-01-001
floor	**noun**	**170-15-099**
floor	NN	157-15-093
Floor	NN-TL	1-01-001
floors	NNS	12-08-010
floor-length	**NN**	**1-01-001**
floor-to-ceiling	**JJ**	**1-01-001**
floorboard	**noun**	**4-03-004**
floorboards	NNS	4-03-004
flooring	**NN**	**7-03-004**
floorshow	**NN**	**1-01-001**
flop	**NN**	**1-01-001**
flop	**verb**	**7-03-006**
flops	VBZ	1-01-001
flopped	VBD	6-03-005
floppy	**JJ**	**1-01-001**
Flor	**NP**	**1-01-001**
flora	**NNS**	**1-01-001**
Floradora	**NP**	**1-01-001**
floral	**JJ**	**3-03-003**
Florence	**NP**	**5-02-003**
Florentine	**JJ**	**3-02-002**
Florentine	**NP**	**1-01-001**
Floresville	**NP**	**1-01-001**
Florican	**NP**	**2-01-001**
florid	**JJ**	**2-02-002**
Florida	**prop. noun**	**32-08-017**
Florida	NP	17-08-012
Fla.	NP	5-01-004
Fla.	NP-HL	5-03-003
Florida	NP-TL	3-03-003
Florida's	NP$	2-01-001
Floridian	**prop. noun**	**2-02-002**
Floridian	NP	1-01-001
Floridians	NPS	1-01-001
florist	**noun**	**3-02-003**
florist	NN	1-01-001
florist's	NN$	2-01-002
Flory	**NP**	**3-01-001**
flotation-type	**JJ**	**1-01-001**
flotilla	**noun**	**1-01-001**
flotillas	NNS	1-01-001
Flotilla	**NP**	**1-01-001**
Flotte	**prop. noun**	**2-01-001**
Flotte	NP	1-01-001
Flotte's	NP$	1-01-001
flounce	**verb**	**1-01-001**
flounced	VBD	1-01-001
flounder	**verb**	**5-04-004**
flounder	VB	1-01-001
flounders	VBZ	1-01-001
floundered	VBN	1-01-001
floundering	VBG	2-02-002
flour	**NN**	**8-05-008**
flour	**verb**	**1-01-001**
floured	VBN	1-01-001
flour-milling	**JJ**	**1-01-001**
flourish	**noun**	**3-03-003**
flourish	NN	1-01-001
flourishes	NNS	2-02-002
flourish	**verb**	**13-09-013**
flourish	VB	4-04-004
flourishes	VBZ	2-02-002
flourished	VBD	6-05-006
flourishing	VBG	1-01-001
flout	**verb**	**1-01-001**
flouted	VBN	1-01-001
flouting	**NN**	**1-01-001**
flow	**noun**	**56-11-032**
flow	NN	55-11-031
flows	NNS	1-01-001
flow	**verb**	**40-11-033**
flow	VB	13-07-013
flows	VBZ	4-03-004
flowed	VBD	4-03-004
flowed	VBN	2-02-002
flowing	VBG	17-08-014
flower	**noun**	**78-13-049**
flower	NN	17-09-016
Flower	NN-TL	4-03-004
flower's	NN$	1-01-001
flowers	NNS	54-13-032
Flowers	NNS-TL	2-02-002
flower	**verb**	**6-05-006**
flower	VB	1-01-001
flowered	VBD	1-01-001
flowered	VBN	2-02-002
flowering	VBG	2-02-002
Flower	**prop. noun**	**2-01-001**
Flower	NP	1-01-001
Flowers	NPS	1-01-001
flower-scented	**JJ**	**1-01-001**
flowering	**NN**	**4-03-004**
flowerpot	**NN**	**2-01-001**
Floyd	**prop. noun**	**4-03-003**
Floyd	NP	1-01-001
Floyd	NP-TL	1-01-001
Floyd's	NP$	2-02-002
flu	**NN**	**8-05-006**
flub	**verb**	**1-01-001**
flubbed	VBD	1-01-001
fluctuate	**verb**	**3-02-003**
fluctuates	VBZ	1-01-001
fluctuating	VBG	2-02-002
fluctuation	**noun**	**1-01-001**
fluctuations	NNS	1-01-001
fluency	**NN**	**1-01-001**
fluent	**JJ**	**5-03-003**
fluently	**RB**	**1-01-001**
fluff	**NN**	**1-01-001**
fluffy	**JJ**	**1-01-001**
Flugel	**NP**	**1-01-001**
fluid	**JJ**	**3-03-003**
fluid	**noun**	**33-06-011**

Word	Tag	Frequency
fluid (cont.):		
fluid	NN	18-06-009
fluids	NNS	14-03-003
fluids	NNS-HL	1-01-001
fluid-filled	**JJ**	**1-01-001**
fluidity	**NN**	**2-02-002**
fluke	**NN**	**1-01-001**
Flumenophobe	**NP**	**1-01-001**
fluoresce	**verb**	**1-01-001**
fluoresces	VBZ	1-01-001
fluorescein	**NN**	**1-01-001**
fluorescein-labeled	**JJ**	**1-01-001**
fluorescence	**noun**	**12-01-001**
fluorescence	NN	11-01-001
fluorescence	NN-HL	1-01-001
fluorescent	**JJ**	**4-03-003**
fluoride	**NN**	**2-01-001**
fluorinate	**verb**	**1-01-001**
fluorinated	VBN	1-01-001
fluorine	**NN**	**1-01-001**
flurry	**NN**	**3-03-003**
flurry	**verb**	**2-02-002**
flurry	VB	1-01-001
flurried	VBD	1-01-001
flush	**JJ**	**5-02-003**
flush	**NN**	**4-03-004**
flush	**RB**	**1-01-001**
flush	**verb**	**8-05-008**
flush	VB	1-01-001
flushed	VBD	1-01-001
flushed	VBN	5-03-005
flushing	VBG	1-01-001
Flushing	**prop. noun**	**4-03-003**
Flushing	NP	2-02-002
Flushing	NP-HL	1-01-001
Flushing	NP-TL	1-01-001
fluster	**verb**	**1-01-001**
flustered	VBN	1-01-001
flute	**NN**	**1-01-001**
flute	**verb**	**1-01-001**
fluted	VBN	1-01-001
fluting	**NN**	**1-01-001**
flutist	**NN**	**1-01-001**
flutter	**NN**	**2-02-002**
flutter	**verb**	**6-05-006**
fluttered	VBD	2-02-002
fluttering	VBG	4-04-004
flux	**noun**	**34-04-008**
flux	NN	26-04-008
flux	NN-HL	4-01-002
fluxes	NNS	4-01-002
fly	**noun**	**23-08-014**
fly	NN	15-08-010
flies	NNS	8-06-006
fly	**verb**	**92-13-056**
fly	VB	18-08-015
flies	VBZ	3-02-003
flies	VBZ-HL	1-01-001
flew	VBD	27-11-024
flown	VBN	4-04-004
flying	VBG	35-11-025
Flying	VBG-TL	4-03-004
fly-boy	**NN**	**1-01-001**
fly-dotted	**JJ**	**1-01-001**
flyaway	**JJ**	**1-01-001**
flyer	**noun**	**7-04-004**
flyer	NN	3-02-002
Flyer	NN-TL	2-01-001
flyers	NNS	2-02-002
flying	**noun**	**4-04-004**
flying	NN	3-03-003
Flying	NN-TL	1-01-001
flying-mount	**NN**	**1-01-001**
Flynn	**prop. noun**	**3-02-002**
Flynn	NP	2-01-001
Flynn's	NP$	1-01-001
flyway	**noun**	**1-01-001**
flyways	NNS	1-01-001
foal	**noun**	**3-01-001**
foal	NN	2-01-001
foals	NNS	1-01-001
foam	**noun**	**59-04-004**
foam	NN	36-04-004
foam's	NN$	1-01-001
foams	NNS	21-01-001
foams	NNS-HL	1-01-001
foam	**verb**	**12-02-002**
foam	VB	1-01-001
foamed	VBD	1-01-001
foam (cont.):		
foamed	VBN	7-01-001
Foamed	VBN-TL	1-01-001
foaming	VBG	2-01-001
foamed-core	**NN**	**1-01-001**
foamed-in-place	**JJ**	**1-01-001**
foaming	**NN**	**4-01-001**
foamy	**JJ**	**3-02-002**
foamy-necked	**JJ**	**1-01-001**
focal	**JJ**	**8-06-006**
focally	**RB**	**1-01-001**
focus	**noun**	**29-11-025**
focus	NN	26-10-023
focus	NN-HL	2-02-002
foci	NNS	1-01-001
focus	**verb**	**34-12-026**
focus	VB	12-06-011
focuses	VBZ	2-01-001
focused	VBD	6-05-006
focussed	VBD	2-02-002
focused	VBN	6-04-006
focussed	VBN	1-01-001
focusing	VBG	5-02-003
focusing	**NN**	**1-01-001**
fodder	**NN**	**1-01-001**
foe	**noun**	**14-06-011**
foe	NN	8-04-006
foes	NNS	6-03-005
fog	**NN**	**25-09-018**
fog	**verb**	**1-01-001**
fogged	VBN	1-01-001
fog-enshrouded	**JJ**	**1-01-001**
Fogelson	**NP**	**1-01-001**
Fogg	**prop. noun**	**26-02-002**
Fogg	NP	23-02-002
Fogg's	NP$	3-01-001
Foggia	**NP**	**1-01-001**
foggy	**adjective**	**5-03-004**
foggy	JJ	3-02-003
Foggy	JJ-TL	2-01-001
fogy	**NN**	**1-01-001**
foible	**noun**	**3-02-003**
foibles	NNS	3-02-003
foil	**noun**	**18-08-008**
foil	NN	17-07-007
Foil	NN-TL	1-01-001
foil	**verb**	**3-02-003**
foil	VB	2-02-002
foiled	VBN	1-01-001
Foiles	**NP**	**1-01-001**
foist	**verb**	**1-01-001**
foisted	VBN	1-01-001
Fokine	**prop. noun**	**1-01-001**
Fokine's	NP$	1-01-001
fold	**noun**	**8-05-006**
fold	NN	5-04-005
folds	NNS	3-02-002
fold	**verb**	**20-07-019**
fold	VB	2-02-002
folded	VBD	5-04-005
folded	VBN	9-05-009
Folded	VBN-TL	1-01-001
folding	VBG	3-03-003
folder	**noun**	**2-02-002**
folder	NN	1-01-001
folders	NNS	1-01-001
Foley	**NP**	**1-01-001**
foliage	**noun**	**12-07-008**
foliage	NN	10-07-008
foliage	NN-HL	1-01-001
Foliage	NN-TL	1-01-001
folk	**noun**	**53-13-033**
folk	NN	33-12-020
Folk	NN-TL	1-01-001
folks	NNS	17-07-012
folks	NNS-HL	1-01-001
folks'	NNS$	1-01-001
folk-dance	**NN**	**1-01-001**
folk-music	**NN**	**1-01-001**
folk-tale	**NN**	**1-01-001**
folklike	**JJ**	**1-01-001**
folklore	**noun**	**30-04-005**
folklore	NN	26-03-003
folk-lore	NN	2-01-001
Folklore	NN-TL	2-02-002
folksong	**noun**	**1-01-001**
folksongs	NNS	1-01-001
Folkston	**NP**	**1-01-001**
folksy	**JJ**	**3-02-002**

Word	Tag	Frequency
follicular	**JJ**	**1-01-001**
follow	**verb**	**540-15-289**
follow	VB	97-15-087
follows	VBZ	75-11-055
followeth	VBZ	1-01-001
follows	VBZ-HL	1-01-001
Follows	VBZ-TL	1-01-001
followed	VBD	91-14-069
followed	VBN	81-14-065
following	VBG	192-15-128
followin'	VBG	1-01-001
follow-through	**NN**	**1-01-001**
follow-up	**JJ**	**6-02-003**
follow-up	**noun**	**3-02-003**
follow-up	NN	2-02-002
follow-ups	NNS	1-01-001
follower	**noun**	**20-08-018**
follower	NN	3-02-003
followers	NNS	17-08-015
following	**IN**	**13-03-009**
following	**NN**	**16-09-014**
folly	**noun**	**12-06-010**
folly	NN	6-04-006
Folly	NN-TL	4-02-002
follies	NNS	2-02-002
Folsom	**NP**	**1-01-001**
fond	**JJ**	**13-09-013**
fonder	**JJR**	**1-01-001**
fondly	**RB**	**4-04-004**
fondness	**NN**	**4-04-004**
fonds	**foreign**	**1-01-001**
fonds	FW-NN	0-00-000
Fonds	FW-NN-TL	1-01-001
Fonta	**NP**	**1-01-001**
Fontainebleau	**NP**	**1-01-001**
Fontana	**NP**	**1-01-001**
fontanel	**NN**	**1-01-001**
food	**noun**	**198-15-071**
food	NN	137-15-062
food	NN-HL	2-02-002
Food	NN-TL	8-06-007
foods	NNS	41-06-012
foods	NNS-HL	3-02-002
Foods	NNS-TL	7-01-001
food-preservation	**NN**	**4-01-001**
food-processing	**JJ**	**1-01-001**
foodstuff	**noun**	**2-02-002**
foodstuffs	NNS	2-02-002
fool	**JJ**	**2-02-002**
fool	**noun**	**35-10-030**
fool	NN	30-09-025
fools	NNS	5-03-005
fool	**verb**	**10-06-010**
fool	VB	5-03-005
fooled	VBN	3-03-003
fooling	VBG	2-02-002
foolhardy	**JJ**	**2-01-002**
fooling	**NN**	**1-01-001**
foolish	**JJ**	**16-08-015**
foolishly	**RB**	**3-03-003**
foolishness	**NN**	**2-01-001**
foolproof	**JJ**	**2-02-002**
foot	**noun**	**361-15-157**
foot	NN	68-11-051
ft.	NN	5-01-001
Foot	NN-TL	2-01-001
feet	NNS	283-15-131
ft.	NNS	3-01-001
foot	**verb**	**2-02-002**
footing	VBG	2-02-002
foot-high	**JJ**	**1-01-001**
foot-loose	**JJ**	**2-02-002**
footage	**NN**	**1-01-001**
football	**noun**	**38-10-020**
football	NN	29-10-019
football	NN-HL	1-01-001
Football	NN-TL	6-01-003
football's	NN$	1-01-001
footballs	NNS	1-01-001
footballer	**noun**	**1-01-001**
footballer's	NN$	1-01-001
footbridge	**NN**	**1-01-001**
Foote	**NP**	**1-01-001**
footfall	**noun**	**2-02-002**
footfall	NN	1-01-001
footfalls	NNS	1-01-001
foothill	**noun**	**2-02-002**
foothill	NN	1-01-001
foothills	NNS	1-01-001

Word	Tag	Frequency
footing	**NN**	**1-01-001**
footman	**NN**	**1-01-001**
footnote	**noun**	**6-04-006**
footnote	NN	3-02-003
footnotes	NNS	2-02-002
footnotes	NNS-HL	1-01-001
footpath	**NN**	**1-01-001**
footstep	**noun**	**11-07-010**
footstep	NN	3-03-003
footsteps	NNS	8-05-007
footstool	**NN**	**1-01-001**
footwear	**NN**	**1-01-001**
footwork	**NN**	**1-01-001**
foppish	**JJ**	**1-01-001**
for	**CS**	**494-15-229**
for	**prep.**	**8996-15-500**
for	IN	8848-15-500
f'r	IN	1-01-001
fer	IN	2-01-001
foh	IN	1-01-001
fur	IN	1-01-001
for	IN-HL	51-07-039
for	IN-NC	3-01-001
For	IN-TL	38-07-024
for	IN-TL	50-09-035
f'ovuh	IN+IN	1-01-001
for	**RB**	**5-03-004**
forage	**noun**	**4-02-002**
forage	NN	3-01-001
forages	NNS	1-01-001
forage	**verb**	**2-02-002**
foraging	VBG	2-02-002
foraging	**NN**	**1-01-001**
Forand	**NP**	**1-01-001**
foray	**noun**	**2-02-002**
foray	NN	1-01-001
forays	NNS	1-01-001
forbear	**verb**	**3-02-003**
forbore	VBD	1-01-001
forborne	VBN	1-01-001
forbearing	VBG	0-00-000
forebearing	VBG	1-01-001
Forbes	**prop. noun**	**10-03-003**
Forbes	NP	9-02-002
Forbes's	NP$	1-01-001
forbid	**verb**	**28-11-027**
forbid	VB	4-04-004
forbids	VBZ	5-05-005
forbade	VBD	1-01-001
forbad	VBD	1-01-001
forbidden	VBN	15-07-015
forbidding	VBG	2-02-002
force	**foreign**	**5-03-004**
force	FW-NN	1-01-001
Force	FW-NN-TL	2-01-001
forces	FW-NNS	0-00-000
Forces	FW-NNS-TL	2-02-002
force	**noun**	**371-15-146**
force	NN	173-15-097
force	NN-HL	2-02-002
Force	NN-TL	28-07-017
force's	NN$	0-00-000
Force's	NN$-TL	1-01-001
forces	NNS	141-12-068
forces	NNS-HL	3-02-002
Forces	NNS-TL	21-04-006
Forces	NNS-TL-HL	2-01-002
force	**verb**	**124-15-096**
force	VB	24-10-020
forces	VBZ	6-04-006
forced	VBD	19-07-017
forced	VBN	62-15-052
forcing	VBG	13-10-012
force-fear	**JJ**	**1-01-001**
force-rate	**NN**	**1-01-001**
forceful	**JJ**	**8-05-007**
forcefulness	**NN**	**1-01-001**
forcibly	**RB**	**3-03-003**
ford	**noun**	**2-01-001**
fords	NNS	2-01-001
Ford	**prop. noun**	**25-08-017**
Ford	NP	20-08-014
Ford	NP-TL	4-03-003
Fords	NPS	1-01-001
fore	**JJ**	**1-01-001**
fore	**NN**	**4-01-004**
fore	**RB**	**1-01-001**
fore-play	**NN**	**1-01-001**
FOREAMI	**NP**	**1-01-001**

Word	Tag	Frequency
forearm	**noun**	**4-03-004**
forearm	NN	3-02-003
forearms	NNS	1-01-001
forebear	**noun**	**3-03-003**
forebears	NNS	1-01-001
forbears	NNS	2-02-002
forebode	**verb**	**1-01-001**
foreboding	VBG	1-01-001
foreboding	**NN**	**3-03-003**
forecast	**noun**	**8-06-008**
forecast	NN	3-02-003
forecasts	NNS	5-04-005
forecast	**verb**	**14-06-009**
forecast	VB	2-02-002
forecast	VBN	5-03-004
forecasting	VBG	7-02-004
forecaster	**noun**	**1-01-001**
forecasters	NNS	1-01-001
forecasting	**NN**	**2-02-002**
foreclose	**verb**	**2-01-002**
foreclosed	VBN	1-01-001
foreclosing	VBG	1-01-001
forefather	**noun**	**1-01-001**
forefathers	NNS	1-01-001
forefinger	**noun**	**7-06-007**
forefinger	NN	6-05-006
forefingers	NNS	1-01-001
forefoot	**noun**	**1-01-001**
forefeet	NNS	1-01-001
forego	**verb**	**12-06-011**
forego	VB	3-03-003
forgo	VB	1-01-001
foregone	VBN	1-01-001
foregoing	VBG	7-03-006
foregoing	**NN**	**4-03-004**
foreground	**NN**	**2-01-001**
forehead	**noun**	**18-07-017**
forehead	NN	16-07-015
foreheads	NNS	2-02-002
foreign	**adjective**	**158-13-083**
foreign	JJ	139-13-077
foreign	JJ-HL	1-01-001
Foreign	JJ-TL	18-05-013
foreign-aid	**NN**	**1-01-001**
foreign-entry-limit	**NN**	**1-01-001**
foreign-policy	**NN**	**2-02-002**
foreign-sounding	**JJ**	**1-01-001**
foreigner	**noun**	**17-07-012**
foreigner	NN	4-02-003
foreigners	NNS	12-06-009
foreigners	NNS-HL	1-01-001
foreknowledge	**NN**	**1-01-001**
foreknown	**JJ**	**1-01-001**
foreleg	**NN**	**1-01-001**
Forellen	**foreign**	**1-01-001**
Forellen	FW-NN	0-00-000
Forellen	FW-NN-TL	1-01-001
foreman	**noun**	**5-04-005**
foreman	NN	4-03-004
foreman's	NN$	1-01-001
foremost	**JJS**	**5-05-005**
foremost	**RB**	**7-04-007**
forensic	**adjective**	**7-02-002**
forensic	JJ	1-01-001
Forensic	JJ-TL	6-01-001
forepart	**NN**	**1-01-001**
forepaw	**noun**	**1-01-001**
forepaws	NNS	1-01-001
forerunner	**noun**	**8-03-005**
forerunner	NN	3-02-003
Forerunner	NN-TL	4-01-001
forerunners	NNS	1-01-001
foresee	**verb**	**14-09-012**
foresee	VB	3-03-003
foresaw	VBD	2-02-002
foreseen	VBN	7-05-006
foreseeing	VBG	2-02-002
foreseeable	**JJ**	**4-04-004**
foreseen	**JJ**	**1-01-001**
foreshorten	**verb**	**1-01-001**
foreshortened	VBN	1-01-001
foreshortening	**NN**	**1-01-001**
foresight	**NN**	**5-05-005**
forest	**noun**	**88-09-026**
forest	NN	40-08-015
Forest	NN-TL	26-05-009
forests	NNS	9-06-008
Forests	NNS-TL	13-02-002
forestall	**VB**	**5-02-005**
forestry	**NN**	**1-01-001**
foretell	**VB**	**1-01-001**
forethought	**NN**	**1-01-001**
forever	**adverb**	**39-14-030**
forever	RB	37-14-028
Forever	RB-TL	2-02-002
forever-Cathy	**NP**	**1-01-001**
forfeit	**verb**	**4-03-003**
forfeit	VB	2-01-001
forfeited	VBN	1-01-001
forfeit	VBN	1-01-001
forge	**noun**	**10-03-003**
forge	NN	4-01-001
Forge	NN-TL	6-02-002
forge	**verb**	**4-04-004**
forged	VBD	1-01-001
forged	VBN	2-02-002
forging	VBG	1-01-001
forgery	**noun**	**2-02-002**
forgery	NN	1-01-001
forgeries	NNS	1-01-001
forget	**verb**	**119-15-088**
forget	VB	53-14-041
forgit	VB	2-01-001
forget	VB-HL	1-01-001
forgot	VBD	17-09-015
forgotten	VBN	37-11-034
forgot	VBN	1-01-001
Forgotten	VBN-TL	1-01-001
forgetting	VBG	7-06-006
forgetful	**adjective**	**3-02-003**
forgetful	JJ	2-01-002
forgitful	JJ	1-01-001
forgetfulness	**NN**	**3-03-003**
forgive	**verb**	**33-10-016**
forgive	VB	24-09-012
forgave	VBD	2-02-002
forgiven	VBN	6-03-003
forgiving	VBG	1-01-001
forgiveness	**NN**	**15-05-006**
forgiving	**JJ**	**1-01-001**
forisque	**FW-RB+CC**	**1-01-001**
fork	**noun**	**20-08-012**
fork	NN	13-08-011
forks	NNS	2-01-001
Forks	NNS-TL	5-01-001
fork	**verb**	**5-02-004**
fork	VB	1-01-001
forked	VBN	3-01-002
Forked	VBN-TL	1-01-001
forklift	**noun**	**2-01-001**
forklift	NN	1-01-001
fork-lift	NN	1-01-001
forlorn	**JJ**	**3-03-003**
form	**noun**	**441-14-172**
form	NN	300-14-142
form	NN-HL	1-01-001
form	NN-NC	1-01-001
Form	NN-TL	17-03-003
forms	NNS	122-13-058
form	**verb**	**153-13-103**
form	VB	51-09-042
forms	VBZ	5-04-005
formed	VBD	19-07-015
formed	VBN	57-11-043
forming	VBG	21-08-019
form-creating	**JJ**	**1-01-001**
form-dictionary	**NN**	**1-01-001**
forma	**NN**	**2-02-002**
formability	**NN**	**1-01-001**
formal	**adjective**	**48-09-035**
formal	JJ	47-09-035
formal	JJ-HL	1-01-001
formalism	**NN**	**2-01-001**
formality	**noun**	**4-04-004**
formality	NN	2-02-002
formalities	NNS	2-02-002
formalize	**verb**	**4-03-004**
formalize	VB	2-02-002
formalized	VBN	2-01-002
formally	**RB**	**18-06-018**
format	**noun**	**10-04-005**
format	NN	4-04-004
format	NN-HL	5-01-002
formats	NNS	1-01-001
formation	**noun**	**44-11-027**
formation	NN	37-11-025
formations	NNS	7-02-004
formative	**JJ**	**1-01-001**

Word	Tag	Frequency
formative	**NN**	**1-01-001**
Formby	**prop. noun**	**2-01-001**
Formby	NP	1-01-001
Formby's	NP$	1-01-001
formed-tooth	**NN**	**1-01-001**
former	**AP**	**131-14-090**
formerly	**RB**	**28-11-024**
formidable	**FW-JJ**	**1-01-001**
formidable	**JJ**	**16-06-015**
formidably	**QL**	**1-01-001**
Formosa	**NP**	**5-02-003**
Formosan	**JJ**	**1-01-001**
formula	**noun**	**86-09-036**
formula	NN	56-07-027
formula	NN-HL	3-02-002
formulas	NNS	22-06-008
formulae	NNS	5-03-004
formulaic	**JJ**	**12-01-001**
formulate	**verb**	**24-07-022**
formulate	VB	9-04-007
formulated	VBD	3-03-003
formulated	VBN	8-05-008
formulating	VBG	4-03-004
formulation	**noun**	**28-05-012**
formulation	NN	17-04-007
formulations	NNS	11-03-007
Forrest	**NP**	**2-02-002**
forsake	**verb**	**4-03-004**
forsake	VB	1-01-001
forsakes	VBZ	1-01-001
forsaken	VBN	2-01-002
forsan	**FW-RB**	**1-01-001**
Forster	**prop. noun**	**1-01-001**
Forster's	NP$	1-01-001
forswear	**verb**	**1-01-001**
forswears	VBZ	1-01-001
Forsythe	**prop. noun**	**7-02-003**
Forsythe	NP	5-01-001
Forsyth	NP	1-01-001
Forsythe	NP-TL	1-01-001
fort	**noun**	**55-10-020**
fort	NN	7-05-005
Fort	NN-TL	42-09-015
Fort	NN-TL-HL	2-01-001
forts	NNS	4-03-003
fort	**VB**	**3-01-002**
Fort	**NP**	**1-01-001**
forte	**NN**	**4-04-004**
Forte	**NP**	**2-02-002**
forte-piano	**noun**	**1-01-001**
forte-pianos	NNS	1-01-001
Fortescue	**NP**	**2-01-001**
forth	**RB**	**71-14-061**
forthcoming	**JJ**	**10-05-009**
forthcoming	**NN**	**1-01-001**
forthright	**JJ**	**6-05-006**
forthrightly	**RB**	**1-01-001**
forthrightness	**NN**	**2-02-002**
Fortier	**NP**	**1-01-001**
fortification	**noun**	**3-02-002**
fortifications	NNS	3-02-002
fortify	**verb**	**9-06-009**
fortify	VB	2-01-002
fortified	VBD	2-02-002
fortified	VBN	5-04-005
Fortin	**NP**	**1-01-001**
fortiori	**FW-JJR**	**1-01-001**
fortitude	**NN**	**3-02-003**
Fortman	**NP**	**2-01-001**
fortnight	**NN**	**1-01-001**
fortress	**noun**	**8-04-007**
fortress	NN	5-02-005
Fortress	NN-TL	1-01-001
fortresses	NNS	2-01-001
fortunate	**JJ**	**22-08-018**
fortunately	**RB**	**20-11-017**
fortune	**noun**	**29-10-020**
fortune	NN	23-09-016
fortunes	NNS	6-05-005
Fortune	**NP**	**2-01-001**
fortune-happy	**JJ**	**1-01-001**
fortune-teller	**noun**	**1-01-001**
fortune-tellers	NNS	1-01-001
forty	**card. num.**	**36-12-031**
forty	CD	35-12-030
Forty	CD-TL	1-01-001
forty	**noun**	**7-04-006**
forties	NNS	6-03-005
Forties	NNS-TL	1-01-001

Word	Tag	Frequency
forty-eight	**CD**	**1-01-001**
forty-fifth	**OD**	**1-01-001**
forty-five	**CD**	**7-06-007**
forty-four	**CD**	**6-03-005**
forty-nine	**CD**	**4-02-002**
forty-niner	**noun**	**1-01-001**
forty-niners	NNS	1-01-001
forty-second	**ord. num.**	**1-01-001**
forty-second	OD	0-00-000
Forty-second	OD-TL	1-01-001
forty-seven	**CD**	**4-02-003**
forty-six	**CD**	**2-02-002**
forty-third	**ord. num.**	**1-01-001**
forty-third	OD	0-00-000
Forty-third	OD-TL	1-01-001
forty-three	**CD**	**2-01-002**
forty-two	**CD**	**2-02-002**
forty-year	**JJ**	**1-01-001**
forum	**noun**	**11-06-007**
forum	NN	7-05-005
Forum	NN-TL	3-03-003
forums	NNS	1-01-001
forward	**JJ**	**18-08-012**
forward	**RB**	**97-14-074**
forward	**verb**	**4-02-004**
forwarded	VBN	3-02-003
forwarding	VBG	1-01-001
forward-moving	**JJ**	**1-01-001**
Fosdick	**prop. noun**	**13-01-001**
Fosdick	NP	10-01-001
Fosdick's	NP$	3-01-001
Foss	**NP**	**3-01-001**
fossilize	**verb**	**3-02-002**
fossilized	VBN	3-02-002
foster	**JJ**	**2-02-002**
foster	**verb**	**14-07-012**
foster	VB	3-03-003
fosters	VBZ	3-02-003
fostered	VBD	1-01-001
fostered	VBN	6-04-006
fostering	VBG	1-01-001
Foster	**prop. noun**	**11-05-006**
Foster	NP	9-04-005
Foster	NP-TL	1-01-001
Foster's	NP$	1-01-001
fostering	**NN**	**1-01-001**
Fosterite	**JJ**	**1-01-001**
Fosterite	**prop. noun**	**1-01-001**
Fosterites	NPS	1-01-001
foul	**JJ**	**3-03-003**
foul	**verb**	**4-03-004**
foul	VB	1-01-001
fouled	VBD	2-02-002
fouling	VBG	1-01-001
foul-smelling	**JJ**	**2-02-002**
foulest	**JJT**	**1-01-001**
fouling	**NN**	**2-01-001**
foully	**RB**	**1-01-001**
found	**verb**	**34-10-024**
found	VB	1-01-001
founded	VBD	6-05-006
founded	VBN	14-07-014
founding	VBG	8-05-008
Founding	VBG-TL	5-01-002
foundation	**noun**	**65-08-031**
foundation	NN	19-07-016
Foundation	NN-TL	19-06-011
foundation's	NN$	1-01-001
Foundation's	NN$-TL	12-01-001
foundations	NNS	14-05-010
foundation-stone	**NN**	**1-01-001**
founder	**noun**	**16-08-014**
founder	NN	10-06-010
founders	NNS	2-02-002
Founders	NNS-TL	4-02-002
founder	**verb**	**1-01-001**
foundering	VBG	1-01-001
founder-conductor	**NN**	**1-01-001**
founder-originator	**NN**	**1-01-001**
founding	**NN**	**3-03-003**
foundling	**NN**	**1-01-001**
foundry	**noun**	**1-01-001**
foundry	NN	0-00-000
Foundry	NN-TL	1-01-001
fountain	**noun**	**22-08-010**
fountain	NN	12-07-009
Fountain	NN-TL	6-02-002
fountains	NNS	4-02-002
fountain-fall	**noun**	**1-01-001**

Word	Tag	Count
fountain-fall (cont.):		
fountain-falls	NNS	1-01-001
fountainhead	**noun**	**2-02-002**
fountainhead	NN	1-01-001
fountain-head	NN	1-01-001
four	**card. num.**	**360-15-215**
four	CD	347-15-211
four	CD-HL	4-03-004
Four	CD-TL	9-07-008
four	**noun**	**1-01-001**
fours	NNS	1-01-001
four-element	**JJ**	**2-01-001**
four-fold	**JJ**	**1-01-001**
four-hour	**JJ**	**3-03-003**
four-jet	**JJ**	**1-01-001**
four-lane	**JJ**	**2-02-002**
four-letter	**JJ**	**2-02-002**
four-o'clock	**NN**	**2-02-002**
four-sided	**JJ**	**1-01-001**
four-story	**JJ**	**1-01-001**
four-syllable	**JJ**	**1-01-001**
four-thirty	**CD**	**1-01-001**
four-wheel-drive	**NN**	**1-01-001**
four-wood	**NN**	**2-01-001**
four-year	**JJ**	**3-02-002**
foursome	**NN**	**1-01-001**
fourteen	**card. num.**	**31-11-027**
fourteen	CD	29-11-025
fourteen	CD-HL	1-01-001
Fourteen	CD-TL	1-01-001
fourteen-nation	**JJ**	**1-01-001**
fourteen-team	**JJ**	**1-01-001**
fourteen-year-old	**JJ**	**1-01-001**
fourteenth	**ord. num.**	**3-02-003**
fourteenth	OD	2-02-002
Fourteenth	OD-TL	1-01-001
fourth	**ord. num.**	**72-12-056**
fourth	OD	62-12-048
fourth	OD-HL	1-01-001
Fourth	OD-TL	9-04-008
fourth	**RB**	**2-01-002**
fourth-century	**NN**	**1-01-001**
fourth-class	**NN**	**1-01-001**
fourth-down	**NN**	**1-01-001**
fourth-flight	**NN**	**1-01-001**
fourth-hand	**RB**	**1-01-001**
Fourth-of-July	**NP**	**1-01-001**
fowl	**NN**	**1-01-001**
Fowler	**prop. noun**	**2-02-002**
Fowler	NP	1-01-001
Fowler	NP-TL	1-01-001
fox	**noun**	**11-06-008**
fox	NN	9-05-006
Fox	NN-TL	1-01-001
fox's	NN$	1-01-001
Fox	**NP**	**3-02-002**
fox-hound	**noun**	**1-01-001**
fox-hounds	NNS	1-01-001
fox-terrier	**NN**	**1-01-001**
foxhole	**noun**	**2-01-002**
foxholes	NNS	2-01-002
Foxx	**NP**	**1-01-001**
Foy	**NP**	**2-01-001**
foyer	**NN**	**3-03-003**
Fra	**NP**	**1-01-001**
fracas	**noun**	**1-01-001**
fracases	NNS	1-01-001
fraction	**noun**	**43-07-016**
fraction	NN	20-07-015
Fraction	NN-TL	3-01-001
fractions	NNS	20-02-005
fractional	**JJ**	**1-01-001**
fractionate	**verb**	**3-01-001**
fractionated	VBD	1-01-001
fractionated	VBN	2-01-001
fractionation	**NN**	**3-01-002**
fractious	**JJ**	**1-01-001**
fracture	**noun**	**2-02-002**
fracture	NN	1-01-001
fractures	NNS	1-01-001
fracture	**verb**	**2-02-002**
fractures	VBZ	1-01-001
fractured	VBN	1-01-001
fragile	**JJ**	**10-07-009**
fragment	**noun**	**16-05-011**
fragment	NN	6-04-006
fragments	NNS	10-04-007
fragment	**verb**	**4-03-003**
fragmented	VBN	3-03-003

Word	Tag	Count
fragment (cont.):		
fragmented	VBN-HL	1-01-001
fragmentarily	**RB**	**1-01-001**
fragmentary	**JJ**	**7-03-006**
fragmentation	**NN**	**5-04-005**
Fragonard	**NP**	**1-01-001**
fragrance	**noun**	**7-03-005**
fragrance	NN	6-03-004
fragrances	NNS	1-01-001
fragrant	**JJ**	**3-03-003**
frail	**JJ**	**8-06-007**
frailest	**JJT**	**1-01-001**
frambesia	**NN**	**1-01-001**
frame	**noun**	**96-12-041**
frame	NN	69-12-038
frame	NN-HL	1-01-001
frames	NNS	26-05-008
frame	**verb**	**23-12-020**
frame	VB	4-03-004
framed	VBD	2-02-002
framed	VBN	12-09-011
framing	VBG	5-05-005
framer	**NN**	**1-01-001**
framework	**NN**	**11-06-010**
framing	**NN**	**5-03-005**
Fran	**prop. noun**	**6-02-002**
Fran	NP	5-02-002
Fran's	NP$	1-01-001
franc	**noun**	**4-02-003**
franc	NN	1-01-001
francs	NNS	3-02-002
francaise	**foreign**	**3-01-002**
francaise	FW-JJ	0-00-000
Francaise	FW-JJ-TL	3-01-002
France	**prop. noun**	**81-12-042**
France	NP	72-12-038
France	NP-TL	3-03-003
France's	NP$	6-06-006
France-Germany	**prop. noun**	**1-01-001**
France-Germany	NP	0-00-000
France-Germany	NP-TL	1-01-001
Frances	**NP**	**2-02-002**
Francesca	**prop. noun**	**9-02-002**
Francesca	NP	8-02-002
Francesca's	NP$	1-01-001
Francesco	**prop. noun**	**2-02-002**
Francesco	NP	1-01-001
Francesco	NP-TL	1-01-001
franchise	**noun**	**6-05-005**
franchise	NN	5-04-004
franchises	NNS	1-01-001
Francie	**prop. noun**	**5-01-001**
Francie	NP	4-01-001
Francie's	NP$	1-01-001
Francis	**NP**	**21-07-018**
Franciscan	**JJ**	**1-01-001**
Franciscan	**prop. noun**	**2-02-002**
Franciscans	NPS	0-00-000
Franciscans	NPS-TL	2-02-002
Francisco	**prop. noun**	**44-11-024**
Francisco	NP	35-11-021
Francisco	NP-HL	1-01-001
Francisco	NP-TL	5-01-003
Francisco's	NP$	3-03-003
Franck	**NP**	**1-01-001**
Franco	**NP**	**2-01-002**
Franco-German	**JJ**	**1-01-001**
Franco-Irishman	**NP**	**1-01-001**
Francois	**NP**	**2-02-002**
Francoisette	**NP**	**1-01-001**
frangipani	**NN**	**1-01-001**
frank	**JJ**	**18-08-016**
frank	**noun**	**12-01-001**
frank	NN	4-01-001
franks	NNS	7-01-001
franks	NNS-HL	1-01-001
Frank	**prop. noun**	**46-10-038**
Frank	NP	45-10-037
Frank	NP-TL	1-01-001
franker	**JJR**	**1-01-001**
frankest	**JJT**	**1-01-001**
Frankford	**prop. noun**	**1-01-001**
Frankford	NP	0-00-000
Frankford	NP-TL	1-01-001
Frankfort	**NP**	**1-01-001**
Frankfurt	**prop. noun**	**7-01-001**
Frankfurt	NP	3-01-001
Frankfurt	NP-TL	4-01-001
frankfurter	**noun**	**16-01-001**

Word	Tag	Frequency
frankfurter (cont.):		
frankfurter	NN	8-01-001
frankfurter	NN-HL	1-01-001
frankfurters	NNS	5-01-001
frankfurters	NNS-HL	2-01-001
Frankfurter	**prop. noun**	**10-01-001**
Frankfurter	NP	8-01-001
Frankfurter's	NP$	2-01-001
Frankie	**NP**	**17-02-002**
Franklin	**prop. noun**	**31-07-019**
Franklin	NP	26-07-017
Franklin	NP-TL	4-01-003
Franklin's	NP$	1-01-001
frankly	**RB**	**13-07-013**
frankness	**NN**	**4-03-004**
franks-in-buns	**NNS**	**1-01-001**
Franny	**prop. noun**	**1-01-001**
Franny	NP	0-00-000
Franny	NP-HL	1-01-001
Frans	**NP**	**2-01-001**
frantic	**JJ**	**11-07-011**
frantically	**RB**	**8-05-007**
Franz	**NP**	**2-02-002**
fraternisation	**NN**	**1-01-001**
fraternity	**noun**	**7-05-006**
fraternity	NN	6-04-005
fraternities	NNS	1-01-001
fraternize	**verb**	**2-01-002**
fraternize	VB	1-01-001
fraternized	VBD	1-01-001
frau	**NN**	**1-01-001**
fraud	**noun**	**13-07-008**
fraud	NN	7-03-004
Fraud	NN-TL	1-01-001
frauds	NNS	4-04-004
Frauds	NNS-TL	1-01-001
Fraud	**prop. noun**	**2-01-001**
Fraud's	NP$	2-01-001
fray	**NN**	**1-01-001**
fray	**verb**	**3-03-003**
frayed	VBN	3-03-003
Frayne	**prop. noun**	**5-01-001**
Frayne	NP	3-01-001
Frayne's	NP$	2-01-001
frazzle	**verb**	**1-01-001**
frazzled	VBN	1-01-001
freak	**noun**	**6-03-005**
freak	NN	4-02-004
freaks	NNS	2-01-001
freakish	**JJ**	**1-01-001**
freckle	**noun**	**3-02-003**
freckles	NNS	3-02-003
freckle	**verb**	**1-01-001**
freckled	VBN	1-01-001
Fred	**prop. noun**	**29-04-010**
Fred	NP	27-04-010
Fred's	NP$	2-01-001
Freddie	**NP**	**2-02-002**
Freddy	**prop. noun**	**24-01-001**
Freddy	NP	20-01-001
Freddy's	NP$	4-01-001
Frederic	**NP**	**1-01-001**
Frederick	**NP**	**19-09-014**
Fredericksburg	**NP**	**1-01-001**
Frederik	**NP**	**1-01-001**
Fredrico	**NP**	**1-01-001**
Fredrik	**NP**	**1-01-001**
Fredrikshall	**NP**	**1-01-001**
free	**adjective**	**238-15-141**
free	JJ	223-15-137
Free	JJ-TL	14-05-009
Free	JJ-TL-HL	1-01-001
free	**RB**	**10-02-003**
free	**verb**	**28-11-025**
free	VB	11-06-011
frees	VBZ	2-02-002
freed	VBD	2-01-002
freed	VBN	10-07-010
freeing	VBG	3-02-003
free-blown	**JJ**	**1-01-001**
free-burning	**JJ**	**1-01-001**
free-buying	**JJ**	**1-01-001**
free-drink	**NN**	**1-01-001**
free-for-all	**JJ**	**1-01-001**
free-lance	**NN**	**2-01-002**
free-wheeling	**JJ**	**1-01-001**
free-will	**noun**	**1-01-001**
free-will	NN	0-00-000
Free-Will	NN-TL	1-01-001

Word	Tag	Frequency
free-world	**NN**	**1-01-001**
freebooter	**noun**	**1-01-001**
freebooters	NNS	1-01-001
freedman	**noun**	**3-02-002**
freedmen	NNS	3-02-002
freedom	**noun**	**133-12-074**
freedom	NN	122-12-070
Freedom	NN-TL	6-05-005
freedom's	NN$	2-01-002
freedoms	NNS	3-03-003
freedom-conscious	**JJ**	**1-01-001**
freedom-loving	**JJ**	**1-01-001**
freehand	**JJ**	**2-01-001**
freehand	**RB**	**1-01-001**
freeholder	**noun**	**5-04-004**
freeholder	NN	0-00-000
Freeholder	NN-TL	1-01-001
freeholders	NNS	3-02-002
free-holders	NNS	1-01-001
freely	**RB**	**22-10-020**
freeman	**NN**	**1-01-001**
Freeman	**prop. noun**	**11-05-007**
Freeman	NP	10-05-007
Freeman's	NP$	1-01-001
Freeport	**NP**	**1-01-001**
freer	**JJR**	**5-03-004**
freest	**JJT**	**2-02-002**
freethinker	**noun**	**1-01-001**
freethinkers	NNS	1-01-001
freeway	**noun**	**10-03-003**
freeway	NN	5-03-003
freeways	NNS	5-02-002
freewheeler	**noun**	**1-01-001**
freewheelers	NNS	1-01-001
freeze	**NN**	**1-01-001**
freeze	**verb**	**53-13-033**
freeze	VB	5-04-004
freezes	VBZ	1-01-001
froze	VBD	1-01-001
frozen	VBN	26-09-017
froze	VBN	4-01-001
frozen	VBN-HL	1-01-001
freezing	VBG	15-07-009
freeze-out	**NN**	**1-01-001**
freezer	**noun**	**2-02-002**
freezer	NN	1-01-001
freezers	NNS	1-01-001
Freida	**NP**	**1-01-001**
freight	**noun**	**30-08-013**
freight	NN	24-08-012
Freight	NN-TL	4-01-001
freight's	NN$	1-01-001
freights	NNS	1-01-001
freight-bum	**noun**	**1-01-001**
freight-bums	NNS	1-01-001
freight-car	**NN**	**1-01-001**
freight-jumper	**NN**	**1-01-001**
freighter	**noun**	**5-02-004**
freighter	NN	4-02-003
freighters	NNS	1-01-001
Freinkel	**NP**	**1-01-001**
Frelinghuysen	**prop. noun**	**5-01-001**
Frelinghuysen	NP	4-01-001
Frelinghuysen's	NP$	1-01-001
French	**adjective**	**108-12-058**
French	JJ	91-11-047
French	JJ-HL	1-01-001
French	JJ-TL	16-07-012
French	**prop. noun**	**32-08-026**
French	NP	14-06-011
French	NPS	18-06-015
French-born	**JJ**	**1-01-001**
French-Canadian	**JJ**	**2-01-002**
French-Canadian	**prop. noun**	**1-01-001**
French-Canadians	NPS	1-01-001
French-polished	**JJ**	**1-01-001**
Frenchman	**prop. noun**	**11-04-008**
Frenchman	NP	8-03-006
Frenchman's	NP$	1-01-001
Frenchmen	NPS	2-02-002
frenetic	**JJ**	**1-01-001**
frenzied	**JJ**	**1-01-001**
frenziedly	**RB**	**1-01-001**
frenzy	**NN**	**6-05-006**
frenzy-free	**JJ**	**1-01-001**
frequency	**noun**	**53-06-016**
frequency	NN	22-05-013
frequencies	NNS	31-06-007
frequency-independent	**JJ**	**1-01-001**

Word	Tag	Frequency
frequency-modulation	**NN**	**1-01-001**
frequent	**JJ**	**32-10-030**
frequent	**verb**	**3-03-003**
frequent	VB	2-02-002
frequented	VBD	1-01-001
frequently	**RB**	**91-13-066**
fresco	**noun**	**12-03-004**
fresco	NN	7-02-002
frescoes	NNS	3-02-002
frescos	NNS	2-01-001
fresco	**verb**	**1-01-001**
frescoed	VBN	1-01-001
frescoing	**NN**	**1-01-001**
fresh	**adjective**	**82-13-061**
fresh	JJ	79-13-060
Fresh	JJ-TL	3-01-001
fresh-ground	**JJ**	**1-01-001**
freshborn	**JJ**	**1-01-001**
freshen	**verb**	**1-01-001**
freshened	VBN	1-01-001
freshly	**RB**	**2-02-002**
freshly-ground	**adjective**	**1-01-001**
freshly-ground	JJ	0-00-000
freshly-ground	JJ-HL	1-01-001
freshman	**noun**	**11-05-008**
freshman	NN	8-05-007
freshmen	NNS	3-02-002
freshness	**NN**	**4-03-003**
Fresnel	**NP**	**3-01-001**
Fresno	**NP**	**1-01-001**
fret	**verb**	**4-04-004**
fret	VB	1-01-001
fretted	VBD	1-01-001
fretting	VBG	2-02-002
Freud	**prop. noun**	**11-03-010**
Freud	NP	9-03-009
Freud's	NP$	2-02-002
Freudian	**JJ**	**3-03-003**
Freya	**NP**	**3-01-001**
friable	**JJ**	**2-01-001**
friar	**noun**	**2-02-002**
friar	NN	0-00-000
Friar	NN-TL	1-01-001
friars	NNS	0-00-000
Friars	NNS-TL	1-01-001
Frick	**prop. noun**	**3-02-003**
Frick	NP	2-01-002
Frick	NP-TL	1-01-001
friction	**noun**	**18-05-011**
friction	NN	16-05-010
friction	NN-HL	1-01-001
frictions	NNS	1-01-001
friction-free	**JJ**	**1-01-001**
frictional	**JJ**	**2-01-001**
Friday	**adv. noun**	**64-10-034**
Friday	NR	55-08-030
Friday	NR-TL	4-04-004
Fridays	NRS	3-02-002
Friday's	NR$	2-01-002
Friday	**NP**	**1-01-001**
Friedenwald	**NP**	**2-01-001**
Friedman	**NP**	**1-01-001**
Friedrich	**NP**	**1-01-001**
friend	**noun**	**294-15-150**
friend	NN	126-14-081
Friend	NN	2-01-001
Friend	NN-TL	2-02-002
friend's	NN$	2-02-002
friends	NNS	146-15-091
friends	NNS-NC	3-01-001
Friends	NNS-TL	12-06-009
friends'	NNS$	0-00-000
Friends'	NNS$-TL	1-01-001
friend	**verb**	**1-01-001**
friend	VB	0-00-000
ffreind	VB	1-01-001
Friend	**NP**	**3-01-001**
friendlier	**comp. adj.**	**2-01-002**
friendlier	JJR	1-01-001
friendlier	JJR-NC	1-01-001
friendlily	**RB**	**1-01-001**
friendliness	**NN**	**4-03-004**
friendly	**adjective**	**61-14-044**
friendly	JJ	59-14-043
friendly	JJ-NC	2-01-001
friendship	**noun**	**31-09-024**
friendship	NN	26-08-020
friendship	NN-NC	1-01-001
friendships	NNS	4-03-004

Word	Tag	Frequency
frieze	**noun**	**16-04-006**
frieze	NN	13-02-004
friezes	NNS	3-03-003
fright	**NN**	**2-02-002**
frighten	**verb**	**51-12-041**
frighten	VB	11-04-005
frightened	VBD	2-02-002
frightened	VBN	24-08-022
frightening	VBG	14-09-014
frighteningly	**RB**	**1-01-001**
frightful	**JJ**	**6-04-006**
frightfully	**RB**	**1-01-001**
frigid	**JJ**	**5-04-005**
frill	**noun**	**3-03-003**
frills	NNS	3-03-003
frilly	**JJ**	**1-01-001**
fringe	**NN**	**16-06-009**
fringe	**verb**	**5-04-004**
fringed	VBN	5-04-004
fringed-wrapped	**JJ**	**1-01-001**
Frisco	**NP**	**3-02-002**
frise	**FW-NN**	**1-01-001**
Frist	**FW-NN**	**1-01-001**
Frito	**NP**	**2-01-001**
fritter	**noun**	**1-01-001**
fritters	NNS	1-01-001
Fritz	**NP**	**2-02-002**
Fritzie	**prop. noun**	**7-01-001**
Fritzie	NP	6-01-001
Fritzie's	NP$	1-01-001
frivolity	**NN**	**2-02-002**
frivolous	**adjective**	**6-02-004**
frivolous	JJ	5-02-004
frivolous	JJ-NC	1-01-001
frizzle	**verb**	**2-02-002**
frizzled	VBN	1-01-001
frizzling	VBG	1-01-001
frock	**NN**	**2-02-002**
frog	**noun**	**2-01-002**
frog	NN	1-01-001
frogs	NNS	1-01-001
frog-eating	**JJ**	**1-01-001**
frog-haiku	**NN**	**1-01-001**
frog-march	**verb**	**1-01-001**
frog-marched	VBN	1-01-001
Frohock	**NP**	**1-01-001**
Froissart	**NP**	**1-01-001**
frolic	**noun**	**3-03-003**
frolic	NN	2-02-002
frolics	NNS	1-01-001
frolic	**verb**	**2-02-002**
frolicking	VBG	2-02-002
from	**prep.**	**4371-15-500**
from	IN	4343-15-500
From	IN	2-02-002
from	IN-HL	20-07-016
From	IN-TL	5-03-005
from	IN-TL	1-01-001
Fromm	**prop. noun**	**30-02-002**
Fromm	NP	15-02-002
Fromm's	NP$	15-01-001
Frondel	**NP**	**1-01-001**
front	**JJ**	**77-14-042**
front	**noun**	**153-13-098**
front	NN	143-13-093
Front	NN-TL	3-03-003
fronts	NNS	7-04-005
front	**verb**	**4-04-004**
fronted	VBD	1-01-001
fronting	VBG	3-03-003
front-back	**JJ**	**1-01-001**
front-line	**NN**	**2-02-002**
front-page	**NN**	**2-02-002**
frontage	**NN**	**7-01-001**
frontal	**JJ**	**3-02-003**
frontier	**noun**	**35-09-026**
frontier	NN	25-08-017
Frontier	NN-TL	5-02-005
frontiers	NNS	5-04-005
frontiersman	**noun**	**2-02-002**
frontiersmen	NNS	2-02-002
frost	**noun**	**4-03-004**
frost	NN	3-03-003
Frost	NN-TL	1-01-001
frost	**verb**	**1-01-001**
frosted	VBD	1-01-001
Frost	**prop. noun**	**5-03-004**
Frost	NP	3-02-002
Frost's	NP$	1-01-001

Word	Tag	Frequency
Frost (cont.):		
Frosts	NPS	1-01-001
frost-bitten	**JJ**	**2-02-002**
frostbite	**NN**	**3-03-003**
frosting	**NN**	**1-01-001**
frosty	**JJ**	**1-01-001**
froth	**NN**	**1-01-001**
froth	**verb**	**2-02-002**
frothing	VBG	2-02-002
frothier	**JJR**	**1-01-001**
Frothingham	**NP**	**2-01-001**
frothy	**JJ**	**2-02-002**
frown	**verb**	**22-08-019**
frown	VB	1-01-001
frowns	VBZ	1-01-001
frowned	VBD	7-03-007
frowned	VBN	1-01-001
frowning	VBG	12-05-010
frowningly	**RB**	**1-01-001**
frowzy	**JJ**	**1-01-001**
frugality	**NN**	**2-02-002**
frugally	**QL**	**1-01-001**
fruit	**noun**	**49-11-027**
fruit	NN	33-10-020
Fruit	NN-TL	2-02-002
fruits	NNS	14-05-010
fruitful	**JJ**	**7-05-007**
fruitfully	**RB**	**1-01-001**
fruitfulness	**NN**	**1-01-001**
fruition	**NN**	**2-02-002**
fruitless	**JJ**	**5-02-005**
fruitlessly	**RB**	**1-01-001**
frustrate	**verb**	**15-06-014**
frustrate	VB	4-03-003
frustrated	VBD	1-01-001
frustrated	VBN	9-04-009
frustrating	VBG	1-01-001
frustrating	**JJ**	**2-02-002**
frustration	**noun**	**15-07-013**
frustration	NN	10-05-009
frustration	NN-HL	1-01-001
frustrations	NNS	4-03-004
fry	**verb**	**8-04-006**
fry	VB	2-02-002
fried	VBN	6-04-005
Fuchs	**NP**	**4-02-002**
fuchsia	**NN**	**1-01-001**
fuck	**noun**	**1-01-001**
fucks	NNS	1-01-001
fuck	**verb**	**10-01-001**
fuck	VB	4-01-001
fucking	VBG	0-00-000
fucken	VBG	6-01-001
Fudo	**prop. noun**	**9-01-001**
Fudo	NP	7-01-001
Fudo's	NP$	2-01-001
Fudomae	**NP**	**3-01-001**
fuel	**NN**	**17-06-011**
fuel	**verb**	**2-01-002**
fuels	VBZ	1-01-001
fueled	VBD	1-01-001
fueloil	**noun**	**3-01-001**
fueloil	NN	2-01-001
Fueloil	NN-TL	1-01-001
fugal	**adjective**	**1-01-001**
fugal	JJ	0-00-000
fugual	JJ	1-01-001
fugitive	**JJ**	**1-01-001**
fugitive	**noun**	**3-03-003**
fugitive	NN	2-02-002
fugitives	NNS	1-01-001
Fuhrer	**NP**	**1-01-001**
Fuhrmann	**prop. noun**	**3-01-001**
Fuhrmann	NP	0-00-000
Fuhrmann	NP-TL	1-01-001
Fuhrmann's	NP$	1-01-001
Furhmann's	NP$	1-01-001
Fuji	**NP**	**1-01-001**
Fujimoto	**NP**	**2-01-001**
Fulbright	**NP**	**2-02-002**
fulfill	**verb**	**25-09-024**
fulfill	VB	9-04-008
fulfills	VBZ	2-02-002
fulfilled	VBD	3-03-003
fulfilled	VBN	8-03-008
fulfilling	VBG	3-03-003
fulfillment	**NN**	**12-05-009**
Fulke	**NP**	**3-01-001**
full	**adjective**	**221-15-164**
full (cont.):		
full	JJ	219-15-163
Full	JJ-TL	2-01-001
full	**NN**	**1-01-001**
full	**QL**	**3-02-003**
full	**RB**	**5-04-005**
full-banded	**JJ**	**1-01-001**
full-blown	**JJ**	**1-01-001**
full-bodied	**JJ**	**1-01-001**
full-clad	**JJ**	**1-01-001**
full-dress	**NN**	**1-01-001**
full-fledged	**JJ**	**2-02-002**
full-grown	**JJ**	**2-02-002**
full-of-the-moon	**NN**	**1-01-001**
full-scale	**JJ**	**2-02-002**
full-sister	**noun**	**1-01-001**
full-sisters	NNS	1-01-001
full-sized	**JJ**	**1-01-001**
full-time	**JJ**	**23-09-014**
full-time	**RB**	**1-01-001**
full-year	**JJ**	**1-01-001**
fullback	**NN**	**2-01-001**
fullbacking	**NN**	**1-01-001**
fuller	**JJR**	**5-04-005**
Fuller	**NP**	**3-01-001**
fullest	**JJT**	**5-04-005**
fullness	**NN**	**4-04-004**
fully	**QL**	**14-07-014**
fully	**adverb**	**66-12-058**
fully	RB	65-12-058
fully	RB-HL	1-01-001
fulminate	**verb**	**2-02-002**
fulminate	VB	1-01-001
fulminating	VBG	1-01-001
Fulton	**prop. noun**	**17-03-003**
Fulton	NP	7-03-003
Fulton	NP-TL	10-01-001
fumble	**NN**	**1-01-001**
fumble	**verb**	**9-06-009**
fumbled	VBD	5-03-005
fumbling	VBG	4-04-004
fume	**noun**	**5-05-005**
fumes	NNS	5-05-005
fume	**verb**	**2-02-002**
fumed	VBD	1-01-001
fuming	VBG	1-01-001
fumed-oak	**NN**	**2-02-002**
Fumio	**prop. noun**	**1-01-001**
Fumio's	NP$	1-01-001
fun	**noun**	**44-12-031**
fun	NN	43-12-030
Fun	NN-TL	1-01-001
fun-filled	**JJ**	**1-01-001**
fun-loving	**JJ**	**2-02-002**
Funari	**NP**	**1-01-001**
function	**noun**	**151-11-065**
function	NN	107-10-049
functions	NNS	41-09-021
functions	NNS-HL	1-01-001
Functions	NNS-TL	2-02-002
function	**verb**	**18-09-015**
function	VB	6-04-006
functions	VBZ	4-03-003
functioned	VBD	2-02-002
functioned	VBN	1-01-001
functioning	VBG	5-05-005
functional	**JJ**	**23-06-015**
functional	**NN**	**1-01-001**
functionalism	**NN**	**2-02-002**
functionally	**RB**	**4-03-004**
functionary	**NN**	**2-02-002**
functioning	**NN**	**7-02-005**
fund	**noun**	**160-11-066**
fund	NN	41-08-025
fund	NN-HL	1-01-001
Fund	NN-TL	20-06-011
fund's	NN$	3-01-002
funds	NNS	91-07-045
funds	NNS-HL	4-03-004
fund	**verb**	**1-01-001**
funding	VBG	1-01-001
fund-raiser	**noun**	**2-01-001**
fund-raiser	NN	1-01-001
fund-raisers	NNS	1-01-001
fund-raising	**NN**	**5-03-004**
fundamental	**adjective**	**50-09-038**
fundamental	JJ	49-09-037
Fundamental	JJ-TL	1-01-001
fundamental	**noun**	**5-05-005**

Word	Tag	Frequency
fundamental (cont.):		
fundamentals	NNS	5-05-005
fundamentalism	**NN**	**1-01-001**
fundamentalist	**JJ**	**2-02-002**
fundamentalist	**NN**	**2-01-002**
fundamentally	**QL**	**1-01-001**
fundamentally	**RB**	**8-05-008**
funeral	**JJ**	**3-02-002**
funeral	**noun**	**31-12-022**
funeral	NN	26-12-020
funeral	NN-HL	1-01-001
Funeral	NN-TL	3-02-003
funerals	NNS	1-01-001
funeral-accessory	**noun**	**1-01-001**
funeral-accessories	NNS	1-01-001
fungal	**JJ**	**1-01-001**
fungicide	**noun**	**1-01-001**
fungicides	NNS	1-01-001
fungus	**NN**	**2-02-002**
Funk	**prop. noun**	**4-02-002**
Funk	NP	3-02-002
Funk	NP-TL	1-01-001
funnel	**noun**	**2-01-002**
funnel	NN	1-01-001
funnels	NNS	1-01-001
funnel	**verb**	**1-01-001**
funneled	VBD	1-01-001
funnier	**JJR**	**1-01-001**
funniest	**JJT**	**2-02-002**
funny	**adjective**	**40-08-024**
funny	JJ	39-08-024
funny	JJ-NC	1-01-001
funny	**RB**	**1-01-001**
Funston	**NP**	**2-01-001**
fur	**noun**	**17-04-009**
fur	NN	11-04-007
Fur	NN-TL	1-01-001
furs	NNS	5-02-003
fur-piece	**NN**	**1-01-001**
furbish	**verb**	**1-01-001**
furbishing	VBG	1-01-001
furious	**adjective**	**8-04-006**
furious	JJ	5-04-005
Furious	JJ-TL	3-01-001
furiouser	**JJR**	**2-01-001**
furiously	**RB**	**12-06-010**
furl	**verb**	**1-01-001**
furled	VBD	1-01-001
furlong	**noun**	**1-01-001**
furlongs	NNS	1-01-001
furlough	**NN**	**2-02-002**
furlough	**verb**	**1-01-001**
furloughed	VBN	1-01-001
furnace	**noun**	**14-03-007**
furnace	NN	11-03-005
furnace's	NN$	1-01-001
furnaces	NNS	1-01-001
Furnaces	NNS-TL	1-01-001
furnish	**verb**	**58-10-040**
furnish	VB	29-08-021
furnishes	VBZ	5-03-004
furnished	VBD	4-03-003
furnished	VBN	19-08-016
furnishing	VBG	1-01-001
furnishing	**noun**	**12-07-009**
furnishing	NN	3-03-003
furnishings	NNS	9-06-008
furniture	**noun**	**39-10-022**
furniture	NN	38-10-022
Furniture	NN-TL	1-01-001
furor	**NN**	**3-02-002**
furrow	**noun**	**6-02-002**
furrow	NN	5-01-001
furrows	NNS	1-01-001
furrow	**verb**	**2-02-002**
furrowed	VBD	1-01-001
furrowed	VBN	1-01-001
further	**AP**	**32-06-021**
further	**JJR**	**74-12-060**
further	**RBR**	**104-14-084**
further	**verb**	**13-07-010**
further	VB	8-06-006
furthered	VBD	2-01-002
furthered	VBN	1-01-001
furthering	VBG	2-01-002
furthermore	**adverb**	**40-12-035**
furthermore	RB	39-12-035
futhermore	RB	1-01-001
furtive	**JJ**	**1-01-001**
furtively	**RB**	**1-01-001**
fury	**noun**	**19-07-012**
fury	NN	14-06-011
Fury	NN-TL	5-01-001
Fury	**prop. noun**	**1-01-001**
Furies	NPS	1-01-001
fuse	**noun**	**6-04-005**
fuse	NN	3-03-003
fuses	NNS	3-02-002
fuse	**verb**	**6-04-006**
fuse	VB	2-01-002
fused	VBD	2-02-002
fused	VBN	1-01-001
fusing	VBG	1-01-001
fuselage	**NN**	**1-01-001**
fusiform	**JJ**	**1-01-001**
fusillade	**noun**	**1-01-001**
fusillades	NNS	1-01-001
fusion	**NN**	**13-06-007**
fuss	**NN**	**2-02-002**
fuss	**verb**	**4-03-003**
fuss	VB	2-01-001
fussing	VBG	2-02-002
fussily	**RB**	**1-01-001**
fussy	**JJ**	**3-03-003**
fusty	**JJ**	**1-01-001**
futile	**JJ**	**6-05-005**
futility	**NN**	**7-05-007**
Futotsu	**NP**	**1-01-001**
future	**adjective**	**119-15-082**
future	JJ	109-14-078
future	JJ-HL	4-03-004
Future	JJ-TL	6-03-003
future	**noun**	**108-14-076**
future	NN	106-14-074
Future	NN-TL	2-02-002
future-day	**JJ**	**1-01-001**
future-time	**JJ**	**1-01-001**
fuzz	**NN**	**3-02-003**
fuzzed	**JJ**	**1-01-001**
fuzzy	**JJ**	**7-06-007**
fy	**noun**	**1-01-001**
fy	NN	0-00-000
fy	NN-NC	1-01-001
Fyodor	**NP**	**1-01-001**

G

Word	Tag	Frequency
G	**prop. noun**	**10-02-006**
G	NP	7-02-003
G	NP-HL	3-02-003
G.	**NP**	**42-08-031**
G.B.S.	**NP**	**1-01-001**
G.O.P.	**NP**	**1-01-001**
Gaafer	**NP**	**1-01-001**
gab	**NN**	**1-01-001**
gabardine	**NN**	**1-01-001**
gabble	**NN**	**1-01-001**
gabble	**verb**	**1-01-001**
gabbling	VBG	1-01-001
gable	**noun**	**5-03-004**
gable (cont.):		
gable	NN	2-02-002
gables	NNS	0-00-000
Gables	NNS-TL	3-02-002
Gabler	**NP**	**1-01-001**
Gables	**NPS**	**1-01-001**
Gabriel	**prop. noun**	**17-02-004**
Gabriel	NP	12-02-003
Gabriel's	NP$	5-02-003
Gabrielle	**prop. noun**	**3-03-003**
Gabrielle	NP	2-02-002
Gabrielle	NP-TL	1-01-001
gadfly	**NN**	**3-03-003**

gadget	**noun**	**11-04-006**
gadget	NN	4-03-003
gadgets	NNS	7-03-005
gadgetry	**NN**	**1-01-001**
Gaetan	**NP**	**1-01-001**
gag	**noun**	**6-03-003**
gag	NN	4-03-003
gags	NNS	2-01-001
gag	**verb**	**2-02-002**
gagged	VBD	1-01-001
gagging	VBG	1-01-001
Gagarin	**NP**	**2-02-002**
gaggle	**NN**	**1-01-001**
gagline	**NN**	**1-01-001**
gagwriter	**noun**	**1-01-001**
gagwriters	NNS	1-01-001
gai	**FW-JJ**	**1-01-001**
gaiety	**noun**	**13-07-009**
gaiety	NN	8-05-006
gayety	NN	1-01-001
gaieties	NNS	0-00-000
Gaieties	NNS-TL	4-02-002
gaily	**RB**	**5-05-005**
gain	**noun**	**69-09-025**
gain	NN	48-09-018
gain	NN-HL	3-01-001
gains	NNS	15-06-011
gains	NNS-HL	3-03-003
gain	**verb**	**77-12-064**
gain	VB	23-08-021
gains	VBZ	1-01-001
gained	VBD	18-09-016
gained	VBN	21-09-019
gaining	VBG	14-08-014
gainer	**noun**	**2-02-002**
gainer	NN	1-01-001
gainers	NNS	1-01-001
Gaines	**prop. noun**	**3-02-002**
Gaines	NP	2-02-002
Gaines'	NP$	1-01-001
Gainesville	**NP**	**1-01-001**
gainful	**JJ**	**1-01-001**
gaining	**NN**	**1-01-001**
gait	**NN**	**8-03-004**
gaited	**JJ**	**1-01-001**
gaiter	**noun**	**1-01-001**
gaiters	NNS	1-01-001
Gaither	**prop. noun**	**1-01-001**
Gaither	NP	0-00-000
Gaither	NP-TL	1-01-001
gal	**noun**	**7-05-006**
gal	NN	3-03-003
Gal	NN-TL	2-01-001
gals	NNS	2-02-002
gala	**adjective**	**4-03-004**
gala	JJ	3-03-003
Gala	JJ-TL	1-01-001
gala	**NN**	**3-01-002**
galactic	**JJ**	**1-01-001**
Galahad	**NP**	**1-01-001**
Galantuomo	**foreign**	**1-01-001**
Galantuomo	FW-NN	0-00-000
Galantuomo	FW-NN-TL	1-01-001
Galapagos	**NP**	**1-01-001**
Galata	**prop. noun**	**1-01-001**
Galata	NP	0-00-000
Galata	NP-TL	1-01-001
Galatian	**prop. noun**	**2-01-001**
Galatians	NPS	0-00-000
Galatians	NPS-TL	2-01-001
galaxy	**noun**	**10-04-004**
galaxy	NN	2-02-002
Galaxy	NN-TL	1-01-001
galaxies	NNS	7-01-001
gale	**NN**	**2-02-002**
Galen	**NP**	**1-01-001**
Galena	**NP**	**2-02-002**
Galilee	**NP**	**2-01-001**
Galina	**NP**	**1-01-001**
Galindez	**NP**	**1-01-001**
gall	**noun**	**8-02-002**
gall	NN	7-01-001
galls	NNS	1-01-001
gall	**verb**	**1-01-001**
galled	VBN	1-01-001
gallant	**JJ**	**5-05-005**
gallant	**noun**	**1-01-001**
gallants	NNS	1-01-001
gallantry	**NN**	**3-02-003**
gallbladder	**NN**	**1-01-001**
gallery	**noun**	**35-09-015**
gallery	NN	18-06-009
Gallery	NN-TL	13-06-007
gallery's	NN$	0-00-000
Gallery's	NN$-TL	3-01-001
galleries	NNS	1-01-001
Gallet	**NP**	**1-01-001**
galley	**noun**	**8-04-005**
galley	NN	4-03-003
galleys	NNS	4-02-002
Galli	**NP**	**3-01-001**
galling	**JJ**	**1-01-001**
gallium	**NN**	**6-01-001**
gallivant	**verb**	**1-01-001**
gallivanting	VBG	0-00-000
gallivantin'	VBG	1-01-001
gallon	**noun**	**11-05-006**
gallon	NN	5-02-003
gallons	NNS	6-04-004
Gallon	**NP**	**2-01-001**
gallonage	**NN**	**1-01-001**
gallop	**NN**	**3-02-003**
gallop	**verb**	**3-02-002**
gallop	VB	1-01-001
galloped	VBN	1-01-001
galloping	VBG	1-01-001
gallows	**NN**	**2-02-002**
gallstone	**noun**	**2-02-002**
gallstone	NN	1-01-001
gallstones	NNS	1-01-001
Gallup	**NP**	**1-01-001**
gallus-snapping	**JJ**	**1-01-001**
Galophone	**NP**	**2-01-001**
Galt	**prop. noun**	**2-02-002**
Galt	NP	0-00-000
Galt	NP-TL	2-02-002
Galtier	**prop. noun**	**2-01-001**
Galtier	NP	1-01-001
Galtier's	NP$	1-01-001
galvanic	**JJ**	**2-02-002**
galvanism	**NN**	**1-01-001**
galvanize	**verb**	**3-03-003**
galvanizing	VBG	3-03-003
Galveston	**NP**	**3-02-003**
Galway	**prop. noun**	**2-02-002**
Galway	NP	1-01-001
Galway	NP-TL	1-01-001
gambit	**noun**	**3-03-003**
gambit	NN	2-02-002
gambits	NNS	1-01-001
gamble	**noun**	**3-02-002**
gamble	NN	2-01-001
gambles	NNS	1-01-001
gamble	**verb**	**17-08-014**
gamble	VB	1-01-001
gambling	VBG	16-08-013
gambler	**noun**	**5-03-003**
gamblers	NNS	5-03-003
gambler-politician	**NN**	**1-01-001**
gambling	**NN**	**1-01-001**
game	**noun**	**180-13-065**
game	NN	121-12-050
Game	NN-TL	1-01-001
game's	NN$	4-01-002
games	NNS	52-12-026
Games	NNS-TL	2-01-002
game	**verb**	**2-02-002**
game	VB	1-01-001
gaming	VBG	1-01-001
game-management	**NN**	**1-01-001**
gamebird	**NN**	**1-01-001**
Gamecock	**NP**	**1-01-001**
gaming-card	**NN**	**2-01-001**
gamma	**noun**	**5-02-002**
gamma	NN	4-01-001
Gamma	NN-TL	1-01-001
gamut	**NN**	**4-03-004**
Ganado	**NP**	**1-01-001**
Gander	**NP**	**1-01-001**
Ganessa	**NP**	**1-01-001**
gang	**noun**	**27-08-013**
gang	NN	20-06-011
gang's	NN$	1-01-001
gangs	NNS	6-04-004
gang	**VB**	**2-02-002**
Ganges	**NP**	**2-02-002**
gangland	**NN**	**1-01-001**
gangling	**JJ**	**1-01-001**

Word	Tag	Frequency
gangplank	**NN**	**1-01-001**
gangster	**noun**	**6-05-006**
gangster	NN	2-02-002
gangsters	NNS	4-03-004
gangway	**NN**	**1-01-001**
Gannett	**prop. noun**	**4-01-001**
Gannett	NP	3-01-001
Gannett's	NP$	1-01-001
Gannon	**prop. noun**	**5-01-001**
Gannon	NP	4-01-001
Gannon's	NP$	1-01-001
Gansevoort	**NP**	**6-01-001**
gantlet	**NN**	**2-01-001**
Gantry	**prop. noun**	**5-01-001**
Gantry	NP	0-00-000
Gantry	NP-TL	5-01-001
gap	**noun**	**19-08-016**
gap	NN	11-06-011
Gap	NN-TL	6-03-003
gaps	NNS	2-02-002
gape	**verb**	**5-04-004**
gaped	VBD	3-02-002
gaping	VBG	2-02-002
gapt	**NN**	**7-01-001**
Gar-Dene	**prop. noun**	**2-01-001**
Gar-Dene	NPS	1-01-001
Gar-Dene	NPS-NC	1-01-001
garage	**noun**	**25-07-012**
garage	NN	19-06-010
garage	NN-NC	1-01-001
garages	NNS	5-03-003
garage	**verb**	**2-01-002**
garage	VB	1-01-001
garaged	VBN	1-01-001
garb	**NN**	**3-03-003**
garb	**verb**	**1-01-001**
garbed	VBN	1-01-001
garbage	**NN**	**7-06-006**
garble	**verb**	**1-01-001**
garbled	VBN	1-01-001
Garcia	**NP**	**3-03-003**
garde	**FW-NN**	**1-01-001**
garden	**noun**	**91-13-047**
garden	NN	46-11-028
Garden	NN-TL	13-05-009
gardens	NNS	19-07-015
Gardens	NNS-TL	13-06-007
garden	**verb**	**3-02-002**
garden	VB	1-01-001
gardened	VBD	1-01-001
gardening	VBG	1-01-001
gardener	**noun**	**5-04-004**
gardener	NN	4-03-003
gardeners	NNS	1-01-001
gardenia	**noun**	**2-02-002**
gardenia	NN	1-01-001
gardenias	NNS	1-01-001
gardening	**noun**	**2-02-002**
gardening	NN	1-01-001
Gardening	NN-TL	1-01-001
Gardner	**prop. noun**	**8-03-004**
Gardner	NP	4-03-003
Gardner's	NP$	4-01-001
gargantuan	**JJ**	**1-01-001**
Gargery	**prop. noun**	**3-01-001**
Gargery	NP	2-01-001
Gargery's	NP$	1-01-001
gargle	**noun**	**2-01-001**
gargle	NN	1-01-001
Gargle	NN-TL	1-01-001
Garibaldi	**prop. noun**	**21-01-002**
Garibaldi	NP	12-01-002
Garibaldi	NP-TL	1-01-001
Garibaldi's	NP$	8-01-002
Garine	**NP**	**1-01-001**
garish	**JJ**	**1-01-001**
garishness	**NN**	**1-01-001**
garland	**NN**	**1-01-001**
garland	**verb**	**1-01-001**
garlanded	VBD	1-01-001
Garland	**NP**	**8-03-004**
garlic	**NN**	**4-03-004**
garment	**noun**	**12-05-007**
garment	NN	6-03-004
garments	NNS	5-03-004
garments	NNS-HL	1-01-001
garner	**VB**	**1-01-001**
garnet	**NN**	**1-01-001**
Garnett	**NP**	**1-01-001**

Word	Tag	Frequency
Garrard	**prop. noun**	**1-01-001**
Garrard's	NP$	1-01-001
Garrett	**NP**	**1-01-001**
Garrick	**prop. noun**	**2-02-002**
Garrick	NP	0-00-000
Garrick	NP-TL	2-02-002
garrison	**NN**	**2-01-002**
garrison	**verb**	**1-01-001**
garrisoned	VBN	1-01-001
Garrison	**NP**	**3-01-002**
Garrisonian	**NP**	**1-01-001**
garrulous	**JJ**	**1-01-001**
Garry	**prop. noun**	**12-03-003**
Garry	NP	5-02-002
Garry	NP-TL	7-01-001
Garryowen	**prop. noun**	**14-01-001**
Garryowen	NP	12-01-001
Garryowen	NP-NC	1-01-001
Garryowen	NP-TL	1-01-001
Garson	**NP**	**9-01-002**
Garstung	**NP**	**1-01-001**
garter	**NN**	**2-01-001**
Garth	**prop. noun**	**19-02-002**
Garth	NP	13-02-002
Garth	NP-TL	1-01-001
Garth's	NP$	4-01-001
Garth's	NP$-TL	1-01-001
Garvier	**NP**	**2-01-001**
Gary	**NP**	**5-02-004**
Garza	**NP**	**1-01-001**
gas	**noun**	**107-13-042**
gas	NN	96-11-036
gasse	NN	0-00-000
Gasse	NN-TL	1-01-001
gas	NN-HL	1-01-001
Gas	NN-TL	2-02-002
gases	NNS	7-05-007
gas	**verb**	**4-04-004**
gas	VB	1-01-001
gassed	VBN	2-02-002
gassing	VBG	1-01-001
gas-fired	**JJ**	**1-01-001**
gas-glass	**NN**	**1-01-001**
Gascony	**NP**	**3-01-001**
gaseous	**JJ**	**2-01-002**
gash	**noun**	**3-02-003**
gash	NN	1-01-001
gashes	NNS	2-02-002
gasket	**noun**	**6-01-002**
gasket	NN	4-01-001
gasket's	NN$	1-01-001
gaskets	NNS	1-01-001
gaslight	**noun**	**1-01-001**
gaslights	NNS	1-01-001
gasoline	**NN**	**12-05-009**
gasp	**noun**	**7-05-007**
gasp	NN	2-02-002
gasps	NNS	5-03-005
gasp	**verb**	**11-06-010**
gasp	VB	1-01-001
gasped	VBD	5-04-005
gasping	VBG	5-04-005
Gaspard	**NP**	**1-01-001**
Gaspee	**prop. noun**	**1-01-001**
Gaspee	NP	0-00-000
Gaspee	NP-TL	1-01-001
gaspingly	**RB**	**1-01-001**
gasser	**NN**	**1-01-001**
Gasset	**NP**	**1-01-001**
gassing	**noun**	**1-01-001**
gassings	NNS	1-01-001
gassy	**JJ**	**1-01-001**
Gaston	**NP**	**2-02-002**
gastrocnemius	**NN**	**4-01-001**
gastrointestinal	**JJ**	**2-02-002**
gastronome	**noun**	**1-01-001**
gastronomes	NNS	1-01-001
gastronomy	**NN**	**1-01-001**
gate	**noun**	**50-10-029**
gate	NN	33-08-018
Gate	NN-TL	4-03-004
gates	NNS	13-07-010
gate-post	**NN**	**1-01-001**
Gates	**NP**	**2-01-001**
gateway	**noun**	**4-04-004**
gateway	NN	2-02-002
Gateway	NN-TL	1-01-001
gateways	NNS	1-01-001
gather	**verb**	**66-14-059**

gather (cont.):		
gather	VB	19-12-019
gather	VB-HL	1-01-001
gathers	VBZ	1-01-001
gathered	VBD	22-10-020
gathered	VBN	10-07-010
gathering	VBG	13-09-013
gathering	**noun**	**22-11-020**
gathering	NN	15-10-014
gatherings	NNS	7-05-007
gathering-in	**NN**	**1-01-001**
Gatlinburg	**NP**	**2-01-001**
Gator	**NP**	**2-01-001**
Gatsby	**prop. noun**	**1-01-001**
Gatsby	NP	0-00-000
Gatsby	NP-TL	1-01-001
gauche	**JJ**	**1-01-001**
gaucherie	**noun**	**2-02-002**
gaucherie	NN	1-01-001
gaucheries	NNS	1-01-001
gaudy	**JJ**	**7-05-007**
Gauer	**NP**	**2-01-001**
gauge	**noun**	**18-07-011**
gauge	NN	10-06-007
gage	NN	4-03-004
gauge	NN-HL	2-01-001
gauges	NNS	0-00-000
gages	NNS	2-02-002
gauge	**verb**	**3-03-003**
gauged	VBD	1-01-001
gauged	VBN	1-01-001
gauging	VBG	0-00-000
gaging	VBG	1-01-001
Gauguin	**NP**	**1-01-001**
Gaul	**NP**	**1-01-001**
Gauleiter	**foreign**	**1-01-001**
Gauleiter	FW-NN	0-00-000
Gauleiter	FW-NN-TL	1-01-001
Gaulle	**NP**	**4-02-002**
gaunt	**JJ**	**6-04-005**
gauntlet	**NN**	**2-02-002**
Gauntley	**NP**	**1-01-001**
gauss	**NN**	**2-01-001**
Gaussian	**JJ**	**2-01-002**
Gautier	**NP**	**1-01-001**
gauze	**NN**	**1-01-001**
Gaveston	**NP**	**1-01-001**
Gavin	**prop. noun**	**25-03-003**
Gavin	NP	15-02-002
Gavin	NP-HL	1-01-001
Gavin's	NP$	9-02-002
gavotte	**noun**	**1-01-001**
gavottes	NNS	1-01-001
gawdamighty	**UH**	**1-01-001**
gawky	**JJ**	**1-01-001**
gay	**adjective**	**28-12-022**
gay	JJ	26-12-022
gay	JJ-NC	2-01-001
Gay	**NP**	**2-01-001**
Gaylor	**prop. noun**	**2-01-001**
Gaylor	NP	1-01-001
Gaylor's	NP$	1-01-001
Gaynor	**NP**	**1-01-001**
gaze	**NN**	**7-05-007**
gaze	**verb**	**21-10-018**
gaze	VB	5-04-005
gazes	VBZ	1-01-001
gazed	VBD	7-05-006
gazing	VBG	8-07-007
gazelle	**NN**	**1-01-001**
gazer	**NN**	**1-01-001**
gazette	**foreign**	**1-01-001**
gazette	FW-NN	0-00-000
Gazette	FW-NN-TL	1-01-001
gazette	**noun**	**10-03-003**
gazette	NN	0-00-000
Gazette	NN-TL	9-03-003
gazettes	NNS	0-00-000
Gazettes	NNS-TL	1-01-001
Gazinosu	**NP**	**1-01-001**
gear	**noun**	**28-06-010**
gear	NN	25-06-009
gear	NN-HL	1-01-001
gears	NNS	2-02-002
gear	**verb**	**4-03-004**
geared	VBN	2-02-002
geered	VBN	1-01-001
gearing	VBG	1-01-001
gear-set	**noun**	**1-01-001**

gear-set (cont.):		
gear-sets	NNS	1-01-001
Geary	**NP**	**1-01-001**
Geatish	**JJ**	**1-01-001**
Geddes	**NP**	**1-01-001**
gee	**exclam.**	**2-02-002**
gee	UH	1-01-001
Gee	UH	1-01-001
Gee	**prop. noun**	**3-01-001**
Gee	NP	2-01-001
Gee's	NP$	1-01-001
geeing	**NN**	**1-01-001**
Geely	**prop. noun**	**8-01-001**
Geely	NP	7-01-001
Geely's	NP$	1-01-001
gegenschein	**FW-NN**	**1-01-001**
Gehrig	**NP**	**5-02-003**
Geiger	**NP**	**1-01-001**
Geisha	**NP**	**1-01-001**
gel	**noun**	**2-01-002**
gel	NN	1-01-001
Gel	NN-TL	1-01-001
gelatin-like	**JJ**	**1-01-001**
gelding	**noun**	**5-03-003**
gelding	NN	4-02-002
geldings	NNS	1-01-001
Gelly	**NP**	**1-01-001**
gem	**noun**	**6-04-006**
gem	NN	4-04-004
gems	NNS	2-01-002
Gemeinschaft	**FW-NN**	**1-01-001**
gemlike	**JJ**	**1-01-001**
gender	**noun**	**3-01-001**
gender	NN	2-01-001
genders	NNS	1-01-001
gene	**noun**	**1-01-001**
genes	NNS	1-01-001
Gene	**NP**	**11-04-008**
genealogy	**noun**	**1-01-001**
genealogies	NNS	1-01-001
general	**adjective**	**378-13-190**
general	JJ	291-13-165
gen.	JJ	0-00-000
Gen.	JJ-TL	4-02-004
general	JJ-HL	7-03-007
General	JJ-TL	76-08-037
general	**noun**	**158-11-052**
general	NN	20-07-015
gen.	NN	0-00-000
Gen.	NN-TL	19-03-008
General	NN-TL	103-10-030
general's	NN$	2-02-002
General's	NN$-TL	4-03-003
generals	NNS	10-05-006
general-appeal	**JJ**	**1-01-001**
general-purpose	**JJ**	**1-01-001**
generale	**foreign**	**4-03-003**
generale	FW-JJ	0-00-000
Generale	FW-JJ-TL	4-03-003
generalist	**noun**	**3-01-001**
generalist	NN	1-01-001
generalists	NNS	2-01-001
generality	**noun**	**4-03-004**
generality	NN	3-03-003
generalities	NNS	1-01-001
generalization	**noun**	**11-05-010**
generalization	NN	4-03-004
generalizations	NNS	7-04-007
generalize	**verb**	**14-04-012**
generalize	VB	5-04-005
generalized	VBN	9-02-007
generally	**QL**	**3-03-003**
generally	**adverb**	**129-14-097**
generally	RB	128-14-097
generally	RB-HL	1-01-001
generate	**verb**	**30-07-021**
generate	VB	7-03-005
generates	VBZ	5-04-005
generated	VBD	2-02-002
generated	VBN	9-03-008
generating	VBG	7-03-006
generation	**noun**	**79-11-054**
generation	NN	53-10-037
Generation	NN-TL	2-02-002
generation's	NN$	1-01-001
generations	NNS	23-07-018
generator	**noun**	**23-04-005**
generator	NN	14-04-005
generators	NNS	9-01-002

Word	Tag	Frequency
generosity	**NN**	**7-06-007**
generous	**JJ**	**25-08-023**
generously	**RB**	**8-05-008**
genesis	**noun**	**4-03-004**
genesis	NN	3-02-003
Genesis	NN-TL	1-01-001
genetic	**JJ**	**5-02-002**
geneticist	**noun**	**3-02-002**
geneticist	NN	1-01-001
Geneticist	NN-TL	2-01-001
Geneva	**prop. noun**	**17-04-008**
Geneva	NP	15-04-007
Geneva	NP-HL	2-01-001
Genevieve	**NP**	**1-01-001**
genial	**JJ**	**5-04-004**
genie	**noun**	**2-02-002**
genie	NN	1-01-001
genii	NN	1-01-001
genius	**noun**	**24-08-017**
genius	NN	23-08-016
geniuses	NNS	1-01-001
Gennaro	**NP**	**1-01-001**
genre	**noun**	**3-03-003**
genre	NN	2-02-002
genres	NNS	1-01-001
genteel	**JJ**	**4-03-003**
gentian	**noun**	**2-02-002**
gentian	NN	1-01-001
gentians	NNS	1-01-001
gentile	**JJ**	**3-01-001**
gentile	**NN**	**1-01-001**
Gentile	**prop. noun**	**10-03-004**
Gentile	NP	9-03-004
Gentiles	NPS	1-01-001
Gentile-Jewish	**JJ**	**5-01-001**
gentility	**NN**	**3-03-003**
gentle	**JJ**	**26-10-024**
gentle	**VB**	**1-01-001**
gentleman	**noun**	**49-14-037**
gentleman	NN	26-11-024
Gentleman	NN	1-01-001
Gentleman	NN-TL	1-01-001
gentlemen	NNS	20-11-017
Gentlemen	NNS-TL	1-01-001
gentlemanly	**JJ**	**1-01-001**
gentleness	**NN**	**2-02-002**
gentler	**JJR**	**3-03-003**
gently	**RB**	**31-10-024**
gentry	**NN**	**1-01-001**
genuine	**JJ**	**34-11-033**
genuinely	**QL**	**8-04-007**
genuinely	**RB**	**2-02-002**
genus	**noun**	**3-01-002**
genus	NN	2-01-001
genera	NNS	1-01-001
geocentric	**JJ**	**2-01-001**
geocentricism	**NN**	**1-01-001**
geochemistry	**noun**	**2-02-002**
geochemistry	NN	1-01-001
geochemistry	NN-HL	1-01-001
geodetic	**adjective**	**1-01-001**
geodetic	JJ	0-00-000
Geodetic	JJ-TL	1-01-001
geographer	**noun**	**1-01-001**
geographers	NNS	1-01-001
geographic	**adjective**	**6-03-005**
geographic	JJ	4-02-004
geographic	JJ-HL	1-01-001
Geographic	JJ-TL	1-01-001
geographical	**JJ**	**16-06-011**
geographically	**RB**	**6-02-005**
geography	**NN**	**5-04-005**
geological	**adjective**	**8-02-003**
geological	JJ	2-01-002
Geological	JJ-TL	6-02-002
geologist	**noun**	**5-04-004**
geologist	NN	2-02-002
geologists	NNS	3-02-002
geology	**noun**	**5-04-004**
geology	NN	4-03-003
Geology	NN-TL	1-01-001
geometric	**adjective**	**17-01-003**
geometric	JJ	1-01-001
Geometric	JJ-TL	16-01-002
geometrical	**JJ**	**1-01-001**
geometrically	**RB**	**1-01-001**
geometry	**NN**	**9-04-006**
geopolitical	**adjective**	**2-02-002**
geopolitical	JJ	1-01-001
geopolitical (cont.):		
geo-political	JJ	1-01-001
George	**prop. noun**	**133-13-069**
George	NP	118-13-066
Geroge	NP	1-01-001
George	NP-NC	6-01-001
George	NP-TL	5-02-003
George's	NP$	3-02-002
George-Barden	**prop. noun**	**3-01-001**
George-Barden	NP	1-01-001
George-Barden	NP-TL	2-01-001
Georges	**NP**	**2-01-002**
Georgetown	**prop. noun**	**4-04-004**
Georgetown	NP	1-01-001
Georgetown	NP-TL	2-02-002
Georgetown's	NP$	1-01-001
Georgi	**NP**	**1-01-001**
Georgia	**prop. noun**	**60-09-021**
Georgia	NP	31-08-014
Ga.	NP	5-03-004
Georgia	NP-HL	1-01-001
Georgia	NP-TL	14-03-007
Georgia's	NP$	9-02-004
Georgia-Pacific	**prop. noun**	**2-01-001**
Georgia-Pacific	NP	0-00-000
Georgia-Pacific	NP-TL	2-01-001
Georgian	**JJ**	**2-02-002**
Georgian	**prop. noun**	**2-02-002**
Georgian	NP	1-01-001
Georgians	NPS	1-01-001
Geraghty	**prop. noun**	**8-01-001**
Geraghty	NP	4-01-001
Geraghty's	NP$	3-01-001
Geraghtys'	NPS$	1-01-001
Gerald	**NP**	**3-01-002**
Geraldine	**NP**	**2-02-002**
Gerby	**NP**	**1-01-001**
Gerhard	**NP**	**1-01-001**
geriatric	**JJ**	**1-01-001**
germ	**noun**	**4-04-004**
germ	NN	3-03-003
germs	NNS	1-01-001
German	**adjective**	**51-10-029**
German	JJ	48-10-028
German	JJ-TL	3-02-003
German	**prop. noun**	**62-10-031**
German	NP	27-07-013
German	NP-HL	1-01-001
German	NP-TL	6-03-005
German's	NP$	1-01-001
Germans	NPS	27-06-016
German-language	**JJ**	**1-01-001**
germane	**JJ**	**2-02-002**
Germania	**NP**	**1-01-001**
Germanic	**JJ**	**9-02-003**
germanium	**NN**	**8-02-002**
Germanize	**verb**	**1-01-001**
Germanized	VBN	1-01-001
Germano-Slavic	**JJ**	**1-01-001**
Germantown	**NP**	**2-02-002**
Germany	**prop. noun**	**83-12-033**
Germany	NP	62-12-026
Germany	NP-HL	1-01-001
Germany	NP-TL	18-05-011
Germany's	NP$	2-01-001
germinal	**JJ**	**1-01-001**
germinate	**VB**	**2-01-001**
Gerome	**NP**	**1-01-001**
Gerosa	**prop. noun**	**4-02-002**
Gerosa	NP	2-01-001
Gerosa's	NP$	2-02-002
Gerry	**NP**	**4-01-001**
Gershwin	**prop. noun**	**3-02-002**
Gershwin	NP	1-01-001
Gershwins	NPS	1-01-001
Gershwins'	NPS$	1-01-001
Gerstacker	**NP**	**1-01-001**
Gertrude	**NP**	**5-02-002**
gerundial	**JJ**	**2-01-001**
Gesamtkunstwerke	**FW-NN**	**1-01-001**
Gesangverein	**foreign**	**1-01-001**
Gesangverein	FW-NN	0-00-000
Gesangverein	FW-NN-TL	1-01-001
Gestapo	**NP**	**1-01-001**
gesticulate	**verb**	**2-02-002**
gesticulated	VBD	1-01-001
gesticulating	VBG	1-01-001
gesture	**noun**	**38-13-029**
gesture	NN	32-12-024

Word	Tag	Count
gesture (cont.):		
gestures	NNS	6-06-006
gesture	**verb**	**5-03-005**
gestures	VBZ	1-01-001
gestured	VBD	3-03-003
gesturing	VBG	1-01-001
Gesualdo	**NP**	**1-01-001**
get	**verb**	**1486-15-344**
get	VB	742-15-273
git	VB	4-04-004
get	VB-HL	2-02-002
get	VB-NC	1-01-001
Get	VB-TL	4-03-004
gets	VBZ	64-12-047
gets	VBZ-HL	2-01-002
got	VBD	338-14-164
Got	VBD-TL	1-01-001
got	VBN	140-12-086
gotten	VBN	16-08-013
Got	VBN-TL	3-02-003
gotta	VBN+TO	5-04-004
getting	VBG	162-15-122
gettin'	VBG	1-01-001
getting	VBG-HL	1-01-001
get-together	**NN**	**2-01-002**
getaway	**NN**	**1-01-001**
getting	**NN**	**2-02-002**
Gettysburg	**NP**	**2-02-002**
Getz	**prop. noun**	**2-01-001**
Getz	NP	1-01-001
Getz's	NP$	1-01-001
Gevurtz	**NP**	**1-01-001**
geyser	**noun**	**2-02-002**
geysers	NNS	2-02-002
geyser	**verb**	**1-01-001**
geysering	VBG	1-01-001
Ghadiali	**NP**	**1-01-001**
Ghana	**NP**	**4-03-004**
ghastly	**JJ**	**6-04-006**
ghazal	**foreign**	**2-01-001**
ghazal	FW-NN	1-01-001
ghazals	FW-NNS	1-01-001
Ghent	**NP**	**1-01-001**
gherkin	**noun**	**1-01-001**
gherkins	NNS	1-01-001
ghetto	**noun**	**16-05-005**
ghetto	NN	11-04-004
ghettos	NNS	5-02-002
Ghiberti	**NP**	**1-01-001**
Ghoreyeb	**NP**	**2-01-001**
Ghormley	**NP**	**1-01-001**
ghost	**noun**	**16-06-013**
ghost	NN	9-06-008
ghost	NN-HL	1-01-001
Ghost	NN-TL	1-01-001
ghosts	NNS	5-04-004
ghost	**verb**	**1-01-001**
ghosted	VBD	1-01-001
ghostlike	**JJ**	**1-01-001**
ghostly	**JJ**	**2-02-002**
ghoul	**noun**	**3-01-001**
ghoul	NN	1-01-001
ghouls	NNS	2-01-001
Giacometti	**NP**	**1-01-001**
Giacomo	**NP**	**1-01-001**
Gianicolo	**NP**	**2-01-001**
giant	**JJ**	**17-10-015**
giant	**noun**	**29-07-015**
giant	NN	6-04-006
giants	NNS	11-03-004
giants	NNS-HL	1-01-001
Giants	NNS-TL	9-01-005
giants'	NNS$	0-00-000
Giants'	NNS$-TL	2-01-001
Giaour	**NP**	**1-01-001**
Gibault	**NP**	**2-01-001**
gibbet	**NN**	**1-01-001**
Gibbon	**NP**	**2-02-002**
Gibbs	**prop. noun**	**7-02-002**
Gibbs	NP	6-02-002
Gibbs	NP-TL	1-01-001
Gibby	**NP**	**7-01-001**
gibe	**noun**	**2-02-002**
gibe	NN	1-01-001
gibes	NNS	1-01-001
giblet	**NN**	**1-01-001**
Gibson	**prop. noun**	**8-04-005**
Gibson	NP	6-04-005
Gibson	NP-TL	2-01-001
giddiness	**NN**	**1-01-001**
Giddings	**NP**	**1-01-001**
giddy	**JJ**	**2-02-002**
Gide	**NP**	**1-01-001**
Giffen	**prop. noun**	**19-01-001**
Giffen	NP	17-01-001
Giffen's	NP$	2-01-001
gift	**noun**	**45-13-038**
gift	NN	32-12-029
Gift	NN-TL	1-01-001
gifts	NNS	11-06-010
guiftes	NNS	1-01-001
gifted	**JJ**	**13-09-013**
gig	**NN**	**1-01-001**
gigantic	**JJ**	**10-10-010**
giggle	**noun**	**5-03-005**
giggle	NN	1-01-001
giggles	NNS	4-03-004
giggle	**verb**	**4-03-004**
giggled	VBD	2-02-002
giggled	VBN	1-01-001
giggling	VBG	1-01-001
Gil	**NP**	**1-01-001**
Gilbert	**NP**	**3-03-003**
Gilborn	**prop. noun**	**19-01-001**
Gilborn	NP	16-01-001
Gilborn's	NP$	3-01-001
gild	**verb**	**3-03-003**
gild	VB	1-01-001
gilded	VBN	2-02-002
Gildas	**NP**	**1-01-001**
Gilels	**NP**	**2-01-001**
Giles	**NP**	**7-02-002**
Gilkson	**NP**	**1-01-001**
Gill	**NP**	**2-02-002**
Gillespie	**NP**	**3-02-002**
Gillis	**NP**	**1-01-001**
Gilman	**NP**	**3-01-001**
Gilmore	**NP**	**1-01-001**
Gilroy	**NP**	**1-01-001**
gilt	**JJ**	**2-02-002**
gilt	**NN**	**1-01-001**
gimbaled	**JJ**	**1-01-001**
Gimbel	**prop. noun**	**2-01-002**
Gimbel	NP	1-01-001
Gimbel	NP-TL	1-01-001
Gimpy	**NP**	**1-01-001**
gin	**noun**	**24-05-006**
gin	NN	17-05-006
Gin	NN-TL	6-01-001
gins	NNS	1-01-001
gin	**verb**	**6-02-002**
ginning	VBG	4-01-001
ginnin'	VBG	1-01-001
Ginning	VBG-TL	1-01-001
ginger	**NN**	**2-02-002**
gingerly	**JJ**	**1-01-001**
gingerly	**RB**	**1-01-001**
gingham	**noun**	**3-03-003**
gingham	NN	2-02-002
ginghams	NNS	1-01-001
ginkgo	**NN**	**1-01-001**
ginmill	**NN**	**2-01-001**
ginner	**noun**	**1-01-001**
ginner's	NN$	0-00-000
Ginner's	NN$-TL	1-01-001
Gino	**NP**	**1-01-001**
Ginsberg	**prop. noun**	**1-01-001**
Ginsberg's	NP$	1-01-001
Gioconda	**NP**	**1-01-001**
Giorgio	**NP**	**3-01-001**
Giovanni	**NP**	**3-02-003**
gird	**VB**	**1-01-001**
girder	**noun**	**1-01-001**
girders	NNS	1-01-001
girdle	**NN**	**2-02-002**
girl	**noun**	**374-15-132**
girl	NN	211-14-098
Girl	NN-TL	9-05-006
girl's	NN$	10-07-007
girls	NNS	139-15-062
girls	NNS-HL	1-01-001
Girls	NNS-TL	2-01-001
girls'	NNS$	1-01-001
Girls'	NNS$-TL	1-01-001
girl-friend	**NN**	**1-01-001**
girl-san	**NN**	**1-01-001**
girlie	**NN**	**1-01-001**
girlish	**JJ**	**5-04-004**

Word	Tag	Frequency
girlishly	**RB**	**2-02-002**
girth	**NN**	**1-01-001**
Gisele	**NP**	**1-01-001**
Giselle	**prop. noun**	**4-02-002**
Giselle	NP	2-01-001
Giselle	NP-TL	2-01-001
Gisors	**NP**	**1-01-001**
gist	**NN**	**1-01-001**
Giubbonari	**NP**	**1-01-001**
Giulietta	**NP**	**1-01-001**
Giuseppe	**NP**	**3-02-003**
Giustiniani	**NP**	**1-01-001**
give	**NN**	**2-01-002**
give	**verb**	**1264-15-428**
give	VB	387-15-248
gimme	VB+PPO	1-01-001
gives	VBZ	114-14-084
giveth	VBZ	2-01-001
gave	VBD	285-15-176
given	VBN	375-15-225
given	VBN-HL	1-01-001
giving	VBG	94-14-081
givin'	VBG	5-01-001
give-and-take	**NN**	**1-01-001**
give-away	**JJ**	**1-01-001**
giveaway	**noun**	**7-05-005**
giveaway	NN	4-04-004
giveaways	NNS	3-01-001
givenness	**NN**	**1-01-001**
giver	**noun**	**2-02-002**
giver	NN	1-01-001
givers	NNS	0-00-000
Givers	NNS-TL	1-01-001
giving	**NN**	**2-02-002**
Gizenga	**prop. noun**	**3-01-002**
Gizenga	NP	2-01-002
Gigenza	NP	1-01-001
glacier	**noun**	**2-02-002**
glacier	NN	1-01-001
glaciers	NNS	1-01-001
glacier-like	**JJ**	**1-01-001**
glad	**JJ**	**38-13-035**
Gladden	**prop. noun**	**5-01-001**
Gladden	NP	3-01-001
Gladden's	NP$	2-01-001
Gladdy	**prop. noun**	**8-01-001**
Gladdy	NP	6-01-001
Gladdy's	NP$	2-01-001
gladiator	**NN**	**1-01-001**
gladius	**foreign**	**2-01-001**
gladius	FW-NN	1-01-001
Gladius	FW-NN-TL	1-01-001
gladly	**RB**	**4-04-004**
gladness	**NN**	**1-01-001**
glamorize	**VB**	**1-01-001**
glamorous	**JJ**	**5-04-005**
glamour	**noun**	**9-06-008**
glamour	NN	5-04-005
glamor	NN	4-03-003
glance	**noun**	**35-09-029**
glance	NN	30-08-026
glances	NNS	5-04-005
glance	**verb**	**43-11-033**
glance	VB	10-07-010
glanced	VBD	25-07-021
glancing	VBG	8-04-008
gland	**noun**	**15-03-005**
gland	NN	9-02-003
glands	NNS	6-03-004
glander	**noun**	**1-01-001**
glanders	NNS	1-01-001
glandular	**JJ**	**1-01-001**
glare	**NN**	**6-03-006**
glare	**verb**	**13-05-011**
glare	VB	1-01-001
glared	VBD	5-03-005
glaring	VBG	7-04-007
glaringly	**RB**	**1-01-001**
Glasgow	**prop. noun**	**2-01-002**
Glasgow	NP	1-01-001
Glasgow	NP-TL	1-01-001
glass	**noun**	**128-15-080**
glass	NN	96-14-060
Glass	NN-TL	3-03-003
glasses	NNS	29-11-022
glass-bottom	**NN**	**1-01-001**
glass-fiber	**NN**	**2-01-001**
glass-like	**JJ**	**1-01-001**
glassless	**JJ**	**1-01-001**
glassy	**JJ**	**2-01-002**
glaucoma	**NN**	**1-01-001**
Glayre	**NP**	**1-01-001**
glaze	**noun**	**12-02-002**
glaze	NN	9-02-002
glazes	NNS	3-01-001
glaze	**verb**	**9-03-005**
glaze	VB	2-01-001
glazed	VBN	5-03-004
glazing	VBG	2-01-002
Glazer	**NP**	**3-02-002**
gleam	**NN**	**3-03-003**
gleam	**verb**	**11-05-010**
gleam	VB	1-01-001
gleamed	VBD	4-03-004
gleaming	VBG	6-03-005
glean	**verb**	**2-01-002**
glean	VB	1-01-001
gleaned	VBN	1-01-001
Gleason	**prop. noun**	**2-01-002**
Gleason	NP	1-01-001
Gleason	NP-TL	1-01-001
glee	**noun**	**4-03-003**
glee	NN	1-01-001
Glee	NN-TL	2-01-001
glees	NNS	1-01-001
glee-club	**NN**	**1-01-001**
gleeful	**JJ**	**1-01-001**
gleefully	**RB**	**1-01-001**
glen	**noun**	**3-03-003**
glen	NN	2-02-002
Glen	NN-TL	1-01-001
Glen	**NP**	**4-02-004**
Glenda	**NP**	**2-01-002**
Glendale	**NP**	**1-01-001**
Glendora	**prop. noun**	**14-01-001**
Glendora	NP	13-01-001
Glendora's	NP$	1-01-001
Glenn	**NP**	**6-03-003**
Glennon	**NP**	**1-01-001**
glib	**JJ**	**1-01-001**
glibly	**RB**	**4-03-004**
glide	**verb**	**4-04-004**
glide	VB	2-02-002
glides	VBZ	1-01-001
glided	VBD	1-01-001
glide-bomb	**verb**	**1-01-001**
glide-bombed	VBD	1-01-001
glider	**noun**	**1-01-001**
gliders	NNS	1-01-001
Glimco	**prop. noun**	**5-01-001**
Glimco	NP	3-01-001
Glimco	NP-HL	1-01-001
Glimco's	NP$	1-01-001
glimmer	**NN**	**3-03-003**
glimmer	**verb**	**1-01-001**
glimmering	VBG	1-01-001
glimpse	**noun**	**19-06-017**
glimpse	NN	14-05-013
glimpse	NN-HL	1-01-001
glimpses	NNS	4-03-004
glimpse	**verb**	**6-05-006**
glimpse	VB	1-01-001
glimpsed	VBD	2-01-002
glimpsed	VBN	3-03-003
glint	**NN**	**2-02-002**
glint	**verb**	**7-04-006**
glinted	VBD	2-01-002
glinting	VBG	5-04-005
Glison	**NP**	**2-01-001**
glissade	**NN**	**1-01-001**
glisten	**NN**	**2-01-002**
glisten	**verb**	**12-05-012**
glisten	VB	2-01-002
glistened	VBD	4-03-004
glistening	VBG	6-03-006
glitter	**NN**	**5-04-005**
glitter	**verb**	**7-05-006**
glittered	VBD	1-01-001
glittering	VBG	6-05-005
gloat	**verb**	**3-03-003**
gloats	VBZ	1-01-001
gloated	VBD	2-02-002
glob-flake	**noun**	**1-01-001**
glob-flakes	NNS	1-01-001
global	**JJ**	**4-02-003**
globally	**RB**	**1-01-001**
globe	**noun**	**14-10-013**
globe	NN	12-09-011

Word	Tag	Frequency
globe (cont.):		
Globe	NN-TL	1-01-001
globes	NNS	1-01-001
Globe-Democrat	**NP**	**1-01-001**
globe-girdling	**JJ**	**1-01-001**
globetrotter	**NN**	**1-01-001**
globigii	**NP**	**1-01-001**
Globocnik	**prop. noun**	**4-01-001**
Globocnik	NP	3-01-001
Globocnik's	NP$	1-01-001
globulin	**noun**	**5-01-002**
globulin	NN	4-01-002
globulins	NNS	1-01-001
Glocester	**NP**	**1-01-001**
glom	**verb**	**1-01-001**
glommed	VBD	1-01-001
glomerular	**JJ**	**2-01-001**
gloom	**NN**	**14-05-013**
gloomily	**RB**	**3-03-003**
gloomy	**JJ**	**3-02-003**
Gloria	**NP**	**1-01-001**
Gloriana	**NP**	**3-01-001**
glorification	**NN**	**1-01-001**
glorify	**verb**	**7-04-006**
glorify	VB	1-01-001
glorify	VB-NC	1-01-001
glorifies	VBZ	1-01-001
glorified	VBN	4-03-004
glorious	**JJ**	**16-06-014**
gloriously	**RB**	**1-01-001**
glory	**noun**	**23-09-015**
glory	NN	18-07-010
Glory	NN-TL	2-02-002
glories	NNS	3-03-003
Glory	**UH**	**1-01-001**
glory	**verb**	**2-02-002**
glories	VBZ	1-01-001
glorying	VBG	1-01-001
gloss	**NN**	**1-01-001**
gloss	**verb**	**1-01-001**
glossed	VBN	1-01-001
glossary	**NN**	**3-02-002**
glossy	**JJ**	**1-01-001**
glottal	**JJ**	**1-01-001**
glottochronological	**JJ**	**3-01-001**
glottochronology	**NN**	**1-01-001**
Gloucester	**prop. noun**	**7-03-003**
Gloucester	NP	5-01-001
Gloucester	NP-TL	2-02-002
glove	**noun**	**16-07-011**
glove	NN	9-04-006
gloves	NNS	6-05-005
Gloves	NNS-TL	1-01-001
glove	**verb**	**2-02-002**
gloved	VBN	2-02-002
glover	**NN**	**1-01-001**
glow	**noun**	**14-08-013**
glow	NN	13-07-012
Glow	NN-TL	1-01-001
glow	**verb**	**19-08-014**
glow	VB	1-01-001
glow	VB-HL	1-01-001
glows	VBZ	1-01-001
glowed	VBD	6-04-005
glowing	VBG	10-06-006
glower	**verb**	**6-03-006**
glowered	VBD	2-02-002
glowered	VBN	1-01-001
glowering	VBG	3-02-003
glue	**NN**	**7-02-002**
glue	**verb**	**20-04-008**
glue	VB	1-01-001
glued	VBD	2-01-001
glued	VBN	17-03-007
glum	**NN**	**1-01-001**
glumly	**RB**	**1-01-001**
glut	**verb**	**1-01-001**
glutted	VBN	1-01-001
glutamic	**JJ**	**1-01-001**
glutinous	**JJ**	**1-01-001**
glutton	**noun**	**3-02-002**
gluttons	NNS	3-02-002
glycerinate	**verb**	**1-01-001**
glycerinated	VBN	1-01-001
glycerine	**noun**	**7-03-004**
glycerine	NN	5-02-002
glycerin	NN	2-02-002
glycerol	**NN**	**2-01-002**
glycerolize	**verb**	**1-01-001**

Word	Tag	Frequency
glycerolize (cont.):		
glycerolized	VBN	1-01-001
glycol	**noun**	**3-01-001**
glycol	NN	2-01-001
glycols	NNS	1-01-001
glycoside	**noun**	**1-01-001**
glycosides	NNS	1-01-001
gnarled	**JJ**	**1-01-001**
gnash	**verb**	**2-02-002**
gnashing	VBG	2-02-002
gnaw	**verb**	**6-03-006**
gnaw	VB	1-01-001
gnawed	VBD	1-01-001
gnawing	VBG	4-03-004
gnome	**noun**	**2-02-002**
gnome	NN	1-01-001
gnomes	NNS	1-01-001
gnomelike	**JJ**	**1-01-001**
gnomon	**NN**	**1-01-001**
go	**NN**	**1-01-001**
go	**verb**	**1844-15-394**
go	VB	613-15-272
go	VB-HL	1-01-001
go	VB-NC	8-01-002
Go	VB-TL	3-03-003
g'ahn	VB+RP	1-01-001
goes	VBZ	89-14-074
went	VBD	508-15-222
gone	VBN	194-15-138
gonne	VBN	1-01-001
Gone	VBN-TL	1-01-001
going	VBG	395-15-194
goin	VBG	4-01-002
goin'	VBG	8-02-005
Going	VBG-TL	1-01-001
gonna	VBG+TO	17-05-007
go-go-go	**NN**	**1-01-001**
go-it-alone	**JJ**	**1-01-001**
go-to-war	**JJ**	**1-01-001**
Goa	**NP**	**1-01-001**
goad	**NN**	**1-01-001**
goad	**verb**	**3-03-003**
goaded	VBD	1-01-001
goaded	VBN	2-02-002
goal	**noun**	**100-12-058**
goal	NN	60-11-044
goals	NNS	38-08-021
Goals	NNS-TL	2-01-001
goal-line	**NN**	**1-01-001**
goal-oriented	**JJ**	**1-01-001**
goal-value	**noun**	**1-01-001**
goal-values	NNS	1-01-001
goat	**noun**	**8-04-004**
goat	NN	6-04-004
goat's	NN$	2-01-001
gob	**NN**	**1-01-001**
gobble	**verb**	**3-03-003**
gobbles	VBZ	1-01-001
gobbled	VBD	2-02-002
gobbledygook	**NN**	**1-01-001**
gobbler	**noun**	**1-01-001**
gobblers	NNS	1-01-001
god	**noun**	**31-10-018**
god	NN	13-05-007
god	NN-HL	4-01-001
gods	NNS	12-07-010
Gods	NNS-TL	2-01-001
God	**UH**	**2-02-002**
God	**prop. noun**	**335-14-095**
God	NP	260-14-084
God	NP-HL	8-01-001
God	NP-TL	29-08-014
God's	NP$	38-11-025
God-curst	**JJ**	**1-01-001**
God-forsaken	**JJ**	**1-01-001**
God-given	**JJ**	**3-02-002**
god-like	**JJ**	**1-01-001**
goddammit	**exclam.**	**4-03-003**
goddammit	UH	2-01-001
godamit	UH	1-01-001
goddamit	UH	1-01-001
goddamn	**adjective**	**10-04-006**
goddamn	JJ	6-03-003
goddam	JJ	4-03-003
goddamn	**QL**	**2-01-001**
goddamn	**UH**	**1-01-001**
goddamn	**verb**	**4-01-003**
goddamn	VB	2-01-002
goddamned	VBN	2-01-001

goddess	**noun**	**5-04-004**
goddess	NN	3-03-003
Goddess	NN-TL	2-01-001
Godfrey	**NP**	**1-01-001**
godhead	**NN**	**1-01-001**
Godkin	**prop. noun**	**4-01-001**
Godkin	NP	2-01-001
Godkin	NP-TL	2-01-001
godless	**JJ**	**2-02-002**
godlike	**JJ**	**1-01-001**
godliness	**NN**	**1-01-001**
Godot	**prop. noun**	**5-01-001**
Godot	NP	1-01-001
Godot	NP-TL	4-01-001
godsend	**NN**	**2-02-002**
Godunov	**prop. noun**	**1-01-001**
Godunov	NP	0-00-000
Godunov	NP-TL	1-01-001
Godwin	**NP**	**4-03-003**
Goering	**NP**	**1-01-001**
Goethe	**prop. noun**	**4-01-001**
Goethe	NP	3-01-001
Goethe's	NP$	1-01-001
Gog	**prop. noun**	**1-01-001**
Gog	NP	0-00-000
Gog	NP-TL	1-01-001
goggle	**noun**	**1-01-001**
goggles	NNS	1-01-001
goggle-eyed	**JJ**	**2-02-002**
Gogh	**NP**	**2-02-002**
Gogo	**NP**	**1-01-001**
Gogol	**prop. noun**	**2-02-002**
Gogol	NP	1-01-001
Gogol's	NP$	1-01-001
going	**noun**	**4-04-004**
going	NN	3-03-003
goings	NNS	1-01-001
going-over	**NN**	**2-02-002**
goitre	**NN**	**3-01-001**
goitrogen	**noun**	**4-01-001**
goitrogen	NN	2-01-001
goitrogens	NNS	2-01-001
gold	**adjective**	**15-06-009**
gold	JJ	12-04-006
Gold	JJ-TL	3-03-003
gold	**noun**	**37-11-030**
gold	NN	36-11-029
Gold	NN-TL	1-01-001
gold-filled	**JJ**	**1-01-001**
gold-phone	**JJ**	**1-01-001**
gold-wire	**NN**	**1-01-001**
Golda	**NP**	**1-01-001**
Goldberg	**NP**	**10-03-006**
golden	**adjective**	**42-11-029**
golden	JJ	24-10-022
golden	JJ-HL	1-01-001
Golden	JJ-TL	17-05-008
golden-crusted	**JJ**	**1-01-001**
goldfish	**NN**	**1-01-001**
goldsmith	**NN**	**1-01-001**
Goldwater	**NP**	**3-02-003**
golf	**noun**	**37-08-015**
golf	NN	27-08-013
Golf	NN-TL	7-05-007
golf's	NN$	2-01-002
golf's	NN$-HL	1-01-001
golf	**verb**	**1-01-001**
golfing	VBG	1-01-001
golfer	**noun**	**7-02-003**
golfer	NN	3-02-002
golfers	NNS	3-01-001
Golfers	NNS-TL	1-01-001
golly	**UH**	**2-01-002**
Gomez	**NP**	**2-02-002**
Gompachi	**NP**	**1-01-001**
Gontran	**NP**	**2-01-001**
Gonzales	**prop. noun**	**9-02-002**
Gonzales	NP	6-02-002
Gonzales	NP-TL	3-01-001
Gonzalez	**NP**	**2-01-001**
good	**adjective**	**731-15-308**
good	JJ	715-15-305
good	JJ-HL	3-02-003
Good	JJ-TL	13-07-010
good	**noun**	**118-13-067**
good	NN	60-11-043
good	NN-HL	1-01-001
goods	NNS	57-10-027
good	**RB**	**13-06-012**

good-bye	**noun**	**3-02-003**
good-bye	NN	0-00-000
goodbye	NN	1-01-001
good-by	NN	2-01-002
good-bye	**exclam.**	**14-08-013**
good-bye	UH	6-05-006
good-by	UH	2-02-002
goodby	UH	0-00-000
goodby	UH-HL	1-01-001
goodbye	UH	5-03-004
good-humoredly	**RB**	**1-01-001**
good-living	**JJ**	**1-01-001**
good-looking	**JJ**	**4-03-004**
good-natured	**JJ**	**4-03-004**
good-news	**NN**	**1-01-001**
good-night	**exclam.**	**2-02-002**
good-night	UH	1-01-001
goodnight	UH	1-01-001
good-size	**JJ**	**1-01-001**
good-will	**NN**	**1-01-001**
Goodbody	**prop. noun**	**2-01-001**
Goodbody	NP	1-01-001
Goodbody	NP-TL	1-01-001
goodie	**noun**	**1-01-001**
goodies	NNS	1-01-001
Goodis	**NP**	**4-01-001**
Goodman	**NP**	**2-02-002**
goodness	**noun**	**17-08-011**
goodness	NN	16-08-010
goodness'	NN$	1-01-001
goodnight	**NN**	**1-01-001**
Goodwill	**NP**	**1-01-001**
Goodwin	**NP**	**2-01-001**
goody	**UH**	**2-01-001**
gooey	**JJ**	**1-01-001**
goof	**verb**	**1-01-001**
goofed	VBD	1-01-001
goolick	**UH**	**1-01-001**
goooolick	**UH**	**1-01-001**
goose	**noun**	**7-05-007**
goose	NN	2-02-002
Goose	NN-TL	2-02-002
geese	NNS	3-03-003
gooshey	**JJ**	**1-01-001**
GOP	**prop. noun**	**1-01-001**
GOP	NP	0-00-000
GOP	NP-HL	1-01-001
Gorboduc	**NP**	**7-01-001**
Gord	**prop. noun**	**2-01-001**
Gord	NP	0-00-000
Gord	NP-TL	2-01-001
Gordin	**prop. noun**	**3-01-001**
Gordin	NP	1-01-001
Gordin	NP-TL	2-01-001
Gordon	**prop. noun**	**12-06-010**
Gordon	NP	10-05-009
Gordon's	NP$	2-02-002
Gore	**prop. noun**	**8-04-004**
Gore	NP	4-03-003
Gore	NP-TL	3-01-001
Gore's	NP$	1-01-001
gorge	**noun**	**2-02-002**
gorge	NN	1-01-001
gorges	NNS	1-01-001
gorge	**verb**	**1-01-001**
gorging	VBG	1-01-001
gorgeous	**JJ**	**7-05-007**
gorgeously	**QL**	**1-01-001**
Gorham	**prop. noun**	**5-01-001**
Gorham	NP	4-01-001
Gorham's	NP$	1-01-001
Gorky	**prop. noun**	**1-01-001**
Gorky	NP	0-00-000
Gorky	NP-TL	1-01-001
Gorshek	**NP**	**1-01-001**
Gorshin	**NP**	**1-01-001**
Gorton	**prop. noun**	**35-01-001**
Gorton	NP	31-01-001
Gorton	NP-TL	1-01-001
Gorton's	NP$	3-01-001
Gortonist	**prop. noun**	**2-01-001**
Gortonists	NPS	2-01-001
gosaimasu	**FW-VB**	**1-01-001**
gosh	**exclam.**	**4-03-004**
gosh	UH	3-03-003
Gosh	UH	1-01-001
gospel	**noun**	**11-03-005**
gospel	NN	9-03-004
Gospel	NN-TL	2-01-001

Word	Tag	Frequency
Gospel	**prop. noun**	**6-04-005**
Gospel	NP	2-01-001
Gospels	NPS	4-03-004
Gospel-singer	**NN**	**1-01-001**
Gospeler	**prop. noun**	**1-01-001**
Gospelers	NPS	1-01-001
gossamer	**NN**	**1-01-001**
gossip	**NN**	**13-06-012**
gossip	**verb**	**3-03-003**
gossiped	VBD	1-01-001
gossiping	VBG	1-01-001
Gossiping	VBG-TL	1-01-001
Gosson	**prop. noun**	**6-01-001**
Gosson	NP	5-01-001
Gosson's	NP$	1-01-001
Gotham	**NP**	**1-01-001**
gothic	**adjective**	**4-02-004**
gothic	JJ	1-01-001
Gothic	JJ-TL	3-01-003
Gothicism	**prop. noun**	**1-01-001**
Gothicism	NP	0-00-000
Gothicism	NP-TL	1-01-001
Gott	**FW-NP**	**1-01-001**
Gotterdammerung	**NP**	**1-01-001**
Gottingen	**NP**	**1-01-001**
gouge	**verb**	**7-03-007**
gouge	VB	1-01-001
gouged	VBD	2-01-002
gouged	VBN	1-01-001
gouging	VBG	3-03-003
Gould	**NP**	**2-02-002**
Goulding	**prop. noun**	**10-01-001**
Goulding	NP	7-01-001
Goulding's	NP$	2-01-001
Gouldings	NPS	1-01-001
gourd	**NN**	**2-01-001**
gourmet	**noun**	**4-02-003**
gourmet	NN	2-01-001
gourmet's	NN$	1-01-001
gourmets	NNS	1-01-001
gout	**NN**	**2-02-002**
goutte	**FW-NN**	**1-01-001**
gouverne	**FW-VBZ**	**1-01-001**
gouvernement	**foreign**	**1-01-001**
gouvernement	FW-NN	0-00-000
Gouvernement	FW-NN-TL	1-01-001
govern	**verb**	**45-09-029**
govern	VB	7-04-006
governs	VBZ	2-02-002
governed	VBD	1-01-001
governed	VBN	14-06-010
governing	VBG	21-08-015
governess	**NN**	**3-03-003**
government	**noun**	**495-13-145**
government	NN	273-13-112
government	NN-HL	4-02-004
Government	NN-TL	141-07-044
government's	NN$	6-03-006
Government's	NN$-TL	10-03-006
governments	NNS	53-09-030
Governments	NNS-TL	8-01-002
Government-blessed	**JJ**	**1-01-001**
government-controlled	**JJ**	**1-01-001**
Government-owned	**JJ**	**1-01-001**
government-supported	**JJ**	**1-01-001**
government-to-government	**JJ**	**1-01-001**
governmental	**JJ**	**23-06-017**
governmentally	**RB**	**1-01-001**
governor	**noun**	**118-08-044**
governor	NN	41-07-020
gov.	NN	0-00-000
Gov.	NN-TL	19-02-011
governor	NN-HL	2-01-001
Governor	NN-TL	27-07-018
governor	NN-TL	2-01-001
Governor	NN-TL-HL	5-01-001
governor's	NN$	9-03-005
Governor's	NN$-TL	5-03-003
governors	NNS	7-04-006
Governors	NNS-TL	1-01-001
governor-general	**noun**	**1-01-001**
governor-general	NN	0-00-000
Governor-General	NN-TL	1-01-001
gown	**noun**	**18-05-014**
gown	NN	16-05-012
gowns	NNS	2-02-002
gowned	**JJ**	**1-01-001**
Goyette	**NP**	**1-01-001**
grab	**noun**	**7-05-006**

Word	Tag	Frequency
grab (cont.):		
grab	NN	4-02-003
grabs	NNS	3-03-003
grab	**verb**	**37-09-028**
grab	VB	12-06-012
grabbed	VBD	19-05-012
grabbed	VBN	1-01-001
grabbing	VBG	4-04-004
grabbin'	VBG	1-01-001
grabbing	**NN**	**1-01-001**
Grabski	**prop. noun**	**6-01-001**
Grabski	NP	5-01-001
Grabski's	NP$	1-01-001
grace	**noun**	**36-09-028**
grace	NN	31-09-024
grace	NN-HL	1-01-001
graces	NNS	4-03-004
grace	**verb**	**1-01-001**
graced	VBN	1-01-001
Grace	**NP**	**8-03-006**
graceful	**JJ**	**10-05-009**
gracefully	**RB**	**8-06-007**
gracias	**FW-NNS**	**2-01-001**
Gracie	**prop. noun**	**2-01-001**
Gracie	NP	1-01-001
Gracie's	NP$	1-01-001
gracious	**JJ**	**9-07-009**
graciously	**RB**	**3-03-003**
grad	**noun**	**4-02-002**
grad	NN	1-01-001
Grad	NN-TL	1-01-001
grads	NNS	2-01-001
gradation	**noun**	**2-02-002**
gradations	NNS	2-02-002
grade	**noun**	**58-10-031**
grade	NN	35-07-022
grades	NNS	23-07-016
grade	**verb**	**3-02-003**
graded	VBN	2-02-002
grading	VBG	1-01-001
grade-A	**NN**	**1-01-001**
grade-constructed	**JJ**	**1-01-001**
grade-equivalent	**noun**	**2-01-001**
grade-equivalent	NN	1-01-001
grade-equivalents	NNS	1-01-001
grader	**NN**	**2-02-002**
gradient	**JJ**	**1-01-001**
gradient	**noun**	**18-02-004**
gradient	NN	13-02-003
gradients	NNS	5-02-003
gradual	**JJ**	**16-07-012**
gradualist	**NN**	**1-01-001**
gradually	**adverb**	**51-14-046**
gradually	RB	50-13-045
gradually	RB-HL	1-01-001
graduate	**JJ**	**5-02-004**
graduate	**noun**	**36-09-026**
graduate	NN	21-09-016
Graduate	NN-TL	1-01-001
graduates	NNS	14-05-012
graduate	**verb**	**25-09-020**
graduate	VB	3-03-003
graduates	VBZ	3-02-002
graduated	VBD	3-03-003
graduated	VBN	10-05-008
graduating	VBG	6-04-005
graduating	**NN**	**1-01-001**
graduation	**NN**	**11-05-006**
Grady	**prop. noun**	**5-01-003**
Grady	NP	1-01-001
Grady	NP-TL	4-01-002
Graff	**NP**	**1-01-001**
graffito	**noun**	**1-01-001**
graffiti	NNS	1-01-001
Grafin	**prop. noun**	**6-01-001**
Grafin	NP	5-01-001
Grafin's	NP$	1-01-001
graft	**NN**	**1-01-001**
Grafton	**NP**	**5-03-003**
graham	**NN**	**2-01-001**
Graham	**prop. noun**	**13-05-006**
Graham	NP	11-05-006
Graham	NP-TL	2-01-001
Grahamstown	**NP**	**1-01-001**
grail	**noun**	**2-02-002**
grail	NN	0-00-000
Grail	NN-TL	2-02-002
grain	**noun**	**47-10-021**
grain	NN	26-10-019

Word	Tag	Frequency
grain (cont.):		
grain	NN-HL	1-01-001
grains	NNS	20-05-006
grain-storage	**NN**	**1-01-001**
graining	**NN**	**1-01-001**
gram	**noun**	**37-02-005**
gram	NN	9-02-003
grams	NNS	18-02-002
gm.	NNS	10-01-001
Gram	**NP**	**1-01-001**
Gram-negative	**JJ**	**1-01-001**
grammar	**NN**	**4-03-003**
grammarian	**noun**	**1-01-001**
grammarians	NNS	1-01-001
grammatical	**JJ**	**9-03-004**
grammatically	**RB**	**1-01-001**
Grammophon	**foreign**	**1-01-001**
Grammophon	FW-NN	0-00-000
Grammophon	FW-NN-TL	1-01-001
Gran	**NP**	**9-01-001**
gran'dad	**NP**	**1-01-001**
granary	**NN**	**2-02-002**
grand	**foreign**	**6-04-004**
grand	FW-JJ	0-00-000
Grand	FW-JJ-TL	3-03-003
grands	FW-JJ	0-00-000
Grands	FW-JJ-TL	3-01-001
grand	**adjective**	**45-12-037**
grand	JJ	30-10-024
Grand	JJ-TL	15-09-015
grand-looking	**JJ**	**1-01-001**
grand-slam	**NN**	**1-01-001**
grandchild	**noun**	**6-04-005**
grandchildren	NNS	6-04-005
granddaughter	**noun**	**4-03-003**
granddaughter	NN	2-02-002
grand-daughter	NN	2-01-001
Grande	**NP**	**2-02-002**
Grande-Bretagne	**prop. noun**	**2-01-001**
Grande-Bretagne	NP	1-01-001
Grande-Bretagne	NP-TL	1-01-001
grander	**JJR**	**1-01-001**
grandeur	**NN**	**6-04-006**
grandfather	**noun**	**13-09-012**
grandfather	NN	12-09-011
grandfathers	NNS	1-01-001
grandfather-father-to-son	**NN**	**1-01-001**
grandiloquent	**JJ**	**1-01-001**
grandiose	**JJ**	**3-03-003**
grandly	**RB**	**1-01-001**
grandma	**noun**	**16-04-005**
grandma	NN	2-02-002
Grandma	NN-TL	11-02-002
grandma's	NN$	0-00-000
Grandma's	NN$-TL	3-01-002
grandmother	**noun**	**14-09-011**
grandmother	NN	8-06-006
Grandmother	NN-TL	1-01-001
grandmother's	NN$	3-03-003
grandmothers	NNS	1-01-001
grandmothers'	NNS$	0-00-000
Grandmothers'	NNS$-TL	1-01-001
grandparent	**noun**	**3-02-002**
grandparents	NNS	3-02-002
grandson	**noun**	**6-05-005**
grandson	NN	3-03-003
Grandson	NN-TL	2-01-001
grandsons	NNS	1-01-001
grandstand	**NN**	**1-01-001**
granite	**noun**	**4-02-002**
granite	NN	2-01-001
Granite	NN-TL	1-01-001
granite's	NN+BEZ	1-01-001
Granny	**prop. noun**	**7-03-003**
Granny	NP	6-03-003
Granny's	NP$	1-01-001
grant	**noun**	**43-05-019**
grant	NN	22-05-015
Grant	NN-TL	1-01-001
grants	NNS	20-04-007
grant	**verb**	**78-12-056**
grant	VB	13-06-013
graunt	VB	1-01-001
grant	VB-HL	1-01-001
granted	VBD	7-05-006
granted	VBN	49-12-038
granting	VBG	7-04-007
Grant	**prop. noun**	**11-04-008**
Grant	NP	10-03-007

Word	Tag	Frequency
Grant (cont.):		
Grant's	NP$	1-01-001
grant-in-aid	**noun**	**6-03-005**
grant-in-aid	NN	3-02-002
grants-in-aid	NNS	3-01-003
Granther	**NP**	**1-01-001**
granting	**NN**	**1-01-001**
granular	**JJ**	**3-01-002**
granular-type	**JJ**	**1-01-001**
granule	**noun**	**1-01-001**
granules	NNS	1-01-001
granulocytic	**JJ**	**1-01-001**
Granville	**NP**	**2-02-002**
grape	**noun**	**10-06-009**
grape	NN	3-02-003
grapes	NNS	5-04-005
Grapes	NNS-TL	2-02-002
grape-arbor	**NN**	**3-01-002**
grapefruit	**noun**	**3-02-003**
grapefruit	NN	1-01-001
Grapefruit	NN-TL	1-01-001
grapefruit	NNS	1-01-001
grapevine	**noun**	**4-03-004**
grapevine	NN	3-03-003
grapevines	NNS	1-01-001
graph	**noun**	**18-01-006**
graph	NN	17-01-005
graphs	NNS	1-01-001
graph	**verb**	**1-01-001**
graphed	VBN	1-01-001
graphic	**adjective**	**6-05-006**
graphic	JJ	5-05-005
Graphic	JJ-TL	1-01-001
graphical	**JJ**	**1-01-001**
graphically	**RB**	**2-02-002**
graphite	**NN**	**5-01-001**
Grappelly	**NP**	**1-01-001**
Grappely	**NP**	**1-01-001**
grapple	**verb**	**5-04-005**
grapple	VB	1-01-001
grappled	VBD	1-01-001
grappling	VBG	3-03-003
grappling	**NN**	**1-01-001**
Gras	**NP**	**2-01-001**
grasp	**NN**	**7-05-007**
grasp	**verb**	**23-10-021**
grasp	VB	10-08-010
grasped	VBD	5-02-004
grasped	VBN	6-04-005
grasping	VBG	2-02-002
grass	**noun**	**55-12-034**
grass	NN	53-12-033
Grass	NN-TL	1-01-001
grasses	NNS	1-01-001
grass	**verb**	**1-01-001**
grassed	VBN	1-01-001
grass-fed	**JJ**	**1-01-001**
grass-green	**JJ**	**1-01-001**
grasser	**noun**	**1-01-001**
grassers	NNS	1-01-001
grassfire	**NN**	**1-01-001**
grasshopper	**noun**	**4-03-003**
grasshoppers	NNS	4-03-003
grassland	**noun**	**7-02-002**
grassland	NN	1-01-001
grasslands	NNS	1-01-001
Grasslands	NNS-TL	5-01-001
grassroots	**pl. noun**	**2-02-002**
grassroots	NNS	1-01-001
grass-roots	NNS	1-01-001
grassroots-fueled	**JJ**	**1-01-001**
grassy	**adjective**	**2-02-002**
grassy	JJ	1-01-001
Grassy	JJ-TL	1-01-001
grata	**FW-JJ**	**1-01-001**
grate	**NN**	**3-02-002**
grate	**verb**	**2-02-002**
grated	VBD	1-01-001
grated	VBN	1-01-001
grateful	**JJ**	**25-13-022**
gratefully	**RB**	**3-02-002**
gratification	**NN**	**4-03-003**
gratify	**verb**	**6-02-006**
gratify	VB	1-01-001
gratified	VBN	4-02-004
gratifying	VBG	1-01-001
gratifying	**JJ**	**2-02-002**
gratifyingly	**QL**	**1-01-001**
grating	**noun**	**2-02-002**

Word	Tag	Frequency
grating (cont.):		
grating	NN	1-01-001
gratings	NNS	1-01-001
gratingly	**RB**	**1-01-001**
gratis	**RB**	**1-01-001**
gratitude	**NN**	**9-05-006**
Gratt	**NP**	**8-01-001**
Grattan	**NP**	**2-01-001**
gratuitous	**JJ**	**3-02-003**
gratuitously	**RB**	**2-02-002**
grave	**JJ**	**19-08-015**
grave	**noun**	**20-08-016**
grave	NN	14-07-012
graves	NNS	6-04-006
gravel	**NN**	**9-03-006**
gravely	**RB**	**7-05-007**
graven	**JJ**	**1-01-001**
graver	**JJR**	**2-02-002**
Graves	**prop. noun**	**5-04-004**
Graves	NP	1-01-001
Graves	NP-TL	2-01-001
Graves'	NP$	1-01-001
Graves'	NP$-TL	1-01-001
Gravesend	**NP**	**1-01-001**
gravest	**sup. adj.**	**4-03-003**
gravest	JJT	3-03-003
gravest	JJT-HL	1-01-001
gravestone	**NN**	**1-01-001**
graveyard	**noun**	**9-05-007**
graveyard	NN	7-05-006
graveyards	NNS	2-02-002
gravid	**JJ**	**2-01-001**
gravitation	**NN**	**3-02-002**
gravitational	**JJ**	**4-01-002**
gravity	**noun**	**7-04-006**
gravity	NN	6-04-005
Gravity	NN-TL	1-01-001
gravy	**NN**	**4-04-004**
gray	**adjective**	**74-13-054**
gray	JJ	59-12-045
grey	JJ	6-05-006
Gray	JJ-TL	9-03-003
gray	**noun**	**6-04-004**
gray	NN	5-03-003
grey	NN	1-01-001
gray	**verb**	**6-03-006**
grayed	VBN	1-01-001
graying	VBG	4-02-004
greying	VBG	1-01-001
Gray	**NP**	**7-05-005**
gray-back	**noun**	**1-01-001**
gray-backs	NNS	1-01-001
gray-haired	**adjective**	**4-04-004**
gray-haired	JJ	3-03-003
grey-haired	JJ	1-01-001
gray-looking	**JJ**	**1-01-001**
gray-thatched	**JJ**	**1-01-001**
graybeard	**noun**	**2-02-002**
graybeard	NN	1-01-001
graybeards	NNS	1-01-001
grayer	**JJR**	**1-01-001**
Grayson	**NP**	**1-01-001**
graze	**verb**	**9-05-007**
graze	VB	1-01-001
grazed	VBD	1-01-001
grazed	VBN	1-01-001
grazing	VBG	3-03-003
grazin'	VBG	3-01-001
grazer	**NN**	**1-01-001**
Grazie	**NP**	**4-01-001**
grease	**noun**	**12-07-009**
grease	NN	9-07-008
greases	NNS	3-01-001
grease	**verb**	**2-02-002**
greased	VBD	1-01-001
greased	VBN	1-01-001
grease-removal	**NN**	**1-01-001**
greasy	**JJ**	**8-02-002**
great	**adjective**	**653-15-287**
great	JJ	599-15-281
gre't	JJ	1-01-001
greate	JJ	1-01-001
gret	JJ	1-01-001
Great	JJ-TL	50-11-029
Great's	JJ$-TL	1-01-001
great	**QL**	**15-09-014**
great	**RB**	**1-01-001**
great-grandfather	**NN**	**2-02-002**
great-grandmother	**NN**	**1-01-001**
great-grandson	**NN**	**1-01-001**
great-niece	**noun**	**1-01-001**
great-nieces	NNS	1-01-001
greatcoat	**NN**	**5-01-002**
greatcoated	**JJ**	**1-01-001**
greater	**comp. adj.**	**188-14-119**
greater	JJR	180-14-115
greater	JJR-HL	2-01-001
Greater	JJR-TL	6-03-005
greatest	**sup. adj.**	**88-13-071**
greatest	JJT	86-13-070
Greatest	JJT-TL	2-02-002
greatly	**RB**	**62-10-054**
greatness	**noun**	**11-08-011**
greatness	NN	10-07-010
Greatness	NN-TL	1-01-001
Grecian	**JJ**	**3-01-003**
Grecian	**prop. noun**	**1-01-001**
Grecian	NP	0-00-000
Grecian	NP-TL	1-01-001
Greece	**prop. noun**	**17-05-011**
Greece	NP	16-04-010
Greece's	NP$	1-01-001
greed	**NN**	**3-02-002**
greedily	**RB**	**1-01-001**
greedy	**JJ**	**5-04-004**
Greek	**adjective**	**46-08-019**
Greek	JJ	44-08-017
Greek	JJ-TL	2-01-002
Greek	**prop. noun**	**20-08-016**
Greek	NP	15-07-012
Greeks	NPS	5-04-005
Greek-born	**JJ**	**1-01-001**
Greek-speaking	**JJ**	**1-01-001**
green	**adjective**	**85-12-060**
green	JJ	75-11-052
green	JJ-HL	2-02-002
Green	JJ-TL	8-05-008
green	**noun**	**25-08-016**
green	NN	20-07-013
Green	NN-TL	1-01-001
greens	NNS	4-03-004
green	**verb**	**2-02-002**
greening	VBG	2-02-002
Green	**prop. noun**	**13-05-009**
Green	NP	10-05-007
Green's	NP$	2-02-002
Greens	NPS	1-01-001
green-brown	**JJ**	**2-01-001**
green-bug	**noun**	**1-01-001**
green-bugs	NNS	1-01-001
green-scaled	**JJ**	**1-01-001**
green-tinted	**JJ**	**1-01-001**
Greenberg	**NP**	**2-01-001**
Greene	**prop. noun**	**13-04-006**
Greene	NP	12-03-005
Greene	NP-TL	1-01-001
greenest	**JJT**	**2-01-002**
Greenfield	**NP**	**2-01-001**
greenhouse	**noun**	**3-03-003**
greenhouse	NN	2-02-002
greenhouses	NNS	1-01-001
greenish	**JJ**	**2-02-002**
Greenland	**NP**	**3-03-003**
Greenleaf	**NP**	**2-02-002**
greenly	**RB**	**1-01-001**
greenness	**NN**	**1-01-001**
Greenock	**NP**	**1-01-001**
greensward	**NN**	**1-01-001**
Greentree	**NP**	**1-01-001**
Greenville	**prop. noun**	**3-01-002**
Greenville	NP	1-01-001
Greenville	NP-TL	2-01-001
greenware	**NN**	**1-01-001**
Greenwich	**prop. noun**	**28-07-009**
Greenwich	NP	4-03-003
Greenwich	NP-TL	24-05-007
Greenwood	**prop. noun**	**1-01-001**
Greenwood	NP	0-00-000
Greenwood	NP-TL	1-01-001
Greer	**NP**	**6-02-002**
greet	**verb**	**28-10-022**
greet	VB	7-05-005
greeted	VBD	15-09-014
greeted	VBN	5-05-005
greeting	VBG	1-01-001
greeting	**noun**	**10-07-010**
greeting	NN	4-03-004
greetings	NNS	6-05-006

Word	Tag	Frequency
Greg	**prop. noun**	**36-02-002**
Greg	NP	26-02-002
Greg's	NP$	10-02-002
gregarious	**JJ**	**4-04-004**
Gregg	**NP**	**3-03-003**
Gregorio	**NP**	**4-01-001**
Gregorius	**NP**	**2-01-001**
Gregory	**prop. noun**	**5-03-004**
Gregory	NP	3-03-003
Gregory	NP-TL	1-01-001
Gregory's	NP$	1-01-001
grenade	**noun**	**9-05-007**
grenade	NN	3-02-002
grenades	NNS	6-05-006
Grenier	**NP**	**2-01-001**
Grenoble	**prop. noun**	**1-01-001**
Grenoble	NP	0-00-000
Grenoble	NP-TL	1-01-001
Grenville	**NP**	**1-01-001**
Gresham	**NP**	**1-01-001**
Gretchen	**NP**	**1-01-001**
Greville	**prop. noun**	**22-01-001**
Greville	NP	14-01-001
Gre.	NP	1-01-001
Grev.	NP	1-01-001
Grevile	NP	1-01-001
Greville's	NP$	4-01-001
Grevyles	NP$	1-01-001
Grey	**prop. noun**	**6-01-001**
Grey	NP	4-01-001
Grey	NP-TL	1-01-001
Grey's	NP$	1-01-001
grey-skied	**JJ**	**1-01-001**
Greyhound	**NP**	**1-01-001**
Greylag	**NP**	**1-01-001**
Gridley	**NP**	**1-01-001**
grief	**NN**	**10-07-008**
grief-stricken	**JJ**	**2-02-002**
grievance	**noun**	**6-04-004**
grievance	NN	3-01-001
grievances	NNS	3-03-003
grieve	**verb**	**3-03-003**
grieving	VBG	3-03-003
grievous	**JJ**	**1-01-001**
grievously	**adverb**	**1-01-001**
grievously	RB	0-00-000
grevouselye	RB	1-01-001
Griffin	**prop. noun**	**5-03-003**
Griffin	NP	4-03-003
Griffin's	NP$	1-01-001
Griffin-Byrd	**NP**	**1-01-001**
Griffith	**prop. noun**	**19-03-004**
Griffith	NP	17-03-004
Griffith	NP-HL	1-01-001
Griffith's	NP$	1-01-001
Griffith-Jones	**NP**	**1-01-001**
Griggs	**NP**	**3-01-001**
Grigori	**prop. noun**	**5-01-001**
Grigori	NP	2-01-001
Grigori's	NP$	3-01-001
Grigorss	**NP**	**5-01-001**
Grigory	**NP**	**1-01-001**
grill	**noun**	**11-02-003**
grill	NN	10-02-002
Grill	NN-TL	1-01-001
grill	**verb**	**3-01-001**
grill	VB	1-01-001
grilled	VBN	2-01-001
grille	**NN**	**3-01-001**
grille-route	**NN**	**1-01-001**
grillwork	**noun**	**3-03-003**
grillwork	NN	2-02-002
grillework	NN	1-01-001
grim	**JJ**	**14-06-014**
grimace	**NN**	**1-01-001**
grimace	**verb**	**4-04-004**
grimace	VB	2-02-002
grimaced	VBD	2-02-002
grime	**verb**	**1-01-001**
grimed	VBN	1-01-001
Grimesby	**NP**	**1-01-001**
grimly	**RB**	**11-05-010**
Grimm	**NP**	**2-02-002**
grimmer	**JJR**	**1-01-001**
grimness	**NN**	**1-01-001**
grin	**noun**	**14-08-013**
grin	NN	12-08-012
grins	NNS	2-02-002
grin	**verb**	**38-07-030**

Word	Tag	Frequency
grin (cont.):		
grin	VB	1-01-001
grinned	VBD	29-07-023
grinned	VBN	1-01-001
grinning	VBG	7-04-007
grind	**verb**	**26-12-018**
grind	VB	2-02-002
grinds	VBZ	1-01-001
ground	VBD	4-03-004
ground	VBN	12-05-007
grinding	VBG	7-04-004
grinder	**noun**	**3-01-001**
grinders	NNS	3-01-001
grinding	**noun**	**2-02-002**
grinding	NN	1-01-001
grindings	NNS	1-01-001
Grindlay	**NP**	**1-01-001**
grindstone	**NN**	**1-01-001**
Grinsfelder	**NP**	**2-01-001**
grip	**noun**	**28-11-025**
grip	NN	19-08-016
grips	NNS	8-04-008
Grips	NNS-TL	1-01-001
grip	**verb**	**19-08-017**
grip	VB	1-01-001
gripped	VBD	9-04-007
gripped	VBN	3-03-003
gripping	VBG	6-04-006
gripe	**noun**	**1-01-001**
gripes	NNS	1-01-001
Gris	**NP**	**1-01-001**
grisly	**JJ**	**2-02-002**
grist	**NN**	**2-02-002**
gristmill	**NN**	**1-01-001**
Griston	**NP**	**1-01-001**
grit	**noun**	**4-03-003**
grit	NN	1-01-001
grits	NNS	1-01-001
Grits	NNS-TL	2-01-001
grit-impregnated	**JJ**	**1-01-001**
gritty	**JJ**	**1-01-001**
gritty-eyed	**JJ**	**1-01-001**
grizzled	**JJ**	**1-01-001**
grizzly	**noun**	**2-02-002**
grizzly	NN	1-01-001
grizzlies'	NNS$	0-00-000
Grizzlies'	NNS$-TL	1-01-001
groan	**NN**	**1-01-001**
groan	**verb**	**4-02-004**
groaned	VBD	3-02-003
groaning	VBG	1-01-001
Groat	**NP**	**1-01-001**
grocer	**noun**	**6-06-006**
grocer	NN	1-01-001
grocer's	NN$	2-02-002
grocers	NNS	3-03-003
grocery	**noun**	**11-06-010**
grocery	NN	8-06-008
Grocery	NN-TL	1-01-001
groceries	NNS	2-02-002
Groggins	**NP**	**4-01-001**
groggy	**JJ**	**1-01-001**
groin	**NN**	**4-02-002**
grok	**verb**	**10-01-001**
grok	VB	5-01-001
grokked	VBD	3-01-001
grokked	VBN	1-01-001
grokking	VBG	1-01-001
grokking	**NN**	**3-01-001**
groom	**noun**	**5-03-003**
groom	NN	4-03-003
grooms	NNS	1-01-001
groom	**verb**	**5-04-005**
groomed	VBN	4-03-004
grooming	VBG	1-01-001
Groom	**NP**	**1-01-001**
Grooms	**NP**	**1-01-001**
groomsman	**noun**	**1-01-001**
groomsmen	NNS	1-01-001
Groot	**NP**	**1-01-001**
groove	**noun**	**5-03-004**
groove	NN	2-02-002
grooves	NNS	3-02-003
groove	**verb**	**1-01-001**
grooved	VBN	1-01-001
grope	**verb**	**12-05-009**
grope	VB	1-01-001
groped	VBD	7-03-006
groping	VBG	4-03-003

Word	Tag	Count
groping	**NN**	**1-01-001**
gross	**adjective**	**30-10-015**
gross	JJ	18-10-015
gross	JJ-HL	1-01-001
Gross	JJ-TL	11-01-001
gross	**NN**	**7-05-005**
Gross	**prop. noun**	**30-02-002**
Gross	NP	27-02-002
Gross	NP-TL	2-01-001
Gross's	NP$	1-01-001
Grosse	**NP**	**9-01-001**
grossly	**QL**	**1-01-001**
grossly	**RB**	**3-03-003**
Grossman	**NP**	**1-01-001**
Grosvenor	**NP**	**2-01-001**
grotesque	**JJ**	**9-04-008**
grotesque	**noun**	**1-01-001**
grotesques	NNS	1-01-001
grotesquely	**QL**	**2-01-002**
grotesquely	**RB**	**2-02-002**
Groth	**prop. noun**	**8-01-001**
Groth	NP	2-01-001
Groth	NP-TL	2-01-001
Groth's	NP$	4-01-001
grotto	**noun**	**1-01-001**
grottoes	NNS	1-01-001
ground	**noun**	**227-15-139**
ground	NN	168-15-101
Ground	NN-TL	1-01-001
grounds	NNS	54-14-043
Grounds	NNS-TL	4-03-004
ground	**verb**	**9-08-009**
ground	VB	1-01-001
grounded	VBD	2-02-002
gruonded	VBD	1-01-001
grounded	VBN	4-04-004
grounding	VBG	1-01-001
ground-glass	**NN**	**1-01-001**
ground-level	**NN**	**1-01-001**
ground-swell	**NN**	**1-01-001**
ground-truck	**NN**	**1-01-001**
grounder	**NN**	**1-01-001**
grounding	**NN**	**1-01-001**
groundless	**JJ**	**1-01-001**
groundwave	**NN**	**6-01-001**
groundwork	**NN**	**3-03-003**
group	**noun**	**512-15-221**
group	NN	378-15-187
Group	NN-TL	8-03-005
group's	NN$	1-01-001
groups	NNS	124-12-073
groups	NNS-HL	1-01-001
group	**verb**	**13-04-011**
group	VB	4-02-004
grouped	VBN	5-02-004
grouping	VBG	4-02-004
grouping	**noun**	**9-04-005**
groupings	NNS	9-04-005
grove	**noun**	**17-07-012**
grove	NN	7-01-004
Grove	NN-TL	4-03-004
Grove	NN-TL-HL	2-02-002
groves	NNS	4-03-003
Grove	**NP**	**1-01-001**
grovel	**verb**	**2-02-002**
grovel	VB	1-01-001
groveling	VBG	1-01-001
grovelike	**JJ**	**1-01-001**
Grover	**NP**	**4-01-001**
Grovers	**prop. noun**	**1-01-001**
Grovers	NP	0-00-000
Grovers	NP-TL	1-01-001
grow	**verb**	**300-15-171**
grow	VB	61-13-049
grow	VB-HL	2-02-002
grows	VBZ	22-09-018
grew	VBD	65-15-051
grown	VBN	43-14-037
growing	VBG	107-15-079
grower	**noun**	**5-03-003**
grower	NN	1-01-001
growers	NNS	3-02-002
growers'	NNS$	1-01-001
growing	**NN**	**1-01-001**
growing-waiting	**NN**	**1-01-001**
growl	**NN**	**4-03-004**
growl	**verb**	**5-03-005**
growled	VBD	4-02-004
growling	VBG	1-01-001
grown-up	**JJ**	**4-03-004**
grownup	**noun**	**4-03-003**
grownups	NNS	3-02-002
grownups'	NNS$	1-01-001
growth	**noun**	**156-11-062**
growth	NN	150-11-060
growth	NN-HL	2-02-002
Growth	NN-TL	3-02-002
growths	NNS	1-01-001
growth-stunting	**JJ**	**1-01-001**
grub	**noun**	**3-02-003**
grub	NN	2-01-002
grubs	NNS	1-01-001
Grubb	**NP**	**3-01-001**
grubby	**JJ**	**2-02-002**
grudge	**noun**	**10-04-007**
grudge	NN	7-04-006
grudges	NNS	3-02-003
grudgingly	**RB**	**6-03-005**
gruesome	**JJ**	**2-02-002**
gruff	**JJ**	**4-03-003**
Gruller	**NP**	**1-01-001**
grumble	**NN**	**1-01-001**
grumble	**verb**	**8-05-007**
grumble	VB	5-04-005
grumbled	VBD	1-01-001
grumbled	VBN	1-01-001
grumbling	VBG	1-01-001
Grumble	**NP**	**1-01-001**
Grunnfeu	**NP**	**1-01-001**
grunt	**NN**	**1-01-001**
grunt	**verb**	**11-05-009**
grunt	VB	1-01-001
grunted	VBD	9-05-008
grunting	VBG	1-01-001
grunting	**NN**	**1-01-001**
Grzesiak	**NP**	**1-01-001**
Guam	**NP**	**12-03-003**
guanidine	**NN**	**1-01-001**
guar	**NN**	**2-01-001**
guarantee	**noun**	**12-07-012**
guarantee	NN	7-06-007
guaranty	NN	1-01-001
guarantees	NNS	4-03-004
guarantee	**verb**	**19-07-017**
guarantee	VB	2-02-002
guarantees	VBZ	4-03-004
guaranteed	VBD	2-02-002
guaranteed	VBN	11-05-010
guaranteed-neutral	**JJ**	**1-01-001**
guard	**noun**	**63-10-035**
guard	NN	27-08-019
Guard	NN-TL	13-04-007
guard's	NN$	4-02-003
guards	NNS	19-07-011
guard	**verb**	**22-09-020**
guard	VB	8-05-008
guarded	VBD	1-01-001
guarded	VBN	4-02-004
guarding	VBG	9-06-009
guard-room	**NN**	**1-01-001**
guardedness	**NN**	**1-01-001**
guardhouse	**NN**	**1-01-001**
Guardia	**prop. noun**	**1-01-001**
Guardia	NP	0-00-000
Guardia	NP-TL	1-01-001
guardian	**noun**	**13-07-011**
guardian	NN	3-03-003
Guardian	NN-TL	6-04-005
guardians	NNS	4-03-004
Guardini	**NP**	**1-01-001**
Guardino	**prop. noun**	**4-01-001**
Guardino	NP	3-01-001
Guardino's	NP+HVZ	1-01-001
Guatemala	**NP**	**3-03-003**
Guatemalan	**JJ**	**1-01-001**
gubernatorial	**JJ**	**7-02-003**
Guerin	**prop. noun**	**2-01-001**
Guerin	NP	1-01-001
Guerin	NP-TL	1-01-001
guerrilla	**noun**	**30-06-013**
guerrilla	NN	12-05-010
guerilla	NN	1-01-001
guerrillas	NNS	17-03-005
guerrilla-th'-wisp	**JJ**	**1-01-001**
guess	**noun**	**6-04-006**
guess	NN	3-02-003
guesses	NNS	3-03-003
guess	**verb**	**77-12-058**

Word	Tag	Count
guess (cont.):		
guess	VB	53-10-041
gay-ess	VB	1-01-001
guessed	VBD	7-04-007
guessed	VBN	8-06-007
guessing	VBG	8-06-007
guest	**noun**	**99-14-051**
guest	NN	35-10-023
guests	NNS	61-13-036
guests	NNS-HL	1-01-001
guests'	NNS$	2-02-002
Guest	**prop. noun**	**4-01-001**
Guest	NP	3-01-001
Guest	NP-TL	1-01-001
Guevara	**NP**	**1-01-001**
guffaw	**noun**	**1-01-001**
guffaws	NNS	1-01-001
Guggenheim	**NP**	**1-01-001**
Guglielmo	**NP**	**1-01-001**
Guiana	**prop. noun**	**2-02-002**
Guiana	NP	0-00-000
Guiana	NP-TL	2-02-002
guidance	**NN**	**40-10-030**
guide	**noun**	**25-08-021**
guide	NN	17-06-014
guide	NN-HL	1-01-001
guide's	NN$	1-01-001
guides	NNS	5-03-005
guides	NNS-HL	1-01-001
guide	**verb**	**51-14-042**
guide	VB	18-09-017
guides	VBZ	3-03-003
guided	VBD	4-03-003
guided	VBN	16-07-014
guiding	VBG	10-09-010
guidebook	**NN**	**2-02-002**
guideline	**noun**	**1-01-001**
guidelines	NNS	1-01-001
guidepost	**noun**	**9-01-001**
guideposts	NNS	0-00-000
Guideposts	NNS-TL	8-01-001
guideposts'	NNS$	0-00-000
Guideposts'	NNS$-TL	1-01-001
Guignol	**prop. noun**	**1-01-001**
Guignol	NP	0-00-000
Guignol	NP-TL	1-01-001
guild	**noun**	**7-03-005**
guild	NN	3-02-003
Guild	NN-TL	4-01-002
guile	**NN**	**1-01-001**
guileless	**JJ**	**1-01-001**
Guilford	**NP**	**1-01-001**
Guilford-Martin	**prop. noun**	**3-01-001**
Guilford-Martin	NP	2-01-001
Guilford-Martin	NP-HL	1-01-001
Guillaume	**NP**	**1-01-001**
guilt	**NN**	**33-10-021**
guiltiness	**NN**	**1-01-001**
guiltless	**JJ**	**1-01-001**
guilty	**JJ**	**29-12-027**
Guimet	**prop. noun**	**1-01-001**
Guimet	NP	0-00-000
Guimet	NP-TL	1-01-001
guinea	**NN**	**1-01-001**
Guinea	**prop. noun**	**2-02-002**
Guinea	NP	1-01-001
Guinea	NP-TL	1-01-001
guise	**noun**	**7-04-007**
guise	NN	6-03-006
guises	NNS	1-01-001
guitar	**noun**	**22-07-011**
guitar	NN	17-05-009
Guitar	NN-TL	2-02-002
guitars	NNS	3-02-002
guitar-strumming	**JJ**	**1-01-001**
guitarist	**NN**	**2-02-002**
Guizot	**NP**	**1-01-001**
gulf	**noun**	**23-09-016**
gulf	NN	5-05-005
Gulf	NN-TL	16-06-010
Gulf	NN-TL-HL	1-01-001
gulf's	NN$	0-00-000
Gulf's	NN$-TL	1-01-001
gull	**NN**	**1-01-001**
gull	**verb**	**2-01-002**
gulled	VBN	1-01-001
gulling	VBG	1-01-001
Gullah	**NP**	**1-01-001**
gullet	**NN**	**1-01-001**

Word	Tag	Count
gullibility	**NN**	**1-01-001**
gullible	**JJ**	**2-02-002**
Gulliver	**prop. noun**	**1-01-001**
Gulliver's	NP$	1-01-001
gully	**noun**	**7-05-005**
gully	NN	5-03-003
gulley	NN	1-01-001
gullies	NNS	1-01-001
gulp	**noun**	**3-03-003**
gulp	NN	2-02-002
gulps	NNS	1-01-001
gulp	**verb**	**3-03-003**
gulped	VBD	3-03-003
gum	**noun**	**18-05-009**
gum	NN	14-04-007
gums	NNS	4-02-003
gum	**verb**	**1-01-001**
gumming	VBG	1-01-001
gum-chewing	**JJ**	**1-01-001**
gummy	**JJ**	**2-02-002**
gumption	**NN**	**1-01-001**
gun	**noun**	**142-11-047**
gun	NN	99-09-032
Gun	NN-TL	1-01-001
guns	NNS	40-10-022
guns	NNS-HL	1-01-001
Guns	NNS-TL	1-01-001
gun	**verb**	**2-02-002**
gun	VB	1-01-001
gunning	VBG	1-01-001
Gun	**prop. noun**	**18-01-001**
Gun	NP	17-01-001
Gun's	NP$	1-01-001
gun-shot	**NN**	**1-01-001**
gun-slinger	**NN**	**1-01-001**
gun-slinging	**JJ**	**1-01-001**
gunbarrel	**NN**	**1-01-001**
gunfight	**noun**	**1-01-001**
gunfights	NNS	1-01-001
gunfighter	**NN**	**1-01-001**
gunfire	**noun**	**7-04-005**
gunfire	NN	6-03-004
gunfire	NN-HL	1-01-001
gunflint	**NN**	**1-01-001**
gunk	**NN**	**1-01-001**
gunman	**noun**	**7-05-005**
gunman	NN	3-03-003
gunmen	NNS	4-02-002
Gunnar	**NP**	**2-01-001**
gunner	**noun**	**3-03-003**
gunner	NN	1-01-001
gunners	NNS	2-02-002
Gunny	**NP**	**6-01-001**
gunplay	**NN**	**1-01-001**
gunpowder	**NN**	**2-02-002**
gunslinger	**NN**	**1-01-001**
Gunther	**NP**	**1-01-001**
gurgle	**NN**	**1-01-001**
Gurion	**NP**	**2-01-001**
Gurkha	**prop. noun**	**1-01-001**
Gurkhas	NPS	1-01-001
Gurla	**NP**	**1-01-001**
Gursel	**NP**	**3-01-001**
guru	**NN**	**1-01-001**
Gus	**NP**	**3-02-003**
gush	**NN**	**1-01-001**
gush	**verb**	**5-04-005**
gushed	VBD	5-04-005
gusher	**NN**	**1-01-001**
gusset	**noun**	**1-01-001**
gussets	NNS	1-01-001
gust	**noun**	**4-03-004**
gust	NN	1-01-001
gusts	NNS	3-02-003
Gustaf	**NP**	**1-01-001**
Gustav	**NP**	**1-01-001**
Gustave	**NP**	**1-01-001**
Gustavus	**NP**	**1-01-001**
gusto	**NN**	**2-02-002**
gusty	**JJ**	**2-02-002**
gut	**noun**	**10-04-008**
gut	NN	1-01-001
guts	NNS	9-04-007
gut	**verb**	**1-01-001**
gutted	VBD	1-01-001
gut-flattening	**JJ**	**1-01-001**
gute	**FW-JJ**	**2-01-001**
Guthman	**NP**	**1-01-001**
Guthrie	**prop. noun**	**2-02-002**

Word	Tag	Frequency
Guthrie (cont.):		
Guthrie	NP	1-01-001
Guthrie's	NP$	1-01-001
gutter	**noun**	**3-03-003**
gutter	NN	1-01-001
gutters	NNS	2-02-002
gutter	**verb**	**1-01-001**
guttered	VBD	1-01-001
Guttman-type	**JJ**	**1-01-001**
guttural	**JJ**	**3-03-003**
Gutzon	**NP**	**1-01-001**
guy	**noun**	**66-12-036**
guy	NN	42-10-024
Guy	NN-TL	1-01-001
guy's	NN+BEZ	1-01-001
guy's	NN+HVZ	1-01-001
guy's	NN$	1-01-001
guys	NNS	20-08-013
guy	**VB**	**1-01-001**
Guy	**prop. noun**	**7-03-004**
Guy	NP	4-03-004
Guy	NP-TL	3-01-001
guzzle	**verb**	**2-02-002**
guzzle	VB	1-01-001
guzzled	VBD	1-01-001
Gwen	**NP**	**1-01-001**
gym	**noun**	**4-02-003**
gym	NN	2-02-002
gyms	NNS	2-01-001
gymnasium	**noun**	**1-01-001**
gymnasium	NN	0-00-000
Gymnasium	NN-TL	1-01-001
gymnast	**noun**	**5-01-001**
gymnast	NN	1-01-001
gymnasts	NNS	4-01-001
gymnastic	**JJ**	**4-01-001**
gymnastics	**noun**	**11-01-001**
gymnastics	NN	8-01-001
gymnastics	NNS	3-01-001
gynecological	**JJ**	**1-01-001**
gynecologist	**noun**	**3-01-002**
gynecologist	NN	1-01-001
gynecologists	NNS	2-01-001
Gyp	**prop. noun**	**7-01-001**
Gyp	NP	6-01-001
Gyp'll	NP+MD	1-01-001
gypsum	**NN**	**2-01-001**
gypsy	**noun**	**5-04-005**
gypsy	NN	4-04-004
gypsies	NNS	1-01-001
gyration	**noun**	**2-02-002**
gyration	NN	1-01-001
gyrations	NNS	1-01-001
gyro	**noun**	**31-01-001**
gyro	NN	26-01-001
gyros	NNS	5-01-001
gyro-platform-servo	**NN**	**1-01-001**
gyro-stabilized	**JJ**	**6-01-001**
gyrocompass	**noun**	**2-01-001**
gyrocompass	NN	1-01-001
gyrocompass	NN-HL	1-01-001
gyroscope	**noun**	**1-01-001**
gyroscopes	NNS	1-01-001

Word	Tag	Frequency
H	**prop. noun**	**8-04-006**
H	NP	6-04-004
H	NP-HL	2-01-002
H.	**prop. noun**	**71-08-044**
H.	NP	70-08-044
H.	NP-HL	1-01-001
H.L.	**NP**	**1-01-001**
H.M.	**NP**	**2-01-001**
H.M.S.	**NP**	**3-02-002**
H.P.R.	**NP**	**1-01-001**
H.W.	**NP**	**1-01-001**
ha	**UH**	**2-01-001**
Haaek	**NP**	**1-01-001**
Haase	**prop. noun**	**1-01-001**
Haase	NP	0-00-000
Haase	NP-TL	1-01-001
habe	**FW-HV**	**1-01-001**
haberdashery	**noun**	**2-02-002**
haberdashery	NN	1-01-001
haberdasheries	NNS	1-01-001
Habib	**NP**	**1-01-001**
habit	**noun**	**44-11-037**
habit	NN	22-08-019
habit	NN-HL	1-01-001
habits	NNS	21-08-018
habitable	**JJ**	**2-02-002**
habitant	**noun**	**4-01-001**
habitants	NNS	4-01-001
habitat	**noun**	**14-04-004**
habitat	NN	13-04-004
habitat	NN-HL	1-01-001
habitual	**JJ**	**5-05-005**
habitually	**RB**	**2-02-002**
habla	**foreign**	**1-01-001**
habla	FW-VB	0-00-000
Habla	FW-VB	1-01-001
Habsburg	**prop. noun**	**1-01-001**
Habsburg	NP	0-00-000
Habsburg	NP-TL	1-01-001
hack	**NN**	**2-01-002**
hack	**verb**	**4-04-004**
hacked	VBD	1-01-001
hacked	VBN	1-01-001
hacking	VBG	2-02-002
Hack	**NP**	**1-01-001**
hacker	**noun**	**1-01-001**
hackers	NNS	1-01-001
Hackett	**NP**	**1-01-001**
Hackettstown	**NP**	**1-01-001**
hackle	**noun**	**1-01-001**
hackles	NNS	1-01-001
Hackmann	**NP**	**1-01-001**
hackneyed	**JJ**	**2-01-002**
hacksaw	**NN**	**1-01-001**
Hackstaff	**NP**	**1-01-001**
hackwork	**NN**	**1-01-001**
Haddix	**NP**	**2-01-001**
haddock	**NN**	**1-01-001**
Hadrian	**NP**	**1-01-001**
haec	**FW-DTS**	**1-01-001**
Haestier	**NP**	**1-01-001**
Hafiz	**NP**	**2-01-001**
haflis	**FW-NNS**	**1-01-001**
Hagerty	**prop. noun**	**1-01-001**
Hagerty's	NP$	1-01-001
haggard	**JJ**	**2-02-002**
haggardly	**RB**	**1-01-001**
haggle	**NN**	**1-01-001**
haggle	**verb**	**3-02-003**
haggling	VBG	3-02-003
Hagner	**NP**	**1-01-001**
Hague	**NP**	**9-01-001**
Haijac	**prop. noun**	**2-01-001**
Haijac	NP	0-00-000
Haijac	NP-TL	2-01-001
hail	**NN**	**4-03-004**
hail	**verb**	**14-07-013**
hail	VB	1-01-001
Hail	VB-TL	5-03-004
hails	VBZ	1-01-001
hailed	VBD	2-02-002
hailed	VBN	4-04-004
hailed	VBN-HL	1-01-001
hailstorm	**NN**	**1-01-001**
hair	**noun**	**160-13-089**
hair	NN	148-13-083
hairs	NNS	12-06-009
hair-raising	**JJ**	**1-01-001**
hair-trigger	**NN**	**1-01-001**
haircut	**noun**	**3-02-003**
haircut	NN	2-01-002
haircuts	NNS	1-01-001
hairdo	**noun**	**1-01-001**
hairdos	NNS	1-01-001
hairier	**JJR**	**1-01-001**
hairless	**JJ**	**1-01-001**

Word	Tag	Frequency
hairpin	**NN**	**1-01-001**
hairshirt	**NN**	**1-01-001**
hairtonic	**NN**	**1-01-001**
hairy	**JJ**	**5-04-005**
Haitian	**JJ**	**1-01-001**
Hajime	**NP**	**1-01-001**
Hal	**prop. noun**	**29-04-006**
Hal	NP	28-04-006
Hal's	NP$	1-01-001
halcyon	**JJ**	**1-01-001**
Halda	**NP**	**1-01-001**
Hale	**prop. noun**	**3-03-003**
Hale	NP	2-02-002
Hale's	NP$	1-01-001
half	**ABN**	**238-15-157**
half	**noun**	**20-06-012**
half	NN	14-04-009
Half	NN-TL	4-01-001
halves	NNS	2-02-002
half	**QL**	**13-10-013**
half	**RB**	**6-04-004**
half-a-dozen	**NN**	**1-01-001**
half-acceptance	**NN**	**1-01-001**
half-acre	**NN**	**1-01-001**
half-aloud	**RB**	**1-01-001**
half-blood	**JJ**	**1-01-001**
half-bottle	**noun**	**1-01-001**
half-bottles	NNS	1-01-001
half-breed	**NN**	**5-01-002**
half-brother	**noun**	**2-02-002**
half-brother	NN	1-01-001
half-brothers	NNS	1-01-001
half-century	**NN**	**2-01-002**
half-city	**NN**	**1-01-001**
half-clad	**JJ**	**1-01-001**
half-closed	**JJ**	**3-03-003**
half-cocked	**JJ**	**1-01-001**
half-conscious	**JJ**	**2-01-002**
half-crazy	**JJ**	**1-01-001**
half-crocked	**JJ**	**1-01-001**
half-darkness	**NN**	**1-01-001**
half-digested	**JJ**	**1-01-001**
half-dozen	**NN**	**3-03-003**
half-dressed	**JJ**	**1-01-001**
half-drunk	**JJ**	**2-02-002**
half-educated	**JJ**	**1-01-001**
half-expressed	**JJ**	**1-01-001**
half-filled	**JJ**	**2-01-002**
half-forgotten	**JJ**	**1-01-001**
half-gainer	**NN**	**1-01-001**
half-gourd	**NN**	**1-01-001**
half-grown	**JJ**	**1-01-001**
half-hearted	**adjective**	**4-03-004**
half-hearted	JJ	3-02-003
halfhearted	JJ	1-01-001
half-heartedly	**RB**	**1-01-001**
half-hour	**NN**	**8-06-007**
half-inch	**NN**	**3-01-001**
half-intensity	**NN**	**2-01-001**
half-life	**NN**	**1-01-001**
half-light	**NN**	**1-01-001**
half-man	**NN**	**9-01-001**
half-melted	**JJ**	**1-01-001**
half-mile	**NN**	**7-03-005**
half-million	**JJ**	**1-01-001**
half-mincing	**JJ**	**1-01-001**
half-moon	**noun**	**1-01-001**
half-moons	NNS	1-01-001
half-murmured	**JJ**	**1-01-001**
half-off	**RB**	**1-01-001**
half-past	**JJ**	**1-01-001**
half-reach	**verb**	**1-01-001**
half-reached	VBD	1-01-001
half-reluctant	**JJ**	**1-01-001**
half-sister	**NN**	**1-01-001**
half-smile	**NN**	**1-01-001**
half-standard	**JJ**	**1-01-001**
half-starved	**JJ**	**1-01-001**
half-straighten	**verb**	**1-01-001**
half-straightened	VBD	1-01-001
half-swamped	**JJ**	**1-01-001**
half-swimming	**JJ**	**1-01-001**
half-time	**RB**	**1-01-001**
half-transparent	**JJ**	**1-01-001**
half-turned	**JJ**	**1-01-001**
half-understand	**verb**	**1-01-001**
half-understood	VBN	1-01-001
half-witted	**JJ**	**1-01-001**
half-year	**NN**	**1-01-001**
halfback	**noun**	**11-01-003**
halfback	NN	10-01-002
halfbacks	NNS	1-01-001
halftime	**noun**	**2-02-002**
halftime	NN	1-01-001
half-time	NN	1-01-001
halfway	**adjective**	**4-04-004**
halfway	JJ	3-03-003
half-way	JJ	1-01-001
halfway	**qualifier**	**2-02-002**
halfway	QL	1-01-001
half-way	QL	1-01-001
halfway	**adverb**	**16-07-014**
halfway	RB	14-07-012
half-way	RB	2-02-002
halfways	**RB**	**1-01-001**
Haliburton	**NP**	**1-01-001**
halide	**noun**	**1-01-001**
halides	NNS	1-01-001
Halkett	**NP**	**1-01-001**
hall	**noun**	**151-14-070**
hall	NN	106-12-050
hall	NN-HL	1-01-001
Hall	NN-TL	39-11-025
hall's	NN$	1-01-001
halls	NNS	3-03-003
Halls	NNS-TL	1-01-001
Hall	**prop. noun**	**7-05-006**
Hall	NP	6-05-005
Hall's	NP$	1-01-001
Hall-Mills	**NP**	**1-01-001**
Halleck	**NP**	**3-02-002**
hallelujah	**noun**	**1-01-001**
hallelujahs	NNS	1-01-001
Hallelujah	**UH**	**1-01-001**
hallmark	**noun**	**6-05-006**
hallmark	NN	2-02-002
hall-mark	NN	1-01-001
Hallmark	NN-TL	1-01-001
hallmarks	NNS	2-02-002
hallow	**verb**	**2-02-002**
hallowed	VBN	2-02-002
Halloween	**NP**	**2-01-001**
Hallowell	**prop. noun**	**1-01-001**
Hallowell's	NP$	1-01-001
hallucinate	**verb**	**1-01-001**
hallucinating	VBG	1-01-001
hallucination	**noun**	**1-01-001**
hallucinations	NNS	1-01-001
hallway	**noun**	**8-04-008**
hallway	NN	7-04-007
hallways	NNS	1-01-001
Halma	**NP**	**1-01-001**
halo	**noun**	**3-02-002**
halo	NN	2-01-001
halos	NNS	1-01-001
halogen	**noun**	**1-01-001**
halogens	NNS	1-01-001
Hals	**NP**	**2-02-002**
halt	**noun**	**4-04-004**
halt	NN	3-03-003
halts	NNS	1-01-001
halt	**verb**	**21-08-016**
halt	VB	7-07-007
halted	VBD	10-04-008
halted	VBN	2-02-002
halting	VBG	2-02-002
halter	**NN**	**1-01-001**
haltingly	**RB**	**2-02-002**
halvah	**NN**	**1-01-001**
ham	**noun**	**16-04-007**
ham	NN	14-03-006
ham	NN-HL	1-01-001
hams	NNS	1-01-001
Ham	**NP**	**4-02-002**
ham-like	**JJ**	**1-01-001**
ham-radio	**NN**	**1-01-001**
Hambric	**NP**	**1-01-001**
hamburger	**noun**	**10-05-005**
hamburger	NN	5-04-004
hamburger	NN-HL	1-01-001
hamburgers	NNS	4-02-002
Hamey	**NP**	**1-01-001**
Hamilton	**prop. noun**	**20-04-008**
Hamilton	NP	17-04-008
Hamilton's	NP$	3-01-001
Hamilton-oriented	**JJ**	**1-01-001**
Hamiltonian	**JJ**	**1-01-001**
Hamiltonian	**prop. noun**	**1-01-001**

Word	Tag	Frequency
Hamiltonian (cont.):		
Hamiltonians	NPS	1-01-001
hamlet	**NN**	**3-02-003**
Hamlet	**NP**	**4-02-002**
Hamm	**prop. noun**	**8-02-003**
Hamm	NP	7-02-002
Hamm's	NP$	1-01-001
Hammarskjold	**prop. noun**	**21-04-007**
Hammarskjold	NP	16-04-007
Hammarskjold's	NP$	5-02-004
hammer	**NN**	**6-04-004**
hammer	**verb**	**4-03-003**
hammer	VB	1-01-001
hammered	VBD	3-02-002
Hammer	**NP**	**2-01-001**
hammerless	**JJ**	**1-01-001**
Hammett	**prop. noun**	**4-02-002**
Hammett	NP	2-02-002
Hammett's	NP$	2-01-001
hamming	**NN**	**1-01-001**
hammock	**NN**	**5-01-001**
Hammond	**NP**	**2-02-002**
Hammons	**NP**	**1-01-001**
hamper	**NN**	**3-02-002**
hamper	**verb**	**6-05-006**
hamper	VB	2-02-002
hampers	VBZ	1-01-001
hampered	VBN	3-03-003
Hampshire	**prop. noun**	**11-06-009**
Hampshire	NP	1-01-001
Hampshire	NP-TL	10-06-008
Hampton	**prop. noun**	**3-03-003**
Hampton	NP	2-02-002
Hampton's	NP$	1-01-001
Hamrick	**prop. noun**	**10-01-001**
Hamrick	NP	8-01-001
Hamrick's	NP$	2-01-001
Han	**prop. noun**	**9-01-001**
Han	NP	8-01-001
Han	NP-TL	1-01-001
Hanch	**NP**	**5-01-001**
Hancock	**NP**	**1-01-001**
hand	**noun**	**717-15-281**
hand	NN	413-15-215
han'	NN	4-01-001
hande	NN	3-01-001
hand	NN-HL	1-01-001
Hand	NN-TL	7-01-001
hands	NNS	285-15-146
hands	NNS-HL	1-01-001
Hands	NNS-TL	3-02-003
hand	**verb**	**52-11-042**
hand	VB	8-08-008
handed	VBD	25-06-018
handed	VBN	13-06-012
handing	VBG	6-05-006
Hand	**NP**	**2-02-002**
hand-blower	**NN**	**1-01-001**
hand-covered	**JJ**	**1-01-001**
hand-crafted	**JJ**	**1-01-001**
hand-file	**verb**	**1-01-001**
hand-filed	VBN	1-01-001
hand-hewn	**JJ**	**1-01-001**
hand-holding	**NN**	**1-01-001**
hand-in-glove	**JJ**	**1-01-001**
hand-in-glove	**RB**	**1-01-001**
hand-level	**NN**	**1-01-001**
hand-me-down	**JJ**	**1-01-001**
hand-painted	**JJ**	**1-01-001**
hand-screened	**JJ**	**1-01-001**
hand-to-hand	**JJ**	**2-02-002**
hand-woven	**JJ**	**2-02-002**
hand-written	**JJ**	**1-01-001**
handbag	**NN**	**3-03-003**
handbook	**noun**	**3-03-003**
handbook	NN	1-01-001
Handbook	NN-TL	1-01-001
handbooks	NNS	1-01-001
handclasp	**NN**	**3-03-003**
handcuff	**noun**	**2-02-002**
handcuffs	NNS	2-02-002
hander	**NN**	**1-01-001**
handful	**noun**	**14-08-014**
handful	NN	13-08-013
handfuls	NNS	1-01-001
handgun	**noun**	**5-01-001**
handgun	NN	3-01-001
handguns	NNS	1-01-001
handguns	NNS-HL	1-01-001

Word	Tag	Frequency
handhold	**NN**	**1-01-001**
handicap	**noun**	**7-05-007**
handicap	NN	6-05-006
handicaps	NNS	1-01-001
handicap	**verb**	**13-03-005**
handicapped	VBN	9-03-004
handicapped	VBN-HL	1-01-001
Handicapped	VBN-TL	3-02-002
handicraft	**noun**	**1-01-001**
handicrafts	NNS	1-01-001
handicraftsman	**NN**	**1-01-001**
handier	**JJR**	**1-01-001**
handiest	**JJT**	**1-01-001**
handiwork	**NN**	**1-01-001**
handkerchief	**noun**	**10-05-007**
handkerchief	NN	9-04-006
handkerchiefs	NNS	1-01-001
handle	**noun**	**22-08-015**
handle	NN	19-07-012
handles	NNS	3-02-003
handle	**verb**	**81-15-063**
handle	VB	34-13-031
handles	VBZ	6-03-006
handled	VBD	6-05-006
handled	VBN	20-09-017
handling	VBG	13-08-012
handling	VBG-HL	1-01-001
Handling	VBG-TL	1-01-001
handlebar	**noun**	**1-01-001**
handlebars	NNS	1-01-001
handler	**noun**	**9-01-001**
handler	NN	0-00-000
Handler	NN-TL	6-01-001
handlers	NNS	0-00-000
handlers	NNS-HL	1-01-001
Handlers	NNS-TL	1-01-001
handlers'	NNS$	0-00-000
Handlers'	NNS$-TL	1-01-001
handless	**JJ**	**1-01-001**
Handley	**NP**	**16-01-001**
handling	**NN**	**23-05-013**
handmade	**adjective**	**3-03-003**
handmade	JJ	2-02-002
hand-made	JJ	1-01-001
handmaiden	**NN**	**1-01-001**
hands-off	**RB**	**1-01-001**
hands-off-all-sweets	**NN**	**1-01-001**
handshake	**NN**	**1-01-001**
handsome	**JJ**	**40-09-029**
handsomely	**RB**	**1-01-001**
handsomer	**JJR**	**2-02-002**
handsomest	**JJT**	**1-01-001**
handspike	**noun**	**3-01-001**
handspikes	NNS	3-01-001
handstand	**noun**	**4-01-001**
handstand	NN	1-01-001
handstands	NNS	2-01-001
handstands	NNS-HL	1-01-001
handwriting	**NN**	**5-05-005**
handy	**JJ**	**13-08-012**
handyman	**noun**	**3-01-002**
handyman	NN	2-01-001
handymen	NNS	1-01-001
handyman-carpenter	**NN**	**1-01-001**
Haney	**prop. noun**	**21-01-001**
Haney	NP	19-01-001
Haney's	NP$	2-01-001
Hanford	**prop. noun**	**16-01-001**
Hanford	NP	10-01-001
Hanford	NP-TL	6-01-001
hang	**verb**	**131-13-088**
hang	VB	26-11-024
hangs	VBZ	4-03-004
hung	VBD	53-09-044
hanged	VBD	1-01-001
hung	VBN	12-07-011
hanged	VBN	6-04-005
hanging	VBG	27-09-024
hangin'	VBG	2-02-002
hangar	**noun**	**2-02-002**
hangar	NN	1-01-001
hangars	NNS	1-01-001
hanger	**noun**	**1-01-001**
hangers	NNS	1-01-001
hanger-on	**noun**	**1-01-001**
hangers-on	NNS	1-01-001
hanging	**NN**	**1-01-001**
hangman	**noun**	**2-01-002**
hangman	NN	1-01-001

Word	Tag	Frequency
hangman (cont.):		
hangman's	NN$	0-00-000
Hangman's	NN$-TL	1-01-001
hangout	**noun**	**1-01-001**
hangouts	NNS	1-01-001
hangover	**noun**	**3-02-002**
hangover	NN	2-01-001
hangovers	NNS	1-01-001
Hank	**NP**	**17-05-007**
hanker	**verb**	**2-01-001**
hankered	VBD	1-01-001
hankering	VBG	0-00-000
hankerin'	VBG	1-01-001
Hannah	**prop. noun**	**2-01-001**
Hannah	NP	1-01-001
Hannah	NP-TL	1-01-001
Hannibal	**NP**	**1-01-001**
Hanover	**prop. noun**	**78-04-004**
Hanover	NP	75-03-003
Hanover	NP-TL	2-02-002
Hanover's	NP$	1-01-001
Hanoverian	**adjective**	**7-02-003**
Hanoverian	JJ	5-02-003
Hanoverian	JJ-TL	2-01-001
Hans	**prop. noun**	**45-05-008**
Hans	NP	31-04-007
Hans	NP-TL	13-02-002
Hans'	NP$	1-01-001
Hansen	**prop. noun**	**12-03-003**
Hansen	NP	10-02-002
Hansen's	NP$	2-02-002
hansom	**NN**	**1-01-001**
Hanukkah	**NP**	**1-01-001**
Hap	**NP**	**1-01-001**
Hapgood	**NP**	**2-01-001**
haphazard	**JJ**	**2-02-002**
haphazardly	**RB**	**1-01-001**
hapless	**JJ**	**2-01-002**
happen	**verb**	**278-15-165**
happen	VB	63-15-049
happens	VBZ	40-12-037
happened	VBD	86-14-067
happened	VBN	63-15-054
happening	VBG	26-10-022
happening	**noun**	**7-05-007**
happening	NN	2-01-002
happenings	NNS	5-04-005
happenstance	**NN**	**2-02-002**
happier	**JJR**	**11-09-011**
happiest	**JJT**	**3-03-003**
happily	**RB**	**20-10-019**
happiness	**noun**	**23-06-014**
happiness	NN	22-06-013
Happiness	NN-TL	1-01-001
happy	**adjective**	**97-14-065**
happy	JJ	92-14-064
Happy	JJ	1-01-001
happy	JJ-HL	1-01-001
Happy	JJ-TL	3-03-003
Happy	**NP**	**1-01-001**
Haqvin	**NP**	**1-01-001**
harangue	**verb**	**3-03-003**
harangued	VBD	1-01-001
haranguing	VBG	2-02-002
harass	**verb**	**9-07-009**
harass	VB	1-01-001
harassed	VBD	2-02-002
harassed	VBN	4-04-004
harassing	VBG	2-02-002
harassment	**noun**	**1-01-001**
harrassment	NN	0-00-000
harrassment	NN	1-01-001
Harbert	**NP**	**2-01-001**
harbor	**noun**	**38-12-021**
harbor	NN	16-07-011
Harbor	NN-TL	18-06-010
harbors	NNS	1-01-001
Harbors	NNS-TL	1-01-001
harbor's	NN$	0-00-000
Harbor's	NN$-TL	2-01-001
harbor	**verb**	**8-04-008**
harbor	VB	3-01-003
harbors	VBZ	1-01-001
harbored	VBD	1-01-001
harbored	VBN	2-02-002
harboring	VBG	1-01-001
Harburg	**prop. noun**	**3-01-001**
Harburg	NP	2-01-001
Harburg's	NP$	1-01-001

Word	Tag	Frequency
Harcourt	**prop. noun**	**6-02-002**
Harcourt	NP	5-02-002
Harcourt	NP-TL	1-01-001
hard	**adjective**	**140-15-109**
hard	JJ	139-15-109
hard	JJ-HL	1-01-001
hard	**RB**	**61-14-053**
Hard	**prop. noun**	**3-01-001**
Hard	NP	2-01-001
Hard's	NP$	1-01-001
hard-bitten	**JJ**	**1-01-001**
hard-boiled	**adjective**	**4-03-003**
hard-boiled	JJ	2-02-002
hardboiled	JJ	2-01-001
hard-come-by	**JJ**	**1-01-001**
hard-earned	**JJ**	**1-01-001**
hard-fought	**JJ**	**2-02-002**
hard-hearted	**adjective**	**1-01-001**
hard-hearted	JJ	0-00-000
Hard-Hearted	JJ-TL	1-01-001
hard-hit	**JJ**	**1-01-001**
hard-liquor	**NN**	**2-01-001**
hard-nosed	**JJ**	**1-01-001**
hard-sell	**NN**	**1-01-001**
hard-surface	**JJ**	**10-01-001**
hard-to-get	**JJ**	**1-01-001**
hard-to-please	**JJ**	**1-01-001**
hard-won	**JJ**	**1-01-001**
hardbake	**NN**	**1-01-001**
hardboard	**NN**	**1-01-001**
Hardee	**prop. noun**	**1-01-001**
Hardee's	NP$	1-01-001
harden	**verb**	**13-05-008**
harden	VB	1-01-001
hardened	VBD	1-01-001
hardened	VBN	11-05-007
hardener	**NN**	**1-01-001**
harder	**JJR**	**9-05-009**
harder	**RBR**	**14-08-012**
hardest	**JJT**	**9-06-008**
hardest	**RBT**	**2-02-002**
Harding	**prop. noun**	**3-02-002**
Harding	NP	2-02-002
Hardings	NPS	1-01-001
hardly	**QL**	**13-07-013**
hardly	**RB**	**93-14-079**
hardness	**NN**	**2-02-002**
Hardscrabble	**NP**	**1-01-001**
Hardshell	**NP**	**1-01-001**
hardship	**noun**	**14-07-013**
hardship	NN	9-05-008
hardships	NNS	5-03-005
hardtack	**NN**	**3-01-001**
hardtack-box	**NN**	**1-01-001**
hardware	**noun**	**11-08-010**
hardware	NN	10-07-009
Hardware	NN-TL	1-01-001
Hardwick	**NP**	**3-02-002**
Hardwicke	**NP**	**1-01-001**
Hardwicke-Etter	**prop. noun**	**2-01-001**
Hardwicke-Etter	NP	1-01-001
Hardwicke-Etter	NP-TL	1-01-001
hardwood	**noun**	**1-01-001**
hardwoods	NNS	1-01-001
hardworking	**JJ**	**1-01-001**
hardy	**JJ**	**6-05-005**
Hardy	**prop. noun**	**51-03-004**
Hardy	NP	36-03-004
Hardy's	NP$	15-01-001
hare	**NN**	**1-01-001**
harelip	**noun**	**1-01-001**
harelips	NNS	1-01-001
harem	**NN**	**2-02-002**
Harford	**prop. noun**	**1-01-001**
Harford	NP	0-00-000
Harford	NP-TL	1-01-001
Hargett	**NP**	**1-01-001**
hark	**verb**	**3-01-002**
hark	VB	0-00-000
Hark	VB-TL	3-01-002
Harlan	**NP**	**1-01-001**
Harlan-Marcia	**NP**	**1-01-001**
Harlem	**prop. noun**	**15-02-003**
Harlem	NP	10-02-002
Harlem	NP-HL	1-01-001
Harlem	NP-TL	3-01-001
Harlem's	NP$	1-01-001
Harley	**prop. noun**	**1-01-001**
Harley's	NP$	1-01-001

Word	Tag	Frequency
Harlingen	**NP**	**1-01-001**
harm	**NN**	**24-13-023**
harm	**verb**	**3-03-003**
harm	VB	1-01-001
harmed	VBN	2-02-002
harmful	**adjective**	**4-02-004**
harmful	JJ	3-02-003
harmful	JJ-HL	1-01-001
harmless	**JJ**	**5-04-005**
harmlessly	**RB**	**1-01-001**
Harmon	**NP**	**1-01-001**
harmonic	**JJ**	**2-02-002**
harmonious	**JJ**	**5-03-005**
harmoniously	**RB**	**1-01-001**
harmonization	**NN**	**1-01-001**
harmony	**noun**	**32-09-019**
harmony	NN	22-08-014
harmony	NN-HL	1-01-001
Harmony	NN-TL	2-02-002
harmonies	NNS	7-05-005
Harmony	**prop. noun**	**9-01-001**
Harmony	NP	8-01-001
Harmony's	NP$	1-01-001
Harnack	**NP**	**1-01-001**
harness	**NN**	**10-04-007**
harness	**verb**	**3-03-003**
harnessed	VBN	2-02-002
harnessing	VBG	1-01-001
Harnick	**NP**	**1-01-001**
Harold	**NP**	**32-06-012**
harp	**NN**	**1-01-001**
harp	**verb**	**1-01-001**
harping	VBG	1-01-001
Harper	**prop. noun**	**10-05-005**
Harper	NP	2-01-001
Harper's	NP$	0-00-000
Harper's	NP$-TL	5-01-001
Harpers	NP$-TL	3-02-002
harping	**NN**	**2-01-001**
harpsichord	**NN**	**1-01-001**
harpsichordist	**NN**	**1-01-001**
harpy	**JJ**	**1-01-001**
Harriet	**prop. noun**	**10-04-005**
Harriet	NP	9-04-005
Harriet's	NP$	1-01-001
Harriman	**NP**	**2-02-002**
Harrington	**prop. noun**	**8-01-002**
Harrington	NP	7-01-002
Harrington's	NP$	1-01-001
Harris	**prop. noun**	**31-09-018**
Harris	NP	24-08-015
Harris	NP-HL	1-01-001
Harris	NP-TL	3-02-003
Harris's	NP$	2-02-002
Harris'	NP$	1-01-001
Harrison	**prop. noun**	**3-03-003**
Harrison	NP	2-02-002
Harrison's	NP$	1-01-001
Harrity	**NP**	**1-01-001**
harro	**UH**	**1-01-001**
harrow	**verb**	**2-02-002**
harrowed	VBN	1-01-001
harrowing	VBG	1-01-001
Harrow	**prop. noun**	**3-01-001**
Harrow	NP	2-01-001
Harrows	NPS	1-01-001
harrowing	**JJ**	**1-01-001**
harrumphing	**NN**	**1-01-001**
harry	**verb**	**2-02-002**
harried	VBD	1-01-001
Harry	**prop. noun**	**35-07-017**
Harry	NP	34-06-016
Harry's	NP$	0-00-000
Harry's	NP$-TL	1-01-001
harsh	**JJ**	**12-07-012**
harshen	**verb**	**1-01-001**
harshened	VBD	1-01-001
harsher	**JJR**	**1-01-001**
harshly	**RB**	**5-03-005**
harshness	**NN**	**1-01-001**
Hart	**NP**	**13-04-005**
Hartford	**prop. noun**	**3-02-003**
Hartford	NP	1-01-001
Hartford	NP-TL	2-02-002
Hartley	**NP**	**1-01-001**
Hartlib	**NP**	**1-01-001**
Hartman	**prop. noun**	**5-02-002**
Hartman	NP	4-02-002

Word	Tag	Frequency
Hartman (cont.):		
Hartman	NP-HL	1-01-001
Hartselle	**NP**	**1-01-001**
Hartsfield	**NP**	**5-01-001**
Hartweger	**NP**	**5-01-001**
Hartwell	**NP**	**1-01-001**
Haruo	**NP**	**1-01-001**
Harvard	**prop. noun**	**35-08-018**
Harvard	NP	21-06-010
Harvard	NP-TL	13-07-009
Harvard's	NP$	1-01-001
Harve	**NP**	**1-01-001**
harvest	**noun**	**12-07-011**
harvest	NN	8-05-007
Harvest	NN-TL	2-02-002
harvests	NNS	2-02-002
harvest	**verb**	**5-04-005**
harvest	VB	2-02-002
harvested	VBN	1-01-001
harvesting	VBG	2-02-002
Harvester	**prop. noun**	**3-02-002**
Harvester	NP	0-00-000
Harvester	NP-TL	3-02-002
harvesting	**NN**	**1-01-001**
Harvey	**prop. noun**	**19-04-006**
Harvey	NP	8-03-005
Harvey	NP-HL	2-02-002
Harvey	NP-TL	8-01-001
Harveys	NPS	1-01-001
Harvie	**NP**	**3-01-001**
hash	**NN**	**1-01-001**
hasher	**NN**	**1-01-001**
Haskell	**NP**	**2-01-001**
Haskins	**NP**	**1-01-001**
hasp	**noun**	**1-01-001**
hasps	NNS	1-01-001
Hasseltine	**NP**	**2-01-001**
haste	**NN**	**9-06-007**
hasten	**verb**	**14-08-013**
hasten	VB	3-03-003
hastened	VBD	6-05-005
hastened	VBN	3-01-003
hastening	VBG	2-02-002
hastily	**RB**	**15-07-013**
hastily-summoned	**JJ**	**1-01-001**
Hastings	**NP**	**1-01-001**
hasty	**JJ**	**5-05-005**
hat	**noun**	**71-11-043**
hat	NN	54-11-036
hat	NN-HL	1-01-001
Hat	NN-TL	1-01-001
hats	NNS	14-08-013
hattes	NNS	1-01-001
hatch	**NN**	**4-03-003**
hatch	**verb**	**7-04-007**
hatch	VB	1-01-001
hatched	VBD	1-01-001
hatched	VBN	1-01-001
hatching	VBG	3-03-003
Hatching	VBG-TL	1-01-001
hatchet	**NN**	**4-02-003**
hatchet-faced	**JJ**	**1-01-001**
hatching	**NN**	**2-02-002**
hatchway	**NN**	**2-01-001**
hate	**noun**	**10-06-009**
hate	NN	9-06-008
hates	NNS	1-01-001
hate	**verb**	**66-11-041**
hate	VB	33-10-022
hates	VBZ	3-02-003
hated	VBD	18-07-016
hated	VBN	10-06-008
hating	VBG	2-02-002
hateful	**JJ**	**3-02-003**
Hatfield	**NP**	**2-01-001**
Hathaway	**NP**	**2-02-002**
hatless	**JJ**	**1-01-001**
hatred	**NN**	**20-08-017**
hatted	**JJ**	**1-01-001**
hatter	**noun**	**1-01-001**
hatters	NNS	0-00-000
Hatters	NNS-TL	1-01-001
Hatteras	**prop. noun**	**1-01-001**
Hatteras	NP	0-00-000
Hatteras	NP-TL	1-01-001
Hattie	**NP**	**1-01-001**
Hattiesburg	**NP**	**1-01-001**
haughtily	**RB**	**1-01-001**
haughtiness	**NN**	**1-01-001**

Word	Tag	Frequency
Haughton	**prop. noun**	**1-01-001**
Haughton's	NP$	1-01-001
haughty	**JJ**	**2-02-002**
haul	**noun**	**3-03-003**
haul	NN	2-02-002
hauls	NNS	1-01-001
haul	**verb**	**17-09-014**
haul	VB	3-02-003
hauls	VBZ	1-01-001
hauled	VBD	3-02-003
hauled	VBN	6-05-006
hauling	VBG	4-03-004
haulage	**NN**	**1-01-001**
Haumd	**prop. noun**	**2-01-001**
Haumd	NP	1-01-001
Haumd's	NP$	1-01-001
haunch	**noun**	**5-04-005**
haunches	NNS	5-04-005
haunt	**noun**	**3-03-003**
haunt	NN	2-02-002
haunts	NNS	1-01-001
haunt	**verb**	**13-06-012**
haunt	VB	2-02-002
haunts	VBZ	1-01-001
haunted	VBD	2-02-002
haunted	VBN	6-05-006
haunting	VBG	2-01-001
haunting	**JJ**	**6-05-006**
Haupts	**prop. noun**	**1-01-001**
Haupts'	NP$	1-01-001
Hausman	**prop. noun**	**2-01-001**
Hausman	NP	1-01-001
Hausman's	NP$	1-01-001
haute	**FW-JJ**	**2-02-002**
Havana	**prop. noun**	**15-03-005**
Havana	NP	13-03-005
Havana	NP-HL	1-01-001
Havana	NP-TL	1-01-001
have	**verb**	**12458-15-500**
have	HV	3925-15-497
hast	HV	1-01-001
hev	HV	1-01-001
o'	HV	1-01-001
have	HV-NC	11-01-001
have	HV-HL	3-02-002
Have	HV-TL	3-01-002
haven't	HV*	38-08-027
ain't	HV*	4-03-004
hafta	HV+TO	3-02-002
've	+HV	244-13-109
've	+HV-TL	1-01-001
coulda	+HV	1-01-001
musta	+HV	1-01-001
shouldda	+HV	1-01-001
woulda	+HV	1-01-001
has	HVZ	2430-15-408
hath	HVZ	3-03-003
has	HVZ-NC	2-01-001
Has	HVZ-TL	4-02-003
hasn't	HVZ*	20-11-014
ain't	HVZ*	2-02-002
's	+HVZ	63-10-046
's	+HVZ-NC	1-01-001
's	+HVZ-TL	1-01-001
had	HVD	4885-15-415
had	HVD-HL	1-01-001
hadn't	HVD*	99-07-057
'd	+HVD	176-09-047
had	HVN	248-15-168
hadd	HVN	1-01-001
having	HVG	279-15-189
hevin	HVG	3-01-001
having	HVG-HL	1-01-001
haven	**noun**	**12-05-011**
haven	NN	5-03-005
Haven	NN-TL	6-03-005
havens	NNS	1-01-001
Haverfield	**NP**	**2-01-001**
Haverhill	**NP**	**2-02-002**
Havilland	**NP**	**1-01-001**
Havisham	**prop. noun**	**4-01-001**
Havisham	NP	3-01-001
Havisham's	NP$	1-01-001
havoc	**NN**	**3-03-003**
haw	**UH**	**1-01-001**
Hawaii	**prop. noun**	**16-03-005**
Hawaii	NP	15-03-005
Hawaii	NP-HL	1-01-001
Hawaiian	**adjective**	**6-03-003**
Hawaiian (cont.):		
Hawaiian	JJ	3-03-003
Hawaiian	JJ-TL	3-01-001
Hawaiian-American	**prop. noun**	**1-01-001**
Hawaiian-Americans	NPS	1-01-001
hawing	**NN**	**1-01-001**
hawk	**NN**	**7-03-003**
hawk	**verb**	**2-02-002**
hawks	VBZ	1-01-001
hawked	VBN	1-01-001
Hawk	**NP**	**7-02-002**
hawk-faced	**JJ**	**1-01-001**
hawker	**noun**	**2-02-002**
hawker	NN	1-01-001
hawkers	NNS	1-01-001
Hawkins	**prop. noun**	**4-03-004**
Hawkins	NP	2-02-002
Hawkins'	NP$	1-01-001
Hawkinses	NPS	1-01-001
Hawksley	**NP**	**10-01-001**
Hawksworth	**NP**	**1-01-001**
Hawthorne	**prop. noun**	**6-04-006**
Hawthorne	NP	5-04-005
Hawthorne	NP-TL	1-01-001
hay	**NN**	**19-05-011**
hay	**verb**	**1-01-001**
haying	VBG	1-01-001
hay-shaker	**noun**	**2-01-001**
hay-shakers	NNS	2-01-001
hay-wagon	**NN**	**1-01-001**
Haydn	**prop. noun**	**3-02-003**
Haydn	NP	2-02-002
Haydn's	NP$	1-01-001
Haydon	**NP**	**1-01-001**
Hayek	**NP**	**1-01-001**
Hayes	**NP**	**5-02-004**
hayfield	**noun**	**1-01-001**
hayfields	NNS	1-01-001
Haynes	**NP**	**1-01-001**
Hays	**prop. noun**	**6-02-003**
Hays	NP	4-02-002
Hays	NP-HL	2-01-001
haystack	**noun**	**2-02-002**
haystack	NN	1-01-001
haystacks	NNS	1-01-001
Hayter	**NP**	**1-01-001**
Hayward	**NP**	**1-01-001**
Haywood	**NP**	**1-01-001**
hazard	**noun**	**20-08-015**
hazard	NN	10-05-009
hazards	NNS	10-07-008
hazard	**VB**	**1-01-001**
Hazard	**NP**	**1-01-001**
hazardous	**JJ**	**5-03-004**
haze	**NN**	**7-04-005**
haze	**verb**	**1-01-001**
hazes	VBZ	1-01-001
hazel	**noun**	**2-02-002**
hazel	NN	1-01-001
Hazel	NN-TL	1-01-001
hazelnut	**noun**	**1-01-001**
hazelnuts	NNS	1-01-001
Hazlitt	**NP**	**2-02-002**
hazy	**JJ**	**5-03-005**
he	**pers. pro.**	**19427-15-451**
he	PPS	9500-15-426
He	PPS	42-06-013
he	PPS-NC	3-02-002
he	PPS-HL	1-01-001
He	PPS-TL	1-01-001
he'd	PPS+HVD	50-05-023
he'd	PPS+MD	48-07-029
he'll	PPS+MD	30-09-019
he's	PPS+BEZ	99-11-058
he's	PPS+BEZ-NC	2-01-001
he's	PPS+HVZ	24-08-020
him	PPO	2572-15-349
'im	PPO	6-01-001
Him	PPO	42-04-009
hym	PPO	2-01-001
him	PPO-NC	4-01-001
Him	PPO-TL	1-01-001
'hi-im	+PPO	1-01-001
his	PP$	6891-15-434
His	PP$	55-07-016
hys	PP$	5-01-001
his	PP$-NC	8-01-001
His	PP$-TL	1-01-001
his	PP$-TL	2-01-001

Word	Tag	Frequency
he (cont.):		
his	PP$$	37-12-027
head	**JJS**	**4-02-003**
head	**noun**	**449-15-195**
head	NN	403-15-182
heade	NN	1-01-001
Head	NN-TL	2-02-002
Head	NN-TL-HL	1-01-001
heads	NNS	41-14-032
head	NNS	1-01-001
head	**verb**	**87-14-060**
head	VB	13-06-013
heads	VBZ	2-02-002
headed	VBD	23-09-019
headed	VBN	36-12-026
heading	VBG	11-06-011
heading	VBG-HL	2-01-001
head-and-shoulders	**QL**	**1-01-001**
head-cold	**NN**	**1-01-001**
head-in-the-clouds	**JJ**	**1-01-001**
head-on	**RB**	**2-02-002**
head-tossing	**NN**	**2-02-002**
headache	**noun**	**11-06-009**
headache	NN	5-04-005
headaches	NNS	6-03-005
headboard	**NN**	**1-01-001**
headdress	**NN**	**1-01-001**
header	**NN**	**1-01-001**
heading	**noun**	**19-03-005**
heading	NN	18-03-004
headings	NNS	1-01-001
headland	**noun**	**2-02-002**
headland	NN	1-01-001
headlands	NNS	1-01-001
headless	**JJ**	**3-02-003**
headlight	**noun**	**8-04-007**
headlights	NNS	8-04-007
headline	**noun**	**11-07-010**
headline	NN	4-03-004
headlines	NNS	7-05-006
headline	**verb**	**1-01-001**
headlining	VBG	1-01-001
headlinese	**NN**	**1-01-001**
headmaster	**NN**	**3-03-003**
headquarters	**noun**	**66-12-041**
headquarters	NN	38-08-023
headquarter	NN	1-01-001
Headquarters	NN-TL	5-03-004
headquarters	NNS	22-08-015
headroom	**NN**	**1-01-001**
headsman	**NN**	**1-01-001**
headstand	**noun**	**2-01-001**
headstand	NN	1-01-001
headstands	NNS	1-01-001
headstone	**noun**	**1-01-001**
headstones	NNS	1-01-001
headwall	**noun**	**2-01-001**
headwalls	NNS	2-01-001
headwater	**noun**	**4-03-003**
headwaters	NNS	4-03-003
heady	**JJ**	**2-02-002**
heal	**verb**	**11-07-007**
heal	VB	2-02-002
healed	VBD	3-02-002
healed	VBN	3-03-003
healing	VBG	3-03-003
healer	**NN**	**2-02-002**
healing	**NN**	**3-02-003**
health	**noun**	**105-12-066**
health	NN	88-12-055
health	NN-HL	1-01-001
Health	NN-TL	16-07-015
healthful	**JJ**	**3-02-003**
healthier	**comp. adj.**	**2-01-002**
healthier	JJR	1-01-001
healthier	JJR-HL	1-01-001
healthiest	**JJT**	**1-01-001**
healthily	**RB**	**2-02-002**
healthy	**JJ**	**33-09-021**
heap	**noun**	**15-07-013**
heap	NN	14-07-012
heaps	NNS	1-01-001
heap	**verb**	**4-03-004**
heaped	VBD	1-01-001
heaped	VBN	3-02-003
hear	**verb**	**433-15-202**
hear	VB	153-14-110
heare	VB	2-01-001
hears	VBZ	7-06-007
hear (cont.):		
hearest	VBZ	1-01-001
heard	VBD	129-12-083
heard	VBN	112-15-087
yeard	VBN	1-01-001
hearing	VBG	28-10-025
Heard	**NP**	**7-01-001**
hearer	**noun**	**4-03-004**
hearer	NN	2-02-002
hearers	NNS	2-02-002
hearing	**noun**	**56-09-022**
hearing	NN	47-09-018
hearing	NN-HL	1-01-001
hearings	NNS	8-04-006
hearing-aid	**NN**	**1-01-001**
Hearn	**NP**	**1-01-001**
hearsay	**noun**	**2-02-002**
hearsay	NN	1-01-001
hearsay	NN-HL	1-01-001
hearse	**NN**	**1-01-001**
Hearst	**prop. noun**	**54-01-002**
Hearst	NP	45-01-002
Hearst	NP-HL	1-01-001
Hearst	NP-TL	2-01-002
Hearst's	NP$	6-01-002
heart	**noun**	**199-15-111**
heart	NN	171-15-096
Heart	NN-TL	2-02-002
heart's	NN$	1-01-001
hearts	NNS	21-10-019
hartes	NNS	2-01-001
Hearts	NNS-TL	2-01-001
heart-measuring	**adjective**	**1-01-001**
heart-measuring	JJ	0-00-000
heart-measuring	JJ-HL	1-01-001
heart-stopping	**JJ**	**1-01-001**
heart-warming	**JJ**	**1-01-001**
heartbeat	**NN**	**4-02-002**
heartbreak	**NN**	**1-01-001**
heartbreaking	**JJ**	**2-02-002**
heartening	**JJ**	**4-04-004**
heartfelt	**JJ**	**1-01-001**
hearth	**NN**	**4-02-003**
heartiest	**JJT**	**1-01-001**
heartily	**RB**	**9-07-009**
heartless	**JJ**	**1-01-001**
hearty	**JJ**	**4-04-004**
heat	**noun**	**93-13-045**
heat	NN	89-13-043
heat	NN-HL	1-01-001
Heat	NN-TL	2-01-002
heat's	NN+BEZ	1-01-001
heat	**verb**	**38-09-020**
heat	VB	5-02-004
heated	VBN	16-08-015
heating	VBG	17-05-007
heat-absorbing	**JJ**	**1-01-001**
heat-denatured	**JJ**	**1-01-001**
heat-processing	**JJ**	**1-01-001**
heatedly	**RB**	**1-01-001**
heater	**noun**	**15-08-010**
heater	NN	14-07-009
heaters	NNS	1-01-001
heathen	**JJ**	**2-02-002**
heathenish	**JJ**	**1-01-001**
heather	**noun**	**2-02-002**
heather	NN	1-01-001
Heather	NN-TL	1-01-001
heating	**NN**	**7-02-004**
Heatwole	**NP**	**1-01-001**
heave	**NN**	**1-01-001**
heave	**verb**	**10-06-010**
heave	VB	1-01-001
heaves	VBZ	1-01-001
heaved	VBD	4-04-004
hove	VBD	1-01-001
heaving	VBG	3-03-003
heaven	**noun**	**53-12-040**
heaven	NN	26-08-020
Heaven	NN-TL	17-10-014
heavens	NNS	9-06-007
heaven's	NN$	0-00-000
Heaven's	NN$-TL	1-01-001
heavenly	**adjective**	**9-05-006**
heavenly	JJ	6-02-003
Heavenly	JJ	1-01-001
Heavenly	JJ-TL	2-02-002
heavenward	**JJ**	**1-01-001**
heaver	**noun**	**2-01-001**

heaver (cont.):

heavers	NNS	2-01-001
heavier	**JJR**	**14-08-012**
heavier	**RBR**	**1-01-001**
heaviest	**JJT**	**2-02-002**
heavily	**QL**	**7-04-007**
heavily	**RB**	**53-13-048**
heavily-upholstered	**JJ**	**1-01-001**
heaviness	**NN**	**2-02-002**
heaving	**NN**	**1-01-001**
heavy	**adjective**	**110-13-086**
heavy	JJ	108-13-084
heavy	JJ-HL	1-01-001
Heavy	JJ-TL	1-01-001
heavy-armed	**JJ**	**1-01-001**
heavy-coated	**JJ**	**1-01-001**
heavy-duty	**NN**	**1-01-001**
heavy-electrical-goods	**NNS**	**2-01-001**
heavy-faced	**JJ**	**1-01-001**
heavy-framed	**JJ**	**1-01-001**
heavy-handed	**JJ**	**1-01-001**
heavy-weight	**NN**	**1-01-001**
hebephrenic	**JJ**	**7-01-001**
Hebraic	**JJ**	**1-01-001**
Hebrew	**adjective**	**3-01-001**
Hebrew	JJ	1-01-001
Hebrew	JJ-TL	2-01-001
Hebrew	**prop. noun**	**8-05-007**
Hebrew	NP	7-05-006
Hebrews	NPS	0-00-000
Hebrews	NPS-TL	1-01-001
hecatomb	**NN**	**1-01-001**
heck	**NN**	**1-01-001**
Heckman	**NP**	**1-01-001**
hectic	**JJ**	**3-03-003**
Hector	**prop. noun**	**2-02-002**
Hector	NP	1-01-001
Hector's	NP$	0-00-000
Hector's	NP$-TL	1-01-001
Hedda	**NP**	**1-01-001**
hedge	**noun**	**4-03-003**
hedge	NN	2-01-001
hedges	NNS	2-02-002
hedge	**verb**	**1-01-001**
hedged	VBN	1-01-001
Hedison	**NP**	**2-01-001**
hedonism	**NN**	**1-01-001**
hedonistic	**JJ**	**2-01-001**
Hee	**NP**	**1-01-001**
heed	**NN**	**1-01-001**
heed	**verb**	**8-06-008**
heed	VB	7-05-007
heeded	VBD	1-01-001
heedless	**JJ**	**2-02-002**
heel	**noun**	**41-10-023**
heel	NN	9-07-008
Heel	NN-TL	9-01-001
heels	NNS	22-08-015
Heels	NNS-TL	1-01-001
heeler	**noun**	**1-01-001**
heelers	NNS	1-01-001
Heenan	**NP**	**1-01-001**
Heffer	**prop. noun**	**1-01-001**
Heffer	NP	0-00-000
Heffer	NP-TL	1-01-001
Heffernan	**NP**	**1-01-001**
heft	**verb**	**1-01-001**
hefted	VBD	1-01-001
hefty	**JJ**	**1-01-001**
Hegel	**prop. noun**	**3-03-003**
Hegel	NP	2-02-002
Hegel's	NP$	1-01-001
Hegelian	**JJ**	**3-01-001**
hegemony	**NN**	**1-01-001**
Heidegger	**prop. noun**	**3-02-002**
Heidegger	NP	1-01-001
Heidegger's	NP$	2-01-001
Heidelberg	**NP**	**1-01-001**
Heideman	**NP**	**1-01-001**
Heidenstam	**prop. noun**	**9-01-001**
Heidenstam	NP	6-01-001
Heidenstam's	NP$	3-01-001
heigh-ho	**UH**	**1-01-001**
height	**noun**	**58-13-041**
height	NN	35-13-028
heights	NNS	12-08-010
Heights	NNS-TL	11-05-005
height-to-diameter	**JJ**	**1-01-001**
heighten	**verb**	**8-05-008**

heighten (cont.):

heighten	VB	1-01-001
heightened	VBD	1-01-001
heightened	VBN	5-04-005
heightening	VBG	1-01-001
heightening	**NN**	**1-01-001**
Heilman	**prop. noun**	**2-01-001**
Heilman	NP	1-01-001
Heilman	NP-TL	1-01-001
Heine	**NP**	**1-01-001**
Heinkel	**NP**	**2-01-001**
Heinze	**prop. noun**	**2-02-002**
Heinze	NP	1-01-001
Heinzes	NPS	1-01-001
heir	**noun**	**9-06-009**
heir	NN	7-05-007
heirs	NNS	2-02-002
heiress	**NN**	**1-01-001**
Heiser	**NP**	**7-01-001**
heist	**verb**	**1-01-001**
heisted	VBD	1-01-001
Heitschmidt	**NP**	**1-01-001**
Helen	**prop. noun**	**14-05-011**
Helen	NP	12-05-010
Helen	NP-TL	2-02-002
Helena	**NP**	**1-01-001**
Helene	**NP**	**1-01-001**
helicopter	**NN**	**1-01-001**
helicopter-borne	**JJ**	**1-01-001**
heliocentric	**JJ**	**1-01-001**
Helion	**prop. noun**	**20-01-001**
Helion	NP	18-01-001
Helion's	NP$	2-01-001
Heliopolis	**NP**	**2-01-001**
heliotrope	**NN**	**1-01-001**
helium	**NN**	**15-03-003**
helium-4	**NN**	**2-01-001**
hell	**noun**	**86-11-049**
hell	NN	78-11-042
hel	NN	1-01-001
Hell	NN-TL	3-02-003
hell's	NN+BEZ	1-01-001
hell's	NN$	2-02-002
hells	NNS	1-01-001
hell	**exclam.**	**14-05-013**
hell	UH	13-05-012
Hell	UH	1-01-001
hell-bound	**JJ**	**1-01-001**
hell-fire	**noun**	**3-02-003**
hell-fire	NN	1-01-001
hellfire	NN	1-01-001
Hellfire	NN-TL	1-01-001
hell-for-leather	**RB**	**1-01-001**
hell-raising	**NN**	**1-01-001**
Hellenic	**JJ**	**6-02-003**
hellion	**noun**	**1-01-001**
hellion	NN	0-00-000
helion	NN	1-01-001
hello	**exclam.**	**11-08-011**
hello	UH	9-07-009
'ello	UH	1-01-001
hello	UH-NC	1-01-001
helluva	**JJ**	**1-01-001**
helm	**NN**	**3-01-003**
Helm	**NP**	**1-01-001**
helmet	**noun**	**3-03-003**
helmet	NN	1-01-001
helmets	NNS	2-02-002
helmsman	**NN**	**1-01-001**
Helmut	**NP**	**1-01-001**
help	**noun**	**99-15-074**
help	NN	93-15-071
help	NN-HL	3-02-003
helps	NNS	2-02-002
Helps	NNS-TL	1-01-001
help	**UH**	**1-01-001**
help	**verb**	**352-15-193**
help	VB	211-15-143
help	VB-HL	3-03-003
helps	VBZ	27-10-021
helps	VBZ-HL	1-01-001
helped	VBD	40-12-031
helped	VBN	26-11-026
helping	VBG	43-11-031
helping	VBG-HL	1-01-001
helper	**noun**	**8-04-005**
helper	NN	6-03-004
helpers	NNS	2-01-001
helpful	**adjective**	**29-11-026**

helpful (cont.):		
helpful	JJ	28-11-026
helpful	JJ-HL	1-01-001
helpfully	**RB**	**4-03-003**
helpfulness	**NN**	**1-01-001**
helpless	**JJ**	**21-10-015**
helplessly	**RB**	**3-03-003**
helplessness	**NN**	**5-03-003**
helpmate	**NN**	**1-01-001**
helsq'iyokom	**FW-NN**	**1-01-001**
Helva	**prop. noun**	**34-01-001**
Helva	NP	26-01-001
Helva's	NP$	8-01-001
hem	**NN**	**4-03-004**
hem	**verb**	**4-03-004**
hemmed	VBN	3-02-003
hemming	VBG	1-01-001
Hemenway	**prop. noun**	**1-01-001**
Hemenway's	NP$	1-01-001
Hemingway	**prop. noun**	**3-01-002**
Hemingway	NP	2-01-002
Hemingway's	NP$	1-01-001
hemisphere	**noun**	**15-05-008**
hemisphere	NN	10-05-007
Hemisphere	NN-TL	4-02-003
hemisphere's	NN$	1-01-001
hemispherical	**JJ**	**1-01-001**
hemlock	**noun**	**1-01-001**
hemlocks	NNS	1-01-001
hemoglobin	**NN**	**4-01-001**
hemolytic	**JJ**	**1-01-001**
hemorrhage	**noun**	**6-03-003**
hemorrhage	NN	5-03-003
hemorrhages	NNS	1-01-001
hemorrhage	**verb**	**2-01-001**
hemorrhaging	VBG	2-01-001
hemorrhoid	**noun**	**1-01-001**
hemorrhoids	NNS	1-01-001
hemosiderin	**NN**	**2-01-001**
Hempel	**NP**	**2-01-001**
Hemphill	**NP**	**8-01-001**
Hempstead	**NP**	**3-02-002**
Hemus	**NP**	**5-01-001**
hen	**noun**	**27-06-009**
hen	NN	21-05-007
hen's	NN$	1-01-001
hens	NNS	4-03-003
hens'	NNS$	1-01-001
hence	**RB**	**58-08-039**
henceforth	**RB**	**4-03-004**
henchman	**noun**	**3-02-002**
henchman	NN	1-01-001
henchmen	NNS	2-02-002
Henderson	**NP**	**3-02-002**
Hendl	**NP**	**3-01-001**
Hendricks	**prop. noun**	**3-01-001**
Hendricks	NP	2-01-001
Hendricks'	NP$	1-01-001
Hendrik	**NP**	**1-01-001**
Hendry	**NP**	**1-01-001**
Heng-Shan	**NP**	**1-01-001**
Hengesbach	**NP**	**9-01-001**
henh	**UH**	**1-01-001**
Henley	**prop. noun**	**2-01-001**
Henley's	NP$	2-01-001
henpeck	**verb**	**1-01-001**
henpecked	VBN	1-01-001
Henri	**prop. noun**	**18-05-005**
Henri	NP	16-05-005
Henri's	NP$	2-01-001
Henrietta	**prop. noun**	**43-02-002**
Henrietta	NP	41-02-002
Henrietta's	NP$	2-01-001
Henrik	**NP**	**1-01-001**
Henry	**prop. noun**	**85-10-052**
Henry	NP	80-10-050
Henry	NP-TL	3-02-003
Henry's	NP$	2-02-002
Heorot	**NP**	**1-01-001**
hepatitis	**NN**	**3-01-001**
Hephzibah	**prop. noun**	**1-01-001**
Hephzibah	NP	0-00-000
Hephzibah	NP-TL	1-01-001
Hepker	**NP**	**1-01-001**
heptachlor	**NN**	**1-01-001**
Heraclitus	**NP**	**1-01-001**
herald	**noun**	**11-07-008**
herald	NN	0-00-000
Herald	NN-TL	11-07-008
herald	**verb**	**2-02-002**
heralded	VBD	1-01-001
heralded	VBN	1-01-001
Herald-Examiner	**NP**	**1-01-001**
herb	**noun**	**6-03-004**
herb	NN	3-01-001
herbs	NNS	3-02-003
Herb	**NP**	**5-03-004**
Herberet	**prop. noun**	**4-01-001**
Herberet	NP	3-01-001
Herberet's	NP$	1-01-001
Herbert	**NP**	**12-07-009**
Hercule	**NP**	**1-01-001**
Herculean	**JJ**	**1-01-001**
Hercules	**NP**	**3-03-003**
herd	**noun**	**26-05-013**
herd	NN	19-04-009
herd	NN-NC	1-01-001
herds	NNS	6-05-005
herd	**verb**	**6-03-004**
herd	VB	2-01-001
herded	VBD	1-01-001
herded	VBN	1-01-001
herding	VBG	1-01-001
herdin'	VBG	1-01-001
herd-owner	**NN**	**1-01-001**
herding	**noun**	**2-01-001**
herding	NN	0-00-000
herdin'	NN	2-01-001
here	**adverb**	**757-15-316**
here	RB	734-15-312
here	RB-HL	5-02-004
here	RB-NC	6-01-001
Here	RB-TL	1-01-001
here's	RB+BEZ	10-06-009
here's	RB+BEZ-HL	1-01-001
here	**RN**	**4-02-002**
hereabouts	**RB**	**2-02-002**
hereafter	**RB**	**4-02-003**
hereby	**RB**	**8-03-004**
hereditary	**JJ**	**2-01-001**
heredity	**NN**	**3-03-003**
Hereford	**NP**	**1-01-001**
herein	**RB**	**3-03-003**
hereinafter	**RB**	**5-02-003**
heresy	**noun**	**2-01-002**
heresy	NN	1-01-001
Heresy	NN-TL	1-01-001
heretic	**JJ**	**1-01-001**
heretic	**noun**	**1-01-001**
heretics	NNS	1-01-001
heretofore	**RB**	**8-05-008**
heretofore-accepted	**JJ**	**1-01-001**
hereunto	**RB**	**7-01-001**
herewith	**RB**	**2-01-002**
Herford	**prop. noun**	**6-01-001**
Herford	NP	5-01-001
Herford's	NP$	1-01-001
Hergesheimer	**NP**	**1-01-001**
heritage	**noun**	**22-09-014**
heritage	NN	15-08-012
Heritage	NN-TL	5-02-002
Heritage	NN-TL-HL	1-01-001
heritages	NNS	1-01-001
Herman	**prop. noun**	**13-07-007**
Herman	NP	10-07-007
Huhmun	NP	2-01-001
Herman's	NP$	1-01-001
Hermanovski	**NP**	**1-01-001**
hermeneutics	**NN**	**1-01-001**
hermetic	**JJ**	**1-01-001**
Hernandez	**NP**	**6-01-001**
hero	**noun**	**70-13-040**
hero	NN	46-12-029
Hero	NN-TL	4-02-002
hero's	NN$	2-02-002
Hero's	NN$-TL	1-01-001
heroes	NNS	17-07-016
Hero	**NP**	**2-01-001**
hero-worship	**NN**	**1-01-001**
hero-worshipper	**noun**	**1-01-001**
hero-worshippers	NNS	1-01-001
heroic	**adjective**	**21-07-017**
heroic	JJ	20-07-017
Heroic	JJ-TL	1-01-001
heroically	**RB**	**1-01-001**
heroics	**NNS**	**2-02-002**
heroin	**NN**	**2-02-002**
heroine	**NN**	**5-02-003**

Word	Tag	Count
heroism	**NN**	**3-03-003**
Herold	**NP**	**4-01-001**
heron	**noun**	**2-01-001**
herons	NNS	2-01-001
Heron	**NP**	**1-01-001**
herpetologist	**noun**	**3-01-001**
herpetologist	NN	1-01-001
herpetologists	NNS	2-01-001
herpetology	**NN**	**1-01-001**
Herr	**NP**	**10-03-003**
Herrick	**NP**	**2-01-002**
Herridge	**NP**	**1-01-001**
Herrin-Murphysboro	**NP**	**1-01-001**
herring	**noun**	**2-02-002**
herring	NN	1-01-001
Herring	NN-TL	1-01-001
herringbone	**NN**	**1-01-001**
Herrington	**NP**	**1-01-001**
Herrmann	**NP**	**1-01-001**
Herry	**prop. noun**	**4-01-001**
Herry	NP	3-01-001
Herry's	NP$	1-01-001
herself	**PPL**	**125-14-069**
Hersey	**NP**	**1-01-001**
Hershel	**NP**	**1-01-001**
Hershey	**prop. noun**	**1-01-001**
Hershey's	NP$	1-01-001
Herter	**NP**	**3-01-001**
Hertz	**NP**	**1-01-001**
Herzfeld	**NP**	**1-01-001**
Herzog	**NP**	**1-01-001**
hesiometer	**noun**	**6-01-001**
hesiometer	NN	0-00-000
Hesiometer	NN-TL	6-01-001
hesitance	**NN**	**1-01-001**
hesitancy	**NN**	**2-02-002**
hesitant	**JJ**	**3-02-003**
hesitantly	**RB**	**2-02-002**
hesitate	**verb**	**33-11-031**
hesitate	VB	10-06-010
hesitates	VBZ	1-01-001
hesitated	VBD	20-07-018
hesitated	VBN	1-01-001
hesitating	VBG	1-01-001
hesitatingly	**RB**	**1-01-001**
hesitation	**NN**	**7-03-006**
Hesperus	**prop. noun**	**12-01-001**
Hesperus	NP	11-01-001
Hesperus'	NP$	1-01-001
Hess	**NP**	**1-01-001**
Hessian	**JJ**	**2-01-001**
Hessian	**prop. noun**	**3-02-003**
Hessians	NPS	3-02-003
Hester	**NP**	**3-01-001**
heterogamous	**JJ**	**1-01-001**
heterogeneous	**JJ**	**4-02-003**
heterozygous	**JJ**	**2-01-001**
Hetman	**prop. noun**	**20-01-001**
Hetman	NP	12-01-001
Hetman's	NP$	8-01-001
Hettie	**NP**	**5-01-001**
Hetty	**prop. noun**	**3-01-001**
Hetty	NP	2-01-001
Hetty's	NP$	1-01-001
Heusen	**NP**	**1-01-001**
heute	**foreign**	**1-01-001**
heute	FW-NR	0-00-000
heute	FW-NR-TL	1-01-001
Heuvelmans	**NP**	**2-01-001**
hew	**verb**	**1-01-001**
hewed	VBN	1-01-001
Hewett	**NP**	**1-01-001**
Hewlett-Woodmere	**NP**	**1-01-001**
Hewlitt	**NP**	**1-01-001**
hex	**NN**	**2-02-002**
hexagon	**NN**	**1-01-001**
hexagonal	**JJ**	**2-01-002**
hexametaphosphate	**noun**	**1-01-001**
hexametaphosphate	NN	0-00-000
hexametaphosphate	NN-HL	1-01-001
hexameter	**NN**	**3-01-002**
Hexen	**FW-NN**	**1-01-001**
hey	**UH**	**15-07-013**
heyday	**NN**	**3-03-003**
Heydrich	**NP**	**3-02-002**
Heywood	**NP**	**5-04-004**
Hez	**NP**	**7-01-001**
hi	**exclam.**	**6-05-006**
hi	UH	4-03-004
hi (cont.):		
Hi	UH-TL	2-02-002
hi-fi	**NN**	**1-01-001**
hi-grader	**noun**	**1-01-001**
hi-graders	NNS	1-01-001
Hiawatha	**prop. noun**	**2-02-002**
Hiawatha	NP	1-01-001
Hiawatha	NP-TL	1-01-001
hibachi	**noun**	**4-01-001**
hibachi	NN	3-01-001
hibachi	NN-HL	1-01-001
hibachi	**VB**	**1-01-001**
hibernate	**VB**	**2-01-001**
hiccup	**noun**	**1-01-001**
hiccups	NNS	1-01-001
hick	**NN**	**1-01-001**
hick-self	**NN**	**1-01-001**
Hickok	**prop. noun**	**1-01-001**
Hickok	NP	0-00-000
Hickok	NP-TL	1-01-001
hickory	**noun**	**7-03-003**
hickory	NN	2-02-002
Hickory	NN-TL	5-01-001
Hicks	**NP**	**1-01-001**
hide	**noun**	**8-06-008**
hide	NN	4-03-004
hides	NNS	4-04-004
hide	**verb**	**61-10-045**
hide	VB	18-08-016
hides	VBZ	1-01-001
hid	VBD	6-03-004
hidden	VBN	20-07-016
hiding	VBG	16-07-011
hide-out	**noun**	**3-02-002**
hide-out	NN	2-01-001
hideout	NN	1-01-001
hideaway	**NN**	**1-01-001**
hideous	**adjective**	**11-06-010**
hideous	JJ	10-06-009
Hideous	JJ-TL	1-01-001
hideously	**RB**	**3-03-003**
hiding	**NN**	**1-01-001**
hierarchy	**noun**	**10-06-010**
hierarchy	NN	9-06-009
hierarchies	NNS	1-01-001
Hieronymus	**NP**	**2-01-001**
hifaluting	**adjective**	**1-01-001**
hifaluting	JJ	0-00-000
hifalutin'	JJ	1-01-001
high	**adjective**	**454-15-238**
high	JJ	423-15-232
high-	JJ	1-01-001
high	JJ-HL	1-01-001
High	JJ-TL	29-08-023
high	**noun**	**13-06-013**
high	NN	10-06-010
high's	NN$	0-00-000
High's	NN$-TL	1-01-001
highs	NNS	2-02-002
high	**RB**	**34-11-025**
high-backed	**JJ**	**1-01-001**
high-ceilinged	**JJ**	**2-02-002**
high-class	**NN**	**1-01-001**
high-cost	**NN**	**1-01-001**
high-current	**NN**	**1-01-001**
high-density	**NN**	**2-02-002**
high-end	**NN**	**1-01-001**
high-energy	**NN**	**4-02-002**
high-gain	**NN**	**4-01-001**
high-interest	**NN**	**1-01-001**
high-legged	**JJ**	**1-01-001**
high-level	**NN**	**4-04-004**
high-minded	**JJ**	**1-01-001**
high-pitched	**JJ**	**7-06-007**
high-positive	**JJ**	**1-01-001**
high-power	**NN**	**1-01-001**
high-powered	**JJ**	**2-02-002**
high-priced	**JJ**	**5-05-005**
high-protein	**NN**	**2-02-002**
high-quality	**NN**	**2-01-001**
high-rep	**JJ**	**2-01-001**
high-resolution	**NN**	**1-01-001**
high-salaried	**JJ**	**1-01-001**
high-school	**noun**	**6-05-006**
high-school	NN	5-05-005
highschool	NN	1-01-001
high-set	**JJ**	**2-01-001**
high-sounding	**JJ**	**2-02-002**
high-speed	**NN**	**5-05-005**

Word	Tag	Frequency
high-spirited	**JJ**	**3-02-002**
high-stepped	**JJ**	**1-01-001**
high-sudsing	**JJ**	**1-01-001**
high-tail	**verb**	**1-01-001**
high-tailed	VBD	1-01-001
high-temperature	**NN**	**1-01-001**
high-tension	**NN**	**1-01-001**
high-topped	**JJ**	**1-01-001**
high-up	**JJ**	**1-01-001**
high-value	**NN**	**3-02-002**
high-velocity	**NN**	**1-01-001**
high-voltage	**NN**	**1-01-001**
high-wage	**NN**	**1-01-001**
high-water	**NN**	**1-01-001**
highball	**NN**	**4-03-003**
highboard	**NN**	**1-01-001**
highboy	**NN**	**1-01-001**
higher	**comp. adj.**	**147-13-080**
higher	JJR	140-13-079
higher-	JJR	1-01-001
higher	JJR-HL	3-02-002
Higher	JJR-TL	3-02-002
higher	**RBR**	**14-06-011**
higher-density	**NN**	**1-01-001**
higher-priced	**JJR**	**1-01-001**
higher-quality	**NN**	**1-01-001**
highest	**sup. adj.**	**59-11-046**
highest	JJT	57-11-045
highest	JJT-HL	1-01-001
Highest	JJT-TL	1-01-001
highest	**RBT**	**4-03-004**
highest-paid	**JJT**	**1-01-001**
Highfield	**NP**	**1-01-001**
highland	**noun**	**8-05-005**
highland	NN	1-01-001
Highland	NN-TL	1-01-001
highlands	NNS	0-00-000
Highlands	NNS-TL	6-03-003
highlight	**noun**	**5-05-005**
highlight	NN	2-02-002
highlights	NNS	3-03-003
highlight	**verb**	**2-02-002**
highlighting	VBG	2-02-002
highly	**QL**	**88-14-069**
highly	**RB**	**6-05-006**
highness	**noun**	**1-01-001**
highness	NN	0-00-000
Highness	NN-TL	1-01-001
highpoint	**NN**	**2-02-002**
highroad	**NN**	**6-01-001**
highway	**noun**	**56-12-027**
highway	NN	32-11-021
Highway	NN-TL	8-03-005
highways	NNS	15-05-011
Highways	NNS-TL	1-01-001
highwayman	**NN**	**1-01-001**
hijack	**verb**	**3-02-002**
hijacked	VBD	1-01-001
hijacked	VBN	1-01-001
hijacking	VBG	1-01-001
hijacker	**noun**	**2-02-002**
hijackers	NNS	2-02-002
hijacking	**NN**	**1-01-001**
hike	**noun**	**7-05-007**
hike	NN	3-03-003
hikes	NNS	4-03-004
hike	**verb**	**3-03-003**
hike	VB	1-01-001
hiked	VBD	1-01-001
hiking	VBG	1-01-001
hiking	**NN**	**1-01-001**
hilar	**JJ**	**4-01-001**
hilarious	**JJ**	**2-01-002**
hilariously	**RB**	**1-01-001**
hilarity	**NN**	**1-01-001**
Hildy	**NP**	**1-01-001**
hill	**noun**	**119-13-074**
hill	NN	36-07-020
hill	NN-HL	1-01-001
Hill	NN-TL	31-07-022
hill	NN-TL	1-01-001
hills	NNS	36-10-028
hills	NNS-HL	1-01-001
Hills	NNS-TL	13-06-009
Hill	**NP**	**3-02-002**
Hillary	**NP**	**1-01-001**
hillbilly	**NN**	**3-02-003**
Hillcrest	**NP**	**1-01-001**
Hillel	**NP**	**1-01-001**
Hilliard	**NP**	**1-01-001**
Hillman	**prop. noun**	**3-01-001**
Hillman	NP	2-01-001
Hillman's	NP$	1-01-001
Hillsboro	**prop. noun**	**11-01-001**
Hillsboro	NP	10-01-001
Hillsboro	NP-HL	1-01-001
Hillsdale	**NP**	**1-01-001**
hillside	**NN**	**9-04-007**
hilltop	**noun**	**1-01-001**
hilltops	NNS	1-01-001
Hillyer	**NP**	**2-02-002**
Hilo	**prop. noun**	**4-01-001**
Hilo	NP	3-01-001
Hilo	NP-TL	1-01-001
Hilprecht	**prop. noun**	**4-01-001**
Hilprecht	NP	3-01-001
Hilprecht's	NP$	1-01-001
hilt	**NN**	**3-02-003**
Hilton	**prop. noun**	**3-02-002**
Hilton	NP	1-01-001
Hilton	NP-TL	2-02-002
hilum	**NN**	**5-01-001**
Himalaya	**prop. noun**	**2-02-002**
Himalayas	NPS	2-02-002
Himmler	**NP**	**1-01-001**
himself	**refl. pro.**	**606-15-246**
himself	PPL	596-15-244
Himself	PPL	4-02-004
himselfe	PPL	1-01-001
hisself	PPL	1-01-001
hymselfe	PPL	1-01-001
himself	PPL-HL	1-01-001
himself	PPL-NC	2-01-001
Hinckley	**prop. noun**	**1-01-001**
Hinckley	NP	0-00-000
Hinckley	NP-TL	1-01-001
hind	**JJ**	**3-03-003**
Hindemith	**prop. noun**	**1-01-001**
Hindemith's	NP$	1-01-001
hinder	**verb**	**5-04-005**
hinders	VBZ	1-01-001
hindered	VBD	2-02-002
hindered	VBN	1-01-001
hindering	VBG	1-01-001
hindmost	**JJT**	**1-01-001**
Hindoo	**NP**	**1-01-001**
hindquarter	**noun**	**1-01-001**
hindquarters	NNS	1-01-001
hindrance	**noun**	**2-02-002**
hindrances	NNS	2-02-002
hindsight	**NN**	**3-01-001**
Hindu	**prop. noun**	**4-03-003**
Hindu	NP	3-03-003
Hindus	NPS	1-01-001
Hinduism	**NP**	**2-02-002**
hinge	**noun**	**4-04-004**
hinge	NN	1-01-001
hinges	NNS	3-03-003
hinge	**verb**	**2-02-002**
hinges	VBZ	1-01-001
hinged	VBN	1-01-001
Hinkle	**NP**	**1-01-001**
Hino	**prop. noun**	**15-01-001**
Hino	NP	13-01-001
Hino's	NP$	2-01-001
Hinsdale	**NP**	**1-01-001**
hint	**noun**	**16-10-015**
hint	NN	8-04-008
hints	NNS	8-06-007
hint	**verb**	**11-05-011**
hint	VB	1-01-001
hints	VBZ	2-01-002
hinted	VBD	1-01-001
hinted	VBN	6-03-006
hinting	VBG	1-01-001
hinterland	**noun**	**1-01-001**
hinterlands	NNS	1-01-001
Hinton	**NP**	**3-01-002**
hip	**JJ**	**1-01-001**
hip	**noun**	**17-10-016**
hip	NN	9-06-008
hips	NNS	8-06-008
hip-pocket	**NN**	**1-01-001**
hipline	**NN**	**1-01-001**
Hippodrome	**NP**	**5-01-001**
hipster	**NN**	**1-01-001**
Hiram	**NP**	**3-03-003**
hire	**verb**	**47-13-033**

Word	Tag	Frequency
hire (cont.):		
hire	VB	15-08-012
hires	VBZ	1-01-001
hired	VBD	6-04-006
hired	VBN	19-09-014
hiring	VBG	6-04-006
hireling	**noun**	**1-01-001**
hirelings	NNS	1-01-001
Hirey	**prop. noun**	**7-01-001**
Hirey	NP	6-01-001
Hirey's	NP$	1-01-001
Hiroshima	**prop. noun**	**11-04-004**
Hiroshima	NP	10-04-004
Hiroshima	NP-HL	1-01-001
Hirsch	**prop. noun**	**3-01-001**
Hirsch	NP	2-01-001
Hirsch's	NP$	1-01-001
Hirschey	**NP**	**1-01-001**
hiss	**NN**	**1-01-001**
hiss	**verb**	**4-04-004**
hissed	VBD	2-02-002
hissing	VBG	2-02-002
Hiss	**NP**	**1-01-001**
hissing	**NN**	**2-02-002**
histochemical	**JJ**	**1-01-001**
histochemistry	**noun**	**3-01-001**
histochemistry	NN	0-00-000
Histochemistry	NN-TL	3-01-001
histology	**NN**	**1-01-001**
historian	**noun**	**53-09-024**
historian	NN	30-06-012
historian's	NN$	3-02-002
historians	NNS	20-06-017
historic	**JJ**	**23-09-016**
historical	**adjective**	**71-10-048**
historical	JJ	70-10-047
Historical	JJ-TL	1-01-001
historically	**RB**	**16-06-013**
historicism	**NN**	**1-01-001**
historicity	**NN**	**1-01-001**
historiography	**NN**	**2-01-001**
history	**noun**	**297-13-140**
history	NN	273-13-133
history	NN-HL	1-01-001
History	NN-TL	12-04-004
histories	NNS	9-05-007
Histories	NNS-TL	2-01-002
histrionics	**NN**	**1-01-001**
hit	**noun**	**27-06-011**
hit	NN	10-05-009
hit	NN-HL	1-01-001
Hit	NN-TL	1-01-001
hits	NNS	14-03-005
Hits	NNS-TL	1-01-001
hit	**verb**	**126-14-070**
hit	VB	38-10-026
hits	VBZ	6-05-005
hits	VBZ-HL	1-01-001
hit	VBD	38-11-032
hit	VBN	26-10-022
hitting	VBG	16-07-014
hitting	VBG-HL	1-01-001
hit-and-miss	**JJ**	**1-01-001**
hit-and-run	**JJ**	**1-01-001**
hit-run	**JJ**	**2-01-001**
hitch	**NN**	**4-03-004**
hitch	**verb**	**6-04-006**
hitched	VBN	3-03-003
hitching	VBG	3-02-003
Hitch	**NP**	**1-01-001**
Hitchcock	**NP**	**2-02-002**
hither	**RB**	**2-02-002**
hitherto	**RB**	**3-02-002**
Hitler	**prop. noun**	**16-08-011**
Hitler	NP	8-04-006
Hitler's	NP$	7-05-006
Hitlers	NPS	1-01-001
hitless	**JJ**	**1-01-001**
hitter	**noun**	**6-02-003**
hitter	NN	2-02-002
hitters	NNS	4-02-002
hive	**NN**	**2-02-002**
hmm	**UH**	**1-01-001**
hmpf	**UH**	**1-01-001**
hoa-whup	**UH**	**1-01-001**
Hoag	**prop. noun**	**23-01-001**
Hoag	NP	21-01-001
Hoag's	NP$	2-01-001
Hoagy	**NP**	**1-01-001**

Word	Tag	Frequency
Hoak	**NP**	**1-01-001**
Hoaps	**NP**	**1-01-001**
hoarse	**JJ**	**5-02-004**
hoarsely	**RB**	**4-02-004**
hoarseness	**NN**	**1-01-001**
hoax	**noun**	**1-01-001**
hoaxes	NNS	0-00-000
hoaxes	NNS-HL	1-01-001
hob	**NN**	**1-01-001**
Hobart	**NP**	**1-01-001**
Hobbes	**prop. noun**	**2-01-001**
Hobbes	NP	1-01-001
Hobbes'	NP$	1-01-001
hobbing	**NN**	**1-01-001**
hobble	**verb**	**3-03-003**
hobble	VB	1-01-001
hobbled	VBN	2-02-002
hobby	**noun**	**7-03-004**
hobby	NN	4-03-004
hobbies	NNS	3-01-001
Hobday	**NP**	**1-01-001**
hobo	**NN**	**1-01-001**
hoc	**FW-DT**	**3-03-003**
hock	**verb**	**1-01-001**
hocking	VBG	1-01-001
Hock	**prop. noun**	**1-01-001**
Hock's	NP$	1-01-001
Hockaday	**prop. noun**	**1-01-001**
Hockaday	NP	0-00-000
Hockaday	NP-TL	1-01-001
Hockett	**NP**	**1-01-001**
hockey	**NN**	**1-01-001**
hodge-podge	**noun**	**2-01-002**
hodge-podge	NN	1-01-001
hodgepodge	NN	1-01-001
Hodges	**prop. noun**	**16-05-006**
Hodges	NP	14-05-006
Hodges'	NP$	2-01-001
Hodgkin	**NP**	**3-01-001**
Hodosh	**NP**	**1-01-001**
hoe	**noun**	**1-01-001**
hoes	NNS	1-01-001
Hoe-Down	**NP**	**1-01-001**
Hoeve	**NP**	**3-01-001**
Hoffa	**NP**	**2-02-002**
Hoffer	**NP**	**1-01-001**
Hoffman	**prop. noun**	**2-02-002**
Hoffman	NP	1-01-001
Hoffman	NP-TL	1-01-001
hog	**noun**	**5-04-005**
hog	NN	2-01-002
hogs	NNS	2-02-002
hog	NNS	1-01-001
hog	**verb**	**1-01-001**
hogging	VBG	1-01-001
Hogan	**prop. noun**	**12-02-003**
Hogan	NP	10-02-003
Hogan	NP-TL	1-01-001
Hogan s	NP$	1-01-001
Hoge	**prop. noun**	**1-01-001**
Hoge's	NP$	1-01-001
Hohlbein	**prop. noun**	**9-01-001**
Hohlbein	NP	7-01-001
Hohlbein	NP-TL	2-01-001
hoi-polloi	**FW-NNS**	**1-01-001**
Hoijer	**prop. noun**	**6-01-001**
Hoijer	NP	3-01-001
Hoijer's	NP$	3-01-001
hoist	**verb**	**3-03-003**
hoist	VB	1-01-001
hoisted	VBD	1-01-001
hoisted	VBN	1-01-001
Hokan	**NP**	**1-01-001**
Holabird	**NP**	**1-01-001**
Holbrook	**NP**	**1-01-001**
hold	**noun**	**28-11-026**
hold	NN	25-11-024
holds	NNS	2-02-002
Holds	NNS-TL	1-01-001
hold	**verb**	**509-15-265**
hold	VB	144-15-100
holds	VBZ	38-10-037
holds	VBZ-HL	1-01-001
held	VBD	125-15-092
held	VBD-HL	1-01-001
held	VBN	134-14-099
held	VBN-HL	4-02-004
holding	VBG	61-12-053
holdin'	VBG	1-01-001

Word	Tag	Count
hold-back	**NN**	**1-01-001**
Holden	**prop. noun**	**11-01-001**
Holden	NP	9-01-001
Holden's	NP$	2-01-001
holder	**noun**	**32-07-008**
holder	NN	25-05-005
holder	NN-HL	2-02-002
holders	NNS	5-03-004
Holderlin	**NP**	**1-01-001**
holding	**noun**	**8-06-008**
holding	NN	4-03-004
holdings	NNS	4-04-004
holdover	**noun**	**1-01-001**
holdovers	NNS	1-01-001
holdup	**noun**	**3-02-002**
holdup	NN	2-01-001
holdups	NNS	1-01-001
hole	**noun**	**95-13-041**
hole	NN	53-10-028
hole	NN-HL	1-01-001
Hole	NN-TL	2-01-001
holes	NNS	38-11-020
Holes	NNS-TL	1-01-001
hole	**verb**	**2-02-002**
hole	VB	1-01-001
holed	VBD	1-01-001
Hole	**NP**	**1-01-001**
holiday	**noun**	**30-09-018**
holiday	NN	16-08-012
holiday	NN-HL	1-01-001
Holiday	NN-TL	1-01-001
holidays	NNS	10-05-007
holidays	NNS-HL	2-01-001
holier-than-thou	**JJ**	**2-02-002**
holiness	**noun**	**2-02-002**
holiness	NN	1-01-001
Holiness	NN-TL	1-01-001
Holland	**prop. noun**	**8-05-006**
Holland	NP	7-05-005
Holland	NP-TL	1-01-001
Hollander	**NP**	**1-01-001**
holler	**verb**	**6-03-005**
hollered	VBD	2-01-002
holored	VBD	1-01-001
hollering	VBG	3-02-002
Holley	**NP**	**1-01-001**
Hollingshead	**NP**	**1-01-001**
hollow	**JJ**	**8-05-005**
hollow	**noun**	**5-04-005**
hollow	NN	4-04-004
hollows	NNS	1-01-001
Holloway	**NP**	**1-01-001**
Hollowell	**NP**	**1-01-001**
hollowness	**NN**	**1-01-001**
hollowware	**NN**	**1-01-001**
hollyhock	**noun**	**2-01-001**
hollyhock	NN	1-01-001
hollyhocks	NNS	1-01-001
Hollywood	**prop. noun**	**27-06-015**
Hollywood	NP	18-06-009
Hollywood	NP-HL	1-01-001
Hollywood	NP-TL	4-03-004
Hollywood's	NP$	4-03-004
Holman	**prop. noun**	**1-01-001**
Holman	NP	0-00-000
Holman	NP-TL	1-01-001
Holmes	**prop. noun**	**39-07-007**
Holmes	NP	37-07-007
Holmes'	NP$	2-01-001
holocaust	**NN**	**5-04-005**
Holstein	**NP**	**1-01-001**
holster	**NN**	**10-02-007**
holster	**verb**	**3-01-002**
holstered	VBD	1-01-001
holstered	VBN	2-01-001
Holt	**prop. noun**	**1-01-001**
Holt's	NP$	0-00-000
Holt's	NP$-TL	1-01-001
Holty	**NP**	**1-01-001**
holy	**adjective**	**48-09-022**
holy	JJ	19-05-008
holy	JJ-HL	1-01-001
Holy	JJ-TL	28-08-016
holy	**noun**	**2-01-001**
holy	NN	0-00-000
Holy	NN-TL	1-01-001
holies	NNS	0-00-000
Holies	NNS-TL	1-01-001
Holyoke	**prop. noun**	**2-02-002**

Word	Tag	Count
Holyoke (cont.):		
Holyoke	NP	1-01-001
Holyoke	NP-TL	1-01-001
holystone	**noun**	**1-01-001**
holystones	NNS	1-01-001
Holzman	**NP**	**1-01-001**
homage	**NN**	**2-02-002**
home	**noun**	**301-11-136**
home	NN	220-10-098
home	NN-HL	1-01-001
home	NN-NC	4-01-001
Home	NN-TL	13-07-010
home's	NN$	1-01-001
homes	NNS	62-10-049
home	**adv. noun**	**308-15-174**
home	NR	303-15-172
home	NR-HL	2-02-002
home	NR-NC	1-01-001
Home	NR-TL	2-02-002
home	**verb**	**2-02-002**
home	VB	1-01-001
homing	VBG	1-01-001
Home	**NP**	**1-01-001**
home-and-home	**JJ**	**1-01-001**
home-blend	**NN**	**1-01-001**
home-bred	**JJ**	**1-01-001**
home-building	**NN**	**1-01-001**
home-city	**NN**	**1-01-001**
home-coming	**noun**	**1-01-001**
home-comings	NNS	1-01-001
home-for-the-night	**NN**	**1-01-001**
home-grown	**JJ**	**2-02-002**
home-keeping	**JJ**	**1-01-001**
home-office	**NN**	**1-01-001**
home-run	**noun**	**3-01-002**
home-run	NN	2-01-001
homerun	NN	1-01-001
homebound	**adjective**	**2-02-002**
homebound	JJ	1-01-001
home-bound	JJ	1-01-001
homebuilder	**noun**	**1-01-001**
homebuilders	NNS	1-01-001
homebuilding	**JJ**	**1-01-001**
homecoming	**noun**	**5-01-001**
homecoming	NN	3-01-001
Homecoming	NN-TL	1-01-001
homecomings	NNS	1-01-001
homefolk	**NNS**	**1-01-001**
homeland	**NN**	**5-01-004**
homely	**JJ**	**9-06-006**
homemade	**adjective**	**5-03-003**
homemade	JJ	3-03-003
home-made	JJ	1-01-001
homemade	JJ-HL	1-01-001
homemaker	**noun**	**6-04-004**
homemaker	NN	3-02-002
homemakers	NNS	1-01-001
Homemakers	NNS-TL	2-01-001
Homemaster	**NP**	**1-01-001**
homeowner	**noun**	**4-02-003**
homeowners	NNS	2-02-002
home-owners	NNS	1-01-001
Homeowners	NNS-TL	1-01-001
homer	**noun**	**12-01-004**
homer	NN	8-01-003
homer	NN-HL	1-01-001
homers	NNS	3-01-002
Homer	**prop. noun**	**8-04-006**
Homer	NP	7-04-005
Homer's	NP$	1-01-001
Homeric	**JJ**	**15-01-002**
Homerist	**prop. noun**	**1-01-001**
Homerists	NPS	1-01-001
homesick	**JJ**	**3-01-001**
homesickness	**NN**	**1-01-001**
homestead	**noun**	**3-03-003**
homestead	NN	1-01-001
Homestead	NN-TL	1-01-001
homesteads	NNS	1-01-001
homesteader	**noun**	**3-01-001**
homesteaders	NNS	3-01-001
homeward	**RB**	**1-01-001**
homewards	**RB**	**1-01-001**
homicidal	**JJ**	**1-01-001**
homicide	**noun**	**6-02-004**
homicide	NN	1-01-001
Homicide	NN-TL	5-02-004
homo	**foreign**	**1-01-001**
homo	FW-NN	0-00-000

Word	Tag	Count
homo (cont.):		
Homo	FW-NN-TL	1-01-001
homogenate	**NN**	**2-01-001**
homogeneity	**NN**	**5-03-004**
homogeneous	**JJ**	**8-03-005**
homogeneously	**QL**	**1-01-001**
homogeneously	**RB**	**1-01-001**
homogenization	**NN**	**1-01-001**
homogenize	**VB**	**1-01-001**
homopolymer	**noun**	**1-01-001**
homopolymers	NNS	1-01-001
homosexual	**JJ**	**2-02-002**
homosexual	**noun**	**3-01-001**
homosexuals	NNS	3-01-001
homozygous	**JJ**	**5-01-001**
hon	**NN**	**2-01-001**
Honan	**NP**	**2-02-002**
Hondo	**prop. noun**	**1-01-001**
Hondo	NP	0-00-000
Hondo	NP-TL	1-01-001
Hone	**prop. noun**	**2-01-001**
Hone	NP	1-01-001
Hone	NP-HL	1-01-001
honest	**JJ**	**47-13-041**
honest-to-Betsy	**UH**	**1-01-001**
honestly	**RB**	**12-07-010**
honesty	**noun**	**10-06-008**
honesty	NN	9-06-008
honesty	NN-HL	1-01-001
honey	**noun**	**25-09-018**
honey	NN	23-08-016
Honey	NN-TL	2-02-002
honey-in-the-sun	**JJ**	**1-01-001**
honeybee	**noun**	**6-01-001**
honeybee	NN	2-01-001
honeybees	NNS	4-01-001
honeycomb	**verb**	**1-01-001**
honeycombed	VBN	1-01-001
honeymoon	**NN**	**10-06-008**
honeymoon	**verb**	**4-03-003**
honeymoon	VB	1-01-001
honeymooned	VBD	1-01-001
honeymooned	VBN	1-01-001
honeymooning	VBG	1-01-001
honeymooner	**noun**	**1-01-001**
honeymooners	NNS	1-01-001
honeysuckle	**noun**	**3-03-003**
honeysuckle	NN	2-02-002
Honeysuckle	NN-TL	1-01-001
Hong	**prop. noun**	**11-04-007**
Hong	NP	10-03-006
Hong	NP-TL	1-01-001
honky-tonk	**noun**	**2-01-002**
honky-tonk	NN	1-01-001
honky-tonks	NNS	0-00-000
honkytonks	NNS	1-01-001
Honolulu	**prop. noun**	**6-02-002**
Honolulu	NP	4-02-002
Honolulu	NP-HL	1-01-001
Honolulu	NP-TL	1-01-001
honor	**noun**	**67-12-049**
honor	NN	48-12-037
honour	NN	2-02-002
honor	NN-HL	1-01-001
Honor	NN-TL	3-03-003
honors	NNS	13-04-009
honor	**verb**	**49-12-036**
honor	VB	13-07-010
honor	VB-HL	1-01-001
honors	VBZ	1-01-001
honors	VBZ-HL	1-01-001
honored	VBD	2-02-002
honored	VBN	22-09-019
honoured	VBN	1-01-001
honoring	VBG	8-03-007
Honor	**NP**	**1-01-001**
honorable	**adjective**	**18-06-011**
honorable	JJ	9-05-008
hon.	JJ	0-00-000
Hon.	JJ-TL	0-00-000
Hon.	JJ-TL-HL	4-01-001
hon'ble	JJ	0-00-000
Hon'ble	JJ-TL	2-01-001
Honorable	JJ-TL	3-03-003
honorably	**RB**	**3-02-002**
honorary	**JJ**	**2-01-002**
honoree	**NN**	**1-01-001**
Honotassa	**NP**	**4-01-001**
Honshu	**NP**	**1-01-001**

Word	Tag	Count
hoo-pig	**UH**	**1-01-001**
hooch	**NN**	**1-01-001**
hood	**noun**	**7-06-006**
hood	NN	4-04-004
hood	NN-HL	1-01-001
hoods	NNS	2-02-002
Hood	**prop. noun**	**3-03-003**
Hood	NP	1-01-001
Hood	NP-TL	1-01-001
Hood's	NP$	1-01-001
hoodlum	**noun**	**6-03-004**
hoodlum	NN	3-02-002
hoodlums	NNS	3-02-003
hoof	**noun**	**11-05-008**
hoof	NN	1-01-001
hoof	NN-NC	1-01-001
hoofs	NNS	7-02-005
hooves	NNS	2-02-002
hoof-and-mouth	**NN**	**1-01-001**
hoofmark	**noun**	**1-01-001**
hoofmarks	NNS	1-01-001
Hooghli	**prop. noun**	**2-01-001**
Hooghli	NP	0-00-000
Hoogli	NP	1-01-001
Hooghli	NP-TL	1-01-001
hook	**noun**	**5-04-005**
hook	NN	3-02-003
hooks	NNS	2-02-002
hook	**verb**	**9-06-009**
hook	VB	1-01-001
hooked	VBD	2-02-002
hooked	VBN	5-05-005
hooking	VBG	1-01-001
Hook	**NP**	**1-01-001**
Hooker	**prop. noun**	**1-01-001**
Hooker's	NP$	1-01-001
hookup	**noun**	**3-03-003**
hookup	NN	2-02-002
hookups	NNS	1-01-001
hookworm	**NN**	**1-01-001**
hooliganism	**NN**	**1-01-001**
hoop	**noun**	**6-04-004**
hoop	NN	3-02-002
hoops	NNS	3-02-002
Hooper	**NP**	**2-01-001**
Hoopla	**NP**	**1-01-001**
hooray	**exclam.**	**1-01-001**
hooray	UH	0-00-000
Hooray	UH-TL	1-01-001
hoosegow	**noun**	**2-01-001**
hoosegow	NN	1-01-001
hoosegows	NNS	1-01-001
Hoosier	**NP**	**1-01-001**
hoot	**noun**	**2-01-002**
hoot	NN	1-01-001
hoots	NNS	1-01-001
hoot	**verb**	**3-03-003**
hoot	VB	1-01-001
hooted	VBD	1-01-001
hooting	VBG	1-01-001
Hoot	**NP**	**7-02-002**
Hoover	**prop. noun**	**8-04-006**
Hoover	NP	7-04-005
Hoover	NP-TL	1-01-001
hop	**noun**	**2-02-002**
hop	NN	1-01-001
hops	NNS	1-01-001
hop	**verb**	**10-06-010**
hop	VB	1-01-001
hopped	VBD	5-05-005
hopping	VBG	4-04-004
hop-skip	**verb**	**1-01-001**
hop-skipped	VBD	1-01-001
hope	**noun**	**136-15-092**
hope	NN	99-15-071
hope	NN-HL	1-01-001
Hope	NN-TL	5-02-003
hopes	NNS	30-13-028
hopes	NNS-HL	1-01-001
hope	**verb**	**164-15-119**
hope	VB	68-13-052
hopes	VBZ	18-06-017
hoped	VBD	33-10-029
hoped	VBN	15-08-014
hoping	VBG	30-11-027
Hope	**prop. noun**	**5-04-004**
Hope	NP	4-04-004
Hope's	NP$	1-01-001
hoped-for	**JJ**	**3-03-003**

Word	Tag	Frequency
Hopedale	**prop. noun**	**1-01-001**
Hopedale	NP	0-00-000
Hopedale	NP-TL	1-01-001
hopeful	**adjective**	**12-09-012**
hopeful	JJ	11-09-011
hopeful	JJ-HL	1-01-001
hopeful	**noun**	**2-02-002**
hopefuls	NNS	2-02-002
hopefully	**RB**	**8-05-007**
Hopei	**NP**	**1-01-001**
hopeless	**JJ**	**14-07-012**
hopelessly	**QL**	**1-01-001**
hopelessly	**RB**	**6-04-004**
hopelessness	**NN**	**3-02-003**
Hopkins	**prop. noun**	**8-04-006**
Hopkins	NP	3-03-003
Hopkins	NP-TL	4-02-002
Hopkins'	NP$	1-01-001
Hopkinsian	**JJ**	**2-01-001**
hopper	**NN**	**2-02-002**
hopple	**noun**	**4-01-001**
hopples	NNS	4-01-001
hopple	**verb**	**1-01-001**
hoppled	VBN	1-01-001
hopscotch	**NN**	**1-01-001**
Horace	**prop. noun**	**6-03-004**
Horace	NP	5-03-004
Horace's	NP$	1-01-001
Horatio	**prop. noun**	**1-01-001**
Horatio's	NP$	1-01-001
Hord	**NP**	**1-01-001**
horde	**noun**	**4-03-004**
horde	NN	2-02-002
hordes	NNS	2-02-002
horizon	**noun**	**33-12-028**
horizon	NN	27-12-022
horizons	NNS	6-04-006
horizontal	**JJ**	**9-04-008**
horizontally	**RB**	**3-02-003**
hormone	**noun**	**15-03-003**
hormone	NN	12-02-002
hormone	NN-HL	1-01-001
hormones	NNS	2-02-002
horn	**noun**	**33-11-021**
horn	NN	14-06-008
Horn	NN-TL	10-04-004
horns	NNS	8-07-008
horns'	NNS$	1-01-001
Horn	**NP**	**7-01-001**
horn-rim	**JJ**	**1-01-001**
horn-rimmed	**JJ**	**1-01-001**
Horne	**prop. noun**	**3-03-003**
Horne	NP	2-02-002
Horne's	NP$	1-01-001
horned	**JJ**	**1-01-001**
horoscope	**NN**	**1-01-001**
Horowitz	**NP**	**3-03-003**
horrible	**JJ**	**15-06-013**
horribly	**QL**	**1-01-001**
horribly	**RB**	**1-01-001**
horrid	**JJ**	**1-01-001**
horrify	**verb**	**4-03-004**
horrified	VBN	4-03-004
horrifying	**JJ**	**3-02-003**
horrifyingly	**RB**	**1-01-001**
horror	**noun**	**21-09-019**
horror	NN	16-09-015
Horror	NN-TL	1-01-001
horrors	NNS	4-03-004
hors	**FW-RB**	**1-01-001**
horse	**noun**	**203-14-065**
horse	NN	112-14-045
hoss	NN	5-01-001
horse	NN-HL	1-01-001
Horse	NN-TL	4-02-002
horse's	NN$	5-04-004
horses	NNS	68-09-033
hosses	NNS	5-01-001
horses'	NNS$	3-03-003
horse-blanket	**NN**	**1-01-001**
horse-chestnut	**NN**	**1-01-001**
horse-playing	**JJ**	**1-01-001**
horse-radish	**NN**	**2-01-001**
horse-trading	**NN**	**1-01-001**
horse-trail	**NN**	**1-01-001**
horseback	**NN**	**3-02-002**
horsedom	**NN**	**1-01-001**
horseflesh	**NN**	**1-01-001**
horsehair	**NN**	**1-01-001**
horselike	**JJ**	**1-01-001**
Horsely	**NP**	**2-01-001**
horseman	**noun**	**4-04-004**
horseman	NN	1-01-001
horsemen	NNS	3-03-003
horsemanship	**NN**	**3-03-003**
horseplay	**NN**	**2-02-002**
horsepower	**noun**	**7-02-003**
horsepower	NN	5-01-002
hp.	NN	2-01-001
horsewoman	**NN**	**1-01-001**
Horstman	**NP**	**1-01-001**
Horton	**NP**	**1-01-001**
Hosaka	**NP**	**2-01-001**
hose	**noun**	**11-05-006**
hose	NN	8-03-004
Hose	NN-TL	1-01-001
hoses	NNS	2-02-002
hospice	**noun**	**1-01-001**
hospice	NN	0-00-000
Hospice	NN-TL	1-01-001
hospitable	**JJ**	**4-03-004**
hospital	**noun**	**130-14-055**
hospital	NN	77-12-038
Hospital	NN-TL	33-08-021
hospitals	NNS	18-09-012
Hospitals	NNS-TL	2-01-001
hospital-care	**NN**	**1-01-001**
hospitality	**NN**	**6-04-006**
hospitalization	**NN**	**4-02-003**
hospitalize	**verb**	**1-01-001**
hospitalized	VBN	1-01-001
host	**noun**	**47-11-030**
host	NN	36-10-024
hoste	NN	1-01-001
host's	NN$	5-04-005
hosts	NN$	1-01-001
hosts	NNS	4-04-004
host-specific	**JJ**	**1-01-001**
hostage	**noun**	**5-03-003**
hostage	NN	1-01-001
Hostage	NN-TL	1-01-001
hostages	NNS	3-01-001
Hostaria	**NP**	**1-01-001**
hostelry	**noun**	**1-01-001**
hostelries	NNS	1-01-001
hostess	**noun**	**11-06-009**
hostess	NN	8-04-007
hostesses	NNS	3-03-003
hostile	**JJ**	**19-07-017**
hostility	**noun**	**11-05-008**
hostility	NN	6-04-006
hostilities	NNS	5-02-002
hostler	**NN**	**2-01-001**
hot	**adjective**	**130-14-077**
hot	JJ	123-14-074
hot	JJ-HL	2-02-002
Hot	JJ-TL	5-03-003
hot-blooded	**JJ**	**1-01-001**
hot-colored	**JJ**	**1-01-001**
hot-honey	**NN**	**1-01-001**
hot-shot	**NN**	**2-02-002**
hot-slough	**JJ**	**1-01-001**
hot-water	**NN**	**1-01-001**
hotbed	**NN**	**1-01-001**
hotdog	**noun**	**1-01-001**
hotdogs	NNS	1-01-001
Hotei	**NP**	**5-01-001**
hotel	**noun**	**147-12-066**
hotel	NN	84-11-042
Hotel	NN-TL	42-10-027
hotel's	NN$	1-01-001
hotels	NNS	20-08-014
hotel-motel	**NN**	**1-01-001**
hotelman	**noun**	**1-01-001**
hotelman's	NN$	1-01-001
Hotham	**NP**	**2-01-001**
hothouse	**NN**	**1-01-001**
hotly	**QL**	**1-01-001**
hotly	**RB**	**1-01-001**
hotrod	**NN**	**1-01-001**
hotter	**JJR**	**7-06-007**
hottest	**JJT**	**4-03-004**
Houdini	**NP**	**1-01-001**
Hough	**prop. noun**	**8-02-002**
Hough	NP	6-02-002
Hough's	NP$	2-01-001
Houghton	**prop. noun**	**5-03-004**
Houghton	NP	3-01-002

Houghton (cont.):		
Houghton	NP-TL	1-01-001
Houghton's	NP$	1-01-001
Houk	**NP**	**3-01-003**
hound	**noun**	**10-05-010**
hound	NN	4-03-004
Hound	NN-TL	3-02-003
hounds	NNS	2-02-002
Hounds	NNS-TL	1-01-001
hour	**noun**	**325-15-184**
hour	NN	145-15-100
hr.	NN	3-01-002
hour's	NN$	1-01-001
hours	NNS	174-15-110
hr.	NNS	1-01-001
hours'	NNS$	1-01-001
hour-long	**JJ**	**2-02-002**
hourly	**JJ**	**2-02-002**
house	**noun**	**662-14-209**
house	NN	388-14-147
howse	NN	2-01-001
house	NN-HL	4-04-004
House	NN-TL	186-13-062
House	NN-TL-HL	1-01-001
house's	NN$	0-00-000
House's	NN$-TL	1-01-001
houses	NNS	80-12-062
house	**verb**	**53-11-032**
house	VB	9-07-009
houses	VBZ	3-03-003
housed	VBD	4-04-004
housed	VBN	8-04-007
housing	VBG	29-07-011
House	**prop. noun**	**4-02-002**
House	NP	2-02-002
House	NP-TL	0-00-000
House	NP-TL-HL	1-01-001
House's	NP$	1-01-001
house-building	**NN**	**1-01-001**
house-cleaning	**NN**	**1-01-001**
houseboat	**noun**	**1-01-001**
houseboats	NNS	1-01-001
housebreak	**verb**	**1-01-001**
housebroken	VBN	1-01-001
housebreaker	**noun**	**1-01-001**
housebreakers	NNS	1-01-001
housebreaking	**NN**	**1-01-001**
household	**noun**	**34-11-028**
household	NN	32-10-026
households	NNS	2-02-002
household-type	**JJ**	**1-01-001**
householder	**noun**	**2-02-002**
householder	NN	1-01-001
householders	NNS	1-01-001
housekeeper	**NN**	**2-02-002**
housekeeping	**noun**	**7-05-006**
housekeeping	NN	6-04-005
Housekeeping	NN-TL	1-01-001
housepaint	**NN**	**1-01-001**
housewife	**noun**	**9-06-008**
housewife	NN	4-03-004
housewives	NNS	5-05-005
housework	**NN**	**2-02-002**
housing	**noun**	**30-06-019**
housing	NN	21-06-014
Housing	NN-TL	9-05-007
Housman	**prop. noun**	**3-01-002**
Housman	NP	1-01-001
Housman's	NP$	2-01-002
Houston	**prop. noun**	**25-05-010**
Houston	NP	24-04-009
Houston	NP-TL	1-01-001
Houtz	**NP**	**2-01-001**
Hovarter	**NP**	**1-01-001**
hovdingar	**foreign**	**1-01-001**
hovdingar	FW-NNS	0-00-000
Hovdingar	FW-NNS-TL	1-01-001
hovel	**NN**	**2-02-002**
hover	**verb**	**7-05-007**
hover	VB	4-03-004
hovers	VBZ	1-01-001
hovered	VBD	1-01-001
hovering	VBG	1-01-001
how	**QL**	**26-07-021**
how	**wh-qual.**	**148-08-090**
how	WQL	143-08-086
How	WQL-TL	5-02-004
how	**wh-adverb**	**675-15-291**
how	WRB	637-15-287

how (cont.):		
howe	WRB	2-01-001
how	WRB-HL	21-04-004
how	WRB-NC	2-02-002
how'd	WRB+DOD	3-01-002
how's	WRB+BEZ	8-05-007
how's	WRB+DOZ	1-01-001
howda	WRB+DO	1-01-001
How-2	**NP**	**1-01-001**
Howard	**prop. noun**	**33-06-017**
Howard	NP	31-06-016
Howard	NP-TL	1-01-001
Howard's	NP$	1-01-001
howdy	**UH**	**1-01-001**
Howe	**prop. noun**	**11-03-004**
Howe	NP	8-02-003
Howe	NP-TL	2-02-002
Howe's	NP$	1-01-001
Howell	**prop. noun**	**1-01-001**
Howell	NP	0-00-000
Howell	NP-TL	1-01-001
however	**RB**	**402-12-206**
however	**WQL**	**33-09-031**
however	**WRB**	**117-14-077**
howl	**noun**	**6-05-006**
howl	NN	3-03-003
Howl	NN-TL	1-01-001
howls	NNS	2-01-002
howl	**verb**	**5-03-005**
howls	VBZ	1-01-001
howled	VBD	1-01-001
howling	VBG	3-03-003
Howorth	**NP**	**2-01-001**
Howry	**NP**	**1-01-001**
howsabout	**WRB**	**1-01-001**
Howsam	**prop. noun**	**2-01-001**
Howsam	NP	1-01-001
Howsam's	NP$	1-01-001
Howser	**NP**	**2-01-001**
howsomever	**RB**	**1-01-001**
Hoxa	**NP**	**1-01-001**
hoy	**foreign**	**1-01-001**
hoy	FW-NR	0-00-000
Hoy	FW-NR-TL	1-01-001
hoydenish	**JJ**	**1-01-001**
Hoyle	**prop. noun**	**1-01-001**
Hoyle's	NP$	1-01-001
Hoyt	**NP**	**4-03-003**
Hrothgar	**prop. noun**	**2-01-001**
Hrothgar	NP	1-01-001
Hrothgar's	NP$	1-01-001
Huai	**NP**	**1-01-001**
Huang-ti	**NP**	**1-01-001**
hub	**noun**	**3-03-003**
hub	NN	1-01-001
hubs	NNS	2-02-002
Hub	**NP**	**10-01-001**
Hubay	**NP**	**1-01-001**
hubba	**UH**	**2-01-001**
Hubbell	**NP**	**1-01-001**
hubbub	**NN**	**1-01-001**
hubby	**NN**	**1-01-001**
Hubermann	**NP**	**1-01-001**
Hubert	**NP**	**3-03-003**
Hubie	**prop. noun**	**1-01-001**
Hubie's	NP$	1-01-001
hubris	**NN**	**1-01-001**
Huck	**NP**	**1-01-001**
huckster	**noun**	**2-01-001**
huckster	NN	1-01-001
huckster's	NN$	1-01-001
huckster	**VB**	**1-01-001**
huddle	**noun**	**4-02-004**
huddle	NN	3-02-003
huddle	NN-HL	1-01-001
huddle	**verb**	**13-05-011**
huddled	VBD	6-03-006
huddled	VBN	4-01-003
huddling	VBG	3-03-003
Hudson	**prop. noun**	**69-08-016**
Hudson	NP	40-06-009
Hudson	NP-TL	13-05-009
Hudson's	NP$	9-02-002
Hudson's	NP$-TL	7-01-001
hue	**noun**	**3-01-002**
hue	NN	1-01-001
hues	NNS	2-01-001
Huey	**NP**	**1-01-001**
Huff	**prop. noun**	**11-01-001**

Word	Tag	Frequency
Huff (cont.):		
Huff	NP	10-01-001
Huff's	NP$	1-01-001
Huffman	**NP**	**1-01-001**
hug	**NN**	**1-01-001**
hug	**verb**	**11-04-011**
hug	VB	2-02-002
hugged	VBD	2-02-002
hugging	VBG	7-02-007
huge	**JJ**	**55-14-043**
hugging	**noun**	**1-01-001**
huggings	NNS	1-01-001
Huggins	**NP**	**1-01-001**
Hugh	**NP**	**8-03-007**
Hughes	**prop. noun**	**29-04-007**
Hughes	NP	25-03-006
Hughes	NP-TL	2-02-002
Hughes'	NP$	2-01-001
Hugo	**prop. noun**	**4-01-001**
Hugo	NP	3-01-001
Hugo's	NP$	1-01-001
huh	**UH**	**5-05-005**
huh-uh	**UH**	**1-01-001**
Huitotoe	**prop. noun**	**1-01-001**
Huitotoes	NPS	1-01-001
hulk	**noun**	**5-04-005**
hulk	NN	2-02-002
hulks	NNS	2-02-002
Hulks	NNS-TL	1-01-001
hulk	**verb**	**2-02-002**
hulking	VBG	2-02-002
hull	**NN**	**10-04-005**
Hull	**NP**	**3-01-001**
hull-first	**RB**	**1-01-001**
Hultberg	**NP**	**1-01-001**
hum	**NN**	**4-03-003**
hum	**verb**	**6-04-006**
hum	VB	1-01-001
hummed	VBD	2-02-002
hummed	VBN	1-01-001
humming	VBG	2-02-002
humaine	**FW-JJ**	**1-01-001**
human	**adjective**	**263-12-110**
human	JJ	261-12-109
Human	JJ-TL	2-02-002
human	**noun**	**45-11-027**
human	NN	36-09-021
humans	NNS	9-07-008
humane	**JJ**	**5-03-005**
humanely	**RB**	**1-01-001**
humanism	**noun**	**5-02-005**
humanism	NN	4-02-004
Humanism	NN-TL	1-01-001
humanist	**JJ**	**2-02-002**
humanist	**noun**	**3-02-003**
humanist	NN	1-01-001
Humanist	NN-TL	1-01-001
humanists	NNS	1-01-001
humanistic	**JJ**	**2-02-002**
humanitarian	**JJ**	**2-02-002**
humanitarian	**NN**	**1-01-001**
humanity	**noun**	**30-09-023**
humanity	NN	26-08-020
Humanity	NN-TL	2-01-001
humanities	NNS	2-01-002
humanize	**VB**	**1-01-001**
humanly	**RB**	**1-01-001**
humanness	**NN**	**2-02-002**
humble	**JJ**	**17-06-015**
humble	**verb**	**2-02-002**
humble	VB	1-01-001
humbled	VBN	1-01-001
humbly	**QL**	**1-01-001**
humbly	**RB**	**3-03-003**
Hume	**prop. noun**	**4-01-002**
Hume	NP	2-01-002
Hume's	NP$	2-01-001
humid	**JJ**	**1-01-001**
humidity	**NN**	**8-03-003**
humiliate	**verb**	**2-02-002**
humiliated	VBN	2-02-002
humiliating	**JJ**	**4-03-004**
humiliatingly	**QL**	**1-01-001**
humiliation	**noun**	**7-05-007**
humiliation	NN	6-04-006
humilation	NN	1-01-001
humility	**noun**	**6-03-003**
humility	NN	5-03-004
humly	NN-NC	1-01-001
humming	**NN**	**4-03-004**
hummock	**noun**	**2-02-002**
hummocks	NNS	2-02-002
humor	**noun**	**45-11-031**
humor	NN	44-11-030
humour	NN	1-01-001
humor	**VB**	**3-02-002**
humorist	**noun**	**2-01-001**
humorists	NNS	2-01-001
humorous	**JJ**	**16-08-012**
hump	**verb**	**1-01-001**
humped	VBD	1-01-001
Hump	**NP**	**2-01-001**
Humphrey	**NP**	**6-03-003**
Humpty	**NP**	**1-01-001**
Hun	**NP**	**2-01-001**
hunch	**noun**	**7-05-005**
hunch	NN	6-05-005
hunches	NNS	1-01-001
hunch	**verb**	**3-02-002**
hunch	VB	1-01-001
hunched	VBD	1-01-001
hunched	VBN	1-01-001
hunched-up	**JJ**	**1-01-001**
hundred	**CD**	**171-14-104**
hundred	**noun**	**44-12-032**
hundreds	NNS	44-12-032
hundred-and-eighty-degree	**JJ**	**1-01-001**
hundred-and-fifty	**CD**	**1-01-001**
hundred-leaf	**JJ**	**1-01-001**
hundred-odd	**CD**	**2-01-002**
hundred-yen	**JJ**	**1-01-001**
hundredth	**OD**	**2-02-002**
Hungarian	**adjective**	**5-03-004**
Hungarian	JJ	3-02-002
Hungarian	JJ-TL	2-02-002
Hungarian	**NP**	**4-03-003**
Hungarian-born	**JJ**	**1-01-001**
Hungary	**NP**	**4-02-003**
Hungary-Suez	**NP**	**1-01-001**
hunger	**noun**	**17-09-012**
hunger	NN	15-09-012
hunger	NN-NC	2-01-001
hungrier	**JJR**	**1-01-001**
hungry	**JJ**	**23-10-017**
hunk	**NN**	**2-02-002**
hunker	**verb**	**2-01-002**
hunkered	VBD	1-01-001
hunkered	VBN	1-01-001
Hunkerish	**JJ**	**1-01-001**
hunt	**noun**	**4-04-004**
hunt	NN	3-03-003
hunts	NNS	1-01-001
hunt	**verb**	**44-12-026**
hunt	VB	5-04-004
hunts	VBZ	1-01-001
hunted	VBD	2-02-002
hunted	VBN	5-03-004
hunting	VBG	30-09-019
hunting	VBG-HL	1-01-001
Hunt	**NP**	**2-02-002**
hunter	**noun**	**17-05-009**
hunter	NN	7-04-004
Hunter	NN-TL	3-01-001
hunter's	NN$	1-01-001
hunters	NNS	5-03-005
Hunters	NNS-TL	1-01-001
Hunter	**prop. noun**	**8-04-006**
Hunter	NP	5-03-003
Hunter	NP-TL	3-02-003
hunter-killer	**NN**	**5-02-002**
hunting	**NN**	**3-01-003**
Huntington	**prop. noun**	**2-01-001**
Huntington	NP	1-01-001
Huntingtons	NPS	1-01-001
Huntley	**NP**	**5-02-002**
Huo-Shan	**NP**	**1-01-001**
hurdle	**noun**	**3-03-003**
hurdle	NN	2-02-002
hurdles	NNS	1-01-001
hurdle	**verb**	**2-01-001**
hurdle	VB	1-01-001
hurdled	VBN	1-01-001
hurl	**verb**	**12-08-011**
hurl	VB	3-03-003
hurled	VBD	3-03-003
hurled	VBN	1-01-001
hurling	VBG	5-05-005
hurler	**noun**	**2-01-001**

Word	Tag	Frequency
hurler (cont.):		
hurler	NN	1-01-001
hurlers	NNS	1-01-001
hurley	**NN**	**1-01-001**
Hurok	**NP**	**4-02-002**
hurrah	**exclam.**	**3-02-002**
hurrah	UH	0-00-000
Hurrah	UH-TL	1-01-001
Hurrah	UH-NC	2-01-001
hurray	**exclam.**	**1-01-001**
hurray	UH	0-00-000
Hurray	UH-TL	1-01-001
Hurrays	**NP**	**3-01-001**
hurricane	**noun**	**8-05-006**
hurricane	NN	7-04-005
Hurricane	NN-TL	1-01-001
hurriedly	**RB**	**2-02-002**
hurry	**NN**	**19-07-015**
hurry	**verb**	**45-10-034**
hurry	VB	18-06-016
hurried	VBD	18-06-015
hurried	VBN	5-03-005
hurrying	VBG	4-04-004
hurt	**JJ**	**1-01-001**
hurt	**noun**	**12-07-012**
hurt	NN	11-07-011
hurts	NNS	1-01-001
hurt	**verb**	**31-09-026**
hurt	VB	15-07-012
hurts	VBZ	3-03-003
hurt	VBD	1-01-001
hurt	VBN	9-05-009
hurting	VBG	1-01-001
hurting	VBG-NC	2-01-001
hurtle	**verb**	**6-04-005**
hurtled	VBD	1-01-001
hurtling	VBG	5-04-004
husband	**noun**	**163-15-077**
husband	NN	131-15-067
husbun	NN	1-01-001
husband's	NN$	17-08-015
husbands	NNS	14-07-010
husband-stealer	**NN**	**1-01-001**
husband-wife	**JJ**	**1-01-001**
husbandry	**NN**	**2-02-002**
hush	**NN**	**2-01-001**
hush	**UH**	**2-01-002**
hush	**verb**	**2-02-002**
hushed	VBN	2-02-002
huskily	**RB**	**1-01-001**
huskiness	**NN**	**1-01-001**
husky	**JJ**	**3-02-003**
husky-voiced	**JJ**	**1-01-001**
hustle	**verb**	**5-03-005**
hustle	VB	2-02-002
hustled	VBD	1-01-001
hustled	VBN	1-01-001
hustling	VBG	1-01-001
hustler	**noun**	**4-03-004**
hustler	NN	2-01-002
hustler	NN-NC	1-01-001
Hustler	NN-TL	1-01-001
Huston	**NP**	**1-01-001**
hut	**noun**	**19-03-007**
hut	NN	13-03-005
huts	NNS	6-02-003
Hutchins	**prop. noun**	**5-01-002**
Hutchins	NP	4-01-002
Hutchins'	NP$	1-01-001
Hutchinson	**NP**	**2-01-001**
hutment	**noun**	**2-01-001**
hutment	NN	1-01-001
hutments	NNS	1-01-001
Hutton	**NP**	**2-02-002**
Huxley	**prop. noun**	**8-03-005**
Huxley	NP	6-03-004
Huxley's	NP$	2-01-002
huzzah	**noun**	**1-01-001**
huzzahs	NNS	1-01-001
Hwa-Shan	**NP**	**1-01-001**
Hwang	**NP**	**4-01-001**
hyacinth	**noun**	**1-01-001**
hyacinths	NNS	1-01-001
hyaline	**NN**	**1-01-001**
hyalinization	**NN**	**1-01-001**
Hyannis	**NP**	**2-01-002**
hybrid	**NN**	**1-01-001**
Hyde	**prop. noun**	**5-01-001**
Hyde	NP	4-01-001

Word	Tag	Frequency
Hyde (cont.):		
Hyde's	NP$	1-01-001
hydrate	**verb**	**1-01-001**
hydrated	VBN	1-01-001
hydraulic	**JJ**	**1-01-001**
hydraulically	**RB**	**1-01-001**
hydraulics	**NN**	**1-01-001**
hydride	**noun**	**5-02-002**
hydride	NN	2-02-002
hydrides	NNS	3-01-001
hydrido	**NN**	**1-01-001**
hydro-electric	**adjective**	**1-01-001**
hydro-electric	JJ	0-00-000
Hydro-Electric	JJ-TL	1-01-001
hydrocarbon	**noun**	**4-01-002**
hydrocarbon	NN	3-01-002
hydrocarbons	NNS	1-01-001
hydrochemistry	**NN**	**1-01-001**
hydrochloride	**NN**	**4-01-001**
hydrogen	**noun**	**42-05-007**
hydrogen	NN	39-05-007
hydrogens	NNS	3-01-001
hydrolysis	**NN**	**5-01-001**
hydrolyze	**verb**	**1-01-001**
hydrolyzed	VBN	1-01-001
hydrophilic	**JJ**	**2-01-001**
hydrophobia	**NN**	**1-01-001**
hydrophobic	**JJ**	**2-01-001**
hydrostatic	**JJ**	**1-01-001**
hydrous	**JJ**	**1-01-001**
hydroxazine	**NN**	**1-01-001**
hydroxide	**noun**	**1-01-001**
hydroxides	NNS	1-01-001
hydroxyl-rich	**JJ**	**2-01-001**
hydroxylation	**NN**	**1-01-001**
hyena	**NN**	**1-01-001**
hygiene	**noun**	**3-02-003**
hygiene	NN	2-02-002
Hygiene	NN-TL	1-01-001
hymen	**noun**	**14-01-001**
hymen	NN	13-01-001
hymens	NNS	1-01-001
hymn	**noun**	**15-04-012**
hymn	NN	7-03-006
Hymn	NN-TL	2-02-002
hymns	NNS	6-04-006
Hyndman	**NP**	**1-01-001**
hyped-up	**JJ**	**1-01-001**
hyperbole	**NN**	**2-01-001**
hyperbolic	**JJ**	**2-02-002**
hyperbolically	**RB**	**1-01-001**
hypercellularity	**NN**	**1-01-001**
hyperemia	**NN**	**2-01-001**
hyperemic	**JJ**	**2-01-001**
hyperfine	**JJ**	**1-01-001**
hyperplasia	**NN**	**1-01-001**
hypertrophy	**NN**	**2-01-001**
hypertrophy	**verb**	**1-01-001**
hypertrophied	VBN	1-01-001
hypervelocity	**NN**	**1-01-001**
hyphenate	**verb**	**2-02-002**
hyphenated	VBN	2-02-002
hypnosis	**NN**	**1-01-001**
hypnotic	**JJ**	**1-01-001**
hypnotically	**RB**	**1-01-001**
hypnotize	**verb**	**1-01-001**
hypnotized	VBN	1-01-001
hypo-	**JJ**	**1-01-001**
hypoactive	**JJ**	**1-01-001**
hypoadrenocorticism	**NN**	**1-01-001**
hypocellularity	**NN**	**1-01-001**
hypocrisy	**noun**	**9-06-008**
hypocrisy	NN	7-06-007
hypocrisies	NNS	2-02-002
hypocrite	**noun**	**4-03-004**
hypocrite	NN	2-02-002
hypocrites	NNS	2-02-002
hypocritical	**JJ**	**2-01-001**
hypodermic	**JJ**	**1-01-001**
hypophyseal	**JJ**	**1-01-001**
hypophysectomise	**verb**	**1-01-001**
hypophysectomised	VBN	1-01-001
hypostatization	**NN**	**1-01-001**
hypothalamic	**adjective**	**22-01-001**
hypothalamic	JJ	21-01-001
hypothalamic	JJ-HL	1-01-001
hypothalamic-cortical	**JJ**	**4-01-001**
hypothalamically	**RB**	**1-01-001**
hypothalamus	**NN**	**19-02-002**

Word	Tag	Frequency
hypothesis	**noun**	**22-04-013**
hypothesis	NN	17-04-012
Hypothesis	NN-TL	1-01-001
hypotheses	NNS	2-02-002
Hypotheses	NNS-TL	2-01-001
hypothesize	**verb**	**4-03-004**
hypothesize	VB	1-01-001
hypothesized	VBN	2-01-002
hypothesize (cont.):		
hypothesizing	VBG	1-01-001
hypothetical	**JJ**	**8-03-007**
hypothyroidism	**NN**	**1-01-001**
hysterectomy	**NN**	**1-01-001**
hysteria	**NN**	**7-04-006**
hysterical	**JJ**	**10-06-009**
hysteron-proteron	**NN**	**1-01-001**

I

Word	Tag	Frequency
I	**pers. pro.**	**8387-15-352**
I	PPSS	5132-15-329
Ah	PPSS	7-01-001
I	PPSS-HL	2-01-002
I	PPSS-NC	24-02-003
I'd	PPSS+HVD	41-06-021
I'd	PPSS+MD	63-08-047
I'll	PPSS+MD	179-12-080
I'll	PPSS+MD-NC	2-01-001
I'm	PPSS+BEM	269-13-112
I've	PPSS+HV	125-12-076
me	PPO	1173-15-232
mee	PPO	5-01-001
Me	PPO-TL	7-04-006
gimme	+PPO	1-01-001
my	PP$	1306-15-248
mah	PP$	2-01-001
mine	PP$	1-01-001
My	PP$	1-01-001
myn	PP$	1-01-001
myne	PP$	1-01-001
My	PP$-TL	8-05-007
mine	PP$$	37-11-030
I	**NP**	**1-01-001**
I.	**NP**	**16-05-012**
I.B.M.	**NP**	**1-01-001**
i.d.	**NN**	**3-01-001**
i.e.	**RB**	**43-10-030**
I.L.	**NP**	**1-01-001**
I.M.F.	**NP**	**1-01-001**
I.Q.	**NP**	**5-02-002**
I.R.S.	**NP**	**2-01-001**
Iberia	**prop. noun**	**1-01-001**
Iberia	NP	0-00-000
Iberia	NP-TL	1-01-001
IBM	**NP**	**1-01-001**
Ibn	**NP**	**1-01-001**
Ibrahim	**NP**	**4-01-001**
Ibsen	**NP**	**1-01-001**
ICBM	**prop. noun**	**1-01-001**
ICBMs	NPS	1-01-001
ice	**NN**	**45-08-028**
ice	**verb**	**1-01-001**
iced	VBN	1-01-001
ice-chest	**NN**	**1-01-001**
ice-cold	**JJ**	**1-01-001**
ice-cube	**noun**	**1-01-001**
ice-cubes	NNS	1-01-001
ice-feeling	**JJ**	**1-01-001**
ice-filled	**JJ**	**2-01-001**
icebox	**NN**	**3-03-003**
Iceland	**NP**	**4-02-002**
Icelandic	**NP**	**1-01-001**
Icelandic-speaking	**JJ**	**1-01-001**
ich	**FW-PPSS**	**1-01-001**
icicle	**NN**	**1-01-001**
icing	**NN**	**1-01-001**
iconoclasm	**NN**	**1-01-001**
icy	**JJ**	**12-09-010**
Ida	**NP**	**2-01-001**
Idaho	**NP**	**3-02-002**
Idal	**NP**	**1-01-001**
idea	**foreign**	**1-01-001**
idea	FW-NN	0-00-000
Idea	FW-NN-TL	1-01-001
idea	**noun**	**337-15-167**
idea	NN	191-15-125
idea	NN-HL	1-01-001
idea	NN-NC	2-01-001
ideas	NNS	143-12-071
idea-exchange	**NN**	**1-01-001**
ideal	**adjective**	**46-08-031**

Word	Tag	Frequency
ideal (cont.):		
ideal	JJ	45-08-030
Ideal	JJ-TL	1-01-001
ideal	**noun**	**31-09-024**
ideal	NN	15-06-013
ideals	NNS	16-08-013
idealism	**NN**	**3-03-003**
idealist	**noun**	**4-02-003**
idealist	NN	3-01-002
Idealist	NN-TL	1-01-001
idealistic	**JJ**	**2-01-002**
idealization	**NN**	**2-02-002**
idealize	**verb**	**4-02-002**
idealized	VBN	4-02-002
ideally	**RB**	**10-05-010**
ideational	**JJ**	**1-01-001**
identical	**adjective**	**31-09-022**
identical	JJ	30-09-022
identical	JJ-HL	1-01-001
identically	**RB**	**1-01-001**
identifiable	**JJ**	**5-05-005**
identification	**noun**	**45-09-028**
identification	NN	42-09-027
Identification	NN-TL	1-01-001
identifications	NNS	2-01-001
identify	**verb**	**81-13-061**
identify	VB	26-07-022
identifies	VBZ	6-05-006
identified	VBD	11-06-009
identified	VBN	35-11-029
identifying	VBG	3-02-003
identity	**noun**	**65-10-031**
identity	NN	55-10-028
identities	NNS	10-03-006
ideological	**JJ**	**21-06-012**
ideologist	**NN**	**1-01-001**
ideology	**noun**	**16-09-013**
ideology	NN	13-07-011
ideologies	NNS	3-03-003
idiocy	**noun**	**1-01-001**
idiocies	NNS	1-01-001
idiom	**noun**	**10-04-008**
idiom	NN	7-04-007
idioms	NNS	3-02-002
idiomatic	**JJ**	**1-01-001**
idiosyncrasy	**noun**	**3-03-003**
idiosyncrasies	NNS	3-03-003
idiosyncratic	**JJ**	**2-02-002**
idiot	**noun**	**3-02-003**
idiot	NN	2-02-002
idiot's	NN$	1-01-001
idiot-grin	**NN**	**1-01-001**
idiotic	**JJ**	**3-02-003**
idiotically	**RB**	**1-01-001**
Idje	**NP**	**3-01-001**
idle	**JJ**	**12-08-010**
idle	**verb**	**4-03-003**
idle	VB	1-01-001
idled	VBD	1-01-001
idling	VBG	2-02-002
idleness	**NN**	**3-03-003**
idler	**noun**	**2-01-001**
idler	NN	1-01-001
idlers	NNS	1-01-001
idly	**RB**	**6-05-006**
idol	**noun**	**10-06-009**
idol	NN	6-05-006
Idol	NN-HL	1-01-001
idols	NNS	1-01-001
idols	NNS-HL	1-01-001
idols'	NNS$	0-00-000
idols'	NNS$-HL	1-01-001

Word	Tag	Frequency
idol-worship	**NN**	**1-01-001**
idolatry	**NN**	**1-01-001**
idolize	**verb**	**2-02-002**
idolize	VB	1-01-001
idolized	VBN	1-01-001
idyll	**NN**	**2-01-001**
idyllic	**JJ**	**4-02-004**
Ierulli	**NP**	**3-01-001**
if	**sub. conj.**	**2199-15-453**
if	CS	2187-15-453
yff	CS	2-01-001
if	CS-HL	10-03-003
Ifni	**NP**	**1-01-001**
Igbo	**NP**	**3-01-001**
Iglehart	**NP**	**1-01-001**
Ignazio	**NP**	**1-01-001**
igneous	**JJ**	**1-01-001**
ignite	**verb**	**3-03-003**
ignite	VB	2-02-002
ignited	VBN	1-01-001
ignition	**noun**	**5-04-004**
ignition	NN	4-04-004
ignition	NN-HL	1-01-001
ignoramus	**NN**	**2-02-002**
ignorance	**NN**	**16-09-015**
ignorant	**JJ**	**12-06-010**
ignore	**verb**	**57-14-050**
ignore	VB	19-09-016
ignores	VBZ	5-03-005
ignored	VBD	13-08-013
ignored	VBN	16-09-015
ignoring	VBG	4-03-004
Igor	**NP**	**3-02-003**
Ihmsen	**NP**	**1-01-001**
Iijima	**NP**	**1-01-001**
IJAL	**NP**	**1-01-001**
Ike	**prop. noun**	**5-04-005**
Ike	NP	2-02-002
Ike	NP-HL	1-01-001
Ike	NP-TL	1-01-001
Ike's	NP+BEZ	1-01-001
ikey-kikey	**JJ**	**1-01-001**
Ikle	**NP**	**1-01-001**
il	**foreign**	**1-01-001**
il	FW-AT	0-00-000
Il	FW-AT-TL	1-01-001
il	**FW-PPS**	**1-01-001**
Il	**prop. noun**	**1-01-001**
Il	NP	0-00-000
Il	NP-TL	1-01-001
ileum	**NN**	**1-01-001**
iliac	**JJ**	**1-01-001**
Iliad	**prop. noun**	**14-01-002**
Iliad	NP	5-01-001
Iliad	NP-TL	9-01-001
Ilka	**NP**	**1-01-001**
ill	**JJ**	**21-07-019**
ill	**noun**	**10-05-008**
ill	NN	1-01-001
ills	NNS	9-05-007
ill	**QL**	**1-01-001**
ill	**RB**	**3-03-003**
ill-conceived	**JJ**	**3-02-003**
ill-equipped	**JJ**	**2-02-002**
ill-fated	**JJ**	**2-02-002**
ill-prepared	**JJ**	**1-01-001**
ill-starred	**JJ**	**4-04-004**
ille	**foreign**	**1-01-001**
ille	FW-NN	0-00-000
Ille	FW-NN-TL	1-01-001
illegal	**JJ**	**9-05-009**
illegally	**RB**	**2-02-002**
illegitimacy	**NN**	**4-02-002**
illegitimate	**JJ**	**3-02-002**
illicit	**JJ**	**3-03-003**
Illinois	**prop. noun**	**54-09-036**
Illinois	NP	26-08-020
Ill.	NP	12-05-009
Ill.	NP-HL	1-01-001
Illinois	NP-HL	1-01-001
Illinois	NP-TL	13-06-010
Illinois'	NP$	1-01-001
illiterate	**JJ**	**8-03-007**
illness	**noun**	**22-11-017**
illness	NN	20-10-016
illnesses	NNS	2-02-002
illogical	**JJ**	**1-01-001**
illuminate	**verb**	**16-07-011**
illuminate	VB	1-01-001

Word	Tag	Frequency
illuminate (cont.):		
illuminated	VBD	1-01-001
illuminated	VBN	13-06-009
illuminating	VBG	1-01-001
illuminating	**JJ**	**4-03-003**
illumination	**noun**	**10-04-008**
illumination	NN	9-04-008
illuminations	NNS	1-01-001
illumine	**verb**	**5-04-004**
illumine	VB	1-01-001
illumines	VBZ	1-01-001
illumined	VBD	2-01-001
illumined	VBN	1-01-001
illusion	**noun**	**43-08-021**
illusion	NN	36-07-016
illusion	NN-HL	1-01-001
illusions	NNS	6-03-006
illusionary	**JJ**	**1-01-001**
illusions	**FW-NNS**	**1-01-001**
illusive	**JJ**	**2-01-002**
illusory	**JJ**	**2-02-002**
illustrate	**verb**	**65-11-053**
illustrate	VB	17-07-016
illustrates	VBZ	7-03-007
illustrated	VBD	1-01-001
illustrated	VBN	33-11-026
Illustrated	VBN-TL	3-01-003
illustrating	VBG	4-04-004
illustration	**noun**	**36-11-023**
illustration	NN	16-10-015
Illustration	NN-TL	6-01-001
Illustration	NN-TL-HL	1-01-001
illustrations	NNS	11-06-009
Illustrations	NNS-TL	2-02-002
illustrative	**JJ**	**6-03-006**
illustrator	**noun**	**2-01-001**
illustrator	NN	1-01-001
illustrators	NNS	1-01-001
illustrious	**JJ**	**3-03-003**
Ilona	**NP**	**1-01-001**
Ilyushin	**NP**	**1-01-001**
image	**noun**	**156-13-058**
image	NN	117-13-046
image	NN-HL	2-01-001
images	NNS	36-06-022
Images	NNS-TL	1-01-001
image-provoking	**JJ**	**1-01-001**
imagery	**NN**	**10-03-008**
imaginary	**adjective**	**17-08-014**
imaginary	JJ	16-07-013
Imaginary	JJ-TL	1-01-001
imagination	**noun**	**67-14-053**
imagination	NN	65-14-051
imagnation	NN	1-01-001
imaginations	NNS	1-01-001
imaginative	**JJ**	**13-07-012**
imaginatively	**RB**	**1-01-001**
imagine	**verb**	**92-13-072**
imagine	VB	61-13-049
imagines	VBZ	3-03-003
imagined	VBD	12-05-012
imagined	VBN	15-07-012
imagining	VBG	1-01-001
imaging	**NN**	**2-01-002**
imagining	**noun**	**1-01-001**
imaginings	NNS	1-01-001
imbalance	**noun**	**2-02-002**
imbalance	NN	1-01-001
imbalances	NNS	1-01-001
imbecile	**NN**	**1-01-001**
imbed	**verb**	**4-04-004**
imbedded	VBD	1-01-001
imbedded	VBN	3-03-003
imbibe	**verb**	**3-03-003**
imbibe	VB	1-01-001
imbibed	VBD	1-01-001
imbibed	VBN	1-01-001
Imboden	**NP**	**1-01-001**
Imbrium	**prop. noun**	**1-01-001**
Imbrium	NP	0-00-000
Imbrium	NP-TL	1-01-001
imbroglio	**NN**	**1-01-001**
imbrue	**verb**	**1-01-001**
imbruing	VBG	1-01-001
imbue	**verb**	**1-01-001**
imbued	VBN	1-01-001
imitate	**verb**	**13-07-009**
imitate	VB	5-04-005
imitates	VBZ	2-01-002

Word	Tag	Frequency
imitate (cont.):		
imitated	VBD	2-02-002
imitated	VBN	2-02-002
imitating	VBG	2-02-002
imitation	**noun**	**26-04-005**
imitation	NN	23-04-005
imitations	NNS	3-01-001
imitation-caning	**NN**	**1-01-001**
imitation-woodgrain	**NN**	**1-01-001**
imitative	**JJ**	**1-01-001**
imitator	**noun**	**2-02-002**
imitators	NNS	2-02-002
immaculate	**JJ**	**5-04-005**
immanent	**JJ**	**3-02-002**
immaterial	**JJ**	**2-02-002**
immature	**JJ**	**7-05-006**
immaturity	**NN**	**1-01-001**
immeasurable	**JJ**	**2-02-002**
immeasurably	**QL**	**1-01-001**
immediacy	**noun**	**9-03-006**
immediacy	NN	8-03-005
immediacies	NNS	1-01-001
immediate	**adjective**	**81-14-071**
immediate	JJ	80-14-070
immediate	JJ-HL	1-01-001
immediately	**QL**	**7-05-006**
immediately	**RB**	**116-15-092**
immemorial	**JJ**	**2-02-002**
immense	**JJ**	**14-07-013**
immensely	**QL**	**4-03-004**
immensely	**RB**	**5-05-005**
immensity	**noun**	**3-02-003**
immensity	NN	2-02-002
immensities	NNS	1-01-001
immerse	**verb**	**4-04-004**
immersed	VBD	1-01-001
immersed	VBN	3-03-003
immersion	**NN**	**2-01-002**
immigrant	**noun**	**14-06-011**
immigrant	NN	4-03-004
immigrants	NNS	10-05-008
immigration	**noun**	**10-04-005**
immigration	NN	7-03-004
Immigration	NN-TL	3-02-002
imminence	**NN**	**1-01-001**
imminent	**JJ**	**3-03-003**
immobility	**NN**	**4-03-003**
immoderate	**JJ**	**1-01-001**
immodest	**JJ**	**1-01-001**
immodesty	**NN**	**1-01-001**
immoral	**JJ**	**5-04-005**
immorality	**noun**	**5-02-002**
immorality	NN	4-02-002
immoralities	NNS	1-01-001
immortal	**adjective**	**7-04-004**
immortal	JJ	6-04-004
Immortal	JJ-TL	1-01-001
immortality	**NN**	**19-03-008**
immortalize	**verb**	**1-01-001**
immortalized	VBN	1-01-001
immovable	**JJ**	**1-01-001**
immunity	**NN**	**7-04-004**
immunization	**NN**	**1-01-001**
immunoelectrophoresis	**NN**	**1-01-001**
immutable	**JJ**	**1-01-001**
impact	**noun**	**70-12-045**
impact	NN	67-12-045
impacts	NNS	3-01-001
impact	**verb**	**2-02-002**
impacted	VBN	2-02-002
impair	**verb**	**11-05-011**
impair	VB	4-04-004
impaired	VBN	7-03-007
impairment	**NN**	**1-01-001**
impale	**verb**	**3-02-003**
impaled	VBN	2-02-002
impaling	VBG	1-01-001
impart	**verb**	**9-06-007**
impart	VB	4-04-004
imparts	VBZ	1-01-001
imparted	VBD	1-01-001
imparted	VBN	3-02-003
impartation	**noun**	**1-01-001**
impartation	NN	0-00-000
impartation	NN-HL	1-01-001
impartial	**JJ**	**8-03-006**
impartiality	**NN**	**2-01-002**
impassable	**JJ**	**2-02-002**
impasse	**NN**	**2-02-002**

Word	Tag	Frequency
impassioned	**JJ**	**8-04-008**
impassive	**JJ**	**1-01-001**
impassively	**RB**	**1-01-001**
impatience	**NN**	**10-08-010**
impatient	**JJ**	**10-06-009**
impatiently	**RB**	**9-04-009**
impeccable	**JJ**	**6-06-006**
impeccably	**QL**	**1-01-001**
impeccably	**RB**	**1-01-001**
impede	**verb**	**5-03-005**
impeded	VBD	1-01-001
impeded	VBN	4-03-004
impediment	**NN**	**1-01-001**
impel	**verb**	**7-03-006**
impelled	VBD	1-01-001
impelled	VBN	5-03-005
impelling	VBG	1-01-001
impend	**verb**	**4-03-004**
impending	VBG	3-02-003
impending	VBG-HL	1-01-001
impenetrable	**JJ**	**1-01-001**
imperative	**JJ**	**8-06-008**
imperative	**NN**	**2-02-002**
imperceptible	**JJ**	**1-01-001**
imperceptibly	**RB**	**1-01-001**
imperfect	**JJ**	**4-04-004**
imperfectibility	**noun**	**1-01-001**
imperfectibility	NN	0-00-000
imperfectability	NN	1-01-001
imperfection	**noun**	**3-02-003**
imperfection	NN	1-01-001
imperfections	NNS	2-01-002
imperfectly	**RB**	**2-01-002**
imperial	**adjective**	**13-08-013**
imperial	JJ	6-04-006
Imperial	JJ-TL	7-06-007
Imperiale	**prop. noun**	**1-01-001**
Imperiales	NPS	1-01-001
imperialism	**NN**	**2-02-002**
imperialist	**noun**	**2-01-002**
imperialist	NN	1-01-001
imperialists	NNS	1-01-001
imperil	**verb**	**3-03-003**
imperil	VB	1-01-001
imperiled	VBN	1-01-001
imperilled	VBN	1-01-001
imperious	**JJ**	**1-01-001**
imperiously	**RB**	**2-02-002**
imperishable	**JJ**	**1-01-001**
impersonal	**adjective**	**14-07-010**
impersonal	JJ	13-07-009
impersonal	JJ-HL	1-01-001
impersonalize	**verb**	**1-01-001**
impersonalized	VBN	1-01-001
impersonally	**RB**	**1-01-001**
impersonate	**verb**	**2-02-002**
impersonates	VBZ	1-01-001
impersonated	VBN	1-01-001
impersonation	**NN**	**2-01-002**
impertinent	**JJ**	**1-01-001**
imperturbable	**JJ**	**1-01-001**
impervious	**JJ**	**2-02-002**
impetuous	**JJ**	**3-03-003**
impetus	**NN**	**6-04-006**
impiety	**NN**	**1-01-001**
impinge	**verb**	**8-04-007**
impinge	VB	3-03-003
impinging	VBG	5-02-004
impious	**JJ**	**2-02-002**
implacable	**JJ**	**3-03-003**
implant	**NN**	**1-01-001**
implant	**verb**	**1-01-001**
implanted	VBN	1-01-001
implantation	**noun**	**1-01-001**
implantation	NN	0-00-000
implantation	NN-HL	1-01-001
implausibly	**RB**	**1-01-001**
implement	**noun**	**6-03-004**
implement	NN	1-01-001
implements	NNS	5-03-003
implement	**verb**	**7-05-007**
implement	VB	3-03-003
implemented	VBN	1-01-001
implementing	VBG	3-02-003
implementation	**NN**	**8-05-007**
implicate	**verb**	**2-02-002**
implicated	VBN	2-02-002
implication	**noun**	**32-10-027**
implication	NN	10-06-010

Word	Tag	Frequency
implication (cont.):		
implications	NNS	22-08-017
implicit	**JJ**	**13-05-011**
implicitly	**RB**	**3-03-003**
implore	**verb**	**4-04-004**
implore	VB	1-01-001
implored	VBD	1-01-001
implored	VBN	1-01-001
imploring	VBG	1-01-001
imply	**verb**	**53-09-041**
imply	VB	13-06-011
implies	VBZ	16-05-015
implied	VBD	5-04-005
implied	VBN	12-04-012
implying	VBG	7-04-006
impolitic	**JJ**	**2-02-002**
imponderable	**JJ**	**1-01-001**
import	**noun**	**28-10-018**
import	NN	14-09-012
imports	NNS	14-06-009
import	**verb**	**12-08-009**
import	VB	3-03-003
imports	VBZ	1-01-001
imported	VBD	2-02-002
imported	VBN	6-03-004
importance	**NN**	**108-13-079**
important	**adjective**	**369-15-211**
important	JJ	368-15-211
important	JJ-HL	1-01-001
important-looking	**JJ**	**1-01-001**
importantly	**RB**	**8-05-007**
importation	**NN**	**2-02-002**
importunately	**adverb**	**1-01-001**
importunately	RB	0-00-000
importunately	RB-NC	1-01-001
importunity	**noun**	**1-01-001**
importunities	NNS	1-01-001
impose	**verb**	**39-12-033**
impose	VB	9-05-008
imposes	VBZ	4-04-004
imposed	VBD	4-03-004
imposed	VBN	15-08-015
imposing	VBG	7-05-007
imposition	**NN**	**5-05-005**
impossibility	**NN**	**1-01-001**
impossible	**JJ**	**85-15-073**
impossibly	**QL**	**1-01-001**
impotence	**NN**	**2-02-002**
impotency	**NN**	**1-01-001**
impotent	**JJ**	**2-02-002**
impoundment	**noun**	**1-01-001**
impoundments	NNS	1-01-001
impoverished	**JJ**	**3-02-003**
impracticable	**JJ**	**1-01-001**
impractical	**JJ**	**5-05-005**
imprecate	**verb**	**1-01-001**
imprecates	VBZ	1-01-001
imprecation	**noun**	**1-01-001**
imprecations	NNS	1-01-001
imprecise	**JJ**	**1-01-001**
imprecisely	**QL**	**3-02-002**
impresario	**NN**	**1-01-001**
impress	**NN**	**1-01-001**
impress	**verb**	**36-11-029**
impress	VB	3-02-003
impresses	VBZ	1-01-001
impressed	VBD	7-04-006
impressed	VBN	23-10-020
impressing	VBG	2-01-002
impresser	**NN**	**1-01-001**
impression	**noun**	**70-13-045**
impression	NN	45-12-036
impressions	NNS	25-09-016
Impressionism	**NP**	**1-01-001**
impressionist	**noun**	**4-03-003**
impressionist	NN	3-02-002
impressionists	NNS	1-01-001
impressionistic	**JJ**	**1-01-001**
impressive	**adjective**	**49-11-042**
impressive	JJ	48-11-041
impressive	JJ-HL	1-01-001
imprimatur	**NN**	**2-02-002**
imprint	**verb**	**2-02-002**
imprint	VB	1-01-001
imprinted	VBN	1-01-001
imprison	**verb**	**5-04-005**
imprisons	VBZ	1-01-001
imprisoned	VBN	4-03-004
imprisonment	**NN**	**6-04-005**
improbable	**JJ**	**2-02-002**
improbably	**RB**	**1-01-001**
impromptu	**JJ**	**2-02-002**
impromptu	**NN**	**1-01-001**
improper	**adjective**	**2-02-002**
improper	JJ	1-01-001
improper	JJ-HL	1-01-001
improperly	**RB**	**2-02-002**
impropriety	**NN**	**1-01-001**
improve	**verb**	**121-12-079**
improve	VB	39-10-033
improves	VBZ	11-03-005
improved	VBD	7-04-005
improved	VBN	46-11-036
improved	VBN-HL	2-02-002
improving	VBG	16-07-015
improvement	**noun**	**60-08-037**
improvement	NN	39-07-025
Improvement	NN-TL	1-01-001
improvements	NNS	18-07-014
improvements	NNS-HL	2-02-002
improvisation	**noun**	**3-03-003**
improvisation	NN	1-01-001
improvisations	NNS	2-02-002
improvise	**verb**	**6-02-004**
improvise	VB	2-02-002
improvises	VBZ	1-01-001
improvised	VBD	2-01-001
improvised	VBN	1-01-001
improviser	**NN**	**1-01-001**
improvising	**NN**	**1-01-001**
imprudently	**RB**	**2-02-002**
impudence	**NN**	**1-01-001**
impudent	**JJ**	**3-03-003**
impudently	**RB**	**1-01-001**
impulse	**noun**	**32-11-028**
impulse	NN	20-09-018
impulses	NNS	12-05-010
impulsive	**JJ**	**1-01-001**
impunity	**NN**	**3-03-003**
impurity	**noun**	**11-02-006**
impurity	NN	2-01-002
impurities	NNS	9-02-006
impurity-doped	**JJ**	**1-01-001**
imputation	**NN**	**2-01-002**
impute	**verb**	**6-04-004**
impute	VB	1-01-001
imputed	VBN	5-03-003
in	**FW-IN**	**1-01-001**
in	**prep.**	**20870-15-500**
in	IN	20732-15-500
in	IN-HL	69-10-045
in	IN-NC	2-02-002
In	IN-TL	42-10-034
in	IN-TL	22-09-017
'n	+IN	3-01-001
in	**NN**	**1-01-001**
in	**adv./part.**	**466-15-236**
in	RP	462-15-235
in	RP-HL	2-01-002
in	RP-NC	2-01-001
in-group	**noun**	**5-04-005**
in-group	NN	4-03-004
in-groups	NNS	1-01-001
in-law	**noun**	**2-02-002**
in-laws	NNS	2-02-002
in-migrant	**noun**	**1-01-001**
in-migrants	NNS	1-01-001
in-person	**NN**	**1-01-001**
in-plant	**JJ**	**1-01-001**
in-state	**RB**	**1-01-001**
inability	**NN**	**17-08-014**
inaccessible	**JJ**	**1-01-001**
inaccuracy	**noun**	**3-02-003**
inaccuracy	NN	2-02-002
inaccuracies	NNS	1-01-001
inaccurate	**JJ**	**5-04-005**
inaction	**NN**	**6-04-005**
inactivate	**VB**	**2-01-001**
inactivation	**NN**	**2-01-002**
inactive	**JJ**	**7-03-005**
inactivity	**NN**	**1-01-001**
inadequacy	**noun**	**5-04-005**
inadequacy	NN	3-03-003
inadequacies	NNS	2-02-002
inadequate	**JJ**	**32-10-029**
inadequately	**RB**	**2-02-002**
inadvertence	**NN**	**1-01-001**
inadvertent	**JJ**	**2-02-002**

Word	Tag	Frequency
inadvertently	**RB**	**2-02-002**
inadvisable	**JJ**	**1-01-001**
inalienable	**JJ**	**2-02-002**
inane	**JJ**	**1-01-001**
inanimate	**JJ**	**2-02-002**
inapplicable	**JJ**	**2-01-001**
inappropriate	**JJ**	**4-04-004**
inappropriateness	**NN**	**1-01-001**
inapt	**JJ**	**1-01-001**
inarticulate	**JJ**	**1-01-001**
inasmuch	**RB**	**1-01-001**
inattentive	**JJ**	**1-01-001**
inaudible	**JJ**	**2-02-002**
inaugural	**JJ**	**2-02-002**
inaugural	**noun**	**6-03-006**
inaugural	NN	3-03-003
Inaugural	NN-TL	3-02-003
inaugurate	**verb**	**5-04-005**
inaugurated	VBD	1-01-001
inaugurated	VBN	3-03-003
inaugurating	VBG	1-01-001
inauguration	**noun**	**8-05-007**
inauguration	NN	3-03-003
Inauguration	NN-TL	5-03-004
inboard	**JJ**	**1-01-001**
inboard	**noun**	**1-01-001**
inboards	NNS	1-01-001
inboard	**RB**	**2-02-002**
inborn	**JJ**	**1-01-001**
inbreed	**verb**	**1-01-001**
inbreeding	VBG	1-01-001
Inca	**NP**	**1-01-001**
incalculable	**JJ**	**1-01-001**
incandescent	**JJ**	**3-03-003**
incant	**verb**	**1-01-001**
incanted	VBD	1-01-001
incantation	**NN**	**2-01-002**
incapable	**JJ**	**11-04-011**
incapacitate	**verb**	**2-02-002**
incapacitated	VBN	2-02-002
incapacity	**NN**	**1-01-001**
incarcerate	**verb**	**1-01-001**
incarcerated	VBN	1-01-001
incarnate	**JJ**	**1-01-001**
incarnate	**VB**	**1-01-001**
incarnation	**noun**	**5-03-005**
incarnation	NN	4-03-004
Incarnation	NN-TL	1-01-001
incautious	**JJ**	**1-01-001**
incendiary	**noun**	**1-01-001**
incendiaries	NNS	1-01-001
incense	**NN**	**2-02-002**
incense	**verb**	**3-03-003**
incensed	VBN	3-03-003
incentive	**noun**	**16-06-010**
incentive	NN	11-06-009
incentive	NN-HL	1-01-001
incentives	NNS	4-02-003
incept	**verb**	**4-01-001**
incepted	VBD	1-01-001
incepting	VBG	3-01-001
inception	**NN**	**6-05-006**
inceptor	**NN**	**1-01-001**
incertain	**JJ**	**1-01-001**
incessant	**JJ**	**4-03-004**
incessantly	**RB**	**2-01-002**
incest	**NN**	**13-02-002**
incestuous	**JJ**	**3-01-002**
inch	**noun**	**129-12-041**
inch	NN	39-08-022
in.	NN	4-02-002
inches	NNS	80-11-025
inches	NNS-HL	6-01-001
inch	**verb**	**1-01-001**
inched	VBD	1-01-001
incidence	**NN**	**7-02-004**
incident	**JJ**	**14-03-005**
incident	**noun**	**46-12-038**
incident	NN	35-11-032
incidents	NNS	11-07-010
incidental	**JJ**	**5-03-005**
incidental	**noun**	**1-01-001**
incidentals	NNS	1-01-001
incidentally	**RB**	**14-06-014**
incinerator	**noun**	**2-01-001**
incinerator	NN	1-01-001
Incinerator	NN-TL	1-01-001
incipience	**NN**	**1-01-001**
incipiency	**NN**	**2-01-001**

Word	Tag	Frequency
incipient	**JJ**	**4-03-004**
incise	**VB**	**1-01-001**
incisive	**JJ**	**4-03-003**
incisiveness	**NN**	**1-01-001**
incite	**verb**	**7-04-005**
incite	VB	3-03-003
incited	VBD	2-01-001
incited	VBN	1-01-001
inciting	VBG	1-01-001
incitement	**noun**	**4-02-003**
incitement	NN	3-01-002
incitements	NNS	1-01-001
inclement	**JJ**	**2-02-002**
inclination	**noun**	**9-06-008**
inclination	NN	8-05-007
inclinations	NNS	1-01-001
incline	**noun**	**4-02-002**
incline	NN	2-02-002
Incline	NN-TL	2-01-001
incline	**verb**	**21-12-017**
inclined	VBN	21-12-017
include	**verb**	**260-13-157**
include	VB	113-09-082
includes	VBZ	45-09-037
included	VBD	41-11-033
included	VBN	56-12-046
including	VBG	5-04-005
including	**IN**	**166-14-124**
inclusion	**noun**	**5-02-004**
inclusion	NN	3-02-003
inclusions	NNS	2-01-001
inclusive	**JJ**	**4-04-004**
inclusiveness	**NN**	**1-01-001**
incoherent	**JJ**	**4-04-004**
incoherently	**RB**	**1-01-001**
income	**noun**	**110-12-036**
income	NN	95-12-036
income	NN-HL	2-01-001
Income	NN-TL	12-01-001
incomes	NNS	1-01-001
incoming	**JJ**	**5-04-005**
incomparable	**adjective**	**5-03-004**
incomparable	JJ	4-03-004
imcomparable	JJ	1-01-001
incomparably	**QL**	**1-01-001**
incomparably	**RB**	**2-02-002**
incompatibility	**NN**	**1-01-001**
incompatible	**JJ**	**2-02-002**
incompatible	**noun**	**1-01-001**
incompatibles	NNS	1-01-001
incompetence	**NN**	**4-03-003**
incompetent	**JJ**	**2-02-002**
incompetent	**noun**	**2-02-002**
incompetents	NNS	2-02-002
incomplete	**adjective**	**14-03-009**
incomplete	JJ	13-03-009
imcomplete	JJ	1-01-001
incompletely	**RB**	**2-02-002**
incompleteness	**NN**	**1-01-001**
incomprehensible	**JJ**	**2-02-002**
incomprehension	**NN**	**1-01-001**
inconceivable	**JJ**	**1-01-001**
inconclusive	**JJ**	**3-03-003**
incongruity	**noun**	**3-03-003**
incongruity	NN	1-01-001
incongruities	NNS	2-02-002
incongruous	**JJ**	**1-01-001**
inconsequential	**JJ**	**3-03-003**
inconsiderable	**JJ**	**1-01-001**
inconsistency	**noun**	**2-02-002**
inconsistency	NN	1-01-001
inconsistencies	NNS	1-01-001
inconsistent	**JJ**	**5-04-005**
inconspicuous	**JJ**	**1-01-001**
inconspicuously	**RB**	**1-01-001**
incontestable	**JJ**	**1-01-001**
incontrovertible	**JJ**	**1-01-001**
inconvenience	**NN**	**3-03-003**
inconvenient	**JJ**	**3-03-003**
inconveniently	**RB**	**1-01-001**
incorporate	**verb**	**39-07-027**
incorporate	VB	2-02-002
incorporates	VBZ	3-03-003
incorporated	VBD	2-02-002
incorporated	VBN	11-04-008
inc.	VBN	0-00-000
Inc.	VBN-TL	20-06-013
incorporating	VBG	1-01-001
incorporation	**NN**	**3-03-003**

Word	Tag	Frequency
incorrect	**adjective**	**5-04-005**
incorrect	JJ	4-04-004
Incorrect	JJ-TL	1-01-001
incorrigible	**JJ**	**1-01-001**
incorruptibility	**NN**	**1-01-001**
incorruptible	**JJ**	**2-02-002**
increase	**noun**	**155-08-061**
increase	NN	112-08-052
increase	NN-HL	1-01-001
increases	NNS	42-06-015
increase	**verb**	**332-15-168**
increase	VB	81-11-060
increase	VB-HL	1-01-001
increases	VBZ	30-06-022
increased	VBD	38-12-033
increased	VBN	105-11-069
increased	VBN-HL	3-02-002
increasing	VBG	72-10-058
increasing	VBG-HL	2-01-002
increasingly	**QL**	**21-08-019**
increasingly	**RB**	**21-10-018**
incredible	**adjective**	**23-11-020**
incredible	JJ	21-11-019
incredible	JJ-NC	2-01-001
incredibly	**QL**	**5-04-005**
incredibly	**RB**	**2-02-002**
incredulity	**NN**	**1-01-001**
incredulously	**RB**	**1-01-001**
incremental	**JJ**	**1-01-001**
incriminate	**verb**	**1-01-001**
incriminating	VBG	1-01-001
incubate	**verb**	**2-01-002**
incubated	VBN	1-01-001
incubating	VBG	1-01-001
incubation	**NN**	**4-02-003**
incubus	**noun**	**2-02-002**
incubus	NN	1-01-001
incubi	NNS	1-01-001
inculcate	**verb**	**2-02-002**
inculcated	VBN	2-02-002
inculcation	**NN**	**2-02-002**
incumbent	**JJ**	**4-02-003**
incumbent	**noun**	**1-01-001**
incumbents	NNS	1-01-001
incur	**verb**	**16-07-013**
incur	VB	5-03-005
incurs	VBZ	1-01-001
incurred	VBD	1-01-001
incurred	VBN	8-05-006
incurring	VBG	1-01-001
incurable	**JJ**	**2-02-002**
incurably	**QL**	**2-02-002**
incursion	**NN**	**1-01-001**
indebted	**JJ**	**10-06-009**
indecent	**JJ**	**6-04-006**
indecipherable	**JJ**	**1-01-001**
indecision	**NN**	**5-04-004**
indecisive	**JJ**	**2-02-002**
indecisively	**RB**	**1-01-001**
indecisiveness	**NN**	**1-01-001**
indeed	**QL**	**1-01-001**
indeed	**QLP**	**13-09-013**
indeed	**RB**	**145-14-108**
indeed	**UH**	**3-01-002**
indefatigable	**JJ**	**1-01-001**
indefensible	**JJ**	**2-02-002**
indefinable	**JJ**	**2-02-002**
indefinite	**JJ**	**7-04-004**
indefinite	**NN**	**1-01-001**
indefinitely	**RB**	**6-05-006**
indefiniteness	**NN**	**1-01-001**
indefinity	**NN**	**1-01-001**
indelible	**adjective**	**5-03-003**
indelible	JJ	4-03-003
indelible	JJ-HL	1-01-001
indelibly	**QL**	**1-01-001**
indelicate	**JJ**	**1-01-001**
indemnity	**noun**	**2-02-002**
indemnity	NN	1-01-001
Indemnity	NN-TL	1-01-001
indentation	**noun**	**1-01-001**
indentations	NNS	1-01-001
indenture	**NN**	**2-02-002**
independence	**noun**	**71-08-032**
independence	NN	46-07-023
independence	NN-HL	1-01-001
Independence	NN-TL	24-05-010
independent	**adjective**	**70-11-047**
independent	JJ	67-11-045

Word	Tag	Frequency
independent (cont.):		
independent	JJ-HL	1-01-001
Independent	JJ-TL	2-02-002
independent	**noun**	**1-01-001**
independents	NNS	1-01-001
independently	**RB**	**12-05-009**
indescribable	**JJ**	**4-04-004**
indestructible	**JJ**	**1-01-001**
indeterminate	**adjective**	**4-04-004**
indeterminate	JJ	3-03-003
Indeterminate	JJ-TL	1-01-001
index	**noun**	**89-08-014**
index	NN	75-08-014
index	NN-HL	1-01-001
Index	NN-TL	4-01-002
indices	NNS	7-01-002
indexes	NNS	2-01-001
index	**verb**	**3-02-003**
index	VB	1-01-001
indexing	VBG	2-01-002
indexing	**NN**	**1-01-001**
India	**prop. noun**	**60-10-020**
India	NP	35-10-017
India	NP-TL	23-04-005
India's	NP$	2-01-001
Indian	**adjective**	**42-14-024**
Indian	JJ	37-13-020
Indian	JJ-TL	5-04-005
Indian	**prop. noun**	**48-09-021**
Indian	NP	9-01-004
Indian	NP-TL	1-01-001
Indian's	NP$	5-01-004
Indians	NPS	28-06-013
Indians	NPS-HL	1-01-001
Indians	NPS-TL	3-03-003
Indians'	NPS$	1-01-001
Indiana	**prop. noun**	**16-06-009**
Indiana	NP	12-05-007
Ind.	NP	1-01-001
Ind.	NP-HL	1-01-001
Indiana	NP-TL	1-01-001
Indiana's	NP$	1-01-001
Indianapolis	**NP**	**6-04-005**
indicate	**verb**	**244-15-148**
indicate	VB	80-12-065
indicates	VBZ	40-08-029
indicated	VBD	59-14-049
indicated	VBN	49-07-042
indicating	VBG	16-09-015
indication	**noun**	**36-10-032**
indication	NN	20-08-020
indications	NNS	15-07-014
indications	NNS-HL	1-01-001
indicative	**JJ**	**6-04-006**
indicator	**noun**	**17-05-010**
indicator	NN	8-04-006
indicators	NNS	9-03-005
indict	**verb**	**2-02-002**
indicted	VBN	2-02-002
indictment	**noun**	**14-05-009**
indictment	NN	12-05-009
indictments	NNS	2-01-002
Indies	**prop. noun**	**9-04-008**
Indies	NPS	5-03-004
Indies	NPS-TL	4-03-004
indifference	**NN**	**17-09-016**
indifferent	**JJ**	**11-07-011**
indigenes	**foreign**	**1-01-001**
indigenes	FW-JJ	0-00-000
Indigenes	FW-JJ-TL	1-01-001
indigenes	**foreign**	**1-01-001**
indigenes	FW-NNS	0-00-000
Indigenes	FW-NNS-TL	1-01-001
indigenous	**JJ**	**3-02-002**
indigent	**JJ**	**1-01-001**
indigestible	**JJ**	**1-01-001**
indigestion	**NN**	**2-02-002**
indignant	**JJ**	**10-07-010**
indignantly	**RB**	**1-01-001**
indignation	**noun**	**10-08-010**
indignation	NN	9-07-009
indigation	NN	1-01-001
indignity	**noun**	**3-03-003**
indignities	NNS	3-03-003
indigo	**adjective**	**1-01-001**
indigo	JJ	0-00-000
Indigo	JJ-TL	1-01-001
indirect	**adjective**	**21-03-007**
indirect	JJ	18-03-006

indirect (cont.):		
indirect	JJ-HL	3-01-002
indirection	**NN**	**1-01-001**
indirectly	**RB**	**17-05-015**
indiscreet	**JJ**	**2-02-002**
indiscriminate	**JJ**	**3-02-003**
indiscriminately	**adverb**	**1-01-001**
indiscriminately	RB	0-00-000
indiscriminantly	RB	1-01-001
indiscriminating	**JJ**	**1-01-001**
indispensable	**adjective**	**16-09-016**
indispensable	JJ	15-09-015
indispensible	JJ	1-01-001
indispose	**verb**	**3-02-002**
indisposed	VBN	3-02-002
indisposition	**NN**	**1-01-001**
indisputably	**QL**	**1-01-001**
indistinct	**JJ**	**1-01-001**
indistinguishable	**JJ**	**3-03-003**
indium	**NN**	**1-01-001**
individual	**AP**	**8-03-007**
individual	**adjective**	**150-09-091**
individual	JJ	147-09-090
individual	JJ-HL	3-02-003
individual	**noun**	**165-11-088**
individual	NN	81-11-052
individual's	NN$	11-03-008
individuals	NNS	73-10-054
individual-contributor	**JJ**	**2-01-001**
individualism	**NN**	**12-01-004**
individualist	**noun**	**5-01-003**
individualist	NN	3-01-001
individualists	NNS	2-01-002
individualistic	**JJ**	**4-02-004**
individuality	**NN**	**4-04-004**
individualize	**verb**	**6-02-006**
individualized	VBN	5-02-005
individualizing	VBG	1-01-001
individually	**RB**	**19-08-018**
individuation	**NN**	**1-01-001**
indivisibility	**NN**	**1-01-001**
indivisible	**JJ**	**1-01-001**
Indochina	**prop. noun**	**3-03-003**
Indochina	NP	1-01-001
Indo-China	NP	1-01-001
Indochina	NP-TL	1-01-001
indoctrinate	**verb**	**1-01-001**
indoctrinated	VBN	1-01-001
indoctrinating	**NN**	**1-01-001**
indoctrination	**NN**	**1-01-001**
indolence	**NN**	**1-01-001**
indolent	**JJ**	**4-02-003**
indolently	**RB**	**1-01-001**
indomitable	**JJ**	**1-01-001**
Indonesia	**prop. noun**	**9-03-005**
Indonesia	NP	7-03-005
Indonesia	NP-TL	2-01-001
Indonesian	**JJ**	**1-01-001**
indoor	**JJ**	**4-04-004**
indoors	**RB**	**5-03-005**
indubitable	**JJ**	**1-01-001**
induce	**verb**	**29-06-020**
induce	VB	9-04-009
induces	VBZ	3-02-002
induced	VBD	1-01-001
induced	VBN	12-04-007
inducing	VBG	4-02-003
inducement	**noun**	**3-03-003**
inducement	NN	2-02-002
inducements	NNS	1-01-001
induct	**verb**	**3-02-002**
inducted	VBN	3-02-002
inductee	**noun**	**1-01-001**
inductees	NNS	1-01-001
induction	**noun**	**7-03-005**
induction	NN	6-03-004
inductions	NNS	1-01-001
indulge	**verb**	**15-07-014**
indulge	VB	9-05-008
indulged	VBD	5-03-005
indulging	VBG	1-01-001
indulgence	**noun**	**6-02-003**
indulgence	NN	4-02-003
Indulgence	NN-TL	1-01-001
indulgences	NNS	1-01-001
indulgent	**JJ**	**2-02-002**
industrial	**adjective**	**143-11-057**
industrial	JJ	113-11-055
industrial	JJ-HL	4-02-003

industrial (cont.):		
Industrial	JJ-TL	26-06-011
industrialism	**NN**	**1-01-001**
industrialist	**noun**	**3-03-003**
industrialist	NN	2-02-002
industrialists	NNS	1-01-001
industrialistes	**foreign**	**1-01-001**
industrialistes	FW-NNS	0-00-000
Industrialistes	FW-NNS-TL	1-01-001
industrialization	**noun**	**3-03-003**
industrialization	NN	2-02-002
industralization	NN	1-01-001
industrialize	**verb**	**9-04-006**
industrialized	VBN	9-04-006
industrially	**RB**	**1-01-001**
industrious	**JJ**	**3-02-003**
industriously	**RB**	**2-02-002**
industry	**noun**	**222-11-063**
industry	NN	161-10-053
industry	NN-HL	5-02-003
Industry	NN-TL	5-03-004
industry's	NN$	14-03-005
industry's	NN$-HL	1-01-001
industries	NNS	28-10-019
Industries	NNS-TL	8-04-004
industry-wide	**JJ**	**1-01-001**
indwell	**verb**	**2-02-002**
indwelling	VBG	2-02-002
ineffable	**JJ**	**1-01-001**
ineffective	**JJ**	**3-03-003**
ineffectively	**RB**	**1-01-001**
ineffectiveness	**NN**	**1-01-001**
ineffectual	**JJ**	**1-01-001**
inefficiency	**NN**	**1-01-001**
inefficient	**JJ**	**7-05-006**
ineligible	**JJ**	**3-03-003**
ineluctable	**JJ**	**1-01-001**
inept	**JJ**	**2-02-002**
ineptly	**RB**	**1-01-001**
ineptness	**NN**	**2-02-002**
inequality	**NN**	**1-01-001**
inert	**JJ**	**5-03-005**
inertia	**NN**	**2-02-002**
inertial	**JJ**	**3-01-001**
inescapable	**JJ**	**8-07-008**
inescapably	**RB**	**1-01-001**
inevitability	**noun**	**3-03-003**
inevitability	NN	2-02-002
inevitabilities	NNS	1-01-001
inevitable	**JJ**	**33-11-025**
inevitably	**RB**	**38-11-035**
inexact	**JJ**	**2-02-002**
inexcusable	**JJ**	**2-02-002**
inexhaustible	**JJ**	**3-03-003**
inexorable	**JJ**	**3-03-003**
inexorably	**RB**	**3-03-003**
inexpensive	**JJ**	**6-03-006**
inexperience	**NN**	**3-03-003**
inexperienced	**JJ**	**7-06-007**
inexpert	**JJ**	**1-01-001**
inexplicable	**JJ**	**6-04-005**
inexplicably	**RB**	**1-01-001**
inexpressible	**JJ**	**1-01-001**
inexpressibly	**QL**	**1-01-001**
inextricable	**JJ**	**1-01-001**
infallible	**JJ**	**3-02-003**
infamous	**JJ**	**4-02-004**
infamy	**NN**	**1-01-001**
infancy	**NN**	**11-04-005**
infant	**JJ**	**1-01-001**
infant	**noun**	**14-08-012**
infant	NN	10-07-010
infant's	NN$	1-01-001
infants	NNS	3-02-002
infantile	**JJ**	**2-02-002**
infantry	**noun**	**16-04-006**
infantry	NN	13-03-004
Infantry	NN-TL	3-03-003
infantryman	**noun**	**3-02-002**
infantryman	NN	2-02-002
infantrymen	NNS	1-01-001
infarct	**NN**	**1-01-001**
infarction	**NN**	**1-01-001**
infatuation	**NN**	**4-02-003**
infect	**verb**	**5-04-004**
infect	VB	1-01-001
infected	VBD	1-01-001
infected	VBN	3-03-003
infection	**noun**	**13-06-008**

infection (cont.):

Word	Tag	Frequency
infection	NN	8-06-008
infections	NNS	5-02-002
infectious	**JJ**	**17-04-005**
infer	**verb**	**4-02-004**
infer	VB	1-01-001
inferred	VBD	2-02-002
inferred	VBN	1-01-001
inference	**noun**	**11-04-009**
inference	NN	7-03-005
inferences	NNS	4-02-004
inferential	**JJ**	**2-01-002**
inferior	**JJ**	**7-04-007**
inferiority	**noun**	**5-03-005**
inferiority	NN	4-03-004
Inferiority	NN-TL	1-01-001
infernally	**RB**	**1-01-001**
inferno	**NN**	**1-01-001**
Inferno	**NP**	**1-01-001**
infertile	**JJ**	**1-01-001**
infest	**verb**	**2-01-001**
infest	VB	1-01-001
infested	VBN	1-01-001
infestation	**noun**	**6-02-002**
infestation	NN	2-02-002
infestations	NNS	4-01-001
infidel	**JJ**	**1-01-001**
infidel	**noun**	**1-01-001**
infidels	NNS	1-01-001
infidelity	**NN**	**2-02-002**
infield	**NN**	**7-03-003**
infighting	**noun**	**2-02-002**
infighting	NN	1-01-001
in-fighting	NN	1-01-001
infiltrate	**verb**	**3-02-002**
infiltrated	VBN	2-01-001
infiltrating	VBG	1-01-001
infiltration	**NN**	**6-03-004**
infinite	**JJ**	**16-09-013**
infinite	**noun**	**3-02-003**
infinite	NN	2-02-002
Infinite	NN-TL	1-01-001
infinitely	**QL**	**1-01-001**
infinitely	**RB**	**2-02-002**
infinitesimal	**JJ**	**3-02-002**
infinitesimally	**QL**	**1-01-001**
infinitive	**NN**	**1-01-001**
infinitum	**FW-NN**	**2-02-002**
infinity	**NN**	**2-02-002**
infirm	**JJ**	**1-01-001**
infirmary	**NN**	**1-01-001**
infirmity	**NN**	**1-01-001**
inflame	**verb**	**2-02-002**
inflame	VB	1-01-001
inflamed	VBD	1-01-001
inflammation	**NN**	**1-01-001**
inflammatory	**JJ**	**1-01-001**
inflate	**verb**	**4-04-004**
inflate	VB	1-01-001
inflated	VBN	3-03-003
inflation	**NN**	**5-04-004**
inflect	**verb**	**4-02-002**
inflected	VBN	3-02-002
inflecting	VBG	1-01-001
inflection	**noun**	**7-04-006**
inflection	NN	3-02-003
inflections	NNS	4-03-004
inflexible	**JJ**	**3-03-003**
inflict	**verb**	**11-08-010**
inflict	VB	4-03-004
inflicted	VBD	3-03-003
inflicted	VBN	1-01-001
inflicting	VBG	3-03-003
infliction	**NN**	**3-02-003**
inflow	**NN**	**2-02-002**
influence	**noun**	**124-12-071**
influence	NN	112-12-066
influence	NN-HL	1-01-001
influences	NNS	10-05-010
influences	NNS-HL	1-01-001
influence	**verb**	**40-10-029**
influence	VB	18-07-014
influence	VB-HL	1-01-001
influences	VBZ	3-02-003
influenced	VBD	1-01-001
influenced	VBN	15-07-014
influencing	VBG	2-02-002
influent	**JJ**	**1-01-001**
influent	**NN**	**1-01-001**

Word	Tag	Frequency
influential	**JJ**	**14-07-012**
influenza	**NN**	**2-01-002**
influenza-pneumonia	**NN**	**1-01-001**
influx	**noun**	**4-04-004**
influx	NN	3-03-003
influx	NN-HL	1-01-001
inform	**verb**	**74-15-056**
inform	VB	7-06-007
informs	VBZ	6-03-005
informed	VBD	22-07-017
informed	VBN	35-12-028
informing	VBG	4-04-004
informal	**JJ**	**18-09-014**
informality	**NN**	**1-01-001**
informally	**RB**	**5-05-005**
informant	**noun**	**3-02-002**
informant	NN	2-01-001
informants	NNS	1-01-001
information	**noun**	**269-14-115**
information	NN	263-14-112
information	NN-HL	1-01-001
Information	NN-TL	5-03-005
information-cell	**NN**	**1-01-001**
information-seeking	**JJ**	**1-01-001**
informational	**JJ**	**2-01-002**
informative	**JJ**	**2-02-002**
infra	**IN**	**1-01-001**
infraction	**NN**	**1-01-001**
infrared	**JJ**	**11-03-005**
infrared	**NN**	**1-01-001**
infrequent	**JJ**	**4-04-004**
infrequently	**RB**	**2-02-002**
infringement	**noun**	**8-01-001**
infringement	NN	7-01-001
infringements	NNS	1-01-001
infuriate	**verb**	**4-04-004**
infuriate	VB	1-01-001
infuriated	VBD	3-03-003
infuriating	**JJ**	**2-02-002**
infuriation	**NN**	**1-01-001**
infusion	**NN**	**1-01-001**
Ingbar	**NP**	**1-01-001**
ingenious	**JJ**	**10-06-010**
ingeniously	**RB**	**1-01-001**
ingenuity	**NN**	**5-03-005**
ingest	**verb**	**4-04-004**
ingested	VBD	2-02-002
ingested	VBN	2-02-002
ingestion	**NN**	**1-01-001**
Ingleside	**prop. noun**	**2-01-001**
Ingleside	NP	0-00-000
Ingleside	NP-TL	1-01-001
Ingleside's	NP$	1-01-001
inglorious	**JJ**	**1-01-001**
Ingo	**NP**	**1-01-001**
ingratiating	**JJ**	**4-03-004**
ingratitude	**noun**	**2-02-002**
ingratitude	NN	1-01-001
ingratitoode	NN	1-01-001
ingredient	**noun**	**15-07-011**
ingredient	NN	6-06-006
ingredients	NNS	9-04-006
inhabit	**verb**	**8-05-007**
inhabit	VB	1-01-001
inhabited	VBN	6-05-005
inhabiting	VBG	1-01-001
inhabitant	**noun**	**13-08-012**
inhabitants	NNS	13-08-012
inhabitation	**NN**	**1-01-001**
inhalation	**NN**	**1-01-001**
inhale	**verb**	**1-01-001**
inhaling	VBG	1-01-001
inharmonious	**JJ**	**1-01-001**
inhere	**verb**	**1-01-001**
inheres	VBZ	1-01-001
inherent	**JJ**	**26-06-022**
inherently	**RB**	**3-02-003**
inherit	**verb**	**22-10-020**
inherit	VB	4-04-004
inherits	VBZ	1-01-001
inherited	VBD	6-06-006
inherited	VBN	10-06-010
inheriting	VBG	1-01-001
inheritance	**noun**	**6-03-005**
inheritance	NN	5-03-004
inheritance	NN-HL	1-01-001
inheritor	**noun**	**1-01-001**
inheritors	NNS	1-01-001
inhibit	**verb**	**17-03-008**

Word	Tag	Frequency
inhibit (cont.):		
inhibit	VB	7-01-004
inhibit	VB-HL	1-01-001
inhibits	VBZ	2-02-002
inhibited	VBD	2-01-001
inhibited	VBN	3-02-003
inhibiting	VBG	2-01-002
inhibition	**noun**	**9-04-008**
inhibition	NN	6-02-005
inhibitions	NNS	3-03-003
inhibitor	**noun**	**4-02-002**
inhibitor	NN	2-01-001
inhibitors	NNS	2-02-002
inhibitory	**JJ**	**2-01-001**
inholding	**noun**	**3-01-001**
inholdings	NNS	3-01-001
inhomogeneous	**JJ**	**1-01-001**
inhospitable	**JJ**	**1-01-001**
inhuman	**JJ**	**7-05-007**
inhumane	**JJ**	**4-03-003**
inhumanity	**noun**	**1-01-001**
inhumanities	NNS	1-01-001
inimical	**JJ**	**1-01-001**
iniquitous	**JJ**	**1-01-001**
iniquity	**noun**	**1-01-001**
iniquities	NNS	1-01-001
initial	**adjective**	**69-11-051**
initial	JJ	67-11-049
intial	JJ	1-01-001
initial	JJ-HL	1-01-001
initial	**noun**	**3-03-003**
initials	NNS	3-03-003
initial	**verb**	**1-01-001**
initialed	VBN	1-01-001
initially	**RB**	**18-06-015**
initiate	**noun**	**1-01-001**
initiates	NNS	1-01-001
initiate	**verb**	**22-09-020**
initiate	VB	5-05-005
initiates	VBZ	1-01-001
initiated	VBD	4-03-004
initiated	VBN	8-04-006
initiating	VBG	4-03-004
initiation	**NN**	**7-05-007**
initiative	**noun**	**32-09-017**
initiative	NN	31-09-017
initiative	NN-HL	1-01-001
initiator	**NN**	**2-01-001**
inject	**verb**	**13-05-007**
inject	VB	6-03-003
injected	VBD	1-01-001
injected	VBN	1-01-001
injecting	VBG	5-02-004
injection	**NN**	**7-04-006**
injection-molded	**JJ**	**1-01-001**
Injun	**prop. noun**	**5-01-001**
Injun	NP	3-01-001
Injun's	NP$	1-01-001
Injuns	NPS	1-01-001
injunction	**noun**	**8-02-002**
injunction	NN	3-01-001
injunctions	NNS	5-02-002
injunctive	**JJ**	**1-01-001**
injure	**verb**	**21-10-019**
injured	VBD	2-01-002
injured	VBN	18-10-017
injuring	VBG	1-01-001
injurious	**JJ**	**2-02-002**
injury	**noun**	**38-10-023**
injury	NN	27-09-018
injuries	NNS	11-05-010
injustice	**noun**	**17-05-009**
injustice	NN	16-05-008
injustices	NNS	1-01-001
ink	**noun**	**8-03-005**
ink	NN	6-03-004
ink	NN-HL	1-01-001
inks	NNS	1-01-001
inkling	**NN**	**1-01-001**
inland	**adjective**	**1-01-001**
inland	JJ	0-00-000
Inland	JJ-TL	1-01-001
inland	**RB**	**3-03-003**
inlay	**verb**	**1-01-001**
inlaid	VBN	1-01-001
inlet	**noun**	**7-05-006**
inlet	NN	4-02-003
inlets	NNS	3-03-003
inmate	**noun**	**7-04-004**
inmate (cont.):		
inmate	NN	1-01-001
inmates	NNS	5-03-003
Inmates	NNS-TL	1-01-001
inn	**noun**	**10-05-009**
inn	NN	5-03-004
Inn	NN-TL	4-01-004
inns	NNS	1-01-001
Inna	**NP**	**3-02-002**
innate	**JJ**	**4-03-004**
inner	**adjective**	**55-12-041**
inner	JJ	53-12-039
Inner	JJ-TL	2-02-002
innermost	**JJS**	**1-01-001**
Innesfree	**NP**	**2-01-001**
inning	**noun**	**16-03-005**
inning	NN	12-03-004
innings	NNS	4-02-003
innocence	**NN**	**28-07-012**
innocent	**JJ**	**37-11-022**
innocent	**noun**	**1-01-001**
innocents	NNS	1-01-001
innocently	**RB**	**3-02-003**
innovate	**VB**	**1-01-001**
innovation	**noun**	**11-07-011**
innovation	NN	7-05-007
innovations	NNS	4-03-004
innovator	**noun**	**1-01-001**
innovators	NNS	1-01-001
innuendo	**noun**	**3-02-003**
innuendo	NN	1-01-001
innuendoes	NNS	1-01-001
innuendos	NNS	1-01-001
innumerable	**JJ**	**6-05-006**
inoculation	**noun**	**3-01-003**
inoculation	NN	2-01-002
inoculations	NNS	1-01-001
inoperable	**JJ**	**1-01-001**
inopportune	**JJ**	**1-01-001**
inordinately	**QL**	**2-01-002**
inorganic	**adjective**	**11-01-004**
inorganic	JJ	10-01-003
inorganic	JJ-HL	1-01-001
inpost	**NN**	**1-01-001**
input	**NN**	**20-02-005**
input/output	**adjective**	**4-01-001**
input/output	JJ	0-00-000
Input/Output	JJ-TL	4-01-001
input/output	**noun**	**1-01-001**
input/output	NN	0-00-000
input/output	NN-HL	1-01-001
inquest	**NN**	**5-02-003**
inquire	**verb**	**28-11-025**
inquire	VB	6-06-006
inquired	VBD	14-07-011
enquired	VBD	1-01-001
inquired	VBN	2-02-002
inquiring	VBG	5-03-005
Inquirer	**prop. noun**	**13-01-001**
Inquirer	NP	0-00-000
Inquirer	NP-HL	13-01-001
inquiry	**noun**	**34-08-021**
inquiry	NN	17-06-013
inquiries	NNS	17-05-009
inquisition	**noun**	**3-03-003**
inquisition	NN	0-00-000
Inquisition	NN-TL	3-03-003
inquisitive	**JJ**	**1-01-001**
inquisitor	**NN**	**1-01-001**
Inquisitor-General	**NP**	**1-01-001**
inroad	**noun**	**3-03-003**
inroads	NNS	3-03-003
insane	**JJ**	**13-07-011**
insanely	**RB**	**1-01-001**
insanity	**NN**	**3-02-002**
insatiable	**JJ**	**1-01-001**
inscribe	**verb**	**7-02-003**
inscribed	VBD	1-01-001
inscribed	VBN	6-02-002
inscription	**noun**	**7-06-006**
inscription	NN	6-05-005
inscriptions	NNS	1-01-001
inscrutability	**NN**	**1-01-001**
inscrutable	**JJ**	**5-03-004**
insect	**noun**	**37-09-016**
insect	NN	14-06-009
insects	NNS	22-07-010
insects	NNS-HL	1-01-001
insecticide	**noun**	**3-01-001**

insecticide (cont.):		
insecticide	NN	1-01-001
insecticides	NNS	2-01-001
insecure	**JJ**	**3-02-002**
insecurity	**NN**	**5-04-005**
insemination	**NN**	**1-01-001**
insensitive	**JJ**	**3-03-003**
inseparable	**JJ**	**4-02-004**
insert	**noun**	**4-02-003**
insert	NN	3-01-002
inserts	NNS	1-01-001
insert	**verb**	**26-10-018**
insert	VB	9-02-005
insert	VB-HL	1-01-001
inserted	VBD	5-04-004
inserted	VBN	11-06-009
insertion	**noun**	**2-01-002**
insertion	NN	1-01-001
insertions	NNS	1-01-001
inset	**noun**	**2-02-002**
inset	NN	1-01-001
insets	NNS	1-01-001
inshore	**JJ**	**1-01-001**
inshore	**RB**	**1-01-001**
inside	**prep.**	**81-15-053**
inside	IN	80-15-052
Inside	IN-TL	1-01-001
inside	**JJ**	**7-04-004**
inside	**noun**	**23-10-017**
inside	NN	18-09-013
inside	NN-HL	1-01-001
insides	NNS	4-03-004
inside	**RB**	**67-10-040**
insider	**noun**	**2-02-002**
insiders	NNS	2-02-002
insidious	**JJ**	**2-02-002**
insidiously	**QL**	**1-01-001**
insidiously	**RB**	**1-01-001**
insight	**noun**	**38-08-027**
insight	NN	22-07-022
insights	NNS	16-06-013
insignificance	**noun**	**2-02-002**
insignificance	NN	1-01-001
insignificances	NNS	1-01-001
insignificant	**JJ**	**5-04-005**
insincere	**JJ**	**1-01-001**
insinuate	**verb**	**3-02-003**
insinuates	VBZ	1-01-001
insinuated	VBD	1-01-001
insinuating	VBG	1-01-001
insinuation	**noun**	**5-03-004**
insinuation	NN	2-02-002
insinuations	NNS	3-03-003
insipid	**JJ**	**1-01-001**
insist	**verb**	**86-15-075**
insist	VB	27-11-026
insists	VBZ	10-06-009
insisted	VBD	39-11-036
insisted	VBN	4-04-004
insisting	VBG	6-05-006
insistence	**NN**	**19-09-017**
insistent	**JJ**	**8-04-008**
insofar	**RB**	**7-04-007**
insolence	**NN**	**6-05-005**
insolent	**JJ**	**2-02-002**
insolently	**RB**	**1-01-001**
insoluble	**JJ**	**12-04-007**
insomma	**UH**	**1-01-001**
insomnia	**NN**	**3-01-001**
insomniac	**noun**	**1-01-001**
insomniacs	NNS	1-01-001
insouciance	**NN**	**1-01-001**
inspect	**verb**	**16-07-013**
inspect	VB	12-07-009
inspected	VBD	1-01-001
inspected	VBN	1-01-001
inspecting	VBG	2-02-002
inspection	**noun**	**24-13-022**
inspection	NN	20-12-019
Inspection	NN-TL	1-01-001
inspections	NNS	2-02-002
Inspections	NNS-TL	1-01-001
inspector	**noun**	**15-06-009**
inspector	NN	5-02-003
Inspector	NN-TL	8-05-005
inspector's	NN$	1-01-001
Inspector's	NN$-TL	1-01-001
inspiration	**noun**	**10-06-008**
inspiration	NN	9-05-007

inspiration (cont.):		
inspirations	NNS	1-01-001
inspirational	**JJ**	**1-01-001**
inspire	**verb**	**33-11-028**
inspire	VB	3-02-003
inspires	VBZ	1-01-001
inspired	VBD	8-06-008
inspired	VBN	17-10-016
inspiring	VBG	4-04-004
inspiring	**JJ**	**4-03-004**
instability	**NN**	**4-04-004**
install	**verb**	**48-12-029**
install	VB	8-03-006
installed	VBD	5-04-005
installed	VBN	30-11-020
installing	VBG	5-02-005
installation	**noun**	**28-04-013**
installation	NN	12-02-007
installations	NNS	16-04-008
installment	**noun**	**8-03-005**
installment	NN	5-02-003
installments	NNS	2-01-002
instalments	NNS	1-01-001
instance	**noun**	**112-15-087**
instance	NN	82-15-068
instances	NNS	30-09-027
instancy	**NN**	**1-01-001**
instant	**adjective**	**7-06-006**
instant	JJ	5-04-004
instant	JJ-HL	1-01-001
Instant	JJ-TL	1-01-001
instant	**noun**	**32-07-021**
instant	NN	31-06-020
instant's	NN$	1-01-001
instantaneous	**adjective**	**5-04-004**
instantaneous	JJ	4-03-003
instantaneous	JJ-HL	1-01-001
instantaneously	**RB**	**2-02-002**
instantly	**QL**	**1-01-001**
instantly	**RB**	**18-10-018**
instead	**adverb**	**174-15-139**
instead	RB	173-15-138
'stead	RB	1-01-001
instigate	**verb**	**2-02-002**
instigate	VB	1-01-001
instigating	VBG	1-01-001
instigation	**NN**	**1-01-001**
instigator	**NN**	**1-01-001**
instillation	**NN**	**1-01-001**
instinct	**noun**	**18-08-014**
instinct	NN	14-05-011
instincts	NNS	4-04-004
instinctive	**JJ**	**2-02-002**
instinctively	**RB**	**10-07-008**
instinctual	**JJ**	**2-02-002**
institut	**foreign**	**1-01-001**
institut	FW-NN	0-00-000
Institut	FW-NN-TL	1-01-001
institute	**noun**	**51-08-027**
institute	NN	4-03-004
Institute	NN-TL	45-08-025
institute's	NN$	0-00-000
Institute's	NN$-TL	1-01-001
institutes	NNS	0-00-000
Institutes	NNS-TL	1-01-001
institute	**verb**	**14-07-012**
institute	VB	1-01-001
instituted	VBD	3-03-003
instituted	VBN	9-04-007
instituting	VBG	1-01-001
institution	**noun**	**140-10-060**
institution	NN	38-09-026
Institution	NN-TL	3-03-003
institution's	NN$	1-01-001
institutions	NNS	97-08-046
Institutions	NNS-TL	1-01-001
institution-wide	**JJ**	**1-01-001**
institutional	**JJ**	**9-05-008**
institutionalization	**NN**	**1-01-001**
institutionalize	**verb**	**3-03-003**
institutionalized	VBN	3-03-003
instruct	**verb**	**23-11-020**
instruct	VB	3-02-003
instructs	VBZ	2-01-001
instructed	VBD	2-02-002
instructed	VBN	14-10-013
instructing	VBG	2-02-002
instruction	**noun**	**61-12-041**
instruction	NN	26-11-020

instruction (cont.):		
instructions	NNS	30-08-022
Instructions	NNS	1-01-001
instructions	NNS-NC	4-01-001
instructional	**JJ**	**3-02-003**
instructive	**JJ**	**3-03-003**
instructor	**noun**	**10-08-009**
instructor	NN	8-06-007
instructor's	NN$	0-00-000
Instructor's	NN$-TL	1-01-001
instructors	NNS	1-01-001
instrument	**noun**	**73-13-048**
instrument	NN	44-10-031
Instrument	NN-TL	3-03-003
instruments	NNS	25-11-017
Instruments	NNS-TL	1-01-001
instrument-jammed	**JJ**	**1-01-001**
instrumental	**foreign**	**1-01-001**
instrumental	FW-JJ	0-00-000
Instrumental	FW-JJ-TL	1-01-001
instrumental	**JJ**	**10-06-007**
instrumental	**noun**	**1-01-001**
instrumentals	NNS	1-01-001
instrumental-reward	**JJ**	**1-01-001**
instrumentalist	**noun**	**3-02-002**
instrumentalists	NNS	3-02-002
instrumentality	**noun**	**3-03-003**
instrumentalities	NNS	3-03-003
instrumentally	**RB**	**3-02-002**
instrumentation	**NN**	**4-02-003**
insubordinate	**JJ**	**2-01-001**
insubordination	**NN**	**2-02-002**
insubstantial	**JJ**	**2-02-002**
insufficient	**JJ**	**7-05-007**
insufficiently	**QL**	**2-02-002**
insufficiently	**RB**	**1-01-001**
insularity	**NN**	**3-03-003**
insulate	**verb**	**8-05-006**
insulate	VB	2-02-002
insulated	VBN	4-04-004
insulating	VBG	2-01-001
insulation	**NN**	**10-03-004**
insulator	**noun**	**2-02-002**
insulator	NN	1-01-001
insulators	NNS	1-01-001
insulin	**NN**	**3-02-002**
insult	**noun**	**8-08-008**
insult	NN	5-05-005
insults	NNS	3-03-003
insult	**verb**	**5-04-005**
insult	VB	2-02-002
insulted	VBD	1-01-001
insulted	VBN	1-01-001
insulting	VBG	1-01-001
insulting	**JJ**	**3-02-003**
insuperable	**JJ**	**2-02-002**
insuperably	**QL**	**1-01-001**
insurance	**noun**	**46-09-017**
insurance	NN	41-09-016
insurance	NN-HL	2-01-001
Insurance	NN-TL	3-03-003
insure	**verb**	**37-09-032**
insure	VB	24-09-023
insures	VBZ	1-01-001
insured	VBD	1-01-001
insured	VBN	5-03-005
insuring	VBG	6-05-006
insurgence	**NN**	**1-01-001**
insurgent	**JJ**	**1-01-001**
insurgent	**noun**	**1-01-001**
insurgents	NNS	1-01-001
insurmountable	**JJ**	**2-02-002**
insurrection	**noun**	**3-02-002**
insurrection	NN	2-01-001
insurrections	NNS	1-01-001
intact	**JJ**	**14-07-012**
intactible	**JJ**	**1-01-001**
intake	**NN**	**7-04-005**
intangible	**JJ**	**6-03-004**
intangible	**noun**	**3-03-003**
intangibles	NNS	3-03-003
integer	**noun**	**5-01-003**
integer	NN	4-01-003
integers	NNS	1-01-001
integral	**JJ**	**13-06-012**
integral	**noun**	**3-02-002**
integrals	NNS	3-02-002
integrate	**verb**	**22-07-017**
integrate	VB	7-04-006

integrate (cont.):		
integrates	VBZ	2-02-002
integrated	VBN	11-07-011
integrating	VBG	2-01-002
integration	**NN**	**48-09-024**
integrative	**JJ**	**1-01-001**
integrity	**NN**	**10-07-009**
intellect	**NN**	**5-03-003**
intellectual	**JJ**	**57-11-038**
intellectual	**noun**	**21-07-016**
intellectual	NN	9-06-008
intellectuals	NNS	12-05-010
intellectual-literary	**JJ**	**1-01-001**
intellectuality	**NN**	**1-01-001**
intellectually	**RB**	**5-04-005**
intellectus	**FW-NN$**	**1-01-001**
intelligence	**noun**	**48-10-024**
intelligence	NN	46-10-023
Intelligence	NN-TL	2-02-002
intelligent	**JJ**	**26-13-022**
intelligently	**RB**	**3-02-003**
intelligentsia	**NN**	**1-01-001**
intelligible	**JJ**	**11-05-010**
intemperance	**NN**	**1-01-001**
intend	**verb**	**67-13-059**
intend	VB	14-10-013
intend	VB-HL	1-01-001
intends	VBZ	6-05-006
intended	VBD	10-07-010
intended	VBN	35-12-030
intending	VBG	1-01-001
intendant	**noun**	**2-01-001**
intendant	NN	1-01-001
intendants	NNS	1-01-001
intense	**JJ**	**40-10-037**
intensely	**QL**	**3-02-003**
intensely	**RB**	**7-05-007**
intensification	**NN**	**8-04-005**
intensifier	**noun**	**12-01-001**
intensifier	NN	5-01-001
intensifier	NN-HL	1-01-001
intensifiers	NNS	5-01-001
intensifiers	NNS-HL	1-01-001
intensify	**verb**	**10-05-010**
intensify	VB	4-03-004
intensified	VBD	1-01-001
intensified	VBN	3-03-003
intensifying	VBG	2-02-002
intensity	**noun**	**61-11-033**
intensity	NN	56-11-031
intensities	NNS	5-03-005
intensive	**JJ**	**15-05-010**
intensively	**RB**	**1-01-001**
intent	**JJ**	**3-03-003**
intent	**NN**	**11-07-011**
intention	**noun**	**58-12-052**
intention	NN	36-10-035
intentions	NNS	22-09-020
intentional	**JJ**	**5-02-004**
intentionally	**RB**	**4-04-004**
intentioned	**JJ**	**1-01-001**
intently	**RB**	**4-03-004**
inter	**FW-IN**	**1-01-001**
inter	**verb**	**1-01-001**
interred	VBN	1-01-001
inter-American	**adjective**	**7-03-005**
Inter-American	JJ	4-03-004
Inter-american	JJ	1-01-001
Inter-american	JJ-HL	1-01-001
Inter-American	JJ-TL	1-01-001
inter-plant	**JJ**	**1-01-001**
inter-species	**adjective**	**2-01-001**
inter-species	JJ	1-01-001
interspecies	JJ	1-01-001
inter-town	**JJ**	**1-01-001**
inter-tribal	**JJ**	**1-01-001**
interact	**verb**	**4-03-004**
interact	VB	2-02-002
interacts	VBZ	1-01-001
interacting	VBG	1-01-001
interaction	**noun**	**20-04-009**
interaction	NN	15-03-008
interaction	NN-HL	2-01-001
interactions	NNS	3-02-003
Interama	**NP**	**4-01-001**
interaxial	**JJ**	**1-01-001**
intercede	**VB**	**1-01-001**
intercept	**noun**	**4-02-004**
intercept	NN	3-02-003

Word	Tag	Frequency
intercept (cont.):		
intercepts	NNS	1-01-001
intercept	**verb**	**6-04-006**
intercept	VB	3-03-003
intercepted	VBD	3-03-003
interceptor	**NN**	**1-01-001**
interchange	**noun**	**8-03-003**
interchange	NN	6-03-003
interchanges	NNS	2-01-001
interchangeable	**JJ**	**3-03-003**
interclass	**JJ**	**1-01-001**
intercollegiate	**adjective**	**4-02-002**
intercollegiate	JJ	3-01-001
Intercollegiate	JJ-TL	1-01-001
interconnect	**verb**	**1-01-001**
interconnected	VBN	1-01-001
interconnectedness	**NN**	**1-01-001**
intercontinental	**JJ**	**5-03-004**
intercourse	**NN**	**9-01-002**
intercrisis	**NN**	**1-01-001**
interdenominational	**JJ**	**2-01-001**
interdepartmental	**JJ**	**1-01-001**
interdependence	**NN**	**6-02-002**
interdependent	**JJ**	**8-04-007**
interest	**noun**	**408-15-185**
interest	NN	323-15-170
interest	NN-HL	3-02-003
Interest	NN-TL	1-01-001
interests	NNS	81-11-047
interest	**verb**	**106-14-076**
interest	VB	3-03-003
interests	VBZ	2-02-002
interested	VBD	3-03-003
interested	VBN	97-14-072
interested	VBN-HL	1-01-001
interested	**JJ**	**4-02-003**
interesting	**JJ**	**82-13-070**
interestingly	**RB**	**3-03-003**
interface	**noun**	**8-01-004**
interface	NN	3-01-002
interfaces	NNS	5-01-002
interfacial	**JJ**	**6-01-004**
interfaith	**JJ**	**7-02-002**
interfere	**verb**	**22-09-022**
interfere	VB	9-08-009
interferes	VBZ	2-02-002
interfered	VBD	4-04-004
interfered	VBN	1-01-001
interfering	VBG	6-05-006
interference	**noun**	**45-07-015**
interference	NN	42-07-014
intereference	NN	1-01-001
Interference	NN-TL	2-01-001
interference-like	**JJ**	**1-01-001**
interferometer	**noun**	**5-02-002**
interferometer	NN	3-02-002
interferometer	NN-HL	1-01-001
interferometers	NNS	1-01-001
interglacial	**JJ**	**1-01-001**
intergovernmental	**JJ**	**1-01-001**
intergroup	**adjective**	**3-01-002**
intergroup	JJ	2-01-002
Intergroup	JJ-TL	1-01-001
interim	**JJ**	**6-03-004**
interim	**NN**	**5-03-005**
interior	**JJ**	**29-03-004**
interior	**noun**	**49-10-020**
interior	NN	16-06-011
interior	NN-HL	1-01-001
Interior	NN-TL	28-06-008
interiors	NNS	4-02-003
interject	**verb**	**1-01-001**
interjected	VBD	1-01-001
interlace	**verb**	**5-04-005**
interlaced	VBN	4-03-004
interlacing	VBG	1-01-001
interlayer	**JJ**	**2-01-001**
interlibrary	**JJ**	**2-01-001**
interlining	**NN**	**2-01-001**
interlobular	**JJ**	**8-01-001**
interlock	**verb**	**9-03-005**
interlocking	VBG	9-03-005
interlocutor	**NN**	**1-01-001**
interlude	**noun**	**7-06-007**
interlude	NN	4-04-004
Interlude	NN-TL	1-01-001
interludes	NNS	2-02-002
intermarriage	**NN**	**1-01-001**
intermediary	**JJ**	**1-01-001**
intermediate	**adjective**	**21-04-013**
intermediate	JJ	19-04-011
Intermediate	JJ-TL	2-02-002
intermediate	**noun**	**5-02-003**
intermediates	NNS	2-01-002
intermediates	NNS-HL	1-01-001
Intermediates	NNS-TL	2-01-001
interment	**NN**	**2-02-002**
intermesh	**verb**	**1-01-001**
intermeshed	VBN	1-01-001
interminable	**JJ**	**4-04-004**
intermission	**noun**	**2-02-002**
intermission	NN	1-01-001
intermissions	NNS	1-01-001
intermittent	**JJ**	**3-03-003**
intermittently	**RB**	**2-01-002**
intermolecular	**JJ**	**1-01-001**
intern	**noun**	**5-04-004**
intern	NN	2-02-002
interne	NN	2-02-002
interns	NNS	1-01-001
intern	**verb**	**1-01-001**
interned	VBN	1-01-001
internal	**adjective**	**62-10-036**
internal	JJ	50-07-030
Internal	JJ-TL	12-05-006
internal-external	**JJ**	**1-01-001**
internalize	**verb**	**2-01-002**
internalized	VBN	2-01-002
internally	**RB**	**6-01-004**
international	**adjective**	**154-09-075**
international	JJ	118-09-059
international	JJ-HL	1-01-001
International	JJ-TL	34-08-026
International	JJ-TL-HL	1-01-001
international	**NN**	**1-01-001**
internationale	**foreign**	**1-01-001**
internationale	FW-JJ	0-00-000
Internationale	FW-JJ-TL	1-01-001
internationalist	**JJ**	**2-02-002**
internationalist	**noun**	**1-01-001**
internationalists	NNS	1-01-001
internationalize	**verb**	**1-01-001**
internationalized	VBN	1-01-001
internationally	**RB**	**4-02-004**
internist	**noun**	**1-01-001**
internist's	NN$	1-01-001
interpenetrate	**verb**	**3-02-002**
interpenetrate	VB	1-01-001
interpenetrates	VBZ	2-01-001
interpeople	**JJ**	**1-01-001**
interpersonal	**adjective**	**3-02-003**
interpersonal	JJ	2-01-002
Interpersonal	JJ-TL	1-01-001
interplanetary	**JJ**	**3-01-001**
interplay	**NN**	**6-03-006**
interpolate	**verb**	**1-01-001**
interpolated	VBD	1-01-001
interpolation	**noun**	**2-02-002**
interpolation	NN	1-01-001
interpolations	NNS	1-01-001
interpose	**verb**	**2-02-002**
interposed	VBN	1-01-001
interposing	VBG	1-01-001
interposition	**NN**	**2-02-002**
interpret	**verb**	**40-11-035**
interpret	VB	11-06-010
interprets	VBZ	3-02-002
interpreted	VBD	3-03-003
interpreted	VBN	21-08-021
interpreting	VBG	2-02-002
interpretable	**JJ**	**1-01-001**
interpretation	**noun**	**66-12-043**
interpretation	NN	51-11-038
Interpretation	NN-TL	3-02-002
interpretations	NNS	12-06-009
interpretative	**JJ**	**1-01-001**
interpreter	**noun**	**9-08-009**
interpreter	NN	8-07-008
interpretor	NN	1-01-001
interregnum	**NN**	**2-02-002**
interrelate	**verb**	**5-02-005**
interrelated	VBN	5-02-005
interrelation	**noun**	**9-05-009**
interrelation	NN	4-04-004
inter-relation	NN	1-01-001
interrelations	NNS	4-02-004
interrelationship	**noun**	**4-02-004**
interrelationship	NN	1-01-001

Word	Tag	Frequency
interrelationship (cont.):		
interrelationships	NNS	2-01-002
inter-relationships	NNS	1-01-001
interrogation	**NN**	**2-02-002**
interrogative	**noun**	**1-01-001**
interrogatives	NNS	1-01-001
interrogator	**NN**	**1-01-001**
interrupt	**verb**	**22-10-019**
interrupt	VB	4-04-004
interrupted	VBD	10-04-009
interrupted	VBN	8-07-008
interruption	**noun**	**11-06-010**
interruption	NN	8-05-008
interruptions	NNS	3-03-003
Interscience	**prop. noun**	**1-01-001**
Interscience	NP	0-00-000
Interscience	NP-TL	1-01-001
intersect	**verb**	**8-02-004**
intersect	VB	6-01-003
intersecting	VBG	2-02-002
intersection	**noun**	**29-05-007**
intersection	NN	17-05-007
intersections	NNS	12-01-002
intersperse	**verb**	**1-01-001**
interspersed	VBN	1-01-001
interstage	**JJ**	**3-01-001**
interstate	**adjective**	**14-04-009**
interstate	JJ	5-03-005
Interstate	JJ-TL	9-04-005
interstellar	**adjective**	**5-02-002**
interstellar	JJ	4-02-002
interstellar	JJ-HL	1-01-001
interstice	**noun**	**1-01-001**
interstices	NNS	1-01-001
interstitial	**JJ**	**2-01-001**
intertwine	**verb**	**4-04-004**
intertwined	VBD	1-01-001
intertwined	VBN	3-03-003
interval	**noun**	**43-11-031**
interval	NN	18-06-010
intervals	NNS	25-09-023
intervene	**verb**	**8-03-006**
intervene	VB	2-02-002
intervenes	VBZ	0-00-000
intervenes	VBZ-HL	1-01-001
intervened	VBD	4-03-003
intervening	VBG	1-01-001
intervention	**NN**	**20-07-013**
interview	**noun**	**50-08-022**
interview	NN	31-08-015
interviews	NNS	19-04-010
interview	**verb**	**19-07-013**
interview	VB	2-01-002
interviewed	VBD	7-03-004
interviewed	VBN	5-05-005
interviewing	VBG	5-03-004
interviewee	**noun**	**2-02-002**
interviewee	NN	1-01-001
interviewees	NNS	1-01-001
interviewer	**noun**	**3-03-003**
interviewer	NN	2-02-002
interviewers	NNS	1-01-001
interviewing	**NN**	**2-01-001**
interweave	**verb**	**5-04-005**
interwoven	VBN	4-03-004
interweaving	VBG	1-01-001
intestine	**noun**	**2-01-001**
intestine	NN	1-01-001
intestines	NNS	1-01-001
intima	**NN**	**3-02-002**
intimacy	**NN**	**3-03-003**
intimal	**JJ**	**1-01-001**
intimate	**JJ**	**20-09-017**
intimate	**NN**	**1-01-001**
intimate	**verb**	**6-05-006**
intimated	VBD	4-04-004
intimated	VBN	1-01-001
intimating	VBG	1-01-001
intimately	**RB**	**6-04-006**
intimation	**noun**	**1-01-001**
intimations	NNS	1-01-001
intimidate	**verb**	**5-05-005**
intimidate	VB	2-02-002
intimidated	VBN	3-03-003
intimidation	**NN**	**5-04-005**
into	**prep.**	**1790-15-464**
into	IN	1781-15-464
inter	IN	1-01-001
into	IN-HL	5-04-005
into (cont.):		
Into	IN-TL	3-01-001
intolerable	**JJ**	**3-02-003**
intolerance	**NN**	**2-01-002**
intolerant	**JJ**	**1-01-001**
intonaco	**FW-NN**	**2-01-001**
intonation	**noun**	**9-03-003**
intonation	NN	8-02-002
intonations	NNS	1-01-001
intone	**verb**	**4-02-003**
intoned	VBD	4-02-003
intoxicate	**verb**	**2-02-002**
intoxicated	VBN	1-01-001
intoxicating	VBG	1-01-001
intra-city	**JJ**	**1-01-001**
intra-company	**JJ**	**1-01-001**
intra-state	**JJ**	**1-01-001**
intra-stellar	**JJ**	**1-01-001**
intractable	**JJ**	**2-01-002**
intradepartmental	**JJ**	**1-01-001**
intraepithelial	**JJ**	**1-01-001**
intramural	**adjective**	**3-02-002**
intramural	JJ	2-01-001
intra-mural	JJ	1-01-001
intramuscularly	**RB**	**1-01-001**
intranasal	**JJ**	**1-01-001**
intransigence	**NN**	**2-01-002**
intransigent	**noun**	**1-01-001**
intransigents	NNS	1-01-001
intrapulmonary	**JJ**	**1-01-001**
intratissue	**JJ**	**1-01-001**
intrepid	**JJ**	**1-01-001**
intricate	**JJ**	**10-07-010**
intricately	**QL**	**1-01-001**
intrigue	**noun**	**7-04-006**
intrigue	NN	4-04-004
intrigues	NNS	3-03-003
intrigue	**verb**	**2-02-002**
intrigued	VBN	2-02-002
intriguing	**JJ**	**3-03-003**
intriguingly	**RB**	**2-02-002**
intrinsic	**JJ**	**5-02-005**
intrinsically	**RB**	**4-03-004**
introduce	**verb**	**76-14-065**
introduce	VB	11-10-011
introduces	VBZ	4-03-004
introduced	VBD	15-09-014
introduced	VBN	37-09-033
introducing	VBG	9-06-008
introduction	**noun**	**40-12-035**
introduction	NN	28-12-026
introduction	NN-HL	6-01-006
Introduction	NN-TL	5-03-004
introductions	NNS	1-01-001
introductory	**JJ**	**3-03-003**
introject	**noun**	**4-01-001**
introject	NN	3-01-001
introjects	NNS	1-01-001
introject	**verb**	**1-01-001**
introjected	VBN	1-01-001
introspection	**NN**	**1-01-001**
introspective	**JJ**	**2-02-002**
introvert	**verb**	**1-01-001**
introverted	VBN	1-01-001
intrude	**verb**	**4-04-004**
intrude	VB	1-01-001
intrudes	VBZ	1-01-001
intruded	VBN	1-01-001
intruding	VBG	1-01-001
intruder	**noun**	**2-02-002**
intruder	NN	1-01-001
intruders	NNS	1-01-001
intrusion	**noun**	**5-03-005**
intrusion	NN	3-02-003
intrusions	NNS	2-02-002
intrusive	**JJ**	**2-02-002**
intuition	**noun**	**19-07-014**
intuition	NN	18-06-013
intuitions	NNS	1-01-001
intuitive	**JJ**	**7-03-006**
intuitively	**RB**	**1-01-001**
inundate	**verb**	**2-02-002**
inundated	VBN	1-01-001
inundating	VBG	1-01-001
inundation	**noun**	**1-01-001**
inundations	NNS	1-01-001
inure	**verb**	**4-04-004**
inure	VB	2-02-002
inured	VBN	2-02-002

Word	Tag	Numbers
invade	**verb**	**15-07-012**
invade	VB	5-03-004
invades	VBZ	1-01-001
invaded	VBD	1-01-001
invaded	VBN	5-05-005
invading	VBG	3-02-002
invader	**noun**	**6-05-006**
invader	NN	1-01-001
invaders	NNS	5-05-005
invalid	**JJ**	**3-03-003**
invalid	**noun**	**5-05-005**
invalid	NN	3-03-003
Invalid	NN-TL	1-01-001
invalids	NNS	1-01-001
invalidate	**verb**	**3-03-003**
invalidate	VB	2-02-002
invalidated	VBN	1-01-001
invalidism	**NN**	**1-01-001**
invaluable	**JJ**	**5-04-005**
invariable	**JJ**	**1-01-001**
invariably	**RB**	**31-13-031**
invariant	**JJ**	**13-01-002**
invasion	**noun**	**26-06-016**
invasion	NN	16-05-014
Invasion	NN-TL	1-01-001
invasions	NNS	9-01-002
inveigh	**VB**	**1-01-001**
invent	**verb**	**21-09-019**
invent	VB	7-04-006
invented	VBD	5-05-005
invented	VBN	8-06-008
inventing	VBG	1-01-001
invention	**noun**	**24-06-012**
invention	NN	20-06-011
inventions	NNS	4-03-003
inventive	**JJ**	**3-03-003**
inventor	**noun**	**11-06-007**
inventor	NN	7-06-007
inventors	NNS	4-01-001
inventory	**noun**	**35-07-017**
inventory	NN	19-06-011
inventory	NN-HL	2-01-002
Inventory	NN-TL	1-01-001
inventories	NNS	12-04-008
inventories	NNS-HL	1-01-001
inventory	**VB**	**1-01-001**
Invercalt	**NP**	**1-01-001**
Inverness	**NP**	**1-01-001**
inverse	**JJ**	**4-01-003**
inverse	**NN**	**1-01-001**
inversely	**RB**	**5-01-004**
inversion	**NN**	**2-02-002**
invert	**verb**	**4-03-004**
invert	VB	1-01-001
inverted	VBN	3-03-003
invest	**verb**	**16-08-012**
invest	VB	3-03-003
invests	VBZ	1-01-001
invested	VBN	11-06-009
investing	VBG	1-01-001
investigate	**verb**	**38-10-029**
investigate	VB	11-06-011
investigates	VBZ	1-01-001
investigated	VBD	2-02-002
investigated	VBN	16-04-010
investigating	VBG	8-06-007
investigation	**noun**	**73-11-046**
investigation	NN	43-11-034
Investigation	NN-TL	8-03-004
investigations	NNS	22-05-013
investigative	**JJ**	**3-03-003**
investigator	**noun**	**17-05-015**
investigator	NN	4-03-004
investigators	NNS	13-03-011
investment	**noun**	**49-08-023**
investment	NN	38-07-019
investment	NN-HL	2-02-002
Investment	NN-TL	3-02-002
investments	NNS	6-05-006
investor	**noun**	**18-05-009**
investor	NN	1-01-001
Investor	NN-TL	1-01-001
investors	NNS	15-05-008
Investors	NNS-TL	1-01-001
inveterate	**JJ**	**3-03-003**
invictus	**foreign**	**1-01-001**
invictus	FW-JJ	0-00-000
Invictus	FW-JJ-TL	1-01-001
invigorate	**verb**	**1-01-001**
invigorate (cont.):		
invigorating	VBG	1-01-001
invigoration	**NN**	**2-02-002**
invincible	**JJ**	**2-02-002**
inviolability	**NN**	**1-01-001**
inviolable	**JJ**	**1-01-001**
inviolate	**JJ**	**3-03-003**
invisible	**adjective**	**8-06-008**
invisible	JJ	7-05-007
Invisible	JJ-TL	1-01-001
invisibly	**RB**	**2-02-002**
invitation	**noun**	**34-10-026**
invitation	NN	18-09-016
Invitation	NN-TL	2-02-002
invitations	NNS	14-07-011
invitational	**JJ**	**1-01-001**
invite	**NN**	**1-01-001**
invite	**verb**	**49-14-042**
invite	VB	10-08-009
invites	VBZ	7-04-006
invited	VBD	11-09-010
invited	VBN	15-11-015
inviting	VBG	6-05-006
invitee	**noun**	**1-01-001**
invitees	NNS	1-01-001
inviting	**JJ**	**2-02-002**
invocation	**NN**	**1-01-001**
invoice	**noun**	**1-01-001**
invoices	NNS	1-01-001
invoke	**verb**	**14-06-013**
invoke	VB	4-03-004
invoked	VBD	1-01-001
invoked	VBN	5-03-005
invoking	VBG	4-03-004
involuntarily	**RB**	**1-01-001**
involuntary	**JJ**	**3-03-003**
involuntary-control	**NN**	**1-01-001**
involution	**noun**	**12-01-001**
involution	NN	9-01-001
involutions	NNS	3-01-001
involutorial	**JJ**	**3-01-001**
involve	**verb**	**249-15-150**
involve	VB	31-09-026
involves	VBZ	41-08-030
involved	VBD	23-08-019
involved	VBN	121-15-089
involved	VBN-HL	3-02-003
involving	VBG	30-08-026
involvement	**noun**	**14-07-011**
involvement	NN	13-07-010
involvements	NNS	1-01-001
involving	**IN**	**3-02-003**
invulnerability	**NN**	**1-01-001**
invulnerable	**JJ**	**1-01-001**
inward	**JJ**	**2-02-002**
inward	**RB**	**7-06-007**
inwardly	**RB**	**3-03-003**
inwardness	**NN**	**2-02-002**
Io	**NP**	**1-01-001**
iodide	**NN**	**8-01-002**
iodide-concentrating	**JJ**	**1-01-001**
iodinate	**verb**	**11-02-002**
iodinate	VB	1-01-001
iodinated	VBN	7-02-002
iodinating	VBG	3-01-001
iodination	**NN**	**2-01-001**
iodine	**noun**	**18-01-002**
iodine	NN	17-01-002
iodine	NN-HL	1-01-001
iodoamino	**NN**	**1-01-001**
iodocompound	**noun**	**1-01-001**
iodocompounds	NNS	1-01-001
iodoprotein	**NN**	**1-01-001**
iodothyronine	**noun**	**1-01-001**
iodothyronines	NNS	1-01-001
iodotyrosine	**noun**	**1-01-001**
iodotyrosines	NNS	1-01-001
ion	**noun**	**14-02-007**
ion	NN	5-01-004
ions	NNS	9-02-004
Ion	**prop. noun**	**1-01-001**
Ion	NP	0-00-000
Ion	NP-TL	1-01-001
Ione	**NP**	**1-01-001**
ionic	**JJ**	**4-01-003**
Ionic	**adjective**	**4-03-003**
Ionic	JJ	2-01-001
Ionic	JJ-TL	2-02-002
ionize	**verb**	**9-02-003**

Word	Tag	Frequency
ionize (cont.):		
ionized	VBN	3-02-002
ionizing	VBG	5-01-001
ionizing	VBG-HL	1-01-001
ionosphere	**NN**	**3-01-001**
Iosola	**NP**	**1-01-001**
iota	**NN**	**1-01-001**
Iowa	**NP**	**4-04-004**
ipso	**FW-JJ**	**1-01-001**
Ira	**NP**	**2-01-002**
Iraj	**NP**	**1-01-001**
Iran	**NP**	**2-02-002**
Iraq	**NP**	**3-03-003**
Iraqw	**prop. noun**	**2-01-001**
Iraqw	NP	0-00-000
Iraqw	NP-TL	2-01-001
irate	**JJ**	**1-01-001**
ire	**NN**	**1-01-001**
Ireland	**prop. noun**	**16-08-012**
Ireland	NP	12-07-009
Ireland	NP-TL	1-01-001
Ireland's	NP$	2-02-002
Irelands'	NPS$	1-01-001
Irenaeus	**prop. noun**	**15-01-001**
Irenaeus	NP	14-01-001
Irenaeus'	NP$	1-01-001
Irene	**prop. noun**	**2-02-002**
Irene	NP	1-01-001
Irene	NP-TL	1-01-001
iridium	**NN**	**1-01-001**
Irina	**NP**	**2-02-002**
Irish	**adjective**	**26-09-015**
Irish	JJ	18-07-010
Irish	JJ-TL	8-03-005
Irish	**prop. noun**	**2-02-002**
Irish	NP	1-01-001
Irish	NPS	1-01-001
Irishman	**prop. noun**	**2-02-002**
Irishman	NP	1-01-001
Irishmen	NPS	1-01-001
irksome	**JJ**	**1-01-001**
Irma	**NP**	**1-01-001**
iron	**adjective**	**3-03-003**
iron	JJ	1-01-001
Iron	JJ-TL	2-02-002
iron	**noun**	**46-12-034**
iron	NN	35-10-027
Iron	NN-TL	4-03-003
irons	NNS	7-04-005
iron	**verb**	**8-04-006**
iron	VB	1-01-001
ironed	VBN	2-02-002
ironing	VBG	3-02-003
ironing	VBG-HL	2-01-001
iron-clad	**JJ**	**1-01-001**
iron-poor	**JJ**	**1-01-001**
iron-shod	**JJ**	**1-01-001**
ironic	**JJ**	**13-04-011**
ironical	**JJ**	**2-02-002**
ironically	**RB**	**6-04-005**
Ironpants	**prop. noun**	**1-01-001**
Ironpants	NP	0-00-000
Ironpants	NP-TL	1-01-001
Ironside	**NP**	**1-01-001**
irony	**noun**	**13-06-012**
irony	NN	12-06-011
ironies	NNS	1-01-001
Iroquois	**prop. noun**	**1-01-001**
Iroquois	NP	0-00-000
Iroquois	NP-TL	1-01-001
irradiate	**verb**	**5-01-001**
irradiated	VBN	5-01-001
irradiation	**noun**	**10-01-001**
irradiation	NN	9-01-001
irradiation	NN-HL	1-01-001
irrational	**JJ**	**8-03-007**
irrationality	**NN**	**1-01-001**
irrationally	**RB**	**1-01-001**
Irrawaddy	**prop. noun**	**1-01-001**
Irrawaddy	NP	0-00-000
Irrawaddy	NP-TL	1-01-001
irreconcilable	**JJ**	**3-03-003**
irredeemable	**JJ**	**2-02-002**
irredeemably	**QL**	**1-01-001**
irredentism	**NN**	**1-01-001**
irreducible	**JJ**	**1-01-001**
irregular	**JJ**	**9-05-008**
irregular	**noun**	**1-01-001**
irregulars	NNS	1-01-001

Word	Tag	Frequency
irregularity	**noun**	**12-07-010**
irregularity	NN	4-04-004
irregularities	NNS	8-06-006
irregularly	**RB**	**5-03-005**
irrelevant	**JJ**	**14-07-013**
irremediable	**JJ**	**2-02-002**
irreparable	**JJ**	**2-02-002**
irreparably	**RB**	**1-01-001**
irreproducibility	**NN**	**2-01-001**
irresistible	**JJ**	**8-04-005**
irresistibly	**RB**	**1-01-001**
irresolute	**JJ**	**2-02-002**
irresolution	**NN**	**1-01-001**
irresolvable	**JJ**	**1-01-001**
irrespective	**JJ**	**3-02-003**
irresponsibility	**NN**	**3-03-003**
irresponsible	**JJ**	**9-07-009**
irreverence	**NN**	**2-02-002**
irreverent	**JJ**	**2-02-002**
irreversible	**JJ**	**2-02-002**
irreversibly	**QL**	**1-01-001**
irrevocable	**JJ**	**2-02-002**
irrevocably	**RB**	**2-02-002**
irrigate	**verb**	**2-02-002**
irrigate	VB	1-01-001
irrigating	VBG	1-01-001
irrigation	**NN**	**3-02-002**
irritability	**NN**	**1-01-001**
irritable	**JJ**	**5-03-004**
irritably	**QL**	**1-01-001**
irritably	**RB**	**2-02-002**
irritant	**NN**	**1-01-001**
irritate	**verb**	**6-04-006**
irritates	VBZ	1-01-001
irritated	VBD	1-01-001
irritated	VBN	4-03-004
irritating	**JJ**	**4-03-004**
irritation	**noun**	**10-05-009**
irritation	NN	7-04-006
irritations	NNS	3-03-003
irruption	**noun**	**1-01-001**
irruptions	NNS	1-01-001
IRSAC	**NP**	**1-01-001**
Irv	**NP**	**1-01-001**
Irvin	**NP**	**1-01-001**
Irving	**prop. noun**	**4-03-003**
Irving	NP	3-03-003
Irving	NP-TL	1-01-001
Irwin	**NP**	**1-01-001**
Isaac	**NP**	**10-05-006**
Isaacs	**prop. noun**	**2-02-002**
Isaacs	NP	1-01-001
Isaacs	NP-TL	1-01-001
Isaacson	**NP**	**1-01-001**
Isabel	**prop. noun**	**1-01-001**
Isabel	NP	0-00-000
Isabel	NP-TL	1-01-001
Isabell	**NP**	**1-01-001**
Isaiah	**NP**	**1-01-001**
Isfahan	**NP**	**4-01-001**
Isham	**NP**	**1-01-001**
Ishii	**NP**	**1-01-001**
Ishtar	**NP**	**1-01-001**
Isis	**prop. noun**	**1-01-001**
Isis	NP	0-00-000
Isis	NP-TL	1-01-001
Islam	**prop. noun**	**4-03-004**
Islam	NP	3-03-003
Islam's	NP$	1-01-001
Islamic	**adjective**	**3-02-002**
Islamic	JJ	2-02-002
Islamic	JJ-TL	1-01-001
island	**noun**	**207-15-067**
island	NN	31-12-023
Island	NN	1-01-001
island	NN-HL	1-01-001
Island	NN-TL	130-14-043
Island	NN-TL-HL	4-01-002
island's	NN$	0-00-000
Island's	NN$-TL	9-03-005
islands	NNS	12-07-011
Islands	NNS-TL	18-05-006
islands'	NNS$	1-01-001
islander	**noun**	**6-03-003**
islanders	NNS	1-01-001
Islanders	NNS-TL	5-02-002
Islandia	**NP**	**1-01-001**
isle	**noun**	**9-06-008**
isle	NN	4-04-004

Word	Tag	Frequency
isle (cont.):		
Isle	NN-TL	1-01-001
isles	NNS	0-00-000
Isles	NNS-TL	4-03-004
isocyanate	**NN**	**2-01-001**
isocyanate-labeled	**JJ**	**1-01-001**
Isodine	**prop. noun**	**1-01-001**
Isodine	NP	0-00-000
Isodine	NP-TL	1-01-001
isolate	**verb**	**48-10-036**
isolate	VB	8-03-007
isolated	VBN	35-08-027
isolating	VBG	5-03-005
isolation	**NN**	**16-03-009**
isolationism	**NN**	**1-01-001**
isolationistic	**JJ**	**1-01-001**
Isolde	**NP**	**1-01-001**
Isoletta	**NP**	**1-01-001**
isomer	**noun**	**1-01-001**
isomers	NNS	1-01-001
isopleth	**noun**	**2-01-001**
isopleths	NNS	2-01-001
isothermal	**JJ**	**1-01-001**
isothermally	**RB**	**1-01-001**
isotonic	**JJ**	**4-01-001**
isotopic	**JJ**	**2-01-002**
isotropic	**JJ**	**3-01-001**
Israel	**prop. noun**	**16-06-007**
Israel	NP	12-05-005
Israel	NP-TL	3-02-002
Israel's	NP$	1-01-001
Israeli	**adjective**	**4-02-002**
Israeli	JJ	1-01-001
Israeli	JJ-TL	3-02-002
Israelite	**prop. noun**	**2-02-002**
Israelite	NP	1-01-001
Israelites	NPS	1-01-001
issuance	**NN**	**7-04-007**
issue	**noun**	**200-12-096**
issue	NN	129-11-075
issue	NN-HL	7-02-002
Issue	NN-TL	1-01-001
issues	NNS	61-10-038
issues	NNS-HL	2-01-002
issue	**verb**	**72-12-048**
issue	VB	14-06-010
issue	VB-HL	1-01-001
issues	VBZ	3-02-003
issued	VBD	20-10-018
issued	VBN	30-08-022
issuing	VBG	4-02-003
ist	**FW-BEZ**	**1-01-001**
Istanbul	**NP**	**5-01-001**
Istiqlal	**prop. noun**	**12-01-001**
Istiqlal	NP	10-01-001
Istiqlal's	NP$	2-01-001
Istiqlal-sponsored	**JJ**	**1-01-001**
Istvan	**NP**	**1-01-001**
it	**pronoun**	**10942-15-500**
it	PPS	5854-15-500
hytt	PPS	1-01-001
it	PPS-NC	3-01-001
it	PPS-HL	18-02-003
It	PPS-TL	5-02-002
'tain't	PPS+BEZ*	1-01-001
it'd	PPS+HVD	1-01-001
it'd	PPS+MD	2-02-002
it'll	PPS+MD	18-08-016
it's	PPS+BEZ	294-14-145
it's	PPS+BEZ-HL	1-01-001
it's	PPS+BEZ-NC	1-01-001
it's	PPS+HVZ	6-04-006
it (cont.):		
it	PPO	2876-15-463
it	PPO-HL	1-01-001
it	PPO-NC	1-01-001
It	PPO-TL	2-01-001
its	PP$	1854-15-426
its	PP$-HL	3-03-003
it	**UH**	**1-01-001**
it-wit	**NN**	**2-01-001**
Italian	**adjective**	**43-11-027**
Italian	JJ	39-11-026
Italian	JJ-TL	4-03-004
Italian	**prop. noun**	**11-06-009**
Italian	NP	4-04-004
Italians	NPS	7-04-006
italic	**noun**	**3-01-002**
italics	NNS	3-01-002
italicize	**verb**	**1-01-001**
italicized	VBN	1-01-001
Italo	**NP**	**1-01-001**
Italo-American	**adjective**	**1-01-001**
Italo-American	JJ	0-00-000
Italo-American	JJ-TL	1-01-001
Italy	**prop. noun**	**36-11-024**
Italy	NP	33-11-022
Italy	NP-TL	1-01-001
Italy's	NP$	2-02-002
Itasca	**prop. noun**	**1-01-001**
Itasca	NP	0-00-000
Itasca	NP-TL	1-01-001
itch	**NN**	**2-02-002**
itch	**verb**	**8-04-005**
itch	VB	3-02-002
itches	VBZ	1-01-001
itching	VBG	4-03-003
item	**noun**	**127-13-050**
item	NN	55-10-020
items	NNS	71-11-039
Items	NNS-TL	1-01-001
item-category	**noun**	**1-01-001**
item-categories	NNS	0-00-000
Item-Categories	NNS-TL	1-01-001
itemization	**NN**	**1-01-001**
itemize	**verb**	**5-02-003**
itemized	VBN	3-01-002
itemizing	VBG	2-02-002
Ithaca	**NP**	**1-01-001**
Ithacan	**JJ**	**1-01-001**
itinerant	**JJ**	**1-01-001**
itinerary	**NN**	**3-03-003**
Ito	**NP**	**1-01-001**
Itoiz	**NP**	**1-01-001**
itself	**PPL**	**304-15-171**
iuvabit	**FW-VB**	**1-01-001**
Ivan	**NP**	**4-02-003**
ivory	**JJ**	**3-02-003**
ivory	**noun**	**14-07-009**
ivory	NN	13-07-008
Ivory	NN-TL	1-01-001
ivory-inlay	**NN**	**1-01-001**
ivy	**noun**	**9-03-005**
ivy	NN	1-01-001
Ivy	NN-TL	8-02-004
Ivy	**prop. noun**	**2-01-001**
Ivies	NPS	2-01-001
ivy-covered	**JJ**	**1-01-001**
Izaak	**prop. noun**	**6-01-001**
Izaak	NP	1-01-001
Izaak	NP-TL	2-01-001
Izaak's	NP$	3-01-001
Izvestia	**NP**	**1-01-001**

J

Word	Tag	Frequency
J	**prop. noun**	**4-03-004**
J	NP	1-01-001
J	NP-HL	2-01-002
J	NP-TL	1-01-001
J.	**prop. noun**	**120-11-064**
J.	NP	117-11-064
J.	NP-TL	3-03-003
J.D.H.	**NP**	**2-01-001**
J.H.	**NP**	**1-01-001**
j'ai	**FW-PPSS+HV**	**1-01-001**
jab	**noun**	**2-01-002**
jab	NN	1-01-001
jabs	NNS	1-01-001
jab	**verb**	**4-02-004**
jabbed	VBD	2-01-002
jabbing	VBG	2-02-002
jabbering	**noun**	**1-01-001**
jabberings	NNS	1-01-001
Jacchia	**NP**	**1-01-001**
Jacinto	**NP**	**1-01-001**
Jack	**prop. noun**	**103-11-034**
Jack	NP	88-10-031
Jack	NP-NC	2-01-001
Jack	NP-TL	2-01-002
Jack's	NP+BEZ	0-00-000
Jack's	NP+BEZ-NC	1-01-001
Jack's	NP$	9-03-004
Jack's	NP$-TL	1-01-001
Jack-an-Apes	**NP**	**1-01-001**
jack-of-all-trades	**noun**	**1-01-001**
jack-of-all-trades	NN	0-00-000
Jack-of-all-trades	NN-TL	1-01-001
jackass	**NN**	**2-01-001**
jackboot	**noun**	**1-01-001**
jackboots	NNS	1-01-001
jackbooted	**JJ**	**1-01-001**
jackdaw	**noun**	**1-01-001**
jackdaws	NNS	1-01-001
jacket	**noun**	**39-10-032**
jacket	NN	33-09-027
jackets	NNS	6-05-006
jacket	**verb**	**3-02-002**
jacketed	VBN	3-02-002
Jackie	**prop. noun**	**5-01-003**
Jackie	NP	4-01-002
Jackie's	NP$	1-01-001
Jackman	**NP**	**1-01-001**
Jackson	**prop. noun**	**40-09-020**
Jackson	NP	33-09-018
Jackson	NP-HL	1-01-001
Jackson	NP-TL	2-02-002
Jackson's	NP$	2-02-002
Jacksons	NPS	2-01-001
Jacksonian	**JJ**	**2-01-002**
Jacksonville	**NP**	**2-02-002**
Jacky	**NP**	**1-01-001**
Jacob	**NP**	**1-01-001**
Jacobean	**JJ**	**1-01-001**
Jacobite	**adjective**	**1-01-001**
Jacobite	JJ	0-00-000
Jacobite	JJ-TL	1-01-001
Jacobs	**NP**	**2-01-001**
Jacoby	**prop. noun**	**7-01-001**
Jacoby	NP	5-01-001
Jacoby's	NP$	2-01-001
Jacopo	**NP**	**2-01-001**
Jacqueline	**NP**	**4-02-002**
Jacquelyn	**prop. noun**	**1-01-001**
Jacquelyn's	NP$	1-01-001
Jacques	**NP**	**8-03-003**
jade	**NN**	**1-01-001**
jade	**verb**	**2-02-002**
jade (cont.):		
jaded	VBN	2-02-002
jade-handled	**JJ**	**1-01-001**
jag	**NN**	**1-01-001**
Jagan	**prop. noun**	**2-01-001**
Jagan	NP	1-01-001
Jagan	NP-HL	1-01-001
Jager	**NP**	**1-01-001**
jagged	**JJ**	**5-04-005**
jaggedly	**RB**	**1-01-001**
Jaggers	**prop. noun**	**4-01-001**
Jaggers	NP	2-01-001
Jaggers'	NP$	2-01-001
Jaguar	**NP**	**5-02-002**
Jahr	**FW-NNS**	**1-01-001**
Jai	**prop. noun**	**1-01-001**
Jai	NP	0-00-000
Jai	NP-TL	1-01-001
jail	**noun**	**24-06-015**
jail	NN	16-06-010
jail	NN-HL	1-01-001
Jail	NN-TL	4-03-004
jails	NNS	3-03-003
jail	**verb**	**2-02-002**
jailed	VBN	2-02-002
Jakarta	**NP**	**1-01-001**
Jake	**NP**	**6-02-002**
jakes	**NN**	**1-01-001**
jalopy	**NN**	**1-01-001**
jam	**noun**	**6-06-006**
jam	NN	4-04-004
jams	NNS	2-02-002
jam	**verb**	**10-06-010**
jam	VB	2-02-002
jammed	VBD	1-01-001
jammed	VBN	7-05-007
Jamaica	**NP**	**2-01-002**
Jamaican	**NP**	**1-01-001**
James	**prop. noun**	**105-12-062**
James	NP	92-12-058
Jas.	NP	1-01-001
James	NP-TL	9-04-004
James's	NP$	2-02-002
James'	NP$	1-01-001
Jameson	**NP**	**1-01-001**
Jamestown	**NP**	**1-01-001**
jammed-together	**JJ**	**1-01-001**
Jan	**NP**	**4-02-002**
Jana	**NP**	**1-01-001**
Jane	**prop. noun**	**36-08-012**
Jane	NP	34-08-011
Jane	NP-TL	1-01-001
Jane's	NP$	1-01-001
Janet	**NP**	**1-01-001**
jangle	**verb**	**2-02-002**
jangling	VBG	2-02-002
Janice	**NP**	**6-02-002**
Janis	**NP**	**1-01-001**
Janissary	**prop. noun**	**1-01-001**
Janissaries	NPS	1-01-001
janitor	**noun**	**11-05-006**
janitor	NN	4-04-004
janitor's	NN$	1-01-001
janitors	NNS	3-02-002
janitors'	NNS$	3-01-001
Janitsch	**NP**	**1-01-001**
Jannequin	**prop. noun**	**3-01-001**
Jannequin	NP	2-01-001
Jannequin's	NP$	1-01-001
Jannsen	**NP**	**1-01-001**
Jansen	**NP**	**1-01-001**
Jansenist	**JJ**	**1-01-001**

Word	Tag	Frequency
Janssen	**NP**	**4-03-003**
January	**prop. noun**	**74-11-045**
January	NP	53-10-032
Jan.	NP	16-03-012
Jan.	NP-HL	4-01-002
January's	NP$	1-01-001
Janus-faced	**JJ**	**1-01-001**
Jap	**prop. noun**	**5-01-001**
Jap's	NP$	1-01-001
Japs	NPS	4-01-001
Japan	**prop. noun**	**38-10-020**
Japan	NP	37-10-020
Japan	NP-TL	1-01-001
Japanese	**adjective**	**40-10-015**
Japanese	JJ	37-09-014
Japanese	JJ-NC	2-01-001
Japanese	JJ-TL	1-01-001
Japanese	**prop. noun**	**13-07-010**
Japanese	NP	5-03-003
Japanese	NPS	8-06-008
jar	**noun**	**19-05-006**
jar	NN	16-05-006
jars	NNS	2-01-001
jars	NNS-HL	1-01-001
jar	**verb**	**2-02-002**
jarred	VBD	1-01-001
jarred	VBN	1-01-001
jardin	**foreign**	**1-01-001**
jardin	FW-NN	0-00-000
Jardin	FW-NN-TL	1-01-001
jargon	**NN**	**4-03-004**
Jaross	**NP**	**1-01-001**
Jarrodsville	**NP**	**6-01-001**
Jarvis	**NP**	**1-01-001**
Jason	**NP**	**5-02-002**
Jasper	**NP**	**1-01-001**
Jastrow	**NP**	**11-01-001**
jaunty	**JJ**	**2-02-002**
java	**NN**	**1-01-001**
Java	**NP**	**3-02-003**
Javert	**NP**	**1-01-001**
jaw	**noun**	**26-07-017**
jaw	NN	16-07-011
jaws	NNS	10-04-007
Jawaharlal	**NP**	**1-01-001**
jawbone	**NN**	**1-01-001**
jay	**NN**	**1-01-001**
Jay	**NP**	**14-04-004**
Jaycee	**prop. noun**	**4-02-002**
Jaycee	NP	1-01-001
Jaycees	NPS	3-01-001
jazz	**JJ**	**1-01-001**
jazz	**noun**	**99-08-016**
jazz	NN	85-08-016
Jazz	NN-TL	13-03-006
Jazz	NN-TL-HL	1-01-001
jazzman	**noun**	**1-01-001**
jazzmen	NNS	1-01-001
jazzy	**JJ**	**1-01-001**
je	**FW-PPSS**	**1-01-001**
jealous	**JJ**	**4-04-004**
jealously	**RB**	**1-01-001**
jealousy	**noun**	**5-04-005**
jealousy	NN	4-03-004
jealousies	NNS	1-01-001
Jean	**NP**	**23-06-014**
Jean-Honore	**NP**	**1-01-001**
Jean-Marie	**NP**	**1-01-001**
Jean-Paul	**NP**	**2-02-002**
Jean-Pierre	**NP**	**1-01-001**
Jeannie	**NP**	**1-01-001**
jeans	**NNS**	**1-01-001**
Jeb	**NP**	**1-01-001**
Jed	**prop. noun**	**9-03-003**
Jed	NP	8-03-003
Jed's	NP$	1-01-001
jeep	**noun**	**16-05-005**
jeep	NN	3-03-003
Jeep	NN-TL	13-02-002
jeepers	**exclam.**	**1-01-001**
jeepers	UH	0-00-000
Jeepers	UH-TL	1-01-001
jeer	**verb**	**1-01-001**
jeers	VBZ	1-01-001
Jeff	**NP**	**3-01-001**
Jefferson	**prop. noun**	**32-07-015**
Jefferson	NP	25-07-013
Jefferson	NP-TL	2-02-002
Jefferson's	NP$	5-02-002

Word	Tag	Frequency
Jeffersonian	**JJ**	**1-01-001**
Jeffersonian	**prop. noun**	**2-01-001**
Jeffersonians	NPS	2-01-001
Jehovah	**prop. noun**	**3-02-002**
Jehovah	NP	1-01-001
Jehovah's	NP$	0-00-000
Jehovah's	NP$-TL	2-01-001
jejunum	**NN**	**3-01-001**
Jelke	**NP**	**7-01-001**
Jellinek	**prop. noun**	**1-01-001**
Jellinek's	NP$	1-01-001
jelly	**noun**	**4-04-004**
jelly	NN	3-03-003
jellies	NNS	1-01-001
Jellyby	**NP**	**1-01-001**
Jemela	**NP**	**1-01-001**
Jen	**NP**	**7-02-002**
Jena	**NP**	**1-01-001**
Jenkins	**prop. noun**	**10-03-003**
Jenkins	NP	9-03-003
Jenkins's	NP$	1-01-001
Jenks	**prop. noun**	**6-02-002**
Jenks	NP	5-02-002
Jenks	NP-TL	1-01-001
Jenni	**prop. noun**	**2-01-001**
Jenni	NP	1-01-001
Jenni's	NP$	1-01-001
Jennie	**prop. noun**	**4-01-001**
Jennie	NP	3-01-001
Jennie's	NP$	1-01-001
Jennifer	**NP**	**1-01-001**
Jennings	**NP**	**3-02-003**
Jenny	**prop. noun**	**9-02-002**
Jenny	NP	8-02-002
Jenny's	NP$	1-01-001
Jens	**NP**	**1-01-001**
Jensen	**NP**	**4-01-001**
jeopardize	**verb**	**5-04-005**
jeopardize	VB	4-03-004
jeopardizing	VBG	1-01-001
jeopardy	**NN**	**4-04-004**
Jerebohm	**prop. noun**	**5-01-001**
Jerebohm	NP	2-01-001
Jerebohms	NPS	3-01-001
Jeremiah	**prop. noun**	**3-03-003**
Jeremiah	NP	2-02-002
Jeremiah	NP-HL	1-01-001
Jerez	**NP**	**1-01-001**
jerk	**noun**	**2-02-002**
jerk	NN	1-01-001
jerks	NNS	1-01-001
jerk	**verb**	**16-06-015**
jerk	VB	1-01-001
jerked	VBD	12-05-011
jerking	VBG	3-03-003
jerking	**noun**	**1-01-001**
jerkings	NNS	1-01-001
jerky	**JJ**	**4-03-004**
Jeroboam	**prop. noun**	**2-02-002**
Jeroboam	NP	1-01-001
Jeroboams	NPS	1-01-001
Jerome	**NP**	**5-03-005**
Jerry	**prop. noun**	**16-05-011**
Jerry	NP	15-05-010
Jerry's	NP$	1-01-001
jersey	**noun**	**3-03-003**
jersey	NN	1-01-001
Jersey	NN-TL	2-02-002
Jersey	**prop. noun**	**24-08-016**
Jersey	NP	2-02-002
Jersey	NP-TL	20-07-013
Jersey's	NP$	2-02-002
Jerusalem	**UH**	**1-01-001**
Jerusalem	**NP**	**6-04-004**
Jervis	**prop. noun**	**1-01-001**
Jervis	NP	0-00-000
Jervis	NP-TL	1-01-001
Jess	**prop. noun**	**47-01-001**
Jess	NP	33-01-001
Jess's	NP$	14-01-001
Jesse	**NP**	**3-01-002**
Jessica	**prop. noun**	**15-01-002**
Jessica	NP	14-01-002
Jessica's	NP$	1-01-001
Jessie	**NP**	**2-01-001**
Jessy	**NP**	**1-01-001**
jest	**NN**	**1-01-001**
jest	**verb**	**2-02-002**
jesting	VBG	2-02-002

Word	Tag	Frequency
Jesuit	**prop. noun**	**4-03-003**
Jesuit	NP	3-02-002
Jesuits	NPS	1-01-001
Jesus	**exclam.**	**6-01-002**
Jesus	UH	5-01-002
Jee-sus	UH	1-01-001
Jesus	**prop. noun**	**61-06-016**
Jesus	NP	57-06-015
Jesus	NP-TL	1-01-001
Jesus's	NP$	1-01-001
Jesus'	NP$	2-02-002
jet	**noun**	**33-09-018**
jet	NN	19-08-012
Jet	NN-TL	10-01-003
jets	NNS	4-04-004
jet	**verb**	**1-01-001**
jetting	VBG	1-01-001
jet-black	**NN**	**1-01-001**
jetliner	**noun**	**1-01-001**
jetliners	NNS	1-01-001
jeunes	**FW-JJ**	**1-01-001**
Jew	**prop. noun**	**81-07-018**
Jew	NP	25-04-010
Jew	NP-TL	1-01-001
Jews	NPS	54-07-014
Jews'	NPS$	1-01-001
Jew-as-enemy	**NN**	**1-01-001**
Jew-baiter	**NN**	**2-01-001**
Jew-hater	**noun**	**1-01-001**
Jew-haters	NNS	1-01-001
jewel	**noun**	**4-04-004**
jewel	NN	1-01-001
jewels	NNS	3-03-003
jewel-bright	**JJ**	**1-01-001**
jeweled	**adjective**	**3-03-003**
jeweled	JJ	2-02-002
jewelled	JJ	1-01-001
jeweler	**noun**	**3-03-003**
jeweler	NN	2-02-002
jeweler's	NN$	1-01-001
jewelry	**NN**	**3-03-003**
Jewett	**NP**	**1-01-001**
Jewish	**adjective**	**74-08-020**
Jewish	JJ	66-07-018
Jewish	JJ-TL	8-03-005
Jewish-Gentile	**JJ**	**1-01-001**
Jewishness	**NN**	**2-01-001**
jibe	**noun**	**1-01-001**
jibes	NNS	1-01-001
Jidge	**NP**	**1-01-001**
jiffy	**adjective**	**1-01-001**
jiffy	JJ	0-00-000
jiffy	JJ-HL	1-01-001
jiffy	**NN**	**1-01-001**
Jiffy-Couch-a-Bed	**NP**	**1-01-001**
jig	**NN**	**8-02-002**
jigger	**NN**	**1-01-001**
jiggle	**verb**	**1-01-001**
jiggling	VBG	1-01-001
jilt	**verb**	**2-02-002**
jilted	VBN	2-02-002
Jim	**prop. noun**	**40-08-017**
Jim	NP	36-08-017
Jim's	NP$	4-02-002
Jimbo	**prop. noun**	**1-01-001**
Jimbo's	NP$	1-01-001
Jimenez	**NP**	**1-01-001**
Jimmie	**NP**	**1-01-001**
jimmy	**verb**	**1-01-001**
jimmied	VBD	1-01-001
Jimmy	**NP**	**11-06-010**
jingle	**verb**	**3-03-003**
jingled	VBD	2-02-002
jingling	VBG	1-01-001
Jinny	**NP**	**1-01-001**
jinx	**NN**	**1-01-001**
jitterbug	**NN**	**1-01-001**
jitters	**NNS**	**2-02-002**
jittery	**JJ**	**1-01-001**
jiu-jitsu	**NN**	**1-01-001**
jive	**verb**	**1-01-001**
jiving	VBG	1-01-001
JNR	**NP**	**1-01-001**
Jo	**NP**	**6-01-001**
Joan	**prop. noun**	**16-04-010**
Joan	NP	14-04-010
Joan's	NP$	2-02-002
Joanne	**NP**	**1-01-001**
Joaquin	**prop. noun**	**1-01-001**
Joaquin (cont.):		
Joaquin	NP	0-00-000
Joaquin	NP-TL	1-01-001
job	**noun**	**302-13-149**
job	NN	233-13-133
job-	NN	1-01-001
job	NN-HL	3-02-003
jobs	NNS	64-10-042
jobs	NNS-HL	1-01-001
Job	**prop. noun**	**2-01-002**
Job	NP	1-01-001
Job	NP-TL	1-01-001
job-seeker	**noun**	**1-01-001**
job-seekers	NNS	1-01-001
jobless	**JJ**	**2-02-002**
joblessness	**noun**	**1-01-001**
joblessness	NN	0-00-000
joblessness	NN-HL	1-01-001
joblot	**NN**	**1-01-001**
jobs-tears	**NNS**	**1-01-001**
Jock	**NP**	**1-01-001**
jockey	**noun**	**5-04-005**
jockey	NN	3-03-003
Jockey	NN-TL	2-02-002
jockey	**verb**	**1-01-001**
jockeying	VBG	1-01-001
jocose	**JJ**	**1-01-001**
jocular	**JJ**	**4-03-003**
jocularly	**RB**	**1-01-001**
jocund	**JJ**	**1-01-001**
Jody	**NP**	**1-01-001**
Joe	**prop. noun**	**60-11-024**
Joe	NP	55-10-023
Joe's	NP$	5-04-004
Joel	**prop. noun**	**14-02-002**
Joel	NP	12-02-002
Joel's	NP$	2-01-001
Joey	**NP**	**2-01-002**
jog	**verb**	**1-01-001**
jogs	VBZ	1-01-001
Johann	**NP**	**1-01-001**
Johannesburg	**NP**	**1-01-001**
Johansen	**NP**	**1-01-001**
john	**noun**	**3-03-003**
john	NN	2-02-002
John	NN-TL	1-01-001
John	**prop. noun**	**381-12-117**
John	NP	303-12-111
John	NP-HL	9-02-003
John	NP-TL	47-10-015
John'll	NP+MD	1-01-001
John's	NP$	15-05-006
John's	NP$-TL	6-04-004
John-and-Linda	**NPS**	**5-01-001**
John-Henry	**NP**	**1-01-001**
Johnnie	**prop. noun**	**27-02-002**
Johnnie	NP	26-02-002
Johnnie's	NP$	1-01-001
Johnny	**prop. noun**	**30-06-016**
Johnny	NP	28-06-014
Johnny	NP-TL	2-02-002
Johns	**prop. noun**	**6-04-004**
Johns	NP	1-01-001
Johns	NP-HL	1-01-001
Johns	NP-TL	4-02-002
Johns-Manville	**prop. noun**	**1-01-001**
Johns-Manville	NP	0-00-000
Johns-Manville	NP-TL	1-01-001
Johnson	**prop. noun**	**44-09-019**
Johnson	NP	34-09-016
Johnson's	NP$	10-03-004
Johnston	**prop. noun**	**21-04-005**
Johnston	NP	17-04-005
Johnston	NP-TL	4-01-002
joie	**FW-NN**	**1-01-001**
join	**verb**	**139-14-089**
join	VB	63-13-045
Join	VB-TL	2-02-002
'jawn	+VB	1-01-001
joins	VBZ	2-01-002
joined	VBD	33-11-025
joined	VBN	23-12-021
joining	VBG	14-08-013
joining	VBG-HL	1-01-001
joiner	**noun**	**4-01-001**
joiner	NN	3-01-001
joiners	NNS	1-01-001
joint	**adjective**	**23-08-019**
joint	JJ	16-08-014

joint (cont.):		
Joint	JJ-TL	7-04-005
joint	**noun**	**28-10-018**
joint	NN	16-08-013
joints	NNS	12-06-008
jointly	**RB**	**7-05-007**
joke	**noun**	**27-11-021**
joke	NN	19-09-014
jokes	NNS	8-06-008
joke	**verb**	**10-06-010**
joke	VB	3-02-003
jokes	VBZ	1-01-001
joked	VBD	1-01-001
joking	VBG	5-05-005
joker	**noun**	**1-01-001**
jokers	NNS	1-01-001
Jolla	**prop. noun**	**2-01-001**
Jolla	NP	1-01-001
Jolla	NP-TL	1-01-001
Jolliffe	**NP**	**4-01-001**
jolly	**adjective**	**4-03-003**
jolly	JJ	3-02-002
Jolly	JJ-TL	1-01-001
jolly	**verb**	**1-01-001**
jollying	VBG	1-01-001
jolt	**NN**	**2-02-002**
jolt	**verb**	**3-03-003**
jolt	VB	2-02-002
jolting	VBG	1-01-001
Jon	**NP**	**2-02-002**
Jonathan	**prop. noun**	**9-03-003**
Jonathan	NP	5-03-003
Jonathan's	NP$	4-01-001
Jones	**prop. noun**	**75-11-025**
Jones	NP	69-11-023
Jones	NP-HL	1-01-001
Jones	NP-TL	2-01-002
Jones's	NP$	1-01-001
Jones'	NP$	1-01-001
Joneses	NPS	1-01-001
Jones-Imboden	**NP**	**1-01-001**
Jonesborough	**NP**	**1-01-001**
Jonquieres	**NP**	**1-01-001**
jonquil	**noun**	**1-01-001**
jonquils	NNS	1-01-001
Joplin	**NP**	**1-01-001**
Jorda	**prop. noun**	**3-01-001**
Jorda	NP	2-01-001
Jorda's	NP$	1-01-001
Jordan	**NP**	**4-03-003**
Jordon	**NP**	**1-01-001**
Jorge	**NP**	**4-02-002**
Jose	**NP**	**2-02-002**
Josef	**NP**	**2-02-002**
Joseph	**prop. noun**	**57-10-036**
Joseph	NP	50-10-031
Joseph	NP-HL	1-01-001
Joseph	NP-TL	4-03-003
Joseph's	NP$	2-02-002
Josephus	**NP**	**1-01-001**
Joshua	**NP**	**4-03-003**
Joshual	**NP**	**1-01-001**
Josiah	**NP**	**2-02-002**
joss	**NN**	**1-01-001**
Jossy	**NP**	**4-01-001**
jostle	**VB**	**1-01-001**
jot	**NN**	**1-01-001**
jot	**verb**	**2-02-002**
jotted	VBN	1-01-001
jotting	VBG	1-01-001
jour	**foreign**	**4-01-001**
jour	FW-NN	2-01-001
Jour	FW-NN-TL	2-01-001
journal	**noun**	**47-10-020**
journal	NN	6-02-004
Journal	NN-TL	36-09-012
journals	NNS	5-04-005
Journal-American	**NP**	**1-01-001**
Journal-Bulletin	**prop. noun**	**2-01-001**
Journal-Bulletin	NP	1-01-001
Journal-Bulletin's	NP$	1-01-001
journalese	**NN**	**2-01-001**
journalism	**noun**	**13-08-011**
journalism	NN	12-07-010
Journalism	NN-TL	1-01-001
journalist	**noun**	**12-07-011**
journalist	NN	10-06-009
journalists	NNS	2-02-002
journey	**noun**	**31-11-025**

journey (cont.):		
journey	NN	24-09-020
journey	NN-HL	1-01-001
Journey	NN-TL	2-01-001
journey's	NN$	2-02-002
journeys	NNS	2-02-002
journey	**verb**	**3-03-003**
journey	VB	1-01-001
journeyed	VBD	2-02-002
joust	**NN**	**1-01-001**
Jouvet	**NP**	**4-01-001**
jovial	**JJ**	**1-01-001**
joviality	**NN**	**1-01-001**
Jovian	**JJ**	**1-01-001**
jowl	**noun**	**6-05-006**
jowl	NN	2-02-002
jowls	NNS	4-03-004
joy	**noun**	**47-12-037**
joy	NN	40-12-032
joys	NNS	7-05-007
Joyce	**NP**	**21-04-006**
joyful	**JJ**	**1-01-001**
joyfully	**RB**	**1-01-001**
joyous	**JJ**	**5-02-004**
joyously	**RB**	**1-01-001**
joyride	**noun**	**2-01-001**
joyride	NN	1-01-001
joyride	NN-HL	1-01-001
Juan	**prop. noun**	**7-05-006**
Juan	NP	6-05-005
Juan	NP-TL	1-01-001
Juanita	**prop. noun**	**16-01-001**
Juanita	NP	15-01-001
Juanita's	NP$	1-01-001
Jubal	**prop. noun**	**12-01-001**
Jubal	NP	9-01-001
Jubal's	NP$	3-01-001
jubilant	**JJ**	**2-01-002**
jubilantly	**RB**	**2-02-002**
jubilation	**NN**	**1-01-001**
Judaism	**NP**	**2-01-001**
Judas	**NP**	**2-02-002**
Jude	**prop. noun**	**3-03-003**
Jude	NP	1-01-001
Jude	NP-TL	2-02-002
Judea	**NP**	**1-01-001**
Judeo-Christian	**JJ**	**1-01-001**
judge	**noun**	**81-10-041**
judge	NN	22-08-018
Judge	NN-TL	38-06-020
judge's	NN$	1-01-001
judges	NNS	18-04-009
Judges	NNS-TL	1-01-001
judges'	NNS$	1-01-001
judge	**verb**	**42-14-029**
judge	VB	15-11-012
Judge	VB	1-01-001
judge	VB-HL	1-01-001
judges	VBZ	0-00-000
judges	VBZ-HL	1-01-001
judged	VBD	3-03-003
judged	VBN	12-05-010
judging	VBG	8-07-008
judging	VBG-HL	1-01-001
judge-made	**JJ**	**1-01-001**
judgement	**noun**	**1-01-001**
judgement	NN	0-00-000
Judgement	NN-TL	1-01-001
judgeship	**NN**	**1-01-001**
judging	**noun**	**6-02-002**
judging	NN	2-02-002
Judging	NN-TL	4-01-001
judgment	**noun**	**88-12-057**
judgment	NN	58-11-047
judgement	NN	1-01-001
Judgment	NN-TL	1-01-001
judgments	NNS	27-08-016
judgements	NNS	1-01-001
judicial	**adjective**	**16-04-009**
judicial	JJ	15-04-009
Judicial	JJ-TL	1-01-001
judiciary	**noun**	**4-02-003**
judiciary	NN	2-01-002
Judiciary	NN-TL	1-01-001
judiciaries	NNS	1-01-001
judicious	**JJ**	**1-01-001**
judiciously	**RB**	**2-02-002**
Judith	**NP**	**4-02-002**
Judson	**prop. noun**	**4-03-003**

Word	Tag	Frequency
Judson (cont.):		
Judson	NP	2-02-002
Judson	NP-TL	1-01-001
Judsons	NPS	1-01-001
Judy	**NP**	**8-03-004**
Juet	**prop. noun**	**11-01-001**
Juet	NP	8-01-001
Juet's	NP$	3-01-001
jug	**NN**	**6-05-005**
juggle	**verb**	**2-02-002**
juggling	VBG	2-02-002
juice	**noun**	**13-06-009**
juice	NN	11-06-008
juices	NNS	2-02-002
juiciest	**JJT**	**1-01-001**
juicy	**JJ**	**6-03-004**
juju	**NN**	**1-01-001**
juke	**NN**	**2-02-002**
julep	**noun**	**3-02-002**
julep	NN	2-02-002
juleps	NNS	1-01-001
Jules	**NP**	**1-01-001**
Julia	**NP**	**27-04-004**
Julian	**NP**	**8-06-008**
Julie	**prop. noun**	**10-02-003**
Julie	NP	9-02-003
Julie	NP-HL	1-01-001
Juliet	**prop. noun**	**1-01-001**
Juliet	NP	0-00-000
Juliet	NP-TL	1-01-001
Julio	**NP**	**1-01-001**
Julius	**NP**	**4-02-003**
July	**prop. noun**	**66-11-040**
July	NP	62-10-036
July	NP-HL	2-02-002
July	NP-TL	2-02-002
jumble	**NN**	**4-03-004**
jumble	**verb**	**3-03-003**
jumbled	VBN	3-03-003
jump	**noun**	**10-06-008**
jump	NN	9-05-007
jumps	NNS	1-01-001
jump	**verb**	**58-14-049**
jump	VB	15-07-014
jumps	VBZ	1-01-001
jumped	VBD	32-10-030
jumped	VBN	3-02-003
jumping	VBG	7-04-006
jumper	**NN**	**1-01-001**
jumping	**NN**	**1-01-001**
jumping	**UH**	**1-01-001**
jumpy	**JJ**	**2-02-002**
junction	**noun**	**7-06-007**
junction	NN	4-04-004
Junction	NN-TL	3-03-003
juncture	**noun**	**6-03-004**
juncture	NN	4-03-004
junctures	NNS	2-01-001
June	**prop. noun**	**99-11-054**
June	NP	93-11-052
June	NP-HL	5-01-001
June	NP-TL	1-01-001
Jungian	**JJ**	**1-01-001**
jungle	**noun**	**24-06-009**
jungle	NN	18-03-006
Jungle	NN-TL	2-02-002
jungles	NNS	4-02-002
junior	**adjective**	**58-09-022**
junior	JJ	20-09-017
Junior	JJ-TL	38-04-008
junior	**noun**	**47-06-011**
junior	NN	8-06-008
Junior	NN-TL	5-01-001
junior's	NN$	1-01-001
Junior's	NN$-TL	1-01-001
juniors	NNS	3-02-003
Juniors	NNS-TL	27-01-001
Juniors	NNS-TL-HL	1-01-001
juniors'	NNS$	0-00-000
Juniors'	NNS$-TL	1-01-001
Junior	**prop. noun**	**81-10-035**
Junior	NP	3-02-003
Jr.	NP	67-09-030
Jr.	NP-HL	8-02-002
junior	NP	1-01-001
Junior's	NP$	0-00-000
Jr.'s	NP$	2-02-002
junior-grade	**JJ**	**1-01-001**
junior-philosophical	**JJ**	**1-01-001**
junior-senior	**JJ**	**1-01-001**
junior-year-abroad	**JJ**	**1-01-001**
junk	**noun**	**8-05-006**
junk	NN	7-05-006
junk	NN-HL	1-01-001
junk	**verb**	**1-01-001**
junks	VBZ	1-01-001
Junkerdom	**NP**	**1-01-001**
Junkers	**prop. noun**	**2-01-001**
Junkers	NP	0-00-000
Junkers	NP-TL	1-01-001
Junkers	NPS	1-01-001
junketeer	**verb**	**1-01-001**
junketeering	VBG	1-01-001
junkie	**noun**	**1-01-001**
junkies	NNS	1-01-001
junta	**NN**	**3-01-001**
Jupiter	**NP**	**9-03-003**
Juras	**NP**	**2-01-001**
jure	**FW-NN**	**3-01-001**
juridical	**JJ**	**1-01-001**
jurisdiction	**noun**	**30-05-012**
jurisdiction	NN	27-04-010
jurisdiction	NN-HL	1-01-001
Jurisdiction	NN-TL	1-01-001
jurisdictions	NNS	1-01-001
jurisdictional	**JJ**	**3-03-003**
jurisprudence	**NN**	**3-02-002**
jurisprudentially	**RB**	**1-01-001**
jurist	**noun**	**7-03-006**
jurist	NN	3-02-003
jurists	NNS	2-02-002
Jurists	NNS-TL	2-01-001
juror	**noun**	**8-01-003**
juror	NN	4-01-001
jurors	NNS	4-01-003
jury	**noun**	**68-08-022**
jury	NN	63-08-021
jury	NN-HL	1-01-001
Jury	NN-TL	3-02-003
juries	NNS	1-01-001
jury-tampering	**NN**	**1-01-001**
Jussel	**NP**	**1-01-001**
just	**JJ**	**21-10-017**
just	**QL**	**64-12-056**
just	**adverb**	**795-15-303**
just	RB	787-15-303
gust	RB	1-01-001
jist	RB	7-03-003
juste	**FW-JJ**	**1-01-001**
justice	**noun**	**104-12-061**
justice	NN	77-12-048
Justice	NN	2-02-002
Justice	NN-TL	20-05-011
justice's	NN$	0-00-000
Justice's	NN$-TL	2-02-002
justices	NNS	1-01-001
Justices	NNS-TL	2-01-001
Justice	**prop. noun**	**17-04-005**
Justice	NP	16-04-005
Justice's	NP$	1-01-001
justifiable	**JJ**	**4-03-003**
justifiably	**RB**	**5-04-005**
justification	**noun**	**19-04-015**
justification	NN	16-04-013
justifications	NNS	3-02-003
justify	**verb**	**52-11-036**
justify	VB	26-10-022
justified	VBD	1-01-001
justified	VBN	22-06-016
justifying	VBG	3-01-002
Justine	**NP**	**1-01-001**
Justinian	**NP**	**4-02-002**
justitia	**FW-NN**	**1-01-001**
Justitia	**NP**	**1-01-001**
justly	**QL**	**1-01-001**
justly	**RB**	**4-03-004**
justness	**NN**	**1-01-001**
jut	**verb**	**2-02-002**
jutting	VBG	2-02-002
Jutish	**JJ**	**1-01-001**
juvenile	**adjective**	**13-06-008**
juvenile	JJ	10-06-007
Juvenile	JJ-TL	3-01-002
juvenile	**NN**	**5-02-005**
juxtapose	**verb**	**2-01-001**
juxtaposed	VBN	2-01-001
juxtaposition	**NN**	**3-02-003**
JYJ	**prop. noun**	**1-01-001**

Word	Tag	Frequency
JYJ (cont.):		
JYJ	NP	0-00-000
JYJ	NP-TL	1-01-001

Word	Tag	Frequency
JYM	**prop. noun**	**1-01-001**
JYM	NP	0-00-000
JYM	NP-TL	1-01-001

Word	Tag	Frequency
K	**prop. noun**	**6-02-002**
K	NP	5-01-001
K	NP-HL	1-01-001
K.	**prop. noun**	**17-07-017**
K.	NP	16-07-016
K.	NP-TL	1-01-001
K.C.	**NP**	**1-01-001**
K.G.	**NP**	**1-01-001**
K.J.P.	**NP**	**1-01-001**
K'ang-si	**NP**	**1-01-001**
Kabalevsky	**prop. noun**	**1-01-001**
Kabalevsky	NP	0-00-000
Kabalevsky	NP-TL	1-01-001
kaboom	**UH**	**1-01-001**
Kaddish	**NP**	**1-01-001**
Kader	**prop. noun**	**1-01-001**
Kader	NP	0-00-000
Kader	NP-TL	1-01-001
Kafka	**NP**	**5-01-001**
Kaganovich	**NP**	**1-01-001**
Kahler	**NP**	**8-01-001**
Kahler-Craft	**prop. noun**	**1-01-001**
Kahler-Craft	NP	0-00-000
Kahler-Craft	NP-TL	1-01-001
Kahn	**prop. noun**	**2-01-001**
Kahn	NP	1-01-001
Kahn's	NP$	1-01-001
Kai-shek	**prop. noun**	**2-02-002**
Kai-shek	NP	1-01-001
Kai-shek's	NP$	1-01-001
Kaiser	**prop. noun**	**5-03-003**
Kaiser	NP	0-00-000
Kaiser	NP-TL	1-01-001
Kaiser's	NP$	0-00-000
Kaiser's	NP$-TL	3-01-001
Kaisers	NPS	1-01-001
Kajar	**NP**	**1-01-001**
Kakutani	**NP**	**1-01-001**
Kalamazoo	**NP**	**1-01-001**
kale	**NN**	**1-01-001**
kaleidoscope	**noun**	**2-02-002**
kaleidoscope	NN	1-01-001
kaleidescope	NN	1-01-001
Kalentiev	**NP**	**1-01-001**
Kali	**NP**	**1-01-001**
Kalmuk	**prop. noun**	**1-01-001**
Kalmuk	NP	0-00-000
Kalmuk	NP-TL	1-01-001
Kalonji	**NP**	**1-01-001**
Kamchatka	**prop. noun**	**1-01-001**
Kamchatka	NP	0-00-000
Kamchatka	NP-TL	1-01-001
Kamens	**NP**	**1-01-001**
Kamieniec	**NP**	**2-01-001**
kamikaze	**FW-NNS**	**1-01-001**
Kaminsky	**NP**	**1-01-001**
Kandinsky	**NP**	**1-01-001**
Kanin	**NP**	**1-01-001**
Kankakee	**NP**	**1-01-001**
Kansas	**prop. noun**	**36-08-019**
Kansas	NP	19-06-012
Kan.	NP	3-02-002
Kans.	NP	1-01-001
Kas.	NP	1-01-001
Kansas	NP-HL	1-01-001
Kansas	NP-TL	11-06-007
Kansas-Nebraska	**prop. noun**	**1-01-001**
Kansas-Nebraska	NP	0-00-000
Kansas-Nebraska	NP-TL	1-01-001
Kant	**NP**	**2-02-002**
Kanto	**NP**	**1-01-001**
Kaola	**NP**	**1-01-001**
Kaplan	**NP**	**1-01-001**
Kapnek	**NP**	**1-01-001**
kapok-filled	**JJ**	**1-01-001**
Kappa	**NP**	**5-02-004**
Karamazov	**prop. noun**	**4-03-003**

Word	Tag	Frequency
Karamazov (cont.):		
Karamazov	NP	3-02-002
Karamazov	NP-TL	1-01-001
Karen	**NP**	**3-02-003**
Karet	**NP**	**1-01-001**
Karipo	**prop. noun**	**5-01-001**
Karipo	NP	4-01-001
Karipo's	NP$	1-01-001
Karl	**NP**	**7-05-005**
KARL	**NP**	**1-01-001**
Karl-Birger	**NP**	**1-01-001**
Karlheinz	**NP**	**1-01-001**
Karlis	**NP**	**1-01-001**
Karns	**prop. noun**	**8-01-001**
Karns	NP	7-01-001
Karns'	NP$	1-01-001
Karol	**NP**	**1-01-001**
Karolinerna	**NP**	**1-01-001**
Karp	**prop. noun**	**1-01-001**
Karp's	NP$	1-01-001
Karshilama	**NP**	**1-01-001**
Karsner	**NP**	**2-01-001**
Kasai	**prop. noun**	**2-01-001**
Kasai	NP	1-01-001
Kasai	NP-TL	1-01-001
Kasavubu	**NP**	**5-01-001**
Kaskaskia	**NP**	**1-01-001**
Kassem	**NP**	**1-01-001**
Kaster	**prop. noun**	**1-01-001**
Kaster's	NP$	0-00-000
Kaster's	NP$-TL	1-01-001
Katanga	**prop. noun**	**21-03-007**
Katanga	NP	18-03-006
Katanga	NP-HL	1-01-001
Katanga	NP-TL	2-01-001
Katangan	**JJ**	**1-01-001**
Katangan	**prop. noun**	**2-01-002**
Katangans	NPS	2-01-002
Kate	**prop. noun**	**45-02-004**
Kate	NP	41-02-004
Kate's	NP+BEZ	1-01-001
Kate's	NP$	3-01-002
Katharine	**prop. noun**	**7-01-001**
Katharine	NP	6-01-001
Katharine's	NP+BEZ	1-01-001
Katherine	**prop. noun**	**6-04-005**
Katherine	NP	5-03-004
Katherine's	NP$	1-01-001
Kathleen	**NP**	**2-02-002**
Kathy	**NP**	**4-03-004**
Katie	**prop. noun**	**17-02-003**
Katie	NP	15-02-003
Katie's	NP$	2-02-002
Katow	**NP**	**1-01-001**
Katya	**NP**	**3-01-001**
Kauffeld	**NP**	**1-01-001**
Kauffmann	**NP**	**1-01-001**
Kaufnabb	**NP**	**1-01-001**
kava	**NN**	**1-01-001**
Kawecki	**prop. noun**	**1-01-001**
Kawecki	NP	0-00-000
Kawecki	NP-TL	1-01-001
Kay	**NP**	**21-03-004**
Kayabashi	**prop. noun**	**11-01-001**
Kayabashi	NP	9-01-001
Kayabashi's	NP$	2-01-001
Kayabashi-san	**NP**	**1-01-001**
kayo	**VB**	**1-01-001**
Kazan	**prop. noun**	**1-01-001**
Kazan	NP	0-00-000
Kazan	NP-TL	1-01-001
kazoo	**NN**	**1-01-001**
Keane	**NP**	**2-01-001**
Kearton	**NP**	**9-01-001**
Keating	**prop. noun**	**1-01-001**
Keating's	NP$	1-01-001
Keats	**prop. noun**	**1-01-001**

Word	Tag	Frequency
Keats (cont.):		
Keats's	NP$	1-01-001
kebob	**NN**	**1-01-001**
keddah	**FW-NN**	**1-01-001**
kedgeree	**noun**	**4-01-001**
kedgeree	NN	3-01-001
Kedgeree	NN-HL	1-01-001
Kedzie	**prop. noun**	**1-01-001**
Kedzie	NP	0-00-000
Kedzie	NP-TL	1-01-001
Keegan	**NP**	**3-01-001**
keel	**NN**	**5-02-002**
keel	**VB**	**1-01-001**
Keeler	**NP**	**3-02-002**
keelson	**NN**	**10-01-001**
keen	**JJ**	**11-08-011**
keen	**verb**	**1-01-001**
keening	VBG	1-01-001
Keene	**NP**	**3-01-001**
keenest	**JJT**	**2-02-002**
keening	**NN**	**1-01-001**
keenly	**QL**	**1-01-001**
keenly	**RB**	**2-02-002**
keep	**noun**	**5-04-005**
keep	NN	3-03-003
keeps	NNS	2-02-002
keep	**verb**	**523-15-274**
keep	VB	257-14-174
keep	VB-HL	2-02-002
keep	VB-NC	1-01-001
Keep	VB-TL	1-01-001
keeps	VBZ	19-09-017
kept	VBD	115-14-084
kept	VBD-HL	1-01-001
kept	VBN	69-12-060
kept	VBN-HL	1-01-001
keeping	VBG	56-14-046
keeping	VBG-HL	1-01-001
keeper	**NN**	**3-01-001**
keeping	**NN**	**3-03-003**
Keeshond	**NP**	**1-01-001**
keg	**noun**	**3-03-003**
keg	NN	2-02-002
kegs	NNS	1-01-001
kegful	**NN**	**1-01-001**
Kegham	**NP**	**2-01-001**
Kehl	**prop. noun**	**11-01-001**
Kehl	NP	10-01-001
Kehl	NP-TL	1-01-001
keine	**FW-AT**	**1-01-001**
Keith	**prop. noun**	**24-02-002**
Keith	NP	21-02-002
Keith's	NP$	3-01-001
Keizer	**NP**	**1-01-001**
Kekisheva	**NP**	**1-01-001**
Kel	**NP**	**1-01-001**
Kelley	**prop. noun**	**1-01-001**
Kelley's	NP$	1-01-001
Kellum	**NP**	**1-01-001**
Kelly	**NP**	**1-01-001**
kelp	**NN**	**2-01-001**
Kelsey	**NP**	**6-01-002**
Kelseyville	**NP**	**1-01-001**
Kelt	**prop. noun**	**1-01-001**
Kelts	NPS	0-00-000
Kelts	NPS-TL	1-01-001
Kemble	**prop. noun**	**7-01-001**
Kemble	NP	5-01-001
Kemble's	NP$	2-01-001
Kemchenjunga	**NP**	**1-01-001**
Kemm	**NP**	**1-01-001**
Kempe	**NP**	**2-02-002**
ken	**NN**	**2-02-002**
Ken	**NP**	**10-03-004**
Keng	**NP**	**1-01-001**
Kenilworth	**NP**	**1-01-001**
Kennan	**prop. noun**	**10-02-002**
Kennan	NP	7-01-001
Kennan's	NP$	3-02-002
Kennard	**NP**	**2-02-002**
Kennedy	**prop. noun**	**166-07-044**
Kennedy	NP	130-07-036
Kennedy	NP-TL	10-03-006
Kennedy's	NP$	26-05-018
kennel	**noun**	**3-01-001**
kennel	NN	0-00-000
Kennel	NN-TL	3-01-001
Kenneth	**NP**	**6-03-003**
Kennett	**prop. noun**	**1-01-001**

Word	Tag	Frequency
Kennett (cont.):		
Kennett	NP	0-00-000
Kennett	NP-TL	1-01-001
kenning	**noun**	**11-01-001**
kenning	NN	1-01-001
kennings	NNS	10-01-001
Kenny	**NP**	**2-01-002**
keno	**NN**	**1-01-001**
Kent	**prop. noun**	**14-06-008**
Kent	NP	3-03-003
Kent	NP-TL	11-05-005
Kentfield	**NP**	**1-01-001**
Kentucky	**prop. noun**	**18-08-014**
Kentucky	NP	14-08-012
Kentuck'	NP	1-01-001
Ky.	NP	2-01-001
Kentucky	NP-TL	1-01-001
Kenyon	**NP**	**2-01-001**
Kenzo	**NP**	**1-01-001**
Keo	**NP**	**4-01-001**
Kepler	**NP**	**1-01-001**
Kerby	**NP**	**1-01-001**
Kercheval	**NP**	**1-01-001**
kerchief	**NN**	**1-01-001**
Kern	**NP**	**8-02-003**
kernel	**noun**	**6-01-001**
kernel	NN	3-01-001
kernels	NNS	3-01-001
kerosene	**NN**	**6-03-003**
Kerr	**prop. noun**	**6-03-003**
Kerr	NP	5-03-003
Kerr's	NP$	1-01-001
Kerrville	**NP**	**1-01-001**
Kerry	**prop. noun**	**1-01-001**
Kerry	NP	0-00-000
Kerry	NP-TL	1-01-001
Kershbaum	**NP**	**1-01-001**
kerygma	**NN**	**3-01-001**
Kestner	**NP**	**1-01-001**
ketch	**noun**	**1-01-001**
ketches	NNS	1-01-001
ketchup	**NN**	**1-01-001**
ketosis	**NN**	**6-01-001**
kettle	**NN**	**3-03-003**
key	**JJS**	**29-08-022**
key	**noun**	**71-12-052**
key	NN	50-12-038
key	NN-HL	3-03-003
Key	NN-TL	2-02-002
keys	NNS	16-07-013
key	**verb**	**4-03-003**
key	VB	1-01-001
keyed	VBN	3-02-002
Key	**NP**	**3-03-003**
key-punch	**verb**	**1-01-001**
key-punched	VBN	1-01-001
keyboard	**NN**	**4-03-003**
keyboarding	**NN**	**1-01-001**
keyhole	**NN**	**3-03-003**
keynote	**noun**	**3-03-003**
keynote	NN	1-01-001
keynotes	NNS	1-01-001
Keynotes	NNS-TL	1-01-001
keynote	**VB**	**3-02-002**
Keys	**prop. noun**	**21-01-001**
Keys	NP	18-01-001
Keys's	NP$	3-01-001
keystone	**noun**	**1-01-001**
keystone	NN	0-00-000
Keystone	NN-TL	1-01-001
Kezziah	**NP**	**1-01-001**
Khaju	**NP**	**3-01-001**
khaki	**JJ**	**1-01-001**
khaki-bound	**JJ**	**1-01-001**
khan	**NN**	**1-01-001**
Khan	**NP**	**1-01-001**
khaneh	**FW-NN**	**1-01-001**
Khartoum	**NP**	**1-01-001**
Khasi	**prop. noun**	**1-01-001**
Khasi	NP	0-00-000
Khasi	NP-TL	1-01-001
Khmer	**NP**	**1-01-001**
Khrushchev	**prop. noun**	**85-07-024**
Khrushchev	NP	68-06-017
Khrush	NP	1-01-001
Khrushchev's	NP$	14-04-010
Khrushchevs	NPS	2-02-002
ki-yi	**verb**	**1-01-001**
ki-yi-ing	VBG	1-01-001

Word	Tag	Frequency
Kiang	**NP**	**1-01-001**
kibbutz	**noun**	**1-01-001**
kibbutzim	NNS	1-01-001
kick	**noun**	**13-08-010**
kick	NN	10-06-008
kick	NN-HL	1-01-001
kicks	NNS	2-02-002
kick	**verb**	**34-11-020**
kick	VB	4-02-002
kicks	VBZ	1-01-001
kicked	VBD	10-05-007
kicked	VBN	8-06-008
kicking	VBG	11-08-010
kick-off	**noun**	**4-03-003**
kick-off	NN	1-01-001
kickoff	NN	2-01-001
kick-offs	NNS	1-01-001
kick-up	**NN**	**1-01-001**
kickback	**noun**	**1-01-001**
kickbacks	NNS	1-01-001
kicking	**NN**	**1-01-001**
kid	**noun**	**104-12-041**
kid	NN	54-09-022
Kid	NN-TL	7-05-006
kid's	NN+BEZ	3-02-002
kid's	NN$	9-03-003
kids	NNS	31-09-024
kid	**verb**	**8-03-007**
kid	VB	1-01-001
kids	VBZ	1-01-001
kidding	VBG	6-03-005
Kidder	**NP**	**1-01-001**
kidding	**NN**	**1-01-001**
kidnap	**verb**	**5-04-005**
kidnaped	VBN	3-03-003
kidnapped	VBN	1-01-001
kidnapping	VBG	1-01-001
kidnapper	**noun**	**4-02-002**
kidnapper	NN	1-01-001
kidnaper	NN	1-01-001
Kidnapper	NN-TL	1-01-001
kidnappers	NNS	1-01-001
kidney	**noun**	**11-04-006**
kidney	NN	6-03-003
kidneys	NNS	5-04-004
Kieffer	**NP**	**2-01-001**
Kiefferm	**NP**	**1-01-001**
Kika	**NP**	**1-01-001**
Kikuyu	**prop. noun**	**4-02-002**
Kikuyu	NP	2-01-001
Kikuyu	NP-TL	1-01-001
Kikuyus	NPS	0-00-000
Kikiyus	NPS	1-01-001
Kilhour	**NP**	**1-01-001**
kill	**noun**	**5-03-005**
kill	NN	3-03-003
kills	NNS	2-02-002
kill	**verb**	**153-15-082**
kill	VB	60-13-039
kills	VBZ	6-05-005
killed	VBD	34-10-023
killed	VBN	41-12-034
killing	VBG	11-07-009
killin'	VBG	1-01-001
killable	**JJ**	**1-01-001**
Killebrew	**NP**	**1-01-001**
killer	**noun**	**22-06-015**
killer	NN	21-06-015
killers	NNS	1-01-001
killing	**NN**	**12-04-007**
Killingsworth	**prop. noun**	**6-01-001**
Killingsworth	NP	3-01-001
Kililngsworth	NP	2-01-001
Killingsworth	NP-HL	1-01-001
Killpath	**prop. noun**	**25-01-001**
Killpath	NP	19-01-001
Killpath's	NP$	6-01-001
kilometer	**noun**	**11-02-003**
kilometer	NN	8-01-001
kilometers	NNS	3-02-003
kiloton	**NN**	**1-01-001**
kilowatt	**noun**	**2-01-001**
kilowatt	NN	1-01-001
kilowatts	NNS	1-01-001
kilowatt-hour	**noun**	**5-01-001**
kilowatt-hour	NN	4-01-001
kilowatt-hours	NNS	1-01-001
kilt	**noun**	**1-01-001**
kilts	NNS	1-01-001

Word	Tag	Frequency
Kimball	**NP**	**1-01-001**
Kimbell-Diamond	**NP**	**1-01-001**
Kimberly	**NP**	**3-01-001**
Kimbolton	**prop. noun**	**1-01-001**
Kimbolton	NP	0-00-000
Kimbolton	NP-TL	1-01-001
Kimmell	**NP**	**4-01-001**
kimono	**NN**	**1-01-001**
Kimpton	**NP**	**4-01-001**
kin	**NN**	**1-01-001**
kind	**adjective**	**17-09-016**
kind	JJ	16-09-015
kind	JJ-HL	1-01-001
kind	**noun**	**333-15-189**
kind	NN	295-15-177
kind	NN-HL	1-01-001
kind's	NN+BEZ	1-01-001
kinds	NNS	36-13-032
kinda	**QL**	**2-02-002**
kinda	**RB**	**3-01-002**
kinder	**JJR**	**1-01-001**
kindergarten	**NN**	**3-03-003**
kindest	**JJT**	**1-01-001**
kindle	**verb**	**1-01-001**
kindled	VBN	1-01-001
kindliness	**NN**	**1-01-001**
kindly	**JJ**	**5-03-005**
kindly	**RB**	**3-03-003**
kindness	**noun**	**6-02-005**
kindness	NN	5-02-004
kindnesses	NNS	1-01-001
kindred	**NN**	**3-03-003**
kinesics	**NN**	**1-01-001**
kinesthetic	**JJ**	**4-01-001**
kinesthetically	**RB**	**1-01-001**
kinetic	**JJ**	**8-01-006**
king	**noun**	**98-14-044**
king	NN	25-06-012
King	NN-TL	52-13-023
king's	NN$	4-03-003
King's	NN$-TL	10-05-008
kings	NNS	2-02-002
Kings	NNS-TL	5-02-002
King	**NP**	**11-02-004**
Kingan	**prop. noun**	**1-01-001**
Kingan	NP	0-00-000
Kingan	NP-TL	1-01-001
kingdom	**noun**	**27-08-016**
kingdom	NN	16-06-009
kingdom	NN-HL	1-01-001
Kingdom	NN-TL	9-05-006
kingdoms	NNS	1-01-001
kingdom-wide	**JJ**	**1-01-001**
kingpin	**NN**	**1-01-001**
Kingsley	**NP**	**2-02-002**
Kingston	**prop. noun**	**5-03-003**
Kingston	NP	3-02-002
Kingston	NP-TL	2-02-002
Kingstown	**prop. noun**	**2-01-001**
Kingstown	NP	0-00-000
Kingstown	NP-TL	2-01-001
Kingwood	**NP**	**1-01-001**
Kinsell	**NP**	**1-01-001**
Kinsey	**NP**	**1-01-001**
kinship	**NN**	**3-03-003**
kiosk	**NN**	**1-01-001**
Kiowa	**NP**	**1-01-001**
Kipling	**prop. noun**	**4-03-003**
Kipling	NP	1-01-001
Kipling's	NP$	3-03-003
Kira	**NP**	**1-01-001**
Kirby	**prop. noun**	**12-02-002**
Kirby	NP	9-02-002
Kirby's	NP$	3-01-001
Kirk	**NP**	**1-01-001**
Kirkland	**NP**	**1-01-001**
Kirkpatrick	**NP**	**2-01-001**
Kirkwood	**NP**	**2-01-001**
Kirov	**prop. noun**	**10-02-004**
Kirov	NP	5-02-002
Kirov	NP-TL	4-02-004
Kirov's	NP$	1-01-001
kiss	**noun**	**11-05-009**
kiss	NN	8-04-007
kisses	NNS	3-03-003
kiss	**verb**	**31-07-021**
kiss	VB	9-05-008
kisses	VBZ	1-01-001
kissed	VBD	15-06-012

Word	Tag	Frequency
kiss (cont.):		
kissing	VBG	6-05-006
Kissak	**NP**	**1-01-001**
kissing	**noun**	**2-02-002**
kissing	NN	0-00-000
kissin'	NN	0-00-000
Kissin'	NN-TL	1-01-001
kissings	NNS	1-01-001
kit	**noun**	**3-02-002**
kit	NN	2-01-001
kits	NNS	1-01-001
kitchen	**noun**	**95-14-058**
kitchen	NN	90-13-054
kitchens	NNS	5-04-005
kitchenette	**NN**	**3-02-002**
Kitchin	**NP**	**1-01-001**
kite	**NN**	**1-01-001**
kitten	**noun**	**10-05-006**
kitten	NN	5-04-004
kittens	NNS	5-02-002
kittenish	**JJ**	**1-01-001**
Kitti	**prop. noun**	**20-01-001**
Kitti	NP	18-01-001
Kitti's	NP$	2-01-001
Kittler	**NP**	**1-01-001**
Kittredge	**NP**	**1-01-001**
Kitty	**prop. noun**	**12-02-002**
Kitty	NP	7-02-002
Kitty's	NP+BEZ	4-01-001
Kitty's	NP$	1-01-001
Kivu	**NP**	**1-01-001**
Kiwanis	**prop. noun**	**2-02-002**
Kiwanis	NP	1-01-001
Kiwanis	NP-TL	1-01-001
Kiz	**NP**	**3-01-001**
Kizzie	**NP**	**5-01-001**
Klan	**NP**	**3-02-002**
Klauber	**NP**	**2-01-001**
Klaus	**NP**	**1-01-001**
klaxon	**NN**	**1-01-001**
Klee	**prop. noun**	**2-01-001**
Klees	NPS	2-01-001
Kleenex	**NP**	**1-01-001**
Kleiber	**NP**	**1-01-001**
Klein	**NP**	**1-01-001**
Kleist	**NP**	**1-01-001**
Klemperer	**prop. noun**	**1-01-001**
Klemperer's	NP$	1-01-001
Klimt	**NP**	**1-01-001**
Kline	**NP**	**1-01-001**
klinico	**foreign**	**1-01-001**
klinico	FW-NN	0-00-000
Klinico	FW-NN-TL	1-01-001
Kloman	**NP**	**1-01-001**
Kluckhohn	**NP**	**1-01-001**
Klux	**NP**	**3-02-002**
knack	**NN**	**4-04-004**
knackwurst	**NN**	**1-01-001**
Knappertsbusch	**NP**	**1-01-001**
Knauer	**NP**	**2-01-001**
knead	**VB**	**1-01-001**
Knecht	**NP**	**1-01-001**
knee	**noun**	**73-12-048**
knee	NN	33-10-021
Knee	NN-TL	2-01-001
knees	NNS	38-10-032
knee-deep	**RB**	**1-01-001**
knee-length	**JJ**	**2-01-001**
knee-type	**JJ**	**2-01-001**
kneecap	**NN**	**1-01-001**
kneel	**verb**	**21-06-016**
kneel	VB	5-04-005
kneels	VBZ	1-01-001
knelt	VBD	7-05-007
kneeled	VBD	2-01-002
knelt	VBN	1-01-001
kneeling	VBG	5-03-005
knick-knack	**noun**	**1-01-001**
knick-knacks	NNS	1-01-001
Knickerbocker	**NP**	**1-01-001**
knife	**noun**	**86-10-024**
knife	NN	72-09-020
knife	NN-HL	2-01-001
Knife	NN-TL	2-02-002
knife's	NN+HVZ	0-00-000
Knife's	NN+HVZ-TL	1-01-001
knife's	NN+BEZ	0-00-000
Knife's	NN+BEZ-TL	1-01-001
knife's	NN$	0-00-000
knife (cont.):		
Knife's	NN$-TL	1-01-001
knives	NNS	7-06-006
knife-edge	**NN**	**1-01-001**
knife-grinder	**noun**	**1-01-001**
knife-grinder	NN	0-00-000
Knife-grinder	NN-TL	1-01-001
knife-man	**noun**	**1-01-001**
knife-men	NNS	1-01-001
knife/coating	**NN**	**1-01-001**
knifelike	**JJ**	**1-01-001**
knight	**noun**	**25-07-013**
knight	NN	7-03-006
Knight	NN-TL	9-02-002
knights	NNS	4-02-004
Knightes	NNS	1-01-001
Knights	NNS-TL	4-04-004
Knight	**prop. noun**	**2-02-002**
Knight	NP	1-01-001
Knight	NP-TL	1-01-001
knight-errant	**NN**	**2-01-001**
knight-errantry	**NN**	**1-01-001**
Knightfall	**NP**	**1-01-001**
knightly	**JJ**	**1-01-001**
Knill	**prop. noun**	**1-01-001**
Knill's	NP$	1-01-001
knit	**noun**	**2-01-001**
knit	NN	0-00-000
knit	NN-HL	2-01-001
knit	**verb**	**18-08-013**
knit	VB	2-02-002
knitted	VBD	1-01-001
knitted	VBN	5-02-002
knit	VBN	6-05-006
knite	VBN	1-01-001
knitted	VBN-HL	2-01-001
knitting	VBG	1-01-001
knob	**noun**	**3-03-003**
knob	NN	2-02-002
knobs	NNS	1-01-001
knobby-knuckled	**JJ**	**1-01-001**
knock	**noun**	**5-03-004**
knock	NN	4-03-003
knocks	NNS	1-01-001
knock	**verb**	**47-11-038**
knock	VB	11-08-010
knocks	VBZ	1-01-001
knocked	VBD	17-07-015
knocked	VBN	14-07-012
knocking	VBG	4-02-002
knock-down	**JJ**	**1-01-001**
knockdown	**NN**	**1-01-001**
knocking	**NN**	**1-01-001**
knoll	**noun**	**2-02-002**
knoll	NN	1-01-001
Knoll	NN-TL	1-01-001
knot	**noun**	**9-06-009**
knot	NN	7-05-007
knott	NN	1-01-001
knots	NNS	1-01-001
knot	**verb**	**5-05-005**
knot	VB	1-01-001
knotted	VBD	1-01-001
knotted	VBN	3-03-003
knot-tying	**JJ**	**1-01-001**
knotty	**JJ**	**2-02-002**
know	**NN**	**3-03-003**
know	**verb**	**1473-15-379**
know	VB	674-15-270
knoe	VB	1-01-001
know	VB-HL	2-01-002
know	VB-NC	4-01-001
'know	+VB	2-01-002
knows	VBZ	99-14-071
knoweth	VBZ	1-01-001
knew	VBD	394-15-170
knew	VBD-NC	1-01-001
known	VBN	245-15-161
knowed	VBN	1-01-001
knowing	VBG	49-14-042
know-how	**NN**	**4-04-004**
know-nothing	**adjective**	**1-01-001**
know-nothing	JJ	0-00-000
Know-Nothing	JJ-TL	1-01-001
Know-nothing	**prop. noun**	**1-01-001**
Know-nothings	NPS	1-01-001
knowing	**JJ**	**1-01-001**
knowingly	**RB**	**4-03-004**
knowledge	**NN**	**145-13-103**

Word	Tag	Frequency
knowledgeable	**JJ**	**2-02-002**
Knowlton	**prop. noun**	**3-01-001**
Knowlton	NP	2-01-001
Knowlton's	NP$	1-01-001
Knox	**NP**	**5-02-004**
Knoxville	**NP**	**1-01-001**
knuckle	**noun**	**9-04-009**
knuckle	NN	2-02-002
knuckles	NNS	7-04-007
knuckle	**verb**	**3-03-003**
knuckle	VB	1-01-001
knuckles	VBZ	1-01-001
knuckled	VBD	1-01-001
knuckle-duster	**NN**	**1-01-001**
knuckleball	**NN**	**1-01-001**
koan	**FW-NN**	**1-01-001**
kob	**NNS**	**1-01-001**
Kobayashi	**NP**	**1-01-001**
Koch	**NP**	**1-01-001**
Kochanek	**prop. noun**	**2-01-001**
Kochanek	NP	1-01-001
Kochaneks	NPS	1-01-001
Kodak	**prop. noun**	**1-01-001**
Kodaks	NPS	1-01-001
Kodama	**NP**	**2-01-001**
Kodiak	**prop. noun**	**3-01-001**
Kodiak	NP	2-01-001
Kodiak	NP-TL	1-01-001
Kodyke	**NP**	**7-01-001**
Koehler	**NP**	**3-01-001**
Koenig	**NP**	**1-01-001**
Koenigsberg	**NP**	**2-01-001**
Kofane	**prop. noun**	**1-01-001**
Kofanes	NPS	1-01-001
Koh	**NP**	**1-01-001**
Kohi	**NP**	**1-01-001**
Kohnstamm	**NP**	**13-01-001**
Kohnstamm-negative	**JJ**	**9-01-001**
Kohnstamm-positive	**JJ**	**13-01-001**
koinonia	**FW-NN**	**2-01-001**
Kok	**NP**	**1-01-001**
Kokoschka	**NP**	**1-01-001**
kola	**NN**	**2-01-001**
Kolb	**NP**	**1-01-001**
kolkhoz	**foreign**	**4-01-001**
kolkhoz	FW-NN	2-01-001
kolkhozes	FW-NNS	2-01-001
Kolpakova	**NP**	**2-02-002**
Kombo	**NP**	**1-01-001**
Komleva	**NP**	**1-01-001**
Komurasaki	**NP**	**1-01-001**
Kong	**prop. noun**	**11-04-007**
Kong	NP	10-03-006
Kong	NP-TL	1-01-001
konga	**NN**	**1-01-001**
Konishi	**NP**	**2-01-001**
Konitz	**NP**	**2-01-001**
Konrad	**NP**	**1-01-001**
Konstantin	**NP**	**1-01-001**
konzerthaus	**foreign**	**1-01-001**
konzerthaus	FW-NN	0-00-000
Konzerthaus	FW-NN-TL	1-01-001
Kook	**prop. noun**	**1-01-001**
Kooks	NPS	1-01-001
Kool-Aid	**NP**	**1-01-001**
Kooning	**NP**	**2-02-002**
Koop	**NP**	**1-01-001**
Kopstein	**NP**	**1-01-001**
Korea	**prop. noun**	**12-03-006**
Korea	NP	10-03-005
Korea	NP-TL	2-01-002
Korean	**adjective**	**11-06-007**
Korean	JJ	5-04-005
Korean	JJ-TL	6-04-004
Korean	**prop. noun**	**5-02-002**
Koreans	NPS	5-02-002
Korman	**NP**	**1-01-001**
Kornbluth	**prop. noun**	**4-01-001**
Kornbluth	NP	1-01-001
Kornbluth's	NP$	3-01-001
Korneyev	**prop. noun**	**2-01-001**
Korneyev	NP	1-01-001
Kornevey	NP	1-01-001
Korneyeva	**NP**	**1-01-001**
Korngold	**NP**	**1-01-001**
Korra	**NP**	**1-01-001**
Koshare	**NP**	**1-01-001**
kosher	**JJ**	**1-01-001**
kotowaza	**FW-NN**	**1-01-001**
Koussevitzky	**prop. noun**	**4-02-002**
Koussevitzky	NP	3-01-001
Koussevitzky's	NP$	1-01-001
Kowalski	**prop. noun**	**19-01-002**
Kowalski	NP	18-01-002
Kowalski's	NP$	1-01-001
Kozintsev	**NP**	**1-01-001**
Kraemer	**NP**	**1-01-001**
kraft	**NN**	**1-01-001**
Krakatoa	**NP**	**1-01-001**
Krakow	**prop. noun**	**1-01-001**
Krakow	NP	0-00-000
Krakow	NP-TL	1-01-001
Krakowiak	**NP**	**1-01-001**
Kramer	**prop. noun**	**1-01-001**
Kramer's	NP$	1-01-001
Krapp	**prop. noun**	**1-01-001**
Krapp's	NP$	0-00-000
Krapp's	NP$-TL	1-01-001
Krasnik	**NP**	**1-01-001**
kraut	**NN**	**1-01-001**
Kraut	**prop. noun**	**1-01-001**
Krauts	NPS	1-01-001
krauthead	**noun**	**1-01-001**
krautheads	NNS	1-01-001
Kreisler	**NP**	**1-01-001**
Kremlin	**prop. noun**	**13-05-012**
Kremlin	NP	11-04-011
Kremlin's	NP$	2-01-001
Kretchmer	**NP**	**2-01-001**
Krim	**prop. noun**	**26-01-001**
Krim	NP	17-01-001
Krim's	NP$	8-01-001
Krims	NPS	1-01-001
Krishna	**NP**	**1-01-001**
Krishnaist	**prop. noun**	**1-01-001**
Krishnaists	NPS	1-01-001
Kriss	**NP**	**1-01-001**
kristallstrukturen	**foreign**	**1-01-001**
kristallstrukturen	FW-NNS	0-00-000
Kristallstrukturen	FW-NNS-TL	1-01-001
Kroening	**NP**	**1-01-001**
Kroger	**prop. noun**	**7-03-003**
Kroger	NP	2-02-002
Kroger's	NP$	1-01-001
Krogers	NPS	3-01-001
Krogers'	NPS$	1-01-001
Kromy	**NP**	**1-01-001**
Kronenberger	**NP**	**1-01-001**
Kruger	**prop. noun**	**7-01-001**
Kruger	NP	5-01-001
Kruger's	NP$	2-01-001
Krumpp	**NP**	**1-01-001**
Krupa	**NP**	**1-01-001**
Krutch	**prop. noun**	**5-01-002**
Krutch	NP	2-01-001
Krutch's	NP$	3-01-002
krystallographie	**foreign**	**4-01-001**
krystallographie	FW-NN	0-00-000
Krystallographie	FW-NN-TL	4-01-001
Krzywy-Rog	**NP**	**1-01-001**
ksu'u'peli'afo	**FW-VB**	**1-01-001**
Ku	**NP**	**3-02-002**
Kubek	**NP**	**1-01-001**
Kuhn	**NP**	**1-01-001**
Kulturbund	**foreign**	**4-01-001**
Kulturbund	FW-NN	0-00-000
Kulturbund	FW-NN-TL	4-01-001
Kunkel	**prop. noun**	**4-01-001**
Kunkel	NP	2-01-001
Kunkel's	NP$	2-01-001
Kupcinet	**NP**	**1-01-001**
Kurd	**NP**	**1-01-001**
Kurigalzu	**NP**	**1-01-001**
Kurt	**NP**	**1-01-001**
Kwame	**NP**	**1-01-001**
Kwango	**prop. noun**	**1-01-001**
Kwango	NP	0-00-000
Kwango	NP-TL	1-01-001
kwashiorkor	**FW-NN**	**1-01-001**
Kyne	**NP**	**2-01-001**
Kyo	**NP**	**1-01-001**
Kyo-zan	**NP**	**1-01-001**
Kyoto	**prop. noun**	**7-01-001**
Kyoto	NP	4-01-001
Kyoto	NP-HL	1-01-001
Kyoto	NP-TL	2-01-001

L

Word	Tag	Frequency
L	**NP**	**6-01-001**
l.	**NN**	**2-01-001**
L.	**prop. noun**	**54-10-035**
L.	NP	53-10-034
L.	NP-HL	1-01-001
L.S.U.	**NP**	**1-01-001**
L-5-vinyl-2-thio-oxazolidone	**NP**	**1-01-001**
l'activite	**foreign**	**1-01-001**
l'activite	FW-AT+NN	0-00-000
l'activite	FW-AT+NN-TL	1-01-001
l'ange	**foreign**	**1-01-001**
l'ange	FW-AT+NN	0-00-000
l'Ange	FW-AT+NN-TL	1-01-001
l'arcade	**foreign**	**1-01-001**
l'arcade	FW-AT+NN	0-00-000
L'Arcade	FW-AT+NN-TL	1-01-001
l'assistance	**foreign**	**1-01-001**
l'assistance	FW-AT+NN	0-00-000
l'Assistance	FW-AT+NN-TL	1-01-001
l'Astree	**foreign**	**1-01-001**
l'Astree	FW-AT+NP	0-00-000
L'Astree	FW-AT+NP-TL	1-01-001
l'identite	**foreign**	**1-01-001**
l'identite	FW-AT+NN	0-00-000
l'identite	FW-AT+NN-TL	1-01-001
l'Imperiale	**foreign**	**1-01-001**
l'Imperiale	FW-AT+NP	0-00-000
L'Imperiale	FW-AT+NP-TL	1-01-001
l'independance	**foreign**	**1-01-001**
l'independance	FW-AT+NN	0-00-000
l'Independance	FW-AT+NN-TL	1-01-001
l'institut	**foreign**	**1-01-001**
l'institut	FW-AT+NN	0-00-000
L'Institut	FW-AT+NN-TL	1-01-001
l'orchestre	**foreign**	**1-01-001**
l'orchestre	FW-AT+NN	0-00-000
L'orchestre	FW-AT+NN-TL	1-01-001
l'osservatore	**foreign**	**1-01-001**
l'osservatore	FW-AT+NN	0-00-000
l'Osservatore	FW-AT+NN-TL	1-01-001
L'Turu	**NP**	**3-01-001**
l'union	**foreign**	**2-01-001**
l'union	FW-AT+NN	0-00-000
L'Union	FW-AT+NN-TL	2-01-001
l'unita	**foreign**	**1-01-001**
l'unita	FW-AT+NN	0-00-000
L'Unita	FW-AT+NN-TL	1-01-001
l'universite	**foreign**	**1-01-001**
l'universite	FW-AT+NN	0-00-000
l'Universite	FW-AT+NN-TL	1-01-001
La	**prop. noun**	**18-07-016**
La	NP	13-06-013
La	NP-TL	5-04-005
lab	**NN**	**3-02-002**
Laban	**prop. noun**	**5-01-001**
Laban	NP	4-01-001
Labans	NPS	1-01-001
label	**noun**	**20-08-014**
label	NN	17-08-013
label	NN-HL	1-01-001
labels	NNS	2-01-001
label	**verb**	**17-09-017**
label	VB	1-01-001
labels	VBZ	1-01-001
labeled	VBD	2-02-002
labeled	VBN	7-03-007
labelled	VBN	2-02-002
labeling	VBG	4-04-004
labile	**JJ**	**1-01-001**
labor	**noun**	**151-11-069**
labor	NN	118-10-056
labour	NN	3-02-002
labor (cont.):		
Labour	NN-TL	1-01-001
labor	NN-HL	3-02-002
Labor	NN-TL	24-06-015
labor's	NN$	1-01-001
labors	NNS	1-01-001
labor	**verb**	**10-04-009**
labor	VB	4-01-004
labors	VBZ	1-01-001
labored	VBD	3-02-003
labored	VBN	2-02-002
labor-based	**JJ**	**1-01-001**
labor-management	**NN**	**7-04-006**
labor-saving	**JJ**	**1-01-001**
laboratory	**noun**	**49-09-026**
laboratory	NN	25-06-016
laboratory	NN-HL	2-01-001
Laboratory	NN-TL	13-05-007
laboratories	NNS	5-03-005
Laboratories	NNS-TL	4-03-004
laborer	**noun**	**12-05-010**
laborer	NN	6-04-005
laborers	NNS	6-03-005
laborious	**JJ**	**1-01-001**
laboriously	**RB**	**2-02-002**
Labothe	**NP**	**1-01-001**
Labouisse	**NP**	**1-01-001**
Labrador	**NP**	**1-01-001**
labyrinth	**NN**	**1-01-001**
lace	**noun**	**8-04-005**
lace	NN	7-03-004
laces	NNS	1-01-001
lace	**verb**	**2-02-002**
laced	VBD	1-01-001
laced	VBN	1-01-001
lace-drawn	**JJ**	**1-01-001**
lacerate	**verb**	**2-02-002**
lacerate	VB	1-01-001
lacerated	VBN	1-01-001
laceration	**noun**	**2-02-002**
lacerations	NNS	2-02-002
lacheln	**FW-VB**	**1-01-001**
lack	**noun**	**97-14-079**
lack	NN	96-14-078
lack	NN-HL	1-01-001
lack	**verb**	**70-12-054**
lack	VB	13-05-011
lacks	VBZ	6-04-005
lacked	VBD	15-07-014
lacked	VBN	4-04-004
lacking	VBG	31-07-027
lacking	VBG-HL	1-01-001
lackadaisical	**JJ**	**1-01-001**
lackey	**noun**	**1-01-001**
lackeys	NNS	1-01-001
lacquer	**NN**	**2-02-002**
lacquer	**verb**	**1-01-001**
lacquered	VBN	1-01-001
lactate	**NN**	**2-02-002**
lactate	**verb**	**2-01-001**
lactating	VBG	2-01-001
lacy	**adjective**	**5-04-004**
lacy	JJ	3-03-003
lacey	JJ	2-01-001
Lacy	**NP**	**1-01-001**
lad	**noun**	**8-07-007**
lad	NN	6-06-006
lad's	NN$	1-01-001
lads	NNS	1-01-001
ladder	**NN**	**19-10-013**
laden	**JJ**	**6-06-006**
Ladgham	**NP**	**2-01-001**

Word	Tag	Frequency
ladle	**NN**	**1-01-001**
lady	**noun**	**122-13-068**
lady	NN	48-13-026
Lady	NN-TL	32-09-015
lady's	NN$	5-04-005
ladies	NNS	28-10-023
ladies'	NNS$	7-06-007
Ladies'	NNS$-TL	2-02-002
Lady	**NP**	**1-01-001**
lady-bug	**noun**	**1-01-001**
lady-bugs	NNS	1-01-001
ladylike	**JJ**	**1-01-001**
laendler	**FW-NN**	**1-01-001**
Lafayette	**prop. noun**	**13-04-004**
Lafayette	NP	7-01-001
Lafayette	NP-TL	6-03-003
Lafe	**NP**	**1-01-001**
lag	**noun**	**3-03-003**
lag	NN	1-01-001
lags	NNS	2-02-002
lag	**verb**	**5-03-004**
lag	VB	2-02-002
lags	VBZ	1-01-001
lagged	VBD	1-01-001
lagged	VBN	1-01-001
lager	**noun**	**1-01-001**
lagers	NNS	1-01-001
Lagerlof	**NP**	**1-01-001**
lagoon	**noun**	**15-03-003**
lagoon	NN	12-03-003
lagoon	NN-HL	1-01-001
lagoons	NNS	2-01-001
Lagoon	**NP**	**2-01-001**
LaGow	**NP**	**1-01-001**
Lagrange	**prop. noun**	**1-01-001**
Lagrange's	NP$	1-01-001
LaGuardia	**prop. noun**	**4-01-001**
LaGuardia	NP	3-01-001
LaGuardia's	NP$	1-01-001
Laguerre	**NP**	**3-01-001**
Laguna	**prop. noun**	**2-02-002**
Laguna	NP	0-00-000
Laguna	NP-TL	2-02-002
laicos	**foreign**	**1-01-001**
laicos	FW-NNS	0-00-000
Laicos	FW-NNS-TL	1-01-001
lair	**noun**	**1-01-001**
lairs	NNS	1-01-001
laissez-faire	**JJ**	**3-02-003**
laissez-faire	**NN**	**2-02-002**
laity	**NN**	**3-01-001**
lake	**noun**	**61-12-026**
lake	NN	11-06-007
Lake	NN-TL	42-11-020
lakes	NNS	6-03-004
lakes	NNS-HL	1-01-001
Lakes	NNS-TL	1-01-001
Lake	**prop. noun**	**2-01-001**
Lake	NP	1-01-001
Lake	NP-HL	1-01-001
Lakewood	**NP**	**1-01-001**
Lalaurie	**prop. noun**	**21-01-001**
Lalaurie	NP	17-01-001
Lalaurie's	NP$	1-01-001
Lalauries	NPS	2-01-001
Lalauries'	NPS$	1-01-001
lam	**verb**	**2-02-002**
lammed	VBD	1-01-001
lamming	VBG	1-01-001
Lamar	**prop. noun**	**3-01-002**
Lamar	NP	1-01-001
Lamar	NP-TL	2-01-002
lamb	**noun**	**14-05-006**
lamb	NN	6-04-004
Lamb	NN-TL	1-01-001
lambs	NNS	5-01-001
lambs	NNS-HL	2-01-001
Lambarene	**NP**	**1-01-001**
Lambert	**NP**	**2-01-002**
Lambeth	**prop. noun**	**3-01-001**
Lambeth	NP	0-00-000
Lambeth	NP-TL	3-01-001
lame	**JJ**	**2-02-002**
lamechian	**JJ**	**1-01-001**
lamechian	**prop. noun**	**1-01-001**
lamechians	NPS	1-01-001
lament	**noun**	**3-02-003**
lament	NN	1-01-001
laments	NNS	2-01-002
lamentation	**noun**	**3-03-003**
lamentation	NN	0-00-000
Lamentation	NN-TL	1-01-001
lamentations	NNS	2-02-002
laminate	**NN**	**3-01-001**
laminate	**verb**	**3-02-002**
laminated	VBN	2-01-001
laminating	VBG	1-01-001
Lammermoor	**NP**	**2-01-002**
Lamon	**NP**	**1-01-001**
lamp	**noun**	**24-09-015**
lamp	NN	18-07-010
lamps	NNS	6-04-006
lamplight	**NN**	**3-03-003**
lampoon	**VB**	**1-01-001**
lana	**foreign**	**2-01-001**
lana	FW-NN	1-01-001
Lana	FW-NN-TL	1-01-001
Lancashire	**prop. noun**	**1-01-001**
Lancashire	NP	0-00-000
Lancashire	NP-TL	1-01-001
Lancaster	**prop. noun**	**2-02-002**
Lancaster	NP	1-01-001
Lancaster	NP-TL	1-01-001
lance	**noun**	**5-03-003**
lance	NN	3-03-003
lances	NNS	2-01-001
lance	**verb**	**1-01-001**
lanced	VBD	1-01-001
Lancret	**NP**	**1-01-001**
land	**noun**	**232-15-107**
land	NN	192-15-094
Land	NN	1-01-001
land	NN-HL	6-03-003
Land	NN-TL	8-04-005
lands	NNS	23-09-016
landes	NNS	1-01-001
Lands	NNS-TL	1-01-001
land	**verb**	**38-09-026**
land	VB	9-06-008
lands	VBZ	1-01-001
landed	VBD	12-06-012
landed	VBN	3-03-003
landing	VBG	13-06-009
Land	**prop. noun**	**3-02-002**
Land	NP	2-01-001
Land's	NP$	1-01-001
land-based	**JJ**	**1-01-001**
land-locked	**JJ**	**1-01-001**
Land-Rover	**NP**	**1-01-001**
landau	**NN**	**1-01-001**
Landau	**NP**	**1-01-001**
Lander	**NP**	**1-01-001**
Landesco	**NP**	**1-01-001**
landing	**noun**	**15-07-010**
landing	NN	12-06-009
Landing	NN-TL	1-01-001
landings	NNS	2-01-001
Landis	**prop. noun**	**4-02-002**
Landis	NP	3-01-001
Landis'	NP$	1-01-001
landlord	**noun**	**15-06-008**
landlord	NN	12-04-006
landlord's	NN$	1-01-001
landlords	NNS	2-02-002
landmark	**noun**	**10-05-007**
landmark	NN	3-03-003
landmarks	NNS	7-04-005
Landon	**NP**	**1-01-001**
landowner	**noun**	**1-01-001**
landowners	NNS	1-01-001
Landrum-Griffin	**prop. noun**	**2-02-002**
Landrum-Griffin	NP	0-00-000
Landrum-Griffin	NP-TL	2-02-002
landscape	**noun**	**25-10-016**
landscape	NN	20-09-013
landscapes	NNS	5-04-004
landscape	**verb**	**4-04-004**
landscaped	VBN	3-03-003
landscaping	VBG	1-01-001
landslide	**noun**	**3-02-003**
landslide	NN	2-02-002
landslides	NNS	1-01-001
lane	**noun**	**24-07-012**
lane	NN	11-05-007
Lane	NN-TL	9-05-005
lanes	NNS	4-03-003
Lane	**prop. noun**	**10-04-006**
Lane	NP	9-03-005

Word	Tag	Frequency
Lane (cont.):		
Lane	NP-TL	1-01-001
lanesmanship	**noun**	**1-01-001**
lanesmanship	NN	0-00-000
Lanesmanship	NN-TL	1-01-001
Lanesville	**NP**	**1-01-001**
Lang	**NP**	**1-01-001**
lange	**FW-JJ**	**1-01-001**
Langeland	**NP**	**1-01-001**
Langer	**NP**	**3-01-001**
Langford	**NP**	**18-01-001**
Langhorne	**NP**	**1-01-001**
Langsdorf	**NP**	**1-01-001**
language	**noun**	**149-13-074**
language	NN	107-13-067
Language	NN-TL	2-02-002
languages	NNS	39-06-016
Languages	NNS-TL	1-01-001
languid	**JJ**	**4-03-004**
languish	**verb**	**2-02-002**
languished	VBD	1-01-001
languishing	VBG	1-01-001
Lanin	**prop. noun**	**1-01-001**
Lanin's	NP$	1-01-001
lanky	**JJ**	**2-02-002**
Lante	**NP**	**1-01-001**
lantern	**noun**	**15-04-008**
lantern	NN	13-03-006
lanterns	NNS	2-02-002
lanthanum	**NN**	**1-01-001**
Lanza	**NP**	**2-01-001**
Lao	**prop. noun**	**17-02-004**
Lao	NP	14-02-004
Lao	NP-TL	3-02-002
Lao-tse	**NP**	**1-01-001**
Laodicean	**JJ**	**1-01-001**
Laodicean	**prop. noun**	**1-01-001**
Laodicean	NP	0-00-000
Laodicean	NP-TL	1-01-001
Laos	**prop. noun**	**64-05-013**
Laos	NP	62-05-013
Laos	NP-HL	1-01-001
Laos	NP-TL	1-01-001
Laotian	**JJ**	**4-02-003**
Laotian	**prop. noun**	**1-01-001**
Laotians	NPS	1-01-001
lap	**noun**	**19-08-013**
lap	NN	17-06-011
Lap	NN-TL	1-01-001
laps	NNS	1-01-001
lap	**verb**	**6-03-004**
lap	VB	1-01-001
laps	VBZ	1-01-001
lapped	VBD	1-01-001
lapped	VBN	1-01-001
lapping	VBG	2-01-002
lapel	**noun**	**3-03-003**
lapel	NN	1-01-001
lapels	NNS	2-02-002
lapidary	**NN**	**1-01-001**
Laplace	**NP**	**1-01-001**
Lappenberg	**NP**	**5-01-001**
Lappenburg-Kemble	**NP**	**1-01-001**
lappet	**noun**	**1-01-001**
lappets	NNS	1-01-001
lapse	**noun**	**7-06-006**
lapse	NN	4-03-003
lapses	NNS	3-03-003
lapse	**verb**	**7-05-007**
lapse	VB	2-02-002
lapses	VBZ	1-01-001
lapsed	VBD	2-02-002
lapsed	VBN	1-01-001
lapsing	VBG	1-01-001
Laramie	**prop. noun**	**3-02-002**
Laramie	NP	1-01-001
Laramie	NP-TL	2-01-001
larceny	**NN**	**2-02-002**
lard	**NN**	**4-02-002**
larder	**NN**	**1-01-001**
Laredo	**NP**	**2-02-002**
large	**JJ**	**354-15-209**
large	**NN**	**2-02-002**
large	**RB**	**5-03-005**
large-area	**NN**	**1-01-001**
large-enough	**JJ**	**1-01-001**
large-package	**noun**	**2-01-001**
large-package	NN	1-01-001
large-package	NN-HL	1-01-001
large-scale	**NN**	**7-04-007**
largely	**QL**	**12-08-011**
largely	**RB**	**56-10-046**
largely-silent	**JJ**	**1-01-001**
larger	**comp. adj.**	**123-15-084**
larger	JJR	122-15-083
larger	JJR-HL	1-01-001
largesse	**NN**	**1-01-001**
largest	**JJT**	**53-11-043**
Larimer	**prop. noun**	**1-01-001**
Larimer	NP	0-00-000
Larimer	NP-TL	1-01-001
lark	**noun**	**4-03-003**
lark	NN	1-01-001
Lark	NN-TL	1-01-001
larks	NNS	2-02-002
Larkin	**prop. noun**	**12-01-002**
Larkin	NP	10-01-002
Larkin's	NP$	1-01-001
Larkins	NPS	1-01-001
larkspur	**noun**	**3-02-002**
larkspur	NN	1-01-001
Larkspur	NN-TL	2-01-001
Larry	**NP**	**9-04-007**
Lars	**NP**	**1-01-001**
Larson	**prop. noun**	**6-02-003**
Larson	NP	5-01-002
Larson's	NP$	1-01-001
larva	**noun**	**6-01-001**
larvae	NNS	6-01-001
larval	**JJ**	**1-01-001**
las	**foreign**	**1-01-001**
las	FW-AT	0-00-000
Las	FW-AT-TL	1-01-001
Las	**NP**	**4-03-004**
LaSalle	**NP**	**2-02-002**
Lascar	**NP**	**1-01-001**
lascivious	**adjective**	**1-01-001**
lascivious	JJ	0-00-000
Lascivious	JJ-TL	1-01-001
lash	**noun**	**4-03-003**
lash	NN	2-01-001
lashes	NNS	2-02-002
lash	**verb**	**9-05-007**
lash	VB	4-04-004
lashed	VBD	3-03-003
lashing	VBG	2-01-001
lashing	**noun**	**1-01-001**
lashings	NNS	1-01-001
lass	**noun**	**3-03-003**
lass	NN	1-01-001
Lass	NN-TL	1-01-001
lasses	NNS	1-01-001
lasso	**NN**	**1-01-001**
lasso	**VB**	**1-01-001**
Lassus	**NP**	**1-01-001**
Lasswitz	**prop. noun**	**1-01-001**
Lasswitz's	NP$	1-01-001
last	**post-det.**	**613-15-276**
last	AP	605-15-274
last	AP-HL	1-01-001
Last	AP-TL	7-04-005
last	**NN**	**8-06-008**
last	**RB**	**32-09-029**
last	**verb**	**48-14-045**
last	VB	23-13-021
lasts	VBZ	1-01-001
lasted	VBD	11-09-011
lasted	VBN	1-01-001
lasting	VBG	12-08-012
last-ditch	**NN**	**1-01-001**
last-mentioned	**JJ**	**1-01-001**
last-minute	**NN**	**2-02-002**
last-named	**JJ**	**2-01-001**
last-round	**NN**	**1-01-001**
lasting	**JJ**	**1-01-001**
lastly	**RB**	**3-03-003**
Laswick	**NP**	**1-01-001**
latch	**NN**	**4-03-003**
latch	**verb**	**3-02-002**
latch	VB	1-01-001
latches	VBZ	1-01-001
latched	VBN	1-01-001
late	**adjective**	**132-15-098**
late	JJ	130-15-097
Late	JJ-TL	2-01-002
late	**RB**	**47-14-041**
late-comer	**noun**	**1-01-001**
late-comers	NNS	1-01-001

Word	Tag	Frequency
late-summer	**NN**	**1-01-001**
Lateiner	**NP**	**1-01-001**
lately	**RB**	**12-05-012**
latent	**JJ**	**9-06-007**
later	**JJR**	**55-10-041**
later	**RBR**	**342-15-208**
lateral	**adjective**	**1-01-001**
lateral	JJ	0-00-000
Lateral	JJ-TL	1-01-001
Lateran	**NP**	**1-01-001**
latest	**JJT**	**35-12-030**
latex	**NN**	**2-01-001**
lath	**NN**	**2-01-001**
lathe	**noun**	**2-02-002**
lathe	NN	1-01-001
lathes	NNS	1-01-001
lather	**NN**	**3-02-002**
lather	**verb**	**3-02-003**
lathered	VBD	1-01-001
lathered	VBN	2-02-002
Latin	**adjective**	**39-11-027**
Latin	JJ	24-09-017
Latin	JJ-TL	15-07-013
Latin	**NP**	**11-05-008**
Latinovich	**NP**	**1-01-001**
latitude	**noun**	**6-04-006**
latitude	NN	5-04-005
latitudes	NNS	1-01-001
latter	**post-det.**	**114-13-083**
latter	AP	113-13-083
Latter	AP-TL	1-01-001
latter	**noun**	**10-09-010**
latter's	NN$	10-09-010
latter-day	**NN**	**1-01-001**
lattice	**NN**	**2-01-002**
Lattimer	**prop. noun**	**4-01-001**
Lattimer	NP	3-01-001
Lattimer's	NP$	1-01-001
Lauchli	**prop. noun**	**5-01-001**
Lauchli	NP	4-01-001
Lauchli's	NP$	1-01-001
laudably	**RB**	**1-01-001**
laudanum	**NN**	**3-02-002**
Laude	**NP**	**1-01-001**
Lauder	**NP**	**1-01-001**
Lauderdale	**prop. noun**	**6-03-003**
Lauderdale	NP	3-02-002
Lauderdale	NP-HL	2-01-001
Lauderdale	NP-TL	1-01-001
Laue	**NP**	**1-01-001**
laugh	**noun**	**22-08-019**
laugh	NN	19-08-017
laughs	NNS	3-02-003
laugh	**verb**	**89-10-056**
laugh	VB	9-04-007
laughs	VBZ	1-01-001
laughed	VBD	46-08-036
laughed	VBN	5-04-005
laughing	VBG	27-07-022
Laughing	VBG-TL	1-01-001
laughingly	**RB**	**1-01-001**
Laughlin	**NP**	**2-01-002**
laughter	**NN**	**22-10-017**
launch	**NN**	**3-02-003**
launch	**verb**	**31-12-023**
launch	VB	7-06-007
launches	VBZ	2-01-002
launched	VBD	3-02-003
launched	VBN	16-08-011
launched	VBN-HL	1-01-001
launching	VBG	2-02-002
launch-control	**NN**	**1-01-001**
launcher	**NN**	**1-01-001**
launching	**noun**	**2-02-002**
launching	NN	1-01-001
launchings	NNS	1-01-001
launder	**verb**	**7-02-002**
laundered	VBN	1-01-001
laundering	VBG	6-02-002
Launder-Ometer	**NP**	**1-01-001**
laundering	**noun**	**2-01-001**
laundering	NN	1-01-001
launderings	NNS	1-01-001
laundry	**NN**	**5-03-003**
laundry-type	**noun**	**1-01-001**
laundry-type	NN	0-00-000
laundry-type	NN-HL	1-01-001
Laura	**NP**	**20-05-007**
Laurance	**NP**	**1-01-001**

Word	Tag	Frequency
laureate	**JJ**	**1-01-001**
laureate	**NN**	**1-01-001**
laurel	**noun**	**5-05-005**
laurel	NN	1-01-001
Laurel	NN-TL	2-02-002
laurels	NNS	2-02-002
Lauren	**NP**	**10-01-002**
Laurence	**NP**	**3-02-003**
Laurentian	**JJ**	**1-01-001**
Laurents	**prop. noun**	**1-01-001**
Laurents'	NP$	1-01-001
Lauri	**NP**	**1-01-001**
Laurie	**NP**	**1-01-001**
Lauritsen	**NP**	**1-01-001**
Lauritz	**NP**	**1-01-001**
Lauro	**NP**	**6-01-001**
Lausanne	**NP**	**1-01-001**
Lautner	**NP**	**3-01-001**
lava	**NN**	**1-01-001**
lava-rock	**noun**	**1-01-001**
lava-rocks	NNS	1-01-001
Lavallade	**NP**	**2-01-001**
Lavato	**NP**	**1-01-001**
lavatory	**NN**	**4-02-002**
Lavaughn	**NP**	**1-01-001**
lavender	**JJ**	**1-01-001**
lavender	**NN**	**4-02-002**
lavish	**JJ**	**3-03-003**
lavish	**verb**	**2-02-002**
lavished	VBD	1-01-001
lavishing	VBG	1-01-001
lavishly	**QL**	**2-02-002**
lavishly	**RB**	**2-02-002**
Lavoisier	**NP**	**1-01-001**
law	**noun**	**387-14-112**
law	NN	279-14-092
Law	NN-TL	20-08-016
laws	NNS	88-12-042
law-abiding	**JJ**	**1-01-001**
law-breaking	**NN**	**1-01-001**
law-enforcement	**NN**	**1-01-001**
law-governed	**JJ**	**1-01-001**
law-unto-itself	**JJ**	**1-01-001**
Lawford	**NP**	**1-01-001**
lawful	**JJ**	**2-02-002**
lawless	**JJ**	**1-01-001**
Lawless	**NP**	**1-01-001**
lawmaker	**noun**	**4-03-003**
lawmakers	NNS	4-03-003
lawmaking	**JJ**	**2-02-002**
lawmaking	**NN**	**1-01-001**
lawman	**noun**	**5-01-003**
lawman	NN	2-01-001
lawman's	NN$	1-01-001
lawmen	NNS	2-01-002
lawn	**noun**	**20-11-015**
lawn	NN	14-09-011
Lawn	NN-TL	1-01-001
lawns	NNS	5-05-005
Lawrence	**prop. noun**	**41-07-023**
Lawrence	NP	35-06-020
Lawrence	NP-TL	4-03-003
Lawrence's	NP$	2-01-001
Lawrenceville	**NP**	**2-01-001**
lawsuit	**noun**	**2-02-002**
lawsuit	NN	1-01-001
lawsuits	NNS	1-01-001
lawyer	**noun**	**69-13-039**
lawyer	NN	43-13-030
lawyer's	NN$	2-02-002
lawyers	NNS	23-08-015
lawyers'	NNS$	1-01-001
lax	**JJ**	**3-03-003**
laxative	**NN**	**1-01-001**
laxness	**NN**	**2-02-002**
lay	**adjective**	**9-06-007**
lay	JJ	7-06-007
Lay	JJ-TL	2-01-001
lay	**noun**	**1-01-001**
lays	NNS	1-01-001
lay	**verb**	**138-15-102**
lay	VB	48-12-039
lays	VBZ	5-04-004
laid	VBD	24-10-024
laid	VBN	53-13-045
laying	VBG	8-06-008
Lay	**NP**	**1-01-001**
lay-off	**noun**	**5-02-002**
lay-offs	NNS	4-02-002

lay-off (cont.):		
lay-offs	NNS-HL	1-01-001
lay-sister	**noun**	**4-01-001**
lay-sisters	NNS	4-01-001
lay-up	**JJ**	**1-01-001**
layer	**noun**	**22-07-013**
layer	NN	12-05-009
layers	NNS	10-05-006
layer	**verb**	**3-01-001**
layered	VBN	1-01-001
layering	VBG	2-01-001
layette	**NN**	**1-01-001**
laying	**noun**	**3-01-003**
laying	NN	2-01-002
Laying	NN-TL	1-01-001
layman	**noun**	**11-07-010**
layman	NN	3-03-003
layman's	NN$	1-01-001
laymen	NNS	6-05-006
laymen's	NNS$	1-01-001
layoff	**noun**	**1-01-001**
layoffs	NNS	1-01-001
layout	**NN**	**6-04-005**
Layton	**NP**	**1-01-001**
Lazarus	**prop. noun**	**1-01-001**
Lazarus	NP	0-00-000
Lazarus	NP-TL	1-01-001
laze	**VB**	**1-01-001**
lazily	**RB**	**1-01-001**
lazy	**JJ**	**9-06-008**
lazybones	**noun**	**2-01-001**
lazybones	NN	0-00-000
Lazybones	NN-TL	2-01-001
Lazzeri	**NP**	**1-01-001**
le	**foreign**	**48-11-027**
le	FW-AT	8-07-007
Le	FW-AT-TL	3-02-003
la	FW-AT	6-03-004
La	FW-AT-TL	24-07-014
la	FW-AT-TL	4-04-004
les	FW-AT	1-01-001
Les	FW-AT-TL	2-02-002
Le	**NP**	**3-03-003**
leach	**noun**	**1-01-001**
leaches	NNS	1-01-001
lead	**noun**	**49-14-036**
lead	NN	47-14-034
leads	NNS	2-02-002
lead	**verb**	**313-15-208**
lead	VB	81-14-062
lead	VB-HL	1-01-001
leads	VBZ	31-11-028
led	VBD	82-14-070
led	VBD-HL	1-01-001
led	VBN	49-13-046
leading	VBG	68-14-060
leaded	**JJ**	**1-01-001**
leaden	**JJ**	**2-01-002**
leader	**noun**	**187-12-093**
leader	NN	66-09-041
leader	NN-NC	3-01-001
Leader	NN-TL	5-02-004
leader's	NN$	6-03-004
leaders	NNS	106-11-064
leaders	NNS-HL	1-01-001
leaderless	**JJ**	**1-01-001**
leadership	**noun**	**92-12-046**
leadership	NN	91-12-046
leadership	NN-HL	1-01-001
leading	**noun**	**1-01-001**
leadings	NNS	1-01-001
leadsman	**NN**	**1-01-001**
leaf	**noun**	**33-08-021**
leaf	NN	12-05-009
leaves	NNS	21-08-015
leaf	**verb**	**1-01-001**
leafed	VBD	1-01-001
leafhopper	**NN**	**1-01-001**
leafiest	**JJT**	**1-01-001**
leaflet	**noun**	**4-03-004**
leaflet	NN	1-01-001
leaflets	NNS	3-03-003
leafmold	**NN**	**1-01-001**
leafy	**JJ**	**1-01-001**
league	**noun**	**81-09-029**
league	NN	23-07-013
league	NN-HL	1-01-001
League	NN-TL	45-07-022
league's	NN$	1-01-001
league (cont.):		
League's	NN$-TL	3-01-003
leagues	NNS	8-04-006
league	**verb**	**1-01-001**
leagued	VBN	1-01-001
leaguer	**noun**	**5-01-004**
leaguer	NN	3-01-002
leaguers	NNS	0-00-000
Leaguers	NNS-TL	2-01-002
leak	**noun**	**5-03-004**
leak	NN	2-02-002
leaks	NNS	3-02-002
leak	**verb**	**5-03-005**
leaked	VBD	4-02-004
leaked	VBN	1-01-001
leakage	**NN**	**1-01-001**
leaky	**JJ**	**2-02-002**
Leale	**NP**	**1-01-001**
Leamington	**NP**	**1-01-001**
lean	**JJ**	**13-07-012**
lean	**verb**	**61-11-043**
lean	VB	7-05-007
leans	VBZ	1-01-001
leaned	VBD	37-10-028
leaned	VBN	1-01-001
leaning	VBG	15-06-014
lean-to	**NN**	**2-01-002**
leap	**noun**	**9-06-008**
leap	NN	6-04-005
leaps	NNS	3-03-003
leap	**verb**	**33-09-028**
leap	VB	8-07-008
leaps	VBZ	1-01-001
leaped	VBD	18-08-015
leapt	VBD	2-02-002
leaped	VBN	2-01-002
leaping	VBG	2-02-002
leapfrog	**NN**	**2-01-002**
Lear	**prop. noun**	**4-01-001**
Lear	NP	1-01-001
Lear	NP-TL	3-01-001
learn	**verb**	**254-15-158**
learn	VB	83-15-068
Learn	VB-TL	1-01-001
learns	VBZ	10-03-008
learned	VBD	54-12-044
learned	VBN	58-15-048
learning	VBG	47-14-036
learning	VBG-HL	1-01-001
learned	**JJ**	**4-02-003**
Learned	**NP**	**1-01-001**
learner	**noun**	**1-01-001**
learners	NNS	1-01-001
learning	**NN**	**12-05-010**
Leary	**NP**	**1-01-001**
lease	**noun**	**9-06-007**
lease	NN	7-05-006
leases	NNS	2-02-002
lease	**verb**	**9-03-005**
lease	VB	3-02-002
leases	VBZ	1-01-001
leased	VBN	2-02-002
leasing	VBG	3-02-003
leash	**noun**	**4-03-003**
leash	NN	3-02-002
leashes	NNS	1-01-001
least	**AP**	**325-15-206**
least	**NN**	**1-01-001**
least	**QL**	**16-07-015**
least	**RBT**	**1-01-001**
leather	**noun**	**26-10-021**
leather	NN	23-09-020
Leather	NN-TL	1-01-001
leathers	NNS	2-01-001
leather	**verb**	**1-01-001**
leathered	VBD	1-01-001
leather-bound	**JJ**	**1-01-001**
leather-hard	**JJ**	**1-01-001**
Leatherman	**NP**	**1-01-001**
Leatherneck	**NP**	**1-01-001**
leathery	**JJ**	**1-01-001**
leave	**noun**	**11-07-009**
leave	NN	8-07-008
leave	NN-HL	1-01-001
leaves	NNS	2-01-001
leave	**verb**	**650-15-299**
leave	VB	191-15-128
leave	VB-NC	4-01-001
leaves	VBZ	26-11-023

Word	Tag	Frequency
leave (cont.):		
left	VBD	157-14-117
left	VBN	181-15-134
leaving	VBG	88-13-073
leavin'	VBG	1-01-001
leavin	VBG	2-01-001
leave-taking	**NN**	**2-02-002**
leaven	**verb**	**1-01-001**
leavened	VBN	1-01-001
leavened	**JJ**	**1-01-001**
leavening	**NN**	**1-01-001**
Leavenworth	**NP**	**1-01-001**
leaving	**noun**	**1-01-001**
leavings	NNS	1-01-001
Leavitt	**prop. noun**	**7-01-001**
Leavitt	NP	6-01-001
Leavitt's	NP$	1-01-001
Lebanese	**JJ**	**1-01-001**
Lebanese	**NPS**	**1-01-001**
lebensraum	**NN**	**1-01-001**
lecher	**NN**	**1-01-001**
Lecky	**NP**	**1-01-001**
LeClair	**NP**	**1-01-001**
lecture	**noun**	**29-14-021**
lecture	NN	13-10-010
Lecture	NN-TL	1-01-001
lectures	NNS	13-06-011
Lectures	NNS-TL	2-01-001
lecture	**verb**	**7-06-006**
lecture	VB	2-02-002
lectured	VBD	1-01-001
lectured	VBN	1-01-001
lecturing	VBG	3-02-002
lecturer	**NN**	**6-05-005**
Ledford	**NP**	**1-01-001**
ledge	**noun**	**7-05-007**
ledge	NN	4-03-004
Ledge	NN-TL	2-02-002
ledges	NNS	1-01-001
ledger	**noun**	**8-05-006**
ledger	NN	7-05-005
ledgers	NNS	1-01-001
Ledoux	**NP**	**4-01-001**
Ledyard	**NP**	**1-01-001**
Lee	**prop. noun**	**37-07-020**
Lee	NP	33-07-020
Lee	NP-HL	1-01-001
Lee's	NP$	3-01-001
Leeds	**prop. noun**	**3-02-002**
Leeds	NP	0-00-000
Leeds	NP-TL	1-01-001
Leeds'	NP$	2-01-001
leer	**verb**	**7-03-007**
leered	VBD	3-02-003
leering	VBG	4-02-004
Lees	**NP**	**1-01-001**
Leesona	**prop. noun**	**8-01-002**
Leesona	NP	4-01-001
Leesona	NP-TL	1-01-001
Leesona's	NP$	3-01-001
Leesona-Holt	**prop. noun**	**2-01-001**
Leesona-Holt	NP	0-00-000
Leesona-Holt	NP-TL	2-01-001
Leet	**NP**	**1-01-001**
leeway	**NN**	**2-02-002**
left	**JJ**	**68-12-043**
left	**noun**	**6-03-004**
left	NN	1-01-001
Left	NN-TL	5-02-002
left	**NR**	**67-12-038**
left-centerfield	**NN**	**1-01-001**
left-front	**NN**	**1-01-001**
left-hand	**NN**	**5-02-004**
left-handed	**RB**	**3-01-001**
left-justify	**verb**	**1-01-001**
left-justified	VBN	1-01-001
left-of-center	**JJ**	**1-01-001**
leftfield	**NN**	**1-01-001**
lefthander	**noun**	**3-01-002**
lefthander	NN	2-01-002
lefthanders	NNS	1-01-001
leftist	**NN**	**1-01-001**
lefty	**noun**	**2-01-001**
lefty	NN	0-00-000
Lefty	NN-TL	2-01-001
leg	**noun**	**126-12-068**
leg	NN	54-10-031
Leg	NN-TL	4-01-001
leg's	NN+BEZ	1-01-001

Word	Tag	Frequency
leg (cont.):		
legs	NNS	67-12-043
leg-split	**NN**	**1-01-001**
legacy	**noun**	**6-02-005**
legacy	NN	5-02-004
legacies	NNS	1-01-001
legal	**adjective**	**72-13-040**
legal	JJ	71-13-040
legal	JJ-HL	1-01-001
legality	**NN**	**1-01-001**
legalize	**verb**	**2-01-001**
legalized	VBN	2-01-001
legally	**RB**	**5-04-005**
legatee	**NN**	**1-01-001**
legation	**noun**	**3-02-002**
legation	NN	1-01-001
legation's	NN$	1-01-001
legations	NNS	1-01-001
legato	**NN**	**1-01-001**
legend	**noun**	**36-08-019**
legend	NN	26-07-018
legends	NNS	10-03-004
legendary	**JJ**	**6-03-005**
Leger	**prop. noun**	**3-02-002**
Leger	NP	2-01-001
Legers	NPS	1-01-001
legged	**JJ**	**1-01-001**
Leggett	**NP**	**1-01-001**
legging	**noun**	**1-01-001**
leggings	NNS	1-01-001
leggy	**JJ**	**1-01-001**
legibility	**NN**	**1-01-001**
legion	**noun**	**8-05-006**
legion	NN	2-02-002
Legion	NN-TL	5-02-003
legions	NNS	1-01-001
legislate	**verb**	**2-01-002**
legislate	VB	1-01-001
legislated	VBN	1-01-001
legislation	**noun**	**46-07-028**
legislation	NN	45-07-027
Legislation	NN-TL	1-01-001
legislation-delaying	**JJ**	**1-01-001**
legislative	**adjective**	**40-07-029**
legislative	JJ	39-07-028
Legislative	JJ-TL	1-01-001
legislator	**noun**	**27-06-013**
legislator	NN	7-03-003
legislators	NNS	19-06-012
legislators	NNS-HL	1-01-001
legislature	**noun**	**43-06-015**
legislature	NN	12-05-007
Legislature	NN-TL	27-03-007
legislature's	NN$	2-01-001
legislatures	NNS	1-01-001
Legislatures	NNS-TL	1-01-001
legitimacy	**NN**	**2-02-002**
legitimate	**JJ**	**16-09-016**
legitimately	**RB**	**2-02-002**
legitimize	**verb**	**3-01-003**
legitimized	VBD	1-01-001
legitimized	VBN	2-01-002
legume	**NN**	**2-02-002**
leguminous	**JJ**	**1-01-001**
Lehman	**NP**	**1-01-001**
Lehmann	**NP**	**1-01-001**
Lehner	**NP**	**1-01-001**
Leibowitz	**prop. noun**	**1-01-001**
Leibowitz	NP	0-00-000
Leibowitz	NP-TL	1-01-001
Leiden	**NP**	**1-01-001**
Leigh	**NP**	**3-01-001**
Leighton	**NP**	**1-01-001**
Leila	**NP**	**1-01-001**
leisure	**noun**	**12-07-012**
leisure	NN	11-07-011
leasure	NN	1-01-001
leisurely	**JJ**	**1-01-001**
leisurely	**RB**	**4-03-004**
leitmotiv	**noun**	**2-02-002**
leitmotiv	NN	1-01-001
leitmotif	NN	1-01-001
Leland	**NP**	**2-02-002**
lemma	**noun**	**8-01-001**
lemma	NN	0-00-000
lemma	NN-HL	1-01-001
Lemma	NN-TL	3-01-001
Lemma	NN-TL-HL	3-01-001
lemmas	NNS	1-01-001

Word	Tag	Frequency
lemon	**noun**	**16-07-012**
lemon	NN	14-06-010
Lemon	NN-TL	1-01-001
lemons	NNS	1-01-001
Lemon	**NP**	**3-01-001**
lemon-meringue	**NN**	**1-01-001**
lemonade	**NN**	**3-03-003**
Lemuel	**NP**	**1-01-001**
Len	**NP**	**3-02-002**
Lena	**NP**	**3-02-002**
lend	**verb**	**29-10-027**
lend	VB	13-09-012
Lend	VB-TL	1-01-001
lends	VBZ	4-04-004
lent	VBD	3-02-003
lent	VBN	2-02-002
lending	VBG	6-03-005
lending	**NN**	**1-01-001**
Lendrum	**NP**	**1-01-001**
length	**noun**	**139-14-079**
length	NN	114-14-073
length	NN-HL	2-01-002
lengths	NNS	23-04-013
lengthen	**verb**	**7-05-007**
lengthen	VB	2-02-002
lengthened	VBN	2-02-002
lengthening	VBG	3-03-003
lengthily	**RB**	**1-01-001**
lengthwise	**JJ**	**2-01-002**
lengthwise	**RB**	**2-01-002**
lengthy	**JJ**	**11-07-011**
Leni	**NP**	**1-01-001**
lenient	**JJ**	**3-03-003**
Lenin	**prop. noun**	**7-02-003**
Lenin	NP	6-01-002
Lenin's	NP$	1-01-001
Leningrad	**prop. noun**	**4-03-004**
Leningrad	NP	1-01-001
Leningrad	NP-TL	2-02-002
Leningrad's	NP$	0-00-000
Leningrad's	NP$-TL	1-01-001
Leningrad-Kirov	**prop. noun**	**1-01-001**
Leningrad-Kirov	NP	0-00-000
Leningrad-Kirov	NP-TL	1-01-001
Leninism-Marxism	**NP**	**1-01-001**
Lennie	**NP**	**1-01-001**
Lenny	**NP**	**1-01-001**
Lenobel	**prop. noun**	**1-01-001**
Lenobel's	NP$	1-01-001
lens	**noun**	**17-06-009**
lens	NN	12-04-005
lenses	NNS	5-05-005
lentil	**noun**	**1-01-001**
lentils	NNS	1-01-001
Lenygon	**prop. noun**	**2-01-001**
Lenygon	NP	1-01-001
Lenygon's	NP$	1-01-001
Leo	**NP**	**7-03-005**
Leon	**prop. noun**	**5-03-005**
Leon	NP	4-03-004
Leon	NP-TL	1-01-001
Leona	**NP**	**5-01-001**
Leonard	**prop. noun**	**10-03-008**
Leonard	NP	9-03-008
Leonard	NP-TL	1-01-001
Leonato	**prop. noun**	**2-01-001**
Leonato	NP	1-01-001
Leonato's	NP$	1-01-001
Leone	**NP**	**1-01-001**
Leonore	**prop. noun**	**1-01-001**
Leonore	NP	0-00-000
Leonore	NP-TL	1-01-001
leopard	**noun**	**2-02-002**
leopards	NNS	1-01-001
leopard's	NN$	0-00-000
Leopard's	NN$-TL	1-01-001
Leopold	**prop. noun**	**2-01-001**
Leopold	NP	1-01-001
Leopold's	NP$	1-01-001
Leopoldville	**NP**	**3-03-003**
leprae	**NN**	**1-01-001**
leprosy	**NN**	**1-01-001**
Lerner	**NP**	**1-01-001**
Leroy	**NP**	**2-02-002**
lesbian	**noun**	**1-01-001**
lesbians	NNS	1-01-001
Lescaut	**prop. noun**	**1-01-001**
Lescaut	NP	0-00-000
Lescaut	NP-TL	1-01-001
lesion	**NN**	**2-01-002**
Leslie	**NP**	**2-02-002**
LeSourd	**NP**	**3-01-001**
less	**post-det.**	**232-15-156**
less	AP	229-15-155
less	AP-HL	3-02-003
less	**QL**	**186-15-129**
less	**RBR**	**19-08-018**
less-developed	**JJ**	**1-01-001**
less-dramatic	**JJ**	**1-01-001**
less-hurried	**JJ**	**1-01-001**
less-indomitable	**JJ**	**1-01-001**
less-than-carload	**JJ**	**1-01-001**
less-traveled	**JJ**	**1-01-001**
lessen	**verb**	**17-09-017**
lessen	VB	5-04-005
lessens	VBZ	1-01-001
lessened	VBD	3-03-003
lessened	VBN	6-04-006
lessening	VBG	2-02-002
lessening	**NN**	**5-02-002**
lesser	**AP**	**1-01-001**
lesser	**JJR**	**18-07-016**
lesser-known	**JJ**	**1-01-001**
Lessing	**NP**	**2-01-001**
lesson	**noun**	**46-12-036**
lesson	NN	28-09-022
lesson	NN-HL	1-01-001
lessons	NNS	16-09-013
Lessons	NNS-TL	1-01-001
lest	**CS**	**17-10-013**
Lester	**prop. noun**	**14-06-008**
Lester	NP	13-06-008
Lester's	NP$	1-01-001
let	**NN**	**7-05-006**
let	**verb**	**482-15-236**
let	VB	334-15-185
let	VB-HL	1-01-001
let's	VB+PPO	69-12-046
lemme	VB+PPO	1-01-001
lets	VBZ	5-03-004
let	VBD	37-09-031
let	VBN	4-04-004
letting	VBG	30-13-030
lettin'	VBG	1-01-001
let-down	**NN**	**1-01-001**
let's-make-your-house-our-club	**JJ**	**1-01-001**
Letch	**prop. noun**	**21-01-001**
Letch	NP	19-01-001
Letch's	NP$	2-01-001
lethal	**JJ**	**5-04-005**
lethality	**NN**	**1-01-001**
lethargy	**noun**	**5-03-005**
lethargy	NN	4-03-004
lethargies	NNS	1-01-001
Letitia	**NP**	**2-01-001**
letter	**noun**	**260-15-105**
letter	NN	140-15-067
Letter	NN	2-01-001
letter	NN-HL	1-01-001
Letter	NN-TL	2-02-002
letters	NNS	113-14-055
letters	NNS-HL	1-01-001
Letters	NNS-TL	1-01-001
letter	**verb**	**2-02-002**
lettered	VBD	1-01-001
lettering	VBG	1-01-001
letterhead	**NN**	**1-01-001**
lettering	**NN**	**3-03-003**
letterman	**noun**	**2-01-002**
letterman	NN	1-01-001
lettermen	NNS	1-01-001
letting	**NN**	**1-01-001**
leukemia	**noun**	**3-03-003**
leukemia	NN	2-02-002
Leukemia	NN-TL	1-01-001
Lev	**NP**	**1-01-001**
levee	**NN**	**1-01-001**
level	**JJ**	**15-05-007**
level	**noun**	**265-13-124**
level	NN	195-12-103
level	NN-HL	1-01-001
level's	NN+BEZ	1-01-001
levels	NNS	67-09-042
levels	NNS-HL	1-01-001
level	**verb**	**27-08-015**
level	VB	2-02-002
levels	VBZ	1-01-001
leveled	VBD	4-03-004

Word	Tag	Frequency
level (cont.):		
leveled	VBN	9-06-007
levelled	VBN	2-01-002
leveling	VBG	8-01-001
leveling	VBG-HL	1-01-001
level-headed	**JJ**	**2-02-002**
leveling	**NN**	**7-01-001**
lever	**noun**	**19-02-005**
lever	NN	13-02-005
levers	NNS	6-01-001
Lever	**NP**	**1-01-001**
lever-action	**NN**	**3-01-001**
leverage	**NN**	**1-01-001**
Leverett	**NP**	**1-01-001**
Leverkuhn	**NP**	**3-01-001**
levi-clad	**JJ**	**1-01-001**
Levin	**NP**	**1-01-001**
Levinger	**prop. noun**	**1-01-001**
Levinger's	NP$	1-01-001
levis	**NNS**	**2-01-002**
levitation	**NN**	**1-01-001**
Levitt	**NP**	**4-02-002**
Levittown	**NP**	**1-01-001**
levity	**NN**	**1-01-001**
levy	**noun**	**6-04-006**
levy	NN	4-04-004
levies	NNS	2-01-002
levy	**verb**	**4-02-002**
levy	VB	3-01-001
levied	VBN	1-01-001
Lew	**prop. noun**	**5-02-002**
Lew	NP	4-02-002
Lew's	NP$	1-01-001
lewd	**JJ**	**3-03-003**
lewdly	**RB**	**1-01-001**
Lewelleyn	**NP**	**1-01-001**
Lewellyn	**NP**	**1-01-001**
Lewis	**prop. noun**	**63-07-012**
Lewis	NP	56-06-010
Lewis	NP-TL	1-01-001
Lewis's	NP$	5-01-002
Lewis'	NP$	1-01-001
Lewisohn	**prop. noun**	**4-01-003**
Lewisohn	NP	0-00-000
Lewisohn	NP-TL	4-01-003
lex	**FW-NN**	**1-01-001**
Lex	**NP**	**1-01-001**
lexical	**JJ**	**2-01-001**
lexicon	**NN**	**2-01-001**
lexicostatistic	**JJ**	**1-01-001**
lexicostatistics	**NN**	**4-01-001**
Lexington	**prop. noun**	**7-05-006**
Lexington	NP	5-05-005
Lexington	NP-TL	2-01-002
Leyden	**NP**	**1-01-001**
Leyte	**prop. noun**	**6-02-002**
Leyte	NP	5-02-002
Leyte	NP-TL	1-01-001
liability	**noun**	**8-05-007**
liability	NN	7-04-006
liabilities	NNS	1-01-001
liable	**JJ**	**6-05-006**
liaison	**noun**	**7-06-007**
liaison	NN	5-05-005
Liaison	NN-TL	1-01-001
liaisons	NNS	1-01-001
liar	**noun**	**5-03-004**
liar	NN	3-02-002
liar's	NN$	1-01-001
liars	NNS	1-01-001
libel	**NN**	**2-01-001**
libellos	**FW-NNS**	**1-01-001**
libelous	**JJ**	**1-01-001**
liber	**foreign**	**1-01-001**
liber	FW-JJ	0-00-000
Liber	FW-JJ-TL	1-01-001
Liberace	**NP**	**2-01-001**
liberal	**adjective**	**57-10-034**
liberal	JJ	53-10-031
Liberal	JJ-TL	4-03-004
liberal	**noun**	**39-04-012**
liberal	NN	8-03-005
Liberal	NN-TL	4-01-003
liberal's	NN$	1-01-001
liberals	NNS	22-03-006
Liberals	NNS-TL	4-02-003
liberal-conservative	**JJ**	**3-02-002**
liberal-led	**JJ**	**1-01-001**
Liberal-Radical	**NP**	**1-01-001**

Word	Tag	Frequency
liberalism	**noun**	**15-03-009**
liberalism	NN	13-02-008
Liberalism	NN-TL	2-02-002
liberality	**NN**	**3-02-002**
liberalize	**verb**	**1-01-001**
liberalizing	VBG	1-01-001
liberally	**RB**	**4-03-004**
liberate	**verb**	**13-06-010**
liberate	VB	4-04-004
liberated	VBD	1-01-001
liberated	VBN	5-03-005
liberated	VBN-HL	2-01-001
liberating	VBG	1-01-001
liberation	**NN**	**5-03-004**
Liberia	**NP**	**1-01-001**
libertarian	**JJ**	**1-01-001**
libertarian	**noun**	**2-02-002**
libertarians	NNS	2-02-002
libertine	**noun**	**3-03-003**
libertine	NN	1-01-001
libertines	NNS	2-02-002
liberty	**noun**	**56-11-029**
liberty	NN	41-11-023
libertie	NN	1-01-001
Liberty	NN	1-01-001
Liberty	NN-TL	4-03-003
liberty's	NN$	0-00-000
Liberty's	NN$-TL	1-01-001
liberties	NNS	7-02-004
Liberties	NNS-TL	1-01-001
liberty-and-union	**noun**	**2-01-001**
liberty-and-union	NN	0-00-000
Liberty-and-Union	NN-TL	2-01-001
libido	**NN**	**2-01-002**
librarian	**noun**	**12-03-004**
librarian	NN	5-02-003
librarian's	NN$	1-01-001
librarians	NNS	6-02-002
librarian-board	**NN**	**1-01-001**
library	**noun**	**90-12-026**
library	NN	48-09-018
Library	NN-TL	14-04-007
libraries	NNS	28-04-006
librettist	**noun**	**1-01-001**
librettists	NNS	1-01-001
libretto	**NN**	**2-02-002**
Libyan	**prop. noun**	**2-01-001**
Libyan	NP	0-00-000
Libyan	NP-TL	2-01-001
license	**noun**	**41-10-024**
license	NN	35-10-022
licenses	NNS	5-03-005
Licenses	NNS-TL	1-01-001
license	**verb**	**12-05-009**
license	VB	1-01-001
licensed	VBN	6-03-004
licensing	VBG	5-04-005
licensee	**NN**	**1-01-001**
licensing	**NN**	**1-01-001**
Lichtenstein	**NP**	**1-01-001**
lick	**verb**	**14-08-012**
lick	VB	3-03-003
licked	VBD	7-06-006
licked	VBN	3-03-003
licking	VBG	1-01-001
lid	**noun**	**24-04-007**
lid	NN	19-03-004
lids	NNS	4-03-004
lids	NNS-HL	1-01-001
lidless	**JJ**	**1-01-001**
lie	**noun**	**9-05-009**
lie	NN	6-04-006
lies	NNS	3-03-003
lie	**verb**	**13-09-013**
lie	VB	1-01-001
'lah	+VB	1-01-001
lied	VBD	5-04-005
Lied	VBD-TL	1-01-001
lying	VBG	5-05-005
lie	**verb**	**211-15-140**
lie	VB	52-12-042
lies	VBZ	41-11-038
lay	VBD	81-13-059
lain	VBN	4-01-003
lying	VBG	31-10-028
lyin'	VBG	1-01-001
laying	VBG	1-01-001
Lieberman	**NP**	**1-01-001**
Liebler	**NP**	**1-01-001**

Word	Tag	Frequency
lied	**noun**	**2-01-001**
lieder	NNS	2-01-001
lien	**noun**	**3-02-002**
lien	NN	1-01-001
lien	NN-HL	1-01-001
liens	NNS	1-01-001
lieu	**NN**	**5-04-004**
lieutenant	**noun**	**44-10-018**
lieutenant	NN	12-07-007
lieut	NN	0-00-000
Lieut	NN	1-01-001
lt.	NN	0-00-000
Lt.	NN-TL	8-04-005
Lieutenant	NN-TL	17-05-007
lieutenant's	NN$	3-01-001
lieutenants	NNS	3-02-003
lieutenant-colonel	**noun**	**1-01-001**
lieutenant-colonel	NN	0-00-000
Lieutenant-Colonel	NN-TL	1-01-001
lieutenant-governor	**noun**	**2-01-001**
lieutenant-governor	NN	1-01-001
Lieutenant-Governor	NN-TL	1-01-001
life	**noun**	**772-15-288**
life	NN	678-15-273
life	NN-HL	4-04-004
Life	NN-TL	32-07-020
Life	NN-TL-HL	1-01-001
life's	NN$	6-03-005
lives	NNS	50-12-039
lives	NNS-NC	1-01-001
life-and-death	**NN**	**1-01-001**
life-contract	**noun**	**1-01-001**
life-contracts	NNS	1-01-001
life-death	**JJ**	**1-01-001**
life-long	**adjective**	**3-03-003**
life-long	JJ	2-02-002
lifelong	JJ	1-01-001
life-preserver	**noun**	**1-01-001**
life-preservers	NNS	1-01-001
life-size	**NN**	**1-01-001**
life-supporting	**JJ**	**1-01-001**
lifeblood	**NN**	**1-01-001**
lifeboat	**noun**	**5-01-001**
lifeboat	NN	3-01-001
Lifeboat	NN-TL	1-01-001
lifeboats	NNS	1-01-001
lifeguard	**noun**	**1-01-001**
lifeguards	NNS	1-01-001
lifeless	**JJ**	**2-02-002**
lifelike	**adjective**	**5-03-005**
lifelike	JJ	3-02-003
life-like	JJ	2-01-002
lifer	**NN**	**1-01-001**
lifetime	**NN**	**10-05-010**
Lifson	**NP**	**1-01-001**
lift	**noun**	**6-06-006**
lift	NN	5-05-005
lifts	NNS	1-01-001
lift	**verb**	**69-14-055**
lift	VB	18-10-014
lifts	VBZ	1-01-001
lifted	VBD	34-09-029
lifted	VBN	9-08-009
lifting	VBG	7-05-007
lifter	**noun**	**4-01-001**
lifters	NNS	4-01-001
lifting	**NN**	**1-01-001**
ligament	**NN**	**1-01-001**
ligand	**noun**	**3-01-001**
ligand	NN	1-01-001
ligands	NNS	2-01-001
Ligget	**prop. noun**	**1-01-001**
Ligget	NP	0-00-000
Ligget	NP-TL	1-01-001
light	**adjective**	**63-13-050**
light	JJ	61-13-048
light	JJ-HL	1-01-001
Light	JJ-TL	1-01-001
light	**noun**	**306-15-150**
light	NN	253-15-131
Light	NN-TL	7-02-002
lights	NNS	46-14-035
light	**verb**	**72-13-053**
light	VB	10-07-010
lights	VBZ	1-01-001
lighted	VBD	6-03-005
lit	VBD	9-06-009
lighted	VBN	23-08-018
lit	VBN	7-06-007

light (cont.):

Word	Tag	Frequency
lighting	VBG	15-08-012
lighting	VBG-HL	1-01-001
light-colored	**JJ**	**2-02-002**
light-duty	**NN**	**1-01-001**
light-flared	**JJ**	**1-01-001**
light-headed	**JJ**	**2-02-002**
light-headedness	**NN**	**1-01-001**
light-mindedness	**NN**	**1-01-001**
light-reflecting	**JJ**	**1-01-001**
light-transmitting	**JJ**	**1-01-001**
light-year	**noun**	**2-01-002**
light-year	NN	1-01-001
light-years	NNS	0-00-000
lightyears	NNS	1-01-001
lighten	**verb**	**5-03-005**
lightens	VBZ	1-01-001
lightened	VBD	2-02-002
lightened	VBN	2-02-002
lighter	**comp. adj.**	**10-05-009**
lighter	JJR	8-05-008
lighter	JJR-HL	1-01-001
lighter'n	JJR+CS	1-01-001
lighter	**noun**	**4-02-003**
lighter	NN	3-02-002
lighters	NNS	1-01-001
lightest	**JJT**	**2-02-002**
Lightfoot	**NP**	**1-01-001**
lighthearted	**adjective**	**3-03-003**
lighthearted	JJ	2-02-002
light-hearted	JJ	1-01-001
lighthouse	**noun**	**1-01-001**
lighthouses	NNS	1-01-001
lighting	**NN**	**7-04-006**
lightly	**QL**	**1-01-001**
lightly	**RB**	**30-11-027**
lightness	**NN**	**1-01-001**
lightning	**NN**	**14-05-010**
lightning-occurrence	**NN**	**1-01-001**
lightweight	**adjective**	**7-05-007**
lightweight	JJ	4-04-004
light-weight	JJ	3-02-003
lightweight	**NN**	**1-01-001**
Ligne	**NP**	**1-01-001**
lignite	**NN**	**4-01-001**
like	**CS**	**1012-15-317**
like	**prep.**	**35-08-023**
like	IN	32-07-020
lahk	IN	1-01-001
lak	IN	1-01-001
Like	IN-TL	1-01-001
like	**JJ**	**36-12-034**
like	**noun**	**1-01-001**
likes	NNS	1-01-001
like	**verb**	**294-15-172**
like	VB	210-15-137
likee	VB	1-01-001
like	VB-HL	1-01-001
likes	VBZ	18-08-015
liked	VBD	45-12-037
liked	VBN	13-07-012
liking	VBG	4-04-004
lyking	VBG	2-01-001
like-minded	**JJ**	**2-01-001**
likelihood	**NN**	**10-09-010**
likely	**JJ**	**126-12-082**
likely	**RB**	**25-10-023**
liken	**verb**	**3-03-003**
likened	VBD	1-01-001
likened	VBN	2-02-002
likeness	**NN**	**3-03-003**
likewise	**RB**	**18-08-016**
liking	**NN**	**7-04-007**
Lil	**NP**	**1-01-001**
Lila	**NP**	**2-01-001**
lilac	**JJ**	**1-01-001**
lilac	**noun**	**4-02-002**
lilac	NN	0-00-000
Lilac	NN-TL	1-01-001
lilacs	NNS	3-01-001
Lilac	**NP**	**2-01-001**
Lili	**NP**	**1-01-001**
Lilian	**NP**	**7-01-001**
Lillian	**prop. noun**	**6-03-004**
Lillian	NP	5-03-004
Lillian's	NP$	1-01-001
lilliputian	**adjective**	**2-01-002**
lilliputian	JJ	0-00-000
Lilliputian	JJ	1-01-001

Word	Tag	Frequency
lilliputian (cont.):		
Liliputian	JJ-TL	1-01-001
Lilly	**prop. noun**	**13-01-001**
Lilly	NP	10-01-001
Lilly's	NP$	3-01-001
lilt	**NN**	**1-01-001**
lilt	**verb**	**3-03-003**
lilting	VBG	3-03-003
lily	**noun**	**1-01-001**
lilies	NNS	1-01-001
Lily	**NP**	**1-01-001**
limb	**noun**	**10-07-010**
limb	NN	4-04-004
limb	NN-HL	1-01-001
limbs	NNS	5-04-005
limber	**JJ**	**1-01-001**
limber	**NN**	**1-01-001**
limbic	**JJ**	**1-01-001**
limbo	**noun**	**2-02-002**
limbo	NN	1-01-001
Limbo	NN-TL	1-01-001
lime	**NN**	**13-03-004**
limelight	**NN**	**1-01-001**
Limerick	**prop. noun**	**1-01-001**
Limerick	NP	0-00-000
Limerick	NP-TL	1-01-001
limit	**noun**	**68-12-059**
limit	NN	31-10-027
limits	NNS	36-09-033
Limits	NNS-TL	1-01-001
limit	**verb**	**143-13-097**
limit	VB	17-08-015
limits	VBZ	4-03-004
limited	VBD	6-05-006
limited	VBN	98-13-076
Ltd.	VBN	0-00-000
Ltd.	VBN-TL	5-03-003
Limited	VBN-TL	2-01-001
limiting	VBG	11-07-009
limitation	**noun**	**38-11-029**
limitation	NN	10-04-009
limitations	NNS	27-09-021
limitations	NNS-HL	1-01-001
limited-time	**NN**	**1-01-001**
limitless	**JJ**	**1-01-001**
limousine	**noun**	**5-03-003**
limousine	NN	4-02-002
limousines	NNS	1-01-001
limp	**JJ**	**11-04-011**
limp	**NN**	**1-01-001**
limp	**verb**	**5-04-004**
limps	VBZ	1-01-001
limped	VBD	1-01-001
limped	VBN	1-01-001
limping	VBG	2-02-002
limp-looking	**JJ**	**1-01-001**
limpid	**JJ**	**1-01-001**
limply	**RB**	**1-01-001**
Lincoln	**prop. noun**	**52-10-023**
Lincoln	NP	39-09-019
Lincoln	NP-TL	8-04-005
Lincoln's	NP$	5-03-004
Linda	**prop. noun**	**45-02-002**
Linda	NP	42-02-002
Linda's	NP$	3-01-001
Lindbergh	**prop. noun**	**1-01-001**
Lindbergh's	NP$	1-01-001
Lindemann	**prop. noun**	**4-01-001**
Lindemann	NP	3-01-001
Lindemanns	NPS	1-01-001
linden	**NN**	**1-01-001**
Linden	**NP**	**6-02-002**
Lindsay	**prop. noun**	**2-02-002**
Lindsay	NP	1-01-001
Lindsay	NP-HL	1-01-001
Lindsey	**prop. noun**	**1-01-001**
Lindsey's	NP$	1-01-001
Lindskog	**NP**	**1-01-001**
Lindy	**NP**	**1-01-001**
line	**noun**	**491-15-218**
line	NN	281-15-143
Line	NN-TL	13-04-009
lines	NNS	196-15-109
Lines	NNS-TL	1-01-001
line	**verb**	**23-12-023**
line	VB	4-03-004
lines	VBZ	1-01-001
lined	VBD	7-06-007
lined	VBN	9-07-009
line (cont.):		
lining	VBG	2-02-002
line-density	**NN**	**1-01-001**
line-drive	**verb**	**1-01-001**
line-driven	VBN	1-01-001
line-drying	**noun**	**1-01-001**
line-drying	NN	0-00-000
line-drying	NN-HL	1-01-001
line-fragment	**noun**	**1-01-001**
line-fragments	NNS	1-01-001
line-pair	**noun**	**1-01-001**
line-pairs	NNS	1-01-001
lineage	**noun**	**3-03-003**
lineage	NN	2-02-002
lineages	NNS	1-01-001
lineal	**JJ**	**1-01-001**
linear	**JJ**	**21-02-006**
linearly	**RB**	**4-01-003**
lineback	**NN**	**2-01-001**
linebacker	**noun**	**1-01-001**
linebackers	NNS	1-01-001
lineman	**NN**	**1-01-001**
linen	**NN**	**6-04-005**
linen-covered	**JJ**	**1-01-001**
liner	**noun**	**5-04-004**
liner	NN	3-02-002
liners	NNS	2-02-002
Liner	**NP**	**1-01-001**
lineup	**noun**	**3-02-002**
lineup	NN	2-02-002
lineup	NN-HL	1-01-001
linger	**verb**	**16-09-016**
linger	VB	7-05-007
lingers	VBZ	2-02-002
lingered	VBD	2-02-002
lingering	VBG	5-05-005
lingerie	**NN**	**2-02-002**
lingo	**noun**	**3-03-003**
lingo	NN	2-02-002
Lingo	NN-TL	1-01-001
linguist	**noun**	**24-03-004**
linguist	NN	9-03-003
linguist	NN-NC	4-01-001
linguists	NNS	11-03-003
linguist-anthropologist	**NN**	**1-01-001**
linguistic	**JJ**	**10-02-005**
linguistically	**RB**	**1-01-001**
linguistics	**NN**	**5-02-002**
liniment	**noun**	**2-02-002**
liniment	NN	1-01-001
liniments	NNS	1-01-001
link	**noun**	**19-10-016**
link	NN	12-09-012
links	NNS	7-05-005
link	**verb**	**25-12-024**
link	VB	4-04-004
linked	VBD	1-01-001
linked	VBN	15-07-014
linking	VBG	5-05-005
linkage	**noun**	**3-01-001**
linkage	NN	2-01-001
linkage	NN-HL	1-01-001
linking	**NN**	**1-01-001**
linoleum	**NN**	**1-01-001**
lint	**noun**	**4-03-003**
lint	NN	3-02-002
Lint	NN-TL	1-01-001
Linus	**NP**	**1-01-001**
Linville	**NP**	**1-01-001**
Linz	**NP**	**1-01-001**
lion	**noun**	**26-07-010**
lion	NN	14-03-004
Lion	NN-TL	3-02-002
lion's	NN$	2-02-002
lions	NNS	4-03-003
Lions	NNS-TL	2-02-002
lions'	NNS$	1-01-001
Lionel	**NP**	**2-02-002**
lioness	**noun**	**6-01-001**
lioness	NN	3-01-001
lioness'	NN$	2-01-001
lionesses	NNS	1-01-001
lionize	**verb**	**2-02-002**
lionized	VBN	2-02-002
lip	**noun**	**87-13-053**
lip	NN	18-11-016
lips	NNS	69-10-044
lip-sucking	**NN**	**1-01-001**
Lipchitz	**NP**	**2-02-002**

Word	Tag	Frequency
Lipowa	**NP**	**1-01-001**
Lippi	**NP**	**1-01-001**
Lippincott	**NP**	**1-01-001**
Lippman	**NP**	**2-02-002**
Lippmann	**NP**	**3-03-003**
Lipson	**NP**	**1-01-001**
lipstick	**NN**	**3-02-003**
Lipton	**NP**	**5-02-002**
liqueur	**NN**	**1-01-001**
liquid	**adjective**	**20-02-006**
liquid	JJ	19-02-006
liquid	JJ-HL	1-01-001
liquid	**noun**	**34-08-017**
liquid	NN	28-07-016
liquids	NNS	6-03-003
liquid-glass	**NN**	**1-01-001**
liquidate	**verb**	**6-03-003**
liquidated	VBD	1-01-001
liquidated	VBN	4-03-003
liquidating	VBG	1-01-001
liquidation	**noun**	**13-05-005**
liquidation	NN	12-05-005
liquidations	NNS	1-01-001
liquidity	**NN**	**1-01-001**
liquor	**noun**	**43-13-030**
liquor	NN	42-13-030
Liquor	NN-TL	1-01-001
liquor-crazed	**JJ**	**1-01-001**
Lisa	**NP**	**4-01-001**
Lisbon	**NP**	**1-01-001**
Lisle	**NP**	**1-01-001**
lisp	**verb**	**1-01-001**
lisping	VBG	1-01-001
Liss	**NP**	**1-01-001**
Lissa	**NP**	**2-01-001**
list	**noun**	**154-15-070**
list	NN	125-15-062
List	NN-TL	1-01-001
lists	NNS	27-08-013
lists	NNS-HL	1-01-001
list	**verb**	**59-11-042**
list	VB	7-05-006
lists	VBZ	5-04-004
lists	VBZ-HL	1-01-001
listed	VBD	11-05-010
listed	VBN	33-11-024
listing	VBG	2-02-002
liste	**FW-NN**	**1-01-001**
listen	**verb**	**123-14-089**
listen	VB	50-13-042
Listen	VB-TL	1-01-001
listens	VBZ	2-02-002
listened	VBD	29-09-025
listened	VBN	1-01-001
listening	VBG	39-11-033
listenin'	VBG	1-01-001
listener	**noun**	**31-07-015**
listener	NN	10-04-005
listener's	NN$	1-01-001
listeners	NNS	20-07-012
listener-supported	**JJ**	**1-01-001**
listing	**noun**	**6-04-005**
listing	NN	5-03-004
listings	NNS	0-00-000
listings	NNS-HL	1-01-001
listless	**JJ**	**1-01-001**
listlessly	**RB**	**1-01-001**
Liston	**NP**	**6-01-001**
lit	**NN**	**1-01-001**
liter	**noun**	**4-01-003**
liter	NN	2-01-002
liters	NNS	2-01-001
literal	**JJ**	**15-03-005**
literalism	**NN**	**1-01-001**
literally	**QL**	**1-01-001**
literally	**RB**	**26-11-024**
literalness	**NN**	**3-01-001**
literary	**adjective**	**78-12-038**
literary	JJ	77-12-038
Literary	JJ-TL	1-01-001
literate	**JJ**	**3-02-002**
literature	**noun**	**134-12-053**
literature	NN	132-12-053
Literature	NN-TL	1-01-001
literatures	NNS	1-01-001
lithe	**JJ**	**4-03-004**
lithograph	**noun**	**2-02-002**
lithograph	NN	1-01-001
lithographs	NNS	1-01-001

Word	Tag	Frequency
litigant	**noun**	**5-03-004**
litigant	NN	2-02-002
litigants	NNS	3-02-003
litigation	**NN**	**13-03-005**
Litowski	**prop. noun**	**1-01-001**
Litowski	NP	0-00-000
Litowski	NP-TL	1-01-001
Litta	**NP**	**1-01-001**
Littau	**NP**	**1-01-001**
litter	**noun**	**6-04-005**
litter	NN	3-03-003
litters	NNS	3-02-002
litter	**verb**	**5-05-005**
littered	VBD	1-01-001
littered	VBN	3-03-003
littering	VBG	1-01-001
litterbug	**NN**	**1-01-001**
little	**post-det.**	**397-15-233**
little	AP	396-15-233
little	AP-HL	1-01-001
little	**adjective**	**318-15-157**
little	JJ	285-15-149
li'l	JJ	0-00-000
Li'l	JJ-TL	1-01-001
little	JJ-HL	2-02-002
Little	JJ-TL	30-09-018
little	**QL**	**111-14-083**
little	**adverb**	**6-05-006**
little	RB	5-04-005
litle	RB	1-01-001
Little	**NP**	**1-01-001**
little-girl	**NN**	**1-01-001**
little-known	**JJ**	**1-01-001**
little-town	**NN**	**1-01-001**
Littlepage	**prop. noun**	**11-01-001**
Littlepage	NP	10-01-001
Littlepage's	NP$	1-01-001
littlest	**JJT**	**1-01-001**
Littleton	**prop. noun**	**1-01-001**
Littleton's	NP$	1-01-001
liturgical	**JJ**	**2-01-001**
Litz	**NP**	**2-01-001**
livability	**NN**	**1-01-001**
livable	**JJ**	**1-01-001**
live	**JJ**	**20-10-016**
live	**verb**	**472-15-238**
live	VB	154-15-108
live	VB-HL	1-01-001
Live	VB-TL	2-02-002
lives	VBZ	29-09-023
lives	VBZ-HL	1-01-001
lived	VBD	72-14-058
lived	VBN	43-11-033
living	VBG	164-15-124
living	VBG-HL	2-02-002
Living	VBG-TL	4-02-003
live-oak	**NN**	**1-01-001**
livelier	**JJR**	**2-01-002**
livelihood	**NN**	**5-05-005**
liveliness	**NN**	**2-02-002**
lively	**JJ**	**22-06-017**
lively	**RB**	**4-02-004**
liver	**noun**	**17-07-010**
liver	NN	16-07-010
livers	NNS	1-01-001
liveried	**JJ**	**1-01-001**
Livermore	**NP**	**1-01-001**
Liverpool	**prop. noun**	**2-02-002**
Liverpool	NP	1-01-001
Liverpool	NP-TL	1-01-001
livery	**NN**	**5-02-004**
livestock	**NN**	**19-04-008**
livid	**JJ**	**1-01-001**
living	**NN**	**24-10-018**
living-room	**NN**	**1-01-001**
Livingston	**NP**	**1-01-001**
livre	**noun**	**3-01-001**
livres	NNS	3-01-001
Livshitz	**NP**	**2-01-001**
Liz	**NP**	**1-01-001**
lizard	**noun**	**2-02-002**
lizard's	NN$	1-01-001
lizards	NNS	1-01-001
Lizzie	**prop. noun**	**18-01-001**
Lizzie	NP	17-01-001
Lizzie's	NP$	1-01-001
Lizzy	**NP**	**2-01-001**
Llewellyn	**NP**	**1-01-001**
Lloyd	**prop. noun**	**13-06-012**

Word	Tag	Frequency
Lloyd (cont.):		
Lloyd	NP	9-05-009
Lloyd	NP-TL	1-01-001
Lloyd's	NP$	0-00-000
Lloyd's	NP$-TL	3-02-002
lo	**UH**	**1-01-001**
Lo	**prop. noun**	**21-01-001**
Lo	NP	19-01-001
Lo	NP-HL	2-01-001
load	**noun**	**52-10-035**
load	NN	42-10-031
loads	NNS	10-04-007
load	**verb**	**30-10-024**
load	VB	3-02-003
loaded	VBD	1-01-001
loaded	VBN	21-09-019
loading	VBG	5-04-005
loader	**noun**	**2-02-002**
loader	NN	1-01-001
loaders	NNS	1-01-001
loading	**noun**	**11-02-005**
loading	NN	6-02-004
loadings	NNS	5-01-003
loaf	**noun**	**8-04-005**
loaf	NN	5-03-003
loaves	NNS	3-03-003
loaf	**verb**	**1-01-001**
loafed	VBD	1-01-001
loan	**noun**	**78-09-023**
loan	NN	41-09-019
loan	NN-HL	2-01-001
Loan	NN-TL	3-02-003
loans	NNS	28-03-009
loans	NNS-HL	3-01-001
Loans	NNS-TL	1-01-001
loan	**verb**	**4-01-002**
loaned	VBN	4-01-002
loath	**JJ**	**3-03-003**
loathe	**verb**	**5-04-005**
loathed	VBD	4-03-004
loathing	VBG	1-01-001
loathing	**NN**	**1-01-001**
loathsome	**JJ**	**4-03-004**
lob	**VB**	**1-01-001**
lobar	**adjective**	**1-01-001**
lobar	JJ	0-00-000
Lobar	JJ-TL	1-01-001
lobby	**noun**	**21-07-014**
lobby	NN	19-06-012
Lobby	NN-TL	1-01-001
lobbies	NNS	1-01-001
lobby	**verb**	**1-01-001**
lobbied	VBN	1-01-001
lobe	**noun**	**8-03-005**
lobe	NN	3-01-003
lobes	NNS	5-03-003
Lobl	**NP**	**1-01-001**
loblolly	**NN**	**1-01-001**
lobo	**NN**	**1-01-001**
lobscouse	**noun**	**3-01-001**
lobscouse	NN	1-01-001
lob-scuse	NN	2-01-001
lobster	**NN**	**1-01-001**
lobster-backed	**JJ**	**1-01-001**
lobular	**JJ**	**1-01-001**
lobularity	**NN**	**1-01-001**
lobule	**noun**	**3-01-001**
lobule	NN	1-01-001
lobules	NNS	2-01-001
local	**adjective**	**279-15-110**
local	JJ	275-15-110
local	JJ-HL	2-02-002
Local	JJ-TL	2-02-002
local	**noun**	**9-02-007**
local	NN	6-02-005
Local	NN-TL	3-01-002
locale	**noun**	**7-04-005**
locale	NN	3-03-003
locales	NNS	4-02-002
localism	**noun**	**1-01-001**
localisms	NNS	1-01-001
locality	**noun**	**9-04-008**
locality	NN	5-02-004
localities	NNS	4-03-004
localization	**NN**	**2-01-001**
localize	**verb**	**2-01-002**
localize	VB	1-01-001
localized	VBN	1-01-001
locally	**RB**	**11-06-010**

Word	Tag	Frequency
locate	**verb**	**92-10-062**
locate	VB	16-07-012
located	VBD	4-03-004
located	VBN	60-09-044
locating	VBG	11-04-010
locatin'	VBG	1-01-001
location	**noun**	**81-08-047**
location	NN	61-07-037
location	NN-HL	1-01-001
Location	NN-TL	1-01-001
locations	NNS	18-05-013
location-minded	**JJ**	**1-01-001**
lock	**noun**	**28-09-014**
lock	NN	21-09-013
locks	NNS	7-03-003
lock	**verb**	**63-11-030**
lock	VB	2-02-002
locked	VBD	9-04-009
locked	VBN	20-10-017
locked	VBN-HL	1-01-001
locking	VBG	30-05-007
locking	VBG-HL	1-01-001
Lock	**NP**	**1-01-001**
lock-out	**noun**	**1-01-001**
lock-outs	NNS	1-01-001
Locke	**prop. noun**	**1-01-001**
Locke's	NP$	1-01-001
locker	**NN**	**9-05-006**
locker-room	**NN**	**2-02-002**
Lockheed	**prop. noun**	**4-03-003**
Lockheed	NP	3-03-003
Lockheed's	NP$	1-01-001
Lockian	**JJ**	**1-01-001**
lockup	**NN**	**2-01-001**
Locky	**prop. noun**	**2-01-001**
Lockies	NPS	2-01-001
locomotive	**noun**	**3-03-003**
locomotive	NN	2-02-002
locomotives	NNS	1-01-001
locus	**NN**	**2-02-002**
locust	**NN**	**6-02-002**
lodge	**noun**	**17-04-006**
lodge	NN	9-02-002
Lodge	NN-TL	6-03-005
lodges	NNS	2-01-001
lodge	**verb**	**7-04-006**
lodge	VB	2-02-002
lodged	VBD	1-01-001
lodging	VBG	4-02-003
Lodge	**NP**	**2-02-002**
lodging	**noun**	**3-03-003**
lodging	NN	1-01-001
lodgings	NNS	2-02-002
lodgment	**NN**	**1-01-001**
Lodley	**NP**	**2-01-001**
Lodowick	**NP**	**1-01-001**
Loeb	**NP**	**1-01-001**
Loen	**NP**	**1-01-001**
Loeser	**NP**	**1-01-001**
Loesser	**prop. noun**	**4-01-002**
Loesser	NP	3-01-002
Loesser's	NP$	1-01-001
Loew	**prop. noun**	**1-01-001**
Loew's	NP$	0-00-000
Loew's	NP$-TL	1-01-001
Loewe	**prop. noun**	**1-01-001**
Loewe	NP	0-00-000
Loewe	NP-TL	1-01-001
loft	**NN**	**2-02-002**
lofty	**JJ**	**5-04-005**
log	**noun**	**19-07-015**
log	NN	11-05-007
logs	NNS	8-04-008
log	**verb**	**6-05-005**
logged	VBN	2-02-002
logging	VBG	4-03-003
log-house	**NN**	**1-01-001**
log-jam	**NN**	**1-01-001**
Logan	**NP**	**2-02-002**
logarithm	**noun**	**2-01-002**
logarithm	NN	1-01-001
logarithms	NNS	1-01-001
logger	**NN**	**1-01-001**
logging	**NN**	**1-01-001**
logic	**NN**	**17-11-016**
logic-rhetoric	**NN**	**1-01-001**
logical	**JJ**	**34-11-026**
logically	**RB**	**12-07-012**
logistic	**JJ**	**2-01-002**

Word	Tag	Frequency
logistical	**JJ**	**1-01-001**
logistics	**NNS**	**4-04-004**
Lohman	**prop. noun**	**1-01-001**
Lohmans	NPS	1-01-001
loin	**noun**	**3-03-003**
loin	NN	1-01-001
loins	NNS	2-02-002
loincloth	**NN**	**1-01-001**
Loire	**prop. noun**	**1-01-001**
Loire	NP	0-00-000
Loire	NP-TL	1-01-001
Lois	**NP**	**2-01-002**
Lola	**prop. noun**	**3-01-002**
Lola	NP	2-01-002
Lola	NP-HL	1-01-001
loll	**verb**	**1-01-001**
lolling	VBG	1-01-001
Lolly	**NP**	**3-01-001**
Lolotte	**prop. noun**	**9-01-001**
Lolotte	NP	8-01-001
Lolotte's	NP$	1-01-001
Lombard	**prop. noun**	**1-01-001**
Lombard	NP	0-00-000
Lombard	NP-TL	1-01-001
London	**prop. noun**	**93-12-051**
London	NP	79-11-046
Lond.	NP	1-01-001
London	NP-HL	2-02-002
London	NP-TL	8-06-008
London's	NP$	3-01-002
London-based	**JJ**	**1-01-001**
London-bred	**JJ**	**1-01-001**
Londonderry	**prop. noun**	**2-01-001**
Londonderry	NP	1-01-001
Londonderry	NP-TL	1-01-001
Londoner	**NP**	**1-01-001**
lone	**JJ**	**8-06-008**
lonelier	**JJR**	**1-01-001**
loneliest	**JJT**	**1-01-001**
loneliness	**noun**	**9-03-007**
loneliness	NN	7-03-006
Loneliness	NN-TL	2-01-001
lonely	**JJ**	**25-08-018**
loner	**noun**	**1-01-001**
loners	NNS	1-01-001
lonesome	**JJ**	**2-01-002**
long	**adjective**	**541-15-266**
long	JJ	521-15-258
long-	JJ	1-01-001
Long	JJ-TL	19-08-014
long	**QL**	**8-04-008**
long	**adverb**	**192-13-134**
long	RB	191-13-133
long	RB-HL	1-01-001
long	**verb**	**16-06-013**
long	VB	3-02-003
longs	VBZ	1-01-001
longed	VBD	4-02-003
longed	VBN	3-02-003
longing	VBG	5-04-005
Long	**prop. noun**	**9-01-001**
Long	NP	8-01-001
Long	NP-HL	1-01-001
long-acting	**JJ**	**1-01-001**
long-awaited	**JJ**	**3-02-003**
long-bodied	**JJ**	**1-01-001**
long-chain	**NN**	**1-01-001**
long-cruise	**NN**	**1-01-001**
long-distance	**NN**	**2-02-002**
long-endurance	**NN**	**1-01-001**
long-established	**JJ**	**2-02-002**
long-familiar	**JJ**	**1-01-001**
long-far	**adjective**	**1-01-001**
long-far	JJ+JJ	0-00-000
long-far	JJ+JJ-NC	1-01-001
long-hair	**NN**	**1-01-001**
long-haul	**NN**	**1-01-001**
long-keeping	**JJ**	**1-01-001**
long-known	**JJ**	**1-01-001**
long-life	**NN**	**1-01-001**
long-line	**NN**	**1-01-001**
long-lived	**JJ**	**2-02-002**
long-overdue	**JJ**	**1-01-001**
long-range	**noun**	**42-07-020**
long-range	NN	41-07-020
long-range	NN-HL	1-01-001
long-run	**noun**	**6-02-004**
long-run	NN	5-01-003
longrun	NN	1-01-001
long-settled	**JJ**	**1-01-001**
long-shanked	**JJ**	**1-01-001**
long-sleeved	**JJ**	**1-01-001**
long-sought	**JJ**	**2-02-002**
long-stemmed	**JJ**	**1-01-001**
long-term	**noun**	**32-05-015**
long-term	NN	28-05-015
long-term	NN-HL	4-01-001
long-time	**noun**	**5-04-005**
long-time	NN	4-04-004
longtime	NN	1-01-001
long-vanished	**JJ**	**1-01-001**
long-view	**NN**	**1-01-001**
longed-for	**JJ**	**1-01-001**
longer	**JJR**	**69-14-055**
longer	**RBR**	**124-14-092**
longer-lived	**JJR**	**2-02-002**
longer-term	**NN**	**2-01-001**
longest	**JJT**	**6-06-006**
longevity	**NN**	**2-02-002**
Longfellow	**prop. noun**	**3-02-002**
Longfellow	NP	1-01-001
Longfellow's	NP$	2-02-002
longhand	**NN**	**2-02-002**
longhorn	**noun**	**9-02-002**
longhorn	NN	2-01-001
Longhorn	NN-TL	2-01-001
longhorns	NNS	1-01-001
Longhorns	NNS-TL	4-01-001
longing	**noun**	**7-03-006**
longing	NN	5-03-004
longings	NNS	2-02-002
Longinotti	**NP**	**1-01-001**
longish	**JJ**	**1-01-001**
longitude	**noun**	**2-02-002**
longitude	NN	1-01-001
longitudes	NNS	1-01-001
longitudinal	**JJ**	**1-01-001**
longshoreman	**noun**	**2-02-002**
longshoremen	NNS	1-01-001
longshoremen's	NNS$	1-01-001
longshot	**NN**	**1-01-001**
longstanding	**JJ**	**3-03-003**
Longstreet	**NP**	**2-01-001**
longsuffering	**JJ**	**1-01-001**
Longue	**NP**	**3-01-001**
Longwood	**prop. noun**	**1-01-001**
Longwood	NP	0-00-000
Longwood	NP-TL	1-01-001
Lonsdale	**prop. noun**	**4-01-001**
Lonsdale	NP	3-01-001
Lonsdale's	NP$	1-01-001
look	**noun**	**105-14-079**
look	NN	96-14-073
looks	NNS	9-05-008
look	**verb**	**910-15-304**
look	VB	302-15-180
looky	VB	1-01-001
look	VB-HL	1-01-001
lookit	VB+IN	3-02-002
looks	VBZ	69-14-055
looked	VBD	327-15-152
looked	VBD-NC	2-01-001
looked	VBN	38-13-035
looking	VBG	165-15-117
looking	VBG-NC	1-01-001
Looking	VBG-TL	1-01-001
look-see	**NN**	**1-01-001**
looking	**JJ**	**3-03-003**
looking	**NN**	**3-03-003**
lookout	**noun**	**2-01-002**
lookout	NN	1-01-001
Lookout	NN-TL	1-01-001
lookup	**NN**	**7-01-001**
loom	**noun**	**6-02-002**
loom	NN	5-02-002
looms	NNS	1-01-001
loom	**verb**	**15-08-014**
loom	VB	1-01-001
looms	VBZ	1-01-001
loomed	VBD	3-03-003
looming	VBG	10-06-010
Loomis	**NP**	**4-01-001**
loon	**noun**	**2-02-002**
loon	NN	1-01-001
Loon	NN-TL	1-01-001
loop	**noun**	**21-06-011**
loop	NN	15-04-007
loop	NN-HL	1-01-001

loop (cont.):		
Loop	NN-TL	5-03-003
loop	**verb**	**2-02-002**
loops	VBZ	1-01-001
looped	VBD	1-01-001
loophole	**noun**	**4-04-004**
loophole	NN	2-02-002
loopholes	NNS	2-02-002
loose	**JJ**	**41-13-035**
loose	**NN**	**1-01-001**
loose	**RB**	**8-05-008**
loose	**VB**	**3-03-003**
loose-jointed	**JJ**	**2-02-002**
loose-jowled	**JJ**	**1-01-001**
loose-knit	**JJ**	**1-01-001**
loose-leaf	**NN**	**1-01-001**
loose-loaded	**JJ**	**1-01-001**
loosely	**QL**	**1-01-001**
loosely	**RB**	**11-08-011**
loosely-taped	**JJ**	**1-01-001**
loosen	**verb**	**9-06-009**
loosen	VB	3-03-003
loosens	VBZ	1-01-001
loosened	VBD	1-01-001
loosened	VBN	3-02-003
loosening	VBG	1-01-001
looseness	**NN**	**2-02-002**
loosest	**JJT**	**1-01-001**
Loosli	**NP**	**1-01-001**
loot	**NN**	**3-03-003**
loot	**verb**	**6-04-006**
looted	VBD	1-01-001
looted	VBN	2-01-002
looting	VBG	3-03-003
lop	**JJ**	**1-01-001**
lop	**verb**	**1-01-001**
lopped	VBD	1-01-001
Lopatnikoff	**prop. noun**	**1-01-001**
Lopatnikoff's	NP$	1-01-001
lope	**NN**	**2-01-001**
lope	**verb**	**1-01-001**
loped	VBD	1-01-001
Loper	**NP**	**3-01-001**
Lopez	**NP**	**2-02-002**
lopsidedly	**RB**	**1-01-001**
loquacious	**JJ**	**2-02-002**
loquacity	**NN**	**1-01-001**
Lorain	**NP**	**1-01-001**
Lorca	**NP**	**1-01-001**
lord	**noun**	**77-11-038**
lord	NN	7-04-005
lorde	NN	0-00-000
Lorde	NN-TL	1-01-001
Lord	NN-TL	66-10-033
lords	NNS	1-01-001
Lords	NNS-TL	2-02-002
Lord	**prop. noun**	**32-06-008**
Lord	NP	20-02-002
Lord's	NP$	8-04-004
Lord's	NP$-TL	4-03-003
lordly	**JJ**	**2-02-002**
lordship	**NN**	**3-02-002**
lore	**NN**	**7-05-007**
Lorelei	**NP**	**1-01-001**
Loren	**NP**	**2-02-002**
Lorena	**NP**	**1-01-001**
Lorenz	**NP**	**2-02-002**
Lorlyn	**NP**	**1-01-001**
Lorrain	**NP**	**1-01-001**
Lorraine	**NP**	**1-01-001**
Los	**prop. noun**	**51-11-032**
Los	NP	42-11-027
Los	NP-TL	9-05-007
lose	**verb**	**274-14-178**
lose	VB	57-13-050
lose	VB-HL	1-01-001
loses	VBZ	12-05-012
loses	VBZ-HL	2-02-002
Loses	VBZ-TL	1-01-001
lost	VBD	49-13-043
lost	VBN	124-14-103
losing	VBG	28-10-028
loser	**noun**	**2-02-002**
loser	NN	1-01-001
losers	NNS	1-01-001
loss	**noun**	**132-13-078**
loss	NN	84-13-062
loss	NN-HL	2-02-002
losses	NNS	46-10-025
lot	**noun**	**165-14-109**
lot	NN	124-14-092
lots	NNS	41-13-033
lot	**QL**	**1-01-001**
Lot	**NP**	**2-01-001**
Lothario	**NP**	**1-01-001**
lotion	**noun**	**9-03-003**
lotion	NN	8-02-002
lotions	NNS	1-01-001
lots	**QL**	**1-01-001**
Lotte	**NP**	**1-01-001**
lottery	**noun**	**1-01-001**
lottery	NN	0-00-000
Lottery	NN-TL	1-01-001
Lottie	**NP**	**1-01-001**
lotus	**noun**	**3-02-002**
lotus	NN	1-01-001
Lotus	NN-TL	2-01-001
Lou	**NP**	**13-05-008**
Louchheim	**NP**	**1-01-001**
loud	**adjective**	**15-08-013**
loud	JJ	14-08-012
Loud	JJ-TL	1-01-001
loud	**RB**	**5-04-005**
loud-voiced	**JJ**	**1-01-001**
louder	**JJR**	**11-05-009**
louder	**RBR**	**1-01-001**
loudest	**JJT**	**3-03-003**
loudest	**RBT**	**1-01-001**
loudly	**RB**	**17-08-014**
Loudon	**prop. noun**	**1-01-001**
Loudon's	NP$	1-01-001
loudspeaker	**noun**	**3-03-003**
loudspeaker	NN	1-01-001
loudspeakers	NNS	2-02-002
Louis	**prop. noun**	**76-12-036**
Louis	NP	60-11-030
Louis	NP-TL	13-07-009
Louis's	NP$	2-02-002
Louis'	NP$	1-01-001
Louisa	**NP**	**1-01-001**
Louise	**NP**	**5-02-004**
Louisiana	**prop. noun**	**38-09-018**
Louisiana	NP	27-08-013
La.	NP	7-03-003
La.	NP-HL	1-01-001
Louisiana	NP-TL	3-03-003
Louisianan	**NP**	**1-01-001**
Louisiane	**prop. noun**	**1-01-001**
Louisiane	NP	0-00-000
Louisiane	NP-TL	1-01-001
Louisville	**prop. noun**	**6-05-006**
Louisville	NP	5-04-005
Louisville	NP-TL	1-01-001
lounge	**noun**	**9-04-005**
lounge	NN	5-02-002
Lounge	NN-TL	3-02-002
lounges	NNS	1-01-001
lounge	**verb**	**8-05-008**
lounge	VB	1-01-001
lounged	VBD	3-03-003
lounging	VBG	4-04-004
louse	**noun**	**4-03-004**
louse	NN	1-01-001
lice	NNS	2-02-002
lise	NNS	1-01-001
louse	**verb**	**3-03-003**
louse	VB	2-02-002
loused	VBD	1-01-001
lousiness	**NN**	**1-01-001**
lousy	**adjective**	**13-06-008**
lousy	JJ	11-05-007
lousie	JJ	0-00-000
Lousie	JJ-TL	1-01-001
lousy	JJ-HL	1-01-001
louver	**noun**	**2-01-001**
louvers	NNS	2-01-001
Louvre	**NP**	**2-01-001**
lovable	**JJ**	**2-02-002**
love	**noun**	**179-14-081**
love	NN	165-14-079
Love	NN-TL	10-04-006
love's	NN$	2-02-002
loves	NNS	2-02-002
love	**verb**	**145-15-086**
love	VB	53-12-038
love	VB-HL	3-02-002
Love	VB-TL	1-01-001
loves	VBZ	17-09-016

Word	Tag	Frequency
love (cont.):		
loved	VBD	45-10-030
loved	VBN	11-07-011
loving	VBG	14-09-013
lovin	VBG	1-01-001
love-in-action	**NN**	**1-01-001**
love-making	**NN**	**4-02-002**
Lovejoy	**prop. noun**	**5-02-002**
Lovejoy	NP	3-01-001
Lovejoy's	NP$	0-00-000
Lovejoy's	NP$-TL	2-01-001
Lovelace	**NP**	**1-01-001**
Loveless	**NP**	**5-01-001**
loveliest	**JJT**	**3-02-003**
loveliness	**NN**	**4-03-003**
lovelorn	**JJ**	**1-01-001**
lovely	**JJ**	**44-12-032**
lovely	**noun**	**1-01-001**
lovelies	NNS	1-01-001
lover	**noun**	**31-09-028**
lover	NN	16-07-014
Lover	NN-TL	3-03-003
lover's	NN$	1-01-001
lovers	NNS	8-07-008
Lovers	NNS-TL	2-02-002
lovers'	NNS$	1-01-001
lovering	**NN**	**1-01-001**
Lovering	**NP**	**1-01-001**
Lovett	**NP**	**1-01-001**
loveway	**noun**	**1-01-001**
loveways	NNS	0-00-000
Loveways	NNS-TL	1-01-001
lovie	**NN**	**1-01-001**
Loving	**NP**	**1-01-001**
lovingly	**RB**	**1-01-001**
Lovingood	**NP**	**1-01-001**
low	**adjective**	**147-14-090**
low	JJ	143-14-089
low	JJ-HL	1-01-001
Low	JJ-TL	3-01-001
low	**noun**	**3-02-003**
low	NN	2-02-002
lows	NNS	1-01-001
low	**RB**	**15-09-012**
Low	**NP**	**9-01-001**
low-boiling	**JJ**	**1-01-001**
low-budget	**NN**	**1-01-001**
low-calorie	**NN**	**1-01-001**
low-ceilinged	**JJ**	**1-01-001**
low-class	**NN**	**2-02-002**
low-cost	**NN**	**6-03-005**
low-down	**adjective**	**2-02-002**
low-down	JJ	1-01-001
lowdown	JJ	1-01-001
low-down	**NN**	**2-02-002**
low-duty	**NN**	**1-01-001**
low-flying	**JJ**	**1-01-001**
low-foam	**NN**	**1-01-001**
low-frequency	**NN**	**1-01-001**
low-grade	**NN**	**2-02-002**
low-heeled	**JJ**	**1-01-001**
low-key	**NN**	**2-02-002**
low-level	**NN**	**2-02-002**
low-lying	**JJ**	**1-01-001**
low-moisture	**NN**	**2-01-001**
low-pass	**NN**	**2-01-001**
low-pitched	**JJ**	**2-02-002**
low-power	**NN**	**1-01-001**
low-priced	**JJ**	**1-01-001**
low-speed	**NN**	**1-01-001**
low-sudsing	**JJ**	**1-01-001**
low-temperature	**NN**	**2-01-002**
low-tension	**NN**	**1-01-001**
low-voltage	**NN**	**1-01-001**
low-wage	**NN**	**3-01-001**
low-water	**NN**	**1-01-001**
Lowe	**prop. noun**	**2-01-002**
Lowe	NP	1-01-001
Lowe's	NP$	1-01-001
Lowell	**prop. noun**	**8-03-005**
Lowell	NP	5-02-004
Lowell	NP-TL	1-01-001
Lowell's	NP$	2-01-001
lower	**comp. adj.**	**110-13-071**
lower	JJR	107-13-068
lower	JJR-HL	1-01-001
Lower	JJR-TL	2-02-002
lower	**noun**	**1-01-001**
lowers	NNS	1-01-001
lower	**RBR**	**5-03-004**
lower	**verb**	**32-09-028**
lower	VB	7-06-006
lowered	VBD	10-04-010
lowered	VBN	11-07-010
lowering	VBG	4-04-004
Lower	**prop. noun**	**1-01-001**
Lower	NP	0-00-000
Lower	NP-TL	1-01-001
lower-class	**NN**	**8-02-003**
lower-cut	**JJR**	**1-01-001**
lower-level	**NN**	**1-01-001**
lower-middle	**adjective**	**4-02-002**
lower-middle	JJ	3-02-002
lower-middle	JJ-HL	1-01-001
lower-middle-class	**NN**	**3-01-002**
lower-paid	**JJR**	**1-01-001**
lower-priced	**JJR**	**1-01-001**
lower-status	**NN**	**2-02-002**
lowering	**NN**	**1-01-001**
lowest	**JJT**	**13-09-013**
lowland	**noun**	**1-01-001**
lowlands	NNS	1-01-001
lowliest	**JJT**	**1-01-001**
lowly	**JJ**	**1-01-001**
Lown	**NP**	**1-01-001**
Loy	**NP**	**1-01-001**
loyal	**JJ**	**18-10-017**
loyalist	**noun**	**4-03-003**
loyalist	NN	1-01-001
Loyalist	NN-TL	1-01-001
loyalists	NNS	2-02-002
loyalty	**noun**	**25-10-020**
loyalty	NN	21-10-018
Loyalty	NN-TL	1-01-001
loyalties	NNS	3-03-003
Luang	**NP**	**2-01-001**
Lubberlander	**prop. noun**	**1-01-001**
Lubberlanders	NPS	1-01-001
Lubbock	**NP**	**2-01-002**
Lubell	**NP**	**2-01-001**
Lublin	**prop. noun**	**17-02-002**
Lublin	NP	12-01-001
Lublin	NP-TL	3-02-002
Lublin's	NP$	2-01-001
lubra	**FW-NN**	**2-01-001**
lubricant	**NN**	**2-01-002**
lubricate	**verb**	**1-01-001**
lubricated	VBN	1-01-001
lubrication	**NN**	**1-01-001**
Lucas	**prop. noun**	**2-02-002**
Lucas	NP	1-01-001
Lucas's	NP$	1-01-001
Lucia	**NP**	**8-02-003**
Lucian	**NP**	**5-03-003**
lucid	**JJ**	**4-03-003**
lucidity	**NN**	**1-01-001**
Lucien	**NP**	**10-01-001**
Lucifer	**prop. noun**	**4-02-002**
Lucifer	NP	3-02-002
Lucifer's	NP$	1-01-001
Lucille	**prop. noun**	**14-02-003**
Lucille	NP	13-02-003
Lucille's	NP+BEZ	1-01-001
Lucius	**NP**	**2-01-001**
luck	**noun**	**48-09-034**
luck	NN	47-09-034
lucks	NNS	1-01-001
luck	**verb**	**1-01-001**
lucked	VBD	1-01-001
luckier	**JJR**	**1-01-001**
luckily	**RB**	**3-03-003**
lucky	**adjective**	**21-09-019**
lucky	JJ	20-09-018
Lucky	JJ-TL	1-01-001
lucrative	**JJ**	**3-03-003**
Lucretia	**NP**	**2-01-001**
Lucretius	**NP**	**2-01-002**
lucy	**NN**	**1-01-001**
Lucy	**prop. noun**	**46-04-004**
Lucy	NP	45-04-004
Lucy's	NP$	1-01-001
ludicrous	**JJ**	**3-03-003**
ludicrousness	**NN**	**1-01-001**
Ludie	**NP**	**13-01-001**
Ludlow	**NP**	**1-01-001**
Ludmilla	**NP**	**1-01-001**
Ludwick	**NP**	**1-01-001**
Ludwig	**NP**	**3-02-003**

Word	Tag	Frequency
Luechtefeld	**NP**	**1-01-001**
Lueger	**prop. noun**	**2-01-001**
Lueger's	NP$	2-01-001
Luette	**NP**	**1-01-001**
Luftwaffe	**NP**	**1-01-001**
lug	**NN**	**1-01-001**
lug	**verb**	**6-03-004**
lug	VB	1-01-001
lugged	VBD	3-03-003
lugged	VBN	2-01-001
Luger	**NP**	**1-01-001**
luggage	**noun**	**10-06-006**
luggage	NN	6-05-005
luggage	NN-NC	4-01-001
lui	**FW-PPO**	**1-01-001**
Luis	**prop. noun**	**10-03-004**
Luis	NP	8-02-003
Luis	NP-TL	1-01-001
Luis's	NP$	1-01-001
Luisa	**prop. noun**	**1-01-001**
Luisa	NP	0-00-000
Luisa	NP-TL	1-01-001
Luise	**NP**	**1-01-001**
Luke	**prop. noun**	**5-04-004**
Luke	NP	2-02-002
Luke	NP-TL	1-01-001
Luke's	NP$	1-01-001
Luke's	NP$-TL	1-01-001
lukewarm	**JJ**	**5-05-005**
Lukuklu	**NP**	**1-01-001**
lull	**noun**	**2-02-002**
lull	NN	1-01-001
lulls	NNS	1-01-001
lull	**verb**	**2-02-002**
lull	VB	1-01-001
lulled	VBN	1-01-001
lullaby	**noun**	**5-03-004**
lullaby	NN	4-03-004
Lullaby	NN-TL	1-01-001
Lullwater	**prop. noun**	**2-01-001**
Lullwater	NP	1-01-001
Lullwater	NP-TL	1-01-001
Lully	**NP**	**1-01-001**
lulu	**NN**	**1-01-001**
lumbar	**JJ**	**1-01-001**
lumber	**noun**	**35-07-010**
lumber	NN	30-07-010
lumber	NN-HL	1-01-001
Lumber	NN-TL	4-03-003
lumber	**verb**	**3-03-003**
lumbered	VBD	1-01-001
lumbering	VBG	2-02-002
lumen	**NN**	**2-02-002**
lumen/watt	**NN**	**1-01-001**
Lumia	**NP**	**1-01-001**
lumiere	**foreign**	**2-01-001**
lumiere	FW-NN	0-00-000
Lumiere	FW-NN-TL	2-01-001
luminary	**noun**	**1-01-001**
luminaries	NNS	1-01-001
luminescence	**NN**	**1-01-001**
luminescent	**JJ**	**1-01-001**
luminosity	**NN**	**1-01-001**
luminous	**JJ**	**12-06-007**
lummox	**NN**	**1-01-001**
Lummus	**prop. noun**	**1-01-001**
Lummus	NP	0-00-000
Lummus	NP-TL	1-01-001
lump	**noun**	**10-05-009**
lump	NN	7-03-006
lumps	NNS	3-03-003
lump	**verb**	**2-02-002**
lumped	VBD	1-01-001
lumped	VBN	1-01-001
Lumpe	**prop. noun**	**4-01-001**
Lumpe	NP	3-01-001
Lumpe	NP-HL	1-01-001
lumpish	**JJ**	**1-01-001**
lumpy	**JJ**	**2-02-002**
Lumumba	**prop. noun**	**15-02-002**
Lumumba	NP	12-02-002
Lumumba's	NP$	3-02-002
lunar	**JJ**	**10-02-003**
lunatic	**JJ**	**1-01-001**
lunatic-fringe	**NN**	**1-01-001**
lunation	**NN**	**2-01-001**
lunch	**NN**	**32-10-027**
lunch	**VB**	**1-01-001**
luncheon	**noun**	**25-07-018**

Word	Tag	Frequency
luncheon (cont.):		
luncheon	NN	23-07-016
luncheons	NNS	2-02-002
luncheon-table	**NN**	**1-01-001**
lunchroom	**NN**	**1-01-001**
lunchtime	**NN**	**2-02-002**
Lund	**NP**	**1-01-001**
Lundeen	**NP**	**1-01-001**
Lundy	**NP**	**1-01-001**
lung	**noun**	**36-09-016**
lung	NN	16-05-006
lungs	NNS	20-06-012
lunge	**noun**	**3-01-001**
lunge	NN	0-00-000
Lunge	NN-TL	3-01-001
lunge	**verb**	**5-03-004**
lunge	VB	1-01-001
lunged	VBD	4-02-003
Lura	**NP**	**1-01-001**
Luray	**prop. noun**	**1-01-001**
Luray	NP	0-00-000
Luray	NP-TL	1-01-001
Lurcat	**NP**	**1-01-001**
lurch	**NN**	**3-02-003**
lurch	**verb**	**7-03-007**
lurched	VBD	5-03-005
lurching	VBG	2-02-002
lure	**NN**	**4-04-004**
lure	**verb**	**7-06-007**
lure	VB	3-03-003
lured	VBD	3-03-003
luring	VBG	1-01-001
lurid	**JJ**	**3-03-003**
lurk	**verb**	**8-05-008**
lurk	VB	1-01-001
lurks	VBZ	1-01-001
lurked	VBD	3-02-003
lurking	VBG	3-03-003
luscious	**JJ**	**2-02-002**
lush	**JJ**	**5-05-005**
lush	**noun**	**1-01-001**
lushes	NNS	1-01-001
Lusignan	**NP**	**1-01-001**
lust	**noun**	**6-06-006**
lust	NN	4-04-004
Lust	NN-TL	1-01-001
lusts	NNS	1-01-001
luster	**noun**	**4-03-003**
luster	NN	2-02-002
lustre	NN	2-02-002
lustful	**JJ**	**1-01-001**
lustily	**RB**	**1-01-001**
lustrous	**JJ**	**1-01-001**
lusty	**adjective**	**4-04-004**
lusty	JJ	3-03-003
Lusty	JJ-TL	1-01-001
lute	**NN**	**1-01-001**
Luther	**prop. noun**	**7-04-005**
Luther	NP	5-04-004
Luther's	NP$	2-02-002
Lutheran	**adjective**	**3-02-002**
Lutheran	JJ	1-01-001
Lutheran	JJ-TL	2-02-002
Luthuli	**NP**	**1-01-001**
lutihaw	**FW-NNS**	**1-01-001**
lutte	**foreign**	**1-01-001**
lutte	FW-NN	0-00-000
Lutte	FW-NN-TL	1-01-001
Luxemburg	**NP**	**4-01-001**
luxuriance	**NN**	**1-01-001**
luxurious	**JJ**	**6-04-004**
luxuriously-upholstered	**adjective**	**1-01-001**
luxuriously-upholstered	JJ	0-00-000
luxuriosly-upholstered	JJ	1-01-001
luxury	**noun**	**24-10-021**
luxury	NN	21-10-019
luxuries	NNS	3-03-003
Luzon	**NP**	**1-01-001**
Lycidas	**NP**	**1-01-001**
Lydia	**NP**	**1-01-001**
Lyford	**prop. noun**	**9-01-001**
Lyford	NP	5-01-001
Lyford's	NP$	4-01-001
Lyle	**prop. noun**	**1-01-001**
Lyle	NP	0-00-000
Lyle	NP-TL	1-01-001
Lyman	**NP**	**1-01-001**
Lymington	**NP**	**1-01-001**
lymph	**NN**	**2-01-001**

lymphocyte	**noun**	**1-01-001**
lymphocytes	NNS	1-01-001
lymphoma	**NN**	**1-01-001**
lynch	**verb**	**1-01-001**
lynched	VBN	1-01-001
Lyndon	**NP**	**3-03-003**
Lynn	**NP**	**5-02-004**
Lyon	**NP**	**3-02-002**
lyophilize	**verb**	**1-01-001**
lyophilized	VBN	1-01-001
lyric	**JJ**	**5-04-004**
lyric	**noun**	**22-04-009**
lyric	NN	7-02-003
lyrics	NNS	15-04-007
lyrical	**JJ**	**7-04-006**
lyricism	**NN**	**2-02-002**
lyricist	**noun**	**6-02-002**
lyricist	NN	2-02-002
lyriist	NN	1-01-001
lyricist's	NN$	1-01-001
lyricists	NNS	2-01-001
Lyttleton	**NP**	**5-01-001**

M

m	**noun**	**1-01-001**
m	NN	0-00-000
M	NN-TL	1-01-001
M	**NP**	**2-01-002**
M.	**prop. noun**	**63-12-045**
M.	NP	60-11-042
M.	NP-HL	1-01-001
M.	NP-TL	1-01-001
M.'s	NP$	1-01-001
M.A.	**NP**	**4-02-002**
M.D.	**NP**	**1-01-001**
M.E.	**prop. noun**	**1-01-001**
M.E.'s	NP$	1-01-001
M.P.	**NP**	**2-02-002**
m.p.h.	**NNS**	**6-03-003**
m-m-m	**UH**	**1-01-001**
ma	**foreign**	**1-01-001**
ma	FW-CC	0-00-000
Ma	FW-CC-TL	1-01-001
ma	**FW-CS**	**1-01-001**
ma	**noun**	**17-03-004**
ma	NN	1-01-001
Ma	NN-TL	16-03-003
Mac	**NP**	**1-01-001**
macabre	**JJ**	**2-01-002**
MacArthur	**NP**	**3-01-001**
Macassar	**NP**	**1-01-001**
Macaulay	**prop. noun**	**3-02-002**
Macaulay	NP	1-01-001
Macaulay's	NP$	2-01-001
Macbeth	**prop. noun**	**6-02-002**
Macbeth	NP	5-02-002
Macbeth	NP-TL	1-01-001
Maccabeus	**NP**	**1-01-001**
MacDonald	**prop. noun**	**3-02-003**
MacDonald	NP	2-01-002
MacDonald's	NP$	1-01-001
Macedon	**NP**	**1-01-001**
MacGregors	**NP**	**1-01-001**
mach't	**FW-VB**	**1-01-001**
Machado	**NP**	**1-01-001**
Machiavelli	**NP**	**1-01-001**
machine	**noun**	**157-12-053**
machine	NN	98-11-035
Machine	NN-TL	5-02-002
machines	NNS	50-09-024
machines	NNS-HL	2-01-001
Machines	NNS-TL	2-01-001
machine-family	**NN**	**1-01-001**
machine-gun	**noun**	**2-02-002**
machine-gun	NN	1-01-001
machinegun	NN	1-01-001
machine-gun	**verb**	**1-01-001**
machine-gunned	VBN	1-01-001
machine-master	**noun**	**1-01-001**
machine-masters	NNS	1-01-001
machinelike	**JJ**	**1-01-001**
machinery	**NN**	**60-08-022**
machinist	**noun**	**8-03-007**
machinist	NN	5-03-005
machinists	NNS	0-00-000
Machinists	NNS-TL	2-02-002
machinists'	NNS$	1-01-001
Macintosh	**NP**	**1-01-001**
MacIsaacs	**prop. noun**	**1-01-001**
MacIsaacs	NP	0-00-000
MacIsaacs	NP-TL	1-01-001
Mack	**prop. noun**	**3-02-002**
Mack	NP	0-00-000
Mack (cont.):		
Mack	NP-TL	1-01-001
Mack's	NP+BEZ	0-00-000
Mack's	NP+BEZ-NC	2-01-001
mackerel	**NN**	**2-01-001**
Mackey	**prop. noun**	**3-02-002**
Mackey	NP	2-01-001
Mackey	NP-TL	1-01-001
Mackinac	**prop. noun**	**3-03-003**
Mackinac	NP	1-01-001
Mackinac	NP-TL	1-01-001
Mackinack	NP-TL	1-01-001
mackinaw	**NN**	**1-01-001**
mackintosh	**NN**	**1-01-001**
Macklin	**prop. noun**	**9-01-001**
Macklin	NP	8-01-001
Macklin's	NP$	1-01-001
MacLean	**NP**	**1-01-001**
MacLeish	**prop. noun**	**1-01-001**
MacLeishes	NPS	1-01-001
Macmillan	**NP**	**1-01-001**
Macneff	**NP**	**7-01-001**
Macon	**prop. noun**	**4-03-004**
Macon	NP	3-03-003
Macon	NP-TL	1-01-001
MacPhail	**NP**	**1-01-001**
MacPherson	**NP**	**3-01-001**
MacReady	**NP**	**2-01-001**
macro-instruction	**noun**	**3-01-001**
macro-instructions	NNS	3-01-001
macromolecular	**adjective**	**2-01-002**
macromolecular	JJ	1-01-001
macromolecular	JJ-HL	1-01-001
macromolecule	**noun**	**2-01-001**
macromolecules	NNS	1-01-001
macromolecules	NNS-HL	1-01-001
macropathological	**adjective**	**2-01-001**
macropathological	JJ	1-01-001
Macropathological	JJ-TL	1-01-001
macropathology	**noun**	**1-01-001**
macropathology	NN	0-00-000
Macropathology	NN-TL	1-01-001
macrophage	**noun**	**1-01-001**
macrophages	NNS	1-01-001
macroscopically	**RB**	**1-01-001**
MacWhorter	**NP**	**1-01-001**
Macwhyte	**prop. noun**	**1-01-001**
Macwhyte	NP	0-00-000
Macwhyte	NP-TL	1-01-001
mad	**adjective**	**38-09-028**
mad	JJ	35-09-027
Mad	JJ-TL	3-02-002
mad	**NNS**	**1-01-001**
Madagascar	**NP**	**1-01-001**
madam	**noun**	**7-05-007**
madam	NN	1-01-001
ma'am	NN	2-02-002
Ma'am	NN-TL	3-02-003
Madam	NN-TL	1-01-001
Madama	**NP**	**1-01-001**
Madame	**prop. noun**	**18-06-008**
Madame	NP	15-06-006
Mme	NP	1-01-001
Madames	NPS	0-00-000
Mrnes.	NPS	2-01-001
Madaripur	**NP**	**1-01-001**
Maddalena	**NP**	**1-01-001**
madden	**verb**	**2-02-002**
maddening	VBG	2-02-002

Word	Tag	Frequency
Madden	**prop. noun**	**21-01-001**
Madden	NP	18-01-001
Madden's	NP$	3-01-001
madding	**adjective**	**1-01-001**
madding	JJ	0-00-000
Madding	JJ-TL	1-01-001
Madeira	**NP**	**1-01-001**
Madeleine	**NP**	**3-01-001**
mademoiselle	**foreign**	**1-01-001**
mademoiselle	FW-NN	0-00-000
Mademoiselle	FW-NN-TL	1-01-001
madhouse	**NN**	**1-01-001**
Madison	**prop. noun**	**24-07-011**
Madison	NP	15-03-004
Madison	NP-TL	8-07-008
Madison's	NP$	1-01-001
madly	**RB**	**4-02-004**
madman	**noun**	**5-03-004**
madman	NN	2-01-002
madmen	NNS	3-03-003
madness	**NN**	**2-02-002**
Madonna	**prop. noun**	**4-03-003**
Madonna	NP	3-03-003
Madonna's	NP$	1-01-001
Madrid	**NP**	**1-01-001**
madrigal	**noun**	**8-01-002**
madrigal	NN	4-01-001
Madrigal	NN-TL	1-01-001
madrigals	NNS	3-01-002
madrigaling	**NN**	**1-01-001**
madstone	**noun**	**1-01-001**
madstones	NNS	1-01-001
Mae	**prop. noun**	**17-02-002**
Mae	NP	16-02-002
Mae's	NP$	1-01-001
Maecker	**NP**	**1-01-001**
maelstrom	**NN**	**1-01-001**
maestro	**noun**	**6-04-004**
maestro	NN	0-00-000
Maestro	NN-TL	4-03-003
maestro's	NN$	1-01-001
Maestro's	NN$-TL	1-01-001
Maeterlinck	**NP**	**1-01-001**
mag	**noun**	**1-01-001**
mag	NN	0-00-000
Mag	NN-TL	1-01-001
Magarrell	**NP**	**1-01-001**
magazine	**noun**	**65-15-039**
magazine	NN	33-13-022
Magazine	NN-TL	6-04-006
magazine's	NN$	1-01-001
magazines	NNS	25-11-014
Magdalene	**NP**	**3-02-003**
Magee	**NP**	**1-01-001**
magenta	**JJ**	**2-02-002**
Maggie	**prop. noun**	**26-02-003**
Maggie	NP	23-02-003
Maggie's	NP$	3-01-001
maggot	**noun**	**3-01-003**
maggot	NN	0-00-000
maget	NN	1-01-001
maggots	NNS	2-01-002
maggoty	**JJ**	**1-01-001**
Magi	**NPS**	**1-01-001**
magic	**JJ**	**21-09-013**
magic	**NN**	**16-07-011**
magic-practicing	**JJ**	**1-01-001**
magical	**JJ**	**12-04-005**
magically	**RB**	**3-03-003**
magician	**noun**	**7-04-004**
magician	NN	4-03-003
magician's	NN$	2-02-002
magicians	NNS	1-01-001
magisterial	**adjective**	**1-01-001**
magisterial	JJ	0-00-000
majesterial	JJ	1-01-001
magistrate	**noun**	**6-03-003**
magistrate	NN	3-01-001
magistrates	NNS	3-02-002
magnanimity	**NN**	**1-01-001**
magnate	**noun**	**2-02-002**
magnate	NN	1-01-001
magnates	NNS	1-01-001
magnet	**NN**	**3-03-003**
magnetic	**adjective**	**25-05-008**
magnetic	JJ	24-05-008
magnetic	JJ-HL	1-01-001
magnetically	**RB**	**1-01-001**
magnetism	**noun**	**9-03-003**
magnetism (cont.):		
magnetism	NN	7-02-002
Magnetism	NN-TL	1-01-001
magnetisms	NNS	1-01-001
magnetize	**verb**	**2-01-001**
magnetized	VBN	2-01-001
magnification	**NN**	**10-04-005**
magnificence	**NN**	**2-02-002**
magnificent	**adjective**	**27-12-026**
magnificent	JJ	26-12-025
magnificent	JJ-HL	1-01-001
magnificently	**QL**	**1-01-001**
magnificently	**RB**	**6-04-006**
magnify	**verb**	**10-09-010**
magnifies	VBZ	1-01-001
magnified	VBD	1-01-001
magnified	VBN	5-05-005
magnifying	VBG	3-03-003
magnitude	**noun**	**30-06-017**
magnitude	NN	29-06-016
magnitudes	NNS	1-01-001
magnolia	**NN**	**1-01-001**
magnum	**noun**	**3-02-002**
magnum	NN	1-01-001
magnums	NNS	0-00-000
Magnums	NNS	2-01-001
Magnum	**prop. noun**	**13-01-001**
Magnum	NP	7-01-001
Magnum	NP-TL	3-01-001
Magnums	NPS	3-01-001
Magog	**prop. noun**	**1-01-001**
Magog	NP	0-00-000
Magog	NP-TL	1-01-001
Magoun	**NP**	**2-01-001**
magpie	**noun**	**3-03-003**
magpie	NN	0-00-000
Magpie	NN-TL	1-01-001
magpies	NNS	2-02-002
Maguire	**prop. noun**	**6-01-001**
Maguire	NP	5-01-001
Maguires	NPS	1-01-001
Magwitch	**prop. noun**	**6-01-001**
Magwitch	NP	2-01-001
Magwitch's	NP$	4-01-001
mah-jongg	**NN**	**1-01-001**
Mahayana	**NP**	**11-01-001**
Mahayanist	**NP**	**1-01-001**
Mahler	**prop. noun**	**7-01-001**
Mahler	NP	3-01-001
Mahler's	NP$	4-01-001
Mahmoud	**NP**	**2-01-001**
mahogany	**NN**	**8-03-004**
Mahone	**NP**	**1-01-001**
mahua	**NN**	**1-01-001**
Mahzeer	**prop. noun**	**16-01-001**
Mahzeer	NP	11-01-001
Mahzeer's	NP+BEZ	2-01-001
Mahzeer's	NP$	3-01-001
mai'teipa	**FW-NN**	**1-01-001**
maid	**noun**	**44-10-021**
maid	NN	27-08-016
Maid	NN-TL	4-02-002
maid's	NN$	1-01-001
maids	NNS	12-07-008
maiden	**noun**	**4-03-004**
maiden	NN	1-01-001
Maiden	NN-TL	1-01-001
maidens	NNS	1-01-001
Maidens	NNS-TL	1-01-001
Maier	**NP**	**1-01-001**
mail	**noun**	**49-08-020**
mail	NN	37-08-017
mail	NN-HL	2-02-002
Mail	NN-TL	3-01-001
mails	NNS	7-04-004
mail	**verb**	**25-10-015**
mail	VB	5-03-004
mailed	VBD	3-03-003
mailed	VBN	13-05-008
mailing	VBG	2-02-002
mailing	VBG-HL	2-01-001
mailbox	**noun**	**5-02-003**
mailbox	NN	1-01-001
mailboxes	NNS	4-01-002
mailed-fist-in-velvet-glove	**JJ**	**1-01-001**
Mailer	**NP**	**2-02-002**
mailing	**noun**	**7-02-002**
mailing	NN	4-01-001
mailings	NNS	2-01-001

Word	Tag	Frequency
mailing (cont.):		
mailings	NNS-HL	1-01-001
mailman	**NN**	**1-01-001**
maim	**verb**	**1-01-001**
maimed	VBN	1-01-001
main	**sem. sup.**	**110-13-090**
main	JJS	99-13-083
Main	JJS-TL	11-05-008
main	**noun**	**11-07-011**
main	NN	10-06-010
mains	NNS	1-01-001
main-d'oeuvre	**foreign**	**1-01-001**
main-d'oeuvre	FW-NN	0-00-000
Main-d'Oeuvre	FW-NN-TL	1-01-001
Maine	**NP**	**9-06-009**
mainland	**noun**	**11-04-005**
mainland	NN	6-03-004
Mainland	NN-TL	5-01-001
Mainliner	**NP**	**1-01-001**
mainly	**QL**	**1-01-001**
mainly	**RB**	**30-11-029**
mainstream	**NN**	**2-01-002**
maintain	**verb**	**152-13-095**
maintain	VB	60-12-046
maintains	VBZ	16-07-013
maintained	VBD	13-07-012
maintained	VBN	35-05-024
maintaining	VBG	28-09-025
maintenance	**noun**	**64-11-034**
maintenance	NN	57-11-031
maintenance	NN-HL	3-03-003
Maintenance	NN-TL	4-02-002
mais	**FW-CC**	**3-03-003**
Maitland	**prop. noun**	**2-02-002**
Maitland	NP	1-01-001
Maitland's	NP$	1-01-001
maitres	**foreign**	**2-02-002**
maitre	FW-NN	1-01-001
maitres	FW-NNS	0-00-000
Maitres	FW-NNS-TL	1-01-001
Majdan-Tartarski	**NP**	**1-01-001**
Majdanek	**NP**	**10-01-001**
majestic	**adjective**	**10-06-009**
majestic	JJ	9-06-008
Majestic	JJ-TL	1-01-001
majestically	**QL**	**1-01-001**
majesty	**noun**	**4-04-004**
majesty	NN	1-01-001
maiestie	NN	1-01-001
majesties	NNS	0-00-000
Majesties	NNS-TL	1-01-001
majesty's	NN$	0-00-000
Majesty's	NN$-TL	1-01-001
major	**adjective**	**224-14-129**
major	JJ	221-14-128
major	JJ-HL	2-01-002
Major	JJ-TL	1-01-001
major	**noun**	**25-06-016**
major	NN	5-02-003
maj.	NN	0-00-000
Maj.	NN-TL	1-01-001
majuh	NN	1-01-001
Major	NN-TL	15-06-011
majors	NNS	3-01-003
major	**verb**	**2-01-002**
major	VB	1-01-001
majored	VBN	1-01-001
Major	**NP**	**2-02-002**
major-league	**noun**	**5-02-003**
major-league	NN	4-02-002
Major-League	NN-TL	1-01-001
major-market	**NN**	**1-01-001**
majority	**noun**	**60-10-041**
majority	NN	57-10-039
majorities	NNS	3-03-003
make	**noun**	**7-05-007**
make	NN	3-03-003
makes	NNS	4-03-004
make	**verb**	**2312-15-479**
make	VB	791-15-365
makes	VBZ	168-15-120
made	VBD	466-15-256
made	VBN	654-15-323
made	VBN-HL	1-01-001
made	VBN-NC	1-01-001
making	VBG	231-15-168
make-believe	**NN**	**1-01-001**
make-ready	**NN**	**1-01-001**
make-up	**noun**	**6-06-006**

Word	Tag	Frequency
make-up (cont.):		
make-up	NN	5-05-005
makeup	NN	1-01-001
make-work	**JJ**	**1-01-001**
Makepeace	**NP**	**1-01-001**
maker	**noun**	**31-06-016**
maker	NN	12-05-008
makers	NNS	18-05-011
Makers	NNS-TL	1-01-001
makeshift	**JJ**	**6-05-006**
makeshift	**noun**	**1-01-001**
makeshifts	NNS	1-01-001
making	**noun**	**28-08-022**
making	NN	21-07-018
Making	NN-TL	3-01-001
makings	NNS	4-03-003
maku	**FW-NN**	**2-01-001**
Mal	**NP**	**1-01-001**
Malabar	**NP**	**1-01-001**
maladaptive	**JJ**	**1-01-001**
maladjusted	**JJ**	**3-01-001**
maladjustment	**noun**	**8-01-001**
maladjustment	NN	5-01-001
maladjustment	NN-HL	1-01-001
maladjustments	NNS	2-01-001
maladroit	**JJ**	**1-01-001**
malady	**noun**	**3-03-003**
malady	NN	1-01-001
maladies	NNS	2-02-002
malaise	**NN**	**9-03-005**
Malamud	**NP**	**1-01-001**
malapropism	**NN**	**1-01-001**
malaria	**NN**	**3-02-003**
Malay	**prop. noun**	**1-01-001**
Malay	NP	0-00-000
Malay	NP-TL	1-01-001
Malcolm	**NP**	**3-03-003**
Malden	**prop. noun**	**1-01-001**
Malden	NP	0-00-000
Malden	NP-TL	1-01-001
male	**JJ**	**13-06-011**
male	**noun**	**43-11-026**
male	NN	24-11-020
males	NNS	19-05-010
malediction	**NN**	**1-01-001**
maleness	**NN**	**3-02-003**
Malenkov	**NP**	**1-01-001**
Malesherbes	**NP**	**1-01-001**
malevolence	**NN**	**2-02-002**
malevolency	**noun**	**1-01-001**
malevolencies	NNS	1-01-001
malevolent	**JJ**	**2-02-002**
malfeasant	**NN**	**1-01-001**
malformation	**noun**	**1-01-001**
malformations	NNS	1-01-001
malformed	**JJ**	**4-02-002**
malfunctioning	**NN**	**1-01-001**
Mali	**NP**	**1-01-001**
Malia	**NP**	**1-01-001**
malice	**NN**	**2-02-002**
malicious	**JJ**	**2-02-002**
maliciously	**RB**	**1-01-001**
malign	**JJ**	**1-01-001**
malign	**verb**	**2-02-002**
maligned	VBD	1-01-001
maligned	VBN	1-01-001
malignancy	**noun**	**2-02-002**
malignancy	NN	1-01-001
malignancies	NNS	1-01-001
malingering	**NN**	**2-02-002**
Malinovsky	**NP**	**1-01-001**
mall	**noun**	**3-02-003**
mall	NN	1-01-001
Mall	NN-TL	2-02-002
malleable	**JJ**	**1-01-001**
Mallinckrodt	**NP**	**1-01-001**
Mallory	**prop. noun**	**2-01-001**
Mallory	NP	1-01-001
Mallory's	NP$	1-01-001
Malmesbury	**NP**	**1-01-001**
Malmros	**NP**	**1-01-001**
Malmud	**NP**	**1-01-001**
malnourished	**JJ**	**1-01-001**
malnutrition	**noun**	**4-03-003**
malnutrition	NN	3-03-003
malnutrition	NN-HL	1-01-001
malocclusion	**NN**	**6-01-001**
Malone	**NP**	**1-01-001**
malposed	**JJ**	**1-01-001**

Word	Tag	Frequency
Malraux	**prop. noun**	**21-01-002**
Malraux	NP	13-01-002
Malraux's	NP$	8-01-001
malt	**NN**	**1-01-001**
malt	**verb**	**1-01-001**
malted	VBN	1-01-001
Malta	**prop. noun**	**3-03-003**
Malta	NP	2-02-002
Malta	NP-TL	1-01-001
Maltese	**adjective**	**3-02-002**
Maltese	JJ	1-01-001
Maltese	JJ-TL	2-01-001
maltreat	**VB**	**1-01-001**
mama	**noun**	**55-04-010**
mama	NN	1-01-001
mamma	NN	0-00-000
Mamma	NN-TL	8-02-002
Mama	NN-TL	43-04-006
mamas	NNS	0-00-000
mammas	NNS	1-01-001
mama's	NN$	0-00-000
Mama's	NN$-TL	2-02-002
Mamaroneck	**NP**	**1-01-001**
Mambo	**NP**	**1-01-001**
Mame	**NP**	**1-01-001**
mammal	**noun**	**4-02-002**
mammal	NN	1-01-001
mammals	NNS	3-01-001
mammalian	**JJ**	**5-02-003**
mammoth	**JJ**	**4-03-004**
man	**noun**	**2110-15-380**
man	NN	1160-15-316
man	NN-HL	2-02-002
man	NN-NC	2-01-001
Man	NN-TL	39-10-024
man's	NN$	117-14-075
Man's	NN$-TL	8-02-004
men	NNS	752-15-245
men	NNS-HL	3-03-003
Men	NNS-TL	8-04-004
men's	NNS$	18-09-018
Men's	NNS$-TL	1-01-001
man	**UH**	**1-01-001**
man	**verb**	**18-08-011**
man	VB	3-02-003
mans	VBZ	1-01-001
manned	VBN	12-06-006
manning	VBG	2-01-002
man-made	**adjective**	**8-06-008**
man-made	JJ	6-06-006
manmade	JJ	2-02-002
man-of-war	**noun**	**1-01-001**
men-of-war	NNS	1-01-001
man-to-man	**RB**	**1-01-001**
mana	**NN**	**2-01-001**
Mana	**NP**	**1-01-001**
manage	**verb**	**68-14-061**
manage	VB	20-11-020
manages	VBZ	4-04-004
managed	VBD	23-11-020
managed	VBN	13-08-013
managing	VBG	7-05-007
Managing	VBG-TL	1-01-001
management	**noun**	**95-08-033**
management	NN	85-08-031
management	NN-HL	3-02-002
Management	NN-TL	3-01-002
management's	NN$	2-02-002
managements	NNS	2-01-002
management-trained	**JJ**	**1-01-001**
manager	**noun**	**114-13-044**
manager	NN	79-12-039
manager	NN-HL	1-01-001
Manager	NN-TL	8-02-003
manager's	NN$	2-01-002
managers	NNS	23-06-009
managers	NNS-HL	1-01-001
managerial	**JJ**	**10-04-004**
Managua	**NP**	**1-01-001**
Manas	**NP**	**4-01-001**
Manassas	**prop. noun**	**2-01-001**
Manassas	NP	1-01-001
Manassas	NP-TL	1-01-001
Manchester	**prop. noun**	**45-06-010**
Manchester	NP	18-03-003
Manchester	NP-TL	26-06-008
Manchester's	NP$	1-01-001
mandamus	**NN**	**1-01-001**
Mandarin	**NP**	**1-01-001**
mandate	**noun**	**7-05-007**
mandate	NN	6-04-006
Mandate	NN-TL	1-01-001
mandate	**verb**	**1-01-001**
mandated	VBN	1-01-001
mandatory	**JJ**	**6-05-006**
Manderscheid	**NP**	**1-01-001**
Mandhata	**NP**	**1-01-001**
Mando	**NP**	**5-01-001**
mandrel	**NN**	**1-01-001**
mane	**noun**	**2-01-002**
manes	NNS	2-01-002
Maneret	**prop. noun**	**1-01-001**
Maneret	NP	0-00-000
Maneret	NP-TL	1-01-001
maneuver	**noun**	**11-05-006**
maneuver	NN	3-03-003
maneuvers	NNS	8-03-003
maneuver	**verb**	**8-07-007**
maneuver	VB	2-02-002
maneuvered	VBD	3-03-003
maneuvering	VBG	3-03-003
maneuverability	**NN**	**1-01-001**
maneuvering	**NN**	**1-01-001**
Manfred	**NP**	**1-01-001**
manganese	**NN**	**1-01-001**
mangle	**verb**	**1-01-001**
mangled	VBN	1-01-001
Manhattan	**prop. noun**	**21-06-010**
Manhattan	NP	16-05-008
Manhattan	NP-TL	4-04-004
Manhattan's	NP$	1-01-001
manhood	**NN**	**6-03-004**
manhour	**noun**	**4-01-002**
manhours	NNS	3-01-001
man-hours	NNS	1-01-001
mania	**NN**	**5-05-005**
maniac	**noun**	**5-04-005**
maniac	NN	4-04-004
maniacs	NNS	1-01-001
maniacal	**JJ**	**1-01-001**
manic	**JJ**	**2-01-001**
manic-depressive	**JJ**	**1-01-001**
maniclike	**JJ**	**1-01-001**
manifest	**JJ**	**5-03-005**
manifest	**verb**	**11-05-010**
manifest	VB	4-03-004
manifested	VBD	3-02-002
manifested	VBN	3-02-003
manifesting	VBG	1-01-001
manifestation	**noun**	**15-07-013**
manifestation	NN	6-05-006
manifestations	NNS	9-05-007
manifestly	**RB**	**5-05-005**
manifold	**JJ**	**2-01-002**
manifold	**NN**	**11-01-001**
manikin	**noun**	**2-02-002**
manikin	NN	1-01-001
manikins	NNS	1-01-001
manila	**NN**	**1-01-001**
Manila	**NP**	**1-01-001**
Manin	**prop. noun**	**2-01-001**
Manin	NP	1-01-001
Manin	NP-TL	1-01-001
manipulate	**verb**	**10-06-009**
manipulate	VB	6-05-006
manipulated	VBD	1-01-001
manipulated	VBN	1-01-001
manipulating	VBG	2-01-002
manipulation	**noun**	**9-05-008**
manipulation	NN	7-05-006
manipulations	NNS	2-01-002
manipulator	**noun**	**1-01-001**
manipulators	NNS	1-01-001
Manitoba	**prop. noun**	**1-01-001**
Manitoba	NP	0-00-000
Manitoba	NP-TL	1-01-001
Manjucri	**NP**	**1-01-001**
mankind	**noun**	**43-08-026**
mankind	NN	37-08-023
mankind	NN-HL	2-02-002
mankind's	NN$	4-03-004
Mankowski	**NP**	**3-01-001**
Manley	**prop. noun**	**7-02-003**
Manley	NP	5-02-003
Manley	NP-TL	1-01-001
Manley's	NP$	0-00-000
Manley's	NP$-TL	1-01-001
manliness	**NN**	**1-01-001**

Word	Tag	Freq.
manly	**JJ**	**2-01-001**
Mann	**prop. noun**	**11-01-002**
Mann	NP	2-01-001
Mann's	NP$	9-01-002
mannequin	**NN**	**1-01-001**
manner	**noun**	**139-15-114**
manner	NN	124-15-101
manners	NNS	14-08-014
Manners	NNS	1-01-001
mannered	**JJ**	**1-01-001**
Mannerhouse	**NP**	**1-01-001**
mannerism	**noun**	**3-02-002**
mannerism	NN	2-02-002
mannerisms	NNS	1-01-001
Manning	**prop. noun**	**5-02-002**
Manning	NP	1-01-001
Manning's	NP$	4-01-001
Manningham	**NP**	**2-01-001**
Manny	**NP**	**2-02-002**
mano	**FW-NN**	**2-01-001**
manometer	**NN**	**6-01-001**
Manon	**prop. noun**	**1-01-001**
Manon	NP	0-00-000
Manon	NP-TL	1-01-001
manor	**noun**	**6-04-005**
manor	NN	3-03-003
Manor	NN-TL	2-02-002
manors	NNS	1-01-001
manpower	**noun**	**14-06-007**
manpower	NN	13-06-007
Manpower	NN-TL	1-01-001
manse	**NN**	**1-01-001**
manservant	**NN**	**3-02-002**
mansion	**noun**	**13-06-007**
mansion	NN	7-03-003
Mansion	NN-TL	1-01-001
mansion's	NN$	0-00-000
Mansion's	NN$-TL	1-01-001
mansions	NNS	4-03-004
manslaughter	**NN**	**4-02-003**
Mantegna	**NP**	**1-01-001**
mantel	**NN**	**3-03-003**
mantelpiece	**noun**	**1-01-001**
mantelpiece	NN	0-00-000
mantlepiece	NN	1-01-001
Manthey	**NP**	**3-01-001**
mantic	**JJ**	**1-01-001**
mantle	**noun**	**3-02-003**
mantle	NN	2-02-002
mantle's	NN$	1-01-001
Mantle	**prop. noun**	**51-01-003**
Mantle	NP	46-01-003
Mantle's	NP$	5-01-002
mantrap	**NN**	**1-01-001**
Manu	**NP**	**5-01-001**
manual	**JJ**	**7-02-006**
manual	**noun**	**6-03-005**
manual	NN	1-01-001
Manual	NN-TL	1-01-001
manuals	NNS	4-03-004
manually	**RB**	**3-01-001**
Manuel	**NP**	**6-02-002**
manufacture	**NN**	**16-06-010**
manufacture	**verb**	**37-09-022**
manufacture	VB	2-01-002
manufactures	VBZ	2-01-002
manufactured	VBD	3-03-003
manufactured	VBN	8-05-007
manufacturing	VBG	20-07-013
Manufacturing	VBG-TL	2-01-002
manufacturer	**noun**	**77-07-029**
manufacturer	NN	23-07-015
manufacturer's	NN$	4-01-003
manufacturers	NNS	41-05-020
Manufacturers	NNS-TL	6-03-005
manufacturers'	NNS$	2-02-002
Manufacturers'	NNS$-TL	1-01-001
manufacturing	**noun**	**3-02-003**
manufacturing	NN	2-02-002
mfg.	NN	0-00-000
Mfg.	NN-TL	1-01-001
manumission	**NN**	**1-01-001**
manumit	**verb**	**1-01-001**
manumitted	VBN	1-01-001
manure	**NN**	**6-03-004**
manure-scented	**JJ**	**1-01-001**
manuscript	**noun**	**12-07-008**
manuscript	NN	6-05-005
Manuscript	NN-TL	2-01-001
manuscript (cont.):		
manuscripts	NNS	4-02-002
Manville	**NP**	**1-01-001**
many	**ABN**	**25-09-020**
many	**post-det.**	**997-15-362**
many	AP	992-15-361
manye	AP	1-01-001
many	AP-HL	3-02-003
many	AP-NC	1-01-001
many	**QL**	**8-06-008**
many-bodied	**JJ**	**1-01-001**
many-faced	**JJ**	**1-01-001**
many-much	**post-det.**	**1-01-001**
many-much	AP + AP	0-00-000
many-much	AP + AP-NC	1-01-001
many-sided	**JJ**	**3-03-003**
many-time	**noun**	**1-01-001**
many-times	NNS	1-01-001
manzanita	**NN**	**1-01-001**
Manzanola	**NP**	**1-01-001**
Mao	**NP**	**7-02-003**
map	**noun**	**25-09-016**
map	NN	11-06-009
Map	NN-TL	1-01-001
maps	NNS	13-06-009
map	**verb**	**6-05-005**
map	VB	1-01-001
mapped	VBN	1-01-001
mapping	VBG	3-03-003
mapping	VBG-HL	1-01-001
maple	**noun**	**10-06-008**
maple	NN	6-03-005
Maple	NN-TL	1-01-001
maples	NNS	3-02-002
Maplecrest	**NP**	**1-01-001**
mapping	**NN**	**3-01-001**
Maquet	**NP**	**1-01-001**
mar	**verb**	**9-07-009**
mar	VB	2-02-002
mars	VBZ	2-02-002
marred	VBN	4-04-004
marring	VBG	1-01-001
Mar	**prop. noun**	**2-01-001**
Mar	NP	1-01-001
Mar	NP-HL	1-01-001
marathon	**NN**	**1-01-001**
marauder	**noun**	**1-01-001**
marauders	NNS	1-01-001
marble	**noun**	**23-08-016**
marble	NN	18-07-013
Marble	NN-TL	2-01-001
marbles	NNS	3-02-002
Marble	**NP**	**1-01-001**
marbleize	**verb**	**2-02-002**
marbleized	VBN	1-01-001
marbleizing	VBG	1-01-001
Marc	**NP**	**2-02-002**
Marcel	**prop. noun**	**2-02-002**
Marcel	NP	1-01-001
Marcel's	NP$	1-01-001
Marcello	**NP**	**1-01-001**
Marcellus	**prop. noun**	**2-02-002**
Marcellus	NP	1-01-001
Marcellus	NP-TL	1-01-001
march	**noun**	**19-08-019**
march	NN	14-07-014
March	NN-TL	4-03-004
marches	NNS	1-01-001
march	**verb**	**37-07-026**
march	VB	10-05-008
marches	VBZ	3-02-003
marched	VBD	6-03-006
marched	VBN	3-02-003
marching	VBG	14-06-010
Marching	VBG-TL	1-01-001
March	**prop. noun**	**100-10-052**
March	NP	84-10-048
Mar.	NP	3-02-002
March	NP-HL	9-02-004
Marches	NPS	4-01-001
Marchand	**NP**	**1-01-001**
marching	**noun**	**1-01-001**
marching	NN	0-00-000
marchin'	NN	1-01-001
Marcile	**NP**	**1-01-001**
Marcius	**NP**	**1-01-001**
Marcmann	**NP**	**1-01-001**
Marcos	**NP**	**1-01-001**
Marcus	**NP**	**7-04-006**

Word	Tag	Frequency
Mardi	**NP**	**2-01-001**
Mardis	**NP**	**1-01-001**
mare	**foreign**	**2-01-001**
mare	FW-NN	0-00-000
Mare	FW-NN-TL	1-01-001
maria	FW-NNS	1-01-001
mare	**noun**	**18-05-006**
mare	NN	12-05-006
Mare	NN-TL	3-01-001
mare's	NN$	1-01-001
Mare's	NN$-TL	1-01-001
mares	NNS	1-01-001
Marella	**NP**	**2-01-001**
Marenzio	**NP**	**1-01-001**
Margaret	**NP**	**10-04-008**
Margaretville	**NP**	**1-01-001**
Margarito	**NP**	**1-01-001**
Margenau	**NP**	**2-01-001**
margin	**noun**	**16-07-012**
margin	NN	9-06-009
margin	NN-HL	1-01-001
margins	NNS	6-03-004
marginal	**JJ**	**26-06-015**
marginality	**NN**	**2-01-001**
marginally	**RB**	**1-01-001**
Margo	**NP**	**1-01-001**
Maria	**NP**	**11-08-011**
Mariano	**NP**	**1-01-001**
Marie	**NP**	**6-04-006**
Marietta	**prop. noun**	**2-01-001**
Marietta	NP	0-00-000
Marietta	NP-TL	2-01-001
marijuana	**NN**	**10-02-002**
Marilyn	**NP**	**1-01-001**
marimba	**NN**	**1-01-001**
Marin	**prop. noun**	**4-01-002**
Marin	NP	2-01-002
Marin	NP-TL	2-01-001
marina	**noun**	**10-02-003**
marina	NN	3-01-002
marinas	NNS	7-02-002
Marina	**NP**	**7-02-002**
marinade	**NN**	**1-01-001**
marinate	**verb**	**2-02-002**
marinated	VBN	1-01-001
marinating	VBG	1-01-001
marine	**JJ**	**6-02-004**
marine	**noun**	**64-08-013**
marine	NN	36-03-003
Marine	NN-TL	13-06-009
marine's	NN$	4-01-001
marines	NNS	10-03-003
Marines	NNS-TL	1-01-001
mariner	**NN**	**1-01-001**
Mario	**NP**	**1-01-001**
Marion	**NP**	**3-02-003**
marionette	**noun**	**1-01-001**
marionettes	NNS	1-01-001
Maris	**prop. noun**	**40-01-002**
Maris	NP	36-01-002
Maris's	NP$	4-01-001
Maritain	**prop. noun**	**1-01-001**
Maritain's	NP$	1-01-001
marital	**JJ**	**10-03-005**
maritime	**adjective**	**4-02-002**
maritime	JJ	0-00-000
Maritime	JJ-TL	3-02-002
Maritime	JJ-TL-HL	1-01-001
Marjorie	**NP**	**1-01-001**
mark	**noun**	**50-13-044**
mark	NN	36-12-032
marks	NNS	14-10-014
mark	**verb**	**126-14-084**
mark	VB	18-06-015
marks	VBZ	14-08-011
marked	VBD	15-08-015
marked	VBN	69-12-047
marking	VBG	9-06-008
marking	VBG-HL	1-01-001
Mark	**prop. noun**	**31-09-015**
Mark	NP	29-09-015
Mark's	NP$	2-01-001
mark-up	**NN**	**1-01-001**
marked	**JJ**	**1-01-001**
markedly	**QL**	**2-02-002**
markedly	**RB**	**2-02-002**
Markel	**NP**	**1-01-001**
marker	**noun**	**6-03-003**
marker	NN	5-03-003

Word	Tag	Frequency
marker (cont.):		
markers	NNS	0-00-000
markers	NNS-HL	1-01-001
market	**noun**	**185-12-063**
market	NN	140-12-051
market	NN-HL	4-02-003
Market	NN-TL	11-05-007
markets	NNS	29-07-017
markets	NNS-HL	1-01-001
market	**verb**	**41-04-010**
markets	VBZ	1-01-001
marketed	VBN	3-03-003
marketing	VBG	32-03-006
marketing	VBG-HL	4-02-002
Marketing	VBG-TL	1-01-001
marketability	**NN**	**1-01-001**
marketable	**JJ**	**4-01-001**
marketing	**noun**	**9-03-006**
marketing	NN	6-02-004
marketings	NNS	3-02-002
marketplace	**noun**	**4-02-004**
marketplace	NN	3-02-003
market-place	NN	1-01-001
marketwise	**RB**	**1-01-001**
marking	**noun**	**3-02-003**
marking	NN	1-01-001
markings	NNS	2-02-002
Markovitz	**NP**	**1-01-001**
marksman	**noun**	**8-02-002**
marksman	NN	7-02-002
marksman's	NN$	1-01-001
marksmanship	**noun**	**4-03-003**
marksmanship	NN	3-03-003
marksmanship	NN-HL	1-01-001
Marlborough	**NP**	**3-01-002**
Marlene	**NP**	**2-02-002**
Marlin	**prop. noun**	**4-01-001**
Marlin	NP	2-01-001
Marlin's	NP$	2-01-001
Marlowe	**prop. noun**	**5-01-003**
Marlowe	NP	4-01-002
Marlowe's	NP$	1-01-001
marmalade	**NN**	**1-01-001**
Marmara	**prop. noun**	**3-01-001**
Marmara	NP	0-00-000
Marmara	NP-TL	3-01-001
Marmee	**NP**	**1-01-001**
Marmi	**NP**	**1-01-001**
Marmon	**prop. noun**	**2-01-001**
Marmon	NP	1-01-001
Marmon	NP-TL	1-01-001
Maroc	**NP**	**1-01-001**
marocaine	**foreign**	**1-01-001**
marocaine	FW-JJ	0-00-000
Marocaine	FW-JJ-TL	1-01-001
maroon	**JJ**	**3-03-003**
maroon	**verb**	**1-01-001**
marooned	VBD	1-01-001
Maroy	**NP**	**1-01-001**
marquee	**noun**	**1-01-001**
marquees	NNS	1-01-001
Marquess	**prop. noun**	**1-01-001**
Marquess	NP	0-00-000
Marquess	NP-TL	1-01-001
Marquet	**NP**	**1-01-001**
Marquette	**NP**	**1-01-001**
Marquis	**prop. noun**	**5-03-003**
Marquis	NP	4-03-003
Marquis'	NP$	1-01-001
Marquita	**NP**	**1-01-001**
Marr	**prop. noun**	**7-01-001**
Marr	NP	6-01-001
Marr's	NP$	1-01-001
marriage	**noun**	**122-14-049**
marriage	NN	92-13-043
marriage	NN-HL	1-01-001
Marriage	NN-TL	2-01-001
marriages	NNS	27-09-012
marrow	**NN**	**5-03-003**
marrowbone	**noun**	**1-01-001**
marrowbones	NNS	1-01-001
marry	**verb**	**130-13-067**
marry	VB	18-06-011
marries	VBZ	3-02-003
married	VBD	22-08-014
Married	VBD-TL	1-01-001
married	VBN	82-13-047
maryed	VBN	1-01-001
marrying	VBG	3-02-003

Word	Tag	Frequency
Mars	**prop. noun**	**19-04-008**
Mars	NP	18-04-008
Mars	NP-TL	1-01-001
Marsden	**NP**	**5-01-001**
Marseilles	**NP**	**1-01-001**
marsh	**noun**	**5-04-005**
marshes	NNS	4-04-004
Marshes	NNS-TL	1-01-001
Marsh	**prop. noun**	**5-02-002**
Marsh	NP	4-02-002
Marsh's	NP$	1-01-001
Marsha	**NP**	**1-01-001**
marshal	**noun**	**26-05-010**
marshal	NN	3-01-002
Marshal	NN-TL	21-05-009
marshal's	NN$	2-01-002
marshal	**verb**	**5-04-004**
marshal	VB	2-02-002
marshalled	VBD	1-01-001
marshaling	VBG	1-01-001
marshalling	VBG	1-01-001
Marshall	**prop. noun**	**28-09-015**
Marshall	NP	22-08-010
Marshall	NP-TL	5-05-005
Marshall's	NP$	1-01-001
marshland	**noun**	**1-01-001**
marshlands	NNS	1-01-001
marshmallow	**noun**	**1-01-001**
marshmallows	NNS	1-01-001
Marsicano	**NP**	**3-02-002**
Marskman	**prop. noun**	**1-01-001**
Marskmen	NPS	1-01-001
Marston	**prop. noun**	**3-02-002**
Marston	NP	2-02-002
Marston	NP-TL	1-01-001
mart	**noun**	**3-03-003**
mart	NN	0-00-000
Mart	NN-TL	2-02-002
marts	NNS	1-01-001
Martha	**prop. noun**	**6-04-004**
Martha	NP	5-03-003
Martha's	NP$	0-00-000
Martha's	NP$-TL	1-01-001
Martian	**JJ**	**5-02-002**
Martian	**prop. noun**	**3-01-001**
Martians	NPS	3-01-001
Martin	**prop. noun**	**56-11-024**
Martin	NP	55-10-023
Martin's	NP$	0-00-000
Martin's	NP$-TL	1-01-001
Martinelli	**NP**	**7-01-001**
Martinez	**NP**	**3-02-002**
martingale	**NN**	**1-01-001**
martini	**noun**	**5-05-005**
martini	NN	2-02-002
Martini	NN-TL	1-01-001
martinis	NNS	2-02-002
Martini	**NP**	**3-03-003**
Martinique	**prop. noun**	**1-01-001**
Martinique	NP	0-00-000
Martinique	NP-NC	1-01-001
Marty	**prop. noun**	**15-02-002**
Marty	NP	14-02-002
Marty's	NP$	1-01-001
martyr	**noun**	**9-03-004**
martyr	NN	8-02-003
martyrs	NNS	0-00-000
Martyrs	NNS-TL	1-01-001
martyrdom	**NN**	**1-01-001**
Marum	**NP**	**1-01-001**
Marv	**NP**	**3-02-002**
marvel	**noun**	**4-04-004**
marvel	NN	3-03-003
marvels	NNS	1-01-001
marvel	**verb**	**6-03-006**
marvel	VB	3-02-003
marveled	VBD	1-01-001
marvelled	VBD	1-01-001
marveled	VBN	1-01-001
marvelous	**adjective**	**11-07-011**
marvelous	JJ	10-06-010
Marvelous	JJ-TL	1-01-001
marvelously	**RB**	**1-01-001**
Marvin	**NP**	**9-03-005**
Marx	**prop. noun**	**12-06-009**
Marx	NP	8-06-007
Marx's	NP$	4-02-003
Marxist	**NP**	**3-02-002**
Marxist-Leninist	**NP**	**1-01-001**

Word	Tag	Frequency
Mary	**prop. noun**	**97-13-037**
Mary	NP	80-13-033
Mary	NP-NC	3-01-001
Mary	NP-TL	4-03-003
Mary's	NP$	9-04-006
Mary's	NP$-TL	1-01-001
Maryinsky	**NP**	**1-01-001**
Maryland	**prop. noun**	**30-09-018**
Maryland	NP	17-08-010
Md.	NP	4-04-004
Md.	NP-HL	1-01-001
Maryland	NP-TL	6-04-004
Maryland's	NP$	2-01-001
Marylander	**prop. noun**	**2-01-001**
Marylanders	NPS	2-01-001
Masaryk	**prop. noun**	**4-01-001**
Masaryk	NP	3-01-001
Masaryk	NP-HL	1-01-001
mascara	**NN**	**1-01-001**
masculine	**JJ**	**7-04-006**
masculinity	**NN**	**1-01-001**
Maser	**NP**	**1-01-001**
mash	**NN**	**1-01-001**
mash	**verb**	**4-03-003**
mashed	VBN	3-02-002
mashing	VBG	1-01-001
mask	**noun**	**11-05-006**
mask	NN	8-04-005
masks	NNS	3-02-002
mask	**verb**	**5-03-004**
mask	VB	1-01-001
masked	VBD	1-01-001
masked	VBN	3-02-002
masker	**noun**	**1-01-001**
maskers'	NNS$	1-01-001
masking	**NN**	**1-01-001**
Mason	**prop. noun**	**28-06-009**
Mason	NP	23-05-007
Mason	NP-TL	1-01-001
Mason's	NP$	1-01-001
Masons	NPS	3-02-002
masonic	**adjective**	**3-01-003**
masonic	JJ	0-00-000
Masonic	JJ-TL	3-01-003
masonry	**JJ**	**1-01-001**
masonry	**noun**	**5-04-004**
masonry	NN	4-04-004
Masonry	NN-TL	1-01-001
Masque	**NP**	**1-01-001**
masquer	**noun**	**1-01-001**
masquers'	NNS$	1-01-001
masquerade	**NN**	**1-01-001**
masquerade	**verb**	**4-03-004**
masquerade	VB	1-01-001
masquerades	VBZ	2-02-002
masquerading	VBG	1-01-001
mass	**JJ**	**6-05-006**
mass	**noun**	**110-14-063**
mass	NN	81-13-045
mass	NN-NC	1-01-001
Mass	NN-TL	7-04-004
masses	NNS	21-09-018
mass	**verb**	**6-05-006**
mass	VB	3-03-003
massed	VBD	1-01-001
massed	VBN	1-01-001
massing	VBG	1-01-001
mass-building	**JJ**	**1-01-001**
mass-distribution	**NN**	**1-01-001**
mass-production	**NN**	**1-01-001**
Massachusetts	**prop. noun**	**65-10-039**
Massachusetts	NP	36-09-022
Mass.	NP	12-04-010
Massachusetts	NP-TL	14-06-011
Massachusetts'	NP$	3-02-002
massacre	**noun**	**1-01-001**
massacres	NNS	1-01-001
massacre	**verb**	**2-02-002**
massacre	VB	1-01-001
massacred	VBD	1-01-001
massage	**NN**	**1-01-001**
massage	**verb**	**2-02-002**
massage	VB	1-01-001
massaging	VBG	1-01-001
masseur	**NN**	**3-01-001**
Massey-Ferguson	**NP**	**1-01-001**
massif	**noun**	**1-01-001**
massifs	NNS	1-01-001
Massimo	**NP**	**1-01-001**

Word	Tag	Frequency
massive	**JJ**	**33-13-029**
Masson	**NP**	**1-01-001**
mast	**noun**	**8-04-005**
mast	NN	6-02-003
masts	NNS	2-02-002
master	**JJS**	**5-05-005**
master	**noun**	**90-14-057**
master	NN	49-13-036
massuh	NN	1-01-001
master	NN-HL	1-01-001
Master	NN-TL	10-06-008
master's	NN$	6-04-005
Master's	NN$-TL	1-01-001
masters	NNS	12-06-011
Masters	NNS-TL	10-01-003
master	**verb**	**13-07-012**
master	VB	7-04-007
mastered	VBD	1-01-001
mastered	VBN	4-03-004
mastering	VBG	1-01-001
master-race	**NN**	**1-01-001**
masterful	**JJ**	**2-02-002**
masterfully	**RB**	**1-01-001**
masterly	**JJ**	**1-01-001**
mastermind	**verb**	**1-01-001**
masterminding	VBG	1-01-001
masterpiece	**noun**	**12-06-011**
masterpiece	NN	10-05-009
masterpieces	NNS	1-01-001
Masterpieces	NNS-TL	1-01-001
Masters	**NP**	**2-01-001**
mastery	**NN**	**10-07-009**
mastic	**NN**	**1-01-001**
mastiff	**NN**	**1-01-001**
mastodon	**noun**	**1-01-001**
mastodons	NNS	1-01-001
mastoideus	**NN**	**1-01-001**
Masu	**prop. noun**	**7-01-001**
Masu	NP	6-01-001
Masu's	NP$	1-01-001
mat	**noun**	**7-03-005**
mat	NN	5-02-004
mats	NNS	2-02-002
Matamoras	**NP**	**1-01-001**
match	**noun**	**24-08-016**
match	NN	15-07-012
matches	NNS	9-04-006
match	**verb**	**77-14-046**
match	VB	26-12-022
matches	VBZ	4-02-004
matched	VBD	2-02-002
matched	VBN	14-06-010
matching	VBG	29-07-018
matching	VBG-HL	2-01-001
match-width	**NN**	**1-01-001**
matching	**JJ**	**2-02-002**
matching-fund	**NN**	**1-01-001**
matchless	**JJ**	**2-02-002**
matchmaker	**NN**	**2-01-001**
matchmaking	**NN**	**1-01-001**
mate	**noun**	**27-08-016**
mate	NN	17-07-010
mates	NNS	10-04-006
mate	**verb**	**16-06-008**
mate	VB	4-02-003
mated	VBN	4-02-002
mating	VBG	8-05-006
Mateo	**NP**	**1-01-001**
mater	**foreign**	**2-02-002**
mater	FW-NN	1-01-001
Mater	FW-NN-TL	1-01-001
material	**JJ**	**4-02-004**
material	**noun**	**269-12-112**
material	NN	166-12-091
material	NN-HL	4-01-001
material's	NN$	1-01-001
materials	NNS	92-08-041
materials	NNS-HL	5-02-005
materials'	NNS$	1-01-001
material-formal	**JJ**	**1-01-001**
materialism	**noun**	**7-03-007**
materialism	NN	6-03-006
Materialism	NN-TL	1-01-001
materialistic	**JJ**	**2-02-002**
materialize	**verb**	**4-04-004**
materialize	VB	3-03-003
materialized	VBN	1-01-001
materially	**QL**	**2-02-002**
materially	**RB**	**3-03-003**

Word	Tag	Frequency
materials-handling	**JJ**	**1-01-001**
materiel	**NN**	**2-02-002**
maternal	**JJ**	**5-05-005**
math	**NN**	**4-03-003**
mathematical	**adjective**	**24-05-009**
mathematical	JJ	23-05-008
Mathematical	JJ-TL	1-01-001
mathematically	**RB**	**5-04-005**
mathematician	**NN**	**2-02-002**
mathematics	**noun**	**20-07-013**
mathematics	NN	18-07-012
Mathematics	NN-TL	1-01-001
mathematics	NNS	1-01-001
Matheson	**NP**	**1-01-001**
Mathewson	**prop. noun**	**1-01-001**
Mathewson	NP	0-00-000
Mathewson	NP-TL	1-01-001
Mathias	**prop. noun**	**3-02-002**
Mathias	NP	2-02-002
Mathias'	NP$	1-01-001
Mathues	**NP**	**1-01-001**
Matilda	**NP**	**6-01-001**
matinals	**FW-JJ**	**1-01-001**
Matisse	**prop. noun**	**2-02-002**
Matisse	NP	1-01-001
Matisses	NPS	1-01-001
Matlowsky	**NP**	**1-01-001**
matriarch	**NN**	**1-01-001**
matriarchal	**JJ**	**1-01-001**
matriculate	**verb**	**5-02-003**
matriculate	VB	2-02-002
matriculated	VBD	1-01-001
matriculated	VBN	2-01-001
matrimonial	**JJ**	**1-01-001**
matrimony	**NN**	**3-03-003**
matrix	**NN**	**1-01-001**
matron	**NN**	**3-03-003**
Matson	**NP**	**8-01-001**
Matsu	**NP**	**1-01-001**
Matsuo	**prop. noun**	**37-01-001**
Matsuo	NP	35-01-001
Matsuo's	NP$	2-01-001
matsyendra	**FW-NN**	**1-01-001**
matt	**NN**	**2-01-001**
Matt	**NP**	**1-01-001**
Mattathias	**NP**	**1-01-001**
Mattei	**NP**	**3-01-001**
matter	**noun**	**342-15-204**
matter	NN	281-15-179
matter	NN-HL	1-01-001
Matter	NN-TL-HL	1-01-001
matters	NNS	59-13-045
matter	**verb**	**35-10-028**
matter	VB	25-10-021
matters	VBZ	5-04-005
mattered	VBD	4-03-004
mattered	VBN	1-01-001
matter-of-factness	**NN**	**1-01-001**
Matthew	**prop. noun**	**4-02-003**
Matthew	NP	2-02-002
Matthew	NP-TL	2-01-001
Mattie	**NP**	**1-01-001**
matting	**NN**	**2-02-002**
mattress	**noun**	**1-01-001**
mattresses	NNS	1-01-001
Matunuck	**NP**	**3-01-001**
maturation	**NN**	**3-03-003**
maturational	**JJ**	**1-01-001**
mature	**JJ**	**24-08-020**
mature	**verb**	**12-05-008**
mature	VB	7-04-005
matured	VBD	1-01-001
matured	VBN	1-01-001
maturing	VBG	3-02-002
maturity	**noun**	**40-06-014**
maturity	NN	36-06-013
Maturity	NN-TL	3-01-001
maturities	NNS	1-01-001
Mauch	**NP**	**2-01-001**
Maude	**prop. noun**	**22-01-001**
Maude	NP	21-01-001
Maude's	NP$	1-01-001
maudlin	**JJ**	**1-01-001**
maul	**verb**	**1-01-001**
mauling	VBG	1-01-001
Mauldin	**NP**	**1-01-001**
mauler	**NN**	**1-01-001**
Maureen	**NP**	**3-01-001**
Mauri	**NP**	**1-01-001**

Word	Tag	Frequency
Maurice	**NP**	**7-04-006**
Maurier	**NP**	**1-01-001**
Maurine	**NP**	**1-01-001**
mausoleum	**NN**	**2-02-002**
mauve	**JJ**	**1-01-001**
mauve-colored	**JJ**	**1-01-001**
maverick	**JJ**	**1-01-001**
maverick	**noun**	**3-02-002**
maverick	NN	2-02-002
mavericks	NNS	1-01-001
Mavis	**NP**	**2-01-001**
maw	**NN**	**2-02-002**
mawkish	**JJ**	**1-01-001**
Mawr	**prop. noun**	**2-01-001**
Mawr	NP	0-00-000
Mawr	NP-TL	2-01-001
Max	**prop. noun**	**14-06-009**
Max	NP	11-06-007
Max	NP-TL	1-01-001
Max's	NP$	2-02-002
Maxentius	**prop. noun**	**1-01-001**
Maxentius	NP	0-00-000
Maxentius	NP-TL	1-01-001
maxim	**NN**	**1-01-001**
Maxim	**prop. noun**	**1-01-001**
Maxim's	NP$	1-01-001
maximal	**JJ**	**3-02-003**
Maximilian	**NP**	**1-01-001**
maximization	**NN**	**7-02-003**
maximize	**verb**	**11-02-005**
maximize	VB	2-01-002
maximizes	VBZ	3-01-002
maximized	VBN	1-01-001
maximizing	VBG	4-02-003
maximizing	VBG-HL	1-01-001
maximum	**adjective**	**67-08-036**
maximum	JJ	66-08-036
maximum	JJ-HL	1-01-001
maximum	**noun**	**14-06-010**
maximum	NN	12-06-009
maximums	NNS	2-01-001
Maxine	**prop. noun**	**3-01-001**
Maxine	NP	2-01-001
Maxine's	NP$	1-01-001
Maxwell	**prop. noun**	**13-03-004**
Maxwell	NP	9-02-003
Maxwell	NP-HL	1-01-001
Maxwell	NP-TL	1-01-001
Maxwell's	NP$	2-01-001
may	**modal aux.**	**1307-15-325**
may	MD	1300-15-324
mai	MD	1-01-001
maye	MD	2-01-001
mayst	MD	1-01-001
may	MD-HL	2-02-002
May	MD-TL	1-01-001
May	**prop. noun**	**98-11-049**
May	NP	89-11-048
May	NP-HL	4-02-002
May	NP-TL	5-04-004
Mayan	**prop. noun**	**1-01-001**
Mayans	NPS	1-01-001
maybe	**RB**	**133-15-074**
Mayer	**NP**	**5-02-003**
Mayfair	**prop. noun**	**2-02-002**
Mayfair	NP	0-00-000
Mayfair	NP-TL	2-02-002
Mayflower	**prop. noun**	**4-03-004**
Mayflower	NP	1-01-001
Mayflower	NP-TL	3-03-003
mayhem	**NN**	**1-01-001**
Maynard	**NP**	**2-02-002**
Maynor	**NP**	**1-01-001**
Mayo	**NP**	**1-01-001**
mayonnaise	**NN**	**2-02-002**
mayor	**noun**	**47-07-017**
mayor	NN	8-04-005
Mayor	NN-TL	29-03-011
Mayor	NN-TL-HL	1-01-001
mayor's	NN$	5-02-003
Mayor's	NN$-TL	4-02-002
mayor-elect	**noun**	**1-01-001**
mayor-elect	NN	0-00-000
Mayor-elect	NN-TL	1-01-001
mayor-nominate	**noun**	**1-01-001**
mayor-nominate	NN	0-00-000
Mayor-nominate	NN-TL	1-01-001
mayoral	**adjective**	**2-02-002**
mayoral	JJ	1-01-001

Word	Tag	Frequency
mayoral (cont.):		
Mayoral	JJ-TL	1-01-001
mayorship	**NN**	**1-01-001**
Mays	**prop. noun**	**15-04-006**
Mays	NP	12-03-005
Mays	NP-TL	1-01-001
Mays'	NP$	2-01-002
maze	**NN**	**6-06-006**
Mazeroski	**NP**	**3-01-002**
Mazowsze	**NP**	**1-01-001**
mazurka	**NN**	**2-01-001**
mc.	**NNS**	**1-01-001**
McAlester	**NP**	**1-01-001**
McAlister	**NP**	**1-01-001**
McAuliffe	**NP**	**4-01-002**
McBride	**NP**	**11-01-001**
McCafferty	**NP**	**1-01-001**
McCarthy	**prop. noun**	**8-04-005**
McCarthy	NP	7-04-005
McCarthy's	NP$	1-01-001
McCauley	**NP**	**2-01-001**
McCay	**NP**	**2-01-001**
McClellan	**prop. noun**	**15-04-005**
McClellan	NP	12-04-005
McClellan	NP-TL	1-01-001
McClellan's	NP$	2-02-002
McCloy	**prop. noun**	**3-02-002**
McCloy	NP	2-01-001
McCloy's	NP$	1-01-001
McCluskey	**NP**	**1-01-001**
McCone	**prop. noun**	**2-01-002**
McCone	NP	1-01-001
McCone's	NP$	1-01-001
McConnell	**prop. noun**	**3-01-002**
McConnell	NP	2-01-002
McConnell's	NP$	1-01-001
McCormack	**prop. noun**	**1-01-001**
McCormack	NP	0-00-000
McCormack	NP-HL	1-01-001
McCormick	**prop. noun**	**8-02-004**
McCormick	NP	7-02-004
McCormick	NP-TL	1-01-001
McCracken	**NP**	**1-01-001**
McCrady	**NP**	**2-01-001**
McCullers	**NP**	**2-01-001**
McCullough	**NP**	**3-01-001**
McDaniel	**NP**	**2-01-002**
McDermott	**NP**	**1-01-001**
McDonnell	**NP**	**1-01-001**
McEachern	**NP**	**1-01-001**
McElvaney	**prop. noun**	**1-01-001**
McElvaney	NP	0-00-000
McElvaney	NP-TL	1-01-001
McElyee	**NP**	**1-01-001**
McEnroe	**prop. noun**	**1-01-001**
McEnroe's	NP$	1-01-001
McFarland	**NP**	**1-01-001**
McFee	**NP**	**1-01-001**
McFeeley	**NP**	**13-01-001**
McFeely	**NP**	**1-01-001**
McGehee	**NP**	**1-01-001**
McGeorge	**NP**	**2-02-002**
McGhie	**NP**	**1-01-001**
McGlynn	**NP**	**1-01-001**
McGovern	**prop. noun**	**1-01-001**
McGovern's	NP$	0-00-000
McGovern's	NP$-TL	1-01-001
McGruder	**NP**	**1-01-001**
McIntosh	**NP**	**1-01-001**
McIntyre	**NP**	**1-01-001**
McIver	**NP**	**3-01-001**
McKee	**NP**	**3-02-002**
McKellar	**prop. noun**	**1-01-001**
McKellar	NP	0-00-000
McKellar	NP-TL	1-01-001
McKenna	**NP**	**1-01-001**
McKenzie	**NP**	**3-01-001**
McKinley	**prop. noun**	**12-05-005**
McKinley	NP	10-03-003
McKinley	NP-TL	1-01-001
McKinley's	NP$	1-01-001
McKinney	**NP**	**1-01-001**
McLauchlin	**NP**	**1-01-001**
McLemore	**NP**	**1-01-001**
McLendon	**NP**	**2-01-001**
McLeod	**NP**	**1-01-001**
McLish	**NP**	**3-01-001**
McN.	**NP**	**1-01-001**
McNair	**NP**	**3-01-001**

Word	Tag	Frequency
McNamara	**NP**	**3-02-002**
McNaughton	**NP**	**2-02-002**
McNear	**NP**	**1-01-001**
McNeil	**prop. noun**	**1-01-001**
McNeil	NP	0-00-000
McNeil	NP-TL	1-01-001
McNeill	**NP**	**1-01-001**
McPherson	**prop. noun**	**2-01-001**
McPherson	NP	1-01-001
McPherson's	NP$	1-01-001
McQuillan	**NP**	**1-01-001**
McRoberts	**NP**	**1-01-001**
McSorley	**prop. noun**	**1-01-001**
McSorley's	NP$	0-00-000
McSorley's	NP$-TL	1-01-001
McWhinney	**NP**	**1-01-001**
me	**FW-PPO**	**1-01-001**
Me'a	**NP**	**1-01-001**
mea	**foreign**	**2-02-002**
mea	FW-PP$	1-01-001
mea	FW-PP$-NC	1-01-001
Mead	**prop. noun**	**2-02-002**
Mead	NP	1-01-001
Mead	NP-TL	1-01-001
meadow	**adjective**	**1-01-001**
meadow	JJ	0-00-000
Meadow	JJ-TL	1-01-001
meadow	**noun**	**23-08-013**
meadow	NN	12-04-006
Meadow	NN-TL	4-03-004
meadows	NNS	5-03-003
Meadows	NNS-TL	2-02-002
meager	**JJ**	**6-05-006**
meal	**noun**	**56-12-034**
meal	NN	30-08-020
meals	NNS	26-10-020
meal-to-meal	**JJ**	**1-01-001**
mealie-meal	**NN**	**1-01-001**
mealtime	**NN**	**2-02-002**
mealynose	**NN**	**1-01-001**
mealynosed	**JJ**	**1-01-001**
mean	**JJ**	**29-08-017**
mean	**noun**	**130-13-084**
mean	NN	12-03-005
means	NNS	115-13-078
meanes	NNS	2-01-001
Means	NNS-TL	1-01-001
mean	**verb**	**376-15-209**
mean	VB	158-14-113
means	VBZ	103-12-078
Means	VBZ-TL	2-01-001
meant	VBD	70-13-047
meant	VBN	30-12-027
meaning	VBG	12-07-010
meanin'	VBG	1-01-001
mean-square	**NN**	**1-01-001**
meander	**verb**	**4-03-004**
meandered	VBD	1-01-001
meandering	VBG	3-02-003
meanest	**JJT**	**1-01-001**
meaning	**noun**	**138-15-071**
meaning	NN	112-15-067
meanin'	NN	1-01-001
meaning	NN-HL	1-01-001
Meaning	NN-TL	2-01-001
meanings	NNS	21-05-008
Meanings	NNS-TL	1-01-001
meaningful	**JJ**	**24-08-020**
meaningfully	**RB**	**1-01-001**
meaningfulness	**NN**	**2-02-002**
meaningless	**JJ**	**15-10-014**
meanness	**NN**	**3-03-003**
means	**noun**	**75-08-053**
means	NN	74-08-053
means	NN-HL	1-01-001
Means	**prop. noun**	**15-02-002**
Means	NP	14-01-001
Means's	NP$	1-01-001
meantime	**NN**	**9-05-009**
meantime	**RB**	**3-02-002**
meanwhile	**RB**	**35-13-035**
Mears	**NP**	**1-01-001**
measles	**NN**	**2-02-002**
measurable	**JJ**	**5-03-004**
measurably	**RB**	**1-01-001**
measure	**noun**	**107-12-076**
measure	NN	60-11-042
Measure	NN-TL	1-01-001
measures	NNS	46-10-037

Word	Tag	Frequency
measure	**verb**	**128-10-053**
measure	VB	28-08-020
measure	VB-HL	2-01-001
measures	VBZ	3-02-003
measured	VBD	7-04-006
measured	VBN	59-09-027
measuring	VBG	27-04-014
measuring	VBG-HL	2-02-002
measurement	**noun**	**88-06-028**
measurement	NN	31-05-016
measurement	NN-HL	2-01-001
Measurement	NN-TL	1-01-001
measurements	NNS	48-05-019
measurements	NNS-HL	5-02-004
Measurements	NNS-TL	1-01-001
meat	**noun**	**57-10-017**
meat	NN	43-10-017
meat	NN-HL	2-02-002
meats	NNS	11-03-003
meats	NNS-HL	1-01-001
meat-wagon	**NN**	**1-01-001**
meaty	**JJ**	**1-01-001**
Mecca	**NP**	**1-01-001**
mechanic	**noun**	**22-10-017**
mechanic	NN	5-05-005
mechanic's	NN$	1-01-001
mechanics	NNS	16-09-012
mechanical	**JJ**	**34-09-023**
mechanically	**RB**	**4-03-004**
mechanics	**noun**	**3-01-003**
mechanics	NN	2-01-002
mechanics	NN-HL	1-01-001
mechanism	**noun**	**46-06-020**
mechanism	NN	26-05-011
mechanism	NN-HL	2-01-001
mechanisms	NNS	18-05-012
mechanist	**NN**	**1-01-001**
mechanistic	**JJ**	**1-01-001**
mechanization	**NN**	**4-04-004**
mechanize	**verb**	**5-02-003**
mechanized	VBN	5-02-003
mechanochemically	**RB**	**1-01-001**
Mecholyl	**NP**	**4-01-001**
mecum	**FW-PPO+IN**	**2-01-002**
med-chemical	**adjective**	**1-01-001**
med-chemical	JJ	0-00-000
Med-Chemical	JJ-TL	1-01-001
medal	**noun**	**11-06-009**
medal	NN	3-02-003
Medal	NN-TL	4-03-004
medals	NNS	4-04-004
medallion	**noun**	**1-01-001**
medallions	NNS	1-01-001
meddle	**verb**	**4-03-003**
meddle	VB	1-01-001
meddling	VBG	3-02-002
meddling	**NN**	**1-01-001**
Medea	**NP**	**1-01-001**
medecine	**foreign**	**1-01-001**
medecine	FW-NN	0-00-000
Medecine	FW-NN-TL	1-01-001
Medfield	**prop. noun**	**4-01-001**
Medfield	NP	2-01-001
Medfield	NP-TL	1-01-001
Medfield's	NP$	1-01-001
mediaevalist	**NN**	**1-01-001**
median	**NN**	**1-01-001**
mediate	**verb**	**1-01-001**
mediating	VBG	1-01-001
medic	**noun**	**1-01-001**
medics	NNS	1-01-001
medical	**adjective**	**162-13-049**
medical	JJ	117-13-044
medical	JJ-HL	2-01-002
Medical	JJ-TL	40-08-010
Medical	JJ-TL-HL	3-01-001
medicale	**foreign**	**1-01-001**
medicale	FW-JJ	0-00-000
Medicale	FW-JJ-TL	1-01-001
medically	**RB**	**2-02-002**
medication	**NN**	**2-02-002**
medicinal	**JJ**	**1-01-001**
medicine	**noun**	**35-11-021**
medicine	NN	25-11-017
Medicine	NN-TL	5-04-004
medicines	NNS	5-03-005
Medicis	**prop. noun**	**2-02-002**
Medicis	NP	1-01-001
Medici	NPS	1-01-001

Word	Tag	Frequency
medico	**noun**	**1-01-001**
medico's	NN$	1-01-001
medico-military	**JJ**	**3-01-001**
medieval	**adjective**	**18-07-010**
medieval	JJ	17-07-010
Medieval	JJ-TL	1-01-001
mediocre	**JJ**	**5-04-005**
mediocrity	**noun**	**2-01-002**
mediocrity	NN	1-01-001
mediocrities	NNS	1-01-001
meditate	**verb**	**4-03-004**
meditate	VB	1-01-001
meditated	VBD	1-01-001
meditating	VBG	2-02-002
meditation	**noun**	**6-03-005**
meditation	NN	2-02-002
meditations	NNS	2-02-002
meditations	NNS-HL	1-01-001
Meditations	NNS-TL	1-01-001
meditative	**JJ**	**2-02-002**
Mediterranean	**prop. noun**	**7-07-007**
Mediterranean	NP	6-06-006
Mediterranean	NP-TL	1-01-001
medium	**JJ**	**9-05-006**
medium	**noun**	**55-10-030**
medium	NN	36-08-021
medium's	NN$	2-01-001
media	NNS	12-07-010
mediums	NNS	4-01-001
media	NNS-HL	1-01-001
medium-sized	**JJ**	**1-01-001**
mediumistic	**JJ**	**3-01-001**
mediumship	**NN**	**1-01-001**
medley	**NN**	**1-01-001**
Medmenham	**prop. noun**	**1-01-001**
Medmenham	NP	0-00-000
Medmenham	NP-TL	1-01-001
Meehan	**NP**	**1-01-001**
meek	**JJ**	**1-01-001**
Meek	**NP**	**9-01-001**
meek-mannered	**JJ**	**1-01-001**
Meeker	**prop. noun**	**17-01-001**
Meeker	NP	9-01-001
Meeker	NP-TL	1-01-001
Meeker's	NP$	7-01-001
meekest	**JJT**	**1-01-001**
meekly	**RB**	**2-02-002**
meet	**noun**	**9-04-004**
meet	NN	7-03-003
meets	NNS	2-01-001
meet	**verb**	**339-14-185**
meet	VB	141-14-100
meet	VB-HL	1-01-001
meets	VBZ	31-08-014
meets	VBZ-HL	1-01-001
Meets	VBZ-TL	1-01-001
met	VBD	80-14-057
met	VBN	49-12-047
meeting	VBG	32-11-029
meetin'	VBG	1-01-001
meeting	VBG-HL	2-01-002
meeting	**noun**	**153-14-074**
meeting	NN	122-14-055
Meeting	NN-TL	3-03-003
meetings	NNS	28-08-025
Meg	**NP**	**2-01-001**
megakaryocytic	**JJ**	**1-01-001**
megalomania	**NN**	**1-01-001**
megalopolis	**noun**	**1-01-001**
megalopolises	NNS	1-01-001
Megarian	**prop. noun**	**1-01-001**
Megarians	NPS	1-01-001
megaton	**noun**	**12-02-003**
megaton	NN	2-02-002
megatons	NNS	10-01-002
megawatt	**NN**	**2-01-001**
Mehitabel	**NP**	**1-01-001**
Meinckian	**JJ**	**1-01-001**
Meinung	**FW-NN**	**1-01-001**
Meir	**NP**	**1-01-001**
Meisenheimer	**NP**	**1-01-001**
Meister	**prop. noun**	**1-01-001**
Meister	NP	0-00-000
Meister	NP-TL	1-01-001
Meistersinger	**foreign**	**1-01-001**
Meistersinger	NPS	0-00-000
Meistersinger	NPS-TL	1-01-001
Mekong	**prop. noun**	**3-02-002**
Mekong	NP	1-01-001

Word	Tag	Frequency
Mekong (cont.):		
Mekong	NP-TL	2-02-002
Mel	**NP**	**8-01-001**
Melamine	**NP**	**2-01-001**
melancholy	**adjective**	**4-02-004**
melancholy	JJ	3-02-003
melancholy	JJ-HL	1-01-001
melancholy	**NN**	**5-05-005**
melanderi	**NP**	**1-01-001**
Melanesian	**NP**	**2-01-001**
melange	**NN**	**1-01-001**
Melbourne	**NP**	**1-01-001**
Melcher	**NP**	**1-01-001**
meld	**VB**	**1-01-001**
melee	**NN**	**3-02-002**
Melies	**NP**	**4-01-001**
melioration	**NN**	**1-01-001**
Melisande	**NP**	**1-01-001**
Melissa	**NP**	**3-01-001**
Mellal	**NP**	**1-01-001**
mellow	**JJ**	**1-01-001**
mellow	**verb**	**2-02-002**
mellowed	VBN	2-02-002
melodic	**JJ**	**5-04-005**
melodically	**QL**	**1-01-001**
melodious	**JJ**	**4-03-004**
melodrama	**NN**	**3-02-003**
melodramatic	**JJ**	**4-04-004**
melody	**noun**	**31-09-018**
melody	NN	20-08-015
Melody	NN-TL	1-01-001
melodies	NNS	10-04-006
melon	**NN**	**1-01-001**
melon-like	**JJ**	**1-01-001**
melt	**verb**	**32-12-022**
melt	VB	4-04-004
melted	VBD	2-02-002
melted	VBN	7-06-007
melting	VBG	18-09-013
melting	VBG-HL	1-01-001
melting	**JJ**	**1-01-001**
melting	**NN**	**2-01-001**
Meltzer	**prop. noun**	**14-01-001**
Meltzer	NP	8-01-001
Meltzer	NP-TL	4-01-001
Meltzer's	NP$	2-01-001
Melville	**NP**	**3-02-003**
Melvin	**prop. noun**	**4-02-004**
Melvin	NP	3-01-003
Melvin	NP-HL	1-01-001
Melzi	**NP**	**4-01-001**
mem	**FW-NN**	**1-01-001**
member	**noun**	**464-15-177**
member	NN	133-14-086
Member	NN-TL	4-02-002
members	NNS	318-14-132
members	NNS-HL	2-02-002
Members	NNS-TL	5-03-004
members'	NNS$	2-02-002
membership	**noun**	**75-07-027**
membership	NN	67-07-025
membership	NN-HL	2-01-001
Membership	NN-TL	4-01-001
memberships	NNS	2-02-002
membrane	**NN**	**6-02-004**
meme	**FW-JJ**	**1-01-001**
memento	**noun**	**4-02-004**
memento	NN	1-01-001
mementos	NNS	1-01-001
mementoes	NNS	1-01-001
momentoes	NNS	1-01-001
meminisse	**FW-VB**	**1-01-001**
memo	**noun**	**2-02-002**
memo	NN	1-01-001
memos	NNS	1-01-001
memoir	**noun**	**6-03-006**
memoir	NN	1-01-001
Memoir	NN-TL	1-01-001
memoirs	NNS	3-02-003
Memoirs	NNS-TL	1-01-001
memorabilia	**NNS**	**2-01-002**
memorable	**JJ**	**11-06-011**
memorandum	**noun**	**4-02-003**
memorandum	NN	3-02-002
memoranda	NNS	1-01-001
memorial	**adjective**	**18-07-016**
memorial	JJ	2-02-002
Memorial	JJ-TL	16-06-014
memorial	**noun**	**8-04-006**

Word	Tag	Frequency
memorial (cont.):		
memorial	NN	2-02-002
Memorial	NN-TL	3-03-003
memorials	NNS	2-01-001
Memorials	NNS-TL	1-01-001
memorialize	**verb**	**1-01-001**
memorialized	VBN	1-01-001
memorization	**NN**	**1-01-001**
memorize	**verb**	**7-07-007**
memorize	VB	3-03-003
memorized	VBD	1-01-001
memorized	VBN	2-02-002
memorizing	VBG	1-01-001
memorizing	**NN**	**1-01-001**
memory	**noun**	**91-14-066**
memory	NN	76-14-056
memories	NNS	15-07-014
memory-image	**noun**	**2-01-001**
memory-images	NNS	2-01-001
memory-picture	**noun**	**2-01-001**
memory-picture	NN	1-01-001
memory-pictures	NNS	1-01-001
Memphis	**NP**	**8-05-006**
menace	**noun**	**10-09-010**
menace	NN	9-08-009
menaces	NNS	0-00-000
minaces	NNS	1-01-001
menace	**verb**	**6-05-005**
menaced	VBN	2-02-002
menacing	VBG	4-04-004
menagerie	**noun**	**1-01-001**
menagerie	NN	0-00-000
Menagerie	NN-TL	1-01-001
menarche	**noun**	**4-01-001**
menarche	NN	3-01-001
menarches	NNS	1-01-001
Menas	**NP**	**1-01-001**
Mencius	**NP**	**1-01-001**
Mencken	**NP**	**3-01-002**
mend	**verb**	**6-05-006**
mend	VB	2-02-002
mended	VBN	1-01-001
mending	VBG	3-03-003
mendacious	**JJ**	**1-01-001**
Mendelssohn	**prop. noun**	**3-01-003**
Mendelssohn	NP	2-01-002
Mendelssohn's	NP$	1-01-001
Menderes	**NP**	**2-01-001**
Mendoza	**NP**	**1-01-001**
Menelaus	**prop. noun**	**1-01-001**
Menelaus'	NP$	1-01-001
Menet	**NP**	**1-01-001**
menfolk	**pl. noun**	**2-02-002**
menfolk	NNS	1-01-001
men-folk	NNS	1-01-001
menial	**JJ**	**1-01-001**
Menilmontant	**NP**	**1-01-001**
Menlo	**prop. noun**	**1-01-001**
Menlo	NP	0-00-000
Menlo	NP-TL	1-01-001
Mennen	**NP**	**1-01-001**
Mennonite	**JJ**	**2-01-001**
Mennonite	**prop. noun**	**1-01-001**
Mennonites	NPS	1-01-001
Menshikov	**NP**	**7-01-001**
menstruation	**NN**	**1-01-001**
mental	**adjective**	**43-14-035**
mental	JJ	41-14-033
mental	JJ-HL	1-01-001
Mental	JJ-TL	1-01-001
mentality	**noun**	**4-03-004**
mentality	NN	3-02-003
mentalities	NNS	1-01-001
mentally	**RB**	**15-08-013**
mention	**noun**	**18-08-017**
mention	NN	17-07-016
mentions	NNS	1-01-001
mention	**verb**	**125-13-100**
mention	VB	33-11-030
mentions	VBZ	6-04-006
mentioned	VBD	18-08-016
mentioned	VBN	61-13-058
mentioning	VBG	7-04-007
mentioning	**NN**	**1-01-001**
mentor	**NN**	**1-01-001**
menu	**noun**	**7-05-006**
menu	NN	5-05-005
menus	NNS	2-02-002
Menuhin	**NP**	**2-02-002**
Mephistopheles	**NP**	**1-01-001**
mEq.	**NN**	**1-01-001**
Merc	**prop. noun**	**2-01-001**
Merc	NP	1-01-001
Merc	NP-TL	1-01-001
Merce	**NP**	**1-01-001**
Mercedes	**NP**	**1-01-001**
mercenary	**noun**	**13-05-006**
mercenary	NN	0-00-000
mercenary	NN-HL	1-01-001
mercenaries	NNS	12-05-006
mercer	**NN**	**1-01-001**
Mercer	**prop. noun**	**79-03-006**
Mercer	NP	67-03-003
Mercer	NP-TL	3-02-003
Mercer's	NP$	8-02-002
Mercers	NPS	1-01-001
merchandise	**noun**	**7-04-006**
merchandise	NN	6-04-005
Merchandise	NN-TL	1-01-001
merchandise	**verb**	**8-03-007**
merchandising	VBG	7-03-006
Merchandising	VBG-TL	1-01-001
merchant	**noun**	**40-09-021**
merchant	NN	12-07-011
Merchant	NN-TL	6-02-002
merchants	NNS	17-05-011
Merchants	NNS-TL	5-01-001
Merchant	**NP**	**2-01-001**
Mercier	**NP**	**1-01-001**
merciful	**JJ**	**2-02-002**
mercifully	**RB**	**4-03-004**
merciless	**JJ**	**3-03-003**
mercilessly	**RB**	**3-03-003**
mercurial	**JJ**	**1-01-001**
mercury	**NN**	**7-04-006**
Mercury	**prop. noun**	**3-03-003**
Mercury	NP	2-02-002
Mercury	NP-TL	1-01-001
mercy	**noun**	**20-11-018**
mercy	NN	19-11-017
Mercy	NN-TL	1-01-001
mere	**JJ**	**47-12-039**
Meredith	**prop. noun**	**20-04-006**
Meredith	NP	18-04-006
Meredith's	NP$	2-01-001
merely	**QL**	**5-03-005**
merely	**RB**	**130-13-097**
merest	**JJT**	**3-03-003**
meretricious	**JJ**	**1-01-001**
merge	**verb**	**20-09-016**
merge	VB	10-08-008
merges	VBZ	2-02-002
merged	VBD	1-01-001
merged	VBN	3-01-003
merging	VBG	4-03-004
merger	**noun**	**26-07-012**
merger	NN	20-06-008
merger	NN-HL	1-01-001
mergers	NNS	5-04-005
merging	**NN**	**1-01-001**
merit	**noun**	**38-10-034**
merit	NN	25-10-023
Merit	NN-TL	2-02-002
merits	NNS	11-06-011
merit	**verb**	**10-07-010**
merit	VB	2-02-002
merits	VBZ	3-03-003
merited	VBD	4-04-004
merited	VBN	1-01-001
meritorious	**JJ**	**2-02-002**
Meriwether	**NP**	**1-01-001**
Merle	**NP**	**1-01-001**
Merleau-Ponty	**NP**	**1-01-001**
mermaid	**NN**	**1-01-001**
Merner	**NP**	**1-01-001**
Merrick	**NP**	**1-01-001**
merriest	**JJT**	**1-01-001**
Merrill	**NP**	**2-02-002**
merrily	**RB**	**2-02-002**
Merrimack	**prop. noun**	**5-02-002**
Merrimack	NP	1-01-001
Merrimac	NP	0-00-000
Merrimac	NP-TL	1-01-001
Merrimack	NP-TL	3-02-002
merriment	**NN**	**3-03-003**
Merritt	**prop. noun**	**2-02-002**
Merritt	NP	1-01-001
Merritt	NP-TL	1-01-001

Word	Tag	Frequency
merry	**adjective**	**8-05-007**
merry	JJ	6-03-005
Merry	JJ-TL	2-02-002
merry-go-round	**noun**	**2-02-002**
merry-go-round	NN	1-01-001
Merry-go-round	NN-TL	1-01-001
merrymaking	**JJ**	**1-01-001**
Merton	**prop. noun**	**1-01-001**
Merton's	NP$	1-01-001
merveilleux	**FW-JJ**	**1-01-001**
Mervin	**NP**	**1-01-001**
Merz	**NP**	**2-01-001**
Mesa	**NP**	**1-01-001**
mesenteric	**JJ**	**1-01-001**
mesh	**NN**	**2-01-002**
mesh	**VB**	**2-02-002**
mesmerize	**verb**	**1-01-001**
mesmerized	VBN	1-01-001
mess	**noun**	**21-08-012**
mess	NN	20-08-011
messes	NNS	1-01-001
mess	**verb**	**5-05-005**
mess	VB	2-02-002
messed	VBD	1-01-001
messing	VBG	2-02-002
message	**noun**	**80-14-043**
message	NN	63-13-038
Message	NN-TL	1-01-001
messages	NNS	16-06-009
messenger	**noun**	**12-06-012**
messenger	NN	8-05-008
Messenger	NN-TL	2-02-002
messengers	NNS	1-01-001
Messengers	NNS-TL	1-01-001
messhall	**NN**	**1-01-001**
Messiah	**prop. noun**	**2-02-002**
Messiah	NP	1-01-001
Messiah	NP-TL	1-01-001
messieurs	**FW-NNS**	**1-01-001**
Messina	**prop. noun**	**1-01-001**
Messina	NP	0-00-000
Messina	NP-TL	1-01-001
Messinesi	**NP**	**1-01-001**
Messrs.	**NPS**	**3-03-003**
messy	**JJ**	**3-03-003**
Mesta	**NP**	**1-01-001**
Met	**prop. noun**	**5-01-001**
Met	NP	2-01-001
Met	NP-HL	1-01-001
Mets	NPS	1-01-001
Mets	NPS-TL	1-01-001
metabolic	**JJ**	**2-02-002**
metabolism	**NN**	**2-02-002**
metabolite	**noun**	**7-01-001**
metabolite	NN	6-01-001
metabolites	NNS	1-01-001
metabolize	**verb**	**1-01-001**
metabolized	VBN	1-01-001
metal	**noun**	**68-14-042**
metal	NN	58-13-038
metal	NN-HL	1-01-001
Metal	NN-TL	2-02-002
metals	NNS	6-03-006
Metals	NNS-TL	1-01-001
metal-cleaning	**JJ**	**1-01-001**
metal-hydrido	**NN**	**1-01-001**
metal-tasting	**JJ**	**1-01-001**
metal-working	**JJ**	**1-01-001**
metallic	**JJ**	**9-06-007**
metalsmith	**noun**	**1-01-001**
metalsmiths	NNS	1-01-001
metalworking	**NN**	**2-01-001**
metamorphic	**JJ**	**1-01-001**
metamorphose	**foreign**	**1-01-001**
metamorphose	FW-NN	0-00-000
Metamorphose	FW-NN-TL	1-01-001
metamorphose	**verb**	**2-01-001**
metamorphosed	VBN	2-01-001
metamorphosis	**NN**	**2-01-002**
metaphor	**noun**	**8-03-006**
metaphor	NN	5-03-004
metaphors	NNS	3-01-003
metaphorical	**JJ**	**2-02-002**
metaphosphate	**noun**	**1-01-001**
metaphosphate	NN	0-00-000
metaphosphate	NN-HL	1-01-001
metaphysic	**NN**	**3-01-001**
metaphysical	**JJ**	**16-06-009**
metaphysical	**noun**	**1-01-001**

Word	Tag	Frequency
metaphysical (cont.):		
metaphysicals	NNS	1-01-001
metaphysics	**NN**	**12-02-005**
mete	**verb**	**2-02-002**
meted	VBD	1-01-001
meted	VBN	1-01-001
meteor	**noun**	**7-02-002**
meteor	NN	3-02-002
meteors	NNS	4-01-001
meteoric	**JJ**	**1-01-001**
meteorite	**noun**	**14-01-002**
meteorite	NN	6-01-001
meteorites	NNS	7-01-002
meteorites	NNS-HL	1-01-001
meteoritic	**JJ**	**7-01-002**
meteorological	**adjective**	**4-02-002**
meteorological	JJ	3-02-002
meterological	JJ	1-01-001
meter	**noun**	**18-05-008**
meter	NN	6-03-004
metre	NN	1-01-001
meters	NNS	11-03-005
meter	**verb**	**6-02-004**
metered	VBN	4-02-003
metering	VBG	2-01-001
methacrylate	**NN**	**1-01-001**
method	**noun**	**284-12-136**
method	NN	130-12-081
method	NN-HL	9-02-004
Method	NN-TL	3-02-002
methods	NNS	133-11-089
methods	NNS-HL	7-04-006
Methods	NNS-TL	2-01-002
methode	**foreign**	**1-01-001**
methode	FW-NN	0-00-000
methode	FW-NN-TL	1-01-001
methodical	**JJ**	**4-04-004**
methodically	**RB**	**6-06-006**
Methodism	**NP**	**1-01-001**
Methodist	**adjective**	**9-06-007**
Methodist	JJ	3-03-003
Methodist	JJ-TL	6-04-005
Methodist	**prop. noun**	**5-03-004**
Methodist	NP	2-02-002
Methodist	NP-TL	2-02-002
Methodists	NPS	1-01-001
methodological	**JJ**	**3-02-002**
methodology	**NN**	**1-01-001**
Methuselah	**prop. noun**	**3-03-003**
Methuselah	NP	1-01-001
Methuselah	NP-TL	1-01-001
Methuselahs	NPS	1-01-001
methyl	**NN**	**2-01-002**
meticulous	**JJ**	**1-01-001**
meticulously	**QL**	**2-02-002**
meticulously	**RB**	**4-04-004**
metier	**FW-NN**	**1-01-001**
metis	**FW-NNS**	**1-01-001**
metrazol	**NN**	**1-01-001**
Metrecal	**NP**	**3-01-001**
metrical	**JJ**	**2-01-002**
metrically	**RB**	**1-01-001**
Metro	**NP**	**3-03-003**
metronome	**noun**	**3-02-002**
metronome	NN	1-01-001
Metronome	NN-TL	2-01-001
metropolis	**NN**	**8-02-002**
metropolitan	**adjective**	**36-08-018**
metropolitan	JJ	23-07-011
metropolian	JJ	0-00-000
Metropolian	JJ-TL	1-01-001
metropolitian	JJ	1-01-001
Metropolitan	JJ-TL	11-05-009
metropolitanization	**NN**	**1-01-001**
mettle	**NN**	**2-01-002**
mettlesome	**JJ**	**1-01-001**
mettwurst	**FW-NN**	**1-01-001**
Meuron	**prop. noun**	**1-01-001**
Meurons	NPS	1-01-001
mew	**verb**	**2-02-002**
mew	VB	1-01-001
mewed	VBD	1-01-001
Mexican	**adjective**	**19-07-010**
Mexican	JJ	17-06-009
Mexican	JJ-TL	2-02-002
Mexican	**prop. noun**	**17-03-004**
Mexican	NP	5-03-004
Mexicans	NPS	12-01-001
Mexico	**prop. noun**	**22-09-015**

Word	Tag	Frequency
Mexico (cont.):		
Mexico	NP	6-04-005
Mexico	NP-TL	13-07-009
Mexico's	NP$	0-00-000
Mexico's	NP$-TL	3-03-003
Meyer	**NP**	**6-03-005**
Meyerbeer	**prop. noun**	**1-01-001**
Meyerbeer's	NP$	1-01-001
Meyers	**NP**	**1-01-001**
Meyle	**NP**	**1-01-001**
Meynell	**prop. noun**	**8-01-001**
Meynell	NP	7-01-001
Meynell's	NP$	1-01-001
Meyner	**prop. noun**	**4-01-001**
Meyner	NP	3-01-001
Meyner's	NP$	1-01-001
mezzo	**NN**	**1-01-001**
mi	**FW-PPO**	**1-01-001**
mi	**noun**	**1-01-001**
mi	NN	0-00-000
Mi	NN-TL	1-01-001
Mi	**NP**	**1-01-001**
Miami	**prop. noun**	**25-04-010**
Miami	NP	8-04-007
Miami	NP-HL	3-02-002
Miami	NP-TL	11-04-006
Miami's	NP$	3-02-002
Miantonomi	**NP**	**2-01-001**
miasmal	**JJ**	**1-01-001**
mica	**NN**	**1-01-001**
Micawber	**NP**	**1-01-001**
micelle	**noun**	**11-01-001**
micelle	NN	6-01-001
micelles	NNS	5-01-001
Michael	**prop. noun**	**13-06-011**
Michael	NP	11-05-010
Michael's	NP$	0-00-000
Michael's	NP$-TL	2-01-001
Michaels	**NP**	**1-01-001**
Michaelson	**NP**	**1-01-001**
Michelangelo	**prop. noun**	**21-03-003**
Michelangelo	NP	20-03-003
Michelangelo's	NP$	1-01-001
Michelson	**NP**	**2-01-001**
Michigan	**prop. noun**	**25-08-016**
Michigan	NP	16-07-011
Mich.	NP	3-02-002
Mich.	NP-HL	1-01-001
Michigan	NP-TL	5-04-004
Michilimackinac	**NP**	**1-01-001**
Mick	**NP**	**1-01-001**
Mickey	**prop. noun**	**32-04-006**
Mickey	NP	29-04-006
Mickey's	NP$	3-02-002
Mickie	**NP**	**4-01-001**
micro-microcurie	**NN**	**1-01-001**
microanalysis	**NN**	**1-01-001**
microbial	**JJ**	**1-01-001**
microchemistry	**NN**	**1-01-001**
microcosm	**NN**	**3-03-003**
microcytochemistry	**NN**	**1-01-001**
microfilm	**NN**	**2-02-002**
microfossil	**noun**	**1-01-001**
microfossils	NNS	1-01-001
micrometeorite	**noun**	**13-01-001**
micrometeorite	NN	6-01-001
micrometeorite	NN-HL	2-01-001
micrometeorites	NNS	5-01-001
micrometeoritic	**JJ**	**2-01-001**
micrometer	**noun**	**3-02-002**
micrometer	NN	2-02-002
micrometers	NNS	1-01-001
micron	**noun**	**5-01-003**
microns	NNS	5-01-003
microorganism	**noun**	**13-02-003**
microorganism	NN	1-01-001
microorganisms	NNS	12-02-003
microphone	**noun**	**8-05-006**
microphone	NN	4-03-004
microphones	NNS	4-03-003
microphoning	**NN**	**1-01-001**
microscope	**noun**	**9-05-005**
microscope	NN	8-04-004
microscopes	NNS	1-01-001
microscopic	**adjective**	**8-03-005**
microscopic	JJ	7-03-005
microscopic	JJ-HL	1-01-001
microscopical	**JJ**	**1-01-001**
microscopically	**RB**	**6-01-001**
microscopy	**noun**	**4-03-003**
microscopy	NN	2-02-002
microscopy	NN-HL	2-02-002
microsecond	**noun**	**4-02-002**
microseconds	NNS	4-02-002
microsomal	**JJ**	**1-01-001**
microwave	**noun**	**3-01-002**
microwave	NN	2-01-001
microwaves	NNS	1-01-001
mid	**JJ**	**2-02-002**
mid-April	**NP**	**1-01-001**
Mid-Atlantic	**NP**	**1-01-001**
mid-century	**NN**	**1-01-001**
mid-continent	**NN**	**1-01-001**
mid-fifties	**NNS**	**2-01-002**
mid-flight	**NN**	**1-01-001**
mid-July	**NP**	**1-01-001**
mid-June	**NP**	**3-02-003**
mid-October	**NP**	**2-01-001**
mid-range	**NN**	**1-01-001**
mid-section	**NN**	**1-01-001**
mid-September	**NP**	**3-03-003**
mid-shimmy	**NN**	**1-01-001**
mid-thirties	**NNS**	**3-02-003**
mid-twentieth	**OD**	**3-02-003**
mid-twentieth-century	**NN**	**1-01-001**
mid-Victorian	**JJ**	**1-01-001**
mid-watch	**NN**	**1-01-001**
mid-1890's	**NNS**	**1-01-001**
mid-19th	**OD**	**1-01-001**
mid-1948	**CD**	**1-01-001**
mid-1950's	**NNS**	**1-01-001**
mid-1958	**CD**	**1-01-001**
mid-1960	**CD**	**1-01-001**
mid-1960's	**NNS**	**1-01-001**
mid-1963	**CD**	**1-01-001**
midair	**noun**	**3-03-003**
midair	NN	2-02-002
mid-air	NN	1-01-001
Midas	**prop. noun**	**1-01-001**
Midas	NP	0-00-000
Midas	NP-TL	1-01-001
midday	**NN**	**5-03-005**
middle	**adjective**	**76-11-044**
middle	JJ	47-09-027
middle-	JJ	4-01-003
middle	JJ-HL	1-01-001
Middle	JJ-TL	24-08-019
middle	**noun**	**47-13-041**
middle	NN	46-13-040
middles	NNS	1-01-001
middle-age	**NN**	**2-02-002**
middle-aged	**adjective**	**8-07-007**
middle-aged	JJ	7-06-006
middle-aged	JJ-HL	1-01-001
middle-class	**NN**	**22-03-005**
Middle-Eastern	**JJ**	**1-01-001**
middle-Gaelic	**NP**	**1-01-001**
middle-range	**NN**	**1-01-001**
middle-school	**NN**	**1-01-001**
middle-sized	**JJ**	**1-01-001**
Middle-South	**adjective**	**3-01-001**
Middle-South	JJ	1-01-001
Middle-South	JJ-TL	2-01-001
Middletown	**NP**	**3-01-002**
Midge	**NP**	**4-02-002**
Midi	**NP**	**1-01-001**
midmorning	**NN**	**1-01-001**
midnight	**NN**	**23-08-019**
midpoint	**NN**	**1-01-001**
midshipman	**noun**	**4-01-001**
midshipman	NN	0-00-000
Midshipman	NN-TL	2-01-001
midshipmen	NNS	2-01-001
midst	**noun**	**20-10-019**
midst	NN	19-10-018
midsts	NNS	1-01-001
midstream	**NN**	**1-01-001**
midsummer	**NN**	**3-03-003**
midway	**NN**	**1-01-001**
midway	**QL**	**1-01-001**
midway	**RB**	**3-03-003**
Midway	**NP**	**3-02-002**
midweek	**noun**	**3-03-003**
midweek	NN	2-02-002
mid-week	NN	1-01-001
Midwest	**prop. noun**	**11-05-005**
Midwest	NP	6-03-003
Midwest	NP-HL	3-02-002

Midwest (cont.):		
Midwest	NP-TL	2-01-001
midwestern	**adjective**	**6-04-005**
midwestern	JJ	4-02-003
Midwestern	JJ-TL	2-02-002
midwesterner	**noun**	**1-01-001**
midwesterners	NNS	0-00-000
Midwesterners	NNS-TL	1-01-001
midwife	**NN**	**1-01-001**
Midwood	**prop. noun**	**1-01-001**
Midwood	NP	0-00-000
Midwood	NP-TL	1-01-001
mien	**NN**	**1-01-001**
miff	**verb**	**1-01-001**
miffed	VBN	1-01-001
Mig	**prop. noun**	**2-01-001**
Mig	NP	1-01-001
Migs	NPS	1-01-001
might	**modal aux.**	**660-15-308**
might	MD	658-15-308
maht	MD	1-01-001
might	MD-HL	1-01-001
might	**noun**	**13-06-012**
might	NN	12-06-012
Might	NN-TL	1-01-001
mightiest	**JJT**	**1-01-001**
mightily	**RB**	**1-01-001**
mighty	**adjective**	**16-08-015**
mighty	JJ	14-07-013
Mighty	JJ-TL	2-02-002
mighty	**QL**	**13-08-012**
Miglia	**NP**	**1-01-001**
Mignon	**NP**	**1-01-001**
migrant	**adjective**	**3-02-002**
migrant	JJ	2-01-001
Migrant	JJ-TL	1-01-001
migrant	**noun**	**2-02-002**
migrants	NNS	2-02-002
migrate	**verb**	**5-04-005**
migrate	VB	1-01-001
migrates	VBZ	1-01-001
migrated	VBD	1-01-001
migrated	VBN	1-01-001
migrating	VBG	1-01-001
migration	**NN**	**5-04-004**
migratory	**JJ**	**3-02-002**
Miguel	**NP**	**2-02-002**
Mij	**NP**	**3-01-001**
Mijbil	**prop. noun**	**5-01-001**
Mijbil	NP	3-01-001
Mijbil's	NP$	2-01-001
mike	**NN**	**1-01-001**
Mike	**prop. noun**	**97-07-010**
Mike	NP	88-07-010
Mike	NP-TL	2-01-001
Mike's	NP$	7-02-002
Mikeen	**NP**	**1-01-001**
Mikhail	**NP**	**1-01-001**
Mikoyan	**NP**	**1-01-001**
mil.	**NNS**	**1-01-001**
Milan	**NP**	**1-01-001**
Milanoff	**NP**	**1-01-001**
Milbankes	**NP**	**1-01-001**
Milcote	**NP**	**2-01-001**
mild	**JJ**	**14-09-014**
mild-mannered	**JJ**	**2-02-002**
mild-voiced	**JJ**	**1-01-001**
mild-winter	**NN**	**1-01-001**
milder	**JJR**	**3-02-003**
mildew	**NN**	**1-01-001**
mildly	**QL**	**2-02-002**
mildly	**RB**	**5-04-005**
mile	**noun**	**217-15-097**
mile	NN	42-11-023
Mile	NN-TL	6-03-004
miles	NNS	169-15-080
mile-long	**JJ**	**1-01-001**
mileage	**noun**	**15-05-005**
mileage	NN	14-05-005
mileage	NN-HL	1-01-001
Milenoff	**prop. noun**	**1-01-001**
Milenoff	NP	0-00-000
Milenoff	NP-TL	1-01-001
Miles	**prop. noun**	**4-02-004**
Miles	NP	3-02-003
Miles	NP-TL	1-01-001
milestone	**noun**	**5-04-005**
milestone	NN	4-03-004
milestones	NNS	1-01-001
Milhaud	**prop. noun**	**2-01-001**
Milhaud	NP	1-01-001
Milhaud's	NP$	1-01-001
miliaris	**noun**	**1-01-001**
miliaris	NN	0-00-000
miliaris	NN-TL	1-01-001
milieu	**NN**	**4-02-003**
militant	**JJ**	**7-04-006**
militant	**NN**	**1-01-001**
militantly	**RB**	**1-01-001**
militarily	**RB**	**3-02-003**
militarism	**noun**	**3-01-001**
militarism	NN	2-01-001
militarism	NN-HL	1-01-001
militarist	**noun**	**3-02-002**
militarist	NN	2-02-002
militarist's	NN$	1-01-001
military	**adjective**	**199-09-070**
military	JJ	186-09-065
military	JJ-HL	3-01-002
Military	JJ-TL	10-05-007
military	**NN**	**13-06-010**
military-medical	**JJ**	**1-01-001**
militate	**verb**	**1-01-001**
militated	VBN	1-01-001
militia	**noun**	**11-02-005**
militia	NN	10-02-005
militia	NNS	0-00-000
Militia	NNS-TL	1-01-001
milk	**noun**	**49-08-026**
milk	NN	48-08-025
Milk	NN-TL	1-01-001
milk	**verb**	**2-02-002**
milks	VBZ	2-02-002
milky	**adjective**	**2-02-002**
milky	JJ	0-00-000
Milky	JJ-TL	2-02-002
mill	**noun**	**24-08-013**
mill	NN	9-05-005
Mill	NN-TL	1-01-001
mills	NNS	11-04-007
Mills	NNS-TL	3-01-001
mill	**verb**	**16-07-009**
milling	VBG	15-07-009
Milling	VBG-TL	1-01-001
Mill	**NP**	**1-01-001**
mill-pond	**NN**	**1-01-001**
mill-wheel	**NN**	**1-01-001**
Millay	**prop. noun**	**3-01-001**
Millay	NP	1-01-001
Millay's	NP$	2-01-001
Mille	**NP**	**2-02-002**
Milledgeville	**prop. noun**	**1-01-001**
Milledgeville	NP	0-00-000
Milledgeville	NP-TL	1-01-001
millenarianism	**NN**	**1-01-001**
millennium	**noun**	**8-04-008**
millennium	NN	3-02-003
millenium	NN	1-01-001
Millennium	NN-TL	1-01-001
millennia	NNS	3-02-003
Miller	**prop. noun**	**28-08-015**
Miller	NP	20-08-012
Miller	NP-TL	2-01-001
Miller's	NP$	6-04-004
milliampere/cell	**noun**	**1-01-001**
milliamperes/cell	NNS	1-01-001
millidegree	**noun**	**6-01-001**
millidegree	NN	3-01-001
millidegrees	NNS	3-01-001
Millie	**NP**	**5-02-002**
milligram	**noun**	**37-03-004**
milligram	NN	5-01-001
mg.	NN	1-01-001
milligrams	NNS	21-02-002
mg.	NNS	10-01-001
milliliter	**noun**	**3-01-002**
milliliter	NN	2-01-001
ml.	NN	1-01-001
millimeter	**noun**	**13-05-007**
millimeter	NN	3-03-003
mm.	NN	6-03-003
millimeters	NNS	0-00-000
mm.	NNS	4-02-003
millinery	**NN**	**1-01-001**
milling	**NN**	**2-02-002**
million	**CD**	**204-14-073**
million	**noun**	**49-12-036**
millions	NNS	49-12-036

Word	Tag	Count
millionaire	**noun**	**3-03-003**
millionaire	NN	2-02-002
millionaires	NNS	1-01-001
millivoltmeter	**NN**	**1-01-001**
Mills	**prop. noun**	**20-06-010**
Mills	NP	15-05-008
Mills	NP-TL	3-03-003
Mills's	NP$	2-01-001
millstone	**noun**	**1-01-001**
millstone	NN	0-00-000
Millstone	NN-TL	1-01-001
Milman	**NP**	**1-01-001**
milord	**FW-NN**	**2-01-001**
milquetoast	**noun**	**2-02-002**
milquetoast	NN	1-01-001
milquetoasts	NNS	0-00-000
Milquetoasts	NNS-TL	1-01-001
Milstein	**NP**	**4-01-001**
Milt	**NP**	**2-01-002**
Milties	**NP**	**1-01-001**
Milton	**prop. noun**	**23-02-006**
Milton	NP	17-02-005
Milton's	NP$	6-01-002
Miltonic	**JJ**	**1-01-001**
Milwaukee	**prop. noun**	**10-03-006**
Milwaukee	NP	9-03-006
Milwaukee's	NP$	1-01-001
mimesis	**noun**	**12-01-001**
mimesis	NN	11-01-001
Mimesis	NN-TL	1-01-001
mimetic	**JJ**	**3-01-001**
mimetically	**RB**	**1-01-001**
Mimi	**NP**	**1-01-001**
Mimieux	**NP**	**1-01-001**
minaret	**noun**	**4-01-001**
minarets	NNS	4-01-001
minber	**FW-NN**	**1-01-001**
mince	**verb**	**8-03-004**
mince	VB	1-01-001
minced	VBN	6-01-002
mincing	VBG	1-01-001
mind	**noun**	**350-15-191**
mind	NN	288-15-165
mind's	NN$	6-06-006
minds	NNS	56-13-046
mind	**verb**	**41-11-034**
mind	VB	38-10-032
minded	VBD	1-01-001
minded	VBN	2-02-002
Mindanao	**NP**	**1-01-001**
mindful	**JJ**	**5-05-005**
mindless	**JJ**	**3-03-003**
mine	**noun**	**49-09-018**
mine	NN	20-07-011
Mine	NN-TL	1-01-001
mines	NNS	28-08-011
mine	**verb**	**12-07-009**
mined	VBD	1-01-001
mined	VBN	2-01-001
mining	VBG	9-06-007
mine-safety	**NN**	**1-01-001**
miner	**noun**	**6-03-003**
miner	NN	1-01-001
miners	NNS	4-02-002
Miners	NNS-TL	1-01-001
mineral	**noun**	**26-08-015**
mineral	NN	11-06-009
Mineral	NN-TL	1-01-001
minerals	NNS	11-06-008
minerals	NNS-HL	1-01-001
Minerals	NNS-TL	2-01-001
mineral-rich	**JJ**	**1-01-001**
mineralize	**verb**	**1-01-001**
mineralized	VBN	1-01-001
mineralogical	**JJ**	**2-01-001**
mineralogy	**noun**	**6-02-002**
mineralogy	NN	1-01-001
Mineralogy	NN-TL	4-01-001
mineralogies	NNS	0-00-000
Mineralogies	NNS-TL	1-01-001
Minerva	**NP**	**2-01-001**
mingle	**verb**	**12-08-012**
mingle	VB	2-02-002
mingles	VBZ	1-01-001
mingled	VBD	3-03-003
mingled	VBN	5-04-005
mingling	VBG	1-01-001
Mingus	**NP**	**1-01-001**
Minh	**NP**	**1-01-001**

Word	Tag	Count
miniature	**JJ**	**4-03-004**
miniature	**noun**	**6-04-004**
miniature	NN	5-03-003
miniatures	NNS	1-01-001
minify	**verb**	**1-01-001**
minifying	VBG	1-01-001
minimal	**JJ**	**27-04-009**
minimally	**RB**	**1-01-001**
minimize	**verb**	**25-06-022**
minimize	VB	16-05-014
minimizes	VBZ	1-01-001
minimized	VBD	2-02-002
minimized	VBN	3-03-003
minimizing	VBG	3-03-003
minimum	**JJ**	**38-06-022**
minimum	**NN**	**30-09-028**
mining	**NN**	**1-01-001**
Mining	**NP**	**2-01-001**
minister	**noun**	**73-11-037**
minister	NN	45-11-020
minister	NN-HL	1-01-001
Minister	NN-TL	15-05-010
minister's	NN$	1-01-001
ministers	NNS	8-04-007
Ministers	NNS-TL	3-03-003
minister	**verb**	**5-03-003**
ministered	VBD	2-02-002
ministering	VBG	3-02-002
ministerial	**JJ**	**2-02-002**
ministration	**noun**	**2-02-002**
ministrations	NNS	2-02-002
ministry	**noun**	**16-05-011**
ministry	NN	7-03-006
Ministry	NN-TL	6-03-003
ministries	NNS	3-02-002
Miniver	**NP**	**1-01-001**
mink	**NN**	**5-04-005**
Minks	**NP**	**1-01-001**
Minkus	**NP**	**2-01-002**
Minneapolis	**prop. noun**	**10-05-008**
Minneapolis	NP	8-05-006
Minneapolis	NP-HL	2-02-002
Minnesota	**prop. noun**	**17-07-012**
Minnesota	NP	9-06-006
Minn.	NP	2-01-001
Minnesota	NP-TL	4-04-004
Minnesota's	NP$	1-01-001
Minnesota's	NP$-TL	1-01-001
Minnett	**NP**	**3-01-001**
Minnie	**NP**	**3-02-003**
Minns	**NP**	**1-01-001**
Minoan-Mycenaean	**JJ**	**1-01-001**
minor	**adjective**	**51-13-045**
minor	JJ	42-13-039
Minor	JJ-TL	7-03-005
minor	JJ-TL	2-01-001
minor	**noun**	**10-05-006**
minor	NN	5-03-003
minors	NNS	3-03-003
minors	NNS-HL	2-01-001
Minor	**NP**	**2-02-002**
minority	**noun**	**25-08-019**
minority	NN	20-06-015
minorities	NNS	5-05-005
Minoso	**NP**	**1-01-001**
Minot	**NP**	**1-01-001**
minstrel	**noun**	**3-02-002**
minstrel	NN	2-01-001
minstrels	NNS	1-01-001
mint	**NN**	**7-06-006**
minter	**NN**	**1-01-001**
minuet	**NN**	**2-02-002**
minus	**CC**	**2-02-002**
minus	**FW-QL**	**1-01-001**
minus	**IN**	**4-02-004**
minus	**NN**	**1-01-001**
minuscule	**adjective**	**1-01-001**
minuscule	JJ	0-00-000
miniscule	JJ	1-01-001
minute	**JJ**	**11-06-011**
minute	**noun**	**242-15-127**
minute	NN	43-12-039
min.	NN	1-01-001
Minute	NN-TL	1-01-001
minute's	NN$	1-01-001
minutes	NNS	193-14-099
Minutes	NNS-TL	3-02-002
minutely	**RB**	**1-01-001**
Minuteman	**prop. noun**	**8-03-004**

Word	Tag	Frequency
Minuteman (cont.):		
Minuteman	NP	3-02-003
Minutemen	NPS	5-01-001
minutiae	**NNS**	**1-01-001**
mio	**foreign**	**1-01-001**
mio	FW-PP$	0-00-000
Mio	FW-PP$-TL	1-01-001
Mira	**NP**	**1-01-001**
miracle	**noun**	**26-09-020**
miracle	NN	15-08-013
Miracle	NN-TL	3-02-002
miracles	NNS	8-06-007
miraculous	**adjective**	**4-03-004**
miraculous	JJ	3-02-003
miraculous	JJ-HL	1-01-001
miraculously	**RB**	**3-01-003**
Miranda	**prop. noun**	**4-03-003**
Miranda	NP	3-03-003
Miranda's	NP$	1-01-001
Miriam	**prop. noun**	**32-01-001**
Miriam	NP	30-01-001
Miriam's	NP$	2-01-001
Miriani	**prop. noun**	**1-01-001**
Miriani's	NP$	1-01-001
Miro	**NP**	**1-01-001**
mirror	**noun**	**27-10-021**
mirror	NN	26-09-020
mirrors	NNS	1-01-001
mirror	**verb**	**5-02-005**
mirror	VB	1-01-001
mirrors	VBZ	3-01-003
mirrored	VBN	1-01-001
Mirsky	**prop. noun**	**1-01-001**
Mirsky's	NP$	1-01-001
mirth	**NN**	**2-02-002**
mirthless	**JJ**	**1-01-001**
mis-read	**verb**	**1-01-001**
mis-reading	VBG	1-01-001
misalignment	**NN**	**2-01-001**
misanthrope	**NN**	**1-01-001**
misbegotten	**pl. noun**	**1-01-001**
misbegotten	NNS	0-00-000
Misbegotten	NNS-TL	1-01-001
misbehavior	**NN**	**3-01-001**
misbrand	**verb**	**1-01-001**
misbranded	VBN	1-01-001
miscalculate	**verb**	**1-01-001**
miscalculated	VBD	1-01-001
miscalculation	**noun**	**3-03-003**
miscalculation	NN	2-02-002
miscalculations	NNS	1-01-001
miscarry	**verb**	**1-01-001**
miscarried	VBN	1-01-001
miscegenation	**NN**	**1-01-001**
miscellaneous	**JJ**	**10-05-008**
miscellany	**noun**	**3-03-003**
miscellany	NN	1-01-001
Miscellany	NN-TL	1-01-001
miscellanies	NNS	1-01-001
Mischa	**NP**	**2-01-001**
mischief	**NN**	**5-03-005**
mischievous	**JJ**	**3-03-003**
misconception	**noun**	**6-04-005**
misconception	NN	4-03-004
misconceptions	NNS	2-02-002
misconstruction	**noun**	**2-02-002**
misconstruction	NN	1-01-001
misconstructions	NNS	1-01-001
misconstrue	**verb**	**2-02-002**
misconstrued	VBD	1-01-001
misconstrued	VBN	1-01-001
miscount	**NN**	**1-01-001**
miscreant	**noun**	**2-01-001**
miscreant	NN	1-01-001
miscreants	NNS	1-01-001
misdeed	**noun**	**5-03-004**
misdeeds	NNS	5-03-004
misdemeanant	**noun**	**1-01-001**
misdemeanants	NNS	1-01-001
misdemeanor	**NN**	**2-02-002**
misdirector	**noun**	**1-01-001**
misdirectors	NNS	1-01-001
miserable	**JJ**	**13-07-011**
miserably	**RB**	**3-02-003**
misery	**noun**	**17-07-015**
misery	NN	15-06-014
miseries	NNS	2-02-002
Mises	**NP**	**1-01-001**
misfire	**verb**	**1-01-001**
misfire (cont.):		
misfired	VBN	1-01-001
misfortune	**noun**	**11-06-011**
misfortune	NN	10-06-010
misfortunes	NNS	1-01-001
misgauge	**verb**	**1-01-001**
misgauged	VBN	1-01-001
misgiving	**noun**	**5-05-005**
misgivings	NNS	5-05-005
misguide	**verb**	**2-02-002**
misguided	VBN	2-02-002
mishap	**NN**	**4-04-004**
misinformation	**NN**	**1-01-001**
misinterpret	**verb**	**4-03-004**
misinterpret	VB	2-02-002
misinterpreted	VBN	2-02-002
misinterpretation	**NN**	**1-01-001**
misinterpreter	**noun**	**1-01-001**
misinterpreters	NNS	1-01-001
misjudge	**verb**	**2-02-002**
misjudged	VBD	1-01-001
misjudged	VBN	1-01-001
mislead	**verb**	**12-06-011**
misleads	VBZ	1-01-001
misled	VBD	1-01-001
misled	VBN	2-02-002
misleading	VBG	8-04-007
misleading	**JJ**	**2-02-002**
mismanage	**verb**	**1-01-001**
mismanaged	VBD	1-01-001
misname	**verb**	**1-01-001**
misnamed	VBN	1-01-001
misnomer	**NN**	**1-01-001**
miso	**FW-NN**	**1-01-001**
misogynist	**NN**	**1-01-001**
misperceive	**verb**	**1-01-001**
misperceives	VBZ	1-01-001
misplace	**verb**	**8-05-005**
misplaced	VBN	7-04-004
misplacing	VBG	1-01-001
misplacement	**noun**	**1-01-001**
misplacements	NNS	1-01-001
mispronunciation	**NN**	**1-01-001**
misquote	**verb**	**1-01-001**
misquoted	VBN	1-01-001
misrelate	**verb**	**1-01-001**
misrelated	VBN	1-01-001
misrepresent	**verb**	**3-03-003**
misrepresents	VBZ	2-02-002
misrepresenting	VBG	1-01-001
misrepresentation	**noun**	**3-02-003**
misrepresentation	NN	2-02-002
misrepresentations	NNS	1-01-001
miss	**noun**	**5-05-005**
miss	NN	1-01-001
Miss	NN-TL	2-02-002
misses	NNS	1-01-001
Misses	NNS-TL	1-01-001
miss	**verb**	**95-13-077**
miss	VB	20-10-017
misses	VBZ	3-02-002
missed	VBD	17-07-015
missed	VBN	22-11-020
missed	VBN-HL	1-01-001
missing	VBG	32-12-027
Miss	**prop. noun**	**233-13-057**
Miss	NP	228-13-057
Miss	NP-TL	5-01-001
missa	**foreign**	**1-01-001**
missa	FW-NN	0-00-000
Missa	FW-NN-TL	1-01-001
Missail	**NP**	**3-01-001**
misshapen	**JJ**	**2-02-002**
missile	**noun**	**81-10-020**
missile	NN	46-09-014
Missile	NN-TL	2-02-002
missile's	NN$	1-01-001
missiles	NNS	31-07-011
Missiles	NNS-TL	1-01-001
missile-type	**JJ**	**1-01-001**
missing	**NN**	**1-01-001**
mission	**noun**	**94-15-052**
mission	NN	64-12-035
mission	NN-HL	2-02-002
Mission	NN-TL	12-08-010
missions	NNS	15-09-011
Missions	NNS-TL	1-01-001
missionary	**JJ**	**4-02-002**
missionary	**noun**	**23-06-009**

Word	Tag	Frequency
missionary (cont.):		
missionary	NN	10-04-005
missionary	NN-HL	1-01-001
Missionary	NN-TL	2-02-002
missionaries	NNS	10-04-004
Mississippi	**prop. noun**	**47-09-024**
Mississippi	NP	32-08-018
Miss.	NP	4-02-003
Miss.	NP-HL	1-01-001
Mississippi	NP-HL	1-01-001
Mississippi	NP-TL	6-05-005
Mississippi's	NP$	3-02-003
Mississippian	**prop. noun**	**1-01-001**
Mississippians	NPS	1-01-001
missive	**NN**	**1-01-001**
Missoula	**NP**	**1-01-001**
Missouri	**prop. noun**	**33-09-023**
Missouri	NP	14-07-011
Mo.	NP	6-03-005
Mo.	NP-HL	1-01-001
Mo.	NP-TL	1-01-001
Missouri	NP-TL	7-05-005
Missouri's	NP$	4-03-003
Missouri-Illinois	**NP**	**1-01-001**
misstep	**NN**	**2-02-002**
missy	**NN**	**1-01-001**
Missy	**NP**	**1-01-001**
mist	**noun**	**16-07-014**
mist	NN	11-06-010
Mist	NN-TL	3-02-002
mists	NNS	2-02-002
mist	**verb**	**1-01-001**
misted	VBD	1-01-001
mist-like	**JJ**	**1-01-001**
mistake	**noun**	**45-13-039**
mistake	NN	30-12-027
mistakes	NNS	15-07-014
mistake	**verb**	**24-11-022**
mistake	VB	4-03-004
mistakes	VBZ	1-01-001
mistook	VBD	1-01-001
mistaken	VBN	17-11-016
mistaking	VBG	1-01-001
mistakenly	**RB**	**3-02-003**
mistaking	**NN**	**1-01-001**
Mister	**prop. noun**	**857-15-155**
Mister	NP	5-05-005
Mis-ter	NP	2-01-001
mister	NP	3-02-002
Mr.	NP	833-15-148
Mr.	NP-HL	11-02-005
Mr.	NP-TL	1-01-001
Mister	NP-TL	2-01-001
mistletoe	**NN**	**1-01-001**
mistress	**NN**	**5-04-005**
mistrial	**NN**	**2-01-002**
mistrust	**NN**	**4-03-003**
mistrust	**verb**	**2-01-001**
mistrusted	VBD	2-01-001
misty	**JJ**	**4-04-004**
Misty	**NP**	**1-01-001**
misty-eyed	**JJ**	**1-01-001**
misunderstand	**verb**	**12-07-011**
misunderstand	VB	1-01-001
misunderstood	VBD	1-01-001
misunderstood	VBN	5-04-005
misunderstanding	VBG	5-04-005
misunderstander	**noun**	**1-01-001**
misunderstanders	NNS	1-01-001
misunderstanding	**noun**	**7-04-007**
misunderstanding	NN	6-04-006
misunderstandings	NNS	1-01-001
misuse	**NN**	**3-02-003**
misuse	**VB**	**2-02-002**
miswrite	**verb**	**1-01-001**
miswritten	VBN	1-01-001
Mitch	**NP**	**2-01-001**
Mitchell	**prop. noun**	**27-06-011**
Mitchell	NP	25-05-009
Mitchell	NP-TL	1-01-001
Mitchell's	NP$	1-01-001
Mite	**NP**	**1-01-001**
mite-box	**NN**	**1-01-001**
miter	**VB**	**1-01-001**
mitigate	**verb**	**5-05-005**
mitigate	VB	1-01-001
mitigates	VBZ	2-02-002
mitigating	VBG	2-02-002
mitigation	**NN**	**1-01-001**
mitral	**JJ**	**1-01-001**
mitre	**NN**	**1-01-001**
Mitropoulos	**NP**	**2-01-001**
mitten	**noun**	**2-02-002**
mittens	NNS	2-02-002
Mityukh	**NP**	**5-01-001**
miuchi	**FW-VB**	**1-01-001**
mix	**NN**	**2-02-002**
mix	**verb**	**56-09-035**
mix	VB	11-06-011
mixed	VBD	1-01-001
mixed	VBN	35-08-023
Mixed	VBN-NC	1-01-001
mixing	VBG	8-04-007
mixer	**noun**	**3-02-002**
mixer	NN	2-01-001
mixers	NNS	1-01-001
mixing	**NN**	**2-01-001**
mixture	**noun**	**34-08-022**
mixture	NN	30-08-022
mixtures	NNS	4-01-003
Miyagi	**prop. noun**	**2-01-001**
Miyagi	NP	1-01-001
Miyagi	NP-TL	1-01-001
Mizell	**NP**	**3-01-001**
mmm	**UH**	**2-01-001**
mmmm	**UH**	**1-01-001**
moan	**verb**	**4-03-004**
moan	VB	1-01-001
moans	VBZ	1-01-001
moaned	VBD	2-01-002
mob	**noun**	**15-08-011**
mob	NN	10-06-007
mob's	NN$	1-01-001
mobs	NNS	4-02-003
mobcap	**noun**	**1-01-001**
mobcaps	NNS	1-01-001
mobile	**JJ**	**26-09-011**
mobile	**noun**	**1-01-001**
mobile	NN	0-00-000
Mobile	NN-TL	1-01-001
Mobile	**NP**	**17-02-002**
mobility	**NN**	**8-04-006**
mobilization	**noun**	**5-04-005**
mobilization	NN	3-03-003
Mobilization	NN-TL	2-01-002
mobilize	**verb**	**9-04-007**
mobilize	VB	2-01-002
mobilized	VBN	4-03-004
mobilizing	VBG	2-01-001
mobilizing	VBG-HL	1-01-001
mobster	**noun**	**1-01-001**
mobsters	NNS	1-01-001
Mobutu	**NP**	**2-01-001**
moccasin	**noun**	**3-03-003**
moccasin	NN	0-00-000
Moccasin	NN-TL	1-01-001
moccasins	NNS	2-02-002
mock	**JJ**	**5-04-005**
mock	**verb**	**11-07-009**
mock	VB	3-03-003
mocked	VBD	1-01-001
mocked	VBN	2-02-002
mocking	VBG	4-04-004
Mocking	VBG-TL	1-01-001
mockery	**NN**	**2-02-002**
mockingly	**RB**	**1-01-001**
modal	**JJ**	**3-01-003**
modality	**NN**	**1-01-001**
mode	**FW-NN**	**1-01-001**
mode	**noun**	**28-04-015**
mode	NN	20-04-010
modes	NNS	8-03-007
model	**JJ**	**3-03-003**
model	**noun**	**120-13-045**
model	NN	57-11-025
model	NN-HL	2-01-001
Model	NN-TL	14-03-004
models	NNS	47-10-025
model	**verb**	**5-05-005**
model	VB	1-01-001
modeled	VBD	1-01-001
modeled	VBN	2-02-002
modeling	VBG	1-01-001
moderate	**JJ**	**22-09-017**
moderate	**noun**	**3-02-003**
moderates	NNS	3-02-003
moderate	**verb**	**2-02-002**
moderates	VBZ	1-01-001

Word	Tag	Frequency
moderate (cont.):		
moderating	VBG	1-01-001
moderate-income	**NN**	**1-01-001**
moderately	**QL**	**5-04-005**
moderately	**RB**	**1-01-001**
moderation	**NN**	**3-02-003**
moderator	**NN**	**4-03-003**
modern	**adjective**	**198-15-116**
modern	JJ	191-15-114
modern	JJ-HL	1-01-001
Modern	JJ-TL	6-05-006
modern	**noun**	**3-03-003**
moderns	NNS	3-03-003
modern-dance	**NN**	**1-01-001**
modernism	**NN**	**2-02-002**
modernist	**noun**	**2-02-002**
modernists	NNS	2-02-002
modernistic	**JJ**	**1-01-001**
modernity	**NN**	**6-03-003**
modernization	**NN**	**13-04-006**
modernize	**verb**	**7-03-004**
modernize	VB	1-01-001
modernized	VBD	1-01-001
modernized	VBN	2-02-002
modernizing	VBG	2-02-002
modernizing	VBG-HL	1-01-001
modernizing	**NN**	**1-01-001**
modest	**adjective**	**29-10-026**
modest	JJ	27-10-026
modest	JJ-HL	2-01-002
modestly	**RB**	**3-03-003**
modesty	**NN**	**4-04-004**
modicum	**NN**	**2-02-002**
modification	**noun**	**10-05-010**
modification	NN	4-03-004
modifications	NNS	6-04-006
modifier	**noun**	**7-03-003**
modifier	NN	5-03-003
modifiers	NNS	2-01-001
modify	**verb**	**25-06-021**
modify	VB	6-04-005
modifies	VBZ	2-02-002
modified	VBN	11-04-010
modified	VBN-HL	2-02-002
modifying	VBG	4-01-003
Modigliani	**NP**	**1-01-001**
modish	**JJ**	**1-01-001**
modular	**adjective**	**4-02-003**
modular	JJ	3-01-002
Modular	JJ-TL	1-01-001
modulate	**verb**	**1-01-001**
modulated	VBN	1-01-001
modulation	**noun**	**5-03-003**
modulation	NN	4-02-002
modulations	NNS	1-01-001
module	**noun**	**1-01-001**
modules	NNS	1-01-001
modus	**FW-NN**	**1-01-001**
Moffett	**NP**	**1-01-001**
Mohammedanism	**NP**	**1-01-001**
moi	**FW-PPO**	**1-01-001**
Moineau	**NP**	**1-01-001**
moire	**NN**	**1-01-001**
Moise	**NP**	**4-02-002**
Moiseyev	**prop. noun**	**2-01-001**
Moiseyev	NP	1-01-001
Moiseyev	NP-TL	1-01-001
Moiseyeva	**NP**	**2-01-001**
moist	**JJ**	**11-07-010**
moisten	**verb**	**5-03-004**
moisten	VB	2-02-002
moistened	VBD	1-01-001
moistened	VBN	1-01-001
moistening	VBG	1-01-001
moisture	**NN**	**10-05-008**
molal	**JJ**	**2-01-001**
molar	**noun**	**2-01-001**
molar	NN	1-01-001
molars	NNS	1-01-001
Molard	**prop. noun**	**1-01-001**
Molard	NP	0-00-000
Molard	NP-TL	1-01-001
molasses	**NN**	**1-01-001**
mold	**noun**	**50-05-009**
mold	NN	43-05-007
molds	NNS	7-02-004
mold	**verb**	**22-06-009**
mold	VB	2-02-002
mould	VB	1-01-001

Word	Tag	Frequency
mold (cont.):		
molded	VBD	1-01-001
molded	VBN	11-03-004
molding	VBG	6-02-002
molding	VBG-HL	1-01-001
Moldavian	**NP**	**1-01-001**
moldboard	**NN**	**1-01-001**
molding	**NN**	**8-02-003**
mole	**NN**	**3-03-003**
Mole	**NP**	**1-01-001**
molecular	**JJ**	**17-03-010**
molecule	**noun**	**15-05-007**
molecule	NN	6-02-004
molecules	NNS	9-05-006
molest	**verb**	**2-02-002**
molest	VB	1-01-001
molesting	VBG	1-01-001
Molesworth	**NP**	**7-01-001**
Moliere	**prop. noun**	**8-02-002**
Moliere	NP	3-02-002
Moliere's	NP$	5-01-001
Molinari	**NP**	**2-02-002**
Moll	**NP**	**5-01-001**
Moller	**NP**	**1-01-001**
Mollie	**prop. noun**	**6-01-001**
Mollie	NP	1-01-001
Mollie	NP-TL	5-01-001
mollify	**verb**	**3-03-003**
mollify	VB	2-02-002
mollified	VBN	1-01-001
mollusk	**noun**	**1-01-001**
mollusks	NNS	1-01-001
Molly	**prop. noun**	**7-05-005**
Molly	NP	4-03-003
Molly	NP-TL	1-01-001
Molly's	NP$	2-02-002
mollycoddle	**NN**	**1-01-001**
Moloch	**NP**	**3-02-002**
Molotov	**prop. noun**	**7-02-002**
Molotov	NP	6-02-002
Molotov	NP-TL	1-01-001
molten	**JJ**	**3-02-003**
Molucca	**prop. noun**	**1-01-001**
Moluccas	NPS	1-01-001
Molvar	**NP**	**3-01-001**
mom	**noun**	**4-03-003**
mom	NN	1-01-001
Mom	NN-TL	2-01-001
mom's	NN$	1-01-001
moment	**noun**	**301-15-172**
moment	NN	244-14-150
moment	NN-NC	2-01-001
moment's	NN$	5-05-005
moments	NNS	48-13-039
moments	NNS-HL	1-01-001
Moments	NNS-TL	1-01-001
momentarily	**RB**	**5-05-005**
momentary	**JJ**	**6-05-006**
momentous	**JJ**	**8-06-007**
momentum	**NN**	**14-05-008**
Momma	**NP**	**2-01-001**
Mommor	**NP**	**1-01-001**
Mommy	**prop. noun**	**2-01-001**
Mommy	NP	1-01-001
Mommy's	NP$	1-01-001
Momoyama	**NP**	**3-01-001**
mon	**FW-PP$**	**1-01-001**
Mon	**NP**	**6-01-001**
Mon-Khmer	**prop. noun**	**2-01-001**
Mon-Khmer	NP	1-01-001
Mon-Khmer	NP-TL	1-01-001
Monagan	**prop. noun**	**2-01-001**
Monagan	NP	0-00-000
Monagan	NP-HL	2-01-001
monarch	**NN**	**3-02-003**
monarque	**foreign**	**1-01-001**
monarque	FW-NN	0-00-000
Monarque	FW-NN-TL	1-01-001
monastery	**noun**	**4-02-004**
monastery	NN	2-02-002
monasteries	NNS	2-02-002
monastic	**JJ**	**7-03-003**
monasticism	**NN**	**1-01-001**
monaural	**JJ**	**1-01-001**
Monday	**adv. noun**	**72-09-032**
Monday	NR	68-08-030
Monday's	NR$	3-01-002
Mondays	NRS	1-01-001
monde	**foreign**	**2-02-002**

Word	Tag	Frequency
monde (cont.):		
monde	FW-NN	1-01-001
Monde	FW-NN-TL	1-01-001
Mondonville	**NP**	**1-01-001**
Mondrian	**NP**	**3-01-001**
Monel	**NP**	**3-01-001**
Monet	**NP**	**3-03-003**
monetary	**JJ**	**9-04-004**
money	**noun**	**275-14-144**
money	NN	262-14-141
monei	NN	5-01-001
Money	NN	2-02-002
money	NN-HL	1-01-001
money's	NN+BEZ	1-01-001
money's	NN$	1-01-001
moneys	NNS	2-02-002
monies	NNS	1-01-001
money-fed	**JJ**	**1-01-001**
money-handling	**NN**	**1-01-001**
money-hungry	**JJ**	**1-01-001**
money-maker	**NN**	**1-01-001**
money-making	**NN**	**1-01-001**
money-minded	**JJ**	**1-01-001**
money-saving	**adjective**	**2-01-002**
money-saving	JJ	1-01-001
money-saving	JJ-HL	1-01-001
money-winner	**NN**	**1-01-001**
moneyed	**JJ**	**1-01-001**
moneymaking	**JJ**	**1-01-001**
Mongi	**NP**	**1-01-001**
Mongolia	**prop. noun**	**2-01-001**
Mongolia	NP	0-00-000
Mongolia	NP-TL	1-01-001
Mongolia's	NP$	1-01-001
monic	**JJ**	**3-01-001**
Monica	**NP**	**2-02-002**
Monilia	**NP**	**1-01-001**
monitor	**noun**	**5-03-004**
monitor	NN	1-01-001
Monitor	NN-TL	2-02-002
monitors	NNS	2-01-001
monitor	**verb**	**10-02-002**
monitored	VBN	1-01-001
monitoring	VBG	9-02-002
monitoring	**NN**	**4-02-002**
Moniuszko	**prop. noun**	**1-01-001**
Moniuszko's	NP$	1-01-001
monk	**noun**	**23-07-010**
monk	NN	13-04-005
monks	NNS	10-06-007
Monk	**NP**	**3-02-002**
monkey	**noun**	**10-03-004**
monkey	NN	9-03-004
monkeys	NNS	1-01-001
monkey-gland	**NN**	**1-01-001**
monkish	**JJ**	**1-01-001**
Monmouth	**prop. noun**	**5-01-001**
Monmouth	NP	3-01-001
Monmouth's	NP$	2-01-001
mono-	**JJ**	**2-01-001**
mono-iodotyrosine	**NN**	**3-01-001**
mono-unsaturated	**JJ**	**2-01-001**
monochrome	**noun**	**1-01-001**
monochromes	NNS	1-01-001
Monocite	**NP**	**1-01-001**
monocle	**noun**	**5-01-001**
monocle	NN	0-00-000
monacle	NN	5-01-001
monoclinic	**JJ**	**1-01-001**
monodisperse	**JJ**	**1-01-001**
monogamous	**JJ**	**1-01-001**
monogamy	**NN**	**1-01-001**
monograph	**noun**	**2-02-002**
monograph	NN	1-01-001
monographs	NNS	1-01-001
monolith	**NN**	**1-01-001**
monolithic	**JJ**	**1-01-001**
monolithically	**RB**	**1-01-001**
monologist	**NN**	**1-01-001**
monologue	**NN**	**3-02-002**
monomer	**noun**	**3-02-003**
monomer	NN	2-02-002
monomers	NNS	1-01-001
mononuclear	**JJ**	**1-01-001**
monophonic	**JJ**	**1-01-001**
monopolist	**noun**	**1-01-001**
monopolists	NNS	1-01-001
monopolistic	**JJ**	**2-01-001**
monopolization	**NN**	**1-01-001**

Word	Tag	Frequency
monopolize	**VB**	**4-03-003**
monopoly	**noun**	**19-07-011**
monopoly	NN	14-07-011
monopolies	NNS	5-02-002
monosyllable	**noun**	**3-03-003**
monosyllable	NN	1-01-001
monosyllables	NNS	2-02-002
monotone	**JJ**	**3-01-001**
monotonous	**JJ**	**8-06-008**
monotony	**NN**	**7-06-007**
Monroe	**prop. noun**	**12-04-004**
Monroe	NP	6-02-002
Monroe	NP-TL	6-02-002
Monsieur	**prop. noun**	**12-05-006**
Monsieur	NP	11-04-005
Monsieur	NP-HL	1-01-001
monsoon	**NN**	**3-02-002**
monsoon-shrouded	**JJ**	**1-01-001**
monster	**noun**	**9-06-009**
monster	NN	5-03-005
Monster	NN-TL	1-01-001
monsters	NNS	3-03-003
monstrosity	**NN**	**3-03-003**
monstrous	**JJ**	**13-06-012**
Mont	**NP**	**1-01-001**
Montaigne	**NP**	**2-01-002**
Montana	**prop. noun**	**3-03-003**
Montana	NP	2-02-002
Mont.	NP	1-01-001
Monte	**prop. noun**	**5-03-005**
Monte	NP	4-02-004
Monte	NP-TL	1-01-001
Montenegrin	**JJ**	**1-01-001**
Monterey	**NP**	**1-01-001**
Montero	**prop. noun**	**15-01-001**
Montero	NP	10-01-001
Montero's	NP$	5-01-001
Monteverdi	**NP**	**2-02-002**
Montevideo	**NP**	**1-01-001**
Montfaucon	**NP**	**1-01-001**
Montgomery	**prop. noun**	**18-06-007**
Montgomery	NP	11-02-002
Montgomery	NP-TL	5-04-005
Montgomery's	NP$	2-02-002
month	**noun**	**327-15-174**
month	NN	130-14-082
month's	NN$	2-02-002
months	NNS	189-15-118
mos.	NNS	1-01-001
months'	NNS$	5-05-005
month-long	**JJ**	**1-01-001**
monthly	**JJ**	**17-07-015**
monthly	**noun**	**3-02-003**
monthly	NN	0-00-000
Monthly	NN-TL	3-02-003
monthly	**RB**	**3-03-003**
Monticello	**prop. noun**	**3-03-003**
Monticello	NP	2-02-002
Monticello	NP-TL	1-01-001
Montmartre	**NP**	**2-01-001**
montmorillonite	**noun**	**1-01-001**
montmorillonites	NNS	1-01-001
Montpelier	**NP**	**7-01-001**
Montrachet	**NP**	**1-01-001**
Montreal	**prop. noun**	**4-02-002**
Montreal	NP	3-02-002
Montreal	NP-TL	1-01-001
Montreux	**NP**	**1-01-001**
Monty	**NP**	**2-01-001**
monument	**noun**	**29-08-018**
monument	NN	18-08-014
monument	NN-HL	1-01-001
Monument	NN-TL	2-02-002
monuments	NNS	8-05-007
monumental	**JJ**	**5-04-005**
monumentality	**NN**	**1-01-001**
monumentally	**RB**	**1-01-001**
moo	**verb**	**1-01-001**
mooed	VBD	1-01-001
mood	**noun**	**45-10-035**
mood	NN	35-09-028
mood	NN-HL	1-01-001
Mood	NN-TL	1-01-001
moods	NNS	7-03-006
Moods	NNS-TL	1-01-001
moodily	**RB**	**1-01-001**
moody	**JJ**	**2-02-002**
Moody	**NP**	**3-02-003**
moon	**noun**	**63-11-026**

Word	Tag	Frequency
moon (cont.):		
moon	NN	46-10-020
moon	NN-HL	2-02-002
Moon	NN-TL	10-05-006
moon's	NN$	2-02-002
moons	NNS	3-02-002
moon	**VB**	**1-01-001**
Moon	**NP**	**1-01-001**
moon-drenched	**JJ**	**1-01-001**
moon-faced	**JJ**	**1-01-001**
moon-round	**JJ**	**1-01-001**
moon-splashed	**JJ**	**1-01-001**
moon-washed	**JJ**	**1-01-001**
Moonan	**NP**	**1-01-001**
mooncurser	**noun**	**1-01-001**
mooncursers	NNS	1-01-001
moonlight	**NN**	**13-04-009**
moonlike	**JJ**	**1-01-001**
moonlit	**JJ**	**2-02-002**
moontrack	**NN**	**1-01-001**
moor	**noun**	**1-01-001**
moors	NNS	1-01-001
moor	**verb**	**3-03-003**
moored	VBD	1-01-001
moored	VBN	1-01-001
mooring	VBG	1-01-001
Moor	**prop. noun**	**1-01-001**
Moors	NPS	1-01-001
Moore	**prop. noun**	**26-07-010**
Moore	NP	24-07-010
Moore's	NP$	2-02-002
Moorish	**JJ**	**2-02-002**
Moos	**prop. noun**	**3-01-001**
Moos	NP	0-00-000
Moos	NP-HL	1-01-001
Moos	NP-TL	2-01-001
Moosilauke	**prop. noun**	**1-01-001**
Moosilauke	NP	0-00-000
Moosilauke	NP-TL	1-01-001
moot	**JJ**	**1-01-001**
mop	**noun**	**2-02-002**
mop	NN	1-01-001
mops	NNS	1-01-001
mop	**verb**	**9-07-009**
mop	VB	2-02-002
mopped	VBD	2-02-002
mopped	VBN	2-02-002
mopping	VBG	3-03-003
moraine	**noun**	**1-01-001**
moraine's	NN$	1-01-001
moral	**adjective**	**137-14-059**
moral	JJ	135-14-059
Moral	JJ-TL	2-02-002
moral	**noun**	**12-05-011**
moral	NN	5-04-005
morals	NNS	7-04-006
morale	**NN**	**17-05-010**
morale-enhancing	**JJ**	**1-01-001**
moralist	**NN**	**2-01-002**
moralistic	**JJ**	**1-01-001**
morality	**noun**	**30-08-019**
morality	NN	29-08-018
moralities	NNS	1-01-001
morally	**RB**	**7-04-006**
morass	**NN**	**1-01-001**
moratorium	**NN**	**1-01-001**
Moravian	**JJ**	**1-01-001**
morbid	**JJ**	**1-01-001**
morbid-minded	**JJ**	**1-01-001**
more	**post-det.**	**990-15-389**
more	AP	978-15-388
mor	AP	1-01-001
more	AP-HL	9-04-009
More	AP-TL	2-01-001
more	**QL**	**1015-15-365**
more	**comp. adv.**	**198-15-145**
more	RBR	196-15-144
more	RBR-NC	1-01-001
more'n	RBR+CS	1-01-001
More	**prop. noun**	**20-02-002**
More	NP	13-02-002
More's	NP$	7-01-001
more-than-average	**JJ**	**1-01-001**
more-than-ordinary	**JJ**	**1-01-001**
Morehouse	**NP**	**1-01-001**
Morel	**NP**	**1-01-001**
Moreland	**NP**	**17-01-001**
moreover	**RB**	**88-13-063**
mores	**NNS**	**7-04-007**

Word	Tag	Frequency
Morgan	**prop. noun**	**78-07-010**
Morgan	NP	71-07-008
Morgan	NP-TL	1-01-001
Morgan's	NP$	5-01-001
Morgan's	NP$-TL	1-01-001
Morgart	**NP**	**1-01-001**
morgen	**foreign**	**1-01-001**
morgen	FW-NR	0-00-000
morgen	FW-NR-TL	1-01-001
Morgenthau	**prop. noun**	**3-02-002**
Morgenthau	NP	0-00-000
Morgenthau	NP-TL	2-01-001
Morgenthau's	NP$	1-01-001
morgue	**NN**	**1-01-001**
Moriarty	**prop. noun**	**7-02-002**
Moriarty	NP	5-02-002
Mor-ee-air-teeeee	NP	1-01-001
Moriarty's	NP$	1-01-001
Morikawa	**NP**	**1-01-001**
Moritz	**NP**	**11-01-001**
Morley	**NP**	**2-02-002**
Mormon	**prop. noun**	**2-02-002**
Mormon	NP	1-01-001
Mormon	NP-TL	1-01-001
morning	**noun**	**222-15-124**
morning	NN	210-15-121
morning's	NN$	2-02-002
mornings	NNS	10-07-010
Morning	**UH**	**1-01-001**
morning-frightened	**JJ**	**1-01-001**
morning-glory	**NN**	**1-01-001**
Morningstar	**NP**	**1-01-001**
Moroccan	**JJ**	**2-01-001**
Moroccan	**NP**	**1-01-001**
Morocco	**prop. noun**	**5-02-003**
Morocco	NP	4-02-002
Morocco	NP-TL	1-01-001
morocco-bound	**JJ**	**1-01-001**
morose	**JJ**	**2-02-002**
morosely	**RB**	**2-02-002**
morphemic	**JJ**	**1-01-001**
morphine	**NN**	**1-01-001**
morphologic	**JJ**	**1-01-001**
morphological	**JJ**	**5-02-002**
morphology	**NN**	**2-01-002**
morphophonemic	**JJ**	**7-01-001**
morphophonemics	**NN**	**9-01-001**
Morris	**prop. noun**	**22-06-013**
Morris	NP	18-05-011
Morris	NP-TL	3-01-001
Morris'	NP$	1-01-001
Morrison	**NP**	**4-02-002**
morrow	**NN**	**2-02-002**
Morse	**prop. noun**	**34-04-005**
Morse	NP	29-04-005
Morse's	NP$	5-01-001
morsel	**noun**	**4-04-004**
morsel	NN	3-03-003
morsels	NNS	1-01-001
Mort	**NP**	**2-02-002**
mortal	**JJ**	**10-06-008**
mortal	**noun**	**2-02-002**
mortals	NNS	1-01-001
Mortals	NNS-TL	1-01-001
mortality	**NN**	**9-05-006**
mortally	**RB**	**1-01-001**
mortar	**noun**	**13-06-006**
mortar	NN	10-04-004
Mortar	NN-TL	1-01-001
mortars	NNS	2-01-001
mortar	**verb**	**3-01-001**
mortared	VBN	2-01-001
mortaring	VBG	1-01-001
mortgage	**noun**	**22-08-013**
mortgage	NN	16-08-009
Mortgage	NN-TL	1-01-001
mortgages	NNS	5-03-005
mortician	**noun**	**1-01-001**
morticians	NNS	1-01-001
mortification	**NN**	**1-01-001**
Morton	**prop. noun**	**16-03-006**
Morton	NP	8-03-006
Morton	NP-TL	7-01-001
Morton's	NP$	1-01-001
mosaic	**JJ**	**1-01-001**
mosaic	**noun**	**4-04-004**
mosaic	NN	3-03-003
mosaics	NNS	1-01-001
mosaic-like	**JJ**	**1-01-001**

Word	Tag	Frequency
Moscone	**NP**	**1-01-001**
Moscow	**prop. noun**	**51-06-020**
Moscow	NP	41-06-018
Moscow	NP-HL	3-02-003
Moscow	NP-TL	3-03-003
Moscow's	NP$	4-03-003
Moscow-allied	**JJ**	**1-01-001**
Mose	**NP**	**6-01-001**
Moses	**prop. noun**	**9-05-008**
Moses	NP	7-04-006
Moses	NP-TL	2-02-002
Mosk	**NP**	**3-01-002**
mosque	**noun**	**12-02-002**
mosque	NN	2-01-001
Mosque	NN-TL	7-01-001
Mosque	NN-TL-HL	1-01-001
mosques	NNS	2-02-002
mosquito	**noun**	**2-02-002**
mosquito	NN	1-01-001
mosquitoes	NNS	1-01-001
mosquito-plagued	**JJ**	**1-01-001**
moss	**NN**	**3-03-003**
Moss	**prop. noun**	**6-03-004**
Moss	NP	5-03-003
Moss	NP-TL	1-01-001
Mossberg	**prop. noun**	**2-01-001**
Mossberg	NP	1-01-001
Mossberg's	NP$	1-01-001
most	**post-det.**	**478-15-268**
most	AP	477-15-268
most	AP-HL	1-01-001
most	**qualifier**	**648-15-306**
most	QL	646-15-306
Most	QL-TL	2-02-002
most	**RB**	**1-01-001**
most	**RBT**	**32-13-029**
most-valuable	**JJ**	**1-01-001**
most-valuable-player	**NN**	**1-01-001**
mostly	**adverb**	**44-15-042**
mostly	RB	43-15-042
mostly	RB-HL	1-01-001
mot	**FW-NN**	**1-01-001**
motel	**noun**	**31-06-011**
motel	NN	19-06-010
motel	NN-HL	1-01-001
Motel	NN-TL	4-02-002
motels	NNS	7-02-003
motel-keeper	**noun**	**1-01-001**
motel-keepers	NNS	1-01-001
motel-keeping	**NN**	**1-01-001**
motet	**noun**	**2-01-001**
motet	NN	1-01-001
motets	NNS	1-01-001
moth	**noun**	**4-03-004**
moth	NN	1-01-001
moth's	NN$	1-01-001
moths	NNS	2-02-002
moth-eaten	**JJ**	**1-01-001**
mother	**noun**	**280-13-106**
mother	NN	192-13-084
mother	NN-HL	1-01-001
Mother	NN-TL	22-07-012
mother's	NN$	34-10-025
Mother's	NN$-TL	2-02-002
mothers	NNS	25-09-013
mothers'	NNS$	3-02-003
Mothers'	NNS$-TL	1-01-001
mother	**verb**	**2-02-002**
mother	VB	1-01-001
mothered	VBN	1-01-001
mother-in-law	**noun**	**2-01-001**
mother-in-law	NN	1-01-001
mothers-in-law	NNS	1-01-001
mother-introject	**NN**	**1-01-001**
mother-naked	**JJ**	**1-01-001**
mother-of-pearl	**NN**	**2-02-002**
motherhood	**NN**	**1-01-001**
motherland	**NN**	**1-01-001**
motherly	**JJ**	**1-01-001**
Motherwell	**NP**	**1-01-001**
motif	**noun**	**13-06-007**
motif	NN	8-05-005
motifs	NNS	5-03-003
motion	**noun**	**72-14-047**
motion	NN	55-14-037
motions	NNS	17-07-012
motion	**verb**	**3-02-002**
motioned	VBD	1-01-001
motioning	VBG	2-01-001

Word	Tag	Frequency
motion-pattern	**NN**	**1-01-001**
motion-picture	**NN**	**3-03-003**
motional	**JJ**	**1-01-001**
motional-modified	**JJ**	**1-01-001**
motionless	**JJ**	**7-06-007**
motivate	**verb**	**16-04-013**
motivate	VB	1-01-001
motivates	VBZ	3-03-003
motivated	VBD	1-01-001
motivated	VBN	8-03-008
motivating	VBG	3-02-003
motivation	**noun**	**16-05-009**
motivation	NN	11-04-005
motivations	NNS	5-04-005
motive	**JJ**	**1-01-001**
motive	**noun**	**41-10-027**
motive	NN	21-05-013
motives	NNS	20-09-016
motley	**JJ**	**3-02-002**
motor	**noun**	**108-11-039**
motor	NN	51-10-030
motor	NN-HL	1-01-001
Motor	NN-TL	3-03-003
motors	NNS	7-04-004
Motors	NNS-TL	43-06-006
motors'	NNS$	0-00-000
Motors'	NNS$-TL	3-01-001
motor	**verb**	**2-02-002**
motor	VB	1-01-001
motoring	VBG	1-01-001
motor-car	**NN**	**1-01-001**
motorist	**noun**	**8-02-005**
motorist	NN	2-01-001
motorists	NNS	5-02-003
motorists'	NNS$	1-01-001
motorscooter	**noun**	**1-01-001**
motorscooters	NNS	1-01-001
mottle	**verb**	**3-01-001**
mottled	VBN	3-01-001
motto	**NN**	**4-03-004**
moulder	**verb**	**1-01-001**
mouldering	VBG	1-01-001
moulding	**NN**	**1-01-001**
Moulton	**prop. noun**	**2-01-001**
Moulton	NP	1-01-001
Moultons	NPS	1-01-001
mound	**noun**	**12-05-008**
mound	NN	8-05-006
Mound	NN-TL	3-02-002
mounds	NNS	1-01-001
mound	**verb**	**2-01-001**
mounded	VBN	2-01-001
Moune	**NP**	**1-01-001**
mount	**noun**	**11-04-008**
mount	NN	6-04-004
mounts	NNS	5-01-004
mount	**verb**	**62-12-040**
mount	VB	4-04-004
mounts	VBZ	3-02-003
mounted	VBD	13-08-011
mounted	VBN	31-07-018
Mounted	VBN-TL	1-01-001
mounting	VBG	9-06-007
mounting	VBG-HL	1-01-001
mountain	**noun**	**98-14-054**
mountain	NN	26-08-018
mount	NN	0-00-000
Mount	NN-TL	16-08-012
mt.	NN	3-02-002
Mt.	NN-TL	2-02-002
mountain	NN-NC	1-01-001
Mountain	NN-TL	6-05-005
mountains	NNS	34-09-023
Mts.	NNS	0-00-000
Mts.	NNS-TL	1-01-001
Mountains	NNS-TL	8-05-005
mountains	NNS-TL	1-01-001
mountaineering	**noun**	**1-01-001**
mountaineering	NN	0-00-000
Mountaineering	NN-TL	1-01-001
mountainous	**JJ**	**6-05-006**
mountainously	**QL**	**1-01-001**
mountainside	**noun**	**5-03-005**
mountainside	NN	4-02-004
mountainsides	NNS	1-01-001
mounting	**noun**	**2-01-002**
mounting	NN	1-01-001
mountings	NNS	1-01-001
mourn	**verb**	**12-05-010**

Word	Tag	Frequency
mourn (cont.):		
mourn	VB	2-02-002
mourned	VBD	2-02-002
mourning	VBG	8-04-006
mourner	**noun**	**2-01-002**
mourners	NNS	2-01-002
mournful	**JJ**	**1-01-001**
mournfully	**RB**	**1-01-001**
mouse	**noun**	**20-08-010**
mouse	NN	9-03-005
Mouse	NN-TL	1-01-001
mice	NNS	9-05-005
mice	NNS-HL	1-01-001
Mousie	**NP**	**7-01-001**
moustache	**NN**	**1-01-001**
mousy	**JJ**	**1-01-001**
mouth	**noun**	**113-13-067**
mouth	NN	103-13-064
mough	NN	2-01-001
mouths	NNS	8-07-008
mouth	**verb**	**3-03-003**
mouthed	VBD	1-01-001
mouthing	VBG	2-02-002
mouth-watering	**JJ**	**1-01-001**
mouthful	**NN**	**3-01-003**
mouthpiece	**noun**	**8-06-007**
mouthpiece	NN	7-05-006
mouthpieces	NNS	1-01-001
mouvement	**foreign**	**1-01-001**
mouvement	FW-NN	0-00-000
Mouvement	FW-NN-TL	1-01-001
movable	**JJ**	**19-04-005**
move	**noun**	**45-12-040**
move	NN	36-10-034
moves	NNS	9-05-007
move	**verb**	**447-15-236**
move	VB	133-13-102
move	VB-HL	2-02-002
moves	VBZ	26-09-024
moves	VBZ-HL	1-01-001
moved	VBD	138-15-095
moved	VBN	43-12-040
moving	VBG	104-13-083
movement	**noun**	**175-15-092**
movement	NN	124-15-075
movement	NN-HL	1-01-001
Movement	NN-TL	3-03-003
movements	NNS	46-11-028
movements	NNS-HL	1-01-001
mover	**noun**	**4-02-002**
movers	NNS	4-02-002
movie	**noun**	**60-12-034**
movie	NN	29-10-020
movies	NNS	30-11-016
movies	NNS-HL	1-01-001
movie-goer	**NN**	**1-01-001**
movie-to-be	**NN**	**1-01-001**
moving	**JJ**	**8-03-007**
moving	**NN**	**2-02-002**
movingly	**RB**	**1-01-001**
mow	**verb**	**1-01-001**
mowed	VBN	1-01-001
Mozart	**prop. noun**	**3-02-002**
Mozart	NP	2-01-001
Mozart's	NP$	1-01-001
Mrs.	**prop. noun**	**536-13-101**
Mrs.	NP	534-13-101
Mrs.	NP-HL	2-02-002
MS	**NN**	**1-01-001**
Msec.	**NNS**	**1-01-001**
Mubarak	**NP**	**1-01-001**
much	**post-det.**	**496-15-278**
much	AP	490-15-278
much	AP-HL	2-01-002
Much	AP-TL	4-01-001
much	**qualifier**	**229-15-157**
much	QL	228-15-157
much	QL-HL	1-01-001
much	**RB**	**212-15-143**
much-copied	**JJ**	**1-01-001**
much-craved	**JJ**	**1-01-001**
much-discussed	**JJ**	**1-01-001**
much-needed	**JJ**	**1-01-001**
much-thumbed	**JJ**	**1-01-001**
mucilage	**NN**	**1-01-001**
muck	**NN**	**1-01-001**
muck	**verb**	**2-02-002**
mucking	VBG	2-02-002
Muck	**prop. noun**	**1-01-001**

Word	Tag	Frequency
Muck (cont.):		
Muck's	NP$	1-01-001
mucker	**NN**	**1-01-001**
mucosa	**NN**	**5-01-001**
mucus	**NN**	**2-02-002**
mud	**noun**	**32-09-021**
mud	NN	31-09-021
Mud	NN-TL	1-01-001
mud-beplastered	**JJ**	**1-01-001**
mud-caked	**JJ**	**1-01-001**
mud-sweat-and-tears	**JJ**	**1-01-001**
muddle	**verb**	**1-01-001**
muddling	VBG	1-01-001
muddleheaded	**JJ**	**1-01-001**
muddy	**JJ**	**10-06-008**
muddy	**verb**	**2-02-002**
muddied	VBN	2-02-002
muddy-tasting	**JJ**	**1-01-001**
mudguard	**NN**	**1-01-001**
mudslinging	**NN**	**1-01-001**
Mudugno	**NP**	**1-01-001**
mudwagon	**NN**	**1-01-001**
muezzin	**NN**	**1-01-001**
muff	**NN**	**1-01-001**
muffin	**noun**	**1-01-001**
muffins	NNS	1-01-001
muffle	**verb**	**12-05-010**
muffled	VBD	1-01-001
muffled	VBN	10-04-008
muffling	VBG	1-01-001
muffler	**NN**	**2-01-001**
mug	**noun**	**3-02-002**
mug	NN	1-01-001
mugs	NNS	2-01-001
mugger	**noun**	**1-01-001**
muggers	NNS	1-01-001
muggy	**JJ**	**1-01-001**
Muhammad	**prop. noun**	**3-03-003**
Muhammad	NP	0-00-000
Mohammad	NP	1-01-001
Mohammed	NP	1-01-001
Muhammad	NP-TL	1-01-001
Muir	**NP**	**1-01-001**
mulatto	**noun**	**1-01-001**
mulatto's	NN$	1-01-001
mulch	**NN**	**6-02-002**
mulch	**verb**	**1-01-001**
mulching	VBG	1-01-001
mule	**noun**	**7-06-007**
mule	NN	4-03-004
mules	NNS	3-03-003
mule-drawn	**JJ**	**1-01-001**
mullah	**NN**	**1-01-001**
Mullen	**NP**	**2-01-001**
Mullenax	**NP**	**2-01-001**
Mullendore	**NP**	**1-01-001**
Muller	**prop. noun**	**12-01-001**
Muller	NP	9-01-001
Muller's	NP$	3-01-001
mullerin	**foreign**	**1-01-001**
mullerin	FW-NN	0-00-000
Mullerin	FW-NN-TL	1-01-001
Mulligan	**prop. noun**	**5-01-001**
Mulligan	NP	1-01-001
Mulligan's	NP$	4-01-001
Mulligatawny	**prop. noun**	**1-01-001**
Mulligatawny	NP	0-00-000
Mulligatawny	NP-HL	1-01-001
mulling	**NN**	**1-01-001**
Mullins	**NP**	**7-01-001**
multi-	**JJ**	**1-01-001**
multi-family	**JJ**	**1-01-001**
multi-lingual	**JJ**	**1-01-001**
multi-million-dollar	**JJ**	**2-02-002**
multi-phase	**JJ**	**1-01-001**
multi-product	**JJ**	**1-01-001**
multi-state	**JJ**	**1-01-001**
multi-valued	**JJ**	**2-01-001**
multi-year	**JJ**	**2-02-002**
multichannel	**JJ**	**1-01-001**
multicolor	**JJ**	**1-01-001**
multicolored	**adjective**	**2-01-002**
multicolored	JJ	1-01-001
multi-colored	JJ	1-01-001
multidimensional	**JJ**	**1-01-001**
multifigure	**NN**	**1-01-001**
multilateral	**JJ**	**1-01-001**
multimegaton	**JJ**	**1-01-001**
multimillionaire	**noun**	**2-02-002**

Word	Tag	Frequency
multimillionaire (cont.):		
multimillionaire	NN	1-01-001
multi-millionaire	NN	1-01-001
multipactor	**NN**	**2-01-001**
multiphastic	**adjective**	**1-01-001**
multiphastic	JJ	0-00-000
Multiphastic	JJ-TL	1-01-001
multiple	**adjective**	**36-09-025**
multiple	JJ	35-08-024
Multiple	JJ-HL	1-01-001
multiple-choice	**NN**	**1-01-001**
multiple-purpose	**NN**	**1-01-001**
multiplication	**NN**	**6-02-003**
multiplicity	**NN**	**8-02-003**
multiply	**verb**	**27-08-015**
multiply	VB	9-04-004
multiply	VB-HL	1-01-001
multiplies	VBZ	2-02-002
multiplied	VBD	2-02-002
multiplied	VBN	5-03-004
multiplying	VBG	8-04-005
multipurpose	**adjective**	**2-02-002**
multipurpose	JJ	1-01-001
multi-purpose	JJ	1-01-001
multistage	**NN**	**1-01-001**
multitude	**noun**	**5-05-005**
multitude	NN	3-03-003
multitudes	NNS	2-02-002
multitudinous	**JJ**	**2-02-002**
multivalent	**JJ**	**1-01-001**
multiversity	**NN**	**1-01-001**
Multnomah	**prop. noun**	**6-01-002**
Multnomah	NP	1-01-001
Multnomah	NP-TL	5-01-002
mum	**JJ**	**1-01-001**
mumble	**NN**	**1-01-001**
mumble	**verb**	**6-04-006**
mumbled	VBD	5-04-005
mumbling	VBG	1-01-001
mumbo-jumbo	**NN**	**1-01-001**
Mumford	**NP**	**1-01-001**
mummify	**verb**	**1-01-001**
mummified	VBN	1-01-001
mummy	**noun**	**1-01-001**
mummies	NNS	1-01-001
munch	**verb**	**3-03-003**
munch	VB	1-01-001
munched	VBD	1-01-001
munching	VBG	1-01-001
mundane	**JJ**	**3-02-003**
Mundt	**prop. noun**	**2-01-001**
Mundt	NP	1-01-001
Mundt's	NP$	1-01-001
Munger	**prop. noun**	**1-01-001**
Munger	NP	0-00-000
Munger	NP-TL	1-01-001
mungus	**NN**	**1-01-001**
Munich	**prop. noun**	**7-03-005**
Munich	NP	5-03-004
Munich	NP-TL	1-01-001
Munich's	NP$	1-01-001
municipal	**adjective**	**29-07-020**
municipal	JJ	27-06-019
muncipal	JJ	0-00-000
Muncipal	JJ-TL	1-01-001
Municipal	JJ-TL	1-01-001
municipality	**noun**	**11-04-006**
municipality	NN	1-01-001
municipality's	NN$	1-01-001
municipalities	NNS	9-03-005
municipally	**RB**	**1-01-001**
municipally-sponsored	**JJ**	**1-01-001**
munitions	**NNS**	**3-03-003**
Munoz	**NP**	**1-01-001**
Munroe	**NP**	**1-01-001**
Muong	**NP**	**1-01-001**
mural	**NN**	**1-01-001**
Murat	**NP**	**1-01-001**
murder	**noun**	**83-10-033**
murder	NN	70-10-031
Murder	NN-TL	1-01-001
murders	NNS	12-04-005
murder	**verb**	**16-08-014**
murder	VB	4-03-003
murdered	VBN	9-05-008
murdering	VBG	3-02-003
murderer	**noun**	**25-09-016**
murderer	NN	19-07-012
murderer's	NN$	1-01-001

Word	Tag	Frequency
murderer (cont.):		
murderers	NNS	5-03-004
murderous	**JJ**	**4-04-004**
Murkland	**NP**	**2-01-001**
murky	**JJ**	**5-05-005**
murmur	**NN**	**2-02-002**
murmur	**verb**	**22-06-018**
murmur	VB	1-01-001
murmured	VBD	17-05-013
murmuring	VBG	4-03-004
Murphy	**prop. noun**	**8-04-005**
Murphy	NP	6-03-004
Murphy	NP-HL	1-01-001
Murphy's	NP$	1-01-001
Murray	**prop. noun**	**9-04-007**
Murray	NP	7-04-007
Murray	NP-TL	1-01-001
Murray's	NP$	1-01-001
Murrin	**NP**	**1-01-001**
Murrow	**NP**	**1-01-001**
Murtaugh	**NP**	**3-01-001**
Murville	**NP**	**1-01-001**
muscle	**noun**	**73-12-032**
muscle	NN	40-08-017
muscle	NN-HL	1-01-001
Muscle	NN-TL	1-01-001
muscles	NNS	31-10-019
muscle	**verb**	**1-01-001**
muscled	VBN	1-01-001
muscle-bound	**JJ**	**1-01-001**
muscle-shaping	**JJ**	**1-01-001**
muscleman	**noun**	**1-01-001**
musclemen	NNS	1-01-001
Muscovy	**prop. noun**	**3-01-001**
Muscovy	NP	0-00-000
Muscovy	NP-TL	3-01-001
muscular	**adjective**	**16-07-011**
muscular	JJ	15-07-011
Muscular	JJ-TL	1-01-001
musculature	**NN**	**1-01-001**
muse	**noun**	**5-04-005**
muse	NN	2-02-002
Muse	NN-TL	2-01-002
muses	NNS	0-00-000
Muses	NNS-TL	1-01-001
muse	**verb**	**5-03-005**
mused	VBD	4-02-004
musing	VBG	1-01-001
musee	**foreign**	**1-01-001**
musee	FW-NN	0-00-000
Musee	FW-NN-TL	1-01-001
museum	**noun**	**42-08-022**
museum	NN	16-06-011
Museum	NN-TL	15-05-009
Museum	NN-TL-HL	1-01-001
museums	NNS	10-04-007
Mushr	**NP**	**1-01-001**
mushroom	**noun**	**4-04-004**
mushroom	NN	2-02-002
mushrooms	NNS	2-02-002
mushroom	**verb**	**1-01-001**
mushrooming	VBG	1-01-001
Musial	**NP**	**3-01-001**
music	**noun**	**216-15-064**
music	NN	201-15-058
music	NN-HL	1-01-001
Music	NN-TL	14-06-013
music-hall	**NN**	**1-01-001**
music-loving	**JJ**	**2-02-002**
music-making	**NN**	**1-01-001**
musica	**foreign**	**1-01-001**
musica	FW-NN	0-00-000
Musica	FW-NN-TL	1-01-001
musical	**adjective**	**81-13-032**
musical	JJ	76-12-030
musical	JJ-HL	1-01-001
Musical	JJ-TL	4-03-003
musical	**noun**	**7-04-006**
musical	NN	4-02-004
musicals	NNS	3-03-003
musicale	**foreign**	**1-01-001**
musicale	FW-JJ	0-00-000
Musicale	FW-JJ-TL	1-01-001
musicality	**NN**	**1-01-001**
musically	**RB**	**3-02-003**
musician	**noun**	**65-08-023**
musician	NN	23-06-011
musicians	NNS	40-08-021
Musicians	NNS-TL	1-01-001

Word	Tag	Frequency
musician (cont.):		
musician's	NN$	0-00-000
Musician's	NN$-TL	1-01-001
musicianship	**NN**	**3-02-003**
musicologist	**noun**	**1-01-001**
musicologists	NNS	1-01-001
Musil	**prop. noun**	**1-01-001**
Musil's	NP$	1-01-001
musing	**noun**	**1-01-001**
musings	NNS	1-01-001
musique	**foreign**	**2-01-001**
musique	FW-NN	0-00-000
Musique	FW-NN-TL	2-01-001
muskadell	**NN**	**1-01-001**
Muskegon	**NP**	**1-01-001**
musket	**noun**	**9-03-005**
musket	NN	6-01-002
muskets	NNS	3-03-003
Muskoka	**NP**	**1-01-001**
Muslim	**adjective**	**5-03-003**
Muslim	JJ	2-01-001
Moslem	JJ	2-01-001
Muslim	JJ-TL	1-01-001
Muslim	**prop. noun**	**4-03-003**
Muslim	NP	0-00-000
Moslem	NP	1-01-001
Muslims	NPS	2-01-001
Moslems	NPS	1-01-001
Musmanno	**prop. noun**	**5-01-001**
Musmanno	NP	4-01-001
Musmanno's	NP$	1-01-001
mussel	**noun**	**2-02-002**
mussels	NNS	2-02-002
Mussett	**NP**	**1-01-001**
Mussolini	**prop. noun**	**3-02-002**
Mussolini	NP	1-01-001
Mussolini's	NP$	1-01-001
Mussolinis	NPS	1-01-001
Mussorgsky	**prop. noun**	**8-01-001**
Mussorgsky	NP	7-01-001
Mussorgsky's	NP$	1-01-001
must	**modal aux.**	**1017-15-347**
must	MD	999-15-345
must	MD-HL	6-05-006
Must	MD-TL	3-03-003
mustn't	MD*	5-03-004
musn't	MD*	1-01-001
must've	MD+HV	2-02-002
musta	MD+HV	1-01-001
must	**noun**	**5-05-005**
must	NN	4-04-004
musts	NNS	1-01-001
mustache	**noun**	**6-03-006**
mustache	NN	5-03-005
mustaches	NNS	1-01-001
mustached	**JJ**	**3-02-003**
mustachioed	**JJ**	**1-01-001**
Mustang	**prop. noun**	**2-01-001**
Mustang	NP	1-01-001
Mustangs	NPS	1-01-001
mustard	**noun**	**19-02-005**
mustard	NN	18-02-005
mustard	NN-HL	1-01-001
mustard	**VB**	**1-01-001**
muster	**NN**	**1-01-001**
muster	**verb**	**4-03-004**
muster	VB	2-02-002
mustered	VBD	1-01-001
mustering	VBG	1-01-001
mustiness	**NN**	**1-01-001**
mutant	**noun**	**1-01-001**
mutants	NNS	1-01-001
mutation	**noun**	**1-01-001**
mutations	NNS	1-01-001
mutational	**JJ**	**1-01-001**
mute	**JJ**	**3-03-003**
mute	**verb**	**3-03-003**
muted	VBN	3-03-003
mutely	**RB**	**2-01-002**
mutilate	**verb**	**3-03-003**
mutilated	VBN	3-03-003
mutilation	**NN**	**1-01-001**
mutineer	**NN**	**1-01-001**
mutiny	**noun**	**4-04-004**
mutiny	NN	3-03-003
mutinies	NNS	1-01-001
mutter	**verb**	**26-08-021**
mutter	VB	1-01-001
mutters	VBZ	1-01-001

Word	Tag	Frequency
mutter (cont.):		
muttered	VBD	16-06-014
muttered	VBN	1-01-001
muttering	VBG	7-04-006
mutterer	**noun**	**1-01-001**
mutterers	NNS	1-01-001
muttering	**NN**	**1-01-001**
mutton	**noun**	**8-02-002**
mutton	NN	3-02-002
Mutton	NN-TL	5-01-001
mutual	**adjective**	**26-08-020**
mutual	JJ	21-08-018
Mutual	JJ-TL	5-02-002
mutual-aid	**NN**	**1-01-001**
mutuality	**NN**	**1-01-001**
mutually	**QL**	**4-02-003**
mutually	**RB**	**9-04-005**
Muzak	**NP**	**1-01-001**
Muzo	**NP**	**1-01-001**
muzyka	**foreign**	**1-01-001**
muzyka	FW-NN	0-00-000
Muzyka	FW-NN-TL	1-01-001
muzzle	**noun**	**11-05-008**
muzzle	NN	10-05-007
muzzles	NNS	1-01-001
my	**UH**	**2-01-001**
My	**NP**	**2-01-001**
Mycenae	**NP**	**2-01-001**
mycobacterium	**noun**	**1-01-001**
mycobacteria	NNS	1-01-001
mycology	**NN**	**1-01-001**
myelofibrosis	**NN**	**1-01-001**
myeloid	**JJ**	**1-01-001**
Myers	**NP**	**3-02-002**
Mylar	**NP**	**2-01-001**
Mynah	**NP**	**1-01-001**
Mynheer	**NP**	**3-01-001**
myocardial	**JJ**	**3-01-001**
myocardium	**NN**	**1-01-001**
myofibril	**noun**	**1-01-001**
myofibrils	NNS	1-01-001
myofibrillae	**NNS**	**2-01-001**
myopia	**NN**	**1-01-001**
myopic	**JJ**	**1-01-001**
myosin	**NN**	**1-01-001**
Myra	**prop. noun**	**31-02-002**
Myra	NP	27-02-002
Myra's	NP+BEZ	1-01-001
Myra's	NP$	3-01-001
myriad	**JJ**	**5-05-005**
myriad	**NN**	**2-02-002**
Myron	**NP**	**1-01-001**
myrrh	**NN**	**2-01-001**
myrtle	**NN**	**1-01-001**
myself	**refl. pro.**	**129-13-077**
myself	PPL	128-13-076
Myself	PPL-TL	1-01-001
mysterious	**adjective**	**26-10-024**
mysterious	JJ	25-10-023
mysterious	JJ-HL	1-01-001
mysteriously	**RB**	**2-02-002**
mystery	**noun**	**46-07-028**
mystery	NN	37-07-022
Mystery	NN-TL	2-02-002
mysteries	NNS	7-03-007
mystery-story	**NN**	**1-01-001**
mystic	**JJ**	**2-02-002**
mystic	**noun**	**4-03-003**
mystic	NN	1-01-001
mystics	NNS	3-03-003
mystical	**JJ**	**5-04-004**
mysticism	**noun**	**3-03-003**
mysticism	NN	2-02-002
mysticisms	NNS	1-01-001
mystification	**NN**	**1-01-001**
mystify	**verb**	**1-01-001**
mystified	VBN	1-01-001
mystique	**NN**	**5-02-003**
myth	**noun**	**41-07-020**
myth	NN	34-07-017
Myth	NN-TL	1-01-001
myths	NNS	6-03-005
myth-making	**NN**	**2-02-002**
mythic	**JJ**	**2-02-002**
mythological	**JJ**	**13-02-005**
mythology	**noun**	**5-02-002**
mythology	NN	3-02-002
mythologies	NNS	2-02-002
Mytton	**NP**	**1-01-001**

N

Word	Tag	Frequency
N	**noun**	**9-02-003**
N	NN	1-01-001
N	NN-TL	8-02-003
N	**NP**	**11-01-005**
n.	**adjective**	**2-01-002**
n.	JJ	0-00-000
N.	JJ-TL	2-01-002
N.	**prop. noun**	**26-08-018**
N.	NP	25-08-017
N.	NP-HL	1-01-001
N.A.	**NP**	**1-01-001**
N.C.	**prop. noun**	**9-04-004**
N.C.	NP	8-04-004
N.C.'s	NP$	1-01-001
N.D.	**NP**	**1-01-001**
N.J.	**NP**	**2-01-002**
N.L.	**NP**	**1-01-001**
N.M.	**NP**	**1-01-001**
N.Y.	**NP**	**13-06-010**
N.Y.U.	**NP**	**1-01-001**
nab	**verb**	**2-01-002**
nab	VB	1-01-001
nabbed	VBN	1-01-001
Nabisco	**NP**	**1-01-001**
Nacht	**FW-NN**	**2-01-001**
Nadine	**prop. noun**	**20-01-001**
Nadine	NP	17-01-001
Nadine's	NP$	3-01-001
nadir	**NN**	**2-01-001**
nae	**RB**	**1-01-001**
nag	**verb**	**6-06-006**
nagged	VBD	1-01-001
nagging	VBG	5-05-005
Nagamo	**NP**	**1-01-001**
Nagasaki	**NP**	**2-02-002**
Nagel	**NP**	**1-01-001**
nagging	**NN**	**4-03-004**
Nagle	**NP**	**1-01-001**
Nagrin	**prop. noun**	**6-01-001**
Nagrin	NP	4-01-001
Nagrin	NP-TL	1-01-001
Nagrin's	NP$	1-01-001
nail	**noun**	**20-09-013**
nail	NN	5-04-005
Nail	NN-TL	1-01-001
nails	NNS	14-06-008
nail	**verb**	**12-08-009**
nailed	VBD	3-03-003
nailed	VBN	8-05-006
nailing	VBG	1-01-001
Nairne	**NP**	**2-01-001**
NAIRO	**NP**	**1-01-001**
Nairobi	**NP**	**1-01-001**
naive	**JJ**	**19-07-013**
naively	**RB**	**1-01-001**
naivete	**NN**	**2-01-002**
Nakamura	**NP**	**3-01-001**
Nakayasu	**NP**	**1-01-001**
naked	**JJ**	**32-09-027**
nakedly	**RB**	**1-01-001**
nakedness	**NN**	**3-03-003**
Nakoma	**prop. noun**	**1-01-001**
Nakoma	NP	0-00-000
Nakoma	NP-TL	1-01-001
Naktong	**prop. noun**	**2-01-001**
Naktong	NP	0-00-000
Naktong	NP-TL	2-01-001
Nam	**prop. noun**	**14-03-006**
Nam	NP	3-02-003
Nam	NP-HL	1-01-001
Nam	NP-TL	9-03-005
Nam's	NP$	0-00-000
Nam (cont.):		
Nam's	NP$-TL	1-01-001
name	**noun**	**365-15-179**
name	NN	256-15-148
name	NN-HL	16-01-001
Name	NN-TL	1-01-001
name's	NN+BEZ	4-02-004
names	NNS	87-14-054
Names	NNS	1-01-001
name	**verb**	**109-14-083**
name	VB	21-09-019
names	VBZ	1-01-001
named	VBD	13-07-011
named	VBN	71-14-057
naming	VBG	3-03-003
name-dropper	**NN**	**1-01-001**
nameless	**adjective**	**2-02-002**
nameless	JJ	1-01-001
Nameless	JJ-TL	1-01-001
namely	**RB**	**33-07-026**
namesake	**NN**	**2-02-002**
naming	**NN**	**1-01-001**
Nan	**NP**	**2-02-002**
Nancy	**NP**	**5-02-005**
Nanook	**prop. noun**	**1-01-001**
Nanook	NP	0-00-000
Nanook	NP-TL	1-01-001
Nantucket	**prop. noun**	**4-03-003**
Nantucket	NP	3-03-003
Nantucket	NP-TL	1-01-001
Naomi	**NP**	**2-01-001**
nap	**noun**	**6-05-005**
nap	NN	4-03-003
naps	NNS	2-02-002
nap	**verb**	**2-02-002**
napped	VBD	1-01-001
napping	VBG	1-01-001
Naphta	**NP**	**1-01-001**
napkin	**noun**	**5-03-005**
napkin	NN	2-02-002
napkin	NN-HL	1-01-001
napkins	NNS	2-01-002
Naples	**NP**	**3-02-002**
Napoleon	**prop. noun**	**9-04-006**
Napoleon	NP	6-03-005
Napoleon	NP-TL	1-01-001
Napoleon's	NP$	2-02-002
Napoleonic	**JJ**	**1-01-001**
Nara	**prop. noun**	**6-01-001**
Nara	NP	5-01-001
Nara	NP-HL	1-01-001
Narbonne	**NP**	**1-01-001**
narcosis	**NN**	**1-01-001**
narcotic	**JJ**	**1-01-001**
narcotic	**noun**	**8-02-002**
narcotic	NN	1-01-001
narcotics	NNS	7-02-002
narcotize	**verb**	**1-01-001**
narcotizes	VBZ	1-01-001
NAREB	**NP**	**1-01-001**
Narragansett	**prop. noun**	**6-03-005**
Narragansett	NP	2-01-001
Narragansett	NP-TL	4-03-004
narrate	**verb**	**1-01-001**
narrated	VBN	1-01-001
narration	**NN**	**2-02-002**
narrative	**adjective**	**4-02-003**
narrative	JJ	3-02-003
narrative	JJ-HL	1-01-001
narrative	**noun**	**23-04-013**
narrative	NN	20-04-011
narratives	NNS	3-01-003

Word	Tag	Frequency
narrator	**NN**	**11-02-002**
narrow	**adjective**	**63-12-049**
narrow	JJ	61-12-048
narrow	JJ-HL	1-01-001
Narrow	JJ-TL	1-01-001
narrow	**verb**	**15-09-015**
narrows	VBZ	3-03-003
narrowed	VBD	3-03-003
narrowed	VBN	6-05-006
narrowing	VBG	3-03-003
narrow-minded	**JJ**	**1-01-001**
narrower	**JJR**	**7-04-007**
narrowing	**NN**	**1-01-001**
narrowly	**RB**	**6-03-005**
narrowness	**NN**	**1-01-001**
nary	**ABN**	**1-01-001**
nasal	**JJ**	**2-01-002**
nasal	**verb**	**1-01-001**
nasaled	VBD	1-01-001
nascent	**JJ**	**1-01-001**
Nashville	**NP**	**7-02-004**
Nassau	**prop. noun**	**15-04-005**
Nassau	NP	10-04-004
Nassau	NP-TL	4-02-002
Nassau's	NP$	1-01-001
Nasser	**prop. noun**	**3-01-002**
Nasser	NP	2-01-002
Nasser's	NP$	1-01-001
nastier	**JJR**	**1-01-001**
nastiest	**JJT**	**1-01-001**
nasty	**JJ**	**5-04-005**
Nat	**NP**	**1-01-001**
natal	**JJ**	**2-02-002**
Natalie	**NP**	**1-01-001**
natch	**RB**	**1-01-001**
Natchez	**NP**	**2-02-002**
Nate	**prop. noun**	**7-01-001**
Nate	NP	5-01-001
Nate's	NP$	2-01-001
Nathan	**NP**	**5-03-005**
Nathanael	**NP**	**1-01-001**
Nathaniel	**NP**	**2-01-002**
nation	**noun**	**351-13-122**
nation	NN	118-13-066
Nation	NN-TL	21-05-011
nation's	NN$	32-08-027
Nation's	NN$-TL	5-03-004
nations	NNS	118-10-043
Nations	NNS-TL	55-09-031
Nations	NNS-TL-HL	2-02-002
nations'	NNS$	0-00-000
Nations'	NNS$-TL	3-01-002
nation-building	**JJ**	**1-01-001**
nation-state	**noun**	**7-02-002**
nation-state	NN	6-01-001
nation-states	NNS	1-01-001
nation-wide	**JJ**	**3-03-003**
national	**foreign**	**1-01-001**
national	FW-JJ	0-00-000
National	FW-JJ-TL	1-01-001
national	**adjective**	**372-13-143**
national	JJ	216-12-104
National	JJ-TL	154-11-072
National	JJ-TL-HL	2-02-002
national	**noun**	**7-04-005**
national	NN	3-03-003
nationals	NNS	4-02-003
Nationalcar	**prop. noun**	**1-01-001**
Nationalcar	NP	0-00-000
Nationalcar	NP-TL	1-01-001
nationalism	**noun**	**37-07-014**
nationalism	NN	35-05-012
nationalisms	NNS	2-02-002
nationalist	**adjective**	**2-02-002**
nationalist	JJ	1-01-001
Nationalist	JJ-TL	1-01-001
nationalist	**noun**	**3-01-003**
nationalist	NN	2-01-002
nationalists	NNS	1-01-001
nationalistic	**adjective**	**4-03-003**
nationalistic	JJ	3-02-002
Nationalistic	JJ-TL	1-01-001
nationality	**NN**	**3-03-003**
nationalize	**verb**	**4-03-004**
nationalize	VB	1-01-001
nationalized	VBD	1-01-001
nationalized	VBN	1-01-001
nationalizing	VBG	1-01-001
nationally	**RB**	**10-06-010**
nationhood	**NN**	**1-01-001**
nationwide	**JJ**	**5-04-005**
native	**JJ**	**36-11-030**
native	**noun**	**21-10-018**
native	NN	10-05-009
natives	NNS	11-07-009
native-born	**JJ**	**1-01-001**
NATO	**NP**	**2-01-001**
Natrona	**prop. noun**	**1-01-001**
Natrona	NP	0-00-000
Natrona	NP-TL	1-01-001
natty	**JJ**	**1-01-001**
natural	**adjective**	**156-14-097**
natural	JJ	152-14-095
natural	JJ-HL	3-02-002
Natural	JJ-TL	1-01-001
natural-law	**NN**	**1-01-001**
naturalism	**NN**	**1-01-001**
naturalist	**NN**	**1-01-001**
naturalistic	**JJ**	**4-03-004**
naturalize	**verb**	**3-03-003**
naturalized	VBN	3-03-003
naturally	**qualifier**	**1-01-001**
naturally	QL	0-00-000
naturally	QL-HL	1-01-001
naturally	**RB**	**69-14-058**
naturalness	**NN**	**2-02-002**
naturam	**foreign**	**1-01-001**
naturam	FW-NN	0-00-000
Naturam	FW-NN-TL	1-01-001
nature	**noun**	**198-15-128**
nature	NN	183-15-123
nature	NN-HL	5-03-003
Nature	NN-TL	3-02-002
nature's	NN$	3-03-003
natures	NNS	4-02-003
naturopath	**NN**	**1-01-001**
naught	**PN**	**2-02-002**
naughtier	**JJR**	**1-01-001**
naughty	**JJ**	**1-01-001**
nausea	**NN**	**3-03-003**
nauseate	**verb**	**2-02-002**
nauseated	VBN	2-02-002
nautical	**JJ**	**2-02-002**
Nautilus	**NP**	**2-01-001**
naval	**adjective**	**33-07-017**
naval	JJ	21-06-010
Naval	JJ-TL	12-05-009
navel	**noun**	**3-03-003**
navel	NN	2-02-002
navels	NNS	1-01-001
navigable	**JJ**	**1-01-001**
navigate	**verb**	**2-01-001**
navigate	VB	1-01-001
navigating	VBG	1-01-001
navigation	**noun**	**6-05-006**
navigation	NN	5-04-005
Navigation	NN-TL	1-01-001
navigator	**noun**	**3-02-002**
navigator	NN	2-02-002
navigators	NNS	1-01-001
Navona	**prop. noun**	**4-01-001**
Navona	NP	3-01-001
Navona	NP-HL	1-01-001
navy	**JJ**	**1-01-001**
navy	**noun**	**48-10-026**
navy	NN	5-04-004
Navy	NN-TL	31-09-020
navy's	NN$	4-01-001
navy's	NN$-HL	1-01-001
Navy's	NN$-TL	7-05-006
navy-blue	**JJ**	**1-01-001**
naw	**RB**	**1-01-001**
Naxos	**NP**	**1-01-001**
nay	**RB**	**2-02-002**
Nazarene	**JJ**	**1-01-001**
Nazarova	**NP**	**1-01-001**
Nazi	**prop. noun**	**25-07-009**
Nazi	NP	13-05-006
Nazis	NPS	12-05-005
Nazi-minded	**JJ**	**1-01-001**
Nazism	**NP**	**1-01-001**
NBC	**NP**	**2-02-002**
Ndola	**NP**	**1-01-001**
ne	**FW-***	**1-01-001**
Neal	**NP**	**4-02-002**
Neanderthal	**NP**	**1-01-001**
Neapolitan	**JJ**	**1-01-001**
Neapolitan	**NP**	**1-01-001**

Word	Tag	Frequency
near	**IN**	**156-14-113**
near	**adjective**	**17-10-014**
near	JJ	16-10-013
Near	JJ-TL	1-01-001
near	**QL**	**1-01-001**
near	**adverb**	**20-09-018**
near	RB	19-09-017
near	RB-HL	1-01-001
near	**verb**	**19-08-017**
near	VB	4-03-003
neared	VBD	3-02-003
nearing	VBG	11-06-011
nearing	VBG-HL	1-01-001
near-absence	**NN**	**1-01-001**
near-at-hand	**JJ**	**1-01-001**
near-at-hand	**RB**	**1-01-001**
near-Balkanization	**NN**	**1-01-001**
near-blind	**JJ**	**1-01-001**
near-Communist	**noun**	**1-01-001**
near-Communists	NNS	1-01-001
near-equivalent	**noun**	**1-01-001**
near-equivalents	NNS	1-01-001
near-miss	**noun**	**1-01-001**
near-misses	NNS	1-01-001
near-mutiny	**NN**	**1-01-001**
near-stranger	**noun**	**1-01-001**
near-strangers	NNS	1-01-001
near-synonym	**noun**	**1-01-001**
near-synonyms	NNS	1-01-001
nearby	**adjective**	**26-08-022**
nearby	JJ	24-08-020
near-by	JJ	2-01-002
nearby	**RB**	**21-08-020**
nearer	**IN**	**2-02-002**
nearer	**JJR**	**4-02-004**
nearer	**RBR**	**8-05-007**
nearest	**IN**	**3-03-003**
nearest	**JJT**	**18-09-012**
nearest	**RBT**	**3-02-003**
nearly	**QL**	**29-08-025**
nearly	**RB**	**112-14-089**
nearness	**noun**	**3-01-002**
nearness	NN	1-01-001
nearness	NN-HL	2-01-001
nearsighted	**JJ**	**1-01-001**
nearsightedly	**RB**	**1-01-001**
neat	**JJ**	**21-11-021**
neatest	**JJT**	**1-01-001**
neatly	**RB**	**19-12-017**
neatness	**NN**	**1-01-001**
Nebraska	**NP**	**6-05-006**
nebula	**NN**	**1-01-001**
nebular	**JJ**	**1-01-001**
nebulous	**JJ**	**3-03-003**
nec	**FW-CC**	**1-01-001**
necessarily	**QL**	**1-01-001**
necessarily	**RB**	**50-09-042**
necessary	**adjective**	**222-14-142**
necessary	JJ	218-14-141
necessary	JJ-HL	4-01-001
necessary	**noun**	**1-01-001**
necessaries	NNS	1-01-001
necessitate	**verb**	**20-06-018**
necessitate	VB	5-04-005
necessitates	VBZ	3-02-003
necessitated	VBD	4-02-003
necessitated	VBN	7-05-007
necessitating	VBG	1-01-001
necessity	**noun**	**53-12-042**
necessity	NN	39-12-036
necessity	NN-HL	1-01-001
necessities	NNS	13-06-009
neck	**noun**	**80-12-054**
neck	NN	76-11-051
Neck	NN-TL	2-01-001
necks	NNS	2-02-002
neck	**verb**	**3-03-003**
neck	VB	2-02-002
necking	VBG	1-01-001
Neck	**NP**	**1-01-001**
necklace	**noun**	**5-04-005**
necklace	NN	2-02-002
Necklace	NN-TL	1-01-001
necklaces	NNS	2-02-002
neckline	**NN**	**3-02-002**
necktie	**NN**	**2-02-002**
necromantic	**JJ**	**1-01-001**
necropsy	**noun**	**2-01-001**
necropsy	NN	1-01-001

Word	Tag	Frequency
necropsy (cont.):		
necropsy	NN-HL	1-01-001
necrosis	**NN**	**3-01-001**
necrotic	**JJ**	**1-01-001**
nectar	**NN**	**3-02-002**
nectareous	**JJ**	**1-01-001**
nectary	**noun**	**1-01-001**
nectaries	NNS	1-01-001
need	**MD**	**38-11-032**
need	**noun**	**253-14-137**
need	NN	155-14-105
need	NN-HL	5-03-004
needs	NNS	90-12-053
needs	NNS-HL	3-02-003
need	**verb**	**413-15-220**
need	VB	160-15-109
Need	VB-TL	2-01-001
needs	VBZ	59-14-047
needed	VBD	57-10-052
needed	VBN	122-14-086
needed	VBN-HL	8-06-007
needing	VBG	5-03-005
Needham	**prop. noun**	**6-01-001**
Needham	NP	5-01-001
Needham's	NP$	1-01-001
needle	**noun**	**21-07-010**
needle	NN	15-05-006
needles	NNS	6-05-005
needle	**verb**	**1-01-001**
needled	VBD	1-01-001
needle-sharp	**JJ**	**1-01-001**
needless	**JJ**	**11-05-009**
needlessly	**RB**	**1-01-001**
needy	**adjective**	**6-03-005**
needy	JJ	5-02-004
Needy	JJ-TL	1-01-001
Neesen	**NP**	**1-01-001**
negate	**VB**	**2-02-002**
negation	**NN**	**5-02-004**
negative	**adjective**	**50-08-033**
negative	JJ	49-08-033
negative	JJ-HL	1-01-001
negative	**NN**	**3-03-003**
negatively	**RB**	**2-02-002**
negativism	**NN**	**1-01-001**
neglect	**NN**	**8-06-007**
neglect	**verb**	**28-10-025**
neglect	VB	4-03-004
neglects	VBZ	1-01-001
neglected	VBD	2-02-002
neglected	VBN	15-09-014
Neglected	VBN-TL	1-01-001
neglecting	VBG	5-02-005
negligence	**NN**	**4-03-003**
negligent	**JJ**	**2-02-002**
negligible	**JJ**	**10-04-006**
negociant	**foreign**	**3-01-001**
negociant	FW-NN	2-01-001
negociants	FW-NNS	1-01-001
negotiate	**verb**	**25-08-015**
negotiate	VB	10-03-005
negotiated	VBD	2-01-001
negotiated	VBN	5-03-004
negotiating	VBG	8-05-007
negotiation	**noun**	**26-06-015**
negotiation	NN	6-04-005
negotiations	NNS	20-05-011
Negro	**prop. noun**	**171-08-038**
Negro	NP	105-08-033
Negro	NP-TL	2-01-001
Negro's	NP$	4-02-002
Negroes	NPS	58-07-016
Negroes	NPS-HL	1-01-001
Negroes'	NPS$	1-01-001
Negro-appeal	**JJ**	**6-01-001**
Negroid	**JJ**	**1-01-001**
Nehf	**NP**	**1-01-001**
Nehru	**prop. noun**	**6-04-005**
Nehru	NP	5-04-005
Nehru's	NP$	1-01-001
neighbor	**noun**	**59-13-037**
neighbor	NN	14-06-008
neighbor's	NN$	3-03-003
neighbors	NNS	40-12-029
neighbours	NNS	1-01-001
neighbors'	NNS$	1-01-001
neighbor	**verb**	**24-09-020**
neighboring	VBG	24-09-020
neighborhood	**noun**	**75-13-041**

Word	Tag	Count
neighborhood (cont.):		
neighborhood	NN	55-12-035
neighbourhood	NN	1-01-001
neighborhood	NN-HL	1-01-001
neighborhood	NN-NC	1-01-001
neighborhoods	NNS	17-07-008
neighborliness	**NN**	**1-01-001**
Neil	**NP**	**3-02-003**
Neilson	**NP**	**1-01-001**
Neiman-Marcus	**prop. noun**	**4-01-002**
Neiman-Marcus	NP	3-01-002
Neiman-Marcus	NP-TL	1-01-001
Neisse	**prop. noun**	**2-01-001**
Neisse	NP	0-00-000
Neisse	NP-TL	2-01-001
Neisse-Oder	**prop. noun**	**1-01-001**
Neisse-Oder	NP	0-00-000
Neisse-Oder	NP-TL	1-01-001
neither	**CC**	**97-15-084**
neither	**dt./d. cj.**	**37-14-036**
neither	DTX	36-14-035
nether	DTX	1-01-001
neither	**RB**	**7-02-004**
Neitzbohr	**NP**	**4-01-001**
Nell	**NP**	**1-01-001**
Nellie	**NP**	**6-02-002**
Nelson	**NP**	**16-07-009**
nemesis	**NN**	**4-02-002**
Nennius	**NP**	**2-01-001**
neo-	**JJ**	**1-01-001**
neo-classicism	**noun**	**2-02-002**
neo-classicism	NN	1-01-001
Neo-Classicism	NN-TL	1-01-001
neo-classicist	**noun**	**1-01-001**
neo-classicists	NNS	0-00-000
Neo-Classicists	NNS-TL	1-01-001
neo-dadaist	**NN**	**1-01-001**
Neo-Ecclesiasticism	**NP**	**1-01-001**
Neo-Jazz	**NP**	**1-01-001**
Neo-Paganism	**NP**	**1-01-001**
Neo-Popularism	**NP**	**1-01-001**
Neo-Romanticism	**NP**	**1-01-001**
neo-stagnationist	**NN**	**1-01-001**
neo-swing	**NN**	**1-01-001**
neocortex	**NN**	**5-01-001**
neocortical-hypothalamic	**JJ**	**2-01-001**
neoliberal	**JJ**	**1-01-001**
neon	**noun**	**14-04-005**
neon	NN	12-04-005
Neon	NN-TL	2-01-001
neon-lighted	**JJ**	**1-01-001**
neon-lit	**JJ**	**2-02-002**
neonatal	**JJ**	**1-01-001**
Nepal	**NP**	**1-01-001**
nephew	**noun**	**14-05-007**
nephew	NN	9-03-005
nephews	NNS	5-02-002
Neptune	**prop. noun**	**3-03-003**
Neptune	NP	2-02-002
Neptune	NP-TL	1-01-001
Nerien	**NP**	**2-01-001**
Nernst	**NP**	**2-01-001**
Nero	**NP**	**3-02-002**
nerve	**noun**	**34-11-032**
nerve	NN	12-09-012
nerves	NNS	22-09-020
nerve-end	**noun**	**1-01-001**
nerve-ends	NNS	1-01-001
nerve-shattering	**JJ**	**2-02-002**
nerveless	**JJ**	**1-01-001**
nervous	**JJ**	**24-12-020**
nervously	**RB**	**3-01-003**
nervousness	**NN**	**2-01-002**
nest	**noun**	**22-07-011**
nest	NN	18-07-009
Nest	NN-TL	1-01-001
nests	NNS	3-02-002
nest	**verb**	**7-03-006**
nest	VB	1-01-001
nested	VBD	2-01-002
nested	VBN	2-01-002
nesting	VBG	2-01-001
nester	**NN**	**2-01-002**
nestle	**verb**	**4-03-004**
nestled	VBD	1-01-001
nestled	VBN	2-02-002
nestling	VBG	1-01-001
nestling	**NN**	**1-01-001**
Nestor	**NP**	**1-01-001**

Word	Tag	Count
net	**JJ**	**13-02-007**
net	**noun**	**24-08-015**
net	NN	21-07-012
nets	NNS	3-02-003
net	**verb**	**2-02-002**
netted	VBD	1-01-001
netting	VBG	1-01-001
net-like	**JJ**	**1-01-001**
Netherlands	**prop. noun**	**3-03-003**
Netherlands	NP	1-01-001
Netherlands	NP-TL	2-02-002
nettle	**verb**	**2-02-002**
nettled	VBD	1-01-001
nettled	VBN	1-01-001
nettlesome	**JJ**	**1-01-001**
network	**noun**	**48-13-022**
network	NN	30-09-016
network's	NN$	1-01-001
networks	NNS	15-06-007
networks	NNS-HL	1-01-001
networks'	NNS$	1-01-001
Neuberger	**NP**	**1-01-001**
Neumann	**NP**	**1-01-001**
neural	**JJ**	**3-01-001**
neuralgia	**NN**	**1-01-001**
neurasthenic	**NN**	**1-01-001**
Neurenschatz	**prop. noun**	**1-01-001**
Neurenschatz	NP	0-00-000
Neurenschatz	NP-TL	1-01-001
neuritis	**NN**	**1-01-001**
neurological	**JJ**	**1-01-001**
neurologist	**NN**	**1-01-001**
neuromuscular	**JJ**	**1-01-001**
neuron	**NN**	**1-01-001**
neuronal	**JJ**	**1-01-001**
neuropathology	**NN**	**1-01-001**
neuropsychiatric	**JJ**	**2-01-001**
neurosis	**noun**	**10-02-003**
neurosis	NN	6-02-003
neuroses	NNS	4-01-001
neurotic	**JJ**	**9-05-007**
neurotic	**NN**	**1-01-001**
Neusteter	**prop. noun**	**2-01-001**
Neusteter	NP	1-01-001
Neusteters	NPS	1-01-001
neuter	**JJ**	**1-01-001**
neutral	**adjective**	**39-07-017**
neutral	JJ	32-07-015
neutral	JJ-HL	2-02-002
Neutral	JJ-TL	5-01-001
neutralism	**NN**	**5-03-003**
neutralist	**JJ**	**4-02-002**
neutralist	**noun**	**6-03-005**
neutralist	NN	4-02-003
neutralists	NNS	2-02-002
neutrality	**NN**	**3-03-003**
neutralization	**NN**	**2-01-001**
neutralize	**verb**	**6-04-006**
neutralize	VB	1-01-001
neutralized	VBN	5-03-005
neutron	**NN**	**1-01-001**
neutrophil	**noun**	**5-01-001**
neutrophils	NNS	5-01-001
Nevada	**prop. noun**	**7-04-006**
Nevada	NP	5-03-004
Nev.	NP	1-01-001
Nevada	NP-TL	1-01-001
Nevah	**prop. noun**	**1-01-001**
Nevah	NP	0-00-000
Nevah	NP-TL	1-01-001
Neveh	**NP**	**1-01-001**
never	**QL**	**3-03-003**
never	**RB**	**694-15-305**
never-predictable	**JJ**	**1-01-001**
never-to-be-forgotten	**JJ**	**1-01-001**
Neversink	**prop. noun**	**3-01-001**
Neversink	NP	2-01-001
Neversink	NP-TL	1-01-001
nevertheless	**RB**	**73-14-063**
Nevsky	**NP**	**1-01-001**
new	**adjective**	**1635-15-388**
new	JJ	1056-15-345
new	JJ-HL	31-06-011
New	JJ-TL	546-14-192
New	JJ-TL-HL	2-02-002
New-England	**prop. noun**	**1-01-001**
New-England	NP	0-00-000
New-England	NP-TL	1-01-001
new-found	**adjective**	**4-04-004**

Word	Tag	Frequency
new-found (cont.):		
new-found	JJ	3-03-003
newfound	JJ	1-01-001
new-house	**NN**	**1-01-001**
new-rich	**JJ**	**1-01-001**
new-spilled	**JJ**	**1-01-001**
New-Waver	**NP**	**1-01-001**
New-York	**prop. noun**	**1-01-001**
New-York	NP	0-00-000
New-York	NP-TL	1-01-001
Newark	**prop. noun**	**8-03-004**
Newark	NP	6-03-004
Newark	NP-TL	2-01-001
Newarker	**NP**	**1-01-001**
Newbery	**NP**	**1-01-001**
Newbiggin	**prop. noun**	**2-01-001**
Newbiggin	NP	1-01-001
Newbiggin's	NP$	1-01-001
Newbold	**NP**	**2-02-002**
newborn	**JJ**	**6-05-006**
Newburger	**NP**	**1-01-001**
Newburgh	**NP**	**1-01-001**
Newbury	**prop. noun**	**4-01-001**
Newbury	NP	3-01-001
Newbury	NP-HL	1-01-001
Newburyport	**NP**	**5-01-001**
Newcastle	**NP**	**1-01-001**
newcomer	**noun**	**14-06-012**
newcomer	NN	7-04-006
newcomers	NNS	7-04-007
newel	**NN**	**1-01-001**
Newell	**prop. noun**	**1-01-001**
Newells	NPS	1-01-001
newer	**JJR**	**20-10-017**
newest	**JJT**	**15-07-014**
Newfoundland	**NP**	**3-02-002**
newly	**JJ**	**2-02-002**
newly	**RB**	**26-08-021**
newly-appointed	**JJ**	**1-01-001**
newly-created	**JJ**	**1-01-001**
newly-emerging	**JJ**	**1-01-001**
newly-married	**JJ**	**1-01-001**
newly-plowed	**JJ**	**1-01-001**
newly-scrubbed	**JJ**	**1-01-001**
newlywed	**noun**	**4-04-004**
newlywed	NN	1-01-001
newlyweds	NNS	2-02-002
newly-weds	NNS	1-01-001
Newman	**prop. noun**	**10-04-005**
Newman	NP	9-03-004
Newman	NP-TL	1-01-001
Newport	**prop. noun**	**28-06-009**
Newport	NP	23-06-009
Newport	NP-TL	4-02-003
Newport's	NP$	1-01-001
Newport-based	**JJ**	**1-01-001**
news	**noun**	**101-15-078**
news	NN	90-15-072
news	NN-HL	2-02-002
news	NN-NC	1-01-001
News	NN-TL	8-03-005
News	**NP**	**1-01-001**
newsboy	**NN**	**2-02-002**
newsletter	**noun**	**5-03-004**
newsletter	NN	4-02-003
newsletters	NNS	1-01-001
newsman	**noun**	**5-01-004**
newsman	NN	1-01-001
newsmen	NNS	4-01-004
Newsom	**NP**	**1-01-001**
newspaper	**noun**	**104-14-063**
newspaper	NN	64-13-043
Newspaper	NN-TL	1-01-001
newspapers	NNS	38-12-030
newspapers'	NNS$	1-01-001
newspaperman	**noun**	**7-04-006**
newspaperman	NN	6-03-005
newspapermen	NNS	1-01-001
newsreel	**NN**	**1-01-001**
newsstand	**NN**	**1-01-001**
Newsweek	**NP**	**1-01-001**
newt	**noun**	**9-01-002**
newt	NN	8-01-001
newts	NNS	0-00-000
Newts	NNS-TL	1-01-001
Newton	**prop. noun**	**9-03-007**
Newton	NP	6-03-005
Newton's	NP$	3-01-002
Newtonian	**JJ**	**2-02-002**
Newtown	**prop. noun**	**1-01-001**
Newtown	NP	0-00-000
Newtown	NP-TL	1-01-001
next	**post-det.**	**305-15-197**
next	AP	301-15-196
next	AP-HL	2-02-002
Next	AP-TL	2-01-001
next	**IN**	**42-11-034**
next	**QL**	**2-02-002**
next	**RB**	**46-11-043**
next-door	**JJ**	**1-01-001**
next-to-last	**AP**	**1-01-001**
ngandlu	**FW-NN**	**1-01-001**
Ngo	**NP**	**1-01-001**
Niagara	**prop. noun**	**2-02-002**
Niagara	NP	0-00-000
Niagara	NP-TL	2-02-002
Nibble	**NP**	**1-01-001**
nibbler	**noun**	**1-01-001**
nibblers	NNS	1-01-001
Nibelungenlied	**prop. noun**	**1-01-001**
Nibelungenlied	NP	0-00-000
Nibelungenlied	NP-TL	1-01-001
nibs	**noun**	**1-01-001**
nibs'	NN$	1-01-001
Nicaragua	**NP**	**2-02-002**
Niccolo	**NP**	**1-01-001**
nice	**adjective**	**76-13-050**
nice	JJ	74-13-049
nahce	JJ	1-01-001
nise	JJ	1-01-001
nice	**RB**	**1-01-001**
Nice	**NP**	**1-01-001**
nice-looking	**JJ**	**1-01-001**
nicely	**RB**	**9-06-009**
nicer	**JJR**	**2-02-002**
nicest	**JJT**	**1-01-001**
nicety	**noun**	**1-01-001**
niceties	NNS	1-01-001
niche	**NN**	**3-03-003**
Nicholas	**prop. noun**	**7-04-004**
Nicholas	NP	5-04-004
Nicholas	NP-TL	2-01-001
Nichols	**NP**	**1-01-001**
Nicholson	**NP**	**1-01-001**
Nichtige	**foreign**	**1-01-001**
Nichtige	FW-NN	0-00-000
Nichtige	FW-NN-TL	1-01-001
nick	**verb**	**1-01-001**
nicked	VBN	1-01-001
Nick	**prop. noun**	**32-03-004**
Nick	NP	25-02-003
Nick's	NP$	7-02-002
nickel	**noun**	**8-04-006**
nickel	NN	7-03-005
nickels	NNS	1-01-001
nickel-iron	**NN**	**2-01-001**
Nicklaus	**NP**	**1-01-001**
nickname	**noun**	**10-03-009**
nickname	NN	9-03-008
nicknames	NNS	1-01-001
nickname	**verb**	**2-02-002**
nickname	VB	1-01-001
nicknamed	VBN	1-01-001
Nicodemus	**NP**	**3-02-002**
Nicolas	**prop. noun**	**17-01-001**
Nicolas	NP	16-01-001
Nicolas's	NP$	1-01-001
nicotine-choked	**JJ**	**1-01-001**
Niebuhr	**NP**	**2-02-002**
niece	**noun**	**9-04-006**
niece	NN	8-04-005
nieces	NNS	1-01-001
Nieman	**prop. noun**	**3-01-001**
Nieman	NP	2-01-001
Nieman	NP-HL	1-01-001
Niepce	**NP**	**1-01-001**
Nietzsche	**NP**	**2-01-001**
nig	**noun**	**1-01-001**
nigs	NNS	1-01-001
niger	**NP**	**1-01-001**
Niger	**NP**	**1-01-001**
Nigeria	**NP**	**1-01-001**
nigger	**noun**	**16-01-003**
nigger	NN	12-01-002
niggers	NNS	3-01-001
nigras	NNS	1-01-001
Niggertown	**NP**	**1-01-001**
nigh	**RB**	**1-01-001**

Word	Tag	Frequency
night	**noun**	**457-15-193**
night	NN	400-15-180
Night	NN-TL	11-06-007
night's	NN$	13-07-012
nights	NNS	31-12-028
Nights	NNS-TL	2-02-002
night-coach	**NN**	**1-01-001**
night-sight	**NN**	**1-01-001**
night-watchman	**NN**	**1-01-001**
nightclub	**noun**	**7-04-004**
nightclub	NN	2-02-002
nightclub's	NN$	1-01-001
nightclubs	NNS	3-02-002
nightclubs	NNS-HL	1-01-001
nightdress	**NN**	**1-01-001**
nighted	**JJ**	**1-01-001**
nighter	**noun**	**1-01-001**
nighters	NNS	1-01-001
nightfall	**NN**	**4-03-004**
nightingale	**noun**	**5-03-004**
nightingale	NN	3-02-002
Nightingale	NN-TL	1-01-001
nightingales	NNS	1-01-001
nightly	**RB**	**3-03-003**
nightmare	**noun**	**10-07-008**
nightmare	NN	9-06-007
nightmares	NNS	1-01-001
nightmarish	**JJ**	**2-02-002**
nightshirt	**NN**	**1-01-001**
nighttime	**JJ**	**12-01-001**
nighttime	**RB**	**1-01-001**
nihilism	**NN**	**1-01-001**
nihilist	**NN**	**2-01-001**
nihilistic	**JJ**	**1-01-001**
Nijinsky	**NP**	**1-01-001**
Nike-Zeus	**NP**	**1-01-001**
Nikita	**NP**	**7-03-004**
Nikko	**NP**	**1-01-001**
Nikolai	**NP**	**2-01-002**
Nikolais	**NP**	**4-02-002**
nil	**NN**	**1-01-001**
Nile	**NP**	**3-02-002**
nilly	**RB**	**1-01-001**
nilpotent	**JJ**	**12-01-001**
Nilsen	**NP**	**1-01-001**
Nilsson	**NP**	**1-01-001**
nimbler	**JJR**	**1-01-001**
nimbly	**RB**	**2-02-002**
Nina	**NP**	**1-01-001**
nine	**card. num.**	**81-13-056**
nine	CD	79-13-056
Nine	CD-TL	2-01-001
nine-chambered	**JJ**	**1-01-001**
nine-game	**JJ**	**1-01-001**
nine-state	**JJ**	**1-01-001**
nine-thirty	**CD**	**2-02-002**
nine-to-five	**JJ**	**1-01-001**
nine-year	**JJ**	**1-01-001**
nineteen	**card. num.**	**18-10-014**
nineteen	CD	13-08-011
Nineteen	CD-TL	5-03-003
nineteen-sixty	**CD**	**1-01-001**
nineteen-year-old	**JJ**	**2-01-001**
nineteenth	**ord. num.**	**42-10-023**
nineteenth	OD	37-10-021
Nineteenth	OD-TL	4-01-003
nineteenth	OD-TL	1-01-001
nineteenth-century	**NN**	**16-06-009**
ninetieth	**OD**	**1-01-001**
ninety	**CD**	**12-05-008**
ninety	**noun**	**3-03-003**
nineties	NNS	2-02-002
Nineties	NNS-TL	1-01-001
ninety-eight	**CD**	**1-01-001**
ninety-five	**CD**	**1-01-001**
ninety-nine	**CD**	**3-03-003**
ninety-six	**CD**	**2-01-001**
Nineveh	**NP**	**1-01-001**
ninth	**ord. num.**	**20-07-013**
ninth	OD	15-04-008
Ninth	OD-TL	5-05-005
Niobe	**NP**	**1-01-001**
nip	**noun**	**3-02-002**
nip	NN	2-02-002
nips	NNS	1-01-001
nip	**verb**	**2-02-002**
nip	VB	1-01-001
nipped	VBD	1-01-001
Nipe	**prop. noun**	**1-01-001**

Word	Tag	Frequency
Nipe (cont.):		
Nipe's	NP$	1-01-001
nipple	**noun**	**1-01-001**
nipples	NNS	1-01-001
Nippur	**NP**	**1-01-001**
nirvana	**NN**	**1-01-001**
Nischwitz	**prop. noun**	**4-01-001**
Nischwitz	NP	3-01-001
Nischwitz'	NP$	1-01-001
nisf-i-jahan	**foreign**	**1-01-001**
nisf-i-jahan	FW-NN	0-00-000
nisf-i-jahan	FW-NN-NC	1-01-001
Nishima	**NP**	**3-01-001**
Nishimo	**NP**	**1-01-001**
nitrate	**noun**	**4-01-002**
nitrate	NN	3-01-001
nitrates	NNS	1-01-001
nitrogen	**NN**	**12-06-007**
nitrogen-mustard	**NN**	**1-01-001**
nitroglycerine	**NN**	**1-01-001**
Niven	**NP**	**1-01-001**
Nixon	**prop. noun**	**26-06-011**
Nixon	NP	25-06-010
Nixon's	NP$	1-01-001
Njust	**NP**	**1-01-001**
Nkrumah	**NP**	**2-01-001**
NMR	**prop. noun**	**1-01-001**
NMR	NP	0-00-000
NMR	NP-HL	1-01-001
nnuolapertar-it-vuh-karti-biri-pitknoumen	**FW-NN**	**1-01-001**
no	**article**	**1821-15-457**
no	AT	1807-15-456
no	AT-HL	6-05-006
No	AT-TL	8-05-005
no	**noun**	**2-02-002**
nos	NNS	1-01-001
noes	NNS	1-01-001
no	**QL**	**137-10-101**
no	**adverb**	**189-13-112**
no	RB	182-13-109
n-no	RB	1-01-001
no-o	RB	1-01-001
no-o-o	RB	1-01-001
nope	RB	1-01-001
no	RB-NC	3-02-002
no-back	**NN**	**1-01-001**
No-Cal	**NP**	**1-01-001**
no-driving	**JJ**	**1-01-001**
no-goal	**NN**	**1-01-001**
no-good	**JJ**	**1-01-001**
no-hit	**NN**	**2-01-002**
no-man's-land	**NN**	**1-01-001**
No-Name	**NP**	**1-01-001**
no-nonsense	**NN**	**2-02-002**
no-one	**PN**	**1-01-001**
no-trading	**JJ**	**1-01-001**
no-valued	**JJ**	**1-01-001**
Noah	**NP**	**1-01-001**
Nob	**prop. noun**	**1-01-001**
Nob	NP	0-00-000
Nob	NP-TL	1-01-001
Nobel	**prop. noun**	**7-04-006**
Nobel	NP	2-02-002
Nobel	NP-TL	5-04-005
nobility	**NN**	**4-03-004**
noble	**JJ**	**23-11-021**
noble	**noun**	**1-01-001**
nobles	NNS	1-01-001
nobleman	**NN**	**2-02-002**
nobler	**JJR**	**1-01-001**
noblesse	**NN**	**1-01-001**
noblest	**JJT**	**5-03-004**
nobody	**nom. pro.**	**79-13-057**
nobody	PN	74-12-052
nobody's	PN$	2-02-002
nobody'd	PN+HVD	1-01-001
nobody's	PN+BEZ	1-01-001
nobody's	PN+HVZ	1-01-001
noces	**foreign**	**1-01-001**
noces	FW-NNS	0-00-000
Noces	FW-NNS-TL	1-01-001
nociceptive	**JJ**	**2-01-001**
Noctiluca	**prop. noun**	**1-01-001**
Noctiluca	NP	0-00-000
Noctiluca	NP-TL	1-01-001
nocturnal	**JJ**	**3-02-003**
nocturne	**noun**	**3-02-002**
nocturne	NN	0-00-000

Word	Tag	Frequency
nocturne (cont.):		
Nocturne	NN-TL	3-02-002
nod	**noun**	**8-06-008**
nod	NN	7-05-007
nods	NNS	1-01-001
nod	**verb**	**62-08-042**
nod	VB	4-03-004
nodded	VBD	49-07-033
nodded	VBN	2-02-002
nodding	VBG	7-04-007
Nod	**prop. noun**	**1-01-001**
Nod	NP	0-00-000
Nod	NP-TL	1-01-001
node	**noun**	**2-01-001**
nodes	NNS	2-01-001
nodular	**JJ**	**1-01-001**
nodule	**noun**	**1-01-001**
nodules	NNS	1-01-001
Noel	**NP**	**8-04-004**
Nogaret	**NP**	**2-01-001**
Nogay	**NP**	**2-01-001**
Nogol	**NP**	**8-01-001**
noir	**foreign**	**2-02-002**
noir	FW-JJ	1-01-001
noire	FW-JJ	1-01-001
noise	**noun**	**43-13-032**
noise	NN	35-13-026
noise	NN-NC	2-01-001
noises	NNS	6-05-006
noiseless	**JJ**	**1-01-001**
noisemaker	**noun**	**2-02-002**
noisemakers	NNS	2-02-002
noisier	**JJR**	**1-01-001**
noisily	**RB**	**4-04-004**
noisy	**JJ**	**6-04-006**
Nolan	**NP**	**1-01-001**
nolens	**FW-VBG**	**1-01-001**
noli	**FW-VB**	**1-01-001**
Noll	**NP**	**1-01-001**
nolle	**VB**	**1-01-001**
nolo	**FW-VB**	**1-01-001**
nomenclature	**noun**	**7-02-002**
nomenclature	NN	2-02-002
nomenclature	NN-HL	5-01-001
nomia	**noun**	**2-01-001**
nomias	NNS	2-01-001
Nomia	**NP**	**1-01-001**
nominal	**JJ**	**11-05-009**
nominally	**RB**	**3-03-003**
nominate	**verb**	**12-05-008**
nominate	VB	3-03-003
nominated	VBD	1-01-001
nominated	VBN	7-03-004
nominating	VBG	1-01-001
nomination	**NN**	**12-04-006**
nominee	**NN**	**3-02-002**
non	**foreign**	**6-04-006**
non	FW-*	4-03-004
non	FW-*-TL	2-02-002
non	**FW-RB**	**3-02-002**
non	**JJ**	**2-02-002**
non-absorbent	**JJ**	**1-01-001**
non-academic	**JJ**	**2-01-001**
non-algebraically	**RB**	**1-01-001**
non-artistic	**JJ**	**1-01-001**
non-authoritative	**JJ**	**1-01-001**
non-bearing	**JJ**	**1-01-001**
non-book	**noun**	**1-01-001**
non-books	NNS	1-01-001
non-Catholic	**JJ**	**2-02-002**
non-Catholic	**prop. noun**	**8-02-002**
non-Catholic	NP	4-01-001
non-Catholics	NPS	1-01-001
Non-Catholics	NPS	3-01-001
non-Christian	**prop. noun**	**2-01-001**
non-Christians	NPS	2-01-001
non-code	**NN**	**1-01-001**
non-college	**NN**	**1-01-001**
non-color	**NN**	**1-01-001**
non-com	**NN**	**1-01-001**
non-commissioned	**adjective**	**2-02-002**
non-commissioned	JJ	1-01-001
noncommissioned	JJ	1-01-001
non-Communist	**JJ**	**1-01-001**
non-comparable	**JJ**	**1-01-001**
non-competitive	**JJ**	**1-01-001**
non-contributory	**JJ**	**2-01-001**
non-dealer	**NN**	**1-01-001**
non-discrimination	**NN**	**1-01-001**
non-dissonant	**adjective**	**1-01-001**
non-dissonant	JJ	0-00-000
Non-Dissonant	JJ-TL	1-01-001
non-drama	**noun**	**1-01-001**
non-dramas	NNS	1-01-001
non-English	**NN**	**1-01-001**
non-enzymatic	**JJ**	**1-01-001**
non-exempt	**JJ**	**1-01-001**
non-farm	**NN**	**1-01-001**
non-Federal	**JJ**	**1-01-001**
non-figurative	**JJ**	**1-01-001**
non-forthcoming	**JJ**	**1-01-001**
non-freezing	**JJ**	**1-01-001**
non-God	**NP**	**2-01-001**
non-Greek	**JJ**	**1-01-001**
non-hydrogen-bonded	**JJ**	**1-01-001**
non-identity	**NN**	**1-01-001**
non-Indian	**NP**	**1-01-001**
non-instinctive	**JJ**	**1-01-001**
non-institutionalized	**JJ**	**1-01-001**
non-intellectual	**JJ**	**1-01-001**
non-interference	**NN**	**1-01-001**
non-itemized	**JJ**	**1-01-001**
non-Jew	**prop. noun**	**3-01-002**
non-Jew	NP	2-01-002
non-Jews	NPS	1-01-001
non-Jewish	**JJ**	**2-02-002**
non-job-connected	**JJ**	**1-01-001**
non-linear	**JJ**	**1-01-001**
non-military	**JJ**	**3-03-003**
non-negative	**JJ**	**1-01-001**
non-newtonian	**adjective**	**1-01-001**
non-newtonian	JJ	0-00-000
non-newtonian	JJ-HL	1-01-001
non-nonsense	**NN**	**1-01-001**
non-object	**noun**	**1-01-001**
non-objects	NNS	1-01-001
non-objective	**JJ**	**1-01-001**
non-party	**NN**	**2-02-002**
non-pathogenic	**JJ**	**1-01-001**
non-poetry	**NN**	**1-01-001**
non-police	**NN**	**1-01-001**
non-political	**JJ**	**2-02-002**
non-polygynous	**JJ**	**1-01-001**
non-productive	**JJ**	**1-01-001**
non-professional	**JJ**	**1-01-001**
non-profit	**adjective**	**4-03-004**
non-profit	JJ	3-02-003
nonprofit	JJ	1-01-001
non-propagandistic	**JJ**	**1-01-001**
non-propagating	**JJ**	**1-01-001**
non-public	**JJ**	**1-01-001**
non-publisher	**noun**	**1-01-001**
non-publishers	NNS	1-01-001
non-reader	**noun**	**1-01-001**
non-readers	NNS	1-01-001
non-repetitious	**JJ**	**1-01-001**
non-representation	**NN**	**1-01-001**
non-resident	**noun**	**1-01-001**
non-residents	NNS	1-01-001
non-resistant	**noun**	**1-01-001**
non-resistants	NNS	1-01-001
non-romantic	**JJ**	**1-01-001**
non-scientific	**JJ**	**1-01-001**
non-scientist	**NN**	**1-01-001**
non-sentimental	**JJ**	**1-01-001**
non-service	**NN**	**1-01-001**
non-service-connected	**JJ**	**4-01-001**
non-skid	**NN**	**1-01-001**
non-social	**JJ**	**1-01-001**
non-Soviet	**JJ**	**1-01-001**
non-stop	**NN**	**1-01-001**
non-success	**NN**	**1-01-001**
non-supervisory	**JJ**	**3-01-001**
non-systematic	**adjective**	**2-01-001**
non-systematic	JJ	1-01-001
nonsystematic	JJ	1-01-001
non-taxable	**JJ**	**3-01-001**
non-thermal	**JJ**	**2-01-001**
non-time	**NN**	**1-01-001**
non-violence	**NN**	**3-02-002**
non-violent	**adjective**	**11-02-002**
non-violent	JJ	10-01-001
nonviolent	JJ	1-01-001
non-violently	**RB**	**1-01-001**
non-volatile	**JJ**	**1-01-001**
non-wage	**NN**	**1-01-001**
non-Western	**JJ**	**1-01-001**
non-writer	**noun**	**1-01-001**

Word	Tag	Frequency
non-writer (cont.):		
non-writers	NNS	1-01-001
nonacid	**JJ**	**1-01-001**
nonagricultural	**JJ**	**1-01-001**
nonce	**NN**	**1-01-001**
nonchalant	**JJ**	**1-01-001**
nonchurchgoing	**JJ**	**1-01-001**
noncombatant	**JJ**	**1-01-001**
noncommittal	**JJ**	**2-02-002**
noncommittally	**RB**	**1-01-001**
noncompliance	**NN**	**2-01-001**
nonconformist	**noun**	**4-03-003**
nonconformist	NN	1-01-001
Nonconformist	NN-TL	1-01-001
nonconformists	NNS	0-00-000
non-conformists	NNS	1-01-001
Nonconformists	NNS-TL	1-01-001
nondefeatist	**NN**	**1-01-001**
nondescript	**JJ**	**5-04-005**
nondescriptly	**RB**	**1-01-001**
nondiscriminatory	**JJ**	**1-01-001**
nondriver	**NN**	**1-01-001**
nondrying	**JJ**	**2-01-001**
none	**PN**	**108-15-095**
nonequivalence	**NN**	**1-01-001**
nonequivalent	**JJ**	**1-01-001**
nonetheless	**RB**	**10-05-010**
nonexistent	**adjective**	**5-04-005**
nonexistent	JJ	3-03-003
non-existent	JJ	2-02-002
nonfiction	**noun**	**7-03-004**
nonfiction	NN	4-02-003
non-fiction	NN	3-01-001
nonfood	**NN**	**1-01-001**
nonfunctional	**JJ**	**1-01-001**
nonionic	**JJ**	**1-01-001**
nonism	**NN**	**1-01-001**
nonlinguistic	**JJ**	**2-01-001**
nonliterary	**adjective**	**2-01-002**
nonliterary	JJ	1-01-001
non-literary	JJ	1-01-001
nonmagical	**JJ**	**1-01-001**
nonmetallic	**JJ**	**4-01-001**
nonmusical	**JJ**	**1-01-001**
nonmythological	**JJ**	**1-01-001**
nonobservant	**JJ**	**1-01-001**
nonoccurrence	**NN**	**1-01-001**
nonogenarian	**NN**	**1-01-001**
nonparticulate	**JJ**	**1-01-001**
nonpartisan	**adjective**	**4-03-003**
nonpartisan	JJ	2-01-001
non-partisan	JJ	2-02-002
nonpayment	**NN**	**1-01-001**
nonpoisonous	**JJ**	**1-01-001**
nonpolitical	**JJ**	**1-01-001**
nonracial	**JJ**	**1-01-001**
nonreactivity	**NN**	**3-01-001**
nonreactor	**noun**	**2-01-001**
nonreactors	NNS	2-01-001
nonresident	**adjective**	**3-01-001**
nonresident	JJ	2-01-001
nonresident	JJ-HL	1-01-001
nonresidential	**JJ**	**2-01-001**
nonsegregated	**JJ**	**1-01-001**
nonsense	**NN**	**13-09-012**
nonsensical	**JJ**	**1-01-001**
nonshifter	**noun**	**1-01-001**
nonshifters	NNS	1-01-001
nonsingular	**JJ**	**3-01-001**
nonspecific	**JJ**	**19-01-001**
nonspecifically	**RB**	**3-01-001**
nonstop	**NN**	**1-01-001**
nonverbal	**adjective**	**5-03-003**
nonverbal	JJ	3-01-001
non-verbal	JJ	2-02-002
nonwhite	**adjective**	**4-03-003**
nonwhite	JJ	3-02-002
non-white	JJ	1-01-001
nook	**noun**	**1-01-001**
nooks	NNS	1-01-001
noon	**noun**	**25-10-023**
noon	NN	24-09-022
Noon	NN-TL	0-00-000
Noon	NN-TL-HL	1-01-001
noontime	**NN**	**1-01-001**
noose	**NN**	**3-02-002**
nor	**CC**	**195-15-138**
noradrenalin	**NN**	**1-01-001**
Noranda	**NP**	**1-01-001**
Norberg	**NP**	**6-01-001**
Norborne	**NP**	**1-01-001**
Nordmann	**NP**	**4-01-001**
Nordstrom	**NP**	**1-01-001**
Nordyke	**prop. noun**	**1-01-001**
Nordyke	NP	0-00-000
Nordyke	NP-TL	1-01-001
Norell	**NP**	**2-01-001**
norethandrolone	**NN**	**1-01-001**
Norfolk	**NP**	**2-02-002**
Nori	**NP**	**1-01-001**
norm	**noun**	**31-05-013**
norm	NN	7-04-007
norms	NNS	23-03-010
norms	NNS-HL	1-01-001
Norm	**NP**	**3-02-003**
Norma	**prop. noun**	**2-01-001**
Norma	NP	1-01-001
Norma	NP-HL	1-01-001
normal	**JJ**	**133-15-072**
normal	**noun**	**1-01-001**
normals	NNS	1-01-001
normal	**RB**	**3-01-002**
normalcy	**NN**	**4-03-003**
normalize	**verb**	**2-02-002**
normalize	VB	1-01-001
normalized	VBN	1-01-001
normally	**QL**	**2-01-001**
normally	**RB**	**34-10-026**
Norman	**NP**	**15-05-015**
Normandy	**NP**	**1-01-001**
normative	**JJ**	**1-01-001**
Norris	**NP**	**1-01-001**
Norris-LaGuardia	**NP**	**1-01-001**
Norristown	**NP**	**1-01-001**
north	**adjective**	**97-13-056**
north	JJ	0-00-000
North	JJ-TL	96-13-055
north	JJ-TL	1-01-001
north	**adv. noun**	**105-10-045**
north	NR	63-10-034
nawth	NR	1-01-001
North	NR-TL	41-05-010
North	**prop. noun**	**6-03-003**
North	NP	5-03-003
Norths	NPS	1-01-001
north-bound	**JJ**	**1-01-001**
north-south	**JJ**	**2-01-001**
Northampton	**NP**	**2-02-002**
northeast	**adjective**	**5-04-004**
northeast	JJ	2-02-002
Northeast	JJ-TL	3-02-002
northeast	**adv. noun**	**11-06-007**
northeast	NR	4-04-004
Northeast	NR-TL	5-03-003
Northeast	NR-TL-HL	2-01-001
northeast	**RB**	**2-02-002**
Northeastern	**JJ**	**1-01-001**
norther	**noun**	**1-01-001**
northers	NNS	1-01-001
northerly	**JJ**	**1-01-001**
northern	**adjective**	**47-12-034**
northern	JJ	24-10-019
Northern	JJ-TL	23-07-016
northerner	**noun**	**10-02-003**
northerner	NN	1-01-001
Northerner	NN-TL	3-01-001
northerners	NNS	1-01-001
Northerners	NNS-TL	4-01-001
Northeners	NNS-TL	1-01-001
northernmost	**JJS**	**1-01-001**
Northfield	**prop. noun**	**3-02-002**
Northfield	NP	2-02-002
Northfield	NP-TL	1-01-001
Northland	**NP**	**2-02-002**
Northrop	**NP**	**1-01-001**
Northumberland	**NP**	**1-01-001**
northward	**RB**	**5-02-004**
northwest	**adjective**	**7-05-007**
northwest	JJ	3-03-003
Northwest	JJ-TL	4-02-004
northwest	**adv. noun**	**20-07-010**
northwest	NR	7-05-007
NW	NR	1-01-001
nw.	NR	0-00-000
nw.	NR-TL	1-01-001
Northwest	NR-TL	11-03-005
northwestern	**adjective**	**4-02-002**
northwestern	JJ	0-00-000

Word	Tag	Counts
northwestern (cont.):		
Northwestern	JJ	2-01-001
Northwestern	JJ-TL	2-02-002
Norton	**prop. noun**	**9-03-004**
Norton	NP	8-03-003
Norton	NP-TL	1-01-001
Norway	**NP**	**2-02-002**
Norwegian	**JJ**	**2-02-002**
nose	**noun**	**65-10-044**
nose	NN	59-10-041
noses	NNS	6-04-006
nose	**verb**	**2-02-002**
nose	VB	1-01-001
nosing	VBG	1-01-001
nosebag	**NN**	**1-01-001**
nosebleed	**NN**	**2-01-001**
Noskova	**NP**	**1-01-001**
nostalgia	**NN**	**8-05-008**
nostalgic	**JJ**	**6-05-006**
nostalgically	**RB**	**1-01-001**
Nostradamus	**NP**	**1-01-001**
nostril	**noun**	**4-03-004**
nostril	NN	1-01-001
nostrils	NNS	3-02-003
not	**neg. adv.**	**6976-15-497**
not	*	4600-15-495
nawt	*	1-01-001
nott	*	2-01-001
not	*-HL	8-05-007
not	*-NC	1-01-001
Not	*-TL	1-01-001
n't	+*	2098-15-228
n't	+*-HL	4-02-003
n't	+*-NC	1-01-001
n't	+*-TL	2-02-002
not	+*	258-14-150
not-A	**NP**	**1-01-001**
not-ace	**NN**	**2-01-001**
not-knowing	**NN**	**1-01-001**
not-less-deadly	**JJ**	**1-01-001**
not-quite-perfect	**JJ**	**1-01-001**
not-so-lonely	**JJ**	**1-01-001**
not-so-pale	**JJ**	**1-01-001**
not-strictly-practical	**JJ**	**1-01-001**
not-yet-married	**JJ**	**1-01-001**
notable	**JJ**	**20-08-020**
notable	**noun**	**2-01-002**
notables	NNS	2-01-002
notably	**QL**	**3-03-003**
notably	**RB**	**13-08-012**
Notarius	**NP**	**1-01-001**
notarize	**verb**	**1-01-001**
notarized	VBN	1-01-001
notation	**NN**	**3-02-003**
notch	**noun**	**12-03-004**
notch	NN	6-03-004
notches	NNS	6-01-001
notch	**verb**	**3-01-001**
notched	VBN	2-01-001
notching	VBG	1-01-001
notched-stick	**NN**	**1-01-001**
note	**noun**	**126-14-084**
note	NN	72-13-056
note	NN-HL	1-01-001
notes	NNS	50-12-034
Notes	NNS-TL	2-02-002
Notes	NNS-TL-HL	1-01-001
note	**verb**	**165-14-119**
note	VB	53-10-041
note	VB-HL	1-01-001
notes	VBZ	4-04-004
noted	VBD	27-12-026
noted	VBN	62-10-044
noted	VBN-HL	1-01-001
noting	VBG	17-08-017
notebook	**noun**	**4-04-004**
notebook	NN	2-02-002
notebooks	NNS	1-01-001
Notebooks	NNS-TL	1-01-001
noteworthy	**JJ**	**7-05-007**
nothing	**noun**	**1-01-001**
nothings	NNS	1-01-001
nothing	**nom. pro.**	**419-15-221**
nothing	PN	408-15-218
nothin	PN	3-02-002
nothin'	PN	4-02-003
nothing	PN-HL	1-01-001
Nothing	PN-TL	2-02-002
nothing's	PN+BEZ	1-01-001
nothing-down	**JJ**	**1-01-001**
nothingness	**NN**	**3-02-003**
notice	**noun**	**39-12-030**
notice	NN	30-12-024
notices	NNS	9-07-007
notice	**verb**	**84-13-063**
notice	VB	29-10-027
noticed	VBD	28-11-022
noticed	VBN	22-08-020
noticing	VBG	5-05-005
noticeable	**JJ**	**11-07-010**
noticeably	**RB**	**2-01-002**
notification	**NN**	**1-01-001**
notify	**verb**	**13-08-010**
notify	VB	8-04-006
notified	VBD	2-02-002
notified	VBN	2-02-002
notifying	VBG	1-01-001
notion	**noun**	**57-11-035**
notion	NN	40-10-027
notions	NNS	17-05-014
notitia	**foreign**	**1-01-001**
notitia	FW-NNS	0-00-000
Notitia	FW-NNS-TL	1-01-001
notoriety	**NN**	**1-01-001**
notorious	**JJ**	**8-05-008**
notoriously	**QL**	**1-01-001**
Notre	**prop. noun**	**6-02-003**
Notre	NP	3-01-002
Notre	NP-TL	3-02-002
Notre-Dame	**NP**	**1-01-001**
Notte	**prop. noun**	**20-02-003**
Notte	NP	13-02-003
Notte	NP-HL	7-01-001
notwithstanding	**IN**	**3-02-002**
notwithstanding	**RB**	**1-01-001**
noun	**noun**	**4-02-003**
noun	NN	1-01-001
nouns	NNS	3-02-002
nourish	**verb**	**7-07-007**
nourishes	VBZ	1-01-001
nourished	VBN	5-05-005
nourishing	VBG	1-01-001
nourishment	**NN**	**1-01-001**
nouvelle	**foreign**	**1-01-001**
nouvelle	FW-JJ	0-00-000
Nouvelle	FW-JJ-TL	1-01-001
Nouvelle-Heloise	**prop. noun**	**1-01-001**
Nouvelle-Heloise	NP	0-00-000
Nouvelle-Heloise	NP-TL	1-01-001
Nova	**prop. noun**	**1-01-001**
Nova	NP	0-00-000
Nova	NP-TL	1-01-001
Novak	**NP**	**1-01-001**
Novaya	**NP**	**1-01-001**
novel	**JJ**	**11-05-008**
novel	**noun**	**71-10-029**
novel	NN	48-09-023
novel's	NN$	1-01-001
novels	NNS	22-08-016
novelist	**noun**	**22-04-014**
novelist	NN	15-02-010
novelist's	NN$	3-02-002
novelists	NNS	4-02-004
novelize	**verb**	**1-01-001**
novelized	VBN	1-01-001
novelty	**noun**	**12-05-012**
novelty	NN	5-03-005
novelties	NNS	7-03-007
November	**prop. noun**	**95-15-050**
November	NP	74-15-042
Nov.	NP	21-04-011
November-December	**NP**	**1-01-001**
novice	**NN**	**3-02-003**
novitiate	**NN**	**1-01-001**
novo	**FW-NN**	**1-01-001**
Novo	**prop. noun**	**1-01-001**
Novo	NP	0-00-000
Novo	NP-TL	1-01-001
Novosibirsk	**NP**	**1-01-001**
Novosti	**NP**	**1-01-001**
now	**adverb**	**1314-15-394**
now	RB	1309-15-393
now	RB-HL	2-02-002
now	RB-NC	3-02-003
now-famous	**JJ**	**1-01-001**
now-historic	**JJ**	**1-01-001**
now-misplaced	**JJ**	**1-01-001**
Nowacki	**NP**	**1-01-001**

nowadays	**RB**	**12-06-011**
nowhere	**NN**	**4-01-003**
nowhere	**RB**	**26-12-024**
noxious	**JJ**	**2-02-002**
Noyes	**NP**	**1-01-001**
Noyon-la-Sainte	**NP**	**1-01-001**
nozze	**foreign**	**1-01-001**
nozze	FW-NNS	0-00-000
Nozze	FW-NNS-TL	1-01-001
nozzle	**noun**	**7-03-005**
nozzle	NN	4-03-004
nozzles	NNS	3-02-002
nuance	**noun**	**4-04-004**
nuance	NN	1-01-001
nuances	NNS	3-03-003
nubbin	**noun**	**1-01-001**
nubbins	NNS	1-01-001
nubile	**JJ**	**1-01-001**
nuclear	**adjective**	**115-10-035**
nuclear	JJ	113-10-034
nuclear	JJ-HL	1-01-001
Nuclear	JJ-TL	1-01-001
nucleate	**verb**	**1-01-001**
nucleated	VBN	1-01-001
nucleic	**JJ**	**1-01-001**
nucleolus	**noun**	**2-01-001**
nucleoli	NNS	2-01-001
nucleotide	**NN**	**2-02-002**
nucleus	**noun**	**24-05-010**
nucleus	NN	11-05-007
nuclei	NNS	13-01-003
nuclide	**NN**	**3-01-001**
nude	**adjective**	**20-06-011**
nude	JJ	19-06-011
Nude	JJ-TL	1-01-001
nude	**noun**	**2-02-002**
nudes	NNS	2-02-002
nudge	**NN**	**1-01-001**
nudge	**verb**	**4-03-003**
nudge	VB	1-01-001
nudged	VBD	2-01-001
nudging	VBG	1-01-001
nudism	**NN**	**1-01-001**
nudist	**NN**	**1-01-001**
nudity	**NN**	**2-01-001**
nuf	**noun**	**1-01-001**
nufs	NNS	1-01-001
Nugent	**prop. noun**	**6-02-003**
Nugent	NP	3-02-003
Nugent	NP-TL	2-01-001
Nugent's	NP$	1-01-001
nugget	**NN**	**1-01-001**
nuisance	**noun**	**6-04-005**
nuisance	NN	5-03-004
nuisances	NNS	1-01-001
nuit	**foreign**	**2-01-001**
nuit	FW-NN	0-00-000
Nuit	FW-NN-TL	2-01-001
null	**JJ**	**10-02-002**
null	**NN**	**3-01-001**
null-type	**JJ**	**1-01-001**
nullifier	**noun**	**1-01-001**
nullifiers	NNS	1-01-001
nullify	**verb**	**3-02-003**
nullify	VB	1-01-001
nullified	VBD	1-01-001
nullified	VBN	1-01-001
nullity	**NN**	**1-01-001**
numb	**JJ**	**4-04-004**
numb	**verb**	**2-01-002**
numbing	VBG	2-01-002
number	**noun**	**658-15-243**
number	NN	461-15-200
no.	NN	1-01-001
no.	NN-HL	9-02-002
No.	NN-TL	53-08-024
Number	NN	1-01-001
number	NN-HL	3-02-002
number	NN-NC	2-01-001
Number	NN-TL	3-02-002
numbers	NNS	124-12-071
nos.	NNS	1-01-001
number	**verb**	**18-11-016**
number	VB	2-02-002
numbers	VBZ	1-01-001
numbered	VBD	3-02-003
numbered	VBN	6-06-006
numbering	VBG	6-04-005
numbering	**NN**	**1-01-001**
numbingly	**RB**	**1-01-001**
numbness	**noun**	**2-01-001**
numbness	NN	1-01-001
numbness	NN-HL	1-01-001
numeral	**noun**	**2-02-002**
numeral	NN	0-00-000
Numeral	NN-TL	1-01-001
numerals	NNS	1-01-001
numerical	**JJ**	**19-04-012**
numerically	**RB**	**2-02-002**
numerological	**JJ**	**1-01-001**
numerology	**NN**	**1-01-001**
numerous	**JJ**	**47-10-041**
numinous	**adjective**	**3-03-003**
numinous	JJ	2-02-002
numenous	JJ	1-01-001
nun	**noun**	**6-04-006**
nun	NN	2-02-002
nuns	NNS	4-04-004
Nunes	**NP**	**1-01-001**
nuovo	**foreign**	**1-01-001**
nuovo	FW-JJ	0-00-000
Nuovo	FW-JJ-TL	1-01-001
nuper	**FW-RB**	**1-01-001**
nurse	**noun**	**24-09-017**
nurse	NN	16-08-014
Nurse	NN-TL	1-01-001
nurse's	NN$	1-01-001
nurses	NNS	4-02-003
nurses'	NNS$	2-02-002
nurse	**verb**	**17-08-012**
nursing	VBG	13-07-010
nursing	VBG-HL	2-01-001
Nursing	VBG-TL	2-02-002
nursery	**noun**	**14-05-008**
nursery	NN	13-05-008
nursery-	NN	1-01-001
nurture	**NN**	**2-02-002**
nurture	**VB**	**2-02-002**
nut	**noun**	**35-09-013**
nut	NN	15-07-009
nuts	NNS	19-05-006
nuts	NNS-HL	1-01-001
nut-house	**NN**	**1-01-001**
nut-like	**JJ**	**1-01-001**
nutcracker	**noun**	**3-01-002**
nutcracker	NN	0-00-000
Nutcracker	NN-TL	3-01-002
nutmeg	**NN**	**4-02-002**
nutrient	**JJ**	**2-02-002**
nutrient	**noun**	**5-02-003**
nutrients	NNS	5-02-003
nutrition	**noun**	**8-01-002**
nutrition	NN	7-01-002
Nutrition	NN-TL	1-01-001
nutritional	**JJ**	**3-03-003**
nutritious	**adjective**	**1-01-001**
nutritious	JJ	0-00-000
nutritious	JJ-HL	1-01-001
nutritive	**JJ**	**2-01-002**
nuts	**JJ**	**1-01-001**
nutshell	**NN**	**1-01-001**
Nuttall	**NP**	**1-01-001**
nux	**NN**	**1-01-001**
nuzzle	**verb**	**1-01-001**
nuzzled	VBD	1-01-001
Nyberg	**NP**	**2-01-001**
nylon	**NN**	**1-01-001**
nymph	**noun**	**2-02-002**
nymph	NN	1-01-001
nymphs	NNS	1-01-001
nymphomaniac	**noun**	**6-05-005**
nymphomaniac	NN	4-03-003
nymphomaniacs	NNS	2-02-002

O

Word	Tag	Frequency
o	**foreign**	**1-01-001**
o	FW-UH	0-00-000
O	FW-UH-TL	1-01-001
o	**exclam.**	**10-04-006**
o	UH	7-03-005
O	UH	3-01-001
O	**NP**	**1-01-001**
O.	**prop. noun**	**29-06-011**
O.	NP	19-06-010
O.	NP-TL	10-02-002
O.E.C.D.	**NP**	**5-02-002**
O.K.	**adjective**	**6-05-006**
O.K.	JJ	0-00-000
OK	JJ	1-01-001
okay	JJ	5-04-005
O.K.	**adverb**	**5-01-003**
O.K.	RB	1-01-001
OK	RB	4-01-002
O.K.	**exclam.**	**23-07-017**
O.K.	UH	7-04-006
OK.	UH	1-01-001
okay	UH	15-05-011
O'Banion	**prop. noun**	**34-01-001**
O'Banion	NP	25-01-001
O'Banion's	NP$	9-01-001
O'Brien	**NP**	**2-02-002**
O'Casey	**NP**	**1-01-001**
o'clock	**adverb**	**40-11-035**
o'clock	RB	38-10-033
O'Clock	RB-TL	2-02-002
O'Connor	**prop. noun**	**6-05-005**
O'Connor	NP	5-04-004
O'Connor's	NP$	1-01-001
O'Donnell	**prop. noun**	**3-01-001**
O'Donnell	NP	2-01-001
O'Donnell's	NP$	1-01-001
O'Dwyer	**NP**	**2-01-001**
O'Dwyers	**NP**	**2-01-001**
O'Gara	**NP**	**1-01-001**
O'Hare	**NP**	**1-01-001**
O'Neill	**NP**	**3-02-002**
O'Sullivan	**NP**	**2-01-001**
oaf	**noun**	**1-01-001**
oafs	NNS	1-01-001
oak	**noun**	**16-09-015**
oak	NN	7-05-007
Oak	NN-TL	7-04-007
Oak	NN-TL-HL	1-01-001
oaks	NNS	1-01-001
oak-log	**NN**	**1-01-001**
oaken	**JJ**	**1-01-001**
Oakes	**NP**	**3-01-001**
Oakland	**prop. noun**	**1-01-001**
Oakland	NP	0-00-000
Oakland	NP-TL	1-01-001
Oakmont	**NP**	**1-01-001**
Oakwood	**prop. noun**	**5-01-001**
Oakwood	NP	0-00-000
Oakwood	NP-TL	5-01-001
oasis	**noun**	**2-02-002**
oases	NNS	2-02-002
oat	**noun**	**8-04-006**
oats	NN	7-03-005
oats's	NN$	0-00-000
Oats's	NN$-TL	1-01-001
oath	**noun**	**10-06-009**
oath	NN	6-04-005
oathe	NN	1-01-001
oaths	NNS	3-03-003
oath-taking	**JJ**	**1-01-001**
oatmeal	**NN**	**1-01-001**
Oatnut	**prop. noun**	**2-01-001**
Oatnut (cont.):		
Oatnut	NP	0-00-000
Oatnut	NP-TL	2-01-001
OBE	**NP**	**1-01-001**
obedience	**noun**	**10-04-008**
obedience	NN	9-04-007
obediences	NNS	1-01-001
obedience-trained	**JJ**	**1-01-001**
obedient	**JJ**	**2-02-002**
obelisk	**noun**	**6-03-003**
obelisk	NN	5-03-003
Obelisk	NN-TL	1-01-001
Oberlin	**NP**	**2-02-002**
obesity	**noun**	**5-01-001**
obesity	NN	4-01-001
obesity	NN-HL	1-01-001
obey	**verb**	**19-08-017**
obey	VB	8-06-008
obeys	VBZ	1-01-001
obeyed	VBD	5-04-005
obeyed	VBN	2-02-002
obeying	VBG	3-03-003
obituary	**noun**	**2-02-002**
obituaries	NNS	2-02-002
object	**noun**	**115-11-063**
object	NN	53-11-037
objects	NNS	62-09-036
object	**verb**	**29-09-022**
object	VB	12-07-008
objects	VBZ	2-02-002
Objects	VBZ-TL	1-01-001
objected	VBD	12-05-012
objected	VBN	1-01-001
objecting	VBG	1-01-001
objectification	**NN**	**2-02-002**
objection	**noun**	**31-12-022**
objection	NN	18-09-011
objections	NNS	13-09-013
objectionable	**JJ**	**3-01-001**
objective	**JJ**	**38-08-023**
objective	**noun**	**92-09-049**
objective	NN	53-07-033
objectives	NNS	39-06-027
objectively	**RB**	**3-03-003**
objectiveness	**NN**	**1-01-001**
objectivity	**NN**	**2-02-002**
objector	**noun**	**3-01-001**
objector	NN	2-01-001
objectors	NNS	1-01-001
objets	**FW-NNS**	**1-01-001**
obligate	**verb**	**4-04-004**
obligated	VBD	1-01-001
obligated	VBN	3-03-003
obligation	**noun**	**37-08-025**
obligation	NN	16-06-013
obligations	NNS	20-07-016
obligations	NNS-HL	1-01-001
obligational	**JJ**	**1-01-001**
oblige	**NN**	**1-01-001**
oblige	**verb**	**21-07-016**
obliged	VBD	3-02-003
obliged	VBN	18-07-014
obligingly	**RB**	**2-02-002**
oblique	**JJ**	**1-01-001**
obliquely	**RB**	**1-01-001**
obliterans	**foreign**	**1-01-001**
obliterans	FW-VBG	0-00-000
obliterans	FW-VBG-TL	1-01-001
obliterate	**verb**	**3-03-003**
obliterate	VB	2-02-002
obliterated	VBN	1-01-001
obliteration	**NN**	**2-02-002**

Word	Tag	Frequency
oblivion	**NN**	**2-02-002**
oblivious	**JJ**	**2-02-002**
oblong	**JJ**	**1-01-001**
obnoxious	**JJ**	**5-03-005**
oboist	**NN**	**1-01-001**
obscene	**JJ**	**2-01-002**
obscenity	**noun**	**3-03-003**
obscenity	NN	1-01-001
obscenities	NNS	2-02-002
obscure	**JJ**	**11-09-011**
obscure	**verb**	**14-08-014**
obscure	VB	6-03-006
obscures	VBZ	1-01-001
obscured	VBD	2-02-002
obscured	VBN	5-05-005
obscurely	**RB**	**1-01-001**
obscurity	**noun**	**6-04-005**
obscurity	NN	5-03-004
obscurities	NNS	1-01-001
obsequious	**JJ**	**2-01-002**
obsequy	**noun**	**1-01-001**
obsequies	NNS	1-01-001
observable	**JJ**	**3-02-003**
observance	**noun**	**7-04-004**
observance	NN	6-03-003
observances	NNS	1-01-001
observant	**JJ**	**3-03-003**
observation	**noun**	**67-09-036**
observation	NN	27-07-021
observations	NNS	38-06-019
observations	NNS-HL	1-01-001
Observations	NNS-TL	1-01-001
observational	**JJ**	**4-02-002**
observatory	**noun**	**3-02-002**
observatory	NN	0-00-000
Observatory	NN-TL	3-02-002
observe	**verb**	**120-15-086**
observe	VB	25-13-022
observes	VBZ	8-03-008
observed	VBD	15-08-013
observed	VBN	59-10-037
observing	VBG	13-07-013
observer	**noun**	**37-09-026**
observer	NN	13-05-011
Observer	NN-TL	3-02-002
observer's	NN$	1-01-001
observers	NNS	20-06-014
obsess	**verb**	**7-03-005**
obsesses	VBZ	2-01-002
obsessed	VBN	5-03-004
obsession	**noun**	**6-05-006**
obsession	NN	4-03-004
obsession	NN-HL	1-01-001
obsessions	NNS	1-01-001
obsessive	**JJ**	**1-01-001**
obsessive-compulsive	**JJ**	**1-01-001**
obsidian	**NN**	**1-01-001**
obsolescent	**JJ**	**2-02-002**
obsolete	**JJ**	**5-02-004**
obsolete	**verb**	**1-01-001**
obsoleting	VBG	1-01-001
obstacle	**noun**	**17-10-017**
obstacle	NN	10-09-010
obstacles	NNS	7-06-007
obstinate	**JJ**	**1-01-001**
obstruct	**verb**	**8-07-008**
obstruct	VB	4-04-004
obstructed	VBD	2-02-002
obstructed	VBN	2-02-002
obstructionist	**NN**	**2-02-002**
obtain	**verb**	**167-09-082**
obtain	VB	42-08-039
obtaine	VB	1-01-001
obtained	VBD	8-06-007
obtained	VBN	107-09-052
obtaining	VBG	9-02-005
obtainable	**JJ**	**11-04-007**
obtrude	**verb**	**2-02-002**
obtrudes	VBZ	2-02-002
obtrusiveness	**NN**	**1-01-001**
obverse	**NN**	**1-01-001**
obvious	**JJ**	**92-14-074**
obviously	**QL**	**2-01-002**
obviously	**RB**	**112-15-087**
obviousness	**NN**	**1-01-001**
ocarina	**NN**	**1-01-001**
occasion	**noun**	**80-15-066**
occasion	NN	58-15-048
occasions	NNS	22-12-020
occasion	**verb**	**5-03-005**
occasioned	VBN	5-03-005
occasional	**JJ**	**37-13-033**
occasionally	**RB**	**48-12-042**
Occident	**NP**	**2-01-001**
occidental	**adjective**	**2-02-002**
occidental	JJ	1-01-001
Occidental	JJ-TL	1-01-001
occipital	**JJ**	**2-01-001**
occlude	**verb**	**4-01-002**
occluded	VBN	4-01-002
occlusion	**NN**	**2-02-002**
occlusive	**JJ**	**1-01-001**
occupancy	**noun**	**5-04-005**
occupancy	NN	4-03-004
occupancies	NNS	1-01-001
occupant	**noun**	**13-06-010**
occupant	NN	4-04-004
occupants	NNS	9-05-007
occupation	**noun**	**28-11-022**
occupation	NN	23-11-019
Occupation	NN-TL	1-01-001
occupation's	NN$	1-01-001
occupations	NNS	3-03-003
occupational	**adjective**	**11-04-005**
occupational	JJ	10-03-004
Occupational	JJ-TL	1-01-001
occupy	**verb**	**63-13-054**
occupy	VB	16-09-016
occupies	VBZ	4-03-004
occupied	VBD	9-08-009
occupied	VBN	27-10-022
occupying	VBG	7-05-007
occur	**verb**	**158-15-099**
occur	VB	43-11-035
occurs	VBZ	27-06-019
occurred	VBD	47-11-037
occurred	VBN	20-08-014
occurring	VBG	21-05-015
occurrence	**noun**	**40-09-018**
occurrence	NN	29-06-012
occurrence	NN-NC	1-01-001
occurrences	NNS	10-04-007
ocean	**noun**	**37-12-023**
ocean	NN	32-12-021
Ocean	NN-TL	2-02-002
oceans	NNS	3-03-003
ocean-going	**JJ**	**1-01-001**
Oceana	**prop. noun**	**1-01-001**
Oceana	NP	0-00-000
Oceana	NP-TL	1-01-001
Oceania	**prop. noun**	**1-01-001**
Oceania	NP	0-00-000
Oceania	NP-TL	1-01-001
oceanographic	**JJ**	**2-01-001**
oceanography	**noun**	**3-02-002**
oceanography	NN	2-01-001
Oceanography	NN-TL	1-01-001
Oceanside	**NP**	**1-01-001**
ocelot	**NN**	**1-01-001**
och	**foreign**	**2-01-001**
och	FW-CC	0-00-000
och	FW-CC-TL	2-01-001
ochre	**noun**	**3-03-003**
ochre	NN	2-02-002
ocher	NN	1-01-001
octagonal	**JJ**	**3-03-003**
octahedron	**NN**	**1-01-001**
octave	**noun**	**4-03-003**
octave	NN	0-00-000
Octave	NN-TL	2-01-001
octaves	NNS	2-02-002
Octavia	**prop. noun**	**1-01-001**
Octavia	NP	0-00-000
Octavia	NP-TL	1-01-001
octet	**noun**	**1-01-001**
octet	NN	0-00-000
Octet	NN-TL	1-01-001
octillion	**card. num.**	**3-01-001**
octillion	CD	2-01-001
octillion	CD-HL	1-01-001
October	**prop. noun**	**79-11-042**
October	NP	51-11-034
Oct.	NP	26-04-010
Oct.	NP-HL	2-01-002
octopus	**NN**	**1-01-001**
octoroon	**noun**	**2-02-002**
octoroon	NN	1-01-001
Octoroon	NN-TL	1-01-001

ocular	**JJ**	**2-02-002**
Oczakov	**NP**	**2-01-001**
odd	**JJ**	**44-12-031**
odd-lot	**NN**	**17-01-001**
oddity	**noun**	**1-01-001**
oddities	NNS	1-01-001
oddly	**RB**	**9-08-009**
odds	**NNS**	**14-09-014**
odds-on	**JJ**	**1-01-001**
Odell	**NP**	**1-01-001**
Oder	**NP**	**3-01-001**
Odessa	**NP**	**1-01-001**
Odilo	**NP**	**1-01-001**
odious	**JJ**	**3-03-003**
Odom	**NP**	**1-01-001**
odor	**noun**	**22-07-017**
odor	NN	14-06-011
odors	NNS	7-04-007
Odors	NNS-TL	1-01-001
Odysseus	**NP**	**1-01-001**
odyssey	**NN**	**1-01-001**
Odyssey	**prop. noun**	**10-01-001**
Odyssey	NP	2-01-001
Odyssey	NP-TL	8-01-001
oedipal	**adjective**	**4-01-001**
oedipal	JJ	3-01-001
Oedipal	JJ-TL	1-01-001
Oedipus	**prop. noun**	**20-01-002**
Oedipus	NP	17-01-002
Oedipus	NP-TL	3-01-002
Oersted	**prop. noun**	**20-01-001**
Oersted	NP	13-01-001
Oersted's	NP$	7-01-001
of	**prep.**	**36432-15-500**
of	IN	35032-15-500
o'	IN	15-04-006
uh	IN	1-01-001
of	IN-HL	207-09-078
of	IN-NC	3-02-002
Of	IN-TL	163-10-075
of	IN-TL	1003-15-252
of	IN-TL-HL	2-01-002
Of	IN-TL-HL	4-02-003
buncha	+IN	1-01-001
outta	+IN	1-01-001
off	**prep.**	**157-14-108**
off	IN	156-14-107
off	IN-HL	1-01-001
off	**adv./part.**	**482-15-233**
off	RP	479-15-233
off	RP-HL	3-02-002
off-beat	**adjective**	**3-03-003**
off-beat	JJ	2-02-002
offbeat	JJ	1-01-001
off-Broadway	**NN**	**2-02-002**
off-Broadway	**RB**	**1-01-001**
off-color	**JJ**	**1-01-001**
off-duty	**JJ**	**3-03-003**
off-farm	**JJ**	**1-01-001**
off-flavor	**noun**	**2-01-001**
off-flavor	NN	1-01-001
off-flavors	NNS	1-01-001
off-key	**JJ**	**1-01-001**
off-level	**JJ**	**1-01-001**
off-road	**JJ**	**1-01-001**
off-the-cuff	**JJ**	**1-01-001**
offal	**NN**	**1-01-001**
Offenbach	**prop. noun**	**1-01-001**
Offenbach's	NP$	1-01-001
offend	**verb**	**8-05-008**
offend	VB	4-03-004
offended	VBD	1-01-001
offended	VBN	2-02-002
offending	VBG	1-01-001
offender	**noun**	**4-04-004**
offender	NN	2-02-002
offenders	NNS	2-02-002
offense	**noun**	**15-05-011**
offense	NN	8-03-007
offenses	NNS	5-02-003
offences	NNS	1-01-001
offenses	NNS-HL	1-01-001
offensive	**adjective**	**8-05-008**
offensive	JJ	7-05-007
Offensive	JJ-TL	1-01-001
offensive	**noun**	**1-01-001**
offensives	NNS	1-01-001
offensively	**RB**	**1-01-001**
offer	**noun**	**13-09-013**

offer (cont.):		
offer	NN	12-09-012
offers	NNS	1-01-001
offer	**verb**	**217-14-143**
offer	VB	68-13-061
offers	VBZ	43-10-032
Offers	VBZ-HL	1-01-001
offered	VBD	43-12-039
offered	VBN	40-12-037
offering	VBG	22-11-018
offering	**noun**	**9-05-007**
offering	NN	6-03-004
offerings	NNS	3-03-003
offhand	**JJ**	**1-01-001**
office	**noun**	**301-14-136**
office	NN	215-13-111
Office	NN-TL	40-09-027
offices	NNS	39-10-025
Offices	NNS-TL	6-02-002
office's	NN$	0-00-000
Office's	NN$-TL	1-01-001
officeholder	**noun**	**1-01-001**
officeholders	NNS	1-01-001
officer	**noun**	**204-13-082**
officer	NN	95-12-048
officer	NN-HL	2-02-002
Officer	NN-TL	4-04-004
officer's	NN$	13-03-004
officers	NNS	82-11-052
offersey	NNS	1-01-001
Officers	NNS-TL	1-01-001
officers'	NNS$	3-03-003
Officers'	NNS$-TL	3-02-002
officer	**verb**	**1-01-001**
officered	VBN	1-01-001
official	**JJ**	**55-13-045**
official	**noun**	**82-10-058**
official	NN	20-09-018
officials	NNS	60-08-047
Officials	NNS-TL	2-02-002
officialdom	**NN**	**1-01-001**
officially	**RB**	**18-08-016**
officiate	**verb**	**5-01-003**
officiate	VB	1-01-001
officiated	VBD	3-01-001
officiating	VBG	1-01-001
officielle	**foreign**	**1-01-001**
officielle	FW-JJ	0-00-000
Officielle	FW-JJ-TL	1-01-001
officio	**FW-NN**	**1-01-001**
officious	**JJ**	**1-01-001**
offing	**NN**	**1-01-001**
offsaddle	**verb**	**1-01-001**
offsaddled	VBD	1-01-001
offset	**verb**	**10-05-008**
offset	VB	7-05-006
offset	VBN	2-01-001
offsetting	VBG	1-01-001
offshore	**JJ**	**1-01-001**
offshore	**adverb**	**3-03-003**
offshore	RB	2-02-002
off-shore	RB	1-01-001
offspring	**noun**	**7-03-005**
offspring	NN	5-02-003
offspring	NNS	2-02-002
offstage	**adverb**	**2-02-002**
offstage	RB	1-01-001
off-stage	RB	1-01-001
Offutt	**prop. noun**	**1-01-001**
Offutt	NP	0-00-000
Offutt	NP-TL	1-01-001
oft	**RB**	**1-01-001**
oft-repeated	**JJ**	**1-01-001**
often	**RB**	**369-15-206**
oftener	**RBR**	**1-01-001**
oftentimes	**RB**	**2-02-002**
Ogden	**prop. noun**	**3-01-001**
Ogden	NP	1-01-001
Ogden	NP-HL	1-01-001
Ogden	NP-TL	1-01-001
ogle	**verb**	**2-02-002**
ogled	VBD	1-01-001
ogled	VBN	1-01-001
Oglethorpe	**prop. noun**	**1-01-001**
Oglethorpe	NP	0-00-000
Oglethorpe	NP-TL	1-01-001
ogress	**NN**	**1-01-001**
oh	**exclam.**	**119-12-069**
oh	UH	117-11-067

oh (cont.):		
Oh	UH	1-01-001
Oh	UH-TL	1-01-001
oh-the-pain-of-it	**UH**	**1-01-001**
Ohio	**prop. noun**	**38-10-025**
Ohio	NP	25-10-021
Ohio	NP-HL	2-02-002
Ohio	NP-TL	11-03-005
ohmic	**JJ**	**1-01-001**
oil	**noun**	**111-12-047**
oil	NN	88-11-042
Oil	NN-TL	8-05-006
oils	NNS	15-03-003
oil	**verb**	**3-02-003**
oiled	VBN	3-02-003
oil-bearing	**JJ**	**2-01-001**
oil-field	**NN**	**1-01-001**
oil-well	**NN**	**1-01-001**
oilcloth	**NN**	**3-02-002**
Oiler	**prop. noun**	**1-01-001**
Oilers	NPS	1-01-001
oilheating	**NN**	**2-01-001**
oilman-rancher	**NN**	**1-01-001**
oilseed	**noun**	**5-01-001**
oilseed	NN	1-01-001
oilseeds	NNS	4-01-001
oily	**JJ**	**10-05-009**
ointment	**NN**	**3-03-003**
Oistrakh	**NP**	**1-01-001**
oiticica	**NN**	**1-01-001**
ok	**verb**	**1-01-001**
oks	VBZ	0-00-000
oks	VBZ-HL	1-01-001
Okada	**NP**	**1-01-001**
Okamoto	**NP**	**2-01-001**
Okinawa	**NP**	**1-01-001**
Oklahoma	**prop. noun**	**17-06-010**
Oklahoma	NP	11-06-009
Okla.	NP	3-01-003
Oklahoma	NP-TL	3-01-002
Olaf	**prop. noun**	**1-01-001**
Olaf	NP	0-00-000
Olaf	NP-TL	1-01-001
Olatunji	**NP**	**1-01-001**
old	**adjective**	**673-15-257**
old	JJ	582-15-241
ol	JJ	3-01-001
ol'	JJ	1-01-001
Ol'	JJ-TL	1-01-001
Olde	JJ	1-01-001
ole	JJ	2-01-001
Ole	JJ-TL	3-01-001
ould	JJ	1-01-001
Old	JJ-TL	79-13-037
old-age	**NN**	**1-01-001**
old-fashioned	**JJ**	**7-05-007**
old-grad-type	**NN**	**1-01-001**
old-line	**NN**	**1-01-001**
old-style	**NN**	**2-02-002**
old-time	**JJ**	**4-03-004**
old-timer	**noun**	**3-01-002**
old-timer	NN	2-01-001
old-timers	NNS	1-01-001
olden	**JJ**	**1-01-001**
Oldenburg	**prop. noun**	**2-01-001**
Oldenburg	NP	1-01-001
Oldenburg's	NP$	1-01-001
older	**comp. adj.**	**93-14-067**
older	JJR	92-14-067
older	JJR-HL	1-01-001
oldest	**JJT**	**14-10-013**
oldie	**noun**	**1-01-001**
oldies	NNS	1-01-001
Oldsmobile	**NP**	**2-02-002**
oldster	**noun**	**2-02-002**
oldsters	NNS	2-02-002
oleander	**noun**	**2-02-002**
oleanders	NNS	2-02-002
Oleg	**NP**	**1-01-001**
oleomargarine	**NN**	**1-01-001**
oleophilic	**JJ**	**3-01-001**
oleophobic	**JJ**	**1-01-001**
Olerichs	**NP**	**1-01-001**
Olga	**NP**	**6-03-004**
Olgivanna	**NP**	**7-01-001**
olim	**FW-RB**	**1-01-001**
olive	**JJ**	**2-02-002**
olive	**noun**	**3-02-002**
olive	NN	2-01-001
olive (cont.):		
olives	NNS	1-01-001
Olive	**NP**	**1-01-001**
olive-flushed	**JJ**	**1-01-001**
olive-green	**JJ**	**1-01-001**
olivefaced	**JJ**	**1-01-001**
Oliver	**prop. noun**	**10-04-005**
Oliver	NP	7-04-005
Oliver's	NP$	3-01-001
Olivet	**prop. noun**	**1-01-001**
Olivet	NP	0-00-000
Olivet	NP-TL	1-01-001
Olivette	**NP**	**1-01-001**
Olivetti	**NP**	**4-01-001**
Olivia	**NP**	**1-01-001**
Olney	**prop. noun**	**1-01-001**
Olney	NP	0-00-000
Olney	NP-TL	1-01-001
ology	**noun**	**1-01-001**
ologies	NNS	1-01-001
Olsen	**NP**	**1-01-001**
Olson	**prop. noun**	**2-02-002**
Olson	NP	1-01-001
Olson's	NP$	1-01-001
Olvey	**NP**	**1-01-001**
Olympian	**JJ**	**1-01-001**
Olympic	**adjective**	**7-04-006**
Olympic	JJ	4-02-004
Olympic	JJ-TL	3-02-003
Olympics	**NPS**	**2-01-001**
Omaha	**NP**	**2-01-001**
Oman	**NP**	**1-01-001**
OME	**NP**	**1-01-001**
Omega	**NP**	**1-01-001**
omelet	**noun**	**3-01-001**
omelet	NN	2-01-001
omelet	NN-HL	1-01-001
omen	**NN**	**2-02-002**
ominous	**JJ**	**12-08-012**
ominously	**RB**	**3-03-003**
omission	**noun**	**7-06-007**
omission	NN	3-03-003
ommission	NN	1-01-001
omissions	NNS	3-03-003
omit	**verb**	**22-08-019**
omit	VB	1-01-001
omits	VBZ	2-02-002
omitted	VBN	13-06-011
omitting	VBG	6-04-005
omnipotence	**NN**	**1-01-001**
omniscient	**JJ**	**1-01-001**
Omsk	**NP**	**1-01-001**
on	**prep.**	**6183-15-499**
on	IN	6105-15-499
on	IN-HL	24-06-019
on	IN-NC	6-02-002
On	IN-TL	15-06-014
on	IN-TL	33-08-026
on	**adv./part.**	**559-15-285**
on	RP	556-15-284
On	RP-TL	1-01-001
g'ahn	+RP	1-01-001
c'mon	+RP	1-01-001
on-again-off-again	**JJ**	**1-01-001**
on-level	**JJ**	**1-01-001**
on-shore	**adjective**	**1-01-001**
on-shore	JJ	0-00-000
on-sure	JJ	1-01-001
on-site	**JJ**	**2-02-002**
on-stage	**JJ**	**1-01-001**
on-the-job	**JJ**	**3-03-003**
on-the-scene	**JJ**	**2-02-002**
on-the-spot	**JJ**	**1-01-001**
on-to-Spokane	**adjective**	**1-01-001**
on-to-Spokane	JJ	0-00-000
On-to-Spokane	JJ-TL	1-01-001
once	**sub. conj.**	**82-14-071**
once	CS	81-14-070
onct	CS	1-01-001
once	**adverb**	**419-15-237**
once	RB	413-15-236
Once	RB	1-01-001
onct	RB	1-01-001
Once	RB-TL	4-02-003
once-a-month	**JJ**	**1-01-001**
once-dry	**JJ**	**1-01-001**
once-in-a-lifetime	**JJ**	**1-01-001**
once-over	**NN**	**1-01-001**
once-over-lightly	**NN**	**1-01-001**

Word	Tag	Frequency
once-popular	**JJ**	**1-01-001**
oncoming	**JJ**	**2-02-002**
one	**card. num.**	**2737-15-490**
one	CD	2712-15-489
one-	CD	5-03-003
one	CD-HL	4-04-004
one	CD-NC	5-01-001
One	CD-TL	11-07-009
one	**DTX**	**2-01-001**
one	**noun**	**117-15-091**
one's	NN$	1-01-001
ones	NNS	113-15-088
ones	NNS-HL	1-01-001
Ones	NNS-TL	2-01-001
one	**nom. pro.**	**622-15-262**
one	PN	557-15-251
one	PN-NC	1-01-001
one's	PN+HVZ	1-01-001
one's	PN$	63-13-039
one-act	**NN**	**1-01-001**
one-act-play	**NN**	**1-01-001**
one-arm	**NN**	**2-02-002**
one-armed	**JJ**	**1-01-001**
one-color	**NN**	**1-01-001**
one-day	**NN**	**1-01-001**
one-digit	**NN**	**2-01-001**
one-dumbbell	**NN**	**1-01-001**
one-eighth	**NN**	**2-01-002**
one-fifth	**NN**	**4-03-004**
one-fourth	**NN**	**6-06-006**
one-gee	**JJ**	**2-01-001**
one-half	**NN**	**9-07-008**
one-horse	**NN**	**1-01-001**
one-inch	**JJ**	**6-01-001**
one-iron	**NN**	**1-01-001**
one-kiloton	**NN**	**1-01-001**
one-leg	**adjective**	**1-01-001**
one-leg	JJ	0-00-000
One-Leg	JJ-TL	1-01-001
one-man	**JJ**	**5-03-004**
one-minute	**NN**	**1-01-001**
one-night	**NN**	**2-02-002**
one-o'clock	**NN**	**1-01-001**
one-over-par	**NN**	**1-01-001**
one-plane	**NN**	**1-01-001**
one-quarter	**NN**	**2-02-002**
one-reel	**NN**	**1-01-001**
one-room	**JJ**	**3-02-003**
one-shot	**JJ**	**8-02-003**
one-sided	**JJ**	**2-02-002**
one-sixteenth	**NN**	**1-01-001**
one-sixth	**NN**	**2-02-002**
one-step	**noun**	**1-01-001**
one-step	NN	0-00-000
One-Step	NN-TL	1-01-001
one-story	**JJ**	**5-03-004**
one-stroke	**NN**	**2-01-001**
one-tenth	**NN**	**5-05-005**
one-third	**NN**	**14-07-010**
one-thirty	**CD**	**2-01-001**
one-thousand-zloty	**NN**	**1-01-001**
one-thousandth	**NN**	**1-01-001**
one-time	**adjective**	**3-03-003**
one-time	JJ	2-02-002
onetime	JJ	1-01-001
one-time	**NN**	**1-01-001**
one-twentieth	**NN**	**2-02-002**
one-two-three	**NN**	**2-01-001**
one-way	**NN**	**1-01-001**
one-week-old	**JJ**	**1-01-001**
one-year	**NN**	**1-01-001**
Oneida	**NP**	**1-01-001**
oneness	**NN**	**2-02-002**
oneself	**PPL**	**5-03-003**
oneupmanship	**NN**	**1-01-001**
onion	**noun**	**19-06-007**
onion	NN	15-04-005
onions	NNS	4-04-004
onlooker	**noun**	**4-04-004**
onlooker	NN	2-02-002
onlookers	NNS	2-02-002
only	**post-det.**	**365-15-230**
only	AP	364-15-230
only	AP-HL	1-01-001
only	**JJ**	**5-03-005**
only	**QL**	**21-09-021**
only	**adverb**	**1360-15-442**
only	RB	1357-15-442
onleh	RB	3-01-001
onrush	**NN**	**4-04-004**
onrushing	**JJ**	**1-01-001**
onset	**noun**	**43-02-003**
onset	NN	15-02-003
Onset	NN-TL	23-01-001
onsets	NNS	0-00-000
Onsets	NNS-TL	5-01-001
onslaught	**noun**	**6-05-006**
onslaught	NN	4-04-004
onslaughts	NNS	2-01-002
Ontario	**prop. noun**	**2-02-002**
Ontario	NP	1-01-001
Ontario's	NP$	1-01-001
onto	**IN**	**61-12-047**
ontological	**JJ**	**8-01-001**
ontologically	**RB**	**1-01-001**
onus	**NN**	**2-02-002**
onward	**RB**	**1-01-001**
onward-driving	**JJ**	**1-01-001**
onwards	**RB**	**1-01-001**
oooo	**UH**	**1-01-001**
oops	**UH**	**1-01-001**
Oopsie-Cola	**NP**	**1-01-001**
ooze	**NN**	**1-01-001**
ooze	**verb**	**3-02-003**
ooze	VB	1-01-001
oozed	VBD	2-02-002
opalescent	**JJ**	**1-01-001**
opaque	**JJ**	**6-03-006**
Opelika	**NP**	**2-02-002**
open	**adjective**	**242-14-155**
open	JJ	238-14-155
open	JJ-HL	2-02-002
Open	JJ-TL	2-02-002
open	**noun**	**12-04-007**
open	NN	4-03-003
Open	NN-TL	8-03-005
open	**RB**	**8-05-007**
open	**verb**	**259-15-158**
open	VB	54-15-045
open	VB-HL	1-01-001
opens	VBZ	16-10-015
open	VBZ	1-01-001
opened	VBD	94-15-069
opened	VBN	37-12-029
opening	VBG	56-13-043
open-air	**NN**	**1-01-001**
open-collared	**JJ**	**1-01-001**
open-end	**NN**	**1-01-001**
open-ended	**JJ**	**1-01-001**
open-face	**NN**	**1-01-001**
open-flame	**NN**	**1-01-001**
open-handed	**JJ**	**1-01-001**
open-meeting	**NN**	**1-01-001**
open-minded	**JJ**	**1-01-001**
open-mouthed	**JJ**	**3-03-003**
open-work	**NN**	**1-01-001**
opener	**NN**	**6-04-006**
opening	**noun**	**34-12-029**
opening	NN	27-12-023
openings	NNS	7-05-006
opening-day	**NN**	**1-01-001**
openly	**QL**	**1-01-001**
openly	**RB**	**33-11-028**
opera	**FW-NN**	**1-01-001**
opera	**noun**	**49-10-022**
opera	NN	28-10-016
Opera	NN-TL	18-04-010
opera's	NN$	0-00-000
Opera's	NN$-TL	1-01-001
operas	NNS	2-01-002
operable	**JJ**	**1-01-001**
operagoer	**noun**	**1-01-001**
operagoers	NNS	1-01-001
operand	**noun**	**17-01-001**
operand	NN	16-01-001
operands	NNS	1-01-001
operate	**verb**	**177-12-091**
operate	VB	48-10-032
operates	VBZ	15-05-013
operated	VBD	8-06-008
operated	VBN	19-07-015
operating	VBG	85-09-042
operating	VBG-HL	1-01-001
Operating	VBG-TL	1-01-001
operatic	**JJ**	**5-03-005**
operation	**noun**	**197-13-090**
operation	NN	104-12-069
operation	NN-HL	3-02-003

Word	Tag	Frequency
operation (cont.):		
Operation	NN-TL	6-05-005
operations	NNS	78-09-040
operations	NNS-HL	3-02-003
Operations	NNS-TL	3-03-003
operational	**JJ**	**25-05-013**
operationally	**RB**	**1-01-001**
operative	**JJ**	**6-03-004**
operator	**noun**	**66-08-022**
operator	NN	49-06-011
operators	NNS	17-05-013
operetta	**NN**	**6-02-002**
ophthalmic	**adjective**	**2-01-001**
ophthalmic	JJ	0-00-000
Ophthalmic	JJ-TL	2-01-001
opiate	**noun**	**1-01-001**
opiates	NNS	1-01-001
opinion	**noun**	**140-13-080**
opinion	NN	95-11-066
Opinion	NN-TL	1-01-001
opinions	NNS	43-10-024
opinions	NNS-HL	1-01-001
opinionated	**JJ**	**2-01-002**
opium	**NN**	**16-02-002**
Oppenheim	**NP**	**1-01-001**
opponent	**noun**	**30-09-019**
opponent	NN	15-06-007
opponent's	NN$	2-01-001
opponents	NNS	13-07-013
opportune	**JJ**	**1-01-001**
opportunism	**NN**	**1-01-001**
opportunistic	**JJ**	**1-01-001**
opportunity	**noun**	**172-14-090**
opportunity	NN	120-14-077
opportunity	NN-HL	1-01-001
opportunities	NNS	50-13-029
opportunities	NNS-HL	1-01-001
oppose	**verb**	**71-10-059**
oppose	VB	15-06-015
opposes	VBZ	2-01-002
opposed	VBD	9-06-009
opposed	VBN	32-08-031
opposing	VBG	13-07-011
opposite	**IN**	**24-09-016**
opposite	**JJ**	**47-10-042**
opposite	**NN**	**7-03-006**
opposite	**RB**	**3-03-003**
opposition	**noun**	**46-09-032**
opposition	NN	45-09-032
opposition	NN-HL	1-01-001
oppress	**verb**	**5-05-005**
oppressed	VBD	1-01-001
oppressed	VBN	4-04-004
oppression	**NN**	**6-05-006**
oppressive	**JJ**	**4-04-004**
oppressor	**noun**	**2-02-002**
oppressors	NNS	2-02-002
opprobrium	**NN**	**1-01-001**
opt	**verb**	**2-01-001**
opted	VBD	2-01-001
optical	**JJ**	**19-03-008**
optically	**RB**	**1-01-001**
optics	**NN**	**1-01-001**
optimal	**JJ**	**28-01-004**
optimality	**NN**	**5-01-001**
optimism	**NN**	**15-10-014**
optimistic	**JJ**	**15-06-013**
optimization	**NN**	**1-01-001**
optimize	**verb**	**1-01-001**
optimizing	VBG	1-01-001
optimo	**FW-JJT**	**1-01-001**
optimum	**JJ**	**13-03-009**
optimum	**NN**	**3-01-002**
option	**noun**	**6-04-006**
option	NN	5-03-005
options	NNS	1-01-001
optional	**JJ**	**4-02-004**
opulent	**JJ**	**1-01-001**
opus	**noun**	**11-04-007**
opus	NN	3-03-003
op.	NN	0-00-000
Op.	NN-TL	8-01-003
or	**co. conj.**	**4204-15-492**
or	CC	4189-15-492
or	CC-HL	12-02-002
or	CC-NC	1-01-001
or	CC-TL	2-02-002
oracle	**noun**	**3-01-003**
oracle	NN	2-01-002
oracle (cont.):		
oracles	NNS	1-01-001
oral	**adjective**	**27-06-007**
oral	JJ	25-05-006
Oral	JJ-TL	2-01-001
orally	**RB**	**2-02-002**
orange	**JJ**	**8-06-008**
orange	**noun**	**15-06-012**
orange	NN	9-04-008
oranges	NNS	4-03-003
Oranges	NNS-TL	2-01-001
Orange	**prop. noun**	**6-04-004**
Orange	NP	1-01-001
Orange	NP-TL	5-03-003
orate	**VB**	**1-01-001**
oratio	**FW-NN**	**1-01-001**
oration	**noun**	**5-04-004**
oration	NN	3-02-002
orations	NNS	2-02-002
orator	**noun**	**7-02-004**
orator	NN	5-02-003
orators	NNS	2-02-002
oratorical	**JJ**	**2-02-002**
oratorio	**NN**	**1-01-001**
oratory	**noun**	**3-03-003**
oratory	NN	2-02-002
Oratory	NN-TL	1-01-001
orb	**NN**	**1-01-001**
orbit	**noun**	**24-09-013**
orbit	NN	15-09-010
orbits	NNS	9-03-004
orbit	**verb**	**4-04-004**
orbit	VB	1-01-001
orbiting	VBG	3-03-003
orbital	**JJ**	**2-01-001**
orchard	**noun**	**8-05-005**
orchard	NN	3-02-002
orchards	NNS	5-04-004
Orchesis	**NP**	**2-01-001**
orchester	**foreign**	**1-01-001**
orchester	FW-NN	0-00-000
Orchester	FW-NN-TL	1-01-001
orchestra	**noun**	**66-12-026**
orchestra	NN	40-10-023
Orchestra	NN-TL	20-05-009
orchestra's	NN$	2-01-002
orchestras	NNS	4-04-004
orchestral	**adjective**	**4-02-003**
orchestral	JJ	3-02-003
Orchestral	JJ-TL	1-01-001
orchestration	**noun**	**5-02-003**
orchestration	NN	3-02-003
orchestrations	NNS	2-01-001
orchestre	**foreign**	**1-01-001**
orchestre	FW-NN	0-00-000
Orchestre	FW-NN-TL	1-01-001
orchid	**noun**	**3-03-003**
orchids	NNS	3-03-003
Orcutt	**NP**	**2-01-001**
ordain	**verb**	**6-03-005**
ordain	VB	2-01-001
ordained	VBN	4-03-004
ordeal	**NN**	**3-02-003**
order	**noun**	**416-15-213**
order	NN	342-15-187
order	NN-HL	4-03-003
Order	NN-TL	13-07-010
orders	NNS	56-14-040
Orders	NNS-TL	1-01-001
order	**verb**	**89-14-066**
order	VB	17-09-017
orders	VBZ	1-01-001
ordered	VBD	28-09-022
ordered	VBN	41-13-033
ordering	VBG	2-02-002
ordering	**noun**	**13-04-008**
ordering	NN	11-04-007
orderings	NNS	2-01-002
orderliness	**NN**	**1-01-001**
orderly	**JJ**	**19-09-015**
orderly	**NN**	**1-01-001**
ordinance	**noun**	**12-06-009**
ordinance	NN	9-04-006
ordinances	NNS	3-03-003
ordinarily	**RB**	**14-07-010**
ordinarius	**FW-NN**	**1-01-001**
ordinary	**JJ**	**69-11-049**
ordinary	**noun**	**4-01-001**
ordinary	NN	1-01-001

Word	Tag	Frequency
ordinary (cont.):		
Ordinary	NN-TL	2-01-001
ordinary's	NN$	1-01-001
ordinate	**noun**	**1-01-001**
ordinates	NNS	1-01-001
ordnance	**NN**	**1-01-001**
ordo	**FW-NN**	**3-01-001**
ore	**noun**	**3-01-001**
ores	NNS	3-01-001
Oregon	**prop. noun**	**14-07-011**
Oregon	NP	7-05-006
Ore.	NP	3-03-003
Oregon	NP-TL	4-02-002
Oregonian	**prop. noun**	**1-01-001**
Oregonians	NPS	1-01-001
Oresme	**prop. noun**	**1-01-001**
Oresme	NP	0-00-000
Oresme	NP-TL	1-01-001
Oresteia	**prop. noun**	**1-01-001**
Oresteia	NP	0-00-000
Oresteia	NP-TL	1-01-001
Orestes	**NP**	**2-01-001**
organ	**noun**	**26-10-019**
organ	NN	12-07-009
organs	NNS	14-06-011
organdy	**NN**	**3-02-003**
organic	**adjective**	**38-05-015**
organic	JJ	37-05-015
Organic	JJ-TL	1-01-001
organically	**RB**	**3-03-003**
organification	**noun**	**5-01-001**
organification	NN	4-01-001
organification	NN-HL	1-01-001
organism	**noun**	**13-03-006**
organism	NN	6-03-004
organisms	NNS	7-02-003
organismic	**JJ**	**1-01-001**
organist	**NN**	**1-01-001**
organization	**noun**	**192-12-094**
organization	NN	106-11-068
organization	NN-HL	4-01-001
Organization	NN-TL	17-05-010
organization	NN-TL	1-01-001
organization's	NN$	3-01-002
organizations	NNS	59-10-034
Organizations	NNS-TL	2-02-002
organization-position	**NN**	**1-01-001**
organizational	**JJ**	**5-04-005**
organizationally	**RB**	**1-01-001**
organize	**verb**	**80-14-062**
organize	VB	14-07-012
organizes	VBZ	1-01-001
organized	VBD	4-03-004
organised	VBD	1-01-001
organized	VBN	52-12-041
organizing	VBG	7-06-007
Organizing	VBG-TL	1-01-001
organizer	**noun**	**3-03-003**
organizers	NNS	3-03-003
orgasm	**noun**	**8-03-003**
orgasm	NN	7-03-003
orgasms	NNS	1-01-001
orgiastic	**JJ**	**2-01-001**
orgone	**NN**	**1-01-001**
orgy	**noun**	**3-02-003**
orgy	NN	1-01-001
orgies	NNS	2-02-002
orient	**verb**	**14-05-011**
oriented	VBN	11-05-008
orienting	VBG	3-02-003
Orient	**NP**	**4-03-004**
oriental	**adjective**	**16-08-013**
oriental	JJ	1-01-001
Oriental	JJ	2-02-002
Oriental	JJ-TL	13-07-010
orientation	**noun**	**17-08-011**
orientation	NN	16-08-011
orientations	NNS	1-01-001
orifice	**noun**	**2-01-001**
orifices	NNS	2-01-001
Origen	**NP**	**3-01-001**
origin	**noun**	**51-10-039**
origin	NN	42-10-035
origin	NN-HL	2-01-001
origins	NNS	7-04-006
origin/destination	**NN**	**1-01-001**
original	**adjective**	**100-14-076**
original	JJ	99-14-075
Original	JJ-TL	1-01-001

Word	Tag	Frequency
original	**noun**	**6-03-004**
original	NN	3-02-003
originals	NNS	3-01-001
originality	**NN**	**6-04-006**
originally	**RB**	**23-10-023**
originate	**verb**	**26-12-023**
originate	VB	6-04-005
originates	VBZ	2-02-002
originated	VBD	10-07-010
originated	VBN	5-05-005
originating	VBG	3-02-002
origination	**NN**	**1-01-001**
Orin	**NP**	**1-01-001**
Orinoco	**NP**	**1-01-001**
oriole	**noun**	**1-01-001**
orioles	NNS	0-00-000
Orioles	NNS-TL	1-01-001
Oriole	**prop. noun**	**16-02-002**
Oriole	NP	5-02-002
Orioles	NPS	10-02-002
Orioles'	NPS$	1-01-001
Orissa	**NP**	**1-01-001**
Orkney	**prop. noun**	**1-01-001**
Orkney	NP	0-00-000
Orkney	NP-TL	1-01-001
Orlando	**prop. noun**	**2-02-002**
Orlando	NP	1-01-001
Orlando	NP-HL	1-01-001
Orleans	**prop. noun**	**44-08-019**
Orleans	NP	1-01-001
Orleans	NP-TL	39-08-019
Orleans'	NP$	0-00-000
Orleans'	NP$-TL	4-01-002
Orlick	**prop. noun**	**6-01-001**
Orlick	NP	3-01-001
Orlick's	NP$	3-01-001
Orly	**NP**	**1-01-001**
Ormoc	**NP**	**2-01-001**
Ormsby	**prop. noun**	**1-01-001**
Ormsby	NP	0-00-000
Ormsby	NP-TL	1-01-001
ornament	**noun**	**7-04-005**
ornament	NN	4-03-003
ornaments	NNS	3-02-003
ornament	**verb**	**3-02-003**
ornamented	VBN	3-02-003
ornamentation	**NN**	**1-01-001**
ornate	**JJ**	**1-01-001**
ornately	**RB**	**1-01-001**
ornerier	**comp. adj.**	**1-01-001**
ornerier	JJR	0-00-000
ornraier	JJR	1-01-001
ornery	**adjective**	**4-02-002**
ornery	JJ	2-02-002
orney	JJ	2-01-001
orphan	**noun**	**2-02-002**
orphan	NN	1-01-001
orphans	NNS	1-01-001
orphan	**verb**	**2-01-001**
orphaned	VBN	2-01-001
orphanage	**NN**	**1-01-001**
Orpheus	**NP**	**2-02-002**
Orphic	**JJ**	**1-01-001**
orso	**foreign**	**1-01-001**
orso	FW-NN	0-00-000
Orso	FW-NN-TL	1-01-001
Ortega	**prop. noun**	**2-01-002**
Ortega	NP	1-01-001
Ortega's	NP$	1-01-001
orthicon	**NN**	**2-01-001**
orthodontic	**JJ**	**9-01-001**
orthodontics	**NN**	**3-01-001**
orthodontist	**noun**	**13-01-001**
orthodontist	NN	9-01-001
orthodontist's	NN$	1-01-001
orthodontists	NNS	3-01-001
orthodox	**adjective**	**19-06-013**
orthodox	JJ	11-04-008
Orthodox	JJ-TL	8-04-005
orthodoxy	**noun**	**3-02-003**
orthodoxy	NN	0-00-000
Orthodoxy	NN-TL	3-02-003
orthographic	**JJ**	**3-01-001**
orthography	**noun**	**8-01-001**
orthography	NN	6-01-001
orthographies	NNS	2-01-001
orthopedic	**adjective**	**3-02-002**
orthopedic	JJ	1-01-001
Orthopedic	JJ-TL	2-01-001

orthophosphate	**noun**	**2-01-001**
orthophosphate	NN	1-01-001
orthophosphates	NNS	1-01-001
orthorhombic	**JJ**	**1-01-001**
Orvil	**NP**	**2-01-001**
Orville	**NP**	**4-01-001**
Orvis	**NP**	**6-01-001**
Orwell	**prop. noun**	**4-02-003**
Orwell	NP	2-02-002
Orwell's	NP$	2-01-002
Orwellian	**JJ**	**1-01-001**
Ory	**prop. noun**	**3-01-001**
Ory	NP	2-01-001
Ory	NP-TL	1-01-001
orzae	**NP**	**1-01-001**
os	**NN**	**1-01-001**
Osaka	**prop. noun**	**6-01-002**
Osaka	NP	4-01-001
Osaka	NP-HL	1-01-001
Osaka	NP-TL	1-01-001
Osbert	**NP**	**1-01-001**
Osborne	**NP**	**2-01-001**
Oscar	**NP**	**9-08-009**
oscillate	**verb**	**1-01-001**
oscillating	VBG	1-01-001
oscillation	**NN**	**3-02-003**
oscillator	**NN**	**1-01-001**
Oshkosh	**NP**	**1-01-001**
Osipenko	**NP**	**1-01-001**
Osis	**NP**	**1-01-001**
Oskar	**NP**	**1-01-001**
Oslo	**prop. noun**	**5-01-001**
Oslo	NP	4-01-001
Oslo	NP-HL	1-01-001
osmium	**NN**	**1-01-001**
osmotic	**JJ**	**3-01-001**
Oso	**prop. noun**	**9-01-001**
Oso	NP	7-01-001
Oso's	NP$	2-01-001
Osram	**NP**	**1-01-001**
Osric	**NP**	**1-01-001**
osseous	**JJ**	**2-01-001**
ossification	**NN**	**6-01-001**
ossify	**VB**	**1-01-001**
ostensible	**JJ**	**3-03-003**
ostensibly	**RB**	**1-01-001**
ostentatious	**JJ**	**2-02-002**
osteoporosis	**NN**	**1-01-001**
ostinato	**FW-JJ**	**1-01-001**
ostracism	**NN**	**1-01-001**
ostracize	**verb**	**1-01-001**
ostracized	VBN	1-01-001
Othello	**NP**	**1-01-001**
other	**post-det.**	**1710-15-462**
other	AP	1688-15-462
other	AP-HL	11-05-010
Other	AP-TL	2-02-002
other's	AP$	9-09-009
other	**noun**	**325-15-213**
others	NNS	320-15-210
others	NNS-HL	3-02-003
others'	NNS$	2-02-002
other-directed	**JJ**	**2-01-001**
otherwise	**RB**	**86-15-069**
otherworldly	**JJ**	**2-01-001**
Othon	**prop. noun**	**10-01-001**
Othon	NP	8-01-001
Othon	NP-TL	1-01-001
Othon's	NP$	1-01-001
Otis	**NP**	**3-03-003**
Ottauquechee	**NP**	**1-01-001**
Ottawa	**NP**	**1-01-001**
otter	**NN**	**5-02-002**
Ottermole	**prop. noun**	**1-01-001**
Ottermole	NP	0-00-000
Ottermole	NP-TL	1-01-001
Otto	**NP**	**1-01-001**
Ottoman	**prop. noun**	**3-02-002**
Ottoman	NP	1-01-001
Ottoman	NP-TL	2-01-001
oud	**FW-NN**	**1-01-001**
ought	**modal aux.**	**70-14-052**
ought	MD	68-14-050
oughta	MD+TO	2-02-002
oui	**FW-RB**	**2-02-002**
Oum	**NP**	**2-02-002**
ounce	**noun**	**8-05-005**
ounce	NN	3-03-003
oz.	NN	2-01-001
ounce (cont.):		
ounces	NNS	3-01-001
Ouray	**NP**	**1-01-001**
ourselves	**PPLS**	**66-12-046**
Ouse	**prop. noun**	**1-01-001**
Ouse	NP	0-00-000
Ouse	NP-TL	1-01-001
oust	**verb**	**5-03-004**
oust	VB	3-01-002
ousted	VBD	1-01-001
ousting	VBG	1-01-001
ouster	**NN**	**1-01-001**
out	**prep.**	**454-14-235**
out	IN	452-14-235
out	IN-HL	2-01-001
out	**noun**	**1-01-001**
outs	NNS	1-01-001
out	**adv./part.**	**1644-15-433**
out	RP	1629-15-430
Out	RP	3-01-001
out	RP-HL	2-02-002
out	RP-NC	3-01-001
Out	RP-TL	5-02-002
outta	RP+IN	2-01-001
out-dated	**JJ**	**1-01-001**
out-group	**NN**	**1-01-001**
out-migrant	**noun**	**2-01-001**
out-migrants	NNS	2-01-001
out-moded	**JJ**	**1-01-001**
out-of-bounds	**JJ**	**1-01-001**
out-of-door	**JJ**	**1-01-001**
out-of-doors	**NN**	**3-03-003**
out-of-doors	**RB**	**2-01-001**
out-of-mind	**NN**	**1-01-001**
out-of-pocket	**JJ**	**3-01-001**
out-of-school	**JJ**	**1-01-001**
out-of-sight	**NN**	**1-01-001**
out-of-state	**JJ**	**5-01-001**
out-of-state	**RB**	**1-01-001**
out-of-step	**JJ**	**1-01-001**
out-of-the-way	**JJ**	**2-02-002**
out-of-town	**JJ**	**6-03-004**
out-reaching	**JJ**	**1-01-001**
outback	**JJ**	**1-01-001**
outback	**NN**	**1-01-001**
outback	**RB**	**1-01-001**
outboard	**JJ**	**6-03-003**
outboard	**noun**	**2-01-001**
outboards	NNS	2-01-001
outboard	**RB**	**1-01-001**
outbreak	**noun**	**5-03-004**
outbreak	NN	2-02-002
outbreaks	NNS	3-02-002
outburst	**noun**	**8-04-006**
outburst	NN	2-02-002
outbursts	NNS	6-03-004
outcast	**noun**	**2-01-002**
outcast	NN	1-01-001
outcasts	NNS	1-01-001
outclass	**verb**	**2-01-002**
outclass	VB	1-01-001
outclassed	VBN	1-01-001
outcome	**noun**	**37-08-019**
outcome	NN	26-08-018
outcomes	NNS	11-02-002
outcrop	**noun**	**1-01-001**
outcrops	NNS	1-01-001
outcry	**NN**	**3-01-002**
outdate	**verb**	**3-03-003**
outdated	VBN	3-03-003
outdistance	**verb**	**4-04-004**
outdistanced	VBD	2-02-002
outdistanced	VBN	1-01-001
outdistancing	VBG	1-01-001
outdo	**VB**	**3-03-003**
outdoor	**adjective**	**27-07-015**
outdoor	JJ	23-07-015
outdoor	JJ-HL	1-01-001
Outdoor	JJ-TL	3-01-001
outdoors	**NN**	**2-02-002**
outdoors	**RB**	**4-03-004**
outdraw	**verb**	**1-01-001**
outdrew	VBD	1-01-001
outer	**adjective**	**32-12-023**
outer	JJ	28-11-021
Outer	JJ-TL	4-03-003
outface	**VB**	**2-01-001**
outfield	**NN**	**3-02-002**
outfielder	**noun**	**5-02-005**

Word	Tag	Frequency
outfielder (cont.):		
outfielder	NN	3-01-003
Outfielder	NN-TL	1-01-001
outfielders	NNS	1-01-001
outfight	**verb**	**1-01-001**
outfought	VBN	1-01-001
outfit	**NN**	**16-08-012**
outfit	**verb**	**1-01-001**
outfitted	VBD	1-01-001
outflow	**NN**	**2-01-002**
outfox	**VB**	**1-01-001**
outgeneral	**verb**	**1-01-001**
outgeneraled	VBN	1-01-001
outgoing	**JJ**	**8-05-008**
outgrip	**VB**	**1-01-001**
outgrow	**VB**	**4-03-004**
outgrowth	**NN**	**1-01-001**
outhouse	**NN**	**1-01-001**
outing	**noun**	**5-01-003**
outing	NN	2-01-002
Outing	NN-TL	3-01-001
outlander	**noun**	**1-01-001**
outlanders	NNS	1-01-001
outlandish	**JJ**	**1-01-001**
outlaw	**noun**	**4-02-002**
outlaw	NN	2-01-001
outlaws	NNS	2-02-002
outlaw	**verb**	**4-03-004**
outlawed	VBN	4-03-004
outlawry	**NN**	**1-01-001**
outlay	**noun**	**3-01-003**
outlay	NN	2-01-002
outlays	NNS	0-00-000
outlays	NNS-HL	1-01-001
outlet	**noun**	**15-07-012**
outlet	NN	9-05-008
outlets	NNS	6-05-005
outline	**noun**	**13-07-013**
outline	NN	8-05-008
outlines	NNS	5-05-005
outline	**verb**	**13-08-011**
outline	VB	4-04-004
outlines	VBZ	1-01-001
outlined	VBD	1-01-001
outlined	VBN	5-04-005
outlining	VBG	2-02-002
outlive	**verb**	**3-02-003**
outlived	VBN	3-02-003
outlook	**noun**	**36-08-026**
outlook	NN	35-08-025
outlook	NN-HL	1-01-001
outlying	**JJ**	**2-02-002**
outmaneuver	**verb**	**1-01-001**
outmaneuvered	VBN	1-01-001
outmatch	**verb**	**1-01-001**
outmatched	VBD	1-01-001
outmoded	**JJ**	**4-04-004**
outnumber	**verb**	**4-03-004**
outnumber	VB	2-02-002
outnumbered	VBD	1-01-001
outnumbered	VBN	1-01-001
outpatient	**NN**	**1-01-001**
outplay	**verb**	**1-01-001**
outplayed	VBD	1-01-001
outpost	**noun**	**4-03-003**
outpost	NN	3-03-003
outposts	NNS	1-01-001
outpouring	**NN**	**1-01-001**
output	**noun**	**40-07-016**
output	NN	35-07-015
outputs	NNS	5-02-003
output	**verb**	**1-01-001**
outputting	VBG	1-01-001
output-axis	**NN**	**1-01-001**
outrage	**noun**	**6-04-006**
outrage	NN	3-03-003
outrages	NNS	3-02-003
outrage	**verb**	**7-06-007**
outrage	VB	1-01-001
outraged	VBD	1-01-001
outraged	VBN	5-04-005
outraged	**JJ**	**1-01-001**
outrageous	**JJ**	**2-01-002**
outreach	**NN**	**5-01-001**
outrigger	**noun**	**5-02-002**
outrigger	NN	3-01-001
outriggers	NNS	2-02-002
outright	**JJ**	**5-03-005**
outright	**RB**	**4-04-004**

Word	Tag	Frequency
outrun	**verb**	**4-04-004**
outrun	VB	3-03-003
outrun	VBN	1-01-001
outscore	**verb**	**1-01-001**
outscoring	VBG	1-01-001
outset	**NN**	**13-08-013**
outside	**IN**	**83-15-064**
outside	**JJ**	**40-11-031**
outside	**noun**	**22-09-016**
outside	NN	21-09-015
outside	NN-HL	1-01-001
outside	**RB**	**65-13-053**
outsider	**noun**	**11-07-010**
outsider	NN	3-03-003
outsiders	NNS	8-06-008
outsized	**JJ**	**1-01-001**
outskirt	**noun**	**4-04-004**
outskirt's	NN$	1-01-001
outskirts	NNS	3-03-003
outsmart	**verb**	**2-02-002**
outsmarted	VBD	1-01-001
outsmarted	VBN	1-01-001
outspoken	**JJ**	**6-04-006**
outspread	**VBN**	**2-01-001**
outstanding	**adjective**	**37-07-030**
outstanding	JJ	36-07-029
Outstanding	JJ-TL	1-01-001
outstandingly	**QL**	**2-01-001**
outstate	**JJ**	**1-01-001**
outstrip	**verb**	**1-01-001**
outstripping	VBG	1-01-001
Outsville	**NP**	**1-01-001**
outward	**JJ**	**3-03-003**
outward	**RB**	**7-05-007**
outwardly	**RB**	**3-02-003**
outweigh	**verb**	**6-05-006**
outweigh	VB	2-02-002
outweighed	VBD	2-02-002
outweighed	VBN	2-02-002
outwit	**VB**	**1-01-001**
outworn	**JJ**	**1-01-001**
Ouzo	**NP**	**1-01-001**
ova	**noun**	**1-01-001**
ova	NN	0-00-000
ova	NN-NC	1-01-001
oval	**JJ**	**5-04-004**
oval	**noun**	**5-03-003**
oval	NN	3-03-003
ovals	NNS	2-01-001
ovation	**NN**	**2-02-002**
oven	**noun**	**8-05-005**
oven	NN	7-05-005
ovens	NNS	1-01-001
over	**prep.**	**843-15-362**
over	IN	835-15-362
o'er	IN	1-01-001
over	IN-HL	4-02-003
Over	IN-TL	2-01-001
'ovuh	+IN	1-01-001
over	**adjective**	**4-02-004**
over	JJ	3-02-003
over-	JJ	1-01-001
over	**adv./part.**	**392-15-225**
over	RP	390-15-223
over	RP-HL	2-02-002
over-achievement	**NN**	**1-01-001**
over-achiever	**noun**	**2-01-001**
over-achievers	NNS	2-01-001
over-all	**adjective**	**45-11-032**
over-all	JJ	33-10-024
overall	JJ	10-04-008
over-all	JJ-HL	2-01-001
over-arranged	**JJ**	**1-01-001**
over-chilling	**NN**	**1-01-001**
over-correct	**verb**	**1-01-001**
over-corrected	VBD	1-01-001
over-emphasize	**verb**	**4-03-004**
over-emphasize	VB	1-01-001
over-emphasized	VBN	2-02-002
overemphasized	VBN	1-01-001
over-large	**JJ**	**1-01-001**
over-occupied	**JJ**	**1-01-001**
over-pretended	**JJ**	**1-01-001**
over-produce	**VB**	**1-01-001**
over-simple	**JJ**	**1-01-001**
over-spend	**verb**	**1-01-001**
over-spent	VBN	1-01-001
over-stitch	**verb**	**1-01-001**
over-stitched	VBN	1-01-001

Word	Tag	Count
over-the-counter	**JJ**	**1-01-001**
over/under	**JJ**	**3-01-001**
overactive	**JJ**	**1-01-001**
overage	**JJ**	**1-01-001**
overaggressive	**JJ**	**1-01-001**
overall	**noun**	**7-02-003**
overall	NN	2-01-002
overalls	NNS	5-02-002
overbear	**verb**	**1-01-001**
overbearing	VBG	1-01-001
overbearing	**JJ**	**1-01-001**
overblown	**JJ**	**1-01-001**
overboard	**RB**	**8-05-007**
overburden	**verb**	**2-02-002**
overburden	VB	1-01-001
overburdened	VBN	1-01-001
overcast	**JJ**	**1-01-001**
overcast	**NN**	**8-03-003**
overcerebral	**JJ**	**1-01-001**
overcoat	**noun**	**6-03-006**
overcoat	NN	5-02-005
overcoats	NNS	1-01-001
overcome	**verb**	**42-13-036**
overcome	VB	17-08-017
overcome	VB-HL	1-01-001
overcomes	VBZ	7-05-006
overcame	VBD	3-03-003
overcome	VBN	8-05-008
overcoming	VBG	6-05-006
overconfident	**JJ**	**1-01-001**
overcook	**verb**	**1-01-001**
overcooked	VBN	1-01-001
overcool	**verb**	**1-01-001**
overcooled	VBN	1-01-001
overcrowd	**verb**	**3-02-003**
overcrowded	VBN	3-02-003
overcrowding	**NN**	**1-01-001**
overcurious	**JJ**	**1-01-001**
overdevelop	**verb**	**3-03-003**
overdeveloped	VBN	3-03-003
overdo	**verb**	**3-02-002**
overdone	VBN	2-01-001
overdoing	VBG	1-01-001
overdrive	**verb**	**1-01-001**
overdriving	VBG	1-01-001
overdue	**JJ**	**2-02-002**
overeager	**JJ**	**1-01-001**
overeat	**verb**	**3-02-002**
overeat	VB	1-01-001
overeating	VBG	2-02-002
overemphasis	**NN**	**1-01-001**
overestimate	**verb**	**2-02-002**
overestimates	VBZ	1-01-001
overestimated	VBN	1-01-001
overestimation	**NN**	**2-02-002**
overexcite	**verb**	**1-01-001**
overexcited	VBN	1-01-001
overexploit	**verb**	**1-01-001**
overexploited	VBN	1-01-001
overexploitation	**NN**	**1-01-001**
overexpose	**VB**	**1-01-001**
overfall	**noun**	**3-01-001**
overfall	NN	0-00-000
Overfall	NN-TL	3-01-001
overfeed	**VB**	**1-01-001**
overfill	**VB**	**1-01-001**
overflow	**NN**	**2-01-002**
overflow	**verb**	**4-03-004**
overflowed	VBD	2-02-002
overflowing	VBG	2-01-002
overgenerous	**JJ**	**1-01-001**
overgraze	**verb**	**1-01-001**
overgrazing	VBG	1-01-001
overgrown	**JJ**	**4-04-004**
overhand	**JJ**	**1-01-001**
overhand	**adverb**	**2-02-002**
overhand	RB	1-01-001
over-hand	RB	1-01-001
overhang	**noun**	**3-02-002**
overhang	NN	1-01-001
overhangs	NNS	2-01-001
overhaul	**NN**	**2-01-001**
overhaul	**verb**	**2-02-002**
overhaul	VB	1-01-001
overhauling	VBG	1-01-001
overhauling	**NN**	**2-02-002**
overhead	**JJ**	**7-06-007**
overhead	**NN**	**4-02-003**
overhead	**RB**	**7-06-007**

Word	Tag	Count
overhear	**verb**	**7-06-007**
overheard	VBD	2-02-002
overheard	VBN	4-04-004
overhearing	VBG	1-01-001
overheat	**verb**	**2-01-002**
overheat	VB	1-01-001
overheated	VBN	1-01-001
overheating	**NN**	**1-01-001**
overindulge	**verb**	**1-01-001**
overindulged	VBD	1-01-001
overland	**RB**	**1-01-001**
overlap	**verb**	**11-06-007**
overlap	VB	4-03-003
overlaps	VBZ	1-01-001
overlapped	VBD	1-01-001
overlapped	VBN	2-02-002
overlapping	VBG	3-03-003
overlay	**NN**	**1-01-001**
overlay	**verb**	**2-02-002**
overlay	VBD	1-01-001
overlaid	VBN	1-01-001
overlie	**verb**	**1-01-001**
overlying	VBG	1-01-001
overload	**NN**	**1-01-001**
overload	**verb**	**3-03-003**
overload	VB	2-02-002
overloaded	VBN	1-01-001
overlook	**verb**	**17-10-016**
overlook	VB	4-04-004
overlooks	VBZ	4-03-003
overlooked	VBD	2-02-002
overlooked	VBN	5-05-005
overlooking	VBG	2-02-002
Overlord	**prop. noun**	**3-01-001**
Overlords	NPS	3-01-001
overloud	**JJ**	**1-01-001**
overly	**QL**	**8-06-008**
overnight	**adjective**	**4-04-004**
overnight	JJ	3-03-003
over-night	JJ	1-01-001
overnight	**NN**	**1-01-001**
overnight	**RB**	**14-06-013**
overnighter	**noun**	**3-01-001**
overnighters	NNS	3-01-001
overpay	**verb**	**1-01-001**
overpaid	VBN	1-01-001
overpayment	**NN**	**4-01-001**
overplay	**verb**	**1-01-001**
overplayed	VBD	1-01-001
overpopulate	**verb**	**1-01-001**
overpopulated	VBN	1-01-001
overpopulation	**NN**	**2-01-002**
overpower	**verb**	**4-04-004**
overpowers	VBZ	1-01-001
overpowered	VBN	2-02-002
overpowering	VBG	1-01-001
overpressure	**NN**	**1-01-001**
overprice	**verb**	**1-01-001**
overpriced	VBN	1-01-001
overprotection	**NN**	**1-01-001**
overprotective	**JJ**	**1-01-001**
overrate	**verb**	**1-01-001**
overrated	VBN	1-01-001
overreach	**verb**	**5-05-005**
overreach	VB	2-02-002
overreaches	VBZ	1-01-001
overreached	VBD	2-02-002
Overreach	**NP**	**1-01-001**
override	**verb**	**5-04-005**
override	VB	1-01-001
overrode	VBD	1-01-001
overridden	VBN	1-01-001
overriding	VBG	2-02-002
overriding	**NN**	**1-01-001**
overrun	**NN**	**2-02-002**
overrun	**verb**	**4-03-004**
overran	VBD	1-01-001
overrun	VBN	3-02-003
overseas	**JJ**	**12-05-007**
overseas	**NN**	**2-02-002**
overseas	**RB**	**8-06-007**
overseer	**NN**	**1-01-001**
overshadow	**verb**	**4-04-004**
overshadow	VB	2-02-002
overshadowed	VBD	1-01-001
overshadowed	VBN	1-01-001
overshoe	**noun**	**2-02-002**
overshoes	NNS	2-02-002
overshoot	**verb**	**2-02-002**

overshoot (cont.):		
overshoots	VBZ	1-01-001
overshot	VBD	1-01-001
oversight	**NN**	**1-01-001**
oversimplification	**noun**	**4-04-004**
oversimplification	NN	3-03-003
over-simplification	NN	1-01-001
oversimplify	**verb**	**4-03-004**
oversimplified	VBN	4-03-004
oversize	**JJ**	**2-01-001**
oversized	**JJ**	**2-02-002**
oversoft	**JJ**	**2-01-001**
oversoftness	**NN**	**1-01-001**
overstep	**verb**	**1-01-001**
overstepping	VBG	1-01-001
overstrain	**verb**	**1-01-001**
overstraining	VBG	1-01-001
oversubscribe	**verb**	**3-02-002**
oversubscribed	VBN	2-02-002
over-subscribed	VBN	1-01-001
overt	**JJ**	**11-04-010**
overtake	**verb**	**6-05-006**
overtake	VB	3-03-003
overtook	VBD	1-01-001
overtaken	VBN	1-01-001
overtaking	VBG	0-00-000
overtakin'	VBG	1-01-001
overtax	**verb**	**1-01-001**
overtaxed	VBN	1-01-001
overthrow	**NN**	**2-02-002**
overthrow	**verb**	**6-03-006**
overthrow	VB	3-02-003
overthrown	VBN	3-02-003
overtime	**noun**	**3-02-002**
overtime	NN	2-02-002
overtime	NN-HL	1-01-001
overtly	**RB**	**3-02-003**
overtone	**noun**	**4-03-004**
overtones	NNS	3-02-003
Overtones	NNS-TL	1-01-001
overture	**noun**	**8-05-008**
overture	NN	1-01-001
Overture	NN-TL	4-01-004
overtures	NNS	3-03-003
overturn	**verb**	**4-04-004**
overturned	VBD	1-01-001
overturned	VBN	1-01-001
overturning	VBG	2-02-002
overvaulting	**JJ**	**1-01-001**
overweight	**JJ**	**3-03-003**
overweight	**NN**	**2-01-002**
overwhelm	**verb**	**5-05-005**
overwhelm	VB	1-01-001
overwhelmed	VBN	4-04-004
overwhelming	**JJ**	**20-09-019**
overwhelmingly	**QL**	**1-01-001**
overwhelmingly	**RB**	**6-04-005**
overwork	**verb**	**1-01-001**
overworked	VBN	1-01-001
overwrite	**verb**	**1-01-001**
overwritten	VBN	1-01-001
oviform	**JJ**	**1-01-001**
owe	**verb**	**34-14-028**
owe	VB	10-07-008
owes	VBZ	5-05-005
owed	VBD	12-06-010
owed	VBN	3-02-003
owing	VBG	4-03-004
Owen	**prop. noun**	**25-06-006**
Owen	NP	24-05-005
Owen	NP-TL	1-01-001
Owens	**NP**	**1-01-001**
owl	**noun**	**6-03-003**
owl	NN	2-02-002
owl's	NN$	1-01-001
Owl's	NN$-TL	1-01-001
owls	NNS	1-01-001
Owls	NNS-TL	1-01-001
own	**adjective**	**751-15-331**
own	JJ	750-15-331
owne	JJ	1-01-001
own	**verb**	**70-14-052**
own	VB	22-12-020
owns	VBZ	13-07-009
owned	VBD	15-06-013
owned	VBN	19-09-017
owning	VBG	1-01-001
owner	**noun**	**72-11-043**
owner	NN	33-10-022
owner's	NN$	2-02-002
owners	NNS	33-11-025
owners	NNS-HL	1-01-001
Owners	NNS-TL	1-01-001
owners'	NNS$	2-02-002
ownership	**noun**	**25-06-016**
ownership	NN	22-06-016
ownerships	NNS	3-02-002
owning	**NN**	**2-01-002**
ownself	**PPL**	**1-01-001**
ox	**noun**	**17-04-008**
ox	NN	6-03-005
oxen	NNS	10-02-003
oxen's	NNS$	1-01-001
oxalate	**NN**	**2-01-001**
oxaloacetic	**JJ**	**1-01-001**
oxcart	**NN**	**2-02-002**
Oxford	**prop. noun**	**19-05-009**
Oxford	NP	17-05-009
Oxford	NP-TL	1-01-001
Oxford's	NP$	1-01-001
oxidation	**noun**	**23-03-004**
oxidation	NN	22-03-004
oxidation	NN-HL	1-01-001
oxide	**noun**	**4-01-003**
oxide	NN	3-01-002
oxides	NNS	1-01-001
oxidise	**verb**	**2-01-001**
oxidised	VBN	2-01-001
Oxnard	**NP**	**1-01-001**
oxygen	**noun**	**47-04-012**
oxygen	NN	43-04-012
oxygen	NN-HL	1-01-001
oxygens	NNS	3-01-001
oxyhydroxide	**noun**	**1-01-001**
oxyhydroxides	NNS	1-01-001
oxytetracycline	**NN**	**3-01-001**
oyabun	**FW-NN**	**4-01-001**
Oyajima	**NP**	**1-01-001**
oyster	**noun**	**16-05-006**
oyster	NN	6-03-003
oysters	NNS	8-02-003
oystchers	NNS	1-01-001
oystchers'll	NNS+MD	1-01-001
Ozagen	**NP**	**4-01-001**
Ozagenian	**prop. noun**	**1-01-001**
Ozagenians	NPS	1-01-001
Ozark	**prop. noun**	**1-01-001**
Ozarks	NPS	1-01-001
Ozon	**NP**	**1-01-001**
ozone	**NN**	**3-01-001**
Ozzie	**NP**	**1-01-001**

P

Word	Tag	Frequency
P	**NP**	**16-01-003**
p.	**JJ**	**1-01-001**
p.	**noun**	**18-06-008**
p.	NN	14-05-007
P.	NN-TL	4-02-002
P.	**prop. noun**	**39-07-029**
P.	NP	37-07-028
P.	NP-HL	1-01-001
P.	NP-TL	1-01-001
P.-T.A.	**NP**	**1-01-001**
P.D.I.	**NP**	**3-01-001**
P.G.	**NP**	**1-01-001**
P.L.	**prop. noun**	**1-01-001**
P.L.	NP	0-00-000
P.L.	NP-TL	1-01-001
p.m.	**adverb**	**63-10-028**
p.m.	RB	53-07-021
P.m.	RB	1-01-001
P.M.	RB	9-06-007
P.S.	**RB**	**1-01-001**
p(Q)	**NN**	**1-01-001**
p(T)	**NN**	**1-01-001**
pa	**noun**	**28-03-003**
pa	NN	4-02-002
Pa	NN-TL	19-02-002
Pa's	NN+BEZ-TL	1-01-001
Pa'd	NN+HVD-TL	1-01-001
pa's	NN$	0-00-000
Pa's	NN$-TL	3-01-001
PABA	**NP**	**1-01-001**
Pablo	**NP**	**1-01-001**
Pabor	**NP**	**1-01-001**
pace	**noun**	**45-12-038**
pace	NN	37-11-032
pace	NN-HL	1-01-001
paces	NNS	7-06-007
pace	**verb**	**19-07-009**
pace	VB	4-02-002
paced	VBD	10-05-006
paced	VBN	1-01-001
pacing	VBG	4-04-004
Pace	**NP**	**1-01-001**
pace-setter	**NN**	**1-01-001**
pacem	**FW-NN**	**1-01-001**
pacemaker	**NN**	**1-01-001**
pacer	**noun**	**4-01-001**
pacer	NN	1-01-001
pacers	NNS	3-01-001
Pachelbel	**NP**	**1-01-001**
pachinko	**FW-NN**	**1-01-001**
Pacific	**adjective**	**24-06-013**
Pacific	JJ	0-00-000
Pacific	JJ-TL	24-06-013
Pacific	**prop. noun**	**7-06-006**
Pacific	NP	4-04-004
Pacific	NP-TL	3-03-003
pacifier	**NN**	**1-01-001**
pacifism	**NN**	**3-02-002**
pacifist	**NN**	**2-02-002**
pacifistic	**JJ**	**1-01-001**
pacify	**verb**	**3-03-003**
pacify	VB	2-02-002
pacifies	VBZ	1-01-001
pacing	**NN**	**3-03-003**
pack	**noun**	**17-07-013**
pack	NN	14-06-010
packs	NNS	2-01-002
Packs	NNS-TL	1-01-001
pack	**verb**	**44-11-033**
pack	VB	11-07-010
packed	VBD	7-04-007
packed	VBN	12-09-012

Word	Tag	Frequency
pack (cont.):		
packing	VBG	14-05-009
package	**noun**	**25-10-016**
package	NN	19-09-014
packages	NNS	6-03-003
package	**verb**	**14-07-010**
package	VB	1-01-001
packaged	VBN	6-05-006
packaging	VBG	7-04-005
Packard	**prop. noun**	**14-02-002**
Packard	NP	12-02-002
Packard	NP-TL	1-01-001
Packards	NPS	1-01-001
Packer	**prop. noun**	**2-01-002**
Packers	NPS	2-01-002
packet	**noun**	**4-03-004**
packet	NN	3-02-003
packets	NNS	1-01-001
packing	**noun**	**3-03-003**
packing	NN	2-02-002
Packing	NN-TL	1-01-001
Packwood	**NP**	**1-01-001**
pact	**noun**	**5-04-005**
pact	NN	1-01-001
pact	NN-HL	1-01-001
Pact	NN-TL	3-03-003
pacta	**FW-NNS**	**1-01-001**
pad	**noun**	**12-03-007**
pad	NN	7-02-004
pads	NNS	5-02-004
pad	**verb**	**8-07-008**
pad	VB	1-01-001
padded	VBN	4-04-004
padded	VBN-HL	1-01-001
padding	VBG	2-02-002
padding	**NN**	**1-01-001**
paddle	**VB**	**1-01-001**
paddock	**NN**	**1-01-001**
paddy	**noun**	**1-01-001**
paddies	NNS	1-01-001
padlock	**NN**	**2-02-002**
padlock	**verb**	**1-01-001**
padlocked	VBD	1-01-001
paean	**noun**	**3-03-003**
paean	NN	2-02-002
paeans	NNS	1-01-001
Paestum	**NP**	**1-01-001**
pagan	**noun**	**5-03-003**
pagan	NN	1-01-001
Pagan	NN-TL	3-01-001
pagans	NNS	1-01-001
Paganini	**NP**	**1-01-001**
paganism	**NN**	**1-01-001**
page	**noun**	**102-15-071**
page	NN	60-14-041
Page	NN	1-01-001
Page	NN-TL	1-01-001
pages	NNS	31-11-026
pp.	NNS	8-03-005
Pp.	NNS-TL	1-01-001
page	**VB**	**1-01-001**
Page	**NP**	**3-02-003**
pageant	**noun**	**12-03-004**
pageant	NN	2-02-002
Pageant	NN-TL	4-01-001
Pageant	NN-TL-HL	1-01-001
pageants	NNS	3-02-002
Pageants	NNS-TL	2-01-001
pageantry	**NN**	**1-01-001**
Paget	**NP**	**1-01-001**
paginate	**verb**	**1-01-001**
paginated	VBN	1-01-001

Word	Tag	Frequency
paging	**NN**	**1-01-001**
Paglieri	**prop. noun**	**1-01-001**
Paglieri's	NP$	0-00-000
Paglieri's	NP$-TL	1-01-001
Pagnol	**prop. noun**	**3-01-001**
Pagnol	NP	1-01-001
Pagnol's	NP$	2-01-001
pagoda	**noun**	**2-02-002**
pagoda	NN	1-01-001
pagodas	NNS	1-01-001
Pah	**NP**	**4-01-001**
pail	**noun**	**8-06-008**
pail	NN	4-03-004
pails	NNS	4-04-004
pain	**noun**	**102-13-052**
pain	NN	88-12-044
pains	NNS	14-07-013
pain	**verb**	**1-01-001**
pained	VBD	1-01-001
Paine	**NP**	**1-01-001**
painful	**JJ**	**25-12-025**
painfully	**QL**	**3-03-003**
painfully	**RB**	**11-08-011**
painless	**JJ**	**3-03-003**
painlessly	**RB**	**1-01-001**
pains	**FW-NNS**	**1-01-001**
painstaking	**adjective**	**2-02-002**
painstaking	JJ	1-01-001
pains-taking	JJ	1-01-001
painstakingly	**RB**	**2-02-002**
paint	**noun**	**24-09-019**
paint	NN	18-09-016
paints	NNS	6-03-004
paint	**verb**	**95-12-045**
paint	VB	19-07-012
paints	VBZ	4-02-004
painted	VBD	9-06-006
painted	VBN	31-12-023
painting	VBG	31-10-018
painting	VBG-NC	1-01-001
paintbrush	**NN**	**1-01-001**
painted-in	**JJ**	**1-01-001**
painter	**noun**	**35-11-018**
painter	NN	21-11-014
painter's	NN$	1-01-001
painters	NNS	13-06-009
Painter	**prop. noun**	**2-01-001**
Painter's	NP$	2-01-001
painteresque	**JJ**	**1-01-001**
painting	**noun**	**63-10-029**
painting	NN	27-08-015
paintings	NNS	36-09-021
pair	**noun**	**64-13-051**
pair	NN	50-13-043
pairs	NNS	14-06-013
pair	**verb**	**6-04-006**
paired	VBD	1-01-001
paired	VBN	5-03-005
paix	**foreign**	**1-01-001**
paix	FW-NN	0-00-000
Paix	FW-NN-TL	1-01-001
pajama	**noun**	**4-03-004**
pajama	NN	1-01-001
pajamas	NNS	3-03-003
Pak	**NP**	**2-01-001**
Pakistan	**prop. noun**	**7-04-005**
Pakistan	NP	6-04-005
Pakistan	NP-TL	1-01-001
Pakistani	**JJ**	**1-01-001**
Pakistani	**prop. noun**	**2-02-002**
Pakistanis	NPS	2-02-002
pal	**noun**	**3-03-003**
pal	NN	2-02-002
pals	NNS	1-01-001
Pal	**prop. noun**	**1-01-001**
Pal's	NP$	0-00-000
Pal's	NP$-TL	1-01-001
palace	**noun**	**45-10-023**
palace	NN	15-07-009
Palace	NN-TL	23-09-012
palace's	NN$	0-00-000
Palace's	NN$-TL	2-01-001
palaces	NNS	4-04-004
Palaces	NNS-TL	1-01-001
Palache	**NP**	**1-01-001**
Palast	**prop. noun**	**1-01-001**
Palasts	NPS	1-01-001
palatability	**NN**	**9-01-001**
palatable	**JJ**	**1-01-001**

Word	Tag	Frequency
palate	**noun**	**3-02-002**
palate	NN	2-02-002
palates	NNS	1-01-001
palazzo	**foreign**	**2-01-001**
palazzo	FW-NN	1-01-001
palazzi	FW-NNS	1-01-001
palazzo	**noun**	**4-02-002**
palazzo	NN	3-01-001
palazzos	NNS	1-01-001
Palazzo	**NP**	**8-01-001**
pale	**JJ**	**57-09-037**
pale	**noun**	**2-02-002**
pale	NN	1-01-001
pales	NNS	1-01-001
pale	**verb**	**2-01-001**
paled	VBN	1-01-001
paling	VBG	1-01-001
pale-blue	**JJ**	**1-01-001**
palely	**RB**	**1-01-001**
paleness	**NN**	**1-01-001**
paleo-	**JJ**	**1-01-001**
paleocortical	**JJ**	**1-01-001**
paleoexplosion	**NN**	**1-01-001**
Palermo	**NP**	**2-02-002**
palest	**JJT**	**1-01-001**
Palestine	**prop. noun**	**7-02-003**
Palestine	NP	6-02-002
Palestine	NP-TL	1-01-001
palette	**NN**	**5-03-003**
Palfrey	**prop. noun**	**35-01-001**
Palfrey	NP	26-01-001
Palfrey's	NP$	9-01-001
palindrome	**noun**	**1-01-001**
palindromes	NNS	1-01-001
palisade	**noun**	**2-02-002**
palisades	NNS	1-01-001
Palisades	NNS-TL	1-01-001
pall	**NN**	**2-02-002**
pall	**VB**	**1-01-001**
Pall	**prop. noun**	**1-01-001**
Pall	NP	0-00-000
Pall	NP-TL	1-01-001
Palladian	**JJ**	**1-01-001**
Palladio	**NP**	**3-02-002**
palladium	**NN**	**1-01-001**
Pallavicini	**prop. noun**	**1-01-001**
Pallavicini	NP	0-00-000
Pallavicini	NP-TL	1-01-001
pallet	**NN**	**1-01-001**
palletize	**verb**	**1-01-001**
palletized	VBN	1-01-001
palliative	**JJ**	**1-01-001**
pallid	**JJ**	**3-03-003**
pallor	**NN**	**2-02-002**
palm	**noun**	**30-09-020**
palm	NN	18-07-009
Palm	NN-TL	4-01-004
palms	NNS	8-05-007
palm	**verb**	**2-02-002**
palmed	VBD	1-01-001
palmed	VBN	1-01-001
palm-lined	**JJ**	**1-01-001**
palm-studded	**JJ**	**1-01-001**
Palmer	**prop. noun**	**62-05-007**
Palmer	NP	56-05-007
Palmer's	NP$	6-01-002
Palo	**NP**	**1-01-001**
Palomar	**prop. noun**	**1-01-001**
Palomar	NP	0-00-000
Palomar	NP-TL	1-01-001
palpable	**JJ**	**2-02-002**
palpably	**RB**	**1-01-001**
palsy	**noun**	**2-02-002**
palsy	NN	1-01-001
Palsy	NN-TL	1-01-001
Pam	**prop. noun**	**9-02-002**
Pam	NP	8-02-002
Pam's	NP$	1-01-001
Pamasu	**NP**	**1-01-001**
Pamela	**prop. noun**	**20-03-003**
Pamela	NP	19-03-003
Pamela's	NP$	1-01-001
Pampa	**NP**	**2-01-001**
pamper	**verb**	**2-02-002**
pamper	VB	1-01-001
pampered	VBN	1-01-001
Pamphili	**NP**	**1-01-001**
pamphlet	**noun**	**11-03-006**
pamphlet	NN	2-01-001

pamphlet (cont.):		
pamphlets	NNS	9-03-006
pan	**adjective**	**2-01-001**
pan	JJ	0-00-000
Pan	JJ-TL	2-01-001
pan	**noun**	**16-09-012**
pan	NN	12-08-010
pan	NN-HL	1-01-001
pans	NNS	3-02-003
pan	**VB**	**1-01-001**
panacea	**noun**	**1-01-001**
panaceas	NNS	1-01-001
Panama	**prop. noun**	**4-04-004**
Panama	NP	2-02-002
Panama	NP-TL	2-02-002
Pancho	**NP**	**1-01-001**
Pancrazio	**NP**	**1-01-001**
pandanus	**NN**	**1-01-001**
Pandelli	**prop. noun**	**1-01-001**
Pandelli's	NP$	1-01-001
pandemic	**NN**	**2-01-001**
pander	**noun**	**1-01-001**
panders	NNS	1-01-001
Pandora	**prop. noun**	**3-01-002**
Pandora	NP	1-01-001
Pandora's	NP$	2-01-001
pane	**noun**	**6-03-005**
pane	NN	3-03-003
panes	NNS	3-03-003
panel	**noun**	**78-10-025**
panel	NN	31-08-017
panel's	NN$	1-01-001
panels	NNS	46-08-013
panel	**verb**	**2-01-001**
paneled	VBN	2-01-001
paneling	**NN**	**6-04-004**
panelization	**NN**	**1-01-001**
panelize	**verb**	**1-01-001**
panelized	VBN	1-01-001
pang	**noun**	**2-02-002**
pangs	NNS	2-02-002
panic	**NN**	**20-08-019**
panic	**verb**	**4-04-004**
panic	VB	2-02-002
panicked	VBD	1-01-001
panicked	VBN	1-01-001
panicky	**JJ**	**1-01-001**
panjandrum	**NN**	**1-01-001**
Pankowski	**NP**	**2-01-001**
panorama	**noun**	**5-04-005**
panorama	NN	4-03-004
panoramas	NNS	1-01-001
panoramic	**JJ**	**1-01-001**
pansy	**noun**	**19-01-001**
pansy	NN	6-01-001
pansies	NNS	13-01-001
pant	**noun**	**9-06-009**
pants	NNS	9-06-009
pant	**verb**	**10-05-009**
panted	VBD	1-01-001
panting	VBG	9-04-008
pant-leg	**noun**	**2-02-002**
pant-legs	NNS	1-01-001
pants-legs	NNS	1-01-001
Pantas	**NP**	**2-01-001**
Pantasaph	**NP**	**1-01-001**
pantheist	**NN**	**1-01-001**
pantheon	**noun**	**3-03-003**
pantheon	NN	2-02-002
pantheon	NN-HL	1-01-001
Pantheon	**prop. noun**	**4-01-001**
Pantheon	NP	2-01-001
Pantheon's	NP$	2-01-001
panther	**noun**	**2-02-002**
panther	NN	0-00-000
Panther	NN-TL	1-01-001
panthers	NNS	1-01-001
pantomime	**NN**	**2-02-002**
pantomime	**verb**	**1-01-001**
pantomimed	VBD	1-01-001
pantomimic	**JJ**	**1-01-001**
pantry	**NN**	**2-02-002**
panty	**noun**	**1-01-001**
panties	NNS	1-01-001
Panyotis	**NP**	**2-01-001**
Panza	**NP**	**3-01-001**
paot	**FW-NN**	**3-01-001**
pap	**NN**	**1-01-001**
pap-pap-pap-hey	**UH**	**1-01-001**
Papa	**prop. noun**	**50-04-008**
Papa	NP	40-04-008
Papa's	NP$	10-02-002
Papa-san	**NP**	**8-01-001**
papal	**adjective**	**7-03-004**
papal	JJ	6-02-003
Papal	JJ	1-01-001
Papanicolaou	**NP**	**1-01-001**
paper	**noun**	**208-15-111**
paper	NN	152-15-086
paper	NN-HL	1-01-001
paper	NN-NC	2-01-001
Paper	NN-TL	1-01-001
paper's	NN$	1-01-001
papers	NNS	50-12-035
Papers	NNS-TL	1-01-001
paper	**VB**	**1-01-001**
paperback	**noun**	**3-02-003**
paperback	NN	2-02-002
paperbacks	NNS	1-01-001
paperwad	**noun**	**1-01-001**
paperwads	NNS	1-01-001
paperweight	**noun**	**2-01-001**
paperweight	NN	1-01-001
paperweight	NN-HL	1-01-001
papery	**JJ**	**1-01-001**
papier-mache	**NN**	**2-02-002**
papiers	**FW-NNS**	**1-01-001**
papillary	**JJ**	**1-01-001**
Papp	**NP**	**2-01-001**
Pappas	**NP**	**1-01-001**
Pappy	**prop. noun**	**1-01-001**
Pappy's	NP$	1-01-001
paprika	**NN**	**2-01-001**
par	**FW-IN**	**4-03-004**
par	**noun**	**12-03-004**
par	NN	9-03-004
pars	NNS	3-01-001
par-3	**NN**	**1-01-001**
par-5	**NN**	**1-01-001**
parable	**noun**	**4-03-004**
parable	NN	3-02-003
parables	NNS	1-01-001
parachute	**noun**	**2-02-002**
parachute	NN	1-01-001
parachutes	NNS	1-01-001
parade	**noun**	**26-10-019**
parade	NN	23-09-016
Parade	NN-TL	1-01-001
parades	NNS	2-02-002
parade	**verb**	**6-04-005**
parade	VB	1-01-001
parades	VBZ	1-01-001
paraded	VBD	1-01-001
paraded	VBN	1-01-001
parading	VBG	2-02-002
paradigm	**noun**	**7-03-004**
paradigm	NN	6-03-004
paradigms	NNS	1-01-001
paradigmatic	**JJ**	**1-01-001**
paradise	**noun**	**12-08-011**
paradise	NN	5-05-005
Paradise	NN-TL	7-05-006
paradox	**NN**	**9-05-008**
paradoxical	**JJ**	**3-02-003**
paradoxically	**RB**	**11-06-010**
paragon	**noun**	**2-02-002**
paragon	NN	1-01-001
Paragon	NN-TL	1-01-001
paragraph	**noun**	**26-07-015**
paragraph	NN	10-06-009
Paragraph	NN-TL	2-02-002
paragraphs	NNS	14-05-007
paragraphing	**NN**	**1-01-001**
parakeet	**noun**	**1-01-001**
parakeets	NNS	1-01-001
paralanguage	**NN**	**2-01-001**
paralinguistic	**JJ**	**1-01-001**
parallel	**JJ**	**14-06-012**
parallel	**noun**	**11-05-008**
parallel	NN	10-05-008
parallels	NNS	1-01-001
parallel	**RB**	**14-03-006**
parallel	**verb**	**8-04-007**
parallel	VB	2-01-002
parallels	VBZ	1-01-001
paralleled	VBD	1-01-001
paralleled	VBN	3-02-003
paralleling	VBG	1-01-001

Word	Tag	Frequency
parallelism	**NN**	**3-02-002**
paralysis	**NN**	**6-03-004**
paralyze	**verb**	**5-03-005**
paralyze	VB	1-01-001
paralyzes	VBZ	2-02-002
paralyzed	VBN	2-02-002
paramagnet	**NN**	**1-01-001**
paramagnetic	**JJ**	**13-02-002**
parameter	**noun**	**15-01-009**
parameter	NN	7-01-004
parameters	NNS	8-01-007
parametric	**JJ**	**2-01-001**
paramilitary	**JJ**	**1-01-001**
paramount	**sem. sup.**	**9-06-009**
paramount	JJS	8-06-008
Paramount	JJS-TL	1-01-001
paranoiac	**NN**	**1-01-001**
paranoid	**JJ**	**2-01-001**
paranormal	**JJ**	**1-01-001**
paraoxon	**NN**	**1-01-001**
parapet	**noun**	**2-02-002**
parapet	NN	1-01-001
parapets	NNS	1-01-001
paraphernalia	**NN**	**1-01-001**
paraphrase	**noun**	**3-02-002**
paraphrase	NN	2-01-001
paraphrases	NNS	1-01-001
paraphrase	**verb**	**1-01-001**
paraphrasing	VBG	1-01-001
parapsychology	**noun**	**3-01-001**
parapsychology	NN	1-01-001
Parapsychology	NN-TL	2-01-001
parasite	**noun**	**5-03-003**
parasite	NN	1-01-001
parasites	NNS	4-03-003
parasitic	**JJ**	**2-01-001**
parasol	**noun**	**5-03-004**
parasol	NN	3-03-003
parasols	NNS	2-01-001
parasympathetic	**adjective**	**9-01-001**
parasympathetic	JJ	8-01-001
parsympathetic	JJ	1-01-001
paratrooper	**noun**	**1-01-001**
paratroopers	NNS	1-01-001
paratroops	**NNS**	**1-01-001**
paraxial	**adjective**	**2-01-001**
paraxial	JJ	1-01-001
paraxial	JJ-HL	1-01-001
Paray	**NP**	**2-01-001**
parboil	**verb**	**1-01-001**
parboiled	VBD	1-01-001
parcel	**noun**	**2-02-002**
parcel	NN	1-01-001
parcels	NNS	1-01-001
parcel	**verb**	**1-01-001**
parceled	VBN	1-01-001
parch	**verb**	**2-02-002**
parched	VBD	1-01-001
parched	VBN	1-01-001
parchment	**NN**	**1-01-001**
pardon	**noun**	**5-05-005**
pardon	NN	4-04-004
pardons	NNS	1-01-001
pardon	**verb**	**6-05-006**
pardon	VB	4-04-004
pardoned	VBN	2-01-002
pardonable	**JJ**	**1-01-001**
pare	**VB**	**2-01-002**
paredon	**FW-NN**	**4-01-001**
Paree	**NP**	**2-02-002**
Parella	**NP**	**1-01-001**
parenchyma	**NN**	**4-01-002**
parent	**noun**	**113-14-058**
parent	NN	14-07-012
parent	NN-HL	1-01-001
parent's	NN$	1-01-001
parents	NNS	89-13-044
Parents	NNS-TL	2-02-002
parents'	NNS$	6-05-006
parent-child	**NN**	**1-01-001**
parent-teacher	**NN**	**1-01-001**
parentage	**NN**	**2-01-001**
parental	**JJ**	**2-02-002**
parenthesis	**noun**	**1-01-001**
parentheses	NNS	1-01-001
parenthetically	**RB**	**1-01-001**
parenthood	**noun**	**6-02-003**
parenthood	NN	3-02-002
Parenthood	NN-TL	3-01-002

Word	Tag	Frequency
pari-mutuel	**JJ**	**1-01-001**
pariah	**NN**	**1-01-001**
Parichy	**NP**	**2-01-001**
Parichy-Hamm	**prop. noun**	**1-01-001**
Parichy-Hamm	NP	0-00-000
Parichy-Hamm	NP-HL	1-01-001
parimutuel	**noun**	**1-01-001**
parimutuels	NNS	1-01-001
paring	**noun**	**2-01-001**
parings	NNS	2-01-001
Parioli	**NP**	**1-01-001**
Paris	**prop. noun**	**68-12-040**
Paris	NP	62-12-037
Paris	NP-HL	1-01-001
Paris	NP-TL	4-04-004
Paris'	NP$	1-01-001
parish	**noun**	**12-04-006**
parish	NN	10-04-006
Parish	NN-TL	1-01-001
parishes	NNS	1-01-001
parishioner	**noun**	**3-03-003**
parishioners	NNS	3-03-003
Parisian	**JJ**	**2-01-001**
Parisian	**NP**	**1-01-001**
Parisina	**prop. noun**	**1-01-001**
Parisina	NP	0-00-000
Parisina	NP-TL	1-01-001
parisology	**NN**	**1-01-001**
park	**noun**	**111-13-049**
park	NN	48-10-024
park	NN-HL	1-01-001
Park	NN-TL	42-08-026
Park	NN-TL-HL	1-01-001
parks	NNS	14-06-011
parks	NNS-HL	1-01-001
Parks	NNS-TL	4-03-003
park	**verb**	**61-11-029**
park	VB	1-01-001
parked	VBD	8-04-008
parked	VBN	25-08-015
parking	VBG	26-07-013
parking	VBG-HL	1-01-001
Park	**NP**	**1-01-001**
Parker	**prop. noun**	**65-06-009**
Parker	NP	63-06-009
Parker's	NP$	2-01-001
Parkersburg	**prop. noun**	**4-02-002**
Parkersburg	NP	3-01-001
Parkersburg	NP-TL	1-01-001
Parkhouse	**NP**	**5-01-001**
parking	**NN**	**4-02-003**
Parkinson	**prop. noun**	**1-01-001**
Parkinson's	NP$	1-01-001
parkish	**JJ**	**1-01-001**
parklike	**JJ**	**1-01-001**
Parks	**NP**	**1-01-001**
parkway	**noun**	**6-02-003**
parkway	NN	3-02-003
parkway	NN-HL	1-01-001
Parkway	NN-TL	2-01-002
parlance	**NN**	**2-02-002**
parlay	**verb**	**1-01-001**
parlayed	VBD	1-01-001
parley	**VB**	**1-01-001**
parliament	**noun**	**17-05-010**
parliament	NN	4-03-004
Parliament	NN-TL	12-03-006
parliaments	NNS	1-01-001
Parliamentarian	**prop. noun**	**1-01-001**
Parliamentarians	NPS	0-00-000
Parliamentarians	NPS-TL	1-01-001
parliamentary	**JJ**	**8-03-006**
parlor	**noun**	**19-07-017**
parlor	NN	18-07-016
parlors	NNS	1-01-001
Parmer	**NP**	**1-01-001**
parochial	**JJ**	**12-06-009**
parody	**noun**	**5-03-004**
parody	NN	4-03-003
parodies	NNS	1-01-001
parody	**verb**	**2-02-002**
parodied	VBD	2-02-002
parole	**NN**	**5-02-003**
parolee	**noun**	**2-01-001**
parolees	NNS	2-01-001
parquet	**NN**	**1-01-001**
Parrillo	**NP**	**3-01-001**
Parris	**NP**	**2-01-001**
parrot	**noun**	**2-02-002**

Word	Tag	Count
parrot (cont.):		
parrot	NN	0-00-000
Parrot	NN-TL	1-01-001
parrots	NNS	1-01-001
parrot	**verb**	**1-01-001**
parroting	VBG	1-01-001
parrot-like	**JJ**	**1-01-001**
parry	**verb**	**1-01-001**
parried	VBD	1-01-001
Parry	**prop. noun**	**2-01-001**
Parry	NP	1-01-001
Parry's	NP$	1-01-001
Parsifal	**prop. noun**	**2-02-002**
Parsifal	NP	1-01-001
Parsifal	NP-TL	1-01-001
parsimonious	**JJ**	**1-01-001**
parsimony	**NN**	**1-01-001**
parsley	**NN**	**1-01-001**
parson	**noun**	**2-02-002**
parson	NN	1-01-001
Parson	NN-TL	1-01-001
parsonage	**NN**	**1-01-001**
Parsons	**NP**	**5-02-002**
part	**noun**	**610-15-321**
part	NN	471-15-296
pt.	NN	0-00-000
Pt.	NN-TL	1-01-001
part	NN-HL	1-01-001
Part	NN-TL	24-02-004
parts	NNS	109-13-074
parts	NNS-HL	1-01-001
Parts	NNS-TL	3-01-001
part	**verb**	**11-06-011**
part	VB	3-03-003
parted	VBD	2-02-002
parted	VBN	3-02-003
parting	VBG	3-03-003
part-time	**JJ**	**24-06-008**
part-time	**RB**	**2-02-002**
partake	**verb**	**5-03-005**
partake	VB	1-01-001
partakes	VBZ	2-02-002
partook	VBD	1-01-001
partaking	VBG	1-01-001
partaker	**NN**	**1-01-001**
Parthenon	**NP**	**6-01-002**
parti	**foreign**	**1-01-001**
parti	FW-NN	0-00-000
Parti	FW-NN-TL	1-01-001
partial	**JJ**	**11-06-011**
partially	**QL**	**5-02-005**
partially	**RB**	**20-12-019**
participant	**noun**	**11-05-010**
participant	NN	4-02-003
participants	NNS	7-05-007
participate	**verb**	**57-11-039**
participate	VB	22-09-016
participates	VBZ	7-04-005
participated	VBD	5-04-005
participated	VBN	8-06-007
participating	VBG	15-06-011
participation	**NN**	**41-09-028**
particle	**noun**	**63-09-017**
particle	NN	21-05-009
particles	NNS	42-06-012
particular	**AP**	**14-02-011**
particular	**JJ**	**160-14-099**
particular	**noun**	**10-07-009**
particular	NN	5-04-004
particulars	NNS	5-05-005
particularistic	**JJ**	**1-01-001**
particularistic-seeming	**JJ**	**1-01-001**
particularity	**NN**	**1-01-001**
particularly	**QL**	**40-10-034**
particularly	**RB**	**106-15-090**
particulate	**JJ**	**3-01-003**
parting	**noun**	**2-01-001**
parting	NN	1-01-001
partings	NNS	1-01-001
partisan	**adjective**	**12-05-009**
partisan	JJ	9-05-008
Partisan	JJ-TL	3-01-001
partisan	**noun**	**10-03-004**
partisan	NN	3-02-003
Partisan	NN-TL	6-01-001
partisans	NNS	1-01-001
partition	**noun**	**7-04-006**
partition	NN	6-04-005
partitions	NNS	1-01-001
Partlow	**prop. noun**	**10-01-001**
Partlow	NP	8-01-001
Partlow	NP-TL	1-01-001
Partlow's	NP$	1-01-001
partly	**QL**	**8-05-007**
partly	**RB**	**41-13-034**
partner	**noun**	**48-13-031**
partner	NN	32-10-022
partners	NNS	16-09-013
partner	**verb**	**1-01-001**
partnered	VBN	1-01-001
partnership	**NN**	**18-05-009**
parts-supplier	**noun**	**1-01-001**
parts-suppliers	NNS	1-01-001
party	**noun**	**283-15-112**
party	NN	191-14-083
party	NN-HL	3-02-003
Party	NN-TL	19-06-014
party	NN-TL	2-01-001
party's	NN$	8-01-005
Party's	NN$-TL	1-01-001
parties	NNS	58-12-038
Parties	NNS-TL	1-01-001
party	**VB**	**1-01-001**
party-line	**NN**	**1-01-001**
Parvenu	**NP**	**2-01-001**
pas	**FW-***	**1-01-001**
pas	**FW-NN**	**5-01-002**
Pasadena	**prop. noun**	**8-04-004**
Pasadena	NP	6-03-003
Pasadena	NP-HL	1-01-001
Pasadena's	NP$	1-01-001
Pascagoula	**NP**	**1-01-001**
Pascal	**NP**	**1-01-001**
Pascataqua	**NP**	**1-01-001**
Paschal	**NP**	**2-01-001**
Paschall	**NP**	**1-01-001**
Pasha	**NP**	**3-01-001**
Pasley	**NP**	**2-01-001**
paso	**FW-NN**	**1-01-001**
Paso	**NP**	**10-02-003**
pass	**noun**	**34-10-015**
pass	NN	23-06-009
passes	NNS	11-08-008
pass	**verb**	**298-15-169**
pass	VB	64-14-053
Pass	VB-TL	2-01-001
passes	VBZ	16-07-013
passed	VBD	91-13-068
passed	VBN	66-14-050
passing	VBG	59-15-048
passable	**JJ**	**1-01-001**
passage	**noun**	**69-12-053**
passage	NN	49-12-041
passages	NNS	20-08-018
passageway	**NN**	**4-03-004**
Passavant	**prop. noun**	**1-01-001**
Passavant	NP	0-00-000
Passavant	NP-TL	1-01-001
passenger	**noun**	**35-12-022**
passenger	NN	14-07-012
passengers	NNS	21-10-016
passerby	**noun**	**3-02-003**
passerby	NN	1-01-001
passer-by	NN	1-01-001
passersby	NNS	0-00-000
passers-by	NNS	1-01-001
passing	**NN**	**6-04-005**
passion	**noun**	**40-09-026**
passion	NN	27-07-021
Passion	NN-TL	1-01-001
passions	NNS	12-03-005
passionate	**JJ**	**12-05-012**
passionately	**RB**	**3-03-003**
passive	**JJ**	**11-07-009**
passively	**RB**	**1-01-001**
passiveness	**NN**	**1-01-001**
passivity	**NN**	**1-01-001**
Passos	**NP**	**1-01-001**
passport	**NN**	**6-03-003**
past	**AP**	**84-12-065**
past	**IN**	**61-11-043**
past	**JJ**	**28-09-024**
past	**noun**	**100-13-075**
past	NN	99-13-075
Past	NN-TL	1-01-001
past	**RB**	**8-04-008**
past-fantasy	**NN**	**1-01-001**
paste	**noun**	**10-05-006**

Word	Tag	Frequency
paste (cont.):		
paste	NN	9-05-006
pastes	NNS	1-01-001
paste	**verb**	**8-03-003**
paste	VB	1-01-001
pasted	VBN	6-02-002
pasting	VBG	1-01-001
pastel	**noun**	**4-03-003**
pastel	NN	3-03-003
pastels	NNS	1-01-001
pastel-like	**JJ**	**1-01-001**
Pastern	**prop. noun**	**10-01-001**
Pastern	NP	9-01-001
Pasterns	NPS	1-01-001
Pasternak	**NP**	**1-01-001**
pasteurization	**NN**	**1-01-001**
pastille	**noun**	**1-01-001**
pastilles	NNS	1-01-001
pastime	**noun**	**5-03-005**
pastime	NN	4-03-004
pastimes	NNS	1-01-001
pastness	**NN**	**1-01-001**
pastor	**noun**	**26-07-011**
pastor	NN	17-06-008
pastor's	NN$	2-02-002
pastors	NNS	6-03-003
pastors'	NNS$	1-01-001
pastoral	**JJ**	**6-03-004**
pastry	**NN**	**4-02-004**
pastry-lined	**JJ**	**1-01-001**
pasture	**noun**	**16-07-010**
pasture	NN	10-05-008
Pasture	NN-TL	4-01-001
pastures	NNS	2-02-002
pasty	**JJ**	**2-01-002**
pat	**NN**	**2-02-002**
pat	**verb**	**12-04-011**
pat	VB	1-01-001
patted	VBD	7-04-007
patting	VBG	4-02-004
Pat	**prop. noun**	**34-05-008**
Pat	NP	32-05-008
Pat's	NP$	2-02-002
Patagonian	**prop. noun**	**1-01-001**
Patagonians	NPS	1-01-001
patch	**noun**	**23-10-020**
patch	NN	13-06-012
patches	NNS	10-07-010
patch	**verb**	**5-04-005**
patched	VBN	5-04-005
Patchen	**prop. noun**	**33-02-002**
Patchen	NP	26-02-002
Patchen's	NP$	7-02-002
patchwork	**NN**	**2-02-002**
pate	**NN**	**1-01-001**
Pate	**NP**	**1-01-001**
patent	**JJ**	**1-01-001**
patent	**noun**	**53-05-013**
patent	NN	33-04-008
Patent	NN-TL	1-01-001
patents	NNS	19-04-007
patent	**verb**	**3-02-003**
patented	VBD	1-01-001
patented	VBN	2-02-002
patent-sharing	**JJ**	**2-01-001**
patentee	**noun**	**1-01-001**
patentees	NNS	0-00-000
Patentees	NNS-TL	1-01-001
patenting	**NN**	**1-01-001**
pater	**foreign**	**2-01-001**
pater	FW-NN	1-01-001
Pater	FW-NN-TL	1-01-001
paternalism	**NN**	**2-01-001**
paternalistic	**JJ**	**1-01-001**
paternally	**RB**	**1-01-001**
pateroller	**noun**	**1-01-001**
paterollers	NNS	1-01-001
Paterson	**NP**	**1-01-001**
path	**noun**	**58-13-040**
path	NN	44-13-033
paths	NNS	14-07-010
Pathet	**NP**	**10-02-004**
pathetic	**JJ**	**8-07-008**
pathless	**JJ**	**1-01-001**
pathogenesis	**NN**	**1-01-001**
pathogenic	**JJ**	**2-01-002**
pathologic	**JJ**	**1-01-001**
pathological	**JJ**	**9-02-004**
pathologist	**NN**	**2-01-001**

Word	Tag	Frequency
pathology	**noun**	**33-02-002**
pathology	NN	7-02-002
Pathology	NN-TL	25-01-001
Pathology	NN-TL-HL	1-01-001
pathos	**NN**	**1-01-001**
pathway	**noun**	**3-01-002**
pathways	NNS	3-01-002
pati	**foreign**	**1-01-001**
pati	FW-VB	0-00-000
Pati	FW-VB-TL	1-01-001
patience	**noun**	**21-11-019**
patience	NN	20-11-019
patience	NN-HL	1-01-001
Patience	**NP**	**1-01-001**
patient	**JJ**	**11-07-010**
patient	**noun**	**132-12-030**
patient	NN	75-10-018
patient's	NN$	21-05-007
patients	NNS	36-12-020
patiently	**RB**	**9-07-009**
Patil	**NP**	**1-01-001**
patina	**noun**	**2-02-002**
patina	NN	1-01-001
patinas	NNS	1-01-001
patio	**NN**	**2-01-002**
patisserie	**noun**	**1-01-001**
patisseries	NNS	1-01-001
Patmore	**NP**	**1-01-001**
patriarch	**noun**	**2-02-002**
patriarch	NN	1-01-001
Patriarch	NN-TL	1-01-001
patriarchal	**JJ**	**1-01-001**
patriarchy	**NN**	**1-01-001**
Patrice	**NP**	**5-02-002**
Patricia	**NP**	**7-01-006**
patrician	**NN**	**1-01-001**
Patrick	**prop. noun**	**4-02-003**
Patrick	NP	1-01-001
Patrick's	NP$	0-00-000
Patrick's	NP$-TL	3-02-002
patrimony	**noun**	**1-01-001**
patrimony	NN	0-00-000
Patrimony	NN-TL	1-01-001
patriot	**noun**	**11-06-008**
patriot	NN	7-05-006
Patriot	NN-TL	3-01-001
patriots	NNS	1-01-001
patriotic	**JJ**	**10-04-009**
patriotism	**NN**	**6-03-005**
patristic	**JJ**	**1-01-001**
patrol	**noun**	**24-08-013**
patrol	NN	18-06-009
Patrol	NN-TL	5-02-004
patrols	NNS	1-01-001
patrol	**verb**	**7-04-006**
patrol	VB	2-01-001
patrolled	VBD	1-01-001
patrolled	VBN	1-01-001
patrolling	VBG	3-03-003
patrolman	**noun**	**15-03-008**
patrolman	NN	8-03-005
Patrolman	NN-TL	4-02-004
patrolman's	NN$	1-01-001
patrolmen	NNS	2-02-002
patron	**noun**	**13-09-011**
patron	NN	4-04-004
patrons	NNS	9-06-007
patronage	**NN**	**10-06-007**
patroness	**NN**	**1-01-001**
patronize	**verb**	**6-04-006**
patronize	VB	1-01-001
patronized	VBD	1-01-001
patronized	VBN	2-02-002
patronizing	VBG	2-02-002
patronne	**foreign**	**4-01-001**
patronne	FW-NN	3-01-001
patronne's	FW-NN$	1-01-001
patsy	**NN**	**1-01-001**
patter	**NN**	**3-02-002**
patter	**verb**	**1-01-001**
pattered	VBD	1-01-001
pattern	**noun**	**159-13-085**
pattern	NN	112-13-067
patterns	NNS	47-10-028
pattern	**verb**	**7-05-007**
pattern	VB	1-01-001
patterned	VBN	6-04-006
Patterson	**prop. noun**	**5-03-003**
Patterson	NP	2-02-002

Word	Tag	Frequency
Patterson (cont.):		
Patterson	NP-HL	1-01-001
Patterson	NP-TL	2-01-001
Patti	**NP**	**1-01-001**
Patton	**NP**	**1-01-001**
patty	**noun**	**2-01-001**
patties	NNS	1-01-001
patties	NNS-HL	1-01-001
Patty	**prop. noun**	**1-01-001**
Patty	NP	0-00-000
Patty	NP-TL	1-01-001
paucity	**NN**	**1-01-001**
Paul	**prop. noun**	**40-10-031**
Paul	NP	37-10-028
Paul	NP-HL	1-01-001
Paul	NP-TL	1-01-001
Paul's	NP$	1-01-001
Paula	**prop. noun**	**21-02-002**
Paula	NP	19-02-002
Paula's	NP$	2-01-001
Paulah	**NP**	**1-01-001**
Pauley	**prop. noun**	**1-01-001**
Pauleys	NPS	1-01-001
Pauling	**prop. noun**	**8-02-002**
Pauling	NP	7-02-002
Pauling's	NP$	1-01-001
Paulus	**NP**	**1-01-001**
paunch	**NN**	**2-02-002**
paunchy	**JJ**	**2-01-002**
pauper	**noun**	**1-01-001**
pauper's	NN$	1-01-001
Paus'l	**NP**	**1-01-001**
pause	**noun**	**17-10-015**
pause	NN	16-10-014
pauses	NNS	1-01-001
pause	**verb**	**40-10-033**
pause	VB	5-04-004
pauses	VBZ	1-01-001
paused	VBD	25-07-022
paused	VBN	3-02-002
pausing	VBG	6-05-006
Pauson	**NP**	**2-01-001**
pave	**verb**	**9-08-009**
pave	VB	2-02-002
paved	VBD	1-01-001
paved	VBN	4-04-004
paving	VBG	2-02-002
pavement	**noun**	**13-06-008**
pavement	NN	11-05-006
pavements	NNS	2-02-002
Pavese	**NP**	**2-01-001**
pavilion	**noun**	**6-01-001**
pavilion	NN	4-01-001
pavilions	NNS	2-01-001
Pavletich	**NP**	**1-01-001**
Pavlov	**NP**	**1-01-001**
Pavlovitch	**NP**	**1-01-001**
Pavlovsky	**NP**	**1-01-001**
paw	**noun**	**5-04-005**
paw	NN	2-02-002
paws	NNS	3-02-003
paw	**verb**	**2-02-002**
paw	VB	1-01-001
pawing	VBG	1-01-001
Pawcatuck	**prop. noun**	**2-01-001**
Pawcatuck	NP	1-01-001
Pawcatuck	NP-TL	1-01-001
pawn	**NN**	**2-02-002**
pawnshop	**NN**	**3-02-002**
Pawtucket	**prop. noun**	**3-03-003**
Pawtucket	NP	2-02-002
Pawtucket's	NP$	1-01-001
Pawtuxet	**NP**	**4-01-001**
pax	**foreign**	**1-01-001**
pax	FW-NN	0-00-000
Pax	FW-NN-TL	1-01-001
pax-ordo	**FW-NN**	**3-01-001**
paxam	**FW-NN**	**1-01-001**
Paxton	**prop. noun**	**7-01-001**
Paxton	NP	6-01-001
Paxton	NP-TL	1-01-001
pay	**noun**	**39-12-026**
pay	NN	38-12-026
pay	NN-HL	1-01-001
pay	**verb**	**325-14-153**
pay	VB	130-13-083
paie	VB	3-01-001
pay	VB-HL	2-02-002
Pay	VB-TL	1-01-001

Word	Tag	Frequency
pay (cont.):		
pays	VBZ	17-09-016
paid	VBD	50-13-043
paid	VBN	94-12-059
paide	VBN	1-01-001
paid	VBN-HL	1-01-001
paying	VBG	26-11-024
payable	**JJ**	**3-02-003**
paycheck	**NN**	**2-01-002**
payday	**NN**	**3-02-003**
paymaster	**NN**	**1-01-001**
payment	**noun**	**102-09-036**
payment	NN	50-08-022
payment	NN-HL	3-02-002
payments	NNS	48-08-018
payments	NNS-HL	1-01-001
Payne	**prop. noun**	**20-03-003**
Payne	NP	16-02-002
Payne's	NP$	3-02-002
Paynes	NPS	1-01-001
payoff	**NN**	**1-01-001**
payroll	**NN**	**16-04-006**
Payson	**NP**	**1-01-001**
PBS	**NP**	**1-01-001**
pea	**noun**	**24-04-007**
peas	NNS	24-04-007
Peabody	**prop. noun**	**2-02-002**
Peabody	NP	1-01-001
Peabody's	NP$	0-00-000
Peabody's	NP$-HL	1-01-001
peace	**noun**	**198-13-086**
peace	NN	134-13-075
peace	NN-HL	2-01-002
Peace	NN-TL	59-06-015
Peace	NN-TL-HL	3-01-001
peace-loving	**JJ**	**2-02-002**
peace-treaty	**NN**	**1-01-001**
peaceable	**adjective**	**3-03-003**
peaceable	JJ	2-02-002
Peaceable	JJ-TL	1-01-001
peaceful	**adjective**	**26-10-020**
peaceful	JJ	25-10-019
Peaceful	JJ-TL	1-01-001
peacefully	**RB**	**5-04-005**
peacemaking	**JJ**	**1-01-001**
peacetime	**NN**	**4-03-004**
peach	**noun**	**4-03-004**
peach	NN	2-02-002
Peach	NN-TL	1-01-001
peaches	NNS	1-01-001
peacock	**noun**	**6-04-004**
peacock	NN	2-02-002
peacocks	NNS	4-02-002
peak	**noun**	**24-07-018**
peak	NN	16-05-013
peaks	NNS	8-07-007
peaked	**JJ**	**7-02-002**
peaky	**JJ**	**1-01-001**
peal	**noun**	**1-01-001**
peals	NNS	1-01-001
Peale	**prop. noun**	**5-03-004**
Peale	NP	3-02-002
Peal	NP	1-01-001
Peale's	NP$	1-01-001
peanut	**noun**	**11-03-004**
peanut	NN	6-03-003
peanuts	NNS	5-01-002
pear	**noun**	**8-04-005**
pear	NN	6-04-004
pears	NNS	2-02-002
pearl	**noun**	**9-07-009**
pearl	NN	3-02-003
Pearl	NN-TL	4-03-004
pearls	NNS	2-02-002
Pearl	**NP**	**2-02-002**
pearl-gray	**JJ**	**1-01-001**
pearly	**JJ**	**1-01-001**
Pearson	**prop. noun**	**12-05-006**
Pearson	NP	7-05-005
Pearson	NP-TL	5-01-001
peasant	**noun**	**19-07-014**
peasant	NN	7-05-007
peasants	NNS	12-06-009
peasanthood	**NN**	**1-01-001**
pebble	**noun**	**5-04-004**
pebble	NN	1-01-001
Pebble	NN-TL	1-01-001
pebbles	NNS	3-02-002
Pebworth	**NP**	**1-01-001**

pecan	**noun**	**2-02-002**
pecan	NN	1-01-001
pecans	NNS	1-01-001
peccadillo	**noun**	**1-01-001**
peccadilloes	NNS	1-01-001
peccavi	**FW-VBD**	**1-01-001**
peck	**NN**	**1-01-001**
peck	**verb**	**3-03-003**
peck	VB	1-01-001
pecked	VBD	2-02-002
Peck	**prop. noun**	**4-03-003**
Peck	NP	3-02-002
Pecks	NPS	1-01-001
Pecorone	**prop. noun**	**1-01-001**
Pecorone	NP	0-00-000
Pecorone	NP-TL	1-01-001
Pecos	**NP**	**1-01-001**
pectoral	**JJ**	**1-01-001**
pectoral	**noun**	**1-01-001**
pectorals	NNS	1-01-001
pectoral-ribcage	**NN**	**1-01-001**
pectoralis	**NN**	**2-01-001**
peculiar	**JJ**	**28-10-028**
peculiarity	**noun**	**5-04-005**
peculiarity	NN	1-01-001
peculiarities	NNS	4-04-004
peculiarly	**QL**	**3-03-003**
peculiarly	**RB**	**5-03-004**
pedagogical	**JJ**	**1-01-001**
pedagogue	**NN**	**1-01-001**
pedal	**noun**	**4-03-004**
pedal	NN	3-02-003
pedals	NNS	1-01-001
pedal	**VB**	**1-01-001**
pedantic	**JJ**	**2-02-002**
peddle	**verb**	**2-02-002**
peddle	VB	1-01-001
peddled	VBN	1-01-001
peddler	**noun**	**7-03-004**
peddler	NN	5-03-004
peddlers	NNS	1-01-001
peddlers	NNS-HL	1-01-001
Peden	**NP**	**1-01-001**
Pedersen	**prop. noun**	**11-01-001**
Pedersen	NP	10-01-001
Pedersen's	NP$	1-01-001
pedestal	**NN**	**5-03-004**
pedestrian	**JJ**	**3-01-001**
pedestrian	**noun**	**5-02-003**
pedestrian	NN	2-01-002
Pedestrian	NN-TL	1-01-001
pedestrians	NNS	2-01-001
pedigree	**NN**	**3-03-003**
pedigreed	**JJ**	**1-01-001**
pedimented	**JJ**	**1-01-001**
Pedro	**NP**	**3-03-003**
pee	**verb**	**1-01-001**
peed	VBN	1-01-001
Pee	**NP**	**2-01-002**
pee-wee	**JJ**	**1-01-001**
peek	**verb**	**3-03-003**
peeked	VBD	1-01-001
peeked	VBN	1-01-001
peeking	VBG	1-01-001
peel	**verb**	**14-08-010**
peel	VB	2-02-002
peels	VBZ	1-01-001
peeled	VBD	2-02-002
peeled	VBN	3-03-003
peeling	VBG	6-03-003
Peel	**NP**	**1-01-001**
peep	**noun**	**2-01-001**
peep	NN	0-00-000
Peep	NN-TL	2-01-001
peep	**verb**	**2-02-002**
peeping	VBG	1-01-001
Peeping	VBG-TL	1-01-001
Peepy	**NP**	**1-01-001**
peer	**noun**	**13-04-007**
peer	NN	6-03-004
peers	NNS	7-04-006
peer	**verb**	**32-07-023**
peer	VB	2-02-002
peers	VBZ	1-01-001
peered	VBD	19-05-015
peered	VBN	1-01-001
peering	VBG	9-05-008
peer-group	**NN**	**1-01-001**
peerless	**adjective**	**4-02-002**

peerless (cont.):		
peerless	JJ	1-01-001
Peerless	JJ-TL	3-01-001
peg	**noun**	**5-03-003**
peg	NN	3-01-001
pegs	NNS	2-02-002
peg	**verb**	**3-03-003**
pegged	VBN	1-01-001
pegging	VBG	1-01-001
peggin'	VBG	1-01-001
Peg	**NP**	**1-01-001**
pegboard	**noun**	**8-01-001**
pegboard	NN	6-01-001
pegboards	NNS	2-01-001
pegged-down	**JJ**	**1-01-001**
Pegler	**NP**	**1-01-001**
Peiping	**NP**	**1-01-001**
Peking	**NP**	**1-01-001**
Pelham	**NP**	**5-01-001**
pellagra	**NN**	**1-01-001**
Pellegrini	**NP**	**1-01-001**
pellet	**noun**	**1-01-001**
pellets	NNS	1-01-001
Pels	**NP**	**6-01-001**
pelt	**noun**	**9-01-001**
pelts	NNS	9-01-001
pelt	**verb**	**2-02-002**
pelting	VBG	2-02-002
peltry	**NN**	**2-01-001**
Peltz	**NP**	**1-01-001**
pelvic	**JJ**	**3-01-001**
pelvis	**NN**	**1-01-001**
Pemberton	**NP**	**1-01-001**
Pembina	**prop. noun**	**4-01-001**
Pembina	NP	3-01-001
Pembina	NP-TL	1-01-001
Pembroke	**NP**	**2-01-002**
pemmican	**NN**	**1-01-001**
pen	**noun**	**18-08-013**
pen	NN	15-07-011
pen	NN-HL	1-01-001
pens	NNS	2-02-002
pen	**verb**	**5-03-005**
pen	VB	1-01-001
penned	VBD	1-01-001
penned	VBN	3-03-003
Pen	**NP**	**1-01-001**
pen-and-ink	**NN**	**2-02-002**
Pena	**NP**	**1-01-001**
penal	**JJ**	**1-01-001**
penalize	**verb**	**3-03-003**
penalized	VBN	3-03-003
penalty	**noun**	**18-10-016**
penalty	NN	14-09-013
penalties	NNS	4-02-003
penance	**NN**	**5-04-005**
penchant	**NN**	**1-01-001**
pencil	**noun**	**38-07-014**
pencil	NN	34-07-014
pencils	NNS	4-01-001
pencil	**verb**	**1-01-001**
penciled	VBN	1-01-001
pencil-and-sepia	**NN**	**1-01-001**
pencil-pusher	**NN**	**1-01-001**
pendant	**foreign**	**1-01-001**
pendant	FW-IN	0-00-000
Pendant	FW-IN-TL	1-01-001
pending	**IN**	**5-05-005**
pending	**JJ**	**9-06-007**
Pendleton	**prop. noun**	**6-02-002**
Pendleton	NP	5-02-002
Pendleton's	NP$	1-01-001
pendulum	**NN**	**2-02-002**
penetrate	**verb**	**17-09-016**
penetrate	VB	7-04-007
penetrated	VBD	5-05-005
penetrated	VBN	3-02-003
penetrating	VBG	2-02-002
penetrating	**JJ**	**12-08-012**
penetration	**NN**	**15-06-008**
Pengally	**NP**	**2-01-001**
penicillin	**NN**	**1-01-001**
peninsula	**noun**	**9-06-009**
peninsula	NN	5-04-005
Peninsula	NN-TL	4-03-004
penman	**NN**	**1-01-001**
Penn	**NP**	**5-03-004**
pennant	**noun**	**10-04-007**
pennant	NN	9-03-006

Word	Tag	Frequency
pennant (cont.):		
pennants	NNS	1-01-001
Pennell	**prop. noun**	**1-01-001**
Pennell	NP	0-00-000
Pennell	NP-TL	1-01-001
penniless	**JJ**	**3-03-003**
Pennock	**NP**	**2-02-002**
Pennsylvania	**prop. noun**	**56-11-039**
Pennsylvania	NP	33-11-024
Pa.	NP	9-05-008
Penna.	NP	1-01-001
Pennsylvania	NP-TL	13-07-011
penny	**noun**	**9-06-008**
penny	NN	4-02-004
pennies	NNS	5-04-004
Penny	**prop. noun**	**24-01-002**
Penny	NP	21-01-002
Penny's	NP+BEZ	2-01-001
Penny's	NP$	1-01-001
penny-wise	**JJ**	**2-02-002**
Penrose	**prop. noun**	**1-01-001**
Penrose	NP	0-00-000
Penrose	NP-TL	1-01-001
Pensacola	**NP**	**4-02-002**
pension	**noun**	**20-06-010**
pension	NN	12-05-007
Pension	NN-TL	1-01-001
pensions	NNS	7-05-007
pensioner	**NN**	**2-02-002**
pensive	**JJ**	**1-01-001**
pentagon	**noun**	**14-08-012**
pentagon	NN	1-01-001
Pentagon	NN-TL	12-07-010
pentagon's	NN$	0-00-000
Pentagon's	NN$-TL	1-01-001
Pentecostal	**JJ**	**1-01-001**
penthouse	**NN**	**1-01-001**
penultimate	**JJ**	**1-01-001**
penurious	**JJ**	**1-01-001**
penury	**NN**	**1-01-001**
Penutian	**NP**	**1-01-001**
peony	**noun**	**2-02-002**
peonies	NNS	2-02-002
Peony	**NP**	**3-01-001**
people	**pl. noun**	**902-15-298**
people	NNS	827-15-287
People	NNS	1-01-001
peoples	NNS	36-09-023
people	NNS-HL	2-01-001
people	NNS-NC	6-01-001
People	NNS-TL	9-05-007
people's	NNS$	14-07-012
peoples'	NNS$	0-00-000
Peoples'	NNS$-TL	1-01-001
poeple's	NNS$	1-01-001
People's	NNS$-TL	5-03-003
people	**verb**	**3-03-003**
people	VB	2-02-002
peopled	VBN	1-01-001
people-oriented	**JJ**	**2-01-001**
pep	**verb**	**1-01-001**
pepping	VBG	1-01-001
Pepinsky	**NP**	**1-01-001**
pepper	**noun**	**13-03-007**
pepper	NN	12-03-007
pepper	NN-HL	1-01-001
pepper	**verb**	**2-01-002**
peppered	VBN	2-01-002
peppermint	**noun**	**2-01-001**
peppermints	NNS	2-01-001
pepperoni	**NN**	**1-01-001**
peppery	**JJ**	**3-02-003**
peptidase	**noun**	**2-01-002**
peptidases	NNS	1-01-001
peptidases	NNS-HL	1-01-001
peptide	**noun**	**3-01-001**
peptide	NN	1-01-001
peptides	NNS	1-01-001
peptides	NNS-HL	1-01-001
peptize	**verb**	**1-01-001**
peptizing	VBG	1-01-001
per	**FW-IN**	**1-01-001**
per	**IN**	**370-09-095**
per-day	**JJ**	**1-01-001**
per-game	**JJ**	**1-01-001**
per-year	**JJ**	**1-01-001**
Peralta	**NP**	**4-01-001**
Perasso	**NP**	**1-01-001**
perceive	**verb**	**29-08-018**

Word	Tag	Frequency
perceive (cont.):		
perceive	VB	13-05-008
perceives	VBZ	3-01-002
perceived	VBD	3-02-002
perceived	VBN	9-05-008
perceiving	VBG	1-01-001
percent	**NN**	**53-08-021**
percentage	**noun**	**52-09-026**
percentage	NN	46-09-026
percentages	NNS	6-04-004
perceptible	**JJ**	**1-01-001**
perception	**noun**	**38-08-023**
perception	NN	27-07-017
Perception	NN-TL	2-02-002
perceptions	NNS	9-03-007
perceptive	**JJ**	**3-03-003**
perceptual	**JJ**	**7-02-006**
perch	**verb**	**5-04-005**
perch	VB	1-01-001
perched	VBD	1-01-001
perched	VBN	3-03-003
perchance	**RB**	**1-01-001**
percolator	**NN**	**1-01-001**
percussion	**noun**	**4-02-002**
percussion	NN	2-02-002
Percussion	NN-TL	2-01-001
percussive	**adjective**	**7-02-003**
percussive	JJ	5-02-003
Percussive	JJ-TL	2-01-001
Percy	**NP**	**2-02-002**
Perdido	**prop. noun**	**3-01-001**
Perdido	NP	0-00-000
Perdido	NP-TL	3-01-001
Perelman	**NP**	**1-01-001**
peremptory	**JJ**	**1-01-001**
perennial	**JJ**	**6-05-006**
perennially	**RB**	**2-02-002**
Perennian	**JJ**	**2-01-001**
Perez	**NP**	**1-01-001**
perfect	**JJ**	**58-13-045**
perfect	**verb**	**8-03-007**
perfected	VBN	5-02-005
perfecting	VBG	3-02-003
perfectibility	**noun**	**2-02-002**
perfectibility	NN	1-01-001
perfectability	NN	1-01-001
perfection	**NN**	**11-05-010**
perfectionism	**NN**	**1-01-001**
perfectionist	**noun**	**1-01-001**
perfectionists	NNS	1-01-001
perfectly	**QL**	**21-08-019**
perfectly	**RB**	**10-07-010**
perfidious	**JJ**	**1-01-001**
perforate	**verb**	**3-02-002**
perforated	VBN	2-02-002
perforated	VBN-HL	1-01-001
perforation	**noun**	**1-01-001**
perforations	NNS	1-01-001
perforce	**RB**	**2-02-002**
perform	**verb**	**85-12-060**
perform	VB	29-10-027
performs	VBZ	4-02-004
performed	VBD	11-08-011
performed	VBN	24-10-020
performing	VBG	17-06-016
performance	**noun**	**155-12-075**
performance	NN	122-12-065
performances	NNS	33-09-022
performance-capacity	**NN**	**1-01-001**
performer	**noun**	**20-08-013**
performer	NN	7-05-005
performers	NNS	13-06-010
perfume	**noun**	**11-06-010**
perfume	NN	10-05-009
perfumes	NNS	1-01-001
perfume	**verb**	**2-02-002**
perfumed	VBN	2-02-002
perfumery	**NN**	**1-01-001**
perfunctorily	**RB**	**1-01-001**
perfunctory	**JJ**	**1-01-001**
perfusion	**NN**	**1-01-001**
Pergamon	**prop. noun**	**1-01-001**
Pergamon	NP	0-00-000
Pergamon	NP-TL	1-01-001
Pergolesi	**prop. noun**	**1-01-001**
Pergolesi's	NP$	1-01-001
perhaps	**adverb**	**307-15-192**
perhaps	RB	306-15-192
perhaps	RB-NC	1-01-001

Word	Tag	Frequency
Periclean	**JJ**	**1-01-001**
Pericles	**NP**	**1-01-001**
Perier	**prop. noun**	**8-01-001**
Perier	NP	6-01-001
Perier's	NP$	2-01-001
peril	**noun**	**10-08-009**
peril	NN	8-06-007
perils	NNS	2-02-002
perilla	**NN**	**1-01-001**
perilous	**JJ**	**8-05-008**
perilously	**QL**	**1-01-001**
perilously	**RB**	**2-02-002**
perimeter	**NN**	**1-01-001**
Perinetti	**NP**	**1-01-001**
period	**noun**	**312-14-163**
period	NN	263-14-147
Period	NN-TL	2-02-002
periods	NNS	47-10-037
periodic	**JJ**	**9-05-009**
periodical	**noun**	**9-07-009**
periodical	NN	4-03-004
periodicals	NNS	5-05-005
periodically	**RB**	**6-04-005**
periodicity	**NN**	**1-01-001**
periodontal	**adjective**	**1-01-001**
periodontal	JJ	0-00-000
peridontal	JJ	1-01-001
peripheral	**JJ**	**8-03-006**
peripherally	**RB**	**2-01-002**
periphery	**NN**	**5-02-005**
periphrastic	**JJ**	**1-01-001**
periscope	**noun**	**1-01-001**
periscopes	NNS	1-01-001
perish	**verb**	**5-03-004**
perish	VB	2-01-001
perishes	VBZ	1-01-001
perished	VBN	1-01-001
perishing	VBG	1-01-001
perishable	**JJ**	**1-01-001**
periwinkle	**noun**	**1-01-001**
periwinkles	NNS	1-01-001
perjury	**NN**	**3-02-002**
perk	**VB**	**1-01-001**
Perken	**NP**	**1-01-001**
Perkins	**prop. noun**	**2-01-002**
Perkins	NP	1-01-001
Perkins	NP-TL	1-01-001
perky	**JJ**	**2-02-002**
Perle	**NP**	**1-01-001**
Perlman	**NP**	**3-01-001**
Perluss	**NP**	**2-01-001**
permanence	**NN**	**2-02-002**
permanent	**JJ**	**40-11-034**
permanently	**RB**	**13-07-012**
permeate	**verb**	**6-04-006**
permeate	VB	1-01-001
permeates	VBZ	2-02-002
permeated	VBN	3-01-003
Permian	**JJ**	**1-01-001**
permissibility	**NN**	**1-01-001**
permissible	**JJ**	**1-01-001**
permission	**NN**	**27-09-016**
permissive	**JJ**	**5-04-005**
permit	**noun**	**13-07-010**
permit	NN	10-06-007
Permit	NN-TL	1-01-001
permits	NNS	2-02-002
permit	**verb**	**157-15-106**
permit	VB	66-12-053
permits	VBZ	25-06-021
permitted	VBD	14-07-013
permitted	VBN	43-12-032
permitting	VBG	9-05-009
pernicious	**JJ**	**1-01-001**
Pernod	**NP**	**1-01-001**
peroxide	**NN**	**2-01-001**
perpendicular	**JJ**	**2-01-001**
perpendicularly	**RB**	**1-01-001**
perpetrate	**verb**	**3-03-003**
perpetrated	VBD	1-01-001
perpetrated	VBN	2-02-002
perpetration	**NN**	**1-01-001**
perpetrator	**NN**	**1-01-001**
perpetual	**JJ**	**8-04-006**
perpetually	**RB**	**3-03-003**
perpetuate	**verb**	**10-03-008**
perpetuate	VB	5-03-004
perpetuated	VBN	1-01-001
perpetuating	VBG	4-03-004
perpetuation	**NN**	**2-02-002**
perplex	**verb**	**3-03-003**
perplex	VB	1-01-001
perplexed	VBN	2-02-002
perplexing	**JJ**	**2-02-002**
perplexity	**NN**	**1-01-001**
Perrin	**prop. noun**	**7-01-001**
Perrin	NP	6-01-001
Perrin's	NP$	1-01-001
Perry	**NP**	**8-04-007**
Perse	**prop. noun**	**2-02-002**
Perse	NP	1-01-001
Perse	NP-TL	1-01-001
persecute	**verb**	**3-03-003**
persecuted	VBN	3-03-003
persecution	**NN**	**7-03-006**
persecutory	**JJ**	**1-01-001**
perseverance	**NN**	**1-01-001**
persevere	**verb**	**2-02-002**
persevere	VB	0-00-000
persevere	VB-HL	1-01-001
perseveres	VBZ	1-01-001
Pershing	**NP**	**1-01-001**
Persia	**NP**	**4-01-001**
Persian	**JJ**	**9-05-005**
Persian	**prop. noun**	**13-01-001**
Persian	NP	1-01-001
Persians	NPS	12-01-001
Persianesque	**JJ**	**1-01-001**
persiflage	**NN**	**1-01-001**
persimmon	**noun**	**1-01-001**
persimmons	NNS	1-01-001
persist	**verb**	**25-11-023**
persist	VB	6-04-005
persists	VBZ	7-04-007
persisted	VBD	8-06-008
persisted	VBN	2-02-002
persisting	VBG	2-02-002
persistence	**NN**	**9-04-006**
persistent	**JJ**	**15-04-014**
persistent	**NN**	**1-01-001**
persistently	**RB**	**3-03-003**
person	**noun**	**299-15-169**
person	NN	170-15-118
Person	NN-TL	4-02-002
person's	NN$	4-04-004
persons	NNS	120-13-076
Persons	NNS	1-01-001
person-to-person	**NN**	**1-01-001**
persona	**FW-NN**	**1-01-001**
persona	**noun**	**2-02-002**
persona	NN	1-01-001
personae	NNS	1-01-001
personage	**noun**	**4-02-003**
personage	NN	1-01-001
personages	NNS	2-01-001
Personages	NNS-TL	1-01-001
personal	**adjective**	**196-15-108**
personal	JJ	192-15-107
personal	JJ-HL	3-02-002
Personal	JJ-TL	1-01-001
personality	**noun**	**63-12-038**
personality	NN	46-12-029
personality	NN-HL	1-01-001
Personality	NN-TL	1-01-001
personalities	NNS	15-08-013
personalize	**verb**	**3-03-003**
personalized	VBN	3-03-003
personally	**RB**	**40-12-032**
personally-owned	**JJ**	**3-01-001**
personification	**NN**	**3-03-003**
personify	**verb**	**5-03-005**
personifies	VBZ	3-02-003
personified	VBN	1-01-001
personifying	VBG	1-01-001
personnel	**FW-JJ**	**1-01-001**
personnel	**noun**	**74-10-043**
personnel	NNS	70-10-041
personnel	NNS-HL	3-01-002
Personnel	NNS-TL	1-01-001
perspective	**noun**	**29-08-022**
perspective	NN	26-08-020
perspectives	NNS	2-01-002
perspectives	NNS-HL	1-01-001
perspiration	**NN**	**1-01-001**
perspire	**verb**	**2-02-002**
perspired	VBD	1-01-001
perspiring	VBG	1-01-001
persuade	**verb**	**42-13-035**

Word	Tag	Frequency
persuade (cont.):		
persuade	VB	17-08-017
persuaded	VBD	6-04-006
persuaded	VBN	15-08-012
persuading	VBG	4-03-004
persuader	**noun**	**1-01-001**
persuaders	NNS	1-01-001
persuading	**NN**	**1-01-001**
persuasion	**noun**	**10-04-009**
persuasion	NN	9-04-008
persuasions	NNS	1-01-001
persuasive	**JJ**	**4-04-004**
persuasively	**QL**	**1-01-001**
persuasively	**RB**	**2-02-002**
pert	**JJ**	**2-02-002**
pertain	**verb**	**13-05-010**
pertain	VB	2-02-002
pertains	VBZ	5-01-003
pertained	VBD	1-01-001
pertaining	VBG	5-04-004
pertinence	**NN**	**2-02-002**
pertinent	**JJ**	**21-07-021**
perturb	**verb**	**1-01-001**
perturbed	VBN	1-01-001
perturbation	**noun**	**3-03-003**
perturbation	NN	1-01-001
perturbations	NNS	2-02-002
Peru	**NP**	**4-03-003**
perusal	**NN**	**2-02-002**
peruse	**verb**	**1-01-001**
perusing	VBG	1-01-001
Peruvian	**JJ**	**2-02-002**
pervade	**verb**	**5-04-005**
pervades	VBZ	2-02-002
pervaded	VBD	1-01-001
pervading	VBG	2-02-002
pervaporation	**NN**	**1-01-001**
pervasive	**JJ**	**4-03-004**
pervasively	**RB**	**1-01-001**
perverse	**JJ**	**5-04-004**
perversely	**QL**	**2-02-002**
perversely	**RB**	**1-01-001**
pervert	**verb**	**1-01-001**
perverted	VBN	1-01-001
Pesce	**NP**	**2-01-001**
pessimism	**NN**	**6-03-005**
pessimist	**noun**	**1-01-001**
pessimists	NNS	1-01-001
pessimistic	**JJ**	**6-04-006**
pest	**noun**	**6-03-003**
pest	NN	4-03-003
pests	NNS	2-01-001
pester	**verb**	**2-02-002**
pester	VB	1-01-001
pestering	VBG	1-01-001
pesticide	**noun**	**1-01-001**
pesticides	NNS	1-01-001
pestilent	**JJ**	**1-01-001**
pestle	**noun**	**1-01-001**
pestle	NN	0-00-000
Pestle	NN-TL	1-01-001
pet	**noun**	**14-06-013**
pet	NN	8-04-008
pets	NNS	5-03-004
pets	NNS-HL	1-01-001
pet	**verb**	**4-03-003**
petted	VBN	2-02-002
petting	VBG	2-02-002
petal	**noun**	**4-03-003**
petals	NNS	4-03-003
Pete	**prop. noun**	**24-04-007**
Pete	NP	23-04-007
Pete's	NP$	1-01-001
peter	**verb**	**1-01-001**
petered	VBN	1-01-001
Peter	**prop. noun**	**46-09-024**
Peter	NP	30-06-016
Peeter	NP	1-01-001
Peter	NP-TL	6-03-003
Peter's	NP$	6-03-003
Peter's	NP$-TL	3-02-002
Peterhouse	**NP**	**2-01-001**
Petermann	**NP**	**1-01-001**
Peters	**NP**	**4-02-002**
Petersburg	**prop. noun**	**5-03-003**
Petersburg	NP	4-03-003
Petersburg	NP-HL	1-01-001
Peterson	**NP**	**8-03-003**
Petey	**NP**	**1-01-001**

Word	Tag	Frequency
Petipa	**NP**	**3-01-002**
Petipa-Tschaikowsky	**prop. noun**	**1-01-001**
Petipa-Tschaikowsky	NP	0-00-000
Petipa-Tschaikowsky	NP-TL	1-01-001
petit	**foreign**	**3-02-003**
petit	FW-JJ	1-01-001
petits	FW-JJ	2-02-002
petite	**JJ**	**1-01-001**
petition	**noun**	**21-06-010**
petition	NN	14-05-008
petitions	NNS	7-02-004
petition	**verb**	**6-05-006**
petition	VB	1-01-001
petitions	VBZ	1-01-001
petitioned	VBD	4-03-004
petitioner	**noun**	**31-02-002**
petitioner	NN	29-02-002
petitioner's	NN$	2-01-001
Petrarchan	**JJ**	**1-01-001**
Petrie	**NP**	**3-01-001**
petrify	**verb**	**2-02-002**
petrified	VBN	2-02-002
Petrini	**NP**	**1-01-001**
petroleum	**NN**	**1-01-001**
Petruchka	**NP**	**1-01-001**
Pettersson	**NP**	**1-01-001**
Pettibone	**NP**	**1-01-001**
Pettigrew	**prop. noun**	**2-01-001**
Pettigrew	NP	1-01-001
Pettigrew's	NP$	1-01-001
pettiness	**noun**	**2-02-002**
pettiness	NN	1-01-001
pettinesses	NNS	1-01-001
Pettit	**NP**	**2-01-001**
petty	**adjective**	**8-06-007**
petty	JJ	6-04-005
Petty	JJ-TL	2-02-002
petulance	**NN**	**1-01-001**
petulant	**JJ**	**1-01-001**
Peugeot	**NP**	**1-01-001**
pew	**noun**	**1-01-001**
pews	NNS	1-01-001
Pezza	**NP**	**3-01-001**
Pfaff	**NP**	**4-01-001**
Pfau	**NP**	**1-01-001**
Pfc.	**NP**	**1-01-001**
pfennig	**NN**	**1-01-001**
pffft	**verb**	**1-01-001**
pfffted	VBD	1-01-001
Pfohl	**NP**	**3-01-001**
phagocyte	**noun**	**1-01-001**
phagocytes	NNS	1-01-001
phalanx	**NN**	**5-03-003**
phantasy	**NN**	**2-01-002**
phantom	**NN**	**2-02-002**
pharmaceutical	**JJ**	**2-02-002**
pharmacist	**NN**	**1-01-001**
pharmacological	**JJ**	**2-01-002**
pharmacopoeia	**noun**	**1-01-001**
pharmacopoeia	NN	0-00-000
Pharmacopoeia	NN-TL	1-01-001
pharmacy	**noun**	**5-02-002**
pharmacy	NN	2-01-001
Pharmacy	NN-TL	3-02-002
pharmical	**adjective**	**1-01-001**
pharmical	JJ	0-00-000
Pharmical	JJ-TL	1-01-001
phase	**noun**	**96-09-049**
phase	NN	64-07-034
phase	NN-HL	2-01-001
Phase	NN-TL	6-03-003
phases	NNS	24-09-020
pheasant	**noun**	**3-02-002**
pheasant	NNS	1-01-001
pheasants	NNS	2-01-001
Phedre	**prop. noun**	**6-02-003**
Phedre	NP	3-01-002
Phedre	NP-TL	3-02-002
Phelan	**NP**	**1-01-001**
Phelps	**NP**	**1-01-001**
phenomenal	**JJ**	**2-02-002**
phenomenological	**JJ**	**1-01-001**
phenomenon	**noun**	**62-09-041**
phenomenon	NN	35-09-027
phenonenon	NN	1-01-001
phenomena	NNS	26-08-020
phenothiazine	**NN**	**4-01-001**
Phi	**NP**	**2-01-002**
Phil	**prop. noun**	**67-04-007**

Word	Tag	Frequency
Phil (cont.):		
Phil	NP	65-04-007
Phil's	NP$	2-01-001
Philadelphia	**prop. noun**	**51-11-026**
Philadelphia	NP	36-11-021
Philadelphia	NP-HL	1-01-001
Philadelphia	NP-TL	13-06-010
Philadelphia's	NP$	1-01-001
philanthropic	**JJ**	**4-04-004**
philanthropist	**noun**	**2-02-002**
philanthropist	NN	1-01-001
philanthropists	NNS	0-00-000
philantropists	NNS	1-01-001
philanthropy	**noun**	**2-02-002**
philanthropy	NN	0-00-000
philantrophy	NN	1-01-001
philanthropies	NNS	1-01-001
Philco	**prop. noun**	**2-02-002**
Philco	NP	1-01-001
Philco	NP-TL	1-01-001
Philco-sponsored	**JJ**	**1-01-001**
philharmonic	**noun**	**10-04-006**
philharmonic	NN	1-01-001
Philharmonic	NN-TL	9-03-005
philharmonique	**foreign**	**1-01-001**
philharmonique	FW-JJ	0-00-000
Philharmonique	FW-JJ-TL	1-01-001
Philibert	**NP**	**1-01-001**
Philip	**prop. noun**	**23-07-012**
Philip	NP	21-07-012
Philip's	NP$	2-01-001
Philippe	**NP**	**1-01-001**
Philippi	**prop. noun**	**5-01-001**
Philippi	NP	4-01-001
Philippi	NP-TL	1-01-001
Philippian	**prop. noun**	**1-01-001**
Philippians	NPS	0-00-000
Philippians	NPS-TL	1-01-001
Philippine	**adjective**	**3-03-003**
Philippine	JJ	2-02-002
Philippine	JJ-TL	1-01-001
Philippine	**prop. noun**	**4-03-003**
Philippines	NPS	4-03-003
Philippoff	**NP**	**2-01-001**
Philistine	**prop. noun**	**2-01-001**
Philistines	NPS	2-01-001
Phillip	**NP**	**2-02-002**
Phillips	**NP**	**11-06-006**
Philly	**prop. noun**	**4-02-003**
Philly	NP	1-01-001
Phillies	NPS	3-01-002
Philmont	**prop. noun**	**4-01-001**
Philmont	NP	1-01-001
Philmont	NP-TL	3-01-001
philological	**JJ**	**2-02-002**
philologist	**noun**	**1-01-001**
philologists	NNS	1-01-001
philology	**NN**	**2-02-002**
philosopher	**noun**	**25-09-017**
philosopher	NN	16-07-012
philosophers	NNS	9-05-007
philosophic	**JJ**	**11-04-006**
philosophical	**adjective**	**26-08-018**
philosophical	JJ	24-07-016
Philosophical	JJ-TL	2-02-002
philosophically	**RB**	**1-01-001**
philosophize	**verb**	**3-02-003**
philosophized	VBD	1-01-001
philosophizing	VBG	2-01-002
philosophy	**noun**	**88-11-037**
philosophy	NN	84-11-034
Philosophy	NN-TL	2-02-002
philosophies	NNS	1-01-001
Philosophies	NNS-TL	1-01-001
Phineoppus	**NP**	**1-01-001**
Phipps	**NP**	**2-01-001**
phis	**FW-NNS**	**1-01-001**
phloem	**NN**	**1-01-001**
phobic-like	**JJ**	**1-01-001**
Phoenix	**prop. noun**	**9-02-004**
Phoenix	NP	8-02-004
Phoenix	NP-TL	1-01-001
phone	**noun**	**53-09-026**
phone	NN	47-08-025
phone	NN-HL	1-01-001
phones	NNS	5-04-004
phone	**verb**	**12-06-009**
phone	VB	5-04-005
phones	VBZ	2-02-002
phone (cont.):		
phoned	VBD	3-03-003
phoned	VBN	2-02-002
Phone	**NP**	**1-01-001**
phoneme	**noun**	**2-01-001**
phonemes	NNS	2-01-001
phonemic	**JJ**	**8-01-001**
phonemics	**NN**	**2-01-001**
phonetic	**JJ**	**2-01-001**
phonetics	**NN**	**1-01-001**
phonic	**JJ**	**1-01-001**
phonograph	**noun**	**4-04-004**
phonograph	NN	3-03-003
phonographs	NNS	1-01-001
phonologic	**JJ**	**10-01-001**
phonology	**NN**	**5-01-001**
phony	**JJ**	**11-04-008**
phony	**noun**	**3-03-003**
phony	NN	1-01-001
phonies	NNS	2-02-002
phosgene	**NN**	**1-01-001**
phosphate	**noun**	**8-02-003**
phosphate	NN	7-02-003
phosphates	NNS	1-01-001
phosphate-buffered	**JJ**	**1-01-001**
phosphide	**NN**	**1-01-001**
phosphine	**noun**	**1-01-001**
phosphines	NNS	1-01-001
phosphor	**noun**	**14-01-001**
phosphor	NN	13-01-001
phosphors	NNS	1-01-001
phosphor-screen	**NN**	**1-01-001**
phosphorescent	**JJ**	**1-01-001**
phosphorus	**NN**	**1-01-001**
phosphorus-bridged	**JJ**	**1-01-001**
Photek	**prop. noun**	**1-01-001**
Photek	NP	0-00-000
Photek	NP-TL	1-01-001
photo	**noun**	**12-03-007**
photo	NN	5-02-003
photos	NNS	7-03-005
photo-montage	**NN**	**1-01-001**
photo-offset	**NN**	**1-01-001**
photocathode	**noun**	**9-01-001**
photocathode	NN	7-01-001
photocathodes	NNS	2-01-001
photochemical	**adjective**	**7-01-001**
photochemical	JJ	5-01-001
photochemical	JJ-HL	2-01-001
photoelectron	**noun**	**1-01-001**
photoelectrons	NNS	1-01-001
photoelectronic	**JJ**	**2-01-001**
photofloodlight	**noun**	**1-01-001**
photofloodlights	NNS	1-01-001
photogenic	**JJ**	**2-01-001**
photograph	**noun**	**29-08-020**
photograph	NN	15-05-009
photographs	NNS	14-06-013
photograph	**verb**	**12-07-009**
photograph	VB	3-01-001
photographs	VBZ	2-02-002
photographed	VBN	4-04-004
photographing	VBG	2-02-002
photographing	VBG-HL	1-01-001
photographer	**noun**	**11-05-007**
photographer	NN	4-04-004
Photographer	NN-TL	1-01-001
photographers	NNS	6-03-005
photographic	**JJ**	**11-05-007**
photographically	**RB**	**1-01-001**
photography	**NN**	**7-04-006**
photoluminescence	**NN**	**1-01-001**
photomicrograph	**NN**	**1-01-001**
photomicrography	**NN**	**1-01-001**
photon-counting	**JJ**	**1-01-001**
photorealism	**NN**	**1-01-001**
photosensitive	**JJ**	**1-01-001**
Phouma	**prop. noun**	**5-02-003**
Phouma	NP	4-02-003
Phouma's	NP$	1-01-001
phrase	**noun**	**51-13-039**
phrase	NN	33-13-032
phrases	NNS	18-07-012
phrase	**verb**	**6-05-006**
phrase	VB	1-01-001
phrased	VBD	1-01-001
phrased	VBN	2-01-002
phrasing	VBG	2-02-002
phrasemaking	**NN**	**1-01-001**

Word	Tag	Count
phraseology	**NN**	**3-02-003**
phrasing	**noun**	**3-02-002**
phrasing	NN	2-01-001
phrasings	NNS	1-01-001
phthalate	**NN**	**1-01-001**
Phyfe	**NP**	**4-01-001**
Phyllis	**NP**	**2-02-002**
phylum	**noun**	**1-01-001**
phyla	NNS	1-01-001
physical	**adjective**	**138-13-083**
physical	JJ	128-13-082
physical	JJ-HL	7-01-003
Physical	JJ-TL	3-02-003
physical-chemical	**JJ**	**1-01-001**
physically	**QL**	**1-01-001**
physically	**RB**	**19-07-017**
physicalness	**NN**	**1-01-001**
physician	**noun**	**22-09-015**
physician	NN	15-07-010
physician's	NN$	1-01-001
physicians	NNS	5-04-005
Physicians	NNS-TL	1-01-001
physicist	**noun**	**7-04-006**
physicist	NN	4-03-003
Physicist	NN-TL	1-01-001
physicists	NNS	2-02-002
physicochemical	**JJ**	**1-01-001**
physics	**noun**	**22-09-012**
physics	NN	18-09-011
physics	NN-HL	1-01-001
Physics	NN-TL	3-02-002
physiochemical	**JJ**	**1-01-001**
physiognomy	**NN**	**2-01-002**
physiologic	**JJ**	**2-01-001**
physiological	**adjective**	**22-05-009**
physiological	JJ	20-05-009
physiological	JJ-HL	1-01-001
Physiological	JJ-TL	1-01-001
physiologically	**RB**	**1-01-001**
physiologist	**noun**	**2-01-001**
physiologist	NN	1-01-001
Physiologist	NN-TL	1-01-001
physiology	**NN**	**2-02-002**
physiotherapist	**NN**	**1-01-001**
physique	**NN**	**2-01-001**
pi	**NN**	**2-01-001**
Pi	**NP**	**1-01-001**
pianism	**NN**	**1-01-001**
pianist	**noun**	**21-05-010**
pianist	NN	14-05-008
pianist's	NN$	4-02-002
pianists	NNS	3-03-003
pianistic	**JJ**	**1-01-001**
piano	**noun**	**39-08-020**
piano	NN	30-08-018
Piano	NN-TL	8-03-006
pianos	NNS	0-00-000
Pianos	NNS-TL	1-01-001
piazza	**foreign**	**2-02-002**
piazza	FW-NN	0-00-000
Piazza	FW-NN-TL	2-02-002
piazza	**noun**	**7-03-003**
piazza	NN	5-02-002
piazza	NN-HL	1-01-001
piazzas	NNS	1-01-001
Piazza	**NP**	**9-01-001**
Piazzo	**NP**	**1-01-001**
Picasso	**prop. noun**	**17-06-006**
Picasso	NP	14-06-006
Picasso's	NP$	3-01-001
picayune	**JJ**	**1-01-001**
Piccadilly	**prop. noun**	**2-02-002**
Piccadilly	NP	1-01-001
Piccadilly	NP-TL	1-01-001
pick	**noun**	**5-03-005**
pick	NN	4-03-004
picks	NNS	1-01-001
pick	**verb**	**143-14-099**
pick	VB	49-13-039
picks	VBZ	3-03-003
picked	VBD	51-10-037
picked	VBN	27-10-025
picking	VBG	13-08-013
Pick	**NP**	**2-01-001**
pick-up	**JJ**	**2-01-001**
pick-up	**NN**	**1-01-001**
pickaxe	**NN**	**1-01-001**
picker	**noun**	**4-01-001**
picker	NN	1-01-001
picker (cont.):		
pickers	NNS	3-01-001
Pickering	**NP**	**1-01-001**
picket	**noun**	**11-06-009**
picket	NN	9-06-008
pickets	NNS	2-01-001
picket	**verb**	**4-02-003**
picketed	VBD	1-01-001
picketed	VBN	1-01-001
picketing	VBG	2-01-001
Pickett	**prop. noun**	**1-01-001**
Pickett's	NP$	0-00-000
Pickett's	NP$-TL	1-01-001
Pickfair	**NP**	**1-01-001**
Pickford	**NP**	**1-01-001**
picking	**noun**	**2-02-002**
picking	NN	1-01-001
pickings	NNS	0-00-000
pickins	NNS	1-01-001
pickle	**noun**	**2-02-002**
pickle	NN	1-01-001
pickles	NNS	1-01-001
pickle	**verb**	**3-01-001**
pickled	VBN	3-01-001
Pickman	**NP**	**1-01-001**
pickoff	**noun**	**4-01-001**
pickoff	NN	3-01-001
pickoffs	NNS	0-00-000
pickoffs	NNS-HL	1-01-001
pickup	**NN**	**14-06-010**
picnic	**noun**	**18-08-011**
picnic	NN	15-06-008
picnics	NNS	3-03-003
picnic	**verb**	**1-01-001**
picnicked	VBD	1-01-001
picnicker	**noun**	**1-01-001**
picnickers	NNS	1-01-001
Picon	**NP**	**1-01-001**
pictorial	**JJ**	**5-03-003**
pictorially	**RB**	**1-01-001**
picture	**noun**	**227-15-126**
picture	NN	160-14-096
pictures	NNS	65-14-045
pictures	NNS-HL	1-01-001
Pictures	NNS-TL	1-01-001
picture	**verb**	**9-05-009**
picture	VB	2-01-002
pictures	VBZ	1-01-001
pictured	VBD	2-02-002
pictured	VBN	2-02-002
picturing	VBG	1-01-001
picturing	VBG-HL	1-01-001
picture-image	**noun**	**1-01-001**
picture-images	NNS	1-01-001
picture-palace	**NN**	**1-01-001**
picturesque	**JJ**	**9-04-008**
picturing	**NN**	**1-01-001**
Piddington	**NP**	**3-01-001**
piddle	**verb**	**1-01-001**
piddling	VBG	1-01-001
pidgin	**NN**	**2-02-002**
pie	**noun**	**19-07-010**
pie	NN	13-07-007
pie	NN-HL	1-01-001
pies	NNS	5-03-004
piece	**FW-NN**	**1-01-001**
piece	**noun**	**219-15-100**
piece	NN	127-14-072
pieces	NNS	92-14-042
piece	**VB**	**1-01-001**
piecemeal	**JJ**	**1-01-001**
piecemeal	**RB**	**1-01-001**
piecewise	**RB**	**1-01-001**
Piedmont	**prop. noun**	**2-02-002**
Piedmont	NP	1-01-001
Piedmont	NP-TL	1-01-001
Piepsam	**prop. noun**	**14-01-001**
Piepsam	NP	13-01-001
Piepsam's	NP$	1-01-001
pier	**noun**	**8-06-006**
pier	NN	3-03-003
piers	NNS	5-04-004
pier-table	**NN**	**1-01-001**
pierce	**verb**	**7-05-007**
pierced	VBD	1-01-001
pierced	VBN	3-02-003
piercing	VBG	3-03-003
Pierce	**NP**	**6-03-004**
Piero	**NP**	**2-02-002**

Word	Tag	Count
Pierpont	**NP**	**1-01-001**
Pierre	**prop. noun**	**17-08-012**
Pierre	NP	16-08-011
Pierre	NP-TL	1-01-001
Piers	**NP**	**1-01-001**
Piersee	**NP**	**1-01-001**
Pierson	**NP**	**2-01-001**
Pieta	**NP**	**2-01-001**
Pietism	**NP**	**1-01-001**
Pietro	**prop. noun**	**3-01-001**
Pietro	NP	2-01-001
Pietro's	NP+BEZ	1-01-001
piety	**NN**	**4-03-004**
piezoelectric	**JJ**	**3-01-002**
piezoelectricity	**NN**	**1-01-001**
pig	**noun**	**14-07-011**
pig	NN	8-05-007
pigs	NNS	6-04-005
pig-drunk	**JJ**	**2-01-001**
pig-infested	**JJ**	**1-01-001**
pigeon	**noun**	**5-03-004**
pigeon	NN	2-01-002
pigen	NN	1-01-001
Pigeon	NN-TL	1-01-001
pigeons	NNS	1-01-001
pigeonhole	**NN**	**1-01-001**
pigment	**noun**	**12-05-007**
pigment	NN	9-03-005
pigments	NNS	3-03-003
pigmented	**JJ**	**1-01-001**
pigpen	**noun**	**1-01-001**
pigpens	NNS	1-01-001
pigskin	**NN**	**1-01-001**
pike	**NN**	**3-01-002**
Pike	**prop. noun**	**40-03-003**
Pike	NP	37-02-002
Pike	NP-TL	1-01-001
Pike's	NP$	2-01-001
Pilate	**prop. noun**	**2-02-002**
Pilate	NP	1-01-001
Pilate's	NP$	1-01-001
pile	**noun**	**23-08-018**
pile	NN	18-07-016
Pile	NN-TL	4-01-001
piles	NNS	1-01-001
pile	**verb**	**26-12-026**
pile	VB	3-03-003
piles	VBZ	1-01-001
piled	VBD	7-04-007
piled	VBN	9-05-009
piling	VBG	6-05-006
pilfer	**verb**	**1-01-001**
pilfering	VBG	1-01-001
pilgrim	**noun**	**11-06-007**
pilgrim	NN	3-03-003
Pilgrim	NN-TL	1-01-001
pilgrim's	NN$	0-00-000
Pilgrim's	NN$-TL	1-01-001
pilgrims	NNS	1-01-001
Pilgrims	NNS-TL	5-01-001
pilgrimage	**noun**	**10-07-009**
pilgrimage	NN	6-04-006
Pilgrimage	NN-TL	3-02-002
pilgrimages	NNS	1-01-001
pill	**noun**	**23-07-009**
pill	NN	15-05-005
pills	NNS	6-03-004
pills	NNS-HL	2-02-002
pillage	**NN**	**1-01-001**
pillage	**verb**	**3-01-001**
pillage	VB	2-01-001
pillaged	VBD	1-01-001
pillar	**noun**	**7-05-007**
pillar	NN	2-01-002
pillars	NNS	5-04-005
pillar	**verb**	**1-01-001**
pillared	VBN	1-01-001
pillared	**JJ**	**1-01-001**
pillory	**verb**	**2-02-002**
pilloried	VBD	1-01-001
pilloried	VBN	1-01-001
pillow	**noun**	**11-05-010**
pillow	NN	8-05-007
pillows	NNS	3-01-003
Pillsbury	**NP**	**1-01-001**
pilot	**noun**	**54-12-019**
pilot	NN	40-10-017
pilot	NN-HL	2-01-001
pilot's	NN$	2-02-002
pilot (cont.):		
pilots	NNS	8-04-004
pilots'	NNS$	2-02-002
pilot	**verb**	**3-02-003**
pilot	VB	2-02-002
piloting	VBG	1-01-001
piloting	**NN**	**1-01-001**
Pils	**NP**	**1-01-001**
Pimen	**prop. noun**	**7-01-001**
Pimen	NP	5-01-001
Pimen's	NP$	2-01-001
pimp	**noun**	**5-03-004**
pimp	NN	3-02-002
pimps	NNS	2-02-002
pimple	**noun**	**1-01-001**
pimples	NNS	1-01-001
pimpled	**JJ**	**1-01-001**
pimplike	**JJ**	**1-01-001**
pin	**noun**	**20-09-016**
pin	NN	14-08-012
pins	NNS	5-04-004
pins	NNS-HL	1-01-001
pin	**verb**	**7-05-006**
pin	VB	2-02-002
pinned	VBD	1-01-001
pinned	VBN	3-03-003
pinning	VBG	1-01-001
pin-curl	**NN**	**1-01-001**
pinafore	**noun**	**1-01-001**
pinafores	NNS	1-01-001
Pinar	**NP**	**2-01-001**
pinball	**NN**	**1-01-001**
pinch	**NN**	**4-02-002**
pinch	**verb**	**11-05-010**
pinch	VB	2-02-002
pinched	VBD	2-02-002
pinched	VBN	5-03-005
pinching	VBG	2-02-002
pinch-hit	**VB**	**1-01-001**
pinch-hitter	**noun**	**2-01-002**
pinch-hitter	NN	1-01-001
pinch-hitters	NNS	1-01-001
Pincian	**adjective**	**2-01-001**
Pincian	JJ	0-00-000
Pincian	JJ-TL	2-01-001
pine	**noun**	**16-07-013**
pine	NN	14-07-011
pines	NNS	2-02-002
pine-knot	**NN**	**1-01-001**
pineapple	**noun**	**9-05-005**
pineapple	NN	8-05-005
pineapple	NN-HL	1-01-001
ping	**verb**	**1-01-001**
pinging	VBG	1-01-001
Ping-pong	**NP**	**1-01-001**
pinhead	**NN**	**1-01-001**
pinhole	**noun**	**1-01-001**
pinholes	NNS	1-01-001
pinion	**verb**	**1-01-001**
pinioned	VBN	1-01-001
pink	**adjective**	**47-13-031**
pink	JJ	46-12-030
Pink	JJ-TL	1-01-001
pink	**noun**	**3-03-003**
pink	NN	1-01-001
pinks	NNS	2-02-002
pink-petticoated	**JJ**	**1-01-001**
Pinkie	**NP**	**1-01-001**
pinkish-white	**JJ**	**1-01-001**
pinkly	**RB**	**1-01-001**
pinnacle	**noun**	**2-02-002**
pinnacle	NN	1-01-001
pinnacles	NNS	1-01-001
pinning	**noun**	**1-01-001**
pinnings	NNS	1-01-001
pinochle	**NN**	**1-01-001**
pinpoint	**noun**	**4-04-004**
pinpoint	NN	2-02-002
pin-point	NN	1-01-001
pinpoints	NNS	1-01-001
pinpoint	**verb**	**4-04-004**
pinpoint	VB	3-03-003
pinpointing	VBG	1-01-001
Pinscher	**NP**	**1-01-001**
Pinsk	**NP**	**1-01-001**
pint	**noun**	**14-05-006**
pint	NN	13-04-005
pynte	NN	1-01-001
pint-sized	**JJ**	**1-01-001**

Word	Tag	Frequency
pinto	**NN**	**1-01-001**
pioneer	**noun**	**23-11-016**
pioneer	NN	17-10-013
Pioneer	NN-TL	2-02-002
pioneer's	NN$	1-01-001
pioneers	NNS	2-01-001
Pioneers	NNS-TL	1-01-001
pioneer	**verb**	**7-05-006**
pioneer	VB	1-01-001
pioneered	VBD	1-01-001
pioneered	VBN	2-02-002
pioneering	VBG	3-02-002
pious	**JJ**	**10-06-008**
piously	**RB**	**1-01-001**
pip	**NN**	**1-01-001**
pip	**UH**	**2-01-001**
Pip	**prop. noun**	**33-01-001**
Pip	NP	20-01-001
Pip's	NP$	13-01-001
pipe	**noun**	**27-09-018**
pipe	NN	20-07-012
pipes	NNS	7-05-007
pipe	**verb**	**5-05-005**
piped	VBD	1-01-001
piped	VBN	1-01-001
piping	VBG	3-03-003
pipeline	**noun**	**6-03-003**
pipeline	NN	4-03-003
Pipeline	NN-TL	2-01-001
piper	**noun**	**1-01-001**
pipers	NNS	1-01-001
Pipgras	**NP**	**1-01-001**
piping	**NN**	**2-01-001**
piquant	**JJ**	**2-02-002**
pique	**NN**	**2-02-002**
piracy	**NN**	**1-01-001**
Piraeus	**NP**	**1-01-001**
Pirandello	**NP**	**1-01-001**
Piranesi	**NP**	**1-01-001**
Piraro	**NP**	**1-01-001**
pirate	**noun**	**17-04-007**
pirate	NN	2-02-002
Pirate	NN-TL	2-01-001
pirates	NNS	4-03-003
Pirates	NNS-TL	8-02-003
pirates'	NNS$	0-00-000
Pirates'	NNS$-TL	1-01-001
Pirie	**NP**	**1-01-001**
pirogue	**noun**	**1-01-001**
pirogues	NNS	1-01-001
pirouette	**NN**	**4-02-003**
Pisces	**NP**	**1-01-001**
piss	**VB**	**1-01-001**
pistachio	**NN**	**1-01-001**
pistol	**noun**	**31-09-017**
pistol	NN	27-08-016
pistols	NNS	4-03-003
pistol-packing	**JJ**	**1-01-001**
pistol-whip	**verb**	**2-02-002**
pistol-whipped	VBD	1-01-001
pistol-whipping	VBG	1-01-001
pistoleer	**noun**	**1-01-001**
pistoleers	NNS	1-01-001
piston	**noun**	**10-01-002**
piston	NN	7-01-001
pistons	NNS	3-01-002
pit	**noun**	**17-07-011**
pit	NN	13-07-009
pits	NNS	4-03-003
pit	**VB**	**1-01-001**
pit-run	**JJ**	**3-01-001**
pitch	**noun**	**27-09-018**
pitch	NN	21-09-016
pitches	NNS	6-03-004
pitch	**verb**	**20-08-015**
pitch	VB	1-01-001
pitched	VBD	4-04-004
pitched	VBN	4-04-004
pitching	VBG	11-05-009
pitcher	**noun**	**29-05-012**
pitcher	NN	21-05-011
pitchers	NNS	7-02-005
pitchers	NNS-HL	1-01-001
pitchfork	**NN**	**2-01-001**
pitching	**NN**	**5-02-004**
piteous	**JJ**	**1-01-001**
pitfall	**noun**	**4-04-004**
pitfall	NN	3-03-003
pitfalls	NNS	1-01-001
pith	**NN**	**1-01-001**
pithy	**JJ**	**1-01-001**
pitiable	**JJ**	**3-03-003**
pitiful	**JJ**	**4-03-004**
pitifully	**RB**	**2-01-002**
pitiless	**JJ**	**2-02-002**
pitilessly	**RB**	**1-01-001**
Pitney-Bowes	**prop. noun**	**1-01-001**
Pitney-Bowes	NP	0-00-000
Pitney-Bowes	NP-TL	1-01-001
Pitt	**NP**	**2-01-001**
Pitt-Rivers	**NP**	**1-01-001**
Pittenger	**NP**	**1-01-001**
Pittsboro	**NP**	**1-01-001**
Pittsburgh	**prop. noun**	**25-08-011**
Pittsburgh	NP	21-08-011
Pittsburgh	NP-TL	4-02-002
Pittsburgher	**prop. noun**	**2-02-002**
Pittsburghers	NPS	2-02-002
pituitary	**adjective**	**6-01-001**
pituitary	JJ	5-01-001
pituitary	JJ-HL	1-01-001
pituitary	**NN**	**5-03-003**
pity	**NN**	**13-06-011**
pity	**verb**	**3-03-003**
pity	VB	1-01-001
pitied	VBD	2-02-002
pityingly	**RB**	**1-01-001**
Pius	**NP**	**2-02-002**
pivot	**NN**	**2-01-001**
pivot	**verb**	**1-01-001**
pivoting	VBG	1-01-001
pivotal	**JJ**	**1-01-001**
Piwen	**NP**	**1-01-001**
pixie	**noun**	**1-01-001**
pixies	NNS	1-01-001
Pizarro	**NP**	**1-01-001**
pizza	**NN**	**3-03-003**
pizzicato	**NN**	**1-01-001**
placate	**verb**	**1-01-001**
placating	VBG	1-01-001
place	**foreign**	**5-02-002**
place	FW-NN	0-00-000
Place	FW-NN-TL	5-02-002
place	**noun**	**584-15-301**
place	NN	474-15-269
pl.	NN	0-00-000
pl.	NN-TL	2-01-002
place	NN-HL	1-01-001
place	NN-NC	1-01-001
Place	NN-TL	14-04-010
places	NNS	91-15-075
places	NNS-HL	1-01-001
place	**verb**	**233-14-154**
place	VB	74-10-046
places	VBZ	8-04-008
placed	VBD	25-12-023
placed	VBN	101-12-081
placing	VBG	25-11-023
Place	**NP**	**1-01-001**
place-kicker	**NN**	**1-01-001**
place-kicking	**NN**	**3-01-001**
place-name	**noun**	**9-01-001**
place-name	NN	6-01-001
place-names	NNS	3-01-001
placeless	**JJ**	**1-01-001**
placement	**NN**	**15-04-011**
Placentia	**NP**	**1-01-001**
placid	**adjective**	**6-05-006**
placid	JJ	4-03-004
Placid	JJ-TL	2-02-002
placing	**NN**	**2-01-001**
plagiarism	**NN**	**1-01-001**
plague	**NN**	**3-03-003**
plague	**verb**	**8-06-008**
plague	VB	3-03-003
plagued	VBD	3-03-003
plagued	VBN	2-02-002
plaid	**noun**	**2-02-002**
plaid	NN	1-01-001
plaids	NNS	1-01-001
plain	**adjective**	**37-12-032**
plain	JJ	36-12-031
Plain	JJ-TL	1-01-001
plain	**noun**	**21-09-014**
plain	NN	7-02-003
plains	NNS	4-04-004
Plains	NNS-TL	10-05-007
plain	**QL**	**2-02-002**

Word	Tag	Frequency
plain	**RB**	**2-01-002**
plain-clothesman	**noun**	**2-01-001**
plain-clothesmen	NNS	2-01-001
plain-out	**RB**	**1-01-001**
plain-spoken	**JJ**	**2-02-002**
plainclothes	**NNS**	**1-01-001**
plainest	**JJT**	**1-01-001**
Plainfield	**prop. noun**	**3-01-002**
Plainfield	NP	2-01-002
Plainfield	NP-HL	1-01-001
plainly	**QL**	**4-02-004**
plainly	**RB**	**14-08-014**
plaintiff	**noun**	**9-02-003**
plaintiff	NN	4-01-001
plaintiff	NN-HL	1-01-001
plaintiff's	NN$	1-01-001
plaintiffs	NNS	3-02-003
plaintive	**JJ**	**2-02-002**
Plainview	**NP**	**1-01-001**
plan	**noun**	**278-15-124**
plan	NN	164-14-077
plan	NN-HL	2-02-002
Plan	NN-TL	9-05-007
plan's	NN$	1-01-001
plans	NNS	98-15-072
plans	NNS-HL	3-03-003
Plans	NNS-TL	1-01-001
plan	**verb**	**200-15-107**
plan	VB	29-10-025
plan	VB-HL	1-01-001
plans	VBZ	11-05-010
planned	VBD	19-10-018
planned	VBN	52-13-039
planned	VBN-HL	1-01-001
Planned	VBN-TL	3-01-002
planning	VBG	68-10-036
planning	VBG-HL	5-03-004
Planning	VBG-TL	11-04-007
planar	**JJ**	**2-01-001**
plane	**noun**	**138-12-044**
plane	NN	112-10-036
planes	NNS	26-11-015
plane	**verb**	**2-01-001**
plane	VB	1-01-001
planed	VBN	1-01-001
Plane	**NP**	**1-01-001**
planeload	**NN**	**1-01-001**
planer	**NN**	**3-01-001**
planet	**noun**	**44-08-015**
planet	NN	21-06-011
planet's	NN$	1-01-001
planets	NNS	22-06-006
planetarium	**NN**	**1-01-001**
planetary	**JJ**	**21-04-005**
Planeten	**foreign**	**1-01-001**
Planeten	FW-NNS	0-00-000
Planeten	FW-NNS-TL	1-01-001
planetoid	**noun**	**2-02-002**
planetoid	NN	1-01-001
planetoids	NNS	1-01-001
plank	**noun**	**11-05-010**
plank	NN	6-03-006
planks	NNS	5-03-004
plank	**VB**	**1-01-001**
planking	**NN**	**8-01-001**
planner	**noun**	**15-07-013**
planner	NN	2-02-002
planners	NNS	13-07-012
planning	**noun**	**45-07-023**
planning	NN	44-07-023
Planning	NN-TL	1-01-001
planoconcave	**JJ**	**1-01-001**
plant	**noun**	**182-12-054**
plant	NN	116-10-041
plant	NN-HL	3-03-003
Plant	NN-TL	2-02-002
plant's	NN$	2-01-002
plants	NNS	58-11-029
plants	NNS-HL	1-01-001
plant	**verb**	**18-09-015**
plant	VB	4-04-004
planted	VBD	5-03-004
planted	VBN	6-05-006
planting	VBG	3-03-003
plant-location	**NN**	**1-01-001**
plantain	**NN**	**1-01-001**
plantation	**noun**	**26-04-007**
plantation	NN	17-03-005
Plantation	NN-TL	2-02-002
plantation (cont.):		
plantations	NNS	0-00-000
Plantations	NNS-TL	7-01-001
planter	**noun**	**10-02-003**
planter	NN	6-02-002
planters	NNS	2-01-001
planters'	NNS$	2-02-002
planting	**noun**	**3-02-002**
planting	NN	2-02-002
plantings	NNS	1-01-001
plaque	**noun**	**6-03-004**
plaque	NN	1-01-001
plaque	NN-HL	1-01-001
plaques	NNS	4-03-003
plasm	**NN**	**1-01-001**
plasma	**NN**	**13-02-006**
plaster	**noun**	**24-06-011**
plaster	NN	23-06-010
plasters	NNS	1-01-001
plaster	**verb**	**5-04-005**
plastered	VBN	5-04-005
plaster-of-Paris	**NN**	**1-01-001**
plasterer	**NN**	**1-01-001**
plastering	**NN**	**1-01-001**
Plasti-Bar	**prop. noun**	**1-01-001**
Plasti-Bars	NPS	1-01-001
plastic	**JJ**	**7-06-007**
plastic	**noun**	**56-06-014**
plastic	NN	23-04-008
Plastic	NN-TL	2-02-002
plastics	NNS	28-04-006
plastics	NNS-HL	2-01-001
Plastics	NNS-TL	1-01-001
plastic-covered	**JJ**	**1-01-001**
plastically	**RB**	**1-01-001**
plasticity	**NN**	**4-02-002**
plastisol	**noun**	**1-01-001**
plastisols	NNS	1-01-001
plat	**verb**	**1-01-001**
platted	VBN	1-01-001
plate	**noun**	**44-11-023**
plate	NN	20-06-011
Plate	NN-TL	1-01-001
plates	NNS	22-10-013
Plates	NNS-TL	1-01-001
plate	**verb**	**1-01-001**
plated	VBN	1-01-001
Plate	**NP**	**1-01-001**
plateau	**noun**	**3-03-003**
plateau	NN	2-02-002
Plateau	NN-TL	1-01-001
platform	**noun**	**77-08-019**
platform	NN	72-08-016
platforms	NNS	5-04-005
platform-controller	**NN**	**1-01-001**
Plath	**NP**	**1-01-001**
platinum	**NN**	**4-03-003**
platitudinous	**JJ**	**1-01-001**
Plato	**prop. noun**	**34-03-007**
Plato	NP	19-02-004
Plato	NP-HL	1-01-001
Plato's	NP$	14-03-006
Platonic	**JJ**	**3-02-003**
Platonica	**foreign**	**1-01-001**
Platonica	FW-JJ	0-00-000
Platonica	FW-JJ-TL	1-01-001
Platonism	**NP**	**4-02-002**
Platonist	**NP**	**2-01-002**
platoon	**noun**	**10-05-005**
platoon	NN	7-02-002
platoons	NNS	3-03-003
platter	**noun**	**3-02-003**
platter	NN	1-01-001
Platter	NN-TL	1-01-001
platters	NNS	1-01-001
plausible	**JJ**	**4-03-004**
play	**noun**	**126-15-049**
play	NN	88-13-044
Play	NN-TL	2-02-002
play's	NN$	3-02-003
plays	NNS	32-08-014
playes	NNS	0-00-000
Playes	NNS-TL	1-01-001
play	**verb**	**333-15-165**
play	VB	110-12-076
plays	VBZ	34-11-031
played	VBD	65-13-048
played	VBD-HL	1-01-001
played	VBN	38-12-032

Word	Tag	Frequency
play (cont.):		
playing	VBG	84-15-055
playin'	VBG	1-01-001
play-act	**verb**	**1-01-001**
play-acting	VBG	1-01-001
play-girl	**NN**	**1-01-001**
Playa	**NP**	**1-01-001**
playable	**JJ**	**1-01-001**
playback	**noun**	**2-02-002**
playback	NN	1-01-001
playbacks	NNS	1-01-001
playboy	**noun**	**2-02-002**
playboy	NN	1-01-001
Playboy	NN-TL	1-01-001
Playboy-Show-Biz	**prop. noun**	**1-01-001**
Playboy-Show-Biz	NP	0-00-000
Playboy-Show-Biz	NP-TL	1-01-001
played-out	**JJ**	**2-02-002**
player	**noun**	**54-10-025**
player	NN	18-07-013
Player	NN-TL	3-02-002
player's	NN$	3-02-003
players	NNS	26-06-013
Players	NNS-TL	3-02-002
players'	NNS$	1-01-001
Player	**prop. noun**	**34-01-001**
Player	NP	30-01-001
Player's	NP$	4-01-001
playful	**JJ**	**3-03-003**
playground	**noun**	**4-03-004**
playground	NN	3-03-003
Playground	NN-TL	1-01-001
playhouse	**noun**	**5-01-003**
playhouse	NN	0-00-000
Playhouse	NN-TL	4-01-002
playhouses	NNS	0-00-000
Playhouses	NNS-TL	1-01-001
playing	**NN**	**17-03-007**
playmate	**noun**	**4-04-004**
playmate	NN	2-02-002
playmates	NNS	2-02-002
playoff	**noun**	**3-02-002**
playoff	NN	2-01-001
play-off	NN	1-01-001
playroom	**NN**	**1-01-001**
playtime	**NN**	**1-01-001**
playwright	**noun**	**4-03-004**
playwright	NN	3-03-003
playwrights	NNS	1-01-001
playwright-director	**NN**	**1-01-001**
playwriting	**NN**	**1-01-001**
plaza	**noun**	**2-02-002**
plaza	NN	0-00-000
Plaza	NN-TL	1-01-001
plazas	NNS	1-01-001
Plaza	**NP**	**1-01-001**
Plazek	**NP**	**1-01-001**
plea	**noun**	**14-08-012**
plea	NN	9-05-008
plea	NN-HL	1-01-001
Plea	NN-TL	1-01-001
pleas	NNS	1-01-001
Pleas	NNS-TL	2-02-002
plead	**verb**	**24-09-020**
plead	VB	5-04-005
pleads	VBZ	1-01-001
pleaded	VBD	7-04-005
pleading	VBG	11-07-009
pleader	**NN**	**1-01-001**
pleading	**NN**	**1-01-001**
pleasance	**NN**	**1-01-001**
pleasant	**adjective**	**35-10-029**
pleasant	JJ	33-10-029
pleasant	JJ-HL	1-01-001
Pleasant	**prop. noun**	**3-02-002**
Pleasant	NP	2-01-001
Pleasant	NP-TL	1-01-001
pleasantly	**QL**	**1-01-001**
pleasantly	**RB**	**9-09-009**
pleasantness	**NN**	**1-01-001**
please	**UH**	**15-05-012**
please	**verb**	**91-14-071**
please	VB	47-13-040
pleases	VBZ	2-01-002
pleased	VBD	11-05-010
pleased	VBN	30-11-028
pleasing	VBG	0-00-000
pleasin'	VBG	1-01-001
pleasing	**JJ**	**10-06-009**

Word	Tag	Frequency
pleasingly	**QL**	**1-01-001**
pleasure	**noun**	**67-13-054**
pleasure	NN	60-12-048
pleasure	NN-HL	1-01-001
pleasures	NNS	6-06-006
pleasure	**VB**	**1-01-001**
pleasure-boat	**NN**	**1-01-001**
pleat	**noun**	**1-01-001**
pleats	NNS	1-01-001
plebeian	**adjective**	**2-01-001**
plebeian	JJ	1-01-001
plebian	JJ-HL	1-01-001
pledge	**noun**	**6-03-004**
pledge	NN	2-02-002
Pledge	NN-TL	1-01-001
pledges	NNS	3-03-003
pledge	**verb**	**5-03-004**
pledged	VBD	2-02-002
pledged	VBN	3-02-002
Plee-Zing	**NP**	**1-01-001**
plenary	**adjective**	**4-02-003**
plenary	JJ	2-02-002
Plenary	JJ-TL	2-01-001
plenipotentiary	**NN**	**1-01-001**
plenitude	**NN**	**1-01-001**
plentiful	**JJ**	**7-05-007**
plenty	**AP**	**1-01-001**
plenty	**NN**	**47-12-039**
plenty	**QL**	**1-01-001**
plenty	**RB**	**6-03-005**
pleura	**NN**	**6-01-001**
pleural	**JJ**	**6-01-001**
Plexiglas	**NP**	**1-01-001**
pliable	**JJ**	**1-01-001**
pliant	**JJ**	**1-01-001**
pliers	**noun**	**1-01-001**
pliers	NNS	1-01-001
plight	**NN**	**7-05-007**
plink	**verb**	**1-01-001**
plinking	VBG	1-01-001
Pliny	**prop. noun**	**1-01-001**
Pliny's	NP$	1-01-001
plod	**verb**	**6-05-006**
plod	VB	1-01-001
plodded	VBD	1-01-001
plodded	VBN	1-01-001
plodding	VBG	3-02-003
plodding	**NN**	**1-01-001**
plop	**verb**	**1-01-001**
plopped	VBD	1-01-001
plot	**noun**	**40-12-033**
plot	NN	32-11-028
plot	NN-HL	1-01-001
plots	NNS	7-05-006
plot	**verb**	**17-08-013**
plot	VB	4-02-002
plots	VBZ	1-01-001
plotted	VBD	2-01-002
plotted	VBN	8-03-006
plotting	VBG	2-02-002
plow	**noun**	**12-05-008**
plow	NN	8-03-004
Plow	NN-TL	1-01-001
plows	NNS	3-03-003
plow	**verb**	**16-08-011**
plow	VB	3-03-003
plowed	VBD	1-01-001
plowed	VBN	4-02-002
plowing	VBG	8-03-006
plowing	**NN**	**3-01-002**
plowman	**noun**	**1-01-001**
plowman's	NN$	0-00-000
Plowman's	NN$-TL	1-01-001
plowshare	**noun**	**1-01-001**
plowshares	NNS	1-01-001
pluck	**NN**	**1-01-001**
pluck	**verb**	**6-04-005**
pluck	VB	1-01-001
plucked	VBD	4-03-004
plucking	VBG	1-01-001
plug	**noun**	**23-05-006**
plug	NN	21-04-005
plugs	NNS	2-02-002
plug	**verb**	**6-04-006**
plug	VB	2-01-002
plugged	VBD	1-01-001
plugged	VBN	2-02-002
plugging	VBG	1-01-001
plugugly	**NN**	**2-02-002**

Word	Tag	Frequency
plum	**NN**	**1-01-001**
plumb	**NN**	**1-01-001**
plumb	**QL**	**4-02-003**
plumb	**verb**	**1-01-001**
plumbed	VBD	1-01-001
plumber	**NN**	**4-03-003**
plumbing	**NN**	**9-05-008**
plume	**NN**	**2-02-002**
plume	**verb**	**1-01-001**
plumed	VBN	1-01-001
Plummer	**NP**	**2-01-001**
plummet	**verb**	**1-01-001**
plummeting	VBG	1-01-001
plump	**JJ**	**4-03-004**
plump	**verb**	**2-02-002**
plumped	VBD	2-02-002
plumpness	**NN**	**4-01-002**
plunder	**NN**	**1-01-001**
plunder	**VB**	**1-01-001**
plunderer	**noun**	**1-01-001**
plunderers	NNS	1-01-001
plundering	**NN**	**1-01-001**
plunge	**noun**	**5-03-003**
plunge	NN	4-03-003
plunges	NNS	1-01-001
plunge	**verb**	**20-09-020**
plunge	VB	1-01-001
plunges	VBZ	1-01-001
plunged	VBD	10-05-010
plunged	VBN	5-04-005
plunging	VBG	3-02-003
plunk	**verb**	**2-02-002**
plunking	VBG	2-02-002
plunker	**noun**	**1-01-001**
plunkers	NNS	1-01-001
pluralism	**NN**	**1-01-001**
pluralistic	**JJ**	**2-02-002**
plus	**CC**	**52-13-042**
plus	**IN**	**17-04-013**
plus	**adverb**	**3-02-002**
plus	RB	0-00-000
Plus	RB-TL	3-02-002
plus-one	**adjective**	**3-01-001**
plus-one	JJ	2-01-001
plus-one	JJ-HL	1-01-001
plush	**JJ**	**1-01-001**
plush	**NN**	**2-02-002**
Plutarch	**NP**	**1-01-001**
ply	**verb**	**2-02-002**
plied	VBD	2-02-002
Plymouth	**NP**	**11-03-004**
Plympton	**NP**	**1-01-001**
plywood	**NN**	**9-01-003**
PM	**NP**	**1-01-001**
PMR	**NP**	**1-01-001**
pneumonia	**NN**	**3-02-003**
Po	**prop. noun**	**1-01-001**
Po	NP	0-00-000
Po	NP-TL	1-01-001
Po'	**NP**	**2-01-001**
poach	**verb**	**2-02-002**
poach	VB	1-01-001
poaches	VBZ	1-01-001
Pocasset	**NP**	**3-01-001**
pocket	**noun**	**59-11-040**
pocket	NN	42-08-027
pockets	NNS	17-09-016
pocket	**verb**	**1-01-001**
pocketed	VBN	1-01-001
Pocket	**prop. noun**	**5-01-001**
Pocket	NP	4-01-001
Pocket's	NP$	1-01-001
pocket-size	**NN**	**1-01-001**
pocketbook	**noun**	**4-03-004**
pocketbook	NN	3-02-003
pocketbooks	NNS	1-01-001
pocketful	**NN**	**1-01-001**
Pockmanster	**prop. noun**	**1-01-001**
Pockmanster's	NP$	1-01-001
Pocono	**prop. noun**	**1-01-001**
Poconos	NPS	1-01-001
pod	**noun**	**1-01-001**
pods	NNS	1-01-001
Pod	**NP**	**3-01-001**
Podger	**prop. noun**	**24-01-001**
Podger	NP	21-01-001
Podger's	NP$	2-01-001
Podgers	NPS	1-01-001
podium	**NN**	**1-01-001**
Podolia	**NP**	**1-01-001**
Poe	**NP**	**4-02-003**
poem	**noun**	**130-07-025**
poem	NN	48-07-019
poems	NNS	77-05-015
Poems	NNS-TL	5-01-001
poem-in-drawing-and-type	**noun**	**1-01-001**
poems-in-drawing-and-type	NNS	1-01-001
Poesy	**prop. noun**	**1-01-001**
Poesy	NP	0-00-000
Poesy	NP-TL	1-01-001
poet	**noun**	**144-12-043**
poet	NN	68-11-036
Poet	NN-TL	31-02-003
poet's	NN$	8-04-008
Poet's	NN$-TL	5-01-001
poets	NNS	32-06-016
poet-painter	**NN**	**1-01-001**
poetic	**JJ**	**31-07-018**
poetically	**RB**	**2-02-002**
poetics	**noun**	**8-01-002**
poetics	NN	0-00-000
Poetics	NN-TL	8-01-002
poetize	**verb**	**2-01-001**
poetizing	VBG	2-01-001
poetry	**noun**	**90-09-025**
poetry	NN	85-08-024
poetrie	NN	0-00-000
Poetrie	NN-TL	1-01-001
Poetry	NN-TL	3-03-003
poetry's	NN$	0-00-000
Poetry's	NN$-TL	1-01-001
poetry-and-jazz	**noun**	**4-01-001**
poetry-and-jazz	NN	3-01-001
poetry-and-jazz	NN-NC	1-01-001
pogrom	**noun**	**2-01-001**
pogroms	NNS	2-01-001
Pogue	**NP**	**1-01-001**
Pohl	**prop. noun**	**14-02-002**
Pohl	NP	11-02-002
Pohl's	NP$	3-02-002
Pohly	**NP**	**2-01-001**
poignancy	**NN**	**2-02-002**
poignant	**JJ**	**6-04-006**
poignantly	**RB**	**1-01-001**
Poindexter	**NP**	**1-01-001**
point	**noun**	**493-15-235**
point	NN	349-14-200
point	NN-HL	1-01-001
Point	NN-TL	19-08-013
points	NNS	124-12-062
point	**verb**	**143-15-113**
point	VB	26-09-022
points	VBZ	19-09-018
pointed	VBD	48-11-045
pointed	VBN	24-10-021
pointing	VBG	26-09-024
point-blank	**RB**	**1-01-001**
pointed	**JJ**	**2-02-002**
pointedly	**RB**	**3-03-003**
pointer	**noun**	**4-03-003**
pointer	NN	2-02-002
Pointer	NN-TL	1-01-001
pointers	NNS	0-00-000
Pointers	NNS-TL	1-01-001
pointless	**JJ**	**1-01-001**
Poirot	**NP**	**2-01-001**
poise	**noun**	**8-07-007**
poise	NN	6-06-006
poises	NNS	2-01-001
poise	**verb**	**12-08-010**
poised	VBD	2-02-002
poised	VBN	8-06-008
Poised	VBN-TL	2-01-001
poison	**noun**	**11-05-008**
poison	NN	9-04-007
poisons	NNS	2-02-002
poison	**verb**	**7-07-007**
poison	VB	1-01-001
poisoned	VBD	2-02-002
poisoned	VBN	2-02-002
poisoning	VBG	2-02-002
poisoning	**NN**	**1-01-001**
poisonous	**JJ**	**5-03-005**
Poitrine	**prop. noun**	**5-01-001**
Poitrine	NP	3-01-001
Poitrine's	NP$	2-01-001
poke	**verb**	**13-06-011**
poke	VB	1-01-001

Word	Tag	Frequency
poke (cont.):		
pokes	VBZ	3-03-003
poked	VBD	3-03-003
poked	VBN	1-01-001
poking	VBG	5-04-005
pokeneu	**FW-NN**	**1-01-001**
poker	**noun**	**6-06-006**
poker	NN	5-05-005
Poker	NN-TL	1-01-001
pokerfaced	**JJ**	**1-01-001**
Poland	**prop. noun**	**35-06-008**
Poland	NP	32-05-007
Poland	NP-TL	1-01-001
Poland's	NP$	2-01-001
polar	**JJ**	**7-04-005**
Polaris	**NP**	**10-04-007**
polarity	**noun**	**6-03-003**
polarity	NN	5-03-003
polarities	NNS	1-01-001
polarization	**NN**	**6-02-003**
polarize	**verb**	**5-03-004**
polarize	VB	1-01-001
polarized	VBN	3-02-002
polarizing	VBG	1-01-001
Polaroid	**NP**	**1-01-001**
Poldowski	**NP**	**1-01-001**
pole	**noun**	**23-10-017**
pole	NN	13-06-010
Pole	NN-TL	2-01-001
poles	NNS	8-06-007
pole	**verb**	**2-01-001**
poling	VBG	2-01-001
Pole	**prop. noun**	**7-02-002**
Pole	NP	3-01-001
Poles	NPS	4-02-002
polecat	**NN**	**1-01-001**
polemic	**noun**	**2-01-001**
polemic	NN	1-01-001
polemics	NNS	1-01-001
polemical	**JJ**	**1-01-001**
police	**noun**	**155-12-056**
police	NN	76-10-038
police	NNS	64-07-026
police	NNS-HL	2-01-002
Police	NNS-TL	13-06-012
police	**verb**	**3-03-003**
policed	VBN	1-01-001
policing	VBG	2-02-002
police-dodging	**NN**	**1-01-001**
policeman	**noun**	**36-08-021**
policeman	NN	18-06-011
Policeman	NN-TL	1-01-001
policeman's	NN$	1-01-001
policemen	NNS	14-06-011
Policemen	NNS-TL	1-01-001
policemen's	NNS$	0-00-000
Policemen's	NNS$-TL	1-01-001
policeman-murderer	**NN**	**1-01-001**
policing	**NN**	**1-01-001**
policy	**noun**	**290-10-087**
policy	NN	216-10-070
policy	NN-HL	5-02-004
Policy	NN-TL	1-01-001
policies	NNS	61-07-035
policies	NNS-HL	7-04-006
policy-maker	**noun**	**3-02-002**
policy-makers	NNS	3-02-002
policy-making	**JJ**	**1-01-001**
policy-oriented	**JJ**	**1-01-001**
polio	**NN**	**1-01-001**
polis	**FW-NN**	**1-01-001**
Polish	**adjective**	**11-07-007**
Polish	JJ	8-06-006
Polish	JJ-TL	3-03-003
polish	**noun**	**5-04-004**
polish	NN	4-04-004
polishes	NNS	1-01-001
polish	**verb**	**20-11-018**
polish	VB	4-02-004
polished	VBD	3-03-003
polished	VBN	11-08-010
polishing	VBG	2-01-001
Politburo	**NP**	**1-01-001**
polite	**adjective**	**8-06-008**
polite	JJ	7-06-007
p'lite	JJ	1-01-001
politely	**RB**	**10-07-009**
politeness	**NN**	**5-04-005**
politic	**JJ**	**4-03-004**
political	**adjective**	**258-13-103**
political	JJ	257-13-103
Political	JJ-TL	1-01-001
politically	**RB**	**11-05-010**
politician	**noun**	**32-09-020**
politician	NN	12-06-008
politician	NN-HL	1-01-001
politicians	NNS	19-08-015
politicking	**NN**	**1-01-001**
politico	**noun**	**2-02-002**
politico	NN	1-01-001
politicos	NNS	1-01-001
politico-sociological	**JJ**	**1-01-001**
politics	**noun**	**69-12-038**
politics	NN	66-12-037
politics	NN-HL	1-01-001
Politics	NN-TL	2-02-002
politics-ridden	**JJ**	**1-01-001**
polity	**noun**	**2-02-002**
polity	NN	1-01-001
polities	NNS	1-01-001
Polk	**prop. noun**	**1-01-001**
Polk's	NP$	1-01-001
polka	**NN**	**1-01-001**
polka-dotted	**JJ**	**1-01-001**
poll	**noun**	**19-06-014**
poll	NN	9-04-007
polls	NNS	10-05-008
poll	**verb**	**4-02-002**
polled	VBN	1-01-001
polling	VBG	3-01-001
pollen	**NN**	**11-03-003**
pollen-and-nectar	**NN**	**1-01-001**
Pollock	**prop. noun**	**9-04-004**
Pollock	NP	8-04-004
Pollock's	NP$	1-01-001
pollute	**verb**	**1-01-001**
polluted	VBN	1-01-001
pollution	**NN**	**6-04-005**
polo	**noun**	**4-02-004**
polo	NN	1-01-001
Polo	NN-TL	3-02-003
Pololu	**prop. noun**	**1-01-001**
Pololu	NP	0-00-000
Pololu	NP-TL	1-01-001
polonaise	**NN**	**1-01-001**
Poltava	**NP**	**2-01-001**
Poltawa	**NP**	**1-01-001**
poly-unsaturated	**JJ**	**2-01-001**
Polyanka	**NP**	**1-01-001**
polybutene	**noun**	**2-01-001**
polybutene	NN	1-01-001
polybutenes	NNS	1-01-001
polychemical	**noun**	**1-01-001**
polychemicals	NNS	0-00-000
Polychemicals	NNS-TL	1-01-001
polycrystalline	**JJ**	**3-01-002**
polyelectrolyte	**noun**	**1-01-001**
polyelectrolytes	NNS	1-01-001
polyester	**noun**	**7-02-002**
polyester	NN	5-02-002
polyesters	NNS	2-01-001
polyether	**noun**	**8-01-001**
polyether	NN	7-01-001
polyethers	NNS	1-01-001
polyether-type	**JJ**	**1-01-001**
polyethylene	**NN**	**4-02-003**
polygynous	**JJ**	**1-01-001**
polyisobutylene	**NN**	**1-01-001**
polyisocyanate	**noun**	**2-01-001**
polyisocyanate	NN	1-01-001
polyisocyanates	NNS	1-01-001
polymer	**noun**	**5-02-002**
polymer	NN	1-01-001
polymers	NNS	3-01-001
polymers	NNS-HL	1-01-001
polymeric	**adjective**	**2-01-001**
polymeric	JJ	1-01-001
polymeric	JJ-HL	1-01-001
polymerization	**noun**	**8-01-002**
polymerization	NN	6-01-002
polymerization	NN-HL	1-01-001
polymerizations	NNS	1-01-001
polymyositis	**NN**	**1-01-001**
polynomial	**JJ**	**1-01-001**
polynomial	**noun**	**37-01-001**
polynomial	NN	27-01-001
polynomials	NNS	10-01-001
polyphosphate	**noun**	**6-01-001**

Word	Tag	Frequency
polyphosphate (cont.):		
polyphosphate	NN	1-01-001
polyphosphates	NNS	5-01-001
polypropylene	**NN**	**3-01-001**
polysiloxanes	**NN**	**1-01-001**
polystyrene	**NN**	**1-01-001**
polytechnic	**adjective**	**1-01-001**
polytechnic	JJ	0-00-000
Polytechnic	JJ-TL	1-01-001
polytonal	**JJ**	**1-01-001**
polyunsaturated	**adjective**	**1-01-001**
polyunsaturated	JJ	0-00-000
polyunsaturated	JJ-HL	1-01-001
pomade	**verb**	**1-01-001**
pomaded	VBN	1-01-001
Pomerania	**NP**	**1-01-001**
Pomham	**NP**	**2-01-001**
pomp	**NN**	**1-01-001**
Pompadour	**NP**	**1-01-001**
Pompano	**prop. noun**	**1-01-001**
Pompano	NP	0-00-000
Pompano	NP-TL	1-01-001
Pompeii	**prop. noun**	**6-01-001**
Pompeii	NP	5-01-001
Pompeii's	NP$	1-01-001
Pompey	**prop. noun**	**2-01-001**
Pompey	NP	1-01-001
Pompey	NP-TL	1-01-001
pompon	**noun**	**1-01-001**
pompons	NNS	1-01-001
pompous	**JJ**	**3-02-002**
pompously	**RB**	**1-01-001**
pompousness	**NN**	**1-01-001**
Ponce	**prop. noun**	**1-01-001**
Ponce	NP	0-00-000
Ponce	NP-TL	1-01-001
Ponchielli	**NP**	**1-01-001**
poncho	**NN**	**3-01-001**
pond	**noun**	**32-05-009**
pond	NN	23-05-008
pond	NN-HL	1-01-001
Pond	NN-TL	1-01-001
ponds	NNS	7-01-001
ponder	**verb**	**7-05-006**
ponder	VB	1-01-001
pondered	VBD	3-02-002
pondered	VBN	1-01-001
pondering	VBG	2-02-002
ponderous	**JJ**	**3-03-003**
Ponkob	**NP**	**1-01-001**
Ponoluu	**NP**	**1-01-001**
Pons	**NP**	**4-01-001**
Pont	**prop. noun**	**50-05-006**
Pont	NP	34-05-005
Pont	NP-TL	1-01-001
Pont's	NP$	15-02-002
Pontchartrain	**prop. noun**	**3-03-003**
Pontchartrain	NP	0-00-000
Pontchartrain	NP-TL	2-02-002
Ponchartrain	NP-TL	1-01-001
Pontiac	**prop. noun**	**1-01-001**
Pontiac	NP	0-00-000
Pontiac	NP-TL	1-01-001
Pontiff	**NP**	**1-01-001**
pontifical	**JJ**	**1-01-001**
pontificate	**verb**	**1-01-001**
pontificates	VBZ	1-01-001
Pontissara	**NP**	**1-01-001**
Pontius	**NP**	**1-01-001**
pony	**noun**	**17-05-008**
pony	NN	7-02-003
Pony	NN-TL	3-03-003
pony's	NN$	1-01-001
ponies	NNS	6-02-002
pooch	**verb**	**1-01-001**
pooched	VBD	1-01-001
poodle	**NN**	**2-02-002**
pooh-pooh	**verb**	**1-01-001**
pooh-poohed	VBD	1-01-001
pool	**noun**	**129-12-031**
pool	NN	105-12-026
pool	NN-HL	2-02-002
Pool	NN-TL	1-01-001
pool's	NN$	6-03-003
pools	NNS	14-05-007
pools	NNS-HL	1-01-001
pool	**verb**	**6-05-006**
pool	VB	3-03-003
pooled	VBN	1-01-001
pool (cont.):		
pooling	VBG	1-01-001
Pooling	VBG-TL	1-01-001
pool-care	**NN**	**1-01-001**
pool-equipment	**NN**	**1-01-001**
pool-owner	**noun**	**1-01-001**
pool-owners	NNS	1-01-001
pool-side	**NN**	**2-01-001**
poor	**adjective**	**113-14-075**
poor	JJ	104-14-075
poor	JJ-NC	1-01-001
Poor	JJ-TL	8-02-002
Poor	**prop. noun**	**1-01-001**
Poor's	NP$	1-01-001
poor-mouth	**RB**	**1-01-001**
poor-white-trash	**NN**	**1-01-001**
poorer	**JJR**	**3-02-003**
poorest	**JJT**	**3-03-003**
poorly	**QL**	**3-03-003**
poorly	**RB**	**8-06-007**
pop	**NN**	**3-03-003**
pop	**verb**	**17-07-015**
pop	VB	2-01-002
Pop	VB-TL	1-01-001
pops	VBZ	2-02-002
popped	VBD	6-04-006
popping	VBG	6-04-005
Pop	**NP**	**1-01-001**
pope	**noun**	**31-08-014**
pope	NN	5-02-002
Pope	NN-TL	23-07-012
pope's	NN$	2-01-001
popes	NNS	0-00-000
Popes	NNS-TL	1-01-001
Pope	**prop. noun**	**13-02-004**
Pope	NP	10-02-004
Pope	NP-HL	1-01-001
Pope	NP-TL	1-01-001
Pope's	NP$	1-01-001
Popish	**adjective**	**2-01-001**
Popish	JJ	1-01-001
Popish	JJ-TL	1-01-001
poplar	**NN**	**1-01-001**
poplin	**NN**	**1-01-001**
poppy	**noun**	**3-02-002**
poppy	NN	2-02-002
poppies	NNS	1-01-001
poppyseed	**NN**	**1-01-001**
Pops	**prop. noun**	**11-01-001**
Pops	NP	10-01-001
Pops's	NP$	1-01-001
populace	**NN**	**4-03-003**
populaire	**foreign**	**2-01-001**
populaire	FW-JJ	0-00-000
Populaire	FW-JJ-TL	1-01-001
populaires	FW-JJ	0-00-000
Populaires	FW-JJ-TL	1-01-001
popular	**adjective**	**99-13-074**
popular	JJ	96-13-072
pop'lar	JJ	1-01-001
Popular	JJ-TL	2-01-002
Popularism	**NP**	**1-01-001**
popularity	**NN**	**17-08-013**
popularly	**RB**	**7-05-007**
populate	**verb**	**13-10-012**
populate	VB	1-01-001
populated	VBD	1-01-001
populated	VBN	11-09-011
population	**noun**	**144-10-058**
population	NN	135-09-053
population	NN-HL	1-01-001
populations	NNS	8-05-007
populous	**JJ**	**5-03-005**
porcelain	**NN**	**2-02-002**
porch	**noun**	**45-09-026**
porch	NN	42-09-025
Porch	NN-TL	1-01-001
porches	NNS	2-01-002
porcupine	**noun**	**1-01-001**
porcupines	NNS	1-01-001
pore	**noun**	**5-04-004**
pore	NN	2-01-001
pores	NNS	3-03-003
pore	**verb**	**1-01-001**
pored	VBD	1-01-001
Porgy	**prop. noun**	**1-01-001**
Porgy	NP	0-00-000
Porgy	NP-TL	1-01-001
pork	**noun**	**14-04-008**

pork (cont.):		
pork	NN	10-04-006
po'k	NN	3-01-001
poark	NN	1-01-001
pork-barrel	**NN**	**1-01-001**
pornographer	**noun**	**1-01-001**
pornographer	NN	0-00-000
Pornographer	NN-TL	1-01-001
pornographic	**JJ**	**1-01-001**
Pornsen	**NP**	**3-01-001**
porosity	**NN**	**2-01-002**
porous	**JJ**	**12-02-003**
porpoise	**noun**	**1-01-001**
porpoises	NNS	1-01-001
porridge	**NN**	**1-01-001**
port	**JJ**	**2-01-002**
port	**noun**	**24-08-018**
port	NN	11-04-008
Port	NN-TL	8-05-007
Port	NN-TL-HL	1-01-001
ports	NNS	4-02-002
Porta	**NP**	**1-01-001**
portable	**JJ**	**13-06-011**
Portage	**NP**	**1-01-001**
Portago	**NP**	**5-01-001**
portal	**NN**	**3-02-002**
portant	**FW-VB**	**1-01-001**
portend	**verb**	**1-01-001**
portended	VBD	1-01-001
portent	**noun**	**1-01-001**
portents	NNS	1-01-001
portentous	**JJ**	**2-02-002**
porter	**NN**	**6-04-005**
Porter	**prop. noun**	**14-04-005**
Porter	NP	10-03-003
Porter	NP-TL	1-01-001
Porter's	NP$	2-01-001
Porters	NPS	1-01-001
Porterhouse	**NP**	**1-01-001**
portfolio	**NN**	**1-01-001**
portfolio-maker	**NN**	**2-01-001**
Portia	**NP**	**1-01-001**
portico	**noun**	**3-03-003**
portico	NN	2-02-002
Portico	NN-TL	1-01-001
portion	**noun**	**73-12-047**
portion	NN	62-12-040
portions	NNS	11-07-011
Portland	**prop. noun**	**26-02-004**
Portland	NP	21-01-003
Portland	NP-TL	3-02-003
Portland's	NP$	2-01-001
portly	**JJ**	**1-01-001**
Porto	**NP**	**3-01-001**
portrait	**noun**	**24-09-022**
portrait	NN	16-07-014
Portrait	NN-TL	1-01-001
portraits	NNS	7-05-007
portraiture	**NN**	**1-01-001**
portray	**verb**	**19-06-016**
portray	VB	6-03-005
portrays	VBZ	5-03-005
portrayed	VBN	5-03-004
portrayed	VBN-HL	1-01-001
portraying	VBG	2-02-002
portrayal	**NN**	**7-05-006**
Portsmouth	**NP**	**4-03-003**
Portugal	**NP**	**4-04-004**
Portuguese	**JJ**	**2-02-002**
Portuguese	**NP**	**1-01-001**
portwatcher	**noun**	**3-01-001**
portwatchers	NNS	2-01-001
portwatchers'	NNS$	0-00-000
Portwatchers'	NNS$-TL	1-01-001
pose	**NN**	**2-02-002**
pose	**verb**	**20-10-018**
pose	VB	9-05-008
poses	VBZ	1-01-001
posed	VBD	3-03-003
posed	VBN	4-04-004
posing	VBG	3-03-003
Poseidon	**NP**	**1-01-001**
poseur	**noun**	**2-02-002**
poseur	NN	1-01-001
poseurs	NNS	1-01-001
Posey	**NP**	**1-01-001**
poshest	**JJT**	**1-01-001**
position	**noun**	**291-15-164**
position	NN	235-15-144

position (cont.):		
position	NN-HL	2-02-002
positions	NNS	54-09-043
position	**verb**	**5-02-004**
position	VB	4-01-003
positioned	VBN	1-01-001
positive	**adjective**	**73-12-050**
positive	JJ	72-12-050
Positive	JJ-TL	1-01-001
positive	**NN**	**1-01-001**
positively	**QL**	**1-01-001**
positively	**RB**	**8-07-008**
positivism	**noun**	**4-01-002**
positivism	NN	3-01-002
positivism	NN-NC	1-01-001
positivist	**noun**	**10-01-001**
positivist	NN	7-01-001
positivists	NNS	3-01-001
posse	**noun**	**13-03-003**
posse	NN	11-03-003
posse's	NN$	2-01-001
posseman	**noun**	**2-01-001**
posseman	NN	1-01-001
possemen	NNS	1-01-001
possess	**verb**	**54-12-037**
possess	VB	17-06-013
possesses	VBZ	8-04-008
possessed	VBD	18-09-015
possessed	VBN	5-02-004
possessing	VBG	6-04-006
possession	**noun**	**32-10-025**
possession	NN	21-09-019
possessions	NNS	11-07-009
possessive	**JJ**	**3-03-003**
possessive	**NN**	**1-01-001**
possessor	**NN**	**1-01-001**
possibility	**noun**	**130-13-092**
possibility	NN	87-13-070
possibilities	NNS	42-09-031
possiblities	NNS	1-01-001
possible	**JJ**	**374-15-226**
possibly	**RB**	**61-14-051**
possum	**NN**	**2-02-002**
possum-hunting	**NN**	**2-01-001**
post	**FW-IN**	**1-01-001**
post	**IN**	**3-02-003**
post	**JJ**	**4-04-004**
post	**noun**	**101-11-049**
post	NN	55-11-035
Post	NN-TL	23-07-013
posts	NNS	22-06-013
post's	NN$	0-00-000
Post's	NN$-TL	1-01-001
post	**verb**	**13-06-011**
post	VB	2-02-002
posted	VBD	3-03-003
posted	VBN	8-05-006
Post	**NP**	**1-01-001**
post-attack	**JJ**	**5-02-002**
post-bellum	**JJ**	**2-01-001**
post-census	**JJ**	**1-01-001**
Post-Dispatch	**NP**	**1-01-001**
post-Inaugural	**JJ**	**1-01-001**
post-independence	**JJ**	**1-01-001**
post-mortem	**NN**	**1-01-001**
post-operative	**JJ**	**1-01-001**
post-reapportionment	**JJ**	**1-01-001**
Post-Serialism	**NP**	**1-01-001**
postage-prepaid	**JJ**	**1-01-001**
postal	**adjective**	**7-02-006**
postal	JJ	4-02-003
postal	JJ-HL	1-01-001
Postal	JJ-TL	2-01-002
postcard	**noun**	**8-05-005**
postcard	NN	7-05-005
postcards	NNS	1-01-001
poster	**noun**	**8-03-006**
poster	NN	3-03-003
Poster	NN-TL	1-01-001
posters	NNS	4-02-004
posterior	**JJ**	**6-02-003**
posterity	**NN**	**6-03-005**
postgraduate	**adjective**	**3-02-002**
postgraduate	JJ	2-01-001
post-graduate	JJ	0-00-000
Post-Graduate	JJ-TL	1-01-001
postgraduate	**NN**	**1-01-001**
posthumous	**JJ**	**2-01-002**
postman	**noun**	**4-03-004**

Word	Tag	Frequency
postman (cont.):		
postman	NN	2-02-002
postmen	NNS	2-02-002
postmark	**NN**	**2-02-002**
postmaster	**noun**	**6-03-005**
postmaster	NN	0-00-000
Postmaster	NN-TL	4-02-004
postmaster's	NN$	0-00-000
Postmaster's	NN$-TL	1-01-001
postmasters	NNS	1-01-001
postpone	**verb**	**19-09-016**
postpone	VB	7-06-006
postponed	VBD	1-01-001
postponed	VBN	8-05-006
postponing	VBG	3-03-003
postponement	**NN**	**2-02-002**
postscript	**noun**	**3-03-003**
postscript	NN	2-02-002
postscript	NN-HL	1-01-001
postulate	**noun**	**1-01-001**
postulates	NNS	1-01-001
postulate	**verb**	**10-04-008**
postulate	VB	3-03-003
postulated	VBN	7-03-006
posture	**noun**	**15-10-015**
posture	NN	13-09-013
postures	NNS	2-02-002
postwar	**adjective**	**19-05-014**
postwar	JJ	11-03-009
post-war	JJ	8-03-005
pot	**noun**	**33-10-023**
pot	NN	27-10-018
pot	NN-HL	1-01-001
pots	NNS	5-04-005
pot	**verb**	**4-04-004**
potted	VBN	3-03-003
potting	VBG	1-01-001
potassium	**NN**	**5-01-003**
potato	**noun**	**30-10-017**
potato	NN	15-05-007
potatoes	NNS	15-09-011
potboiler	**noun**	**3-02-002**
potboiler	NN	2-02-002
potboilers	NNS	1-01-001
Potemkin	**prop. noun**	**7-01-001**
Potemkin	NP	4-01-001
Potemkin's	NP$	3-01-001
potency	**NN**	**6-04-005**
potent	**JJ**	**9-06-008**
potential	**JJ**	**39-09-026**
potential	**noun**	**32-09-023**
potential	NN	28-09-021
potentials	NNS	4-02-003
potentiality	**noun**	**11-06-010**
potentiality	NN	3-03-003
potentialities	NNS	8-05-008
potentially	**RB**	**7-04-006**
potentiometer	**NN**	**1-01-001**
pothole	**NN**	**1-01-001**
potion	**noun**	**1-01-001**
potions	NNS	1-01-001
Potlatch	**prop. noun**	**1-01-001**
Potlatches	NPS	1-01-001
Potomac	**prop. noun**	**2-02-002**
Potomac	NP	1-01-001
Potomac	NP-TL	1-01-001
Potowomut	**NP**	**2-01-001**
potpourri	**NN**	**1-01-001**
Potsdam	**prop. noun**	**1-01-001**
Potsdam	NP	0-00-000
Potsdam	NP-TL	1-01-001
Pottawatomie	**prop. noun**	**1-01-001**
Pottawatomie	NP	0-00-000
Pottawatomie	NP-TL	1-01-001
potter	**noun**	**8-02-002**
potters	NNS	8-02-002
Potter	**NP**	**4-02-003**
pottery	**noun**	**16-04-005**
pottery	NN	15-04-005
pottery	NN-HL	1-01-001
pouch	**noun**	**4-03-004**
pouch	NN	2-02-002
pouches	NNS	2-02-002
Poughkeepsie	**NP**	**2-02-002**
Pouilly-Fuisse	**NP**	**1-01-001**
poultice	**noun**	**5-01-002**
poultice	NN	3-01-001
poultices	NNS	2-01-002
poultry	**noun**	**11-04-005**

Word	Tag	Frequency
poultry (cont.):		
poultry	NN	10-04-005
poultry	NN-HL	1-01-001
poultry-loving	**JJ**	**1-01-001**
pound	**noun**	**96-11-032**
pound	NN	26-07-008
lb.	NN	3-01-001
lb.	NN-HL	1-01-001
pounds	NNS	43-07-020
lbs.	NNS	6-02-002
lb.	NNS	15-02-003
pounds	NNS-HL	1-01-001
pounds'	NNS$	1-01-001
pound	**verb**	**11-07-011**
pound	VB	2-02-002
pounded	VBD	4-04-004
pounding	VBG	5-05-005
pound-foolish	**JJ**	**1-01-001**
pound-of-flesh	**NN**	**1-01-001**
pounding	**NN**	**1-01-001**
Poupin	**NP**	**1-01-001**
pour	**foreign**	**2-01-001**
pour	FW-IN	0-00-000
pour	FW-IN-TL	2-01-001
pour	**verb**	**48-13-040**
pour	VB	7-06-007
pours	VBZ	2-02-002
poured	VBD	21-09-021
poured	VBN	8-05-007
pouring	VBG	9-06-009
poring	VBG	1-01-001
Poussin	**prop. noun**	**4-02-003**
Poussin	NP	2-02-002
Poussin's	NP$	1-01-001
Poussins	NPS	1-01-001
pout	**NN**	**1-01-001**
pout	**verb**	**1-01-001**
pouted	VBD	1-01-001
poverty	**NN**	**20-08-018**
poverty-stricken	**JJ**	**2-02-002**
powder	**noun**	**33-06-015**
powder	NN	28-06-013
powders	NNS	5-02-003
powder	**verb**	**7-03-004**
powdered	VBN	7-03-004
powderpuff	**NN**	**1-01-001**
powdery	**JJ**	**3-03-003**
Powell	**prop. noun**	**17-04-006**
Powell	NP	14-04-006
Powell	NP-TL	1-01-001
Powell's	NP$	2-01-001
power	**noun**	**404-15-174**
power	NN	321-15-155
Power	NN	1-01-001
power	NN-HL	5-03-005
Power	NN-TL	11-03-005
powers	NNS	66-13-039
power	**verb**	**5-04-005**
power	VB	2-02-002
powers	VBZ	1-01-001
powered	VBN	2-02-002
Power	**prop. noun**	**3-01-001**
Power	NP	2-01-001
Power's	NP$	1-01-001
power-hungry	**JJ**	**1-01-001**
Power-Seek	**NP**	**1-01-001**
power-starved	**JJ**	**1-01-001**
powerful	**JJ**	**63-14-054**
powerfully	**RB**	**4-02-004**
powerfulness	**NN**	**1-01-001**
powerless	**JJ**	**3-03-003**
powerplant	**noun**	**1-01-001**
powerplants	NNS	1-01-001
Powers	**NP**	**6-01-001**
powers-that-be	**NNS**	**1-01-001**
Powicke	**NP**	**1-01-001**
Poynting-Robertson	**NP**	**5-01-001**
Pozzatti	**NP**	**5-01-001**
Prabang	**NP**	**2-01-001**
practicability	**NN**	**1-01-001**
practicable	**JJ**	**6-02-004**
practical	**adjective**	**68-11-052**
practical	JJ	67-11-052
practical	JJ-HL	1-01-001
practicality	**NN**	**2-02-002**
practically	**QL**	**10-05-010**
practically	**RB**	**43-13-039**
practice	**noun**	**132-12-080**
practice	NN	80-11-060

practice (cont.):		
practices	NNS	46-09-028
practices	NNS-HL	5-01-002
Practices	NNS-TL	1-01-001
practice	**verb**	**40-13-032**
practice	VB	12-07-010
practice	VB-HL	2-01-001
practices	VBZ	1-01-001
practiced	VBD	2-02-002
practiced	VBN	6-05-006
practised	VBN	2-02-002
practicing	VBG	14-09-012
practising	VBG	1-01-001
practicing	**NN**	**1-01-001**
practitioner	**noun**	**8-04-007**
practitioner	NN	2-01-002
practitioners	NNS	6-04-006
Prado	**NP**	**1-01-001**
pragmatic	**JJ**	**4-03-004**
pragmatism	**noun**	**2-02-002**
pragmatism	NN	1-01-001
Pragmatism	NN-TL	1-01-001
Prague	**NP**	**3-01-002**
prairie	**noun**	**13-06-008**
prairie	NN	9-05-007
Prairie	NN-TL	3-02-002
Prairie	NN-TL-HL	1-01-001
Prairie	**NP**	**8-02-002**
praise	**NN**	**13-09-013**
praise	**verb**	**21-07-019**
praise	VB	4-04-004
praises	VBZ	1-01-001
praises	VBZ-HL	1-01-001
praised	VBD	8-05-007
praised	VBN	5-03-005
praising	VBG	2-01-001
Praisegod	**NP**	**3-01-001**
pram	**noun**	**2-02-002**
pram	NN	1-01-001
prams	NNS	1-01-001
prance	**verb**	**3-03-003**
prancing	VBG	3-03-003
Prandtl	**NP**	**1-01-001**
pranha	**NN**	**1-01-001**
prank	**noun**	**2-02-002**
prank	NN	1-01-001
pranks	NNS	1-01-001
pratakku	**FW-NN**	**1-01-001**
Pratt	**prop. noun**	**11-04-006**
Pratt	NP	5-02-003
Pratt	NP-TL	5-03-003
Pratt's	NP$	0-00-000
Pratt's	NP$-TL	1-01-001
Prattville	**NP**	**1-01-001**
pray	**verb**	**30-12-020**
pray	VB	12-07-009
prai	VB	1-01-001
prayed	VBD	8-05-006
prayed	VBN	4-04-004
praying	VBG	3-03-003
prayin'	VBG	2-01-001
prayer	**noun**	**41-11-027**
prayer	NN	24-09-018
Prayer	NN-TL	4-03-003
prayers	NNS	13-06-010
prayer-request	**noun**	**1-01-001**
prayer-requests	NNS	1-01-001
prayer-time	**NN**	**1-01-001**
prayerbook	**noun**	**1-01-001**
prayerbooks	NNS	1-01-001
prayerful	**JJ**	**1-01-001**
prayerfully	**RB**	**1-01-001**
pre	**JJ**	**4-03-004**
pre-academic	**JJ**	**1-01-001**
pre-Anglo-Saxon	**JJ**	**1-01-001**
pre-assault	**JJ**	**1-01-001**
pre-attack	**JJ**	**1-01-001**
pre-cast	**JJ**	**1-01-001**
pre-cooled	**JJ**	**1-01-001**
pre-decoration	**NN**	**1-01-001**
pre-drill	**verb**	**1-01-001**
pre-drilled	VBN	1-01-001
pre-Easter	**JJ**	**1-01-001**
pre-eminent	**JJ**	**1-01-001**
pre-employment	**adjective**	**2-01-001**
pre-employment	JJ	1-01-001
preemployment	JJ	1-01-001
pre-empting	**JJ**	**1-01-001**
pre-emption	**NN**	**1-01-001**
pre-existence	**NN**	**1-01-001**
pre-existent	**JJ**	**1-01-001**
pre-Fair	**JJ**	**1-01-001**
pre-Han	**JJ**	**1-01-001**
pre-history	**NN**	**2-02-002**
pre-inaugural	**adjective**	**1-01-001**
pre-inaugural	JJ	0-00-000
pre-inaugural	JJ-HL	1-01-001
pre-legislative	**adjective**	**2-01-001**
pre-legislative	JJ	1-01-001
Pre-Legislative	JJ-TL	1-01-001
pre-nuptial	**JJ**	**1-01-001**
pre-packed	**JJ**	**1-01-001**
pre-penicillin	**JJ**	**1-01-001**
pre-planning	**NN**	**1-01-001**
pre-primary	**NN**	**2-01-001**
pre-Revolutionary	**JJ**	**1-01-001**
pre-season	**JJ**	**2-02-002**
pre-sell	**verb**	**1-01-001**
pre-selling	VBG	1-01-001
pre-selling	**NN**	**1-01-001**
pre-set	**JJ**	**1-01-001**
pre-shaped	**adjective**	**2-01-001**
pre-shaped	JJ	1-01-001
pre-shaped	JJ-HL	1-01-001
pre-war	**adjective**	**7-06-006**
pre-war	JJ	6-05-005
prewar	JJ	1-01-001
pre-World-War-	**JJ**	**1-01-001**
pre-1960	**JJ**	**1-01-001**
preach	**verb**	**26-11-022**
preach	VB	8-06-008
preaches	VBZ	1-01-001
preached	VBD	6-04-006
preached	VBN	2-02-002
preaching	VBG	9-07-008
preacher	**noun**	**13-06-009**
preacher	NN	11-04-007
preachers	NNS	2-02-002
preacher-singer	**NN**	**1-01-001**
preaching	**NN**	**8-04-005**
preamble	**noun**	**7-04-004**
preamble	NN	3-03-003
Preamble	NN-TL	1-01-001
preambles	NNS	1-01-001
Preambles	NNS-TL	2-01-001
prearrange	**verb**	**1-01-001**
prearranged	VBN	1-01-001
precarious	**JJ**	**8-06-007**
precariously	**RB**	**3-03-003**
precaution	**noun**	**15-08-014**
precaution	NN	8-06-008
precautions	NNS	7-04-007
precautionary	**JJ**	**2-02-002**
precede	**verb**	**51-11-041**
precede	VB	3-03-003
precedes	VBZ	1-01-001
preceded	VBD	9-07-009
preceded	VBN	6-03-006
preceeded	VBN	1-01-001
preceding	VBG	29-09-022
preceeding	VBG	2-01-001
precedence	**NN**	**3-02-003**
precedent	**noun**	**12-06-010**
precedent	NN	8-04-006
precedent	NN-HL	1-01-001
precedents	NNS	3-03-003
precedent-based	**JJ**	**1-01-001**
preceding	**NN**	**1-01-001**
precept	**noun**	**4-03-004**
precept	NN	1-01-001
precepts	NNS	3-03-003
prechlorination	**NN**	**1-01-001**
precinct	**noun**	**13-03-005**
precinct	NN	6-02-002
Precinct	NN-TL	2-01-001
precincts	NNS	5-02-003
precious	**adjective**	**30-13-022**
precious	JJ	22-12-021
Precious	JJ-TL	8-02-002
precipice	**NN**	**1-01-001**
precipice-walled	**JJ**	**1-01-001**
precipitate	**NN**	**1-01-001**
precipitate	**verb**	**11-03-008**
precipitated	VBD	3-02-002
precipitated	VBN	6-03-006
precipitating	VBG	2-01-002
precipitin	**NN**	**1-01-001**
precise	**adjective**	**33-09-028**

Word	Tag	Frequency
precise (cont.):		
precise	JJ	32-08-027
precise	JJ-HL	1-01-001
precisely	**QL**	**2-01-002**
precisely	**RB**	**46-11-037**
precision	**JJ**	**2-02-002**
precision	**noun**	**44-09-026**
precision	NN	43-09-026
Precision	NN-TL	1-01-001
preclude	**verb**	**5-04-005**
preclude	VB	4-04-004
precluded	VBD	1-01-001
precocious	**JJ**	**3-03-003**
precociously	**QL**	**1-01-001**
precocity	**NN**	**1-01-001**
preconceive	**verb**	**2-01-002**
preconceived	VBN	2-01-002
preconception	**noun**	**2-02-002**
preconceptions	NNS	2-02-002
precondition	**noun**	**3-02-002**
precondition	NN	1-01-001
preconditions	NNS	1-01-001
pre-conditions	NNS	1-01-001
precondition	**verb**	**2-01-001**
preconditioned	VBN	2-01-001
preconscious	**adjective**	**2-02-002**
preconscious	JJ	1-01-001
pre-conscious	JJ	1-01-001
precook	**verb**	**1-01-001**
precooked	VBN	1-01-001
precut	**VBN**	**1-01-001**
predecessor	**noun**	**11-06-011**
predecessor	NN	5-05-005
predecessors	NNS	6-04-006
predestine	**verb**	**1-01-001**
predestined	VBN	1-01-001
predetermine	**verb**	**4-03-004**
predetermined	VBN	3-03-003
pre-determined	VBN	1-01-001
predicament	**NN**	**3-02-003**
predicator	**NN**	**2-01-001**
predict	**verb**	**35-12-029**
predict	VB	8-05-006
predicts	VBZ	3-03-003
predicted	VBD	5-03-005
predicted	VBN	13-05-010
predicting	VBG	6-05-006
predictability	**NN**	**1-01-001**
predictable	**JJ**	**8-07-008**
predictably	**RB**	**2-02-002**
predicting-machine	**noun**	**1-01-001**
predicting-machines	NNS	1-01-001
prediction	**noun**	**13-07-011**
prediction	NN	10-05-009
predictions	NNS	3-03-003
predictive	**JJ**	**3-02-003**
predictor	**noun**	**1-01-001**
predictors	NNS	1-01-001
predigest	**verb**	**1-01-001**
predigested	VBN	1-01-001
predilection	**noun**	**1-01-001**
predilections	NNS	1-01-001
predispose	**verb**	**1-01-001**
predisposed	VBN	1-01-001
predisposition	**noun**	**13-03-003**
predisposition	NN	4-02-002
predispositions	NNS	9-02-002
prednisone	**NN**	**3-01-001**
predominance	**NN**	**2-01-002**
predominant	**JJ**	**1-01-001**
predominantly	**QL**	**2-02-002**
predominantly	**adverb**	**6-03-006**
predominantly	RB	5-02-005
predominately	RB	1-01-001
predominate	**verb**	**3-02-003**
predominates	VBZ	1-01-001
predominated	VBD	1-01-001
predominating	VBG	1-01-001
predomination	**NN**	**1-01-001**
preen	**verb**	**1-01-001**
preening	VBG	1-01-001
prefab	**JJ**	**1-01-001**
prefabricate	**verb**	**2-01-002**
prefabricated	VBN	2-01-002
preface	**noun**	**3-01-003**
preface	NN	2-01-002
Preface	NN-TL	1-01-001
preface	**verb**	**2-01-002**
prefaced	VBD	1-01-001
preface (cont.):		
prefaced	VBN	1-01-001
prefecture	**noun**	**2-01-001**
prefecture	NN	0-00-000
Prefecture	NN-TL	1-01-001
prefectures	NNS	1-01-001
prefer	**verb**	**60-13-055**
prefer	VB	27-09-025
prefuh	VB	1-01-001
prefers	VBZ	5-04-005
preferred	VBD	16-08-016
preferred	VBN	10-05-008
preferring	VBG	1-01-001
preferable	**JJ**	**6-06-006**
preferably	**RB**	**14-07-014**
preference	**noun**	**16-07-015**
preference	NN	9-05-009
preferences	NNS	7-04-006
preferential	**JJ**	**4-02-003**
preferentially	**RB**	**2-01-002**
preferment	**NN**	**1-01-001**
prefix	**noun**	**1-01-001**
prefixes	NNS	1-01-001
preflight	**JJ**	**2-01-001**
pregnancy	**NN**	**4-01-001**
pregnant	**JJ**	**8-06-007**
prehistoric	**adjective**	**3-03-003**
prehistoric	JJ	2-02-002
pre-historic	JJ	1-01-001
preisolate	**verb**	**1-01-001**
preisolated	VBN	1-01-001
prejudge	**verb**	**2-01-001**
prejudged	VBN	2-01-001
prejudice	**noun**	**13-07-011**
prejudice	NN	8-04-007
Prejudice	NN-TL	1-01-001
prejudices	NNS	4-04-004
prejudice	**verb**	**6-03-006**
prejudice	VB	2-01-002
prejudiced	VBN	4-03-004
prejudicial	**adjective**	**4-03-003**
prejudicial	JJ	3-03-003
prejudicial	JJ-HL	1-01-001
preliminary	**JJ**	**23-09-019**
preliminary	**noun**	**3-02-003**
preliminary	NN	1-01-001
preliminaries	NNS	2-01-002
preliterate	**adjective**	**2-02-002**
preliterate	JJ	1-01-001
pre-literate	JJ	1-01-001
prelude	**noun**	**6-05-005**
prelude	NN	3-03-003
Prelude	NN-TL	2-02-002
preludes	NNS	0-00-000
Preludes	NNS-TL	1-01-001
premarital	**adjective**	**4-02-002**
premarital	JJ	3-02-002
pre-marital	JJ	1-01-001
premature	**JJ**	**3-03-003**
prematurely	**RB**	**3-02-003**
premier	**noun**	**26-03-009**
premier	NN	2-01-001
Premier	NN-TL	24-03-008
premiere	**noun**	**9-04-005**
premiere	NN	5-03-004
premieres	NNS	4-03-003
premise	**noun**	**15-07-012**
premise	NN	7-04-006
premises	NNS	8-06-007
premium	**noun**	**14-05-011**
premium	NN	11-04-009
Premium	NN-TL	1-01-001
premiums	NNS	2-02-002
premix	**NN**	**3-01-001**
premonition	**noun**	**3-02-003**
premonition	NN	2-02-002
premonitions	NNS	1-01-001
premonitory	**JJ**	**1-01-001**
Prence	**NP**	**1-01-001**
Prentice	**prop. noun**	**1-01-001**
Prentice's	NP$	1-01-001
Prentice-Hall	**prop. noun**	**1-01-001**
Prentice-Hall	NP	0-00-000
Prentice-Hall	NP-TL	1-01-001
Prentiss	**prop. noun**	**1-01-001**
Prentiss'	NP$	1-01-001
preoccupation	**noun**	**10-07-009**
preoccupation	NN	9-06-008
preoccupations	NNS	1-01-001

Word	Tag	Frequency
preoccupy	**verb**	**12-07-012**
preoccupies	VBZ	1-01-001
preoccupied	VBN	11-06-011
preordainment	**NN**	**1-01-001**
prep	**NN**	**2-02-002**
prepackage	**verb**	**2-02-002**
prepackaged	VBN	2-02-002
preparation	**noun**	**69-11-038**
preparation	NN	48-09-029
preparation	NN-HL	4-02-003
Preparation	NN-TL	2-02-002
preparations	NNS	14-08-012
preparations	NNS-HL	1-01-001
Preparation-Inquirer	**prop. noun**	**1-01-001**
Preparation-Inquirers'	NP$	0-00-000
Preparation-Inquirers'	NP$-TL	1-01-001
preparative	**JJ**	**3-01-002**
preparatory	**JJ**	**7-05-005**
prepare	**verb**	**163-14-113**
prepare	VB	35-12-029
prepares	VBZ	4-04-004
prepared	VBD	12-07-012
prepared	VBN	90-12-065
preparing	VBG	22-11-022
preparedness	**NN**	**2-02-002**
prepayment	**NN**	**1-01-001**
prepolymer	**noun**	**4-01-001**
prepolymer	NN	3-01-001
prepolymer	NN-HL	1-01-001
preponderance	**NN**	**2-02-002**
preponderantly	**RB**	**1-01-001**
preponderate	**verb**	**1-01-001**
preponderating	VBG	1-01-001
preposition	**NN**	**2-01-001**
prepositional	**JJ**	**3-01-001**
preposterous	**JJ**	**5-04-004**
preprepare	**verb**	**2-01-001**
preprepared	VBN	2-01-001
preprint	**verb**	**1-01-001**
preprinting	VBG	1-01-001
prepubescent	**JJ**	**1-01-001**
prepublication	**NN**	**1-01-001**
prepupal	**JJ**	**1-01-001**
preradiation	**NN**	**1-01-001**
prerequisite	**NN**	**2-01-002**
prerogative	**noun**	**3-03-003**
prerogative	NN	1-01-001
prerogatives	NNS	2-02-002
presage	**verb**	**2-02-002**
presage	VB	1-01-001
presaged	VBD	1-01-001
Presbyterian	**JJ**	**2-02-002**
Presbyterian	**prop. noun**	**10-04-007**
Presbyterian	NP	2-01-002
Presbyterian	NP-TL	8-04-006
Presbyterianism	**NP**	**1-01-001**
preschool	**adjective**	**2-02-002**
preschool	JJ	1-01-001
pre-school	JJ	1-01-001
prescribe	**verb**	**20-08-016**
prescribe	VB	5-03-003
prescribes	VBZ	1-01-001
prescribed	VBD	2-02-002
prescribed	VBN	12-06-011
prescription	**noun**	**7-05-007**
prescription	NN	5-04-005
prescriptions	NNS	2-02-002
prescriptive	**JJ**	**1-01-001**
presence	**noun**	**78-14-062**
presence	NN	75-14-059
Presence	NN-TL	1-01-001
presences	NNS	2-02-002
present	**post-det.**	**5-01-002**
present	AP	4-01-001
present	AP-HL	1-01-001
present	**JJ**	**225-14-145**
present	**noun**	**50-10-035**
present	NN	43-10-031
Present	NN-TL	1-01-001
presents	NNS	6-03-004
present	**adverb**	**65-11-051**
present	RB	64-11-050
presente	RB	1-01-001
present	**verb**	**158-14-116**
present	VB	39-11-038
presents	VBZ	27-08-022
presented	VBD	16-08-015
presented	VBN	66-12-055
presenting	VBG	10-08-010
present-day	**JJ**	**17-06-013**
present-time	**JJ**	**2-01-001**
presentable	**JJ**	**2-02-002**
presentation	**noun**	**39-09-029**
presentation	NN	33-08-026
presentations	NNS	6-04-005
presentational	**JJ**	**1-01-001**
presenter	**NN**	**1-01-001**
presently	**adverb**	**36-14-032**
presently	RB	35-14-031
presentlye	RB	1-01-001
presentment	**noun**	**1-01-001**
presentments	NNS	1-01-001
presentness	**NN**	**1-01-001**
preservation	**noun**	**17-06-008**
preservation	NN	16-06-008
preservation	NN-HL	1-01-001
preserve	**noun**	**12-06-008**
preserve	NN	3-02-003
Preserve	NN-TL	1-01-001
preserves	NNS	8-05-005
preserve	**verb**	**63-13-050**
preserve	VB	31-13-028
preserves	VBZ	3-03-003
preserved	VBD	2-02-002
preserved	VBN	17-07-016
preserving	VBG	8-05-006
preserving	VBG-HL	2-01-001
preside	**verb**	**14-08-011**
preside	VB	2-02-002
presides	VBZ	1-01-001
presided	VBD	1-01-001
presiding	VBG	6-06-006
Presiding	VBG-TL	4-01-001
presidency	**noun**	**11-05-010**
presidency	NN	2-02-002
presidency	NN-HL	1-01-001
Presidency	NN-TL	8-03-007
president	**noun**	**424-13-112**
president	NN	126-12-055
President	NN-TL	256-12-072
president's	NN$	5-02-002
President's	NN$-TL	23-05-013
presidents	NNS	6-04-004
Presidents	NNS-TL	8-06-006
president-elect	**noun**	**5-01-002**
president-elect	NN	0-00-000
President-elect	NN-TL	5-01-002
presidential	**adjective**	**34-10-020**
presidential	JJ	12-06-009
Presidential	JJ-TL	22-08-011
Presley	**NP**	**1-01-001**
press	**noun**	**107-11-051**
press	NN	80-09-041
press	NN-HL	1-01-001
Press	NN-TL	18-08-012
Press	NN-TL-HL	1-01-001
presses	NNS	7-03-004
press	**verb**	**82-13-058**
press	VB	27-10-016
presses	VBZ	2-02-002
pressed	VBD	12-06-012
pressed	VBN	16-09-015
pressed	VBN-HL	1-01-001
pressing	VBG	22-11-021
pressing	VBG-HL	2-02-002
pressed-paper	**NN**	**1-01-001**
presser	**noun**	**3-01-001**
presser	NN	0-00-000
presser	NN-HL	2-01-001
Presser	NN-TL	1-01-001
pressing	**JJ**	**1-01-001**
pressure	**noun**	**222-14-096**
pressure	NN	181-14-083
pressure	NN-HL	3-02-002
pressures	NNS	37-11-022
pressures	NNS-HL	1-01-001
pressure	**VB**	**1-01-001**
pressure-cooker	**NN**	**1-01-001**
pressure-formed	**JJ**	**1-01-001**
pressure-happy	**JJ**	**1-01-001**
pressure-measuring	**JJ**	**1-01-001**
pressure-sensing	**JJ**	**1-01-001**
pressure-volume-temperature	**NN**	**1-01-001**
prestidigitator	**NN**	**1-01-001**
prestige	**noun**	**29-09-017**
prestige	NN	28-09-017
prestige	NN-HL	1-01-001
presto	**foreign**	**1-01-001**

Word	Tag	Frequency
presto (cont.):		
presto	FW-JJ	0-00-000
Presto	FW-JJ-TL	1-01-001
presto	**UH**	**1-01-001**
Preston	**NP**	**2-02-002**
presumably	**RB**	**40-09-035**
presume	**verb**	**20-08-017**
presume	VB	3-01-001
presumes	VBZ	3-03-003
presumed	VBD	2-02-002
presumed	VBN	10-04-009
presuming	VBG	2-02-002
presumption	**noun**	**4-01-002**
presumption	NN	3-01-001
presumptions	NNS	1-01-001
presumptuous	**JJ**	**4-03-004**
presuppose	**verb**	**4-03-003**
presuppose	VB	1-01-001
presupposes	VBZ	2-02-002
presupposed	VBN	1-01-001
presupposition	**noun**	**2-01-001**
presupposition	NN	1-01-001
presuppositions	NNS	1-01-001
pretend	**adjective**	**1-01-001**
pretend	JJ	0-00-000
pretend	JJ-HL	1-01-001
pretend	**verb**	**27-10-024**
pretend	VB	7-05-007
pretends	VBZ	2-02-002
pretended	VBD	3-02-003
pretended	VBN	3-01-003
pretending	VBG	12-06-010
pretender	**noun**	**2-02-002**
pretender	NN	0-00-000
Pretender	NN-TL	2-02-002
pretense	**noun**	**11-04-011**
pretense	NN	6-02-006
pretence	NN	4-03-004
pretenses	NNS	1-01-001
pretension	**noun**	**1-01-001**
pretensions	NNS	1-01-001
pretentious	**JJ**	**6-03-005**
pretest	**noun**	**1-01-001**
pretest	NN	0-00-000
pretest	NN-HL	1-01-001
pretext	**noun**	**5-03-005**
pretext	NN	3-03-003
pretexts	NNS	2-02-002
pretrial	**JJ**	**1-01-001**
prettier	**JJR**	**4-02-003**
prettiest	**sup. adj.**	**5-03-005**
prettiest	JJT	4-03-004
purtiest	JJT	1-01-001
prettily	**RB**	**2-02-002**
prettiness	**NN**	**1-01-001**
pretty	**adjective**	**41-11-028**
pretty	JJ	39-11-028
pretty	JJ-NC	2-01-001
pretty	**QL**	**63-14-054**
Pretty	**NP**	**3-01-001**
Prettyman	**NP**	**2-01-001**
prevail	**verb**	**41-11-033**
prevail	VB	7-04-007
prevaile	VB	1-01-001
prevayle	VB	1-01-001
prevails	VBZ	7-03-005
prevailed	VBD	7-06-007
prevailing	VBG	17-06-015
prevailin'	VBG	1-01-001
prevalence	**NN**	**4-04-004**
prevalent	**JJ**	**5-04-005**
prevent	**verb**	**130-14-084**
prevent	VB	83-12-061
prevents	VBZ	10-07-009
prevented	VBD	11-07-010
prevented	VBN	16-08-014
preventing	VBG	10-06-007
prevention	**noun**	**27-06-009**
prevention	NN	26-06-008
prevention	NN-HL	1-01-001
preventive	**JJ**	**15-06-007**
preview	**NN**	**1-01-001**
previous	**AP**	**8-02-005**
previous	**JJ**	**76-12-071**
previous	**RB**	**2-02-002**
previously	**RB**	**58-11-049**
prevision	**noun**	**5-01-001**
prevision	NN	2-01-001
pre-vision	NN	1-01-001

Word	Tag	Frequency
prevision (cont.):		
previsions	NNS	2-01-001
Prevost	**NP**	**1-01-001**
Prevot	**NP**	**9-01-001**
Prexy	**NP**	**1-01-001**
prey	**NN**	**7-05-007**
prey	**verb**	**1-01-001**
preying	VBG	1-01-001
Priam	**NP**	**2-01-001**
price	**noun**	**164-12-055**
price	NN	101-12-040
price	NN-HL	1-01-001
Price	NN-TL	1-01-001
prices	NNS	61-07-025
price	**verb**	**10-05-008**
price	VB	1-01-001
priced	VBN	4-02-003
pricing	VBG	5-03-004
Price	**prop. noun**	**4-02-003**
Price	NP	2-01-002
Price	NP-HL	2-01-001
price-consciousness	**noun**	**3-01-001**
price-consciousness	NN	2-01-001
price-consciousness	NN-HL	1-01-001
price-cutting	**NN**	**1-01-001**
price-earning	**noun**	**3-02-002**
price-earnings	NNS	3-02-002
price-level	**NN**	**1-01-001**
price-setting	**NN**	**1-01-001**
price-wise	**RB**	**1-01-001**
priceless	**JJ**	**5-04-005**
pricing	**NN**	**2-02-002**
prick	**noun**	**2-01-001**
prick	NN	1-01-001
pricks	NNS	1-01-001
prick	**verb**	**3-03-003**
prick	VB	1-01-001
pricked	VBN	1-01-001
pricking	VBG	1-01-001
prickly	**JJ**	**1-01-001**
prickly	**RB**	**1-01-001**
Priddy	**NP**	**1-01-001**
pride	**noun**	**45-15-038**
pride	NN	39-14-034
Pride	NN-TL	5-03-003
pride's	NN$	1-01-001
pride	**verb**	**3-03-003**
pride	VB	1-01-001
prides	VBZ	2-02-002
prie-dieu	**FW-NN**	**1-01-001**
priest	**noun**	**33-09-018**
priest	NN	16-06-008
priest's	NN$	1-01-001
priests	NNS	16-07-011
priestly	**JJ**	**1-01-001**
Prieur	**NP**	**6-01-001**
prim	**JJ**	**1-01-001**
prima-facie	**JJ**	**2-02-002**
primacy	**NN**	**5-04-005**
primal	**JJ**	**1-01-001**
primarily	**RB**	**64-09-045**
primary	**adjective**	**81-11-056**
primary	JJ	79-11-056
primary	JJ-HL	2-01-001
primary	**noun**	**17-05-007**
primary	NN	15-03-005
primaries	NNS	2-02-002
primate	**noun**	**1-01-001**
primates	NNS	1-01-001
Primate	**NP**	**1-01-001**
prime	**adjective**	**42-09-024**
prime	JJ	36-09-021
prime	JJ-HL	1-01-001
Prime	JJ-TL	5-03-003
prime	**noun**	**3-02-002**
prime	NN	1-01-001
primes	NNS	2-01-001
prime	**verb**	**3-02-003**
primed	VBN	2-02-002
priming	VBG	1-01-001
Prime	**NP**	**2-01-001**
primer	**noun**	**1-01-001**
primers	NNS	1-01-001
primeval	**JJ**	**5-04-005**
priming	**NN**	**1-01-001**
primitive	**JJ**	**37-11-029**
primitive	**NN**	**1-01-001**
primitive-eclogue	**NN**	**1-01-001**
primitivism	**NN**	**1-01-001**

Word	Tag	Count
primly	**RB**	**2-02-002**
primp	**verb**	**1-01-001**
primping	VBG	1-01-001
prince	**noun**	**40-06-015**
prince	NN	2-02-002
Prince	NN	1-01-001
Prince	NN-TL	29-06-013
Prince	NN-TL-HL	1-01-001
prince's	NN$	0-00-000
Prince's	NN$-TL	3-01-001
princes	NNS	2-01-002
Princes	NNS-TL	1-01-001
princes'	NNS$	0-00-000
Princes'	NNS$-TL	1-01-001
princess	**noun**	**12-06-008**
princess	NN	5-04-004
Princess	NN-TL	7-04-005
princess-in-a-carriage	**NN**	**1-01-001**
princesse	**NN**	**2-01-001**
Princeton	**prop. noun**	**7-03-004**
Princeton	NP	6-03-004
Princeton	NP-TL	1-01-001
principal	**sup. adj.**	**71-11-053**
principal	JJS	70-11-052
principle	JJS	1-01-001
principal	**noun**	**26-09-014**
principal	NN	21-07-011
Principal	NN-TL	1-01-001
principals	NNS	4-03-004
principally	**RB**	**10-08-010**
principia	**foreign**	**1-01-001**
principia	FW-NNS	0-00-000
Principia	FW-NNS-TL	1-01-001
principle	**noun**	**179-14-095**
principle	NN	106-12-059
principle	NN-HL	1-01-001
Principle	NN-TL	1-01-001
principles	NNS	67-11-047
principles	NNS-HL	2-02-002
Principles	NNS-TL	2-02-002
print	**noun**	**24-09-021**
print	NN	14-08-012
prints	NNS	10-05-009
print	**verb**	**53-12-032**
print	VB	4-03-003
printed	VBD	9-05-007
printed	VBN	22-07-019
printed	VBN-HL	4-01-001
Printed	VBN-TL	1-01-001
printing	VBG	10-05-005
Printing	VBG-TL	3-02-002
printable	**JJ**	**1-01-001**
printemps	**foreign**	**1-01-001**
printemps	FW-NN	0-00-000
Printemps	FW-NN-TL	1-01-001
printer	**noun**	**4-01-003**
printer	NN	3-01-002
printer's	NN$	1-01-001
printing	**NN**	**5-03-004**
printmaking	**NN**	**1-01-001**
prior	**JJ**	**7-05-007**
prior	**RB**	**40-10-029**
prior-year	**NN**	**1-01-001**
priority	**noun**	**23-06-016**
priority	NN	18-05-014
priorities	NNS	5-03-004
priory	**noun**	**1-01-001**
priory	NN	0-00-000
Priory	NN-TL	1-01-001
Pripet	**prop. noun**	**1-01-001**
Pripet	NP	0-00-000
Pripet	NP-TL	1-01-001
Prisca	**prop. noun**	**1-01-001**
Prisca	NP	0-00-000
Prisca	NP-TL	1-01-001
prison	**noun**	**46-10-028**
prison	NN	41-09-024
Prison	NN-TL	2-02-002
prisons	NNS	3-02-003
prisoner	**noun**	**31-08-014**
prisoner	NN	7-05-006
prisoners	NNS	20-06-011
Prisoners	NNS-TL	1-01-001
prisoners'	NNS$	3-02-002
prissy	**adjective**	**1-01-001**
prissy	JJ	0-00-000
Prissy	JJ-TL	1-01-001
pristine	**JJ**	**2-02-002**
privacy	**NN**	**12-08-010**

Word	Tag	Count
private	**adjective**	**185-14-100**
private	JJ	183-14-099
private	JJ-HL	1-01-001
Private	JJ-TL	1-01-001
private	**noun**	**6-04-004**
private	NN	4-04-004
Private	NN-TL	2-01-001
private-eye	**NN**	**1-01-001**
private-school	**NN**	**1-01-001**
privately	**RB**	**13-07-011**
privately-owned	**JJ**	**1-01-001**
privation	**noun**	**2-02-002**
privations	NNS	2-02-002
privet	**NN**	**1-01-001**
privilege	**noun**	**28-09-022**
privilege	NN	18-08-015
privileges	NNS	10-05-008
privileged	**JJ**	**10-07-009**
privy	**adjective**	**3-01-001**
privy	JJ	0-00-000
Privy	JJ-TL	3-01-001
privy	**noun**	**2-01-002**
privy	NN	1-01-001
privies	NNS	1-01-001
prix	**foreign**	**2-02-002**
prix	FW-NN	0-00-000
Prix	FW-NN-TL	2-02-002
prize	**noun**	**34-09-020**
prize	NN	18-09-013
Prize	NN-TL	10-06-008
prizes	NNS	6-04-005
prize	**verb**	**3-02-003**
prize	VB	1-01-001
prized	VBN	2-01-002
prize-fight	**NN**	**1-01-001**
prize-winning	**JJ**	**1-01-001**
pro	**foreign**	**3-01-001**
pro	FW-IN	0-00-000
Pro	FW-IN-TL	3-01-001
pro	**prep.**	**5-03-005**
pro	IN	4-03-004
pro	IN-HL	1-01-001
pro	**JJ**	**4-02-004**
pro	**noun**	**7-03-005**
pro	NN	5-02-004
pros	NNS	2-02-002
pro-ball	**NN**	**1-01-001**
pro-Castro	**JJ**	**1-01-001**
pro-Communist	**JJ**	**5-04-005**
pro-Europe	**JJ**	**1-01-001**
pro-Hearst	**JJ**	**1-01-001**
pro-neutralist	**JJ**	**1-01-001**
pro-tem	**JJ**	**1-01-001**
pro-Trujillo	**JJ**	**1-01-001**
pro-U.N.F.P.	**JJ**	**1-01-001**
pro-Western	**JJ**	**12-04-008**
pro-Yankee	**JJ**	**1-01-001**
probabilistic	**JJ**	**1-01-001**
probability	**noun**	**55-08-015**
probability	NN	35-07-013
probabilities	NNS	18-04-004
probabilities	NNS-HL	2-02-002
probable	**adjective**	**25-10-023**
probable	JJ	24-10-022
probable	JJ-HL	1-01-001
probably	**adverb**	**263-15-184**
probably	RB	261-15-183
probl'y	RB	1-01-001
probly	RB	1-01-001
probate	**NN**	**2-02-002**
probation	**NN**	**7-02-004**
probe	**noun**	**4-02-002**
probe	NN	1-01-001
probes	NNS	3-01-001
probe	**verb**	**13-08-013**
probe	VB	5-04-005
probed	VBD	3-02-003
probing	VBG	5-05-005
probing	**noun**	**1-01-001**
probings	NNS	1-01-001
probity	**NN**	**1-01-001**
problem	**noun**	**560-15-213**
problem	NN	309-15-152
problem	NN-HL	3-02-003
Problem	NN-TL	1-01-001
problems	NNS	240-14-135
problems	NNS-HL	7-03-005
problem-solving	**JJ**	**2-02-002**
problematic	**JJ**	**3-02-002**

Word	Tag	Frequency
problematical	**JJ**	**1-01-001**
procaine	**NN**	**1-01-001**
procedural	**JJ**	**7-04-005**
procedure	**noun**	**140-13-065**
procedure	NN	71-13-041
procedure	NN-HL	6-01-002
Procedure	NN-TL	2-02-002
procedures	NNS	59-08-033
procedures	NNS-HL	2-01-002
proceed	**verb**	**56-12-050**
proceed	VB	18-06-018
proceeds	VBZ	6-05-006
proceeded	VBD	22-10-019
proceeded	VBN	3-03-003
proceeding	VBG	7-03-006
proceeding	**noun**	**23-07-016**
proceeding	NN	5-02-002
proceedings	NNS	18-07-014
proceeds	**NNS**	**10-04-010**
process	**noun**	**252-15-100**
process	NN	191-14-086
process	NN-HL	3-02-002
Process	NN-TL	1-01-001
processes	NNS	56-10-030
processes	NNS-HL	1-01-001
process	**verb**	**34-06-013**
process	VB	1-01-001
processed	VBN	12-03-006
processing	VBG	17-04-009
processing	VBG-HL	2-01-002
Processing	VBG-TL	2-01-001
process-server	**NN**	**1-01-001**
processing	**NN**	**17-06-010**
procession	**NN**	**5-04-005**
processional	**NN**	**1-01-001**
processor	**noun**	**5-02-003**
processor	NN	4-01-002
processors	NNS	1-01-001
proclaim	**verb**	**30-10-018**
proclaim	VB	13-06-007
proclaims	VBZ	4-03-004
proclaimed	VBD	5-05-005
proclaimed	VBN	4-04-004
proclaiming	VBG	4-03-003
proclamation	**noun**	**17-06-008**
proclamation	NN	6-04-004
proclamation	NN-HL	6-01-001
Proclamation	NN-TL	1-01-001
Proclamation	NN-TL-HL	1-01-001
proclamations	NNS	3-03-003
proclivity	**noun**	**1-01-001**
proclivities	NNS	1-01-001
procrastinate	**VB**	**1-01-001**
procrastination	**NN**	**1-01-001**
procreation	**NN**	**5-02-002**
procreative	**JJ**	**2-02-002**
procreativity	**NN**	**1-01-001**
proctor	**noun**	**4-02-002**
proctor	NN	3-02-002
proctors	NNS	1-01-001
Proctor	**NP**	**1-01-001**
procure	**verb**	**8-03-005**
procure	VB	4-01-002
procured	VBN	4-03-004
procurement	**noun**	**21-04-009**
procurement	NN	20-04-009
procurement	NN-HL	1-01-001
procurer	**NN**	**3-02-002**
prod	**NN**	**1-01-001**
prod	**verb**	**5-05-005**
prod	VB	1-01-001
prodded	VBN	3-03-003
prodding	VBG	1-01-001
prodigal	**JJ**	**1-01-001**
prodigal	**noun**	**1-01-001**
prodigal	NN	0-00-000
Prodigall	NN-TL	1-01-001
prodigally	**RB**	**1-01-001**
prodigious	**JJ**	**4-04-004**
prodigy	**noun**	**4-03-004**
prodigy	NN	3-02-003
prodigies	NNS	1-01-001
produce	**NN**	**9-07-009**
produce	**verb**	**217-14-130**
produce	VB	73-11-056
produces	VBZ	19-07-017
produced	VBD	28-10-025
produced	VBN	62-10-044
producing	VBG	34-09-030

Word	Tag	Frequency
produce (cont.):		
producin'	VBG	1-01-001
producer	**noun**	**31-10-023**
producer	NN	16-09-014
producers	NNS	14-08-009
producers'	NNS$	1-01-001
producer-hubby	**NN**	**1-01-001**
producing	**NN**	**1-01-001**
product	**noun**	**195-10-065**
product	NN	80-09-043
product	NN-HL	4-03-003
Product	NN-TL	3-01-002
products	NNS	95-08-037
Products	NNS-TL	13-03-009
production	**noun**	**155-12-076**
production	NN	146-12-071
production	NN-HL	1-01-001
Production	NN-TL	1-01-001
productions	NNS	6-04-006
Productions	NNS-TL	1-01-001
productive	**JJ**	**25-07-015**
productivity	**NN**	**17-06-011**
productivity-share	**NN**	**1-01-001**
profane	**JJ**	**1-01-001**
profanity	**NN**	**4-04-004**
profess	**verb**	**13-06-012**
profess	VB	5-04-005
professes	VBZ	1-01-001
professed	VBD	4-03-004
professed	VBN	1-01-001
professing	VBG	2-02-002
professedly	**RB**	**3-03-003**
professeur	**FW-NN**	**1-01-001**
profession	**noun**	**42-12-031**
profession	NN	36-11-029
profession	NN-HL	1-01-001
professions	NNS	5-03-004
professional	**adjective**	**99-15-060**
professional	JJ	96-15-059
Professional	JJ-TL	3-02-002
professional	**noun**	**16-10-012**
professional	NN	6-04-004
professionals	NNS	10-09-009
professionalism	**noun**	**2-01-001**
professionalism	NN	1-01-001
professionalism	NN-HL	1-01-001
professionally	**RB**	**5-05-005**
professor	**noun**	**78-11-047**
professor	NN	28-08-023
prof.	NN	0-00-000
Prof.	NN-TL	4-03-003
professor	NN-HL	1-01-001
Professor	NN-TL	28-10-018
professor's	NN$	1-01-001
professors	NNS	14-08-012
Professors	NNS-TL	2-01-001
professorship	**NN**	**1-01-001**
proffer	**verb**	**3-02-003**
proffered	VBD	2-01-002
proffered	VBN	1-01-001
proficiency	**NN**	**3-02-003**
proficient	**JJ**	**5-04-005**
profile	**noun**	**18-04-007**
profile	NN	7-03-005
Profile	NN-TL	8-01-001
profiles	NNS	3-02-002
Profili	**NP**	**1-01-001**
profit	**noun**	**46-08-027**
profit	NN	24-08-015
profet	NN	1-01-001
profits	NNS	21-07-013
profit	**verb**	**7-06-007**
profit	VB	4-04-004
profited	VBD	1-01-001
profited	VBN	2-01-002
profit-maximizing	**JJ**	**3-01-001**
profit-motivated	**JJ**	**1-01-001**
profit-sharing	**JJ**	**1-01-001**
profitability	**NN**	**1-01-001**
profitable	**JJ**	**14-07-014**
profitably	**RB**	**4-01-002**
profound	**JJ**	**27-11-027**
profoundest	**JJT**	**1-01-001**
profoundly	**QL**	**3-02-003**
profoundly	**RB**	**5-04-004**
profundity	**noun**	**4-04-004**
profundity	NN	3-03-003
profoundity	NN	1-01-001
profuse	**JJ**	**2-02-002**

profusely	**RB**	**3-03-003**
profusion	**NN**	**2-01-002**
progeny	**NN**	**2-02-002**
prognosis	**noun**	**3-03-003**
prognosis	NN	2-02-002
prognoses	NNS	1-01-001
prognostication	**NN**	**1-01-001**
prognosticator	**NN**	**1-01-001**
program	**noun**	**529-13-132**
program	NN	367-13-113
program	NN-HL	4-04-004
Program	NN-TL	17-06-014
program's	NN$	1-01-001
programs	NNS	137-10-056
programmes	NNS	1-01-001
programs	NNS-HL	2-02-002
program	**verb**	**21-07-015**
program	VB	5-04-005
programed	VBN	2-02-002
programmed	VBN	3-03-003
programing	VBG	8-02-003
programming	VBG	3-01-003
programing	**noun**	**7-04-004**
programing	NN	5-02-002
programming	NN	2-02-002
programmer	**NN**	**3-01-001**
progress	**noun**	**116-12-077**
progress	NN	108-12-072
progress	NN-HL	1-01-001
Progress	NN-TL	7-04-006
progress	**verb**	**25-10-023**
progress	VB	4-04-004
progresses	VBZ	6-04-005
progressed	VBD	10-06-009
progressed	VBN	3-03-003
progressing	VBG	2-02-002
progression	**noun**	**5-04-004**
progression	NN	2-02-002
progressions	NNS	3-02-002
progressive	**JJ**	**17-07-010**
progressively	**QL**	**1-01-001**
progressively	**RB**	**5-03-005**
progressivism	**noun**	**3-01-002**
progressivism	NN	1-01-001
Progressivism	NN-TL	2-01-001
prohibit	**verb**	**15-07-012**
prohibit	VB	2-02-002
prohibits	VBZ	1-01-001
prohibited	VBD	2-02-002
prohibited	VBN	6-06-006
prohibiting	VBG	4-03-004
prohibition	**noun**	**14-06-010**
prohibition	NN	10-06-007
prohibiton	NN	1-01-001
Prohibition	NN-TL	3-01-002
prohibitive	**JJ**	**1-01-001**
project	**noun**	**145-13-062**
project	NN	79-13-051
Project	NN-TL	2-01-001
projects	NNS	60-07-022
projects	NNS-HL	1-01-001
Projects	NNS-TL	3-02-002
project	**verb**	**36-10-029**
project	VB	12-08-009
projects	VBZ	4-02-004
projected	VBD	2-02-002
projected	VBN	12-06-011
projecting	VBG	6-05-005
projectile	**noun**	**2-01-002**
projectile	NN	1-01-001
projectiles	NNS	1-01-001
projection	**noun**	**19-04-012**
projection	NN	9-03-008
projections	NNS	10-03-006
projective	**JJ**	**2-02-002**
projector	**NN**	**1-01-001**
Prokofieff	**prop. noun**	**39-02-004**
Prokofieff	NP	33-02-004
Prokofieff's	NP$	6-01-001
proletariat	**NN**	**3-02-003**
proliferate	**verb**	**1-01-001**
proliferated	VBD	1-01-001
proliferation	**NN**	**5-04-005**
prolific	**JJ**	**2-02-002**
prolixity	**NN**	**2-01-001**
prolong	**verb**	**20-08-018**
prolong	VB	1-01-001
prolongs	VBZ	1-01-001
prolonged	VBN	16-08-015
prolong (cont.):		
prolonging	VBG	2-02-002
prolongation	**NN**	**1-01-001**
prolusion	**noun**	**9-01-001**
prolusion	NN	3-01-001
Prolusion	NN-TL	2-01-001
prolusions	NNS	4-01-001
promazine	**NN**	**1-01-001**
promenade	**noun**	**4-01-001**
promenade	NN	3-01-001
promenades	NNS	1-01-001
Prometheus	**NP**	**1-01-001**
prominence	**NN**	**5-05-005**
prominent	**JJ**	**40-13-032**
prominently	**QL**	**1-01-001**
prominently	**RB**	**7-04-006**
promise	**noun**	**46-11-034**
promise	NN	36-11-026
promises	NNS	10-05-009
promise	**verb**	**68-14-059**
promise	VB	9-06-009
promises	VBZ	10-07-010
promised	VBD	26-11-023
promised	VBN	19-09-018
promising	VBG	4-03-004
promising	**JJ**	**20-08-017**
promote	**verb**	**61-10-044**
promote	VB	32-08-023
promotes	VBZ	4-04-004
promoted	VBD	1-01-001
promoted	VBN	11-07-010
promoting	VBG	13-06-011
promoter	**noun**	**5-04-005**
promoter	NN	1-01-001
promoters	NNS	4-03-004
promotion	**noun**	**26-09-014**
promotion	NN	23-08-013
promotion	NN-HL	2-02-002
Promotion	NN-TL	1-01-001
promotional	**JJ**	**6-03-004**
prompt	**adjective**	**9-05-007**
prompt	JJ	6-04-006
Prompt	JJ-TL	3-01-001
prompt	**verb**	**11-09-011**
prompt	VB	2-02-002
prompts	VBZ	2-02-002
prompted	VBD	3-02-003
prompted	VBN	4-03-004
prompting	**noun**	**1-01-001**
promptings	NNS	1-01-001
promptly	**RB**	**28-12-025**
promulgate	**verb**	**3-03-003**
promulgated	VBN	2-02-002
promulgating	VBG	1-01-001
promulgator	**noun**	**1-01-001**
promulgators	NNS	1-01-001
prone	**JJ**	**11-05-009**
prone	**RB**	**3-03-003**
proneness	**NN**	**1-01-001**
pronoun	**noun**	**8-04-005**
pronoun	NN	4-02-002
pronouns	NNS	3-02-003
pronouns	NNS-HL	1-01-001
pronounce	**verb**	**21-09-019**
pronounce	VB	2-02-002
pronounced	VBD	2-02-002
pronounced	VBN	16-09-015
pronouncing	VBG	1-01-001
pronouncement	**noun**	**5-04-005**
pronouncement	NN	3-02-003
pronouncements	NNS	2-02-002
pronto	**RB**	**1-01-001**
proof	**noun**	**40-12-027**
proof	NN	33-12-026
proof	NN-HL	7-02-003
prop	**noun**	**8-07-008**
prop	NN	2-02-002
props	NNS	6-06-006
prop	**verb**	**6-05-006**
prop	VB	2-02-002
propped	VBN	3-03-003
propping	VBG	1-01-001
propaganda	**noun**	**30-08-021**
propaganda	NN	28-08-021
propaganda	NN-HL	1-01-001
Propaganda	NN-TL	1-01-001
propagandist	**noun**	**8-03-004**
propagandist	NN	3-03-003
progandist	NN	1-01-001

Word	Tag	Frequency
propagandist (cont.):		
propagandists	NNS	4-01-002
propagandistic	**JJ**	**4-01-001**
propagate	**verb**	**2-02-002**
propagate	VB	1-01-001
propagated	VBN	1-01-001
propagation	**NN**	**8-03-004**
propel	**verb**	**6-05-006**
propel	VB	4-03-004
propelled	VBD	1-01-001
propelling	VBG	1-01-001
propeller	**NN**	**2-02-002**
propeller-driven	**JJ**	**1-01-001**
proper	**JJ**	**95-14-071**
properly	**RB**	**55-14-046**
Propertius	**NP**	**1-01-001**
property	**noun**	**222-14-077**
property	NN	148-13-059
property	NN-HL	6-02-003
Property	NN-TL	2-02-002
properties	NNS	57-10-031
properties	NNS-HL	9-02-005
prophecy	**noun**	**6-05-006**
prophecy	NN	5-04-005
prophecies	NNS	1-01-001
prophesy	**verb**	**5-03-005**
prophesies	VBZ	1-01-001
prophesied	VBD	1-01-001
prophesied	VBN	3-03-003
prophet	**noun**	**9-05-008**
prophet	NN	4-02-004
Prophet	NN-TL	1-01-001
prophets	NNS	4-03-004
prophetic	**JJ**	**2-02-002**
prophetically	**RB**	**3-03-003**
propionate	**NN**	**2-01-002**
propitiate	**VB**	**1-01-001**
propitious	**JJ**	**2-01-002**
proponent	**noun**	**8-04-005**
proponent	NN	2-02-002
proponents	NNS	6-03-003
proportion	**noun**	**47-11-037**
proportion	NN	29-09-021
proportions	NNS	18-08-017
proportional	**JJ**	**14-01-006**
proportionality	**NN**	**1-01-001**
proportionally	**RB**	**1-01-001**
proportionate	**JJ**	**9-05-007**
proportionately	**QL**	**1-01-001**
proportionately	**RB**	**8-04-006**
proposal	**noun**	**70-12-044**
proposal	NN	40-12-032
proposal	NN-HL	1-01-001
proposals	NNS	28-05-016
proposals	NNS-HL	1-01-001
propose	**verb**	**110-13-068**
propose	VB	13-08-011
proposes	VBZ	7-04-007
proposed	VBD	19-09-017
proposed	VBN	63-09-039
proposed	VBN-HL	2-02-002
proposing	VBG	6-05-006
proposition	**noun**	**18-08-015**
proposition	NN	16-07-013
propositions	NNS	2-02-002
proposition	**verb**	**1-01-001**
propositioned	VBN	1-01-001
proprietary	**adjective**	**1-01-001**
proprietary	JJ	0-00-000
proprietory	JJ	1-01-001
proprietor	**noun**	**21-08-013**
proprietor	NN	11-06-007
prop.	NN	1-01-001
Prop.	NN-TL	2-01-001
proprieter	NN	2-02-002
proprietors	NNS	5-04-004
proprietorship	**noun**	**12-02-002**
proprietorship	NN	9-02-002
proprietorships	NNS	3-01-001
propriety	**NN**	**7-05-006**
propulsion	**noun**	**7-03-004**
propulsion	NN	6-03-004
propulsions	NNS	1-01-001
Propylaea	**NP**	**1-01-001**
propylthiouracil	**NN**	**1-01-001**
prorate	**VB**	**1-01-001**
prosaic	**JJ**	**2-02-002**
proscenium	**noun**	**1-01-001**
prosceniums	NNS	1-01-001
proscribe	**verb**	**2-02-002**
proscribe	VB	1-01-001
proscribed	VBN	1-01-001
proscription	**NN**	**3-02-002**
prose	**noun**	**14-04-010**
prose	NN	13-03-009
Prose	NN-TL	1-01-001
prosecute	**verb**	**10-07-009**
prosecute	VB	2-02-002
prosecuted	VBN	5-03-004
prosecuting	VBG	3-03-003
prosecution	**noun**	**11-06-008**
prosecution	NN	9-05-007
prosecution's	NN$	1-01-001
prosecutions	NNS	1-01-001
prosecutor	**noun**	**10-03-006**
prosecutor	NN	2-01-002
Prosecutor	NN-TL	6-03-003
prosecutors	NNS	2-01-001
proselytize	**verb**	**1-01-001**
proselytizing	VBG	1-01-001
prosodic	**JJ**	**3-01-002**
prosody	**noun**	**1-01-001**
prosodies	NNS	1-01-001
Prosopopoeia	**NP**	**1-01-001**
prospect	**noun**	**49-12-036**
prospect	NN	25-10-019
prospects	NNS	24-10-019
prospective	**JJ**	**21-08-019**
prosper	**verb**	**7-05-006**
prosper	VB	3-02-003
prospers	VBZ	1-01-001
prospered	VBD	1-01-001
prospered	VBN	1-01-001
prospering	VBG	1-01-001
prosperity	**NN**	**14-08-011**
prosperous	**JJ**	**8-04-006**
pross	**verb**	**1-01-001**
prossed	VBN	1-01-001
Prosser	**NP**	**1-01-001**
prostate	**NN**	**2-02-002**
prostitute	**noun**	**8-03-004**
prostitute	NN	5-01-001
prostitutes	NNS	3-03-003
prostitute	**VB**	**1-01-001**
prostitution	**NN**	**10-04-006**
prostrate	**JJ**	**2-02-002**
protagonist	**NN**	**2-02-002**
protease	**noun**	**5-01-001**
protease	NN	1-01-001
proteases	NNS	4-01-001
protect	**verb**	**72-13-058**
protect	VB	34-09-030
protects	VBZ	4-02-004
protected	VBD	5-04-005
protected	VBN	25-09-021
protected	VBN-HL	1-01-001
protecting	VBG	3-02-003
protection	**noun**	**68-11-035**
protection	NN	64-11-035
protection	NN-HL	4-01-001
protective	**JJ**	**14-09-013**
protectively	**RB**	**1-01-001**
Protectorate	**NP**	**1-01-001**
protege	**NN**	**1-01-001**
protein	**noun**	**35-05-009**
protein	NN	21-05-008
proteins	NNS	12-02-005
proteins	NNS-HL	2-01-001
protein-bound	**JJ**	**1-01-001**
proteolysis	**NN**	**2-01-001**
proteolytic	**JJ**	**1-01-001**
protest	**noun**	**25-10-023**
protest	NN	17-07-015
protests	NNS	8-05-008
protest	**verb**	**29-10-025**
protest	VB	6-06-006
protests	VBZ	3-01-003
protested	VBD	11-05-010
protested	VBN	2-02-002
protesting	VBG	7-05-007
Protestant	**adjective**	**48-06-014**
Protestant	JJ	43-05-010
Protestant	JJ-TL	5-03-005
Protestant	**prop. noun**	**17-04-008**
Protestant	NP	3-03-003
Protestants	NPS	14-03-006
Protestant-dominated	**JJ**	**1-01-001**
Protestantism	**prop. noun**	**11-03-004**

Word	Tag	Frequency
Protestantism (cont.):		
Protestantism	NP	10-03-004
Protestantism	NP-TL	1-01-001
protestation	**noun**	**3-02-003**
protestations	NNS	3-02-003
Protitch	**NP**	**1-01-001**
proto-Athabascan	**NP**	**1-01-001**
proto-senility	**NN**	**1-01-001**
proto-Yokuts	**NP**	**1-01-001**
protocol	**NN**	**3-03-003**
Protogeometric	**JJ**	**3-01-001**
proton	**noun**	**6-02-003**
proton	NN	3-02-002
protons	NNS	3-02-002
protoplasm	**NN**	**1-01-001**
protoplasmic	**JJ**	**1-01-001**
prototype	**NN**	**3-02-003**
prototypical	**JJ**	**1-01-001**
protozoan	**JJ**	**1-01-001**
protozoon	**noun**	**7-01-001**
protozoa	NNS	7-01-001
protract	**verb**	**1-01-001**
protracted	VBN	1-01-001
protrude	**verb**	**8-04-006**
protrude	VB	1-01-001
protruded	VBD	4-03-004
protruding	VBG	3-03-003
protrusion	**NN**	**1-01-001**
protuberance	**NN**	**1-01-001**
proud	**JJ**	**50-12-045**
prouder	**JJR**	**1-01-001**
proudest	**JJT**	**1-01-001**
Proudhon	**NP**	**1-01-001**
proudly	**RB**	**9-06-009**
Proust	**NP**	**1-01-001**
prove	**verb**	**156-14-117**
prove	VB	53-14-044
proves	VBZ	16-10-015
proved	VBD	48-12-041
proved	VBN	23-09-023
proven	VBN	11-05-011
proving	VBG	5-03-005
provenance	**NN**	**1-01-001**
proverb	**noun**	**6-04-006**
proverb	NN	5-04-005
proverbs	NNS	1-01-001
proverbial	**JJ**	**4-04-004**
provide	**verb**	**486-14-206**
provide	VB	216-13-123
provides	VBZ	81-10-056
provided	VBD	29-10-023
provided	VBN	103-11-066
provdied	VBN	1-01-001
providing	VBG	55-12-048
providing	VBG-HL	1-01-001
providence	**NN**	**3-02-003**
Providence	**prop. noun**	**78-08-017**
Providence	NP	38-07-014
Providence	NP-HL	1-01-001
Providence	NP-TL	38-04-008
Providence's	NP$	1-01-001
providential	**JJ**	**1-01-001**
providing	**CS**	**3-03-003**
province	**noun**	**27-08-019**
province	NN	14-06-011
Province	NN-TL	1-01-001
provinces	NNS	9-06-007
Provinces	NNS-TL	3-02-002
Provincetown	**NP**	**1-01-001**
provincial	**adjective**	**9-05-008**
provincial	JJ	8-05-008
Provincial	JJ-TL	1-01-001
provincialism	**NN**	**3-01-003**
provision	**noun**	**87-10-046**
provision	NN	47-10-034
provisions	NNS	39-09-019
provisons	NNS	1-01-001
provision	**verb**	**1-01-001**
provisioned	VBN	1-01-001
provisional	**adjective**	**7-05-005**
provisional	JJ	5-03-003
Provisional	JJ-TL	2-02-002
proviso	**NN**	**3-03-003**
provocateur	**noun**	**1-01-001**
provocateurs	NNS	1-01-001
provocation	**NN**	**5-03-004**
provocative	**JJ**	**7-05-007**
provocatively	**RB**	**1-01-001**
provoke	**verb**	**14-08-013**

Word	Tag	Frequency
provoke (cont.):		
provoke	VB	3-03-003
provokes	VBZ	4-04-004
provoked	VBD	5-04-005
provoked	VBN	2-02-002
provost	**noun**	**2-02-002**
provost	NN	0-00-000
Provost	NN-TL	2-02-002
prow	**NN**	**1-01-001**
prowazwki	**NP**	**1-01-001**
prowess	**NN**	**2-02-002**
prowl	**NN**	**1-01-001**
prowl	**verb**	**4-03-004**
prowl	VB	1-01-001
prowled	VBD	1-01-001
prowling	VBG	2-02-002
prowler	**noun**	**1-01-001**
prowlers	NNS	1-01-001
proximal	**JJ**	**2-01-002**
proximate	**JJ**	**3-02-002**
proximity	**NN**	**5-03-005**
Proxmire	**NP**	**1-01-001**
proxy	**NN**	**7-02-003**
prudence	**noun**	**3-03-003**
prudence	NN	2-02-002
Prudence	NN-HL	1-01-001
Prudence	**NP**	**3-01-002**
prudent	**adjective**	**2-02-002**
prudent	JJ	1-01-001
Prudent	JJ-TL	1-01-001
prudential	**JJ**	**1-01-001**
prudentially	**RB**	**1-01-001**
prudently	**RB**	**1-01-001**
prune	**noun**	**2-02-002**
prune	NN	1-01-001
prunes	NNS	1-01-001
prune	**verb**	**1-01-001**
pruned	VBD	1-01-001
prurient	**JJ**	**1-01-001**
Prussia	**prop. noun**	**2-01-001**
Prussia	NP	0-00-000
Prussia	NP-TL	2-01-001
Prussian	**JJ**	**1-01-001**
pruta	**FW-NNS**	**1-01-001**
pry	**verb**	**7-06-007**
pry	VB	6-05-006
prying	VBG	1-01-001
psalm	**noun**	**4-01-002**
psalm	NN	1-01-001
Psalm	NN-TL	3-01-002
psalmist	**NN**	**5-01-001**
pseudo	**JJ**	**1-01-001**
pseudo-anthropological	**JJ**	**2-01-001**
pseudo-capitalism	**NN**	**2-01-001**
pseudo-emotion	**NN**	**1-01-001**
pseudo-feeling	**NN**	**1-01-001**
pseudo-glamorous	**JJ**	**2-01-001**
pseudo-happiness	**NN**	**1-01-001**
pseudo-patriotism	**NN**	**1-01-001**
pseudo-question	**noun**	**1-01-001**
pseudo-questions	NNS	1-01-001
pseudo-scientific	**JJ**	**1-01-001**
pseudo-sophistication	**NN**	**1-01-001**
pseudo-symmetric	**JJ**	**1-01-001**
pseudo-thinking	**NN**	**2-01-001**
pseudo-willing	**NN**	**1-01-001**
Pseudomonas	**NP**	**1-01-001**
pseudonym	**noun**	**2-02-002**
pseudonym	NN	1-01-001
pseudynom	NN	1-01-001
pseudophloem	**NN**	**6-01-001**
Psithyrus	**NP**	**5-01-001**
psyche	**noun**	**7-04-006**
psyche	NN	6-04-006
psyches	NNS	1-01-001
Psyche	**NP**	**1-01-001**
psychiatric	**JJ**	**5-02-003**
psychiatrist	**noun**	**9-04-007**
psychiatrist	NN	4-03-004
psychiatrists	NNS	5-02-004
psychiatry	**NN**	**3-02-002**
psychic	**JJ**	**3-03-003**
psychical	**JJ**	**4-02-002**
psychically	**RB**	**2-01-001**
psychically-blind	**JJ**	**1-01-001**
psycho-physiology	**NN**	**1-01-001**
psychoactive	**JJ**	**2-01-001**
psychoanalysis	**NN**	**5-01-003**
psychoanalyst	**NN**	**1-01-001**

Word	Tag	Frequency
psychoanalytic	**adjective**	**7-02-005**
psychoanalytic	JJ	6-02-005
Psychoanalytic	JJ-TL	1-01-001
psychological	**JJ**	**41-08-028**
psychological-intellectual	**JJ**	**1-01-001**
psychologically	**RB**	**4-03-004**
psychologist	**noun**	**21-05-011**
psychologist	NN	10-03-007
psychologists	NNS	11-04-007
psychology	**noun**	**14-06-013**
psychology	NN	13-06-012
Psychology	NN-TL	1-01-001
psychopath	**NN**	**2-02-002**
psychopathic	**JJ**	**3-02-003**
psychopharmacological	**JJ**	**1-01-001**
psychopomp	**NN**	**1-01-001**
psychosomatic	**JJ**	**1-01-001**
psychotherapeutic	**JJ**	**1-01-001**
psychotherapist	**noun**	**1-01-001**
psychotherapists	NNS	1-01-001
psychotherapy	**noun**	**6-03-005**
psychotherapy	NN	4-03-004
psychotherapy	NN-HL	1-01-001
Psychotherapy	NN-TL	1-01-001
psychotic	**JJ**	**1-01-001**
psyllium	**NN**	**3-01-001**
pterygia	**NN**	**1-01-001**
Ptolemaic	**JJ**	**12-01-002**
Ptolemaist	**prop. noun**	**1-01-001**
Ptolemaists	NPS	1-01-001
Ptolemy	**prop. noun**	**14-01-001**
Ptolemy	NP	8-01-001
Ptolemy's	NP$	6-01-001
Pualani	**NP**	**1-01-001**
pub	**noun**	**2-02-002**
pub	NN	1-01-001
pubs	NNS	1-01-001
puberty	**NN**	**1-01-001**
pubescent	**JJ**	**3-01-001**
public	**adjective**	**306-13-152**
public	JJ	272-13-142
publick	JJ	1-01-001
Publick	JJ-TL	2-01-001
public	JJ-HL	1-01-001
Public	JJ-TL	30-08-025
public	**noun**	**141-14-077**
public	NN	135-14-075
public's	NN$	6-03-006
public-address	**NN**	**1-01-001**
public-limit	**NN**	**8-01-001**
public-opinion	**NN**	**2-01-001**
public-school	**NN**	**2-02-002**
public-spirited	**JJ**	**3-03-003**
publication	**noun**	**78-08-037**
publication	NN	49-07-029
publication	NN-HL	4-01-001
Publication	NN-TL	1-01-001
Publication	NN-TL-HL	1-01-001
publications	NNS	11-03-008
publications	NNS-HL	3-01-002
Publications	NNS-TL	9-03-003
publicist	**noun**	**1-01-001**
publicists	NNS	1-01-001
publicity	**NN**	**27-12-023**
publicize	**verb**	**8-06-008**
publicized	VBN	6-05-006
publicizing	VBG	2-02-002
publicly	**adverb**	**28-13-026**
publicly	RB	27-13-025
publically	RB	1-01-001
publique	**foreign**	**2-01-001**
publique	FW-JJ	0-00-000
Publique	FW-JJ-TL	2-01-001
publish	**verb**	**108-13-064**
publish	VB	3-03-003
publishes	VBZ	4-04-004
published	VBD	11-05-009
published	VBN	78-11-047
publishing	VBG	11-07-009
Publishing	VBG-TL	1-01-001
publisher	**noun**	**20-07-013**
publisher	NN	9-05-006
publishers	NNS	10-06-008
Publishers	NNS-TL	1-01-001
publishing	**NN**	**2-01-001**
Puccini	**prop. noun**	**3-01-001**
Puccini's	NP$	3-01-001
pucker	**verb**	**3-03-003**
puckered	VBN	2-02-002
pucker (cont.):		
puckering	VBG	1-01-001
puckish	**JJ**	**1-01-001**
pudding	**noun**	**1-01-001**
puddings	NNS	1-01-001
Puddingstone	**NP**	**1-01-001**
puddle	**noun**	**3-03-003**
puddle	NN	1-01-001
puddles	NNS	2-02-002
pueri	**FW-NNS**	**1-01-001**
puerile	**JJ**	**1-01-001**
Puerto	**prop. noun**	**24-05-009**
Puerto	NP	21-05-008
Puerto	NP-HL	1-01-001
Puerto	NP-TL	2-01-001
puff	**verb**	**8-06-007**
puff	VB	1-01-001
puffs	VBZ	1-01-001
puffed	VBD	2-02-002
puffed	VBN	2-02-002
puffing	VBG	2-02-002
puffy	**JJ**	**2-02-002**
pug-nosed	**JJ**	**1-01-001**
pugh	**UH**	**2-01-001**
puissant	**JJ**	**2-02-002**
puke	**NN**	**1-01-001**
Pulaski	**prop. noun**	**1-01-001**
Pulaski	NP	0-00-000
Pulaski	NP-TL	1-01-001
Pulitzer	**prop. noun**	**3-02-002**
Pulitzer	NP	0-00-000
Pulitzer	NP-TL	3-02-002
pull	**noun**	**13-07-011**
pull	NN	12-06-010
pulls	NNS	1-01-001
pull	**verb**	**145-14-090**
pull	VB	39-12-035
pulls	VBZ	8-04-006
pulled	VBD	54-10-043
pulled	VBN	19-07-015
pulling	VBG	24-08-018
pulling	VBG-HL	1-01-001
Pullen	**NP**	**4-02-002**
pulley	**noun**	**5-02-002**
pulley	NN	3-01-001
pulleys	NNS	2-01-001
Pulley	**NP**	**8-01-001**
Pullings	**NP**	**2-01-001**
Pullman	**prop. noun**	**3-02-002**
Pullman	NP	0-00-000
Pullman	NP-TL	1-01-001
Pullman's	NP$	1-01-001
Pullmans	NPS	1-01-001
pullover	**noun**	**2-01-001**
pullover	NN	0-00-000
Pullover	NN-TL	2-01-001
pulmonary	**JJ**	**33-01-002**
Pulova	**NP**	**2-01-001**
pulp	**NN**	**5-03-004**
pulpit	**noun**	**5-04-005**
pulpit	NN	4-04-004
pulpits	NNS	1-01-001
pulsate	**verb**	**3-03-003**
pulsating	VBG	3-03-003
pulsation	**noun**	**3-03-003**
pulsation	NN	2-02-002
pulsations	NNS	1-01-001
pulse	**NN**	**8-06-008**
pulse	**verb**	**4-03-003**
pulse	VB	1-01-001
pulsed	VBN	1-01-001
pulsing	VBG	2-02-002
pulse-jet	**NN**	**1-01-001**
pulse-timing	**JJ**	**1-01-001**
pulverize	**verb**	**3-02-003**
pulverized	VBD	1-01-001
pulverized	VBN	1-01-001
pulverizing	VBG	1-01-001
Pumblechook	**prop. noun**	**3-01-001**
Pumblechook	NP	1-01-001
Pumblechook's	NP$	2-01-001
pummel	**verb**	**1-01-001**
pummeled	VBD	1-01-001
pump	**noun**	**15-06-010**
pump	NN	8-03-006
pump	NN-HL	1-01-001
Pump	NN-TL	1-01-001
pumps	NNS	5-04-004
pump	**verb**	**12-06-010**

Word	Tag	Count
pump (cont.):		
pump	VB	1-01-001
pumped	VBD	2-02-002
pumped	VBN	1-01-001
pumping	VBG	8-05-008
pump-action	**NN**	**2-01-001**
pump-priming	**NN**	**1-01-001**
pumpkin	**noun**	**2-02-002**
pumpkin	NN	1-01-001
Pumpkin	NN-TL	1-01-001
pun	**NN**	**1-01-001**
punch	**noun**	**5-04-004**
punch	NN	4-03-003
punches	NNS	1-01-001
punch	**verb**	**3-03-003**
punch	VB	1-01-001
punched	VBD	1-01-001
punching	VBG	1-01-001
punchbowl	**NN**	**1-01-001**
punched-card	**NN**	**1-01-001**
puncher	**NN**	**3-01-002**
punching	**NN**	**1-01-001**
punctuality	**NN**	**1-01-001**
punctually	**RB**	**2-02-002**
punctuate	**verb**	**4-03-004**
punctuated	VBN	4-03-004
punctuation	**NN**	**2-02-002**
puncture	**verb**	**4-04-004**
punctured	VBN	3-03-003
puncturing	VBG	1-01-001
pundit	**noun**	**1-01-001**
pundits	NNS	1-01-001
punditry	**NN**	**1-01-001**
pungency	**NN**	**1-01-001**
pungent	**JJ**	**4-04-004**
pungently	**QL**	**1-01-001**
Punic	**JJ**	**1-01-001**
punish	**verb**	**14-06-013**
punish	VB	3-02-003
punishes	VBZ	1-01-001
punished	VBD	0-00-000
punnished	VBD	1-01-001
punished	VBN	7-04-007
punnished	VBN	1-01-001
punishing	VBG	1-01-001
punishable	**JJ**	**1-01-001**
punishment	**noun**	**23-08-019**
punishment	NN	21-07-017
punishments	NNS	2-02-002
punitive	**JJ**	**1-01-001**
punk	**noun**	**3-03-003**
punk	NN	2-02-002
punks	NNS	1-01-001
punster	**NN**	**1-01-001**
punt	**verb**	**1-01-001**
punted	VBD	1-01-001
puny	**JJ**	**6-03-003**
pup	**noun**	**4-04-004**
pup	NN	2-02-002
pups	NNS	2-02-002
pupate	**verb**	**2-01-001**
pupates	VBZ	1-01-001
pupated	VBN	1-01-001
pupil	**noun**	**45-11-017**
pupil	NN	18-06-007
pupil	NN-HL	2-01-002
pupils	NNS	24-08-012
Pupils	NNS-TL	1-01-001
puppet	**noun**	**12-03-003**
puppet	NN	6-03-003
puppet's	NN$	1-01-001
puppets	NNS	5-01-001
puppy	**noun**	**3-03-003**
puppy	NN	2-02-002
puppies	NNS	1-01-001
puppyish	**JJ**	**1-01-001**
Purcell	**NP**	**1-01-001**
purchase	**noun**	**50-09-023**
purchase	NN	31-08-017
purchase	NN-HL	3-01-002
Purchase	NN-TL	2-01-001
purchases	NNS	13-04-009
Purchases	NNS-TL	1-01-001
purchase	**verb**	**48-11-035**
purchase	VB	11-06-011
purchases	VBZ	2-02-002
purchased	VBD	4-03-003
purchased	VBN	16-08-015
purchasing	VBG	13-05-009

Word	Tag	Count
purchase (cont.):		
purchasing	VBG-HL	1-01-001
Purchasing	VBG-TL	1-01-001
purchaser	**noun**	**5-03-003**
purchaser's	NN$	1-01-001
purchasers	NNS	4-03-003
purchasing	**noun**	**2-02-002**
purchasing	NN	1-01-001
Purchasing	NN-TL	1-01-001
Purdew	**NP**	**12-01-001**
Purdue	**prop. noun**	**1-01-001**
Purdue's	NP$	1-01-001
pure	**adjective**	**56-11-040**
pure	JJ	55-11-039
Pure	JJ-TL	1-01-001
purely	**QL**	**21-07-020**
purely	**RB**	**9-07-009**
purest	**JJT**	**3-03-003**
purgation	**NN**	**2-01-002**
purgatory	**NN**	**1-01-001**
Purgatory	**NP**	**1-01-001**
purge	**noun**	**3-03-003**
purge	NN	1-01-001
purges	NNS	2-02-002
purge	**verb**	**5-03-003**
purge	VB	1-01-001
purges	VBZ	1-01-001
purged	VBN	2-02-002
purging	VBG	1-01-001
purging	**NN**	**1-01-001**
purification	**noun**	**4-02-004**
purification	NN	3-02-003
purification	NN-HL	1-01-001
purify	**verb**	**13-04-008**
purify	VB	2-02-002
purified	VBN	10-03-007
purifying	VBG	1-01-001
purism	**NN**	**1-01-001**
purist	**noun**	**1-01-001**
purists	NNS	1-01-001
puritan	**adjective**	**5-03-005**
puritan	JJ	1-01-001
Puritan	JJ-TL	4-03-004
Puritan	**prop. noun**	**3-01-002**
Puritans	NPS	3-01-002
puritanical	**JJ**	**1-01-001**
purity	**NN**	**12-07-012**
purl	**verb**	**3-02-003**
purled	VBD	1-01-001
purled	VBN	1-01-001
purling	VBG	1-01-001
purloin	**verb**	**1-01-001**
purloined	VBN	1-01-001
purple	**adjective**	**11-06-008**
purple	JJ	8-06-007
purple	JJ-HL	1-01-001
Purple	JJ-TL	1-01-001
Purple	JJ-TL-HL	1-01-001
purple	**NN**	**2-02-002**
purple	**verb**	**1-01-001**
purpling	VBG	1-01-001
purple-black	**JJ**	**1-01-001**
purport	**verb**	**10-05-010**
purport	VB	2-02-002
purports	VBZ	2-01-002
purported	VBD	3-02-003
purported	VBN	1-01-001
purporting	VBG	2-02-002
purportedly	**RB**	**1-01-001**
purpose	**noun**	**239-14-142**
purpose	NN	146-14-104
purpose	NN-HL	1-01-001
Purpose	NN-TL	2-01-002
purposes	NNS	89-13-055
purposes	NNS-HL	1-01-001
purpose	**verb**	**1-01-001**
purposed	VBN	1-01-001
purposeful	**JJ**	**3-02-003**
purposefully	**RB**	**1-01-001**
purposeless	**JJ**	**1-01-001**
purposely	**RB**	**5-05-005**
purposive	**JJ**	**3-01-002**
purposively	**RB**	**1-01-001**
purr	**verb**	**3-02-003**
purring	VBG	3-02-003
purse	**noun**	**15-10-014**
purse	NN	12-09-012
Purse	NN-TL	2-01-001
purses	NNS	1-01-001

purse	**verb**	**3-02-003**
pursed	VBD	3-02-003
Pursewarden	**NP**	**1-01-001**
pursuant	**IN**	**20-01-003**
pursuant	**JJ**	**7-01-001**
pursue	**verb**	**45-12-042**
pursue	VB	20-07-018
pursues	VBZ	2-02-002
pursued	VBD	3-03-003
pursued	VBN	11-06-011
pursuing	VBG	9-08-009
pursuer	**noun**	**4-04-004**
pursuer	NN	2-02-002
pursuers	NNS	2-02-002
pursuit	**noun**	**19-09-016**
pursuit	NN	15-08-012
Pursuit	NN-TL	1-01-001
pursuits	NNS	3-02-003
purveyor	**noun**	**2-01-002**
purveyor	NN	1-01-001
purveyors	NNS	1-01-001
Purvis	**NP**	**4-01-001**
push	**noun**	**8-05-007**
push	NN	7-05-006
pushes	NNS	1-01-001
push	**verb**	**102-12-082**
push	VB	30-10-025
pushes	VBZ	2-02-002
pushed	VBD	31-10-027
pushed	VBN	22-10-020
pushing	VBG	16-10-016
pushin'	VBG	1-01-001
Push-Pull	**NP**	**9-01-001**
push-up	**noun**	**7-02-002**
push-up	NN	3-01-001
push-ups	NNS	2-01-001
push-ups	NNS-HL	2-02-002
push-up	**VB**	**1-01-001**
pusher	**noun**	**3-01-001**
pushers	NNS	3-01-001
pushing	**JJ**	**1-01-001**
pushing	**noun**	**1-01-001**
pushing	NN	0-00-000
pushin'	NN	1-01-001
Pushup	**NP**	**2-01-001**
pussy	**NN**	**5-02-002**
pussycat	**NN**	**1-01-001**
put	**verb**	**513-15-278**
put	VB	196-15-139
put	VB-HL	1-01-001
puts	VBZ	20-11-019
put	VBD	130-15-098
put	VBD-NC	1-01-001
put	VBN	110-14-089
putting	VBG	54-14-050
put (cont.):		
Puttin'	VBG-TL	1-01-001
put-upon	**JJ**	**1-01-001**
putains	**FW-NNS**	**1-01-001**
putas	**foreign**	**1-01-001**
putas	FW-NNS	0-00-000
Putas	FW-NNS-TL	1-01-001
putout	**NN**	**1-01-001**
putt	**NN**	**5-01-001**
putt	**verb**	**2-01-001**
putt	VB	1-01-001
putted	VBD	1-01-001
Putt	**NP**	**1-01-001**
puttana	**FW-NN**	**1-01-001**
putter	**NN**	**1-01-001**
putter	**verb**	**2-02-002**
puttering	VBG	2-02-002
putty	**NN**	**1-01-001**
putty-like	**JJ**	**1-01-001**
puzzle	**noun**	**10-06-008**
puzzle	NN	6-05-005
puzzles	NNS	3-02-002
puzzles	NNS-HL	1-01-001
puzzle	**verb**	**24-11-022**
puzzle	VB	4-04-004
puzzled	VBD	2-02-002
puzzled	VBN	17-08-015
puzzling	VBG	1-01-001
puzzlement	**NN**	**1-01-001**
puzzler	**NN**	**1-01-001**
puzzling	**JJ**	**8-03-007**
Pye	**NP**	**1-01-001**
pyknotic	**JJ**	**2-01-001**
pyocanea	**NP**	**1-01-001**
pyorrhea	**NN**	**1-01-001**
pyramid	**noun**	**2-02-002**
pyramid	NN	1-01-001
pyramids	NNS	1-01-001
pyramid	**VB**	**1-01-001**
pyramidal	**JJ**	**1-01-001**
pyre	**NN**	**1-01-001**
Pyrex	**NP**	**5-01-001**
pyrometer	**noun**	**4-01-001**
pyrometer	NN	2-01-001
Pyrometer	NN-TL	1-01-001
pyrometers	NNS	1-01-001
pyrophosphate	**NN**	**1-01-001**
Pyrrhic	**adjective**	**1-01-001**
Pyrrhic	JJ	0-00-000
Pyhrric	JJ	1-01-001
pyschiatrist	**NN**	**1-01-001**
Pythagorean	**prop. noun**	**1-01-001**
Pythagoreans	NPS	1-01-001
python	**NN**	**14-01-001**

Q

Q	**NP**	**7-01-005**
Q.	**NP**	**2-02-002**
qua	**FW-WDT**	**2-02-002**
quack	**noun**	**18-01-001**
quack	NN	9-01-001
quacks	NNS	9-01-001
quack	**verb**	**1-01-001**
quacked	VBD	1-01-001
quackery	**NN**	**6-01-002**
quadratic	**JJ**	**2-01-001**
quadrennial	**JJ**	**1-01-001**
quadric	**JJ**	**6-01-001**
quadric	**NN**	**1-01-001**
quadriceps	**NNS**	**1-01-001**
quadrille	**noun**	**1-01-001**
quadrille	NN	0-00-000
Quadrille	NN-TL	1-01-001
quadrillion	**CD**	**1-01-001**
quadripartite	**JJ**	**1-01-001**
quadruple	**verb**	**2-02-002**
quadruple	VB	1-01-001
quadrupled	VBN	1-01-001
quadrupling	**NN**	**1-01-001**
quagmire	**NN**	**1-01-001**
quaint	**JJ**	**12-08-012**
quake	**noun**	**3-01-001**
quake	NN	2-01-001
quake's	NN$	1-01-001
quake	**verb**	**1-01-001**
quaking	VBG	1-01-001
Quaker	**prop. noun**	**10-06-008**
Quaker	NP	5-04-004
Quaker	NP-TL	1-01-001
Quakers	NPS	4-03-004
Quakeress	**NP**	**1-01-001**
qualification	**noun**	**24-10-018**
qualification	NN	8-05-008
qualifications	NNS	16-10-013
qualify	**verb**	**42-10-034**
qualify	VB	15-07-013
qualifies	VBZ	2-02-002
qualified	VBD	2-02-002
qualified	VBN	22-10-019
qualifying	VBG	1-01-001
qualitative	**JJ**	**6-03-005**
qualitatively	**RB**	**2-02-002**
quality	**noun**	**159-14-095**
quality	NN	114-13-071
qualities	NNS	44-10-035
Qualities	NNS-TL	1-01-001

Word	Tag	Frequency
qualm	**noun**	**1-01-001**
qualms	NNS	1-01-001
quam	**FW-CS**	**1-01-001**
quantitative	**JJ**	**9-04-007**
quantitatively	**RB**	**4-02-004**
quantity	**noun**	**44-12-033**
quantity	NN	33-11-026
quantities	NNS	11-06-010
quantum	**NN**	**5-01-002**
quarrel	**noun**	**17-07-013**
quarrel	NN	14-05-010
quarrels	NNS	3-03-003
quarrel	**verb**	**16-09-014**
quarrel	VB	6-05-006
quarrels	VBZ	1-01-001
quarreled	VBD	2-02-002
quarreled	VBN	2-02-002
quarreling	VBG	5-05-005
quarrelsome	**JJ**	**2-01-002**
quarry	**NN**	**7-04-006**
quarryman	**noun**	**1-01-001**
quarrymen	NNS	1-01-001
quart	**noun**	**4-04-004**
quart	NN	3-03-003
quarts	NNS	1-01-001
quarter	**noun**	**62-15-053**
quarter	NN	31-13-026
Quarter	NN-TL	3-02-002
quarters	NNS	28-11-026
quarter-century	**NN**	**2-02-002**
quarter-century-old	**JJ**	**1-01-001**
quarter-inch	**NN**	**1-01-001**
quarter-mile	**NN**	**2-02-002**
quarter-to-quarter	**JJ**	**1-01-001**
quarterback	**noun**	**6-01-003**
quarterback	NN	4-01-003
Quarterback	NN-TL	1-01-001
quarterbacks	NNS	1-01-001
quarterly	**JJ**	**4-02-003**
quarterly	**noun**	**2-02-002**
quarterly	NN	0-00-000
Quarterly	NN-TL	2-02-002
quarterly	**RB**	**1-01-001**
quartermaster	**noun**	**1-01-001**
quartermaster	NN	0-00-000
Quartermaster	NN-TL	1-01-001
quartet	**noun**	**9-04-005**
quartet	NN	2-01-002
Quartet	NN-TL	7-03-003
quartz	**NN**	**1-01-001**
quash	**verb**	**1-01-001**
quashed	VBN	1-01-001
quasi-folk	**JJ**	**1-01-001**
quasi-governmental	**JJ**	**1-01-001**
quasi-mechanistic	**JJ**	**1-01-001**
quasi-performer	**NN**	**1-01-001**
quasi-recitative	**JJ**	**1-01-001**
Quasimodo	**prop. noun**	**5-01-001**
Quasimodo	NP	3-01-001
Quasimodo's	NP$	2-01-001
quatrain	**NN**	**2-02-002**
quaver	**NN**	**1-01-001**
quaver	**verb**	**3-03-003**
quavered	VBD	1-01-001
quavering	VBG	2-02-002
que	**FW-WDT**	**1-01-001**
queasiness	**NN**	**1-01-001**
Quebec	**prop. noun**	**3-03-003**
Quebec	NP	1-01-001
Quebec	NP-TL	1-01-001
Quebec's	NP$	1-01-001
queen	**noun**	**51-09-019**
queen	NN	20-07-009
queen	NN-HL	1-01-001
Queen	NN-TL	20-09-013
queen's	NN$	0-00-000
Queen's	NN$-TL	1-01-001
queens	NNS	7-01-001
queens'	NNS$	0-00-000
Queens'	NNS$-TL	2-02-002
Queens	**NP**	**3-02-002**
queer	**JJ**	**6-03-006**
queerer	**JJR**	**1-01-001**
queerest	**JJT**	**1-01-001**
Quelch	**NP**	**1-01-001**
quell	**verb**	**3-03-003**
quell	VB	2-02-002
quelling	VBG	1-01-001
Quell	**NP**	**1-01-001**
Quemoy	**NP**	**2-02-002**
quench	**VB**	**1-01-001**
quenching	**NN**	**1-01-001**
querulous	**JJ**	**1-01-001**
querulously	**RB**	**1-01-001**
query	**noun**	**4-03-004**
query	NN	1-01-001
queries	NNS	3-03-003
query	**verb**	**4-04-004**
queried	VBD	1-01-001
queried	VBN	2-02-002
querying	VBG	1-01-001
quest	**noun**	**16-06-011**
quest	NN	15-06-011
quest	NN-HL	1-01-001
question	**noun**	**378-15-184**
question	NN	232-15-137
question	NN-HL	4-03-004
Question	NN-TL	4-04-004
questions	NNS	135-14-092
questions	NNS-HL	1-01-001
Questions	NNS-TL	2-02-002
question	**verb**	**67-12-054**
question	VB	17-10-016
questions	VBZ	1-01-001
questions	VBZ-HL	1-01-001
questioned	VBD	8-07-008
questioned	VBN	21-07-020
questioning	VBG	19-10-016
question-and-answer	**NN**	**1-01-001**
questionable	**JJ**	**9-06-008**
questioner	**noun**	**3-02-003**
questioner	NN	2-02-002
questioners	NNS	1-01-001
questioning	**NN**	**2-02-002**
questioningly	**RB**	**1-01-001**
questionnaire	**noun**	**44-03-006**
questionnaire	NN	33-03-005
questionaire	NN	1-01-001
questionnaire	NN-HL	4-01-001
questionnaires	NNS	6-01-002
quetzal	**NN**	**2-01-001**
queue	**verb**	**1-01-001**
queued	VBN	1-01-001
qui	**FW-WPS**	**1-01-001**
quibble	**VB**	**1-01-001**
quibusdam	**FW-WPO**	**1-01-001**
quick	**JJ**	**58-13-052**
quick	**NN**	**1-01-001**
quick	**adverb**	**9-05-008**
quick	RB	8-04-007
quick	RB-HL	1-01-001
quick-drying	**JJ**	**1-01-001**
quick-freeze	**verb**	**1-01-001**
quick-frozen	VBN	1-01-001
quick-handling	**JJ**	**1-01-001**
quick-kill	**NN**	**1-01-001**
Quick-Wate	**NP**	**1-01-001**
quicken	**verb**	**4-03-004**
quicken	VB	1-01-001
quickened	VBN	1-01-001
quickening	VBG	2-02-002
quicker	**JJR**	**5-04-004**
quicker	**RBR**	**1-01-001**
quickest	**JJT**	**1-01-001**
quickie	**NN**	**2-02-002**
quickly	**RB**	**89-14-071**
quickness	**NN**	**1-01-001**
quicksilver	**NN**	**2-02-002**
quickstep	**NN**	**1-01-001**
quickstep	**VB**	**1-01-001**
quiescent	**JJ**	**2-02-002**
quiet	**adjective**	**65-14-051**
quiet	JJ	63-14-051
quiet	JJ-HL	1-01-001
Quiet	JJ-TL	1-01-001
quiet	**NN**	**9-06-009**
quiet	**verb**	**5-05-005**
quiet	VB	2-02-002
quieted	VBD	2-02-002
quieted	VBN	1-01-001
quiet-spoken	**JJ**	**1-01-001**
quieter	**JJR**	**4-03-004**
Quietism	**NP**	**2-01-001**
Quietist	**JJ**	**2-01-001**
quietly	**RB**	**49-12-042**
quietness	**NN**	**3-02-002**
quill	**NN**	**9-02-002**
quilt	**verb**	**1-01-001**

Word	Tag	Frequency
quilt (cont.):		
quilted	VBN	1-01-001
quince	**NN**	**2-01-001**
Quincy	**NP**	**4-03-004**
Quiney	**prop. noun**	**25-01-001**
Quiney	NP	22-01-001
Quiney	NP-TL	1-01-001
Quiney's	NP$	2-01-001
Quint	**prop. noun**	**13-01-001**
Quint	NP	11-01-001
Quint's	NP$	2-01-001
Quintana	**NP**	**1-01-001**
quintet	**noun**	**4-02-003**
quintet	NN	1-01-001
Quintet	NN-TL	2-02-002
quintets	NNS	1-01-001
quintillion	**CD**	**1-01-001**
quintus	**foreign**	**2-01-001**
quintus	FW-OD	0-00-000
quintus	FW-OD-NC	1-01-001
Quintus	FW-OD-TL	1-01-001
Quintus	**prop. noun**	**1-01-001**
Quintus	NP	0-00-000
Quintus	NP-TL	1-01-001
Quinzaine	**prop. noun**	**4-01-001**
Quinzaine	NP	2-01-001
Quinzaine	NP-TL	2-01-001
quip	**noun**	**1-01-001**
quips	NNS	0-00-000
quibs	NNS	1-01-001
quip	**verb**	**1-01-001**
quipping	VBG	1-01-001
Quirinal	**prop. noun**	**1-01-001**
Quirinal	NP	0-00-000
Quirinal	NP-TL	1-01-001
quirk	**noun**	**2-02-002**
quirk	NN	1-01-001
quirks	NNS	1-01-001
quirk	**verb**	**1-01-001**
quirking	VBG	1-01-001
quirt	**NN**	**8-01-002**
quit	**verb**	**20-09-016**
quit	VB	12-06-011
quits	VBZ	1-01-001
quit	VBD	2-02-002
quit	VBN	1-01-001
quitting	VBG	4-03-004
quite	**ABL**	**42-13-037**
quite	**QL**	**224-15-152**
quite	**RB**	**15-09-013**
quiver	**noun**	**1-01-001**
quivers	NNS	1-01-001
quiver	**verb**	**9-04-008**
quivered	VBD	1-01-001
quivering	VBG	8-04-007
Quixote	**NP**	**4-01-002**
quixotic	**JJ**	**2-02-002**
quiz	**NN**	**2-02-002**
quizzical	**adjective**	**2-02-002**
quizzical	JJ	1-01-001
Quizzical	JJ-TL	1-01-001
quo	**FW-WDT**	**11-05-010**
quod	**FW-WDT**	**1-01-001**
quok	**FW-WDT**	**1-01-001**
quota	**noun**	**7-04-005**
quota	NN	3-03-003
Quota	NN-TL	1-01-001
quotas	NNS	3-01-001
quotation	**noun**	**9-06-008**
quotation	NN	4-02-003
quotations	NNS	5-04-005
quote	**NN**	**2-02-002**
quote	**verb**	**48-12-039**
quote	VB	15-05-013
quotes	VBZ	4-03-004
quoted	VBD	8-04-008
quoted	VBN	18-10-016
quoting	VBG	3-03-003
Quyne	**NP**	**1-01-001**
Quyney	**NP**	**1-01-001**

Word	Tag	Frequency
R	**NP**	**15-04-006**
R.	**prop. noun**	**62-10-039**
R.	NP	57-10-038
R.	NP-HL	1-01-001
R.	NP-TL	3-01-003
R.'s	NPS	1-01-001
R.A.F.	**NP**	**1-01-001**
R.H.	**NP**	**2-01-001**
R.L.	**NP**	**1-01-001**
r.p.m.	**noun**	**2-01-001**
r.p.m.	NNS	0-00-000
r.p.m.	NNS-HL	2-01-001
Rabat	**NP**	**1-01-001**
Rabaul	**NP**	**1-01-001**
Rabb	**NP**	**2-01-001**
rabbeting	**NN**	**1-01-001**
rabbi	**noun**	**14-02-003**
rabbi	NN	6-02-003
Rabbi	NN-TL	7-02-002
rabbi's	NN$	0-00-000
Rabbi's	NN$-TL	1-01-001
rabbit	**noun**	**16-08-012**
rabbit	NN	11-05-007
rabbits	NNS	5-05-005
rabble	**NN**	**2-02-002**
rabid	**JJ**	**2-01-002**
rabies	**NNS**	**1-01-001**
Raccoon	**NP**	**1-01-001**
race	**noun**	**120-12-060**
race	NN	94-12-052
race	NN-HL	2-02-002
Race	NN-TL	3-02-002
races	NNS	20-10-015
races	NNS-HL	1-01-001
race	**verb**	**30-10-022**
race	VB	4-04-004
raced	VBD	11-06-011
raced	VBN	1-01-001
racing	VBG	13-07-010
racin'	VBG	0-00-000
race (cont.):		
Racin'	VBG-TL	1-01-001
race-driver	**noun**	**7-01-001**
race-driver	NN	3-01-001
race-drivers	NNS	4-01-001
racer	**noun**	**1-01-001**
racers	NNS	1-01-001
racetrack	**NN**	**2-01-002**
raceway	**noun**	**2-01-001**
raceway	NN	0-00-000
Raceway	NN-TL	2-01-001
Rachel	**prop. noun**	**44-05-005**
Rachel	NP	42-05-005
Rachel's	NP$	2-01-001
Rachmaninoff	**NP**	**2-01-002**
racial	**JJ**	**25-06-013**
racially	**RB**	**1-01-001**
Racie	**NP**	**1-01-001**
Racine	**prop. noun**	**4-02-003**
Racine	NP	2-01-001
Racine's	NP$	2-02-002
racing	**noun**	**9-05-006**
racing	NN	8-04-005
Racing	NN-TL	1-01-001
racist	**noun**	**1-01-001**
racists	NNS	1-01-001
rack	**noun**	**9-05-009**
rack	NN	7-04-007
racks	NNS	1-01-001
racks	NNS-HL	1-01-001
rack	**verb**	**4-04-004**
rack	VB	2-02-002
racked	VBN	1-01-001
racking	VBG	1-01-001
racket	**noun**	**7-06-007**
racket	NN	4-04-004
rackets	NNS	3-03-003
racket	**VB**	**1-01-001**
racketeer	**noun**	**5-02-005**
racketeer	NN	2-02-002

Word	Tag	Frequency
racketeer (cont.):		
racketeers	NNS	3-01-003
rackety	**JJ**	**2-02-002**
Rackmil	**NP**	**1-01-001**
Racquet	**NP**	**1-01-001**
racy	**JJ**	**2-02-002**
radar	**NN**	**23-09-013**
radar-controlled	**JJ**	**3-01-001**
radar-type	**NN**	**1-01-001**
Radetzky	**NP**	**1-01-001**
Radhakrishnan	**NP**	**1-01-001**
radial	**adjective**	**5-03-005**
radial	JJ	4-03-004
radial	JJ-HL	1-01-001
radiance	**NN**	**3-03-003**
radiant	**JJ**	**8-05-006**
radiate	**verb**	**7-05-006**
radiate	VB	1-01-001
radiates	VBZ	1-01-001
radiated	VBD	2-02-002
radiated	VBN	2-02-002
radiating	VBG	1-01-001
radiation	**noun**	**100-06-013**
radiation	NN	95-06-012
radiation	NN-HL	2-01-001
radiations	NNS	3-02-002
radiation-produced	**JJ**	**1-01-001**
radiator	**noun**	**6-04-005**
radiator	NN	4-04-004
radiators	NNS	2-01-002
Radic	**NP**	**4-01-001**
radical	**JJ**	**22-07-019**
radical	**noun**	**12-04-005**
radical	NN	7-03-003
Radical	NN-TL	1-01-001
radicals	NNS	4-03-003
radicalism	**NN**	**4-03-004**
radically	**QL**	**3-03-003**
radically	**RB**	**10-06-010**
radio	**noun**	**126-14-047**
radio	NN	111-14-040
radio	NN-HL	1-01-001
Radio	NN-TL	7-06-006
radios	NNS	7-04-006
radio	**verb**	**3-02-002**
radio	VB	1-01-001
radioed	VBD	1-01-001
radioed	VBN	1-01-001
radio-transmitter	**noun**	**1-01-001**
radio-transmitter	NN	0-00-000
radio-transmitter	NN-HL	1-01-001
radio-TV	**NN**	**3-03-003**
radioactive	**JJ**	**10-05-007**
radioactivity	**NN**	**3-03-003**
radiocarbon	**NN**	**1-01-001**
radiochlorine	**NN**	**3-01-001**
radioclast	**NN**	**1-01-001**
radiography	**NN**	**1-01-001**
radioman	**noun**	**1-01-001**
radiomen	NNS	1-01-001
radionic	**JJ**	**1-01-001**
radiopasteurization	**NN**	**9-01-001**
radiosterilization	**NN**	**6-01-001**
radiosterilize	**verb**	**1-01-001**
radiosterilized	VBN	1-01-001
radish	**NN**	**8-01-001**
radius	**noun**	**13-04-007**
radius	NN	9-03-005
radii	NNS	4-02-003
Rae	**NP**	**2-02-002**
Raesz	**NP**	**1-01-001**
Rafael	**NP**	**1-01-001**
Rafer	**NP**	**1-01-001**
raffish	**JJ**	**1-01-001**
raft	**noun**	**5-03-005**
raft	NN	3-02-003
Raft	NN-TL	1-01-001
rafts	NNS	1-01-001
rafter	**noun**	**1-01-001**
rafters	NNS	1-01-001
Rafter	**NP**	**1-01-001**
raftered	**JJ**	**1-01-001**
rag	**noun**	**17-08-013**
rag	NN	7-04-006
Rag	NN-TL	3-01-001
rags	NNS	7-05-007
rag	**verb**	**2-01-001**
ragging	VBG	2-01-001
rage	**noun**	**17-08-015**
rage (cont.):		
rage	NN	16-08-014
rages	NNS	1-01-001
rage	**verb**	**10-07-010**
raged	VBD	7-05-007
raged	VBN	1-01-001
raging	VBG	2-02-002
ragged	**JJ**	**9-06-009**
raggedness	**NN**	**1-01-001**
raid	**noun**	**14-04-007**
raid	NN	9-04-005
raids	NNS	5-03-005
raid	**verb**	**4-03-004**
raid	VB	1-01-001
raided	VBN	1-01-001
raiding	VBG	2-02-002
raider	**noun**	**2-02-002**
raiders	NNS	1-01-001
raiders'	NNS$	0-00-000
Raiders'	NNS$-TL	1-01-001
rail	**noun**	**25-10-019**
rail	NN	16-10-015
rails	NNS	9-05-006
rail-mobile	**JJ**	**1-01-001**
railbird	**noun**	**1-01-001**
railbirds	NNS	1-01-001
railhead	**NN**	**2-02-002**
railing	**NN**	**3-03-003**
raillery	**NN**	**1-01-001**
railroad	**noun**	**77-10-030**
railroad	NN	47-10-024
Railroad	NN-TL	11-05-008
railroad's	NN$	2-02-002
Railroad's	NN$-TL	1-01-001
railroads	NNS	15-06-009
Railroads	NNS-TL	1-01-001
railroader	**NN**	**1-01-001**
railroading	**NN**	**1-01-001**
railway	**noun**	**14-08-011**
railway	NN	10-06-008
ry.	NN	0-00-000
Ry.	NN-TL	1-01-001
Railway	NN-TL	2-02-002
railways	NNS	1-01-001
railway-based	**JJ**	**1-01-001**
Raimu	**NP**	**1-01-001**
rain	**noun**	**73-10-040**
rain	NN	66-10-035
Rain	NN-TL	2-02-002
rain's	NN+HVZ	1-01-001
rains	NNS	4-04-004
rain	**verb**	**14-08-013**
rain	VB	2-02-002
rains	VBZ	1-01-001
rained	VBD	2-02-002
rained	VBN	2-02-002
raining	VBG	7-04-007
rain-slick	**JJ**	**1-01-001**
rainbow	**noun**	**4-03-003**
rainbow	NN	2-02-002
Rainbow	NN-TL	2-01-001
rainbow-hued	**JJ**	**1-01-001**
raincoat	**noun**	**2-02-002**
raincoats	NNS	2-02-002
raindrop	**noun**	**1-01-001**
raindrops	NNS	1-01-001
Raine	**NP**	**1-01-001**
rainfall	**NN**	**3-02-003**
Rainier	**prop. noun**	**1-01-001**
Rainier	NP	0-00-000
Rainier	NP-TL	1-01-001
rainless	**JJ**	**1-01-001**
rainstorm	**NN**	**2-02-002**
rainy	**JJ**	**4-03-003**
Rainy	**NP**	**1-01-001**
raise	**noun**	**8-04-006**
raise	NN	4-03-003
Raise	NN-TL	1-01-001
raises	NNS	3-01-002
raise	**verb**	**188-15-137**
raise	VB	47-12-036
raises	VBZ	13-07-013
raised	VBD	42-13-038
raised	VBN	57-12-049
raised	VBN-HL	2-02-002
raising	VBG	26-11-024
a-raising	VBG	1-01-001
raiser	**NN**	**1-01-001**
raisin	**NN**	**1-01-001**

raising	**NN**	**8-04-007**
rajah	**NN**	**1-01-001**
Rak	**NP**	**1-01-001**
rake	**NN**	**8-01-001**
rake	**verb**	**6-05-006**
rake	VB	2-02-002
raked	VBD	3-03-003
raked	VBN	1-01-001
Rake	**NP**	**1-01-001**
Rakestraw	**NP**	**1-01-001**
rakish	**JJ**	**1-01-001**
rakishly	**RB**	**1-01-001**
Rall	**NP**	**5-02-002**
rally	**noun**	**7-03-007**
rally	NN	5-02-005
rallies	NNS	2-02-002
rally	**verb**	**8-05-008**
rally	VB	5-04-005
rallies	VBZ	1-01-001
rallied	VBD	1-01-001
rallying	VBG	1-01-001
rallying	**NN**	**1-01-001**
Ralph	**NP**	**22-06-016**
ram	**NN**	**1-01-001**
ram	**verb**	**6-04-004**
ram	VB	1-01-001
rammed	VBD	3-03-003
ramming	VBG	1-01-001
rammin'	VBG	1-01-001
ramble	**verb**	**5-04-005**
ramble	VB	2-02-002
Ramble	VB-TL	1-01-001
rambles	VBZ	1-01-001
rambling	VBG	1-01-001
rambling	**noun**	**2-02-002**
rambling	NN	1-01-001
ramblings	NNS	1-01-001
Rameau	**prop. noun**	**6-02-002**
Rameau	NP	2-02-002
Rameau's	NP$	4-02-002
Ramey	**prop. noun**	**31-01-001**
Ramey	NP	28-01-001
Ramey's	NP$	3-01-001
ramification	**noun**	**4-03-004**
ramification	NN	1-01-001
ramifications	NNS	3-03-003
Ramillies	**prop. noun**	**2-01-001**
Ramillies	NP	1-01-001
Ramillies	NP-TL	1-01-001
Ramirez	**NP**	**2-01-001**
ramp	**noun**	**7-05-006**
ramp	NN	6-04-005
ramps	NNS	1-01-001
rampage	**NN**	**1-01-001**
rampant	**JJ**	**4-04-004**
rampart	**NN**	**2-01-001**
Ramsey	**NP**	**10-02-003**
Ramsperger	**NP**	**1-01-001**
Ranavan	**prop. noun**	**1-01-001**
Ranavan	NP	0-00-000
Ranavan	NP-TL	1-01-001
ranch	**noun**	**28-06-016**
ranch	NN	26-06-015
Ranch	NN-TL	1-01-001
ranches	NNS	1-01-001
ranch	**verb**	**1-01-001**
ranches	VBZ	1-01-001
rancher	**noun**	**22-04-008**
rancher	NN	14-04-006
Rancher	NN-TL	1-01-001
ranchers	NNS	7-02-005
rancho	**NN**	**1-01-001**
rancidity	**NN**	**1-01-001**
rancor	**NN**	**3-02-003**
rancorous	**JJ**	**2-02-002**
Rand	**NP**	**1-01-001**
Randall	**NP**	**1-01-001**
Randolph	**NP**	**9-01-001**
random	**adjective**	**33-06-016**
random	JJ	31-05-015
random	JJ-HL	1-01-001
Random	JJ-TL	1-01-001
random	**NN**	**5-04-005**
random-storage	**NN**	**1-01-001**
randomization	**NN**	**1-01-001**
randomly	**RB**	**2-01-002**
Randy	**NP**	**1-01-001**
range	**noun**	**152-15-083**
range	NN	141-15-080
range (cont.):		
range	NN-HL	2-02-002
range	NN-NC	1-01-001
Range	NN-TL	1-01-001
ranges	NNS	7-05-006
range	**verb**	**63-11-049**
range	VB	12-06-011
ranges	VBZ	3-03-003
ranged	VBD	16-06-011
ranged	VBN	2-02-002
ranging	VBG	30-10-028
rangeland	**noun**	**2-01-001**
rangelands	NNS	2-01-001
ranger	**noun**	**2-02-002**
rangers	NNS	1-01-001
Rangers	NNS-TL	1-01-001
Ranger	**prop. noun**	**2-01-001**
Ranger	NP	0-00-000
Ranger	NP-TL	2-01-001
Rangoni	**prop. noun**	**8-01-001**
Rangoni	NP	6-01-001
Rangoni's	NP$	2-01-001
rangy	**JJ**	**2-02-002**
rank	**JJ**	**2-02-002**
rank	**noun**	**41-11-029**
rank	NN	22-08-017
ranks	NNS	19-09-016
rank	**verb**	**9-04-008**
ranks	VBZ	1-01-001
ranked	VBD	2-02-002
ranked	VBN	2-02-002
ranking	VBG	3-03-003
ranking	VBG-HL	1-01-001
rank-and-file	**NN**	**1-01-001**
Ranke	**NP**	**1-01-001**
rankest	**JJT**	**1-01-001**
Rankin	**prop. noun**	**10-02-002**
Rankin	NP	9-02-002
Rankin's	NP$	1-01-001
ranking	**NN**	**1-01-001**
rankle	**verb**	**1-01-001**
rankles	VBZ	1-01-001
ransack	**verb**	**6-04-005**
ransack	VB	2-02-002
ransacked	VBD	1-01-001
ransacked	VBN	2-02-002
ransacking	VBG	1-01-001
ransom	**noun**	**4-04-004**
ransom	NN	3-03-003
Ransom	NN-TL	1-01-001
Ransom	**NP**	**1-01-001**
Ransy	**NP**	**1-01-001**
rant	**verb**	**1-01-001**
ranted	VBD	1-01-001
Ranyard	**NP**	**1-01-001**
Raoul	**NP**	**2-02-002**
rap	**NN**	**2-02-002**
rap	**verb**	**6-03-005**
rapped	VBD	2-02-002
rapped	VBN	2-02-002
rapping	VBG	2-01-001
rape	**noun**	**3-03-003**
rape	NN	1-01-001
rape	NN-NC	1-01-001
rapes	NNS	1-01-001
rape	**verb**	**6-05-005**
rape	VB	3-03-003
raped	VBN	2-02-002
raping	VBG	1-01-001
Raphael	**prop. noun**	**6-04-004**
Raphael	NP	4-02-002
Raphael's	NP$	1-01-001
Raphaels	NPS	1-01-001
rapid	**adjective**	**43-10-037**
rapid	JJ	42-10-037
rapid	JJ-HL	1-01-001
rapid-fire	**NN**	**1-01-001**
rapid-transit	**NN**	**1-01-001**
rapidity	**NN**	**4-03-004**
rapidly	**QL**	**1-01-001**
rapidly	**RB**	**64-14-054**
rapidly-diminishing	**JJ**	**1-01-001**
rapier	**NN**	**1-01-001**
rapist	**noun**	**2-02-002**
rapists	NNS	2-02-002
Rapoport	**NP**	**1-01-001**
rapping	**NN**	**1-01-001**
rapport	**foreign**	**1-01-001**
rapport	FW-NN	0-00-000

Word	Tag	Frequency
rapport (cont.):		
Rapport	FW-NN-TL	1-01-001
rapport	**NN**	**3-02-003**
rapprochement	**NN**	**1-01-001**
rapt	**JJ**	**1-01-001**
rapture	**noun**	**4-04-004**
rapture	NN	3-03-003
raptures	NNS	1-01-001
Rapunzel	**NP**	**1-01-001**
rare	**JJ**	**41-11-036**
rarely	**adverb**	**41-11-034**
rarely	RB	39-11-033
rarely	RB-NC	2-01-001
rarer	**JJR**	**1-01-001**
rarify	**verb**	**1-01-001**
rarified	VBN	1-01-001
rarity	**NN**	**2-02-002**
rasa	**FW-VBN**	**2-01-001**
rascal	**noun**	**2-02-002**
rascal	NN	1-01-001
rascals	NNS	1-01-001
rash	**JJ**	**1-01-001**
rasp	**noun**	**3-03-003**
rasp	NN	2-02-002
rasps	NNS	1-01-001
rasp	**verb**	**2-02-002**
rasped	VBD	1-01-001
rasping	VBG	1-01-001
raspberry	**JJ**	**1-01-001**
Rastus	**NP**	**1-01-001**
rat	**noun**	**10-06-008**
rat	NN	6-05-006
rat's	NN$	1-01-001
rats	NNS	3-02-002
rat-a-tat-tatty	**JJ**	**1-01-001**
Rat-face	**NP**	**1-01-001**
rat-hole	**noun**	**1-01-001**
rat-holes	NNS	1-01-001
rata	**FW-NNS**	**2-02-002**
ratable	**adjective**	**2-01-002**
ratable	JJ	1-01-001
rateable	JJ	1-01-001
Ratcliff	**NP**	**3-01-001**
Ratcliffe	**NP**	**1-01-001**
rate	**noun**	**303-12-095**
rate	NN	205-11-081
rates	NNS	97-09-036
rates	NNS-HL	1-01-001
rate	**verb**	**21-05-014**
rate	VB	4-04-004
rates	VBZ	4-03-004
rated	VBN	9-03-007
rating	VBG	3-02-002
rating	VBG-HL	1-01-001
Rathbone	**prop. noun**	**3-02-002**
Rathbone	NP	2-01-001
Rathbones	NPS	1-01-001
rather	**ABL**	**5-04-005**
rather	**IN**	**119-13-086**
rather	**QL**	**108-13-083**
rather	**RB**	**141-14-105**
ratification	**NN**	**5-03-003**
ratify	**verb**	**5-04-005**
ratify	VB	1-01-001
ratified	VBD	1-01-001
ratified	VBN	3-02-003
rating	**noun**	**15-03-008**
rating	NN	6-03-004
ratings	NNS	9-02-005
ratio	**noun**	**54-06-022**
ratio	NN	34-04-018
ratio	NN-HL	2-01-001
ratios	NNS	18-04-007
ratiocinate	**verb**	**1-01-001**
ratiocinating	VBG	1-01-001
ration	**noun**	**14-06-007**
ration	NN	9-05-005
ration	NN-HL	1-01-001
rations	NNS	3-03-003
rations	NNS-HL	1-01-001
ration	**verb**	**4-04-004**
rationed	VBN	3-03-003
rationing	VBG	1-01-001
rational	**JJ**	**25-04-016**
rationale	**NN**	**6-05-005**
rationalism	**NN**	**4-01-002**
rationalist	**JJ**	**1-01-001**
rationalist	**NN**	**2-02-002**
rationalistic	**JJ**	**1-01-001**

Word	Tag	Frequency
rationality	**NN**	**1-01-001**
rationalization	**noun**	**3-03-003**
rationalization	NN	2-02-002
rationalizations	NNS	1-01-001
rationalize	**verb**	**6-03-005**
rationalize	VB	5-03-004
rationalized	VBN	1-01-001
rationally	**QL**	**2-02-002**
rationally	**RB**	**1-01-001**
rationing	**NN**	**2-01-001**
Raton	**NP**	**3-02-002**
rator	**NN**	**1-01-001**
rattail	**NN**	**1-01-001**
rattle	**NN**	**5-04-005**
rattle	**verb**	**9-05-008**
rattles	VBZ	1-01-001
rattled	VBD	2-02-002
rattling	VBG	6-03-006
rattler	**noun**	**2-02-002**
rattler	NN	1-01-001
rattlers	NNS	1-01-001
rattlesnake	**noun**	**8-03-003**
rattlesnake	NN	3-02-002
rattlesnakes	NNS	5-03-003
rattling	**NN**	**1-01-001**
Ratto	**NP**	**1-01-001**
Rattzhenfuut	**NP**	**1-01-001**
raucous	**JJ**	**7-05-007**
raucously	**RB**	**1-01-001**
Rauschenberg	**NP**	**1-01-001**
Rauschenbusch	**NP**	**1-01-001**
ravage	**noun**	**2-02-002**
ravages	NNS	2-02-002
rave	**verb**	**1-01-001**
raving	VBG	1-01-001
Ravel-like	**JJ**	**1-01-001**
Ravencroft	**NP**	**1-01-001**
ravenous	**JJ**	**2-01-002**
ravine	**noun**	**2-02-002**
ravine	NN	0-00-000
Ravine	NN-TL	1-01-001
ravines	NNS	1-01-001
raving	**NN**	**1-01-001**
raving	**QL**	**1-01-001**
raw	**JJ**	**43-13-028**
rawboned	**JJ**	**1-01-001**
rawhide	**NN**	**1-01-001**
Rawlings	**NP**	**4-01-001**
Rawlins	**NP**	**3-01-001**
Rawson	**NP**	**3-02-003**
ray	**noun**	**10-06-010**
ray	NN	3-03-003
rays	NNS	7-04-007
Ray	**NP**	**16-07-013**
Rayburn	**prop. noun**	**47-04-007**
Rayburn	NP	39-04-006
Rayburn's	NP$	8-02-003
Rayburn-Johnson	**NP**	**1-01-001**
Raymond	**NP**	**17-06-014**
Raymondville	**NP**	**1-01-001**
Raymont	**NP**	**1-01-001**
Raynal	**NP**	**1-01-001**
raze	**verb**	**1-01-001**
razing	VBG	1-01-001
razor	**NN**	**15-03-005**
razor-edged	**JJ**	**1-01-001**
razor-sharp	**JJ**	**1-01-001**
razorback	**NN**	**1-01-001**
rbi's	**NNS**	**1-01-001**
RCA	**NP**	**4-03-003**
RDWS	**NP**	**1-01-001**
re	**foreign**	**1-01-001**
re	FW-NN	0-00-000
Re	FW-NN-TL	1-01-001
re	**noun**	**1-01-001**
re	NN	0-00-000
Re	NN-TL	1-01-001
re-adopt	**VB**	**1-01-001**
re-argue	**verb**	**1-01-001**
re-arguing	VBG	1-01-001
re-assume	**verb**	**1-01-001**
re-assumed	VBN	1-01-001
re-creation	**NN**	**1-01-001**
re-declare	**verb**	**1-01-001**
re-declared	VBD	1-01-001
re-echo	**VB**	**1-01-001**
re-elect	**verb**	**4-02-004**
re-elected	VBN	3-02-003
reelected	VBN	1-01-001

Word	Tag	Frequency
re-election	**noun**	**4-02-003**
re-election	NN	2-01-001
reelection	NN	2-02-002
re-emergence	**NN**	**1-01-001**
re-emphasize	**verb**	**1-01-001**
re-emphasize	VB	0-00-000
re-emphasise	VB	1-01-001
re-enactment	**noun**	**3-02-002**
re-enactment	NN	2-02-002
re-enactments	NNS	1-01-001
re-enforce	**verb**	**1-01-001**
re-enforces	VBZ	1-01-001
re-enter	**verb**	**6-03-003**
re-enter	VB	5-02-002
re-entered	VBD	0-00-000
reentered	VBD	1-01-001
re-establish	**verb**	**1-01-001**
re-establishing	VBG	1-01-001
re-evaluate	**VB**	**1-01-001**
re-examine	**verb**	**7-04-007**
re-examine	VB	4-02-004
reexamine	VB	1-01-001
re-examines	VBZ	1-01-001
re-examined	VBD	1-01-001
re-explore	**VB**	**1-01-001**
re-export	**NN**	**1-01-001**
re-incorporate	**verb**	**1-01-001**
re-incorporated	VBN	1-01-001
re-introduction	**NN**	**1-01-001**
re-moralize	**verb**	**1-01-001**
re-moralizing	VBG	1-01-001
re-run	**noun**	**1-01-001**
re-runs	NNS	1-01-001
re-run	**VBN**	**1-01-001**
re-schedule	**verb**	**1-01-001**
re-scheduled	VBN	1-01-001
re-set	**VB**	**1-01-001**
re-sharpening	**NN**	**2-01-001**
re-use	**verb**	**2-01-002**
re-use	VB	1-01-001
re-used	VBD	1-01-001
re-vision	**NN**	**1-01-001**
reach	**noun**	**18-10-017**
reach	NN	14-08-013
reaches	NNS	4-04-004
reach	**verb**	**324-15-189**
reach	VB	91-13-073
reaches	VBZ	21-07-018
reached	VBD	106-14-076
reached	VBN	63-13-052
reaching	VBG	43-14-036
reacquaint	**verb**	**1-01-001**
reacquainted	VBN	1-01-001
react	**verb**	**32-09-027**
react	VB	15-07-013
reacts	VBZ	1-01-001
reacted	VBD	12-06-010
reacting	VBG	4-03-004
reactant	**noun**	**3-01-001**
reactants	NNS	3-01-001
reaction	**noun**	**166-12-061**
reaction	NN	120-11-048
reaction	NN-HL	4-02-002
reactions	NNS	42-07-021
reactionary	**adjective**	**14-04-006**
reactionary	JJ	12-04-006
reactionary	JJ-NC	1-01-001
Reactionary	JJ-TL	1-01-001
reactionary	**noun**	**8-03-005**
reactionary	NN	6-03-004
reactionaries	NNS	2-02-002
reactivate	**verb**	**3-01-003**
reactivate	VB	0-00-000
re-activate	VB	1-01-001
reactivated	VBN	2-01-002
reactivity	**NN**	**19-01-004**
reactor	**noun**	**13-03-005**
reactor	NN	7-02-003
reactors	NNS	6-03-004
read	**verb**	**274-15-154**
read	VB	89-15-067
reads	VBZ	15-07-012
reads	VBZ-NC	1-01-001
read	VBD	36-13-029
read	VBN	47-13-038
reading	VBG	84-15-059
reading	VBG-NC	2-01-001
Read	**prop. noun**	**3-02-003**
Read	NP	2-02-002

Word	Tag	Frequency
Read (cont.):		
Read's	NP$	1-01-001
readable	**JJ**	**2-02-002**
readapt	**verb**	**1-01-001**
readapting	VBG	1-01-001
reader	**noun**	**84-12-048**
reader	NN	43-10-027
reader's	NN$	2-01-002
Reader's	NN$-TL	2-02-002
readers	NNS	37-11-026
readily	**QL**	**2-02-002**
readily	**RB**	**41-09-033**
readiness	**NN**	**15-08-014**
reading	**noun**	**71-11-033**
reading	NN	52-11-028
reading	NN-HL	1-01-001
reading	NN-NC	1-01-001
readings	NNS	17-08-011
Reading	**NP**	**1-01-001**
reading-room	**noun**	**1-01-001**
reading-rooms	NNS	1-01-001
readjust	**verb**	**3-03-003**
readjust	VB	2-02-002
readjusted	VBN	1-01-001
readjustment	**NN**	**2-02-002**
ready	**JJ**	**141-14-109**
ready	**verb**	**3-03-003**
ready	VB	2-02-002
readying	VBG	1-01-001
ready-made	**JJ**	**5-04-005**
reaffirm	**verb**	**6-04-005**
reaffirm	VB	2-02-002
reaffirms	VBZ	1-01-001
reaffirmed	VBD	2-02-002
reaffirmed	VBN	1-01-001
reaffirmation	**NN**	**2-02-002**
reagent	**noun**	**4-01-001**
reagent	NN	1-01-001
reagents	NNS	3-01-001
real	**adjective**	**241-15-145**
real	JJ	234-15-145
real	JJ-NC	2-01-001
Real	JJ-TL	5-02-002
real	**QL**	**17-09-015**
real-analytic	**JJ**	**1-01-001**
real-life	**NN**	**2-01-001**
realer	**JJR**	**1-01-001**
realest	**JJT**	**1-01-001**
realign	**verb**	**1-01-001**
realigning	VBG	1-01-001
realism	**noun**	**24-08-015**
realism	NN	23-07-014
Realism	NN-TL	1-01-001
realismo	**FW-NN**	**1-01-001**
realist	**NN**	**2-01-002**
realistic	**JJ**	**34-08-026**
realistically	**QL**	**1-01-001**
realistically	**RB**	**7-05-006**
reality	**noun**	**94-13-056**
reality	NN	79-11-049
realities	NNS	15-08-013
realization	**NN**	**24-11-022**
realize	**verb**	**153-15-118**
realize	VB	69-14-058
realizes	VBZ	3-03-003
realized	VBD	49-11-039
realized	VBN	20-09-019
realizing	VBG	12-07-012
really	**QL**	**49-11-044**
really	**adverb**	**226-15-147**
really	RB	225-15-147
Really	RB-TL	1-01-001
realm	**noun**	**21-07-019**
realm	NN	19-07-017
realms	NNS	2-02-002
realness	**NN**	**1-01-001**
realtor	**noun**	**25-02-002**
realtor	NN	4-01-001
Realtor	NN-TL	1-01-001
realtor's	NN$	1-01-001
realtors	NNS	18-01-001
Realtors	NNS-TL	1-01-001
realty	**noun**	**2-02-002**
realty	NN	1-01-001
Realty	NN-TL	1-01-001
ream	**noun**	**2-02-002**
reams	NNS	2-02-002
Reama	**NP**	**5-01-001**
reap	**verb**	**5-04-005**

Word	Tag	Frequency
reap (cont.):		
reap	VB	3-03-003
reaped	VBN	1-01-001
reaping	VBG	1-01-001
reappear	**verb**	**9-06-009**
reappear	VB	2-02-002
reappears	VBZ	3-03-003
reappeared	VBD	2-02-002
reappeared	VBN	1-01-001
reappearing	VBG	1-01-001
reappearance	**NN**	**2-02-002**
reapportion	**verb**	**1-01-001**
reapportioned	VBN	1-01-001
reapportionment	**NN**	**1-01-001**
reappraisal	**noun**	**3-02-003**
reappraisal	NN	2-02-002
reappraisals	NNS	1-01-001
rear	**JJ**	**29-08-018**
rear	**NN**	**19-07-015**
rear	**verb**	**14-06-010**
rear	VB	3-03-003
reared	VBD	7-03-004
reared	VBN	3-02-003
rearing	VBG	1-01-001
rear-looking	**JJ**	**1-01-001**
rearguard	**noun**	**2-02-002**
rearguard	NN	1-01-001
rear-guard	NN	1-01-001
rearing	**NN**	**1-01-001**
rearm	**verb**	**1-01-001**
rearmed	VBN	1-01-001
rearrange	**verb**	**5-04-004**
rearrange	VB	3-02-002
rearranged	VBD	1-01-001
rearranging	VBG	1-01-001
reason	**noun**	**340-15-211**
reason	NN	237-15-167
Reason	NN-TL	1-01-001
reasons	NNS	99-11-076
reasons	NNS-HL	3-02-002
reason	**verb**	**12-06-012**
reason	VB	3-03-003
reasons	VBZ	1-01-001
reasoned	VBD	4-04-004
reasoning	VBG	4-03-004
reasonable	**adjective**	**65-12-052**
reasonable	JJ	64-12-051
resonable	JJ	1-01-001
reasonably	**QL**	**17-07-016**
reasonably	**RB**	**17-09-017**
reasoning	**noun**	**12-08-012**
reasoning	NN	11-08-011
Reasoning	NN-TL	1-01-001
reassemble	**verb**	**4-04-004**
reassemble	VB	3-03-003
reassembled	VBN	1-01-001
reassert	**verb**	**2-02-002**
reassert	VB	1-01-001
reasserting	VBG	1-01-001
reassign	**VB**	**1-01-001**
reassurance	**NN**	**8-06-007**
reassure	**verb**	**12-06-012**
reassure	VB	1-01-001
reassured	VBD	3-02-003
reassured	VBN	2-01-002
reassuring	VBG	6-04-006
reassuring	**JJ**	**1-01-001**
reassuringly	**RB**	**2-02-002**
Reavey	**prop. noun**	**3-01-001**
Reavey	NP	1-01-001
Reavey's	NP$	2-01-001
reawaken	**VB**	**1-01-001**
Reb	**prop. noun**	**7-02-002**
Reb	NP	2-01-001
Rebs	NPS	5-02-002
Rebecca	**NP**	**1-01-001**
rebel	**noun**	**31-07-017**
rebel	NN	8-05-007
Rebel	NN-TL	7-02-003
rebels	NNS	11-05-010
Rebels	NNS-TL	5-02-002
rebel	**verb**	**11-08-011**
rebel	VB	3-03-003
rebels	VBZ	1-01-001
rebelled	VBD	2-02-002
rebelled	VBN	2-01-002
rebelling	VBG	3-03-003
rebellion	**noun**	**14-07-012**
rebellion	NN	13-07-011

Word	Tag	Frequency
rebellion (cont.):		
rebellions	NNS	1-01-001
rebellious	**JJ**	**2-02-002**
rebelliously	**RB**	**3-03-003**
rebirth	**noun**	**3-02-002**
rebirth	NN	1-01-001
re-birth	NN	0-00-000
Re-Birth	NN-TL	2-01-001
reborn	**JJ**	**3-03-003**
rebound	**NN**	**1-01-001**
rebound	**VB**	**1-01-001**
rebuff	**NN**	**4-03-004**
rebuff	**verb**	**4-04-004**
rebuffed	VBD	1-01-001
rebuffed	VBN	3-03-003
rebuild	**verb**	**15-10-012**
rebuild	VB	5-05-005
rebuilds	VBZ	1-01-001
rebuilt	VBN	4-03-003
rebuilding	VBG	5-05-005
rebuilding	**NN**	**1-01-001**
rebuke	**verb**	**3-03-003**
rebuke	VB	2-02-002
rebuked	VBD	1-01-001
rebut	**verb**	**8-03-003**
rebut	VB	6-02-002
rebutted	VBD	1-01-001
rebutted	VBN	1-01-001
rebuttal	**NN**	**2-01-001**
recalcitrant	**JJ**	**2-01-002**
recalculate	**verb**	**1-01-001**
recalculated	VBN	1-01-001
recalculation	**NN**	**1-01-001**
recall	**NN**	**4-04-004**
recall	**verb**	**78-13-066**
recall	VB	35-11-031
recalls	VBZ	12-08-012
recalled	VBD	19-09-019
recalled	VBN	7-06-007
recalling	VBG	5-04-005
recalling	**NN**	**2-01-002**
recant	**verb**	**1-01-001**
recanted	VBN	1-01-001
recapitulate	**VB**	**1-01-001**
recapitulation	**NN**	**2-02-002**
recapture	**verb**	**4-04-004**
recapture	VB	3-03-003
recaptured	VBN	1-01-001
recede	**verb**	**10-06-009**
recede	VB	3-03-003
receded	VBD	1-01-001
receded	VBN	1-01-001
receding	VBG	5-03-004
receipt	**noun**	**11-05-009**
receipt	NN	4-02-003
receipts	NNS	7-05-006
receive	**verb**	**294-15-169**
receive	VB	76-13-056
receave	VB	1-01-001
receives	VBZ	20-07-019
received	VBD	65-14-052
received	VBN	96-14-067
received	VBN-HL	2-02-002
receiving	VBG	34-12-032
receiver	**noun**	**18-06-012**
receiver	NN	13-05-010
receivers	NNS	5-03-003
recent	**adjective**	**179-13-120**
recent	JJ	178-13-119
recent	JJ-HL	1-01-001
recently	**RB**	**123-14-101**
recently-passed	**JJ**	**1-01-001**
receptacle	**NN**	**1-01-001**
reception	**noun**	**39-11-029**
reception	NN	34-10-027
reception	NN-HL	1-01-001
Reception	NN-TL	3-02-002
receptions	NNS	1-01-001
receptionist	**noun**	**6-02-002**
receptionist	NN	5-02-002
receptionist's	NN$	1-01-001
receptive	**JJ**	**2-02-002**
recess	**NN**	**1-01-001**
recess	**verb**	**3-03-003**
recess	VB	1-01-001
recessed	VBN	2-02-002
recession	**NN**	**7-03-006**
rechartering	**NN**	**1-01-001**
recheck	**VB**	**1-01-001**

Word	Tag	Frequency
recherche	**foreign**	**2-02-002**
recherche	FW-NN	0-00-000
Recherche	FW-NN-TL	1-01-001
recherches	FW-NNS	0-00-000
Recherches	FW-NNS-TL	1-01-001
recipe	**noun**	**9-05-007**
recipe	NN	8-04-006
recipes	NNS	1-01-001
recipient	**JJ**	**1-01-001**
recipient	**noun**	**11-04-009**
recipient	NN	6-04-006
recipients	NNS	5-03-004
reciprocal	**JJ**	**8-04-004**
reciprocate	**VB**	**1-01-001**
recit	**FW-NN**	**1-01-001**
recital	**noun**	**11-03-010**
recital	NN	6-03-006
Recital	NN-TL	2-01-001
recitals	NNS	3-03-003
recitation	**NN**	**3-03-003**
recitative	**NN**	**2-01-001**
recite	**verb**	**6-04-004**
recite	VB	2-02-002
recited	VBD	1-01-001
recited	VBN	1-01-001
reciting	VBG	2-02-002
reckless	**JJ**	**9-07-008**
recklessly	**RB**	**2-02-002**
recklessness	**NN**	**1-01-001**
reckon	**verb**	**13-06-011**
reckon	VB	7-04-006
reckons	VBZ	1-01-001
reckoned	VBD	0-00-000
recond	VBD	1-01-001
recooned	VBD	1-01-001
reckoned	VBN	3-02-003
reckoning	**noun**	**4-03-004**
reckoning	NN	3-02-003
reckonings	NNS	1-01-001
reclaim	**verb**	**4-04-004**
reclaim	VB	2-02-002
reclaimed	VBN	2-02-002
reclassification	**NN**	**1-01-001**
reclassify	**verb**	**2-01-001**
reclassified	VBD	1-01-001
reclassified	VBN	1-01-001
recline	**verb**	**3-03-003**
reclining	VBG	3-03-003
recluse	**NN**	**2-02-002**
recognition	**NN**	**44-09-033**
recognizable	**JJ**	**7-04-007**
recognize	**verb**	**163-15-116**
recognize	VB	62-12-047
recognizes	VBZ	10-05-010
recognized	VBD	30-11-023
recognised	VBD	1-01-001
recognized	VBN	50-08-041
recognizing	VBG	10-08-010
recoil	**NN**	**4-02-002**
recoil	**verb**	**2-02-002**
recoil	VB	1-01-001
recoiled	VBD	1-01-001
recoilless	**JJ**	**2-01-001**
recollect	**verb**	**2-02-002**
recollect	VB	1-01-001
recollected	VBD	1-01-001
recollection	**noun**	**8-04-006**
recollection	NN	5-03-004
recollections	NNS	3-03-003
recommence	**VB**	**1-01-001**
recommend	**verb**	**81-15-057**
recommend	VB	25-10-022
recommends	VBZ	2-02-002
recommended	VBD	17-07-012
recommended	VBN	29-10-023
recommending	VBG	8-05-007
recommendation	**noun**	**46-09-025**
recommendation	NN	24-09-011
recommendations	NNS	22-06-017
recompense	**noun**	**2-02-002**
recompense	NN	1-01-001
recompence	NN	1-01-001
reconcile	**verb**	**9-04-009**
reconcile	VB	4-02-004
reconciles	VBZ	1-01-001
reconciled	VBN	3-03-003
reconciling	VBG	1-01-001
reconciliation	**NN**	**1-01-001**
recondite	**JJ**	**1-01-001**
recondition	**verb**	**1-01-001**
reconditioning	VBG	1-01-001
reconnaissance	**noun**	**10-05-005**
reconnaissance	NN	9-04-004
reconnaissanace	NN	1-01-001
reconsider	**verb**	**8-05-006**
reconsider	VB	4-03-004
reconsidered	VBN	4-02-002
reconsideration	**NN**	**4-03-004**
reconstruct	**verb**	**10-03-008**
reconstruct	VB	6-03-006
reconstructs	VBZ	1-01-001
reconstructed	VBD	1-01-001
reconstructed	VBN	2-01-001
reconstruction	**noun**	**11-06-009**
reconstruction	NN	8-06-007
Reconstruction	NN-TL	3-02-002
recontamination	**NN**	**1-01-001**
reconvene	**verb**	**2-01-002**
reconvenes	VBZ	1-01-001
reconvened	VBN	1-01-001
reconvention	**NN**	**1-01-001**
reconvert	**verb**	**1-01-001**
reconverting	VBG	1-01-001
recopy	**verb**	**1-01-001**
recopied	VBN	1-01-001
record	**noun**	**214-15-113**
record	NN	124-14-075
Record	NN-TL	3-03-003
records	NNS	82-13-051
records	NNS-HL	2-02-002
Records	NNS-TL	3-03-003
record	**verb**	**74-12-051**
record	VB	11-05-010
records	VBZ	4-02-004
recorded	VBD	8-06-008
recorded	VBN	35-11-029
recording	VBG	15-06-011
Recording	VBG-TL	1-01-001
record-high	**JJ**	**1-01-001**
record-tying	**JJ**	**1-01-001**
recorder	**NN**	**7-05-005**
recording	**noun**	**26-08-013**
recording	NN	14-06-008
Recording	NN-TL	1-01-001
recordings	NNS	10-07-009
Recordings	NNS-TL	1-01-001
recount	**verb**	**10-07-009**
recount	VB	2-02-002
recounts	VBZ	3-02-003
recounted	VBD	2-02-002
recounting	VBG	3-03-003
recoup	**verb**	**1-01-001**
recouped	VBN	1-01-001
recourse	**NN**	**6-04-006**
recover	**verb**	**25-11-023**
recover	VB	11-06-010
recovers	VBZ	1-01-001
recovered	VBD	2-02-002
recovered	VBN	7-06-006
recovering	VBG	4-03-004
recoverable	**JJ**	**1-01-001**
recovery	**JJ**	**1-01-001**
recovery	**noun**	**28-08-017**
recovery	NN	26-08-016
Recovery	NN-TL	2-02-002
recreate	**verb**	**7-04-006**
recreate	VB	1-01-001
recreates	VBZ	1-01-001
re-creates	VBZ	1-01-001
recreated	VBN	1-01-001
re-created	VBN	2-02-002
recreating	VBG	1-01-001
recreation	**noun**	**43-07-015**
recreation	NN	36-07-013
recreation	NN-HL	1-01-001
Recreation	NN-TL	5-03-003
Recreation	NN-TL-HL	1-01-001
recreational	**JJ**	**8-04-006**
recrimination	**noun**	**4-04-004**
recrimination	NN	1-01-001
recriminations	NNS	3-03-003
recruit	**noun**	**9-06-007**
recruit	NN	1-01-001
recruits	NNS	8-06-006
recruit	**verb**	**17-07-010**
recruit	VB	9-03-003
recruited	VBD	1-01-001
recruited	VBN	3-02-003

Word	Tag	Frequency
recruit (cont.):		
recruiting	VBG	4-04-004
recruiter	**NN**	**1-01-001**
recruitment	**NN**	**7-02-002**
rectangle	**NN**	**4-02-003**
rectangular	**adjective**	**5-03-004**
rectangular	JJ	4-03-004
rectangular	JJ-HL	1-01-001
rectifier	**NN**	**3-02-002**
rectilinear	**JJ**	**1-01-001**
rectitude	**NN**	**1-01-001**
rectlinearly	**RB**	**1-01-001**
rector	**NN**	**7-02-002**
Rector	**prop. noun**	**29-02-002**
Rector	NP	26-02-002
Rector's	NP$	3-01-001
recumbent	**JJ**	**1-01-001**
recuperate	**verb**	**1-01-001**
recuperating	VBG	1-01-001
recur	**verb**	**11-02-009**
recur	VB	2-02-002
recurred	VBD	2-02-002
recurred	VBN	1-01-001
recurring	VBG	6-02-006
recurrence	**NN**	**1-01-001**
recurrent	**JJ**	**4-02-004**
recurrently	**RB**	**1-01-001**
recursive	**JJ**	**1-01-001**
recusant	**NN**	**1-01-001**
red	**adjective**	**169-15-093**
red	JJ	119-13-071
Red	JJ-TL	49-10-025
Red	JJ-TL-HL	1-01-001
red	**noun**	**11-06-009**
red	NN	6-04-006
Red	NN-TL	1-01-001
reds	NNS	2-02-002
Reds	NNS-TL	2-01-001
Red	**prop. noun**	**22-05-006**
Red	NP	21-05-006
Red's	NP$	1-01-001
red-and-yellow	**JJ**	**1-01-001**
red-bellied	**JJ**	**1-01-001**
red-blooded	**JJ**	**1-01-001**
red-clay	**NN**	**2-01-001**
red-faced	**JJ**	**1-01-001**
red-haired	**JJ**	**3-01-002**
red-light	**NN**	**2-01-001**
red-necked	**JJ**	**1-01-001**
Red-prone	**JJ**	**1-01-001**
red-rimmed	**JJ**	**1-01-001**
red-tailed	**JJ**	**1-01-001**
red-tile	**NN**	**1-01-001**
red-turbaned	**JJ**	**1-01-001**
red-visored	**JJ**	**1-01-001**
redaction	**noun**	**1-01-001**
redactions	NNS	1-01-001
redactor	**NN**	**2-01-001**
Redbird	**prop. noun**	**4-01-001**
Redbirds	NPS	3-01-001
Redbirds'	NPS$	1-01-001
redcoat	**noun**	**15-02-002**
redcoat	NN	6-01-001
redcoats	NNS	9-02-002
redden	**verb**	**1-01-001**
reddened	VBD	1-01-001
redder	**JJR**	**3-02-003**
Redding	**NP**	**1-01-001**
reddish	**JJ**	**3-03-003**
redecorate	**verb**	**5-03-004**
redecorated	VBN	2-01-001
redecorating	VBG	3-02-003
redecoration	**NN**	**2-01-001**
rededicate	**VB**	**1-01-001**
redeem	**verb**	**5-03-005**
redeem	VB	2-02-002
redeemed	VBN	1-01-001
redeeming	VBG	1-01-001
redeemin'	VBG	1-01-001
redefine	**verb**	**1-01-001**
redefined	VBD	1-01-001
redefinition	**NN**	**1-01-001**
redemption	**NN**	**4-02-004**
redemptive	**JJ**	**1-01-001**
redeposition	**NN**	**3-01-002**
redeveloper	**noun**	**1-01-001**
redevelopers	NNS	1-01-001
redevelopment	**noun**	**5-03-003**
redevelopment	NN	1-01-001
redevelopment (cont.):		
Redevelopment	NN-TL	4-02-002
redhead	**noun**	**8-03-004**
redhead	NN	7-03-004
redheads	NNS	1-01-001
redheaded	**JJ**	**1-01-001**
redheader	**NN**	**1-01-001**
Redhook	**NP**	**1-01-001**
redirect	**verb**	**2-02-002**
redirect	VB	1-01-001
redirecting	VBG	1-01-001
rediscover	**verb**	**2-02-002**
rediscover	VB	1-01-001
rediscovering	VBG	1-01-001
rediscovery	**NN**	**2-02-002**
redistribute	**verb**	**2-02-002**
redistributed	VBN	2-02-002
redistrict	**verb**	**1-01-001**
redistricting	VBG	1-01-001
redneck	**NN**	**1-01-001**
redo	**VB**	**1-01-001**
Redondo	**prop. noun**	**2-01-001**
Redondo	NP	0-00-000
Redondo	NP-TL	2-01-001
redouble	**verb**	**3-03-003**
redoubled	VBD	1-01-001
redoubled	VBN	2-02-002
redoute	**foreign**	**3-01-001**
redoute	FW-NN	0-00-000
Redoute	FW-NN-TL	3-01-001
redress	**NN**	**1-01-001**
redress	**verb**	**2-02-002**
redress	VB	1-01-001
redressed	VBN	1-01-001
Redstone	**NP**	**1-01-001**
reduce	**verb**	**179-12-097**
reduce	VB	62-08-044
reduces	VBZ	7-02-005
reduced	VBD	10-05-008
reduced	VBN	69-11-058
reducing	VBG	31-08-022
reducer	**noun**	**1-01-001**
reducer	NN	0-00-000
reducer	NN-HL	1-01-001
reduction	**noun**	**46-07-030**
reduction	NN	41-07-026
reduction	NN-HL	1-01-001
reductions	NNS	4-03-004
redundancy	**NN**	**4-03-004**
redundant	**adjective**	**4-03-003**
redundant	JJ	3-03-003
Redundant	JJ-TL	1-01-001
redwood	**noun**	**4-01-001**
redwood	NN	2-01-001
redwoods	NNS	2-01-001
Ree	**prop. noun**	**2-01-001**
Rees	NPS	2-01-001
Reed	**NP**	**5-05-005**
reedbuck	**NNS**	**1-01-001**
Reeder	**NP**	**1-01-001**
Reedville	**NP**	**1-01-001**
reedy	**JJ**	**2-02-002**
reef	**noun**	**12-01-002**
reef	NN	0-00-000
Reef	NN-TL	11-01-001
reefs	NNS	1-01-001
reek	**NN**	**1-01-001**
reek	**verb**	**3-03-003**
reek	VB	1-01-001
reeked	VBD	1-01-001
reeking	VBG	1-01-001
reel	**noun**	**3-02-002**
reel	NN	2-01-001
reels	NNS	0-00-000
Reels	NNS-TL	1-01-001
reel	**verb**	**3-01-002**
reeled	VBD	2-01-001
reeling	VBG	1-01-001
reemerge	**verb**	**2-01-001**
reemerged	VBD	1-01-001
re-emerged	VBD	1-01-001
reenact	**verb**	**4-03-003**
reenact	VB	2-02-002
reenacted	VBN	0-00-000
re-enacted	VBN	1-01-001
reenacting	VBG	0-00-000
re-enacting	VBG	1-01-001
Reese	**NP**	**3-01-001**
reestablish	**verb**	**2-02-002**

Word	Tag	Frequency
reestablish (cont.):		
reestablish	VB	1-01-001
re-establish	VB	1-01-001
reevaluation	**noun**	**2-02-002**
reevaluation	NN	1-01-001
re-evaluation	NN	1-01-001
Reeves-type	**JJ**	**1-01-001**
reexamination	**NN**	**1-01-001**
refashion	**VB**	**1-01-001**
refectory	**noun**	**1-01-001**
refectories	NNS	1-01-001
refer	**verb**	**109-15-072**
refer	VB	27-09-024
refers	VBZ	18-06-016
referred	VBD	14-07-013
referred	VBN	31-10-024
referring	VBG	18-06-015
referrin'	VBG	1-01-001
referee	**NN**	**1-01-001**
reference	**noun**	**87-14-049**
reference	NN	67-13-043
ref.	NN	0-00-000
Ref.	NN-TL	4-01-001
references	NNS	16-07-010
reference-point	**noun**	**1-01-001**
reference-points	NNS	1-01-001
referendum	**NN**	**1-01-001**
referent	**NN**	**1-01-001**
referral	**noun**	**14-01-002**
referral	NN	6-01-002
referrals	NNS	8-01-001
refill	**verb**	**4-02-002**
refill	VB	3-01-001
refilled	VBN	1-01-001
refinance	**VB**	**1-01-001**
refine	**verb**	**11-05-011**
refine	VB	3-02-003
refined	VBN	6-04-006
refining	VBG	2-01-002
refinement	**noun**	**10-06-010**
refinement	NN	5-05-005
refinements	NNS	5-05-005
reflect	**verb**	**107-14-077**
reflect	VB	25-08-021
reflects	VBZ	23-07-020
reflected	VBD	13-06-010
reflected	VBN	29-09-022
reflecting	VBG	17-10-015
reflectance	**NN**	**1-01-001**
reflectance-measuring	**JJ**	**1-01-001**
reflection	**noun**	**39-10-027**
reflection	NN	32-10-023
reflections	NNS	6-04-005
Reflections	NNS-TL	1-01-001
reflective	**JJ**	**6-04-006**
reflector	**noun**	**8-02-002**
reflector	NN	5-02-002
reflectors	NNS	3-01-001
reflex	**noun**	**10-05-007**
reflex	NN	4-03-004
reflexes	NNS	6-03-004
reflexly	**RB**	**2-01-001**
refocusing	**NN**	**1-01-001**
refold	**verb**	**1-01-001**
refolded	VBD	1-01-001
reform	**noun**	**41-07-020**
reform	NN	23-07-014
reform	NN-HL	1-01-001
Reform	NN-TL	3-01-001
reforms	NNS	14-06-012
reform	**verb**	**7-05-006**
reform	VB	3-03-003
reformed	VBN	0-00-000
Reformed	VBN-TL	3-01-002
reforming	VBG	1-01-001
reformation	**noun**	**5-01-004**
reformation	NN	3-01-003
Reformation	NN-TL	2-01-002
reformatory	**NN**	**2-02-002**
reformer	**noun**	**5-03-004**
reformer	NN	3-03-003
reformers	NNS	2-01-001
reformism	**NN**	**1-01-001**
reformulate	**verb**	**1-01-001**
reformulated	VBN	1-01-001
refract	**verb**	**1-01-001**
refracted	VBN	1-01-001
refraction	**NN**	**1-01-001**
refractive	**JJ**	**1-01-001**

Word	Tag	Frequency
refractory	**JJ**	**1-01-001**
refrain	**NN**	**4-01-003**
refrain	**verb**	**7-05-006**
refrain	VB	6-04-005
refrained	VBD	1-01-001
refresh	**verb**	**7-05-006**
refresh	VB	1-01-001
refreshed	VBD	1-01-001
refreshed	VBN	3-03-003
refreshed	VBN-NC	1-01-001
refreshing	VBG	1-01-001
refresher	**NN**	**1-01-001**
refreshing	**JJ**	**5-03-005**
refreshingly	**QL**	**1-01-001**
refreshingly	**RB**	**1-01-001**
refreshment	**noun**	**4-03-003**
refreshment	NN	2-02-002
refreshments	NNS	2-02-002
refrigerate	**verb**	**5-02-002**
refrigerated	VBN	5-02-002
refrigeration	**NN**	**13-03-005**
refrigerator	**noun**	**25-07-009**
refrigerator	NN	23-07-009
refrigerators	NNS	2-02-002
refuel	**verb**	**4-03-004**
refuel	VB	2-02-002
refueling	VBG	2-02-002
refuge	**NN**	**7-05-007**
refugee	**noun**	**14-05-009**
refugee	NN	7-03-004
refugees	NNS	7-04-006
refund	**noun**	**24-02-002**
refund	NN	19-02-002
refund	NN-HL	2-02-002
Refund	NN-TL	1-01-001
refunds	NNS	1-01-001
refunds	NNS-HL	1-01-001
refund	**verb**	**1-01-001**
refunded	VBN	1-01-001
refurbish	**verb**	**2-01-001**
refurbished	VBN	2-01-001
refurbishing	**NN**	**1-01-001**
refusal	**NN**	**15-09-014**
refuse	**NN**	**1-01-001**
refuse	**verb**	**91-15-069**
refuse	VB	15-07-015
refuses	VBZ	5-04-005
refuses	VBZ-HL	1-01-001
refused	VBD	44-12-035
refused	VBN	16-08-015
refusing	VBG	10-08-009
refuse-littered	**JJ**	**1-01-001**
refute	**verb**	**4-03-003**
refute	VB	1-01-001
refuted	VBD	2-02-002
refuted	VBN	0-00-000
refuted	VBN-HL	1-01-001
regain	**verb**	**9-04-009**
regain	VB	1-01-001
regains	VBZ	1-01-001
regained	VBD	3-01-003
regained	VBN	1-01-001
regaining	VBG	3-03-003
regal	**JJ**	**2-02-002**
regale	**verb**	**1-01-001**
regaled	VBD	1-01-001
regalia	**NNS**	**1-01-001**
regard	**noun**	**55-11-042**
regard	NN	53-10-040
regards	NNS	2-02-002
regard	**verb**	**100-15-076**
regard	VB	36-11-030
regards	VBZ	5-03-005
regarded	VBD	12-08-012
regarded	VBN	44-10-036
regarding	VBG	3-03-003
regarding	**IN**	**37-11-030**
regardless	**RB**	**38-10-032**
regatta	**noun**	**1-01-001**
regattas	NNS	1-01-001
regency	**noun**	**1-01-001**
regency	NN	0-00-000
Regency	NN-TL	1-01-001
regenerate	**verb**	**2-02-002**
regenerates	VBZ	1-01-001
regenerating	VBG	1-01-001
regeneration	**NN**	**1-01-001**
regent	**noun**	**2-02-002**
regents	NNS	2-02-002

Word	Tag	Frequency
regi	**FW-NN**	**1-01-001**
regime	**noun**	**25-08-019**
regime	NN	23-07-018
regimes	NNS	2-01-001
regimen	**NN**	**1-01-001**
regiment	**noun**	**28-06-009**
regiment	NN	21-05-007
Regiment	NN-TL	4-03-003
regiment's	NN$	1-01-001
regiments	NNS	2-02-002
regiment	**verb**	**1-01-001**
regimented	VBN	1-01-001
regimentation	**NN**	**1-01-001**
Regina	**NP**	**1-01-001**
Reginald	**NP**	**1-01-001**
region	**noun**	**119-11-061**
region	NN	71-11-047
Region	NN-TL	5-01-002
region's	NN$	3-02-003
regions	NNS	35-08-023
Regions	NNS-TL	5-02-002
regional	**adjective**	**42-07-023**
regional	JJ	38-07-022
Regional	JJ-TL	4-02-002
regionalism	**noun**	**1-01-001**
regionalism	NN	0-00-000
Regionalism	NN-TL	1-01-001
regionally	**RB**	**1-01-001**
register	**noun**	**22-10-014**
register	NN	11-10-010
Register	NN-TL	7-03-003
registers	NNS	4-02-002
register	**verb**	**36-14-031**
register	VB	8-07-008
registers	VBZ	1-01-001
registered	VBD	7-05-006
registered	VBN	16-08-014
registering	VBG	4-04-004
registrant	**noun**	**8-01-003**
registrant	NN	4-01-001
registrant's	NN$	2-01-001
registrants	NNS	1-01-001
registrants'	NNS$	1-01-001
registrar	**NN**	**1-01-001**
registration	**noun**	**25-06-010**
registration	NN	23-06-009
registrations	NNS	2-02-002
registry	**noun**	**11-03-004**
registry	NN	2-02-002
Registry	NN-TL	4-01-002
Registry	NN-TL-HL	1-01-001
registries	NNS	4-01-001
Regius	**prop. noun**	**2-02-002**
Regius	NP	0-00-000
Regius	NP-TL	2-02-002
regression	**NN**	**7-01-003**
regret	**noun**	**4-04-004**
regret	NN	3-03-003
regrets	NNS	1-01-001
regret	**verb**	**19-10-018**
regret	VB	6-05-006
regrets	VBZ	1-01-001
regrets	VBZ-HL	1-01-001
regretted	VBD	7-04-007
regretted	VBN	4-03-004
regretfully	**RB**	**1-01-001**
regrettable	**JJ**	**1-01-001**
regrettably	**QL**	**1-01-001**
regrettably	**RB**	**1-01-001**
regrind	**verb**	**1-01-001**
reground	VBN	1-01-001
regroup	**verb**	**1-01-001**
regrouped	VBD	1-01-001
regrouping	**NN**	**1-01-001**
regular	**adjective**	**83-15-063**
regular	JJ	79-15-061
Regular	JJ-TL	4-02-002
regular	**noun**	**6-04-005**
regulars	NNS	6-04-005
regular-featured	**JJ**	**1-01-001**
regularity	**NN**	**2-02-002**
regularly	**adverb**	**22-10-021**
regularly	RB	21-10-020
regularly	RB-HL	1-01-001
regulate	**verb**	**13-06-010**
regulate	VB	2-02-002
regulated	VBD	2-02-002
regulated	VBN	5-04-004
regulating	VBG	4-03-003
regulation	**noun**	**43-09-025**
regulation	NN	8-04-007
Regulation	NN-TL	6-01-001
regulations	NNS	28-07-020
Regulations	NNS-TL	1-01-001
regulative	**JJ**	**2-01-001**
regulator	**NN**	**1-01-001**
regulatory	**JJ**	**5-04-004**
regulus	**noun**	**10-01-001**
regulus	NN	9-01-001
reguli	NNS	1-01-001
Regulus	**prop. noun**	**1-01-001**
Regulus	NP	0-00-000
Regulus	NP-TL	1-01-001
rehabilitate	**verb**	**1-01-001**
rehabilitating	VBG	1-01-001
rehabilitation	**noun**	**23-05-009**
rehabilitation	NN	20-04-008
Rehabilitation	NN-TL	2-01-001
rehabilitations	NNS	1-01-001
reharmonization	**NN**	**1-01-001**
rehash	**NN**	**1-01-001**
rehash	**VB**	**1-01-001**
rehear	**verb**	**1-01-001**
rehearing	VBG	1-01-001
rehearsal	**noun**	**8-06-006**
rehearsal	NN	4-04-004
rehearsals	NNS	4-02-002
rehearse	**verb**	**9-05-006**
rehearse	VB	1-01-001
rehearsed	VBN	7-04-004
rehearsing	VBG	1-01-001
Reich	**prop. noun**	**6-02-003**
Reich	NP	5-02-003
Reich	NP-TL	1-01-001
Reichenberg	**NP**	**2-01-001**
Reichstag	**NP**	**1-01-001**
Reid	**NP**	**3-02-002**
Reifenrath	**NP**	**1-01-001**
reign	**NN**	**6-04-005**
reign	**verb**	**6-04-006**
reign	VB	1-01-001
reigns	VBZ	1-01-001
reigned	VBD	1-01-001
reigning	VBG	3-03-003
Reik	**NP**	**1-01-001**
Reilly	**NP**	**1-01-001**
Reily	**prop. noun**	**1-01-001**
Reily's	NP$	1-01-001
reimbursable	**adjective**	**2-01-001**
reimburseable	JJ	0-00-000
reimburseable	JJ	2-01-001
reimburse	**verb**	**3-01-003**
reimburse	VB	1-01-001
reimburses	VBZ	1-01-001
reimbursed	VBN	1-01-001
reimbursement	**noun**	**4-01-002**
reimbursement	NN	2-01-002
reimbursements	NNS	2-01-001
rein	**noun**	**12-06-011**
rein	NN	3-03-003
reins	NNS	9-04-008
rein	**verb**	**3-02-002**
reined	VBD	3-02-002
reincarnate	**verb**	**1-01-001**
reincarnated	VBD	1-01-001
reine	**foreign**	**2-02-002**
reine	FW-NN	0-00-000
Reine	FW-NN-TL	2-02-002
reinforce	**verb**	**22-08-015**
reinforce	VB	10-05-007
reinforces	VBZ	3-02-003
reinforced	VBD	1-01-001
reinforced	VBN	6-04-005
reinforcing	VBG	2-02-002
reinforcement	**noun**	**5-03-003**
reinforcement	NN	2-02-002
reinforcements	NNS	3-01-001
Reinhard	**prop. noun**	**2-01-001**
Reinhard	NP	0-00-000
Reinhard	NP-TL	2-01-001
Reinhardt	**NP**	**2-01-001**
reinstall	**VB**	**1-01-001**
reinstate	**verb**	**1-01-001**
reinstated	VBN	1-01-001
reinstitution	**NN**	**1-01-001**
reinterpret	**verb**	**2-01-001**
reinterpret	VB	1-01-001
reinterpreted	VBN	1-01-001

Word	Tag	Frequency
reintroduce	**verb**	**1-01-001**
reintroduces	VBZ	1-01-001
reinvestigation	**NN**	**1-01-001**
reinvigoration	**NN**	**1-01-001**
reipublicae	**FW-NN**	**1-01-001**
Reiss	**NP**	**1-01-001**
reissue	**NN**	**2-01-001**
reiterate	**verb**	**5-03-005**
reiterate	VB	1-01-001
reiterates	VBZ	1-01-001
reiterated	VBN	2-02-002
reiterating	VBG	1-01-001
reject	**verb**	**58-12-047**
reject	VB	10-06-009
rejects	VBZ	11-05-009
rejected	VBD	12-06-012
rejected	VBN	21-10-020
rejecting	VBG	4-03-004
rejection	**noun**	**12-05-011**
rejection	NN	11-05-010
rejections	NNS	1-01-001
rejoice	**verb**	**6-06-006**
rejoice	VB	1-01-001
rejoices	VBZ	1-01-001
rejoiced	VBD	1-01-001
rejoicing	VBG	3-03-003
rejoicing	**NN**	**1-01-001**
rejoin	**verb**	**3-02-003**
rejoin	VB	2-02-002
rejoining	VBG	1-01-001
rejoinder	**NN**	**1-01-001**
rekindling	**NN**	**1-01-001**
relate	**verb**	**137-10-088**
relate	VB	7-03-007
relates	VBZ	8-04-008
related	VBD	9-05-008
related	VBN	92-09-064
related	VBN-HL	1-01-001
relating	VBG	20-06-014
relatedness	**NN**	**1-01-001**
relation	**noun**	**165-11-100**
relation	NN	62-08-042
relation	NN-HL	1-01-001
relations	NNS	92-11-059
relations	NNS-HL	1-01-001
Relations	NNS-TL	9-04-008
relational	**JJ**	**1-01-001**
relationship	**noun**	**126-14-082**
relationship	NN	87-14-062
relationship	NN-HL	1-01-001
relationships	NNS	37-09-028
relationships	NNS-HL	1-01-001
relationship-building	**JJ**	**1-01-001**
relative	**JJ**	**45-09-037**
relative	**noun**	**23-08-018**
relative	NN	1-01-001
relatives	NNS	20-08-017
relatives	NNS-NC	2-01-001
relatively	**QL**	**76-09-061**
relatively	**RB**	**9-06-009**
relativism	**NN**	**2-01-002**
relativist	**NN**	**1-01-001**
relativistic	**JJ**	**3-03-003**
relativity	**NN**	**3-03-003**
relax	**verb**	**41-11-029**
relax	VB	19-08-013
relaxes	VBZ	3-03-003
relaxed	VBD	6-03-006
relaxed	VBN	8-06-008
relaxing	VBG	5-05-005
relaxation	**NN**	**7-04-006**
relay	**NN**	**2-02-002**
relay	**verb**	**3-02-002**
relayed	VBN	2-01-001
relaying	VBG	1-01-001
relearn	**verb**	**1-01-001**
relearns	VBZ	1-01-001
release	**noun**	**34-12-023**
release	NN	27-09-019
Release	NN-TL	1-01-001
releases	NNS	6-05-005
release	**verb**	**39-13-033**
release	VB	9-06-007
releases	VBZ	2-02-002
released	VBD	7-04-006
released	VBN	19-09-016
releasing	VBG	2-02-002
relegate	**verb**	**6-06-006**
relegated	VBD	1-01-001
relegate (cont.):		
relegated	VBN	5-05-005
relent	**verb**	**3-03-003**
relented	VBD	1-01-001
relented	VBN	2-02-002
relentless	**JJ**	**5-05-005**
relentlessly	**QL**	**1-01-001**
relentlessly	**RB**	**4-04-004**
relentlessness	**NN**	**2-02-002**
relevance	**NN**	**10-03-007**
relevancy	**NN**	**2-02-002**
relevant	**JJ**	**23-06-020**
reliability	**NN**	**2-02-002**
reliable	**JJ**	**22-06-020**
reliably	**RB**	**1-01-001**
reliance	**NN**	**7-03-007**
relic	**NN**	**6-05-005**
relict	**NN**	**1-01-001**
relief	**NN**	**66-15-052**
relieve	**verb**	**40-12-033**
relieve	VB	13-09-012
relieves	VBZ	2-02-002
relieved	VBD	3-02-003
relieved	VBN	21-08-018
relieving	VBG	1-01-001
religion	**noun**	**137-14-049**
religion	NN	116-14-044
religion	NN-HL	1-01-001
Religion	NN-TL	2-01-001
religions	NNS	18-07-008
religionist	**noun**	**1-01-001**
religionists	NNS	1-01-001
religiosity	**NN**	**1-01-001**
religious	**adjective**	**165-12-061**
religious	JJ	161-12-060
religious	JJ-HL	1-01-001
Religious	JJ-TL	3-02-002
religiously	**RB**	**4-02-003**
religiousness	**NN**	**1-01-001**
relinquish	**verb**	**13-07-010**
relinquish	VB	6-04-005
relinquished	VBD	3-03-003
relinquished	VBN	1-01-001
relinquishing	VBG	3-02-003
relinquishing	**NN**	**1-01-001**
relish	**noun**	**7-03-005**
relish	NN	5-03-005
relishes	NNS	2-01-001
relish	**verb**	**4-03-004**
relish	VB	3-02-003
relishing	VBG	1-01-001
relive	**verb**	**4-02-004**
relive	VB	2-02-002
relives	VBZ	1-01-001
reliving	VBG	1-01-001
reliving	**noun**	**2-02-002**
reliving	NN	1-01-001
re-living	NN	1-01-001
reload	**verb**	**2-02-002**
reloaded	VBD	1-01-001
reloaded	VBN	1-01-001
relocation	**NN**	**1-01-001**
reluctance	**NN**	**5-03-005**
reluctant	**JJ**	**15-09-014**
reluctantly	**RB**	**7-05-007**
rely	**verb**	**30-11-029**
rely	VB	13-09-013
relies	VBZ	4-03-004
relied	VBD	2-01-002
relied	VBN	6-04-006
relying	VBG	5-03-005
relyric	**verb**	**1-01-001**
relyriced	VBD	1-01-001
remain	**verb**	**314-15-210**
remain	VB	92-15-073
remain	VB-HL	1-01-001
remains	VBZ	72-11-069
remains	VBZ-HL	2-02-002
remained	VBD	84-15-070
remained	VBN	22-10-021
remaining	VBG	41-11-035
remainder	**NN**	**19-10-019**
remains	**NNS**	**10-07-008**
remake	**verb**	**3-03-003**
remake	VB	2-02-002
remaking	VBG	0-00-000
remaking	VBG-HL	1-01-001
remand	**verb**	**3-02-002**
remanded	VBD	1-01-001

Word	Tag	Frequency
remand (cont.):		
remanded	VBN	1-01-001
remanding	VBG	1-01-001
remark	**noun**	**75-13-048**
remark	NN	29-09-017
remarks	NNS	41-12-033
remarks	NNS-HL	5-02-002
remark	**verb**	**43-12-033**
remark	VB	2-01-002
remarks	VBZ	7-05-007
remarked	VBD	25-10-019
remarked	VBN	7-03-007
remarking	VBG	2-02-002
remarkable	**adjective**	**47-11-040**
remarkable	JJ	46-11-040
remarkable	JJ-HL	1-01-001
remarkably	**QL**	**9-05-008**
remarkably	**RB**	**9-05-008**
Remarque	**prop. noun**	**9-01-001**
Remarque	NP	3-01-001
Remarque's	NP$	6-01-001
remarry	**verb**	**4-03-003**
remarry	VB	1-01-001
remarried	VBD	1-01-001
remarried	VBN	1-01-001
remarrying	VBG	1-01-001
Rembrandt	**prop. noun**	**3-03-003**
Rembrandt	NP	1-01-001
Rembrandt's	NP$	2-02-002
remedial	**JJ**	**1-01-001**
remedy	**noun**	**16-05-012**
remedy	NN	10-02-007
remedies	NNS	6-04-006
remedy	**VB**	**3-03-003**
remember	**verb**	**250-15-154**
remember	VB	138-15-099
remembers	VBZ	13-05-011
remembered	VBD	52-08-039
remembered	VBN	31-12-028
remembering	VBG	16-09-014
remembering	**NN**	**1-01-001**
remembrance	**noun**	**3-02-003**
remembrance	NN	2-01-002
remembrances	NNS	1-01-001
remind	**verb**	**57-13-047**
remind	VB	15-08-013
reminds	VBZ	8-04-007
reminded	VBD	19-06-016
reminded	VBN	10-07-010
reminding	VBG	5-04-004
reminder	**noun**	**10-07-010**
reminder	NN	8-07-008
reminders	NNS	2-02-002
Remington	**NP**	**5-01-001**
reminisce	**verb**	**3-03-003**
reminisces	VBZ	1-01-001
reminisced	VBD	1-01-001
reminiscing	VBG	1-01-001
reminiscence	**noun**	**3-03-003**
reminiscence	NN	2-02-002
reminiscences	NNS	1-01-001
reminiscent	**JJ**	**4-03-004**
remission	**noun**	**1-01-001**
remissions	NNS	1-01-001
remit	**verb**	**1-01-001**
remitted	VBN	1-01-001
remnant	**noun**	**4-04-004**
remnant	NN	2-02-002
remnants	NNS	2-02-002
remodel	**verb**	**3-03-003**
remodeled	VBD	1-01-001
remodeling	VBG	2-02-002
remold	**verb**	**1-01-001**
remolding	VBG	1-01-001
remonstrate	**verb**	**3-03-003**
remonstrate	VB	1-01-001
remonstrated	VBD	2-02-002
remorse	**NN**	**1-01-001**
remorseful	**JJ**	**1-01-001**
remorseless	**JJ**	**2-02-002**
remote	**JJ**	**32-11-026**
remotely	**RB**	**4-04-004**
remoteness	**NN**	**2-02-002**
remoter	**JJR**	**1-01-001**
remotest	**JJT**	**1-01-001**
remount	**verb**	**1-01-001**
remounting	VBG	1-01-001
removable	**JJ**	**1-01-001**
removal	**NN**	**41-08-019**

Word	Tag	Frequency
remove	**verb**	**146-15-100**
remove	VB	58-11-042
removes	VBZ	5-02-004
removed	VBD	11-08-010
removed	VBN	64-14-050
removing	VBG	8-06-008
Remphan	**NP**	**1-01-001**
remuda	**NN**	**1-01-001**
remuneration	**NN**	**2-02-002**
remunerative	**JJ**	**1-01-001**
Remus	**NP**	**1-01-001**
Remy	**NP**	**1-01-001**
Rena	**NP**	**1-01-001**
renaissance	**noun**	**15-07-011**
renaissance	NN	5-02-004
renaissance	NN-HL	1-01-001
Renaissance	NN-TL	9-05-006
renal	**JJ**	**1-01-001**
rename	**verb**	**3-02-003**
renamed	VBN	3-02-003
renaturation	**NN**	**1-01-001**
Renault	**prop. noun**	**1-01-001**
Renaults	NPS	1-01-001
rend	**VB**	**1-01-001**
render	**verb**	**47-11-034**
render	VB	11-06-009
renders	VBZ	2-01-002
rendered	VBD	5-04-005
rendered	VBN	23-07-016
rendering	VBG	6-05-005
rendering	**noun**	**6-06-006**
rendering	NN	5-05-005
renderings	NNS	1-01-001
rendezvous	**NN**	**7-05-006**
rendition	**noun**	**4-03-003**
rendition	NN	1-01-001
renditions	NNS	3-02-002
renew	**verb**	**23-12-020**
renew	VB	4-04-004
renews	VBZ	1-01-001
renewed	VBD	3-03-003
renewed	VBN	14-09-012
renewing	VBG	1-01-001
renewable	**JJ**	**1-01-001**
renewal	**noun**	**8-04-007**
renewal	NN	7-04-007
renewal	NN-NC	1-01-001
Renfrew	**NP**	**1-01-001**
Renfro	**NP**	**1-01-001**
Rennell	**prop. noun**	**1-01-001**
Rennell	NP	0-00-000
Rennell	NP-TL	1-01-001
Reno	**NP**	**8-03-004**
Renoir	**NP**	**3-03-003**
renounce	**verb**	**1-01-001**
renouncing	VBG	1-01-001
renovate	**verb**	**3-02-003**
renovated	VBN	3-02-003
renovation	**NN**	**2-02-002**
Renovo	**NP**	**1-01-001**
renown	**NN**	**1-01-001**
renowned	**JJ**	**2-02-002**
Rensselaer	**NP**	**2-02-002**
Rensselaerwyck	**NP**	**1-01-001**
rent	**noun**	**12-08-011**
rent	NN	8-05-008
rents	NNS	3-03-003
rents	NNS-HL	1-01-001
rent	**verb**	**25-08-014**
rent	VB	12-05-005
rented	VBN	7-05-006
rent	VBN	1-01-001
renting	VBG	5-03-004
rental	**JJ**	**7-03-003**
rental	**noun**	**10-06-008**
rental	NN	7-05-006
Rental	NN-TL	1-01-001
rentals	NNS	2-02-002
renunciation	**noun**	**2-02-002**
renunciation	NN	1-01-001
renunciations	NNS	1-01-001
Renville	**NP**	**1-01-001**
reopen	**verb**	**3-03-003**
reopen	VB	1-01-001
reopened	VBN	1-01-001
reopening	VBG	1-01-001
reorder	**VB**	**1-01-001**
reorganization	**noun**	**29-04-006**
reorganization	NN	26-04-005

Word	Tag	Frequency
reorganization (cont.):		
Reorganization	NN-TL	1-01-001
reorganizations	NNS	2-01-001
reorganize	**verb**	**6-05-006**
reorganize	VB	1-01-001
reorganized	VBN	4-03-004
reorganizing	VBG	1-01-001
reorient	**verb**	**1-01-001**
reoriented	VBN	1-01-001
reorientation	**NN**	**2-01-002**
rep	**noun**	**1-01-001**
reps	NNS	1-01-001
repaint	**verb**	**1-01-001**
repainting	VBG	1-01-001
repainting	**NN**	**1-01-001**
repair	**noun**	**23-12-018**
repair	NN	15-10-014
repairs	NNS	8-06-007
repair	**verb**	**17-06-013**
repair	VB	5-04-005
repaired	VBD	2-01-002
repaired	VBN	9-05-006
repairing	VBG	1-01-001
repairing	**NN**	**1-01-001**
repairman	**noun**	**2-02-002**
repairmen	NNS	2-02-002
reparation	**NN**	**1-01-001**
repartee	**NN**	**1-01-001**
repay	**verb**	**10-06-007**
repay	VB	7-06-006
repaid	VBN	3-02-002
repayable	**JJ**	**2-02-002**
repayment	**noun**	**3-01-002**
repayment	NN	2-01-002
repayment	NN-HL	1-01-001
repeal	**noun**	**7-02-003**
repeal	NN	6-02-003
repeal	NN-HL	1-01-001
repeal	**verb**	**3-03-003**
repealed	VBN	3-03-003
repeat	**NN**	**3-02-003**
repeat	**verb**	**95-15-075**
repeat	VB	23-12-020
repeats	VBZ	4-03-004
repeated	VBD	18-09-017
repeated	VBN	39-12-032
repeated	VBN-HL	2-02-002
repeating	VBG	9-06-009
repeatedly	**RB**	**18-10-018**
repeater	**NN**	**1-01-001**
repel	**verb**	**14-06-011**
repel	VB	8-05-007
repels	VBZ	1-01-001
repelled	VBN	5-04-005
repellent	**NN**	**1-01-001**
repent	**VB**	**3-03-003**
repentance	**NN**	**2-02-002**
repentant	**JJ**	**1-01-001**
repercussion	**noun**	**1-01-001**
repercussions	NNS	1-01-001
repertoire	**NN**	**2-02-002**
repertory	**noun**	**5-04-005**
repertory	NN	4-03-004
Repertory	NN-TL	1-01-001
repetition	**noun**	**16-10-014**
repetition	NN	13-10-013
repetitions	NNS	3-01-001
repetitious	**JJ**	**2-02-002**
repetitive	**JJ**	**1-01-001**
rephrase	**verb**	**1-01-001**
rephrased	VBN	1-01-001
replace	**verb**	**87-13-067**
replace	VB	30-07-027
replaces	VBZ	6-02-005
replaced	VBD	12-07-012
replaced	VBN	30-09-024
replacing	VBG	9-05-009
replacement	**noun**	**23-09-018**
replacement	NN	20-09-016
replacement	NN-HL	1-01-001
replacements	NNS	2-02-002
replant	**verb**	**1-01-001**
replanted	VBN	1-01-001
replenish	**verb**	**6-04-005**
replenish	VB	4-02-003
replenished	VBD	2-02-002
replenishment	**NN**	**1-01-001**
replete	**JJ**	**1-01-001**
replica	**NN**	**1-01-001**
replication	**NN**	**1-01-001**
reply	**noun**	**35-11-026**
reply	NN	24-09-021
reply	NN-HL	4-01-001
replies	NNS	7-05-006
reply	**verb**	**75-14-051**
reply	VB	14-08-012
replies	VBZ	2-02-002
replies	VBZ-HL	1-01-001
replied	VBD	55-13-036
replied	VBN	2-02-002
replying	VBG	1-01-001
Repnin	**NP**	**2-01-001**
report	**noun**	**205-14-099**
report	NN	114-12-052
report	NN-HL	2-02-002
Report	NN-TL	19-04-007
reports	NNS	69-13-052
Reports	NNS-TL	1-01-001
report	**verb**	**184-14-112**
report	VB	37-12-033
report	VB-HL	2-01-002
reports	VBZ	13-08-012
reports	VBZ-HL	1-01-001
reported	VBD	51-12-040
reported	VBN	67-11-048
reported	VBN-HL	1-01-001
reporting	VBG	12-07-012
reportage	**NN**	**1-01-001**
reportedly	**RB**	**9-06-009**
reporter	**noun**	**54-10-024**
reporter	NN	19-08-010
Reporter	NN-TL	1-01-001
reporters	NNS	34-09-019
reporting	**NN**	**5-03-005**
reportorial	**JJ**	**1-01-001**
repose	**NN**	**2-02-002**
repose	**verb**	**1-01-001**
reposed	VBN	1-01-001
repository	**noun**	**5-05-005**
repository	NN	4-04-004
repositories	NNS	1-01-001
reprehensible	**JJ**	**2-02-002**
represent	**verb**	**163-14-107**
represent	VB	38-10-031
represents	VBZ	39-08-029
represented	VBD	15-08-012
represented	VBN	41-09-031
representing	VBG	30-07-025
representation	**noun**	**28-06-017**
representation	NN	18-05-011
representations	NNS	10-04-006
representational	**NN**	**2-01-001**
representative	**adjective**	**18-08-017**
representative	JJ	17-08-016
Representative	JJ-TL	1-01-001
representative	**noun**	**85-09-051**
representative	NN	23-08-022
rep.	NN	0-00-000
Rep.	NN-TL	13-02-004
Representative	NN-TL	6-04-005
representatives	NNS	28-07-022
reps.	NNS	0-00-000
Reps.	NNS-TL	2-01-002
Representatives	NNS-TL	13-04-008
repress	**verb**	**4-03-003**
repress	VB	1-01-001
repressed	VBN	3-03-003
repression	**noun**	**7-04-007**
repression	NN	6-03-006
repressions	NNS	1-01-001
repressive	**JJ**	**2-02-002**
reprieve	**NN**	**2-02-002**
reprimand	**verb**	**2-02-002**
reprimanded	VBN	2-02-002
reprint	**noun**	**3-03-003**
reprints	NNS	3-03-003
reprint	**verb**	**2-02-002**
reprinted	VBD	1-01-001
reprinted	VBN	1-01-001
reprisal	**noun**	**5-04-004**
reprisal	NN	3-03-003
reprisals	NNS	2-02-002
reproach	**NN**	**2-02-002**
reproach	**verb**	**2-02-002**
reproach	VB	1-01-001
reproaches	VBZ	1-01-001
reprobate	**NN**	**1-01-001**
reprobate	**verb**	**1-01-001**

reprobate (cont.):		
reprobating	VBG	1-01-001
reproduce	**verb**	**19-11-017**
reproduce	VB	7-06-007
reproduces	VBZ	3-03-003
reproduced	VBN	7-05-007
reproducing	VBG	2-02-002
reproducibility	**noun**	**2-02-002**
reproducibility	NN	1-01-001
reproducibilities	NNS	1-01-001
reproducible	**JJ**	**5-02-003**
reproducibly	**RB**	**1-01-001**
reproduction	**noun**	**8-04-006**
reproduction	NN	6-03-004
reproductions	NNS	2-01-002
reproductive	**JJ**	**1-01-001**
reproof	**NN**	**1-01-001**
reprovingly	**RB**	**1-01-001**
republic	**noun**	**49-11-030**
republic	NN	7-05-007
republic	NN-NC	1-01-001
Republic	NN-TL	35-11-020
republics	NNS	2-01-002
Republics	NNS-TL	4-02-003
Republican	**adjective**	**13-04-005**
Republican	JJ	9-03-003
Republican	JJ-TL	4-02-003
Republican	**prop. noun**	**71-06-024**
Republican	NP	32-05-013
Republican	NP-TL	9-04-005
Republicans	NPS	28-06-016
Republicans	NPS-HL	1-01-001
Republicans'	NPS$	1-01-001
Republican-controlled	**JJ**	**1-01-001**
Republicanism	**NP**	**4-02-002**
repudiate	**verb**	**5-04-005**
repudiate	VB	1-01-001
repudiated	VBD	1-01-001
repudiated	VBN	2-02-002
repudiating	VBG	1-01-001
repudiation	**NN**	**4-02-002**
repugnance	**NN**	**1-01-001**
repugnant	**JJ**	**1-01-001**
repulse	**verb**	**1-01-001**
repulsed	VBN	1-01-001
repulsion	**noun**	**3-03-003**
repulsion	NN	1-01-001
repulsions	NNS	2-02-002
repulsive	**JJ**	**4-03-003**
reputable	**JJ**	**7-04-005**
reputation	**noun**	**30-11-027**
reputation	NN	27-10-025
rep'tation	NN	1-01-001
reputation's	NN$	1-01-001
reputations	NNS	1-01-001
repute	**NN**	**2-02-002**
repute	**verb**	**5-03-005**
reputed	VBN	5-03-005
reputedly	**RB**	**4-03-003**
request	**noun**	**54-12-036**
request	NN	42-11-030
requests	NNS	12-06-011
request	**verb**	**29-08-025**
request	VB	7-05-007
requests	VBZ	2-02-002
requested	VBD	5-05-005
requested	VBN	7-05-006
requesting	VBG	8-05-007
requester	**noun**	**1-01-001**
requesters	NNS	1-01-001
require	**verb**	**340-14-171**
require	VB	86-10-066
requires	VBZ	55-11-049
requires	VBZ-HL	2-02-002
required	VBD	31-09-025
required	VBN	149-11-091
required	VBN-HL	1-01-001
requiring	VBG	16-06-014
requirement	**noun**	**110-09-069**
requirement	NN	27-07-022
requirements	NNS	78-09-050
requirements	NNS-HL	5-03-004
requisite	**noun**	**1-01-001**
requisites	NNS	1-01-001
requisition	**NN**	**1-01-001**
requisition	**verb**	**2-02-002**
requisitioned	VBD	1-01-001
requisitioned	VBN	1-01-001
reread	**verb**	**4-04-004**

reread (cont.):		
reread	VB	3-03-003
reread	VBN	1-01-001
resale	**NN**	**2-01-001**
rescind	**verb**	**3-02-002**
rescind	VB	2-01-001
rescinded	VBN	1-01-001
rescue	**noun**	**9-06-006**
rescue	NN	8-06-006
Rescue	NN-TL	1-01-001
rescue	**verb**	**14-09-014**
rescue	VB	6-05-006
rescued	VBD	1-01-001
rescued	VBN	5-05-005
rescuing	VBG	2-02-002
reseal	**verb**	**1-01-001**
resealed	VBN	1-01-001
research	**noun**	**172-11-072**
research	NN	137-11-066
research	NN-HL	9-04-008
Research	NN-TL	25-06-014
researches	NNS	1-01-001
research	**verb**	**1-01-001**
researching	VBG	1-01-001
research-staff	**NN**	**3-01-001**
researchable	**JJ**	**1-01-001**
researcher	**noun**	**7-05-007**
researcher	NN	3-02-003
researchers	NNS	4-04-004
resemblance	**NN**	**13-07-012**
resemble	**verb**	**27-12-021**
resemble	VB	8-06-008
resembles	VBZ	9-05-007
resembled	VBD	8-07-007
resembling	VBG	2-02-002
resent	**verb**	**16-08-015**
resent	VB	8-04-008
resented	VBD	5-04-005
resented	VBN	3-03-003
resentful	**JJ**	**3-02-002**
resentment	**NN**	**18-08-014**
reserpine	**NN**	**1-01-001**
reservation	**noun**	**17-07-013**
reservation	NN	7-05-005
reservation	NN-HL	1-01-001
reservations	NNS	9-04-007
reserve	**noun**	**34-07-016**
reserve	NN	19-07-012
Reserve	NN-TL	11-04-005
reserves	NNS	4-02-003
reserve	**verb**	**39-09-031**
reserve	VB	7-03-005
reserves	VBZ	1-01-001
reserved	VBD	3-03-003
reserved	VBN	24-09-019
reserving	VBG	4-03-004
reservoir	**noun**	**13-05-010**
reservoir	NN	10-05-009
reservoirs	NNS	3-03-003
resettle	**verb**	**1-01-001**
resettling	VBG	1-01-001
resettlement	**NN**	**1-01-001**
reshape	**verb**	**2-01-002**
reshapes	VBZ	1-01-001
reshaped	VBD	1-01-001
reside	**verb**	**15-06-013**
reside	VB	2-02-002
resides	VBZ	4-02-004
resided	VBD	3-02-003
residing	VBG	6-04-005
residence	**noun**	**31-10-022**
residence	NN	29-10-021
residences	NNS	2-02-002
resident	**adjective**	**5-04-005**
resident	JJ	4-04-004
Resident	JJ-TL	1-01-001
resident	**noun**	**28-09-022**
resident	NN	8-06-008
residents	NNS	20-05-015
residential	**adjective**	**45-09-018**
residential	JJ	43-09-017
Residential	JJ-TL	2-01-001
residentially	**RB**	**1-01-001**
residual	**JJ**	**1-01-001**
residue	**noun**	**11-04-007**
residue	NN	8-04-006
residues	NNS	3-02-002
resift	**verb**	**1-01-001**
resifted	VBN	1-01-001

resign	**verb**	**13-06-012**
resign	VB	2-02-002
resigns	VBZ	1-01-001
resigned	VBD	7-03-006
resigned	VBN	2-02-002
resigning	VBG	1-01-001
resignation	**noun**	**8-05-008**
resignation	NN	7-04-007
resignations	NNS	1-01-001
resignedly	**RB**	**1-01-001**
resilience	**NN**	**1-01-001**
resin	**noun**	**11-03-005**
resin	NN	9-02-003
resins	NNS	2-02-002
resin-saturated	**JJ**	**2-01-001**
resinlike	**JJ**	**1-01-001**
resiny	**JJ**	**1-01-001**
resist	**verb**	**36-11-033**
resist	VB	22-08-021
resists	VBZ	1-01-001
resisted	VBD	4-03-004
resisted	VBN	5-03-005
resisting	VBG	4-04-004
resistance	**FW-NN**	**1-01-001**
resistance	**noun**	**48-10-022**
resistance	NN	43-10-021
resistance	NN-HL	3-03-003
Resistance	NN-TL	1-01-001
resistances	NNS	1-01-001
resistant	**JJ**	**4-04-004**
resistive	**JJ**	**1-01-001**
resistor	**noun**	**10-02-003**
resistor	NN	3-02-002
resistors	NNS	7-01-002
Resnik	**NP**	**2-01-001**
resolute	**JJ**	**3-03-003**
Resolute	**NP**	**1-01-001**
resolutely	**RB**	**2-02-002**
resolution	**noun**	**70-08-024**
resolution	NN	61-08-018
resolution	NN-HL	2-01-001
Resolution	NN-TL	1-01-001
resolutions	NNS	6-04-006
resolve	**noun**	**2-02-002**
resolve	NN	1-01-001
Resolve	NN-TL	1-01-001
resolve	**verb**	**38-11-028**
resolve	VB	11-06-011
resolves	VBZ	2-02-002
Resolves	VBZ-TL	1-01-001
resolved	VBD	3-03-003
resolved	VBN	18-06-014
resolving	VBG	3-03-003
resonance	**noun**	**17-05-006**
resonance	NN	13-04-004
resonance	NN-HL	1-01-001
resonances	NNS	3-01-002
resonant	**JJ**	**4-02-002**
resorcinol	**NN**	**3-02-002**
resort	**noun**	**7-05-007**
resort	NN	6-05-006
resorts	NNS	1-01-001
resort	**verb**	**14-07-013**
resort	VB	6-04-006
resorted	VBD	1-01-001
resorted	VBN	4-02-003
resorting	VBG	3-02-003
resound	**verb**	**2-02-002**
resounds	VBZ	1-01-001
resounding	VBG	1-01-001
resounding	**JJ**	**1-01-001**
resource	**noun**	**81-12-044**
resource	NN	9-07-008
resources	NNS	69-11-040
resources	NNS-HL	3-01-002
resource-use	**NN**	**1-01-001**
resourceful	**adjective**	**3-02-002**
resourceful	JJ	2-02-002
resourceful	JJ-HL	1-01-001
resourcefully	**RB**	**1-01-001**
resourcefulness	**NN**	**2-02-002**
respect	**noun**	**139-13-091**
respect	NN	119-13-076
respect	NN-HL	1-01-001
respects	NNS	19-06-019
respect	**verb**	**22-10-021**
respect	VB	5-05-005
respects	VBZ	3-02-003
respected	VBD	5-03-005

respect (cont.):		
respected	VBN	6-04-006
respecting	VBG	3-03-003
respectability	**NN**	**5-04-005**
respectable	**JJ**	**21-10-020**
respectful	**JJ**	**4-03-004**
respectfully	**RB**	**2-02-002**
respecting	**IN**	**2-02-002**
respective	**JJ**	**19-07-018**
respectively	**RB**	**31-06-021**
respiration	**NN**	**2-01-002**
respirator	**noun**	**1-01-001**
respirators	NNS	1-01-001
respiratory	**adjective**	**17-03-005**
respiratory	JJ	16-03-005
Respiratory	JJ-TL	1-01-001
respite	**NN**	**2-02-002**
resplendent	**JJ**	**1-01-001**
respond	**verb**	**54-13-045**
respond	VB	21-09-018
responds	VBZ	7-03-007
responded	VBD	13-09-012
responded	VBN	7-06-007
responding	VBG	6-04-005
respondent	**noun**	**22-01-001**
respondent	NN	8-01-001
respondent's	NN$	1-01-001
respondents	NNS	8-01-001
respondents'	NNS$	5-01-001
response	**noun**	**105-14-065**
response	NN	77-13-056
responses	NNS	28-08-016
responsibility	**noun**	**143-13-070**
responsibility	NN	116-11-058
responsibility	NN-HL	1-01-001
Responsibility	NN-TL	1-01-001
responsibilities	NNS	25-10-020
responsible	**adjective**	**71-15-059**
responsible	JJ	70-15-059
responsible	JJ-HL	1-01-001
responsibly	**RB**	**1-01-001**
responsive	**JJ**	**4-03-004**
responsively	**RB**	**1-01-001**
responsiveness	**NN**	**4-02-002**
rest	**noun**	**140-15-102**
rest	NN	135-15-099
rest	NN-HL	1-01-001
Rest	NN-TL	2-02-002
rests	NNS	2-01-001
rest	**verb**	**77-15-064**
rest	VB	25-10-023
rests	VBZ	16-07-014
rested	VBD	12-09-011
rested	VBN	5-05-005
resting	VBG	19-12-016
rest-room	**NN**	**1-01-001**
restate	**verb**	**2-02-002**
restates	VBZ	1-01-001
restating	VBG	1-01-001
restatement	**NN**	**4-02-003**
restaurant	**noun**	**53-11-030**
restaurant	NN	37-08-020
Restaurant	NN-TL	4-02-002
restaurants	NNS	12-09-012
restaurateur	**NN**	**1-01-001**
restful	**JJ**	**3-03-003**
restitution	**NN**	**1-01-001**
restive	**JJ**	**1-01-001**
restively	**RB**	**1-01-001**
restless	**adjective**	**13-08-013**
restless	JJ	12-08-012
restless	JJ-HL	1-01-001
restlessly	**RB**	**2-02-002**
restlessness	**NN**	**2-02-002**
restock	**VB**	**1-01-001**
restorability	**NN**	**3-01-001**
restoration	**noun**	**11-06-009**
restoration	NN	8-05-007
Restoration	NN-TL	3-02-002
restorative	**adjective**	**8-01-001**
restorative	JJ	6-01-001
restorative	JJ-HL	2-01-001
restore	**verb**	**28-12-024**
restore	VB	9-06-009
restored	VBD	3-03-003
restored	VBN	10-05-009
restored	VBN-HL	1-01-001
restoring	VBG	5-04-004
restorer	**noun**	**1-01-001**

Word	Tag	Frequency
restorer (cont.):		
restorers	NNS	1-01-001
restoring	**NN**	**1-01-001**
restrain	**verb**	**31-10-024**
restrain	VB	10-08-009
restrains	VBZ	1-01-001
restrained	VBN	12-04-009
restrained	VBN-HL	1-01-001
restraining	VBG	7-03-005
restraint	**noun**	**18-07-013**
restraint	NN	11-06-011
restraints	NNS	7-03-003
restrict	**verb**	**31-12-028**
restrict	VB	11-05-010
restricts	VBZ	2-02-002
restricted	VBN	15-11-015
restricting	VBG	3-02-002
restricting	**JJ**	**1-01-001**
restriction	**noun**	**35-11-031**
restriction	NN	8-05-008
restrictions	NNS	27-10-024
restrictive	**JJ**	**7-03-005**
restructure	**verb**	**1-01-001**
restructured	VBN	1-01-001
restudy	**NN**	**1-01-001**
restudy	**verb**	**1-01-001**
restudy	VB	0-00-000
restudy	VB-HL	1-01-001
resublime	**verb**	**1-01-001**
resublimed	VBN	1-01-001
result	**noun**	**329-15-186**
result	NN	197-13-129
results	NNS	127-11-081
results	NNS-HL	5-02-005
result	**verb**	**144-09-093**
result	VB	47-09-037
results	VBZ	17-04-014
resulted	VBD	32-07-029
resulted	VBN	5-04-005
resulting	VBG	43-07-034
resultant	**JJ**	**11-06-010**
resultant	**noun**	**6-03-004**
resultant	NN	1-01-001
resultants	NNS	5-02-003
resume	**NN**	**6-04-004**
resume	**verb**	**37-11-027**
resume	VB	10-05-009
resumed	VBD	12-09-012
resumed	VBN	11-07-011
resuming	VBG	3-03-003
resuming	VBG-HL	1-01-001
resumption	**NN**	**9-03-005**
resurgence	**noun**	**3-02-002**
resurgence	NN	2-02-002
resurgence	NN-HL	1-01-001
resurgent	**JJ**	**1-01-001**
resurrect	**verb**	**2-02-002**
resurrected	VBN	1-01-001
resurrecting	VBG	1-01-001
resurrection	**NN**	**1-01-001**
resuspend	**verb**	**3-01-001**
resuspended	VBN	3-01-001
resuspension	**NN**	**1-01-001**
retail	**adjective**	**11-05-008**
retail	JJ	10-05-007
Retail	JJ-TL	1-01-001
retail	**NN**	**8-02-004**
retail	**verb**	**3-03-003**
retail	VB	1-01-001
retailing	VBG	2-02-002
retailer	**noun**	**6-03-004**
retailer	NN	1-01-001
retailers	NNS	5-03-004
retailing	**NN**	**3-01-001**
retain	**verb**	**49-11-042**
retain	VB	11-07-011
retains	VBZ	9-05-008
retained	VBD	4-03-004
retained	VBN	18-10-016
retaining	VBG	7-06-007
retainer	**noun**	**1-01-001**
retainers	NNS	1-01-001
retaliate	**verb**	**3-03-003**
retaliate	VB	1-01-001
retaliated	VBD	1-01-001
retaliating	VBG	1-01-001
retaliation	**NN**	**6-04-006**
retaliatory	**JJ**	**2-02-002**
retard	**verb**	**11-07-010**

Word	Tag	Frequency
retard (cont.):		
retard	VB	3-03-003
retarded	VBN	6-04-006
retarded	VBN-HL	1-01-001
retarding	VBG	1-01-001
retardation	**NN**	**3-01-002**
retch	**VB**	**1-01-001**
retching	**NN**	**1-01-001**
retell	**verb**	**2-02-002**
retell	VB	1-01-001
retold	VBD	1-01-001
retelling	**NN**	**2-02-002**
retention	**NN**	**12-04-007**
retentive	**JJ**	**2-02-002**
retentiveness	**NN**	**1-01-001**
rethink	**verb**	**3-02-002**
rethink	VB	2-02-002
rethinking	VBG	0-00-000
re-thinking	VBG	1-01-001
reticulate	**JJ**	**3-01-001**
retie	**verb**	**1-01-001**
retied	VBD	1-01-001
retina	**NN**	**1-01-001**
retinal	**JJ**	**3-01-001**
retinue	**NN**	**1-01-001**
retire	**verb**	**54-12-036**
retire	VB	9-07-009
retires	VBZ	2-02-002
retired	VBD	10-05-010
retired	VBN	25-10-018
retiring	VBG	8-03-007
retirement	**noun**	**27-07-015**
retirement	NN	24-07-014
retirement	NN-HL	2-01-001
retirements	NNS	1-01-001
retort	**NN**	**2-02-002**
retort	**verb**	**5-04-005**
retort	VB	2-02-002
retorted	VBD	3-03-003
retouching	**NN**	**1-01-001**
retrace	**NN**	**1-01-001**
retrace	**verb**	**2-02-002**
retraced	VBD	1-01-001
retracing	VBG	1-01-001
retract	**verb**	**3-03-003**
retracted	VBN	3-03-003
retraction	**NN**	**1-01-001**
retrain	**verb**	**1-01-001**
retraining	VBG	1-01-001
retranslate	**verb**	**1-01-001**
retranslated	VBN	1-01-001
retreat	**noun**	**12-07-010**
retreat	NN	11-07-010
retreats	NNS	1-01-001
retreat	**verb**	**16-07-015**
retreat	VB	3-02-003
retreated	VBD	6-03-005
retreated	VBN	2-02-002
retreating	VBG	5-04-005
retrench	**verb**	**1-01-001**
retrenching	VBG	1-01-001
retribution	**NN**	**4-04-004**
retrieval	**NN**	**1-01-001**
retrieve	**verb**	**12-05-006**
retrieve	VB	2-01-002
retrieved	VBD	1-01-001
retrieved	VBN	9-03-003
retriever	**NN**	**1-01-001**
retrogradation	**noun**	**1-01-001**
retrogradations	NNS	1-01-001
retrograde	**JJ**	**2-01-001**
retrograde	**VB**	**1-01-001**
retrogressive	**JJ**	**1-01-001**
retrospect	**NN**	**3-03-003**
retrospective	**NN**	**1-01-001**
retrovision	**NN**	**1-01-001**
return	**JJ**	**2-01-002**
return	**noun**	**130-15-063**
return	NN	103-15-058
return	NN-NC	1-01-001
returns	NNS	22-06-008
returns	NNS-HL	4-03-003
return	**verb**	**232-15-154**
return	VB	74-14-065
returns	VBZ	8-04-007
returned	VBD	81-12-066
returned	VBN	34-12-031
returning	VBG	35-14-033
Reub	**NP**	**1-01-001**

Reuben	**NP**	**3-03-003**
reunion	**noun**	**13-08-011**
reunion	NN	11-06-009
Reunion	NN-TL	1-01-001
reunions	NNS	1-01-001
reunite	**verb**	**4-04-004**
reunite	VB	1-01-001
reunited	VBN	2-02-002
reuniting	VBG	1-01-001
reupholster	**verb**	**1-01-001**
reupholstering	VBG	1-01-001
Reuther	**NP**	**1-01-001**
Reuveni	**NP**	**5-01-001**
rev	**verb**	**1-01-001**
revved	VBD	1-01-001
Rev	**prop. noun**	**2-01-001**
Rev's	NP$	2-01-001
revaluation	**NN**	**1-01-001**
revamp	**verb**	**4-03-003**
revamped	VBD	1-01-001
revamped	VBN	1-01-001
revamped	VBN-HL	1-01-001
revamping	VBG	1-01-001
reveal	**verb**	**97-13-061**
reveal	VB	29-11-025
reveal	VB-HL	1-01-001
reveals	VBZ	21-05-014
revealed	VBD	21-10-018
revealed	VBN	18-05-015
revealing	VBG	7-05-007
revealing	**JJ**	**4-03-004**
revel	**noun**	**3-03-003**
revel	NN	2-02-002
revels	NNS	1-01-001
revel	**verb**	**4-03-004**
revel	VB	1-01-001
reveled	VBD	1-01-001
reveling	VBG	1-01-001
revelling	VBG	1-01-001
revelation	**noun**	**17-07-016**
revelation	NN	11-05-010
Revelation	NN-TL	3-02-003
revelations	NNS	3-02-003
revelatory	**JJ**	**1-01-001**
reveller	**noun**	**1-01-001**
revellers	NNS	1-01-001
revelling	**noun**	**1-01-001**
revellings	NNS	1-01-001
revelry	**NN**	**1-01-001**
revenge	**NN**	**7-05-007**
revenge-seeking	**JJ**	**1-01-001**
revenue	**noun**	**61-08-022**
revenue	NN	19-07-014
revenue	NN-HL	1-01-001
Revenue	NN-TL	15-04-006
revenues	NNS	26-03-006
revenuer	**noun**	**1-01-001**
revenuers	NNS	1-01-001
reverberate	**verb**	**2-02-002**
reverberated	VBD	2-02-002
reverberation	**noun**	**2-02-002**
reverberation	NN	1-01-001
reverberations	NNS	1-01-001
Reverdy	**NP**	**1-01-001**
revere	**verb**	**5-03-005**
revered	VBN	5-03-005
Revere	**NP**	**2-02-002**
reverence	**NN**	**4-03-004**
reverence	**VB**	**1-01-001**
Reverend	**prop. noun**	**55-09-022**
Reverend	NP	21-06-012
Rev	NP	11-01-001
Rev.	NP	22-05-011
rev'rend	NP	1-01-001
reverent	**JJ**	**3-02-003**
reverently	**RB**	**1-01-001**
reverie	**noun**	**2-01-002**
reverie	NN	1-01-001
revery	NN	1-01-001
reversal	**noun**	**2-02-002**
reversal	NN	1-01-001
reversal	NN-HL	1-01-001
reverse	**JJ**	**3-01-003**
reverse	**NN**	**4-04-004**
reverse	**verb**	**27-10-023**
reverse	VB	11-07-010
reverses	VBZ	2-02-002
reversed	VBN	8-03-007
reversing	VBG	5-03-004

reverse (cont.):		
reversing	VBG-HL	1-01-001
reverse-surface	**NN**	**1-01-001**
reversibility	**NN**	**1-01-001**
reversible	**JJ**	**6-03-005**
revert	**verb**	**5-03-005**
revert	VB	3-02-003
reverted	VBD	2-02-002
revetment	**noun**	**1-01-001**
revetments	NNS	1-01-001
review	**noun**	**52-07-030**
review	NN	35-06-025
review	NN-HL	1-01-001
Review	NN-TL	10-02-006
reviews	NNS	6-02-003
review	**verb**	**36-10-033**
review	VB	10-06-010
reviews	VBZ	3-02-002
reviewed	VBD	3-03-003
reviewed	VBN	10-05-009
reviewing	VBG	10-05-009
reviewer	**noun**	**4-02-004**
reviewer	NN	2-02-002
reviewers	NNS	2-01-002
revile	**verb**	**1-01-001**
reviled	VBN	1-01-001
revise	**verb**	**22-08-017**
revise	VB	5-03-005
revised	VBD	5-03-005
revised	VBN	9-06-007
Revised	VBN-TL	2-01-001
revising	VBG	1-01-001
revision	**noun**	**17-06-014**
revision	NN	8-05-008
revisions	NNS	9-06-008
revisionist	**NN**	**1-01-001**
revisit	**verb**	**1-01-001**
revisited	VBN	0-00-000
Revisited	VBN-TL	1-01-001
revitalize	**VB**	**1-01-001**
revival	**noun**	**13-06-009**
revival	NN	8-06-007
revivals	NNS	5-02-003
revivalism	**NN**	**2-01-001**
revive	**verb**	**16-08-015**
revive	VB	8-05-008
revived	VBD	3-03-003
revived	VBN	3-02-003
reviving	VBG	2-02-002
revivify	**verb**	**1-01-001**
revivified	VBN	1-01-001
revoke	**verb**	**1-01-001**
revoked	VBN	1-01-001
revolt	**noun**	**10-05-008**
revolt	NN	8-05-007
revolts	NNS	2-01-001
revolt	**verb**	**1-01-001**
revolted	VBD	1-01-001
revolting	**JJ**	**2-02-002**
revolution	**noun**	**78-08-041**
revolution	NN	42-07-027
revolution	NN-HL	1-01-001
Revolution	NN-TL	27-06-013
revolution's	NN$	0-00-000
Revolution's	NN$-TL	1-01-001
revolutions	NNS	7-06-006
revolutionary	**adjective**	**20-07-015**
revolutionary	JJ	19-07-015
Revolutionary	JJ-TL	1-01-001
revolutionary	**noun**	**2-02-002**
revolutionary	NN	1-01-001
revolutionaries	NNS	0-00-000
Revolutionaries	NNS-TL	1-01-001
revolutionibus	**foreign**	**3-01-001**
revolutionibus	FW-NNS	0-00-000
Revolutionibus	FW-NNS-TL	3-01-001
revolutionist	**noun**	**1-01-001**
revolutionists	NNS	1-01-001
revolutionize	**verb**	**3-03-003**
revolutionized	VBD	1-01-001
revolutionized	VBN	2-02-002
revolve	**verb**	**12-08-010**
revolve	VB	1-01-001
revolves	VBZ	1-01-001
revolved	VBD	3-03-003
revolved	VBN	1-01-001
revolving	VBG	5-03-005
revolving	VBG-HL	1-01-001
revolver	**NN**	**14-05-008**

Word	Tag	Count
revulsion	**noun**	**10-07-007**
revulsion	NN	5-05-005
revulsion	NN-HL	1-01-001
Revulsion	NN-TL	4-01-001
reward	**noun**	**17-11-016**
reward	NN	13-11-013
rewards	NNS	4-03-004
reward	**verb**	**5-04-005**
reward	VB	2-02-002
rewarded	VBN	3-02-003
rewarding	**JJ**	**4-04-004**
rewrite	**NN**	**2-01-001**
rewrite	**verb**	**6-03-005**
rewrite	VB	2-02-002
rewrites	VBZ	1-01-001
rewritten	VBN	1-01-001
rewriting	VBG	2-02-002
Rex	**NP**	**5-03-004**
Rexroth	**prop. noun**	**7-01-001**
Rexroth	NP	6-01-001
Rexroth's	NP$	1-01-001
Rey	**prop. noun**	**2-02-002**
Rey	NP	1-01-001
Rey	NP-TL	1-01-001
Reyes	**prop. noun**	**1-01-001**
Reyes	NP	0-00-000
Reyes	NP-TL	1-01-001
Reynolds	**NP**	**5-02-004**
Rhea	**prop. noun**	**1-01-001**
Rhea's	NP$	1-01-001
Rheims	**NP**	**1-01-001**
Rheinholdt	**prop. noun**	**2-01-001**
Rheinholdt	NP	1-01-001
Rheinholdt's	NP$	1-01-001
Rhenish	**JJ**	**1-01-001**
rhenium	**NN**	**1-01-001**
rhetoric	**NN**	**5-02-005**
rhetorician	**noun**	**1-01-001**
rhetoricians	NNS	1-01-001
rheum	**NN**	**1-01-001**
rheumatic	**JJ**	**2-01-002**
rheumatic	**noun**	**1-01-001**
rheumatics	NNS	1-01-001
rheumatism	**noun**	**3-02-002**
rheumatism	NN	2-02-002
Rheumatism	NN-TL	1-01-001
Rhine	**prop. noun**	**7-02-002**
Rhine	NP	5-02-002
Rhine	NP-TL	2-01-001
Rhine-Main	**NP**	**1-01-001**
Rhine-Westphalia	**prop. noun**	**1-01-001**
Rhine-Westphalia	NP	0-00-000
Rhine-Westphalia	NP-TL	1-01-001
rhinestone	**noun**	**1-01-001**
rhinestones	NNS	1-01-001
rhino	**noun**	**2-01-001**
rhinos	NNS	2-01-001
rhinoceros	**NN**	**3-02-002**
rhinotracheitis	**NN**	**2-01-001**
Rhode	**prop. noun**	**105-08-019**
Rhode	NP	0-00-000
Rhode	NP-TL	100-08-019
Rhode	NP-TL-HL	5-01-003
Rhodes	**prop. noun**	**8-04-004**
Rhodes	NP	3-02-002
Rhodes	NP-TL	5-03-003
Rhodesia	**prop. noun**	**1-01-001**
Rhodesia	NP	0-00-000
Rhodesia	NP-TL	1-01-001
rhododendron	**NN**	**1-01-001**
rhubarb	**noun**	**2-01-001**
rhubarb	NN	0-00-000
rhu-beb	NN	1-01-001
rhu-beb-ni-ice	NN	1-01-001
rhyme	**noun**	**3-02-003**
rhyme	NN	2-01-002
rhymes	NNS	1-01-001
rhyme	**verb**	**2-02-002**
rhyme	VB	1-01-001
rhyming	VBG	1-01-001
rhythm	**noun**	**35-09-023**
rhythm	NN	21-09-016
Rhythm	NN-TL	2-02-002
rhythms	NNS	11-04-009
Rhythms	NNS-TL	1-01-001
rhythm-and-blues	**NNS**	**1-01-001**
rhythmic	**JJ**	**11-07-009**
rhythmical	**JJ**	**1-01-001**
rhythmically	**RB**	**2-02-002**
rib	**noun**	**12-06-010**
rib	NN	1-01-001
ribs	NNS	11-05-009
ribald	**JJ**	**1-01-001**
Ribas	**NP**	**1-01-001**
ribbing	**NN**	**1-01-001**
ribbon	**noun**	**18-07-013**
ribbon	NN	12-05-009
ribbons	NNS	6-04-005
ribcage	**NN**	**1-01-001**
Ribes	**NP**	**2-01-001**
riboflavin	**NN**	**1-01-001**
ribonucleic	**JJ**	**1-01-001**
Rican	**adjective**	**1-01-001**
Rican	JJ	0-00-000
Rican	JJ-TL	1-01-001
Rican	**prop. noun**	**2-01-002**
Ricans	NPS	2-01-002
Ricci	**NP**	**1-01-001**
Ricco	**NP**	**4-01-001**
rice	**NN**	**24-09-012**
Rice	**NP**	**9-02-002**
rich	**JJ**	**70-13-056**
rich	**NN**	**1-01-001**
Rich	**NP**	**3-03-003**
Richard	**prop. noun**	**76-09-038**
Richard	NP	69-09-035
Richard	NP-TL	2-01-002
Richard's	NP$	5-03-003
Richards	**prop. noun**	**11-04-006**
Richards	NP	10-03-005
Richards'	NP$	1-01-001
Richardson	**prop. noun**	**13-04-006**
Richardson	NP	12-04-005
Richardson's	NP$	1-01-001
richer	**JJR**	**5-04-005**
Richert	**NP**	**5-01-001**
riches	**NNS**	**2-02-002**
richest	**JJT**	**5-04-005**
Richey	**NP**	**1-01-001**
richly	**QL**	**3-01-003**
richly	**RB**	**2-02-002**
Richmond	**prop. noun**	**12-09-010**
Richmond	NP	11-08-009
Richmond	NP-TL	1-01-001
Richmond-Petersburg	**NP**	**1-01-001**
richness	**NN**	**5-03-004**
Richter-Haaser	**NP**	**1-01-001**
Rickards	**NP**	**4-01-001**
Rickenbaugh	**NP**	**2-01-001**
Rickettsia	**NP**	**1-01-001**
rickety	**JJ**	**1-01-001**
Rickey	**prop. noun**	**1-01-001**
Rickey's	NP$	1-01-001
Rickshaw	**NP**	**1-01-001**
Rico	**prop. noun**	**21-03-006**
Rico	NP	18-03-005
Rico	NP-HL	1-01-001
Rico	NP-TL	2-01-001
ricochet	**verb**	**1-01-001**
ricocheted	VBD	1-01-001
rid	**JJ**	**15-07-015**
rid	**verb**	**6-06-006**
rid	VB	3-03-003
rid	VBD	1-01-001
ridding	VBG	2-02-002
riddance	**NN**	**1-01-001**
riddle	**noun**	**3-03-003**
riddle	NN	1-01-001
riddles	NNS	2-02-002
riddle	**verb**	**4-04-004**
riddled	VBN	2-02-002
riddling	VBG	2-02-002
ride	**noun**	**21-08-019**
ride	NN	14-06-014
Ride	NN-TL	1-01-001
rides	NNS	6-04-005
ride	**verb**	**126-13-066**
ride	VB	32-09-022
Ride	VB-TL	2-01-001
rides	VBZ	4-03-003
ridden	VBN	6-03-006
rode	VBD	40-09-026
riding	VBG	42-10-027
rider	**noun**	**28-09-015**
rider	NN	11-05-006
Rider	NN-TL	2-02-002
Rider	NN-TL-HL	1-01-001
rider's	NN$	2-02-002

Word	Tag	Frequency
rider (cont.):		
riders	NNS	6-04-006
Riders	NNS-TL	6-03-003
Rider	**NP**	**2-01-001**
rider-fashion	**RB**	**1-01-001**
ridge	**noun**	**22-08-018**
ridge	NN	12-04-011
Ridge	NN-TL	6-04-005
ridges	NNS	4-03-003
Ridgefield	**NP**	**1-01-001**
Ridgway	**NP**	**1-01-001**
ridicule	**NN**	**2-02-002**
ridicule	**verb**	**7-04-006**
ridicule	VB	3-02-003
ridiculed	VBN	2-02-002
ridiculing	VBG	2-02-002
ridiculous	**JJ**	**19-08-016**
ridiculously	**QL**	**1-01-001**
ridiculously	**RB**	**1-01-001**
riding	**noun**	**3-02-002**
riding	NN	2-01-001
Riding	NN-TL	1-01-001
Ridpath	**NP**	**1-01-001**
Riefling	**NP**	**3-01-001**
Riegger	**NP**	**2-01-001**
Riemann	**prop. noun**	**1-01-001**
Riemann's	NP$	1-01-001
Riesman	**NP**	**1-01-001**
riffle	**VB**	**1-01-001**
rifle	**noun**	**87-09-027**
rifle	NN	61-09-020
Rifle	NN-TL	2-02-002
rifle's	NN$	1-01-001
rifles	NNS	21-06-012
rifles	NNS-HL	1-01-001
Rifles	NNS-TL	1-01-001
rifle	**verb**	**1-01-001**
rifled	VBN	1-01-001
rifle-shotgun	**NN**	**1-01-001**
rifleman	**noun**	**12-03-004**
rifleman	NN	4-03-003
rifleman's	NN$	1-01-001
riflemen	NNS	6-01-001
riflemen's	NNS$	1-01-001
rifleman-ranger	**noun**	**1-01-001**
riflemen-rangers	NNS	1-01-001
rifling	**NN**	**1-01-001**
rift	**NN**	**1-01-001**
rig	**noun**	**8-04-006**
rig	NN	4-03-004
rigs	NNS	4-03-003
rig	**verb**	**5-02-003**
rig	VB	1-01-001
rigged	VBN	3-02-002
rigging	VBG	1-01-001
Rig-Veda	**NP**	**1-01-001**
rigger	**noun**	**2-01-001**
rigger	NN	1-01-001
riggers	NNS	1-01-001
rigging	**NN**	**1-01-001**
Riggs	**NP**	**1-01-001**
right	**adjective**	**224-15-135**
right	JJ	222-14-134
right	JJ-HL	1-01-001
Right	JJ-TL	1-01-001
right	**noun**	**204-14-109**
right	NN	122-13-072
Right	NN	1-01-001
right	NN-HL	1-01-001
Right	NN-TL	3-02-003
rights	NNS	69-14-045
Rights	NNS-TL	8-03-006
right	**adv. noun**	**57-11-029**
right	NR	56-11-028
right	NR-TL	1-01-001
right	**QL**	**127-15-094**
right	**RB**	**79-11-057**
right-angle	**NN**	**1-01-001**
right-angled	**JJ**	**1-01-001**
right-hand	**NN**	**6-03-004**
right-handed	**RB**	**1-01-001**
right-of-entry	**NN**	**2-01-001**
right-of-way	**noun**	**1-01-001**
rights-of-way	NNS	1-01-001
right-wing	**NN**	**1-01-001**
righteous	**JJ**	**5-03-004**
righteousness	**noun**	**6-04-006**
righteousness	NN	5-04-005
righteousness	NN-HL	1-01-001
rightfield	**NN**	**3-01-001**
rightful	**JJ**	**4-03-004**
rightfully	**RB**	**3-02-003**
righthander	**NN**	**2-01-001**
rightist	**NN**	**1-01-001**
rightly	**QL**	**1-01-001**
rightly	**RB**	**3-03-003**
rightness	**NN**	**2-02-002**
rigid	**JJ**	**24-09-017**
rigid	**noun**	**1-01-001**
rigids	NNS	1-01-001
rigidity	**NN**	**2-01-001**
rigidly	**RB**	**8-06-008**
rigor	**noun**	**4-04-004**
rigors	NNS	4-04-004
rigorous	**JJ**	**7-04-007**
rigorously	**RB**	**4-03-004**
Rilke	**NP**	**1-01-001**
Rilly	**NP**	**1-01-001**
rim	**noun**	**6-05-006**
rim	NN	4-04-004
Rim	NN-TL	1-01-001
rims	NNS	1-01-001
rim	**verb**	**2-02-002**
rimmed	VBD	1-01-001
rimmed	VBN	1-01-001
rim-fire	**adjective**	**1-01-001**
rim-fire	JJ	0-00-000
Rim-Fire	JJ-TL	1-01-001
rim-fire	**noun**	**5-01-001**
rim-fire	NN	2-01-001
rim-fires	NNS	3-01-001
Rimanelli	**NP**	**3-01-001**
Rimbaud	**NP**	**1-01-001**
rime	**NN**	**1-01-001**
Rimini	**NP**	**1-01-001**
rimless	**JJ**	**1-01-001**
Rinascimento	**NP**	**2-01-001**
ring	**noun**	**43-14-027**
ring	NN	34-13-022
Ring	NN-TL	3-01-002
Ring	NN-TL-HL	1-01-001
rings	NNS	5-04-004
ring	**verb**	**39-12-030**
ring	VB	7-06-007
Ring	VB-TL	1-01-001
rings	VBZ	1-01-001
rang	VBD	21-05-017
rung	VBN	1-01-001
ringing	VBG	8-05-007
ring	**verb**	**2-02-002**
ringed	VBN	2-02-002
Ring	**NP**	**1-01-001**
ring-around-a-rosy	**NN**	**1-01-001**
ring-around-the-rosie	**NN**	**1-01-001**
ring-labeled	**JJ**	**1-01-001**
Ringel	**NP**	**1-01-001**
ringer	**noun**	**1-01-001**
ringers	NNS	1-01-001
ringing	**noun**	**4-04-004**
ringing	NN	3-03-003
ringings	NNS	1-01-001
Ringler	**prop. noun**	**1-01-001**
Ringler's	NP$	1-01-001
ringlet	**noun**	**1-01-001**
ringlets	NNS	1-01-001
ringside	**NN**	**1-01-001**
ringsider	**noun**	**1-01-001**
ringsiders	NNS	1-01-001
rink	**noun**	**2-01-001**
rink	NN	0-00-000
Rink	NN-TL	2-01-001
Rinker	**NP**	**2-01-001**
rinse	**NN**	**5-01-001**
rinse	**verb**	**6-02-003**
rinse	VB	1-01-001
rinsing	VBG	5-01-002
Rio	**NP**	**4-03-003**
riot	**noun**	**8-06-007**
riot	NN	7-05-006
riots	NNS	1-01-001
riot	**verb**	**2-02-002**
rioted	VBD	1-01-001
rioting	VBG	1-01-001
rioter	**noun**	**2-01-001**
rioters	NNS	2-01-001
riotous	**JJ**	**2-02-002**
rip	**verb**	**14-06-013**
rip	VB	5-04-005

Word	Tag	Frequency
rip (cont.):		
ripped	VBD	5-03-005
ripped	VBN	1-01-001
ripping	VBG	3-03-003
Rip	**NP**	**1-01-001**
rip-roaring	**JJ**	**2-01-001**
ripa	**foreign**	**1-01-001**
ripa	FW-NN	0-00-000
Ripa	FW-NN-TL	1-01-001
ripe	**adjective**	**14-05-010**
ripe	JJ	11-05-010
Ripe	JJ-TL	3-01-001
ripen	**verb**	**4-04-004**
ripened	VBD	1-01-001
ripened	VBN	1-01-001
ripening	VBG	2-02-002
ripening	**NN**	**1-01-001**
ripple	**noun**	**9-05-005**
ripple	NN	4-03-003
ripples	NNS	5-03-003
ripple	**verb**	**5-04-005**
ripple	VB	1-01-001
rippled	VBD	1-01-001
rippling	VBG	3-02-003
rise	**noun**	**55-09-040**
rise	NN	53-09-039
rises	NNS	2-02-002
rise	**verb**	**199-14-121**
rise	VB	48-12-038
Rise	VB-TL	1-01-001
rises	VBZ	17-06-013
Rises	VBZ-TL	1-01-001
rose	VBD	60-12-047
risen	VBN	10-08-009
rising	VBG	61-13-043
Rising	VBG-TL	1-01-001
risk	**noun**	**47-11-031**
risk	NN	42-10-027
risks	NNS	4-04-004
risks	NNS-HL	1-01-001
risk	**verb**	**17-09-016**
risk	VB	11-08-011
Risk	VB-TL	1-01-001
risked	VBD	2-02-002
risked	VBN	2-02-002
risking	VBG	1-01-001
risky	**JJ**	**3-02-003**
Ritchie	**NP**	**4-01-002**
rite	**noun**	**12-06-009**
rite	NN	3-02-003
Rite	NN-TL	5-01-002
rites	NNS	4-03-004
Ritschl	**NP**	**1-01-001**
Rittenhouse	**NP**	**1-01-001**
Ritter	**prop. noun**	**10-01-002**
Ritter	NP	9-01-002
Ritter's	NP$	1-01-001
ritual	**JJ**	**2-02-002**
ritual	**noun**	**27-08-012**
ritual	NN	23-07-011
rituals	NNS	4-02-002
rituality	**noun**	**1-01-001**
rituality	NN	0-00-000
ritiuality	NN	1-01-001
ritualize	**verb**	**1-01-001**
ritualized	VBN	1-01-001
Ritz	**NP**	**1-01-001**
rival	**adjective**	**6-04-006**
rival	JJ	5-03-005
Rival	JJ-TL	1-01-001
rival	**noun**	**6-05-006**
rival	NN	3-03-003
rival	NN-HL	1-01-001
rival's	NN$	1-01-001
rivals	NNS	1-01-001
rival	**verb**	**5-03-004**
rival	VB	2-02-002
rivaled	VBD	2-01-001
rivalled	VBD	1-01-001
rivalry	**noun**	**9-05-007**
rivalry	NN	5-04-004
rivalry	NN-HL	1-01-001
rivalries	NNS	3-02-003
rive	**verb**	**1-01-001**
riven	VBN	1-01-001
river	**noun**	**183-13-072**
river	NN	78-11-043
River	NN-TL	85-12-038
River	NN-TL-HL	2-02-002

Word	Tag	Frequency
river (cont.):		
river's	NN$	1-01-001
rivers	NNS	15-06-009
Rivers	NNS-TL	2-02-002
riverbank	**noun**	**5-03-003**
riverbank	NN	3-02-002
riverbanks	NNS	2-02-002
Riverboat	**NP**	**1-01-001**
Riverside	**prop. noun**	**11-03-004**
Riverside	NP	8-02-002
Riverside	NP-TL	2-02-002
Riverside's	NP$	1-01-001
Riverview	**NP**	**1-01-001**
rivet	**verb**	**1-01-001**
rivets	VBZ	1-01-001
Riviera	**prop. noun**	**2-02-002**
Riviera	NP	1-01-001
Riviera	NP-TL	1-01-001
rivulet	**noun**	**1-01-001**
rivulets	NNS	1-01-001
Rizzuto	**NP**	**1-01-001**
roach	**NN**	**1-01-001**
Roach	**NP**	**1-01-001**
road	**noun**	**262-14-102**
road	NN	179-14-076
rd.	NN	0-00-000
Rd.	NN-TL	3-01-003
road	NN-HL	1-01-001
Road	NN-TL	15-06-010
Road	NN-TL-HL	2-01-001
road's	NN$	4-02-002
roads	NNS	53-10-026
roads	NNS-HL	2-02-002
Roads	NNS-TL	3-02-002
road-circuit	**NN**	**1-01-001**
road-crossing	**NN**	**1-01-001**
road-show	**NN**	**1-01-001**
road-shy	**JJ**	**1-01-001**
roadbed	**NN**	**1-01-001**
roadblock	**NN**	**3-03-003**
roadbuilding	**NN**	**1-01-001**
roadhouse	**NN**	**1-01-001**
roadside	**NN**	**4-04-004**
roadster	**NN**	**1-01-001**
roadway	**noun**	**6-05-005**
roadway	NN	5-04-004
roadways	NNS	1-01-001
roam	**verb**	**10-07-009**
roam	VB	6-04-005
roamed	VBD	1-01-001
roaming	VBG	3-03-003
roar	**NN**	**12-04-010**
roar	**verb**	**27-09-019**
roar	VB	1-01-001
roars	VBZ	1-01-001
roared	VBD	18-06-014
roaring	VBG	7-05-007
roaring	**NN**	**2-01-002**
roaringest	**JJT**	**1-01-001**
roast	**noun**	**8-03-004**
roast	NN	7-03-004
roasts	NNS	1-01-001
roast	**verb**	**8-05-007**
roast	VB	2-02-002
roasted	VBD	1-01-001
roasted	VBN	4-02-003
roast	VBN	1-01-001
rob	**verb**	**15-08-015**
rob	VB	2-02-002
robs	VBZ	1-01-001
robbed	VBD	2-02-002
robbed	VBN	8-06-008
robbing	VBG	2-02-002
Rob	**prop. noun**	**18-03-003**
Rob	NP	17-03-003
Rob's	NP+BEZ	1-01-001
Robards	**prop. noun**	**9-01-001**
Robards	NP	8-01-001
Robards'	NP$	1-01-001
robber	**noun**	**8-04-004**
robber	NN	2-02-002
robbers	NNS	6-02-002
robbery	**noun**	**13-03-005**
robbery	NN	6-02-003
Robbery	NN-TL	4-01-001
robberies	NNS	3-03-003
Robbie	**NP**	**3-02-002**
Robbins	**NP**	**6-03-004**
Robby	**prop. noun**	**2-01-001**

Word	Tag	Count
Robby (cont.):		
Robby	NP	0-00-000
Robby	NP-HL	1-01-001
Robby's	NP$	1-01-001
robe	**noun**	**10-09-010**
robe	NN	6-05-006
robes	NNS	4-04-004
robe	**verb**	**1-01-001**
robed	VBN	1-01-001
Robert	**prop. noun**	**83-12-056**
Robert	NP	81-12-055
Robert	NP-TL	2-02-002
Roberta	**NP**	**6-01-001**
Roberto	**NP**	**1-01-001**
Roberts	**prop. noun**	**49-07-008**
Roberts	NP	37-07-007
Roberts'	NP$	12-02-002
Robertson	**prop. noun**	**3-03-003**
Robertson	NP	2-02-002
Robertsons	NPS	1-01-001
robin	**NN**	**1-01-001**
Robin	**NP**	**1-01-001**
Robinson	**prop. noun**	**39-05-009**
Robinson	NP	37-05-009
Robinson	NP-HL	1-01-001
Robinson's	NP$	1-01-001
Robinsonville	**NP**	**1-01-001**
robot	**noun**	**4-01-001**
robot	NN	1-01-001
robots	NNS	3-01-001
robotism	**NN**	**1-01-001**
robustness	**NN**	**1-01-001**
Rocco	**NP**	**2-01-001**
Rochdale	**NP**	**2-01-001**
Rochester	**NP**	**2-02-002**
Rochford	**NP**	**2-01-001**
rock	**noun**	**91-14-046**
rock	NN	52-13-030
Rock	NN-TL	17-07-009
rocks	NNS	22-08-015
rock	**verb**	**20-08-013**
rock	VB	3-02-002
Rock	VB-TL	1-01-001
rocks	VBZ	1-01-001
rocked	VBD	7-05-005
rocked	VBN	1-01-001
rocking	VBG	5-04-005
Rocking	VBG-TL	2-01-001
Rock	**NP**	**2-01-001**
rock-and-roll	**noun**	**3-03-003**
rock-and-roll	NN	2-02-002
rock'n'roll	NN	1-01-001
rock-carved	**JJ**	**1-01-001**
rock-ribbed	**JJ**	**1-01-001**
rock-steady	**JJ**	**1-01-001**
rock-strewn	**adjective**	**2-02-002**
rock-strewn	JJ	1-01-001
rockstrewn	JJ	1-01-001
rockabye	**exclam.**	**1-01-001**
rockabye	UH	0-00-000
Rockabye	UH-TL	1-01-001
Rockaway	**prop. noun**	**1-01-001**
Rockaways	NPS	1-01-001
rockbound	**JJ**	**1-01-001**
Rockefeller	**prop. noun**	**12-05-010**
Rockefeller	NP	7-04-006
Rockefeller	NP-TL	5-04-005
rocker	**noun**	**5-04-005**
rocker	NN	4-03-004
rockers	NNS	1-01-001
rocket	**noun**	**22-09-012**
rocket	NN	7-05-006
rocket's	NN$	2-01-001
rockets	NNS	13-06-008
rocket-bomb	**noun**	**2-01-001**
rocket-bomb	NN	1-01-001
rocket-bombs	NNS	1-01-001
Rockette	**prop. noun**	**1-01-001**
Rockettes	NPS	0-00-000
Rockettes	NPS-TL	1-01-001
Rockfork	**prop. noun**	**3-01-001**
Rockfork	NP	2-01-001
Rockfork	NP-TL	1-01-001
Rockhall	**NP**	**1-01-001**
rocking	**adjective**	**1-01-001**
rocking	JJ	0-00-000
rockin'	JJ	1-01-001
rocking	**NN**	**6-01-002**
rocklike	**adjective**	**3-02-002**

Word	Tag	Count
rocklike (cont.):		
rocklike	JJ	2-01-001
rock-like	JJ	1-01-001
Rockport	**NP**	**2-02-002**
Rockville	**NP**	**1-01-001**
rocky	**JJ**	**9-06-009**
Rocky	**prop. noun**	**4-03-003**
Rocky	NP	1-01-001
Rockies	NPS	3-02-002
rococo	**JJ**	**4-02-002**
rococo	**NN**	**2-02-002**
rod	**noun**	**9-05-008**
rod	NN	5-03-004
rods	NNS	4-04-004
rod	**verb**	**3-01-001**
rodding	VBG	3-01-001
Rod	**prop. noun**	**14-01-001**
Rod	NP	13-01-001
Rod's	NP$	1-01-001
rodder	**NN**	**3-01-001**
rodding	**NN**	**1-01-001**
rodent	**noun**	**6-03-003**
rodent	NN	3-02-002
rodents	NNS	3-02-002
rodeo	**noun**	**2-01-001**
rodeo	NN	1-01-001
rodeos	NNS	1-01-001
Rodeph	**prop. noun**	**1-01-001**
Rodeph	NP	0-00-000
Rodeph	NP-TL	1-01-001
Rodgers	**prop. noun**	**7-01-001**
Rodgers	NP	6-01-001
Rodgers'	NP$	1-01-001
Rodney	**NP**	**6-01-001**
Roe	**NP**	**1-01-001**
Roebuck	**NP**	**9-01-001**
roemer	**NN**	**1-01-001**
roger	**UH**	**1-01-001**
Roger	**prop. noun**	**15-04-011**
Roger	NP	13-03-009
Roger	NP-TL	1-01-001
Rogers	NPS	1-01-001
Rogers	**prop. noun**	**8-05-006**
Rogers	NP	7-05-006
Rogers	NP-HL	1-01-001
rogue	**noun**	**4-04-004**
rogue	NN	1-01-001
rogues	NNS	2-02-002
rogues'	NNS$	0-00-000
Rogues'	NNS$-TL	1-01-001
roi	**FW-NN**	**1-01-001**
roil	**verb**	**3-02-002**
roiling	VBG	3-02-002
ROK	**prop. noun**	**1-01-001**
ROK's	NP$	1-01-001
Roland	**prop. noun**	**4-03-003**
Roland	NP	3-02-002
Roland	NP-TL	1-01-001
role	**noun**	**138-13-077**
role	NN	104-13-064
roles	NNS	34-08-025
role-experiment	**VB**	**1-01-001**
role-experimentation	**NN**	**1-01-001**
roleplay	**verb**	**1-01-001**
roleplayed	VBD	1-01-001
roleplaying	**NN**	**16-01-001**
Rolette	**NP**	**1-01-001**
roll	**noun**	**23-12-019**
roll	NN	15-09-012
rolls	NNS	8-05-007
roll	**verb**	**88-13-060**
roll	VB	18-09-016
Roll	VB-TL	1-01-001
rolls	VBZ	2-02-002
rolled	VBD	34-09-026
rolled	VBN	14-06-008
rolling	VBG	19-10-019
rolled-up	**JJ**	**1-01-001**
roller	**NN**	**3-03-003**
rollick	**verb**	**1-01-001**
rollicking	VBG	1-01-001
rollickingly	**RB**	**1-01-001**
Rollie	**NP**	**1-01-001**
Rollins	**NP**	**1-01-001**
Rolls	**NP**	**1-01-001**
Rolls-Royce	**prop. noun**	**4-02-003**
Rolls-Royce	NP	3-02-002
Rolls-Royces	NPS	1-01-001
Rolnick	**NP**	**1-01-001**

Word	Tag	Frequency
Roloff	**NP**	**1-01-001**
Romagnosi	**NP**	**1-01-001**
Roman	**adjective**	**58-11-026**
Roman	JJ	41-10-021
Roman	JJ-TL	17-06-012
Roman	**prop. noun**	**10-05-008**
Romans	NPS	9-05-008
Romans	NPS-TL	1-01-001
Roman-camp	**JJ**	**1-01-001**
romance	**noun**	**15-07-012**
romance	NN	13-07-010
romances	NNS	1-01-001
Romances	NNS-HL	1-01-001
romance	**verb**	**1-01-001**
romancing	VBG	1-01-001
romancer	**noun**	**1-01-001**
romancers	NNS	1-01-001
Romaniuk	**NP**	**1-01-001**
Romano	**foreign**	**1-01-001**
Romano	FW-JJ	0-00-000
Romano	FW-JJ-TL	1-01-001
romantic	**adjective**	**32-08-024**
romantic	JJ	30-08-022
romantick	JJ	1-01-001
Romantic	JJ-TL	1-01-001
romantic	**noun**	**6-02-003**
romantic	NN	1-01-001
romantics	NNS	5-02-003
romantically	**RB**	**1-01-001**
romanticism	**NN**	**2-02-002**
romanticize	**VB**	**2-01-002**
romanticizing	**NN**	**1-01-001**
Romanza	**foreign**	**2-01-001**
Romanza	FW-NN	0-00-000
Romanza	FW-NN-TL	2-01-001
Rome	**prop. noun**	**72-10-027**
Rome	NP	66-10-026
Rome	NP-TL	4-03-004
Rome's	NP$	2-01-001
Romeo	**prop. noun**	**4-03-003**
Romeo	NP	2-02-002
Romeo	NP-TL	1-01-001
Romeo's	NP$	1-01-001
Rommel	**prop. noun**	**1-01-001**
Rommel's	NP$	0-00-000
Rommel's	NP$-TL	1-01-001
romp	**NN**	**1-01-001**
romp	**verb**	**2-02-002**
romped	VBD	1-01-001
romping	VBG	1-01-001
Romulo	**NP**	**1-01-001**
Ron	**NP**	**4-02-004**
Ronald	**NP**	**5-02-003**
rondo	**foreign**	**1-01-001**
rondo	FW-NN	0-00-000
Rondo	FW-NN-TL	1-01-001
ronnel	**NN**	**1-01-001**
Ronnie	**NP**	**5-02-002**
roof	**noun**	**64-13-034**
roof	NN	58-12-032
Roof	NN-TL	1-01-001
roofs	NNS	5-05-005
roof	**verb**	**1-01-001**
roofed	VBN	1-01-001
roofer	**noun**	**2-02-002**
roofer	NN	1-01-001
roofer's	NN$	1-01-001
roofing	**NN**	**1-01-001**
rooftop	**noun**	**3-02-003**
rooftop	NN	2-02-002
rooftops	NNS	1-01-001
rooftree	**NN**	**1-01-001**
rookie	**noun**	**13-05-008**
rookie	NN	8-04-006
Rookie	NN-TL	1-01-001
rookies	NNS	4-03-004
rookie-of-the-year	**NN**	**1-01-001**
room	**noun**	**439-15-173**
room	NN	364-15-153
room	NN-HL	1-01-001
Room	NN-TL	18-06-013
room's	NN$	1-01-001
rooms	NNS	54-11-039
Rooms	NNS-TL	1-01-001
room	**verb**	**4-02-003**
room	VB	1-01-001
rooming	VBG	3-01-002
Roomberg	**NP**	**1-01-001**
roomful	**NN**	**1-01-001**
roommate	**noun**	**3-01-002**
roommate	NN	1-01-001
roommates	NNS	1-01-001
roommates	NNS-HL	1-01-001
roomy	**JJ**	**1-01-001**
Rooney	**NP**	**7-01-001**
Roos	**NP**	**2-01-001**
Roosevelt	**prop. noun**	**33-08-020**
Roosevelt	NP	24-07-015
Roosevelt	NP-TL	4-04-004
Roosevelt's	NP$	5-03-004
Rooseveltian	**JJ**	**1-01-001**
roost	**NN**	**1-01-001**
rooster	**noun**	**6-05-006**
rooster	NN	3-03-003
rooster's	NN$	1-01-001
roosters	NNS	2-02-002
root	**noun**	**53-10-033**
root	NN	26-10-020
roots	NNS	21-06-016
Roots	NNS-TL	6-01-002
root	**verb**	**13-06-006**
root	VB	3-01-001
rooted	VBD	1-01-001
rooted	VBN	7-03-003
rooting	VBG	2-01-001
Root	**prop. noun**	**1-01-001**
Root	NP	0-00-000
Root	NP-TL	1-01-001
rootless	**JJ**	**2-01-002**
rope	**noun**	**19-06-013**
rope	NN	15-06-012
ropes	NNS	4-02-003
rope	**verb**	**1-01-001**
roped	VBD	1-01-001
roper	**noun**	**1-01-001**
ropers	NNS	1-01-001
Roquemore	**NP**	**2-01-001**
Rorschach	**NP**	**1-01-001**
Rosa	**NP**	**4-01-001**
Rosabelle	**prop. noun**	**1-01-001**
Rosabelle	NP	0-00-000
Rosabelle	NP-TL	1-01-001
Rosalie	**NP**	**1-01-001**
rosary	**noun**	**3-02-003**
rosaries	NNS	3-02-003
Rosburg	**NP**	**4-01-001**
rose	**JJ**	**1-01-001**
rose	**noun**	**18-06-016**
rose	NN	9-05-008
Rose	NN-TL	2-02-002
roses	NNS	7-03-006
Rose	**prop. noun**	**17-07-010**
Rose	NP	14-07-010
Rose's	NP$	3-01-001
rose-of-Sharon	**NN**	**1-01-001**
rose-pink	**JJ**	**1-01-001**
rose-tea	**NN**	**1-01-001**
rosebud	**noun**	**4-02-002**
rosebuds	NNS	4-02-002
rosebush	**NN**	**1-01-001**
Rosella	**NP**	**1-01-001**
Rosemary	**NP**	**1-01-001**
Rosen	**NP**	**2-01-001**
Rosenberg	**prop. noun**	**4-02-003**
Rosenberg	NP	3-02-002
Rosenberg	NP-TL	1-01-001
Rosenmueller	**NP**	**1-01-001**
rosette	**noun**	**1-01-001**
rosettes	NNS	1-01-001
Rosie	**NP**	**1-01-001**
Roslev	**NP**	**1-01-001**
Ross	**NP**	**11-05-006**
Rossi	**NP**	**2-02-002**
Rossilini	**prop. noun**	**1-01-001**
Rossilini's	NP$	1-01-001
Rossoff	**NP**	**6-01-001**
Rostagno	**prop. noun**	**2-01-001**
Rostagno	NP	1-01-001
Rostagnos	NPS	1-01-001
roster	**NN**	**2-02-002**
rostrum	**NN**	**2-02-002**
Roswell	**NP**	**1-01-001**
rosy	**adjective**	**8-07-008**
rosy	JJ	7-07-007
Rosy	JJ-TL	1-01-001
rosy-fingered	**JJ**	**1-01-001**
rot	**NN**	**6-04-004**
rot	**verb**	**8-05-008**

Word	Tag	Frequency
rot (cont.):		
rot	VB	2-02-002
rots	VBZ	3-03-003
rotting	VBG	3-02-003
Rotarian	**prop. noun**	**1-01-001**
Rotarians	NPS	1-01-001
rotary	**adjective**	**8-06-006**
rotary	JJ	4-02-002
rotary	JJ-HL	1-01-001
Rotary	JJ-TL	3-03-003
Rotary	**prop. noun**	**2-01-002**
Rotary	NP	1-01-001
Rotary	NP-TL	1-01-001
rotate	**verb**	**21-05-011**
rotate	VB	2-02-002
rotates	VBZ	2-01-002
rotated	VBD	2-02-002
rotated	VBN	4-03-004
rotating	VBG	10-02-006
rotating	VBG-HL	1-01-001
rotation	**noun**	**12-05-008**
rotation	NN	11-05-007
rotations	NNS	1-01-001
rotationally	**RB**	**1-01-001**
Rotelli	**NP**	**1-01-001**
rotenone	**NN**	**1-01-001**
Rothko	**NP**	**1-01-001**
rotogravure	**noun**	**1-01-001**
rotogravures	NNS	1-01-001
Rotonda	**NP**	**1-01-001**
rotor	**NN**	**6-01-001**
rotten	**JJ**	**2-01-002**
Rottger	**NP**	**2-01-001**
Rottosei	**NP**	**1-01-001**
rotund	**JJ**	**1-01-001**
rotunda	**noun**	**6-04-004**
rotunda	NN	3-03-003
Rotunda	NN-TL	3-01-001
rotundity	**NN**	**1-01-001**
Rouben	**NP**	**1-01-001**
rouge	**FW-NN**	**1-01-001**
rouge	**NN**	**1-01-001**
Rouge	**prop. noun**	**5-04-004**
Rouge	NP	4-03-003
Rouge	NP-HL	1-01-001
rough	**JJ**	**40-10-035**
rough	**verb**	**2-02-002**
rough	VB	1-01-001
roughed	VBN	1-01-001
rough-and-tumble	**JJ**	**1-01-001**
rough-hewn	**JJ**	**1-01-001**
rough-housing	**NN**	**1-01-001**
rough-sand	**verb**	**2-01-001**
rough-sanded	VBN	2-01-001
rough-tough	**JJ**	**1-01-001**
roughcast	**NN**	**3-01-001**
roughen	**verb**	**2-02-002**
roughened	VBN	2-02-002
rougher	**JJR**	**1-01-001**
roughest	**JJT**	**1-01-001**
roughish	**JJ**	**1-01-001**
roughly	**QL**	**3-02-003**
roughly	**RB**	**22-10-020**
roughneck	**NN**	**1-01-001**
roughness	**NN**	**3-03-003**
roughshod	**JJ**	**1-01-001**
roulette	**noun**	**5-04-004**
roulette	NN	4-04-004
roulette's	NN+BEZ	1-01-001
round	**IN**	**4-01-004**
round	**adjective**	**32-11-025**
round	JJ	28-11-023
round	JJ-HL	1-01-001
Round	JJ-TL	3-02-002
round	**noun**	**32-10-016**
round	NN	18-07-009
Round	NN-TL	1-01-001
rounds	NNS	13-07-008
round	**RB**	**14-08-010**
round	**verb**	**25-11-024**
round	VB	6-04-006
rounded	VBD	5-05-005
rounded	VBN	10-08-010
rounding	VBG	4-04-004
Round	**prop. noun**	**1-01-001**
Round's	NP$	1-01-001
round-bottom	**NN**	**1-01-001**
round-eyed	**JJ**	**1-01-001**
round-faced	**JJ**	**1-01-001**
round-table	**NN**	**1-01-001**
round-the-clock	**JJ**	**1-01-001**
round-tipped	**JJ**	**1-01-001**
roundabout	**JJ**	**2-02-002**
roundhead	**NN**	**3-01-001**
roundhouse	**NN**	**2-02-002**
rounding	**NN**	**1-01-001**
roundly	**QL**	**1-01-001**
roundly	**RB**	**1-01-001**
roundness	**NN**	**1-01-001**
roundup	**noun**	**4-04-004**
roundup	NN	3-03-003
roundups	NNS	1-01-001
Rourke	**prop. noun**	**22-01-002**
Rourke	NP	19-01-002
Rourke's	NP$	3-01-001
rouse	**verb**	**5-04-005**
rouse	VB	2-02-002
roused	VBD	2-02-002
rousing	VBG	1-01-001
rousing	**JJ**	**7-03-006**
Rousseau	**prop. noun**	**22-02-005**
Rousseau	NP	19-02-003
Rousseau's	NP$	3-01-003
Rousseauan	**JJ**	**1-01-001**
route	**FW-NN**	**4-03-004**
route	**noun**	**48-09-030**
route	NN	29-07-019
rewt	NN	1-01-001
rte.	NN	0-00-000
Rte.	NN-TL	2-02-002
Route	NN-TL	10-06-007
routes	NNS	6-04-004
route	**verb**	**1-01-001**
routed	VBD	1-01-001
routine	**JJ**	**17-09-015**
routine	**noun**	**21-12-019**
routine	NN	18-10-016
routines	NNS	3-03-003
routinely	**RB**	**1-01-001**
routing	**noun**	**1-01-001**
routings	NNS	1-01-001
Routo-Jig	**NP**	**1-01-001**
rove	**verb**	**4-04-004**
rove	VB	1-01-001
roved	VBD	1-01-001
roving	VBG	2-02-002
rover	**noun**	**3-01-001**
rover	NN	0-00-000
Rover	NN-TL	3-01-001
Rover	**prop. noun**	**1-01-001**
Rover	NP	0-00-000
Rover	NP-TL	1-01-001
row	**noun**	**48-12-034**
row	NN	31-09-023
Row	NN-TL	1-01-001
rows	NNS	16-09-012
row	**verb**	**5-05-005**
row	VB	3-03-003
rowed	VBN	2-02-002
rowdy	**JJ**	**3-02-003**
rowdy	**NN**	**1-01-001**
Rowlands	**prop. noun**	**1-01-001**
Rowlands'	NP$	1-01-001
Rowley	**NP**	**2-02-002**
Rowswell	**NP**	**1-01-001**
Roxy	**prop. noun**	**1-01-001**
Roxy	NP	0-00-000
Roxy	NP-TL	1-01-001
Roy	**prop. noun**	**38-06-010**
Roy	NP	37-06-010
Roy's	NP$	1-01-001
royal	**adjective**	**45-09-027**
royal	JJ	27-08-017
Royal	JJ-TL	18-05-012
Royal	**NP**	**3-03-003**
Royale	**NP**	**1-01-001**
royalty	**noun**	**9-04-005**
royalty	NN	7-04-004
royalties	NNS	1-01-001
royalties	NNS-HL	1-01-001
royalty-free	**JJ**	**1-01-001**
royaux	**foreign**	**1-01-001**
royaux	FW-JJ	0-00-000
Royaux	FW-JJ-TL	1-01-001
Royce	**NP**	**3-02-002**
Roylott	**prop. noun**	**1-01-001**
Roylott's	NP$	1-01-001
Rozella	**NP**	**1-01-001**

Word	Tag	Frequency
Rozelle	**NP**	**1-01-001**
Ruanda-Urundi	**prop. noun**	**8-01-001**
Ruanda-Urundi	NP	7-01-001
Ruanda-Urundi	NP-TL	1-01-001
Ruark	**prop. noun**	**1-01-001**
Ruark's	NP$	1-01-001
rub	**NN**	**2-02-002**
rub	**verb**	**34-10-023**
rub	VB	4-04-004
rubbed	VBD	13-06-010
rubbed	VBN	5-04-005
rubbing	VBG	11-05-008
rubbin'	VBG	1-01-001
rubber	**noun**	**15-07-013**
rubber	NN	13-07-011
Rubber	NN-TL	2-01-002
rubber-like	**JJ**	**1-01-001**
rubberize	**verb**	**1-01-001**
rubberized	VBN	1-01-001
rubbery	**JJ**	**1-01-001**
rubbish	**NN**	**4-03-004**
rubble	**NN**	**1-01-001**
rubdown	**NN**	**1-01-001**
Rube	**NP**	**1-01-001**
Rubens	**NP**	**1-01-001**
rubicund	**JJ**	**1-01-001**
rubric	**NN**	**1-01-001**
ruby	**noun**	**1-01-001**
rubies	NNS	1-01-001
Rucellai	**NP**	**1-01-001**
ruckus	**NN**	**1-01-001**
rudder	**NN**	**1-01-001**
rudderless	**JJ**	**1-01-001**
ruddiness	**NN**	**1-01-001**
ruddy	**JJ**	**2-02-002**
ruddy	**QL**	**1-01-001**
rude	**adjective**	**6-05-006**
rude	JJ	5-04-005
rude	JJ-HL	1-01-001
rudely	**RB**	**2-02-002**
rudeness	**NN**	**1-01-001**
rudimentary	**JJ**	**4-04-004**
Rudkoebing	**NP**	**1-01-001**
Rudolf	**NP**	**1-01-001**
Rudolph	**NP**	**3-01-001**
Rudy	**NP**	**4-02-003**
Rudyard	**NP**	**1-01-001**
rue	**foreign**	**4-03-003**
rue	FW-NN	0-00-000
Rue	FW-NN-TL	4-03-003
rue	**NN**	**2-02-002**
ruefully	**RB**	**3-03-003**
ruefulness	**NN**	**1-01-001**
ruffian	**noun**	**3-03-003**
ruffian	NN	2-02-002
ruffians	NNS	1-01-001
ruffle	**verb**	**4-03-004**
ruffles	VBZ	1-01-001
ruffled	VBD	1-01-001
ruffled	VBN	2-02-002
Rufus	**NP**	**1-01-001**
rug	**noun**	**17-08-013**
rug	NN	13-08-011
rugs	NNS	4-03-004
Ruger	**prop. noun**	**5-01-001**
Ruger	NP	4-01-001
Ruger's	NP$	1-01-001
rugged	**JJ**	**19-07-015**
ruggedly	**RB**	**1-01-001**
Ruggiero	**NP**	**1-01-001**
ruh	**FW-NN**	**2-01-001**
Ruidoso	**NP**	**1-01-001**
ruin	**noun**	**17-07-015**
ruin	NN	9-05-008
ruins	NNS	8-04-007
ruin	**verb**	**22-08-018**
ruin	VB	5-04-005
ruined	VBN	16-08-013
ruining	VBG	1-01-001
ruinous	**JJ**	**1-01-001**
Ruiz	**NP**	**1-01-001**
rule	**noun**	**148-13-075**
rule	NN	58-12-042
rule	NN-HL	3-01-001
Rule	NN-TL	5-02-002
rules	NNS	72-13-035
rules	NNS-HL	1-01-001
Rules	NNS-TL	9-01-002
rule	**verb**	**53-10-041**

Word	Tag	Frequency
rule (cont.):		
rule	VB	7-05-006
rules	VBZ	3-02-003
ruled	VBD	13-08-011
ruled	VBN	18-07-016
ruling	VBG	11-03-008
ruling	VBG-HL	1-01-001
ruler	**noun**	**13-07-011**
ruler	NN	3-03-003
rulers	NNS	8-05-007
Rulers	NNS-TL	1-01-001
rulers'	NNS$	1-01-001
ruling	**noun**	**16-04-008**
ruling	NN	8-03-006
rul.	NN	0-00-000
Rul.	NN-TL	1-01-001
Ruling	NN-TL	4-01-001
ruling's	NN$	1-01-001
rulings	NNS	2-01-002
ruling-class	**NN**	**1-01-001**
rum	**noun**	**3-03-003**
rum	NN	2-02-002
Rum	NN-TL	1-01-001
rum-tum-tum	**UH**	**1-01-001**
Rumania	**NP**	**1-01-001**
Rumanian	**JJ**	**1-01-001**
Rumanian	**prop. noun**	**1-01-001**
Rumanians	NPS	1-01-001
rumble	**NN**	**2-02-002**
rumble	**verb**	**5-03-004**
rumbles	VBZ	1-01-001
rumbled	VBD	2-01-001
rumbling	VBG	2-02-002
rumdum	**NN**	**2-01-001**
rumen	**NN**	**2-01-001**
Rumford	**NP**	**2-02-002**
ruminant	**noun**	**1-01-001**
ruminants	NNS	0-00-000
ruminants	NNS-HL	1-01-001
rummage	**verb**	**4-04-004**
rummaged	VBD	1-01-001
rummaging	VBG	3-03-003
Rummel	**NP**	**1-01-001**
rummy	**NN**	**1-01-001**
rumor	**noun**	**14-07-009**
rumor	NN	8-05-006
rumors	NNS	6-04-004
rumor	**verb**	**2-02-002**
rumored	VBN	2-02-002
rump	**NN**	**2-01-002**
rumple	**verb**	**2-02-002**
rumpled	VBN	2-02-002
rumpus	**NN**	**1-01-001**
Rumscheidt	**NP**	**1-01-001**
run	**noun**	**94-11-036**
run	NN	52-11-027
Run	NN-TL	3-02-002
runs	NNS	39-06-012
run	**verb**	**431-15-226**
run	VB	126-15-102
runs	VBZ	16-10-015
ran	VBD	134-14-084
run	VBD	1-01-001
run	VBN	31-11-026
running	VBG	120-15-080
runing	VBG	1-01-001
runnin'	VBG	2-01-001
run-down	**adjective**	**2-02-002**
run-down	JJ	1-01-001
rundown	JJ	1-01-001
run-of-the-mine	**JJ**	**1-01-001**
run-scoring	**JJ**	**1-01-001**
run-up	**JJ**	**1-01-001**
run-up	**noun**	**2-01-001**
run-up	NN	1-01-001
run-ups	NNS	1-01-001
run/chamber	**VBN**	**1-01-001**
runabout	**NN**	**1-01-001**
runaway	**JJ**	**4-02-002**
runaway	**NN**	**1-01-001**
Rundfunk	**foreign**	**1-01-001**
Rundfunk	FW-NP	0-00-000
Rundfunk	FW-NP-TL	1-01-001
Rundfunk-Sinfonie-Orchester	**NP**	**1-01-001**
Rundfunkchor	**NP**	**1-01-001**
rundown	**NN**	**2-01-002**
rune	**noun**	**1-01-001**
runes	NNS	1-01-001
rung	**NN**	**2-01-002**

Word	Tag	Frequency
runner	**noun**	**6-04-005**
runner	NN	1-01-001
runners	NNS	5-04-004
runner-up	**NN**	**2-02-002**
running	**NN**	**3-03-003**
runoff	**NN**	**2-02-002**
runt	**NN**	**1-01-001**
runway	**noun**	**8-04-006**
runway	NN	4-02-004
runways	NNS	4-02-002
Runyon	**prop. noun**	**4-01-001**
Runyon	NP	3-01-001
Runyon's	NP$	1-01-001
rupee	**noun**	**20-01-001**
rupee	NN	6-01-001
rupees	NNS	12-01-001
rupees	NNS-HL	2-01-001
Ruppert	**NP**	**1-01-001**
rupture	**NN**	**3-01-001**
rupture	**verb**	**2-01-002**
ruptured	VBN	2-01-002
rural	**adjective**	**54-09-027**
rural	JJ	46-09-023
Rural	JJ-TL	7-04-006
Rural	JJ-TL-HL	1-01-001
ruse	**NN**	**2-02-002**
rush	**noun**	**17-09-017**
rush	NN	16-09-016
rushes	NNS	1-01-001
rush	**verb**	**42-14-033**
rush	VB	3-03-003
rushes	VBZ	2-02-002
rushed	VBD	20-11-018
rushed	VBN	7-04-005
rushing	VBG	10-05-006
Rush	**NP**	**1-01-001**
Rushall	**NP**	**1-01-001**
Rushmore	**prop. noun**	**1-01-001**
Rushmore	NP	0-00-000
Rushmore	NP-TL	1-01-001
Rusk	**prop. noun**	**13-04-007**
Rusk	NP	9-04-006
Rusk	NP-HL	1-01-001
Rusk's	NP$	3-01-001
Russ	**NP**	**21-02-002**
russe	**NN**	**1-01-001**
Russell	**prop. noun**	**19-05-009**
Russell	NP	12-05-009
Russell's	NP$	7-02-002
russet	**JJ**	**1-01-001**
russet-colored	**JJ**	**1-01-001**
Russia	**prop. noun**	**86-11-046**
Russia	NP	66-11-044
Russia	NP-HL	1-01-001
Russia	NP-TL	5-03-003
Russia's	NP$	14-05-010
Russian	**adjective**	**69-11-034**
Russian	JJ	67-11-033
Russian	JJ-TL	2-01-002
Russian	**prop. noun**	**43-09-027**
Russian	NP	11-05-007
Russians	NPS	29-09-021
Russians	NPS-HL	1-01-001
Russian (cont.):		
Russians	NPS-TL	1-01-001
Russians'	NPS$	1-01-001
Russian-dominated	**JJ**	**1-01-001**
Russo-American	**JJ**	**1-01-001**
rust	**NN**	**7-02-004**
rust	**verb**	**2-02-002**
rust	VB	1-01-001
rusted	VBN	1-01-001
Rust	**NP**	**2-01-001**
rustic	**JJ**	**3-02-003**
rusting	**NN**	**1-01-001**
rustle	**NN**	**2-02-002**
rustle	**verb**	**13-03-006**
rustle	VB	2-01-001
rustled	VBD	1-01-001
rustled	VBN	1-01-001
rustling	VBG	9-02-003
rustler	**noun**	**5-02-002**
rustler	NN	3-02-002
rustler	NN-NC	1-01-001
rustlers	NNS	1-01-001
rustler-hunter	**NN**	**1-01-001**
rustling	**noun**	**2-02-002**
rustling	NN	1-01-001
rustlin'	NN	1-01-001
rustproof	**JJ**	**1-01-001**
rusty	**adjective**	**8-05-006**
rusty	JJ	7-04-005
Rusty	JJ-TL	1-01-001
rut	**noun**	**3-03-003**
rut	NN	1-01-001
ruts	NNS	2-02-002
rut	**verb**	**1-01-001**
rutted	VBN	1-01-001
rutabaga	**noun**	**2-02-002**
rutabaga	NN	1-01-001
rutabagas	NNS	1-01-001
Ruth	**prop. noun**	**31-05-009**
Ruth	NP	21-05-007
Ruth	NP-TL	2-02-002
Ruth's	NP$	8-02-003
ruthenium	**NN**	**1-01-001**
Rutherford	**NP**	**1-01-001**
ruthless	**JJ**	**7-06-007**
ruthlessly	**RB**	**2-02-002**
ruthlessness	**NN**	**3-03-003**
Rutstein	**NP**	**1-01-001**
Ruysch	**NP**	**1-01-001**
Ryan	**NP**	**15-02-002**
Rychard	**prop. noun**	**2-01-001**
Rychard	NP	1-01-001
Ryc'	NP	1-01-001
Ryder	**NP**	**1-01-001**
rye	**noun**	**3-02-003**
rye	NN	2-01-002
Rye	NN-TL	1-01-001
Rye	**NP**	**1-01-001**
Ryerson	**NP**	**1-01-001**
Rylie	**NP**	**1-01-001**
Ryne	**NP**	**1-01-001**
Ryusenji	**NP**	**8-01-001**

S

Word	Tag	Frequency
S	**NP**	**11-02-003**
s.	**adjective**	**2-01-001**
s.	JJ	0-00-000
S.	JJ-TL	2-01-001
S.	**prop. noun**	**114-11-062**
S.	NP	74-09-044
S.	NP-HL	2-01-002
S.	NP-TL	38-08-022
S.C.	**NP**	**2-02-002**
S.K.	**NP**	**5-01-001**
S.P.C.A.	**prop. noun**	**1-01-001**
S.P.C.A.	NP	0-00-000
S.P.C.A.	NP-TL	1-01-001
S.S.	**NP**	**1-01-001**
S.S.R.	**NP**	**1-01-001**
s'accuse	**FW-PPL+VBZ**	**1-01-001**
s'excuse	**FW-PPL+VBZ**	**1-01-001**
Saabye	**NP**	**1-01-001**
Saadi	**NP**	**1-01-001**
SAAMI	**prop. noun**	**2-01-001**
SAAMI's	NP$	2-01-001
Saba	**NP**	**1-01-001**
Sabbath	**NP**	**2-02-002**
Sabella	**NP**	**7-01-001**
Sabina	**NP**	**2-01-001**
sabinas	**foreign**	**1-01-001**
sabinas	FW-NNS	0-00-000
sabinas	FW-NNS-NC	1-01-001
Sabine	**NP**	**2-02-002**
sable	**noun**	**3-02-002**
sable	NN	2-02-002
sables	NNS	1-01-001
Sabol	**NP**	**1-01-001**
sabotage	**NN**	**3-02-002**
Sabra	**prop. noun**	**1-01-001**
Sabras	NPS	1-01-001

Word	Tag	Frequency
sabre	**noun**	**3-03-003**
sabre	NN	2-02-002
saber	NN	1-01-001
sabre-rattling	**NN**	**1-01-001**
sachem	**noun**	**3-02-002**
sachems	NNS	2-02-002
sachems'	NNS$	1-01-001
Sacheverell	**NP**	**1-01-001**
sack	**noun**	**10-05-008**
sack	NN	6-04-006
Sack	NN-TL	2-01-001
sacks	NNS	1-01-001
sackes	NNS	1-01-001
sack	**verb**	**1-01-001**
sacking	VBG	1-01-001
sacker	**NN**	**1-01-001**
sacral	**JJ**	**1-01-001**
sacrament	**noun**	**3-03-003**
sacrament	NN	1-01-001
sacraments	NNS	2-02-002
Sacramento	**NP**	**3-03-003**
sacre	**foreign**	**1-01-001**
sacre	FW-NN	0-00-000
Sacre	FW-NN-TL	1-01-001
sacred	**adjective**	**38-09-028**
sacred	JJ	34-09-026
Sacred	JJ-TL	4-01-002
sacredness	**NN**	**4-01-002**
Sacrestia	**NP**	**1-01-001**
sacrifice	**noun**	**26-10-023**
sacrifice	NN	19-10-018
Sacrifice	NN-TL	1-01-001
sacrifices	NNS	5-04-005
sacrifices	NNS-HL	1-01-001
sacrifice	**verb**	**14-06-012**
sacrifice	VB	10-04-008
sacrificed	VBN	2-01-002
sacrificing	VBG	2-02-002
sacrificial	**JJ**	**2-02-002**
sacrificium	**FW-NN**	**2-01-001**
sacrilege	**NN**	**2-02-002**
sacrosanct	**JJ**	**1-01-001**
sad	**JJ**	**35-12-025**
sadden	**verb**	**1-01-001**
saddened	VBN	1-01-001
sadder	**JJR**	**1-01-001**
saddle	**noun**	**26-06-014**
saddle	NN	22-04-011
Saddle	NN-TL	2-01-001
saddles	NNS	2-02-002
saddle	**verb**	**5-04-005**
saddle	VB	1-01-001
saddled	VBD	1-01-001
saddled	VBN	3-03-003
saddlebag	**noun**	**3-01-001**
saddlebags	NNS	3-01-001
Sadie	**NP**	**5-01-001**
sadism	**NN**	**3-03-003**
sadist	**NN**	**1-01-001**
sadistic	**JJ**	**2-02-002**
sadly	**RB**	**12-06-011**
sadness	**NN**	**6-06-006**
safari	**NN**	**2-02-002**
Safavid	**prop. noun**	**1-01-001**
Safavids	NPS	1-01-001
safe	**JJ**	**51-13-046**
safe	**NN**	**7-03-004**
safe-conduct	**NN**	**1-01-001**
safe-cracking	**JJ**	**1-01-001**
safe-driving	**NN**	**1-01-001**
safeguard	**noun**	**4-04-004**
safeguard	NN	3-03-003
safeguards	NNS	1-01-001
safeguard	**VB**	**2-01-002**
safekeeping	**JJ**	**1-01-001**
safely	**RB**	**13-09-013**
safer	**JJR**	**5-05-005**
safest	**JJT**	**4-04-004**
safety	**noun**	**48-10-028**
safety	NN	46-10-027
Safety	NN-TL	1-01-001
safeties	NNS	1-01-001
saffron	**NN**	**1-01-001**
sag	**noun**	**1-01-001**
sags	NNS	1-01-001
sag	**verb**	**11-07-010**
sag	VB	4-04-004
sagged	VBD	3-03-003
sagging	VBG	4-02-004
saga	**noun**	**7-04-007**
saga	NN	6-03-006
Saga	NN-TL	1-01-001
Sagami	**prop. noun**	**1-01-001**
Sagami	NP	0-00-000
Sagami	NP-TL	1-01-001
sage	**noun**	**3-03-003**
sage	NN	2-02-002
sages	NNS	1-01-001
sagebrush	**NN**	**1-01-001**
sago	**NN**	**1-01-001**
Sahara	**prop. noun**	**2-02-002**
Sahara	NP	0-00-000
Sahara	NP-TL	2-02-002
Saigon	**NP**	**1-01-001**
sail	**noun**	**7-04-006**
sail	NN	4-03-003
Sail	NN-TL	1-01-001
sails	NNS	2-02-002
sail	**verb**	**33-10-019**
sail	VB	6-03-003
Sail	VB-TL	1-01-001
sailed	VBD	7-03-005
sailed	VBN	3-01-002
sailing	VBG	16-08-013
sailboat	**noun**	**4-02-002**
sailboat	NN	1-01-001
sailboats	NNS	3-01-001
sailing	**NN**	**4-02-002**
sailor	**noun**	**13-07-008**
sailor	NN	4-04-004
Sailor	NN-TL	1-01-001
sailors	NNS	8-06-006
sailorly	**JJ**	**1-01-001**
saint	**noun**	**103-14-048**
saint	NN	10-08-009
st.	NN	0-00-000
St.	NN-TL	82-12-032
Saint	NN-TL	5-05-005
saints	NNS	4-03-004
Saints	NNS-TL	2-02-002
Saint	**prop. noun**	**65-12-030**
Saint	NP	3-03-003
St.	NP	47-11-023
St.	NP-HL	3-01-003
St.	NP-TL	11-05-008
Saint	NP-TL	1-01-001
Saint-Saens	**NP**	**1-01-001**
sainted	**adjective**	**1-01-001**
sainted	JJ	0-00-000
Sainted	JJ-TL	1-01-001
sainthood	**NN**	**1-01-001**
saintliness	**NN**	**1-01-001**
Saintsbury	**NP**	**1-01-001**
sake	**FW-NN**	**6-02-002**
sake	**NN**	**34-12-030**
sake	**UH**	**1-01-001**
Sakellariadis	**prop. noun**	**3-01-001**
Sakellariadis	NP	2-01-001
Sakellariadises	NPS	1-01-001
Sako	**NP**	**1-01-001**
SAKOS	**foreign**	**1-01-001**
SAKOS	FW-NN	0-00-000
SAKOS	FW-NN-NC	1-01-001
salable	**JJ**	**1-01-001**
salacious	**JJ**	**2-02-002**
salad	**noun**	**12-05-008**
salad	NN	9-05-006
salads	NNS	3-02-002
salamander	**noun**	**2-01-001**
salamander	NN	1-01-001
Salamander	NN-TL	1-01-001
salami	**NN**	**7-03-003**
salaried	**JJ**	**1-01-001**
salary	**noun**	**51-12-029**
salary	NN	41-12-025
salary	NN-HL	2-01-002
salaries	NNS	8-06-008
sale	**noun**	**177-12-058**
sale	NN	44-11-032
sales	NNS	127-08-035
Sales	NNS	1-01-001
sales	NNS-HL	3-02-003
Sales	NNS-TL	2-02-002
Saledo	**NP**	**3-01-001**
Salem	**prop. noun**	**19-04-008**
Salem	NP	17-04-008
Salem	NP-HL	2-01-002
sales-building	**JJ**	**1-01-001**

Word	Tag	Frequency
sales-conscious	**JJ**	**1-01-001**
salesgirl	**NN**	**1-01-001**
saleslady	**NN**	**3-01-001**
salesman	**noun**	**32-09-016**
salesman	NN	12-07-010
salesman's	NN$	1-01-001
salesmen	NNS	18-06-006
salesmen	NNS-HL	1-01-001
salesmanship	**noun**	**6-03-003**
salesmanship	NN	5-03-003
salesmanship	NN-HL	1-01-001
SalFininistas	**prop. noun**	**2-01-001**
SalFininistas	NP	1-01-001
SalFininistas	NP-HL	1-01-001
Salida	**NP**	**1-01-001**
salient	**JJ**	**4-03-003**
saline	**adjective**	**8-02-002**
saline	JJ	7-02-002
saline	JJ-NC	1-01-001
saline	**NN**	**23-01-003**
Salinger	**NP**	**4-03-003**
Salisbury	**prop. noun**	**5-02-002**
Salisbury	NP	4-02-002
Salisbury	NP-TL	1-01-001
Salish	**NP**	**1-01-001**
saliva	**NN**	**4-02-002**
salivary	**JJ**	**1-01-001**
salivate	**VB**	**1-01-001**
Salk	**NP**	**1-01-001**
Salle	**prop. noun**	**2-02-002**
Salle	NP	0-00-000
Salle	NP-TL	2-02-002
sallow	**JJ**	**1-01-001**
sally	**noun**	**1-01-001**
sallies	NNS	1-01-001
Sally	**prop. noun**	**16-05-005**
Sally	NP	14-05-005
Sally's	NP$	2-01-001
sallying	**NN**	**1-01-001**
salmon	**NN**	**2-02-002**
Salmon	**NP**	**1-01-001**
Salomonovich	**NP**	**1-01-001**
salon	**noun**	**4-03-003**
salon	NN	1-01-001
salons	NNS	3-02-002
saloon	**noun**	**20-07-013**
saloon	NN	10-05-008
Saloon	NN-TL	2-02-002
saloons	NNS	8-05-005
saloonkeeper	**NN**	**1-01-001**
Salpetriere	**NP**	**1-01-001**
Salsich	**NP**	**1-01-001**
salt	**noun**	**52-12-027**
salt	NN	44-11-024
salt	NN-HL	1-01-001
Salt	NN-TL	1-01-001
salts	NNS	6-03-005
salt	**verb**	**6-05-005**
salted	VBN	4-03-003
salting	VBG	2-02-002
salt-crusted	**JJ**	**1-01-001**
salt-edged	**JJ**	**1-01-001**
salt-fractionation	**NN**	**1-01-001**
saltbush	**NN**	**1-01-001**
Salter	**prop. noun**	**10-02-002**
Salter	NP	9-02-002
Salter's	NP$	1-01-001
Saltis-McErlane	**NP**	**1-01-001**
Salton	**NP**	**1-01-001**
Saltonstall	**NP**	**1-01-001**
salty	**JJ**	**4-03-004**
Salu	**NP**	**1-01-001**
salubrious	**JJ**	**2-02-002**
salutaris	**FW-JJ**	**1-01-001**
salutary	**JJ**	**5-04-005**
salutation	**NN**	**1-01-001**
salute	**NN**	**2-02-002**
salute	**verb**	**4-04-004**
salute	VB	1-01-001
saluted	VBD	2-02-002
saluted	VBN	1-01-001
Salvador	**NP**	**3-02-002**
salvage	**NN**	**3-03-003**
salvage	**verb**	**4-03-004**
salvage	VB	2-02-002
salvaging	VBG	2-02-002
salvation	**noun**	**32-04-015**
salvation	NN	29-03-013
Salvation	NN-TL	3-02-002
Salvatore	**NP**	**1-01-001**
salve	**noun**	**4-02-003**
salve	NN	3-02-003
salves	NNS	1-01-001
salvo	**noun**	**3-03-003**
salvo	NN	2-02-002
salvos	NNS	1-01-001
Salyer	**prop. noun**	**3-01-001**
Salyer's	NP$	0-00-000
Salyer's	NP$-TL	3-01-001
Sam	**prop. noun**	**83-09-027**
Sam	NP	76-08-024
Sam	NP-HL	2-01-002
Sam	NP-TL	1-01-001
Sam's	NP$	4-02-004
Samar	**NP**	**1-01-001**
samba	**foreign**	**1-01-001**
samba	FW-NN	0-00-000
Samba	FW-NN-TL	1-01-001
sambur	**NN**	**1-01-001**
same	**post-det.**	**686-15-336**
same	AP	684-15-336
same	AP-HL	1-01-001
Same	AP-TL	1-01-001
sameness	**NN**	**4-02-002**
Sammartini	**NP**	**1-01-001**
Sammy	**NP**	**1-01-001**
Samoa	**prop. noun**	**1-01-001**
Samoa	NP	0-00-000
Samoa	NP-TL	1-01-001
SAMOS	**NP**	**2-02-002**
samovar	**NN**	**2-01-001**
sample	**noun**	**85-09-029**
sample	NN	54-08-022
sample	NN-HL	2-01-001
samples	NNS	27-05-012
samples	NNS-HL	2-01-002
sample	**verb**	**20-04-008**
sample	VB	1-01-001
sampled	VBD	1-01-001
sampled	VBN	6-04-005
sampling	VBG	12-01-003
sampler	**noun**	**1-01-001**
samplers	NNS	1-01-001
sampling	**NN**	**10-03-006**
Sampson	**NP**	**2-01-001**
Samuel	**prop. noun**	**34-08-022**
Samuel	NP	32-08-021
Samuel	NP-HL	1-01-001
Samuel	NP-TL	1-01-001
Samuels	**NP**	**1-01-001**
San	**prop. noun**	**70-14-039**
San	NP	57-13-034
San	NP-HL	1-01-001
San	NP-TL	12-06-008
sana	**FW-JJ**	**1-01-001**
SanAntonio	**NP**	**1-01-001**
sanatorium	**noun**	**2-02-002**
sanatorium	NN	1-01-001
Sanatorium	NN-TL	1-01-001
Sanchez	**NP**	**1-01-001**
Sancho	**NP**	**3-01-001**
sanctam	**foreign**	**1-01-001**
sanctam	FW-JJ	0-00-000
Sanctam	FW-JJ-TL	1-01-001
sanctify	**verb**	**1-01-001**
sanctified	VBN	1-01-001
sanctimonious	**JJ**	**2-02-002**
sanction	**noun**	**14-05-009**
sanction	NN	7-04-006
sanctions	NNS	6-02-004
sanctions	NNS-HL	1-01-001
sanction	**verb**	**10-05-008**
sanction	VB	4-04-004
sanctions	VBZ	2-01-001
sanctioned	VBN	4-03-004
sanctity	**NN**	**3-02-003**
sanctuary	**noun**	**10-06-006**
sanctuary	NN	8-06-006
Sanctuary	NN-TL	1-01-001
sanctuary's	NN$	1-01-001
sand	**noun**	**37-11-024**
sand	NN	28-10-018
sands	NNS	7-05-006
Sands	NNS-TL	2-02-002
sand	**verb**	**2-01-002**
sanding	VBG	2-01-002
sandal	**noun**	**5-03-004**
sandals	NNS	5-03-004

Word	Tag	Frequency
Sandalphon	**NP**	**3-01-001**
sandalwood	**noun**	**2-02-002**
sandalwood	NN	1-01-001
Sandalwood	NN-TL	1-01-001
sandbar	**noun**	**1-01-001**
sandbars	NNS	1-01-001
Sandburg	**prop. noun**	**27-03-004**
Sandburg	NP	22-02-002
Sandburg's	NP$	3-03-003
Sandburgs	NPS	2-02-002
Sande	**prop. noun**	**1-01-001**
Sande's	NP$	1-01-001
sander	**NN**	**1-01-001**
Sanderson	**NP**	**2-01-001**
Sandman	**NP**	**5-01-001**
sandpaper	**NN**	**1-01-001**
Sandra	**NP**	**1-01-001**
Sands	**NP**	**1-01-001**
sandwich	**noun**	**13-05-011**
sandwich	NN	9-05-008
sandwiches	NNS	4-02-004
Sandwich	**NP**	**1-01-001**
sandwich-type	**JJ**	**1-01-001**
sandy	**JJ**	**6-05-006**
sane	**adjective**	**8-05-005**
sane	JJ	5-04-004
Sane	JJ-TL	3-01-001
saner	**JJR**	**1-01-001**
sanest	**JJT**	**1-01-001**
Sanford	**prop. noun**	**2-01-001**
Sanford's	NP$	0-00-000
Sanford's	NP$-TL	2-01-001
sang	**FW-NN**	**1-01-001**
sang-froid	**NN**	**1-01-001**
Sangallo	**prop. noun**	**2-01-001**
Sangallo	NP	1-01-001
Sangallo's	NP$	1-01-001
sangaree	**NN**	**1-01-001**
Sanger-Harris	**NP**	**1-01-001**
sanguineous	**JJ**	**1-01-001**
sanguineum	**NP**	**1-01-001**
sanhedrin	**NN**	**1-01-001**
sanipractor	**NN**	**2-01-001**
sanitaire	**FW-JJ**	**1-01-001**
sanitarium	**NN**	**1-01-001**
sanitary	**adjective**	**4-03-004**
sanitary	JJ	1-01-001
Sanitary	JJ-TL	3-02-003
sanitation	**noun**	**11-06-010**
sanitation	NN	8-05-007
Sanitation	NN-TL	3-03-003
sanity	**NN**	**4-04-004**
sans	**foreign**	**2-02-002**
sans	FW-IN	0-00-000
Sans	FW-IN-TL	2-02-002
Sansom	**NP**	**12-01-001**
Sansome	**NP**	**1-01-001**
Santa	**prop. noun**	**37-08-014**
Santa	NP	24-06-011
Sant'	NP	1-01-001
Sant'	NP-TL	2-01-001
Sante	NP	5-01-001
Santa	NP-HL	1-01-001
Santa	NP-TL	3-02-002
Santa's	NP$	1-01-001
Santayana	**prop. noun**	**4-02-002**
Santayana	NP	3-02-002
Santayana's	NP$	1-01-001
Santo	**NP**	**2-01-001**
sap	**NN**	**1-01-001**
sap	**verb**	**5-03-005**
saps	VBZ	1-01-001
sapped	VBD	1-01-001
sapped	VBN	2-02-002
sapping	VBG	1-01-001
Sapio	**NP**	**3-02-002**
sapling	**NN**	**2-02-002**
saponin	**noun**	**1-01-001**
saponins	NNS	1-01-001
sappy	**JJ**	**1-01-001**
Sara	**prop. noun**	**5-01-001**
Sara	NP	4-01-001
Sara's	NP$	1-01-001
Saracen	**prop. noun**	**2-02-002**
Saracens	NPS	2-02-002
Sarah	**prop. noun**	**30-04-005**
Sarah	NP	26-04-005
Sarah's	NP$	4-01-001
Saran	**prop. noun**	**1-01-001**
Saran (cont.):		
Saran	NP	0-00-000
Saran	NP-HL	1-01-001
Sarasate	**NP**	**1-01-001**
Sarason	**NP**	**1-01-001**
Sarasota	**NP**	**1-01-001**
Saratoga	**NP**	**4-04-004**
sarcasm	**noun**	**2-02-002**
sarcasm	NN	1-01-001
sarcasms	NNS	1-01-001
sarcastic	**JJ**	**1-01-001**
sarcastically	**RB**	**1-01-001**
sarcolemmal	**JJ**	**1-01-001**
Sardanapalus	**NP**	**1-01-001**
sardine	**noun**	**2-02-002**
sardines	NNS	2-02-002
sardonic	**JJ**	**2-02-002**
Sargent	**NP**	**5-04-005**
sari	**NN**	**1-01-001**
Sarkees	**NP**	**2-01-001**
Sarmi	**NP**	**1-01-001**
Sarpsis	**NP**	**2-01-001**
sarsaparilla	**noun**	**1-01-001**
sarsaparilla	NN	0-00-000
Sarsaparilla	NN-TL	1-01-001
Sarti	**NP**	**1-01-001**
Sartoris	**NP**	**3-01-002**
Sartre	**NP**	**2-02-002**
Sarum	**prop. noun**	**1-01-001**
Sarum's	NP$	0-00-000
Sarum's	NP$-TL	1-01-001
sash	**NN**	**3-02-003**
sashay	**verb**	**1-01-001**
sashayed	VBD	1-01-001
sashimi	**NN**	**1-01-001**
sassafras	**NN**	**2-01-002**
sassing	**NN**	**1-01-001**
Satan	**prop. noun**	**4-03-004**
Satan	NP	3-03-003
Satan's	NP$	0-00-000
Satan's	NP$-TL	1-01-001
satellite	**noun**	**15-07-009**
satellite	NN	7-05-006
satellite	NN-HL	1-01-001
satellites	NNS	7-04-004
satiate	**VB**	**1-01-001**
satiety	**NN**	**2-02-002**
satin	**NN**	**5-02-003**
satin-covered	**JJ**	**1-01-001**
satire	**noun**	**12-05-007**
satire	NN	9-04-006
satires	NNS	0-00-000
Satires	NNS-TL	3-01-001
satiric	**JJ**	**4-03-003**
satirical	**JJ**	**3-03-003**
satirically	**RB**	**1-01-001**
satirist	**NN**	**1-01-001**
satirize	**verb**	**1-01-001**
satirizes	VBZ	1-01-001
Satis	**prop. noun**	**2-01-001**
Satis	NP	0-00-000
Satis	NP-TL	2-01-001
satisfaction	**noun**	**32-13-030**
satisfaction	NN	28-12-026
satisfactions	NNS	4-04-004
satisfactorily	**RB**	**11-06-007**
satisfactory	**JJ**	**39-08-036**
satisfy	**verb**	**63-13-054**
satisfy	VB	16-09-015
satisfies	VBZ	3-01-001
satisfied	VBD	5-04-005
satisfied	VBN	31-09-029
satisfying	VBG	8-07-008
satisfying	**JJ**	**5-03-004**
Satterfield	**NP**	**1-01-001**
saturate	**verb**	**7-04-005**
saturated	VBN	7-04-005
saturation	**NN**	**5-03-004**
Saturday	**adv. noun**	**72-10-041**
Saturday	NR	65-10-038
Saturday	NR-HL	1-01-001
Saturday	NR-TL	1-01-001
Saturday's	NR$	3-02-003
Saturdays	NRS	2-02-002
Saturday-night	**JJ**	**1-01-001**
Saturn	**NP**	**3-01-001**
sauce	**noun**	**24-03-004**
sauce	NN	17-02-003
sauce	NN-HL	2-01-002

Word	Tag	Frequency
sauce (cont.):		
sauces	NNS	5-02-002
sauce	**VB**	**1-01-001**
saucepan	**NN**	**3-01-002**
saucer	**noun**	**2-02-002**
saucers	NNS	2-02-002
saucy	**JJ**	**1-01-001**
Saud	**prop. noun**	**2-01-001**
Saud	NP	1-01-001
Saud's	NP$	1-01-001
Saudi	**NP**	**2-01-001**
Saudi-American	**JJ**	**1-01-001**
sauerkraut	**NN**	**4-02-002**
Saul	**NP**	**2-02-002**
Saunders	**NP**	**1-01-001**
sausage	**noun**	**6-03-003**
sausage	NN	1-01-001
sausages	NNS	5-02-002
sausage-meat	**NN**	**1-01-001**
saute	**VB**	**1-01-001**
sauterne	**JJ**	**1-01-001**
Sauterne	**prop. noun**	**1-01-001**
Sauternes	NPS	1-01-001
savage	**JJ**	**19-09-019**
savage	**noun**	**7-04-004**
savage	NN	1-01-001
savages	NNS	6-03-003
Savage	**prop. noun**	**2-02-002**
Savage	NP	1-01-001
Savage	NP-TL	1-01-001
savagely	**QL**	**1-01-001**
savagely	**RB**	**2-02-002**
savagery	**NN**	**1-01-001**
Savannah	**prop. noun**	**9-05-005**
Savannah	NP	8-04-004
Savannah	NP-TL	1-01-001
Savannakhet	**NP**	**2-01-001**
save	**IN**	**7-04-007**
save	**verb**	**121-15-086**
save	VB	53-12-040
save	VB-HL	2-02-002
saves	VBZ	4-04-004
saves	VBZ-HL	1-01-001
saved	VBD	11-07-011
saved	VBN	32-11-024
saving	VBG	18-10-018
saver	**NN**	**1-01-001**
saving	**noun**	**24-05-021**
saving	NN	3-02-003
savings	NNS	17-05-014
Savings	NNS-TL	4-01-004
savings	**NN**	**2-01-002**
savior	**noun**	**15-03-006**
savior	NN	2-02-002
saviour	NN	0-00-000
saviour	NN-HL	1-01-001
Saviour	NN-TL	8-01-002
Savior	NN-TL	4-01-003
Savonarola	**NP**	**1-01-001**
savor	**NN**	**1-01-001**
savor	**verb**	**6-06-006**
savored	VBD	2-02-002
savored	VBN	1-01-001
savoring	VBG	3-03-003
savory	**JJ**	**4-03-003**
Savoy	**prop. noun**	**4-01-002**
Savoy	NP	2-01-001
Savoy	NP-TL	2-01-002
Savoyard	**prop. noun**	**2-01-001**
Savoyards	NPS	2-01-001
savvy	**VB**	**1-01-001**
saw	**noun**	**8-05-006**
saw	NN	4-02-003
Saw	NN-TL	1-01-001
saws	NNS	3-02-002
saw	**VB**	**9-06-009**
saw-horse	**NN**	**1-01-001**
Sawallisch	**prop. noun**	**2-01-001**
Sawallisch	NP	1-01-001
Sawalisch	NP	1-01-001
sawdust	**NN**	**3-03-003**
sawed-off	**JJ**	**1-01-001**
sawing	**NN**	**1-01-001**
sawmill	**NN**	**1-01-001**
Sawnders	**NP**	**1-01-001**
sawtimber	**NN**	**3-01-001**
Sawyer	**NP**	**1-01-001**
sax	**NN**	**6-02-002**
Saxon	**prop. noun**	**25-01-001**

Word	Tag	Frequency
Saxon (cont.):		
Saxon	NP	4-01-001
Saxon	NP-TL	14-01-001
Saxons	NPS	4-01-001
Saxons	NPS-TL	3-01-001
Saxony	**NP**	**1-01-001**
saxophone	**NN**	**4-01-001**
saxophonist	**NN**	**1-01-001**
Saxton	**prop. noun**	**3-02-002**
Saxton	NP	2-01-001
Saxton's	NP$	0-00-000
Saxton's	NP$-TL	1-01-001
say	**FW-VB**	**1-01-001**
say	**noun**	**7-06-007**
say	NN	4-03-004
says	NNS	3-03-003
say	**UH**	**15-06-013**
say	**verb**	**2765-15-392**
say	VB	482-15-231
say	VB-NC	1-01-001
Say	VB-TL	1-01-001
says	VBZ	197-14-112
saith	VBZ	4-03-004
sez	VBZ	0-00-000
Sez	VBZ-TL	1-01-001
said	VBD	1748-15-265
sayed	VBD	1-01-001
sed	VBD	1-01-001
said	VBN	213-15-150
sed	VBN	1-01-001
said	VBN-HL	1-01-001
saying	VBG	112-14-089
sayin	VBG	1-01-001
sayin'	VBG	1-01-001
say-so	**NN**	**1-01-001**
say-speak	**verb**	**1-01-001**
say-speak	VB+VB	0-00-000
say-speak	VB+VB-NC	1-01-001
Sayers	**NP**	**1-01-001**
saying	**noun**	**5-03-003**
saying	NN	1-01-001
sayin'	NN	3-01-001
sayings	NNS	1-01-001
sayonara	**foreign**	**1-01-001**
sayonara	FW-UH	0-00-000
sayonara	FW-UH-NC	1-01-001
SBA	**NP**	**8-01-001**
scab	**verb**	**1-01-001**
scabbed	VBN	1-01-001
scabbard	**NN**	**5-02-003**
scabrous	**JJ**	**1-01-001**
scaffold	**NN**	**6-04-005**
scaffolding	**noun**	**4-03-003**
scaffolding	NN	3-02-002
scaffoldings	NNS	1-01-001
Scala	**NP**	**1-01-001**
scalar	**JJ**	**2-01-001**
scald	**verb**	**3-02-003**
scald	VB	1-01-001
scalded	VBN	1-01-001
scalding	VBG	1-01-001
scale	**noun**	**62-10-037**
scale	NN	52-10-036
scale	NN-HL	1-01-001
Scale	NN-TL	5-01-001
scales	NNS	4-02-004
scale	**verb**	**4-02-004**
scale	VB	1-01-001
scales	VBZ	1-01-001
scaled	VBN	2-02-002
scallop	**noun**	**1-01-001**
scallops	NNS	1-01-001
scallop	**verb**	**2-02-002**
scalloped	VBN	2-02-002
scalp	**NN**	**4-02-003**
scamper	**verb**	**1-01-001**
scampering	VBG	1-01-001
Scampini	**NP**	**1-01-001**
scan	**noun**	**3-02-002**
scan	NN	2-02-002
scans	NNS	1-01-001
scan	**verb**	**17-10-014**
scan	VB	3-03-003
scans	VBZ	1-01-001
scanned	VBD	9-05-008
scanned	VBN	1-01-001
scanning	VBG	3-02-002
scandal	**noun**	**15-06-008**
scandal	NN	5-04-005

Word	Tag	Frequency
scandal (cont.):		
scandal	NN-HL	1-01-001
Scandal	NN-TL	2-01-001
scandals	NNS	7-03-003
scandalize	**verb**	**3-02-003**
scandalized	VBD	2-01-002
scandalized	VBN	1-01-001
scandalizing	**JJ**	**1-01-001**
Scandinavia	**NP**	**1-01-001**
Scandinavian	**JJ**	**2-02-002**
Scandinavian	**prop. noun**	**1-01-001**
Scandinavians	NPS	1-01-001
scanner	**noun**	**1-01-001**
scanners	NNS	1-01-001
scanning	**NN**	**1-01-001**
scant	**JJ**	**5-03-005**
scanty	**JJ**	**4-04-004**
scapegoat	**noun**	**2-02-002**
scapegoat	NN	1-01-001
scapegoats	NNS	1-01-001
Scapin	**prop. noun**	**4-01-001**
Scapin	NP	3-01-001
Scapin	NP-TL	1-01-001
scapular	**noun**	**1-01-001**
scapulars	NNS	1-01-001
scar	**noun**	**20-09-014**
scar	NN	10-05-006
scars	NNS	10-07-009
scar	**verb**	**2-02-002**
scarred	VBN	2-02-002
Scarborough	**NP**	**1-01-001**
scarce	**JJ**	**6-05-006**
scarcely	**QL**	**3-02-003**
scarcely	**RB**	**21-10-020**
scarcely-tapped	**JJ**	**1-01-001**
scarcity	**NN**	**3-03-003**
scare	**NN**	**1-01-001**
scare	**verb**	**26-07-016**
scare	VB	2-02-002
scared	VBD	3-02-003
scared	VBN	18-06-011
scairt	VBN	1-01-001
Scared	VBN-TL	1-01-001
scaring	VBG	1-01-001
scarecrowish	**JJ**	**1-01-001**
scarf	**NN**	**4-02-004**
Scarface	**NP**	**1-01-001**
scarify	**VB**	**1-01-001**
scarlet	**adjective**	**3-03-003**
scarlet	JJ	1-01-001
Scarlet	JJ-TL	2-02-002
Scarsdale	**NP**	**2-02-002**
scary	**JJ**	**2-02-002**
scathe	**verb**	**1-01-001**
scathing	VBG	1-01-001
scathingly	**QL**	**1-01-001**
scatter	**NN**	**2-01-001**
scatter	**verb**	**29-11-027**
scatters	VBZ	1-01-001
scattered	VBD	7-04-006
scattered	VBN	20-10-020
scattering	VBG	1-01-001
scatterbrained	**JJ**	**2-01-001**
scattergun	**NN**	**2-01-001**
scavenge	**verb**	**1-01-001**
scavenging	VBG	1-01-001
scavenger	**NN**	**1-01-001**
scenario	**noun**	**2-02-002**
scenario	NN	1-01-001
scenarios	NNS	1-01-001
scene	**noun**	**135-14-077**
scene	NN	102-14-065
Scene	NN-TL	4-02-002
scenes	NNS	29-09-023
scenery	**noun**	**15-07-014**
scenery	NN	14-06-013
sceneries	NNS	1-01-001
scenic	**adjective**	**9-03-004**
scenic	JJ	8-03-004
scenic	JJ-HL	1-01-001
scenic	**noun**	**1-01-001**
scenics	NNS	1-01-001
scent	**NN**	**6-04-006**
scent	**verb**	**5-02-005**
scented	VBN	5-02-005
sceptical	**JJ**	**3-01-001**
scepticism	**NN**	**5-01-002**
Schaack	**NP**	**3-01-001**
Schaefer	**NP**	**4-01-001**

Word	Tag	Frequency
Schaeffer	**NP**	**2-01-001**
Schaffner	**NP**	**9-01-001**
Schang	**NP**	**1-01-001**
Schapiro	**NP**	**1-01-001**
schedule	**noun**	**44-09-034**
schedule	NN	34-06-025
schedules	NNS	10-07-010
schedule	**verb**	**41-13-034**
schedule	VB	2-02-002
scheduled	VBD	2-02-002
scheduled	VBN	36-11-030
scheduling	VBG	1-01-001
scheduling	**NN**	**1-01-001**
Scheherazade	**prop. noun**	**2-02-002**
Scheherazade	NP	1-01-001
Scheherazade	NP-TL	1-01-001
Schelling	**NP**	**2-02-002**
schema	**noun**	**4-02-002**
schema	NN	3-01-001
schemata	NNS	1-01-001
schematic	**JJ**	**3-01-003**
schematically	**RB**	**3-01-001**
scheme	**noun**	**39-12-029**
scheme	NN	33-12-024
schemes	NNS	6-05-006
scheme	**verb**	**3-03-003**
scheming	VBG	3-03-003
Schenk	**NP**	**2-01-001**
Scherer	**NP**	**2-01-001**
scherzo	**NN**	**1-01-001**
Schiele	**prop. noun**	**7-01-001**
Schiele	NP	4-01-001
Schiele's	NP$	3-01-001
Schilling	**NP**	**1-01-001**
Schillinger	**NP**	**4-01-001**
schism	**NN**	**1-01-001**
schizophrenic	**JJ**	**5-01-001**
schizophrenic	**NN**	**1-01-001**
Schleiermacher	**NP**	**1-01-001**
Schlek	**NP**	**2-01-001**
Schlesinger	**NP**	**2-01-001**
Schley	**NP**	**1-01-001**
Schlieren	**NP**	**1-01-001**
Schmalma	**NP**	**1-01-001**
Schmalzried	**NP**	**1-01-001**
Schmidl-Seeberg	**NP**	**1-01-001**
Schmidt	**NP**	**1-01-001**
Schmitt	**NP**	**2-01-001**
Schnabel	**prop. noun**	**13-01-001**
Schnabel	NP	7-01-001
Schnabel's	NP$	6-01-001
Schnabelian	**JJ**	**1-01-001**
schnapps	**NN**	**1-01-001**
schnook	**noun**	**1-01-001**
schnooks	NNS	1-01-001
Schockler	**NP**	**1-01-001**
scholar	**noun**	**42-08-018**
scholar	NN	11-06-008
Scholar	NN-TL	4-02-002
scholars	NNS	26-07-012
Scholars	NNS-TL	1-01-001
scholar-businessman	**NN**	**1-01-001**
scholarly	**JJ**	**8-05-007**
scholarship	**noun**	**44-10-022**
scholarship	NN	35-10-020
Scholarship	NN-TL	1-01-001
scholarships	NNS	8-05-006
scholastic	**JJ**	**9-06-007**
scholastic	**noun**	**1-01-001**
scholastics	NNS	1-01-001
Scholastica	**NP**	**1-01-001**
scholastically	**RB**	**1-01-001**
Schonberg	**prop. noun**	**3-01-001**
Schonberg	NP	2-01-001
Schonberg's	NP$	1-01-001
schone	**foreign**	**1-01-001**
schone	FW-JJ	0-00-000
Schone	FW-JJ-TL	1-01-001
school	**noun**	**687-15-158**
school	NN	413-15-120
school	NN-HL	3-02-003
School	NN-TL	72-12-046
school	NN-TL	1-01-001
school's	NN$	3-02-003
schools	NNS	189-12-058
schools	NNS-HL	2-02-002
Schools	NNS-TL	4-03-003
school	**verb**	**7-07-007**
school	VB	4-04-004

school (cont.):		
schooled	VBN	1-01-001
schooling	VBG	2-02-002
school-age	**NN**	**1-01-001**
school-leaving	**JJ**	**1-01-001**
schoolbook	**noun**	**1-01-001**
schoolbooks	NNS	1-01-001
schoolboy	**noun**	**4-03-004**
schoolboy	NN	3-03-003
schoolboys	NNS	1-01-001
schoolchild	**noun**	**1-01-001**
schoolchildren	NNS	1-01-001
schoolday	**noun**	**1-01-001**
schooldays	NNS	1-01-001
schooler	**noun**	**1-01-001**
schoolers	NNS	1-01-001
schoolgirl	**noun**	**2-02-002**
schoolgirl	NN	1-01-001
schoolgirls	NNS	1-01-001
schoolgirlish	**JJ**	**1-01-001**
schoolhouse	**NN**	**11-03-003**
schooling	**NN**	**3-03-003**
schoolmarm	**noun**	**1-01-001**
schoolmarm	NN	0-00-000
Schoolmarm	NN-TL	1-01-001
schoolmaster	**noun**	**4-02-003**
schoolmaster	NN	3-01-002
schoolmaster's	NN$	1-01-001
schoolmate	**noun**	**3-02-002**
schoolmate	NN	1-01-001
schoolmates	NNS	2-01-001
schoolroom	**NN**	**3-01-002**
schoolwork	**NN**	**1-01-001**
schooner	**NN**	**3-02-002**
Schopenhauer	**prop. noun**	**2-01-001**
Schopenhauer	NP	1-01-001
Schopenhauer's	NP$	1-01-001
Schott	**NP**	**1-01-001**
Schraffts	**NP**	**1-01-001**
Schramm	**NP**	**2-01-001**
Schrunk	**NP**	**1-01-001**
Schubert	**prop. noun**	**7-03-004**
Schubert	NP	3-03-003
Schubert's	NP$	4-03-003
Schubert-Beethoven-Mozart	**NP**	**1-01-001**
Schultz	**NP**	**2-01-001**
Schulz	**NP**	**1-01-001**
Schuman	**prop. noun**	**2-01-001**
Schuman	NP	1-01-001
Schuman's	NP$	1-01-001
Schumann	**prop. noun**	**1-01-001**
Schumann's	NP$	1-01-001
Schutz	**NP**	**1-01-001**
Schuyler	**prop. noun**	**4-02-002**
Schuyler	NP	2-01-001
Schuyler	NP-TL	1-01-001
Schuyler's	NP$	1-01-001
Schuylkill	**prop. noun**	**7-03-003**
Schuylkill	NP	3-03-003
Schuylkill	NP-TL	4-02-002
Schwab	**NP**	**2-01-001**
Schwada	**NP**	**1-01-001**
Schwartz	**NP**	**6-03-005**
Schwarzen	**FW-JJ**	**1-01-001**
Schwarzkopf	**NP**	**6-01-001**
Schweitzer	**prop. noun**	**10-05-006**
Schweitzer	NP	9-04-005
Schweitzers	NPS	1-01-001
Schweizer	**NP**	**1-01-001**
sciatica	**noun**	**4-02-002**
sciatica	NN	3-02-002
sciatica	NN-HL	1-01-001
science	**noun**	**167-13-059**
science	NN	111-11-037
Science	NN-TL	20-10-018
science's	NN$	1-01-001
sciences	NNS	30-07-013
Sciences	NNS-TL	5-03-004
science-fiction	**NN**	**8-01-001**
scientific	**adjective**	**86-09-047**
scientific	JJ	81-09-043
scientific	JJ-HL	1-01-001
Scientific	JJ-TL	4-03-004
scientifically	**RB**	**4-03-004**
scientifically-trained	**JJ**	**1-01-001**
scientifique	**foreign**	**1-01-001**
scientifique	FW-JJ	0-00-000
Scientifique	FW-JJ-TL	1-01-001
scientist	**noun**	**53-13-035**
scientist (cont.):		
scientist	NN	16-08-011
scientist	NN-HL	1-01-001
scientists	NNS	36-10-026
scimitar	**noun**	**2-02-002**
scimitar	NN	1-01-001
scimitars	NNS	1-01-001
scimitar-wielding	**JJ**	**1-01-001**
scintillate	**verb**	**1-01-001**
scintillating	VBG	1-01-001
scion	**noun**	**2-02-002**
scion	NN	1-01-001
scions	NNS	1-01-001
scissoring	**NN**	**1-01-001**
scissors	**NNS**	**1-01-001**
sclerosis	**NN**	**2-02-002**
sclerotic	**JJ**	**1-01-001**
Scobee-Frazier	**prop. noun**	**1-01-001**
Scobee-Frazier	NP	0-00-000
Scobee-Frazier	NP-TL	1-01-001
scoff	**verb**	**3-02-003**
scoffed	VBD	1-01-001
scoffed	VBN	2-02-002
scoffing	**NN**	**1-01-001**
Scolatti	**NP**	**1-01-001**
scold	**verb**	**2-02-002**
scolding	VBG	2-02-002
scoop	**NN**	**4-03-003**
scoop	**verb**	**5-04-005**
scoop	VB	1-01-001
scooped	VBD	3-03-003
scooping	VBG	1-01-001
scoot	**verb**	**5-04-005**
scooted	VBD	4-03-004
scooting	VBG	1-01-001
scop	**noun**	**2-01-001**
scop	NN	1-01-001
scops	NNS	1-01-001
scope	**noun**	**28-08-026**
scope	NN	26-08-024
scope	NN-HL	1-01-001
scopes	NNS	1-01-001
scoped	**JJ**	**1-01-001**
scorch	**verb**	**2-01-002**
scorched	VBD	1-01-001
scorched	VBN	1-01-001
scorcher	**NN**	**1-01-001**
score	**noun**	**65-12-038**
score	NN	50-11-033
scores	NNS	15-04-006
score	**verb**	**35-06-013**
score	VB	16-04-008
scored	VBD	9-05-006
scored	VBN	6-02-003
scoring	VBG	4-03-004
scoreboard	**noun**	**5-02-004**
scoreboard	NN	4-02-004
scoreboards	NNS	1-01-001
scorecard	**NN**	**1-01-001**
scoreless	**JJ**	**2-01-001**
scoring	**NN**	**1-01-001**
scorn	**NN**	**4-04-004**
scorn	**verb**	**2-02-002**
scorned	VBD	1-01-001
scorned	VBN	1-01-001
scornful	**JJ**	**5-03-004**
scornfully	**RB**	**2-02-002**
Scot	**prop. noun**	**9-03-004**
Scot	NP	1-01-001
Scots	NPS	7-03-003
Scots	NPS-TL	1-01-001
scot-free	**JJ**	**1-01-001**
scotch	**adjective**	**4-02-002**
scotch	JJ	0-00-000
Scotch	JJ-TL	4-02-002
Scotch	**prop. noun**	**2-02-002**
Scotch	NP	1-01-001
Scotch	NP-TL	1-01-001
Scotch-and-soda	**NP**	**1-01-001**
Scotch-Irish-Scandinavian	**NP**	**1-01-001**
Scotchgard	**NP**	**1-01-001**
Scotchman	**NP**	**1-01-001**
Scotian	**adjective**	**1-01-001**
Scotian	JJ	0-00-000
Scotian	JJ-TL	1-01-001
Scotland	**prop. noun**	**13-05-009**
Scotland	NP	8-05-008
Scotland	NP-TL	5-02-003
Scott	**prop. noun**	**17-07-013**

Word	Tag	Frequency
Scott (cont.):		
Scott	NP	16-06-012
Scott's	NP$	1-01-001
Scottish	**adjective**	**10-04-006**
Scottish	JJ	5-03-004
Scottish	JJ-TL	5-01-002
Scotty	**prop. noun**	**43-02-002**
Scotty	NP	32-01-001
Scotty's	NP$	9-01-001
Scotty's	NP$-TL	2-01-001
scoundrel	**noun**	**2-02-002**
scoundrel	NN	1-01-001
scoundrels	NNS	1-01-001
scour	**verb**	**7-06-007**
scour	VB	1-01-001
scoured	VBN	3-03-003
scouring	VBG	3-03-003
scourge	**NN**	**2-02-002**
scouring	**NN**	**1-01-001**
scours	**NN**	**5-01-001**
scout	**noun**	**10-03-005**
scout	NN	5-02-002
Scout	NN-TL	2-02-002
scout's	NN$	1-01-001
scouts	NNS	2-02-002
scout	**verb**	**6-03-006**
scout	VB	1-01-001
scouted	VBD	1-01-001
scouting	VBG	3-03-003
skouting	VBG	1-01-001
scowl	**verb**	**6-05-005**
scowled	VBD	4-04-004
scowling	VBG	2-02-002
scraggly	**JJ**	**2-02-002**
scramble	**noun**	**2-01-001**
scramble	NN	1-01-001
scramble	NN-HL	1-01-001
scramble	**verb**	**10-05-009**
scrambled	VBD	8-04-008
scrambled	VBN	1-01-001
scrambling	VBG	1-01-001
scrap	**noun**	**11-09-011**
scrap	NN	8-07-008
scraps	NNS	3-03-003
scrap	**verb**	**1-01-001**
scrapped	VBN	1-01-001
scrapbook	**NN**	**1-01-001**
scrape	**NN**	**1-01-001**
scrape	**verb**	**18-09-016**
scrape	VB	2-02-002
scrapes	VBZ	1-01-001
scraped	VBD	6-04-006
scraped	VBN	2-02-002
scraping	VBG	7-05-006
scraping	**noun**	**1-01-001**
scrapings	NNS	1-01-001
Scrapiron	**prop. noun**	**1-01-001**
Scrapiron	NP	0-00-000
Scrapiron	NP-TL	1-01-001
scratch	**noun**	**12-06-009**
scratch	NN	6-04-006
scratches	NNS	6-03-003
scratch	**verb**	**22-07-016**
scratch	VB	3-02-003
scratched	VBD	4-02-004
scratched	VBN	3-03-003
scratching	VBG	12-05-007
scratchiness	**NN**	**1-01-001**
scratchy	**JJ**	**1-01-001**
scrawl	**verb**	**5-03-004**
scrawled	VBD	3-02-002
scrawled	VBN	2-02-002
scrawny	**JJ**	**4-04-004**
scream	**noun**	**8-03-007**
scream	NN	6-02-005
screams	NNS	2-02-002
scream	**verb**	**40-08-029**
scream	VB	7-04-007
screamed	VBD	14-06-012
screamed	VBN	3-03-003
screaming	VBG	16-08-015
screaming	**NN**	**1-01-001**
screech	**noun**	**2-02-002**
screech	NN	1-01-001
screeches	NNS	1-01-001
screech	**verb**	**12-04-008**
screeched	VBD	5-03-004
screeching	VBG	7-04-006
screechy	**JJ**	**1-01-001**

Word	Tag	Frequency
screen	**noun**	**53-12-032**
screen	NN	42-10-025
screen	NN-HL	1-01-001
screens	NNS	10-03-007
screen	**verb**	**8-05-007**
screen	VB	5-03-005
screened	VBD	1-01-001
screened	VBN	1-01-001
screening	VBG	1-01-001
screening	**noun**	**5-04-005**
screening	NN	3-02-003
screening	NN-HL	1-01-001
screenings	NNS	1-01-001
screenland	**NN**	**1-01-001**
screenplay	**NN**	**1-01-001**
Screvane	**prop. noun**	**3-01-001**
Screvane	NP	2-01-001
Screvane	NP-HL	1-01-001
screw	**noun**	**30-05-008**
screw	NN	19-04-005
Screw	NN-TL	1-01-001
screws	NNS	10-01-004
screw	**verb**	**15-05-006**
screw	VB	1-01-001
screwed	VBD	1-01-001
screwed	VBN	13-04-005
screw-loose	**JJ**	**1-01-001**
screwball	**NN**	**1-01-001**
scribble	**verb**	**1-01-001**
scribbled	VBN	1-01-001
scribe	**NN**	**1-01-001**
scribe	**verb**	**4-01-001**
scribe	VB	3-01-001
scribing	VBG	1-01-001
scrim	**NN**	**1-01-001**
scrimmage	**NN**	**1-01-001**
scrimmage	**verb**	**1-01-001**
scrimmaged	VBD	1-01-001
Scripps	**prop. noun**	**2-02-002**
Scripps	NP	1-01-001
Scripps	NP-TL	1-01-001
script	**noun**	**12-08-010**
script	NN	11-08-009
script's	NN$	1-01-001
scriptural	**adjective**	**2-02-002**
scriptural	JJ	1-01-001
Scriptural	JJ-TL	1-01-001
scripture	**noun**	**15-06-011**
scripture	NN	1-01-001
Scripture	NN-TL	3-02-003
scriptures	NNS	4-03-003
Scriptures	NNS-TL	7-03-004
scrivener	**noun**	**3-01-002**
scrivener	NN	1-01-001
Scrivener	NN-TL	2-01-001
Scrooge-like	**JJ**	**1-01-001**
scrounge	**verb**	**1-01-001**
scrounging	VBG	1-01-001
scrub	**JJ**	**1-01-001**
scrub	**NN**	**2-02-002**
scrub	**verb**	**9-06-008**
scrub	VB	6-05-005
scrubbed	VBD	1-01-001
scrubbing	VBG	2-02-002
scrubbing	**NN**	**1-01-001**
scrumptious	**JJ**	**1-01-001**
scrupulosity	**NN**	**1-01-001**
scrupulous	**JJ**	**1-01-001**
scrupulously	**QL**	**1-01-001**
scrutin	**FW-NN**	**2-01-001**
scrutinize	**verb**	**6-05-006**
scrutinized	VBD	2-02-002
scrutinized	VBN	1-01-001
scrutinizing	VBG	3-03-003
scrutiny	**NN**	**14-06-013**
scud	**verb**	**2-02-002**
scudding	VBG	2-02-002
scuff	**VB**	**1-01-001**
scuffle	**NN**	**1-01-001**
sculpt	**verb**	**1-01-001**
sculpted	VBN	1-01-001
sculptor	**noun**	**8-05-005**
sculptor	NN	6-03-003
sculptor's	NN$	1-01-001
sculptors	NNS	1-01-001
sculptural	**JJ**	**2-01-001**
sculpture	**noun**	**18-06-011**
sculpture	NN	11-05-007
sculptures	NNS	7-04-005

Word	Tag	Frequency
sculpture	**verb**	**5-04-004**
sculptured	VBN	5-04-004
scurrilous	**JJ**	**1-01-001**
scurry	**verb**	**3-02-003**
scurried	VBD	3-02-003
scurvy	**NN**	**1-01-001**
scuttle	**verb**	**3-03-003**
scuttled	VBD	1-01-001
scuttled	VBN	1-01-001
scuttling	VBG	1-01-001
se	**foreign**	**9-05-008**
se	FW-PPL	8-04-007
Se	FW-PPL	1-01-001
sea	**noun**	**104-15-056**
sea	NN	78-14-045
Sea	NN-TL	15-07-010
sea's	NN$	0-00-000
Sea's	NN$-TL	1-01-001
seas	NNS	9-05-007
seas	NNS-HL	1-01-001
sea-beach	**NN**	**1-01-001**
sea-blessed	**JJ**	**1-01-001**
sea-damp	**NN**	**1-01-001**
sea-horse	**noun**	**2-02-002**
sea-horse	NN	0-00-000
seahorse	NN	1-01-001
sea-horses	NNS	1-01-001
sea-road	**NN**	**1-01-001**
sea-village	**NN**	**1-01-001**
seaboard	**noun**	**4-01-001**
seaboard	NN	0-00-000
Seaboard	NN-TL	4-01-001
Seaborg	**NP**	**1-01-001**
Seabrook	**NP**	**1-01-001**
seacoast	**NN**	**3-03-003**
seafarer	**noun**	**2-02-002**
seafarers	NNS	2-02-002
seafaring	**JJ**	**1-01-001**
seafood	**noun**	**4-03-003**
seafood	NN	2-02-002
sea-food	NN	1-01-001
seafood	NN-HL	1-01-001
Seagoville	**NP**	**1-01-001**
seagull	**noun**	**1-01-001**
seagulls	NNS	1-01-001
seal	**noun**	**17-07-008**
seal	NN	14-05-005
seals	NNS	3-02-003
seal	**verb**	**20-08-014**
seal	VB	3-03-003
seals	VBZ	1-01-001
sealed	VBN	13-05-010
sealing	VBG	3-03-003
sealing	**NN**	**1-01-001**
seam	**noun**	**18-06-006**
seam	NN	7-03-003
seam	NN-HL	2-01-001
seams	NNS	7-04-004
seams	NNS-HL	2-01-001
seaman	**noun**	**9-04-005**
seaman	NN	2-01-001
Seaman	NN-TL	5-02-002
seamen	NNS	2-02-002
seamanship	**NN**	**1-01-001**
seamless	**JJ**	**1-01-001**
Sean	**NP**	**2-02-002**
seaport	**noun**	**2-01-002**
seaports	NNS	2-01-002
seaquake	**NN**	**1-01-001**
Seaquarium	**NP**	**2-01-001**
sear	**verb**	**4-02-003**
sear	VB	2-01-001
searing	VBG	2-01-002
search	**noun**	**59-12-045**
search	NN	58-12-044
searches	NNS	1-01-001
search	**verb**	**41-14-038**
search	VB	8-06-008
searches	VBZ	2-02-002
searched	VBD	7-05-007
searched	VBN	2-02-002
searching	VBG	22-11-020
searching	**noun**	**2-02-002**
searching	NN	1-01-001
searchings	NNS	1-01-001
searchingly	**RB**	**1-01-001**
searchlight	**noun**	**3-01-001**
searchlight	NN	2-01-001
searchlights	NNS	1-01-001

Word	Tag	Frequency
Searles	**NP**	**1-01-001**
Sears	**NP**	**2-01-001**
seashore	**noun**	**5-04-005**
seashore	NN	4-04-004
Seashore	NN-TL	1-01-001
seaside	**NN**	**2-02-002**
season	**noun**	**125-13-057**
season	NN	105-12-050
season's	NN$	3-03-003
seasons	NNS	17-09-015
season	**verb**	**5-03-004**
seasoned	VBN	5-03-004
seasonal	**JJ**	**8-07-007**
seasonally	**RB**	**1-01-001**
seasoning	**NN**	**2-01-002**
seat	**noun**	**68-11-040**
seat	NN	53-10-034
seats	NNS	14-08-011
seats	NNS-HL	1-01-001
seat	**verb**	**31-11-021**
seat	VB	1-01-001
seated	VBD	2-01-001
seated	VBN	23-10-017
seating	VBG	5-03-003
SEATO	**NP**	**1-01-001**
Seaton	**prop. noun**	**3-01-001**
Seaton	NP	1-01-001
Seaton's	NP+BEZ	1-01-001
Seaton's	NP$	1-01-001
Seattle	**NP**	**7-03-006**
seaweed	**NN**	**3-02-002**
secant	**noun**	**28-01-001**
secant	NN	12-01-001
secants	NNS	16-01-001
secco	**FW-NN**	**3-01-001**
secede	**verb**	**14-02-003**
secede	VB	10-02-002
seceded	VBN	2-01-001
seceding	VBG	2-01-002
Secesh	**NP**	**1-01-001**
secession	**NN**	**2-02-002**
secessionist	**noun**	**3-03-003**
secessionist	NN	2-02-002
secessionists	NNS	1-01-001
seclude	**verb**	**2-02-002**
seclude	VB	1-01-001
secluded	VBN	1-01-001
seclusion	**NN**	**3-03-003**
second	**noun**	**57-12-043**
second	NN	27-09-023
Second	NN-TL	1-01-001
seconds	NNS	27-12-020
sec.	NNS	2-02-002
second	**ord. num.**	**334-15-202**
second	OD	320-15-195
second-	OD	2-02-002
second	OD-HL	2-02-002
Second	OD-TL	10-06-010
second	**QL**	**1-01-001**
second	**RB**	**12-05-010**
second-class	**NN**	**1-01-001**
second-degree	**NN**	**2-01-002**
second-echelon	**NN**	**1-01-001**
second-floor	**NN**	**1-01-001**
second-half	**NN**	**2-02-002**
second-level	**NN**	**1-01-001**
second-look	**NN**	**1-01-001**
second-order	**NN**	**1-01-001**
second-place	**NN**	**1-01-001**
second-rate	**JJ**	**5-03-003**
second-stage	**NN**	**1-01-001**
second-story	**NN**	**1-01-001**
secondarily	**RB**	**3-02-003**
secondary	**JJ**	**31-08-023**
secondhand	**noun**	**2-01-002**
secondhand	NN	1-01-001
second-hand	NN	1-01-001
secondly	**RB**	**5-03-005**
secrecy	**NN**	**9-05-008**
secret	**JJ**	**46-12-035**
secret	**noun**	**52-12-031**
secret	NN	32-10-025
secrets	NNS	20-06-008
secretarial	**JJ**	**4-04-004**
secretariat	**noun**	**5-04-005**
secretariat	NN	0-00-000
Secretariat	NN-TL	5-04-005
secretariate	**noun**	**1-01-001**
secretariate	NN	0-00-000

Word	Tag	Frequency
secretariate (cont.):		
Secretariate	NN-TL	1-01-001
secretary	**noun**	**210-13-074**
secretary	NN	41-12-030
Secretary	NN-TL	150-07-043
secretary's	NN$	4-04-004
Secretary's	NN$-TL	5-01-001
secretaries	NNS	6-05-006
Secretaries	NNS-TL	3-03-003
secretaries'	NNS$	1-01-001
secretary-designate	**noun**	**1-01-001**
secretary-designate	NN	0-00-000
Secretary-designate	NN-TL	1-01-001
secretary-general	**noun**	**2-01-001**
secretary-general	NN	0-00-000
Secretary-General	NN-TL	2-01-001
secretary-treasurer	**NN**	**2-02-002**
secrete	**verb**	**1-01-001**
secreted	VBN	1-01-001
secretion	**noun**	**5-01-002**
secretion	NN	3-01-002
secretion	NN-HL	1-01-001
secretions	NNS	1-01-001
secretly	**RB**	**6-06-006**
sect	**noun**	**4-03-004**
sect	NN	2-02-002
sects	NNS	2-02-002
sectarian	**JJ**	**1-01-001**
section	**foreign**	**1-01-001**
section	FW-NN	0-00-000
Section	FW-NN-TL	1-01-001
section	**noun**	**276-14-094**
section	NN	140-14-069
sec.	NN	1-01-001
Sec.	NN-TL	0-00-000
Sec.	NN-TL-HL	16-01-002
Section	NN-TL	47-06-018
Section	NN-TL-HL	1-01-001
sections	NNS	69-09-022
sections	NNS-HL	1-01-001
Sections	NNS-TL	1-01-001
sectionalize	**verb**	**1-01-001**
sectionalized	VBN	1-01-001
sector	**noun**	**23-08-016**
sector	NN	13-07-010
sectors	NNS	10-06-009
secular	**JJ**	**15-06-010**
secular	**NN**	**1-01-001**
secularism	**NN**	**1-01-001**
secularist	**JJ**	**1-01-001**
secularist	**noun**	**1-01-001**
secularists	NNS	1-01-001
secularize	**verb**	**3-02-002**
secularized	VBN	3-02-002
secure	**JJ**	**14-06-011**
secure	**verb**	**33-12-030**
secure	VB	16-08-015
secured	VBD	1-01-001
secured	VBN	10-07-010
securing	VBG	6-03-006
securely	**RB**	**5-04-005**
securing	**NN**	**1-01-001**
security	**noun**	**99-11-054**
security	NN	74-11-041
Security	NN-TL	17-06-013
securities	NNS	7-02-004
Securities	NNS-TL	1-01-001
sedan	**noun**	**6-03-003**
sedan	NN	2-02-002
sedans	NNS	4-01-001
sedate	**JJ**	**2-02-002**
sedately	**RB**	**2-02-002**
sedative	**NN**	**1-01-001**
sedentary	**JJ**	**1-01-001**
Sedgwick	**NP**	**3-01-001**
sediment	**noun**	**7-03-003**
sediment	NN	3-01-001
sediments	NNS	4-02-002
sedimentary	**JJ**	**1-01-001**
sedimentation	**NN**	**2-01-002**
sedition	**NN**	**1-01-001**
seditious	**JJ**	**1-01-001**
seduce	**verb**	**1-01-001**
seduced	VBN	1-01-001
seducer	**NN**	**1-01-001**
seduction	**noun**	**3-03-003**
seduction	NN	2-02-002
seduction	NN-NC	1-01-001
seductive	**JJ**	**2-02-002**
sedulously	**RB**	**1-01-001**
see	**UH**	**1-01-001**
see	**verb**	**1513-15-399**
see	VB	771-15-336
sea	VB	2-01-001
sees	VBZ	35-11-027
sees	VBZ-HL	1-01-001
saw	VBD	337-15-176
Saw	VBD	1-01-001
seen	VBN	279-15-180
seed	VBN	1-01-001
seeing	VBG	84-15-064
seein'	VBG	1-01-001
Seeing	VBG-TL	1-01-001
see-through	**JJ**	**1-01-001**
Seebohm	**prop. noun**	**5-01-001**
Seebohm	NP	4-01-001
Seebohm's	NP$	1-01-001
seed	**noun**	**82-10-017**
seed	NN	39-09-013
seed	NN-HL	1-01-001
seeds	NNS	42-04-006
seed-bearing	**JJ**	**1-01-001**
seed-pod	**noun**	**1-01-001**
seed-pods	NNS	1-01-001
seedbed	**NN**	**2-01-001**
seedcoat	**noun**	**2-01-001**
seedcoat	NN	1-01-001
seedcoats	NNS	1-01-001
seedless	**JJ**	**1-01-001**
seedling	**noun**	**1-01-001**
seedlings	NNS	1-01-001
seeing	**CS**	**1-01-001**
seek	**verb**	**179-14-130**
seek	VB	69-13-057
seeks	VBZ	9-06-009
seeks	VBZ-HL	1-01-001
sought	VBD	35-12-029
sought	VBN	19-09-018
sought	VBN-HL	1-01-001
seeking	VBG	44-12-040
seekin'	VBG	1-01-001
seeker	**noun**	**4-04-004**
seeker	NN	1-01-001
seekers	NNS	3-03-003
seekingly	**RB**	**1-01-001**
Seekonk	**NP**	**2-01-001**
Seeley	**NP**	**1-01-001**
seem	**verb**	**831-15-325**
seem	VB	229-15-154
seems	VBZ	259-15-146
seemed	VBD	311-14-178
seemed	VBN	22-10-022
seeming	VBG	10-06-010
seeming	**JJ**	**4-04-004**
seemingly	**QL**	**3-03-003**
seemingly	**RB**	**14-09-014**
seep	**verb**	**6-05-006**
seep	VB	2-02-002
seeped	VBD	1-01-001
seeped	VBN	1-01-001
seeping	VBG	2-02-002
seepage	**NN**	**2-02-002**
seer	**noun**	**1-01-001**
seers	NNS	1-01-001
Seerey	**NP**	**1-01-001**
seersucker	**NN**	**1-01-001**
Segal	**prop. noun**	**1-01-001**
Segal's	NP$	1-01-001
segment	**noun**	**20-07-015**
segment	NN	10-05-009
segments	NNS	10-03-006
segmental	**JJ**	**2-01-002**
Segovia	**prop. noun**	**4-01-001**
Segovia	NP	3-01-001
Segovia's	NP$	1-01-001
segregate	**verb**	**17-05-009**
segregate	VB	1-01-001
segregated	VBN	15-05-009
segregating	VBG	1-01-001
segregation	**NN**	**10-04-005**
segregationist	**NN**	**3-03-003**
Segur	**NP**	**1-01-001**
Segura	**NP**	**1-01-001**
Seidel	**NP**	**2-01-001**
Seigner	**NP**	**5-01-001**
seismic	**JJ**	**1-01-001**
seismograph	**noun**	**2-01-001**
seismograph	NN	1-01-001

Word	Tag	Frequency
seismograph (cont.):		
seismographs	NNS	1-01-001
seismological	**JJ**	**1-01-001**
seize	**verb**	**33-11-026**
seize	VB	5-04-005
Seize	VB-TL	1-01-001
seized	VBD	12-06-010
seized	VBN	12-08-011
seizing	VBG	1-01-001
seizin'	VBG	2-01-001
seizure	**NN**	**6-04-005**
Selden	**NP**	**15-01-001**
Seldes	**NP**	**1-01-001**
seldom	**RB**	**34-13-030**
select	**JJ**	**5-04-004**
select	**verb**	**112-12-076**
select	VB	18-08-017
selects	VBZ	5-04-005
selected	VBD	8-06-008
selected	VBN	66-09-044
selecting	VBG	13-05-012
selecting	VBG-HL	2-02-002
selection	**noun**	**54-08-032**
selection	NN	39-08-026
selections	NNS	15-05-009
selection-rejection	**NN**	**1-01-001**
selective	**adjective**	**19-08-014**
selective	JJ	18-07-013
see-lective	JJ	1-01-001
selectively	**RB**	**2-02-002**
selectivity	**NN**	**1-01-001**
selectman	**noun**	**1-01-001**
selectmen	NNS	0-00-000
Selectmen	NNS-TL	1-01-001
selector	**noun**	**1-01-001**
selectors	NNS	1-01-001
Selena	**NP**	**4-01-001**
self	**noun**	**41-12-027**
self	NN	34-11-025
Self	NN-TL	2-02-002
self's	NN$	1-01-001
selves	NNS	4-02-003
Self	**NP**	**3-01-001**
self-acceptance	**NN**	**1-01-001**
self-aggrandizement	**noun**	**2-02-002**
self-aggrandizement	NN	1-01-001
self-aggrandisement	NN	1-01-001
self-analysis	**NN**	**1-01-001**
self-appointed	**JJ**	**3-03-003**
self-assertion	**NN**	**1-01-001**
self-assertive	**JJ**	**2-01-001**
self-awareness	**NN**	**1-01-001**
self-betrayal	**NN**	**1-01-001**
self-centered	**JJ**	**2-01-002**
self-certainty	**NN**	**7-01-001**
self-completion	**NN**	**1-01-001**
self-conceited	**JJ**	**1-01-001**
self-confidence	**NN**	**4-04-004**
self-confident	**JJ**	**3-02-003**
self-congratulation	**NN**	**1-01-001**
self-conscious	**JJ**	**5-03-005**
self-consciously	**RB**	**3-03-003**
self-consciousness	**NN**	**5-04-005**
self-consistent	**JJ**	**1-01-001**
self-consuming	**JJ**	**1-01-001**
self-contained	**JJ**	**5-03-005**
self-content	**JJ**	**1-01-001**
self-control	**NN**	**3-02-003**
self-correcting	**JJ**	**1-01-001**
self-crimination	**NN**	**1-01-001**
self-critical	**JJ**	**1-01-001**
self-criticism	**NN**	**2-02-002**
self-deceiving	**JJ**	**1-01-001**
self-deception	**noun**	**3-03-003**
self-deception	NN	2-02-002
self-deceptions	NNS	1-01-001
self-defeat	**NN**	**1-01-001**
self-defeating	**JJ**	**2-02-002**
self-defense	**NN**	**3-02-003**
self-deluded	**JJ**	**1-01-001**
self-delusion	**NN**	**2-02-002**
self-deprecation	**NN**	**1-01-001**
self-destruction	**NN**	**3-03-003**
self-destructive	**JJ**	**3-03-003**
self-determination	**NN**	**7-03-004**
self-dictate	**NN**	**1-01-001**
self-discipline	**NN**	**5-02-002**
self-discovery	**NN**	**2-02-002**
self-dramatization	**NN**	**1-01-001**

Word	Tag	Frequency
self-effacement	**NN**	**1-01-001**
self-effacing	**adjective**	**2-02-002**
self-effacing	JJ	1-01-001
selfeffacing	JJ	1-01-001
self-employed	**JJ**	**2-02-002**
self-enclosed	**JJ**	**1-01-001**
self-energizing	**JJ**	**1-01-001**
self-esteem	**NN**	**4-03-004**
self-evident	**JJ**	**5-03-005**
self-examination	**NN**	**5-03-003**
self-exile	**NN**	**1-01-001**
self-extinguishing	**JJ**	**1-01-001**
self-flagellation	**NN**	**1-01-001**
self-government	**NN**	**2-01-001**
self-help	**noun**	**15-03-003**
self-help	NN	11-03-003
self-help	NN-HL	4-01-001
self-image	**noun**	**2-02-002**
self-image	NN	1-01-001
self-images	NNS	1-01-001
self-imposed	**JJ**	**4-03-004**
self-indulgence	**NN**	**4-02-003**
self-insurance	**NN**	**1-01-001**
self-interest	**NN**	**2-01-002**
self-judging	**JJ**	**1-01-001**
self-locking	**JJ**	**1-01-001**
self-mastery	**NN**	**1-01-001**
self-observation	**NN**	**1-01-001**
self-ordained	**JJ**	**1-01-001**
self-pacification	**NN**	**1-01-001**
self-perceived	**JJ**	**1-01-001**
self-pity	**NN**	**3-02-003**
self-pitying	**JJ**	**1-01-001**
self-plagiarism	**noun**	**1-01-001**
self-plagiarisms	NNS	1-01-001
self-portrait	**noun**	**2-02-002**
self-portrait	NN	1-01-001
self-portraits	NNS	1-01-001
self-preservation	**NN**	**2-02-002**
self-proclaimed	**JJ**	**1-01-001**
self-protection	**NN**	**1-01-001**
self-realized	**JJ**	**1-01-001**
self-redefinition	**NN**	**1-01-001**
self-reliance	**NN**	**1-01-001**
self-reliant	**JJ**	**3-02-002**
self-respect	**NN**	**4-04-004**
self-restraint	**NN**	**1-01-001**
self-righteousness	**NN**	**1-01-001**
self-rule	**NN**	**1-01-001**
self-sacrifice	**NN**	**2-02-002**
self-sacrificing	**JJ**	**1-01-001**
self-satisfaction	**NN**	**4-03-004**
self-seeking	**JJ**	**1-01-001**
self-serve	**NN**	**1-01-001**
self-serve	**verb**	**1-01-001**
self-served	VBD	1-01-001
self-styled	**JJ**	**2-02-002**
self-sufficiency	**noun**	**2-02-002**
self-sufficiency	NN	1-01-001
self-sufficiency	NN-HL	1-01-001
self-sufficient	**JJ**	**3-02-003**
self-sustaining	**JJ**	**5-02-002**
self-unloading	**JJ**	**4-01-002**
self-victimized	**JJ**	**1-01-001**
self-will	**NN**	**2-02-002**
selfish	**JJ**	**8-06-007**
selfishness	**NN**	**1-01-001**
selfless	**JJ**	**2-02-002**
selflessness	**NN**	**1-01-001**
Selkirk	**prop. noun**	**16-01-001**
Selkirk	NP	11-01-001
Selkirk	NP-TL	1-01-001
Selkirk's	NP$	4-01-001
Selkirker	**prop. noun**	**1-01-001**
Selkirkers	NPS	1-01-001
sell	**NN**	**1-01-001**
sell	**verb**	**128-14-073**
sell	VB	39-13-031
selle	VB	1-01-001
sells	VBZ	13-06-011
sold	VBD	20-09-013
sold	VBN	27-08-021
selling	VBG	27-09-018
Selling	VBG-TL	1-01-001
Sell	**NP**	**1-01-001**
seller	**noun**	**8-04-005**
seller	NN	6-04-005
seller's	NN$	1-01-001
sellers'	NNS$	1-01-001

Word	Tag	Frequency
Sellers	**NP**	**1-01-001**
selling	**JJ**	**1-01-001**
selling	**noun**	**3-03-003**
selling	NN	2-02-002
sellin'	NN	1-01-001
sellout	**NN**	**1-01-001**
Selma	**NP**	**2-02-002**
semantic	**JJ**	**7-01-004**
semantically	**RB**	**2-01-001**
semblance	**NN**	**2-01-002**
Semenov	**NP**	**1-01-001**
semester	**noun**	**12-04-004**
semester	NN	10-03-003
semester's	NN$	2-02-002
semi-abstract	**JJ**	**1-01-001**
semi-abstraction	**noun**	**1-01-001**
semi-abstractions	NNS	1-01-001
semi-ambiguous	**JJ**	**1-01-001**
semi-autonomous	**JJ**	**1-01-001**
semi-catatonic	**JJ**	**1-01-001**
semi-circle	**NN**	**1-01-001**
semi-city	**NN**	**1-01-001**
semi-conductor	**noun**	**1-01-001**
semi-conductors	NNS	1-01-001
semi-conscious	**JJ**	**1-01-001**
semi-height	**noun**	**1-01-001**
semi-heights	NNS	1-01-001
semi-independent	**JJ**	**1-01-001**
semi-inflated	**JJ**	**1-01-001**
semi-isolated	**JJ**	**1-01-001**
semi-literate	**JJ**	**2-02-002**
semi-major	**JJ**	**2-01-001**
semi-minor	**JJ**	**1-01-001**
semi-nude	**JJ**	**1-01-001**
semi-precious	**JJ**	**1-01-001**
semi-private	**JJ**	**1-01-001**
semi-processed	**JJ**	**1-01-001**
semi-professionally	**RB**	**1-01-001**
semi-rigid	**JJ**	**2-01-001**
semi-serious	**JJ**	**1-01-001**
semi-skilled	**JJ**	**2-01-002**
semi-special	**JJ**	**1-01-001**
semiarid	**JJ**	**1-01-001**
semiautomatic	**JJ**	**1-01-001**
semicircular	**JJ**	**1-01-001**
semidry	**verb**	**1-01-001**
semidrying	VBG	1-01-001
semiempirical	**JJ**	**1-01-001**
seminal	**JJ**	**1-01-001**
seminar	**noun**	**4-03-004**
seminar	NN	3-02-003
Seminar	NN-TL	1-01-001
seminarian	**noun**	**1-01-001**
seminarians	NNS	1-01-001
Seminario	**NP**	**1-01-001**
seminary	**noun**	**10-04-005**
seminary	NN	2-02-002
Seminary	NN-TL	8-04-004
Seminole	**NP**	**1-01-001**
semipublic	**adjective**	**2-02-002**
semipublic	JJ	1-01-001
semi-public	JJ	1-01-001
semiquantitative	**JJ**	**1-01-001**
Semiramis	**prop. noun**	**1-01-001**
Semiramis	NP	0-00-000
Semiramis	NP-TL	1-01-001
semisecret	**JJ**	**1-01-001**
semitrance	**NN**	**1-01-001**
semitropical	**JJ**	**1-01-001**
Semmes	**NP**	**1-01-001**
semper	**FW-RB**	**1-01-001**
Semple-Lisle	**NP**	**1-01-001**
Semra	**NP**	**1-01-001**
senate	**noun**	**66-06-026**
senate	NN	4-04-004
senate	NN-HL	1-01-001
Senate	NN-TL	57-06-024
senate's	NN$	0-00-000
Senate's	NN$-TL	4-00-000
senator	**noun**	**82-10-034**
senator	NN	3-01-003
sen.	NN	0-00-000
Sen.	NN-TL	30-02-012
Senator	NN-TL	37-10-024
senator's	NN$	1-01-001
senators	NNS	5-01-003
sens.	NNS	0-00-000
Sens.	NNS-TL	1-01-001
senators	NNS-HL	1-01-001

Word	Tag	Frequency
senator (cont.):		
Senators	NNS-TL	4-02-002
senatorial	**JJ**	**3-03-003**
send	**verb**	**253-15-153**
send	VB	73-12-062
Send	VB-TL	1-01-001
sends	VBZ	4-04-004
sent	VBD	69-14-055
sent	VBN	75-12-061
sent	VBN-HL	1-01-001
sending	VBG	30-11-025
sender	**noun**	**1-01-001**
senders	NNS	1-01-001
sending	**NN**	**4-03-004**
Senesac	**NP**	**1-01-001**
Senese	**NP**	**1-01-001**
senile	**JJ**	**2-02-002**
senilis	**JJ**	**1-01-001**
senior	**adjective**	**29-07-021**
senior	JJ	26-07-021
senior	JJ-HL	1-01-001
Senior	JJ-TL	2-01-001
senior	**noun**	**6-04-006**
senior	NN	5-04-005
seniors	NNS	1-01-001
Senior	**prop. noun**	**7-03-004**
Senior	NP	0-00-000
Sr.	NP	7-03-004
senior-graduate	**JJ**	**1-01-001**
senioritatis	**FW-NN$**	**2-01-001**
seniority	**NN**	**2-02-002**
senium	**foreign**	**1-01-001**
senium	FW-NN	0-00-000
Senium	FW-NN-TL	1-01-001
Senor	**NP**	**2-01-001**
senora	**NN**	**1-01-001**
Senora	**NP**	**1-01-001**
sensation	**noun**	**24-08-015**
sensation	NN	14-08-012
sensations	NNS	10-04-007
sensational	**JJ**	**6-05-005**
sensationalism	**NN**	**2-02-002**
sense	**noun**	**313-15-156**
sense	NN	300-15-153
sense	NN-HL	1-01-001
senses	NNS	12-06-010
sense	**verb**	**35-13-031**
sense	VB	10-08-010
senses	VBZ	3-03-003
sensed	VBD	16-07-014
sensed	VBN	1-01-001
sensing	VBG	5-04-005
senseless	**JJ**	**6-05-006**
senselessly	**RB**	**1-01-001**
sensibility	**noun**	**14-04-011**
sensibility	NN	8-03-006
sensibilities	NNS	6-02-005
sensible	**JJ**	**14-07-013**
sensibly	**RB**	**4-04-004**
sensing	**NN**	**3-01-003**
sensitive	**JJ**	**59-10-043**
sensitive	**noun**	**2-01-001**
sensitives	NNS	2-01-001
sensitive-area	**NN**	**1-01-001**
sensitively	**RB**	**1-01-001**
sensitivity	**noun**	**29-08-017**
sensitivity	NN	28-08-017
sensitivities	NNS	1-01-001
sensitize	**verb**	**2-01-001**
sensitized	VBN	2-01-001
sensor	**noun**	**9-01-002**
sensor	NN	3-01-002
sensors	NNS	6-01-001
sensory	**JJ**	**9-04-006**
sensual	**JJ**	**6-05-006**
sensuality	**NN**	**5-04-004**
sensuous	**JJ**	**2-01-002**
sentence	**noun**	**47-11-029**
sentence	NN	33-11-022
Sentence	NN-TL	1-01-001
sentences	NNS	13-08-010
sentence	**verb**	**9-05-008**
sentenced	VBN	8-05-007
sentencing	VBG	1-01-001
sentence-structure	**NN**	**1-01-001**
sentient	**JJ**	**2-01-002**
sentiment	**noun**	**31-10-025**
sentiment	NN	22-09-020
sentiment	NN-HL	1-01-001

Word	Tag	Frequency
sentiment (cont.):		
sentiments	NNS	8-04-007
sentimental	**JJ**	**15-07-014**
sentimentalist	**noun**	**1-01-001**
sentimentalists	NNS	1-01-001
sentimentality	**NN**	**1-01-001**
sentimentalize	**VB**	**1-01-001**
sentinel	**noun**	**4-02-004**
sentinel	NN	2-02-002
sentinels	NNS	2-02-002
sentry	**noun**	**7-04-006**
sentry	NN	5-03-005
Sentry	NN-TL	1-01-001
sentry's	NN$	1-01-001
Seoul	**NP**	**1-01-001**
separable	**JJ**	**2-02-002**
separate	**adjective**	**65-12-050**
separate	JJ	64-12-050
separate	JJ-HL	1-01-001
separate	**verb**	**67-14-051**
separate	VB	14-08-013
separates	VBZ	3-02-002
separated	VBD	6-05-006
separated	VBN	37-10-030
separating	VBG	7-05-007
separately	**RB**	**13-05-012**
separateness	**NN**	**2-02-002**
separation	**noun**	**18-07-013**
separation	NN	17-07-012
separations	NNS	1-01-001
separator	**noun**	**1-01-001**
separators	NNS	1-01-001
sepia	**NN**	**1-01-001**
Sept	**NP**	**1-01-001**
septation	**NN**	**1-01-001**
September	**prop. noun**	**90-13-043**
September	NP	56-12-038
Sept.	NP	34-06-010
September-October	**NP**	**1-01-001**
septic	**JJ**	**3-01-001**
septillion	**CD**	**1-01-001**
septuagenarian	**noun**	**1-01-001**
septuagenarian's	NN$	1-01-001
septum	**noun**	**7-02-002**
septum	NN	1-01-001
septa	NNS	6-01-001
sepulchre	**verb**	**1-01-001**
sepulchred	VBN	1-01-001
seq.	**FW-VBG**	**1-01-001**
sequel	**NN**	**1-01-001**
sequence	**noun**	**41-07-024**
sequence	NN	35-07-020
sequences	NNS	6-03-005
sequence	**verb**	**1-01-001**
sequenced	VBN	1-01-001
sequestration	**NN**	**1-01-001**
sequin	**noun**	**1-01-001**
sequins	NNS	1-01-001
Sequoia	**prop. noun**	**2-02-002**
Sequoia	NP	0-00-000
Sequoia	NP-TL	2-02-002
Serafin	**NP**	**1-01-001**
seraph	**noun**	**1-01-001**
seraphim	NNS	1-01-001
Serbantian	**JJ**	**1-01-001**
serenade	**NN**	**1-01-001**
serenade	**verb**	**2-02-002**
serenaded	VBD	1-01-001
serenaded	VBN	1-01-001
serene	**JJ**	**8-06-008**
Serene	**NP**	**2-01-001**
serenely	**RB**	**1-01-001**
Serenissimus	**NP**	**3-01-001**
serenity	**NN**	**6-04-006**
serf	**noun**	**1-01-001**
serfs	NNS	1-01-001
serge	**NN**	**1-01-001**
Serge	**NP**	**4-01-001**
sergeant	**noun**	**31-06-014**
sergeant	NN	10-05-007
s-s-sahjunt	NN	1-01-001
sahjunt	NN	0-00-000
Sahjunt	NN-TL	1-01-001
Sergeant	NN-TL	18-04-009
sergeants	NNS	1-01-001
Sergei	**NP**	**2-01-002**
serial	**JJ**	**2-02-002**
serial	**noun**	**5-02-003**
serial	NN	4-02-003

Word	Tag	Frequency
serial (cont.):		
Serial	NN-TL	1-01-001
series	**noun**	**120-12-073**
series	NN	113-12-071
Series	NN-TL	7-04-006
series	**pl. noun**	**10-04-009**
series	NNS	9-04-008
Series	NNS-TL	1-01-001
serieuses	**foreign**	**1-01-001**
serieuses	FW-JJ	0-00-000
Serieuses	FW-JJ-TL	1-01-001
Serif	**NP**	**1-01-001**
serious	**adjective**	**116-14-088**
serious	JJ	114-14-088
serious	JJ-NC	2-01-001
serious-minded	**JJ**	**1-01-001**
seriously	**QL**	**3-03-003**
seriously	**RB**	**43-13-038**
seriousness	**NN**	**8-06-007**
sermon	**noun**	**14-06-011**
sermon	NN	10-05-007
Sermon	NN-TL	2-02-002
sermons	NNS	2-02-002
serological	**adjective**	**2-01-001**
serological	JJ	1-01-001
serological	JJ-HL	1-01-001
serpent	**noun**	**5-05-005**
serpent	NN	2-02-002
serpents	NNS	3-03-003
serpentine	**adjective**	**1-01-001**
serpentine	JJ	0-00-000
Serpentine	JJ-TL	1-01-001
Serra	**prop. noun**	**1-01-001**
Serra	NP	0-00-000
Serra	NP-TL	1-01-001
serratus	**NN**	**2-01-001**
serum	**noun**	**37-01-004**
serum	NN	18-01-004
sera	NNS	19-01-003
servanda	**FW-VBG**	**1-01-001**
servant	**noun**	**41-12-025**
servant	NN	18-08-012
Servant	NN-TL	1-01-001
servants	NNS	22-09-015
Servatius	**NP**	**1-01-001**
serve	**verb**	**300-15-169**
serve	VB	107-15-084
serves	VBZ	37-08-033
served	VBD	52-09-041
served	VBD-HL	1-01-001
served	VBN	66-12-049
serving	VBG	37-10-032
service	**foreign**	**1-01-001**
service	FW-NN	0-00-000
Service	FW-NN-TL	1-01-001
service	**noun**	**448-14-155**
service	NN	242-13-098
service	NN-HL	1-01-001
Service	NN-TL	66-11-039
Service	NN-TL-HL	1-01-001
services	NNS	126-10-065
services	NNS-HL	3-03-003
Services	NNS-TL	9-03-008
service	**verb**	**7-02-005**
service	VB	4-02-004
services	VBZ	1-01-001
servicing	VBG	2-02-002
service-connected	**JJ**	**3-01-001**
serviceable	**JJ**	**4-04-004**
serviceman	**noun**	**1-01-001**
servicemen	NNS	1-01-001
servicing	**NN**	**2-02-002**
serviette	**noun**	**1-01-001**
serviettes	NNS	1-01-001
servile	**JJ**	**2-02-002**
serving	**noun**	**2-02-002**
serving	NN	1-01-001
servings	NNS	1-01-001
servitor	**noun**	**1-01-001**
servitors	NNS	1-01-001
servo	**NN**	**5-01-001**
sesame	**noun**	**7-04-004**
sesame	NN	6-03-003
Sesame	NN-TL	1-01-001
Sesshu	**NP**	**1-01-001**
session	**noun**	**106-12-053**
session	NN	77-11-042
session	NN-HL	2-02-002
Session	NN-TL	1-01-001

Word	Tag	Frequency
session (cont.):		
sessions	NNS	26-09-018
set	**noun**	**137-14-076**
set	NN	86-13-058
set	NN-HL	2-02-002
Set	NN-TL	1-01-001
set's	NN$	1-01-001
sets	NNS	47-07-022
set	**verb**	**372-15-223**
set	VB	92-15-070
sets	VBZ	14-07-014
sets	VBZ-HL	1-01-001
set	VBD	71-14-061
set	VBN	159-14-122
set	VBN-HL	2-02-002
Set	VBN-TL	1-01-001
setting	VBG	32-13-029
setback	**noun**	**6-04-005**
setback	NN	3-02-003
setbacks	NNS	3-03-003
Sethness	**NP**	**2-01-001**
Seton	**NP**	**1-01-001**
Setter	**prop. noun**	**2-01-001**
Setter	NP	0-00-000
Setter	NP-TL	2-01-001
setting	**noun**	**37-10-030**
setting	NN	28-09-023
settings	NNS	9-05-008
settle	**verb**	**105-14-083**
settle	VB	23-11-022
settles	VBZ	2-02-002
settled	VBD	31-09-028
settled	VBN	38-11-033
settling	VBG	11-08-011
settlement	**noun**	**32-09-016**
settlement	NN	25-08-013
Settlement	NN-TL	1-01-001
settlements	NNS	4-03-004
Settlements	NNS-TL	2-02-002
settler	**noun**	**15-05-007**
settler	NN	3-02-002
settlers	NNS	12-05-006
setup	**noun**	**12-08-012**
setup	NN	7-06-007
set-up	NN	3-03-003
set-up	NN-HL	1-01-001
setup	NN-HL	1-01-001
Seurat	**NP**	**1-01-001**
seven	**card. num.**	**114-15-076**
seven	CD	102-15-072
seven-	CD	1-01-001
seven	CD-HL	2-01-002
Seven	CD-TL	9-03-004
seven-concert	**JJ**	**1-01-001**
seven-hit	**JJ**	**1-01-001**
seven-inch	**JJ**	**1-01-001**
seven-iron	**NN**	**1-01-001**
seven-o'clock	**NN**	**1-01-001**
seven-shot	**JJ**	**1-01-001**
seven-stories	**JJ**	**1-01-001**
seven-thirty	**CD**	**1-01-001**
seven-week	**JJ**	**1-01-001**
seven-word	**JJ**	**1-01-001**
seventeen	**card. num.**	**24-08-019**
seventeen	CD	23-08-019
Seventeen	CD-TL	1-01-001
seventeen-inch	**JJ**	**1-01-001**
seventeen-year-old	**JJ**	**1-01-001**
seventeenth	**ord. num.**	**11-05-006**
seventeenth	OD	9-04-005
Seventeenth	OD-TL	2-01-001
seventeenth-century	**NN**	**2-02-002**
seventh	**ord. num.**	**31-11-021**
seventh	OD	14-06-012
Seventh	OD-TL	17-07-009
seventy	**CD**	**4-03-004**
seventy	**noun**	**2-01-002**
seventies	NNS	1-01-001
Seventies	NNS-TL	1-01-001
seventy-eight	**CD**	**1-01-001**
seventy-fifth	**OD**	**1-01-001**
seventy-five	**CD**	**1-01-001**
seventy-five-foot	**JJ**	**1-01-001**
seventy-foot	**JJ**	**1-01-001**
seventy-four	**CD**	**1-01-001**
seventy-fourth	**ord. num.**	**1-01-001**
seventy-fourth	OD	0-00-000
Seventy-fourth	OD-TL	1-01-001
seventy-odd	**CD**	**1-01-001**
seventy-six	**CD**	**1-01-001**
seventy-two	**CD**	**1-01-001**
sever	**verb**	**9-07-009**
sever	VB	3-03-003
severed	VBD	1-01-001
severed	VBN	5-04-005
several	**AP**	**378-15-234**
severally	**RB**	**1-01-001**
severalty	**NN**	**1-01-001**
severe	**JJ**	**38-11-032**
Severe	**NP**	**1-01-001**
severe-looking	**JJ**	**1-01-001**
severely	**qualifier**	**3-03-003**
severely	QL	2-02-002
severly	QL	1-01-001
severely	**RB**	**14-08-014**
severing	**NN**	**1-01-001**
severity	**NN**	**5-03-003**
Severna	**prop. noun**	**1-01-001**
Severna	NP	0-00-000
Severna	NP-TL	1-01-001
Severs	**NP**	**1-01-001**
Sevigli	**prop. noun**	**1-01-001**
Sevigli	NP	0-00-000
Sevigli	NP-TL	1-01-001
sew	**verb**	**18-07-007**
sew	VB	4-01-001
sew	VB-HL	2-01-001
sewed	VBN	1-01-001
sewn	VBN	1-01-001
sewing	VBG	9-05-005
sewing	VBG-HL	1-01-001
sewage	**NN**	**29-05-007**
Sewanee	**NP**	**1-01-001**
Seward	**prop. noun**	**8-01-001**
Seward	NP	5-01-001
Seward's	NP$	3-01-001
sewer	**noun**	**15-05-010**
sewer	NN	9-04-006
Sewer	NN-TL	1-01-001
sewer's	NN$	1-01-001
sewers	NNS	4-03-004
Sewickley	**NP**	**1-01-001**
sex	**noun**	**95-12-032**
sex	NN	84-12-030
sexes	NNS	11-05-008
sex-manual	**noun**	**1-01-001**
sex-manuals	NNS	1-01-001
sextet	**noun**	**4-02-003**
sextet	NN	2-01-002
Sextet	NN-TL	2-01-001
sextillion	**CD**	**1-01-001**
sexton	**noun**	**2-02-002**
sexton	NN	1-01-001
Sexton	NN-TL	1-01-001
Sexton	**NP**	**1-01-001**
sextuor	**foreign**	**1-01-001**
sextuor	FW-NN	0-00-000
Sextuor	FW-NN-TL	1-01-001
sexual	**adjective**	**59-07-018**
sexual	JJ	58-07-018
Sexual	JJ-TL	1-01-001
sexuality	**NN**	**4-03-003**
sexualize	**verb**	**1-01-001**
sexualized	VBN	1-01-001
sexually	**RB**	**6-02-002**
sexy	**JJ**	**2-02-002**
Seymour	**NP**	**1-01-001**
Seynes	**NP**	**2-01-001**
sforzando	**NN**	**1-01-001**
Sforzt	**NP**	**1-01-001**
Shabbat	**NP**	**1-01-001**
shabbily	**RB**	**2-02-002**
shabby	**JJ**	**5-04-005**
shack	**noun**	**2-02-002**
shack	NN	1-01-001
shacks	NNS	1-01-001
shack	**verb**	**1-01-001**
shacked	VBN	1-01-001
shack-up	**JJ**	**1-01-001**
shackle	**noun**	**2-01-001**
shackles	NNS	2-01-001
shackle	**verb**	**2-01-001**
shackled	VBN	2-01-001
shade	**noun**	**39-11-027**
shade	NN	25-10-018
shade	NN-HL	1-01-001
shades	NNS	11-07-009
Shades	NNS-TL	2-01-001

Word	Tag	Frequency
shade	**verb**	**10-06-008**
shade	VB	2-02-002
shaded	VBD	1-01-001
shaded	VBN	5-04-005
shading	VBG	2-02-002
shade-darkened	**JJ**	**1-01-001**
shading	**noun**	**3-03-003**
shading	NN	2-02-002
shadings	NNS	1-01-001
shadow	**noun**	**54-14-041**
shadow	NN	27-10-021
shadow	NN-HL	1-01-001
Shadow	NN-TL	6-04-004
shadows	NNS	20-09-019
shadow	**verb**	**9-03-006**
shadow	VB	2-01-001
shadowed	VBN	3-02-003
shadowing	VBG	4-03-003
shadowing	**NN**	**1-01-001**
shadowy	**JJ**	**1-01-001**
shady	**JJ**	**1-01-001**
Shaefer	**prop. noun**	**8-01-001**
Shaefer	NP	7-01-001
Shaefer's	NP$	1-01-001
Shafer	**prop. noun**	**7-01-001**
Shafer	NP	6-01-001
Shafer's	NP$	1-01-001
Shaffner	**NP**	**1-01-001**
shaft	**noun**	**13-08-010**
shaft	NN	11-07-008
shafts	NNS	2-02-002
shag	**NN**	**1-01-001**
shaggy	**JJ**	**2-02-002**
shah	**noun**	**2-01-001**
shah	NN	0-00-000
Shah	NN-TL	2-01-001
Shahn	**NP**	**1-01-001**
shake	**noun**	**3-03-003**
shake	NN	2-02-002
shakes	NNS	1-01-001
shake	**verb**	**107-13-078**
shake	VB	15-09-013
shakes	VBZ	4-02-003
shook	VBD	57-08-044
shaken	VBN	11-06-011
shaking	VBG	19-08-018
Shaking	VBG	1-01-001
shaker	**noun**	**5-02-003**
shaker	NN	2-01-001
shakers	NNS	3-02-003
Shakespeare	**prop. noun**	**43-08-013**
Shakespeare	NP	28-06-011
Sha.	NP	1-01-001
Shak.	NP	1-01-001
Shakespeare	NP-TL	2-02-002
Shakespeare's	NP$	11-04-007
Shakespearean	**adjective**	**7-02-002**
Shakespearean	JJ	6-01-001
Shakespearian	JJ	1-01-001
shakily	**RB**	**2-02-002**
shaking	**NN**	**1-01-001**
shaky	**JJ**	**5-04-005**
Shakya	**NP**	**1-01-001**
shall	**modal aux.**	**269-15-109**
shall	MD	266-15-107
shall	MD-NC	1-01-001
Shall	MD-TL	1-01-001
shan't	MD*	1-01-001
shallow	**JJ**	**14-07-011**
shallower	**JJR**	**1-01-001**
shallowness	**NN**	**1-01-001**
Shalom	**prop. noun**	**1-01-001**
Shalom	NP	0-00-000
Shalom	NP-TL	1-01-001
sham	**noun**	**2-02-002**
sham	NN	1-01-001
shams	NNS	1-01-001
shamble	**verb**	**2-02-002**
shambled	VBN	1-01-001
shambling	VBG	1-01-001
shame	**noun**	**21-07-018**
shame	NN	20-07-017
shames	NNS	1-01-001
shame	**verb**	**2-02-002**
shame	VB	1-01-001
shamed	VBN	1-01-001
shamefacedly	**RB**	**1-01-001**
shameful	**JJ**	**2-02-002**
shampoo	**NN**	**2-01-002**
shamrock	**noun**	**3-02-002**
shamrock	NN	1-01-001
Shamrock	NN-TL	2-01-001
Shan	**NP**	**3-01-001**
Shangri-La	**NP**	**1-01-001**
shank	**NN**	**1-01-001**
Shann	**prop. noun**	**10-01-001**
Shann	NP	9-01-001
Shann's	NP$	1-01-001
Shannon	**prop. noun**	**1-01-001**
Shannon	NP	0-00-000
Shannon	NP-TL	1-01-001
Shansi	**NP**	**1-01-001**
Shantung	**NP**	**1-01-001**
shantung-like	**JJ**	**1-01-001**
shanty	**noun**	**4-03-003**
shanty	NN	3-03-003
shanties	NNS	0-00-000
Shanties	NNS-TL	1-01-001
Shantz	**NP**	**1-01-001**
shape	**noun**	**104-14-063**
shape	NN	77-13-056
shape	NN-HL	1-01-001
Shape	NN-TL	1-01-001
shapes	NNS	25-08-017
shape	**verb**	**34-12-031**
shape	VB	6-04-006
shapes	VBZ	4-03-004
shaped	VBD	3-02-002
shaped	VBN	14-08-014
shaping	VBG	7-04-006
shape-up	**JJ**	**1-01-001**
shapeless	**JJ**	**5-04-005**
shapely	**JJ**	**2-02-002**
shaping	**NN**	**1-01-001**
shard	**noun**	**1-01-001**
shards	NNS	1-01-001
share	**noun**	**100-12-040**
share	NN	56-12-036
Share	NN-TL	2-01-001
shares	NNS	41-05-009
shares	NNS-HL	1-01-001
share	**verb**	**105-14-080**
share	VB	40-11-032
shares	VBZ	4-03-003
shared	VBD	19-09-019
shared	VBN	21-07-017
sharing	VBG	21-10-018
sharecrop	**NN**	**1-01-001**
shareholder	**noun**	**5-03-003**
shareholder	NN	1-01-001
shareholders	NNS	3-02-002
share-holders	NNS	1-01-001
sharer	**noun**	**1-01-001**
sharers	NNS	1-01-001
Shari	**NP**	**1-01-001**
sharing	**NN**	**2-02-002**
shark	**noun**	**4-04-004**
shark's	NN$	1-01-001
sharks	NNS	3-03-003
shark-infested	**JJ**	**1-01-001**
Sharkey	**NP**	**1-01-001**
Sharon	**NP**	**3-02-002**
sharp	**JJ**	**71-15-058**
Sharp	**NP**	**1-01-001**
sharp-limbed	**JJ**	**1-01-001**
Sharpe	**prop. noun**	**33-03-003**
Sharpe	NP	7-02-002
Sharpe	NP-TL	23-01-001
Sharpe's	NP$	1-01-001
Sharpe's	NP$-TL	2-02-002
sharpen	**verb**	**7-05-007**
sharpen	VB	1-01-001
sharpened	VBD	1-01-001
sharpened	VBN	4-03-004
sharpening	VBG	1-01-001
sharpening	**NN**	**2-02-002**
sharper	**JJR**	**3-03-003**
sharpest	**JJT**	**1-01-001**
sharply	**QL**	**3-02-003**
sharply	**RB**	**35-13-032**
sharpness	**NN**	**1-01-001**
sharpshooter	**noun**	**1-01-001**
sharpshooters	NNS	1-01-001
Shartzer	**prop. noun**	**1-01-001**
Shartzer's	NP$	1-01-001
Shatilov	**NP**	**1-01-001**
shatter	**verb**	**22-08-019**
shatter	VB	2-02-002

Word	Tag	Frequency
shatter (cont.):		
shatters	VBZ	1-01-001
shattered	VBD	6-04-006
shattered	VBN	7-05-006
shattering	VBG	6-03-005
shatteringly	**QL**	**1-01-001**
shatterproof	**JJ**	**1-01-001**
shave	**verb**	**23-09-018**
shave	VB	6-05-006
shaved	VBD	4-02-003
shaved	VBN	5-05-005
shaven	VBN	2-02-002
shaving	VBG	6-03-004
shaving	**noun**	**1-01-001**
shavings	NNS	1-01-001
Shaw	**prop. noun**	**11-03-004**
Shaw	NP	9-03-004
Shaw's	NP$	2-01-001
Shawano	**NP**	**1-01-001**
shawl	**noun**	**5-02-002**
shawl	NN	3-02-002
shawls	NNS	2-01-001
Shawnee	**prop. noun**	**2-02-002**
Shawnee	NP	1-01-001
Shawnee	NP-TL	1-01-001
Shawomet	**NP**	**3-01-001**
Shay	**NP**	**1-01-001**
Shayne	**prop. noun**	**29-01-001**
Shayne	NP	27-01-001
Shayne's	NP$	2-01-001
Shayol	**NP**	**4-01-001**
she	**pers. pro.**	**6039-15-275**
she	PPS	2857-15-228
she	PPS-NC	3-02-002
she'd	PPS+HVD	32-05-013
she'd	PPS+MD	36-03-014
she'll	PPS+MD	10-05-009
she's	PPS+BEZ	35-09-027
she's	PPS+HVZ	13-05-012
her	PPO	1107-14-173
her	PP$	1925-15-236
hir	PP$	1-01-001
her	PP$-NC	4-01-001
hers	PP$$	16-07-012
She'arim	**NP**	**1-01-001**
shea	**NN**	**1-01-001**
Shea	**prop. noun**	**10-01-001**
Shea	NP	9-01-001
Shea's	NP$	1-01-001
sheaf	**NN**	**3-03-003**
shear	**NN**	**38-01-002**
shear	**verb**	**6-02-003**
shear	VB	2-01-001
shearing	VBG	4-01-002
Shearing	**prop. noun**	**4-01-001**
Shearing	NP	2-01-001
Shearing	NP-HL	1-01-001
Shearing's	NP$	1-01-001
Shearn	**NP**	**1-01-001**
sheath	**NN**	**4-02-004**
sheathing	**NN**	**2-01-001**
Sheckley	**prop. noun**	**1-01-001**
Sheckley's	NP$	1-01-001
shed	**noun**	**5-02-002**
shed	NN	4-01-001
sheds	NNS	1-01-001
shed	**verb**	**12-08-012**
shed	VB	2-02-002
sheds	VBZ	3-03-003
shed	VBD	3-02-003
shed	VBN	2-02-002
shedding	VBG	2-02-002
sheen	**NN**	**2-02-002**
sheep	**noun**	**24-08-012**
sheep	NN	15-07-009
sheep	NN-HL	1-01-001
sheep	NNS	4-03-003
sheepe	NNS	1-01-001
sheep	NNS-HL	3-01-001
sheep-lined	**JJ**	**1-01-001**
sheepskin	**NN**	**3-03-003**
sheer	**JJ**	**14-09-014**
sheer	**verb**	**1-01-001**
sheered	VBD	1-01-001
Sheer	**NP**	**1-01-001**
Sheeran	**NP**	**3-01-001**
sheet	**noun**	**71-14-041**
sheet	NN	45-12-027
sheets	NNS	26-10-019

Word	Tag	Frequency
sheet	**verb**	**1-01-001**
sheeted	VBN	1-01-001
sheet-metal	**NN**	**1-01-001**
sheeting	**NN**	**1-01-001**
Sheets	**NP**	**4-01-001**
sheik	**NN**	**4-01-001**
Sheila	**NP**	**1-01-001**
Shelagh	**NP**	**1-01-001**
Shelby	**NP**	**1-01-001**
Sheldon	**prop. noun**	**8-04-006**
Sheldon	NP	7-04-006
Sheldon	NP-HL	1-01-001
shelf	**noun**	**20-10-015**
shelf	NN	12-07-009
shelves	NNS	8-06-008
shell	**noun**	**36-10-016**
shell	NN	21-06-009
shells	NNS	15-08-010
shell	**verb**	**1-01-001**
shelled	VBN	1-01-001
Shell	**NP**	**1-01-001**
shell-psychology	**NN**	**1-01-001**
Shelley	**prop. noun**	**19-04-006**
Shelley	NP	12-04-006
Shelley's	NP$	7-02-003
shelter	**noun**	**94-10-020**
shelter	NN	64-07-012
shelter	NN-HL	5-02-002
shelters	NNS	23-07-009
shelters	NNS-HL	2-01-002
shelter	**verb**	**5-04-005**
shelter	VB	1-01-001
sheltered	VBN	4-04-004
shelve	**verb**	**1-01-001**
shelved	VBN	1-01-001
Shenandoah	**prop. noun**	**1-01-001**
Shenandoah	NP	0-00-000
Shenandoah	NP-TL	1-01-001
shenanigan	**noun**	**3-02-003**
shenanigans	NNS	3-02-003
Shensi	**NP**	**1-01-001**
Shep	**NP**	**1-01-001**
Shepard	**NP**	**2-02-002**
shepherd	**noun**	**5-04-004**
shepherd	NN	1-01-001
Shepherd	NN-TL	1-01-001
shepherd's	NN$	1-01-001
shepherds	NNS	1-01-001
Shepherds	NNS-TL	1-01-001
shepherd	**VB**	**1-01-001**
Sheraton-Biltmore	**prop. noun**	**3-02-003**
Sheraton-Biltmore	NP	0-00-000
Sheraton-Biltmore	NP-TL	3-02-003
Sheraton-Dallas	**prop. noun**	**2-01-002**
Sheraton-Dallas	NP	0-00-000
Sheraton-Dallas	NP-TL	2-01-002
sherbet-colored	**JJ**	**1-01-001**
Sheridan	**prop. noun**	**2-02-002**
Sheridan	NP	1-01-001
Sheridan	NP-TL	1-01-001
sheriff	**noun**	**28-06-013**
sheriff	NN	15-05-008
Sheriff	NN-TL	5-03-004
sheriff's	NN$	5-04-005
sheriffs	NNS	3-03-003
Sherlock	**NP**	**6-01-001**
Sherman	**prop. noun**	**36-04-009**
Sherman	NP	25-02-006
Sherman	NP-TL	4-02-003
Sherman's	NP$	7-02-002
Sherrill	**NP**	**2-01-001**
sherry	**noun**	**6-04-004**
sherry	NN	4-03-003
Sherry	NN-TL	2-01-001
Sherry	**NP**	**2-01-001**
Sherwood	**prop. noun**	**3-03-003**
Sherwood	NP	2-02-002
Sherwood	NP-TL	1-01-001
Shevchenko	**NP**	**1-01-001**
shh	**UH**	**1-01-001**
shibboleth	**noun**	**3-02-003**
shibboleth	NN	2-02-002
shibboleths	NNS	1-01-001
shield	**noun**	**8-05-006**
shield	NN	6-03-004
shields	NNS	2-02-002
shield	**verb**	**7-06-006**
shield	VB	2-02-002
shielded	VBN	5-04-004

Word	Tag	Frequency
shielding	**NN**	**5-02-002**
Shietz	**NP**	**1-01-001**
Shiflett	**NP**	**2-01-001**
shift	**noun**	**41-09-029**
shift	NN	25-07-019
shift	NN-HL	1-01-001
shifts	NNS	15-07-011
shift	**verb**	**47-13-035**
shift	VB	15-08-013
shifts	VBZ	2-02-002
shifted	VBD	12-07-008
shifted	VBN	6-05-006
shifting	VBG	11-06-010
shifting	VBG-HL	1-01-001
Shifte	**NP**	**1-01-001**
shifter	**noun**	**1-01-001**
shifters	NNS	1-01-001
shiftless	**JJ**	**1-01-001**
shifty	**JJ**	**1-01-001**
Shih	**NP**	**1-01-001**
shill	**noun**	**2-01-001**
shill	NN	1-01-001
shills	NNS	1-01-001
shilling	**noun**	**1-01-001**
shillings	NNS	1-01-001
Shillong	**NP**	**1-01-001**
Shiloh	**NP**	**2-02-002**
shim	**noun**	**1-01-001**
shims	NNS	1-01-001
shim	**verb**	**2-01-001**
shim	VB	1-01-001
shimming	VBG	1-01-001
shimmer	**NN**	**1-01-001**
shimmer	**verb**	**3-03-003**
shimmering	VBG	3-03-003
shimmy	**VB**	**2-02-002**
shin	**NN**	**3-03-003**
shinbone	**NN**	**1-01-001**
shine	**noun**	**3-02-002**
shine	NN	2-01-001
Shine	NN-TL	1-01-001
shine	**verb**	**32-13-029**
shine	VB	2-02-002
shines	VBZ	4-04-004
shone	VBD	5-04-005
shining	VBG	21-09-019
shingle	**noun**	**5-04-004**
shingles	NNS	5-04-004
shiningly	**RB**	**1-01-001**
Shintoism	**NP**	**1-01-001**
shiny	**JJ**	**3-03-003**
ship	**noun**	**126-14-050**
ship	NN	76-13-030
Ship	NN-TL	1-01-001
ship's	NN$	5-03-003
ships	NNS	43-11-023
ships'	NNS$	1-01-001
ship	**verb**	**28-08-016**
ship	VB	6-05-006
shipped	VBD	1-01-001
shipped	VBN	5-03-004
shipping	VBG	15-04-006
shippin'	VBG	1-01-001
ship-to-surface	**JJ**	**1-01-001**
shipboard	**NN**	**1-01-001**
shipbuilding	**NN**	**3-03-003**
Shipley	**NP**	**1-01-001**
Shipman	**NP**	**1-01-001**
shipmate	**noun**	**3-02-002**
shipmate	NN	2-02-002
shipmates	NNS	1-01-001
shipment	**noun**	**18-06-012**
shipment	NN	2-02-002
shipments	NNS	16-05-010
shipper	**noun**	**4-01-001**
shipper	NN	3-01-001
shippers	NNS	1-01-001
shipping	**NN**	**4-04-004**
shipshape	**JJ**	**1-01-001**
shipwreck	**NN**	**2-02-002**
shipwreck	**verb**	**1-01-001**
shipwrecked	VBN	1-01-001
shipyard	**noun**	**1-01-001**
shipyards	NNS	1-01-001
Shires	**prop. noun**	**3-01-001**
Shires	NP	2-01-001
Shires	NP-TL	1-01-001
shirk	**verb**	**2-02-002**
shirking	VBG	2-02-002

Word	Tag	Frequency
Shirl	**NP**	**3-01-001**
Shirley	**prop. noun**	**6-03-004**
Shirley	NP	5-02-003
Shirley's	NP$	1-01-001
shirt	**noun**	**29-07-022**
shirt	NN	26-05-020
Shirt	NN-TL	1-01-001
shirts	NNS	2-02-002
shirt-sleeved	**JJ**	**1-01-001**
shirtfront	**NN**	**1-01-001**
shirtsleeve	**NN**	**1-01-001**
shish	**NN**	**1-01-001**
shit	**noun**	**4-02-003**
shit	NN	2-01-002
shits	NNS	0-00-000
sh-ts	NNS	1-01-001
shitts	NNS	0-00-000
Shitts	NNS-TL	1-01-001
shit-sick	**JJ**	**1-01-001**
shiver	**NN**	**2-02-002**
shiver	**verb**	**17-08-015**
shiver	VB	2-02-002
shivered	VBD	3-02-003
shivered	VBN	1-01-001
shivering	VBG	11-05-009
shivery	**JJ**	**1-01-001**
shoal	**noun**	**3-02-003**
shoals	NNS	2-02-002
Shoals	NNS-TL	1-01-001
shock	**noun**	**33-11-027**
shock	NN	28-11-023
shock	NN-HL	1-01-001
shocks	NNS	4-04-004
shock	**verb**	**23-10-022**
shock	VB	2-02-002
shocks	VBZ	1-01-001
shocked	VBD	2-02-002
shocked	VBN	17-08-016
shocking	VBG	1-01-001
shocker	**NN**	**1-01-001**
shocking	**JJ**	**3-03-003**
shockingly	**QL**	**3-03-003**
shockwave	**NN**	**2-02-002**
shoddy	**JJ**	**1-01-001**
shoe	**noun**	**58-12-044**
shoe	NN	14-11-013
shoes	NNS	44-10-036
shoe	**verb**	**2-02-002**
shod	VBN	2-02-002
shoelace	**noun**	**2-02-002**
shoelace	NN	1-01-001
shoelaces	NNS	1-01-001
shoestring	**noun**	**3-03-003**
shoestring	NN	1-01-001
shoe-string	NN	1-01-001
shoestrings	NNS	1-01-001
Shoettle	**NP**	**2-01-001**
shoji	**NN**	**1-01-001**
Sholom	**prop. noun**	**1-01-001**
Sholom	NP	0-00-000
Sholom	NP-TL	1-01-001
shoo	**verb**	**1-01-001**
shooing	VBG	1-01-001
shoot	**NN**	**1-01-001**
shoot	**verb**	**117-13-052**
shoot	VB	26-09-020
shute	VB	1-01-001
shot	VBD	18-09-017
shot	VBN	34-11-021
shooting	VBG	36-08-013
shootin'	VBG	2-02-002
shoot-down	**NN**	**2-01-001**
shooter	**noun**	**4-02-002**
shooter	NN	3-01-001
shooters	NNS	1-01-001
Shooter	**NP**	**1-01-001**
shooting	**noun**	**13-06-009**
shooting	NN	11-06-008
Shooting	NN-TL	1-01-001
shootings	NNS	1-01-001
shop	**noun**	**75-12-052**
shop	NN	49-11-035
Shop	NN-TL	7-04-004
shop's	NN$	1-01-001
Shop's	NN$-TL	1-01-001
shops	NNS	16-10-016
Shops	NNS-TL	1-01-001
shop	**verb**	**26-11-018**
shop	VB	7-06-006

Word	Tag	Frequency
shop (cont.):		
shopping	VBG	19-08-015
shopkeeper	**noun**	**1-01-001**
shopkeepers	NNS	1-01-001
shopper	**NN**	**1-01-001**
shopping	**noun**	**8-07-007**
shopping	NN	7-06-006
Shopping	NN-TL	1-01-001
shopping-center	**NN**	**1-01-001**
shopworn	**JJ**	**1-01-001**
shore	**noun**	**66-12-030**
shore	NN	41-11-022
Shore	NN-TL	15-04-004
shores	NNS	9-05-007
shores'	NNS$	1-01-001
shore	**VB**	**1-01-001**
Shore	**NP**	**3-01-001**
shoreline	**noun**	**7-05-005**
shoreline	NN	6-05-005
shorelines	NNS	1-01-001
short	**adjective**	**195-15-147**
short	JJ	190-15-144
short	JJ-HL	3-01-003
Short	JJ-TL	2-02-002
short	**RB**	**14-08-014**
Short	**prop. noun**	**4-01-001**
Short	NP	3-01-001
Short's	NP$	1-01-001
short-barrel	**NN**	**1-01-001**
short-change	**verb**	**1-01-001**
short-changing	VBG	1-01-001
short-contact	**NN**	**2-01-001**
short-cut	**JJ**	**1-01-001**
short-cut	**verb**	**1-01-001**
short-cutting	VBG	1-01-001
short-lived	**JJ**	**3-03-003**
short-of-war	**JJ**	**2-01-001**
short-range	**NN**	**1-01-001**
short-run	**NN**	**3-02-003**
short-skirted	**JJ**	**1-01-001**
short-story	**NN**	**1-01-001**
short-term	**NN**	**14-03-007**
short-time	**NN**	**1-01-001**
shortage	**noun**	**19-08-014**
shortage	NN	14-07-011
shortage	NN-HL	2-01-001
shortages	NNS	3-03-003
shortcoming	**noun**	**5-04-005**
shortcomings	NNS	5-04-005
shortcut	**noun**	**3-02-002**
shortcut	NN	1-01-001
shortcuts	NNS	1-01-001
shortcuts	NNS-HL	1-01-001
shorten	**verb**	**14-07-014**
shorten	VB	4-04-004
shortened	VBN	7-04-007
shortening	VBG	3-03-003
shorter	**JJR**	**18-09-017**
Shorter	**NP**	**1-01-001**
shortest	**JJT**	**3-03-003**
shorthand	**NN**	**2-02-002**
shortly	**RB**	**34-11-029**
shortness	**NN**	**1-01-001**
shorts	**pl. noun**	**29-05-005**
shorts	NNS	28-05-005
shorts	NNS-HL	1-01-001
shortsighted	**JJ**	**5-03-004**
shortsightedness	**NN**	**1-01-001**
shortstop	**noun**	**7-03-004**
shortstop	NN	6-03-004
Shortstop	NN-TL	1-01-001
shot	**noun**	**90-12-037**
shot	NN	60-11-031
shot	NN-HL	1-01-001
shots	NNS	29-08-016
shotgun	**noun**	**9-04-005**
shotgun	NN	8-04-005
shotguns	NNS	0-00-000
shotguns	NNS-HL	1-01-001
shotgun-type	**JJ**	**1-01-001**
shotshell	**noun**	**1-01-001**
shotshells	NNS	1-01-001
Shotwell	**NP**	**1-01-001**
should	**modal aux.**	**915-15-327**
should	MD	883-15-320
shuld	MD	3-01-001
shulde	MD	1-01-001
should	MD-HL	3-02-002
Should	MD-TL	2-02-002
should (cont.):		
shouldda	MD+HV	1-01-001
shouldn't	MD*	22-08-019
shoulder	**noun**	**112-13-076**
shoulder	NN	60-12-042
shoulders	NNS	51-13-044
shouders	NNS	1-01-001
shoulder	**verb**	**5-03-004**
shoulder	VB	1-01-001
shouldered	VBD	3-03-003
shouldering	VBG	1-01-001
shoulder-high	**JJ**	**1-01-001**
shoulder-to-shoulder	**RB**	**1-01-001**
Shoup	**NP**	**4-01-002**
shout	**noun**	**5-04-005**
shout	NN	3-03-003
shouts	NNS	2-02-002
shout	**verb**	**77-14-050**
shout	VB	5-03-005
shouts	VBZ	3-03-003
shouted	VBD	36-08-026
shouted	VBN	4-04-004
shouting	VBG	29-10-021
shouting	**NN**	**3-03-003**
shove	**verb**	**16-04-014**
shove	VB	2-02-002
shoved	VBD	8-03-007
shoving	VBG	6-04-006
shovel	**noun**	**8-04-005**
shovel	NN	5-03-004
shovels	NNS	3-02-002
shovel	**verb**	**2-02-002**
shoveled	VBD	1-01-001
shoveled	VBN	1-01-001
show	**noun**	**108-14-054**
show	NN	72-14-043
shewe	NN	1-01-001
show	NN-HL	2-01-002
Show	NN-TL	10-04-004
Show	NN-TL-HL	2-02-002
shows	NNS	21-07-014
show	**verb**	**640-15-295**
show	VB	202-15-159
shows	VBZ	72-10-057
shows	VBZ-HL	1-01-001
showed	VBD	138-15-099
shown	VBN	166-13-091
showed	VBN	3-03-003
showing	VBG	57-11-039
showin'	VBG	1-01-001
show-offy	**JJ**	**1-01-001**
showcase	**NN**	**3-02-003**
showdown	**noun**	**5-04-005**
showdown	NN	4-03-004
show-down	NN	1-01-001
shower	**noun**	**15-06-009**
shower	NN	13-05-007
showers	NNS	2-02-002
shower	**verb**	**8-04-007**
shower	VB	2-02-002
showered	VBD	4-02-003
showered	VBN	1-01-001
showering	VBG	1-01-001
showerhead	**NN**	**1-01-001**
Showers	**NP**	**1-01-001**
showing	**noun**	**6-04-006**
showing	NN	4-03-004
showings	NNS	2-02-002
showman	**noun**	**4-02-003**
showman	NN	3-02-003
showmen	NNS	1-01-001
showmanship	**noun**	**11-02-002**
showmanship	NN	3-02-002
Showmanship	NN-TL	8-01-001
showpiece	**NN**	**1-01-001**
showroom	**NN**	**1-01-001**
showy	**JJ**	**1-01-001**
shrapnel	**NN**	**2-01-002**
shred	**noun**	**6-04-005**
shred	NN	1-01-001
shreds	NNS	5-03-004
shred	**verb**	**4-03-004**
shred	VB	2-02-002
shredded	VBN	1-01-001
shredding	VBG	1-01-001
shredder	**NN**	**1-01-001**
Shreveport	**NP**	**3-01-002**
shrewd	**JJ**	**8-04-007**
shrewdest	**JJT**	**1-01-001**

Word	Tag	Frequency
shrewdly	**RB**	**2-02-002**
shrewish	**JJ**	**2-02-002**
shriek	**NN**	**4-03-004**
shriek	**verb**	**5-03-004**
shriek	VB	1-01-001
shrieked	VBD	4-02-003
shrieking	**NN**	**1-01-001**
shrill	**JJ**	**7-04-006**
shrill	**verb**	**3-02-003**
shrilled	VBD	2-01-002
shrilling	VBG	1-01-001
shrillness	**NN**	**1-01-001**
shrilly	**RB**	**3-03-003**
shrimp	**NN**	**2-02-002**
shrine	**noun**	**11-05-011**
shrine	NN	5-03-005
Shrine	NN-TL	2-02-002
shrines	NNS	4-03-004
shrink	**verb**	**12-08-012**
shrink	VB	5-04-005
shrinks	VBZ	2-02-002
shrank	VBD	1-01-001
shrunken	VBN	1-01-001
shrinking	VBG	3-03-003
shrinkage	**noun**	**3-02-002**
shrinkage	NN	1-01-001
shrinkage	NN-HL	2-01-001
shrivel	**verb**	**3-03-003**
shriveled	VBN	3-03-003
Shriver	**NP**	**5-03-004**
shroud	**verb**	**1-01-001**
shrouded	VBN	1-01-001
Shrove	**NP**	**1-01-001**
shrub	**noun**	**5-04-004**
shrub	NN	1-01-001
shrubs	NNS	4-03-003
shrub-covered	**JJ**	**1-01-001**
shrubbery	**NN**	**1-01-001**
shrubbery-lined	**JJ**	**1-01-001**
shrug	**noun**	**4-03-003**
shrug	NN	2-02-002
shrugs	NNS	2-01-001
shrug	**verb**	**18-06-015**
shrugged	VBD	18-06-015
Shu	**prop. noun**	**21-01-001**
Shu	NP	19-01-001
Shu	NP-HL	2-01-001
shucks	**NNS**	**1-01-001**
shucks	**UH**	**2-01-002**
shudder	**verb**	**13-06-012**
shudder	VB	5-03-005
shuddered	VBD	5-04-005
shuddering	VBG	3-03-003
shuddery	**JJ**	**1-01-001**
shuffle	**NN**	**2-02-002**
shuffle	**verb**	**6-03-006**
shuffle	VB	1-01-001
shuffled	VBD	2-02-002
shuffling	VBG	3-02-003
Shuiski	**NP**	**1-01-001**
shun	**verb**	**5-04-005**
shun	VB	1-01-001
shuns	VBZ	2-02-002
shunned	VBD	1-01-001
shunning	VBG	1-01-001
shunt	**noun**	**6-01-002**
shunt	NN	1-01-001
shunts	NNS	5-01-001
shunt	**verb**	**1-01-001**
shunted	VBN	1-01-001
shut	**verb**	**50-10-040**
shut	VB	15-08-014
shu-tt	VB	1-01-001
shuts	VBZ	1-01-001
shut	VBD	7-04-006
shut	VBN	24-08-022
shutting	VBG	2-02-002
shutdown	**noun**	**6-02-002**
shutdown	NN	3-01-001
shutdowns	NNS	3-02-002
shutter	**noun**	**10-03-005**
shutter	NN	5-01-001
shutters	NNS	5-02-004
shutter	**verb**	**2-02-002**
shuttered	VBN	2-02-002
shuttle	**verb**	**2-02-002**
shuttled	VBD	1-01-001
shuttling	VBG	1-01-001
Shuz	**NP**	**1-01-001**
shy	**adjective**	**11-06-011**
shy	JJ	10-06-010
Shy	JJ-TL	1-01-001
shy	**verb**	**6-04-006**
shy	VB	2-02-002
shies	VBZ	1-01-001
shied	VBD	3-02-003
Shylock	**NP**	**7-01-001**
Shylockian	**JJ**	**1-01-001**
shyly	**RB**	**4-03-004**
Si	**NP**	**1-01-001**
Siamese	**JJ**	**4-02-003**
Siberia	**NP**	**6-04-005**
Siberian	**JJ**	**1-01-001**
sibilant	**JJ**	**1-01-001**
Sibley	**NP**	**1-01-001**
Sibling	**NP**	**1-01-001**
Sibly	**NP**	**1-01-001**
Sibyl	**prop. noun**	**1-01-001**
Sibyls	NPS	1-01-001
Sibylla	**prop. noun**	**5-01-001**
Sibylla	NP	4-01-001
Sibylla's	NP$	1-01-001
sic	**FW-RB**	**2-02-002**
Sicilian	**JJ**	**3-03-003**
Sicilian	**prop. noun**	**2-01-001**
Sicilians	NPS	2-01-001
Siciliana	**foreign**	**1-01-001**
Siciliana	FW-JJ	0-00-000
Siciliana	FW-JJ-TL	1-01-001
Sicily	**NP**	**3-02-003**
sick	**JJ**	**51-12-035**
sicken	**verb**	**6-03-005**
sickened	VBD	1-01-001
sickened	VBN	3-02-002
sickening	VBG	2-02-002
sicker	**JJR**	**2-02-002**
sickish	**JJ**	**1-01-001**
sickly	**JJ**	**2-02-002**
sickly-tolerant	**JJ**	**1-01-001**
sickness	**NN**	**6-05-006**
sickroom	**NN**	**1-01-001**
Sicurella	**prop. noun**	**1-01-001**
Sicurella	NP	0-00-000
Sicurella	NP-TL	1-01-001
Sid	**prop. noun**	**1-01-001**
Sid	NP	0-00-000
Sid	NP-TL	1-01-001
Siddo	**NP**	**7-01-001**
side	**JJ**	**6-04-004**
side	**noun**	**476-15-219**
side	NN	363-15-194
side	NN-HL	2-02-002
Side	NN-TL	10-04-006
sides	NNS	98-13-067
sides	NNS-HL	1-01-001
Sides	NNS-TL	1-01-001
side's	NN$	0-00-000
Side's	NN$-TL	1-01-001
side	**verb**	**2-02-002**
sided	VBN	1-01-001
siding	VBG	1-01-001
side-conclusion	**noun**	**1-01-001**
side-conclusions	NNS	1-01-001
side-effect	**noun**	**1-01-001**
side-effects	NNS	1-01-001
side-looking	**JJ**	**1-01-001**
side-rack	**NN**	**1-01-001**
side-step	**verb**	**4-04-004**
side-step	VB	1-01-001
side-steps	VBZ	0-00-000
sidesteps	VBZ	1-01-001
side-stepped	VBD	1-01-001
side-stepped	VBN	1-01-001
sidearm	**noun**	**2-02-002**
sidearm	NN	0-00-000
side-arm	NN	1-01-001
sidearms	NNS	1-01-001
sideboard	**noun**	**2-02-002**
sideboard	NN	1-01-001
sideboards	NNS	1-01-001
sidechair	**noun**	**1-01-001**
sidechairs	NNS	1-01-001
sidelight	**NN**	**1-01-001**
sideline	**noun**	**2-02-002**
sideline	NN	1-01-001
sidelines	NNS	1-01-001
sidelong	**JJ**	**1-01-001**
sideman	**noun**	**1-01-001**

Word	Tag	Frequency
sideman (cont.):		
sidemen	NNS	1-01-001
sideshow	**NN**	**1-01-001**
sidewalk	**noun**	**26-08-020**
sidewalk	NN	20-08-016
sidewalk	NN-HL	1-01-001
sidewalks	NNS	5-03-004
sideways	**JJ**	**1-01-001**
sideways	**RB**	**2-02-002**
sidewinder	**NN**	**1-01-001**
sidewise	**RB**	**6-04-006**
siding	**NN**	**4-03-003**
sidle	**verb**	**3-03-003**
sidle	VB	1-01-001
sidled	VBD	2-02-002
Sidney	**prop. noun**	**11-04-006**
Sidney	NP	9-04-006
Sidney's	NP$	2-01-001
sie	**FW-PPSS**	**1-01-001**
sieben	**FW-CD**	**1-01-001**
Siebern	**prop. noun**	**3-01-001**
Siebern	NP	2-01-001
Siebern	NP-HL	1-01-001
siecle	**foreign**	**2-01-001**
siecle	FW-NN	0-00-000
Siecle	FW-NN-TL	1-01-001
siecles	FW-NNS	0-00-000
Siecles	FW-NNS-TL	1-01-001
siege	**noun**	**6-04-006**
siege	NN	5-03-005
Siege	NN-TL	1-01-001
Siegfried	**NP**	**1-01-001**
Sienkiewicz	**NP**	**1-01-001**
sienna	**NN**	**2-01-001**
Siepi	**NP**	**2-01-001**
Sierra	**prop. noun**	**4-03-003**
Sierra	NP	2-02-002
Sierras	NPS	2-01-001
siesta	**NN**	**2-01-001**
sieve	**NN**	**1-01-001**
Sievers	**NP**	**1-01-001**
sift	**verb**	**3-03-003**
sifted	VBD	2-02-002
sifted	VBN	1-01-001
sifting	**NN**	**1-01-001**
Sigemund	**NP**	**1-01-001**
sigh	**noun**	**11-08-011**
sigh	NN	10-08-010
sighs	NNS	1-01-001
sigh	**verb**	**28-08-024**
sigh	VB	1-01-001
sighed	VBD	22-08-020
sighing	VBG	5-02-004
sight	**noun**	**97-13-072**
sight	NN	82-13-064
sights	NNS	15-07-011
sight	**verb**	**10-05-008**
sight	VB	1-01-001
sighted	VBD	2-02-002
sighted	VBN	4-03-004
sighted	VBN-HL	1-01-001
sighting	VBG	2-02-002
sight-see	**verb**	**3-02-003**
sight-seeing	VBG	2-01-002
sightseeing	VBG	1-01-001
sighting	**NN**	**1-01-001**
sightseer	**noun**	**1-01-001**
sightseers	NNS	1-01-001
Sigma	**NP**	**1-01-001**
Sigmen	**prop. noun**	**4-01-001**
Sigmen	NP	3-01-001
Sigmen	NP-TL	1-01-001
Sigmund	**NP**	**1-01-001**
sign	**noun**	**142-14-071**
sign	NN	73-13-043
Sign	NN-TL	3-01-001
signs	NNS	66-10-035
sign	**verb**	**62-12-051**
sign	VB	18-07-016
signs	VBZ	2-02-002
signed	VBD	15-06-014
signed	VBN	22-10-018
signing	VBG	5-04-005
signal	**noun**	**87-12-037**
signal	NN	52-11-023
Signal	NN-TL	7-04-005
signals	NNS	28-09-016
signal	**verb**	**10-07-010**
signal	VB	4-03-004

Word	Tag	Frequency
signal (cont.):		
signals	VBZ	1-01-001
signaled	VBD	2-02-002
signaling	VBG	3-03-003
signal-intensity	**NN**	**1-01-001**
signal-to-noise	**JJ**	**1-01-001**
signaling	**NN**	**2-02-002**
signalize	**verb**	**1-01-001**
signalizes	VBZ	1-01-001
signature	**noun**	**11-05-008**
signature	NN	6-05-006
signatures	NNS	5-01-002
signboard	**NN**	**1-01-001**
signer	**noun**	**1-01-001**
signers	NNS	1-01-001
significance	**noun**	**66-11-051**
significance	NN	65-11-051
significance	NN-HL	1-01-001
significant	**adjective**	**86-09-067**
significant	JJ	85-09-067
Significant	JJ-TL	1-01-001
significant	**noun**	**1-01-001**
significants	NNS	0-00-000
Significants	NNS-TL	1-01-001
significantly	**QL**	**6-01-003**
significantly	**RB**	**11-06-010**
signify	**verb**	**5-04-004**
signify	VB	2-02-002
signifies	VBZ	1-01-001
signified	VBD	1-01-001
signified	VBN	1-01-001
signing	**NN**	**2-02-002**
Signor	**NP**	**2-01-001**
signora	**FW-NN**	**1-01-001**
Signora	**NP**	**2-01-001**
Signore	**NP**	**1-01-001**
signpost	**noun**	**3-03-003**
signpost	NN	2-02-002
signposts	NNS	1-01-001
sigue	**FW-VBZ**	**1-01-001**
Sihanouk	**prop. noun**	**2-01-001**
Sihanouk	NP	1-01-001
Sihanouk's	NP$	1-01-001
Silas	**NP**	**1-01-001**
silence	**noun**	**54-10-041**
silence	NN	49-10-038
Silence	NN-TL	2-02-002
silences	NNS	3-03-003
silence	**verb**	**7-05-007**
silence	VB	1-01-001
silenced	VBD	2-02-002
silenced	VBN	3-02-003
silencing	VBG	1-01-001
silent	**JJ**	**49-11-043**
silently	**RB**	**17-07-016**
Silesia	**NP**	**2-02-002**
silhouette	**noun**	**9-04-004**
silhouette	NN	4-03-003
silhouettes	NNS	5-02-002
silhouette	**verb**	**3-03-003**
silhouetted	VBN	3-03-003
silica	**NN**	**2-01-001**
silica-glass	**NN**	**1-01-001**
silicate	**JJ**	**1-01-001**
silicate	**noun**	**1-01-001**
silicates	NNS	1-01-001
silicon	**NN**	**2-02-002**
silicone	**NN**	**1-01-001**
silk	**noun**	**13-06-012**
silk	NN	11-05-010
silke	NN	1-01-001
Silk	NN-TL	1-01-001
silken	**JJ**	**1-01-001**
silkworm	**noun**	**1-01-001**
silkworms	NNS	0-00-000
Silkworms	NNS-TL	1-01-001
silky	**JJ**	**1-01-001**
sill	**NN**	**4-03-004**
silliest	**sup. adj.**	**1-01-001**
silliest	JJT	0-00-000
silliest	JJT-NC	1-01-001
silly	**JJ**	**15-07-012**
silo	**noun**	**3-03-003**
silo	NN	1-01-001
silos	NNS	2-02-002
Silone	**NP**	**1-01-001**
silvas	**FW-NNS**	**1-01-001**
silver	**adjective**	**7-06-007**
silver	JJ	6-05-006

Word	Tag	Frequency
silver (cont.):		
Silver	JJ-TL	1-01-001
silver	**NN**	**22-10-020**
silver-gray	**JJ**	**1-01-001**
silver-painted	**JJ**	**1-01-001**
Silvers	**NP**	**1-01-001**
silvery	**JJ**	**2-02-002**
Silvio	**NP**	**1-01-001**
Simak	**prop. noun**	**1-01-001**
Simak's	NP$	1-01-001
Simba	**NP**	**1-01-001**
Simca	**NP**	**1-01-001**
similar	**adjective**	**157-14-113**
similar	JJ	156-14-113
similar	JJ-HL	1-01-001
similarity	**noun**	**12-05-012**
similarity	NN	9-05-009
similarities	NNS	3-02-003
similarly	**JJ**	**1-01-001**
similarly	**RB**	**35-09-028**
simile	**NN**	**1-01-001**
similitude	**NN**	**6-01-001**
Simmel	**NP**	**1-01-001**
simmer	**verb**	**6-02-003**
simmer	VB	5-02-003
simmered	VBN	1-01-001
Simmons	**prop. noun**	**11-02-002**
Simmons	NP	10-02-002
Simmons'	NP$	1-01-001
Simmonsville	**NP**	**1-01-001**
Simms	**NP**	**17-03-003**
Simon	**prop. noun**	**5-03-005**
Simon	NP	4-03-004
Simon's	NP$	1-01-001
Simonelli	**NP**	**1-01-001**
Simonson	**prop. noun**	**1-01-001**
Simonson's	NP$	1-01-001
Simpkins	**prop. noun**	**7-01-001**
Simpkins	NP	6-01-001
Simpkins	NP-HL	1-01-001
simple	**adjective**	**160-15-113**
simple	JJ	158-15-113
simple	JJ-HL	2-01-002
simple	**noun**	**1-01-001**
simples	NNS	1-01-001
simple-minded	**JJ**	**2-02-002**
simple-seeming	**JJ**	**1-01-001**
simpler	**JJR**	**18-06-011**
simplest	**JJT**	**10-08-010**
simpleton	**NN**	**1-01-001**
Simplex	**NP**	**1-01-001**
simpliciter	**FW-RB**	**1-01-001**
simplicitude	**NN**	**1-01-001**
simplicity	**noun**	**18-06-011**
simplicity	NN	16-06-009
simplicities	NNS	2-01-002
simplify	**verb**	**20-05-014**
simplify	VB	9-04-008
simplifies	VBZ	2-02-002
simplified	VBN	9-03-006
simplistic	**JJ**	**2-01-001**
simply	**RB**	**171-15-125**
Simpson	**prop. noun**	**7-02-005**
Simpson	NP	5-02-004
Simpson's	NP$	2-02-002
Sims	**NP**	**3-01-002**
simulate	**verb**	**11-03-005**
simulate	VB	4-02-003
simulated	VBN	7-02-003
simulation	**NN**	**2-02-002**
simultaneous	**adjective**	**9-05-008**
simultaneous	JJ	8-04-007
simultaneous	JJ-HL	1-01-001
simultaneously	**QL**	**1-01-001**
simultaneously	**RB**	**37-10-030**
sin	**noun**	**67-10-030**
sin	NN	50-08-022
sin	NN-HL	1-01-001
sins	NNS	16-06-013
sin	**verb**	**10-04-007**
sin	VB	2-01-001
sinned	VBD	0-00-000
sin-ned	VBD	1-01-001
sinned	VBN	5-03-004
sinned	VBN-HL	1-01-001
sinning	VBG	1-01-001
Sinai	**NP**	**1-01-001**
Sinan	**NP**	**1-01-001**
Sinatra	**NP**	**4-03-003**
since	**sub. conj.**	**420-15-238**
since	CS	419-15-238
synce	CS	1-01-001
since	**IN**	**180-14-116**
since	**RB**	**29-10-026**
sincere	**JJ**	**15-09-014**
sincerely	**RB**	**7-03-006**
sincerest	**JJT**	**1-01-001**
sincerity	**NN**	**13-06-012**
sind	**FW-BER**	**1-01-001**
sine	**FW-IN**	**3-02-003**
sine	**NN**	**1-01-001**
sinew	**noun**	**1-01-001**
sinews	NNS	1-01-001
sinewy	**JJ**	**2-02-002**
sinfonica	**foreign**	**1-01-001**
sinfonica	FW-JJ	0-00-000
Sinfonica	FW-JJ-TL	1-01-001
sinful	**JJ**	**3-03-003**
sinfulness	**NN**	**3-02-002**
sing	**verb**	**120-15-055**
sing	VB	27-10-019
Sing	VB-TL	4-03-003
sings	VBZ	9-03-005
sings	VBZ-HL	1-01-001
sang	VBD	28-07-021
sung	VBN	18-08-015
singing	VBG	32-10-023
Singing	VBG-TL	1-01-001
Sing	**prop. noun**	**4-03-003**
Sing	NP	3-02-002
Sing's	NP$	1-01-001
sing-song	**NN**	**1-01-001**
singe	**verb**	**1-01-001**
singed	VBD	1-01-001
singer	**noun**	**23-04-012**
singer	NN	8-02-005
singer's	NN$	1-01-001
singers	NNS	13-04-009
singers'	NNS$	1-01-001
Singer	**NP**	**2-02-002**
singing	**NN**	**14-04-009**
single	**post-det.**	**160-13-108**
single	AP	158-13-108
single	AP-HL	2-01-001
single	**JJ**	**4-04-004**
single	**NN**	**7-01-002**
single	**verb**	**13-05-008**
single	VB	1-01-001
singles	VBZ	0-00-000
singles	VBZ-HL	1-01-001
singled	VBD	7-02-003
singled	VBN	3-02-003
singling	VBG	1-01-001
single-barrel	**NN**	**1-01-001**
single-color	**noun**	**1-01-001**
single-color	NN	0-00-000
single-color	NN-HL	1-01-001
single-crystal	**NN**	**1-01-001**
single-dose	**NN**	**1-01-001**
single-foot	**VB**	**1-01-001**
single-handed	**JJ**	**1-01-001**
single-handedly	**adverb**	**3-02-003**
single-handedly	RB	2-02-002
singlehandedly	RB	1-01-001
single-lane	**NN**	**1-01-001**
single-minded	**JJ**	**1-01-001**
single-seeded	**JJ**	**1-01-001**
single-shot	**NN**	**5-01-002**
single-spaced	**JJ**	**1-01-001**
single-step	**noun**	**3-01-001**
single-step	NN	2-01-001
single-step	NN-HL	1-01-001
single-valued	**JJ**	**6-01-001**
singleness	**NN**	**1-01-001**
singly	**RB**	**6-05-006**
singsong	**verb**	**1-01-001**
singsonged	VBD	1-01-001
singular	**JJ**	**14-06-008**
singularity	**NN**	**1-01-001**
singularly	**RB**	**1-01-001**
sinister	**JJ**	**13-07-012**
sink	**NN**	**12-06-008**
sink	**verb**	**40-12-033**
sink	VB	11-07-011
sank	VBD	18-09-015
sunk	VBN	6-05-006
sinking	VBG	5-05-005
sinkhole	**NN**	**1-01-001**

sinking	**NN**	**1-01-001**
sinkt	**FW-VBZ**	**1-01-001**
sinless	**JJ**	**3-02-003**
sinner	**noun**	**11-04-007**
sinner	NN	4-03-004
Sinner	NN-TL	3-01-001
sinners	NNS	4-03-003
Sino-Soviet	**NP**	**1-01-001**
sinter	**verb**	**1-01-001**
sintered	VBN	1-01-001
Sinton	**NP**	**1-01-001**
sinuous	**JJ**	**2-02-002**
sinuously	**RB**	**1-01-001**
sinuousness	**NN**	**1-01-001**
sinus	**noun**	**2-02-002**
sinus	NN	1-01-001
sinuses	NNS	1-01-001
sinusoid	**noun**	**2-01-001**
sinusoids	NNS	2-01-001
sinusoidal	**JJ**	**2-01-002**
Sioux	**prop. noun**	**9-03-004**
Sioux	NPS	8-03-004
Sieux	NPS	0-00-000
Sieux	NPS-TL	1-01-001
sip	**NN**	**2-02-002**
sip	**verb**	**10-06-008**
sipped	VBD	2-02-002
sipping	VBG	8-05-006
siphon	**verb**	**1-01-001**
siphoned	VBD	1-01-001
sipper	**noun**	**1-01-001**
sippers	NNS	1-01-001
sir	**noun**	**39-10-022**
sir	NN	37-10-020
sirs	NNS	1-01-001
Sirs	NNS-TL	1-01-001
sir	**UH**	**1-01-001**
Sir	**prop. noun**	**57-08-022**
Sir	NP	56-07-021
Sir	NP-TL	1-01-001
sire	**verb**	**3-02-003**
sired	VBN	3-02-003
siren	**noun**	**3-03-003**
siren	NN	1-01-001
sirens	NNS	2-02-002
Sirinjani	**NP**	**1-01-001**
sirloin	**noun**	**1-01-001**
sirloin	NN	0-00-000
serloin	NN	1-01-001
Sis	**NP**	**3-02-002**
Sisk	**NP**	**2-01-001**
sister	**noun**	**55-10-035**
sister	NN	35-09-026
Sister	NN-TL	3-02-003
sister's	NN$	2-02-002
sisters	NNS	10-06-008
sisters	NNS-NC	2-01-001
Sisters	NNS-TL	1-01-001
sisters'	NNS$	0-00-000
sisters'	NNS$-NC	2-01-001
sister-in-law	**noun**	**3-03-003**
sister-in-law	NN	2-02-002
sisters-in-law	NNS	1-01-001
Sistine	**adjective**	**1-01-001**
Sistine	JJ	0-00-000
Sistine	JJ-TL	1-01-001
sit	**FW-BE**	**1-01-001**
sit	**verb**	**314-15-142**
sit	VB	66-14-049
sits	VBZ	6-04-005
sat	VBD	139-14-075
sat	VBN	11-07-010
sitting	VBG	92-13-069
sit-down	**NN**	**1-01-001**
sit-in	**noun**	**2-02-002**
sit-in	NN	1-01-001
sit-ins	NNS	1-01-001
site	**noun**	**80-09-029**
site	NN	63-08-024
site	NN-HL	1-01-001
sites	NNS	16-07-010
sitter	**noun**	**28-05-005**
sitter	NN	24-04-004
sitter's	NN$	2-01-001
sitters	NNS	2-02-002
sitting	**noun**	**6-02-002**
sitting	NN	4-02-002
sittings	NNS	2-01-001
situ	**FW-NN**	**1-01-001**

situate	**verb**	**19-07-011**
situated	VBN	19-07-011
situation	**noun**	**247-15-138**
situation	NN	196-15-126
situations	NNS	51-11-032
situs	**noun**	**5-01-001**
situs	NN	4-01-001
situs	NN-HL	1-01-001
Sitwell	**NP**	**3-03-003**
Siva	**NP**	**1-01-001**
six	**card. num.**	**220-15-147**
six	CD	213-15-144
six	CD-HL	3-02-002
Six	CD-TL	4-03-004
Six	**NP**	**1-01-001**
six-dollar	**JJ**	**1-01-001**
six-foot	**JJ**	**2-02-002**
six-four	**CD**	**1-01-001**
six-gallon	**JJ**	**1-01-001**
six-inch	**JJ**	**1-01-001**
six-man	**JJ**	**1-01-001**
six-month	**JJ**	**1-01-001**
six-point	**JJ**	**2-02-002**
six-shooter	**NN**	**1-01-001**
six-thirty	**CD**	**1-01-001**
six-ton	**JJ**	**1-01-001**
sixteen	**card. num.**	**20-10-019**
sixteen	CD	19-09-018
sixteen	CD-HL	1-01-001
sixteen-year-old	**JJ**	**1-01-001**
sixteenth	**ord. num.**	**12-06-010**
sixteenth	OD	10-05-008
Sixteenth	OD-TL	2-02-002
sixth	**ord. num.**	**26-08-018**
sixth	OD	20-07-013
Sixth	OD-TL	6-04-005
sixth-grade	**NN**	**1-01-001**
sixth-sense	**NN**	**1-01-001**
sixty	**CD**	**21-11-021**
sixty	**noun**	**23-08-008**
sixties	NNS	11-06-006
Sixties	NNS-TL	11-02-002
sixties'	NNS$	0-00-000
Sixties'	NNS$-HL	1-01-001
sixty-day	**JJ**	**1-01-001**
sixty-eight	**CD**	**1-01-001**
sixty-eighth	**ord. num.**	**1-01-001**
sixty-eighth	OD	0-00-000
Sixty-eighth	OD-TL	1-01-001
sixty-five	**CD**	**9-04-006**
sixty-five-mile	**JJ**	**1-01-001**
sixty-nine	**CD**	**1-01-001**
sixty-one	**CD**	**8-02-002**
sixty-seven	**CD**	**1-01-001**
sixty-two	**CD**	**2-02-002**
sizable	**adjective**	**16-08-015**
sizable	JJ	15-07-014
sizeable	JJ	1-01-001
size	**noun**	**148-15-086**
size	NN	133-15-080
size	NN-HL	3-02-003
sizes	NNS	12-05-010
size	**verb**	**5-04-005**
size	VB	2-02-002
sized	VBD	2-02-002
sized	VBN	1-01-001
sized	**JJ**	**1-01-001**
Sizova	**NP**	**1-01-001**
sizzle	**verb**	**5-04-005**
sizzle	VB	1-01-001
sizzled	VBD	2-02-002
sizzling	VBG	2-02-002
skate	**noun**	**1-01-001**
skates	NNS	1-01-001
skate	**verb**	**3-03-003**
skate	VB	1-01-001
skating	VBG	1-01-001
Skating	VBG-TL	1-01-001
skeet	**NN**	**2-02-002**
skeletal	**adjective**	**13-01-002**
skeletal	JJ	4-01-002
Skeletal	JJ-TL	9-01-001
skeleton	**noun**	**3-02-003**
skeleton	NN	2-02-003
skeletons	NNS	1-01-001
skeptic	**noun**	**3-02-003**
skeptics	NNS	3-02-003
skeptical	**JJ**	**7-04-005**
skeptically	**RB**	**1-01-001**

Word	Tag	Frequency
skepticism	**NN**	**5-03-004**
sketch	**noun**	**32-08-015**
sketch	NN	15-06-010
sketches	NNS	17-05-007
sketch	**verb**	**11-04-008**
sketch	VB	1-01-001
sketches	VBZ	2-02-002
sketched	VBD	2-02-002
sketched	VBN	2-02-002
sketching	VBG	4-03-004
sketchbook	**NN**	**2-01-001**
skewer	**NN**	**1-01-001**
ski	**JJ**	**1-01-001**
ski	**noun**	**7-03-004**
ski	NN	2-02-002
Ski	NN-TL	2-01-001
skis	NNS	1-01-001
skiis	NNS	2-02-002
ski	**verb**	**5-02-003**
skiing	VBG	5-02-003
ski-jor	**verb**	**1-01-001**
ski-joring	VBG	1-01-001
skid	**noun**	**3-02-003**
skid	NN	1-01-001
Skid	NN-TL	1-01-001
skids	NNS	1-01-001
skid	**verb**	**4-02-004**
skidded	VBD	2-01-002
skidding	VBG	2-02-002
skiddy	**JJ**	**1-01-001**
skiff	**noun**	**14-02-002**
skiff	NN	9-02-002
skiff's	NN$	1-01-001
skiffs	NNS	4-01-001
skiing	**NN**	**2-01-001**
skill	**noun**	**79-11-047**
skill	NN	41-10-030
Skill	NN-TL	1-01-001
skills	NNS	37-08-021
skilled	**adjective**	**30-08-018**
skilled	JJ	29-08-017
skilled	JJ-HL	1-01-001
skillet	**NN**	**2-01-001**
skillful	**adjective**	**10-06-009**
skillful	JJ	9-06-008
skilful	JJ	1-01-001
skillfully	**adverb**	**6-05-006**
skillfully	RB	5-04-005
skilfully	RB	1-01-001
skillfulness	**NN**	**1-01-001**
skim	**verb**	**8-06-008**
skimmed	VBD	2-02-002
skimmed	VBN	3-02-003
skimming	VBG	3-03-003
skimming	**NN**	**1-01-001**
skimpy	**JJ**	**1-01-001**
skin	**noun**	**53-11-038**
skin	NN	47-10-033
skins	NNS	6-04-006
skin	**verb**	**2-01-002**
skins	VBZ	1-01-001
skinning	VBG	0-00-000
skinnin'	VBG	1-01-001
skin-perceptiveness	**NN**	**1-01-001**
skindive	**verb**	**2-02-002**
skindive	VB	1-01-001
skindiving	VBG	1-01-001
skinfold	**noun**	**1-01-001**
skinfolds	NNS	1-01-001
skinless	**JJ**	**4-01-001**
Skinner	**NP**	**1-01-001**
skinny	**JJ**	**8-05-008**
Skinny	**NP**	**1-01-001**
skip	**verb**	**17-08-014**
skip	VB	4-03-003
skips	VBZ	1-01-001
skipped	VBD	6-04-006
skipped	VBN	2-02-002
skipping	VBG	4-03-004
Skip	**NP**	**1-01-001**
Skipjack	**prop. noun**	**5-01-001**
Skipjack	NP	4-01-001
Skipjack's	NP$	1-01-001
skipper	**noun**	**3-02-002**
skipper	NN	1-01-001
skippers	NNS	2-01-001
skirmish	**noun**	**5-04-005**
skirmish	NN	4-04-004
skirmishes	NNS	1-01-001
skirmish	**verb**	**2-02-002**
skirmished	VBD	1-01-001
skirmishing	VBG	1-01-001
skirmisher	**noun**	**1-01-001**
skirmishers	NNS	1-01-001
skirmishing	**NN**	**1-01-001**
skirt	**noun**	**22-07-015**
skirt	NN	19-07-013
skirts	NNS	3-03-003
skirt	**verb**	**5-05-005**
skirt	VB	2-02-002
skirts	VBZ	1-01-001
skirted	VBD	1-01-001
skirting	VBG	1-01-001
skit	**noun**	**2-01-002**
skit	NN	1-01-001
skits	NNS	1-01-001
Skiway	**NP**	**1-01-001**
Skolkau	**prop. noun**	**1-01-001**
Skolkau	NP	0-00-000
Skolkau	NP-TL	1-01-001
Skolman	**prop. noun**	**5-01-001**
Skolman	NP	3-01-001
Skolman's	NP+HVZ	1-01-001
Skolman's	NP$	1-01-001
Skolovsky	**prop. noun**	**5-01-001**
Skolovsky	NP	4-01-001
Skolovsky's	NP$	1-01-001
Skopas	**NP**	**4-01-001**
Skorich	**NP**	**10-01-001**
skulk	**VB**	**1-01-001**
skull	**noun**	**5-04-005**
skull	NN	3-03-003
skulls	NNS	2-01-002
skull-bashing	**noun**	**1-01-001**
skull-bashings	NNS	1-01-001
skullcap	**NN**	**3-02-002**
skunk	**noun**	**1-01-001**
skunks	NNS	1-01-001
sky	**noun**	**72-14-050**
sky	NN	56-13-042
Sky	NN-TL	2-01-001
sky's	NN+BEZ	2-01-001
skies	NNS	9-05-007
Skies	NNS-TL	3-01-001
sky-carving	**JJ**	**1-01-001**
Sky-god	**prop. noun**	**1-01-001**
Sky-god	NP	0-00-000
Sky-god	NP-TL	1-01-001
sky-reaching	**JJ**	**1-01-001**
sky-tapping	**JJ**	**1-01-001**
Skybolt	**NP**	**1-01-001**
Skye	**NP**	**1-01-001**
skyjack	**verb**	**1-01-001**
skyjacked	VBN	1-01-001
skyjacker	**noun**	**1-01-001**
skyjackers	NNS	1-01-001
skylark	**noun**	**1-01-001**
skylark	NN	0-00-000
Skylark	NN-TL	1-01-001
skylark	**verb**	**1-01-001**
skylarking	VBG	1-01-001
skylight	**noun**	**3-01-001**
skylight	NN	1-01-001
skylights	NNS	2-01-001
skyline	**noun**	**5-05-005**
skyline	NN	1-01-001
Skyline	NN-TL	4-04-004
Skyros	**prop. noun**	**22-01-001**
Skyros	NP	20-01-001
Skyros'	NP$	2-01-001
skyscraper	**noun**	**3-03-003**
skyscraper	NN	2-02-002
skyscrapers	NNS	1-01-001
skywave	**noun**	**32-01-001**
skywave	NN	31-01-001
Skywave	NN-TL	1-01-001
skyway	**noun**	**1-01-001**
skyway	NN	0-00-000
Skyway	NN-TL	1-01-001
slab	**NN**	**9-04-005**
slack	**JJ**	**6-05-006**
slack	**noun**	**9-06-007**
slack	NN	2-02-002
slacks	NNS	7-04-005
slack	**verb**	**1-01-001**
slacking	VBG	1-01-001
Slack	**NP**	**1-01-001**
slacken	**verb**	**5-05-005**

Word	Tag	Count
slacken (cont.):		
slackened	VBD	1-01-001
slackened	VBN	2-02-002
slackening	VBG	2-02-002
sladang	**NN**	**1-01-001**
slake	**verb**	**3-01-001**
slaked	VBN	3-01-001
slam	**NN**	**3-01-002**
slam	**verb**	**20-07-017**
slammed	VBD	13-04-012
slammed	VBN	3-03-003
slamming	VBG	4-03-004
slander	**noun**	**1-01-001**
slanders	NNS	1-01-001
slanderer	**NN**	**3-01-001**
slanderous	**JJ**	**1-01-001**
slang	**NN**	**2-02-002**
slant	**noun**	**3-03-003**
slant	NN	2-02-002
slants	NNS	1-01-001
slant	**verb**	**8-07-008**
slant	VB	1-01-001
slanted	VBD	1-01-001
slanted	VBN	2-02-002
slanting	VBG	4-03-004
slant-wise	**RB**	**1-01-001**
slap	**verb**	**17-08-015**
slap	VB	2-02-002
slaps	VBZ	1-01-001
slapped	VBD	6-03-005
slapped	VBN	2-01-002
slapping	VBG	6-06-006
slapstick	**NN**	**2-02-002**
slash	**noun**	**1-01-001**
slashes	NNS	1-01-001
slash	**verb**	**18-07-014**
slash	VB	3-03-003
slashed	VBD	6-05-005
slashed	VBN	4-03-003
slashing	VBG	5-03-005
Slash-B	**NP**	**2-01-001**
slash-mouthed	**JJ**	**1-01-001**
slat	**noun**	**3-02-002**
slat	NN	2-01-001
slats	NNS	1-01-001
slate	**noun**	**10-04-006**
slate	NN	5-04-005
Slate	NN-TL	5-01-001
slate	**verb**	**3-03-003**
slated	VBN	3-03-003
Slater	**prop. noun**	**6-01-001**
Slater	NP	5-01-001
Slater's	NP$	1-01-001
slatted	**JJ**	**1-01-001**
slaughter	**NN**	**8-07-007**
slaughter	**verb**	**4-04-004**
slaughtered	VBD	1-01-001
slaughtered	VBN	2-02-002
slaughtering	VBG	1-01-001
Slaughter	**prop. noun**	**2-01-002**
Slaughter	NP	1-01-001
Slaughter	NP-TL	1-01-001
Slav	**prop. noun**	**1-01-001**
Slavs	NPS	1-01-001
slave	**noun**	**75-10-018**
slave	NN	30-09-012
slave's	NN$	1-01-001
slaves	NNS	44-07-014
slave-laborer	**noun**	**1-01-001**
slave-laborers	NNS	1-01-001
slave-owner	**noun**	**1-01-001**
slave-owners	NNS	1-01-001
slaver	**verb**	**1-01-001**
slavered	VBD	1-01-001
slavery	**noun**	**33-04-015**
slavery	NN	32-04-014
Slavery	NN-TL	1-01-001
Slavic	**JJ**	**2-01-001**
slavish	**JJ**	**1-01-001**
slay	**verb**	**1-01-001**
slaying	VBG	1-01-001
slaying	**NN**	**2-01-002**
sledding	**NN**	**2-02-002**
sleek	**JJ**	**2-02-002**
sleek-headed	**JJ**	**1-01-001**
sleep	**NN**	**34-09-022**
sleep	**verb**	**97-14-061**
sleep	VB	31-08-023
sleeps	VBZ	1-01-001

Word	Tag	Count
sleep (cont.):		
slept	VBD	18-07-015
slept	VBN	9-03-008
sleeping	VBG	36-14-031
Sleeping	VBG-TL	2-02-002
sleep-wakefulness	**NN**	**1-01-001**
sleeper	**noun**	**3-02-003**
sleeper	NN	0-00-000
Sleeper	NN-TL	1-01-001
sleeper's	NN$	1-01-001
sleepers	NNS	0-00-000
Sleepers	NNS-TL	1-01-001
sleepily	**RB**	**3-02-003**
sleeping	**NN**	**1-01-001**
sleepless	**JJ**	**1-01-001**
sleeplessly	**RB**	**1-01-001**
sleepwalker	**NN**	**1-01-001**
sleepy	**JJ**	**6-03-006**
sleepy-eyed	**JJ**	**1-01-001**
sleet	**NN**	**1-01-001**
sleeve	**noun**	**19-08-015**
sleeve	NN	11-05-009
sleeves	NNS	7-06-006
sleeves	NNS-HL	1-01-001
Sleight	**NP**	**1-01-001**
Slenczynka	**NP**	**1-01-001**
slender	**JJ**	**19-08-018**
slender-waisted	**JJ**	**1-01-001**
slenderer	**JJR**	**1-01-001**
sleuthing	**NN**	**1-01-001**
slice	**noun**	**12-06-010**
slice	NN	10-05-009
slices	NNS	2-02-002
slice	**verb**	**7-05-006**
slice	VB	3-03-003
sliced	VBD	3-03-003
sliced	VBN	1-01-001
slick	**JJ**	**6-03-006**
slick	**NN**	**1-01-001**
slick-headed	**JJ**	**1-01-001**
slicker	**noun**	**5-03-003**
slicker	NN	4-03-003
slickers	NNS	1-01-001
slide	**noun**	**17-09-012**
slide	NN	12-07-008
slides	NNS	5-04-005
slide	**verb**	**43-10-032**
slide	VB	8-05-006
slid	VBD	24-08-019
sliding	VBG	11-08-011
slide-lock	**NN**	**1-01-001**
slight	**adjective**	**51-13-042**
slight	JJ	50-13-041
slight	JJ-HL	1-01-001
slight	**noun**	**3-03-003**
slight	NN	2-02-002
slights	NNS	1-01-001
slighter	**JJR**	**1-01-001**
slightest	**JJT**	**13-08-013**
slightly	**QL**	**32-11-031**
slightly	**RB**	**51-13-043**
slightly-smoking	**JJ**	**1-01-001**
slim	**JJ**	**10-07-009**
Slim	**NP**	**10-03-003**
slim-waisted	**JJ**	**1-01-001**
slime	**verb**	**1-01-001**
slimed	VBN	1-01-001
slimly	**RB**	**1-01-001**
slimmer	**JJR**	**1-01-001**
sling	**noun**	**2-01-001**
sling	NN	1-01-001
slings	NNS	1-01-001
sling	**verb**	**3-03-003**
slung	VBD	1-01-001
slung	VBN	1-01-001
slinging	VBG	1-01-001
slingshot	**NN**	**1-01-001**
slip	**noun**	**19-08-009**
slip	NN	12-07-007
slips	NNS	7-03-003
slip	**verb**	**47-11-041**
slip	VB	7-06-007
slips	VBZ	1-01-001
slipped	VBD	26-08-024
slipped	VBN	6-05-006
slipping	VBG	7-05-007
slippage	**NN**	**1-01-001**
slipper	**noun**	**10-05-007**
slipper	NN	3-03-003

Word	Tag	Frequency
slipper (cont.):		
slippers	NNS	7-04-006
slippery	**JJ**	**5-05-005**
slipstream	**NN**	**1-01-001**
slit	**noun**	**5-02-004**
slit	NN	3-02-003
slits	NNS	2-01-001
slit	**verb**	**3-02-003**
slit	VB	2-02-002
slit	VBN	1-01-001
slitter	**noun**	**2-01-001**
slitter	NN	1-01-001
slitters	NNS	1-01-001
slivery	**JJ**	**1-01-001**
Slo-Flo	**prop. noun**	**1-01-001**
Slo-Flo	NP	0-00-000
Slo-Flo	NP-TL	1-01-001
Sloan	**prop. noun**	**20-03-003**
Sloan	NP	14-03-003
Sloan	NP-TL	1-01-001
Sloan's	NP$	5-01-001
Sloanaker	**NP**	**5-01-001**
Sloane	**NP**	**3-01-001**
slob	**NN**	**4-03-004**
Slocum	**prop. noun**	**5-02-002**
Slocum	NP	2-01-001
Slocum	NP-TL	1-01-001
Slocum's	NP$	2-01-001
sloe	**NN**	**2-01-001**
slogan	**noun**	**12-04-009**
slogan	NN	6-03-005
slogan	NN-HL	1-01-001
slogans	NNS	5-04-004
sloganeer	**verb**	**1-01-001**
sloganeering	VBG	1-01-001
sloop	**NN**	**1-01-001**
slop	**NN**	**1-01-001**
slop	**verb**	**4-03-003**
slop	VB	1-01-001
slopped	VBD	1-01-001
slopping	VBG	2-02-002
slope	**noun**	**27-11-021**
slope	NN	19-10-014
slope's	NN$	1-01-001
slopes	NNS	7-05-007
slope	**verb**	**7-04-007**
sloping	VBG	7-04-007
sloppily	**RB**	**1-01-001**
sloppy	**JJ**	**3-03-003**
slosh	**verb**	**1-01-001**
sloshed	VBD	1-01-001
slot	**noun**	**11-05-007**
slot	NN	6-04-005
slots	NNS	4-03-004
slots	NNS-HL	1-01-001
slot	**verb**	**1-01-001**
slotted	VBN	1-01-001
slothful	**JJ**	**1-01-001**
slouch	**NN**	**1-01-001**
slouch	**verb**	**1-01-001**
slouches	VBZ	1-01-001
Slough	**NP**	**1-01-001**
slovenliness	**NN**	**1-01-001**
slovenly	**JJ**	**3-01-002**
slow	**adjective**	**49-11-038**
slow	JJ	48-11-037
slow	JJ-HL	1-01-001
slow	**RB**	**3-03-003**
slow	**verb**	**30-10-024**
slow	VB	8-04-006
slowed	VBD	12-06-011
slowed	VBN	5-04-005
slowing	VBG	5-04-004
slow-acting	**JJ**	**1-01-001**
slow-baked	**JJ**	**1-01-001**
slow-bouncing	**JJ**	**1-01-001**
slow-firing	**JJ**	**1-01-001**
slow-growing	**JJ**	**1-01-001**
slow-moving	**JJ**	**1-01-001**
slow-scrambling	**JJ**	**1-01-001**
slower	**JJR**	**7-03-006**
slower	**RBR**	**2-02-002**
slowest	**JJT**	**2-02-002**
slowing	**NN**	**1-01-001**
slowly	**RB**	**115-13-078**
slowly-mending	**JJ**	**1-01-001**
slowness	**NN**	**4-03-004**
sludge	**NN**	**4-01-001**
slug	**noun**	**12-06-008**
slug (cont.):		
slug	NN	8-05-005
slugs	NNS	4-04-004
slug	**verb**	**9-04-008**
slug	VB	2-02-002
slugged	VBD	3-02-003
slugged	VBN	1-01-001
slugging	VBG	3-03-003
slugger	**noun**	**6-02-005**
slugger	NN	4-02-003
sluggers	NNS	2-01-002
sluggish	**JJ**	**2-02-002**
sluggishly	**RB**	**2-02-002**
sluice	**noun**	**4-03-004**
sluice	NN	2-02-002
sluices	NNS	2-02-002
sluice	**verb**	**3-02-003**
sluiced	VBD	1-01-001
sluiced	VBN	1-01-001
sluicing	VBG	1-01-001
sluicehouse	**NN**	**1-01-001**
slum	**noun**	**16-08-011**
slum	NN	8-04-005
slums	NNS	7-06-006
Slums	NNS-TL	1-01-001
slumber	**NN**	**3-03-003**
slumber	**verb**	**1-01-001**
slumbered	VBD	1-01-001
slump	**NN**	**5-02-005**
slump	**verb**	**11-04-009**
slump	VB	3-02-002
slumped	VBD	6-03-005
slumped	VBN	2-02-002
slurp	**verb**	**1-01-001**
slurped	VBD	1-01-001
slurry	**noun**	**1-01-001**
slurries	NNS	1-01-001
sly	**JJ**	**5-05-005**
slyly	**RB**	**2-01-002**
slyness	**NN**	**1-01-001**
smack	**verb**	**7-04-005**
smack	VB	4-03-003
smacks	VBZ	1-01-001
smacked	VBD	2-02-002
small	**adjective**	**537-15-241**
small	JJ	521-15-241
small	JJ-HL	4-01-002
Small	JJ-TL	12-01-001
small	**NN**	**1-01-001**
Small	**NP**	**4-02-002**
small-arm	**noun**	**1-01-001**
small-arms	NNS	1-01-001
small-boat	**NN**	**1-01-001**
small-car	**NN**	**1-01-001**
small-game	**NN**	**2-02-002**
small-scale	**NN**	**1-01-001**
small-town	**noun**	**6-06-006**
small-town	NN	5-05-005
small-town	NN-NC	1-01-001
smaller	**comp. adj.**	**78-14-064**
smaller	JJR	77-14-063
smaller	JJR-NC	1-01-001
smaller-size	**NN**	**1-01-001**
smallest	**JJT**	**13-05-009**
smallish	**JJ**	**1-01-001**
smallness	**NN**	**2-02-002**
smallpox	**NN**	**2-02-002**
smalltime	**NN**	**1-01-001**
Smallwood	**NP**	**4-02-002**
smart	**JJ**	**20-08-017**
smart	**RB**	**1-01-001**
smart	**verb**	**1-01-001**
smarted	VBD	1-01-001
smarter	**JJR**	**2-02-002**
smartly	**RB**	**4-03-004**
smash	**NN**	**2-02-002**
smash	**verb**	**18-10-016**
smash	VB	2-02-002
smashed	VBD	11-08-010
smashed	VBN	4-03-004
smashing	VBG	1-01-001
smash-'em-down	**JJ**	**1-01-001**
smashed-out	**JJ**	**1-01-001**
smattering	**noun**	**1-01-001**
smatterings	NNS	1-01-001
smear	**NN**	**2-01-001**
smear	**verb**	**2-02-002**
smeared	VBN	2-02-002
smell	**noun**	**27-09-021**

Word	Tag	Frequency
smell (cont.):		
smell	NN	25-08-019
smells	NNS	2-02-002
smell	**verb**	**43-11-034**
smell	VB	9-05-008
smells	VBZ	7-04-005
smelled	VBD	15-06-013
smelt	VBD	3-02-002
smelled	VBN	4-03-004
smelling	VBG	5-04-005
smelt	**noun**	**1-01-001**
smelts	NNS	1-01-001
Smerdyakov	**NP**	**1-01-001**
smile	**noun**	**56-12-045**
smile	NN	48-11-038
smiles	NNS	8-06-008
smile	**verb**	**122-12-070**
smile	VB	10-05-010
smiles	VBZ	3-03-003
smiled	VBD	68-08-047
smiled	VBN	3-03-003
smiling	VBG	35-10-026
smilin'	VBG	0-00-000
Smilin'	VBG-TL	2-01-001
Smiling	VBG-TL	1-01-001
smilingly	**RB**	**2-01-002**
smirk	**NN**	**2-02-002**
smirk	**verb**	**2-02-002**
smirk	VB	1-01-001
smirked	VBD	1-01-001
smite	**verb**	**1-01-001**
smitten	VBN	1-01-001
Smith	**prop. noun**	**59-11-038**
Smith	NP	47-09-029
Smith	NP-TL	7-06-007
Smith's	NP$	5-04-004
Smith-Colmer	**NP**	**1-01-001**
Smith-Hughes	**prop. noun**	**3-02-002**
Smith-Hughes	NP	2-02-002
Smith-Hughes	NP-TL	1-01-001
smithereens	**NNS**	**2-01-002**
Smithfield	**NP**	**3-02-002**
Smithsonian	**prop. noun**	**3-01-001**
Smithsonian	NP	2-01-001
Smithsonian	NP-TL	1-01-001
Smithtown	**NP**	**1-01-001**
smithy	**NN**	**1-01-001**
smog	**NN**	**1-01-001**
smoke	**noun**	**33-10-027**
smoke	NN	32-10-026
Smoke	NN-TL	1-01-001
smoke	**verb**	**26-07-022**
smoke	VB	8-04-006
smokes	VBZ	1-01-001
smoked	VBD	6-03-006
smoked	VBN	3-03-003
smoking	VBG	8-05-008
smoke-filled	**JJ**	**1-01-001**
smoke-stained	**JJ**	**1-01-001**
smokehouse	**NN**	**2-01-001**
smoker	**noun**	**1-01-001**
smokers	NNS	1-01-001
smokescreen	**NN**	**1-01-001**
smoky	**adjective**	**4-02-002**
smoky	JJ	1-01-001
Smoky	JJ-TL	3-01-001
Smoky	**prop. noun**	**2-02-002**
Smoky	NP	1-01-001
Smokies	NPS	0-00-000
Smokies	NPS-TL	1-01-001
smolder	**verb**	**5-05-005**
smolders	VBZ	1-01-001
smoldered	VBD	2-02-002
smoldering	VBG	1-01-001
Smoldering	VBG-TL	1-01-001
smolderingly	**RB**	**1-01-001**
smooch	**verb**	**1-01-001**
smooching	VBG	1-01-001
smooth	**JJ**	**36-11-026**
smooth	**verb**	**15-07-012**
smooth	VB	6-02-003
smoothed	VBD	4-03-004
smoothed	VBN	3-03-003
smoothing	VBG	2-02-002
smoothbore	**NN**	**1-01-001**
smoother	**JJR**	**3-02-003**
smoothest	**JJT**	**1-01-001**
smoothly	**RB**	**12-06-012**
smoothness	**NN**	**5-03-004**

Word	Tag	Frequency
smother	**verb**	**7-05-006**
smothered	VBD	2-02-002
smothered	VBN	4-03-004
smothering	VBG	1-01-001
SMU	**NP**	**1-01-001**
smudge	**verb**	**1-01-001**
smudged	VBN	1-01-001
smug	**JJ**	**7-05-006**
smuggle	**verb**	**5-04-005**
smuggle	VB	1-01-001
smuggled	VBN	3-02-003
smuggling	VBG	1-01-001
smuggler	**noun**	**2-01-001**
smugglers	NNS	1-01-001
smugglers'	NNS$	1-01-001
Smythe	**NP**	**4-02-003**
snack	**noun**	**9-04-006**
snack	NN	6-04-005
snacks	NNS	2-01-002
snacks	NNS-HL	1-01-001
snag	**noun**	**1-01-001**
snags	NNS	1-01-001
snag	**VB**	**3-02-002**
snail	**noun**	**3-03-003**
snail	NN	1-01-001
snail's	NN$	1-01-001
snails	NNS	1-01-001
snake	**noun**	**70-08-014**
snake	NN	42-07-011
Snake	NN-TL	2-02-002
snakes	NNS	26-03-003
snake	**verb**	**3-02-003**
snaked	VBD	3-02-003
snake-like	**JJ**	**1-01-001**
snake-rail	**NN**	**1-01-001**
snakestrike	**NN**	**1-01-001**
snap	**NN**	**1-01-001**
snap	**verb**	**38-12-032**
snap	VB	11-06-009
snapped	VBD	17-06-016
snapped	VBN	2-02-002
snapping	VBG	8-04-007
snap-in	**JJ**	**1-01-001**
snapback	**NN**	**1-01-001**
snapdragon	**noun**	**1-01-001**
snapdragons	NNS	1-01-001
snapper	**NN**	**1-01-001**
snapping	**NN**	**1-01-001**
snappy	**JJ**	**1-01-001**
snapshot	**noun**	**1-01-001**
snapshots	NNS	1-01-001
snare	**NN**	**1-01-001**
snare	**verb**	**1-01-001**
snared	VBN	1-01-001
snarl	**verb**	**11-05-009**
snarled	VBD	8-04-006
snarling	VBG	3-03-003
snatch	**noun**	**2-01-001**
snatches	NNS	2-01-001
snatch	**verb**	**17-07-015**
snatch	VB	4-04-004
snatches	VBZ	1-01-001
snatched	VBD	9-04-008
snatched	VBN	2-02-002
snatching	VBG	1-01-001
snazzy	**JJ**	**1-01-001**
Snead	**NP**	**2-01-001**
sneak	**NN**	**1-01-001**
sneak	**verb**	**11-05-010**
sneak	VB	1-01-001
sneaks	VBZ	1-01-001
sneaked	VBD	4-03-004
snuck	VBD	1-01-001
sneaked	VBN	2-02-002
sneaking	VBG	2-01-002
sneaker	**noun**	**5-03-004**
sneaker	NN	2-01-001
sneakers	NNS	3-02-003
sneaky	**JJ**	**2-02-002**
Sneed	**NP**	**1-01-001**
sneer	**noun**	**2-02-002**
sneer	NN	1-01-001
sneers	NNS	1-01-001
sneer	**verb**	**3-02-003**
sneers	VBZ	1-01-001
sneered	VBD	1-01-001
sneering	VBG	1-01-001
sneeze	**verb**	**3-02-003**
sneezed	VBD	1-01-001

Word	Tag	Frequency
sneeze (cont.):		
sneezed	VBN	1-01-001
sneezing	VBG	1-01-001
Snelling	**prop. noun**	**7-01-001**
Snelling	NP	3-01-001
Snelling	NP-TL	4-01-001
Snellville	**NP**	**2-01-001**
snick	**NN**	**1-01-001**
snicker	**verb**	**2-02-002**
snickered	VBD	2-02-002
sniff	**verb**	**10-05-010**
sniff	VB	2-02-002
sniffed	VBD	6-03-006
sniffing	VBG	2-02-002
Sniffle	**NP**	**1-01-001**
snigger	**verb**	**1-01-001**
sniggered	VBD	1-01-001
snip	**noun**	**1-01-001**
snips	NNS	1-01-001
sniper	**noun**	**2-02-002**
sniper	NN	1-01-001
sniper's	NN$	1-01-001
sniping	**NN**	**1-01-001**
snippy	**JJ**	**1-01-001**
sniveling	**noun**	**1-01-001**
snivelings	NNS	1-01-001
snob	**noun**	**1-01-001**
snobs	NNS	1-01-001
snob-clannish	**JJ**	**1-01-001**
snobbery	**NN**	**4-03-003**
snobbish	**JJ**	**2-02-002**
snobbishly	**RB**	**1-01-001**
Snodgrass	**NP**	**2-02-002**
Snook	**NP**	**1-01-001**
snoop	**verb**	**2-02-002**
snoop	VB	1-01-001
snooping	VBG	1-01-001
Snopes	**NP**	**4-01-002**
snore	**verb**	**4-02-003**
snoring	VBG	4-02-003
snoring	**NN**	**2-01-002**
snorkle	**NN**	**2-01-001**
snort	**NN**	**1-01-001**
snort	**verb**	**6-03-005**
snort	VB	2-01-001
snorted	VBD	4-03-004
snout	**NN**	**1-01-001**
snow	**noun**	**56-13-028**
snow	NN	52-12-025
snow	NN-HL	1-01-001
Snow	NN-TL	1-01-001
snows	NNS	2-01-001
snow	**verb**	**12-05-005**
snow	VB	1-01-001
snows	VBZ	1-01-001
snows	VBZ-NC	4-01-001
snowed	VBD	2-01-001
snowing	VBG	4-04-004
Snow	**prop. noun**	**7-03-003**
Snow	NP	4-03-003
Snow's	NP$	3-02-002
snow-covered	**JJ**	**1-01-001**
snow-fence	**NN**	**1-01-001**
snow-white	**JJ**	**1-01-001**
snowball	**noun**	**3-01-002**
snowball	NN	1-01-001
Snowball	NN-TL	1-01-001
snowballs	NNS	1-01-001
snowball	**verb**	**1-01-001**
snowballs	VBZ	1-01-001
snowfall	**NN**	**2-02-002**
snowflake	**noun**	**1-01-001**
snowflakes	NNS	1-01-001
snowstorm	**NN**	**3-03-003**
snowy	**JJ**	**4-04-004**
snub	**verb**	**4-03-004**
snubbed	VBN	3-03-003
snubbing	VBG	1-01-001
snuff	**verb**	**1-01-001**
snuffed	VBD	1-01-001
snuffbox	**noun**	**1-01-001**
snuffboxes	NNS	1-01-001
snuffer	**NN**	**1-01-001**
snug	**JJ**	**2-02-002**
snug-fitting	**JJ**	**1-01-001**
Snug-Grip	**NP**	**1-01-001**
snuggle	**verb**	**4-02-004**
snuggled	VBD	4-02-004
snugly	**RB**	**2-02-002**
Snyder	**prop. noun**	**2-02-002**
Snyder	NP	1-01-001
Snyder's	NP$	1-01-001
so	**CS**	**479-15-250**
so	**qualifier**	**932-15-356**
so	QL	931-15-356
So	QL-TL	1-01-001
so	**adverb**	**574-15-298**
so	RB	573-15-298
soe	RB	1-01-001
so	**UH**	**1-01-001**
so-called	**JJ**	**32-12-029**
so-far	**RB**	**1-01-001**
so-so	**JJ**	**3-02-003**
so-so	**RB**	**1-01-001**
so's	**CS**	**4-02-003**
soak	**verb**	**18-06-012**
soak	VB	7-04-005
soaked	VBD	1-01-001
soaked	VBN	5-03-005
soaking	VBG	5-03-004
soaking	**NN**	**1-01-001**
soaking	**QL**	**3-01-002**
soap	**noun**	**25-06-010**
soap	NN	21-06-010
soap	NN-HL	1-01-001
soaps	NNS	3-02-002
soapsuds	**NNS**	**1-01-001**
soapy	**JJ**	**1-01-001**
Soapy	**NP**	**1-01-001**
soar	**verb**	**9-06-009**
soared	VBD	3-02-003
soared	VBN	1-01-001
soaring	VBG	5-04-005
sob	**noun**	**3-03-003**
sobs	NNS	3-03-003
sob	**verb**	**3-02-003**
sobbed	VBD	1-01-001
sobbed	VBN	1-01-001
sobbing	VBG	1-01-001
soba	**FW-NN**	**1-01-001**
sobbingly	**RB**	**1-01-001**
sober	**JJ**	**16-09-014**
sober	**verb**	**6-03-006**
sobered	VBN	3-01-003
sobering	VBG	3-02-003
Sober	**NP**	**3-01-001**
soberly	**RB**	**4-03-004**
Sobibor	**NP**	**1-01-001**
sobriety	**NN**	**1-01-001**
sobriquet	**noun**	**3-02-003**
sobriquet	NN	2-02-002
soubriquet	NN	1-01-001
soccer	**noun**	**3-01-001**
soccer	NN	1-01-001
Soccer	NN-TL	1-01-001
Soccer	NN-TL-HL	1-01-001
Sochi	**NP**	**2-01-001**
sociability	**NN**	**2-02-002**
sociable	**JJ**	**1-01-001**
social	**adjective**	**380-15-122**
social	JJ	361-15-116
socal	JJ	1-01-001
social	JJ-HL	3-01-003
Social	JJ-TL	15-06-015
social	**NN**	**1-01-001**
social-class	**NN**	**8-01-001**
social-climbing	**JJ**	**1-01-001**
social-economic	**JJ**	**3-02-002**
social-political-economical	**JJ**	**1-01-001**
social-register	**NN**	**1-01-001**
social-role	**NN**	**1-01-001**
social-welfare	**NN**	**1-01-001**
socialism	**noun**	**20-06-010**
socialism	NN	17-05-008
socialism	NN-HL	1-01-001
Socialism	NN-TL	2-02-002
socialist	**adjective**	**14-04-008**
socialist	JJ	2-01-002
Socialist	JJ-TL	12-04-006
socialist	**noun**	**7-03-006**
socialist	NN	4-02-004
Socialist	NN-TL	3-02-002
socialistic	**JJ**	**3-01-003**
sociality	**NN**	**1-01-001**
socialization	**noun**	**6-03-003**
socialization	NN	5-03-003
socialization	NN-HL	1-01-001
socialize	**verb**	**5-03-005**

socialize (cont.):		
socialize	VB	1-01-001
socializes	VBZ	1-01-001
socialized	VBN	3-02-003
socially	**RB**	**15-08-013**
socially-oriented	**JJ**	**1-01-001**
societal	**JJ**	**4-02-002**
societe	**foreign**	**1-01-001**
societe	FW-NN	0-00-000
Societe	FW-NN-TL	1-01-001
society	**noun**	**281-14-109**
society	NN	194-14-080
Society	NN-TL	42-11-030
Society	NN-TL-HL	1-01-001
society's	NN$	3-02-003
societies	NNS	38-08-023
societies	NNS-HL	2-01-001
Societies	NNS-TL	1-01-001
Socinianism	**NP**	**1-01-001**
socio-archaeological	**JJ**	**1-01-001**
socio-political	**JJ**	**1-01-001**
socio-structural	**JJ**	**1-01-001**
socioeconomic	**adjective**	**6-03-003**
socioeconomic	JJ	2-01-001
socio-economic	JJ	3-02-002
socioeconomic	JJ-HL	1-01-001
sociological	**JJ**	**11-05-009**
sociologically	**RB**	**1-01-001**
sociologist	**noun**	**3-02-003**
sociologist	NN	2-02-002
sociologists	NNS	1-01-001
sociology	**NN**	**15-02-002**
sock	**noun**	**10-08-009**
sock	NN	3-03-003
socks	NNS	7-05-006
sock	**verb**	**2-02-002**
sock	VB	1-01-001
socked	VBD	1-01-001
sockdologize	**verb**	**1-01-001**
sockdologizing	VBG	1-01-001
socket	**noun**	**4-03-003**
socket	NN	3-03-003
sockets	NNS	1-01-001
Socola	**NP**	**1-01-001**
Soconoco	**NP**	**1-01-001**
sod	**noun**	**4-02-004**
sod	NN	3-01-003
sods	NNS	1-01-001
soda	**NN**	**3-02-002**
sodden	**JJ**	**2-02-002**
soddenly	**RB**	**1-01-001**
soddy	**noun**	**1-01-001**
soddies	NNS	1-01-001
sodium	**noun**	**12-02-005**
sodium	NN	10-02-004
sodium	NN-HL	2-01-001
Soeren	**NP**	**1-01-001**
sofa	**noun**	**9-04-005**
sofa	NN	6-03-003
sofas	NNS	3-02-002
sofar	**RB**	**1-01-001**
soft	**adjective**	**60-11-049**
soft	JJ	59-11-048
soft-	JJ	1-01-001
soft	**RB**	**2-02-002**
soft-drink	**noun**	**2-02-002**
soft-drink	NN	1-01-001
soft-drinks	NNS	1-01-001
soft-headed	**JJ**	**1-01-001**
soft-heartedness	**NN**	**1-01-001**
soft-looking	**JJ**	**1-01-001**
soft-shell	**NN**	**1-01-001**
soft-shoe	**NN**	**1-01-001**
soft-spoken	**JJ**	**1-01-001**
soften	**verb**	**16-08-015**
soften	VB	4-03-004
softens	VBZ	1-01-001
softened	VBD	3-03-003
softened	VBN	4-04-004
softening	VBG	4-03-004
softener	**noun**	**2-01-001**
softener	NN	1-01-001
softener	NN-HL	1-01-001
softening	**NN**	**2-02-002**
softer	**JJR**	**5-04-005**
softest	**JJT**	**1-01-001**
softly	**QL**	**1-01-001**
softly	**RB**	**30-08-023**
softness	**NN**	**5-03-004**

softwood	**NN**	**1-01-001**
soggy	**JJ**	**3-02-003**
Sohn	**NP**	**1-01-001**
soignee	**JJ**	**1-01-001**
soil	**noun**	**67-11-021**
soil	NN	51-11-021
soil	NN-HL	1-01-001
soils	NNS	15-02-003
soil	**verb**	**9-03-004**
soil	VB	2-02-002
soiled	VBN	7-01-002
soil-bearing	**JJ**	**1-01-001**
soil-removal	**NN**	**1-01-001**
soiree	**foreign**	**1-01-001**
soiree	FW-NN	0-00-000
Soiree	FW-NN-TL	1-01-001
soiree	**noun**	**1-01-001**
soirees	NNS	1-01-001
sojourn	**NN**	**5-02-005**
sojourner	**noun**	**2-02-002**
sojourner	NN	1-01-001
sojourners	NNS	1-01-001
Sojourner	**NP**	**2-01-001**
Sokol	**NP**	**4-01-001**
Sokolev	**NP**	**1-01-001**
Sokolov	**NP**	**2-01-001**
Sokolsky	**NP**	**2-02-002**
Sol	**NP**	**3-03-003**
solace	**NN**	**5-04-005**
solace	**verb**	**2-02-002**
solace	VB	1-01-001
solaced	VBN	1-01-001
solar	**adjective**	**16-04-008**
solar	JJ	14-04-007
Solar	JJ-TL	2-02-002
solar-corpuscular-radiation	**NN**	**1-01-001**
solar-electromagnetic-	**JJ**	**1-01-001**
solar-radiation	**NN**	**1-01-001**
solar-wind	**NN**	**1-01-001**
sold-out	**JJ**	**1-01-001**
solder	**NN**	**1-01-001**
solder	**verb**	**5-01-001**
solder	VB	3-01-001
soldered	VBN	1-01-001
soldering	VBG	1-01-001
soldier	**noun**	**98-11-045**
soldier	NN	38-08-018
Soldier	NN-TL	1-01-001
soldier's	NN$	1-01-001
soldiers	NNS	55-08-029
Soldiers	NNS-TL	1-01-001
soldiers'	NNS$	2-01-001
soldier	**verb**	**1-01-001**
soldiering	VBG	1-01-001
soldier-master	**noun**	**1-01-001**
soldier-masters	NNS	1-01-001
soldierly	**JJ**	**1-01-001**
soldiery	**NN**	**1-01-001**
sole	**foreign**	**1-01-001**
sole	FW-NN	0-00-000
Sole	FW-NN-TL	1-01-001
sole	**JJ**	**15-10-015**
sole	**noun**	**7-04-006**
sole	NN	2-02-002
soles	NNS	5-02-004
solely	**QL**	**2-02-002**
solely	**RB**	**18-06-016**
solemn	**adjective**	**12-08-012**
solemn	JJ	11-08-011
solemn	JJ-NC	1-01-001
solemnis	**foreign**	**1-01-001**
solemnis	FW-JJ	0-00-000
Solemnis	FW-JJ-TL	1-01-001
solemnity	**NN**	**1-01-001**
solemnly	**RB**	**9-06-008**
solenoid	**NN**	**1-01-001**
Solesmes	**prop. noun**	**1-01-001**
Solesmes	NP	0-00-000
Solesmes	NP-TL	1-01-001
solicit	**verb**	**5-04-004**
solicit	VB	1-01-001
solicits	VBZ	1-01-001
solicited	VBD	1-01-001
solicited	VBN	1-01-001
soliciting	VBG	1-01-001
solicitor	**noun**	**6-03-004**
solicitor	NN	3-02-002
Solicitor	NN-TL	3-02-003
solicitous	**JJ**	**2-02-002**

Word	Tag	Frequency
solicitousness	**NN**	**1-01-001**
solicitude	**NN**	**3-03-003**
solid	**adjective**	**70-14-056**
solid	JJ	69-14-055
solid	JJ-HL	1-01-001
solid	**noun**	**20-04-006**
solid	NN	7-04-004
solids	NNS	13-01-002
solid-fueled	**JJ**	**1-01-001**
solid-state	**NN**	**1-01-001**
solidarity	**NN**	**13-05-009**
solidify	**verb**	**1-01-001**
solidifies	VBZ	1-01-001
solidity	**NN**	**4-03-003**
solidly	**RB**	**10-05-007**
solipsism	**NN**	**1-01-001**
solitary	**JJ**	**13-07-013**
solitary	**NN**	**1-01-001**
solitude	**noun**	**3-03-003**
solitude	NN	2-02-002
solitudes	NNS	1-01-001
solitudinem	**FW-NN**	**1-01-001**
Solly	**NP**	**2-01-001**
solo	**noun**	**8-04-008**
solo	NN	6-04-006
solos	NNS	2-02-002
solo	**verb**	**2-01-001**
solo	VB	1-01-001
solos	VBZ	1-01-001
soloist	**noun**	**15-05-012**
soloist	NN	9-03-007
soloists	NNS	5-03-005
soloists'	NNS$	1-01-001
Solomon	**prop. noun**	**3-03-003**
Solomon	NP	2-02-002
Solomon's	NP$	1-01-001
Soloviev	**NP**	**2-02-002**
Soloviev-Sedoi	**NP**	**1-01-001**
solstice	**NN**	**1-01-001**
soluble	**JJ**	**3-02-003**
solution	**noun**	**88-11-062**
solution	NN	56-11-046
Solution	NN-TL	3-01-001
solutions	NNS	29-06-019
solution-type	**JJ**	**1-01-001**
solvate	**verb**	**1-01-001**
solvating	VBG	1-01-001
solve	**verb**	**49-12-041**
solve	VB	18-09-017
solve	VB-HL	2-02-002
solves	VBZ	2-01-002
solved	VBD	1-01-001
solved	VBN	18-09-017
solving	VBG	8-05-006
solvency	**NN**	**1-01-001**
solvent	**noun**	**8-01-002**
solvent	NN	5-01-001
solvents	NNS	3-01-002
soma	**NN**	**1-01-001**
somatic	**JJ**	**2-01-001**
Somay	**NP**	**1-01-001**
sombre	**adjective**	**5-04-005**
sombre	JJ	2-01-002
somber	JJ	3-03-003
some	**sg/pl det.**	**1594-15-440**
some	DTI	1589-15-440
some	DTI-HL	4-02-004
some	DTI-TL	1-01-001
some	**QL**	**1-01-001**
some	**RB**	**23-07-019**
somebody	**nom. pro.**	**65-12-047**
somebody	PN	56-11-039
somebody	PN-HL	1-01-001
Somebody	PN-TL	1-01-001
somebody's	PN+BEZ	1-01-001
somebody's	PN+HVZ	1-01-001
somebody'll	PN+MD	1-01-001
somebody's	PN$	4-04-004
someday	**RB**	**12-06-012**
somehow	**RB**	**72-15-062**
someone	**nom. pro.**	**100-14-074**
someone	PN	94-14-068
someone'll	PN+MD	1-01-001
someone's	PN+BEZ	1-01-001
someone's	PN$	4-04-004
someplace	**NN**	**1-01-001**
someplace	**RB**	**5-04-005**
Somers	**prop. noun**	**7-02-002**
Somers	NP	1-01-001
Somers (cont.):		
Somers	NP-TL	6-01-001
somersault	**noun**	**5-02-002**
somersault	NN	2-01-001
somersaults	NNS	2-01-001
somersaults	NNS-HL	1-01-001
somersault	**verb**	**1-01-001**
somersaulting	VBG	1-01-001
Somerset	**prop. noun**	**3-01-001**
Somerset	NP	2-01-001
Somerset	NP-HL	1-01-001
Somerville	**NP**	**2-01-001**
something	**nom. pro.**	**454-15-223**
something	PN	449-15-222
somethin	PN	1-01-001
somethin'	PN	2-01-002
sompin	PN	1-01-001
Something	PN-TL	1-01-001
sometime	**RB**	**11-08-011**
sometimes	**RB**	**221-15-131**
sometimes-necessary	**JJ**	**1-01-001**
somewhat	**QL**	**99-13-068**
somewhat	**RB**	**28-12-028**
somewhere	**NN**	**9-05-009**
somewhere	**adverb**	**51-13-042**
somewhere	RB	49-13-040
somewhere	RB-HL	1-01-001
Somewhere	RB-TL	1-01-001
somewheres	**RB**	**1-01-001**
sommelier	**NN**	**1-01-001**
Sommers	**NP**	**3-01-001**
somnolence	**NN**	**1-01-001**
somnolent	**JJ**	**2-02-002**
son	**foreign**	**2-01-001**
son	FW-NN	0-00-000
Son	FW-NN-TL	2-01-001
son	**noun**	**202-14-096**
son	NN	141-14-076
son	NN-HL	1-01-001
Son	NN-TL	21-05-008
son's	NN$	9-07-008
sons	NNS	18-09-015
suns	NNS	1-01-001
Sons	NNS-TL	11-06-007
son-in-law	**NN**	**4-01-002**
sonambula	**foreign**	**1-01-001**
sonambula	FW-NN	0-00-000
Sonambula	FW-NN-TL	1-01-001
sonar	**noun**	**7-01-001**
sonar	NN	6-01-001
sonar	NN-HL	1-01-001
sonata	**noun**	**15-03-006**
sonata	NN	1-01-001
Sonata	NN-TL	8-01-003
sonatas	NNS	3-02-002
Sonatas	NNS-TL	3-01-002
sonates	**foreign**	**1-01-001**
sonates	FW-NNS	0-00-000
Sonates	FW-NNS-TL	1-01-001
Sonenberg	**NP**	**1-01-001**
song	**noun**	**129-13-045**
song	NN	56-11-025
Song	NN-TL	12-06-009
song's	NN$	1-01-001
Song's	NN$-TL	1-01-001
songs	NNS	58-10-023
Songs	NNS-TL	1-01-001
Song	**NP**	**2-01-001**
song-writing	**JJ**	**1-01-001**
Songau	**NP**	**4-01-001**
songbag	**noun**	**1-01-001**
songbag	NN	0-00-000
Songbag	NN-TL	1-01-001
songbook	**NN**	**1-01-001**
songful	**JJ**	**1-01-001**
sonic	**JJ**	**2-01-002**
sonnet	**noun**	**5-02-003**
sonnet	NN	3-02-002
sonnets	NNS	2-02-002
sonny	**NN**	**1-01-001**
Sonny	**NP**	**1-01-001**
sonny-boy	**NN**	**1-01-001**
sonofabitch	**noun**	**6-03-006**
sonofabitch	NN	4-03-004
son-of-a-bitch	NN	2-02-002
sonogram	**NN**	**1-01-001**
Sonoma	**NP**	**1-01-001**
Sonora	**NP**	**1-01-001**
sonority	**noun**	**2-02-002**

Word	Tag	Frequency
sonority (cont.):		
sonority	NN	1-01-001
sonorities	NNS	1-01-001
sonorous	**JJ**	**1-01-001**
sonuvabitch	**UH**	**1-01-001**
soon	**adverb**	**200-15-147**
soon	RB	199-15-146
soon's	RB+CS	1-01-001
sooner	**RBR**	**17-09-016**
soot	**NN**	**1-01-001**
soothe	**verb**	**8-04-008**
soothe	VB	2-02-002
soothed	VBD	2-02-002
soothing	VBG	4-02-004
soothingly	**RB**	**1-01-001**
soothsayer	**noun**	**3-03-003**
soothsayer	NN	0-00-000
Soothsayer	NN-TL	1-01-001
soothsayers	NNS	2-02-002
sop	**noun**	**2-02-002**
sop	NN	1-01-001
sops	NNS	1-01-001
Sophia	**prop. noun**	**9-02-002**
Sophia	NP	0-00-000
Sophia	NP-TL	7-01-001
Sophia's	NP$	1-01-001
Sophias	NPS	0-00-000
Sophias	NPS-TL	1-01-001
Sophie	**NP**	**2-01-002**
sophisticate	**noun**	**2-02-002**
sophisticate	NN	1-01-001
sophisticates	NNS	1-01-001
sophisticated	**JJ**	**26-09-021**
sophistication	**noun**	**8-04-006**
sophistication	NN	7-04-006
sophistication	NN-HL	1-01-001
Sophoclean	**JJ**	**1-01-001**
Sophocles	**NP**	**3-02-002**
sophomore	**noun**	**6-04-004**
sophomore	NN	5-03-003
sophomores	NNS	1-01-001
sopping	**JJ**	**1-01-001**
soprano	**noun**	**7-03-006**
soprano	NN	6-03-005
sopranos	NNS	1-01-001
Sopsaisana	**NP**	**1-01-001**
sorb	**verb**	**8-01-001**
sorbed	VBN	8-01-001
sorcery	**noun**	**1-01-001**
sorcery	NN	0-00-000
sorcery	NN-HL	1-01-001
sordid	**JJ**	**3-01-003**
sore	**JJ**	**10-06-009**
sore	**noun**	**3-02-002**
sores	NNS	3-02-002
sore-ridden	**JJ**	**1-01-001**
sorely	**RB**	**3-03-003**
soreness	**NN**	**1-01-001**
sorest	**JJT**	**1-01-001**
sorghum	**NN**	**3-01-001**
sorority	**noun**	**2-01-001**
sorority	NN	1-01-001
sororities	NNS	1-01-001
sorption	**NN**	**1-01-001**
sorption-desorption	**NN**	**1-01-001**
sorrel	**adjective**	**2-02-002**
sorrel	JJ	1-01-001
sor'l	JJ	1-01-001
sorrel	**NN**	**1-01-001**
Sorrentine	**prop. noun**	**2-01-001**
Sorrentine	NP	0-00-000
Sorrentine	NP-TL	1-01-001
Sorrentine's	NP$	1-01-001
Sorrentino	**NP**	**3-01-001**
sorriest	**JJT**	**1-01-001**
sorrow	**noun**	**11-07-011**
sorrow	NN	9-06-009
sorrows	NNS	2-02-002
sorry	**adjective**	**48-11-036**
sorry	JJ	47-11-036
Sorry	JJ-NC	1-01-001
sort	**noun**	**169-13-122**
sort	NN	157-13-115
sorts	NNS	12-07-012
sort	**RB**	**2-02-002**
sort	**verb**	**10-07-009**
sort	VB	5-03-004
sorted	VBD	1-01-001
sorted	VBN	3-03-003
sort (cont.):		
sorting	VBG	1-01-001
sortie	**NN**	**2-01-002**
Sotun	**NP**	**1-01-001**
sou	**FW-NN**	**1-01-001**
souci	**foreign**	**1-01-001**
souci	FW-NN	0-00-000
Souci	FW-NN-TL	1-01-001
souffle	**NN**	**1-01-001**
Soukhouma	**NP**	**1-01-001**
soul	**noun**	**73-11-045**
soul	NN	47-10-033
soul's	NN$	3-02-003
souls	NNS	21-07-014
souls	NNS-HL	1-01-001
souls'	NNS$	1-01-001
soul-searching	**JJ**	**1-01-001**
Soule	**NP**	**1-01-001**
soulful	**JJ**	**1-01-001**
soulfully	**RB**	**1-01-001**
sound	**adjective**	**50-11-043**
sound	JJ	49-11-042
sound	JJ-HL	1-01-001
sound	**noun**	**163-14-091**
sound	NN	126-14-071
Sound	NN-TL	2-02-002
sounds	NNS	35-09-030
sound	**QL**	**1-01-001**
sound	**verb**	**82-13-063**
sound	VB	25-10-021
sounds	VBZ	20-07-016
sounded	VBD	29-11-027
sounded	VBN	6-06-006
sounding	VBG	2-02-002
sound-truck	**NN**	**1-01-001**
sounder	**JJR**	**4-03-003**
Sounder	**NP**	**1-01-001**
sounding	**JJ**	**1-01-001**
soundly	**RB**	**3-03-003**
soundness	**NN**	**1-01-001**
soundproof	**JJ**	**1-01-001**
Sounion	**NP**	**3-01-001**
soup	**NN**	**16-08-012**
Souphanouvong	**NP**	**1-01-001**
sour	**adjective**	**2-02-002**
sour	JJ	1-01-001
Sour	JJ-TL	1-01-001
sour	**verb**	**3-03-003**
sour	VB	1-01-001
sours	VBZ	1-01-001
soured	VBD	0-00-000
sowered	VBD	1-01-001
source	**noun**	**182-12-100**
source	NN	90-12-068
source	NN-HL	1-01-001
Source	NN-TL	3-01-001
sources	NNS	80-09-051
sources	NNS-HL	8-02-004
sourdough	**NN**	**2-01-002**
sourly	**RB**	**3-03-003**
Sousa	**NP**	**1-01-001**
soutane	**NN**	**1-01-001**
south	**adjective**	**76-13-050**
south	JJ	2-02-002
South	JJ-TL	74-13-048
south	**adv. noun**	**167-14-058**
south	NR	54-12-037
south	NR-HL	1-01-001
South	NR-TL	105-10-024
South	NR-TL-HL	1-01-001
south's	NR$	0-00-000
South's	NR$-TL	5-03-004
souths	NRS	0-00-000
Souths	NRS-TL	1-01-001
south	**RB**	**3-01-001**
South-Asian	**JJ**	**1-01-001**
south-central	**JJ**	**1-01-001**
Southampton	**NP**	**2-01-001**
southbound	**JJ**	**1-01-001**
southeast	**adjective**	**19-06-014**
southeast	JJ	1-01-001
south-east	JJ	0-00-000
South-East	JJ-TL	1-01-001
Southeast	JJ-TL	16-04-012
Southeast	JJ-TL-HL	1-01-001
southeast	**adv. noun**	**10-05-009**
southeast	NR	9-05-008
Southeast	NR-TL	1-01-001
southeastern	**adjective**	**6-05-005**

Word	Tag	Frequency
southeastern (cont.):		
southeastern	JJ	4-03-003
south-eastern	JJ	1-01-001
Southeastern	JJ-TL	1-01-001
southern	**adjective**	**138-12-054**
southern	JJ	30-09-025
suhthuhn	JJ	1-01-001
Southern	JJ-TL	107-10-035
southern-central	**JJ**	**1-01-001**
Southern-Republican	**NP**	**1-01-001**
southerner	**noun**	**35-04-010**
southerner	NN	0-00-000
Southerner	NN-TL	8-03-005
southerner's	NN$	0-00-000
Southerner's	NN$-TL	1-01-001
southerners	NNS	0-00-000
Southerners	NNS-TL	26-04-009
southernism	**noun**	**1-01-001**
southernisms	NNS	1-01-001
Southey	**NP**	**1-01-001**
Southfield	**NP**	**1-01-001**
Southland	**prop. noun**	**1-01-001**
Southland	NP	0-00-000
Southland	NP-TL	1-01-001
southpaw	**NN**	**5-01-003**
southward	**JJ**	**1-01-001**
southward	**RB**	**7-05-005**
southwest	**adjective**	**5-04-004**
southwest	JJ	0-00-000
Southwest	JJ-TL	5-04-004
southwest	**adv. noun**	**11-06-011**
southwest	NR	4-03-004
Southwest	NR-TL	7-05-007
southwestern	**adjective**	**2-01-002**
southwestern	JJ	0-00-000
Southwestern	JJ	1-01-001
Southwestern	JJ-TL	1-01-001
Souvanna	**NP**	**6-02-003**
souvenir	**noun**	**3-03-003**
souvenir	NN	2-02-002
souvenirs	NNS	1-01-001
sovereign	**JJ**	**17-02-005**
sovereign	**noun**	**16-03-005**
sovereign	NN	11-03-004
Sovereign	NN-TL	2-01-001
sovereigns	NNS	3-02-002
sovereignty	**NN**	**28-05-008**
soviet	**noun**	**99-06-026**
soviet	NN	1-01-001
Soviet	NN-TL	98-06-025
Soviet	**prop. noun**	**44-08-018**
Soviet	NP	16-04-008
Soviet	NP-TL	14-04-006
Soviet's	NP$	1-01-001
Soviets	NPS	11-04-007
Soviets	NPS-HL	1-01-001
Soviets'	NPS$	1-01-001
Soviet-Chinese	**JJ**	**2-01-001**
Soviet-Western	**JJ**	**1-01-001**
sovietskaya	**foreign**	**1-01-001**
sovietskaya	FW-JJ	0-00-000
Sovietskaya	FW-JJ-TL	1-01-001
sow	**verb**	**6-04-005**
sow	VB	3-02-002
sown	VBN	3-03-003
sowbelly	**NN**	**2-02-002**
sowing	**NN**	**1-01-001**
Sox	**prop. noun**	**13-02-004**
Sox	NPS	2-01-001
Sox	NPS-TL	11-02-004
Soxhlet	**NP**	**1-01-001**
soy	**NN**	**1-01-001**
soyaburger	**noun**	**1-01-001**
soyaburgers	NNS	1-01-001
soybean	**noun**	**11-02-002**
soybean	NN	5-01-001
soybeans	NNS	6-02-002
spa	**noun**	**2-01-001**
spa	NN	1-01-001
Spa	NN-TL	1-01-001
space	**noun**	**194-14-083**
space	NN	173-14-080
space	NN-HL	1-01-001
Space	NN-TL	9-03-005
spaces	NNS	11-05-008
space	**verb**	**11-05-008**
space	VB	1-01-001
spaced	VBN	8-05-007
spacing	VBG	2-01-001
space-time	**NN**	**1-01-001**
spacecraft	**NN**	**3-01-001**
spacer	**noun**	**7-01-001**
spacer	NN	2-01-001
spacers	NNS	5-01-001
spaceship	**NN**	**2-01-001**
spacesuit	**noun**	**2-01-002**
spacesuit	NN	1-01-001
spacesuits	NNS	1-01-001
spacing	**noun**	**5-03-005**
spacing	NN	4-03-004
spacings	NNS	1-01-001
spacious	**JJ**	**9-06-008**
spaciousness	**NN**	**3-03-003**
Spada	**NP**	**2-01-001**
spade	**noun**	**7-03-004**
spade	NN	3-03-003
spades	NNS	4-01-001
spade	**VB**	**1-01-001**
Spade	**NP**	**6-01-002**
spaghetti	**NN**	**1-01-001**
spagna	**foreign**	**1-01-001**
spagna	FW-NP	0-00-000
Spagna	FW-NP-TL	1-01-001
Spahn	**prop. noun**	**6-01-002**
Spahn	NP	5-01-002
Spahn's	NP$	1-01-001
Spahnie	**NP**	**1-01-001**
Spain	**prop. noun**	**7-06-006**
Spain	NP	4-04-004
Spain	NP-TL	3-03-003
Spalding	**NP**	**1-01-001**
span	**noun**	**17-08-014**
span	NN	11-06-010
Span	NN	3-01-001
span	NN-HL	1-01-001
spans	NNS	2-02-002
span	**verb**	**10-05-006**
span	VB	4-02-002
spans	VBZ	3-03-003
spanned	VBN	2-01-001
spanning	VBG	1-01-001
spandrel	**noun**	**1-01-001**
spandrels	NNS	1-01-001
spangle	**NN**	**1-01-001**
spangled	**adjective**	**1-01-001**
spangled	JJ	0-00-000
Spangled	JJ-TL	1-01-001
spaniel	**noun**	**1-01-001**
spaniel's	NN$	1-01-001
spaniel-like	**JJ**	**1-01-001**
Spanish	**adjective**	**31-12-025**
Spanish	JJ	21-10-016
Spanish	JJ-TL	9-06-009
Spanish	JJ-HL	1-01-001
Spanish	**NP**	**5-03-003**
Spanish-American	**adjective**	**2-02-002**
Spanish-American	JJ	0-00-000
Spanish-American	JJ-TL	2-02-002
Spanish-born	**NP**	**1-01-001**
spar	**verb**	**3-03-003**
sparring	VBG	3-03-003
spare	**JJ**	**15-09-013**
spare	**verb**	**19-10-018**
spare	VB	8-05-008
spares	VBZ	1-01-001
spared	VBD	3-03-003
spared	VBN	6-06-006
sparing	VBG	1-01-001
spark	**noun**	**12-05-009**
spark	NN	8-04-006
Spark	NN-TL	1-01-001
sparks	NNS	3-02-003
spark	**verb**	**7-05-007**
spark	VB	2-02-002
sparks	VBZ	2-02-002
sparked	VBD	1-01-001
sparked	VBN	2-02-002
Spark	**NP**	**1-01-001**
sparkle	**NN**	**4-04-004**
sparkle	**verb**	**6-03-006**
sparkles	VBZ	1-01-001
sparkled	VBD	1-01-001
sparkling	VBG	4-03-004
sparkling	**JJ**	**1-01-001**
Sparky	**NP**	**3-01-001**
Sparling	**prop. noun**	**2-01-001**
Sparling	NP	1-01-001
Sparling's	NP$	1-01-001

Word	Tag	Frequency
sparrow	**noun**	**1-01-001**
sparrow's	NN$	1-01-001
sparrow-size	**NN**	**1-01-001**
sparse	**JJ**	**5-05-005**
sparsely	**RB**	**2-02-002**
Sparta	**NP**	**1-01-001**
Spartan	**NP**	**2-02-002**
spasm	**noun**	**4-04-004**
spasm	NN	3-03-003
spasms	NNS	1-01-001
spat	**noun**	**2-01-001**
spat	NN	1-01-001
spats	NNS	1-01-001
spat	**VB**	**1-01-001**
spate	**NN**	**2-02-002**
spatial	**JJ**	**10-02-003**
spatiality	**NN**	**1-01-001**
spatially	**RB**	**2-01-002**
spatter	**NN**	**1-01-001**
spatter	**verb**	**2-02-002**
spattered	VBN	2-02-002
spavined	**JJ**	**1-01-001**
speak	**verb**	**274-15-158**
speak	VB	110-14-078
speaks	VBZ	17-07-012
speaks	VBZ-HL	1-01-001
spoke	VBD	86-13-063
speaking	VBG	58-13-053
speakin'	VBG	1-01-001
Speaking	VBG-TL	1-01-001
speak-easy	**NN**	**1-01-001**
speaker	**noun**	**67-11-031**
speaker	NN	22-07-014
speaker	NN-HL	2-02-002
Speaker	NN-TL	25-05-009
speaker's	NN$	1-01-001
Speaker's	NN$-TL	3-03-003
speakers	NNS	14-09-012
speakership	**noun**	**1-01-001**
speakership	NN	0-00-000
Speakership	NN-TL	1-01-001
speaking	**NN**	**3-02-002**
spear	**NN**	**5-03-003**
spear	**verb**	**3-02-002**
spear	VB	2-01-001
speared	VBD	1-01-001
spear-throwing	**JJ**	**1-01-001**
spearhead	**VB**	**1-01-001**
special	**adjective**	**245-14-150**
special	JJ	230-14-145
special	JJ-HL	6-03-005
Special	JJ-TL	9-05-006
special	**noun**	**7-05-006**
special	NN	4-03-004
sp.	NN	0-00-000
sp.	NN-HL	2-01-001
Special	NN-TL	1-01-001
special-interest	**NN**	**1-01-001**
specialist	**noun**	**35-13-025**
specialist	NN	15-07-013
Specialist	NN-TL	1-01-001
specialists	NNS	19-10-014
specialization	**NN**	**10-07-009**
specialize	**verb**	**26-10-021**
specialize	VB	3-03-003
specializes	VBZ	1-01-001
specialized	VBD	2-02-002
specialized	VBN	16-07-012
specializing	VBG	4-03-004
specially	**RB**	**9-05-008**
specialty	**noun**	**9-07-009**
specialty	NN	4-03-004
specialties	NNS	4-04-004
Specialties	NNS-TL	1-01-001
specie	**FW-NN**	**2-02-002**
species	**noun**	**37-07-018**
species	NN	23-07-014
species	NNS	14-01-008
species-dependent	**JJ**	**1-01-001**
specific	**adjective**	**115-11-076**
specific	JJ	114-11-075
specific	JJ-HL	1-01-001
specific	**noun**	**1-01-001**
specifics	NNS	1-01-001
specifically	**QL**	**1-01-001**
specifically	**RB**	**37-11-034**
specification	**noun**	**12-04-008**
specification	NN	3-01-001
specifications	NNS	6-04-006
specification (cont.):		
Specifications	NNS-TL	3-02-002
specificity	**noun**	**10-02-004**
specificity	NN	9-02-004
specificity	NN-HL	1-01-001
specify	**verb**	**46-08-029**
specify	VB	11-04-009
specifies	VBZ	4-03-004
specified	VBN	28-07-020
specifying	VBG	3-02-003
specimen	**noun**	**37-08-012**
specimen	NN	23-05-006
specimen	NN-HL	1-01-001
specimens	NNS	13-05-007
specimentalia	**NN**	**1-01-001**
specious	**JJ**	**2-01-002**
speck	**noun**	**9-05-007**
speck	NN	6-04-006
speck	NN-HL	1-01-001
specks	NNS	2-02-002
speckle	**noun**	**1-01-001**
speckles	NNS	1-01-001
speckle	**verb**	**1-01-001**
speckled	VBN	1-01-001
spectacle	**noun**	**21-08-019**
spectacle	NN	18-07-016
spectacles	NNS	3-03-003
spectacular	**JJ**	**22-06-018**
spectacularly	**RB**	**2-02-002**
spectator	**noun**	**22-08-020**
spectator	NN	9-07-009
spectators	NNS	13-07-011
spectator-type	**JJ**	**1-01-001**
specter	**noun**	**5-05-005**
specter	NN	3-03-003
spectre	NN	1-01-001
specters	NNS	1-01-001
Spector	**NP**	**1-01-001**
spectral	**JJ**	**6-02-003**
spectrally	**RB**	**1-01-001**
spectrometer	**NN**	**2-01-001**
spectrometric	**JJ**	**1-01-001**
spectrophotometer	**NN**	**1-01-001**
spectrophotometric	**JJ**	**1-01-001**
spectroscopy	**NN**	**3-01-001**
spectrum	**noun**	**32-05-011**
spectrum	NN	14-05-009
spectra	NNS	17-02-003
spectra	NNS-HL	1-01-001
speculate	**verb**	**13-05-013**
speculate	VB	7-03-007
speculated	VBD	2-02-002
speculating	VBG	4-03-004
speculation	**noun**	**7-07-007**
speculation	NN	3-03-003
speculations	NNS	4-04-004
speculative	**JJ**	**8-04-006**
speculatively	**RB**	**1-01-001**
speculator	**noun**	**3-03-003**
speculator	NN	1-01-001
speculators	NNS	2-02-002
speech	**noun**	**82-14-060**
speech	NN	61-14-045
speeches	NNS	21-10-020
speech-making	**NN**	**1-01-001**
speechless	**JJ**	**3-02-003**
speechlessness	**NN**	**2-02-002**
speed	**noun**	**89-13-048**
speed	NN	74-12-046
speed	NN-HL	2-02-002
speeds	NNS	12-05-005
speeds	NNS-HL	1-01-001
speed	**verb**	**22-12-018**
speed	VB	5-04-004
speeds	VBZ	1-01-001
sped	VBD	9-06-007
speeded	VBD	3-03-003
speeding	VBG	4-03-004
Speed	**NP**	**2-02-002**
speedboat	**NN**	**1-01-001**
speedily	**RB**	**3-03-003**
speedometer	**NN**	**1-01-001**
speedup	**noun**	**1-01-001**
speedup	NN	0-00-000
Speedup	NN-TL	1-01-001
speedy	**adjective**	**6-06-006**
speedy	JJ	5-05-005
Speedy	JJ-TL	1-01-001
Speer	**NP**	**1-01-001**

Word	Tag	Frequency
Spegititgninino	**prop. noun**	**1-01-001**
Spegititgninino	NP	0-00-000
Spegititgninino	NP-TL	1-01-001
Speidel	**prop. noun**	**1-01-001**
Speidel	NP	0-00-000
Speidel	NP-TL	1-01-001
spell	**NN**	**14-08-011**
spell	**verb**	**14-07-012**
spell	VB	5-04-005
spells	VBZ	2-02-002
spelled	VBD	1-01-001
spelled	VBN	5-05-005
spelling	VBG	1-01-001
spell-binding	**JJ**	**1-01-001**
spellbind	**verb**	**1-01-001**
spellbound	VBN	1-01-001
spelling	**noun**	**3-02-003**
spelling	NN	2-02-002
Spelling	NN-TL	1-01-001
Spelman	**prop. noun**	**11-01-001**
Spelman	NP	9-01-001
Spelman	NP-TL	2-01-001
Spencer	**prop. noun**	**29-02-002**
Spencer	NP	23-02-002
Spencer's	NP$	6-01-001
Spencerian	**JJ**	**1-01-001**
spend	**verb**	**194-15-136**
spend	VB	53-15-045
spends	VBZ	8-07-008
spent	VBD	40-12-037
spent	VBN	64-13-056
spending	VBG	29-10-022
spender	**noun**	**1-01-001**
spenders	NNS	1-01-001
spending	**NN**	**12-04-005**
Spenglerian	**JJ**	**1-01-001**
spew	**verb**	**1-01-001**
spewing	VBG	1-01-001
spewing	**noun**	**1-01-001**
spewings	NNS	1-01-001
sphere	**noun**	**26-09-016**
sphere	NN	22-09-015
spheres	NNS	3-01-002
spheres	NNS-HL	1-01-001
spherical	**JJ**	**8-03-007**
spherule	**noun**	**1-01-001**
spherules	NNS	1-01-001
Sphinx	**NP**	**1-01-001**
sphynx	**noun**	**1-01-001**
sphynxes	NNS	1-01-001
spic	**JJ**	**1-01-001**
spice	**noun**	**5-04-005**
spice	NN	2-01-002
spices	NNS	3-03-003
spice	**verb**	**5-02-003**
spice	VB	2-02-002
spiced	VBN	3-01-001
spice-laden	**JJ**	**1-01-001**
Spice-Nice	**NP**	**3-01-001**
spicy	**JJ**	**1-01-001**
spider	**NN**	**2-02-002**
spider-leg	**NN**	**1-01-001**
spidery	**JJ**	**1-01-001**
spigot	**noun**	**1-01-001**
spigots	NNS	1-01-001
spike	**noun**	**3-02-002**
spike	NN	1-01-001
spikes	NNS	2-01-001
spike	**verb**	**3-03-003**
spike	VB	1-01-001
spiked	VBN	2-02-002
spike-haired	**JJ**	**1-01-001**
Spikes	**NP**	**1-01-001**
spill	**verb**	**9-06-008**
spill	VB	1-01-001
spills	VBZ	2-02-002
spilled	VBD	2-02-002
spilled	VBN	1-01-001
spilling	VBG	3-03-003
Spillane	**prop. noun**	**1-01-001**
Spillane's	NP$	1-01-001
Spiller	**NP**	**1-01-001**
spin	**NN**	**3-01-002**
spin	**verb**	**31-09-021**
spin	VB	4-04-004
spun	VBD	14-07-012
spun	VBN	2-01-001
spinning	VBG	11-06-008
spinach	**NN**	**2-02-002**

Word	Tag	Frequency
Spinco	**NP**	**4-01-001**
spindle	**NN**	**8-02-003**
spine	**NN**	**6-05-006**
spine-chilling	**JJ**	**2-01-001**
spineless	**JJ**	**2-01-002**
Spinley	**prop. noun**	**1-01-001**
Spinley's	NP$	1-01-001
spinnability	**NN**	**1-01-001**
spinneret	**NN**	**1-01-001**
Spinrad	**NP**	**1-01-001**
spiral	**NN**	**7-02-002**
spiral	**verb**	**3-01-002**
spiral	VB	1-01-001
spiraled	VBD	1-01-001
spiraling	VBG	1-01-001
spiralis	**NP**	**1-01-001**
spire	**noun**	**8-04-005**
spire	NN	5-03-003
spires	NNS	3-02-002
spirit	**noun**	**226-14-109**
spirit	NN	161-14-086
Spirit	NN	1-01-001
spirit	NN-HL	1-01-001
Spirit	NN-TL	19-04-009
spirits	NNS	42-10-025
Spirits	NNS-TL	2-01-001
spirit	**verb**	**7-04-006**
spirited	VBN	7-04-006
spirit-gum	**NN**	**1-01-001**
spirited	**JJ**	**1-01-001**
spirito	**foreign**	**1-01-001**
spirito	FW-NN	0-00-000
Spirito	FW-NN-TL	1-01-001
Spirito	**NP**	**2-01-001**
spiritual	**adjective**	**64-10-032**
spiritual	JJ	62-10-032
spiritual	JJ-HL	2-01-001
spiritual	**noun**	**2-01-001**
spirituals	NNS	1-01-001
Spirituals	NNS-TL	1-01-001
spirituality	**NN**	**1-01-001**
spiritually	**adverb**	**7-03-006**
spiritually	RB	6-03-005
spiritually	RB-HL	1-01-001
spit	**NN**	**2-01-001**
spit	**verb**	**21-08-016**
spit	VB	6-04-005
spat	VBD	7-04-007
spit	VBD	3-03-003
spitting	VBG	5-04-004
spite	**IN**	**8-04-008**
spite	**NN**	**48-10-041**
spittle	**NN**	**2-02-002**
splash	**noun**	**4-04-004**
splash	NN	3-03-003
splashes	NNS	1-01-001
splash	**verb**	**7-05-007**
splashes	VBZ	1-01-001
splashed	VBD	3-03-003
splashing	VBG	3-03-003
splashy	**JJ**	**1-01-001**
splatter	**verb**	**1-01-001**
splattered	VBN	1-01-001
splay	**verb**	**1-01-001**
splayed	VBD	1-01-001
spleen	**NN**	**2-02-002**
spleen-crushing	**JJ**	**1-01-001**
splendid	**JJ**	**20-08-017**
Splendide	**NP**	**1-01-001**
splendidly	**QL**	**1-01-001**
splendidly	**RB**	**3-03-003**
splendor	**noun**	**7-05-006**
splendor	NN	6-05-006
splendor	NN-HL	1-01-001
splenetic	**JJ**	**1-01-001**
splenomegaly	**NN**	**1-01-001**
splice	**NN**	**1-01-001**
splice	**verb**	**1-01-001**
spliced	VBN	1-01-001
splicing	**NN**	**1-01-001**
splinter	**noun**	**4-02-002**
splinter	NN	3-01-001
splinters	NNS	1-01-001
splinter	**verb**	**3-03-003**
splinter	VB	1-01-001
splintered	VBD	1-01-001
splintered	VBN	1-01-001
splintery	**JJ**	**1-01-001**
splinting	**noun**	**1-01-001**

splinting (cont.):		
splinting	NN	0-00-000
Splinting	NN-TL	1-01-001
split	**noun**	**9-04-005**
split	NN	8-04-004
splits	NNS	1-01-001
split	**verb**	**26-09-024**
split	VB	2-02-002
splits	VBZ	1-01-001
split	VBD	5-03-005
split	VBN	15-07-014
splitting	VBG	3-03-003
split-bamboo	**NN**	**1-01-001**
split-level	**NN**	**1-01-001**
splotch	**noun**	**1-01-001**
splotches	NNS	1-01-001
splotch	**verb**	**2-01-001**
splotched	VBN	2-01-001
splurge	**NN**	**1-01-001**
Spofford	**NP**	**1-01-001**
spoil	**noun**	**1-01-001**
spoils	NNS	1-01-001
spoil	**verb**	**10-07-010**
spoil	VB	3-03-003
spoiled	VBD	1-01-001
spoiled	VBN	5-04-005
spoiling	VBG	1-01-001
spoilable	**noun**	**1-01-001**
spoilables	NNS	1-01-001
spoilage	**noun**	**8-02-002**
spoilage	NN	7-02-002
spoilage	NN-HL	1-01-001
Spokane	**NP**	**2-01-001**
spoke	**noun**	**3-02-002**
spoke	NN	1-01-001
spokes	NNS	2-02-002
spoke	**verb**	**37-14-028**
spoken	VBN	36-14-028
Spoken	VBN-TL	1-01-001
spokesman	**noun**	**26-07-020**
spokesman	NN	13-05-010
spokesmen	NNS	13-06-010
sponge	**noun**	**6-05-005**
sponge	NN	4-04-004
Sponge	NN-TL	1-01-001
sponges	NNS	1-01-001
sponge	**verb**	**4-01-002**
sponge	VB	2-01-002
sponged	VBN	2-01-001
sponging	**NN**	**1-01-001**
spongy	**JJ**	**2-02-002**
sponsor	**noun**	**23-09-013**
sponsor	NN	8-05-006
Sponsor	NN-TL	7-01-001
sponsor's	NN$	1-01-001
sponsors	NNS	7-06-006
sponsor	**verb**	**43-10-033**
sponsor	VB	7-05-007
sponsors	VBZ	3-02-002
sponsored	VBD	7-05-006
sponsored	VBN	23-08-020
sponsoring	VBG	3-03-003
sponsorship	**NN**	**5-03-004**
spontaneity	**NN**	**7-03-005**
spontaneous	**JJ**	**17-06-017**
spontaneously	**RB**	**9-04-007**
spoof	**NN**	**1-01-001**
spooky	**JJ**	**2-01-001**
spoon	**NN**	**6-05-006**
spoon	**verb**	**1-01-001**
spooned	VBD	1-01-001
spoonful	**NN**	**1-01-001**
sporadic	**JJ**	**7-03-006**
spore	**noun**	**3-02-002**
spores	NNS	3-02-002
sport	**noun**	**65-11-038**
sport	NN	17-08-013
sports	NNS	44-10-027
Sports	NNS-TL	4-01-004
sport	**verb**	**14-07-008**
sports	VBZ	1-01-001
sporting	VBG	8-06-006
sportin'	VBG	4-01-001
Sporting	VBG-TL	1-01-001
Sport-King	**NP**	**1-01-001**
sportiest	**JJT**	**1-01-001**
sportsman	**noun**	**12-03-008**
sportsman	NN	3-03-003
Sportsman	NN-TL	2-01-002

sportsman (cont.):		
sportsmen	NNS	6-01-003
sportsmen's	NNS$	0-00-000
Sportsmen's	NNS$-TL	1-01-001
sportsmanship	**NN**	**1-01-001**
sportswriter	**NN**	**3-02-002**
Sposato	**NP**	**4-01-001**
spot	**noun**	**85-12-064**
spot	NN	53-12-045
spots	NNS	30-12-025
spots	NNS-HL	1-01-001
Spots	NNS-TL	1-01-001
spot	**verb**	**22-09-018**
spot	VB	4-04-004
spotted	VBD	9-04-008
spotted	VBN	7-04-005
spotting	VBG	2-02-002
spot-news	**NN**	**1-01-001**
spot-promote	**verb**	**1-01-001**
spot-promoted	VBN	1-01-001
spotless	**JJ**	**3-01-003**
spotlight	**NN**	**6-04-006**
spotlight	**verb**	**1-01-001**
spotlights	VBZ	1-01-001
spotty	**JJ**	**1-01-001**
spouse	**noun**	**7-05-006**
spouse	NN	3-03-003
spouses	NNS	4-03-004
spout	**NN**	**1-01-001**
spout	**verb**	**4-04-004**
spouted	VBD	2-02-002
spouted	VBN	1-01-001
spouting	VBG	1-01-001
Sprague	**prop. noun**	**4-01-001**
Sprague	NP	3-01-001
Sprague's	NP$	1-01-001
sprain	**noun**	**1-01-001**
sprains	NNS	1-01-001
sprain	**verb**	**2-01-002**
sprained	VBN	2-01-002
sprawl	**NN**	**1-01-001**
sprawl	**verb**	**18-08-015**
sprawl	VB	2-02-002
sprawled	VBD	2-02-002
sprawled	VBN	9-06-007
sprawling	VBG	5-03-005
spray	**noun**	**15-07-010**
spray	NN	13-07-010
spray	NN-HL	1-01-001
sprays	NNS	1-01-001
spray	**verb**	**14-06-010**
spray	VB	2-02-002
sprayed	VBD	3-03-003
sprayed	VBN	3-02-002
spraying	VBG	6-03-004
spray-dried	**JJ**	**1-01-001**
spraying	**NN**	**2-01-001**
spread	**noun**	**18-08-013**
spread	NN	16-08-013
spread	NN-HL	1-01-001
spreads	NNS	1-01-001
spread	**verb**	**90-14-075**
spread	VB	27-11-023
spreads	VBZ	9-06-009
spread	VBD	18-07-017
spread	VBN	21-09-020
spreading	VBG	15-09-015
spread-eagle	**verb**	**1-01-001**
spread-eagled	VBN	1-01-001
spread-out	**JJ**	**1-01-001**
spreader	**NN**	**1-01-001**
spreading	**NN**	**1-01-001**
spree	**NN**	**4-03-004**
sprig	**NN**	**1-01-001**
sprightly	**JJ**	**1-01-001**
spring	**noun**	**138-12-080**
spring	NN	102-12-060
Spring	NN-TL	16-08-012
springs	NNS	7-04-006
Springs	NNS-TL	13-06-008
spring	**verb**	**30-10-028**
spring	VB	6-04-006
springs	VBZ	1-01-001
sprang	VBD	13-07-012
sprung	VBN	8-05-008
springing	VBG	2-02-002
Spring	**NP**	**2-02-002**
spring-back	**JJ**	**1-01-001**
spring-joint	**noun**	**1-01-001**

Word	Tag	Frequency
spring-joint (cont.):		
spring-joints	NNS	1-01-001
spring-training	**NN**	**1-01-001**
springboard	**NN**	**2-02-002**
Springfield	**prop. noun**	**4-03-003**
Springfield	NP	3-03-003
Springfield's	NP+BEZ	1-01-001
springtime	**NN**	**4-04-004**
Sprinkel	**NP**	**3-01-001**
sprinkle	**NN**	**2-02-002**
sprinkle	**verb**	**11-06-006**
sprinkle	VB	5-03-003
sprinkled	VBD	3-02-002
sprinkled	VBN	1-01-001
sprinkling	VBG	2-02-002
sprinkling	**NN**	**5-02-005**
sprint	**verb**	**2-02-002**
sprinted	VBD	2-02-002
Sprite	**NP**	**1-01-001**
sprout	**verb**	**8-05-006**
sprout	VB	1-01-001
sprouted	VBD	1-01-001
sprouted	VBN	2-01-001
sprouting	VBG	4-03-003
sprouting	**NN**	**2-01-001**
spruce	**noun**	**5-04-004**
spruce	NN	2-02-002
Spruce	NN-TL	3-02-002
spruce	**verb**	**1-01-001**
spruced	VBN	1-01-001
sprue	**NN**	**2-02-002**
spume	**NN**	**1-01-001**
Spumoni	**prop. noun**	**1-01-001**
Spumoni's	NP$	1-01-001
spur	**noun**	**13-07-011**
spur	NN	10-06-009
spurs	NNS	3-03-003
spur	**verb**	**10-08-010**
spur	VB	3-03-003
spurred	VBD	4-04-004
spurred	VBN	2-02-002
spurring	VBG	1-01-001
Spurdle	**NP**	**3-01-001**
spurious	**JJ**	**2-02-002**
spurn	**verb**	**2-02-002**
spurns	VBZ	1-01-001
spurned	VBN	1-01-001
spurt	**NN**	**2-02-002**
sputnik	**noun**	**3-03-003**
sputnik	NN	1-01-001
Sputnik	NN-TL	1-01-001
sputniks	NNS	1-01-001
sputter	**verb**	**2-02-002**
sputter	VB	1-01-001
sputtered	VBD	1-01-001
Spuyten	**NP**	**1-01-001**
spy	**noun**	**9-06-007**
spy	NN	8-06-006
spies	NNS	1-01-001
spy	**verb**	**4-03-003**
spy	VB	1-01-001
spies	VBZ	1-01-001
spying	VBG	2-01-001
Spycket	**prop. noun**	**1-01-001**
Spycket	NP	0-00-000
Spycket	NP-TL	1-01-001
squabble	**noun**	**3-03-003**
squabbles	NNS	3-03-003
squabbling	**NN**	**1-01-001**
squad	**noun**	**20-05-010**
squad	NN	16-05-008
squad	NN-HL	1-01-001
Squad	NN-TL	1-01-001
squads	NNS	2-02-002
squadron	**noun**	**5-04-004**
squadron	NN	2-02-002
Squadron	NN-TL	1-01-001
squadrons	NNS	1-01-001
Squadrons	NNS-TL	1-01-001
squadroom	**NN**	**1-01-001**
squalid	**JJ**	**1-01-001**
squall	**noun**	**8-02-002**
squall	NN	7-01-001
squalls	NNS	1-01-001
squander	**verb**	**2-02-002**
squandered	VBN	2-02-002
square	**adjective**	**30-08-022**
square	JJ	26-08-022
sq.	JJ	4-01-001
square	**noun**	**121-15-052**
square	NN	75-15-038
square	NN-HL	3-02-002
Square	NN-TL	29-09-016
square's	NN$	0-00-000
Square's	NN$-TL	1-01-001
squares	NNS	13-06-007
square	**RB**	**1-01-001**
square	**verb**	**14-07-010**
square	VB	9-05-007
squared	VBN	5-02-003
square-built	**JJ**	**1-01-001**
square-mile	**NN**	**1-01-001**
squarely	**RB**	**11-08-011**
Squaresville	**NP**	**1-01-001**
squash	**NN**	**2-01-001**
squash	**verb**	**2-02-002**
squashed	VBN	1-01-001
squashing	VBG	1-01-001
squashed-looking	**JJ**	**1-01-001**
squashy	**JJ**	**1-01-001**
squat	**JJ**	**2-02-002**
squat	**noun**	**5-04-005**
squat	NN	4-03-004
squats	NNS	0-00-000
Squats	NNS-TL	1-01-001
squat	**verb**	**12-05-010**
squat	VB	1-01-001
squatted	VBD	4-03-004
squatting	VBG	6-03-005
Squatting	VBG-TL	1-01-001
squat-style	**JJ**	**1-01-001**
squatter	**noun**	**1-01-001**
squatter's	NN$	1-01-001
squaw	**NN**	**1-01-001**
squawk	**VB**	**1-01-001**
squeak	**NN**	**1-01-001**
squeak	**verb**	**2-01-001**
squeaked	VBD	2-01-001
squeaking	**NN**	**1-01-001**
squeaky	**JJ**	**1-01-001**
squeal	**noun**	**2-02-002**
squeal	NN	1-01-001
squeals	NNS	1-01-001
squeal	**verb**	**3-03-003**
squealed	VBD	1-01-001
squealed	VBN	1-01-001
squealing	VBG	1-01-001
squeamish	**JJ**	**1-01-001**
squeamishness	**NN**	**1-01-001**
squeeze	**NN**	**3-03-003**
squeeze	**verb**	**30-11-026**
squeeze	VB	8-05-006
squeezed	VBD	8-04-007
squeezed	VBN	10-05-010
squeezing	VBG	4-03-003
squelch	**verb**	**1-01-001**
squelched	VBN	1-01-001
Squibb	**prop. noun**	**2-01-001**
Squibb	NP	1-01-001
Squibb	NP-TL	1-01-001
squint	**verb**	**6-03-006**
squinted	VBD	3-02-003
squinting	VBG	3-02-003
Squint	**NP**	**1-01-001**
squire	**noun**	**4-03-003**
squire	NN	3-02-002
squires	NNS	1-01-001
Squire	**prop. noun**	**4-02-002**
Squire	NP	2-01-001
Squire's	NP$	2-02-002
squirm	**verb**	**3-03-003**
squirms	VBZ	1-01-001
squirmed	VBD	1-01-001
squirmed	VBN	1-01-001
squirrel	**NN**	**1-01-001**
squirt	**NN**	**1-01-001**
squirt	**verb**	**2-02-002**
squirted	VBD	1-01-001
squirting	VBG	1-01-001
SR	**NP**	**2-01-001**
SS	**NP**	**1-01-001**
SS.	**NP**	**1-01-001**
sssshoo	**UH**	**1-01-001**
St.-Pol	**NP**	**2-01-001**
stab	**noun**	**4-04-004**
stab	NN	3-03-003
stabs	NNS	1-01-001
stab	**verb**	**2-02-002**

Word	Tag	Frequency
stab (cont.):		
stabbed	VBD	1-01-001
stabbed	VBN	1-01-001
stabat	**foreign**	**1-01-001**
stabat	FW-VBD	0-00-000
Stabat	FW-VBD-TL	1-01-001
stability	**noun**	**14-06-013**
stability	NN	13-06-012
stabilities	NNS	1-01-001
stabilization	**NN**	**3-02-002**
stabilize	**verb**	**8-04-008**
stabilize	VB	2-02-002
stabilizes	VBZ	1-01-001
stabilized	VBN	1-01-001
stabilizing	VBG	4-02-004
stabilizer	**noun**	**1-01-001**
stabilizers	NNS	1-01-001
stabilizing-conserving	**JJ**	**1-01-001**
stable	**JJ**	**16-04-013**
stable	**noun**	**17-05-009**
stable	NN	14-04-007
stables	NNS	3-03-003
stable	**verb**	**1-01-001**
stabled	VBD	1-01-001
stable-garage	**NN**	**1-01-001**
stableman	**NN**	**1-01-001**
staccato	**JJ**	**1-01-001**
staccato	**noun**	**5-05-005**
staccato	NN	4-04-004
staccatos	NNS	1-01-001
Stacey	**NP**	**2-01-001**
stack	**noun**	**8-05-008**
stack	NN	7-05-007
stacks	NNS	1-01-001
stack	**verb**	**11-08-010**
stacked	VBD	1-01-001
stacked	VBN	8-07-008
stacking	VBG	2-02-002
Stack	**NP**	**2-02-002**
Stacy	**prop. noun**	**10-02-002**
Stacy	NP	9-01-001
Stacy	NP-TL	1-01-001
stadium	**noun**	**25-03-013**
stadium	NN	5-03-004
stadium	NN-HL	1-01-001
Stadium	NN-TL	19-03-010
stadtisches	**foreign**	**2-01-001**
stadtisches	FW-JJ	0-00-000
Stadtisches	FW-JJ-TL	2-01-001
staff	**noun**	**120-12-067**
staff	NN	100-12-057
staff	NN-HL	2-01-001
Staff	NN-TL	9-03-006
staff's	NN$	1-01-001
staffs	NNS	8-04-007
staff	**verb**	**6-03-006**
staff	VB	2-02-002
staffed	VBN	3-03-003
staffing	VBG	1-01-001
Staffe	**NP**	**4-01-001**
Stafford	**NP**	**1-01-001**
Staffordshire	**NP**	**1-01-001**
stag	**noun**	**9-04-006**
stag	NN	8-03-005
stags	NNS	1-01-001
stage	**noun**	**224-14-097**
stage	NN	169-14-083
stage	NN-HL	2-01-001
Stage	NN-TL	2-01-001
stages	NNS	51-09-024
stage	**verb**	**21-05-016**
stage	VB	2-02-002
staged	VBD	5-03-005
staged	VBN	11-03-009
staging	VBG	3-03-003
stage-play	**noun**	**1-01-001**
stage-plays	NNS	1-01-001
stagecoach	**noun**	**3-01-001**
stagecoach	NN	1-01-001
Stagecoach	NN-TL	2-01-001
stager	**NN**	**1-01-001**
stagger	**verb**	**17-08-016**
stagger	VB	2-02-002
staggered	VBD	9-05-009
staggered	VBN	3-02-003
staggering	VBG	3-02-003
staggering	**JJ**	**3-03-003**
staggeringly	**QL**	**1-01-001**
staggeringly	**RB**	**1-01-001**

Word	Tag	Frequency
staginess	**NN**	**1-01-001**
stagnant	**JJ**	**5-05-005**
stagnation	**NN**	**1-01-001**
Staiger	**NP**	**1-01-001**
stain	**noun**	**13-05-010**
stain	NN	4-02-004
stains	NNS	9-05-007
stain	**verb**	**45-08-015**
stain	VB	2-02-002
stains	VBZ	1-01-001
stained	VBD	4-02-002
stained	VBN	24-06-012
staining	VBG	12-01-001
staining	VBG-HL	2-01-001
stained-glass	**NN**	**1-01-001**
staining	**NN**	**23-01-001**
stainless	**JJ**	**2-01-001**
stainless-steel	**NN**	**1-01-001**
stair	**noun**	**49-08-027**
stair	NN	2-02-002
stairs	NNS	46-08-026
Stairs	NNS-TL	1-01-001
stair-step	**NN**	**1-01-001**
staircase	**noun**	**9-06-008**
staircase	NN	8-05-007
staircases	NNS	1-01-001
stairway	**noun**	**8-07-008**
stairway	NN	6-06-006
stairways	NNS	2-02-002
stairwell	**noun**	**2-02-002**
stairwell	NN	0-00-000
stair-well	NN	1-01-001
stairwells	NNS	1-01-001
stake	**noun**	**22-09-017**
stake	NN	18-06-013
stakes	NNS	3-03-003
Stakes	NNS-TL	1-01-001
stake	**verb**	**5-05-005**
stake	VB	2-02-002
stakes	VBZ	1-01-001
staked	VBD	1-01-001
staked	VBN	1-01-001
stake-out	**NN**	**3-01-001**
Stalag	**NP**	**4-01-001**
stale	**JJ**	**4-03-004**
stalemate	**NN**	**2-02-002**
Staley	**NP**	**1-01-001**
Stalin	**prop. noun**	**21-05-007**
Stalin	NP	15-03-004
Stalin's	NP$	5-03-004
Stalins	NPS	1-01-001
Stalingrad	**prop. noun**	**1-01-001**
Stalingrad	NP	0-00-000
Stalingr	NP	1-01-001
Stalinist	**NP**	**1-01-001**
Stalinist-corrupted	**JJ**	**1-01-001**
stalk	**verb**	**9-05-008**
stalked	VBD	6-03-005
stalked	VBN	1-01-001
stalking	VBG	2-02-002
stall	**noun**	**20-05-009**
stall	NN	17-05-007
stalls	NNS	3-03-003
stall	**verb**	**6-04-006**
stalled	VBD	3-02-003
stalled	VBN	1-01-001
stalling	VBG	1-01-001
stalling	VBG-HL	1-01-001
Stall	**NP**	**1-01-001**
Stallard	**NP**	**1-01-001**
Stallings	**NP**	**1-01-001**
stallion	**noun**	**5-01-001**
stallion	NN	3-01-001
stallion's	NN$	2-01-001
stalwart	**JJ**	**4-04-004**
stamen	**noun**	**1-01-001**
stamens	NNS	1-01-001
Stamford	**prop. noun**	**4-02-003**
Stamford	NP	3-02-003
Stamford	NP-TL	1-01-001
stamina	**NN**	**2-02-002**
staminate	**JJ**	**2-01-001**
stammer	**verb**	**5-04-004**
stammered	VBD	4-04-004
stammering	VBG	1-01-001
stamp	**noun**	**7-06-007**
stamp	NN	3-03-003
stamps	NNS	4-03-004
stamp	**verb**	**16-09-016**

Word	Tag	Frequency
stamp (cont.):		
stamp	VB	5-04-005
stamped	VBD	2-01-002
stamped	VBN	5-05-005
stamping	VBG	4-04-004
stampede	**NN**	**2-02-002**
stampede	**verb**	**3-01-002**
stampede	VB	2-01-001
stampeded	VBD	1-01-001
stamping	**NN**	**1-01-001**
Stan	**NP**	**3-02-002**
Stanbury	**NP**	**2-01-001**
stance	**noun**	**7-05-007**
stance	NN	6-04-006
stances	NNS	1-01-001
stanch	**JJ**	**1-01-001**
stanchest	**JJT**	**1-01-001**
stand	**noun**	**58-14-044**
stand	NN	39-12-034
stands	NNS	16-08-010
Stands	NNS-TL	3-01-001
stand	**verb**	**468-15-236**
stand	VB	108-14-090
stand	VB-HL	1-01-001
stands	VBZ	48-14-043
standeth	VBZ	1-01-001
stands	VBZ-HL	1-01-001
stood	VBD	198-15-108
stood	VBN	14-07-012
standing	VBG	95-13-070
standin'	VBG	1-01-001
Standing	VBG-TL	1-01-001
stand-in	**noun**	**3-01-001**
stand-ins	NNS	3-01-001
stand-up	**noun**	**1-01-001**
stand-ups	NNS	0-00-000
stand-ups	NNS-HL	1-01-001
standard	**adjective**	**79-11-044**
standard	JJ	66-09-037
standard	JJ-HL	1-01-001
Standard	JJ-TL	12-06-008
standard	**noun**	**105-09-063**
standard	NN	29-08-022
Standard	NN-TL	2-01-001
standards	NNS	72-09-045
Standards	NNS-TL	2-02-002
Standard-Times	**prop. noun**	**1-01-001**
Standard-Times	NP	0-00-000
Standard-Times	NP-TL	1-01-001
standard-weight	**NN**	**1-01-001**
standardize	**verb**	**5-03-005**
standardized	VBN	4-02-004
standardizing	VBG	1-01-001
standby	**JJ**	**1-01-001**
standby	**NN**	**2-02-002**
standing	**NN**	**5-05-005**
standpoint	**NN**	**13-06-010**
standstill	**NN**	**1-01-001**
Stanford	**prop. noun**	**1-01-001**
Stanford	NP	0-00-000
Stanford	NP-TL	1-01-001
Stanhope	**NP**	**1-01-001**
Stanislas	**prop. noun**	**2-01-001**
Stanislas	NP	1-01-001
Stanislas'	NP$	1-01-001
Stanley	**prop. noun**	**39-07-011**
Stanley	NP	34-06-009
Stanley	NP-TL	1-01-001
Stanley's	NP$	4-02-002
Stannard	**NP**	**1-01-001**
Stans	**prop. noun**	**2-01-001**
Stans	NP	1-01-001
Stans	NP-HL	1-01-001
Stansbery	**NP**	**1-01-001**
Stanton	**prop. noun**	**4-04-004**
Stanton	NP	3-03-003
Stanton	NP-TL	1-01-001
stanza-form	**NN**	**1-01-001**
staple	**noun**	**2-02-002**
staple	NN	1-01-001
staples	NNS	1-01-001
stapling	**NN**	**1-01-001**
star	**noun**	**58-12-042**
star	NN	16-07-013
starre	NN	1-01-001
Star	NN-TL	9-06-008
star's	NN$	0-00-000
Star's	NN$-TL	3-01-001
stars	NNS	26-09-021
star (cont.):		
stars	NNS-HL	1-01-001
Stars	NNS-TL	2-02-002
star	**verb**	**4-03-004**
starred	VBN	2-02-002
starring	VBG	2-02-002
star-spangled	**adjective**	**1-01-001**
star-spangled	JJ	0-00-000
Star-Spangled	JJ-TL	1-01-001
Starbird	**NP**	**4-01-001**
starboard	**JJ**	**1-01-001**
starch	**NN**	**4-01-001**
starch	**verb**	**2-02-002**
starched	VBN	2-02-002
starchy	**JJ**	**2-01-001**
Stardel	**NP**	**2-01-001**
stardom	**NN**	**2-01-002**
stare	**noun**	**6-05-006**
stare	NN	5-05-005
stares	NNS	1-01-001
stare	**verb**	**95-10-066**
stare	VB	9-06-008
stared	VBD	58-09-044
stared	VBN	2-02-002
staring	VBG	26-07-023
stark	**JJ**	**3-02-003**
stark	**QL**	**1-01-001**
Stark	**NP**	**3-02-002**
Starkey	**NP**	**1-01-001**
starkly	**RB**	**1-01-001**
starlet	**NN**	**2-01-002**
Starlette	**NP**	**2-01-001**
starlight	**NN**	**1-01-001**
starling	**noun**	**1-01-001**
starlings	NNS	1-01-001
Starr	**NP**	**1-01-001**
start	**noun**	**61-13-045**
start	NN	50-13-039
start	NN-HL	1-01-001
starts	NNS	10-03-008
start	**verb**	**386-15-208**
start	VB	102-15-077
start	VB-HL	1-01-001
starts	VBZ	21-08-020
started	VBD	139-14-088
started	VBN	55-13-046
starting	VBG	67-13-053
startin'	VBG	1-01-001
starter	**noun**	**3-03-003**
starter	NN	2-02-002
Starter	NN-TL	1-01-001
starting	**NN**	**1-01-001**
startle	**verb**	**22-08-020**
startle	VB	1-01-001
startled	VBD	3-03-003
startled	VBN	18-05-016
startled-horse	**NN**	**1-01-001**
startling	**JJ**	**19-11-016**
startlingly	**QL**	**2-02-002**
startlingly	**RB**	**2-02-002**
startup	**noun**	**1-01-001**
startups	NNS	1-01-001
starvation	**NN**	**7-05-007**
starve	**verb**	**10-04-007**
starve	VB	1-01-001
starved	VBN	3-02-003
starving	VBG	6-03-006
stash	**verb**	**1-01-001**
stashed	VBN	1-01-001
stasis	**NN**	**3-02-002**
state	**noun**	**1421-15-258**
state	NN	528-14-152
state	NN-HL	5-03-004
State	NN-TL	250-12-085
State	NN-TL-HL	1-01-001
State	NN-TL-NC	3-01-002
state's	NN$	19-06-013
State's	NN$-TL	19-02-002
states	NNS	140-11-059
states	NNS-HL	3-02-003
States	NNS-TL	439-13-147
States	NNS-TL-HL	2-02-002
States	NNS-TL-NC	3-01-002
states'	NNS$	5-03-003
States'	NNS$-TL	4-02-004
state	**verb**	**138-14-090**
state	VB	20-10-020
states	VBZ	17-06-014
stated	VBD	38-09-022

Word	Tag	Frequency
state (cont.):		
stated	VBN	47-09-033
stating	VBG	16-09-015
state-administered	**JJ**	**1-01-001**
state-law	**NN**	**1-01-001**
state-local	**adjective**	**3-01-002**
state-local	JJ	2-01-001
State-Local	JJ-TL	1-01-001
state-owned	**JJ**	**12-01-001**
state-sponsored	**JJ**	**1-01-001**
state-supported	**JJ**	**1-01-001**
state's-responsibility	**NN**	**1-01-001**
stateless	**JJ**	**1-01-001**
stately	**JJ**	**4-04-004**
statement	**noun**	**209-15-104**
statement	NN	141-15-083
statements	NNS	67-12-037
statements	NNS-HL	1-01-001
Staten	**prop. noun**	**5-04-005**
Staten	NP	0-00-000
Staten	NP-TL	5-04-005
stateroom	**NN**	**2-02-002**
statesman	**noun**	**20-06-014**
statesman	NN	11-04-007
Statesman	NN-TL	1-01-001
statesmen	NNS	8-04-008
statesmanlike	**JJ**	**1-01-001**
statesmanship	**NN**	**2-02-002**
statewide	**JJ**	**11-04-007**
statewide	**RB**	**2-01-001**
static	**JJ**	**12-07-012**
static	**NN**	**1-01-001**
station	**noun**	**195-13-060**
station	NN	92-13-047
station	NN-HL	1-01-001
Station	NN-TL	12-06-009
station's	NN$	4-03-004
stations	NNS	85-09-019
stations'	NNS$	1-01-001
station	**verb**	**5-03-004**
stationed	VBN	5-03-004
stationary	**JJ**	**2-01-002**
stationery	**NN**	**2-01-002**
stationmaster	**NN**	**1-01-001**
statistic	**noun**	**22-09-015**
statistics	NNS	22-09-015
statistical	**adjective**	**16-06-011**
statistical	JJ	15-06-011
Statistical	JJ-TL	1-01-001
statistically	**QL**	**1-01-001**
statistically	**RB**	**3-02-003**
statistician	**noun**	**1-01-001**
statisticians	NNS	1-01-001
statistique	**foreign**	**1-01-001**
statistique	FW-JJ	0-00-000
Statistique	FW-JJ-TL	1-01-001
stator	**NN**	**1-01-001**
statu	**FW-NN**	**1-01-001**
statuary	**NN**	**2-02-002**
statue	**noun**	**25-08-014**
statue	NN	16-05-008
Statue	NN-TL	1-01-001
statues	NNS	8-06-007
statuette	**NN**	**1-01-001**
stature	**NN**	**15-08-012**
status	**noun**	**99-10-058**
status	NN	94-10-056
status	NN-HL	2-01-002
Status	NN-TL	1-01-001
statuses	NNS	2-02-002
status-conscious	**JJ**	**2-02-002**
status-role	**noun**	**2-01-001**
status-roles	NNS	1-01-001
status-roles	NNS-HL	1-01-001
statute	**noun**	**24-06-014**
statute	NN	12-02-005
stat.	NN	0-00-000
Stat.	NN-TL	4-01-003
Statute	NN-TL	1-01-001
statutes	NNS	7-06-006
statuto	**foreign**	**1-01-001**
statuto	FW-NN	0-00-000
Statuto	FW-NN-TL	1-01-001
statutory	**JJ**	**13-03-005**
staunch	**JJ**	**3-03-003**
staunchest	**JJT**	**3-02-003**
Staunton	**prop. noun**	**1-01-001**
Staunton	NP	0-00-000
Staunton	NP-TL	1-01-001
stave	**verb**	**3-02-003**
stave	VB	2-02-002
staved	VBN	1-01-001
Stavropoulos	**prop. noun**	**4-01-001**
Stavropoulos	NP	3-01-001
Stavropoulos'	NP$	1-01-001
stay	**noun**	**16-09-013**
stay	NN	14-09-012
stays	NNS	2-02-002
stay	**verb**	**195-15-121**
stay	VB	97-13-072
Stay	VB-TL	2-02-002
stays	VBZ	3-03-003
stayed	VBD	60-13-051
stayed	VBN	15-09-014
staid	VBN	1-01-001
staying	VBG	17-07-014
stead	**NN**	**4-02-004**
steadfastly	**RB**	**1-01-001**
steadier	**JJR**	**3-03-003**
steadily	**RB**	**22-10-021**
steadiness	**NN**	**1-01-001**
steady	**JJ**	**37-11-032**
steady	**RB**	**3-03-003**
steady	**verb**	**3-01-003**
steady	VB	1-01-001
steadied	VBD	2-01-002
steady-state	**NN**	**1-01-001**
steak	**noun**	**14-06-009**
steak	NN	8-05-007
Steak	NN-TL	2-01-001
steaks	NNS	4-03-003
steal	**verb**	**39-12-032**
steal	VB	5-05-005
steals	VBZ	1-01-001
stole	VBD	10-04-010
stolen	VBN	18-10-015
stealing	VBG	4-03-004
stealin'	VBG	1-01-001
stealer	**NN**	**1-01-001**
stealing	**NN**	**2-02-002**
stealth	**NN**	**5-05-005**
stealthily	**RB**	**1-01-001**
steam	**noun**	**17-08-011**
steam	NN	16-08-011
steam	NN-HL	1-01-001
steam	**verb**	**11-08-011**
steamed	VBD	1-01-001
steamed	VBN	5-05-005
steaming	VBG	5-05-005
steam-bath	**noun**	**1-01-001**
steam-baths	NNS	1-01-001
steam-generation	**NN**	**1-01-001**
steamboat	**noun**	**3-02-002**
steamboat	NN	2-02-002
Steamboat	NN-TL	1-01-001
steamer	**NN**	**1-01-001**
steamily	**QL**	**1-01-001**
steamship	**NN**	**3-03-003**
Stearns	**prop. noun**	**3-01-001**
Stearns	NP	1-01-001
Stearns	NPS	2-01-001
steed	**NN**	**1-01-001**
steel	**noun**	**48-12-031**
steel	NN	38-12-026
Steel	NN-TL	6-03-006
steel's	NN$	0-00-000
Steel's	NN$-TL	1-01-001
steels	NNS	3-01-001
steel	**verb**	**1-01-001**
steeled	VBN	1-01-001
Steel	**NP**	**1-01-001**
steel-edged	**JJ**	**1-01-001**
Steele	**prop. noun**	**33-01-002**
Steele	NP	20-01-002
Steele	NP-TL	1-01-001
Steele's	NP$	12-01-001
Steeler	**prop. noun**	**2-01-001**
Steelers	NPS	2-01-001
steelmaker	**noun**	**2-01-001**
steelmaker	NN	1-01-001
steelmakers'	NNS$	1-01-001
steely	**RB**	**1-01-001**
steep	**JJ**	**7-05-006**
steep	**NN**	**6-04-005**
steep	**verb**	**5-03-004**
steeped	VBN	5-03-004
steeper	**JJR**	**2-01-001**
steepest	**JJT**	**1-01-001**

steeple	**noun**	**13-03-005**
steeple	NN	9-01-003
steeples	NNS	4-03-003
steeply	**RB**	**1-01-001**
steer	**noun**	**7-02-002**
steer	NN	6-02-002
steers	NNS	1-01-001
steer	**verb**	**16-08-013**
steer	VB	3-03-003
steered	VBD	4-03-003
steering	VBG	9-06-008
Steeves	**NP**	**1-01-001**
Steffens	**NP**	**1-01-001**
Steichen	**NP**	**10-02-002**
stein	**NN**	**2-02-002**
Stein	**prop. noun**	**20-04-005**
Stein	NP	16-04-005
Stein's	NP$	4-01-001
Steinbeck	**prop. noun**	**2-01-001**
Steinbeck's	NP$	1-01-001
Steinbecks	NPS	1-01-001
Steinberg	**NP**	**15-02-002**
Steiner	**prop. noun**	**2-02-002**
Steiner	NP	1-01-001
Steiners	NPS	0-00-000
Steiners	NPS-NC	1-01-001
Steinhager	**NP**	**3-01-001**
Steinkerque	**NP**	**1-01-001**
Stella	**NP**	**1-01-001**
stellar	**JJ**	**1-01-001**
stem	**noun**	**44-05-007**
stem	NN	25-03-005
stems	NNS	18-03-005
Stems	NNS-TL	1-01-001
stem	**verb**	**22-10-022**
stem	VB	5-04-005
stems	VBZ	14-07-014
stemmed	VBD	3-03-003
stench	**NN**	**1-01-001**
Stendhal	**NP**	**2-02-002**
Stendler	**NP**	**1-01-001**
Stengel	**prop. noun**	**8-02-005**
Stengel	NP	6-01-004
Stengel's	NP$	2-02-002
Stennis	**NP**	**1-01-001**
stenography	**NN**	**1-01-001**
Stenton	**NP**	**1-01-001**
step	**noun**	**228-14-129**
step	NN	109-14-077
step	NN-HL	1-01-001
steps	NNS	114-12-068
steps	NNS-HL	1-01-001
Steps	NNS-TL	3-02-003
step	**verb**	**71-14-062**
step	VB	20-11-019
Step	VB-TL	1-01-001
steps	VBZ	1-01-001
stepped	VBD	33-10-028
stepped	VBN	7-06-007
stepping	VBG	9-07-008
step-by-step	**JJ**	**2-02-002**
step-cone	**NN**	**1-01-001**
Stepanovich	**NP**	**2-01-001**
stepchild	**NN**	**1-01-001**
Stephane	**NP**	**1-01-001**
Stephanie	**NP**	**2-01-001**
stephanotis	**NN**	**2-01-001**
Stephen	**prop. noun**	**19-07-013**
Stephen	NP	18-07-012
Stephen's	NP$	0-00-000
Stephen's	NP$-TL	1-01-001
Stephens	**prop. noun**	**7-02-002**
Stephens	NP	5-02-002
Stephens's	NP$	2-01-001
Stephenson	**NP**	**2-01-002**
stepladder	**noun**	**1-01-001**
stepladders	NNS	1-01-001
stepmother	**noun**	**5-02-002**
stepmother	NN	3-02-002
stepmothers	NNS	2-01-001
steppe	**noun**	**2-01-002**
steppes	NNS	2-01-002
stepped-up	**JJ**	**3-02-003**
steprelationship	**NN**	**1-01-001**
stepson	**noun**	**3-02-002**
stepson	NN	2-02-002
stepson	NN-HL	1-01-001
stepwise	**JJ**	**1-01-001**
stepwise	**RB**	**2-01-002**

stereo	**JJ**	**1-01-001**
stereo	**NN**	**11-03-006**
stereophonic	**JJ**	**1-01-001**
stereotype	**noun**	**14-04-008**
stereotype	NN	12-04-006
stereotypes	NNS	2-01-002
stereotype	**verb**	**6-03-004**
stereotyped	VBN	5-03-004
steoreotyped	VBN	1-01-001
sterile	**JJ**	**9-06-008**
sterility	**NN**	**2-02-002**
sterilization	**noun**	**5-01-001**
sterilization	NN	4-01-001
sterilization	NN-NC	1-01-001
sterilize	**verb**	**4-03-004**
sterilize	VB	1-01-001
sterilized	VBN	1-01-001
sterilizing	VBG	2-02-002
sterios	**foreign**	**1-01-001**
sterios	FW-JJ	0-00-000
sterios	FW-JJ-NC	1-01-001
sterling	**JJ**	**2-02-002**
Sterling	**prop. noun**	**5-03-003**
Sterling	NP	2-02-002
Sterling	NP-TL	3-01-001
stern	**JJ**	**13-06-012**
stern	**noun**	**10-06-007**
stern	NN	8-04-005
stern	NN-HL	1-01-001
sterns	NNS	1-01-001
Stern	**NP**	**1-01-001**
stern-faced	**JJ**	**1-01-001**
stern-to	**RB**	**1-01-001**
sternal	**JJ**	**1-01-001**
sternly	**RB**	**3-03-003**
sterno-cleido	**NN**	**1-01-001**
sternum	**NN**	**1-01-001**
steroid	**noun**	**3-01-001**
steroid	NN	1-01-001
steroids	NNS	2-01-001
steroid-induced	**JJ**	**1-01-001**
stethoscope	**NN**	**2-01-001**
Stetson	**prop. noun**	**3-02-003**
Stetson	NP	2-02-002
Stetsons	NPS	1-01-001
Stettin	**NP**	**4-02-002**
Steuben	**NP**	**2-02-002**
Steve	**NP**	**3-02-003**
stevedore	**NN**	**1-01-001**
Stevens	**prop. noun**	**19-05-007**
Stevens	NP	17-05-006
Stevens	NP-TL	1-01-001
Stevenses'	NPS$	1-01-001
Stevenson	**prop. noun**	**17-05-008**
Stevenson	NP	15-05-008
Stevenson's	NP$	2-02-002
Stevie	**NP**	**18-01-001**
stew	**noun**	**6-04-004**
stew	NN	5-04-004
stews	NNS	1-01-001
stew	**verb**	**1-01-001**
stewed	VBN	1-01-001
steward	**noun**	**4-03-004**
steward	NN	1-01-001
Steward	NN-TL	1-01-001
stewards	NNS	2-01-002
stewardess	**noun**	**3-01-001**
stewardess	NN	2-01-001
stewardesses	NNS	1-01-001
stewardship	**NN**	**1-01-001**
Stewart	**prop. noun**	**7-03-003**
Stewart	NP	5-03-003
Stewart	NP-TL	1-01-001
Stewart's	NP$	1-01-001
stick	**noun**	**42-10-025**
stick	NN	23-08-012
sticks	NNS	19-09-014
stick	**verb**	**50-13-042**
stick	VB	16-08-014
sticks	VBZ	3-02-003
stuck	VBD	13-07-012
stuck	VBN	10-06-010
sticking	VBG	8-08-008
stickler	**noun**	**2-02-002**
stickler	NN	1-01-001
stickler	NN-HL	1-01-001
stickman	**NN**	**1-01-001**
Stickney	**NP**	**5-02-002**
stickpin	**NN**	**1-01-001**

Word	Tag	Frequency
sticky	**JJ**	**9-06-007**
sticky-fingered	**JJ**	**1-01-001**
sticle	**VB**	**1-01-001**
Stidger	**NP**	**2-01-001**
stiff	**JJ**	**19-09-016**
stiff	**noun**	**3-02-002**
stiff	NN	2-01-001
stiffs	NNS	1-01-001
stiff-backed	**JJ**	**1-01-001**
stiffen	**verb**	**11-07-011**
stiffens	VBZ	2-02-002
stiffened	VBD	7-04-007
stiffened	VBN	1-01-001
stiffening	VBG	1-01-001
stiffening	**NN**	**3-02-003**
stiffer	**JJR**	**1-01-001**
stiffly	**RB**	**9-03-007**
stiffness	**NN**	**1-01-001**
stifle	**verb**	**6-06-006**
stifle	VB	2-02-002
stifled	VBD	1-01-001
stifled	VBN	1-01-001
stifling	VBG	2-02-002
stigma	**noun**	**2-02-002**
stigma	NN	1-01-001
stigmata	NNS	1-01-001
Stiles	**NP**	**1-01-001**
stiletto	**NN**	**1-01-001**
still	**JJ**	**24-09-020**
still	**noun**	**4-03-003**
still	NN	2-01-001
stills	NNS	2-02-002
still	**QL**	**28-12-027**
still	**QLP**	**1-01-001**
still	**RB**	**724-15-335**
still	**VB**	**2-02-002**
Still	**NP**	**1-01-001**
still-building	**JJ**	**1-01-001**
still-dark	**JJ**	**1-01-001**
stillbirth	**noun**	**1-01-001**
stillbirths	NNS	1-01-001
stillness	**NN**	**9-06-008**
Stillwell	**NP**	**1-01-001**
stilt	**noun**	**2-02-002**
stilts	NNS	2-02-002
stilted	**JJ**	**2-02-002**
Stilts	**NP**	**1-01-001**
Stimson	**NP**	**1-01-001**
stimulant	**noun**	**2-02-002**
stimulant	NN	1-01-001
stimulants	NNS	1-01-001
stimulate	**verb**	**20-07-018**
stimulate	VB	6-04-006
stimulates	VBZ	1-01-001
stimulates	VBZ-NC	2-01-001
stimulated	VBD	3-03-003
stimulated	VBN	4-03-004
stimulating	VBG	4-03-004
stimulating	**JJ**	**5-03-004**
stimulation	**noun**	**14-07-010**
stimulation	NN	13-06-009
stimulations	NNS	1-01-001
stimulatory	**JJ**	**1-01-001**
stimulus	**noun**	**20-05-015**
stimulus	NN	15-05-012
stimuli	NNS	5-03-004
sting	**noun**	**5-04-004**
sting	NN	3-03-003
stings	NNS	2-01-001
sting	**verb**	**6-04-005**
sting	VB	2-01-002
stung	VBD	1-01-001
stung	VBN	1-01-001
stinging	VBG	2-02-002
stingy	**JJ**	**1-01-001**
stink	**NN**	**2-01-001**
stink	**verb**	**4-03-004**
stink	VB	1-01-001
stunk	VBD	1-01-001
stinking	VBG	2-02-002
stinkpotter	**noun**	**1-01-001**
stinkpotters	NNS	1-01-001
Stinky	**NP**	**1-01-001**
stint	**NN**	**6-05-006**
stipulate	**verb**	**4-03-004**
stipulate	VB	2-02-002
stipulates	VBZ	2-02-002
stipulation	**NN**	**1-01-001**
stir	**verb**	**39-12-034**
stir (cont.):		
stir	VB	7-05-007
stirs	VBZ	3-02-003
stirred	VBD	7-05-007
stirred	VBN	8-04-007
stirring	VBG	13-05-011
stirrin	VBG	1-01-001
stirling	**JJ**	**1-01-001**
Stirling	**NP**	**2-02-002**
stirring	**JJ**	**2-02-002**
stirring	**noun**	**2-02-002**
stirring	NN	1-01-001
stirrings	NNS	1-01-001
stirringly	**RB**	**1-01-001**
stirrup	**noun**	**2-02-002**
stirrup	NN	1-01-001
stirrups	NNS	0-00-000
stirups	NNS	1-01-001
stirrup-guard	**NN**	**1-01-001**
stitch	**noun**	**7-04-004**
stitch	NN	3-02-002
stitches	NNS	4-03-003
stitch	**verb**	**1-01-001**
stitched	VBD	1-01-001
Stober	**prop. noun**	**1-01-001**
Stober's	NP$	1-01-001
stochastic	**JJ**	**1-01-001**
stock	**noun**	**164-14-068**
stock	NN	139-14-059
Stock	NN-TL	6-02-003
stock's	NN$	1-01-001
stocks	NNS	16-03-010
stocks	NNS-HL	1-01-001
Stocks	NNS-TL	1-01-001
stock	**verb**	**3-02-003**
stock	VB	2-02-002
stocking	VBG	1-01-001
stock-market	**NN**	**1-01-001**
stockade	**NN**	**12-03-004**
stockbroker	**NN**	**1-01-001**
stockgrower	**noun**	**1-01-001**
stockgrowers'	NNS$	0-00-000
Stockgrowers'	NNS$-TL	1-01-001
Stockhausen	**NP**	**1-01-001**
stockholder	**noun**	**28-06-009**
stockholder	NN	2-02-002
stockholders	NNS	26-06-007
stocking	**noun**	**6-03-006**
stockings	NNS	5-02-005
stockynges	NNS	1-01-001
stockpiling	**NN**	**1-01-001**
stockroom	**NN**	**2-02-002**
stocky	**JJ**	**2-02-002**
stodgy	**JJ**	**1-01-001**
Stoic	**prop. noun**	**4-02-002**
Stoic	NP	3-02-002
Stoics	NPS	1-01-001
Stoic-patristic	**JJ**	**1-01-001**
stoicism	**noun**	**5-03-003**
stoicism	NN	2-01-001
Stoicism	NN-TL	3-02-002
stoke	**verb**	**1-01-001**
stoked	VBN	1-01-001
stoker	**NN**	**1-01-001**
stolid	**JJ**	**1-01-001**
stolidly	**RB**	**2-02-002**
Stoll	**NP**	**1-01-001**
Stolzenbach	**NP**	**1-01-001**
stomach	**noun**	**41-11-033**
stomach	NN	37-10-029
stomack	NN	1-01-001
stomachs	NNS	3-03-003
stomach-belly	**noun**	**1-01-001**
stomach-belly	NN+NN	0-00-000
stomach-belly	NN+NN-NC	1-01-001
stomp	**verb**	**4-04-004**
stomp	VB	0-00-000
stooooomp	VB	1-01-001
stomped	VBD	1-01-001
stomped	VBN	1-01-001
stomping	VBG	1-01-001
stone	**noun**	**66-13-043**
stone	NN	47-12-033
Stone	NN-TL	7-03-003
stones	NNS	12-05-009
stone	**verb**	**2-02-002**
stoned	VBN	2-02-002
Stone	**prop. noun**	**6-01-004**
Stone	NP	4-01-003

Word	Tag	Frequency
Stone (cont.):		
Stone's	NP$	2-01-002
stone-blind	**JJ**	**1-01-001**
stone-gray	**JJ**	**1-01-001**
stone-still	**JJ**	**1-01-001**
Stonehenge	**prop. noun**	**1-01-001**
Stonehenge	NP	0-00-000
Stonehenge	NP-TL	1-01-001
Stonestown	**NP**	**1-01-001**
stoneware	**NN**	**3-01-001**
stonily	**RB**	**1-01-001**
stony	**JJ**	**5-04-004**
stony-meteorite	**NN**	**1-01-001**
Stooge	**prop. noun**	**1-01-001**
Stooges	NPS	1-01-001
stool	**NN**	**8-03-005**
stoop	**NN**	**1-01-001**
stoop	**verb**	**11-06-010**
stoop	VB	3-03-003
stooped	VBD	3-03-003
stooping	VBG	4-03-003
a-stoopin'	VBG	1-01-001
stop	**noun**	**31-11-025**
stop	NN	26-09-020
stops	NNS	5-04-005
stop	**verb**	**240-15-146**
stop	VB	94-13-070
stops	VBZ	2-02-002
Stops	VBZ-TL	1-01-001
stopped	VBD	103-13-077
stopped	VBN	26-11-026
stopping	VBG	14-11-014
stopover	**noun**	**3-03-003**
stopover	NN	1-01-001
stopovers	NNS	1-01-001
stop-overs	NNS	1-01-001
stoppage	**noun**	**2-01-002**
stoppage	NN	1-01-001
stoppages	NNS	1-01-001
stopper	**NN**	**2-01-001**
stopping-point	**NN**	**1-01-001**
storage	**NN**	**41-06-021**
store	**noun**	**102-14-053**
store	NN	65-12-037
Store	NN-TL	2-02-002
stores	NNS	34-10-019
Stores	NNS-TL	1-01-001
store	**verb**	**47-11-026**
store	VB	7-03-006
stored	VBD	1-01-001
stored	VBN	35-11-019
storing	VBG	4-03-003
stored-up	**JJ**	**1-01-001**
storefront	**noun**	**2-02-002**
storefront	NN	1-01-001
store-front	NN	1-01-001
storehouse	**noun**	**4-02-002**
storehouse	NN	3-01-001
storehouses	NNS	1-01-001
storekeeper	**noun**	**1-01-001**
storekeepers	NNS	1-01-001
Storeria	**NP**	**1-01-001**
storeroom	**NN**	**1-01-001**
storied	**JJ**	**1-01-001**
storm	**noun**	**31-11-022**
storm	NN	24-11-018
storm	NN-HL	1-01-001
storms	NNS	6-06-006
storm	**verb**	**5-05-005**
storm	VB	1-01-001
stormed	VBD	3-03-003
storming	VBG	1-01-001
stormbound	**JJ**	**1-01-001**
stormy	**adjective**	**5-05-005**
stormy	JJ	4-04-004
Stormy	JJ-TL	1-01-001
Stormy	**NP**	**3-01-001**
story	**noun**	**212-15-103**
story	NN	149-15-078
st-story	NN	1-01-001
Story	NN-TL	3-03-003
stories	NNS	59-12-040
Story	**NP**	**1-01-001**
story-book	**NN**	**1-01-001**
storyline	**noun**	**3-01-001**
storyline	NN	2-01-001
storylines	NNS	1-01-001
storyteller	**noun**	**5-04-005**
storyteller	NN	4-03-004

Word	Tag	Frequency
storyteller (cont.):		
storyteller's	NN$	1-01-001
stout	**JJ**	**2-02-002**
Stout	**prop. noun**	**2-02-002**
Stout	NP	1-01-001
Stout's	NP$	1-01-001
stoutly	**RB**	**1-01-001**
stove	**noun**	**17-09-014**
stove	NN	15-08-012
stoves	NNS	2-02-002
stow	**verb**	**2-02-002**
stowed	VBN	2-02-002
Stowe	**prop. noun**	**2-02-002**
Stowe	NP	1-01-001
Stowe's	NP$	1-01-001
Stowey	**NP**	**5-01-001**
straddle	**verb**	**5-04-005**
straddled	VBD	1-01-001
straddled	VBN	1-01-001
straddling	VBG	3-03-003
Strafaci	**NP**	**1-01-001**
strafe	**FW-VB**	**2-01-001**
strafe	**verb**	**1-01-001**
strafing	VBG	1-01-001
straggle	**verb**	**5-05-005**
straggle	VB	2-02-002
straggled	VBD	1-01-001
straggling	VBG	2-02-002
straggler	**noun**	**2-01-002**
stragglers	NNS	2-01-002
straight	**JJ**	**56-12-041**
straight	**QL**	**5-03-005**
straight	**RB**	**53-12-042**
straight-A	**JJ**	**1-01-001**
straight-arm	**adjective**	**1-01-001**
straight-arm	JJ	0-00-000
Straight-Arm	JJ-TL	1-01-001
straight-arm	**verb**	**1-01-001**
straight-armed	VBD	1-01-001
straight-backed	**JJ**	**2-01-001**
straight-haired	**JJ**	**2-01-001**
straight-line	**NN**	**1-01-001**
straight-out	**JJ**	**1-01-001**
straightaway	**NN**	**1-01-001**
straightaway	**RB**	**1-01-001**
straighten	**verb**	**33-09-026**
straighten	VB	7-06-006
straightens	VBZ	1-01-001
straightened	VBD	15-04-013
straightened	VBN	4-03-003
straightening	VBG	5-04-005
straightening	VBG-HL	1-01-001
straightforward	**JJ**	**8-05-007**
straightway	**RB**	**1-01-001**
strain	**noun**	**38-10-035**
strain	NN	30-10-028
strains	NNS	8-06-008
strain	**verb**	**20-08-018**
strain	VB	1-01-001
strained	VBD	8-04-006
strained	VBN	3-03-003
straining	VBG	7-06-007
strainin'	VBG	1-01-001
strait	**noun**	**8-03-003**
strait	NN	3-02-002
Strait	NN-TL	2-01-001
straits	NNS	0-00-000
Straits	NNS-TL	3-03-003
strait-laced	**JJ**	**1-01-001**
Stram	**prop. noun**	**5-01-001**
Stram	NP	4-01-001
Stram's	NP$	1-01-001
stramonium	**NN**	**1-01-001**
Stranahan	**prop. noun**	**1-01-001**
Stranahan	NP	0-00-000
Stranahan	NP-TL	1-01-001
strand	**noun**	**10-06-007**
strand	NN	7-04-004
strands	NNS	3-03-003
strand	**verb**	**8-06-007**
stranded	VBN	7-05-006
stranding	VBG	1-01-001
Strang	**NP**	**1-01-001**
strange	**JJ**	**84-13-068**
strange-sounding	**JJ**	**1-01-001**
strangely	**QL**	**2-02-002**
strangely	**RB**	**6-06-006**
strangeness	**NN**	**2-02-002**
stranger	**comp. adj.**	**2-01-001**

Word	Tag	Frequency
stranger (cont.):		
stranger	JJR	0-00-000
stranger	JJR-NC	2-01-001
stranger	**noun**	**50-09-028**
stranger	NN	38-09-021
stranger's	NN$	3-02-003
strangers	NNS	8-02-007
strangers'	NNS$	1-01-001
strangest	**JJT**	**1-01-001**
strangle	**verb**	**6-05-005**
strangled	VBD	1-01-001
strangled	VBN	5-04-004
strangulation	**NN**	**1-01-001**
strap	**noun**	**3-02-003**
strap	NN	1-01-001
straps	NNS	2-02-002
strap	**verb**	**4-02-002**
strap	VB	1-01-001
strapped	VBN	1-01-001
strapping	VBG	2-01-001
strapping	**JJ**	**1-01-001**
Strasbourg	**prop. noun**	**8-01-001**
Strasbourg	NP	6-01-001
Strasbourg	NP-TL	2-01-001
Strasny	**NP**	**1-01-001**
stratagem	**noun**	**2-02-002**
stratagem	NN	1-01-001
stratagems	NNS	1-01-001
strategic	**adjective**	**23-06-012**
strategic	JJ	19-06-010
strategic	JJ-HL	1-01-001
Strategic	JJ-TL	3-02-003
strategically	**QL**	**1-01-001**
strategically	**RB**	**1-01-001**
strategist	**noun**	**4-02-004**
strategists	NNS	4-02-004
strategy	**NN**	**22-10-016**
Stratford	**prop. noun**	**8-01-002**
Stratford	NP	6-01-002
Stratforde	NP	1-01-001
Stratford's	NP$	1-01-001
stratification	**NN**	**2-02-002**
stratify	**verb**	**3-02-003**
stratify	VB	1-01-001
stratified	VBN	2-01-002
stratosphere	**NN**	**1-01-001**
Stratton	**prop. noun**	**3-02-002**
Stratton	NP	1-01-001
Stratton	NP-HL	2-01-001
stratum	**noun**	**5-03-003**
stratum	NN	3-01-001
strata	NNS	2-02-002
Strauss	**prop. noun**	**3-03-003**
Strauss	NP	2-02-002
Strauss	NP-TL	1-01-001
Stravinsky	**prop. noun**	**9-02-002**
Stravinsky	NP	8-02-002
Stravinsky's	NP$	1-01-001
straw	**noun**	**18-08-013**
straw	NN	15-07-012
straws	NNS	3-02-002
straw-colored	**JJ**	**1-01-001**
straw-hat	**NN**	**1-01-001**
strawberry	**noun**	**2-02-002**
strawberries	NNS	2-02-002
stray	**JJ**	**7-06-006**
stray	**noun**	**7-04-004**
stray	NN	1-01-001
strays	NNS	6-03-003
stray	**verb**	**5-05-005**
stray	VB	4-04-004
strayed	VBD	1-01-001
streak	**noun**	**16-05-013**
streak	NN	10-03-009
streaks	NNS	6-04-006
streak	**verb**	**4-04-004**
streaked	VBD	3-03-003
streaked	VBN	1-01-001
stream	**noun**	**61-10-038**
stream	NN	49-09-031
stream's	NN$	0-00-000
Stream's	NN$-TL	1-01-001
streams	NNS	11-06-009
stream	**verb**	**12-06-011**
stream	VB	2-02-002
streamed	VBD	2-02-002
streamed	VBN	1-01-001
streaming	VBG	7-05-006
stream-of-consciousness	**NN**	**1-01-001**

Word	Tag	Frequency
streamer	**NN**	**1-01-001**
streamline	**verb**	**4-03-003**
streamlined	VBN	4-03-003
streamliner	**NN**	**1-01-001**
streamside	**NN**	**1-01-001**
street	**noun**	**323-14-137**
street	NN	147-13-074
st.	NN	0-00-000
St.	NN-TL	18-03-011
Street	NN-TL	96-12-050
Street	NN-TL-HL	1-01-001
street's	NN$	0-00-000
Street's	NN$-TL	1-01-001
streets	NNS	57-11-046
Streets	NNS-TL	3-02-003
streetcar	**noun**	**15-05-007**
streetcar	NN	13-05-006
streetcars	NNS	2-02-002
Streeter	**prop. noun**	**1-01-001**
Streeters	NPS	1-01-001
streetlight	**NN**	**1-01-001**
strength	**noun**	**141-14-080**
strength	NN	132-14-078
strength	NN-HL	4-02-002
Strength	NN-TL	1-01-001
strengths	NNS	4-02-003
strengthen	**verb**	**36-08-027**
strengthen	VB	16-07-012
strengthens	VBZ	4-03-003
strengthens	VBZ-HL	1-01-001
strengthened	VBD	1-01-001
strengthened	VBN	5-05-005
strengtened	VBN	1-01-001
strengthening	VBG	8-06-008
strengthening	**NN**	**4-03-004**
strenuous	**JJ**	**11-06-011**
strenuously	**RB**	**2-02-002**
Streptococcus	**NP**	**1-01-001**
stress	**noun**	**111-10-031**
stress	NN	96-08-026
stresses	NNS	15-08-010
stress	**verb**	**43-12-036**
stress	VB	11-06-010
stresses	VBZ	4-03-004
stressed	VBD	11-07-009
stressed	VBN	12-08-010
stressing	VBG	4-02-004
stressing	VBG-HL	1-01-001
stress-temperature	**NN**	**1-01-001**
stressful	**JJ**	**2-01-001**
stretch	**noun**	**24-09-016**
stretch	NN	18-08-011
stretch	NN-HL	1-01-001
stretches	NNS	5-04-005
stretch	**verb**	**61-14-051**
stretch	VB	7-06-007
stretches	VBZ	4-02-004
stretched	VBD	21-07-018
stretched	VBN	13-08-013
stretching	VBG	16-09-014
stretcher	**NN**	**1-01-001**
stretching	**NN**	**1-01-001**
strew	**verb**	**6-04-005**
strewn	VBN	6-04-005
Strickland	**NP**	**1-01-001**
strict	**JJ**	**11-08-011**
strictest	**JJT**	**2-02-002**
strictly	**QL**	**8-03-007**
strictly	**RB**	**25-09-023**
stricture	**noun**	**1-01-001**
strictures	NNS	1-01-001
stride	**noun**	**19-09-017**
stride	NN	12-06-010
strides	NNS	7-05-007
stride	**verb**	**15-07-014**
stride	VB	4-04-004
strode	VBD	10-05-009
striding	VBG	1-01-001
strife	**NN**	**6-06-006**
strike	**noun**	**37-07-018**
strike	NN	25-06-012
strikes	NNS	12-05-009
strike	**verb**	**108-15-074**
strike	VB	22-10-018
Strike	VB-TL	3-01-001
strikes	VBZ	8-06-008
struck	VBD	40-12-033
struck	VBN	19-09-017
stricken	VBN	5-04-005

Word	Tag	Frequency
strike (cont.):		
Stricken	VBN-TL	1-01-001
striking	VBG	10-04-009
strikebreaker	**noun**	**1-01-001**
strikebreakers	NNS	1-01-001
striking	**JJ**	**28-08-025**
striking	**NN**	**1-01-001**
strikingly	**QL**	**1-01-001**
strikingly	**RB**	**7-04-007**
Strindberg	**prop. noun**	**2-01-001**
Strindberg	NP	1-01-001
Strindberg's	NP$	1-01-001
string	**noun**	**34-12-025**
string	NN	18-10-015
strings	NNS	12-07-009
strings	NNS-HL	2-02-002
Strings	NNS-TL	2-01-002
string	**verb**	**7-05-007**
string	VB	1-01-001
strung	VBD	1-01-001
strung	VBN	3-03-003
stringed	VBN	1-01-001
stringing	VBG	1-01-001
stringently	**RB**	**1-01-001**
stringy	**JJ**	**3-03-003**
strip	**noun**	**39-08-021**
strip	NN	24-08-016
Strip	NN-TL	1-01-001
strips	NNS	14-05-009
strip	**verb**	**22-08-020**
strip	VB	5-04-005
stripped	VBD	7-04-007
stripped	VBN	10-05-009
stripe	**noun**	**9-06-007**
stripe	NN	4-02-002
stripes	NNS	4-03-004
Stripes	NNS-TL	1-01-001
stripe	**verb**	**5-03-004**
striped	VBN	5-03-004
stripper	**noun**	**2-02-002**
strippers	NNS	2-02-002
striptease	**NN**	**1-01-001**
Stritch	**NP**	**1-01-001**
strive	**verb**	**18-10-017**
strive	VB	7-06-006
strives	VBZ	3-02-003
strove	VBD	4-04-004
striven	VBN	1-01-001
striving	VBG	3-03-003
striving	**noun**	**4-02-003**
striving	NN	1-01-001
strivings	NNS	3-02-002
stroke	**noun**	**30-08-017**
stroke	NN	18-07-013
strokes	NNS	12-03-006
stroke	**verb**	**5-04-005**
stroke	VB	1-01-001
stroked	VBD	2-01-002
stroked	VBN	1-01-001
stroking	VBG	1-01-001
stroking	**NN**	**1-01-001**
stroll	**NN**	**4-03-004**
stroll	**verb**	**8-05-007**
strolled	VBD	4-04-004
strolling	VBG	4-03-004
strong	**adjective**	**198-14-130**
strong	JJ	197-14-129
Strong	JJ-TL	1-01-001
strong	**RB**	**3-03-003**
Strong	**NP**	**1-01-001**
strong-made	**JJ**	**1-01-001**
stronger	**JJR**	**37-11-029**
strongest	**JJT**	**20-08-018**
Strongheart	**NP**	**1-01-001**
stronghold	**noun**	**6-03-004**
stronghold	NN	3-03-003
Stronghold	NN-TL	3-01-001
strongly	**QL**	**2-01-002**
strongly	**RB**	**35-13-030**
strongroom	**noun**	**1-01-001**
strongrooms	NNS	1-01-001
strop	**verb**	**2-01-001**
stropped	VBD	1-01-001
stropping	VBG	1-01-001
strophe	**NN**	**1-01-001**
structural	**adjective**	**25-05-017**
structural	JJ	22-05-015
Structural	JJ-TL	3-02-002
structurally	**RB**	**2-02-002**
structure	**noun**	**121-12-073**
structure	NN	87-12-061
structure	NN-HL	3-02-003
structures	NNS	28-07-022
Structures	NNS-TL	3-01-001
structure	**verb**	**16-02-004**
structure	VB	1-01-001
structured	VBN	14-02-003
structuring	VBG	1-01-001
struggle	**noun**	**57-12-047**
struggle	NN	55-12-045
struggles	NNS	2-02-002
struggle	**verb**	**36-12-033**
struggle	VB	7-06-007
struggles	VBZ	1-01-001
struggled	VBD	7-06-007
struggled	VBN	1-01-001
struggling	VBG	20-09-018
Strukturbericht	**foreign**	**1-01-001**
Strukturbericht	FW-NN	0-00-000
Strukturbericht	FW-NN-NC	1-01-001
strum	**verb**	**1-01-001**
strumming	VBG	1-01-001
strut	**NN**	**2-02-002**
strut	**verb**	**4-04-004**
strut	VB	0-00-000
Strut	VB-TL	1-01-001
strutted	VBD	2-02-002
strutting	VBG	1-01-001
strychnine	**NN**	**4-02-002**
Stuart	**prop. noun**	**16-05-009**
Stuart	NP	14-05-008
Stuart	NP-TL	2-01-001
Stuart-family	**JJ**	**1-01-001**
stub	**noun**	**5-05-005**
stub	NN	3-03-003
stubs	NNS	2-02-002
stub	**verb**	**1-01-001**
stubbed	VBN	1-01-001
stubble	**NN**	**2-01-001**
Stubblefield	**prop. noun**	**8-01-001**
Stubblefield	NP	4-01-001
Stubblefields	NPS	4-01-001
stubborn	**JJ**	**12-09-012**
stubbornly	**RB**	**3-02-003**
stubbornness	**NN**	**2-02-002**
Stubbs	**NP**	**1-01-001**
stubby	**JJ**	**3-03-003**
stucco	**NN**	**4-03-003**
stuck-up	**adjective**	**3-02-002**
stuck-up	JJ	1-01-001
Stuck-up	JJ-TL	2-01-001
stud	**noun**	**10-02-002**
stud	NN	6-02-002
stud	NN-HL	1-01-001
studs	NNS	3-01-001
stud	**verb**	**4-03-004**
studded	VBN	4-03-004
Studebaker	**NP**	**1-01-001**
student	**noun**	**351-14-087**
student	NN	112-11-048
student	NN-HL	5-03-003
Student	NN-TL	14-04-006
student's	NN$	3-03-003
students	NNS	211-13-062
students	NNS-HL	1-01-001
Students	NNS-TL	1-01-001
students'	NNS$	3-03-003
Students'	NNS$-TL	1-01-001
student-directed	**JJ**	**1-01-001**
student-loan	**NN**	**1-01-001**
student-physicist	**noun**	**1-01-001**
student-physicists	NNS	1-01-001
studio	**noun**	**33-10-019**
studio	NN	28-09-014
Studio	NN-TL	3-03-003
studios	NNS	2-02-002
studious	**JJ**	**1-01-001**
studiously	**QL**	**1-01-001**
studiously	**RB**	**1-01-001**
study	**noun**	**305-13-119**
study	NN	200-13-099
Study	NN-TL	3-03-003
studies	NNS	95-12-052
studies	NNS-HL	3-01-001
Studies	NNS-TL	4-02-002
study	**verb**	**163-14-117**
study	VB	40-12-029
study	VB-HL	1-01-001

Word	Tag	Frequency
study (cont.):		
Study	VB-TL	2-02-002
studies	VBZ	1-01-001
studied	VBD	34-13-031
studied	VBN	44-11-040
studied	VBN-HL	1-01-001
studying	VBG	40-11-037
stuff	**noun**	**29-10-026**
stuff	NN	28-10-025
Stuff	NN-TL	1-01-001
stuff	**verb**	**10-07-010**
stuff	VB	3-02-003
stuffed	VBD	1-01-001
stuffed	VBN	4-04-004
stuffing	VBG	2-02-002
stuffy	**JJ**	**2-02-002**
stultify	**verb**	**1-01-001**
stultifying	VBG	1-01-001
stumble	**verb**	**31-10-025**
stumble	VB	1-01-001
stumbles	VBZ	1-01-001
stumbled	VBD	18-08-016
stumbled	VBN	3-03-003
stumbling	VBG	8-04-008
stumbling-block	**NN**	**1-01-001**
stump	**noun**	**7-05-006**
stump	NN	2-01-001
stumps	NNS	5-05-005
stump	**verb**	**2-02-002**
stumped	VBN	1-01-001
stumping	VBG	1-01-001
stumpage	**NN**	**1-01-001**
stumpy	**JJ**	**1-01-001**
stun	**verb**	**8-05-007**
stunned	VBD	1-01-001
stunned	VBN	7-05-006
stunning	**JJ**	**6-03-006**
stunningly	**RB**	**1-01-001**
stunt	**noun**	**2-01-001**
stunts	NNS	2-01-001
stunt	**VB**	**1-01-001**
stupefy	**verb**	**1-01-001**
stupefying	VBG	1-01-001
stupendous	**JJ**	**3-03-003**
stupid	**JJ**	**24-08-020**
stupidest	**JJT**	**1-01-001**
stupidity	**noun**	**9-06-009**
stupidity	NN	8-06-008
stupidities	NNS	1-01-001
stupidly	**RB**	**2-02-002**
stupor	**NN**	**4-03-004**
Sturbridge	**prop. noun**	**1-01-001**
Sturbridge	NP	0-00-000
Sturbridge	NP-TL	1-01-001
Sturch	**NP**	**2-01-001**
sturdy	**JJ**	**16-09-015**
sturgeon	**NN**	**1-01-001**
Sturley	**prop. noun**	**11-01-001**
Sturley	NP	10-01-001
Sturley's	NP$	1-01-001
Stuttgart	**NP**	**1-01-001**
Styka	**NP**	**16-01-001**
style	**noun**	**117-13-065**
style	NN	98-13-054
styles	NNS	18-06-014
styles	NNS-HL	1-01-001
style	**verb**	**3-02-003**
styled	VBD	1-01-001
styled	VBN	2-02-002
stylemark	**NN**	**1-01-001**
Styles	**NP**	**1-01-001**
styling	**NN**	**1-01-001**
stylish	**JJ**	**1-01-001**
stylist	**NN**	**3-03-003**
stylistic	**JJ**	**1-01-001**
stylization	**NN**	**2-02-002**
stylize	**verb**	**2-02-002**
stylized	VBN	2-02-002
stymie	**verb**	**1-01-001**
stymied	VBN	1-01-001
styrene	**noun**	**9-02-002**
styrene	NN	7-02-002
styrene's	NN$	1-01-001
styrenes	NNS	1-01-001
Styron	**NP**	**2-01-001**
styryl-lithium	**NN**	**1-01-001**
suability	**NN**	**1-01-001**
suable	**JJ**	**1-01-001**
suave	**JJ**	**2-02-002**
suavity	**NN**	**1-01-001**
sub	**IN**	**1-01-001**
sub	**noun**	**6-02-002**
sub	NN	4-01-001
subs	NNS	2-02-002
sub	**verb**	**1-01-001**
subbing	VBG	1-01-001
sub-assembly	**NN**	**1-01-001**
sub-chief	**noun**	**1-01-001**
sub-chiefs	NNS	1-01-001
sub-chiefdom	**NN**	**1-01-001**
sub-Christian	**JJ**	**1-01-001**
sub-conscious-level	**NN**	**1-01-001**
sub-freezing	**JJ**	**1-01-001**
sub-human	**JJ**	**1-01-001**
sub-interval	**NN**	**3-01-001**
sub-station	**NN**	**1-01-001**
sub-test	**noun**	**2-01-001**
sub-tests	NNS	2-01-001
sub-zero	**NN**	**1-01-001**
subaltern	**NN**	**1-01-001**
subatomic	**JJ**	**1-01-001**
subcommittee	**noun**	**5-03-004**
subcommittee	NN	4-02-003
Subcommittee	NN-TL	1-01-001
subconscious	**JJ**	**3-02-002**
subconscious	**NN**	**1-01-001**
subconsciously	**RB**	**4-03-004**
subcontinent	**NN**	**1-01-001**
subcontract	**verb**	**1-01-001**
subcontracting	VBG	1-01-001
subdivision	**noun**	**12-04-006**
subdivision	NN	8-04-005
Subdivision	NN-TL	2-01-001
Subdivision	NN-TL-HL	1-01-001
subdivisions	NNS	1-01-001
subdue	**verb**	**12-07-011**
subdue	VB	2-02-002
subdues	VBZ	1-01-001
subdued	VBN	8-06-008
subduing	VBG	1-01-001
subfigure	**noun**	**1-01-001**
subfigures	NNS	1-01-001
subgross	**JJ**	**2-01-001**
subgroup	**noun**	**8-01-003**
subgroup	NN	0-00-000
sub-group	NN	1-01-001
subgroups	NNS	7-01-002
subhumanity	**NN**	**1-01-001**
Subic	**NP**	**2-01-001**
subject	**JJ**	**39-06-023**
subject	**noun**	**203-15-106**
subject	NN	121-15-084
subject's	NN$	1-01-001
subjects	NNS	79-10-032
subjects	NNS-HL	1-01-001
subjects'	NNS$	1-01-001
subject	**verb**	**26-10-019**
subject	VB	1-01-001
subjects	VBZ	1-01-001
subjected	VBN	22-10-018
subjected	VBN-HL	2-01-001
subjective	**JJ**	**18-03-013**
subjectively	**QL**	**1-01-001**
subjectively	**RB**	**5-03-003**
subjectivist	**noun**	**3-01-001**
subjectivist	NN	2-01-001
subjectivists	NNS	1-01-001
subjectivity	**NN**	**1-01-001**
subjugate	**VB**	**1-01-001**
subjugation	**NN**	**3-02-003**
sublease	**NN**	**1-01-001**
sublimate	**NN**	**1-01-001**
sublimate	**VB**	**1-01-001**
sublime	**JJ**	**1-01-001**
sublime	**NN**	**2-01-001**
sublime	**verb**	**1-01-001**
sublimed	VBN	1-01-001
subliterary	**JJ**	**1-01-001**
sublunary	**JJ**	**1-01-001**
submachine	**JJ**	**3-03-003**
submarine	**JJ**	**11-01-001**
submarine	**noun**	**35-05-010**
submarine	NN	15-04-005
submarines	NNS	20-05-010
submarine-ball	**NN**	**1-01-001**
submariner	**noun**	**1-01-001**
submariners	NNS	1-01-001
submerge	**verb**	**8-05-007**

Word	Tag	Frequency
submerge (cont.):		
submerged	VBN	7-05-007
submerging	VBG	1-01-001
submission	**noun**	**5-03-004**
submission	NN	4-03-003
submissions	NNS	1-01-001
submissive	**JJ**	**4-02-002**
submit	**verb**	**47-11-038**
submit	VB	18-08-018
submits	VBZ	3-02-002
submitted	VBD	10-07-008
submitted	VBN	11-06-010
submitting	VBG	5-02-004
submitting	**NN**	**1-01-001**
submucosa	**NN**	**2-01-001**
subnormal	**JJ**	**1-01-001**
subordinate	**JJ**	**4-04-004**
subordinate	**noun**	**10-06-008**
subordinate	NN	1-01-001
subordinates	NNS	9-06-007
subordinate	**verb**	**5-03-004**
subordinate	VB	1-01-001
subordinated	VBN	4-03-003
subordinator	**NN**	**2-01-001**
subparagraph	**NN**	**1-01-001**
subpart	**noun**	**1-01-001**
subparts	NNS	1-01-001
subpoena	**FW-NN**	**1-01-001**
subpoena	**noun**	**2-01-001**
subpoenas	NNS	0-00-000
subpenas	NNS	1-01-001
subpoenas	NNS-HL	1-01-001
subpoena	**verb**	**1-01-001**
subpoenaed	VBN	0-00-000
subpenaed	VBN	1-01-001
subrogation	**NN**	**1-01-001**
subroutine	**noun**	**2-01-001**
subroutine	NN	1-01-001
subroutines	NNS	1-01-001
subscribe	**verb**	**6-05-005**
subscribe	VB	1-01-001
subscribed	VBD	1-01-001
subscribed	VBN	2-02-002
subscribing	VBG	2-02-002
subscriber	**noun**	**7-04-004**
subscribers	NNS	6-04-004
Subscribers	NNS	1-01-001
subscript	**noun**	**1-01-001**
subscripts	NNS	1-01-001
subscription	**NN**	**4-04-004**
subsection	**noun**	**16-01-003**
subsection	NN	13-01-003
subsections	NNS	3-01-002
subsequent	**JJ**	**28-08-026**
subsequent	**RB**	**1-01-001**
subsequently	**RB**	**11-06-011**
subservience	**NN**	**1-01-001**
subservient	**JJ**	**3-03-003**
subside	**verb**	**7-05-007**
subside	VB	2-02-002
subsided	VBD	4-03-004
subsided	VBN	1-01-001
subsidiary	**JJ**	**1-01-001**
subsidiary	**noun**	**8-03-005**
subsidiary	NN	5-03-004
subsidiary	NN-HL	1-01-001
subsidiaries	NNS	2-02-002
subsidize	**verb**	**8-06-007**
subsidize	VB	4-03-003
subsidized	VBD	1-01-001
subsidized	VBN	3-02-003
subsidy	**noun**	**7-05-006**
subsidy	NN	3-03-003
subsidies	NNS	2-02-002
subsedies	NNS	1-01-001
subsidies	NNS-HL	1-01-001
subsist	**VB**	**1-01-001**
subsistence	**NN**	**10-05-008**
subsistent	**JJ**	**1-01-001**
subsoil	**NN**	**1-01-001**
subspace	**noun**	**8-01-001**
subspace	NN	7-01-001
subspaces	NNS	1-01-001
subspecies	**noun**	**3-01-001**
subspecies	NNS	3-01-001
substance	**noun**	**56-11-033**
substance	NN	31-11-026
Substance	NN-TL	2-02-002
substances	NNS	18-03-007
substance (cont.):		
substances	NNS-HL	5-01-001
substantial	**JJ**	**66-09-046**
substantially	**QL**	**5-05-005**
substantially	**RB**	**31-06-023**
substantiate	**verb**	**3-03-003**
substantiate	VB	2-02-002
substantiates	VBZ	1-01-001
substantiation	**NN**	**1-01-001**
substantive	**adjective**	**3-03-003**
substantive	JJ	2-02-002
Substantive	JJ-TL	1-01-001
substantively	**RB**	**1-01-001**
substerilization	**JJ**	**1-01-001**
substitute	**JJ**	**5-04-005**
substitute	**noun**	**17-09-015**
substitute	NN	12-06-011
substitutes	NNS	5-03-004
substitute	**verb**	**24-10-022**
substitute	VB	5-03-005
substituted	VBD	3-03-003
substituted	VBN	12-05-011
substituting	VBG	4-04-004
substitution	**noun**	**3-03-003**
substitution	NN	2-02-002
substitutions	NNS	1-01-001
substitutionary	**JJ**	**1-01-001**
substrate	**noun**	**26-01-005**
substrate	NN	23-01-005
substrates	NNS	3-01-002
substratum	**NN**	**1-01-001**
substructure	**NN**	**1-01-001**
subsume	**verb**	**1-01-001**
subsumed	VBN	1-01-001
subsurface	**adjective**	**2-01-002**
subsurface	JJ	1-01-001
sub-surface	JJ	1-01-001
subsystem	**noun**	**12-01-002**
subsystem	NN	2-01-002
subsystems	NNS	9-01-002
subsystems	NNS-HL	1-01-001
subtend	**verb**	**2-01-001**
subtends	VBZ	1-01-001
subtended	VBN	1-01-001
subterfuge	**noun**	**1-01-001**
subterfuges	NNS	1-01-001
subtilis	**NP**	**2-02-002**
subtitle	**verb**	**3-03-003**
subtitled	VBN	3-03-003
subtle	**JJ**	**25-08-022**
subtler	**JJR**	**1-01-001**
subtlety	**noun**	**5-02-005**
subtlety	NN	1-01-001
subtleties	NNS	4-02-004
subtly	**QL**	**2-02-002**
subtly	**RB**	**4-04-004**
subtract	**verb**	**9-04-005**
subtract	VB	2-02-002
subtracted	VBD	1-01-001
subtracted	VBN	3-02-002
subtracting	VBG	3-02-002
subtraction	**NN**	**6-01-001**
subtype	**noun**	**4-01-001**
subtype	NN	3-01-001
subtypes	NNS	1-01-001
suburb	**noun**	**31-10-022**
suburb	NN	13-06-011
suburbs	NNS	16-08-012
suburbs	NNS-HL	1-01-001
Suburbs	NNS-TL	1-01-001
suburban	**JJ**	**29-08-016**
suburbanite	**JJ**	**1-01-001**
suburbanite	**noun**	**2-01-001**
suburbanite	NN	1-01-001
suburbanites	NNS	1-01-001
suburbanize	**verb**	**1-01-001**
suburbanized	VBN	1-01-001
suburbia	**NN**	**1-01-001**
subversion	**NN**	**1-01-001**
subversive	**JJ**	**2-01-002**
subversive	**noun**	**1-01-001**
subversives	NNS	1-01-001
subvert	**verb**	**2-01-002**
subverted	VBN	1-01-001
subverting	VBG	1-01-001
subway	**noun**	**8-05-006**
subway	NN	6-04-005
subway	NN-HL	1-01-001
subways	NNS	1-01-001

Word	Tag	Frequency
succeed	**verb**	**61-15-054**
succeed	VB	14-08-014
Succeed	VB-TL	1-01-001
succeeds	VBZ	8-05-008
succeeded	VBD	18-12-017
succeeded	VBN	15-09-013
succeeding	VBG	5-04-004
succeeding	**JJ**	**1-01-001**
success	**noun**	**116-11-065**
success	NN	91-11-061
sucess	NN	1-01-001
success	NN-HL	1-01-001
success	NN-NC	1-01-001
successes	NNS	21-07-011
successes	NNS-HL	1-01-001
success-oriented	**JJ**	**1-01-001**
successful	**adjective**	**95-12-073**
successful	JJ	94-12-072
Successful	JJ-TL	1-01-001
successfully	**RB**	**31-09-027**
succession	**noun**	**25-10-015**
succession	NN	20-10-015
Succession	NN-TL	5-01-002
successive	**JJ**	**12-08-012**
successively	**RB**	**2-01-002**
successor	**noun**	**22-06-014**
successor	NN	16-06-010
successors	NNS	6-04-006
successor-in-spirit	**noun**	**1-01-001**
successors-in-spirit	NNS	1-01-001
successorship	**NN**	**1-01-001**
succinct	**JJ**	**1-01-001**
succinctly	**RB**	**2-02-002**
succor	**NN**	**1-01-001**
succumb	**verb**	**7-04-007**
succumb	VB	1-01-001
succumbed	VBD	1-01-001
succumbed	VBN	4-04-004
succumbing	VBG	1-01-001
such	**ABL**	**310-15-194**
such	**JJ**	**978-15-349**
such	**QL**	**15-08-015**
suck	**NN**	**1-01-001**
suck	**verb**	**18-06-015**
suck	VB	4-03-004
sucked	VBD	5-02-005
sucked	VBN	1-01-001
sucking	VBG	8-04-007
sucker	**noun**	**1-01-001**
suckers	NNS	1-01-001
sucker-rolling	**JJ**	**1-01-001**
suction	**NN**	**1-01-001**
Sudanese	**JJ**	**1-01-001**
sudden	**JJ**	**37-11-028**
sudden	**NN**	**1-01-001**
sudden-end	**JJ**	**1-01-001**
suddenly	**RB**	**153-13-098**
suddenness	**NN**	**2-02-002**
Sudier	**NP**	**1-01-001**
suds	**NNS**	**9-02-002**
suds	**verb**	**1-01-001**
sudsing	VBG	1-01-001
sue	**verb**	**19-06-007**
sue	VB	12-04-004
sue	VB-HL	1-01-001
sues	VBZ	1-01-001
sued	VBD	2-02-002
sued	VBN	2-02-002
suing	VBG	1-01-001
Sue	**NP**	**5-04-005**
suey	**NN**	**1-01-001**
Suez	**NP**	**2-02-002**
Suez-Hungary	**NP**	**2-01-001**
suffer	**verb**	**110-13-077**
suffer	VB	33-09-027
suffers	VBZ	5-04-005
suffered	VBD	22-10-022
suffered	VBN	20-08-018
suffering	VBG	30-07-020
sufferer	**noun**	**5-03-004**
sufferer	NN	4-03-004
sufferers	NNS	1-01-001
suffering	**noun**	**18-05-010**
suffering	NN	14-05-006
sufferings	NNS	4-02-004
suffice	**VB**	**5-04-005**
sufficiency	**NN**	**1-01-001**
sufficient	**JJ**	**63-08-050**
sufficiently	**QL**	**26-07-022**
sufficiently	**RB**	**16-10-016**
suffix	**noun**	**2-01-002**
suffix	NN	1-01-001
suffixes	NNS	1-01-001
suffocate	**verb**	**5-03-005**
suffocated	VBN	1-01-001
suffocating	VBG	4-02-004
suffocating	**NN**	**1-01-001**
suffocation	**NN**	**1-01-001**
suffrage	**NN**	**5-04-005**
suffragette	**noun**	**1-01-001**
suffragettes	NNS	1-01-001
suffuse	**verb**	**6-04-005**
suffuse	VB	1-01-001
suffused	VBD	4-03-004
suffused	VBN	1-01-001
sugar	**noun**	**34-09-016**
sugar	NN	33-09-016
sugar	NN-HL	1-01-001
sugar	**verb**	**1-01-001**
sugared	VBD	1-01-001
suggest	**verb**	**200-15-139**
suggest	VB	54-12-047
suggests	VBZ	29-06-027
suggested	VBD	48-13-042
suggested	VBN	55-09-048
suggested	VBN-HL	1-01-001
suggesting	VBG	13-09-013
suggested	**JJ**	**1-01-001**
suggestibility	**NN**	**3-01-001**
suggestion	**noun**	**57-12-048**
suggestion	NN	33-09-029
suggestion	NN-NC	1-01-001
suggestions	NNS	21-09-018
suggestions	NNS-HL	1-01-001
suggestions	NNS-NC	1-01-001
suggestive	**JJ**	**9-02-008**
Suggs	**NP**	**1-01-001**
suicide	**noun**	**19-10-016**
suicide	NN	17-10-015
suicides	NNS	2-01-002
suit	**noun**	**64-13-040**
suit	NN	40-12-031
suits	NNS	24-08-014
suit	**verb**	**31-09-026**
suit	VB	8-02-008
suits	VBZ	1-01-001
suited	VBD	3-03-003
suited	VBN	19-08-015
suitability	**NN**	**1-01-001**
suitable	**adjective**	**34-09-031**
suitable	JJ	33-09-030
suitable	JJ-HL	1-01-001
suitably	**QL**	**1-01-001**
suitably	**RB**	**2-02-002**
suitably-loaded	**JJ**	**1-01-001**
suitcase	**noun**	**25-06-012**
suitcase	NN	20-04-009
suitcases	NNS	5-02-003
suite	**FW-NN**	**1-01-001**
suite	**noun**	**31-07-017**
suite	NN	19-05-010
Suite	NN-TL	7-03-004
suite's	NN$	1-01-001
suites	NNS	4-04-004
suitor	**noun**	**4-02-003**
suitor	NN	1-01-001
suitors	NNS	3-02-003
Sukarno	**prop. noun**	**5-03-004**
Sukarno	NP	4-02-003
Sukarno's	NP$	1-01-001
Sukuma	**NP**	**1-01-001**
Sulamite	**NP**	**1-01-001**
Sulamith	**NP**	**1-01-001**
Sulcer	**NP**	**1-01-001**
sulfaquinoxaline	**NN**	**1-01-001**
sulfide	**NN**	**1-01-001**
sulk	**noun**	**1-01-001**
sulks	NNS	1-01-001
sulk	**verb**	**3-03-003**
sulked	VBD	2-02-002
sulking	VBG	1-01-001
sulkily	**RB**	**1-01-001**
sulky	**JJ**	**4-04-004**
sulky	**noun**	**1-01-001**
sulky's	NN$	1-01-001
Sullam	**NP**	**3-01-001**
sullen	**JJ**	**9-05-009**
sullenly	**RB**	**2-02-002**

Word	Tag	Frequency
Sullivan	**NP**	**8-03-005**
sully	**verb**	**1-01-001**
sullying	VBG	1-01-001
sulphur	**noun**	**4-04-004**
sulphur	NN	2-02-002
sulfur	NN	1-01-001
Sulphur	NN-TL	1-01-001
sulphur	**verb**	**1-01-001**
sulphured	VBN	1-01-001
sultan	**noun**	**7-02-002**
sultan	NN	0-00-000
Sultan	NN-TL	3-01-001
sultans	NNS	3-02-002
Sultans	NNS-TL	1-01-001
sultane	**foreign**	**1-01-001**
sultane	FW-NN	0-00-000
Sultane	FW-NN-TL	1-01-001
sultry	**JJ**	**1-01-001**
Sulzberger	**prop. noun**	**5-02-002**
Sulzberger	NP	3-01-001
Sulzberger's	NP$	2-02-002
sum	**noun**	**59-11-042**
sum	NN	43-10-030
Sum	NN-TL	1-01-001
sums	NNS	15-06-014
sum	**verb**	**11-06-011**
sum	VB	1-01-001
sums	VBZ	2-02-002
summed	VBD	4-02-004
summed	VBN	3-03-003
summing	VBG	1-01-001
sumac	**NN**	**1-01-001**
Sumatra	**NP**	**1-01-001**
summarization	**NN**	**1-01-001**
summarize	**verb**	**16-04-013**
summarize	VB	2-02-002
summarize	VB-HL	1-01-001
summarizes	VBZ	1-01-001
summarized	VBD	1-01-001
summarized	VBN	8-03-008
summarizing	VBG	3-01-003
summary	**noun**	**21-05-016**
summary	NN	14-05-013
summary	NN-HL	2-01-002
Summary	NN-TL	5-01-001
summate	**VB**	**2-01-002**
summation	**NN**	**3-03-003**
summer	**noun**	**151-15-084**
summer	NN	131-15-076
summer	NN-HL	1-01-001
Summer	NN-TL	2-02-002
summer's	NN+HVZ	1-01-001
summer's	NN$	6-04-006
summers	NNS	10-07-008
summer-winter	**JJ**	**1-01-001**
Summerdale	**NP**	**2-01-002**
Summers	**NP**	**7-01-001**
Summerspace	**NP**	**1-01-001**
summertime	**NN**	**4-04-004**
summit	**noun**	**12-04-005**
summit	NN	11-03-004
Summit	NN-TL	1-01-001
summitry	**NN**	**1-01-001**
summon	**verb**	**13-08-012**
summon	VB	3-03-003
summoned	VBD	5-04-005
summoned	VBN	4-04-004
summoned	VBN-HL	1-01-001
summons	**NN**	**1-01-001**
Sumner	**NP**	**2-02-002**
sumptuous	**JJ**	**4-02-002**
Sumter	**prop. noun**	**2-02-002**
Sumter	NP	0-00-000
Sumter	NP-TL	2-02-002
sun	**noun**	**117-14-069**
sun	NN	101-14-059
Sun	NN-TL	10-05-007
sun'll	NN+MD	1-01-001
sun's	NN+BEZ	1-01-001
sun's	NN$	3-03-003
suns	NNS	0-00-000
Suns	NNS-TL	1-01-001
sun	**verb**	**2-01-002**
sun	VB	1-01-001
sunning	VBG	1-01-001
sun-bleached	**JJ**	**1-01-001**
sun-browned	**JJ**	**1-01-001**
sun-burned	**JJ**	**1-01-001**
sun-inflamed	**JJ**	**1-01-001**
sun-suit	**NN**	**1-01-001**
sun-tanned	**JJ**	**1-01-001**
Sun-Times	**NP**	**1-01-001**
sun-warmed	**JJ**	**1-01-001**
Sunay	**NP**	**1-01-001**
sunbaked	**adjective**	**2-02-002**
sunbaked	JJ	1-01-001
sun-baked	JJ	1-01-001
sunbonnet	**NN**	**1-01-001**
sunburn	**NN**	**5-01-002**
sunburn	**verb**	**1-01-001**
sunburned	VBN	0-00-000
sunburnt	VBN	1-01-001
Sunday	**adv. noun**	**116-13-059**
Sunday	NR	93-13-050
Sunday	NR-HL	1-01-001
Sunday	NR-TL	7-03-005
Sunday's	NR$	6-03-006
Sundays	NRS	9-08-009
Sunday-school	**JJ**	**1-01-001**
sunder	**VB**	**1-01-001**
sundial	**noun**	**1-01-001**
sundials	NNS	1-01-001
sundown	**NN**	**6-04-006**
sundry	**JJ**	**5-04-005**
Sung-Shan	**NP**	**1-01-001**
sunken	**adjective**	**3-02-003**
sunken	JJ	2-01-002
Sunken	JJ-TL	1-01-001
sunlight	**NN**	**17-07-011**
Sunman	**prop. noun**	**1-01-001**
Sunman	NP	0-00-000
Sunman	NP-TL	1-01-001
sunny	**JJ**	**12-06-010**
Sunny	**NP**	**1-01-001**
Sunnyvale	**NP**	**3-01-001**
sunrise	**noun**	**10-03-004**
sunrise	NN	8-02-002
Sunrise	NN-TL	2-01-002
sunset	**noun**	**14-04-006**
sunset	NN	12-03-004
Sunset	NN-TL	2-01-002
sunshade	**noun**	**2-01-001**
sunshades	NNS	2-01-001
sunshield	**NN**	**1-01-001**
sunshine	**noun**	**8-06-008**
sunshine	NN	7-05-007
Sunshine	NN-TL	1-01-001
sunshiny	**JJ**	**1-01-001**
sunspot	**NN**	**1-01-001**
sunt	**FW-BER**	**1-01-001**
suntan	**noun**	**2-02-002**
suntan	NN	1-01-001
sun-tan	NN	1-01-001
sup	**VB**	**1-01-001**
super	**FW-IN**	**1-01-001**
super	**adjective**	**6-05-006**
super	JJ	5-04-005
Super	JJ-TL	1-01-001
super	**noun**	**1-01-001**
super	NN	0-00-000
super	NN-HL	1-01-001
super-charged	**JJ**	**1-01-001**
super-city	**NN**	**1-01-001**
super-condamine	**NN**	**4-01-001**
super-empirical	**JJ**	**1-01-001**
super-experiment	**NN**	**1-01-001**
super-Herculean	**JJ**	**1-01-001**
super-high	**JJ**	**1-01-001**
Super-Protein	**NP**	**1-01-001**
super-secret	**JJ**	**1-01-001**
Super-Set	**prop. noun**	**10-01-001**
Super-Set	NP	7-01-001
Super-Sets	NPS	3-01-001
superb	**JJ**	**14-05-011**
superbly	**QL**	**4-02-004**
superbly	**RB**	**5-05-005**
supercilious	**JJ**	**1-01-001**
supercritical	**JJ**	**1-01-001**
superego	**NN**	**1-01-001**
superficial	**JJ**	**7-05-007**
superficiality	**NN**	**1-01-001**
superficially	**RB**	**3-02-003**
superfluous	**JJ**	**3-03-003**
superhighway	**noun**	**1-01-001**
superhighways	NNS	1-01-001
superhuman	**JJ**	**2-02-002**
superieure	**foreign**	**1-01-001**
superieure	FW-JJ	0-00-000

Word	Tag	Frequency
superieure (cont.):		
superieure	FW-JJ-TL	1-01-001
superimpose	**verb**	**13-04-011**
superimpose	VB	4-03-003
superimposes	VBZ	1-01-001
superimposed	VBN	6-03-006
super-imposed	VBN	1-01-001
superimposing	VBG	1-01-001
superintend	**VB**	**1-01-001**
superintendent	**noun**	**23-06-013**
superintendent	NN	13-04-006
supt.	NN	0-00-000
Supt.	NN-TL	2-01-002
Superintendent	NN-TL	4-02-003
superintendent's	NN$	2-02-002
superintendents	NNS	2-01-001
superior	**adjective**	**45-10-033**
superior	JJ	30-10-028
Superior	JJ-TL	15-02-005
superior	**noun**	**5-02-002**
superior	NN	1-01-001
superiors	NNS	4-01-001
superiority	**NN**	**14-06-012**
superlative	**adjective**	**3-03-003**
superlative	JJ	2-02-002
Superlative	JJ-TL	1-01-001
superlative	**noun**	**1-01-001**
superlatives	NNS	1-01-001
superlunary	**JJ**	**1-01-001**
supermachine	**NN**	**1-01-001**
supermarket	**noun**	**5-04-004**
supermarket	NN	1-01-001
Supermarket	NN-TL	1-01-001
supermarkets	NNS	3-02-002
Supermatic	**prop. noun**	**1-01-001**
Supermatic	NP	0-00-000
Supermatic	NP-TL	1-01-001
supernatant	**NN**	**1-01-001**
supernatural	**JJ**	**14-04-005**
supernatural	**NN**	**3-01-002**
supernaturalism	**NN**	**4-02-003**
supernormal	**JJ**	**1-01-001**
superpose	**verb**	**1-01-001**
superposed	VBN	0-00-000
Superposed	VBN-TL	1-01-001
superposition	**NN**	**1-01-001**
supersede	**verb**	**6-04-006**
superseded	VBD	1-01-001
superseded	VBN	4-03-004
superceded	VBN	1-01-001
supersensitive	**JJ**	**1-01-001**
supersonic	**JJ**	**4-02-002**
superstition	**noun**	**10-05-007**
superstition	NN	8-05-007
superstitions	NNS	2-02-002
superstitious	**JJ**	**1-01-001**
superstructure	**NN**	**1-01-001**
supervene	**verb**	**1-01-001**
supervened	VBN	1-01-001
supervise	**verb**	**14-09-013**
supervise	VB	5-05-005
supervises	VBZ	2-02-002
supervised	VBD	3-03-003
supervised	VBN	1-01-001
supervising	VBG	3-03-003
supervision	**NN**	**19-08-013**
supervisor	**noun**	**13-05-009**
supervisor	NN	3-03-003
Supervisor	NN-TL	2-02-002
supervisor's	NN$	2-02-002
supervisors	NNS	4-04-004
Supervisors	NNS-TL	1-01-001
supervisors'	NNS$	1-01-001
supervisory	**JJ**	**2-01-001**
supine	**JJ**	**1-01-001**
supinely	**RB**	**1-01-001**
supper	**noun**	**38-10-026**
supper	NN	32-09-022
Supper	NN-TL	5-03-003
suppers	NNS	1-01-001
supplant	**verb**	**5-03-005**
supplant	VB	3-02-003
supplanted	VBN	1-01-001
supplanting	VBG	1-01-001
supplement	**noun**	**21-06-013**
supplement	NN	11-05-008
Supplement	NN-TL	2-02-002
supplements	NNS	8-04-007
supplement	**verb**	**16-10-015**

Word	Tag	Frequency
supplement (cont.):		
supplement	VB	7-06-007
supplemented	VBD	2-02-002
supplemented	VBN	4-02-004
supplementing	VBG	3-03-003
supplemental	**JJ**	**3-03-003**
supplementary	**JJ**	**9-03-006**
suppleness	**NN**	**1-01-001**
supplicate	**verb**	**2-02-002**
supplicating	VBG	2-02-002
supplier	**noun**	**7-03-005**
supplier	NN	6-02-004
suppliers	NNS	1-01-001
supply	**noun**	**95-14-059**
supply	NN	54-11-038
Supply	NN-TL	5-03-004
supplies	NNS	35-12-025
Supplies	NNS-TL	1-01-001
supply	**verb**	**103-13-074**
supply	VB	43-10-037
supplies	VBZ	11-05-010
supplied	VBD	9-06-009
supplied	VBN	27-10-023
supplying	VBG	13-06-011
support	**noun**	**132-12-083**
support	NN	124-12-079
support	NN-HL	1-01-001
Support	NN-TL	1-01-001
supports	NNS	6-05-006
support	**verb**	**144-14-099**
support	VB	54-09-047
supports	VBZ	8-04-007
supports	VBZ-HL	1-01-001
supported	VBD	17-09-017
supported	VBN	37-09-034
supporting	VBG	26-08-021
supporting	VBG-HL	1-01-001
supporter	**noun**	**11-04-009**
supporter	NN	3-01-002
supporters	NNS	8-04-007
supportive	**JJ**	**7-01-002**
suppose	**verb**	**163-15-114**
suppose	VB	97-14-072
supposes	VBZ	1-01-001
supposed	VBD	8-06-008
supposed	VBN	57-14-049
supposedly	**RB**	**12-08-011**
supposing	**sub. conj.**	**3-03-003**
supposing	CS	2-02-002
s'posin'	CS	1-01-001
supposition	**noun**	**3-02-002**
suppositions	NNS	3-02-002
suppress	**verb**	**10-09-010**
suppress	VB	6-05-006
suppressed	VBD	1-01-001
suppressed	VBN	3-03-003
suppression	**NN**	**7-03-004**
supra	**RB**	**3-01-001**
Supra-Expressionism	**NP**	**1-01-001**
supra-personal	**JJ**	**1-01-001**
supranational	**JJ**	**1-01-001**
supranationalism	**NN**	**1-01-001**
supremacy	**NN**	**5-04-004**
supreme	**adjective**	**51-11-033**
supreme	JJ	18-08-016
Supreme	JJ-TL	33-08-020
supremely	**QL**	**2-02-002**
supremely	**RB**	**2-02-002**
sur	**foreign**	**3-03-003**
sur	FW-IN	1-01-001
Sur	FW-IN-TL	2-02-002
surcease	**NN**	**1-01-001**
Surcliffe	**prop. noun**	**2-01-001**
Surcliffe	NP	1-01-001
Surcliffes'	NPS$	1-01-001
sure	**adjective**	**225-15-151**
sure	JJ	224-15-151
Sure	JJ-TL	1-01-001
sure	**adverb**	**39-10-031**
sure	RB	37-10-029
shore	RB	1-01-001
sho'	RB	1-01-001
sure	**verb**	**1-01-001**
sure	VB	0-00-000
sure	VB-NC	1-01-001
sure-enough	**JJ**	**1-01-001**
sure-sure	**UH**	**2-01-001**
surely	**QL**	**1-01-001**
surely	**RB**	**46-13-040**

Word	Tag	Frequency
surf	**NN**	**1-01-001**
surface	**JJ**	**7-02-004**
surface	**noun**	**221-14-077**
surface	NN	193-13-073
surfaces	NNS	28-06-015
surface	**verb**	**1-01-001**
surfaced	VBN	1-01-001
surface-active	**JJ**	**7-01-001**
surface-analyzer	**NN**	**1-01-001**
surface-declaring	**JJ**	**1-01-001**
surfaceness	**NN**	**1-01-001**
surfactant	**noun**	**3-01-001**
surfactant	NN	1-01-001
surfactants	NNS	2-01-001
surfeit	**verb**	**2-02-002**
surfeit	VB	1-01-001
surfeited	VBN	1-01-001
surge	**NN**	**8-06-008**
surge	**verb**	**10-07-010**
surge	VB	1-01-001
surged	VBD	7-05-007
surging	VBG	2-02-002
surgeon	**noun**	**12-04-008**
surgeon	NN	11-03-007
surgeons	NNS	0-00-000
Surgeons	NNS-TL	1-01-001
surgery	**noun**	**6-05-005**
surgery	NN	4-04-004
Surgery	NN-TL	2-01-001
surgical	**JJ**	**1-01-001**
surly	**JJ**	**2-02-002**
surmise	**noun**	**2-02-002**
surmises	NNS	2-02-002
surmise	**verb**	**3-01-003**
surmise	VB	1-01-001
surmised	VBD	1-01-001
surmised	VBN	1-01-001
surmount	**verb**	**3-02-003**
surmount	VB	1-01-001
surmounted	VBD	1-01-001
surmounted	VBN	1-01-001
surname	**NN**	**3-01-001**
surpass	**verb**	**3-03-003**
surpass	VB	1-01-001
surpassed	VBN	2-02-002
surplus	**JJ**	**3-01-002**
surplus	**noun**	**28-08-020**
surplus	NN	24-08-017
surpluses	NNS	4-03-003
surprise	**adjective**	**2-01-001**
surprise	JJ	1-01-001
surprise	JJ-HL	1-01-001
surprise	**noun**	**49-14-045**
surprise	NN	44-13-040
surprises	NNS	5-04-005
surprise	**verb**	**76-12-058**
surprise	VB	5-05-005
surprised	VBD	9-04-007
surprised	VBN	49-11-040
surprising	VBG	13-07-013
surprising	**JJ**	**17-08-016**
surprisingly	**QL**	**4-02-004**
surprisingly	**RB**	**14-08-014**
surrealism	**NN**	**1-01-001**
surrealist	**JJ**	**1-01-001**
surrealist	**noun**	**2-01-001**
surrealists	NNS	2-01-001
surrender	**NN**	**15-08-011**
surrender	**verb**	**18-06-015**
surrender	VB	7-05-006
surrendered	VBD	6-02-005
surrendered	VBN	1-01-001
surrendering	VBG	4-03-004
surreptitious	**JJ**	**1-01-001**
surreptitiously	**RB**	**3-03-003**
surround	**verb**	**53-15-050**
surround	VB	5-05-005
surrounded	VBD	4-04-004
surrounded	VBN	17-09-017
surrounding	VBG	27-11-024
surrounding	**noun**	**8-06-008**
surroundings	NNS	8-06-008
surtout	**NN**	**1-01-001**
surveillance	**NN**	**6-05-006**
survey	**noun**	**45-10-030**
survey	NN	28-09-021
Survey	NN-TL	6-05-005
surveys	NNS	11-04-007
survey	**verb**	**21-07-013**

Word	Tag	Frequency
survey (cont.):		
survey	VB	3-03-003
surveys	VBZ	1-01-001
surveyed	VBD	2-02-002
surveyed	VBN	6-02-004
surveyed	VBN-HL	1-01-001
surveying	VBG	7-02-003
surveying	VBG-HL	1-01-001
survey-type	**JJ**	**2-01-001**
surveyor	**NN**	**5-04-004**
survivability	**NN**	**1-01-001**
survival	**noun**	**33-09-024**
survival	NN	29-09-022
survival	NN-HL	1-01-001
Survival	NN-TL	2-02-002
survivals	NNS	1-01-001
survivalist	**noun**	**3-01-001**
survivalist	NN	1-01-001
survivalists	NNS	2-01-001
survive	**verb**	**62-14-048**
survive	VB	33-13-027
survives	VBZ	1-01-001
survived	VBD	5-05-005
survived	VBN	9-07-009
surviving	VBG	13-06-010
Surviving	VBG-TL	1-01-001
survivor	**noun**	**15-05-012**
survivor	NN	1-01-001
survivors	NNS	13-05-010
survivors'	NNS$	1-01-001
Susan	**prop. noun**	**39-06-008**
Susan	NP	37-06-008
Susan's	NP$	2-01-001
susceptibility	**NN**	**2-01-002**
susceptible	**JJ**	**6-06-006**
sushi	**FW-NN**	**2-02-002**
Susie	**prop. noun**	**6-02-002**
Susie	NP	4-01-001
Susie	NP-TL	1-01-001
Susie's	NP$	1-01-001
suspect	**JJ**	**3-02-003**
suspect	**NN**	**7-03-003**
suspect	**verb**	**47-13-043**
suspect	VB	20-10-020
suspects	VBZ	4-03-004
suspected	VBD	12-05-010
suspected	VBN	9-08-009
suspecting	VBG	2-02-002
suspend	**verb**	**33-11-021**
suspend	VB	3-02-003
suspended	VBD	1-01-001
suspended	VBN	29-10-017
suspender	**noun**	**1-01-001**
suspenders	NNS	1-01-001
suspense	**NN**	**6-05-006**
suspension	**noun**	**14-05-011**
suspension	NN	12-05-009
suspensions	NNS	2-02-002
suspensor	**NN**	**2-01-001**
suspicion	**noun**	**34-11-028**
suspicion	NN	27-10-025
suspicions	NNS	7-05-006
suspicious	**JJ**	**13-09-012**
suspiciously	**RB**	**4-03-004**
Sussex	**prop. noun**	**2-02-002**
Sussex	NP	1-01-001
Sussex	NP-TL	1-01-001
sustain	**verb**	**32-10-027**
sustain	VB	14-08-012
sustains	VBZ	1-01-001
sustained	VBD	1-01-001
sustained	VBN	14-05-013
sustaining	VBG	2-02-002
sustenance	**NN**	**3-02-003**
Sut	**NP**	**1-01-001**
Sutherland	**NP**	**6-02-002**
Sutpen	**NP**	**1-01-001**
Suvorov	**prop. noun**	**8-01-001**
Suvorov	NP	6-01-001
Suvorov's	NP$	2-01-001
Suzanne	**NP**	**1-01-001**
suzerain	**NN**	**2-01-001**
suzerainty	**NN**	**1-01-001**
Suzuki	**NP**	**1-01-001**
svelte	**JJ**	**1-01-001**
Svenskarna	**foreign**	**1-01-001**
Svenskarna	FW-NPS	0-00-000
Svenskarna	FW-NPS-TL	1-01-001
Svevo	**NP**	**1-01-001**

Word	Tag	Frequency
swab	**verb**	**1-01-001**
swabbed	VBD	1-01-001
Swadesh	**prop. noun**	**10-01-001**
Swadesh	NP	8-01-001
Swadesh's	NP$	2-01-001
swagger	**verb**	**4-03-004**
swaggered	VBD	3-02-003
swaggering	VBG	1-01-001
Swahili	**NP**	**1-01-001**
swallow	**noun**	**7-04-007**
swallow	NN	4-03-004
Swallow	NN-TL	1-01-001
swallows	NNS	2-02-002
swallow	**verb**	**20-10-019**
swallow	VB	5-05-005
swallowed	VBD	6-05-006
swallowed	VBN	6-05-006
swallowing	VBG	3-02-003
Swallow-Barn	**NP**	**1-01-001**
swami	**NN**	**1-01-001**
swamp	**noun**	**7-03-003**
swamp	NN	5-02-002
swamps	NNS	2-01-001
swamp	**verb**	**2-02-002**
swamped	VBD	1-01-001
swamping	VBG	1-01-001
swampy	**JJ**	**1-01-001**
swan	**noun**	**4-04-004**
swan	NN	2-02-002
Swan	NN-TL	1-01-001
swans	NNS	1-01-001
swank	**JJ**	**1-01-001**
swanky	**JJ**	**1-01-001**
swanlike	**JJ**	**1-01-001**
swap	**VB**	**2-02-002**
swarm	**noun**	**3-03-003**
swarm	NN	2-02-002
swarms	NNS	1-01-001
swarm	**verb**	**7-05-007**
swarm	VB	1-01-001
swarmed	VBD	3-03-003
swarming	VBG	3-03-003
swart	**JJ**	**1-01-001**
swarthy	**JJ**	**4-02-003**
Swartz	**prop. noun**	**1-01-001**
Swartz	NP	0-00-000
Swartz	NP-TL	1-01-001
swastika	**NN**	**1-01-001**
swatch	**noun**	**3-02-002**
swatches	NNS	3-02-002
swath	**NN**	**1-01-001**
swathe	**verb**	**1-01-001**
swathed	VBN	1-01-001
swathing	**noun**	**1-01-001**
swathings	NNS	1-01-001
sway	**NN**	**4-03-003**
sway	**verb**	**13-08-010**
sway	VB	1-01-001
swayed	VBD	7-04-006
swayed	VBN	2-02-002
swaying	VBG	3-03-003
sway-backed	**JJ**	**1-01-001**
swear	**verb**	**33-07-025**
swear	VB	10-04-009
swears	VBZ	2-02-002
swore	VBD	14-05-010
sworn	VBN	5-03-005
swearing	VBG	2-02-002
swearing	**noun**	**2-02-002**
swearing	NN	1-01-001
swearinge	NN	1-01-001
swearing-in	**NN**	**1-01-001**
sweat	**NN**	**22-06-018**
sweat	**verb**	**6-04-006**
sweat	VB	1-01-001
sweated	VBD	1-01-001
sweating	VBG	4-04-004
sweat-saturated	**JJ**	**1-01-001**
sweat-soaked	**JJ**	**1-01-001**
sweat-suit	**noun**	**1-01-001**
sweat-suits	NNS	1-01-001
sweatband	**NN**	**1-01-001**
sweater	**noun**	**18-07-008**
sweater	NN	14-05-006
sweaters	NNS	4-04-004
sweathruna	**foreign**	**1-01-001**
sweathruna	FW-NN	0-00-000
sweathruna	FW-NN-NC	1-01-001
sweatshirt	**NN**	**2-01-001**

Word	Tag	Frequency
sweaty	**JJ**	**5-03-004**
Sweazey	**NP**	**1-01-001**
Swede	**prop. noun**	**2-01-001**
Swedes	NPS	2-01-001
Sweden	**prop. noun**	**13-03-005**
Sweden	NP	10-02-004
Sweden's	NP$	3-02-002
Swedish	**JJ**	**7-02-002**
Sweeney	**prop. noun**	**7-01-001**
Sweeney	NP	3-01-001
Sweeney	NP-TL	1-01-001
Sweeneys	NPS	3-01-001
sweep	**NN**	**8-07-008**
sweep	**verb**	**54-13-046**
sweep	VB	7-05-007
swept	VBD	19-09-016
swept	VBN	15-08-013
sweeping	VBG	13-09-013
sweeping	**noun**	**1-01-001**
sweepings	NNS	1-01-001
sweepingly	**RB**	**1-01-001**
sweepstake	**noun**	**2-01-002**
sweepstakes	NNS	1-01-001
Sweepstakes	NNS-TL	1-01-001
sweet	**adjective**	**68-11-038**
sweet	JJ	65-10-036
sweet	JJ-NC	2-01-001
Sweet	JJ-TL	1-01-001
sweet	**noun**	**2-02-002**
sweets	NNS	2-02-002
sweet	**RB**	**1-01-001**
sweet-clover	**NN**	**1-01-001**
sweet-faced	**JJ**	**1-01-001**
sweet-shrub	**NN**	**1-01-001**
sweet-smelling	**JJ**	**2-02-002**
sweet-sounding	**JJ**	**1-01-001**
sweet-sour	**adjective**	**3-01-001**
sweet-sour	JJ	2-01-001
sweet-sour	JJ-HL	1-01-001
sweet-throated	**JJ**	**1-01-001**
sweet-tongued	**JJ**	**1-01-001**
sweeter	**JJR**	**2-01-002**
sweetest	**JJT**	**2-01-002**
sweetheart	**noun**	**10-06-006**
sweetheart	NN	9-06-006
sweethearts	NNS	1-01-001
sweetheart-secretary	**NN**	**1-01-001**
sweetish	**JJ**	**1-01-001**
sweetly	**RB**	**6-04-006**
Sweetmite	**NP**	**1-01-001**
sweetness	**NN**	**3-03-003**
sweetpea	**noun**	**1-01-001**
sweetpeas	NNS	1-01-001
swell	**JJ**	**3-02-003**
swell	**noun**	**5-03-003**
swell	NN	1-01-001
swells	NNS	4-03-003
swell	**verb**	**20-09-019**
swell	VB	3-03-003
swelled	VBD	3-03-003
swollen	VBN	4-03-004
swelling	VBG	9-04-009
swelling	VBG-HL	1-01-001
swelling	**noun**	**3-02-002**
swelling	NN	1-01-001
swellings	NNS	2-01-001
swelter	**verb**	**1-01-001**
sweltering	VBG	1-01-001
swerve	**NN**	**1-01-001**
swerve	**verb**	**5-05-005**
swerve	VB	1-01-001
swerved	VBD	2-02-002
swerving	VBG	2-02-002
swift	**JJ**	**13-10-013**
Swift	**prop. noun**	**22-04-006**
Swift	NP	19-04-005
Swift	NP-TL	1-01-001
Swift's	NP$	2-01-002
swift-footed	**JJ**	**1-01-001**
swift-striding	**JJ**	**1-01-001**
swiftest	**JJT**	**1-01-001**
swiftly	**RB**	**15-07-013**
swiftness	**NN**	**1-01-001**
swig	**NN**	**2-02-002**
swim	**NN**	**1-01-001**
swim	**verb**	**55-11-029**
swim	VB	10-06-007
Swim	VB-TL	1-01-001
swam	VBD	6-03-005

swim (cont.):		
swum	VBN	1-01-001
swimming	VBG	37-09-020
Swim	**prop. noun**	**3-01-001**
Swim	NP	2-01-001
Swim	NP-HL	1-01-001
swimmer	**noun**	**3-01-001**
swimmers	NNS	2-01-001
swimmers'	NNS$	1-01-001
swimsuit	**NN**	**1-01-001**
Swinburne	**NP**	**2-02-002**
swindle	**verb**	**2-02-002**
swindled	VBD	1-01-001
swindling	VBG	1-01-001
swine	**NNS**	**3-02-002**
swing	**noun**	**13-08-011**
swing	NN	8-05-007
Swing	NN-TL	2-01-001
swings	NNS	3-03-003
swing	**verb**	**77-11-052**
swing	VB	11-07-011
swung	VBD	43-10-029
swung	VBN	5-04-005
swinging	VBG	16-07-014
swingin'	VBG	1-01-001
swingin'	VBG-HL	1-01-001
Swing	**NP**	**3-01-001**
swingy	**JJ**	**1-01-001**
swipe	**NN**	**2-02-002**
swipe	**verb**	**2-02-002**
swiped	VBD	1-01-001
swiping	VBG	1-01-001
swirl	**NN**	**2-02-002**
swirl	**verb**	**9-05-008**
swirled	VBD	5-03-005
swirling	VBG	4-03-003
swish	**verb**	**4-02-004**
swished	VBD	3-02-003
swished	VBN	1-01-001
Swiss	**JJ**	**9-05-006**
Swiss	**prop. noun**	**5-02-002**
Swiss	NPS	5-02-002
Swiss-born	**JJ**	**1-01-001**
switch	**noun**	**63-09-016**
switch	NN	37-09-014
Switch	NN-TL	1-01-001
switches	NNS	23-03-003
Switches	NNS	1-01-001
switches	NNS-HL	1-01-001
switch	**verb**	**28-12-019**
switch	VB	5-04-004
switches	VBZ	1-01-001
switched	VBD	10-06-007
switched	VBN	6-03-005
switching	VBG	6-04-006
switch-hitter	**NN**	**1-01-001**
switchblade	**NN**	**1-01-001**
switchboard	**NN**	**1-01-001**
switchgear	**noun**	**2-01-001**
switchgear	NN	1-01-001
Switchgear	NN-TL	1-01-001
switching	**NN**	**1-01-001**
Switzer	**NP**	**1-01-001**
Switzerland	**NP**	**12-04-010**
swivel	**JJ**	**1-01-001**
swivel	**NN**	**3-02-003**
swivel	**verb**	**2-02-002**
swivel	VB	1-01-001
swivels	VBZ	1-01-001
swollen	**JJ**	**8-04-007**
swollen-looking	**JJ**	**1-01-001**
swoop	**noun**	**3-03-003**
swoop	NN	2-02-002
swoops	NNS	1-01-001
swoop	**verb**	**9-06-008**
swoops	VBZ	1-01-001
swooped	VBD	4-04-004
swooped	VBN	1-01-001
swooping	VBG	3-02-003
sword	**noun**	**12-06-011**
sword	NN	6-06-006
sworde	NN	1-01-001
Sword	NN-TL	1-01-001
swords	NNS	4-03-004
Sybert	**NP**	**1-01-001**
Sybil	**NP**	**2-01-001**
sycophant	**noun**	**1-01-001**
sycophants	NNS	1-01-001
sycophantic	**JJ**	**1-01-001**

sycophantically	**RB**	**1-01-001**
Sydney	**NP**	**5-03-005**
syllabicity	**noun**	**2-01-001**
syllabicity	NN	1-01-001
Syllabicity	NN-TL	1-01-001
syllabification	**noun**	**1-01-001**
syllabification	NN	0-00-000
syllabification	NN-HL	1-01-001
syllable	**noun**	**10-01-002**
syllable	NN	1-01-001
syllables	NNS	9-01-002
Sylphide	**NP**	**1-01-001**
sylvan	**JJ**	**1-01-001**
Sylvania	**NP**	**2-01-001**
Sylvie	**prop. noun**	**1-01-001**
Sylvie	NP	0-00-000
Sylvie	NP-TL	1-01-001
symbol	**noun**	**90-13-050**
symbol	NN	54-13-035
symbols	NNS	31-08-018
symbols	NNS-HL	5-01-001
symbolic	**JJ**	**35-05-013**
symbolic-sounding	**JJ**	**1-01-001**
symbolical	**JJ**	**1-01-001**
symbolically	**RB**	**5-03-005**
symbolism	**NN**	**8-04-007**
symbolist	**noun**	**1-01-001**
symbolists	NNS	1-01-001
symbolize	**verb**	**25-07-018**
symbolize	VB	9-04-008
symbolizes	VBZ	3-02-003
symbolized	VBD	6-05-006
symbolized	VBN	5-03-004
symbolizing	VBG	2-01-001
Symes	**prop. noun**	**1-01-001**
Symes's	NP$	1-01-001
Symington	**NP**	**2-02-002**
symmetric	**JJ**	**7-01-001**
symmetrical	**JJ**	**2-02-002**
symmetrically	**RB**	**1-01-001**
symmetry	**NN**	**7-03-003**
Symonds	**NP**	**1-01-001**
sympathetic	**JJ**	**35-09-024**
sympathetically	**RB**	**5-03-005**
sympathique	**FW-JJ**	**1-01-001**
sympathize	**verb**	**9-06-009**
sympathize	VB	7-06-007
sympathized	VBD	1-01-001
sympathizing	VBG	1-01-001
sympathy	**noun**	**44-11-031**
sympathy	NN	35-11-024
Sympathy	NN-TL	1-01-001
sympathies	NNS	8-05-007
symphonic	**JJ**	**7-03-003**
symphony	**noun**	**37-09-019**
symphony	NN	10-07-010
Symphony	NN-TL	23-05-011
symphony's	NN$	1-01-001
symphonies	NNS	3-03-003
symposium	**noun**	**9-02-005**
symposium	NN	2-01-002
symposium	NN-HL	1-01-001
Symposium	NN-TL	6-01-003
symptom	**noun**	**19-07-012**
symptom	NN	5-03-004
symptoms	NNS	14-07-009
symptomatic	**JJ**	**7-04-006**
synagogue	**noun**	**5-04-005**
synagogue	NN	3-02-003
synagogues	NNS	2-02-002
synapse	**noun**	**1-01-001**
synapses	NNS	1-01-001
synchronism	**NN**	**1-01-001**
synchronize	**verb**	**3-03-003**
synchronize	VB	1-01-001
synchronized	VBN	2-02-002
synchronizer	**noun**	**2-01-001**
synchronizers	NNS	2-01-001
synchronous	**JJ**	**2-02-002**
synchrony	**NN**	**2-01-001**
syndic	**noun**	**1-01-001**
syndic	NN	0-00-000
Syndic	NN-TL	1-01-001
syndicate	**noun**	**8-05-007**
syndicate	NN	5-03-005
Syndicate	NN-TL	1-01-001
syndicate's	NN$	1-01-001
syndicates	NNS	1-01-001
syndicate	**verb**	**2-02-002**

syndicate (cont.):		
syndicated	VBN	1-01-001
Syndicated	VBN-TL	1-01-001
syndication	**NN**	**1-01-001**
syndrome	**NN**	**2-01-002**
synergism	**NN**	**1-01-001**
synergistic	**JJ**	**1-01-001**
synod	**noun**	**1-01-001**
synod	NN	0-00-000
Synod	NN-TL	1-01-001
synonym	**noun**	**6-04-005**
synonym	NN	3-03-003
synonyms	NNS	3-02-002
synonymous	**JJ**	**4-03-004**
synonymy	**NN**	**1-01-001**
syntactic	**JJ**	**1-01-001**
syntactical	**JJ**	**1-01-001**
syntactically	**RB**	**1-01-001**
syntax	**NN**	**6-03-005**
synthesis	**noun**	**16-03-009**
synthesis	NN	15-03-009
synthesis	NN-HL	1-01-001
synthesize	**verb**	**5-03-005**
synthesize	VB	1-01-001
synthesizes	VBZ	1-01-001
synthesized	VBN	2-01-002
synthesised	VBN	1-01-001
synthesizine	**NN**	**1-01-001**
synthetic	**adjective**	**12-02-007**
synthetic	JJ	10-02-007
synthetic	JJ-HL	1-01-001
Synthetic	JJ-TL	1-01-001
synthetic	**noun**	**1-01-001**
synthetics	NNS	1-01-001
Syracuse	**NP**	**1-01-001**
Syria	**NP**	**2-02-002**
Syrian	**JJ**	**1-01-001**
Syrian	**prop. noun**	**1-01-001**
Syrians	NPS	1-01-001
syringa	**NN**	**1-01-001**
syringe	**NN**	**1-01-001**
syrup	**NN**	**4-03-003**
syrupy	**JJ**	**2-02-002**
system	**noun**	**548-15-148**
system	NN	392-14-130
system	NN-HL	1-01-001
System	NN-TL	23-06-011
system's	NN$	2-01-001
System's	NN$-TL	1-01-001
systems	NNS	126-12-051
systems	NNS-HL	1-01-001
Systems	NNS-TL	2-02-002
systematic	**JJ**	**18-04-013**
systematically	**QL**	**1-01-001**
systematically	**RB**	**9-06-009**
systematically-simple	**JJ**	**1-01-001**
systematization	**NN**	**1-01-001**
systematize	**verb**	**4-03-004**
systematized	VBN	2-02-002
systematizing	VBG	2-02-002
systeme	**foreign**	**1-01-001**
systeme	FW-NN	0-00-000
Systeme	FW-NN-TL	1-01-001
systemic	**adjective**	**3-01-001**
systemic	JJ	2-01-001
systemic	JJ-HL	1-01-001
systemization	**NN**	**1-01-001**
Szelenyi	**NP**	**1-01-001**
Szold	**prop. noun**	**17-01-001**
Szold	NP	11-01-001
Szolds	NPS	4-01-001
Szolds'	NPS$	2-01-001

T

T	**NP**	**36-02-007**
T.	**NP**	**27-09-025**
T.B.	**NP**	**1-01-001**
T.W.	**NP**	**2-01-001**
T'ai-Shan	**NP**	**1-01-001**
T'ien	**NP**	**1-01-001**
tab	**NN**	**1-01-001**
tab-lifter	**NN**	**1-01-001**
tabac	**NN**	**1-01-001**
Tabb	**NP**	**1-01-001**
Tabellen	**foreign**	**1-01-001**
Tabellen	FW-NNS	0-00-000
Tabellen	FW-NNS-TL	1-01-001
tabernacle	**noun**	**2-02-002**
tabernacle	NN	0-00-000
Tabernacle	NN-TL	1-01-001
tabernacles	NNS	1-01-001
Tabit	**NP**	**1-01-001**
table	**noun**	**242-15-118**
table	NN	147-14-089
Table	NN-TL	50-05-020
table's	NN$	1-01-001
tables	NNS	39-10-026
Tables	NNS-TL	5-01-003
table	**VB**	**1-01-001**
table-tennis	**NN**	**1-01-001**
table-top	**NN**	**1-01-001**
tableau	**NN**	**1-01-001**
tablecloth	**noun**	**1-01-001**
tablecloths	NNS	1-01-001
tableland	**NN**	**1-01-001**
tablespoon	**noun**	**13-02-003**
tablespoon	NN	6-02-002
tablespoons	NNS	7-01-002
tablespoonful	**noun**	**4-01-001**
tablespoonful	NN	3-01-001
tablespoonfuls	NNS	1-01-001
tablet	**noun**	**4-03-003**
tablet	NN	3-02-002
tablets	NNS	1-01-001
tabloid	**noun**	**1-01-001**
tabloids	NNS	1-01-001
taboo	**JJ**	**2-01-002**
taboo	**noun**	**2-02-002**
taboo (cont.):		
taboo	NN	1-01-001
taboos	NNS	1-01-001
tabula	**FW-NN**	**2-01-001**
tabulate	**verb**	**5-03-005**
tabulate	VB	1-01-001
tabulated	VBD	1-01-001
tabulated	VBN	3-02-003
tabulation	**noun**	**4-01-004**
tabulation	NN	2-01-002
tabulations	NNS	2-01-002
tacit	**JJ**	**2-02-002**
tacitly	**RB**	**2-02-002**
Tacitus	**NP**	**1-01-001**
tack	**NN**	**4-02-003**
tack	**verb**	**4-04-004**
tacked	VBD	1-01-001
tacked	VBN	1-01-001
tacking	VBG	2-02-002
tack-solder	**VB**	**2-01-001**
tackle	**noun**	**7-04-005**
tackle	NN	5-03-004
Tackle	NN-TL	1-01-001
tackles	NNS	1-01-001
tackle	**VB**	**4-04-004**
Tacloban	**NP**	**2-01-001**
tact	**NN**	**6-04-006**
tactful	**JJ**	**2-01-002**
tactic	**noun**	**24-09-020**
tactic	NN	4-03-004
tactics	NNS	19-08-016
tactics	NNS-HL	1-01-001
tactical	**JJ**	**8-04-006**
tactically	**RB**	**1-01-001**
tactile	**JJ**	**2-01-001**
tactlessness	**NN**	**1-01-001**
tactual	**JJ**	**8-01-001**
tactually	**RB**	**1-01-001**
tadpole	**noun**	**1-01-001**
tadpoles	NNS	1-01-001
taffeta	**NN**	**2-01-001**
taffy	**NN**	**1-01-001**
taffycolored	**JJ**	**1-01-001**
Taft	**NP**	**1-01-001**

Word	Tag	Frequency
Taft-Hartley	**prop. noun**	**3-02-002**
Taft-Hartley	NP	1-01-001
Taft-Hartley	NP-TL	2-02-002
tag	**noun**	**6-04-004**
tag	NN	5-04-004
tags	NNS	1-01-001
tag	**verb**	**7-06-006**
tagged	VBD	1-01-001
tagged	VBN	5-05-005
tagging	VBG	1-01-001
tagua	**NN**	**1-01-001**
Tahiti	**NP**	**2-02-002**
Tahoe	**prop. noun**	**4-03-003**
Tahoe	NP	2-02-002
Tahoe	NP-TL	2-02-002
Tahse	**prop. noun**	**2-01-001**
Tahse	NP	1-01-001
Tahse's	NP$	1-01-001
Tai	**prop. noun**	**1-01-001**
Tai	NP	0-00-000
Tai	NP-TL	1-01-001
tail	**noun**	**31-11-019**
tail	NN	24-10-015
tails	NNS	7-04-004
tailback	**NN**	**1-01-001**
tailgate	**NN**	**2-01-002**
tailing	**noun**	**4-01-001**
tailing	NN	0-00-000
tailin'	NN	3-01-001
tailings	NNS	0-00-000
tailin's	NNS	0-00-000
tailin's	NNS-NC	1-01-001
tailor	**NN**	**2-02-002**
tailor	**verb**	**9-07-009**
tailored	VBN	9-07-009
tailor-make	**verb**	**4-03-004**
tailor-make	VB	1-01-001
tailor-made	VBN	3-03-003
taint	**NN**	**1-01-001**
taint	**verb**	**1-01-001**
tainted	VBN	1-01-001
Taipei	**NP**	**1-01-001**
Taiwan	**NP**	**7-02-002**
take	**NN**	**4-03-004**
take	**verb**	**1575-15-449**
take	VB	605-15-296
take	VB-HL	1-01-001
takes	VBZ	85-14-077
takes	VBZ-HL	1-01-001
took	VBD	426-15-227
tooke	VBD	2-01-001
taken	VBN	281-15-198
taking	VBG	170-15-141
takin	VBG	2-02-002
takin'	VBG	2-02-002
take-up	**adjective**	**4-01-001**
take-up	JJ	3-01-001
take-up	JJ-HL	1-01-001
takeoff	**noun**	**8-03-004**
takeoff	NN	2-02-002
take-off	NN	4-03-004
takeoffs	NNS	2-01-001
takeover	**NN**	**2-02-002**
taking	**noun**	**7-04-007**
taking	NN	4-04-004
takeing	NN	1-01-001
takings	NNS	2-02-002
Taksim	**prop. noun**	**1-01-001**
Taksim	NP	0-00-000
Taksim	NP-TL	1-01-001
Talbott	**prop. noun**	**1-01-001**
Talbott's	NP$	1-01-001
tale	**noun**	**41-11-031**
tale	NN	21-10-015
tales	NNS	19-07-016
Tales	NNS-TL	1-01-001
talent	**noun**	**68-12-053**
talent	NN	39-12-031
talent	NN-HL	1-01-001
talents	NNS	28-09-024
talented	**JJ**	**7-03-007**
Taliesin	**NP**	**11-01-001**
talismanic	**JJ**	**1-01-001**
talk	**noun**	**55-12-046**
talk	NN	40-12-035
talks	NNS	15-05-013
talk	**verb**	**275-15-149**
talk	VB	114-15-081
talks	VBZ	3-03-003

Word	Tag	Frequency
talk (cont.):		
talked	VBD	41-12-036
talked	VBN	17-09-015
talking	VBG	99-14-078
talkin'	VBG	1-01-001
talk-aboutiveness	**NN**	**1-01-001**
talkative	**JJ**	**4-03-004**
talker	**NN**	**1-01-001**
talking	**NN**	**1-01-001**
talky	**JJ**	**1-01-001**
tall	**JJ**	**55-10-045**
tall-growing	**JJ**	**1-01-001**
tall-masted	**JJ**	**1-01-001**
tall-tale	**NN**	**1-01-001**
Tallahassee	**NP**	**1-01-001**
Tallahoosa	**prop. noun**	**1-01-001**
Tallahoosa	NP	0-00-000
Tallahoosa	NP-TL	1-01-001
Tallchief	**NP**	**1-01-001**
taller	**JJR**	**7-03-006**
Talleyrand	**NP**	**1-01-001**
tallow	**NN**	**1-01-001**
tally	**noun**	**4-01-003**
tally	NN	2-01-002
tallies	NNS	2-01-002
tally	**VB**	**2-02-002**
tallyho	**NN**	**7-01-001**
Talmud	**NP**	**4-03-003**
talon	**noun**	**1-01-001**
talons	NNS	1-01-001
tam-o'-shanter	**NN**	**1-01-001**
tamale	**NN**	**1-01-001**
tambourine	**NN**	**2-02-002**
tame	**JJ**	**4-03-004**
tame	**verb**	**2-02-002**
tame	VB	1-01-001
taming	VBG	1-01-001
Tamiris	**prop. noun**	**3-01-001**
Tamiris	NP	1-01-001
Tamiris'	NP$	2-01-001
Tammany	**prop. noun**	**7-02-002**
Tammany	NP	4-02-002
Tammany	NP-TL	3-02-002
tamp	**VB**	**1-01-001**
tamper	**verb**	**3-02-003**
tamper	VB	1-01-001
tampering	VBG	2-02-002
tan	**JJ**	**5-04-005**
tan	**noun**	**3-03-003**
tan	NN	2-02-002
Tan	NN-TL	1-01-001
tan	**verb**	**7-03-005**
tan	VB	0-00-000
Tan	VB-TL	1-01-001
tanned	VBN	6-02-004
tandem	**NN**	**1-01-001**
Taney	**prop. noun**	**1-01-001**
Taney's	NP$	1-01-001
tang	**NN**	**4-02-004**
Tanganika	**NP**	**1-01-001**
tangency	**NN**	**3-01-001**
tangent	**JJ**	**22-01-002**
tangent	**noun**	**10-01-001**
tangent	NN	4-01-001
tangents	NNS	6-01-001
tangential	**JJ**	**1-01-001**
tangere	**FW-VB**	**1-01-001**
tangible	**JJ**	**19-07-009**
tangibly	**QL**	**1-01-001**
tangle	**NN**	**7-06-006**
tangle	**verb**	**6-04-006**
tangle	VB	1-01-001
tangled	VBD	1-01-001
tangled	VBN	4-02-004
tango	**noun**	**3-03-003**
tango	NN	2-02-002
tangos	NNS	1-01-001
tangy	**JJ**	**1-01-001**
tanin	**FW-NNS**	**1-01-001**
tank	**noun**	**30-10-019**
tank	NN	12-08-010
tanks	NNS	18-07-011
tanker	**noun**	**2-02-002**
tankers	NNS	2-02-002
Tanker	**NP**	**1-01-001**
Tannenbaum	**NP**	**1-01-001**
Tanner	**NP**	**2-01-001**
Tannhaeuser	**prop. noun**	**2-01-001**
Tannhaeuser	NP	0-00-000

Word	Tag	Frequency
Tannhaeuser (cont.):		
Tannhaeuser	NP-TL	2-01-001
tannin	**NN**	**1-01-001**
Tanny	**NP**	**1-01-001**
tansy	**NN**	**1-01-001**
tantalize	**verb**	**4-04-004**
tantalizing	VBG	4-04-004
tantalizingly	**RB**	**1-01-001**
tantamount	**JJ**	**3-02-002**
tantrum	**noun**	**4-03-004**
tantrum	NN	2-02-002
tantrums	NNS	2-02-002
Tao	**NP**	**4-01-002**
Taoism	**NP**	**4-02-002**
Taoist	**JJ**	**3-01-001**
Taoist	**prop. noun**	**2-01-001**
Taoists	NPS	2-01-001
Taos	**NP**	**1-01-001**
tap	**noun**	**9-07-008**
tap	NN	8-06-007
taps	NNS	1-01-001
tap	**verb**	**19-10-013**
tap	VB	10-04-005
tapped	VBD	2-02-002
tapped	VBN	5-05-005
tapping	VBG	1-01-001
tapping	VBG-HL	1-01-001
tapdance	**NN**	**1-01-001**
tape	**noun**	**39-09-016**
tape	NN	31-08-013
Tape	NN-TL	4-02-002
tapes	NNS	4-02-003
tape	**verb**	**1-01-001**
taped	VBN	1-01-001
taper	**NN**	**2-02-002**
taper	**verb**	**10-06-009**
taper	VB	1-01-001
tapered	VBN	7-04-006
tapering	VBG	2-02-002
tapestry	**noun**	**7-05-005**
tapestry	NN	5-04-004
tapestries	NNS	2-02-002
tapis	**NN**	**1-01-001**
Tapley	**NP**	**1-01-001**
Tappan	**NP**	**2-01-001**
tappet	**noun**	**28-01-001**
tappet	NN	15-01-001
tappets	NNS	12-01-001
tappets	NNS-HL	1-01-001
tapping	**NN**	**4-03-003**
tar	**noun**	**12-02-003**
tar	NN	2-02-002
Tar	NN-TL	10-01-001
tar	**verb**	**1-01-001**
tarred	VBN	1-01-001
tar-soaked	**JJ**	**1-01-001**
Tara	**prop. noun**	**1-01-001**
Tara	NP	0-00-000
Tara	NP-TL	1-01-001
Taraday	**NP**	**1-01-001**
tarantara	**UH**	**1-01-001**
Taras	**prop. noun**	**4-02-003**
Taras	NP	2-02-002
Taras	NP-TL	2-01-001
tardily	**RB**	**1-01-001**
tardiness	**NN**	**1-01-001**
tardy	**JJ**	**1-01-001**
Tareytown	**prop. noun**	**1-01-001**
Tareytown	NP	0-00-000
Tareytown	NP-TL	1-01-001
target	**noun**	**68-11-029**
target	NN	45-11-025
target's	NN$	1-01-001
targets	NNS	22-07-009
target-hunting	**JJ**	**1-01-001**
target-language	**NN**	**1-01-001**
Targo	**NP**	**3-01-001**
Tarheelia	**NP**	**1-01-001**
tariff	**NN**	**5-05-005**
tariff-free	**JJ**	**1-01-001**
Tarkington	**NP**	**1-01-001**
tarnish	**verb**	**3-03-003**
tarnished	VBN	3-03-003
tarpaper	**verb**	**1-01-001**
tarpapered	VBN	1-01-001
tarpaulin	**noun**	**2-02-002**
tarpaulin	NN	1-01-001
tarpaulins	NNS	1-01-001
tarpon	**NN**	**1-01-001**
Tarrant	**NP**	**1-01-001**
tarry	**VB**	**1-01-001**
tart	**JJ**	**6-03-006**
tart	**NN**	**1-01-001**
Tartar	**NP**	**1-01-001**
Tartarughe	**NP**	**1-01-001**
Tartary	**NP**	**2-01-001**
tartly	**RB**	**1-01-001**
Tartuffe	**prop. noun**	**4-01-001**
Tartuffe	NP	3-01-001
Tartuffe	NP-TL	1-01-001
Taruffi	**NP**	**1-01-001**
Tarzan	**NP**	**4-01-001**
task	**noun**	**89-13-062**
task	NN	58-13-048
task	NN-HL	1-01-001
Task	NN-TL	1-01-001
tasks	NNS	29-08-019
taskmaster	**NN**	**1-01-001**
Tasmania	**NP**	**2-02-002**
TASS	**NP**	**1-01-001**
tassel	**noun**	**1-01-001**
tassels	NNS	1-01-001
Tasso	**NP**	**1-01-001**
taste	**noun**	**60-12-047**
taste	NN	53-12-040
Taste	NN-TL	1-01-001
tastes	NNS	5-05-005
Tastes	NNS-TL	1-01-001
taste	**verb**	**22-10-019**
taste	VB	5-05-005
tastes	VBZ	4-03-004
tasted	VBD	7-06-007
tasted	VBN	3-03-003
tasting	VBG	2-01-002
tasting	VBG-HL	1-01-001
tasteful	**JJ**	**2-02-002**
tasteless	**JJ**	**1-01-001**
Tasti-Freeze	**NP**	**1-01-001**
tasty	**JJ**	**2-01-001**
tat	**VB**	**1-01-001**
Tate	**prop. noun**	**2-02-002**
Tate	NP	1-01-001
Tate	NP-TL	1-01-001
Tatian	**NP**	**1-01-001**
Tatler	**prop. noun**	**1-01-001**
Tatler	NP	0-00-000
Tatler	NP-TL	1-01-001
Tatra	**prop. noun**	**1-01-001**
Tatras	NPS	1-01-001
tatter	**verb**	**5-04-004**
tattered	VBN	5-04-004
tattle-tale	**NN**	**1-01-001**
tattoo	**verb**	**1-01-001**
tattooed	VBN	1-01-001
Tau	**NP**	**1-01-001**
Taui	**NP**	**1-01-001**
taunt	**noun**	**5-05-005**
taunt	NN	3-03-003
taunts	NNS	2-02-002
taunt	**verb**	**4-04-004**
taunt	VB	1-01-001
taunted	VBD	1-01-001
taunted	VBN	1-01-001
taunting	VBG	1-01-001
tauntingly	**RB**	**1-01-001**
Taurida	**NP**	**1-01-001**
Taurog	**NP**	**2-01-001**
Taussig	**NP**	**2-01-002**
taut	**JJ**	**7-05-006**
taut	**RB**	**1-01-001**
taut-nerved	**JJ**	**1-01-001**
tavern	**noun**	**6-06-006**
tavern	NN	2-02-002
taverns	NNS	4-04-004
tawdry	**JJ**	**2-02-002**
Tawes	**NP**	**2-01-001**
Tawney	**NP**	**1-01-001**
tawny	**JJ**	**4-03-004**
tax	**noun**	**241-10-046**
tax	NN	181-10-039
tax	NN-HL	6-02-005
Tax	NN-TL	9-02-005
taxes	NNS	43-08-024
taxes	NNS-HL	1-01-001
Taxes	NNS-TL	1-01-001
tax	**verb**	**27-06-008**
tax	VB	5-02-002
taxed	VBD	1-01-001

Word	Tag	Frequency
tax (cont.):		
taxed	VBN	12-03-004
taxing	VBG	6-04-004
taxing	VBG-HL	3-02-002
tax-aided	**JJ**	**1-01-001**
tax-avoidance	**NN**	**1-01-001**
tax-exempt	**JJ**	**6-02-004**
tax-exemption	**NN**	**2-01-001**
tax-free	**adjective**	**9-02-003**
tax-free	JJ	8-02-003
tax-free	JJ-HL	1-01-001
tax-freedom	**NN**	**1-01-001**
taxable	**adjective**	**8-02-004**
taxable	JJ	7-02-003
Taxable	JJ-TL	1-01-001
taxation	**noun**	**11-04-006**
taxation	NN	10-04-005
Taxation	NN-TL	1-01-001
taxi	**noun**	**19-08-017**
taxi	NN	16-07-015
taxis	NNS	3-03-003
taxi	**verb**	**2-02-002**
taxied	VBD	1-01-001
taxiing	VBG	1-01-001
taxi-way	**noun**	**1-01-001**
taxi-ways	NNS	1-01-001
taxicab	**NN**	**1-01-001**
taxpayer	**noun**	**36-08-020**
taxpayer	NN	11-06-009
taxpayer's	NN$	2-02-002
taxpayers	NNS	21-06-013
taxpayers'	NNS$	2-01-002
taxpaying	**adjective**	**2-01-002**
taxpaying	JJ	1-01-001
tax-paying	JJ	1-01-001
Taylor	**prop. noun**	**24-06-013**
Taylor	NP	17-05-010
Taylor	NP-TL	4-02-002
Taylor's	NP$	2-02-002
Taylors	NPS	1-01-001
Tchaikovsky	**NP**	**3-01-003**
tchalo	**FW-UH**	**1-01-001**
TCU	**prop. noun**	**1-01-001**
TCU's	NP$	1-01-001
tea	**noun**	**29-09-021**
tea	NN	28-09-020
teas	NNS	1-01-001
tea-drinking	**JJ**	**1-01-001**
tea-leaf	**NN**	**1-01-001**
teacart	**NN**	**2-01-001**
teach	**verb**	**153-13-087**
teach	VB	41-11-035
teaches	VBZ	11-08-009
taught	VBD	19-09-017
taught	VBN	31-10-025
teaching	VBG	48-09-028
teaching	VBG-HL	3-02-002
teacher	**noun**	**152-13-052**
teacher	NN	77-11-037
Teacher	NN	1-01-001
teacher	NN-HL	2-01-002
teacher's	NN$	2-02-002
teachers	NNS	67-11-027
Teachers	NNS-TL	2-02-002
teachers'	NNS$	1-01-001
teacher-employee	**NN**	**1-01-001**
teaching	**noun**	**22-07-017**
teaching	NN	15-06-010
Teaching	NN-TL	1-01-001
teachings	NNS	6-04-006
Teagarden	**NP**	**1-01-001**
teahouse	**noun**	**3-02-002**
teahouse	NN	2-02-002
teahouses	NNS	1-01-001
teakettle	**NN**	**1-01-001**
teakwood	**NN**	**1-01-001**
team	**noun**	**108-11-042**
team	NN	81-11-035
Team	NN-TL	2-01-001
team's	NN$	2-01-001
teams	NNS	21-07-012
Teams	NNS	1-01-001
teams'	NNS$	1-01-001
team	**verb**	**3-03-003**
teamed	VBD	2-02-002
teaming	VBG	1-01-001
teammate	**noun**	**7-02-003**
teammate	NN	2-01-001
team-mate	NN	1-01-001
teammate (cont.):		
teammate's	NN$	1-01-001
teammates	NNS	2-01-002
teammates'	NNS$	1-01-001
teamster	**noun**	**9-03-005**
teamster	NN	1-01-001
teamsters	NNS	6-02-004
teamsters	NNS-HL	1-01-001
Teamsters	NNS-TL	1-01-001
teamwork	**NN**	**1-01-001**
tear	**noun**	**36-10-029**
tear	NN	2-01-002
tears	NNS	34-10-027
tear	**verb**	**58-13-044**
tear	VB	9-07-009
tore	VBD	15-08-014
torn	VBN	25-10-021
tearing	VBG	9-05-009
tear-filled	**JJ**	**1-01-001**
tear-soaked	**JJ**	**1-01-001**
teardrop	**NN**	**1-01-001**
tearfully	**RB**	**2-02-002**
Tearle	**NP**	**1-01-001**
tease	**NN**	**2-02-002**
tease	**verb**	**8-05-007**
tease	VB	4-03-003
teased	VBD	2-02-002
teasing	VBG	2-02-002
teasing	**NN**	**1-01-001**
teaspoon	**noun**	**7-01-001**
teaspoon	NN	4-01-001
teaspoons	NNS	3-01-001
teaspoonful	**noun**	**3-02-002**
teaspoonful	NN	2-02-002
teaspoonfuls	NNS	1-01-001
teat	**noun**	**2-01-001**
teats	NNS	2-01-001
Teatro	**NP**	**1-01-001**
Tech	**prop. noun**	**9-03-006**
Tech	NP	8-03-006
Tech's	NP$	1-01-001
Tech.	**NP**	**2-02-002**
technical	**adjective**	**120-13-062**
technical	JJ	117-13-060
technical	JJ-HL	1-01-001
Technical	JJ-TL	2-02-002
technical-ladder	**NN**	**1-01-001**
technicality	**noun**	**2-02-002**
technicalities	NNS	2-02-002
technically	**RB**	**9-07-008**
technician	**noun**	**18-07-014**
technician	NN	5-04-004
Technician	NN-TL	1-01-001
technicians	NNS	10-04-008
Technicians	NNS-TL	2-01-001
technique	**noun**	**159-11-083**
technique	NN	56-09-041
technique	NN-HL	3-01-003
Technique	NN-TL	1-01-001
techniques	NNS	96-11-053
techniques	NNS-HL	2-02-002
Techniques	NNS-TL	1-01-001
technological	**JJ**	**18-04-014**
technologically	**RB**	**1-01-001**
technology	**noun**	**43-08-027**
technology	NN	34-06-020
technology	NN-NC	1-01-001
Technology	NN-TL	8-05-008
tecum	**FW-PPO+IN**	**1-01-001**
Ted	**NP**	**7-03-005**
teddy	**NN**	**2-01-001**
Teddy	**NP**	**2-01-002**
tedious	**JJ**	**6-03-006**
tediously	**RB**	**2-02-002**
tedium	**NN**	**1-01-001**
tee	**noun**	**5-01-002**
tee	NN	4-01-002
Tee	NN-TL	1-01-001
Tee-wah	**NP**	**2-01-001**
teem	**verb**	**2-02-002**
teems	VBZ	1-01-001
teeming	VBG	1-01-001
teen	**noun**	**11-05-006**
teen	NN	2-01-001
Teen	NN-TL	4-01-001
teens	NNS	4-04-004
teens	NNS-HL	1-01-001
teenage	**adjective**	**8-06-008**
teenage	JJ	4-04-004

Word	Tag	Frequency
teenage (cont.):		
teen-age	JJ	4-04-004
teenager	**noun**	**22-08-011**
teenager	NN	2-02-002
teen-ager	NN	2-02-002
teenagers	NNS	5-03-004
teen-agers	NNS	12-04-004
teenagers'	NNS$	0-00-000
teen-agers'	NNS$	1-01-001
teensy	**JJ**	**1-01-001**
teeter	**verb**	**2-02-002**
teetering	VBG	2-02-002
teethe	**verb**	**1-01-001**
teething	VBG	1-01-001
teetotaler	**NN**	**2-02-002**
Teheran	**NP**	**2-01-001**
tektite	**noun**	**6-01-001**
tektite	NN	1-01-001
tektites	NNS	4-01-001
tektites	NNS-HL	1-01-001
Tel	**NP**	**1-01-001**
Telefunken	**NP**	**1-01-001**
telegram	**noun**	**10-04-008**
telegram	NN	8-02-006
telegrams	NNS	2-02-002
telegraph	**noun**	**20-04-006**
telegraph	NN	6-04-004
telegraph	NN-HL	1-01-001
Telegraph	NN-TL	13-02-003
telegraph	**verb**	**4-04-004**
telegraph	VB	1-01-001
telegraphed	VBD	2-02-002
telegraphing	VBG	1-01-001
telegrapher	**noun**	**9-03-003**
telegrapher	NN	3-01-001
telegrapher's	NN$	1-01-001
telegraphers	NNS	4-02-002
Telegraphers	NNS-TL	1-01-001
telegraphic	**JJ**	**3-02-002**
telegraphie	**foreign**	**1-01-001**
telegraphie	FW-NN	0-00-000
Telegraphie	FW-NN-TL	1-01-001
telegraphy	**NN**	**1-01-001**
Telemann	**NP**	**1-01-001**
teleological	**JJ**	**1-01-001**
teleology	**NN**	**1-01-001**
telepathically	**RB**	**1-01-001**
telepathy	**noun**	**3-02-003**
telepathy	NN	2-01-002
telepathy	NN-HL	1-01-001
telephone	**noun**	**79-12-046**
telephone	NN	67-11-043
telephone	NN-HL	1-01-001
Telephone	NN-TL	5-03-003
telephones	NNS	6-03-005
telephone	**verb**	**21-10-015**
telephone	VB	3-03-003
telephoned	VBD	13-06-008
telephoned	VBN	3-02-003
telephoning	VBG	2-02-002
telephone-booth	**NN**	**1-01-001**
telephoning	**NN**	**1-01-001**
Teleprompter	**NP**	**1-01-001**
telescope	**noun**	**4-04-004**
telescope	NN	3-03-003
telescopes	NNS	1-01-001
telescope	**verb**	**4-03-004**
telescope	VB	1-01-001
telescoped	VBN	2-02-002
telescoping	VBG	1-01-001
telescopic	**JJ**	**1-01-001**
teletype	**noun**	**3-03-003**
teletype	NN	2-02-002
teletypes	NNS	0-00-000
Teletypes	NNS	1-01-001
televise	**verb**	**4-03-004**
televised	VBN	4-03-004
television	**noun**	**51-11-037**
television	NN	50-11-036
televison	NN	1-01-001
television-electronics	**noun**	**1-01-001**
television-electronics	NN	0-00-000
Television-Electronics	NN-TL	1-01-001
tell	**verb**	**759-15-263**
tell	VB	262-15-152
tell	VB-NC	5-01-001
Tell	VB-TL	1-01-001
tells	VBZ	34-14-030
told	VBD	286-14-140

Word	Tag	Frequency
tell (cont.):		
tole	VBD	1-01-001
told	VBN	127-15-093
telling	VBG	43-13-037
tell-tale	**JJ**	**3-03-003**
teller	**noun**	**2-02-002**
tellers	NNS	2-02-002
Teller	**NP**	**4-02-002**
Telli	**NP**	**1-01-001**
telling	**JJ**	**4-03-004**
telling	**NN**	**5-03-005**
telomeric	**JJ**	**1-01-001**
temerity	**NN**	**1-01-001**
tempeh	**FW-NN**	**1-01-001**
temper	**noun**	**14-06-012**
temper	NN	12-06-010
tempers	NNS	2-02-002
temper	**verb**	**1-01-001**
tempered	VBN	1-01-001
tempera	**NN**	**1-01-001**
temperament	**NN**	**7-07-007**
temperance	**NN**	**1-01-001**
temperate	**JJ**	**2-02-002**
temperately	**RB**	**1-01-001**
temperature	**noun**	**161-11-036**
temperature	NN	131-09-032
temperature	NN-HL	3-02-002
Temperature	NN-TL	1-01-001
temperatures	NNS	26-06-013
tempest	**noun**	**2-02-002**
tempest	NN	1-01-001
Tempest	NN-TL	1-01-001
template	**NN**	**5-01-001**
temple	**noun**	**41-09-021**
temple	NN	22-07-010
Temple	NN-TL	15-05-010
temples	NNS	4-04-004
Temple	**NP**	**1-01-001**
Templeman	**NP**	**2-01-001**
tempo	**noun**	**6-03-006**
tempo	NN	3-02-003
tempo	NN-HL	1-01-001
tempos	NNS	2-02-002
temporal	**JJ**	**5-02-002**
temporally	**RB**	**1-01-001**
temporarily	**RB**	**20-07-016**
temporary	**adjective**	**32-10-028**
temporary	JJ	31-10-028
Temporary	JJ-TL	1-01-001
tempore	**noun**	**1-01-001**
tempore	NN	0-00-000
tempore	NN-HL	1-01-001
temporize	**VB**	**1-01-001**
tempt	**verb**	**18-08-018**
tempt	VB	2-02-002
tempts	VBZ	1-01-001
tempted	VBN	13-07-013
tempting	VBG	2-01-002
temptation	**noun**	**18-07-013**
temptation	NN	12-07-010
temptations	NNS	6-02-003
tempter	**noun**	**1-01-001**
tempter	NN	0-00-000
Tempter	NN-TL	1-01-001
temptingly	**QL**	**1-01-001**
ten	**card. num.**	**163-15-118**
ten	CD	162-15-117
Ten	CD-TL	1-01-001
ten	**noun**	**1-01-001**
tens	NNS	1-01-001
Ten	**NP**	**1-01-001**
ten-by-ten-mile	**JJ**	**1-01-001**
ten-concert	**JJ**	**1-01-001**
ten-day	**JJ**	**1-01-001**
ten-fifty-five	**CD**	**1-01-001**
ten-foot	**JJ**	**3-02-003**
ten-gallon	**adjective**	**2-01-001**
ten-gallon	JJ	1-01-001
ten-gallon	JJ-HL	1-01-001
ten-hour	**JJ**	**1-01-001**
ten-minute	**JJ**	**1-01-001**
ten-month	**JJ**	**1-01-001**
ten-thousand-dollar	**JJ**	**1-01-001**
ten-twelve	**CD**	**1-01-001**
ten-year	**JJ**	**3-02-002**
ten-year-old	**JJ**	**1-01-001**
tenable	**JJ**	**4-04-004**
tenacious	**JJ**	**1-01-001**
tenaciously	**RB**	**1-01-001**

Word	Tag	Count
tenacity	**NN**	**5-04-005**
tenancy	**NN**	**2-02-002**
tenant	**noun**	**14-07-010**
tenant	NN	5-04-005
tenants	NNS	9-05-007
tend	**verb**	**104-11-078**
tend	VB	43-09-034
tends	VBZ	34-08-028
tended	VBD	15-08-014
tended	VBN	9-06-009
tending	VBG	3-03-003
Tenda	**NP**	**1-01-001**
tendency	**noun**	**54-10-041**
tendency	NN	49-10-040
tendencies	NNS	5-03-005
tender	**JJ**	**11-05-010**
tender	**verb**	**1-01-001**
tendered	VBN	1-01-001
tenderfoot	**noun**	**3-02-002**
tenderfoot	NN	2-01-001
Tenderfoot	NN-TL	1-01-001
Tenderloin	**NP**	**1-01-001**
tenderly	**QL**	**1-01-001**
tenderly	**RB**	**3-03-003**
tenderness	**NN**	**4-04-004**
tending	**NN**	**1-01-001**
tendon	**noun**	**2-02-002**
tendons	NNS	2-02-002
tenebrous	**JJ**	**1-01-001**
tenement	**noun**	**5-04-005**
tenement	NN	2-02-002
tenements	NNS	3-03-003
tenet	**noun**	**2-02-002**
tenets	NNS	2-02-002
tenfold	**RB**	**1-01-001**
Tenite	**NP**	**2-01-001**
Tennessee	**prop. noun**	**25-10-014**
Tennessee	NP	20-08-011
Tenn.	NP	1-01-001
Tennessee	NP-TL	3-03-003
Tennessee's	NP$	1-01-001
tennis	**noun**	**15-07-008**
tennis	NN	12-07-008
Tennis	NN-TL	3-02-002
Tennyson	**NP**	**2-02-002**
tenor	**noun**	**7-05-007**
tenor	NN	6-04-006
tenors	NNS	1-01-001
tense	**JJ**	**10-06-009**
tense	**noun**	**6-03-003**
tense	NN	5-03-003
tenses	NNS	1-01-001
tense	**verb**	**1-01-001**
tensed	VBD	1-01-001
tensely	**RB**	**4-03-004**
tensile	**adjective**	**5-02-002**
tensile	JJ	4-02-002
tensile	JJ-HL	1-01-001
Tensing	**NP**	**1-01-001**
tension	**noun**	**78-14-050**
tension	NN	55-14-037
tension	NN-HL	3-02-002
Tension	NN-TL	1-01-001
tensions	NNS	18-06-014
Tensions	NNS-TL	1-01-001
tension	**verb**	**2-01-001**
tensioning	VBG	2-01-001
tensional	**JJ**	**1-01-001**
tensionless	**JJ**	**1-01-001**
tenspot	**NN**	**1-01-001**
tent	**noun**	**30-04-007**
tent	NN	20-04-006
tents	NNS	10-02-002
tent	**verb**	**1-01-001**
tenting	VBG	1-01-001
tentacle	**noun**	**3-03-003**
tentacle	NN	1-01-001
tentacles	NNS	2-02-002
tentative	**JJ**	**15-06-013**
tentatively	**RB**	**6-05-006**
tenth	**noun**	**1-01-001**
tenths	NNS	1-01-001
tenth	**ord. num.**	**7-06-007**
tenth	OD	5-05-005
Tenth	OD-TL	2-02-002
tenuous	**JJ**	**6-03-005**
tenuously	**RB**	**1-01-001**
tenure	**noun**	**12-05-006**
tenure	NN	11-05-006

Word	Tag	Count
tenure (cont.):		
tenure	NN-HL	1-01-001
tepee	**noun**	**1-01-001**
tepees	NNS	1-01-001
tepid	**JJ**	**1-01-001**
Ter-Arutunian	**NP**	**1-01-001**
Ter-Stepanova	**NP**	**1-01-001**
teratology	**noun**	**1-01-001**
teratologies	NNS	1-01-001
Teresa	**NP**	**1-01-001**
Terg-O-Tometer	**NP**	**1-01-001**
Terka	**NP**	**1-01-001**
term	**noun**	**236-15-158**
term	NN	75-11-054
term	NN-HL	1-01-001
terms	NNS	159-15-117
Terms	NNS	1-01-001
term	**verb**	**22-10-022**
term	VB	3-02-003
terms	VBZ	3-01-003
termed	VBD	3-02-003
termed	VBN	11-08-011
termed	VBN-HL	1-01-001
terming	VBG	1-01-001
term-end	**NN**	**1-01-001**
terminal	**JJ**	**9-01-004**
terminal	**noun**	**7-06-007**
terminal	NN	3-03-003
terminals	NNS	4-03-004
terminate	**verb**	**18-06-017**
terminate	VB	12-06-012
terminates	VBZ	1-01-001
terminated	VBN	4-03-004
terminating	VBG	1-01-001
termination	**NN**	**8-03-004**
Terminiello	**prop. noun**	**1-01-001**
Terminiello	NP	0-00-000
Terminiello	NP-TL	1-01-001
terminology	**NN**	**6-04-006**
terminus	**noun**	**5-02-003**
terminus	NN	2-01-001
termini	NNS	3-02-002
Terper	**prop. noun**	**2-01-001**
Terpers	NPS	1-01-001
Terpers	NPS-HL	1-01-001
terra	**foreign**	**2-02-002**
terra	FW-NN	1-01-001
terram	FW-NN	1-01-001
terra-cotta-colored	**JJ**	**1-01-001**
terrace	**noun**	**17-06-010**
terrace	NN	7-04-007
ter.	NN	0-00-000
Ter.	NN-TL	1-01-001
Terrace	NN-TL	2-02-002
terraces	NNS	7-02-002
terrace	**verb**	**2-02-002**
terraced	VBN	2-02-002
terrain	**noun**	**9-04-008**
terrain	NN	8-04-007
terrains	NNS	1-01-001
Terral	**NP**	**1-01-001**
Terramycin	**NP**	**1-01-001**
terrestrial	**adjective**	**8-04-007**
terrestrial	JJ	7-04-006
terrestial	JJ	1-01-001
terrible	**FW-JJ**	**1-01-001**
terrible	**adjective**	**44-12-037**
terrible	JJ	43-11-036
Terrible	JJ-TL	1-01-001
terribly	**QL**	**7-05-006**
terribly	**RB**	**11-07-010**
terrier	**noun**	**7-05-005**
terrier	NN	4-03-003
Terrier	NN-TL	2-01-001
terriers	NNS	1-01-001
terrific	**JJ**	**5-04-004**
terrify	**verb**	**14-07-012**
terrifies	VBZ	2-01-001
terrified	VBN	7-05-007
terrifying	VBG	5-04-005
terrifying	**JJ**	**2-02-002**
territoire	**FW-NN**	**1-01-001**
territorial	**adjective**	**14-04-009**
territorial	JJ	12-04-008
Territorial	JJ-TL	2-02-002
territory	**noun**	**40-11-028**
territory	NN	27-09-021
Territory	NN-TL	4-02-003
territories	NNS	8-05-007

Word	Tag	Frequency
territory (cont.):		
Territories	NNS-TL	1-01-001
terror	**noun**	**26-11-023**
terror	NN	24-10-021
Terror	NN-TL	1-01-001
terrors	NNS	0-00-000
terrours	NNS	1-01-001
terror-stricken	**JJ**	**1-01-001**
terrorist	**noun**	**1-01-001**
terrorists	NNS	1-01-001
terrorize	**verb**	**4-03-004**
terrorized	VBD	1-01-001
terrorized	VBN	2-02-002
terrorizing	VBG	1-01-001
terry	**NN**	**1-01-001**
Terry	**NP**	**6-02-006**
terry-cloth	**NN**	**2-02-002**
terse	**JJ**	**2-02-002**
tersely	**RB**	**2-02-002**
tertian	**NN**	**1-01-001**
tertiary	**JJ**	**1-01-001**
tertre	**foreign**	**1-01-001**
tertre	FW-NN	0-00-000
Tertre	FW-NN-TL	1-01-001
Tess	**NP**	**1-01-001**
Tessie	**NP**	**7-01-001**
test	**noun**	**161-13-076**
test	NN	94-13-057
test	NN-HL	4-02-003
Test	NN-TL	2-01-002
Test	NN-TL-HL	1-01-001
tests	NNS	57-10-027
tests	NNS-HL	2-02-002
Tests	NNS-TL-HL	1-01-001
test	**verb**	**67-12-043**
test	VB	18-10-018
tests	VBZ	1-01-001
tested	VBD	3-03-003
tested	VBN	34-06-020
testing	VBG	11-05-007
test-like	**JJ**	**1-01-001**
test-run	**NN**	**1-01-001**
testament	**noun**	**31-09-022**
testament	NN	6-04-006
Testament	NN-TL	23-08-016
testaments	NNS	1-01-001
Testaments	NNS-TL	1-01-001
testicle	**NN**	**2-01-002**
testicular	**adjective**	**1-01-001**
testicular	JJ	0-00-000
Testicular	JJ-TL	1-01-001
testify	**verb**	**23-06-018**
testify	VB	8-05-008
testifies	VBZ	3-01-003
testifies	VBZ-HL	1-01-001
testified	VBD	9-04-007
testified	VBN	2-01-001
testily	**RB**	**1-01-001**
testimonial	**JJ**	**1-01-001**
testimonial	**noun**	**2-02-002**
testimonial	NN	1-01-001
testimonials	NNS	1-01-001
testimony	**NN**	**47-08-025**
testing	**noun**	**22-05-013**
testing	NN	21-04-012
testings	NNS	1-01-001
tetanus	**NN**	**1-01-001**
Teter	**prop. noun**	**1-01-001**
Teter	NP	0-00-000
Teter	NP-TL	1-01-001
tether	**noun**	**1-01-001**
tethers	NNS	1-01-001
tether	**verb**	**3-02-003**
tethered	VBD	1-01-001
tethered	VBN	2-02-002
tetrachloride	**NN**	**19-01-001**
tetragonal	**JJ**	**1-01-001**
tetrahalide	**noun**	**1-01-001**
tetrahalides	NNS	1-01-001
Tetrameron	**NP**	**1-01-001**
tetrasodium	**NN**	**1-01-001**
Teutonic	**JJ**	**1-01-001**
Tewfik	**NP**	**1-01-001**
Tex	**NP**	**1-01-001**
Texan	**JJ**	**1-01-001**
Texan	**prop. noun**	**13-04-005**
Texan	NP	3-02-002
Texan	NP-TL	1-01-001
Texans	NPS	9-02-003

Word	Tag	Frequency
Texas	**prop. noun**	**79-09-031**
Texas	NP	44-08-022
Tex.	NP	6-02-005
Tex.	NP-HL	1-01-001
Texas	NP-HL	8-01-002
Texas	NP-TL	17-05-009
Texas'	NP$	3-01-002
Texoma	**prop. noun**	**2-01-001**
Texoma	NP	0-00-000
Texoma	NP-TL	2-01-001
text	**noun**	**64-10-024**
text	NN	59-10-020
Text	NN-TL	1-01-001
texts	NNS	4-04-004
text-form	**NN**	**10-01-001**
text-lookup	**NN**	**1-01-001**
text-ordered	**JJ**	**1-01-001**
textbook	**noun**	**5-03-005**
textbook	NN	4-03-004
textbooks	NNS	1-01-001
textile	**JJ**	**2-02-002**
textile	**noun**	**42-07-013**
textile	NN	24-04-005
Textile	NN-TL	2-02-002
textile's	NN$	0-00-000
Textile's	NN$-TL	1-01-001
textiles	NNS	15-05-008
textile-exporting	**JJ**	**1-01-001**
textile-importing	**JJ**	**1-01-001**
textile-producing	**JJ**	**2-01-001**
Textron	**prop. noun**	**1-01-001**
Textron	NP	0-00-000
Textron	NP-TL	1-01-001
textual	**JJ**	**2-02-002**
texture	**noun**	**21-09-014**
texture	NN	15-09-013
textures	NNS	6-03-003
textured	**JJ**	**2-01-001**
Thackeray	**NP**	**2-02-002**
Thaddeus	**NP**	**1-01-001**
Thai	**NP**	**1-01-001**
Thailand	**NP**	**4-03-003**
Thakhek	**NP**	**1-01-001**
Thalberg	**prop. noun**	**1-01-001**
Thalbergs	NPS	1-01-001
Thames	**NP**	**3-01-001**
Thamnophis	**NP**	**1-01-001**
than	**sub. conj.**	**1297-15-414**
than	CS	1290-15-414
then	CS	2-01-001
than	CS-HL	1-01-001
than	CS-NC	2-01-001
'n	+CS	2-02-002
than	**prep.**	**497-15-261**
than	IN	496-15-260
than	IN-NC	1-01-001
thank	**verb**	**45-12-038**
thank	VB	35-11-031
thank	VB-NC	1-01-001
thanked	VBD	5-03-004
thanked	VBN	1-01-001
thanking	VBG	3-03-003
thankful	**JJ**	**6-03-004**
thankfulness	**NN**	**2-02-002**
thankless	**JJ**	**1-01-001**
thanks	**pl. noun**	**37-12-032**
thanks	NNS	36-12-032
thanks	NNS-HL	1-01-001
thanksgiving	**noun**	**8-03-003**
thanksgiving	NN	1-01-001
Thanksgiving	NN-TL	6-03-003
Thanksgiving	NN-TL-HL	1-01-001
Thant	**prop. noun**	**5-01-001**
Thant	NP	4-01-001
Thant	NP-HL	1-01-001
that	**sub. conj.**	**6468-15-497**
that	CS	6463-15-497
thatt	CS	1-01-001
thet	CS	1-01-001
that	CS-HL	1-01-001
that	CS-NC	2-01-001
that	**sing. det.**	**2455-15-456**
that	DT	2260-15-454
thet	DT	1-01-001
that	DT-HL	1-01-001
that	DT-NC	6-02-002
That	DT-TL	5-03-003
that'll	DT+MD	2-02-002
that's	DT+BEZ	178-14-096

Word	Tag	Frequency
that (cont.):		
thet's	DT+BEZ	1-01-001
that's	DT+BEZ-NC	1-01-001
that	**QL**	**57-13-048**
that	**s. wh-pro.**	**1674-15-414**
that	WPS	1654-15-414
that	WPS-HL	2-01-002
that	WPS-NC	3-01-001
That	WPS-TL	3-02-002
that'd	WPS+MD	1-01-001
that'll	WPS+MD	3-03-003
that's	WPS+BEZ	7-05-006
that's	WPS+HVZ	1-01-001
that	**o. wh-pro.**	**136-11-087**
that	WPO	135-11-086
that	WPO-NC	1-01-001
that-a-way	**RB**	**1-01-001**
thatch	**noun**	**1-01-001**
thatches	NNS	1-01-001
thatched-roof	**NN**	**1-01-001**
thaw	**NN**	**3-02-003**
thaw	**verb**	**8-06-008**
thaw	VB	3-03-003
thawed	VBN	3-02-003
thawing	VBG	2-02-002
Thaxter	**prop. noun**	**3-01-001**
Thaxter	NP	2-01-001
Thaxters	NPS	1-01-001
Thayer	**prop. noun**	**14-03-003**
Thayer	NP	11-01-001
Thayer	NP-TL	2-01-001
Thayer's	NP$	0-00-000
Thayer's	NP$-TL	1-01-001
the	**article**	**69975-15-500**
the	AT	69016-15-500
th'	AT	1-01-001
The	AT	2-01-001
the	AT-HL	253-10-083
the	AT-NC	26-02-002
The	AT-TL	454-15-141
the	AT-TL	222-14-098
the	AT-TL-HL	1-01-001
Thea	**NP**	**1-01-001**
theater	**noun**	**92-12-045**
theater	NN	38-08-021
theatre	NN	19-07-013
Theatre	NN-TL	9-04-006
theater	NN-HL	1-01-001
Theater	NN-TL	13-06-009
theaters	NNS	11-04-005
theatres	NNS	1-01-001
theater-going	**NN**	**1-01-001**
theatergoer	**noun**	**3-02-003**
theatergoer	NN	1-01-001
theatregoer	NN	1-01-001
theatergoers	NNS	1-01-001
theatergoing	**JJ**	**1-01-001**
theatre	**foreign**	**1-01-001**
theatre	FW-NN	0-00-000
Theatre	FW-NN-TL	1-01-001
Theatre-by-the-Sea	**NP**	**2-01-001**
theatrical	**JJ**	**12-09-012**
theatrical	**noun**	**2-01-001**
theatricals	NNS	2-01-001
theatrically	**RB**	**2-01-002**
theft	**NN**	**10-06-008**
theistic	**JJ**	**1-01-001**
Thelma	**prop. noun**	**7-01-001**
Thelma	NP	6-01-001
Thelma's	NP$	1-01-001
thematic	**JJ**	**1-01-001**
theme	**noun**	**63-08-038**
theme	NN	55-08-034
themes	NNS	8-03-007
themselves	**refl. pro.**	**271-15-177**
themselves	PPLS	270-15-176
'emselves	PPLS	1-01-001
then	**JJ**	**26-12-024**
then	**adverb**	**1348-15-406**
then	RB	1344-15-406
then	RB-HL	1-01-001
then	RB-NC	3-01-001
then	**RN**	**3-01-002**
thence	**RB**	**6-04-006**
thenceforth	**RB**	**2-02-002**
theocracy	**NN**	**1-01-001**
Theodor	**NP**	**1-01-001**
Theodore	**prop. noun**	**14-06-012**
Theodore	NP	12-06-011
Theodore (cont.):		
Theodore	NP-TL	2-02-002
Theodosian	**JJ**	**1-01-001**
Theodosius	**prop. noun**	**1-01-001**
Theodosius	NP	0-00-000
Theodosius	NP-TL	1-01-001
theologian	**noun**	**14-06-009**
theologian	NN	5-02-004
theologians	NNS	9-05-007
theologian-philosopher	**noun**	**1-01-001**
theologian-philosophers	NNS	1-01-001
theological	**adjective**	**27-05-016**
theological	JJ	24-05-014
Theological	JJ-TL	3-02-002
theology	**noun**	**20-05-010**
theology	NN	18-04-009
Theology	NN-TL	1-01-001
theology's	NN$	1-01-001
Theon	**prop. noun**	**1-01-001**
Theon's	NP$	1-01-001
theorem	**noun**	**18-01-002**
theorem	NN	8-01-002
theorem	NN-HL	3-01-001
Theorem	NN-TL	6-01-001
Theorem	NN-TL-HL	1-01-001
theoretical	**adjective**	**21-05-015**
theoretical	JJ	19-05-015
theoretical	JJ-HL	2-01-001
theoretically	**RB**	**5-02-005**
theoretician	**noun**	**2-02-002**
theoreticians	NNS	1-01-001
theoriticians	NNS	1-01-001
theorist	**noun**	**2-01-002**
theorists	NNS	2-01-002
theorize	**VB**	**2-01-002**
theorizing	**NN**	**1-01-001**
theory	**noun**	**150-11-051**
theory	NN	127-11-048
theory	NN-HL	2-02-002
Theory	NN-TL	1-01-001
theories	NNS	19-04-014
Theories	NNS-TL	1-01-001
therapeutic	**JJ**	**13-04-007**
therapist	**noun**	**23-02-002**
therapist	NN	19-02-002
therapist's	NN$	2-02-002
therapists	NNS	2-01-001
therapy	**noun**	**13-02-006**
therapy	NN	12-02-006
therapies	NNS	1-01-001
there	**ex. subj.**	**2280-15-457**
there	EX	2162-15-454
theare	EX	1-01-001
ther	EX	1-01-001
there	EX-HL	1-01-001
there	EX-NC	1-01-001
there'd	EX+HVD	3-03-003
there'd	EX+MD	1-01-001
there'll	EX+MD	3-02-002
there's	EX+BEZ	105-12-072
there's	EX+HVZ	2-02-002
there	**adverb**	**571-15-249**
there	RB	561-15-247
dere	RB	1-01-001
thar	RB	2-01-001
ther	RB	2-01-001
there	RB-HL	3-01-002
there's	RB+BEZ	1-01-001
there's	RB+BEZ-NC	1-01-001
thereabouts	**RB**	**1-01-001**
thereafter	**RB**	**20-08-020**
thereby	**RB**	**34-09-030**
therefor	**RB**	**1-01-001**
therefore	**noun**	**1-01-001**
therefores	NNS	1-01-001
therefore	**RB**	**205-15-135**
therefrom	**RB**	**5-03-004**
therein	**RB**	**9-05-008**
thereof	**RB**	**16-04-009**
thereon	**RB**	**1-01-001**
Theresa	**NP**	**24-01-001**
thereto	**RB**	**11-02-005**
theretofore	**RB**	**2-01-002**
thereunder	**RB**	**1-01-001**
thereupon	**RB**	**5-05-005**
therewith	**RB**	**3-03-003**
thermal	**adjective**	**33-03-010**
thermal	JJ	31-03-010
thermal	JJ-HL	2-01-002

Word	Tag	Frequency
thermally	**RB**	**1-01-001**
thermistor	**NN**	**1-01-001**
thermocouple	**noun**	**6-01-001**
thermocouple	NN	3-01-001
thermocouples	NNS	3-01-001
thermodynamic	**JJ**	**2-01-001**
thermodynamically	**RB**	**2-02-002**
thermodynamics	**NN**	**2-01-001**
thermoelectric	**JJ**	**2-01-001**
thermoform	**verb**	**3-01-001**
thermoformed	VBN	1-01-001
thermoforming	VBG	2-01-001
thermogravimetric	**JJ**	**1-01-001**
thermometer	**noun**	**16-04-004**
thermometer	NN	10-04-004
thermometers	NNS	5-01-001
thermometers	NNS-HL	1-01-001
thermometric	**JJ**	**1-01-001**
thermometry	**noun**	**3-01-001**
thermometry	NN	2-01-001
thermometry	NN-HL	1-01-001
thermonuclear	**JJ**	**2-01-001**
thermopile	**NN**	**1-01-001**
thermoplastic	**NN**	**1-01-001**
Thermopylae	**NP**	**1-01-001**
thermos	**NN**	**1-01-001**
thermostat	**noun**	**7-02-003**
thermostat	NN	6-02-003
thermostats	NNS	1-01-001
thermostated	**JJ**	**1-01-001**
thermostatics	**NN**	**1-01-001**
thesaurus	**NN**	**1-01-001**
these	**pl. det.**	**1575-15-413**
these	DTS	1572-15-413
thease	DTS	1-01-001
thees	DTS	1-01-001
these	DTS-HL	1-01-001
thesis	**noun**	**11-05-009**
thesis	NN	9-05-008
thesis	NN-HL	1-01-001
theses	NNS	1-01-001
thespian	**noun**	**1-01-001**
thespians	NNS	1-01-001
Thevenow	**NP**	**1-01-001**
they	**pers. pro.**	**8284-15-499**
they	PPSS	3621-15-483
dey	PPSS	1-01-001
thay	PPSS	1-01-001
thei	PPSS	1-01-001
they	PPSS-HL	2-02-002
They	PPSS-TL	1-01-001
they'd	PPSS+HVD	13-04-012
they'd	PPSS+MD	17-07-016
they'll	PPSS+MD	32-10-018
they're	PPSS+BER	65-13-039
they've	PPSS+HV	16-06-010
them	PPO	1774-15-427
'em	PPO	41-09-020
em	PPO	4-01-001
thum	PPO	1-01-001
um	PPO	1-01-001
them	PPO-HL	1-01-001
their	PP$	2666-15-465
ther	PP$	2-01-001
Their	PP$-TL	2-02-002
theirs	PP$$	21-08-019
their's	PP$$	1-01-001
thiamin	**NN**	**1-01-001**
thick	**JJ**	**63-11-046**
thick	**NN**	**2-02-002**
thick	**RB**	**2-02-002**
thick-skulled	**JJ**	**1-01-001**
thick-walled	**JJ**	**2-01-001**
thicken	**verb**	**8-06-007**
thicken	VB	1-01-001
thickens	VBZ	1-01-001
thickened	VBD	2-02-002
thickened	VBN	3-01-002
thickening	VBG	1-01-001
thickener	**noun**	**1-01-001**
thickeners	NNS	1-01-001
thicker	**JJR**	**5-04-004**
thickest	**JJT**	**1-01-001**
thicket	**noun**	**3-03-003**
thicket	NN	1-01-001
thickets	NNS	2-02-002
thickly	**RB**	**5-05-005**
thickness	**noun**	**46-04-013**
thickness	NN	43-04-012
thickness (cont.):		
thicknesses	NNS	3-02-002
THIDIU	**NP**	**1-01-001**
thief	**noun**	**18-09-014**
thief	NN	8-06-007
theaf	NN	1-01-001
thieves	NNS	9-06-007
thieve	**verb**	**6-03-005**
thieving	VBG	4-03-004
thefin	VBG	1-01-001
thievin	VBG	1-01-001
thigh	**noun**	**16-07-011**
thigh	NN	9-06-006
thighs	NNS	7-03-006
thigh-bone	**NN**	**1-01-001**
thill	**noun**	**1-01-001**
thills	NNS	1-01-001
thimble	**NN**	**1-01-001**
thimble-sized	**JJ**	**1-01-001**
thin	**JJ**	**90-14-061**
thin	**verb**	**4-03-004**
thin	VB	2-01-002
thinned	VBD	1-01-001
thinning	VBG	1-01-001
thin-lipped	**JJ**	**2-02-002**
thin-soled	**JJ**	**1-01-001**
thing	**noun**	**702-15-293**
thing	NN	326-15-202
thiihng	NN	1-01-001
thing	NN-NC	5-01-001
Thing	NN-TL	2-01-001
things	NNS	362-15-198
things	NNS-HL	1-01-001
things	NNS-NC	3-01-001
Things	NNS-TL	2-02-002
think	**verb**	**982-15-319**
think	VB	433-15-219
thinke	VB	2-01-002
thynke	VB	1-01-001
thinks	VBZ	23-12-021
thought	VBD	340-15-157
thout	VBD	1-01-001
thought	VBN	74-13-063
thinking	VBG	105-15-079
thinkin	VBG	3-02-002
thinker	**noun**	**12-06-011**
thinker	NN	6-04-006
thinkers	NNS	6-04-006
thinking	**NN**	**40-12-031**
thinly	**RB**	**3-03-003**
thinner	**JJR**	**6-03-003**
thinness	**NN**	**1-01-001**
thinning	**NN**	**1-01-001**
thiocyanate-perchlorate-fluoroboride	**NN**	**1-01-001**
Thiot	**NP**	**1-01-001**
thiouracil	**NN**	**3-01-001**
third	**noun**	**6-04-005**
third	NN	2-02-002
thirds	NNS	4-03-003
third	**ord. num.**	**184-15-126**
third	OD	174-15-118
third-	OD	1-01-001
Third	OD-TL	9-07-008
third	**RB**	**5-03-004**
third-dimensional	**JJ**	**2-01-001**
third-dimensionality	**NN**	**1-01-001**
third-grade	**NN**	**4-01-001**
third-inning	**NN**	**1-01-001**
third-rate	**JJ**	**1-01-001**
third-shift	**NN**	**1-01-001**
third-story	**NN**	**1-01-001**
thirdly	**RB**	**1-01-001**
thirst	**NN**	**4-04-004**
thirst	**verb**	**1-01-001**
thirsted	VBN	1-01-001
thirsty	**JJ**	**4-03-004**
thirteen	**CD**	**11-08-010**
thirteenth	**OD**	**2-02-002**
thirteenth-century	**NN**	**1-01-001**
thirtieth	**OD**	**1-01-001**
thirty	**CD**	**59-12-047**
thirty	**noun**	**7-05-006**
thirties	NNS	4-03-003
Thirties	NNS-TL	3-03-003
thirty-caliber	**JJ**	**1-01-001**
thirty-eight	**CD**	**1-01-001**
thirty-eighth	**ord. num.**	**2-02-002**
thirty-eighth	OD	1-01-001

Word	Tag	Frequency
thirty-eighth (cont.):		
Thirty-eighth	OD-TL	1-01-001
thirty-five	**card. num.**	**14-09-013**
thirty-five	CD	13-08-012
thirty-five	CD-HL	1-01-001
thirty-foot	**JJ**	**1-01-001**
thirty-four	**card. num.**	**7-05-006**
thirty-four	CD	6-04-005
thirty-four	CD-HL	1-01-001
thirty-fourth	**ord. num.**	**2-02-002**
thirty-fourth	OD	1-01-001
Thirty-fourth	OD-TL	1-01-001
thirty-mile	**JJ**	**1-01-001**
thirty-nine	**CD**	**2-01-002**
thirty-ninth	**ord. num.**	**1-01-001**
thirty-ninth	OD	0-00-000
Thirty-ninth	OD-TL	1-01-001
thirty-one	**CD**	**3-03-003**
thirty-seven	**CD**	**1-01-001**
thirty-six	**card. num.**	**4-04-004**
thirty-six	CD	3-03-003
thirty-six	CD-HL	1-01-001
thirty-sixth	**OD**	**1-01-001**
thirty-three	**card. num.**	**2-01-002**
thirty-three	CD	1-01-001
thirty-three	CD-HL	1-01-001
thirty-two	**CD**	**3-03-003**
thirty-year	**JJ**	**1-01-001**
this	**sing. det.**	**5145-15-495**
this	DT	5138-15-495
this	DT-HL	1-01-001
this	DT-NC	1-01-001
This	DT-TL	4-03-003
this'll	DT+MD	1-01-001
this	**QL**	**1-01-001**
thither	**RB**	**1-01-001**
Thom	**prop. noun**	**6-01-001**
Thom	NP	5-01-001
Thom's	NP$	1-01-001
Thomas	**prop. noun**	**112-08-048**
Thomas	NP	95-08-046
Thomas	NP-TL	5-02-002
Thomas'	NP$	6-02-002
Thomas's	NP$	6-01-001
Thompson	**prop. noun**	**43-05-012**
Thompson	NP	38-05-011
Thompson's	NP$	5-01-002
Thomson	**NP**	**2-01-001**
thong	**NN**	**1-01-001**
Thor	**prop. noun**	**13-03-003**
Thor	NP	9-03-003
Thor's	NP$	4-01-001
Thoreau	**prop. noun**	**2-02-002**
Thoreau	NP	1-01-001
Thoreau's	NP$	1-01-001
thoriate	**verb**	**1-01-001**
thoriated	VBN	1-01-001
thorn	**noun**	**4-03-003**
thorn	NN	3-02-002
thorns	NNS	1-01-001
Thornburg	**NP**	**8-02-002**
Thornton	**NP**	**1-01-001**
thorny	**JJ**	**2-02-002**
thorough	**JJ**	**21-08-021**
Thoroughbred	**prop. noun**	**1-01-001**
Thoroughbred	NP	0-00-000
Thoroughbred	NP-TL	1-01-001
thoroughfare	**noun**	**4-04-004**
thoroughfare	NN	3-03-003
thoroughfares	NNS	1-01-001
thoroughgoing	**JJ**	**2-01-002**
thoroughly	**QL**	**10-07-010**
thoroughly	**RB**	**30-11-026**
thoroughness	**NN**	**1-01-001**
Thorp	**NP**	**2-01-001**
Thorpe	**NP**	**4-01-001**
Thorstein	**NP**	**1-01-001**
those	**pl. det.**	**864-15-369**
those	DTS	849-15-367
them	DTS	12-04-005
them's	DTS+BEZ	2-02-002
those	DTS-HL	1-01-001
thou	**pers. pro.**	**44-08-014**
thou	PPSS	13-04-006
Thou	PPSS	1-01-001
thee	PPS	0-00-000
thee	PPS	1-01-001
thee	PPO	16-06-009
thy	PP$	8-03-005

Word	Tag	Frequency
thou (cont.):		
Thy	PP$	4-01-001
thine	PP$	1-01-001
though	**CC**	**1-01-001**
though	**sub. conj.**	**407-15-230**
though	CS	406-15-230
tho'	CS	1-01-001
though	**RB**	**32-11-026**
thought	**noun**	**157-14-108**
thought	NN	103-13-080
thoughts	NNS	51-12-042
Thoughts	NNS-TL	3-01-002
thoughtful	**JJ**	**11-09-011**
thoughtfully	**RB**	**14-07-014**
thoughtfulness	**NN**	**1-01-001**
thoughtless	**JJ**	**3-02-003**
thoughtlessly	**RB**	**1-01-001**
thousand	**card. num.**	**97-15-065**
thousand	CD	95-15-063
Thousand	CD-TL	2-01-002
thousand	**noun**	**47-12-035**
thousands	NNS	47-12-035
thousand-fold	**NN**	**1-01-001**
thousand-legged	**JJ**	**1-01-001**
thousandth	**noun**	**1-01-001**
thousandths	NNS	1-01-001
thousandth	**OD**	**3-02-002**
thrash	**verb**	**4-03-004**
thrash	VB	1-01-001
thrashed	VBD	2-01-002
thrashed	VBN	1-01-001
thread	**noun**	**20-09-015**
thread	NN	13-07-009
threads	NNS	7-06-007
thread	**verb**	**9-05-008**
thread	VB	2-01-001
threaded	VBN	4-02-004
threading	VBG	3-03-003
threadbare	**JJ**	**3-03-003**
threat	**noun**	**56-11-044**
threat	NN	40-10-033
threat	NN-HL	2-01-002
threats	NNS	14-10-013
threaten	**verb**	**67-14-057**
threaten	VB	11-07-010
threatens	VBZ	5-05-005
threatened	VBD	15-07-015
threatened	VBN	14-08-013
threatening	VBG	22-09-020
threatening	**JJ**	**4-03-004**
threateningly	**RB**	**1-01-001**
three	**card. num.**	**610-15-288**
three	CD	588-15-285
three	CD-HL	3-02-003
Three	CD-TL	18-08-015
Three	CD-TL-HL	1-01-001
three	**noun**	**3-02-002**
threes	NNS	3-02-002
three-axis	**JJ**	**1-01-001**
three-bedroom	**JJ**	**1-01-001**
three-body	**JJ**	**1-01-001**
three-building	**JJ**	**1-01-001**
three-day	**JJ**	**3-03-003**
three-dice	**NN**	**1-01-001**
three-dimensional	**adjective**	**11-06-008**
three-dimensional	JJ	10-05-007
three-dimentional	JJ	1-01-001
three-dimensionality	**NN**	**2-01-001**
three-family	**JJ**	**1-01-001**
three-fifths	**NNS**	**2-01-001**
three-foot	**JJ**	**1-01-001**
three-fourths	**NNS**	**2-02-002**
three-front	**JJ**	**1-01-001**
three-hour	**JJ**	**3-03-003**
three-hundred-foot	**JJ**	**1-01-001**
three-inch	**JJ**	**1-01-001**
three-inch-wide	**JJ**	**3-01-001**
three-inning	**JJ**	**1-01-001**
three-judge	**JJ**	**1-01-001**
three-man	**JJ**	**3-03-003**
three-masted	**JJ**	**1-01-001**
three-men-and-a-helper	**JJ**	**1-01-001**
three-month	**JJ**	**4-02-003**
three-night	**JJ**	**1-01-001**
three-panel	**JJ**	**1-01-001**
three-part	**adjective**	**5-04-004**
three-part	JJ	4-04-004
three-part	JJ-HL	1-01-001
three-power	**JJ**	**1-01-001**

Word	Tag	Frequency
three-quarters	**NNS**	**4-04-004**
three-room	**JJ**	**1-01-001**
three-round	**JJ**	**2-01-001**
three-sectioned	**JJ**	**1-01-001**
three-story	**JJ**	**1-01-001**
three-way	**JJ**	**2-02-002**
three-week	**JJ**	**1-01-001**
three-wood	**JJ**	**1-01-001**
three-year	**JJ**	**5-03-004**
threefold	**adjective**	**5-04-004**
threefold	JJ	3-02-002
three-fold	JJ	2-02-002
threes-fulfilled	**JJ**	**1-01-001**
threesome	**NN**	**3-03-003**
thresh	**verb**	**2-02-002**
threshed	VBD	1-01-001
threshing	VBG	1-01-001
threshold	**noun**	**16-06-010**
threshold	NN	14-05-008
threshhold	NN	1-01-001
Threshold	NN-TL	1-01-001
thrice	**RB**	**1-01-001**
thrift	**noun**	**5-01-001**
thrift	NN	0-00-000
Thrift	NN-TL	5-01-001
thrifty	**JJ**	**3-03-003**
thrill	**noun**	**6-06-006**
thrill	NN	4-04-004
thrills	NNS	2-02-002
thrill	**verb**	**4-03-004**
thrill	VB	1-01-001
thrilled	VBD	2-01-002
thrilled	VBN	1-01-001
thriller	**noun**	**1-01-001**
thrillers	NNS	1-01-001
thrilling	**JJ**	**4-03-004**
thrive	**verb**	**11-07-011**
thrive	VB	1-01-001
thrives	VBZ	1-01-001
thrived	VBD	4-03-004
thrived	VBN	1-01-001
thriving	VBG	4-04-004
throat	**noun**	**63-11-034**
throat	NN	40-11-030
Throat	NN-TL	11-01-001
throat's	NN+BEZ	1-01-001
throat's	NN$	0-00-000
Throat's	NN$-TL	5-01-001
throats	NNS	6-04-006
throaty	**JJ**	**1-01-001**
throb	**verb**	**5-04-005**
throbbed	VBD	3-03-003
throbbing	VBG	2-02-002
throbbing	**NN**	**1-01-001**
throe	**noun**	**2-02-002**
throes	NNS	2-02-002
thrombosed	**JJ**	**1-01-001**
thrombosis	**NN**	**1-01-001**
thrombus	**noun**	**1-01-001**
thrombi	NNS	1-01-001
throne	**noun**	**6-04-004**
throne	NN	3-03-003
Throne	NN-TL	2-01-001
thrones	NNS	1-01-001
Throneberry	**prop. noun**	**5-01-001**
Throneberry	NP	4-01-001
Throneberry's	NP$	1-01-001
throng	**NN**	**2-02-002**
throng	**VB**	**1-01-001**
throttle	**NN**	**6-03-003**
throttle	**verb**	**2-02-002**
throttled	VBN	1-01-001
throttling	VBG	1-01-001
through	**prep.**	**926-15-369**
through	IN	905-15-365
thru	IN	16-04-009
through	IN-HL	2-02-002
Through	IN-TL	3-02-002
through	**RP**	**61-14-047**
throughout	**IN**	**133-14-101**
throughout	**RB**	**8-04-007**
throughput	**NN**	**1-01-001**
throw	**noun**	**7-05-007**
throw	NN	6-05-006
Throw	NN-TL	1-01-001
throw	**verb**	**150-15-102**
throw	VB	35-13-032
throws	VBZ	5-04-004
throws	VBZ-HL	1-01-001

throw (cont.):

Word	Tag	Frequency
threw	VBD	46-13-036
throwed	VBD	2-01-001
thrown	VBN	40-12-032
throwing	VBG	17-10-016
throwin'	VBG	4-01-001
throw-rug	**NN**	**1-01-001**
thrower	**NN**	**2-02-002**
thrum	**verb**	**1-01-001**
thrumming	VBG	1-01-001
thrush	**noun**	**2-02-002**
thrush	NN	1-01-001
Thrush	NN-TL	1-01-001
thrust	**noun**	**11-08-010**
thrust	NN	7-05-006
thrusts	NNS	4-04-004
thrust	**verb**	**23-09-021**
thrust	VB	3-02-002
thrusts	VBZ	1-01-001
thrust	VBD	9-04-008
thrust	VBN	3-02-003
thrusting	VBG	7-06-007
thrust-to-weight	**JJ**	**3-01-001**
thrusting	**NN**	**1-01-001**
Thruston	**NP**	**1-01-001**
thruway	**noun**	**2-02-002**
thruway	NN	1-01-001
thruways	NNS	1-01-001
thud	**noun**	**3-03-003**
thud	NN	2-02-002
thuds	NNS	1-01-001
thud	**verb**	**2-02-002**
thud	VB	1-01-001
thudding	VBG	1-01-001
thug	**noun**	**3-03-003**
thug	NN	1-01-001
thugs	NNS	2-02-002
Thuggee	**NP**	**1-01-001**
Thule	**NP**	**1-01-001**
thumb	**noun**	**14-06-013**
thumb	NN	10-06-010
thumb-	NN	1-01-001
thumbs	NNS	3-03-003
thumb	**verb**	**2-01-001**
thumbed	VBD	1-01-001
thumbing	VBG	1-01-001
thumb-sucking	**NN**	**1-01-001**
thumbnail	**NN**	**1-01-001**
thump	**NN**	**2-02-002**
thump	**verb**	**6-03-006**
thump	VB	1-01-001
thumped	VBD	1-01-001
thumping	VBG	4-02-004
thumping	**NN**	**1-01-001**
thunder	**noun**	**12-06-008**
thunder	NN	11-06-007
Thunder	NN-TL	1-01-001
thunder	**verb**	**6-06-006**
thunder	VB	2-02-002
thundered	VBD	2-02-002
thundering	VBG	2-02-002
thunder-purple	**JJ**	**1-01-001**
thunderclap	**noun**	**1-01-001**
thunderclaps	NNS	1-01-001
thunderous	**JJ**	**2-01-002**
thunk	**NN**	**1-01-001**
Thurber	**prop. noun**	**8-01-001**
Thurber	NP	6-01-001
Thurber's	NP$	2-01-001
Thurman	**NP**	**1-01-001**
Thursday	**adv. noun**	**34-11-024**
Thursday	NR	32-11-022
Thursday	NR-TL	1-01-001
Thursday's	NR$	1-01-001
Thursday-night	**JJ**	**1-01-001**
thus	**QL**	**12-06-011**
thus	**RB**	**299-13-171**
Thutmose	**NP**	**1-01-001**
thwack	**NN**	**1-01-001**
thwart	**NN**	**1-01-001**
thwart	**verb**	**7-07-007**
thwart	VB	2-02-002
thwarted	VBN	4-04-004
thwarting	VBG	1-01-001
thwump	**NN**	**1-01-001**
Thynne	**prop. noun**	**3-01-001**
Thynne	NP	2-01-001
Thynnes	NPS	1-01-001
thyratron	**NN**	**1-01-001**

Word	Tag	Frequency
thyroglobulin	**noun**	**17-01-001**
thyroglobulin	NN	16-01-001
thyroglobulin	NN-HL	1-01-001
thyroid	**noun**	**39-02-003**
thyroid	NN	37-02-003
thyroid	NN-HL	1-01-001
thyroids	NNS	1-01-001
thyroid-stimulating	**adjective**	**4-01-001**
thyroid-stimulating	JJ	2-01-001
thyroid-stimulating	JJ-HL	2-01-001
thyroidal	**JJ**	**1-01-001**
thyronine	**NN**	**1-01-001**
thyrotoxic	**JJ**	**1-01-001**
thyrotrophic	**JJ**	**1-01-001**
thyrotrophin	**NP**	**1-01-001**
thyroxine	**NN**	**8-01-001**
thyroxine-binding	**JJ**	**1-01-001**
Ti	**NP**	**1-01-001**
Tiao	**NP**	**1-01-001**
Tiber	**NP**	**2-01-001**
Tibet	**NP**	**7-03-003**
Tibetan	**JJ**	**3-03-003**
Tibetan-like	**JJ**	**1-01-001**
tibialis	**FW-NN**	**1-01-001**
Tiburon	**NP**	**1-01-001**
Tic-Tac-Toe	**NP**	**1-01-001**
tick	**noun**	**3-03-003**
tick	NN	1-01-001
ticks	NNS	2-02-002
tick	**verb**	**5-05-005**
tick	VB	2-02-002
ticked	VBD	2-02-002
ticking	VBG	1-01-001
Ticker	**NP**	**1-01-001**
ticket	**noun**	**30-08-018**
ticket	NN	16-06-011
tickets	NNS	14-06-009
tickle	**verb**	**2-01-002**
tickled	VBD	1-01-001
tickled	VBN	1-01-001
ticklebrush	**NN**	**1-01-001**
Ticonderoga	**prop. noun**	**4-01-001**
Ticonderoga	NP	3-01-001
Ticonderoga	NP-TL	1-01-001
tidal	**JJ**	**1-01-001**
tidbit	**noun**	**3-03-003**
tidbit	NN	1-01-001
tidbits	NNS	2-02-002
tide	**noun**	**14-08-012**
tide	NN	8-06-008
Tide	NN	1-01-001
tide	NN-HL	1-01-001
tides	NNS	4-02-003
tide	**VB**	**1-01-001**
tideland	**noun**	**1-01-001**
tidelands	NNS	1-01-001
tidewater	**noun**	**3-01-002**
tidewater	NN	1-01-001
Tidewater	NN-TL	2-01-002
tidiness	**NN**	**1-01-001**
tidings	**NNS**	**3-03-003**
tidy	**JJ**	**1-01-001**
tidy	**verb**	**2-02-002**
tidied	VBD	1-01-001
tidying	VBG	1-01-001
tie	**noun**	**27-10-021**
tie	NN	14-06-010
ties	NNS	13-08-011
tie	**verb**	**50-12-038**
tie	VB	9-07-008
ties	VBZ	2-02-002
tied	VBD	13-06-012
tied	VBN	21-11-017
tying	VBG	5-04-004
tie-in	**NN**	**1-01-001**
Tieck	**NP**	**1-01-001**
tiefes	**FW-JJ**	**1-01-001**
Tieken	**NP**	**1-01-001**
Tien	**prop. noun**	**2-02-002**
Tien	NP	1-01-001
Tien	NP-TL	1-01-001
Tiepolo	**NP**	**3-01-001**
tier	**noun**	**3-03-003**
tiers	NNS	3-03-003
tiered	**JJ**	**1-01-001**
Tift	**NP**	**1-01-001**
Tigard	**NP**	**2-01-001**
tiger	**noun**	**9-06-007**
tiger	NN	5-04-004

tiger (cont.):

Word	Tag	Frequency
Tiger	NN-TL	2-02-002
tiger's	NN$	1-01-001
tigers	NNS	0-00-000
Tigers	NNS-TL	1-01-001
tight	**JJ**	**22-09-020**
tight	**RB**	**6-05-006**
tight-turn	**NN**	**1-01-001**
tighten	**verb**	**12-06-011**
tighten	VB	3-02-003
tightened	VBD	6-02-005
tightening	VBG	3-03-003
tightening	**NN**	**1-01-001**
tighter	**RBR**	**1-01-001**
tightest	**JJT**	**2-02-002**
tightest-fitting	**JJT**	**1-01-001**
tightly	**QL**	**2-02-002**
tightly	**RB**	**13-08-011**
tigress	**NN**	**1-01-001**
Tigris	**NP**	**1-01-001**
Tijuana	**prop. noun**	**1-01-001**
Tijuana	NP	0-00-000
Tijuana	NP-TL	1-01-001
Tikopia	**NP**	**1-01-001**
tile	**noun**	**22-06-010**
tile	NN	16-04-006
tiles	NNS	5-04-004
tiles	NNS-HL	1-01-001
tile	**verb**	**4-04-004**
tiled	VBN	4-04-004
Tilghman	**prop. noun**	**29-01-001**
Tilghman	NP	25-01-001
Tilghman's	NP$	4-01-001
till	**CS**	**44-09-027**
till	**IN**	**4-04-004**
till	**verb**	**2-02-002**
till	VB	1-01-001
tilled	VBN	1-01-001
tiller	**NN**	**1-01-001**
Tillet	**NP**	**1-01-001**
Tillich	**NP**	**1-01-001**
Tillie	**prop. noun**	**3-01-001**
Tillie	NP	2-01-001
Tillie's	NP$	1-01-001
tilling	**NN**	**1-01-001**
Tillotson	**NP**	**2-01-001**
tilt	**NN**	**3-01-002**
tilt	**verb**	**17-09-015**
tilt	VB	2-02-002
tilts	VBZ	2-02-002
tilted	VBD	6-04-006
tilted	VBN	6-05-005
tilting	VBG	1-01-001
tilt-top	**NN**	**1-01-001**
tilth	**NN**	**1-01-001**
Tim	**prop. noun**	**27-02-003**
Tim	NP	25-02-003
Tim's	NP+HVZ	1-01-001
Tim's	NP$	1-01-001
timber	**noun**	**24-07-014**
timber	NN	19-07-010
timbers	NNS	5-04-004
timber	**verb**	**2-01-001**
timbered	VBN	2-01-001
timberland	**noun**	**3-01-001**
timberlands	NNS	3-01-001
timbre	**NN**	**2-02-002**
time	**noun**	**1901-15-465**
time	NN	1567-15-447
tyme	NN	2-01-001
time	NN-HL	8-04-005
Time	NN-TL	23-08-013
time's	NN$	2-02-002
Time's	NN$-TL	2-02-002
times	NNS	260-15-179
Times	NNS	2-01-001
Times	NNS-TL	29-08-018
Times	NNS-TL-HL	5-01-001
times'	NNS$	0-00-000
Times'	NNS$-TL	1-01-001
time	**verb**	**16-09-014**
time	VB	1-01-001
times	VBZ	1-01-001
timed	VBD	2-02-002
timed	VBN	7-04-006
timing	VBG	5-03-005
time-&-motion	**NN**	**2-01-001**
time-cast	**JJ**	**1-01-001**
time-consuming	**JJ**	**1-01-001**

Word	Tag	Frequency
time-delay	**NN**	**1-01-001**
time-honored	**JJ**	**3-02-002**
Time-Life	**NP**	**1-01-001**
time-on-the-job	**NN**	**1-01-001**
time-server	**noun**	**2-01-001**
time-servers	NNS	2-01-001
time-span	**NN**	**2-02-002**
time-temperature	**NN**	**2-01-001**
timeless	**JJ**	**2-02-002**
timeliness	**NN**	**2-02-002**
timely	**JJ**	**8-04-007**
timely	**RB**	**1-01-001**
Timen	**prop. noun**	**1-01-001**
Timen	NP	0-00-000
Timen	NP-TL	1-01-001
timepiece	**NN**	**1-01-001**
timer	**noun**	**1-01-001**
timers	NNS	1-01-001
times	**IN**	**3-03-003**
Times-Picayune	**prop. noun**	**1-01-001**
Times-Picayune	NP	0-00-000
Times-Picayune	NP-TL	1-01-001
timetable	**noun**	**5-02-005**
timetable	NN	4-02-004
timetables	NNS	1-01-001
timeworn	**JJ**	**1-01-001**
Timex	**prop. noun**	**2-01-001**
Timex	NP	1-01-001
Timex	NP-TL	1-01-001
timid	**JJ**	**5-04-005**
timidity	**NN**	**1-01-001**
timidly	**RB**	**1-01-001**
timing	**NN**	**6-03-004**
Timmy	**NP**	**1-01-001**
Timon	**prop. noun**	**1-01-001**
Timon	NP	0-00-000
Timon	NP-TL	1-01-001
Timothy	**NP**	**11-02-002**
Tims	**NP**	**1-01-001**
tin	**noun**	**12-08-009**
tin	NN	11-07-008
Tin	NN-TL	1-01-001
tincture	**NN**	**1-01-001**
Tindal	**NP**	**1-01-001**
tinder	**NN**	**1-01-001**
tine	**noun**	**2-01-001**
tines	NNS	2-01-001
tingle	**verb**	**6-05-005**
tingling	VBG	6-05-005
tiniest	**JJT**	**3-03-003**
tinker	**noun**	**1-01-001**
tinkers	NNS	1-01-001
tinker	**verb**	**1-01-001**
tinkering	VBG	1-01-001
tinkering	**NN**	**1-01-001**
tinkle	**verb**	**3-02-002**
tinkled	VBD	1-01-001
tinkling	VBG	2-01-001
tinning	**NN**	**1-01-001**
tinplate	**verb**	**1-01-001**
tinplated	VBN	1-01-001
tinsel	**NN**	**2-01-001**
tint	**noun**	**2-02-002**
tint	NN	1-01-001
tints	NNS	1-01-001
tint	**verb**	**1-01-001**
tinted	VBN	1-01-001
tintable	**JJ**	**2-01-001**
Tintoretto	**NP**	**1-01-001**
tintype	**NN**	**1-01-001**
tiny	**adjective**	**50-13-042**
tiny	JJ	49-13-041
Tiny	JJ-TL	1-01-001
tip	**noun**	**33-10-024**
tip	NN	20-09-015
tips	NNS	12-06-010
tips	NNS-HL	1-01-001
tip	**verb**	**7-06-007**
tip	VB	2-02-002
tipped	VBD	4-04-004
tipping	VBG	1-01-001
tip-toe	**NN**	**1-01-001**
Tipoff	**prop. noun**	**1-01-001**
Tipoff	NP	0-00-000
Tipoff	NP-TL	1-01-001
Tippecanoe	**NP**	**1-01-001**
Tipperary	**NP**	**1-01-001**
tipple	**VB**	**1-01-001**
tipsy	**JJ**	**2-02-002**
tiptoe	**verb**	**2-02-002**
tiptoeing	VBG	2-02-002
tirade	**noun**	**1-01-001**
tirades	NNS	1-01-001
tire	**noun**	**31-08-014**
tire	NN	20-05-006
tires	NNS	11-05-008
tire	**verb**	**46-09-038**
tire	VB	2-02-002
tires	VBZ	1-01-001
tired	VBD	4-04-004
tired	VBN	35-09-028
tiring	VBG	4-04-004
tired	**JJ**	**9-04-008**
tiredly	**RB**	**2-02-002**
tiredness	**NN**	**1-01-001**
tireless	**JJ**	**4-02-004**
tirelessly	**RB**	**1-01-001**
tiresome	**JJ**	**3-03-003**
tissue	**noun**	**54-07-015**
tissue	NN	41-06-012
tissues	NNS	13-02-005
tit	**noun**	**2-01-001**
tits	NNS	2-01-001
Titan	**prop. noun**	**8-03-005**
Titan	NP	7-02-004
Titans	NPS	1-01-001
titanic	**adjective**	**3-03-003**
titanic	JJ	2-02-002
Titanic	JJ-TL	1-01-001
titanium	**NN**	**2-02-002**
Titche	**prop. noun**	**1-01-001**
Titche's	NP$	1-01-001
titer	**noun**	**8-01-002**
titer	NN	4-01-002
titers	NNS	4-01-001
tithe	**noun**	**1-01-001**
tithes	NNS	1-01-001
Titian	**NP**	**2-02-002**
titian-haired	**JJ**	**1-01-001**
titillate	**verb**	**1-01-001**
titillating	VBG	1-01-001
title	**noun**	**94-13-052**
title	NN	51-13-040
title	NN-HL	1-01-001
Title	NN-TL	25-03-005
titles	NNS	16-07-011
Titles	NNS-TL	1-01-001
title	**verb**	**12-06-010**
titled	VBD	1-01-001
titled	VBN	11-06-010
title-holder	**NN**	**1-01-001**
Tito	**NP**	**2-02-002**
titration	**NN**	**1-01-001**
titre	**FW-NN**	**2-02-002**
titter	**noun**	**1-01-001**
titters	NNS	1-01-001
titter	**VB**	**1-01-001**
titular	**JJ**	**1-01-001**
Titus	**NP**	**2-01-001**
Tiveden	**NP**	**1-01-001**
Tizard	**prop. noun**	**1-01-001**
Tizard	NP	0-00-000
Tizard	NP-TL	1-01-001
Tjokorda	**NP**	**1-01-001**
to	**prep.**	**11165-15-500**
to	IN	11052-15-500
to	IN-HL	68-06-028
to	IN-NC	8-01-001
To	IN-TL	24-06-018
to	IN-TL	12-07-011
t'hi-im	IN + PPO	1-01-001
to	**inf. mark.**	**15025-15-500**
to	TO	14913-15-500
t'	TO	1-01-001
to	TO-HL	55-06-023
to	TO-NC	13-01-002
To	TO-TL	10-06-008
t'lah	TO + VB	1-01-001
t'jawn	TO + VB	1-01-001
gonna	+ TO	17-05-007
gotta	+ TO	5-04-004
hafta	+ TO	3-02-002
oughta	+ TO	2-02-002
wanna	+ TO	3-02-002
wanta	+ TO	1-01-001
to-and-fro	**RB**	**1-01-001**
to-do	**NN**	**1-01-001**
to-the-death	**JJ**	**1-01-001**

Word	Tag	Count
toad	**NN**	**4-03-003**
toady	**noun**	**1-01-001**
toadies	NNS	1-01-001
toadyism	**NN**	**1-01-001**
toast	**noun**	**14-09-010**
toast	NN	13-08-009
Toast	NN-TL	1-01-001
toast	**verb**	**9-05-005**
toast	VB	5-03-003
toasted	VBD	1-01-001
toasted	VBN	1-01-001
toasting	VBG	2-02-002
toasted-nut	**NN**	**1-01-001**
tobacco	**noun**	**19-08-011**
tobacco	NN	15-08-011
Tobacco	NN-TL	2-01-001
Tobacco	NN-TL-HL	2-01-001
tobacco-juice	**NN**	**1-01-001**
Tobin	**NP**	**2-02-002**
toccata	**noun**	**1-01-001**
toccata	NN	0-00-000
Toccata	NN-TL	1-01-001
Toch	**NP**	**1-01-001**
today	**adv. noun**	**330-14-174**
today	NR	282-14-160
to-day	NR	4-01-002
today	NR-HL	1-01-001
Today	NR-TL	1-01-001
today'll	NR+MD	1-01-001
today's	NR$	38-10-029
Today's	NR$-TL	3-01-001
Todd	**NP**	**2-02-002**
toddler	**noun**	**1-01-001**
toddlers	NNS	1-01-001
Todman	**prop. noun**	**11-01-001**
Todman	NP	10-01-001
Todman's	NP$	1-01-001
toe	**noun**	**26-10-019**
toe	NN	7-06-006
toes	NNS	19-09-015
toe	**VB**	**2-02-002**
toe-tip	**noun**	**1-01-001**
toe-tips	NNS	1-01-001
toed	**adjective**	**1-01-001**
toed	JJ	0-00-000
tode	JJ	1-01-001
toffee	**NN**	**1-01-001**
Toffenetti	**prop. noun**	**1-01-001**
Toffenetti's	NP$	1-01-001
tofu	**FW-NN**	**1-01-001**
tog	**noun**	**1-01-001**
togs	NNS	1-01-001
together	**adverb**	**268-15-193**
together	RB	265-15-191
t'gethuh	RB	1-01-001
together	RB-HL	1-01-001
Together	RB-TL	1-01-001
togetherness	**noun**	**1-01-001**
togetherness	NN	0-00-000
togetherness	NN-HL	1-01-001
toil	**NN**	**1-01-001**
toil	**verb**	**1-01-001**
toiled	VBN	1-01-001
toilet	**noun**	**17-07-009**
toilet	NN	13-06-007
toilets	NNS	4-02-002
toilsome	**JJ**	**1-01-001**
Tojo	**prop. noun**	**1-01-001**
Tojos	NPS	1-01-001
token	**JJ**	**6-03-004**
token	**noun**	**6-05-006**
token	NN	4-04-004
tokens	NNS	2-02-002
tokenish	**JJ**	**1-01-001**
Tokyo	**prop. noun**	**18-05-007**
Tokyo	NP	14-05-007
Tokyo	NP-HL	2-01-001
Tokyo	NP-TL	2-01-001
Toland	**NP**	**1-01-001**
Tolek	**NP**	**1-01-001**
tolerable	**JJ**	**3-03-003**
tolerance	**NN**	**9-07-009**
tolerant	**JJ**	**9-05-007**
tolerate	**verb**	**11-08-011**
tolerate	VB	4-03-004
tolerated	VBN	6-06-006
tolerating	VBG	1-01-001
toleration	**NN**	**1-01-001**
toll	**noun**	**19-07-010**

toll (cont.):

Word	Tag	Count
toll	NN	13-07-009
tole	NN	1-01-001
Toll	NN	1-01-001
Toll	NN-TL	1-01-001
tolls	NNS	2-01-001
Tolls	NNS-TL	1-01-001
toll	**verb**	**2-02-002**
toll	VB	1-01-001
tolled	VBN	1-01-001
toll-rate	**NN**	**1-01-001**
toll-road	**NN**	**8-01-001**
Tolley	**prop. noun**	**9-01-001**
Tolley	NP	6-01-001
Tolley's	NP$	3-01-001
tollgate	**NN**	**1-01-001**
tollhouse	**NN**	**1-01-001**
Tolstoy	**prop. noun**	**2-02-002**
Tolstoy	NP	1-01-001
Tolstoy's	NP$	1-01-001
Tolubeyev	**NP**	**1-01-001**
tolylene	**NN**	**1-01-001**
Tom	**prop. noun**	**67-10-019**
Tom	NP	62-08-017
Tom	NP-TL	1-01-001
Tom's	NP$	3-02-002
Tom's	NP$-TL	1-01-001
Tomas	**NP**	**4-01-001**
tomato	**noun**	**7-04-007**
tomato	NN	4-02-004
tomatoes	NNS	3-02-003
tomato-red	**JJ**	**1-01-001**
tomb	**noun**	**13-06-011**
tomb	NN	11-06-009
tombs	NNS	2-02-002
Tombigbee	**NP**	**2-01-001**
tomblike	**JJ**	**2-01-002**
tombstone	**noun**	**3-02-003**
tombstone	NN	2-02-002
tombstones	NNS	1-01-001
tome	**noun**	**1-01-001**
tomes	NNS	1-01-001
Tomkins	**NP**	**1-01-001**
Tommie	**NP**	**1-01-001**
Tommy	**prop. noun**	**19-04-004**
Tommy	NP	18-04-004
Tommy's	NP$	1-01-001
Tomonggong	**NP**	**1-01-001**
tomorrow	**adv. noun**	**67-11-042**
tomorrow	NR	62-11-039
to-morrow	NR	1-01-001
tomorrow	NR-HL	1-01-001
tomorrow's	NR$	3-03-003
ton	**noun**	**41-11-024**
ton	NN	13-05-006
tons	NNS	28-10-019
ton-mile	**NN**	**1-01-001**
tonal	**JJ**	**9-03-004**
tonality	**noun**	**1-01-001**
tonalities	NNS	1-01-001
tonally	**RB**	**1-01-001**
tone	**noun**	**97-14-047**
tone	NN	77-13-038
tones	NNS	15-08-013
Tones	NNS-TL	5-01-001
tone	**VB**	**1-01-001**
toneless	**JJ**	**1-01-001**
toner	**NN**	**3-01-001**
tong	**noun**	**1-01-001**
tongs	NNS	1-01-001
Tong	**NP**	**1-01-001**
tongue	**noun**	**39-12-025**
tongue	NN	35-11-023
tongues	NNS	4-03-004
tongue	**verb**	**1-01-001**
tongued	VBD	1-01-001
tongue-in-cheek	**JJ**	**2-02-002**
tongue-thrusting	**NN**	**1-01-001**
tongue-tied	**JJ**	**1-01-001**
tongue-twister	**NN**	**1-01-001**
Toni	**NP**	**1-01-001**
tonic	**noun**	**3-03-003**
tonic	NN	1-01-001
tonics	NNS	2-02-002
tonight	**adv. noun**	**40-10-029**
tonight	NR	38-10-029
tonight's	NR$	2-01-002
Tonio	**NP**	**1-01-001**
tonsil	**NN**	**2-01-001**

Word	Tag	Count
Tony	**prop. noun**	**11-04-007**
Tony	NP	8-04-006
Tony	NP-TL	3-01-001
too	**qualifier**	**550-15-272**
too	QL	547-15-271
to	QL	1-01-001
too	QL-HL	1-01-001
Too	QL-TL	1-01-001
too	**adverb**	**285-15-180**
too	RB	283-15-178
too	RB-HL	1-01-001
too	RB-NC	1-01-001
too-expensive	**JJ**	**1-01-001**
too-hearty	**JJ**	**1-01-001**
too-large	**JJ**	**2-02-002**
too-naked	**JJ**	**1-01-001**
too-shiny	**JJ**	**1-01-001**
too-simple-to-be-true	**JJ**	**1-01-001**
Toobin	**NP**	**2-01-001**
Toodle	**NP**	**2-01-001**
tool	**JJ**	**1-01-001**
tool	**noun**	**73-12-034**
tool	NN	37-09-019
Tool	NN-TL	2-01-001
tools	NNS	33-10-019
tools	NNS-HL	1-01-001
tool	**verb**	**5-05-005**
tooling	VBG	5-05-005
tool-and-die	**NN**	**2-01-001**
tool-kit	**NN**	**1-01-001**
toolmaker	**NN**	**1-01-001**
Toomey	**NP**	**1-01-001**
Toonker	**NP**	**1-01-001**
toot	**exclam.**	**3-02-002**
toot	UH	0-00-000
Toot	UH	1-01-001
Toot	UH-TL	2-01-001
Toot-toot	**UH**	**1-01-001**
tooth	**noun**	**123-12-039**
tooth	NN	19-05-005
tooth	NN-HL	1-01-001
teeth	NNS	102-11-036
teeth	NNS-HL	1-01-001
tooth-hurty	**NN**	**1-01-001**
tooth-straightening	**NN**	**1-01-001**
toothbrush	**NN**	**6-02-002**
toothpaste	**noun**	**2-02-002**
toothpaste	NN	1-01-001
tooth-paste	NN	1-01-001
tootley-toot-tootle	**verb**	**1-01-001**
tootley-toot-tootled	VBD	1-01-001
Tootsie	**prop. noun**	**1-01-001**
Tootsie	NP	0-00-000
Tootsie	NP-TL	1-01-001
top	**sem. sup.**	**72-13-051**
top	JJS	70-13-050
top	JJS-HL	1-01-001
Top	JJS-TL	1-01-001
top	**noun**	**136-15-090**
top	NN	129-15-088
tops	NNS	7-04-005
top	**verb**	**13-07-011**
top	VB	3-03-003
tops	VBZ	1-01-001
topped	VBD	3-02-002
topped	VBN	4-03-004
topping	VBG	2-01-002
top-drawer	**NN**	**2-02-002**
top-grade	**NN**	**2-02-002**
top-heavy	**JJ**	**1-01-001**
top-level	**NN**	**3-02-002**
top-notch	**noun**	**2-02-002**
top-notch	NN	1-01-001
topnotch	NN	1-01-001
top-priority	**NN**	**1-01-001**
top-quality	**NN**	**2-01-002**
top-ranking	**JJ**	**1-01-001**
top-tang	**NN**	**2-01-001**
topcoat	**noun**	**3-02-002**
topcoat	NN	2-01-001
topcoats	NNS	1-01-001
Topeka	**NP**	**1-01-001**
topgallant	**NN**	**2-01-001**
topic	**noun**	**19-07-017**
topic	NN	9-05-008
topics	NNS	10-05-010
topical	**JJ**	**4-02-003**
Topkapi	**prop. noun**	**1-01-001**
Topkapi	NP	0-00-000
Topkapi (cont.):		
Topkapi	NP-TL	1-01-001
topmost	**JJS**	**1-01-001**
topographic	**JJ**	**1-01-001**
topography	**noun**	**6-03-003**
topography	NN	4-02-002
topography	NN-HL	2-02-002
Topper	**prop. noun**	**1-01-001**
Toppers	NPS	0-00-000
Toppers	NPS-TL	1-01-001
topping	**noun**	**1-01-001**
toppings	NNS	1-01-001
topple	**verb**	**4-03-004**
topple	VB	1-01-001
toppled	VBD	1-01-001
toppled	VBN	1-01-001
toppling	VBG	1-01-001
toppling	**NN**	**1-01-001**
tops	**JJS**	**2-02-002**
topsoil	**NN**	**1-01-001**
Topsy	**NP**	**1-01-001**
topsy-turvy	**JJ**	**1-01-001**
Torah	**NP**	**1-01-001**
torch	**noun**	**4-03-003**
torch	NN	2-02-002
torches	NNS	2-01-001
Torino	**NP**	**2-01-001**
Torkin	**NP**	**1-01-001**
torment	**NN**	**4-03-004**
torment	**verb**	**5-04-004**
tormented	VBN	2-02-002
tormented	VBN-HL	1-01-001
tormenting	VBG	2-02-002
tormenter	**noun**	**1-01-001**
tormenters	NNS	1-01-001
tornado	**noun**	**2-02-002**
tornado	NN	1-01-001
tornadoes	NNS	1-01-001
Toronto	**prop. noun**	**6-04-005**
Toronto	NP	5-04-004
Toronto	NP-TL	1-01-001
torpedo	**noun**	**2-02-002**
torpedo	NN	1-01-001
torpedoes	NNS	1-01-001
Torpetius	**NP**	**1-01-001**
torpid	**JJ**	**1-01-001**
torpor	**NN**	**2-02-002**
Torquato	**NP**	**1-01-001**
torque	**NN**	**5-01-001**
Torquemada	**NP**	**1-01-001**
torquer	**noun**	**9-01-001**
torquer	NN	5-01-001
torquers	NNS	4-01-001
Torrence	**NP**	**2-01-001**
torrent	**noun**	**6-04-006**
torrent	NN	4-04-004
torrents	NNS	2-02-002
torrid	**adjective**	**5-01-001**
torrid	JJ	0-00-000
Torrid	JJ-TL	5-01-001
Torrio	**NP**	**12-01-001**
Torrio-Capone	**NP**	**2-01-001**
torsion	**NN**	**1-01-001**
torso	**noun**	**10-06-006**
torso	NN	7-05-005
torsos	NNS	3-02-002
torso-defining	**JJ**	**1-01-001**
tortoise	**noun**	**4-02-002**
tortoise	NN	3-02-002
tortoises	NNS	0-00-000
Tortoises	NNS-TL	1-01-001
tortuous	**JJ**	**3-03-003**
torture	**noun**	**4-04-004**
torture	NN	3-03-003
tortures	NNS	1-01-001
torture	**verb**	**10-07-010**
tortures	VBZ	1-01-001
tortured	VBD	1-01-001
tortured	VBN	8-06-008
Tory	**prop. noun**	**18-02-005**
Tory	NP	11-01-004
Tory	NP-TL	1-01-001
Tories	NPS	6-02-002
Tosca	**NP**	**1-01-001**
Toscanini	**prop. noun**	**3-02-002**
Toscanini	NP	2-02-002
Toscanini's	NP$	1-01-001
toss	**noun**	**5-02-003**
toss	NN	3-02-002

Word	Tag	Frequency
toss (cont.):		
tosses	NNS	2-02-002
toss	**verb**	**41-10-030**
toss	VB	6-05-005
tossed	VBD	22-09-019
tossed	VBN	9-04-004
tossing	VBG	4-04-004
tossing	**NN**	**1-01-001**
tot	**verb**	**1-01-001**
totted	VBN	1-01-001
total	**adjective**	**74-10-035**
total	JJ	72-10-034
total	JJ-HL	2-02-002
total	**noun**	**134-09-079**
total	NN	131-09-079
totals	NNS	3-03-003
total	**verb**	**25-07-021**
total	VB	6-04-006
totals	VBZ	3-03-003
totaled	VBD	6-03-006
totalled	VBD	3-01-001
totaled	VBN	1-01-001
totaling	VBG	6-04-006
total-cost	**NN**	**2-01-001**
totalistic	**JJ**	**1-01-001**
totalitarian	**JJ**	**6-06-006**
totalitarianism	**noun**	**3-01-003**
totalitarianism	NN	2-01-002
Totalitarianism	NN-TL	1-01-001
totality	**NN**	**2-02-002**
totally	**QL**	**7-06-007**
totally	**RB**	**15-09-015**
tote	**VB**	**1-01-001**
totemic	**JJ**	**1-01-001**
toto	**NN**	**1-01-001**
totter	**verb**	**1-01-001**
tottering	VBG	1-01-001
touch	**noun**	**64-14-044**
touch	NN	54-13-036
Touch	NN-TL	1-01-001
touches	NNS	9-06-009
touch	**verb**	**91-15-075**
touch	VB	32-14-029
touches	VBZ	5-04-005
touched	VBD	24-08-022
touched	VBN	18-09-017
touching	VBG	12-05-011
touchdown	**noun**	**7-02-003**
touchdown	NN	6-02-003
touchdowns	NNS	1-01-001
touching	**JJ**	**3-03-003**
touchstone	**noun**	**2-02-002**
touchstone	NN	1-01-001
touchstones	NNS	1-01-001
touchy	**JJ**	**1-01-001**
Tougas	**NP**	**1-01-001**
tough	**adjective**	**36-12-031**
tough	JJ	35-12-030
tough	JJ-NC	1-01-001
tough	**noun**	**3-02-002**
toughs	NNS	3-02-002
tough-looking	**JJ**	**1-01-001**
tougher	**JJR**	**9-05-008**
tougher	**RBR**	**1-01-001**
toughest	**JJT**	**2-02-002**
toughness	**NN**	**6-05-005**
toujours	**FW-RB**	**1-01-001**
Toulouse	**prop. noun**	**1-01-001**
Toulouse	NP	0-00-000
Toulouse	NP-TL	1-01-001
Toulouse-Lautrec	**NP**	**1-01-001**
tour	**foreign**	**3-02-003**
tour	FW-NN	1-01-001
Tour	FW-NN-TL	2-02-002
tour	**noun**	**48-10-028**
tour	NN	38-09-024
tour	NN-HL	1-01-001
tours	NNS	9-04-007
tour	**verb**	**10-06-008**
tour	VB	1-01-001
toured	VBD	2-02-002
touring	VBG	6-04-005
Touring	VBG-TL	1-01-001
tourist	**noun**	**31-09-024**
tourist	NN	15-05-012
Tourist	NN-TL	1-01-001
tourist's	NN$	2-02-002
tourists	NNS	12-08-012
tourists'	NNS$	1-01-001
tournament	**noun**	**25-04-007**
tournament	NN	18-04-007
Tournament	NN-TL	2-01-002
tournaments	NNS	5-03-004
Tours	**NP**	**1-01-001**
tousle	**verb**	**2-02-002**
tousled	VBN	2-02-002
tout	**FW-RB**	**1-01-001**
tow	**NN**	**1-01-001**
tow	**verb**	**1-01-001**
towed	VBD	1-01-001
toward	**prep.**	**386-15-216**
toward	IN	384-15-216
toward	IN-HL	2-01-002
towards	**prep.**	**65-14-040**
towards	IN	63-14-038
towardes	IN	1-01-001
Towards	IN-TL	1-01-001
towboat	**noun**	**1-01-001**
towboats	NNS	1-01-001
towel	**noun**	**17-06-011**
towel	NN	6-05-005
towels	NNS	11-04-006
toweling	**NN**	**1-01-001**
tower	**noun**	**16-08-013**
tower	NN	12-05-009
towers	NNS	4-03-004
tower	**verb**	**12-06-011**
towers	VBZ	1-01-001
towering	VBG	11-06-010
Tower	**prop. noun**	**2-02-002**
Tower	NP	1-01-001
Tower's	NP$	1-01-001
town	**noun**	**281-14-110**
town	NN	198-14-098
towne	NN	4-01-001
Towne	NN-TL	1-01-001
town	NN-HL	1-01-001
town	NN-NC	2-01-001
Town	NN-TL	11-04-006
town's	NN$	14-06-010
towns	NNS	50-11-021
Towne	**NP**	**4-01-001**
Townley	**NP**	**1-01-001**
Townsend	**NP**	**1-01-001**
township	**noun**	**8-04-005**
township	NN	3-02-002
Township	NN-TL	4-02-002
townships	NNS	1-01-001
townsman	**noun**	**3-02-002**
townsman	NN	1-01-001
townsmen	NNS	2-01-001
Towsley	**NP**	**2-01-001**
toxic	**JJ**	**3-01-001**
toxin	**NN**	**1-01-001**
toy	**noun**	**14-05-006**
toy	NN	4-03-004
toys	NNS	9-04-004
Toys	NNS-TL	1-01-001
toy	**verb**	**2-02-002**
toys	VBZ	1-01-001
toying	VBG	1-01-001
Toynbee	**NP**	**9-03-003**
TR	**NP**	**1-01-001**
TR.	**prop. noun**	**1-01-001**
TR.'s	NP$	1-01-001
Trabb	**NP**	**1-01-001**
trace	**JJ**	**2-01-001**
trace	**noun**	**22-09-020**
trace	NN	13-08-012
trace	NN-HL	1-01-001
traces	NNS	8-06-008
trace	**verb**	**36-11-023**
trace	VB	7-05-007
traces	VBZ	1-01-001
traced	VBD	2-02-002
traced	VBN	10-05-008
tracing	VBG	16-06-007
traceable	**JJ**	**3-02-003**
tracer	**noun**	**2-02-002**
tracers	NNS	2-02-002
trachea	**NN**	**2-02-002**
tracing	**noun**	**2-02-002**
tracing	NN	1-01-001
tracings	NNS	1-01-001
track	**noun**	**48-13-034**
track	NN	34-12-024
track	NN-HL	1-01-001
Track	NN-TL	1-01-001

Word	Tag	Frequency
track (cont.):		
tracks	NNS	12-08-011
track	**verb**	**8-06-007**
track	VB	2-02-002
tracked	VBD	2-01-002
tracked	VBN	1-01-001
tracking	VBG	3-02-002
track-signal	**NN**	**1-01-001**
Trackdown	**NP**	**1-01-001**
trackless	**JJ**	**1-01-001**
tract	**noun**	**22-09-017**
tract	NN	15-08-012
Tract	NN-TL	2-01-001
tracts	NNS	5-05-005
Tractarian	**prop. noun**	**1-01-001**
Tractarians	NPS	1-01-001
tractor	**noun**	**31-06-008**
tractor	NN	23-03-005
Tractor	NN-TL	1-01-001
tractors	NNS	7-05-005
tractor-trailer	**NN**	**1-01-001**
trade	**noun**	**138-13-069**
trade	NN	121-13-062
Trade	NN-TL	9-04-007
trades	NNS	8-05-006
trade	**verb**	**47-08-021**
trade	VB	13-08-011
trades	VBZ	1-01-001
traded	VBD	3-02-002
traded	VBN	5-03-003
trading	VBG	24-07-012
Trading	VBG-TL	1-01-001
trade-preparatory	**JJ**	**1-01-001**
trademark	**noun**	**5-04-005**
trademark	NN	3-03-003
trade-mark	NN	1-01-001
trademarks	NNS	1-01-001
trader	**noun**	**35-04-006**
trader	NN	6-02-003
Trader	NN-TL	2-01-001
traders	NNS	26-03-005
traders'	NNS$	1-01-001
tradesman	**noun**	**1-01-001**
tradesmen	NNS	1-01-001
tradition	**noun**	**115-11-061**
tradition	NN	93-09-052
Tradition	NN-TL	1-01-001
traditions	NNS	21-05-016
tradition-minded	**JJ**	**1-01-001**
traditional	**JJ**	**78-10-058**
traditionalism	**noun**	**3-02-002**
traditionalism	NN	2-02-002
Traditionalism	NN-TL	1-01-001
traditionalist	**noun**	**5-02-002**
traditionalist	NN	3-01-001
Traditionalist	NN-TL	1-01-001
traditionalists	NNS	0-00-000
Traditionalists	NNS-TL	1-01-001
traditionalistic	**JJ**	**1-01-001**
traditionalize	**verb**	**1-01-001**
traditionalized	VBN	1-01-001
traditionally	**RB**	**10-08-010**
traditionnel	**FW-JJ**	**1-01-001**
traffic	**noun**	**68-11-035**
traffic	NN	65-11-034
traffic	NN-HL	1-01-001
Traffic	NN-TL	2-02-002
traffic	**verb**	**1-01-001**
trafficked	VBD	1-01-001
Trafton	**prop. noun**	**4-01-001**
Trafton	NP	3-01-001
Trafton's	NP$	1-01-001
tragedian	**noun**	**2-01-002**
tragedians	NNS	2-01-002
tragedy	**noun**	**56-11-028**
tragedy	NN	47-10-022
tragedy	NN-NC	1-01-001
Tragedy	NN-TL	1-01-001
tragedies	NNS	7-06-007
Trager	**NP**	**2-02-002**
tragic	**JJ**	**33-08-026**
tragically	**RB**	**1-01-001**
tragicomic	**adjective**	**2-02-002**
tragicomic	JJ	1-01-001
tragi-comic	JJ	1-01-001
trail	**noun**	**45-12-019**
trail	NN	27-09-015
Trail	NN-TL	2-01-001
trails	NNS	15-04-005

Word	Tag	Frequency
trail (cont.):		
trails	NNS-HL	1-01-001
trail	**verb**	**17-10-017**
trail	VB	2-02-002
trailed	VBD	6-03-006
trailed	VBN	2-01-002
trailing	VBG	7-07-007
trail-worn	**JJ**	**1-01-001**
trailer	**noun**	**23-04-007**
trailer	NN	11-02-004
trailers	NNS	12-03-004
train	**noun**	**86-13-046**
train	NN	67-13-034
Train	NN-TL	4-02-002
trains	NNS	15-07-014
train	**verb**	**130-14-067**
train	VB	10-08-009
trains	VBZ	1-01-001
trained	VBD	2-02-002
trained	VBN	52-11-041
training	VBG	63-11-028
Training	VBG-TL	2-01-001
Train	**NP**	**1-01-001**
traineeship	**noun**	**1-01-001**
traineeships	NNS	1-01-001
training	**noun**	**91-11-042**
training	NN	84-11-040
Training	NN-TL	7-03-005
trainman	**NN**	**1-01-001**
traipse	**verb**	**1-01-001**
traipsing	VBG	1-01-001
trait	**noun**	**9-06-009**
trait	NN	3-02-003
traits	NNS	5-04-005
Traits	NNS-TL	1-01-001
traitor	**noun**	**6-04-004**
traitor	NN	2-01-001
traitors	NNS	4-03-003
traitorous	**JJ**	**1-01-001**
trajectory	**NN**	**2-02-002**
trammel	**VB**	**1-01-001**
tramp	**NN**	**1-01-001**
tramp	**verb**	**2-02-002**
tramped	VBD	2-02-002
trample	**verb**	**4-04-004**
trample	VB	3-03-003
trampled	VBN	1-01-001
trampling	**NN**	**1-01-001**
tramway	**NN**	**1-01-001**
trance	**noun**	**6-04-005**
trance	NN	4-03-003
trances	NNS	2-02-002
tranquil	**JJ**	**2-02-002**
tranquilizer	**noun**	**5-04-004**
tranquilizer	NN	1-01-001
tranquilizers	NNS	4-03-003
tranquillity	**noun**	**5-04-004**
tranquillity	NN	1-01-001
tranquility	NN	3-02-002
Tranquility	NN-TL	1-01-001
trans-illuminated	**adjective**	**6-01-001**
trans-illuminated	JJ	5-01-001
trans-illuminated	JJ-HL	1-01-001
trans-illumination	**NN**	**1-01-001**
trans-lingually	**RB**	**1-01-001**
trans-political	**JJ**	**1-01-001**
transact	**VB**	**3-03-003**
transaction	**noun**	**10-04-007**
transaction	NN	5-03-004
transactions	NNS	5-03-004
transaminase	**NN**	**1-01-001**
transatlantic	**adjective**	**2-02-002**
transatlantic	JJ	1-01-001
trans-Atlantic	JJ	1-01-001
transcend	**verb**	**11-05-008**
transcend	VB	1-01-001
transcends	VBZ	6-02-005
transcended	VBD	1-01-001
transcending	VBG	3-03-003
transcendence	**NN**	**2-02-002**
transcendent	**adjective**	**3-02-003**
transcendent	JJ	2-02-002
transcendant	JJ	1-01-001
transcendental	**adjective**	**3-02-003**
transcendental	JJ	2-01-002
Transcendental	JJ-TL	1-01-001
transcendentalism	**noun**	**2-01-001**
transcendentalism	NN	0-00-000
Transcendentalism	NN-TL	2-01-001

Word	Tag	Frequency
transcendentalist	**noun**	**1-01-001**
transcendentalists	NNS	0-00-000
Transcendentalists	NNS-TL	1-01-001
transcribe	**verb**	**4-03-004**
transcribe	VB	1-01-001
transcribed	VBN	3-02-003
transcript	**noun**	**6-03-003**
transcript	NN	4-03-003
transcripts	NNS	2-02-002
transcription	**NN**	**2-01-002**
transcultural	**JJ**	**1-01-001**
transducer	**noun**	**12-02-002**
transducer	NN	9-02-002
transducer	NN-HL	1-01-001
transducers	NNS	2-01-001
transfer	**noun**	**43-11-016**
transfer	NN	31-08-012
transfer	NN-HL	1-01-001
Transfer	NN-TL	1-01-001
transfers	NNS	9-05-005
transfers	NNS-HL	1-01-001
transfer	**verb**	**38-13-024**
transfer	VB	6-05-006
transfers	VBZ	1-01-001
transferred	VBD	2-02-002
transferred	VBN	27-09-016
transfered	VBN	1-01-001
transferring	VBG	1-01-001
transferee	**NN**	**2-01-001**
transference	**NN**	**2-01-001**
transferor	**noun**	**16-01-001**
transferor	NN	11-01-001
transferor	NN-HL	1-01-001
transferor's	NN$	3-01-001
transferors	NNS	1-01-001
transferral	**NN**	**1-01-001**
transform	**verb**	**37-06-017**
transform	VB	7-03-007
transforms	VBZ	3-01-002
transformed	VBD	4-03-004
transformed	VBN	21-03-006
transforming	VBG	2-02-002
transformation	**NN**	**20-04-012**
transformer	**noun**	**3-01-003**
transformer	NN	1-01-001
transformers	NNS	2-01-002
transfusion	**noun**	**4-02-002**
transfusions	NNS	4-02-002
transgress	**verb**	**1-01-001**
transgressed	VBD	1-01-001
transgression	**NN**	**1-01-001**
transience	**NN**	**1-01-001**
transient	**JJ**	**3-02-002**
transient	**noun**	**1-01-001**
transients	NNS	1-01-001
transistor	**noun**	**2-02-002**
transistor	NN	1-01-001
transistors	NNS	1-01-001
transit	**noun**	**16-04-007**
transit	NN	13-03-005
transit	NN-HL	2-02-002
Transit	NN-TL	1-01-001
transition	**noun**	**37-10-023**
transition	NN	31-10-020
transition	NN-HL	1-01-001
transitions	NNS	5-03-005
transitional	**adjective**	**5-03-003**
transitional	JJ	4-03-003
transitional	JJ-HL	1-01-001
translate	**verb**	**34-12-029**
translate	VB	15-11-014
translates	VBZ	1-01-001
translated	VBD	1-01-001
translated	VBN	15-09-013
translating	VBG	2-02-002
translation	**noun**	**19-06-014**
translation	NN	16-06-012
translations	NNS	3-03-003
translator	**NN**	**1-01-001**
translucence	**NN**	**1-01-001**
translucency	**NN**	**1-01-001**
translucent	**adjective**	**4-03-003**
translucent	JJ	3-02-002
transluscent	JJ	1-01-001
transmissible	**JJ**	**1-01-001**
transmission	**NN**	**16-05-011**
transmit	**verb**	**13-06-011**
transmit	VB	3-03-003
transmits	VBZ	1-01-001

Word	Tag	Frequency
transmit (cont.):		
transmitted	VBN	8-05-008
transmitting	VBG	1-01-001
transmittable	**JJ**	**1-01-001**
transmitter	**NN**	**4-02-002**
transmitting	**NN**	**1-01-001**
transmutation	**NN**	**3-02-002**
transmute	**verb**	**4-04-004**
transmuted	VBN	4-04-004
transoceanic	**JJ**	**1-01-001**
transom	**noun**	**19-03-004**
transom	NN	17-02-002
transoms	NNS	2-02-002
transparency	**NN**	**2-02-002**
transparent	**JJ**	**13-06-010**
transpirate	**verb**	**1-01-001**
transpirating	VBG	1-01-001
transpiration	**noun**	**4-01-001**
transpiration	NN	3-01-001
transpiration	NN-HL	1-01-001
transpire	**verb**	**7-02-004**
transpired	VBD	1-01-001
transpired	VBN	2-01-002
transpiring	VBG	4-01-001
transplant	**verb**	**4-02-003**
transplant	VB	2-01-001
transplanted	VBN	1-01-001
transplanting	VBG	1-01-001
transplantable	**JJ**	**1-01-001**
transport	**noun**	**19-08-013**
transport	NN	14-06-010
transport	NN-HL	1-01-001
transports	NNS	4-04-004
transport	**verb**	**12-06-009**
transport	VB	3-02-003
transports	VBZ	1-01-001
transported	VBD	1-01-001
transported	VBN	4-04-004
transporting	VBG	3-03-003
transportation	**noun**	**43-07-026**
transportation	NN	40-07-024
transportation	NN-HL	1-01-001
Transportation	NN-TL	2-02-002
transpose	**verb**	**5-04-005**
transposed	VBN	5-04-005
transposition	**NN**	**1-01-001**
transshipment	**NN**	**2-01-001**
transversally	**RB**	**1-01-001**
transverse	**JJ**	**4-02-002**
transversely	**RB**	**1-01-001**
transversus	**NN**	**2-01-001**
transvestitism	**NN**	**1-01-001**
Transylvania	**prop. noun**	**2-01-001**
Transylvania	NP	0-00-000
Transylvania	NP-TL	2-01-001
trap	**noun**	**27-09-017**
trap	NN	19-08-013
Trap	NN-TL	1-01-001
traps	NNS	7-04-005
trap	**verb**	**10-07-010**
traps	VBZ	1-01-001
trapped	VBN	7-06-007
trapping	VBG	2-02-002
trapdoor	**noun**	**2-02-002**
trapdoor	NN	1-01-001
trapdoors	NNS	1-01-001
trapezoid	**NN**	**1-01-001**
Trapp	**NP**	**1-01-001**
trapper	**noun**	**3-01-001**
trapper	NN	2-01-001
trapper's	NN$	1-01-001
trapping	**noun**	**3-03-003**
trappings	NNS	3-03-003
trash	**NN**	**2-02-002**
Trastevere	**NP**	**3-03-003**
trauma	**NN**	**1-01-001**
traumatic	**JJ**	**1-01-001**
Travancore	**NP**	**1-01-001**
travel	**noun**	**37-08-027**
travel	NN	30-08-022
travel	NN-HL	1-01-001
Travel	NN-TL	2-02-002
travels	NNS	2-02-002
Travels	NNS-TL	2-02-002
travel	**verb**	**80-12-058**
travel	VB	28-10-023
travels	VBZ	1-01-001
traveled	VBD	13-09-013
travelled	VBD	2-02-002

Word	Tag	Frequency
travel (cont.):		
traveled	VBN	9-07-009
travelled	VBN	2-02-002
traveling	VBG	18-08-017
travelling	VBG	4-04-004
travelin'	VBG	2-01-001
Traveling	VBG-TL	1-01-001
traveler	**noun**	**21-08-018**
traveler	NN	7-04-006
traveller	NN	3-02-003
Traveler	NN-TL	1-01-001
travelers	NNS	7-05-007
travellers	NNS	1-01-001
Travellers	NNS	1-01-001
Travelers	NNS-TL	1-01-001
travelogue	**noun**	**3-03-003**
travelogue	NN	2-02-002
travelogues	NNS	1-01-001
travelogue-like	**JJ**	**1-01-001**
traverse	**verb**	**12-07-010**
traverse	VB	2-02-002
Traverse	VB-TL	3-01-001
traversed	VBD	2-02-002
traversed	VBN	4-02-004
traversing	VBG	1-01-001
travesty	**VB**	**1-01-001**
trawler	**NN**	**1-01-001**
Traxel	**NP**	**1-01-001**
tray	**noun**	**21-08-012**
tray	NN	18-07-010
trays	NNS	3-03-003
treacherous	**JJ**	**6-03-006**
treachery	**noun**	**1-01-001**
treacheries	NNS	1-01-001
tread	**NN**	**3-02-003**
tread	**verb**	**3-03-003**
tread	VB	2-02-002
treading	VBG	1-01-001
treadmill	**NN**	**1-01-001**
Treadwell	**NP**	**1-01-001**
treason	**NN**	**6-04-004**
treasonable	**JJ**	**1-01-001**
treasonous	**JJ**	**1-01-001**
treasure	**noun**	**10-08-010**
treasure	NN	3-03-003
Treasure	NN-TL	1-01-001
treasures	NNS	6-06-006
treasure	**verb**	**2-02-002**
treasured	VBN	2-02-002
treasurer	**noun**	**14-05-010**
treasurer	NN	13-04-009
Treasurer	NN-TL	1-01-001
treasury	**noun**	**42-08-017**
treasury	NN	2-02-002
Treasury	NN-TL	38-08-015
treasury's	NN$	0-00-000
Treasury's	NN$-TL	1-01-001
treasuries	NNS	1-01-001
treat	**noun**	**4-03-004**
treat	NN	2-02-002
treats	NNS	2-02-002
treat	**verb**	**122-13-071**
treat	VB	24-09-019
treats	VBZ	12-07-009
treated	VBD	11-06-010
treated	VBN	64-12-040
treating	VBG	11-05-009
treatise	**NN**	**1-01-001**
treatment	**noun**	**138-11-055**
treatment	NN	124-11-049
treatment	NN-HL	1-01-001
Treatment	NN-TL	2-02-002
treatments	NNS	11-04-006
treaty	**noun**	**24-08-012**
treaty	NN	13-04-006
Treaty	NN-TL	7-03-004
treaties	NNS	4-03-003
treaty-making	**NN**	**1-01-001**
treble	**JJ**	**1-01-001**
treble	**NN**	**1-01-001**
Tredding	**NP**	**1-01-001**
tree	**noun**	**160-13-077**
tree	NN	56-10-029
Tree	NN-TL	2-02-002
trees	NNS	95-12-056
Trees	NNS-TL	6-01-001
trees'	NNS$	1-01-001
Tree	**NP**	**1-01-001**
tree-clump	**noun**	**2-01-001**
tree-clump (cont.):		
tree-clumps	NNS	2-01-001
Treece	**NP**	**1-01-001**
treelike	**JJ**	**1-01-001**
treetop	**noun**	**1-01-001**
treetops	NNS	1-01-001
Tregnum	**prop. noun**	**1-01-001**
Tregnums	NPS	1-01-001
trek	**NN**	**2-02-002**
trek	**verb**	**1-01-001**
trekked	VBD	1-01-001
trellis	**noun**	**1-01-001**
trellises	NNS	1-01-001
tremble	**verb**	**42-09-032**
tremble	VB	10-06-010
trembles	VBZ	1-01-001
trembled	VBD	5-03-005
trembling	VBG	26-08-021
tremendous	**JJ**	**37-12-033**
tremendously	**QL**	**5-03-004**
tremendously	**RB**	**5-05-005**
tremor	**NN**	**2-02-002**
Trempler	**NP**	**1-01-001**
tremulously	**RB**	**1-01-001**
trench	**noun**	**3-02-003**
trench	NN	2-01-002
trenches	NNS	1-01-001
trenchant	**JJ**	**4-02-003**
Trenchard	**NP**	**2-01-002**
trencherman	**noun**	**1-01-001**
trenchermen	NNS	1-01-001
trend	**noun**	**67-09-047**
trend	NN	45-09-034
trend	NN-HL	1-01-001
trends	NNS	20-09-014
Trends	NNS-TL	1-01-001
trend-following	**JJ**	**1-01-001**
Trenton	**prop. noun**	**4-02-002**
Trenton	NP	2-02-002
Trenton	NP-HL	2-01-001
trespass	**noun**	**3-01-001**
trespasses	NNS	3-01-001
trespass	**verb**	**3-03-003**
trespassed	VBD	1-01-001
trespassed	VBN	2-02-002
trestle	**noun**	**2-02-002**
trestle	NN	1-01-001
trestles	NNS	1-01-001
Trevelyan	**prop. noun**	**29-01-001**
Trevelyan	NP	17-01-001
Trevelyan's	NP$	12-01-001
tri-iodothyronine	**NN**	**4-01-001**
tri-motor	**NN**	**1-01-001**
tri-state	**adjective**	**12-02-002**
tri-state	JJ	0-00-000
Tri-State	JJ-TL	12-02-002
triad	**NN**	**1-01-001**
trial	**noun**	**173-14-045**
trial	NN	117-14-039
trial	NN-HL	1-01-001
trial	NN-NC	1-01-001
Trial	NN-TL	15-01-001
trials	NNS	34-06-011
trials	NNS-HL	5-01-001
trial-book	**NN**	**1-01-001**
triamcinolone	**NN**	**4-01-001**
Triandos	**NP**	**3-01-001**
triangle	**noun**	**5-04-005**
triangle	NN	4-03-004
triangles	NNS	1-01-001
triangular	**JJ**	**5-04-005**
Trianon	**prop. noun**	**1-01-001**
Trianon	NP	0-00-000
Trianon	NP-TL	1-01-001
tribal	**JJ**	**6-05-006**
tribe	**noun**	**17-05-011**
tribe	NN	4-04-004
tribe's	NN$	0-00-000
Tribe's	NN$-TL	1-01-001
tribes	NNS	11-04-006
Tribes	NNS-TL	1-01-001
tribesman	**noun**	**2-02-002**
tribesmen	NNS	2-02-002
tribulation	**NN**	**1-01-001**
Tribuna	**NP**	**1-01-001**
tribunal	**noun**	**9-05-007**
tribunal	NN	5-03-005
tribunals	NNS	4-03-003
tribune	**noun**	**16-08-010**

Word	Tag	Frequency
tribune (cont.):		
tribune	NN	0-00-000
Tribune	NN-TL	15-08-010
tribune's	NN$	0-00-000
Tribune's	NN$-TL	1-01-001
tribute	**noun**	**25-08-020**
tribute	NN	23-08-019
tribute	NN-HL	1-01-001
tributes	NNS	1-01-001
Trichieri	**NP**	**1-01-001**
Trichinella	**NP**	**1-01-001**
trichloroacetic	**JJ**	**1-01-001**
trichrome	**JJ**	**1-01-001**
trick	**noun**	**23-10-020**
trick	NN	15-06-012
tricks	NNS	7-06-007
Tricks	NNS-TL	1-01-001
trick	**verb**	**2-02-002**
tricked	VBN	2-02-002
trickle	**NN**	**2-02-002**
trickle	**verb**	**2-02-002**
trickling	VBG	2-02-002
trickster	**noun**	**2-02-002**
trickster	NN	1-01-001
Trickster	NN-TL	1-01-001
tricky	**JJ**	**1-01-001**
tricolor	**NN**	**1-01-001**
trifle	**NN**	**9-07-009**
trifle	**verb**	**2-02-002**
trifling	VBG	2-02-002
Trig	**prop. noun**	**11-01-001**
Trig	NP	10-01-001
Trig's	NP$	1-01-001
Trigg	**NP**	**1-01-001**
trigger	**NN**	**11-04-009**
trigger	**verb**	**8-05-007**
trigger	VB	1-01-001
triggered	VBN	7-05-007
trigger-happy	**JJ**	**2-01-002**
trigonal	**JJ**	**2-01-002**
Trikojus	**NP**	**1-01-001**
trill	**NN**	**3-02-002**
trill	**verb**	**1-01-001**
trilled	VBD	1-01-001
trillion	**CD**	**1-01-001**
trilogy	**NN**	**4-01-003**
trim	**JJ**	**4-04-004**
trim	**noun**	**6-05-005**
trim	NN	5-04-004
trims	NNS	1-01-001
trim	**verb**	**16-05-010**
trim	VB	11-04-006
trimmed	VBN	4-03-004
trimming	VBG	1-01-001
trim-your-own-franks	**NNS**	**1-01-001**
Trimble	**NP**	**3-01-002**
trimester	**NN**	**1-01-001**
Trimmer	**NP**	**2-01-001**
trimming	**noun**	**5-03-004**
trimming	NN	1-01-001
trimmings	NNS	4-03-003
Trinidad	**NP**	**1-01-001**
Trinitarian	**JJ**	**1-01-001**
Trinitarian	**prop. noun**	**1-01-001**
Trinitarians	NPS	1-01-001
Trinity	**prop. noun**	**5-03-005**
Trinity	NP	4-03-004
Trinity	NP-TL	1-01-001
trinket	**noun**	**2-02-002**
trinket	NN	1-01-001
trinkets	NNS	1-01-001
trio	**noun**	**9-04-007**
trio	NN	8-04-006
Trio	NN-TL	1-01-001
triol	**NN**	**1-01-001**
triomphe	**foreign**	**1-01-001**
triomphe	FW-NN	0-00-000
Triomphe	FW-NN-TL	1-01-001
trip	**noun**	**109-15-075**
trip	NN	78-13-057
trip	NN-NC	2-01-001
trips	NNS	29-09-023
trip	**verb**	**6-05-006**
trip	VB	1-01-001
tripped	VBD	2-02-002
tripping	VBG	2-02-002
trippin'	VBG	1-01-001
trip-hammer	**NN**	**1-01-001**
tripartite	**JJ**	**1-01-001**
Tripe	**NP**	**1-01-001**
triphenylarsine	**NN**	**1-01-001**
triphenylphosphine	**NN**	**1-01-001**
triphenylstibine	**NN**	**1-01-001**
triphosphopyridine	**NN**	**1-01-001**
triple	**JJ**	**1-01-001**
triple	**NN**	**4-01-004**
triple	**verb**	**4-03-004**
tripled	VBD	1-01-001
tripled	VBN	3-03-003
triple-checked	**JJ**	**1-01-001**
triple-crown	**NN**	**1-01-001**
triple-tank	**NN**	**1-01-001**
triplet	**noun**	**4-02-002**
triplet	NN	1-01-001
triplets	NNS	3-01-001
triplication	**NN**	**1-01-001**
tripod	**noun**	**4-02-002**
tripod	NN	3-02-002
tripods	NNS	1-01-001
Tripoli	**NP**	**1-01-001**
tripolyphosphate	**NN**	**2-01-001**
triptych	**noun**	**2-02-002**
triptych	NN	1-01-001
Triptych	NN-TL	1-01-001
Tris	**NP**	**2-01-001**
tris(hydroxymethyl)-aminomethane	**NN**	**1-01-001**
triservice	**NN**	**2-01-001**
trisodium	**NN**	**1-01-001**
Tristan	**NP**	**1-01-001**
Tristano	**NP**	**4-02-002**
trite	**JJ**	**2-02-002**
triumph	**noun**	**24-08-022**
triumph	NN	21-08-019
triumphs	NNS	3-02-003
triumph	**VB**	**1-01-001**
triumphant	**JJ**	**5-04-004**
triumphantly	**RB**	**8-07-008**
trivia	**noun**	**2-02-002**
trivia	NNS	1-01-001
Trivia	NNS-TL	1-01-001
trivial	**JJ**	**11-07-011**
triviality	**NN**	**2-02-002**
Troeltsch	**NP**	**1-01-001**
Trohan	**NP**	**1-01-001**
troika	**FW-NN**	**1-01-001**
troll	**noun**	**1-01-001**
trolls	NNS	1-01-001
trolley	**NN**	**5-04-005**
trollop	**NN**	**1-01-001**
trombonist	**NN**	**1-01-001**
trompe-l'oeil	**FW-NN**	**1-01-001**
troop	**noun**	**69-09-030**
troop	NN	9-04-005
Troop	NN-TL	7-02-002
troops	NNS	52-09-027
Troops	NNS-TL	1-01-001
trooper	**noun**	**13-05-006**
trooper	NN	6-02-002
Trooper	NN-TL	1-01-001
troopers	NNS	6-04-004
troopship	**noun**	**2-02-002**
troopship	NN	1-01-001
troopships	NNS	1-01-001
Tropez	**NP**	**1-01-001**
tropho-	**JJ**	**1-01-001**
trophy	**noun**	**10-02-005**
trophy	NN	2-02-002
Trophy	NN-TL	6-02-004
trophies	NNS	2-01-001
tropic	**noun**	**4-03-003**
tropic	NN	0-00-000
Tropic	NN-TL	3-02-002
tropics	NNS	1-01-001
tropical	**JJ**	**11-08-009**
tropidoclonion	**NN**	**1-01-001**
tropocollagen	**NN**	**1-01-001**
trot	**NN**	**6-03-003**
trot	**verb**	**13-05-006**
trot	VB	6-01-002
trotted	VBD	5-04-004
trotted	VBN	2-02-002
Trotsky	**NP**	**1-01-001**
trotter	**NN**	**1-01-001**
trouble	**noun**	**154-15-108**
trouble	NN	130-15-095
troubie	NN	1-01-001
troubles	NNS	21-10-018

Word	Tag	Counts
trouble (cont.):		
trobles	NNS	1-01-001
troubles	NNS-HL	1-01-001
trouble	**verb**	**37-13-034**
trouble	VB	4-03-004
troubled	VBD	8-05-007
troubled	VBN	23-11-023
troubling	VBG	2-02-002
trouble-free	**JJ**	**2-02-002**
troubleshooter	**noun**	**2-02-002**
troubleshooter	NN	1-01-001
trouble-shooter	NN	1-01-001
troublesome	**JJ**	**7-03-007**
trough	**noun**	**4-02-003**
trough	NN	3-02-002
troughs	NNS	1-01-001
Troup	**NP**	**2-01-001**
troupe	**noun**	**5-04-005**
troupe	NN	3-03-003
troup	NN	1-01-001
troupes	NNS	1-01-001
trouser	**noun**	**10-05-009**
trouser	NN	3-03-003
trousers	NNS	7-03-006
trousers-pockets	**NNS**	**1-01-001**
trout	**noun**	**4-02-002**
trout	NN	1-01-001
Trout	NN-TL	3-01-001
Troy	**prop. noun**	**3-03-003**
Troy	NP	1-01-001
Troy	NP-TL	2-02-002
Troyes	**NP**	**1-01-001**
truant	**JJ**	**1-01-001**
truce	**NN**	**5-04-005**
truck	**noun**	**80-10-035**
truck	NN	56-10-024
Truck	NN-TL	1-01-001
truck's	NN$	1-01-001
trucks	NNS	21-06-013
trucks	NNS-HL	1-01-001
truck	**verb**	**3-02-003**
truck	VB	1-01-001
trucked	VBN	1-01-001
trucking	VBG	1-01-001
truckdriver	**NN**	**1-01-001**
Truckee	**prop. noun**	**1-01-001**
Truckee	NP	0-00-000
Truckee	NP-TL	1-01-001
trucker	**noun**	**2-02-002**
trucker	NN	1-01-001
truckers	NNS	1-01-001
trucking	**NN**	**1-01-001**
truculence	**NN**	**1-01-001**
truculent	**JJ**	**1-01-001**
trudge	**verb**	**4-04-004**
trudged	VBD	4-04-004
true	**adjective**	**220-15-149**
true	JJ	218-15-149
true	JJ-NC	1-01-001
True	JJ-TL	1-01-001
true	**NN**	**1-01-001**
true	**RB**	**10-07-010**
true-false	**JJ**	**1-01-001**
truer	**JJR**	**2-02-002**
truest	**JJT**	**2-02-002**
truism	**NN**	**3-02-003**
Trujillo	**prop. noun**	**16-01-003**
Trujillo	NP	11-01-002
Trujillo	NP-HL	1-01-001
Trujillo's	NP$	2-01-002
Trujillos	NPS	2-01-002
truly	**QL**	**25-13-024**
truly	**RB**	**32-13-031**
Truman	**prop. noun**	**16-05-012**
Truman	NP	12-05-010
Truman	NP-TL	1-01-001
Truman's	NP$	3-02-003
Trumbull	**prop. noun**	**1-01-001**
Trumbull	NP	0-00-000
Trumbull	NP-TL	1-01-001
trump	**noun**	**1-01-001**
trumps	NNS	1-01-001
trump	**VB**	**1-01-001**
trumped-up	**JJ**	**1-01-001**
trumpet	**NN**	**6-04-005**
trumpet	**VB**	**1-01-001**
trumpeter	**NN**	**1-01-001**
truncate	**verb**	**3-03-003**
truncated	VBN	3-03-003
trundle	**NN**	**1-01-001**
trundle	**verb**	**1-01-001**
trundling	VBG	1-01-001
trunk	**noun**	**13-06-008**
trunk	NN	8-01-003
trunks	NNS	5-05-005
truss	**noun**	**2-01-001**
trusses	NNS	2-01-001
trust	**noun**	**32-11-023**
trust	NN	25-10-021
Trust	NN-TL	2-02-002
trusts	NNS	4-02-003
trusts	NNS-HL	1-01-001
trust	**verb**	**42-13-032**
trust	VB	23-10-018
trust	VB-HL	1-01-001
trust	VB-NC	1-01-001
trusts	VBZ	2-02-002
trusteth	VBZ	2-01-001
trusted	VBD	2-02-002
trusted	VBN	9-05-009
trusting	VBG	2-02-002
trustee	**noun**	**37-07-017**
trustee	NN	7-02-004
Trustee	NN-TL	2-02-002
trustee's	NN$	1-01-001
trustees	NNS	15-06-007
Trustees	NNS-TL	10-03-004
trustees'	NNS$	1-01-001
Trustees'	NNS$-TL	1-01-001
trusteeship	**NN**	**1-01-001**
trustful	**adjective**	**1-01-001**
trustful	JJ	0-00-000
Trustful	JJ-TL	1-01-001
trustfully	**RB**	**1-01-001**
trusting	**JJ**	**2-02-002**
trustingly	**RB**	**1-01-001**
trustworthy	**JJ**	**3-02-002**
truth	**noun**	**130-15-079**
truth	NN	123-15-077
truth	NN-HL	1-01-001
Truth	NN-TL	2-01-002
truths	NNS	4-03-004
truth-packed	**JJ**	**1-01-001**
truth-revealing	**JJ**	**1-01-001**
truthful	**JJ**	**1-01-001**
truthfully	**RB**	**5-05-005**
truthfulness	**NN**	**2-02-002**
try	**noun**	**8-05-005**
try	NN	3-03-003
tries	NNS	5-02-002
try	**verb**	**472-15-257**
try	VB	136-15-103
try	VB-HL	1-01-001
tries	VBZ	8-05-008
tried	VBD	120-15-092
tried	VBN	50-12-047
trying	VBG	154-15-115
tryin	VBG	2-01-001
Trying	VBG-TL	1-01-001
trying	**JJ**	**7-03-006**
Tsar	**prop. noun**	**3-02-002**
Tsar	NP	1-01-001
Tsar's	NP$	2-01-001
Tsarevich	**NP**	**1-01-001**
Tsarism	**NP**	**1-01-001**
Tschilwyk	**NP**	**1-01-001**
TSEM	**NP**	**2-01-001**
TSH	**NP**	**1-01-001**
Tshombe	**NP**	**7-02-003**
Tshombe-Gizenga-Goa-Ghana	**NP**	**1-01-001**
Tsitouris	**NP**	**1-01-001**
Tsou	**NP**	**1-01-001**
tsunami	**noun**	**21-01-001**
tsunami	NN	16-01-001
tsunami	NNS	5-01-001
tsunami-warning	**JJ**	**1-01-001**
Tsvetkov	**NP**	**1-01-001**
Tualatin	**NP**	**1-01-001**
tub	**noun**	**18-05-010**
tub	NN	13-05-009
tubs	NNS	5-02-002
tuba	**NN**	**1-01-001**
tube	**noun**	**55-08-016**
tube	NN	30-06-011
Tube	NN-TL	1-01-001
tubes	NNS	24-06-009
tube-nosed	**JJ**	**1-01-001**
tuber	**noun**	**1-01-001**

Word	Tag	Frequency
tuber (cont.):		
tubers	NNS	1-01-001
tuberculosis	**noun**	**6-04-004**
tuberculosis	NN	5-03-003
Tuberculosis	NN-TL	1-01-001
tubing	**NN**	**6-03-003**
Tuborg	**NP**	**1-01-001**
tubular	**JJ**	**4-03-004**
tubule	**noun**	**1-01-001**
tubules	NNS	1-01-001
tuck	**verb**	**9-07-009**
tuck	VB	1-01-001
tucked	VBD	4-03-004
tucked	VBN	2-02-002
tucking	VBG	2-02-002
Tuck	**prop. noun**	**1-01-001**
Tuck	NP	0-00-000
Tuck	NP-TL	1-01-001
Tucker	**prop. noun**	**6-04-005**
Tucker	NP	4-02-003
Tucker	NP-TL	1-01-001
Tucker's	NP$	1-01-001
Tucson	**NP**	**3-02-002**
Tudor	**NP**	**4-03-003**
Tudor-style	**JJ**	**1-01-001**
Tuesday	**adv. noun**	**59-09-030**
Tuesday	NR	53-08-029
Tuesday	NR-HL	1-01-001
Tuesday	NR-NC	3-01-001
Tuesday	NR-TL	1-01-001
Tuesday's	NR$	1-01-001
tuft	**noun**	**1-01-001**
tufts	NNS	1-01-001
tug	**NN**	**2-02-002**
tug	**verb**	**4-03-004**
tug	VB	1-01-001
tugged	VBD	2-02-002
tugging	VBG	1-01-001
tug-of-war	**noun**	**3-02-003**
tug-of-war	NN	2-02-002
tug-o'-war	NN	1-01-001
Tugaru	**NP**	**1-01-001**
TuHulHulZote	**NP**	**2-01-001**
tuition	**NN**	**5-03-004**
Tulane	**NP**	**1-01-001**
tularemia	**NN**	**2-01-001**
tulip	**noun**	**6-05-006**
tulip	NN	3-02-003
Tulip	NN-TL	1-01-001
tulips	NNS	2-02-002
tulip-shaped	**JJ**	**1-01-001**
tulle	**NN**	**1-01-001**
Tullio	**NP**	**1-01-001**
Tulln	**NP**	**1-01-001**
Tulsa	**NP**	**1-01-001**
tultul	**FW-NN**	**4-01-001**
tumble	**noun**	**3-02-002**
tumble	NN	1-01-001
tumble	NN-HL	1-01-001
tumbles	NNS	1-01-001
tumble	**verb**	**17-06-015**
tumble	VB	1-01-001
tumbled	VBD	7-04-007
tumbled	VBN	6-04-006
tumbling	VBG	3-03-003
tumbler	**NN**	**2-02-002**
tumbrel	**noun**	**1-01-001**
tumbrels	NNS	1-01-001
tumefaciens	**NP**	**1-01-001**
tumor	**noun**	**26-06-007**
tumor	NN	13-05-005
Tumor	NN-TL	4-01-001
tumors	NNS	8-02-002
tumours	NNS	1-01-001
tumultuous	**JJ**	**1-01-001**
tune	**noun**	**15-08-013**
tune	NN	7-05-007
Tune	NN-TL	1-01-001
tunes	NNS	7-04-006
tune	**verb**	**6-06-006**
tune	VB	2-02-002
tuned	VBN	3-03-003
tuning	VBG	1-01-001
tune-belly	**NN**	**1-01-001**
tuneful	**JJ**	**1-01-001**
tunefulness	**NN**	**1-01-001**
tunelessly	**RB**	**1-01-001**
tung	**NN**	**2-01-001**
tungsten	**NN**	**4-01-003**

Word	Tag	Frequency
tunic	**NN**	**1-01-001**
tuning	**NN**	**2-01-001**
Tunis	**NP**	**1-01-001**
Tunisia	**NP**	**3-02-003**
Tunisian	**JJ**	**3-01-001**
Tunnard	**NP**	**1-01-001**
tunnel	**noun**	**12-07-007**
tunnel	NN	9-04-004
tunnels	NNS	3-03-003
tunnel	**verb**	**2-02-002**
tunnel	VB	1-01-001
tunneled	VBD	1-01-001
Tuohy	**NP**	**1-01-001**
Turandot	**NP**	**1-01-001**
turban	**NN**	**2-01-001**
turbinate	**noun**	**1-01-001**
turbinates	NNS	1-01-001
turbine	**noun**	**7-03-004**
turbine	NN	5-02-003
Turbine	NN-TL	1-01-001
turbines	NNS	1-01-001
turbofan	**NN**	**1-01-001**
turbulence	**NN**	**3-03-003**
turbulent	**JJ**	**4-02-003**
turf	**NN**	**3-03-003**
Turin	**NP**	**2-01-001**
Turk	**prop. noun**	**10-04-006**
Turk	NP	3-03-003
Turk	NP-TL	2-01-002
Turks	NPS	5-02-003
turkey	**noun**	**4-02-003**
turkey	NN	3-02-003
turkeys	NNS	1-01-001
Turkey	**prop. noun**	**6-03-005**
Turkey	NP	5-03-005
Turkey	NP-HL	1-01-001
Turkish	**adjective**	**12-05-006**
Turkish	JJ	8-04-005
Turkish	JJ-TL	4-02-002
turmoil	**noun**	**12-06-012**
turmoil	NN	11-05-011
turmoil	NN-HL	1-01-001
turn	**noun**	**96-14-079**
turn	NN	88-14-074
turns	NNS	8-05-008
turn	**verb**	**566-15-274**
turn	VB	144-15-107
turne	VB	1-01-001
turn	VB-HL	1-01-001
turns	VBZ	29-10-027
turns	VBZ-HL	1-01-001
turned	VBD	253-15-144
turned	VBN	67-14-059
turning	VBG	70-13-059
turnaround	**NN**	**1-01-001**
Turner	**prop. noun**	**6-04-006**
Turner	NP	4-04-004
Turner	NP-TL	2-01-002
turnery	**NN**	**1-01-001**
turning	**noun**	**6-05-006**
turning	NN	5-05-005
turnings	NNS	1-01-001
turnip	**noun**	**1-01-001**
turnips	NNS	1-01-001
turnkey	**noun**	**1-01-001**
turnkey	NN	0-00-000
Turnkey	NN-TL	1-01-001
turnoff	**NN**	**1-01-001**
turnout	**noun**	**6-03-003**
turnout	NN	2-02-002
turn-out	NN	1-01-001
Turnout	NN-TL	1-01-001
turnouts	NNS	2-01-001
turnover	**NN**	**2-02-002**
turnpike	**noun**	**25-04-004**
turnpike	NN	6-02-002
Turnpike	NN-TL	9-03-003
turnpikes	NNS	10-01-001
turntable	**NN**	**1-01-001**
turpentine	**NN**	**4-01-001**
turquoise	**JJ**	**2-02-002**
turquoise	**NN**	**1-01-001**
turret	**noun**	**4-02-002**
turret	NN	3-01-001
turrets	NNS	1-01-001
turtle	**noun**	**9-04-005**
turtle	NN	8-03-004
turtles	NNS	1-01-001
turtleback	**noun**	**1-01-001**

Word	Tag	Frequency
turtleback (cont.):		
turtlebacks	NNS	1-01-001
turtleneck	**noun**	**3-02-002**
turtleneck	NN	2-01-001
turtle-neck	NN	1-01-001
Tuscany	**NP**	**2-02-002**
tusk	**noun**	**3-03-003**
tusks	NNS	3-03-003
Tuskegee	**NP**	**1-01-001**
Tussaud	**prop. noun**	**1-01-001**
Tussaud's	NP$	0-00-000
Tussard's	NP$	1-01-001
Tussle	**NP**	**4-01-001**
tutor	**noun**	**5-04-004**
tutor	NN	4-03-003
tutors	NNS	1-01-001
tutor	**verb**	**1-01-001**
tutoring	VBG	1-01-001
tutorial	**noun**	**1-01-001**
tutorials	NNS	1-01-001
tutoring	**NN**	**1-01-001**
Tuttle	**prop. noun**	**5-01-002**
Tuttle	NP	4-01-002
Tuttle's	NP$	1-01-001
Tuxapoka	**NP**	**5-01-001**
tuxedoed	**JJ**	**1-01-001**
TV	**prop. noun**	**3-02-002**
TV	NP	2-02-002
TV	NP-TL	1-01-001
Twain	**prop. noun**	**2-02-002**
Twain	NP	1-01-001
Twain's	NP$	1-01-001
tweed	**NN**	**5-03-005**
tweedy	**JJ**	**1-01-001**
tweeze	**verb**	**1-01-001**
tweezed	VBN	1-01-001
twelfth	**OD**	**5-05-005**
twelve	**CD**	**48-12-042**
twelve-hour	**JJ**	**2-02-002**
twelve-year	**JJ**	**1-01-001**
twelve-year-old	**JJ**	**1-01-001**
twentieth	**ord. num.**	**20-08-018**
twentieth	OD	13-06-012
Twentieth	OD-TL	7-04-006
Twentieth-Century	**JJ**	**1-01-001**
twentieth-century	**NN**	**9-05-007**
twenty	**CD**	**80-15-067**
twenty	**noun**	**10-06-007**
twenties	NNS	6-05-005
Twenties	NNS-TL	4-02-003
twenty-dollar	**JJ**	**1-01-001**
twenty-eight	**CD**	**5-03-005**
twenty-eighth	**OD**	**1-01-001**
twenty-fifth	**OD**	**1-01-001**
twenty-first	**OD**	**3-02-003**
twenty-first-century	**NN**	**1-01-001**
twenty-five	**CD**	**25-10-021**
twenty-five-dollar	**JJ**	**1-01-001**
twenty-five-year-old	**JJ**	**1-01-001**
twenty-four	**CD**	**14-07-013**
twenty-mile	**JJ**	**1-01-001**
twenty-nine	**CD**	**2-02-002**
twenty-nine-foot-wide	**JJ**	**1-01-001**
twenty-one	**CD**	**8-05-006**
twenty-one-year-old	**JJ**	**1-01-001**
twenty-page	**JJ**	**1-01-001**
twenty-second	**ord. num.**	**3-01-002**
twenty-second	OD	0-00-000
Twenty-second	OD-TL	3-01-002
twenty-seven	**CD**	**1-01-001**
twenty-six	**CD**	**5-04-005**
twenty-three	**CD**	**7-05-006**
twenty-two	**CD**	**8-06-007**
twenty-year	**JJ**	**2-02-002**
twice	**adverb**	**75-13-059**
twice	RB	74-13-059
twise	RB	1-01-001
twice-a-year	**JJ**	**1-01-001**
twice-around	**NN**	**1-01-001**
twig	**noun**	**1-01-001**
twigs	NNS	1-01-001
twig	**verb**	**1-01-001**
twigged	VBD	1-01-001
twilight	**noun**	**4-03-003**
twilight	NN	3-02-002
Twilight	NN-TL	1-01-001
twin	**JJ**	**1-01-001**
twin	**noun**	**19-07-011**
twin	NN	6-04-005
twin (cont.):		
twins	NNS	7-04-005
Twins	NNS-TL	5-02-002
twins'	NNS$	1-01-001
twine	**verb**	**4-04-004**
twined	VBD	3-03-003
twined	VBN	1-01-001
twinge	**noun**	**4-03-004**
twinge	NN	3-03-003
twinges	NNS	1-01-001
twinkle	**NN**	**3-02-002**
twinkle	**verb**	**2-02-002**
twinkling	VBG	2-02-002
twirl	**verb**	**6-04-005**
twirled	VBN	1-01-001
twirling	VBG	5-03-004
twirler	**NN**	**3-02-002**
twirlingly	**RB**	**1-01-001**
twist	**noun**	**19-11-016**
twist	NN	12-09-010
Twist	NN-TL	1-01-001
twists	NNS	5-03-005
twists	NNS-HL	1-01-001
twist	**verb**	**34-10-026**
twist	VB	5-04-005
twisted	VBD	12-05-008
twisted	VBN	7-05-006
twisting	VBG	10-06-010
twister	**noun**	**4-02-002**
twister	NN	3-02-002
twister	NN-HL	1-01-001
twister-coner	**noun**	**1-01-001**
twister-coners	NNS	1-01-001
twisting	**NN**	**1-01-001**
twisty	**JJ**	**1-01-001**
twitch	**NN**	**3-03-003**
twitch	**verb**	**6-03-006**
twitched	VBD	4-03-004
twitching	VBG	2-02-002
twitter	**verb**	**2-02-002**
twittered	VBD	1-01-001
twittering	VBG	1-01-001
two	**card. num.**	**1412-15-429**
two	CD	1398-15-428
two	CD-HL	6-04-006
Two	CD-TL	8-06-007
two	**noun**	**2-02-002**
twos	NNS	2-02-002
two-and-a-half-mile	**JJ**	**1-01-001**
two-bedroom	**JJ**	**1-01-001**
two-bits	**pl. noun**	**1-01-001**
two-bits'	NNS$	1-01-001
two-burner	**JJ**	**1-01-001**
two-by-four	**noun**	**2-02-002**
two-by-four	NN	1-01-001
two-by-fours	NNS	1-01-001
two-class	**adjective**	**1-01-001**
two-class	JJ	0-00-000
two-class	JJ-HL	1-01-001
two-color	**JJ**	**1-01-001**
two-colored	**JJ**	**1-01-001**
two-component	**JJ**	**1-01-001**
two-day	**JJ**	**4-03-004**
two-digit	**JJ**	**5-01-001**
two-dimensional	**JJ**	**1-01-001**
two-disc	**JJ**	**1-01-001**
two-family	**JJ**	**1-01-001**
two-fisted	**JJ**	**1-01-001**
two-fold	**JJ**	**1-01-001**
two-game	**JJ**	**1-01-001**
Two-Head	**NP**	**1-01-001**
two-hour	**JJ**	**4-03-004**
two-inch	**JJ**	**1-01-001**
two-inch	**noun**	**1-01-001**
two-inches	NNS	1-01-001
two-lane	**JJ**	**1-01-001**
two-line	**JJ**	**1-01-001**
two-mile	**JJ**	**1-01-001**
two-nosed	**JJ**	**1-01-001**
two-part	**JJ**	**1-01-001**
two-record	**JJ**	**1-01-001**
two-room	**JJ**	**1-01-001**
two-run	**JJ**	**2-01-001**
two-season	**JJ**	**2-02-002**
two-seater	**noun**	**1-01-001**
two-seaters	NNS	1-01-001
two-stem	**adjective**	**1-01-001**
two-stem	JJ	0-00-000
Two-Stem	JJ-TL	1-01-001

two-step	**JJ**	**1-01-001**
two-story	**JJ**	**8-05-006**
two-system	**JJ**	**2-01-001**
two-tail	**JJ**	**1-01-001**
two-term	**JJ**	**1-01-001**
two-thirds	**NNS**	**10-05-009**
two-thirds	**QL**	**1-01-001**
two-time	**verb**	**3-03-003**
two-timed	VBN	1-01-001
two-timing	VBG	1-01-001
twotiming	VBG	1-01-001
two-to-three	**CD**	**1-01-001**
two-valued	**JJ**	**1-01-001**
two-way	**JJ**	**1-01-001**
two-week	**JJ**	**1-01-001**
two-weeks	**NNS**	**1-01-001**
two-year	**JJ**	**5-03-004**
two-year-old	**NN**	**1-01-001**
twofold	**JJ**	**2-02-002**
twofold	**adverb**	**2-01-002**
twofold	RB	1-01-001
two-fold	RB	1-01-001
twosome	**NN**	**1-01-001**
Tyburn	**NP**	**1-01-001**
tycoon	**NN**	**1-01-001**
Tygartis	**prop. noun**	**1-01-001**
Tygartis	NP	0-00-000
Tygartis	NP-TL	1-01-001
Tyler	**NP**	**2-01-002**
type	**noun**	**314-15-141**
type	NN	191-13-112
type	NN-HL	5-01-002
Type	NN-TL	2-01-002
types	NNS	113-10-068
types	NNS-HL	3-02-002
type	**verb**	**12-06-009**

type (cont.):		
type	VB	2-01-002
typed	VBD	1-01-001
typed	VBN	2-01-002
typing	VBG	7-05-005
typescript	**NN**	**1-01-001**
typesetting	**NN**	**1-01-001**
typewriter	**noun**	**11-05-009**
typewriter	NN	10-05-009
typewriters	NNS	1-01-001
typewriting	**NN**	**1-01-001**
typewritten	**JJ**	**1-01-001**
typhoid	**NN**	**2-02-002**
typhoon	**NN**	**1-01-001**
typhus	**NN**	**3-01-001**
typical	**JJ**	**65-10-052**
typicality	**NN**	**3-01-001**
typically	**RB**	**16-06-014**
typify	**verb**	**4-02-004**
typify	VB	1-01-001
typified	VBN	2-01-002
typifying	VBG	1-01-001
typographic	**JJ**	**1-01-001**
typography	**NN**	**3-01-001**
typology	**NN**	**1-01-001**
tyrannical	**JJ**	**1-01-001**
tyrannis	**FW-NNS**	**1-01-001**
tyrannize	**VB**	**1-01-001**
tyranny	**noun**	**11-07-011**
tyranny	NN	10-06-010
Tyranny	NN-TL	1-01-001
tyrant	**noun**	**3-02-003**
tyrant	NN	2-02-002
tyrants	NNS	1-01-001
tyrosine	**NN**	**3-01-001**
Tyson	**NP**	**1-01-001**

U

U	**prop. noun**	**9-02-003**
U	NP	8-02-003
U	NP-HL	1-01-001
u.	**noun**	**4-02-002**
u.	NN	1-01-001
U.	NN-TL	1-01-001
U.	NN-TL	1-01-001
u.'s	NN$	0-00-000
U.'s	NN$-TL	1-01-001
U.	**prop. noun**	**60-08-027**
U.	NP	24-04-008
U.	NP-TL	36-07-020
U.M.C.I.A.	**NP**	**3-01-001**
U.M.T.	**NP**	**1-01-001**
U.N.	**prop. noun**	**56-05-016**
U.N.	NP	47-05-015
U.N.	NP-HL	2-01-002
U.N.	NP-TL	3-02-002
U.N.'s	NP$	3-02-003
U.N's	NP$-HL	1-01-001
U.N.-chartered	**JJ**	**1-01-001**
U.N.F.P.	**NP**	**5-01-001**
U.S.	**prop. noun**	**163-11-058**
U.S.	NP	101-09-038
U.s.	NP	0-00-000
U.s.	NP-TL	1-01-001
U.S.	NP-HL	4-03-004
U.S.	NP-TL	56-09-031
U.S.'s	NP$	1-01-001
U.S.-Soviet	**JJ**	**1-01-001**
U.S.A.	**NP**	**4-02-003**
U.S.C.	**prop. noun**	**2-01-002**
U.S.C.	NP	1-01-001
U.S.C.	NP-TL	1-01-001
U.S.S.R.	**prop. noun**	**8-04-006**
U.S.S.R.	NP	7-03-005
U.S.S.R.'s	NP$	1-01-001
Ubermenschen	**FW-NNS**	**1-01-001**
ubiquitous	**JJ**	**2-02-002**
Udall	**prop. noun**	**7-02-002**
Udall	NP	6-02-002
Udall's	NP$	1-01-001
udon	**FW-NN**	**1-01-001**
ugh	**UH**	**1-01-001**

uglier	**JJR**	**2-01-001**
ugliness	**NN**	**7-05-007**
ugly	**JJ**	**21-08-015**
uh	**UH**	**5-03-004**
uh-huh	**UH**	**5-04-004**
uh-uh	**UH**	**1-01-001**
uhhu	**UH**	**4-01-001**
Uhles	**NP**	**1-01-001**
Ukrainian	**adjective**	**3-03-003**
Ukrainian	JJ	2-02-002
Ukrainian	JJ-TL	1-01-001
Ukrainian	**prop. noun**	**1-01-001**
Ukrainians	NPS	1-01-001
Ulany	**prop. noun**	**3-01-001**
Ulanys	NPS	3-01-001
Ulbricht	**NP**	**2-01-001**
ulcer	**NN**	**5-03-003**
ulcerate	**verb**	**1-01-001**
ulcerated	VBN	1-01-001
ulceration	**noun**	**1-01-001**
ulcerations	NNS	1-01-001
Ullman	**NP**	**1-01-001**
ultimate	**JJ**	**59-13-042**
ultimately	**QL**	**1-01-001**
ultimately	**RB**	**22-09-020**
ultimatum	**NN**	**3-03-003**
ultra-efficient	**JJ**	**1-01-001**
ultra-fast	**JJ**	**1-01-001**
ultra-high-speed	**JJ**	**1-01-001**
ultra-liberal	**JJ**	**1-01-001**
ultracentrifugally	**RB**	**1-01-001**
ultracentrifugation	**noun**	**5-01-001**
ultracentrifugation	NN	4-01-001
ultracentrifugation	NN-HL	1-01-001
ultracentrifuge	**NN**	**3-01-002**
ultramarine	**JJ**	**1-01-001**
ultramodern	**adjective**	**2-02-002**
ultramodern	JJ	1-01-001
ultra-modern	JJ	1-01-001
ultrasonic	**JJ**	**8-01-001**
ultrasonically	**RB**	**1-01-001**
ultravehement	**JJ**	**1-01-001**
ultraviolet	**adjective**	**18-04-007**
ultraviolet	JJ	13-02-003

Word	Tag	Frequency
ultraviolet (cont.):		
ultra-violet	JJ	4-03-004
ultraviolet	JJ-HL	1-01-001
Ulyate	**NP**	**15-01-001**
um	**FW-RB**	**1-01-001**
um	**UH**	**2-02-002**
umber	**NN**	**4-02-002**
umbrella	**noun**	**11-05-009**
umbrella	NN	8-04-006
umbrellas	NNS	3-02-003
umm	**UH**	**1-01-001**
umpire	**NN**	**1-01-001**
Umschlagplatz	**NP**	**1-01-001**
un	**foreign**	**2-02-002**
un	FW-AT	0-00-000
un	FW-AT-TL	1-01-001
une	FW-AT	1-01-001
un-American	**adjective**	**4-03-004**
un-American	JJ	2-01-002
Un-American	JJ-TL	2-02-002
un-English	**JJ**	**2-01-001**
unabashed	**JJ**	**3-03-003**
unabated	**JJ**	**2-02-002**
unable	**JJ**	**54-13-047**
unabridged	**JJ**	**1-01-001**
unacceptable	**JJ**	**1-01-001**
unaccompanied	**JJ**	**3-02-002**
unaccountable	**JJ**	**1-01-001**
unaccountably	**QL**	**1-01-001**
unaccountably	**RB**	**1-01-001**
unaccustomed	**JJ**	**1-01-001**
unachievable	**JJ**	**1-01-001**
unachieved	**JJ**	**1-01-001**
unacknowledged	**JJ**	**1-01-001**
unacquainted	**JJ**	**2-02-002**
unadjusted	**JJ**	**12-01-001**
unadorned	**JJ**	**1-01-001**
unadulterated	**JJ**	**1-01-001**
unaffected	**JJ**	**3-03-003**
unafraid	**JJ**	**4-03-004**
unaggressive	**JJ**	**1-01-001**
unagi	**FW-NN**	**1-01-001**
unaided	**JJ**	**4-03-004**
unalienable	**JJ**	**1-01-001**
unallocable	**JJ**	**3-01-001**
unalloyed	**JJ**	**1-01-001**
unalterable	**JJ**	**1-01-001**
unam	**foreign**	**1-01-001**
unam	FW-CD	0-00-000
Unam	FW-CD-TL	1-01-001
unambiguity	**NN**	**1-01-001**
unambiguous	**JJ**	**3-02-003**
unambiguously	**RB**	**2-01-002**
unamused	**JJ**	**1-01-001**
unanalyzed	**JJ**	**3-01-001**
unanimity	**NN**	**5-03-004**
unanimous	**JJ**	**5-04-005**
unanimously	**RB**	**11-08-010**
unannounced	**JJ**	**2-02-002**
unanswered	**JJ**	**1-01-001**
unappeasable	**JJ**	**1-01-001**
unappeasably	**QL**	**1-01-001**
unappreciated	**JJ**	**1-01-001**
unarmed	**JJ**	**4-03-003**
unashamedly	**RB**	**1-01-001**
unasked	**JJ**	**2-02-002**
unassisted	**JJ**	**2-02-002**
unasterisked	**JJ**	**1-01-001**
unattached	**JJ**	**2-02-002**
unattainable	**JJ**	**1-01-001**
unattended	**JJ**	**2-01-002**
unattractive	**JJ**	**3-03-003**
unauthentic	**JJ**	**1-01-001**
unauthorized	**JJ**	**2-02-002**
unavailable	**JJ**	**7-05-005**
unavailing	**JJ**	**1-01-001**
unavoidable	**JJ**	**7-04-005**
unavoidably	**QL**	**1-01-001**
unavoidably	**RB**	**2-01-002**
unaware	**JJ**	**13-06-012**
unawareness	**NN**	**3-03-003**
unbalance	**NN**	**1-01-001**
unbalance	**verb**	**3-02-002**
unbalanced	VBN	3-02-002
unbearable	**JJ**	**6-04-006**
unbearably	**QL**	**1-01-001**
unbeknownst	**JJ**	**1-01-001**
unbelievable	**JJ**	**4-03-004**
unbelievably	**RB**	**1-01-001**
unbelieving	**JJ**	**1-01-001**
unbend	**verb**	**1-01-001**
unbent	VBN	1-01-001
unbidden	**JJ**	**1-01-001**
unbind	**verb**	**1-01-001**
unbound	VBN	1-01-001
unblemished	**JJ**	**1-01-001**
unblinkingly	**RB**	**2-01-002**
unblushing	**JJ**	**1-01-001**
unborn	**JJ**	**4-03-004**
unbounded	**JJ**	**1-01-001**
unbreakable	**JJ**	**5-03-005**
unbridle	**verb**	**2-01-002**
unbridled	VBN	2-01-002
unbroken	**JJ**	**7-05-007**
unburden	**verb**	**1-01-001**
unburdened	VBN	1-01-001
unburned	**JJ**	**1-01-001**
uncalled	**JJ**	**1-01-001**
uncanny	**JJ**	**5-04-004**
uncap	**VB**	**1-01-001**
Uncas	**prop. noun**	**1-01-001**
Uncas	NP	0-00-000
Uncas	NP-TL	1-01-001
uncaused	**JJ**	**1-01-001**
unceasing	**JJ**	**1-01-001**
unceasingly	**RB**	**1-01-001**
uncertain	**JJ**	**22-10-021**
uncertainly	**RB**	**2-02-002**
uncertainty	**noun**	**22-08-019**
uncertainty	NN	17-08-014
uncertainties	NNS	5-05-005
uncertified	**JJ**	**1-01-001**
unchallenged	**JJ**	**2-02-002**
unchangeable	**JJ**	**1-01-001**
unchanged	**JJ**	**9-07-009**
unchanging	**JJ**	**2-02-002**
uncharged	**JJ**	**4-01-001**
uncharted	**JJ**	**3-02-002**
unchecked	**JJ**	**1-01-001**
unchristian	**JJ**	**1-01-001**
uncircumcision	**NN**	**1-01-001**
uncivil	**JJ**	**1-01-001**
unclaimed	**JJ**	**2-02-002**
unclasp	**verb**	**1-01-001**
unclasping	VBG	1-01-001
uncle	**noun**	**58-10-026**
uncle	NN	17-10-013
unckle	NN	0-00-000
Unckle	NN-TL	1-01-001
Uncle	NN-TL	32-04-011
uncle's	NN$	2-02-002
Uncle's	NN$-TL	3-02-002
uncles	NNS	3-03-003
Uncle	**prop. noun**	**8-06-007**
Uncle	NP	7-05-006
Uncle	NP-TL	1-01-001
unclean	**JJ**	**4-04-004**
unclear	**JJ**	**2-02-002**
unclench	**verb**	**1-01-001**
unclenched	VBN	1-01-001
unclouded	**JJ**	**2-02-002**
uncluttered	**JJ**	**1-01-001**
uncoil	**verb**	**1-01-001**
uncoiling	VBG	1-01-001
uncolored	**JJ**	**1-01-001**
uncombable	**JJ**	**1-01-001**
uncomfortable	**JJ**	**14-09-014**
uncomfortably	**QL**	**1-01-001**
uncomfortably	**RB**	**2-01-002**
uncomforted	**JJ**	**1-01-001**
uncommitted	**JJ**	**3-03-003**
uncommon	**JJ**	**8-07-008**
uncommonly	**QL**	**1-01-001**
uncommunicative	**JJ**	**1-01-001**
uncomplainingly	**RB**	**1-01-001**
uncompromising	**JJ**	**5-03-004**
unconcern	**NN**	**1-01-001**
unconcerned	**JJ**	**8-07-008**
unconcernedly	**RB**	**1-01-001**
unconditional	**JJ**	**4-03-003**
unconditionally	**RB**	**2-02-002**
unconditioned	**JJ**	**1-01-001**
unconnected	**JJ**	**2-02-002**
unconquerable	**JJ**	**1-01-001**
unconscionable	**JJ**	**1-01-001**
unconscious	**JJ**	**26-05-015**
unconscious	**noun**	**4-03-003**
unconscious	NN	3-03-003

unconscious (cont.):		
Unconscious	NN-TL	1-01-001
unconsciously	**RB**	**10-06-009**
unconstitutional	**JJ**	**2-02-002**
uncontrollable	**JJ**	**2-02-002**
uncontrolled	**JJ**	**4-03-004**
unconventional	**JJ**	**3-03-003**
unconvincing	**JJ**	**1-01-001**
unconvincing	**NN**	**1-01-001**
uncooperative	**adjective**	**3-02-003**
uncooperative	JJ	2-02-002
unco-operative	JJ	1-01-001
uncork	**verb**	**2-02-002**
uncorked	VBD	1-01-001
uncorked	VBN	1-01-001
uncounted	**JJ**	**3-01-002**
uncourageous	**JJ**	**1-01-001**
uncousinly	**JJ**	**1-01-001**
uncover	**verb**	**11-05-011**
uncover	VB	4-02-004
uncovered	VBN	7-05-007
uncritical	**JJ**	**3-02-003**
uncritically	**RB**	**1-01-001**
unction	**NN**	**1-01-001**
uncurl	**verb**	**1-01-001**
uncurled	VBD	1-01-001
und	**foreign**	**3-02-003**
und	FW-CC	2-01-002
und	FW-CC-TL	1-01-001
undamaged	**JJ**	**1-01-001**
undaunted	**JJ**	**1-01-001**
undeclared	**JJ**	**1-01-001**
undecorated	**JJ**	**1-01-001**
undedicated	**JJ**	**1-01-001**
undefined	**JJ**	**4-04-004**
undemocratic	**JJ**	**1-01-001**
undeniable	**JJ**	**5-03-005**
undeniably	**RB**	**1-01-001**
undependable	**JJ**	**2-02-002**
undepicted	**JJ**	**4-01-001**
under	**prep.**	**688-15-328**
under	IN	686-15-327
under	IN-HL	1-01-001
Under	IN-TL	1-01-001
under	**adjective**	**5-05-005**
under	JJ	2-02-002
Under	JJ-TL	3-03-003
under	**RB**	**14-05-009**
under-achievement	**NN**	**3-01-001**
underachiever	**noun**	**2-01-001**
underachievers	NNS	1-01-001
under-achievers	NNS	1-01-001
underarm	**NN**	**1-01-001**
underbedding	**NN**	**1-01-001**
underbelly	**NN**	**1-01-001**
underbracing	**NN**	**1-01-001**
underbrush	**NN**	**1-01-001**
underclassman	**NN**	**1-01-001**
underclothes	**NNS**	**1-01-001**
undercover	**JJ**	**1-01-001**
undercurrent	**NN**	**3-02-002**
undercut	**JJ**	**1-01-001**
undercut	**NN**	**1-01-001**
underdeveloped	**adjective**	**12-06-011**
underdeveloped	JJ	10-06-010
under-developed	JJ	2-01-001
underdog	**NN**	**2-01-001**
undereducated	**JJ**	**1-01-001**
underestimate	**verb**	**6-05-006**
underestimate	VB	4-04-004
underestimated	VBN	2-02-002
underfoot	**RB**	**4-03-004**
undergirding	**NN**	**1-01-001**
undergo	**verb**	**34-13-030**
undergo	VB	8-06-007
undergoes	VBZ	2-02-002
underwent	VBD	2-02-002
undergone	VBN	10-07-009
undergoing	VBG	12-06-011
undergraduate	**JJ**	**7-04-004**
undergraduate	**noun**	**13-05-006**
undergraduate	NN	4-02-002
undergraduates	NNS	8-04-005
undergraduates	NNS-HL	1-01-001
underground	**adjective**	**13-07-009**
underground	JJ	12-07-009
underground	JJ-HL	1-01-001
underground	**NN**	**2-02-002**
underground	**RB**	**4-03-004**
undergrowth	**NN**	**1-01-001**
underhanded	**JJ**	**1-01-001**
underhandedness	**NN**	**1-01-001**
underlie	**verb**	**24-07-020**
underlie	VB	2-01-001
underlay	VBD	1-01-001
underlies	VBZ	1-01-001
underlying	VBG	19-06-018
underlying	VBG-HL	1-01-001
underline	**verb**	**6-03-004**
underline	VB	2-02-002
underlined	VBN	2-02-002
underlining	VBG	2-01-002
underling	**NN**	**1-01-001**
undermine	**verb**	**11-06-011**
undermine	VB	8-05-008
undermined	VBN	2-02-002
undermining	VBG	1-01-001
underneath	**IN**	**9-06-008**
underneath	**RB**	**2-02-002**
underpaid	**JJ**	**1-01-001**
underpin	**verb**	**1-01-001**
underpins	VBZ	1-01-001
underpinning	**NN**	**1-01-001**
underplay	**verb**	**1-01-001**
underplayed	VBN	1-01-001
underprivileged	**JJ**	**3-03-003**
underrate	**verb**	**2-02-002**
underrate	VB	1-01-001
underrated	VBN	1-01-001
underscore	**verb**	**4-04-004**
underscore	VB	1-01-001
underscored	VBD	1-01-001
underscored	VBN	2-02-002
undersea	**JJ**	**3-03-003**
undersecretary	**noun**	**2-02-002**
undersecretary	NN	0-00-000
Undersecretary	NN-TL	1-01-001
undersecretary's	NN+BEZ	1-01-001
undershirt	**NN**	**3-01-003**
underside	**NN**	**5-04-005**
undersize	**JJ**	**1-01-001**
undersized	**JJ**	**1-01-001**
understand	**verb**	**240-15-155**
understand	VB	137-15-105
understands	VBZ	6-06-006
understood	VBD	20-08-019
understood	VBN	38-12-036
understanded	VBN	1-01-001
understanding	VBG	38-10-030
understandable	**JJ**	**13-09-013**
understandably	**RB**	**3-03-003**
understanding	**JJ**	**1-01-001**
understanding	**noun**	**83-11-059**
understanding	NN	82-11-058
understandings	NNS	1-01-001
understandingly	**RB**	**3-03-003**
understate	**verb**	**2-02-002**
understates	VBZ	1-01-001
understated	VBN	1-01-001
understatement	**NN**	**4-04-004**
understructure	**NN**	**1-01-001**
undertake	**verb**	**41-10-035**
undertake	VB	13-07-013
undertakes	VBZ	3-03-003
undertook	VBD	7-07-007
undertaken	VBN	18-06-015
undertaker	**NN**	**1-01-001**
undertaking	**noun**	**9-06-008**
undertaking	NN	5-04-005
undertakings	NNS	3-02-002
undertakings	NNS-HL	1-01-001
undertow	**NN**	**1-01-001**
underwater	**adjective**	**12-06-008**
underwater	JJ	10-06-007
Underwater	JJ-TL	2-01-001
underwater	**RB**	**3-03-003**
underway	**RB**	**3-03-003**
underwear	**NN**	**3-02-003**
Underwood	**prop. noun**	**3-01-001**
Underwood	NP	2-01-001
Underwood's	NP$	1-01-001
underworld	**NN**	**6-05-005**
underwrite	**verb**	**4-04-004**
underwrite	VB	3-03-003
underwriting	VBG	1-01-001
underwriter	**noun**	**5-03-004**
underwriter	NN	1-01-001
underwriters	NNS	3-02-003

Word	Tag	Count
underwriter (cont.):		
Underwriters	NNS-TL	1-01-001
underwriting	**NN**	**1-01-001**
undeserved	**JJ**	**1-01-001**
undesirable	**JJ**	**10-04-008**
undetectable	**JJ**	**1-01-001**
undetected	**JJ**	**1-01-001**
undetermined	**JJ**	**2-02-002**
undeveloped	**JJ**	**4-04-004**
undifferentiated	**JJ**	**1-01-001**
undigested	**JJ**	**1-01-001**
undiluted	**JJ**	**1-01-001**
undiminished	**JJ**	**3-03-003**
undimmed	**JJ**	**1-01-001**
undisciplined	**JJ**	**3-02-003**
undisclosed	**JJ**	**1-01-001**
undisguised	**JJ**	**1-01-001**
undismayed	**JJ**	**1-01-001**
undisputed	**JJ**	**2-02-002**
undisrupted	**JJ**	**1-01-001**
undistinguished	**JJ**	**3-03-003**
undisturbed	**JJ**	**3-03-003**
undivided	**JJ**	**1-01-001**
undo	**verb**	**9-06-008**
undo	VB	3-03-003
undid	VBD	1-01-001
undone	VBN	4-03-003
undoing	VBG	1-01-001
undoing	**NN**	**1-01-001**
undoubtedly	**RB**	**24-11-020**
undreamed	**adjective**	**2-01-002**
undreamed	JJ	1-01-001
undreamt	JJ	1-01-001
undress	**verb**	**5-03-005**
undressed	VBD	2-01-002
undressing	VBG	3-03-003
undrinkable	**JJ**	**1-01-001**
undue	**JJ**	**13-08-013**
undulate	**verb**	**2-02-002**
undulated	VBD	1-01-001
undulating	VBG	1-01-001
unduly	**QL**	**5-05-005**
unduly	**RB**	**1-01-001**
undying	**JJ**	**1-01-001**
une	**FW-CD**	**1-01-001**
unearned	**JJ**	**2-02-002**
unearth	**verb**	**3-03-003**
unearth	VB	1-01-001
unearthed	VBD	1-01-001
unearthed	VBN	1-01-001
unease	**NN**	**1-01-001**
uneasily	**RB**	**6-05-006**
uneasiness	**NN**	**5-03-004**
uneasy	**adjective**	**23-09-021**
uneasy	JJ	22-08-020
oneasy	JJ	1-01-001
uneconomic	**JJ**	**1-01-001**
uneconomical	**JJ**	**3-02-003**
uneducated	**JJ**	**1-01-001**
unemotional	**JJ**	**2-02-002**
unemployed	**JJ**	**5-02-004**
unemployment	**noun**	**16-05-010**
unemployment	NN	15-05-010
Unemployment	NN-TL	1-01-001
unending	**JJ**	**3-03-003**
unendurable	**JJ**	**1-01-001**
unenforcible	**JJ**	**1-01-001**
unenthusiastic	**JJ**	**2-02-002**
unenunciated	**JJ**	**1-01-001**
unenviable	**JJ**	**1-01-001**
unenvied	**JJ**	**1-01-001**
unequal	**JJ**	**1-01-001**
unequaled	**adjective**	**2-02-002**
unequaled	JJ	1-01-001
unequalled	JJ	1-01-001
unequally	**RB**	**2-01-001**
unequivocally	**QL**	**1-01-001**
unequivocally	**RB**	**4-02-004**
unerring	**JJ**	**2-02-002**
unerringly	**RB**	**1-01-001**
uneven	**JJ**	**6-04-006**
unexamined	**JJ**	**1-01-001**
unexpected	**JJ**	**23-08-021**
unexpectedly	**RB**	**11-09-011**
unexpended	**JJ**	**1-01-001**
unexplainable	**JJ**	**1-01-001**
unexplained	**JJ**	**4-04-004**
unexplored	**JJ**	**4-04-004**
unfailing	**JJ**	**2-01-002**

Word	Tag	Count
unfailingly	**QL**	**1-01-001**
unfailingly	**RB**	**1-01-001**
unfair	**JJ**	**13-08-013**
unfairly	**RB**	**2-02-002**
unfaithful	**JJ**	**1-01-001**
unfalteringly	**RB**	**1-01-001**
unfamiliar	**JJ**	**10-07-009**
unfasten	**verb**	**1-01-001**
unfastened	VBD	1-01-001
unfathomable	**JJ**	**1-01-001**
unfavorable	**JJ**	**5-05-005**
unfelt	**JJ**	**1-01-001**
unfenced	**JJ**	**2-02-002**
unfertile	**JJ**	**1-01-001**
unfertilized	**JJ**	**1-01-001**
unfettered	**JJ**	**4-02-004**
unfinished	**JJ**	**2-02-002**
unfired	**JJ**	**2-01-001**
unfit	**JJ**	**1-01-001**
unfitting	**JJ**	**3-01-001**
unfixed	**JJ**	**1-01-001**
unflagging	**JJ**	**1-01-001**
unflattering	**JJ**	**1-01-001**
unfold	**verb**	**15-05-012**
unfold	VB	2-02-002
unfolds	VBZ	4-02-002
unfolded	VBD	2-02-002
unfolded	VBN	2-02-002
unfolding	VBG	5-02-005
unfoldment	**NN**	**1-01-001**
unforeseen	**adjective**	**3-03-003**
unforeseen	JJ	2-02-002
unforseen	JJ	1-01-001
unforgettable	**JJ**	**3-03-003**
unforgivable	**JJ**	**1-01-001**
unformed	**JJ**	**1-01-001**
unfortunate	**JJ**	**18-08-017**
unfortunate	**noun**	**5-03-003**
unfortunate	NN	4-02-002
unfortunates	NNS	1-01-001
unfortunately	**RB**	**33-11-031**
unfounded	**JJ**	**2-02-002**
unfreeze	**verb**	**2-01-001**
unfrozen	VBN	2-01-001
unfriendly	**JJ**	**6-04-005**
unfrocking	**NN**	**1-01-001**
unfrosted	**JJ**	**1-01-001**
unfulfilled	**JJ**	**1-01-001**
unfunnily	**RB**	**1-01-001**
unfunny	**JJ**	**1-01-001**
unfurl	**verb**	**1-01-001**
unfurled	VBN	1-01-001
ungainly	**JJ**	**2-01-002**
ungallant	**JJ**	**1-01-001**
Ungava	**prop. noun**	**1-01-001**
Ungava	NP	0-00-000
Ungava	NP-TL	1-01-001
unglamorous	**JJ**	**1-01-001**
unglazed	**JJ**	**1-01-001**
unglued	**JJ**	**1-01-001**
ungodly	**JJ**	**2-01-001**
ungoverned	**JJ**	**1-01-001**
ungracious	**JJ**	**1-01-001**
ungrateful	**JJ**	**2-02-002**
ungratified	**JJ**	**1-01-001**
unguided	**JJ**	**1-01-001**
unhappiest	**JJT**	**1-01-001**
unhappily	**QL**	**1-01-001**
unhappily	**RB**	**8-06-008**
unhappiness	**NN**	**6-04-006**
unhappy	**JJ**	**26-09-024**
unharmonious	**JJ**	**1-01-001**
unhealthy	**JJ**	**4-02-002**
unheard	**JJ**	**3-02-002**
unheard-of	**JJ**	**2-02-002**
unheated	**JJ**	**2-02-002**
unheeded	**JJ**	**2-01-002**
unheeding	**JJ**	**1-01-001**
unhesitant	**JJ**	**1-01-001**
unhesitatingly	**RB**	**3-02-003**
unhinge	**verb**	**1-01-001**
unhinged	VBN	1-01-001
unhitch	**verb**	**2-02-002**
unhitched	VBD	1-01-001
unhitched	VBN	1-01-001
unhook	**VB**	**1-01-001**
unhurried	**JJ**	**3-02-002**
unhurriedly	**RB**	**2-02-002**
unhurt	**JJ**	**1-01-001**

uni-directional	**JJ**	**1-01-001**
Uniconer	**prop. noun**	**5-01-001**
Uniconer	NP	4-01-001
Uniconer	NP-HL	1-01-001
unidentified	**JJ**	**1-01-001**
unidirectional	**JJ**	**1-01-001**
unification	**noun**	**10-04-006**
unification	NN	9-04-005
unifications	NNS	1-01-001
Unifil	**prop. noun**	**5-01-001**
Unifil	NP	4-01-001
Unifil	NP-HL	1-01-001
uniform	**JJ**	**28-04-012**
uniform	**noun**	**37-13-032**
uniform	NN	23-12-020
uniforms	NNS	14-09-014
uniformed	**JJ**	**7-06-007**
uniformity	**noun**	**11-04-006**
uniformity	NN	10-04-006
uniformity	NN-HL	1-01-001
uniformly	**RB**	**6-04-006**
unify	**verb**	**20-06-013**
unify	VB	2-02-002
unifies	VBZ	3-01-001
unified	VBN	11-04-009
unifying	VBG	4-03-004
unilateral	**JJ**	**3-02-003**
unilaterally	**RB**	**1-01-001**
unimaginable	**JJ**	**2-02-002**
unimaginative	**JJ**	**1-01-001**
unimpaired	**JJ**	**2-02-002**
unimpassioned	**JJ**	**1-01-001**
unimpeachable	**JJ**	**2-02-002**
unimpeachably	**QL**	**1-01-001**
unimportant	**JJ**	**9-06-008**
unimposing	**JJ**	**1-01-001**
unimpressed	**JJ**	**4-03-003**
unimpressive	**JJ**	**2-02-002**
unimproved	**JJ**	**2-02-002**
uninfluenced	**JJ**	**1-01-001**
uninhibited	**JJ**	**4-02-004**
uninitiate	**NN**	**1-01-001**
uninitiated	**JJ**	**2-02-002**
uninjectable	**JJ**	**1-01-001**
uninjured	**JJ**	**2-01-001**
uninominal	**JJ**	**1-01-001**
unintelligible	**JJ**	**1-01-001**
unintended	**JJ**	**2-02-002**
unintentionally	**RB**	**2-02-002**
uninterested	**JJ**	**1-01-001**
uninteresting	**JJ**	**1-01-001**
uninterrupted	**JJ**	**5-05-005**
uninterruptedly	**RB**	**1-01-001**
uninvited	**JJ**	**1-01-001**
uninvolved	**JJ**	**1-01-001**
union	**noun**	**213-13-076**
union	NN	78-08-030
union	NN-HL	2-02-002
Union	NN-TL	102-11-047
union's	NN$	2-01-002
unions	NNS	29-06-013
union-industry	**NN**	**1-01-001**
unique	**JJ**	**58-13-046**
unique-ingrown-screwedup	**JJ**	**1-01-001**
uniquely	**RB**	**10-05-009**
uniqueness	**noun**	**5-05-005**
uniqueness	NN	4-04-004
Uniqueness	NN-TL	1-01-001
unison	**NN**	**3-03-003**
unit	**noun**	**190-11-082**
unit	NN	96-10-050
Unit	NN-TL	7-05-005
units	NNS	81-10-044
units	NNS-HL	6-01-002
Unitarian	**adjective**	**8-02-003**
Unitarian	JJ	7-02-002
Unitarian	JJ-TL	1-01-001
Unitarian	**prop. noun**	**2-01-002**
Unitarians	NPS	2-01-002
Unitarianism	**NP**	**2-01-002**
unite	**verb**	**495-13-156**
unite	VB	10-06-009
unites	VBZ	1-01-001
united	VBD	3-03-003
united	VBN	16-07-012
United	VBN-TL	456-11-144
United	VBN-TL-HL	4-03-004
United	VBN-TL-NC	3-01-002
uniting	VBG	2-02-002

unitize	**verb**	**5-01-001**
unitized	VBN	5-01-001
unity	**noun**	**72-10-037**
unity	NN	66-10-037
Unity	NN-TL	5-02-002
unities	NNS	1-01-001
univalent	**JJ**	**1-01-001**
universal	**adjective**	**45-08-026**
universal	JJ	40-08-023
Universal	JJ-TL	5-03-004
universal	**noun**	**1-01-001**
universals	NNS	1-01-001
universal-international	**adjective**	**1-01-001**
universal-international	JJ	0-00-000
Universal-International	JJ-TL	1-01-001
universalistic	**JJ**	**1-01-001**
universality	**NN**	**3-02-003**
universalize	**VB**	**1-01-001**
universally	**QL**	**1-01-001**
universally	**RB**	**5-04-005**
universe	**noun**	**71-09-025**
universe	NN	63-08-020
Universe	NN-TL	8-04-006
university	**noun**	**256-13-094**
university	NN	90-11-035
University	NN-TL	123-12-066
University	NN-TL-HL	1-01-001
university's	NN$	5-04-004
University's	NN$-TL	5-03-003
universities	NNS	30-07-018
Universities	NNS-TL	2-02-002
university-educated	**JJ**	**1-01-001**
university-trained	**JJ**	**1-01-001**
university-wide	**JJ**	**1-01-001**
unjacketed	**JJ**	**1-01-001**
unjust	**JJ**	**3-02-002**
unjustifiable	**JJ**	**2-02-002**
unjustified	**JJ**	**1-01-001**
unkempt	**JJ**	**1-01-001**
unkind	**JJ**	**3-02-003**
unknowing	**JJ**	**1-01-001**
unknowingly	**RB**	**1-01-001**
unknown	**JJ**	**43-14-040**
unknown	**noun**	**5-03-004**
unknown	NN	4-02-003
unknowns	NNS	1-01-001
unlace	**verb**	**2-02-002**
unlaced	VBD	1-01-001
unlacing	VBG	1-01-001
unlamented	**JJ**	**1-01-001**
unlash	**verb**	**1-01-001**
unlashed	VBD	1-01-001
unlaundered	**JJ**	**1-01-001**
unlawful	**JJ**	**1-01-001**
unleash	**verb**	**5-05-005**
unleash	VB	1-01-001
unleashed	VBD	1-01-001
unleashed	VBN	2-02-002
unleashing	VBG	1-01-001
unleavened	**JJ**	**2-01-001**
unless	**sub. conj.**	**101-14-076**
unless	CS	100-14-075
unless	CS-NC	1-01-001
unleveled	**JJ**	**1-01-001**
unlicensed	**JJ**	**1-01-001**
unlike	**IN**	**42-12-040**
unlikely	**JJ**	**21-12-019**
unlimited	**JJ**	**13-06-010**
unlined	**JJ**	**3-02-002**
unlink	**verb**	**1-01-001**
unlinked	VBN	1-01-001
unliterary	**JJ**	**1-01-001**
unload	**verb**	**18-08-009**
unload	VB	7-03-003
unloads	VBZ	1-01-001
unloaded	VBN	5-05-005
unloading	VBG	5-04-004
unlock	**verb**	**18-08-015**
unlock	VB	3-03-003
unlocks	VBZ	2-02-002
unlocked	VBD	5-02-004
unlocked	VBN	7-04-005
unlocking	VBG	1-01-001
unlovely	**JJ**	**1-01-001**
unluckily	**RB**	**1-01-001**
unlucky	**JJ**	**2-01-002**
unmagnified	**JJ**	**1-01-001**
unmalicious	**JJ**	**1-01-001**
unmanageable	**JJ**	**1-01-001**

Word	Tag	Frequency
unmanageably	QL	1-01-001
unmanaged	JJ	1-01-001
unmarked	JJ	1-01-001
unmarried	JJ	6-04-006
unmask	verb	1-01-001
unmasked	VBN	1-01-001
unmatched	JJ	2-02-002
unmated	JJ	1-01-001
unmeritorious	JJ	1-01-001
unmeshed	JJ	1-01-001
unmethodical	JJ	1-01-001
unmindful	JJ	1-01-001
unmistakable	JJ	7-06-007
unmistakably	RB	5-04-005
unmixed	JJ	1-01-001
unmodified	JJ	1-01-001
unmolested	JJ	1-01-001
unmotivated	JJ	1-01-001
unmoved	JJ	3-03-003
unmurmuring	JJ	1-01-001
unnameable	JJ	1-01-001
unnamed	JJ	4-03-004
unnatural	JJ	8-03-006
unnaturally	RB	1-01-001
unnaturalness	NN	1-01-001
unnecessarily	RB	3-03-003
unnecessary	JJ	16-11-016
unneeded	JJ	1-01-001
unnerve	verb	1-01-001
unnerving	VBG	1-01-001
unnnt	UH	1-01-001
unnoticed	adjective	4-04-004
unnoticed	JJ	3-03-003
unnoticed	JJ-HL	1-01-001
unnourished	JJ	1-01-001
unnumbered	JJ	1-01-001
Uno	prop. noun	2-01-001
Uno	NP	1-01-001
Uno's	NP$	1-01-001
unobtainable	JJ	3-03-003
unobtrusive	JJ	3-03-003
unobtrusively	QL	1-01-001
unobtrusively	RB	1-01-001
unoccupied	JJ	3-03-003
unofficial	JJ	5-04-005
unofficially	RB	1-01-001
unopened	JJ	1-01-001
unoriginal	noun	2-01-001
unoriginals	NNS	1-01-001
unoriginals	NNS-HL	1-01-001
unorthodox	JJ	6-05-005
unpack	verb	2-02-002
unpack	VB	1-01-001
unpacking	VBG	1-01-001
unpadded	JJ	1-01-001
unpaid	adjective	9-04-006
unpaid	JJ	7-04-005
unpaid	JJ-HL	1-01-001
Unpaid	JJ-TL	1-01-001
unpaintable	JJ	1-01-001
unpaired	JJ	4-01-001
unparalleled	JJ	2-02-002
unpartisan	JJ	1-01-001
unpatriotic	JJ	2-01-002
unpatronizing	JJ	1-01-001
unpaved	JJ	1-01-001
unperceived	JJ	1-01-001
unperformed	JJ	1-01-001
unphysical	JJ	1-01-001
unpicturesque	JJ	1-01-001
unplagued	JJ	1-01-001
unpleasant	JJ	15-09-014
unpleasantly	RB	1-01-001
unpleasantness	NN	1-01-001
unpleased	JJ	1-01-001
unplowed	JJ	2-02-002
unplumbed	JJ	1-01-001
unpopular	JJ	6-03-004
unprecedented	JJ	11-07-010
unpredictability	NN	2-02-002
unpredictable	JJ	2-01-001
unpredictably	RB	2-01-002
unpremeditated	JJ	1-01-001
unprepared	JJ	6-06-006
unpretentious	JJ	1-01-001
unproblematic	JJ	1-01-001
unprocurable	JJ	1-01-001
unproductive	JJ	1-01-001
unprofessional	JJ	1-01-001
unprofitable	JJ	1-01-001
unpromising	JJ	1-01-001
unprotected	JJ	2-02-002
unproved	JJ	1-01-001
unprovocative	JJ	1-01-001
unpublished	JJ	3-03-003
unpunished	JJ	1-01-001
unqualified	JJ	2-02-002
unqualifiedly	QL	1-01-001
unquenched	JJ	1-01-001
unquestionable	JJ	1-01-001
unquestionably	RB	11-07-011
unquestioningly	RB	1-01-001
unquiet	JJ	1-01-001
unravel	VB	1-01-001
unready	JJ	1-01-001
unreal	JJ	6-04-004
unrealism	NN	1-01-001
unrealistic	JJ	3-03-003
unrealistically	RB	1-01-001
unreality	NN	2-02-002
unreason	NN	1-01-001
unreasonable	JJ	3-02-003
unreasonably	QL	1-01-001
unreasoning	JJ	1-01-001
unreassuringly	RB	1-01-001
unrecognizable	JJ	2-02-002
unrecognized	JJ	2-02-002
unreconstructed	JJ	5-01-001
unrecoverable	JJ	1-01-001
unredeemed	JJ	1-01-001
unreel	verb	1-01-001
unreeling	VBG	1-01-001
unreflective	JJ	1-01-001
unrehearsed	JJ	1-01-001
unrelated	JJ	7-03-005
unreleased	JJ	1-01-001
unrelenting	JJ	1-01-001
unreliability	NN	1-01-001
unreliable	JJ	4-03-003
unrelieved	JJ	4-04-004
unremarkable	JJ	1-01-001
unremitting	JJ	1-01-001
unrepentant	JJ	1-01-001
unrequited	JJ	1-01-001
unreservedly	RB	1-01-001
unresolved	JJ	2-02-002
unresponsive	JJ	2-02-002
unrest	NN	5-05-005
unrestricted	JJ	3-03-003
unrestrictedly	RB	1-01-001
unrevealing	JJ	1-01-001
unrewarding	JJ	2-02-002
unrifled	JJ	1-01-001
unripe	JJ	1-01-001
unroll	verb	1-01-001
unrolled	VBN	1-01-001
unromantic	JJ	1-01-001
unruffled	JJ	1-01-001
unruly	JJ	2-02-002
unsafe	JJ	1-01-001
unsalted	JJ	2-01-001
unsatisfactory	JJ	8-05-007
unsaturated	JJ	2-01-001
unsavory	JJ	1-01-001
unscathed	JJ	2-02-002
unscientific	JJ	2-02-002
unscramble	VB	1-01-001
unscrew	verb	3-03-003
unscrew	VB	1-01-001
unscrewed	VBD	2-02-002
unscrupulous	JJ	5-04-005
unseal	verb	1-01-001
unsealed	VBN	1-01-001
unseasonable	JJ	1-01-001
unsee	VB	1-01-001
unseemly	JJ	1-01-001
unseen	JJ	5-04-005
unself-conscious	JJ	1-01-001
unselfconsciousness	NN	1-01-001
unselfish	JJ	1-01-001
unselfishly	RB	1-01-001
unservile	JJ	1-01-001
unsettle	verb	5-04-005
unsettled	VBN	4-03-004
unsettling	VBG	1-01-001
unshakable	adjective	2-02-002
unshakable	JJ	1-01-001
unshakeable	JJ	1-01-001

Word	Tag	Frequency
unsharpened	**JJ**	**1-01-001**
unshaved	**JJ**	**1-01-001**
unshaven	**JJ**	**1-01-001**
unsheathe	**verb**	**2-02-002**
unsheathe	VB	1-01-001
unsheathing	VBG	1-01-001
unshed	**JJ**	**1-01-001**
unshelled	**JJ**	**1-01-001**
unsheltered	**JJ**	**1-01-001**
unshielded	**JJ**	**1-01-001**
unsightly	**JJ**	**1-01-001**
unsigned	**JJ**	**3-03-003**
unsinkable	**adjective**	**4-02-002**
unsinkable	JJ	0-00-000
Unsinkable	JJ-TL	4-02-002
unskilled	**JJ**	**3-02-002**
unsloped	**JJ**	**1-01-001**
unsmiling	**JJ**	**2-01-002**
unsmilingly	**RB**	**1-01-001**
unsold	**JJ**	**3-02-002**
unsolder	**VB**	**1-01-001**
unsolved	**JJ**	**3-03-003**
unsophisticated	**JJ**	**1-01-001**
unspeakable	**JJ**	**5-04-005**
unspecified	**JJ**	**4-02-003**
unspectacular	**JJ**	**1-01-001**
unspoken	**JJ**	**3-03-003**
unsprayed	**JJ**	**1-01-001**
unstable	**JJ**	**8-04-005**
unstained	**JJ**	**3-01-002**
unstapled	**JJ**	**1-01-001**
unstaring	**JJ**	**1-01-001**
unsteadily	**RB**	**1-01-001**
unsteady	**JJ**	**2-02-002**
unstilted	**JJ**	**1-01-001**
unstressed	**JJ**	**4-01-001**
unstring	**verb**	**2-02-002**
unstrung	VBN	2-02-002
unstructured	**JJ**	**12-01-001**
unstuck	**JJ**	**1-01-001**
unstuffy	**JJ**	**1-01-001**
unsuccessful	**JJ**	**9-05-009**
unsuccessfully	**RB**	**1-01-001**
unsuitable	**JJ**	**3-03-003**
unsuitably	**RB**	**1-01-001**
unsuited	**JJ**	**1-01-001**
unsung	**JJ**	**3-03-003**
unsupportable	**JJ**	**1-01-001**
unsupported	**JJ**	**1-01-001**
unsure	**JJ**	**1-01-001**
unsurmountable	**JJ**	**1-01-001**
unsurpassed	**JJ**	**1-01-001**
unsuspecting	**JJ**	**1-01-001**
unsympathetic	**JJ**	**3-02-002**
Untch	**NP**	**1-01-001**
unteach	**VB**	**1-01-001**
untellable	**JJ**	**1-01-001**
untenable	**JJ**	**2-02-002**
untenanted	**JJ**	**1-01-001**
unthaw	**VB**	**1-01-001**
unthematic	**JJ**	**1-01-001**
unthinkable	**JJ**	**3-02-003**
unthinking	**JJ**	**1-01-001**
untidiness	**NN**	**1-01-001**
untidy	**JJ**	**1-01-001**
untie	**verb**	**3-02-003**
untie	VB	2-02-002
untied	VBD	1-01-001
until	**CS**	**338-15-216**
until	**prep.**	**125-13-094**
until	IN	124-13-093
'till	IN	1-01-001
untimely	**JJ**	**1-01-001**
unto	**prep.**	**16-05-009**
unto	IN	14-05-009
unto	IN-HL	2-02-002
untold	**JJ**	**2-02-002**
untouched	**JJ**	**9-06-009**
untoward	**JJ**	**1-01-001**
untracked	**JJ**	**1-01-001**
untraditional	**JJ**	**1-01-001**
untrained	**JJ**	**1-01-001**
untrammeled	**JJ**	**4-03-004**
untreated	**JJ**	**1-01-001**
untrue	**JJ**	**2-02-002**
untrustworthiness	**NN**	**1-01-001**
untruth	**NN**	**2-02-002**
unused	**JJ**	**3-02-003**
unusual	**JJ**	**63-15-052**
unusually	**QL**	**5-04-005**
unusually	**RB**	**6-03-006**
unutterably	**RB**	**1-01-001**
unuttered	**JJ**	**2-02-002**
unvarying	**JJ**	**1-01-001**
unveil	**verb**	**3-02-003**
unveiled	VBD	1-01-001
unveiled	VBN	2-01-002
unventilated	**JJ**	**1-01-001**
unwanted	**JJ**	**6-05-006**
unwarrantable	**JJ**	**2-01-001**
unwarranted	**JJ**	**4-04-004**
unwavering	**adjective**	**1-01-001**
unwavering	JJ	0-00-000
unwaivering	JJ	1-01-001
unwaveringly	**RB**	**1-01-001**
unwed	**JJ**	**12-02-002**
unwelcome	**JJ**	**5-05-005**
unwholesome	**JJ**	**2-02-002**
unwilling	**JJ**	**7-04-007**
unwillingly	**RB**	**1-01-001**
unwillingness	**NN**	**5-03-005**
unwind	**verb**	**1-01-001**
unwinding	VBG	1-01-001
unwire	**verb**	**2-01-001**
unwire	VB	1-01-001
unwired	VBD	1-01-001
unwise	**JJ**	**3-02-003**
unwisely	**RB**	**2-02-002**
unwitting	**JJ**	**1-01-001**
unwittingly	**RB**	**5-05-005**
unwomanly	**JJ**	**1-01-001**
unworkable	**JJ**	**1-01-001**
unworn	**JJ**	**1-01-001**
unworthy	**JJ**	**5-04-005**
unwounded	**JJ**	**1-01-001**
unwrinkled	**JJ**	**1-01-001**
unyielding	**JJ**	**1-01-001**
up	**prep.**	**179-14-118**
up	IN	177-14-117
up	IN-NC	2-01-001
up	**noun**	**2-01-001**
ups	NNS	2-01-001
up	**adv./part.**	**1712-15-424**
up	RP	1703-13-424
up-pp	RP	1-01-001
up	RP-HL	4-03-004
up	RP-NC	1-01-001
Up	RP-TL	3-01-001
up	**verb**	**2-02-002**
upped	VBD	1-01-001
upped	VBN	1-01-001
up-and-coming	**JJ**	**1-01-001**
up-jutting	**JJ**	**1-01-001**
up-to-date	**JJ**	**3-03-003**
upbeat	**JJ**	**1-01-001**
upbringing	**NN**	**1-01-001**
upcoming	**JJ**	**1-01-001**
update	**verb**	**4-04-004**
update	VB	1-01-001
updated	VBN	3-03-003
upgrade	**verb**	**5-03-005**
upgrade	VB	3-02-003
upgraded	VBN	1-01-001
upgrading	VBG	1-01-001
upgrading	**NN**	**1-01-001**
upheaval	**NN**	**3-03-003**
uphill	**JJ**	**1-01-001**
uphold	**verb**	**18-08-018**
uphold	VB	7-06-007
upholds	VBZ	0-00-000
Upholds	VBZ-HL	1-01-001
upheld	VBD	5-04-005
upheld	VBN	1-01-001
upholding	VBG	4-02-004
upholder	**noun**	**1-01-001**
upholders	NNS	1-01-001
upholster	**verb**	**1-01-001**
upholstered	VBN	1-01-001
upholstery	**NN**	**3-02-003**
UPI	**prop. noun**	**5-01-004**
UPI	NP	1-01-001
UPI	NP-HL	4-01-003
upkeep	**NN**	**6-04-006**
upland	**JJ**	**1-01-001**
upland	**noun**	**3-02-002**
uplands	NNS	1-01-001
Uplands	NNS-TL	2-01-001
upland	**RB**	**1-01-001**

Word	Tag	Frequency
uplift	**NN**	**1-01-001**
upon	**prep.**	**454-15-216**
upon	IN	449-15-215
uppon	IN	3-01-001
Upon	IN-TL	2-01-001
upon	**RB**	**44-09-043**
upper	**adjective**	**65-14-047**
upper	JJ	57-14-042
upper-	JJ	3-01-001
Upper	JJ-TL	5-05-005
upper	**JJR**	**10-01-005**
upper-class	**NN**	**2-01-001**
upper-level	**NN**	**1-01-001**
upper-lower	**JJ**	**1-01-001**
upper-middle	**adjective**	**3-01-002**
upper-middle	JJ	1-01-001
upper-middle-	JJ	2-01-001
upper-middle-class	**NN**	**5-02-002**
upperclassman	**noun**	**1-01-001**
upperclassmen	NNS	1-01-001
uppercut	**NN**	**1-01-001**
uppermost	**JJS**	**1-01-001**
uppermost	**RBT**	**2-02-002**
upraise	**verb**	**1-01-001**
upraised	VBN	1-01-001
upright	**JJ**	**3-03-003**
upright	**NN**	**6-05-006**
upright	**RB**	**5-04-005**
uprising	**noun**	**3-03-003**
uprising	NN	0-00-000
Uprising	NN-TL	1-01-001
uprisings	NNS	2-02-002
upriver	**JJ**	**1-01-001**
uproar	**NN**	**2-02-002**
uproariously	**RB**	**1-01-001**
uproot	**verb**	**1-01-001**
uprooted	VBN	1-01-001
upset	**noun**	**2-02-002**
upset	NN	1-01-001
upsets	NNS	1-01-001
upset	**verb**	**16-11-015**
upset	VB	2-02-002
upsets	VBZ	2-02-002
upset	VBD	1-01-001
upset	VBN	10-07-010
upsetting	VBG	1-01-001
upshot	**noun**	**2-02-002**
upshot	NN	1-01-001
upshots	NNS	1-01-001
upside	**RB**	**8-06-007**
Upson	**NP**	**1-01-001**
upstairs	**JJ**	**4-04-004**
upstairs	**NN**	**1-01-001**
upstairs	**RB**	**23-07-019**
upstanding	**JJ**	**1-01-001**
upstate	**RB**	**1-01-001**
upstream	**JJ**	**2-01-001**
upstream	**RB**	**3-02-002**
upsurge	**NN**	**3-03-003**
upswing	**NN**	**2-02-002**
uptake	**NN**	**5-01-003**
Upton	**NP**	**18-01-001**
uptown	**JJ**	**2-01-001**
uptown	**NN**	**2-02-002**
uptown	**RB**	**1-01-001**
uptrend	**NN**	**1-01-001**
upturn	**NN**	**7-04-005**
upturned	**JJ**	**1-01-001**
upward	**JJ**	**3-02-003**
upward	**RB**	**24-10-017**
upward-mobile	**JJ**	**2-01-001**
upwards	**RB**	**6-05-005**
uranium	**NN**	**6-02-002**
uranyl	**NN**	**2-01-001**
urban	**adjective**	**42-09-022**
urban	JJ	41-09-021
Urban	JJ-TL	1-01-001
urban-fringe	**NN**	**1-01-001**
Urbana	**NP**	**1-01-001**
urbanism	**NN**	**2-01-001**
urbanization	**NN**	**8-02-002**
urbanize	**verb**	**4-03-004**
urbanized	VBN	4-03-004
Urbano	**NP**	**1-01-001**
urea	**NN**	**1-01-001**
uremia	**NN**	**1-01-001**
urethane	**noun**	**28-01-001**
urethane	NN	25-01-001
urethane	NN-HL	1-01-001
urethane (cont.):		
urethanes	NNS	1-01-001
urethanes	NNS-HL	1-01-001
urethra	**NN**	**1-01-001**
urge	**noun**	**10-05-007**
urge	NN	8-05-006
urges	NNS	2-01-001
urge	**verb**	**64-14-056**
urge	VB	13-08-013
urges	VBZ	6-06-006
urged	VBD	21-10-018
urged	VBN	12-09-012
urged	VBN-HL	2-01-002
urging	VBG	10-06-010
urgency	**noun**	**13-07-012**
urgency	NN	12-07-011
urgencies	NNS	1-01-001
urgent	**JJ**	**21-13-019**
urgently	**RB**	**6-03-005**
urging	**noun**	**2-02-002**
urgings	NNS	2-02-002
Urich	**NP**	**1-01-001**
Urielite	**prop. noun**	**1-01-001**
Urielites	NPS	1-01-001
urinal	**noun**	**1-01-001**
urinals	NNS	1-01-001
urinary	**JJ**	**2-01-002**
urine	**NN**	**1-01-001**
urn	**noun**	**3-03-003**
urn	NN	1-01-001
urns	NNS	2-02-002
Urn	**NP**	**1-01-001**
Ursuline	**prop. noun**	**1-01-001**
Ursuline	NP	0-00-000
Ursuline	NP-TL	1-01-001
Uruguay	**NP**	**1-01-001**
usable	**adjective**	**9-06-009**
usable	JJ	8-05-008
useable	JJ	1-01-001
usage	**noun**	**17-05-011**
usage	NN	14-04-008
usages	NNS	3-02-003
use	**noun**	**389-14-171**
use	NN	352-14-168
yuse	NN	1-01-001
use	NN-HL	9-03-004
uses	NNS	25-05-015
uses	NNS-HL	2-02-002
use	**verb**	**1016-15-342**
use	VB	228-15-150
use	VB-HL	2-02-002
uses	VBZ	32-06-025
used	VBD	137-15-100
used	VBN	474-15-177
using	VBG	143-15-094
useful	**JJ**	**58-11-045**
usefully	**RB**	**1-01-001**
usefulness	**NN**	**11-05-009**
useless	**JJ**	**17-07-015**
uselessly	**QL**	**1-01-001**
uselessly	**RB**	**2-02-002**
uselessness	**NN**	**2-02-002**
user	**noun**	**10-05-010**
user	NN	4-03-004
users	NNS	6-03-006
usher	**NN**	**1-01-001**
usher	**verb**	**3-03-003**
usher	VB	1-01-001
ushered	VBD	2-02-002
using	**adjective**	**2-02-002**
using	JJ	0-00-000
using	JJ-NC	2-02-002
USN.	**NP**	**1-01-001**
usual	**JJ**	**92-15-075**
usual	**RB**	**4-03-003**
usually	**RB**	**206-15-137**
usurious	**JJ**	**1-01-001**
usurp	**verb**	**2-02-002**
usurp	VB	1-01-001
usurped	VBN	1-01-001
Utah	**prop. noun**	**6-04-004**
Utah	NP	5-04-004
Utah	NP-HL	1-01-001
utensil	**noun**	**3-03-003**
utensils	NNS	3-03-003
utilitarian	**JJ**	**3-02-003**
utility	**noun**	**36-07-022**
utility	NN	28-07-019
utility	NN-HL	1-01-001

Word	Tag	Frequency
utility (cont.):		
utilities	NNS	7-04-005
utility-cost	**NN**	**1-01-001**
utilization	**NN**	**9-03-006**
utilize	**verb**	**32-06-025**
utilize	VB	10-06-010
utilizes	VBZ	4-03-004
utilized	VBD	1-01-001
utilized	VBN	9-04-007
utilizing	VBG	8-04-007
utmost	**JJS**	**5-05-005**
utmost	**NN**	**2-02-002**
Uto-Aztecan	**NP**	**2-01-001**
utopia	**noun**	**4-01-002**
utopia	NN	3-01-002
utopias	NNS	1-01-001
Utopia	**prop. noun**	**21-03-003**
Utopia	NP	2-02-002
Utopia	NP-TL	19-02-002
utopian	**adjective**	**19-02-005**
utopian	JJ	7-02-004
Utopian	JJ	12-01-001
utopian	**noun**	**4-01-003**
utopian	NN	2-01-002
utopians	NNS	2-01-002
Utopian	**prop. noun**	**3-01-001**
Utopians	NPS	3-01-001
utopianism	**NN**	**1-01-001**
utter	**JJ**	**10-05-009**
utter	**verb**	**11-05-010**
utter	VB	3-03-003
uttuh	VB	1-01-001
uttered	VBD	3-03-003
uttered	VBN	2-02-002
uttering	VBG	2-02-002
utterance	**noun**	**6-04-005**
utterance	NN	5-03-004
utterances	NNS	1-01-001
utterly	**QL**	**17-08-017**
utterly	**RB**	**10-06-008**
uttermost	**NN**	**1-01-001**
Uxbridge	**NP**	**1-01-001**

V

Word	Tag	Frequency
V	**NP**	**5-02-003**
V.	**NP**	**14-06-013**
vacancy	**noun**	**8-04-007**
vacancy	NN	4-03-003
vacancy	NN-HL	1-01-001
Vacancy	NN-TL	1-01-001
vacancies	NNS	2-02-002
vacant	**JJ**	**11-07-008**
vacate	**verb**	**5-04-005**
vacate	VB	1-01-001
vacated	VBD	1-01-001
vacated	VBN	3-02-003
vacation	**noun**	**55-10-021**
vacation	NN	46-10-019
vacations	NNS	7-03-004
vacations	NNS-HL	2-01-001
vacation	**verb**	**4-02-003**
vacation	VB	1-01-001
vacationing	VBG	3-02-003
vacationer	**noun**	**1-01-001**
vacationers	NNS	1-01-001
vacationland	**NN**	**1-01-001**
vaccinate	**verb**	**1-01-001**
vaccinating	VBG	1-01-001
vaccination	**NN**	**2-02-002**
vaccine	**NN**	**1-01-001**
Vachell	**NP**	**1-01-001**
vacuolate	**verb**	**1-01-001**
vacuolated	VBN	1-01-001
vacuolization	**NN**	**2-01-001**
vacuous	**JJ**	**1-01-001**
vacuum	**noun**	**21-09-011**
vacuum	NN	20-09-011
vacuum-	NN	1-01-001
vacuum	**verb**	**3-02-002**
vacuumed	VBN	1-01-001
vacuuming	VBG	2-01-001
vacuum-formed	**JJ**	**2-01-001**
vade	**FW-VB**	**2-01-002**
Vadim	**NP**	**1-01-001**
Vadstena	**NP**	**1-01-001**
vagabond	**noun**	**3-03-003**
vagabond	NN	2-02-002
vagabonds	NNS	0-00-000
Vagabonds	NNS-TL	1-01-001
vagary	**noun**	**1-01-001**
vagaries	NNS	1-01-001
vagina	**NN**	**10-01-001**
vaginal	**JJ**	**6-01-001**
vaginal	**NN**	**1-01-001**
vagrant	**JJ**	**1-01-001**
vague	**JJ**	**25-11-024**
vaguely	**QL**	**2-02-002**
vaguely	**RB**	**15-07-015**
vaguely-imagined	**JJ**	**1-01-001**
vagueness	**NN**	**3-03-003**
vaguest	**JJT**	**1-01-001**
Vail	**prop. noun**	**3-01-001**
Vail (cont.):		
Vail	NP	1-01-001
Vail	NP-TL	2-01-001
vain	**JJ**	**10-05-010**
vainly	**RB**	**2-02-002**
Vale	**NP**	**4-01-001**
valedictorian	**noun**	**1-01-001**
valedictorian	NN	0-00-000
Valedictorian	NN-TL	1-01-001
Valente	**NP**	**1-01-001**
Valentine	**prop. noun**	**2-02-002**
Valentine	NP	1-01-001
Valentine	NP-TL	1-01-001
Valerie	**NP**	**1-01-001**
Valery	**NP**	**3-02-002**
valet	**NN**	**2-01-002**
valeur	**FW-NN**	**1-01-001**
valiant	**JJ**	**1-01-001**
valiantly	**RB**	**1-01-001**
valid	**JJ**	**22-06-019**
validate	**verb**	**4-04-004**
validate	VB	2-02-002
validated	VBD	1-01-001
validating	VBG	1-01-001
validation	**NN**	**1-01-001**
validity	**NN**	**15-07-014**
validly	**RB**	**1-01-001**
Valle	**prop. noun**	**1-01-001**
Valle	NP	0-00-000
Valle	NP-TL	1-01-001
Vallee	**NP**	**1-01-001**
valley	**noun**	**79-11-036**
valley	NN	48-07-019
Valley	NN-TL	25-11-019
valley's	NN$	1-01-001
valleys	NNS	5-04-004
Vallfart	**foreign**	**1-01-001**
Vallfart	FW-NN	0-00-000
Vallfart	FW-NN-TL	1-01-001
Valmet	**NP**	**1-01-001**
Valois	**prop. noun**	**1-01-001**
Valois	NP	0-00-000
Valois	NP-TL	1-01-001
valor	**NN**	**1-01-001**
valuable	**adjective**	**45-13-039**
valuable	JJ	44-13-038
Valuable	JJ-TL	1-01-001
valuation	**noun**	**9-05-006**
valuation	NN	7-05-005
valuations	NNS	2-02-002
value	**noun**	**383-14-128**
value	NN	197-12-101
valewe	NN	1-01-001
value	NN-HL	2-02-002
values	NNS	182-11-062
Values	NNS-TL	1-01-001
value	**verb**	**18-09-014**
value	VB	1-01-001

Word	Tag	Frequency
value (cont):		
values	VBZ	3-03-003
valued	VBD	1-01-001
valued	VBN	13-05-009
value-judgment	**noun**	**1-01-001**
value-judgments	NNS	1-01-001
value-orientation	**noun**	**1-01-001**
value-orientations	NNS	1-01-001
value-problem	**noun**	**1-01-001**
value-problems	NNS	1-01-001
value-system	**NN**	**1-01-001**
valueless	**JJ**	**1-01-001**
valve	**noun**	**7-03-007**
valve	NN	3-03-003
valves	NNS	4-02-004
vamp	**noun**	**1-01-001**
vamp	NN	0-00-000
Vamp	NN-TL	1-01-001
vampire	**noun**	**1-01-001**
vampires	NNS	1-01-001
van	**NN**	**2-02-002**
Van	**NP**	**30-09-020**
Vance	**prop. noun**	**1-01-001**
Vance's	NP$	1-01-001
vandal	**noun**	**1-01-001**
vandals	NNS	1-01-001
vandalism	**NN**	**1-01-001**
Vandervoort	**NP**	**1-01-001**
Vandiver	**NP**	**6-02-002**
Vandringsar	**foreign**	**1-01-001**
Vandringsar	FW-NNS	0-00-000
Vandringsar	FW-NNS-TL	1-01-001
vanguard	**noun**	**3-03-003**
vanguard	NN	1-01-001
Vanguard	NN-TL	2-02-002
vanilla	**NN**	**1-01-001**
vanish	**verb**	**25-10-022**
vanish	VB	5-04-005
vanishes	VBZ	1-01-001
vanished	VBD	9-05-008
vanished	VBN	6-05-005
vanishing	VBG	4-03-004
vanity	**noun**	**8-06-008**
vanity	NN	7-06-007
vanities	NNS	1-01-001
vantage	**NN**	**6-05-006**
vantage-point	**noun**	**1-01-001**
vantage-points	NNS	1-01-001
vapor	**noun**	**12-03-004**
vapor	NN	11-03-004
vapor	NN-HL	1-01-001
vapor-pressure	**NN**	**3-01-001**
vaporization	**NN**	**1-01-001**
vaquero	**NN**	**1-01-001**
var.	**NN**	**1-01-001**
Varani	**NP**	**2-01-001**
variability	**NN**	**3-02-002**
variable	**JJ**	**25-06-017**
variable	**noun**	**37-03-012**
variable	NN	11-01-003
variables	NNS	25-03-011
variables	NNS-HL	1-01-001
variable-speed	**NN**	**1-01-001**
Varian	**JJ**	**2-01-001**
variance	**NN**	**1-01-001**
variant	**NN**	**4-04-004**
variation	**noun**	**54-08-034**
variation	NN	32-06-018
variations	NNS	21-07-017
Variations	NNS-TL	1-01-001
variations	**foreign**	**1-01-001**
variations	FW-NNS	0-00-000
Variations	FW-NNS-TL	1-01-001
varicolored	**JJ**	**1-01-001**
variegate	**verb**	**1-01-001**
variegated	VBN	1-01-001
variety	**noun**	**93-13-077**
variety	NN	84-12-070
Variety	NN-TL	1-01-001
varieties	NNS	8-06-007
Varigrad	**NP**	**1-01-001**
various	**AP**	**56-04-031**
various	**adjective**	**145-14-106**
various	JJ	144-14-105
Various	JJ-TL	1-01-001
variously	**RB**	**5-05-005**
varitinted	**JJ**	**1-01-001**
varitype	**verb**	**1-01-001**
varityping	VBG	1-01-001

Word	Tag	Frequency
Varlaam	**prop. noun**	**6-01-001**
Varlaam	NP	4-01-001
Varlaam's	NP$	2-01-001
varmint	**NN**	**2-01-001**
Varner	**NP**	**1-01-001**
Varnessa	**NP**	**1-01-001**
varnish	**noun**	**3-01-001**
varnish	NN	1-01-001
varnishes	NNS	2-01-001
Varviso	**NP**	**1-01-001**
vary	**verb**	**127-13-085**
vary	VB	34-08-028
varies	VBZ	11-04-010
varied	VBD	7-03-006
varied	VBN	35-09-028
varying	VBG	39-11-033
varying	VBG-HL	1-01-001
varying	**JJ**	**2-02-002**
vasa	**NN**	**2-01-001**
Vasa	**NP**	**1-01-001**
Vasady	**NP**	**1-01-001**
vascular	**JJ**	**3-01-002**
vase	**noun**	**15-04-004**
vase	NN	4-03-003
vases	NNS	10-02-002
vases	NNS-HL	1-01-001
Vasilievitch	**NP**	**1-01-001**
Vaska	**NP**	**1-01-001**
vasorum	**NN**	**2-01-001**
vassal	**NN**	**1-01-001**
vast	**JJ**	**61-13-054**
vaster	**JJR**	**1-01-001**
vastly	**QL**	**7-05-007**
vastly	**RB**	**3-03-003**
Vatican	**prop. noun**	**4-04-004**
Vatican	NP	3-03-003
Vatican	NP-TL	1-01-001
Vattern	**prop. noun**	**1-01-001**
Vattern	NP	0-00-000
Vattern	NP-TL	1-01-001
vaudeville	**NN**	**5-02-002**
Vaudois	**NP**	**1-01-001**
Vaughan	**NP**	**3-02-002**
Vaughn	**NP**	**2-01-001**
vault	**noun**	**8-02-003**
vault	NN	2-02-002
vaults	NNS	6-01-001
vault	**verb**	**2-02-002**
vaulting	VBG	2-02-002
vaulting	**NN**	**1-01-001**
veal	**NN**	**1-01-001**
Veblen	**NP**	**1-01-001**
Vecchio	**NP**	**8-02-002**
vector	**noun**	**26-02-005**
vector	NN	19-02-004
vectors	NNS	7-01-004
VecTrol	**prop. noun**	**4-01-001**
VecTrol	NP	2-01-001
VecTrol's	NP$	2-01-001
Veeck	**prop. noun**	**1-01-001**
Veeck's	NP$	1-01-001
veer	**verb**	**8-05-008**
veer	VB	2-01-002
veers	VBZ	1-01-001
veered	VBD	3-02-003
veering	VBG	2-02-002
Vegas	**NP**	**5-03-005**
vegetable	**noun**	**26-07-014**
vegetable	NN	10-05-009
vegetables	NNS	16-05-007
vegetarian	**NN**	**1-01-001**
vegetation	**NN**	**3-03-003**
vehemence	**NN**	**3-03-003**
vehement	**JJ**	**2-02-002**
vehemently	**RB**	**1-01-001**
vehicle	**noun**	**88-11-031**
vehicle	NN	33-09-019
vehicle	NN-HL	2-01-001
vehicles	NNS	51-09-015
vehicles	NNS-HL	1-01-001
Vehicles	NNS-TL	1-01-001
vehicular	**JJ**	**1-01-001**
veil	**noun**	**11-08-009**
veil	NN	8-07-007
veils	NNS	3-03-003
veil	**verb**	**7-04-006**
veiled	VBN	6-03-005
veiling	VBG	1-01-001
vein	**noun**	**31-11-020**

Word	Tag	Frequency
vein (cont.):		
vein	NN	25-09-014
veins	NNS	6-05-006
vein	**verb**	**3-02-003**
veined	VBN	1-01-001
veining	VBG	2-02-002
Velasquez	**NP**	**1-01-001**
veldt	**NN**	**1-01-001**
vellum	**NN**	**1-01-001**
velociter	**FW-RB**	**1-01-001**
velocity	**noun**	**32-06-014**
velocity	NN	26-06-013
velocities	NNS	6-02-003
Velon	**prop. noun**	**1-01-001**
Velon	NP	0-00-000
Velon	NP-HL	1-01-001
velour	**noun**	**2-02-002**
velour	NN	1-01-001
velours	NN	1-01-001
velvet	**NN**	**4-03-004**
velvety	**JJ**	**3-02-002**
Venable	**prop. noun**	**1-01-001**
Venable	NP	0-00-000
Venable	NP-TL	1-01-001
vend	**verb**	**6-02-002**
vending	VBG	6-02-002
Vendome	**prop. noun**	**1-01-001**
Vendome	NP	0-00-000
Vendome	NP-TL	1-01-001
vendor	**noun**	**3-03-003**
vendor	NN	1-01-001
vendors	NNS	2-02-002
veneer	**NN**	**1-01-001**
venerable	**adjective**	**5-05-005**
venerable	JJ	4-04-004
Venerable	JJ-TL	1-01-001
venerate	**verb**	**2-02-002**
venerated	VBN	2-02-002
veneration	**NN**	**3-03-003**
venereal	**JJ**	**3-01-001**
Venetian	**adjective**	**6-03-004**
Venetian	JJ	5-03-004
Venetian	JJ-TL	1-01-001
Veneto	**prop. noun**	**1-01-001**
Veneto	NP	0-00-000
Veneto	NP-TL	1-01-001
Venezuela	**NP**	**3-02-003**
Venezuelan	**JJ**	**2-01-001**
vengeance	**NN**	**10-06-009**
Venice	**prop. noun**	**7-02-005**
Venice	NP	2-02-002
Venice	NP-TL	5-01-003
venison	**NN**	**1-01-001**
Venn	**NP**	**2-01-001**
venom	**NN**	**2-02-002**
venomous	**JJ**	**2-02-002**
vent	**noun**	**12-06-009**
vent	NN	8-05-008
vents	NNS	4-02-002
vent	**verb**	**3-03-003**
vent	VB	2-02-002
vented	VBN	1-01-001
Venti	**NP**	**1-01-001**
ventilate	**verb**	**3-03-003**
ventilates	VBZ	1-01-001
ventilated	VBN	1-01-001
ventilating	VBG	1-01-001
ventilation	**noun**	**6-03-005**
ventilation	NN	5-03-004
Ventilation	NN-TL	1-01-001
ventilator	**NN**	**1-01-001**
ventricle	**noun**	**4-02-002**
ventricle	NN	3-02-002
ventricles	NNS	1-01-001
Ventura	**NP**	**1-01-001**
venture	**noun**	**17-10-015**
venture	NN	13-09-011
ventures	NNS	4-04-004
venture	**verb**	**11-07-010**
venture	VB	6-03-005
ventured	VBD	2-02-002
ventured	VBN	3-03-003
venturesome	**JJ**	**1-01-001**
Venturi	**NP**	**1-01-001**
Venus	**NP**	**12-05-006**
Venusian	**prop. noun**	**1-01-001**
Venusians	NPS	1-01-001
Vera	**NP**	**2-02-002**
veracious	**JJ**	**1-01-001**
veracity	**NN**	**3-03-003**
veranda	**noun**	**11-04-007**
veranda	NN	8-02-004
vuhranduh	NN	1-01-001
verandah	NN	1-01-001
verandas	NNS	1-01-001
verb	**noun**	**11-04-006**
verb	NN	4-03-004
verbs	NNS	7-04-005
verbal	**adjective**	**21-05-017**
verbal	JJ	20-05-016
Verbal	JJ-TL	1-01-001
verbally	**RB**	**5-04-005**
verbatim	**RB**	**2-01-002**
verbena	**noun**	**3-01-001**
verbenas	NNS	3-01-001
Verboort	**NP**	**1-01-001**
verboten	**FW-VBN**	**1-01-001**
verdant	**JJ**	**1-01-001**
Verdi	**prop. noun**	**5-04-004**
Verdi	NP	3-02-002
Verdi's	NP$	2-02-002
verdict	**NN**	**15-03-005**
Vere	**NP**	**1-01-001**
verge	**NN**	**2-02-002**
Verges	**NP**	**1-01-001**
Vergessen	**FW-NN**	**1-01-001**
veridical	**JJ**	**1-01-001**
verification	**NN**	**4-03-004**
verify	**verb**	**11-05-011**
verify	VB	5-04-005
verified	VBN	6-03-006
verisimilitude	**NN**	**1-01-001**
veritable	**JJ**	**4-04-004**
verity	**NN**	**1-01-001**
Verloop	**prop. noun**	**3-01-001**
Verloop	NP	2-01-001
Verloop's	NP$	1-01-001
Vermeersch	**NP**	**1-01-001**
vermeil	**FW-JJ**	**1-01-001**
Vermejo	**NP**	**7-01-001**
vermilion	**NN**	**3-03-003**
Vermont	**prop. noun**	**23-08-011**
Vermont	NP	16-07-010
Vermont	NP-TL	5-02-002
Vermont's	NP$	2-02-002
vermouth	**NN**	**1-01-001**
Vern	**prop. noun**	**1-01-001**
Vern	NP	0-00-000
Vern	NP-TL	1-01-001
vernacular	**JJ**	**1-01-001**
vernacular	**NN**	**1-01-001**
vernal	**JJ**	**1-01-001**
Vernava	**NP**	**3-01-001**
Verne	**NP**	**1-01-001**
Verner	**NP**	**1-01-001**
vernier	**noun**	**2-01-001**
vernier	NN	1-01-001
Vernier	NN-TL	1-01-001
Vernon	**prop. noun**	**24-05-009**
Vernon	NP	18-04-006
Vernon	NP-TL	3-03-003
Vernon's	NP$	3-01-001
Vernor	**prop. noun**	**1-01-001**
Vernor	NP	0-00-000
Vernor	NP-TL	1-01-001
Vero	**prop. noun**	**2-01-001**
Vero	NP	0-00-000
Vero	NP-TL	2-01-001
veronica	**NN**	**1-01-001**
Verplanck	**prop. noun**	**1-01-001**
Verplanck's	NP$	0-00-000
Verplanck's	NP$-TL	1-01-001
Verreau	**NP**	**2-01-001**
Verrone	**NP**	**1-01-001**
versa	**RB**	**6-03-005**
Versailles	**NP**	**2-01-001**
versatile	**JJ**	**3-03-003**
versatility	**NN**	**4-02-003**
verse	**noun**	**37-08-018**
verse	NN	28-06-013
verses	NNS	9-05-008
versed	**JJ**	**2-02-002**
version	**noun**	**62-11-034**
version	NN	47-10-030
Version	NN-TL	6-01-001
versions	NNS	9-04-008
Verstandig	**NP**	**1-01-001**
verstrichen	**FW-VBN**	**1-01-001**

Word	Tag	Frequency
versus	**prep.**	**42-10-021**
versus	IN	9-04-006
v.	IN	3-02-003
v.	IN-TL	14-02-003
vs.	IN	14-06-009
vs.	IN-HL	1-01-001
Vs.	IN-TL	1-01-001
vertebra	**noun**	**1-01-001**
vertebrae	NNS	1-01-001
vertebral	**JJ**	**3-01-001**
vertebrate	**noun**	**2-01-002**
vertebrate	NN	1-01-001
vertebrates	NNS	1-01-001
vertex	**NN**	**19-01-002**
vertical	**JJ**	**16-06-011**
vertical-takeoff-and-landing	**NN**	**1-01-001**
vertically	**RB**	**2-02-002**
vertigo	**NN**	**1-01-001**
verve	**NN**	**4-03-004**
very	**AP**	**93-14-079**
very	**JJ**	**1-01-001**
very	**qualifier**	**703-15-316**
very	QL	700-15-316
verie	QL	1-01-001
very	QL-NC	2-01-001
vesicular	**JJ**	**1-01-001**
Vesole	**NP**	**5-01-001**
vessel	**noun**	**28-08-016**
vessel	NN	15-06-009
Vessel	NN-TL	1-01-001
vessels	NNS	12-05-009
vest	**noun**	**4-03-004**
vest	NN	3-02-003
vests	NNS	1-01-001
vest	**verb**	**4-04-004**
vest	VB	1-01-001
vested	VBN	3-03-003
vestibule	**NN**	**2-01-001**
vestige	**NN**	**2-02-002**
vestment	**noun**	**1-01-001**
vestments	NNS	1-01-001
Vesuvio	**prop. noun**	**1-01-001**
Vesuvio's	NP$	1-01-001
vet	**NN**	**1-01-001**
veteran	**JJ**	**8-05-007**
veteran	**noun**	**38-09-023**
veteran	NN	19-08-016
veteran's	NN$	1-01-001
veterans	NNS	11-04-004
Veterans	NNS-TL	5-04-004
veterans'	NNS$	1-01-001
Veterans'	NNS$-TL	1-01-001
veterinarian	**noun**	**3-02-003**
veterinarian	NN	2-01-002
veterinarians	NNS	1-01-001
veterinary	**adjective**	**4-03-003**
veterinary	JJ	3-02-002
Veterinary	JJ-TL	1-01-001
veto	**NN**	**9-04-007**
veto	**verb**	**2-02-002**
veto	VB	1-01-001
vetoed	VBD	1-01-001
Vevay	**NP**	**1-01-001**
vex	**verb**	**6-06-006**
vex	VB	1-01-001
vexes	VBZ	1-01-001
vexed	VBN	2-02-002
vexing	VBG	2-02-002
vexatious	**JJ**	**1-01-001**
via	**foreign**	**1-01-001**
via	FW-NN	0-00-000
Via	FW-NN-TL	1-01-001
via	**IN**	**17-07-014**
Via	**prop. noun**	**32-02-002**
Via	NP	27-02-002
Via	NP-TL	3-01-001
Via's	NP$	2-01-001
viability	**NN**	**3-02-002**
viable	**JJ**	**5-03-004**
Viale	**NP**	**1-01-001**
Viall	**NP**	**2-01-001**
Viareggio	**NP**	**1-01-001**
viator	**foreign**	**1-01-001**
viator	FW-NN	0-00-000
Viator	FW-NN-TL	1-01-001
vibe	**noun**	**1-01-001**
vibes	NNS	1-01-001
vibrancy	**NN**	**2-02-002**
vibrant	**JJ**	**6-04-006**
vibrate	**verb**	**2-02-002**
vibrated	VBD	1-01-001
vibrating	VBG	1-01-001
vibration	**NN**	**5-03-005**
vibrato	**NN**	**1-01-001**
vibrionic	**JJ**	**1-01-001**
Vic	**prop. noun**	**5-03-003**
Vic	NP	4-03-003
Vic's	NP$	1-01-001
vicar	**NN**	**4-02-004**
vicarious	**JJ**	**2-02-002**
vice	**adjective**	**15-05-009**
vice	JJ	0-00-000
Vice	JJ-TL	15-05-009
vice	**noun**	**25-09-021**
vice	NN	20-08-016
vices	NNS	5-04-005
vice	**RB**	**6-03-005**
vice-chairman	**NN**	**1-01-001**
vice-chancellor	**NN**	**1-01-001**
vice-president	**noun**	**15-05-009**
vice-president	NN	11-04-006
vice-president	NN	0-00-000
Vice-President	NN-TL	3-02-003
vice-presidents	NNS	1-01-001
vice-regent	**NN**	**1-01-001**
Vicenza	**NP**	**2-01-001**
Viceroy	**prop. noun**	**1-01-001**
Viceroy	NP	0-00-000
Viceroy	NP-TL	1-01-001
Vichy	**NP**	**1-01-001**
vicinity	**NN**	**6-05-006**
vicious	**JJ**	**17-06-016**
viciousness	**NN**	**2-02-002**
vicissitude	**noun**	**1-01-001**
vicissitudes	NNS	1-01-001
Vickers	**prop. noun**	**1-01-001**
Vickers	NP	0-00-000
Vickers	NP-TL	1-01-001
Vickery	**NP**	**3-02-002**
Vicksburg	**NP**	**3-03-003**
Vicky	**NP**	**3-01-001**
Vicolo	**NP**	**1-01-001**
victim	**noun**	**50-12-037**
victim	NN	27-08-023
victim's	NN$	4-04-004
victims	NNS	19-08-016
victimize	**verb**	**3-03-003**
victimize	VB	1-01-001
victimized	VBN	2-02-002
victor	**noun**	**8-04-006**
victor	NN	1-01-001
Victor	NN-TL	7-03-005
Victor	**prop. noun**	**17-04-009**
Victor	NP	16-04-009
Victor's	NP$	1-01-001
Victoria	**prop. noun**	**9-03-003**
Victoria	NP	7-02-002
Victoria	NP-TL	1-01-001
Victoria's	NP$	1-01-001
Victorian	**JJ**	**8-05-008**
Victorian	**prop. noun**	**1-01-001**
Victorians	NPS	1-01-001
victorious	**JJ**	**1-01-001**
victoriously	**RB**	**1-01-001**
victory	**noun**	**68-11-037**
victory	NN	55-11-033
Victory	NN-TL	6-03-003
victories	NNS	7-04-006
Victrola	**NP**	**1-01-001**
victual	**noun**	**1-01-001**
victuals	NNS	1-01-001
Vida	**NP**	**1-01-001**
Vidal	**prop. noun**	**2-02-002**
Vidal	NP	1-01-001
Vidal's	NP$	1-01-001
video	**NN**	**2-02-002**
vie	**verb**	**5-04-005**
vies	VBZ	1-01-001
vied	VBN	1-01-001
vying	VBG	3-03-003
vielleicht	**FW-RB**	**1-01-001**
Vienna	**prop. noun**	**24-07-012**
Vienna	NP	19-05-010
Vienna	NP-HL	1-01-001
Vienna	NP-TL	3-03-003
Vienna's	NP$	1-01-001
Vienne	**NP**	**1-01-001**
Viennese	**JJ**	**1-01-001**

Word	Tag	Frequency
Vienot	**NP**	**1-01-001**
Vientiane	**NP**	**7-02-002**
Viet	**prop. noun**	**16-03-007**
Viet	NP	5-02-004
Viet	NP-HL	1-01-001
Viet	NP-TL	10-03-005
Vieth	**NP**	**3-01-001**
Vietnam	**prop. noun**	**3-03-003**
Vietnam	NP	0-00-000
Vietnam	NP-TL	3-03-003
Vietnamese	**JJ**	**2-01-001**
Vietnamese	**NPS**	**4-02-003**
vieux	**foreign**	**1-01-001**
vieux	FW-JJ	0-00-000
Vieux	FW-JJ-TL	1-01-001
Vieux	**NP**	**1-01-001**
view	**noun**	**217-14-138**
view	NN	166-14-119
View	NN-TL	2-01-002
views	NNS	47-09-034
views	NNS-HL	2-01-002
view	**verb**	**55-12-043**
view	VB	18-09-016
views	VBZ	2-01-002
viewed	VBD	2-02-002
viewed	VBN	23-10-021
viewing	VBG	10-05-007
viewer	**noun**	**7-04-007**
viewer	NN	4-03-004
viewers	NNS	3-02-003
viewless	**JJ**	**2-01-001**
viewpoint	**noun**	**19-07-012**
viewpoint	NN	16-06-010
viewpoints	NNS	3-02-002
vigil	**NN**	**1-01-001**
vigilance	**NN**	**4-03-003**
vigilant	**JJ**	**2-02-002**
vigilantism	**NN**	**1-01-001**
vignette	**NN**	**1-01-001**
vigor	**NN**	**14-09-013**
vigorous	**JJ**	**29-09-028**
vigorously	**RB**	**13-07-012**
Vigreux	**NP**	**1-01-001**
Viking	**prop. noun**	**3-01-001**
Vikings	NPS	3-01-001
Vikulov	**NP**	**1-01-001**
Vilas	**prop. noun**	**1-01-001**
Vilas	NP	0-00-000
Vilas	NP-TL	1-01-001
vile	**JJ**	**5-04-005**
vilify	**verb**	**1-01-001**
vilifying	VBG	1-01-001
villa	**NN**	**3-02-003**
Villa	**NP**	**3-02-002**
village	**noun**	**84-14-048**
village	NN	47-12-033
Village	NN-TL	25-09-014
villages	NNS	12-05-009
villager	**noun**	**2-01-001**
villager	NN	1-01-001
villagers	NNS	1-01-001
villain	**noun**	**7-05-007**
villain	NN	3-03-003
villains	NNS	4-03-004
villainous	**JJ**	**1-01-001**
Vince	**NP**	**11-01-001**
Vincent	**NP**	**19-06-011**
vindicate	**verb**	**4-03-004**
vindicate	VB	1-01-001
vindicated	VBD	1-01-001
vindicated	VBN	1-01-001
vindicated	VBN-HL	1-01-001
vindication	**NN**	**4-03-004**
vindictive	**JJ**	**2-02-002**
vine	**noun**	**12-07-010**
vine	NN	4-04-004
vines	NNS	8-05-007
vine-crisscrossed	**JJ**	**1-01-001**
vine-embowered	**JJ**	**1-01-001**
vine-shaded	**JJ**	**1-01-001**
vinegar	**noun**	**9-03-004**
vinegar	NN	8-02-003
Vinegar	NN-TL	1-01-001
vineyard	**noun**	**7-04-005**
vineyard	NN	1-01-001
Vineyard	NN-TL	1-01-001
vineyards	NNS	5-02-003
Vinnicum	**NP**	**1-01-001**
Vinogradoff	**NP**	**1-01-001**
Vinson	**NP**	**1-01-001**
vintage	**NN**	**3-02-003**
vintner	**NN**	**1-01-001**
vinyl	**NN**	**4-02-002**
Viola	**prop. noun**	**15-01-001**
Viola	NP	10-01-001
Viola	NP-HL	1-01-001
Viola's	NP$	3-01-001
Viola's	NP$-HL	1-01-001
violate	**verb**	**17-06-015**
violate	VB	7-04-007
violates	VBZ	2-02-002
violated	VBD	2-02-002
violated	VBN	2-02-002
violating	VBG	4-04-004
violation	**noun**	**20-08-017**
violation	NN	17-07-014
violations	NNS	3-02-003
violence	**noun**	**46-09-030**
violence	NN	44-09-030
Violence	NN-TL	2-01-001
violent	**adjective**	**33-12-029**
violent	JJ	32-12-029
violent	JJ-NC	1-01-001
violently	**RB**	**12-07-012**
violet	**noun**	**4-03-004**
violet	NN	2-02-002
violets	NNS	2-02-002
Violet	**NP**	**5-01-001**
violin	**noun**	**13-04-010**
violin	NN	10-03-007
vioiln	NN	1-01-001
Violin	NN-TL	1-01-001
violins	NNS	1-01-001
violinist	**noun**	**5-03-004**
violinist	NN	4-02-003
violinists	NNS	1-01-001
Viphakone	**NP**	**1-01-001**
Virdon	**NP**	**2-01-001**
Virgil	**NP**	**2-02-002**
Virgilia	**NP**	**1-01-001**
virgin	**adjective**	**6-05-005**
virgin	JJ	4-04-004
Virgin	JJ-TL	2-02-002
virgin	**noun**	**29-08-013**
virgin	NN	5-02-002
Virgin	NN-TL	24-07-012
Virginia	**prop. noun**	**85-11-033**
Virginia	NP	62-09-027
Va.	NP	7-04-005
Virginia	NP-TL	13-08-010
Virginia's	NP$	3-02-002
Virginian	**prop. noun**	**5-02-004**
Virginian	NP	3-01-002
Virginian	NP-TL	1-01-001
Virginians	NPS	1-01-001
virginity	**NN**	**4-02-002**
virile	**JJ**	**4-04-004**
virility	**NN**	**3-02-003**
Virsaladze	**NP**	**1-01-001**
virtual	**JJ**	**5-03-005**
virtually	**QL**	**5-04-005**
virtually	**RB**	**36-10-029**
virtue	**noun**	**45-09-033**
virtue	NN	30-09-021
virtues	NNS	15-07-014
virtuosi	**FW-NNS**	**1-01-001**
virtuosity	**NN**	**1-01-001**
virtuoso	**NN**	**3-02-003**
virtuous	**JJ**	**6-04-005**
virulence	**NN**	**3-03-003**
virulent	**JJ**	**1-01-001**
virus	**noun**	**13-04-005**
virus	NN	12-04-005
virus	NN-HL	1-01-001
vis-a-vis	**IN**	**2-01-002**
visa	**NN**	**5-02-002**
visage	**NN**	**2-02-002**
viscera	**noun**	**2-02-002**
viscera	NNS	1-01-001
Viscera	NNS-TL	1-01-001
visceral	**JJ**	**4-01-002**
viscoelastic	**adjective**	**4-01-002**
viscoelastic	JJ	3-01-002
viscoelastic	JJ-HL	1-01-001
viscoelasticity	**noun**	**3-01-001**
viscoelasticity	NN	2-01-001
viscoelasticity	NN-HL	1-01-001
viscometer	**NN**	**1-01-001**

Word	Tag	Frequency
viscosity	**NN**	**10-02-003**
Viscount	**NP**	**3-02-002**
viscous	**JJ**	**1-01-001**
vise	**NN**	**1-01-001**
viselike	**adjective**	**2-02-002**
viselike	JJ	1-01-001
vicelike	JJ	1-01-001
visibility	**NN**	**5-03-005**
visible	**JJ**	**34-11-029**
visibly	**RB**	**6-06-006**
Visigoth	**prop. noun**	**1-01-001**
Visigoths	NPS	1-01-001
vision	**noun**	**63-14-044**
vision	NN	55-13-038
Vision	NN-TL	1-01-001
visions	NNS	7-03-007
visit	**noun**	**74-13-055**
visit	NN	59-12-048
visits	NNS	15-06-009
visit	**verb**	**129-15-094**
visit	VB	50-13-039
visits	VBZ	1-01-001
visits	VBZ-HL	1-01-001
visited	VBD	24-10-020
visited	VBN	17-10-017
visiting	VBG	34-13-034
visiting	VBG-NC	2-01-001
visitation	**noun**	**3-02-002**
visitation	NN	0-00-000
Visitation	NN-TL	2-01-001
visitations	NNS	1-01-001
visitor	**noun**	**49-14-042**
visitor	NN	13-08-013
visitors	NNS	36-13-029
visrhanik	**noun**	**1-01-001**
visrhanik	NN	0-00-000
visrhanik	NN-NC	1-01-001
vista	**noun**	**5-02-005**
vista	NN	2-02-002
vistas	NNS	3-02-003
Vista	**prop. noun**	**1-01-001**
Vista	NP	0-00-000
Vista	NP-TL	1-01-001
visual	**JJ**	**40-08-014**
visualization	**NN**	**1-01-001**
visualize	**verb**	**6-05-006**
visualize	VB	3-03-003
visualizes	VBZ	1-01-001
visualized	VBD	1-01-001
visualized	VBN	1-01-001
visually	**RB**	**4-03-004**
vita	**foreign**	**5-01-002**
vita	FW-NN	0-00-000
Vita	FW-NN-TL	5-01-002
vital	**JJ**	**56-11-043**
vital	**noun**	**2-02-002**
vitals	NNS	2-02-002
vitality	**NN**	**17-09-017**
vitally	**QL**	**6-06-006**
vitally	**RB**	**3-03-003**
vitamin	**noun**	**15-05-008**
vitamin	NN	5-04-004
vitamins	NNS	10-05-006
vitamin-and-iron	**NN**	**1-01-001**
vitiate	**verb**	**2-02-002**
vitiates	VBZ	1-01-001
vitiated	VBN	1-01-001
vitriol	**NN**	**1-01-001**
vitriolic	**JJ**	**2-02-002**
vitro	**NN**	**4-01-002**
Vittorio	**NP**	**2-01-001**
Vitus	**NP**	**1-01-001**
viva	**FW-JJ**	**1-01-001**
vivacious	**JJ**	**3-03-003**
vivacity	**NN**	**2-02-002**
Vivaldi	**NP**	**1-01-001**
vive	**FW-VB**	**1-01-001**
Vivian	**prop. noun**	**12-01-001**
Vivian	NP	11-01-001
Vivian's	NP$	1-01-001
vivid	**JJ**	**25-08-022**
vividly	**RB**	**9-04-006**
vividness	**NN**	**1-01-001**
Vivier	**NP**	**1-01-001**
vivify	**verb**	**2-02-002**
vivify	VB	1-01-001
vivified	VBN	1-01-001
vivo	**NN**	**4-01-002**
Viyella	**NP**	**1-01-001**
viz.	**RB**	**1-01-001**
Vladilen	**NP**	**1-01-001**
vocabularianism	**noun**	**1-01-001**
vocabularianism	NN	0-00-000
Vocabularianism	NN-TL	1-01-001
vocabulary	**noun**	**15-07-011**
vocabulary	NN	12-06-010
Vocabulary	NN-TL	1-01-001
vocabularies	NNS	2-02-002
vocal	**JJ**	**14-07-009**
vocal	**noun**	**1-01-001**
vocals	NNS	1-01-001
vocalic	**JJ**	**1-01-001**
vocalism	**NN**	**1-01-001**
vocalist	**noun**	**4-02-003**
vocalist	NN	2-02-002
vocalists	NNS	2-01-002
vocalization	**NN**	**1-01-001**
vocalize	**VB**	**1-01-001**
vocally	**RB**	**1-01-001**
vocation	**NN**	**3-03-003**
vocational	**adjective**	**76-06-011**
vocational	JJ	70-06-010
vocational	JJ-HL	1-01-001
Vocational	JJ-TL	5-04-004
vocational	**NN**	**1-01-001**
vocational-advancement	**NN**	**2-01-001**
vocationally	**RB**	**1-01-001**
voce	**FW-NN**	**1-01-001**
vociferous	**JJ**	**3-02-003**
vociferously	**RB**	**1-01-001**
vociferousness	**NN**	**1-01-001**
Voegelin	**NP**	**2-01-002**
vogue	**noun**	**6-04-006**
vogue	NN	4-04-004
Vogue	NN-TL	2-01-002
voice	**noun**	**265-15-143**
voice	NN	220-15-127
Voice	NN-TL	6-03-004
voice's	NN$	1-01-001
voices	NNS	37-10-031
voices	NNS-HL	1-01-001
voice	**verb**	**5-04-005**
voiced	VBD	4-04-004
voiced	VBN	1-01-001
voiceless	**JJ**	**1-01-001**
void	**JJ**	**2-02-002**
void	**NN**	**8-04-006**
void	**verb**	**1-01-001**
voids	VBZ	1-01-001
Voiture	**prop. noun**	**1-01-001**
Voiture	NP	0-00-000
Voiture	NP-TL	1-01-001
Volare	**NP**	**1-01-001**
volatile	**JJ**	**5-02-003**
volatilization	**NN**	**1-01-001**
volcanic	**JJ**	**2-01-002**
volcano	**noun**	**3-03-003**
volcano	NN	2-02-002
volcanos	NNS	1-01-001
volens	**FW-VBG**	**1-01-001**
volition	**NN**	**2-02-002**
Volkenstein	**NP**	**1-01-001**
Volker	**NP**	**1-01-001**
Volksgeist	**FW-NN**	**1-01-001**
Volkswagen	**prop. noun**	**1-01-001**
Volkswagens	NPS	1-01-001
volley	**NN**	**6-05-005**
volley-ball	**noun**	**3-02-002**
volley-ball	NN	2-01-001
volleyball	NN	1-01-001
Volney	**NP**	**1-01-001**
Volstead	**prop. noun**	**2-01-002**
Volstead	NP	1-01-001
Volstead	NP-TL	1-01-001
volt	**noun**	**1-01-001**
volts	NNS	1-01-001
Volta	**prop. noun**	**2-01-001**
Volta	NP	1-01-001
Volta's	NP$	1-01-001
voltage	**noun**	**20-03-006**
voltage	NN	16-03-006
voltages	NNS	4-01-002
voltaic	**JJ**	**7-01-001**
Voltaire	**prop. noun**	**11-02-002**
Voltaire	NP	9-02-002
Voltaire's	NP$	2-01-001
voltmeter	**NN**	**1-01-001**
voluble	**JJ**	**2-02-002**

Word	Tag	Frequency
volume	**noun**	**182-13-066**
volume	NN	116-11-048
vol.	NN	0-00-000
Vol.	NN-TL	2-01-002
voume	NN	1-01-001
volume	NN-HL	1-01-001
Volume	NN-TL	18-02-002
volumes	NNS	41-11-022
Volumes	NNS-TL	3-02-002
volumetric	**JJ**	**2-01-002**
volumetrically	**RB**	**1-01-001**
voluminous	**JJ**	**3-03-003**
voluntarily	**RB**	**9-05-009**
voluntary	**JJ**	**22-06-016**
voluntary-control	**NN**	**1-01-001**
volunteer	**noun**	**34-10-021**
volunteer	NN	3-02-003
volunteer	NN-HL	1-01-001
Volunteer	NN-TL	1-01-001
volunteers	NNS	25-07-015
Volunteers	NNS-TL	4-03-003
volunteer	**verb**	**11-07-009**
volunteer	VB	4-03-003
volunteered	VBD	2-02-002
volunteered	VBN	3-03-003
volunteering	VBG	2-01-001
voluptuous	**JJ**	**3-02-002**
Vom	**NP**	**1-01-001**
vomica	**NN**	**1-01-001**
vomit	**verb**	**3-03-003**
vomiting	VBG	3-03-003
von	**foreign**	**3-02-002**
von	FW-IN	0-00-000
Von	FW-IN-TL	3-02-002
Von	**prop. noun**	**6-03-004**
Von	NP	5-03-004
von	NP	1-01-001
Vonnegut	**prop. noun**	**2-01-001**
Vonnegut's	NP$	2-01-001
voodoo	**NN**	**2-02-002**
Voorhees	**NP**	**1-01-001**
vopos	**FW-NNS**	**1-01-001**
voraciously	**RB**	**1-01-001**
Voroshilov	**NP**	**1-01-001**
vortex	**NN**	**1-01-001**
vos	**FW-PP$**	**1-01-001**
vote	**noun**	**66-10-033**
vote	NN	48-09-025
vote	NN-HL	1-01-001
votes	NNS	17-07-013
vote	**verb**	**79-09-046**
vote	VB	26-05-019
votes	VBZ	3-03-003
voted	VBD	22-07-018
voted	VBN	5-03-004

Word	Tag	Frequency
vote (cont.):		
voting	VBG	23-07-016
voter	**noun**	**24-05-016**
voter	NN	4-03-004
voters	NNS	19-04-013
Voters	NNS-TL	1-01-001
voting	**NN**	**7-02-004**
votive	**JJ**	**2-02-002**
vouch	**verb**	**1-01-001**
vouching	VBG	1-01-001
voucher	**noun**	**1-01-001**
vouchers	NNS	1-01-001
vouchsafe	**verb**	**1-01-001**
vouchsafes	VBZ	1-01-001
Vouillemont	**NP**	**1-01-001**
voulez	**FW-VB**	**1-01-001**
vous	**FW-PPSS**	**3-02-002**
vow	**noun**	**6-03-004**
vow	NN	2-02-002
vows	NNS	4-02-002
vow	**verb**	**8-05-008**
vows	VBZ	1-01-001
vowed	VBD	5-04-005
vowing	VBG	2-02-002
vowel	**noun**	**10-03-004**
vowel	NN	6-02-003
Vowel	NN-TL	1-01-001
vowels	NNS	3-02-002
vowel-length	**noun**	**1-01-001**
vowel-length	NN	0-00-000
Vowel-Length	NN-TL	1-01-001
voyage	**FW-NN**	**1-01-001**
voyage	**noun**	**17-04-006**
voyage	NN	16-04-006
voyages	NNS	1-01-001
voyager	**NN**	**1-01-001**
voyageurs	**FW-NNS**	**4-02-003**
vrai	**FW-JJ**	**1-01-001**
Vrilium	**prop. noun**	**1-01-001**
Vrilium	NP	0-00-000
Vrilium	NP-TL	1-01-001
Vroman	**NP**	**1-01-001**
VTOL	**NP**	**1-01-001**
vue	**FW-VBN**	**7-01-001**
Vue	**NP**	**3-01-001**
vulcanize	**verb**	**1-01-001**
vulcanized	VBN	1-01-001
vulgar	**JJ**	**7-05-007**
vulnerability	**NN**	**7-02-002**
vulnerable	**JJ**	**14-09-012**
vulpine	**JJ**	**1-01-001**
vulture	**NN**	**4-03-003**
vulture-like	**JJ**	**1-01-001**
Vulturidae	**NPS**	**1-01-001**

Word	Tag	Frequency
W	**NP**	**3-02-002**
w.	**adjective**	**2-02-002**
w.	JJ	0-00-000
w.	JJ-HL	1-01-001
W.	JJ-TL	1-01-001
W.	**prop. noun**	**82-11-055**
W.	NP	79-11-054
W.	NP-HL	1-01-001
W.	NP-TL	2-02-002
W.'s	**NP+BEZ**	**1-01-001**
W.G.	**NP**	**1-01-001**
W.H.	**NP**	**1-01-001**
W.M.	**NP**	**1-01-001**
W.R.	**NP**	**1-01-001**
Waal	**prop. noun**	**1-01-001**
Waal's	NP$	1-01-001
Wabash	**prop. noun**	**4-02-002**
Wabash	NP	3-01-001
Wabash	NP-TL	1-01-001
Wacker	**prop. noun**	**2-01-001**
Wacker	NP	1-01-001
Wackers'	NPS$	1-01-001
Wacklin	**NP**	**1-01-001**
wacky	**JJ**	**1-01-001**
Waco	**NP**	**5-01-001**

Word	Tag	Frequency
wad	**noun**	**1-01-001**
wads	NNS	1-01-001
wad	**verb**	**2-02-002**
wadded	VBD	2-02-002
Waddell	**prop. noun**	**15-02-002**
Waddell	NP	14-01-001
Waddell	NP-TL	1-01-001
wade	**verb**	**4-03-004**
wade	VB	2-02-002
waded	VBD	2-01-002
Wade-Evans	**NP**	**4-01-001**
waffle	**noun**	**1-01-001**
waffles	NNS	1-01-001
waffle-pattern	**JJ**	**1-01-001**
wag	**verb**	**4-04-004**
wagged	VBD	2-02-002
wagging	VBG	2-02-002
wage	**noun**	**95-11-021**
wage	NN	53-06-008
wages	NNS	42-09-017
wage	**verb**	**11-07-011**
wage	VB	3-03-003
waged	VBD	1-01-001
waged	VBN	6-05-006
waging	VBG	1-01-001

Word	Tag	Count
wage-earning	**JJ**	**1-01-001**
wage-price	**NN**	**5-01-001**
wage-rate	**noun**	**2-01-001**
wage-rate	NN	1-01-001
wage-rates	NNS	1-01-001
wage-setter	**NN**	**1-01-001**
wager	**NN**	**1-01-001**
wager	**VB**	**2-01-001**
Waggin	**NP**	**1-01-001**
waggle	**verb**	**2-02-002**
waggled	VBD	1-01-001
waggling	VBG	1-01-001
Wagner	**prop. noun**	**23-06-009**
Wagner	NP	19-05-007
Wagner	NP-TL	2-02-002
Wagner's	NP$	2-02-002
Wagner-Peyser	**prop. noun**	**9-01-001**
Wagner-Peyser	NP	0-00-000
Wagner-Peyser	NP-TL	9-01-001
wagon	**noun**	**72-10-033**
wagon	NN	52-07-024
Wagon	NN-TL	3-02-002
wagons	NNS	17-07-010
wail	**noun**	**5-03-004**
wail	NN	3-02-003
wails	NNS	2-01-001
wail	**verb**	**8-07-008**
wailed	VBD	3-03-003
wailing	VBG	5-05-005
Wailbri	**NP**	**1-01-001**
wainscoted	**JJ**	**1-01-001**
waist	**NN**	**11-06-010**
waist-high	**adjective**	**1-01-001**
waist-high	JJ	0-00-000
Waist-High	JJ-TL	1-01-001
waist-length	**JJ**	**1-01-001**
waistcoat	**NN**	**1-01-001**
wait	**NN**	**7-05-006**
wait	**verb**	**263-15-146**
wait	VB	82-12-057
wait	VB-NC	1-01-001
waits	VBZ	2-02-002
waited	VBD	68-09-054
waited	VBN	2-02-002
waiting	VBG	103-15-079
waitin	VBG	1-01-001
Waiting	VBG-TL	4-01-001
Wait	**NP**	**5-01-001**
Waite	**NP**	**1-01-001**
waiter	**noun**	**15-03-006**
waiter	NN	10-02-004
waiters	NNS	5-02-004
waiting	**NN**	**3-03-003**
waitress	**noun**	**3-03-003**
waitress	NN	2-02-002
waitresses	NNS	1-01-001
waive	**verb**	**2-02-002**
waive	VB	1-01-001
waived	VBN	1-01-001
wake	**NN**	**7-06-007**
wake	**verb**	**45-11-033**
wake	VB	16-08-012
wakes	VBZ	1-01-001
Wakes	VBZ-TL	1-01-001
woke	VBD	14-07-013
waked	VBD	1-01-001
waked	VBN	1-01-001
waking	VBG	11-08-010
wakeful	**JJ**	**5-02-002**
wakefulness	**NN**	**3-01-001**
waken	**verb**	**2-02-002**
wakened	VBN	1-01-001
wakening	VBG	1-01-001
Walbridge	**NP**	**1-01-001**
Walcott	**prop. noun**	**1-01-001**
Walcott	NP	0-00-000
Walcott	NP-TL	1-01-001
Waldensian	**JJ**	**1-01-001**
Waldo	**NP**	**2-02-002**
Waldorf-Astoria	**prop. noun**	**2-01-002**
Waldorf-Astoria	NP	0-00-000
Waldorf-Astoria	NP-TL	2-01-002
wale	**noun**	**2-01-001**
wales	NNS	2-01-001
Wales	**prop. noun**	**9-05-006**
Wales	NP	6-04-004
Wales	NP-TL	2-02-002
Wales'	NP$	1-01-001
Walford	**NP**	**1-01-001**

Word	Tag	Count
Walitzee	**NP**	**5-01-001**
walk	**noun**	**40-09-031**
walk	NN	33-07-027
Walk	NN-TL	1-01-001
walks	NNS	6-04-005
walk	**verb**	**287-14-141**
walk	VB	66-12-048
walks	VBZ	7-04-007
walked	VBD	143-13-084
walked	VBN	16-09-014
walking	VBG	54-11-047
walkin'	VBG	1-01-001
walk-to	**JJ**	**1-01-001**
walk-up	**NN**	**1-01-001**
walker	**NN**	**1-01-001**
Walker	**prop. noun**	**17-04-009**
Walker	NP	16-04-009
Walkers	NPS	1-01-001
walkout	**NN**	**1-01-001**
walkover	**NN**	**1-01-001**
walkway	**noun**	**2-02-002**
walkway	NN	0-00-000
walk-way	NN	1-01-001
walkways	NNS	1-01-001
wall	**noun**	**224-14-109**
wall	NN	138-14-074
Wall	NN-TL	16-08-013
walls	NNS	70-13-046
wall	**verb**	**3-02-002**
wall	VB	2-01-001
walled	VBN	1-01-001
Wall	**NP**	**4-01-001**
wall-flower	**noun**	**1-01-001**
wall-flowers	NNS	1-01-001
wall-stabilized	**JJ**	**1-01-001**
wall-switch	**NN**	**1-01-001**
Wall-Tex	**NP**	**1-01-001**
wall-to-wall	**JJ**	**2-02-002**
Wallace	**NP**	**6-04-005**
wallboard	**NN**	**1-01-001**
Walle	**NP**	**1-01-001**
Wallenstein	**NP**	**2-01-001**
wallet	**NN**	**6-05-005**
Wallingford	**NP**	**1-01-001**
wallop	**NN**	**1-01-001**
wallop	**verb**	**2-01-002**
walloped	VBD	1-01-001
walloping	VBG	1-01-001
wallow	**verb**	**3-03-003**
wallow	VB	1-01-001
wallowed	VBD	1-01-001
wallowing	VBG	1-01-001
wallpaper	**noun**	**8-02-004**
wallpaper	NN	7-02-004
wallpapers	NNS	1-01-001
Wally	**prop. noun**	**28-03-003**
Wally	NP	25-03-003
Wally's	NP+BEZ	1-01-001
Wally's	NP+HVZ	1-01-001
Wally's	NP$	1-01-001
walnut	**noun**	**16-06-009**
walnut	NN	4-02-003
Walnut	NN-TL	7-02-002
walnuts	NNS	5-03-004
Walpole	**NP**	**1-01-001**
walrus	**NN**	**1-01-001**
Walsh	**prop. noun**	**3-03-003**
Walsh	NP	2-02-002
Walsh's	NP$	1-01-001
Walt	**NP**	**5-04-004**
Walter	**prop. noun**	**42-09-028**
Walter	NP	40-09-028
Walter's	NP$	2-02-002
Walters	**NP**	**2-02-002**
Waltham	**NP**	**1-01-001**
Walton	**NP**	**9-01-001**
waltz	**NN**	**1-01-001**
wan	**JJ**	**2-02-002**
wand	**NN**	**1-01-001**
wander	**verb**	**24-10-020**
wander	VB	7-05-007
Wander	VB-TL	1-01-001
wanders	VBZ	2-02-002
wandered	VBD	7-05-007
wandered	VBN	1-01-001
wandering	VBG	6-05-006
wander-year	**noun**	**2-01-001**
wander-years	NNS	0-00-000
Wander-Years	NNS-TL	2-01-001

wanderer	**noun**	**2-02-002**
wanderer	NN	1-01-001
wanderers	NNS	1-01-001
wandering	**noun**	**4-03-004**
wandering	NN	1-01-001
wanderings	NNS	3-02-003
Wanderjahr	**FW-NN**	**1-01-001**
wane	**verb**	**4-03-004**
waned	VBD	1-01-001
waned	VBN	1-01-001
waning	VBG	2-02-002
Wangeman	**prop. noun**	**1-01-001**
Wangemans	NPS	1-01-001
Wangenheim	**NP**	**2-01-001**
wangle	**verb**	**1-01-001**
wangled	VBD	1-01-001
Wansee	**prop. noun**	**1-01-001**
Wansee	NP	0-00-000
Wansee	NP-TL	1-01-001
Wansley	**NP**	**1-01-001**
want	**noun**	**17-08-014**
want	NN	9-05-008
wants	NNS	8-06-007
want	**verb**	**631-15-258**
want	VB	318-15-166
want	VB-NC	1-01-001
wanna	VB+AT	2-01-002
wanna	VB+TO	3-02-002
wanta	VB+TO	1-01-001
wants	VBZ	64-15-053
wanted	VBD	204-14-121
wanted	VBD-NC	1-01-001
wanted	VBN	21-11-020
wanting	VBG	16-08-015
wanting-to-be-alone	**JJ**	**1-01-001**
wanton	**JJ**	**3-03-003**
Wappinger	**prop. noun**	**1-01-001**
Wappinger	NP	0-00-000
Wappinger	NP-TL	1-01-001
war	**noun**	**492-15-172**
war	NN	301-15-125
war	NN-HL	4-03-003
War	NN-TL	158-14-091
war's	NN$	3-03-003
wars	NNS	25-10-023
Wars	NNS-TL	1-01-001
war	**verb**	**3-03-003**
war	VB	1-01-001
warred	VBD	1-01-001
warring	VBG	0-00-000
Warring	VBG-TL	1-01-001
war-dirty	**JJ**	**1-01-001**
war-ridden	**JJ**	**2-02-002**
warble	**verb**	**1-01-001**
warbling	VBG	1-01-001
ward	**noun**	**25-05-008**
ward	NN	22-05-007
wards	NNS	2-02-002
wards	NNS-HL	1-01-001
Ward	**prop. noun**	**4-03-004**
Ward	NP	2-02-002
Ward	NP-TL	1-01-001
Ward's	NP$	1-01-001
ward-heeler	**noun**	**1-01-001**
ward-heelers	NNS	1-01-001
ward-personnel	**NNS**	**1-01-001**
warden	**noun**	**6-02-002**
warden	NN	4-02-002
wardens	NNS	2-01-001
wardrobe	**NN**	**8-04-006**
wardroom	**NN**	**1-01-001**
ware	**noun**	**3-03-003**
ware	NN	1-01-001
wares	NNS	1-01-001
warys	NNS	1-01-001
warehouse	**noun**	**8-06-007**
warehouse	NN	4-04-004
warehouses	NNS	4-02-003
warehouse	**verb**	**1-01-001**
warehousing	VBG	1-01-001
warehouseman	**noun**	**1-01-001**
warehouseman's	NN$	1-01-001
warfare	**noun**	**43-07-024**
warfare	NN	42-07-024
warfare	NN-HL	1-01-001
Warfield	**NP**	**1-01-001**
warfront	**NN**	**1-01-001**
warhead	**NN**	**2-02-002**
warily	**RB**	**2-02-002**
warless	**JJ**	**1-01-001**
warlike	**JJ**	**5-05-005**
warm	**JJ**	**64-14-053**
warm	**verb**	**23-10-018**
warm	VB	3-02-002
warms	VBZ	1-01-001
warmed	VBD	6-04-006
warmed	VBN	4-04-004
warming	VBG	9-06-008
warm-blooded	**JJ**	**1-01-001**
warm-toned	**JJ**	**1-01-001**
warm-up	**noun**	**2-02-002**
warm-up	NN	1-01-001
warmup	NN	1-01-001
warmed-over	**JJ**	**1-01-001**
warmer	**JJR**	**4-03-003**
warmhearted	**JJ**	**1-01-001**
warmish	**JJ**	**1-01-001**
warmly	**QL**	**1-01-001**
warmly	**RB**	**7-04-007**
warmongering	**JJ**	**1-01-001**
warmth	**NN**	**28-12-025**
warn	**verb**	**62-11-040**
warn	VB	11-07-010
warns	VBZ	3-03-003
warned	VBD	14-08-011
warned	VBN	8-06-007
warning	VBG	26-08-018
Warner	**NP**	**1-01-001**
warning	**noun**	**27-07-023**
warning	NN	16-06-014
warning	NN-HL	1-01-001
Warning	NN-TL	1-01-001
warnings	NNS	9-05-008
warningly	**RB**	**1-01-001**
warp	**noun**	**4-01-001**
warp	NN	3-01-001
warp	NN-HL	1-01-001
warp	**verb**	**7-03-005**
warped	VBN	3-02-003
warping	VBG	4-01-002
warrant	**noun**	**14-05-009**
warrant	NN	9-04-008
warrants	NNS	5-03-003
warrant	**verb**	**14-05-014**
warrant	VB	11-05-011
warranted	VBD	1-01-001
warranted	VBN	2-02-002
warranty	**NN**	**1-01-001**
warren	**NN**	**1-01-001**
Warren	**prop. noun**	**51-07-019**
Warren	NP	46-07-018
Warren	NP-TL	4-02-003
Warren's	NP$	1-01-001
Warrenton	**NP**	**1-01-001**
warrior	**noun**	**12-03-004**
warrior	NN	5-02-003
warriors	NNS	7-02-002
Warsaw	**prop. noun**	**12-02-003**
Warsaw	NP	9-02-002
Warsaw	NP-TL	1-01-001
Warsaw's	NP$	2-01-001
warship	**noun**	**2-02-002**
warships	NNS	2-02-002
wart	**noun**	**16-05-005**
wart	NN	11-02-002
warts	NNS	5-04-004
wart-hog	**NN**	**1-01-001**
wartime	**noun**	**8-06-008**
wartime	NN	6-04-006
wahtahm	NN	1-01-001
war-time	NN	1-01-001
wartorn	**JJ**	**1-01-001**
warty	**JJ**	**1-01-001**
Warwick	**prop. noun**	**21-05-008**
Warwick	NP	11-04-005
Warwick	NP-TL	10-05-006
Warwickshire	**NP**	**1-01-001**
wary	**JJ**	**7-06-007**
wash	**noun**	**28-07-008**
wash	NN	21-07-008
wash	NN-HL	2-01-001
washes	NNS	5-01-001
wash	**verb**	**83-09-034**
wash	VB	10-06-008
washed	VBD	10-04-010
washed	VBN	25-07-012
washing	VBG	36-07-013
washing	VBG-HL	2-01-002

Word	Tag	Frequency
wash-out	**noun**	**1-01-001**
wash-outs	NNS	1-01-001
wash-up	**NN**	**1-01-001**
washbasin	**NN**	**1-01-001**
washboard	**NN**	**1-01-001**
washbowl	**NN**	**1-01-001**
washed-out	**JJ**	**1-01-001**
washer	**NN**	**2-02-002**
washing	**noun**	**8-04-006**
washing	NN	6-04-004
washings	NNS	2-01-002
Washington	**prop. noun**	**217-11-092**
Washington	NP	163-11-080
Wash.	NP	4-02-003
Washington	NP-HL	15-03-009
Washington	NP-TL	28-08-013
Washington's	NP$	7-05-007
Washington-Alexandria	**prop. noun**	**1-01-001**
Washington-Alexandria	NP	0-00-000
Washington-Alexandria	NP-TL	1-01-001
Washington-Oregon	**NP**	**1-01-001**
Washizu	**prop. noun**	**4-01-001**
Washizu	NP	3-01-001
Washizu's	NP$	1-01-001
Washoe	**prop. noun**	**1-01-001**
Washoe	NP	0-00-000
Washoe	NP-TL	1-01-001
wasp	**NN**	**2-01-001**
waspish	**JJ**	**3-01-001**
waspishly	**RB**	**1-01-001**
Wasson	**NP**	**1-01-001**
wastage	**NN**	**1-01-001**
waste	**noun**	**31-08-026**
waste	NN	25-08-022
wastes	NNS	6-04-004
waste	**verb**	**31-10-025**
waste	VB	8-04-007
waste	VB-HL	2-01-001
wasted	VBD	5-02-005
wasted	VBN	11-07-010
wasting	VBG	5-04-005
wastebasket	**NN**	**2-01-001**
wasteful	**JJ**	**7-05-006**
wasteland	**NN**	**3-03-003**
wastewater	**NN**	**2-01-001**
wastrel	**NN**	**1-01-001**
watch	**noun**	**31-11-026**
watch	NN	27-08-022
Watch	NN-TL	1-01-001
watches	NNS	3-03-003
watch	**verb**	**209-15-129**
watch	VB	53-12-046
watches	VBZ	1-01-001
watched	VBD	68-10-050
watched	VBN	13-09-013
watching	VBG	74-13-060
watch-spring	**NN**	**1-01-001**
watchdog	**NN**	**3-03-003**
watcher	**noun**	**2-02-002**
watchers	NNS	1-01-001
Watchers	NNS-TL	1-01-001
watchful	**JJ**	**2-01-002**
watching	**noun**	**3-03-003**
watching	NN	2-02-002
watchings	NNS	1-01-001
watchmaker	**NN**	**2-02-002**
watchman	**noun**	**1-01-001**
watchmen	NNS	1-01-001
water	**noun**	**486-14-145**
water	NN	426-14-132
water	NN-HL	2-02-002
water	NN-NC	9-02-002
Water	NN-TL	6-04-005
Water	NN-TL-HL	1-01-001
water's	NN+BEZ	1-01-001
water's	NN$	4-04-004
waters	NNS	36-10-028
Waters	NNS-TL	1-01-001
water	**verb**	**12-07-012**
water	VB	1-01-001
watered	VBD	4-03-004
watered	VBN	3-03-003
watering	VBG	4-03-004
water-balance	**NN**	**1-01-001**
water-cooled	**JJ**	**1-01-001**
water-filled	**JJ**	**1-01-001**
water-holding	**JJ**	**1-01-001**
water-ski	**NN**	**1-01-001**
water-soluble	**JJ**	**2-02-002**
water-washed	**NN**	**1-01-001**
Waterbury	**NP**	**1-01-001**
watercolor	**noun**	**15-01-001**
watercolor	NN	9-01-001
Watercolor	NN-TL	3-01-001
watercolors	NNS	3-01-001
watercolorist	**noun**	**4-01-001**
watercolorist	NN	2-01-001
watercolorists	NNS	2-01-001
waterfall	**noun**	**3-03-003**
waterfall	NN	2-02-002
waterfalls	NNS	1-01-001
waterflow	**noun**	**1-01-001**
waterflows	NNS	1-01-001
waterfront	**NN**	**10-07-008**
waterline	**noun**	**2-02-002**
waterline	NN	1-01-001
water-line	NN	1-01-001
Waterloo	**NP**	**1-01-001**
watermelon	**NN**	**1-01-001**
waterproof	**adjective**	**3-03-003**
waterproof	JJ	2-02-002
water-proof	JJ	1-01-001
waterproofing	**NN**	**1-01-001**
Waters	**prop. noun**	**5-02-002**
Waters	NP	4-02-002
Waters	NP-TL	1-01-001
watershed	**noun**	**7-03-003**
watershed	NN	3-01-001
watersheds	NNS	4-02-002
waterside	**NN**	**1-01-001**
waterski	**verb**	**1-01-001**
waterskiing	VBG	1-01-001
waterway	**noun**	**5-03-004**
waterway	NN	2-02-002
waterways	NNS	3-02-003
watery	**JJ**	**3-03-003**
Watling	**prop. noun**	**1-01-001**
Watling	NP	0-00-000
Watling	NP-TL	1-01-001
Watson	**prop. noun**	**50-04-006**
Watson	NP	45-04-006
Watson's	NP$	5-02-002
Watson-Watt	**prop. noun**	**3-01-001**
Watson-Watt	NP	1-01-001
Watson-Watt's	NP$	2-01-001
watt	**NN**	**2-01-001**
Wattenberg	**NP**	**1-01-001**
Watterson	**NP**	**1-01-001**
wattle	**noun**	**2-01-001**
wattles	NNS	2-01-001
wave	**noun**	**95-13-035**
wave	NN	43-12-021
wave	NN-HL	1-01-001
waves	NNS	51-08-017
wave	**verb**	**30-11-029**
wave	VB	2-02-002
waved	VBD	16-09-016
waving	VBG	12-06-012
wave-particle	**NN**	**1-01-001**
wave-setting	**JJ**	**1-01-001**
wave-travel	**NN**	**1-01-001**
Waveland	**NP**	**1-01-001**
wavelength	**noun**	**12-04-004**
wavelength	NN	4-02-002
wave-length	NN	2-01-001
wavelengths	NNS	6-02-002
waver	**noun**	**2-02-002**
waver	NN	1-01-001
wavers	NNS	1-01-001
waver	**VB**	**2-02-002**
waving	**NN**	**1-01-001**
wavy	**JJ**	**2-01-002**
wavy-haired	**JJ**	**1-01-001**
wax	**NN**	**13-05-007**
wax	**verb**	**6-06-006**
wax	VB	1-01-001
waxed	VBD	3-03-003
waxed	VBN	1-01-001
waxing	VBG	1-01-001
waxen	**JJ**	**1-01-001**
waxwork	**noun**	**1-01-001**
waxworks	NNS	0-00-000
Waxworks	NNS-TL	1-01-001
waxy	**JJ**	**2-02-002**
way	**noun**	**1027-15-385**
way	NN	882-15-358
way	NN-HL	1-01-001
Way	NN-TL	16-08-013

way (cont.):		
ways	NNS	126-15-102
Ways	NNS-TL	2-02-002
way	**QL**	**6-03-005**
way	**RB**	**3-01-002**
Way	**prop. noun**	**2-01-001**
Way	NP	1-01-001
Way's	NP$	0-00-000
Way's	NP$-TL	1-01-001
way-out	**JJ**	**1-01-001**
waylay	**verb**	**1-01-001**
waylaid	VBN	1-01-001
Waymouth	**NP**	**1-01-001**
Wayne	**prop. noun**	**12-04-009**
Wayne	NP	9-03-007
Wayne	NP-HL	1-01-001
Wayne	NP-TL	2-01-001
wayside	**NN**	**2-02-002**
wayward	**JJ**	**3-03-003**
WBAI	**NP**	**2-01-001**
we	**pers. pro.**	**4865-15-427**
we	PPSS	2628-15-364
wee	PPSS	1-01-001
we	PPSS-HL	20-04-004
We	PPSS-TL	4-03-004
we'd	PPSS+HVD	18-05-010
we'd	PPSS+MD	14-07-011
we'll	PPSS+MD	64-10-038
we're	PPSS+BER	59-10-045
We're	PPSS+BER	1-01-001
we're	PPSS+BER-NC	1-01-001
we've	PPSS+HV	34-11-027
us	PPO	668-15-232
we'uns	PPO	1-01-001
us	PPO-HL	2-01-002
Us	PPO-TL	1-01-001
's	+PPO	69-12-046
our	PP$	1233-15-277
out	PP$	1-01-001
our	PP$-NC	1-01-001
our	PP$-HL	3-03-003
Our	PP$-TL	15-06-007
ours	PP$$	27-12-023
weak	**JJ**	**32-11-023**
weaken	**verb**	**15-10-015**
weaken	VB	7-05-007
weakens	VBZ	1-01-001
weakened	VBD	1-01-001
weakened	VBN	5-05-005
weakening	VBG	1-01-001
weakening	**NN**	**5-03-004**
weaker	**JJR**	**8-06-007**
weakest	**JJT**	**3-03-003**
weakly	**RB**	**3-03-003**
weakness	**noun**	**52-12-032**
weakness	NN	46-12-027
weaknesses	NNS	6-05-005
wealth	**noun**	**22-08-017**
wealth	NN	20-08-015
Wealth	NN-TL	2-02-002
wealthiest	**JJT**	**1-01-001**
wealthy	**JJ**	**12-06-009**
wean	**verb**	**3-03-003**
weaned	VBN	1-01-001
weaning	VBG	1-01-001
Weaning	VBG-TL	1-01-001
weapon	**noun**	**103-13-055**
weapon	NN	42-12-028
weapons	NNS	61-12-035
weaponry	**NN**	**1-01-001**
wear	**NN**	**3-03-003**
wear	**verb**	**174-14-104**
wear	VB	32-13-028
wears	VBZ	5-04-005
wears	VBZ-HL	1-01-001
wore	VBD	65-11-047
worn	VBN	23-10-022
wearing	VBG	46-11-040
wearin'	VBG	1-01-001
Wearing	VBG-TL	1-01-001
wearily	**RB**	**7-05-007**
weariness	**NN**	**2-01-002**
wearisome	**JJ**	**2-02-002**
weary	**adjective**	**17-09-016**
weary	JJ	15-08-015
weary	JJ-HL	1-01-001
Weary	JJ-TL	1-01-001
weary	**verb**	**3-02-002**
wearied	VBD	1-01-001

weary (cont.):		
wearying	VBG	2-02-002
weasel	**NN**	**1-01-001**
weasel-worded	**JJ**	**1-01-001**
weather	**noun**	**70-11-053**
weather	NN	66-11-052
Weather	NN-TL	3-02-002
weathers	NNS	0-00-000
Weathers	NNS-TL	1-01-001
weather	**verb**	**2-01-001**
weathering	VBG	2-01-001
weather-resistant	**JJ**	**2-01-001**
weather-royal	**JJ**	**1-01-001**
weatherbeaten	**JJ**	**1-01-001**
Weatherford	**NP**	**2-01-001**
weatherproof	**JJ**	**3-02-003**
weatherstrip	**VB**	**1-01-001**
weave	**noun**	**3-01-001**
weave	NN	1-01-001
weaves	NNS	2-01-001
weave	**verb**	**20-06-013**
weave	VB	2-01-002
weave	VB-HL	1-01-001
wove	VBD	3-02-003
woven	VBN	7-05-006
woven	VBN-HL	2-01-001
weaving	VBG	4-01-002
weaving	VBG-HL	1-01-001
Weaver	**NP**	**4-01-003**
web	**NN**	**6-04-005**
Webb	**NP**	**1-01-001**
Webber	**NP**	**1-01-001**
Weber	**NP**	**2-02-002**
Webster	**prop. noun**	**6-03-005**
Webster	NP	4-03-004
Webster	NP-TL	1-01-001
Webster's	NP$	1-01-001
Websterville	**prop. noun**	**2-01-001**
Websterville	NP	1-01-001
Websterville	NP-TL	1-01-001
Wechsler	**prop. noun**	**1-01-001**
Wechsler	NP	0-00-000
Wechsler	NP-TL	1-01-001
wed	**verb**	**6-04-006**
wed	VB	1-01-001
wedded	VBN	4-03-004
wed	VBN	1-01-001
wedding	**noun**	**34-10-022**
wedding	NN	31-08-020
Wedding	NN-TL	1-01-001
weddings	NNS	2-02-002
wedge	**NN**	**4-03-004**
wedge	**verb**	**2-02-002**
wedged	VBN	2-02-002
wedge-shaped	**JJ**	**2-02-002**
wedlock	**noun**	**2-01-002**
wedlock	NN	1-01-001
wedlock	NN-NC	1-01-001
Wednesday	**adv. noun**	**37-10-028**
Wednesday	NR	35-09-027
Wednesday's	NR$	1-01-001
Wednesdays	NRS	1-01-001
wee	**JJ**	**1-01-001**
Wee	**NP**	**2-01-002**
weed	**noun**	**5-04-005**
weeds	NNS	5-04-005
weed	**verb**	**2-02-002**
weed	VB	1-01-001
weeded	VBN	1-01-001
Weede	**NP**	**1-01-001**
week	**noun**	**425-15-187**
week	NN	257-15-134
week	NN-HL	1-01-001
Week	NN-TL	14-04-008
Week	NN-TL-HL	3-01-001
week's	NN$	8-03-007
weeks	NNS	140-13-095
weeks'	NNS$	2-02-002
week-long	**JJ**	**3-02-002**
week-old	**JJ**	**1-01-001**
weekday	**NN**	**2-02-002**
weekend	**noun**	**42-11-034**
weekend	NN	27-08-021
week-end	NN	6-05-006
weekends	NNS	7-04-006
week-ends	NNS	2-01-001
weekly	**JJ**	**14-10-012**
weekly	**noun**	**6-04-004**
weekly	NN	3-03-003

Word	Tag	Frequency
weekly (cont.):		
weeklies	NNS	3-02-002
weekly	**RB**	**7-06-006**
Weeks	**NP**	**1-01-001**
Weems	**prop. noun**	**1-01-001**
Weems's	NP$	1-01-001
weep	**verb**	**28-10-022**
weep	VB	13-07-013
Weep	VB-TL	1-01-001
wept	VBD	7-05-005
wept	VBN	2-02-002
weeping	VBG	5-04-005
weeping	**NN**	**3-03-003**
Wegener	**NP**	**1-01-001**
wei	**FW-NN**	**2-01-001**
Weider	**prop. noun**	**6-01-001**
Weider	NP	5-01-001
Weider	NP-TL	1-01-001
Weidman	**NP**	**1-01-001**
Weigand	**NP**	**4-01-001**
Weigel	**prop. noun**	**2-01-001**
Weigel's	NP$	2-01-001
weigh	**verb**	**33-08-023**
weigh	VB	4-04-004
weighs	VBZ	4-03-003
weighed	VBD	11-03-007
weighed	VBN	5-04-005
weighing	VBG	9-04-008
weight	**noun**	**101-11-055**
weight	NN	91-11-053
weights	NNS	10-03-007
weight	**verb**	**5-04-005**
weights	VBZ	1-01-001
weighted	VBD	1-01-001
weighted	VBN	3-03-003
weight-height	**NN**	**1-01-001**
weighting	**NN**	**1-01-001**
weightlessness	**NN**	**2-02-002**
weighty	**JJ**	**4-04-004**
Weigle	**NP**	**1-01-001**
Weil	**NP**	**1-01-001**
Weinberg	**NP**	**1-01-001**
Weinstein	**prop. noun**	**3-01-001**
Weinstein	NP	2-01-001
Weinstein's	NP$	1-01-001
weir	**noun**	**3-02-003**
weir	NN	2-02-002
weirs	NNS	1-01-001
weird	**adjective**	**10-06-007**
weird	JJ	9-06-006
Weird	JJ-TL	1-01-001
weirdly	**RB**	**1-01-001**
weirdy	**NN**	**1-01-001**
Weiss	**NP**	**1-01-001**
Weissman	**NP**	**1-01-001**
Weissmuller	**NP**	**1-01-001**
Welborn	**NP**	**1-01-001**
Welch	**prop. noun**	**20-01-001**
Welch	NP	14-01-001
Welch's	NP$	5-01-001
Welch's	NP$-TL	1-01-001
welcome	**adjective**	**19-10-018**
welcome	JJ	18-10-018
welcome	JJ-NC	1-01-001
welcome	**noun**	**13-07-010**
welcome	NN	12-07-009
Welcome	NN-TL	1-01-001
welcome	**exclam.**	**3-01-001**
welcome	UH	0-00-000
Welcome	UH-TL	3-01-001
welcome	**verb**	**33-12-029**
welcome	VB	15-08-013
welcomes	VBZ	1-01-001
welcomed	VBD	6-05-006
welcomed	VBN	6-05-006
welcoming	VBG	5-04-005
weld	**verb**	**5-04-005**
weld	VB	1-01-001
welded	VBN	3-03-003
welding	VBG	1-01-001
Weld	**NP**	**3-01-001**
welding	**NN**	**1-01-001**
Weldon	**NP**	**1-01-001**
Weldwood	**prop. noun**	**2-01-001**
Weldwood	NP	1-01-001
Weldwood	NP-TL	1-01-001
welfare	**noun**	**53-08-037**
welfare	NN	46-08-033
welfare	NN-HL	1-01-001

Word	Tag	Frequency
welfare (cont.):		
Welfare	NN-TL	6-04-005
well	**adjective**	**15-09-014**
well	JJ	14-08-013
Well	JJ-TL	1-01-001
well	**noun**	**22-09-017**
well	NN	17-08-013
wells	NNS	4-03-004
Wells	NNS-TL	1-01-001
well	**qualifier**	**69-09-055**
well	QL	68-09-054
well	QL-HL	1-01-001
well	**adverb**	**656-15-341**
well	RB	653-15-339
Well	RB-TL	1-01-001
well's	RB+CS	2-01-001
well	**exclam.**	**138-13-079**
well	UH	136-13-079
Well	UH	2-01-002
well	**verb**	**6-05-006**
well	VB	4-03-004
welled	VBD	1-01-001
welling	VBG	1-01-001
well-adjusted	**JJ**	**2-02-002**
well-administered	**JJ**	**1-01-001**
well-armed	**JJ**	**1-01-001**
well-baby	**NN**	**1-01-001**
well-balanced	**JJ**	**1-01-001**
well-being	**noun**	**10-07-009**
well-being	NN	9-06-008
wellbeing	NN	1-01-001
well-bound	**JJ**	**1-01-001**
well-braced	**JJ**	**1-01-001**
well-bred	**JJ**	**1-01-001**
well-brushed	**JJ**	**1-01-001**
well-cemented	**JJ**	**1-01-001**
well-defined	**JJ**	**3-02-003**
well-deserved	**JJ**	**2-02-002**
well-designed	**JJ**	**2-02-002**
well-developed	**JJ**	**2-01-002**
well-dressed	**JJ**	**1-01-001**
well-educated	**JJ**	**4-02-003**
well-equipped	**JJ**	**1-01-001**
well-established	**JJ**	**3-03-003**
well-fed	**JJ**	**3-03-003**
well-fleshed	**JJ**	**1-01-001**
well-grooved	**JJ**	**1-01-001**
well-house	**NN**	**1-01-001**
well-informed	**JJ**	**6-04-006**
well-kept	**JJ**	**4-04-004**
well-known	**adjective**	**18-09-017**
well-known	JJ	17-08-016
wellknown	JJ	1-01-001
well-made	**JJ**	**3-03-003**
well-meaning	**JJ**	**3-03-003**
well-modulated	**JJ**	**1-01-001**
well-molded	**JJ**	**1-01-001**
well-nigh	**QL**	**1-01-001**
well-organized	**JJ**	**1-01-001**
well-oriented	**JJ**	**1-01-001**
well-planned	**JJ**	**1-01-001**
well-played	**JJ**	**1-01-001**
well-prepared	**JJ**	**1-01-001**
well-publicized	**JJ**	**1-01-001**
well-read	**JJ**	**1-01-001**
well-received	**JJ**	**1-01-001**
well-regulated	**JJ**	**1-01-001**
well-rounded	**JJ**	**1-01-001**
well-ruled	**JJ**	**1-01-001**
well-spring	**noun**	**1-01-001**
well-springs	NNS	1-01-001
well-stocked	**JJ**	**1-01-001**
well-stretched	**JJ**	**1-01-001**
well-stuffed	**JJ**	**1-01-001**
well-to-do	**JJ**	**2-02-002**
well-trained	**JJ**	**2-02-002**
well-understood	**JJ**	**1-01-001**
well-wedged	**JJ**	**1-01-001**
well-wisher	**noun**	**1-01-001**
well-wishers	NNS	1-01-001
well-wishing	**NN**	**1-01-001**
well-worn	**JJ**	**1-01-001**
well-written	**JJ**	**1-01-001**
Wellesley	**prop. noun**	**4-02-003**
Wellesley	NP	2-02-002
Wellsley	NP	0-00-000
Wellsley	NP-TL	1-01-001
Wellesley	NP-TL	1-01-001
Wellington	**NP**	**1-01-001**

Word	Tag	Count
Wellman	**NP**	**1-01-001**
Wells	**prop. noun**	**11-07-008**
Wells	NP	6-06-006
Wells's	NP$	5-02-002
Wellsville	**NP**	**1-01-001**
Welmers	**NP**	**1-01-001**
Welsh	**JJ**	**4-02-002**
welt	**noun**	**1-01-001**
welts	NNS	1-01-001
Weltanschauung	**FW-NN**	**1-01-001**
welter	**NN**	**2-01-001**
Welton	**NP**	**1-01-001**
Wemmick	**NP**	**2-01-001**
Wendell	**prop. noun**	**9-03-003**
Wendell	NP	8-03-003
Wendells	NPS	1-01-001
Wentworth	**NP**	**2-01-001**
Wergeland	**NP**	**1-01-001**
Werner	**prop. noun**	**6-02-003**
Werner	NP	5-02-003
Werner	NP-HL	1-01-001
Wert	**prop. noun**	**3-01-001**
Wert	NP	2-01-001
Wert's	NP$	1-01-001
Werther	**prop. noun**	**2-02-002**
Werther	NP	1-01-001
Werther	NP-TL	1-01-001
Wes	**NP**	**1-01-001**
Wesker	**prop. noun**	**4-01-001**
Wesker	NP	2-01-001
Wesker's	NP$	2-01-001
Wesley	**prop. noun**	**3-03-003**
Wesley	NP	1-01-001
Wesley	NP-TL	1-01-001
Wesley's	NP$	1-01-001
Wesleyan	**prop. noun**	**3-02-002**
Wesleyan	NP	2-02-002
Wesleyan	NP-TL	1-01-001
Wesson	**prop. noun**	**1-01-001**
Wesson	NP	0-00-000
Wesson	NP-TL	1-01-001
west	**adjective**	**96-14-054**
west	JJ	1-01-001
West	JJ-TL	95-14-053
west	**adv. noun**	**142-13-073**
west	NR	49-12-037
west	NR-HL	1-01-001
West	NR-TL	87-11-041
West	NR-TL-HL	2-02-002
West's	NR$-TL	3-03-003
West	**NP**	**2-01-002**
Westbrook	**NP**	**2-01-001**
Westchester	**prop. noun**	**4-03-003**
Westchester	NP	1-01-001
Westchester	NP-TL	3-03-003
westerly	**JJ**	**2-02-002**
westerly	**RB**	**1-01-001**
Westerly	**NP**	**2-02-002**
western	**adjective**	**137-15-075**
western	JJ	34-11-026
Western	JJ	1-01-001
Western	JJ-TL	102-13-051
western-style	**adjective**	**2-02-002**
western-style	JJ	1-01-001
Western-style	JJ-TL	1-01-001
westerner	**noun**	**3-02-002**
westerner	NN	0-00-000
Westerner	NN-TL	2-02-002
westerners	NNS	0-00-000
Westerners	NNS-TL	1-01-001
Westfield	**prop. noun**	**6-02-002**
Westfield	NP	4-02-002
Westfield	NP-TL	2-01-001
Westhampton	**NP**	**1-01-001**
Westinghouse	**prop. noun**	**3-02-003**
Westinghouse	NP	2-02-002
Westinghouse	NP-TL	1-01-001
Westminster	**prop. noun**	**23-05-006**
Westminster	NP	20-04-005
Westminster	NP-HL	1-01-001
Westminster	NP-TL	2-02-002
Westmore	**prop. noun**	**2-01-001**
Westmore	NP	0-00-000
Westmore	NP-TL	2-01-001
Weston	**NP**	**8-02-003**
Westphalia	**NP**	**2-01-001**
Westport	**NP**	**2-01-001**
westward	**RB**	**8-05-007**
westwards	**RB**	**1-01-001**

Word	Tag	Count
Westwood	**prop. noun**	**1-01-001**
Westwood	NP	0-00-000
Westwood	NP-TL	1-01-001
wet	**JJ**	**47-11-038**
wet	**verb**	**9-06-008**
wet	VB	3-03-003
wet	VBD	2-02-002
wet	VBN	1-01-001
wetting	VBG	3-02-003
wetland	**noun**	**1-01-001**
wetlands	NNS	1-01-001
wetly	**RB**	**1-01-001**
wetness	**NN**	**1-01-001**
Wetter	**NP**	**1-01-001**
wetting	**NN**	**1-01-001**
Wexler	**NP**	**6-01-001**
Weybosset	**prop. noun**	**1-01-001**
Weybosset	NP	0-00-000
Weybosset	NP-TL	1-01-001
whack	**NN**	**1-01-001**
whack	**verb**	**2-02-002**
whacked	VBD	2-02-002
whale	**verb**	**1-01-001**
whaling	VBG	1-01-001
wharf	**noun**	**4-03-003**
wharf	NN	2-01-001
wharves	NNS	2-02-002
Wharf	**NP**	**2-01-001**
Wharton	**NP**	**1-01-001**
what	**wh-det.**	**1955-15-422**
what	WDT	1865-15-421
what	WDT-HL	29-05-012
what	WDT-NC	4-01-001
what'd	WDT+DOD	1-01-001
what're	WDT+BER	1-01-001
what's	WDT+BEZ	47-12-034
what's	WDT+BEZ-HL	1-01-001
what's	WDT+BEZ-NC	2-01-001
What's	WDT+BEZ-TL	1-01-001
what's	WDT+HVZ	2-02-002
whaddya	WDT+DO+PPSS	1-01-001
whaddya	WDT+BER+PPSS	1-01-001
what	**s. wh-pro.**	**7-05-005**
what	WPS	2-02-002
What	WPS-TL	5-03-003
what	**o. wh-pro.**	**3-02-002**
what	WPO	0-00-000
What	WPO-TL	3-02-002
what-not	**noun**	**1-01-001**
what-nots	NNS	1-01-001
what's-his-name	**NN**	**3-01-001**
whatever	**RB**	**1-01-001**
whatever	**WDT**	**111-15-087**
Whatman	**NP**	**1-01-001**
whatsoever	**RB**	**3-02-002**
whatsoever	**WPS**	**3-02-003**
wheat	**NN**	**9-03-005**
wheat-germ	**NN**	**2-01-001**
Wheaton	**NP**	**2-01-002**
whee	**UH**	**1-01-001**
wheedle	**verb**	**1-01-001**
wheedled	VBN	1-01-001
wheel	**noun**	**77-12-039**
wheel	NN	52-09-026
wheel	NN-HL	2-01-001
Wheel	NN-TL	2-02-002
wheels	NNS	21-09-016
wheel	**verb**	**11-07-010**
wheeled	VBD	7-06-007
wheeled	VBN	3-02-003
wheeling	VBG	1-01-001
Wheelan	**prop. noun**	**1-01-001**
Wheelan's	NP$	1-01-001
Wheeler	**prop. noun**	**5-04-005**
Wheeler	NP	4-03-004
Wheeler's	NP$	1-01-001
Wheeling	**NP**	**1-01-001**
Wheelock	**prop. noun**	**4-02-002**
Wheelock	NP	3-02-002
Wheelock's	NP$	1-01-001
wheeze	**noun**	**1-01-001**
wheezes	NNS	1-01-001
wheeze	**verb**	**2-02-002**
wheezed	VBD	1-01-001
wheezing	VBG	1-01-001
Whelan	**NP**	**1-01-001**
when	**wh-adverb**	**2333-15-468**

Word	Tag	Frequency
when (cont.):		
when	WRB	2322-15-468
when	WRB-HL	5-03-004
when	WRB-NC	2-02-002
When	WRB-TL	4-02-004
whence	**WRB**	**3-02-002**
whenever	**WRB**	**43-13-038**
where	**wh-adverb**	**949-15-374**
where	WRB	925-15-371
wheare	WRB	1-01-001
wher	WRB	1-01-001
where	WRB-HL	6-03-004
Where	WRB-TL	5-02-003
where'd	WRB+DOD	3-02-003
where'd	WRB+MD	1-01-001
where're	WRB+BER	1-01-001
where's	WRB+BEZ	3-03-003
Where's	WRB+BEZ-TL	3-01-001
whereabouts	**NN**	**5-04-005**
whereas	**CS**	**41-09-035**
whereby	**WRB**	**19-07-019**
wherefore	**noun**	**1-01-001**
wherefores	NNS	1-01-001
wherefore	**WRB**	**3-02-002**
wherein	**WRB**	**5-04-004**
whereof	**WRB**	**8-01-002**
whereon	**WRB**	**1-01-001**
whereupon	**CS**	**6-04-005**
wherever	**wh-adverb**	**28-12-026**
wherever	WRB	27-12-026
whereever	WRB	1-01-001
wherewith	**WRB**	**1-01-001**
whet	**verb**	**1-01-001**
whetted	VBN	1-01-001
whether	**CS**	**286-15-170**
which	**wh-det.**	**3560-15-474**
which	WDT	3556-15-474
which	WDT-HL	1-01-001
which	WDT-NC	3-01-001
whichever	**WDT**	**6-05-006**
whichever-the-hell	**WDT**	**1-01-001**
whiff	**NN**	**1-01-001**
Whig	**prop. noun**	**12-02-005**
Whig	NP	6-01-002
Whigs	NPS	2-02-002
Whigs	NPS-TL	4-01-002
while	**sub. conj.**	**600-15-305**
while	CS	599-15-305
while	CS-HL	1-01-001
while	**NN**	**78-14-062**
while	**VB**	**2-02-002**
whim	**noun**	**3-03-003**
whim	NN	2-02-002
whims	NNS	1-01-001
whimper	**verb**	**2-02-002**
whimper	VB	1-01-001
whimpering	VBG	1-01-001
Whimsey	**NP**	**1-01-001**
whimsical	**JJ**	**1-01-001**
whine	**NN**	**2-01-002**
whine	**verb**	**9-05-006**
whine	VB	2-02-002
whined	VBD	1-01-001
whining	VBG	6-03-003
whinny	**NN**	**1-01-001**
whinny	**verb**	**2-01-001**
whinnied	VBD	2-01-001
whip	**noun**	**16-06-007**
whip	NN	14-06-007
whip's	NN$	1-01-001
whips	NNS	1-01-001
whip	**verb**	**24-11-019**
whip	VB	5-04-004
whipped	VBD	7-05-007
whipped	VBN	5-04-004
whipping	VBG	7-05-006
whiplash	**noun**	**2-02-002**
whiplash	NN	1-01-001
whiplashes	NNS	1-01-001
Whippet	**NP**	**1-01-001**
whipping-boy	**noun**	**1-01-001**
whipping-boys	NNS	1-01-001
Whipple	**prop. noun**	**8-02-003**
Whipple	NP	7-02-003
Whipple's	NP$	1-01-001
whipsaw	**verb**	**1-01-001**
whipsawed	VBN	1-01-001
Whipsnade	**NP**	**2-01-001**
whir	**NN**	**3-03-003**

Word	Tag	Frequency
whir	**verb**	**2-02-002**
whirring	VBG	2-02-002
whirl	**NN**	**1-01-001**
whirl	**verb**	**17-10-013**
whirl	VB	2-02-002
whirled	VBD	6-04-004
whirling	VBG	8-06-008
Whirling	VBG-TL	1-01-001
whirling	**NN**	**1-01-001**
Whirlpool	**prop. noun**	**1-01-001**
Whirlpool	NP	0-00-000
Whirlpool	NP-TL	1-01-001
whirlwind	**noun**	**3-02-002**
whirlwind	NN	1-01-001
Whirlwind	NN-TL	1-01-001
whirlwind's	NN$	0-00-000
Whirlwind's	NN$-TL	1-01-001
whisk	**verb**	**3-03-003**
whisked	VBD	1-01-001
whisked	VBN	1-01-001
whisking	VBG	1-01-001
whisker	**noun**	**3-02-002**
whiskers	NNS	3-02-002
whiskered	**JJ**	**1-01-001**
whisky	**noun**	**40-08-022**
whisky	NN	22-06-010
whiskey	NN	16-06-012
Whiskey	NN-TL	1-01-001
whisky	NN-HL	1-01-001
whisky-on-the-rocks	**NN**	**1-01-001**
whisper	**noun**	**12-05-011**
whisper	NN	8-04-007
whispers	NNS	4-02-004
whisper	**verb**	**31-08-024**
whisper	VB	4-04-004
whispered	VBD	20-06-015
whispered	VBN	3-03-003
whispering	VBG	4-04-004
whispering	**noun**	**2-02-002**
whispering	NN	1-01-001
whisperings	NNS	1-01-001
whistle	**NN**	**3-03-003**
whistle	**verb**	**12-06-012**
whistle	VB	1-01-001
whistled	VBD	6-05-006
whistling	VBG	5-05-005
whit	**NN**	**1-01-001**
Whitcomb	**NP**	**1-01-001**
white	**adjective**	**334-14-146**
white	JJ	252-14-123
White	JJ-TL	82-10-031
white	**noun**	**27-07-015**
white	NN	8-04-005
White	NN-TL	3-01-003
whites	NNS	16-05-007
White	**prop. noun**	**24-07-010**
White	NP	19-05-008
White	NP-TL	1-01-001
White's	NP$	4-02-002
white-clad	**JJ**	**3-03-003**
white-collar	**NN**	**1-01-001**
white-columned	**JJ**	**1-01-001**
white-dominated	**JJ**	**1-01-001**
white-shirted	**JJ**	**1-01-001**
white-stucco	**NN**	**1-01-001**
white-suited	**JJ**	**1-01-001**
white-topped	**JJ**	**2-02-002**
whiteface	**NN**	**2-01-001**
whitehaired	**JJ**	**1-01-001**
Whitehall	**NP**	**1-01-001**
Whitehead	**prop. noun**	**9-04-006**
Whitehead	NP	7-03-004
Whitehead's	NP$	2-02-002
Whiteleaf	**NP**	**1-01-001**
Whiteley	**NP**	**1-01-001**
whitely	**RB**	**1-01-001**
Whiteman	**NP**	**4-01-001**
Whitemarsh	**NP**	**3-01-001**
whiten	**verb**	**5-02-004**
whitens	VBZ	1-01-001
whitened	VBD	1-01-001
whitened	VBN	2-01-001
whitening	VBG	1-01-001
whiteness	**NN**	**2-02-002**
whitetail	**noun**	**2-01-001**
whitetail	NN	1-01-001
whitetail	NNS	1-01-001
whitewash	**verb**	**1-01-001**
whitewashed	VBN	1-01-001

Word	Tag	Frequency
Whitey	**NP**	**6-02-003**
Whitfield	**NP**	**1-01-001**
Whiting	**NP**	**2-01-001**
Whitman	**prop. noun**	**3-02-003**
Whitman	NP	2-02-002
Whitman's	NP$	1-01-001
Whitney	**prop. noun**	**4-03-003**
Whitney	NP	3-02-002
Whitney	NP-TL	1-01-001
Whitrow	**NP**	**2-01-001**
Whittaker	**NP**	**1-01-001**
Whittier	**prop. noun**	**2-02-002**
Whittier	NP	1-01-001
Whittier's	NP$	1-01-001
whiz	**NN**	**2-01-002**
whiz	**verb**	**3-03-003**
whizzed	VBD	2-02-002
whizzing	VBG	1-01-001
who	**wh-pronoun**	**2678-15-438**
who	WPS	2246-15-419
Who	WPS	1-01-001
whoe	WPS	2-01-001
Who	WPS-TL	4-03-004
who'd	WPS+HVD	6-03-004
who'd	WPS+MD	3-01-003
who'll	WPS+MD	1-01-001
who's	WPS+BEZ	14-07-012
who's	WPS+BEZ-NC	2-01-001
Who's	WPS+BEZ-TL	1-01-001
who's	WPS+HVZ	1-01-001
whom	WPO	144-15-094
who	WPO	1-01-001
Whom	WPO-TL	1-01-001
whose	WP$	251-15-171
whoa	**UH**	**1-01-001**
whodunnit	**NN**	**1-01-001**
whoever	**WPS**	**13-07-012**
whole	**adjective**	**259-15-163**
whole	JJ	258-15-163
whole	JJ-HL	1-01-001
whole	**noun**	**52-13-041**
whole	NN	50-13-040
wholes	NNS	2-01-001
whole-house	**NN**	**1-01-001**
whole-wheat	**noun**	**7-01-001**
whole-wheat	NN	6-01-001
wholewheat	NN	1-01-001
whole-word	**NN**	**1-01-001**
wholeheartedly	**adverb**	**2-02-002**
wholeheartedly	RB	1-01-001
whole-heartedly	RB	1-01-001
wholeness	**NN**	**2-01-001**
wholesale	**JJ**	**7-06-006**
wholesaler	**noun**	**1-01-001**
wholesalers	NNS	1-01-001
wholesome	**adjective**	**11-05-008**
wholesome	JJ	10-05-007
wholesome	JJ-HL	1-01-001
wholly	**QL**	**11-05-011**
wholly	**RB**	**13-09-012**
wholly-owned	**JJ**	**2-02-002**
whoop	**NN**	**1-01-001**
whoop	**verb**	**2-02-002**
whooping	VBG	2-02-002
whoosh	**UH**	**1-01-001**
whopper	**noun**	**1-01-001**
whoppers	NNS	1-01-001
whopping	**JJ**	**1-01-001**
whore	**noun**	**3-02-002**
whore	NN	2-01-001
whores	NNS	1-01-001
whorl	**noun**	**1-01-001**
whorls	NNS	1-01-001
whosever	**WP$**	**1-01-001**
whosoever	**WPS**	**3-02-002**
why	**UH**	**3-02-003**
why	**wh-adverb**	**404-15-200**
why	WRB	393-15-196
whah	WRB	1-01-001
Why	WRB	1-01-001
why	WRB-HL	4-03-004
why	WRB-NC	3-02-002
why'n	WRB+IN	1-01-001
whyn't	WRB+DOD*	1-01-001
whyfore	**noun**	**1-01-001**
whyfores	NNS	1-01-001
Wichita	**NP**	**1-01-001**
wick	**NN**	**2-02-002**
Wick	**NP**	**2-02-002**
wicked	**adjective**	**9-05-009**
wicked	JJ	8-05-008
Wicked	JJ-TL	1-01-001
wickedly	**RB**	**2-02-002**
wickedness	**NN**	**3-03-003**
wicker	**NN**	**4-04-004**
wicket	**noun**	**2-02-002**
wicket	NN	1-01-001
wickets	NNS	1-01-001
Wickham	**NP**	**1-01-001**
wide	**adjective**	**118-15-089**
wide	JJ	115-15-089
w-i-d-e	JJ	1-01-001
wide	JJ-HL	2-02-002
wide	**QL**	**3-02-003**
wide	**RB**	**5-04-004**
wide-awake	**JJ**	**1-01-001**
wide-cut	**JJ**	**1-01-001**
wide-door	**NN**	**1-01-001**
wide-eyed	**JJ**	**1-01-001**
wide-grip	**noun**	**2-01-001**
wide-grip	NN	1-01-001
widegrip	NN	1-01-001
wide-open	**JJ**	**1-01-001**
wide-ranging	**JJ**	**3-03-003**
wide-shouldered	**JJ**	**1-01-001**
wide-sweeping	**JJ**	**1-01-001**
wide-winged	**JJ**	**1-01-001**
widely	**QL**	**3-03-003**
widely	**RB**	**49-11-039**
widen	**verb**	**11-08-009**
widen	VB	5-04-004
widens	VBZ	1-01-001
widened	VBD	2-02-002
widened	VBN	3-03-003
Widener	**NP**	**1-01-001**
wider	**comp. adj.**	**17-07-015**
wider	JJR	16-07-014
wider	JJR-HL	1-01-001
widespread	**JJ**	**29-10-025**
widespread	**RB**	**1-01-001**
widest	**JJT**	**3-03-003**
widow	**noun**	**27-11-019**
widow	NN	24-09-016
Widow	NN-TL	2-02-002
widows	NNS	1-01-001
widow	**verb**	**5-04-005**
widowed	VBN	5-04-005
widower	**NN**	**1-01-001**
widowhood	**NN**	**1-01-001**
Widsith	**prop. noun**	**1-01-001**
Widsith	NP	0-00-000
Widsith	NP-TL	1-01-001
width	**noun**	**19-03-013**
width	NN	14-03-012
widths	NNS	5-01-003
widthwise	**JJ**	**1-01-001**
wiederum	**FW-RB**	**1-01-001**
Wieland	**NP**	**1-01-001**
wield	**verb**	**4-04-004**
wield	VB	1-01-001
wielded	VBD	2-02-002
wielded	VBN	1-01-001
wielder	**NN**	**1-01-001**
wiener	**noun**	**2-01-001**
wieners	NNS	1-01-001
wieners'	NNS$	1-01-001
wife	**noun**	**265-15-123**
wife	NN	227-15-115
Wife	NN-TL	1-01-001
wife's	NN+BEZ	1-01-001
wife's	NN$	14-07-011
wives	NNS	17-06-010
Wives	NNS-TL	4-01-001
wives'	NNS$	0-00-000
wive's	NNS$	1-01-001
wife-to-be	**NN**	**1-01-001**
wifely	**JJ**	**1-01-001**
wig	**NN**	**1-01-001**
wiggle	**NN**	**1-01-001**
wiggle	**verb**	**5-04-004**
wiggled	VBD	3-03-003
wiggling	VBG	2-02-002
wigmaker	**NN**	**2-01-001**
Wilbur	**NP**	**2-02-002**
Wilcke	**NP**	**1-01-001**
Wilcox	**NP**	**2-01-001**
wild	**adjective**	**54-13-043**
wild	JJ	51-13-041

Word	Tag	Frequency
wild (cont.):		
Wild	JJ-TL	3-03-003
wild	**adverb**	**2-02-002**
wild	RB	1-01-001
wild	RB-HL	1-01-001
wild-eyed	**JJ**	**1-01-001**
wild-sounding	**JJ**	**1-01-001**
wildcat	**noun**	**4-03-003**
wildcat	NN	3-02-002
Wildcat	NN-TL	1-01-001
wildcatter	**NN**	**1-01-001**
Wilde	**NP**	**1-01-001**
Wildenstein	**NP**	**1-01-001**
Wilder	**prop. noun**	**2-01-001**
Wilder	NP	1-01-001
Wilder's	NP$	1-01-001
wilderness	**noun**	**11-06-010**
wilderness	NN	9-06-008
Wilderness	NN-TL	2-02-002
wildest	**JJT**	**1-01-001**
Wildhack	**NP**	**1-01-001**
wildlife	**noun**	**19-04-006**
wildlife	NN	18-04-006
wildlife	NN-HL	1-01-001
wildly	**QL**	**1-01-001**
wildly	**RB**	**24-09-023**
wildness	**NN**	**1-01-001**
wile	**noun**	**2-02-002**
wiles	NNS	2-02-002
Wiley	**prop. noun**	**6-03-004**
Wiley	NP	3-03-003
Wiley	NP-TL	3-01-001
Wilfred	**NP**	**1-01-001**
Wilfrid	**NP**	**1-01-001**
wilfully	**RB**	**2-02-002**
Wilhelm	**prop. noun**	**4-03-004**
Wilhelm	NP	3-03-003
Wilhelm	NP-TL	1-01-001
Wilhelmina	**NP**	**2-01-001**
Wiligis	**NP**	**1-01-001**
Wilkes	**prop. noun**	**2-01-002**
Wilkes	NP	1-01-001
Wilkes	NP-TL	1-01-001
Wilkes-Barre	**NP**	**1-01-001**
Wilkey	**NP**	**1-01-001**
Wilkinson	**NP**	**1-01-001**
will	**modal aux.**	**2686-15-429**
will	MD	2130-15-392
wil	MD	1-01-001
wilt	MD	1-01-001
will	MD-HL	6-03-004
won't	MD*	105-13-074
willya	MD+PPSS	1-01-001
'll	+MD	440-00-000
'll	+MD-NC	2-01-001
will	**noun**	**105-14-075**
will	NN	99-14-073
Will	NN-TL	5-02-004
wills	NNS	1-01-001
will	**verb**	**7-05-007**
will	VB	1-01-001
willed	VBD	3-03-003
willed	VBN	3-02-003
Will	**NP**	**4-03-003**
will-to-power	**NN**	**1-01-001**
Willa	**NP**	**1-01-001**
Willamette	**prop. noun**	**3-01-002**
Willamette	NP	0-00-000
Willamette	NP-TL	3-01-002
Willard	**NP**	**4-02-003**
Willcox	**prop. noun**	**2-01-001**
Willcox	NP	1-01-001
Willcox	NP-TL	1-01-001
Willem	**NP**	**1-01-001**
Willett	**NP**	**1-01-001**
willful	**JJ**	**1-01-001**
willfully	**RB**	**1-01-001**
william	**NN**	**1-01-001**
William	**prop. noun**	**155-13-076**
William	NP	145-13-076
Wm.	NP	2-01-001
William	NP-HL	1-01-001
William	NP-TL	1-01-001
William's	NP$	6-02-002
Williams	**prop. noun**	**35-09-018**
Williams	NP	32-09-016
Williams's	NP$	2-02-002
Williams'	NP$	1-01-001
Williamsburg	**NP**	**1-01-001**
Williamson	**prop. noun**	**1-01-001**
Williamson's	NP$	1-01-001
Willie	**prop. noun**	**15-03-007**
Willie	NP	11-03-007
Willie's	NP$	4-01-003
willing	**adjective**	**70-14-057**
willing	JJ	69-14-056
willinge	JJ	1-01-001
willingly	**RB**	**4-04-004**
willingness	**NN**	**11-06-009**
Willings	**NP**	**7-01-001**
Willis	**prop. noun**	**18-01-001**
Willis	NP	16-01-001
Willis'	NP$	2-01-001
willow	**noun**	**10-03-004**
willow	NN	8-02-002
Willow	NN-TL	1-01-001
willows	NNS	0-00-000
Willows	NNS-TL	1-01-001
willow-lined	**JJ**	**1-01-001**
willowy	**JJ**	**1-01-001**
willy	**RB**	**1-01-001**
Willy	**NP**	**4-03-003**
willy-nilly	**RB**	**4-03-003**
Wilmette	**prop. noun**	**4-02-003**
Wilmette	NP	3-01-002
Wilmette	NP-HL	1-01-001
Wilmington	**prop. noun**	**6-03-004**
Wilmington	NP	5-03-004
Wilmington	NP-TL	1-01-001
Wilshire	**prop. noun**	**2-01-001**
Wilshire	NP	1-01-001
Wilshire	NP-TL	1-01-001
Wilson	**prop. noun**	**65-09-021**
Wilson	NP	60-09-018
Wilson	NP-HL	1-01-001
Wilson	NP-TL	1-01-001
Wilson's	NP$	3-02-003
Wilsonian	**JJ**	**1-01-001**
wilt	**NN**	**1-01-001**
wilt	**verb**	**2-01-002**
wilt	VB	1-01-001
wilted	VBN	1-01-001
wily	**adjective**	**3-02-003**
wily	JJ	2-01-002
Wily	JJ-TL	1-01-001
Wimsatt	**NP**	**1-01-001**
win	**noun**	**4-02-002**
win	NN	0-00-000
win	NN-HL	1-01-001
wins	NNS	3-01-001
win	**verb**	**159-13-086**
win	VB	53-11-037
wynne	VB	1-01-001
win	VB-HL	1-01-001
wins	VBZ	5-04-004
won	VBD	45-07-030
won	VBD-HL	1-01-001
won	VBN	22-08-019
winning	VBG	31-09-024
wince	**verb**	**5-03-005**
winced	VBD	4-03-004
wincing	VBG	1-01-001
winch	**noun**	**1-01-001**
winches	NNS	1-01-001
Winchell	**NP**	**1-01-001**
Winchester	**NP**	**12-05-006**
wind	**noun**	**74-14-049**
wind	NN	54-14-036
Wind	NN-TL	2-02-002
winds	NNS	16-07-013
Winds	NNS-TL	2-01-001
wind	**verb**	**29-10-025**
wind	VB	7-06-007
winds	VBZ	3-03-003
wound	VBD	7-04-007
wound	VBN	3-03-003
winding	VBG	9-06-007
wind	**verb**	**2-02-002**
winded	VBN	2-02-002
wind-and-water	**NN**	**1-01-001**
wind-blown	**JJ**	**2-02-002**
wind-swept	**JJ**	**2-02-002**
wind-velocity	**NN**	**1-01-001**
windbag	**NN**	**1-01-001**
windbreak	**noun**	**1-01-001**
windbreaks	NNS	1-01-001
winder	**noun**	**4-01-001**
winder	NN	3-01-001

winder (cont.):		
winders	NNS	1-01-001
windfall	**NN**	**2-02-002**
Windham	**prop. noun**	**2-01-001**
Windham	NP	1-01-001
Windham	NP-TL	1-01-001
winding-clothes	**NNS**	**1-01-001**
windless	**JJ**	**1-01-001**
windmill	**NN**	**1-01-001**
window	**noun**	**172-14-090**
window	NN	119-14-066
windows	NNS	53-13-038
window-washing	**NN**	**1-01-001**
windowless	**JJ**	**3-03-003**
windowpane	**noun**	**2-01-002**
windowpanes	NNS	2-01-002
windshield	**NN**	**6-03-004**
Windsor	**NP**	**2-02-002**
windstorm	**NN**	**1-01-001**
windup	**NN**	**1-01-001**
windy	**JJ**	**2-02-002**
wine	**JJ**	**1-01-001**
wine	**noun**	**97-12-024**
wine	NN	71-12-023
wine-	NN	1-01-001
wine's	NN$	1-01-001
wines	NNS	24-02-002
winehead	**NN**	**1-01-001**
Winfield	**NP**	**1-01-001**
wing	**noun**	**44-13-032**
wing	NN	16-06-013
Wing	NN-TL	1-01-001
wings	NNS	24-11-017
Wings	NNS-TL	3-03-003
wing	**verb**	**5-05-005**
wing	VB	1-01-001
winged	VBD	2-02-002
winged	VBN	1-01-001
winging	VBG	1-01-001
wing-shooting	**NN**	**1-01-001**
wingback	**NN**	**1-01-001**
wingman	**NN**	**2-01-001**
wink	**NN**	**4-03-004**
wink	**verb**	**18-06-011**
wink	VB	3-02-002
winked	VBD	7-05-006
winked	VBN	1-01-001
winking	VBG	7-03-004
winless	**JJ**	**2-01-001**
winner	**noun**	**12-04-009**
winner	NN	6-03-006
Winner	NN-TL	2-01-001
winners	NNS	3-02-002
winners	NNS-HL	1-01-001
Winnetka	**NP**	**1-01-001**
winning	**noun**	**3-02-002**
winnings	NNS	3-02-002
Winnipeg	**NP**	**1-01-001**
Winnipesaukee	**prop. noun**	**1-01-001**
Winnipesaukee	NP	0-00-000
Winnipesaukee	NP-TL	1-01-001
winnow	**VB**	**1-01-001**
wino	**noun**	**1-01-001**
winos	NNS	1-01-001
Winooski	**prop. noun**	**4-02-002**
Winooski	NP	2-01-001
Winooski	NP-TL	2-02-002
Winsett	**NP**	**1-01-001**
Winslow	**prop. noun**	**13-01-001**
Winslow	NP	11-01-001
Winslow's	NP$	2-01-001
winsome	**JJ**	**1-01-001**
Winsor	**NP**	**2-02-002**
Winston	**NP**	**40-04-005**
winter	**noun**	**82-14-052**
winter	NN	77-14-051
Winter	NN-TL	3-03-003
winters	NNS	2-02-002
winter	**verb**	**3-03-003**
wintered	VBN	2-02-002
wintering	VBG	1-01-001
Winter	**NP**	**3-01-001**
wintertime	**NN**	**1-01-001**
Winthrop	**NP**	**3-02-002**
wintry	**JJ**	**2-02-002**
wipe	**verb**	**35-10-032**
wipe	VB	10-07-010
wiped	VBD	11-03-010
wiped	VBN	8-06-008

wipe (cont.):		
wiping	VBG	6-04-006
wire	**noun**	**55-12-037**
wire	NN	41-12-028
Wire	NN-TL	1-01-001
wires	NNS	13-07-013
wire	**verb**	**11-07-011**
wired	VBD	4-03-004
wired	VBN	7-06-007
wire-haired	**JJ**	**1-01-001**
wiring	**NN**	**2-02-002**
wiry	**JJ**	**8-05-007**
Wisconsin	**prop. noun**	**21-07-012**
Wisconsin	NP	14-07-009
Wis.	NP	1-01-001
Wisconsin	NP-TL	5-03-004
Wisconsin's	NP$	0-00-000
Wisconsin's	NP$-TL	1-01-001
wisdom	**noun**	**44-12-035**
wisdom	NN	42-12-033
Wisdom	NN-TL	2-02-002
wise	**JJ**	**33-11-027**
wise	**verb**	**1-01-001**
wised	VBN	1-01-001
Wise	**prop. noun**	**3-03-003**
Wise	NP	2-02-002
Wise	NP-TL	1-01-001
wisecrack	**verb**	**2-02-002**
wisecracked	VBD	2-02-002
wisely	**RB**	**8-05-008**
wisenheimer	**NN**	**1-01-001**
wiser	**JJR**	**7-06-007**
wisest	**JJT**	**1-01-001**
wish	**noun**	**34-12-029**
wish	NN	23-10-020
wishes	NNS	11-07-011
wish	**verb**	**161-15-123**
wish	VB	87-15-071
wishes	VBZ	13-06-011
wished	VBD	52-11-044
wished	VBN	4-04-004
wishing	VBG	5-04-005
Wishart	**NP**	**1-01-001**
wishful	**JJ**	**9-05-009**
Wisman	**prop. noun**	**15-01-001**
Wisman	NP	9-01-001
Wisman's	NP$	6-01-001
wisp	**noun**	**3-03-003**
wisp	NN	2-02-002
wisps	NNS	1-01-001
wispy	**JJ**	**2-02-002**
Wissahickon	**prop. noun**	**1-01-001**
Wissahickon	NP	0-00-000
Wissahickon	NP-TL	1-01-001
Wister	**NP**	**2-02-002**
wistful	**JJ**	**2-02-002**
wistfully	**RB**	**4-04-004**
wit	**noun**	**25-10-020**
wit	NN	20-08-015
wits	NNS	5-04-005
witch	**noun**	**13-06-007**
witch	NN	5-03-003
witches	NNS	8-04-005
with	**prep.**	**7286-15-500**
with	IN	7261-15-500
with	IN-HL	12-05-010
with	IN-NC	4-02-002
With	IN-TL	9-04-007
with	**RB**	**3-03-003**
with-but-after	**IN**	**1-01-001**
withal	**RB**	**1-01-001**
withdraw	**verb**	**25-10-023**
withdraw	VB	8-05-007
withdrew	VBD	9-06-009
withdrawn	VBN	4-04-004
withdrawing	VBG	4-03-004
withdrawal	**NN**	**6-06-006**
withe	**noun**	**1-01-001**
withes	NNS	1-01-001
wither	**verb**	**5-05-005**
wither	VB	2-02-002
withered	VBN	2-02-002
withering	VBG	1-01-001
Witherspoon	**NP**	**1-01-001**
withhold	**verb**	**14-07-012**
withhold	VB	2-02-002
withheld	VBD	1-01-001
withheld	VBN	7-04-007
withholding	VBG	3-02-002

Word	Tag	Frequency
withhold (cont.):		
withholding	VBG-HL	1-01-001
withholding	**NN**	**4-02-003**
within	**IN**	**351-15-194**
within	**RB**	**8-05-006**
without	**prep.**	**583-15-312**
without	IN	574-15-310
without	IN-HL	3-02-002
without	IN-NC	4-01-001
Without	IN-TL	2-02-002
withstand	**verb**	**7-05-006**
withstand	VB	3-03-003
withstands	VBZ	1-01-001
withstood	VBD	1-01-001
withstood	VBN	2-01-002
witness	**noun**	**40-11-029**
witness	NN	18-07-015
witness	NN-HL	1-01-001
witnesses	NNS	19-07-015
Witnesses	NNS-TL	2-01-001
witness	**verb**	**28-10-025**
witness	VB	9-05-009
witnessed	VBD	7-06-007
witnessed	VBN	6-06-006
witnessing	VBG	6-05-006
Witold	**NP**	**1-01-001**
Witt	**prop. noun**	**2-02-002**
Witt	NP	1-01-001
Witt	NP-TL	1-01-001
Witter	**NP**	**1-01-001**
wittingly	**RB**	**1-01-001**
witty	**JJ**	**10-05-007**
wizard	**noun**	**3-03-003**
wizard	NN	2-02-002
Wizard	NN-TL	1-01-001
wobble	**verb**	**6-05-006**
wobble	VB	3-03-003
wobbled	VBD	2-01-002
wobbling	VBG	1-01-001
wobbly	**JJ**	**2-01-002**
Woburn	**NP**	**1-01-001**
woe	**NN**	**5-03-005**
woebegone	**JJ**	**1-01-001**
woeful	**JJ**	**1-01-001**
woefully	**QL**	**1-01-001**
woefully	**RB**	**1-01-001**
wohaw	**foreign**	**3-01-001**
wohaw	FW-NN	1-01-001
wohaw	FW-NN-NC	1-01-001
wohaws	FW-NNS	1-01-001
Wolcott	**NP**	**1-01-001**
Wolcyrz	**NP**	**1-01-001**
wolf	**noun**	**9-04-007**
wolf	NN	4-02-004
Wolf	NN-TL	1-01-001
wolves	NNS	4-04-004
Wolf	**NP**	**1-01-001**
Wolfe	**prop. noun**	**10-02-006**
Wolfe	NP	8-02-005
Wolfe's	NP$	1-01-001
Wolfes	NPS	1-01-001
Wolff	**prop. noun**	**4-03-003**
Wolff	NP	2-01-001
Wolff's	NP$	2-02-002
Wolfgang	**NP**	**1-01-001**
wolfishly	**RB**	**1-01-001**
Wollman	**prop. noun**	**4-01-001**
Wollman	NP	2-01-001
Wollman	NP-TL	2-01-001
Wolpe	**prop. noun**	**2-01-001**
Wolpe	NP	1-01-001
Wolpe's	NP$	1-01-001
Wolstenholme	**NP**	**1-01-001**
Wolverton	**NP**	**1-01-001**
woman	**noun**	**467-15-169**
woman	NN	216-15-106
Woman	NN-TL	7-01-001
woman's	NN$	19-11-018
Woman's	NN$-TL	3-03-003
women	NNS	184-15-094
women	NNS-NC	1-01-001
Women	NNS-TL	10-06-009
women's	NNS$	15-06-014
Women's	NNS$-TL	11-05-008
Women's	NNS$-TL-HL	1-01-001
woman	**VB**	**1-01-001**
womanhood	**NN**	**1-01-001**
womanly	**JJ**	**1-01-001**
womb	**NN**	**1-01-001**

Word	Tag	Frequency
womb-to-tomb	**JJ**	**1-01-001**
women-trodden	**JJ**	**1-01-001**
won-lost	**JJ**	**1-01-001**
wonder	**JJ**	**1-01-001**
wonder	**noun**	**34-11-029**
wonder	NN	28-10-024
wonders	NNS	6-05-006
wonder	**verb**	**119-14-076**
wonder	VB	38-13-031
wonduh	VB	1-01-001
wonders	VBZ	2-02-002
wondered	VBD	55-08-035
wondered	VBN	3-03-003
wondering	VBG	20-08-019
wonder-working	**JJ**	**1-01-001**
wonderful	**JJ**	**53-14-044**
wonderfully	**QL**	**10-04-010**
wonderfully	**RB**	**1-01-001**
wonderfulness	**NN**	**1-01-001**
wondering	**NN**	**1-01-001**
wonderingly	**RB**	**1-01-001**
Wonderland	**NP**	**1-01-001**
wondrous	**JJ**	**1-01-001**
wondrously	**QL**	**1-01-001**
wont	**JJ**	**2-02-002**
woo	**verb**	**4-04-004**
woo	VB	3-03-003
wooed	VBN	1-01-001
wood	**noun**	**76-13-052**
wood	NN	51-13-040
woods	NNS	24-10-017
Woods	NNS-TL	1-01-001
Wood	**NP**	**4-01-003**
wood-grained	**JJ**	**1-01-001**
wood-oil	**NN**	**1-01-001**
Woodberry	**prop. noun**	**1-01-001**
Woodberry	NP	0-00-000
Woodberry	NP-TL	1-01-001
Woodbury	**prop. noun**	**3-01-001**
Woodbury	NP	2-01-001
Woodbury's	NP$	1-01-001
woodcarver	**NN**	**1-01-001**
Woodcock	**prop. noun**	**2-01-001**
Woodcock	NP	1-01-001
Woodcock's	NP$	1-01-001
woodcutter	**noun**	**1-01-001**
woodcutters	NNS	1-01-001
wooded	**JJ**	**5-02-004**
wooden	**JJ**	**50-11-030**
wooden-leg	**NN**	**1-01-001**
woodgraining	**NN**	**1-01-001**
Woodin	**NP**	**1-01-001**
woodland	**noun**	**2-02-002**
woodland	NN	1-01-001
Woodland	NN-TL	1-01-001
Woodman	**prop. noun**	**1-01-001**
Woodman's	NP$	0-00-000
Woodman's	NP$-TL	1-01-001
woodpecker	**NN**	**1-01-001**
Woodrow	**NP**	**4-03-004**
Woodruff	**prop. noun**	**32-01-001**
Woodruff	NP	30-01-001
Woodruff's	NP$	2-01-001
Woods	**prop. noun**	**1-01-001**
Woods's	NP$	1-01-001
woodshed	**NN**	**1-01-001**
Woodside	**NP**	**3-02-002**
woodsmoke	**NN**	**3-03-003**
Woodward	**prop. noun**	**5-03-003**
Woodward	NP	2-02-002
Woodward	NP-TL	1-01-001
Woodwards	NPS	2-01-001
woodwind	**NN**	**2-02-002**
woodwork	**NN**	**5-04-004**
woodwork	**verb**	**2-02-002**
woodworking	VBG	2-02-002
Woodyard	**prop. noun**	**1-01-001**
Woodyard	NP	0-00-000
Woodyard	NP-TL	1-01-001
wool	**NN**	**10-07-010**
woolen	**JJ**	**2-02-002**
woolen	**NN**	**2-02-002**
woolgather	**VB**	**1-01-001**
Woollcott	**NP**	**1-01-001**
woolly	**JJ**	**3-03-003**
woolly-headed	**JJ**	**1-01-001**
woolly-minded	**JJ**	**1-01-001**
woolworker	**noun**	**1-01-001**
woolworkers	NNS	1-01-001

Word	Tag	Frequency
Woolworth	**prop. noun**	**1-01-001**
Woolworth's	NP$	1-01-001
woomera	**NN**	**1-01-001**
Woonasquatucket	**prop. noun**	**1-01-001**
Woonasquatucket	NP	0-00-000
Woonasquatucket	NP-TL	1-01-001
Woonsocket	**prop. noun**	**4-02-002**
Woonsocket	NP	1-01-001
Woonsocket	NP-TL	3-01-001
wooooosh	**NN**	**1-01-001**
wop	**verb**	**2-01-001**
wop	VB	1-01-001
wops	VBZ	1-01-001
Worcester	**NP**	**2-02-002**
Worcestershire	**NP**	**3-01-002**
word	**noun**	**549-15-237**
word	NN	263-15-151
wohd	NN	1-01-001
word	NN-HL	2-01-001
Word	NN-NC	1-01-001
Word	NN-TL	8-02-006
words	NNS	270-15-153
words	NNS-HL	1-01-001
Words	NNS-TL	3-02-003
word	**verb**	**5-03-005**
worded	VBN	4-03-004
wording	VBG	1-01-001
word-game	**noun**	**1-01-001**
word-games	NNS	1-01-001
wording	**NN**	**3-03-003**
wordlessly	**RB**	**2-02-002**
Wordsworth	**NP**	**2-01-001**
wordy	**JJ**	**1-01-001**
work	**noun**	**680-15-274**
work	NN	578-15-265
work	NN-HL	4-04-004
work	NN-NC	1-01-001
work's	NN$	1-01-001
works	NNS	89-13-055
works	NNS-HL	1-01-001
Works	NNS-TL	6-04-006
work	**verb**	**496-15-255**
work	VB	179-15-126
works	VBZ	34-14-027
worked	VBD	76-15-063
wrought	VBD	1-01-001
worked	VBN	52-11-043
wrought	VBN	2-02-002
working	VBG	149-14-113
workin'	VBG	1-01-001
working	VBG-HL	1-01-001
Working	VBG-TL	1-01-001
work-paralysis	**NN**	**1-01-001**
work-satisfaction	**NN**	**1-01-001**
work-study	**NN**	**1-01-001**
work-success	**NN**	**1-01-001**
work-weary	**JJ**	**1-01-001**
workable	**JJ**	**9-06-009**
workbench	**NN**	**8-01-001**
workday	**NN**	**1-01-001**
worker	**noun**	**123-13-046**
worker	NN	30-08-018
worker's	NN$	4-03-003
workers	NNS	81-11-035
workers	NNS-HL	1-01-001
Workers	NNS-TL	4-02-004
workers'	NNS$	3-03-003
working	**noun**	**6-05-005**
workings	NNS	6-05-005
working-class	**NN**	**3-01-001**
workingman	**noun**	**1-01-001**
workingmen	NNS	1-01-001
workman	**noun**	**9-06-007**
workman	NN	1-01-001
workman's	NN$	1-01-001
workmen	NNS	7-05-005
workmanlike	**JJ**	**2-02-002**
workmanship	**NN**	**6-04-004**
workout	**noun**	**12-03-006**
workout	NN	6-03-006
work-out	NN	2-01-001
workouts	NNS	3-01-002
work-outs	NNS	1-01-001
workpiece	**NN**	**1-01-001**
worksheet	**NN**	**1-01-001**
workshop	**noun**	**30-06-016**
workshop	NN	18-05-011
workshop	NN-HL	1-01-001
Workshop	NN-TL	5-03-004
workshop (cont.):		
workshops	NNS	6-03-005
worktable	**NN**	**1-01-001**
world	**noun**	**832-15-273**
world	NN	686-15-248
world	NN-HL	2-02-002
World	NN-TL	102-12-061
world's	NN$	32-11-029
World's	NN$-TL	3-02-002
worlds	NNS	5-05-005
Worlds	NNS-TL	2-01-001
world-at-large	**NN**	**1-01-001**
world-famous	**JJ**	**3-02-003**
world-ignoring	**JJ**	**1-01-001**
world-oriented	**JJ**	**1-01-001**
world-renowned	**JJ**	**3-03-003**
world-shaking	**JJ**	**2-02-002**
world-shattering	**JJ**	**1-01-001**
world-wide	**adjective**	**11-03-007**
world-wide	JJ	10-03-007
worldwide	JJ	1-01-001
world-wide	**RB**	**2-02-002**
worlder	**noun**	**1-01-001**
worlders	NNS	0-00-000
Worlders	NNS-TL	1-01-001
worldly	**JJ**	**9-05-007**
worm	**noun**	**8-05-007**
worm	NN	4-03-004
worms	NNS	4-03-004
Worms	**prop. noun**	**1-01-001**
Worms	NP	0-00-000
Worms	NP-TL	1-01-001
wormy	**JJ**	**1-01-001**
worn-faced	**JJ**	**1-01-001**
worn-out	**adjective**	**2-02-002**
worn-out	JJ	1-01-001
wornout	JJ	1-01-001
Worrell	**NP**	**1-01-001**
worriedly	**RB**	**1-01-001**
worrisome	**JJ**	**2-01-002**
worry	**noun**	**27-07-019**
worry	NN	12-07-012
worries	NNS	15-05-008
worry	**verb**	**89-14-063**
worry	VB	43-12-035
worries	VBZ	5-03-004
worried	VBD	7-07-007
worried	VBN	28-09-023
worrying	VBG	5-02-005
worryin'	VBG	1-01-001
worse	**comp. adj.**	**50-12-045**
worse	JJR	49-12-044
wus	JJR	1-01-001
worse	**RBR**	**1-01-001**
worsen	**verb**	**2-02-002**
worsens	VBZ	1-01-001
worsened	VBD	1-01-001
worship	**noun**	**31-12-019**
worship	NN	29-12-019
Worship	NN-TL	2-01-001
worship	**verb**	**12-05-010**
worship	VB	5-04-005
worshiped	VBD	0-00-000
worshipped	VBD	1-01-001
worshiped	VBN	1-01-001
worshipped	VBN	1-01-001
worshiping	VBG	3-01-002
worshipping	VBG	1-01-001
worshipful	**JJ**	**2-02-002**
worshipper	**noun**	**1-01-001**
worshippers	NNS	1-01-001
worst	**JJT**	**34-11-030**
worst-marked	**JJ**	**1-01-001**
worsted	**NN**	**2-02-002**
worth	**adjective**	**71-14-063**
worth	JJ	70-14-062
worth	JJ-HL	1-01-001
worth	**NN**	**20-09-016**
Worth	**NP**	**3-01-002**
worth-waiting-for	**JJ**	**1-01-001**
worthiest	**JJT**	**2-02-002**
worthless	**JJ**	**3-02-003**
worthlessness	**NN**	**1-01-001**
worthwhile	**adjective**	**9-07-009**
worthwhile	JJ	8-07-008
worth-while	JJ-HL	1-01-001
worthy	**adjective**	**26-07-022**
worthy	JJ	25-07-021
Worthy	JJ-TL	1-01-001

Word	Tag	Frequency
Worthy	**NP**	**2-01-001**
would	**modal aux.**	**3062-15-450**
would	MD	2711-15-448
wod	MD	1-01-001
wold	MD	1-01-001
wolde	MD	1-01-001
would	MD-HL	4-02-004
'd	+MD	214-11-088
woulda	MD+HV	1-01-001
wouldn't	MD*	128-13-076
wouldn't	MD*-HL	1-01-001
would-be	**adjective**	**6-05-006**
would-be	JJ	5-05-005
wouldbe	JJ	1-01-001
wound	**noun**	**24-08-012**
wound	NN	16-06-009
wounds	NNS	8-04-005
wound	**verb**	**26-06-018**
wound	VB	2-02-002
wounded	VBD	1-01-001
wounded	VBN	22-05-014
wounding	VBG	1-01-001
wound-tumor	**NN**	**1-01-001**
woven-root	**JJ**	**1-01-001**
wow	**UH**	**1-01-001**
Wozzek	**NP**	**1-01-001**
wrack	**NN**	**1-01-001**
wrack	**verb**	**2-02-002**
wracked	VBN	1-01-001
wracking	VBG	1-01-001
Wragge	**NP**	**1-01-001**
wraith-like	**JJ**	**2-01-002**
wrangle	**verb**	**2-02-002**
wrangled	VBD	2-02-002
wrangler	**noun**	**6-03-003**
wrangler	NN	3-02-002
Wrangler	NN-TL	3-01-001
wrap	**noun**	**2-02-002**
wraps	NNS	2-02-002
wrap	**verb**	**23-09-016**
wrap	VB	5-04-005
wrapped	VBD	2-02-002
wrapped	VBN	12-08-011
wrapping	VBG	3-03-003
wrappin'	VBG	1-01-001
wrapper	**noun**	**3-03-003**
wrapper	NN	2-02-002
wrappers	NNS	1-01-001
wrapping	**NN**	**3-03-003**
wrath	**noun**	**9-04-009**
wrath	NN	8-03-008
Wrath	NN-TL	1-01-001
wrathful	**JJ**	**1-01-001**
Wratten	**prop. noun**	**1-01-001**
Wratten	NP	0-00-000
Wratten	NP-TL	1-01-001
wreak	**VB**	**1-01-001**
wreath	**noun**	**11-04-006**
wreath	NN	8-03-004
wreaths	NNS	3-02-003
wreathe	**verb**	**1-01-001**
wreathed	VBN	1-01-001
wreck	**NN**	**6-05-006**
wreck	**verb**	**13-06-009**
wreck	VB	2-02-002
wrecked	VBD	2-01-002
wrecked	VBN	4-03-003
wrecking	VBG	5-03-003
wreckage	**NN**	**2-01-002**
wrench	**noun**	**1-01-001**
wrenches	NNS	1-01-001
wrench	**verb**	**4-04-004**
wrenches	VBZ	1-01-001
wrenched	VBD	2-02-002
wrenching	VBG	1-01-001
wrest	**VB**	**1-01-001**
wrestle	**noun**	**1-01-001**
wrestles	NNS	1-01-001
wrestle	**verb**	**3-03-003**
wrestle	VB	2-02-002
wrestling	VBG	1-01-001
wrestler	**noun**	**1-01-001**
wrestler's	NN$	1-01-001
wrestling	**noun**	**1-01-001**
wrestlings	NNS	1-01-001
wretch	**NN**	**1-01-001**
wretched	**JJ**	**7-03-006**
wretchedness	**NN**	**1-01-001**
Wright	**prop. noun**	**55-05-006**
Wright (cont.):		
Wright	NP	46-05-005
Wright's	NP$	7-02-002
Wright's	NP$-HL	2-01-001
Wrigley	**NP**	**3-02-002**
wring	**verb**	**3-03-003**
wring	VB	2-02-002
wrings	VBZ	1-01-001
wrinkle	**noun**	**9-06-008**
wrinkle	NN	2-02-002
wrinkles	NNS	7-06-007
wrinkle	**verb**	**12-05-011**
wrinkled	VBD	4-03-004
wrinkled	VBN	8-04-008
wrist	**noun**	**16-07-013**
wrist	NN	9-04-006
Wrist	NN-TL	1-01-001
wrists	NNS	6-06-006
wristwatch	**NN**	**2-02-002**
writ	**noun**	**6-02-004**
writ	NN	5-02-003
writs	NNS	1-01-001
write	**verb**	**561-15-198**
write	VB	106-14-074
writes	VBZ	40-09-026
Writes	VBZ-TL	1-01-001
wrote	VBD	179-14-081
wrote	VBD-NC	2-01-001
written	VBN	154-14-097
writ	VBN	2-01-002
writing	VBG	77-11-050
writer	**noun**	**151-13-065**
writer	NN	71-11-042
Writer	NN-TL	2-02-002
writer's	NN$	1-01-001
writers	NNS	71-11-031
Writers	NNS-TL	2-02-002
writers'	NNS$	3-03-003
Writers'	NNS$-TL	1-01-001
writer-turned-painter	**NN**	**1-01-001**
writhe	**verb**	**8-04-008**
writhe	VB	2-02-002
writhed	VBD	1-01-001
writhing	VBG	5-03-005
writhing	**NN**	**1-01-001**
writing	**noun**	**55-11-042**
writing	NN	37-11-028
Writing	NN	1-01-001
Writing	NN-TL	2-02-002
writings	NNS	15-06-014
writing-like	**JJ**	**1-01-001**
wrong	**adjective**	**117-15-085**
wrong	JJ	115-15-083
wrong	JJ-HL	1-01-001
wrong	JJ-NC	1-01-001
wrong	**noun**	**14-06-011**
wrong	NN	8-04-007
wrongs	NNS	5-03-004
wrongs	NNS-HL	1-01-001
wrong	**RB**	**4-03-004**
wrong	**verb**	**1-01-001**
wronged	VBN	1-01-001
wrong-headed	**JJ**	**1-01-001**
wrong-o	**NN**	**1-01-001**
wrongdoer	**NN**	**1-01-001**
wrongdoing	**NN**	**2-02-002**
wrongful	**JJ**	**1-01-001**
wrongly	**RB**	**1-01-001**
wrought-iron	**NN**	**1-01-001**
wry	**JJ**	**5-04-005**
wry-faced	**JJ**	**1-01-001**
wryly	**RB**	**3-03-003**
Wu	**NP**	**1-01-001**
Wustman	**NP**	**1-01-001**
Wyatt	**NP**	**3-03-003**
Wyckoff	**NP**	**1-01-001**
Wycliffe	**NP**	**1-01-001**
Wycoff	**prop. noun**	**2-01-001**
Wycoff	NP	1-01-001
Wycoff's	NP$	1-01-001
Wycombe	**prop. noun**	**1-01-001**
Wycombe	NP	0-00-000
Wycombe	NP-TL	1-01-001
Wylie	**NP**	**2-01-001**
Wyman	**NP**	**1-01-001**
Wyn	**NP**	**1-01-001**
Wyndham	**prop. noun**	**2-01-001**
Wyndham's	NP$	2-01-001
Wynn	**NP**	**1-01-001**

Word	Tag	Frequency
Wynston	**NP**	**1-01-001**
Wyoming	**NP**	**9-06-007**

Word	Tag	Frequency
X	**NP**	**3-01-001**
x-ray	**noun**	**16-04-009**
x-ray	NN	8-02-003
X-ray	NN-TL	4-02-003
x-rays	NNS	2-01-002
X-rays	NNS-TL	2-02-002
X-Tru-Coat	**NP**	**1-01-001**
Xavier	**prop. noun**	**2-01-001**
Xavier	NP	1-01-001
Xavier's	NP$	1-01-001
Xenia	**NP**	**1-01-001**
xenon	**NN**	**1-01-001**
xenophobia	**NN**	**2-02-002**
Ximenez-Vargas	**prop. noun**	**1-01-001**
Ximenez-Vargas	NP	0-00-000
Ximenez-Vargas	NP-TL	1-01-001
Xydis	**prop. noun**	**6-01-001**
Xydis	NP	5-01-001
Xydis'	NP$	1-01-001
xylem	**NN**	**4-01-001**
xylophone	**noun**	**1-01-001**
xylophones	NNS	1-01-001

Word	Tag	Frequency
y	**FW-CC**	**1-01-001**
Y	**NP**	**1-01-001**
Y.	**prop. noun**	**7-04-006**
Y.	NP	6-04-005
Y.	NP-HL	1-01-001
Y.M.C.A.	**NP**	**1-01-001**
Y.M.H.A.	**NP**	**1-01-001**
Y.W.C.A.	**NP**	**1-01-001**
yacht	**noun**	**7-05-005**
yacht	NN	1-01-001
Yacht	NN-TL	3-02-002
yachts	NNS	3-03-003
yacht	**verb**	**2-02-002**
yachting	VBG	2-02-002
yachtel	**noun**	**3-01-001**
yachtel	NN	2-01-001
yachtels	NNS	1-01-001
yachter	**noun**	**1-01-001**
yachters	NNS	1-01-001
yachtsman	**noun**	**2-02-002**
yachtsman	NN	1-01-001
yachtsmen	NNS	1-01-001
Yaddo	**NP**	**1-01-001**
Yahwe	**NP**	**1-01-001**
yak	**noun**	**1-01-001**
yaks	NNS	1-01-001
Yakima	**NP**	**1-01-001**
Yakov	**NP**	**1-01-001**
Yalagaloo	**UH**	**1-01-001**
Yale	**prop. noun**	**14-06-011**
Yale	NP	7-03-005
Yale	NP-TL	6-05-006
Yale's	NP$	1-01-001
Yale-Army	**NP**	**1-01-001**
Yalie	**prop. noun**	**1-01-001**
Yalies	NPS	1-01-001
Yalta	**prop. noun**	**14-02-002**
Yalta	NP	10-02-002
Yalta	NP-TL	4-02-002
Yamabe	**NP**	**1-01-001**
Yamata	**NP**	**1-01-001**
Yancy-6	**NP**	**2-01-001**
Yang	**prop. noun**	**12-01-002**
Yang	NP	11-01-002
Yang	NP-HL	1-01-001
yank	**NN**	**1-01-001**
yank	**verb**	**7-04-007**
yank	VB	1-01-001
yanked	VBD	4-02-004
yanked	VBN	1-01-001
yanking	VBG	1-01-001
Yank	**prop. noun**	**10-03-005**
Yank	NP	5-02-002
Yanks	NPS	4-02-003
Yanks'	NPS$	1-01-001
Yankee	**adjective**	**8-05-008**
Yankee	JJ	5-04-005
Yankee (cont.):		
Yankee	JJ-TL	3-02-003
Yankee	**prop. noun**	**40-07-014**
Yankee	NP	8-05-008
Yankee	NP-TL	2-02-002
Yankees	NPS	23-04-007
Yankees	NPS-TL	5-02-004
Yankees'	NPS$	1-01-001
Yankees'	NPS$-TL	1-01-001
Yankee-hatred	**NN**	**1-01-001**
Yankeefication	**prop. noun**	**2-01-001**
Yankeefication	NP	1-01-001
Yankeefication	NP-TL	1-01-001
Yankton	**NP**	**1-01-001**
yap	**verb**	**1-01-001**
yapping	VBG	1-01-001
Yaqui	**NP**	**1-01-001**
yard	**noun**	**100-11-051**
yard	NN	33-08-023
Yard	NN-TL	2-01-001
yards	NNS	63-10-027
yd.	NNS	1-01-001
Yards	NNS-TL	1-01-001
yardage	**NN**	**2-01-001**
yardstick	**NN**	**2-02-002**
Yardumian	**NP**	**1-01-001**
yarn	**noun**	**20-04-004**
yarn	NN	12-03-003
yarn	NN-HL	2-02-002
yarns	NNS	6-02-002
Yarrow	**NP**	**4-01-001**
yassuh	**noun**	**1-01-001**
yassuhs	NNS	1-01-001
yaw	**noun**	**1-01-001**
yaws	NNS	1-01-001
yawl	**NN**	**1-01-001**
yawn	**NN**	**1-01-001**
yawn	**verb**	**3-02-003**
yawn	VB	1-01-001
yawning	VBG	2-01-002
ye	**article**	**1-01-001**
ye	AT	0-00-000
Ye	AT-TL	1-01-001
yea	**RB**	**3-02-003**
yeah	**adverb**	**26-04-014**
yeah	RB	24-04-013
yehhh	RB	2-01-001
year	**noun**	**1661-15-379**
year	NN	641-15-208
yeah	NN	1-01-001
year	NN-HL	6-03-005
Year	NN-TL	9-04-008
year's	NN$	36-11-027
Year's	NN$-TL	7-05-006
years	NNS	946-15-346
yrs.	NNS	4-01-001
years	NNS-HL	3-03-003

year (cont.):		
years'	NNS$	8-06-007
year-earlier	**JJR**	**2-02-002**
year-end	**JJ**	**1-01-001**
year-long	**JJ**	**1-01-001**
year-old	**JJ**	**1-01-001**
year-round	**adjective**	**8-03-006**
year-round	JJ	4-03-004
year-'round	JJ	4-01-002
year-to-year	**JJ**	**2-01-001**
yearbook	**noun**	**2-02-002**
yearbook	NN	1-01-001
Yearbook	NN-TL	1-01-001
yearly	**adjective**	**6-05-006**
yearly	JJ	5-04-005
Yearly	JJ-TL	1-01-001
yearly	**RB**	**6-05-006**
yearn	**verb**	**4-04-004**
yearn	VB	1-01-001
yearned	VBD	2-02-002
yearned	VBN	1-01-001
yearning	**noun**	**9-09-009**
yearning	NN	7-07-007
yearnings	NNS	2-02-002
yearningly	**RB**	**1-01-001**
yeast	**noun**	**4-03-004**
yeast	NN	3-02-003
yeasts	NNS	1-01-001
Yeats	**NP**	**1-01-001**
Yedisan	**NP**	**1-01-001**
Yehudi	**NP**	**1-01-001**
yell	**NN**	**6-04-004**
yell	**verb**	**31-06-020**
yell	VB	3-01-002
yelled	VBD	21-05-014
yelled	VBN	1-01-001
yelling	VBG	5-02-004
yellin'	VBG	1-01-001
yelling	**NN**	**1-01-001**
yellow	**adjective**	**52-12-041**
yellow	JJ	48-11-039
yeller	JJ	2-01-001
Yellow	JJ-TL	2-02-002
yellow	**NN**	**4-04-004**
yellow	**verb**	**4-03-004**
yellow	VB	1-01-001
yellowed	VBN	1-01-001
yellowing	VBG	2-01-002
yellow-bellied	**JJ**	**1-01-001**
yellow-brown	**JJ**	**1-01-001**
yellow-dwarf	**NN**	**3-01-001**
yellow-green	**JJ**	**3-02-002**
yellowish	**adjective**	**2-02-002**
yellowish	JJ	1-01-001
yellerish	JJ	1-01-001
yelp	**noun**	**3-03-003**
yelp	NN	2-02-002
yelps	NNS	1-01-001
yelp	**verb**	**2-02-002**
yelped	VBD	1-01-001
yelping	VBG	1-01-001
yen	**NN**	**2-02-002**
Yen	**NP**	**1-01-001**
Yeni	**NP**	**1-01-001**
yes	**adverb**	**144-14-089**
yes	RB	140-13-085
Yes	RB	1-01-001
yes	RB-NC	1-01-001
Yes	RB-NC	1-01-001
Yes	RB-TL	1-01-001
yesiree	**UH**	**1-01-001**
yesterday	**adv. noun**	**89-11-041**
yesterday	NR	83-11-038
yesterday's	NR$	6-06-006
yesteryear	**NN**	**3-03-003**
yet	**CC**	**133-10-090**
yet	**QL**	**3-02-002**
yet	**RB**	**283-15-186**
Yiddish	**JJ**	**2-02-002**
Yiddish	**NP**	**2-01-001**
yield	**noun**	**21-06-010**
yield	NN	19-06-009
yields	NNS	2-02-002
yield	**verb**	**41-11-033**
yield	VB	16-07-014
yields	VBZ	5-03-005
yielded	VBD	7-05-006
yielded	VBN	5-03-005
yielding	VBG	8-05-007

yielding	**NN**	**1-01-001**
yielding-Mediterranean-woman-flesh-of-water	**NN**	**1-01-001**
Yin	**prop. noun**	**8-01-002**
Yin	NP	7-01-002
Yin	NP-HL	1-01-001
Yin-Yang	**NP**	**2-01-001**
Yinger	**NP**	**1-01-001**
yip	**NN**	**1-01-001**
yodel	**NN**	**1-01-001**
yodel	**verb**	**2-01-001**
yodeling	VBG	2-01-001
yoga	**NN**	**1-01-001**
Yogi	**NP**	**2-01-002**
yoke	**NN**	**3-03-003**
yokel	**noun**	**2-02-002**
yokel	NN	1-01-001
yokels	NNS	1-01-001
Yokel	**NP**	**1-01-001**
Yoknapatawpha	**prop. noun**	**2-01-001**
Yoknapatawpha	NP	0-00-000
Yoknapatawpha	NP-TL	2-01-001
Yokosuka	**NP**	**3-01-001**
Yokuts	**prop. noun**	**8-01-001**
Yokuts	NP	7-01-001
Yok.	NP	1-01-001
yolk	**NN**	**1-01-001**
yon	**RB**	**1-01-001**
yonder	**RB**	**1-01-001**
Yoneda	**NP**	**2-01-001**
Yonkers	**NP**	**1-01-001**
yooee	**UH**	**1-01-001**
Yoorick	**NP**	**1-01-001**
yore	**NN**	**1-01-001**
yori	**FW-NNS**	**1-01-001**
York	**prop. noun**	**312-13-127**
York	NP	1-01-001
York	NP-TL	304-13-125
York's	NP$	0-00-000
York's	NP$-TL	7-07-007
Yorker	**prop. noun**	**10-06-007**
Yorker	NP	0-00-000
Yorker	NP-TL	7-05-005
Yorker's	NP$	1-01-001
Yorkers	NPS	1-01-001
Yorkers	NPS-TL	1-01-001
Yorktown	**prop. noun**	**2-02-002**
Yorktown	NP	1-01-001
Yorktown	NP-TL	1-01-001
Yosemite	**prop. noun**	**3-01-001**
Yosemite	NP	2-01-001
Yosemite	NP-TL	1-01-001
Yoshimoto	**prop. noun**	**1-01-001**
Yoshimoto's	NP$	1-01-001
you	**pers. pro.**	**4620-15-313**
you	PPSS	2378-15-281
y'all	PPSS	5-02-002
ya	PPSS	3-03-003
ye	PPSS	9-05-006
you'uns	PPSS	1-01-001
yow	PPSS	5-01-001
yuh	PPSS	2-02-002
you	PPSS-HL	1-01-001
you	PPSS-NC	7-02-003
You	PPSS-TL	4-03-003
you'd	PPSS+HVD	11-05-009
you'd	PPSS+MD	25-08-022
you'll	PPSS+MD	90-10-055
you're	PPSS+BER	148-12-074
y're	PPSS+BER	2-01-001
ye're	PPSS+BER	2-01-001
You're	PPSS+BER	1-01-001
you're	PPSS+BER-NC	1-01-001
You're	PPSS+BER-TL	1-01-001
you's	PPSS+BEZ	1-01-001
you've	PPSS+HV	66-11-040
You've	PPSS+HV-TL	1-01-001
y'know	PPSS+VB	2-01-002
'you	+PPSS	1-01-001
whaddya	+PPSS	2-01-001
willya	+PPSS	1-01-001
you	PPO	890-15-212
u	PPO	1-01-001
ya	PPO	1-01-001
ye	PPO	1-01-001
you	PPO-HL	1-01-001
you	PPO-NC	4-01-002
You	PPO-TL	2-02-002
your	PP$	912-15-199

Word	Tag	Count
you (cont.):		
y'r	PP$	1-01-001
yore	PP$	1-01-001
your	PP$-HL	4-02-004
Your	PP$-TL	7-04-007
yours	PP$$	25-11-020
young	**adjective**	**375-15-187**
young	JJ	363-15-183
young	JJ-NC	2-01-001
Young	JJ-TL	10-04-008
young	**noun**	**3-03-003**
young	NN	2-02-002
Young	NN-TL	1-01-001
Young	**prop. noun**	**10-04-006**
Young	NP	7-03-004
Young's	NP$	3-03-003
younger	**comp. adj.**	**44-13-035**
younger	JJR	41-13-033
younguh	JJR	1-01-001
younger	JJR-HL	1-01-001
Younger	JJR-TL	1-01-001
Younger	**NP**	**1-01-001**
youngest	**sup. adj.**	**14-06-013**
youngest	JJT	12-06-011
yongst	JJT	1-01-001
Youngest	JJT-TL	1-01-001
youngish	**JJ**	**2-02-002**
youngster	**noun**	**27-08-018**
youngster	NN	8-06-006
youngster's	NN$	1-01-001
youngsters	NNS	16-06-014
youngsters	NNS-HL	2-02-002
yourself	**PPL**	**67-12-052**
yourselves	**PPLS**	**8-05-005**
youth	**noun**	**93-14-050**
youth	NN	76-14-042
Youth	NN-TL	5-02-003
youth's	NN$	0-00-000
Youths	NN$-TL	1-01-001
youth	NNS	1-01-001
youths	NNS	10-05-006
youthful	**JJ**	**12-06-010**
Yuba	**prop. noun**	**2-01-001**
Yuba	NP	0-00-000
Yuba	NP-TL	2-01-001
Yucatan	**prop. noun**	**1-01-001**
Yucatan	NP	0-00-000
Yucatan	NP-TL	1-01-001
yucca	**NN**	**1-01-001**
Yugoslav	**adjective**	**7-01-001**
Yugoslav	JJ	0-00-000
Yugoslav	JJ-TL	7-01-001
Yugoslav	**NP**	**1-01-001**
Yugoslavia	**prop. noun**	**5-04-004**
Yugoslavia	NP	3-03-003
Yugoslavia	NP-TL	2-01-001
Yujobo	**NP**	**1-01-001**
Yuki	**NP**	**1-01-001**
Yum-Yum	**prop. noun**	**1-01-001**
Yum-Yum	NP	0-00-000
Yum-Yum	NP-TL	1-01-001
Yuri	**NP**	**6-03-004**
Yurochka	**NP**	**1-01-001**
Yvette	**NP**	**2-02-002**

Z

Word	Tag	Count
Zabel	**NP**	**1-01-001**
Zachrisson	**prop. noun**	**2-01-001**
Zachrisson	NP	1-01-001
Zachrisson's	NP$	1-01-001
Zadel	**NP**	**1-01-001**
Zamiatin	**prop. noun**	**1-01-001**
Zamiatin's	NP$	1-01-001
Zanzibar	**NP**	**1-01-001**
Zapala	**NP**	**1-01-001**
Zaporogian	**JJ**	**1-01-001**
Zara	**NP**	**1-01-001**
Zaroubin	**NP**	**1-01-001**
zeal	**noun**	**8-06-008**
zeal	NN	7-06-007
zeal	NN-HL	1-01-001
Zealand	**prop. noun**	**3-03-003**
Zealand	NP	0-00-000
Zealand	NP-TL	3-03-003
zealot	**NN**	**1-01-001**
zealous	**JJ**	**4-02-003**
zealously	**QL**	**1-01-001**
zealously	**RB**	**2-02-002**
Zebek	**NP**	**1-01-001**
zebra	**NN**	**1-01-001**
Zeffirelli	**NP**	**1-01-001**
Zeising	**NP**	**1-01-001**
Zeiss	**NP**	**2-01-001**
Zeitgeist	**FW-NN**	**1-01-001**
Zeme	**prop. noun**	**1-01-001**
Zeme	NP	0-00-000
Zeme	NP-TL	1-01-001
Zemlinsky	**NP**	**2-01-001**
Zemlya	**NP**	**1-01-001**
Zen	**NP**	**26-03-003**
Zend-Avesta	**NP**	**1-01-001**
Zendo	**NP**	**2-01-001**
zenith	**noun**	**6-02-002**
zenith	NN	1-01-001
Zenith	NN-TL	5-01-001
Zennist	**NP**	**1-01-001**
zero	**CD**	**17-04-009**
zero	**noun**	**9-03-005**
zero	NN	6-03-004
Zero	NN-TL	1-01-001
zeros	NNS	2-02-002
zero	**verb**	**1-01-001**
zeroed	VBN	1-01-001
zero-magnitude	**NN**	**2-01-001**
zest	**NN**	**5-04-005**
Zhitkov	**NP**	**1-01-001**
Zhitzhakli	**NP**	**1-01-001**
Zhok	**NP**	**1-01-001**
Ziegfeld	**prop. noun**	**2-01-001**
Ziegfeld	NP	0-00-000
Ziegfeld	NP-TL	2-01-001
Ziffren	**NP**	**2-01-001**
Ziggy	**NP**	**1-01-001**
zigzag	**verb**	**4-02-004**
zigzagging	VBG	4-02-004
Ziminska-Sygietynska	**NP**	**1-01-001**
Zimmerman	**NP**	**3-01-001**
zinc	**NN**	**10-04-005**
zing	**NP**	**8-01-001**
zingggg-O	**UH**	**1-01-001**
Zinman	**NP**	**1-01-001**
Zion	**prop. noun**	**6-03-003**
Zion	NP	5-02-002
Zion	NP-TL	1-01-001
Zionism	**NP**	**1-01-001**
Zionist	**prop. noun**	**1-01-001**
Zionists	NPS	1-01-001
zip	**verb**	**2-02-002**
zip	VB	1-01-001
zipped	VBD	1-01-001
zipper	**NN**	**1-01-001**
Ziraldo	**NP**	**1-01-001**
zloty	**noun**	**1-01-001**
zlotys	NNS	1-01-001
zodiacal	**JJ**	**3-02-002**
Zoe	**NP**	**1-01-001**
zombie	**noun**	**2-02-002**
zombie	NN	1-01-001
zombies	NNS	1-01-001
zone	**noun**	**14-06-010**
zone	NN	10-05-007
Zone	NN-TL	1-01-001
zones	NNS	3-03-003
zone	**verb**	**6-04-005**
zoned	VBN	1-01-001
zoning	VBG	4-03-004
Zoning	VBG-TL	1-01-001
zoning	**NN**	**1-01-001**
zoo	**noun**	**9-05-007**
zoo	NN	6-03-005
Zoo	NN-TL	3-02-002
Zooey	**prop. noun**	**1-01-001**

Zooey (cont.):		
Zooey	NP	0-00-000
Zooey	NP-HL	1-01-001
zoologist	**NN**	**2-02-002**
zoology	**NN**	**1-01-001**
zoom	**verb**	**3-02-003**
zooms	VBZ	1-01-001
zoomed	VBD	1-01-001
zooming	VBG	1-01-001
zoooop	**UH**	**1-01-001**
zorrillas	**FW-NNS**	**1-01-001**
zounds	**UH**	**2-01-001**
zu	**FW-RB**	**1-01-001**
Zubkovskaya	**NP**	**2-02-002**
zur	**foreign**	**1-01-001**
zur	FW-IN+AT	0-00-000
Zur	FW-IN+AT-TL	1-01-001
zur	**FW-NN**	**1-01-001**
Zurcher	**NP**	**2-01-001**
Zurich	**NP**	**2-01-001**
zwei	**foreign**	**1-01-001**
zwei	FW-CD	0-00-000
Zwei	FW-CD-TL	1-01-001
Zworykin	**NP**	**2-01-001**

IV

Rank List

This section presents the rank list of lemmas, i.e., a list, in descending order of frequency, of the set of grammatical words belonging to the same major word class. As in Section III, each lemma is represented here by a single entry form, as defined in Section I. The reader should note especially that this rank list gives no information about the frequency of individual grammatical forms belonging to the respective lemmas. So, for example, the lemma represented by the entry GO gives the total frequency for all forms, i.e., the base *go*, the third person singular of the present tense *goes*, the past tense *went*, the participle or gerund *going*, and the past participle *gone*, with their spelling variants. The total frequency for the entry GO in the rank list is thus the same as the frequency listed opposite the lemma entry in the alphabetical lemmatized list in Section III, namely 1844.

The reader interested in the frequency of individual forms can, of course, locate them in the frequency list in Section III, where the lemmas appear in alphabetic order. Although a rank list of the frequencies of all forms has not been included in this book because it would have required several hundred additional pages, such a list is available to all interested readers on computer-processible magnetic tape or in printout form; for full information see the Concluding Remarks at the end of this book.

In assembling any rank list, even from a representative corpus consisting of a wide variety of samples and genre categories, the question arises of whether the actual frequency of an item in the data base should be considered in the ranking process without further adjustments, or whether its frequency distribution among the various subdivisions of the data base should also be taken into account. To illustrate the nature of the problem, let us assume that there are two lemmas with exactly the same overall frequency, for example 300. Let us further assume that one lemma is distributed evenly among all the genres of the corpus, i.e., has the same *relative* frequency in each genre subdivision. (It is relative frequency, i.e., the percentage of the text accounted for by a particular lemma, rather than the absolute frequency in a genre that is important in considering distribution. The reason for this, of course, lies in the fact that the genre subdivisions are not equal in size.) And let us assume, on the other hand, that all of the 300 ocurrences of the second lemma are found in a single genre. Because of the structure of our data base and the selection process used in assembling it, extreme cases like these do not actually occur in our corpus. Nevertheless, when it comes to lemmas of somewhat lower frequency, as for example 40, distributional differences become quite apparent. There are altogether 62 different lemmas of frequency 40 in the corpus; two of them, the nouns ELECTRON and DESEGREGATION, occur in only four genres, while five lemmas of this frequency are each found in 13 of the 15 genres represented in the corpus. These are the verbs DESIRE and PRACTICE, the adjectives PROMINENT and ATTRACTIVE, and the numeral ELEVEN. Even a high frequency word may sometimes fail to occur in a particular genre. For example, the noun HOUSE, which has a frequency of 662 in the corpus, occurs in only 14 genres.

Distributional facts like these raise the question of how these differences should be reflected in a rank list of lemmas, or if they should affect the structure of the rank list at all. In other words, the question of calculating an *adjusted frequency* for each lemma, reflecting the dispersion of the lemma in the data base, needs careful consideration. If a frequency rank list is to be, in some sense, an indicator of the "usefulness" of a particular word, whether for general purposes in the investigation of linguistic performance and in dictionary construction, or for more specialized reasons, such as psycholinguistic experiments or pedagogical considerations in language teaching, then dispersion requires attention.

The problem of adjusting the actual frequencies of an item to reflect its distribution in the various subsections of the sampled data has been extensively discussed by linguists interested in the statistical properties of language. The most satisfactory approaches have been proposed by Juilland and Chang-Rodriguez (1964) in their work on the frequency of Spanish vocabulary and by Rosengren (1972) in her study of the vocabulary frequency in German newspapers.

The adjusted frequency, as computed by Juilland and Chang-Rodriguez, is the product of the actual frequency of an item and the dispersion value D. The dispersion D is calculated as follows:

$$D = 1 - \frac{s}{\bar{x}\,(n - 1)^{1/2}}$$

where s = the standard deviation of the distribution, $\bar{x}$ = the mean frequency per category, and n = the number of categories taken into consideration in determining the dispersion of the item.

As can be seen from the formula, the dispersion value D is based on the coefficient of variation $s/\bar{x}$, which is independent of the actual frequency figure. This coefficient is then divided by $(n\text{-}1)^{1/2}$, which assures that D will have values ranging from 0 to 1. Since this result is then subtracted from 1, the maximum value of the dispersion D, i.e., 1, will be obtained when the occurrences of the item are evenly distributed among the subcategories n; this will then represent the optimal situation as far as the usage of the item is concerned. Conversely, D will be 0 only if the distribution is maximally skewed; this will be the case if all the occurrences of the given item are found in a single subcategory of the data base.

In order to come up with a *coefficient of usage* of an item, and thus its proper place in a rank list, Juilland and Chang-Rodriguez multiply the actual frequency F of an item in the data base by D. The final result is then the adjusted frequency $U = FD$.

Of the possible problems that this calculation of adjusted frequency can present, the most obvious is the fact that U will have the value of 0 whenever the distribution is maximally skewed, i.e., whenever all occurrences of a given item are found in only one subcategory of the examined data base. This will be the case regardless of the actual frequency of the item under consideration. It is thus theoretically possible that U can equal 0 both for an item with a frequency of 50 and an item with a frequency of 1 in the data base, the former because all of its 50 occurrences happen to be in the same subcategory and the latter (the item with but a single occurrence) by definition. No such case actually occurs in our corpus, but there are lemmas in our data base with a frequency of 20 or more (e.g., the noun POLYNOMIAL with 37 occurrences) that are found in a single genre only and for which U would thus have the value of 0 if dispersion were calculated over genres. This property of the U measure is not particularly desirable.

More subtle but perhaps more serious is another defect of the adjusted frequency U. As Muller (1965) pointed out, U does not differentiate between two distributions in which the frequencies are comparable in all categories but one, differing markedly in this last category. To illustrate this point, consider the following example: Assume a data base with five subcategories, with all subcategories equal in size (i.e., in the total number of word tokens), and a series of items with the following distributions:

2	2	2	2	2
3	2	2	2	2
4	2	2	2	2
100	2	2	2	2
.				
.				
.				
n	2	2	2	2

It turns out that for all of the above distributions U will have exactly the same value, namely 10, regardless of the frequency figure in the first category. The reason for this anomaly lies in the fact that the Juilland—Chang-Rodriguez measure actually represents the subtraction from the actual frequency F of the standard deviation s, multiplied by the constant value $n/(n\text{-}1)^{1/2}$, which depends only on the number of categories. This can be shown in the following way: Since $\bar{x} = F/n$ (assuming subcategories of equal size), then it is the case that

$$U = FD$$

$$U = F\left(1 - \frac{s}{\bar{x}\,(n - 1)^{1/2}}\right)$$

$$U = F - \frac{n}{(n - 1)^{1/2}}\,s$$

In the case of 5 categories, the constant $n/(n-1)^{1/2} = 5/(4)^{1/2} = 2.5$. The standard deviation s increases by 0.4 for each frequency increase of 1 in the first (variable) category; for the distribution given above, the standard deviation values are 0, 0.4, 0.8, 1.2, etc. Multiplying the standard deviation by the 2.5 constant yields a value identical to the increase of the frequency in the first category. A subtraction of this value from the actual frequency F then must give the same result for all such distributions, namely 10 in the example cited above.

Muller also pointed out that the U measure does not differentiate between certain distributions where the differences may be important to usage, such as

4-2-1-1-0 versus 3-3-2-0-0

both of which have the U value of 4.61. Moreover, U will reach the actual frequency of an item in a data base only if this actual frequency is some multiple of the number of categories (in our example, a multiple of 5). So, for example, a distribution such as

9 9 9 9 9

will give a U value of 45 (i.e., equal to the actual frequency) but a distribution such as

9 9 9 9 8

a U value of only 43, i.e., 1 less than the actual frequency, which is 44.

Some of the shortcomings of the Juilland—Chang-Rodriguez adjusted frequency value are absent from the "corrected frequency" measure proposed by Rosengren (1972) and attributed by the author to her statistical advisor, J. Lanke of the University of Lund. This measure, which we shall label AF (for *adjusted frequency*), has—in cases of categories of equal size—the following form:

$$AF = \frac{1}{n}\left(\sum_{i=1}^{n} x_i^{1/2}\right)^2$$

where x_i = the frequency of the item in category i, and n = the number of categories.

AF will reach its maximum value when the item has the same frequency in every category; in such a case, the adjusted frequency AF will be exactly the same as the actual frequency of the item in the data base. Whenever the distribution is not even, AF will be smaller than the actual frequency of the item in the data base.

A more general form of the AF measure is required whenever the various categories into which the data base is divided are not of equal size, which is, of course, the case in our corpus. In such cases, we then have

$$AF = \left(\sum_{i=1}^{n} (d_i x_i)^{1/2}\right)^2$$

where d_i = the relative size of category i, x_i = the frequency of an item in category i, and n = the number of categories.

The maximum possible value of AF is the actual frequency of the item, and is reached (as will be shown below) only if the item's distribution is uniform among categories; the minimum value, on the other hand, is never 0, even if the distribution is maximally skewed (because even if the item occurs exclusively in one category in the corpus, then $AF = x_i d_i$, which is never 0). That the maximum value of AF is the actual frequency of the item in the corpus can be shown on the basis of the principle of Schwartz's inequality which, for any two sequences of n elements a and b has the form

$$\left(\sum_{i=1}^{n} a_i b_i\right)^2 \leq \left(\sum_{i=1}^{n} a_i^2\right)\left(\sum_{i=1}^{n} b_i^2\right)$$

Applying this to our AF formula, where $a_i = d_i^{1/2}$ and $b_i = x_i^{1/2}$, we can write:

$$\left(\sum_{i=1}^{n} d_i^{1/2} x_i^{1/2}\right) \leq \left(\sum_{i=1}^{n} d_i\right)\left(\sum_{i=1}^{n} x_i\right)$$

Since $\left(\sum_{i=1}^{n} d_i^{1/2} x_i^{1/2}\right)^2 = AF$, we get

$$AF \leq \left(\sum_{i=1}^{n} d_i\right)\left(\sum_{i=1}^{n} x_i\right)$$

By definition, $\sum_{i=1}^{n} d_i = 1$ because the sum of the relative proportions of the categories must be equal to 1; since $\sum_{i=1}^{n} x_i = F$, we have $AF \leq F$.

Furthermore, in the case where the adjusted frequency equals the actual frequency of the item in the corpus, then the distribution of this item is uniform among the categories. This may be shown as follows. Since, as noted above, the sum of the relative proportions of the categories must equal 1, then $\left(\sum_{i=1}^{n} d_i\right)^2$ must also equal 1, and in the case where $AF = F$, then the following holds true:

$$AF = F\left(\sum_{i=1}^{n} d_i\right)^2$$

$$AF = \left(F^{1/2}\sum_{i=1}^{n} d_i\right)^2$$

$$AF = \left(\sum_{i=1}^{n} d_i F^{1/2}\right)^2$$

$$AF = \left(\sum_{i=1}^{n} (d_i^2\, F)^{1/2}\right)^2$$

$$AF = \left(\sum_{i=1}^{n} (d_i(d_iF))^{1/2}\right)^2$$

Thus $x_i = d_iF$, which means that the number of occurrences of the item in each category is equal to the relative size of that category multiplied by the total frequency of the item in the corpus, and consequently the item occurs with a uniform distribution.

As Rosengren has shown in detail, the *AF* measure also differentiates among distributions with comparable frequency in all categories but one where *U* gives counterintuitive results, as shown above. Nor is *AF* distorted when the actual frequency is not an exact multiple of the number of categories in the data base.

Since the *AF* measure, used by Rosengren, has some advantages over the *U* value proposed by Juilland and Chang-Rodriguez, we have calculated it for all lemmas. The calculation is based on the fifteen genre categories of the corpus, as described in Section I, taking the unequal size of the categories into account.

The rank table, which follows, is organized in two parallel columns: in each column, the rank of each lemma and its entry form, as well as the actual and adjusted frequencies, are given. Whenever two or more lemmas have the same rank (because both their actual and adjusted frequencies are identical), they are given the same rank number and listed alphabetically. In the left hand column, the frequency which determines the rank of a lemma is the actual frequency, and in the right hand column it is the adjusted frequency. The reader can thus determine at a glance how the dispersion of the lemmas among the genres changes their relative ranking.

The rank table, in both columns, includes all items that have an adjusted frequency of 5 or more. It was felt that the ranking of lemmas with *AF* values of less than 5 is not useful enough to justify the expansion of the book by several hundred pages, since the relative rank order of these low frequency items can be assumed to be idiosyncratic to this particular corpus. However, readers interested in the ranking of the 30,000-odd remaining lemmas can obtain the complete list on computer tape or in printout form as noted in the Concluding Remarks.

1	the	article	69975	69792.94
2	be	verb	39175	39109.95
3	of	prep.	36432	35786.01
4	and	co. conj.	28872	28821.11
5	a	article	23073	22984.95
6	in	prep.	20870	20685.17
7	he	pers. pro.	19427	17280.77
8	to	inf. mark.	15025	14990.82
9	have	verb	12458	12192.06
10	to	prep.	11165	11129.57
11	it	pronoun	10942	10836.51
12	for	prep.	8996	8899.55
13	I	pers. pro.	8387	6885.48
14	they	pers. pro.	8284	8162.08
15	with	prep.	7286	7267.37
16	not	neg. adv.	6976	6739.48
17	that	sub. conj.	6468	6373.68
18	on	prep.	6183	6151.18
19	she	pers. pro.	6039	4378.51
20	as	sub. conj.	6029	5982.09
21	at	prep.	5377	5317.20
22	by	prep.	5246	5066.04
23	this	sing. det.	5145	5064.57
24	we	pers. pro.	4865	4699.87
25	you	pers. pro.	4620	3644.51
26	from	prep.	4371	4358.51
27	do	verb	4367	4141.96
28	but	co. conj.	4226	4123.17
29	or	co. conj.	4204	4064.58
30	an	article	3727	3695.88
31	which	wh-det.	3560	3435.25
32	would	modal aux.	3062	2896.00
33	say	verb	2765	2331.97
34	all	pre-quant.	2758	2733.03
35	one	card. num.	2737	2714.29
36	will	modal aux.	2686	2579.81
37	who	wh-pronoun	2678	2592.16
38	that	sing. det.	2455	2328.14
39	when	wh-adverb	2333	2297.18
40	make	verb	2312	2300.46
41	there	ex. subj.	2280	2255.21
42	if	sub. conj.	2199	2165.12
43	can	modal aux.	2192	2121.73
44	man	noun	2110	1954.28
45	what	wh-det.	1955	1874.09
46	time	noun	1901	1885.00
47	go	verb	1844	1584.22
48	no	article	1821	1783.66
49	into	prep.	1790	1746.84
50	could	modal aux.	1782	1635.56
51	up	adv./part.	1712	1578.76
52	other	post-det.	1710	1674.54
53	that	s. wh-pro.	1674	1645.14
54	year	noun	1661	1543.23
55	out	adv./part.	1644	1538.81
56	new	adjective	1635	1537.72
57	some	sg/pl det.	1594	1577.21
58	take	verb	1575	1533.65
59	these	pl. det.	1575	1474.37
60	come	verb	1561	1454.25
61	see	verb	1513	1416.71
62	get	verb	1486	1253.99
63	know	verb	1473	1339.58
64	state	noun	1421	1125.84
65	two	card. num.	1412	1395.39
66	only	adverb	1360	1331.14
67	then	adverb	1348	1276.77
68	any	sg/pl det.	1335	1316.50
69	now	adverb	1314	1265.00
70	may	modal aux.	1307	1142.10
71	than	sub. conj.	1297	1263.93
72	give	verb	1264	1254.43
73	about	prep.	1242	1164.29
74	as	qualifier	1101	1091.71
75	day	noun	1077	1039.88
76	also	adverb	1070	997.80
77	find	verb	1033	1013.11
78	first	ord. num.	1031	1008.71
79	way	noun	1027	1005.38
80	must	modal aux.	1017	991.58
81	use	verb	1016	934.78
82	more	qualifier	1015	969.96
83	like	sub. conj.	1012	887.59
84	even	adverb	997	972.22
85	many	post-det.	997	954.14
86	more	post-det.	990	968.81
87	think	verb	982	842.43
88	such	adjective	978	874.55
89	where	wh-adverb	949	932.76

1	the	article	69975	69792.94
2	be	verb	39175	39109.95
3	of	prep.	36432	35786.01
4	and	co. conj.	28872	28821.11
5	a	article	23073	22984.95
6	in	prep.	20870	20685.17
7	he	pers. pro.	19427	17280.77
8	to	inf. mark.	15025	14990.82
9	have	verb	12458	12192.06
10	to	prep.	11165	11129.57
11	it	pronoun	10942	10836.51
12	for	prep.	8996	8899.55
13	they	pers. pro.	8284	8162.08
14	with	prep.	7286	7267.37
15	I	pers. pro.	8387	6885.48
16	not	neg. adv.	6976	6739.48
17	that	sub. conj.	6468	6373.68
18	on	prep.	6183	6151.18
19	as	sub. conj.	6029	5982.09
20	at	prep.	5377	5317.20
21	by	prep.	5246	5066.04
22	this	sing. det.	5145	5064.57
23	we	pers. pro.	4865	4699.87
24	she	pers. pro.	6039	4378.51
25	from	prep.	4371	4358.51
26	do	verb	4367	4141.96
27	but	co. conj.	4226	4123.17
28	or	co. conj.	4204	4064.58
29	an	article	3727	3695.88
30	you	pers. pro.	4620	3644.51
31	which	wh-det.	3560	3435.25
32	would	modal aux.	3062	2896.00
33	all	pre-quant.	2758	2733.03
34	one	card. num.	2737	2714.29
35	who	wh-pronoun	2678	2592.16
36	will	modal aux.	2686	2579.81
37	say	verb	2765	2331.97
38	that	sing. det.	2455	2328.14
39	make	verb	2312	2300.46
40	when	wh-adverb	2333	2297.18
41	there	ex. subj.	2280	2255.21
42	if	sub. conj.	2199	2165.12
43	can	modal aux.	2192	2121.73
44	man	noun	2110	1954.28
45	time	noun	1901	1885.00
46	what	wh-det.	1955	1874.09
47	no	article	1821	1783.66
48	into	prep.	1790	1746.84
49	other	post-det.	1710	1674.54
50	that	s. wh-pro.	1674	1645.14
51	could	modal aux.	1782	1635.56
52	go	verb	1844	1584.22
53	up	adv./part.	1712	1578.76
54	some	sg/pl det.	1594	1577.21
55	year	noun	1661	1543.23
56	out	adv./part.	1644	1538.81
57	new	adjective	1635	1537.72
58	take	verb	1575	1533.65
59	these	pl. det.	1575	1474.37
60	come	verb	1561	1454.25
61	see	verb	1513	1416.71
62	two	card. num.	1412	1395.39
63	know	verb	1473	1339.58
64	only	adverb	1360	1331.14
65	any	sg/pl det.	1335	1316.50
66	then	adverb	1348	1276.77
67	now	adverb	1314	1265.00
68	than	sub. conj.	1297	1263.93
69	give	verb	1264	1254.43
70	get	verb	1486	1253.99
71	about	prep.	1242	1164.29
72	may	modal aux.	1307	1142.10
73	state	noun	1421	1125.84
74	as	qualifier	1101	1091.71
75	day	noun	1077	1039.88
76	find	verb	1033	1013.11
77	first	ord. num.	1031	1008.71
78	way	noun	1027	1005.38
79	also	adverb	1070	997.80
80	must	modal aux.	1017	991.58
81	even	adverb	997	972.22
82	more	qualifier	1015	969.96
83	more	post-det.	990	968.81
84	many	post-det.	997	954.14
85	use	verb	1016	934.78
86	where	wh-adverb	949	932.76
87	through	prep.	926	914.60
88	so	qualifier	932	888.17
89	like	sub. conj.	1012	887.59

90	so	qualifier	932	888.17
91	through	prep.	926	914.60
92	should	modal aux.	915	876.39
93	people	pl. noun	902	867.35
94	each	sing. det.	878	840.99
95	those	pl. det.	864	855.84
96	Mister	prop. noun	857	713.49
97	over	prep.	843	826.80
98	world	noun	832	759.96
99	seem	verb	831	789.28
100	just	adverb	795	703.32
101	life	noun	772	715.94
102	become	verb	765	733.03
103	tell	verb	759	644.23
104	here	adverb	757	724.92
105	own	adjective	751	732.76
106	back	adverb	734	607.46
107	both	p.q./d.cj.	731	719.52
108	good	adjective	731	691.20
109	between	prep.	729	696.83
110	still	adverb	724	696.59
111	hand	noun	717	660.18
112	because	sub. conj.	712	690.78
113	very	qualifier	703	689.07
114	thing	noun	702	649.53
115	after	prep.	699	688.15
116	down	adv./part.	698	603.66
117	never	adverb	694	639.15
118	another	sing. det.	690	678.92
119	under	prep.	688	663.48
120	school	noun	687	597.74
121	same	post-det.	686	668.66
122	work	noun	680	662.45
123	how	wh-adverb	675	634.90
124	old	adjective	673	600.59
125	house	noun	662	607.23
126	might	modal aux.	660	632.64
127	number	noun	658	568.15
128	well	adverb	656	645.65
129	great	adjective	653	629.85
130	leave	verb	650	604.80
131	most	qualifier	648	618.18
132	feel	verb	643	569.61
133	show	verb	640	607.36
134	want	verb	631	557.07
135	call	verb	627	605.98
136	against	prep.	625	605.11
137	one	nom. pro.	622	575.56
138	child	noun	620	577.41
139	last	post-det.	613	550.16
140	ask	verb	612	543.69
141	part	noun	610	593.62
142	three	card. num.	610	591.47
143	himself	refl. pro.	606	533.04
144	few	post-det.	601	588.03
145	while	sub. conj.	600	596.14
146	during	prep.	588	548.84
147	place	noun	584	567.77
148	begin	verb	583	573.71
149	without	prep.	583	571.82
150	again	adverb	580	532.63
151	so	adverb	574	553.56
152	about	adv./part.	574	552.44
153	there	adverb	571	475.17
154	turn	verb	566	503.78
155	area	noun	562	458.95
156	write	verb	561	497.18
157	problem	noun	560	500.28
158	on	adv./part.	559	513.93
159	too	qualifier	550	520.74
160	word	noun	549	521.38
161	system	noun	548	419.77
162	long	adjective	541	494.24
163	follow	verb	540	523.58
164	small	adjective	537	519.17
165	Mrs.	prop. noun	536	355.71
166	American	adjective	535	455.26
167	fact	noun	534	495.47
168	program	noun	529	365.85
169	course	noun	527	511.35
170	eye	noun	524	392.40
171	keep	verb	523	495.33
172	city	noun	521	476.78
173	put	verb	513	488.46
174	group	noun	512	469.39
175	hold	verb	509	500.01
176	case	noun	503	468.73
177	than	prep.	497	465.44
178	much	post-det.	496	489.80

90	should	modal aux.	915	876.39
91	such	adjective	978	874.55
92	people	pl. noun	902	867.35
93	those	pl. det.	864	855.84
94	think	verb	982	842.43
95	each	sing. det.	878	840.99
96	over	prep.	843	826.80
97	seem	verb	831	789.28
98	world	noun	832	759.96
99	become	verb	765	733.03
100	own	adjective	751	732.76
101	here	adverb	757	724.92
102	both	p.q./d.cj.	731	719.52
103	life	noun	772	715.94
104	Mister	prop. noun	857	713.49
105	just	adverb	795	703.32
106	between	prep.	729	696.83
107	still	adverb	724	696.59
108	good	adjective	731	691.20
109	because	sub. conj.	712	690.78
110	very	qualifier	703	689.07
111	after	prep.	699	688.15
112	another	sing. det.	690	678.92
113	same	post-det.	686	668.66
114	under	prep.	688	663.48
115	work	noun	680	662.45
116	hand	noun	717	660.18
117	thing	noun	702	649.53
118	well	adverb	656	645.65
119	tell	verb	759	644.23
120	never	adverb	694	639.15
121	how	wh-adverb	675	634.90
122	might	modal aux.	660	632.64
123	great	adjective	653	629.85
124	most	qualifier	648	618.18
125	back	adverb	734	607.46
126	show	verb	640	607.36
127	house	noun	662	607.23
128	call	verb	627	605.98
129	against	prep.	625	605.11
130	leave	verb	650	604.80
131	down	adv./part.	698	603.66
132	old	adjective	673	600.59
133	school	noun	687	597.74
134	while	sub. conj.	600	596.14
135	part	noun	610	593.62
136	three	card. num.	610	591.47
137	few	post-det.	601	588.03
138	child	noun	620	577.41
139	one	nom. pro.	622	575.56
140	begin	verb	583	573.71
141	without	prep.	583	571.82
142	feel	verb	643	569.61
143	number	noun	658	568.15
144	place	noun	584	567.77
145	want	verb	631	557.07
146	so	adverb	574	553.56
147	about	adv./part.	574	552.44
148	last	post-det.	613	550.16
149	during	prep.	588	548.84
150	ask	verb	612	543.69
151	himself	refl. pro.	606	533.04
152	again	adverb	580	532.63
153	follow	verb	540	523.58
154	word	noun	549	521.38
155	too	qualifier	550	520.74
156	small	adjective	537	519.17
157	on	adv./part.	559	513.93
158	course	noun	527	511.35
159	turn	verb	566	503.78
160	problem	noun	560	500.28
161	hold	verb	509	500.01
162	write	verb	561	497.18
163	fact	noun	534	495.47
164	keep	verb	523	495.33
165	long	adjective	541	494.24
166	much	post-det.	496	489.80
167	put	verb	513	488.46
168	every	article	492	483.02
169	work	verb	496	479.15
170	city	noun	521	476.78
171	there	adverb	571	475.17
172	bring	verb	488	472.92
173	for	sub. conj.	494	472.78
174	group	noun	512	469.39
175	case	noun	503	468.73
176	than	prep.	497	465.44
177	area	noun	562	458.95
178	line	noun	491	458.40

179	work	verb	496	479.15
180	government	noun	495	357.13
181	unite	verb	495	349.86
182	for	sub. conj.	494	472.78
183	point	noun	493	455.60
184	every	article	492	483.02
185	war	noun	492	441.24
186	line	noun	491	458.40
187	country	noun	491	448.02
188	bring	verb	488	472.92
189	water	noun	486	428.09
190	provide	verb	486	398.90
191	let	verb	482	440.57
192	off	adv./part.	482	423.12
193	so	sub. conj.	479	452.58
194	most	post-det.	478	455.41
195	side	noun	476	431.15
196	live	verb	472	446.44
197	try	verb	472	430.25
198	stand	verb	468	414.33
199	woman	noun	467	404.83
200	member	noun	464	387.18
201	away	adverb	458	401.89
202	night	noun	457	376.12
203	always	adverb	456	421.76
204	high	adjective	454	430.29
205	upon	prep.	454	422.30
206	something	nom. pro.	454	394.86
207	out	prep.	454	348.21
208	company	noun	453	403.12
209	church	noun	451	288.53
210	before	sub. conj.	450	430.07
211	head	noun	449	375.79
212	service	noun	448	337.45
213	move	verb	447	417.20
214	form	noun	441	370.29
215	room	noun	439	374.98
216	hear	verb	433	364.93
217	run	verb	431	396.88
218	week	noun	425	373.59
219	president	noun	424	292.71
220	end	noun	423	416.20
221	since	sub. conj.	420	400.61
222	once	adverb	419	384.00
223	nothing	nom. pro.	419	382.73
224	order	noun	416	389.25
225	need	verb	413	396.84
226	business	noun	412	358.85
227	boy	noun	409	336.87
228	before	prep.	408	395.94
229	interest	noun	408	377.56
230	though	sub. conj.	407	389.14
231	family	noun	405	384.86
232	why	wh-adverb	404	358.28
233	power	noun	404	349.89
234	however	adverb	402	287.36
235	little	post-det.	397	370.28
236	car	noun	393	295.62
237	over	adv./part.	392	361.91
238	figure	noun	389	343.31
239	use	noun	389	309.36
240	law	noun	387	332.03
241	toward	prep.	386	368.47
242	start	verb	386	358.34
243	value	noun	383	294.62
244	John	prop. noun	381	316.24
245	social	adjective	380	317.95
246	face	noun	379	290.87
247	several	post-det.	378	361.55
248	question	noun	378	356.72
249	general	adjective	378	307.34
250	development	noun	377	253.97
251	mean	verb	376	357.43
252	young	adjective	375	350.04
253	possible	adjective	374	348.36
254	girl	noun	374	320.58
255	set	verb	372	363.93
256	national	adjective	372	296.79
257	force	noun	371	324.90
258	per	prep.	370	247.95
259	among	prep.	369	354.41
260	important	adjective	369	342.45
261	often	adverb	369	338.89
262	only	post-det.	365	355.39
263	name	noun	365	354.62
264	foot	noun	361	323.93
265	after	sub. conj.	360	348.19
266	four	card. num.	360	337.00
267	action	noun	359	325.12

179	point	noun	493	455.60
180	most	post-det.	478	455.41
181	American	adjective	535	455.26
182	so	sub. conj.	479	452.58
183	country	noun	491	448.02
184	live	verb	472	446.44
185	war	noun	492	441.24
186	let	verb	482	440.57
187	side	noun	476	431.15
188	high	adjective	454	430.29
189	try	verb	472	430.25
190	before	sub. conj.	450	430.07
191	water	noun	486	428.09
192	off	adv./part.	482	423.12
193	upon	prep.	454	422.30
194	always	adverb	456	421.76
195	system	noun	548	419.77
196	move	verb	447	417.20
197	end	noun	423	416.20
198	stand	verb	468	414.33
199	woman	noun	467	404.83
200	company	noun	453	403.12
201	away	adverb	458	401.89
202	since	sub. conj.	420	400.61
203	provide	verb	486	398.90
204	run	verb	431	396.88
205	need	verb	413	396.84
206	before	prep.	408	395.94
207	something	nom. pro.	454	394.86
208	eye	noun	524	392.40
209	order	noun	416	389.25
210	though	sub. conj.	407	389.14
211	member	noun	464	387.18
212	family	noun	405	384.86
213	once	adverb	419	384.00
214	nothing	nom. pro.	419	382.73
215	interest	noun	408	377.56
216	night	noun	457	376.12
217	head	noun	449	375.79
218	room	noun	439	374.98
219	week	noun	425	373.59
220	form	noun	441	370.29
221	little	post-det.	397	370.28
222	toward	prep.	386	368.47
223	program	noun	529	365.85
224	hear	verb	433	364.93
225	set	verb	372	363.93
226	over	adv./part.	392	361.91
227	several	post-det.	378	361.55
228	business	noun	412	358.85
229	start	verb	386	358.34
230	why	wh-adverb	404	358.28
231	mean	verb	376	357.43
232	government	noun	495	357.13
233	question	noun	378	356.72
234	Mrs.	prop. noun	536	355.71
235	only	post-det.	365	355.39
236	name	noun	365	354.62
237	among	prep.	369	354.41
238	young	adjective	375	350.04
239	power	noun	404	349.89
240	unite	verb	495	349.86
241	possible	adjective	374	348.36
242	out	prep.	454	348.21
243	after	sub. conj.	360	348.19
244	figure	noun	389	343.31
245	important	adjective	369	342.45
246	help	verb	352	341.34
247	often	adverb	369	338.89
248	service	noun	448	337.45
249	four	card. num.	360	337.00
250	boy	noun	409	336.87
251	large	adjective	354	333.67
252	later	comp. adv.	342	333.55
253	law	noun	387	332.03
254	matter	noun	342	331.99
255	reason	noun	340	331.88
256	meet	verb	339	330.31
257	appear	verb	353	330.30
258	until	sub. conj.	338	327.22
259	action	noun	359	325.12
260	within	prep.	351	325.01
261	force	noun	371	324.90
262	continue	verb	342	324.39
263	foot	noun	361	323.93
264	body	noun	342	323.43
265	second	ord. num.	334	323.40
266	kind	noun	333	322.29
267	field	noun	333	322.19

268	big	adjective	359	304.03
269	large	adjective	354	333.67
270	nation	noun	354	275.84
271	appear	verb	353	330.30
272	help	verb	352	341.34
273	within	prep.	351	325.01
274	student	noun	351	290.12
275	mind	noun	350	317.36
276	doctor	noun	349	285.99
277	cost	noun	349	221.42
278	door	noun	348	240.33
279	example	noun	345	291.81
280	later	comp. adv.	342	333.55
281	matter	noun	342	331.99
282	continue	verb	342	324.39
283	body	noun	342	323.43
284	reason	noun	340	331.88
285	require	verb	340	265.63
286	meet	verb	339	330.31
287	until	sub. conj.	338	327.22
288	ever	adverb	337	312.95
289	idea	noun	337	307.21
290	believe	verb	336	321.85
291	expect	verb	335	316.09
292	God	prop. noun	335	203.11
293	second	ord. num.	334	323.40
294	white	adjective	334	299.55
295	kind	noun	333	322.29
296	field	noun	333	322.19
297	play	verb	333	288.29
298	increase	verb	332	280.03
299	first	adverb	330	318.31
300	today	adv. noun	330	299.48
301	result	noun	329	282.25
302	around	prep.	327	302.29
303	month	noun	327	300.42
304	other	noun	325	321.01
305	least	post-det.	325	316.74
306	hour	noun	325	308.26
307	pay	verb	325	293.97
308	reach	verb	324	310.53
309	although	sub. conj.	323	307.17
310	street	noun	323	273.57
311	develop	verb	322	277.57
312	little	adjective	318	275.25
313	consider	verb	317	284.48
314	remain	verb	314	305.76
315	type	noun	314	240.97
316	sit	verb	314	235.73
317	lead	verb	313	304.22
318	sense	noun	313	282.33
319	different	adjective	312	288.01
320	York	prop. noun	312	259.53
321	period	noun	312	254.12
322	such	pre-qual.	310	297.89
323	home	adv. noun	308	252.54
324	college	noun	308	250.52
325	perhaps	adverb	307	291.23
326	effect	noun	307	272.57
327	light	noun	306	284.69
328	experience	noun	306	263.35
329	public	adjective	306	251.37
330	next	post-det.	305	296.53
331	study	noun	305	248.59
332	carry	verb	304	297.25
333	itself	refl. pro.	304	282.94
334	rate	noun	303	205.23
335	job	noun	302	276.23
336	office	noun	301	267.16
337	moment	noun	301	252.40
338	home	noun	301	230.14
339	grow	verb	300	280.22
340	serve	verb	300	275.68
341	person	noun	299	289.47
342	thus	adverb	299	232.12
343	pass	verb	298	286.71
344	history	noun	297	237.91
345	receive	verb	294	267.87
346	like	verb	294	266.11
347	friend	noun	294	259.91
348	best	sup. adj.	292	283.03
349	book	noun	292	256.92
350	class	noun	292	236.89
351	add	verb	291	271.49
352	position	noun	291	270.72
353	policy	noun	290	199.74
354	five	card. num.	287	274.39
355	walk	verb	287	210.22
356	whether	sub. conj.	286	276.16

268	believe	verb	336	321.85
269	other	noun	325	321.01
270	girl	noun	374	320.58
271	first	adverb	330	318.31
272	social	adjective	380	317.95
273	mind	noun	350	317.36
274	least	post-det.	325	316.74
275	John	prop. noun	381	316.24
276	expect	verb	335	316.09
277	ever	adverb	337	312.95
278	reach	verb	324	310.53
279	use	noun	389	309.36
280	hour	noun	325	308.26
281	general	adjective	378	307.34
282	idea	noun	337	307.21
283	although	sub. conj.	323	307.17
284	remain	verb	314	305.76
285	lead	verb	313	304.22
286	big	adjective	359	304.03
287	around	prep.	327	302.29
288	month	noun	327	300.42
289	white	adjective	334	299.55
290	today	adv. noun	330	299.48
291	such	pre-qual.	310	297.89
292	carry	verb	304	297.25
293	national	adjective	372	296.79
294	next	post-det.	305	296.53
295	car	noun	393	295.62
296	value	noun	383	294.62
297	pay	verb	325	293.97
298	president	noun	424	292.71
299	example	noun	345	291.81
300	perhaps	adverb	307	291.23
301	face	noun	379	290.87
302	student	noun	351	290.12
303	person	noun	299	289.47
304	church	noun	451	288.53
305	play	verb	333	288.29
306	different	adjective	312	288.01
307	however	adverb	402	287.36
308	pass	verb	298	286.71
309	doctor	noun	349	285.99
310	light	noun	306	284.69
311	consider	verb	317	284.48
312	best	sup. adj.	292	283.03
313	itself	refl. pro.	304	282.94
314	sense	noun	313	282.33
315	result	noun	329	282.25
316	grow	verb	300	280.22
317	increase	verb	332	280.03
318	develop	verb	322	277.57
319	job	noun	302	276.23
320	whether	sub. conj.	286	276.16
321	nation	noun	354	275.84
322	serve	verb	300	275.68
323	little	adjective	318	275.25
324	five	card. num.	287	274.39
325	street	noun	323	273.57
326	effect	noun	307	272.57
327	add	verb	291	271.49
328	position	noun	291	270.72
329	receive	verb	294	267.87
330	already	adverb	272	267.84
331	office	noun	301	267.16
332	like	verb	294	266.11
333	require	verb	340	265.63
334	read	verb	274	265.51
335	yet	adverb	283	264.02
336	experience	noun	306	263.35
337	friend	noun	294	259.91
338	York	prop. noun	312	259.53
339	almost	adverb	276	258.89
340	together	adverb	268	258.05
341	themselves	refl. pro.	271	257.92
342	happen	verb	278	257.56
343	town	noun	281	257.37
344	book	noun	292	256.92
345	too	adverb	285	256.63
346	probably	adverb	263	255.79
347	period	noun	312	254.12
348	development	noun	377	253.97
349	lose	verb	274	253.61
350	home	adv. noun	308	252.54
351	moment	noun	301	252.40
352	party	noun	283	251.71
353	speak	verb	274	251.59
354	public	adjective	306	251.37
355	age	noun	275	251.08
356	college	noun	308	250.52

357	court	noun	286	225.93
358	too	adverb	285	256.63
359	board	noun	285	225.81
360	death	noun	284	245.03
361	change	noun	284	244.70
362	method	noun	284	212.88
363	yet	adverb	283	264.02
364	party	noun	283	251.71
365	town	noun	281	257.37
366	society	noun	281	242.12
367	anything	nom. pro.	281	241.78
368	mother	noun	280	214.34
369	local	adjective	279	233.18
370	happen	verb	278	257.56
371	plan	noun	278	245.34
372	almost	adverb	276	258.89
373	section	noun	276	191.73
374	age	noun	275	251.08
375	money	noun	275	249.80
376	talk	verb	275	232.41
377	community	noun	275	214.69
378	read	verb	274	265.51
379	lose	verb	274	253.61
380	speak	verb	274	251.59
381	determine	verb	274	228.08
382	already	adverb	272	267.84
383	effort	noun	272	247.23
384	department	noun	272	179.40
385	themselves	refl. pro.	271	257.92
386	condition	noun	271	227.75
387	information	noun	269	213.20
388	material	noun	269	207.14
389	shall	modal aux.	269	206.07
390	together	adverb	268	258.05
391	wife	noun	265	218.78
392	level	noun	265	215.69
393	voice	noun	265	205.80
394	probably	adverb	263	255.79
395	wait	verb	263	186.80
396	human	adjective	263	183.08
397	art	noun	262	213.77
398	road	noun	262	213.69
399	center	noun	261	246.02
400	air	noun	260	249.56
401	letter	noun	260	239.08
402	include	verb	260	206.53
403	whole	adjective	259	249.96
404	open	verb	259	232.00
405	across	prep.	258	232.24
406	political	adjective	258	200.33
407	university	noun	256	200.98
408	far	adverb	254	246.93
409	early	adjective	254	243.40
410	learn	verb	254	242.37
411	century	noun	254	212.56
412	send	verb	253	232.76
413	need	noun	253	228.88
414	process	noun	252	199.29
415	remember	verb	250	218.19
416	involve	verb	249	233.43
417	build	verb	249	227.06
418	situation	noun	247	229.80
419	enough	post-qual.	247	229.53
420	federal	adjective	247	159.23
421	ago	adverb	246	223.66
422	available	adjective	246	185.24
423	special	adjective	245	221.20
424	cut	verb	245	214.71
425	indicate	verb	244	213.50
426	economic	adjective	243	173.27
427	open	adjective	242	225.63
428	minute	noun	242	215.91
429	table	noun	242	215.50
430	all	qualifier	242	202.74
431	real	adjective	241	228.44
432	tax	noun	241	124.37
433	understand	verb	240	229.78
434	father	noun	240	215.83
435	stop	verb	240	199.13
436	around	adverb	240	180.17
437	fall	verb	239	226.82
438	purpose	noun	239	202.72
439	better	comp. adj.	238	228.93
440	half	pre-quant.	238	222.74
441	free	adjective	238	222.51
442	act	noun	237	191.80
443	term	noun	236	214.01
444	place	verb	233	210.51
445	Miss	prop. noun	233	171.73

357	whole	adjective	259	249.96
358	money	noun	275	249.80
359	air	noun	260	249.56
360	study	noun	305	248.59
361	per	prep.	370	247.95
362	effort	noun	272	247.23
363	far	adverb	254	246.93
364	center	noun	261	246.02
365	plan	noun	278	245.34
366	death	noun	284	245.03
367	change	noun	284	244.70
368	early	adjective	254	243.40
369	learn	verb	254	242.37
370	society	noun	281	242.12
371	anything	nom. pro.	281	241.78
372	type	noun	314	240.97
373	door	noun	348	240.33
374	letter	noun	260	239.08
375	history	noun	297	237.91
376	class	noun	292	236.89
377	sit	verb	314	235.73
378	involve	verb	249	233.43
379	local	adjective	279	233.18
380	send	verb	253	232.76
381	talk	verb	275	232.41
382	across	prep.	258	232.24
383	thus	adverb	299	232.12
384	open	verb	259	232.00
385	home	noun	301	230.14
386	situation	noun	247	229.80
387	understand	verb	240	229.78
388	enough	post-qual.	247	229.53
389	better	comp. adj.	238	228.93
390	need	noun	253	228.88
391	real	adjective	241	228.44
392	determine	verb	274	228.08
393	condition	noun	271	227.75
394	build	verb	249	227.06
395	fall	verb	239	226.82
396	court	noun	286	225.93
397	board	noun	285	225.81
398	open	adjective	242	225.63
399	ago	adverb	246	223.66
400	half	pre-quant.	238	222.74
401	free	adjective	238	222.51
402	cost	noun	349	221.42
403	special	adjective	245	221.20
404	wife	noun	265	218.78
405	remember	verb	250	218.19
406	change	verb	225	218.07
407	minute	noun	242	215.91
408	much	qualifier	229	215.90
409	father	noun	240	215.83
410	level	noun	265	215.69
411	table	noun	242	215.50
412	step	noun	228	215.24
413	return	verb	232	215.02
414	ground	noun	227	214.77
415	cut	verb	245	214.71
416	community	noun	275	214.69
417	full	adjective	221	214.55
418	mother	noun	280	214.34
419	able	adjective	217	214.10
420	term	noun	236	214.01
421	art	noun	262	213.77
422	road	noun	262	213.69
423	indicate	verb	244	213.50
424	break	verb	228	213.39
425	six	card. num.	220	213.37
426	land	noun	232	213.28
427	information	noun	269	213.20
428	quite	qualifier	224	213.01
429	method	noun	284	212.88
430	century	noun	254	212.56
431	less	post-det.	232	212.37
432	draw	verb	222	212.19
433	picture	noun	227	211.42
434	place	verb	233	210.51
435	walk	verb	287	210.22
436	certain	adjective	221	209.21
437	enter	verb	213	208.03
438	true	adjective	220	207.19
439	sometimes	adverb	221	207.16
440	material	noun	269	207.14
441	include	verb	260	206.53
442	shall	modal aux.	269	206.07
443	voice	noun	265	205.80
444	rate	noun	303	205.23
445	offer	verb	217	205.22

446	return	verb	232	215.02
447	land	noun	232	213.28
448	less	post-det.	232	212.37
449	activity	noun	231	196.89
450	behind	prep.	231	195.09
451	much	qualifier	229	215.90
452	step	noun	228	215.24
453	break	verb	228	213.39
454	difference	noun	228	186.86
455	ground	noun	227	214.77
456	picture	noun	227	211.42
457	really	adverb	226	201.22
458	spirit	noun	226	174.16
459	change	verb	225	218.07
460	sure	adjective	225	191.01
461	present	adjective	225	190.00
462	quite	qualifier	224	213.01
463	right	adjective	224	201.31
464	wall	noun	224	198.86
465	major	adjective	224	186.27
466	stage	noun	224	176.39
467	draw	verb	222	212.19
468	necessary	adjective	222	195.53
469	pressure	noun	222	188.25
470	morning	noun	222	182.13
471	property	noun	222	160.44
472	industry	noun	222	150.06
473	full	adjective	221	214.55
474	certain	adjective	221	209.21
475	sometimes	adverb	221	207.16
476	surface	noun	221	153.99
477	six	card. num.	220	213.37
478	true	adjective	220	207.19
479	control	noun	220	192.06
480	piece	noun	219	178.77
481	able	adjective	217	214.10
482	offer	verb	217	205.22
483	mile	noun	217	198.92
484	view	noun	217	197.12
485	arm	noun	217	183.95
486	produce	verb	217	181.66
487	America	prop. noun	217	176.52
488	Washington	prop. noun	217	158.03
489	music	noun	216	163.10
490	education	noun	215	169.18
491	record	noun	214	193.24
492	enter	verb	213	208.03
493	union	noun	213	169.49
494	much	adverb	212	190.44
495	story	noun	212	164.61
496	lie	verb	211	191.56
497	bear	verb	211	190.99
498	common	adjective	211	180.71
499	apply	verb	210	169.83
500	secretary	noun	210	155.62
501	allow	verb	209	191.23
502	statement	noun	209	177.51
503	watch	verb	209	159.40
504	paper	noun	208	191.81
505	evidence	noun	208	170.17
506	usually	adverb	206	189.42
507	decide	verb	205	194.03
508	therefore	adverb	205	177.84
509	report	noun	205	172.22
510	right	noun	204	183.98
511	officer	noun	204	162.06
512	million	card. num.	204	153.16
513	subject	noun	203	174.85
514	drive	verb	203	172.18
515	horse	noun	203	156.10
516	cover	verb	202	186.76
517	exist	verb	202	169.82
518	son	noun	202	165.84
519	soon	adverb	200	190.03
520	suggest	verb	200	183.46
521	describe	verb	200	165.99
522	plan	verb	200	165.08
523	issue	noun	200	156.31
524	rise	verb	199	190.54
525	heart	noun	199	174.06
526	military	adjective	199	133.54
527	along	prep.	198	192.89
528	strong	adjective	198	188.85
529	more	comp. adv.	198	187.04
530	modern	adjective	198	177.09
531	food	noun	198	176.36
532	nature	noun	198	173.29
533	peace	noun	198	144.88
534	operation	noun	197	144.67

446	God	prop. noun	335	203.11
447	all	qualifier	242	202.74
448	purpose	noun	239	202.72
449	right	adjective	224	201.31
450	really	adverb	226	201.22
451	university	noun	256	200.98
452	political	adjective	258	200.33
453	policy	noun	290	199.74
454	process	noun	252	199.29
455	stop	verb	240	199.13
456	mile	noun	217	198.92
457	wall	noun	224	198.86
458	view	noun	217	197.12
459	activity	noun	231	196.89
460	necessary	adjective	222	195.53
461	behind	prep.	231	195.09
462	decide	verb	205	194.03
463	record	noun	214	193.24
464	along	prep.	198	192.89
465	control	noun	220	192.06
466	paper	noun	208	191.81
467	act	noun	237	191.80
468	section	noun	276	191.73
469	lie	verb	211	191.56
470	allow	verb	209	191.23
471	sure	adjective	225	191.01
472	bear	verb	211	190.99
473	short	adjective	195	190.73
474	rise	verb	199	190.54
475	much	adverb	212	190.44
476	soon	adverb	200	190.03
477	present	adjective	225	190.00
478	usually	adverb	206	189.42
479	strong	adjective	198	188.85
480	clear	adjective	196	188.38
481	pressure	noun	222	188.25
482	nor	co. conj.	195	187.76
483	more	comp. adv.	198	187.04
484	difference	noun	228	186.86
485	wait	verb	263	186.80
486	cover	verb	202	186.76
487	spend	verb	194	186.54
488	major	adjective	224	186.27
489	available	adjective	246	185.24
490	raise	verb	188	184.96
491	right	noun	204	183.98
492	arm	noun	217	183.95
493	suggest	verb	200	183.46
494	human	adjective	263	183.08
495	morning	noun	222	182.13
496	produce	verb	217	181.66
497	common	adjective	211	180.71
498	around	adverb	240	180.17
499	finally	adverb	191	179.78
500	department	noun	272	179.40
501	above	prep.	188	178.94
502	piece	noun	219	178.77
503	therefore	adverb	205	177.84
504	statement	noun	209	177.51
505	accept	verb	193	177.47
506	modern	adjective	198	177.09
507	alone	adverb	187	176.76
508	America	prop. noun	217	176.52
509	stage	noun	224	176.39
510	food	noun	198	176.36
511	feeling	noun	192	175.28
512	fill	verb	184	175.24
513	subject	noun	203	174.85
514	attention	noun	180	174.21
515	spirit	noun	226	174.16
516	heart	noun	199	174.06
517	third	ord. num.	184	173.88
518	enough	post-det.	181	173.33
519	nature	noun	198	173.29
520	economic	adjective	243	173.27
521	report	noun	205	172.22
522	drive	verb	203	172.18
523	either	co. conj.	189	171.95
524	choose	verb	177	171.74
525	Miss	prop. noun	233	171.73
526	cause	verb	186	171.36
527	long	adverb	192	171.19
528	evidence	noun	208	170.17
529	apply	verb	210	169.83
530	exist	verb	202	169.82
531	except	prep.	174	169.66
532	union	noun	213	169.49
533	explain	verb	177	169.25
534	less	qualifier	186	169.19

535	clear	adjective	196	188.38	535	education	noun	215	169.18
536	personal	adjective	196	165.37	536	fire	noun	195	169.15
537	short	adjective	195	190.73	537	instead	adverb	174	168.87
538	nor	co. conj.	195	187.76	538	building	noun	187	168.55
539	fire	noun	195	169.15	539	seek	verb	179	167.74
540	stay	verb	195	163.53	540	event	noun	182	166.19
541	establish	verb	195	149.30	541	describe	verb	200	165.99
542	station	noun	195	140.11	542	son	noun	202	165.84
543	product	noun	195	121.60	543	personal	adjective	196	165.37
544	spend	verb	194	186.54	544	plan	verb	200	165.08
545	space	noun	194	159.69	545	story	noun	212	164.61
546	accept	verb	193	177.47	546	since	prep.	180	164.52
547	feeling	noun	192	175.28	547	stay	verb	195	163.53
548	long	adverb	192	171.19	548	music	noun	216	163.10
549	organization	noun	192	150.76	549	simply	adverb	171	162.99
550	county	noun	192	139.52	550	officer	noun	204	162.06
551	down	prep.	192	129.02	551	everything	nom. pro.	188	161.05
552	finally	adverb	191	179.78	552	close	verb	174	160.53
553	back	noun	190	134.77	553	property	noun	222	160.44
554	unit	noun	190	133.47	554	create	verb	177	159.95
555	either	co. conj.	189	171.95	555	beyond	prep.	163	159.83
556	no	adverb	189	119.93	556	space	noun	194	159.69
557	raise	verb	188	184.96	557	watch	verb	209	159.40
558	above	prep.	188	178.94	558	private	adjective	185	159.31
559	everything	nom. pro.	188	161.05	559	federal	adjective	247	159.23
560	greater	comp. adj.	188	159.23	560	greater	comp. adj.	188	159.23
561	contain	verb	188	153.56	561	die	verb	183	158.81
562	committee	noun	188	109.72	562	Washington	prop. noun	217	158.03
563	alone	adverb	187	176.76	563	color	noun	184	157.55
564	building	noun	187	168.55	564	movement	noun	175	157.23
565	leader	noun	187	140.45	565	issue	noun	200	156.31
566	cause	verb	186	171.36	566	opportunity	noun	172	156.18
567	less	qualifier	186	169.19	567	horse	noun	203	156.10
568	private	adjective	185	159.31	568	actually	adverb	165	155.64
569	else	adverb	185	154.67	569	secretary	noun	210	155.62
570	market	noun	185	143.28	570	else	adverb	185	154.67
571	fill	verb	184	175.24	571	recognize	verb	163	154.10
572	third	ord. num.	184	173.88	572	surface	noun	221	153.99
573	color	noun	184	157.55	573	decision	noun	173	153.90
574	report	verb	184	152.54	574	contain	verb	188	153.56
575	basis	noun	184	147.80	575	study	verb	163	153.48
576	die	verb	183	158.81	576	million	card. num.	204	153.16
577	river	noun	183	140.85	577	ten	card. num.	163	152.77
578	event	noun	182	166.19	578	report	verb	184	152.54
579	source	noun	182	142.87	579	recent	adjective	179	152.17
580	volume	noun	182	139.57	580	prepare	verb	163	152.01
581	plant	noun	182	119.05	581	red	adjective	169	151.92
582	enough	post-det.	181	173.33	582	hope	verb	164	151.82
583	cent	noun	181	128.14	583	almost	qualifier	157	151.35
584	attention	noun	180	174.21	584	better	comp. adv.	166	151.24
585	since	prep.	180	164.52	585	difficult	adjective	161	150.97
586	defense	noun	180	149.07	586	organization	noun	192	150.76
587	game	noun	180	127.95	587	hundred	card. num.	171	150.47
588	seek	verb	179	167.74	588	industry	noun	222	150.06
589	recent	adjective	179	152.17	589	up	prep.	179	149.62
590	up	prep.	179	149.62	590	direction	noun	163	149.61
591	principle	noun	179	148.92	591	establish	verb	195	149.30
592	love	noun	179	142.05	592	including	prep.	166	149.15
593	reduce	verb	179	132.00	593	defense	noun	180	149.07
594	club	noun	178	131.23	594	principle	noun	179	148.92
595	choose	verb	177	171.74	595	complete	adjective	163	148.66
596	explain	verb	177	169.25	596	realize	verb	153	148.39
597	create	verb	177	159.95	597	simple	adjective	160	148.15
598	operate	verb	177	125.20	598	note	verb	165	148.05
599	sale	noun	177	105.24	599	prove	verb	156	148.00
600	factor	noun	176	129.98	600	basis	noun	184	147.80
601	district	noun	176	114.87	601	act	verb	159	147.02
602	movement	noun	175	157.23	602	earth	noun	167	146.64
603	except	prep.	174	169.66	603	concern	verb	161	145.75
604	instead	adverb	174	168.87	604	wish	verb	161	145.70
605	close	verb	174	160.53	605	floor	noun	170	145.57
606	wear	verb	174	133.32	606	sort	noun	169	145.51
607	datum	noun	174	96.55	607	suppose	verb	163	145.34
608	decision	noun	173	153.90	608	peace	noun	198	144.88
609	trial	noun	173	126.70	609	along	adverb	157	144.85
610	opportunity	noun	172	156.18	610	summer	noun	151	144.79
611	window	noun	172	128.47	611	operation	noun	197	144.67
612	research	noun	172	121.71	612	face	verb	152	144.12
613	simply	adverb	171	162.99	613	dead	adjective	166	143.47
614	hundred	card. num.	171	150.47	614	market	noun	185	143.28
615	because	adverb	171	138.36	615	present	verb	158	143.20
616	basic	adjective	171	123.60	616	source	noun	182	142.87
617	Negro	prop. noun	171	102.93	617	love	noun	179	142.05
618	floor	noun	170	145.57	618	permit	verb	157	141.25
619	red	adjective	169	151.92	619	near	prep.	156	141.12
620	sort	noun	169	145.51	620	single	post-det.	160	141.09
621	administration	noun	169	90.33	621	river	noun	183	140.85
622	association	noun	168	132.04	622	lot	noun	165	140.46
623	earth	noun	167	146.64	623	leader	noun	187	140.45

624	science	noun	167	139.28
625	south	adv. noun	167	127.34
626	equipment	noun	167	123.11
627	obtain	verb	167	110.22
628	better	comp. adv.	166	151.24
629	including	prep.	166	149.15
630	dead	adjective	166	143.47
631	amount	noun	166	119.88
632	reaction	noun	166	101.58
633	Kennedy	prop. noun	166	63.87
634	actually	adverb	165	155.64
635	note	verb	165	148.05
636	lot	noun	165	140.46
637	religious	adjective	165	130.76
638	relation	noun	165	130.33
639	black	adjective	165	129.34
640	central	adjective	165	127.71
641	individual	noun	165	126.18
642	hope	verb	164	151.82
643	stock	noun	164	139.44
644	price	noun	164	125.89
645	beyond	prep.	163	159.83
646	recognize	verb	163	154.10
647	study	verb	163	153.48
648	ten	card. num.	163	152.77
649	prepare	verb	163	152.01
650	direction	noun	163	149.61
651	complete	adjective	163	148.66
652	suppose	verb	163	145.34
653	husband	noun	163	133.94
654	represent	verb	163	133.63
655	sound	noun	163	118.91
656	U.S.	prop. noun	163	97.01
657	buy	verb	162	137.66
658	medical	adjective	162	118.49
659	difficult	adjective	161	150.97
660	concern	verb	161	145.75
661	wish	verb	161	145.70
662	test	noun	161	118.62
663	temperature	noun	161	83.00
664	simple	adjective	160	148.15
665	single	post-det.	160	141.09
666	assume	verb	160	138.07
667	particular	adjective	160	137.90
668	before	adverb	160	137.54
669	tree	noun	160	125.26
670	dark	adjective	160	118.65
671	hair	noun	160	103.51
672	fund	noun	160	99.35
673	act	verb	159	147.02
674	quality	noun	159	132.76
675	drop	verb	159	131.77
676	pattern	noun	159	126.89
677	win	verb	159	125.04
678	element	noun	159	119.39
679	technique	noun	159	111.21
680	present	verb	158	143.20
681	occur	verb	158	135.83
682	foreign	adjective	158	114.72
683	general	noun	158	99.42
684	almost	qualifier	157	151.35
685	along	adverb	157	144.85
686	permit	verb	157	141.25
687	off	prep.	157	135.93
688	thought	noun	157	128.23
689	similar	adjective	157	128.01
690	machine	noun	157	116.61
691	England	prop. noun	157	113.82
692	prove	verb	156	148.00
693	near	prep.	156	141.12
694	natural	adjective	156	140.39
695	image	noun	156	121.15
696	growth	noun	156	119.54
697	fight	verb	155	135.14
698	attitude	noun	155	133.21
699	William	prop. noun	155	123.48
700	performance	noun	155	112.06
701	production	noun	155	110.84
702	police	noun	155	97.93
703	increase	noun	155	84.87
704	trouble	noun	154	137.72
705	list	noun	154	130.61
706	character	noun	154	126.95
707	international	adjective	154	106.96
708	realize	verb	153	148.39
709	form	verb	153	137.49
710	teach	verb	153	129.91
711	front	noun	153	124.67
712	kill	verb	153	121.23

624	natural	adjective	156	140.39
625	station	noun	195	140.11
626	volume	noun	182	139.57
627	county	noun	192	139.52
628	stock	noun	164	139.44
629	point	verb	143	139.30
630	science	noun	167	139.28
631	final	adjective	146	139.27
632	agree	verb	150	138.76
633	chance	noun	152	138.73
634	anyone	nom. pro.	146	138.37
635	because	adverb	171	138.36
636	assume	verb	160	138.07
637	particular	adjective	160	137.90
638	fail	verb	142	137.77
639	trouble	noun	154	137.72
640	buy	verb	162	137.66
641	answer	noun	145	137.65
642	before	adverb	160	137.54
643	form	verb	153	137.49
644	throw	verb	150	136.98
645	off	prep.	157	135.93
646	occur	verb	158	135.83
647	charge	noun	151	135.63
648	entire	adjective	149	135.63
649	hard	adjective	140	135.26
650	especially	adverb	141	135.20
651	fight	verb	155	135.14
652	knowledge	noun	145	134.95
653	manner	noun	139	134.87
654	back	noun	190	134.77
655	indeed	adverb	145	134.49
656	remove	verb	146	134.07
657	rest	noun	140	133.95
658	husband	noun	163	133.94
659	range	noun	152	133.69
660	certainly	adverb	143	133.65
661	represent	verb	163	133.63
662	military	adjective	199	133.54
663	unit	noun	190	133.47
664	wear	verb	174	133.32
665	attitude	noun	155	133.21
666	quality	noun	159	132.76
667	association	noun	168	132.04
668	reduce	verb	179	132.00
669	drop	verb	159	131.77
670	club	noun	178	131.23
671	religious	adjective	165	130.76
672	list	noun	154	130.61
673	relation	noun	165	130.33
674	strength	noun	141	130.16
675	factor	noun	176	129.98
676	teach	verb	153	129.91
677	black	adjective	165	129.34
678	down	prep.	192	129.02
679	teacher	noun	152	128.81
680	end	verb	140	128.76
681	cold	adjective	147	128.62
682	window	noun	172	128.47
683	thought	noun	157	128.23
684	cent	noun	181	128.14
685	similar	adjective	157	128.01
686	game	noun	180	127.95
687	central	adjective	165	127.71
688	support	verb	144	127.68
689	but	prep.	131	127.58
690	late	adjective	132	127.43
691	south	adv. noun	167	127.34
692	character	noun	154	126.95
693	pattern	noun	159	126.89
694	trial	noun	173	126.70
695	join	verb	139	126.61
696	higher	comp. adj.	147	126.58
697	army	noun	152	126.37
698	individual	noun	165	126.18
699	price	noun	164	125.89
700	lay	verb	138	125.84
701	rule	noun	148	125.65
702	degree	noun	148	125.30
703	tree	noun	160	125.26
704	operate	verb	177	125.20
705	west	adv. noun	142	125.19
706	maintain	verb	152	125.10
707	win	verb	159	125.04
708	hope	noun	136	125.01
709	western	adjective	137	124.94
710	front	noun	153	124.67
711	tax	noun	241	124.37
712	low	adjective	147	124.32

713	meeting	noun	153	117.44	713	evening	noun	149	124.26
714	suddenly	adverb	153	115.31	714	ready	adjective	141	123.99
715	Congress	prop. noun	153	96.87	715	various	adjective	145	123.84
716	face	verb	152	144.12	716	basic	adjective	171	123.60
717	chance	noun	152	138.73	717	William	prop. noun	155	123.48
718	range	noun	152	133.69	718	equipment	noun	167	123.11
719	teacher	noun	152	128.81	719	fine	adjective	150	122.69
720	army	noun	152	126.37	720	opinion	noun	140	122.12
721	maintain	verb	152	125.10	721	limit	verb	143	121.75
722	summer	noun	151	144.79	722	research	noun	172	121.71
723	charge	noun	151	135.63	723	product	noun	195	121.60
724	addition	noun	151	118.99	724	dollar	noun	144	121.43
725	writer	noun	151	117.51	725	rather	adverb	141	121.36
726	hall	noun	151	113.54	726	bad	adjective	134	121.34
727	labor	noun	151	111.32	727	kill	verb	153	121.23
728	function	noun	151	87.43	728	top	noun	136	121.23
729	agree	verb	150	138.76	729	image	noun	156	121.15
730	throw	verb	150	136.98	730	size	noun	148	120.69
731	fine	adjective	150	122.69	731	corner	noun	134	120.34
732	individual	adjective	150	106.57	732	no	adverb	189	119.93
733	theory	noun	150	95.54	733	amount	noun	166	119.88
734	entire	adjective	149	135.63	734	state	verb	138	119.88
735	evening	noun	149	124.26	735	spring	noun	138	119.85
736	language	noun	149	110.92	736	visit	verb	129	119.84
737	rule	noun	148	125.65	737	growth	noun	156	119.54
738	degree	noun	148	125.30	738	force	verb	124	119.54
739	size	noun	148	120.69	739	element	noun	159	119.39
740	how	wh-qual.	148	94.27	740	plant	noun	182	119.05
741	cold	adjective	147	128.62	741	addition	noun	151	118.99
742	higher	comp. adj.	147	126.58	742	sound	noun	163	118.91
743	low	adjective	147	124.32	743	express	verb	135	118.88
744	dog	noun	147	117.24	744	prevent	verb	130	118.84
745	hotel	noun	147	109.26	745	dark	adjective	160	118.65
746	final	adjective	146	139.27	746	test	noun	161	118.62
747	anyone	nom. pro.	146	138.37	747	medical	adjective	162	118.49
748	remove	verb	146	134.07	748	public	noun	141	118.12
749	catch	verb	146	111.50	749	mention	verb	125	117.89
750	cell	noun	146	63.49	750	physical	adjective	138	117.63
751	answer	noun	145	137.65	751	writer	noun	151	117.51
752	knowledge	noun	145	134.95	752	directly	adverb	133	117.50
753	indeed	adverb	145	134.49	753	meeting	noun	153	117.44
754	various	adjective	145	123.84	754	dog	noun	147	117.24
755	love	verb	145	116.82	755	love	verb	145	116.82
756	pull	verb	145	108.27	756	throughout	prep.	133	116.82
757	project	noun	145	93.80	757	answer	verb	133	116.67
758	support	verb	144	127.68	758	machine	noun	157	116.61
759	dollar	noun	144	121.43	759	until	prep.	125	116.45
760	population	noun	144	99.78	760	even	qualifier	119	116.40
761	yes	adverb	144	97.05	761	responsibility	noun	143	116.27
762	poet	noun	144	93.92	762	detail	noun	128	116.08
763	result	verb	144	91.58	763	loss	noun	132	115.90
764	point	verb	143	139.30	764	authority	noun	135	115.83
765	certainly	adverb	143	133.65	765	scene	noun	135	115.74
766	limit	verb	143	121.75	766	couple	noun	136	115.47
767	responsibility	noun	143	116.27	767	suddenly	adverb	153	115.31
768	pick	verb	143	109.27	768	brother	noun	135	115.24
769	industrial	adjective	143	96.84	769	apparently	adverb	124	115.02
770	fail	verb	142	137.77	770	district	noun	176	114.87
771	west	adv. noun	142	125.19	771	enjoy	verb	128	114.79
772	sign	noun	142	105.36	772	length	noun	139	114.78
773	gun	noun	142	91.30	773	mark	verb	126	114.78
774	especially	adverb	141	135.20	774	foreign	adjective	158	114.72
775	strength	noun	141	130.16	775	meaning	noun	138	114.60
776	ready	adjective	141	123.99	776	sell	verb	128	114.54
777	rather	adverb	141	121.36	777	discover	verb	123	114.07
778	public	noun	141	118.12	778	England	prop. noun	157	113.82
779	fear	noun	141	99.27	779	hall	noun	151	113.54
780	hard	adjective	140	135.26	780	generally	adverb	129	113.39
781	rest	noun	140	133.95	781	clearly	adverb	122	113.08
782	end	verb	140	128.76	782	approach	noun	125	112.93
783	opinion	noun	140	122.12	783	account	noun	120	112.70
784	procedure	noun	140	100.60	784	one	noun	117	112.24
785	institution	noun	140	95.41	785	as	prep.	121	112.14
786	manner	noun	139	134.87	786	performance	noun	155	112.06
787	join	verb	139	126.61	787	glass	noun	128	111.96
788	length	noun	139	114.78	788	former	post-det.	131	111.70
789	respect	noun	139	110.55	789	possibility	noun	130	111.62
790	bed	noun	139	104.79	790	distance	noun	127	111.53
791	lay	verb	138	125.84	791	catch	verb	146	111.50
792	state	verb	138	119.88	792	save	verb	121	111.37
793	spring	noun	138	119.85	793	labor	noun	151	111.32
794	physical	adjective	138	117.63	794	technique	noun	159	111.21
795	meaning	noun	138	114.60	795	according	prep.	128	111.05
796	trade	noun	138	109.59	796	language	noun	149	110.92
797	role	noun	138	108.38	797	note	noun	126	110.92
798	plane	noun	138	108.21	798	extend	verb	127	110.90
799	treatment	noun	138	99.63	799	production	noun	155	110.84
800	southern	adjective	138	94.41	800	far	qualifier	131	110.82
801	well	exclam.	138	81.19	801	doubt	noun	115	110.62

802	western	adjective	137	124.94
803	set	noun	137	107.09
804	farm	noun	137	106.42
805	religion	noun	137	105.12
806	no	qualifier	137	97.11
807	moral	adjective	137	96.76
808	relate	verb	137	95.02
809	hope	noun	136	125.01
810	top	noun	136	121.23
811	couple	noun	136	115.47
812	that	o. wh-pro.	136	100.24
813	design	noun	136	91.23
814	express	verb	135	118.88
815	authority	noun	135	115.83
816	scene	noun	135	115.74
817	brother	noun	135	115.24
818	bad	adjective	134	121.34
819	corner	noun	134	120.34
820	total	noun	134	89.89
821	literature	noun	134	89.50
822	directly	adverb	133	117.50
823	throughout	prep.	133	116.82
824	answer	verb	133	116.67
825	normal	adjective	133	110.32
826	achieve	verb	133	108.69
827	George	prop. noun	133	107.74
828	freedom	noun	133	106.05
829	bill	noun	133	100.14
830	yet	co. conj.	133	95.13
831	maybe	adverb	133	87.04
832	late	adjective	132	127.43
833	loss	noun	132	115.90
834	support	noun	132	101.10
835	practice	noun	132	100.40
836	patient	noun	132	99.60
837	feed	verb	132	84.77
838	but	prep.	131	127.58
839	former	post-det.	131	111.70
840	far	qualifier	131	110.82
841	audience	noun	131	99.12
842	hang	verb	131	96.03
843	corporation	noun	131	81.48
844	Christian	adjective	131	80.78
845	prevent	verb	130	118.84
846	possibility	noun	130	111.62
847	hot	adjective	130	110.53
848	return	noun	130	110.10
849	merely	adverb	130	108.91
850	train	verb	130	108.54
851	truth	noun	130	108.37
852	marry	verb	130	108.27
853	mean	noun	130	107.08
854	hospital	noun	130	101.66
855	base	verb	130	100.11
856	poem	noun	130	65.06
857	visit	verb	129	119.84
858	generally	adverb	129	113.39
859	animal	noun	129	108.79
860	effective	adjective	129	98.48
860	myself	refl. pro.	129	98.48
862	aid	noun	129	85.58
863	song	noun	129	85.31
864	inch	noun	129	75.78
865	pool	noun	129	74.98
866	Brown	prop. noun	129	70.44
867	detail	noun	128	116.08
868	enjoy	verb	128	114.79
869	sell	verb	128	114.54
870	glass	noun	128	111.96
871	according	prep.	128	111.05
872	American	prop. noun	128	102.33
873	measure	verb	128	80.82
874	election	noun	128	70.12
875	distance	noun	127	111.53
876	extend	verb	127	110.90
877	beautiful	adjective	127	105.24
878	right	qualifier	127	99.55
879	vary	verb	127	97.47
880	film	noun	127	87.63
881	item	noun	127	82.88
882	mark	verb	126	114.78
883	note	noun	126	110.92
884	relationship	noun	126	108.54
885	radio	noun	126	103.99
886	play	noun	126	99.59
887	blue	adjective	126	99.55
888	discussion	noun	126	98.94
889	likely	adjective	126	96.76
890	ride	verb	126	95.42

802	respect	noun	139	110.55
803	hot	adjective	130	110.53
804	square	noun	121	110.37
805	normal	adjective	133	110.32
806	obtain	verb	167	110.22
807	return	noun	130	110.10
808	committee	noun	188	109.72
809	trade	noun	138	109.59
810	pick	verb	143	109.27
811	hotel	noun	147	109.26
812	longer	comp. adv.	124	109.11
813	merely	adverb	130	108.91
814	animal	noun	129	108.79
815	achieve	verb	133	108.69
816	train	verb	130	108.54
817	relationship	noun	126	108.54
818	role	noun	138	108.38
819	truth	noun	130	108.37
820	recently	adverb	123	108.30
821	pull	verb	145	108.27
822	marry	verb	130	108.27
823	plane	noun	138	108.21
824	difficulty	noun	123	108.09
825	blood	noun	122	107.90
826	George	prop. noun	133	107.74
827	seven	card. num.	114	107.61
828	immediately	adverb	116	107.32
829	set	noun	137	107.09
830	mean	noun	130	107.08
831	international	adjective	154	106.96
832	observe	verb	120	106.74
833	individual	adjective	150	106.57
834	farm	noun	137	106.42
835	treat	verb	122	106.35
836	wrong	adjective	117	106.31
837	enemy	noun	123	106.08
838	freedom	noun	133	106.05
839	wide	adjective	118	105.50
840	sign	noun	142	105.36
841	serious	adjective	116	105.30
842	sale	noun	177	105.24
843	beautiful	adjective	127	105.24
844	religion	noun	137	105.12
845	marriage	noun	122	104.97
846	bed	noun	139	104.79
847	easy	adjective	111	104.21
848	larger	comp. adj.	123	104.10
849	whatever	wh-det.	111	104.08
850	radio	noun	126	103.99
851	hair	noun	160	103.51
852	future	adjective	119	103.34
853	citizen	noun	120	103.17
854	Negro	prop. noun	171	102.93
855	main	sem. sup.	110	102.58
856	concern	noun	115	102.42
857	American	prop. noun	128	102.33
858	arrive	verb	108	102.27
859	discuss	verb	113	101.77
860	hospital	noun	130	101.66
861	forget	verb	119	101.63
862	finish	verb	120	101.61
863	reaction	noun	166	101.58
864	deal	verb	124	101.45
865	instance	noun	112	101.42
866	poor	adjective	113	101.33
867	series	noun	120	101.31
868	support	noun	132	101.10
869	Europe	prop. noun	121	100.71
870	obviously	adverb	112	100.64
871	procedure	noun	140	100.60
872	practice	noun	132	100.40
873	that	o. wh-pro.	136	100.24
874	nearly	adverb	112	100.22
875	bill	noun	133	100.14
876	base	verb	130	100.11
877	none	nom. pro.	108	100.08
878	artist	noun	125	100.00
879	ahead	adverb	109	99.98
880	population	noun	144	99.78
881	particularly	adverb	106	99.70
882	parent	noun	113	99.69
883	treatment	noun	138	99.63
884	patient	noun	132	99.60
885	play	noun	126	99.59
886	right	qualifier	127	99.55
887	blue	adjective	126	99.55
888	general	noun	158	99.42
889	trip	noun	109	99.39
890	fund	noun	160	99.35

891	ship	noun	126	95.27
892	hit	verb	126	90.17
893	leg	noun	126	87.22
894	mention	verb	125	117.89
895	until	prep.	125	116.45
896	approach	noun	125	112.93
897	artist	noun	125	100.00
898	herself	refl. pro.	125	83.74
899	season	noun	125	78.87
900	force	verb	124	119.54
901	apparently	adverb	124	115.02
902	longer	comp. adv.	124	109.11
903	deal	verb	124	101.45
904	influence	noun	124	95.03
905	claim	noun	124	80.79
906	division	noun	124	79.29
907	discover	verb	123	114.07
908	recently	adverb	123	108.30
909	difficulty	noun	123	108.09
910	enemy	noun	123	106.08
911	larger	comp. adj.	123	104.10
912	demand	noun	123	95.24
913	listen	verb	123	90.19
914	worker	noun	123	89.35
915	ball	noun	123	77.53
916	boat	noun	123	75.92
917	tooth	noun	123	66.56
918	clearly	adverb	122	113.08
919	blood	noun	122	107.90
920	treat	verb	122	106.35
921	marriage	noun	122	104.97
922	eat	verb	122	99.24
923	design	verb	122	97.10
924	lady	noun	122	96.00
925	conference	noun	122	93.65
926	afternoon	noun	122	88.02
927	experiment	noun	122	75.98
928	smile	verb	122	60.50
929	as	prep.	121	112.14
930	save	verb	121	111.37
931	square	noun	121	110.37
932	Europe	prop. noun	121	100.71
933	choice	noun	121	95.67
934	structure	noun	121	93.83
935	director	noun	121	93.78
936	improve	verb	121	91.29
937	agreement	noun	121	73.84
938	analysis	noun	121	63.20
939	account	noun	120	112.70
940	observe	verb	120	106.74
941	citizen	noun	120	103.17
942	finish	verb	120	101.61
943	series	noun	120	101.31
944	date	noun	120	98.91
945	staff	noun	120	93.52
946	technical	adjective	120	89.68
947	additional	adjective	120	87.34
948	race	noun	120	87.14
949	sing	verb	120	83.78
950	J.	prop. noun	120	79.95
951	model	noun	120	78.78
952	fiscal	adjective	120	26.19
953	even	qualifier	119	116.40
954	future	adjective	119	103.34
955	forget	verb	119	101.63
956	attend	verb	119	90.05
957	hill	noun	119	89.61
958	region	noun	119	86.44
959	rather	prep.	119	85.37
960	wonder	verb	119	83.00
961	oh	exclam.	119	58.66
962	wide	adjective	118	105.50
963	good	noun	118	97.50
964	agency	noun	118	79.85
965	governor	noun	118	67.97
966	one	noun	117	112.24
967	wrong	adjective	117	106.31
968	affair	noun	117	95.67
969	sun	noun	117	93.75
970	style	noun	117	90.39
971	shoot	verb	117	87.97
972	bridge	noun	117	76.71
973	commission	noun	117	74.08
974	however	wh-adverb	117	69.45
975	immediately	adverb	116	107.32
976	serious	adjective	116	105.30
977	announce	verb	116	96.36
978	success	noun	116	94.70
979	progress	noun	116	93.37

891	future	noun	108	99.35
892	fear	noun	141	99.27
893	eat	verb	122	99.24
894	audience	noun	131	99.12
895	direct	adjective	114	99.12
896	discussion	noun	126	98.94
897	date	noun	120	98.91
898	name	verb	109	98.82
899	little	qualifier	111	98.54
900	effective	adjective	129	98.48
900	myself	refl. pro.	129	98.48
902	police	noun	155	97.93
903	deny	verb	109	97.92
904	share	verb	105	97.64
905	good	noun	118	97.50
906	vary	verb	127	97.47
907	fix	verb	109	97.40
908	no	qualifier	137	97.11
909	design	verb	122	97.10
910	yes	adverb	144	97.05
911	U.S.	prop. noun	163	97.01
912	Congress	prop. noun	153	96.87
913	industrial	adjective	143	96.84
914	moral	adjective	137	96.76
915	likely	adjective	126	96.76
916	heavy	adjective	110	96.69
917	datum	noun	174	96.55
918	announce	verb	116	96.36
919	early	adverb	107	96.11
920	hang	verb	131	96.03
921	lady	noun	122	96.00
922	further	comp. adv.	104	95.76
923	choice	noun	121	95.67
924	affair	noun	117	95.67
925	easily	adverb	104	95.59
926	theory	noun	150	95.54
927	ride	verb	126	95.42
928	institution	noun	140	95.41
929	ship	noun	126	95.27
930	demand	noun	123	95.24
931	yet	co. conj.	133	95.13
932	influence	noun	124	95.03
933	relate	verb	137	95.02
934	success	noun	116	94.70
935	reflect	verb	107	94.68
936	latter	post-det.	114	94.65
937	southern	adjective	138	94.41
938	settle	verb	105	94.40
939	how	wh-qual.	148	94.27
940	refer	verb	109	94.06
941	interest	verb	106	93.95
942	poet	noun	144	93.92
943	will	noun	105	93.88
944	structure	noun	121	93.83
945	project	noun	145	93.80
946	director	noun	121	93.78
947	sun	noun	117	93.75
948	conference	noun	122	93.65
949	page	noun	102	93.57
950	staff	noun	120	93.52
951	strike	verb	108	93.43
952	progress	noun	116	93.37
953	suffer	verb	110	93.31
954	mass	noun	110	93.30
955	regard	verb	100	93.22
956	weapon	noun	103	93.10
957	feature	noun	105	92.96
958	lower	comp. adj.	110	92.71
959	help	noun	99	92.54
960	edge	noun	114	92.53
961	circumstance	noun	99	92.42
962	shape	noun	104	92.35
963	store	noun	102	92.22
964	professional	adjective	99	91.84
965	result	verb	144	91.58
966	despite	prep.	104	91.56
967	aspect	noun	111	91.43
968	gun	noun	142	91.30
969	improve	verb	121	91.29
970	design	noun	136	91.23
971	burn	verb	103	91.19
972	eight	card. num.	104	91.06
973	cause	noun	109	91.04
974	publish	verb	108	90.82
975	unless	sub. conj.	101	90.56
976	neither	co. conj.	97	90.51
977	usual	adjective	92	90.49
978	exactly	adverb	97	90.48
979	attempt	noun	102	90.44

980	due	adjective	116	89.86	980	rather	qualifier	108	90.41
981	Sunday	adv. noun	116	76.90	981	style	noun	117	90.39
982	firm	noun	116	76.67	982	complete	verb	107	90.39
983	bar	noun	116	73.14	983	administration	noun	169	90.33
984	doubt	noun	115	110.62	984	sea	noun	104	90.22
985	concern	noun	115	102.42	985	lack	noun	97	90.21
986	slowly	adverb	115	89.67	986	listen	verb	123	90.19
987	specific	adjective	115	84.89	987	hit	verb	126	90.17
988	object	noun	115	84.56	988	attend	verb	119	90.05
989	tradition	noun	115	79.98	989	total	noun	134	89.89
990	council	noun	115	73.70	990	due	adjective	116	89.86
991	nuclear	adjective	115	71.46	991	energy	noun	111	89.86
992	Christ	prop. noun	115	59.97	992	technical	adjective	120	89.68
993	seven	card. num.	114	107.61	993	slowly	adverb	115	89.67
994	direct	adjective	114	99.12	994	hill	noun	119	89.61
995	latter	post-det.	114	94.65	995	literature	noun	134	89.50
996	edge	noun	114	92.53	996	approach	verb	95	89.41
997	compare	verb	114	89.00	997	worker	noun	123	89.35
998	manager	noun	114	86.76	998	compare	verb	114	89.00
999	S.	prop. noun	114	77.42	999	newspaper	noun	104	88.80
1000	discuss	verb	113	101.77	1000	somewhat	qualifier	99	88.68
1001	poor	adjective	113	101.33	1001	close	adverb	97	88.24
1002	parent	noun	113	99.69	1002	depend	verb	106	88.12
1003	mouth	noun	113	77.22	1003	afternoon	noun	122	88.02
1004	instance	noun	112	101.42	1004	shoot	verb	117	87.97
1005	obviously	adverb	112	100.64	1005	news	noun	101	87.92
1006	nearly	adverb	112	100.22	1006	care	verb	108	87.89
1007	select	verb	112	84.59	1007	turn	noun	96	87.67
1008	shoulder	noun	112	73.33	1008	film	noun	127	87.63
1009	concept	noun	112	72.40	1009	original	adjective	100	87.52
1010	Thomas	prop. noun	112	66.02	1010	function	noun	151	87.43
1011	communist	noun	112	50.79	1011	additional	adjective	120	87.34
1012	easy	adjective	111	104.21	1012	leg	noun	126	87.22
1013	whatever	wh-det.	111	104.08	1013	race	noun	120	87.14
1014	little	qualifier	111	98.54	1014	maybe	adverb	133	87.04
1015	aspect	noun	111	91.43	1015	measure	noun	107	86.98
1016	energy	noun	111	89.86	1016	manager	noun	114	86.76
1017	park	noun	111	79.59	1017	youth	noun	93	86.70
1018	facility	noun	111	78.33	1018	region	noun	119	86.44
1019	oil	noun	111	71.53	1019	obvious	adjective	92	86.38
1020	stress	noun	111	58.62	1020	push	verb	102	86.19
1021	main	sem. sup.	110	102.58	1021	advantage	noun	101	86.17
1022	heavy	adjective	110	96.69	1022	claim	verb	99	86.15
1023	suffer	verb	110	93.31	1023	forward	adverb	97	86.15
1024	mass	noun	110	93.30	1024	supply	noun	95	86.04
1025	lower	comp. adj.	110	92.71	1025	thousand	card. num.	97	86.01
1026	propose	verb	110	84.46	1026	response	noun	105	85.98
1027	faith	noun	110	77.61	1027	repeat	verb	95	85.98
1028	bank	noun	110	73.00	1028	bit	noun	105	85.78
1029	extent	noun	110	71.93	1029	consist	verb	109	85.72
1030	A.	prop. noun	110	70.15	1030	aid	noun	129	85.58
1031	requirement	noun	110	68.10	1031	health	noun	105	85.54
1032	income	noun	110	63.01	1032	older	comp. adj.	93	85.53
1033	ahead	adverb	109	99.98	1033	hardly	adverb	93	85.42
1034	trip	noun	109	99.39	1034	rather	prep.	119	85.37
1035	name	verb	109	98.82	1035	song	noun	129	85.31
1036	deny	verb	109	97.92	1036	past	noun	100	85.26
1037	fix	verb	109	97.40	1037	finger	noun	106	85.25
1038	refer	verb	109	94.06	1038	refuse	verb	91	85.19
1039	cause	noun	109	91.04	1039	care	noun	89	85.09
1040	consist	verb	109	85.72	1040	assure	verb	92	85.08
1041	English	adjective	109	74.33	1041	avoid	verb	91	84.95
1042	democratic	adjective	109	62.31	1042	specific	adjective	115	84.89
1043	employee	noun	109	58.20	1043	increase	noun	155	84.87
1044	arrive	verb	108	102.27	1044	deal	noun	99	84.86
1045	none	nom. pro.	108	100.08	1045	importance	noun	108	84.83
1046	future	noun	108	99.35	1046	king	noun	98	84.80
1047	strike	verb	108	93.43	1047	feed	verb	132	84.77
1048	publish	verb	108	90.82	1048	fall	noun	94	84.72
1049	rather	qualifier	108	90.41	1049	control	verb	95	84.63
1050	care	verb	108	87.89	1050	select	verb	112	84.59
1051	importance	noun	108	84.83	1051	object	noun	115	84.56
1052	contribute	verb	108	84.29	1052	destroy	verb	104	84.55
1053	French	adjective	108	79.51	1053	propose	verb	110	84.46
1054	Chicago	prop. noun	108	78.78	1054	tend	verb	104	84.44
1055	team	noun	108	78.16	1055	order	verb	89	84.41
1056	show	noun	108	73.95	1056	supply	verb	103	84.40
1057	motor	noun	108	58.02	1057	contribute	verb	108	84.29
1058	early	adverb	107	96.11	1058	duty	noun	95	84.27
1059	reflect	verb	107	94.68	1059	sing	verb	120	83.78
1060	complete	verb	107	90.39	1060	herself	refl. pro.	125	83.74
1061	measure	noun	107	86.98	1061	base	noun	102	83.69
1062	column	noun	107	83.02	1062	fit	verb	91	83.60
1063	press	noun	107	80.43	1063	Charles	prop. noun	104	83.48
1064	existence	noun	107	80.20	1064	popular	adjective	99	83.18
1065	gas	noun	107	78.21	1065	column	noun	107	83.02
1066	shake	verb	107	71.46	1066	temperature	noun	161	83.00
1067	particularly	adverb	106	99.70	1067	wonder	verb	119	83.00
1068	interest	verb	106	93.95	1068	very	post-det.	93	82.90

1069	depend	verb	106	88.12
1070	finger	noun	106	85.25
1071	session	noun	106	69.16
1072	share	verb	105	97.64
1073	settle	verb	105	94.40
1074	will	noun	105	93.88
1075	feature	noun	105	92.96
1076	response	noun	105	85.98
1077	bit	noun	105	85.78
1078	health	noun	105	85.54
1079	look	noun	105	78.32
1080	James	prop. noun	105	73.78
1081	north	adv. noun	105	73.28
1082	standard	noun	105	72.31
1083	Rhode	prop. noun	105	38.14
1084	further	comp. adv.	104	95.76
1085	easily	adverb	104	95.59
1086	shape	noun	104	92.35
1087	despite	prep.	104	91.56
1088	eight	card. num.	104	91.06
1089	sea	noun	104	90.22
1090	newspaper	noun	104	88.80
1091	destroy	verb	104	84.55
1092	tend	verb	104	84.44
1093	Charles	prop. noun	104	83.48
1094	justice	noun	104	76.67
1095	kid	noun	104	61.18
1096	weapon	noun	103	93.10
1097	burn	verb	103	91.19
1098	supply	verb	103	84.40
1099	saint	noun	103	81.55
1100	corps	noun	103	67.13
1101	Jack	prop. noun	103	54.41
1102	page	noun	102	93.57
1103	store	noun	102	92.22
1104	attempt	noun	102	90.44
1105	push	verb	102	86.19
1106	base	noun	102	83.69
1107	pain	noun	102	78.13
1108	crisis	noun	102	75.74
1109	payment	noun	102	49.06
1110	unless	sub. conj.	101	90.56
1111	news	noun	101	87.92
1112	advantage	noun	101	86.17
1113	post	noun	101	78.28
1114	British	adjective	101	76.81
1115	weight	noun	101	75.31
1116	regard	verb	100	93.22
1117	original	adjective	100	87.52
1118	past	noun	100	85.26
1119	goal	noun	100	81.84
1120	someone	nom. pro.	100	78.79
1121	dinner	noun	100	77.36
1122	yard	noun	100	70.27
1123	editor	noun	100	68.72
1124	behavior	noun	100	64.26
1124	March	prop. noun	100	64.26
1126	share	noun	100	57.58
1127	radiation	noun	100	37.53
1128	help	noun	99	92.54
1129	circumstance	noun	99	92.42
1130	professional	adjective	99	91.84
1131	somewhat	qualifier	99	88.68
1132	claim	verb	99	86.15
1133	deal	noun	99	84.86
1134	popular	adjective	99	83.18
1135	guest	noun	99	82.47
1136	status	noun	99	75.44
1137	security	noun	99	74.99
1138	June	prop. noun	99	74.02
1139	article	noun	99	68.20
1140	actual	adjective	99	65.07
1141	captain	noun	99	55.52
1142	jazz	noun	99	39.37
1143	soviet	noun	99	32.97
1144	king	noun	98	84.80
1145	mountain	noun	98	81.57
1146	block	noun	98	81.17
1147	everyone	nom. pro.	98	78.67
1148	May	prop. noun	98	71.23
1149	apartment	noun	98	69.52
1150	construction	noun	98	69.05
1151	east	adjective	98	63.28
1152	soldier	noun	98	61.63
1153	neither	co. conj.	97	90.51
1154	exactly	adverb	97	90.48
1155	lack	noun	97	90.21
1156	close	adverb	97	88.24
1157	forward	adverb	97	86.15

1069	item	noun	127	82.88
1070	spread	verb	90	82.70
1071	fellow	noun	90	82.67
1072	mission	noun	94	82.48
1073	guest	noun	99	82.47
1074	reveal	verb	97	82.32
1075	belong	verb	88	82.28
1076	goal	noun	100	81.84
1077	November	prop. noun	95	81.75
1078	chapter	noun	97	81.60
1079	mountain	noun	98	81.57
1080	saint	noun	103	81.55
1081	corporation	noun	131	81.48
1082	well	exclam.	138	81.19
1083	block	noun	98	81.17
1084	measure	verb	128	80.82
1085	claim	noun	124	80.79
1086	Christian	adjective	131	80.78
1087	proper	adjective	95	80.59
1088	desire	noun	88	80.56
1089	press	noun	107	80.43
1090	successful	adjective	95	80.34
1091	existence	noun	107	80.20
1092	insist	verb	86	80.12
1093	admit	verb	91	80.07
1094	tradition	noun	115	79.98
1095	affect	verb	93	79.98
1096	J.	prop. noun	120	79.95
1097	impossible	adjective	85	79.93
1098	agency	noun	118	79.85
1099	quickly	adverb	89	79.83
1100	park	noun	111	79.59
1101	expense	noun	97	79.52
1102	French	adjective	108	79.51
1103	master	noun	90	79.45
1104	deep	adjective	87	79.34
1105	division	noun	124	79.29
1106	encourage	verb	95	79.02
1107	please	verb	91	78.99
1108	frequently	adverb	91	78.90
1109	season	noun	125	78.87
1110	someone	nom. pro.	100	78.79
1111	model	noun	120	78.78
1112	Chicago	prop. noun	108	78.78
1113	connection	noun	86	78.74
1114	everyone	nom. pro.	98	78.67
1115	California	prop. noun	88	78.34
1116	facility	noun	111	78.33
1117	look	noun	105	78.32
1118	post	noun	101	78.28
1119	gas	noun	107	78.21
1120	team	noun	108	78.16
1121	pain	noun	102	78.13
1122	highly	qualifier	88	78.10
1123	touch	verb	91	78.03
1124	otherwise	adverb	86	77.93
1125	variety	noun	93	77.85
1126	regular	adjective	83	77.83
1127	miss	verb	95	77.81
1128	capacity	noun	88	77.81
1129	occasion	noun	80	77.81
1130	faith	noun	110	77.61
1131	ball	noun	123	77.53
1132	demand	verb	92	77.51
1133	S.	prop. noun	114	77.42
1134	communication	noun	95	77.42
1135	dinner	noun	100	77.36
1136	mouth	noun	113	77.22
1137	attack	noun	97	77.19
1138	beginning	noun	92	77.12
1139	battle	noun	91	77.06
1140	symbol	noun	90	76.95
1141	Sunday	adv. noun	116	76.90
1142	outside	prep.	83	76.82
1143	British	adjective	101	76.81
1144	bridge	noun	117	76.71
1145	firm	noun	116	76.67
1146	justice	noun	104	76.67
1147	east	adv. noun	85	76.64
1148	greatest	sup. adj.	88	76.36
1149	happy	adjective	97	76.15
1150	handle	verb	81	76.08
1151	circle	noun	91	76.04
1152	experiment	noun	122	75.98
1153	boat	noun	123	75.92
1154	attempt	verb	87	75.81
1155	inch	noun	129	75.78
1156	aware	adjective	84	75.76
1157	crisis	noun	102	75.74

1158	thousand	card. num.	97	86.01
1159	reveal	verb	97	82.32
1160	chapter	noun	97	81.60
1161	expense	noun	97	79.52
1162	attack	noun	97	77.19
1163	happy	adjective	97	76.15
1164	sight	noun	97	75.72
1165	tone	noun	97	75.27
1166	north	adjective	97	71.94
1167	Mary	prop. noun	97	69.97
1168	sleep	verb	97	64.57
1169	wine	noun	97	43.93
1170	cattle	noun	97	42.28
1171	Mike	prop. noun	97	29.44
1172	turn	noun	96	87.67
1173	considerable	adjective	96	74.50
1174	west	adjective	96	73.23
1175	pound	noun	96	68.71
1176	frame	noun	96	63.64
1177	phase	noun	96	63.52
1178	approach	verb	95	89.41
1179	supply	noun	95	86.04
1180	repeat	verb	95	85.98
1181	control	verb	95	84.63
1182	duty	noun	95	84.27
1183	November	prop. noun	95	81.75
1184	proper	adjective	95	80.59
1185	successful	adjective	95	80.34
1186	encourage	verb	95	79.02
1187	miss	verb	95	77.81
1188	communication	noun	95	77.42
1189	conclusion	noun	95	74.29
1190	paint	verb	95	73.34
1191	declare	verb	95	71.98
1192	wave	noun	95	69.21
1193	sex	noun	95	66.75
1194	hole	noun	95	65.01
1195	kitchen	noun	95	64.86
1196	wage	noun	95	59.93
1197	stare	verb	95	44.24
1198	distribution	noun	95	44.15
1199	management	noun	95	43.48
1200	fall	noun	94	84.72
1201	mission	noun	94	82.48
1202	direct	verb	94	74.53
1203	title	noun	94	71.01
1204	reality	noun	94	70.38
1205	campaign	noun	94	69.80
1206	civil	adjective	94	69.18
1207	expression	noun	94	67.05
1208	dance	noun	94	61.40
1209	run	noun	94	58.06
1210	shelter	noun	94	38.17
1211	youth	noun	93	86.70
1212	older	comp. adj.	93	85.53
1213	hardly	adverb	93	85.42
1214	very	post-det.	93	82.90
1215	affect	verb	93	79.98
1216	variety	noun	93	77.85
1217	bottom	noun	93	75.35
1218	failure	noun	93	72.81
1219	heat	noun	93	72.58
1220	drink	verb	93	67.71
1221	London	prop. noun	93	67.28
1222	application	noun	93	67.09
1223	usual	adjective	92	90.49
1224	obvious	adjective	92	86.38
1225	assure	verb	92	85.08
1226	demand	verb	92	77.51
1227	beginning	noun	92	77.12
1228	device	noun	92	74.07
1229	imagine	verb	92	72.18
1230	collection	noun	92	71.47
1231	fly	verb	92	70.47
1232	leadership	noun	92	68.33
1233	locate	verb	92	65.87
1234	annual	adjective	92	63.82
1235	camp	noun	92	63.61
1236	C.	prop. noun	92	63.40
1237	theater	noun	92	60.78
1238	objective	noun	92	60.47
1239	certain	post-det.	92	25.06
1240	refuse	verb	91	85.19
1241	avoid	verb	91	84.95
1242	fit	verb	91	83.60
1243	admit	verb	91	80.07
1244	please	verb	91	78.99
1245	frequently	adverb	91	78.90
1246	touch	verb	91	78.03

1158	sight	noun	97	75.72
1159	broad	adjective	83	75.71
1160	memory	noun	91	75.68
1161	belief	noun	87	75.47
1162	status	noun	99	75.44
1163	bottom	noun	93	75.35
1164	weight	noun	101	75.31
1165	tone	noun	97	75.27
1166	village	noun	84	75.10
1167	security	noun	99	74.99
1168	pool	noun	129	74.98
1169	rock	noun	91	74.93
1170	ability	noun	87	74.73
1171	atmosphere	noun	84	74.72
1172	direct	verb	94	74.53
1173	considerable	adjective	96	74.50
1174	English	adjective	109	74.33
1175	replace	verb	87	74.32
1176	conclusion	noun	95	74.29
1177	commission	noun	117	74.08
1178	device	noun	92	74.07
1179	June	prop. noun	99	74.02
1180	once	sub. conj.	82	74.00
1181	show	noun	108	73.95
1182	close	adjective	80	73.93
1183	fresh	adjective	82	73.89
1184	agreement	noun	121	73.84
1185	carefully	adverb	87	73.80
1186	James	prop. noun	105	73.78
1187	council	noun	115	73.70
1188	active	adjective	88	73.56
1189	cross	verb	84	73.45
1190	interesting	adjective	82	73.44
1191	twenty	card. num.	80	73.40
1192	paint	verb	95	73.34
1193	shoulder	noun	112	73.33
1194	north	adv. noun	105	73.28
1195	west	adjective	96	73.23
1196	bar	noun	116	73.14
1197	famous	adjective	89	73.12
1198	bank	noun	110	73.00
1199	task	noun	89	72.99
1200	danger	noun	86	72.91
1200	English	prop. noun	86	72.91
1202	collect	verb	78	72.88
1203	failure	noun	93	72.81
1204	equal	adjective	83	72.76
1205	speech	noun	82	72.72
1206	heat	noun	93	72.58
1207	message	noun	80	72.52
1208	concept	noun	112	72.40
1209	standard	noun	105	72.31
1210	imagine	verb	92	72.18
1211	moreover	adverb	88	72.12
1212	rest	verb	77	72.06
1213	thin	adjective	90	72.04
1214	declare	verb	95	71.98
1215	garden	noun	91	71.96
1216	north	adjective	97	71.94
1217	extent	noun	110	71.93
1218	argue	verb	78	71.79
1219	organize	verb	80	71.64
1220	oil	noun	111	71.53
1221	collection	noun	92	71.47
1222	nuclear	adjective	115	71.46
1223	shake	verb	107	71.46
1224	May	prop. noun	98	71.23
1225	spot	noun	85	71.15
1226	judgment	noun	88	71.06
1227	dream	noun	88	71.05
1228	title	noun	94	71.01
1229	inform	verb	74	70.78
1230	immediate	adjective	81	70.71
1231	tension	noun	78	70.53
1232	fly	verb	92	70.47
1233	Brown	prop. noun	129	70.44
1234	reality	noun	94	70.38
1235	winter	noun	82	70.31
1236	yard	noun	100	70.27
1237	charge	verb	82	70.16
1238	A.	prop. noun	110	70.15
1239	election	noun	128	70.12
1240	twice	adverb	75	70.03
1241	past	post-det.	84	69.99
1242	Mary	prop. noun	97	69.97
1243	campaign	noun	94	69.80
1244	signal	noun	87	69.75
1245	balance	noun	83	69.74
1246	identify	verb	81	69.74

1247	battle	noun	91	77.06
1248	circle	noun	91	76.04
1249	memory	noun	91	75.68
1250	rock	noun	91	74.93
1251	garden	noun	91	71.96
1252	conduct	verb	91	69.64
1253	training	noun	91	66.73
1254	daughter	noun	91	63.95
1255	clay	noun	91	33.43
1256	spread	verb	90	82.70
1257	fellow	noun	90	82.67
1258	master	noun	90	79.45
1259	symbol	noun	90	76.95
1260	thin	adjective	90	72.04
1261	shot	noun	90	62.98
1262	September	prop. noun	90	62.24
1263	capital	noun	90	61.91
1264	poetry	noun	90	47.79
1265	library	noun	90	47.31
1266	bond	noun	90	46.90
1267	bottle	noun	90	44.91
1268	care	noun	89	85.09
1269	order	verb	89	84.41
1270	quickly	adverb	89	79.83
1271	famous	adjective	89	73.12
1272	task	noun	89	72.99
1273	speed	noun	89	68.45
1274	chair	noun	89	67.63
1275	worry	verb	89	64.69
1276	clothes	pl. noun	89	57.02
1277	yesterday	adv. noun	89	45.65
1278	laugh	verb	89	39.02
1279	index	noun	89	26.03
1280	belong	verb	88	82.28
1281	desire	noun	88	80.56
1282	California	prop. noun	88	78.34
1283	highly	qualifier	88	78.10
1284	capacity	noun	88	77.81
1285	greatest	sup. adj.	88	76.36
1286	active	adjective	88	73.56
1287	moreover	adverb	88	72.12
1288	judgment	noun	88	71.06
1289	dream	noun	88	71.05
1290	solution	noun	88	65.80
1291	check	verb	88	65.43
1292	roll	verb	88	64.00
1293	philosophy	noun	88	59.55
1294	vehicle	noun	88	49.58
1295	forest	noun	88	48.26
1296	measurement	noun	88	32.32
1297	deep	adjective	87	79.34
1298	attempt	verb	87	75.81
1299	belief	noun	87	75.47
1300	ability	noun	87	74.73
1301	replace	verb	87	74.32
1302	carefully	adverb	87	73.80
1303	signal	noun	87	69.75
1304	reference	noun	87	69.54
1305	head	verb	87	65.98
1306	provision	noun	87	53.24
1307	lip	noun	87	47.12
1308	assistance	noun	87	45.07
1309	file	verb	87	44.04
1310	rifle	noun	87	41.64
1311	insist	verb	86	80.12
1312	connection	noun	86	78.74
1313	otherwise	adverb	86	77.93
1314	danger	noun	86	72.91
1314	English	prop. noun	86	72.91
1316	train	noun	86	67.22
1317	above	adverb	86	60.86
1318	significant	adjective	86	60.51
1319	address	noun	86	60.44
1320	scientific	adjective	86	60.34
1321	financial	adjective	86	60.27
1322	Russia	prop. noun	86	58.97
1323	knife	noun	86	52.20
1324	formula	noun	86	48.95
1325	hell	noun	86	44.99
1326	impossible	adjective	85	79.93
1327	east	adv. noun	85	76.64
1328	spot	noun	85	71.15
1329	Virginia	prop. noun	85	68.59
1330	perform	verb	85	67.06
1331	green	adjective	85	66.00
1332	economy	noun	85	60.09
1333	Henry	prop. noun	85	58.80
1334	E.	prop. noun	85	52.64
1335	representative	noun	85	48.60

1247	divide	verb	83	69.73
1248	conduct	verb	91	69.64
1249	box	noun	82	69.64
1250	travel	verb	80	69.58
1251	press	verb	82	69.57
1252	reference	noun	87	69.54
1253	apartment	noun	98	69.52
1254	however	wh-adverb	117	69.45
1255	wave	noun	95	69.21
1256	civil	adjective	94	69.18
1257	session	noun	106	69.16
1258	construction	noun	98	69.05
1259	introduce	verb	76	68.96
1260	experience	verb	82	68.81
1261	editor	noun	100	68.72
1262	pound	noun	96	68.71
1263	career	noun	82	68.66
1264	Virginia	prop. noun	85	68.59
1265	speed	noun	89	68.45
1266	leadership	noun	92	68.33
1267	article	noun	99	68.20
1268	requirement	noun	110	68.10
1269	below	prep.	80	68.03
1270	recommend	verb	81	68.01
1271	governor	noun	118	67.97
1272	presence	noun	78	67.85
1273	drink	verb	93	67.71
1274	chair	noun	89	67.63
1275	smaller	comp. adj.	78	67.60
1276	arrange	verb	71	67.59
1277	contact	noun	79	67.55
1278	London	prop. noun	93	67.28
1279	train	noun	86	67.22
1280	corps	noun	103	67.13
1281	wind	noun	74	67.13
1282	application	noun	93	67.09
1283	arrangement	noun	72	67.07
1284	perform	verb	85	67.06
1285	expression	noun	94	67.05
1286	familiar	adjective	73	66.97
1287	gain	verb	77	66.93
1288	bright	adjective	81	66.86
1289	inside	prep.	81	66.80
1290	sex	noun	95	66.75
1291	training	noun	91	66.73
1292	tooth	noun	123	66.56
1293	nine	card. num.	81	66.33
1294	recall	verb	78	66.06
1295	Thomas	prop. noun	112	66.02
1296	green	adjective	85	66.00
1297	head	verb	87	65.98
1298	previous	adjective	76	65.95
1299	locate	verb	92	65.87
1300	solution	noun	88	65.80
1301	match	verb	77	65.75
1302	remark	noun	75	65.55
1303	check	verb	88	65.43
1304	combination	noun	76	65.26
1305	actual	adjective	99	65.07
1306	poem	noun	130	65.06
1307	hole	noun	95	65.01
1308	sharp	adjective	71	64.95
1309	appearance	noun	71	64.87
1310	kitchen	noun	95	64.86
1311	sound	verb	82	64.85
1312	worry	verb	89	64.69
1313	motion	noun	72	64.65
1314	forth	adverb	71	64.65
1315	agent	noun	84	64.60
1316	nevertheless	adverb	73	64.60
1317	employ	verb	77	64.59
1318	sleep	verb	97	64.57
1319	understanding	noun	83	64.49
1320	arise	verb	75	64.45
1321	behavior	noun	100	64.26
1321	March	prop. noun	100	64.26
1323	reply	verb	75	64.22
1324	beauty	noun	77	64.04
1325	roll	verb	88	64.00
1326	daughter	noun	91	63.95
1327	call	noun	76	63.88
1328	responsible	adjective	71	63.88
1329	Kennedy	prop. noun	166	63.87
1330	annual	adjective	92	63.82
1331	argument	noun	78	63.80
1332	bird	noun	83	63.79
1333	flower	noun	78	63.67
1334	wood	noun	76	63.66
1335	frame	noun	96	63.64

1336	sample	noun	85	36.07
1337	Khrushchev	prop. noun	85	22.70
1338	aware	adjective	84	75.76
1339	village	noun	84	75.10
1340	atmosphere	noun	84	74.72
1341	cross	verb	84	73.45
1342	past	post-det.	84	69.99
1343	agent	noun	84	64.60
1344	current	adjective	84	61.88
1345	reader	noun	84	61.84
1346	strange	adjective	84	61.10
1347	notice	verb	84	60.87
1348	achievement	noun	84	59.17
1349	assign	verb	84	58.08
1350	regular	adjective	83	77.83
1351	outside	prep.	83	76.82
1352	broad	adjective	83	75.71
1353	equal	adjective	83	72.76
1354	balance	noun	83	69.74
1355	divide	verb	83	69.73
1356	understanding	noun	83	64.49
1357	bird	noun	83	63.79
1358	Germany	prop. noun	83	60.88
1359	Robert	prop. noun	83	55.53
1360	murder	noun	83	54.06
1361	W.	prop. noun	83	50.82
1362	wash	verb	83	50.75
1363	Sam	prop. noun	83	45.22
1364	Catholic	adjective	83	33.88
1365	once	sub. conj.	82	74.00
1366	fresh	adjective	82	73.89
1367	interesting	adjective	82	73.44
1368	speech	noun	82	72.72
1369	winter	noun	82	70.31
1370	charge	verb	82	70.16
1371	box	noun	82	69.64
1372	press	verb	82	69.57
1373	experience	verb	82	68.81
1374	career	noun	82	68.66
1375	sound	verb	82	64.85
1376	official	noun	82	57.82
1377	seed	noun	82	37.18
1378	senator	noun	82	35.71
1379	handle	verb	81	76.08
1380	immediate	adjective	81	70.71
1381	identify	verb	81	69.74
1382	recommend	verb	81	68.01
1383	bright	adjective	81	66.86
1384	inside	prep.	81	66.80
1385	nine	card. num.	81	66.33
1386	primary	adjective	81	62.62
1387	resource	noun	81	59.07
1388	France	prop. noun	81	58.23
1389	consideration	noun	81	54.46
1390	attorney	noun	81	51.26
1391	musical	adjective	81	49.50
1392	define	verb	81	49.24
1393	judge	noun	81	49.02
1394	missile	noun	81	48.52
1395	location	noun	81	45.22
1396	league	noun	81	36.98
1397	Junior	prop. noun	81	35.90
1398	Jew	prop. noun	81	35.50
1399	occasion	noun	80	77.81
1400	close	adjective	80	73.93
1401	twenty	card. num.	80	73.40
1402	message	noun	80	72.52
1403	organize	verb	80	71.64
1404	travel	verb	80	69.58
1405	below	prep.	80	68.03
1406	decade	noun	80	63.39
1407	error	noun	80	60.94
1408	baby	noun	80	52.33
1409	neck	noun	80	51.08
1410	assignment	noun	80	48.13
1411	truck	noun	80	45.35
1412	component	noun	80	42.24
1413	site	noun	80	37.38
1414	Berlin	prop. noun	80	29.83
1415	contact	noun	79	67.55
1416	skill	noun	79	61.53
1417	telephone	noun	79	61.47
1418	December	prop. noun	79	60.32
1419	standard	adjective	79	54.21
1420	generation	noun	79	53.17
1421	October	prop. noun	79	51.94
1422	estimate	verb	79	51.91
1423	driver	noun	79	51.12
1424	vote	verb	79	49.93

1336	camp	noun	92	63.61
1337	phase	noun	96	63.52
1338	background	noun	74	63.50
1339	cell	noun	146	63.49
1340	devote	verb	76	63.49
1341	aside	adverb	67	63.47
1342	C.	prop. noun	92	63.40
1343	decade	noun	80	63.39
1344	shop	noun	75	63.34
1345	east	adjective	98	63.28
1346	analysis	noun	121	63.20
1347	visit	noun	74	63.18
1348	income	noun	110	63.01
1349	shot	noun	90	62.98
1350	own	verb	70	62.84
1351	essential	adjective	78	62.68
1352	primary	adjective	81	62.62
1353	fashion	noun	70	62.56
1354	grant	verb	78	62.50
1355	relief	noun	66	62.43
1356	solid	adjective	70	62.33
1357	democratic	adjective	109	62.31
1358	September	prop. noun	90	62.24
1359	neighborhood	noun	75	62.12
1360	instrument	noun	73	62.08
1361	earlier	comp. adj.	76	61.99
1362	capital	noun	90	61.91
1363	current	adjective	84	61.88
1364	gather	verb	66	61.87
1365	reader	noun	84	61.84
1366	while	noun	78	61.67
1367	soldier	noun	98	61.63
1368	accomplish	verb	71	61.63
1369	manage	verb	68	61.54
1370	skill	noun	79	61.53
1371	telephone	noun	79	61.47
1372	deliver	verb	71	61.44
1373	dance	noun	94	61.40
1374	intend	verb	67	61.37
1375	kid	noun	104	61.18
1376	somehow	adverb	72	61.16
1377	ancient	adjective	68	61.15
1378	worth	adjective	71	61.11
1379	strange	adjective	84	61.10
1380	error	noun	80	60.94
1381	Germany	prop. noun	83	60.88
1382	notice	verb	84	60.87
1383	above	adverb	86	60.86
1384	theater	noun	92	60.78
1385	fire	verb	78	60.76
1386	emerge	verb	68	60.65
1387	significant	adjective	86	60.51
1388	smile	verb	122	60.50
1389	willing	adjective	70	60.50
1390	objective	noun	92	60.47
1391	address	noun	86	60.44
1392	scientific	adjective	86	60.34
1393	December	prop. noun	79	60.32
1394	financial	adjective	86	60.27
1395	rich	adjective	70	60.23
1396	escape	verb	69	60.14
1397	economy	noun	85	60.09
1398	fourth	ord. num.	72	60.08
1399	professor	noun	78	60.01
1400	Christ	prop. noun	115	59.97
1401	step	verb	71	59.96
1402	wage	noun	95	59.93
1403	fair	adjective	70	59.62
1404	examine	verb	70	59.60
1405	philosophy	noun	88	59.55
1406	legal	adjective	72	59.26
1407	achievement	noun	84	59.17
1408	fifty	card. num.	68	59.15
1409	south	adjective	76	59.13
1410	resource	noun	81	59.07
1411	Russia	prop. noun	86	58.97
1412	advance	verb	71	58.84
1413	Henry	prop. noun	85	58.80
1414	impression	noun	70	58.76
1415	brief	adjective	64	58.74
1416	oh	exclam.	119	58.66
1417	contrast	noun	78	58.63
1418	stress	noun	111	58.62
1419	accompany	verb	63	58.59
1420	threaten	verb	67	58.57
1421	earlier	comp. adv.	70	58.54
1422	imagination	noun	67	58.42
1423	sheet	noun	71	58.34
1424	naturally	adverb	69	58.28

1425	nobody	nom. pro.	79	49.21
1426	valley	noun	79	47.45
1427	B.	prop. noun	79	45.81
1428	right	adverb	79	41.97
1429	Texas	prop. noun	79	31.74
1430	Mercer	prop. noun	79	14.23
1431	collect	verb	78	72.88
1432	argue	verb	78	71.79
1433	tension	noun	78	70.53
1434	presence	noun	78	67.85
1435	smaller	comp. adj.	78	67.60
1436	recall	verb	78	66.06
1437	argument	noun	78	63.80
1438	flower	noun	78	63.67
1439	essential	adjective	78	62.68
1440	grant	verb	78	62.50
1441	while	noun	78	61.67
1442	fire	verb	78	60.76
1443	professor	noun	78	60.01
1444	contrast	noun	78	58.63
1445	traditional	adjective	78	57.31
1446	revolution	noun	78	46.28
1447	literary	adjective	78	44.43
1448	Providence	prop. noun	78	43.83
1449	coffee	noun	78	43.45
1450	faculty	noun	78	43.24
1451	publication	noun	78	42.41
1452	panel	noun	78	41.27
1453	beside	prep.	78	41.24
1454	engineer	noun	78	39.56
1455	loan	noun	78	33.38
1456	atom	noun	78	29.46
1457	Morgan	prop. noun	78	27.56
1458	Hanover	prop. noun	78	15.11
1459	anode	noun	78	12.48
1460	rest	verb	77	72.06
1461	gain	verb	77	66.93
1462	match	verb	77	65.75
1463	employ	verb	77	64.59
1464	beauty	noun	77	64.04
1465	everybody	nom. pro.	77	57.49
1466	August	prop. noun	77	57.38
1467	wheel	noun	77	57.36
1468	railroad	noun	77	54.36
1469	author	noun	77	53.45
1470	front	adjective	77	52.11
1471	shout	verb	77	51.68
1472	emotion	noun	77	49.32
1473	swing	verb	77	48.99
1474	guess	verb	77	47.90
1475	lord	noun	77	42.11
1476	platform	noun	77	36.60
1477	manufacturer	noun	77	36.26
1478	chairman	noun	77	32.97
1479	introduce	verb	76	68.96
1480	previous	adjective	76	65.95
1481	combination	noun	76	65.26
1482	call	noun	76	63.88
1483	wood	noun	76	63.66
1484	devote	verb	76	63.49
1485	earlier	comp. adj.	76	61.99
1486	south	adjective	76	59.13
1487	middle	adjective	76	56.89
1488	surprise	verb	76	56.14
1489	Louis	prop. noun	76	52.99
1490	relatively	qualifier	76	51.64
1491	nice	adjective	76	48.07
1492	characteristic	noun	76	42.54
1493	vocational	adjective	76	37.53
1494	Richard	prop. noun	76	37.32
1495	twice	adverb	75	70.03
1496	remark	noun	75	65.55
1497	arise	verb	75	64.45
1498	reply	verb	75	64.22
1499	shop	noun	75	63.34
1500	neighborhood	noun	75	62.12
1501	benefit	noun	75	53.64
1502	means	noun	75	46.11
1503	Jones	prop. noun	75	45.36
1504	slave	noun	75	44.30
1505	drink	noun	75	44.22
1506	membership	noun	75	30.17
1507	inform	verb	74	70.78
1508	wind	noun	74	67.13
1509	background	noun	74	63.50
1510	visit	noun	74	63.18
1511	further	comp. adj.	74	58.22
1512	record	verb	74	55.90
1513	gray	adjective	74	54.04

1425	coast	noun	67	58.28
1426	San	prop. noun	70	58.25
1427	France	prop. noun	81	58.23
1428	further	comp. adj.	74	58.22
1429	employee	noun	109	58.20
1430	careful	adjective	62	58.16
1431	weather	noun	70	58.11
1432	assign	verb	84	58.08
1433	lack	verb	70	58.07
1434	run	noun	94	58.06
1435	motor	noun	108	58.02
1436	hero	noun	70	57.88
1437	official	noun	82	57.82
1438	issue	verb	72	57.61
1439	share	noun	100	57.58
1440	everybody	nom. pro.	77	57.49
1441	desire	verb	71	57.47
1442	promise	verb	68	57.40
1443	August	prop. noun	77	57.38
1444	wheel	noun	77	57.36
1445	traditional	adjective	78	57.31
1446	engage	verb	66	57.22
1447	key	noun	71	57.17
1448	lawyer	noun	69	57.15
1449	ordinary	adjective	69	57.10
1450	ought	modal aux.	70	57.09
1451	clothes	pl. noun	89	57.02
1452	unusual	adjective	63	57.02
1453	knee	noun	73	57.01
1454	excellent	adjective	68	57.00
1455	touch	noun	64	56.92
1456	middle	adjective	76	56.89
1457	powerful	adjective	63	56.83
1458	capable	adjective	66	56.81
1459	top	sem. sup.	72	56.68
1460	favor	noun	63	56.61
1461	quarter	noun	62	56.59
1462	limit	noun	68	56.56
1463	preserve	verb	63	56.40
1464	possibly	adverb	61	56.38
1465	upper	adjective	65	56.36
1466	pair	noun	64	56.34
1467	portion	noun	73	56.32
1468	protect	verb	71	56.28
1469	satisfy	verb	63	56.28
1470	distinguish	verb	71	56.21
1471	passage	noun	69	56.19
1472	fully	adverb	66	56.16
1473	surprise	verb	76	56.14
1474	quiet	adjective	65	56.14
1475	rapidly	adverb	64	56.11
1476	succeed	verb	61	56.10
1477	owner	noun	72	56.06
1478	exception	noun	66	55.92
1479	record	verb	74	55.90
1480	honor	noun	67	55.84
1481	separate	verb	67	55.79
1482	principal	sup. adj.	71	55.72
1483	separate	adjective	65	55.68
1484	count	verb	65	55.67
1485	metal	noun	68	55.64
1486	positive	adjective	73	55.58
1487	Robert	prop. noun	83	55.53
1488	captain	noun	99	55.52
1489	dozen	noun	63	55.52
1490	comment	noun	64	55.34
1491	sky	noun	72	55.33
1492	closely	adverb	65	55.27
1493	adopt	verb	71	55.21
1494	cloud	noun	64	55.18
1495	survive	verb	62	55.01
1496	appeal	noun	72	54.83
1497	impact	noun	70	54.75
1498	investigation	noun	73	54.57
1499	vast	adjective	61	54.55
1500	either	dt./d. cj.	64	54.51
1501	entirely	adverb	61	54.49
1502	friendly	adjective	61	54.47
1503	consideration	noun	81	54.46
1504	Jack	prop. noun	103	54.41
1505	railroad	noun	77	54.36
1506	prefer	verb	60	54.30
1507	contract	noun	73	54.27
1508	chief	sem. sup.	66	54.26
1509	light	adjective	63	54.26
1510	urge	verb	64	54.23
1511	standard	adjective	79	54.21
1512	depth	noun	72	54.21
1513	conviction	noun	70	54.19

1514	January	prop. noun	74	53.51
1515	beach	noun	74	53.22
1516	automobile	noun	74	52.33
1517	associate	verb	74	51.96
1518	command	noun	74	49.89
1519	communism	noun	74	44.93
1520	personnel	noun	74	44.63
1521	total	adjective	74	39.43
1522	Jewish	adjective	74	32.47
1523	familiar	adjective	73	66.97
1524	nevertheless	adverb	73	64.60
1525	instrument	noun	73	62.08
1526	knee	noun	73	57.01
1527	portion	noun	73	56.32
1528	positive	adjective	73	55.58
1529	investigation	noun	73	54.57
1530	contract	noun	73	54.27
1531	minister	noun	73	53.84
1532	muscle	noun	73	53.63
1533	rain	noun	73	52.17
1534	demonstrate	verb	73	47.68
1535	candidate	noun	73	46.93
1536	avenue	noun	73	46.65
1537	soul	noun	73	45.42
1538	tool	noun	73	45.31
1539	arrangement	noun	72	67.07
1540	motion	noun	72	64.65
1541	somehow	adverb	72	61.16
1542	fourth	ord. num.	72	60.08
1543	legal	adjective	72	59.26
1544	issue	verb	72	57.61
1545	top	sem. sup.	72	56.68
1546	owner	noun	72	56.06
1547	sky	noun	72	55.33
1548	appeal	noun	72	54.83
1549	depth	noun	72	54.21
1550	light	verb	72	52.83
1551	exchange	noun	72	51.56
1552	disease	noun	72	51.26
1553	dry	verb	72	50.83
1554	combine	verb	72	49.30
1555	Rome	prop. noun	72	45.79
1556	unity	noun	72	42.81
1557	detective	noun	72	34.84
1558	wagon	noun	72	34.24
1559	Saturday	adv. noun	72	32.25
1560	Monday	adv. noun	72	20.72
1561	arrange	verb	71	67.59
1562	sharp	adjective	71	64.95
1563	appearance	noun	71	64.87
1564	forth	adverb	71	64.65
1565	responsible	adjective	71	63.88
1566	accomplish	verb	71	61.63
1567	deliver	verb	71	61.44
1568	worth	adjective	71	61.11
1569	step	verb	71	59.96
1570	advance	verb	71	58.84
1571	sheet	noun	71	58.34
1572	desire	verb	71	57.47
1573	key	noun	71	57.17
1574	protect	verb	71	56.28
1575	distinguish	verb	71	56.21
1576	principal	sup. adj.	71	55.72
1577	adopt	verb	71	55.21
1578	average	noun	71	53.47
1579	oppose	verb	71	52.76
1580	reading	noun	71	52.58
1581	April	prop. noun	71	48.86
1582	culture	noun	71	48.28
1583	historical	adjective	71	47.19
1584	novel	noun	71	45.14
1585	independence	noun	71	44.89
1586	hat	noun	71	44.87
1587	H.	prop. noun	71	44.09
1588	aircraft	noun	71	36.62
1589	Republican	prop. noun	71	32.47
1590	universe	noun	71	32.09
1591	own	verb	70	62.84
1592	fashion	noun	70	62.56
1593	solid	adjective	70	62.33
1594	willing	adjective	70	60.50
1595	rich	adjective	70	60.23
1596	fair	adjective	70	59.62
1597	examine	verb	70	59.60
1598	impression	noun	70	58.76
1599	earlier	comp. adv.	70	58.54
1600	San	prop. noun	70	58.25
1601	weather	noun	70	58.11
1602	lack	verb	70	58.07

1514	attack	verb	63	54.16
1515	crowd	noun	63	54.15
1516	question	verb	67	54.09
1517	murder	noun	83	54.06
1518	gray	adjective	74	54.04
1519	pretty	qualifier	63	54.01
1520	talent	noun	68	53.99
1521	completely	adverb	63	53.88
1522	minister	noun	73	53.84
1523	test	verb	67	53.84
1524	reasonable	adjective	65	53.68
1525	customer	noun	69	53.67
1526	benefit	noun	75	53.64
1527	muscle	noun	73	53.63
1528	politics	noun	69	53.62
1529	January	prop. noun	74	53.51
1530	average	noun	71	53.47
1531	dust	noun	68	53.47
1532	author	noun	77	53.45
1533	ignore	verb	57	53.40
1534	provision	noun	87	53.24
1535	towards	prep.	65	53.24
1536	beach	noun	74	53.22
1537	band	noun	64	53.20
1538	generation	noun	79	53.17
1539	de	foreign	67	53.16
1540	present	adverb	65	53.02
1541	Louis	prop. noun	76	52.99
1542	just	qualifier	64	52.85
1543	light	verb	72	52.83
1544	Paris	prop. noun	68	52.83
1545	oppose	verb	71	52.76
1546	acquire	verb	66	52.74
1547	independent	adjective	70	52.71
1548	E.	prop. noun	85	52.64
1549	establishment	noun	60	52.64
1550	occupy	verb	63	52.62
1551	explanation	noun	58	52.59
1552	reading	noun	71	52.58
1553	pleasure	noun	67	52.35
1554	baby	noun	80	52.33
1555	automobile	noun	74	52.33
1556	headquarters	noun	66	52.32
1557	vision	noun	63	52.30
1558	initial	adjective	69	52.23
1559	knife	noun	86	52.20
1560	rain	noun	73	52.17
1561	daily	adjective	67	52.13
1562	front	adjective	77	52.11
1563	longer	comp. adj.	69	52.09
1564	lift	verb	69	52.08
1565	stand	noun	58	51.98
1566	left	adjective	68	51.97
1567	associate	verb	74	51.96
1568	October	prop. noun	79	51.94
1569	estimate	verb	79	51.91
1570	suit	noun	64	51.91
1571	magazine	noun	65	51.90
1572	contribution	noun	67	51.72
1573	shout	verb	77	51.68
1574	relatively	qualifier	76	51.64
1575	height	noun	58	51.62
1576	through	adv./part.	61	51.60
1577	shore	noun	66	51.58
1578	exchange	noun	72	51.56
1579	practical	adjective	68	51.56
1580	interpretation	noun	66	51.56
1581	constant	adjective	61	51.48
1582	narrow	adjective	63	51.46
1583	expand	verb	64	51.40
1584	attorney	noun	81	51.26
1585	disease	noun	72	51.26
1586	path	noun	58	51.15
1587	electric	adjective	60	51.13
1588	driver	noun	79	51.12
1589	warm	adjective	64	51.09
1590	neck	noun	80	51.08
1591	traffic	noun	68	51.05
1592	range	verb	63	51.01
1593	quick	adjective	58	51.01
1594	dry	verb	72	50.83
1595	W.	prop. noun	83	50.82
1596	communist	noun	112	50.79
1597	ourselves	refl. pro.	66	50.79
1598	wash	verb	83	50.75
1599	outside	adverb	65	50.65
1600	consequence	noun	65	50.64
1601	dramatic	adjective	63	50.60
1602	convince	verb	57	50.56

1603	hero	noun	70	57.88	1603	significance	noun	66	50.37
1604	ought	modal aux.	70	57.09	1604	ear	noun	67	50.19
1605	impact	noun	70	54.75	1605	fifteen	card. num.	56	50.17
1606	conviction	noun	70	54.19	1606	dress	noun	63	50.08
1607	independent	adjective	70	52.71	1607	stretch	verb	61	49.98
1608	birth	noun	70	48.33	1608	taste	noun	60	49.98
1609	educational	adjective	70	48.28	1609	vote	verb	79	49.93
1610	proposal	noun	70	47.60	1610	mount	verb	62	49.93
1611	resolution	noun	70	40.03	1611	Russian	adjective	69	49.90
1612	snake	noun	70	30.96	1612	command	noun	74	49.89
1613	escape	verb	69	60.14	1613	unable	adjective	54	49.89
1614	naturally	adverb	69	58.28	1614	personality	noun	63	49.84
1615	lawyer	noun	69	57.15	1615	by	adverb	61	49.83
1616	ordinary	adjective	69	57.10	1616	Boston	prop. noun	63	49.81
1617	passage	noun	69	56.19	1617	conclude	verb	60	49.78
1618	customer	noun	69	53.67	1618	illustrate	verb	65	49.77
1619	politics	noun	69	53.62	1619	enable	verb	57	49.75
1620	initial	adjective	69	52.23	1620	ultimate	adjective	59	49.65
1621	longer	comp. adj.	69	52.09	1621	branch	noun	63	49.62
1622	lift	verb	69	52.08	1622	vehicle	noun	88	49.58
1623	Russian	adjective	69	49.90	1623	warn	verb	62	49.54
1624	desk	noun	69	49.21	1624	surround	verb	53	49.52
1625	preparation	noun	69	47.98	1625	musical	adjective	81	49.50
1626	well	qualifier	69	45.90	1626	eliminate	verb	67	49.44
1627	gain	noun	69	43.27	1627	stream	noun	61	49.42
1628	engine	noun	69	42.09	1628	flight	noun	60	49.41
1629	troop	noun	69	38.45	1629	search	noun	59	49.39
1630	drug	noun	69	30.03	1630	emotion	noun	77	49.32
1631	Hudson	prop. noun	69	28.24	1631	combine	verb	72	49.30
1632	manage	verb	68	61.54	1632	define	verb	81	49.24
1633	ancient	adjective	68	61.15	1633	nobody	nom. pro.	79	49.21
1634	emerge	verb	68	60.65	1634	desk	noun	69	49.21
1635	fifty	card. num.	68	59.15	1635	roof	noun	64	49.16
1636	promise	verb	68	57.40	1636	afford	verb	58	49.07
1637	excellent	adjective	68	57.00	1637	payment	noun	102	49.06
1638	limit	noun	68	56.56	1638	judge	noun	81	49.02
1639	metal	noun	68	55.64	1639	swing	verb	77	48.99
1640	talent	noun	68	53.99	1640	confidence	noun	58	48.97
1641	dust	noun	68	53.47	1641	formula	noun	86	48.95
1642	Paris	prop. noun	68	52.83	1642	apparent	adjective	57	48.95
1643	left	adjective	68	51.97	1643	April	prop. noun	71	48.86
1644	practical	adjective	68	51.56	1644	February	prop. noun	67	48.86
1645	traffic	noun	68	51.05	1645	instruction	noun	61	48.73
1646	target	noun	68	48.61	1646	left	adv. noun	67	48.63
1647	victory	noun	68	45.12	1647	target	noun	68	48.61
1648	sweet	adjective	68	44.78	1648	representative	noun	85	48.60
1649	protection	noun	68	42.71	1649	cost	verb	62	48.56
1650	seat	noun	68	41.44	1650	missile	noun	81	48.52
1651	bomb	noun	68	41.10	1651	respond	verb	54	48.50
1652	emotional	adjective	68	38.32	1652	beat	verb	66	48.48
1653	electronic	adjective	68	32.67	1653	credit	noun	67	48.47
1654	jury	noun	68	30.12	1654	description	noun	64	48.44
1655	artery	noun	68	16.81	1655	confront	verb	55	48.43
1656	aside	adverb	67	63.47	1656	birth	noun	70	48.33
1657	intend	verb	67	61.37	1657	hard	adverb	61	48.33
1658	threaten	verb	67	58.57	1658	culture	noun	71	48.28
1659	imagination	noun	67	58.42	1659	educational	adjective	70	48.28
1660	coast	noun	67	58.28	1660	forest	noun	88	48.26
1661	honor	noun	67	55.84	1661	apart	adverb	57	48.25
1662	separate	verb	67	55.79	1662	eventually	adverb	55	48.23
1663	question	verb	67	54.09	1663	soft	adjective	60	48.20
1664	test	verb	67	53.84	1664	drive	noun	60	48.15
1665	de	foreign	67	53.16	1665	assignment	noun	80	48.13
1666	pleasure	noun	67	52.35	1666	advance	noun	60	48.13
1667	daily	adjective	67	52.13	1667	nice	adjective	76	48.07
1668	contribution	noun	67	51.72	1668	onto	prep.	61	48.07
1669	ear	noun	67	50.19	1669	suggestion	noun	57	48.04
1670	eliminate	verb	67	49.44	1670	amount	verb	56	48.02
1671	February	prop. noun	67	48.86	1671	properly	adverb	55	48.00
1672	left	adv. noun	67	48.63	1672	preparation	noun	69	47.98
1673	credit	noun	67	48.47	1673	moon	noun	63	47.98
1674	soil	noun	67	47.92	1674	below	adverb	65	47.95
1675	trend	noun	67	47.91	1675	thirty	card. num.	59	47.94
1676	appropriate	adjective	67	46.69	1676	soil	noun	67	47.92
1677	etcetera	adverb	67	45.12	1677	trend	noun	67	47.91
1678	speaker	noun	67	43.65	1678	guess	verb	77	47.90
1679	inside	adverb	67	41.76	1679	poetry	noun	90	47.79
1680	yourself	refl. pro.	67	41.56	1680	greatly	adverb	62	47.78
1681	tomorrow	adv. noun	67	39.93	1681	stone	noun	66	47.74
1682	farmer	noun	67	38.66	1682	demonstrate	verb	73	47.68
1683	observation	noun	67	38.12	1683	attract	verb	51	47.65
1684	maximum	adjective	67	36.54	1684	brown	adjective	66	47.62
1685	dress	verb	67	35.90	1685	proposal	noun	70	47.60
1686	Tom	prop. noun	67	35.44	1686	valley	noun	79	47.45
1687	sin	noun	67	31.23	1687	intention	noun	58	47.43
1688	Phil	prop. noun	67	10.77	1688	expert	noun	57	47.37
1689	relief	noun	66	62.43	1689	library	noun	90	47.31
1690	gather	verb	66	61.87	1690	fight	noun	58	47.23
1691	engage	verb	66	57.22	1691	historical	adjective	71	47.19

1692	capable	adjective	66	56.81
1693	fully	adverb	66	56.16
1694	exception	noun	66	55.92
1695	chief	sem. sup.	66	54.26
1696	acquire	verb	66	52.74
1697	headquarters	noun	66	52.32
1698	shore	noun	66	51.58
1699	interpretation	noun	66	51.56
1700	ourselves	refl. pro.	66	50.79
1701	significance	noun	66	50.37
1702	beat	verb	66	48.48
1703	stone	noun	66	47.74
1704	brown	adjective	66	47.62
1705	adequate	adjective	66	47.13
1706	being	noun	66	46.95
1707	July	prop. noun	66	44.92
1708	hate	verb	66	41.87
1709	substantial	adjective	66	41.00
1710	orchestra	noun	66	39.76
1711	guy	noun	66	37.64
1712	vote	noun	66	34.56
1713	operator	noun	66	31.27
1714	China	prop. noun	66	29.65
1715	senate	noun	66	25.97
1716	upper	adjective	65	56.36
1717	quiet	adjective	65	56.14
1718	separate	adjective	65	55.68
1719	count	verb	65	55.67
1720	closely	adverb	65	55.27
1721	reasonable	adjective	65	53.68
1722	towards	prep.	65	53.24
1723	present	adverb	65	53.02
1724	magazine	noun	65	51.90
1725	outside	adverb	65	50.65
1726	consequence	noun	65	50.64
1727	illustrate	verb	65	49.77
1728	below	adverb	65	47.95
1729	typical	adjective	65	46.02
1730	score	noun	65	45.74
1731	Saint	prop. noun	65	44.91
1732	Massachusetts	prop. noun	65	44.60
1733	identity	noun	65	42.86
1734	D.	prop. noun	65	42.72
1735	entitle	verb	65	42.62
1736	derive	verb	65	42.24
1737	somebody	nom. pro.	65	42.14
1738	sport	noun	65	42.12
1739	foundation	noun	65	38.29
1740	nose	noun	65	37.73
1741	approximately	adverb	65	36.23
1742	climb	verb	65	35.37
1743	Wilson	prop. noun	65	34.89
1744	cousin	noun	65	34.26
1745	musician	noun	65	33.29
1746	dominant	adjective	65	29.05
1747	Parker	prop. noun	65	28.50
1748	congregation	noun	65	22.34
1749	feed	noun	65	19.96
1750	brief	adjective	64	58.74
1751	touch	noun	64	56.92
1752	pair	noun	64	56.34
1753	rapidly	adverb	64	56.11
1754	comment	noun	64	55.34
1755	cloud	noun	64	55.18
1756	either	dt./d. cj.	64	54.51
1757	urge	verb	64	54.23
1758	band	noun	64	53.20
1759	just	qualifier	64	52.85
1760	suit	noun	64	51.91
1761	expand	verb	64	51.40
1762	warm	adjective	64	51.09
1763	roof	noun	64	49.16
1764	description	noun	64	48.44
1765	primarily	adverb	64	45.11
1766	brain	noun	64	44.91
1767	empty	adjective	64	44.88
1768	average	adjective	64	44.29
1769	maintenance	noun	64	41.47
1770	cry	verb	64	41.17
1771	assumption	noun	64	35.95
1772	text	noun	64	34.21
1773	spiritual	adjective	64	34.00
1774	Friday	adv. noun	64	32.45
1775	concert	noun	64	30.53
1776	completion	noun	64	30.16
1777	curve	noun	64	27.08
1778	marine	noun	64	20.34
1779	Laos	prop. noun	64	19.51
1780	accompany	verb	63	58.59

1692	adequate	adjective	66	47.13
1693	lip	noun	87	47.12
1694	slight	adjective	51	47.12
1695	struggle	noun	57	47.09
1696	highest	sup. adj.	59	47.06
1697	sweep	verb	54	47.03
1698	being	noun	66	46.95
1699	candidate	noun	73	46.93
1700	bond	noun	90	46.90
1701	view	verb	55	46.87
1702	huge	adjective	55	46.84
1703	gradually	adverb	51	46.75
1704	appropriate	adjective	67	46.69
1705	M.	prop. noun	63	46.68
1706	avenue	noun	73	46.65
1707	heavily	adverb	53	46.65
1708	entrance	noun	57	46.61
1709	guide	verb	51	46.43
1710	lake	noun	61	46.32
1711	revolution	noun	78	46.28
1712	threat	noun	56	46.27
1713	absence	noun	56	46.26
1714	unique	adjective	58	46.25
1715	proceed	verb	56	46.23
1716	conversation	noun	60	46.22
1717	sign	verb	62	46.16
1718	straight	adjective	56	46.12
1719	check	noun	53	46.12
1720	means	noun	75	46.11
1721	majority	noun	60	46.08
1722	typical	adjective	65	46.02
1723	chain	noun	60	45.98
1724	talk	noun	55	45.97
1725	emphasis	noun	60	45.91
1726	well	qualifier	69	45.90
1727	B.	prop. noun	79	45.81
1728	Rome	prop. noun	72	45.79
1729	score	noun	65	45.74
1730	clean	verb	58	45.73
1731	yesterday	adv. noun	89	45.65
1732	list	verb	59	45.53
1733	tear	verb	58	45.53
1734	reject	verb	58	45.52
1735	perfect	adjective	58	45.49
1736	wire	noun	55	45.49
1737	soul	noun	73	45.42
1738	jump	verb	58	45.41
1739	invite	verb	49	45.37
1740	Jones	prop. noun	75	45.36
1741	evident	adjective	56	45.36
1742	truck	noun	80	45.35
1743	conflict	noun	58	45.35
1744	tool	noun	73	45.31
1745	vital	adjective	56	45.26
1746	painting	noun	63	45.24
1747	Sam	prop. noun	83	45.22
1748	location	noun	81	45.22
1749	participate	verb	57	45.18
1750	novel	noun	71	45.14
1751	victory	noun	68	45.12
1752	etcetera	adverb	67	45.12
1753	primarily	adverb	64	45.11
1754	safe	adjective	51	45.11
1755	assistance	noun	87	45.07
1756	start	noun	61	45.07
1757	bay	noun	60	45.04
1758	concerning	prep.	62	45.03
1759	visitor	noun	49	45.01
1760	hell	noun	86	44.99
1761	alive	adjective	57	44.96
1762	communism	noun	74	44.93
1763	remind	verb	57	44.93
1764	inner	adjective	55	44.93
1765	July	prop. noun	66	44.92
1766	bottle	noun	90	44.91
1767	Saint	prop. noun	65	44.91
1768	brain	noun	64	44.91
1769	independence	noun	71	44.89
1770	empty	adjective	64	44.88
1771	hat	noun	71	44.87
1772	firm	adjective	50	44.79
1773	sweet	adjective	68	44.78
1774	pilot	noun	54	44.71
1775	intensity	noun	61	44.68
1776	personnel	noun	74	44.63
1777	competition	noun	63	44.63
1778	Massachusetts	prop. noun	65	44.60
1779	useful	adjective	58	44.55
1780	busy	adjective	57	44.55

1781	unusual	adjective	63	57.02
1782	powerful	adjective	63	56.83
1783	favor	noun	63	56.61
1784	preserve	verb	63	56.40
1785	satisfy	verb	63	56.28
1786	dozen	noun	63	55.52
1787	light	adjective	63	54.26
1788	attack	verb	63	54.16
1789	crowd	noun	63	54.15
1790	pretty	qualifier	63	54.01
1791	completely	adverb	63	53.88
1792	occupy	verb	63	52.62
1793	vision	noun	63	52.30
1794	narrow	adjective	63	51.46
1795	range	verb	63	51.01
1796	dramatic	adjective	63	50.60
1797	dress	noun	63	50.08
1798	personality	noun	63	49.84
1799	Boston	prop. noun	63	49.81
1800	branch	noun	63	49.62
1801	moon	noun	63	47.98
1802	M.	prop. noun	63	46.68
1803	painting	noun	63	45.24
1804	competition	noun	63	44.63
1805	guard	noun	63	44.40
1806	thick	adjective	63	44.04
1807	sufficient	adjective	63	42.95
1808	theme	noun	63	37.98
1809	lock	verb	63	37.67
1810	dancer	noun	63	34.77
1811	switch	noun	63	34.35
1812	p.m.	adverb	63	28.33
1813	throat	noun	63	27.03
1814	particle	noun	63	25.20
1815	Lewis	prop. noun	63	23.16
1816	careful	adjective	62	58.16
1817	quarter	noun	62	56.59
1818	survive	verb	62	55.01
1819	mount	verb	62	49.93
1820	warn	verb	62	49.54
1821	cost	verb	62	48.56
1822	greatly	adverb	62	47.78
1823	sign	verb	62	46.16
1824	concerning	prep.	62	45.03
1825	adjust	verb	62	44.26
1826	German	prop. noun	62	43.61
1827	internal	adjective	62	43.50
1828	domestic	adjective	62	42.30
1829	scale	noun	62	39.43
1830	R.	prop. noun	62	39.39
1831	chief	noun	62	38.23
1832	phenomenon	noun	62	37.88
1833	Bill	prop. noun	62	37.83
1834	version	noun	62	33.90
1835	Eisenhower	prop. noun	62	30.96
1836	baseball	noun	62	29.33
1837	nod	verb	62	24.91
1838	billion	card. num.	62	23.49
1839	budget	noun	62	19.79
1840	Palmer	prop. noun	62	14.30
1841	possibly	adverb	61	56.38
1842	succeed	verb	61	56.10
1843	vast	adjective	61	54.55
1844	entirely	adverb	61	54.49
1845	friendly	adjective	61	54.47
1846	through	adv./part.	61	51.60
1847	constant	adjective	61	51.48
1848	stretch	verb	61	49.98
1849	by	adverb	61	49.83
1850	stream	noun	61	49.42
1851	instruction	noun	61	48.73
1852	hard	adverb	61	48.33
1853	onto	prep.	61	48.07
1854	lake	noun	61	46.32
1855	start	noun	61	45.07
1856	intensity	noun	61	44.68
1857	card	noun	61	42.37
1858	hide	verb	61	39.48
1859	Britain	prop. noun	61	39.04
1860	assembly	noun	61	38.19
1861	past	prep.	61	37.84
1862	promote	verb	61	37.66
1863	lean	verb	61	37.20
1864	arm	verb	61	36.38
1865	park	verb	61	35.89
1866	revenue	noun	61	31.17
1867	angle	noun	61	29.61
1868	Jesus	prop. noun	61	15.48
1869	prefer	verb	60	54.30

1781	literary	adjective	78	44.43
1782	guard	noun	63	44.40
1783	factory	noun	56	44.33
1784	slave	noun	75	44.30
1785	average	adjective	64	44.29
1786	advice	noun	52	44.28
1787	adjust	verb	62	44.26
1788	stare	verb	95	44.24
1789	drink	noun	75	44.22
1790	distribution	noun	95	44.15
1791	sum	noun	59	44.15
1792	detail	verb	53	44.11
1793	H.	prop. noun	71	44.09
1794	distinction	noun	56	44.08
1795	file	verb	87	44.04
1796	thick	adjective	63	44.04
1797	mark	noun	50	43.95
1798	wine	noun	97	43.93
1799	necessity	noun	53	43.92
1800	folk	noun	53	43.91
1801	flat	adjective	52	43.85
1802	Providence	prop. noun	78	43.83
1803	whole	noun	52	43.83
1804	official	adjective	55	43.76
1805	neighbor	noun	59	43.74
1806	speaker	noun	67	43.65
1807	previously	adverb	58	43.63
1808	German	prop. noun	62	43.61
1809	internal	adjective	62	43.50
1810	management	noun	95	43.48
1811	coffee	noun	78	43.45
1812	afraid	adjective	57	43.42
1813	meal	noun	56	43.35
1814	late	adverb	47	43.33
1815	gain	noun	69	43.27
1816	Pennsylvania	prop. noun	56	43.27
1817	faculty	noun	78	43.24
1818	critical	adjective	58	43.24
1819	largely	adverb	56	43.04
1820	sensitive	adjective	59	42.97
1821	sufficient	adjective	63	42.95
1822	identity	noun	65	42.86
1823	bitter	adjective	53	42.84
1824	pride	noun	45	42.82
1825	unity	noun	72	42.81
1826	cover	noun	52	42.80
1827	slightly	adverb	51	42.78
1828	twelve	card. num.	48	42.77
1829	D.	prop. noun	65	42.72
1830	fear	verb	53	42.72
1831	protection	noun	68	42.71
1832	entitle	verb	65	42.62
1833	commit	verb	50	42.60
1834	characteristic	noun	76	42.54
1835	retire	verb	54	42.53
1836	solve	verb	49	42.42
1837	publication	noun	78	42.41
1838	regard	noun	55	42.41
1839	snow	noun	56	42.38
1840	card	noun	61	42.37
1841	pure	adjective	56	42.35
1842	domestic	adjective	62	42.30
1843	cattle	noun	97	42.28
1844	bind	verb	51	42.28
1845	weakness	noun	52	42.26
1846	component	noun	80	42.24
1847	derive	verb	65	42.24
1848	somebody	nom. pro.	65	42.14
1849	last	verb	48	42.14
1850	best	sup. adv.	51	42.13
1851	sport	noun	65	42.12
1852	lord	noun	77	42.11
1853	engine	noun	69	42.09
1854	furnish	verb	58	42.09
1855	mostly	adverb	44	42.04
1856	right	adverb	79	41.97
1857	shadow	noun	54	41.95
1858	hate	verb	66	41.87
1859	steel	noun	48	41.80
1860	wild	adjective	54	41.78
1861	inside	adverb	67	41.76
1862	approve	verb	56	41.71
1863	complex	adjective	59	41.66
1864	rifle	noun	87	41.64
1865	appoint	verb	50	41.63
1866	yourself	refl. pro.	67	41.56
1867	file	noun	59	41.48
1868	maintenance	noun	64	41.47
1869	advertise	verb	49	41.47

1870	establishment	noun	60	52.64
1871	electric	adjective	60	51.13
1872	taste	noun	60	49.98
1873	conclude	verb	60	49.78
1874	flight	noun	60	49.41
1875	soft	adjective	60	48.20
1876	drive	noun	60	48.15
1877	advance	noun	60	48.13
1878	conversation	noun	60	46.22
1879	majority	noun	60	46.08
1880	chain	noun	60	45.98
1881	emphasis	noun	60	45.91
1882	bay	noun	60	45.04
1883	Joe	prop. noun	60	41.07
1884	movie	noun	60	40.40
1885	improvement	noun	60	36.96
1886	U.	prop. noun	60	29.82
1887	machinery	noun	60	29.52
1888	Georgia	prop. noun	60	29.21
1889	India	prop. noun	60	28.42
1890	dealer	noun	60	26.46
1891	builder	noun	60	23.55
1892	award	noun	60	21.03
1893	Congo	prop. noun	60	18.15
1894	Du	prop. noun	60	15.89
1895	ultimate	adjective	59	49.65
1896	search	noun	59	49.39
1897	thirty	card. num.	59	47.94
1898	highest	sup. adj.	59	47.06
1899	list	verb	59	45.53
1900	sum	noun	59	44.15
1901	neighbor	noun	59	43.74
1902	sensitive	adjective	59	42.97
1903	complex	adjective	59	41.66
1904	file	noun	59	41.48
1905	Smith	prop. noun	59	41.29
1906	pocket	noun	59	38.76
1907	European	adjective	59	38.61
1908	dance	verb	59	38.23
1909	contemporary	adjective	59	37.82
1910	commercial	adjective	59	35.99
1911	F.	prop. noun	59	34.53
1912	Bible	prop. noun	59	32.27
1913	cool	verb	59	27.48
1914	sexual	adjective	59	24.97
1915	Tuesday	adv. noun	59	24.59
1916	dictionary	noun	59	17.63
1917	foam	noun	59	14.48
1918	explanation	noun	58	52.59
1919	stand	noun	58	51.98
1920	height	noun	58	51.62
1921	path	noun	58	51.15
1922	quick	adjective	58	51.01
1923	afford	verb	58	49.07
1924	confidence	noun	58	48.97
1925	intention	noun	58	47.43
1926	fight	noun	58	47.23
1927	unique	adjective	58	46.25
1928	clean	verb	58	45.73
1929	tear	verb	58	45.53
1930	reject	verb	58	45.52
1931	perfect	adjective	58	45.49
1932	jump	verb	58	45.41
1933	conflict	noun	58	45.35
1934	useful	adjective	58	44.55
1935	previously	adverb	58	43.63
1936	critical	adjective	58	43.24
1937	furnish	verb	58	42.09
1938	grade	noun	58	40.08
1939	shoe	noun	58	38.81
1940	star	noun	58	37.58
1941	Roman	adjective	58	36.34
1942	cup	noun	58	35.76
1943	hence	adverb	58	32.25
1944	uncle	noun	58	30.57
1945	junior	adjective	58	25.18
1946	commerce	noun	58	24.70
1947	Dallas	prop. noun	58	11.68
1948	ignore	verb	57	53.40
1949	convince	verb	57	50.56
1950	enable	verb	57	49.75
1951	apparent	adjective	57	48.95
1952	apart	adverb	57	48.25
1953	suggestion	noun	57	48.04
1954	expert	noun	57	47.37
1955	struggle	noun	57	47.09
1956	entrance	noun	57	46.61
1957	participate	verb	57	45.18
1958	alive	adjective	57	44.96

1870	seat	noun	68	41.44
1871	liberal	adjective	57	41.43
1872	tie	verb	50	41.43
1873	precede	verb	51	41.37
1874	largest	sem. sup.	53	41.31
1875	Smith	prop. noun	59	41.29
1876	panel	noun	78	41.27
1877	beside	prep.	78	41.24
1878	expose	verb	47	41.20
1879	confuse	verb	52	41.18
1880	cry	verb	64	41.17
1881	bomb	noun	68	41.10
1882	Joe	prop. noun	60	41.07
1883	substantial	adjective	66	41.00
1884	possess	verb	54	41.00
1885	yellow	adjective	52	40.73
1886	secret	noun	52	40.65
1887	intellectual	adjective	57	40.62
1888	house	verb	53	40.61
1889	bone	noun	53	40.53
1890	minor	adjective	51	40.53
1891	middle	noun	47	40.53
1892	construct	verb	56	40.47
1893	prospect	noun	49	40.46
1894	movie	noun	60	40.40
1895	De	prop. noun	56	40.37
1896	honest	adjective	47	40.31
1897	back	verb	57	40.30
1898	wonderful	adjective	53	40.30
1899	suspect	verb	47	40.27
1900	beneath	prep.	55	40.26
1901	restaurant	noun	53	40.26
1902	connect	verb	44	40.21
1903	stick	verb	50	40.17
1904	track	noun	48	40.16
1905	cultural	adjective	55	40.13
1906	lead	noun	49	40.13
1907	sister	noun	55	40.09
1908	grade	noun	58	40.08
1909	confusion	noun	48	40.06
1910	flow	noun	56	40.04
1911	shift	verb	47	40.04
1912	resolution	noun	70	40.03
1913	defend	verb	56	40.01
1914	phrase	noun	51	39.96
1915	tomorrow	adv. noun	67	39.93
1916	comfort	noun	46	39.93
1917	comparison	noun	54	39.89
1918	row	noun	48	39.85
1919	blow	verb	52	39.84
1920	orchestra	noun	66	39.76
1921	clear	verb	48	39.75
1922	figure	verb	53	39.74
1923	chest	noun	57	39.64
1924	brilliant	adjective	50	39.64
1925	disappear	verb	54	39.60
1926	account	verb	49	39.60
1927	million	noun	49	39.59
1928	engineer	noun	78	39.56
1929	screen	noun	53	39.50
1930	hide	verb	61	39.48
1931	gentleman	noun	49	39.48
1932	compose	verb	50	39.45
1933	discovery	noun	55	39.44
1934	total	adjective	74	39.43
1935	scale	noun	62	39.43
1936	pace	noun	45	39.42
1937	R.	prop. noun	62	39.39
1938	acceptance	noun	49	39.39
1939	jazz	noun	99	39.37
1940	scientist	noun	53	39.34
1941	retain	verb	49	39.30
1942	firmly	adverb	48	39.24
1943	worse	comp. adj.	50	39.20
1944	seriously	adverb	43	39.10
1945	conscious	adjective	46	39.06
1946	Britain	prop. noun	61	39.04
1947	that	qualifier	57	39.04
1948	laugh	verb	89	39.02
1949	justify	verb	52	38.98
1950	highway	noun	56	38.95
1951	plus	co. conj.	52	38.94
1952	later	comp. adj.	55	38.87
1953	advise	verb	47	38.84
1954	shoe	noun	58	38.81
1955	present	noun	50	38.77
1956	pocket	noun	59	38.76
1957	rise	noun	55	38.73
1957	writing	noun	55	38.73

1959	remind	verb	57	44.93
1960	busy	adjective	57	44.55
1961	afraid	adjective	57	43.42
1962	liberal	adjective	57	41.43
1963	intellectual	adjective	57	40.62
1964	back	verb	57	40.30
1965	chest	noun	57	39.64
1966	that	qualifier	57	39.04
1967	content	noun	57	38.62
1968	right	adv. noun	57	38.54
1969	meat	noun	57	37.83
1970	second	noun	57	36.79
1971	notion	noun	57	36.78
1972	Joseph	prop. noun	57	35.29
1973	bedroom	noun	57	32.82
1974	chemical	noun	57	29.88
1975	pale	adjective	57	27.24
1976	Sir	prop. noun	57	24.64
1977	fifteen	card. num.	56	50.17
1978	amount	verb	56	48.02
1979	threat	noun	56	46.27
1980	absence	noun	56	46.26
1981	proceed	verb	56	46.23
1982	straight	adjective	56	46.12
1983	evident	adjective	56	45.36
1984	vital	adjective	56	45.26
1985	factory	noun	56	44.33
1986	distinction	noun	56	44.08
1987	meal	noun	56	43.35
1988	Pennsylvania	prop. noun	56	43.27
1989	largely	adverb	56	43.04
1990	snow	noun	56	42.38
1991	pure	adjective	56	42.35
1992	approve	verb	56	41.71
1993	construct	verb	56	40.47
1994	De	prop. noun	56	40.37
1995	flow	noun	56	40.04
1996	defend	verb	56	40.01
1997	highway	noun	56	38.95
1998	substance	noun	56	38.17
1999	tragedy	noun	56	36.03
2000	mix	verb	56	35.03
2001	concentration	noun	56	35.02
2002	estate	noun	56	34.70
2003	smile	noun	56	33.53
2004	Martin	prop. noun	56	29.94
2005	hearing	noun	56	26.20
2006	U.N.	prop. noun	56	23.07
2007	plastic	noun	56	17.46
2008	various	post-det.	56	14.92
2009	confront	verb	55	48.43
2010	eventually	adverb	55	48.23
2011	properly	adverb	55	48.00
2012	view	verb	55	46.87
2013	huge	adjective	55	46.84
2014	talk	noun	55	45.97
2015	wire	noun	55	45.49
2016	inner	adjective	55	44.93
2017	official	adjective	55	43.76
2018	regard	noun	55	42.41
2019	beneath	prep.	55	40.26
2020	cultural	adjective	55	40.13
2021	sister	noun	55	40.09
2022	discovery	noun	55	39.44
2023	later	comp. adj.	55	38.87
2024	rise	noun	55	38.73
2024	writing	noun	55	38.73
2026	grass	noun	55	37.78
2027	swim	verb	55	37.23
2028	code	noun	55	37.21
2029	tall	adjective	55	35.61
2030	Reverend	prop. noun	55	35.39
2031	medium	noun	55	34.57
2032	chamber	noun	55	34.46
2033	adjustment	noun	55	33.96
2034	breakfast	noun	55	33.84
2035	childhood	noun	55	33.31
2036	David	prop. noun	55	32.28
2037	daily	adverb	55	31.77
2038	expenditure	noun	55	28.82
2039	tube	noun	55	28.52
2040	finance	verb	55	28.29
2041	fort	noun	55	27.85
2042	probability	noun	55	26.79
2043	vacation	noun	55	26.24
2044	Wright	prop. noun	55	18.57
2045	Alfred	prop. noun	55	16.53
2046	mama	noun	55	15.06
2047	unable	adjective	54	49.89

1959	emphasize	verb	45	38.73
1960	surprise	noun	49	38.70
1961	farmer	noun	67	38.66
1962	content	noun	57	38.62
1963	European	adjective	59	38.61
1964	exercise	verb	50	38.55
1965	right	adv. noun	57	38.54
1966	dry	adjective	53	38.47
1967	abandon	verb	47	38.46
1968	troop	noun	69	38.45
1969	fairly	qualifier	50	38.45
1970	rule	verb	53	38.37
1971	emotional	adjective	68	38.32
1972	foundation	noun	65	38.29
1973	salary	noun	51	38.27
1974	chief	noun	62	38.23
1975	dance	verb	59	38.23
1976	assembly	noun	61	38.19
1977	shelter	noun	94	38.17
1978	substance	noun	56	38.17
1979	skin	noun	53	38.15
1980	Rhode	prop. noun	105	38.14
1981	observation	noun	67	38.12
1982	encounter	verb	47	38.08
1983	practically	adverb	43	38.04
1984	pour	verb	48	38.01
1985	stress	verb	43	37.99
1986	theme	noun	63	37.98
1987	surely	adverb	46	37.98
1988	crime	noun	49	37.97
1989	print	verb	53	37.94
1990	dangerous	adjective	46	37.92
1991	phenomenon	noun	62	37.88
1992	tiny	adjective	50	37.87
1993	past	prep.	61	37.84
1994	Bill	prop. noun	62	37.83
1995	meat	noun	57	37.83
1996	contemporary	adjective	59	37.82
1997	rural	adjective	54	37.79
1998	grass	noun	55	37.78
1999	lesson	noun	46	37.75
2000	nose	noun	65	37.73
2001	unknown	adjective	43	37.70
2002	lock	verb	63	37.67
2003	promote	verb	61	37.66
2004	guy	noun	66	37.64
2005	occasionally	adverb	48	37.61
2006	salt	noun	52	37.60
2007	star	noun	58	37.58
2008	sound	adjective	50	37.57
2009	radiation	noun	100	37.53
2010	vocational	adjective	76	37.53
2011	quote	verb	48	37.53
2012	straight	adverb	53	37.49
2013	really	qualifier	49	37.48
2014	liquor	noun	43	37.45
2014	raw	adjective	43	37.45
2016	site	noun	80	37.38
2017	mistake	noun	45	37.33
2018	Richard	prop. noun	76	37.32
2019	frighten	verb	51	37.32
2020	network	noun	48	37.31
2021	slow	adjective	49	37.28
2022	thousand	noun	47	37.28
2023	iron	noun	46	37.28
2024	widely	adverb	49	37.27
2025	partner	noun	48	37.26
2026	freeze	verb	53	37.25
2027	swim	verb	55	37.23
2028	code	noun	55	37.21
2029	lean	verb	61	37.20
2030	seed	noun	82	37.18
2031	request	noun	54	37.18
2032	extra	adjective	48	37.18
2033	hire	verb	47	37.16
2034	valuable	adjective	45	37.13
2035	tendency	noun	54	37.12
2036	mental	adjective	43	37.09
2037	pursue	verb	45	37.07
2038	remarkable	adjective	47	37.02
2039	league	noun	81	36.98
2040	improvement	noun	60	36.96
2041	chicken	noun	49	36.94
2042	burden	noun	50	36.82
2043	second	noun	57	36.79
2044	honor	verb	49	36.79
2045	notion	noun	57	36.78
2046	hundred	noun	44	36.75
2047	academic	adjective	53	36.71

2048	respond	verb	54	48.50
2049	sweep	verb	54	47.03
2050	pilot	noun	54	44.71
2051	retire	verb	54	42.53
2052	shadow	noun	54	41.95
2053	wild	adjective	54	41.78
2054	possess	verb	54	41.00
2055	comparison	noun	54	39.89
2056	disappear	verb	54	39.60
2057	rural	adjective	54	37.79
2058	request	noun	54	37.18
2059	tendency	noun	54	37.12
2060	constitute	verb	54	35.85
2061	reporter	noun	54	35.15
2062	L.	prop. noun	54	34.83
2063	acre	noun	54	34.70
2064	player	noun	54	34.62
2065	copy	noun	54	34.40
2066	breath	noun	54	33.34
2067	silence	noun	54	33.31
2068	exercise	noun	54	32.83
2069	Illinois	prop. noun	54	32.65
2070	selection	noun	54	31.81
2071	variation	noun	54	30.46
2072	tissue	noun	54	24.45
2073	Democrat	prop. noun	54	23.84
2074	ratio	noun	54	23.45
2075	Hearst	prop. noun	54	8.10
2076	surround	verb	53	49.52
2077	heavily	adverb	53	46.65
2078	check	noun	53	46.12
2079	detail	verb	53	44.11
2080	necessity	noun	53	43.92
2081	folk	noun	53	43.91
2082	bitter	adjective	53	42.84
2083	fear	verb	53	42.72
2084	largest	sem. sup.	53	41.31
2085	house	verb	53	40.61
2086	bone	noun	53	40.53
2087	wonderful	adjective	53	40.30
2088	restaurant	noun	53	40.26
2089	figure	verb	53	39.74
2090	screen	noun	53	39.50
2091	scientist	noun	53	39.34
2092	dry	adjective	53	38.47
2093	rule	verb	53	38.37
2094	skin	noun	53	38.15
2095	print	verb	53	37.94
2096	straight	adverb	53	37.49
2097	freeze	verb	53	37.25
2098	academic	adjective	53	36.71
2099	root	noun	53	35.98
2100	estimate	noun	53	35.72
2101	critic	noun	53	35.52
2102	imply	verb	53	34.51
2103	extreme	adjective	53	34.45
2104	efficiency	noun	53	32.58
2105	heaven	noun	53	32.49
2106	welfare	noun	53	31.47
2107	phone	noun	53	29.93
2108	historian	noun	53	29.07
2109	percent	noun	53	27.07
2110	Edward	prop. noun	53	26.40
2111	frequency	noun	53	24.72
2112	administrative	adjective	53	24.50
2113	constitution	noun	53	21.42
2114	diameter	noun	53	17.57
2115	patent	noun	53	16.91
2116	B	prop. noun	53	12.08
2117	advice	noun	52	44.28
2118	flat	adjective	52	43.85
2119	whole	noun	52	43.83
2120	cover	noun	52	42.80
2121	weakness	noun	52	42.26
2122	confuse	verb	52	41.18
2123	yellow	adjective	52	40.73
2124	secret	noun	52	40.65
2125	blow	verb	52	39.84
2126	justify	verb	52	38.98
2127	plus	co. conj.	52	38.94
2128	salt	noun	52	37.60
2129	load	noun	52	36.29
2130	percentage	noun	52	34.55
2131	coat	noun	52	34.25
2132	Lincoln	prop. noun	52	33.93
2133	hand	verb	52	31.47
2134	Arthur	prop. noun	52	31.18
2135	abroad	adverb	52	31.03
2136	flesh	noun	52	27.46

2048	aircraft	noun	71	36.62
2049	curious	adjective	46	36.62
2050	platform	noun	77	36.60
2051	wing	noun	44	36.60
2052	maximum	adjective	67	36.54
2053	victim	noun	50	36.45
2054	completely	qualifier	47	36.39
2055	arm	verb	61	36.38
2056	gate	noun	50	36.36
2057	alter	verb	42	36.35
2058	Roman	adjective	58	36.34
2059	supreme	adjective	51	36.33
2060	republic	noun	49	36.33
2061	younger	comp. adj.	44	36.30
2062	load	noun	52	36.29
2063	executive	noun	50	36.29
2064	manufacturer	noun	77	36.26
2065	cooperation	noun	51	36.26
2066	approximately	adverb	65	36.23
2067	impressive	adjective	49	36.19
2068	overcome	verb	42	36.09
2069	creation	noun	50	36.08
2070	sample	noun	85	36.07
2071	tragedy	noun	56	36.03
2072	conceive	verb	45	36.00
2073	commercial	adjective	59	35.99
2074	root	noun	53	35.98
2075	search	verb	41	35.98
2076	assumption	noun	64	35.95
2077	Junior	prop. noun	81	35.90
2078	dress	verb	67	35.90
2079	park	verb	61	35.89
2080	constitute	verb	54	35.85
2081	numerous	adjective	47	35.85
2082	prominent	adjective	40	35.84
2083	proud	adjective	50	35.83
2084	next	adverb	46	35.79
2085	approval	noun	51	35.77
2086	cup	noun	58	35.76
2087	estimate	noun	53	35.72
2088	senator	noun	82	35.71
2089	rush	verb	42	35.71
2090	fundamental	adjective	50	35.67
2091	tall	adjective	55	35.61
2092	concentrate	verb	49	35.59
2093	incident	noun	46	35.54
2094	critic	noun	53	35.52
2095	Jew	prop. noun	81	35.50
2096	Tom	prop. noun	67	35.44
2097	German	adjective	51	35.43
2098	unlike	prep.	42	35.41
2099	Reverend	prop. noun	55	35.39
2100	queen	noun	51	35.39
2101	climb	verb	65	35.37
2102	gift	noun	45	35.36
2103	precisely	adverb	46	35.35
2104	submit	verb	47	35.33
2105	easier	comp. adj.	45	35.31
2106	cook	verb	50	35.30
2107	Joseph	prop. noun	57	35.29
2108	northern	adjective	47	35.28
2108	opposite	adjective	47	35.28
2110	move	noun	45	35.26
2111	reporter	noun	54	35.15
2112	conventional	adjective	51	35.04
2113	mix	verb	56	35.03
2114	concentration	noun	56	35.02
2115	practice	verb	40	34.97
2116	employment	noun	48	34.90
2117	Wilson	prop. noun	65	34.89
2118	joy	noun	47	34.89
2119	detective	noun	72	34.84
2120	Philadelphia	prop. noun	51	34.84
2121	L.	prop. noun	54	34.83
2122	le	foreign	48	34.82
2123	judge	verb	42	34.81
2124	dancer	noun	63	34.77
2125	elsewhere	adverb	42	34.77
2126	whenever	wh-adverb	43	34.76
2127	profession	noun	42	34.75
2128	superior	adjective	45	34.74
2129	emergency	noun	46	34.73
2130	estate	noun	56	34.70
2131	acre	noun	54	34.70
2132	anybody	nom. pro.	45	34.70
2133	ring	noun	43	34.69
2134	origin	noun	51	34.68
2134	somewhere	adverb	51	34.68
2136	display	verb	45	34.68

2137	review	noun	52	27.25
2138	attract	verb	51	47.65
2139	slight	adjective	51	47.12
2140	gradually	adverb	51	46.75
2141	guide	verb	51	46.43
2142	safe	adjective	51	45.11
2143	slightly	adverb	51	42.78
2144	bind	verb	51	42.28
2145	best	sup. adv.	51	42.13
2146	precede	verb	51	41.37
2147	minor	adjective	51	40.53
2148	phrase	noun	51	39.96
2149	salary	noun	51	38.27
2150	frighten	verb	51	37.32
2151	supreme	adjective	51	36.33
2152	cooperation	noun	51	36.26
2153	approval	noun	51	35.77
2154	German	adjective	51	35.43
2155	queen	noun	51	35.39
2156	conventional	adjective	51	35.04
2157	Philadelphia	prop. noun	51	34.84
2158	origin	noun	51	34.68
2158	somewhere	adverb	51	34.68
2160	sick	adjective	51	34.40
2161	criticism	noun	51	34.14
2162	Angeles	prop. noun	51	33.97
2162	Los	prop. noun	51	33.97
2164	television	noun	51	33.82
2165	institute	noun	51	28.93
2166	bag	noun	51	28.86
2167	Warren	prop. noun	51	25.26
2168	doctrine	noun	51	24.85
2169	Moscow	prop. noun	51	21.73
2170	Hardy	prop. noun	51	12.25
2171	firm	adjective	50	44.79
2172	mark	noun	50	43.95
2173	commit	verb	50	42.60
2174	appoint	verb	50	41.63
2175	tie	verb	50	41.43
2176	stick	verb	50	40.17
2177	brilliant	adjective	50	39.64
2178	compose	verb	50	39.45
2179	worse	comp. adj.	50	39.20
2180	present	noun	50	38.77
2181	exercise	verb	50	38.55
2182	fairly	qualifier	50	38.45
2183	tiny	adjective	50	37.87
2184	sound	adjective	50	37.57
2185	burden	noun	50	36.82
2186	victim	noun	50	36.45
2187	gate	noun	50	36.36
2188	executive	noun	50	36.29
2189	creation	noun	50	36.08
2190	proud	adjective	50	35.83
2191	fundamental	adjective	50	35.67
2192	cook	verb	50	35.30
2193	female	noun	50	34.27
2194	bend	verb	50	33.53
2195	wooden	adjective	50	33.39
2196	necessarily	adverb	50	33.20
2197	cool	adjective	50	32.65
2198	expansion	noun	50	31.72
2199	shut	verb	50	29.62
2200	negative	adjective	50	27.60
2201	interview	noun	50	27.48
2202	stranger	noun	50	25.87
2203	Charlie	prop. noun	50	25.44
2204	purchase	noun	50	22.74
2205	fiber	noun	50	18.44
2206	Papa	prop. noun	50	14.64
2207	mold	noun	50	13.29
2208	Watson	prop. noun	50	12.56
2209	A	prop. noun	50	10.41
2210	Pont	prop. noun	50	8.92
2211	invite	verb	49	45.37
2212	visitor	noun	49	45.01
2213	solve	verb	49	42.42
2214	advertise	verb	49	41.47
2215	prospect	noun	49	40.46
2216	lead	noun	49	40.13
2217	account	verb	49	39.60
2218	million	noun	49	39.59
2219	gentleman	noun	49	39.48
2220	acceptance	noun	49	39.39
2221	retain	verb	49	39.30
2222	surprise	noun	49	38.70
2223	crime	noun	49	37.97
2224	really	qualifier	49	37.48
2225	slow	adjective	49	37.28

2137	creative	adjective	49	34.64
2138	player	noun	54	34.62
2139	quite	pre-qual.	42	34.58
2140	medium	noun	55	34.57
2141	vote	noun	66	34.56
2142	percentage	noun	52	34.55
2143	F.	prop. noun	59	34.53
2144	imply	verb	53	34.51
2145	sentence	noun	47	34.48
2146	chamber	noun	55	34.46
2147	interior	noun	49	34.46
2148	extreme	adjective	53	34.45
2149	sympathy	noun	44	34.42
2150	copy	noun	54	34.40
2151	sick	adjective	51	34.40
2152	noise	noun	43	34.38
2153	absorb	verb	41	34.38
2154	interval	noun	43	34.37
2155	spite	noun	48	34.36
2156	switch	noun	63	34.35
2157	blind	adjective	43	34.30
2158	plenty	noun	47	34.28
2159	accident	noun	41	34.28
2160	personally	adverb	40	34.28
2161	female	noun	50	34.27
2162	cousin	noun	65	34.26
2163	coat	noun	52	34.25
2164	wagon	noun	72	34.24
2165	text	noun	64	34.21
2166	dare	verb	45	34.21
2167	attach	verb	44	34.21
2168	scholarship	noun	44	34.17
2169	slip	verb	47	34.16
2170	criticism	noun	51	34.14
2171	mere	adjective	47	34.09
2172	scheme	noun	39	34.06
2173	deserve	verb	40	34.04
2174	spiritual	adjective	64	34.00
2175	mine	noun	49	33.98
2176	Angeles	prop. noun	51	33.97
2176	Los	prop. noun	51	33.97
2178	adjustment	noun	55	33.96
2179	definite	adjective	37	33.94
2180	Lincoln	prop. noun	52	33.93
2181	version	noun	62	33.90
2182	briefly	adverb	38	33.89
2183	Catholic	adjective	83	33.88
2184	favor	verb	49	33.87
2185	pupil	noun	45	33.87
2186	breakfast	noun	55	33.84
2187	fruit	noun	49	33.83
2188	closer	comp. adv.	43	33.83
2189	television	noun	51	33.82
2190	attractive	adjective	40	33.80
2191	partly	adverb	41	33.76
2192	purchase	verb	48	33.71
2193	Indian	adjective	42	33.65
2194	risk	noun	47	33.55
2195	Asia	prop. noun	44	33.55
2196	smile	noun	56	33.53
2197	bend	verb	50	33.53
2198	rare	adjective	41	33.50
2199	resistance	noun	48	33.49
2200	loose	adjective	41	33.49
2201	persuade	verb	42	33.45
2202	clay	noun	91	33.43
2203	cite	verb	44	33.41
2204	adult	noun	47	33.40
2204	wet	adjective	47	33.40
2206	wooden	adjective	50	33.39
2207	odd	adjective	44	33.39
2208	loan	noun	78	33.38
2209	breath	noun	54	33.34
2210	formation	noun	44	33.33
2211	childhood	noun	55	33.31
2212	silence	noun	54	33.31
2213	musician	noun	65	33.29
2214	necessarily	adverb	50	33.20
2215	register	verb	36	33.20
2216	clean	adjective	48	33.17
2217	accuse	verb	45	33.16
2218	consult	verb	41	33.15
2219	notice	noun	39	33.13
2220	release	verb	39	33.09
2221	mood	noun	45	33.05
2222	spoke	verb	37	33.05
2223	integration	noun	48	33.04
2224	confirm	verb	41	33.04
2225	journal	noun	47	33.01

2226	widely	adverb	49	37.27
2227	chicken	noun	49	36.94
2228	honor	verb	49	36.79
2229	republic	noun	49	36.33
2230	impressive	adjective	49	36.19
2231	concentrate	verb	49	35.59
2232	creative	adjective	49	34.64
2233	interior	noun	49	34.46
2234	mine	noun	49	33.98
2235	favor	verb	49	33.87
2236	fruit	noun	49	33.83
2237	drama	noun	49	32.55
2238	mail	noun	49	32.45
2239	quietly	adverb	49	31.73
2240	bullet	noun	49	30.25
2241	investment	noun	49	29.93
2242	milk	noun	49	29.27
2243	silent	adjective	49	28.78
2244	laboratory	noun	49	27.55
2245	Cuba	prop. noun	49	25.42
2246	opera	noun	49	25.39
2247	authorize	verb	49	24.06
2248	stair	noun	49	18.86
2249	equation	noun	49	17.03
2250	Roberts	prop. noun	49	12.92
2251	twelve	card. num.	48	42.77
2252	last	verb	48	42.14
2253	steel	noun	48	41.80
2254	track	noun	48	40.16
2255	confusion	noun	48	40.06
2256	row	noun	48	39.85
2257	clear	verb	48	39.75
2258	firmly	adverb	48	39.24
2259	pour	verb	48	38.01
2260	occasionally	adverb	48	37.61
2261	quote	verb	48	37.53
2262	network	noun	48	37.31
2263	partner	noun	48	37.26
2264	extra	adjective	48	37.18
2265	employment	noun	48	34.90
2266	le	foreign	48	34.82
2267	spite	noun	48	34.36
2268	purchase	verb	48	33.71
2269	resistance	noun	48	33.49
2270	clean	adjective	48	33.17
2271	integration	noun	48	33.04
2272	formal	adjective	48	32.57
2273	safety	noun	48	32.21
2274	install	verb	48	31.88
2275	isolate	verb	48	31.75
2276	anger	noun	48	31.66
2277	route	noun	48	31.55
2278	navy	noun	48	31.11
2279	consumer	noun	48	30.45
2280	intelligence	noun	48	29.85
2281	Alexander	prop. noun	48	27.77
2282	luck	noun	48	26.44
2283	Indian	prop. noun	48	25.77
2284	tour	noun	48	25.21
2285	holy	adjective	48	23.48
2286	sorry	adjective	48	23.45
2287	arc	noun	48	21.60
2288	editorial	noun	48	20.04
2289	Protestant	adjective	48	15.80
2290	late	adverb	47	43.33
2291	expose	verb	47	41.20
2292	middle	noun	47	40.53
2293	honest	adjective	47	40.31
2294	suspect	verb	47	40.27
2295	shift	verb	47	40.04
2296	advise	verb	47	38.84
2297	abandon	verb	47	38.46
2298	encounter	verb	47	38.08
2299	thousand	noun	47	37.28
2300	hire	verb	47	37.16
2301	remarkable	adjective	47	37.02
2302	completely	qualifier	47	36.39
2303	numerous	adjective	47	35.85
2304	submit	verb	47	35.33
2305	northern	adjective	47	35.28
2305	opposite	adjective	47	35.28
2307	joy	noun	47	34.89
2308	sentence	noun	47	34.48
2309	plenty	noun	47	34.28
2310	slip	verb	47	34.16
2311	mere	adjective	47	34.09
2312	risk	noun	47	33.55
2313	adult	noun	47	33.40
2313	wet	adjective	47	33.40

2225	proportion	noun	47	33.01
2227	quantity	noun	44	32.99
2228	flow	verb	40	32.98
2229	soviet	noun	99	32.97
2230	chairman	noun	77	32.97
2231	promise	noun	46	32.91
2232	impose	verb	39	32.90
2233	complain	verb	41	32.88
2234	exercise	noun	54	32.83
2235	bedroom	noun	57	32.82
2236	grand	adjective	45	32.80
2237	occasional	adjective	37	32.77
2238	correct	adjective	40	32.74
2239	yield	verb	41	32.73
2240	relieve	verb	40	32.70
2241	electronic	adjective	68	32.67
2242	everywhere	adverb	43	32.67
2243	Illinois	prop. noun	54	32.65
2244	cool	adjective	50	32.65
2245	efficiency	noun	53	32.58
2246	formal	adjective	48	32.57
2247	drama	noun	49	32.55
2248	dimension	noun	44	32.53
2249	heaven	noun	53	32.49
2250	aim	verb	42	32.49
2251	gesture	noun	38	32.48
2252	Jewish	adjective	74	32.47
2253	Republican	prop. noun	71	32.47
2254	dirt	noun	43	32.47
2255	prison	noun	46	32.46
2256	servant	noun	41	32.46
2257	Friday	adv. noun	64	32.45
2258	mail	noun	49	32.45
2259	profit	noun	46	32.39
2260	measurement	noun	88	32.32
2261	David	prop. noun	55	32.28
2262	presently	adverb	36	32.28
2263	Bible	prop. noun	59	32.27
2264	pack	verb	44	32.26
2265	Saturday	adv. noun	72	32.25
2266	hence	adverb	58	32.25
2267	safety	noun	48	32.21
2268	tale	noun	41	32.17
2269	palace	noun	45	32.14
2270	plain	adjective	37	32.12
2271	universe	noun	71	32.09
2272	camera	noun	46	32.09
2273	color	verb	44	32.07
2274	neither	dt./d. cj.	37	32.06
2275	Francisco	prop. noun	44	32.04
2276	flee	verb	40	32.00
2277	anticipate	verb	38	31.93
2278	rank	noun	41	31.92
2279	install	verb	48	31.88
2280	thinking	noun	40	31.88
2281	secret	adjective	46	31.87
2282	trust	verb	42	31.84
2283	selection	noun	54	31.81
2284	Italian	adjective	43	31.81
2285	rough	adjective	40	31.81
2286	daily	adverb	55	31.77
2287	isolate	verb	48	31.75
2288	entry	noun	45	31.75
2289	Texas	prop. noun	79	31.74
2290	quietly	adverb	49	31.73
2291	expansion	noun	50	31.72
2292	host	noun	47	31.72
2293	anger	noun	48	31.66
2294	prevail	verb	41	31.64
2295	aim	noun	40	31.63
2296	proof	noun	40	31.61
2297	constantly	adverb	41	31.58
2298	route	noun	48	31.55
2299	render	verb	47	31.51
2300	plate	noun	44	31.50
2301	welfare	noun	53	31.47
2302	hand	verb	52	31.47
2303	owe	verb	34	31.40
2304	appreciate	verb	39	31.38
2305	earn	verb	45	31.30
2305	over-all	adjective	45	31.30
2307	rarely	adverb	41	31.30
2308	Latin	adjective	39	31.30
2309	operator	noun	66	31.27
2310	sin	noun	67	31.23
2311	bother	verb	45	31.21
2312	command	verb	39	31.20
2313	Arthur	prop. noun	52	31.18
2314	revenue	noun	61	31.17

2315	journal	noun	47	33.01
2315	proportion	noun	47	33.01
2317	host	noun	47	31.72
2318	render	verb	47	31.51
2319	fat	adjective	47	30.56
2320	knock	verb	47	30.28
2321	category	noun	47	30.19
2322	Mississippi	prop. noun	47	29.97
2323	store	verb	47	29.66
2324	trade	verb	47	29.28
2325	grain	noun	47	29.19
2326	extremely	qualifier	47	29.08
2327	egg	noun	47	28.96
2328	pink	adjective	47	28.51
2329	edition	noun	47	28.26
2330	testimony	noun	47	27.45
2331	environment	noun	47	26.97
2332	colonel	noun	47	24.23
2333	mayor	noun	47	16.18
2334	coating	noun	47	13.02
2335	junior	noun	47	11.76
2336	oxygen	noun	47	11.11
2337	Rayburn	prop. noun	47	10.11
2338	comfort	noun	46	39.93
2339	conscious	adjective	46	39.06
2340	surely	adverb	46	37.98
2341	dangerous	adjective	46	37.92
2342	lesson	noun	46	37.75
2343	iron	noun	46	37.28
2344	curious	adjective	46	36.62
2345	next	adverb	46	35.79
2346	incident	noun	46	35.54
2347	precisely	adverb	46	35.35
2348	emergency	noun	46	34.73
2349	promise	noun	46	32.91
2350	prison	noun	46	32.46
2351	profit	noun	46	32.39
2352	camera	noun	46	32.09
2353	secret	adjective	46	31.87
2354	opposition	noun	46	31.12
2355	violence	noun	46	30.87
2356	aid	verb	46	29.88
2357	calculate	verb	46	29.68
2358	ideal	adjective	46	29.59
2359	cow	noun	46	29.51
2360	fence	noun	46	29.03
2361	recommendation	noun	46	28.88
2362	Frank	prop. noun	46	28.85
2363	Greek	adjective	46	28.20
2364	legislation	noun	46	27.35
2365	tire	verb	46	27.20
2366	atomic	adjective	46	26.59
2367	reduction	noun	46	26.46
2368	civilization	noun	46	26.08
2369	specify	verb	46	25.79
2370	Peter	prop. noun	46	25.38
2371	electrical	adjective	46	23.89
2372	Adams	prop. noun	46	23.02
2373	insurance	noun	46	22.31
2374	fiction	noun	46	21.40
2375	anyway	adverb	46	21.24
2376	mystery	noun	46	20.59
2377	mechanism	noun	46	20.29
2378	composer	noun	46	19.03
2379	Anne	prop. noun	46	16.64
2380	thickness	noun	46	14.65
2381	Adam	prop. noun	46	13.52
2382	Lucy	prop. noun	46	9.24
2383	pride	noun	45	42.82
2384	pace	noun	45	39.42
2385	emphasize	verb	45	38.73
2386	mistake	noun	45	37.33
2387	valuable	adjective	45	37.13
2388	pursue	verb	45	37.07
2389	conceive	verb	45	36.00
2390	gift	noun	45	35.36
2391	easier	comp. adj.	45	35.31
2392	move	noun	45	35.26
2393	superior	adjective	45	34.74
2394	anybody	nom. pro.	45	34.70
2395	display	verb	45	34.68
2396	dare	verb	45	34.21
2397	pupil	noun	45	33.87
2398	accuse	verb	45	33.16
2399	mood	noun	45	33.05
2400	grand	adjective	45	32.80
2401	palace	noun	45	32.14
2402	entry	noun	45	31.75
2403	earn	verb	45	31.30

2315	rapid	adjective	43	31.15
2316	opposition	noun	46	31.12
2317	navy	noun	48	31.11
2318	abroad	adverb	52	31.03
2319	sharply	adverb	35	31.00
2320	particularly	qualifier	40	30.99
2321	snake	noun	70	30.96
2322	Eisenhower	prop. noun	62	30.96
2323	continuous	adjective	44	30.96
2324	violence	noun	46	30.87
2325	eleven	card. num.	40	30.86
2326	plot	noun	40	30.75
2327	royal	adjective	45	30.72
2328	stronger	comp. adj.	37	30.67
2329	govern	verb	45	30.64
2330	thank	verb	45	30.59
2331	tough	adjective	36	30.59
2332	uncle	noun	58	30.57
2333	fat	adjective	47	30.56
2334	like	adjective	36	30.56
2335	identification	noun	45	30.55
2336	concert	noun	64	30.53
2337	double	adjective	39	30.51
2338	bureau	noun	44	30.49
2339	variation	noun	54	30.46
2340	intense	adjective	40	30.46
2341	consumer	noun	48	30.45
2342	address	verb	40	30.43
2343	survey	noun	45	30.36
2344	introduction	noun	40	30.34
2345	trouble	verb	37	30.34
2346	hunt	verb	44	30.31
2347	crack	verb	41	30.31
2348	automatically	adverb	36	30.31
2349	knock	verb	47	30.28
2350	bullet	noun	49	30.25
2351	display	noun	44	30.22
2352	need	modal aux.	38	30.22
2353	category	noun	47	30.19
2354	crowd	verb	39	30.19
2355	membership	noun	75	30.17
2356	completion	noun	64	30.16
2357	relax	verb	41	30.14
2358	stir	verb	39	30.14
2359	cloth	noun	43	30.13
2360	jury	noun	68	30.12
2361	recognition	noun	44	30.12
2362	o'clock	adverb	41	30.11
2363	strongly	adverb	35	30.09
2364	urban	adjective	42	30.06
2365	outside	adjective	40	30.06
2366	drug	noun	69	30.03
2367	habit	noun	44	30.03
2368	Mississippi	prop. noun	47	29.97
2369	expensive	adjective	44	29.97
2370	territory	noun	40	29.97
2371	Martin	prop. noun	56	29.94
2372	phone	noun	53	29.93
2373	investment	noun	49	29.93
2374	chemical	noun	57	29.88
2375	aid	verb	46	29.88
2376	tremendous	adjective	37	29.88
2377	assemble	verb	39	29.86
2378	intelligence	noun	48	29.85
2379	Berlin	prop. noun	80	29.83
2380	U.	prop. noun	60	29.82
2381	terrible	adjective	44	29.82
2382	undergo	verb	34	29.70
2383	massive	adjective	33	29.70
2384	calculate	verb	46	29.68
2385	store	verb	47	29.66
2386	China	prop. noun	66	29.65
2387	remark	verb	43	29.65
2388	shut	verb	50	29.62
2389	angle	noun	61	29.61
2390	ideal	adjective	46	29.59
2391	extensive	adjective	44	29.59
2392	regulation	noun	43	29.54
2393	machinery	noun	60	29.52
2394	cow	noun	46	29.51
2395	schedule	noun	44	29.48
2396	atom	noun	78	29.46
2397	Mike	prop. noun	97	29.44
2398	witness	noun	40	29.40
2399	schedule	verb	41	29.39
2400	wisdom	noun	44	29.37
2401	meanwhile	adverb	35	29.36
2402	definition	noun	44	29.35
2403	baseball	noun	62	29.33

2403	over-all	adjective	45	31.30
2405	bother	verb	45	31.21
2406	royal	adjective	45	30.72
2407	govern	verb	45	30.64
2408	thank	verb	45	30.59
2409	identification	noun	45	30.55
2410	survey	noun	45	30.36
2411	virtue	noun	45	28.83
2412	fast	adverb	45	28.70
2413	relative	adjective	45	28.69
2414	Africa	prop. noun	45	28.58
2415	universal	adjective	45	28.13
2416	finding	noun	45	27.97
2417	trail	noun	45	27.35
2418	enterprise	noun	45	26.63
2419	angry	adjective	45	26.52
2420	residential	adjective	45	25.89
2421	ice	noun	45	25.71
2422	clerk	noun	45	25.66
2423	wake	verb	45	25.63
2424	dream	verb	45	25.45
2425	humor	noun	45	25.30
2426	planning	noun	45	24.03
2427	Carl	prop. noun	45	23.08
2428	human	noun	45	23.06
2429	dear	adjective	45	22.93
2430	hurry	verb	45	22.49
2431	fee	noun	45	21.53
2432	porch	noun	45	21.32
2433	ballet	noun	45	20.08
2434	stain	verb	45	19.95
2435	angel	noun	45	19.54
2436	Manchester	prop. noun	45	17.13
2437	interference	noun	45	16.69
2438	C	prop. noun	45	14.35
2439	Hans	prop. noun	45	11.10
2440	Linda	prop. noun	45	5.12
2441	mostly	adverb	44	42.04
2442	connect	verb	44	40.21
2443	hundred	noun	44	36.75
2444	wing	noun	44	36.60
2445	younger	comp. adj.	44	36.30
2446	sympathy	noun	44	34.42
2447	attach	verb	44	34.21
2448	scholarship	noun	44	34.17
2449	Asia	prop. noun	44	33.55
2450	cite	verb	44	33.41
2451	odd	adjective	44	33.39
2452	formation	noun	44	33.33
2453	quantity	noun	44	32.99
2454	dimension	noun	44	32.53
2455	pack	verb	44	32.26
2456	color	verb	44	32.07
2457	Francisco	prop. noun	44	32.04
2458	plate	noun	44	31.50
2459	continuous	adjective	44	30.96
2460	bureau	noun	44	30.49
2461	hunt	verb	44	30.31
2462	display	noun	44	30.22
2463	recognition	noun	44	30.12
2464	habit	noun	44	30.03
2465	expensive	adjective	44	29.97
2466	terrible	adjective	44	29.82
2467	extensive	adjective	44	29.59
2468	schedule	noun	44	29.48
2469	wisdom	noun	44	29.37
2470	definition	noun	44	29.35
2471	maid	noun	44	28.63
2472	Soviet	prop. noun	44	27.57
2473	core	noun	44	27.46
2474	lovely	adjective	44	27.45
2475	fun	noun	44	27.35
2476	extension	noun	44	26.78
2477	assert	verb	44	25.81
2478	till	sub. conj.	44	25.75
2479	precision	noun	44	25.53
2480	fabric	noun	44	24.96
2481	characteristic	adjective	44	24.40
2482	Johnson	prop. noun	44	23.00
2483	Orleans	prop. noun	44	22.83
2484	planet	noun	44	17.51
2485	thou	pers. pro.	44	14.86
2486	stem	noun	44	13.92
2487	Rachel	prop. noun	44	11.82
2488	questionnaire	noun	44	9.28
2489	seriously	adverb	43	39.10
2490	practically	adverb	43	38.04
2491	stress	verb	43	37.99
2492	unknown	adjective	43	37.70

2404	fifth	ord. num.	37	29.30
2405	trade	verb	47	29.28
2406	inevitably	adverb	38	29.28
2407	milk	noun	49	29.27
2408	painter	noun	35	29.24
2409	Georgia	prop. noun	60	29.21
2410	grain	noun	47	29.19
2411	prime	adjective	42	29.18
2412	release	noun	34	29.16
2413	compete	verb	41	29.11
2414	extremely	qualifier	47	29.08
2415	historian	noun	53	29.07
2416	dominant	adjective	65	29.05
2417	undertake	verb	41	29.05
2418	enormous	adjective	37	29.05
2419	fence	noun	46	29.03
2420	self	noun	41	29.02
2421	egg	noun	47	28.96
2422	ton	noun	41	28.96
2423	institute	noun	51	28.93
2424	seldom	adverb	34	28.92
2425	satisfaction	noun	32	28.91
2426	recommendation	noun	46	28.88
2427	interpret	verb	40	28.87
2428	bag	noun	51	28.86
2429	struggle	verb	36	28.86
2430	Frank	prop. noun	46	28.85
2431	resolve	verb	38	28.85
2432	virtue	noun	45	28.83
2433	expenditure	noun	55	28.82
2434	anywhere	adverb	39	28.80
2435	silent	adjective	49	28.78
2436	sink	verb	40	28.78
2437	prayer	noun	41	28.77
2438	forever	adverb	39	28.75
2439	Italy	prop. noun	36	28.71
2440	fast	adverb	45	28.70
2441	relative	adjective	45	28.69
2442	latest	sem. sup.	35	28.66
2443	maid	noun	44	28.63
2444	effectively	adverb	37	28.62
2445	Africa	prop. noun	45	28.58
2446	forty	card. num.	36	28.57
2447	resist	verb	36	28.56
2448	external	adjective	43	28.53
2449	tube	noun	55	28.52
2450	pink	adjective	47	28.51
2451	Parker	prop. noun	65	28.50
2452	steal	verb	39	28.50
2453	Paul	prop. noun	40	28.47
2453	permanent	adjective	40	28.47
2455	contrary	adjective	41	28.45
2456	distinct	adjective	42	28.44
2457	versus	prep.	42	28.43
2458	India	prop. noun	60	28.42
2459	transfer	verb	38	28.41
2460	sense	verb	35	28.41
2461	influence	verb	40	28.38
2462	visible	adjective	34	28.38
2463	p.m.	adverb	63	28.33
2464	thanks	pl. noun	37	28.30
2465	finance	verb	55	28.29
2466	guidance	noun	40	28.28
2467	edition	noun	47	28.26
2468	Hudson	prop. noun	69	28.24
2469	decline	verb	37	28.24
2470	Greek	adjective	46	28.20
2471	shade	noun	39	28.19
2472	universal	adjective	45	28.13
2473	uniform	noun	37	28.12
2474	conduct	noun	36	28.12
2475	glad	adjective	38	28.09
2476	strain	noun	38	28.08
2477	golden	adjective	42	28.07
2478	shift	noun	41	28.07
2479	regarding	prep.	37	28.05
2480	determination	noun	41	28.04
2481	bread	noun	41	28.03
2482	finding	noun	45	27.97
2483	accurate	adjective	35	27.90
2484	sake	noun	34	27.90
2485	fort	noun	55	27.85
2486	Jackson	prop. noun	40	27.82
2487	translate	verb	34	27.82
2488	reception	noun	39	27.79
2489	Alexander	prop. noun	48	27.77
2490	Walter	prop. noun	42	27.76
2491	genuine	adjective	34	27.76
2492	toss	verb	41	27.73

2493	liquor	noun	43	37.45
2493	raw	adjective	43	37.45
2495	mental	adjective	43	37.09
2496	whenever	wh-adverb	43	34.76
2497	ring	noun	43	34.69
2498	noise	noun	43	34.38
2499	interval	noun	43	34.37
2500	blind	adjective	43	34.30
2501	closer	comp. adv.	43	33.83
2502	everywhere	adverb	43	32.67
2503	dirt	noun	43	32.47
2504	Italian	adjective	43	31.81
2505	rapid	adjective	43	31.15
2506	cloth	noun	43	30.13
2507	remark	verb	43	29.65
2508	regulation	noun	43	29.54
2509	external	adjective	43	28.53
2510	i.e.	adverb	43	27.27
2511	glance	verb	43	27.10
2512	male	noun	43	26.89
2513	Russian	prop. noun	43	26.72
2514	sponsor	verb	43	26.65
2515	technology	noun	43	26.63
2516	smell	verb	43	25.98
2517	warfare	noun	43	25.76
2518	illusion	noun	43	25.11
2519	transfer	noun	43	23.52
2520	darkness	noun	43	23.36
2521	anxiety	noun	43	20.99
2522	transportation	noun	43	20.57
2523	mankind	noun	43	20.39
2524	slide	verb	43	20.29
2525	Shakespeare	prop. noun	43	17.47
2526	legislature	noun	43	17.23
2527	fraction	noun	43	17.08
2528	Thompson	prop. noun	43	15.71
2529	grant	noun	43	15.35
2530	recreation	noun	43	15.00
2531	Henrietta	prop. noun	43	8.60
2532	onset	noun	43	8.18
2533	alter	verb	42	36.35
2534	overcome	verb	42	36.09
2535	rush	verb	42	35.71
2536	unlike	prep.	42	35.41
2537	judge	verb	42	34.81
2538	elsewhere	adverb	42	34.77
2539	profession	noun	42	34.75
2540	quite	pre-qual.	42	34.58
2541	Indian	adjective	42	33.65
2542	persuade	verb	42	33.45
2543	aim	verb	42	32.49
2544	trust	verb	42	31.84
2545	urban	adjective	42	30.06
2546	prime	adjective	42	29.18
2547	distinct	adjective	42	28.44
2548	versus	prep.	42	28.43
2549	golden	adjective	42	28.07
2550	Walter	prop. noun	42	27.76
2551	elect	verb	42	27.64
2552	scholar	noun	42	27.46
2553	weekend	noun	42	27.16
2554	cat	noun	42	26.97
2555	alternative	noun	42	26.80
2556	differ	verb	42	26.77
2557	qualify	verb	42	26.64
2558	museum	noun	42	26.61
2559	next	prep.	42	26.24
2560	nineteenth	ord. num.	42	26.18
2561	G.	prop. noun	42	25.70
2562	stick	noun	42	25.68
2563	bus	noun	42	25.41
2564	bench	noun	42	24.37
2565	evil	noun	42	23.42
2566	treasury	noun	42	22.75
2567	regional	adjective	42	22.48
2568	tremble	verb	42	20.51
2569	long-range	noun	42	18.64
2570	textile	noun	42	18.18
2571	disk	noun	42	16.03
2572	hydrogen	noun	42	12.32
2573	search	verb	41	35.98
2574	absorb	verb	41	34.38
2575	accident	noun	41	34.28
2576	partly	adverb	41	33.76
2577	rare	adjective	41	33.50
2578	loose	adjective	41	33.49
2579	consult	verb	41	33.15
2580	confirm	verb	41	33.04
2581	complain	verb	41	32.88

2493	creature	noun	35	27.67
2494	distant	adjective	37	27.65
2495	indication	noun	36	27.65
2496	elect	verb	42	27.64
2497	burst	verb	37	27.63
2498	negative	adjective	50	27.60
2499	Soviet	prop. noun	44	27.57
2500	opening	noun	34	27.57
2501	Morgan	prop. noun	78	27.56
2502	laboratory	noun	49	27.55
2503	destruction	noun	38	27.54
2504	horizon	noun	33	27.52
2505	most	sup. adv.	32	27.52
2506	reserve	verb	39	27.51
2507	primitive	adjective	37	27.50
2508	cool	verb	59	27.48
2509	interview	noun	50	27.48
2510	flesh	noun	52	27.46
2511	core	noun	44	27.46
2512	scholar	noun	42	27.46
2513	severe	adjective	38	27.46
2514	testimony	noun	47	27.45
2515	lovely	adjective	44	27.45
2516	gold	noun	37	27.44
2517	focus	verb	34	27.44
2518	harbor	noun	38	27.43
2519	merit	noun	38	27.40
2520	pretty	adjective	41	27.37
2521	legislation	noun	46	27.35
2522	trail	noun	45	27.35
2523	fun	noun	44	27.35
2524	distribute	verb	39	27.35
2525	delay	verb	34	27.33
2526	i.e.	adverb	43	27.27
2527	wise	adjective	33	27.26
2528	review	noun	52	27.25
2529	pale	adjective	57	27.24
2530	tire	verb	46	27.20
2531	belt	noun	36	27.19
2532	weekend	noun	42	27.16
2533	ocean	noun	37	27.16
2534	glance	verb	43	27.10
2535	curve	noun	64	27.08
2536	percent	noun	53	27.07
2537	investigate	verb	38	27.04
2538	throat	noun	63	27.03
2539	specialist	noun	35	27.00
2540	stomach	noun	41	26.99
2541	environment	noun	47	26.97
2542	cat	noun	42	26.97
2543	specifically	adverb	37	26.92
2544	trace	verb	36	26.91
2545	resume	verb	37	26.90
2546	male	noun	43	26.89
2547	string	noun	34	26.89
2548	license	noun	41	26.86
2549	alternative	noun	42	26.80
2550	probability	noun	55	26.79
2551	steady	adjective	37	26.79
2552	extension	noun	44	26.78
2553	participation	noun	41	26.78
2554	dignity	noun	35	26.78
2555	differ	verb	42	26.77
2556	furthermore	adverb	40	26.77
2557	injury	noun	38	26.77
2558	high	adverb	34	26.73
2559	Russian	prop. noun	43	26.72
2560	smooth	adjective	36	26.71
2561	simultaneously	adverb	37	26.68
2562	sponsor	verb	43	26.65
2563	project	verb	36	26.65
2564	qualify	verb	42	26.64
2565	merchant	noun	40	26.64
2566	enterprise	noun	45	26.63
2567	technology	noun	43	26.63
2568	limitation	noun	38	26.63
2569	wish	noun	34	26.63
2570	downtown	adv. noun	41	26.62
2571	examination	noun	38	26.62
2572	museum	noun	42	26.61
2573	atomic	adjective	46	26.59
2574	admire	verb	32	26.59
2575	cash	noun	32	26.54
2576	angry	adjective	45	26.52
2577	dealer	noun	60	26.46
2578	reduction	noun	46	26.46
2579	luck	noun	48	26.44
2580	Edward	prop. noun	53	26.40
2581	corn	noun	38	26.32

2582	yield	verb	41	32.73
2583	servant	noun	41	32.46
2584	tale	noun	41	32.17
2585	rank	noun	41	31.92
2586	prevail	verb	41	31.64
2587	constantly	adverb	41	31.58
2588	rarely	adverb	41	31.30
2589	crack	verb	41	30.31
2590	relax	verb	41	30.14
2591	o'clock	adverb	41	30.11
2592	schedule	verb	41	29.39
2593	compete	verb	41	29.11
2594	undertake	verb	41	29.05
2595	self	noun	41	29.02
2596	ton	noun	41	28.96
2597	prayer	noun	41	28.77
2598	contrary	adjective	41	28.45
2599	shift	noun	41	28.07
2600	determination	noun	41	28.04
2601	bread	noun	41	28.03
2602	toss	verb	41	27.73
2603	pretty	adjective	41	27.37
2604	stomach	noun	41	26.99
2605	license	noun	41	26.86
2606	participation	noun	41	26.78
2607	downtown	adv. noun	41	26.62
2608	heel	noun	41	26.22
2609	conscience	noun	41	26.05
2610	far	adjective	41	25.39
2611	conception	noun	41	24.98
2612	readily	adverb	41	24.94
2613	temple	noun	41	24.86
2614	removal	noun	41	24.67
2615	sequence	noun	41	24.54
2616	reform	noun	41	24.12
2617	psychological	adjective	41	23.83
2618	comparable	adjective	41	23.57
2619	whereas	sub. conj.	41	23.53
2620	mind	verb	41	23.16
2621	allowance	noun	41	22.82
2622	motive	noun	41	22.53
2623	Lawrence	prop. noun	41	20.99
2624	storage	noun	41	20.21
2625	myth	noun	41	19.59
2626	compute	verb	41	17.33
2627	Bob	prop. noun	41	16.28
2628	comedy	noun	41	15.11
2629	market	verb	41	8.66
2630	prominent	adjective	40	35.84
2631	practice	verb	40	34.97
2632	personally	adverb	40	34.28
2633	deserve	verb	40	34.04
2634	attractive	adjective	40	33.80
2635	flow	verb	40	32.98
2636	correct	adjective	40	32.74
2637	relieve	verb	40	32.70
2638	flee	verb	40	32.00
2639	thinking	noun	40	31.88
2640	rough	adjective	40	31.81
2641	aim	noun	40	31.63
2642	proof	noun	40	31.61
2643	particularly	qualifier	40	30.99
2644	eleven	card. num.	40	30.86
2645	plot	noun	40	30.75
2646	intense	adjective	40	30.46
2647	address	verb	40	30.43
2648	introduction	noun	40	30.34
2649	outside	adjective	40	30.06
2650	territory	noun	40	29.97
2651	witness	noun	40	29.40
2652	interpret	verb	40	28.87
2653	sink	verb	40	28.78
2654	Paul	prop. noun	40	28.47
2654	permanent	adjective	40	28.47
2656	influence	verb	40	28.38
2657	guidance	noun	40	28.28
2658	Jackson	prop. noun	40	27.82
2659	furthermore	adverb	40	26.77
2660	merchant	noun	40	26.64
2661	prior	adverb	40	25.56
2662	presumably	adverb	40	24.61
2663	legislative	adjective	40	24.51
2664	walk	noun	40	23.88
2665	Japanese	adjective	40	23.79
2666	handsome	adjective	40	23.68
2667	a.m.	adverb	40	23.43
2668	pause	verb	40	23.41
2669	coal	noun	40	23.12
2670	drag	verb	40	22.97

2582	tongue	noun	39	26.27
2583	vacation	noun	55	26.24
2584	next	prep.	42	26.24
2585	heel	noun	41	26.22
2586	pay	noun	39	26.22
2587	hearing	noun	56	26.20
2588	fiscal	adjective	120	26.19
2589	nineteenth	ord. num.	42	26.18
2590	welcome	verb	33	26.17
2591	medicine	noun	35	26.13
2592	border	noun	30	26.13
2593	reflection	noun	39	26.11
2594	observer	noun	37	26.11
2595	bigger	comp. adj.	34	26.10
2596	civilization	noun	46	26.08
2597	conscience	noun	41	26.05
2598	lecture	noun	29	26.05
2599	index	noun	89	26.03
2600	drop	noun	34	25.99
2601	smell	verb	43	25.98
2602	senate	noun	66	25.97
2603	sand	noun	37	25.96
2604	illustration	noun	36	25.94
2605	potential	adjective	39	25.92
2606	channel	noun	38	25.92
2607	residential	adjective	45	25.89
2608	stranger	noun	50	25.87
2609	assert	verb	44	25.81
2610	specify	verb	46	25.79
2611	Indian	prop. noun	48	25.77
2612	warfare	noun	43	25.76
2613	till	sub. conj.	44	25.75
2614	so-called	adjective	32	25.75
2615	blanket	noun	39	25.74
2616	shape	verb	34	25.72
2617	ice	noun	45	25.71
2618	G.	prop. noun	42	25.70
2619	disturb	verb	38	25.70
2620	besides	adverb	35	25.70
2620	predict	verb	35	25.70
2622	stick	noun	42	25.68
2623	regardless	adverb	38	25.68
2624	clerk	noun	45	25.66
2625	truly	adverb	32	25.66
2626	wake	verb	45	25.63
2627	satisfactory	adjective	39	25.59
2628	prior	adverb	40	25.56
2629	setting	noun	37	25.56
2630	precision	noun	44	25.53
2631	impress	verb	36	25.52
2632	dream	verb	45	25.45
2633	melt	verb	32	25.45
2634	Charlie	prop. noun	50	25.44
2635	cease	verb	32	25.43
2636	Cuba	prop. noun	49	25.42
2637	bus	noun	42	25.41
2638	date	verb	36	25.41
2639	deeply	adverb	29	25.40
2640	opera	noun	49	25.39
2641	far	adjective	41	25.39
2642	Peter	prop. noun	46	25.38
2643	secure	verb	33	25.38
2644	sudden	adjective	37	25.33
2645	violent	adjective	33	25.33
2646	humor	noun	45	25.30
2647	restriction	noun	35	25.27
2648	outer	adjective	32	25.27
2649	Warren	prop. noun	51	25.26
2650	enforce	verb	35	25.24
2651	desirable	adjective	36	25.22
2652	thereby	adverb	34	25.22
2653	tour	noun	48	25.21
2654	weak	adjective	32	25.21
2655	particle	noun	63	25.20
2656	worship	noun	31	25.19
2657	junior	adjective	58	25.18
2658	badly	adverb	31	25.16
2659	illusion	noun	43	25.11
2660	objection	noun	31	25.10
2661	publicly	adverb	28	25.10
2662	comfortable	adjective	37	25.09
2663	nerve	noun	34	25.07
2664	certain	post-det.	92	25.06
2665	shortly	adverb	34	25.02
2666	convention	noun	37	24.99
2667	blame	verb	32	24.99
2668	conception	noun	41	24.98
2669	shock	noun	33	24.98
2670	sexual	adjective	59	24.97

2671	visual	adjective	40	21.96
2672	actor	noun	40	20.96
2673	prince	noun	40	20.89
2674	tonight	adv. noun	40	20.60
2675	scream	verb	40	20.18
2676	passion	noun	40	18.91
2677	maturity	noun	40	18.78
2678	output	noun	40	18.54
2679	occurrence	noun	40	18.47
2680	bride	noun	40	18.02
2681	whisky	noun	40	15.91
2682	Jim	prop. noun	40	14.11
2683	Yankee	prop. noun	40	13.97
2684	desegregation	noun	40	12.59
2685	funny	adjective	40	11.53
2686	electron	noun	40	11.11
2687	Pike	prop. noun	40	9.46
2688	Winston	prop. noun	40	6.22
2689	scheme	noun	39	34.06
2690	notice	noun	39	33.13
2691	release	verb	39	33.09
2692	impose	verb	39	32.90
2693	appreciate	verb	39	31.38
2694	Latin	adjective	39	31.30
2695	command	verb	39	31.20
2696	double	adjective	39	30.51
2697	crowd	verb	39	30.19
2698	stir	verb	39	30.14
2699	assemble	verb	39	29.86
2700	anywhere	adverb	39	28.80
2701	forever	adverb	39	28.75
2702	steal	verb	39	28.50
2703	shade	noun	39	28.19
2704	reception	noun	39	27.79
2705	reserve	verb	39	27.51
2706	distribute	verb	39	27.35
2707	tongue	noun	39	26.27
2708	pay	noun	39	26.22
2709	reflection	noun	39	26.11
2710	potential	adjective	39	25.92
2711	blanket	noun	39	25.74
2712	satisfactory	adjective	39	25.59
2713	dependent	adjective	39	24.86
2714	presentation	noun	39	24.68
2715	furniture	noun	39	24.14
2716	automatic	adjective	39	23.62
2717	essentially	adverb	39	23.06
2718	evil	adjective	39	23.03
2719	tape	noun	39	22.82
2720	crew	noun	39	22.78
2721	neutral	adjective	39	22.38
2722	strip	noun	39	22.00
2723	P.	prop. noun	39	21.77
2724	fist	noun	39	21.49
2725	ring	verb	39	21.40
2726	jacket	noun	39	21.35
2727	incorporate	verb	39	20.44
2728	subject	adjective	39	20.40
2729	ally	noun	39	20.14
2730	exceed	verb	39	20.08
2731	sir	noun	39	19.48
2732	sure	adverb	39	19.05
2733	Holmes	prop. noun	39	17.18
2734	Atlanta	prop. noun	39	17.02
2735	piano	noun	39	16.46
2736	fellowship	noun	39	14.07
2737	Robinson	prop. noun	39	13.99
2738	Stanley	prop. noun	39	12.77
2739	liberal	noun	39	12.13
2740	Susan	prop. noun	39	11.25
2741	calendar	noun	39	10.66
2742	Castro	prop. noun	39	9.90
2743	thyroid	noun	39	8.01
2744	briefly	adverb	38	33.89
2745	gesture	noun	38	32.48
2746	anticipate	verb	38	31.93
2747	need	modal aux.	38	30.22
2748	inevitably	adverb	38	29.28
2749	resolve	verb	38	28.85
2750	transfer	verb	38	28.41
2751	glad	adjective	38	28.09
2752	strain	noun	38	28.08
2753	destruction	noun	38	27.54
2754	severe	adjective	38	27.46
2755	harbor	noun	38	27.43
2756	merit	noun	38	27.40
2757	investigate	verb	38	27.04
2758	injury	noun	38	26.77
2759	limitation	noun	38	26.63

2671	fabric	noun	44	24.96
2672	readily	adverb	41	24.94
2673	complicate	verb	33	24.92
2674	nod	verb	62	24.91
2675	era	noun	34	24.90
2676	outlook	noun	36	24.87
2677	temple	noun	41	24.86
2678	dependent	adjective	39	24.86
2679	doctrine	noun	51	24.85
2680	Canada	prop. noun	35	24.83
2681	insure	verb	37	24.80
2682	storm	noun	31	24.76
2683	review	verb	36	24.74
2684	frequency	noun	53	24.72
2685	logical	adjective	34	24.71
2686	commerce	noun	58	24.70
2687	presentation	noun	39	24.68
2688	removal	noun	41	24.67
2689	colony	noun	36	24.67
2690	Sir	prop. noun	57	24.64
2691	presumably	adverb	40	24.61
2692	efficient	adjective	32	24.60
2693	Tuesday	adv. noun	59	24.59
2694	dominate	verb	37	24.55
2695	sequence	noun	41	24.54
2696	legislative	adjective	40	24.51
2697	administrative	adjective	53	24.50
2698	possession	noun	32	24.50
2699	educate	verb	31	24.50
2700	tissue	noun	54	24.45
2701	capture	verb	33	24.44
2702	ambition	noun	34	24.42
2703	temporary	adjective	32	24.41
2704	characteristic	adjective	44	24.40
2705	behave	verb	32	24.40
2706	invariably	adverb	31	24.39
2707	bench	noun	42	24.37
2708	native	adjective	36	24.34
2709	mainly	adverb	30	24.32
2710	seventh	ord. num.	31	24.31
2711	admission	noun	36	24.30
2712	dish	noun	36	24.24
2713	colonel	noun	47	24.23
2714	equivalent	adjective	36	24.23
2715	wherever	wh-adverb	28	24.23
2716	guilty	adjective	29	24.22
2717	commander	noun	35	24.20
2718	wonder	noun	34	24.20
2719	rely	verb	30	24.18
2720	furniture	noun	39	24.14
2721	reform	noun	41	24.12
2722	insect	noun	37	24.09
2723	sad	adjective	35	24.09
2724	guilt	noun	33	24.09
2725	restrain	verb	31	24.09
2726	favorite	adjective	37	24.08
2727	authorize	verb	49	24.06
2728	planning	noun	45	24.03
2729	household	noun	34	24.03
2730	electrical	adjective	46	23.89
2731	walk	noun	40	23.88
2732	beer	noun	36	23.88
2733	favorable	adjective	33	23.85
2734	Democrat	prop. noun	54	23.84
2735	multiple	adjective	36	23.84
2736	openly	adverb	33	23.84
2737	psychological	adjective	41	23.83
2738	virtually	adverb	36	23.80
2739	suitable	adjective	34	23.80
2740	Japanese	adjective	40	23.79
2741	cooperate	verb	28	23.72
2742	worst	sem. sup.	34	23.71
2743	strengthen	verb	36	23.69
2744	slightly	qualifier	32	23.69
2745	handsome	adjective	40	23.68
2746	frequent	adjective	32	23.68
2746	inadequate	adjective	32	23.68
2748	inevitable	adjective	33	23.65
2749	architect	noun	33	23.63
2750	automatic	adjective	39	23.62
2751	sympathetic	adjective	35	23.62
2752	dig	verb	32	23.60
2753	comparable	adjective	41	23.57
2754	builder	noun	60	23.55
2755	whereas	sub. conj.	41	23.53
2756	transfer	noun	43	23.52
2757	billion	card. num.	62	23.49
2758	holy	adjective	48	23.48
2759	ratio	noun	54	23.45

2760	examination	noun	38	26.62
2761	corn	noun	38	26.32
2762	channel	noun	38	25.92
2763	disturb	verb	38	25.70
2764	regardless	adverb	38	25.68
2765	complex	noun	38	23.40
2766	land	verb	38	23.33
2767	objective	adjective	38	23.07
2768	Ohio	prop. noun	38	23.04
2769	veteran	noun	38	22.72
2770	brush	verb	38	22.24
2771	sacred	adjective	38	22.09
2772	Japan	prop. noun	38	21.89
2773	heat	verb	38	21.77
2774	snap	verb	38	21.75
2775	perception	noun	38	21.67
2776	Louisiana	prop. noun	38	21.55
2777	football	noun	38	21.28
2778	supper	noun	38	21.00
2779	insight	noun	38	20.99
2780	pencil	noun	38	19.19
2781	mad	adjective	38	19.04
2782	Chinese	adjective	38	18.52
2783	agricultural	adjective	38	17.57
2784	cigarette	noun	38	17.53
2785	Roy	prop. noun	38	16.51
2786	organic	adjective	38	16.45
2787	minimum	adjective	38	15.44
2788	axis	noun	38	14.52
2789	grin	verb	38	13.51
2790	experimental	adjective	38	13.50
2791	shear	noun	38	6.08
2792	definite	adjective	37	33.94
2793	spoke	verb	37	33.05
2794	occasional	adjective	37	32.77
2795	plain	adjective	37	32.12
2796	neither	dt./d. cj.	37	32.06
2797	stronger	comp. adj.	37	30.67
2798	trouble	verb	37	30.34
2799	tremendous	adjective	37	29.88
2800	fifth	ord. num.	37	29.30
2801	enormous	adjective	37	29.05
2802	effectively	adverb	37	28.62
2803	thanks	pl. noun	37	28.30
2804	decline	verb	37	28.24
2805	uniform	noun	37	28.12
2806	regarding	prep.	37	28.05
2807	distant	adjective	37	27.65
2808	burst	verb	37	27.63
2809	primitive	adjective	37	27.50
2810	gold	noun	37	27.44
2811	ocean	noun	37	27.16
2812	specifically	adverb	37	26.92
2813	resume	verb	37	26.90
2814	steady	adjective	37	26.79
2815	simultaneously	adverb	37	26.68
2816	observer	noun	37	26.11
2817	sand	noun	37	25.96
2818	setting	noun	37	25.56
2819	sudden	adjective	37	25.33
2820	comfortable	adjective	37	25.09
2821	convention	noun	37	24.99
2822	insure	verb	37	24.80
2823	dominate	verb	37	24.55
2824	insect	noun	37	24.09
2825	favorite	adjective	37	24.08
2826	innocent	adjective	37	23.42
2827	equip	verb	37	23.41
2828	transition	noun	37	23.25
2829	obligation	noun	37	22.76
2830	blue	noun	37	22.20
2831	outstanding	adjective	37	22.18
2832	strike	noun	37	21.28
2833	symphony	noun	37	20.44
2834	nationalism	noun	37	20.14
2835	travel	noun	37	20.02
2836	Santa	prop. noun	37	19.94
2837	crop	noun	37	19.81
2838	Wednesday	adv. noun	37	19.77
2839	specimen	noun	37	19.68
2840	outcome	noun	37	19.52
2841	manufacture	verb	37	19.07
2842	charter	noun	37	19.05
2843	dispute	noun	37	18.84
2844	transform	verb	37	18.79
2845	Lee	prop. noun	37	18.44
2846	verse	noun	37	18.41
2847	golf	noun	37	18.17
2848	march	verb	37	17.49

2760	sorry	adjective	48	23.45
2761	found	verb	34	23.45
2762	survival	noun	33	23.45
2763	a.m.	adverb	40	23.43
2764	evil	noun	42	23.42
2765	innocent	adjective	37	23.42
2766	restrict	verb	31	23.42
2767	pause	verb	40	23.41
2768	equip	verb	37	23.41
2769	reply	noun	35	23.41
2770	crucial	adjective	30	23.41
2771	complex	noun	38	23.40
2772	passenger	noun	35	23.40
2773	darkness	noun	43	23.36
2774	count	noun	31	23.34
2774	funeral	noun	31	23.34
2776	land	verb	38	23.33
2777	fate	noun	36	23.33
2778	excitement	noun	32	23.30
2779	challenge	verb	29	23.30
2780	Spanish	adjective	31	23.27
2781	transition	noun	37	23.25
2782	besides	prep.	31	23.24
2783	pray	verb	30	23.23
2784	lightly	adverb	30	23.22
2785	attain	verb	35	23.21
2786	Lewis	prop. noun	63	23.16
2787	mind	verb	41	23.16
2788	similarly	adverb	35	23.15
2789	balance	verb	32	23.14
2790	coal	noun	40	23.12
2791	remote	adjective	32	23.12
2792	Carl	prop. noun	45	23.08
2793	U.N.	prop. noun	56	23.07
2794	objective	adjective	38	23.07
2795	human	noun	45	23.06
2796	essentially	adverb	39	23.06
2797	classical	adjective	33	23.06
2798	Ohio	prop. noun	38	23.04
2799	arouse	verb	30	23.04
2800	evil	adjective	39	23.03
2801	Adams	prop. noun	46	23.02
2802	Johnson	prop. noun	44	23.00
2803	comment	verb	31	23.00
2804	analyze	verb	36	22.99
2804	brush	noun	36	22.99
2806	enthusiasm	noun	29	22.99
2807	effect	verb	32	22.98
2808	drag	verb	40	22.97
2809	round	adjective	32	22.97
2810	drawing	noun	33	22.96
2811	nowhere	adverb	26	22.95
2812	wedding	noun	34	22.94
2813	dear	adjective	45	22.93
2814	shine	verb	32	22.91
2815	launch	verb	31	22.88
2816	pass	noun	34	22.87
2817	inspire	verb	33	22.84
2818	Orleans	prop. noun	44	22.83
2819	allowance	noun	41	22.82
2820	tape	noun	39	22.82
2821	beg	verb	34	22.81
2822	awareness	noun	32	22.80
2823	vein	noun	31	22.79
2824	crew	noun	39	22.78
2825	obligation	noun	37	22.76
2826	fourteen	card. num.	31	22.76
2827	treasury	noun	42	22.75
2828	harmony	noun	32	22.75
2829	purchase	noun	50	22.74
2830	residence	noun	31	22.74
2831	gay	adjective	28	22.74
2831	hold	noun	28	22.74
2833	veteran	noun	38	22.72
2834	Khrushchev	prop. noun	85	22.70
2835	unfortunately	adverb	33	22.69
2836	cope	verb	30	22.66
2837	assist	verb	36	22.63
2838	scatter	verb	29	22.62
2839	successfully	adverb	31	22.61
2840	still	qualifier	28	22.61
2841	normally	adverb	34	22.60
2842	sustain	verb	32	22.58
2843	exclusive	adjective	27	22.58
2844	center	verb	34	22.57
2845	realistic	adjective	34	22.56
2846	tip	noun	33	22.55
2847	motive	noun	41	22.53
2848	equally	qualifier	33	22.52

2849	grab	verb	37	17.05
2850	context	noun	37	16.83
2851	trustee	noun	37	16.52
2852	crawl	verb	37	15.51
2853	species	noun	37	13.44
2854	variable	noun	37	9.01
2855	milligram	noun	37	8.13
2856	gram	noun	37	7.87
2857	polynomial	noun	37	5.92
2857	serum	noun	37	5.92
2859	register	verb	36	33.20
2860	presently	adverb	36	32.28
2861	tough	adjective	36	30.59
2862	like	adjective	36	30.56
2863	automatically	adverb	36	30.31
2864	struggle	verb	36	28.86
2865	Italy	prop. noun	36	28.71
2866	forty	card. num.	36	28.57
2867	resist	verb	36	28.56
2868	conduct	noun	36	28.12
2869	indication	noun	36	27.65
2870	belt	noun	36	27.19
2871	trace	verb	36	26.91
2872	smooth	adjective	36	26.71
2873	project	verb	36	26.65
2874	illustration	noun	36	25.94
2875	impress	verb	36	25.52
2876	date	verb	36	25.41
2877	desirable	adjective	36	25.22
2878	outlook	noun	36	24.87
2879	review	verb	36	24.74
2880	colony	noun	36	24.67
2881	native	adjective	36	24.34
2882	admission	noun	36	24.30
2883	dish	noun	36	24.24
2884	equivalent	adjective	36	24.23
2885	beer	noun	36	23.88
2886	multiple	adjective	36	23.84
2887	virtually	adverb	36	23.80
2888	strengthen	verb	36	23.69
2889	fate	noun	36	23.33
2890	analyze	verb	36	22.99
2890	brush	noun	36	22.99
2892	assist	verb	36	22.63
2893	debate	noun	36	22.28
2894	tear	noun	36	22.11
2895	lung	noun	36	21.95
2896	graduate	noun	36	21.91
2897	utility	noun	36	21.70
2898	cotton	noun	36	21.10
2899	Clark	prop. noun	36	20.95
2900	Kansas	prop. noun	36	19.22
2901	grace	noun	36	19.01
2902	dirty	adjective	36	18.66
2903	metropolitan	adjective	36	18.63
2904	accuracy	noun	36	18.41
2905	legend	noun	36	18.28
2906	taxpayer	noun	36	17.11
2907	evaluation	noun	36	16.64
2908	policeman	noun	36	16.55
2909	Jane	prop. noun	36	16.28
2910	commissioner	noun	36	15.82
2911	shell	noun	36	15.64
2912	capability	noun	36	15.45
2913	Sherman	prop. noun	36	11.87
2914	T	prop. noun	36	6.25
2915	binomial	adjective	36	5.76
2916	sharply	adverb	35	31.00
2917	strongly	adverb	35	30.09
2918	meanwhile	adverb	35	29.36
2919	painter	noun	35	29.24
2920	latest	sem. sup.	35	28.66
2921	sense	verb	35	28.41
2922	accurate	adjective	35	27.90
2923	creature	noun	35	27.67
2924	specialist	noun	35	27.00
2925	dignity	noun	35	26.78
2926	medicine	noun	35	26.13
2927	besides	adverb	35	25.70
2927	predict	verb	35	25.70
2929	restriction	noun	35	25.27
2930	enforce	verb	35	25.24
2931	Canada	prop. noun	35	24.83
2932	commander	noun	35	24.20
2933	sad	adjective	35	24.09
2934	sympathetic	adjective	35	23.62
2935	reply	noun	35	23.41
2936	passenger	noun	35	23.40
2937	attain	verb	35	23.21

2849	hurry	verb	45	22.49
2850	regional	adjective	42	22.48
2851	deeper	comp. adj.	29	22.48
2852	cross	noun	29	22.46
2853	et	foreign	29	22.44
2854	thoroughly	adverb	30	22.43
2855	excite	verb	28	22.41
2856	composition	noun	35	22.40
2857	neutral	adjective	39	22.38
2858	fault	noun	29	22.37
2859	congregation	noun	65	22.34
2860	seize	verb	33	22.34
2861	originate	verb	26	22.34
2862	horn	noun	33	22.32
2863	eastern	adjective	32	22.32
2864	since	adverb	29	22.32
2865	insurance	noun	46	22.31
2866	lend	verb	29	22.30
2867	occupation	noun	28	22.30
2868	courage	noun	32	22.29
2869	debate	noun	36	22.28
2870	dine	verb	32	22.27
2870	impulse	noun	32	22.27
2872	brush	verb	38	22.24
2873	blue	noun	37	22.20
2874	outstanding	adjective	37	22.18
2875	healthy	adjective	33	22.17
2876	suit	verb	31	22.14
2877	tear	noun	36	22.11
2878	however	wh-qual.	33	22.11
2879	suburb	noun	31	22.11
2880	sacred	adjective	38	22.09
2881	depart	verb	28	22.07
2882	Missouri	prop. noun	33	22.01
2883	strip	noun	39	22.00
2884	presidential	adjective	34	21.99
2885	visual	adjective	40	21.96
2886	lung	noun	36	21.95
2887	free	verb	28	21.93
2888	graduate	noun	36	21.91
2889	borrow	verb	31	21.90
2890	Japan	prop. noun	38	21.89
2891	rhythm	noun	35	21.87
2892	somewhat	adverb	28	21.81
2893	lower	verb	32	21.79
2894	implication	noun	32	21.78
2895	slope	noun	27	21.78
2896	P.	prop. noun	39	21.77
2897	heat	verb	38	21.77
2898	snap	verb	38	21.75
2899	expectation	noun	34	21.74
2900	Moscow	prop. noun	51	21.73
2901	French	prop. noun	32	21.73
2902	bath	noun	31	21.73
2902	extraordinary	adjective	31	21.73
2904	suspend	verb	33	21.71
2905	utility	noun	36	21.70
2906	rub	verb	34	21.70
2907	volunteer	noun	34	21.68
2908	perception	noun	38	21.67
2909	sleep	noun	34	21.65
2910	focus	noun	29	21.65
2911	promptly	adverb	28	21.64
2912	hesitate	verb	33	21.62
2913	arc	noun	48	21.60
2914	equally	adverb	29	21.57
2915	Louisiana	prop. noun	38	21.55
2916	fee	noun	45	21.53
2917	fish	noun	33	21.51
2918	fist	noun	39	21.49
2919	consequently	adverb	31	21.49
2920	opponent	noun	30	21.47
2921	constitution	noun	53	21.42
2922	employer	noun	34	21.41
2923	controversy	noun	30	21.41
2924	fiction	noun	46	21.40
2925	ring	verb	39	21.40
2926	forbid	verb	28	21.36
2927	jacket	noun	39	21.35
2928	back	adjective	29	21.35
2929	react	verb	32	21.34
2930	sentiment	noun	31	21.34
2931	porch	noun	45	21.32
2932	inquiry	noun	34	21.31
2933	potential	noun	32	21.30
2934	entertain	verb	34	21.29
2935	engagement	noun	30	21.29
2935	entirely	qualifier	30	21.29
2937	football	noun	38	21.28

2938 similarly	adverb	35	23.15
2939 composition	noun	35	22.40
2940 rhythm	noun	35	21.87
2941 Harvard	prop. noun	35	21.08
2942 cut	noun	35	20.13
2943 frontier	noun	35	20.02
2944 gallery	noun	35	19.94
2945 cry	noun	35	19.78
2946 wipe	verb	35	19.57
2947 matter	verb	35	18.68
2948 Harry	prop. noun	35	18.17
2949 fool	noun	35	17.13
2950 submarine	noun	35	17.02
2951 nut	noun	35	16.79
2952 Williams	prop. noun	35	16.60
2953 glance	noun	35	15.79
2954 inventory	noun	35	15.27
2955 Poland	prop. noun	35	15.19
2956 symbolic	adjective	35	14.01
2957 protein	noun	35	13.86
2958 score	verb	35	13.80
2959 like	prep.	35	13.11
2960 lumber	noun	35	11.84
2961 southerner	noun	35	11.72
2962 Black	prop. noun	35	11.70
2963 Catholic	prop. noun	35	10.99
2964 trader	noun	35	10.73
2965 bunk	noun	35	8.67
2966 Gorton	prop. noun	35	5.25
2967 owe	verb	34	31.40
2968 undergo	verb	34	29.70
2969 release	noun	34	29.16
2970 seldom	adverb	34	28.92
2971 visible	adjective	34	28.38
2972 sake	noun	34	27.90
2973 translate	verb	34	27.82
2974 genuine	adjective	34	27.76
2975 opening	noun	34	27.57
2976 focus	verb	34	27.44
2977 delay	verb	34	27.33
2978 string	noun	34	26.89
2979 high	adverb	34	26.73
2980 wish	noun	34	26.63
2981 bigger	comp. adj.	34	26.10
2982 drop	noun	34	25.99
2983 shape	verb	34	25.72
2984 thereby	adverb	34	25.22
2985 nerve	noun	34	25.07
2986 shortly	adverb	34	25.02
2987 era	noun	34	24.90
2988 logical	adjective	34	24.71
2989 ambition	noun	34	24.42
2990 wonder	noun	34	24.20
2991 household	noun	34	24.03
2992 suitable	adjective	34	23.80
2993 worst	sem. sup.	34	23.71
2994 found	verb	34	23.45
2995 wedding	noun	34	22.94
2996 pass	noun	34	22.87
2997 beg	verb	34	22.81
2998 normally	adverb	34	22.60
2999 center	verb	34	22.57
3000 realistic	adjective	34	22.56
3001 presidential	adjective	34	21.99
3002 expectation	noun	34	21.74
3003 rub	verb	34	21.70
3004 volunteer	noun	34	21.68
3005 sleep	noun	34	21.65
3006 employer	noun	34	21.41
3007 inquiry	noun	34	21.31
3008 entertain	verb	34	21.29
3009 suspicion	noun	34	21.12
3010 twist	verb	34	21.07
3011 kick	verb	34	21.01
3012 invitation	noun	34	20.90
3013 pleasant	adjective	34	20.55
3014 prize	noun	34	20.38
3015 currently	adverb	34	20.34
3016 campus	noun	34	20.19
3017 liquid	noun	34	20.07
3018 mechanical	adjective	34	20.03
3019 mixture	noun	34	19.95
3020 crazy	adjective	34	19.91
3021 Thursday	adv. noun	34	19.56
3022 Samuel	prop. noun	34	19.23
3023 appointment	noun	34	18.58
3024 sugar	noun	34	17.94
3025 reserve	noun	34	17.77
3026 fan	noun	34	17.73

2938 strike	noun	37	21.28
2939 anyway	adverb	46	21.24
2940 restore	verb	28	21.21
2941 Roosevelt	prop. noun	33	21.20
2942 cast	verb	28	21.16
2943 delicate	adjective	27	21.13
2944 suspicion	noun	34	21.12
2945 anxious	adjective	29	21.12
2946 cotton	noun	36	21.10
2947 squeeze	verb	30	21.10
2948 arrival	noun	26	21.10
2949 Harvard	prop. noun	35	21.08
2950 twist	verb	34	21.07
2951 blow	noun	28	21.07
2952 specialize	verb	26	21.07
2953 link	verb	25	21.07
2954 lunch	noun	32	21.05
2955 truly	qualifier	25	21.04
2956 award	noun	60	21.03
2957 magnificent	adjective	27	21.02
2958 kick	verb	34	21.01
2959 supper	noun	38	21.00
2960 anxiety	noun	43	20.99
2961 Lawrence	prop. noun	41	20.99
2962 insight	noun	38	20.99
2963 journey	noun	31	20.97
2964 actor	noun	40	20.96
2965 precise	adjective	33	20.96
2965 weigh	verb	33	20.96
2967 Clark	prop. noun	36	20.95
2968 discipline	noun	29	20.94
2969 invitation	noun	34	20.90
2970 prince	noun	40	20.89
2971 either	adverb	32	20.89
2972 excessive	adjective	30	20.88
2973 dismiss	verb	23	20.87
2974 waste	noun	31	20.86
2975 client	noun	33	20.82
2976 resemble	verb	27	20.79
2977 precious	adjective	30	20.75
2978 convert	verb	31	20.74
2979 vague	adjective	25	20.74
2980 Monday	adv. noun	72	20.72
2981 protest	verb	29	20.72
2982 drift	verb	27	20.72
2983 though	adverb	32	20.70
2984 jet	noun	33	20.69
2985 cling	verb	30	20.68
2986 canvas	noun	27	20.66
2987 tank	noun	30	20.63
2988 tonight	adv. noun	40	20.60
2989 doubt	verb	28	20.60
2990 mystery	noun	46	20.59
2991 round	noun	32	20.59
2992 transportation	noun	43	20.57
2993 ceiling	noun	32	20.56
2994 pleasant	adjective	34	20.55
2995 painful	adjective	25	20.54
2996 pot	noun	33	20.52
2997 characterize	verb	32	20.52
2997 trust	noun	32	20.52
2999 acknowledge	verb	27	20.52
3000 tremble	verb	42	20.51
3001 seat	verb	31	20.47
3002 incorporate	verb	39	20.44
3003 symphony	noun	37	20.44
3004 break	noun	26	20.44
3005 stop	noun	31	20.41
3006 subject	adjective	39	20.40
3007 mankind	noun	43	20.39
3008 prize	noun	34	20.38
3009 marine	noun	64	20.34
3010 currently	adverb	34	20.34
3011 recover	verb	25	20.33
3012 mechanism	noun	46	20.29
3013 slide	verb	43	20.29
3014 intelligent	adjective	26	20.26
3015 inspection	noun	24	20.25
3016 fast	adjective	31	20.24
3017 storage	noun	41	20.21
3018 grip	noun	28	20.20
3019 line	verb	23	20.20
3020 campus	noun	34	20.19
3021 scream	verb	40	20.18
3022 document	noun	30	20.17
3023 reverse	verb	27	20.16
3024 ally	noun	39	20.14
3025 nationalism	noun	37	20.14
3026 square	adjective	30	20.14

3027	process	verb	34	13.95
3028	Chandler	prop. noun	34	13.31
3029	Plato	prop. noun	34	10.59
3030	flux	noun	34	9.97
3031	Baker	prop. noun	34	9.47
3032	Morse	prop. noun	34	8.88
3033	Pat	prop. noun	34	7.98
3034	massive	adjective	33	29.70
3035	horizon	noun	33	27.52
3036	wise	adjective	33	27.26
3037	welcome	verb	33	26.17
3038	secure	verb	33	25.38
3039	violent	adjective	33	25.33
3040	shock	noun	33	24.98
3041	complicate	verb	33	24.92
3042	capture	verb	33	24.44
3043	guilt	noun	33	24.09
3044	favorable	adjective	33	23.85
3045	openly	adverb	33	23.84
3046	inevitable	adjective	33	23.65
3047	architect	noun	33	23.63
3048	survival	noun	33	23.45
3049	classical	adjective	33	23.06
3050	drawing	noun	33	22.96
3051	inspire	verb	33	22.84
3052	unfortunately	adverb	33	22.69
3053	tip	noun	33	22.55
3054	equally	qualifier	33	22.52
3055	seize	verb	33	22.34
3056	horn	noun	33	22.32
3057	healthy	adjective	33	22.17
3058	however	wh-qual.	33	22.11
3059	Missouri	prop. noun	33	22.01
3060	suspend	verb	33	21.71
3061	hesitate	verb	33	21.62
3062	fish	noun	33	21.51
3063	Roosevelt	prop. noun	33	21.20
3064	precise	adjective	33	20.96
3064	weigh	verb	33	20.96
3066	client	noun	33	20.82
3067	jet	noun	33	20.69
3068	pot	noun	33	20.52
3069	smoke	noun	33	20.11
3070	sail	verb	33	19.71
3071	artistic	adjective	33	19.43
3072	beam	noun	33	18.62
3073	studio	noun	33	18.49
3074	tragic	adjective	33	18.24
3075	namely	adverb	33	18.14
3076	leaf	noun	33	18.06
3077	naval	adjective	33	17.93
3078	swear	verb	33	17.81
3079	priest	noun	33	17.65
3080	straighten	verb	33	16.92
3081	leap	verb	33	16.70
3082	basement	noun	33	16.60
3083	powder	noun	33	16.44
3084	barn	noun	33	15.72
3085	forgive	verb	33	15.44
3086	density	noun	33	15.28
3087	random	adjective	33	14.87
3088	cheek	noun	33	14.43
3088	damn	verb	33	14.43
3090	fluid	noun	33	13.05
3091	slavery	noun	33	12.88
3092	designer	noun	33	11.75
3093	Howard	prop. noun	33	11.71
3094	fat	noun	33	10.31
3095	thermal	adjective	33	8.13
3096	Coolidge	prop. noun	33	7.68
3097	chlorine	noun	33	6.79
3098	Patchen	prop. noun	33	6.25
3099	Dartmouth	prop. noun	33	5.87
3100	Pip	prop. noun	33	5.28
3100	pulmonary	adjective	33	5.28
3102	satisfaction	noun	32	28.91
3103	most	sup. adv.	32	27.52
3104	admire	verb	32	26.59
3105	cash	noun	32	26.54
3106	so-called	adjective	32	25.75
3107	truly	adverb	32	25.66
3108	melt	verb	32	25.45
3109	cease	verb	32	25.43
3110	outer	adjective	32	25.27
3111	weak	adjective	32	25.21
3112	blame	verb	32	24.99
3113	efficient	adjective	32	24.60
3114	possession	noun	32	24.50
3115	temporary	adjective	32	24.41

3027	cut	noun	35	20.13
3028	object	verb	29	20.13
3029	smoke	noun	33	20.11
3030	vigorous	adjective	29	20.11
3030	widespread	adjective	29	20.11
3032	terror	noun	26	20.09
3033	ballet	noun	45	20.08
3034	exceed	verb	39	20.08
3035	liquid	noun	34	20.07
3036	editorial	noun	48	20.04
3037	explore	verb	29	20.04
3038	mechanical	adjective	34	20.03
3039	modest	adjective	29	20.03
3040	travel	noun	37	20.02
3041	frontier	noun	35	20.02
3042	peculiar	adjective	28	20.02
3043	key	sup. adj.	29	20.01
3044	undoubtedly	adverb	24	19.99
3045	feed	noun	65	19.96
3046	stain	verb	45	19.95
3047	mixture	noun	34	19.95
3048	producer	noun	31	19.95
3049	shop	verb	26	19.95
3050	Santa	prop. noun	37	19.94
3051	gallery	noun	35	19.94
3052	chart	noun	30	19.93
3053	spring	verb	30	19.92
3054	crazy	adjective	34	19.91
3055	witness	verb	28	19.90
3056	round	verb	25	19.87
3057	tie	noun	27	19.86
3058	Maryland	prop. noun	30	19.85
3059	harm	noun	24	19.83
3060	crop	noun	37	19.81
3061	fewer	post-det.	30	19.81
3062	sophisticated	adjective	26	19.81
3063	budget	noun	62	19.79
3064	cry	noun	35	19.78
3065	Wednesday	adv. noun	37	19.77
3066	ideal	noun	31	19.76
3067	god	noun	31	19.75
3068	wind	verb	29	19.75
3069	damage	noun	30	19.73
3069	minimum	noun	30	19.73
3071	attraction	noun	24	19.73
3072	sail	verb	33	19.71
3073	secondary	adjective	31	19.70
3074	specimen	noun	37	19.68
3075	reputation	noun	30	19.68
3076	persist	verb	25	19.68
3077	effectiveness	noun	32	19.67
3078	assistant	noun	32	19.66
3079	absolute	adjective	29	19.66
3080	flame	noun	27	19.66
3081	literally	adverb	26	19.64
3082	prestige	noun	29	19.63
3083	circuit	noun	27	19.63
3084	frame	verb	23	19.61
3085	deliberately	adverb	30	19.60
3086	myth	noun	41	19.59
3087	wipe	verb	35	19.57
3088	fish	verb	30	19.57
3089	Thursday	adv. noun	34	19.56
3090	Van	prop. noun	30	19.56
3091	tail	noun	31	19.55
3092	companion	noun	27	19.55
3093	angel	noun	45	19.54
3094	outcome	noun	37	19.52
3095	withdraw	verb	25	19.52
3096	Laos	prop. noun	64	19.51
3097	barrel	noun	32	19.51
3098	testament	noun	31	19.50
3099	sir	noun	39	19.48
3100	colleague	noun	32	19.46
3101	announcement	noun	30	19.46
3102	monument	noun	29	19.44
3103	arrest	verb	27	19.44
3103	profound	adjective	27	19.44
3105	artistic	adjective	33	19.43
3106	exact	adjective	27	19.41
3107	await	verb	26	19.40
3108	enthusiastic	adjective	24	19.38
3109	clue	noun	25	19.36
3110	widow	noun	27	19.35
3111	helpful	adjective	29	19.32
3112	convey	verb	27	19.31
3113	grind	verb	26	19.30
3114	e.g.	adverb	32	19.28
3115	Samuel	prop. noun	34	19.23

3116	behave	verb	32	24.40
3117	slightly	qualifier	32	23.69
3118	frequent	adjective	32	23.68
3118	inadequate	adjective	32	23.68
3120	dig	verb	32	23.60
3121	excitement	noun	32	23.30
3122	balance	verb	32	23.14
3123	remote	adjective	32	23.12
3124	effect	verb	32	22.98
3125	round	adjective	32	22.97
3126	shine	verb	32	22.91
3127	awareness	noun	32	22.80
3128	harmony	noun	32	22.75
3129	sustain	verb	32	22.58
3130	eastern	adjective	32	22.32
3131	courage	noun	32	22.29
3132	dine	verb	32	22.27
3132	impulse	noun	32	22.27
3134	lower	verb	32	21.79
3135	implication	noun	32	21.78
3136	French	prop. noun	32	21.73
3137	react	verb	32	21.34
3138	potential	noun	32	21.30
3139	lunch	noun	32	21.05
3140	either	adverb	32	20.89
3141	though	adverb	32	20.70
3142	round	noun	32	20.59
3143	ceiling	noun	32	20.56
3144	characterize	verb	32	20.52
3144	trust	noun	32	20.52
3146	effectiveness	noun	32	19.67
3147	assistant	noun	32	19.66
3148	barrel	noun	32	19.51
3149	colleague	noun	32	19.46
3150	e.g.	adverb	32	19.28
3151	settlement	noun	32	19.02
3152	initiative	noun	32	18.95
3153	romantic	adjective	32	18.94
3154	salesman	noun	32	18.92
3155	politician	noun	32	18.58
3156	ceremony	noun	32	18.45
3157	sketch	noun	32	18.28
3158	Christian	prop. noun	32	18.21
3159	last	adverb	32	18.14
3160	congressman	noun	32	17.93
3161	naked	adjective	32	17.81
3162	entertainment	noun	32	17.52
3163	utilize	verb	32	17.33
3164	mud	noun	32	17.14
3165	beef	noun	32	16.58
3166	divine	adjective	32	15.98
3167	bomber	noun	32	15.71
3168	velocity	noun	32	15.26
3169	Florida	prop. noun	32	14.87
3170	contest	noun	32	14.82
3171	Jefferson	prop. noun	32	14.54
3172	holder	noun	32	14.43
3173	devil	noun	32	14.09
3174	further	post-det.	32	13.25
3175	instant	noun	32	13.19
3176	counter	noun	32	13.09
3177	Harold	prop. noun	32	12.31
3178	long-term	noun	32	12.17
3179	spectrum	noun	32	12.15
3180	peer	verb	32	11.22
3181	engineer	verb	32	11.04
3182	pond	noun	32	10.75
3183	Lord	prop. noun	32	9.04
3184	Dave	prop. noun	32	8.46
3185	Mickey	prop. noun	32	8.04
3186	carbon	noun	32	7.73
3186	salvation	noun	32	7.73
3188	cop	noun	32	7.61
3189	electronics	noun	32	5.91
3190	Felix	prop. noun	32	5.72
3191	emission	noun	32	5.12
3191	fallout	noun	32	5.12
3193	worship	noun	31	25.19
3194	badly	adverb	31	25.16
3195	objection	noun	31	25.10
3196	storm	noun	31	24.76
3197	educate	verb	31	24.50
3198	invariably	adverb	31	24.39
3199	seventh	ord. num.	31	24.31
3200	restrain	verb	31	24.09
3201	restrict	verb	31	23.42
3202	count	noun	31	23.34
3202	funeral	noun	31	23.34
3204	Spanish	adjective	31	23.27

3116	Kansas	prop. noun	36	19.22
3117	exhibit	verb	31	19.22
3118	morality	noun	30	19.20
3119	eager	adjective	27	19.20
3120	pencil	noun	38	19.19
3121	grateful	adjective	25	19.19
3122	rail	noun	25	19.16
3123	roll	noun	23	19.16
3124	spin	verb	31	19.15
3125	probable	adjective	25	19.14
3126	switch	verb	28	19.13
3127	manufacture	verb	37	19.07
3128	sure	adverb	39	19.05
3129	charter	noun	37	19.05
3130	mad	adjective	38	19.04
3131	composer	noun	46	19.03
3132	condemn	verb	30	19.03
3133	request	verb	29	19.03
3134	Christmas	prop. noun	27	19.03
3135	settlement	noun	32	19.02
3136	grace	noun	36	19.01
3137	exciting	adjective	27	18.98
3138	alert	adjective	25	18.98
3139	identical	adjective	31	18.97
3140	initiative	noun	32	18.95
3141	pile	verb	26	18.95
3142	romantic	adjective	32	18.94
3143	challenge	noun	23	18.94
3144	salesman	noun	32	18.92
3145	nearly	qualifier	29	18.92
3146	likely	adverb	25	18.92
3147	passion	noun	40	18.91
3148	false	adjective	28	18.89
3148	resident	noun	28	18.89
3150	ease	verb	25	18.87
3151	stair	noun	49	18.86
3152	potato	noun	30	18.86
3153	dispute	noun	37	18.84
3154	greet	verb	28	18.80
3155	transform	verb	37	18.79
3156	climate	noun	27	18.79
3157	maturity	noun	40	18.78
3158	warmth	noun	28	18.74
3159	friendship	noun	31	18.73
3160	preach	verb	26	18.72
3161	neglect	verb	28	18.70
3162	boil	verb	27	18.69
3163	matter	verb	35	18.68
3164	holiday	noun	30	18.67
3165	dirty	adjective	36	18.66
3166	split	verb	26	18.65
3167	long-range	noun	42	18.64
3168	breathe	verb	31	18.64
3169	metropolitan	adjective	36	18.63
3170	collective	adjective	31	18.63
3171	beam	noun	33	18.62
3172	Miller	prop. noun	28	18.62
3173	joint	noun	28	18.61
3174	adventure	noun	27	18.60
3175	appointment	noun	34	18.58
3176	politician	noun	32	18.58
3177	gently	adverb	31	18.58
3178	Wright	prop. noun	55	18.57
3179	race	verb	30	18.55
3180	output	noun	40	18.54
3181	exert	verb	29	18.54
3182	Chinese	adjective	38	18.52
3183	studio	noun	33	18.49
3184	occurrence	noun	40	18.47
3185	departure	noun	24	18.47
3186	ceremony	noun	32	18.45
3187	Tennessee	prop. noun	25	18.45
3188	fiber	noun	50	18.44
3189	Lee	prop. noun	37	18.44
3190	melody	noun	31	18.43
3191	verse	noun	37	18.41
3192	accuracy	noun	36	18.41
3193	realization	noun	24	18.41
3194	correspondence	noun	25	18.40
3195	considering	prep.	24	18.40
3196	endure	verb	31	18.39
3197	pitch	noun	27	18.36
3198	privilege	noun	28	18.35
3199	mirror	noun	27	18.33
3200	formerly	adverb	28	18.30
3201	then	adjective	26	18.30
3202	legend	noun	36	18.28
3203	sketch	noun	32	18.28
3204	current	noun	29	18.28

3205	besides	prep.	31	23.24
3206	comment	verb	31	23.00
3207	launch	verb	31	22.88
3208	vein	noun	31	22.79
3209	fourteen	card. num.	31	22.76
3210	residence	noun	31	22.74
3211	successfully	adverb	31	22.61
3212	suit	verb	31	22.14
3213	suburb	noun	31	22.11
3214	borrow	verb	31	21.90
3215	bath	noun	31	21.73
3215	extraordinary	adjective	31	21.73
3217	consequently	adverb	31	21.49
3218	sentiment	noun	31	21.34
3219	journey	noun	31	20.97
3220	waste	noun	31	20.86
3221	convert	verb	31	20.74
3222	seat	verb	31	20.47
3223	stop	noun	31	20.41
3224	fast	adjective	31	20.24
3225	producer	noun	31	19.95
3226	ideal	noun	31	19.76
3227	god	noun	31	19.75
3228	secondary	adjective	31	19.70
3229	tail	noun	31	19.55
3230	testament	noun	31	19.50
3231	exhibit	verb	31	19.22
3232	spin	verb	31	19.15
3233	identical	adjective	31	18.97
3234	friendship	noun	31	18.73
3235	breathe	verb	31	18.64
3236	collective	adjective	31	18.63
3237	gently	adverb	31	18.58
3238	melody	noun	31	18.43
3239	endure	verb	31	18.39
3240	waste	verb	31	18.22
3241	lover	noun	31	18.20
3242	Mark	prop. noun	31	18.10
3243	maker	noun	31	17.88
3244	Harris	prop. noun	31	17.76
3245	watch	noun	31	17.61
3246	Franklin	prop. noun	31	16.87
3247	poetic	adjective	31	16.85
3248	tourist	noun	31	16.74
3249	hurt	verb	31	16.48
3250	rebel	noun	31	16.43
3251	classic	adjective	31	16.41
3252	evaluate	verb	31	16.28
3253	accordingly	adverb	31	16.26
3254	tire	noun	31	14.82
3255	prisoner	noun	31	14.79
3256	substantially	adverb	31	14.73
3257	stumble	verb	31	14.65
3258	pistol	noun	31	14.52
3259	decrease	verb	31	14.49
3260	pope	noun	31	14.03
3261	beard	noun	31	13.97
3262	Ann	prop. noun	31	13.85
3263	crystal	noun	31	13.63
3264	norm	noun	31	13.45
3265	whisper	verb	31	13.36
3266	suite	noun	31	13.28
3267	amendment	noun	31	12.96
3268	respectively	adverb	31	12.49
3269	festival	noun	31	11.96
3270	champion	noun	31	11.86
3271	listener	noun	31	11.85
3272	sergeant	noun	31	11.27
3273	motel	noun	31	11.03
3274	competitive	adjective	31	10.67
3275	kiss	verb	31	10.36
3276	Ruth	prop. noun	31	9.48
3277	tractor	noun	31	9.35
3278	Christianity	prop. noun	31	9.19
3279	yell	verb	31	8.37
3280	Eddie	prop. noun	31	7.12
3281	border	noun	30	26.13
3282	mainly	adverb	30	24.32
3283	rely	verb	30	24.18
3284	crucial	adjective	30	23.41
3285	pray	verb	30	23.23
3286	lightly	adverb	30	23.22
3287	arouse	verb	30	23.04
3288	cope	verb	30	22.66
3289	thoroughly	adverb	30	22.43
3290	opponent	noun	30	21.47
3291	controversy	noun	30	21.41
3292	engagement	noun	30	21.29
3292	entirely	qualifier	30	21.29

3205	African	adjective	24	18.25
3206	tragic	adjective	33	18.24
3207	detect	verb	28	18.23
3208	waste	verb	31	18.22
3209	Christian	prop. noun	32	18.21
3210	lover	noun	31	18.20
3211	consciousness	noun	30	18.19
3212	publicity	noun	27	18.19
3213	textile	noun	42	18.18
3214	proclaim	verb	30	18.18
3215	golf	noun	37	18.17
3216	Harry	prop. noun	35	18.17
3217	conversion	noun	27	18.17
3218	appreciation	noun	23	18.16
3219	Congo	prop. noun	60	18.15
3220	namely	adverb	33	18.14
3221	last	adverb	32	18.14
3222	commitment	noun	29	18.14
3223	Mark	prop. noun	31	18.10
3224	demonstration	noun	29	18.10
3225	unhappy	adjective	26	18.07
3226	leaf	noun	33	18.06
3227	bride	noun	40	18.02
3228	load	verb	30	17.98
3229	barely	adverb	25	17.97
3229	fighter	noun	25	17.97
3231	chore	noun	23	17.96
3232	humanity	noun	30	17.95
3233	sugar	noun	34	17.94
3234	naval	adjective	33	17.93
3235	congressman	noun	32	17.93
3236	nearby	adjective	26	17.93
3237	bore	verb	26	17.92
3238	maker	noun	31	17.88
3239	senior	adjective	29	17.84
3240	sacrifice	noun	26	17.83
3241	swear	verb	33	17.81
3242	naked	adjective	32	17.81
3243	subsequent	adjective	28	17.78
3244	reserve	noun	34	17.77
3245	Harris	prop. noun	31	17.76
3246	municipal	adjective	29	17.74
3247	trap	noun	27	17.74
3248	fan	noun	34	17.73
3249	comprise	verb	25	17.71
3250	gathering	noun	22	17.71
3251	progress	verb	25	17.70
3252	permission	noun	27	17.67
3253	dedicate	verb	25	17.66
3254	priest	noun	33	17.65
3255	dictionary	noun	59	17.63
3256	eternal	adjective	29	17.62
3257	watch	noun	31	17.61
3258	boundary	noun	30	17.61
3259	striking	adjective	28	17.58
3260	incline	verb	21	17.58
3261	diameter	noun	53	17.57
3262	agricultural	adjective	38	17.57
3263	parade	noun	26	17.57
3264	making	noun	28	17.56
3265	depression	noun	27	17.56
3266	fortune	noun	29	17.55
3267	cheap	adjective	23	17.55
3268	gross	adjective	30	17.54
3269	elaborate	adjective	26	17.54
3270	cigarette	noun	38	17.53
3271	entertainment	noun	32	17.52
3272	surplus	noun	28	17.52
3273	planet	noun	44	17.51
3274	march	verb	37	17.49
3275	wave	verb	30	17.49
3276	Shakespeare	prop. noun	43	17.47
3277	plastic	noun	56	17.46
3278	mail	verb	25	17.46
3279	loyalty	noun	25	17.45
3280	subject	verb	26	17.44
3281	flood	noun	24	17.42
3282	boss	noun	28	17.39
3283	absent	adjective	26	17.38
3284	originally	adverb	23	17.38
3285	compute	verb	41	17.33
3286	utilize	verb	32	17.33
3287	altogether	adverb	26	17.33
3287	draft	noun	26	17.33
3289	nervous	adjective	24	17.33
3290	float	verb	23	17.33
3291	noble	adjective	23	17.31
3292	dull	adjective	27	17.27
3293	recovery	noun	28	17.26

3294	squeeze	verb	30	21.10
3295	excessive	adjective	30	20.88
3296	precious	adjective	30	20.75
3297	cling	verb	30	20.68
3298	tank	noun	30	20.63
3299	document	noun	30	20.17
3300	square	adjective	30	20.14
3301	chart	noun	30	19.93
3302	spring	verb	30	19.92
3303	Maryland	prop. noun	30	19.85
3304	fewer	post-det.	30	19.81
3305	damage	noun	30	19.73
3305	minimum	noun	30	19.73
3307	reputation	noun	30	19.68
3308	deliberately	adverb	30	19.60
3309	fish	verb	30	19.57
3310	Van	prop. noun	30	19.56
3311	announcement	noun	30	19.46
3312	morality	noun	30	19.20
3313	condemn	verb	30	19.03
3314	potato	noun	30	18.86
3315	holiday	noun	30	18.67
3316	race	verb	30	18.55
3317	consciousness	noun	30	18.19
3318	proclaim	verb	30	18.18
3319	load	verb	30	17.98
3320	humanity	noun	30	17.95
3321	boundary	noun	30	17.61
3322	gross	adjective	30	17.54
3323	wave	verb	30	17.49
3324	cycle	noun	30	17.17
3325	abstract	adjective	30	17.00
3326	skilled	adjective	30	16.78
3327	coordinate	verb	30	16.66
3328	cabin	noun	30	16.57
3329	freight	noun	30	16.11
3330	palm	noun	30	15.85
3331	disaster	noun	30	15.77
3332	slow	verb	30	15.71
3333	stroke	noun	30	15.64
3334	generate	verb	30	15.63
3335	propaganda	noun	30	15.09
3336	Johnny	prop. noun	30	14.51
3337	boot	noun	30	14.44
3338	Atlantic	adjective	30	14.38
3339	magnitude	noun	30	13.38
3340	jurisdiction	noun	30	13.25
3341	ticket	noun	30	12.78
3342	softly	adverb	30	12.67
3343	Brooklyn	prop. noun	30	12.43
3344	housing	noun	30	12.16
3345	assessment	noun	30	11.69
3346	guerrilla	noun	30	11.25
3347	workshop	noun	30	10.14
3348	tent	noun	30	10.04
3349	coach	noun	30	8.30
3350	drill	verb	30	6.66
3351	Gross	prop. noun	30	6.50
3352	Fromm	prop. noun	30	6.46
3353	folklore	noun	30	5.82
3354	Faulkner	prop. noun	30	5.74
3355	screw	noun	30	5.73
3356	Sarah	prop. noun	30	5.54
3357	lecture	noun	29	26.05
3358	deeply	adverb	29	25.40
3359	guilty	adjective	29	24.22
3360	challenge	verb	29	23.30
3361	enthusiasm	noun	29	22.99
3362	scatter	verb	29	22.62
3363	deeper	comp. adj.	29	22.48
3364	cross	noun	29	22.46
3365	et	foreign	29	22.44
3366	fault	noun	29	22.37
3367	since	adverb	29	22.32
3368	lend	verb	29	22.30
3369	focus	noun	29	21.65
3370	equally	adverb	29	21.57
3371	back	adjective	29	21.35
3372	anxious	adjective	29	21.12
3373	discipline	noun	29	20.94
3374	protest	verb	29	20.72
3375	object	verb	29	20.13
3376	vigorous	adjective	29	20.11
3376	widespread	adjective	29	20.11
3378	explore	verb	29	20.04
3379	modest	adjective	29	20.03
3380	key	sup. adj.	29	20.01
3381	wind	verb	29	19.75
3382	absolute	adjective	29	19.66

3294	map	noun	25	17.24
3295	pole	noun	23	17.24
3296	legislature	noun	43	17.23
3297	celebrate	verb	25	17.22
3298	regularly	adverb	22	17.22
3299	brick	noun	24	17.21
3300	inquire	verb	28	17.19
3301	Holmes	prop. noun	39	17.18
3302	casual	adjective	22	17.18
3302	considerably	qualifier	22	17.18
3304	cycle	noun	30	17.17
3305	perspective	noun	29	17.17
3306	tactic	noun	24	17.17
3307	mud	noun	32	17.14
3308	devise	verb	25	17.14
3309	Manchester	prop. noun	45	17.13
3310	fool	noun	35	17.13
3311	doubtful	adjective	22	17.13
3312	succession	noun	25	17.12
3313	taxpayer	noun	36	17.11
3314	repair	noun	23	17.11
3315	escape	noun	24	17.09
3316	fraction	noun	43	17.08
3317	interfere	verb	22	17.08
3318	grab	verb	37	17.05
3319	scope	noun	28	17.04
3320	upward	adverb	24	17.04
3321	airplane	noun	21	17.04
3322	equation	noun	49	17.03
3323	desert	noun	21	17.03
3324	Atlanta	prop. noun	39	17.02
3325	submarine	noun	35	17.02
3326	stuff	noun	29	17.02
3327	abstract	adjective	30	17.00
3328	renew	verb	23	16.96
3329	landscape	noun	25	16.95
3330	bare	adjective	28	16.94
3330	custom	noun	28	16.94
3332	designate	verb	24	16.93
3333	straighten	verb	33	16.92
3334	joke	noun	27	16.92
3335	patent	noun	53	16.91
3336	Franklin	prop. noun	31	16.87
3337	eighth	ord. num.	23	16.87
3338	dilemma	noun	27	16.86
3339	poetic	adjective	31	16.85
3340	substitute	verb	24	16.85
3341	assurance	noun	22	16.85
3342	context	noun	37	16.83
3343	noon	noun	25	16.82
3344	urgent	adjective	21	16.82
3345	artery	noun	68	16.81
3346	pioneer	noun	23	16.81
3347	Alabama	prop. noun	29	16.80
3348	inside	noun	23	16.80
3349	nut	noun	35	16.79
3350	T.	prop. noun	27	16.79
3351	skilled	adjective	30	16.78
3352	Albert	prop. noun	29	16.78
3352	tea	noun	29	16.78
3354	import	noun	28	16.78
3355	access	noun	25	16.78
3356	incredible	adjective	23	16.76
3357	continually	adverb	25	16.75
3358	biggest	sem. sup.	24	16.75
3359	tourist	noun	31	16.74
3360	qualification	noun	24	16.74
3361	leap	verb	33	16.70
3362	organ	noun	26	16.70
3363	interference	noun	45	16.69
3364	exposure	noun	27	16.69
3365	coordinate	verb	30	16.66
3366	bundle	noun	26	16.66
3367	Anne	prop. noun	46	16.64
3368	evaluation	noun	36	16.64
3369	term	verb	22	16.64
3370	fulfill	verb	25	16.63
3371	fade	verb	24	16.62
3371	neighbor	verb	24	16.62
3373	businessman	noun	24	16.61
3374	Williams	prop. noun	35	16.60
3375	basement	noun	33	16.60
3376	philosopher	noun	25	16.60
3377	beef	noun	32	16.58
3378	sensitivity	noun	29	16.58
3379	clarity	noun	28	16.58
3380	cabin	noun	30	16.57
3381	policeman	noun	36	16.55
3382	strictly	adverb	25	16.55

3383	prestige	noun	29	19.63
3384	monument	noun	29	19.44
3385	helpful	adjective	29	19.32
3386	request	verb	29	19.03
3387	nearly	qualifier	29	18.92
3388	exert	verb	29	18.54
3389	current	noun	29	18.28
3390	commitment	noun	29	18.14
3391	demonstration	noun	29	18.10
3392	senior	adjective	29	17.84
3393	municipal	adjective	29	17.74
3394	eternal	adjective	29	17.62
3395	fortune	noun	29	17.55
3396	perspective	noun	29	17.17
3397	stuff	noun	29	17.02
3398	Alabama	prop. noun	29	16.80
3399	Albert	prop. noun	29	16.78
3399	tea	noun	29	16.78
3401	sensitivity	noun	29	16.58
3402	perceive	verb	29	16.28
3403	commonly	adverb	29	16.25
3404	ally	verb	29	15.80
3405	suburban	adjective	29	15.69
3406	corresponding	adjective	29	15.57
3407	ethical	adjective	29	15.39
3408	ambassador	noun	29	15.05
3409	apparatus	noun	29	14.93
3410	delight	noun	29	14.87
3411	rear	adjective	29	14.63
3412	depending	prep.	29	14.60
3413	giant	noun	29	13.93
3414	induce	verb	29	13.75
3415	Davis	prop. noun	29	13.68
3416	mean	adjective	29	13.10
3417	sewage	noun	29	12.20
3418	virgin	noun	29	12.19
3419	photograph	noun	29	12.15
3420	Delaware	prop. noun	29	10.93
3421	shirt	noun	29	10.53
3422	O.	prop. noun	29	10.27
3423	reorganization	noun	29	10.04
3424	Fred	prop. noun	29	9.96
3425	pitcher	noun	29	9.33
3426	intersection	noun	29	9.27
3427	detergent	noun	29	8.16
3428	shorts	pl. noun	29	5.73
3429	Hughes	prop. noun	29	5.53
3430	publicly	adverb	28	25.10
3431	wherever	wh-adverb	28	24.23
3432	cooperate	verb	28	23.72
3433	gay	adjective	28	22.74
3433	hold	noun	28	22.74
3435	still	qualifier	28	22.61
3436	excite	verb	28	22.41
3437	occupation	noun	28	22.30
3438	depart	verb	28	22.07
3439	free	verb	28	21.93
3440	somewhat	adverb	28	21.81
3441	promptly	adverb	28	21.64
3442	forbid	verb	28	21.36
3443	restore	verb	28	21.21
3444	cast	verb	28	21.16
3445	blow	noun	28	21.07
3446	doubt	verb	28	20.60
3447	grip	noun	28	20.20
3448	peculiar	adjective	28	20.02
3449	witness	verb	28	19.90
3450	switch	verb	28	19.13
3451	false	adjective	28	18.89
3451	resident	noun	28	18.89
3453	greet	verb	28	18.80
3454	warmth	noun	28	18.74
3455	neglect	verb	28	18.70
3456	Miller	prop. noun	28	18.62
3457	joint	noun	28	18.61
3458	privilege	noun	28	18.35
3459	formerly	adverb	28	18.30
3460	detect	verb	28	18.23
3461	subsequent	adjective	28	17.78
3462	striking	adjective	28	17.58
3463	making	noun	28	17.56
3464	surplus	noun	28	17.52
3465	boss	noun	28	17.39
3466	recovery	noun	28	17.26
3467	inquire	verb	28	17.19
3468	scope	noun	28	17.04
3469	bare	adjective	28	16.94
3469	custom	noun	28	16.94
3471	import	noun	28	16.78

3383	roughly	adverb	22	16.54
3384	Alfred	prop. noun	55	16.53
3385	trustee	noun	37	16.52
3386	exhaust	verb	21	16.52
3387	Roy	prop. noun	38	16.51
3388	academy	noun	28	16.50
3389	denial	noun	22	16.50
3390	hurt	verb	31	16.48
3391	piano	noun	39	16.46
3392	silver	noun	22	16.46
3393	sixty	card. num.	21	16.46
3394	organic	adjective	38	16.45
3395	powder	noun	33	16.44
3396	guide	noun	25	16.44
3397	rebel	noun	31	16.43
3398	newly	adverb	26	16.43
3399	classic	adjective	31	16.41
3400	compel	verb	25	16.37
3401	mistake	verb	24	16.36
3402	rider	noun	28	16.34
3403	initiate	verb	22	16.34
3404	descend	verb	24	16.33
3405	illness	noun	22	16.33
3406	deck	noun	28	16.31
3407	mate	noun	27	16.30
3408	honey	noun	25	16.30
3409	paint	noun	24	16.29
3410	Bob	prop. noun	41	16.28
3411	Jane	prop. noun	36	16.28
3412	evaluate	verb	31	16.28
3413	perceive	verb	29	16.28
3414	evidently	adverb	25	16.27
3415	freely	adverb	22	16.27
3416	accordingly	adverb	31	16.26
3417	cottage	noun	25	16.26
3418	commonly	adverb	29	16.25
3419	discourage	verb	25	16.25
3420	vessel	noun	28	16.24
3421	pipe	noun	27	16.24
3422	leather	noun	26	16.23
3423	attribute	verb	24	16.20
3424	mayor	noun	47	16.18
3425	even	verb	28	16.18
3426	Michigan	prop. noun	25	16.18
3427	peaceful	adjective	26	16.17
3428	twenty-five	card. num.	25	16.17
3429	tract	noun	22	16.15
3430	mysterious	adjective	26	16.12
3431	freight	noun	30	16.11
3432	associate	noun	21	16.11
3433	gentle	adjective	26	16.04
3434	disk	noun	42	16.03
3435	strategy	noun	22	16.03
3436	clock	noun	28	16.01
3437	benefit	verb	24	16.01
3438	generous	adjective	25	16.00
3439	instruct	verb	23	16.00
3440	uncertain	adjective	22	16.00
3441	divine	adjective	32	15.98
3442	calm	adjective	22	15.97
3442	Mexico	prop. noun	22	15.97
3444	Baltimore	prop. noun	24	15.96
3445	preliminary	adjective	23	15.96
3446	creep	verb	27	15.95
3447	bite	verb	26	15.95
3448	considerably	adverb	22	15.95
3449	luxury	noun	24	15.94
3450	flash	verb	28	15.93
3451	whisky	noun	40	15.91
3452	Du	prop. noun	60	15.89
3453	Marshall	prop. noun	28	15.89
3454	bowl	noun	26	15.87
3455	palm	noun	30	15.85
3456	stem	verb	22	15.85
3457	partially	adverb	20	15.85
3458	commissioner	noun	36	15.82
3459	excess	noun	26	15.81
3460	Protestant	adjective	48	15.80
3461	ally	verb	29	15.80
3462	N.	prop. noun	26	15.80
3463	glance	noun	35	15.79
3464	replacement	noun	23	15.79
3465	affection	noun	22	15.78
3466	disaster	noun	30	15.77
3467	decline	noun	26	15.77
3468	concede	verb	23	15.76
3469	anniversary	noun	22	15.76
3470	sixth	ord. num.	26	15.75
3471	barn	noun	33	15.72

3472	clarity	noun	28	16.58
3473	academy	noun	28	16.50
3474	rider	noun	28	16.34
3475	deck	noun	28	16.31
3476	vessel	noun	28	16.24
3477	even	verb	28	16.18
3478	clock	noun	28	16.01
3479	flash	verb	28	15.93
3480	Marshall	prop. noun	28	15.89
3481	ease	noun	28	15.46
3482	conservative	adjective	28	15.43
3483	past	adjective	28	15.26
3484	weep	verb	28	14.70
3485	consistent	adjective	28	14.69
3486	bounce	verb	28	14.55
3487	ship	verb	28	14.26
3488	wash	noun	28	13.89
3489	innocence	noun	28	13.51
3490	costume	noun	28	13.30
3491	diplomatic	adjective	28	13.29
3492	lock	noun	28	13.28
3493	representation	noun	28	13.06
3494	ranch	noun	28	12.53
3495	sheriff	noun	28	12.21
3496	concrete	noun	28	11.97
3497	formulation	noun	28	11.87
3498	D	prop. noun	28	11.74
3498	sigh	verb	28	11.74
3500	mode	noun	28	11.71
3501	stockholder	noun	28	11.68
3502	conductor	noun	28	11.40
3503	Mason	prop. noun	28	10.93
3504	installation	noun	28	10.74
3505	Newport	prop. noun	28	10.40
3506	sovereignty	noun	28	10.22
3507	regiment	noun	28	10.16
3508	commodity	noun	28	9.94
3509	gear	noun	28	8.94
3510	Greenwich	prop. noun	28	8.86
3511	uniform	adjective	28	6.74
3512	sitter	noun	28	5.52
3513	exclusive	adjective	27	22.58
3514	slope	noun	27	21.78
3515	delicate	adjective	27	21.13
3516	magnificent	adjective	27	21.02
3517	resemble	verb	27	20.79
3518	drift	verb	27	20.72
3519	canvas	noun	27	20.66
3520	acknowledge	verb	27	20.52
3521	reverse	verb	27	20.16
3522	tie	noun	27	19.86
3523	flame	noun	27	19.66
3524	circuit	noun	27	19.63
3525	companion	noun	27	19.55
3526	arrest	verb	27	19.44
3526	profound	adjective	27	19.44
3528	exact	adjective	27	19.41
3529	widow	noun	27	19.35
3530	convey	verb	27	19.31
3531	eager	adjective	27	19.20
3532	Christmas	prop. noun	27	19.03
3533	exciting	adjective	27	18.98
3534	climate	noun	27	18.79
3535	boil	verb	27	18.69
3536	adventure	noun	27	18.60
3537	pitch	noun	27	18.36
3538	mirror	noun	27	18.33
3539	publicity	noun	27	18.19
3540	conversion	noun	27	18.17
3541	trap	noun	27	17.74
3542	permission	noun	27	17.67
3543	depression	noun	27	17.56
3544	dull	adjective	27	17.27
3545	joke	noun	27	16.92
3546	dilemma	noun	27	16.86
3547	T.	prop. noun	27	16.79
3548	exposure	noun	27	16.69
3549	mate	noun	27	16.30
3550	pipe	noun	27	16.24
3551	creep	verb	27	15.95
3552	level	verb	27	15.60
3553	essay	noun	27	15.23
3554	multiply	verb	27	15.14
3555	appeal	verb	27	14.98
3556	kingdom	noun	27	14.92
3557	white	noun	27	14.90
3558	province	noun	27	14.84
3559	behind	adverb	27	14.72
3560	warning	noun	27	14.57

3472	defeat	verb	25	15.72
3473	Thompson	prop. noun	43	15.71
3474	bomber	noun	32	15.71
3475	slow	verb	30	15.71
3476	routine	noun	21	15.70
3477	suburban	adjective	29	15.69
3478	philosophical	adjective	26	15.69
3479	print	noun	24	15.69
3480	unlikely	adjective	21	15.68
3481	unexpected	adjective	23	15.67
3482	shell	noun	36	15.64
3483	stroke	noun	30	15.64
3484	exaggerate	verb	25	15.64
3485	opposite	prep.	24	15.64
3486	generate	verb	30	15.63
3487	radar	noun	23	15.63
3488	level	verb	27	15.60
3489	corresponding	adjective	29	15.57
3490	inherit	verb	22	15.57
3491	defeat	noun	26	15.56
3492	vanish	verb	25	15.56
3493	guard	verb	22	15.56
3494	clarify	verb	25	15.55
3495	sixteen	card. num.	20	15.55
3496	Ford	prop. noun	25	15.54
3497	patience	noun	21	15.54
3498	crawl	verb	37	15.51
3499	declaration	noun	26	15.49
3500	physics	noun	22	15.49
3501	Jesus	prop. noun	61	15.48
3502	ease	noun	28	15.46
3503	capability	noun	36	15.45
3504	minimum	adjective	38	15.44
3505	forgive	verb	33	15.44
3506	desperate	adjective	26	15.44
3507	bubble	noun	25	15.44
3508	diminish	verb	24	15.44
3509	conservative	adjective	28	15.43
3510	mobile	adjective	26	15.43
3511	increasingly	adverb	21	15.41
3512	ethical	adjective	29	15.39
3513	grant	noun	43	15.35
3514	mercy	noun	20	15.35
3515	mineral	noun	26	15.34
3516	age	verb	24	15.34
3517	lamp	noun	24	15.33
3518	cape	noun	24	15.32
3519	density	noun	33	15.28
3520	Irish	adjective	26	15.28
3521	inventory	noun	35	15.27
3522	productive	adjective	25	15.27
3523	velocity	noun	32	15.26
3524	past	adjective	28	15.26
3525	just	adjective	21	15.25
3525	respectable	adjective	21	15.25
3527	essay	noun	27	15.23
3528	cafe	noun	25	15.23
3528	vivid	adjective	25	15.23
3530	clothing	noun	20	15.22
3531	Poland	prop. noun	35	15.19
3532	cherish	verb	23	15.19
3533	puzzle	verb	24	15.18
3534	bury	verb	24	15.16
3535	multiply	verb	27	15.14
3536	well	noun	22	15.13
3537	sufficiently	qualifier	26	15.12
3538	steadily	adverb	22	15.12
3539	Hanover	prop. noun	78	15.11
3540	comedy	noun	41	15.11
3541	propaganda	noun	30	15.09
3542	accelerate	verb	24	15.08
3543	statistic	noun	22	15.07
3544	mama	noun	55	15.06
3545	full-time	adjective	23	15.06
3546	ambassador	noun	29	15.05
3547	sector	noun	23	15.05
3548	graduate	verb	25	15.03
3549	sphere	noun	26	15.02
3550	grasp	verb	23	15.02
3551	rigid	adjective	24	15.01
3552	link	noun	19	15.01
3553	recreation	noun	43	15.00
3554	toe	noun	26	15.00
3555	protest	noun	25	14.99
3556	appeal	verb	27	14.98
3557	blade	noun	26	14.98
3558	moderate	adjective	22	14.94
3559	apparatus	noun	29	14.93
3560	various	post-det.	56	14.92

3561	cocktail	noun	27	14.38
3562	aunt	noun	27	14.29
3563	continuity	noun	27	14.28
3564	Carolina	prop. noun	27	14.27
3565	erect	verb	27	14.21
3566	smell	noun	27	14.10
3567	pretend	verb	27	13.75
3568	legislator	noun	27	13.13
3569	retirement	noun	27	12.59
3570	deputy	noun	27	12.55
3571	gang	noun	27	12.49
3572	youngster	noun	27	12.14
3573	bee	noun	27	11.91
3574	ritual	noun	27	11.78
3575	roar	verb	27	11.74
3576	worry	noun	27	11.63
3577	oral	adjective	27	11.58
3578	clinical	adjective	27	11.51
3579	prevention	noun	27	11.06
3580	tax	verb	27	11.04
3581	butter	noun	27	10.67
3582	Mitchell	prop. noun	27	10.32
3583	minimal	adjective	27	10.03
3584	cellar	noun	27	9.61
3585	asleep	adverb	27	9.57
3586	hit	noun	27	9.51
3587	outdoor	adjective	27	9.49
3588	theological	adjective	27	9.45
3589	Hollywood	prop. noun	27	8.29
3590	hen	noun	27	7.98
3591	bastard	noun	27	7.13
3592	Sandburg	prop. noun	27	6.88
3593	Eugene	prop. noun	27	6.58
3594	anti-trust	adjective	27	6.09
3595	Julia	prop. noun	27	5.75
3596	Aristotle	prop. noun	27	5.13
3597	nowhere	adverb	26	22.95
3598	originate	verb	26	22.34
3599	arrival	noun	26	21.10
3600	specialize	verb	26	21.07
3601	break	noun	26	20.44
3602	intelligent	adjective	26	20.26
3603	terror	noun	26	20.09
3604	shop	verb	26	19.95
3605	sophisticated	adjective	26	19.81
3606	literally	adverb	26	19.64
3607	await	verb	26	19.40
3608	grind	verb	26	19.30
3609	pile	verb	26	18.95
3610	preach	verb	26	18.72
3611	split	verb	26	18.65
3612	then	adjective	26	18.30
3613	unhappy	adjective	26	18.07
3614	nearby	adjective	26	17.93
3615	bore	verb	26	17.92
3616	sacrifice	noun	26	17.83
3617	parade	noun	26	17.57
3618	elaborate	adjective	26	17.54
3619	subject	verb	26	17.44
3620	absent	adjective	26	17.38
3621	altogether	adverb	26	17.33
3621	draft	noun	26	17.33
3623	organ	noun	26	16.70
3624	bundle	noun	26	16.66
3625	newly	adverb	26	16.43
3626	leather	noun	26	16.23
3627	peaceful	adjective	26	16.17
3628	mysterious	adjective	26	16.12
3629	gentle	adjective	26	16.04
3630	bite	verb	26	15.95
3631	bowl	noun	26	15.87
3632	excess	noun	26	15.81
3633	N.	prop. noun	26	15.80
3634	decline	noun	26	15.77
3635	sixth	ord. num.	26	15.75
3636	philosophical	adjective	26	15.69
3637	defeat	noun	26	15.56
3638	declaration	noun	26	15.49
3639	desperate	adjective	26	15.44
3640	mobile	adjective	26	15.43
3641	mineral	noun	26	15.34
3642	Irish	adjective	26	15.28
3643	sufficiently	qualifier	26	15.12
3644	sphere	noun	26	15.02
3645	toe	noun	26	15.00
3646	blade	noun	26	14.98
3647	constitutional	adjective	26	14.79
3648	dawn	noun	26	14.66
3649	merger	noun	26	14.46

3561	kingdom	noun	27	14.92
3562	white	noun	27	14.90
3563	neat	adjective	21	14.90
3564	diet	noun	24	14.88
3565	random	adjective	33	14.87
3566	Florida	prop. noun	32	14.87
3567	delight	noun	29	14.87
3568	only	qualifier	21	14.87
3569	thou	pers. pro.	44	14.86
3570	continent	noun	24	14.86
3571	province	noun	27	14.84
3572	newer	comp. adj.	20	14.83
3573	contest	noun	32	14.82
3574	tire	noun	31	14.82
3575	green	noun	25	14.82
3576	speed	verb	22	14.81
3577	prisoner	noun	31	14.79
3578	constitutional	adjective	26	14.79
3579	cook	noun	22	14.77
3580	block	verb	20	14.77
3581	package	noun	25	14.76
3582	discharge	noun	25	14.74
3583	polish	verb	20	14.74
3584	substantially	adverb	31	14.73
3585	historic	adjective	23	14.73
3586	behind	adverb	27	14.72
3587	craft	noun	25	14.72
3588	farther	comp. adv.	23	14.72
3589	weep	verb	28	14.70
3590	consistent	adjective	28	14.69
3591	dawn	noun	26	14.66
3592	fly	noun	23	14.66
3593	thickness	noun	46	14.65
3594	stumble	verb	31	14.65
3595	competent	adjective	21	14.65
3596	Papa	prop. noun	50	14.64
3597	rear	adjective	29	14.63
3598	stake	noun	22	14.61
3599	depending	prep.	29	14.60
3600	mature	adjective	24	14.60
3600	plead	verb	24	14.60
3602	shock	verb	23	14.60
3603	respect	verb	22	14.60
3604	pronounce	verb	21	14.59
3605	warning	noun	27	14.57
3606	earliest	sem. sup.	22	14.56
3607	bounce	verb	28	14.55
3608	discrimination	noun	23	14.55
3609	Jefferson	prop. noun	32	14.54
3610	axis	noun	38	14.52
3611	pistol	noun	31	14.52
3612	Johnny	prop. noun	30	14.51
3613	contrast	verb	22	14.50
3614	decrease	verb	31	14.49
3615	foam	noun	59	14.48
3616	injure	verb	21	14.48
3617	rent	verb	25	14.47
3618	merger	noun	26	14.46
3619	accurately	adverb	24	14.45
3620	texture	noun	21	14.45
3621	boot	noun	30	14.44
3622	complaint	noun	22	14.44
3623	cheek	noun	33	14.43
3623	damn	verb	33	14.43
3625	holder	noun	32	14.43
3626	execute	verb	22	14.43
3627	twist	noun	19	14.43
3628	mill	noun	24	14.42
3629	telephone	verb	21	14.40
3630	administer	verb	22	14.39
3631	Atlantic	adjective	30	14.38
3632	cocktail	noun	27	14.38
3633	heritage	noun	22	14.37
3634	C	prop. noun	45	14.35
3635	contend	verb	24	14.35
3636	remainder	noun	19	14.35
3637	wander	verb	24	14.33
3638	sensation	noun	24	14.32
3639	negotiate	verb	25	14.31
3640	mortgage	noun	22	14.31
3641	Palmer	prop. noun	62	14.30
3642	continuously	adverb	23	14.30
3643	aunt	noun	27	14.29
3644	continuity	noun	27	14.28
3645	vice	noun	25	14.28
3646	disclose	verb	24	14.28
3646	orbit	noun	24	14.28
3648	Carolina	prop. noun	27	14.27
3649	ship	verb	28	14.26

3650	barrier	noun	26	14.24
3650	miracle	noun	26	14.24
3652	but	adverb	26	14.22
3653	drunk	adjective	26	14.16
3654	exploration	noun	26	14.15
3655	electricity	noun	26	14.12
3656	beat	noun	26	14.09
3657	insert	verb	26	14.08
3658	promotion	noun	26	14.06
3659	auto	noun	26	13.93
3660	principal	noun	26	13.92
3661	inherent	adjective	26	13.91
3662	bless	verb	26	13.71
3663	worthy	adjective	26	13.55
3664	sidewalk	noun	26	13.51
3665	paragraph	noun	26	13.47
3666	drum	noun	26	13.46
3667	spokesman	noun	26	13.43
3668	bathe	verb	26	13.19
3669	mutual	adjective	26	12.89
3670	correspond	verb	26	12.72
3671	empire	noun	26	12.46
3672	delightful	adjective	26	12.14
3673	mutter	verb	26	11.98
3674	unconscious	adjective	26	11.62
3675	emperor	noun	26	11.41
3676	wound	verb	26	11.40
3677	vegetable	noun	26	11.33
3678	average	verb	26	11.30
3679	negotiation	noun	26	11.08
3680	pastor	noun	26	11.05
3681	invasion	noun	26	10.94
3682	tumor	noun	26	10.57
3683	lion	noun	26	10.37
3683	scare	verb	26	10.37
3685	recording	noun	26	10.34
3686	cavalry	noun	26	10.26
3687	smoke	verb	26	10.08
3688	marginal	adjective	26	9.91
3689	cast	noun	26	9.88
3690	exhibit	noun	26	9.69
3691	jaw	noun	26	9.61
3692	Moore	prop. noun	26	8.92
3693	plantation	noun	26	8.80
3694	how	qualifier	26	8.61
3695	herd	noun	26	8.16
3696	Nixon	prop. noun	26	8.05
3697	Billy	prop. noun	26	7.96
3698	imitation	noun	26	7.65
3698	saddle	noun	26	7.65
3700	marshal	noun	26	7.60
3701	yeah	adverb	26	5.48
3702	link	verb	25	21.07
3703	truly	qualifier	25	21.04
3704	vague	adjective	25	20.74
3705	painful	adjective	25	20.54
3706	recover	verb	25	20.33
3707	round	verb	25	19.87
3708	persist	verb	25	19.68
3709	withdraw	verb	25	19.52
3710	clue	noun	25	19.36
3711	grateful	adjective	25	19.19
3712	rail	noun	25	19.16
3713	probable	adjective	25	19.14
3714	alert	adjective	25	18.98
3715	likely	adverb	25	18.92
3716	ease	verb	25	18.87
3717	Tennessee	prop. noun	25	18.45
3718	correspondence	noun	25	18.40
3719	barely	adverb	25	17.97
3719	fighter	noun	25	17.97
3721	comprise	verb	25	17.71
3722	progress	verb	25	17.70
3723	dedicate	verb	25	17.66
3724	mail	verb	25	17.46
3725	loyalty	noun	25	17.45
3726	map	noun	25	17.24
3727	celebrate	verb	25	17.22
3728	devise	verb	25	17.14
3729	succession	noun	25	17.12
3730	landscape	noun	25	16.95
3731	noon	noun	25	16.82
3732	access	noun	25	16.78
3733	continually	adverb	25	16.75
3734	fulfill	verb	25	16.63
3735	philosopher	noun	25	16.60
3736	strictly	adverb	25	16.55
3737	guide	noun	25	16.44
3738	compel	verb	25	16.37

3650	spare	verb	19	14.26
3651	trace	noun	22	14.25
3652	barrier	noun	26	14.24
3652	miracle	noun	26	14.24
3654	Mercer	prop. noun	79	14.23
3655	formulate	verb	24	14.23
3656	but	adverb	26	14.22
3657	erect	verb	27	14.21
3658	whip	verb	24	14.20
3659	dispose	verb	23	14.19
3660	wealth	noun	22	14.19
3661	enact	verb	23	14.18
3662	drunk	adjective	26	14.16
3663	perfectly	qualifier	21	14.16
3664	fantastic	adjective	20	14.16
3665	exploration	noun	26	14.15
3666	electricity	noun	26	14.12
3667	Pittsburgh	prop. noun	25	14.12
3668	Jim	prop. noun	40	14.11
3669	smell	noun	27	14.10
3670	devil	noun	32	14.09
3671	beat	noun	26	14.09
3672	insert	verb	26	14.08
3673	fellowship	noun	39	14.07
3674	promotion	noun	26	14.06
3675	fog	noun	25	14.05
3676	correct	verb	21	14.05
3676	thorough	adjective	21	14.05
3678	invent	verb	21	14.04
3679	pope	noun	31	14.03
3680	register	noun	22	14.03
3681	flash	noun	24	14.02
3682	symbolic	adjective	35	14.01
3683	tribute	noun	25	14.00
3684	Robinson	prop. noun	39	13.99
3685	minority	noun	25	13.98
3686	Yankee	prop. noun	40	13.97
3687	beard	noun	31	13.97
3688	abrupt	adjective	18	13.97
3689	lawn	noun	20	13.96
3690	process	verb	34	13.95
3691	criterion	noun	22	13.94
3692	giant	noun	29	13.93
3693	auto	noun	26	13.93
3694	stem	noun	44	13.92
3695	principal	noun	26	13.92
3696	inherent	adjective	26	13.91
3697	dissolve	verb	23	13.91
3698	battery	noun	22	13.90
3699	execution	noun	18	13.90
3700	wash	noun	28	13.89
3701	curiosity	noun	23	13.88
3701	gulf	noun	23	13.88
3703	assess	verb	25	13.87
3704	proprietor	noun	21	13.87
3705	protein	noun	35	13.86
3706	portrait	noun	24	13.86
3707	Ann	prop. noun	31	13.85
3708	fortunately	adverb	20	13.85
3709	strip	verb	22	13.83
3710	across	adv./part.	24	13.82
3711	patch	noun	23	13.82
3712	marble	noun	23	13.81
3713	score	verb	35	13.80
3714	laughter	noun	22	13.79
3715	abuse	noun	22	13.78
3715	mechanic	noun	22	13.78
3717	induce	verb	29	13.75
3718	pretend	verb	27	13.75
3719	chorus	noun	20	13.74
3720	endless	adjective	20	13.73
3721	bless	verb	26	13.71
3722	pursuit	noun	19	13.71
3723	net	noun	24	13.70
3724	delivery	noun	19	13.70
3725	Davis	prop. noun	29	13.68
3726	disposal	noun	20	13.68
3727	confess	verb	25	13.67
3728	crash	verb	23	13.67
3729	finance	noun	19	13.67
3730	reinforce	verb	22	13.65
3731	overlook	verb	17	13.65
3732	deadly	adjective	19	13.64
3733	crystal	noun	31	13.63
3734	agriculture	noun	24	13.63
3735	live	adjective	20	13.62
3736	coincide	verb	24	13.59
3737	worthy	adjective	26	13.55
3738	embarrass	verb	19	13.55

3739	honey	noun	25	16.30
3740	evidently	adverb	25	16.27
3741	cottage	noun	25	16.26
3742	discourage	verb	25	16.25
3743	Michigan	prop. noun	25	16.18
3744	twenty-five	card. num.	25	16.17
3745	generous	adjective	25	16.00
3746	defeat	verb	25	15.72
3747	exaggerate	verb	25	15.64
3748	vanish	verb	25	15.56
3749	clarify	verb	25	15.55
3750	Ford	prop. noun	25	15.54
3751	bubble	noun	25	15.44
3752	productive	adjective	25	15.27
3753	cafe	noun	25	15.23
3753	vivid	adjective	25	15.23
3755	graduate	verb	25	15.03
3756	protest	noun	25	14.99
3757	green	noun	25	14.82
3758	package	noun	25	14.76
3759	discharge	noun	25	14.74
3760	craft	noun	25	14.72
3761	rent	verb	25	14.47
3762	negotiate	verb	25	14.31
3763	vice	noun	25	14.28
3764	Pittsburgh	prop. noun	25	14.12
3765	fog	noun	25	14.05
3766	tribute	noun	25	14.00
3767	minority	noun	25	13.98
3768	assess	verb	25	13.87
3769	confess	verb	25	13.67
3770	subtle	adjective	25	13.47
3771	wit	noun	25	13.42
3772	even	adjective	25	13.35
3773	debt	noun	25	13.27
3774	double	verb	25	13.18
3775	chin	noun	25	13.15
3775	modify	verb	25	13.15
3777	D.C.	prop. noun	25	13.10
3778	statue	noun	25	13.09
3779	faint	adjective	25	13.08
3780	many	pre-quant.	25	12.95
3781	regime	noun	25	12.79
3782	charm	noun	25	12.67
3783	registration	noun	25	12.65
3784	knight	noun	25	12.64
3785	dome	noun	25	12.54
3786	minimize	verb	25	12.28
3787	destiny	noun	25	12.27
3788	total	verb	25	12.22
3789	destructive	adjective	25	12.10
3790	racial	adjective	25	12.07
3791	symbolize	verb	25	11.78
3792	murderer	noun	25	11.72
3793	Nazi	prop. noun	25	11.70
3794	ownership	noun	25	11.60
3795	soap	noun	25	11.25
3796	democracy	noun	25	11.18
3797	garage	noun	25	11.06
3798	major	noun	25	11.05
3799	exhibition	noun	25	10.90
3800	flexible	adjective	25	10.79
3801	magnetic	adjective	25	10.61
3802	coverage	noun	25	10.50
3803	Broadway	prop. noun	25	10.49
3804	classification	noun	25	10.48
3805	rational	adjective	25	10.44
3806	blonde	adjective	25	10.31
3807	variable	adjective	25	10.19
3808	luncheon	noun	25	10.02
3809	belly	noun	25	9.82
3810	operational	adjective	25	9.57
3811	lonely	adjective	25	9.44
3812	refrigerator	noun	25	9.16
3813	structural	adjective	25	9.07
3814	Dean	prop. noun	25	9.06
3815	denomination	noun	25	8.65
3816	Houston	prop. noun	25	8.22
3817	suitcase	noun	25	8.00
3818	denote	verb	25	7.88
3819	ward	noun	25	7.29
3820	Owen	prop. noun	25	7.05
3821	tournament	noun	25	6.57
3822	Miami	prop. noun	25	6.29
3823	turnpike	noun	25	5.38
3824	inspection	noun	24	20.25
3825	undoubtedly	adverb	24	19.99
3826	harm	noun	24	19.83
3827	attraction	noun	24	19.73

3739	dislike	verb	22	13.54
3740	pose	verb	20	13.54
3741	ultimately	adverb	22	13.53
3742	consume	verb	21	13.53
3743	Adam	prop. noun	46	13.52
3744	amazing	adjective	20	13.52
3745	grin	verb	38	13.51
3746	innocence	noun	28	13.51
3747	sidewalk	noun	26	13.51
3748	experimental	adjective	38	13.50
3749	native	noun	21	13.48
3750	paragraph	noun	26	13.47
3751	subtle	adjective	25	13.47
3752	underlie	verb	24	13.47
3753	drum	noun	26	13.46
3754	norm	noun	31	13.45
3755	award	verb	22	13.45
3756	species	noun	37	13.44
3757	spokesman	noun	26	13.43
3758	anticipation	noun	23	13.43
3759	number	verb	18	13.43
3760	wit	noun	25	13.42
3761	acceptable	adjective	21	13.40
3761	colonial	adjective	21	13.40
3763	uncertainty	noun	22	13.39
3764	magnitude	noun	30	13.38
3765	Vermont	prop. noun	23	13.38
3766	carve	verb	23	13.37
3767	whisper	verb	31	13.36
3768	logic	noun	17	13.36
3769	even	adjective	25	13.35
3770	omit	verb	22	13.35
3771	joint	adjective	23	13.32
3771	warm	verb	23	13.32
3773	teaching	noun	22	13.32
3774	Chandler	prop. noun	34	13.31
3775	sixty	noun	23	13.31
3776	exclusively	adverb	21	13.31
3777	midst	noun	20	13.31
3778	costume	noun	28	13.30
3779	mold	noun	50	13.29
3780	diplomatic	adjective	28	13.29
3781	charming	adjective	24	13.29
3782	startling	adjective	19	13.29
3783	suite	noun	31	13.28
3784	lock	noun	28	13.28
3785	devotion	noun	21	13.28
3786	debt	noun	25	13.27
3787	still	adjective	24	13.27
3788	accommodate	verb	19	13.26
3789	further	post-det.	32	13.25
3790	jurisdiction	noun	30	13.25
3791	Allen	prop. noun	21	13.24
3792	revise	verb	22	13.20
3793	instant	noun	32	13.19
3794	bathe	verb	26	13.19
3795	dark	noun	22	13.19
3796	definitely	adverb	21	13.19
3797	shelf	noun	20	13.19
3798	double	verb	25	13.18
3799	thrust	verb	23	13.18
3800	broaden	verb	22	13.18
3801	grave	noun	20	13.18
3802	outside	noun	22	13.16
3803	chin	noun	25	13.15
3803	modify	verb	25	13.15
3805	ruin	verb	22	13.15
3806	meaningful	adjective	24	13.14
3807	legislator	noun	27	13.13
3808	layer	noun	22	13.12
3809	insistence	noun	19	13.12
3810	like	prep.	35	13.11
3811	mean	adjective	29	13.10
3812	D.C.	prop. noun	25	13.10
3813	counter	noun	32	13.09
3814	statue	noun	25	13.09
3815	faint	adjective	25	13.08
3816	living	noun	24	13.08
3817	eighteenth	ord. num.	23	13.08
3817	trick	noun	23	13.08
3819	representation	noun	28	13.06
3820	physician	noun	22	13.06
3821	commence	verb	18	13.06
3821	repeatedly	adverb	18	13.06
3823	fluid	noun	33	13.05
3824	valid	adjective	22	13.05
3825	fortunate	adjective	22	13.04
3826	prospective	adjective	21	13.04
3827	reproduce	verb	19	13.04

3828	enthusiastic	adjective	24	19.38
3829	departure	noun	24	18.47
3830	realization	noun	24	18.41
3831	considering	prep.	24	18.40
3832	African	adjective	24	18.25
3833	flood	noun	24	17.42
3834	nervous	adjective	24	17.33
3835	brick	noun	24	17.21
3836	tactic	noun	24	17.17
3837	escape	noun	24	17.09
3838	upward	adverb	24	17.04
3839	designate	verb	24	16.93
3840	substitute	verb	24	16.85
3841	biggest	sem. sup.	24	16.75
3842	qualification	noun	24	16.74
3843	fade	verb	24	16.62
3843	neighbor	verb	24	16.62
3845	businessman	noun	24	16.61
3846	mistake	verb	24	16.36
3847	descend	verb	24	16.33
3848	paint	noun	24	16.29
3849	attribute	verb	24	16.20
3850	benefit	verb	24	16.01
3851	Baltimore	prop. noun	24	15.96
3852	luxury	noun	24	15.94
3853	print	noun	24	15.69
3854	opposite	prep.	24	15.64
3855	diminish	verb	24	15.44
3856	age	verb	24	15.34
3857	lamp	noun	24	15.33
3858	cape	noun	24	15.32
3859	puzzle	verb	24	15.18
3860	bury	verb	24	15.16
3861	accelerate	verb	24	15.08
3862	rigid	adjective	24	15.01
3863	diet	noun	24	14.88
3864	continent	noun	24	14.86
3865	mature	adjective	24	14.60
3865	plead	verb	24	14.60
3867	accurately	adverb	24	14.45
3868	mill	noun	24	14.42
3869	contend	verb	24	14.35
3870	wander	verb	24	14.33
3871	sensation	noun	24	14.32
3872	disclose	verb	24	14.28
3872	orbit	noun	24	14.28
3874	formulate	verb	24	14.23
3875	whip	verb	24	14.20
3876	flash	noun	24	14.02
3877	portrait	noun	24	13.86
3878	across	adv./part.	24	13.82
3879	net	noun	24	13.70
3880	agriculture	noun	24	13.63
3881	coincide	verb	24	13.59
3882	underlie	verb	24	13.47
3883	charming	adjective	24	13.29
3884	still	adjective	24	13.27
3885	meaningful	adjective	24	13.14
3886	living	noun	24	13.08
3887	triumph	noun	24	12.99
3888	invention	noun	24	12.87
3889	bear	noun	24	12.76
3890	realism	noun	24	12.71
3891	nurse	noun	24	12.66
3892	stretch	noun	24	12.61
3893	explicit	adjective	24	12.40
3894	cooperative	adjective	24	12.38
3895	patrol	noun	24	12.31
3896	seventeen	card. num.	24	12.22
3897	treaty	noun	24	12.15
3898	Taylor	prop. noun	24	12.10
3899	peak	noun	24	12.06
3900	sheep	noun	24	12.03
3901	Madison	prop. noun	24	12.02
3902	condition	verb	24	11.87
3903	port	noun	24	11.85
3904	lane	noun	24	11.76
3905	envelope	noun	24	11.71
3906	genius	noun	24	11.70
3907	Vienna	prop. noun	24	11.67
3908	dose	noun	24	11.26
3909	rice	noun	24	11.19
3910	cancer	noun	24	11.14
3911	wildly	adverb	24	10.85
3912	nucleus	noun	24	10.76
3913	aesthetic	adjective	24	10.74
3913	feature	verb	24	10.74
3915	wound	noun	24	10.71
3916	Pacific	adjective	24	10.57

3828	successor	noun	22	13.03
3829	coating	noun	47	13.02
3830	Frederick	prop. noun	19	13.02
3831	triumph	noun	24	12.99
3832	colorful	adjective	22	12.99
3833	amendment	noun	31	12.96
3834	many	pre-quant.	25	12.95
3835	worth	noun	20	12.94
3836	Roberts	prop. noun	49	12.92
3837	candle	noun	23	12.92
3838	increasingly	qualifier	21	12.92
3839	mutual	adjective	26	12.89
3840	despair	noun	20	12.89
3841	slavery	noun	33	12.88
3842	invention	noun	24	12.87
3843	Ben	prop. noun	22	12.87
3844	overwhelming	adjective	20	12.87
3845	communicate	verb	22	12.86
3846	nearby	adverb	21	12.86
3847	entity	noun	21	12.84
3848	chiefly	adverb	22	12.82
3849	swell	verb	20	12.81
3850	regime	noun	25	12.79
3851	ticket	noun	30	12.78
3852	Stanley	prop. noun	39	12.77
3853	rocket	noun	22	12.77
3854	bear	noun	24	12.76
3855	function	verb	18	12.76
3856	spot	verb	22	12.74
3857	adapt	verb	20	12.73
3858	correspond	verb	26	12.72
3859	publisher	noun	20	12.72
3860	realism	noun	24	12.71
3861	governmental	adjective	23	12.70
3862	compensation	noun	20	12.70
3863	scarcely	adverb	21	12.69
3864	well-known	adjective	18	12.69
3865	softly	adverb	30	12.67
3866	charm	noun	25	12.67
3867	divorce	noun	23	12.67
3868	taste	verb	22	12.67
3869	thereafter	adverb	20	12.67
3870	nurse	noun	24	12.66
3871	purely	qualifier	21	12.66
3872	registration	noun	25	12.65
3873	knight	noun	25	12.64
3874	integrate	verb	22	12.64
3875	relative	noun	23	12.63
3876	temporarily	adverb	20	12.63
3877	stretch	noun	24	12.61
3878	ill	adjective	21	12.61
3879	airport	noun	23	12.60
3880	episode	noun	18	12.60
3881	desegregation	noun	40	12.59
3882	retirement	noun	27	12.59
3883	chapel	noun	22	12.59
3884	conform	verb	18	12.59
3885	nineteen	card. num.	18	12.57
3886	Watson	prop. noun	50	12.56
3887	hazard	noun	20	12.56
3888	embrace	verb	18	12.56
3888	informal	adjective	18	12.56
3888	shorter	comp. adj.	18	12.56
3891	deputy	noun	27	12.55
3892	merge	verb	20	12.55
3893	welcome	adjective	19	12.55
3894	dome	noun	25	12.54
3895	ranch	noun	28	12.53
3896	unnecessary	adjective	16	12.53
3897	crown	noun	19	12.52
3898	cap	noun	22	12.51
3899	strongest	sem. sup.	20	12.51
3900	respectively	adverb	31	12.49
3901	gang	noun	27	12.49
3902	shortage	noun	19	12.49
3903	anode	noun	78	12.48
3904	reward	noun	17	12.48
3905	ridge	noun	22	12.47
3906	empire	noun	26	12.46
3907	pin	noun	20	12.45
3908	Brooklyn	prop. noun	30	12.43
3909	gaze	verb	21	12.43
3910	thread	noun	20	12.42
3911	aggressive	adjective	17	12.42
3912	explicit	adjective	24	12.40
3913	cooperative	adjective	24	12.38
3914	Connecticut	prop. noun	21	12.38
3915	march	noun	19	12.38
3916	explode	verb	22	12.36

3917	stupid	adjective	24	10.52
3918	compound	noun	24	10.24
3919	match	noun	24	10.22
3920	statute	noun	24	10.15
3921	cold	noun	24	10.11
3922	Communist	adjective	24	10.08
3923	embassy	noun	24	10.06
3924	voter	noun	24	9.80
3925	mathematical	adjective	24	9.41
3925	timber	noun	24	9.41
3927	jail	noun	24	9.40
3928	plaster	noun	24	9.29
3929	astronomy	noun	24	9.26
3930	adviser	noun	24	8.92
3931	conspiracy	noun	24	8.88
3932	part-time	adjective	24	8.64
3933	Vernon	prop. noun	24	8.52
3934	White	prop. noun	24	8.44
3935	saving	noun	24	7.84
3936	gin	noun	24	6.62
3937	diffusion	noun	24	6.43
3938	Puerto	prop. noun	24	6.16
3939	linguist	noun	24	6.15
3940	jungle	noun	24	5.53
3941	dive	noun	24	5.44
3942	refund	noun	24	5.13
3943	dismiss	verb	23	20.87
3944	line	verb	23	20.20
3945	frame	verb	23	19.61
3946	roll	noun	23	19.16
3947	challenge	noun	23	18.94
3948	appreciation	noun	23	18.16
3949	chore	noun	23	17.96
3950	cheap	adjective	23	17.55
3951	originally	adverb	23	17.38
3952	float	verb	23	17.33
3953	noble	adjective	23	17.31
3954	pole	noun	23	17.24
3955	repair	noun	23	17.11
3956	renew	verb	23	16.96
3957	eighth	ord. num.	23	16.87
3958	pioneer	noun	23	16.81
3959	inside	noun	23	16.80
3960	incredible	adjective	23	16.76
3961	instruct	verb	23	16.00
3962	preliminary	adjective	23	15.96
3963	replacement	noun	23	15.79
3964	concede	verb	23	15.76
3965	unexpected	adjective	23	15.67
3966	radar	noun	23	15.63
3967	cherish	verb	23	15.19
3968	full-time	adjective	23	15.06
3969	sector	noun	23	15.05
3970	grasp	verb	23	15.02
3971	historic	adjective	23	14.73
3972	farther	comp. adv.	23	14.72
3973	fly	noun	23	14.66
3974	shock	verb	23	14.60
3975	discrimination	noun	23	14.55
3976	continuously	adverb	23	14.30
3977	dispose	verb	23	14.19
3978	enact	verb	23	14.18
3979	dissolve	verb	23	13.91
3980	curiosity	noun	23	13.88
3980	gulf	noun	23	13.88
3982	patch	noun	23	13.82
3983	marble	noun	23	13.81
3984	crash	verb	23	13.67
3985	anticipation	noun	23	13.43
3986	Vermont	prop. noun	23	13.38
3987	carve	verb	23	13.37
3988	joint	adjective	23	13.32
3988	warm	verb	23	13.32
3990	sixty	noun	23	13.31
3991	thrust	verb	23	13.18
3992	eighteenth	ord. num.	23	13.08
3992	trick	noun	23	13.08
3994	candle	noun	23	12.92
3995	governmental	adjective	23	12.70
3996	divorce	noun	23	12.67
3997	relative	noun	23	12.63
3998	airport	noun	23	12.60
3999	hungry	adjective	23	12.35
3999	relevant	adjective	23	12.35
4001	pile	noun	23	12.33
4002	some	adverb	23	12.06
4003	functional	adjective	23	11.97
4003	uneasy	adjective	23	11.97
4005	glory	noun	23	11.64

3917	value	verb	18	12.36
3918	hungry	adjective	23	12.35
3918	relevant	adjective	23	12.35
3920	odor	noun	22	12.34
3921	spectacle	noun	21	12.34
3922	pile	noun	23	12.33
3923	hydrogen	noun	42	12.32
3924	Harold	prop. noun	32	12.31
3925	patrol	noun	24	12.31
3926	affirm	verb	21	12.31
3927	hatred	noun	20	12.31
3928	lest	sub. conj.	17	12.31
3929	elephant	noun	18	12.30
3930	minimize	verb	25	12.28
3931	horror	noun	21	12.28
3932	destiny	noun	25	12.27
3933	pertinent	adjective	21	12.27
3934	routine	adjective	17	12.27
3934	substitute	noun	17	12.27
3936	Hardy	prop. noun	51	12.25
3937	label	verb	17	12.24
3938	carrier	noun	20	12.23
3939	regret	verb	19	12.23
3940	total	verb	25	12.22
3941	seventeen	card. num.	24	12.22
3942	convenience	noun	22	12.22
3943	consistency	noun	18	12.22
3943	representative	adjective	18	12.22
3945	sheriff	noun	28	12.21
3946	sewage	noun	29	12.20
3947	virgin	noun	29	12.19
3948	long-term	noun	32	12.17
3949	lucky	adjective	21	12.17
3950	less	comp. adv.	19	12.17
3951	supplement	verb	16	12.17
3952	housing	noun	30	12.16
3953	gap	noun	19	12.16
3954	spectrum	noun	32	12.15
3955	photograph	noun	29	12.15
3956	treaty	noun	24	12.15
3957	fountain	noun	22	12.15
3958	oblige	verb	21	12.15
3959	swallow	verb	20	12.15
3960	neatly	adverb	19	12.15
3961	youngster	noun	27	12.14
3962	delightful	adjective	26	12.14
3963	liberal	noun	39	12.13
3964	combat	noun	22	12.13
3965	confine	verb	21	12.12
3966	certainty	noun	21	12.11
3967	destructive	adjective	25	12.10
3968	Taylor	prop. noun	24	12.10
3969	tap	verb	19	12.09
3970	B	prop. noun	53	12.08
3971	racial	adjective	25	12.07
3972	risk	verb	17	12.07
3973	peak	noun	24	12.06
3974	some	adverb	23	12.06
3975	cabinet	noun	22	12.06
3976	follower	noun	20	12.05
3977	supervision	noun	19	12.05
3978	sheep	noun	24	12.03
3979	voluntary	adjective	22	12.03
3980	Madison	prop. noun	24	12.02
3981	selective	adjective	19	12.00
3982	celebration	noun	17	12.00
3983	mutter	verb	26	11.98
3984	lessen	verb	17	11.98
3985	concrete	noun	28	11.97
3986	functional	adjective	23	11.97
3986	uneasy	adjective	23	11.97
3988	especially	qualifier	21	11.97
3989	festival	noun	31	11.96
3990	intervention	noun	20	11.94
3990	splendid	adjective	20	11.94
3992	bar	verb	17	11.94
3992	near	adjective	17	11.94
3994	classify	verb	21	11.93
3994	couple	verb	21	11.93
3994	traveler	noun	21	11.93
3997	near	verb	19	11.93
3998	dedication	noun	21	11.92
3999	bee	noun	27	11.91
4000	stimulate	verb	20	11.91
4001	crush	verb	17	11.91
4001	giant	adjective	17	11.91
4003	Columbia	prop. noun	20	11.90
4003	promising	adjective	20	11.90
4005	collapse	verb	18	11.88

4006	monk	noun	23	11.62
4006	shave	verb	23	11.62
4008	sponsor	noun	23	11.57
4009	midnight	noun	23	11.52
4010	civic	adjective	23	11.48
4011	die	noun	23	11.45
4012	wrap	verb	23	11.37
4013	punishment	noun	23	11.30
4014	bell	noun	23	11.19
4015	Philip	prop. noun	23	11.07
4016	Douglas	prop. noun	23	10.72
4017	excuse	noun	23	10.71
4018	classroom	noun	23	10.64
4019	testify	verb	23	10.56
4020	missionary	noun	23	10.48
4021	curse	verb	23	10.35
4022	happiness	noun	23	10.34
4023	priority	noun	23	10.17
4024	superintendent	noun	23	10.08
4025	plug	noun	23	9.92
4026	strategic	adjective	23	9.89
4027	availability	noun	23	9.79
4028	proceeding	noun	23	9.59
4029	narrative	noun	23	9.35
4030	handling	noun	23	9.10
4031	meadow	noun	23	8.74
4032	bat	verb	23	8.65
4033	displacement	noun	23	8.56
4034	Jean	prop. noun	23	8.40
4035	Wagner	prop. noun	23	8.13
4036	upstairs	adverb	23	7.60
4037	O.K.	exclam.	23	7.56
4038	abstraction	noun	23	7.54
4039	deduction	noun	23	7.09
4040	rehabilitation	noun	23	6.87
4041	empirical	adjective	23	6.41
4041	pill	noun	23	6.41
4043	generator	noun	23	6.07
4044	E	prop. noun	23	5.79
4045	Englishman	prop. noun	23	5.73
4046	therapist	noun	23	5.56
4047	oxidation	noun	23	5.43
4048	Westminster	prop. noun	23	5.33
4049	centimeter	noun	23	5.29
4050	Milton	prop. noun	23	5.20
4051	gathering	noun	22	17.71
4052	regularly	adverb	22	17.22
4053	casual	adjective	22	17.18
4053	considerably	qualifier	22	17.18
4055	doubtful	adjective	22	17.13
4056	interfere	verb	22	17.08
4057	assurance	noun	22	16.85
4058	term	verb	22	16.64
4059	roughly	adverb	22	16.54
4060	denial	noun	22	16.50
4061	silver	noun	22	16.46
4062	initiate	verb	22	16.34
4063	illness	noun	22	16.33
4064	freely	adverb	22	16.27
4065	tract	noun	22	16.15
4066	strategy	noun	22	16.03
4067	uncertain	adjective	22	16.00
4068	calm	adjective	22	15.97
4068	Mexico	prop. noun	22	15.97
4070	considerably	adverb	22	15.95
4071	stem	verb	22	15.85
4072	affection	noun	22	15.78
4073	anniversary	noun	22	15.76
4074	inherit	verb	22	15.57
4075	guard	verb	22	15.56
4076	physics	noun	22	15.49
4077	well	noun	22	15.13
4078	steadily	adverb	22	15.12
4079	statistic	noun	22	15.07
4080	moderate	adjective	22	14.94
4081	speed	verb	22	14.81
4082	cook	noun	22	14.77
4083	stake	noun	22	14.61
4084	respect	verb	22	14.60
4085	earliest	sem. sup.	22	14.56
4086	contrast	verb	22	14.50
4087	complaint	noun	22	14.44
4088	execute	verb	22	14.43
4089	administer	verb	22	14.39
4090	heritage	noun	22	14.37
4091	mortgage	noun	22	14.31
4092	trace	noun	22	14.25
4093	wealth	noun	22	14.19
4094	register	noun	22	14.03

4006	Sherman	prop. noun	36	11.87
4007	formulation	noun	28	11.87
4008	condition	verb	24	11.87
4009	champion	noun	31	11.86
4010	helpless	adjective	21	11.86
4011	listener	noun	31	11.85
4012	port	noun	24	11.85
4013	survey	verb	21	11.85
4014	strive	verb	18	11.85
4015	lumber	noun	35	11.84
4016	tilt	verb	17	11.84
4017	coin	noun	18	11.83
4017	plant	verb	18	11.83
4019	Rachel	prop. noun	44	11.82
4020	Detroit	prop. noun	22	11.82
4021	artificial	adjective	17	11.82
4022	presume	verb	20	11.81
4023	interrupt	verb	22	11.80
4024	brave	adjective	21	11.79
4025	glow	verb	19	11.79
4025	twin	noun	19	11.79
4027	ritual	noun	27	11.78
4028	symbolize	verb	25	11.78
4029	tight	adjective	22	11.78
4030	Greek	prop. noun	20	11.78
4031	spread	noun	18	11.77
4032	junior	noun	47	11.76
4033	lane	noun	24	11.76
4034	segment	noun	20	11.76
4035	designer	noun	33	11.75
4036	realm	noun	21	11.75
4037	D	prop. noun	28	11.74
4037	sigh	verb	28	11.74
4039	roar	verb	27	11.74
4040	quarrel	verb	16	11.74
4041	orderly	adjective	19	11.73
4042	southerner	noun	35	11.72
4043	murderer	noun	25	11.72
4044	differently	adverb	16	11.72
4045	Howard	prop. noun	33	11.71
4046	mode	noun	28	11.71
4047	envelope	noun	24	11.71
4048	Black	prop. noun	35	11.70
4049	Nazi	prop. noun	25	11.70
4050	genius	noun	24	11.70
4051	grave	adjective	19	11.70
4052	knit	verb	18	11.70
4053	assessment	noun	30	11.69
4054	Dallas	prop. noun	58	11.68
4055	stockholder	noun	28	11.68
4056	exclude	verb	21	11.68
4057	twentieth	ord. num.	20	11.68
4058	Vienna	prop. noun	24	11.67
4059	shame	noun	21	11.67
4060	individually	adverb	19	11.67
4061	scar	noun	20	11.66
4062	desert	verb	20	11.65
4063	glory	noun	23	11.64
4064	worry	noun	27	11.63
4065	curtain	noun	21	11.63
4066	unconscious	adjective	26	11.62
4067	monk	noun	23	11.62
4067	shave	verb	23	11.62
4069	authentic	adjective	20	11.62
4069	half	noun	20	11.62
4069	quit	verb	20	11.62
4072	ownership	noun	25	11.60
4073	poverty	noun	20	11.59
4074	oral	adjective	27	11.58
4075	prescribe	verb	20	11.58
4076	sponsor	noun	23	11.57
4077	concrete	adjective	20	11.57
4078	breeze	noun	17	11.56
4079	mathematics	noun	20	11.55
4080	funny	adjective	40	11.53
4081	near	adverb	20	11.53
4082	midnight	noun	23	11.52
4083	tile	noun	22	11.52
4084	tobacco	noun	19	11.52
4085	clinical	adjective	27	11.51
4086	plain	noun	21	11.50
4087	delight	verb	20	11.50
4088	plunge	verb	20	11.49
4088	prolong	verb	20	11.49
4090	civic	adjective	23	11.48
4091	postpone	verb	19	11.48
4092	disappointment	noun	17	11.48
4093	span	noun	17	11.47
4094	die	noun	23	11.45

4095	criterion	noun	22	13.94
4096	battery	noun	22	13.90
4097	strip	verb	22	13.83
4098	laughter	noun	22	13.79
4099	abuse	noun	22	13.78
4099	mechanic	noun	22	13.78
4101	reinforce	verb	22	13.65
4102	dislike	verb	22	13.54
4103	ultimately	adverb	22	13.53
4104	award	verb	22	13.45
4105	uncertainty	noun	22	13.39
4106	omit	verb	22	13.35
4107	teaching	noun	22	13.32
4108	revise	verb	22	13.20
4109	dark	noun	22	13.19
4110	broaden	verb	22	13.18
4111	outside	noun	22	13.16
4112	ruin	verb	22	13.15
4113	layer	noun	22	13.12
4114	physician	noun	22	13.06
4115	valid	adjective	22	13.05
4116	fortunate	adjective	22	13.04
4117	successor	noun	22	13.03
4118	colorful	adjective	22	12.99
4119	Ben	prop. noun	22	12.87
4120	communicate	verb	22	12.86
4121	chiefly	adverb	22	12.82
4122	rocket	noun	22	12.77
4123	spot	verb	22	12.74
4124	taste	verb	22	12.67
4125	integrate	verb	22	12.64
4126	chapel	noun	22	12.59
4127	cap	noun	22	12.51
4128	ridge	noun	22	12.47
4129	explode	verb	22	12.36
4130	odor	noun	22	12.34
4131	convenience	noun	22	12.22
4132	fountain	noun	22	12.15
4133	combat	noun	22	12.13
4134	cabinet	noun	22	12.06
4135	voluntary	adjective	22	12.03
4136	Detroit	prop. noun	22	11.82
4137	interrupt	verb	22	11.80
4138	tight	adjective	22	11.78
4139	tile	noun	22	11.52
4140	arbitrary	adjective	22	11.43
4140	convenient	adjective	22	11.43
4140	spectator	noun	22	11.43
4143	shatter	verb	22	11.38
4144	handle	noun	22	11.34
4145	radical	adjective	22	11.24
4146	choke	verb	22	11.20
4147	reliable	adjective	22	10.95
4148	calculation	noun	22	10.91
4149	teenager	noun	22	10.72
4150	mold	verb	22	10.66
4151	autumn	noun	22	10.59
4152	congressional	adjective	22	10.38
4153	spectacular	adjective	22	10.22
4154	guitar	noun	22	10.12
4155	skirt	noun	22	10.10
4156	frown	verb	22	9.97
4157	advisory	adjective	22	9.89
4158	ambiguous	adjective	22	9.83
4159	nest	noun	22	9.82
4160	dot	noun	22	9.25
4161	laugh	noun	22	9.15
4161	lively	adjective	22	9.15
4163	Ralph	prop. noun	22	9.11
4164	startle	verb	22	8.93
4165	alliance	noun	22	8.91
4166	scratch	verb	22	8.81
4167	capitol	noun	22	8.80
4168	hypothesis	noun	22	8.78
4169	Don	prop. noun	22	8.75
4170	Morris	prop. noun	22	8.73
4171	above	adjective	22	8.57
4172	sweat	noun	22	8.22
4173	killer	noun	22	8.08
4174	testing	noun	22	7.84
4175	middle-class	noun	22	7.70
4176	rancher	noun	22	7.52
4177	doll	noun	22	7.51
4178	physiological	adjective	22	7.12
4179	crouch	verb	22	7.04
4180	Arnold	prop. noun	22	6.62
4181	economical	adjective	22	6.44
4182	Swift	prop. noun	22	6.22
4183	murmur	verb	22	6.18

4095	contour	noun	21	11.45
4096	forward	adjective	18	11.45
4097	orientation	noun	17	11.44
4098	arbitrary	adjective	22	11.43
4098	convenient	adjective	22	11.43
4098	spectator	noun	22	11.43
4101	violation	noun	20	11.42
4102	basket	noun	19	11.42
4102	viewpoint	noun	19	11.42
4104	emperor	noun	26	11.41
4105	conductor	noun	28	11.40
4106	wound	verb	26	11.40
4107	feather	noun	19	11.40
4108	man	verb	18	11.40
4109	trail	verb	17	11.40
4110	ample	adjective	16	11.39
4111	shatter	verb	22	11.38
4112	wrap	verb	23	11.37
4113	happily	adverb	20	11.37
4114	hip	noun	17	11.37
4115	encounter	noun	19	11.36
4116	frank	adjective	18	11.36
4117	soften	verb	16	11.35
4118	well	adjective	15	11.35
4119	handle	noun	22	11.34
4120	guarantee	verb	19	11.34
4121	vegetable	noun	26	11.33
4122	proposition	noun	18	11.33
4123	vitality	noun	17	11.33
4124	Francis	prop. noun	21	11.32
4124	heroic	adjective	21	11.32
4126	whirl	verb	17	11.32
4127	average	verb	26	11.30
4128	punishment	noun	23	11.30
4129	broader	comp. adj.	19	11.30
4130	thief	noun	18	11.30
4131	Mexican	adjective	19	11.29
4131	obey	verb	19	11.29
4133	sergeant	noun	31	11.27
4134	necessitate	verb	20	11.27
4135	corporate	adjective	19	11.27
4136	dose	noun	24	11.26
4137	criticize	verb	20	11.26
4138	due	adverb	19	11.26
4138	stride	noun	19	11.26
4140	Susan	prop. noun	39	11.25
4141	guerrilla	noun	30	11.25
4142	soap	noun	25	11.25
4143	radical	adjective	22	11.24
4144	uphold	verb	18	11.24
4145	peer	verb	32	11.22
4146	consistently	adverb	20	11.22
4147	choke	verb	22	11.20
4148	extreme	noun	18	11.20
4148	smash	verb	18	11.20
4150	legitimate	adjective	16	11.20
4151	rice	noun	24	11.19
4152	bell	noun	23	11.19
4153	democracy	noun	25	11.18
4154	hunger	noun	17	11.17
4155	deep	adverb	16	11.15
4155	stay	noun	16	11.15
4157	cancer	noun	24	11.14
4158	topic	noun	19	11.13
4159	bunch	noun	18	11.12
4160	oxygen	noun	47	11.11
4161	electron	noun	40	11.11
4162	Hans	prop. noun	45	11.10
4163	bearing	noun	14	11.09
4164	negotiation	noun	26	11.08
4165	fatal	adjective	19	11.08
4166	Philip	prop. noun	23	11.07
4167	taxi	noun	19	11.07
4168	prevention	noun	27	11.06
4169	garage	noun	25	11.06
4170	magic	adjective	21	11.06
4171	pastor	noun	26	11.05
4172	major	noun	25	11.05
4173	exploit	verb	18	11.05
4174	engineer	verb	32	11.04
4175	tax	verb	27	11.04
4176	rock	verb	20	11.04
4177	invest	verb	16	11.04
4178	motel	noun	31	11.03
4179	professional	noun	16	11.03
4180	acquaint	verb	15	11.03
4181	suicide	noun	19	11.02
4182	closer	comp. adj.	18	11.02
4183	desperately	adverb	20	11.01

4184	alienation	noun	22	6.11
4185	Cromwell	prop. noun	22	5.90
4186	Red	prop. noun	22	5.84
4187	novelist	noun	22	5.24
4188	lyric	noun	22	5.17
4189	incline	verb	21	17.58
4190	airplane	noun	21	17.04
4191	desert	noun	21	17.03
4192	urgent	adjective	21	16.82
4193	exhaust	verb	21	16.52
4194	sixty	card. num.	21	16.46
4195	associate	noun	21	16.11
4196	routine	noun	21	15.70
4197	unlikely	adjective	21	15.68
4198	patience	noun	21	15.54
4199	increasingly	adverb	21	15.41
4200	just	adjective	21	15.25
4200	respectable	adjective	21	15.25
4202	neat	adjective	21	14.90
4203	only	qualifier	21	14.87
4204	competent	adjective	21	14.65
4205	pronounce	verb	21	14.59
4206	injure	verb	21	14.48
4207	texture	noun	21	14.45
4208	telephone	verb	21	14.40
4209	perfectly	qualifier	21	14.16
4210	correct	verb	21	14.05
4210	thorough	adjective	21	14.05
4212	invent	verb	21	14.04
4213	proprietor	noun	21	13.87
4214	consume	verb	21	13.53
4215	native	noun	21	13.48
4216	acceptable	adjective	21	13.40
4216	colonial	adjective	21	13.40
4218	exclusively	adverb	21	13.31
4219	devotion	noun	21	13.28
4220	Allen	prop. noun	21	13.24
4221	definitely	adverb	21	13.19
4222	prospective	adjective	21	13.04
4223	increasingly	qualifier	21	12.92
4224	nearby	adverb	21	12.86
4225	entity	noun	21	12.84
4226	scarcely	adverb	21	12.69
4227	purely	qualifier	21	12.66
4228	ill	adjective	21	12.61
4229	gaze	verb	21	12.43
4230	Connecticut	prop. noun	21	12.38
4231	spectacle	noun	21	12.34
4232	affirm	verb	21	12.31
4233	horror	noun	21	12.28
4234	pertinent	adjective	21	12.27
4235	lucky	adjective	21	12.17
4236	oblige	verb	21	12.15
4237	confine	verb	21	12.12
4238	certainty	noun	21	12.11
4239	especially	qualifier	21	11.97
4240	classify	verb	21	11.93
4240	couple	verb	21	11.93
4240	traveler	noun	21	11.93
4243	dedication	noun	21	11.92
4244	helpless	adjective	21	11.86
4245	survey	verb	21	11.85
4246	brave	adjective	21	11.79
4247	realm	noun	21	11.75
4248	exclude	verb	21	11.68
4249	shame	noun	21	11.67
4250	curtain	noun	21	11.63
4251	plain	noun	21	11.50
4252	contour	noun	21	11.45
4253	Francis	prop. noun	21	11.32
4253	heroic	adjective	21	11.32
4255	magic	adjective	21	11.06
4256	vacuum	noun	21	10.98
4257	mess	noun	21	10.93
4258	loop	noun	21	10.92
4259	Baptist	prop. noun	21	10.88
4260	ideological	adjective	21	10.58
4261	halt	verb	21	10.56
4262	Wisconsin	prop. noun	21	10.38
4263	ride	noun	21	10.35
4264	behalf	noun	21	10.13
4265	ugly	adjective	21	10.08
4266	enjoyment	noun	21	10.07
4267	cowboy	noun	21	10.01
4268	program	verb	21	9.94
4269	yield	noun	21	9.92
4270	kneel	verb	21	9.87
4271	praise	verb	21	9.84
4272	deficiency	noun	21	9.83

4183	pitch	verb	20	11.01
4185	penalty	noun	18	11.01
4186	rush	noun	17	11.00
4187	indispensable	adjective	16	11.00
4188	Catholic	prop. noun	35	10.99
4189	surprising	adjective	17	10.99
4190	vacuum	noun	21	10.98
4191	revolutionary	adjective	20	10.96
4192	reliable	adjective	22	10.95
4193	invasion	noun	26	10.94
4194	Delaware	prop. noun	29	10.93
4195	Mason	prop. noun	28	10.93
4196	mess	noun	21	10.93
4197	loop	noun	21	10.92
4198	resentment	noun	18	10.92
4199	useless	adjective	17	10.92
4200	calculation	noun	22	10.91
4201	pen	noun	18	10.91
4202	exhibition	noun	25	10.90
4203	separation	noun	18	10.90
4204	whereby	wh-adverb	19	10.89
4205	Baptist	prop. noun	21	10.88
4206	penetrate	verb	17	10.87
4207	want	noun	17	10.86
4208	repetition	noun	16	10.86
4209	narrow	verb	15	10.86
4210	wildly	adverb	24	10.85
4211	intimate	adjective	20	10.84
4212	catastrophe	noun	16	10.83
4213	damage	verb	17	10.82
4213	economics	noun	17	10.82
4215	monopoly	noun	19	10.81
4216	obstacle	noun	17	10.81
4217	flexible	adjective	25	10.79
4218	Phil	prop. noun	67	10.77
4219	confident	adjective	17	10.77
4220	nucleus	noun	24	10.76
4221	pie	noun	19	10.76
4222	pond	noun	32	10.75
4223	installation	noun	28	10.74
4224	aesthetic	adjective	24	10.74
4224	feature	verb	24	10.74
4226	trader	noun	35	10.73
4227	accomplishment	noun	17	10.73
4228	Douglas	prop. noun	23	10.72
4229	teenager	noun	22	10.72
4230	wound	noun	24	10.71
4231	excuse	noun	23	10.71
4232	performer	noun	20	10.71
4233	nail	noun	20	10.70
4234	exclaim	verb	20	10.68
4235	competitive	adjective	31	10.67
4236	butter	noun	27	10.67
4237	calendar	noun	39	10.66
4238	mold	verb	22	10.66
4239	comprehensive	adjective	19	10.66
4240	boast	verb	18	10.65
4240	nearest	sem. sup.	18	10.65
4242	enlist	verb	17	10.65
4243	classroom	noun	23	10.64
4244	bush	noun	20	10.63
4245	contemplate	verb	19	10.63
4246	earnest	adjective	15	10.62
4247	protective	adjective	14	10.62
4248	magnetic	adjective	25	10.61
4249	savage	adjective	19	10.60
4250	Plato	prop. noun	34	10.59
4251	autumn	noun	22	10.59
4252	panic	noun	20	10.59
4253	ideological	adjective	21	10.58
4254	exceptional	adjective	19	10.58
4255	officially	adverb	18	10.58
4255	unfortunate	adjective	18	10.58
4257	tumor	noun	26	10.57
4258	Pacific	adjective	24	10.57
4259	seal	verb	20	10.57
4260	inability	noun	17	10.57
4261	sizable	adjective	16	10.57
4262	testify	verb	23	10.56
4263	halt	verb	21	10.56
4264	fascinating	adjective	20	10.56
4265	label	noun	20	10.55
4266	reservation	noun	17	10.55
4267	chemistry	noun	17	10.54
4268	decoration	noun	16	10.54
4268	ignorance	noun	16	10.54
4270	shirt	noun	29	10.53
4271	curriculum	noun	20	10.53
4272	competence	noun	18	10.53

4273	verbal	adjective	21	9.74
4274	bold	adjective	21	9.49
4275	spit	verb	21	9.47
4276	supplement	noun	21	9.45
4277	rate	verb	21	9.42
4278	bulletin	noun	21	9.35
4279	theoretical	adjective	21	9.22
4280	expedition	noun	21	9.00
4281	psychologist	noun	21	8.77
4282	planetary	adjective	21	8.75
4283	summary	noun	21	8.65
4284	petition	noun	21	8.63
4285	Cook	prop. noun	21	8.39
4286	contract	verb	21	8.18
4287	tray	noun	21	8.01
4288	lobby	noun	21	7.75
4289	intermediate	adjective	21	7.72
4290	complement	noun	21	7.71
4291	Warwick	prop. noun	21	7.49
4292	needle	noun	21	7.43
4293	Di	prop. noun	21	6.99
4294	rotate	verb	21	6.93
4295	delegate	noun	21	6.89
4296	Stalin	prop. noun	21	6.80
4297	pianist	noun	21	6.63
4298	stage	verb	21	6.29
4299	Manhattan	prop. noun	21	6.21
4300	Hammarskjold	prop. noun	21	6.18
4301	indirect	adjective	21	5.89
4302	Utopia	prop. noun	21	5.58
4303	Johnston	prop. noun	21	5.51
4304	drill	noun	21	5.46
4305	partially	adverb	20	15.85
4306	sixteen	card. num.	20	15.55
4307	mercy	noun	20	15.35
4308	clothing	noun	20	15.22
4309	newer	comp. adj.	20	14.83
4310	block	verb	20	14.77
4311	polish	verb	20	14.74
4312	fantastic	adjective	20	14.16
4313	lawn	noun	20	13.96
4314	fortunately	adverb	20	13.85
4315	chorus	noun	20	13.74
4316	endless	adjective	20	13.73
4317	disposal	noun	20	13.68
4318	live	adjective	20	13.62
4319	pose	verb	20	13.54
4320	amazing	adjective	20	13.52
4321	midst	noun	20	13.31
4322	shelf	noun	20	13.19
4323	grave	noun	20	13.18
4324	worth	noun	20	12.94
4325	despair	noun	20	12.89
4326	overwhelming	adjective	20	12.87
4327	swell	verb	20	12.81
4328	adapt	verb	20	12.73
4329	publisher	noun	20	12.72
4330	compensation	noun	20	12.70
4331	thereafter	adverb	20	12.67
4332	temporarily	adverb	20	12.63
4333	hazard	noun	20	12.56
4334	merge	verb	20	12.55
4335	strongest	sem. sup.	20	12.51
4336	pin	noun	20	12.45
4337	thread	noun	20	12.42
4338	hatred	noun	20	12.31
4339	carrier	noun	20	12.23
4340	swallow	verb	20	12.15
4341	follower	noun	20	12.05
4342	intervention	noun	20	11.94
4342	splendid	adjective	20	11.94
4344	stimulate	verb	20	11.91
4345	Columbia	prop. noun	20	11.90
4345	promising	adjective	20	11.90
4347	presume	verb	20	11.81
4348	Greek	prop. noun	20	11.78
4349	segment	noun	20	11.76
4350	twentieth	ord. num.	20	11.68
4351	scar	noun	20	11.66
4352	desert	verb	20	11.65
4353	authentic	adjective	20	11.62
4353	half	noun	20	11.62
4353	quit	verb	20	11.62
4356	poverty	noun	20	11.59
4357	prescribe	verb	20	11.58
4358	concrete	adjective	20	11.57
4359	mathematics	noun	20	11.55
4360	near	adverb	20	11.53
4361	delight	verb	20	11.50

4273	stupid	adjective	24	10.52
4274	bitterness	noun	18	10.52
4275	refusal	noun	15	10.51
4276	coverage	noun	25	10.50
4277	fever	noun	19	10.50
4278	reach	noun	18	10.50
4279	ambitious	adjective	16	10.50
4280	Broadway	prop. noun	25	10.49
4281	denounce	verb	17	10.49
4281	venture	noun	17	10.49
4283	classification	noun	25	10.48
4284	missionary	noun	23	10.48
4285	decent	adjective	20	10.47
4286	toll	noun	19	10.46
4287	accustom	verb	15	10.45
4288	foresee	verb	14	10.45
4288	supervise	verb	14	10.45
4290	rational	adjective	25	10.44
4291	countless	adjective	14	10.44
4292	enlarge	verb	17	10.42
4293	A	prop. noun	50	10.41
4294	Newport	prop. noun	28	10.40
4295	congressional	adjective	22	10.38
4296	Wisconsin	prop. noun	21	10.38
4297	loyal	adjective	18	10.38
4298	lion	noun	26	10.37
4298	scare	verb	26	10.37
4300	accordance	noun	20	10.37
4301	kind	adjective	17	10.37
4302	kiss	verb	31	10.36
4303	curse	verb	23	10.35
4304	ride	noun	21	10.35
4305	basically	adverb	19	10.35
4306	recording	noun	26	10.34
4307	happiness	noun	23	10.34
4308	founder	noun	16	10.34
4309	Daniel	prop. noun	17	10.33
4310	stamp	verb	16	10.33
4311	Mitchell	prop. noun	27	10.32
4312	oriental	adjective	16	10.32
4313	fat	noun	33	10.31
4314	blonde	adjective	25	10.31
4315	slip	noun	19	10.30
4316	ruin	noun	17	10.30
4317	ideology	noun	16	10.30
4317	steer	verb	16	10.30
4317	sufficiently	adverb	16	10.30
4320	favorite	noun	16	10.29
4321	birthday	noun	18	10.28
4321	equivalent	noun	18	10.28
4323	costly	adjective	16	10.28
4324	O.	prop. noun	29	10.27
4325	imaginary	adjective	17	10.27
4326	cavalry	noun	26	10.26
4327	respective	adjective	19	10.26
4328	restraint	noun	18	10.26
4329	apprentice	noun	18	10.25
4329	foil	noun	18	10.25
4331	compound	noun	24	10.24
4332	weave	verb	20	10.23
4333	sovereignty	noun	28	10.22
4334	match	noun	24	10.22
4335	spectacular	adjective	22	10.22
4336	notable	adjective	20	10.22
4337	elementary	adjective	19	10.22
4338	afterward	adverb	16	10.22
4339	Arkansas	prop. noun	19	10.21
4340	complexity	noun	18	10.21
4341	coming	noun	16	10.20
4342	feel	noun	15	10.20
4343	variable	adjective	25	10.19
4344	circular	adjective	18	10.19
4345	rebuild	verb	15	10.19
4346	confession	noun	19	10.18
4346	ladder	noun	19	10.18
4348	priority	noun	23	10.17
4349	regiment	noun	28	10.16
4350	statute	noun	24	10.15
4351	spontaneous	adjective	17	10.15
4352	workshop	noun	30	10.14
4353	discharge	verb	15	10.14
4354	behalf	noun	21	10.13
4355	guitar	noun	22	10.12
4356	skip	verb	17	10.12
4357	circulation	noun	16	10.12
4358	low	adverb	15	10.12
4359	Rayburn	prop. noun	47	10.11
4360	cold	noun	24	10.11
4361	daylight	noun	17	10.11

4362	plunge	verb	20	11.49
4362	prolong	verb	20	11.49
4364	violation	noun	20	11.42
4365	happily	adverb	20	11.37
4366	necessitate	verb	20	11.27
4367	criticize	verb	20	11.26
4368	consistently	adverb	20	11.22
4369	rock	verb	20	11.04
4370	desperately	adverb	20	11.01
4370	pitch	verb	20	11.01
4372	revolutionary	adjective	20	10.96
4373	intimate	adjective	20	10.84
4374	performer	noun	20	10.71
4375	nail	noun	20	10.70
4376	exclaim	verb	20	10.68
4377	bush	noun	20	10.63
4378	panic	noun	20	10.59
4379	seal	verb	20	10.57
4380	fascinating	adjective	20	10.56
4381	label	noun	20	10.55
4382	curriculum	noun	20	10.53
4383	decent	adjective	20	10.47
4384	accordance	noun	20	10.37
4385	weave	verb	20	10.23
4386	notable	adjective	20	10.22
4387	administrator	noun	20	10.06
4388	distinctive	adjective	20	9.91
4389	smart	adjective	20	9.90
4390	button	noun	20	9.84
4390	dynamic	adjective	20	9.84
4392	ninth	ord. num.	20	9.82
4393	unify	verb	20	9.81
4394	mouse	noun	20	9.79
4394	stimulus	noun	20	9.79
4396	strain	verb	20	9.71
4397	fork	noun	20	9.57
4398	breast	noun	20	9.54
4398	fold	verb	20	9.54
4400	counterpart	noun	20	9.08
4401	female	adjective	20	9.01
4402	Dick	prop. noun	20	8.91
4402	statesman	noun	20	8.91
4404	cure	verb	20	8.84
4405	anyhow	adverb	20	8.82
4406	acquisition	noun	20	8.56
4407	saloon	noun	20	8.38
4408	banker	noun	20	8.31
4409	pension	noun	20	8.17
4410	B.C.	prop. noun	20	8.12
4411	brand	noun	20	8.04
4412	socialism	noun	20	7.79
4413	simplify	verb	20	7.63
4414	experiment	verb	20	7.58
4415	slam	verb	20	7.49
4416	Anglo-Saxon	adjective	20	7.48
4417	Donald	prop. noun	20	7.42
4418	nude	adjective	20	7.18
4419	transformation	noun	20	7.06
4420	sample	verb	20	6.92
4421	arrow	noun	20	6.85
4422	biological	adjective	20	6.84
4423	Mills	prop. noun	20	6.82
4424	Byron	prop. noun	20	6.68
4425	Austin	prop. noun	20	6.38
4426	Hamilton	prop. noun	20	6.34
4426	telegraph	noun	20	6.34
4428	squad	noun	20	6.32
4429	cubic	adjective	20	6.19
4430	interaction	noun	20	6.11
4431	bishop	noun	20	5.85
4432	solid	noun	20	5.52
4433	glue	verb	20	5.23
4434	stall	noun	20	5.15
4435	link	noun	19	15.01
4436	twist	noun	19	14.43
4437	remainder	noun	19	14.35
4438	spare	verb	19	14.26
4439	pursuit	noun	19	13.71
4440	delivery	noun	19	13.70
4441	finance	noun	19	13.67
4442	deadly	adjective	19	13.64
4443	embarrass	verb	19	13.55
4444	startling	adjective	19	13.29
4445	accommodate	verb	19	13.26
4446	insistence	noun	19	13.12
4447	reproduce	verb	19	13.04
4448	Frederick	prop. noun	19	13.02
4449	welcome	adjective	19	12.55
4450	crown	noun	19	12.52

4362	common	noun	16	10.11
4363	weaken	verb	15	10.11
4364	skirt	noun	22	10.10
4365	utterly	qualifier	17	10.10
4366	sole	adjective	15	10.09
4367	smoke	verb	26	10.08
4368	Communist	adjective	24	10.08
4369	superintendent	noun	23	10.08
4370	ugly	adjective	21	10.08
4371	slide	noun	17	10.08
4372	enjoyment	noun	21	10.07
4373	embassy	noun	24	10.06
4374	administrator	noun	20	10.06
4375	unpleasant	adjective	15	10.06
4376	customary	adjective	14	10.05
4377	tent	noun	30	10.04
4378	reorganization	noun	29	10.04
4379	linger	verb	16	10.04
4380	minimal	adjective	27	10.03
4381	luncheon	noun	25	10.02
4382	cowboy	noun	21	10.01
4383	optimism	noun	15	10.01
4383	reluctant	adjective	15	10.01
4385	mention	noun	18	10.00
4386	pause	noun	17	10.00
4387	fame	noun	19	9.99
4388	Elizabeth	prop. noun	15	9.99
4389	decisive	adjective	19	9.98
4390	formally	adverb	18	9.98
4391	flux	noun	34	9.97
4392	frown	verb	22	9.97
4393	Fred	prop. noun	29	9.96
4394	physically	adverb	19	9.96
4395	scan	verb	17	9.96
4396	margin	noun	16	9.96
4397	illuminate	verb	16	9.95
4398	commodity	noun	28	9.94
4399	program	verb	21	9.94
4400	eighteen	card. num.	17	9.94
4401	carpet	noun	17	9.93
4402	readiness	noun	15	9.93
4403	plug	noun	23	9.92
4404	yield	noun	21	9.92
4405	marginal	adjective	26	9.91
4406	distinctive	adjective	20	9.91
4407	reasonably	qualifier	17	9.91
4408	humorous	adjective	16	9.91
4409	Castro	prop. noun	39	9.90
4410	smart	adjective	20	9.90
4411	strategic	adjective	23	9.89
4412	advisory	adjective	22	9.89
4413	correspondent	noun	17	9.89
4414	cast	noun	26	9.88
4415	backward	adverb	17	9.88
4416	following	noun	16	9.88
4417	deliberate	adjective	15	9.88
4418	deed	noun	14	9.88
4419	kneel	verb	21	9.87
4420	mild	adjective	14	9.87
4421	indifference	noun	17	9.86
4422	praise	verb	21	9.84
4423	button	noun	20	9.84
4423	dynamic	adjective	20	9.84
4425	medieval	adjective	18	9.84
4426	ambiguous	adjective	22	9.83
4427	deficiency	noun	21	9.83
4428	stove	noun	17	9.83
4429	belly	noun	25	9.82
4430	nest	noun	22	9.82
4431	ninth	ord. num.	20	9.82
4432	caution	noun	18	9.82
4432	solely	adverb	18	9.82
4434	unify	verb	20	9.81
4435	interview	verb	19	9.81
4435	symptom	noun	19	9.81
4437	voter	noun	24	9.80
4438	adjoin	verb	17	9.80
4438	weary	adjective	17	9.80
4440	availability	noun	23	9.79
4441	mouse	noun	20	9.79
4441	stimulus	noun	20	9.79
4443	K.	prop. noun	17	9.79
4444	popularity	noun	17	9.78
4445	translation	noun	19	9.76
4446	gradual	adjective	16	9.76
4446	soup	noun	16	9.76
4448	verbal	adjective	21	9.74
4449	naive	adjective	19	9.72
4450	oldest	sem. sup.	14	9.72

4451	shortage	noun	19	12.49
4452	march	noun	19	12.38
4453	regret	verb	19	12.23
4454	less	comp. adv.	19	12.17
4455	gap	noun	19	12.16
4456	neatly	adverb	19	12.15
4457	tap	verb	19	12.09
4458	supervision	noun	19	12.05
4459	selective	adjective	19	12.00
4460	near	verb	19	11.93
4461	glow	verb	19	11.79
4461	twin	noun	19	11.79
4463	orderly	adjective	19	11.73
4464	grave	adjective	19	11.70
4465	individually	adverb	19	11.67
4466	tobacco	noun	19	11.52
4467	postpone	verb	19	11.48
4468	basket	noun	19	11.42
4468	viewpoint	noun	19	11.42
4470	feather	noun	19	11.40
4471	encounter	noun	19	11.36
4472	guarantee	verb	19	11.34
4473	broader	comp. adj.	19	11.30
4474	Mexican	adjective	19	11.29
4474	obey	verb	19	11.29
4476	corporate	adjective	19	11.27
4477	due	adverb	19	11.26
4477	stride	noun	19	11.26
4479	topic	noun	19	11.13
4480	fatal	adjective	19	11.08
4481	taxi	noun	19	11.07
4482	suicide	noun	19	11.02
4483	whereby	wh-adverb	19	10.89
4484	monopoly	noun	19	10.81
4485	pie	noun	19	10.76
4486	comprehensive	adjective	19	10.66
4487	contemplate	verb	19	10.63
4488	savage	adjective	19	10.60
4489	exceptional	adjective	19	10.58
4490	fever	noun	19	10.50
4491	toll	noun	19	10.46
4492	basically	adverb	19	10.35
4493	slip	noun	19	10.30
4494	respective	adjective	19	10.26
4495	elementary	adjective	19	10.22
4496	Arkansas	prop. noun	19	10.21
4497	confession	noun	19	10.18
4497	ladder	noun	19	10.18
4499	fame	noun	19	9.99
4500	decisive	adjective	19	9.98
4501	physically	adverb	19	9.96
4502	interview	verb	19	9.81
4502	symptom	noun	19	9.81
4504	translation	noun	19	9.76
4505	naive	adjective	19	9.72
4506	peasant	noun	19	9.70
4507	amateur	noun	19	9.55
4507	portray	verb	19	9.55
4507	sue	verb	19	9.55
4510	intuition	noun	19	9.51
4511	rugged	adjective	19	9.50
4512	hay	noun	19	9.46
4513	Stephen	prop. noun	19	9.45
4514	transport	noun	19	9.30
4515	poll	noun	19	9.28
4515	stiff	adjective	19	9.28
4517	excess	adjective	19	9.24
4518	ridiculous	adjective	19	9.23
4519	situate	verb	19	9.21
4520	log	noun	19	9.20
4521	continental	adjective	19	9.16
4522	glimpse	noun	19	9.09
4523	dim	adjective	19	8.95
4523	postwar	adjective	19	8.95
4525	lap	noun	19	8.90
4526	rope	noun	19	8.88
4527	extract	verb	19	8.86
4528	brass	noun	19	8.78
4529	fury	noun	19	8.75
4530	grip	verb	19	8.55
4531	cream	noun	19	8.52
4532	Russell	prop. noun	19	8.51
4533	slender	adjective	19	8.41
4534	evoke	verb	19	8.33
4535	Vincent	prop. noun	19	8.21
4536	orthodox	adjective	19	8.18
4537	commute	verb	19	8.10
4538	drift	noun	19	8.03
4539	hostile	adjective	19	8.00

4451	strain	verb	20	9.71
4452	peasant	noun	19	9.70
4453	thirty-five	card. num.	14	9.70
4454	exhibit	noun	26	9.69
4455	accent	noun	14	9.69
4456	initially	adverb	18	9.68
4457	likewise	adverb	18	9.66
4458	endurance	noun	16	9.66
4459	misery	noun	17	9.65
4460	upset	verb	16	9.65
4461	contempt	noun	15	9.65
4462	conceal	verb	18	9.64
4463	familiarity	noun	14	9.64
4464	deem	verb	17	9.63
4465	cellar	noun	27	9.61
4466	jaw	noun	26	9.61
4467	consumption	noun	18	9.60
4468	chaos	noun	17	9.60
4469	proceeding	noun	23	9.59
4470	cancel	verb	17	9.59
4471	meaningless	adjective	15	9.58
4472	asleep	adverb	27	9.57
4473	operational	adjective	25	9.57
4474	fork	noun	20	9.57
4475	defect	noun	16	9.57
4476	amateur	noun	19	9.55
4476	portray	verb	19	9.55
4476	sue	verb	19	9.55
4479	breast	noun	20	9.54
4479	fold	verb	20	9.54
4481	reasonably	adverb	17	9.53
4482	tempt	verb	18	9.52
4483	credit	verb	16	9.52
4484	hit	noun	27	9.51
4485	intuition	noun	19	9.51
4486	purse	noun	15	9.51
4487	rugged	adjective	19	9.50
4488	candy	noun	18	9.50
4489	productivity	noun	17	9.50
4490	divorce	verb	14	9.50
4491	outdoor	adjective	27	9.49
4492	bold	adjective	21	9.49
4493	Ruth	prop. noun	31	9.48
4494	Baker	prop. noun	34	9.47
4495	spit	verb	21	9.47
4496	time	verb	16	9.47
4497	lowest	sem. sup.	13	9.47
4498	Pike	prop. noun	40	9.46
4499	hay	noun	19	9.46
4500	theological	adjective	27	9.45
4501	supplement	noun	21	9.45
4502	Stephen	prop. noun	19	9.45
4503	La	prop. noun	18	9.45
4504	progressive	adjective	17	9.45
4505	lonely	adjective	25	9.44
4506	adaptation	noun	17	9.44
4507	suspicious	adjective	13	9.44
4508	posture	noun	15	9.43
4509	rate	verb	21	9.42
4510	bet	verb	18	9.42
4511	vigor	noun	14	9.42
4512	mathematical	adjective	24	9.41
4512	timber	noun	24	9.41
4514	oak	noun	16	9.41
4515	jail	noun	24	9.40
4516	incur	verb	16	9.40
4517	contradiction	noun	18	9.39
4518	coordination	noun	17	9.39
4519	such	qualifier	15	9.37
4520	catalogue	noun	16	9.36
4520	infinite	adjective	16	9.36
4522	tractor	noun	31	9.35
4523	narrative	noun	23	9.35
4524	bulletin	noun	21	9.35
4525	flavor	noun	18	9.35
4526	geographical	adjective	16	9.35
4527	pitcher	noun	29	9.33
4528	lesser	comp. adj.	18	9.33
4529	terminate	verb	18	9.32
4530	foolish	adjective	16	9.31
4531	transport	noun	19	9.30
4532	tribune	noun	16	9.30
4533	weekly	adjective	14	9.30
4534	plaster	noun	24	9.29
4535	questionnaire	noun	44	9.28
4536	poll	noun	19	9.28
4536	stiff	adjective	19	9.28
4538	intersection	noun	29	9.27
4539	sober	adjective	16	9.27

4540	tangible	adjective	19	7.96
4541	corridor	noun	19	7.88
4542	Oxford	prop. noun	19	7.81
4543	enforcement	noun	19	7.69
4544	justification	noun	19	7.67
4545	fasten	verb	19	7.53
4546	axe	noun	19	7.51
4547	rear	noun	19	7.49
4548	earning	noun	19	7.41
4549	sleeve	noun	19	7.38
4550	cure	noun	19	7.36
4551	onion	noun	19	7.27
4552	parlor	noun	19	7.26
4553	numerical	adjective	19	7.20
4554	hurry	noun	19	7.11
4555	bathroom	noun	19	7.04
4556	chip	noun	19	6.97
4557	dentist	noun	19	6.89
4558	export	noun	19	6.86
4559	bid	noun	19	6.83
4560	ace	noun	19	6.45
4560	Salem	prop. noun	19	6.45
4562	projection	noun	19	6.23
4563	Harvey	prop. noun	19	6.14
4564	acceleration	noun	19	6.09
4565	heading	noun	19	5.95
4566	livestock	noun	19	5.67
4567	southeast	adjective	19	5.64
4568	consultant	noun	19	5.63
4569	allocation	noun	19	5.37
4569	pace	verb	19	5.37
4571	Stevens	prop. noun	19	5.32
4572	constant	noun	19	5.24
4573	dairy	noun	19	5.17
4574	movable	adjective	19	5.09
4575	jar	noun	19	5.06
4576	Mars	prop. noun	19	5.00
4577	abrupt	adjective	18	13.97
4578	execution	noun	18	13.90
4579	number	verb	18	13.43
4580	commence	verb	18	13.06
4580	repeatedly	adverb	18	13.06
4582	function	verb	18	12.76
4583	well-known	adjective	18	12.69
4584	episode	noun	18	12.60
4585	conform	verb	18	12.59
4586	nineteen	card. num.	18	12.57
4587	embrace	verb	18	12.56
4587	informal	adjective	18	12.56
4587	shorter	comp. adj.	18	12.56
4590	value	verb	18	12.36
4591	elephant	noun	18	12.30
4592	consistency	noun	18	12.22
4592	representative	adjective	18	12.22
4594	collapse	verb	18	11.88
4595	strive	verb	18	11.85
4596	coin	noun	18	11.83
4596	plant	verb	18	11.83
4598	spread	noun	18	11.77
4599	knit	verb	18	11.70
4600	forward	adjective	18	11.45
4601	man	verb	18	11.40
4602	frank	adjective	18	11.36
4603	proposition	noun	18	11.33
4604	thief	noun	18	11.30
4605	uphold	verb	18	11.24
4606	extreme	noun	18	11.20
4606	smash	verb	18	11.20
4608	bunch	noun	18	11.12
4609	exploit	verb	18	11.05
4610	closer	comp. adj.	18	11.02
4611	penalty	noun	18	11.01
4612	resentment	noun	18	10.92
4613	pen	noun	18	10.91
4614	separation	noun	18	10.90
4615	boast	verb	18	10.65
4615	nearest	sem. sup.	18	10.65
4617	officially	adverb	18	10.58
4617	unfortunate	adjective	18	10.58
4619	competence	noun	18	10.53
4620	bitterness	noun	18	10.52
4621	reach	noun	18	10.50
4622	loyal	adjective	18	10.38
4623	birthday	noun	18	10.28
4623	equivalent	noun	18	10.28
4625	restraint	noun	18	10.26
4626	apprentice	noun	18	10.25
4626	foil	noun	18	10.25
4628	complexity	noun	18	10.21

4540	astronomy	noun	24	9.26
4541	goodness	noun	17	9.26
4542	dot	noun	22	9.25
4543	Dickens	prop. noun	18	9.25
4544	depict	verb	17	9.25
4545	Lucy	prop. noun	46	9.24
4546	excess	adjective	19	9.24
4547	ridiculous	adjective	19	9.23
4548	plot	verb	17	9.23
4549	theoretical	adjective	21	9.22
4550	fit	noun	18	9.22
4550	instinct	noun	18	9.22
4552	rag	noun	17	9.22
4553	situate	verb	19	9.21
4554	defensive	adjective	17	9.21
4555	commend	verb	15	9.21
4556	log	noun	19	9.20
4557	rob	verb	15	9.20
4558	Christianity	prop. noun	31	9.19
4559	beloved	adjective	18	9.19
4560	surrender	verb	18	9.18
4561	aboard	adverb	17	9.18
4562	Ireland	prop. noun	16	9.17
4563	refrigerator	noun	25	9.16
4564	continental	adjective	19	9.16
4565	nurse	verb	17	9.16
4566	athlete	noun	16	9.16
4567	laugh	noun	22	9.15
4567	lively	adjective	22	9.15
4569	essence	noun	17	9.15
4570	humble	adjective	17	9.14
4571	sturdy	adjective	16	9.13
4572	Ralph	prop. noun	22	9.11
4573	handling	noun	23	9.10
4574	ethic	noun	18	9.10
4575	totally	adverb	15	9.10
4576	glimpse	noun	19	9.09
4577	Pierre	prop. noun	17	9.09
4578	surprisingly	adverb	14	9.09
4579	counterpart	noun	20	9.08
4580	ribbon	noun	18	9.08
4581	structural	adjective	25	9.07
4582	anchor	noun	17	9.07
4583	alarm	noun	15	9.07
4584	Dean	prop. noun	25	9.06
4585	memorial	adjective	18	9.05
4586	Scott	prop. noun	17	9.05
4587	tune	noun	15	9.05
4588	Lord	prop. noun	32	9.04
4589	explosive	adjective	16	9.04
4590	loud	adjective	15	9.04
4591	board	verb	15	9.03
4591	crude	adjective	15	9.03
4593	explosion	noun	16	9.02
4593	hint	noun	16	9.02
4595	variable	noun	37	9.01
4596	female	adjective	20	9.01
4597	plainly	adverb	14	9.01
4597	seemingly	adverb	14	9.01
4599	expedition	noun	21	9.00
4600	damp	adjective	16	8.99
4601	severely	adverb	14	8.98
4602	British	prop. noun	17	8.97
4603	great	qualifier	15	8.96
4604	dim	adjective	19	8.95
4604	postwar	adjective	19	8.95
4606	obscure	verb	14	8.95
4607	gear	noun	28	8.94
4608	pack	noun	17	8.94
4609	startle	verb	22	8.93
4610	preference	noun	16	8.93
4611	railway	noun	14	8.93
4612	outset	noun	13	8.93
4613	Pont	prop. noun	50	8.92
4614	Moore	prop. noun	26	8.92
4615	adviser	noun	24	8.92
4616	present-day	adjective	17	8.92
4617	intact	adjective	14	8.92
4618	alliance	noun	22	8.91
4619	Dick	prop. noun	20	8.91
4619	statesman	noun	20	8.91
4621	absolutely	qualifier	17	8.91
4622	lap	noun	19	8.90
4623	rage	noun	17	8.90
4624	vulnerable	adjective	14	8.90
4625	carriage	noun	17	8.89
4626	dwelling	noun	15	8.89
4626	frustration	noun	15	8.89
4628	Morse	prop. noun	34	8.88

4629	circular	adjective	18	10.19
4630	mention	noun	18	10.00
4631	formally	adverb	18	9.98
4632	medieval	adjective	18	9.84
4633	caution	noun	18	9.82
4633	solely	adverb	18	9.82
4635	initially	adverb	18	9.68
4636	likewise	adverb	18	9.66
4637	conceal	verb	18	9.64
4638	consumption	noun	18	9.60
4639	tempt	verb	18	9.52
4640	candy	noun	18	9.50
4641	La	prop. noun	18	9.45
4642	bet	verb	18	9.42
4643	contradiction	noun	18	9.39
4644	flavor	noun	18	9.35
4645	lesser	comp. adj.	18	9.33
4646	terminate	verb	18	9.32
4647	Dickens	prop. noun	18	9.25
4648	fit	noun	18	9.22
4648	instinct	noun	18	9.22
4650	beloved	adjective	18	9.19
4651	surrender	verb	18	9.18
4652	ethic	noun	18	9.10
4653	ribbon	noun	18	9.08
4654	memorial	adjective	18	9.05
4655	sew	verb	18	8.85
4656	flag	noun	18	8.83
4657	compromise	noun	18	8.80
4658	applicable	adjective	18	8.67
4659	instantly	adverb	18	8.66
4660	unlock	verb	18	8.56
4661	simpler	comp. adj.	18	8.55
4662	scrape	verb	18	8.53
4663	simplicity	noun	18	8.51
4664	applicant	noun	18	8.50
4665	receiver	noun	18	8.46
4666	cosmic	adjective	18	8.42
4666	friction	noun	18	8.42
4668	picnic	noun	18	8.39
4669	diagram	noun	18	8.30
4669	suffering	noun	18	8.30
4671	unload	verb	18	8.29
4672	p.	noun	18	8.26
4673	systematic	adjective	18	8.25
4673	temptation	noun	18	8.25
4675	doorway	noun	18	8.23
4676	tub	noun	18	8.17
4677	accumulate	verb	18	8.01
4678	gauge	noun	18	7.93
4679	straw	noun	18	7.77
4680	assault	noun	18	7.59
4681	continuation	noun	18	7.51
4682	broadcast	noun	18	7.43
4683	meter	noun	18	7.37
4684	rose	noun	18	7.33
4685	technician	noun	18	7.23
4686	honorable	adjective	18	7.21
4687	deviation	noun	18	7.15
4688	sculpture	noun	18	7.12
4689	forehead	noun	18	7.10
4690	subjective	adjective	18	7.09
4691	suck	verb	18	6.97
4692	autonomy	noun	18	6.83
4693	profile	noun	18	6.81
4694	shipment	noun	18	6.75
4695	technological	adjective	18	6.66
4696	fantasy	noun	18	6.64
4697	correlation	noun	18	6.56
4698	bat	noun	18	6.55
4699	asset	noun	18	6.54
4699	athletic	adjective	18	6.54
4701	gum	noun	18	6.53
4702	sprawl	verb	18	6.44
4703	abruptly	adverb	18	6.39
4704	soak	verb	18	6.30
4705	aluminum	noun	18	6.19
4705	Tokyo	prop. noun	18	6.19
4707	Biblical	adjective	18	6.11
4708	ambiguity	noun	18	6.08
4709	ammunition	noun	18	6.03
4710	brightness	noun	18	5.99
4711	computer	noun	18	5.97
4712	bleed	verb	18	5.94
4713	slash	verb	18	5.92
4714	dean	noun	18	5.83
4714	partnership	noun	18	5.83
4716	gown	noun	18	5.82
4716	Madame	prop. noun	18	5.82

4629	conspiracy	noun	24	8.88
4630	rope	noun	19	8.88
4631	offer	noun	13	8.88
4632	Greenwich	prop. noun	28	8.86
4633	extract	verb	19	8.86
4634	revision	noun	17	8.86
4635	sew	verb	18	8.85
4636	praise	noun	13	8.85
4637	cure	verb	20	8.84
4638	haul	verb	17	8.84
4639	flag	noun	18	8.83
4640	bulk	noun	13	8.83
4640	cruelty	noun	13	8.83
4642	anyhow	adverb	20	8.82
4643	scratch	verb	22	8.81
4644	via	prep.	17	8.81
4645	patron	noun	13	8.81
4646	plantation	noun	26	8.80
4647	capitol	noun	22	8.80
4648	compromise	noun	18	8.80
4649	retreat	verb	16	8.80
4650	rescue	verb	14	8.80
4651	analogy	noun	17	8.79
4652	delay	noun	15	8.79
4653	hypothesis	noun	22	8.78
4654	brass	noun	19	8.78
4655	grandmother	noun	14	8.78
4655	impersonal	adjective	14	8.78
4655	shallow	adjective	14	8.78
4655	twenty-four	card. num.	14	8.78
4659	psychologist	noun	21	8.77
4660	rabbit	noun	16	8.77
4661	Don	prop. noun	22	8.75
4662	planetary	adjective	21	8.75
4663	fury	noun	19	8.75
4664	meadow	noun	23	8.74
4665	globe	noun	14	8.74
4666	Morris	prop. noun	22	8.73
4667	Greece	prop. noun	17	8.73
4668	plow	verb	16	8.73
4669	drown	verb	14	8.72
4670	diplomacy	noun	17	8.70
4671	real	qualifier	17	8.69
4672	bunk	noun	35	8.67
4673	applicable	adjective	18	8.67
4674	Cambridge	prop. noun	15	8.67
4675	market	verb	41	8.66
4676	instantly	adverb	18	8.66
4677	criminal	adjective	15	8.66
4678	denomination	noun	25	8.65
4679	bat	verb	23	8.65
4680	summary	noun	21	8.65
4681	one-third	noun	14	8.65
4682	part-time	adjective	24	8.64
4683	petition	noun	21	8.63
4684	absurd	adjective	17	8.63
4685	odds	pl. noun	14	8.63
4685	sheer	adjective	14	8.63
4687	anonymous	adjective	17	8.62
4687	conjunction	noun	17	8.62
4689	how	qualifier	26	8.61
4690	restless	adjective	13	8.61
4691	Henrietta	prop. noun	43	8.60
4692	apprehension	noun	16	8.60
4693	toilet	noun	17	8.58
4694	profitable	adjective	14	8.58
4695	above	adjective	22	8.57
4696	liver	noun	17	8.57
4696	recruit	verb	17	8.57
4698	validity	noun	15	8.57
4699	displacement	noun	23	8.56
4700	acquisition	noun	20	8.56
4701	unlock	verb	18	8.56
4702	grip	verb	19	8.55
4703	simpler	comp. adj.	18	8.55
4704	institute	verb	14	8.55
4705	prosperity	noun	14	8.54
4706	scrape	verb	18	8.53
4707	mighty	adjective	16	8.53
4707	pan	noun	16	8.53
4709	Vernon	prop. noun	24	8.52
4710	cream	noun	19	8.52
4711	Russell	prop. noun	19	8.51
4712	simplicity	noun	18	8.51
4713	applicant	noun	18	8.50
4714	discrepancy	noun	16	8.49
4715	infant	noun	14	8.48
4716	lie	verb	13	8.48
4717	attic	noun	15	8.47

4718 investor	noun	18	5.74
4719 seam	noun	18	5.64
4720 mare	noun	18	5.43
4721 sweater	noun	18	5.40
4722 ultraviolet	adjective	18	5.19
4723 Montgomery	prop. noun	18	5.05
4724 adolescence	noun	18	5.01
4725 overlook	verb	17	13.65
4726 logic	noun	17	13.36
4727 reward	noun	17	12.48
4728 aggressive	adjective	17	12.42
4729 lest	sub. conj.	17	12.31
4730 routine	adjective	17	12.27
4730 substitute	noun	17	12.27
4732 label	verb	17	12.24
4733 risk	verb	17	12.07
4734 celebration	noun	17	12.00
4735 lessen	verb	17	11.98
4736 bar	verb	17	11.94
4736 near	adjective	17	11.94
4738 crush	verb	17	11.91
4738 giant	adjective	17	11.91
4740 tilt	verb	17	11.84
4741 artificial	adjective	17	11.82
4742 breeze	noun	17	11.56
4743 disappointment	noun	17	11.48
4744 span	noun	17	11.47
4745 orientation	noun	17	11.44
4746 trail	verb	17	11.40
4747 hip	noun	17	11.37
4748 vitality	noun	17	11.33
4749 whirl	verb	17	11.32
4750 hunger	noun	17	11.17
4751 rush	noun	17	11.00
4752 surprising	adjective	17	10.99
4753 useless	adjective	17	10.92
4754 penetrate	verb	17	10.87
4755 want	noun	17	10.86
4756 damage	verb	17	10.82
4756 economics	noun	17	10.82
4758 obstacle	noun	17	10.81
4759 confident	adjective	17	10.77
4760 accomplishment	noun	17	10.73
4761 enlist	verb	17	10.65
4762 inability	noun	17	10.57
4763 reservation	noun	17	10.55
4764 chemistry	noun	17	10.54
4765 denounce	verb	17	10.49
4765 venture	noun	17	10.49
4767 enlarge	verb	17	10.42
4768 kind	adjective	17	10.37
4769 Daniel	prop. noun	17	10.33
4770 ruin	noun	17	10.30
4771 imaginary	adjective	17	10.27
4772 spontaneous	adjective	17	10.15
4773 skip	verb	17	10.12
4774 daylight	noun	17	10.11
4775 utterly	qualifier	17	10.10
4776 slide	noun	17	10.08
4777 pause	noun	17	10.00
4778 scan	verb	17	9.96
4779 eighteen	card. num.	17	9.94
4780 carpet	noun	17	9.93
4781 reasonably	qualifier	17	9.91
4782 correspondent	noun	17	9.89
4783 backward	adverb	17	9.88
4784 indifference	noun	17	9.86
4785 stove	noun	17	9.83
4786 adjoin	verb	17	9.80
4786 weary	adjective	17	9.80
4788 K.	prop. noun	17	9.79
4789 popularity	noun	17	9.78
4790 misery	noun	17	9.65
4791 deem	verb	17	9.63
4792 chaos	noun	17	9.60
4793 cancel	verb	17	9.59
4794 reasonably	adverb	17	9.53
4795 productivity	noun	17	9.50
4796 progressive	adjective	17	9.45
4797 adaptation	noun	17	9.44
4798 coordination	noun	17	9.39
4799 goodness	noun	17	9.26
4800 depict	verb	17	9.25
4801 plot	verb	17	9.23
4802 rag	noun	17	9.22
4803 defensive	adjective	17	9.21
4804 aboard	adverb	17	9.18
4805 nurse	verb	17	9.16
4806 essence	noun	17	9.15

4717 vocabulary	noun	15	8.47
4719 Dave	prop. noun	32	8.46
4720 receiver	noun	18	8.46
4721 swift	adjective	13	8.46
4722 bull	noun	16	8.45
4723 harder	comp. adv.	14	8.45
4724 White	prop. noun	24	8.44
4725 acute	adjective	13	8.44
4726 wider	comp. adj.	17	8.43
4727 evolve	verb	16	8.43
4728 cosmic	adjective	18	8.42
4728 friction	noun	18	8.42
4730 ensue	verb	13	8.42
4731 slender	adjective	19	8.41
4732 satellite	noun	15	8.41
4733 spell	verb	14	8.41
4734 Jean	prop. noun	23	8.40
4735 Cook	prop. noun	21	8.39
4736 picnic	noun	18	8.39
4737 saloon	noun	20	8.38
4738 loudly	adverb	17	8.38
4739 close	noun	16	8.38
4740 apt	adjective	15	8.38
4740 socially	adverb	15	8.38
4742 yell	verb	31	8.37
4743 resent	verb	16	8.37
4744 alert	verb	13	8.37
4744 safely	adverb	13	8.37
4746 steam	noun	17	8.36
4747 frustrate	verb	15	8.36
4747 planner	noun	15	8.36
4749 preferably	adverb	14	8.36
4750 inhabitant	noun	13	8.35
4751 stimulation	noun	14	8.34
4752 evoke	verb	19	8.33
4753 banker	noun	20	8.31
4754 ash	noun	17	8.31
4755 ingredient	noun	15	8.31
4755 mob	noun	15	8.31
4757 further	verb	13	8.31
4758 prompt	verb	11	8.31
4759 coach	noun	30	8.30
4760 diagram	noun	18	8.30
4760 suffering	noun	18	8.30
4762 spare	adjective	15	8.30
4763 Hollywood	prop. noun	27	8.29
4764 unload	verb	18	8.29
4765 Minnesota	prop. noun	17	8.29
4765 rug	noun	17	8.29
4767 slightest	sem. sup.	13	8.29
4768 invoke	verb	14	8.28
4768 rumor	noun	14	8.28
4770 cockpit	noun	17	8.27
4771 p.	noun	18	8.26
4772 Anthony	prop. noun	17	8.26
4773 short	adverb	14	8.26
4774 systematic	adjective	18	8.25
4774 temptation	noun	18	8.25
4776 sunlight	noun	17	8.25
4777 constructive	adjective	15	8.25
4777 echo	noun	15	8.25
4779 disposition	noun	14	8.25
4780 Richmond	prop. noun	12	8.25
4781 blast	noun	16	8.24
4782 doorway	noun	18	8.23
4783 preservation	noun	17	8.23
4784 deprive	verb	14	8.23
4785 Houston	prop. noun	25	8.22
4786 sweat	noun	22	8.22
4787 constituent	noun	15	8.22
4787 driveway	noun	15	8.22
4789 wholly	adverb	13	8.22
4790 Vincent	prop. noun	19	8.21
4791 Raymond	prop. noun	17	8.21
4792 good-bye	exclam.	14	8.21
4793 bow	verb	13	8.21
4794 afterwards	adverb	14	8.20
4795 grandfather	noun	13	8.20
4796 calf	noun	17	8.19
4797 manifestation	noun	15	8.19
4798 onset	noun	43	8.18
4799 contract	verb	21	8.18
4800 orthodox	adjective	19	8.18
4801 fleet	noun	16	8.18
4802 pension	noun	20	8.17
4803 tub	noun	18	8.17
4804 preside	verb	14	8.17
4805 detergent	noun	29	8.16
4806 herd	noun	26	8.16

4807	humble	adjective	17	9.14
4808	Pierre	prop. noun	17	9.09
4809	anchor	noun	17	9.07
4810	Scott	prop. noun	17	9.05
4811	British	prop. noun	17	8.97
4812	pack	noun	17	8.94
4813	present-day	adjective	17	8.92
4814	absolutely	qualifier	17	8.91
4815	rage	noun	17	8.90
4816	carriage	noun	17	8.89
4817	revision	noun	17	8.86
4818	haul	verb	17	8.84
4819	via	prep.	17	8.81
4820	analogy	noun	17	8.79
4821	Greece	prop. noun	17	8.73
4822	diplomacy	noun	17	8.70
4823	real	qualifier	17	8.69
4824	absurd	adjective	17	8.63
4825	anonymous	adjective	17	8.62
4825	conjunction	noun	17	8.62
4827	toilet	noun	17	8.58
4828	liver	noun	17	8.57
4828	recruit	verb	17	8.57
4830	wider	comp. adj.	17	8.43
4831	loudly	adverb	17	8.38
4832	steam	noun	17	8.36
4833	ash	noun	17	8.31
4834	Minnesota	prop. noun	17	8.29
4834	rug	noun	17	8.29
4836	cockpit	noun	17	8.27
4837	Anthony	prop. noun	17	8.26
4838	sunlight	noun	17	8.25
4839	preservation	noun	17	8.23
4840	Raymond	prop. noun	17	8.21
4841	calf	noun	17	8.19
4842	slap	verb	17	8.15
4843	indirectly	adverb	17	8.13
4844	foreigner	noun	17	8.12
4845	sooner	comp. adv.	17	8.11
4846	quarrel	noun	17	8.07
4846	seal	noun	17	8.07
4848	Cleveland	prop. noun	17	8.04
4849	segregate	verb	17	7.99
4850	elbow	noun	17	7.90
4851	terrace	noun	17	7.86
4852	processing	noun	17	7.83
4853	acid	noun	17	7.80
4854	investigator	noun	17	7.79
4855	vicious	adjective	17	7.78
4856	clever	adjective	17	7.77
4857	silently	adverb	17	7.70
4858	resonance	noun	17	7.69
4859	monthly	adjective	17	7.65
4860	lens	noun	17	7.60
4861	parliament	noun	17	7.59
4862	stagger	verb	17	7.58
4862	violate	verb	17	7.58
4864	injustice	noun	17	7.45
4865	gamble	verb	17	7.44
4866	shiver	verb	17	7.38
4867	crack	noun	17	7.21
4868	revelation	noun	17	7.17
4868	usage	noun	17	7.17
4870	bloom	verb	17	7.12
4870	educator	noun	17	7.12
4872	Rose	prop. noun	17	7.05
4873	pit	noun	17	7.02
4874	Picasso	prop. noun	17	6.94
4875	snatch	verb	17	6.93
4876	Burma	prop. noun	17	6.89
4877	Stevenson	prop. noun	17	6.88
4878	tribe	noun	17	6.83
4879	repair	verb	17	6.78
4880	indicator	noun	17	6.65
4880	proclamation	noun	17	6.65
4882	pop	verb	17	6.60
4883	ashamed	adjective	17	6.57
4883	comparative	adjective	17	6.57
4885	morale	noun	17	6.42
4886	confrontation	noun	17	6.39
4887	Brooks	prop. noun	17	6.23
4888	Denver	prop. noun	17	6.11
4889	zero	card. num.	17	6.06
4890	tumble	verb	17	6.02
4891	antenna	noun	17	5.98
4891	Victor	prop. noun	17	5.98
4893	Cooper	prop. noun	17	5.80
4894	grove	noun	17	5.65
4895	demon	noun	17	5.63

4807	Indiana	prop. noun	16	8.16
4808	slap	verb	17	8.15
4809	disapproval	noun	15	8.14
4810	peel	verb	14	8.14
4811	milligram	noun	37	8.13
4812	thermal	adjective	33	8.13
4813	Wagner	prop. noun	23	8.13
4814	indirectly	adverb	17	8.13
4815	dwell	verb	15	8.13
4816	prediction	noun	13	8.13
4817	B.C.	prop. noun	20	8.12
4818	foreigner	noun	17	8.12
4819	sooner	comp. adv.	17	8.11
4820	loom	verb	15	8.11
4820	penetration	noun	15	8.11
4820	reside	verb	15	8.11
4823	Hearst	prop. noun	54	8.10
4824	commute	verb	19	8.10
4825	supposedly	adverb	12	8.10
4826	comply	verb	14	8.09
4827	killer	noun	22	8.08
4828	handful	noun	14	8.08
4829	flourish	verb	13	8.08
4830	quarrel	noun	17	8.07
4830	seal	noun	17	8.07
4832	finish	noun	16	8.07
4833	prohibit	verb	15	8.07
4834	detach	verb	13	8.07
4834	half	qualifier	13	8.07
4834	outline	verb	13	8.07
4834	spur	noun	13	8.07
4838	imperial	adjective	13	8.06
4838	unfair	adjective	13	8.06
4840	Nixon	prop. noun	26	8.05
4841	top	verb	13	8.05
4842	Mickey	prop. noun	32	8.04
4843	brand	noun	20	8.04
4844	Cleveland	prop. noun	17	8.04
4845	entail	verb	13	8.04
4846	drift	noun	19	8.03
4847	ghost	noun	16	8.03
4848	indulge	verb	15	8.03
4849	undue	adjective	13	8.03
4850	breakdown	noun	16	8.02
4850	revive	verb	16	8.02
4852	rebellion	noun	14	8.02
4853	thyroid	noun	39	8.01
4854	tray	noun	21	8.01
4855	accumulate	verb	18	8.01
4856	typically	adverb	16	8.01
4857	consent	noun	15	8.01
4858	pentagon	noun	14	8.01
4859	suitcase	noun	25	8.00
4860	hostile	adjective	19	8.00
4861	segregate	verb	17	7.99
4862	distress	noun	16	7.99
4862	walnut	noun	16	7.99
4864	Pat	prop. noun	34	7.98
4865	hen	noun	27	7.98
4866	chill	noun	15	7.98
4866	hastily	adverb	15	7.98
4868	enclose	verb	14	7.98
4868	hasten	verb	14	7.98
4870	nonsense	noun	13	7.98
4871	largely	qualifier	12	7.98
4872	shorten	verb	14	7.97
4873	Billy	prop. noun	26	7.96
4874	tangible	adjective	19	7.96
4875	notably	adverb	13	7.96
4876	Colorado	prop. noun	16	7.95
4877	gauge	noun	18	7.93
4878	quest	noun	16	7.93
4879	coincidence	noun	13	7.93
4880	historically	adverb	16	7.92
4880	muscular	adjective	16	7.92
4880	pasture	noun	16	7.92
4883	ego	noun	14	7.92
4883	resort	verb	14	7.92
4885	probe	verb	13	7.92
4886	brood	verb	15	7.91
4887	provoke	verb	14	7.91
4888	correctly	adverb	13	7.91
4889	elbow	noun	17	7.90
4890	disastrous	adjective	16	7.90
4891	disrupt	verb	13	7.90
4892	mill	verb	16	7.89
4893	disturbing	adjective	14	7.89
4894	denote	verb	25	7.88
4895	corridor	noun	19	7.88

4896	curl	verb	17	5.59
4896	fuel	noun	17	5.59
4898	towel	noun	17	5.48
4899	and/or	co. conj.	17	5.45
4900	fur	noun	17	5.44
4901	clergyman	noun	17	5.38
4901	plus	prep.	17	5.38
4903	infectious	adjective	17	5.37
4904	hunter	noun	17	5.04
4905	Walker	prop. noun	17	5.01
4906	unnecessary	adjective	16	12.53
4907	supplement	verb	16	12.17
4908	quarrel	verb	16	11.74
4909	differently	adverb	16	11.72
4910	ample	adjective	16	11.39
4911	soften	verb	16	11.35
4912	legitimate	adjective	16	11.20
4913	deep	adverb	16	11.15
4913	stay	noun	16	11.15
4915	invest	verb	16	11.04
4916	professional	noun	16	11.03
4917	indispensable	adjective	16	11.00
4918	repetition	noun	16	10.86
4919	catastrophe	noun	16	10.83
4920	sizable	adjective	16	10.57
4921	decoration	noun	16	10.54
4921	ignorance	noun	16	10.54
4923	ambitious	adjective	16	10.50
4924	founder	noun	16	10.34
4925	stamp	verb	16	10.33
4926	oriental	adjective	16	10.32
4927	ideology	noun	16	10.30
4927	steer	verb	16	10.30
4927	sufficiently	adverb	16	10.30
4930	favorite	noun	16	10.29
4931	costly	adjective	16	10.28
4932	afterward	adverb	16	10.22
4933	coming	noun	16	10.20
4934	circulation	noun	16	10.12
4935	common	noun	16	10.11
4936	linger	verb	16	10.04
4937	margin	noun	16	9.96
4938	illuminate	verb	16	9.95
4939	humorous	adjective	16	9.91
4940	following	noun	16	9.88
4941	gradual	adjective	16	9.76
4941	soup	noun	16	9.76
4943	endurance	noun	16	9.66
4944	upset	verb	16	9.65
4945	defect	noun	16	9.57
4946	credit	verb	16	9.52
4947	time	verb	16	9.47
4948	oak	noun	16	9.41
4949	incur	verb	16	9.40
4950	catalogue	noun	16	9.36
4950	infinite	adjective	16	9.36
4952	geographical	adjective	16	9.35
4953	foolish	adjective	16	9.31
4954	tribune	noun	16	9.30
4955	sober	adjective	16	9.27
4956	Ireland	prop. noun	16	9.17
4957	athlete	noun	16	9.16
4958	sturdy	adjective	16	9.13
4959	explosive	adjective	16	9.04
4960	explosion	noun	16	9.02
4960	hint	noun	16	9.02
4962	damp	adjective	16	8.99
4963	preference	noun	16	8.93
4964	retreat	verb	16	8.80
4965	rabbit	noun	16	8.77
4966	plow	verb	16	8.73
4967	apprehension	noun	16	8.60
4968	mighty	adjective	16	8.53
4968	pan	noun	16	8.53
4970	discrepancy	noun	16	8.49
4971	bull	noun	16	8.45
4972	evolve	verb	16	8.43
4973	close	noun	16	8.38
4974	resent	verb	16	8.37
4975	blast	noun	16	8.24
4976	fleet	noun	16	8.18
4977	Indiana	prop. noun	16	8.16
4978	finish	noun	16	8.07
4979	ghost	noun	16	8.03
4980	breakdown	noun	16	8.02
4980	revive	verb	16	8.02
4982	typically	adverb	16	8.01
4983	distress	noun	16	7.99
4983	walnut	noun	16	7.99

4896	gram	noun	37	7.87
4897	Hitler	prop. noun	16	7.87
4898	terrace	noun	17	7.86
4899	bound	verb	13	7.86
4899	fearful	adjective	13	7.86
4899	gifted	adjective	13	7.86
4899	vigorously	adverb	13	7.86
4903	metaphysical	adjective	16	7.85
4904	fashion	verb	13	7.85
4905	saving	noun	24	7.84
4906	testing	noun	22	7.84
4907	sincere	adjective	15	7.84
4908	processing	noun	17	7.83
4909		noun	16	7.83
4910	relinquish	verb	13	7.83
4911	brutality	noun	14	7.82
4912	Oxford	prop. noun	19	7.81
4913	inspect	verb	16	7.81
4914	package	verb	14	7.81
4915	acid	noun	17	7.80
4916	motivation	noun	16	7.80
4917	socialism	noun	20	7.79
4918	investigator	noun	17	7.79
4919	chew	verb	16	7.79
4919	Ray	prop. noun	16	7.79
4921	optimistic	adjective	15	7.79
4921	spray	noun	15	7.79
4923	immense	adjective	14	7.79
4924	vicious	adjective	17	7.78
4925	mist	noun	16	7.78
4925	threshold	noun	16	7.78
4927	straw	noun	18	7.77
4928	clever	adjective	17	7.77
4929	container	noun	14	7.77
4930	farewell	noun	13	7.77
4931	capitalism	noun	14	7.76
4932	lobby	noun	21	7.75
4933	carbon	noun	32	7.73
4933	salvation	noun	32	7.73
4935	slum	noun	16	7.73
4936	examiner	noun	15	7.73
4937	indeed	post-qual.	13	7.73
4937	ruler	noun	13	7.73
4939	intermediate	adjective	21	7.72
4940	competitor	noun	13	7.72
4940	doubtless	adverb	13	7.72
4942	complement	noun	21	7.71
4943	middle-class	noun	22	7.70
4944	silently	adverb	17	7.70
4945	secular	adjective	15	7.70
4946	enforcement	noun	19	7.69
4947	resonance	noun	17	7.69
4948	applause	noun	14	7.69
4948	heavier	comp. adj.	14	7.69
4950	theatrical	adjective	12	7.69
4951	Coolidge	prop. noun	33	7.68
4952	justification	noun	19	7.67
4953	architecture	noun	12	7.67
4954	elderly	adjective	13	7.66
4954	imitate	verb	13	7.66
4956	augment	verb	12	7.66
4957	imitation	noun	26	7.65
4957	saddle	noun	26	7.65
4959	monthly	adjective	17	7.65
4960	stature	noun	15	7.65
4961	solemn	adjective	12	7.65
4962	disguise	verb	15	7.64
4963	stability	noun	14	7.64
4964	fond	adjective	13	7.64
4965	successive	adjective	12	7.64
4966	simplify	verb	20	7.63
4967	tide	noun	14	7.63
4968	mentally	adverb	15	7.62
4969	alike	adverb	14	7.62
4969	foster	verb	14	7.62
4971	elevate	verb	12	7.62
4972	cop	noun	32	7.61
4973	Bryan	prop. noun	14	7.61
4973	Columbus	prop. noun	14	7.61
4975	marshal	noun	26	7.60
4976	upstairs	adverb	23	7.60
4977	lens	noun	17	7.60
4978	consciously	adverb	12	7.60
4978	consultation	noun	12	7.60
4978	water	verb	12	7.60
4981	assault	noun	18	7.59
4982	parliament	noun	17	7.59
4983	collector	noun	16	7.59
4984	experiment	verb	20	7.58

4985	Colorado	prop. noun	16	7.95
4986	quest	noun	16	7.93
4987	historically	adverb	16	7.92
4987	muscular	adjective	16	7.92
4987	pasture	noun	16	7.92
4990	disastrous	adjective	16	7.90
4991	mill	verb	16	7.89
4992	Hitler	prop. noun	16	7.87
4993	metaphysical	adjective	16	7.85
4994		noun	16	7.83
4995	inspect	verb	16	7.81
4996	motivation	noun	16	7.80
4997	chew	verb	16	7.79
4997	Ray	prop. noun	16	7.79
4999	mist	noun	16	7.78
4999	threshold	noun	16	7.78
5001	slum	noun	16	7.73
5002	collector	noun	16	7.59
5003	mate	verb	16	7.58
5004	halfway	adverb	16	7.57
5005	tower	noun	16	7.54
5005	Truman	prop. noun	16	7.54
5007	least	qualifier	16	7.52
5008	pine	noun	16	7.46
5009	murder	verb	16	7.45
5010	arch	noun	16	7.44
5011	cultivate	verb	16	7.41
5012	ministry	noun	16	7.31
5013	counsel	noun	16	7.30
5013	vertical	adjective	16	7.30
5015	compatible	adjective	16	7.25
5016	cake	noun	16	7.23
5016	glove	noun	16	7.23
5018	convict	verb	16	7.21
5018	incentive	noun	16	7.21
5020	stable	adjective	16	7.16
5021	wrist	noun	16	7.15
5022	cardinal	noun	16	7.09
5023	drain	verb	16	7.07
5024	creator	noun	16	7.05
5025	motivate	verb	16	6.90
5026	finest	sem. sup.	16	6.88
5027	remedy	noun	16	6.82
5028	conformity	noun	16	6.79
5028	judicial	adjective	16	6.79
5030	ghetto	noun	16	6.68
5031	x-ray	noun	16	6.66
5032	fragment	noun	16	6.54
5033	Nelson	prop. noun	16	6.47
5034	analyst	noun	16	6.45
5035	long	verb	16	6.39
5035	transmission	noun	16	6.39
5037	dusty	adjective	16	6.35
5038	lemon	noun	16	6.32
5039	angular	adjective	16	6.31
5039	magic	noun	16	6.31
5041	Stuart	prop. noun	16	6.28
5042	trim	verb	16	6.20
5043	thigh	noun	16	6.18
5044	formidable	adjective	16	6.16
5045	outfit	noun	16	6.12
5045	statistical	adjective	16	6.12
5045	unemployment	noun	16	6.12
5048	isolation	noun	16	6.04
5049	I.	prop. noun	16	5.99
5050	compound	verb	16	5.95
5051	frieze	noun	16	5.90
5052	bass	noun	16	5.83
5053	synthesis	noun	16	5.75
5054	sovereign	noun	16	5.74
5055	pottery	noun	16	5.72
5056	manufacture	noun	16	5.65
5057	glorious	adjective	16	5.64
5057	jerk	verb	16	5.64
5059	Israel	prop. noun	16	5.62
5060	ballad	noun	16	5.57
5061	bargaining	noun	16	5.55
5062	ruling	noun	16	5.47
5063	infantry	noun	16	5.43
5064	streak	noun	16	5.42
5065	civilian	adjective	16	5.41
5066	summarize	verb	16	5.34
5067	whip	noun	16	5.28
5068	transit	noun	16	5.24
5069	solar	adjective	16	5.23
5070	flexibility	noun	16	5.13
5071	fringe	noun	16	5.07
5072	well	adjective	15	11.35
5073	acquaint	verb	15	11.03
4985	stagger	verb	17	7.58
4985	violate	verb	17	7.58
4987	mate	verb	16	7.58
4988	compartment	noun	12	7.58
4989	halfway	adverb	16	7.57
4990	allege	verb	14	7.57
4991	O.K.	exclam.	23	7.56
4992	harvest	noun	12	7.56
4993	corruption	noun	14	7.55
4993	fully	qualifier	14	7.55
4995	abstraction	noun	23	7.54
4996	tower	noun	16	7.54
4996	Truman	prop. noun	16	7.54
4998	vaguely	adverb	15	7.54
4999	singular	adjective	14	7.54
5000	ancestor	noun	13	7.54
5001	fasten	verb	19	7.53
5002	rancher	noun	22	7.52
5003	least	qualifier	16	7.52
5004	doll	noun	22	7.51
5005	axe	noun	19	7.51
5006	continuation	noun	18	7.51
5007	Arizona	prop. noun	14	7.51
5008	dazzle	verb	13	7.51
5009	irregularity	noun	12	7.50
5010	Warwick	prop. noun	21	7.49
5011	slam	verb	20	7.49
5012	rear	noun	19	7.49
5013	imaginative	adjective	13	7.49
5013	swing	noun	13	7.49
5015	Anglo-Saxon	adjective	20	7.48
5016	currency	noun	15	7.48
5016	quite	adverb	15	7.48
5018	influential	adjective	14	7.48
5018	pig	noun	14	7.48
5020	bitterly	adverb	14	7.47
5020	incidentally	adverb	14	7.47
5022	faster	comp. adv.	13	7.47
5023	pine	noun	16	7.46
5024	prejudice	noun	13	7.46
5025	likelihood	noun	10	7.46
5026	injustice	noun	17	7.45
5027	murder	verb	16	7.45
5028	Egypt	prop. noun	14	7.45
5028	sensible	adjective	14	7.45
5030	traverse	verb	12	7.45
5031	tolerate	verb	11	7.45
5032	gamble	verb	17	7.44
5033	arch	noun	16	7.44
5034	needle	noun	21	7.43
5035	broadcast	noun	18	7.43
5036	enroll	verb	15	7.43
5037	Donald	prop. noun	20	7.42
5038	precaution	noun	15	7.42
5039	unanimously	adverb	11	7.42
5040	earning	noun	19	7.41
5041	cultivate	verb	16	7.41
5042	feasible	adjective	15	7.41
5042	rubber	noun	15	7.41
5044	diagnosis	noun	14	7.41
5044	immigrant	noun	14	7.41
5044	Yale	prop. noun	14	7.41
5047	compress	verb	13	7.41
5047	earnestly	adverb	13	7.41
5049	embody	verb	14	7.40
5049	scrutiny	noun	14	7.40
5051	abide	verb	14	7.39
5051	encouragement	noun	14	7.39
5051	involvement	noun	14	7.39
5054	sleeve	noun	19	7.38
5055	shiver	verb	17	7.38
5056	meter	noun	18	7.37
5057	flat	noun	13	7.37
5058	cure	noun	19	7.36
5059	alteration	noun	14	7.36
5059	secure	adjective	14	7.36
5061	collar	noun	14	7.35
5061	spell	noun	14	7.35
5063	sinister	adjective	13	7.35
5064	landing	noun	15	7.34
5065	rose	noun	18	7.33
5066	abundance	noun	13	7.33
5067	hopeless	adjective	14	7.32
5068	portable	adjective	13	7.32
5069	ministry	noun	16	7.31
5070	premise	noun	15	7.31
5071	awful	adjective	14	7.31
5072	drainage	noun	13	7.31
5072	expend	verb	13	7.31

5074	narrow	verb	15	10.86
5075	earnest	adjective	15	10.62
5076	refusal	noun	15	10.51
5077	accustom	verb	15	10.45
5078	feel	noun	15	10.20
5079	rebuild	verb	15	10.19
5080	discharge	verb	15	10.14
5081	low	adverb	15	10.12
5082	weaken	verb	15	10.11
5083	sole	adjective	15	10.09
5084	unpleasant	adjective	15	10.06
5085	optimism	noun	15	10.01
5085	reluctant	adjective	15	10.01
5087	Elizabeth	prop. noun	15	9.99
5088	readiness	noun	15	9.93
5089	deliberate	adjective	15	9.88
5090	contempt	noun	15	9.65
5091	meaningless	adjective	15	9.58
5092	purse	noun	15	9.51
5093	posture	noun	15	9.43
5094	such	qualifier	15	9.37
5095	commend	verb	15	9.21
5096	rob	verb	15	9.20
5097	totally	adverb	15	9.10
5098	alarm	noun	15	9.07
5099	tune	noun	15	9.05
5100	loud	adjective	15	9.04
5101	board	verb	15	9.03
5101	crude	adjective	15	9.03
5103	great	qualifier	15	8.96
5104	dwelling	noun	15	8.89
5104	frustration	noun	15	8.89
5106	delay	noun	15	8.79
5107	Cambridge	prop. noun	15	8.67
5108	criminal	adjective	15	8.66
5109	validity	noun	15	8.57
5110	attic	noun	15	8.47
5110	vocabulary	noun	15	8.47
5112	satellite	noun	15	8.41
5113	apt	adjective	15	8.38
5113	socially	adverb	15	8.38
5115	frustrate	verb	15	8.36
5115	planner	noun	15	8.36
5117	ingredient	noun	15	8.31
5117	mob	noun	15	8.31
5119	spare	adjective	15	8.30
5120	constructive	adjective	15	8.25
5120	echo	noun	15	8.25
5122	constituent	noun	15	8.22
5122	driveway	noun	15	8.22
5124	manifestation	noun	15	8.19
5125	disapproval	noun	15	8.14
5126	dwell	verb	15	8.13
5127	loom	verb	15	8.11
5127	penetration	noun	15	8.11
5127	reside	verb	15	8.11
5130	prohibit	verb	15	8.07
5131	indulge	verb	15	8.03
5132	consent	noun	15	8.01
5133	chill	noun	15	7.98
5133	hastily	adverb	15	7.98
5135	brood	verb	15	7.91
5136	sincere	adjective	15	7.84
5137	optimistic	adjective	15	7.79
5137	spray	noun	15	7.79
5139	examiner	noun	15	7.73
5140	secular	adjective	15	7.70
5141	stature	noun	15	7.65
5142	disguise	verb	15	7.64
5143	mentally	adverb	15	7.62
5144	vaguely	adverb	15	7.54
5145	currency	noun	15	7.48
5145	quite	adverb	15	7.48
5147	enroll	verb	15	7.43
5148	precaution	noun	15	7.42
5149	feasible	adjective	15	7.41
5149	rubber	noun	15	7.41
5151	landing	noun	15	7.34
5152	premise	noun	15	7.31
5153	intensive	adjective	15	7.26
5154	assistant	adjective	15	7.20
5155	outlet	noun	15	7.15
5156	cave	noun	15	7.13
5157	arch	verb	15	7.10
5158	invade	verb	15	7.08
5159	creek	noun	15	7.07
5159	renaissance	noun	15	7.07
5161	sentimental	adjective	15	7.05
5162	cemetery	noun	15	7.02

5072	outline	noun	13	7.31
5075	counsel	noun	16	7.30
5075	vertical	adjective	16	7.30
5077	V.	prop. noun	14	7.30
5078	ward	noun	25	7.29
5079	discount	noun	13	7.28
5080	shrink	verb	12	7.28
5081	onion	noun	19	7.27
5082	parlor	noun	19	7.26
5083	intensive	adjective	15	7.26
5084	resemblance	noun	13	7.26
5085	compatible	adjective	16	7.25
5086	confer	verb	10	7.25
5087	dictate	verb	14	7.24
5088	liberate	verb	13	7.24
5088	reunion	noun	13	7.24
5090	technician	noun	18	7.23
5091	cake	noun	16	7.23
5091	glove	noun	16	7.23
5093	transmit	verb	13	7.23
5094	penetrating	adjective	12	7.23
5095	hardship	noun	14	7.22
5096	solitary	adjective	13	7.22
5097	honorable	adjective	18	7.21
5098	crack	noun	17	7.21
5099	convict	verb	16	7.21
5099	incentive	noun	16	7.21
5101	calm	verb	14	7.21
5102	frankly	adverb	13	7.21
5102	mighty	qualifier	13	7.21
5104	numerical	adjective	19	7.20
5105	assistant	adjective	15	7.20
5106	urgency	noun	13	7.20
5107	scrap	noun	11	7.20
5108	nude	adjective	20	7.18
5109	advocate	verb	14	7.18
5110	confide	verb	13	7.18
5111	revelation	noun	17	7.17
5111	usage	noun	17	7.17
5113	stable	adjective	16	7.16
5114	defy	verb	13	7.16
5115	deviation	noun	18	7.15
5116	wrist	noun	16	7.15
5117	outlet	noun	15	7.15
5118	grease	noun	12	7.15
5119	dialect	noun	14	7.14
5120	ominous	adjective	12	7.14
5121	bastard	noun	27	7.13
5122	cave	noun	15	7.13
5123	Eddie	prop. noun	31	7.12
5124	physiological	adjective	22	7.12
5125	sculpture	noun	18	7.12
5126	bloom	verb	17	7.12
5126	educator	noun	17	7.12
5128	hurry	noun	19	7.11
5129	understandable	adjective	13	7.11
5130	forehead	noun	18	7.10
5131	arch	verb	15	7.10
5132	irrelevant	adjective	14	7.10
5133	eagerly	adverb	13	7.10
5134	static	adjective	12	7.10
5135	deduction	noun	23	7.09
5136	subjective	adjective	18	7.09
5137	cardinal	noun	16	7.09
5138	adequately	adverb	14	7.09
5139	misunderstand	verb	12	7.09
5140	invade	verb	15	7.08
5141	endeavor	noun	14	7.08
5142	tightly	adverb	13	7.08
5143	drain	verb	16	7.07
5144	creek	noun	15	7.07
5144	renaissance	noun	15	7.07
5146	beautifully	adverb	14	7.07
5147	bound	noun	13	7.07
5148	transformation	noun	20	7.06
5149	hardware	noun	11	7.06
5150	Owen	prop. noun	25	7.05
5151	Rose	prop. noun	17	7.05
5152	creator	noun	16	7.05
5153	sentimental	adjective	15	7.05
5154	spray	verb	14	7.05
5155	populate	verb	13	7.05
5155	privately	adverb	13	7.05
5157	hopeful	adjective	12	7.05
5158	crouch	verb	22	7.04
5159	bathroom	noun	19	7.04
5160	superiority	noun	14	7.04
5161	idle	adjective	12	7.04
5162	pit	noun	17	7.02

5163	heater	noun	15	7.01	5163	cemetery	noun	15	7.02
5164	ankle	noun	15	6.90	5164	heater	noun	15	7.01
5165	distort	verb	15	6.84	5165	round	adverb	14	7.01
5166	boulevard	noun	15	6.80	5166	commonplace	adjective	13	7.01
5167	criminal	noun	15	6.78	5167	ordinarily	adverb	14	7.00
5168	cruel	adjective	15	6.74	5168	loosely	adverb	11	7.00
5169	level	adjective	15	6.73	5169	Di	prop. noun	21	6.99
5170	scenery	noun	15	6.69	5170	glow	noun	14	6.98
5171	breed	noun	15	6.68	5171	echo	verb	12	6.98
5172	cult	noun	15	6.66	5172	chip	noun	19	6.97
5173	surrender	noun	15	6.62	5173	suck	verb	18	6.97
5174	streetcar	noun	15	6.59	5174	hardly	qualifier	13	6.97
5175	horrible	adjective	15	6.55	5174	monstrous	adjective	13	6.97
5176	compile	verb	15	6.53	5176	classic	noun	14	6.95
5177	domination	noun	15	6.50	5176	terrify	verb	14	6.95
5178	orange	noun	15	6.45	5178	Picasso	prop. noun	17	6.94
5179	heap	noun	15	6.44	5179	uncomfortable	adjective	14	6.94
5180	disappoint	verb	15	6.40	5180	underground	adjective	13	6.94
5181	romance	noun	15	6.37	5181	rotate	verb	21	6.93
5182	preventive	adjective	15	6.30	5182	snatch	verb	17	6.93
5183	say	exclam.	15	6.27	5183	lick	verb	14	6.93
5184	vice-president	noun	15	6.25	5184	sample	verb	20	6.92
5185	rid	adjective	15	6.23	5185	reasoning	noun	12	6.91
5186	duck	verb	15	6.21	5185	retreat	noun	12	6.91
5187	stride	verb	15	6.20	5187	thrust	noun	11	6.91
5188	federation	noun	15	6.19	5188	latter	noun	10	6.91
5189	survivor	noun	15	6.16	5189	motivate	verb	16	6.90
5190	persistent	adjective	15	6.11	5190	ankle	noun	15	6.90
5191	executive	adjective	15	6.10	5191	delegate	noun	21	6.89
5192	sewer	noun	15	6.07	5192	dentist	noun	19	6.89
5193	gold	adjective	15	6.05	5193	Burma	prop. noun	17	6.89
5194	cleaning	noun	15	6.03	5194	donate	verb	12	6.89
5195	newest	sem. sup.	15	5.98	5195	Sandburg	prop. noun	27	6.88
5196	molecule	noun	15	5.95	5196	Stevenson	prop. noun	17	6.88
5197	diamond	noun	15	5.91	5197	finest	sem. sup.	16	6.88
5198	curb	noun	15	5.90	5198	warrant	noun	14	6.88
5199	tentative	adjective	15	5.89	5199	aide	noun	13	6.88
5200	tennis	noun	15	5.78	5199	welcome	noun	13	6.88
5201	crash	noun	15	5.76	5201	durable	adjective	12	6.88
5202	hey	exclam.	15	5.75	5202	rehabilitation	noun	23	6.87
5203	aspiration	noun	15	5.72	5203	Oregon	prop. noun	14	6.87
5204	vitamin	noun	15	5.68	5204	aggression	noun	13	6.87
5205	alcohol	noun	15	5.61	5204	integral	adjective	13	6.87
5206	smooth	verb	15	5.58	5206	export	noun	19	6.86
5207	settler	noun	15	5.56	5207	arrow	noun	20	6.85
5208	hymn	noun	15	5.50	5208	subdue	verb	12	6.85
5209	bake	verb	15	5.44	5209	tropical	adjective	11	6.85
5209	cab	noun	15	5.44	5210	biological	adjective	20	6.84
5211	pump	noun	15	5.43	5211	distort	verb	15	6.84
5212	clearer	comp. adj.	15	5.33	5212	elegant	adjective	14	6.84
5213	R	prop. noun	15	5.16	5213	bid	noun	19	6.83
5214	coalition	noun	15	5.15	5214	autonomy	noun	18	6.83
5215	contact	verb	15	5.10	5215	tribe	noun	17	6.83
5216	attribute	noun	15	5.04	5216	Lester	prop. noun	14	6.83
5217	drain	noun	15	5.03	5217	duration	noun	12	6.83
5218	apple	noun	15	5.01	5218	Mills	prop. noun	20	6.82
5219	bearing	noun	14	11.09	5219	remedy	noun	16	6.82
5220	protective	adjective	14	10.62	5220	leisure	noun	12	6.82
5221	foresee	verb	14	10.45	5221	crown	verb	11	6.82
5221	supervise	verb	14	10.45	5222	profile	noun	18	6.81
5223	countless	adjective	14	10.44	5223	wrong	noun	14	6.81
5224	customary	adjective	14	10.05	5224	Stalin	prop. noun	21	6.80
5225	deed	noun	14	9.88	5225	boulevard	noun	15	6.80
5226	mild	adjective	14	9.87	5226	cripple	verb	12	6.80
5227	oldest	sem. sup.	14	9.72	5226	honestly	adverb	12	6.80
5228	thirty-five	card. num.	14	9.70	5228	wire	verb	11	6.80
5229	accent	noun	14	9.69	5229	chlorine	noun	33	6.79
5230	familiarity	noun	14	9.64	5230	conformity	noun	16	6.79
5231	divorce	verb	14	9.50	5230	judicial	adjective	16	6.79
5232	vigor	noun	14	9.42	5232	master	verb	13	6.79
5233	weekly	adjective	14	9.30	5233	mingle	verb	12	6.79
5234	surprisingly	adverb	14	9.09	5234	repair	verb	17	6.78
5235	plainly	adverb	14	9.01	5235	criminal	noun	15	6.78
5235	seemingly	adverb	14	9.01	5236	shed	verb	12	6.77
5237	severely	adverb	14	8.98	5237	suppress	verb	10	6.77
5238	obscure	verb	14	8.95	5238	deposit	noun	14	6.76
5239	railway	noun	14	8.93	5238	experimentation	noun	14	6.76
5240	intact	adjective	14	8.92	5238	ripe	adjective	14	6.76
5241	vulnerable	adjective	14	8.90	5238	temper	noun	14	6.76
5242	rescue	verb	14	8.80	5242	squarely	adverb	11	6.76
5243	grandmother	noun	14	8.78	5243	shipment	noun	18	6.75
5243	impersonal	adjective	14	8.78	5244	evidence	verb	14	6.75
5243	shallow	adjective	14	8.78	5245	uniform	adjective	28	6.74
5243	twenty-four	card. num.	14	8.78	5246	cruel	adjective	15	6.74
5247	globe	noun	14	8.74	5247	paradise	noun	12	6.74
5248	drown	verb	14	8.72	5248	inflict	verb	11	6.74
5249	one-third	noun	14	8.65	5248	innovation	noun	11	6.74
5250	odds	pl. noun	14	8.63	5250	level	adjective	15	6.73
5250	sheer	adjective	14	8.63	5251	balloon	noun	13	6.73

5252	profitable	adjective	14	8.58
5253	institute	verb	14	8.55
5254	prosperity	noun	14	8.54
5255	infant	noun	14	8.48
5256	harder	comp. adv.	14	8.45
5257	spell	verb	14	8.41
5258	preferably	adverb	14	8.36
5259	stimulation	noun	14	8.34
5260	invoke	verb	14	8.28
5260	rumor	noun	14	8.28
5262	short	adverb	14	8.26
5263	disposition	noun	14	8.25
5264	deprive	verb	14	8.23
5265	good-bye	exclam.	14	8.21
5266	afterwards	adverb	14	8.20
5267	preside	verb	14	8.17
5268	peel	verb	14	8.14
5269	comply	verb	14	8.09
5270	handful	noun	14	8.08
5271	rebellion	noun	14	8.02
5272	pentagon	noun	14	8.01
5273	enclose	verb	14	7.98
5273	hasten	verb	14	7.98
5275	shorten	verb	14	7.97
5276	ego	noun	14	7.92
5276	resort	verb	14	7.92
5278	provoke	verb	14	7.91
5279	disturbing	adjective	14	7.89
5280	brutality	noun	14	7.82
5281	package	verb	14	7.81
5282	immense	adjective	14	7.79
5283	container	noun	14	7.77
5284	capitalism	noun	14	7.76
5285	applause	noun	14	7.69
5285	heavier	comp. adj.	14	7.69
5287	stability	noun	14	7.64
5288	tide	noun	14	7.63
5289	alike	adverb	14	7.62
5289	foster	verb	14	7.62
5291	Bryan	prop. noun	14	7.61
5291	Columbus	prop. noun	14	7.61
5293	allege	verb	14	7.57
5294	corruption	noun	14	7.55
5294	fully	qualifier	14	7.55
5296	singular	adjective	14	7.54
5297	Arizona	prop. noun	14	7.51
5298	influential	adjective	14	7.48
5298	pig	noun	14	7.48
5300	bitterly	adverb	14	7.47
5300	incidentally	adverb	14	7.47
5302	Egypt	prop. noun	14	7.45
5302	sensible	adjective	14	7.45
5304	diagnosis	noun	14	7.41
5304	immigrant	noun	14	7.41
5304	Yale	prop. noun	14	7.41
5307	embody	verb	14	7.40
5307	scrutiny	noun	14	7.40
5309	abide	verb	14	7.39
5309	encouragement	noun	14	7.39
5309	involvement	noun	14	7.39
5312	alteration	noun	14	7.36
5312	secure	adjective	14	7.36
5314	collar	noun	14	7.35
5314	spell	noun	14	7.35
5316	hopeless	adjective	14	7.32
5317	awful	adjective	14	7.31
5318	V.	prop. noun	14	7.30
5319	dictate	verb	14	7.24
5320	hardship	noun	14	7.22
5321	calm	verb	14	7.21
5322	advocate	verb	14	7.18
5323	dialect	noun	14	7.14
5324	irrelevant	adjective	14	7.10
5325	adequately	adverb	14	7.09
5326	endeavor	noun	14	7.08
5327	beautifully	adverb	14	7.07
5328	spray	verb	14	7.05
5329	superiority	noun	14	7.04
5330	round	adverb	14	7.01
5331	ordinarily	adverb	14	7.00
5332	glow	noun	14	6.98
5333	classic	noun	14	6.95
5333	terrify	verb	14	6.95
5335	uncomfortable	adjective	14	6.94
5336	lick	verb	14	6.93
5337	warrant	noun	14	6.88
5338	Oregon	prop. noun	14	6.87
5339	elegant	adjective	14	6.84
5340	Lester	prop. noun	14	6.83
5251	standpoint	noun	13	6.73
5253	prohibition	noun	14	6.72
5254	rebel	verb	11	6.72
5255	speculate	verb	13	6.71
5256	thoughtful	adjective	11	6.71
5257	Max	prop. noun	14	6.70
5258	scenery	noun	15	6.69
5259	grim	adjective	14	6.69
5259	parallel	adjective	14	6.69
5261	youthful	adjective	12	6.69
5262	Byron	prop. noun	20	6.68
5263	ghetto	noun	16	6.68
5264	breed	noun	15	6.68
5265	beckon	verb	12	6.68
5266	stack	verb	11	6.68
5267	drill	verb	30	6.66
5268	technological	adjective	18	6.66
5269	x-ray	noun	16	6.66
5270	cult	noun	15	6.66
5271	exchange	verb	13	6.66
5271	flood	verb	13	6.66
5273	transport	verb	12	6.66
5274	indicator	noun	17	6.65
5274	proclamation	noun	17	6.65
5276	newcomer	noun	14	6.65
5277	fantasy	noun	18	6.64
5278	kick	noun	13	6.64
5278	shaft	noun	13	6.64
5280	pianist	noun	21	6.63
5281	handy	adjective	13	6.63
5281	liquidation	noun	13	6.63
5283	gin	noun	24	6.62
5284	Arnold	prop. noun	22	6.62
5285	surrender	noun	15	6.62
5286	import	verb	12	6.62
5287	toast	noun	14	6.61
5288	content	verb	12	6.61
5289	pop	verb	17	6.60
5290	noticeable	adjective	11	6.60
5291	streetcar	noun	15	6.59
5292	Eugene	prop. noun	27	6.58
5293	maximum	noun	14	6.58
5294	cluster	noun	13	6.58
5294	infection	noun	13	6.58
5296	tournament	noun	25	6.57
5297	ashamed	adjective	17	6.57
5297	comparative	adjective	17	6.57
5299	sport	verb	14	6.57
5300	correlation	noun	18	6.56
5301	pump	verb	12	6.56
5302	bat	noun	18	6.55
5303	horrible	adjective	15	6.55
5304	forecast	verb	14	6.55
5305	implicit	adjective	13	6.55
5306	wage	verb	11	6.55
5307	asset	noun	18	6.54
5307	athletic	adjective	18	6.54
5309	fragment	noun	16	6.54
5310	culminate	verb	11	6.54
5310	facet	noun	11	6.54
5312	gum	noun	18	6.53
5313	compile	verb	15	6.53
5314	Kent	prop. noun	14	6.53
5315	journalism	noun	13	6.53
5315	permanently	adverb	13	6.53
5317	grin	noun	14	6.52
5317	higher	comp. adv.	14	6.52
5317	raid	noun	14	6.52
5320	pertain	verb	13	6.52
5321	conflict	verb	12	6.52
5322	unexpectedly	adverb	11	6.51
5323	Gross	prop. noun	30	6.50
5324	domination	noun	15	6.50
5325	wheel	verb	11	6.50
5326	dividend	noun	14	6.49
5327	descent	noun	11	6.49
5328	Nelson	prop. noun	16	6.47
5329	Australia	prop. noun	11	6.47
5330	Fromm	prop. noun	30	6.46
5331	awaken	verb	13	6.46
5332	principally	adverb	10	6.46
5333	ace	noun	19	6.45
5333	Salem	prop. noun	19	6.45
5335	analyst	noun	16	6.45
5336	orange	noun	15	6.45
5337	gaiety	noun	13	6.45
5338	economical	adjective	22	6.44
5339	sprawl	verb	18	6.44
5340	heap	noun	15	6.44

5341	wrong	noun	14	6.81
5342	deposit	noun	14	6.76
5342	experimentation	noun	14	6.76
5342	ripe	adjective	14	6.76
5342	temper	noun	14	6.76
5346	evidence	verb	14	6.75
5347	prohibition	noun	14	6.72
5348	Max	prop. noun	14	6.70
5349	grim	adjective	14	6.69
5349	parallel	adjective	14	6.69
5351	newcomer	noun	14	6.65
5352	toast	noun	14	6.61
5353	maximum	noun	14	6.58
5354	sport	verb	14	6.57
5355	forecast	verb	14	6.55
5356	Kent	prop. noun	14	6.53
5357	grin	noun	14	6.52
5357	higher	comp. adv.	14	6.52
5357	raid	noun	14	6.52
5360	dividend	noun	14	6.49
5361	repel	verb	14	6.44
5362	zone	noun	14	6.43
5363	ivory	noun	14	6.40
5363	rain	verb	14	6.40
5363	withhold	verb	14	6.40
5363	youngest	sup. adj.	14	6.40
5367	theologian	noun	14	6.38
5368	manpower	noun	14	6.33
5369	sacrifice	verb	14	6.32
5370	punish	verb	14	6.27
5371	thoughtfully	adverb	14	6.26
5372	rear	verb	14	6.21
5373	comrade	noun	14	6.19
5374	amaze	verb	14	6.14
5375	Churchill	prop. noun	14	6.12
5376	auditorium	noun	14	6.08
5377	ad	noun	14	6.07
5377	plea	noun	14	6.07
5379	annually	adverb	14	6.06
5379	disorder	noun	14	6.06
5381	alien	adjective	14	6.04
5381	stereotype	noun	14	6.04
5383	equal	verb	14	6.02
5384	discipline	verb	14	6.00
5385	warrant	verb	14	5.95
5386	ah	exclam.	14	5.93
5387	dash	verb	14	5.92
5388	attendant	noun	14	5.89
5388	foe	noun	14	5.89
5390	lamb	noun	14	5.85
5391	square	verb	14	5.84
5392	pickup	noun	14	5.81
5393	fisherman	noun	14	5.80
5394	toy	noun	14	5.78
5395	Theodore	prop. noun	14	5.76
5396	orient	verb	14	5.75
5397	psychology	noun	14	5.74
5398	treasurer	noun	14	5.72
5399	overnight	adverb	14	5.70
5400	amid	prep.	14	5.67
5401	advertising	noun	14	5.64
5402	reactionary	adjective	14	5.60
5403	vocal	adjective	14	5.58
5404	evolution	noun	14	5.55
5404	sanction	noun	14	5.55
5406	canyon	noun	14	5.48
5406	Helen	prop. noun	14	5.48
5408	Belgian	adjective	14	5.47
5409	disable	verb	14	5.45
5410	generalize	verb	14	5.40
5411	engineering	noun	14	5.38
5411	hail	verb	14	5.38
5411	suspension	noun	14	5.38
5414	excellence	noun	14	5.37
5415	momentum	noun	14	5.33
5415	refugee	noun	14	5.33
5417	chancellor	noun	14	5.30
5418	pork	noun	14	5.25
5419	dump	verb	14	5.19
5420	incomplete	adjective	14	5.16
5421	controller	noun	14	5.10
5422	sensibility	noun	14	5.06
5423	appetite	noun	14	5.05
5423	premium	noun	14	5.05
5423	thumb	noun	14	5.05
5426	diversity	noun	14	5.04
5426	pet	noun	14	5.04
5428	lowest	sem. sup.	13	9.47
5429	suspicious	adjective	13	9.44

5341	repel	verb	14	6.44
5342	Day	prop. noun	13	6.44
5342	motif	noun	13	6.44
5342	permit	noun	13	6.44
5342	unlimited	adjective	13	6.44
5346	diffusion	noun	24	6.43
5347	zone	noun	14	6.43
5348	thus	qualifier	12	6.43
5349	morale	noun	17	6.42
5350	venture	verb	11	6.42
5351	empirical	adjective	23	6.41
5351	pill	noun	23	6.41
5353	mock	verb	11	6.41
5354	disappoint	verb	15	6.40
5355	ivory	noun	14	6.40
5355	rain	verb	14	6.40
5355	withhold	verb	14	6.40
5355	youngest	sup. adj.	14	6.40
5359	civilize	verb	12	6.40
5360	abruptly	adverb	18	6.39
5361	confrontation	noun	17	6.39
5362	long	verb	16	6.39
5362	transmission	noun	16	6.39
5364	accumulation	noun	11	6.39
5364	intent	noun	11	6.39
5366	Austin	prop. noun	20	6.38
5367	theologian	noun	14	6.38
5368	mortar	noun	13	6.38
5369	amuse	verb	12	6.38
5369	comfortably	adverb	12	6.38
5371	romance	noun	15	6.37
5372	revolve	verb	12	6.37
5373	undermine	verb	11	6.37
5374	disagreement	noun	13	6.36
5375	dusty	adjective	16	6.35
5376	Hamilton	prop. noun	20	6.34
5376	telegraph	noun	20	6.34
5378	mislead	verb	12	6.34
5378	photograph	verb	12	6.34
5380	painfully	adverb	11	6.34
5380	trivial	adjective	11	6.34
5382	manpower	noun	14	6.33
5383	wealthy	adjective	12	6.33
5384	squad	noun	20	6.32
5385	lemon	noun	16	6.32
5386	sacrifice	verb	14	6.32
5387	advocate	noun	12	6.32
5387	stubborn	adjective	12	6.32
5389	angular	adjective	16	6.31
5389	magic	noun	16	6.31
5391	guarantee	noun	12	6.31
5392	soak	verb	18	6.30
5393	preventive	adjective	15	6.30
5394	contrary	noun	11	6.30
5395	Miami	prop. noun	25	6.29
5396	stage	verb	21	6.29
5397	fan	verb	13	6.29
5397	Graham	prop. noun	13	6.29
5399	beyond	adverb	12	6.29
5399	tin	noun	12	6.29
5401	prosecute	verb	10	6.29
5402	Stuart	prop. noun	16	6.28
5403	emotionally	adverb	13	6.28
5404	manuscript	noun	12	6.28
5404	script	noun	12	6.28
5406	acreage	noun	11	6.28
5406	eventual	adjective	11	6.28
5408	say	exclam.	15	6.27
5409	punish	verb	14	6.27
5410	thoughtfully	adverb	14	6.26
5411	root	verb	13	6.26
5412	purity	noun	12	6.26
5413	restoration	noun	11	6.26
5414	particular	noun	10	6.26
5414	simplest	sem. sup.	10	6.26
5416	T	prop. noun	36	6.25
5417	Patchen	prop. noun	33	6.25
5418	vice-president	noun	15	6.25
5419	black	noun	11	6.25
5420	cumulative	adjective	13	6.24
5420	delegation	noun	13	6.24
5420	tomb	noun	13	6.24
5423	rite	noun	12	6.24
5424	happier	comp. adj.	11	6.24
5424	paradoxically	adverb	11	6.24
5426	projection	noun	19	6.23
5427	Brooks	prop. noun	17	6.23
5428	rid	adjective	15	6.23
5429	Winston	prop. noun	40	6.22

5430	outset	noun	13	8.93
5431	offer	noun	13	8.88
5432	praise	noun	13	8.85
5433	bulk	noun	13	8.83
5433	cruelty	noun	13	8.83
5435	patron	noun	13	8.81
5436	restless	adjective	13	8.61
5437	lie	verb	13	8.48
5438	swift	adjective	13	8.46
5439	acute	adjective	13	8.44
5440	ensue	verb	13	8.42
5441	alert	verb	13	8.37
5441	safely	adverb	13	8.37
5443	inhabitant	noun	13	8.35
5444	further	verb	13	8.31
5445	slightest	sem. sup.	13	8.29
5446	wholly	adverb	13	8.22
5447	bow	verb	13	8.21
5448	grandfather	noun	13	8.20
5449	prediction	noun	13	8.13
5450	flourish	verb	13	8.08
5451	detach	verb	13	8.07
5451	half	qualifier	13	8.07
5451	outline	verb	13	8.07
5451	spur	noun	13	8.07
5455	imperial	adjective	13	8.06
5455	unfair	adjective	13	8.06
5457	top	verb	13	8.05
5458	entail	verb	13	8.04
5459	undue	adjective	13	8.03
5460	nonsense	noun	13	7.98
5461	notably	adverb	13	7.96
5462	coincidence	noun	13	7.93
5463	probe	verb	13	7.92
5464	correctly	adverb	13	7.91
5465	disrupt	verb	13	7.90
5466	bound	verb	13	7.86
5466	fearful	adjective	13	7.86
5466	gifted	adjective	13	7.86
5466	vigorously	adverb	13	7.86
5470	fashion	verb	13	7.85
5471	relinquish	verb	13	7.83
5472	farewell	noun	13	7.77
5473	indeed	post-qual.	13	7.73
5473	ruler	noun	13	7.73
5475	competitor	noun	13	7.72
5475	doubtless	adverb	13	7.72
5477	elderly	adjective	13	7.66
5477	imitate	verb	13	7.66
5479	fond	adjective	13	7.64
5480	ancestor	noun	13	7.54
5481	dazzle	verb	13	7.51
5482	imaginative	adjective	13	7.49
5482	swing	noun	13	7.49
5484	faster	comp. adv.	13	7.47
5485	prejudice	noun	13	7.46
5486	compress	verb	13	7.41
5486	earnestly	adverb	13	7.41
5488	flat	noun	13	7.37
5489	sinister	adjective	13	7.35
5490	abundance	noun	13	7.33
5491	portable	adjective	13	7.32
5492	drainage	noun	13	7.31
5492	expend	verb	13	7.31
5492	outline	noun	13	7.31
5495	discount	noun	13	7.28
5496	resemblance	noun	13	7.26
5497	liberate	verb	13	7.24
5497	reunion	noun	13	7.24
5499	transmit	verb	13	7.23
5500	solitary	adjective	13	7.22
5501	frankly	adverb	13	7.21
5501	mighty	qualifier	13	7.21
5503	urgency	noun	13	7.20
5504	confide	verb	13	7.18
5505	defy	verb	13	7.16
5506	understandable	adjective	13	7.11
5507	eagerly	adverb	13	7.10
5508	tightly	adverb	13	7.08
5509	bound	noun	13	7.07
5510	populate	verb	13	7.05
5510	privately	adverb	13	7.05
5512	commonplace	adjective	13	7.01
5513	hardly	qualifier	13	6.97
5513	monstrous	adjective	13	6.97
5515	underground	adjective	13	6.94
5516	aide	noun	13	6.88
5516	welcome	noun	13	6.88
5518	aggression	noun	13	6.87
5430	Swift	prop. noun	22	6.22
5431	Manhattan	prop. noun	21	6.21
5432	duck	verb	15	6.21
5433	rear	verb	14	6.21
5434	fashionable	adjective	12	6.21
5435	economically	adverb	11	6.21
5436	trim	verb	16	6.20
5437	stride	verb	15	6.20
5438	cleaner	noun	13	6.20
5438	post	verb	13	6.20
5440	elite	noun	12	6.20
5441	applaud	verb	11	6.20
5442	cubic	adjective	20	6.19
5443	aluminum	noun	18	6.19
5443	Tokyo	prop. noun	18	6.19
5445	federation	noun	15	6.19
5446	comrade	noun	14	6.19
5447	male	adjective	13	6.19
5447	might	noun	13	6.19
5449	murmur	verb	22	6.18
5450	Hammarskjold	prop. noun	21	6.18
5451	thigh	noun	16	6.18
5452	underdeveloped	adjective	12	6.18
5453	lengthy	adjective	11	6.18
5454	Italian	prop. noun	11	6.17
5455	Puerto	prop. noun	24	6.16
5456	formidable	adjective	16	6.16
5457	survivor	noun	15	6.16
5458	biography	noun	13	6.16
5459	linguist	noun	24	6.15
5460	strict	adjective	11	6.15
5461	Harvey	prop. noun	19	6.14
5462	amaze	verb	14	6.14
5463	anecdote	noun	13	6.14
5464	Dwight	prop. noun	12	6.14
5465	unaware	adjective	13	6.13
5466	partial	adjective	11	6.13
5467	outfit	noun	16	6.12
5467	statistical	adjective	16	6.12
5467	unemployment	noun	16	6.12
5470	Churchill	prop. noun	14	6.12
5471	preoccupy	verb	12	6.12
5472	patriot	noun	11	6.12
5473	alienation	noun	22	6.11
5474	interaction	noun	20	6.11
5475	Biblical	adjective	18	6.11
5476	Denver	prop. noun	17	6.11
5477	persistent	adjective	15	6.11
5478	foliage	noun	12	6.11
5479	executive	adjective	15	6.10
5480	Japanese	prop. noun	13	6.10
5481	quaint	adjective	12	6.10
5482	moist	adjective	11	6.10
5483	pilgrimage	noun	10	6.10
5484	anti-trust	adjective	27	6.09
5485	acceleration	noun	19	6.09
5486	casually	adverb	13	6.09
5487	shear	noun	38	6.08
5488	ambiguity	noun	18	6.08
5489	auditorium	noun	14	6.08
5490	gigantic	adjective	10	6.08
5491	generator	noun	23	6.07
5492	sewer	noun	15	6.07
5493	ad	noun	14	6.07
5493	plea	noun	14	6.07
5495	dissatisfaction	noun	10	6.07
5495	traditionally	adverb	10	6.07
5497	zero	card. num.	17	6.06
5498	annually	adverb	14	6.06
5498	disorder	noun	14	6.06
5500	conservation	noun	13	6.06
5501	comparatively	qualifier	12	6.06
5502	gold	adjective	15	6.05
5503	rotation	noun	12	6.05
5504	isolation	noun	16	6.04
5505	alien	adjective	14	6.04
5505	stereotype	noun	14	6.04
5507	stern	adjective	13	6.04
5508	learning	noun	12	6.04
5509	Easter	prop. noun	11	6.04
5510	ammunition	noun	18	6.03
5511	cleaning	noun	15	6.03
5512	tumble	verb	17	6.02
5513	equal	verb	14	6.02
5514	circulate	verb	11	6.02
5514	impair	verb	11	6.02
5516	spur	verb	10	6.02
5517	chill	verb	12	6.01
5517	scratch	noun	12	6.01

5518	integral	adjective	13	6.87
5520	master	verb	13	6.79
5521	balloon	noun	13	6.73
5521	standpoint	noun	13	6.73
5523	speculate	verb	13	6.71
5524	exchange	verb	13	6.66
5524	flood	verb	13	6.66
5526	kick	noun	13	6.64
5526	shaft	noun	13	6.64
5528	handy	adjective	13	6.63
5528	liquidation	noun	13	6.63
5530	cluster	noun	13	6.58
5530	infection	noun	13	6.58
5532	implicit	adjective	13	6.55
5533	journalism	noun	13	6.53
5533	permanently	adverb	13	6.53
5535	pertain	verb	13	6.52
5536	awaken	verb	13	6.46
5537	gaiety	noun	13	6.45
5538	Day	prop. noun	13	6.44
5538	motif	noun	13	6.44
5538	permit	noun	13	6.44
5538	unlimited	adjective	13	6.44
5542	mortar	noun	13	6.38
5543	disagreement	noun	13	6.36
5544	fan	verb	13	6.29
5544	Graham	prop. noun	13	6.29
5546	emotionally	adverb	13	6.28
5547	root	verb	13	6.26
5548	cumulative	adjective	13	6.24
5548	delegation	noun	13	6.24
5548	tomb	noun	13	6.24
5551	cleaner	noun	13	6.20
5551	post	verb	13	6.20
5553	male	adjective	13	6.19
5553	might	noun	13	6.19
5555	biography	noun	13	6.16
5556	anecdote	noun	13	6.14
5557	unaware	adjective	13	6.13
5558	Japanese	prop. noun	13	6.10
5559	casually	adverb	13	6.09
5560	conservation	noun	13	6.06
5561	stern	adjective	13	6.04
5562	Birmingham	prop. noun	13	5.97
5563	diverse	adjective	13	5.92
5564	single	verb	13	5.83
5565	summon	verb	13	5.82
5566	ethnic	adjective	13	5.80
5567	high	noun	13	5.74
5568	disadvantage	noun	13	5.73
5568	sway	verb	13	5.73
5570	everyday	adjective	13	5.72
5571	guardian	noun	13	5.71
5571	undergraduate	noun	13	5.71
5573	notify	verb	13	5.70
5573	transparent	adjective	13	5.70
5575	bark	noun	13	5.69
5576	fatigue	noun	13	5.66
5577	favorably	adverb	13	5.65
5578	modernization	noun	13	5.64
5579	sailor	noun	13	5.63
5580	supervisor	noun	13	5.58
5581	ant	noun	13	5.57
5582	pull	noun	13	5.54
5583	reservoir	noun	13	5.52
5584	Scotland	prop. noun	13	5.51
5585	Lloyd	prop. noun	13	5.50
5586	Herman	prop. noun	13	5.48
5586	resign	verb	13	5.48
5588	miserable	adjective	13	5.46
5589	cane	noun	13	5.45
5589	Kremlin	prop. noun	13	5.45
5589	superimpose	verb	13	5.45
5592	drawer	noun	13	5.43
5593	lean	adjective	13	5.41
5594	irony	noun	13	5.40
5595	drunk	noun	13	5.39
5596	Michael	prop. noun	13	5.37
5596	separately	adverb	13	5.37
5598	solidarity	noun	13	5.35
5599	allot	verb	13	5.34
5600	inject	verb	13	5.30
5601	peer	noun	13	5.29
5601	therapeutic	adjective	13	5.29
5603	ordering	noun	13	5.28
5604	profess	verb	13	5.27
5604	stain	noun	13	5.27
5606	reckon	verb	13	5.26
5607	juvenile	adjective	13	5.22
5519	discipline	verb	14	6.00
5520	brightness	noun	18	5.99
5521	I.	prop. noun	16	5.99
5522	antenna	noun	17	5.98
5522	Victor	prop. noun	17	5.98
5524	newest	sem. sup.	15	5.98
5525	edge	verb	12	5.98
5525	logically	adverb	12	5.98
5527	comfort	verb	11	5.98
5528	discard	verb	9	5.98
5529	computer	noun	18	5.97
5530	Birmingham	prop. noun	13	5.97
5531	escort	verb	11	5.96
5531	greatness	noun	11	5.96
5531	passive	adjective	11	5.96
5534	heading	noun	19	5.95
5535	compound	verb	16	5.95
5536	molecule	noun	15	5.95
5537	warrant	verb	14	5.95
5538	nominate	verb	12	5.95
5538	sixteenth	ord. num.	12	5.95
5540	bleed	verb	18	5.94
5541	blame	noun	11	5.94
5541	prosecution	noun	11	5.94
5543	ah	exclam.	14	5.93
5544	forego	verb	12	5.93
5545	freshman	noun	11	5.93
5546	polynomial	noun	37	5.92
5546	serum	noun	37	5.92
5548	slash	verb	18	5.92
5549	dash	verb	14	5.92
5550	diverse	adjective	13	5.92
5551	Polish	adjective	11	5.92
5552	treasure	noun	10	5.92
5552	well-being	noun	10	5.92
5554	electronics	noun	32	5.91
5555	diamond	noun	15	5.91
5556	harsh	adjective	12	5.91
5557	obscure	adjective	11	5.91
5558	Cromwell	prop. noun	22	5.90
5559	frieze	noun	16	5.90
5560	curb	noun	15	5.90
5561	fulfillment	noun	12	5.90
5561	Herbert	prop. noun	12	5.90
5563	stoop	verb	11	5.90
5564	indirect	adjective	21	5.89
5565	tentative	adjective	15	5.89
5566	attendant	noun	14	5.89
5566	foe	noun	14	5.89
5568	elemental	adjective	11	5.89
5568	veil	noun	11	5.89
5570	Dartmouth	prop. noun	33	5.87
5571	stream	verb	12	5.87
5572	absolutely	adverb	10	5.87
5573	despise	verb	12	5.86
5573	precedent	noun	12	5.86
5575	diversion	noun	11	5.86
5575	picket	noun	11	5.86
5577	intricate	adjective	10	5.86
5577	trap	verb	10	5.86
5579	bishop	noun	20	5.85
5580	lamb	noun	14	5.85
5581	Byrd	prop. noun	12	5.85
5582	overlap	verb	11	5.85
5583	Red	prop. noun	22	5.84
5584	square	verb	14	5.84
5585	vacant	adjective	11	5.84
5586	magnify	verb	10	5.84
5587	dean	noun	18	5.83
5587	partnership	noun	18	5.83
5589	bass	noun	16	5.83
5590	single	verb	13	5.83
5591	folklore	noun	30	5.82
5592	gown	noun	18	5.82
5592	Madame	prop. noun	18	5.82
5594	summon	verb	13	5.82
5595	dispatch	verb	12	5.82
5595	privacy	noun	12	5.82
5597	pickup	noun	14	5.81
5598	empty	verb	12	5.81
5599	Cooper	prop. noun	17	5.80
5600	fisherman	noun	14	5.80
5601	ethnic	adjective	13	5.80
5602	ordinance	noun	12	5.80
5602	princess	noun	12	5.80
5604	satisfactorily	adverb	11	5.80
5605	E	prop. noun	23	5.79
5606	red	noun	11	5.79
5606	sum	verb	11	5.79

5607	Richardson	prop. noun	13	5.22
5609	dough	noun	13	5.20
5609	gossip	noun	13	5.20
5611	depreciation	noun	13	5.12
5611	N.Y.	prop. noun	13	5.12
5611	wreck	verb	13	5.12
5614	financing	noun	13	5.11
5615	sincerity	noun	13	5.07
5616	Green	prop. noun	13	5.04
5617	witch	noun	13	5.03
5618	ironic	adjective	13	5.02
5619	chord	noun	13	5.01
5620	depress	verb	13	5.00
5621	Richmond	prop. noun	12	8.25
5622	supposedly	adverb	12	8.10
5623	largely	qualifier	12	7.98
5624	theatrical	adjective	12	7.69
5625	architecture	noun	12	7.67
5626	augment	verb	12	7.66
5627	solemn	adjective	12	7.65
5628	successive	adjective	12	7.64
5629	elevate	verb	12	7.62
5630	consciously	adverb	12	7.60
5630	consultation	noun	12	7.60
5630	water	verb	12	7.60
5633	compartment	noun	12	7.58
5634	harvest	noun	12	7.56
5635	irregularity	noun	12	7.50
5636	traverse	verb	12	7.45
5637	shrink	verb	12	7.28
5638	penetrating	adjective	12	7.23
5639	grease	noun	12	7.15
5640	ominous	adjective	12	7.14
5641	static	adjective	12	7.10
5642	misunderstand	verb	12	7.09
5643	hopeful	adjective	12	7.05
5644	idle	adjective	12	7.04
5645	echo	verb	12	6.98
5646	reasoning	noun	12	6.91
5646	retreat	noun	12	6.91
5648	donate	verb	12	6.89
5649	durable	adjective	12	6.88
5650	subdue	verb	12	6.85
5651	duration	noun	12	6.83
5652	leisure	noun	12	6.82
5653	cripple	verb	12	6.80
5653	honestly	adverb	12	6.80
5655	mingle	verb	12	6.79
5656	shed	verb	12	6.77
5657	paradise	noun	12	6.74
5658	youthful	adjective	12	6.69
5659	beckon	verb	12	6.68
5660	transport	verb	12	6.66
5661	import	verb	12	6.62
5662	content	verb	12	6.61
5663	pump	verb	12	6.56
5664	conflict	verb	12	6.52
5665	thus	qualifier	12	6.43
5666	civilize	verb	12	6.40
5667	amuse	verb	12	6.38
5667	comfortably	adverb	12	6.38
5669	revolve	verb	12	6.37
5670	mislead	verb	12	6.34
5670	photograph	verb	12	6.34
5672	wealthy	adjective	12	6.33
5673	advocate	noun	12	6.32
5673	stubborn	adjective	12	6.32
5675	guarantee	noun	12	6.31
5676	beyond	adverb	12	6.29
5676	tin	noun	12	6.29
5678	manuscript	noun	12	6.28
5678	script	noun	12	6.28
5680	purity	noun	12	6.26
5681	rite	noun	12	6.24
5682	fashionable	adjective	12	6.21
5683	elite	noun	12	6.20
5684	underdeveloped	adjective	12	6.18
5685	Dwight	prop. noun	12	6.14
5686	preoccupy	verb	12	6.12
5687	foliage	noun	12	6.11
5688	quaint	adjective	12	6.10
5689	comparatively	qualifier	12	6.06
5690	rotation	noun	12	6.05
5691	learning	noun	12	6.04
5692	chill	verb	12	6.01
5692	scratch	noun	12	6.01
5694	edge	verb	12	5.98
5694	logically	adverb	12	5.98
5696	nominate	verb	12	5.95
5608	tennis	noun	15	5.78
5609	toy	noun	14	5.78
5610	pigment	noun	12	5.77
5611	consolidate	verb	10	5.77
5611	robe	noun	10	5.77
5613	binomial	adjective	36	5.76
5614	crash	noun	15	5.76
5615	Theodore	prop. noun	14	5.76
5616	ferry	noun	12	5.76
5616	independently	adverb	12	5.76
5618	Julia	prop. noun	27	5.75
5619	synthesis	noun	16	5.75
5620	hey	exclam.	15	5.75
5621	orient	verb	14	5.75
5622	domain	noun	12	5.75
5622	icy	adjective	12	5.75
5622	mine	verb	12	5.75
5625	akin	adjective	10	5.75
5626	Faulkner	prop. noun	30	5.74
5627	investor	noun	18	5.74
5628	sovereign	noun	16	5.74
5629	psychology	noun	14	5.74
5630	high	noun	13	5.74
5631	Benjamin	prop. noun	12	5.74
5632	potentiality	noun	11	5.74
5633	yearning	noun	9	5.74
5634	screw	noun	30	5.73
5635	shorts	pl. noun	29	5.73
5636	Englishman	prop. noun	23	5.73
5637	disadvantage	noun	13	5.73
5637	sway	verb	13	5.73
5639	slug	noun	12	5.73
5640	verify	verb	11	5.73
5641	menace	noun	10	5.73
5641	peril	noun	10	5.73
5643	Felix	prop. noun	32	5.72
5644	pottery	noun	16	5.72
5645	aspiration	noun	15	5.72
5646	treasurer	noun	14	5.72
5647	everyday	adjective	13	5.72
5648	nowadays	adverb	12	5.72
5648	Marx	prop. noun	12	5.72
5650	Wells	prop. noun	11	5.72
5651	guardian	noun	13	5.71
5651	undergraduate	noun	13	5.71
5653	framework	noun	11	5.71
5654	dense	adjective	9	5.71
5655	overnight	adverb	14	5.70
5656	notify	verb	13	5.70
5656	transparent	adjective	13	5.70
5658	bark	noun	13	5.69
5659	willingness	noun	11	5.69
5660	vitamin	noun	15	5.68
5661	ache	verb	11	5.68
5662	livestock	noun	19	5.67
5663	amid	prep.	14	5.67
5664	novelty	noun	12	5.67
5665	merit	verb	10	5.67
5666	fatigue	noun	13	5.66
5667	grove	noun	17	5.65
5668	manufacture	noun	16	5.65
5669	favorably	adverb	13	5.65
5670	steam	verb	11	5.65
5671	southeast	adjective	19	5.64
5672	seam	noun	18	5.64
5673	glorious	adjective	16	5.64
5673	jerk	verb	16	5.64
5675	advertising	noun	14	5.64
5676	modernization	noun	13	5.64
5677	any	qualifier	12	5.64
5677	campaign	verb	12	5.64
5677	copper	noun	12	5.64
5677	diplomat	noun	12	5.64
5677	similarity	noun	12	5.64
5682	consultant	noun	19	5.63
5683	demon	noun	17	5.63
5684	sailor	noun	13	5.63
5685	bid	verb	10	5.63
5686	Israel	prop. noun	16	5.62
5687	ninety	card. num.	12	5.62
5688	alarm	verb	11	5.62
5688	sometime	adverb	11	5.62
5690	alcohol	noun	15	5.61
5691	predecessor	noun	11	5.61
5692	reactionary	adjective	14	5.60
5693	heal	verb	11	5.60
5693	outsider	noun	11	5.60
5695	curl	verb	17	5.59
5695	fuel	noun	17	5.59

5696	sixteenth	ord. num.	12	5.95
5698	forego	verb	12	5.93
5699	harsh	adjective	12	5.91
5700	fulfillment	noun	12	5.90
5700	Herbert	prop. noun	12	5.90
5702	stream	verb	12	5.87
5703	despise	verb	12	5.86
5703	precedent	noun	12	5.86
5705	Byrd	prop. noun	12	5.85
5706	dispatch	verb	12	5.82
5706	privacy	noun	12	5.82
5708	empty	verb	12	5.81
5709	ordinance	noun	12	5.80
5709	princess	noun	12	5.80
5711	pigment	noun	12	5.77
5712	ferry	noun	12	5.76
5712	independently	adverb	12	5.76
5714	domain	noun	12	5.75
5714	icy	adjective	12	5.75
5714	mine	verb	12	5.75
5717	Benjamin	prop. noun	12	5.74
5718	slug	noun	12	5.73
5719	Marx	prop. noun	12	5.72
5719	nowadays	adverb	12	5.72
5721	novelty	noun	12	5.67
5722	any	qualifier	12	5.64
5722	campaign	verb	12	5.64
5722	copper	noun	12	5.64
5722	diplomat	noun	12	5.64
5722	similarity	noun	12	5.64
5727	ninety	card. num.	12	5.62
5728	economist	noun	12	5.59
5728	messenger	noun	12	5.59
5730	turmoil	noun	12	5.57
5730	Venus	prop. noun	12	5.57
5732	equality	noun	12	5.56
5732	violently	adverb	12	5.56
5734	title	verb	12	5.54
5735	sword	noun	12	5.51
5736	blindness	noun	12	5.49
5736	can	noun	12	5.49
5738	enhance	verb	12	5.48
5739	rein	noun	12	5.47
5739	setup	noun	12	5.47
5741	vent	noun	12	5.44
5742	charity	noun	12	5.43
5743	journalist	noun	12	5.42
5744	garment	noun	12	5.41
5745	elevator	noun	12	5.40
5746	edit	verb	12	5.38
5747	lately	adverb	12	5.35
5748	vine	noun	12	5.32
5749	decay	noun	12	5.30
5749	endorse	verb	12	5.30
5751	Switzerland	prop. noun	12	5.29
5752	luminous	adjective	12	5.26
5753	crossroad	noun	12	5.24
5753	smoothly	adverb	12	5.24
5755	furnishing	noun	12	5.21
5755	hurl	verb	12	5.21
5755	tower	verb	12	5.21
5755	tunnel	noun	12	5.21
5759	deepest	sem. sup.	12	5.19
5759	reassure	verb	12	5.19
5759	type	verb	12	5.19
5762	dispel	verb	12	5.14
5762	rib	noun	12	5.14
5764	sunny	adjective	12	5.13
5765	mourn	verb	12	5.09
5766	duke	noun	12	5.05
5766	second	adverb	12	5.05
5768	compass	noun	12	5.03
5769	nail	verb	12	5.02
5770	Andrew	prop. noun	12	5.01
5770	attendance	noun	12	5.01
5772	prompt	verb	11	8.31
5773	tolerate	verb	11	7.45
5774	unanimously	adverb	11	7.42
5775	scrap	noun	11	7.20
5776	hardware	noun	11	7.06
5777	loosely	adverb	11	7.00
5778	thrust	noun	11	6.91
5779	tropical	adjective	11	6.85
5780	crown	verb	11	6.82
5781	wire	verb	11	6.80
5782	squarely	adverb	11	6.76
5783	inflict	verb	11	6.74
5783	innovation	noun	11	6.74
5785	rebel	verb	11	6.72

5697	economist	noun	12	5.59
5697	messenger	noun	12	5.59
5699	one-half	noun	9	5.59
5699	unchanged	adjective	9	5.59
5701	Utopia	prop. noun	21	5.58
5702	smooth	verb	15	5.58
5703	vocal	adjective	14	5.58
5704	supervisor	noun	13	5.58
5705		adjective	11	5.58
5706	ballad	noun	16	5.57
5707	ant	noun	13	5.57
5708	turmoil	noun	12	5.57
5708	Venus	prop. noun	12	5.57
5710	cautious	adjective	10	5.57
5710	doing	noun	10	5.57
5710	indignation	noun	10	5.57
5710	true	adverb	10	5.57
5714	therapist	noun	23	5.56
5715	settler	noun	15	5.56
5716	equality	noun	12	5.56
5716	violently	adverb	12	5.56
5718	bargaining	noun	16	5.55
5719	evolution	noun	14	5.55
5719	sanction	noun	14	5.55
5721	flame	verb	11	5.55
5722	Sarah	prop. noun	30	5.54
5723	pull	noun	13	5.54
5724	title	verb	12	5.54
5725	frantic	adjective	11	5.54
5725	prone	adjective	11	5.54
5727	Hughes	prop. noun	29	5.53
5728	jungle	noun	24	5.53
5729	pave	verb	9	5.53
5730	sitter	noun	28	5.52
5731	solid	noun	20	5.52
5732	reservoir	noun	13	5.52
5733	Johnston	prop. noun	21	5.51
5734	Scotland	prop. noun	13	5.51
5735	sword	noun	12	5.51
5736	sort	verb	10	5.51
5737	harass	verb	9	5.51
5738	hymn	noun	15	5.50
5739	Lloyd	prop. noun	13	5.50
5740	blindness	noun	12	5.49
5740	can	noun	12	5.49
5742	preoccupation	noun	10	5.49
5743	yeah	adverb	26	5.48
5744	towel	noun	17	5.48
5745	canyon	noun	14	5.48
5745	Helen	prop. noun	14	5.48
5747	Herman	prop. noun	13	5.48
5747	resign	verb	13	5.48
5749	enhance	verb	12	5.48
5750	fascinate	verb	11	5.48
5750	hostility	noun	11	5.48
5752	curse	noun	10	5.48
5753	ruling	noun	16	5.47
5754	Belgian	adjective	14	5.47
5755	rein	noun	12	5.47
5755	setup	noun	12	5.47
5757	reconstruction	noun	11	5.47
5757	thrive	verb	11	5.47
5759	delegate	verb	10	5.47
5760	drill	noun	21	5.46
5761	miserable	adjective	13	5.46
5762	photographic	adjective	11	5.46
5763	ideally	adverb	10	5.46
5764	and/or	co. conj.	17	5.45
5765	disable	verb	14	5.45
5766	cane	noun	13	5.45
5766	Kremlin	prop. noun	13	5.45
5766	superimpose	verb	13	5.45
5769	intelligible	adjective	11	5.45
5770	dive	noun	24	5.44
5771	fur	noun	17	5.44
5772	bake	verb	15	5.44
5772	cab	noun	15	5.44
5774	vent	noun	12	5.44
5775	array	noun	11	5.44
5775	perfume	noun	11	5.44
5775	usefulness	noun	11	5.44
5775	volunteer	verb	11	5.44
5779	oxidation	noun	23	5.43
5780	mare	noun	18	5.43
5781	infantry	noun	16	5.43
5782	pump	noun	15	5.43
5783	drawer	noun	13	5.43
5784	charity	noun	12	5.43
5785	streak	noun	16	5.42

5786	thoughtful	adjective	11	6.71
5787	stack	verb	11	6.68
5788	noticeable	adjective	11	6.60
5789	wage	verb	11	6.55
5790	culminate	verb	11	6.54
5790	facet	noun	11	6.54
5792	unexpectedly	adverb	11	6.51
5793	wheel	verb	11	6.50
5794	descent	noun	11	6.49
5795	Australia	prop. noun	11	6.47
5796	venture	verb	11	6.42
5797	mock	verb	11	6.41
5798	accumulation	noun	11	6.39
5798	intent	noun	11	6.39
5800	undermine	verb	11	6.37
5801	painfully	adverb	11	6.34
5801	trivial	adjective	11	6.34
5803	contrary	noun	11	6.30
5804	acreage	noun	11	6.28
5804	eventual	adjective	11	6.28
5806	restoration	noun	11	6.26
5807	black	noun	11	6.25
5808	happier	comp. adj.	11	6.24
5808	paradoxically	adverb	11	6.24
5810	economically	adverb	11	6.21
5811	applaud	verb	11	6.20
5812	lengthy	adjective	11	6.18
5813	Italian	prop. noun	11	6.17
5814	strict	adjective	11	6.15
5815	partial	adjective	11	6.13
5816	patriot	noun	11	6.12
5817	moist	adjective	11	6.10
5818	Easter	prop. noun	11	6.04
5819	circulate	verb	11	6.02
5819	impair	verb	11	6.02
5821	comfort	verb	11	5.98
5822	escort	verb	11	5.96
5822	greatness	noun	11	5.96
5822	passive	adjective	11	5.96
5825	blame	noun	11	5.94
5825	prosecution	noun	11	5.94
5827	freshman	noun	11	5.93
5828	Polish	adjective	11	5.92
5829	obscure	adjective	11	5.91
5830	stoop	verb	11	5.90
5831	elemental	adjective	11	5.89
5831	veil	noun	11	5.89
5833	diversion	noun	11	5.86
5833	picket	noun	11	5.86
5835	overlap	verb	11	5.85
5836	vacant	adjective	11	5.84
5837	satisfactorily	adverb	11	5.80
5838	red	noun	11	5.79
5838	sum	verb	11	5.79
5840	potentiality	noun	11	5.74
5841	verify	verb	11	5.73
5842	Wells	prop. noun	11	5.72
5843	framework	noun	11	5.71
5844	willingness	noun	11	5.69
5845	ache	verb	11	5.68
5846	steam	verb	11	5.65
5847	alarm	verb	11	5.62
5847	sometime	adverb	11	5.62
5849	predecessor	noun	11	5.61
5850	heal	verb	11	5.60
5850	outsider	noun	11	5.60
5852	three-dimensional	adjective	11	5.58
5853	flame	verb	11	5.55
5854	frantic	adjective	11	5.54
5854	prone	adjective	11	5.54
5856	fascinate	verb	11	5.48
5856	hostility	noun	11	5.48
5858	reconstruction	noun	11	5.47
5858	thrive	verb	11	5.47
5860	photographic	adjective	11	5.46
5861	intelligible	adjective	11	5.45
5862	array	noun	11	5.44
5862	perfume	noun	11	5.44
5862	usefulness	noun	11	5.44
5862	volunteer	verb	11	5.44
5866	eighty	card. num.	11	5.42
5867	locally	adverb	11	5.41
5868	thirteen	card. num.	11	5.40
5869	nominal	adjective	11	5.36
5869	resultant	adjective	11	5.36
5869	rhythmic	adjective	11	5.36
5872	subsequently	adverb	11	5.34
5873	engender	verb	11	5.33
5874	widen	verb	11	5.32

5786	journalist	noun	12	5.42
5787	eighty	card. num.	11	5.42
5788	unconsciously	adverb	10	5.42
5789	attachment	noun	9	5.42
5790	civilian	adjective	16	5.41
5791	lean	adjective	13	5.41
5792	garment	noun	12	5.41
5793	locally	adverb	11	5.41
5794	sweater	noun	18	5.40
5795	generalize	verb	14	5.40
5796	irony	noun	13	5.40
5797	elevator	noun	12	5.40
5798	thirteen	card. num.	11	5.40
5799	amazement	noun	10	5.40
5799	wool	noun	10	5.40
5801	drunk	noun	13	5.39
5802	drape	verb	9	5.39
5802	sever	verb	9	5.39
5804	turnpike	noun	25	5.38
5805	clergyman	noun	17	5.38
5805	plus	prep.	17	5.38
5807	engineering	noun	14	5.38
5807	hail	verb	14	5.38
5807	suspension	noun	14	5.38
5810	edit	verb	12	5.38
5811	luggage	noun	10	5.38
5812	interpreter	noun	9	5.38
5813	allocation	noun	19	5.37
5813	pace	verb	19	5.37
5815	infectious	adjective	17	5.37
5816	excellence	noun	14	5.37
5817	Michael	prop. noun	13	5.37
5817	separately	adverb	13	5.37
5819	disperse	verb	10	5.37
5819	privileged	adjective	10	5.37
5821	nominal	adjective	11	5.36
5821	resultant	adjective	11	5.36
5821	rhythmic	adjective	11	5.36
5824	inclination	noun	9	5.36
5825	solidarity	noun	13	5.35
5826	lately	adverb	12	5.35
5827	integrity	noun	10	5.35
5828	accord	verb	9	5.35
5829	summarize	verb	16	5.34
5830	allot	verb	13	5.34
5831	subsequently	adverb	11	5.34
5832	Westminster	prop. noun	23	5.33
5833	clearer	comp. adj.	15	5.33
5834	momentum	noun	14	5.33
5834	refugee	noun	14	5.33
5836	engender	verb	11	5.33
5837	Stevens	prop. noun	19	5.32
5838	vine	noun	12	5.32
5839	widen	verb	11	5.32
5840	hierarchy	noun	10	5.31
5841	chancellor	noun	14	5.30
5842	inject	verb	13	5.30
5843	decay	noun	12	5.30
5843	endorse	verb	12	5.30
5845	centimeter	noun	23	5.29
5846	peer	noun	13	5.29
5846	therapeutic	adjective	13	5.29
5848	Switzerland	prop. noun	12	5.29
5849	seventeenth	ord. num.	11	5.29
5850	refinement	noun	10	5.29
5851	irresponsible	adjective	9	5.29
5851	untouched	adjective	9	5.29
5853	Pip	prop. noun	33	5.28
5853	pulmonary	adjective	33	5.28
5855	whip	noun	16	5.28
5856	ordering	noun	13	5.28
5857	collaborate	verb	11	5.28
5857	excuse	verb	11	5.28
5859	abolition	noun	10	5.28
5859	indignant	adjective	10	5.28
5861	profess	verb	13	5.27
5861	stain	noun	13	5.27
5863	refine	verb	11	5.27
5864	reckon	verb	13	5.26
5865	luminous	adjective	12	5.26
5866	disregard	verb	9	5.26
5867	Gorton	prop. noun	35	5.25
5868	pork	noun	14	5.25
5869	spoil	verb	10	5.25
5869	surge	verb	10	5.25
5871	novelist	noun	22	5.24
5872	constant	noun	19	5.24
5873	transit	noun	16	5.24
5874	crossroad	noun	12	5.24

5875	seventeenth	ord. num.	11	5.29
5876	collaborate	verb	11	5.28
5876	excuse	verb	11	5.28
5878	refine	verb	11	5.27
5879	Korean	adjective	11	5.24
5879	leave	noun	11	5.24
5881	inventor	noun	11	5.22
5882	boost	verb	11	5.18
5883	decency	noun	11	5.17
5884	occupational	adjective	11	5.16
5884	transcend	verb	11	5.16
5886	darken	verb	11	5.14
5886	parallel	noun	11	5.14
5886	wilderness	noun	11	5.14
5889	layman	noun	11	5.10
5890	sociological	adjective	11	5.09
5891	ascertain	verb	11	5.05
5891	Jimmy	prop. noun	11	5.05
5893	indifferent	adjective	11	5.04
5893	sanitation	noun	11	5.04
5895	ardent	adjective	11	5.03
5896	actively	adverb	11	5.01
5896	awake	verb	11	5.01
5898	blank	adjective	11	5.00
5898	bluff	noun	11	5.00
5898	keen	adjective	11	5.00
5901	likelihood	noun	10	7.46
5902	confer	verb	10	7.25
5903	latter	noun	10	6.91
5904	suppress	verb	10	6.77
5905	principally	adverb	10	6.46
5906	prosecute	verb	10	6.29
5907	particular	noun	10	6.26
5907	simplest	sem. sup.	10	6.26
5909	pilgrimage	noun	10	6.10
5910	gigantic	adjective	10	6.08
5911	dissatisfaction	noun	10	6.07
5911	traditionally	adverb	10	6.07
5913	spur	verb	10	6.02
5914	treasure	noun	10	5.92
5914	well-being	noun	10	5.92
5916	absolutely	adverb	10	5.87
5917	intricate	adjective	10	5.86
5917	trap	verb	10	5.86
5919	magnify	verb	10	5.84
5920	consolidate	verb	10	5.77
5920	robe	noun	10	5.77
5922	akin	adjective	10	5.75
5923	menace	noun	10	5.73
5923	peril	noun	10	5.73
5925	merit	verb	10	5.67
5926	bid	verb	10	5.63
5927	cautious	adjective	10	5.57
5927	doing	noun	10	5.57
5927	indignation	noun	10	5.57
5927	true	adverb	10	5.57
5931	sort	verb	10	5.51
5932	preoccupation	noun	10	5.49
5933	curse	noun	10	5.48
5934	delegate	verb	10	5.47
5935	ideally	adverb	10	5.46
5936	unconsciously	adverb	10	5.42
5937	amazement	noun	10	5.40
5937	wool	noun	10	5.40
5939	luggage	noun	10	5.38
5940	disperse	verb	10	5.37
5940	privileged	adjective	10	5.37
5942	integrity	noun	10	5.35
5943	hierarchy	noun	10	5.31
5944	refinement	noun	10	5.29
5945	abolition	noun	10	5.28
5945	indignant	adjective	10	5.28
5947	spoil	verb	10	5.25
5947	surge	verb	10	5.25
5949	instructor	noun	10	5.23
5950	civilian	noun	10	5.22
5950	ray	noun	10	5.22
5952	alas	exclam.	10	5.21
5952	cheer	noun	10	5.21
5954	sanction	verb	10	5.20
5955	thoroughly	qualifier	10	5.19
5956	puzzle	noun	10	5.18
5957	assertion	noun	10	5.15
5958	stuff	verb	10	5.14
5959	majestic	adjective	10	5.12
5960	grief	noun	10	5.10
5961	debate	verb	10	5.09
5962	subordinate	noun	10	5.08
5963	attainment	noun	10	5.05

5874	smoothly	adverb	12	5.24
5876	Korean	adjective	11	5.24
5876	leave	noun	11	5.24
5878	compact	adjective	9	5.24
5879	glue	verb	20	5.23
5880	solar	adjective	16	5.23
5881	instructor	noun	10	5.23
5882	juvenile	adjective	13	5.22
5882	Richardson	prop. noun	13	5.22
5884	inventor	noun	11	5.22
5885	civilian	noun	10	5.22
5885	ray	noun	10	5.22
5887	furnishing	noun	12	5.21
5887	hurl	verb	12	5.21
5887	tower	verb	12	5.21
5887	tunnel	noun	12	5.21
5891	alas	exclam.	10	5.21
5891	cheer	noun	10	5.21
5893	Milton	prop. noun	23	5.20
5894	dough	noun	13	5.20
5894	gossip	noun	13	5.20
5896	sanction	verb	10	5.20
5897	ultraviolet	adjective	18	5.19
5898	dump	verb	14	5.19
5899	deepest	sem. sup.	12	5.19
5899	reassure	verb	12	5.19
5899	type	verb	12	5.19
5902	thoroughly	qualifier	10	5.19
5903	patiently	adverb	9	5.19
5904	boost	verb	11	5.18
5905	puzzle	noun	10	5.18
5906	bargain	noun	9	5.18
5906	periodical	noun	9	5.18
5908	lyric	noun	22	5.17
5909	dairy	noun	19	5.17
5910	decency	noun	11	5.17
5911	R	prop. noun	15	5.16
5912	incomplete	adjective	14	5.16
5913	occupational	adjective	11	5.16
5913	transcend	verb	11	5.16
5915	stall	noun	20	5.15
5916	coalition	noun	15	5.15
5917	assertion	noun	10	5.15
5918	dispel	verb	12	5.14
5918	rib	noun	12	5.14
5920	darken	verb	11	5.14
5920	parallel	noun	11	5.14
5920	wilderness	noun	11	5.14
5923	stuff	verb	10	5.14
5924	Aristotle	prop. noun	27	5.13
5925	refund	noun	24	5.13
5926	flexibility	noun	16	5.13
5927	sunny	adjective	12	5.13
5928	Linda	prop. noun	45	5.12
5929	emission	noun	32	5.12
5929	fallout	noun	32	5.12
5931	depreciation	noun	13	5.12
5931	N.Y.	prop. noun	13	5.12
5931	wreck	verb	13	5.12
5934	majestic	adjective	10	5.12
5935	purely	adverb	9	5.12
5936	financing	noun	13	5.11
5937	contact	verb	15	5.10
5938	controller	noun	14	5.10
5939	layman	noun	11	5.10
5940	grief	noun	10	5.10
5941	movable	adjective	19	5.09
5942	mourn	verb	12	5.09
5943	sociological	adjective	11	5.09
5944	debate	verb	10	5.09
5945	potent	adjective	9	5.09
5946	shopping	noun	8	5.09
5947	subordinate	noun	10	5.08
5948	challenging	adjective	9	5.08
5949	fringe	noun	16	5.07
5950	sincerity	noun	13	5.07
5951	jar	noun	19	5.06
5952	sensibility	noun	14	5.06
5953	sticky	adjective	9	5.06
5954	Montgomery	prop. noun	18	5.05
5955	appetite	noun	14	5.05
5955	premium	noun	14	5.05
5955	thumb	noun	14	5.05
5958	duke	noun	12	5.05
5958	second	adverb	12	5.05
5960	ascertain	verb	11	5.05
5960	Jimmy	prop. noun	11	5.05
5962	attainment	noun	10	5.05
5963	hunter	noun	17	5.04

5964	rat	noun	10	5.03
5964	torture	verb	10	5.03
5966	convict	noun	10	5.02
5967	appraisal	noun	10	5.01
5967	mastery	noun	10	5.01
5969	chip	verb	10	5.00
5970	discard	verb	9	5.98
5971	yearning	noun	9	5.74
5972	dense	adjective	9	5.71
5973	one-half	noun	9	5.59
5973	unchanged	adjective	9	5.59
5975	pave	verb	9	5.53
5976	harass	verb	9	5.51
5977	attachment	noun	9	5.42
5978	drape	verb	9	5.39
5978	sever	verb	9	5.39
5980	interpreter	noun	9	5.38
5981	inclination	noun	9	5.36
5982	accord	verb	9	5.35
5983	irresponsible	adjective	9	5.29
5983	untouched	adjective	9	5.29
5985	disregard	verb	9	5.26
5986	compact	adjective	9	5.24
5987	patiently	adverb	9	5.19
5988	bargain	noun	9	5.18
5988	periodical	noun	9	5.18
5990	purely	adverb	9	5.12
5991	potent	adjective	9	5.09
5992	challenging	adjective	9	5.08
5993	sticky	adjective	9	5.06
5994	collision	noun	9	5.02
5994	paramount	sem. sup.	9	5.02
5996	shopping	noun	8	5.09

5964	attribute	noun	15	5.04
5965	diversity	noun	14	5.04
5965	pet	noun	14	5.04
5967	Green	prop. noun	13	5.04
5968	indifferent	adjective	11	5.04
5968	sanitation	noun	11	5.04
5970	drain	noun	15	5.03
5971	witch	noun	13	5.03
5972	compass	noun	12	5.03
5973	ardent	adjective	11	5.03
5974	rat	noun	10	5.03
5974	torture	verb	10	5.03
5976	ironic	adjective	13	5.02
5977	nail	verb	12	5.02
5978	convict	noun	10	5.02
5979	collision	noun	9	5.02
5979	paramount	sem. sup.	9	5.02
5981	adolescence	noun	18	5.01
5982	Walker	prop. noun	17	5.01
5983	apple	noun	15	5.01
5984	chord	noun	13	5.01
5985	Andrew	prop. noun	12	5.01
5985	attendance	noun	12	5.01
5987	actively	adverb	11	5.01
5987	awake	verb	11	5.01
5989	appraisal	noun	10	5.01
5989	mastery	noun	10	5.01
5991	Mars	prop. noun	19	5.00
5992	depress	verb	13	5.00
5993	blank	adjective	11	5.00
5993	bluff	noun	11	5.00
5993	keen	adjective	11	5.00
5996	chip	verb	10	5.00

V

Frequency of Word Classes

This section presents data on the frequency and distribution of word classes and morphological forms in the corpus and in its genres. The results of the frequency analysis are given in several tables which provide various degrees of detail about the frequency distribution of individual tags. Table 5.1 gives the basic information on the size of the genres of the corpus, and Table 5.2 detailed information about the frequency of tags and tag combinations in each genre. Table 5.3 summarizes this information and presents the distribution of the word classes and forms in the two major subdivisions of the corpus, *Informative Prose* and *Imaginative Prose*. Table 5.4 lists the types and frequencies of the contractions which occur in the two subdivisions. In Table 5.5, the major word classes are ordered by their decreasing frequency of occurrence, and Table 5.6 provides information on the relative effect of genre properties on word-class frequency.

Genre Size

Table 5.1 gives the basic information on the absolute size of each of the fifteen genre categories comprising the corpus. The number of grammatical words (as defined in Section I) and the number of punctuation marks are given for each genre as well as for the entire corpus. Words with complex tags (i.e., with hyphenated tags or those signaling merged words) are counted only once in Table 5.1. So, for example, all 105 forms of *there's*, which have the tag EX+BEZ, contribute only 105 occurrences to the total number of grammatical words. Later in this section, specifically in Tables 5.3 and 5.5, contractions are counted separately from the words to which they are attached in order to give full frequency figures for all word classes and morphological forms, whether they occur in their full or contracted versions.

Table 5.1: Genre Size

Genre	Number of: Words	Punct. Marks
A. Press: Reportage	88690	10208
B. Press: Editorial	54505	6023
C. Press: Reviews	35346	4410
D. Religion	34590	4001
E. Skills and Hobbies	72590	8801
F. Popular Lore	97223	11175
G. Belles Lettres, etc.	152064	17441
H. Miscellaneous	62477	7014
J. Learned	162211	17592
Subtotal: Informative	759696	86665
K. General Fiction	58380	8187
L. Mystery and Detective	48208	6965
M. Science Fiction	12042	1799
N. Adventure and Western	58416	8397
P. Romance and Love Story	58625	8655
R. Humor	18277	2542
Subtotal: Imaginative	253948	36545
TOTAL CORPUS	1013644	123210

Frequency of Tags

Table 5.2 gives the frequency figures of the complete set of grammatical tags and tag combinations for each of the 15 genres of the corpus and for the corpus as a whole. Although the total inventory of tags used in our analysis is 87 (including the 6 punctuation tags and 4 discourse tags), the number of frequency entries in Table 5.2 is more than double this number, amounting to 179 entries. This is due to the separate listing of certain complex tags, primarily those that are used to annotate merged words, i.e., graphic words containing two distinct word components, one or both of which are given in a reduced graphic form; so, for example, *there's* is tagged as EX+BEZ and *isn't* as BEZ*. Secondly, the number of tag types is enlarged by the existence of hyphenated tags that specify the occurrence of a particular word class in a headline, a title, a metalinguistic citation, or identify a foreign word. In the lemmatized list, a singular common noun, for example, is tagged as NN when it occurs in the text proper, but as NN-HL when in a headline, as NN-NC when used as a cited form, and as NN-TL when in a title. Hyphenated tags of this type are not counted separately in Table 5.2 but are merged with their nonhyphenated equivalents. However, the total numbers of all hyphenated tags of the three types indicating occurrence in headlines, as cited forms, or in titles (i.e., -HL, -NC, and -TL) are given at the end of the table. Similarly, all foreign words, which are identified in the lemmatized list by the prefix FW- followed by a word-class designation, have been collapsed in Table 5.2 into a single entry, FW-.

The list of tags in Table 5.2 is ordered alphabetically, with the punctuation tags listed first. The tag *, designating *not*, and the hyphenated tags are given at the end of the list. Each tag symbol is followed by four lines of data, with separate entries on each line for the fifteen genres of the corpus. The first line of a tag entry gives the actual frequency of the tag in each genre (the "observed frequency *O*"); the second line contains a hypothetical frequency figure which one would expect to occur if the distribution of the respective tag throughout the fifteen genres were completely uniform (the "expected frequency *E*"). This expected frequency is computed by dividing the total corpus frequency of the tag by the proportional size of the genre. The third line gives the relative frequency of the tag in each genre, i.e., the percentage of the text accounted for by words with the relevant tag. And, finally, the fourth line of each entry lists the total tag frequency in the corpus and the chi-square value of the frequency distribution among the fifteen genres, as well as the adjusted chi-square value for large numbers, proposed by Mosteller and Rourke (1973) and discussed below.

The chi-square measure is calculated according to the usual formula:

$$\chi^2 = \sum_{i=1}^{n} \frac{(O_i - E_i)^2}{E_i}$$

where O_i is the observed (i.e., actual) frequency per genre and E_i the expected frequency. The chi-square value can be used to judge whether the differences in the relative frequencies of a tag in the various genres of the corpus are such that they can be ascribed to chance. Our results indicate that, disregarding tag combinations of very low frequency, all the chi-square values in Table 5.2 are statistically significant, even at the 1% level of significance, with the exception of the tag RBT. (At $P = 0.01$ for 14 degrees of freedom the critical value of $\chi^2 = 29.1$.) For the tag RBT, designating superlative adverbs, the chi-square value is significant at the 5% level (where the critical value of $\chi^2 = 23.68$). The hypothesis that the uneven distribution of the tags among the genres of the corpus is due to chance thus has to be rejected. Rather, it is reasonable to assume that style and content characteristics of the genres affect significantly the frequency of occurrence of almost all the grammatically encoded forms that we employed in our analysis. The reader should be cautioned, however, that some of the chi-square values which we include for reasons of consistency of presentation in Table 5.2 cannot be considered to be statistically sound. This is the case with those tags whose frequency in some of the genres is very low (five or less) or zero. Chi-square measures calculated for such defective distributions are generally not considered to be reliable statistical indicators. In Table 5.2, of course, the number of instances of this kind is very small; for most tags, the chi-square values are based on entirely sufficient frequency data.

In spite of the significance of all chi-square values, it is possible to draw some conclusions about individual tags and about how much they depart from a random distribution by using the Mosteller-Rourke interpretation of chi-square values for large numbers. (Cf. Mosteller and Rourke 1973: 186-191). A summary of the conclusions, based on the Mosteller-Rourke argument, is given at the end of this section, in the discussion of Table 5.6.

Table 5.2: Frequency of Tags

	A	B	C	D	E	F	G	H	J	K	L	M	N	P	R
.	4253	2745	1693	1636	3916	4798	7124	2748	7405	4225	3821	931	4583	4371	1042
	4837.75	2973.07	1928.01	1886.77	3959.55	5303.20	8294.60	3407.92	8848.08	3184.44	2629.59	656.85	3186.40	3197.80	996.95
	4.7954	5.0362	4.7898	4.7297	5.3947	4.9350	4.6849	4.3984	4.5650	7.2371	7.9261	7.7313	7.8454	7.4559	5.7012
		TOTAL:	55291			CHI SQUARE:		2765.926			(1000×CHI SQUARE)÷TOTAL:				50.025
(	165	95	101	101	283	164	246	340	777	23	22	8	24	21	31
	210.08	129.10	83.72	81.93	171.94	230.29	360.19	147.99	384.23	138.28	114.19	28.52	138.37	138.86	43.29
	0.1860	0.1743	0.2857	0.2920	0.3899	0.1687	0.1618	0.5442	0.4790	0.0394	0.0456	0.0664	0.0411	0.0358	0.1696
		TOTAL:	2401			CHI SQUARE:		1187.709			(1000×CHI SQUARE)÷TOTAL:				494.672
)	167	95	100	127	280	168	247	342	776	23	22	8	22	21	31
	212.53	130.61	84.70	82.89	173.95	232.98	364.39	149.71	388.71	139.90	115.52	28.86	139.98	140.48	43.80
	0.1883	0.1743	0.2829	0.3672	0.3857	0.1728	0.1624	0.5474	0.4784	0.0394	0.0456	0.0664	0.0377	0.0358	0.1696
		TOTAL:	2429			CHI SQUARE:		1192.412			(1000×CHI SQUARE)÷TOTAL:				490.906
--	299	191	141	109	294	395	452	123	314	176	268	52	212	290	67
	296.00	181.91	117.97	115.44	242.27	324.48	507.51	208.51	541.37	194.84	160.89	40.19	194.96	195.66	61.00
	0.3371	0.3504	0.3989	0.3151	0.4050	0.4063	0.2972	0.1969	0.1936	0.3015	0.5559	0.4318	0.3629	0.4947	0.3666
		TOTAL:	3383			CHI SQUARE:		292.516			(1000×CHI SQUARE)÷TOTAL:				86.467
,	5175	2752	2310	1909	3837	5504	9097	3356	8126	3656	2805	790	3485	3896	1331
	5077.31	3120.30	2023.48	1980.20	4155.62	5565.81	8705.34	3576.68	9286.24	3342.13	2759.81	689.38	3344.19	3356.16	1046.32
	5.8349	5.0491	6.5354	5.5189	5.2859	5.6612	5.9823	5.3716	5.0095	6.2624	5.8185	6.5604	5.9658	6.6456	7.2824
		TOTAL:	58029			CHI SQUARE:		504.914			(1000×CHI SQUARE)÷TOTAL:				8.701
:	149	145	65	119	191	146	275	105	194	84	27	10	71	56	40
	146.73	90.17	58.48	57.23	120.09	160.85	251.58	103.36	268.37	96.59	79.76	19.92	96.64	96.99	30.24
	0.1680	0.2660	0.1839	0.3440	0.2631	0.1502	0.1808	0.1681	0.1196	0.1439	0.0560	0.0830	0.1215	0.0955	0.2189
		TOTAL:	1677			CHI SQUARE:		235.584			(1000×CHI SQUARE)÷TOTAL:				140.479
ABL	21	15	13	28	19	25	49	17	90	19	17	4	12	22	6
	31.24	19.20	12.45	12.18	25.57	34.24	53.56	22.00	57.13	20.56	16.98	4.24	20.57	20.65	6.44
	0.0237	0.0275	0.0368	0.0809	0.0262	0.0257	0.0322	0.0272	0.0555	0.0325	0.0353	0.0332	0.0205	0.0375	0.0328
		TOTAL:	357			CHI SQUARE:		53.275			(1000×CHI SQUARE)÷TOTAL:				149.230
ABN	184	155	155	128	234	268	472	175	373	196	154	65	179	223	61
	264.41	162.50	105.38	103.12	216.41	289.85	453.35	186.26	483.60	174.05	143.72	35.90	174.16	174.78	54.49
	0.2075	0.2844	0.4385	0.3700	0.3224	0.2757	0.3104	0.2801	0.2299	0.3357	0.3194	0.5398	0.3064	0.3804	0.3338
		TOTAL:	3022			CHI SQUARE:		125.294			(1000×CHI SQUARE)÷TOTAL:				41.461
ABX	73	30	27	20	42	79	120	62	148	29	27	2	33	30	9
	63.96	39.31	25.49	24.94	52.35	70.11	109.66	45.06	116.98	42.10	34.77	8.68	42.13	42.28	13.18
	0.0823	0.0550	0.0764	0.0578	0.0579	0.0813	0.0789	0.0992	0.0912	0.0497	0.0560	0.0166	0.0565	0.0512	0.0492
		TOTAL:	731			CHI SQUARE:		41.121			(1000×CHI SQUARE)÷TOTAL:				56.253
AP	931	610	359	325	799	920	1382	649	1715	389	381	115	407	433	168
	838.48	515.29	334.16	327.01	686.27	919.15	1437.61	590.66	1533.54	551.93	455.76	113.85	552.27	554.24	172.79
	1.0497	1.1192	1.0157	0.9396	1.1007	0.9463	0.9088	1.0388	1.0573	0.6663	0.7903	0.9550	0.6967	0.7386	0.9192
		TOTAL:	9583			CHI SQUARE:		202.614			(1000×CHI SQUARE)÷TOTAL:				21.143
AP+AP	0	0	0	0	0	0	0	0	1	0	0	0	0	0	0
	0.09	0.05	0.03	0.03	0.07	0.10	0.15	0.06	0.16	0.06	0.05	0.01	0.06	0.06	0.02
	0.0000	0.0000	0.0000	0.0000	0.0000	0.0000	0.0000	0.0000	0.0006	0.0000	0.0000	0.0000	0.0000	0.0000	0.0000
		TOTAL:	1			CHI SQUARE:		5.249			(1000×CHI SQUARE)÷TOTAL:				5248.914
AP$	1	1	0	0	1	1	0	0	0	1	1	1	1	1	0
	0.79	0.48	0.31	0.31	0.64	0.86	1.35	0.55	1.44	0.52	0.43	0.11	0.52	0.52	0.16
	0.0011	0.0018	0.0000	0.0000	0.0014	0.0010	0.0000	0.0000	0.0000	0.0017	0.0021	0.0083	0.0017	0.0017	0.0000
		TOTAL:	9			CHI SQUARE:		14.514			(1000×CHI SQUARE)÷TOTAL:				1612.638
AT	8962	5449	3551	3391	6989	10001	15159	5873	16994	5457	4322	1044	5535	4685	1674
	8669.64	5327.98	3455.15	3381.25	7095.83	9503.76	14864.60	6107.27	15856.49	5706.77	4712.44	1177.13	5710.29	5730.72	1786.62
	10.1049	9.9972	10.0464	9.8034	9.6280	10.2867	9.9688	9.4003	10.4765	9.3474	8.9653	8.6697	9.4751	7.9915	9.1590
		TOTAL:	99086			CHI SQUARE:		400.975			(1000×CHI SQUARE)÷TOTAL:				4.047
BE	526	422	154	243	524	570	843	601	1363	257	234	80	187	292	79
	557.79	342.79	222.30	217.54	456.53	611.45	956.36	392.93	1020.18	367.16	303.19	75.73	367.39	368.70	114.95
	0.5931	0.7742	0.4357	0.7025	0.7219	0.5863	0.5544	0.9620	0.8403	0.4402	0.4854	0.6643	0.3201	0.4981	0.4322
		TOTAL:	6375			CHI SQUARE:		460.531			(1000×CHI SQUARE)÷TOTAL:				72.240
BED	253	109	87	92	106	349	525	126	633	241	157	59	252	214	84
	287.60	176.75	114.62	112.17	235.39	315.27	493.11	202.60	526.01	189.31	156.33	39.05	189.43	190.11	59.27
	0.2853	0.2000	0.2461	0.2660	0.1460	0.3590	0.3452	0.2017	0.3902	0.4128	0.3257	0.4900	0.4314	0.3650	0.4596
		TOTAL:	3287			CHI SQUARE:		226.228			(1000×CHI SQUARE)÷TOTAL:				68.825
BED*	1	0	2	0	0	2	0	0	0	2	2	1	3	9	0
	1.92	1.18	0.77	0.75	1.58	2.11	3.30	1.36	3.52	1.27	1.05	0.26	1.27	1.27	0.40
	0.0011	0.0000	0.0057	0.0000	0.0000	0.0021	0.0000	0.0000	0.0000	0.0034	0.0041	0.0083	0.0051	0.0154	0.0000
		TOTAL:	22			CHI SQUARE:		67.194			(1000×CHI SQUARE)÷TOTAL:				3054.256
BEDZ	717	310	227	214	265	961	1470	223	1115	1092	828	200	919	999	276
	858.86	527.82	342.29	334.97	702.95	941.49	1472.57	605.02	1570.83	565.34	466.84	116.61	565.69	567.72	176.99
	0.8084	0.5688	0.6422	0.6187	0.3651	0.9884	0.9667	0.3569	0.6874	1.8705	1.7176	1.6609	1.5732	1.7041	1.5101
		TOTAL:	9816			CHI SQUARE:		2275.907			(1000×CHI SQUARE)÷TOTAL:				231.857
BEDZ*	3	2	1	0	2	6	14	0	1	11	32	4	18	52	8
	13.47	8.28	5.37	5.26	11.03	14.77	23.10	9.49	24.64	8.87	7.32	1.83	8.87	8.91	2.78
	0.0034	0.0037	0.0028	0.0000	0.0028	0.0062	0.0092	0.0000	0.0006	0.0188	0.0664	0.0332	0.0308	0.0887	0.0438
		TOTAL:	154			CHI SQUARE:		384.007			(1000×CHI SQUARE)÷TOTAL:				2493.554
BEG	57	45	29	28	37	54	138	41	117	31	20	9	17	50	13
	60.02	36.89	23.92	23.41	49.13	65.80	102.91	42.28	109.78	39.51	32.63	8.15	39.53	39.68	12.37
	0.0643	0.0826	0.0820	0.0809	0.0510	0.0555	0.0908	0.0656	0.0721	0.0531	0.0415	0.0747	0.0291	0.0853	0.0711
		TOTAL:	686			CHI SQUARE:		43.871			(1000×CHI SQUARE)÷TOTAL:				63.952
BEM	13	19	3	15	5	19	58	10	13	22	7	7	9	20	8
	19.95	12.26	7.95	7.78	16.33	21.87	34.20	14.05	36.49	13.13	10.84	2.71	13.14	13.19	4.11
	0.0147	0.0349	0.0085	0.0434	0.0069	0.0195	0.0381	0.0160	0.0080	0.0377	0.0145	0.0581	0.0154	0.0341	0.0438
		TOTAL:	228			CHI SQUARE:		79.640			(1000×CHI SQUARE)÷TOTAL:				349.296

Table 5.2: Frequency of Tags (cont.)

	A	B	C	D	E	F	G	H	J	K	L	M	N	P	R
BEM*	0	0	0	0	0	0	0	0	0	1	3	0	5	0	0
	0.79	0.48	0.31	0.31	0.64	0.86	1.35	0.55	1.44	0.52	0.43	0.11	0.52	0.52	0.16
	0.0000	0.0000	0.0000	0.0000	0.0000	0.0000	0.0000	0.0000	0.0000	0.0017	0.0062	0.0000	0.0086	0.0000	0.0000
		TOTAL:	9			CHI SQUARE:		62.156			(1000×CHI SQUARE)÷TOTAL:				6906.230
BEN	212	151	70	76	115	235	376	130	409	157	152	40	131	179	39
	216.29	132.92	86.20	84.36	177.03	237.10	370.84	152.36	395.59	142.37	117.57	29.37	142.46	142.97	44.57
	0.2390	0.2770	0.1980	0.2197	0.1584	0.2417	0.2473	0.2081	0.2521	0.2689	0.3153	0.3322	0.2243	0.3053	0.2134
		TOTAL:	2472			CHI SQUARE:		58.113			(1000×CHI SQUARE)÷TOTAL:				23.508
BER	330	298	195	197	532	482	649	416	993	52	52	28	54	79	44
	385.07	236.65	153.46	150.18	315.17	422.12	660.23	271.26	704.28	253.47	209.31	52.28	253.63	254.54	79.35
	0.3721	0.5467	0.5517	0.5695	0.7329	0.4958	0.4268	0.6658	0.6122	0.0891	0.1079	0.2325	0.0924	0.1348	0.2407
		TOTAL:	4401			CHI SQUARE:		986.649			(1000×CHI SQUARE)÷TOTAL:				224.187
BER*	4	5	1	0	4	3	3	0	3	1	7	1	9	6	1
	4.20	2.58	1.67	1.64	3.44	4.60	7.20	2.96	7.68	2.76	2.28	0.57	2.77	2.78	0.87
	0.0045	0.0092	0.0028	0.0000	0.0055	0.0031	0.0020	0.0000	0.0018	0.0017	0.0145	0.0083	0.0154	0.0102	0.0055
		TOTAL:	48			CHI SQUARE:		42.109			(1000×CHI SQUARE)÷TOTAL:				877.272
BEZ	733	752	513	537	970	1016	1817	656	2413	151	120	50	102	158	121
	884.50	543.57	352.50	344.96	723.93	969.60	1516.52	623.08	1617.72	582.22	480.77	120.09	582.58	584.66	182.28
	0.8265	1.3797	1.4514	1.5525	1.3363	1.0450	1.1949	1.0500	1.4876	0.2587	0.2489	0.4152	0.1746	0.2695	0.6620
		TOTAL:	10109			CHI SQUARE:		2183.359			(1000×CHI SQUARE)÷TOTAL:				215.982
BEZ*	8	7	3	2	7	4	7	0	0	7	17	7	18	25	5
	10.24	6.29	4.08	3.99	8.38	11.22	17.55	7.21	18.72	6.74	5.56	1.39	6.74	6.77	2.11
	0.0090	0.0128	0.0085	0.0058	0.0096	0.0041	0.0046	0.0000	0.0000	0.0120	0.0353	0.0581	0.0308	0.0426	0.0274
		TOTAL:	117			CHI SQUARE:		157.041			(1000×CHI SQUARE)÷TOTAL:				1342.230
CC	2718	1862	1453	1353	2948	3793	5953	2559	5783	2260	1696	416	2174	2469	712
	3337.89	2051.32	1330.26	1301.81	2731.96	3659.03	5723.00	2351.35	6104.89	2197.16	1814.33	453.21	2198.52	2206.38	687.86
	3.0646	3.4162	4.1108	3.9115	4.0612	3.9013	3.9148	4.0959	3.5651	3.8712	3.5181	3.4546	3.7216	4.2115	3.8956
		TOTAL:	38149			CHI SQUARE:		257.421			(1000×CHI SQUARE)÷TOTAL:				6.748
CD	2195	722	477	510	1457	1269	1567	1617	3195	446	473	79	467	321	154
	1307.98	803.83	521.27	510.13	1070.54	1433.82	2242.61	921.40	2392.25	860.98	710.96	177.59	861.51	864.59	269.54
	2.4749	1.3246	1.3495	1.4744	2.0072	1.3052	1.0305	2.5882	1.9697	0.7640	0.9812	0.6560	0.7994	0.5475	0.8426
		TOTAL:	14949			CHI SQUARE:		2676.477			(1000×CHI SQUARE)÷TOTAL:				179.040
CD$	2	0	0	0	2	0	0	1	0	0	0	0	1	0	0
	0.52	0.32	0.21	0.20	0.43	0.58	0.90	0.37	0.96	0.35	0.29	0.07	0.35	0.35	0.11
	0.0023	0.0000	0.0000	0.0000	0.0028	0.0000	0.0000	0.0016	0.0000	0.0000	0.0000	0.0000	0.0017	0.0000	0.0000
		TOTAL:	6			CHI SQUARE:		16.525			(1000×CHI SQUARE)÷TOTAL:				2754.120
CS	1509	1197	676	971	1379	2180	3843	1175	3870	1161	1061	269	1152	1280	451
	1940.14	1192.33	773.21	756.67	1587.94	2126.80	3326.48	1366.72	3548.45	1277.09	1054.58	263.43	1277.88	1282.45	399.82
	1.7014	2.1961	1.9125	2.8072	1.8997	2.2423	2.5272	1.8807	2.3858	1.9887	2.2009	2.2338	1.9721	2.1834	2.4676
		TOTAL:	22174			CHI SQUARE:		363.479			(1000×CHI SQUARE)÷TOTAL:				16.392
DO	64	111	40	55	125	116	187	51	136	95	102	26	99	121	36
	119.34	73.34	47.56	46.55	97.68	130.83	204.62	84.07	218.28	78.56	64.87	16.20	78.61	78.89	24.59
	0.0722	0.2037	0.1132	0.1590	0.1722	0.1193	0.1230	0.0816	0.0838	0.1627	0.2116	0.2159	0.1695	0.2064	0.1970
		TOTAL:	1364			CHI SQUARE:		166.274			(1000×CHI SQUARE)÷TOTAL:				121.901
DOD	64	36	23	34	25	91	179	18	111	127	55	38	90	127	30
	91.70	56.35	36.54	35.76	75.05	100.52	157.22	64.59	167.71	60.36	49.84	12.45	60.40	60.61	18.90
	0.0722	0.0660	0.0651	0.0983	0.0344	0.0936	0.1177	0.0288	0.0684	0.2175	0.1141	0.3156	0.1541	0.2166	0.1641
		TOTAL:	1048			CHI SQUARE:		331.199			(1000×CHI SQUARE)÷TOTAL:				316.030
DOD*	15	5	5	4	3	16	24	0	1	54	77	5	72	104	18
	35.26	21.67	14.05	13.75	28.86	38.65	60.46	24.84	64.49	23.21	19.17	4.79	23.22	23.31	7.27
	0.0169	0.0092	0.0141	0.0116	0.0041	0.0165	0.0158	0.0000	0.0006	0.0925	0.1597	0.0415	0.1233	0.1774	0.0985
		TOTAL:	403			CHI SQUARE:		796.002			(1000×CHI SQUARE)÷TOTAL:				1975.190
DOZ	26	44	32	35	50	46	93	16	98	7	10	3	6	13	6
	42.44	26.08	16.91	16.55	34.73	46.52	72.76	29.89	77.61	27.93	23.07	5.76	27.95	28.05	8.75
	0.0293	0.0807	0.0905	0.1012	0.0689	0.0473	0.0612	0.0256	0.0604	0.0120	0.0207	0.0249	0.0103	0.0222	0.0328
		TOTAL:	485			CHI SQUARE:		127.457			(1000×CHI SQUARE)÷TOTAL:				262.797
DOZ*	13	10	7	0	8	4	4	0	2	7	8	3	10	12	2
	7.87	4.84	3.14	3.07	6.45	8.63	13.50	5.55	14.40	5.18	4.28	1.07	5.19	5.21	1.62
	0.0147	0.0183	0.0198	0.0000	0.0110	0.0041	0.0026	0.0000	0.0012	0.0120	0.0166	0.0249	0.0171	0.0205	0.0109
		TOTAL:	90			CHI SQUARE:		63.217			(1000×CHI SQUARE)÷TOTAL:				702.409
DO +PPSS	0	0	0	0	0	0	0	0	0	0	0	0	1	0	0
	0.09	0.05	0.03	0.03	0.07	0.10	0.15	0.06	0.16	0.06	0.05	0.01	0.06	0.06	0.02
	0.0000	0.0000	0.0000	0.0000	0.0000	0.0000	0.0000	0.0000	0.0000	0.0000	0.0000	0.0000	0.0017	0.0000	0.0000
		TOTAL:	1			CHI SQUARE:		16.352			(1000×CHI SQUARE)÷TOTAL:				16352.141
DO*	17	24	5	0	44	30	27	1	4	64	83	13	80	86	10
	42.70	26.24	17.02	16.65	34.95	46.81	73.21	30.08	78.09	28.11	23.21	5.80	28.12	28.22	8.80
	0.0192	0.0440	0.0141	0.0000	0.0606	0.0309	0.0178	0.0016	0.0025	0.1096	0.1722	0.1080	0.1369	0.1467	0.0547
		TOTAL:	488			CHI SQUARE:		599.703			(1000×CHI SQUARE)÷TOTAL:				1228.900
DT	590	507	291	393	671	813	1359	612	1569	476	432	118	490	493	166
	785.72	482.87	313.13	306.44	643.08	861.31	1347.15	553.49	1437.05	517.20	427.08	106.68	517.51	519.37	161.92
	0.6652	0.9302	0.8233	1.1362	0.9244	0.8362	0.8937	0.9796	0.9673	0.8153	0.8961	0.9799	0.8388	0.8409	0.9082
		TOTAL:	8980			CHI SQUARE:		105.744			(1000×CHI SQUARE)÷TOTAL:				11.776
DTI	207	187	86	127	198	302	471	211	513	144	149	39	115	141	39
	256.28	157.50	102.13	99.95	209.75	280.93	439.40	180.53	468.72	168.69	139.30	34.80	168.80	169.40	52.81
	0.2334	0.3431	0.2433	0.3672	0.2728	0.3106	0.3097	0.3377	0.3163	0.2467	0.3091	0.3239	0.1969	0.2405	0.2134
		TOTAL:	2929			CHI SQUARE:		69.025			(1000×CHI SQUARE)÷TOTAL:				23.566
DTS	136	140	61	121	210	243	400	218	564	82	49	22	67	89	34
	213.14	130.99	84.94	83.13	174.45	233.65	365.44	150.15	389.83	140.30	115.85	28.94	140.39	140.89	43.92
	0.1533	0.2569	0.1726	0.3498	0.2893	0.2499	0.2630	0.3489	0.3477	0.1405	0.1016	0.1827	0.1147	0.1518	0.1860
		TOTAL:	2436			CHI SQUARE:		296.097			(1000×CHI SQUARE)÷TOTAL:				121.551

Table 5.2: Frequency of Tags (cont.)

	A	B	C	D	E	F	G	H	J	K	L	M	N	P	R
DTS+BEZ	0	0	0	0	0	0	0	0	0	0	0	0	1	1	0
	0.17	0.11	0.07	0.07	0.14	0.19	0.30	0.12	0.32	0.12	0.10	0.02	0.12	0.12	0.04
	0.0000	0.0000	0.0000	0.0000	0.0000	0.0000	0.0000	0.0000	0.0000	0.0000	0.0000	0.0000	0.0017	0.0017	0.0000
		TOTAL:	2			CHI SQUARE:		15.321			(1000×CHI SQUARE)÷TOTAL:				7660.613
DTX	8	5	4	3	8	7	15	4	14	5	14	4	11	1	1
	9.10	5.59	3.63	3.55	7.45	9.98	15.60	6.41	16.64	5.99	4.95	1.24	5.99	6.01	1.88
	0.0090	0.0092	0.0113	0.0087	0.0110	0.0072	0.0099	0.0064	0.0086	0.0086	0.0290	0.0332	0.0188	0.0017	0.0055
		TOTAL:	104			CHI SQUARE:		34.290			(1000×CHI SQUARE)÷TOTAL:				329.713
DT+BEZ	12	1	3	3	5	13	8	0	4	23	30	4	31	38	5
	15.75	9.68	6.28	6.14	12.89	17.26	27.00	11.09	28.80	10.37	8.56	2.14	10.37	10.41	3.25
	0.0135	0.0018	0.0085	0.0087	0.0069	0.0134	0.0053	0.0000	0.0025	0.0394	0.0622	0.0332	0.0531	0.0648	0.0274
		TOTAL:	180			CHI SQUARE:		249.492			(1000×CHI SQUARE)÷TOTAL:				1386.068
DT+MD	0	0	0	0	0	0	0	0	0	1	0	0	0	2	0
	0.26	0.16	0.10	0.10	0.21	0.29	0.45	0.18	0.48	0.17	0.14	0.04	0.17	0.17	0.05
	0.0000	0.0000	0.0000	0.0000	0.0000	0.0000	0.0000	0.0000	0.0000	0.0017	0.0000	0.0000	0.0000	0.0034	0.0000
		TOTAL:	3			CHI SQUARE:		25.841			(1000×CHI SQUARE)÷TOTAL:				8613.777
DT$	1	0	0	0	0	1	1	0	0	1	1	0	0	0	0
	0.44	0.27	0.17	0.17	0.36	0.48	0.75	0.31	0.80	0.29	0.24	0.06	0.29	0.29	0.09
	0.0011	0.0000	0.0000	0.0000	0.0000	0.0010	0.0007	0.0000	0.0000	0.0017	0.0021	0.0000	0.0000	0.0000	0.0000
		TOTAL:	5			CHI SQUARE:		8.382			(1000×CHI SQUARE)÷TOTAL:				1676.410
EX	161	97	86	92	114	187	312	96	392	140	161	37	112	146	33
	189.52	116.47	75.53	73.91	155.11	207.75	324.94	133.50	346.62	124.75	103.01	25.73	124.83	125.27	39.06
	0.1815	0.1780	0.2433	0.2660	0.1570	0.1923	0.2052	0.1537	0.2417	0.2398	0.3340	0.3073	0.1917	0.2490	0.1806
		TOTAL:	2166			CHI SQUARE:		88.511			(1000×CHI SQUARE)÷TOTAL:				40.864
EX+BEZ	2	4	1	0	12	7	7	0	0	7	16	7	25	13	4
	9.19	5.65	3.66	3.58	7.52	10.07	15.75	6.47	16.80	6.05	4.99	1.25	6.05	6.07	1.89
	0.0023	0.0073	0.0028	0.0000	0.0165	0.0072	0.0046	0.0000	0.0000	0.0120	0.0332	0.0581	0.0428	0.0222	0.0219
		TOTAL:	105			CHI SQUARE:		163.885			(1000×CHI SQUARE)÷TOTAL:				1560.811
EX+HVD	0	0	0	0	0	0	0	0	0	1	1	0	1	0	0
	0.26	0.16	0.10	0.10	0.21	0.29	0.45	0.18	0.48	0.17	0.14	0.04	0.17	0.17	0.05
	0.0000	0.0000	0.0000	0.0000	0.0000	0.0000	0.0000	0.0000	0.0000	0.0017	0.0021	0.0000	0.0017	0.0000	0.0000
		TOTAL:	3			CHI SQUARE:		15.580			(1000×CHI SQUARE)÷TOTAL:				5193.496
EX+HVZ	0	0	0	0	0	0	0	0	0	0	1	0	1	0	0
	0.17	0.11	0.07	0.07	0.14	0.19	0.30	0.12	0.32	0.12	0.10	0.02	0.12	0.12	0.04
	0.0000	0.0000	0.0000	0.0000	0.0000	0.0000	0.0000	0.0000	0.0000	0.0000	0.0021	0.0000	0.0017	0.0000	0.0000
		TOTAL:	2			CHI SQUARE:		17.189			(1000×CHI SQUARE)÷TOTAL:				8594.648
EX+MD	0	0	0	0	0	0	2	0	0	0	1	0	0	0	1
	0.35	0.22	0.14	0.14	0.29	0.38	0.60	0.25	0.64	0.23	0.19	0.05	0.23	0.23	0.07
	0.0000	0.0000	0.0000	0.0000	0.0000	0.0000	0.0013	0.0000	0.0000	0.0000	0.0021	0.0000	0.0000	0.0000	0.0055
		TOTAL:	4			CHI SQUARE:		21.788			(1000×CHI SQUARE)÷TOTAL:				5446.883
FW-	92	44	108	21	84	97	294	33	179	83	17	14	36	71	54
	107.36	65.98	42.79	41.87	87.87	117.69	184.07	75.63	196.35	70.67	58.36	14.58	70.71	70.96	22.12
	0.1037	0.0807	0.3056	0.0607	0.1157	0.0998	0.1933	0.0528	0.1104	0.1422	0.0353	0.1163	0.0616	0.1211	0.2955
		TOTAL:	1227			CHI SQUARE:		308.787			(1000×CHI SQUARE)÷TOTAL:				251.660
HV	265	275	124	194	376	396	634	223	551	169	222	61	135	264	56
	345.17	212.13	137.56	134.62	282.51	378.38	591.82	243.15	631.31	227.21	187.62	46.87	227.35	228.16	71.13
	0.2988	0.5045	0.3508	0.5609	0.5180	0.4073	0.4169	0.3569	0.3397	0.2895	0.4605	0.5066	0.2311	0.4503	0.3064
		TOTAL:	3945			CHI SQUARE:		183.269			(1000×CHI SQUARE)÷TOTAL:				46.456
HVD	264	120	65	76	71	431	768	46	319	707	503	135	581	668	144
	428.56	263.37	170.79	167.14	350.76	469.79	734.78	301.89	783.81	282.10	232.94	58.19	282.27	283.28	88.32
	0.2977	0.2202	0.1839	0.2197	0.0978	0.4433	0.5051	0.0736	0.1967	1.2110	1.0434	1.1211	0.9946	1.1394	0.7879
		TOTAL:	4898			CHI SQUARE:		2905.069			(1000×CHI SQUARE)÷TOTAL:				593.113
HVD*	2	0	0	0	0	0	9	0	0	14	27	0	14	30	3
	8.66	5.32	3.45	3.38	7.09	9.50	14.85	6.10	15.84	5.70	4.71	1.18	5.71	5.73	1.79
	0.0023	0.0000	0.0000	0.0000	0.0000	0.0000	0.0059	0.0000	0.0000	0.0240	0.0560	0.0000	0.0240	0.0512	0.0164
		TOTAL:	99			CHI SQUARE:		292.702			(1000×CHI SQUARE)÷TOTAL:				2956.582
HVG	14	19	6	11	17	29	61	6	38	13	13	4	18	24	10
	24.76	15.22	9.87	9.66	20.27	27.14	42.45	17.44	45.29	16.30	13.46	3.36	16.31	16.37	5.10
	0.0158	0.0349	0.0170	0.0318	0.0234	0.0298	0.0401	0.0096	0.0234	0.0223	0.0270	0.0332	0.0308	0.0409	0.0547
		TOTAL:	283			CHI SQUARE:		33.993			(1000×CHI SQUARE)÷TOTAL:				120.117
HVN	18	12	6	8	15	32	41	3	12	22	17	8	11	27	5
	20.74	12.74	8.26	8.09	16.97	22.73	35.55	14.61	37.93	13.65	11.27	2.82	13.66	13.71	4.27
	0.0203	0.0220	0.0170	0.0231	0.0207	0.0329	0.0270	0.0048	0.0074	0.0377	0.0353	0.0664	0.0188	0.0461	0.0274
		TOTAL:	237			CHI SQUARE:		63.913			(1000×CHI SQUARE)÷TOTAL:				269.677
HVZ	301	261	195	112	235	226	405	153	430	28	17	9	15	26	26
	213.40	131.15	85.05	83.23	174.66	233.93	365.89	150.33	390.31	140.47	116.00	28.98	140.56	141.06	43.98
	0.3394	0.4789	0.5517	0.3238	0.3237	0.2325	0.2663	0.2449	0.2651	0.0480	0.0353	0.0747	0.0257	0.0443	0.1423
		TOTAL:	2439			CHI SQUARE:		747.665			(1000×CHI SQUARE)÷TOTAL:				306.546
HVZ*	1	6	0	0	1	1	1	0	1	2	1	0	2	5	1
	1.92	1.18	0.77	0.75	1.58	2.11	3.30	1.36	3.52	1.27	1.05	0.26	1.27	1.27	0.40
	0.0011	0.0110	0.0000	0.0000	0.0014	0.0010	0.0007	0.0000	0.0006	0.0034	0.0021	0.0000	0.0034	0.0085	0.0055
		TOTAL:	22			CHI SQUARE:		40.084			(1000×CHI SQUARE)÷TOTAL:				1821.978
HV+TO	0	0	0	0	0	0	0	0	0	2	1	0	0	0	0
	0.26	0.16	0.10	0.10	0.21	0.29	0.45	0.18	0.48	0.17	0.14	0.04	0.17	0.17	0.05
	0.0000	0.0000	0.0000	0.0000	0.0000	0.0000	0.0000	0.0000	0.0000	0.0034	0.0021	0.0000	0.0000	0.0000	0.0000
		TOTAL:	3			CHI SQUARE:		27.159			(1000×CHI SQUARE)÷TOTAL:				9053.078
HV*	0	0	1	0	2	2	3	0	0	3	8	0	10	13	0
	3.67	2.26	1.46	1.43	3.01	4.03	6.30	2.59	6.72	2.42	2.00	0.50	2.42	2.43	0.76
	0.0000	0.0000	0.0028	0.0000	0.0028	0.0021	0.0020	0.0000	0.0000	0.0051	0.0166	0.0000	0.0171	0.0222	0.0000
		TOTAL:	42			CHI SQUARE:		109.083			(1000×CHI SQUARE)÷TOTAL:				2597.202

Table 5.2: Frequency of Tags (cont.)

Tag	A	B	C	D	E	F	G	H	J	K	L	M	N	P	R
IN	10851	6416	4156	4364	8693	12223	19370	9046	22068	6043	4695	1182	5915	5638	1941
	10727.11	6592.42	4275.13	4183.68	8779.81	11759.19	18392.25	7556.64	19619.54	7061.10	5830.79	1456.49	7065.46	7090.73	2210.62
	12.2347	11.7714	11.7580	12.6164	11.9755	12.5721	12.7381	14.4789	13.6045	10.3511	9.7390	9.8156	10.1256	9.6171	10.6199
		TOTAL:	122601			CHI SQUARE:		1625.088			(1000×CHI SQUARE)÷TOTAL:				13.255
IN+IN	0	0	0	0	0	0	0	0	0	0	0	0	1	0	0
	0.09	0.05	0.03	0.03	0.07	0.10	0.15	0.06	0.16	0.06	0.05	0.01	0.06	0.06	0.02
	0.0000	0.0000	0.0000	0.0000	0.0000	0.0000	0.0000	0.0000	0.0000	0.0000	0.0000	0.0000	0.0017	0.0000	0.0000
		TOTAL:	1			CHI SQUARE:		16.352			(1000×CHI SQUARE)÷TOTAL:				16352.141
IN+PPO	0	0	0	0	0	0	0	0	0	0	0	0	1	0	0
	0.09	0.05	0.03	0.03	0.07	0.10	0.15	0.06	0.16	0.06	0.05	0.01	0.06	0.06	0.02
	0.0000	0.0000	0.0000	0.0000	0.0000	0.0000	0.0000	0.0000	0.0000	0.0000	0.0000	0.0000	0.0017	0.0000	0.0000
		TOTAL:	1			CHI SQUARE:		16.352			(1000×CHI SQUARE)÷TOTAL:				16352.141
JJ	5141	4047	2948	2508	5251	6943	11063	4732	12844	3090	2158	761	2754	3276	1120
	6005.38	3690.65	2393.35	2342.16	4915.22	6583.17	10296.57	4230.45	10983.65	3953.03	3264.27	815.39	3955.47	3969.62	1237.57
	5.7966	7.4250	8.3404	7.2506	7.2338	7.1413	7.2752	7.5740	7.9181	5.2929	4.4764	6.3195	4.7145	5.5881	6.1279
		TOTAL:	68636			CHI SQUARE:		1837.592			(1000×CHI SQUARE)÷TOTAL:				26.773
JJR	154	106	69	63	216	184	278	101	436	86	80	25	81	87	29
	174.55	107.27	69.57	68.08	142.87	191.35	299.28	122.96	319.25	114.90	94.88	23.70	114.97	115.38	35.97
	0.1736	0.1945	0.1952	0.1821	0.2976	0.1893	0.1828	0.1617	0.2688	0.1473	0.1659	0.2076	0.1387	0.1484	0.1587
		TOTAL:	1995			CHI SQUARE:		116.710			(1000×CHI SQUARE)÷TOTAL:				58.501
JJR+CS	0	0	0	0	0	1	0	0	0	0	0	0	0	0	0
	0.09	0.05	0.03	0.03	0.07	0.10	0.15	0.06	0.16	0.06	0.05	0.01	0.06	0.06	0.02
	0.0000	0.0000	0.0000	0.0000	0.0000	0.0010	0.0000	0.0000	0.0000	0.0000	0.0000	0.0000	0.0000	0.0000	0.0000
		TOTAL:	1			CHI SQUARE:		9.426			(1000×CHI SQUARE)÷TOTAL:				9425.965
JJS	51	24	18	10	32	54	59	28	59	12	9	1	8	14	2
	33.34	20.49	13.29	13.00	27.28	36.54	57.16	23.48	60.97	21.94	18.12	4.53	21.96	22.04	6.87
	0.0575	0.0440	0.0509	0.0289	0.0441	0.0555	0.0388	0.0448	0.0364	0.0206	0.0187	0.0083	0.0137	0.0239	0.0109
		TOTAL:	381			CHI SQUARE:		49.571			(1000×CHI SQUARE)÷TOTAL:				130.107
JJT	102	67	55	38	102	106	175	62	120	42	35	8	45	38	21
	88.90	54.63	35.43	34.67	72.76	97.45	152.42	62.62	162.59	58.52	48.32	12.07	58.55	58.76	18.32
	0.1150	0.1229	0.1556	0.1099	0.1405	0.1090	0.1151	0.0992	0.0740	0.0719	0.0726	0.0664	0.0770	0.0648	0.1149
		TOTAL:	1016			CHI SQUARE:		63.443			(1000×CHI SQUARE)÷TOTAL:				62.444
JJ+JJ	0	0	0	0	0	0	0	0	2	0	0	0	0	0	0
	0.17	0.11	0.07	0.07	0.14	0.19	0.30	0.12	0.32	0.12	0.10	0.02	0.12	0.12	0.04
	0.0000	0.0000	0.0000	0.0000	0.0000	0.0000	0.0000	0.0000	0.0012	0.0000	0.0000	0.0000	0.0000	0.0000	0.0000
		TOTAL:	2			CHI SQUARE:		10.498			(1000×CHI SQUARE)÷TOTAL:				5248.914
MD	1037	872	302	501	992	1073	1746	998	2068	698	535	192	573	727	155
	1090.99	670.47	434.80	425.50	892.94	1195.96	1870.56	768.54	1995.38	718.14	593.01	148.13	718.58	721.16	224.83
	1.1692	1.5999	0.8544	1.4484	1.3666	1.1036	1.1482	1.5974	1.2749	1.1956	1.1098	1.5944	0.9809	1.2401	0.8481
		TOTAL:	12469			CHI SQUARE:		290.741			(1000×CHI SQUARE)÷TOTAL:				23.317
MD+HV	1	0	0	0	0	0	0	0	0	0	3	0	2	1	0
	0.61	0.38	0.24	0.24	0.50	0.67	1.05	0.43	1.12	0.40	0.33	0.08	0.40	0.40	0.13
	0.0011	0.0000	0.0000	0.0000	0.0000	0.0000	0.0000	0.0000	0.0000	0.0000	0.0062	0.0000	0.0034	0.0017	0.0000
		TOTAL:	7			CHI SQUARE:		34.052			(1000×CHI SQUARE)÷TOTAL:				4864.605
MD +PPSS	0	0	0	0	0	0	0	0	0	1	0	0	0	0	0
	0.09	0.05	0.03	0.03	0.07	0.10	0.15	0.06	0.16	0.06	0.05	0.01	0.06	0.06	0.02
	0.0000	0.0000	0.0000	0.0000	0.0000	0.0000	0.0000	0.0000	0.0000	0.0017	0.0000	0.0000	0.0000	0.0000	0.0000
		TOTAL:	1			CHI SQUARE:		16.363			(1000×CHI SQUARE)÷TOTAL:				16362.805
MD+TO	0	0	0	0	0	0	0	0	0	1	0	0	0	0	1
	0.17	0.11	0.07	0.07	0.14	0.19	0.30	0.12	0.32	0.12	0.10	0.02	0.12	0.12	0.04
	0.0000	0.0000	0.0000	0.0000	0.0000	0.0000	0.0000	0.0000	0.0000	0.0017	0.0000	0.0000	0.0000	0.0000	0.0055
		TOTAL:	2			CHI SQUARE:		34.411			(1000×CHI SQUARE)÷TOTAL:				17205.727
MD*	44	63	13	24	44	51	85	14	60	59	110	18	95	147	40
	75.86	46.62	30.23	29.59	62.09	83.16	130.06	53.44	138.74	49.93	41.23	10.30	49.96	50.14	15.63
	0.0496	0.1156	0.0368	0.0694	0.0606	0.0525	0.0559	0.0224	0.0370	0.1011	0.2282	0.1495	0.1626	0.2507	0.2189
		TOTAL:	867			CHI SQUARE:		524.872			(1000×CHI SQUARE)÷TOTAL:				605.388
NN	15828	9027	5742	5405	13617	16071	23595	12115	31052	8249	6746	1648	8275	7484	2714
	14661.55	9010.36	5843.13	5718.16	12000.03	16072.17	25138.07	10328.23	26815.50	9650.94	7969.38	1990.69	9656.89	9691.44	3021.42
	17.8464	16.5618	16.2451	15.6259	18.7588	16.5300	15.5165	19.3911	19.1430	14.1298	13.9935	13.6854	14.1656	12.7659	14.8493
		TOTAL:	167568			CHI SQUARE:		2585.022			(1000×CHI SQUARE)÷TOTAL:				15.427
NNS	5503	3214	2005	1807	5413	6109	7941	5140	11228	2407	1455	558	2334	2069	806
	5073.81	3118.15	2022.09	1978.84	4152.76	5561.97	8699.34	3574.21	9279.84	3339.83	2757.90	688.90	3341.89	3353.84	1045.60
	6.2048	5.8967	5.6725	5.2241	7.4569	6.2835	5.2221	8.2270	6.9218	4.1230	3.0182	4.6338	3.9955	3.5292	4.4099
		TOTAL:	57989			CHI SQUARE:		3403.635			(1000×CHI SQUARE)÷TOTAL:				58.694
NNS+MD	0	0	0	0	0	0	0	0	0	0	0	0	1	1	0
	0.17	0.11	0.07	0.07	0.14	0.19	0.30	0.12	0.32	0.12	0.10	0.02	0.12	0.12	0.04
	0.0000	0.0000	0.0000	0.0000	0.0000	0.0000	0.0000	0.0000	0.0000	0.0000	0.0000	0.0000	0.0017	0.0017	0.0000
		TOTAL:	2			CHI SQUARE:		15.321			(1000×CHI SQUARE)÷TOTAL:				7660.613
NNS$	72	25	10	12	23	34	30	29	35	16	7	2	17	19	3
	29.22	17.96	11.65	11.40	23.92	32.04	50.11	20.59	53.45	19.24	15.88	3.97	19.25	19.32	6.02
	0.0812	0.0459	0.0283	0.0347	0.0317	0.0350	0.0197	0.0464	0.0216	0.0274	0.0145	0.0166	0.0291	0.0324	0.0164
		TOTAL:	334			CHI SQUARE:		91.943			(1000×CHI SQUARE)÷TOTAL:				275.279
NN+BEZ	0	0	0	0	1	1	0	0	0	7	7	0	9	10	1
	3.15	1.94	1.26	1.23	2.58	3.45	5.40	2.22	5.76	2.07	1.71	0.43	2.07	2.08	0.65
	0.0000	0.0000	0.0000	0.0000	0.0014	0.0010	0.0000	0.0000	0.0000	0.0120	0.0145	0.0000	0.0154	0.0171	0.0055
		TOTAL:	36			CHI SQUARE:		105.541			(1000×CHI SQUARE)÷TOTAL:				2931.698
NN+HVD	0	0	0	0	0	0	0	0	0	1	0	0	0	0	0
	0.09	0.05	0.03	0.03	0.07	0.10	0.15	0.06	0.16	0.06	0.05	0.01	0.06	0.06	0.02
	0.0000	0.0000	0.0000	0.0000	0.0000	0.0000	0.0000	0.0000	0.0000	0.0017	0.0000	0.0000	0.0000	0.0000	0.0000
		TOTAL:	1			CHI SQUARE:		16.363			(1000×CHI SQUARE)÷TOTAL:				16362.805

Table 5.2: Frequency of Tags (cont.)

	A	B	C	D	E	F	G	H	J	K	L	M	N	P	R
NN+HVZ	0	0	0	0	1	0	0	0	0	0	0	0	2	2	1
	0.52	0.32	0.21	0.20	0.43	0.58	0.90	0.37	0.96	0.35	0.29	0.07	0.35	0.35	0.11
	0.0000	0.0000	0.0000	0.0000	0.0014	0.0000	0.0000	0.0000	0.0000	0.0000	0.0000	0.0000	0.0034	0.0034	0.0055
		TOTAL:	6			CHI SQUARE:		28.666			(1000×CHI SQUARE)÷TOTAL:				4777.605
NN+IN	0	0	0	0	0	0	0	0	0	1	0	0	0	0	0
	0.09	0.05	0.03	0.03	0.07	0.10	0.15	0.06	0.16	0.06	0.05	0.01	0.06	0.06	0.02
	0.0000	0.0000	0.0000	0.0000	0.0000	0.0000	0.0000	0.0000	0.0000	0.0017	0.0000	0.0000	0.0000	0.0000	0.0000
		TOTAL:	1			CHI SQUARE:		16.363			(1000×CHI SQUARE)÷TOTAL:				16362.805
NN+MD	0	0	0	0	0	1	0	0	0	0	0	0	1	0	0
	0.17	0.11	0.07	0.07	0.14	0.19	0.30	0.12	0.32	0.12	0.10	0.02	0.12	0.12	0.04
	0.0000	0.0000	0.0000	0.0000	0.0000	0.0010	0.0000	0.0000	0.0000	0.0000	0.0000	0.0000	0.0017	0.0000	0.0000
		TOTAL:	2			CHI SQUARE:		11.889			(1000×CHI SQUARE)÷TOTAL:				5944.531
NN+NN	0	0	0	0	0	0	0	0	1	0	0	0	0	0	0
	0.09	0.05	0.03	0.03	0.07	0.10	0.15	0.06	0.16	0.06	0.05	0.01	0.06	0.06	0.02
	0.0000	0.0000	0.0000	0.0000	0.0000	0.0000	0.0000	0.0000	0.0006	0.0000	0.0000	0.0000	0.0000	0.0000	0.0000
		TOTAL:	1			CHI SQUARE:		5.249			(1000×CHI SQUARE)÷TOTAL:				5248.914
NN$	279	105	82	32	116	192	236	152	184	112	81	16	134	98	38
	162.48	99.85	64.75	63.37	132.99	178.11	278.58	114.46	297.17	106.95	88.32	22.06	107.02	107.40	33.48
	0.3146	0.1926	0.2320	0.0925	0.1598	0.1975	0.1552	0.2433	0.1134	0.1918	0.1680	0.1329	0.2294	0.1672	0.2079
		TOTAL:	1857			CHI SQUARE:		179.864			(1000×CHI SQUARE)÷TOTAL:				96.857
NP	7800	2298	2245	1076	1736	3475	6177	1851	3126	2176	1815	425	2007	2185	644
	3415.50	2099.02	1361.19	1332.08	2795.48	3744.11	5856.07	2406.02	6246.84	2248.25	1856.52	463.74	2249.63	2257.68	703.86
	8.7947	4.2161	6.3515	3.1107	2.3915	3.5743	4.0621	2.9627	1.9271	3.7273	3.7649	3.5293	3.4357	3.7271	3.5236
		TOTAL:	39036			CHI SQUARE:		8436.035			(1000×CHI SQUARE)÷TOTAL:				216.109
NPS	234	119	66	92	47	231	275	19	74	55	10	18	56	40	23
	118.91	73.08	47.39	46.38	97.32	130.35	203.87	83.76	217.48	78.27	64.63	16.14	78.32	78.60	24.50
	0.2638	0.2183	0.1867	0.2660	0.0647	0.2376	0.1808	0.0304	0.0456	0.0942	0.0207	0.1495	0.0959	0.0682	0.1258
		TOTAL:	1359			CHI SQUARE:		544.464			(1000×CHI SQUARE)÷TOTAL:				400.636
NPS$	18	4	1	2	0	4	5	0	0	5	0	1	2	3	0
	3.94	2.42	1.57	1.54	3.22	4.32	6.75	2.77	7.20	2.59	2.14	0.53	2.59	2.60	0.81
	0.0203	0.0073	0.0028	0.0058	0.0000	0.0041	0.0033	0.0000	0.0000	0.0086	0.0000	0.0083	0.0034	0.0051	0.0000
		TOTAL:	45			CHI SQUARE:		71.071			(1000×CHI SQUARE)÷TOTAL:				1579.355
NP+BEZ	1	1	0	0	0	0	0	0	3	1	6	0	9	6	1
	2.45	1.51	0.98	0.96	2.01	2.69	4.20	1.73	4.48	1.61	1.33	0.33	1.61	1.62	0.50
	0.0011	0.0018	0.0000	0.0000	0.0000	0.0000	0.0000	0.0000	0.0018	0.0017	0.0124	0.0000	0.0154	0.0102	0.0055
		TOTAL:	28			CHI SQUARE:		77.143			(1000×CHI SQUARE)÷TOTAL:				2755.123
NP+HVZ	0	0	0	0	0	0	0	0	1	0	5	0	0	1	0
	0.61	0.38	0.24	0.24	0.50	0.67	1.05	0.43	1.12	0.40	0.33	0.08	0.40	0.40	0.13
	0.0000	0.0000	0.0000	0.0000	0.0000	0.0000	0.0000	0.0000	0.0006	0.0000	0.0104	0.0000	0.0000	0.0017	0.0000
		TOTAL:	7			CHI SQUARE:		71.457			(1000×CHI SQUARE)÷TOTAL:				10208.160
NP+MD	0	0	0	0	0	0	0	0	0	0	0	0	1	1	0
	0.17	0.11	0.07	0.07	0.14	0.19	0.30	0.12	0.32	0.12	0.10	0.02	0.12	0.12	0.04
	0.0000	0.0000	0.0000	0.0000	0.0000	0.0000	0.0000	0.0000	0.0000	0.0000	0.0000	0.0000	0.0017	0.0017	0.0000
		TOTAL:	2			CHI SQUARE:		15.321			(1000×CHI SQUARE)÷TOTAL:				7660.613
NP$	293	169	164	54	104	208	618	61	252	172	175	23	208	155	64
	237.99	146.26	94.85	92.82	194.79	260.89	408.05	167.65	435.27	156.66	129.36	32.31	156.75	157.31	49.04
	0.3304	0.3101	0.4640	0.1561	0.1433	0.2139	0.4064	0.0976	0.1554	0.2946	0.3630	0.1910	0.3561	0.2644	0.3502
		TOTAL:	2720			CHI SQUARE:		430.620			(1000×CHI SQUARE)÷TOTAL:				158.316
NR	511	84	95	49	127	199	222	62	102	99	112	5	85	113	29
	165.72	101.84	66.04	64.63	135.63	181.66	284.13	116.74	303.09	109.08	90.08	22.50	109.15	109.54	34.15
	0.5762	0.1541	0.2688	0.1417	0.1750	0.2047	0.1460	0.0992	0.0629	0.1696	0.2323	0.0415	0.1455	0.1928	0.1587
		TOTAL:	1894			CHI SQUARE:		940.000			(1000×CHI SQUARE)÷TOTAL:				496.304
NRS	0	1	3	1	1	1	3	0	3	2	0	0	0	2	0
	1.49	0.91	0.59	0.58	1.22	1.63	2.55	1.05	2.72	0.98	0.81	0.20	0.98	0.98	0.31
	0.0000	0.0018	0.0085	0.0029	0.0014	0.0010	0.0020	0.0000	0.0018	0.0034	0.0000	0.0000	0.0000	0.0034	0.0000
		TOTAL:	17			CHI SQUARE:		17.426			(1000×CHI SQUARE)÷TOTAL:				1025.042
NR+MD	0	0	0	0	0	0	0	0	0	1	0	0	0	0	0
	0.09	0.05	0.03	0.03	0.07	0.10	0.15	0.06	0.16	0.06	0.05	0.01	0.06	0.06	0.02
	0.0000	0.0000	0.0000	0.0000	0.0000	0.0000	0.0000	0.0000	0.0000	0.0017	0.0000	0.0000	0.0000	0.0000	0.0000
		TOTAL:	1			CHI SQUARE:		16.363			(1000×CHI SQUARE)÷TOTAL:				16362.805
NR$	25	6	5	0	11	2	11	4	6	4	1	0	2	0	0
	6.74	4.14	2.69	2.63	5.51	7.39	11.55	4.75	12.32	4.43	3.66	0.91	4.44	4.45	1.39
	0.0282	0.0110	0.0141	0.0000	0.0152	0.0021	0.0072	0.0064	0.0037	0.0069	0.0021	0.0000	0.0034	0.0000	0.0000
		TOTAL:	77			CHI SQUARE:		77.809			(1000×CHI SQUARE)÷TOTAL:				1010.509
OD	340	113	105	59	159	236	354	120	349	69	62	21	70	66	22
	187.68	115.34	74.80	73.20	153.61	205.74	321.79	132.21	343.26	123.54	102.01	25.48	123.62	124.06	38.68
	0.3834	0.2073	0.2971	0.1706	0.2190	0.2427	0.2328	0.1921	0.2152	0.1182	0.1286	0.1744	0.1198	0.1126	0.1204
		TOTAL:	2145			CHI SQUARE:		245.888			(1000×CHI SQUARE)÷TOTAL:				114.633
PN	90	108	99	83	83	206	412	42	226	222	270	48	232	378	83
	225.92	138.84	90.03	88.11	184.90	247.65	387.34	159.14	413.19	148.71	122.80	30.67	148.80	149.33	46.56
	0.1015	0.1981	0.2801	0.2400	0.1143	0.2119	0.2709	0.0672	0.1393	0.3803	0.5601	0.3986	0.3972	0.6448	0.4541
		TOTAL:	2582			CHI SQUARE:		973.143			(1000×CHI SQUARE)÷TOTAL:				376.895
PN+BEZ	0	0	0	0	0	0	0	0	0	2	2	0	1	2	0
	0.61	0.38	0.24	0.24	0.50	0.67	1.05	0.43	1.12	0.40	0.33	0.08	0.40	0.40	0.13
	0.0000	0.0000	0.0000	0.0000	0.0000	0.0000	0.0000	0.0000	0.0000	0.0034	0.0041	0.0000	0.0017	0.0034	0.0000
		TOTAL:	7			CHI SQUARE:		27.296			(1000×CHI SQUARE)÷TOTAL:				3899.390
PN+HVD	0	0	0	0	0	0	0	0	0	0	0	0	0	1	0
	0.09	0.05	0.03	0.03	0.07	0.10	0.15	0.06	0.16	0.06	0.05	0.01	0.06	0.06	0.02
	0.0000	0.0000	0.0000	0.0000	0.0000	0.0000	0.0000	0.0000	0.0000	0.0000	0.0000	0.0000	0.0000	0.0017	0.0000
		TOTAL:	1			CHI SQUARE:		16.290			(1000×CHI SQUARE)÷TOTAL:				16290.281

Table 5.2: Frequency of Tags (cont.)

	A	B	C	D	E	F	G	H	J	K	L	M	N	P	R
PN+HVZ	1	0	0	0	0	0	0	0	0	1	0	0	1	0	0
	0.26	0.16	0.10	0.10	0.21	0.29	0.45	0.18	0.48	0.17	0.14	0.04	0.17	0.17	0.05
	0.0011	0.0000	0.0000	0.0000	0.0000	0.0000	0.0000	0.0000	0.0000	0.0017	0.0000	0.0000	0.0017	0.0000	0.0000
		TOTAL:	3			CHI SQUARE:		12.381			(1000×CHI SQUARE)÷TOTAL:				4127.117
PN+MD	0	0	0	0	0	0	0	0	0	2	1	0	0	0	0
	0.26	0.16	0.10	0.10	0.21	0.29	0.45	0.18	0.48	0.17	0.14	0.04	0.17	0.17	0.05
	0.0000	0.0000	0.0000	0.0000	0.0000	0.0000	0.0000	0.0000	0.0000	0.0034	0.0021	0.0000	0.0000	0.0000	0.0000
		TOTAL:	3			CHI SQUARE:		27.159			(1000×CHI SQUARE)÷TOTAL:				9053.078
PN$	1	2	8	5	1	21	22	4	6	7	4	0	1	6	1
	7.79	4.79	3.10	3.04	6.37	8.54	13.35	5.49	14.24	5.13	4.23	1.06	5.13	5.15	1.60
	0.0011	0.0037	0.0226	0.0145	0.0014	0.0216	0.0145	0.0064	0.0037	0.0120	0.0083	0.0000	0.0017	0.0102	0.0055
		TOTAL:	89			CHI SQUARE:		55.482			(1000×CHI SQUARE)÷TOTAL:				623.397
PPL	36	57	48	55	48	84	257	21	115	123	82	26	115	139	31
	108.23	66.52	43.13	42.21	88.59	118.65	185.57	76.24	197.95	71.24	58.83	14.70	71.29	71.54	22.30
	0.0406	0.1046	0.1358	0.1590	0.0661	0.0864	0.1690	0.0336	0.0709	0.2107	0.1701	0.2159	0.1969	0.2371	0.1696
		TOTAL:	1237			CHI SQUARE:		334.203			(1000×CHI SQUARE)÷TOTAL:				270.172
PPLS	21	26	13	30	19	32	88	26	47	5	9	3	7	11	8
	30.19	18.55	12.03	11.77	24.71	33.09	51.76	21.26	55.21	19.87	16.41	4.10	19.88	19.95	6.22
	0.0237	0.0477	0.0368	0.0867	0.0262	0.0329	0.0579	0.0416	0.0290	0.0086	0.0187	0.0249	0.0120	0.0188	0.0438
		TOTAL:	345			CHI SQUARE:		90.735			(1000×CHI SQUARE)÷TOTAL:				263.000
PPO	412	457	206	398	491	826	1599	203	629	1230	1207	252	1502	1502	295
	980.74	602.72	390.86	382.50	802.71	1075.10	1681.54	690.88	1793.75	645.57	533.09	133.16	645.97	648.28	202.11
	0.4645	0.8385	0.5828	1.1506	0.6764	0.8496	1.0515	0.3249	0.3878	2.1069	2.5037	2.0927	2.5712	2.5620	1.6140
		TOTAL:	11209			CHI SQUARE:		5525.156			(1000×CHI SQUARE)÷TOTAL:				492.921
PPS	1056	782	494	454	612	1524	2743	428	1384	2089	1767	336	1996	2200	424
	1600.22	983.42	637.74	624.10	1309.73	1754.18	2743.66	1127.26	2926.74	1053.34	869.81	217.27	1053.99	1057.76	329.77
	1.1907	1.4347	1.3976	1.3125	0.8431	1.5675	1.8038	0.6851	0.8532	3.5783	3.6654	2.7902	3.4169	3.7527	2.3199
		TOTAL:	18289			CHI SQUARE:		6064.883			(1000×CHI SQUARE)÷TOTAL:				331.614
PPS	32	23	16	0	44	23	25	1	6	39	78	5	61	70	11
+BEZ	37.97	23.34	15.13	14.81	31.08	41.63	65.11	26.75	69.45	25.00	20.64	5.16	25.01	25.10	7.83
	0.0361	0.0422	0.0453	0.0000	0.0606	0.0237	0.0164	0.0016	0.0037	0.0668	0.1618	0.0415	0.1044	0.1194	0.0602
		TOTAL:	434			CHI SQUARE:		437.609			(1000×CHI SQUARE)÷TOTAL:				1008.316
PPS	0	0	0	0	0	1	1	0	0	10	19	0	20	32	0
+HVD	7.26	4.46	2.89	2.83	5.94	7.96	12.45	5.12	13.28	4.78	3.95	0.99	4.78	4.80	1.50
	0.0000	0.0000	0.0000	0.0000	0.0000	0.0010	0.0007	0.0000	0.0000	0.0171	0.0394	0.0000	0.0342	0.0546	0.0000
		TOTAL:	83			CHI SQUARE:		326.518			(1000×CHI SQUARE)÷TOTAL:				3933.955
PPS	4	3	0	0	0	0	2	0	0	7	7	0	7	11	2
+HVZ	3.76	2.31	1.50	1.47	3.08	4.12	6.45	2.65	6.88	2.48	2.05	0.51	2.48	2.49	0.78
	0.0045	0.0055	0.0000	0.0000	0.0000	0.0000	0.0013	0.0000	0.0000	0.0120	0.0145	0.0000	0.0120	0.0188	0.0109
		TOTAL:	43			CHI SQUARE:		83.098			(1000×CHI SQUARE)÷TOTAL:				1932.504
PPS+MD	8	2	0	0	0	10	4	0	0	30	38	2	18	29	3
	12.60	7.74	5.02	4.91	10.31	13.81	21.60	8.88	23.04	8.29	6.85	1.71	8.30	8.33	2.60
	0.0090	0.0037	0.0000	0.0000	0.0000	0.0103	0.0026	0.0000	0.0000	0.0514	0.0788	0.0166	0.0308	0.0495	0.0164
		TOTAL:	144			CHI SQUARE:		334.770			(1000×CHI SQUARE)÷TOTAL:				2324.790
PPSS	604	676	224	612	909	1040	2137	435	1139	1136	1118	283	1375	1692	494
	1213.92	746.02	483.79	473.44	993.56	1330.71	2081.34	855.14	2220.22	799.06	659.83	164.82	799.55	802.42	250.16
	0.6810	1.2403	0.6337	1.7693	1.2522	1.0697	1.4053	0.6963	0.7022	1.9459	2.3191	2.3501	2.3538	2.8861	2.7029
		TOTAL:	13874			CHI SQUARE:		3481.225			(1000×CHI SQUARE)÷TOTAL:				250.917
PPSS	18	2	1	1	2	5	9	0	0	28	53	12	51	77	11
+BEM	23.62	14.52	9.41	9.21	19.34	25.90	40.50	16.64	43.21	15.55	12.84	3.21	15.56	15.62	4.87
	0.0203	0.0037	0.0028	0.0029	0.0028	0.0051	0.0059	0.0000	0.0000	0.0480	0.1099	0.0997	0.0873	0.1313	0.0602
		TOTAL:	270			CHI SQUARE:		633.135			(1000×CHI SQUARE)÷TOTAL:				2344.946
PPSS	20	12	2	3	19	5	5	0	5	26	50	6	62	50	16
+BER	24.59	15.11	9.80	9.59	20.12	26.95	42.15	17.32	44.97	16.18	13.36	3.34	16.19	16.25	5.07
	0.0226	0.0220	0.0057	0.0087	0.0262	0.0051	0.0033	0.0000	0.0031	0.0445	0.1037	0.0498	0.1061	0.0853	0.0875
		TOTAL:	281			CHI SQUARE:		447.511			(1000×CHI SQUARE)÷TOTAL:				1592.565
PPSS	0	0	0	0	0	0	0	0	0	0	0	0	1	0	0
+BEZ	0.09	0.05	0.03	0.03	0.07	0.10	0.15	0.06	0.16	0.06	0.05	0.01	0.06	0.06	0.02
	0.0000	0.0000	0.0000	0.0000	0.0000	0.0000	0.0000	0.0000	0.0000	0.0000	0.0000	0.0000	0.0017	0.0000	0.0000
		TOTAL:	1			CHI SQUARE:		16.352			(1000×CHI SQUARE)÷TOTAL:				16352.141
PPSS	0	0	0	0	0	0	0	0	0	0	0	0	1	0	0
+BEZ*	0.09	0.05	0.03	0.03	0.07	0.10	0.15	0.06	0.16	0.06	0.05	0.01	0.06	0.06	0.02
	0.0000	0.0000	0.0000	0.0000	0.0000	0.0000	0.0000	0.0000	0.0000	0.0000	0.0000	0.0000	0.0017	0.0000	0.0000
		TOTAL:	1			CHI SQUARE:		16.352			(1000×CHI SQUARE)÷TOTAL:				16352.141
PPSS	19	6	2	1	15	7	12	0	0	24	50	10	42	45	9
+HV	21.17	13.01	8.44	8.26	17.33	23.21	36.30	14.92	38.73	13.94	11.51	2.87	13.95	14.00	4.36
	0.0214	0.0110	0.0057	0.0029	0.0207	0.0072	0.0079	0.0000	0.0000	0.0411	0.1037	0.0830	0.0719	0.0768	0.0492
		TOTAL:	242			CHI SQUARE:		380.525			(1000×CHI SQUARE)÷TOTAL:				1572.417
PPSS	1	1	0	0	0	0	1	0	0	10	27	1	20	22	0
+HVD	7.26	4.46	2.89	2.83	5.94	7.96	12.45	5.12	13.28	4.78	3.95	0.99	4.78	4.80	1.50
	0.0011	0.0018	0.0000	0.0000	0.0000	0.0000	0.0007	0.0000	0.0000	0.0171	0.0560	0.0083	0.0342	0.0375	0.0000
		TOTAL:	83			CHI SQUARE:		308.503			(1000×CHI SQUARE)÷TOTAL:				3716.905
PPSS	31	7	1	2	37	14	16	0	3	43	107	8	98	111	8
+MD	42.52	26.13	16.95	16.58	34.80	46.61	72.91	29.96	77.77	27.99	23.11	5.77	28.01	28.11	8.76
	0.0350	0.0128	0.0028	0.0058	0.0510	0.0144	0.0105	0.0000	0.0018	0.0737	0.2220	0.0664	0.1678	0.1893	0.0438
		TOTAL:	486			CHI SQUARE:		946.963			(1000×CHI SQUARE)÷TOTAL:				1948.483
PPSS	0	0	0	0	0	0	0	0	0	0	0	0	2	0	0
+VB	0.17	0.11	0.07	0.07	0.14	0.19	0.30	0.12	0.32	0.12	0.10	0.02	0.12	0.12	0.04
	0.0000	0.0000	0.0000	0.0000	0.0000	0.0000	0.0000	0.0000	0.0000	0.0000	0.0000	0.0000	0.0034	0.0000	0.0000
		TOTAL:	2			CHI SQUARE:		32.704			(1000×CHI SQUARE)÷TOTAL:				16352.141

Table 5.2: Frequency of Tags (cont.)

	A	B	C	D	E	F	G	H	J	K	L	M	N	P	R
PP$	1052	776	501	591	998	1454	3089	728	1425	1504	1000	272	1644	1478	418
	1481.31	910.35	590.35	577.73	1212.41	1623.83	2539.79	1043.50	2709.27	975.07	805.18	201.13	975.67	979.16	305.26
	1.1862	1.4237	1.4174	1.7086	1.3748	1.4955	2.0314	1.1652	0.8785	2.5762	2.0743	2.2588	2.8143	2.5211	2.2870
		TOTAL:	16930				CHI SQUARE:	2149.291			(1000×CHI SQUARE)÷TOTAL:				126.952
PP$$	3	10	5	8	7	8	30	0	16	14	12	5	7	30	9
	14.35	8.82	5.72	5.60	11.74	15.73	24.60	10.11	26.24	9.45	7.80	1.95	9.45	9.49	2.96
	0.0034	0.0183	0.0141	0.0231	0.0096	0.0082	0.0197	0.0000	0.0099	0.0240	0.0249	0.0415	0.0120	0.0512	0.0492
		TOTAL:	164				CHI SQUARE:	97.858			(1000×CHI SQUARE)÷TOTAL:				596.693
QL	469	541	450	343	725	922	1562	348	1453	405	372	105	379	494	180
	765.42	470.39	305.04	298.52	626.47	839.06	1312.35	539.19	1399.92	503.83	416.05	103.93	504.14	505.95	157.74
	0.5288	0.9926	1.2731	0.9916	0.9988	0.9483	1.0272	0.5570	0.8957	0.6937	0.7717	0.8719	0.6488	0.8426	0.9848
		TOTAL:	8748				CHI SQUARE:	400.443			(1000×CHI SQUARE)÷TOTAL:				45.775
QLP	12	15	8	4	23	15	33	3	39	20	20	9	20	29	11
	22.84	14.03	9.10	8.91	18.69	25.03	39.15	16.09	41.77	15.03	12.41	3.10	15.04	15.10	4.71
	0.0135	0.0275	0.0226	0.0116	0.0317	0.0154	0.0217	0.0048	0.0240	0.0343	0.0415	0.0747	0.0342	0.0495	0.0602
		TOTAL:	261				CHI SQUARE:	65.221			(1000×CHI SQUARE)÷TOTAL:				249.888
RB	2187	1819	1286	1321	2318	3500	5214	1552	5580	2479	2454	522	2845	2727	757
	3198.95	1965.93	1274.89	1247.62	2618.24	3506.72	5484.77	2253.47	5850.77	2105.70	1738.81	434.34	2107.00	2114.54	659.23
	2.4659	3.3373	3.6383	3.8190	3.1933	3.6000	3.4288	2.4841	3.4400	4.2463	5.0904	4.3348	4.8702	4.6516	4.1418
		TOTAL:	36561				CHI SQUARE:	1442.634			(1000×CHI SQUARE)÷TOTAL:				39.458
RBR	88	44	38	33	90	133	186	49	157	64	83	21	95	87	15
	103.51	63.61	41.25	40.37	84.72	113.47	177.47	72.92	189.31	68.13	56.26	14.05	68.18	68.42	21.33
	0.0992	0.0807	0.1075	0.0954	0.1240	0.1368	0.1223	0.0784	0.0968	0.1096	0.1722	0.1744	0.1626	0.1484	0.0821
		TOTAL:	1183				CHI SQUARE:	61.301			(1000×CHI SQUARE)÷TOTAL:				51.818
RBR+CS	0	0	0	0	0	0	0	0	0	0	0	0	1	0	0
	0.09	0.05	0.03	0.03	0.07	0.10	0.15	0.06	0.16	0.06	0.05	0.01	0.06	0.06	0.02
	0.0000	0.0000	0.0000	0.0000	0.0000	0.0000	0.0000	0.0000	0.0000	0.0000	0.0000	0.0000	0.0017	0.0000	0.0000
		TOTAL:	1				CHI SQUARE:	16.352			(1000×CHI SQUARE)÷TOTAL:				16352.141
RBT	5	5	3	2	18	11	16	10	10	5	3	1	7	2	3
	8.84	5.43	3.52	3.45	7.23	9.69	15.15	6.23	16.16	5.82	4.80	1.20	5.82	5.84	1.82
	0.0056	0.0092	0.0085	0.0058	0.0248	0.0113	0.0105	0.0160	0.0062	0.0086	0.0062	0.0083	0.0120	0.0034	0.0164
		TOTAL:	101				CHI SQUARE:	27.630			(1000×CHI SQUARE)÷TOTAL:				273.568
RB+BEZ	1	0	0	0	5	0	0	0	1	1	2	0	1	1	1
	1.14	0.70	0.45	0.44	0.93	1.25	1.95	0.80	2.08	0.75	0.62	0.15	0.75	0.75	0.23
	0.0011	0.0000	0.0000	0.0000	0.0069	0.0000	0.0000	0.0000	0.0006	0.0017	0.0041	0.0000	0.0017	0.0017	0.0055
		TOTAL:	13				CHI SQUARE:	29.950			(1000×CHI SQUARE)÷TOTAL:				2303.826
RB+CS	0	0	0	0	0	0	0	0	0	0	0	0	1	2	0
	0.26	0.16	0.10	0.10	0.21	0.29	0.45	0.18	0.48	0.17	0.14	0.04	0.17	0.17	0.05
	0.0000	0.0000	0.0000	0.0000	0.0000	0.0000	0.0000	0.0000	0.0000	0.0000	0.0000	0.0000	0.0017	0.0034	0.0000
		TOTAL:	3				CHI SQUARE:	25.838			(1000×CHI SQUARE)÷TOTAL:				8612.586
RB$	1	3	1	1	0	0	2	0	0	0	0	0	0	0	1
	0.79	0.48	0.31	0.31	0.64	0.86	1.35	0.55	1.44	0.52	0.43	0.11	0.52	0.52	0.16
	0.0011	0.0055	0.0028	0.0029	0.0000	0.0000	0.0013	0.0000	0.0000	0.0000	0.0000	0.0000	0.0000	0.0000	0.0055
		TOTAL:	9				CHI SQUARE:	26.434			(1000×CHI SQUARE)÷TOTAL:				2937.159
RN	0	3	1	0	0	0	0	0	0	0	3	0	0	2	0
	0.79	0.48	0.31	0.31	0.64	0.86	1.35	0.55	1.44	0.52	0.43	0.11	0.52	0.52	0.16
	0.0000	0.0055	0.0028	0.0000	0.0000	0.0000	0.0000	0.0000	0.0000	0.0000	0.0062	0.0000	0.0000	0.0034	0.0000
		TOTAL:	9				CHI SQUARE:	41.495			(1000×CHI SQUARE)÷TOTAL:				4610.516
RP	486	234	159	127	349	498	601	134	444	633	694	100	751	667	154
	527.69	324.29	210.30	205.80	431.90	578.46	904.75	371.73	965.13	347.35	286.83	71.65	347.56	348.81	108.74
	0.5480	0.4293	0.4498	0.3672	0.4808	0.5122	0.3952	0.2145	0.2737	1.0843	1.4396	0.8304	1.2856	1.1377	0.8426
		TOTAL:	6031				CHI SQUARE:	2235.137			(1000×CHI SQUARE)÷TOTAL:				370.608
RP+IN	0	0	0	0	0	0	0	0	0	1	0	0	1	2	0
	0.35	0.22	0.14	0.14	0.29	0.38	0.60	0.25	0.64	0.23	0.19	0.05	0.23	0.23	0.07
	0.0000	0.0000	0.0000	0.0000	0.0000	0.0000	0.0000	0.0000	0.0000	0.0017	0.0000	0.0000	0.0017	0.0034	0.0000
		TOTAL:	4				CHI SQUARE:	21.969			(1000×CHI SQUARE)÷TOTAL:				5492.254
TO	1245	954	403	505	1022	1550	2341	935	2131	937	798	192	773	912	299
	1312.18	806.41	522.95	511.76	1073.98	1438.43	2249.81	924.36	2399.93	863.74	713.24	178.16	864.27	867.36	270.41
	1.4038	1.7503	1.1402	1.4600	1.4079	1.5943	1.5395	1.4965	1.3137	1.6050	1.6553	1.5944	1.3233	1.5556	1.6359
		TOTAL:	14997				CHI SQUARE:	135.498			(1000×CHI SQUARE)÷TOTAL:				9.035
TO+VB	0	0	0	0	0	0	0	0	0	0	0	0	2	0	0
	0.17	0.11	0.07	0.07	0.14	0.19	0.30	0.12	0.32	0.12	0.10	0.02	0.12	0.12	0.04
	0.0000	0.0000	0.0000	0.0000	0.0000	0.0000	0.0000	0.0000	0.0000	0.0000	0.0000	0.0000	0.0034	0.0000	0.0000
		TOTAL:	2				CHI SQUARE:	32.704			(1000×CHI SQUARE)÷TOTAL:				16352.141
UH	13	12	20	19	8	23	47	0	12	99	75	25	107	138	31
	55.04	33.82	21.93	21.46	45.04	60.33	94.36	38.77	100.66	36.23	29.91	7.47	36.25	36.38	11.34
	0.0147	0.0220	0.0566	0.0549	0.0110	0.0237	0.0309	0.0000	0.0074	0.1696	0.1556	0.2076	0.1832	0.2354	0.1696
		TOTAL:	629				CHI SQUARE:	914.702			(1000×CHI SQUARE)÷TOTAL:				1454.216
VB	2474	2158	902	1283	3014	3088	4848	1856	4398	2177	2033	495	2170	2404	656
	2971.02	1825.86	1184.05	1158.73	2431.69	3256.87	5093.98	2092.91	5433.89	1955.67	1614.92	403.39	1956.87	1963.88	612.26
	2.7895	3.9593	2.5519	3.7092	4.1521	3.1762	3.1881	2.9707	2.7113	3.7290	4.2171	4.1106	3.7147	4.1006	3.5892
		TOTAL:	33956				CHI SQUARE:	887.517			(1000×CHI SQUARE)÷TOTAL:				26.137
VBD	2533	701	507	511	617	2273	3503	405	1492	3032	2645	531	3702	3048	699
	2292.31	1408.76	913.56	894.03	1876.19	2512.86	3930.30	1614.80	4192.56	1508.91	1246.00	311.24	1509.84	1515.24	472.39
	2.8560	1.2861	1.4344	1.4773	0.8500	2.3379	2.3036	0.6482	0.9198	5.1936	5.4866	4.4096	6.3373	5.1991	3.8245
		TOTAL:	26199				CHI SQUARE:	12391.559			(1000×CHI SQUARE)÷TOTAL:				472.978
VBG	1426	906	525	477	1554	1706	2136	1058	2656	1385	989	203	1475	1336	361
	1591.82	978.26	634.39	620.83	1302.85	1744.97	2729.26	1121.34	2911.38	1047.81	865.24	216.13	1048.46	1052.21	328.04
	1.6078	1.6622	1.4853	1.3790	2.1408	1.7547	1.4047	1.6934	1.6374	2.3724	2.0515	1.6858	2.5250	2.2789	1.9752
		TOTAL:	18193				CHI SQUARE:	659.406			(1000×CHI SQUARE)÷TOTAL:				36.245

Table 5.2: Frequency of Tags (cont.)

	A	B	C	D	E	F	G	H	J	K	L	M	N	P	R
VBG+TO	0	0	0	0	1	0	0	0	1	2	0	0	9	4	0
	1.49	0.91	0.59	0.58	1.22	1.63	2.55	1.05	2.72	0.98	0.81	0.20	0.98	0.98	0.31
	0.0000	0.0000	0.0000	0.0000	0.0014	0.0000	0.0000	0.0000	0.0006	0.0034	0.0000	0.0000	0.0154	0.0068	0.0000
		TOTAL:	17			CHI SQUARE:		87.226			(1000×CHI SQUARE)÷TOTAL:				5130.910
VBN	2412	1588	904	952	2288	2880	4288	2397	6120	1504	1163	321	1279	1364	480
	2619.64	1609.91	1044.01	1021.68	2144.09	2871.67	4491.51	1845.38	4791.22	1724.37	1423.92	355.68	1725.43	1731.61	539.85
	2.7196	2.9135	2.5576	2.7522	3.1519	2.9623	2.8199	3.8366	3.7729	2.5762	2.4125	2.6657	2.1895	2.3267	2.6263
		TOTAL:	29940			CHI SQUARE:		872.134			(1000×CHI SQUARE)÷TOTAL:				29.129
VBN+TO	0	0	0	0	1	0	0	0	0	0	1	0	2	1	0
	0.44	0.27	0.17	0.17	0.36	0.48	0.75	0.31	0.80	0.29	0.24	0.06	0.29	0.29	0.09
	0.0000	0.0000	0.0000	0.0000	0.0014	0.0000	0.0000	0.0000	0.0000	0.0000	0.0021	0.0000	0.0034	0.0017	0.0000
		TOTAL:	5			CHI SQUARE:		19.338			(1000×CHI SQUARE)÷TOTAL:				3867.572
VBZ	558	564	531	355	678	775	1410	424	1585	111	116	26	75	134	127
	653.51	401.62	260.45	254.88	534.88	716.38	1120.48	460.36	1195.25	430.17	355.22	88.73	430.44	431.98	134.67
	0.6292	1.0348	1.5023	1.0263	0.9340	0.7971	0.9272	0.6786	0.9771	0.1901	0.2406	0.2159	0.1284	0.2286	0.6949
		TOTAL:	7469			CHI SQUARE:		1589.614			(1000×CHI SQUARE)÷TOTAL:				212.828
VB+AT	0	0	0	0	0	0	0	0	0	0	0	0	2	0	0
	0.17	0.11	0.07	0.07	0.14	0.19	0.30	0.12	0.32	0.12	0.10	0.02	0.12	0.12	0.04
	0.0000	0.0000	0.0000	0.0000	0.0000	0.0000	0.0000	0.0000	0.0000	0.0000	0.0000	0.0000	0.0034	0.0000	0.0000
		TOTAL:	2			CHI SQUARE:		32.704			(1000×CHI SQUARE)÷TOTAL:				16352.141
VB+IN	0	0	0	0	1	0	0	0	0	2	0	0	0	0	0
	0.26	0.16	0.10	0.10	0.21	0.29	0.45	0.18	0.48	0.17	0.14	0.04	0.17	0.17	0.05
	0.0000	0.0000	0.0000	0.0000	0.0014	0.0000	0.0000	0.0000	0.0000	0.0034	0.0000	0.0000	0.0000	0.0000	0.0000
		TOTAL:	3			CHI SQUARE:		24.805			(1000×CHI SQUARE)÷TOTAL:				8268.359
VB+JJ	0	0	0	0	0	0	0	0	1	0	0	0	0	0	0
	0.09	0.05	0.03	0.03	0.07	0.10	0.15	0.06	0.16	0.06	0.05	0.01	0.06	0.06	0.02
	0.0000	0.0000	0.0000	0.0000	0.0000	0.0000	0.0000	0.0000	0.0006	0.0000	0.0000	0.0000	0.0000	0.0000	0.0000
		TOTAL:	1			CHI SQUARE:		5.249			(1000×CHI SQUARE)÷TOTAL:				5248.914
VB+PPO	1	1	0	0	3	4	2	0	1	6	13	2	21	15	2
	6.21	3.82	2.48	2.42	5.08	6.81	10.65	4.38	11.36	4.09	3.38	0.84	4.09	4.11	1.28
	0.0011	0.0018	0.0000	0.0000	0.0041	0.0041	0.0013	0.0000	0.0006	0.0103	0.0270	0.0166	0.0359	0.0256	0.0109
		TOTAL:	71			CHI SQUARE:		163.297			(1000×CHI SQUARE)÷TOTAL:				2299.964
VB+RP	0	0	0	0	0	1	0	0	0	0	0	0	1	0	0
	0.17	0.11	0.07	0.07	0.14	0.19	0.30	0.12	0.32	0.12	0.10	0.02	0.12	0.12	0.04
	0.0000	0.0000	0.0000	0.0000	0.0000	0.0010	0.0000	0.0000	0.0000	0.0000	0.0000	0.0000	0.0017	0.0000	0.0000
		TOTAL:	2			CHI SQUARE:		11.889			(1000×CHI SQUARE)÷TOTAL:				5944.531
VB+TO	0	0	0	0	0	0	0	0	0	2	0	0	2	0	0
	0.35	0.22	0.14	0.14	0.29	0.38	0.60	0.25	0.64	0.23	0.19	0.05	0.23	0.23	0.07
	0.0000	0.0000	0.0000	0.0000	0.0000	0.0000	0.0000	0.0000	0.0000	0.0034	0.0000	0.0000	0.0034	0.0000	0.0000
		TOTAL:	4			CHI SQUARE:		30.715			(1000×CHI SQUARE)÷TOTAL:				7678.738
VB+VB	0	0	0	0	0	0	0	0	1	0	0	0	0	0	0
	0.09	0.05	0.03	0.03	0.07	0.10	0.15	0.06	0.16	0.06	0.05	0.01	0.06	0.06	0.02
	0.0000	0.0000	0.0000	0.0000	0.0000	0.0000	0.0000	0.0000	0.0006	0.0000	0.0000	0.0000	0.0000	0.0000	0.0000
		TOTAL:	1			CHI SQUARE:		5.249			(1000×CHI SQUARE)÷TOTAL:				5248.914
WDT	343	310	182	293	367	447	1021	321	1031	315	213	78	259	285	111
	487.88	299.83	194.44	190.28	399.31	534.82	836.50	343.68	892.31	321.15	265.19	66.24	321.34	322.49	100.54
	0.3867	0.5688	0.5149	0.8471	0.5056	0.4598	0.6714	0.5138	0.6356	0.5396	0.4418	0.6477	0.4434	0.4861	0.6073
		TOTAL:	5576			CHI SQUARE:		210.418			(1000×CHI SQUARE)÷TOTAL:				37.736
WDT +BER	0	0	0	0	0	0	0	0	0	0	0	0	1	0	0
	0.09	0.05	0.03	0.03	0.07	0.10	0.15	0.06	0.16	0.06	0.05	0.01	0.06	0.06	0.02
	0.0000	0.0000	0.0000	0.0000	0.0000	0.0000	0.0000	0.0000	0.0000	0.0000	0.0000	0.0000	0.0017	0.0000	0.0000
		TOTAL:	1			CHI SQUARE:		16.352			(1000×CHI SQUARE)÷TOTAL:				16352.141
WDT+BER +PPS	0	0	0	0	1	0	0	0	0	0	0	0	0	0	0
	0.09	0.05	0.03	0.03	0.07	0.10	0.15	0.06	0.16	0.06	0.05	0.01	0.06	0.06	0.02
	0.0000	0.0000	0.0000	0.0000	0.0014	0.0000	0.0000	0.0000	0.0000	0.0000	0.0000	0.0000	0.0000	0.0000	0.0000
		TOTAL:	1			CHI SQUARE:		12.964			(1000×CHI SQUARE)÷TOTAL:				12963.957
WDT +BEZ	1	3	2	0	1	1	0	0	3	5	8	3	12	10	2
	4.46	2.74	1.78	1.74	3.65	4.89	7.65	3.14	8.16	2.94	2.43	0.61	2.94	2.95	0.92
	0.0011	0.0055	0.0057	0.0000	0.0014	0.0010	0.0000	0.0000	0.0018	0.0086	0.0166	0.0249	0.0205	0.0171	0.0109
		TOTAL:	51			CHI SQUARE:		93.335			(1000×CHI SQUARE)÷TOTAL:				1830.092
WDT+DO +PPSS	0	0	0	0	0	0	0	0	0	0	0	0	1	0	0
	0.09	0.05	0.03	0.03	0.07	0.10	0.15	0.06	0.16	0.06	0.05	0.01	0.06	0.06	0.02
	0.0000	0.0000	0.0000	0.0000	0.0000	0.0000	0.0000	0.0000	0.0000	0.0000	0.0000	0.0000	0.0017	0.0000	0.0000
		TOTAL:	1			CHI SQUARE:		16.352			(1000×CHI SQUARE)÷TOTAL:				16352.141
WDT +DOD	0	0	0	0	0	0	0	0	0	1	0	0	0	0	0
	0.09	0.05	0.03	0.03	0.07	0.10	0.15	0.06	0.16	0.06	0.05	0.01	0.06	0.06	0.02
	0.0000	0.0000	0.0000	0.0000	0.0000	0.0000	0.0000	0.0000	0.0000	0.0017	0.0000	0.0000	0.0000	0.0000	0.0000
		TOTAL:	1			CHI SQUARE:		16.363			(1000×CHI SQUARE)÷TOTAL:				16362.805
WDT +HVZ	0	0	0	0	0	1	0	0	0	1	0	0	0	0	0
	0.17	0.11	0.07	0.07	0.14	0.19	0.30	0.12	0.32	0.12	0.10	0.02	0.12	0.12	0.04
	0.0000	0.0000	0.0000	0.0000	0.0000	0.0010	0.0000	0.0000	0.0000	0.0017	0.0000	0.0000	0.0000	0.0000	0.0000
		TOTAL:	2			CHI SQUARE:		11.894			(1000×CHI SQUARE)÷TOTAL:				5947.203
WPO	9	15	12	18	9	29	106	16	39	15	4	2	2	5	4
	24.94	15.32	9.94	9.73	20.41	27.34	42.75	17.57	45.61	16.41	13.55	3.39	16.42	16.48	5.14
	0.0101	0.0275	0.0340	0.0520	0.0124	0.0298	0.0697	0.0256	0.0240	0.0257	0.0083	0.0166	0.0034	0.0085	0.0219
		TOTAL:	285			CHI SQUARE:		147.136			(1000×CHI SQUARE)÷TOTAL:				516.265
WPS	396	268	244	195	239	427	755	140	430	195	162	28	201	169	92
	344.82	211.91	137.42	134.48	282.23	378.00	591.22	242.91	630.67	226.98	187.43	46.82	227.12	227.93	71.06
	0.4465	0.4917	0.6903	0.5637	0.3292	0.4392	0.4965	0.2241	0.2651	0.3340	0.3360	0.2325	0.3441	0.2883	0.5034
		TOTAL:	3941			CHI SQUARE:		338.045			(1000×CHI SQUARE)÷TOTAL:				85.777

Table 5.2: Frequency of Tags (cont.)

	A	B	C	D	E	F	G	H	J	K	L	M	N	P	R
WPS +BEZ	2	0	2	0	0	0	1	0	3	2	6	0	5	2	1
	2.10	1.29	0.84	0.82	1.72	2.30	3.60	1.48	3.84	1.38	1.14	0.29	1.38	1.39	0.43
	0.0023	0.0000	0.0057	0.0000	0.0000	0.0000	0.0007	0.0000	0.0018	0.0034	0.0124	0.0000	0.0086	0.0034	0.0055
		TOTAL:	24			CHI SQUARE:		43.007			(1000×CHI SQUARE)÷TOTAL:				1791.949
WPS +HVD	0	0	0	0	0	0	0	0	0	1	0	0	2	3	0
	0.52	0.32	0.21	0.20	0.43	0.58	0.90	0.37	0.96	0.35	0.29	0.07	0.35	0.35	0.11
	0.0000	0.0000	0.0000	0.0000	0.0000	0.0000	0.0000	0.0000	0.0000	0.0017	0.0000	0.0000	0.0034	0.0051	0.0000
		TOTAL:	6			CHI SQUARE:		34.397			(1000×CHI SQUARE)÷TOTAL:				5732.891
WPS +HVZ	0	0	0	0	0	0	0	0	0	1	1	0	0	0	0
	0.17	0.11	0.07	0.07	0.14	0.19	0.30	0.12	0.32	0.12	0.10	0.02	0.12	0.12	0.04
	0.0000	0.0000	0.0000	0.0000	0.0000	0.0000	0.0000	0.0000	0.0000	0.0017	0.0021	0.0000	0.0000	0.0000	0.0000
		TOTAL:	2			CHI SQUARE:		17.195			(1000×CHI SQUARE)÷TOTAL:				8597.313
WPS+MD	0	0	0	0	0	1	0	0	0	1	3	1	1	0	1
	0.70	0.43	0.28	0.27	0.57	0.77	1.20	0.49	1.28	0.46	0.38	0.10	0.46	0.46	0.14
	0.0000	0.0000	0.0000	0.0000	0.0000	0.0010	0.0000	0.0000	0.0000	0.0017	0.0062	0.0083	0.0017	0.0000	0.0055
		TOTAL:	8			CHI SQUARE:		38.752			(1000×CHI SQUARE)÷TOTAL:				4843.977
WP$	22	11	17	9	14	32	60	14	39	11	1	3	2	9	8
	22.05	13.55	8.79	8.60	18.05	24.17	37.80	15.53	40.33	14.51	11.98	2.99	14.52	14.57	4.54
	0.0248	0.0202	0.0481	0.0260	0.0193	0.0329	0.0395	0.0224	0.0240	0.0188	0.0021	0.0249	0.0034	0.0154	0.0438
		TOTAL:	252			CHI SQUARE:		51.323			(1000×CHI SQUARE)÷TOTAL:				203.661
WQL	1	0	9	12	32	35	39	12	24	15	1	0	0	1	0
	15.84	9.73	6.31	6.18	12.96	17.36	27.15	11.16	28.96	10.42	8.61	2.15	10.43	10.47	3.26
	0.0011	0.0000	0.0255	0.0347	0.0441	0.0360	0.0256	0.0192	0.0148	0.0257	0.0021	0.0000	0.0000	0.0017	0.0000
		TOTAL:	181			CHI SQUARE:		115.379			(1000×CHI SQUARE)÷TOTAL:				637.451
WRB	328	263	132	135	307	463	613	151	536	415	332	75	326	365	122
	399.24	245.36	159.11	155.71	326.77	437.66	684.53	281.25	730.21	262.80	217.01	54.21	262.96	263.91	82.28
	0.3698	0.4825	0.3735	0.3903	0.4229	0.4762	0.4031	0.2417	0.3304	0.7109	0.6887	0.6228	0.5581	0.6226	0.6675
		TOTAL:	4563			CHI SQUARE:		373.525			(1000×CHI SQUARE)÷TOTAL:				81.859
WRB +BER	0	0	0	0	0	0	0	0	0	0	0	0	1	0	0
	0.09	0.05	0.03	0.03	0.07	0.10	0.15	0.06	0.16	0.06	0.05	0.01	0.06	0.06	0.02
	0.0000	0.0000	0.0000	0.0000	0.0000	0.0000	0.0000	0.0000	0.0000	0.0000	0.0000	0.0000	0.0017	0.0000	0.0000
		TOTAL:	1			CHI SQUARE:		16.352			(1000×CHI SQUARE)÷TOTAL:				16352.141
WRB +BEZ	0	0	3	0	0	2	1	0	0	2	2	0	1	3	0
	1.22	0.75	0.49	0.48	1.00	1.34	2.10	0.86	2.24	0.81	0.67	0.17	0.81	0.81	0.25
	0.0000	0.0000	0.0085	0.0000	0.0000	0.0021	0.0007	0.0000	0.0000	0.0034	0.0041	0.0000	0.0017	0.0051	0.0000
		TOTAL:	14			CHI SQUARE:		31.214			(1000×CHI SQUARE)÷TOTAL:				2229.541
WRB+DO	0	0	0	0	0	0	0	0	0	0	1	0	0	0	0
	0.09	0.05	0.03	0.03	0.07	0.10	0.15	0.06	0.16	0.06	0.05	0.01	0.06	0.06	0.02
	0.0000	0.0000	0.0000	0.0000	0.0000	0.0000	0.0000	0.0000	0.0000	0.0000	0.0021	0.0000	0.0000	0.0000	0.0000
		TOTAL:	1			CHI SQUARE:		20.026			(1000×CHI SQUARE)÷TOTAL:				20026.410
WRB +DOD	0	0	0	0	0	0	0	0	0	0	2	0	4	0	0
	0.52	0.32	0.21	0.20	0.43	0.58	0.90	0.37	0.96	0.35	0.29	0.07	0.35	0.35	0.11
	0.0000	0.0000	0.0000	0.0000	0.0000	0.0000	0.0000	0.0000	0.0000	0.0000	0.0041	0.0000	0.0068	0.0000	0.0000
		TOTAL:	6			CHI SQUARE:		54.290			(1000×CHI SQUARE)÷TOTAL:				9048.340
WRB +DOD*	0	0	0	0	0	0	0	0	0	0	0	0	1	0	0
	0.09	0.05	0.03	0.03	0.07	0.10	0.15	0.06	0.16	0.06	0.05	0.01	0.06	0.06	0.02
	0.0000	0.0000	0.0000	0.0000	0.0000	0.0000	0.0000	0.0000	0.0000	0.0000	0.0000	0.0000	0.0017	0.0000	0.0000
		TOTAL:	1			CHI SQUARE:		16.352			(1000×CHI SQUARE)÷TOTAL:				16352.141
WRB +DOZ	0	0	0	0	0	0	0	0	0	0	0	0	1	0	0
	0.09	0.05	0.03	0.03	0.07	0.10	0.15	0.06	0.16	0.06	0.05	0.01	0.06	0.06	0.02
	0.0000	0.0000	0.0000	0.0000	0.0000	0.0000	0.0000	0.0000	0.0000	0.0000	0.0000	0.0000	0.0017	0.0000	0.0000
		TOTAL:	1			CHI SQUARE:		16.352			(1000×CHI SQUARE)÷TOTAL:				16352.141
WRB+IN	0	0	0	0	0	0	0	0	0	0	1	0	0	0	0
	0.09	0.05	0.03	0.03	0.07	0.10	0.15	0.06	0.16	0.06	0.05	0.01	0.06	0.06	0.02
	0.0000	0.0000	0.0000	0.0000	0.0000	0.0000	0.0000	0.0000	0.0000	0.0000	0.0021	0.0000	0.0000	0.0000	0.0000
		TOTAL:	1			CHI SQUARE:		20.026			(1000×CHI SQUARE)÷TOTAL:				20026.410
WRB+MD	0	0	0	0	0	0	0	0	0	0	1	0	0	0	0
	0.09	0.05	0.03	0.03	0.07	0.10	0.15	0.06	0.16	0.06	0.05	0.01	0.06	0.06	0.02
	0.0000	0.0000	0.0000	0.0000	0.0000	0.0000	0.0000	0.0000	0.0000	0.0000	0.0021	0.0000	0.0000	0.0000	0.0000
		TOTAL:	1			CHI SQUARE:		20.026			(1000×CHI SQUARE)÷TOTAL:				20026.410
*	257	307	156	236	223	420	834	208	783	314	219	95	204	273	84
	403.62	248.05	160.86	157.42	330.35	442.45	692.03	284.33	738.21	265.68	219.39	54.80	265.85	266.80	83.18
	0.2898	0.5633	0.4414	0.6823	0.3072	0.4320	0.5485	0.3329	0.4827	0.5379	0.4543	0.7889	0.3492	0.4657	0.4596
		TOTAL:	4613			CHI SQUARE:		247.820			(1000×CHI SQUARE)÷TOTAL:				53.722
-HL	982	825	193	397	925	229	48	1578	1661	12	5	7	8	0	19
	602.76	370.43	240.22	235.08	493.34	660.75	1033.47	424.61	1102.43	396.77	327.63	81.84	397.01	398.43	124.22
	1.1072	1.5136	0.5460	1.1477	1.2743	0.2355	0.0316	2.5257	1.0240	0.0206	0.0104	0.0581	0.0137	0.0000	0.1040
		TOTAL:	6889			CHI SQUARE:		7560.742			(1000×CHI SQUARE)÷TOTAL:				1097.509
-NC	7	2	2	1	1	24	34	14	530	11	6	0	4	2	4
	56.17	34.52	22.39	21.91	45.98	61.58	96.31	39.57	102.74	36.98	30.53	7.63	37.00	37.13	11.58
	0.0079	0.0037	0.0057	0.0029	0.0014	0.0247	0.0224	0.0224	0.3267	0.0188	0.0124	0.0000	0.0068	0.0034	0.0219
		TOTAL:	642			CHI SQUARE:		2126.046			(1000×CHI SQUARE)÷TOTAL:				3311.598
-TL	4960	2522	1764	1047	2038	2753	4479	4481	3113	850	487	239	443	669	303
	2637.83	1621.10	1051.27	1028.78	2158.99	2891.62	4522.71	1858.20	4824.51	1736.35	1433.81	358.16	1737.42	1743.64	543.60
	5.5925	4.6271	4.9907	3.0269	2.8075	2.8316	2.9455	7.1722	1.9191	1.4560	1.0102	1.9847	0.7584	1.1412	1.6578
		TOTAL:	30148			CHI SQUARE:		10201.965			(1000×CHI SQUARE)÷TOTAL:				338.396

Frequency Distribution of Word Classes

The data presented in Table 5.3 give the frequency figures for word classes and morphological forms in the two major subdivisions of the corpus, Informative Prose (INFO) and Imaginative Prose (IMAG). The 179 tag frequencies, listed in the previous table, are here collapsed into a set of twenty part-of-speech classifications, some of which are further subdivided according to function or morphological form; all are presented with their generally used grammatical designations rather than with tag symbols.

In contrast with the two previous tables, contracted forms are counted separately in Table 5.3, and the figures given are thus those of the total number of occurrences of a particular class, whether occurring in a full or in a contracted form. The types and frequency of all contractions encountered in the corpus are summarized in Table 5.4.

In addition to the absolute frequency figures for the two subdivisions and for the corpus as a whole, Table 5.3 also gives a normalized ratio value (*NR*) of the distribution of each grammatical category among the Informative and Imaginative Prose sections. Since these two sections of the corpus differ in size, the ratio of Informative Prose to Imaginative Prose being 2.955:1, the values of word-class distribution are normalized to take this fact into account. Consequently, an *NR* value of 1 indicates that the distribution of a particular word class or morphological form among the two subdivisions is proportionately equal. An *NR* value of more than 1 indicates a preponderance of occurrences of the class in Informative Prose, while a value of less than 1 points to a higher relative occurrence in Imaginative Prose. The greater the deviation of the normalized ratio from 1, the greater the clustering of the occurrences of the respective word class in one of the subdivisions of the corpus.

Table 5.3: Word Frequency in Two Major Subdivisions

	INFO	IMAG	*NR*	Total
Common Nouns				
Singular	133836	35637	1.27	169473
Plural	48630	9695	1.70	58325
Total	182466	45332	1.36	227798
Proper Nouns				
Singular	31713	10080	1.07	41793
Plural	1191	213	1.89	1404
Total	32904	10293	1.08	43197
Adverbial Nouns				
Singular	1521	451	1.14	1972
Plural	13	4	1.10	17
Total	1534	455	1.14	1989
All nouns	216904	56080	1.31	272984
Pronouns				
Personal, non-reflexive				
nominative	17744	16493	0.36	34237
objective	5233	6048	0.29	11281
Personal, reflexive				
singular	721	516	0.47	1237
plural	302	43	2.38	345
Possessive,				
first	10614	6316	0.57	16930
second	87	77	0.38	164
Nominal	1420	1265	0.38	2685
Total	36121	30758	0.40	66879
Adjectives				
Base form	55482	13159	1.43	68641
Comparative	1608	388	1.40	1996
Superlative	827	189	1.48	1016
Semantic superlative	335	46	2.47	381
Total	58252	13782	1.43	72034
Numerals and Quantifiers				
Cardinal	13014	1941	2.27	14955
Ordinal	1835	310	2.00	2145
Quantifiers	2745	1008	0.92	3753
Total	17594	3259	1.82	20853
Articles and Determiners				
Articles	76369	22719	1.14	99088
Determiners	19016	5217	1.23	24233
Total	95385	27936	1.16	123321
***Wh*- words**				
Wh- pronoun,				
nominative	3103	878	1.20	3981
objective	253	32	2.68	285
possessive	218	34	2.17	252

Wh- det.	4328	1305	1.12	5633
Wh- qualifier	164	17	3.27	181
Wh- adverb	2934	1655	0.60	4589
Total	11000	3921	0.95	14921

Prepositions

Total	97188	25425	1.29	122613

The Verb BE

Base form	5246	1129	1.57	6375
AM	193	314	0.21	507
IS	9736	1386	2.38	11122
ARE	4187	546	2.60	4733
WAS	5531	4439	0.42	9970
WERE	2285	1024	0.76	3309
BEING	546	140	1.32	686
BEEN	1774	698	0.86	2472
Total	29498	9676	1.03	39174

The Verb HAVE

Base form	3109	1130	0.93	4239
HAS	2342	184	4.31	2526
HAD (past)	2176	2998	0.25	5174
HAVING	201	82	0.83	283
HAD (participle)	147	90	0.55	237
Total	7975	4484	0.60	12459

The Verb DO

Base form	1037	818	0.43	1855
DOES	488	88	1.88	576
DID	654	805	0.28	1459
Total	2179	1711	0.43	3890

Modals

Total	10127	3875	0.88	14002

Main Verbs

Base form	24038	10007	0.81	34045
3rd singular present	6880	589	3.95	7469
Past tense	12542	13657	0.31	26199
-ING form	12446	5764	0.73	18210
Past participle	23830	6115	1.32	29945
Total	79736	36132	0.75	115868
All verbs	129515	55878	0.78	185393

Adverbs

Base Form	24792	11794	0.71	36586
Comparative	818	366	0.76	1184
Superlative	80	21	1.29	101
Nominal	4	5	0.27	9
Adverb or particle	3033	3004	0.34	6037
Total	28727	15190	0.64	43917

Qualifiers

Total	7242	2124	1.15	9366

Conjunctions

Coord.	28422	9727	0.99	38149
Subord.	16801	5378	1.06	22179
Total	45223	15105	1.01	60328

Existential THERE

Total	1572	708	0.75	2280

NOT

Total	4220	2756	0.52	6976

Infinitival TO

Total	11089	3941	0.95	15030

Interjections

Total	154	475	0.11	629

Foreign Words

Total	952	275	1.17	1227
All Words (including contractions)	761138	257613	1.00	1018751
Contractions (cf. Table 5.4)	1442	3665	0.13	5107
Grammatical Words	759696	253948		1013644

Punctuation

Sentence closer	36318	18973	0.65	55291
Comma	42066	15963	0.89	58029
Colon	1389	288	1.63	1677

Left parenthesis	2272	129	5.96	2401
Right parenthesis	2302	127	6.13	2429
Dash	1218	1065	0.74	3383
Total	88665	36545	0.80	123210

As already pointed out, the discrepancy in the number of grammatical words (which includes words with complex tags) and the number of words listed in Table 5.3 is due to the fact that in the latter table contractions are counted as separate frequency entries. Subtracting contractions from the total number of words then yields the number of grammatical words. The types of contractions occurring in the corpus and their frequency are given in Table 5.4.

Table 5.4: Contractions

	INFO	IMAG	Ratio (*NR*)	Total
-n't (not)	796	1567	0.17	2363
'm (am)	38	232	0.06	270
're (are)	72	212	0.12	284
's (is)	291	605	0.16	896
've (have)	63	186	0.12	249
'd (had)	5	172	0.01	177
's (has)	13	52	0.09	65
'll (will) or 'd (would)	139	517	0.09	656
object pronoun	12	60	0.07	72
infinitive	3	28	0.04	31
others	10	34	0.10	44
Total	1442	3665	0.13	5107

Stylistic Implications

A number of differences between Informative Prose and Imaginative Prose are reflected in Table 5.3, particularly in the normalized ratio (*NR*) values given for individual entries. *NR* values considerably in excess of 1 point to a significant preponderance of that particular word class in Informative Prose. Taking into account only those instances in which the *NR* value exceeds 1 by 20% or more, the following word classes can be listed as being particularly characteristic of Informative Prose:

Nouns:	*NR* = 1.31
Adjectives:	*NR* = 1.43
Numerals:	*NR* = 2.23

In the Imaginative Prose subdivision, on the other hand, we find the following word classes to have *NR* values lower than the expected figure of 1 by 20% or more:

Verbs: (including auxiliaries and modals)	*NR* = 0.78
Adverbs	*NR* = 0.64
Pronouns:	*NR* = 0.40
Existential THERE	*NR* = 0.75
NOT	*NR* = 0.52

These differences clearly point to the more nominal character of Informative Prose, evidenced in the relatively large number of nouns and adjectives, as against the more verbal character of Imaginative Prose, signaled by the relatively larger number of occurrences of verbs and adverbs. Imaginative Prose is also characterized by a greater number of anaphoric devices, as evidenced by the strikingly larger relative number of pronouns. This suggests that pronominal anaphora provides the major means for the signaling of textual cohesion in the Imaginative Prose style. The reader should be cautioned, however, that some samples of Informative Prose with a low frequency of pronouns, particularly newspaper reportage, editorials, and reviews (i.e., genres A, B, and C), are composed of several unrelated selections. Because many of the selected newspaper passages were quite short, it was often necessary to combine several of them to attain the needed sample length of 2,000 words. (For details, cf. Francis and Kučera 1979). The heterogeneity of such samples affects, among other things, their lexical character, generally increasing the number of distinct words (types) and thus resulting in a higher type/token ratio. (A detailed study of these lexical properties of various samples can be found in Kučera 1968). Sample heterogeneity also has some effect on word-class frequencies, particularly with regard to those classes which signal textual cohesion.

The striking preponderance of contractions in Imaginative Prose is hardly surprising, except perhaps for the fact that the total number of contractions in the Informative Prose section is very small, pointing to a rather conservative usage in the types of writing represented in this subdivision.

Word-Class Rank and Contextuality

The Word-Class Rank Table 5.5 gives the absolute frequencies of the word classes and the percentage of the text that each of them accounts for in Informative Prose, in

Imaginative Prose, and in the corpus as a whole. The classes are ranked in order of their decreasing frequency in the corpus, but rank figures for each of the two subdivisions are given as well. In constructing Table 5.5, the grammatical tags were collapsed into even more general classes than was the case in Table 5.3; so, for example, all nouns (common, proper, and adverbial, both singular and plural) are listed under the heading *Nouns*, and all verbs, including auxiliaries and modals, under the heading *Verbs*. Articles and determiners are combined under the heading *Determiners*, numerals and quantifiers under *Quantifiers*, and adverbs and qualifiers under the heading *Adverbs*.

Table 5.5: Word-class Rank Table

Class	INFO	%	Rank	IMAG	%	Rank	Corpus	%	Rank
Nouns	216904	28.50	1	56080	21.77	1	272984	26.80	1
Verbs	129515	17.02	2	55878	21.69	2	185393	18.20	2
Determiners	95385	12.53	4	27939	10.84	4	123321	12.11	3
Prepositions	97188	12.77	3	25425	9.87	5	122613	12.04	4
Adjectives	58252	7.65	5	13782	5.35	8	72034	7.07	5
Pronouns	36121	4.75	7	30758	11.94	3	66879	6.56	6
Conjunctions	45223	5.94	6	15105	5.86	7	60328	5.92	7
Adverbs	35969	4.73	8	17314	6.72	6	53283	5.23	8
Quantifiers	17594	2.31	9	3259	1.27	11	20853	2.05	9
Infinitival TO	11089	1.46	10	3941	1.53	9	15030	1.48	10
Wh- words	11000	1.44	11	3921	1.52	10	14921	1.46	11
NOT	4220	0.55	12	2756	1.07	12	6976	0.68	12
THERE	1572	0.21	13	708	0.28	13	2280	0.22	13
Foreign words	922	0.12	14	275	0.11	15	1227	0.12	14
Interjections	154	0.02	15	475	0.18	14	629	0.06	15
Total	761138	100.00		257613	100.00		1018751	100.00	

The somewhat different ranking of the word classes in INFO and in IMAG reflects the stylistic differences already indicated by the normalized ratios in Table 5.3. However, the percentage figures are of additional interest. While nouns are more frequent than verbs in both subdivisions, the differences in relative frequencies are striking. In INFO, nouns exceed verbs by more than eleven percentage points in relative frequency, while in IMAG nouns and verbs have almost identical frequencies, the difference between them being a mere 0.08%. The other discrepancies to be noted are in the rank of adjectives (fifth in INFO but only eighth in IMAG) and quantifiers (ninth in INFO, eleventh in IMAG). Conversely, pronouns rank third in IMAG but only seventh in INFO, and adverbs occupy the sixth rank in IMAG but only the eighth in INFO.

Finally, we shall turn to some considerations of the frequency distribution of word classes across the different genres of the corpus. Since we know the frequency distribution of individual tags in the 15 genres, we can determine how evenly any word class is distributed throughout the genres. Applying the chi-square test to the frequency data of each word class in the 15 genres (i.e., computing chi-squares with 14 degrees of freedom in the usual way), we found that the chi-square values were significant, at the 5% level, for all tags. All chi-square figures were given earlier in this section, in Table 5.2.

It is possible, however, to draw some conclusions about individual tags and about how much they depart from a random distribution by using the Mosteller-Rourke adjustment for chi-square for large numbers (Cf. Mosteller and Rourke 1973:186-191). This allows us to say that some tags are more "contextual" than others, i.e., that their rates vary more from genre to genre than do others. It should be emphasized that this adjusted value is not a significance measure and thus in no way affects the conclusions about the distribution of the individual tags. What it does do is allow us to compare how much the individual tags depart from a random distribution. The Mosteller-Rourke modification (which the authors originally applied to the high-frequency words of the Brown Corpus) is computed as

$$1000\chi^2/n$$

where n is the frequency of a given tag in the entire corpus.

Using this measure, we have ranked the major tag classes in Table 5.6 according to increasing degree of their contextuality. The 29 tags of the highest frequency, each of which occurs more than 5000 times, have been ranked.

Table 5.6: Contextuality of Tags

Rank	Class	M-R Measure
1.	Articles	4.047
2.	Coordinating conjunctions	6.748
3.	Infinitival TO	9.035
4.	Determiners	11.776
5.	Prepositions	13.255
6.	Common nouns, singular	15.427
7.	Subordinating conjunctions	16.392
8.	Post-determiners	21.143
9.	Modals	23.317
10.	Main verbs, base form	26.137
11.	Adjectives	26.773
12.	Past participle of main verbs	29.129
13.	-ING form of main verbs	36.245
14.	*Wh-* determiners	37.736
15.	Adverbs	39.458
16.	Qualifiers	45.775
17.	Common nouns, plural	58.694
18.	BE, base form	72.240
19.	Possessive personal pronouns	126.952
20.	Cardinal numerals	179.040
21.	3rd sg. pres. of main verbs	212.828
22.	IS	215.982
23.	Proper nouns, singular	216.109
24.	WAS	231.857
25.	Nominative pronouns (except 3rd singular)	250.917
26.	Nominative pronouns (3rd singular)	331.614
27.	Adverb or Particle	370.608
28.	Past tense of main verbs	472.978
29.	Objective personal pronouns	492.921

The figures calculated according to the Mosteller-Rourke formula show that, in general, function words are the least contextual tags, while tags that belong to an inflectional paradigm and designate grammatical categories are most affected by genre characteristics. The first five tags in Table 5.6, i.e., the least contextual, are all function words: articles, coordinating conjunctions, the infinitival marker TO, determiners, and prepositions. On the other hand, four of the last five tags in Table 5.6, i.e., the most contextual ones, signal grammatical categories: the two classes of nominative personal pronouns, the past tense of verbs, and the objective form of personal pronouns. In the middle range of contextuality, the pattern is similar, with inflected forms clustering towards the second half of Table 5.6: forms of the 3rd person singular present of main verbs and of the verb *be* occupy ranks 21 and 22 respectively, and the singular past tense of *be* rank 24. This shows not only the genre-dependence of such categories as tense and case, but also points out the futility of trying to find some stable frequency relationship between such oppositions as past versus present tense, or nominative versus objective case, as has sometimes been attempted in studies dealing with the markedness of morphological categories and the correlation between markedness and frequency (cf., for example, the discussion in Greenberg 1966).

Somewhat surprising is the relatively low contextuality of conjunctions: coordinating conjunctions occupy second rank in Table 5.6, and subordinating conjuctions rank seven. Since conjunctions, particularly subordinating ones, can be viewed as indicators of the occurrence of various types of sentence embeddings, the relatively low contextuality of these function words indicates that stylistic differences among the genres with regard to phrasal sentence complexity are not as pronounced as one might expect. This fact is confirmed by the study of sentence complexity, defined in terms of predicational structures, which is presented in Section VI of this book.

VI

Sentence Length and Sentence Structure

This section presents a summary of the results of a computational analysis of sentence length and of the structure and complexity of sentences in the corpus, focusing on the type of predications that occur in the different genres and the two major subdivisions.

If we disregard headlines and other headings, the corpus contains 54,718 sentences, with the mean sentence length of 18.40 words. However, as is shown in detail in Table 6.1 below, both sentence length and sentence structure vary considerably among the fifteen genres of writing. In general, sentence length differs significantly between Informative Prose and Imaginative Prose, the former exhibiting a substantially higher mean sentence length. Altogether there are 374 samples in the nine genres of Informative Prose; since each sample is approximately 2,000 words long, this part of the corpus—not counting headlines and other headings—consists of 752,858 words. There are 126 samples of Imaginative Prose, again of about 2,000 words each, accounting for 253,897 words. The entire corpus without headlines and other headings thus consists of 500 samples of texts and contains 1,006,755 running words (graphic-word tokens).

All genres of the Informative Prose portion of the corpus have a higher mean sentence length than any of the genres in the Imaginative Prose portion. The mean sentence length in Informative Prose ranges from a high of 24.07 words (in Miscellaneous) to 18.53 words (in Skills and Hobbies). In Imaginative Prose, on the other hand, the highest mean is only 17.52 words (in Humor) and the low is 12.62 words (in Mystery and Detective Fiction). This difference is, to some extent, due to the percentage of quoted material in the two sections of the corpus. While no genre of Informative Prose has more than 11.9% of quoted material, with Belles Lettres having this highest percentage and the Learned samples the lowest of only 2.8%, the percentage of quoted material in Imaginative Prose ranges from a low of 14.9% (General Fiction) to a high of 26.8% (Science Fiction). Moreover, there is a difference in the nature of the quoted material: in Informative Prose it is a mixture of representations of spoken material and quotations from other written sources; while in Imaginative Prose virtually all quoted material is fictional dialogue. Two facts should be noted in this regard, however: first, that no sample consisting of more than 50% of quoted material was included in the corpus; and second, that the correlation between sentence length and the percentage of dialogue is by no means exact. Several discrepancies in such correlation are discussed in an essay by Marckworth and Bell (in Kučera and Francis 1967:368-405), who studied sentence-length distribution in the corpus in detail.

Sentence-length distribution, of course, is bound to have some effect on the syntactic complexity of a text. Clearly, a sentence consisting of two words cannot be considered to be syntactically complex by any reasonable standard of measurement unless, of course, one is willing to posit an extremely abstract and complex underlying structure of sentences and freely allow deletion rules in the grammar. However, neither in theory nor—as we shall demonstrate below—in practice can sentence length be viewed as a reliable indicator of some common-sense notion of syntactic complexity which might be useful either in the study of performance in general or in stylistic syntactic characterizations. Consider, for example, the length in words and the syntactic properties of the following two sentences:

(1) John's grandfather left all his oil paintings to the Metropolitan Museum of Fine Arts.

(2) Tom planned to ask Alice to dance.

The first sentence has fourteen words (by conventional graphic count), the second exactly half that, i.e., seven words. But while the first sentence has only one verbal form, *left*, the second has three: one finite, *planned*, and two infinitives, *to ask* and *to dance*. In the fairly conservative versions of transformational grammar of the 1960's (known as the "standard theory"), the first sentence would have had an underlying phrase marker ("deep structure") consisting of one S, and thus not very different from the actual sentence. The second sentence, on the other hand, would have had an underlying phrase marker consisting of three S's, supposed to represent the three underlying predications which could be informally given as 'Tom PAST plan', 'Tom ask Alice', 'Alice dance'. In other linguistic theories, of course, the situation might be quite different, with a much more elaborate initial phrase marker in a generative semantic representation, for example. More recently, on the other hand, syntactic solutions have been proposed in which no sentential source at all is assumed for infinitival phrases (cf., for example, Kaplan and Bresnan 1982). In this kind of syntactic treatment the infinitival phrases are directly generated as VP's.

No matter which theoretical stance one adopts, the number of predications contained in a sentence can be viewed as a useful measure of its syntactic complexity. In this section, we will first discuss the algorithm for the retrieval of verbal constructions from the tagged data base, and then summarize the results obtained in the analysis of sentential complexity in the entire corpus as well as in the individual genres.

The data analyzed in this study are the actual sentences of the corpus, which were encoded in the usual standard English graphic form, with each word assigned its grammatical tag. There is no direct information in the data base about "underlying" structure or even about any syntactic bracketing of the surface string. We will therefore avoid the use of the term "surface structure" entirely in referring to our data. Surface structure, in all those linguistic theories that have utilized this concept, includes at least some labeled bracketing of the terminal string. In the "revised extended standard theory" of transformational grammar (cf., for example, Chomsky 1980), surface structure is that level of representation which is not only enriched by the so-called traces, but has yet to pass through the deletion rules, the filter component of the grammar, and, of course, the stylistic rules. In our tagged corpus, however, the only information besides the actual sentences is the accompanying sequence of grammatical tags.

Our basic definition of sentence complexity in the present study is simply the number of predications per sentence. We shall report these results for each of the fifteen genres as well as for the corpus as a whole. Given the form of the analyzed data, the reader should also be aware that our use of the term "predication" is broader than is usually the case in linguistic literature or in general usage. As is customary, we shall consider a predication to be, first of all, any verb or verbal group with a tensed verb having a grammatical subject. We will refer to these verbal constructions as "finite predications." In addition to that, however, we will include in our analysis what we shall call "nonfinite predications." These include infinitives, gerunds, and participles.

Our basic taxonomy of verbal groups is thus quite similar to that adopted by structuralist linguists in the analysis of the English verb. All verbs or verbal groups exhibiting a surface subject, including the subject *it* (as in *it is raining*), will be counted as finite predications, as will interrogatives; those that do not satisfy these conditions will be considered to be nonfinite. Our only departure from some structuralist treatments lies in the inclusion of all imperatives in the class of finite predications. This allows us to place imperatives with and without an overt subject (e.g., *Don't worry!* and *Don't you worry!*) in the same class of predications.

When it comes to complex verbal strings involving a quasi-auxiliary plus infinitive (such as *going to*, *supposed to*, *used to* + infinitive), we shall follow here the consistent—although perhaps somewhat controversial—approach of Joos (1964). Joos treats all quasi-auxiliaries differently from "true" auxiliaries (such as *will* or *may*), pointing out that they exhibit different syntactic properties. Joos also argues that including only some of the quasi-auxiliaries with the class of auxiliary verbs would make the whole English verbal system "incomprehensible." Our adoption of Joos's approach means that in our analysis a sentence such as *He used to play tennis* has two predications, one finite and one nonfinite.

As already mentioned, verbal constructions from all the sentences of the corpus have been included in this analysis, with the exception of those occurring in headlines and other headings. Headlines and headings, which are identified by a special symbol in the tagged corpus (the hyphenated tag -HL), were not included because of the particular nature of English "headline grammar," which often omits verbs entirely, e.g., *Actor in Critical Condition after Explosion*, or omits some verb form, particularly the finite one, e.g., *President to Meet Brezhnev in Vienna*. All sentences outside headlines are included, however, even those that do not contain any verb at all (e.g., *Just our luck!*). The number of sentences with a zero predication is small: there are 1,872 of them in the entire corpus, accounting for only 3.42% of the corpus sentences. Nevertheless, they have been included in computing the statistics.

Verbal constructions of both types, finite and nonfinite, may consist of a single verbal form (e.g., *likes* or *to like*) or of one or more auxiliaries plus the main verb. The longest possible finite verbal group in English can have five elements, e.g., *may (might) have been being considered*; the longest active finite verbal group can have only four elements, e.g., *may (might) have been considering*. A nonfinite verbal group can consist of a maximum of four verbal elements, e.g., *(to) have been being considered*. Of these, the maximum finite passive verbal group with five elements does not occur in the corpus at all, nor does the maximum nonfinite group with four verbal elements. However, the maximum finite active group with four elements, i.e., the type *may have been considering*, occurs 10 times; of the second longest passive groups, only the type *may have been considered* occurs, 74 times. The situation is similar with regard to nonfinite groups: the one of maximum possible length, i.e., the type *(to) have been being considered*, does not occur at all. In three-element verbal groups, i.e., the type *(to) have been considered* or *(to) have been considering*, only the first (passive) form occurs, 22 times; there are no occurrences of the active type of this four-element group.

Complex verbal groups may be continuous, i.e., not interrupted by a nonverbal element, or discontinuous, i.e., so interrupted. Discontinuous verbal constructions exhibit a different pattern in declarative sentences on the one hand, and in *wh-* questions and *yes/no* questions on the other. In declaratives, the number of word classes that can interrupt a complex verbal group is relatively small: it consists primarily of adverbs, e.g., *He will probably consider ...*, *He has indeed been asked*, but also some phrasal adverbial expressions, e.g., *He had in fact said something like it*. One of the important facts that an algorithm for predication retrieval has to consider is that, due to various deletion rules under conditions of identity, an English verbal group may appear in a truncated form. Consider, for example, the following sentences:

(3) Teddy could not be elected but his cousin could (be (elected)).

(4) Teddy could not have been elected but his cousin could (have (been (elected))).

(The forms in parentheses indicate optional deletions.)

It is because of this possible truncation phenomenon that the retrieval algorithm needs to allow for the possibility that a verbal group may end in an auxiliary.

The situation is more complex when it comes to the retrieval of verbal groups in *wh-* questions, *yes/no* questions, or in conditional constructions beginning with *had*, e.g., *Had her husband known it...* Because of the auxiliary inversion in such cases, a large number of word-class representatives, including complex noun phrases, can be embedded within a verbal group in such sentences. Our retrieval of complex verb groups thus needs to take into account a number of variables. In the parsing procedure, particular attention must be paid to the fact that an incomplete verbal group may represent either a truncated string or a discontinuous predication which continues later in the sentence.

The retrieval algorithm for all verbal groups, finite and nonfinite, and continuous and discontinuous, scanned the tag sequence in each sentence from left to right, without backtracking. The retrieval was thus essentially accomplished by a finite-state automaton (FSA). The complete FSA that can properly handle both continuous and discontinuous verbal constructions (including truncated ones) is quite complicated. The reader interested in details can find a description of the retrieval procedure in Kučera 1980. The retrieval program identified correctly over 99% of all predications in the corpus.

The basic results obtained in our analysis of predications are summarized in Table 6.1. All figures in this table as well as in subsequent tables in this section are based on the analysis of all corpus text except for headlines and headings. Three figures are given for each of the fifteen genres and for the corpus as a whole: mean sentence length in graphic words (i.e., word tokens), mean number of predications per sentence, and the average number of words of text per predication.

Table 6.1: Sentence Length and Predications

Genre	Words per Sentence	Predications per Sentence	Words per Predication
A. Press: Reportage	20.72	2.63	7.88
B. Press: Editorials	19.66	2.73	7.21
C. Press: Reviews	21.06	2.62	8.03
D. Religion	21.21	2.90	7.33
E. Skills and Hobbies	18.53	2.59	7.15
F. Popular Lore	20.26	2.81	7.22
G. Belles Lettres	21.35	2.93	7.29
H. Miscellaneous	24.07	2.80	8.59
J. Learned	22.31	2.84	7.85
K. General Fiction	13.82	2.41	5.74
L. Mystery and Detective	12.62	2.29	5.50
M. Science Fiction	12.94	2.23	5.81
N. Adventure and Western	12.75	2.30	5.54
P. Romance and Love Story	13.41	2.44	5.49
R. Humor	17.52	2.82	6.21
CORPUS	18.40	2.64	6.96

The three sets of figures, taken jointly, throw a considerable light on the nature of the principal differences among the genres. Particularly revealing is the comparison of the genres of Informative Prose (A through J—INFO) as a group with the group encompassing Imaginative Prose (K through R—IMAG). As already mentioned—and certainly not unexpectedly—the mean sentence length, measured in graphic-word tokens, is much larger in INFO than in IMAG. The reader should notice especially that all genres of INFO have their sentence-length mean above the corpus mean, while all genres of IMAG are below the corpus mean.

The situation is different, in interesting ways, when it comes to predications. Here, too, the number of predications per sentence tends to be greater in INFO than in IMAG, but not consistently so and certainly not to the extent that the differences in sentence length would lead one to expect. No longer are all INFO genres above corpus mean and all IMAG below it. Within INFO, genres A (Press: Reportage), C (Press: Reviews), and E (Skills and Hobbies) are below the corpus mean. On the other hand, in IMAG, genre R (Humor) is well above the corpus mean.

The lack of correlation between sentence length and the number of predications per sentence, i.e., sentence complexity in our definition, is displayed in a particularly striking manner in the third set of figures, which give the mean number of words per predication. In this case, all genres of INFO show a much larger number of words per predication than do the genres of IMAG. As a matter of fact, in this instance all genres of INFO are above the corpus mean, and all genres of IMAG below it. Table 6.2, which summarizes all the relevant data for the two groups of prose and for the corpus, shows these results quite clearly.

Table 6.2: Informative and Imaginative Prose

Measure	INFO	IMAG	CORPUS
Words/Sentence	21.06	13.38	18.40
Predications/Sentence	2.78	2.38	2.64
Words/Predication	7.57	5.62	6.96

While Table 6.2 simply confirms that sentence length is highly genre-dependent, it also demonstrates that the predications/sentence figure is not directly correlated with sentence length. The words/predication figures show, in essence, that the number of words needed to express a predication is considerably smaller in those styles of writing in which sentences tend to be shorter. This fact also implies some interesting facts about the overall structure of sentences in INFO as compared to IMAG. Since, aside from the verbal groups, the other major constituents of a sentence are the nominal groups (i.e., NP's), the statistics presented in Table 6.2 clearly suggest that nominal groups in INFO generally tend to be longer (and thus, in some sense more complex) than those in IMAG. It should be recalled in this connection that the relative frequency of pronouns is substantially higher in INFO than in IMAG (cf. Table 5.3 above). This fact also contributes to the shorter average length of nominal groups and thus helps to lower the words/predication ratio in Imaginative Prose.

The two subdivisions of the corpus also show interesting differences in the ratio of finite and nonfinite predications. The results of this analysis are given in Table 6.3, where the symbols F and NF stand for finite and nonfinite predications respectively, and P/S stands for predications per sentence.

Table 6.3: Finite and Nonfinite Predications

Group	Type	Number	P/S	%
INFO	F	68304	1.91	68.66
	NF	31171	0.87	31.34
	Total	99475	2.78	100.00
IMAG	F	34454	1.82	76.32
	NF	10693	0.56	23.68
	Total	45147	2.38	100.00
CORPUS	F	102758	1.88	71.05
	NF	41864	0.77	28.95
	Total	144622	2.64	100.00

A further breakdown of the figures in Table 6.3 shows that the greater percentage of nonfinite predications in INFO (31.36%) than in IMAG (23.68%) is due largely, although not exclusively, to the greater frequency of gerunds and participles in the INFO texts. There are, on the average, 0.56 gerundival and participial predications per sentence in INFO and only 0.36 in IMAG; the mean for the corpus is 0.49. The difference is less pronounced with regard to infinitives: INFO has a mean of 0.31 infinitives per sentence, IMAG 0.21; the corpus mean is 0.27 infinitives per sentence.

As far as predicational structure is concerned, the syntactic style of Informative Prose, compared to Imaginative Prose, can be summarized by these three characteristics: longer sentences (in graphic-word tokens), a relatively larger number of words required for the completion of a predication (pointing to more complex nominal groups), and a larger proportion of nonfinite predications. In contrast to this, the texts of Imaginative Prose exhibit shorter sentences, a significantly smaller number of word tokens per predication (pointing to less complex nominal groups) and a smaller percentage of nonfinite predications, particularly gerunds and participles.

Types of Finite Predications

Tables 6.4 through 6.8 provide information on some of the principal characteristics of finite predications in the corpus and its genres, and give figures on the frequency distribution of complex verbal forms which signal voice, tense and aspect. Specifically, Table 6.4 gives the frequency of active and passive constructions in the individual genres, and Table 6.5 a summary of this information in the Informative and Imaginative Prose subdivisions. Table 6.6 gives a summary of the occurrence frequencies of the perfect-tense forms, and Table 6.7 of the frequency of the so-called progressive aspect. Finally, Table 6.8 summarizes the frequency variations of the various verbal forms among the genres and gives statistical values for their distribution. Additional information about the usage of simple verbal forms can be found in the preceding section of this book, particularly in Tables 5.2 and 5.3, where the frequency of individual tags and of grammatical forms is given in detail.

Table 6.4: Active and Passive Predications

Genre	Number of Actives	Number of Passives	Per cent of Actives	Per cent of Passives
A. Press: Reportage	6902	1000	87.34	12.66
B. Press: Editorial	4662	586	88.83	11.17
C. Press: Reviews	2863	293	90.72	9.28
D. Religion	3007	401	88.23	11.77
E. Skills and Hobbies	5680	944	85.75	14.25
F. Popular Lore	8145	1165	87.49	12.51
G. Belles Lettres	13446	1589	89.43	10.57
H. Miscellaneous	3244	1033	75.85	24.15
J. Learned	10415	2929	78.05	21.95
K. General Fiction	7194	362	95.21	4.79
L. Mystery and Detective	6540	259	96.19	3.81
M. Science Fiction	1501	106	93.40	6.60
N. Adventure and Western	7798	290	96.41	3.59
P. Romance and Love Story	7961	273	96.68	3.32
R. Humor	2021	149	93.13	6.87
CORPUS	91379	11379	88.93	11.07

Active versus Passive

Adopting a simple formal definition of finite passive predications as consisting of a finite form of *be* plus a past participle, the results for the frequency of the usage of the voice forms can be summarized as shown in Table 6.4. Table 6.4 points out the striking difference in the use of the passive in Informative and in Imaginative Prose. All genres of IMAG are well below the corpus mean in their average number of passive predications. Interestingly enough, the converse is not quite the case; although most genres of INFO are above the corpus mean, two are below (Press: Reviews, and Belles Lettres) while two (Press: Editorial, and Religion) are only slightly above the corpus mean. At the same time, the genres that contain a great number of samples of a technical nature (Miscellaneous, which includes government documents and various kinds of reports, and Learned) have a strikingly large percentage of passive predications, exceeding most of the other INFO genres by approximately ten percentage points. There are thus essentially three types of genres in the corpus as far the use of the passive is concerned: the two technical genres with an extremely high frequency of the passive voice (over 20%), the other genres of Informative Prose with an intermediate frequency (ranging between 9% and 16%), and all the genres of Imaginative Prose in which the frequency of finite passive constructions is quite low (in the range of 3% to 7%). Comparing the two major subdivisions, the basic distribution of active/passive predications emerges in a striking manner, as Table 6.5 shows.

Table 6.5: Voice in Informative and Imaginative Prose

Group Type	Number of Active	Number of Passive	Per cent of Active	Per cent of Passive
INFO	58364	9940	85.45	14.55
IMAG	33015	1439	95.82	4.18
CORPUS	91379	11379	88.93	11.07

The results in Table 6.5 indicate that there is more than a ten-percentage-point difference between the proportion of passive predications in Informative Prose and those in Imaginative Prose.

The active versus passive distribution of predications has clear relevance for semantic processing strategies. But a word of caution is necessary here. It can be plausibly argued that—in general—the mapping of semantic relations is more direct in syntactically active sentences than in passive ones: the surface subject of an active sentence is much more likely to correspond to the semantic agent than is the case in passive sentences, where agency will remain either unexpressed or will be expressed by other types of phrases (such as the *by* phrase in English). Thus the active sentence expresses on the surface the underlying thematic relations between the predicate and its arguments more directly than does the passive sentence. In traditional linguistic terminology, the "logical subject" of the active sentence coincides with the surface subject, something which is not the case in passive constructions. However, the relation between the set of syntactic concepts, such as "logical subject," and semantic ones, such as "semantic agent," is far from being isomorphic. There are many predicates with which the "logical subject" may serve other functions than that of agency; quite commonly it serves the function of a beneficiary or recipient (as in *Tom got a good grade in this course*, or *This situation requires special care*), as instrument (*This key will open the back door*), and other functions as well. Nevertheless, the mapping between the semantic function and syntactic structures is bound to be more direct, at least statistically, in data bases such as fiction, in which passive constructions have a low probability of occurrence, than in those such as scientific writing or official documents, where they are relatively common.

The Perfect Tenses

Table 6.6 gives the distribution of the perfect tenses in the individual genres and in the corpus as a whole. All forms, regardless of their degree of complexity, that include a non-participial form of *have* (i.e., *has, have* or *had*) plus a past participle have been included.

Table 6.6: The Perfect Tenses

Genre	Perfect Forms: Number	%
A. Press: Reportage	469	5.94
B. Press: Editorial	367	6.99
C. Press: Reviews	188	5.96
D. Religion	210	6.16
E. Skills and Hobbies	326	4.92
F. Popular Lore	588	6.32
G. Belles Lettres	1075	7.15
H. Miscellaneous	233	5.45
J. Learned	739	5.54
K. General Fiction	563	7.45
L. Mystery and Detective	511	7.52
M. Science Fiction	109	6.78
N. Adventure and Western	518	6.40
P. Romance and Love Story	601	7.30
R. Humor	148	6.82
CORPUS	6645	6.47

All the genres with low frequencies of the perfective tenses (under 6 per cent) are in the Informative Prose subsection, with Miscellaneous (which includes various types of documents and reports) and Learned having the lowest relative frequencies of the perfect, 5.45% and 5.54% respectively. The highest relative occurrence of the perfect tenses, on the other hand, can be found in Mystery and Detective Fiction, with 7.52%, and in General Fiction, with 7.45%. Since the principal function of the English perfect is to signal the connection of the event or activity, denoted by the perfect, to another reference point (for example, the speech moment, in the case of the present perfect), the more frequent use of the perfect in fiction is not unexpected.

Nevertheless, the division between Informative Prose and Imaginative Prose, in terms of the frequency of usage of the perfect tenses, is not without some exceptions: Belles Lettres and Press: Editorial have a higher percentage of perfect forms than three fiction genres. On the whole, however, the total occurrences in Informative Prose (a total of 4195) represent only 6.14% of all finite predications, while those in Imaginative Prose (2450 occurrences) account for 7.11% of all finite predications in this subsection.

The Progressive Aspect

Table 6.7 presents frequency figures on the occurrence of the so-called progressive aspect in finite predications, i.e., the occurrence of a finite form of BE plus the -ING form of a verb.

The frequency distribution of the progressive forms groups together the fiction genres and the first two newspaper genres (Reportage and Editorial), in which the usage of these forms is relatively high (above 3.2%), against the other informative genres, in which the finite -ING forms account for only 1.57% to 2.29% of all finite predications. Again, the usage is lowest in the most descriptive (and prescriptive) of the genres, in J (Learned) and H (Miscellaneous), where it accounts for only 1.57% and 2.10% of all finite predications respectively. The genre differences in the usage of these forms are thus substantial: the relative frequency of the progressive is almost three times greater in General Fiction than in the Learned selections.

The primary function of the progressive forms in English is the signalling of ongoing activities (e.g., *Mary is reading*); in the past tense, these forms often serve as a temporal frame for another event (e.g. *When Paul left, Jane was playing the piano* vs. *When Paul left, Jane played the piano*). The -ING forms can also function to denote short-duration states, e.g., *John is playing a lot of tennis this summer.* All of these usages are clearly more appropriate to genres in which dynamic situations and temporary states of affairs prevail, and less useful for static descriptions and statements of more permanent validity.

Table 6.7: The Progressive Forms

Genre	Progressive Forms: Number	%
A. Press: Reportage	297	3.76
B. Press: Editorial	231	4.40
C. Press: Reviews	88	2.79
D. Religion	73	2.14
E. Skills and Hobbies	142	2.14
F. Popular Lore	251	2.70
G. Belles Lettres	362	2.41
H. Miscellaneous	90	2.10
J. Learned	210	1.57
K. General Fiction	320	4.24
L. Mystery and Detective	268	3.94
M. Science Fiction	52	3.24
N. Adventure and Western	328	4.06
P. Romance and Love Story	348	4.23
R. Humor	83	3.82
CORPUS	3143	3.06

Because only two genres of the Informative Prose category, namely Press: Reportage and Press: Editorial, have a relatively high utilization of the finite -ING constructions, the overall percentage of the progressive forms in the entire Informative Prose subsection is much lower, i.e. 2.55% of all predications, than it is in the Imaginative Prose subsections, where it reaches 4.06%.

Frequency Variations in the Use of Grammatical Forms

As already pointed out in the discussion of the frequency distribution of tags in Section V, the frequency of grammatical categories, such as case and tense, is highly genre dependent. This is confirmed by the frequency distribution of the passive and the tense forms as summarized in Table 6.8 below. In this table, chi-square values for the genre distribution of the passive voice and of four major tense and aspect forms, namely the simple present and the simple past of main verbs, the perfect, and the progressive, are included. The table also gives the figures of the chi-square adjustment proposed by Mosteller and Rourke (1973:186-191) which makes it possible to judge the degree of relative genre dependence of the various forms under consideration. The higher this value, the more "contextual" the usage of these forms. The forms in Table 6.8 are ranked by increasing values of this adjusted chi-square computation, identified as M-R.

Table 6.8: Frequency Variation of Grammatical Forms

Form	Chi-Square	M-R Measure
Present tense	840.35	39.29
Perfect	634.00	95.41
Passive	1665.32	146.35
Progressive	806.70	256.67
Past tense	12391.56	472.98

All the chi-square values are highly significant, even at the 1% level of significance (at $P = 0.01$ for 14 degrees of freedom, the critical value of $\chi^2 = 29.1$).

The measure of "contextuality", as reflected in the Mosteller-Rourke adjustment of the chi-square values, shows that of the five grammatical categories compared, the simple present of main verbs is least affected in its frequency distribution by genre style. The perfect and the passive follow, while the progressive and, especially, the simple past tense of main verbs are the most genre dependent.

The usage of voice, aspect, and tense forms also depends on the lexical character of the verbs to which the appropriate forms are applied. So, for example, stative verbs, such as *like, hate* or *know*, only infrequently appear in the progressive form, although such constructions as *Johnny is really liking school now* do occur. Similar and often quite complex constraints on the interaction of the lexical verb and the grammatical forms function in other instances as well. Consequently, it would be of interest to study the statistical distribution of the frequencies of grammatical categories in conjunction with the lexical and semantic classification of the verbs that occur in the individual genres. But even the figures that we have presented here clearly demonstrate that grammatical categories in general are greatly influenced, in their frequency of occurrence, by genre and style characteristics, and that no reliable statements about their frequency can be made without a specific reference to the genre properties of the sample.

Concluding Remarks

In order to keep this book to manageable size, a number of results of our frequency analysis could not be included. So, for example, we were able to give, in Section IV, only the rank list of lemmas of adjusted frequency of five or more, but not the complete rank list of all grammatical words. Such a list would have added several hundred pages. However, all the lists in this book as well as much additional information not contained here—such as the full rank lists—are available on computer tapes to those readers who may wish to pursue the analysis of the data base further. The complete tagged version of the corpus on tape is also available in an easily processible format, with each of the one million words, its tag, and a unique location marker constituting a separate logical record.

Those interested in the tapes of the frequency lists should contact the the Reference Division, Houghton Mifflin Company, Two Park Street, Boston, Massachusetts 02108. Those desiring additional information about the corpus itself should contact one of the authors at Box E, Brown University, Providence, Rhode Island 02912.

References and Bibliography

This bibliography includes all items referred to in the text, together with a selection of studies based on or making use of the Brown Corpus. Those interested in a more complete list are referred to the bibliography in *ICAME News* 2, listed below.

Brown Corpus bibliography. *ICAME News* 2.9-12.

Card, William, and Virginia McDavid 1966. English words of very high frequency. *College English* 27.596-604.

Chomsky, Noam 1980. On binding. *Linguistic Inquiry* 11.1-46.

Dubois, Betty Lou 1972. Meaning and distribution of the perfect in present-day American English prose. Unpublished Ph.D. dissertation, University of New Mexico. (DAI 33/12 - A, pp. 6892f.)

Ehrman, Madeline 1966. *The meanings of the modals in present-day American English.* Janua linguarum, series practica 45. The Hague: Mouton.

Ellegård, Alvar 1978. *The syntactic structure of English texts: a computer-based study of four kinds of text in the Brown University Corpus.* Göteborg: Acta Universitatis Gothoburgensis.

Filipović, Rudolf 1969- . *The Yugoslav Serbo-Croatian - English contrastive project.*
A. Reports, vols. 1-
B. Studies, vols 1-
C. Pedagogical materials, vols. 1-
Zagreb: Institute of Linguistics; Washington: Center for Applied Linguistics.

Francis, W. Nelson, and Henry Kučera 1964, 1971, 1979. *Manual of information to accompany a standard sample of present-day edited American English, for use with digital computers.* Revised ed. 1971; revised and augmented (with Henry Kučera) 1979. Providence: Department of Linguistics, Brown University.

Francis, W, Nelson 1964a. *A standard sample of present-day English for use with digital computers.* Report to the U.S. Office of Education on Cooperative Research Project No. E-007. Providence: Brown University.

Francis, W. Nelson 1965. A standard corpus of edited present-day American English for computer use. *Literary Data Processing Conference Proceedings, September 9,10,11 1964,* edited by Jess B. Bessinger, Jr., Stephen M. Parrish, and Harry F. Arader. Armonk, NY: IBM Corporation; pp. 79-89. Slightly revised version: *College English* 26.267-73.

Francis, W. Nelson 1979. Problems in assembling, describing, and computerizing corpora. Paper for Skylark I: a Workshop on Southwestern English, El Paso, Texas, 17 Oct. 1974;

published in *Papers in Southwest English: research techniques and prospects*, ed. by Betty Lou Dubois and Bates Hoffer; San Antonio: Trinity University, 1975. Revised version, Problems of assembling and computerizing large corpora, in *Empirische Textwissenschaft, Aufbau und Auswertung von Text-Corpora*, ed. by H. Bergenholtz and B. Schaeder. Koenigstein: Scriptor Verlag; pp. 110-23.

Francis, W. Nelson 1980. A tagged corpus—problems and prospects. In *Studies in English linguistics, for Randolph Quirk*, ed. by S. Greenbaum, G. Leech, and J. Svartvik. London and New York: Longman; pp. 192-209.

Geens, Dirk 1978. On measurement of lexical differences by means of frequency. In *Glottometrika* 1, ed. by G. Altman. Bochum: Studienverlag Dr. N. Brockmeier; pp. 46-72.

Greenberg, Joseph H. 1966. Language universals. In *Current Trends in Linguistics*, vol. III *Theoretical Foundations*, ed. by Thomas A. Sebeok. The Hague: Mouton; pp. 61-112.

Greene, Barbara B., and Gerald M. Rubin 1971. *Automatic grammatical tagging of English*. Providence: Department of Linguistics, Brown University.

Hauge, Jostein, and Knut Hofland 1978. Microfiche version of the Brown University Corpus of Present-Day American English. Bergen: NAVF's EDB-Senter for Humanistisk Forskning.

Hofland, Knut, and Stig Johansson 1980. LOB Corpus: KWIC Concordance (microfiche). Bergen: NAVF's EDB-Senter for Humanistisk Forskning.

ICAME News. 1978- . Newsletter of the International Computer Archive of Modern English. Bergen: NAVF's EDB-Senter for Humanistisk Forskning.

Jahr, Mette-Cathrine. 1981. The s-genitive with non-personal nouns in present-day British and American English. *ICAME News* 5.14-31.

Johansson, Stig 1978. *Some aspects of the vocabulary of learned and scientific English*. Gothenburg Studies in English 42. Göteborg: Acta Universitatis Gothoburgensis.

Johansson, Stig 1979. The use of a corpus in register analysis: the case of learned and scientific English. In *Empirische Textwissenschaft, Aufbau und Auswertung von Text-Corpora*, ed. by H. Bergenholtz and B. Schaeder. Koenigstein: Scriptor Verlag; pp. 281-93.

Johansson, Stig 1980a. Corpus-based studies of British and American English. In *Papers from the Scandinavian Symposium on Syntactic Variation, Stockholm, May 18-19, 1979*, ed. by S. Jacobson. Stockholm Studies in English 52. Stockholm: Almqvist & Wiksell; pp. 85-100.

Johansson, Stig 1980b. Word frequencies in British and American English. In *ALVAR. A linguistically varied assortment of readings; studies presented to Alvar Ellegård on the occasion of his 60th birthday* , ed. by J. Allwood and M. Ljung. Stockholm papers in English language and literature 1. Stockholm: Department of English, University of Stockholm; pp. 56-74.

Johansson, Stig 1980c. The LOB Corpus of British English Texts: presentation and comments. *ALLC Journal* 1.25-36.

Johansson, Stig 1980d. Some thoughts on the use of computers in linguistic research. *Humanistiske data* (Bergen) 1.31-39.

Johansson, Stig 1981. Word frequencies in different types of English text. *ICAME News* 5.1-13.

Johansson, Stig, G. Leech, and H. Goodluck 1978. *Manual of information to accompany the Lancaster - Oslo/Bergen Corpus of British English, for use with digital computers*. Oslo: Department of English, University of Oslo.

Johansson, Stig, and Knut Hofland (forthcoming). *Word frequencies in British and American English.* Bergen: Norwegian Computing Center for the Humanities.

Joos, Martin 1964. *The English Verb.* Madison: The University of Wisconsin Press.

Juilland, Alphonse, and Eugenio Chang-Rodriguez 1964. *Frequency dictionary of Spanish words.* The Hague: Mouton.

Kaplan, Ronald M., and Joan W. Bresnan (1982). Lexical-functional grammar: a formal system for grammatical representation. Forthcoming in *The mental representation of grammatical relations,* ed. by Joan Bresnan. Cambridge: MIT Press.

Krogvig, Inger, and Stig Johansson. 1981. *Shall, will, should,* and *would* in British and American English. *ICAME News* 5.32-56.

Kučera, Henry 1968. Some quantitative lexical analyses of Russian, Czech, and English. In *American contributions to the Sixth International Congress of Slavists, I,* ed. by H. Kučera. The Hague: Mouton; pp.155-98.

Kučera, Henry 1969. Computers in language analysis and in lexicography. In *The American Heritage dictionary of the English language,* ed. by William Morris. New York: American Heritage and Houghton Mifflin; pp. xxxviii-xl.

Kučera, Henry 1980. Computational analysis of predicational structures in English. In *Proceedings of the Eighth International Conference on Computational Linguistics,* Tokyo; pp. 32-37.

Kučera, Henry, and W. Nelson Francis 1967. *Computational analysis of present-day American English.* Providence: Brown University Press.

Leech, Geoffrey, and Rosemary Leonard 1974. A computer corpus of British English. *Hamburger Phonetische Beiträge* 13.41-57.

Maegaard, Bente, and Hanne Ruus 1980. DANwORD: a linguistic data base for frequency studies of modern Danish. *Nordic Journal of Linguistics* 3.131-46.

Marchand, H. 1969. *The categories and types of present-day English word-formation,* 2nd ed. München: C.H.Beck.

Marckworth, Mary L., and Laura M. Bell 1967. Sentence-length distribution in the corpus. In Kučera and Francis 1967, pp. 368-405.

Meijs, Willem 1981. Exploring 'Brown' with 'Query.' Paper given at Seminar in Computer Corpora in Research and Teaching, Bergen. Forthcoming in *Proceedings.*

Meyers, Walter E. 1972. A study of usage items based on an examination of the Brown Corpus. *College Composition and Communication* 23.155-69.

Monroe, George K. 1965. Phonemic transcription of graphic post-base affixes in English: a computer problem. Unpublished Ph.D. dissertation, Brown University. (DA 26/08, p. 4648.)

Mosteller, Frederick, and Robert E. K. Rourke 1973. *Sturdy statistics.* Reading, Massachusetts: Addison-Wesley Publishing Company.

Muller, Charles 1965. Frequence, dispersion, et usage. *Cahiers de lexicologie* 7.33-42.

Rosengren, Inger 1972. *Ein Frequenzwörterbuch der deutschen Zeitungssprache.* Lund: CWK Gleerup.

Schaeder, Burkhard 1979. Maschinenlesbare Text-Corpora des Deutschen und Englischen: eine Dokumentation. In *Empirische Textwissenschaft, Aufbau und Auswertung von Text-Corpora,* ed. by H. Bergenholtz and B. Schaeder. Koenigstein: Scriptor Verlag; pp. 325-36.

Shastri, S.V. 1980. A computer corpus of present-day Indian English. *ICAME News* 4.9-10.

Smith, Donald A. 1971. An automatic parsing procedure for simple noun- and verb-phrases. M.A. thesis in Linguistics, Brown University.

Smith, Raoul N. 1973. *Probabilistic performance models of language.* Janua linguarum, series minor 150. The Hague: Mouton.

Solso, R.L., and J.F. King 1976. Frequency and versatility of letters in the English language. *Behavior Research Methods & Instrumentation* 8(3).283-86.

Solso, R.L., P.F. Barbuto, Jr., and C.L. Juel 1979. Bigram and trigram frequencies and versatilities in the English language. *Behavior Research Methods & Instrumentation* 11(5).475-84.

Solso, R.L., and C.L. Juel 1980. Positional frequency of bigrams for two- through nine-letter English words. *Behavior Research Methods & Instrumentation* 12(3).297-343.

Tanaka, Harumi 1971. A statistical study on selectional features of transitive verbs in present-day American English. Unpublished Ph.D. dissertation, Brown University. (DAI 32/10-A, p. 5769.)

Zettersten, Arne 1969. *A statistical study of the graphic system of present-day American English.* Lund: Studentenlitteratur.

Zettersten, Arne 1969a. *A word-frequency list of scientific English.* Lund: Studentenlitteratur.

ABCDEFGHIJ-H-898765432

RALPH P. BARRETT